1 MONTH OF
FREE
READING

at

www.ForgottenBooks.com

By purchasing this book you are eligible for one month membership to ForgottenBooks.com, giving you unlimited access to our entire collection of over 1,000,000 titles via our web site and mobile apps.

To claim your free month visit:
www.forgottenbooks.com/free784299

ISBN 978-0-364-44854-0
PIBN 10784299

THE

POEMS AND DRAMAS

OF

LORD BYRON

WITH BIOGRAPHICAL MEMOIR, EXPLANATORY
NOTES, ETC.

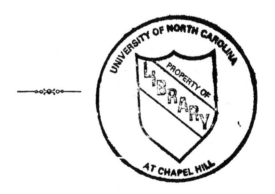

NEW YORK
THOMAS Y. CROWELL & CO.
PUBLISHERS

keenly felt the loneliness of his position. He was almost unknown to society at large; there was no peer to introduce him; and his mortification led him to receive with ungracious coldness the welcome of the lord-chancellor. His unfriended situation inspired him with disgust, and chilled his incipient longing for parliamentary distinction; and even a few days after taking his seat he retired to Newstead Abbey, and engaged with his friend Mr. (now Sir J. C.) Hobhouse to travel together on the Continent. About the end of June the friends sailed together from Falmouth to Lisbon; travelled through part of Portugal and the south of Spain to Gibraltar; sailed thence to Malta and afterwards to Albania, in which country they landed on the 29th of September. From this time till the middle of the spring of 1811, Lord Byron was engaged in visiting many parts of Greece, Turkey, and Asia Minor; staying long at Athens, Constantinople, and Smyrna. He touched again on his return at Malta, quitted it on the 2d of June, and early in July, after two years absence, landed in England. His affairs during this period had fallen into disorder, and it became advisable to sell either Rochdale or Newstead. The latter he was then most anxious to retain, and professed that it was his "only tie" to England, "if he parted with that he should remain abroad." In a letter to a friend, written during his homeward voyage, he thus expresses his melancholy sense of his condition: "Embarrassed in my private affairs, indifferent to public, — solitary without a wish to be social, — with a body a little enfeebled by a succession of fevers, but a spirit I trust yet unbroken, — I am returning home, without a hope and almost without a desire." This gloom was still deepened by numerous afflictions. His mother died on the 1st of August, without his having seen her again since his return to England, and he was deprived by death of five other relatives and friends between that and the end of August. " In the short space of one month," he says, " I have lost her who gave me being, and most of those who made that being tolerable." Amongst the latter were Wingfield, and Matthews, the brother of the author of *The Diary of an Invalid.* At this period of distress, he was approaching unsuspectingly a remarkable epoch of his fame. He had composed while abroad two poems, very different in character, and which he regarded with strangely misplaced feelings; the one called *Hints from Horace*, a weak imitation of his former satire; the other, the first two cantos of *Childe Harold.* The former he intended to publish immediately; but the latter he thought of so disparagingly (owing probably to the injudicious comments of the single friend who had hitherto seen it), that it might probably have never become known to the public but for the wise advice of Mr. Dallas. In compliance with the request of that gentleman, he withheld the *Hints from Horace*, which would have been injurious rather than beneficial to his fame; and allowed *Childe Harold* to be offered for publication. He received from his publisher, Mr. Murray, £600 for the copyright, which he gave to Mr. Dallas. The publication was long delayed; for, though placed in the publisher's hands in August, it did not appear till the beginning of March, 1812. It, however, received during this interval considerable improvements; and the fears of the author were allayed by the approbation of Mr. Gifford, the translator of Juvenal, and then editor of the *Quarterly Review.* The success of the poem exceeded even the anticipation of this able critic; and Lord Byron emerged at once from a state of loneliness and neglect, unusual for one in his sphere of life, to be the magnet and idol of society. As he tersely says in his memoranda, " I awoke one morning and found myself famous." A few days before the publication of *Childe Harold*, he attracted attention, but in a minor degree, by his first speech in the House of Lords on the subject of the housebreaking bill. He opposed it, and with ability; and his first oratorical effort was much commended by Sheridan, Sir F. Burdett, and Lords Grenville and Holland. He had prepared himself, by having committed the whole of his speech to writing. It was well received, and he was extremely gratified by its success. He might perhaps have been incited by the praises it received to seek political distinction; but the greater success which attended his poem turned his ambitious feelings into a different channel. He nevertheless spoke again about six weeks afterwards, on a motion of Lord Donoughmore, in favor of the claims of the Roman Catholics, but less successfully than before. Less clearness was displayed in the matter of his speech, and his delivery was considered as theatrical. In the autumn of this year he wrote an address, at the request of the Drury Lane Committee, to be spoken at the reopening of the theatre; and not long afterwards he became a member of that committee. The same autumn he engaged to sell Newstead for £140,000, of which £60,000 was to remain in mortgage on the estate for three years; but this purchase was never completed. In May, 1813, appeared his *Giaour*, a wildly poetical fragment, of which the story was founded on an event that had occurred at Athens while he was there, and in which he was personally concerned. It was written rapidly, and with such additions during the course of printing as to be more than trebled in length, and swelled from about four hundred lines to upwards of fourteen hundred. On the 2d of June in this year he spoke for the last time in the House of Lords, on presenting a petition from Major Cartwright. He had now apparently ceased to regard parliamentary distinction as a primary object of ambition.

In his journal of November, 1813, is the following entry: "I have declined presenting the debtors' petition, being sick of parliamentary mummeries. I have spoken thrice, but I doubt my ever becoming an orator; my first was liked, my second and third, I don't know whether they succeeded or not; I have never set to it *con amore*." In November he had finished his *Bride of Abydos* (written in a week), and it was published the following month. *The Corsair*, a poem of still higher merit and popularity, appeared in less than three months afterwards; it was written in the astonishingly short space of ten days. During the year 1813 he appeared to have first entertained a serious intention of marriage, and became a suitor to Miss Milbanke, only daughter and heiress of Sir Ralph Milbanke. His first proposal was rejected; but the parties continued on the footing of friendship, and maintained a correspondence, of which, and of that lady, he thus speaks, and it may be presumed with the most perfect sincerity, in his private journal: "Yesterday a very pretty letter from Annabella, which I answered. What an odd situation and friendship is ours! without one spark of love on either side, and produced by circumstances which in general lead to coldness on one side and aversion on the other. She is a very superior woman, and very little spoiled, which is strange in an heiress—a girl of twenty,—peeress, that is to be in her own right,—an only child, and a *savante*, who has always had her own way. She is a poetess, a mathematician, a metaphysician, and yet withal very kind, generous, and gentle, with very little pretensions: any other head would be turned with half her acquisitions and a tenth of her advantages." In September, 1814, he made a second proposal by letter, which was accepted; and on the 2d of January, 1815, he was married to Miss Milbanke, at Seaham, the country-seat of her father. The only issue of this marriage, Augusta Ada, was born on the 10th of December, of that year. We cannot lift the veil of their domestic life; we can only state the unfortunate results. On the 15th of January, 1816, Lady Byron left London for Kirkby Mallory, the residence of her parents, whither Lord Byron was to follow her. She had, with the concurrence of some of Lord Byron's relatives, previously consulted Dr. Baillie respecting the supposed insanity of her husband, and by the advice of that gentleman had written to him in a kind and soothing tone. Lady Byron's impressions of the insanity of Lord Byron were soon removed, but were followed by a resolution on her part to obtain a separation. Conformably to this resolution, Sir Ralph Milbanke wrote to Lord Byron on the 2d of February, proposing such a measure. This proposal Lord Byron at first rejected, but afterwards consented to sign a deed to that effect. Dr. Lushington, the legal adviser of Lady Byron, has stated in a published letter, that he "considered reconciliation impossible." Of the circumstances which led to such an event, and on which Dr. Lushington founded such an opinion, the public is at present uninformed. We are, therefore, in absence of full and satisfying evidence, bound to suspend our judgment on the merits of this melancholy case, and dismiss it with the foregoing statement of the leading facts.

In the course of the spring he published *The Siege of Corinth*, and *Parisina*. He also wrote two copies of verses, which appeared in the public papers, *Fare thee well*, and *A Sketch, from Private Life;* of which his separation from his wife, and the instrumentality which he imputes to an humble individual in conducing to that separation, were the themes. This private circumstance had become the subject of general comment. The majority of those who filled the circles in which Lord Byron had lately lived declared against him, and society withdrew its countenance. Lord Byron, deeply stung by its verdict, hastily resolved to leave the country; and on the 25th of April, 1816, he quitted England for the last time. His course was through Flanders and along the Rhine to Switzerland, where, at a villa called Diodati, in the neighborhood of Geneva, he resided during the summer. From thence he made two excursions, one in the central part of Switzerland in company with Mr. Hobhouse, and another shorter excursion with a celebrated poetical compeer, Mr. Shelley, with whom he became acquainted soon after his arrival at Geneva. He remained in Switzerland till October, during which time he had composed some of his most powerful works, the third canto of *Childe Harold*, *The Prisoner of Chillon*, *Darkness*, *The Dream*, part of *Manfred*, and a few minor poems. In October, he quitted Switzerland in company with Mr. Hobhouse, and proceeded by Milan and Verona to Venice. Here he resided from the middle of November, 1816, to the middle of April, 1817. During this period his principal literary occupation was the completion of *Manfred*, of which he rewrote the third act. He visited Rome for about a month in the spring, and then returned to Venice, at which city, or at La Mira, in its immediate vicinity, he resided almost uninterruptedly from this time till 1819. He wrote during this period *The Lament of Tasso, Beppo*, the fourth canto of *Childe Harold, Marino Faliero, The Foscari, Mazeppa*, and part of *Don Juan*. The licentious character of his life while at Venice corresponded but too well with the tone of that production. His able biographer and friend, Mr. Moore, after adverting to his *liaison* with a married Italian woman, says: " Highly censurable in point of morality and decorum as was his course of life while under the roof of Madame ——, it was (with pain I am forced to confess) venial in comparison with the strange headlong career of license to which, when weaned from that connection, he so unrestrainedly, and, it may be added, defyingly, abandoned himself." This course of unbridled libertinism received its first check from the growth of an attachment, which, as it was still unhallowed, not even the good which it may seem to have done, in the substitution of a purer sentiment, will enable us to regard with satisfaction. In April, 1819, he first became acquainted with the Countess Guiccioli, the young and newly married wife of an elderly Italian nobleman. A mutual attachment, which appears to have commenced on the part of the lady, soon arose between Lord Byron and the Countess Guiccioli. Their passion was augmented by occasional separation, the interest excited by her severe illness during one of their forced absences, and the imprudent complaisance of the husband in leaving them much in the society of each other. They long lived together in a half-permitted state of intimacy, the lady appearing with the consent of her husband to share his protection with that of Lord Byron. But this equivocal position soon terminated in the separation of the Count and Countess Guiccioli. The lady then went to reside with her father; and under his sanction, during the next three or four years, she and Lord Byron enjoyed the intimate possession of each other's society. In December, 1819, Lord Byron quitted Venice for Ravenna, where he remained till the end of October, 1821. During this period he wrote part of *Don Juan, The Prophecy of Dante, Sardanapalus*, a translation of the first Canto of *Pulci's Morgante Maggiore*, and the mysteries, *Heaven and Earth*, and *Cain ;* the latter of which may be justly considered as among the most faulty in principle, and powerful in execution, of the productions of his genius. He also wrote a letter on Mr. Bowles's strictures on Pope, dated 7th February, 1821, in which he defends the poet against his commentator; and an answer to an article in Blackwood's Magazine, entitled " Remarks on Don Juan; " but this was never published.

During this period an insurrectionary spirit broke out in Italy; the Carbonari appeared; and secret societies began to be formed. The brother of the Countess Guiccioli, Count Pietro Gamba, espoused the cause of the insurgents, and through his means Lord Byron became implicated in the proceedings of that party. In his private journal of 16th February, 1821, Lord Byron complains of the conduct of that gentleman and others, in sending to his house, without apprising him, arms, with which he had a short time previously furnished them at their request, and thereby endangering his safety, and exposing him to the vengeance of the government, which had lately issued a severe ordinance against all persons having arms concealed. In July, 1821, the father and brother of Madame Guiccioli were ordered to quit Ravenna, and repaired with that lady first to Florence, and afterwards to Pisa, where they were joined in October by Lord Byron. He remained at Pisa till September, 1822, Madame Guiccioli still living with him under the sanction of her father, who, in consequence of one of the conditions of her separation from her husband, was always to reside with her under the same roof. While here he lost his illegitimate daughter Allegra, and his friend Shelley, who was drowned in July, 1822, in the Bay of Spezzia. The body was burned, and Lord Byron assisted at this singular rite. His principal associates during this time had been the Gambas, Shelley, Captain Medwyn, and Mr. Trelawney. He had also become associated with the brothers John and Leigh Hunt, in a periodical paper called *The Liberal ;* a transaction certainly disinterested, inasmuch as it does not appear that he expected either profit or fame to accrue to himself from the undertaking; and he seems to have allowed his name to be connected with it from a desire to serve the Hunts, of whom Leigh Hunt with his wife and family received an asylum in his house. An affray with a serjeant-major at Pisa rendered his residence in that city less agreeable; and his removal from it was at length determined by an order from the Tuscan government to the Gambas to quit the territory. Accordingly, in September, 1822, he removed with them to Genoa. While at Pisa he had written, besides his contributions to *The Liberal, Werner, The Deformed Transformed*, and the remainder of *Don Juan*.

In April, 1823, he commenced a correspondence with the Greek committee, through Messrs. Bla-quiere and Bowring, and began to interest himself warmly in the cause of the Greeks. In May he de-cided to go to Greece; and in July he sailed from Genoa in an English brig, taking with him Count Gamba, Mr. Trelawney, Dr. Burns, an Italian physician, and eight domestics; five horses, arms, ammu-nition, and medicine. The money which he had raised for this expedition was 50,000 crowns; 10,000 in specie; and the rest in bills of exchange. In August he arrived at Argostoli, the chief port of Cephalo-nia, in which island he established his residence till the end of December. His first feelings of exagger-ated enthusiasm appear to have been soon cooled. Even as early as October he uses, in letters to Madame Guiccioli, such expressions as, "I was a fool to come here;" and, "Of the Greeks I can't say much good hitherto; and I do not like to speak ill of them, though they do of one another." During the latter part of this year we find him endeavoring to compose the dissensions of the Greeks among them-selves, and assisting them with a loan of £4,000. About the end of December, 1823, he sailed from Argostoli in a Greek mistico, and, after narrowly escaping capture by a Turkish frigate, landed on the 5th of January, 1824, at Missolonghi. His reception here was enthusiastic. The whole population came out to welcome him; salutes were fired; and he was met and conducted into the town by Prince Mavrocordato, and all the troops and dignitaries of the place. But the disorganization which reigned in this town soon depressed his spirits, which had been raised by this reception, and filled his mind with reasonable misgivings of the success of the Greek cause. Nevertheless his resolution did not seem to fail, nor did he relax in his devotion to that cause, and in his efforts to advance it. About the end of January, 1824, he received his commission from the Greek government as commander of the expedition against Lepanto, with full powers, both civil and military. He was to be assisted by a military council, with Bozzari at its head. Great difficulties attended the arrangement of this expedition, arising principally from the dissensions and jealousies of the native leaders, and the mutinous spirit of the Suliote troops; with which latter, on the 14th of February, Lord Byron came to a rupture, in conse-quence of their demand, that about a third part of the number should be raised from common soldiers to the rank of officers. Lord Byron was firm, and they submitted on the following day. Difficulties in the civil department harassed him at the same time, aggravated by a difference of opinion between him-self and Colonel Stanhope, on the subject of a free press, which the latter was anxious to introduce, and for which, on the other hand, Lord Byron considered that Greece was not yet ripe. On the 15th of Feb-ruary, the day of the professed submission of the Suliotes, he was seized with a convulsive fit, and for many days was seriously ill. While he was on a sick-bed, the mutinous Suliotes burst into his room, de-manding what they called their rights; and, though his firmness then controlled them, it soon after-wards became necessary to get rid of these lawless soldiers, by a bribe of a month's pay in advance, — and with their dismissal vanished the hopes of the expedition against Lepanto. After this he turned his mind chiefly to the fortification of Missolonghi, the formation of a brigade, and the composition of the differences among the Greek chieftains. Since his attack in February he had never been entirely well. Early in April, he caught a severe cold, through exposure to rain. His fever increased, and, in conse-quence of his prejudice against bleeding, that remedy was delayed till it was too late to be effectual. On the 17th, (the second day after he had been bled,) appearances of inflammation in the brain pre-sented themselves. The following day he became insensible, and, about twenty-four hours afterwards, at a quarter past six in the evening of the 19th of April, 1824, Lord Byron breathed his last. Public honors were decreed to his memory by the authorities of Greece, where his loss was deeply lamented. The body was conveyed to England, and on the 16th of July was deposited in the family vault, in the parish church of Hucknell, near Newstead, in the county of Notts. By his will, dated 29th July, 1815, Lord Byron bequeathed to his half-sister, Mrs. Leigh, during her life, and after her death to her children, the moneys arising from the sale of all such property, real and personal, as was not settled upon Lady Byron and his issue by her. The executors were Mr. Hobhouse, and Mr. Hanson, Lord Byron's solici-tor.

The personal appearance of Lord Byron was prepossessing. His height was five feet eight and a half inches; his head small; his complexion pale; hair dark brown, and curly; forehead high; features regular and good, and somewhat Grecian; eyes light gray, but capable of much expression. He was lame in the right foot, owing, it is said, to an accident at his birth; which circumstance seems always to have been to him a source of deep mortification, little warranted by its real importance. It did not prevent him from being active in his habits, and excelling in various manly exercises. He was a very good swimmer; successfully crossed the Hellespont in emulation of Leander; swam across the Tagus, a still greater feat; and, greatest of all, at Venice, in 1818, from Lido to the opposite end of the grand canal, having been four hours and twenty minutes in the water without touching ground. In his younger days he was fond of sparring; and pistol shooting, in which he excelled, was his favorite diversion while in Italy. In riding, for which he professed fondness, he did not equally excel. He was nervous, both on horseback and in a carriage, though his conduct in Greece, and at other times, proved his unquestionable courage on great occasions. He had always a fondness for animals, and seemed to have preferred those which were of a ferocious kind. A bear, a wolf, and sundry bull-dogs, were at various times among his pets. The habits of his youth, after the period of boyhood, were not literary and intellectual; nor were his amusements of a refined or poetical character. He was always shy, and fond of solitude; but when in society, lively and animated, gentle, playful, and attractive in manner; and he possessed the power of quickly conciliating the friendship of those with whom he associated. He was very susceptible of attachment to women. The objects of his strongest passions appear to have been Miss Chaworth, afterwards Mrs. Musters, and the Countess Guiccioli. His amours were numerous, and there was in his character a too evident proneness to libertinism. His constitution does not seem ever to have been strong, and his health was probably impaired by his modes of life. He was abstemious in eating, sometimes touching neither meat nor fish. Sometimes also he abstained entirely from wine or spirits, which at other times he drank to excess, seldom preserving a wholesome moderation and regularity of system. His temper was irascible, yet placable. He was quickly alive to tender and generous emotions, and performed many acts of disinterested liberality, even toward those whom he could not esteem, and in spite of parsimonious feelings, which latterly gained hold upon him. He was a man of a morbid acuteness of feeling, arising partly from original temperament, and partly from circumstances and habits. He had been ill educated; he had been severely tried; his early attachments, and his first literary efforts, had equally been unfortunate; he had encountered the extremes of neglect and admiration; pecuniary distresses, domestic afflictions, and the unnerving tendency of dissipated habits, had all conspired to aggravate the waywardness of his excitable disposition. It is evident, that, in spite of his assumed indifference, he was always keenly alive to the applause and censure of the world; and its capricious treatment of him more than ordinarily encouraged that vanity and egotism which were conspicuous traits in his character.

The religious opinions of Lord Byron appear, by his own account of them, to have been " unfixed; " but he expressly disclaimed being one of those infidels who deny the Scriptures, and wish to remain " in unbelief." In politics he was liberal, but his opinions were much influenced by his feelings; and, though professedly a lover of free institutions, he could not withhold his admiration even from tyranny when his imagination was wrought upon by its grandeur. He would not view Napoleon as the enslaver of France: he viewed him only as the most extraordinary being of his age, and he sincerely deplored his fall.

Lord Byron's prose compositions were so inconsiderable that they may almost be overlooked in the view of his literary character. His letters, nevertheless, must not pass wholly unnoticed. Careless as they are, and hastily written, they are among the most lively, spirited, and pointed specimens of epistolary writing in our language, and would alone suffice to indicate the possession of superior talent. The critical theories of Lord Byron were remarkably at variance with his practice. The most brilliant supporter of a new school of poetry, he was the professed admirer of a school that was superseded. The most powerful and original poet of the nineteenth century, he was a timid critic of the eighteenth. In theory he preferred polish to originality or vigor. He evidently thought Pope the first of our poets; he defended the unities; praised Shakspeare grudgingly; saw little merit in Spenser; preferred his own *Hints from Horace* to his *Childe Harold's Pilgrimage;* and assigned his contemporaries, Coleridge and Wordsworth, a place far inferior to that which public opinion has more justly accorded to them.

The poetry of Lord Byron produced an immediate effect unparalleled in our literary annals. Of this influence much may be attributed, not only to the real power of his poetry, but also to the impressive identification of its principal characteristics with that which, whether truly or falsely, the world chose to regard as the character of the author. He seemed to have unbosomed himself to the public, and admitted them to view the full intensity of feelings which had never before been poured forth with such eloquent directness. His poems were as tales of the confessional, portraitures of real passion, not tamely feigned, but fresh and glowing from the breast of the writer. The emotions which he excelled in displaying were those of the most stormy character, — hate, scorn, rage, despair, indomitable pride, and the dark spirit of misanthropy. It was a narrow circle, but in that he stood without a rival. His descriptive powers were eminently great. His works abound with splendid examples; among which the Venetian night-scene from Lioni's balcony, Terni, the coliseum viewed by moonlight, and the shipwreck in Don Juan will probably rise foremost in the memories of many readers. In description he was never too minute. He selected happily, and sketched freely, rapidly, and bodily. He seized the most salient images, and brought them directly and forcibly to the eye at once. There was, however, in his descriptive talent, the same absence of versatility and variety which characterized other departments of his genius. His writings do not reflect nature in all its infinite change of climate, scenery, and season. He portrayed with surprising truth and force only such objects as were adapted to the sombre coloring of his pencil. The mountain, the cataract, the glacier, the ruin, — objects inspiring awe and melancholy, — seemed more congenial to his poetical disposition than those which led to joy or gratitude.

His genius was not dramatic; vigorously as he portrayed emotions, he was not successful in drawing characters; he was not master of variety; all his most prominent personages are strictly resolvable into one. There were diversities, but they were diversities of age, clime, and circumstance, not of character. They were merely such as would have appeared in the same individual when placed in different situations. Even the lively and the serious moods belonged alike to that one being; but there was a bitter recklessness in the mirth of his lively personages, which seems only the temporary relaxation of that proud misanthropic gloom that is exhibited in his serious heroes; and each might easily become the other. It may also be objected to many of his personages, that, if tried by the standard of nature, they were essentially false. They were sublime monstrosities; — strange combinations of virtue and vice, such as had never really existed. In his representations of corsairs and renegades, he exaggerates the good feelings which may, by a faint possibility, belong to such characters, and suppresses the brutality and faithlessness which would more probably be found in them, and from which it is not possible that they should have been wholly exempt. His plan was highly conducive to poetical effect; but its incorrectness must not be overlooked in an estimate of his delineation of human character. In his tragedies there is much vigor; but their finest passages are either soliloquies or descriptions, and their highest beauties are seldom of a strictly dramatic nature. Many of his dialogues are scarcely more than interrupted soliloquies; many of his arguments such as one mind would hold with itself. In fact, in his characters, there is seldom that degree of variety and contrast which is requisite for dramatic effect. The opposition was rather that of situation than of sentiment; and we feel that the interlocutors, if transposed, might still have uttered the same things.

It is to be deplored that scarcely any moral good is derivable from the splendid poetry of Lord Byron. The tendency of his works is to shake our confidence in virtue, and to diminish our abhorrence of vice; — to palliate crime, and to unsettle our notions of right and wrong. Even many of the virtuous sentiments which occur in his writings are assigned to characters so worthless, or placed in such close juxtaposition with vicious sentiments, as to induce a belief that there exists no real, definable boundary; and it may perhaps be said with truth, that it would have been better for the cause of morality if even those virtuous sentiments had been omitted. Our sympathy is frequently solicited in the behalf of crime. Alp, Conrad, Juan, Parisina, Hugo, Lara, and Manfred may be cited as examples. They are all interesting and vicious. In the powerful drama of *Cain*, the heroes are Lucifer and the first murderer; and the former is depicted, not like the Satan of Milton, who believes and trembles, but as the compassionate friend of mankind. Resistance to the will of the Creator is represented as dignified and commendable; obedience and faith as mean, slavish, and contemptible. It is implied that it was unmerciful to have created such as we are, and that we owe the Supreme Being neither gratitude nor duty. Such sentiments are clearly deducible from this drama. Whether they were those of Lord Byron is not certain; but he must be held accountable for their promulgation.

CONTENTS.

HOURS OF IDLENESS:

A SERIES OF POEMS, ORIGINAL AND TRANSLATED.

[FIRST PUBLISHED IN 1807.]

" Μήτ' ἄρ με μάλ' αἴνεε μήτε τι νείκει." — HOMER, *Iliad*, x. 249.
" He whistled as he went, for want of thought." — DRYDEN.
" Virginibus puerisque canto." — HORACE, lib. 3, ode 1.

———

TO THE RIGHT HONORABLE

FREDERICK, EARL OF CARLISLE,

KNIGHT OF THE GARTER, ETC., ETC.,

THE SECOND EDITION OF THESE POEMS IS INSCRIBED,

BY HIS

OBLIGING WARD AND AFFECTIONATE KINSMAN,[1]

THE AUTHOR.

———

PREFACE TO THE FIRST EDITION.[2]

IN submitting to the public eye the following collection, I have not only to combat the difficulties that writers of verse generally encounter, but may incur the charge of presumption for obtruding myself on the world, when, without doubt, I might be, at my age, more usefully employed.

These productions are the fruits of the lighter hours of a young man who has lately completed his nineteenth year. As they bear the internal evidence of a boyish mind, this is, perhaps, unnecessary information. Some few were written during the disadvantages of illness and depression of spirits; under the former influence, "CHILDISH RECOLLECTIONS," in particular, were composed. This consideration, though it cannot excite the voice of praise, may at least arrest the arm of censure. A considerable portion of these poems has been privately printed, at the request and for the perusal of my friends. I am sensible that the partial and frequently injudicious admiration of a social circle is not the criterion by which poetical genius is to be estimated, yet "to do greatly," we must "dare greatly;" and I have hazarded my reputation and feelings in publishing this volume. "I have crossed the Rubicon," and must

---

[1] Isabel, daughter of William, fourth Lord Byron (great-great uncle of the Poet), became, in 1742, the wife of Henry, fourth Earl of Carlisle, and was the mother of the fifth Earl, to whom this dedication was addressed. The lady was a poetess in her way. The Fairy's Answer to Mrs. Greville's "Prayer of Indifference," in Pearch's Collection, is usually ascribed to her.
[2] This preface was omitted in the second edition.

stand or fall by the "cast of the die." In the latter event, I shall submit without a murmur; for, though not without solicitude for the fate of these effusions, my expectations are by no means sanguine. It is probable that I may have dared much, and done little; for, in the words of Cowper, "it is one thing to write what may please our friends, who, because they are such, are apt to be a little biased in our favor, and another to write what may please everybody; because they who have no connection, or even knowledge, of the author, will be sure to find fault if they can." To the truth of this, however, I do not wholly subscribe: on the contrary, I feel convinced that these trifles will not be treated with injustice. Their merit, if they possess any, will be liberally allowed: their numerous faults, on the other hand, cannot expect that favor which has been denied to others of maturer years, decided character, and far greater ability.

I have not aimed at exclusive originality, still less have I studied any particular model for imitation: some translations are given, of which many are paraphrastic. In the original pieces, there may appear a casual coincidence with authors whose works I have been accustomed to read; but I have not been guilty of intentional plagiarism. To produce anything entirely new, in an age so fertile in rhyme, would be a Herculean task, as every subject has already been treated to its utmost extent. Poetry, however, is not my primary vocation; to divert the dull moments of indisposition, or the monotony of a vacant hour, urged me "to this sin:" little can be expected from so unpromising a muse. My wreath, scanty as it must be, is all I shall derive from these productions; and I shall never attempt to replace its fading leaves, or pluck a single additional sprig from groves where I am, at best, an intruder. Though accustomed in my younger days to rove, a careless mountaineer, on the Highlands of Scotland, I have not, of late years, had the benefit of such pure air or so elevated a residence, as might enable me to enter the lists with genuine bards, who have enjoyed both these advantages. But they derive considerable fame, and a few not less profit, from their productions; while I shall expiate my rashness as an interloper, certainly without the latter, and in all probability with a very slight share of the former. I leave to others "virûm volitare per ora." I look to the few who will hear with patience "dulce est desipere in loco." To the former worthies I resign, without repining, the hope of immortality, and content myself with the not very magnificent prospect of ranking amongst "the mob of gentlemen who write;" — my readers must determine whether I dare say "with ease," or the honor of a posthumous page in "The Catalogue of Royal and Noble Authors," — a work to which the Peerage is under infinite obligations, inasmuch as many names of considerable length, sound, and antiquity, are thereby rescued from the obscurity which unluckily overshadows several voluminous productions of their illustrious bearers.

With slight hopes, and some fears, I publish this first and last attempt. To the dictates of young ambition may be ascribed many actions more criminal and equally absurd. To a few of my own age the contents may afford amusement: I trust they will, at least, be found harmless. It is highly improbable, from my situation and pursuits hereafter, that I should ever obtrude myself a second time on the public, nor even, in the very doubtful event of present indulgence, shall I be tempted to commit a future trespass of the same nature. The opinion of Dr. Johnson on the Poems of a noble relation of mine,[1] "That when a man of rank appeared in the character of an autnor, he deserved to have his merit handsomely allowed," can have little weight with verbal, and still less with periodical, censors; but were it otherwise, I should be loth to avail myself of the privilege, and would rather incur the bitterest censure of anonymous criticism, than triumph in honors granted solely to a title.

[1] The Earl of Carlisle, whose works have long received the meed of public applause, tc which, by their intrinsic worth, they were well entitled.

HOURS OF IDLENESS.

ᴏN THE DEATH OF A YOUNG LADY,
COUSIN TO THE AUTHOR, AND VERY
DEAR TO HIM.[1]

ʜUSH'ᴅ are the winds, and still the evening
    gloom,
  Not e'en a zephyr wanders through the grove,
Whilst I return, to view my Margaret's tomb,
  And scatter flowers on the dust I love.

Within this narrow cell reclines her clay,
  That clay, where once such animation
    beam'd;
The King of Terrors seized her as his prey,
  Not worth, nor beauty, have her life re-
    deem'd.

Oh! could that King of Terrors pity feel,
  Or Heaven reverse the dread decrees of fate!
Not here the mourner would his grief reveal,
  Not here the muse her virtues would relate.

But wherefore weep? Her matchless spirit
    soars
  Beyond where splendid shines the orb of
    day;
And weeping angels lead her to those bowers
  Where endless pleasures virtue's deeds re-
    pay.

And shall presumptuous mortals Heaven ar-
    raign,
  And, madly, godlike Providence accuse?
Ah! no, far fly from me attempts so vain; —
  I'll ne'er submission to my God refuse.

Yet is remembrance of those virtues dear,
  Yet fresh the memory of that beauteous face;
Still they call forth my warm affection's tear,
  Still in my heart retain their wonted place.

1802.[2]

TO E——.[3]

LET Folly smile, to view the names
  Of thee and me in friendship twined;
Yet Virtue will have greater claims
  To love, than rank with vice combined.

And though unequal is thy fate,
  Since title decked my higher birth!
Yet envy not this gaudy state;
  Thine is the pride of modest worth.

Our souls at least congenial meet,
  Nor can thy lot my rank disgrace;
Our intercourse is not less sweet,
  Since worth of rank supplies the place.

· November, 1802.

TO D——.

IN thee, I fondly hoped to clasp
  A friend, whom death alone could sever;
Till envy, with malignant grasp,
  Detached thee from my breast for ever.

[1] The author claims the indulgence of the reader more for this piece than, perhaps, any other in the collection; but as it was written at an earlier period than the rest (being composed at the age of fourteen), and his first essay, he preferred submitting it to the indulgence of his friends in its present state, to making either addition or alteration.

[2] ["My first dash into poetry was as early as 1800. It was the ebullition of a passion for my first cousin, Margaret Parker (daughter and grand-daughter of the two Admirals Parker), one of the most beauti-

ful of evanescent beings. I have long forgotten the verse; but it would be difficult for me to forget her — her dark eyes — her long eye-lashes — her completely Greek cast of face and figure! I was then about twelve — she rather older, perhaps a year. She died about a year or two afterwards, in consequence of a fall, which injured her spine, and induced consumption. Her sister Augusta (by some thought still more beautiful) died of the same malady; and it was, indeed, in attending her, that Margaret met with the accident which occasioned her death. My sister told me, that when she went to see her, shortly before her death, upon accidentally mentioning my name, Margaret colored, throughout the paleness of mortality, to the eyes, to the great astonishment of my sister, who knew nothing of our attachment, nor could conceive why my name should affect her at such a time. I knew nothing of her illness — being at Harrow and in the country — till she was gone. Some years after, I made an attempt at an elegy — a very dull one. I do not recollect scarcely any thing equal to the transparent beauty of my cousin, or to the sweetness of her temper, during the short period of our intimacy. She looked as if she had been made out of a rainbow — all beauty and peace." — *Byron's Diary*, 1821.]

[3] [This little poem, and some others in the collection, refer to a boy of Byron's own age, son of one of his tenants at Newstead, for whom he had formed

True, she has forced thee from my breast,
  Yet, in my heart thou keep'st thy seat;
There, there thine image still must rest,
  Until that heart shall cease to beat.

And, when the grave restores her dead,
  When life again to dust is given,
On thy dear breast I'll lay my head—
  Without thee, where would be my heaven?

                     February, 1803.

EPITAPH ON A FRIEND.

"Ἀστὴρ πρὶν μὲν ἔλαμπες ἐνὶ ζωοῖσιν ἐῷος."
                          LAERTIUS.

OH Friend! for ever loved, for ever dear!
What fruitless tears have bathed thy honored
    bier!
What sighs re-echoed to thy parting breath,
Whilst thou wast struggling in the pangs of
    death!
Could tears retard the tyrant in his course;
Could sighs avert his dart's relentless force;
Could youth and virtue claim a short delay,
Or beauty charm the spectre from his prey;
Thou still hadst lived to bless my aching sight,
Thy comrade's honor and thy friend's delight[1]
If yet thy gentle spirit hover nigh
The spot where now thy mouldering ashes lie,
Here wilt thou read, recorded on my heart,
A grief too deep to trust the sculptor's art.
No marble marks thy couch of lowly sleep,
But living statues there are seen to weep;
Affliction's semblance bends not o'er thy tomb,

---

a romantic attachment, previous to any of his school
intimacies.]

  [1] From this point the lines in the private edition
were entirely different:
"Though low thy lot, since in a cottage born
  No titles did thy humble name adorn,
  To me, far dearer was thy artless love
  Than all the joys wealth, fame, and friends
    could prove:
For thee alone I lived, or wished to live;
Oh God! if impious, this rash word forgive!
Heart-broken now, I wait an equal doom,
Content to join thee in thy turf-clad tomb;
Where, this frail form composed in endless rest,
I'll make my last cold pillow on thy breast;
That breast where oft in life I've laid my head,
Will yet receive me mouldering with the dead;
This life resigned, without one parting sigh,
Together in one bed of earth we'll lie!
Together share the fate to mortals given;
Together mix our dust, and hope for heaven."
  The epitaph is supposed to commemorate the
youth who is the subject of the verses " To
E——." The latter piece was omitted in the
published volume, which, coupled with the oblit-
eration of every allusion to his humble origin in
the epitaph, led Moore to infer that growing pride
of rank made Byron ashamed of the plebeian
friendship.]

Affliction's self deplores thy youthful doom.
What though thy sire lament his failing line,
A father's sorrows cannot equal mine!
Though none, like thee, his dying hour will
    cheer,
Yet other offspring soothe his anguish here:
But, who with me shall hold thy former place?
Thine image, what new friendship can efface?
Ah, none!—a father's tears will cease to flow,
Time will assuage an infant brother's woe;
To all, save one, is consolation known,
While solitary friendship sighs alone.
                         1802.

A FRAGMENT.

WHEN, to their airy hall, my fathers' voice
Shall call my spirit, joyful in their choice;
When, poised upon the gale, my form shall ride,
Or, dark in mist, descend the mountain's side;
Oh! may my shade behold no sculptured urns
To mark the spot where earth to earth returns!
No lengthened scroll, no praise-encumbered
    stone;
My epitaph shall be my name alone:[2]
If *that* with honor fail to crown my clay,
Oh! may no other fame my deeds repay!
That, only *that*, shall single out the spot;
By that remembered, or with that forgot.
                         1803

ON LEAVING NEWSTEAD ABBEY.[3]

  " Why dost thou build the hall, son of the winged
days? Thou lookest from thy tower to-day: yet a
few years, and the blast of the desert comes, it howls
in thy empty court." — OSSIAN.

THROUGH thy battlements, Newstead, the
    hollow winds whistle;
Thou, the hall of my fathers, art gone to
    decay;
In thy once smiling garden, the hemlock and
    thistle
Have choked up the rose which late
    bloomed in the way.

---

  [2] [By his will, drawn up in 1811, Byron directed,
that "no inscription, save his name and age, should
be written on his tomb;" and, in 1819, he wrote
thus to Mr. Murray:—"Some of the epitaphs at
the Cartosa cemetery, at Ferrara, pleased me more
than the more splendid monuments at Bologna;
for instance —
           'Martini Luigi
           Implora pace.'
Can any thing be more full of pathos? I hope who-
ever may survive me will see those two words, and
no more. put over me."]

  [3] [The priory of Newstead, or de Novo Loco, in
Sherwood, was founded about the year 1170, by
Henry II. On the dissolution of the monasteries, it

Of the mail-covered Barons, who proudly to battle
  Led their vassals from Europe to Palestine's plain,[1]
The escutcheon and shield, which with every blast rattle,   •
  Are the only sad vestiges now that remain.

No more doth old Robert, with harp-stringing numbers,
  Raise a flame in the breast for the war-laurelled wreath;
Near Askalon's towers, John of Horistan[2] slumbers,
  Unnerved is the hand of his minstrel by death.

Paul and Hubert, too, sleep in the valley of Cressy;[3]
  For the safety of Edward and England they fell;
My father! the tears of your country redress ye;
  How you fought, how you died, still her annals can tell.

On Marston,[4] with Rupert, 'gainst traitors contending,
  Four brothers enriched with their blood the bleak field;
For the rights of a monarch their country defending,
  Till death their attachment to royalty sealed.

Shades of heroes, farewell! your descendant departing
  From the seat of his ancestors, bids you adieu!
Abroad, or at home, your remembrance imparting
  New courage, he'll think upon glory and you.

Though a tear dim his eye at this sad separation,
  'Tis nature, not fear, that excites his regret;

Far distant he goes, with the same emulation,
  The fame of his fathers he ne'er can forget.

That fame, and that memory, still will he cherish;
  He vows that he ne'er will disgrace your renown;
Like you will he live, or like you will he perish:
  When decayed, may he mingle his dust with your own!   1803.

LINES,

WRITTEN IN "LETTERS OF AN ITALIAN NUN
AND AN ENGLISH GENTLEMAN: BY J. J.
ROUSSEAU: FOUNDED ON FACTS."

"AWAY, away, your flattering arts
May now betray some simpler hearts;
And you will smile at their believing,
And they shall weep at your deceiving."

ANSWER TO THE FOREGOING, ADDRESSED
TO MISS ——.

Dear, simple girl, those flattering arts,
From which thou'dst guard frail female hearts,
Exist but in imagination, —
Mere phantoms of thine own creation;
For he who views that witching grace,
That perfect form, that lovely face,
With eyes admiring, oh! believe me,
He never wishes to deceive thee:
Once in thy polished mirror glance,
Thou'lt there descry that elegance
Which from our sex demands such praises,
But envy in the other raises:
Then he who tells thee of thy beauty,
Believe me, only does his duty:
Ah! fly not from the candid youth;
It is not flattery, — 'tis truth.
                                July, 1804.

ADRIAN'S ADDRESS TO HIS SOUL
WHEN DYING.

[ANIMULA! vagula, blandula,
Hospes, comesque corporis,
Quæ nunc abibis in loca —
Pallidula, rigida, nudula,
Nec, ut soles, dabis jocos?]

AH! gentle, fleeting, wavering sprite,
Friend and associate of this clay!
  To what unknown region borne,
Wilt thou now wing thy distant flight?
No more with wonted humor gay,
  But pallid, cheerless, and forlorn.

---

was granted by Henry VIII. to "Sir John Byron the Little, with the great beard," whose portrait is still preserved at Newstead.]

  [1] [There is no record of the Byrons having been engaged in the Holy Wars, and Moore conjectures, that the only authority for the notion was some groups of heads, which appear to represent Christian soldiers and Saracens on the old panel-work at Newstead.]

  [2] [Horistan Castle in Derbyshire was an ancient seat of the Byrons. Some ruins of it are yet visible in the park of Horseley.]

  [3] [Two of the family of Byron are enumerated as serving with distinction in the siege of Calais, under Edward III., and as among the knights who fell on the glorious field of Cressy.]

  [4] The battle of Marston Moor, where the adherents of Charles I. were defeated.

TRANSLATION FROM CATULLUS.

AD LESBIAM.

EQUAL to Jove that youth must be —
Greater than Jove he seems to me —
Who, free from Jealousy's alarms,
Securely views thy matchless charms.
That cheek, which ever dimpling glows,
That mouth, from whence such music flows
To him, alike, are always known,
Reserved for him, and him alone.
Ah! Lesbia! though 'tis death to me,
I cannot choose but look on thee;
But, at the sight, my senses fly;
I needs must gaze, but, gazing, die;
Whilst trembling with a thousand fears,
Parched to the throat my tongue adheres,
My pulse beats quick, my breath heaves short,
My limbs deny their slight support,
Cold dews my pallid face o'erspread,
With deadly languor droops my head,
My ears with tingling echoes ring,
And life itself is on the wing;
My eyes refuse the cheering light,
Their orbs are veiled in starless night:
Such pangs my nature sinks beneath,
And feels a temporary death.

TRANSLATION OF THE EPITAPH ON VIRGIL AND TIBULLUS.

BY DOMITIUS MARSUS.

HE who sublime in epic numbers rolled
   And he who struck the softer lyre of love,
By Death's [1] unequal hand alike controlled,
   Fit comrades in Elysian regions move!

IMITATION OF TIBULLUS.

"Sulpicia ad Cerinthum." — *Lib.* 4.

CRUEL Cerinthus! does the fell disease
Which racks my breast your fickle bosom
   please?
Alas! I wished but to o'ercome the pain,
That I might live for love and you again:
But now I scarcely shall bewail my fate:
By death alone I can avoid your hate.

TRANSLATION FROM CATULLUS.

[Lugete, Veneres, Cupidinesque, etc.]

YE Cupids, droop each little head
Nor let your wings with joy be spread,

My Lesbia's favorite bird is dead,
   Whom dearer than her eyes she loved;
For he was gentle, and so true,
Obedient to her call he flew,
No fear, no wild alarm he knew,
   But lightly o'er her bosom moved:

And softly fluttering here and there,
He never sought to cleave the air,
But chirrupped oft, and, free from care,
   Tuned to her ear his grateful strain.
Now having passed the gloomy bourne
From whence he never can return,
His death and Lesbia's grief I mourn,
   Who sighs, alas! but sighs in vain.

Oh! curst be thou, devouring grave!
Whose jaws eternal victims crave,
From whom no earthly power can save,
   For thou hast ta'en the bird away:
From thence the flow my Lesbia's eyes o'erflow,
Her swollen cheeks with weeping glow;
Thou art the cause of all her woe,
   Receptacle of life's decay.

IMITATED FROM CATULLUS.

TO ELLEN.

OH! might I kiss those eyes of fire,
A million scarce would quench desire:
Still would I steep my lips in bliss,
And dwell an age on every kiss:
Nor then my soul should sated be;
Still would I kiss and cling to thee:
Nought should my kiss from thine dissever;
Still would we kiss, and kiss for ever;
E'en though the numbers did exceed
The yellow harvest's countless seed.
To part would be a vain endeavor:
Could I desist? — ah! never — never!

TRANSLATION FROM HORACE.

[Justum et tenacem propositi virum, etc.]

THE man of firm and noble soul
No factious clamors can control,
No threat'ning tyrant's darkling brow
   Can swerve him from his just intent:
Gales the warring waves which plough,
   By Auster on the billows sent
To curb the Adriatic main,
Would awe his fixed determined mind in vain.

Ay, and the red right arm of Jove,
Hurtling his lightnings from above,
With all his terrors there unfurled,
   He would, unmoved, unawed behold.
The flames of an expiring world,

---

[1] [The hand of Death is said to be unjust or unequal, as Virgil was considerably older than Tibullus at his decease.]

Again in crashing chaos rolled,
In vast promiscuous ruin hurled,
Might light his glorious funeral pile:
Still dauntless 'midst the wreck of earth he'd
  smile.

FROM ANACREON.

[θέλω λέγειν 'Ατρείδας, κ. τ. λ.]

I WISH to tune my quivering lyre
To deeds of fame and notes of fire;
To echo, from its rising swell,
How heroes fought and nations fell,
When Atreus' sons advanced to war,
Or Tyrian Cadmus roved afar;
But still, to martial strains unknown,
My lyre recurs to love alone.
Fired with the hope of future fame,
I seek some nobler hero's name;
The dying chords are strung anew,
To war, to war, my harp is due:
With glowing strings, the epic strain
To Jove's great son I raise again:
Alcides and his glorious deeds,
Beneath whose arm the Hydra bleeds.
All, all in vain; my wayward lyre
Wakes silver notes of soft desire.
Adieu, ye chiefs renowned in arms!
Adieu the clang of war's alarms!
To other deeds my soul is strung,
And sweeter notes shall now be sung;
My harp shall all its powers reveal,
To tell the tale my heart must feel;
Love, Love alone, my lyre shall claim,
In songs of bliss and sighs of flame.

FROM ANACREON.

[Μεσονυκτίαις ποθ' ώραις, κ. τ. λ.]

TWAS now the hour when Night had driven
Her car half round yon sable heaven;
Boötes, only, seemed to roll
His arctic charge around the pole;
While mortals, lost in gentle sleep,
Forgot to smile, or ceased to weep,
At this lone hour, the Paphian boy,
Descending from the realms of joy,
Quick to my gate directs his course,
And knocks with all his little force.
My visions fled, alarmed I rose, —
"What stranger breaks my blest repose?"
"Alas!" replies the wily child
In faltering accents sweetly mild,
"A hapless infant here I roam,
Far from my dear maternal home.
Oh! shield me from the wintry blast!
The nightly storm is pouring fast.
No prowling robber lingers here.

A wandering baby who can fear?"
I heard his seeming artless tale,
I heard his sighs upon the gale:
My breast was never pity's foe,
But felt for all the baby's woe.
I drew the bar, and by the light
Young Love, the infant, met my sight;
His bow across his shoulders flung,
And thence his fatal quiver hung
(Ah! little did I think the dart
Would rankle soon within my heart).
With care I tend my weary guest,
His little fingers chill my breast;
His glossy curls, his azure wing,
Which droop with nightly showers, I wring,
His shivering limbs the embers warm;
And now reviving from the storm,
Scarce had he felt his wonted glow,
Than swift he seized his slender bow: —
" I fain would know, my gentle host,"
He cried, " if this its strength has lost;
I fear, relaxed with midnight dews,
The strings their former aid refuse."
With poison tipt, his arrow flies,
Deep in my tortured heart it lies;
Then loud the joyous urchin laughed: —
" My bow can still impel the shaft:
'Tis firmly fixed, thy sighs reveal it;
Say, courteous host, canst thou not feel it?"

FROM THE PROMETHEUS VINCTUS
OF ÆSCHYLUS.

[Μηδάμ' ὁ πάντα νέμων, κ. τ. λ.]

GREAT Jove, to whose almighty throne
  Both gods and mortals homage pay,
Ne'er may my soul thy power disown,
  Thy dread behests ne'er disobey.
Oft shall the sacred victim fall
In sea-girt Ocean's mossy hall;
My voice shall raise no impious strain
'Gainst him who rules the sky and azure main.

How different now thy joyless fate,
  Since first Hesione thy bride,
When placed aloft in godlike state,
  The blushing beauty by thy side,
Thou sat'st, while reverend Ocean smiled,
And mirthful strains the hours beguiled,
The Nymphs and Tritons danced around,
Nor yet thy doom was fixed, nor Jove relent-
  less frowned.[1]

HARROW, Dec. 1, 1804.

---

[1] [" My first Harrow verses, (that is, English, as
Exercises,) a translation of a chorus from the Pro-
metheus of Æschylus, were received by Dr. Drury,
my grand patron (our head-master), but coolly. No
one had, at that time, the least notion that I should
subside into poesy." — *Byron's Diary.*]

TO EMMA.

SINCE now the hour is come at last,
  When you must quit your anxious lover;
Since now our dream of bliss is past,
  One pang, my girl, and all is over.

Alas! that pang will be severe,
  Which bids us part to meet no more;
Which tears me far from one so dear,
  Departing for a distant shore.

Well! we have passed some happy hours,
  And joy will mingle with our tears;
When thinking on these ancient towers,
  The shelter of our infant years;

Where from this Gothic casement's height,
  We viewed the lake, the park, the dell,
And still, though tears obstruct our sight,
  We lingering look a last farewell,

O'er fields through which we used to run,
  And spend the hours in childish play;
O'er shades where, when our race was done,
  Reposing on my breast you lay;

Whilst I, admiring, too remiss,
  Forgot to scare the hovering flies,
Yet envied every fly the kiss
  It dared to give your slumbering eyes:

See still the little painted bark,
  In which I rowed you o'er the lake;
See there, high waving o'er the park,
  The elm I clambered for your sake.

These times are past—our joys are gone,
  You leave me, leave this happy vale;
These scenes I must retrace alone:
  Without thee what will they avail?

Who can conceive, who has not proved,
  The anguish of a last embrace?
When, torn from all you fondly loved,
  You bid a long adieu to peace.

This is the deepest of our woes,
  For this these tears our cheeks bedew:
This is of love the final close,
  Oh, God! the fondest, last adieu!

TO M. S. G.

WHENE'ER I view those lips of thine,
  Their hue invites my fervent kiss;
Yet, I forego that bliss divine,
  Alas! it were unhallowed bliss.

Whene'er I dream of that pure breast,
  How could I dwell upon its snows!
Yet is the daring wish represt,
  For that,—would banish its repose.

A glance from thy soul-searching eye
  Can raise with hope, depress with fear;

Yet I conceal my love,—and why?
  I would not force a painful tear.

I ne'er have told my love, yet thou
  Hast seen my ardent flame too well;
And shall I plead my passion now,
  To make thy bosom's heaven a hell?

No! for thou never canst be mine,
  United by the priest's decree:
By any ties but those divine,
  Mine, my beloved, thou ne'er shalt be.

Then let the secret fire consume,
  Let it consume, thou shalt not know:
With joy I court a certain doom,
  Rather than spread its guilty glow.

I will not ease my tortured heart,
  By driving dove-eyed peace from thine;
Rather than such a sting impart,
  Each thought presumptuous I resign.

Yes! yield those lips, for which I'd brave
  More than I here shall dare to tell;
Thy innocence and mine to save,—
  I bid thee now a last farewell.

Yes! yield that breast, to seek despair,
  And hope no more thy soft embrace;
Which to obtain my soul would dare
  All, all reproach, but thy disgrace.

At least from guilt shalt thou be free,
  No matron shall thy shame reprove;
Though cureless pangs may prey on me,
  No martyr shalt thou be to love.

TO CAROLINE.

THINK'ST thou I saw thy beauteous eyes,
  Suffused in tears, implore to stay,
And heard unmoved thy plenteous sighs,
  Which said far more than words can say?

Though keen the grief thy tears exprest,
  When love and hope lay both o'erthrown;
Yet still, my girl, this bleeding breast
  Throbbed with deep sorrow as thine own.

But when our cheeks with anguish glowed,
  When our sweet lips were joined to mine,
The tears that from my eyelids flowed
  Were lost in those which fell from thine.

Thou could'st not feel my burning cheek,
  Thy gushing tears had quenched its flame,
And as thy tongue essayed to speak,
  In sighs alone it breathed my name.

And yet, my girl, we weep in vain,
  In vain our fate in sighs deplore;
Remembrance only can remain,—
  But that will make us weep the more.

Again, thou best beloved, adieu!
  Ah! if thou canst, o'ercome **regret**,
Nor let thy mind past joys review, —
  Our only hope is to forget!

TO CAROLINE.

WHEN I hear you express an affection so warm,
  Ne'er think, my beloved, that I do not
    believe;
For your lip would the soul of suspicion disarm,
  And your eye beams a ray which can never
    deceive.

Yet, still, this fond bosom regrets, while adoring,
  That love, like the leaf, must fall into the
    sear;
That age will come on, when remembrance,
  deploring,
  Contemplates the scenes of her youth with
    a tear;

That the time must arrive, when, no longer
  retaining
  Their auburn, those locks must wave thin
    to the breeze,
When a few silver hairs of those tresses re-
  maining,
  Prove nature a prey to decay and disease.

'Tis this. my beloved, which spreads gloom
  o'er my features,
  Though I ne'er shall presume to arraign
    the decree
Which God has proclaimed as the fate of his
  creatures,
  In the death which one day will deprive
    you of me.

Mistake not, sweet sceptic, the cause of emotion,
  No doubt can the mind of your lover in-
    vade;
He worships each look with such faithful de-
  votion,
  A smile can enchant, or a tear can dissuade.

But as death, my beloved, soon or late shall
  o'ertake us,
  And our breasts, which alive with such
    sympathy glow,
Will sleep in the grave till the blast shall
  awake us,
  When calling the dead in earth's bosom
    laid low, —

Oh! then let us drain, while we may, draughts
  of pleasure,
  Which from passion like ours may un-
    ceasingly flow;
Let us pass round the cup of love's bliss in
  full measure,
  And quaff the contents as our nectar below.
                    1805.

TO CAROLINE.

OH! when shall the grave hide for ever my
  sorrow?
  Oh! when shall my soul wing her flight
    from this clay?
The present is hell, and the coming to-morrow
  But brings, with new torture, the curse of
    to-day.

From my eye flows no tear from my lips flow
  no curses,
  I blast not the fiends who have hurled me
    from bliss;
For poor is the soul which bewailing rehearses
  Its querulous grief, when in anguish like
    this.

Was my eye, 'stead of tears, with red fury
  flakes bright'ning,
  Would my lips breathe a flame which no
    stream could assuage,
On our foes should my glance launch in
  vengeance its lightning,
  With transport my tongue give a loose to
    its rage.

But now tears and curses, alike unavailing,
  Would add to the souls of our tyrants de-
    light;
Could they view us our sad separation be-
  wailing,
  Their merciless hearts would rejoice at the
    sight.

Yet still, though we bend with a feigned resig-
  nation,
  Life beams not for us with one ray that can
    cheer;
Love and hope upon earth bring no more
  consolation,
  In the grave is our hope, for in life is our
    fear.

Oh! when, my adored, in the tomb will they
  place me,
  Since, in life, love and friendship for ever
    are fled?
If again in the mansion of death I embrace
  thee,
  Perhaps they will leave unmolested the
    dead.   1805.

STANZAS TO A LADY,

WITH THE POEMS OF CAMOENS.[1]

THIS votive pledge of fond esteem,
  Perhaps, dear girl! for me thou'lt prize;
It sings of Love's enchanting dream,
  A theme we never can despise.

---

[1] [Lord Strangford's translation of Camoens's
Amatory Poems was at this period a favorite study
with Byron.]

Who blames it but the envious fool,
  The old and disappointed maid;
Or pupil of the prudish school,
  In single sorrow doomed to fade?

Then read, dear girl! with feeling read,
  For thou wilt ne'er be one of those;
To thee in vain I shall not plead
  In pity for the poet's woes.

He was in sooth a genuine bard;
  His was no faint, fictitious flame:
Like his, may love be thy reward,
  But not thy hapless fate the same.[1]

THE FIRST KISS OF LOVE.

'Α βάρβιτος δὲ χορδαῖς
'Ερωτα μοῦνον ἠχεῖ. — ANACREON.

AWAY with your fictions of flimsy romance;
  Those tissues of falsehood which folly has
    wove!
Give me the mild beam of the soul-breathing
    glance,
  Or the rapture which dwells on the first kiss
    of love.

Ye rhymers, whose bosoms with phantasy glow,
  Whose pastoral passions are made for the
    grove;
From what blest inspiration your sonnets
    would flow,
  Could you ever have tasted the first kiss of
    love!

If Apollo should e'er his assistance refuse,
  Or the Nine be disposed from your service
    to rove,
Invoke them no more, bid adieu to the muse,
  And try the effect of the first kiss of love.

I hate you, ye cold compositions of art:
  Though prudes may condemn me, and big-
    ots reprove,
I court the effusions that spring from the heart,
  Which throbs with delight to the first kiss
    of love.

Your shepherds, your flocks, those fantastical
    themes,
  Perhaps may amuse, yet they never can
    move:
Arcadia displays but a region of dreams;
  What are visions like these to the first kiss
    of love?

Oh! cease to affirm that man, since his birth,
  From Adam till now, has with wretchedness
    strove;
Some portion of paradise still is on earth,
  And Eden revives in the first kiss of love.

---

[1] [Camoens ended in an alms-house a life of mis-
fortunes.]

When age chills the blood, when our pleas-
    ures are past —
For years fleet away with the wings of the
    dove —
The dearest remembrance will still be the last,
  Our sweetest memorial the first kiss of love.

ON A CHANGE OF MASTERS AT A GREAT PUBLIC SCHOOL.[2]

WHERE are those honors, Ida! once your
    own,
When Probus filled your magisterial throne?
As ancient Rome, fast falling to disgrace,
Hailed a barbarian in her Cæsar's place,
So you, degenerate, share as hard a fate,
And seat Pomposus where your Probus sate.
Of narrow brain, yet of a narrower soul,
Pomposus holds you in his harsh control;
Pomposus, by no social virtue swayed,
With florid jargon, and with vain parade;
With noisy nonsense, and new-fangled rules,
Such as were ne'er before enforced in schools,
Mistaking pedantry for learning's laws,
He governs, sanctioned but by self-applause.
With him, the same dire fate attending Rome,
Ill-fated Ida! soon must stamp your doom:
Like her o'erthrown, for ever lost to fame,
No trace of science left you, but the name.
                              July, 1805.

TO THE DUKE OF DORSET.[3]

DORSET! whose early steps with mine have
    strayed,
Exploring every path of Ida's glade;
Whom still affection taught me to defend,
And made me less a tyrant than a friend,

[2] [In March, 1805, Dr. Drury, the "Probus" of
this piece, retired from his situation of head-master
at Harrow, and was succeeded by Dr. Butler, the
"Pomposus." Of the former Byron says in his
Diary, "Dr. Drury, whom I plagued sufficiently,
was the best, the kindest (and yet strict, too) friend
I ever had; and I look upon him still as a father."
Of Dr. Butler he says, — "I treated him rebel-
liously, and have been sorry ever since."]

[3] In looking over my papers to select a few addi-
tional poems for this second edition, I found the
above lines, which I had totally forgotten, composed
in the summer of 1805, a short time previous to my
departure from Harrow. They were addressed to a
young schoolfellow of high rank, who had been my
frequent companion in some rambles through the
neighboring country: however, he never saw the
lines, and most probably never will. As, on a re-
perusal, I found them not worse than some other
pieces in the collection, I have now published them,
for the first time, after a slight revision.
[George-John-Frederick, fourth Duke of Dorset,
born November 15, 1793, was killed by a fall from
his horse, while hunting near Dublin, February 22
1815.]

Though the harsh custom of our youthful band
Bade *thee* obey, and gave *me* to command;[1]
Thee, on whose head a few short years will
    shower
The gift of riches and the pride of power;
E'en now a name illustrious is thine own,
Renowned in rank, not far beneath the throne.
Yet, Dorset, let not this seduce thy soul
To shun fair science, or evade control,
Though passive tutors,[2] fearful to dispraise
The titled child, whose future breath may raise,
View ducal errors with indulgent eyes,
And wink at faults they tremble to chastise.
    When youthful parasites, who bend the knee
To wealth, their golden idol, not to thee, —
And even in simple boyhood's opening dawn
Some slaves are found to flatter and to fawn, —
When these declare, "that pomp alone should
    wait
On one by birth predestined to be great;
That books were only meant for drudging
    fools,
That gallant spirits scorn the common rules;"
Believe them not; — they point the path to
    shame,
And seek to blast the honors of thy name.
Turn to the few in Ida's early throng,
Whose souls disdain not to condemn the
    wrong;
Or if, amidst the comrades of thy youth,
None dare to raise the sterner voice of truth,
Ask thine own heart; 'twill bid thee, boy, for-
    bear;
For *well* I know that virtue lingers there.
    Yes! I have marked thee many a passing
    day,
But now new scenes invite me far away;
Yes! I have marked within that generous mind
A soul, if well matured, to bless mankind.
Ah! though myself, by nature haughty, wild,
Whom Indiscretion hailed her favorite child;
Though every error stamps me for her own,
And dooms my fall, I fain would fall alone;
Though my proud heart no precept now can
    tame,
I love the virtues which I cannot claim.
    'Tis not enough, with other sons of power,
To gleam the lambent meteor of an hour;
To swell some peerage page in feeble pride,
With long-drawn names that grace no page
    beside;
Then share with titled crowds the common
    lot—

In life just gazed at, in the grave forgot;
While nought divides thee from the vulgar
    dead,
Except the dull cold stone that hides thy head,
The mouldering 'scutcheon, or the herald's
    roll,
That well-emblazoned but neglected scroll,
Where lords, unhonored, in the tomb may find
One spot, to leave a worthless name behind.
There sleep, unnoticed as the gloomy vaults
That veil their dust, their follies, and their
    faults,
A race, with old armorial lists o'erspread,
In records destined never to be read.
Fain would I view thee, with prophetic eyes,
Exalted more among the good and wise,
A glorious and a long career pursue,
As first in rank, the first in talent too:
Spurn every vice, each little meanness shun;
Not Fortune's minion, but her noblest son.
    Turn to the annals of a former day;
Bright are the deeds thine earlier sires dis-
    play.
One, though a courtier, lived a man of worth,
And called, proud boast! the British drama
    forth.[3]
Another view, not less renowned for wit;
Alike for courts, and camps, or senates fit;
Bold in the field, and favored by the Nine;
In every splendid part ordained to shine;
Far, far distinguished from the glittering
    throng,
The pride of princes, and the boast of song.[4]
Such were thy fathers; thus preserve their
    name;
Not heir to titles only, but to fame.
The hour draws nigh, a few brief days will
    close,
To me, this little scene of joys and woes;
Each knell of Time now warns me to resign
Shades where Hope, Peace, and Friendship all
    were mine:
Hope, that could vary like the rainbow's hue,
And gild their pinions as the moments flew;
Peace, that reflection never frowned away,
By dreams of ill to cloud some future day;
Friendship, whose truth let childhood only tell;

---

[1] At every public school the junior boys are completely subservient to the upper forms till they attain a seat in the higher classes. From this state of probation, very properly no rank is exempt: but after a certain period, they command in turn those who succeed.

[2] Allow me to disclaim any personal allusions, even the most distant. I merely mention generally what is too often the weakness of preceptors.

[3] ["Thomas Sackville, Lord Buckhurst, created Earl of Dorset by James I., was one of the earliest and brightest ornaments to the poetry of his country, and the first who produced a regular drama." — *Anderson's Poets.*]

[4] ["Charles Sackville, Earl of Dorset, born in 1637, and died in 1706, esteemed the most accomplished man of his day, was alike distinguished in the voluptuous court of Charles II. and the gloomy one of William III. He behaved with great gallantry in the sea-fight with the Dutch in 1665; on the day previous to which he composed his celebrated song, 'To all you Ladies now at Land.' His character has been drawn in the highest colors by Dryden, Pope, Prior, and Congreve." — *Anderson's Poets.*]

Alas! they love not long, who love so well.
To these adieu! nor let me linger o'er
Scenes hailed, as exiles hail their native shore,
Receding slowly through the dark-blue deep,
Beheld by eyes that mourn, yet cannot weep.
Dorset, farewell! I will not ask one part
Of sad remembrance in so young a heart;
The coming morrow from thy youthful mind
Will sweep my name, nor leave a trace behind.
And yet, perhaps, in some maturer year,
Since chance has thrown us in the self-same sphere,
Since the same senate, nay, the same debate,
May one day claim our suffrage for the state,
We hence may meet, and pass each other by
With faint regard, or cold and distant eye.
For me, in future, neither friend nor foe,
A stranger to thyself, thy weal or woe,
With thee no more again I hope to trace
The recollection of our early race;
No more, as once, in social hours rejoice,
Or hear, unless in crowds, thy well-known voice:
Still, if the wishes of a heart untaught
To veil those feelings which perchance it ought,
If these, — but let me cease the lengthened strain, —
Oh! if these wishes are not breathed in vain,
The guardian seraph who directs thy fate
Will leave thee glorious, as he found thee great.[1]

1805.

FRAGMENT.

WRITTEN SHORTLY AFTER THE MARRIAGE OF MISS CHAWORTH.[2]

HILLS of Annesley, bleak and barren,
  Where my thoughtless childhood strayed,
How the northern tempests, warring,
  Howl above thy tufted shade!

Now no more, the hours beguiling,
  Former favorite haunts I see;
Now no more my Mary smiling
  Makes ye seem a heaven to me. 1805.

---

[1] [I have just been, or rather ought to be, very much shocked by the death of the Duke of Dorset. We were at school together, and there I was passionately attached to him. Since, we have never met, but once, I think, since 1805 — and it would be a paltry affectation to pretend that I had any feeling for him worth the name. But there was a time in my life when this event would have broken my heart; and all I can say for it now is, that — it is not worth breaking. — *Byron's Letters*, 1815.]

[2] [Miss Chaworth was married to John Musters, Esq., in August, 1805.]

GRANTA. A MEDLEY.

Ἀργυρέαις λόγχαισι μάχου, καὶ πάντα κρατήσεις

OH! could Le Sage's[3] demon's gift
  Be realized at my desire,
This night my trembling form he'd lift
  To place it on St. Mary's spire.

Then would, unroofed, old Granta's halls
  Pedantic inmates full display;
Fellows who dream on lawn or stalls,
  The price of venal votes to pay.

Then would I view each rival wight,
  Petty and Palmerston survey;
Who canvass there with all their might,
  Against the next elective day.[4]

Lo! candidates and voters lie,
  All lulled in sleep, a goodly number:
A race renowned for piety,
  Whose conscience won't disturb their slumber.

Lord Hawke, indeed, may not demur;
  Fellows are sage reflecting men:
They know preferment can occur
  But very seldom, — now and then.

They know the Chancellor has got
  Some pretty livings in disposal:
Each hopes that one may be his lot,
  And therefore smiles on his proposal.

Now from the soporific scene
  I'll turn mine eye, as night grows later.
To view, unheeded and unseen,
  The studious sons of Alma Mater.

There, in apartments small and damp,
  The candidate for college prizes
Sits poring by the midnight lamp;
  Goes late to bed, yet early rises.

He surely well deserves to gain them,
  With all the honors of his college,
Who, striving hardly to obtain them,
  Thus seeks unprofitable knowledge·

Who sacrifices hours of rest
  To scan precisely metres attic;
Or agitates his anxious breast
  In solving problems mathematic.

Who reads false quantities in Seale,-
  Or puzzles o'er the deep triangle;

---

[3] The Diable Boiteux of Le Sage, where Asmodeus, the demon, places Don Cleofas on an elevated situation, and unroofs the houses for inspection.

[4] [On the death of Mr. Pitt, in January, 1806, Lord Henry Petty and Lord Palmerston were candidates to represent the University of Cambridge in Parliament.]

[5] Seale's publication on Greek Metres displays considerable talent and ingenuity, but, as might be

Deprived of many a wholesome meal;
  In barbarous Latin [1] doomed to wrangle:

Renouncing every pleasing page
  From authors of historic use;
Preferring to the lettered sage,
  The square of the hypothenuse.[2]

Still, harmless are these occupations,
  That hurt none but the hapless student,
Compared with other recreations,
  Which bring together the imprudent;

Whose daring revels shock the sight,
  When vice and infamy combine,
When drunkenness and dice invite,
  As every sense is steeped in wine.

Not so the methodistic crew,
  Who plans of reformation lay:
In humble attitude they sue,
  And for the sins of others pray:

Forgetting that their pride of spirit,
  Their exultation in their trial,
Detracts most largely from the merit
  Of all their boasted self-denial.

'Tis morn:—from these I turn my sight.
  What scene is this which meets the eye?
A numerous crowd, arrayed in white,[3]
  Across the green in numbers fly.

Loud rings in air the chapel bell;
  'Tis hushed:—what sounds are these I hear?
The organ's soft celestial swell
  Rolls deeply on the listening ear.

To this is joined the sacred song,
  The royal minstrel's hallowed strain;
Though he who hears the music long
  Will never wish to hear again.

Our choir would scarcely be excused,
  Even as a band of raw beginners;
All mercy now must be refused
  To such a set of croaking sinners.

If David, when his toils were ended,
  Had heard these blockheads sing before him,
To us his psalms had ne'er descended,—
  In furious mood he would have tore 'em.

The luckless Israelites, when taken
  By some inhuman tyrant's order,

Were asked to sing, by joy forsaken,
  On Babylonian river's border.

Oh! had they sung in notes like these,
  Inspired by stratagem or fear,
They might have set their hearts at ease,
  The devil a soul had stayed to hear.

But if I scribble longer now,
  The deuce a soul will stay to read:
My pen is blunt, my ink is low;
  'Tis almost time to stop, indeed.

Therefore, farewell, old Granta's spires!
  No more, like Cleofas, I fly;
No more thy theme my muse inspires:
  The reader's tired, and so am I.   1806.

ON A DISTANT VIEW OF THE VILLAGE AND SCHOOL OF HARROW ON THE HILL.

Oh! mihi præteritos referat si Jupiter annos.
                               VIRGIL.

YE scenes of my childhood, whose loved recollection
  Embitters the present, compared with the past;
Where science first dawned on the powers of reflection,
  And friendships were formed, too romantic to last;[4]

Where fancy yet joys to retrace the resemblance
  Of comrades, in friendship and mischief allied;
How welcome to me your ne'er fading remembrance,
  Which rests in the bosom, though hope is denied!

Again I revisit the hills where we sported,
  The streams where we swam, and the fields where we fought;[5]
The school where, loud warned by the bell, we resorted,
  To pore o'er the precepts by pedagogues taught.

Again I behold where for hours I have pondered,
  As reclining, at eve, on yon tombstone[6] I lay;

---

expected in so difficult a work, is not remarkable for accuracy.

  [1] The Latin of the schools is of the *canine species,* and not very intelligible.

  [2] The discovery of Pythagoras, that the square of the hypothenuse is equal to the squares of the other two sides of a right angled triangle.

  [3] On a saint's day, the students wear surplices in chapel.

  [4] ["My school-friendships were with me *passions* (for I was always violent), but I do not know that there is one which has endured (to be sure some have been cut short by death) till now." — *Byron's Diary*, 1821.]

  [5] ["At Harrow I fought my way very fairly. I think I lost but one battle out of seven." — *Ibid.*]

  [6] A tomb in the churchyard at Harrow was so

Or round the steep brow of the churchyard I
    wandered,
  To catch the last gleam of the sun's setting
    ray.

I once more view the room, with spectators
    surrounded,
  Where, as Zanga,[1] I trod on Alonzo o'er-
    thrown;
While, to swell my young pride, such ap-
    plauses resounded,
  I fancied that Mossop[2] himself was out-
    shone:

Or, as Lear, I poured forth the deep impre-
    cation,
  By my daughters, of kingdom and reason
    deprived;
Till, fired by loud plaudits[3] and self-adulation,
  I regarded myself as a Garrick revived.

Ye dreams of my boyhood, how much I re-
    gret you!
  Unfaded your memory dwells in my breast;
Though sad and deserted, I ne'er can forget
    you:
  Your pleasures may still be in fancy possest.

To Ida full oft may remembrance restore me,
  While fate shall the shades of the future
    unroll!
Since darkness o'ershadows the prospect be-
    fore me,
  More dear is the beam of the past to my soul.

But if, through the course of the years which
    await me,
  Some new scene of pleasure should open to
    view,
I will say, while with rapture the thought shall
    elate me,
  ' Oh! such were the days which my infancy
    knew.''   1806.

———

TO M——.

OH! did those eyes, instead of fire,
  With bright but mild affection shine,
Though they might kindle less desire,
  Love, more than mortal, would be thine.

For thou art formed so heavenly fair,
  Howe'er those orbs may wildly beam,
We must admire, but still despair;
  That fatal glance forbids esteem.

When Nature stamped thy beauteous birth,
  So much perfection in thee shone,
She feared that, too divine for earth,
  The skies might claim thee for their own·

Therefore, to guard her dearest work,
  Lest angels might dispute the prize,
She bade a secret lightning lurk
  Within those once celestial eyes.

These might the boldest sylph appall,
  When gleaming with meridian blaze;
Thy beauty must enrapture all;
  But who can dare thine ardent gaze?

'Tis said that Berenice's hair
  In stars adorns the vault of heaven;
But they would ne'er permit thee there,
  Thou wouldst so far outshine the seven.

For did those eyes as planets roll,
  Thy sister-lights would scarce appear:
E'en suns, which systems now control,
  Would twinkle dimly through their sphere.[4]
                                         1800.

———

TO WOMAN.

WOMAN! experience might have told me
That all must love thee who behold thee:
Surely experience might have taught
Thy firmest promises are nought;
But, placed in all thy charms before me,
All I forget, but to adore thee.
Oh memory! thou choicest blessing
When joined with hope, when still possessing;
But how much cursed by every lover
When hope is fled and passion's over.
Woman, that fair and fond deceiver,
How prompt are striplings to believe her!
How throbs the pulse when first we view
The eye that rolls in glossy blue,
Or sparkles black, or mildly throws
A beam from under hazel brows!
How quick we credit every oath,
And hear her plight the willing troth!
Fondly we hope 'twill last for aye,
When, lo! she changes in a day.
This record will for ever stand,
  " Woman, thy vows are traced in sand."[5]

---

well known to be his favorite resting-place, that the
boys called it " Byron's Tomb;" and here, they
say, he used to sit for hours, wrapt up in thought. —
Moore.]
  [1] [For the display of his declamatory powers, on
the speech-days, he selected always the most vehe-
ment passages; such as the speech of Zanga over
the body of Alonzo, and Lear's address to the storm.
— *Moore.*]
  [2] Mossop, a contemporary of Garrick, famous for
his performance of Zanga.
  [3] "My grand patron, Dr. Drury, had a great
notion that I should turn out an orator, from my

fluency, my turbulence, my voice, my copiousness
of declamation, and my action." — *Diary.*
  [4] " Two of the fairest stars in all the heaven,
      Having some business, do intreat her eyes
      To twinkle in their spheres till they return."
                                      SHAKSPEARE.
  [5] The last line is almost a literal translation from a
Spanish proverb.

TO M. S. G.

WHEN I dream that you love me, you'll surely
    forgive;
    Extend not your anger to sleep;
For in visions alone your affection can live,—
    I rise, and it leaves me to weep.

Then, Morpheus! envelop my faculties fast,
    Shed o'er me your languor benign;
Should the dream of to-night but resemble the
    last,
    What rapture celestial is mine!

They tell us that slumber, the sister of death,
    Mortality's emblem is given;
To fate how I long to resign my frail breath,
    If this be a foretaste of heaven!

Ah! frown not, sweet lady, unbend your soft
    brow,
    Nor deem me too happy in this;
If I sin in my dream, I atone for it now,
    Thus doomed but to gaze upon bliss.

Though in visions, sweet lady, perhaps you
    may smile,
    Oh! think not my penance deficient!
When dreams of your presence my slumbers
    beguile,
    To awake will be torture sufficient.

———

TO MARY,

ON RECEIVING HER PICTURE.[1]

THIS faint resemblance of thy charms,
    Though strong as mortal art could give,
My constant heart of fear disarms,
    Revives my hopes, and bids me live.

Here I can trace the locks of gold
    Which round thy snowy forehead wave,
The cheeks which sprung from beauty's mould,
    The lips which made me beauty's slave.

Here I can trace—ah, no! that eye,
    Whose azure floats in liquid fire,
Must all the painter's art defy,
    And bid him from the task retire.

Here I behold its beauteous hue;
    But where's the beam so sweetly straying
Which gave a lustre to its blue,
    Like Luna o'er the ocean playing?

Sweet copy! far more dear to me,
    Lifeless, unfeeling as thou art,

Than all the living forms could be,
    Save her who placed thee next my heart.

She placed it, sad, with needless fear,
    Lest time might shake my wavering soul,
Unconscious that her image there
    Held every sense in fast control.

Through hours, through years, through time
    'twill cheer;
    My hope, in gloomy moments, raise;
In life's last conflict 'twill appear,
    And meet my fond expiring gaze.

———

TO LESBIA.

LESBIA! since far from you I've ranged,
    Our souls with fond affection glow not;
You say 'tis I, not you, have changed,
    I'd tell you why,—but yet I know not.

Your polished brow no cares have crost;
    And, Lesbia! we are not much older
Since, trembling, first my heart I lost,
    Or told my love, with hope grown bolder.

Sixteen was then our utmost age,
    Two years have lingering past away, love!
And now new thoughts our minds engage,
    At least I feel disposed to stray, love!

'Tis I that am alone to blame,
    I, that am guilty of love's treason;
Since your sweet breast is still the same,
    Caprice must be my only reason.

I do not, love! suspect your truth,
    With jealous doubt my bosom heaves not
Warm was the passion of my youth,
    One trace of dark deceit it leaves not.

No, no, my flame was not pretended;
    For, oh! I loved you most sincerely;
And—though our dream at last is ended—
    My bosom still esteems you dearly.

No more we meet in yonder bowers;
    Absence has made me prone to roving;
But older, firmer hearts than ours
    Have found monotony in loving.

Your cheek's soft bloom is unimpaired,
    New beauties still are daily bright'ning,
Your eye for conquest beams prepared,
    The forge of love's resistless lightning.

Armed thus, to make their bosoms bleed,
    Many will throng to sigh like me, love!
More constant they may prove, indeed;
    Fonder, alas! they ne'er can be, love!

———

[1] [Of this "Mary," who is not to be confounded with the heiress of Annesley, or "Mary" of Aberdeen, all I can record is, that she was of an humble, if not equivocal, station in life,—and that she had long light golden hair, of which he used to show a lock as well as her picture, among his friends.—*Moore.*]

LINES ADDRESSED TO A YOUNG LADY.

[As the author was discharging his pistols in a garden, two ladies passing near the spot were alarmed by the sound of a bullet hissing near them; to one of whom the following stanzas were addressed the next morning.] [1]

DOUBTLESS, sweet girl! the hissing lead,
    Wafting destruction o'er thy charms,
And hurtling o'er thy lovely head,
    Has filled that breast with fond alarms.

Surely some envious demon's force,
    Vexed to behold such beauty here,
Impelled the bullet's viewless course,
    Diverted from its first career.

Yes! in that nearly fatal hour
    The ball obeyed some hell-born guide;
But Heaven, with interposing power,
    In pity turned the death aside.

Yet, as perchance one trembling tear
    Upon that thrilling bosom fell;
Which I, th' unconscious cause of fear,
    Extracted from its glistening cell:

Say, what dire penance can atone
    For such an outrage done to thee?
Arraigned before thy beauty's throne,
    What punishment wilt thou decree?

Might I perform the judge's part,
    The sentence I should scarce deplore;
It only would restore a heart
    Which but belonged to thee before.

The least atonement I can make
    Is to become no longer free;
Henceforth I breathe but for thy sake,
    Thou shalt be all in all to me.

But thou, perhaps, may'st now reject
    Such expiation of my guilt:
Come then, some other mode elect;
    Let it be death, or what thou wilt.

Choose then, relentless! and I swear
    Nought shall thy dread decree prevent;
Yet hold — one little word forbear!
    Let it be aught but banishment.

LOVE'S LAST ADIEU.

'Αεί, δ' ἀεί με φεύγει. — ANACREON.

THE roses of love glad the garden of life,
    Though nurtured 'mid weeds dropping pestilent dew,

[1] [The occurrence took place at Southwell, and the beautiful lady to whom the lines were addressed was Miss Houson.]

Till time crops the leaves with unmerciful knife,
    Or prunes them for ever, in love's last adieu!

In vain with endearments we soothe the sad heart,
    In vain do we vow for an age to be true;
The chance of an hour may command us to part,
    Or death disunite us in love's last adieu!

Still Hope, breathing peace through the grief-swollen breast,
    Will whisper, "Our meeting we yet may renew:"
With this dream of deceit half our sorrow's represt,
    Nor taste we the poison of love's last adieu!

Oh! mark you yon pair: in the sunshine of youth
    Love twined round their childhood his flowers as they grew;
They flourish awhile in the season of truth,
    Till chilled by the winter of love's last adieu!

Sweet lady! why thus doth a tear steal its way
    Down a cheek which outrivals thy bosom in hue?
Yet why do I ask? — to distraction a prey
    Thy reason has perished with love's last adieu!

Oh! who is yon misanthrope, shunning mankind?
    From cities to caves of the forest he flew:
There, raving, he howls his complaint to the wind;
    The mountains reverberate love's last adieu!

Now hate rules a heart which in love's easy chains
    Once passion's tumultuous blandishments knew;
Despair now inflames the dark tide of his veins;
    He ponders in frenzy on love's last adieu!

How he envies the wretch with a soul wrapt in steel!
    His pleasures are scarce, yet his troubles are few,
Who laughs at the pang that he never can feel,
    And dreads not the anguish of love's last adieu!

Youth flies, life decays, even hope is o'ercast;
    No more with love's former devotion we sue:
He spreads his young wing, he retires with the blast;
    The shroud of affection is love's last adieu!

In this life of probation for rapture divine,
    Astrea declares that some penance is due:

From him who has worshipped at love's gen-
  tle shrine,
  The atonement is ample in love's last adieu!

Who kneels to the god, on his altar of light
  Must myrtle and cypress alternately strew:
His myrtle, an emblem of purest delight;
  His cypress the garland of love's last adieu!

DAMÆTAS.

IN law an infant,[1] and in years a boy,
In mind a slave to every vicious joy;
From every sense of shame and virtue weaned;
In lies an adept, in deceit a fiend;
Versed in hypocrisy, while yet a child;
Fickle as wind, of inclinations wild;
Woman his dupe, his heedless friend a tool;
Old in the world, though scarcely broke from
  school;
Damætas ran through all the maze of sin,
And found the goal when others just begin:
Even still conflicting passions shake his soul,
And bid him drain the dregs of pleasure's
  bowl;
But, palled with vice, he breaks his former
  chain,
And what was once his bliss appears his bane.[2]

TO MARION.

MARION! why that pensive brow?
What disgust to life hast thou?
Change that discontented air;
Frowns become not one so fair.
'Tis not love disturbs thy rest,
Love's a stranger to thy breast;
He in dimpling smiles appears,
Or mourns in sweetly timid tears,
Or bends the languid eyelid down,

---

[1] In law every person is an infant who has not
attained the age of twenty-one.

[2] ["When I went up to Trinity, in 1805, at the
age of seventeen and a half, I was miserable and
untoward to a degree. I was wretched at leaving
Harrow — wretched at going to Cambridge instead
of Oxford — wretched from some private domestic
circumstances of different kinds; and, consequently,
about as unsocial as a wolf taken from the troop."
— *Diary*. Moore adds, "The sort of life which
young Byron led at this period, between the dissi-
pations of London and of Cambridge, without a
home to welcome, or even the roof of a single rela-
tive to receive him, was but little calculated to ren-
der him satisfied either with himself or the world.
Unrestricted as he was by deference to any will but
his own, even the pleasures to which he was natu-
rally most inclined prematurely palled upon him,
for want of those best zests of all enjoyment — rarity
and restraint." Byron evidently meant Damætas
for a portrait of himself.]

But shuns the cold forbidding frown.
Then resume thy former fire,
Some will love, and all admire;
While that icy aspect chills us,
Nought but cool indifference thrills us.
Wouldst thou wandering hearts beguile,
Smile at least, or seem to smile.
Eyes like thine were never meant
To hide their orbs in dark restraint;
Spite of all thou fain wouldst say,
Still in truant beams they play.
Thy lips — but here my modest Muse
Her impulse chaste must needs refuse:
She blushes, curt'sies, frowns, — in short she
Dreads lest the subject should transport me;
And flying off in search of reason,
Brings prudence back in proper season.
All I shall therefore say (whate'er
I think, is neither here nor there)
Is, that such lips, of looks endearing,
Were formed for better things than sneering.
Of soothing compliments divested,
Advice at least's disinterested;
Such is my artless song to thee,
From all the flow of flattery free;
Counsel like mine is as a brother's,
My heart is given to some others;
That is to say, unskilled to cozen,
It shares itself among a dozen.
Marion, adieu! oh, pr'ythee slight not
This warning, though it may delight not;
And, lest my precepts be displeasing
To those who think remonstrance teasing,
At once I'll tell thee our opinion
Concerning woman's soft dominion:
Howe'er we gaze with admiration
On eyes of blue or lips carnation,
Howe'er the flowing locks attract us,
Howe'er those beauties may distract us,
Still fickle, we are prone to rove,
These cannot fix our souls to love:
It is not too severe a stricture
To say they form a pretty picture;
But wouldst thou see the secret chain
Which binds us in your humble train,
To hail you queens of all creation,
Know, in a word, 'tis ANIMATION.

TO A LADY

WHO PRESENTED TO THE AUTHOR A LOCK
OF HAIR BRAIDED WITH HIS OWN, AND
APPOINTED A NIGHT IN DECEMBER TO
MEET HIM IN THE GARDEN.[3]

THESE locks, which fondly thus entwine,
In firmer chains our hearts confine,
Than all th' unmeaning protestations
Which swell with nonsense love orations.

---

[3] See *ante*, p. 15, note.

Our love is fixed, I think we've proved it,
Nor time, nor place, nor art have moved it;
Then wherefore should we sigh and whine,
With groundless jealousy repine,
With silly whims and fancies frantic,
Merely to make our love romantic?
Why should you weep like Lydia Languish,
And fret with self-created anguish?
Or doom the lover you have chosen,
On winter nights to sigh half frozen;
In leafless shades to sue for pardon,
Only because the scene's a garden?
For gardens seem, by one consent,
Since Shakspeare set the precedent,
Since Juliet first declared her passion,
To form the place of assignation.[1]
Oh! would some modern muse inspire,
And seat her by a sea-coal fire;
Or had the bard at Christmas written,
And laid the scene of love in Britain,
He surely, in commiseration,
Had changed the place of declaration.
In Italy I've no objection;
Warm nights are proper for reflection;
But here our climate is so rigid,
That love itself is rather frigid:
Think on our chilly situation,
And curb this rage for imitation;
Then let us meet, as oft we've done,
Beneath the influence of the sun;   .
Or, if at midnight I must meet you,
Within your mansion let me greet you:
There we can love for hours together,
Much better, in such snowy weather,
Than placed in all th' Arcadian groves
That ever witnessed rural loves;
Then, if my passion fail to please,
Next night I'll be content to freeze;
No more I'll give a loose to laughter,
But curse my fate for ever after.[2]

---

[1] In the above little piece the author has been accused by some *candid readers* of introducing the name of a lady from whom he was some hundred miles distant at the time this was written; and poor Juliet, who has slept so long in " the tomb of all the Capulets," has been converted, with a trifling alteration of her name, into an English damsel, walking in a garden of their own creation, during the month of *December*, in a village where the author never passed a winter. Such has been the candor of some ingenious critics. We would advise these *liberal* commentators on taste and arbiters of decorum to read *Shakspeare.*

[2] Having heard that a very severe and indelicate censure has been passed on the above poem, I beg leave to reply in a quotation from an admired work, " Carr's Stranger in France." — " As we were contemplating a painting on a large scale, in which, among other figures, is the uncovered whole length of a warrior, a prudish-looking lady, who seemed to have touched the age of desperation, after having attentively surveyed it through her glass, observed to her party, that there was a great deal of indecorum in that picture. Madame S. shrewdly whis-

OSCAR OF ALVA.[3]

A TALE.

How sweetly shines through azure skies,
    The lamp of heaven on Lora's shore;
Where Alva's hoary turrets rise,
    And hear the din of arms no more.

But often has yon rolling moon
    On Alva's casques of silver played;
And viewed, at midnight's silent noon,
    Her chiefs in gleaming mail arrayed:

And on the crimsoned rocks beneath,
    Which scowl o'er ocean's sullen flow,
Pale in the scattered ranks of death,
    She saw the gasping warrior low;

While many an eye which ne'er again
    Could mark the rising orb of day,
Turned feebly from the gory plain,
    Beheld in death her fading ray.

Once to those eyes the lamp of Love,
    They blest her dear propitious light;
But now she glimmered from above,
    A sad, funereal torch of night.

Faded is Alva's noble race,
    And gray her towers are seen afar;
No more her heroes urge the chase,
    Or roll the crimson tide of war.

But, who was last of Alva's clan?
    Why grows the moss on Alva's stone?
Her towers resound no steps of man,
    They echo to the gale alone.

And when that gale is fierce and high,
    A sound is heard in yonder hall;
It rises hoarsely through the sky,
    And vibrates o'er the mouldering wall.

Yes, when the eddying tempest sighs,
    It shakes the shield of Oscar brave;
But there no more his banners rise,
    No more his plumes of sable wave.

Fair shone the sun on Oscar's birth,
    When Angus hailed his eldest born;
The vassals round their chieftain's hearth
    Crowd to applaud the happy morn.

They feast upon the mountain deer,
    The pibroch raised its piercing note;[4]

---

pered in my ear, ' that the indecorum was in the remark.' "

[3] The catastrophe of this tale was suggested by the story of " Jeronyme and Lorenzo," in the first volume of Schiller's "Armenian, or the Ghost-Seer." It also bears some resemblance to a scene in the third act of " Macbeth."

[4] [Byron falls into a very common error, that of mistaking *pibroch*, which means a particular sort of tune, for the instrument on which it is played, the bagpipe.]

To gladden more their highland cheer,
  The strains in martial numbers float:

And they who heard the war-notes wild
  Hoped that one day the pibroch's strain
Should play before the hero's child
  While he should lead the tartan train.

Another year is quickly past,
  And Angus hails another son;
His natal day is like the last,
  Nor soon the jocund feast was done.

Taught by their sire to bend the bow,
  On Alva's dusky hills of wind,
The boys in childhood chased the roe,
  And left their hounds in speed behind.

But ere their years of youth are o'er,
  They mingle in the ranks of war;
They lightly wheel the bright claymore,
  And send the whistling arrow far.

Dark was the flow of Oscar's hair,
  Wildly it streamed along the gale;
But Allan's locks were bright and fair,
  And pensive seemed his cheek, and pale.

But Oscar owned a hero's soul,
  His dark eye shone through beams of truth;
Allan had early learned control,
  And smooth his words had been from youth.

Both, both were brave; the Saxon spear
  Was shivered oft beneath their steel;
And Oscar's bosom scorned to fear,
  But Oscar's bosom knew to feel;

While Allan's soul belied his form,
  Unworthy with such charms to dwell:
Keen as the lightning of the storm,
  On foes his deadly vengeance fell.

From high Southannon's distant tower
  Arrived a young and noble dame;
With Kenneth's lands to form her dower,
  Glenalvon's blue-eyed daughter came;

And Oscar claimed the beauteous bride,
  And Angus on his Oscar smiled:
It soothed the father's feudal pride
  Thus to obtain Glenalvon's child.

Hark to the pibroch's pleasing note!
  Hark to the swelling nuptial song;
In joyous strains the voices float,
  And still the choral peal prolong.

See how the heroes' blood-red plumes
  Assembled wave in Alva's hall!
Each youth his varied plaid assumes,
  Attending on their chieftain's call.

It is not war their aid demands,
  The pibroch plays the song of peace;
To Oscar's nuptials throng the bands,
  Nor yet the sounds of pleasure cease.

But where is Oscar? sure 'tis late:
  Is this a bridegroom's ardent flame?
While thronging guests and ladies wait,
  Nor Oscar nor his brother came.

At length young Allan joined the bride:
  "Why comes not Oscar," Angus said:
"Is he not here?" the youth replied;
  "With me he roved not o'er the glade:

"Perchance, forgetful of the day,
  'Tis his to chase the bounding roe;
Or ocean's waves prolong his stay;
  Yet Oscar's bark is seldom slow."

"Oh, no!" the anguished sire rejoined,
  "Nor chase, nor wave, my boy delay;
Would he to Mora seem unkind?
  Would aught to her impede his way?

"Oh, search, ye chiefs! oh, search around!
  Allan, with these through Alva fly;
Till Oscar, till my son is found,
  Haste, haste, nor dare attempt reply."

All is confusion — through the vale
  The name of Oscar hoarsely rings,
It rises on the murmuring gale,
  Till night expands her dusky wings;

It breaks the stillness of the night,
  But echoes through her shades in vain,
It sounds through morning's misty light,
  But Oscar comes not o'er the plain.

Three days, three sleepless nights, the Chief
  For Oscar searched each mountain cave;
Then hope is lost; in boundless grief,
  His locks in gray-torn ringlets wave.

"Oscar! my son! — thou God of Heaven
  Restore the prop of sinking age!
Or if that hope no more is given,
  Yield his assassin to my rage.

"Yes, on some desert rocky shore
  My Oscar's whitened bones must lie;
Then grant, thou God! I ask no more
  With him his frantic sire may die!

"Yet he may live, — away, despair!
  Be calm, my soul! he yet may live;
T' arraign my fate, my voice forbear!
  O God! my impious prayer forgive.

"What, if he live for me no more,
  I sink forgotten in the dust,
The hope of Alva's age is o'er:
  Alas! can pangs like these be just?"

Thus did the hapless parent mourn,
  Till Time, who soothes severest woe,
Had bade serenity return,
  And made the tear-drop cease to flow.

For still some latent hope survived
  That Oscar might once more appear;

His hope now drooped and now revived,
  Till Time had told a tedious year.

Days rolled along, the orb of light
  Again had run his destined race;
No Oscar blessed his father's sight,
  And sorrow left a fainter trace.

For youthful Allan still remained,
  And now his father's only joy:
And Mora's heart was quickly gained,
  For beauty crowned the fair-haired boy.

She thought that Oscar low was laid,
  And Allan's face was wondrous fair;
If Oscar lived, some other maid
  Had claimed his faithless bosom's care.

And Angus said, if one year more
  In fruitless hope was passed away,
His fondest scruples should be o'er,
  And he would name their nuptial day.

Slow rolled the moons, but blest at last
  Arrived the dearly destined morn;
The year of anxious trembling past,
  What smiles the lovers' cheeks adorn!

Hark to the pibroch's pleasing note!
  Hark to the swelling nuptial song!
In joyous strains the voices float,
  And still the choral peal prolong.

Again the clan, in festive crowd,
  Throng through the gate of Alva's hall;
The sounds of mirth reëcho loud,
  And all their former joy recall.

But who is he, whose darkened brow
  Glooms in the midst of general mirth?
Before his eyes' far fiercer glow
  The blue flames curdle o'er the hearth.

Dark is the robe which wraps his form,
  And tall his plume of gory red;
His voice is like the rising storm,
  But light and trackless is his tread.

'Tis noon of night, the pledge goes round,
  The bridegroom's health is deeply quaffed;
With shouts the vaulted roofs resound,
  And all combine to hail the draught.

Sudden the stranger-chief arose,
  And all the clamorous crowd are hushed;
And Angus' cheek with wonder glows,
  And Mora's tender bosom blushed.

"Old man!" he cried, "this pledge is done;
  Thou saw'st 'twas duly drank by me;
It hailed the nuptials of thy son:
  Now will I claim a pledge from thee.

"While all around is mirth and joy,
  To bless thy Allan's happy lot,
Say, had'st thou ne'er another boy?
  Say, why should Oscar be forgot?"

"Alas!" the hapless sire replied,
  The big tears starting as he spoke,
"When Oscar left my hall, or died,
  This aged heart was almost broke.

"Thrice has the earth revolved her course
  Since Oscar's form has blest my sight;
And Allan is my last resource,
  Since martial Oscar's death or flight."

"'Tis well," replied the stranger stern,
  And fiercely flashed his rolling eye;
"Thy Oscar's fate I fain would learn;
  Perhaps the hero did not die.

"Perchance, if those whom most he loved
  Would call, thy Oscar might return;
Perchance the chief has only roved;
  For him thy Beltane [1] yet may burn.

"Fill high the bowl the table round,
  We will not claim the pledge by stealth;
With wine let every cup be crowned;
  Pledge me departed Oscar's health."

"With all my soul," old Angus said,
  And filled his goblet to the brim;
"Here's to my boy! alive or dead,
  I ne'er shall find a son like him."

"Bravely, old man, this health has sped;
  But why does Allan trembling stand?
Come, drink remembrance of the dead,
  And raise thy cup with firmer hand."

The crimson glow of Allan's face
  Was turned at once to ghastly hue;
The drops of death each other chase
  Adown in agonizing dew.

Thrice did he raise the goblet high,
  And thrice his lips refused to taste;
For thrice he caught the stranger's eye
  On his with deadly fury placed.

"And is it thus a brother hails
  A brother's fond remembrance here?
If thus affection's strength prevails,
  What might we not expect from fear?"

Roused by the sneer, he raised the bowl,
  "Would Oscar now could share our mirth!"
Internal fear appalled his soul;
  He said, and dashed the cup to earth.

"'Tis he! I hear my murderer's voice!"
  Loud shrieks a darkly gleaming form;
"A murderer's voice!" the roof replies,
  And deeply swells the bursting storm.

The tapers wink, the chieftains shrink,
  The stranger's gone, — amidst the crew

---

[1] Beltane Tree, a Highland festival on the first
of May, held near fires lighted for the occasion.
  [*Beal-tain* means the fire of Baal, and the name
still preserves the primeval origin of this Celtic
superstition.]

A form was seen in tartan green,
And tall the shade terrific grew.

His waist was bound with a broad belt round,
His plume of sable streamed on high;
But his breast was bare, with the red wounds there,
And fixed was the glare of his glassy eye.

And thrice he smiled, with his eye so wild,
On Angus bending low the knee;
And thrice he frowned on a chief on the ground,
Whom shivering crowds with horror see.

The bolts loud roll, from pole to pole,
The thunders through the welkin ring,
And the gleaming form, through the mist of the storm,
Was borne on high by the whirlwind's wing.

Cold was the feast, the revel ceased.
Who lies upon the stony floor?
Oblivion pressed old Angus' breast,
At length his life-pulse throbs once more.

"Away, away! let the leech essay
To pour the light on Allan's eyes:"
His sand is done,—his race is run;
Oh! never more shall Allan rise!

But Oscar's breast is cold as clay,
His locks are lifted by the gale;
And Allan's barbed arrow lay
With him in dark Glentanar's vale.

And whence the dreadful stranger came,
Or who, no mortal wight can tell;
But no one doubts the form of flame,
For Alva's sons knew Oscar well.

Ambition nerved young Allan's hand,
Exulting demons winged his dart;
While Envy waved her burning brand,
And poured her venom round his heart.

Swift is the shaft from Allan's bow;
Whose streaming life-blood stains his side?
Dark Oscar's sable crest is low,
The dart has drunk his vital tide.

And Mora's eye could Allan move,
She bade his wounded pride rebel;
Alas! that eyes which beam'd with love
Should urge the soul to deeds of hell.

Lo! seest thou not a lonely tomb
Which rises o'er a warrior dead?
It glimmers through the twilight gloom;
Oh! that is Allan's nuptial bed.

Far, distant far, the noble grave
Which held his clan's great ashes stood;
And o'er his corse no banners wave,
For they were stained with kindred blood.

What minstrel gray, what hoary bard,
Shall Allan's deeds on harp-strings raise?
The song is glory's chief reward,
But who can strike a murderer's praise?

Unstrung, untouched, the harp must stand,
No minstrel dare the theme awake;
Guilt would benumb his palsied hand,
His harp in shuddering chords would break.

No lyre of fame, no hallowed verse,
Shall sound his glories high in air:
A dying father's bitter curse,
A brother's death-groan echoes there.

THE EPISODE OF NISUS AND EURYALUS.

A PARAPHRASE FROM THE ÆNEID, LIB. IX.

NISUS the guardian of the portal, stood,
Eager to gild his arms with hostile blood;
Well skilled in fight the quivering lance to wield,
Or pour his arrows through th' embattled field:
From Ida torn, he left his sylvan cave,
And sought a foreign home, a distant grave.
To watch the movements of the Daunian host,
With him Euryalus sustains the post;
No lovelier mien adorned the ranks of Troy,
And beardless bloom yet graced the gallant boy,
Though few the seasons of his youthful life,
As yet a novice in the martial strife,
'Twas his, with beauty, valor's gifts to share—
A soul heroic, as his form was fair:
These burn with one pure flame of generous love;
In peace, in war, united still they move;
Friendship and glory form their joint reward;
And now combined they hold their nightly guard.

"What God," exclaimed the first, "instils this fire?
Or, in itself a god, what great desire?
My laboring soul, with anxious thought oppressed,
Abhors this station of inglorious rest;
The love of fame with this can ill accord,
Be't mine to seek for glory with my sword.
Seest thou yon camp, with torches twinkling dim,
Where drunken slumbers wrap each lazy limb?
Where confidence and ease the watch disdain,
And drowsy Silence holds her sable reign?
Then hear my thought:—In deep and sullen grief
Our troops and leaders mourn their absent chief:

Now could the gifts and promised prize be
    thine
(The deed, the danger, and the fame be mine),
Were this decreed, beneath yon rising mound,
Methinks, an easy path perchance were found;
Which past, I speed my way to Pallas' walls,
And lead Æneas from Evander's halls."

With equal ardor fired, and warlike joy,
His glowing friend addressed the Dardan
    boy:—
"These deeds, my Nisus, shalt thou dare
    alone?
Must all the fame, the peril, be thine own?
Am I by thee despised, and left afar,
As one unfit to share the toils of war?
Not thus his son the great Opheltes taught;
Not thus my sire in Argive combats fought;
Not thus, when Ilion fell by heavenly hate,
I tracked Æneas through the walks of fate:
Thou know'st my deeds, my breast devoid of
    fear,
And hostile life-drops dim my gory spear.
Here is a soul with hope immortal burns,
And life, ignoble life, for *glory* spurns.
Fame, fame is cheaply earned by fleeting
    breath:
The price of honor is the sleep of death."

Then Nisus,—"Calm thy bosom's fond
    alarms:
Thy heart beats fiercely to the din of arms.
More dear thy worth and valor than my own,
I swear by him who fills Olympus' throne!
So may I triumph, as I speak the truth,
And clasp again the comrade of my youth!
But should I fall,—and he who dares advance
Through hostile legions must abide by
    chance,—
If some Rutulian arm, with adverse blow,
Should lay the friend who ever loved thee low,
Live thou; such beauties I would fain pre-
    serve,
Thy budding years a lengthened term deserve.
When humbled in the dust, let some one be,
Whose gentle eyes will shed one tear for me;
Whose manly arm may snatch me back by
    force,
Or wealth redeem from foes my captive corse;
Or, if my destiny these last deny,
If in the spoiler's power my ashes lie,
Thy pious care may raise a simple tomb,
To mark thy love, and signalize my doom.
Why should thy doting wretched mother weep
Her only boy, reclined in endless sleep?
Who, for thy sake, the tempest's fury dared,
Who, for thy sake, war's deadly peril shared;
Who braved what woman never braved before,
And left her native for the Latian shore."
"In vain you damp the ardor of my soul,"
Replied Euryalus; 'It scorns control!
Hence, let us haste!"—Their brother guards
    arose,

Roused by their call, nor court again repose;
The pair, buoyed up on Hope's exulting wing,
Their stations leave, and speed to seek the
    king.

Now o'er the earth a solemn stillness ran,
And lulled alike the cares of brute and man;
Save where the Dardan leaders nightly hold
Alternate converse, and their plans unfold.
On one great point the council are agreed,
An instant message to their prince decreed;
Each leaned upon the lance he well could
    wield,
And poised with easy arm his ancient shield;
When Nisus and his friend their leave request
To offer something to their high behest.
With anxious tremors, yet unawed by fear,
The faithful pair before the throne appear:
Iulus greets them; at his kind command,
The elder first addressed the hoary band.

"With patience" (thus Hyrtacides began)
"Attend, nor judge from youth our humble
    plan.
Where yonder beacons half expiring beam,
Our slumbering foes of future conquest dream,
Nor heed that we a secret path have traced,
Between the ocean and the portal placed,
Beneath the covert of the blackening smoke,
Whose shade securely our design will cloak!
If you, ye chiefs, and fortune will allow,
We'll bend our course to yonder mountain's
    brow,
Where Pallas' walls at distance meet the sight,
Seen o'er the glade, when not obscured by
    night:
Then shall Æneas in his pride return,
While hostile matrons raise their offspring's
    urn;
And Latian spoils and purpled heaps of dead
Shall mark the havoc of our hero's tread.
Such is our purpose, not unknown the way;
Where yonder torrent's devious waters stray,
Oft have we seen, when hunting by the stream,
The distant spires above the valleys gleam."

Mature in years, for sober wisdom famed,
Moved by the speech, Alethes here exclaimed,
"Ye parent gods! who rule the fate of Troy,
Still dwells the Dardan spirit in the boy;
When minds like these in striplings thus ye
    raise,
Yours is the godlike act, be yours the praise;
In gallant youth, my fainting hopes revive,
And Ilion's wonted glories still survive."
Then in his warm embrace the boys he pressed,
And, quivering, strained them to his aged
    breast;
With tears the burning cheek of each bedewed,
And, sobbing, thus his first discourse renewed:
"What gift, my countrymen, what martial prize
Can we bestow, which you may not despise?
Our deities the first best boon have given—

Internal virtues are the gift of Heaven.
What poor rewards can bless your deeds on
   earth,
Doubtless await such young, exalted worth.
Æneas and Ascanius shall combine
To yield applause far, far surpassing mine."
Iulus then: — "By all the powers above!
By those Penates who my country love!
By hoary Vesta's sacred fane, I swear,
My hopes are all in you, ye generous pair!
Restore my father to my grateful sight,
And all my sorrows yield to one delight.
Nisus! two silver goblets are thine own,
Saved from Arisba's stately domes o'erthrown!
My sire secured them on that fatal day,
Nor left such bowls an Argive robber's prey:
Two massy tripods, also, shall be thine;
Two talents polished from the glittering mine;
An ancient cup, which Tyrian Dido gave,
While yet our vessels pressed the Punic wave:
But when the hostile chiefs at length bow
   down,
When great Æneas wears Hesperia's crown,
The casque, the buckler, and the fiery steed
Which Turnus guides with more than mortal
   speed,
Are thine; no envious lot shall then be cast,
I pledge my word, irrevocably past:
Nay more, twelve slaves, and twice six captive
   dames
To soothe thy softer hours with amorous
   flames,
And all the realms which now the Latins sway
The labors of to-night shall well repay.
But thou, my generous youth, whose tender
   years
Are near my own, whose worth my heart
   reveres,
Henceforth affection, sweetly thus begun,
Shall join our bosoms and our souls in one;
Without thy aid, no glory shall be mine;
Without thy dear advice, no great design;
Alike through life esteemed, thou godlike boy,
In war my bulwark, and in peace my joy."

To him Euryalus: — "No day shall shame
The rising glories which from this I claim.
Fortune may favor, or the skies may frown,
But valor, spite of fate, obtains renown.
Yet, ere from hence our eager steps depart,
One boon I beg, the nearest to my heart:
My mother, sprung from Priam's royal line,
Like thine ennobled, hardly less divine,
Nor Troy nor king Acestes' realms restrain
Her feeble age from dangers of the main;
Alone she came, all selfish fears above,
A bright example of maternal love.
Unknown the secret enterprise I brave,
Lest grief should bend my parent to the grave;
From this alone no fond adieus I seek,
No fainting mother's lips have pressed my
   cheek;

By gloomy night and thy right hand I vow
Her parting tears would shake my purpose
   now:
Do thou, my prince, her failing age sustain
In thee her much-loved child may live again·
Her dying hours with pious conduct bless,
Assist her wants, relieve her fond distress:
So dear a hope must all my soul inflame,
To rise in glory, or to fall in fame."
Struck with a filial care so deeply felt,
In tears at once the Trojan warriors melt:
Faster than all, Iulus' eyes o'erflow;
Such love was his, and such had been his woe.
"All thou hast asked, receive," the prince re-
   plied;
"Nor this alone, but many a gift beside.
To cheer thy mother's years shall be my aim,
Creusa's [1] style but wanting to the dame.
Fortune an adverse wayward course may run,
But bless'd thy mother in so dear a son.
Now, by my life! — my sire's most sacred
   oath —
To thee I pledge my full; my firmest troth,
All the rewards which once to thee were vowed,
If thou shouldst fall, on her shall be bestowed."
Thus spoke the weeping prince, then forth to
   View
A gleaming falchion from the sheath he drew;
Lycaon's utmost skill had graced the steel,
For friends to envy and for foes to feel:
A tawny hide, the Moorish lion's spoil,
Slain 'midst the forest, in the hunter's toil,
Mnestheus to guard the elder youth bestows,
And old Alethes' casque defends his brows.
Armed, thence they go, while all th' assembled
   train
To aid their cause, implore the gods in vain.
More than a boy, in wisdom and in grace,
Iulus holds amidst the chiefs his place:
His prayer he sends; but what can prayers
   avail,
Lost in the murmurs of the sighing gale!

The trench is passed, and, favored by the
   night,
Through sleeping foes they wheel their wary
   flight.
When shall the sleep of many a foe be o'er?
Alas! some slumber who shall wake no more!
Chariots and bridles, mixed with arms, are
   seen;
And flowing flasks, and scattered troops be-
   tween:
Bacchus and Mars to rule the camp combine;
A mingled chaos this of war and wine.
"Now," cries the first, "for deeds of blood
   prepare,
With me the conquest and the labor share:
Here lies our path; lest any hand arise,

[1] The mother of Iulus, lost on the night when
Troy was taken.

Watch thou, while many a dreaming chieftain
   dies:
I'll carve our passage through the heedless foe,
And clear thy road with many a deadly blow."
His whispering accents then the youth re-
   pressed,
And pierced proud Rhamnes through his
   panting breast:
Stretched at his ease, th' incautious king re-
   posed;
Debauch, and not fatigue, his eyes had closed:
To Turnus dear, a prophet and a prince,
His omens more than augur's skill evince;
But he, who thus foretold the fate of all,
Could not avert his own untimely fall.
Next Remus' armor-bearer, hapless, fell,
And three unhappy slaves the carnage swell;
The charioteer along his courser's sides
Expires, the steel his severed neck divides;
And, last, his lord is numbered with the dead:
Bounding convulsive, flies the gasping head;
From the swollen veins the blackening tor-
   rents pour;
Stained is the couch and earth with clotting
   gore.
Young Lamyrus and Lamus next expire,
And gay Serranus, filled with youthful fire;
Half the long night in childish games was
   passed;
Lulled by the potent grape, he slept at last:
Ah! happier far had he the morn surveyed,
And till Aurora's dawn his skill displayed.

   In slaughtered folds, the keepers lost in
      sleep,
His hungry fangs a lion thus may steep;
Mid the sad flock, at dead of night he prowls,
With murder glutted, and in carnage rolls:
Insatiate still, through teeming herds he
   roams;
In seas of gore the lordly tyrant foams.

   Nor less the other's deadly vengeance came,
But falls on feeble crowds without a name;
His wound unconscious Fadus scarce can feel,
Yet wakeful Rhæsus sees the threatening steel;
His coward breast behind a jar he hides,
And vainly in the weak defence confides;
Full in his heart, the falchion searched his
   veins,
The reeking weapon bears alternate stains;
Through wine and blood, commingling as
   they flow,
One feeble spirit seeks the shades below.
Now where Messapus dwelt they bend their
   way,
Whose fires emit a faint and trembling ray;
There, unconfined, behold each grazing steed,
Unwatched, unheeded, on the herbage feed:
Brave Nisus here arrests his comrade's arm,
Too flushed with carnage, and with conquest
      warm:

"Hence let us haste, the dangerous path is
   passed;
Full foes enough to-night have breathed their
   last:
Soon will the day those eastern clouds adorn;
Now let us speed, nor tempt the rising morn."

   What silver arms, with various art embossed,
What bowls and mantles in confusion tossed,
They leave regardless! yet one glittering prize
Attracts the younger hero's wandering eyes;
The gilded harness Rhamnes' coursers felt,
The gems which stud the monarch's golden
   belt
This from the pallid corse was quickly torn,
Once by a line of former chieftains worn.
Th' exulting boy the studded girdle wears,
Messapus' helm his head in triumph bears;
Then from the tents their cautious steps they
   bend,
To seek the vale where safer paths extend.

   Just at this hour, a band of Latian horse
To Turnus' camp pursue their destined
   course:
While the slow foot their tardy march delay,
The knights, impatient, spur along the way:
Three hundred mail-clad men, by Volscens led,
To Turnus with their master's promise sped:
Now they approach the trench, and view the
   walls,
When, on the left, a light reflection falls;
The plundered helmet, through the waning
   night,
Sheds forth a silver radiance, glancing bright.
Volscens with question loud the pair alarms:—
"Stand, stragglers! stand! why early thus in
   arms?
From whence, to whom?"—He meets with
   no reply:
Trusting the covert of the night, they fly:
The thicket's depth with hurried pace they
   tread,
While round the wood the hostile squadron
   spread.

   With brakes entangled, scarce a path be-
      tween,
Dreary and dark appears the sylvan scene:
Euryalus his heavy spoils impede,
The boughs and winding turns his steps mis-
   lead;
But Nisus scours along the forest's maze
To where Latinus' steeds in safety graze,
Then backward o'er the plain his eyes extend,
On every side they seek his absent friend.
"O God! my boy," he cries, "of me bereft,
In what impending perils art thou left!"
Listening he runs—above the waving trees,
Tumultuous voices swell the passing breeze;
The war-cry rises, thundering hoofs around
Wake the dark echoes of the trembling ground.

Again he turns, of footsteps hears the noise;
The sound elates, the sight his hope destroys:
The hapless boy a ruffian train surround,
While lengthening shades his weary way con-
  found.
Him with loud shouts the furious knights pur-
  sue,
Struggling in vain, a captive to the crew.
What can his friend 'gainst thronging num-
  bers dare?
Ah! must he rush, his comrade's fate to
  share?
What force, what aid, what stratagem essay,
Back to redeem the Latian spoiler's prey?
His life a votive ransom nobly give,
Or die with him for whom he wished to live?
Poising with strength his lifted lance on high,
On Luna's orb he cast his frenzied eye:—
"Goddess serene, transcending every star!
Queen of the sky, whose beams are seen afar!
By night heaven owns thy sway, by day the
  grove,
When, as chaste Dian, here thou deign'st to
  rove;
If e'er myself, or sire, have sought to grace
Thine altars with the produce of the chase,
Speed, speed my dart to pierce yon vaunting
  crowd,
To free my friend, and scatter far the proud."
Thus having said, the hissing dart he flung;
Through parted shades the hurtling weapon
  sung;
The thirsty point in Sulmo's entrails lay,
Transfixed his heart, and stretched him on the
  clay.
He sobs, he dies,—the troop in wild amaze,
Unconscious whence the death, with horror
  gaze.
While pale they stare, through Tagus' temples
  riven,
A second shaft with equal force is driven.
Fierce Volscens rolls around his lowering
  eyes;
Veiled by the night, secure the Trojan lies.
Burning with wrath, he viewed his soldiers
  fall.
"Thou youth accurst, thy life shall pay for
  all!"
Quick from the sheath his flaming glaive he
  drew,
And, raging, on the boy defenceless flew.
Nisus no more the blackening shade conceals,
Forth, forth he starts, and all his love reveals;
Aghast, confused, his fears to madness rise,
And pour these accents, shrieking as he flies:
" Me, me,—your vengeance hurl on me alone;
Here sheathe the steel, my blood is all your
  own.
Ye starry spheres! thou conscious Heaven!
  attest!
He could not—durst not—lo! the guile con-
  fest!

All, all was mine,—his early fate suspend;
He only loved too well his hapless friend:
Spare, spare, ye chiefs! from him your rage
  remove,
His fault was friendship, all his crime was
  love."
He prayed in vain; the dark assassin's sword
Pierced the fair side, the snowy bosom gored;
Lowly to earth inclines his plume-clad crest,
And sanguine torrents mantle o'er his breast:
As some young rose, whose blossom scents
  the air,
Languid in death, expires beneath the share;
Or crimson poppy, sinking with the shower,
Declining gently, falls a fading flower;
Thus sweetly drooping, bends his lovely head,
And lingering beauty hovers round the dead.

But fiery Nisus stems the battle's tide,
Revenge his leader, and despair his guide;
Volscens he seeks amidst the gathering host,
Volscens must soon appease his comrade's
  ghost;
Steel, flashing, pours on steel, foe crowds on
  foe;
Rage nerves his arm, fate gleams in every
  blow;
In vain beneath unnumbered wounds he
  bleeds,
Nor wounds, nor death, distracted Nisus
  heeds;
In viewless circles wheeled, his falchion flies,
Nor quits the hero's grasp till Volscens dies;
Deep in his throat its end the weapon found,
The tyrant's soul fled groaning through the
  · wound.
Thus Nisus all his fond affection proved—
Dying, revenged the fate of him he loved;
Then on his bosom sought his wonted place,
And death was heavenly in his friend's em-
  brace!

Celestial pair! if aught my verse can claim,
Wafted on Time's broad pinion, yours is
  fame!
Ages on ages shall your fate admire,
No future day shall see your names expire,
While stands the Capitol, immortal dome!
And vanquished millions hail their empress,
  Rome!

TRANSLATION FROM THE MEDEA OF EURIPIDES.

[Ἔρωτες ὑπὲρ μὲν ἄγαν, κ. τ. λ.]

WHEN fierce conflicting passions urge
  The breast where love is wont to glow,
What mind can stem the stormy surge
  Which rolls the tide of human woe?
The hope of praise, the dread of shame,
  Can rouse the tortured breast no more·

The wild desire, the guilty flame,
　Absorbs each wish it felt before.

But if affection gently thrills
　The soul by purer dreams possest,
The pleasing balm of mortal ills
　In love can soothe the aching breast:
If thus thou comest in disguise,
　Fair Venus! ʼfrom thy native heaven,
What heart unfeeling would despise
　The sweetest boon the gods have given?

But never from thy golden bow
　May I beneath the shaft expire!
Whose creeping venom, sure and slow,
　Awakes an all-consuming fire:
Ye racking doubts! ye jealous fears!
　With others wage internal war;
Repentance, source of future tears,
　From me be ever distant far!

May no distracting thoughts destroy
　The holy calm of sacred love!
May all the hours be winged with joy,
　Which hover faithful hearts above!
Fair Venus! on thy myrtle shrine
　May I with some fond lover sigh,
Whose heart may mingle pure with mine —
　With me to live, with me to die!

My native soil! beloved before,
　Now dearer as my peaceful home,
Ne'er may I quit thy rocky shore,
　A hapless banished wretch to roam!
This very day, this very hour,
　May I resign this fleeting breath!
Nor quit my silent humble bower;
　A doom to me far worse than death.

Have I not heard the exile's sigh,
　And seen the exile's silent tear,
Through distant climes condemned to fly,
　A pensive weary wanderer here?
Ah! hapless dame![1] no sire bewails,
　No friend thy wretched fate deplores,
No kindred voice with rapture hails
　Thy steps within a stranger's doors.

Perish the fiend whose iron heart,
　To fair affection's truth unknown,
Bids her he fondly loved depart,
　Unpitied, helpless, and alone;
Who ne'er unlocks with silver key[2]
　The milder treasures of his soul, —
May such a friend be far from me,
　And ocean's storms between us roll!

THOUGHTS SUGGESTED BY A COLLEGE EXAMINATION.

HIGH in the midst, surrounded by his peers,
MAGNUS[3] his ample front sublime uprears:
Placed on his chair of state, he seems a god,
While Sophs and Freshmen tremble at his nod.
As all around sit wrapt in speechless gloom,
His voice in thunder shakes the sounding dome
Denouncing dire reproach to luckless fools,
Unskilled to plod in mathematic rules.

Happy the youth in Euclid's axioms tried,
Though little versed in any art beside;
Who, scarcely skilled an English line to pen,
Scans Attic metres with a critic's ken.
What, though he knows not how his fathers bled,
When civil discord piled the fields with dead,
When Edward bade his conquering bands advance,
Or Henry trampled on the crest of France;
Though marvelling at the name of Magna Charta,
Yet well he recollects the laws of Sparta;
Can tell what edicts sage Lycurgus made,
While Blackstone's on the shelf neglected laid;
Of Grecian dramas vaunts the deathless fame,
Of Avon's bard remembering scarce the name.

Such is the youth whose scientific pate
Class-honors, medals, fellowships, await;
Or even, perhaps, the declamation prize,
If to such glorious height he lifts his eyes.
But lo! no common orator can hope
The envied silver cup within his scope.
Not that our heads much eloquence require,
Th' ATHENIAN'S[4] glowing style, or Tully's fire.
A manner clear or warm is useless, since
We do not try by speaking to convince.
Be other orators of pleasing proud:
We speak to please ourselves, not move the crowd:
Our gravity prefers the muttering tone,
A proper mixture of the squeak and groan:
No borrowed grace of action must be seen,

[1] Medea, who accompanied Jason to Corinth, was deserted by him for the daughter of Creon, king of that city. The chorus from which this is taken here addresses Medea; though a considerable liberty is taken with the original, by expanding the idea, as also in some other parts of the translation.

[2] The original is " Καθαρὰν ἀνοίξαντι κλῇδα φρενῶν; " literally " disclosing the bright key of the mind."

[3] No reflection is here intended against the person mentioned under the name of Magnus. He is merely represented as performing an unavoidable function of his office. Indeed, such an attempt could only recoil upon myself; as that gentleman is now as much distinguished by his eloquence, and the dignified propriety with which he fills his situation, as he was in his younger days for wit and conviviality.

[By " Magnus " Byron meant Dr. William Lort Mansel, Master of Trinity College, Cambridge, and afterwards Bishop of Bristol. He died in 1820.]

[4] Demosthenes.

The slightest motion would displease the
Dean; [1]
Whilst every staring graduate would prate
Against what he could never imitate.

The man who hopes t' obtain the promised
cup
Must in one posture stand, and ne'er look up;
Nor stop, but rattle over every word—
No matter what, so it can *not* be heard.
Thus let him hurry on, nor think to rest:
Who speaks the fastest's sure to speak the
best;
Who utters most within the shortest space
May safely hope to win the wordy race.

The sons of science these, who, thus repaid,
Linger in ease in Granta's sluggish shade;
Where on Cam's sedgy banks supine they lie
Unknown, unhonored live, unwept for die:
Dull as the pictures which adorn their halls,
They think all learning fixed within their walls:
In manners rude, in foolish forms precise,
All modern arts affecting to despise,
Yet prizing Bentley's, Brunck's, or Porson's [2]
note,
More than the verse on which the critic wrote:
Vain as their honors, heavy as their ale,
Sad as their wit, and tedious as their tale;
To friendship dead, though not untaught to
feel
When Self and Church demand a bigot zeal.
With eager haste they court the lord of power,
Whether 'tis Pitt or Petty rules the hour; [3]

---

[1] [In most colleges, the Fellow who superintends the chapel service is called *Dean*.]
[2] The present Greek professor at Trinity College, Cambridge, a man whose powers of mind and writings may, perhaps, justify their preference.
["I remember to have seen Porson at Cambridge, in the hall of our college, and in private parties; and I never can recollect him except as drunk or brutal, and generally both: I mean in an evening; for in the hall, he dined at the Dean's table, and I at the Vice-master's; — and he then and there appeared sober in his demeanor; but I have seen him, in a private party of undergraduates, take up a poker to them, and heard him use language as blackguard as his action. Of all the disgusting brutes, sulky, abusive, and intolerable, Porson was the most bestial, as far as the few times I saw him went. He was tolerated in this state amongst the young men for his talents; as the Turks think a madman inspired, and bear with him. He used to recite, or rather vomit, pages of all languages, and could hiccup Greek like a Helot: and certainly Sparta never shocked her children with a grosser exhibition than this man's intoxication." — *Byron's Letters*, 1818.]
[3] Since this was written, Lord Henry Petty has lost his place, and subsequently (I had almost said consequently) the honor of representing the University. A fact so glaring requires no comment. [Lord Henry Petty became in 1809 the Marquess of Lansdowne.]

To him, with suppliant smiles, they bend the
head,
While distant mitres to their eyes are spread.
But should a storm o'erwhelm him with dis-
grace,
They'd fly to seek the next who filled his place,
Such are the men who learning's treasures
guard!
Such is their practice, such is their reward!
This much, at least, we may presume to say—
The premium can't exceed the price they pay.
1806.

TO A BEAUTIFUL QUAKER.

SWEET girl! though only once we met,
That meeting I shall ne'er forget;
And though we ne'er may meet again,
Remembrance will thy form retain.
I would not say, " I love," but still
My senses struggle with my will:
In vain, to drive thee from my breast,
My thoughts are more and more represt;
In vain I check the rising sighs,
Another to the last replies:
Perhaps this is not love, but yet
Our meeting I can ne'er forget.

What though we never silence broke,
Our eyes a sweeter language spoke;
The tongue in flattering falsehood deals,
And tells a tale it never feels:
Deceit the guilty lips impart;
And hush the mandates of the heart;
But soul's interpreters, the eyes,
Spurn such restraint, and scorn disguise.
As thus our glances oft conversed,
And all our bosoms felt rehearsed,
No spirit, from within, reproved us,
Say rather, " 'twas the spirit moved us."
Though what they uttered I repress,
Yet conceive thou'lt partly guess;
For as on thee my memory ponders,
Perchance to me thine also wanders.
This for myself, at least, I'll say,
Thy form appears through night, through day;
Awake, with it my fancy teems;
In sleep, it smiles in fleeting dreams;
The vision charms the hours away,
And bids me curse Aurora's ray
For breaking slumbers of delight,
Which make me wish for endless night.
Since, oh! whate'er my future fate,
Shall joy or woe my steps await,
Tempted by love, by storms beset,
Thine image I can ne'er forget.

Alas! again no more we meet,
No more our former looks repeat;
Then let me breathe this parting prayer,
The dictate of my bosom's care:

"May Heaven so guard my lovely quaker,
That anguish never can o'ertake her;
That peace and virtue ne'er forsake her,
But bliss be aye her heart's partaker!
Oh! may the happy mortal, fated
To be, by dearest ties, related,
For her each hour new joys discover,
And lose the husband in the lover!
May that fair bosom never know
What 'tis to feel the restless woe
Which stings the soul, with vain regret,
Of him who never can forget!"

1806.

THE CORNELIAN.[1]

No specious splendor of this stone
  Endears it to my memory ever;
With lustre only once it shone,
  And blushes modest as the giver.

Some, who can sneer at friendship's ties,
  Have, for my weakness, oft reproved me;
Yet still the simple gift I prize, —
  For I am sure the giver loved me.

He offered it with downcast look,
  As fearful that I might refuse it;
I told him when the gift I took,
  My only fear should be to lose it.

This pledge attentively I viewed,
  And sparkling as I held it near,
Methought one drop the stone bedewed,
  And ever since I've loved a tear.

Still, to adorn his humble youth,
  Nor wealth nor birth their treasures yield;
But he who seeks the flowers of truth,
  Must quit the garden for the field.

'Tis not the plant upreared in sloth,
  Which beauty shows, and sheds perfume;
The flowers which yield the most of both
  In Nature's wild luxuriance bloom.

---

1 [The cornelian of these verses was given to Byron by the Cambridge chorister, Eddlestone, whose musical talents first introduced him to the acquaintance of the poet, who entertained for him a sentiment of the most romantic friendship.

On leaving his choir, Eddlestone entered into a mercantile house in the metropolis, and died of a consumption, in 1811. Byron wrote to Mrs. Pigot, of Southwell, on hearing of his death, "You may remember a cornelian, which some years ago I consigned to Miss Pigot, indeed gave to her, and now I am about to make the most selfish and rude of requests. The person who gave it to me, when I was very young, is dead, and though a long time has elapsed since we met, as it was the only memorial I possessed of that person (in whom I was very much interested), it has acquired a value by this event I could have wished it never to have borne in my eyes. If, therefore, Miss Pigot should

Had Fortune aided Nature's care,
  For once forgetting to be blind,
His would have been an ample share,
  If well proportioned to his mind.

But had the goddess clearly seen,
  His form had fixed her fickle breast;
Her countless hoards would his have been,
  And none remained to give the rest.

AN OCCASIONAL PROLOGUE,

DELIVERED PREVIOUS TO THE PERFORM-
ANCE OF "THE WHEEL OF FORTUNE" AT
A PRIVATE THEATRE.[2]

SINCE the refinement of this polished age
Has swept immoral raillery from the stage;
Since taste has now expunged licentious wit,
Which stamped disgrace on all an author writ;
Since now to please with purest scenes we seek,
Nor dare to call the blush from Beauty's cheek;
Oh! let the modest Muse some pity claim,
And meet indulgence, though she find not
  fame.
Still, not for her alone we wish respect,
Others appear more conscious of defect:
To-night no veteran Roscii you behold,
In all the arts of scenic action old;
No Cooke, no Kemble, can salute you here,
No Siddons draw the sympathetic tear;
To-night you throng to witness the *début*
Of embryo actors, to the Drama new:
Here, then, our almost unfledged wings we try;
Clip not our pinions ere the birds can fly:
Failing in this our first attempt to soar,
Drooping, alas! we fall to rise no more.
Not one poor trembler only fear betrays,
Who hopes, yet almost dreads, to meet your
  praise;
But all our dramatis personæ wait

---

have preserved it, I must, under these circum-
stances, beg her to excuse my requesting it to be
transmitted to me, and I will replace it by some-
thing she may remember me by equally well."
The cornelian heart was returned accordingly; and,
indeed, Miss Pigot reminded Byron that he had left
it with her as a deposit, not a gift.]

2 ["When I was a youth, I was reckoned a good
actor. Besides Harrow speeches, in which I shone,
I enacted Penruddock, in the 'Wheel of Fortune,'
and Tristram Fickle, in the farce of ' The Weather-
cock,' for three nights, in some private theatricals
at Southwell, in 1806, with great applause. The
occasional prologue for our volunteer play was also of
my composition. The other performers were young
ladies and gentlemen of the neighborhood; and the
whole went off with great effect upon our good-
natured audience." — *Byron's Diary*, 1821. This
prologue was written by the young poet, between
stages, on his way from Harrowgate. On getting
into the carriage at Chesterfield he said to his com-
panion, "Now, Pigot, I'll spin a prologue for our

In fond suspense this crisis of their fate.
No venal views our progress can retard,
Your generous plaudits are our sole reward.
For these, each Hero all his power displays,
Each timid Heroine shrinks before your gaze.
Surely the last will some protection find;
None to the softer sex can prove unkind:
While Youth and Beauty form the female
shield,
The sternest censor to the fair must yield.
Yet, should our feeble efforts nought avail,
Should, after all, our best endeavors fail,
Still let some mercy in your bosoms live,
And, if you can't applaud, at least forgive.

ON THE DEATH OF MR. FOX,

THE FOLLOWING ILLIBERAL IMPROMPTU
APPEARED IN A MORNING PAPER.

"OUR nation's foes lament on FOX's death,
But bless the hour when PITT resigned his
breath:
These feelings wide, let sense and truth unclue,
We give the palm where Justice points its
due."

TO WHICH THE AUTHOR OF THESE PIECES
SENT THE FOLLOWING REPLY.

OH factious viper! whose envenomed tooth
Would mangle still the dead, perverting truth;
What though our "nation's foes" lament the
fate,
With generous feeling, of the good and great,
Shall dastard tongues essay to blast the name
Of him whose meed exists in endless fame?
When PITT expired in plenitude of power,
Though ill success obscured his dying hour,
Pity her dewy wings before him spread,
For noble spirits "war not with the dead:"
His friends, in tears, a last sad requiem gave,
As all his errors slumbered in the grave;
He sunk, an Atlas bending 'neath the weight
Of cares o'erwhelming our conflicting state:
When, lo! a Hercules in FOX appeared,
Who for a time the ruined fabric reared:
He, too, is fallen, who Britain's loss supplied,
With him our fast-reviving hopes have died;
Not one great people only raise his urn,
All Europe's far-extended regions mourn.
"These feelings wide, let sense and truth
unclue,
To give the palm where Justice points its
due;"

---

play;" and before they reached Mansfield he had
completed his task, — interrupting, only once, his
rhyming reverie, to ask the proper pronunciation of
the French word "*début*," and, on being answered
(not, it would seem, very correctly), exclaiming,
"Ay, that will do for rhyme to '*new*.'" — *Moore.*]

Yet let not cankered Calumny assail,
Or round our statesmen wind her gloomy
veil.
FOX! o'er whose corse a mourning world
must weep,
Whose dear remains in honored marble sleep;
For whom, at last, e'en hostile nations groan,
While friends and foes alike his talents own;
Fox shall in Britain's future annals shine,.
Nor e'en to PITT the patriot's palm resign;
Which Envy, wearing Candor's sacred mask,
For PITT, and PITT alone, has dared to ask.[1]

THE TEAR.

"O lachrymarum fons, tenero sacros
Ducentium ortus ex animo! quater
Felix, in imo qui scatentem
Pectore te, pia Nympha, sensit." — GRAY.

WHEN Friendship or Love our sympathies
move,
When Truth in a glance should appear,
The lips may beguile with a dimple or smile,
But the test of affection's a Tear.

Too oft is a smile but the hypocrite's wile,
To mask detestation or fear;
Give me the soft sigh, whilst the soul-telling
eye
Is dimmed for a time with a Tear.

Mild Charity's glow, to us mortals below,
Shows the soul from barbarity clear;
Compassion will melt where this virtue is felt,
And its dew is diffused in a Tear.

The man doomed to sail with the blast of the
gale,
Through billows Atlantic to steer,
As he bends o'er the wave which may soon be
his grave,
The green sparkles bright with a Tear.

The soldier braves death for a fanciful wreath
In Glory's romantic career;
But he raises the foe when in battle laid low,
And bathes every wound with a Tear.

If with high-bounding pride he return to his
bride,
Renouncing the gore-crimsoned spear,
All his toils are repaid when, embracing the
maid,
From her eyelid he kisses the Tear.

Sweet scene of my youth![2] seat of Friendship
and Truth,
Where love chased each fast-fleeting year,

---

[1] [The "illiberal impromptu" appeared in the
Morning Post and Byron's "reply" in the Morning
Chronicle.]
[2] Harrow.

Loth to leave thee, I mourned, for a last look
   I turned,
    But thy spire was scarce seen through a
    Tear.

Though my vows I can pour to my Mary no
   more,
   My Mary to Love once so dear,
In the shade of her bower I remember the
   hour
    She rewarded those vows with a Tear.

By another possest, may she live ever blest!
   Her name still my heart must revere:
With a sigh I resign what I once thought was
   mine,
    And forgive her deceit with a Tear.

Ye friends of my heart, ere from you I depart,
   This hope to my breast is most near:
If again we shall meet in this rural retreat,
    May we meet, as we part, with a Tear.

When my soul wings her flight to the regions
   of night,
   And my corse shall recline on its bier,
As ye pass by the tomb where my ashes con-
   sume,
    Oh! moisten their dust with a Tear.

May no marble bestow the splendor of woe
   Which the children of vanity rear;
No fiction of fame shall blazon my name,
    All I ask — all I wish — is a Tear.

               October 26, 1806.

REPLY

TO SOME VERSES OF J. M. B. PIGOT, ESQ., ON
THE CRUELTY OF HIS MISTRESS.

WHY, Pigot, complain of this damsel's dis-
   dain,
   Why thus in despair do you fret?
For months you may try, yet, believe me, a
   sigh
    Will never obtain a coquette.

Would you teach her to love? for a time seem
   to rove;
   At first she may frown in a pet;
But leave her awhile, she shortly will smile,
    And then you may kiss your coquette.

For such are the airs of these fanciful fairs,
   They think all our homage a debt:
Yet a partial neglect soon takes an effect,
    And humbles the proudest coquette.

Dissemble your pain, and lengthen your chain,
   And seem her hauteur to regret:
If again you shall sigh, she no more will deny
    That yours is the rosy coquette.

If still, from false pride, your pangs she deride,
   This whimsical virgin forget;
Some other admire, who will melt with your
   fire,
    And laugh at the little coquette.

For me, I adore some twenty or more,
   And love them most dearly; but yet,
Though my heart they enthrall, I'd abandon
   them all,
    Did they act like your blooming coquette.

No longer repine, adopt this design,
   And break through her slight-woven net;
Away with despair, no longer forbear
    To fly from the captious coquette.

Then quit her, my friend! your bosom defend,
   Ere quite with her snares you're beset:
Lest your deep-wounded heart, when incensed
   by the smart,
    Should lead you to curse the coquette.

               October 27, 1806.

TO THE SIGHING STREPHON.

YOUR pardon, my friend, if my rhymes did
   offend,
   Your pardon, a thousand times o'er;
From friendship I strove your pangs to re-
   move,
    But I swear I will do so no more.

Since your beautiful maid your flame has
   repaid,
   No more I your folly regret;
She's now most divine, and I bow at the shrine
    Of this quickly reformed coquette.

Yet still, I must own, I should never have
   known
   From your verses, what else she deserved;
Your pain seemed so great, I pitied your fate
    As your fair was so devilish reserved.

Since the balm-breathing kiss of this magical
   miss
   Can such wonderful transports produce;
Since the "world you forget, when your lips
   once have met,"
    My counsel will get but abuse.

You say, when "I rove, I know nothing of
   love;"
   'Tis true, I am given to range:
If I rightly remember, I've loved a good
   number,
    Yet there's pleasure, at least, in a change.

I will not advance, by the rules of romance,
   To humor a whimsical fair;
Though a smile may delight, yet a frown won't
   affright,
    Or drive me to dreadful despair.

While my blood is thus warm I ne'er shall
  reform,
    To mix in the Platonists' school;
Of this I am sure, was my passion so pure,
  Thy mistress would think me a fool.

And if I should shun every woman for one,
  Whose image must fill my whole breast—
Whom I must prefer, and sigh but for her—
  What an insult 'twould be to the rest!

Now, Strephon, good bye; I cannot deny
  Your passion appears most absurd;
Such love as you plead is pure love indeed,
  For it only consists in the word.

TO ELIZA.[1]

ELIZA, what fools are the Mussulman sect,
  Who to woman deny the soul's future exist-
    ence;
Could they see thee, Eliza, they'd own their
  defect,
  And this doctrine would meet with a general
    resistance.

Had their prophet possessed half an atom of
  sense,
He ne'er would have women from paradise
  driven;
Instead of his houris, a flimsy pretence,
  With women alone he had peopled his
    heaven.

Yet still, to increase your calamities more,
  Not content with depriving your bodies of
    spirit,
He allots one poor husband to share amongst
  four!—
  With souls you'd dispense; but this last,
  who could bear it?

His religion to please neither party is made;
  On husbands 'tis hard, to the wives most
    uncivil;
Still I can't contradict, what so oft has been
  said,
  "Though women are angels, yet wedlock's
  the devil."

LACHIN Y GAIR.[2]

AWAY, ye gay landscapes, ye gardens of roses!
  In you let the minions of luxury rove;
Restore me the rocks, where the snow-flake
  reposes,

Though still they are sacred to freedom and
  love; .
Yet, Caledonia, beloved are thy mountains,
  Round their white summits though elements
    war;
Though cataracts foam 'stead of smooth-flow-
  ing fountains,
  I sigh for the valley of dark Loch na Garr.

Ah! there my young footsteps in infancy
  wandered;
  My cap was the bonnet, my cloak was the
  plaid;[3]
On chieftains long perished my memory pon-
  dered,
  As daily I strode through the pine-covered
    glade:
I sought not my home till the day's dying
  glory
  Gave place to the rays of the bright polar
    star;
For fancy was cheered by traditional story,
  Disclosed by the natives of dark Loch na
    Garr.

"Shades of the dead! have I not heard your
  voices
  Rise on the night-rolling breath of the
  gale?
Surely the soul of the hero rejoices,
  And rides on the wind, o'er his own High-
    land vale.
Round Loch na Garr while the stormy mist
  gathers,
  Winter presides in his cold icy car:
Clouds there encircle the forms of my
  . fathers;
  They dwell in the tempests of dark Loch
  na Garr.

"Ill-starred,[4] though brave, did no visions
  foreboding
  Tell you that fate had forsaken your
    cause?"

------

our modern tourists mentions it as the highest
mountain, perhaps, in Great Britain. Be this as it
may, it is certainly one of the most sublime and
picturesque amongst our "Caledonian Alps." Its
appearance is of a dusky hue, but the summit is the
seat of eternal snows. Near Lachin y Gair I spent
some of the early part of my life, the recollection of
which has given birth to these stanzas.

[3] This word is erroneously pronounced *plad:* the
proper pronunciation (according to the Scotch) is
shown by the orthography.

[4] I allude here to my maternal ancestors, "the
Gordons," many of whom fought for the unfortu-
nate Prince Charles, better known by the name of
the Pretender. This branch was nearly allied by
blood, as well as attachment, to the Stuarts.
George, the second Earl of Huntley, married the
Princess Annabella Stuart, daughter of James the
First of Scotland. By her he left four sons: the
third, Sir William Gordon, I have the honor to
claim as one of my progenitors.

------

[1] [Miss Elizabeth Pigot, of Southwell, to whom
several of Byron's earliest letters were addressed.]

[2] *Lachin y Gair,* or, as it is pronounced in the
Erse, *Loch na Garr,* towers proudly preëminent in
the Northern Highlands near Invercauld. One of

Ah! were you destined to die at Culloden,[1]
  Victory crowned not your fall with applause:
Still were you happy in death's earthy slumber,
  You rest with your clan in the caves of Braemar;[2]
The pibroch resounds, to the piper's loud number,
  Your deeds on the echoes of dark Loch na Garr.

Years have rolled on, Loch na Garr, since I left you,
  Years must elapse ere I tread you again:
Nature of verdure and flowers has bereft you,
  Yet still are you dearer than Albion's plain.
England! thy beauties are tame and domestic
  To one who has roved on the mountains afar:
Oh for the crags that are wild and majestic!
  The steep frowning glories of dark Loch na Garr![3]

TO ROMANCE.

PARENT of golden dreams, Romance!
  Auspicious queen of childish joys,
Who lead'st along, in airy dance,
  Thy votive train of girls and boys;

---

[1] Whether any perished in the battle of Culloden, I am not certain; but, as many fell in the insurrection, I have used the name of the principal action, "pars pro toto."

[2] A tract of the Highlands so called. There is also a castle of Braemar.

[3] [In the "Island," a poem written a year or two before Byron's death, are these lines: —
"He who first met the Highlands' swelling blue
Will love each peak that shows a kindred hue,
Hail in each crag a friend's familiar face,
And clasp the mountain in his mind's embrace.
Long have I roamed through lands which are not mine,
Adored the Alp, and loved the Apennine,
Revered Parnassus, and beheld the steep
Jove's Ida and Olympus crown the deep:
But 'twas not all long ages' lore, nor all
Their nature held me in their thrilling thrall;
The infant rapture still survived the boy,
And Loch na Garr with Ida looked o'er Troy,
Mixed Celtic memories with the Phrygian mount,
And Highland linns with Castalie's clear fount."
"When very young," (he adds in a note,) "about eight years of age, after an attack of the scarlet fever at Aberdeen, I was removed, by medical advice, into the Highlands, and from this period I date my love of mountainous countries. I can never forget the effect, a few years afterwards, in England, of the only thing I had long seen, even in miniature, of a mountain, in the Malvern Hills. After I returned to Cheltenham, I used to watch them every afternoon, at sunset, with a sensation which I cannot describe."]

At length, in spells no longer bound,
  I break the fetters of my youth;
No more I tread thy mystic round,
  But leave thy realms for those of Truth.

And yet 'tis hard to quit the dreams
  Which haunt the unsuspicious soul,
Where every nymph a goddess seems,
  Whose eyes through rays immortal roll.
While Fancy holds her boundless reign,
  And all assume a varied hue;
When virgins seem no longer vain,
  And even woman's smiles are true.

And must we own thee but a name,
  And from thy hall of clouds descend?
Nor find a sylph in every dame,
  A Pylades[4] in every friend?
But leave at once thy realms of air
  To mingling bands of fairy elves;
Confess that woman's false as fair,
  And friends have feeling for — themselves?

With shame I own I've felt thy sway,
  Repentant, now thy reign is o'er:
No more thy precepts I obey,
  No more on fancied pinions soar.
Fond fool! to love a sparkling eye,
  And think that eye to truth was dear,
To trust a passing wanton's sigh,
  And melt beneath a wanton's tear!

Romance! disgusted with deceit,
  Far from thy motley court I fly,
Where Affectation holds her seat,
  And sickly Sensibility;
Whose silly tears can never flow
  For any pangs excepting thine;
Who turns aside from real woe,
  To steep in dew thy gaudy shrine.

Now join with sable Sympathy,
  With cypress crowned, arrayed in weeds,
Who heaves with thee her simple sigh,
  Whose breast for every bosom bleeds;
And call thy sylvan female choir,
  To mourn a swain for ever gone,
Who once could glow with equal fire,
  But bends not now before thy throne.

Ye genial nymphs, whose ready tears
  On all occasions swiftly flow;
Whose bosoms heave with fancied fears,
  With fancied flames and phrensy glow;
Say, will you mourn my absent name,
  Apostate from your gentle train?

---

[4] It is hardly necessary to add, that Pylades was the companion of Orestes, and a partner in one of those friendships which, with those of Achilles and Patroclus, Nisus and Euryalus, Damon and Pythias, have been handed down to posterity as remarkable instances of attachments, which in all probability never existed beyond the imagination of the poet, or the page of an historian, or modern novelist.

An infant bard at least may claim
From you a sympathetic strain.

Adieu, fond race! a long adieu!
The hour of fate is hovering nigh;
E'en now the gulf appears in view,
Where unlamented you must lie:
Oblivion's blackening lake is seen,
Convulsed by gales you cannot weather;
Where you, and eke your gentle queen,
Alas! must perish altogether.

ANSWER

TO SOME ELEGANT VERSES SENT BY A FRIEND TO THE AUTHOR, COMPLAINING THAT ONE OF HIS DESCRIPTIONS WAS RATHER TOO WARMLY DRAWN.

" But if any old lady, knight, priest, or physician,
   Should condemn me for printing a second edition;
   If good Madam Squintum my work should abuse,
   May I venture to give her a smack of my muse?"
                                    New Bath Guide.

CANDOR compels me, BECHER![1] to commend
The verse which blends the censor with the friend,
Your strong yet just reproof extorts applause
From me, the heedless and imprudent cause.
For this wild error which pervades my strain,
I sue for pardon,—must I sue in vain?
The wise sometimes from Wisdom's ways depart:
Can youth then hush the dictates of the heart?
Precepts of prudence curb, but can't control,
The fierce emotions of the flowing soul.
When Love's delirium haunts the glowing mind,
Limping Decorum lingers far behind:
Vainly the dotard mends her prudish pace,
Outstripped and vanquished in the mental chase.
The young, the old, have worn the chains of love:
Let those they ne'er confined my lay reprove:
Let those whose souls contemn the pleasing power
Their censures on the hapless victim shower.
Oh! how I hate the nerveless, frigid song,
The ceaseless echo of the rhyming throng,
Whose labored lines in chilling numbers flow,
To paint a pang the author ne'er can know!

---

[1] [The Rev. John Becher, prebendary of South-well, the author of several philanthropic plans for the amelioration of the condition of the poor. In this gentleman the youthful poet found not only an honest and judicious critic, but a sincere friend. To his care the superintendence of the second edition of "Hours of Idleness," during its progress through a country press, was intrusted, and at his suggestion several corrections and omissions were made.]

The artless Helicon I boast is youth;—
My lyre, the heart; my muse, the simple truth.
Far be 't from me the "virgin's mind" to "taint:"
Seduction's dread is here no slight restraint.
The maid whose virgin breast is void of guile,
Whose wishes dimple in a modest smile,
Whose downcast eye disdains the wanton leer,
Firm in her virtue's strength, yet not severe—
She whom a conscious grace shall thus refine
Will ne'er be "tainted" by a strain of mine.
But for the nymph whose premature desires
Torment her bosom with unholy fires,
No net to snare her willing heart is spread;
She would have fallen, though she ne'er had read.
For me, I fain would please the chosen few,
Whose souls, to feeling and to nature true,
Will spare the childish verse, and not destroy
The light effusions of a heedless boy.
I seek not glory from the senseless crowd;
Of fancied laurels I shall ne'er be proud:
Their warmest plaudits I would scarcely prize,
Their sneers or censures I alike despise.

November 26, 1806.

ELEGY ON NEWSTEAD ABBEY.

" It is the voice of years that are gone! they roll before me with all their deeds."—OSSIAN.

NEWSTEAD! fast-falling, once-resplendent dome!
   Religion's shrine! repentant HENRY'S[2] pride!
Of warriors, monks, and dames the cloistered tomb,
   Whose pensive shades around thy ruins glide,

Hail to thy pile! more honored in thy fall
   Than modern mansions in their pillared state;
Proudly majestic frowns thy vaulted hall,
   Scowling defiance on the blasts of fate.

No mail-clad serfs, obedient to their lord,
   In grim array the crimson cross[3] demand;
Or gay assemble round the festive board
   Their chief's retainers, an immortal band:

Else might inspiring Fancy's magic eye
   Retrace their progress through the lapse of time,
Marking each ardent youth, ordained to die,
   A votive pilgrim in Judea's clime.

But not from thee, dark pile! departs the chief;
   His feudal realm in other regions lay:

---

[2] Henry II. founded Newstead soon after the murder of Thomas à Becket.
[3] The red cross was the badge of the crusaders.

In thee the wounded conscience courts relief,
  Retiring from the garish blaze of day.
Yes! in thy gloomy cells and shades profound
  The monk abjured a world he ne'er could
    view;
Or blood-stained guilt repenting solace found,
  Or innocence from stern oppression flew.

A monarch bade thee from that wild arise,
  Where Sherwood's outlaws once were wont
    to prowl,
And Superstition's crimes, of various dyes,
  Sought shelter in the priest's protecting
    cowl.

Where now the grass exhales a murky dew,
  The humid pall of life-extinguished clay,
In sainted fame the sacred fathers grew,
  Nor raised their pious voices but to pray.

Where now the bats their wavering wings
    extend
  Soon as the gloaming [1] spreads her waning
    shade,
The choir did oft their mingling vespers blend,
  Or matin orisons to Mary [2] paid.

Years roll on years; to ages, ages yield;
  Abbots to abbots, in a line, succeed:
Religion's charter their protecting shield
  Till royal sacrilege their doom decreed.

One holy HENRY reared the gothic walls,
  And bade the pious inmates rest in peace;
Another HENRY [3] the kind gift recalls,
  And bids devotion's hallowed echoes cease.

Vain is each threat or supplicating prayer;
  He drives them exiles from their blest abode,
To roam a dreary world in deep despair —
  No friend, no home, no refuge, but their God.

Hark how the hall, resounding to the strain,
  Shakes with the martial music's novel din!
The heralds of a warrior's haughty reign,
  High crested banners wave thy walls within.

Of changing sentinels the distant hum,
  The mirth of feasts, the clang of burnished
    arms,
The braying trumpet and the hoarser drum,
  Unite in concert with increased alarms.

An abbey once, a regal fortress [4] now,
  Encircled by insulting rebel powers,

War's dread machines o'erhang thy threaten-
    ing brow,
  And dart destruction in sulphureous show-
    ers.

Ah vain defence! the hostile traitor's siege,
  Though oft repulsed, by guile o'ercomes
    the brave;
His thronging foes oppress the faithful liege,
  Rebellion's reeking standards o'er him wave.

Not unavenged the raging baron yields;
  The blood of traitors smears the purple
    plain;
Unconquered still, his falchion there he wields,
  And days of glory yet for him remain.

Still in that hour the warrior wished to strew
  Self-gathered laurels on a self-sought grave;
But Charles' protecting genius hither flew,
  The monarch's friend, the monarch's hope,
    to save.

Trembling, she snatched him [5] from th' une-
    qual strife,
  In other fields the torrent to repel;
For nobler combats, here, reserved his life,
  To lead the band where godlike FALK-
    LAND [6] fell.

From thee, poor pile! to lawless plunder
    given,
  While dying groans their painful requiem
    sound,
Far different incense now ascends to heaven,
  Such victims wallow on the gory ground.

There many a pale and ruthless robber's corse,
  Noisome and ghast, defiles thy sacred sod;
O'er mingling man, and horse commixed with
    horse,
  Corruption's heap, the savage spoilers trod.

Graves, long with rank and sighing weeds
    o'erspread,
  Ransacked, resign perforce their mortal
    mould:
From ruffian fangs escape not e'en the dead,
  Raked from repose in search for buried
    gold.

Hushed is the harp, unstrung the warlike lyre,
  The minstrel's palsied hand reclines in
    death;
No more he strikes the quivering chords with
    fire,
  Or sings the glories of the martial wreath.

---

[1] As "gloaming," the Scottish word for twilight, is far more poetical, and has been recommended by many eminent literary men, particularly by Dr. Moore in his Letters to Burns, I have ventured to use it on account of its harmony.

[2] The priory was dedicated to the Virgin.

[3] At the dissolution of the monasteries, Henry VIII. bestowed Newstead Abbey on Sir John Byron.

[4] Newstead sustained a considerable siege in the war between Charles I. and his parliament.

[5] Lord Byron, and his brother Sir William, held high commands in the royal army. The former was general in chief in Ireland, lieutenant of the Tower, and governor to James, Duke of York, afterwards the unhappy James II.; the latter had a principal share in many actions.

[6] Lucius Cary, Lord Viscount Falkland, the most accomplished man of his age, was killed at the bat-

At length the sated murderers, gorged with
    prey,
  Retire; the clamor of the fight is o'er;
Silence again resumes her awful sway,
  And sable Horror guards the massy door.

Here Desolation holds her dreary court:
  What satellites declare her dismal reign!
Shrieking their dirge, ill-omened birds resort,
  To flit their vigils in the hoary fane.

Soon a new morn's restoring beams dispel
  The clouds of anarchy from Britain's skies;
The fierce usurper seeks his native hell,
  And Nature triumphs as the tyrant dies.

With storms she welcomes his expiring
    groans;
  Whirlwinds, responsive, greet his laboring
    breath;
Earth shudders as her caves receive his bones,
  Loathing the offering of so dark a death.[1]

The legal ruler[2] now resumes the helm,
  He guides through gentle seas the prow of
    state;
Hope cheers, with wonted smiles, the peaceful
    realm,
  And heals the bleeding wounds of wearied
    hate.

The gloomy tenants, Newstead! of thy cells,
  Howling, resign their violated nest;
Again the master on his tenure dwells,
  Enjoyed, from absence, with enraptured zest.

Vassals, within thy hospitable pale,
  Loudly carousing, bless their lord's return;
Culture again adorns the gladdening vale,
  And matrons, once lamenting, cease to
    mourn.

A thousand songs on tuneful echo float,
  Unwonted foliage mantles o'er the tree;
And hark! the horns proclaim a mellow note,
  The hunters' cry hangs lengthening on the
    breeze.

Beneath their coursers' hoofs the valleys
    shake:
  What fears, what anxious hopes, attend the
    chase!
The dying stag seeks refuge in the Lake;
  Exulting shouts announce the finished race.

Ah happy days! too happy to endure!
  Such simple sports our plain forefathers
    knew:
No splendid vices glittered to allure;
  Their joys were many, as their cares were
    few.

From these descending, sons to sires suc-
    ceed;
  Time steals along, and Death uprears his
    dart;
Another chief impels the foaming steed,
  Another crowd pursue the panting hart.

Newstead! what saddening change of scene is
    thine!
  Thy yawning arch betokens slow decay;
The last and youngest of a noble line
  Now holds thy mouldering turrets in his
    sway.

Deserted now, he scans thy gray worn
    towers;
  Thy vaults, where dead of feudal ages
    sleep;
Thy cloisters, pervious to the wintry show-
    ers;
  These, these he views, and views them but
    to weep.

Yet are his tears no emblem of regret:
  Cherished affection only bids them flow.
Pride, hope, and love, forbid him to forget,
  But warm his bosom with impassioned
    glow.

Yet he prefers thee to the gilded domes
  Or gewgaw grottos of the vainly great;
Yet lingers 'mid thy damp and mossy tombs,
  Nor breathes a murmur 'gainst the will of
    fate.[3]

Haply thy sun, emerging, yet may shine,
  Thee to irradiate with meridian ray;
Hours splendid as the past may still be
    thine,
  And bless thy future as thy former day.[4]

[3] ["Come what may," wrote Byron to his mother, in March, 1809, "Newstead and I stand or fall together. I have now lived on the spot; I have fixed my heart upon it; and no pressure, present or future, shall induce me to barter the last vestige of our inheritance. I have that pride within me which will enable me to support difficulties. I can endure privations; but could I obtain, in exchange for Newstead Abbey, the first fortune in the country, I would reject the proposition. Set your mind at ease on that score; I feel like a man of honor, and I will not sell Newstead."]

[4] [Those who turn from this Elegy to the stanzas on Newstead Abbey, in the thirteenth canto of Don Juan, cannot fail to remark how frequently the thoughts in the two pieces are the same; or to be interested, in comparing the juvenile sketch with the bold touches and mellow coloring of the master's picture.]

tle of Newbury, charging in the ranks of Lord Byron's regiment of cavalry.
[1] This is an historical fact. A violent tempest occurred immediately subsequent to the death or interment of Cromwell, which occasioned many disputes between his partisans and the cavaliers: both interpreted the circumstance into divine interposition: but whether as approbation or condemnation, we leave to the casuists of that age to decide. I have made such use of the occurrence as suited the subject of my poem.
[2] Charles II.

CHILDISH RECOLLECTIONS.[1]

> " I cannot but remember such things were,
> And were most dear to me."

WHEN slow Disease, with all her host of pains,
Chills the warm tide which flows along the
　　veins;
When Health, affrighted, spreads her rosy
　　wing,
And flies with every changing gale of spring;
Not to the aching frame alone confined,
Unyielding pangs assail the drooping mind:
What grisly forms, the spectre-train of woe,
Bid shuddering Nature shrink beneath the
　　blow,
With Resignation wage relentless strife,
While Hope retires appalled, and clings to
　　life.
Yet less the pang when, through the tedious
　　hour,
Remembrance sheds around her genial power,
Calls back the vanished days to rapture given,
When love was bliss, and Beauty formed our
　　heaven;
Or, dear to youth, portrays each childish scene,
Those fairy bowers, where all in turn have
　　been.
As when through clouds that pour the summer
　　storm
The orb of day unveils his distant form,
Gilds with faint beams the crystal dews of rain,
And dimly twinkles o'er the watery plain;
Thus, while the future dark and cheerless
　　gleams,
The sun of memory, glowing through my
　　dreams,
Though sunk the radiance of his former blaze,
To scenes far distant points his paler rays;
Still rules my senses with unbounded sway,
The past confounding with the present day.

---

[1] [These verses were composed while Byron was suffering under severe illness and depression of spirits. " I was laid," he says, " on my back, when that schoolboy thing was written, or rather dictated — expecting to rise no more, my physician having taken his sixteenth fee." In the private volume the poem opened with the following lines: —

" Hence! thou unvarying song of varied loves,
　Which youth commends, maturer age reproves;
　Which every rhyming bard repeats by rote,
　By thousands echoed to the self-same note!
　Tired of the dull, unceasing, copious strain,
　My soul is panting to be free again.
　Farewell! ye nymphs propitious to my verse,
　Some other Damon will your charms rehearse;
　Some other paint his pangs, in hope of bliss,
　Or dwell in rapture on your nectared kiss.
　Those beauties, grateful to my ardent sight,
　No more entrance my senses in delight;
　Those bosoms, formed of animated snow,
　Alike are tasteless, and unfeeling now.
　These to some happier lover I resign —
　The memory of those joys alone is mine.

Oft does my heart indulge the rising thought,
Which still recurs, unlooked for and unsought;
My soul to Fancy's fond suggestion yields,
And roams romantic o'er her airy fields:
Scenes of my youth, developed, crowd to view,
To which I long have bade a last adieu!
Seats of delight, inspiring youthful themes;
Friends lost to me for aye, except in dreams;
Some who in marble prematurely sleep,
Whose forms I now remember but to weep;
Some who yet urge the same scholastic course
Of early science, future fame the source;
Who, still contending in the studious race,
In quick rotation fill the senior place.
These with a thousand visions now unite,
To dazzle, though they please, my aching
　　sight.
IDA! blest spot, where Science holds her
　　reign,
How joyous once I joined thy youthful train!
Bright in idea gleams thy lofty spire,
Again I mingle with thy playful quire;
Our tricks of mischief, every childish game,
Unchanged by time or distance, seem the
　　same;
Through winding paths along the glade, I
　　trace
The social smile of every welcome face;
My wonted haunts, my scenes of joy and woe,
Each early boyish friend, or youthful foe,
Our feuds dissolved, but not my friendship
　　past: —
I bless the former, and forgive the last.
Hours of my youth! when, nurtured in my
　　breast,
To love a stranger, friendship made me
　　blest; —
Friendship, the dear peculiar bond of youth,
When every artless bosom throbs with truth;
Untaught by worldly wisdom how to feign,
And check each impulse with prudential rein;
When all we feel, our honest souls disclose —
In love to friends, in open hate to foes;
No varnished tales the lips of youth repeat,
No dear-bought knowledge purchased by
　　deceit.

Censure no more shall brand my humble name,
The child of passion and the fool of fame.
Weary of love, of life, devoured with spleen,
I rest a perfect Timon, not nineteen.
World! I renounce thee! all my hope's o'ercast:
One sigh I give thee, but that sigh's the last.
Friends, foes, and females, now alike adieu!
Would I could add, remembrance of you too!
Yet though the future dark and cheerless gleams,
The curse of memory, hovering in my dreams,
Depicts with glowing pencil all those years,
Ere yet my cup, empoisoned, flowed with tears;
Still rules my senses with tyrannic sway,
The past confounding with the present day.
　" Alas! in vain I check the maddening thought,
It still recurs, unlooked for and unsought;
My soul to Fancy's," etc., etc., as at line 29.]

Hypocrisy, the gift of lengthened years,
Matured by age, the garb of prudence wears.
When now the boy is ripened into man,
His careful sire chalks forth some wary plan;
Instructs his son from candor's path to shrink,
Smoothly to speak, and cautiously to think;
Still to assent, and never to deny—
A patron's praise can well reward the lie:
And who, when Fortune's warning voice is heard,
Would lose his opening prospects for a word?
Although against that word his heart rebel,
And truth indignant all his bosom swell.

    Away with themes like this! not mine the task
From flattering fiends to tear the hateful mask;
Let keener bards delight in satire's sting;
My fancy soars not on Detraction's wing:
Once, and but once, she aimed a deadly blow,
To hurl defiance on a secret foe;
But when that foe, from feeling or from shame,
The cause unknown, yet still to me the same,
Warned by some friendly hint, perchance, retired,
With this submission all her rage expired.
From dreaded pangs that feeble foe to save,
She hushed her young resentment, and forgave;
Or, if my muse a pedant's portrait drew,
POMPOSUS'[1] virtues are but known to few:
I never feared the young usurper's nod,
And he who wields must sometimes feel the rod.
If since on Granta's failings, known to all
Who share the converse of a college hall,
She sometimes trifled in a lighter strain,
'Tis past, and thus she will not sin again,
Soon must her early song for ever cease,
And all may rail when I shall rest in peace.

    Here first remembered be the joyous band,
Who hailed me chief,[2] obedient to command;
Who joined with me in every boyish sport—
Their first adviser, and their last resort;
Nor shrunk beneath the upstart pedant's frown,
Or all the sable glories of his gown;
Who, thus transplanted from his father's school—
Unfit to govern, ignorant of rule—
Succeeded him, whom all unite to praise,
The dear preceptor of my early days;
PROBUS,[3] the pride of science, and the boast,
To IDA now, alas! for ever lost.
With him, for years, we searched the classic page,
And feared the master, though we loved the sage:
Retired at last, his small yet peaceful seat,
From learning's labor is the blest retreat.
POMPOSUS fills his magisterial chair;
POMPOSUS governs,—but, my muse, forbear:[4]
Contempt, in silence, be the pendant's lot;
His name and precepts be alike forgot;
No more his mention shall my verse degrade,—
To him my tribute is already paid.

[1] [Dr. Butler, head-master of Harrow school. Had Byron published another edition of these poems, it was his intention, instead of the four lines beginning—"Or, if my muse a pedant's portrait drew," to insert—

"If once my muse a harsher portrait drew,
  Warm with her wrongs, and deemed the likeness true,
By cooler judgment taught, her fault she owns,—
With noble minds a fault confessed, atones."]

[2] [On the retirement of Dr. Drury, three candidates presented themselves for the vacant chair, Messrs. Drury, Evans, and Butler. On the first movement to which this contest gave rise in the school, young Wildman was at the head of the party for Mark Drury, while Byron held himself aloof from any. Anxious, however, to have him as an ally, one of the Drury faction said to Wildman—"Byron, I know, will not join, because he does not choose to act second to any one, but, by giving up the leadership to him, you may at once secure him." This Wildman accordingly did, and Byron took the command. — *Moore.*]

[3] Dr Drury. This most able and excellent man retired from his situation in March, 1805, after having resided thirty-five years at Harrow; the last twenty as head-master; an office he held with equal honor to himself and advantage to the very extensive school over which he presided. Panegyric would here be superfluous: it would be useless to enumerate qualifications which were never doubted. A considerable contest took place between three rival candidates for his vacant chair: of this I can only say,

Si mea cum vestris valuissent vota, Pelasgi!
Non foret ambiguus tanti certaminis hæres.

[Such was Byron's parting eulogy on Dr. Drury. It may be interesting to see by the side of it the Doctor's own account of his pupil, when first committed to his care:—"I took," says the Doctor, "my young disciple into my study, and endeavored to bring him forward by inquiries as to his former amusements, employments, and associates, but with little or no effect; and I soon found that a wild mountain colt had been submitted to my management. But there was mind in his eye. His manner and temper soon convinced me, that he might be led by a silken string to a point, rather than by a cable;—and on that principle I acted."]

[4] [To this passage, had Byron published another edition of Hours of Idleness, it was his intention to give the following turn:—

"Another fills his magisterial chair;
Reluctant Ida owns a stranger's care;
Oh! may like honors crown his future name:
If such his virtues, such shall be his fame."]

High, through those elms, with hoary branches crowned,
Fair IDA's bower adorns the landscape round;
There Science, from her favored seat, surveys
The vale where rural Nature claims her praise;
To her awhile resigns her youthful train,
Who move in joy, and dance along the plain;
In scattered groups each favored haunt pursue;
Repeat old pastimes, and discover new;
Flushed with his rays, beneath the noontide sun,
In rival bands, between the wickets run,
Drive o'er the sward the ball with active force,
Or chase with nimble feet its rapid course.
But these with slower steps direct their way,
Where Brent's cool waves in limpid currents stray;
While yonder few search out some green retreat,
And arbors shade them from the summer heat:
Others, again, a pert and lively crew,
Some rough and thoughtless stranger placed in view,
With frolic quaint their antic jests expose,
And tease the grumbling rustic as he goes;
Nor rest with this, but many a passing fray
Tradition treasures for a future day:
"'Twas here the gathered swains for vengeance fought,
And here we earned the conquest dearly bought;
Here have we fled before superior might,
And here renewed the wild tumultuous fight."
While thus our souls with early passions swell,
In lingering tones resounds the distant bell;
Th' allotted hour of daily sport is o'er,
And Learning beckons from her temple's door.
No splendid tablets grace her simple hall,
But ruder records fill the dusky wall;
There, deeply carved, behold! each tyro's name
Secures its owner's academic fame;
Here mingling view the names of sire and son —
The one long graved, the other just begun:
These shall survive alike when son and sire
Beneath one common stroke of fate expire:[1]
Perhaps their last memorial these alone,
Denied in death a monumental stone,
Whilst to the gale in mournful cadence wave
The sighing weeds that hide their nameless grave.
And here my name, and many an early friend's,

Along the wall in lengthened line extends.
Though still our deeds amuse the youthful race,
Who tread our steps, and fill our former place,
Who young, obeyed their lords in silent awe,
Whose nod commanded, and whose voice was law;
And now, in turn, possess the reins of power,
To rule the little tyrants of an hour; —
Though sometimes, with the tales of ancient day,
They pass the dreary winter's eve away —
"And thus our former rulers stemmed the tide,
And thus they dealt the combat side by side;
Just in this place the mouldering walls they scaled,
Nor bolts nor bars against their strength availed;[2]
Here PROBUS came, the rising fray to quell,
And here he faltered forth his last farewell;
And here one night abroad they dared to roam,
While bold POMPOSUS bravely staid at home;" —
While thus they speak, the hour must soon arrive,
When names of these, like ours, alone survive:
Yet a few years, one general wreck will whelm
The faint remembrance of our fairy realm.

Dear honest race! though now we meet no more,
One last long look on what we were before —
Our first kind greetings, and our last adieu —
Drew tears from eyes unused to weep with you.
Through splendid circles, fashion's gaudy world,
Where folly's glaring standard waves unfurled,
I plunged to drown in noise my fond regret,
And all I sought or hoped was to forget.
Vain wish! if chance some well-remembered face,
Some old companion of my early race,
Advanced to claim his friend with honest joy,
My eyes, my heart, proclaimed me still a boy;
The glittering scene, the fluttering groups around,
Were quite forgotten when my friend was found;
The smiles of beauty — (for, alas! I've known
What 'tis to bend before Love's mighty throne) —

---

[1] [During a rebellion at Harrow, the poet prevented the school-room from being burnt down, by pointing out to the boys the names of their fathers and grandfathers on the walls.]

[2] [Byron elsewhere thus describes his usual course of life while at Harrow — "always cricketing, rebelling, *rowing,* and in all manner of mischiefs." One day, in a fit of defiance, he tore down all the gratings from the window of the hall; and when called upon by Dr. Butler to say why he had committed this outrage, coolly answered, "because they darkened the room."]

The smiles of beauty, though those smiles were
    dear,
Could hardly charm me, when that friend
    was near;
My thoughts bewildered in the fond surprise,
The woods of IDA danced before my eyes;
I saw the sprightly wanderers pour along,
I saw and joined again the joyous throng;
Panting, again I traced her lofty grove,
And friendship's feelings triumphed over
    love.[1]

Yet, why should I alone with such delight,
Retrace the circuit of my former flight?
Is there no cause beyond the common claim
Endeared to all in childhood's very name?
Ah! sure some stronger impulse vibrates here,
Which whispers friendship will be doubly
    dear,
To one who thus for kindred hearts must
    roam,
And seek abroad the love denied at home.
Those hearts, dear IDA, have I found in thee—
A home, a world, a paradise to me.
Stern Death forbade my orphan youth to share
The tender guidance of a father's care.
Can rank, or e'en a guardian's name, supply
The love which glistens in a father's eye?
For this can wealth or title's sound atone,
Made, by a parent's early loss, my own?
What brother springs a brother's love to seek?
What sister's gentle kiss has prest my cheek?
For me how dull the vacant moments rise,
To no fond bosom linked by kindred ties!
Oft in the progress of some fleeting dream,
Fraternal smiles collected round me seem;
While still the visions to my heart are prest,

The voice of love will murmur in my rest:
I hear—I wake—and in the sound rejoice;
I hear again,—but, ah! no brother's voice.
A hermit, 'midst of crowds, I fain must stray
Alone, though thousand pilgrims fill the way;
While these a thousand kindred wreaths en-
    twine,
I cannot call one single blossom mine:
What then remains? in solitude to groan,
To mix in friendship, or to sigh alone.
Thus must I cling to some endearing hand
And none more dear than IDA'S social band.

ALONZO![2] best and dearest of my friends,
Thy name ennobles him who thus commends:
From this fond tribute thou canst gain no
    praise;
The praise is his who now that tribute pays.
Oh! in the promise of thy early youth,
If hope anticipate the words of truth,
Some loftier bard shall sing thy glorious name,
To build his own upon thy deathless fame.
Friend of my heart, and foremost of the list
Of those with whom I lived supremely blest,
Oft have we drained the font of ancient lore;
Though drinking deeply, thirsting still the
    more.
Yet, when confinement's lingering hour was
    done,
Our sports, our studies, and our souls were
    one:
Together we impelled the flying ball;
Together waited in our tutor's hall;
Together joined in cricket's manly toil,
Or shared the produce of the river's spoil;
Or, plunging from the green declining shore,
Our pliant limbs the buoyant billows bore;
In every element, unchanged, the same,
All, all that brothers should be, but the name,

Nor yet are you forgot, my jocund boy!
DAVUS,[3] the harbinger of childish joy;
For ever foremost in the ranks of fun,
The laughing herald of the harmless pun;
Yet with a breast of such materials made—
Anxious to please, of pleasing half afraid—
Candid and liberal, with a heart of steel
In danger's path though not untaught to feel,
Still I remember, in the factious strife,
The rustic's musket aimed against my life:[4]
High poised in air the massy weapon hung,

[1] [This description of what the young poet felt in 1806, on encountering any of his former schoolfellows, falls far short of the page in which he records an accidental meeting with Lord Clare, on the road between Imola and Bologna in 1821. "This meeting," he says, "annihilated for a moment all the years between the present time and the days of Harrow. It was a new and inexplicable feeling, like rising from the grave, to me. Clare too was much agitated — more in appearance than was myself; for I could feel his heart beat to his fingers' ends, unless, indeed, it was the pulse of my own which made me think so. We were but five minutes together, and on the public road; but I hardly recollect an hour of my existence which could be weighed against them."—We may also quote the following interesting sentences of Madame Guiccioli: — "In 1822 (says she), a few days before leaving Pisa, we were one evening seated in the garden of the Palazzo Lanfranchi. At this moment a servant announced Mr. Hobhouse. The slight shade of melancholy diffused over Lord Byron's face, gave instant place to the liveliest joy; but it was so great that it almost deprived him of strength. A fearful paleness came over his cheeks, and his eyes were filled with tears as he embraced his friend: his emotion was so great that he was forced to sit down."]

[2] [The Hon. John Wingfield, of the Coldstream Guards. He died of a fever, in his twentieth year, at Coimbra, May 14th, 1811. — "Of all human beings," says Byron, "I was, perhaps, at one time, the most attached to poor Wingfield. I had known him the better half of his life, and the happiest part of mine."]

[3] [The Rev. John Cecil Tattersall, B. A., of Christ Church, Oxford; who died Dec. 8, 1812, at Hall's Place, Kent, aged twenty-four.]

[4] [The "factious strife" was brought on by the breaking up of school, and the dismissal of some

A cry of horror burst from every tongue;
Whilst I, in combat with another foe,
Fought on, unconscious of th'impending blow;
Your arm, brave boy, arrested his career—
Forward you sprung, insensible to fear;
Disarmed and baffled by your conquering hand,
The grovelling savage rolled upon the sand:
An act like this, can simple thanks repay?
Or all the labors of a grateful lay?
Oh no! whene'er my breast forgets the deed,
That instant, DAVUS, it deserves to bleed.

LYCUS![1] on me thy claims are justly great:
Thy milder virtues could my muse relate,
To thee alone, unrivalled, would belong
The feeble efforts of my lengthened song.[2]
Well canst thou boast, to lead in senates fit,
A Spartan firmness with Athenian wit:
Though yet in embryo these perfections shine,
LYCUS! thy father's fame will soon be thine.
Where learning nurtures the superior mind,
What may we hope from genius thus refined!
When time at length matures thy growing years,
How wilt thou tower above thy fellow peers!
Prudence and sense, a spirit bold and free,
With honor's soul, united beam in thee.

Shall fair EURYALUS[3] pass by unsung?
From ancient lineage, not unworthy sprung:
What though one sad dissension bade us part,
That name is yet embalmed within my heart;

Yet at the mention does that heart rebound,
And palpitate, responsive to the sound.
Envy dissolved our ties, and not our will:
We once were friends,—I'll think we are so still.[4]
A form unmatched in nature's partial mould,
A heart untainted, we in thee behold:
Yet not the senate's thunder thou shalt wield,
Nor seek for glory in the tented field;
To minds of ruder texture these be given—
Thy soul shall nearer soar its native heaven.
Haply, in polished courts might be thy seat,
But that thy tongue could never forge deceit:
The courtier's supple bow and sneering smile,
The flow of compliment, the slippery wile,
Would make that breast with indignation burn,
And all the glittering snares to tempt thee spurn.
Domestic happiness will stamp thy fate;
Sacred to love, unclouded e'er by hate;
The world admire thee, and thy friends adore;—
Ambition's slave alone would toil for more.

Now last, but nearest, of the social band,
See honest, open, generous CLEON[5] stand;
With scarce one speck to cloud the pleasing scene,
No vice degrades that purest soul serene.
On the same day our studious race begun,
On the same day our studious race was run;
Thus side by side we passed our first career,
Thus side by side we strove for many a year;
At last concluded our scholastic life,
We neither conquered in the classic strife:

---

volunteers from drill, at the same hour. The butt-end of a musket was aimed at Byron's head, and would have felled him to the ground, but for the interposition of Tattersall.—*Moore.*]

[1] [John Fitzgibbon, second Earl of Clare. "I never," Byron says, in 1821, "hear the word '*Clare*,' without a beating of the heart even *now;* and I write it with the feelings of 1803-4-5, ad infinitum." In 1822 he said of Clare, "I have always loved him better than any *male* thing in the world."]

[2] [In the private volume, the following lines conclude this character:—
"For ever to possess a friend in thee,
Was bliss unhoped, though not unsought by me.
Thy softer soul was formed for love alone,
To ruder passions and to hate unknown:
Thy mind, in union with thy beauteous form,
Was gentle, but unfit to stem the storm.
That face, an index of celestial worth,
Proclaimed a heart abstracted from the earth.
Oft, when depressed with sad foreboding gloom,
I sat reclined upon our favorite tomb,
I've seen those sympathetic eyes o'erflow
With kind compassion for thy comrade's woe;
Or when less mournful subjects formed our themes,
We tried a thousand fond romantic schemes,
Oft hast thou sworn, in friendship's soothing tone,
Whatever wish was mine must be thine own."]

[3] George-John, fifth Earl Delawarr:—
"Harrow, October 25, 1804.—I am happy enough and comfortable here. My friends are not numerous, but select. Among the principal, I rank Lord Del-

awarr, who is very amiable, and my particular friend." "Nov. 2, 1804.—Lord Delawarr is considerably younger than me, but the most good-tempered, amiable, clever fellow in the universe. To all which he adds the quality (a good one in the eyes of women) of being remarkably handsome. Delawarr and myself are, in a manner, connected; for one of my forefathers, in Charles the First's time, married into their family."—*Byron's Letters.*]

[4] ["You will be astonished to hear I have lately written to Delawarr, for the purpose of explaining (as far as possible, without involving some *old friends* of mine in the business), the cause of my behavior to him during my last residence at Harrow, which you will recollect was rather *en cavalier*. Since that period I have discovered he was treated with injustice, both by those who misrepresented his conduct, and by me in consequence of their suggestions. I have, therefore, made all the reparation in my power, by apologizing for my mistake, though with very faint hopes of success. However, I have eased my own conscience by the atonement, which is humiliating enough to one of my disposition; yet I could not have slept satisfied with the reflection of having, even unintentionally, injured any individual. I have done all that could be done to repair the injury."—*Byron's Letter to Lord Clare,* 1807.]

[5] [Edward Noel Long, Esq.]

As speakers[1] each supports an equal name,
And crowds allow to both a partial fame:
To soothe a youthful rival's early pride,
Though Cleon's candor would the palm divide,
Yet candor's self compels me now to own,
Justice awards it to my friend alone.

Oh! friends regretted, scenes for ever dear,
Remembrance hails you with her warmest
   tear!
Drooping, she bends o'er pensive Fancy's urn,
To trace the hours which never can return;
Yet with the retrospection loves to dwell,
And soothe the sorrows of her last farewell!
Yet greets the triumph of my boyish mind,
As infant laurels round my head were twined,
When PROBUS' praise repaid my lyric song,
Or placed me higher in the studious throng;
Or when my first harangue received applause,[2]
His sage instruction the primeval cause,
What gratitude to him my soul possest,
While hope of dawning honors filled my
   breast!
For all my humble fame, to him alone
The praise is due, who made that fame my
   own.[3]

Oh! could I soar above these feeble lays,
These young effusions of my early days,
To him my muse her noblest strain would give:
The song might perish, but the theme might
   live.
Yet why for him the needless verse essay?
His honored name requires no vain display:
By every son of grateful IDA blest,
It finds an echo in each youthful breast;
A fame beyond the glories of the proud,
Or all the plaudits of the venal crowd.

IDA! not yet exhausted is the theme,
Nor closed the progress of my youthful dream.
How many a friend deserves the grateful strain!
What scenes of childhood still unsung remain!

---

[1] This alludes to the public speeches delivered at the school where the author was educated.

[2] [" I remember that my first declamation astonished Dr. Drury into some unwonted (for he was economical of such) and sudden compliments, before the declaimers at our first rehearsal." — *Byron's Diary.*]
[" I certainly was much pleased with Lord Byron's attitude, gesture, and delivery, as well as with his composition. All who spoke on that day adhered, as usual, to the letter of their composition, as in the earlier part of his delivery did Lord Byron. But, to my surprise, he suddenly diverged from the written composition, with a boldness and rapidity sufficient to alarm me, lest he should fail in memory as to the conclusion. There was no failure; — he came round to the close of his composition without discovering any impediment and irregularity on the whole. I questioned him, why he had altered his declamation? He declared he had made no alteration, and did not know, in speaking, that he had deviated from it one letter. I believed him, and from a knowledge of his temperament am convinced, that, fully impressed with the sense and substance of the subject, he was hurried on to expressions and colorings more striking than what his pen had expressed." — *Dr. Drury.*]

[3] [In the private volume the poem concludes thus: —
' When, yet a novice in the mimic art,
I feigned the transports of a vengeful heart —
When as the Royal Slave I trod the stage,
To vent in Zanga more than mortal rage —
The praise of Probus made me feel more proud
Than all the plaudits of the listening crowd.
" Ah! vain endeavor in this childish strain
To soothe the woes of which I thus complain!
What can avail this fruitless loss of time,
To measure sorrow in a jingling rhyme!

No social solace from a friend is near,
And heartless strangers drop no feeling tear.
I seek not joy in woman's sparkling eye:
The smiles of beauty cannot check the sigh.
Adieu, thou world! thy pleasure's still a dream,
Thy virtue but a visionary theme;
Thy years of vice on years of folly roll,
Till grinning death assigns the destined goal —
Where all are hastening to the dread abode,
To meet the judgment of a righteous God;
Mixed in the concourse of the thoughtless throng,
A mourner midst of mirth, I glide along;
A wretched, isolated, gloomy thing,
Curst by reflection's deep corroding sting;
But not that mental sting which stabs within,
The dark avenger of unpunished sin;
The silent shaft which goads the guilty wretch
Extended on a rack's untiring stretch:
Conscience that sting, that shaft to him supplies —
His mind the rack from which he ne'er can rise.
For me, whate'er my folly, or my fear,
One cheerful comfort still is cherished here:
No dread internal haunts my hours of rest,
No dreams of injured innocence infest; *
Of hope, of peace, of almost all bereft,
Conscience, my last but welcome guest is left.
Slander's empoisoned breath may blast my name,
Envy delights to blight the buds of fame;
Deceit may chill the current of my blood,
And freeze affection's warm impassioned flood;
Presaging horror darken every sense; —
Even here will conscience be my best defence.
My bosom feeds no ' worm which ne'er can die: ' †
Not crimes I mourn, but happiness gone by.
Thus crawling on with many a reptile vile,
My heart is bitter, though my cheek may smile:
No more with former bliss my heart is glad;
Hope yields to anguish, and my soul is sad;
From fond regret no future joy can save;
Remembrance slumbers only in the grave."]

* [" I am not a Joseph," said Byron, in 1821, "nor a Scipio; but I can safely affirm, that I never in my life seduced any woman."
† [" We know enough even of Lord Byron's private history to give our warrant that, though his youth may have shared somewhat too largely in the indiscretions of those left too early masters of their own actions and fortunes, falsehood and malice alone can impute to him any real cause for hopeless remorse, or gloomy melancholy." — *Sir Walter Scott.*]

Yet let me hush this echo of the past,
This parting song, the dearest and the last;
And brood in secret o'er those hours of joy,
To me a silent and a sweet employ,
While future hope and fear alike unknown,
I think with pleasure on the past alone;
Yes, to the past alone my heart confine,
And chase the phantom of what once was mine.

IDA! still o'er thy hills in joy preside,
And proudly steer through time's eventful tide;
Still may thy blooming sons thy name revere,
Smile in thy bower, but quit thee with a tear; —
That tear, perhaps, the fondest which will flow,
O'er their last scene of happiness below.
Tell me, ye hoary few, who glide along,
The feeble veterans of some former throng,
Whose friends, like autumn leaves by tempests
    whirled,
Are swept for ever from this busy world;
Revolve the fleeting moments of your youth,
While Care as yet withheld her venomed tooth;
Say if remembrance days like these endears
Beyond the rapture of succeeding years?
Say can ambition's fevered dream bestow
So sweet a balm to soothe your hours of woe?
Can treasures, hoarded for some thankless son,
Can royal smiles, or wreaths by slaughter won,
Can stars or ermine, man's maturer toys,
(For glittering baubles are not left to boys)
Recall one scene so much beloved to view,
As those where Youth her garland twined for
    you?
Ah, no! amidst the gloomy calm of age
You turn with faltering hand life's varied page;
Peruse the record of your days on earth,
Unsullied only where it marks your birth;
Still lingering pause above each chequered
    leaf,
And blot with tears the sable lines of grief;
Where Passion o'er the theme her mantle
    threw,
Or weeping Virtue sighed a faint adieu;
But bless the scroll which fairer words adorn,
Traced by the rosy finger of the morn;
When Friendship bowed before the shrine of
    truth,
And Love, without his pinion,[1] smiled on
    youth.

ANSWER TO A BEAUTIFUL POEM ENTITLED "THE COMMON LOT."[2]

MONTGOMERY! true, the common lot
    Of mortals lies in Lethe's wave;
Yet some shall never be forgot —
    Some shall exist beyond the grave.

"Unknown the region of his birth,"
    The hero[3] rolls the tide of war;
Yet not unknown his martial worth,
    Which glares a meteor from afar.

His joy or grief, his weal or woe,
    Perchance may 'scape the page of fame;
Yet nations now unborn will know
    The record of his deathless name.

The patriot's and the poet's frame
    Must share the common tomb of all:
Their glory will not sleep the same;
    That will arise, though empires fall.

The lustre of a beauty's eye
    Assumes the ghastly stare of death;
The fair, the brave, the good must die,
    And sink the yawning grave beneath.

Once more the speaking eye revives,
    Still beaming through the lover's strain;
For Petrarch's Laura still survives:
    She died, but ne'er will die again.

The rolling seasons pass away,
    And Time, untiring, waves his wing;
Whilst honor's laurels ne'er decay,
    But bloom in fresh, unfading spring.

All, all must sleep in grim repose,
    Collected in the silent tomb;
The old and young, with friends and foes,
    Festering alike in shrouds, consume.

The mouldering marble lasts its day,
    Yet falls at length an useless fane;
To ruin's ruthless fangs a prey,
    The wrecks of pillared pride remain.

What, though the sculpture be destroyed,
    From dark oblivion meant to guard;
A bright renown shall be enjoyed
    By those whose virtues claim reward.

Then do not say the common lot
    Of all lies deep in Lethe's wave;
Some few who ne'er will be forgot
    Shall burst the bondage of the grave.
                                        1806.

TO A LADY

WHO PRESENTED THE AUTHOR WITH THE
VELVET BAND WHICH BOUND HER
TRESSES.

THIS Band, which bound thy yellow hair,
    Is mine, sweet girl! thy pledge of love;
It claims my warmest, dearest care,
    Like relics left of saints above.

------

[1] "L'Amitié est l'Amour sans ailes," is a French
proverb.
[2] Written by James Montgomery, author of
"The Wanderer in Switzerland," etc.

[3] No particular hero is here alluded to. The
exploits of Bayard, Nemours, Edward the Black
Prince, and, in more modern times, the fame of

Oh! I will wear it next my heart;
  'Twill bind my soul in bonds to thee;
From me again 'twill ne'er depart,
  But mingle in the grave with me.

The dew I gather from thy lip
  Is not so dear to me as this;
That I but for a moment sip,
  And banquet on a transient bliss:

This will recall each youthful scene,
  E'en when our lives are on the wane;
The leaves of Love will still be green
  When Memory bids them bud again.

Oh! little lock of golden hue,
  In gently waving ringlet curled,
By the dear head on which you grew,
  I would not lose you for a world.

Not though a thousand more adorn
  The polished brow where once you shone,
Like rays which gild a cloudless morn,
  Beneath Columbia's fervid zone.

1806.

REMEMBRANCE.

'TIS done!—I saw it in my dreams:
No more with Hope the future beams;
  My days of happiness are few:
Chilled by misfortune's wintry blast,
My dawn of life is overcast,
  Love, Hope, and Joy, alike adieu!—
Would I could add Remembrance too!—

1806.

LINES

ADDRESSED TO THE REV. J. T. BECHER, ON HIS ADVISING THE AUTHOR TO MIX MORE WITH SOCIETY.

DEAR Becher, you tell me to mix with mankind;—
I cannot deny such a precept is wise;
But retirement accords with the tone of my mind:
I will not descend to a world I despise.

Did the senate or camp my exertions require,
Ambition might prompt me, at once, to go forth;
When infancy's years of probation expire,
Perchance I may strive to distinguish my birth.

The fire in the cavern of Etna concealed,
Still mantles unseen in its secret recess;—

Marlborough, Frederick the Great, Count Saxe, Charles of Sweden, etc., are familiar to every historical reader, but the exact places of their birth are known to a very small proportion of their admirers.

At length, in a volume terrific revealed,
  No torrent can quench it, no bounds can repress.

Oh! thus, the desire in my bosom for fame
  Bids me live but to hope for posterity's praise.
Could I soar with the phœnix on pinions of flame,
  With him I would wish to expire in the blaze.

For the life of a Fox, of a Chatham the death,
  What censure, what danger, what woe would I brave!
Their lives did not end when they yielded their breath;
  Their glory illumines the gloom of their grave.

Yet why should I mingle in Fashion's full herd?
  Why crouch to her leaders, or cringe to her rules?
Why bend to the proud, or applaud the absurd?
  Why search for delight in the friendship of fools?

I have tasted the sweets and the bitters of love;
  In friendship I early was taught to believe;
My passion the matrons of prudence reprove;
  I have found that a friend may profess, yet deceive.

To me what is wealth? it may pass in an hour,
  If tyrants prevail, or if Fortune should frown;
To me what is title?—the phantom of power;
  To me what is fashion?—I seek but renown.

Deceit is a stranger as yet to my soul;
  I still am unpractised to varnish the truth:
Then why should I live in a hateful control?
  Why waste upon folly the days of my youth?

1806.

THE DEATH OF CALMAR AND ORLA.

AN IMITATION OF MACPHERSON'S OSSIAN.[1]

DEAR are the days of youth! Age dwells on their remembrance through the mist of time. In the twilight he recalls the sunny hours of morn. He lifts his spear with trembling hand. "Not thus feebly did I raise the steel before my fathers!" Past is the race of

[1] It may be necessary to observe, that the story, though considerably varied in the catastrophe, is

heroes! But their fame rises on the harp; their souls ride on the wings of the wind; they hear the sound through the sighs of the storm, and rejoice in their hall of clouds! Such is Calmar. The gray stone marks his narrow house. He looks down from eddying tempests: he rolls his form in the whirlwind, and hovers on the blast of the mountain.

In Morven dwelt the chief; a beam of war to Fingal. His steps in the field were marked in blood. Lochlin's sons had fled before his angry spear; but mild was the eye of Calmar; soft was the flow of his yellow locks: they streamed like the meteor of the night. No maid was the sigh of his soul: his thoughts were given to friendship, — to dark-haired Orla, destroyer of heroes! Equal were their swords in battle; but fierce was the pride of Orla: — gentle alone to Calmar. Together they dwelt in the cave of Oithona.

From Lochlin, Swaran bounded o'er the blue waves. Erin's sons fell beneath his might. Fingal roused his chiefs to combat. Their ships cover the ocean. Their hosts throng on the green hills. They come to the aid of Erin.

Night rose in clouds. Darkness veils the armies, but the blazing oaks gleam through the valley. The sons of Lochlin slept: their dreams were of blood. They lift the spear in thought, and Fingal flies. Not so the host of Morven. To watch was the post of Orla. Calmar stood by his side. Their spears were in their hands. Fingal called his chiefs: they stood around. The king was in the midst. Gray were his locks, but strong was the arm of the king. Age withered not his powers. "Sons of Morven," said the hero, "to-morrow we meet the foe. But where is Cuthullin, the shield of Erin? He rests in the halls· of Tura; he knows not of our coming. Who will speed through Lochlin to the hero, and call the chief to arms? The path is by the swords of foes; but many are my heroes. They are thunderbolts of war. Speak, ye chiefs! Who will arise?"

"Son of Trenmor! mine be the deed," said dark-haired Orla, "and mine alone. What is death to me? I love the sleep of the mighty, but little is the danger. The sons of Lochlin dream. I will seek car-borne Cuthullin. If I fall, raise the song of bards; and lay me by the stream of Lubar."—"And shalt thou fall alone?" said fair-haired Calmar. "Wilt thou leave thy friend afar? Chief of Oithona! not feeble is my arm in fight. Could I see thee die, and not lift the spear? No, Orla! ours has been the chase

taken from "Nisus and Euryalus," of which epi-
sode a translation is already given in the present
volume.

of the roebuck, and the feast of shells; ours be the path of danger: ours has been the cave of Oithona; ours be the narrow dwelling on the banks of Lubar." "Calmar," said the chief of Oithona, "why should thy yellow locks be darkened in the dust of Erin? Let me fall alone. My father dwells in his hall of air: he will rejoice in his boy; but the blue-eyed Mora spreads the feast for her son in Morven. She listens to the steps of the hunter on the heath, and thinks it is the tread of Calmar. Let him not say, 'Calmar has fallen by the steel of Lochlin: he died with gloomy Orla, the chief of the dark brow.' Why should tears dim the azure eye of Mora? Why should her voice curse Orla, the destroyer of Calmar? Live, Calmar! Live to raise my stone of moss; live to revenge me in the blood of Lochlin. Join the song of bards above my grave. Sweet will be the song of death to Orla, from the voice of Calmar. My ghost shall smile on the notes of praise." "Orla," said the son of Mora, " could I raise the song of death to my friend? Could I give his fame to the winds? No, my heart would speak in sighs: faint and broken are the sounds of sorrow. Orla! our souls shall hear the song together. One cloud shall be ours on high: the bards will mingle the names of Orla and Calmar."

They quit the circle of the chiefs. Their steps are to the host of Lochlin. The dying blaze of oak dim twinkles through the night. The northern star points the path to Tura. Swaran, the king, rests on his lonely hill. Here the troops are mixed: they frown in sleep; their shields beneath their heads. Their swords gleam at distance in heaps. The fires are faint; their embers fail in smoke. All is hushed; but the gale sighs on the rocks above. Lightly wheel the heroes through the slumbering band. Half the journey is past, when Mathon, resting on his shield, meets the eye of Orla. It rolls in flame, and glistens through the shade. His spear is raised on high. "Why dost thou bend thy brow, chief of Oithona?" said fair-haired Calmar: "we are in the midst of foes. Is this a time for delay?" "It is a time for vengeance," saiʲ Orla of the gloomy brow. "Mathon of Lochliɴ sleeps: seest thou his spear? Its point is dim with the gore of my father. The blood of Mathon shall reek on mine; but shall I slay him sleeping, son of Mora? No! he shall feel his wound: my fame shall not soar on the blood of slumber. Rise, Mathon, rise! The son of Conna calls; thy life is his; rise to combat." Mathon starts from sleep; but did he rise alone? No: the gathering chiefs bound on the plain. "Fly! Calmar, fly!" said dark-haired Orla. "Mathon is mine. I shall die in joy: but Lochlin crowds around. Fly through the shade of night." Orla turns,

The helm of Mathon is cleft; his shield falls
from his arm: he shudders in his blood. He
rolls by the side of the blazing oak. Strumon
sees him fall: his wrath rises: his weapon
glitters on the head of Orla: but a spear
pierced his eye. His brain gushes through
the wound, and foams on the spear of Cal-
mar. As roll the waves of the Ocean on two
mighty barks of the north, so pour the men of
Lochlin on the chiefs. As, breaking the surge
in foam, proudly steer the barks of the north,
so rise the chiefs of Morven on the scattered
crests of Lochlin. The din of arms came to
the ear of Fingal. He strikes his shield; his
sons throng around; the people pour along
the heath. Ryno bounds in joy. Ossian
stalks in his arms. Oscar shakes the spear.
The eagle wing of Fillan floats on the wind.
Dreadful is the clang of death! many are the
widows of Lochlin! Morven prevails in its
strength.

Morn glimmers on the hills: no living foe
is seen; but the sleepers are many; grim they
lie on Erin. The breeze of ocean lifts their
locks; yet they do not awake. The hawks
scream above their prey.

Whose yellow locks wave o'er the breast of
a chief? Bright as the gold of the stranger,
they mingle with the dark hair of his friend.
'Tis Calmar: he lies on the bosom of Orla.
Theirs is one stream of blood. Fierce is the
look of the gloomy Orla. He breathes not;
but his eye is still a flame. It glares in death
unclosed. His hand is grasped in Calmar's;
but Calmar lives! he lives, though low.
"Rise," said the king, "rise, son of Mora:
'tis mine to heal the wounds of heroes. Cal-
mar may yet bound on the hills of Morven."

"Never more shall Calmar chase the deer
of Morven with Orla," said the hero. "What
were the chase to me alone? Who would
share the spoils of battle with Calmar? Orla
is at rest! Rough was thy soul, Orla! yet
soft to me as the dew of morn It glared on
others in lightning: to me a sliver beam of
night. Bear my sword to blue eyed Mora;
let it hang in my empty hall. It is not pure
from blood: but it could not save Orla. Lay
me with my friend. Raise the song when I
am dark!"

They are laid by the stream of Lubar. Four
gray stones mark the dwelling of Orla and
Calmar. When Swaran was bound, our sails
rose on the blue waves. The winds gave our
barks to Morven:—the bards raised the song.

"What form rises on the roar of clouds?
Whose dark ghost gleams on the red streams
of tempests? His voice rolls on the thunder.
'Tis Orla, the brown chief of Oithona. He
was unmatched in war. Peace to thy soul,
Orla! thy fame will not perish. Nor thine,
Calmar! Lovely wast thou, son of blue-eyed
Mora; but not harmless was thy sword. It
hangs in thy cave. The ghosts of Lochlin
shriek around its steel. Hear thy praise, Cal-
mar! It dwells on the voice of the mighty.
Thy name shakes on the echoes of Morven.
Then raise thy fair locks, son of Mora. Spread
them on the arch of the rainbow; and smile
through the tears of the storm."[1]

L'AMITIÉ EST L'AMOUR SANS AILES.

[WRITTEN DECEMBER, 1806.]

WHY should my anxious breast repine,
　Because my youth is fled?
Days of delight may still be mine;
　Affection is not dead.
In tracing back the years of youth,
One firm record, one lasting truth
　Celestial consolation brings;
Bear it, ye breezes, to the seat,
Where first my heart responsive beat,—
　"Friendship is Love without his wings!"

Through few, but deeply chequered years,
　What moments have been mine!
Now half obscured by clouds of tears,
　Now bright in rays divine;
Howe'er my future doom be cast,
My soul, enraptured with the past,
　To one idea fondly clings;
Friendship! that thought is all thine own,
Worth worlds of bliss, that thought alone—
　"Friendship is Love without his wings!"

Where yonder yew-trees lightly wave
　Their branches on the gale,
Unheeded heaves a simple grave,
　Which tells the common tale;
Round this unconscious schoolboys stray,
Till the dull knell of childish play
　From yonder studious mansion rings;
But here whene'er my footsteps move,
My silent tears too plainly prove
　"Friendship is Love without his wings!"

Oh Love! before thy glowing shrine
　My early vows were paid;
My hopes, my dreams, my heart was thine,
　But these are now decayed;
For thine are pinions like the wind,
No trace of thee remains behind,

<hr>

[1] I fear Laing's late edition has completely over-
thrown every hope that Macpherson's Ossian might
prove the translation of a series of poems complete
in themselves; but, while the imposture is discov-
ered, the merit of the work remains undisputed,
though not without faults—particularly, in some
parts, turgid and bombastic diction.—The present
humble imitation will be pardoned by the admirers
of the original as an attempt, however inferior,
which evinces an attachment to their favorite author.

Except, alas! thy jealous stings.
Away, away! delusive power,
Thou shalt not haunt my coming hour;
  Unless, indeed, without thy wings.

Seat of my youth![1] thy distant spire
  Recalls each scene of joy;
My bosom glows with former fire,—
  In mind again a boy.
Thy grove of elms, thy verdant hill,
Thy every path delights me still,
  Each flower a double fragrance flings;
Again, as once, in converse gay,
Each dear associate seems to say
  "Friendship is Love without his wings!"

My Lycus![2] wherefore dost thou weep?
  Thy falling tears restrain;
Affection for a time may sleep,
  But, oh, 'twill wake again.
Think, think, my friend, when next we meet,
Our long-wished interview, how sweet!
  From this my hope of rapture springs;
While youthful hearts thus fondly swell,
Absence, my friend, can only tell,
  "Friendship is Love without his wings!"

In one, and one alone deceived,
  Did I my error mourn?
No—from oppressive bonds relieved,
  I left the wretch to scorn.
I turned to those my childhood knew,
With feelings warm, with bosoms true,
  Twined with my heart's according strings;
And till those vital chords shall break,
For none but these my breast shall wake
  Friendship, the power deprived of wings!

Ye few! my soul, my life is yours,
  My memory and my hope;
Your worth a lasting love insures,
  Unfettered in its scope;
From smooth deceit and terror sprung,
With aspect fair and honeyed tongue,
  Let Adulation wait on kings;
With joy elate, by snares beset,
We, we, my friends, can ne'er forget
  "Friendship is Love without his wings!"

Fictions and dreams inspire the bard
  Who rolls the epic song;
Friendship and Truth be my reward—
  To me no bays belong;
If laurelled Fame but dwells with lies,
Me the enchantress ever flies,
  Whose heart and not whose fancy sings;
Simple and young, I dare not feign;
Mine be the rude yet heartfelt strain,
  "Friendship is Love without his wings!"

[1] Harrow.
[2] The Earl of Clare.

THE PRAYER OF NATURE.[3]

[WRITTEN DECEMBER 29, 1806.]

FATHER of Light! great God of Heaven!
  Hear'st thou the accents of despair?
Can guilt like man's be e'er forgiven?
  Can vice atone for crimes by prayer?

Father of Light, on thee I call!
  Thou see'st my soul is dark within;
Thou who canst mark the sparrow's fall,
  Avert from me the death of sin.

No shrine I seek, to sects unknown;
  Oh point to me the path of truth!
Thy dread omnipotence I own;
  Spare, yet amend, the faults of youth.

Let bigots rear a gloomy fane,
  Let superstition hail the pile,
Let priests, to spread their sable reign,
  With tales of mystic rights beguile.

Shall man confine his Maker's sway
  To Gothic domes of mouldering stone?
Thy temple is the face of day;
  Earth, ocean, heaven thy boundless throne.

Shall man condemn his race to hell,
  Unless they bend in pompous form?
Tell us that all, for one who fell,
  Must perish in the mingling storm?

Shall each pretend to reach the skies,
  Yet doom his brother to expire,
Whose soul a different hope supplies,
  Or doctrines less severe inspire?

Shall these, by creeds they can't expound,
  Prepare a fancied bliss or woe?
Shall reptiles, grovelling on the ground,
  Their great Creator's purpose know?

Shall those, who live for self alone,
  Whose years float on in daily crime—
Shall they by Faith for guilt atone,
  And live beyond the bounds of Time?

Father! no prophet's laws I seek,—
  Thy laws in Nature's works appear;—
I own myself corrupt and weak,
  Yet will I pray, for thou wilt hear!

Thou, who canst guide the wandering star
  Through trackless realms of æther's space;
Who calm'st the elemental war,
  Whose hand from pole to pole I trace:—

[3] [It is difficult to conjecture for what reason these stanzas, which surpass any thing that Byron had yet written, were not included in the publication of 1807. Written when the author was not nineteen years of age, "this remarkable poem shows," says Moore, "how early the struggle between natural piety and doubt began in his mind."]

Thou, who in wisdom placed me here,
  Who, when thou wilt, can take me hence,
Ah! whilst I tread this earthly sphere,
  Extend to me thy wide defence.

To Thee, my God, to thee I call!
  Whatever weal or woe betide,
By thy command I rise or fall,
  In thy protection I confide.

If when this dust to dust's restored,
  My soul shall float on airy wing,
How shall thy glorious name adored
  Inspire her feeble voice to sing!

But, if this fleeting spirit share
  With clay the grave's eternal bed,
While life yet throbs I raise my prayer,
  Though doomed no more to quit the dead.

To Thee I breathe my humble strain,
  Grateful for all thy mercies past,
And hope, my God, to thee again
  This erring life may fly at last.

TO EDWARD NOEL LONG, ESQ.[1]

" Nil ego contulerim jucundo sanus amico."
                                        HORACE.

DEAR Long, in this sequestered scene,
  While all around in slumber lie,
The joyous days which ours have been
  Come rolling fresh on Fancy's eye;
Thus if amidst the gathering storm,
While clouds the darkened noon deform,
Yon heaven assumes a varied glow,
I hail the sky's celestial bow,
Which spreads the sign of future peace,
And bids the war of tempests cease.
Ah! though the present brings me pain,
I think those days may come again;
Or if, in melancholy mood,
Some lurking envious fear intrude,
To check my bosom's fondest thought,
  And interrupt the golden dream,
I crush the fiend with malice fraught,
  And still indulge my wonted theme.
Although we ne'er again can trace,
  In Granta's vale, the pedant's lore;
Nor through the groves of Ida chase
  Our raptured visions as before,

------

[1] [This gentleman, who was with Byron both at Harrow and Cambridge, entered the Guards, and served in the expedition to Copenhagen. He was drowned in 1809, when on his way to join the army in the Peninsula; the transport in which he sailed being run down in the night by another of the convoy. " Long's father," says Byron, " wrote to me to write his son's epitaph. I promised — but I had not the heart to complete it. He was such a good, amiable being as rarely remains long in this world; with talent and accomplishments, too, to make him the more regretted." — *Diary*, 1821.]

Though Youth has flown on rosy pinion,
And Manhood claims his stern dominion —
Age will not every hope destroy,
But yield some hours of sober joy.

  Yes, I will hope that Time's broad wing
Will shed around some dews of spring:
But if his scythe must sweep the flowers
Which bloom among the fairy bowers,
Where smiling Youth delights to dwell,
And hearts with early rapture swell;
If frowning Age, with cold control,
Confines the current of the soul,
Congeals the tear of Pity's eye,
Or checks the sympathetic sigh,
Or hears unmoved misfortune's groan,
And bids me feel for self alone;
Oh! may my bosom never learn
  To soothe its wonted heedless flow;
Still, still despise the censor stern,
  But ne'er forget another's woe.
Yes, as you knew me in the days
O'er which Remembrance yet delays,
Still may I rove, untutored, wild,
And even in age at heart a child.

  Though now on airy visions borne,
  To you my soul is still the same.
Oft has it been my fate to mourn,
  And all my former joys are tame.
But, hence! ye hours of sable hue!
  Your frowns are gone, my sorrows o'er:
By every bliss my childhood knew,
  I'll think upon your shade no more.
Thus when the whirlwind's rage is past,
  And caves their sullen roar enclose,
We heed no more the wintry blast,
  When lulled by zephyr to repose.

  Full often has my infant Muse
  Attuned to love her languid lyre;
But now, without a theme to choose,
  The strains in stolen sighs expire.
My youthful nymphs, alas! are flown;
  E—— is a wife, and C—— a mother,
And Carolina sighs alone,
  And Mary's given to another;
And Cora's eye, which rolled on me,
  Can now no more my love recall:
In truth, dear LONG, 'twas time to flee;
  For Cora's eye will shine on all.
And though the sun, with genial rays,
His beams alike to all displays,
And every lady's eye's a *sun*,
These last should be confined to one.
The soul's meridian don't become her,
Whose sun displays a general *summer!*
Thus faint is every former flame,
And passion's self is now a name.
As, when the ebbing flames are low,
  The aid which once improved their light,
And bade them burn with fiercer glow,
  Now quenches all their sparks in night;

Thus has it been with passion's fires,
  As many a boy and girl remembers,
While all the force of love expires,
  Extinguished with the dying embers.

But now, dear LONG, 'tis midnight's noon,
And clouds obscure the watery moon,
Whose beauties I shall not rehearse,
Described in every stripling's verse;
For why should I the path go o'er,
Which every bard has trod before?
Yet ere yon silver lamp of night
  Has thrice performed her stated round,
Has thrice retraced her path of light,
  And chased away the gloom profound,
I trust that we, my gentle friend,
Shall see her rolling orbit wend
Above the dear-loved peaceful seat
Which once contained our youth's retreat;
And then with those our childhood knew,
We'll mingle in the festive crew;
While many a tale of former day
Shall wing the laughing hours away;
And all the flow of souls shall pour
The sacred intellectual shower,
Nor cease till Luna's waning horn
Scarce glimmers through the mist of morn.

TO A LADY.[1]

OH! had my fate been joined with thine,
  As once this pledge appeared a token,
These follies had not then been mine,
  For then my peace had not been broken.[2]

To thee these early faults I owe,
  To thee, the wise and old reproving:
They know my sins, but do not know
  'Twas thine to break the bonds of loving.

For once my soul, like thine, was pure,
  And all its rising fires could smother;
But now thy vows no more endure,
  Bestowed by thee upon another.

Perhaps his peace I could destroy,
  And spoil the blisses that await him;
Yet let my rival smile in joy,
  For thy dear sake I cannot hate him.

Ah! since thy angel form is gone,
  My heart no more can rest with any;
But what it sought in thee alone,
  Attempts, alas! to find in many.

Then fare thee well, deceitful maid!
  'Twere vain and fruitless to regret thee;

---

[1] [Mrs. Musters.]
[2] ["Our union would have healed feuds in which
blood had been shed by our fathers — it would have
joined lands broad and rich — it would have joined
at least *one* heart, and two persons not ill matched

Nor Hope, nor Memory yield their aid,
  But Pride may teach me to forget thee.

Yet all this giddy waste of years,
  This tiresome round of palling pleasure:
These varied loves, these matron's fears,
  These thoughtless strains to passion's meas-
    ures —

If thou wert mine, had all been hushed :·
  This cheek, now pale from early riot,
With passion's hectic ne'er had flushed,
  But bloomed in calm domestic quiet.

Yes, once the rural scene was sweet,
  For Nature seemed to smile before thee; [3]
And once my breast abhorred deceit, —
  For then it beat but to adore thee.

But now I seek for other joys:
  To think would drive my soul to madness
In thoughtless throngs and empty noise,
  I conquer half my bosom's sadness.

Yet, even in these a thought will steal
  In spite of every vain endeavor, —
And fiends might pity what I feel, —
  To know that thou art lost for ever.

I WOULD I WERE A CARELESS CHILD.

I WOULD I were a careless child,
  Still dwelling in my Highland cave,
Or roaming through the dusky wild,
  Or bounding o'er the dark blue wave;
The cumbrous pomp of Saxon[4] pride
  Accords not with the freeborn soul,
Which loves the mountain's craggy side,
  And seeks the rocks where billows roll.

Fortune! take back these cultured lands,
  Take back this name of splendid sound!
I hate the touch of servile hands,
  I hate the slaves that cringe around.
Place me among the rocks I love,
  Which sound to Ocean's wildest roar;
I ask but this — again to rove
  Through scenes my youth hath known be-
    fore.

---

in years (she is two years my elder), and — and —
and — *what* has been the result?"] —*Diary*, 1821.
  [3] ["Our meetings," says Byron in 1822, "were
stolen ones, and a gate leading from Mr. Chaworth's
grounds to those of my mother was the place of our
interviews. But the ardor was all on my side. I
was serious; she was volatile: she liked me as a
younger brother, and treated and laughed at me as a
boy; she, however, gave me her picture, and that
was something to make verses upon. Had I mar-
ried her, perhaps the whole tenor of my life would
have been different."]
  [4] Sassenach, or Saxon, a Gaelic word, signifying
either Lowland or English.

Few are my years, and yet I feel
　The world was ne'er designed for me:
Ah! why do darkening shades conceal
　The hour when man must cease to be?

Once I beheld a splendid dream,
　A visionary scene of bliss:
Truth! — wherefore did thy hated beam
　Awake me to a world like this?

I loved — but those I loved are gone,
　Had friends — my early friends are fled:
How cheerless feels the heart alone
　When all its former hopes are dead!
Though gay companions o'er the bowl
　Dispel awhile the sense of ill;
Though pleasure stirs the maddening soul,
　The heart — the heart — is lonely still.

How dull! to hear the voice of those
　Whom rank or chance, whom wealth or power,
Have made, though neither friends nor foes,
　Associates of the festive hour.
Give me again a faithful few,
　In years and feelings still the same,
And I will fly the midnight crew,
　Where boisterous joy is but a name.

And woman, lovely woman! thou,
　My hope, my comforter, my all!
How cold must be my bosom now,
　When e'en thy smiles begin to pall!
Without a sigh would I resign
　This busy scene of splendid woe,
To make that calm contentment mine,
　Which virtue knows, or seems to know.

Fain would I fly the haunts of men —
　I seek to shun, not hate mankind;
My breast requires the sullen glen,
　Whose gloom may suit a darkened mind.
Oh! that to me the wings were given
　Which bear the turtle to her nest!
Then would I cleave the vault of heaven,
　To flee away, and be at rest.[1]

WHEN I ROVED A YOUNG HIGH-
LANDER.

WHEN I roved a young Highlander o'er the
　dark heath,
And climbed thy steep summit, oh Morven
　of snow![2]

----

[1] " And I said, Oh! that I had wings like a dove;
for then would I fly away, and be at rest." — *Psalm*
lv. 6. This verse also constitutes a part of the
most beautiful anthem in our language.
[2] Morven, a lofty mountain in Aberdeenshire.
" Gormal of snow," is an expression frequently to
be found in Ossian.

To gaze on the torrent that thundered beneath,
　Or the mist of the tempest that gathered
　below,[3]

Untutored by science, a stranger to fear,
　And rude as the rocks where my infancy
　grew,
No feeling, save one, to my bosom was dear;
　Need I say, my sweet Mary,[4] 'twas centred
　in you?

Yet it could not be love, for I knew not the
　name, —
　What passion can dwell in the heart of a
　child?
But still I perceive an emotion the same
　As I felt, when a boy, on the crag-covered
　wild.

One image alone on my bosom impressed,
　I loved my bleak regions, nor panted for
　new;
And few were my wants, for my wishes were
　blessed;
　And pure were my thoughts, for my soul
　was with you.

----

[3] This will not appear extraordinary to those who
have been accustomed to the mountains. It is by
no means uncommon, on attaining the top of Ben-e-
vis, Ben-y-bourd, etc., to perceive, between the
summit and the valley, clouds pouring down rain,
and occasionally accompanied by lightning, while
the spectator literally looks down upon the storm,
perfectly secure from its effects.

[4] [In Byron's Diary for 1813, he says, " I have
been thinking lately a good deal of Mary Duff.
How very odd that I should have been so utterly,
devotedly fond of that girl, at an age when I could
neither feel passion, nor know the meaning of the
word. And the effect! My mother used always to
rally me about this childish amour; and, at last,
many years after, when I was sixteen, she told me
one day; ' Oh, Byron, I have had a letter from
Edinburgh, from Miss Abercromby, and your old
sweetheart, Mary Duff, is married to a Mr. Cock-
burn.' [Robert Cockburn, Esq., of Edinburgh.]
And what was my answer? I really cannot explain
or account for my feelings at that moment; but they
nearly threw me into convulsions — to the horror of
my mother and the astonishment of everybody.
And it is a phenomenon in my existence (for I was
not eight years old), which has puzzled, and will
puzzle me to the latest hour of it." — Again, in
January, 1815, a few days after his marriage, in a
letter to his friend Captain Hay, the poet thus
speaks of his childish attachment: — " Pray tell me
more — or as much as you like, of your cousin
Mary. I believe I told you our story some years
ago. I was twenty-seven a few days ago, and I
have never seen her since we were children, and
young children too; but I never forget her, nor ever
can. You will oblige me with presenting her with
my best respects, and all good wishes. It may
seem ridiculous — but it is at any rate, I hope, not
offensive to her nor hers — in me to pretend to rec-
ollect any thing about her, at so early a period of
both our lives, almost, if not quite, in our nur-
series; — but it was a pleasant dream, which she

I arose with the dawn; with my dog as my
  guide,
From mountain to mountain I bounded
  along;
I breasted the billows of Dee's[1] rushing tide,
And heard at a distance the Highlander's
  song:
At eve, on my heath-covered couch of repose,
  No dreams, save of Mary, were spread to
  my view;
And warm to the skies my devotions arose,
  For the first of my prayers was a blessing
  on you.

I left my bleak home, and my visions are gone;
  The mountains are vanished, my youth is
  no more;
As the last of my race, I must wither alone,
  And delight but in days I have witnessed
  before:
Ah! splendor has raised, but embittered my
  lot;
  More dear were the scenes which my in-
  fancy knew:
Though my hopes may have failed, yet they
  are not forgot;
  Though cold is my heart, still it lingers with
  you.

When I see some dark hill point its crest to
  the sky,
  I think of the rocks that o'ershadow Col-
  bleen;[2]
When I see the soft blue of a love-speaking eye,
  I think of those eyes that endeared the rude
  scene;
When, haply, some light-waving locks I be-
  hold,
  That faintly resemble my Mary's in hue,
I think on the long flowing ringlets of gold,
  The locks that were sacred to beauty, and
  you.

Yet the day may arrive when the mountains
  once more
  Shall rise to my sight in their mantles of snow:
But while these soar above me, unchanged as
  before,
  Will Mary be there to receive me?—ah, no!
Adieu, then, ye hills, where my childhood was
  bred!
  Thou sweet flowing Dee, to thy waters adieu!
No home in the forest shall shelter my head,—
  Ah! Mary, what home could be mine but
  with you?

must pardon me for remembering. Is she pretty
still?   I have the most perfect idea of her person, as
a child; but Time, I suppose, has played the devil
with us both."]
  [1] The Dee is a beautiful river, which rises near
Mar Lodge and falls into the sea at New Aberdeen.
  [2] Colbleen is a mountain near the verge of the
Highlands, not far from the ruins of Dee Castle.

TO GEORGE, EARL DELAWARR.

Oh! yes, I will own we were dear to each other;
  The friendships of childhood, though fleet-
  ing, are true;
The love which you felt was the love of a
  brother,
  Nor less the affection I cherished for you.

But Friendship can vary her gentle dominion;
  The attachment of years in a moment ex-
  pires:
Like Love, too, she moves on a swift-waving
  pinion,
  But glows not, like Love, with unquenchable
  fires.

Full oft have we wandered through Ida to-
  gether,
  And blest were the scenes of our youth, I
  allow:
In the spring of our life, how serene is the
  weather!
  But winter's rude tempests are gathering
  now.

No more with affection shall memory blend-
  ing,
  The wonted delights of our childhood re-
  trace:
When pride steels the bosom, the heart is un-
  bending,
  And what would be justice appears a dis-
  grace.

However, dear George, for I still must esteem
  you—
  The few whom I love I can never up-
  braid—
The chance which has lost may in future re-
  deem you,
  Repentance will cancel the vow you have
  made.

I will not complain, and though chilled is
  affection,
  With me no corroding resentment shall live:
My bosom is calmed by the simple reflection,
  That both may be wrong, and that both
  should forgive.

You knew that my soul, that my heart, my
  existence
  If danger demanded, were wholly your own;
You knew me unaltered by years or by dis-
  tance,
  Devoted to love and to friendship alone.

You knew,—but away with the vain retro
  spection!
  The bond of affection no longer endures;
Too late you may droop o'er the fond recol-
  lection,
  And sigh for the friend who was formerly
  yours.

For the present, we part, — I will hope not for
　　ever
For time and regret will restore you at last:
To forget our dissension we both should en-
　　deavor,
I ask no atonement, but days like the past.

———

TO THE EARL OF CLARE.

"Tu semper amoris
Sis memor, et cari comitis n? abscedat imago."
　　　　　　　　　　　　　　VAL. FLAC.

FRIEND of my youth! when young we roved,
Like striplings, mutually beloved,
　　With friendship's purest glow,
The bliss which winged those rosy hours
Was such as pleasure seldom showers
　　On mortals here below.

The recollection seems alone
Dearer than all the joys I've known,
　　When distant far from you:
Though pain, 'tis still a pleasing pain,
To trace those 'lays and hours again,
　　And sigh again, adieu!

My pensive memory lingers o'er
Those scenes to be enjoyed no more,
　　Those scenes regretted ever;
The measure of our youth is full,
Life's evening dreary is dark and dull,
　　And we may meet — ah! never!

As when one parent spring supplies
Two streams which from one fountain rise,
　　Together joined in vain;
How soon, diverging from their source,
Each, murmuring, seeks another course,
　　Till mingled in the main!

Our vital streams of weal or woe,
Though near, alas! distinctly flow,
　　Nor mingle as before:
Now swift or slow, now black or clear
Till death's unfathomed gulf appear,
　　And both shall quit the shore.

Our souls, my friend! which once supplied
One wish, nor breathed a thought beside,
　　Now flow in different channels:
Disdaining humbler rural sports,
'Tis yours to mix in polished courts,
　　And shine in fashion's annals;

'Tis mine to waste on love my time,
Or vent my reveries in rhyme,
　　Without the aid of reason;
For sense and reason (critics know it)
Have quitted every amorous poet,
　　Nor left a thought to seize on.

Poor LITTLE! sweet, melodious bard!
Of late esteemed it monstrous hard

That he, who sang before all, —
He who the lore of love expanded, —
By dire reviewers should be branded
　　As void of wit and moral.[1]

And yet, while Beauty's praise is thine,
Harmonious favorite of the Nine!
　　Repine not at thy lot.
Thy soothing lays may still be read,
When Persecution's arm is dead,
　　And critics are forgot.

Still I must yield those worthies merit,
Who chasten, with unsparing spirit,
　　Bad rhymes, and those who write them,
And though myself may be the next,
By criticism to be vext,
　　I really will not fight them.[2]

Perhaps they would do quite as well
To break the rudely sounding shell
　　Of such a young beginner.
He who offends at pert nineteen,
Ere thirty may become, I ween,
　　A very hardened sinner.

Now, Clare, I must return to you;
And, sure, apologies are due:
　　Accept, then, my concession.
In truth, dear Clare, in fancy's flight
I soar along from left to right;
　　My muse admires digression.

I think I said 'twould be your fate
To add one star to royal state; —
　　May regal smiles attend you!
And should a noble monarch reign,
You will not seek his smiles in vain,
　　If worth can recommend you.

Yet since in danger courts abound,
Where specious rivals glitter round,
　　From snares may saints preserve you;
And grant your love or friendship ne'er
From any claim a kindred care,
　　But those who best deserve you!

Not for a moment may you stray
From truth's secure, unerring way!
　　May no delights decoy!
O'er roses may your footsteps move,
Your smiles be ever smiles of love,
　　Your tears be tears of joy!

———

[1] These stanzas were written soon after the ap-
pearance of a severe critique, in a northern review,
on a new publication of the British Anacreon. — [See
Edinburgh Review, July, 1807, article on "Epistles,
Odes, and other Poems, by Thomas Little, Esq."]
[2] A bard [Moore] (horresco referens) defied his
reviewer [Jeffrey] to mortal combat. If this exam-
ple becomes prevalent, our periodical censors must
be dipped in the river Styx; for what else can secure
them from the numerous host of their enraged as-
sailants?

Oh! if you wish that happiness
Your coming days and years may bless,
　And virtues crown your brow;
Be still as you were wont to be,
Spotless as you've been known to me,—
　Be still as you are now.[1]

And though some trifling share of praise,
To cheer my last declining days,
　To me were doubly dear;
Whilst blessing your beloved name,
I'd wave at once a *poet's* fame,
　To prove a *prophet* here.

LINES WRITTEN BENEATH AN ELM IN THE CHURCHYARD OF HARROW.[2]

SPOT of my youth! whose hoary branches sigh,
Swept by the breeze that fans thy cloudless sky;
Where now alone I muse, who oft have trod,
With those I loved, thy soft and verdant sod;

With those who, scattered far, perchance deplore,
Like me, the happy scenes they knew before:
Oh! as I trace again thy winding hill,
Mine eyes admire, my heart adores thee still,
Thou drooping Elm! beneath whose boughs I lay,
And frequent mused the twilight hours away;
Where, as they once were wont, my limbs recline,
But, ah! without the thoughts which then were mine:
How do thy branches, moaning to the blast,
Invite the bosom to recall the past,
And seem to whisper, as they gently swell,
" Take, while thou canst, a lingering, last farewell!"
　When fate shall chill, at length, this fevered breast,
And calm its cares and passions into rest,
Oft have I thought, 'twould soothe my dying hour,—
If aught may soothe when life resigns her power,—
To know some humble grave, some narrow cell,
Would hide my bosom where it loved to dwell;
With this fond dream, methinks, 'twere sweet to die—
And here it lingered, here my heart might lie;
Here might I sleep where all my hopes arose,
Scene of my youth, and couch of my repose;
For ever stretched beneath this mantling shade,
Pressed by the turf where once my childhood played,
Wrapt by the soil that veils the spot I loved,
Mixed with the earth o'er which my footsteps moved,
Blest by the tongues that charmed my youthful ear,
Mourned by the few my soul acknowledged here;
Deplored by those in early days allied,
And unremembered by the world beside.

September 2, 1807.

---

[1] [" Of all I have ever known, Clare has always been the least altered in every thing from the excellent qualities and kind affections which attached me to him so strongly at school. I should hardly have thought it possible for society (or the world, as it is called) to leave a being with so little of the leaven of bad passions. I do not speak from personal experience only, but from all I have ever heard of him from others, during absence and distance."— *Byron's Diary*, 1821.]

[2] [On losing his natural daughter, Allegra, in April, 1822, Byron sent her remains to be buried at Harrow, "where," he says, in a letter to Mr. Murray, "I once hoped to have laid my own." "There is," he adds, "a spot in the *churchyard*, near the footpath, on the brow of the hill looking towards Windsor, and a tomb under a large tree (bearing the name of Peachie, or Peachey), where I used to sit for hours and hours when a boy. This was my favorite spot; but as I wish to erect a tablet to her memory, the body had better be deposited in the *church*." — and it was so accordingly.]

OCCASIONAL PIECES.

FROM 1807 TO 1824.

THE ADIEU.

WRITTEN UNDER THE IMPRESSION THAT
THE AUTHOR WOULD SOON DIE.

ADIEU, thou Hill![1] where early joy
Spread roses o'er my brow;
Where Science seeks each loitering boy
With knowledge to endow.
Adieu my youthful friends or foes,
Partners of former bliss or woes;
No more through Ida's paths we stray;
Soon must I share the gloomy cell,
Whose ever-slumbering inmates dwell
Unconscious of the day.

Adieu, ye hoary Regal Fanes,
Ye spires of Granta's vale,
Where Learning robed in sable reigns,
And Melancholy pale.
Ye comrades of the jovial hour,
Ye tenants of the classic bower,
On Cama's verdant margin placed,
Adieu! while memory still is mine,
For, offerings on Oblivion's shrine,
These scenes must be effaced.

Adieu, ye mountains of the clime
Where grew my youthful years
Where Loch na Garr in snows sublime
His giant summit rears.
Why did my childhood wander forth
From you, ye regions of the North,
With sons of pride to roam?
Why did I quit my Highland cave,
Marr's dusky heath, and Dee's clear wave,
To seek a Sotheron home?

Hall of my Sires! a long farewell—
Yet why to thee adieu?
Thy vaults will echo back my knell,
Thy towers my tomb will view:
The faltering tongue which sung thy fall,
And former glories of thy Hall[2]
Forgets its wonted simple note—
But yet the Lyre retains the strings,
And sometimes, on Æolian wings,
In dying strains may float.

---

[1] Harrow.
[2] See *ante*, pp. 4, 33.

Fields, which surround yon rustic **cot,**
While yet I linger here,
Adieu! you are not now forgot,
To retrospection dear.
Streamlet![3] along whose rippling surge,
My youthful limbs were wont to urge
At noontide heat their pliant course;
Plunging with ardor from the shore,
Thy springs will lave these limbs no more,
Deprived of active force.

And shall I here forget the scene,
Still nearest to my breast?
Rocks rise, and rivers roll between
The spot which passion blest;
Yet, Mary,[4] all thy beauties seem
Fresh as in Love's bewitching dream,
To me in smiles displayed:
Till slow disease resigns his prey
To Death, the parent of decay,
Thine image cannot fade.

And thou, my Friend![5] whose gentle love
Yet thrills my bosom's chords,
How much thy friendship was above
Description's power of words!
Still near my breast thy gift I wear,
Which sparkled once with Feeling's tear,
Of Love the pure, the sacred gem;
Our souls were equal, and our lot
In that dear moment quite forgot;
Let Pride alone condemn!

All, all, is dark and cheerless now!
No smile of Love's deceit,
Can warm my veins with wonted glow,
Can bid Life's pulses beat:
Not e'en the hope of future fame,
Can wake my faint, exhausted frame,
Or crown with fancied wreaths my head.
Mine is a short inglorious race,—
To humble in the dust my face,
And mingle with the dead.

Oh Fame! thou goddess of my heart;
On him who gains thy praise,

---

[3] [The river Grete, at Southwell.]
[4] Mary Duff. See *ante*, p. 49, note.
[5] Eddlestone, the Cambridge chorister. See *ante*,
p. 28.

Pointless must fall the Spectre's dart,
  Consumed in Glory's blaze;
But me she beckons from the earth,
My name obscure, unmarked my birth,
  My life a short and vulgar dream;
Lost in the dull, ignoble crowd,
My hopes recline within a shroud,
  My fate is Lethe's stream.

When I repose beneath the sod,
  Unheeded in the clay,
Where once my playful footsteps trod,
  Where now my head must lay;
The meed of Pity will be shed
In dew-drops o'er my narrow bed,
  By nightly skies, and storms alone;
No mortal eye will deign to steep
With tears the dark sepulchral deep
  Which hides a name unknown.

Forget this world, my restless sprite,
  Turn, turn thy thoughts to Heaven:
There must thou soon direct thy flight,
  If errors are forgiven.
To bigots and to sects unknown,
Bow down beneath the Almighty's Throne;
  To Him address thy trembling prayer:
He, who is merciful and just,
Will not reject a child of dust,
  Although his meanest care.

Father of Light! to Thee I call,
  My soul is dark within:
Thou, who canst mark the sparrow's fall,
  Avert the death of sin.
Thou, who canst guide the wandering star,
Who calm'st the elemental war,
  Whose mantle is yon boundless sky,
My thoughts, my words, my crimes forgive;
And, since I soon must cease to live,
  Instruct me how to die.   1807.

TO A VAIN LADY.

AH, heedless girl! why thus disclose
  What ne'er was meant for other ears:
Why thus destroy thine own repose,
  And dig the source of future tears?

Oh, thou wilt weep, imprudent maid,
  While lurking envious foes will smile,
For all the follies thou hast said
  Of those who spoke but to beguile.

Vain girl! thy lingering woes are nigh,
  If thou believ'st what striplings say:
Oh, from the deep temptation fly,
  Nor fall the specious spoiler's prey.

Dost thou repeat, in childish boast,
  The words man utters to deceive?
Thy peace, thy hope, thy all is lost,
  If thou canst venture to believe.

While now amongst thy female peers
  Thou tell'st again the soothing tale,
Canst thou not mark the rising sneers
  Duplicity in vain would veil?

These tales in secret silence hush,
  Nor make thyself the public gaze:
What modest maid without a blush
  Recounts a flattering coxcomb's praise?

Will not the laughing boy despise
  Her who relates each fond conceit'—
Who, thinking Heaven is in her eyes
  Yet cannot see the slight deceit?

For she who takes a soft delight
  These amorous nothings in revealing,
Must credit all we say or write,
  While vanity prevents concealing.

Cease, if you prize your beauty's reign!
  No jealousy bids me reprove:
One, who is thus from nature vain,
  I pity, but I cannot love.
                    January 15, 1807.

TO ANNE.

OH, Anne! your offences to me have been
    grievous;
  I thought from my wrath no atonement could
    save you;
But woman is made to command and deceive
    us—
  I looked in your face, and I almost forgave you.

I vowed I could ne'er for a moment respect you,
  Yet thought that a day's separation was long:
When we met, I determined again to suspect
    you—
  Your smile soon convinced me suspicion was
    wrong.

I swore, in a transport of young indignation,
  With fervent contempt evermore to disdain
    you:
I saw you—my anger became admiration;
  And now, all my wish, all my hope, 's to re-
    gain you.

With beauty like yours, oh, how vain the con-
    tention!
  Thus lowly I sue for forgiveness before
    you;—
At once to conclude such a fruitless dissension,
  Be false, my sweet Anne, when I cease to
    adore you!   January 16, 1807.

TO THE SAME.

OH say not, sweet Anne, that the Fates have
    decreed
  The heart which adores you should wish to
    dissever;

Such Fates were to me most unkind ones in-
   deed,—
   To bear me from love and from beauty for
   ever.

Your frowns, lovely girl, are the Fates which
   alone
Could bid me from fond admiration refrain;
By these, every hope, every wish were o'er-
   thrown,
   Till smiles should restore me to rapture
   again.

As the ivy and oak, in the forest entwined,
   The rage of the tempest united must weather,
My love and my life were by nature designed
   To flourish alike, or to perish together.

Then say not, sweet Anne, that the Fates have
   decreed
   Your lover should bid you a lasting adieu;
Till Fate can ordain that his bosom shall bleed,
   His soul, his existence, are centred in you.

1807.

TO THE AUTHOR OF A SONNET
BEGINNING

*"'SAD IS MY VERSE,' YOU SAY, 'AND YET
NO TEAR.'"*

THY verse is "sad" enough, no doubt:
   A devilish deal more sad than witty!
Why we should weep, I can't find out,
   Unless, for *thee* we weep in pity.

Yet there is one I pity more;
   And much, alas! I think he needs it:
For he, I'm sure, will suffer sore,
   Who, to his own misfortune, reads it.

Thy rhymes, without the aid of magic,
   May *once* be read—but never after:
Yet their effect's by no means tragic,
   Although by far too dull for laughter.

But would you make our bosoms bleed,
   And of no common pang complain—
If you would make us weep indeed,
   Tell us, you'll read them o'er again.

March 8, 1807.

ON FINDING A FAN.

IN one who felt as once he felt,
   This might, perhaps, have fanned the flame;
But now his heart no more will melt,
   Because that heart is not the same.

As when the ebbing flames are low,
   The aid which once improved their light,
And bade them burn with fiercer glow,
   Now quenches all their blaze in night,

Thus has it been with passion's fires—
   As many a boy and girl remembers—
While every hope of love expires,
   Extinguished with the dying embers.

The *first*, though not a spark survive,
   Some careful hand may teach to burn;
The *last*, alas! can ne'er·revive;
   No touch can bid its warmth return.

Or, if it chance to wake again,
   Not always doomed its heat to smother,
It sheds (so wayward fates ordain)
   Its former warmth around another.   1807.

FAREWELL TO THE MUSE.

THOU Power! who hast ruled me through in-
   fancy's days,
   Young offspring of Fancy, 'tis time we should
   part;
Then rise on the gale this the last of my lays,
   The coldest effusion which springs from my
   heart.

This bosom, responsive to rapture no more,
   Shall hush thy wild notes, nor implore thee
   to sing;
The feelings of childhood, which taught thee
   to soar,
   Are wafted far distant on Apathy's wing.

Though simple the themes of my rude flow-
   ing Lyre,
   Yet even these themes are departed for ever;
No more beam the eyes which my dream could
   inspire,
   My visions are flown, to return,—alas, never I

When drained is the nectar which gladdens the
   bowl,
   How vain is the effort delight to prolong!
When cold is the beauty which dwelt in my soul,
   What magic of Fancy can lengthen my song?

Can the lips sing of Love in the desert alone,
   Of kisses and smiles which they now must
   resign?
Or dwell with delight on the hours that are
   flown?
   Ah, no! for these hours can no longer be
   mine.

Can they speak of the friends that I lived but
   to love?
   Ah, surely affection ennobles the strain!
But how can my numbers in sympathy move,
   When I scarcely can hope to behold them
   again?

Can I sing of the deeds which my Fathers have
   done,
   And raise my loud harp to the fame of my
   Sires?

For glories like theirs, oh, how faint is my tone!
For Heroes' exploits how unequal my fires!
Untouched, then, my Lyre shall reply to the
　　blast —
　'Tis hushed; and my feeble endeavors are
　　o'er;
And those who have heard it will pardon the
　　past,
　When they know that its murmurs shall vi-
　　brate no more.

And soon shall its wild erring notes be forgot,
　Since early affection and love is o'ercast:
Oh! blest had my fate been, and happy my lot,
　Had the first strain of love been the dearest,
　　the last.

Farewell, my young Muse! since we now can
　　ne'er meet;
　If our songs have been languid, they surely
　　are few:
Let us hope that the present at least will be
　　sweet —
　The present — which seals our eternal
　　Adieu.　　　　　　　　　　　　　　1807.

TO AN OAK AT NEWSTEAD.[1]

YOUNG Oak! when I planted thee deep in
　　the ground,
　I hoped that thy days would be longer than
　　mine;
That thy dark-waving branches would flourish
　　around,
　And ivy thy trunk with its mantle entwine.

Such, such was my hope, when, in infancy's
　　years,
　On the land of my fathers I reared thee
　　with pride:
They are past, and I water thy stem with my
　　tears, —
　Thy decay not the weeds that surround
　　thee can hide.

I left thee, my Oak, and, since that fatal hour,
　A stranger has dwelt in the hall of my sire;
Till manhood shall crown me, not mine is the
　　power,
　But his, whose neglect may have bade thee
　　expire.

[1] [Byron, on his first arrival at Newstead, in 1798,
planted an oak in the garden, and nourished the
fancy, that as the tree flourished so should he. On
revisiting the abbey, he found the oak choked up
by weeds, and almost destroyed; — hence these
lines. Shortly after Colonel Wildman took posses-
sion, he one day noticed it, and said to the servant
who was with him, " Here is a fine young oak; but
it must be cut down, as it grows in an improper
place." — " I hope not, sir," replied the man; " for
it's the one that my lord was so fond of, because he
set it himself." The tree, of course, was spared,
and is shown to strangers as the BYRON OAK.]

Oh! hardy thou wert — even now little care
　Might revive thy young head, and thy
　　wounds gently heal:
But thou wert not fated affection to share —
　For who could suppose that a Stranger
　　would feel?

Ah, droop not, my Oak! lift thy head for a
　　while;
　Ere twice round yon Glory this planet shall
　　run,
The hand of thy Master will teach thee to smile,
　When Infancy's years of probation are done.

Oh, live then, my Oak! tower aloft from the
　　weeds,
　That clog thy young growth, and assist thy
　　decay,
For still in thy bosom are life's early seeds,
　And still may thy branches their beauty dis-
　　play.

Oh! yet, if maturity's years may be thine,
　Though *I* shall lie low in the cavern of
　　death,
On thy leaves yet the day-beam of ages may
　　shine,
　Uninjured by time, or the rude winter's
　　breath.

For centuries still may thy boughs lightly
　　wave
　O'er the corse of thy lord in thy canopy laid;
While the branches thus gratefully shelter his
　　grave,
　The chief who survives may recline in thy
　　shade.

And as he, with his boys, shall revisit this spot,
　He will tell them in whispers more softly to
　　tread.
Oh! surely, by these I shall ne'er be forgot:
　Remembrance still hallows the dust of the
　　dead.

And here, will they say, when in life's glowing
　　prime,
　Perhaps he has poured forth his young
　　simple lay,
And here must he sleep, till the moments of
　　time
　Are lost in the hours of Eternity's day.
　　　　　　　　　　　　　　　　　　　1807.

ON REVISITING HARROW.[2]

HERE once engaged the stranger's view
　Young Friendship's record simply traced;
Few were her words, — but yet, though few,
　Resentment's hand the line defaced.

[2] Some years ago, when at Harrow, a friend of
the author engraved on a particular spot the names
of both, with a few additional words, as a memorial.

Deeply she cut — but not erased,
  The characters were still so plain,
That Friendship once returned, and gazed, —
  Till Memory hailed the words again.

Repentance placed them as before;
  Forgiveness joined her gentle name;
So fair the inscription seemed once more,
  That Friendship thought it still the same.

Thus might the Record now have been;
  But, ah, in spite of Hope's endeavor,
Or Friendship's tears, Pride rushed between,
  And blotted out the line for ever!

September, 1807.

EPITAPH ON JOHN ADAMS, OF SOUTHWELL,

A CARRIER, WHO DIED OF DRUNKENNESS.

JOHN ADAMS lies here, of the parish of
    Southwell,
A *Carrier* who *carried* his can to his mouth
    well;
He *carried* so much, and he *carried* so fast,
He could *carry* no more — so was *carried* at
    last;
For, the liquor he drank, being too much for
    one,
He could not *carry* off, — so he's now *carri-on*.

September, 1807.

TO MY SON.[1]

THOSE flaxen locks, those eyes of blue,
Bright as thy mother's in their hue;
Those rosy lips, whose dimples play
And smile to steal the heart away,
Recall a scene of former joy,
And touch thy father's heart, my Boy!

And thou canst lisp a father's name —
Ah, William, were thine own the same, —
No self-reproach — but, let me cease —
My care for thee shall purchase peace;
Thy mother's shade shall smile in joy,
And pardon all the past, my Boy!

Her lowly grave the turf has prest,
And thou hast known a stranger's breast.
Derision sneers upon thy birth,
And yields thee scarce a name on earth;
Yet shall not these one hope destroy, —
A Father's heart is thine, my Boy!

Afterwards, on receiving some real or imagined in-
jury, the author destroyed the frail record before he
left Harrow. On revisiting the place in 1807, he
wrote under it these stanzas.
  [1] [Moore in his Life of Byron questions the ex-
istence of this son, whom he considers merely a con-
venient fiction of the poet. But from a passage in

Why, let the world unfeeling frown,
Must I fond Nature's claim disown?
Ah, no — though moralists reprove,
I hail thee, dearest child of love,
Fair cherub, pledge of youth and joy —
A Father guards thy birth, my Boy!

Oh, 'twill be sweet in thee to trace,
Ere age has wrinkled o'er my face,
Ere half my glass of life is run,
At once a brother and a son;
And all my wane of years employ
In justice done to thee, my Boy!

Although so young thy heedless sire,
Youth will not damp parental fire;
And, wert thou still less dear to me,
While Helen's form revives in thee,
The breast, which beat to former joy,
Will ne'er desert its pledge, my Boy!

1807.

FAREWELL! IF EVER FONDEST PRAYER.

FAREWELL! if ever fondest prayer
  For other's weal availed on high,
Mine will not all be lost in air,
  But waft thy name beyond the sky.
'Twere vain to speak, to weep, to sigh:
  Oh! more than tears of blood can tell,
When wrung from guilt's expiring eye,
  Are in that word — Farewell! — Farewell!

These lips are mute, these eyes are dry;
  But in my breast and in my brain,
Awake the pangs that pass not by,
  The thought that ne'er shall sleep again.
My soul nor deigns nor dares complain,
  Though grief and passion there rebel:
I only know we loved in vain —
  I only feel — Farewell! — Farewell!

1808.

BRIGHT BE THE PLACE OF THY SOUL.

BRIGHT be the place of thy soul!
  No lovelier spirit than thine
E'er burst from its mortal control,
  In the orbs of the blessed to shine.

On earth thou wert all but divine,
  As thy soul shall immortally be;
And our sorrow may cease to repine,
  When we know that thy God is with thee.

Light be the turf of thy tomb!
  May its verdure like emeralds be:

Don Juan (canto XVI. stanza 61), there is reason to
believe that Moore was mistaken.]

There should not be the shadow of gloom
  In aught that reminds us of thee.

Young flowers and an evergreen tree
  May spring from the spot of thy rest:
But nor cypress nor yew let us see;
  For why should we mourn for the blest?

1808.

WHEN WE TWO PARTED.

WHEN we two parted
  In silence and tears,
Half broken-hearted
  To sever for years,
Pale grew thy cheek and cold,
  Colder thy kiss;
Truly that hour foretold
  Sorrow to this.

The dew of the morning
  Sunk chill on my brow —
It felt like the warning
  Of what I feel now.
Thy vows are all broken,
  And light is thy fame;
I hear thy name spoken,
  And share in its shame.

They name thee before me,
  A knell to mine ear;
A shudder comes o'er me —
  Why wert thou so dear?
They know not I knew thee,
  Who knew thee too well: —
Long, long shall I rue thee,
  Too deeply to tell.

In secret we met—
  In silence I grieve,
That thy heart could forget,
  Thy spirit deceive.
If I should meet thee
  After long years,
How should I greet thee? —
  With silence and tears.

1808.

TO A YOUTHFUL FRIEND.

FEW years have passed since thou and I
  Were firmest friends, at least in name,
And childhood's gay sincerity
  Preserved our feelings long the same.

But now, like me, too well thou knowest
  What trifles oft the heart recall;
And those who once have loved the most
  Too soon forget they loved at all.

And such the change the heart displays,
  So frail is early friendship's reign,

A month's brief lapse, perhaps a day's,
  Will view thy mind estranged again.

If so, it never shall be mine
  To mourn the loss of such a heart;
The fault was Nature's fault, not thine,
  Which made thee fickle as thou art.

As rolls the ocean's changing tide,
  So human feelings ebb and flow;
And who would in a breast confide,
  Where stormy passions ever glow?

It boots not that, together bred,
  Our childish days were days of joy:
My spring of life has quickly fled;
  Thou, too, hast ceased to be a boy.

And when we bid adieu to youth,
  Slaves to the specious world's control,
We sigh a long farewell to truth;
  That world corrupts the noblest soul.

Ah, joyous season! when the mind
  Dares all things boldly but to lie;
When thought ere spoke is unconfined,
  And sparkles in the placid eye.

Not so in Man's maturer years,
  When Man himself is but a tool;
When interest sways our hopes and fears,
  And all must love and hate by rule.

With fools in kindred vice the same,
  We learn at length our faults to blend;
And those, and those alone, may claim
  The prostituted name of friend.

Such is the common lot of man:
  Can we then 'scape from folly free?
Can we reverse the general plan,
  Nor be what all in turn must be?

No; for myself, so dark my fate
  Through every turn of life hath been;
Man and the world so much I hate,
  I care not when I quit the scene.

But thou, with spirit frail and light,
  Wilt shine awhile, and pass away;
As glow-worms sparkle through the night,
  But dare not stand the test of day.

Alas! whenever folly calls
  Where parasites and princes meet,
(For cherished first in royal halls,
  The welcome vices kindly greet)

Ev'n now thou'rt nightly seen to add
  One insect to the fluttering crowd;
And still thy trifling heart is glad
  To join the vain, and court the proud.

There dost thou glide from fair to fair,
  Still simpering on with eager haste,
As flies along the gay parterre,
  That taint the flowers they scarcely taste.

But say, what nymph will prize the flame
  Which seems, as marshy vapors move,
To flit along from dame to dame,
  An ignis-fatuus gleam of love?

What friend for thee, howe'er inclined,
  Will deign to own a kindred care?
Who will debase his manly mind,
  For friendship every fool may share!

In time forbear; amidst the throng
  No more so base a thing be seen;
No more so idly pass along:
  Be something, any thing, but—mean.[1]
                          1808.

LINES INSCRIBED UPON A CUP FORMED FROM A SKULL.

START not—nor deem my spirit fled:
  In me behold the only skull,
From which, unlike a living head,
  Whatever flows is never dull.

I lived, I loved, I quaffed, like thee;
  I died: let earth my bones resign:
Fill up—thou canst not injure me;
  The worm hath fouler lips than thine.

Better to hold the sparkling grape,
  Than nurse the earth-worm's slimy brood;
And circle in the goblet's shape
  The drink of Gods, than reptile's food.

Where once my wit, perchance, hath shone,
  In aid of others' let me shine;
And when, alas! our brains are gone,
  What nobler substitute than wine?

Quaff while thou canst: another race,
  When thou and thine like me are sped,
May rescue thee from earth's embrace,
  And rhyme and revel with the dead.

Why not? since through life's little day
  Our heads such sad effects produce;
Redeemed from worms and wasting clay,
  This chance is theirs, to be of use.[2]
                  NEWSTEAD ABBEY, 1808.

----

[1] [This copy of verses, and several of the poems which follow it, originally appeared in a volume published in 1809 by Mr. Hobhouse, under the title of "Imitations and Translations, together with Original Poems," and bearing the modest epigraph—"Nos hæc novimus esse nihil."]

[2] [Byron gives the following account of this cup:—"The gardener, in digging, discovered a skull that had probably belonged to some jolly friar or monk of the Abbey, about the time it was demonasteried. Observing it to be of giant size, and in a perfect state of preservation, a strange fancy seized me of having it set and mounted as a drinking cup. I accordingly sent it to town, and it returned with a very high polish, and of a mottled color like tortoise-shell."]

WELL! THOU ART HAPPY.[3]

WELL! thou art happy, and I feel
  That I should thus be happy too;
For still my heart regards thy weal
  Warmly, as it was wont to do.

Thy husband's blest—and 'twill impart
  Some pangs to view his happier lot:
But let them pass—Oh! how my heart
  Would hate him, if he loved thee not!

When late I saw thy favorite child,
  I thought my jealous heart would break;
But when the unconscious infant smiled,
  I kissed it for its mother's sake.

I kissed it,—and repressed my sighs,
  Its father in its face to see;
But then it had its mother's eyes,
  And they were all to love and me.

Mary, adieu! I must away:
  While thou art blest I'll not repine;
But near thee I can never stay;
  My heart would soon again be thine.

I deemed that time, I deemed that pride
  Had quenched at length my boyish flame,
Nor knew, till seated by thy side,
  My heart in all,—save hope,—the same.

Yet was I calm: I knew the time
  My breast would thrill before thy look;
But now to tremble were a crime—
  We met,—and not a nerve was shook.

I saw thee gaze upon my face,
  Yet meet with no confusion there:
One only feeling could'st thou trace;
  The sullen calmness of despair.

Away! away! my early dream
  Remembrance never must awake:
Oh! where is Lethe's fabled stream?
  My foolish heart be still, or break.
                  November 2, 1808.

INSCRIPTION ON THE MONUMENT OF A NEWFOUNDLAND DOG.[4]

WHEN some proud son of man returns to earth,
Unknown to glory, but upheld by birth,
The sculptor's art exhausts the pomp of woe,
And storied urns record who rests below;
When all is done, upon the tomb is seen,
Not what he was, but what he should have been:
But the poor dog, in life the firmest friend,
The first to welcome, foremost to defend,

----

[3] [A few days before this poem was written, the poet had been invited to dine at Annesley. On the infant daughter of his fair hostess being brought into the room, he started involuntarily, and with difficulty suppressed his emotion.]

[4] [This monument is still a conspicuous ornament

Whose honest heart is still his master's own,
Who labors, fights, lives, breathes for him
    alone,
Unhonored falls, unnoticed all his worth,
Denied in heaven the soul he held on earth :
While man, vain insect ! hopes to be forgiven,
And claims himself a sole exclusive heaven.
Oh man ! thou feeble tenant of an hour,
Debased by slavery, or corrupt by power,
Who knows thee well must quit thee with dis-
    gust,
Degraded mass of animated dust !
Thy love is lust, thy friendship all a cheat,
Thy smiles hypocrisy, thy words deceit !
By nature vile, ennobled but by name,
Each kindred brute might bid thee blush for
    shame.
Ye ! who perchance behold this simple urn,
Pass on — it honors none you wish to mourn :
To mark a friend's remains these stones arise ;
I never knew but one, — and here he lies.

    NEWSTEAD ABBEY, November 30, 1808.

TO A LADY, ON BEING ASKED MY REASON FOR QUITTING ENGLAND IN THE SPRING.

WHEN Man, expelled from Eden's bowers,
    A moment lingered near the gate,
Each scene recalled the vanished hours,
    And bade him curse his future fate.

But, wandering on through distant climes,
    He learnt to bear his load of grief;
Just gave a sigh to other times,
    And found in busier scenes relief.

---

in the garden of Newstead. The following is the
inscription by which the verses are preceded : —
    " Near this spot
    Are deposited the Remains of one
    Who possessed Beauty without Vanity,
    Strength without Insolence,
    Courage without Ferocity,
    And all the Virtues of Man without his Vices.
This Praise, which would be unmeaning Flattery
    If inscribed over human ashes,
    Is but a just tribute to the Memory of
    BOATSWAIN, a Dog,
    Who was born at Newfoundland, May, 1803,
    And died at Newstead Abbey, Nov. 18, 1808."
Byron thus announced the death of his favorite to
Mr. Hodgson : — " Boatswain is dead ! — he expired
in a state of madness, on the 18th, after suffering
much, yet retaining all the gentleness of his nature
to the last ; never attempting to do the least injury
to any one near him. I have now lost every thing
except old Murray." By the will which he exe-
cuted in 1811, he directed that his own body should
be buried in a vault in the garden near his faithful
dog.]

Thus, lady ! [1] will it be with me,
    And I must view thy charms no more ;
For, while I linger near to thee,
    I sigh for all I knew before.

In flight I shall be surely wise,
    Escaping from temptation's snare ;
I cannot view my paradise,
    Without the wish of dwelling there.[2]
               December 2, 1808.

REMIND ME NOT, REMIND ME NOT.

REMIND me not, remind me not,
    Of those beloved, those vanished hours
      When all my soul was given to thee ;
Hours that may never be forgot,
    Till time unnerves our vital powers,
      And thou and I shall cease to be.

Can I forget — canst thou forget,
    When playing with thy golden hair,
      How quick thy fluttering heart did move ?
Oh ! by my soul, I see thee yet,
    With eyes so languid, breast so fair,
      And lips, though silent, breathing love.

When thus reclining on my breast,
    Those eyes threw back a glance so sweet,
      As half reproached yet raised desire,
And still we near and nearer prest,
    And still our glowing lips would meet,
      As if in kisses to expire.

And then those pensive eyes would close,
    And bid their lids each other seek,
      Veiling the azure orbs below ;
While their long lashes' darkened gloss
    Seemed stealing o'er thy brilliant cheek,
      Like raven's plumage smoothed on snow,

---

[1] [In the first copy, " Thus, Mary ! " — (Mrs.
Musters).]

[2] [Originally this line stood, — " Without a wish
to enter there." The following is an extract from a
letter of Byron's, written in 1823, only three days
previous to his leaving Italy for Greece : — " Miss
Chaworth was two years older than myself. She
married a man of an ancient and respectable family,
but her marriage was not a happier one than my own.
Her conduct, however, was irreproachable ; but there
was not sympathy between their characters. I had
not seen her for many years, when an occasion of-
fered. I was upon the point, with her consent, of
paying her a visit, when my sister, who has always
had more influence over me than any one else, per-
suaded me not to do it. ' For,' said she, ' if you go
you will fall in love again, and then there will be a
scene ; one step will lead to another, *et cela fera
un éclat.*' I was guided by those reasons, and
shortly after married, — with what success it is use-
less to say."]

I dreamt last night our love returned,
  And, sooth to say, that very dream
    Was sweeter in its phantasy,
Than if for other hearts I burned,
  For eyes that ne'er like thine could beam
    In rapture's wild reality.

Then tell me not, remind me not,
  Of hours which, though for ever gone,
    Can still a pleasing dream restore,
Till thou and I shall be forgot,
  And senseless as the mouldering stone
    Which tells that we shall be no more.

THERE WAS A TIME, I NEED NOT NAME.

THERE was a time, I need not name,
  Since it will ne'er forgotten be,
When all our feelings were the same
  As still my soul hath been to thee.

And from that hour when first thy tongue
  Confessed a love which equalled mine,
Though many a grief my heart hath wrung,
  Unknown and thus unfelt by thine,

None, none hath sunk so deep as this—
  To think how all that love hath flown;
Transient as every faithless kiss,
  But transient in thy breast alone.

And yet my heart some solace knew,
  When late I heard thy lips declare,
In accents once imagined true,
  Remembrance of the days that were.

Yes! my adored, yet most unkind!
  Though thou wilt never love again,
To me 'tis doubly sweet to find
  Remembrance of that love remain.

Yes! 'tis a glorious thought to me,
  Nor longer shall my soul repine,
Whate'er thou art or e'er shalt be,
  Thou hast been dearly, solely mine

AND WILT THOU WEEP WHEN I AM LOW?

AND wilt thou weep when I am low?
  Sweet lady! speak those words again:
Yet if they grieve thee, say not so—
  I would not give that bosom pain.

My heart is sad, my hopes are gone,
  My blood runs coldly through my breast;
And when I perish, thou alone
  Wilt sigh above my place of rest.

And yet, methinks, a gleam of peace
  Doth through my cloud of anguish shine;

And for awhile my sorrows cease,
  To know thy heart hath felt for mine.

Oh lady! blessed be that tear—
  It falls for one who cannot weep:
Such precious drops are doubly dear
  To those whose eyes no tear may steep.

Sweet lady! once my heart was warm
  With every feeling soft as thine;
But beauty's self hath ceased to charm
  A wretch created to repine.

Yet wilt thou weep when I am low?
  Sweet lady! speak those words again;
Yet if they grieve thee, say not so—
  I would not give that bosom pain.

FILL THE GOBLET AGAIN.

A SONG.

FILL the goblet again! for I never before
Felt the glow which now gladdens my heart
  to its core;
Let us drink!—who would not?—since,
through life's varied round,
In the goblet alone no deception is found.

I have tried in its turn all that life can supply;
I have basked in the beam of a dark rolling
  eye;
I have loved!—who has not?—but what
  heart can declare,
That pleasure existed while passion was there?

In the days of my youth, when the heart's in
  its spring,
And dreams that affection can never take
  wing,
I had friends!—who has not?—but what
  tongue will avow,
That friends, rosy wine! are so faithful as
  thou?

The heart of a mistress some boy may es-
  trange,
Friendship shifts with the sunbeam—thou
  never canst change:
Thou grow'st old—who does not?—but on
  earth what appears,
Whose virtues, like thine, still increase with
  its years?

Yet if blest to the utmost that love can bestow,
Should a rival bow down to our idol below,
We are jealous!—who's not?—thou hast no
  such alloy;
For the more that enjoy thee, the more we
  enjoy.

Then the season of youth and its vanities
  past,
For refuge we fly to the goblet at last;

There we find — do we not? — in the flow of
the soul,
That truth, as of yore, is confined to the bowl.

When the box of Pandora was opened on
earth,
And Misery's triumph commenced over Mirth,
Hope was left, — was she not? — but the gob-
let we kiss,
And care not for Hope, who are certain of
bliss.

Long life to the grape! for when summer is
flown,
The age of our nectar shall gladden our own:
We must die — who shall not? — May our
sins be forgiven,
And Hebe shall never be idle in heaven.

STANZAS TO A LADY,[1] ON LEAV-ING ENGLAND.

'TIS done — and shivering in the gale
The bark unfurls her snowy sail;
And whistling o'er the bending mast,
Loud sings on high the freshening blast;
And I must from this land be gone,
Because I cannot love but one.

But could I be what I have been,
And could I see what I have seen —
Could I repose upon the breast
Which once my warmest wishes blest —
I should not seek another zone
Because I cannot love but one.

'Tis long since I beheld that eye
Which gave me bliss or misery;
And I have striven, but in vain,
Never to think of it again:
For though I fly from Albion,
I still can only love but one.

As some lone bird, without a mate,
My weary heart is desolate;
I look around, and cannot trace
One friendly smile or welcome face,
And ev'n in crowds am still alone,
Because I cannot love but one.

And I will cross the whitening foam,
And I will seek a foreign home;
Till I forget a false fair face,
I ne'er shall find a resting-place.
My own dark thoughts I cannot shun,
But ever love, and love but one.

The poorest, veriest wretch on earth
Still finds some hospitable hearth,
Where friendship's or love's softer glow
May smile in joy or soothe in woe;

But frien⸱ ⸱r leman I have none,
Because I cannot love but one.

I go — but wheresoe'er I flee,
There's not an eye will weep for me;
There's not a kind congenial heart,
Where I can claim the meanest part;
Nor thou, who hast my hopes undone,
Wilt sigh, although I love but one.

To think of every early scene,
Of what we are, and what we've been,
Would whelm some softer hearts with woe-
But mine, alas! has stood the blow;
Yet still beats on as it begun,
And never truly loves but one.

And who that dear loved one may be
Is not for vulgar eyes to see,
And why that early love was crost,
Thou know'st the best, I feel the most;
But few that dwell beneath the sun
Have loved so long, and loved but one.

I've tried another's fetters too,
With charms perchance as fair to view;
And I would fain have loved as well,
But some unconquerable spell
Forbade my bleeding breast to own
A kindred care for aught but one.

'Twould soothe to take one lingering view,
And bless thee in my last adieu;
Yet wish I not those eyes to weep
For him that wanders o'er the deep;
His home, his hope, his youth are gone,
Yet still he loves, and loves but one.[2]

1809.

LINES WRITTEN IN AN ALBUM AT MALTA.

As o'er the cold sepulchral stone
    Some name arrests the passer-by;
Thus, when thou view'st this page alone,
    May mine attract thy pensive eye!

And when by thee that name is read,
    Perchance in some succeeding year,
Reflect on me as on the dead,
    And think my heart is buried here.

September 14, 1809.

TO FLORENCE.[3]

OH Lady! when I left the shore,
    The distant shore which gave me birth,

----

[1] [Mrs. Musters.]

[2] [Thus corrected by himself; the two last lines
being originally —
    "Though wheresoe'er my bark may run,
        I love but thee, I love but one."]

[3] [These lines were written at Malta. The lady

I hardly thought to grieve once more,
  To quit another spot on earth:

Yet here, amidst this barren isle,
  Where panting Nature droops the head,
Where only thou art seen to smile,
  I view my parting hour with dread.

Though far from Albion's craggy shore,
  Divided by the dark-blue main;
A few, brief, rolling seasons o'er,
  Perchance I view her cliffs again:

But wheresoe'er I now may roam,
  Through scorching clime, and varied sea,
Though Time restore me to my home,
  I ne'er shall bend mine eyes on thee:

On thee, in whom at once conspire
  All charms which heedless hearts can move,
Whom but to see is to admire,
  And, oh! forgive the word—to love.

Forgive the word, in one who ne'er
  With such a word can more offend;
And since thy heart I cannot share,
  Believe me, what I am, thy friend.

And who so cold as look on thee,
  Thou lovely wanderer, and be less?
Nor be, what man should ever be,
  The friend of Beauty in distress?

Ah! who would think that form had past
  Through Danger's most destructive path,
Had braved the death-winged tempest's blast,
  And 'scaped a tyrant's fiercer wrath?

Lady! when I shall view the walls
  Where free Byzantium once arose,
And Stamboul's Oriental halls
  The Turkish tyrants now inclose;

Though mightiest in the lists of fame,
  That glorious city still shall be;
On me 'twill hold a dearer claim,
  As spot of thy nativity:

And though I bid thee now farewell,
  When I behold that wondrous scene,
Since where thou art, I may not dwell,
  'Twill soothe to be where thou hast been.

September, 1809.

STANZAS

COMPOSED DURING A THUNDERSTORM.[1]

CHILL and mirk is the nightly blast,
  Where Pindus' mountains rise,
And angry clouds are pouring fast
  The vengeance of the skies.

Our guides are gone, our hope is lost,
  And lightnings, as they play,
But show where rocks our path have crost,
  Or gild the torrent's spray.

Is yon a cot I saw, though low?
  When lightning broke the gloom—
How welcome were its shade!—ah, no!
  'Tis but a Turkish tomb.

Through sounds of foaming waterfalls,
  I hear a voice exclaim—
My way-worn countryman, who calls
  On distant England's name.

A shot is fired—by foe or friend?
  Another—'tis to tell
The mountain-peasants to descend,
  And lead us where they dwell.

Oh! who in such a night will dare
  To tempt the wilderness?

to whom they were addressed, and whom he afterwards apostrophizes in the stanzas on the thunderstorm of Zitza and in Childe Harold, is thus mentioned in a letter to his mother:—"This letter is committed to the charge of a very extraordinary lady, whom you have doubtless heard of, Mrs. Spencer Smith, of whose escape the Marquis de Salvo published a narrative a few years ago. She has since been shipwrecked; and her life has been from its commencement so fertile in remarkable incidents, that in a romance they would appear improbable. She was born at Constantinople, where her father, Baron Herbert, was Austrian ambassador; married unhappily, yet has never been impeached in point of character; excited the vengeance of Bonaparte, by taking a part in some conspiracy; several times risked her life; and is not yet five and twenty. She is here on her way to England to join her husband, being obliged to leave Trieste, where she was paying a visit to her mother, by the approach of the French, and embarks soon in a ship of war. Since my arrival here I have had scarcely any other companion. I have found her very pretty, very accomplished, and extremely eccentric. Bonaparte is even now so incensed against her, that her life would be in danger if she were taken prisoner a second time."]

[1] [This thunderstorm occurred during the night of the 11th October, 1809, when Byron's guides had lost the road to Zitza, near the range of mountains formerly called Pindus, in Albania. Mr. Hobhouse, who had rode on before the rest of the party, and arrived at Zitza just as the evening set in, describes the thunder as "roaring without intermission, the echoes of one peal not ceasing to roll in the mountains, before another tremendous crash burst over our heads; whilst the plains and the distant hills appeared in a perpetual blaze." "The tempest," he says, "was altogether terrific, and worthy of the Grecian Jove. My Friend, with the priest and the servants, did not enter our hut till three in the morning. I now learnt from him that they had lost their way, and that, after wandering up and down in total ignorance of their position, they had stopped at last near some Turkish tombstones and a torrent, which they saw by the flashes of lightning. They had been thus exposed for nine hours. It was long before we ceased to talk of the thunderstorm in the plain of Zitza."]

And who 'mid thunder peals can hear
Our signal of distress ?

And who that heard our shouts would rise
To try the dubious road ?
Nor rather deem from nightly cries
That outlaws were abroad.

Clouds burst, skies flash, oh, dreadful hour !
More fiercely pours the storm !
Yet here one thought has still the power
To keep my bosom warm.

While wandering through each broken path,
O'er brake and craggy brow;
While elements exhaust their wrath
Sweet Florence, where art thou ?

Not on the sea, not on the sea,
Thy bark hath long been gone :
Oh, may the storm that pours on me,
Bow down my head alone !

Full swiftly blew the swift Siroc,
When last I pressed thy lip;
And long ere now, with foaming shock,
Impelled thy gallant ship.

Now thou art safe ; nay, long ere now
Hast trod the shore of Spain ;
'Twere hard if aught so fair as thou
Should linger on the main.

And since I now remember thee
In darkness and in dread,
As in those hours of revelry
Which mirth and music sped ;[1]

Do thou, amid the fair white walls,
If Cadiz yet be free,
At times from out her latticed halls
Look o'er the dark blue sea;

Then think upon Calypso's isles,
Endeared by days gone by;
To others give a thousand smiles,
To me a single sigh.

And when the admiring circle mark
The paleness of thy face,
A half-formed tear, a transient spark
Of melancholy grace,

Again thou'lt smile, and blushing shun
Some coxcomb's raillery;
Nor own for once thou thought'st of one,
Who ever thinks on thee.

Though smile and sigh alike are vain,
When severed hearts repine,
My spirit flies o'er mount and main,
And mourns in search of thine.

[1] ["This and the two following stanzas have a music in them, which, independently of all meaning, is enchanting." — *Moore*.]

STANZAS

WRITTEN IN PASSING THE AMBRACIAN GULF.

THROUGH cloudless skies, in silvery sheen,
Full beams the moon on Actium's coast,
And on these waves, for Egypt's queen,
The ancient world was won and lost.

And now upon the scene I look,
The azure grave of many a Roman;
Where stern Ambition once forsook
His wavering crown to follow woman.

Florence ! whom I will love as well
As ever yet was said or sung,
(Since Orpheus sang his spouse from hell)
Whilst thou art fair and I am young;

Sweet Florence ! those were pleasant times,
When worlds were staked for ladies' eyes :
Had bards as many realms as rhymes,
Thy charms might raise new Antonies.

Though Fate forbids such things to be,
Yet, by thine eyes and ringlets curled !
I cannot lose a world for thee,
But would not lose thee for a world.
November 14, 1809.

THE SPELL IS BROKE, THE CHARM IS FLOWN !

WRITTEN AT ATHENS, JANUARY 16, 1810.

THE spell is broke, the charm is flown !
Thus is it with life's fitful fever:
We madly smile when we should groan;
Delirium is our best deceiver.

Each lucid interval of thought
Recalls the woes of Nature's charter,
And he that acts as wise men ought,
But lives, as saints have died, a martyr.

WRITTEN AFTER SWIMMING FROM SESTOS TO ABYDOS.[2]

IF, in the month of dark December,
Leander, who was nightly wont
(What maid will not the tale remember ?)
To cross thy stream, broad Hellespont !

If, when the wintry tempest roared,
He sped to Hero, nothing loth,
And thus of old thy current poured,
Fair Venus ! how I pity both !

[2] On the 3d of May, 1810, while the Salsette (Captain Bathurst) was lying in the Dardanelles, Lieutenant Ekenhead, of that frigate and the writer of these rhymes swam from the European shore to

For *me*, degenerate modern wretch,
  Though in the genial month of May,
My dripping limbs I faintly stretch,
  And think I've done a feat to-day.

But since he crossed the rapid tide,
  According to the doubtful story,
To woo, — and — Lord knows what beside,
  And swam for Love, as I for Glory;

'Twere hard to say who fared the best:
  Sad mortals! thus the Gods still plague you!
He lost his labor, I my jest:
  For he was drowned, and I've the ague.[1]

  May 9, 1810.

MAID OF ATHENS, ERE WE PART.

Ζώη μοῦ, σάς ἀγαπῶ.

MAID of Athens,[2] ere we part,
Give, oh, give me back my heart!
Or, since that has left my breast,
Keep it now, and take the rest;

Hear my vow before I go,
Ζώη μοῦ, σάς ἀγαπῶ.[3]

By those tresses unconfined,
Wooed by each Ægean wind;
By those lids whose jetty fringe,
Kiss thy soft cheeks' blooming tinge;
By those wild eyes like the roe,
Ζώη μοῦ, σάς ἀγαπῶ.

By that lip I long to taste;
By that zone-encircled waist;
By all the token-flowers [4] that tell
What words can never speak so well,
By love's alternate joy and woe,
Ζώη μοῦ, σάς ἀγαπῶ.

Maid of Athens! I am gone:
Think of me, sweet! when alone.
Though I fly to Istambol,[5]
Athens holds my heart and soul:
Can I cease to love thee ? No!
Ζώη μοῦ, σάς ἀγαπῶ.

  ATHENS, 1810.

MY EPITAPH.

YOUTH, Nature, and relenting Jove,
To keep my lamp *in* strongly strove;
But Romanelli was so stout,
He beat all three — and *blew* it *out*.[6]

  October, 1810.

---

the Asiatic — by the by, from Abydos to Sestos would have been more correct. The whole distance, from the place whence we started to our landing on the other side, including the length we were carried by the current, was computed by those on board the frigate at upwards of four English miles; though the actual breadth is barely one. The rapidity of the current is such that no boat can row directly across, and it may, in some measure, be estimated from the circumstance of the whole distance being accomplished by one of the parties in an hour and five, and by the other in an hour and ten minutes. The water was extremely cold, from the melting of the mountain snows. About three weeks before, in April, we had made an attempt; but, having ridden all the way from the Troad the same morning, and the water being of an icy chillness, we found it necessary to postpone the completion till the frigate anchored below the castles, when we swam the straits, as just stated; entering a considerable way above the European, and landing below the Asiatic, fort. Chevalier says that a young Jew swam the same distance for his mistress; and Oliver mentions its having been done by a Neapolitan; but our consul, Tarragona, remembered neither of these circumstances, and tried to dissuade us from the attempt. A number of the Salsette's crew were known to have accomplished a greater distance; and the only thing that surprised me was, that, as doubts had been entertained of the truth of Leander's story, no traveller had ever endeavored to ascertain its practicability.
  [1] [" My companion," says Mr. Hobhouse, " had before made a more perilous, but less celebrated passage; for I recollect that, when we were in Portugal, he swam from Old Lisbon to Belem Castle, and having to contend with a tide and counter current, the wind blowing freshly, was but little less than two hours in crossing."]
  [2] " Theresa, the Maid of Athens, and her sisters Catinco, and Mariana, are of middle stature. The two eldest have black, or dark, hair and eyes; their visage oval, and complexion somewhat pale, with

teeth of dazzling whiteness. Their cheeks are rounded, and noses straight, rather inclined to aquiline. The youngest, Mariana, is very fair, her face not so finely rounded, but has a gayer expression than her sisters', whose countenances, except when the conversation has something of mirth in it, may be said to be rather pensive. Their persons are elegant, and their manners pleasing and ladylike, such as would be fascinating in any country. They possess very considerable powers of conversation, and their minds seem to be more instructed than those of the Greek women in general." — *Williams' Travels in Greece.*
  [3] Romaic expression of tenderness: If I translate it, I shall affront the gentlemen, as it may seem that I supposed they could not; and if I do not, I may affront the ladies. For fear of any misconstruction on the part of the latter, I shall do so, begging pardon of the learned. It means, " My life, I love you!" which sounds very prettily in all languages, and is as much in fashion in Greece at this day as, Juvenal tells us, the two first words were amongst the Roman ladies, whose erotic expressions were all Hellenised.
  [4] In the East (where ladies are not taught to write, lest they should scribble assignations) flowers, cinders, pebbles, etc., convey the sentiments of the parties by that universal deputy of Mercury — an old woman. A cinder says, " I burn for thee;" a bunch of flowers tied with hair, " Take me and fly;" but a pebble declares — what nothing else can.
  [5] Constantinople.
  [6] [" I have just escaped from a physician and a fever. In spite of my teeth and tongue, the Eng

SUBSTITUTE FOR AN EPITAPH.

KIND Reader! take your choice to cry or laugh;
Here Harold lies — but where's his Epitaph?
If such you seek, try Westminster, and view
Ten thousand just as fit for him as you.

ATHENS.

LINES IN THE TRAVELLERS' BOOK AT ORCHOMENUS.

IN THIS BOOK A TRAVELLER HAD WRITTEN: —

FAIR Albion, smiling, sees her son depart
To trace the birth and nursery of art:
Noble his object, glorious is his aim;
He comes to Athens, and he writes his name.

BENEATH WHICH LORD BYRON INSERTED THE FOLLOWING: —

THE modest bard, like many a bard unknown,
Rhymes on our names, but wisely hides his own;
But yet, whoe'er he be, to say no worse,
His name would bring more credit than his verse.

1810.

TRANSLATION OF THE FAMOUS GREEK WAR-SONG.

"Δεῦτε παῖδες τῶν Ἑλλήνων." [1]

SONS of the Greeks, arise!
The glorious hour's gone forth,
And, worthy of such ties,
Display who gave us birth.

CHORUS.

Sons of Greeks! let us go
In arms against the foe,
Till their hated blood shall flow
In a river past our feet.

Then manfully despising
The Turkish tyrant's yoke,
Let your country see you rising,
And all her chains are broke.
Brave shades of chiefs and sages,
Behold the coming strife!
Hellénes of past ages,
Oh, start again to life!

At the sound of my trumpet, breaking
Your sleep, oh, join with me!
And the seven-hilled [2] city seeking,
Fight, conquer, till we're free.

Sons of Greeks, etc.

Sparta, Sparta, why in slumbers
Lethargic dost thou lie?
Awake, and join thy numbers
With Athens, old ally!
Leonidas recalling,
That chief of ancient song,
Who saved ye once from falling,
The terrible! the strong!
Who made that bold diversion
In old Thermopylæ,
And warring with the Persian
To keep his country free;
With his three hundred waging
The battle, long he stood,
And like a lion raging,
Expired in seas of blood.

Sons of Greeks, etc. [!]

TRANSLATION OF THE ROMAIC SONG,

"Μπαίνω μέσ' 'ς τὸ περιβόλι
Ὡραιότατη Χαϊδή," etc. [4]

I ENTER thy garden of roses,
Beloved and fair Haidée,
Each morning where Flora reposes,
For surely I see her in thee.
Oh, Lovely! thus low I implore thee,
Receive this fond truth from my tongue,
Which utters its song to adore thee,
Yet trembles for what it has sung;
As the branch, at the bidding of Nature,
Adds fragrance and fruit to the tree,
Through her eyes, through her every feature,
Shines the soul of the young Haidée.

But the loveliest garden grows hateful
When Love has abandoned the bowers;
Bring me hemlock — since mine is ungrateful,

---

lish consul, my Tartar, Albanian, dragoman, forced a physician upon me, and in three days brought me to the last gasp. In this state I made my epitaph."] — *Byron to Mr. Hodgson, October* 3, 1810.

[1] The song Δεῦτε παῖδες, etc., was written by Riga, who perished in the attempt to revolutionize Greece. This translation is as literal as the author could make it in verse. It is of the same measure as that of the original.

[2] Constantinople. "Ἑπτάλοφος."

[3] [Riga was a Thessalian, and passed the first part of his youth among his native mountains, in teaching ancient Greek to his countrymen. On the outbreak of the French Revolution, he and some other enthusiasts perambulated Greece, rousing the bold, and encouraging the timid by their minstrelsy. He afterwards went to Vienna to solicit aid for a rising, but was given up by the Austrian government to the Turks, who vainly endeavored by torture to force from him the names of the other conspirators.]

[4] The song from which this is taken is a great favorite with the young girls of Athens of all classes. Their manner of singing it is by verses in rotation, the whole number present joining in the chorus. I have heard it frequently at our "χόροι," in the winter of 1810-11 The air is plaintive and pretty,

That herb is more fragrant than flowers.
The poison, when poured from the chalice,
  Will deeply embitter the bowl;
But when drunk to escape from thy malice,
  The draught shall be sweet to my soul.
Too cruel! in vain I implore thee
  My heart from these horrors to save:
Will nought to my bosom restore thee?
  Then open the gates of the grave.

As the chief who to combat advances
  Secure of his conquest before,
Thus thou, with those eyes for thy lances,
  Hast pierced through my heart to its core.
Ah, tell me, my soul! must I perish
  By pangs which a smile would dispel?
Would the hope, which thou once bad'st me cherish,
  For torture repay me too well?
Now sad is the garden of roses,
  Beloved but false Haidée!
There Flora all withered reposes,
  And mourns o'er thine absence with me.

LINES WRITTEN BENEATH A
PICTURE.

DEAR object of defeated care!
  Though now of Love and thee bereft,
To reconcile me with despair,
  Thine image and my tears are left.

'Tis said with Sorrow Time can cope;
  But this I feel can ne'er be true:
For by the death-blow of my Hope
  My Memory immortal grew.

ATHENS, January, 1811.

ON PARTING.

THE kiss, dear maid! thy lip has left,
  Shall never part from mine,
Till happier hours restore the gift
  Untainted back to thine.

Thy parting glance, which fondly beams,
  An equal love may see:
The tear that from thine eyelid streams,
  Can weep no change in me.

I ask no pledge to make me blest
  In gazing when alone;
Nor one memorial for a breast,
  Whose thoughts are all thine own.

Nor need I write — to tell the tale
  My pen were doubly weak:
Oh! what can idle words avail,
  Unless the heart could speak?

By day or night, in weal or woe,
  That heart, no longer free,
Must bear the love it cannot show,
  And silent ache for thee.

March, 1811.

EPITAPH FOR JOSEPH BLACKETT
LATE POET AND SHOEMAKER.[1]

STRANGER! behold, interred together,
The *souls* of learning and of leather.
Poor Joe is gone, but left his *all*:
You'll find his relics in a *stall*.
His works were neat, and often found
Well stitched, and with *morocco* bound.
Tread lightly — where the bard is laid
He cannot mend the shoe he made;
Yet is he happy in his hole,
With verse immortal as his *sole*.
But still to business he held fast,
And stuck to Phœbus to the last.
Then who shall say so good a fellow
Was only " leather and prunella ? "
For character — he did not lack it;
And if he did, 'twere shame to " Black-it."

MALTA, May 16, 1811.

FAREWELL TO MALTA.

ADIEU, ye joys of La Valette!
Adieu, sirocco, sun, and sweat!
Adieu, thou palace rarely entered!
Adieu, ye mansions where — I've ventured!
Adieu, ye cursed streets of stairs!
(How surely he who mounts you swears!)
Adieu, ye merchants often failing!
Adieu, thou mob for ever railing!
Adieu, ye packets — without letters!
Adieu, ye fools — who ape your betters!
Adieu, thou damned'st quarantine,
That gave me fever, and the spleen!
Adieu that stage which makes us yawn, Sirs,
Adieu his Excellency's dancers!
Adieu to Peter — whom no fault's in,
But could not teach a colonel waltzing;
Adieu, ye females fraught with graces!
Adieu red coats, and redder faces!
Adieu the supercilious air
Of all that strut " en militaire! "
I go — but God knows when, or why,
To smoky towns and cloudy sky,
To things (the honest truth to say)
As bad — but in a different way. —

Farewell to these, but not adieu,
Triumphant sons of truest blue!
While either Adriatic shore,

---

[1] [He died in 1810, and his works have followed him.]

And fallen chiefs, and fleets no more,
And nightly smiles, and daily dinners,
Proclaim you war and women's winners.
Pardon my Muse, who apt to prate is,
And take my rhyme — because 'tis " gratis."

And now I've got to Mrs. Fraser,
Perhaps you think I mean to praise her —
And were I vain enough to think
My praise was worth this drop of ink,
A line — or two — were no hard matter,
As here, indeed, I need not flatter:
But she must be content to shine
In better praises than in mine,
With lively air and open heart,
And fashion's ease, without its art;
Her hours can gaily glide along,
Nor ask the aid of idle song. —

And now, O Malta! since thou'st got us,
Thou little military hothouse!
I'll not offend with words uncivil,
And wish thee rudely at the Devil,
But only stare from out my casement,
And ask, for what is such a place meant?
Then, in my solitary nook,
Return to scribbling or a book,
Or take my physic while I'm able
(Two spoonfuls hourly by the label),
Prefer my nightcap to my beaver,
And bless the gods — I've got a fever!

                              May 26, 1811.

TO DIVES.

A FRAGMENT.

UNHAPPY DIVES! in an evil hour
'Gainst Nature's voice seduced to deeds ac-
    curst!
Once Fortune's minion, now thou feel'st her
    power;
Wrath's viol on thy lofty head hath burst.
In Wit, in Genius, as in Wealth the first,
How wond'rous bright thy blooming morn
    arose!
But thou wert smitten with th' unhallowed
    thirst
Of Crime un-named, and thy sad noon must
    close
In scorn, and solitude unsought, the worst of
    woes.   1811.

ON MOORE'S LAST OPERATIC FARCE,
OR FARCICAL OPERA.

GOOD plays are scarce,
So Moore writes farce:
The poet's fame grows brittle —

We knew before
That *Little's* Moore,
But now 'tis *Moore* that's *little*.

                       September 14, 1811.[1]

EPISTLE TO A FRIEND,[2]

IN ANSWER TO SOME LINES EXHORTING
THE AUTHOR TO BE CHEERFUL, AND
TO " BANISH CARE."

" OH! banish care " — such ever be
The motto of *thy* revelry!
Perchance of *mine*, when wassail nights
Renew those riotous delights,
Wherewith the children of Despair
Lull the lone heart, and " banish care."
But not in morn's reflecting hour,
When present, past, and future lower,
When all I loved is changed or gone,
Mock with such taunts the woes of one,
Whose every thought — but let them pass — ·
Thou know'st I am not what I was.
But, above all, if thou wouldst hold
Place in a heart that ne'er was cold,
By all the powers that men revere,
By all unto thy bosom dear,
Thy joys below, thy hopes above,
Speak — speak of any thing but love.

'Twere long to tell, and vain to hear,
The tale of one who scorns a tear;
And there is little in that tale
Which better bosoms would bewail.
But mine has suffered more than well
'Twould suit philosophy to tell.
I've seen my bride another's bride, —
Have seen her seated by his side, —
Have seen the infant, which she bore,
Wear the sweet smile the mother wore,
When she and I in youth have smiled,
As fond and faultless as her child; —
Have seen her eyes, in cold disdain,
Ask if I felt no secret pain;
And *I* have acted well my part,
And made my cheek belie my heart,
Returned the freezing glance she gave,
Yet felt the while *that* woman's slave; —
Have kissed, as if without design,
The babe which ought to have been mine,
And showed, alas! in each caress
Time had not made me love the less.[3]

----

[1] [The farce was called " M. P.; or, the Blue Stocking."]
[2] [Francis Hodgson.]
[3] [These lines will show with what gloomy fidelity, even while under the pressure of recent sorrow, the poet reverted to the disappointment of his early affection, as the chief source of all his sufferings and errors, present and to come. — *Moore.*]

But let this pass — I'll whine no more,
Nor seek again an eastern shore;
The world befits a busy brain, —
I'll hie me to its haunts again.
But if, in some succeeding year,
When Britain's " May is in the sere,"
Thou hear'st of one, whose deepening crimes,
Suit with the sablest of the times,
Of one, whom love nor pity sways,
Nor hope of fame, nor good men's praise,
One, who in stern ambition's pride,
Perchance not blood shall turn aside,
One ranked in some recording page
With the worst anarchs of the age,
Him wilt thou *know* — and *knowing* pause,
Nor with the *effect* forget the cause.[1]

NEWSTEAD ABBEY, October 11, 1811.

TO THYRZA.

WITHOUT a stone to mark the spot,
And say, what Truth might well have said,
By all, save one, perchance forgot,
Ah! wherefore art thou lowly laid?

By many a shore and many a sea
Divided, yet beloved in vain;
The past, the future fled to thee
To bid us meet — no — ne'er again!

Could this have been — a word, a look
That softly said, '' We part in peace,"
Had taught my bosom how to brook,
With fainter sighs, thy soul's release.

And didst thou not, since Death for thee
Prepared a light and pangless dart,
Once long for him thou ne'er shalt see,
Who held, and holds thee in his heart?

Oh! who like him had watched thee here?
Or sadly marked thy glazing eye,
In that dread hour ere death appear,
When silent sorrow fears to sigh,

Till all was past? But when no more
'Twas thine to reck of human woe,
Affection's heart-drops, gushing o'er,
Had flowed as fast — as now they flow.

Shall they not flow, when many a day
In these, to me, deserted towers,
Ere called but for a time away,
Affection's mingling tears were ours?

Ours too the glance none saw beside;
The smile none else might understand;
The whispered thought of hearts allied,
The pressure of the thrilling hand;

The kiss, so guiltless and refined
That Love each warmer wish forbore;
Those eyes proclaimed so pure a mind,
Even passion blushed to plead for more.

The tone, that taught me to rejoice,
When prone, unlike thee, to repine;
The song, celestial from thy voice,
But sweet to me from none but thine;

The pledge we wore — I wear it still,
But where is thine? — Ah! where art thou?
Oft have I borne the weight of ill,
But never bent beneath till now!

Well hast thou left in life's best bloom
The cup of woe for me to drain.
If rest alone be in the tomb,
I would not wish thee here again;

But if in worlds more blest than this
Thy virtues seek a fitter sphere,
Impart some portion of thy bliss,
To wean me from mine anguish here.

Teach me — too early taught by thee!
To bear, forgiving and forgiven:
On earth thy love was such to me;
It fain would form my hope in heaven!

October 11, 1811.[2]

---

[1] [The anticipations of his own future career in these concluding lines are of a nature, it must be owned, to awaken more of horror than of interest,

were we not prepared, by so many instances of his exaggeration in this respect, not to be startled at any lengths to which the spirit of self-libelling would carry him. — *Moore.*]

[2] [Moore considers " Thyrza " a mere creature of the poet's brain. " It was," he says, " about the time when he was thus bitterly feeling, and expressing, the blight which his heart had suffered from a *real* object of affection, that his poems on the death of an *imaginary* one were written; — nor is it any wonder, when we consider the peculiar circumstances under which those beautiful effusions flowed from his fancy, that of all his strains of pathos, they should be the most touching and most pure. They were, indeed, the essence, the abstract spirit, as it were, of many griefs; — a confluence of sad thoughts from many sources of sorrow, refined and warmed in their passage through his fancy, and forming thus one deep reservoir of mournful feeling." It is a pity to disturb a sentiment thus beautifully expressed: but Byron, in a letter to Mr. Dallas, bearing the exact date of these lines, namely, Oct. 11, 1811, writes as follows: — " I have been again shocked with a death, and have lost one very dear to me in happier times: but ' I have almost forgot the taste of grief,' and ' supped full of horrors,' till I have become callous; nor have I a tear left for an event which, five years ago, would have bowed my head to the earth." In his reply to this letter, Mr. Dallas says, — " I thank you for your *confidential* communication. How truly do I wish that that being had lived, and lived yours! What your obligations to her would have been in that case is inconceivable." Several years after the series of poems on Thyrza were written, Byron, on being asked to whom they referred, by a person in whose tenderness he never ceased to confide, refused to answer, with marks of

AWAY, AWAY! YE NOTES OF WOE!

AWAY, away, ye notes of woe!
  Be silent, thou once soothing strain,
Or I must flee from hence — for, oh!
  I dare not trust those sounds again.
To me they speak of brighter days —
  But lull the chords, for now, alas!
I must not think, I may not gaze
  On what I am — on what I was.

The voice that made those sounds more sweet
  Is hushed, and all their charms are fled;
And now their softest notes repeat
  A dirge, an anthem o'er the dead!
Yes, Thyrza! yes, they breathe of thee,
  . Beloved dust! since dust thou art;
And all that once was harmony
  Is worse than discord to my heart!

'Tis silent all! — but on my ear
  The well remembered echoes thrill;
I hear a voice I would not hear,
  A voice that now might well be still:
Yet oft my doubting soul 'twill shake;
  Even slumber owns its gentle tone,
Till consciousness will vainly wake
  To listen, though the dream be flown.

Sweet Thyrza! waking as in sleep,
  Thou art but now a lovely dream;
A star that trembled o'er the deep,
  Then turned from earth its tender beam.
But he who through life's dreary way
  Must pass, when heaven is veiled in wrath,
Will long lament the vanished ray
  That scattered gladness o'er his path.

               December 6, 1811. [1]

ONE STRUGGLE MORE AND I AM FREE.

ONE struggle more, and I am free
  From pangs that rend my heart in twain;
One last long sigh to love and thee,
  Then back to busy life again.
It suits me well to mingle now
  With things that never pleased before:
Though every joy is fled below,
  What future grief can touch me more?

Then bring me wine, the banquet bring;
  Man was not formed to live alone:
I'll be that light, unmeaning thing
  That smiles with all, and weeps with none.

agitation, such as rendered recurrence to the subject
impossible. The five following pieces are all de-
voted to Thyrza.]
  [1] ["I wrote this a day or two ago, on hearing a
song of former days." — *Byron's Letters*, Dec. 8,
1811.]

It was not thus in days more dear,
  It never would have been, but thou
Hast fled, and left me lonely here;
  Thou'rt nothing, — all are nothing now.

In vain my lyre would lightly breathe!
  The smile that sorrow fain would wear
But mocks the woe that lurks beneath,
  Like roses o'er a sepulchre.
Though gay companions o'er the bowl
  Dispel awhile the sense of ill;
Though pleasure fires the maddening soul.
  The heart — the heart is lonely still!

On many a lone and lovely night
  It soothed to gaze upon the sky;
For then I deemed the heavenly light
  Shone sweetly on thy pensive eye:
And oft I thought at Cynthia's noon,
  When sailing o'er the Ægean wave,
"Now Thyrza gazes on that moon —"
  Alas, it gleamed upon her grave!

When stretched on fever's sleepless bed,
  And sickness shrunk my throbbing veins,
"'Tis comfort still," I faintly said,
  "That Thyrza cannot know my pains:'
Like freedom to the time-worn slave,
  A boon 'tis idle then to give,
Relenting Nature vainly gave
  My life, when Thyrza ceased to live!

My Thyrza's pledge in better days,
  When love and life alike were new!
How different now thou meet'st my gaze!
  How tinged by time with sorrow's hue!
The heart that gave itself with thee
  Is silent — ah, were mine as still!
Though cold as e'en the dead can be,
  It feels, it sickens with the chill.

Thou bitter pledge! thou mournful token!
  Though painful, welcome to my breast!
Still, still, preserve that love unbroken,
  Or break the heart to which thou'rt pressed
Time tempers love, but not removes,
  More hallowed when its hope is fled:
Oh! what are thousand living loves
  To that which cannot quit the dead?

EUTHANASIA.

WHEN Time, or soon or late, shall bring
  The dreamless sleep that lulls the dead,
Oblivion! may thy languid wing
  Wave gently o'er my dying bed!

No band of friends or heirs be there,
  To weep, or wish the coming blow:
No maiden, with dishevelled hair,
  To feel, or feign, decorous woe.

But silent let me sink to earth,
    With no officious mourners near;
I would not mar one hour of mirth,
    Nor startle friendship with a fear.

Yet Love, if Love in such an hour
    Could nobly check its useless sighs,
Might then exert its latest power
    In her who lives and him who dies.

'Twere sweet, my Psyche! to the last
    Thy features still serene to see:
Forgetful of its struggles past,
    E'en Pain itself should smile on thee.

But vain the wish — for Beauty still
    Will shrink, as shrinks the ebbing breath;
And woman's tears, produced at will,
    Deceive in life, unman in death.

Then lonely be my latest hour,
    Without regret, without a groan;
For thousands Death hath ceased to lower,
    And pain been transient or unknown.

"Ay, but to die, and go," alas!
    Where all have gone, and all must go!
To be the nothing that I was
    Ere born to life and living woe!

Count o'er the joys thine hours have seen,
    Count o'er thy days from anguish free,
And know, whatever thou hast been,
    'Tis something better not to be.

AND THOU ART DEAD, AS YOUNG AND FAIR.

"*Heu, quanto minus est cum reliquis versari quam
    tui meminisse!*"

AND thou art dead, as young and fair
    As aught of mortal birth;
And form so soft, and charms so rare,
    Too soon returned to Earth!
Though Earth received them in her bed,
And o'er the spot the crowd may tread
    In carelessness or mirth,
There is an eye which could not brook
A moment on that grave to look.

I will not ask where thou liest low,
    Nor gaze upon the spot;
There flowers or weeds at will may grow,
    So I behold them not:
It is enough for me to prove
That what I loved and long must love,
    Like common earth can rot;
To me there needs no stone to tell,
'Tis Nothing that I loved so well.

Yet did I love thee to the last
    As fervently as thou,
Who didst not change through all the past,
    And canst not alter now.

The love where Death has set his seal,
Nor age can chill, nor rival steal,
    Nor falsehood disavow:
And, what were worse, thou canst not see
Or wrong, or change, or fault in me.

The better days of life were ours;
    The worst can be but mine:
The sun that cheers, the storm that lowers,
    Shall never more be thine.
The silence of that dreamless sleep
I envy now too much to weep;
    Nor need I to repine
That all those charms have passed away,
I might have watched through long decay.

The flower in ripened bloom unmatched
    Must fall the earliest prey;
Though by no hand untimely snatched,
    The leaves must drop away:
And yet it were a greater grief
To watch it withering, leaf by leaf,
    Than see it plucked to-day;
Since earthly eye but ill can bear
To trace the change to foul from fair.

I know not if I could have borne
    To see thy beauties fade;
The night that followed such a morn
    Had worn a deeper shade:
Thy day without a cloud hath passed,
And thou wert lovely to the last;
    Extinguished, not decayed;
As stars that shoot along the sky
Shine brightest as they fall from high.

As once I wept, if I could weep,
    My tears might well be shed,
To think I was not near to keep
    One vigil o'er thy bed;
To gaze, how fondly! on thy face,
To fold thee in a faint embrace,
    Uphold thy drooping head;
And show that love, however vain,
Nor thou nor I can feel again.

Yet how much less it were to gain,
    Though thou hast left me free,
The loveliest things that still remain,
    Than thus remember thee!
The all of thine that cannot die
Through dark and dread Eternity
    Returns again to me,
And more thy buried love endears
Than aught, except its living years.

                    February, 1812.

IF SOMETIMES IN THE HAUNTS OF MEN.

IF sometimes in the haunts of men
    Thine image from my breast may fade
The lonely hour presents again

The semblance of thy gentle shade:
And now that sad and silent hour
  Thus much of thee can still restore,
And sorrow unobserved may pour
  The plaint she dare not speak before.

Oh, pardon that in crowds awhile
  I waste one thought I owe to thee,
And, self-condemned, appear to smile,
  Unfaithful to thy Memory!
Nor deem that memory less dear,
  That then I seem not to repine;
I would not fools should overhear
  One sigh that should be wholly *thine.*

If not the goblet passed unquaffed,
  It is not drained to banish care;
The cup must hold a deadlier draught,
  That brings a Lethe for despair.
And could Oblivion set my soul
  From all her troubled visions free,
I'd dash to earth the sweetest bowl
  That drowned a single thought of thee.

For wert thou vanished from my mind,
  Where could my vacant bosom turn?
And who would then remain behind
  To honor thine abandoned Urn?
No, no — it is my sorrow's pride
  That last dear duty to fulfil;
Though all the world forget beside,
  'Tis meet that I remember still.

For well I know, that such had been,
  Thy gentle care for him, who now
Unmourned shall quit this mortal scene,
  Where none regarded him, but thou:
And, oh! I feel in *that* was given
  A blessing never meant for me;
Thou wert too like a dream of Heaven,
  For earthly Love to merit thee.
               March 14, 1812.

FROM THE FRENCH.

ÆGLE, beauty and poet, has two little crimes;
She makes her own face, and does not make
  her rhymes.

ON A CORNELIAN HEART WHICH WAS BROKEN.

ILL-FATED Heart! and can it be
  That thou should'st thus be rent in twain?
Have years of care for thine and thee
  Alike been all employed in vain?

Yet precious seems each shattered part,
  And every fragment dearer grown,
Since he who wears thee feels thou art
  A fitter emblem of *his own.*
               March 16, 1812.

LINES TO A LADY WEEPING.[1]

WEEP, daughter of a royal line,
  A Sire's disgrace, a realm's decay,
Ah! happy if each tear of thine
  Could wash a father's fault away!

Weep — for thy tears are Virtue's tears —
  Auspicious to these suffering isles;
And be each drop in future years
  Repaid thee by thy people's smiles!
               March, 1819.

THE CHAIN I GAVE.

FROM THE TURKISH.

THE chain I gave was fair to view,
  The lute I added sweet in sound;
The heart that offered both was true,
  And ill deserved the fate it found.

These gifts were charmed by secret spell
  Thy truth in absence to divine;
And they have done their duty well, —
  Alas! they could not teach thee thine.

That chain was firm in every link,
  But not to bear a stranger's touch;
That lute was sweet — till thou could'st think
  In other hands its notes were such.

Let him, who from thy neck unbound
  The chain which shivered in his grasp,
Who saw that lute refuse to sound,
  Restring the chords, renew the clasp.

When thou wert changed, they altered too;
  The chain is broke, the music mute.
'Tis past — to them and thee adieu —
  False heart, frail chain, and silent lute.

LINES WRITTEN ON A BLANK LEAF OF THE "PLEASURES OF MEMORY."

ABSENT or present, still to thee,
  My friend, what magic spells belong!
As all can tell, who share, like me,
  In turn thy converse, and thy song.

---

[1] [This impromptu owed its birth to an *on dit*, that the Princess Charlotte of Wales burst into tears on hearing that the Whigs had found it impossible to form a cabinet, at the period of Perceval's death. They were appended to the first edition of the "Corsair," and excited a sensation marvellously disproportionate to their length, — or, we may add, their merit. The ministerial prints raved for two months on end, in the most foul-mouthed vituperation of the poet, — the Morning Post even announced a motion in the House of Lords — "and all this," Byron

But when the dreaded hour shall come,
By Friendship ever deemed too nigh,
And "MEMORY" o'er her Druid's tomb[1]
Shall weep that aught of thee can die,

How fondly will she then repay
Thy homage offered at her shrine,
And blend, while ages roll away,
Her name immortally with *thine!*

April 19, 1812.

ADDRESS,

SPOKEN AT THE OPENING OF DRURY-LANE
THEATRE, SATURDAY, OCT. 10, 1812.[2]

IN one dread night our city saw, and sighed,
Bowed to the dust, the Drama's tower of pride;
In one short hour beheld the blazing fane,
Apollo sink, and Shakspeare cease to reign.

Ye who beheld, (oh! sight admired and
mourned,
Whose radiance mocked the ruin it adorned!)
Through clouds of fire the massy fragments
riven,
Like Israel's pillar, chase the night from
heaven;
Saw the long column of revolving flames
Shake its red shadow o'er the startled
Thames.[3]

While thousands, thronged around the burn‑
ing dome,
Shrank back appalled, and trembled for their
home,
As glared the volumed blaze, and ghastly
shone
The skies, with. lightnings awful as their
own,
Till blackening ashes and the lonely wall
Usurped the Muse's realm, and marked her
fall;
Say — shall this new, nor less aspiring pile,
Reared where once rose the mightiest in our
isle,
Know the same favor which the former knew,
A shrine for Shakspeare — worthy him and
you?

Yes — it shall be — the magic of that name
Defies the scythe of time, the torch of flame;
On the same spot still consecrates the scene,
And bids the Drama *be* where she hath *been:*
This fabric's birth attests the potent spell —
Indulge our honest pride, and say, *How Well!*

As soars this fane to emulate the last,
Oh! might we draw our omens from the past,
Some hour propitious to our prayers may
boast
Names such as hallow still the dome we lost.
On Drury first your Siddons' thrilling art
O'erwhelmed the gentlest, stormed the stern‑
est heart.
On Drury, Garrick's latest laurels grew;
Here your last tears retiring Roscius drew,
Sighed his last thanks, and wept his last adieu:
But still for living wit the wreaths may bloom
That only waste their odors o'er the tomb.
Such Drury claimed and claims — nor you
refuse
One tribute to revive his slumbering muse;
With garlands deck your own Menander's
head!
Nor hoard your honors idly for the dead!

Dear are the days which made our annals
bright,
Ere Garrick fled, or Brinsley[4] ceased to write.
Heirs to their labors, like all high-born heirs,
Vain of *our* ancestry as they of *theirs.*

---

writes to Moore, " as Bedreddin in the Arabian
Nights remarks, for making a cream tart with pep‑
per: how odd, that eight lines should have given
birth, I really think, to eight thousand!"]

[1] [" When Rogers does talk, he talks well; and,
on all subjects of taste, his delicacy of expression is
pure as his poetry. If you enter his house — his
drawing-room — his library — you of yourself say,
this is not the dwelling of a common mind. There is
not a gem, a coin, a book thrown aside on his chim‑
ney-piece, his sofa, his table, that does not bespeak
an almost fastidious elegance in the possessor." —
Byron's Diary, 1813.]

[2] The theatre in Drury Lane, which was opened
in 1747, with Dr. Johnson's masterly address, and
witnessed the last glories of Garrick, having fallen
into decay, was rebuilt in 1794. The new building
perished by fire in 1811; and the Managers, in their
anxiety that the opening of the present edifice should
be distinguished by some composition of at least
equal merit, advertised in the newspapers for a gen‑
eral competition. Scores of addresses, not one tol‑
erable, showered on their desk, and they were in sad
despair, when Lord Holland interfered, and not
without difficulty, prevailed on Byron to write these
verses — " at the risk," as he said, " of offending a
hundred scribblers and a discerning public." The
admirable *jeu d'esprit* of the Messrs. Smith will
long preserve the memory of the " Rejected Ad‑
dresses."]

[3] [" By the by, the best view of the said fire
(which I myself saw from a house-top in Covent
Garden) was at Westminster Bridge from the reflec‑
tion of the Thames." — *Byron to Lord Holland.*]

[4] [Originally, " Ere Garrick *died*," etc., — " By
the by one of my corrections in the copy sent yes‑
terday has dived into the bathos some sixty fathom —
' When Garrick died, and Brinsley ceased to write.'
Ceasing to *live* is a much more serious concern, and
ought not to be first. Second thoughts in every
thing are best; but, in rhyme, third and fourth don't
come amiss. I always scrawl in this way, and
smooth as fast as I can, but never sufficiently; and,
latterly, I can weave a nine line stanza faster than
a couplet, for which measure I have not the cunning.
When I began ' Childe Harold,' I had never tried
Spenser's measure, and now I cannot scribble in
any other." — *Byron to Lord Holland.*]

While thus Remembrance borrows Banquo's
    glass
To claim the sceptred shadows as they pass,
And we the mirror hold, where imaged shine
Immortal names emblazoned on our line,
Pause—ere their feebler offspring you con-
    demn,
Reflect how hard the task to rival them!

Friends of the stage! to whom both Play-
    ers and Plays
Must sue alike for pardon or for praise,
Whose judging voice and eye alone direct
The boundless power to cherish or reject;
If e'er frivolity has led to fame,
And made us blush that you forbore to blame;
If e'er the sinking stage could condescend
To soothe the sickly taste it dare not mend,
All past reproach may present scenes refute,
And censure, wisely loud, be justly mute![1]
Oh! since your fiat stamps the Drama's laws,
Forbear to mock us with misplaced applause;
So pride shall doubly nerve the actor's powers,
And reason's voice be echoed back by ours!

This greeting o'er, the ancient rule obeyed,
The Drama's homage by her herald paid,
Receive *our* welcome too, whose every tone
Springs from our hearts, and fain would win
    your own.
The curtain rises—may our stage unfold
Scenes not unworthy Drury's days of old!
Britons our judges, Nature for our guide,
Still may *we* please—long, long may *you*
    preside!

PARENTHETICAL ADDRESS.[2]

BY DR. PLAGIARY.

Half stolen, with acknowledgements, to be spoken
in an inarticulate voice by Master P. at the opening
of the next new theatre. Stolen parts marked with
the inverted commas of quotation — thus "——"

"WHEN energizing objects men pursue,"
Then Lord knows what is writ by Lord knows
    who.

---

[1] [The following lines were omitted by the Com-
mittee —
"Nay, lower still, the Drama yet deplores
  That late she deigned to crawl all-fours.
  When Richard roars in Bosworth for a horse,
  If you command, the steed must come in course.
  If you decree, the stage must condescend
  To soothe the sickly taste we dare not mend.
  Blame not our judgment should we acquiesce,
  And gratify you more by showing less.
  The past reproach let present scenes refute,
  Nor shift from man to babe, from babe to brute."
"Is Whitbread," said Byron, "determined to
castrate all my *cavalry* lines? I do implore, for my
own gratification, one lash on those accursed quadru-
peds — 'a long shot, Sir Lucius, if you love me.'"]

[2] [Among the addresses sent in to the Drury Lane

"A modest monologue you here survey,"
Hissed from the theatre the "other day,"
As if Sir Fretful wrote "the slumberous" verse,
And gave his son "the rubbish" to rehearse.
"Yet at the thing you'd never be amazed,"
Knew you the rumpus which the author raised;
"Nor even here your smiles would be represt,"
Knew you these lines — the badness of the best.
"Flame! fire! and flame!!" (words borrowed
    from Lucretius,)
"Dread metaphors which open wounds" like
    issues
"And sleeping pangs awake—and—but
    away"
(Confound me if I know what next to say).
"Lo Hope reviving re-expands her wings,"
And Master G— recites what Doctor Busby
    sings!—
"If mighty things with small we may compare,"
(Translated from the grammar for the fair!)
Dramatic "spirit drives a conquering car,"
And burned poor Moscow like a tub of "tar."
"This spirit Wellington has shown in Spain,"
To furnish melodrames for Drury Lane.
"Another Marlborough points to Blenheim's
    story,"
And George and I will dramatize it for ye.

"In arts and sciences our isle hath shone"
(This deep discovery is mine alone).
"Oh British poesy, whose powers inspire"
My verse — or I'm a fool — and Fame's a liar,
"Theeave invoke, your sister arts implore"
With "smiles," and "lyres," and "pencils,"
    and much more.
These, if we win the Graces, too, we gain
Disgraces, too! "inseparable train!"
"Three who have stolen their witching airs
    from Cupid"
(You all know what I mean, unless you're
    stupid):
"Harmonious throng" that I have kept in
    petto,
Now to produce in a "divine *sestetto*"!!
"While Poesy," with these delightful doxies,
"Sustains her part" in all the "upper" boxes!
"Thus lifted gloriously, you'll soar along,"
Borne in the vast balloon of Busby's song;
"Shine in your farce, masque, scenery, and
    play"
(For this last line George had a holiday).
"Old Drury never, never soared so high,"
So says the manager, and so says I.
"But hold, you say, this self-complacent
    boast;"
Is this the poem which the public lost?

Committee was one by Dr. Busby, entitled "A
Monologue," of which the above is a parody. It
began:—

    "When energizing objects men pursue,
    What are the prodigies they cannot do?
    A magic edifice you here survey,
    Shot from the ruins of the other day, etc."]

" True — true — that lowers at once our mount-
　ing pride ;"
But lo ! — the papers print what you deride.
" 'Tis ours to look on you — you hold the prize,"
'Tis *twenty guineas*, as they advertise !
" A double blessing your rewards impart " —
I wish I had them, then, with all my heart.
" Our *twofold* feeling *owns* its twofold cause,"
Why son and I both beg for your applause.
" When in your fostering beams you bid us
　live,"
My next subscription list shall say how much
　you give !　　　　　　　October, 1812.

VERSES FOUND IN A SUMMER HOUSE AT HALES-OWEN.[1]

WHEN Dryden's fool, " unknowing what he
　sought,"
His hours in whistling spent, " for want of
　thought," [2]
This guiltless oaf his vacancy of sense
Supplied, and amply too by innocence ;
Did modern swains, possessed of Cymon's
　powers,
In Cymon's manner waste their leisure hours,
Th' offended guests would not, with blushing,
　see
These fair green walks disgraced by infamy.
Severe the fate of modern fools, alas !
When vice and folly mark them as they pass.
Like noxious reptiles o'er the whitened wall,
The filth they leave still points out where they
　crawl.

REMEMBER THEE! REMEMBER THEE!

REMEMBER thee ! remember thee !
　Till Lethe quench life's burning stream !
Remorse and shame shall cling to thee,
　And haunt thee like a feverish dream !

Remember thee ! Ay, doubt it not.
　Thy husband too shall think of thee :
By neither shalt thou be forgot,
　Thou *false* to him, thou *fiend* to me ! [3]

TO TIME.

TIME ! on whose arbitrary wing
　The varying hours must flag or fly,
Whose tardy winter, fleeting spring,
　But drag or drive us on to die —

Hail thou ! who on my birth bestowed
　Those boons to all that know thee known
Yet better I sustain thy load,
　For now I bear the weight alone.

I would not one fond heart should share
　The bitter moments thou hast given ;
And pardon thee, since thou could'st spare
　All that I loved, to peace or heaven ;

To them be joy or rest, on me
　Thy future ills shall press in vain ;
I nothing owe but years to thee,
　A debt already paid in pain.

Yet even that pain was some relief ;
　It felt, but still forgot thy power :
The active agony of grief
　Retards, but never counts the hour.

In joy I've sighed to think thy flight
　Would soon subside from swift to slow ;
Thy cloud could overcast the light,
　But could not add a night to woe ;

For then, however drear and dark,
　My soul was suited to thy sky ;
One star alone shot forth a spark
　To prove thee — not Eternity.

That beam hath sunk, and now thou art
　A blank ; a thing to count and curse
Through each dull tedious trifling part,
　Which all regret, yet all rehearse.

One scene even thou canst not deform ;
　The limit of thy sloth or speed
When future wanderers bear the storm
　Which we shall sleep too sound to heed :

And I can smile to think how weak
　Thine efforts shortly shall be shown,
When all the vengeance thou canst wreak
　Must fall upon — a nameless stone.

TRANSLATION OF A ROMAIC LOVE SONG.

AH ! Love was never yet without
The pang, the agony, the doubt,
Which rends my heart with ceaseless sigh,
While day and night roll darkling by.

Without one friend to hear my woe,
I faint, I die beneath the blow.

---

1 [In Warwickshire.]
2 [See Cymon and Iphigenia.]
3 [On the cessation of a temporary *liaison* formed by Lord Byron during his London career, the fair one called one morning at her quondam lover's apartments. His Lordship was from home : but finding *Vathek* on the table, the lady wrote in the first page of the volume the words " Remember me ! " Byron immediately wrote under the ominous warning these two stanzas. — *Medwin*.]

That Love had arrows, well I knew;
Alas! I find them poisoned too.

Birds, yet in freedom, shun the net
Which Love around your haunts hath set;
Or, circled by his fatal fire,
Your hearts shall burn, your hopes expire.

A bird of free and careless wing
Was I, through many a smiling spring;
But caught within the subtle snare,
I burn, and feebly flutter there.

Who ne'er have loved, and loved in vain,
Can neither feel nor pity pain,
The cold repulse, the look askance,
The lightning of Love's angry glance.

In flattering dreams I deemed thee mine;
Now hope, and he who hoped, decline;
Like melting wax, or withering flower,
I feel my passion, and thy power.

My light of life! ah, tell me why
That pouting lip, and altered eye?
My bird of love! my beauteous mate!
And art thou changed, and canst thou hate?

Mine eyes like wintry streams o'erflow:
What wretch with me would barter woe?
My bird! relent: one note could give
A charm, to bid thy lover live.

My curdling blood, my maddening brain,
In silent anguish I sustain;
And still thy heart, without partaking
One pang, exults — while mine is breaking.

Pour me the poison; fear not thou!
Thou canst not murder more than now:
I've lived to curse my natal day,
And Love, that thus can lingering slay.

My wounded soul, my bleeding breast,
Can patience preach them into rest?
Alas! too late, I dearly know
That joy is harbinger of woe.

————

THOU ART NOT FALSE, BUT THOU ART FICKLE.

THOU art not false, but thou art fickle,
  To those thyself so fondly sought;
The tears that thou hast forced to trickle
  Are doubly bitter from that thought:
'Tis this which breaks the heart thou grievest,
Too well thou lov'st — too soon thou leavest.

The wholly false the heart despises,
  And spurns deceiver and deceit;
But she who not a thought disguises,
  Whose love is as sincere as sweet, —
When she can change who loved so truly,
It feels what mine has felt so newly.

To dream of joy and wake to sorrow
  Is doomed to all who love or live;
And if, when conscious on the morrow,
  We scarce our fancy can forgive,
That cheated us in slumber only,
To leave the waking soul more lonely,

What must they feel whom no false vision
  But truest, tenderest passion warmed?
Sincere, but swift in sad transition;
  As if a dream alone had charmed?
Ah! sure such grief is fancy's scheming,
And all thy change can be but dreaming!

————

ON BEING ASKED WHAT WAS THE "ORIGIN OF LOVE."

THE "Origin of Love!"—Ah, why
  That cruel question ask of me,
When thou mayst read in many an eye
  He starts to life on seeing thee?

And shouldst thou seek his *end* to know:
  My heart forebodes, my fears foresee,
He'll linger long in silent woe;
  But live — until I cease to be.

————

REMEMBER HIM, WHOM PASSION'S POWER.

REMEMBER him, whom passion's power
  Severely, deeply, vainly proved:
Remember thou that dangerous hour
  When neither fell, though both were loved.

That yielding breast, that melting eye,
  Too much invited to be blessed:
That gentle prayer, that pleading sigh,
  The wilder wish reproved, repressed.

Oh! let me feel that all I lost
  But saved thee all that conscience fears;
And blush for every pang it cost
  To spare the vain remorse of years.

Yet think of this when many a tongue,
  Whose busy accents whisper blame,
Would do the heart that loved thee wrong,
  And brand a nearly blighted name.

Think that, whate'er to others, thou
  Hast seen each selfish thought subdued:
I bless thy purer soul even now,
  Even now, in midnight solitude.

Oh, God! that we had met in time,
  Our hearts as fond, thy hand more free;
When thou hadst loved without a crime,
  And I been less unworthy thee!

Far may thy days, as heretofore,
　From this our gaudy world be past!
And that too bitter moment o'er,
　Oh! may such trial be thy last!

This heart, alas! perverted long,
　Itself destroyed might there destroy;
To meet thee in the glittering throng,
　Would wake Presumption's hope of joy.

Then to the things whose bliss or woe,
　Like mine, is wild and worthless all,
That world resign — such scenes forego,
　Where those who feel must surely fall.

Thy youth, thy charms, thy tenderness,
　Thy soul from long seclusion pure;
From what even here hath passed, may guess
　What there thy bosom must endure.

Oh! pardon that imploring tear,
　Since not by Virtue shed in vain,
My frenzy drew from eyes so dear;
　For me they shall not weep again.

Though long and mournful must it be,
　The thought that we no more may meet;
Yet I deserve the stern decree,
　And almost deem the sentence sweet.

Still, had I loved thee less, my heart
　Had then less sacrificed to thine;
It felt not half so much to part,
　As if its guilt had made thee mine.

　　　　　　　　　　　　　1813.

ON LORD THURLOW'S POEMS.[1]

WHEN Thurlow this damned nonsense sent,
(I hope I am not violent)
Nor men nor gods knew what he meant.

And since not even our Rogers' praise
To common sense his thoughts could raise —
Why *would* they let him print his lays?

　　*　　*　　*　　*　　*

　　*　　*　　*　　*　　*

To me divine Apollo, grant — O!
Hermilda's first and second canto,
I'm fitting up a new portmanteau;

And thus to furnish decent lining,
My own and other's bays I'm twining —
So, gentle Thurlow, throw me thine in.

---

[1] [One evening, in 1813, Byron and Moore were ridiculing a volume of poetry which they chanced to take up at the house of Rogers. While their host was palliating faults and pointing out beauties, their mirth received a fresh impulse by the discovery of a piece, in which the author had loudly sung the praises of Rogers himself. "The opening line of the poem," says Moore, "was 'When Rogers o'er this labor bent;' and Lord Byron undertook to read it aloud;

TO LORD THURLOW.

"I lay my branch of laurel down,
　Then thus to form Apollo's crown
Let every other bring his own."
　　　Lord Thurlow's lines to Mr. Rogers.

"*I lay my branch of laurel down.*"
Thou "lay thy branch of *laurel* down!"
　Why, what thou'st stole is not enow;
And, were it lawfully thine own,
　Does Rogers want it most, or thou?
Keep to thyself thy withered bough,
　Or send it back to Doctor Donne!
Were justice done to both, I trow,
　He'd have but little, and thou — none.

"*Then thus to form Apollo's crown.*"
A crown! why, twist it how you will,
　Thy chaplet must be foolscap still.
When next you visit Delphi's town,
　Enquire amongst your fellow-lodgers,
They'll tell you Phœbus gave his crown,
　Some years before your birth, to Rogers.

"*Let every other bring his own.*"
When coals to Newcastle are carried,
　And owls sent to Athens, as wonders,
From his spouse when the Regent's unmarried,
　Or Liverpool weeps o'er his blunders;
When Tories and Whigs cease to quarrel,
　When Castlereagh's wife has an heir,
Then Rogers shall ask us for laurel,
　And thou shalt have plenty to spare.

TO THOMAS MOORE.

WRITTEN THE EVENING BEFORE HIS VISIT
TO MR. LEIGH HUNT IN HORSEMONGER
LANE GAOL, MAY 19, 1813.

OH you, who in all names can tickle the town,
Anacreon, Tom Little, Tom Moore, or Tom
　Brown, —
For hang me if I know of which you may most
　brag,
Your Quarto two-pounds, or your Two-penny
　Post Bag;

　　*　　*　　*　　*　　*

But now to my letter — to *yours* 'tis an answer —
To-morrow be with me, as soon as you can, sir,
All ready and dressed for proceeding to spunge
　on
(According to compact) the wit in the dun-
　geon —

— but he found it impossible to get beyond the first two words. Our laughter had now increased to such a pitch that nothing could restrain it, till even Mr. Rogers himself found it impossible not to join us. A day or two after, Lord Byron sent me the following: 'My dear Moore, "When Rogers" must not see the inclosed, which I send for your perusal.'"]

Pray Phœbus at length our political malice
May not get us lodgings within the same
  palace!
I suppose that to-night you're engaged with
  some codgers,
And for Sotheby's Blues have deserted Sam
  Rogers·
And I, though with cold I have nearly my
  death got,
Must put on my breeches, and wait on the
  Heathcote,
But to-morrow, at four, we will both play the
  Scurra,
And you'll be Catullus, the Regent Mamurra.[1]

IMPROMPTU, IN REPLY TO A FRIEND.

WHEN, from the heart where Sorrow sits,
  Her dusky shadow mounts too high,
And o'er the changing aspect flits,
  And clouds the brow, or fills the eye;
Heed not that gloom, which soon shall sink:
  My thoughts their dungeon know too well;
Back to my breast the wanderers shrink,
  And droop within their silent cell.[2]

September, 1813.

SONNET, TO GENEVRA.

THINE eyes' blue tenderness, thy long fair hair,
  And the wan lustre of thy features — caught
  From   contemplation — where   serenely
    wrought,
Seems Sorrow's softness charmed from its de-
    spair —
Have thrown such speaking sadness in thine
    air,
  That'—but I know thy blessed bosom fraught
  With   mines   of   unalloyed   and   stainless
    thought—
I should have deemed thee doomed to earthly
    care.
With such an aspect, by his colors blent,
  When from his beauty-breathing pencil
    born,
(Except that *thou* hast nothing to repent)

[1] [The reader who wishes to understand the full force of this scandalous insinuation is referred to Muretus's notes on a celebrated poem of Catullus, entitled *In Cæsarem ;* but consisting, in fact, of savagely scornful abuse of the favorite *Mamurra :* —

  "Quis hoc potest videre ? quis potest pati,
  Nisi impudicus et vorax et helluo ?
  Mamurram habere quod comata Gallia
  Habebat unctum, et ultima Britannia ? " etc.—]

[2] [These verses are said to have dropped from the poet's pen to excuse a transient expression of melancholy which overclouded the general gaiety.— *Sir Walter Scott.*]

The Magdalen of Guido saw the morn —
Such seem'st thou — but how much more ex·
  cellent!
With nought Remorse can claim — nor Vir·
  tue scorn.   December 17, 1813.[3]

SONNET, TO THE SAME.

THY cheek is pale with thought, but not from
    woe,
  And yet so lovely, that if Mirth could flush
  Its rose of whiteness with the brightest blush,
My heart would wish away that ruder glow :
And dazzle not thy deep-blue eyes — but, oh l
  While gazing on them sterner eyes will gush,
  And into mine my mother's weakness rush,
Soft as the last drops round heaven's airy bow.
For, through thy long dark lashes low depend·
    ing,
  The soul of melancholy Gentleness
Gleams like a seraph from the sky descending,
  Above all pain, yet pitying all distress ;
At once such majesty with sweetness blending,
  I worship more, but cannot love thee less.

December 17, 1813.

FROM THE PORTUGUESE.

"TU ME CHAMAS."

IN moments to delight devoted,
  " My life ! " with tenderest tone, you cry;
Dear words! on which my heart had doted,
  If youth could neither fade nor die.

To death even hours like these must roll,
  Ah! then repeat those accents never;
Or change " my life ! " into " my soul l "
  Which, like my love, exists for ever.

ANOTHER VERSION.

You call me still your *life.* — Oh l change the
  word —
Life is as transient as the inconstant sigh :
Say rather I'm your soul ; more just that name,
For, like the soul, my love can never die.

THE DEVIL'S DRIVE;

AN UNFINISHED RHAPSODY.[4]

THE Devil returned to hell by two,
  And he staid at home till five ;

[3] [" Read some Italian, and wrote two sonnets. I never wrote but one sonnet before, and that was not in earnest, and many years ago, as an exercise — and I will never write another. They are the most puling, petrifying, stupidly Platonic compositions." — *Byron's Diary,* 1813.]

[4] [" I have lately written a wild, rambling, unfin·

When he dined on some homicides done in
  ragoût,
And a rebel or so in an *Irish* stew,
And sausages made of a self-slain Jew—
And bethought himself what next to do,
"And," quoth he, "I'll take a drive.
I walked in the morning, I'll ride to-night;
In darkness my children take most delight,
And I'll see how my favorites thrive.

"And what shall I ride in?" quoth Lucifer
  then—
"If I followed my taste, indeed,
I should mount in a wagon of wounded men,
  And smile to see them bleed.
But these will be furnished again and again,
  And at present my purpose is speed;
To see my manor as much as I may,
And watch that no souls shall be poached away.

"I have a state-coach at Carlton House,
  A chariot in Seymour Place;
But they're lent to two friends, who make me
  · amends
By driving my favorite pace:
And they handle their reins with such a grace,
I have something for both at the end of their
  race.

"So now for the earth to take my chance."
  Then up to the earth sprung he;
And making a jump from Moscow to France,
He stepped across the sea,
And rested his hoof on a turnpike road,
No very great way from a bishop's abode.

But first as he flew, I forgot to say,
That he hovered a moment upon his way
To look upon Leipsic plain;
And so sweet to his eye was its sulphury glare,
And so soft to his ear was the cry of despair,
That he perched on a mountain of slain;
And he gazed with delight from its growing
  height,
Nor often on earth had he seen such a sight,
  Nor his work done half as well:
For the field ran so red with the blood of the
  dead,
  That it blushed like the waves of hell!
Then loudly, and wildly, and long laughed he:
"Methinks they have here little need of *me!*"
*   *   *   *   *

ished rhapsody, called 'The Devil's Drive,' the
notion of which I took from Porson's 'Devil's
Walk.'"—*Byron's Diary*, 1813.—"Of this
strange, wild poem," says Moore, "the only copy
that Lord Byron, I believe, ever wrote, he pre-
sented to Lord Holland. Though with a good
deal of vigor and imagination, it is, for the most
part, rather clumsily executed, wanting the point
and condensation of those clever verses of Mr.
Coleridge, which Lord Byron, adopting a notion
long prevalent, has attributed to Professor Por-
son."] The "Devil's Walk" is principally South-
ey's. See Southey's Poems, vol. iii. 75.

But the softest note that soothed his ear
  Was the sound of a widow sighing;
And the sweetest sight was the icy tear,
Which horror froze in the blue eye clear
  Of a maid by her lover lying—
As round her fell her long fair hair;
And she looked to heaven with that frenzied
  air,
Which seemed to ask if a God were there!
And, stretched by the wall of a ruined hut,
With its hollow cheek, and eyes half shut,
  A child of famine dying:
And the carnage begun, when resistance is
  done,
  And the fall of the vainly flying.
*   *   *   *   *

But the Devil has reached our cliffs so white,
  And what did he there, I pray?
If his eyes were good, he but saw by night
  What we see every day:
But he made a tour, and kept a journal
Of all the wondrous sights nocturnal,
And he sold it in shares to the *Men* of the *Row*,
Who bid pretty well—but they *cheated* him,
  though.

The Devil first saw, as he thought, the *Mail*,
  Its coachman and his coat;
So instead of a pistol he cocked his tail,
  And seized him by the throat:
"Aha!" quoth he, "what have we here?
'Tis a new barouche, and an ancient peer!"

So he sat him on his box again,
  And bade him have no fear,
But be true to his club, and stanch to his rein,
  His brothel, and his beer;
"Next to seeing a lord at the council board,
  I would rather see him here."
*   *   *   *   *

The Devil gat next to Westminster,
  And he turned to "the room" of the Com-
  mons;
But he heard as he purposed to enter in there,
  That "the Lords" had received a summons;
And he thought, as a "*quondam* aristocrat,"
He might peep at the peers, though to *hear*
  them were flat;
And he walked up the house so like one of our
  own,
That they say that he stood pretty near the
  throne.

He saw the Lord Liverpool seemingly wise,
  The Lord Westmoreland certainly silly,
And Johnny of Norfolk—a man of some
  size—
  And Chatham, so like his friend Billy;
And he saw the tears in Lord Eldon's eyes,
  Because the Catholics would *not* rise,
  In spite of his prayers and his prophecies;
And he heard—which set Satan himself a
  staring—

A certain Chief Justice say something like
  swearing.
And the Devil was shocked — and quoth he,
  " I must go,
For I find we have much better manners be-
  low :
If thus he harangues when he passes my
  border,
I shall hint to friend Moloch to call him to
  order.''

WINDSOR POETICS.

LINES COMPOSED ON THE OCCASION OF HIS
ROYAL HIGHNESS THE PRINCE REGENT
BEING SEEN STANDING BETWEEN THE
COFFINS OF HENRY VIII. AND CHARLES
I., IN THE ROYAL VAULT AT WINDSOR.

FAMED for the contemptuous breach of sacred
  ties,
By headless Charles see heartless Henry lies;
Between them stands another sceptred thing—
It moves, it reigns — in all but name, a king :

Charles to his people, Henry to his wife,
— In him the double tyrant starts to life :
Justice and death have mixed their dust in vain,
Each royal vampire wakes to life again.
Ah, what can tombs avail ! — since these dis-
  gorge
The blood and dust of both — to mould a
  George.

STANZAS FOR MUSIC.

[" I SPEAK NOT, I TRACE NOT," ETC.][1]

I SPEAK not, I trace not, I breathe not thy
  name,
There is grief in the sound, there is guilt in
  the fame ;
But the tear which now burns on my cheek
  may impart
The deep thoughts that dwell in that silence
  of heart.

Too brief for our passion, too long for our
  peace
Were those hours — can their joy or their bit-
  terness cease ?
We repent — we abjure — we will break from
  our chain, —
We will part, — we will fly to — unite it again !
Oh ! thine be the gladness, and mine be the
  guilt !

---

[1] [" Thou hast asked me for a song, and I enclose
you an experiment, which has cost me something
more than trouble, and is, therefore, less likely to be
worth your taking any in your proposed setting.
Now, if it be so, throw it into the fire without
phrase." — *Byron to Moore,* May 10, 1814.]

Forgive me, adored one ! — forsake, if thou
  wilt ; —
But the heart which is thine shall expire unde-
  based,
And *man* shall not break it — whatever *thou*
  mayst.

And stern to the haughty, but humble to thee,
This soul, in its bitterest blackness, shall be ;
And our days seem as swift, and our moments
  more sweet,
With thee by my side, than with worlds at our
  feet.
One sigh of thy sorrow, one look of thy love,
Shall turn me or fix, shall reward or reprove ;
And the heartless may wonder at all I resign —
Thy lip shall reply, not to them, but to *mine.*

                                May, 1814.

ADDRESS INTENDED TO BE RE-
CITED AT THE CALEDONIA
MEETING.

WHO hath not glowed above the page where
  fame
Hath fixed high Caledon's unconquered name ;
The mountain-land which spurned the Roman
  chain,
And baffled back the fiery-crested Dane,
Whose bright claymore and hardihood of
  hand
No foe could tame — no tyrant could com-
  mand ?
That race is gone — but still their children
  breathe,
And glory crowns them with redoubled wreath :
O'er Gael and Saxon mingling banners shine,
And, England ! add their stubborn strength to
  thine.
The blood which flowed with Wallace flows
  as free,
But now 'tis only shed for fame and thee !
Oh ! pass not by the northern veteran's claim,
But give support — the world hath given him
  fame.
The humbler ranks, the lowly brave, who bled
While cheerly following where the mighty
  led —
Who sleep beneath the undistinguished sod
Where happier comrades in their triumph trod,
To us bequeath — 'tis all their fate allows —
The sireless offspring and the lonely spouse :
She on high Albyn's dusky hills may raise
The tearful eye in melancholy gaze,
Or view, while shadowy auguries disclose
The Highland seer's anticipated woes,
The bleeding phantom of each martial form
Dim in the cloud, or darkling in the storm ;
While sad, she chants the solitary song,
The soft lament for him who tarries long —

For him, whose distant relics vainly crave
The Coronach's wild requiem to the brave!
'Tis Heaven—not man—must charm away
   the woe
Which bursts when Nature's feelings newly
   flow;
Yet tenderness and time may rob the tear
Of half its bitterness for one so dear;
A nation's gratitude perchance may spread
A thornless pillow for the widowed head;
May lighten well her heart's maternal care,
And wean from penury the soldier's heir.

May, 1814.

FRAGMENT OF AN EPISTLE TO
THOMAS MOORE.

"WHAT say *I?*"—not a syllable further in
   prose;
I'm your man "of all measures," dear Tom,
   — so, here goes!
Here goes, for a swim on the stream of old
   Time,
On those buoyant supporters, the bladders of
   rhyme.
If our weight breaks them down, and we sink
   in the flood,
We are smothered, at least, in respectable mud,
Where the Divers of Bathos lie drowned in a
   heap,
And Southey's last Pæan has pillowed his
   sleep;—
That "Felo de se" who, half drunk with his
   malmsey,
Walked out of his depth and was lost in a calm
   sea,
Singing "Glory to God" in a spick and span
   stanza,
The like (since Tom Sternhold was choked)
   never man saw.

The papers have told you, no doubt, of the
   fusses,
The fêtes, and the gapings to get at these
   Russes,—
Of his Majesty's suite, up from coachman to
   Hetman,—
And what dignity decks the flat face of the
   great man.
I saw him, last week, at two balls and a party,—
For a prince, his demeanor was rather too
   hearty.
You know, *we* are used to quite different
   graces.

*   *   *   *   *

The Czar's look, I own, was much brighter and
   brisker,
But then he is sadly deficient in whisker;
And wore but a starless blue coat, and in
   kersey-

mere breeches whisked round, in a waltz with
   the Jersey,
Who, lovely as ever, seemed just as delighted
With majesty's presence as those she invited.

*   *   *   *   *

June, 1814.

CONDOLATORY ADDRESS TO SA-
RAH, COUNTESS OF JERSEY, ON
THE PRINCE REGENT'S RETURN-
ING HER PICTURE TO MRS. MEE.[1]

WHEN the vain triumph of the imperial lord,
Whom servile Rome obeyed, and yet abhorred,
Gave to the vulgar gaze each glorious bust,
That left a likeness of the brave, or just;
What most admired each scrutinizing eye
Of all that decked that passing pageantry?
What spread from face to face that wondering
   air?
The thought of Brutus—for his was not there!
That absence proved his worth,—that absence
   fixed
His memory on the longing mind, unmixed;
And more decreed his glory to endure,
Than all a gold Colossus could secure.
If thus, fair Jersey, our desiring gaze
Search for thy form, in vain and mute amaze,
Amidst those pictured charms, whose loveli-
   ness,
Bright though they be, thine own had ren-
   dered less;
If he, that vain old man, whom truth admits
Heir of his father's crown, and of his wits,
If his corrupted eye, and withered heart,
Could with thy gentle image bear depart;
That tasteless shame be *his*, and ours the grief,
To gaze on Beauty's band without its chief:
Yet comfort still one selfish thought imparts,
We lose the portrait, but preserve our hearts.
What can his vaulted gallery now disclose?
A garden with all flowers—except the rose;—
A fount that only wants its living stream;
A night, with every star, save Dian's beam.
Lost to our eyes the present forms shall be,
That turn from tracing them to dream of thee;
And more on that recalled resemblance pause,
Than all he *shall* not force on our applause.
Long may thy yet meridian lustre shine,
With all that Virtue asks of Homage thine:
The symmetry of youth—the grace of mien—
The eye that gladdens—and the brow serene;

---

[1] ["The newspapers have got hold (I know not
how) of the Condolatory Address to Lady Jersey on
the picture-abduction by our Regent, and have pub-
lished them—with my name, too, smack—without
even asking leave, or inquiring whether or no! D—n
their impudence, and d—n every thing. It has put
me out of patience, and so—I shall say no more
about it." — *Byron's Letters.*]

The glossy darkness of that clustering hair,
Which shades, yet shows that forehead more
    than fair !
Each glance that wins us, and the life that
    throws
A spell which will not let our looks repose,
But turn to gaze again, and find anew
Some charm that well rewards another view.
These are not lessened, these are still as bright,
Albeit too dazzling for a dotard's sight;
And those must wait till every charm is gone,
To please the paltry heart that pleases none ; —
That dull cold sensualist, whose sickly eye
In envious dimness passed thy portrait by;
Who racked his little spirit to combine
Its hate of *Freedom's* loveliness, and *thine.*

                        August, 1814.

TO BELSHAZZAR.

BELSHAZZAR ! from the banquet turn,
    Nor in thy sensual fulness fall ;
Behold ! while yet before thee burn
    The graven words, the glowing wall,
Many a despot men miscall
    Crowned and anointed from on high ;
But thou, the weakest, worst of all —
    Is it not written, thou must die ?

Go ! dash the roses from thy brow —
    Gray hairs but poorly wreathe with them ;
Youth's garlands misbecome thee now,
    More than thy very diadem,
Where thou hast tarnished every gem : —
    Then throw the worthless bauble by,
Which, worn by thee, even slaves contemn,
    And learn like better men to die !

Oh ! early in the balance weighed,
    And ever light of word and worth,
Whose soul expired ere youth decayed,
    And left thee but a mass of earth.
To see thee moves the scorner's mirth :
    But tears in Hope's averted eye
Lament that even thou hadst birth —
    Unfit to govern, live, or die.

ELEGIAC STANZAS ON THE DEATH
OF SIR PETER PARKER, BART.[1]

THERE is a tear for all that die,
    A mourner o'er the humblest grave ;
But nations swell the funeral cry,
    And Triumph weeps above the brave.

For them is Sorrow's purest sigh
    O'er Ocean's heaving bosom sent :
In vain their bones unburied lie,
    All earth becomes their monument !

A tomb is theirs on every page,
    An epitaph on every tongue :
The present hours, the future age,
    For them bewail, to them belong.

For them the voice of festal mirth
    Grows hushed, *their name* the only sound
While deep Remembrance pours to Worth
    The goblet's tributary round.

A theme to crowds that knew them not,
    Lamented by admiring foes,
Who would not share their glorious lot ?
    Who would not die the death they chose ?

And, gallant Parker ! thus enshrined
    Thy life, thy fall, thy fame shall be ;
And early valor, glowing, find
    A model in thy memory.

But there are breasts that bleed with thee
    In woe, that glory cannot quell ;
And shuddering hear of victory,
    Where one so dear, so dauntless, fell.

Where shall they turn to mourn thee less ?
    When cease to hear thy cherished name ?
Time cannot teach forgetfulness,
    While Grief's full heart is fed by Fame.

Alas ! for them, though not for thee,
    They cannot choose but weep the more ;
Deep for the dead the grief must be,
    Who ne'er gave cause to mourn before.

                        October, 1814.

STANZAS FOR MUSIC.[2]

[" THERE'S NOT A JOY THE WORLD CAN
          GIVE," ETC.]

    " O Lachrymarum fons, tenero sacros
    Ducentium ortus ex animo: quater
    Felix ! in imo qui scatentem
    Pectore te, pia Nympha, sensit."
                        GRAY'S *Poemata.*

THERE's not a joy the world can give like that
        it takes away,
When the glow of early thought declines in
        feeling's dull decay;
'Tis not on youth's smooth cheek the blush
        alone, which fades so fast,
But the tender bloom of heart is gone, ere
        youth itself be past.

Then the few whose spirits float above the
    wreck of happiness
Are driven o'er the shoals of guilt, or ocean
    of excess:
The magnet of their course is gone, or only
    points in vain
The shore to which their shivered sail shall
    never stretch again.

Then the mortal coldness of the soul like
    death itself comes down;
It cannot feel for others' woes, it dare not
    dream its own;
That heavy chill has frozen o'er the fountain
    of our tears,
And though the eye may sparkle still, 'tis
    where the ice appears.

Though wit may flash from fluent lips, and
    mirth distract the breast,
Through midnight hours that yield no more
    their former hope of rest;
'Tis but as ivy-leaves around the ruined tur-
    ret wreathe,
All green and wildly fresh without, but worn
    and gray beneath.

Oh could I feel as I have felt, — or be what I
    have been,
Or weep as I could once have wept, o'er many
    a vanished scene;
As springs in deserts found seem sweet, all
    brackish though they be,
So, midst the withered waste of life, those
    tears would flow to me.[1]
                        March, 1815.

STANZAS FOR MUSIC.

["THERE BE NONE OF BEAUTY'S
DAUGHTERS."]

THERE be none of Beauty's daughters
    With a magic like thee;
And like music on the waters
    Is thy sweet voice to me:
When, as if its sound were causing
The charmed ocean's pausing
The waves lie still and gleaming,
And the lulled winds seem dreaming.

And the midnight moon is weaving
    Her bright chain o'er the deep;
Whose breast is gently heaving,
    As an infant's asleep:

So the spirit bows before thee,
To listen and adore thee;
With a full but soft emotion,
Like the swell of Summer's ocean.

ON NAPOLEON'S ESCAPE FROM ELBA.

ONCE fairly set out on his party of pleasure,
Taking towns at his liking, and crowns at his
    leisure,
From Elba to Lyons and Paris he goes,
Making *balls for* the ladies, and *bows to* his foes.
                  March 27, 1815.

ODE FROM THE FRENCH.

["WE DO NOT CURSE THEE, WATERLOO!"]

I.

WE do not curse thee, Waterloo!
Though Freedom's blood thy plain bedew;
There 'twas shed, but is not sunk —
Rising from each gory trunk,
Like the water-spout from ocean,
With a strong and growing motion —
It soars, and mingles in the air,
With that of lost Labedoyère —
With that of him whose honored grave
Contains the " bravest of the brave."
A crimson cloud it spreads and glows,
But shall return to whence it rose;
When 'tis full 'twill burst asunder —
Never yet was heard such thunder
As then shall shake the world with wonder —
Never yet was seen such lightning
As o'er heaven shall then be bright'ning!
Like the Wormwood Star foretold
By the sainted Seer of old,
Show'ring down a fiery flood,
Turning rivers into blood.[2]

II.

The Chief has fallen, but not by you,
Vanquishers of Waterloo!
When the soldier citizen
Swayed not o'er his fellow-men —
Save in deeds that led them on
Where Glory smiled on Freedom's son —

now, but could not — set me pondering, and finally
into the train of thought which you have in your
hands."] — *Byron to Moore.*
[1] ["Do you remember the lines I sent you early
last year? I don't wish (like Mr. Fitzgerald) to
claim the character of 'Vates,' in all its transla-
tions, — but were they not a little prophetic? I
mean those beginning, 'There's not a joy the world
can give,' etc., on which I pique myself as being
the *truest*, though the most melancholy, I ever
wrote." — *Byron's Letters*, March, 1816.]
[2] See Rev. chap. viii. *v.* 7, etc. "The first angel
sounded, and there followed hail and fire mingled
with blood," etc. *v.* 8. "And the second angel
sounded, and as it were a great mountain burning
with fire was cast into the sea; and the third part
of the sea became blood," etc. *v.* 10. "And the
third angel sounded, and there fell a great star from

Who, of all the despots banded,
  With that youthful chief competed?
  Who could boast o'er France defeated,
Till lone Tyranny commanded?
Till, goaded by ambition's sting,
The Hero sunk into the King?
Then he fell:—so perish all,
Who would men by man enthrall!

III.

And thou, too, of the snow-white plume!
Whose realm refused thee even a tomb;[1]
Better hadst thou still been leading
France o'er hosts of hirelings bleeding,
Than sold thyself to death and shame
For a meanly royal name;
Such as he of Naples wears,
Who thy blood-bought title bears.
Little didst thou deem, when dashing
  On thy war-horse through the ranks
  Like a stream which burst its banks,
While helmets cleft, and sabres clashing,
Shone and shivered fast around thee—
Of the fate at last which found thee:
Was that haughty plume laid low
By a slave's dishonest blow?
Once—as the Moon sways o'er the tide,
It rolled in air, the warrior's guide;
Through the smoke-created night
Of the black and sulphurous fight,
The soldier raised his seeking eye
To catch that crest's ascendency,—
And, as it onward rolling rose,
So moved his heart upon our foes.
There, where death's brief pang was quickest,
And the battle's wreck lay thickest,
Strewed beneath the advancing banner
  Of the eagle's burning crest—
(There with thunder-clouds to fan her,
  Who could then her wing arrest—
  Victory beaming from her breast?)
While the broken line enlarging
  Fell, or fled along the plain;
There be sure was Murat charging!
There he ne'er shall charge again!

IV.

O'er glories gone the invaders march,
Weeps Triumph o'er each levelled arch—
But let Freedom rejoice,

heaven, burning as it were a lamp; and it fell upon
the third part of the rivers, and upon the fountains
of waters." *v.* 11. "And the name of the star is
called *Wormwood:* and the third part of the wa-
ters became *wormwood;* and many men died of
the waters, because they were made bitter."
[1] ["Murat's remains are said to have been torn
from the grave and burnt. Poor dear Murat, what
an end! His white plume used to be a rallying
point in battle, like Henry the Fourth's. He re-
fused a confessor and a bandage; so would neither
suffer his soul nor body to be bandaged."—*Byron's
Letters.*]

With her heart in her voice;
But, her hand on her sword,
Doubly shall she be adored;
France hath twice too well been taught
The "moral lesson" dearly bought—
Her safety sits not on a throne,
With Capet or Napoleon!
But in equal rights and laws,
Hearts and hands in one great cause—
Freedom, such as God hath given
Unto all beneath his heaven,
With their breath, and from their birth,
Though Guilt would sweep it from the earth;
With a fierce and lavish hand
Scattering nations' wealth like sand;
Pouring nations' blood like water,
In imperial seas of slaughter!

V.

But the heart and the mind,
And the voice of mankind,
Shall arise in communion—
And who shall resist that proud union?
The time is past when swords subdued—
Man may die—the soul's renewed:
Even in this low world of care
Freedom ne'er shall want an heir;
Millions breathe but to inherit
Her for ever bounding spirit—
When once more her hosts assemble,
Tyrants shall believe and tremble—
Smile they at this idle threat?
Crimson tears will follow yet.[2]

FROM THE FRENCH.

["MUST THOU GO, MY GLORIOUS CHIEF?"][3]

I.

MUST thou go, my glorious Chief,
  Severed from thy faithful few?
Who can tell thy warrior's grief,
  Maddening o'er that long adieu?
Woman's love, and friendship's zeal,
  Dear as both have been to me—
What are they to all I feel,
  With a soldier's faith for thee?

[2] ["Talking of politics, pray look at the conclu-
sion of my 'Ode on Waterloo,' written in the year
1815, and, comparing it with the Duke de Berri's
catastrophe in 1820, tell me if I have not as good a
right to the character of '*Vates*,' in both senses of
the word, as Fitzgerald and Coleridge?—
  'Crimson tears will follow yet;'
and have they not?"—*Byron's Letters*, 1820.]

[3] "All wept, but particularly Savary, and a Polish
officer who had been exalted from the ranks by Bona-
parte. He clung to his master's knees; wrote a letter
to Lord Keith, entreating permission to accompany
him, even in the most menial capacity, which could
not be admitted."

II.

Idol of the soldier's soul!
  First in fight, but mightiest now:
Many could a world control;
  Thee alone no doom can bow.
By thy side for years I dared
  Death; and envied those who fell,
When their dying shout was heard,
  Blessing him they served so well.[1]

III.

Would that I were cold with those,
  Since this hour I live to see;
When the doubts of coward foes
  Scarce dare trust a man with thee,
Dreading each should set thee free!
  Oh! although in dungeons pent,
All their chains were light to me,
  Gazing on thy soul unbent.

IV.

Would the sycophants of him
  Now so deaf to duty's prayer,
Were his borrowed glories dim,
  In his native darkness share?
Were that world this hour his own,
  All thou calmly dost resign,
Could he purchase with that throne
  Hearts like those which still are thine?

V.

My chief, my king, my friend, adieu!
  Never did I droop before;
Never to my sovereign sue,
  As his foes I now implore:
All I ask is to divide
  Every peril he must brave;
Sharing by the hero's side
  His fall, his exile, and his grave.

ON THE STAR OF "THE LEGION OF HONOR."

[FROM THE FRENCH.]

STAR of the brave!—whose beam hath shed
Such glory o'er the quick and dead—
Thou radiant and adored deceit!
Which millions rushed in arms to greet,—
Wild meteor of immortal birth!
Why rise in Heaven to set on Earth?

Souls of slain heroes formed thy rays;
Eternity flashed through thy blaze;

---

[1] " At Waterloo, one man was seen, whose left arm was shattered by a cannon ball, to wrench it off with the other, and throwing it up in the air, exclaimed to his comrades, ' Vive l'Empereur, jusqu' à la mort!' There were many other instances of the like: this you may, however, depend on as true." — *Private Letter from Brussels.*

The music of thy martial sphere
Was fame on high and honor here;
And thy light broke on human eyes,
Like a volcano of the skies.

Like lava rolled thy stream of blood,
And swept down empires with its flood;
Earth rocked beneath thee to her base,
As thou didst lighten through all space
And the shorn Sun grew dim in air,
And set while thou wert dwelling there.

Before thee rose, and with thee grew,
A rainbow of the loveliest hue
Of three bright colors,[2] each divine,
And fit for that celestial sign;
For Freedom's hand had blended them,
Like tints in an immortal gem.

One tint was of the sunbeam's dyes;
One, the blue depth of Seraph's eyes;
One, the pure Spirit's veil of white
Had robed in radiance of its light:
The three so mingled did beseem
The texture of a heavenly dream.

Star of the brave! thy ray is pale,
And darkness must again prevail!
But, oh thou Rainbow of the free!
Our tears and blood must flow for thee.
When thy bright promise fades away,
Our life is but a load of clay.

And Freedom hallows with her tread
The silent cities of the dead;
For beautiful in death are they
Who proudly fall in her array;
And soon, oh Goddess! may we be
For evermore with them or thee!

NAPOLEON'S FAREWELL.

[FROM THE FRENCH.]

I.

FAREWELL to the Land, where the gloom of
  my Glory
Arose and o'ershadowed the earth with her
  name—
She abandons me now—but the page of her
  story,
The brightest or blackest, is filled with my
  fame.
I have warred with a world which vanquished
  me only
When the meteor of conquest allured me too
  far;
I have coped with the nations which dread me
  thus lonely,
The last single Captive to millions in war.

---

[2] The tricolor.

II.

Farewell to thee, France! when thy diadem
  crowned me,
I made thee the gem and the wonder of
  earth, —
But thy weakness decrees I should leave as
  I found thee,
Decayed in thy glory, and sunk in thy worth.
Oh! for the veteran hearts that were wasted
In strife with the storm, when their battles were
  won —
Then the Eagle, whose gaze in that moment
  was blasted,
Had still soared with eyes fixed on victory's
  sun!

III.

Farewell to thee, France! — but when Liberty
  rallies
Once more in thy regions, remember me
  then, —
The violet still grows in the depth of thy
  valleys;
Though withered, thy tear will unfold it
  again —
Yet, yet, I may baffle the hosts that surround
  us,
And yet may thy heart leap awake to my
  voice —
There are links which must break in the
  chain that has bound us,
Then turn thee and call on the Chief of thy
  choice!

ENDORSEMENT TO THE DEED OF SEPARATION, IN THE APRIL OF 1816.

A YEAR ago you swore, fond she!
  " To love, to honor," and so forth:
Such was the vow you pledged to me,
  And here's exactly what 'tis worth.

DARKNESS.[1]

I HAD a dream, which was not all a dream.
The bright sun was extinguished, and the stars
Did wander darkling in the eternal space,
Rayless, and pathless, and the icy earth
Swung blind and blackening in the moonless
  air;
Morn came and went — and came, and brought
  no day,
And men forgot their passions in the dread
Of this their desolation; and all hearts
Were chilled into a selfish prayer for light:
And they did live by watchfires — and the
  thrones,

---

[1] [In the original MS. — " A Dream."]

The palaces of crowned kings — the huts,
The habitations of all things which dwell,
Were burnt for beacons; cities were con-
  sumed,
And men were gathered round their blazing
  homes
To look once more into each other's face;
Happy were those who dwelt within the eye
Of the volcanos, and their mountain-torch:
A fearful hope was all the world contained;
Forests were set on fire — but hour by hour
They fell and faded — and the crackling trunks
Extinguished with a crash — and all was black.
The brows of men by the despairing light
Wore an unearthly aspect, as by fits
The flashes fell upon them; some lay down
And hid their eyes and wept; and some did
  rest
Their chins upon their clenched hands, and
  smiled;
And others hurried to and fro, and fed
Their funeral piles with fuel, and looked up
With mad disquietude on the dull sky,
The pall of a past world; and then again
With curses cast them down upon the dust,
And gnashed their teeth and howled: the wild
  birds shrieked,
And, terrified, did flutter on the ground,
And flap their useless wings; the wildest brutes
Came tame and tremulous; and vipers crawled
And twined themselves among the multitude,
Hissing, but stingless — they were slain for
  food:
And War, which for a moment was no more,
Did glut himself again: — a meal was bought
With blood, and each sate sullenly apart
Gorging himself in gloom: no love was left;
All earth was but one thought — and that was
  death,
Immediate and inglorious; and the pang
Of famine fed upon all entrails — men
Died, and their bones were tombless as their
  flesh;
The meagre by the meagre were devoured,
Even dogs assailed their masters, all save one,
And he was faithful to a corse, and kept
The birds and beasts and famished men at bay,
Till hunger clung them, or the dropping dead
Lured their lank jaws; himself sought out no
  food,
But with a piteous and perpetual moan,
And a quick desolate cry, licking the hand
Which answered not with a caress — he died.
The crowd was famished by degrees; but two
Of an enormous city did survive,
And they were enemies: they met beside
The dying embers of an altar-place
Where had been heaped a mass of holy things
For an unholy usage; they raked up,
And shivering scraped with their cold skeleton
  hands
The feeble ashes, and their feeble breath

Blew for a little life, and made a flame
Which was a mockery; then they lifted up
Their eyes as it grew lighter, and beheld
Each other's aspects — saw, and shrieked, and
 died —
Even of their mutual hideousness they died,
Unknowing who he was upon whose brow
Famine had written Fiend. The world was
 void,
The populous and the powerful was a lump,
Seasonless, herbless, treeless, manless, life-
 less —
A lump of death — a chaos of hard clay.
The rivers, lakes, and ocean all stood still,
And nothing stirred within their silent depths;
Ships sailorless lay rotting on the sea,
And their masts fell down piecemeal; as they
 dropped
They slept on the abyss without a surge —
The waves were dead; the tides were in their
 grave,
The Moon, their mistress, had expired before;
The winds were withered in the stagnant air,
And the clouds perished; Darkness had no
 need
Of aid from them — She was the Universe.[1]

 DIODATI, July, 1816.

CHURCHILL'S GRAVE;[2]

A FACT LITERALLY RENDERED.

I STOOD beside the grave of him who blazed
 The comet of a season, and I saw
The humblest of all sepulchres, and gazed
 With not the less of sorrow and of awe
On that neglected turf and quiet stone,

With name no clearer than the names un-
 known,
Which lay unread around it; and I asked
 The Gardener of that ground, why it might
 be
That for this plant strangers his memory tasked
 Through the thick deaths of half a century;
And thus he answered — "Well, I do not know
Why frequent travellers turn to pilgrims so;
 He died before my day of Sextonship,
And I had not the digging of this grave."
And is this all? I thought, — and do we rip
 The veil of Immortality? and crave
I know not what of honor and of light
 Through unborn ages, to endure this blight?
So soon, and so successless? As I said,
 The Architect of all on which we tread,
For Earth is but a tombstone, did essay
 To extricate remembrance from the clay,
Whose minglings might confuse a Newton's
 thought,
Were it not that all life must end in one,
Of which we are but dreamers; — as he caught
 As 'twere the twilight of a former Sun,
Thus spoke he, — "I believe the man of whom
You wot, who lies in this selected tomb,
 Was a most famous writer in his day,
And therefore travellers step from out their way
To pay him honor, — and myself whate'er
 Your honor pleases," — then most pleased
 I shook[3]
From out my pocket's avaricious nook
Some certain coins of silver, which as 'twere
Perforce I gave this man, though I could spare
So much but inconveniently : — Ye smile,
I see ye, ye profane ones! all the while,
Because my homely phrase the truth would tell.
You are the fools, not I — for I did dwell
With a deep thought, and with a softened eye,
On that Old Sexton's natural homily,
In which there was Obscurity and Fame, —
The Glory and the Nothing of a Name.[4]

 DIODATI, 1816.

[1] ["Darkness" is a grand and gloomy sketch of the supposed consequences of the final extinction of the Sun and the heavenly bodies; executed, undoubtedly, with great and fearful force, but with something of German exaggeration, and a fantastical solution of incidents. The very conception is terrible above all conception of known calamity, and is too oppressive to the imagination to be contemplated with pleasure, even in the faint reflection of poetry. — *Jeffrey.*]

[2] [On the sheet containing the original draught of these lines, Byron has written: — " The following poem (as most that I have endeavored to write) is founded on a fact; and this detail is an attempt at a serious imitation of the style of a great poet — its beauties and its defects: I say, the *style;* for the thoughts I claim as my own. In this, if there be any thing ridiculous, let it be attributed to me, at least as much as to Mr. Wordsworth; of whom there can exist few greater admirers than myself. I have blended what I would deem to be the beauties as well as defects, of his style; and it ought to be remembered, that, in such things, whether there be praise or dispraise, there is always what is called a compliment, however unintentional."]

[3] [Originally —
 —— "then most pleased, I shook
 My inmost pocket's most retired nook,
 And out fell five and sixpence."]

[4] [The grave of Churchill might have called from Lord Byron a deeper commemoration; for, though they generally differed in character and genius, there was a resemblance between their history and character. The satire of Churchill flowed with a more profuse, though not a more embittered, stream; while, on the other hand, he cannot be compared to Lord Byron in point of tenderness or imagination. But both these poets held themselves above the opinion of the world, and both were followed by the fame and popularity which they seemed to despise. The writings of both exhibit an inborn, though sometimes ill-regulated generosity of mind, and a spirit of proud independence, frequently pushed to extremes. Both carried their hatred of hypocrisy beyond the verge of prudence, and indulged their vein

PROMETHEUS.

I.

TITAN! to whose immortal eyes
　The sufferings of mortality,
　　Seen in their sad reality,
Were not as things that gods despise;
What was thy pity's recompense?
A silent suffering, and intense;
The rock, the vulture, and the chain,
All that the proud can feel of pain,
The agony they do not show,
The suffocating sense of woe,
　Which speaks but in its loneliness,
And then is jealous lest the sky
Should have a listener, nor will sigh
　Until his voice is echoless.

II.

Titan! to thee the strife was given
　Between the suffering and the will,
　　Which torture where they cannot kill;
And the inexorable Heaven,
And the deaf tyranny of Fate,
The ruling principle of Hate,
Which for its pleasure doth create
The things it may annihilate,
Refused thee even the boon to die:
The wretched gift eternity
Was thine — and thou hast borne it well.
All that the Thunderer wrung from thee
Was but the menace which flung back
On him the torments of thy rack;
The fate thou didst so well foresee,
But would not to appease him tell;
And in thy Silence was his Sentence,
And in his Soul a vain repentance,
And evil dread so ill dissembled
That in his hand the lightnings trembled.

III.

Thy Godlike crime was to be kind,
　To render with thy precepts less
　　The sum of human wretchedness,
And strengthen Man with his own mind;
But baffled as thou wert from high,
Still in thy patient energy,
In the endurance, and repulse
　Of thine impenetrable Spirit,
Which Earth and Heaven could not convulse,
　A mighty lesson we inherit:
Thou art a symbol and a sign
　To Mortals of their fate and force;
Like thee, Man is in part divine,
　A troubled stream from a pure source;
And Man in portions can foresee
His own funereal destiny;
His wretchedness, and his resistance,
And his sad unallied existence:

of satire to the borders of licentiousness. Both died
in the flower of their age in a foreign land. — *Sir
Walter Scott.*]

To which his Spirit may oppose
Itself — and equal to all woes,
　And a firm will, and a deep sense
Which even in torture can descry
　Its own concentred recompense,
Triumphant where it dares defy,
And making Death a Victory.

　　　　　　　　　DIODATI, July, 1816.

A FRAGMENT.

["COULD I REMOUNT," ETC.]

COULD I remount the river of my years
To the first fountain of our smiles and tears,
I would not trace again the stream of hours
Between their outworn banks of withered flow
　ers,
But bid it flow as now — until it glides
Into the number of the nameless tides.

* 　 * 　 * 　 * 　 *

What is this Death? — a quiet of the heart?
The whole of that of which we are a part?
For life is but a vision — what I see
Of all which lives alone is life to me,
And being so — the absent are the dead,
Who haunt us from tranquillity, and spread
A dreary shroud around us, and invest
With sad remembrancers our hours of rest.
　The absent are the dead — for they are cold,
And ne'er can be what once we did behold;
And they are changed, and cheerless, — or if
　yet
The unforgotten do not all forget,
Since thus divided — equal must it be
If the deep barrier be of earth, or sea;
It may be both — but one day end it must
In the dark union of insensate dust.
　The under-earth inhabitants — are they
But mingled millions decomposed to clay?
The ashes of a thousand ages spread
Wherever man has trodden or shall tread?
Or do they in their silent cities dwell
Each in his incommunicative cell?
Or have they their own language? and a
　sense
Of breathless being? — darkened and intense
As midnight in her solitude? — Oh Earth!
Where are the past? — and wherefore had they
　birth?
The dead are thy inheritors — and we
But bubbles on thy surface; and the key
Of thy profundity is in the grave,
The ebon portal of thy peopled cave,
Where I would walk in spirit, and behold
Our elements resolved to things untold,
And fathom hidden wonders, and explore
The essence of great bosoms now no more.

* 　 * 　 * 　 * 　 *

　　　　　　　　　DIODATI, July, 1816.

SONNET TO LAKE LEMAN.

ROUSSEAU — Voltaire — our Gibbon — and
  De Staël —
Leman![1] these names are worthy of thy
  shore,
Thy shore of names like these! wert thou
  no more,
Their memory thy remembrance would recall:
To them thy banks were lovely as to all,
  But they have made them lovelier, for the
   lore
Of mighty minds doth hallow in the core
Of human hearts the ruin of a wall
  Where dwelt the wise and wondrous; but
   by *thee*
How much more, Lake of Beauty! do we feel,
  In sweetly gliding o'er thy crystal sea,
The wild glow of that not ungentle zeal,
  Which of the heirs of immortality
Is proud, and makes the breath of glory real!

              DIODATI, July, 1816.

---

[1] Geneva, Ferney, Copet, Lausanne.

STANZAS FOR MUSIC.

["BRIGHT BE THE PLACE OF THY SOUL!"]

I.

BRIGHT be the place of thy soul!
  No lovelier spirit than thine
E'er burst from its mortal control,
  In the orbs of the blessed to shine.
On earth thou wert all but divine,
  As thy soul shall immortally be;
And our sorrow may cease to repine
  When we know that thy God is with thee

II.

Light be the turf of thy tomb!
  May its verdure like emeralds be!
There should not be the shadow of gloom,
  In aught that reminds us of thee.
Young flowers and an evergreen tree
  May spring from the spot of thy rest:
But nor cypress nor yew let us see;
  For why should we mourn for the blest?

ROMANCE MUY DOLOROSO

DEL

SITIO Y TOMA DE ALHAMA.

El qual dezia en Aravigo assi.

I.

PASSEAVASE el Rey Moro
Por la ciudad de Granada,
Desde las puertas de Elvira
Hasta las de Bivarambla.
    Ay de mi, Alhama!

II.

Cartas le fueron venidas
Que Alhama era ganada.
Las cartas echò en el fuego,
Y al mensagero matava.
    Ay de mi, Alhama!

III.

Descavalga de una mula,
Y en un cavallo cavalga.
Por el Zacatin arriba
Subido se avia al Alhambra.
    Ay de mi, Alhama!

IV.

Como en el Alhambra estuvo,
Al mismo punto mandava

A VERY MOURNFUL BALLAD[1]

ON THE

SIEGE AND CONQUEST OF ALHAMA.

*Which, in the Arabic language, is to the follow-
ing purport.*

I.

THE Moorish King rides up and down
Through Granada's royal town;
From Elvira's gates to those
Of Bivarambla on he goes.
    Woe is me, Alhama!

II.

Letters to the monarch tell
How Alhama's city fell:
In the fire the scroll he threw,
And the messenger he slew.
    Woe is me, Alhama!

III.

He quits his mule, and mounts his horse,
And through the street directs his course;
Through the street of Zacatin
To the Alhambra spurring in.
    Woe is me, Alhama!

IV.

When the Alhambra walls he gained,
On the moment he ordained

---

[1] The effect of the original ballad — which existed both in Spanish and Arabic — was such, that it was forbidden to be sung by the Moors, on pain of death, within Granada.

Que se toquen las trompetas
Con añafiles de plata.
      Ay de mi, Alhama!

V.

Y que atambores de guerra
Apriessa toquen alarma;
Por que lo oygan sus Moros,
Los de la Vega y Granada.
      Ay de mi, Alhama!

VI.

Los Moros que el son oyeron,
Que al sangriento Marte llama,
Uno a uno, y dos a dos,
Un gran esquadron formavan.
      Ay de mi, Alhama!

VII.

Alli habló un Moro viejo;
Desta manera hablava : —
Par que nos llamas, Rey?
Para que es este llamada?
      Ay de mi, Alhama!

VIII.

Aveys de saber, amigos,
Una nueva desdichada :
Que Christianos, con braveza,
Ya nos han tomado Alhama.
      Ay de mi, Alhama!

IX.

Alli habló un viejo Alfaqui,
De barba crecida y cana : —
Bien se te emplea, buen Rey,
Buen Rey; bien se te empleava.
      Ay de mi, Alhama!

X.

Mataste los 'Bencerrages,
Que era la flor de Granada;
Cogiste los tornadizos
De Cordova la nombrada.
      Ay de mi, Alhama!

XI.

Por esso mereces, Rey,
Una pene bien doblada;
Que te pierdas tu y el reyno,
Y que se pierda Granada.
      Ay de mi, Alhama!

XII.

Si no se respetan leyes,
Es ley que todo se pierda;
Y que se pierdas Granada,
Y que te pierdas en ella.
      Ay de mi, Alhama!

XIII.

Fuego por los ojos vierte,
El Rey que esto oyera.

That the trumpet straight should sound
With the silver clarion round.
      Woe is me, Alhama!

V.

And when the hollow drums of war
Beat the loud alarm afar,
That the Moors of town and plain
Might answer to the martial strain,
      Woe is me, Alhama!

VI.

Then the Moors, by this aware
That bloody Mars recalled them there,
One by one, and two by two,
To a mighty squadron grew.
      Woe is me, Alhama!

VII.

Out then spake an aged Moor
In these words the king before,
" Wherefore call on us, oh King?
What may mean this gathering?"
      Woe is me, Alhama!

VIII.

" Friends! ye have, alas! to know
Of a most disastrous blow,
That the Christians, stern and bold,
Have obtained Alhama's hold."
      Woe is me, Alhama!

IX.

Out then spake Old Alfaqui,
With his beard so white to see,
" Good King! thou art justly served,
Good King! this thou hast deserved.
      Woe is me, Alhama!

X.

" By thee were slain, in evil hour,
The Abencerrage, Granada's flower;
And strangers were received by thee
Of Cordova the Chivalry.
      Woe is me, Alhama!

XI.

" And for this, oh King! is sent
On thee a double chastisement:
Thee and thine, thy crown and realm,
One last wreck shall overwhelm.
      Woe is me, Alhama!

XII.

" He who holds no laws in awe,
He must perish by the law;
And Granada must be won,
And thyself with her undone."
      Woe is me, Alhama!

XIII.

Fire flashed from out the old Moor's eyes
The Monarch's wrath began to rise,

Y como cl otro de leyes
De leyes tambien hablava.   .
    Ay de mi, Alhama!

XIV.

Sabe un Rey que no ay leyes
De darle a Reyes disgusto—
Esso dize el Rey Moro
Relinchando de colera.
    Ay de mi, Alhama!

XV.

Moro Alfaqui, Moro Alfaqui,
El de la vellida barba,
El Rey te manda prender,
Por la perdida de Alhama.
    Ay de mi, Alhama!

XVI.

Y cortarte la cabeza,
Y ponerla en el Alhambra,
Por que a ti castigo sea,
Y otros tiemblen en miralla.
    Ay de mi, Alhama!

XVII.

Cavalleros, hombres buenos,
Dezid de mi parte al Rey,
Al Rey Moro de Granada,
Como no le devo nada.
    Ay de mi, Alhama!

XVIII.

De averse Alhama perdido
A mi me pesa en el alma.
Que si el·Rey perdiò su tierra,
Otro mucho mas perdiera.
    Ay de mi, Alhama!

XIX.

Perdieran hijos padres,
Y casados las casadas:
Las cosas que mas amara
Perdiò l'un y el otro fama.
    Ay de mi, Alhama!

XX.

Perdi una hija donzella
Que era la flor d' esta tierra,
Cien doblas dava por ella,
No me las estimo en nada.
    Ay de mi, Alhama!

XXI.

Diziendo assi al hacen Alfaqui,
Le cortaron la cabeça,
Y la elevan al Alhambra,
Assi come el Rey lo manda.
    Ay de mi, Alhama!

XXII.

Hombres, niños y mugeres,
Lloran tan grande perdida.

Because he answered, and because
He spake exceeding well of laws.
    Woe is me, Alhama!

XIV.

" There is no law to say such things
As may disgust the ear of kings :"—
Thus, snorting with his choler, said
The Moorish King, and doomed him dead.
    Woe is me, Alhama!

XV.   .

Moor Alfaqui! Moor Alfaqui!
Though thy beard so hoary be,
The King hath sent to have thee seized,
For Alhama's loss displeased.
    Woe is me, Alhama!

XVI.

And to fix thy head upon
High Alhambra's loftiest stone;
That this for thee should be the law,
And others tremble when they saw.
    Woe is me, Alhama!

XVII.

" Cavalier, and man of worth!
Let these words of mine go forth;
Let the Moorish Monarch know,
That to him I nothing owe.
    Woe is me, Alhama!

XVIII.

" But on my soul Alhama weighs,
And on my inmost spirit preys;
And if the King his land hath lost,
Yet others may have lost the most.
    Woe is me, Alhama!

XIX.

" Sires have lost their children, wives
Their lords, and valiant men their lives;
One what best his love might claim
Hath lost, another wealth, or fame.
    Woe is me, Alhama!

XX.

" I lost a damsel in that hour,
Of all the land the loveliest flower;
Doubloons a hundred I would pay,
And think her ransom cheap that day."
    Woe is me, Alhama!

XXI.

And as these things the old Moor said,
They severed from the trunk his head;
And to the Alhambra's wall with speed
'Twas carried, as the King decreed-
    Woe is me, Alhama!

XXII.

And men and infants therein weep
Their loss, so heavy and so deep;

Lloravan todas las damas
Quantas en Granada avia.
        Ay de mi, Alhama!

XXIII.

Por las calles y ventanas
Mucho luto parecia;
Llora el Rey como fembra,
Qu' es mucho lo que perdia.
        Ay de mi, Alhama!

Granada's ladies, all she rears
Within her walls, burst into tears.
        Woe is me, Alhama!

XXIII.

And from the windows o'er the walls
The sable web of mourning falls;
The King weeps as a woman o'er
His loss, for it is much and sore.
        Woe is me, Alhama!

SONETTO DI VITTORELLI.

PER MONACA.

Sonetto composto in nome di un genitore, a cui
ra morta poco innanzi una figlia appena maritata,
diretto al genitore della sacra sposa.

)l due vaghe donzelle, oneste, accorte,
  Lieti e miseri padri il ciel ne feo,
  Il ciel, che degne di più nobil sorte
  L' una e l' altra veggendo, ambo chiedeo.
La mia fu tolta da veloce morte
  A le fumanti tede d' imeneo :
  La tua, Francesco, in sugellate porte
  Eterna prigioniera or si rendeo.
Ma tu almeno potrai de la gelosa
  Irremeabil soglia, ove s' asconde,
  La sua tenera udir voce pietosa.
Io verso un fiume d' amarissim' onde,
  Corro a quel marmo, in cui la figlia or posa,
  Batto, e ribatto, ma nessun risponde.

TRANSLATION FROM VITTORELLI.

ON A NUN.

Sonnet composed in the name of a father, whose
daughter had recently died shortly after her mar-
riage; and addressed to the father of her who had
lately taken the veil.

OF two fair virgins, modest, though admired,
  Heaven made us happy; and now, wretched
    sires,
  Heaven for a nobler doom their worth de-
    sires,
  And gazing upon *either*, *both* required.
Mine, while the torch of Hymen newly fired
  Becomes extinguished, soon — too soon —
    expires;
  But thine, within the closing grate retired,
  Eternal captive, to her God aspires.
But *thou* at least from out the jealous door,
  Which shuts between your never-meeting
    eyes,
  May'st hear her sweet and pious voice once
    more;
I to the marble, where *my daughter* lies,
  Rush, — the swoln flood of bitterness I pour,
  And knock, and knock, and knock — but
    none replies.

ON THE BUST OF HELEN BY CANOVA.[1]

IN this beloved marble view,
  Above the works and thoughts of man,
What nature *could*, but *would not*, do,
  And beauty and Canova *can!*
Beyond imagination's power,
  Beyond the Bard's defeated art,
With immortality her dower,
  Behold the *Helen* of the *heart!*

---

[1] [" The Helen of Canova (a bust which is in the
house of Madame the Countess d'Albrizzi) is," says
Byron, " without exception, to my mind, the most
perfectly beautiful of human conceptions, and far be-
yond my ideas of human execution."]

STANZAS FOR MUSIC.

["THEY SAY THAT HOPE IS HAPPINESS."]

I.

THEY say that Hope is happiness;
  But genuine Love must prize the past,
And Memory wakes the thoughts that bless:
  They rose the first — they set the last;

II.

And all that Memory loves the most
  Was once our only Hope to be,
And all that Hope adored and lost
  Hath melted into Memory.

III.

Alas! it is delusion all:
  The future cheats us from afar,
Nor can we be what we recall,
  Nor dare we think on what we are.

SONG FOR THE LUDDITES.

I.

As the Liberty lads o'er the sea
Bought their freedom, and cheaply, with
      blood,
    So we, boys, we
    Will *die* fighting, or *live* free,
And down with all kings but King Ludd!

II.

When the web that we weave is complete,
And the shuttle exchanged for the sword,
    We will fling the winding sheet
    O'er the despot at our feet,
And dye it deep in the gore he has poured.

III.

Though black as his heart its hue,
Since his veins are corrupted to mud,
    Yet this is the dew
    Which the tree shall renew
Of Liberty, planted by Ludd!

December, 1816.

VERSICLES.[1]

I READ the " Christabel;"
    Very well:
I read the " Missionary;"
    Pretty— very:
I tried at " Ilderim;"
    Ahem!
I read a sheet of " Marg'ret of *Anjou;* "[2]
    Can you?
I turned a page of Scott's " Waterloo;"
    Pooh! pooh!
I looked at Wordsworth's milk-white " Ryl-
        stone Doe;"
    Hillo!
            Etc., etc., etc.
                    March, 1817.

---

[1] [" I have been ill with a slow fever, which at
last took to flying, and became as quick as need be.
But, at length, after a week of half delirium, burning
skin, thirst, hot headache, horrible pulsation, and no
sleep, by the blessing of barley water, and refusing
to see my physician, I recovered. It is an epi-
demic of the place. Here are some versicles, which
I made one sleepless night. " — *Byron's Letters.*
Venice, March, 1817.]
[2] [The " Missionary," was written by Mr. Bowles;
" Ilderim " by Mr. Gally Knight; and " Margaret
of Anjou " by Miss Holford.]

SO WE'LL GO NO MORE A ROVING.

I.

So we'll go no more a roving
    So late into the night,
Though the heart be still as loving,
    And the moon be still as bright.

II.

For the sword outwears its sheath,
    And the soul wears out the breast,
And the heart must pause to breathe,
    And love itself have rest.

III.

Though the night was made for loving,
    And the day returns too soon,
Yet we'll go no more a roving
    By the light of the moon.   1817

TO THOMAS MOORE.

WHAT are you doing now,
    Oh Thomas Moore?
What are you doing now,
    Oh Thomas Moore?
Sighing or suing now,
Rhyming or wooing now,
Billing or cooing now,
    Which, Thomas Moore?

But the Carnival's coming,
    Oh Thomas Moore!
The Carnival's coming,
    Oh Thomas Moore!
Masking and humming,
Fifing and drumming,
Guitarring and strumming,
    Oh Thomas Moore!

. TO MR. MURRAY.

To hook the reader, you, John Murray,
    Have published " Anjou's Margaret,"
Which won't be sold off in a hurry
    (At least, it has not been as yet);
And then, still further to bewilder 'em,
Without remorse you set up " Ilderim;"
    So mind you don't get into debt,
Because as how, if you should fail,
These books would be but baddish bail.

And mind you do *not* let escape
    These rhymes to Morning Post or Perry,
Which would be *very* treacherous — *very,*
    And get me into such a scrape!
For, firstly, I should have to sally,
    All in my little boat, against a *Galley;*

And, should I chance to slay the Assyrian
     wight,
Have next to combat with the female knight.

March 25, 1817.

TO THOMAS MOORE.

I.

My boat is on the shore,
     And my bark is on the sea;
But, before I go, Tom Moore,
     Here's a double health to thee!

II.

Here's a sigh to those who love me,
     And a smile to those who hate;
And, whatever sky's above me,
     Here's a heart for every fate.

III.

Though the ocean roar around me,
     Yet it still shall bear me on;
Though a desert should surround me,
     It hath springs that may be won.

IV.

Were't the last drop in the well,
     As I gasped upon the brink,
Ere my fainting spirit fell,
     'Tis to thee that I would drink.

V.

With that water, as this wine,
     The libation I would pour
Should be — peace to thine and mine,
     And a health to thee, Tom Moore.

July, 1817.

EPISTLE FROM MR. MURRAY TO DR. POLIDORI.[1]

Dear Doctor, I have read your play,
Which is a good one in its way, —
Purges the eyes and moves the bowels,
And drenches handkerchiefs like towels
With tears, that, in a flux of grief,
Afford hysterical relief
To shattered nerves and quickened pulses,
Which your catastrophe convulses.

[1] ["I never," says Byron, "was much more disgusted with any human production than with the eternal nonsense, and tracasseries, and emptiness, and ill-humor, and vanity of this young person; but he has some talent, and is a man of honor, and has dispositions of amendment. Therefore use your interest for him, for he is improved and improvable. You want a 'civil and delicate declension' for the medical tragedy? Take it. " — *Byron to Mr. Murray*, August 21, 1817.]

I like your moral and machinery;
Your plot, too, has such scope for scenery;
Your dialogue is apt and smart;
The play's concoction full of art;
Your hero raves, your heroine cries,
All stab, and every body dies.
In short, your tragedy would be
The very thing to hear and see:
And for a piece of publication,
If I decline on this occasion,
It is not that I am not sensible
To merits in themselves ostensible,
But — and I grieve to speak it — plays
Are drugs — mere drugs, sir — now-a-days.
I had a heavy loss by " Manuel," —
Too lucky if it prove not annual, —
And Sotheby, with his " Orestes,"
(Which, by the by, the author's best is,)
Has lain so very long on hand
That I despair of all demand.
I've advertised, but see my books,
Or only watch my shopman's looks; —
Still Ivan, Ina, and such lumber,
My back-shop glut, my shelves encumber.

There's Byron too, who once did better,
Has sent me, folded in a letter,
A sort of — it's no more a drama
Than Darnley, Ivan, or Kehama;
So altered since last year his pen is,
I think he's lost his wits at Venice.
In short, sir, what with one and t'other,
I dare not venture on another.
I write in haste; excuse each blunder;
The coaches through the streets so thunder!
My room's so full — we've Gifford here
Reading MS., with Hookham Frere,
Pronouncing on the nouns and particles
Of some of our forthcoming Articles.

The Quarterly — Ah, sir, if you
Had but the genius to review! —
A smart critique upon St. Helena,
Or if you only would but tell in a
Short compass what — but, to resume:
As I was saying, sir, the room —
The room's so full of wits and bards,
Crabbes, Campbells, Crockers, Freres, and
     Wards
And others, neither bards nor wits: —
My humble tenement admits
All persons in the dress of gent.,
From Mr. Hammond to Dog Dent.

A party dines with me to-day,
All clever men, who make their way;
Crabbe, Malcolm, Hamilton, and Chantrey,
Are all partakers of my pantry.
They're at this moment in discussion
On poor De Staël's late dissolution.
Her book, they say, was in advance —
Pray Heaven, she tell the truth of France!
Thus run our time and tongues away. —

But, to return, sir, to your play:
Sorry, sir, but I can not deal,
Unless 'twere acted by O'Neill.
My hands so full, my head so busy,
I'm almost dead, and always dizzy;
And so, with endless truth and hurry,
Dear Doctor, I am yours,
     JOHN MURRAY.

EPISTLE TO MR. MURRAY.

MY dear Mr. Murray,
You're in a damned hurry
 To set up this ultimate Canto;[1]
But (if they don't rob us)
You'll see Mr. Hobhouse
 Will bring it safe in his portmanteau.

For the Journal you hint of,
As ready to print off,
 No doubt you do right to commend it;
But as yet I have writ off
The devil a bit of
 Our " Beppo : "—when copied, I'll send it.

Then you've * * * 's Tour,—
No great things, to be sure,—
 You could hardly begin with a less work;
For the pompous rascallion,
Who don't speak Italian
 Nor French, must have scribbled by guess-
  work.

You can make any loss up
With " Spence " and his gossip,
 A work which must surely succeed;
Then Queen Mary's Epistle-craft,
With the new " Fytte " of " Whistlecraft,"
 Must make people purchase and read.

Then you've General Gordon,
Who girded his sword on,
 To serve with a Muscovite master,
And help him to polish
A nation so owlish,
 They thought shaving their beards a dis-
  aster.

For the man, " poor and shrewd," [2]
With whom you'd conclude
 A compact without more delay,
Perhaps some such pen is
Still extant in Venice;
 But please, sir, to mention *your pay*.
    VENICE, January 8, 1818.

TO MR. MURRAY.

STRAHAN, Tonson, Lintot of the times,
Patron and publisher of rhymes,

---

[1] [The fourth Canto of " Childe Harold."]
[2] *Vide* your letter.

For thee the bard up Pindus climbs,
  My Murray.

To thee, with hope and terror dumb,
The unfledged MS. authors come;
Thou printest all — and sellest some —
  My Murray.

Upon thy table's baize so green
The last new Quarterly is seen, —
But where is thy new Magazine,
  My Murray ?

Along thy sprucest bookshelves shine
The works thou deemest most divine —
The " Art of Cookery," and mine,
  My Murray.

Tours, Travels, Essays, too, I wist,
And Sermons to thy mill bring grist:
And then thou hast the " Navy List,"
  My Murray.

And Heaven forbid I should conclude
Without " the Board of Longitude,"
Although this narrow paper would,
  My Murray !
    VENICE, March 25, 1818.

ON THE BIRTH OF JOHN WIL-LIAM RIZZO HOPPNER.

HIS father's sense, his mother's grace,
 In him, I hope, will always fit so;
With — still to keep him in good case —
 The health and appetite of Rizzo.[3]

STANZAS TO THE PO.

[About the middle of April, 1819, Byron travelled from Venice to Ravenna, at which last city he expected to find the Countess Guiccioli. The following stanzas, which have been as much admired as any of the kind he ever wrote, were composed, according to Madame Guiccioli's statement, during this journey, and while Byron was actually sailing on the Po. In transmitting them to England, in May, 1820, he says, — " They must not be published: pray recollect this, as they are mere verses of society, and written upon private feelings and passions." They were first printed in 1824.]

---

[3] [On the birth of this child, the son of the British vice-consul at Venice, Byron wrote these lines. They are in no other respect remarkable, than that they were thought worthy of being metrically translated into no less than ten different languages; namely, Greek, Latin, Italian (also in the Venetian dialect), German, French, Spanish, Illyrian, Hebrew, Armenian, and Samaritan. The original lines, with the different versions above mentioned, were printed, in a small neat volume, in the seminary of Padua.]

I.

RIVER, that rollest by the ancient walls,[1]
  Where dwells the lady of my love, when she
Walks by thy brink, and there perchance re-
    calls
  A faint and fleeting memory of me;

II.

What if thy deep and ample stream should be
  A mirrow of my heart, where she may read
'The thousand thoughts I now betray to thee,
  Wild as thy wave, and headlong as thy
    pe'd.

III.

What do I say — a mirror of my heart?
  Are not thy waters sweeping, dark, and
    strong?
Such as my feelings were and are, thou art;
  And such as thou art were my passions long.

IV.

Time may have somewhat tamed them, — not
    for ever;
  Thou overflow'st thy banks, and not for aye
Thy bosom overboils, congenial river!
  Thy floods subside, and mine have sunk
    away.

V.

But left long wrecks behind, and now again,
  Borne in our old unchanged career, we
    move;
Thou tendest wildly onwards to the main,
  And I — to loving *one* I should not love.

VI.

The current I behold will sweep beneath
  Her native walls and murmur at her feet;
Her eyes will look on thee, when she shall
    breathe
  The twilight air, unharmed by summer's
    heat.

VII.

She will look on thee, — I have looked on thee,
  Full of that thought; and from that moment,
    ne'er
Thy waters could I dream of, name, or see,
  Without the inseparable sigh for her!

VIII.

Her bright eyes will be imaged in thy stream, —
  Yes! they will meet the wave I gaze on now:
Mine cannot witness, even in a dream,
  That happy wave repass me in its flow!

IX.

The wave that bears my tears returns no more:
  Will she return by whom that wave shall
    sweep? —

---

[1] [Ravenna — a city to which Byron afterwards

Both tread thy banks, both wander on thy
    shore,
  I by thy source, she by the dark-blue deep.

X.

But that which keepeth us apart is not
  Distance, nor depth of wave, nor space of
    earth,
But the distraction of a various lot,
  As various as the climates of our birth.

XI.

A stranger loves the lady of the land,
  Born far beyond the mountains, but his
    blood
Is all meridian, as if never fanned
  By the black wind that chills the polar flood.

XII.

My blood is all meridian; were it not,
  I had not left my clime, nor should I be,
In spite of tortures, ne'er to be forgot,
  A slave again of love, — at least of thee.

XIII.

'Tis vain to struggle — let me perish young —
  Live as I lived, and love as I have loved;
To dust if I return, from dust I sprung,
  And then, at least, my heart can ne'er be
    moved.   April, 1819.

EPIGRAM.

FROM THE FRENCH OF RULHIÈRES.

IF, for silver or for gold,
  You could melt ten thousand pimples
  Into half a dozen dimples,
Then your face we might behold,
  Looking, doubtless, much more snugly;
  Yet even *then* 'twould be d —— d ugly.
            August 12, 1819.

SONNET TO GEORGE THE FOURTH,

ON THE REPEAL OF LORD EDWARD FITZGERALD'S FORFEITURE.

TO be the father of the fatherless,
  To stretch the hand from the throne's height,
    and raise
His offspring, who expired in other days
To make thy sire's sway by a kingdom less, —
This is to be a monarch, and repress
  Envy into unutterable praise.

  Dismiss thy guard, and trust thee to such
    traits,

---

declared himself more attached than to any other
place, except Greece. He resided in it rather more
than two years.]

For who would lift a hand, except to bless ?
 Were it not easy, sir, and is't not sweet
To make thyself beloved ? and to be
Omnipotent by mercy's means ? for thus
 Thy sovereignty would grow but more com-
 plete,
A despot thou, and yet thy people free,
 And by the heart, not hand, enslaving us.

BOLOGNA, August 12, 1819.[1]

STANZAS.[2]

["COULD LOVE FOREVER."]

I.

COULD Love forever
Run like a river,
And Time's endeavor
 Be tried in vain —
No other pleasure
With this could measure;
And like a treasure
 We'd hug the chain.
But since our sighing
Ends not in dying,
And, formed for flying,
 Love plumes his wing;
Then for this reason
Let's love a season;
But let that season be only Spring.

II.

When lovers parted
Feel broken-hearted,
And, all hopes thwarted,
 Expect to die;
A few years older,
Ah! how much colder
They might behold her
 For whom they sigh!
When linked together,
In every weather,
They pluck Love's feather
 From out his wing —

He'll stay forever,
 But sadly shiver
Without his plumage, when past the Spring.[3]

III.

Like Chiefs of Faction,
His life is action —
A formal paction
 That curbs his reign,
Obscures his glory,
Despot no more, he
Such territory
 Quits with disdain.
Still, still advancing,
With banners glancing,
His power enhancing,
 He must move on —
Repose but cloys him,
Retreat destroys him,
Love brooks not a degraded throne.

IV.

Wait not, fond lover!
Till years are over,
And then recover,
 As from a dream.
While each bewailing
The other's failing,
With wrath and railing,
 All hideous seem —
While first decreasing,
Yet not quite ceasing,
Wait not till teasing
 All passion blight:
If once diminished
Love's reign is finished —
Then part in friendship, — and bid good-
 night.[4]

V.

So shall Affection
To recollection
The dear connection
 Bring back with joy:
You had not waited
Till, tired or hated,
Your passions sated
 Began to cloy.
Your last embraces
Leave no cold traces —
The same fond faces
 As through the past;
And eyes, the mirrors
Of your sweet errors,
Reflect but rapture — not least though last.

VI.

True, separations
Ask more than patience;

[1] ["So the prince has been repealing Lord Fitz-
gerald's forfeiture ? Ecco un' sonetto ? There, you
dogs! there's a sonnet for you: you wont have such
as that in a hurry from Fitzgerald. You may pub-
lish it with my name, an' ye wool. He deserves all
praise, bad and good: it was a very noble piece of
principality." — *Byron to Mr. Murray.*]
[2] [A friend of Byron's, who was with him at Ra-
venna when he wrote these stanzas, says, — "They
were composed, like many others, with no view of
publication, but merely to relieve himself in a mo-
ment of suffering. He had been painfully excited
by some circumstances which appeared to make it
necessary that he should immediately quit Italy;
and in the day and the hour that he wrote the song
was laboring under an access of fever."]

[3] [V. L. — "That sped his Spring."]
[4] [V. L. — "One last embrace, then, and bid good-
night."]

What desperations
From such have risen!
But yet remaining,
What is't but chaining
Hearts which, once waning,
Beat 'gainst their prison?
Time can but cloy love,
And use destroy love:
The winged boy, Love,
Is but for boys —
You'll find it torture
Though sharper, shorter,
To wean, and not wear out your joys.
          1819.

ON MY WEDDING DAY.

HERE'S a happy new year! but with reason
I beg you'll permit me to say —
Wish *me many* returns of the *season*,
But as *few* as you please of the *day*.
         January 2, 1820.

EPITAPH FOR WILLIAM PITT.

WITH death doomed to grapple
  Beneath this cold slab, he
Who lied in the Chapel
  Now lies in the Abbey.
         January, 1820.

EPIGRAM.

IN digging up your bones, Tom Paine,
  Will. Cobbett has done well:
You visit him on earth again,
  He'll visit you in hell.
         January, 1820.

STANZAS.

WHEN a man hath no freedom to fight for at
    home,
Let him combat for that of his neighbors;
Let him think of the glories of Greece and of
    Rome,
And get knocked on the head for his labors.

To do good to mankind is the chivalrous plan,
  And is always as nobly requited;
Then battle for freedom wherever you can,
  And, if not shot or hanged, you'll get
    knighted.   November, 1820.

EPIGRAM.

THE world is a bundle of hay,
  Mankind are the asses who pull;
Each tugs it a different way,
  And the greatest of all is John Bull.

THE CHARITY BALL.

WHAT matter the pangs of a husband and
    father,
  If his sorrows in exile be great or be small,
So the Pharisee's glories around her she
    gather,
  And the saint patronizes her "charity ball!"
What matters — a heart which, though faulty,
    was feeling,
  Be driven to excesses which once could ap-
    pall —
That the sinner should suffer is only fair deal-
    ing,
  As the saint keeps her charity back for "the
    ball!"[1]

EPIGRAM,

ON THE BRAZIERS' COMPANY HAVING RE-
SOLVED TO PRESENT AN ADDRESS TO
QUEEN CAROLINE.[2]

THE braziers, it seems, are preparing to pass
An address, and present it themselves all in
    brass; —
A superfluous pageant — for, by the Lord
    Harry!
They'll find where they're going much more
    than they carry.[3]

EPIGRAM ON MY WEDDING DAY.

TO PENELOPE.

THIS day, of all our days, has done
  The worse for me and you: —
'Tis just *six* years since we were *one*,
  And *five* since we were *two*.
         January 2, 1821.

ON MY THIRTY-THIRD BIRTH-DAY.

JANUARY 22, 1821.[4]

THROUGH life's dull road, so dim and dirty,
I have dragged to three and thirty.
What have these years left to me?
Nothing — except thirty-three.

---

[1] These lines were written on reading in the news-papers, that Lady Byron had been patroness of a ball in aid of some charity at Hinckley.

[2] [The procession of the Braziers to Brandenburgh House was one of the fooleries of the time of Queen Caroline's trial.]

[3] [There is an epigram for you, is it not? — worthy Of Wordsworth, the grand metaquizzical poet, A man of vast merit, though few people know it; The perusal of whom (as I told you at Mestri), I owe, in great part, to my passion for pastry."
    Byron's Letters, January 22, 1821.]

[4] [In Byron's MS. Diary of the preceding day

MARTIAL, LIB. I. EPIG. I.

Hic est, quem legis, ille, quem requiris,
Tota notus in orbe Martialis, etc.

HE unto whom thou art so partial,
Oh, reader! is the well-known Martial,
The Epigrammatist: while living,
Give him the fame thou wouldst be giving;
So shall he hear, and feel, and know it —
Post-obits rarely reach a poet.

———

NEW DUET

To the tune of " Why, how now, saucy jade ?"

WHY, how now, saucy Tom ?
  If you thus must ramble,
I will publish some
  Remarks on Mister Campbell.

ANSWER.

Why, how now, Billy Bowles ?
  Sure the priest is maudlin !
(*To the public*) How can you, d—n your souls,
  Listen to his twaddling ?
                   February 22, 1821.

EPIGRAMS.

OH, Castlereagh! thou art a patriot now;
Cato died for his country, so didst thou:
He perished rather than see Rome enslaved,
Thou cutt'st thy throat that Britain may be
  saved;

———

So Castlereagh has cut his throat ! — The
  worst
Of this is, — that his own was not the first.

———

So *He* has cut his throat at last! — He!
  Who?
The man who cut his country's long ago.

———

EPITAPH.

POSTERITY will ne'er survey
  A nobler grave than this:
Here lie the bones of Castlereagh:
  Stop, traveller ———

———

the following entry: — " To-morrow is my birth-day
— that is to say, at twelve o' the clock, midnight:
i.e. in twelve minutes, I shall have completed thirty
and three years of age !!! — and I go to my bed with
a heaviness of heart at having lived so long, and to
so little purpose.   *   *   *   *
It is three minutes past twelve — ' 'Tis the middle
of night by the castle-clock,' and I am now thirty-
three ! —

JOHN KEATS.[1]

Who killed John Keats ?
  " I, " says the Quarterly,
  So savage and Tartarly;
  " ' Twas one of my feats."

Who shot the arrow ?
  " The poet priest Milman
  (So ready to kill man),
  " Or Southey, or Barrow."
                  July. 1822.

———

THE CONQUEST.

[This fragment was found amongst Byron's pa-
pers, after his departure from Genoa for Greece.]
               March 8-9, 1823.

THE Son of Love and Lord of War I sing;
  Him who bade England bow to Nor-
    mandy,
And left the name of conqueror more than
  king
  To his unconquerable dynasty.
Not fanned alone by Victory's fleeting wing,
  He reared his bold and brilliant throne on
    high:
The Bastard kept, like lions, his prey fast,
And Britain's bravest victor was the last.

———

TO MR. MURRAY.

FOR Orford [2] and for Waldegrave [3]
You give much more than me you gave;
Which is not fairly to behave,
           My Murray.

Because if a live dog, 'tis said,
Be worth a lion fairly sped,
A *live lord* must be worth *two* dead,
           My Murray.

And if, as the opinion goes,
Verse hath a better sale than prose —
Certes, I should have more than those,
           My Murray.

———

' Eheu, fugaces, Posthume, Posthume,
  Labuntur anni; ' —
but I don't regret them so much for what I have
done, as for what I might have done."]

[1] [It was pretended at the time, that the death of
Keats was occasioned by a sarcastic article on his
poetry in the Quarterly Review. All the world
knows now that he died of consumption, and not of
criticism.]

[2] [Horace Walpole's Memoirs of the last nine
Years of the Reign of George II.]

[3] [Memoirs by James Earl Waldegrave, Gov-
ernor of George III. when Prince of Wales.]

But now this sheet is nearly crammed,
So, if *you will, I* shan't be shammed,
And if you *won't, you* may be damned,
    My Murray.[1]

THE IRISH AVATAR.

"And Ireland, like a bastinadoed elephant, kneeling to receive the paltry rider." — CURRAN.

I.

ERE the daughter of Brunswick is cold in her
    grave,
And her ashes still float to their home o'er
    the tide,
Lo! George the triumphant speeds over the
    wave,
To the long-cherished isle which he loved
    like his — bride.

II.

True, the great of her bright and brief era are
    gone,
The rainbow-like epoch where Freedom
    could pause
For the few little years, out of centuries won,
Which betrayed not, or crushed not, or wept
    not her cause.

III.

True, the chains of the Catholic clank o'er his
    rags,
The castle still stands, and the senate's no
    more,
And the famine which dwelt on her freedom-
    less crags
Is extending its steps to her desolate shore.

IV.

To her desolate shore — where the emigrant
    stands
For a moment to gaze ere he flies from his
    hearth;
Tears fall on his chain, though it drops from
    his hands,
For the dungeon he quits is the place of
    his birth.

V.

But he comes! the Messiah of royalty comes!
Liks a goodly Leviathan rolled from the
    waves!

1 ["Can't accept your courteous offer. These matters must be arranged with Mr. Douglas Kinnaird. He is my trustee, and a man of honor. To him you can state all your mercantile reasons, which you might not like to state to me personally, such as 'heavy season' — 'flat public' — 'don't go off' — 'lordship writes too much' — 'won't take advice' — 'declining popularity' — 'deduction for the trade' — 'make very little' — 'generally lose by him' — 'pirated edition' — 'foreign edition' — 'severe criticisms,' etc., with other hints and howls for an oration which I leave Douglas, who is an orator, to answer." — *Byron to Mr. Murray.*]

Then receive him as best such an advent be-
    comes,
With a legion of cooks, and an army of
    slaves!

VI.

He comes in the promise and bloom of three-
    score,
To perform in the pageant the sovereign's
    part—
But long live the shamrock which shadows him
    o'er!
Could the green in his *hat* be transferred to
    his *heart!*

VII.

Could that long-withered spot but be verdant
    again,
And a new spring of noble affections
    arise —
Then might freedom forgive thee this dance in
    thy chain,
And this shout of thy slavery which saddens
    the skies.

VIII.

Is it madness or meanness which clings to thee
    now?
Were he God — as he is but the commonest
    clay,
With scarce fewer wrinkles than sins on his
    brow —
Such servile devotion might shame him
    away.

IX.

Ay, roar in his train! let thine orators lash
Their fanciful spirits to pamper his pride —
Not thus did thy Grattan indignantly flash
His soul o'er the freedom implored and de-
    nied.

X.

Ever glorious Grattan! the best of the
    good!
So simple in heart, so sublime in the rest!
With all which Demosthenes wanted endued,
And his rival or victor in all he possessed.

XI.

Ere Tully arose in the zenith of Rome,
Though unequalled, preceded, the task was
    begun—
But Grattan sprung up like a god from the
    tomb
Of ages, the first, last, the saviour, the *one!*

XII.

With the skill of an Orpheus to soften the
    brute:
With the fire of Prometheus to kindle man-
    kind;
Even Tyranny listening sate melted or mute,
And Corruption shrunk scorched from the
    glance of his mind.

XIII.

But back to our theme! Back to despots and
slaves!
Feasts furnished by Famine! rejoicings by
Pain;
True freedom but *welcomes,* while slavery still
raves,
When a week's saturnalia hath loosened her
chain.

XIV.

Let the poor squalid splendor thy wreck can
afford
(As the bankrupt's profusion his ruin would
hide)
Gild over the palace, Lo! Erin, thy lord!
Kiss his foot with thy blessing, his blessings
denied!

XV.

Or *if* freedom past hope be extorted at last,
If the idol of brass find his feet are of clay,
Must what terror or policy wring forth be
classed
. With what monarchs ne'er give, but as
wolves yield their prey?

XVI.

Each brute hath its nature, a king is to *reign,* —
To *reign!* in that word see, ye ages, com-
prised
The cause of the curses all annals contain,
From Cæsar the dreaded to George the de-
spised!

XVII.

Wear, Fingal, thy trapping! O'Connell, pro-
claim
His accomplishments! *His!!!* and thy
country convince
Half an age's contempt was an error of fame,
And that " Hal is the rascaliest, sweetest
young prince!"

XVIII.

Will thy yard of blue riband, poor Fingal, recall
The fetters from millions of Catholic limbs?
Or, has it not bound thee the fastest of all
The slaves, who now hail their betrayer with
hymns?

XIX.

Ay! "Build him a dwelling!" let each give
his mite!
Till, like Babel, the new royal dome hath
arisen!
Let thy beggars and helots their pittance
unite —
And a palace bestow for a poor-house and
prison!

XX.

Spread — spread, for Vitellius, the royal repast,
Till the gluttonous despot be stuffed to the
gorge!

And the roar of his drunkards proclaim him
at last
The Fourth of the fools and oppressors
called "George!"

XXI.

Let the tables be loaded with feasts till they
groan!
Till they *groan* like thy people, through ages
of woe!
Let the wine flow around the old Bacchanal's
throne,
Like their blood which has flowed, and
which yet has to flow.

XXII.

But let not *his* name be thine idol alone —
On his right hand behold a Sejanus appears!
Thine own Castlereagh! let him still be thine
own!
A wretch, never named but with curses and
jeers!

XXIII.

Till now, when the isle which should blush for
his birth,
Deep, deep as the gore which he shed on
her soil,
Seems proud of the reptile which crawled
from her earth,
And for murder repays him with shouts
and a smile!

XXIV.

Without one single ray of her genius, without
The fancy, the manhood, the fire of her
race —
The miscreant who well might plunge Erin
in doubt
If *she* ever gave birth to a being so base.

XXV.

If she did — let her long-boasted proverb be
hushed,
Which proclaims that from Erin no reptile
can spring —
See the cold-blooded serpent, with venom full
flushed,
Still warming its folds in the breast of a king!

XXVI.

Shout, drink, feast, and flatter! Oh! Erin,
how low
Wert thou sunk by misfortune and tyranny,
till
Thy welcome of tyrants hath plunged thee
below
The depth of thy deep in a deeper gulf still.

XXVII.

My voice, though but humble, was raised for
thy right,
My vote, as a freeman's, still voted thee free,

This hand, though but feeble, would arm in thy fight,
　And this heart, though outworn, had a throb still for *thee!*

XXVIII.

Yes, I loved thee and thine, though thou art not my land,
　I have known noble hearts and great souls in thy sons,
And I wept with the world o'er the patriot band
　Who are gone, but I weep them no longer as once.

XXIX.

For happy are they now reposing afar,—
　Thy Grattan, thy Curran, thy Sheridan, all
Who, for years, were the chiefs in the eloquent war,
　And redeemed, if they have not retarded, thy fall.

XXX.

Yes, happy are they in their cold English graves!
　Their shades cannot start to thy shouts of to-day—
Nor the steps of enslavers, and chain-kissing slaves
　Be stamped in the turf o'er their fetterless clay.

XXXI.

Till now I had envied thy sons and their shore,
　Though their virtues were hunted, their liberties fled;
There was something so warm and sublime in the core
　Of an Irishman's heart, that I envy—thy *dead.*

XXXII.

Or, if aught in my bosom can quench for an hour
　My contempt for a nation so servile, though sore,
Which though trod like the worm will not turn upon power,
　'Tis the glory of Grattan, and genius of Moore![1]

────────

STANZAS WRITTEN ON THE ROAD BETWEEN FLORENCE AND PISA.

I.

OH, talk not to me of a name great in story;
The days of our youth are the days of our glory;

And the myrtle and ivy of sweet two-and-twenty
Are worth all your laurels, though ever so plenty.

II.

What are garlands and crowns to the brow that is wrinkled?
'Tis but as a dead-flower with May-dew besprinkled.
Then away with all such from the head that is hoary!
What care I for the wreaths that can *only* give glory?

III.

Oh FAME!—if I e'er took delight in thy praises,
'Twas less for the sake of thy high-sounding phrases,
Than to see the bright eyes of the dear one discover
She thought that I was not unworthy to love her.

IV.

There chiefly I sought thee, *there* only I found thee;
Her glance was the best of the rays that surround thee;
When it sparkled o'er aught that was bright in my story,
I knew it was love, and I felt it was glory.[2]

────────

STANZAS:

TO A HINDOO AIR.

[These verses were written by Byron a little before he left Italy for Greece. They were meant to suit the Hindostanee air — "Alla Malla Punca," which the Countess Guiccioli was fond of singing.]

OH!—my lonely—lonely—lonely—Pillow!
Where is my lover? where is my lover?
Is it his bark which my dreary dreams discover?
Far—far away! and alone along the billow?

Oh! my lonely—lonely—lonely—Pillow!
Why must my head ache where his gentle brow lay?
How the long night flags lovelessly and slowly,
And my head droops over thee like the willow.—

Oh! thou, my sad and solitary Pillow!
Send me kind dreams to keep my heart from breaking;

────────

1 ["The enclosed lines, as you will directly perceive, are written by the Rev. W. L. Bowles. Of course it is for *him* to deny them, if they are not."—*Lord B. to Mr. Moore*, September 17, 1821.]

2 ["I composed these stanzas (except the fourth, added now) a few days ago, on the road from Florence to Pisa."—*Byron's Diary*, Pisa, 6th November, 1821.]

In return for the tears I shed upon thee
waking,
Let me not die till he comes back o'er the bil-
low. —

Then if thou wilt — no more my *lonely*
Pillow,
In one embrace let these arms again enfold
him,
And then expire of the joy — but to behold
him !
Oh ! my lone bosom ! — oh ! my lonely Pillow !

———

IMPROMPTU.[1]

BENEATH Blessington's eyes
The Reclaimed Paradise
Should be free as the former from evil;
But if the new Eve
For an Apple should grieve,
What mortal would not play the Devil ?[2]

1823.

———

TO THE COUNTESS OF BLESS-
INGTON.

YOU have asked for a verse : — the request
In a rhymer 'twere strange to deny;
But my Hippocrene was but my breast,
And my feelings (its fountain) are dry.

Were I now as I was, I had sung
What Lawrence has painted so well;
But the strain would expire on my tongue,
And the theme is too soft for my shell.

I am ashes where once I was fire,
And the bard in my bosom is dead;
What I loved I now merely admire,
And my heart is as gray as my head.

My life is not dated by years —
There are moments which act as a plough,
And there is not a furrow appears
But is deep in my soul as my brow.

Let the young and brilliant aspire
To sing what I gaze on in vain;
For sorrow has torn from my lyre
The string which was worthy the strain.

ON THIS DAY I COMPLETE MY
THIRTY-SIXTH YEAR.

MISSOLONGHI, January 22, 1824.[3]

I.

'TIS time this heart should be unmoved,
Since others it hath ceased to move :
Yet, though I cannot be beloved,
Still let me love !

II.

My days are in the yellow leaf;
The flowers and fruits of love are gone;
The worm, the canker, and the grief
Are mine alone !

III.

The fire that on my bosom preys
Is lone as some volcanic isle;
No torch is kindled at its blaze —
A funeral pile !

IV.

The hope, the fear, the jealous care
The exalted portion of the pain
And power of love, I cannot share,
But wear the chain.

V.

But 'tis not *thus* — and 'tis not *here* —
Such thoughts should shake my soul, *not
now,*
Where glory decks the hero's bier,
Or binds his brow.

VI.

The sword, the banner, and the field,
Glory and Greece, around me see !
The Spartan, borne upon his shield,
Was not more free.

VII.

Awake ! (not Greece — she *is* awake !)
Awake, my spirit ! Think through *whom*
Thy life-blood tracks its parent lake,
And then strike home !

VIII.

Tread those reviving passions down,
Unworthy manhood ! — unto thee

———

[1] [This impromptu was uttered by Byron on going
with Lord and Lady Blessington to a villa at Genoa
called "*Il Paradiso,*" which his companions thought
of renting.]
[2] [The Genoese wits had already applied this
threadbare jest to himself. Taking it into their
heads that this villa had been the one fixed on for
his own residence, they said, " Il Diavolo è ancora
entrato in Paradiso." — *Moore.*]

[3] [This morning Lord Byron came from his bed-
room into the apartment where Colonel Stanhope
and some friends were assembled, and said with a
smile — " You were complaining, the other day,
that I never write any poetry now. This is my
birth-day, and I have just finished something which,
I think, is better than what I usually write." He
then produced these noble and affecting verses. —
Count Gamba.]

Indifferent should the smile or frown
    Of beauty be.

IX.

If thou regret'st thy youth, *why live?*
    The land of honorable death
Is here : — up to the field, and give
    Away thy breath !

X.

Seek out — less often sought than found —
    A soldier's grave, for thee the best;

Then look around, and choose thy ground,
    And take thy rest.[1]

---

[1] [Taking into consideration every thing connected with these verses, — the last tender aspirations of a loving spirit which they breathe, the self-devotion to a noble cause which they so nobly express, and that consciousness of a near grave glimmering sadly through the whole, — there is perhaps no production within the range of mere human composition, round which the circumstances and feelings under which it was written cast so touching an interest. — *Moore.*]

ENGLISH BARDS AND SCOTCH REVIEWERS:

A SATIRE.

" I had rather be a kitten, and cry mew!
  Than one of these same metre ballad-mongers."
                SHAKESPEARE.

" Such shameless bards we have; and yet 'tis true,
  There are as mad, abandoned critics too."
                POPE.

[The first edition of this satire, which then began with what is now the ninety-seventh line (*"Time was, ere yet,"* etc.), appeared in March, 1809. A second, to which the author prefixed his name, followed in October of that year; and a third and fourth were called for during his first *pilgrimage,* in 1810 and 1811. On his return to England, a fifth edition was prepared for the press by himself, with considerable care, but suppressed, and, except one copy, destroyed, when on the eve of publication. The text is now printed from the copy that escaped; on casually meeting with which, in 1816, he reperused the whole, and wrote on the margin some annotations, which in this edition are distinguished by the insertion of their date, from those affixed to the prior editions.

    The first of these MS. notes of 1816 appears on the fly-leaf, and runs thus: — " The binding of this volume is considerably too valuable for the contents; and nothing but the consideration of its being the property of another, prevents me from consigning this miserable record of misplaced anger and indiscriminate acrimony to the flames."]

PREFACE.[1]

ALL my friends, learned and unlearned, have urged me not to publish this Satire with my name. If I were to be " turned from the career of my humor by quibbles quick, and paper bullets of the brain," I should have complied with their counsel. But I am not to be terrified by abuse, or bullied by reviewers, with or without arms. I can safely say that I have attacked none personally, who did not commence on the offensive. An author's works are public property: he who purchases may judge, and publish his opinion if he pleases; and the authors I have endeavored to commemorate may do by me as I have done by them. I dare say they will succeed better in condemning my scribblings, than in mending their own. But my object is not to prove that I can write well, but, if possible, to make others write better.

    As the poem has met with far more success than I expected, I have endeavored in this edition to make some additions and alterations, to render it more worthy of public perusal.

[1] This preface was written for the second edition, and printed with it. The noble author had left this country previous to the publication of that edition, and is not yet returned. — *Note to the fourth edition,* 1811. — ["He is, and gone again." — *Byron,* 1816.]

In the first edition of this satire, published anonymously, fourteen lines on the subject of Bowles's Pope were written by, and inserted at the request of, an ingenious friend of mine,[1] who has now in the press a volume of poetry. In the present edition they are erased, and some of my own substituted in their stead; my only reason for this being that which I conceive would operate with any other person in the same manner, — a determination not to publish with my name any production, which was not entirely and exclusively my own composition.

With[2] regard to the real talents of many of the poetical persons whose performances are mentioned or alluded to in the following pages, it is presumed by the author that there can be little difference of opinion in the public at large; though, like other sectaries, each has his separate tabernacle of proselytes, by whom his abilities are overrated, his faults overlooked, and his metrical canons received without scruple and without consideration. But the unquestionable possession of considerable genius by several of the writers here censured renders their mental prostitution more to be regretted. Imbecility may be pitied, or, at worst, laughed at and forgotten; perverted powers demand the most decided reprehension. No one can wish more than the author that some known and able writer had undertaken their exposure; but Mr. Gifford has devoted himself to Massinger, and, in the absence of the regular physician, a country practitioner may, in cases of absolute necessity, be allowed to prescribe his nostrum to prevent the extension of so deplorable an epidemic, provided there be no quackery in his treatment of the malady. A caustic is here offered; as it is to be feared nothing short of actual cautery can recover the numerous patients afflicted with the present prevalent and distressing *rabies* for rhyming. — As to the Edinburgh Reviewers,[3] it would indeed require an Hercules to crush the Hydra; but if the author succeeds in merely "bruising one of the heads of the serpent," though his own hand should suffer in the encounter, he will be amply satisfied.[4]

[1] [Mr. Hobhouse.]
[2] [Here the preface to the first edition commenced.]
[3] ["I well recollect the effect which the critique of the Edinburgh Reviewers, on my first poem, had upon me — it was rage and resistance, and redress, but not despondency nor despair. A savage review is hemlock to a sucking author, and the one on me (which produced the English Bards, etc.) knocked me down — but I got up again. That critique was a master-piece of low wit, a tissue of scurrilous abuse. I remember there was a great deal of vulgar trash, about people being 'thankful for what they could get,' — 'not looking a gift horse in the mouth,' and such stable expressions. But so far from their bullying me, or deterring me from writing, I was bent on falsifying their raven predictions, and determined to show them, croak as they would, that it was not the last time they should hear from me." — *Byron*, 1821.]
[4] ["The severity of the criticism," Sir Egerton Brydges has observed, "touched Lord Byron in the point where his original strength lay: it wounded his pride, and roused his bitter indignation. He published 'English Bards and Scotch Reviewers,' and bowed down those who had hitherto held a despotic victory over the public mind. There was, after all, more in the boldness of the enterprise, in the fearlessness of the attack, than in its intrinsic force. But the moral effect of the gallantry of the assault, and of the justice of the cause, made it victorious and triumphant. This was one of those lucky developments which cannot often occur; and which fixed Lord Byron's fame. From that day he engaged the public notice as a writer of undoubted talent and energy both of intellect and temper."]

STILL must I hear?[1] — shall hoarse Fitzgerald [2] bawl
His creaking couplets in a tavern hall,[3]
And I not sing, lest, haply, Scotch reviews
Should dub me scribbler, and denounce my muse?

Prepare for rhyme — I'll publish, right or wrong:
Fools are my theme, let satire be my song.

Oh! nature's noblest gift — my gray goosequill!
Slave of my thoughts, obedient to my will,

[1] IMIT. "Semper ego auditor tantum? nunquamne reponam,
Vexatus toties rauci Theseide Codri?"
Juv. Sat. I.
[2] ["*Hoarse Fitzgerald.*" — "Right enough; but why notice such a mountebank." — *Byron*, 1816.]
[3] Mr. Fitzgerald. facetiously termed by Cobbett the "Small Beer Poet," inflicts his annual tribute of verse on the Literary Fund: not content with writing, he spouts in person, after the company have imbibed a reasonable quantity of bad port, to enable them to sustain the operation. — [For the long period of thirty-two years, this harmless poetaster was an attendant at the anniversary dinners of the Literary Fund, and constantly honored the occasion with an ode, which he himself recited with most comical dignity of emphasis.]

Torn from thy parent bird to form a pen,
That mighty instrument of little men!
The pen! foredoomed to aid the mental throes
Of brains that labor, big with verse or prose,
Though nymphs forsake, and critics may deride
The lover's solace, and the author's pride.
What wits! what poets dost thou daily raise!
How frequent is thy use, how small thy praise!
Condemned at length to be forgotten quite,
With all the pages which 'twas thine to write.
But thou, at least, mine own special pen!
Once laid aside, but now assumed again,
Our task complete, like Hamet's [1] shall be free;
Though spurned by others, yet beloved by me:
Then let us soar to-day; no common theme,
No eastern vision, no distempered dream [2]
Inspires — our path, though full of thorns, is plain;
Smooth be the verse, and easy be the strain.

When Vice triumphant holds her sovereign sway,
Obeyed by all who nought beside obey;
When Folly, frequent harbinger of crime,
Bedecks her cap with bells of every clime;
When knaves and fools combined o'er all prevail,
And weigh their justice in a golden scale;
E'en then the boldest start from public sneers,
Afraid of shame, unknown to other fears,
More darkly sin, by satire kept in awe,
And shrink from ridicule, though not from law.

Such is the force of wit! but not belong
To me the arrows of satiric song;
The royal vices of our age demand
A keener weapon, and a mightier hand.
Still there are follies, e'en for me to chase,
And yield at least amusement in the race:
Laugh when I laugh, I seek no other fame;
The cry is up, and scribblers are my game.
Speed, Pegasus! — ye strains of great and small,
Ode, epic, elegy, have at you all!
I too can scrawl, and once upon a time
I poured along the town a flood of rhyme,
A schoolboy freak, unworthy praise or blame;
I printed — older children do the same.
'Tis pleasant, sure, to see one's name in print;
A book's a book, although there's nothing in't.
Not that a title's sounding charm can save
Or scrawl or scribbler from an equal grave:
This Lambe must own, since his patrician name
Failed to preserve the spurious farce from shame. [3]

No matter, George continues still to write, [4]
Though now the name is veiled from public sight.
Moved by the great example, I pursue
The self-same road, but make my own review:
Not seek great Jeffrey's, yet, like him, will be
Self-constituted judge of poesy.

A man must serve his time to every trade
Save censure — critics all are ready made.
Take hackneyed jokes from Miller, got by rote,
With just enough of learning to misquote;
A mind well skilled to find or forge a fault;
A turn for punning, call it Attic salt;
To Jeffrey go, be silent and discreet,
His pay is just ten sterling pounds per sheet:
Fear not to lie, 'twill seem a sharper hit;
Shrink not from blasphemy, 'twill pass for wit;
Care not for feeling — pass your proper jest,
And stand a critic, hated yet caressed.

And shall we own such judgment? no — as soon
Seek roses in December — ice in June;
Hope constancy in wind, or corn in chaff;
Believe a woman or an epitaph,
Or any other thing that's false, before
You trust in critics, who themselves are sore;
Or yield one single thought to be misled
By Jeffrey's heart, or Lambe's Bœotian head. [5]
To these young tyrants, [6] by themselves misplaced,
Combined usurpers on the throne of taste;
To these, when authors bend in humble awe,
And hail their voice as truth, their word as law —
While these are censors, 'twould be sin to spare;
While such are critics, why should I forbear?
But yet, so near all modern worthies run,
'Tis doubtful whom to seek, or whom to shun;
Nor know we when to spare, or where to strike,
Our bards and censors are so much alike.

Then should you ask me, [7] why I venture o'er
The path which Pope and Gifford trod before;

<hr/>

[1] Cid Hamet Benengeli promises repose to his pen, in the last chapter of Don Quixote. Oh! that our voluminous gentry would follow the example of Cid Hamet Benengeli.

[2] ["This must have been written in the spirit of prophecy." — *Byron*, 1816.]

[3] This ingenious youth is mentioned more particularly, with his production, in another place.

[4] In the Edinburgh Review. — ["He's a very good fellow, and, except his mother and sister, the best of the set, to my mind." — *Byron*, 1816.]

[5] Messrs. Jeffrey and Lambe are the alpha and omega, the first and last of the Edinburgh Review; the others are mentioned hereafter.
["This was not just. Neither the heart nor the head of these gentlemen are at all what they are here represented. At the time this was written, I was personally unacquainted with either." — *Byron*, 1816.]

[6] IMIT. "Stulta est Clementia, cum tot ubique
——occurras peritura parcere chartæ."
Juv. Sat. I.

[7] IMIT. "Cur tamen hoc libeat potius decurrere campo
Per quem magnus equos Auruncæ flexit alumnus:
Si vacat, et placidi rationem admittitis, edam."
Juv. Sat. I.

If not yet sickened, you can still proceed:
Go on; my rhyme will tell you as you read.
" But hold ! " exclaims a friend, — " here's some
   neglect:
This — that — and t'other line seem incorrect."
.What then ? the self-same blunder Pope has
   got,—
And careless Dryden — " Ay, but Pye has
   not : " —
Indeed ! — 'tis granted, faith ! — but what care
   I ?
Better to err with Pope, than shine with Pye.

Time was, ere yet in these degenerate days [1]
Ignoble themes obtained mistaken praise,
When sense and wit with poesy allied,
No fabled graces, flourished side by side;
From the same fount their inspiration drew,
And, reared by taste, bloomed fairer as they
   grew.
Then, in this happy isle, a Pope's pure strain
Sought the rapt soul to charm, nor sought in
   vain;
A polished nation's praise aspired to claim,
And raised the people's, as the poet's fame.
Like him great Dryden poured the tide of song,

In stream less smooth, indeed, yet doubly
   strong.
Then Congreve's scenes could cheer, or Ot·
   way's melt—
For nature then an English audience felt.
But why these namès, or greater still, retrace,
When all to feebler bards resign their place ?
Yet to such times our lingering looks are cast,
When taste and reason with those times are
   past.
Now look around, and turn each trifling page,
Survey the precious works that please the age ;
This truth at least let satire's self allow,
No dearth of bards can be complained of now.[2]
The loaded press beneath her labor groans,
And printers' devils shake their weary bones ;
While Southey's epics cram the creaking
   shelves,
And Little's lyrics shine in hot-pressed twelves.
Thus saith the preacher: " Nought beneath
   the sun
Is new ; " yet still from change to change we
   run :
What varied wonders tempt us as they pass.
The cow-pox, tractors, galvanism, and gas,
In turns appear, to make the vulgar stare,
Till the swoln bubble bursts — and all is air !
Nor less new schools of Poetry arise,
Where dull pretenders grapple for the prize :
O'er taste awhile these pseudo-bards prevail ;
Each country book-club bows the knee to Baal,
And, hurling lawful genius from the throne,
Erects a shrine and idol of its own ; [3]
Some leaden calf — but whom it matters not,
From soaring Southey down to grovelling
   Stött.[4]

Behold ! in various throngs the scribbling
   crew,

---

[1] [The first edition of the Satire opened with this line, and Byron's original intention was to prefix the following —

" ARGUMENT.

' The poet considereth times past, and their po-esy — makes a sudden transition to times present — is incensed against bookmakers — revileth Walter Scott for cupidity and ballad-mongering, with notable remarks on Master Southey — complaineth that Master Southey hath inflicted three poems, epic and otherwise, on the public — inveigheth against William Wordsworth, but laudeth Mister Coleridge and his elegy on a young ass — is disposed to vituperate Mr. Lewis — and greatly rebuketh Thomas Little (the late) and the Lord Strangford — recommendeth Mr. Hayley to turn his attention to prose — and exhorteth the Moravians to glorify Mr. Grahame — sympathizeth with the Reverend ——— Bowles — and deploreth the melancholy fate of James Montgomery — breaketh out into invective against the Edinburgh Reviewers — calleth them hard names, harpies and the like — apostrophizeth Jeffrey, and prophesieth. — Episode of Jeffrey and Moore, their jeopardy and deliverance; portents on the morn of the combat; the Tweed, Tolbooth, Frith of Forth, severally shocked; descent of a goddess to save Jeffrey; incorporation of the bullets with his sinciput and occiput. — Edinburgh Reviewers *en masse.* — Lord Aberdeen, Herbert, Scott, Hallam, Fillans, Lambe, Sydney Smith, Brougham, etc. — The Lord Holland applauded for dinners and translations. — The Drama; Skeffington, Hook, Reynolds, Kenney, Cherry, etc. — Sheridan, Colman, and Cumberland called upon to write. — Return to poesy — scribblers of all sorts — lords sometimes rhyme; much better not — Hafiz, Rosa Matilda, and X. Y. Z. — Rogers, Campbell, Gifford, etc., true poets — Translators of the Greek Anthology — Crabbe — Darwin's style — Cambridge — Seatonian Prize — Smythe — Hodgson — Oxford — Richards — Poeta loquitur — Conclusion."]

[2] [" One of my notions is, that the present is not a high age of English poetry. There are *more* poets (soi-disant) than ever there were, and proportionably *less* poetry. This thesis I have maintained for some years; but, strange to say, it meeteth not with favor from my brethren of the shell." — *Byron's Diary,* 1821.]

[3] [" With regard to poetry in general, I am convinced that we are all upon a wrong revolutionary poetical system, not worth a damn in itself, and from which none but Rogers and Crabbe are free. I am the more confirmed in this by having lately gone over some of our classics, particularly Pope, whom I tried in this way : — I took Moore's poems, and my own, and some others, and went over them side by side with Pope's, and I was really astonished and mortified at the ineffable distance, in point of sense, learning, effect, and even imagination, passion, and invention, between the little Queen Anne's man, and us of the Lower Empire. Depend upon it, it is all Horace then, and Claudian now, among us: and if I had to begin again, I would mould myself accordingly." — *Byron's Diary,* 1817.]

[4] Stött, better known in the " Morning Post" by the name of Hafiz. This personage is at present

For notice eager, pass in long review:
Each spurs his jaded Pegasus apace,
And rhyme and blank maintain an equal race;
Sonnets on sonnets crowd, and ode on ode;
And tales of terror jostle on the road;
Immeasurable measures move along;
For simpering folly loves a varied song,
To strange mysterious dulness still the friend,
Admires the strain she cannot comprehend.
Thus Lays of Minstrels [1] — may they be the last! —
On half-strung harps whine mournful to th'
blast.
While mountain spirits prate to river sprites,
That dames may listen to the sound at nights;
And goblin brats, of Gilpin Horner's brood,
Decoy young border-nobles though the wood,
And skip at every step, Lord knows how high,
And frighten foolish babes, the Lord knows why;
While high-born ladies in their magic cell,
Forbidding knights to read who cannot spell,
Despatch a courier to a wizard's grave,
And fight with honest men to shield a knave.

the most profound explorer of the bathos. I remember, when the reigning family left Portugal, a special ode of Master Stott's beginning thus: — *Stott loquitur quoad Hibernia.* —

　　"Princely offspring of Braganza,
　　　Erin greets thee with a stanza," etc.

Also a Sonnet to Rats, well worthy of the subject, and a most thundering Ode, commencing as follows: —

　　"Oh! for a Lay! loud as the surge
　　　That lashes Lapland's sounding shore."
Lord have mercy on us! the "Lay of the Last Minstrel" was nothing to this.

[1] See the "Lay of the Last Minstrel," *passim.* Never was any plan so incongruous and absurd as the groundwork of this production. The entrance of Thunder and Lightning, prologuizing to Bayes' tragedy unfortunately takes away the merit of originality from the dialogue between Messieurs the Spirits of Flood and Fell in the first canto. Then we have the amiable William of Deloraine, "a stark moss-trooper," videlicet, a happy compound of poacher, sheep-stealer, and highwayman. The propriety of his magical lady's injunction not to read can only be equalled by his candid acknowledgment of his independence of the trammels of spelling, although, to use his own elegant phrase, "'twas his neck-verse at Harribee," i.e. the gallows. — The biography of Gilpin Horner, and the marvellous pedestrian page, who travelled twice as fast as his master's horse, without the aid of seven-leagued boots, are *chefs-d'œuvre* in the improvement of taste. For incident we have the invisible, but by no means sparing box on the ear bestowed on the page, and the entrance of a knight and charger into the castle, under the very natural disguise of a wain of hay. Marmion, the hero of the latter romance, is exactly what William of Deloraine would have been, had he been able to read and write. The poem was manufactured for Messrs. Constable, Murray, and Miller, worshipful booksellers, in consideration of the receipt of a sum of money; and

　　Next view in state, proud prancing on his roan,
The golden-crested haughty Marmion,
Now forging scrolls, now foremost in the fight,
Not quite a felon, yet but half a knight,
The gibbet or the field prepared to grace;
A mighty mixture of the great and base.
And thinkest thou, Scott! [2] by vain conceit perchance
On public taste to foist thy stale romance,
Though Murray with his Miller may combine
　To yield thy muse just half-a-crown per line?
No! when the sons of song descend to trade,
Their bays are sear, their former laurels fade.
Let such forego the poet's sacred name,
Who rack their brains for lucre, [3] not for fame:
Still for stern Mammon may they toil in vain!
And sadly gaze on gold they cannot gain!
Such be their meed, such still the just reward
Of prostituted muse and hireling bard!
For this we spurn Apollo's venal son,
And bid a long "good night to Marmion." [4]

　These are the themes that claim our plaudits now;
These are the bards to whom the muse must bow;
While Milton, Dryden, Pope, alike forgot,
Resign their hallowed bays to Walter Scott.

　The time has been, when yet the muse was young,
When Homer swept the lyre, and Maro sung,
An epic scarce ten centuries could claim,

truly, considering the inspiration, it is a very creditable production. If Mr. Scott will write for hire, let him do his best for his paymasters, but not disgrace his genius, which is undoubtedly great, by a repetition of black-letter ballad imitations.

[2] ["When Byron wrote his famous satire, I had my share of flagellation among my betters. My crime was having written a poem for a thousand pounds; which was no otherwise true, than that I sold the copyright for that sum. Now, not to mention that an author can hardly be censured for accepting such a sum as the booksellers are willing to give him, especially as the gentlemen of the trade made no complaints of their bargain, I thought the interference with my private affairs was rather beyond the limits of literary satire. I was, however, so far from having anything to do with the offensive criticism in the Edinburgh, that I remonstrated against it with the editor, because I thought the "Hours of Idleness" treated with undue severity. They were written, like all juvenile poetry, rather from the recollection of what had pleased the author in others, than what had been suggested by his own imagination; but, nevertheless, I thought they contained passages of noble promise." — *Sir Walter Scott.*]

[3] [Byron set out with the determination never to receive money for his writings. This notion, however, he soon got rid of.]

[4] "Good night to Marmion"— the pathetic and also prophetic exclamation of Henry Blount, Esquire, on the death of honest Marmion.

While awe-struck nations hailed the magic name;
The work of each immortal bard appears
The single wonder of a thousand years.[1]
Empires have mouldered from the face of earth,
Tongues have expired with those who gave them birth
Without the glory such a strain can give,
As even in ruin bids the language live.
Not so with us, though minor bards content,
On one great work a life of labor spent:
With eagle pinion soaring to the skies,
Behold the ballad-monger Southey rise!
To him let Camoens, Milton, Tasso yield,
Whose annual strains, like armies, take the field.
First in the ranks see Joan of Arc advance,
The scourge of England and the boast of France!
Though burnt by wicked Bedford for a witch,
Behold her statue placed in glory's niche;
Her fetters burst, and just released from prison,
A virgin phœnix from her ashes risen.
Next see tremendous Thalaba come on,[2]
Arabia's monstrous, wild, and wond'rous son;[3]
Domdaniel's dread destroyer, who o'erthrew
More mad magicians than the world e'er knew.
Immortal hero! all thy foes o'ercome,
For ever reign—the rival of Tom Thumb!
Since startled metre fled before thy face,
Well wert thou doomed the last of all thy race!
Well might triumphant genii bear thee hence,
Illustrious conqueror of common sense!
Now, last and greatest, Madoc spreads his sails,
Cacique in Mexico, and prince in Wales;
Tells us strange tales, as other travellers do,
More old than Mandeville's, and not so true.
Oh, Southey! Southey![4] cease thy varied song!
A bard may chant too often and too long:

As thou art strong in verse, in mercy, spare!
A fourth, alas! were more than we could bear.
But if, in spite of all the world can say,
Thou still wilt verseward plod thy weary way;
If still in Berkley ballads most uncivil,
Thou wilt devote old women to the devil,[5]
The babe unborn thy dread intent may rue:
"God help thee," Southey,[6] and thy readers too.[7]

Next comes the dull disciple of thy school,
That mild apostate from poetic rule,
The simple Wordsworth, framer of a lay
As soft as evening in his favorite May,[8]
Who warns his friend "to shake off toil and trouble,
And quit his books, for fear of growing double;"[9]

Why is epic degraded? and by whom? Certainly the late romaunts of Masters Cottle, Laureat Pye, Ogilvy, Hoole, and gentle Mistress Cowley, have not exalted the epic muse; but as Mr. Southey's poem "disdains the appellation," allow us to ask—has he substituted any thing better in its stead? or must he be content to rival Sir Richard Blackmore in the quantity as well as quality of his verse?

[8] See "The old women of Berkley," a ballad, by Mr. Southey, wherein an aged gentlewoman is carried away by Beelzebub, on a "high-trotting horse."

[6] The last line, "God help thee," is an evident plagiarism from the Anti-Jacobin to Mr. Southey, on his Dactylics. — [Byron here alludes to Gifford's parody on Southey's Dactylics, which ends thus: —
"Ne'er talk of ears again! look at thy spelling-book:
Dilworth and Dyche are both mad at thy quantities —
Dactylics, call'st thou 'em? — 'God help thee, silly one.'"]

[7] [Byron on being introduced to Southey in 1813, at Holland House, describes him, "as the best looking bard he had seen for a long time." — "To have that poet's head and shoulders, I would," he says, "almost have written his Sapphics. He is certainly a prepossessing person to look on, and a man of talent, and all that, and there is his eulogy." In his Journal, of the same year, he says—"Southey I have not seen much of. His appearance is *epic*, and he is the only existing entire man of letters. All the others have some pursuit annexed to their authorship. His manners are mild, but not those of a man of the world, and his talents of the first order. His prose is perfect. Of his poetry there are various opinions: there is, perhaps, too much of it for the present generation—posterity will probably select. He has passages equal to any thing. At present, he has a *party*, but no public—except for his prose writings. His Life of Nelson is beautiful." Elsewhere and later, Byron pronounces Southey's Don Roderick, "the first poem of our time."]

[8] ["*Unjust.*" — *Byron*, 1816.]

[9] Lyrical Ballads, p. 4. — "The Tables Turned." Stanza 1.
"Up, up, my friend, and clear your looks;

---

[1] As the Odyssey is so closely connected with the story of the Iliad, they may almost be classed as one grand historical poem. In alluding to Milton and Tasso, we consider the "Paradise Lost," and "Gierusalemme Liberata," as their standard efforts; since neither the "Jerusalem Conquered" of the Italian, nor the "Paradise Regained" of the English bard, obtained a proportionate celebrity to their former poems. Query: which of Mr. Southey's will survive?

[2] "Thalaba," Mr. Southey's second poem, is written in open defiance of precedent and poetry. Mr. S. wished to produce something novel, and succeeded to a miracle. "Joan of Arc" was marvellous enough, but "Thalaba" was one of those poems "which," in the words of Porson, "will be read when Homer and Virgil are forgotten, but—*not till then.*"

[3] ["Of Thalaba, the wild and wondrous song."— *Southey's Madoc.*]

[4] We beg Mr. Southey's pardon: "Madoc disdains the degraded title of epic." See his preface.

Who, both by precept and example, shows
That prose is verse, and verse is merely prose;
Convincing all, by demonstration plain,
Poetic souls delight in prose insane;
And Christmas stories tortured into rhyme
Contain the essence of the true sublime.
Thus, when he tells the tale of Betty Foy,
The idiot mother of "an idiot boy;"
A moon-struck, silly lad, who lost his way,
And, like his bard, confounded night with day;[1]
So close on each pathetic part he dwells,
And each adventure so sublimely tells,
That all who view the "idiot in his glory,"
Conceive the bard the hero of the story.

Shall gentle Coleridge pass unnoticed here,
To turgid ode and tumid stanza dear?
Though themes of innocence amuse him best,
Yet still obscurity's a welcome guest.
If Inspiration should her aid refuse
To him who takes a pixy for a muse,[2]
Yet none in lofty numbers can surpass
The bard who soars to elegize an ass.
So well the subject suits his noble mind,
He brays,[3] the laureate of the long-eared kind.[4]

Oh! wonderworking Lewis![5] monk, or bard,
Who fain wouldst make Parnassus a church-
yard!

Why all this toil and trouble?
Up, up, my friend, and quit your books,
Or surely you'll grow double."

[1] Mr. W. in his preface labors hard to prove, that prose and verse are much the same; and certainly his precepts and practice are strictly conformable: —

"And thus to Betty's questions he
Made answer, like a traveller bold.
The cock did crow, to-whoo, to-whoo,
And the sun did shine so cold," etc. etc.,
p. 129.

[2] Coleridge's Poems, p. 11, Songs of the Pixies, i.e. Devonshire fairies; p. 42, we have, "Lines to a young Lady:" and, p. 52, "Lines to a young Ass."

[3] [Thus altered by Byron, in his last revision of the satire. In all former editions the line stood,
"A fellow-feeling makes us wond'rous kind."]

[4] ["Unjust," says Byron in 1816. — In a letter to Coleridge, written in 1815, he says, — "You mention my 'Satire,' lampoon, or whatever you or others please to call it. I can only say, that it was written when I was very young and very angry, and has been a thorn in my side ever since: more particularly as almost all the persons animadverted upon became subsequently my acquaintances, and some of them my friends; which is 'heaping fire upon an enemy's head,' and forgiving me too readily to permit me to forgive myself. The part applied to you is pert, and petulant, and shallow enough; but, although I have long done every thing in my power to suppress the circulation of the whole thing, I shall always regret the wantonness or generality of many of its attempted attacks."]

[5] [Matthew Gregory Lewis, M. P. for Hindon,

Lo! wreaths of yew, not laurel, bind thy brow,
Thy muse a sprite, Apollo's sexton thou!
Whether on ancient tombs thou takest thy stand,
By gibbering spectres hailed, thy kindred band;
Or tracest chaste descriptions on thy page,
To please the females of our modest age;
All hail, M. P.![6] from whose infernal brain
Thin sheeted phantoms glide, a grisly train;
At whose command "grim women" throng in crowds,
And kings of fire, of water, and of clouds,
With "small grey men," "wild yagers," and what not,
To crown with honor thee and Walter Scott;
Again all hail! if tales like thine may please,
St. Luke alone can vanquish the disease;
Even Satan's self with thee might dread to dwell,
And in thy skull discern a deeper hell.

never distinguished himself in Parliament, but, mainly in consequence of the clever use he made of his knowledge of the German language, then a rare accomplishment, attracted much notice in the literary world, at a very early period of his life. His Tales of Terror; the drama of the Castle Spectre; and the romance called the Bravo of Venice (which is, however, little more than a version from the Swiss Zschokke); but above all, the libidinous and impious novel of The Monk, invested the name of Lewis with an extraordinary degree of celebrity, during the poor period which intervened between the obscuration of Cowper, and the full display of Sir Walter Scott's talents in the "Lay of the Last Minstrel,"—a period which is sufficiently characterized by the fact that Hayley then passed for a Poet. Next to that solemn coxcomb, Lewis was for several years the fashionable versifier of his time; but his plagiarisms, perhaps more audacious than had ever before been resorted to by a man of real talents, were by degrees unveiled, and writers of greater original genius, as well as of purer taste and morals, successively emerging, Monk Lewis, dying young, had already outlived his reputation. In society he was to the last a favorite; and Byron, who had become well acquainted with him during his experience of London life, thus notices his death, which occurred at sea in 1818: — "Lewis was a good man, a clever man, but a bore. My only revenge or consolation used to be setting him by the ears with some vivacious person who hated bores especially, — Madame de Staël or Hobhouse, for example. But I liked Lewis: he was the jewel of a man, had he been better set; — I don't mean personally, but less tiresome, for he was tedious, as well as contradictory to every thing and every body. Poor fellow! he died a martyr to his new riches — of a second visit to Jamaica: —
"I'd give the lands of Deloraine,
Dark Musgrave were alive again!"
That is, —
"I would give many a sugar cane,
Mat Lewis were alive again!"]

[6] "For every one knows, little Matt's an M. P." — See a poem to Mr. Lewis, in "The Statesman," supposed to be written by Mr. Jekyll.

Who in soft guise, surrounded by a choir
Of virgins melting, not to Vesta's fire,
With sparkling eyes, and cheek by passion
    flushed,
Strikes his wild lyre, whilst listening dames are
    hushed?
'Tis Little! young Catullus of his day,
As sweet, but as immoral, in his lay!
Grieved to condemn,[1] the muse must still be
    just,
Nor spare melodious advocates of lust.
Pure is the flame which o'er her altar burns;
From grosser incense with disgust she turns;
Yet kind to youth, this expiation o'er,
She bids thee "mend thy line, and sin no
    more."

For thee, translator of the tinsel song,
To whom such glittering ornaments belong,
Hibernian Strangford! with thine eyes of
    blue,[2]
And boasted locks of red or auburn hue,
Whose plaintive strain each love-sick miss ad-
    mires,
And o'er harmonious fustian half expires,
Learn, if thou canst, to yield thine author's
    sense,
Nor vend thy sonnets on a false pretence.
Think'st thou to gain thy verse a higher place,
By dressing Camoëns[3] in a suit of lace?
Mend, Strangford! mend thy morals and thy
    taste;
Be warm, but pure; be amorous, but be chaste:
Cease to deceive; thy pilfered harp restore,
Nor teach the Lusian bard to copy Moore.

Behold!—ye tarts! one moment spare the
    text—
Hayley's last work, and worst—until his next;
Whether he spin poor couplets into plays,
Or damn the dead with purgatorial praise,
His style in youth or age is still the same,
For ever feeble and for ever tame.
Triumphant first see "Temper's Triumphs"
    shine;
At least I'm sure they triumphed over mine.

Of "Music's Triumphs," all who read may
    swear
That luckless music never triumphed there.[4]

Moravians, rise! bestow some meet reward
On dull devotion—Lo! the Sabbath bard,
Sepulchral Grahame,[5] pours his notes sublime
In mangled prose, nor e'en aspires to rhyme;
Breaks into blank the Gospel of St. Luke,
And boldly pilfers from the Pentateuch;
And, undisturbed by conscientious qualms,
Perverts the Prophets, and purloins the
    Psalms.

Hail, Sympathy! thy soft idea brings[6]
A thousand visions of a thousand things,
And shows, still whimpering through three-
    score of years,
The maudlin prince of mournful sonneteers.
And art thou not their prince, harmonious
    Bowles!
Thou first, great oracle of tender souls?
Whether thou sing'st with equal ease, and grief,
The fall of empires, or a yellow leaf;
Whether thy muse most lamentably tells
What merry sounds proceed from Oxford
    bells,[7]

---

[1] [In very early life, "Little's Poems" were Byron's favorite study. "Heigho!" he exclaims in 1820, in a letter to Moore, "I believe all the mischief I have ever done or sung has been owing to that confounded book of yours."]

[2] The reader, who may wish for an explanation of this may refer to "Strangford's Camoëns," p. 127, note to p. 56, or to the last page of the Edinburgh Review of Strangford's Camoëns. [Lord Strangford, after declaring "auburn locks and eyes of blue" to be "the essence of loveliness," and indicative of the most amiable disposition and the warmest heart, proceeded to intimate that he was personally possessed of all these advantages.]

[3] It is also to be remarked, that the things given to the public as poems of Camoëns are no more to be found in the original Portuguese, than in the Song of Solomon.

[4] Hayley's two most notorious verse productions are "Triumphs of Temper," and "The triumph of Music." He has also written much comedy in rhyme, epistles, etc. etc. As he is rather an elegant writer of notes and biography, let us recommend Pope's advice to Wycherley to Mr. H.'s consideration, namely, "to convert his poetry into prose," which may be easily done by taking away the final syllable of each couplet.

[5] Mr. Grahame has poured forth two volumes of cant, under the name of "Sabbath Walks," and "Biblical Pictures."—[This amiable man, and pleasing poet, began life as an advocate at the Edinburgh bar, where he had little success, and being of a melancholy and devout temperament, entered into holy orders, and died in 1811.]

[6] [In the MS. immediately before this line, we find the following, which Byron omitted, at the request of Mr. Dallas, who was, no doubt, a friend of the scribbler they referred to:—

"In verse most stale, unprofitable, flat—
    Come, let us change the scene, and '*glean*'
        with Pratt:
In him an author's luckless lot behold,
Condemned to make the books which once he
    sold:
Degraded man! again resume thy trade—
The votaries of the Muse are ill repaid,
Though daily puffs once more invite to buy
A new edition of thy 'Sympathy.'"

To which this note was appended:—"Mr. Pratt, once a Bath bookseller, now a London author, has written as much, to as little purpose, as any of his scribbling contemporaries. Mr. P.'s 'Sympathy' is in rhyme; but his prose productions are the most voluminous." The more popular of these last were entitled "Gleanings."]

[7] See Bowles's "Sonnet to Oxford," and "Stanzas on hearing the Bells of Ostend."

Or, still in bells delighting, finds a friend
In every chime that jingled from Ostend;
Ah! how much juster were thy muse's hap,
If to thy bells thou wouldst but add a cap!
Delightful Bowles! still blessing and still blest,
All love thy strain, but children like it best.
'Tis thine, with gentle Little's moral song,
To soothe the mania of the amorous throng!
With thee our nursery damsels shed their tears,
Ere miss as yet completes her infant years:
But in her teens thy whining powers are vain;
She quits poor Bowles for Little's purer strain.
Now to soft themes thou scornest to confine
The lofty numbers of a harp like thine;
"Awake a louder and a loftier strain," [1]
Such as none heard before, or will again!
Where all Discoveries jumbled from the flood,
Since first the leaky ark reposed in mud,
By more or less, are sung in every book,
From Captain Noah down to Captain Cook.
Nor this alone; but, pausing on the road,
The bard sighs forth a gentle episode; [2]
And gravely tells — attend, — each beauteous
    miss! —
When first Madeira trembled to a kiss.
Bowles! in thy memory let this precept dwell.
Stick to thy sonnets, man! — at least they sell.
But if some new-born whim, or larger bribe,
Prompt thy crude brain, and claim thee for a
    scribe;
If chance some bard, though once by dunces
    feared,
Now, prone in dust, can only be revered;
If Pope, whose fame and genius, from the first,
Have foiled the best of critics, needs the worst,
Do thou essay: each fault, each failing scan;
The first of poets was, alas! but man.
Rake from each ancient dunghill every pearl,
Consult Lord Fanny, and confide in Curll; [3]

Let all the scandals of a former age
Perch on thy pen, and flutter o'er thy page;
Affect a candor which thou canst not feel,
Clothe envy in the garb of honest zeal;
Write, as if St. John's soul could still inspire,
And do from hate what Mallet [4] did for hire.
Oh! hadst thou lived in that congenial time,
To rave with Dennis, and with Ralph to
    rhyme; [5]
Thronged with the rest around his living head,
Not raised thy hoof against the lion dead; [6]
A meet reward had crowned thy glorious gains,
And linked thee to the Dunciad for thy pains.[7]

Another epic! Who inflicts again
More books of blank upon the sons of men?
Bœotian Cottle, rich Bristowa's boast,
Imports old stories from the Cambrian coast,
And sends his goods to market — all alive!
Lines forty thousand, cantos twenty-five!
Fresh fish from Helicon! [8] who'll buy? who'll
    buy?
The precious bargain's cheap — in faith, not I.
Your turtle-feeder's verse must needs be flat,
Though Bristol bloat him with the verdant fat;
If Commerce fills the purse, she clogs the
    brain,
And Amos Cottle strikes the lyre in vain.
In him an author's luckless lot behold,
Condemned to make the books which once
    he sold.
Oh, Amos Cottle! — Phœbus! what a name
To fill the speaking trump of future fame! —

---

[1] "Awake a louder," etc., is the first line in Bowles's "Spirit of Discovery;" a very spirited and pretty dwarf-epic. Among other exquisite lines we have the following: —
    "A kiss
Stole on the list'ning silence, never yet
Here heard; they trembled even as if the power,"
etc. etc.
That is, the woods of Madeira trembled to a kiss; very much astonished, as well they might be, at such a phenomenon. — ["Misquoted and misunderstood by me; but not intentionally. It was not the "woods," but the people in them who trembled — why, Heaven only knows — unless they were overheard making the prodigious smack." — *Byron*, 1816.]

[2] The episode above alluded to is the story of "Robert à Machin" and "Anna d' Arfet," a pair of constant lovers, who performed the kiss above mentioned, that startled the woods of Madeira.

[3] Curll is one of the heroes of the Dunciad, and was a bookseller. Lord Fanny is the poetical name of Lord Hervey, author of "Lines to the Imitator of Horace."

[4] Lord Bolingbroke hired Mallet to traduce Pope after his decease, because the poet had retained some copies of a work by Lord Bolingbroke — the "Patriot King," — which that splendid, but malignant, genius had ordered to be destroyed. — ["Bolingbroke's thirst of vengeance," says Dr. Johnson, "incited him to blast the memory of the man over whom he had wept in his last struggles; and he employed Mallet, another friend of Pope, to tell the tale to the public, with all its aggravations."]

[5] Dennis the critic, and Ralph the rhymester. —
"Silence, ye wolves! while Ralph to Cynthia howls,
    Making night hideous: answer him, ye owls!"
                                        Dunciad.

[6] See Bowles's late edition of Pope's works, for which he received three hundred pounds. Thus Mr. B. has experienced how much easier it is to profit by the reputation of another, than to elevate his own.

[7] [Byron's MS. note of 1816 on this passage is, — "Too savage all this on Bowles:" and well might he say so. For in spite of all the criticism to which his injudicious edition of Pope exposed Bowles afterwards, there can be no doubt that Byron, in his calmer moments, did justice to that exquisite poetical genius which, by their own confession, originally inspired both Wordsworth and Coleridge.]

[8] ["Fresh fish from Helicon!" — "Helicon" is a mountain and not a fish pond. It should have been "Hippocrene." — *Byron*, 1816.]

Oh, Amos Cottle! for a moment think
What meagre profits spring from pen and ink!
When thus devoted to poetic dreams,
Who will peruse thy prostituted reams?
Oh pen perverted! paper misapplied!
Had Cottle[1] still adorned the counter's side,
Bent o'er the desk, or, born to useful toils,
Been taught to make the paper which he soils,
Ploughed, delved, or plied the oar with lusty
    limb,
He had not sung of Wales, nor I of him.[2]

As Sisyphus against the infernal steep
Rolls the huge rock whose motions ne'er may
    sleep,
So up thy hill, ambrosial Richmond, heaves
Dull Maurice[3] all his granite weight of leaves:
Smooth, solid monuments of mental pain!
The petrifactions of a plodding brain,
That, ere they reach the top, fall lumbering
    back again.

With broken lyre, and cheek serenely pale,
Lo! sad Alcæus wanders down the vale;
Though fair they rose, and might have
    bloomed at last,
His hopes have perished by the northern
    blast:
Nipped in the bud by Caledonian gales,
His blossoms wither as the blast prevails!
O'er his lost works let *classic* Sheffield weep;
May no rude hand disturb their early sleep![4]

Yet say! why should the bard at once re-
    sign
His claim to favor from the sacred nine?

For ever startled by the mingled howl
Of northern wolves, that still in darkness
    prowl;
A coward brood, which mangle as they prey,
By hellish instinct, all that cross their way;
Aged or young, the living or the dead,
No mercy find — these harpies[5] must be fed.
Why do the injured unresisting yield
The calm possession of their native field?
Why tamely thus before their fangs retreat,
Nor hunt the bloodhounds back to Arthur's
    Seat?[6]

Health to immortal Jeffrey! once, in name,
England could boast a judge almost the same;
In soul so like, so merciful, yet just,
Some think that Satan has resigned his trust,
And given the spirit to the world again,
To sentence letters, as he sentenced men.
With hand less mighty, but with heart as black,
With voice as willing to decree the rack;
Bred in the courts betimes, though all that law
As yet hath taught him is to find a flaw;
Since well instructed in the patriot school
To rail at party, though a party tool,
Who knows, if chance his patrons should re-
    store
Back to the sway they forfeited before,
His scribbling toils some recompense may
    meet,
And raise this Daniel to the judgment-seat?[7]
Let Jeffries' shade indulge the pious hope,
And greeting thus, present him with a rope:
"Heir to my virtues! man of equal mind!
Skilled to condemn as to traduce mankind,
This cord receive, for thee reserved with care,
To wield in judgment, and at length to wear."

Health to great Jeffrey! Heaven preserve
    his life,
To flourish on the fertile shores of Fife,
And guard it sacred in its future wars,
Since authors sometimes seek the field of
    Mars!
Can none remember that eventful day,[8]

---

[1] Mr. Cottle, Amos, Joseph, I don't know which, but one or both, once sellers of books they did not write, and now writers of books they do not sell, have published a pair of epics. "Alfred," — (poor Alfred! Pye has been at him too!) — "Alfred," and the "Fall of Cambria."

[2] "All right. I saw some letters of this fellow (Joseph Cottle) to an unfortunate poetess, whose productions, which the poor woman by no means thought vainly of, he attacked so roughly and bitterly, that I could hardly resist assailing him, even were it unjust, which it is not — for verily he is an ass." — *Byron*, 1816.

[3] Mr. Maurice hath manufactured the component parts of a ponderous quarto, upon the beauties of "Richmond Hill," and the like: — it also takes in a charming view of Turnham Green, Hammersmith, Brentford, Old and New, and the parts adjacent. — [The Rev. Thomas Maurice wrote "Westminster Abbey," and other poems, the "History of Ancient and Modern Hindostan," etc., and his own "Memoirs;" — a very amusing piece of autobiography. He died in 1824, at his apartments in the British Museum; where he had been for some years assistant keeper of MSS.]

[4] Poor Montgomery, though praised by every English Review, has been bitterly reviled by the Edinburgh. After all, the bard of Sheffield is a man of considerable genius. His "Wanderer of Switzerland" is worth a thousand "Lyrical Ballads," and at least fifty "degraded epics."

[5] [In a MS. critique on this satire, by the late Reverend William Crowe, public orator at Oxford, the incongruity of these metaphors is thus noticed: "Within the space of three or four couplets he transforms a man into as many different animals · allow him but the compass of three lines, and he will metamorphose him from a wolf into a harpy, and in three more he will make him a bloodhound." On seeing Mr. Crowe's remarks, Byron desired Mr. Murray to substitute, in the copy in his possession, for "*hellish* instinct," "*brutal* instinct," for "*harpies*," "*felons*," and for "*blood-hounds*," "*hell-hounds*."]

[6] Arthur's Seat; the hill which overhangs Edinburgh.

[7] ["Too ferocious — this is mere insanity." — *Byron*, 1816.]

[8] ["All this is bad, because personal." — *Byron* 1816.]

That ever glorious, almost fatal fray,
When Little's leadless pistol met his eye,
And Bow-street myrmidons stood laughing
    by ?[1]
Oh, day disastrous! On her firm-set rock,
Dunedin's castle felt a secret shock;
Dark rolled the sympathetic waves of Forth,
Low groaned the startled whirlwinds of the
    north;
Tweed ruffled half his waves to form a tear,
The other half pursued its calm career;[2]
Arthur's steep summit nodded to its base,
The surly Tolbooth scarcely kept her place.
The Tolbooth felt — for marble sometimes
    can,
On such occasions, feel as much as man —
The Tolbooth felt defrauded of his charms,
If Jeffrey died, except within her arms:[3]
Nay last, not least, on that portentous morn,
The sixteenth story, where himself was born,
His patrimonial garret, fell to ground,
And pale Edina shuddered at the sound:
Strewed were the streets around with milk-
    white reams,
Flowed all the Canongate with inky streams;
This of his candor seemed the sable dew,
That of his valor showed the bloodless hue;
And all with justice deemed the two combined
The mingled emblems of his mighty mind.
But Caledonia's goddess hovered o'er
The field, and saved him from the wrath of
    Moore;
From either pistol snatched the vengeful lead,

And straight restored it to her favorite's head;
That head, with greater than magnetic power,
Caught it, as Danaë caught the golden shower,
And, though the thickening dross will scarce
    refine,
Augments its ore, and is itself a mine.
"My son," she cried,"ne'er thirst for gore again.
Resign the pistol, and resume the pen;
O'er politics and poesy preside,
Boast of thy country, and Britannia's guide!
For long as Albion's heedless sons submit,
Or Scottish taste decides on English wit,
So long shall last thine unmolested reign,
Nor any dare to take thy name in vain.
Behold, a chosen band shall aid thy plan,
And own thee chieftain of the critic clan.
First in the oat-fed phalanx shall be seen
The travelled thane, Athenian Aberdeen.[4]
Herbert shall wield Thor's hammer,[5] and
    sometimes,
In gratitude, thou'lt praise his rugged rhymes.
Smug Sydney[6] too thy bitter page shall seek,
And classic Hallam,[7] much renowned for
    Greek;

[1] In 1806, Messrs. Jeffrey and Moore met at
Chalk-Farm. The duel was prevented by the in-
terference of the magistracy; and, on examination,
the balls of the pistols were found to have evapo-
rated. This incident gave occasion to much wag-
gery in the daily prints.
    [For this note Moore sent Byron a challenge,
which resulted in explanations and friendship, in-
stead of a duel. The note was then omitted from
the fifth edition, and the following substituted in its
place.] — "I am informed that Mr. Moore pub-
lished at the time a disavowal of the statements in
the newspapers, as far as regarded himself; and, in
justice to him, I mention this circumstance. As I
never heard of it before, I cannot state the particu-
lars, and was only made acquainted with the fact
very lately. — November 4, 1811."
[2] The Tweed here behaved with proper decorum;
it would have been highly reprehensible in the
English half of the river to have shown the smallest
symptom of apprehension.
[3] This display of sympathy on the part of the
Tolbooth (the principal prison in Edinburgh),
which truly seems to have been most affected
on this occasion, is much to be commended. It
was to be apprehended, that the many unhappy
criminals executed in the front might have ren-
dered the edifice more callous. She is said to be of
the softer sex because her delicacy of feeling on
this day was truly feminine, though, like most fem-
inine impulses, perhaps a little selfish.

[4] His lordship has been much abroad, is a mem-
ber of the Athenian Society, and reviewer of " Gell's
Topography of Troy." — [In 1822, the Earl of Ab-
erdeen published an " Inquiry into the Principles of
Beauty in Grecian Architecture."]
[5] Mr. Herbert is a translator of Icelandic and
other poetry. One of the principal pieces is a
" Song on the Recovery of Thor's Hammer: " the
translation is a pleasant chant in the vulgar tongue,
and endeth thus: —
    " Instead of money and rings, I wot,
        The hammer's bruises were her lot.
        Thus Odin's son his hammer got."
[The Hon. William Herbert, brother to the Earl of
Carnarvon. He also published, in 1811, " Helga,"
a poem in seven cantos.]
[6] The Rev. Sydney Smith, the reputed author of
Peter Plymley's Letters and sundry criticisms.
[7] Mr. Hallam reviewed Payne Knight's " Taste,"
and was exceedingly severe on some Greek verses
therein. It was not discovered that the lines were
Pindar's till the press rendered it impossible to
cancel the critique, which still stands an everlast-
ing monument of Hallam's ingenuity.
    Note added to second edition. — The said Hal-
lam is incensed because he is falsely accused, seeing
that he never dineth at Holland House. If this be
true, I am sorry — not for having said so, but on
his account, as I understand his lordship's feasts
are preferable to his compositions. — If he did not
review Lord Holland's performance, I am glad, be-
cause it must have been painful to read, and irk-
some to praise it. If Mr. Hallam will tell me who
did review it, the real name shall find a place in the
text; provided, nevertheless, the said name be of
two orthodox musical syllables, and will come into
the verse: till then, Hallam must stand for want of
a better. — [It is not necessary to vindicate the au-
thor of the " Middle Ages " and the " Constitutional
History of England " from the insinuations of the
juvenile poet.]

Scott may perchance his name and influence
lend,
And paltry Pillans[1] shall traduce his friend;
While gay Thalia's luckless votary, Lambe,[2]
Damned like the devil, and devil-like will
damn.
Known be thy name, unbounded be thy sway!
Thy Holland's banquets shall each toil repay;
While grateful Britain yields the praise she
owes
To Holland's hirelings and to learning's foes.
Yet mark one caution ere thy next Review
Spread its light wings of saffron and of blue,
Beware lest blundering Brougham[3] destroy the
sale,
Turn beef to bannocks, cauliflowers to kail."
Thus having said, the kilted goddess kist
Her son, and vanished in a Scottish mist.[4]
Then prosper, Jeffrey! pertest of the train
Whom Scotland pampers with her fiery grain!
Whatever blessing waits a genuine Scot,
In double portion swells thy glorious lot;
For thee Edina culls her evening sweets,

And showers their odors on thy candid sheets.
Whose hue and fragrance to thy work ad-
here —
This scents its pages, and that gilds its rear.[5]
Lo! blushing Itch, coy nymph, enamoured
grown,
Forsakes the rest, and cleaves to thee alone;
And, too unjust to other Pictish men,
Enjoys thy person, and inspires thy pen!

Illustrious Holland! hard would be his lot,
His hirelings mentioned, and himself forgot![6]
Holland, with Henry Petty[7] at his back,
The whipper-in and huntsman of the pack.
Blest be the banquets spread at Holland
House,[8]
Where Scotchmen feed, and critics may ca-
rouse!
Long, long beneath that hospitable roof
Shall Grub-street dine, while duns are kept
aloof.
See honest Hallam lay aside his fork,
Resume his pen, review his Lordship's work,
And, grateful for the dainties on his plate,
Declare his landlord can at least translate![9]
Dunedin! view thy children with delight,
They write for food — and feed because they
write;
And lest, when heated with the unusual grape,
Some glowing thoughts should to the press es-
cape,
And tinge with red the female reader's cheek,
My lady skims the cream of each critique;
Breathes o'er the page her purity of soul,
Reforms each error, and refines the whole.[10]

---

[1] Pillans is a tutor at Eton. — [Mr. Pillans became afterwards Rector of the High School at Edinburgh. There was not, it is believed, the slightest foundation for the charge in the text.]

[2] The Hon. George Lambe reviewed "Beresford's Miseries," and is moreover, author of a farce enacted with much applause at the Priory, Stanmore; and damned with great expedition at the late theatre, Covent Garden. It was entitled "Whistle for It." — [The reviewer of "Beresford's Miseries" was Sir Walter Scott. In 1821, Mr. Lambe published a translation of Catullus. In 1832, he was Under Secretary of State for the Home Department. He died in 1833.]

[3] Mr. Brougham, in No. XXV. of the Edinburgh Review, throughout the article concerning Don Pedro de Cevallos, has displayed more politics than policy; many of the worthy burgesses of Edinburgh being so incensed at the infamous principles it evinces, as to have withdrawn their subscriptions. — [Here followed, in the first edition, — "The name of this personage is pronounced Broom in the south, but the truly northern and *musical* pronunciation is BROUGH-AM, in two syllables;" but for this, Byron substituted in the second edition: — "It seems that Mr. Brougham is not a Pict, as I supposed, but a Borderer, and his name is pronounced Broom, from Trent to Tay: — so be it." — The Cevallos article was written by Jeffrey.]

[4] I ought to apologize to the worthy deities for introducing a new goddess with short petticoats to their notice; but, alas! what was to be done? I could not say Caledonia's genius, it being well known there is no such genius to be found from Clackmanan to Caithness: yet, without supernatural agency, how was Jeffrey to be saved? The national "kelpies" are too unpoetical, and the "brownies" and "gude neighbors" (spirits of a good disposition) refused to extricate him. A goddess, therefore, has been called for the purpose; and great ought to be the gratitude of Jeffrey, seeing it is the only communication he ever held, or is likely to hold, with any thing heavenly.

[5] See the color of the back binding of the Edinburgh Review.

[6] ["Bad enough, and on mistaken grounds too." — *Byron*, 1816.]

[7] [Lord Henry Petty; — now(1855) Marquess of Lansdowne.]

[8] [In 1813, Byron dedicated the Bride of Abydos to Lord Holland; and we find in his Journal (Nov. 17th) this passage: — "I have had a most kind letter from Lord Holland on the Bride of Abydos, which he likes, and so does Lady H. This is very good-natured in both, from whom I don't deserve any quarter. Yet I *did* think at the time that my cause of enmity proceeded from Holland House, and am glad I was wrong, and wish I had not been in such a hurry with that confounded Satire, of which I would suppress even the memory; but people, now they can't get it, make a fuss, I verily believe out of contradiction."]

[9] Lord Holland has translated some specimens of Lope de Vega, inserted in his life of the author. Both are bepraised by his *disinterested* guests. — [Lord Holland afterwards published a very good version of the 28th canto of the Orlando Furioso, in an appendix to one of Stewart Rose's volumes.]

[10] Certain it is, her ladyship is suspected of having displayed her matchless wit in the Edinburgh Review. However that may be, we know, from good authority, that the manuscripts are submitted to her perusal — no doubt, for correction.

Now to the Drama turn — Oh! motley sight!
What precious scenes the wondering eyes in-
vite!
Puns, and a prince within a barrel pent,[1]
And Dibdin's nonsense yield complete content.
Though now, thank Heaven! the Koscio-
mania's o'er,[2]
And full-grown actors are endured once more;
Yet what avail their vain attempts to please,
While British critics suffer scenes like these;
While Reynolds vents his "dammes!"
" poohs!" and "zounds!"[3]
And common-place and common sense con-
founds?
While Kenney's "World" — ah! where is
Kenney's wit? —
Tires the sad gallery, lulls the listless pit;
And Beaumont's pilfered Caratach affords
A tragedy complete in all but words?[4]
Who but must mourn, while these are all the
rage,
The degradation of our vaunted stage!
Heavens! is all sense of shame and talent gone?
Have we no living bard of merit? — none!
Awake, George Colman![5] Cumberland,[6] a-
wake!

Ring the alarum bell! let folly quake!
Oh, Sheridan! if aught can move thy pen,
Let Comedy assume her throne again;
Abjure the mummery of the German schools;
Leave new Pizarros to translating fools;
Give, as thy last memorial to the age,
One classic drama, and reform the stage.
Gods! o'er those boards shall Folly rear her
head,
Where Garrick trod, and Siddons lives to
tread?[7]
On those shall Farce display Buffoon'ry's
mask,
And Hook concealed his heroes in a cask?
Shall sapient managers new scenes produce
From Cherry, Skeffington, and Mother
Goose?
While Shakspeare, Otway, Massinger, forgot,
On stalls must moulder, or in closets rot?
Lo! with what pomp the daily prints proclaim
The rival candidates for Attic fame!
In grim array though Lewis' spectres rise,
Still Skeffington and Goose divide the prize.[8]
And sure *great* Skeffington must claim our
praise,
For skirtless coats and skeletons of plays
Renowned alike; whose genius ne'er confines
Her flight to garnish Greenwood's gay de-
signs;[9]
Nor sleeps with "Sleeping Beauties," but anon
In five facetious acts comes thundering on,[10]
While poor John Bull, bewildered with the
scene,
Stares, wondering what the devil it can mean;
But as some hands applaud, a venal few!
Rather than sleep, why John applauds it too.

Such are we now. Ah! wherefore should
we turn
To what our fathers were, unless to mourn?
Degenerate Britons! are ye dead to shame,
Or, kind to dulness, do you fear to blame?
Well may the nobles of our present race

---

[1] In the melo-drama of Tekeli, that heroic prince is clapt into a barrel on the stage; a new asylum for distressed heroes. — [In the original MS. the note stands thus: — " In the melo-drama of Tekeli, that heroic prince is clapt into a barrel on the stage, and Count Évrard in the fortress hides himself in a green-house built expressly for the occasion. 'Tis a pity that Theodore Hook, who is really a man of talent, should confine his genius to such paltry pro-ductions as the ' Fortress,' ' Music Mad,' etc. etc." — This extraordinary humorist was a mere boy at the date of Byron's satire.]

[2] [Master Betty, " the young Roscius," had a lit-tle before been the rage with the play-going public.]

[3] All these are favorite expressions of Mr. Rey-nolds, and prominent in his comedies, living and defunct.

[4] Mr. T. Sheridan, the new manager of Drury Lane theatre, stripped the tragedy of Bonduca of the dialogue, and exhibited the scenes as the spec-tacle of Caractacus. Was this worthy of his sire? or of himself? — [Thomas Sheridan, who united much of the convivial wit of his parent to many amiable qualities, was afterwards made colonial paymaster at the Cape of Good Hope, where he died in September, 1817, leaving a widow whose novel of "Carwell" obtained much approbation, and several children; among others, the Honorable Mrs. Norton.]

[5] [Byron entertained a high opinion of George Colman's conversational powers. — " If I had," he says, " to choose, and could not have both at a time, I should say, ' Let me begin the evening with Sheridan, and finish it with Colman.' Sheridan for dinner, and Colman for supper; Sheridan for claret or port, but Colman for every thing. Sheridan was a grenadier company of life-guards, but Col-man a whole regiment — *of light infantry*, to be sure, but still a regiment."]

[6] [Richard Cumberland, the author of the " West

Indian," the " Observer," and one of the most inter-esting of autobiographies, died in 1811.]

[7] [In all editions previous to the fifth, it was, " Kemble lives to tread." Byron used to say, that, " of actors, Cooke was the most natural, Kemble the most supernatural, Kean the medium between the two; but that Mrs. Siddons was worth them all put together." Such effect, however, had Kean's acting on his mind, that once, on seeing him play Sir Giles Overreach, he was seized with a fit.]

[8] [Dibdin's pantomime of Mother Goose had a run of nearly a hundred nights, and brought more than twenty thousand pounds to the treasury of Covent Garden theatre.]

[9] Mr Greenwood is, we believe, scene-painter to Drury Lane theatre — as such, Mr. Skeffington is much indebted to him.

[10] Mr. [afterwards Sir Lumley] Skeffington is the illustrious author of the " Sleeping Beauty; " and some comedies, particularly " Maids and Bache-lors:" Baccalaurii baculo magis quam lauro digni.

Watch each distortion of a Naldi's face;
Well may they smile on Italy's buffoons,
And worship Catalani's pantaloons,[1]
Since their own drama yields no fairer trace
Of wit than puns, of humor than grimace.[2]

Then let Ausonia, skilled in every art
To soften manners, but corrupt the heart,
Pour her exotic follies o'er the town,
To sanction Vice, and hunt Decorum down:
Let wedded strumpets languish o'er Deshayes,
And bless the promise which his form displays;
While Gayton bounds before th' enraptured looks
Of hoary marquises and stripling dukes:
Let high-born lechers eye the lively Prêsle
Twirl her light limbs, that spurn the needless veil;
Let Angiolini bare her breast of snow,
Wave the white arm, and point the pliant toe;
Collini trill her love-inspiring song,
Strain her fair neck, and charm the listening throng!
Whet not your scythe, suppressors of our vice!
Reforming saints! too delicately nice!
By whose decrees, our sinful souls to save,
No Sunday tankards foam, no barbers shave;
And beer undrawn, and beards unmown, display
Your holy reverence for the Sabbath-day.

Or hail at once the patron and the pile
Of vice and folly, Greville and Argyle![3]

Where yon proud palace, Fashion's hallowed fane,
Spreads wide her portals for the motley train,
Behold the new Petronius[4] of the day,
Our arbiter of pleasure and of play!
There the hired eunuch, the Hesperian choir,
The melting lute, the soft lascivious lyre,
The song from Italy, the step from France,
The midnight orgy, and the mazy dance,
The smile of beauty, and the flush of wine,
For fops, fools, gamesters; knaves, and lords combine
Each to his humor — Comus all allows;
Champagne, dice, music, or your neighbor's spouse.
Talk not to us, ye starving sons of trade!
Of piteous ruin, which ourselves have made;
In Plenty's sunshine Fortune's minions bask,
Nor think of poverty, except "en masque,"
When for the night some lately titled ass
Appears the beggar which his grandsire was,
The curtain dropped, the gay burletta o'er,
The audience take their turn upon the floor;
Now round the room the circling dow'gers sweep,
Now in loose waltz the thin-clad daughters leap;
The first in lengthened line majestic swim,
The last display the free unfettered limb!
Those for Hibernia's lusty sons repair
With art the charms which nature could not spare;
These after husbands wing their eager flight,
Nor leave much mystery for the nuptial night.

Oh! blest retreats of infamy and ease,
Where, all forgotten but the power to please,
Each maid may give a loose to genial thought,
Each swain may teach new systems, or be taught:
There the blithe youngster, just returned from Spain,
Cuts the light pack, or calls the rattling main;
The jovial caster's set, and seven's the nick,
Or — done! — a thousand on the coming trick!
If, mad with loss, existence 'gins to tire,
And all your hope or wish is to expire,
Here's Powell's pistol ready for your life,
And, kinder still, two Pagets for your wife;[5]
Fit consummation of an earthly race,
Begun in folly, ended in disgrace;
While none but menials o'er the bed of death,
Wash thy red wounds, or watch thy wavering breath;
Traduced by liars, and forgot by all,
The mangled victim of a drunken brawl,
To live like Clodius, and like Falkland fall.[6]

---

[1] Naldi and Catalani require little notice; for the visage of the one and the salary of the other, will enable us long to recollect these amusing vagabonds. Besides, we are still black and blue from the squeeze on the first night of the lady's appearance in trousers.

[2] [The following twenty lines were struck off one night after Byron's return from the Opera, and sent the next morning to the printer.]

[3] To prevent any blunder, such as mistaking a street for a man, I beg leave to state, that it is the institution, and not the duke of that name, which is here alluded to. A gentleman, with whom I am slightly acquainted, lost in the Argyle Rooms several thousand pounds at backgammon.* It is but justice to the manager in this instance to say, that some degree of disapprobation was manifested: but why are the implements of gambling allowed in a place devoted to the society of both sexes? A pleasant thing for the wives and daughters of those who are blest or cursed with such connections, to hear the billiard tables rattling in one room, and the dice in another! That this is the case I myself can testify, as a late unworthy member of an institution which materially affects the morals of the higher orders, while the lower may not even move to the sound of a tabor and fiddle, without a chance of indictment for riotous behavior.

* [" True. It was Billy Way who lost the money. I knew him, and was a subscriber to the Argyle at the time of the event." — *Byron*, 1816.]

[4] Petronius "Arbiter Elegantiarum" to Nero, " and a very pretty fellow in his day," as Mr. Congreve's " Old Bachelor " saith of Hannibal.

[5] [The original reading was, " a Paget for your wife."]

[6] I knew the late Lord Falkland well. On Sun-

Truth! rouse some genuine bard, and guide his hand
To drive this pestilence from out the land.
E'en I — least thinking of a thoughtless throng,
Just skilled to know the right and choose the wrong,
Freed at that age when reason's shield is lost,
To fight my course through passion's countless host, [1]
Whom every path of pleasure's flowery way
Has lured in turn, and all have led astray —
E'en I must raise my voice, e'en I must feel
Such scenes, such men, destroy the public weal;
Although some kind, censorious friend will say,
"What art thou better, meddling fool, [2] than they?"
And every brother rake will smile to see
That miracle, a moralist in me.
No matter — when some bard in virtue strong,
Gifford perchance, shall raise the chastening song,
Then sleep my pen for ever! and my voice
Be only heard to hail him, and rejoice;
Rejoice, and yield my feeble praise, though I
May feel the lash that Virtue must apply.

As for the smaller fry, who swarm in shoals
From silly Hafiz up to simple Bowles, [3]
Why should we call them from their dark abode,
In broad St. Giles's or in Tottenham-road?
Or (since some men of fashion nobly dare
To scrawl in verse) from Bond-street or the Square?
If things of ton their harmless lays indite,
Most wisely doomed to shun the public sight,

What harm?   In spite of every critic elf,
Sir T. may read his stanzas to himself;
Miles Andrews [4] still his strength in couplets try,
And live in prologues, though his dramas die.
Lords too are bards, such things at times befall,
And 'tis some praise in peers to write at all.
Yet, did or taste or reason sway the times,
Ah! who would take their titles with their rhymes? [5]
Roscommon! Sheffield! with your spirits fled,
No future laurels deck a noble head;
No muse will cheer, with renovating smile,
The paralytic puling of Carlisle. [6]
The puny schoolboy and his early lay
Men pardon, if his follies pass away;
But who forgives the senior's ceaseless verse,
Whose hairs grow hoary as his rhymes grow worse?
What heterogeneous honors deck the peer!
Lord, rhymester, petit-maître, pamphleteer! [7]
So dull in youth, so drivelling in his age,
His scenes alone had damned our sinking stage;
But managers for once cried, "Hold, enough!"
Nor drugged their audience with the tragic stuff.
Yet at their judgment let his lordship laugh,
And case his volumes in congenial calf;
Yes! doff that covering, where morocco shines,
And hang a calf-skin [8] on those recreant lines. [9]

---

day night I beheld him presiding at his own table, in all the honest pride of hospitality; on Wednesday morning, at three o'clock, I saw stretched before me all that remained of courage, feeling, and a host of passions. He was a gallant and successful officer: his faults were the faults of a sailor — as such, Britons will forgive them. He died like a brave man in a better cause; for had he fallen in like manner on the deck of the frigate to which he was just appointed, his last moments would have been held up by his countrymen as an example to succeeding heroes. — [Lord Falkland was killed in a duel by Mr. Powell, in 1809. Though his own difficulties pressed on him at the time, Byron gave five hundred pounds to the widow and children of his friend.]

[1] ["Yes: and a precious chase they led me." — *Byron*, 1816.]

[2] ["*Fool* enough, certainly, then, and no wiser since." — *Byron*, 1816.]

[3] What would be the sentiments of the Persian Anacreon, Hafiz, could he rise from his splendid sepulchre at Sheeraz, (where he reposes with Ferdousi and Sadi, the oriental Homer and Catullus,) and behold his name assumed by one Stott of Dromore, the most impudent and execrable of literary poachers for the daily prints?

[4] [Miles Peter Andrews, many years M. P., Colonel of the Prince of Wales's Volunteers, author of numerous prologues, epilogues, and farces, and one the heroes of the Baviad. He died in 1814.]

[5] [In the original manuscript we find these lines: —
"In these, our times, with daily wonders big,
A lettered peer is like a lettered pig;
Both know their alphabet, but who, from thence
Infers that peers or pigs have manly sense?
Still less that such should woo the graceful nine:
Parnassus was not made for lords and swine."]

[6] [On being told that it was believed he alluded to Lord Carlisle's nervous disorder in this line, Byron exclaimed, — "I thank heaven I did not know it; and would not, could not, if I had. I must naturally be the last person to be pointed on defects or maladies."]

[7] The Earl of Carlisle has lately published an eighteen-penny pamphlet on the state of the stage, and offers his plan for building a new theatre. It is to be hoped his lordship will be permitted to bring forward any thing for the stage — except his own tragedies.

[8]   "Doff that lion's hide,
And hang a calf-skin on those recreant limbs."
Shakspeare: King John.

Lord Carlisle's works, most resplendently bound, form a conspicuous ornament to his book-shelves: —
"The rest is all but leather and prunella."

[9] ["Wrong also — the provocation was not sufficient to justify the acerbity." — *Byron*, 1816. —

With you, ye Druids! rich in native lead,
Who daily scribble for your daily bread;
With you I war not: Gifford's heavy hand
Has crushed, without remorse, your numer-
ous band.
On "all the talents" vent your venal spleen;
Want is your plea, let pity be your screen.
Let monodies on Fox regale your crew,
And Melville's Mantle [1] prove a blanket too!
One common Lethe waits each hapless bard,
And, peace be with you! 'tis your best reward.
Such damning fame as Dunciads only give
Could bid your lines beyond a morning live;
But now at once your fleeting labors close,
With names of greater note in blest repose.
Far be't from me unkindly to upbraid
The lovely Rosa's prose in masquerade,
Whose strains, the faithful echoes of her mind,
Leave wondering comprehension far behind. [2]
Though Crusca's bards no more our journals
fill,
Some stragglers skirmish round the columns
still;
Last of the howling host which once was Bell's,
Matilda snivels yet, and Hafiz yells;
And Merry's metaphors appear anew,
Chained to the signature of O. P. Q. [3]

Byron greatly regretted the sarcasms he had pub-
lished against his noble relation, under the mis-
taken impression that Lord Carlisle had intention-
ally slighted him. In a letter to Mr. Rogers, written
in 1814, he asks, — "Is there any chance or possi-
bility of making it up with Lord Carlisle, as I feel
disposed to do any thing reasonable or unreasona-
ble to effect it?" And in the third canto of Childe
Harold, he thus adverts to the fate of the Hon.
Frederick Howard, Lord Carlisle's youngest son,
one of those who fell gloriously at Waterloo: —

"Their praise is hymned by loftier harps than
mine:
Yet one I would select from that proud throng,
Partly because they blend me with his line,
And partly that I did his Sire some wrong,
And partly that bright names will hallow song;
And his was of the bravest, and when show-
ered,
The death-bolts deadliest the thinned files
along,
Even where the thickest of war's tempests
lowered,
They reached no nobler breast than thine, young,
gallant Howard!"]

[1] "Melville's Mantle," a parody on "Elijah's
Mantle," a poem.

[2] This lovely little Jessica, the daughter of the
noted Jew King, seems to be a follower of the Della
Crusca school, and has published two volumes of
very respectable absurdities in rhyme, as times go;
besides sundry novels in the style of the first edition
of the Monk. — ["She since married the Morning
Post — an exceeding good match; and is now dead
— which is better." — *Byron*, 1816.]

[3] These are the signatures of various worthies who
figure in the poetical departments of the newspapers.

When some brisk youth, the tenant of a
stall, [4]
Employs a pen less pointed than his awl,
Leaves his snug shop, forsakes his store of
shoes,
St. Crispin quits, and cobbles for the muse,
Heavens! how the vulgar stare! how crowds
applaud!
How ladies read, and literari laud! [5]
If chance some wicked wag should pass his
jest,
'Tis sheer ill-nature — don't the world know
best?
Genius must guide when wits admire the
rhyme,
And Capel Lofft [6] declares 'tis quite sublime.
Hear, then, ye happy sons of needless trade!
Swains! quit the plough, resign the useless
spade!
Lo! Burns [7] and Bloomfield, nay, a greater
far,

[4] [Joseph Blackett, the shoemaker. He died at
Seaham, in 1810. His poems were afterwards col-
lected by Pratt; and, oddly enough, his principal
patroness was Miss Milbanke, then a stranger to
Byron. In a letter written to Dallas, on board the
Volage frigate at sea, in June, 1811, Byron says, —
"I see that yours and Pratt's protégé, Blackett the
cobbler is dead, and in spite of his rhymes, and is proba-
bly one of the instances where death has saved a
man from damnation. You were the ruin of that
poor fellow amongst you: had it not been for his
patrons, he might now have been in very good
plight, shoe- (not verse-) making: but you have
made him immortal with a vengeance: who would
think that anybody would be such a blockhead as
to sin against an express proverb, — ' Ne sutor ultra
crepidam!'
' But spare him, ye Critics, his follies are past,
  For the Cobbler is come, as he ought, to his *last*.' —
Which two lines, with a scratch under *last*, to show
where the joke lies, I beg that you will prevail on
Miss Milbanke to have inserted on the tomb of her
departed Blackett."]

[5] ["This was meant for poor Blackett, who was
then patronized by A. J. B." (Lady Byron); "but
that I did not know, or this would not have been
written, at least I think not." — *Byron*, 1816.]

[6] Capel Lofft, Esq., the Mæcenas of shoemakers,
and preface-writer-general to distressed versemen; a
kind of gratis accoucheur to those who wish to be
delivered of rhyme, but do not know how to bring
forth. — [Bloomfield owed his first celebrity to the
notice of Capel Lofft and Thomas Hill, who recom-
mended his "Farmer's Boy" to a publisher, and by
their influence attracted attention to its merits. The
public sympathy did not rest permanently on the
amiable poet, who died in extreme poverty in 1823.]

[7] ["Read Burns to-day. What would he have
been if a patrician? We should have had more
polish — less force — just as much verse, but no im-
mortality — a divorce and a duel or two, the which
had he survived, as his potations must have been
less spirituous, he might have lived as long as Sheri-
dan, and outlived as much as poor Brinsley." — *By-
ron's Journal*, 1813.]

Gifford was born beneath an adverse star,
Forsook the labors of a servile state,
Stemmed the rude storm, and triumphed over
   fate:
Then why no more? if Phœbus smiled on
   you,
Bloomfield! why not on brother Nathan too? [1]
Him too the mania, not the muse, has seized;
Not inspiration, but a mind diseased:
And now no boor can seek his last abode,
No common be inclosed without an ode.
Oh! since increased refinement deigns to
   smile
On Britain's sons, and bless our genial isle,
Let poesy go forth, pervade the whole,
Alike the rustic, and mechanic soul!
Ye tuneful cobblers! still your notes prolong,
Compose at once a slipper and a song;
So shall the fair your handywork peruse,
Your sonnets sure shall please — perhaps your
   shoes.
May Moorland weavers [2] boast Pindaric skill,
And tailors' lays be longer than their bill!
While punctual beaux reward the grateful
   notes,
And pay for poems — when they pay for coats.

To the famed throng now paid the tribute
   due,
Neglected genius! let me turn to you.
Come forth, oh Campbell! [3] give thy talents
   scope;
Who dares aspire if thou must cease to hope?
And thou, melodious Rogers! [4] rise at last,
Recall the pleasing memory of the past;
Arise! let blest remembrance still inspire,

And strike to wonted tones thy hallowed lyre;
Restore Apollo to his vacant throne,
Assert thy country's honor and thine own.
What! must deserted Poesy still weep
Where her last hopes with pious Cowper
   sleep?
Unless, perchance, from his cold bier she
   turns,
To deck the turf that wraps her minstrel,
   Burns!
No! though contempt hath marked the spu-
   rious brood,
The race who rhyme from folly, or for food,
Yet still some genuine sons 'tis hers to boast,
Who, least affecting, still affect the most:
Feel as they write, and write but as they feel —
Bear witness Gifford,[5] Sotheby,[6] Macneil.[7]

" Why slumbers Gifford?" once was asked
   in vain;
Why slumbers Gifford? let us ask again.
Are there no follies for his pen to purge? [8]
Are there no fools whose backs demand the
   scourge?
Are there no sins for satire's bard to greet?
Stalks not gigantic Vice in every street?
Shall peers or princes tread pollution's path,
And 'scape alike the law's and muse's wrath?
Nor blaze with guilty glare through future time,
Eternal beacons of consummate crime?
Arouse thee, Gifford! be thy promise claimed,
Make bad men better, or at least ashamed.

---

[1] See Nathaniel Bloomfield's ode, elegy, or what-
ever he or any one else chooses to call it, on the in-
closure of " Honington Green."

[2] Vide " Recollections of a Weaver in the Moor-
lands of Staffordshire."

[3] It would be superfluous to recall to the mind of
the reader the authors of " The Pleasures of Mem-
ory " and " The Pleasures of Hope," the most beau-
tiful didactic poems in our language, if we except
Pope's " Essay on Man: " but so many poetasters
have started up, that even the names of Campbell
and Rogers are become strange. — [Beneath this
note Byron scribbled, in 1816, —

    Pretty Miss Jaqueline
    Had a nose aquiline,
    And would assert rude
    Things of Miss Gertrude,
    While Mr. Marmion
    Led a great army on,
    Making Kehama look
    Like a fierce Mameluke.]

[4] [" I have been reading," says Byron in 1813,
" Memory again, and Hope together, and retain all
my preference of the former. His elegance is really
wonderful — there is no such a thing as a vulgar line
in his book." In 1816, Byron wrote — " Rogers has
not fulfilled the promise of his first poems, but has
still very great merit."]

[5] Gifford, author of the Baviad and Mæviad, the
first satires of the day, and translator of Juvenal. —
[The opinion of Mr. Gifford had always great weight
with Byron. " Any suggestion of yours," he says
in a letter written in 1813, " even were it conveyed
in the less tender shape of the text of the Baviad, or
a Monk Mason note in Massinger, would be obeyed."
A few weeks before his death, on hearing from Eng-
land of a report that he had written a satire on Mr.
Gifford, he wrote instantly to Mr. Murray: — " Who-
ever asserts that I am the author or abetter of any
thing of the kind lies in his throat. It is not true
that I ever did, will, would, could, or should write
a satire against Gifford, or a hair of his head. I
always considered him as my literary father, and
myself as his ' prodigal' son; and if I have allowed
his ' fatted calf' to grow to an ox before he kills it
on my return, it is only because I prefer beef to
veal."]

[6] Sotheby, translator of Wieland's Oberon and
Virgil's Georgics, and author of " Saul," an epic
poem.

[7] Macneil, whose poems are deservedly popular,
particularly " Scotland's Scaith," and the " Waes of
War," of which ten thousand copies were sold in
one month. — [Hector Macneil died in 1818.]

[8] Mr. Gifford promised publicly that the Baviad
and Mæviad should not be his last original works:
let him remember " Mox in reluctantes dracones."
— [Mr. Gifford became the editor of the Quarterly
Review, — which thenceforth occupied most of his
time, — a few months after the first appearance of
English Bards and Scotch Reviewers.]

Unhappy White![1] while life was in its
spring,
And thy young muse just waved her· joyous
wing,
The spoiler swept that soaring lyre away,
Which else had sounded an immortal lay.
Oh! what a noble heart was here undone,
When Science' self destroyed her favorite son!
Yes, she too much indulged thy fond pursuit,
She sowed the seeds, but death has reaped
the fruit.
'Twas thine own genius gave the final blow,
And helped to plant the wound that laid thee
low:
So the struck eagle, stretched upon the plain,
No more through rolling clouds to soar again,
Viewed his own feather on the fatal dart,[2]
And winged the shaft that quivered in his
heart;
Keen were his pangs, but keener far to feel
He nursed the pinion which impelled the
steel;
While the same plumage that had warmed his
nest
Drank the last life-drop of his bleeding
breast.

There be, who say, in these enlightened
days,
That splendid lies are all the poet's praise;
That strained invention, ever on the wing,
Alone impels the modern bard to sing:
'Tis true, that all who rhyme — nay, all who
write,
Shrink from that fatal word to genius — trite;

Yet Truth sometimes will lend her noblest
fires,
And decorate the verse herself inspires:
This fact in Virtue's name let Crabbe attest;
Though nature's sternest painter, yet the
best.[3]

And here let Shee [4] and Genius find a place,
Whose pen and pencil yield an equal grace;
To guide whose hand the sister arts combine,
And trace the poet's or the painter's line;
Whose magic touch can bid the canvas glow
Or pour the easy rhyme's harmonious flow;
While honors, doubly merited, attend
The poet's rival, but the painter's friend.

Blest is the man who dares approach the
bower
Where dwelt the muses at their natal hour;
Whose steps have pressed, whose eye has
marked afar
The clime that nursed the sons of song and
war,
The scenes which glory still must hover o'er,
Her place of birth, her own Achaian shore.
But doubly blest is he whose heart expands
With hallowed feelings for those classic lands;
Who rends the veil of ages long gone by,
And views their remnants with a poet's eye!
Wright![5] 'twas thy happy lot at once to view
Those shores of glory, and to sing them too;
And sure no common muse inspired thy pen
To hail the land of gods and godlike men.

And you, associate bards![6] who snatched
to light
Those gems too long withheld from modern
sight;
Whose mingling taste combined to cull the
wreath
Where Attic flowers Aonian odors breathe,
And all their renovated fragrance flung,
To grace the beauties of your native tongue;
Now let those minds, that nobly could trans-
fuse
The glorious spirit of the Grecian muse,
Though soft the echo, scorn a borrowed tone:
Resign Achaia's lyre, and strike your own.

[1] Henry Kirke White died at Cambridge, in Octo-
ber, 1806, in consequence of too much exertion in
the pursuit of studies that would have matured a
mind which disease and poverty could not impair,
and which death itself destroyed rather than sub-
dued. His poems abound in such beauties as must
impress the reader with the liveliest regret that so
short a period was allotted to talents which would
have dignified even the sacred functions he was des-
tined to assume. — [In a letter to Mr. Dallas, in
1811, Byron says, — "I am sorry you don't like
Harry White; with a great deal of cant, which in
him was sincere (indeed it killed him, as you killed
Joe Blackett), certes there is poesy and genius. I
don't say this on account of my simile and rhymes;
but surely he was beyond all the Bloomfields and
Blacketts, and their collateral cobblers, whom Lofft
and Pratt have or may kidnap from their calling into
the service of the trade. Setting aside bigotry, he
surely ranks next to Chatterton. It is astonishing
how little he was known; and at Cambridge no one
thought or heard of such a man till his death ren-
dered all notices useless. For my part, I should
have been most proud of such an acquaintance: his
very prejudices were respectable."]

[2] [That eagle's fate and mine are one,
    Which on the shaft that made him die,
    Espied a feather of his own
    Wherewith he wont to soar on high.
                               Waller.]

[3] [" I consider Crabbe and Coleridge as the first
of these times, in point of power and genius."—
Byron, 1816.]

[4] Mr. Shee, author of "Rhymes on Art," and
"Elements of Art." — [Afterwards Sir Martin Shee,
and President of the Royal Academy.]

[5] Waller Rodwell Wright, late consul-general for
the Seven Islands, is author of a very beautiful poem,
just published: it is entitled "Horæ Ionicæ," and
is descriptive of the isles and the adjacent coast of
Greece.

[6] The translators of the Anthology, Bland and
Merivale, have since published separate poems,
which evince genius that only requires opportu-
nity to attain eminence.

Let these, or such as these, with just applause
Restore the muse's violated laws;
But not in flimsy Darwin's pompous chime,
That mighty master of unmeaning rhyme,
Whose gilded cymbals, more adorned than clear,
The eye delighted, but fatigued the ear;
In show the simple lyre could once surpass,
But now, worn down, appear in native brass;
While all his train of hovering sylphs around
Evaporate in similes and sound:
Him let them shun, with him let tinsel die:
False glare attracts, but more offends the eye.[1]

Yet let them not to vulgar Wordsworth stoop,
The meanest object of the lowly group,
Whose verse, of all but childish prattle void,
Seems blessed harmony to Lamb and Lloyd:[2]
Let them — but hold, my muse, nor dare to teach
A strain far, far beyond thy humble reach:
The native genius with their being given
Will point the path, and peal their notes to heaven.

And thou, too, Scott![3] resign to minstrels rude
The wilder slogan of a border feud:
Let others spin their meagre lines for hire;
Enough for genius if itself inspire!
Let Southey sing, although his teeming muse,
Prolific every spring, be too profuse;
Let simple Wordsworth[4] chime his childish verse,
And Brother Coleridge lull the babe at nurse;
Let spectre-mongering Lewis aim, at most,
To rouse the galleries, or to raise a ghost;
Let Moore still sigh; let Strangford steal from Moore,
And swear that Camoëns sang such notes of yore;
Let Hayley hobble on, Montgomery rave,
And godly Grahame chant a stupid stave;
Let sonneteering Bowles his strains refine,
And whine and whimper to the fourteenth line;
Let Stott, Carlisle,[5] Matilda, and the rest

Of Grub-street, and of Grosvenor-place the best,
Scrawl on, till death release us from the strain,
Or Common Sense assert her rights again.
But thou, with powers that mock the aid of praise,
Shouldst leave to humbler bards ignoble lays:
Thy country's voice, the voice of all the nine,
Demand a hallowed harp — that harp is thine.
Say! will not Caledonia's annals yield
The glorious record of some nobler field,
Than the vile foray of a plundering clan,
Whose proudest deeds disgrace the name of man?
Or Marmion's acts of darkness, fitter food
For Sherwood's outlaw tales of Robin Hood?
Scotland! still proudly claim thy native bard,
And be thy praise his first, his best reward!
Yet not with thee alone his name should live,
But own the vast renown a world can give;
Be known, perchance, when Albion is no more,
And tell the tale of what she was before;
To future times her faded fame recall,
And save her glory, though his country fall.

Yet what avails the sanguine poet's hope,
To conquer ages, and with time to cope?
New eras spread their wings, new nations rise,
And other victors fill the applauding skies;
A few brief generations fleet along,
Whose sons forget the poet and his song:

---

[1] The neglect of the "Botanic Garden" is some proof of returning taste. The scenery is its sole recommendation.

[2] Messrs. Lamb and Lloyd, the most ignoble followers of Southey and Co. — [In 1798, Charles Lamb and Charles Lloyd published in conjunction a volume, entitled, "Poems in Blank Verse."]

[3] By the by, I hope that in Mr. Scott's next poem, his hero or heroine will be less addicted to "Gramarye," and more to grammar, than the Lady of the Lay and her bravo, William of Deloraine.

[4] ["Unjust." — *Byron*, 1816.]

[5] It may be asked, why I have censured the Earl of Carlisle, my guardian and relative, to whom I dedicated a volume of puerile poems a few years ago? — The guardianship was nominal, at least as far as I have been able to discover; the relationship

I cannot help, and am very sorry for it; but as his lordship seemed to forget it on a very essential occasion to me, I shall not burden my memory with the recollection. I do not think that personal differences sanction the unjust condemnation of a brother scribbler; but I see no reason why they should act as a preventive, when the author, noble, or ignoble, has, for a series of years, beguiled a "discerning public" (as the advertisements have it) with divers reams of most orthodox, imperial nonsense. Besides, I do not step aside to vituperate the earl: no — his works come fairly in review with those of other patrician literati. If, before I escaped from my teens, I said any thing in favor of his lordship's paper books, it was in the way of dutiful dedication, and more from the advice of others than my own judgment, and I seize the first opportunity of pronouncing my sincere recantation. I have heard that some persons conceive me to be under obligations to Lord Carlisle: if so, I shall be most particularly happy to learn what they are, and when conferred, that they may be duly appreciated and publicly acknowledged. What I have humbly advanced as an opinion on his printed things, I am prepared to support, if necessary, by quotations from elegies, eulogies, odes, episodes, and certain facetious and dainty tragedies bearing his name and mark: —

"What can ennoble knaves, or fools, or cowards?
Alas! not all the blood of all the Howards."

So says Pope. Amen! — ["Much too savage, whatever the foundation might be." — ..... 1816.]

E'en now, what once-loved minstrel scarce
may claim
The transient mention of a dubious name!
When fame's loud trump hath blown its no-
blest blast,
Though long the sound, the echo sleeps at
last; .
And glory, like the phœnix [1] 'midst her fires,
Exhales her odors, blazes, and expires.

Shall hoary Granta call her sable sons,
Expert in science, more expert at puns ?
Shall these approach the muse ? ah, no ! she
flies,
Even from the tempting ore of Seaton's prize ;
Though printers condescend the press to soil
With rhyme by Hoare,[2] and epic blank by
Hoyle : [3]
Not him whose page, if still upheld by whist,
Requires no sacred theme to bid us list.[4]
Ye! who in Granta's honors would surpass,
Must mount her Pegasus, a full-grown ass ;
A foal well worthy of her ancient dam,
Whose Helicon is duller than her Cam.

There Clarke, still striving piteously "to
please,"
Forgetting doggrel leads not to degrees,
A would-be satirist, a hired buffoon,
A monthly scribbler of some low lampoon,[5]
Condemned to drudge, the meanest of the
mean,
And furbish falsehoods for a magazine,
Devotes to scandal his congenial mind ;
Himself a living libel on mankind.[6]

Oh! dark asylum of a Vandal race![7]
At once the boast of learning, and disgrace!

[1] [" The devil take that phœnix! How came it
there?" — *Byron,* 1816.]
[2] [The Rev. Charles James Hoare published, in
1808, the "Shipwreck of St. Paul," a Seatonian
prize poem.]
[3] [The Rev. Charles Hoyle, author of "Exo-
dus," an epic in thirteen books, and several other
Seatonian prize poems.]
[4] The "Games of Hoyle," well known to the
votaries of whist, chess, etc., are not to be super-
seded by the vagaries of Hoyle's poetical namesake,
whose poem comprised, as expressly stated in the
advertisement, all the "plagues of Egypt."
[5] [" Right enough: this was well deserved, and
well laid on." — *Byron,* 1816.]
[6] This person, who has lately betrayed the most
rabid symptoms of confirmed authorship, is writer
of a poem denominated the "Art of Pleasing," as
"lucus a non lucendo," containing little pleasantry
and less poetry. He also acts as monthly stipendi-
ary and collector of calumnies for the " Satirist."
If this unfortunate young man would exchange the
magazines for the mathematics, and endeavor to
take a decent degree in his university, it might
eventually prove more serviceable than his present
salary. — [Mr. Hewson Clarke was also the author
of " The Saunterer," and a " History of the Cam-
paign in Russia."]
[7] " Into Cambridgeshire the Emperor Probus

So lost to Phœbus, that nor Hodgson's [8] verse
Can make thee better, nor poor Hewson's [9]
worse.
But where fair Isis rolls her purer wave,
The partial muse delighted loves to lave ;
On her green banks a greener wreath she
wove,
To crown the bards that haunt her classic
grove ;
Where Richards wakes a genuine poet's fires,
And modern Britons glory in their sires.[10]

For me, who, thus unasked, have dared to
tell
My country, what her sons should know too
well,
Zeal for her honor bade me here engage
The host of idiots that infest her age ;
No just applause her honored name shall lose,
As first in freedom, dearest to the muse.
Oh! would thy bards but emulate thy fame,
And rise more worthy, Albion, of thy name!
What Athens was in science, Rome in power,
What Tyre appeared in her meridian hour,
'Tis thine at once, fair Albion! to have been —
Earth's chief dictatress, ocean's lovely queen :
But Rome decayed, and Athens strewed the
plain,
And Tyre's proud piers lie shattered in the
main ;
Like these, thy strength may sink, in ruin
hurled,
And Britain fall, the bulwark of the world.
But let me cease, and dread Cassandra's fate,
With warning ever scoffed at, till too late ;
To themes less lofty still my lay confine,
And urge thy bards to gain a name like thine.[11]

Then, hapless Britain! be thy rulers blest,
The senate's oracles, the people's jest!
Still hear thy motley orators dispense
The flowers of rhetoric, though not of sense,
While Canning's colleagues hate him for his wit,

transported a considerable body of Vandals."—
Gibbons' Decline and Fall, vol. ii. p. 83. There is
no reason to doubt the truth of this assertion ; the
breed is still in high perfection.
[8] This gentleman's name requires no praise: the
man who in translation displays unquestionable ge-
nius may be well expected to excel in original com-
position, of which it is to be hoped we shall soon
see a splendid specimen. — [Besides a translation
of Juvenal, Mr. Hodgson published " Lady Jane.
Grey," " Sir Edgar," and " The Friends," a poem
in four books. He also translated, in conjunction
with Dr. Butler, Lucien Bonaparte's unreadable
epic of " Charlemagne."]
[9] Hewson Clarke, *Esq.,* as it is written.
[10] The "Aboriginal Britons," an excellent poem by
Richards. [The Rev. George Richards, D. D., au-
thor of " Songs of the Aboriginal Bards of Britain,"
" Modern France," two volumes of Miscellaneous
Poems, and Bampton Lectures " On the Divine Ori-
gin of Prophecy."]
[11] [With this verse the Satire originally ended.]

And old dame Portland[1] fills the place of Pitt.
Yet once again, adieu! ere this the rail
That wafts me hence is shivering in the gale;
And Afric's coast and Calpe's adverse height,
And Stamboul's minarets must greet my sight:
Thence shall I stray through beauty's native
   clime,[2]
Where Kaff[3] is clad in rocks, and crowned
   with snows sublime.
But should I back return, no tempting press[4]
Shall drag my journal from the desk's recess:
Let coxcombs, printing as they come from far,
Snatch his own wreath of ridicule from Carr;[5]
Let Aberdeen and Elgin[6] still pursue
The shade of fame through regions of virtù;
Waste useless thousands on their Phidian
   freaks,
Misshapen monuments and maimed antiques;
And make their grand saloons a general mart
For all the mutilated blocks of art.
Of Dardan tours let dilettanti tell,
I leave topography to rapid[7] Gell;[8]

[1] A friend of mine being asked, why his Grace
of Portland was likened to an old woman? replied,
" he supposed it was because he was past bearing."
— His Grace is now gathered to his grandmothers,
where he sleeps as sound as ever: but even his
sleep was better than his colleagues' waking. 1811.

[2] Georgia.   [3] Mount Caucasus.

[4] [These four lines originally stood, —
" But should I back return, no lettered sage
  Shall drag my common-place book on the stage:
  Let vain Valentia* rival luckless Carr,†
  And equal him whose work he sought to mar."]

[5] [In a letter written from Gibraltar to his friend
Hodgson, Byron says, — " I have seen Sir John
Carr at Seville and Cadiz, and, like Swift's barber,
have been down on my knees to beg he would not
put me into black and white."]

[6] Lord Elgin would fain persuade us that all the
figures, with and without noses, in his stoneshop are
the work of Phidias! " Credat Judæus!"

[7] [The original epithet was " classic." Byron
altered it in the fifth edition, and added this note —
" ' Rapid,' indeed! He topographized and typo-
graphized King Priam's dominions in three days!
I called him ' classic' before I saw the Troad, but
since have learned better than to tack to his name
what don't belong to it."]

[8] Mr. Gell's Topography of Troy and Ithaca can-

* Lord Valentia (whose tremendous travels are
forthcoming with due decorations, graphical, topo-
graphical, typographical) deposed, on Sir John
Carr's unlucky suit, that Mr. Dubois's satire pre-
vented his purchase of the " Stranger in Ireland."
— Oh, fie, my lord! has your lordship no more feel-
ing for a fellow-tourist? — but " two of a trade,"
they say, etc.
† [From the many tours he made, Sir John was
called " The Jaunting Car." Edward Dubois hav-
ing severely lashed him in a publication, called
" My Pocket Book; or Hints for a Ryght Merrie
and Conceited Tour," Sir John brought an action
of damages against the publisher; but as the work
contained only what the court deemed legitimate
criticism, the knight was nonsuited.]

And, quite content, no more shall interpose
To stun the public ear — at least with prose.[9]

Thus far I've held my undisturbed career,
Prepared for rancor, steeled 'gainst selfish fear:
This thing of rhyme I ne'er disdained to own —
Though not obtrusive, yet not quite unknown:
My voice was heard again, though not so loud,
My page, though nameless, never disavowed;
And now at once I tear the veil away: —
Cheer on the pack! the quarry stands at bay,
Unscared by all the din of Melbourne house,[10]
By Lambe's resentment, or by Holland's
   spouse,
By Jeffrey's harmless pistol, Hallam's rage,
Edina's brawny sons and brimstone page.
Our men in buckram shall have blows enough,
And feel they too are " penetrable stuff: "
And though I hope not hence unscathed to go,
Who conquers me shall find a stubborn foe.
The time hath been, when no harsh sound
   would fall
From lips that now may seem inbued with gall;
Nor fools nor follies tempt me to despise
The meanest thing that crawled beneath my
   eyes:
But now, so callous grown, so changed since
   youth,
I've learned to think, and sternly speak the
   truth;
Learned to deride the critic's starch decree,
And break him on the wheel he meant for me;
To spurn the rod a scribbler bids me kiss,
Nor care if courts and crowds applaud or hiss:
Nay more, though all my rival rhymesters
   frown,
I too can hunt a poetaster down;
And, armed in proof, the gauntlet cast at once
To Scotch marauder, and to southern dunce.
Thus much I've dared; if my incondite lay
Hath wronged these righteous times, let others
   say:

not fail to insure the approbation of every man pos-
sessed of classical taste, as well for the information
Mr. Gell conveys to the mind of the reader, as for the
ability and research the respective works display. —
[" Since seeing the plain of Troy, my opinions are
somewhat changed as to the above note. Gell's
survey was hasty and superficial." — *Byron*, 1816.
Shortly after his return from Greece, in 1811, Byron
wrote a critique on Sir William Gell's works for
the Monthly Review.]
[9] [Byron set out on his travels with the determi-
nation to keep no journal. In a letter to his friend
Henry Drury, when on the point of sailing, he
pleasantly says, — " Hobhouse has made woundy
preparations for a book on his return : — one hun-
dred pens, two gallons of japan ink, and several
volumes of best blank, is no bad provision for a dis-
cerning public. I have laid down my pen, but have
promised to contribute a chapter on the state of
morals, etc. etc."]
[10] [" Singular enough, and din enough, God
knows." — *Byron*, 1816.]

This, let the world, which knows not how to spare,
Yet rarely blames unjustly, now declare.[1]

1 [" The greater part of this satire I most sincerely wish had never been written — not only on account of the injustice of much of the critical, and some of the personal part of it — but the tone and temper are such as I cannot approve." — *Byron*, July 14, 1816. *Diodati. Geneva.*]

POSTSCRIPT TO THE SECOND EDITION..

I HAVE been informed, since the present edition went to the press, that my trusty and well-beloved cousins, the Edinburgh Reviewers, are preparing a most vehement critique on my poor, gentle, *unresisting*, Muse, whom they have already so be-deviled with their ungodly ribaldry:

" Tantæne animis cœlestibus iræ ! "

I suppose I must say of Jeffrey, as Sir Andrew Aguecheek saith, " an I had known he was so cunning of fence, I had seen him damned ere I had fought him." What a pity it is that I shall be beyond the Bosphorus before the next number has passed the Tweed ! But I yet hope to light my pipe with it in Persia.

My northern friends have accused me, with justice, of personality towards their great literary anthropophagus, Jeffrey; but what else was to be done with him and his dirty pack, who feed by " lying and slandering," and slake their thirst by " evil speaking ? " I have adduced facts already well known, and of Jeffrey's mind I have stated my free opinion, nor has he thence sustained any injury; — what scavenger was ever soiled by being pelted with mud ? It may be said that I quit England because I have censured there " persons of honor and wit about town;" but I am coming back again, and their vengeance will keep hot till my return. Those who know me can testify that my motives for leaving England are very different from fears, literary or personal : those who do not, may one day be convinced. Since the publication of this thing, my name has not been concealed; I have been mostly in London, ready to answer for my transgressions, and in daily expectation of sundry cartels; but, alas! " the age of chivalry is over," or, in the vulgar tongue, there is no spirit now-a-days.

There is a youth ycleped Hewson Clarke (subaudi *esquire*), a sizer of Emanuel College, and, I believe, a denizen of Berwick-upon-Tweed, whom I have introduced in these pages to much better company than he has been accustomed to meet; he is, notwithstanding, a very sad dog, and for no reason that I can discover, except a personal quarrel with a bear, kept by me at Cambridge to sit for a fellowship, and whom the jealousy of his Trinity contemporaries prevented from success, has been abusing me, and, what is worse, the defenceless innocent above mentioned, in " The Satirist " for one year and some months. I am utterly unconscious of having given him any provocation; indeed, I am guiltless of having heard his name till coupled with " The Satirist." He has therefore no reason to complain, and I dare say that, like Sir Fretful Plagiary, he is rather *pleased* than otherwise. I have now mentioned all who have done me the honor to notice me and mine, that is, my bear and my book, except the editor of " The Satirist," who, it seems, is a gentleman — God wot! I wish he could impart a little of his gentility to his subordinate scribblers. I hear that Mr. Jerningham is about to take up the cudgels for his Mæcenas, Lord Carlisle. I hope not : he was one of the few, who, in the very short intercourse I had with him, treated me with kindness when a boy; and whatever he may say or do, " pour on, I will endure." I have nothing further to add, save a general note of thanksgiving to readers, purchasers, and publishers, and, in the words of Scott, I wish

" To all and each a fair good night,
And rosy dreams and slumbers light."

[The article referred to in the beginning of the above Postscript never appeared in the Edinburgh Review, and in the " Hints from Horace," Byron has triumphantly taunted Jeffrey with a silence which seemed to indicate that the critic was beaten from the field.]

HINTS FROM HORACE:

BEING AN ALLUSION IN ENGLISH VERSE TO THE EPISTLE "AD PISONES, DE ARTE POETICA," AND INTENDED AS A SEQUEL TO " ENGLISH BARDS AND SCOTCH REVIEWERS."

―――― " Ergo fungar vice cotis, acutum
Reddere quæ ferrum valet, exsors ipsa secandi."
HORACE'S *De Arte Poet.*

" Rhymes are difficult things — they are stubborn things, sir."
FIELDING'S *Amelia.*

[Byron wrote "Hints from Horace" at Athens, in 1811, and brought it home in the same desk with the first two cantos of Childe Harold. He professed to think it superior to Childe Harold and was with apparent difficulty persuaded by his friends to forego its publication. The favorable reception of Childe Harold by the public seems to have softened his feelings towards the critics, and as he soon became personally acquainted with some of the persons whom he had satirized in the " Hints," he did not insist upon its publication until 1820, when he wrote thus to Mr. Murray : — " Get from Mr. Hobhouse and send me a proof of my ' Hints from Horace :' it has now the *nonum prematur in annum* complete for its production. I have a notion that with some omissions of names and passages it will do; and I could put my late observations *for* Pope amongst the notes. As far as versification goes, it is good; and in looking back at what I wrote about that period, I am astonished to see how little I have trained on. I wrote better then than now; but that comes of my having fallen into the atrocious bad taste of the times." On hearing, however, that in Mr. Hobhouse's opinion the verses would require " a good deal of slashing " to suit the times, the notion of printing them was once more abandoned. They were first published in 1831, seven years after the author's death. The editor of Murray's edition remarks : — " No part of the poem is much above mediocrity, and not a little is below it. The versification, which Lord Byron singles out for praise, has no distinguishing excellence, and was surpassed by his later iambics in every metrical quality, — in majesty, in melody, in freedom, and in spirit. Authors are frequently as bad judges of their own works as men in general are, proverbially, in their own cause, and of all the literary hallucinations upon record there are none which exceed the mistaken preferences of Lord Byron. Shortly after the appearance of ' The Corsair,' he fancied that ' English Bards ' was still his masterpiece ; when all his greatest works had been produced, he contended that his translation from Pulci was his ' grand performance, — the best thing he ever did in his life ; ' and throughout the whole of his literary career he regarded these ' Hints from Horace ' with the fondness which parents are said to feel for their least favored offspring."]

ATHENS, Capuchin Convent,
March 12, 1811.

WHO would not laugh, if Lawrence, hired to grace
His costly canvas with each flattered face,
Abused his art, till Nature, with a blush,
Saw cits grow centaurs underneath his brush ?
Or, should some limner join, for show or sale,
A maid of honor to a mermaid's tail ?
Or low Dubost[1] — as once the world has seen —

Degrade God's creatures in his graphic spleen ?
Not all that forced politeness, which defends
Fools in their faults, could gag his grinning friends.

[1] In an English newspaper, which finds its way abroad wherever there are Englishmen, I read an account of this dirty dauber's caricature of Mr.

H―― as a "beast," and the consequent action, etc. The circumstance is, probably, too well known to require further comment. — [Thomas Hope, the author of " Anastasius," having offended Dubost, that painter revenged himself by a picture called " Beauty and the Beast," in which Mr. Hope and his lady were represented according to the well-known fairy story. The exhibition of it is said to have fetched thirty pounds in a day. A brother of Mrs. Hope thrust his sword through the canvas;

Believe me, Moschus,[1] like that picture seems
The book which, sillier than a sick man's
   dreams,
Displays a crowd of figures incomplete,
Poetic nightmares, without head or feet.

Poets and painters, as all artists[2] know,
May shoot a little with a lengthened bow;
We claim this mutual mercy for our task,
And grant in turn the pardon which we ask;
But make not monsters spring from gentle
   dams —
Birds breed not vipers, tigers nurse not lambs.

A labored, long exordium, sometimes tends
(Like patriot speeches) but to paltry ends;
And nonsense in a lofty note goes down,
As pertness passes with a legal gown:
Thus many a bard describes in pompous strain
The clear brook babbling through the goodly
   plain:
The groves of Granta, and her gothic halls,
King's Coll., Cam's stream, stained windows,
   and old walls;
Or, in adventurous numbers, neatly aims
To paint a rainbow, or — the river Thames.[3]

You sketch a tree, and so perhaps may
   shine —
But daub a shipwreck like an alehouse sign;
You plan a *vase* — it dwindles to a *pot*;
Then glide down Grub-street — fasting and
   forgot,
Laughed into Lethe by some quaint Review,
Whose wit is never troublesome till — true.[4]

In fine, to whatsoever you aspire,
Let it at least be simple and entire.

The greater portion of the rhyming tribe
(Give ear, my friend, for thou hast been a
   scribe)
Are led astray by some peculiar lure.
I labor to be brief — become obscure;
One falls while following elegance too fast;
Another soars, inflated with bombast;
Too low a third crawls on, afraid to fly,
He spins his subject to satiety;
Absurdly varying, he at last engraves
Fish in the woods, and boars beneath the
   waves!

Unless your care's exact, your judgment
   nice,
The flight from folly leads but into vice;

None are complete, all wanting in some part,
Like certain tailors, limited in art.
For galligaskins Slowshears is your man;
But coats must claim another artisan.[5]
Now this to me, I own, seems much the same
As Vulcan's feet to bear Apollo's frame: [6]
Or, with a fair complexion, to expose
Black eyes, black ringlets, but — a bottle nose!

Dear authors! suit your topics to your
   strength,
And ponder well your subject, and its length;
Nor lift your load, before you're quite aware
What weight your shoulders will, or will not,
   bear.
But lucid Order, and Wit's siren voice,
Await the poet, skilful in his choice;
With native eloquence he soars along,
Grace in his thoughts, and music in his song.

Let judgment teach him wisely to combine
With future parts the now omitted line:
This shall the author choose, or that reject,
Precise in style, and cautious to select;
Nor slight applause will candid pens afford
To him who furnishes a wanting word.
Then fear not if 'tis needful to produce
Some term unknown, or obsolete in use,
(As Pitt [7] has furnished us a word or two,
Which lexicographers declined to do;)
So you indeed, with care, — (but be content
To take this license rarely) — may invent.
New words find credit in these latter days
If neatly grafted on a Gallic phrase.
What Chaucer, Spenser did, we scarce refuse
To Dryden's or to Pope's maturer muse.
If you can add a little, say why not,
As well as William Pitt, and Walter Scott?
Since they, by force of rhyme and force of
   lungs,
Enriched our island's ill-united tongues;
'Tis then — and shall be — lawful to present
Reform in writing, as in parliament.

As forests shed their foliage by degrees,
So fade expressions which in season please;
And we and ours, alas! are due to fate,
And works and words but dwindle to a date.
Though as a monarch nods, and commerce
   calls,
Impetuous rivers stagnate in canals;

---

and M. Dubost had the consolation to get five
pounds damages. The affair made much noise at
the time.]
  [1] ["Moschus." — In the original MS., "Hob-
house."]
  [2] ["All artists." — Originally, "We scribblers."]
  [3] "Where pure description held the place of
sense." — *Pope.*
  [4] [This is pointed, and felicitously expressed. —
More.]

  [5] Mere common mortals were commonly content
with one tailor and with one bill, but the more par-
ticular gentlemen found it impossible to confide
their lower garments to the makers of their body
clothes. I speak of the beginning of 1809: what
reform may have since taken place I neither know,
nor desire to know.
  [6] [MS. "As one leg perfect, and the other
lame."]
  [7] Mr. Pitt was liberal in his additions to our par-
liamentary tongue: as may be seen in many publi-
cations, particularly the Edinburgh Review.

Though swamps subdued, and marshes
  drained, sustain
The heavy ploughshare and the yellow grain,
And rising ports along the busy shore
Protect the vessel from old Ocean's roar,
All, all must perish; but, surviving last,
The love of letters half preserves the past.
True, some decay, yet not a few revive; [1]
Though those shall sink, which now appear
  to thrive,
As custom arbitrates, whose shifting sway
Our life and language must alike obey.

The immortal wars which gods and angels
  wage,
Are they not shown in Milton's sacred page?
His strain will teach what numbers best be-
  long
To themes celestial told in epic song.

The slow, sad stanza will correctly paint
The lover's anguish, or the friend's complaint.
But which deserves the laurel — rhyme or
  blank?
Which holds on Helicon the higher rank?
Let squabbling critics by themselves dispute
This point, as puzzling as a Chancery suit.

Satiric rhyme first sprang from selfish
  spleen.
You doubt — see Dryden, Pope, St. Patrick's
  dean.[2]

Blank verse [3] is now, with one consent, allied
To Tragedy, and rarely quits her side.
Though mad Almanzor rhymed in Dryden's
  days,
No sing-song hero rants in modern plays;

While modest Comedy her verse foregoes
For jest and *pun* [4] in very middling prose.
Not that our Bens or Beaumonts show the
  worse,
Or lose one point, because they wrote in verse.
But so Thalia pleases to appear,
Poor virgin! damned some twenty times a
  year!

Whate'er the scene, let this advice have
  weight: —
Adapt your language to your hero's state.
At times Melpomene forgets to groan,
And brisk Thalia takes a serious tone;
Nor unregarded will the act pass by
Where angry Townly [5] lifts his voice on high.
Again, our Shakspeare limits verse to kings,
When common prose will serve for common
  things;
And lively Hal resigns heroic ire,
To "hollowing Hotspur" [6] and the sceptred
  sire.

'Tis not enough, ye bards, with all your art,
To polish poems; — they must touch the heart:
Where'er the scene be laid, whate'er the song,
Still let it bear the hearer's soul along;
Command your audience or to smile or weep,
Whiche'er may please you — any thing but
  sleep.
The poet claims our tears; but, by his leave,
Before I shed them, let me see him grieve.

If banished Romeo feigned nor sigh nor tear,
Lulled by his languor, I should sleep or sneer.
Sad words, no doubt, become a serious face,
And men look angry in the proper place.
At double meanings folks seem wondrous sly,
And sentiment prescribes a pensive eye;
For nature formed at first the inward man,
And actors copy nature — when they can.
She bids the beating heart with rapture bound,
Raised to the stars, or levelled with the ground;
And for expression's aid, 'tis said, or sung,

---

[1] Old ballads, old plays, and old women's stories, are at present in as much request as old wine or new speeches. In fact, this is the millennium of black letter: thanks to our Hebers, Webers, and Scotts! — [There was a good deal of malice in thus putting *Weber*, a poor German hack, a mere aman-uensis of Sir Walter Scott, between the two other names.]

[2] "Mac Flecknoe," the "Dunciad," and all Swift's lampooning ballads. Whatever their other works may be, these originated in personal feelings, and angry retort on unworthy rivals; and though the ability of these satires elevates the poetical, their poignancy detracts from the personal character of the writers.

[3] [Like Dr. Johnson, Byron maintained the excellence of rhyme over blank verse in English poetry. "Blank verse," he says, in his long lost letter to the editor of Blackwood's Magazine, "unless in the drama, no one except Milton ever wrote who could rhyme. I am aware that Johnson has said, after some hesitation, that he could not 'prevail upon himself to wish that Milton had been a rhymer.' The opinions of that truly great man, whom, like Pope, it is the present fashion to decry, will ever be received by me with that deference which time will restore to him from all; but, with all humility, I am not persuaded that the 'Paradise Lost' would

not have been more nobly conveyed to posterity, not perhaps in heroic couplets, — although even they could sustain the subject, if well balanced, — but in the stanza of Spenser, or of Tasso, or in the terza rima of Dante, which the powers of Milton could easily have grafted on our language. The 'Seasons' of Thomson would have been better in rhyme, although still inferior to his 'Castle of Indolence;' and Mr. Southey's 'Joan of Arc' no worse."]

[4] With all the vulgar applause and critical abhorrence of *puns*, they have Aristotle on their side; who permits them to orators, and gives them consequence by a grave disquisition. ["Cicero also," says Addison, "has sprinkled several of his works with them; and, in his book on Oratory, quotes abundance of sayings as pieces of wit, which, upon examination, prove arrant puns."]

[5] [In Vanbrugh's comedy of the "Provoked Husband."]

[6] "And in his ear I'll hollow, Mortimer!" — *1 Henry IV.*

She gave our mind's interpreter — the tongue,
Who, worn with use, of late would fain dispense
(At least in theatres) with common sense;
O'erwhelm with sound the boxes, gallery, pit,
And raise a laugh with any thing — but wit.

To skilful writers it will much import,
Whence spring their scenes, from common
    life or court;
Whether they seek applause by smile or tear,
To draw a "Lying Valet," or a "Lear,"
A sage, or rakish youngster wild from school,
A wandering "Peregrine," or plain "John
    Bull;"
All persons please when nature's voice prevails,
Scottish or Irish, born in Wilts or Wales.

Or follow common fame, or forge a plot.
Who cares if mimic heroes lived or not ?
One precept serves to regulate the scene : —
Make it appear as if it *might* have *been.*

If some Drawcansir [1] you aspire to draw,
Present him raving, and above all law :
If female furies in your scheme are planned,
Macbeth's fierce dame is ready to your hand;
For tears and treachery, for good or evil,
Constance, King Richard, Hamlet, and the
    Devil!
But if a new design you dare essay,
And freely wander from the beaten way,
True to your characters, till all be past,
Preserve consistency from first to last.

'Tis hard to venture where our betters fail,
Or lend fresh interest to a twice-told tale;
And yet, perchance, 'tis wiser to prefer
A hackneyed plot, than choose a new, and err ;
Yet copy not too closely, but record,
More justly, thought for thought than word
    for word,
Nor trace your prototype through narrow ways,
But only follow where he merits praise.

For you, young bard! whom luckless fate
    may lead
To tremble on the nod of all who read,
Ere your first score of cantos time unrolls,
Beware — for God's sake, don't begin like
    Bowles! [2]

[1] [" *Johnson.* Pray, Mr. Bayes, who is that
Drawcansir?
    "*Bayes.* Why, Sir, a great hero, that frights
his mistress, snubs up kings, baffles armies, and
does what he will without regard to numbers, good
sense, or justice." — *Rehearsal.*]
[2] About two years ago a young man, named
Townsend, was announced by Mr. Cumberland [*]

[*] [Cumberland died in May, 1811, and had the
honor to be buried in Westminster Abbey, and to
be eulogized, while the company stood round the
grave, in the following manly style by the then
dean, Dr. Vincent, his schoolfellow, and through
life his friend. — "Good people! the person you

"Awake a louder and a loftier strain," —
And pray, what follows from his boiling
    brain? —
He sinks to Southey's level in a trice,
Whose epic mountains never fail in mice!
Not so of yore awoke your mighty sire,
The tempered warblings of his master-lyre;
Soft as the gentler breathing of the lute,
"Of man's first disobedience and the fruit"

(in a review † since deceased) as being engaged in
an epic poem to been titled "Armageddon." The
plan and specimen promise much; but I hope
neither to offend Mr. Townsend, nor his friends, by
recommending to his attention the lines of Horace
to which these rhymes allude. If Mr. Townsend
succeeds in his undertaking, as there is reason to
hope, how much will the world be indebted to Mr.
Cumberland for bringing him before the public!
But, till that eventful day arrives, it may be doubted
whether the premature display of his plan (sublime
as the ideas confessedly are) has not, — by raising
expectation too high, or diminishing curiosity, by
developing his argument, — rather incurred the
hazard of injuring Mr. Townsend's future pros-
pects. Mr. Cumberland (whose talents I shall not
depreciate by the humble tribute of my praise) and
Mr. Townsend must not suppose me actuated by
unworthy motives in this suggestion. I wish the
author all the success he can wish himself, and
shall be truly happy to see epic poetry weighed up
from the bathos where it lies sunken with Southey,
Cottle, Cowley (Mrs. or Abraham), Ogilvy, Wilkie,
Pye, and all the "dull of past and present days."
Even if he is not a *Milton,* he may be better than
Blackmore; if not a *Homer,* an *Antimachus.*
I should deem myself presumptuous, as a young
man, in offering advice, were it not addressed to one

see now deposited is Richard Cumberland, an au-
thor of no small merit: his writings were chiefly for
the stage, but of strict moral tendency: they were
not without faults, but they were not gross, abound-
ing with oaths and libidinous expressions, as, I am
shocked to observe, is the case of many of the pres-
ent day. He wrote as much as any one: few wrote
better; and his works will be held in the highest es-
timation, as long as the English language will be
understood. He considered the theatre a school
for moral improvement, and his remains are truly
worthy of mingling with the illustrious dead which
surround us. Read his prose subjects on divinity!
there you will find the true Christian spirit of a man
who trusted in our Lord and Saviour Jesus Christ.
May God forgive him his sins; and, at the resur-
rection of the just, receive him into everlasting
glory!"]
    † [The "London Review," set up in 1809, under
Mr. Cumberland's editorial care, did not outlive
many numbers. He spoke great things in the pro-
spectus, about the distinguishing feature of the jour-
nal, namely, its having the writer's name affixed to
the articles. This plan has succeeded pretty well
both in France and Germany, but has failed utterly
as often as it has been tried in England. It is need-
less, however, to go into any speculation on the
principle *here;* for the "London Review," whether
sent into the world with or without names, must
soon have died of the original disease of dulness.]

He speaks, but, as his subject swells along,
Earth, Heaven, and Hades echo with the song.[1]
Still to the midst of things he hastens on,
As if we witnessed all already done;
Leaves on his path whatever seems too mean
To raise the subject, or adorn the scene;
Gives, as each page improves upon the sight,
Not smoke from brightness, but from dark-
      ness — light;
And truth and fiction with such art compounds,
We know not where to fix their several bounds.
If you would please the public, deign to hear
What soothes the many-headed monster's ear;
If your heart triumph when the hands of all
Applaud in thunder at the curtain's fall,
Deserve those plaudits — study nature's page,
And sketch the striking traits of every age;
While varying man and varying years unfold
Life's little tale, so oft, so vainly told.
Observe his simple childhood's dawning days,
His pranks, his prate, his playmates, and his
      plays;
Till time at length the mannish tyro weans,
And prurient vice outstrips his tardy teens!

Behold him Freshman! forced no more to
      groan
O'er Virgil's [2] devilish verses and — his own;
Prayers are too tedious, lectures too abstruse,
He flies from Tavell's frown to "Fordham's
      Mews;"

still younger. Mr. Townsend has the greatest dif-
ficulties to encounter: but in conquering them he
will find employment; in having conquered them,
his reward. I know too well "the scribbler's scoff,
the critic's contumely;" and I am afraid time will
teach Mr. Townsend to know them better. Those
who succeed, and those who do not, must bear this
alike, and it is hard to say which have most of it.
I trust that Mr. Townsend's share will be from
envy; — he will soon know mankind well enough
not to attribute this expression to malice. — [This
note Byron says was written at Athens before he
had heard of the death of Cumberland, who died in
May, 1811. On his return to England Byron wrote
to a friend : — "There is a sucking epic poet at
Granta, a Mr. Townsend, protégé of the late Cum-
berland. Did you ever hear of him and his 'Arma-
geddon'? I think his plan (the man I don't know)
borders on the sublime; though, perhaps, the anti-
cipation of the 'Last Day' is a little too daring: at
least, it looks like telling the Almighty what he is
to do; and might remind an ill-natured person of
the line —

' And fools rush in where angels fear to tread.' "

Mr. Townsend, in 1815, was induced to publish
eight of the twelve books of which his poem was to
consist. Their reception realized Byron's ominous
predictions.]

[1] [There is more of poetry in these verses upon
Milton than in any other passage throughout the
paraphrase. — *Moore.*]

[2] Harvey, the *circulator* of the *circulation* of
the blood, used to fling away Virgil in his ecstasy

(Unlucky Tavell! [3] doomed to daily cares
By pugilistic pupils, and by bears,) [4]
Fines, tutors, tasks, conventions threat in vain,
Before hounds, hunters, and Newmarket plain;
Rough with his elders, with his equals rash,
Civil to sharpers, prodigal of cash;
Constant to nought — save hazard and a whore,
Yet cursing both — for both have made him
      sore;
Unread (unless, since books beguile disease,
The p—x becomes his passage to degrees);
Fooled, pillaged, dunned, he wastes his term
      away,
And, unexpelled perhaps, retires M. A.;
Master of arts! as *hells* and *clubs* [5] proclaim,
Where scarce a blackleg bears a brighter
      name!

Launched into life, extinct his early fire,
He apes the selfish prudence of his sire;
Marries for money, chooses friends for rank,
Buys land, and shrewdly trusts not to the Bank;
Sits in the Senate; gets a son and heir;
Sends him to Harrow, for himself was there.
Mute, though he votes, unless when called to
      cheer,
His son's so sharp — he'll see the dog a peer!

Manhood declines — age palsies every limb;
He quits the scene — or else the scene quits
      him;
Scrapes wealth, o'er each departing penny
      grieves,
And avarice seizes all ambition leaves;
Counts cent per cent, and smiles, or vainly frets,
O'er hoards diminished by young Hopeful's
      debts;
Weighs well and wisely what to sell or buy,
Complete in all life's lessons — but to die;
Peevish and spiteful, doting, hard to please,

of admiration, and say, "the book had a devil."
Now, such a character as I am copying would prob-
ably fling it away also, but rather wish that the
devil had the book; not from any dislike to the
poet, but a well-founded horror of hexameters. In-
deed, the public school penance of "Long and
Short" is enough to beget an antipathy to poetry
for the residue of a man's life, and, perhaps, so far
may be an advantage.

[3] "Infandum, regina, jubes renovare dolorem."
I dare say Mr. Tavell (to whom I mean no affront)
will understand me; and it is no matter whether
any one else does or no. — To the above events,
"quæque ipse miserrima vidi, et quorum pars mag-
na fui," all *times* and *terms* bear testimony.

[4] [The Rev. G. F. Tavell was a fellow and tutor
of Trinity College, Cambridge, during Byron's res-
idence, and owed this notice to the zeal with which
he had protested against his juvenile vagaries.

[5] "Hell," a gaming-house so called, where you
risk little, and are cheated a good deal. "Club," a
pleasant purgatory where you lose more, and are
not supposed to be cheated at all.

Commending every time, save times like these;
Crazed, querulous, forsaken, half forgot,
Expires unwept — is buried — let him rot!

But from the Drama let me not digress,
Nor spare my precepts, though they please
    you less.
Though woman weep, and hardest hearts are
    stirred
When what is done is rather seen than heard,
Yet many deeds preserved in history's page
Are better told than acted on the stage;
The ear sustains what shocks the timid eye,
And horror thus subsides to sympathy.
True Briton all beside, I here am French·—
Bloodshed 'tis surely better to retrench;
The gladiatorial gore we teach to flow
In tragic scenes disgusts, though but in show;
We hate the carnage while we see the trick,
And find small sympathy in being sick.
Not on the stage the regicide Macbeth
Appals an audience with a monarch's death;
To gaze when sable Hubert threats to sear
Young Arthur's eyes, can *ours* or *nature* bear?
A haltered heroine [1] Johnson sought to slay —
We saved Irene, but half damned the play,
And (Heaven be praised!) our tolerating times
Stint metamorphoses to pantomimes;
And Lewis' self, with all his sprites, would
    quake
To change Earl Osmond's negro to a snake!
Because, in scenes exciting joy or grief,
We loathe the action which exceeds belief:
And yet, God knows! what may not authors do,
Whose postscripts prate of dyeing "heroines
    blue?" [2]

Above all things, *Dan* Poet, if you can,
Eke out your acts, I pray, with mortal man;
Nor call a ghost, unless some cursed scrape
Must open ten trap-doors for your escape.
Of all the monstrous things I'd fain forbid,
I loathe an opera worse than Dennis did; [3]
Where good and evil persons, right or wrong,
Rage, love, and aught but moralize, in song.

Hail, last memorial of our foreign friends
Which Gaul allows, and still Hesperia lends!
Napoleon's edicts no embargo lay
On whores, spies, singers wisely shipped away.
Our giant capital, whose squares are spread
Where rustics earned, and now may beg, their
    bread,
In all iniquity is grown so nice,
It scorns amusements which are not of price:
Hence the pert shopkeeper, whose throbbing
    ear
Aches with orchestras which he pays to hear,
Whom shame, not sympathy, forbids to snore,
His anguish doubling by his own "encore;"
Squeezed in "Fop's Alley," jostled by the
    beaux,
Teased with his hat, and trembling for his toes;
Scarce wrestles through the night, nor tastes
    of ease
Till the dropped curtain gives a glad release:
Why this, and more, he suffers — can ye
    guess? —
Because it costs him dear, and makes him
    dress!

So prosper eunuchs from Etruscan schools;
Give us but fiddlers, and they're sure of fools!
Ere scenes were played by many a reverend
    clerk [4]
(What harm, if David danced before the
    ark?) [5]
In Christmas revels, simple country folks
Were pleased with morrice-mumm'ry and
    coarse jokes.
Improving years, with things no longer known,
Produced blithe Punch and merry Madame
    Joan,
Who still frisk on with feats so lewdly low,
'Tis strange Benvolio [6] suffers such a show; [7]
Suppressing peer! to whom each vice gives
    place,
Oaths, boxing, begging, — all, save rout and
    race.

---

[1] "Irene had to speak two lines with the bow-string round her neck; but the audience cried out 'Murder!' and she was obliged to go off the stage alive." — *Boswell's Johnson*. [These two lines were afterwards struck out, and Irene was carried off, to be put to death behind the scenes.]

[2] In the postscript to the "Castle Sceptre," Mr. Lewis tells us, that though blacks were unknown in England at the period of his action, yet he has made the anachronism to set off the scene: and if he could have produced the effect "by making his heroine blue," — I quote him — "blue he would have made her!"

[3] [In 1706, Dennis, the critic, wrote an "Essay on the Operas after the Italian manner, which are about to be established on the English Stage;" to show that they were more immoral than the most licentious play.]

[4] "The first theatrical representations, entitled 'Mysteries and Moralities,' were generally enacted at Christmas, by monks (as the only persons who could read), and latterly by the clergy and students of the universities. The dramatis personæ were usually Adam, Pater Cœlestis, Faith, Vice," etc. etc. — See *Warton's History of English Poetry*.

[5] Here follows, in the original MS. —
"Who did what Vestris — yet, at least, cannot,
And cut his kingly capers sans culotte."

[6] Benvolio does not bet; but every man who maintains race-horses is a promoter of all the con comitant evils of the turf. Avoiding to bet is a lit tle pharisaical. Is it an exculpation? I think not I never yet heard a bawd ;raised for chastity because *she herself* did not commit fornication.

[7] [For Benvolio the original MS. had "Earl Grosvenor;" and for the next couplet —
"Suppressing peer! to whom each vice gives place,
Save gambling — for his Lordship loves a race."]

Farce followed Comedy, and reached her
  prime
In ever-laughing Foote's fantastic time:
Mad wag! who pardoned none, nor spared
  the best,
And turned some very serious things to jest.
Nor church nor state escaped his public sneers,
Arms nor the gown, priests, lawyers, volun-
  teers:
"Alas, poor Yorick!" now for ever mute!
Whoever loves a laugh must sigh for Foote.

We smile, perforce, when histrionic scenes
Ape the swoln dialogue of kings and queens,
When "Chrononhotonthologos must die,"
And Arthur struts in mimic majesty.

Moschus! with whom once more I hope to
  sit
And smile at folly, if we can't at wit;
Yes, friend! for thee I'll quit my cynic cell,
And bear Swift's motto, "Vive la bagatelle!"
Which charmed our days in each Ægean
  clime,
As oft at home, with revelry and rhyme.[1]
Then may Euphrosyne, who sped the past,
Soothe thy life's scenes, nor leave thee in the
  last;
But find in thine, like pagan Plato's bed,[2]
Some merry manuscript of mimes, when dead.

Now to the Drama let us bend our eyes,
Where fettered by whig Walpole low she lies;[3]
Corruption foiled her, for she feared her
  glance;
Decorum left her for an opera dance!
Yet Chesterfield,[4] whose polished pen inveighs
'Gainst laughter, fought for freedom to our
  plays;

Unchecked by megrims of patrician brains,
And damning dulness of lord chamberlains.
Repeal that act! again let Humor roam
Wild o'er the stage — we've time for tears at
  home;
Let "Archer" plant the horns on "Sullen's"
  brows,
And "Estifania" gull her "Copper"[5] spouse;
The moral's scant — but that may be excused,
Men go not to be lectured, but amused.
He whom our plays dispose to good or ill
Must wear a head in want of Willis' skill;[6]
Ay, but Macheath's example — psha! — no
  more!
It formed no thieves — the thief was formed
  before;
And, spite of puritans and Collier's curse,[7]
Plays make mankind no better, and no worse.
Then spare our stage, ye methodistic men!
Nor burn damned Drury if it rise again.
But why to brain-scorched bigots thus appeal
Can heavenly mercy dwell with earthly zeal'
For times of fire and fagot let them hope!
Times dear alike to puritan or pope.
As pious Calvin saw Servetus blaze,
So would new sects on newer victims gaze.
E'en now the songs of Solyma begin;
Faith cants, perplexed apologist of sin!
While the Lord's servant chastens whom he
  loves,
And Simeon[8] kicks, where Baxter only
  "shoves."[9]

Whom nature guides, so writes, that every
  dunce,
Enraptured, thinks to do the same at once;
But after inky thumbs and bitten nails,
And twenty scattered quires, the coxcomb fails.

Let Pastoral be dumb; for who can hope
To match the youthful eclogues of our Pope;
Yet his and Phillips' faults, of different kind,
For art too rude, for nature too refined,
Instruct how hard the medium 'tis to hit
'Twixt too much polish and too coarse a wit.

A vulgar scribbler, certes, stands disgraced
In this nice age, when all aspire to taste;

---

[1] [In dedicating the fourth canto of "Childe Harold" to his fellow traveller, Hobhouse, Byron describes him as "one to whom he was indebted for the social advantages of an enlightened friendship; one whom he had long known and accompanied far, whom he had found wakeful over his sickness and kind in his sorrow, glad in his prosperity and firm in his adversity, true in counsel and trusty in peril;" — while Hobhouse, in describing a short tour to Negroponte, in which his noble friend was unable to accompany him, regrets the absence of a companion, "who, to quickness of observation and ingenuity of remark, united that gay good humor which keeps alive the attention under the pressure of fatigue, and softens the aspect of every difficulty and danger."]

[2] Under Plato's pillow a volume of the *Mimes* of Sophron was found the day he died. — *Vide* Barthélémi, De Pauw, or Diogenes Laërtius, if agreeable. De Pauw calls it a jest-book. Cumberland, in his Observer, terms it moral, like the sayings of Publius Syrus.

[3] The English Act of Parliament regulating and restraining theatres was introduced in 1737 by Sir Robert Walpole.

[4] His speech on the Licensing Act is one of his most eloquent efforts.

[5] Michael Perez, the "Copper Captain," in "Rule a Wife and have a Wife."

[6] [Willis was the physician who had charge of George III. in the earlier stages of his insanity.]

[7] Jerry Collier's controversy with Congreve, etc. on the subject of the drama, is too well known to require further comment.

[8] Mr. Simeon is the very bully of beliefs, and castigator of "good works." He is ably supported by John Stickles, a laborer in the same vineyard: — but I say no more, for, according to Johnny in full congregation. "*No hopes for them as laughs.*" — [The Rev. Charles Simeon, — a zealous Calvinist, had several warm disputations with other divines.]

[9] "Baxter's Shove to heavy-a—d Christians" — the veritable title of a book once in good repute, and likely enough to be so again.

The dirty language, and the noisome jest,
Which pleased in Swift of yore, we now
　　detest;
Proscribed not only in the world polite,
But even too nasty for a city knight!

　　Peace to Swift's faults! his wit hath made
　　　them pass,
Unmatched by all, save matchless Hudibras!
Whose author is perhaps the first we meet,
Who from our couplet lopped to final feet;
Nor less in merit than the longer line,
This measure moves a favorite of the Nine.
Though at first view eight feet may seem in vain
Formed, save in ode, to bear a serious strain,
Yet Scott has shown our wondering isle of late
This measure shrinks not from a theme of
　　weight,
And, varied skilfully, surpasses far
Heroic rhyme, but most in love and war,
Whose fluctuations, tender or sublime,
Are curbed too much by long-recurring rhyme.

　　But many a skilful judge abhors to see,
What few admire — irregularity.
This some vouchsafe to pardon; but 'tis hard
When such a word contents a British bard.

　　And must the bard his glowing thoughts
　　　confine,
Lest censure hover o'er some faulty line ?
Remove whate'er a critic may suspect,
To gain the paltry suffrage of "*correct?*"
Or prune the spirit of each daring phrase,
To fly from error, not to merit praise ?

　　Ye, who seek finished models, never cease,
By day and night, to read the works of Greece.
But our good fathers never bent their brains
To heathen Greek, content with native strains.
The few who read a page, or used a pen,
Were satisfied with Chaucer and old Ben;
The jokes and numbers suited to their taste
Were quaint and careless, any thing but
　　chaste;
Yet whether right or wrong the ancient rules,
It will not do to call our fathers fools!
Though you and I, who eruditely know
To separate the elegant and low,
Can also, when a hobbling line appears,
Detect with fingers, in default of ears.

　　In sooth I do not know, or greatly care
To learn, who our first English strollers were;
Or if, till roofs received the vagrant art,
Our Muse, like that of Thespis, kept a cart;
But this is certain, since our Shakspeare's days,
There's pomp enough, if little else in plays;
Nor will Melpomene ascend her throne
Without high heels, white plume, and Bristol
　　stone.

　　Old comedies still meet with much applause,
Though too licentious for dramatic laws:

At least, we moderns, wisely, 'tis confest,
Curtail, or silence, the lascivious jest.

　　Whate'er their follies, and their faults be-
　　　side,
Our enterprising bards pass nought untried;
Nor do they merit slight applause who choose
An English subject for an English muse,
And leave to minds which never dare invent
French flippancy and German sentiment.
Where is that living language which could
　　claim
Poetic more, as philosophic, fame,
If all our bards, more patient of delay,
Would stop, like Pope,[1] to polish by the way?

　　Lords of the quill, whose critical assaults
Overthrow whole quartos with their quires of
　　faults,
Who soon detect, and mark where'er we fail,
And prove our marble with too nice a nail!
Democritus himself was not so bad;
He only *thought*, but *you* would make, us mad!

　　But truth to say, most rhymers rarely guard
Against that ridicule they deem so hard;
In person negligent, they wear, from sloth,
Beards of a week, and nails of annual growth;
Reside in garrets, fly from those they hate,
And walk in alleys, rather than the street.

　　With little rhyme, less reason, if you please,
The name of poet may be got with ease,
So that not tuns of helleboric juice
Shall ever turn your head to any use;
Write but like Wordsworth, live beside a
　　Lake,[2]

---

[1] [" They support Pope, I see, in the Quarterly,"
—wrote Byron in 1820, from Ravenna—" it is a
sin, and a shame, and a *damnation*, that Pope!!
should require it: but he does. Those miserable
mountebanks of the day, the poets, disgrace them-
selves, and deny God, in running down Pope, the
most faultless of poets." Again, in 1821:—"Nei-
ther time, nor distance, nor grief, nor age, can ever
diminish my veneration for him who is the great
moral poet of all times, of all climes, of all feelings,
and of all stages of existence. The delight of my
boyhood, the study of my manhood, perhaps (if
allowed to me to attain it) he may be the conso-
lation of my age. His poetry is the book of life.
Without canting, and yet without neglecting relig-
ion, he has assembled all that a good and great man
can gather together of moral wisdom clothed in con-
summate beauty. Sir William Temple observes,
' that of all the members of mankind that live within
the compass of a thousand years, for one man that
is born capable of making a *great poet*, there may
be a *thousand* born capable of making as great
generals and ministers of state as any in story.'
Here is a statesman's opinion of poetry; it is hon-
orable to him and to the art. Such a ' poet of a
thousand years' was Pope. A thousand years will
roll away before such another can be hoped for in
our literature. But it can *want* them: he is him-
self a literature."]

[2] [" That this is the age of the decline of English

And keep your bushy locks a year from Blake;[1]
Then print your book, once more return to town,
And boys shall hunt your bardship up and down.

Am I not wise, if such some poets' plight,
To purge in spring — like Bayes[2] — before I write?
If this precaution softened not my bile,
I know no scribbler with a madder style;
But since (perhaps my feelings are too nice)
I cannot purchase fame at such a price,
I'll labor gratis as a grinder's wheel,
And, blunt myself, give edge to others' steel,
Nor write at all, unless to teach the art
To those rehearsing for the poet's part;

poetry, will be doubted by few who have calmly considered the subject. That there are men of genius among the present poets, makes little against the fact; because it has been well said, that, ' next to him who forms the taste of his country, the greatest genius is he who corrupts it.' No one has ever denied genius to Marini, who corrupted, not merely the taste of Italy, but that of all Europe, for nearly a century. The great cause of the present deplorable state of English poetry is to be attributed to that absurd and systematic depreciation of Pope, in which, for the last few years, there has been a kind of epidemic concurrence. The Lakers and their school, and everybody else with their school, and even Moore without a school, and dilettanti lecturers at institutions, and elderly gentlemen who translate and imitate, and young ladies who listen and repeat, and baronets who draw indifferent frontispieces for bad poets, and noblemen who let them dine with them in the country, the small body of the wits and the great body of the blues, have latterly united in a depreciation, of which their forefathers would have been as much ashamed as their children will be. In the mean time what have we got instead? The Lake School, which began with an epic poem ' written in six weeks,' (so ' Joan of Arc' proclaimed herself,) and finished with a ballad composed in twenty years, as ' Peter Bell's ' creator takes care to inform the few who will inquire. What have we got instead? A deluge of flimsy and unintelligible romances, imitated from Scott and myself, who have both made the best of our bad materials and erroneous system. What have we got instead? Madoc, which is neither an epic nor any thing else, Thalaba, Kehama, Gebir, and such gibberish, written in all metres, and in no language." — *Byron's Letters*, 1819.]

[1] As famous a tonsor as Licinus himself, and better paid, and may, like him, be one day a senator, having a better qualification than one half of the heads he crops, namely, — independence.

[2] ["*Bayes.* If I am to write familiar things, as sonnets to Armida, and the like, I make use of stewed prunes only; but when I have a grand design in hand, I ever take physic and let blood: for when you have pure swiftness of thought, and fiery flights of fancy, you must have a care of the pensive part. In fine, you must purge." — *The Rehearsal.*]

From Horace show the pleasing paths of song,
And from my own example — what is wrong.

Though modern practice sometimes differs quite,
'Tis just as well to think before you write;
Let every book that suits your theme be read,
So shall you trace it to the fountain-head.

He who has learned the duty which he owes
To friends and country, and to pardon foes;
Who models his deportment as may best
Accord with brother, sire, or stranger guest;
Who takes our laws and worship as they are,
Nor roars reform for senate, church, and bar;
In practice, rather than loud precept, wise,
Bids not his tongue, but heart philosophize:
Such is the man the poet should rehearse,
As joint exemplar of his life and verse.

Sometimes a sprightly wit, and tale well told,
Without much grace, or weight, or art, will hold
A longer empire o'er the public mind
Than sounding trifles, empty, though refined.

Unhappy Greece! thy sons of ancient days
The muse may celebrate with perfect praise,
Whose generous children narrowed not their hearts
With commerce, given alone to arms and arts.
Our boys (save those whom public schools compel
To "long and short " before they're taught to spell)
From frugal fathers soon imbibe by rote,
" A penny saved, my lad, 's a penny got."
Babe of a city birth! from sixpence take
The third, how much will the remainder make? —
" A groat." — "Ah, bravo! Dick hath done the sum!
He'll swell my fifty thousand to a plum."

They whose young souls receive this rust betimes,
'Tis clear, are fit for any thing but rhymes;
And Locke will tell you, that the father's right
Who hides all verses from his children's sight;
For poets (says this sage,[3] and many more,)
Make sad mechanics with their lyric lore;
And Delphi now, however rich of old

[3] I have not the original by me, but the Italian translation runs as follows: — " E una cosa a mio credere molto stravagante, che un padre des;der;, o permetta, che suo figliuolo, coltivi e perfezioni questo talento." A little further on: " Si trovano di rado nel Parnaso le miniere d' oro e d' argento." — *Educazione dei Fanciulli del Signor Locke.* [" If the child have a poetic vein, it is to me the strangest thing in the world, that the father should desire or suffer it to be cherished or improved." — " It is very seldom seen, that any one discovers mines of gold or silver on Parnassus."]

Discovers little silver, and less gold,
Because Parnassus, though a mount divine,
Is poor as Irus,[1] or an Irish mine.[2]

Two objects always should the poet move,
Or one or both, — to please or to improve.
Whate'er you teach, be brief, if you design
For our remembrance your didactic line;
Redundance places memory on the rack,
For brains may be o'erloaded, like the back.

Fiction does best when taught to look like truth,
And fairy fables bubble none but youth:
Expect no credit for too wondrous tales,
Since Jonas only springs alive from whales!

Young men with aught but elegance dispense;
Maturer years require a little sense.
To end at once ; — that bard for all is fit
Who mingles well instruction with his wit;
For him reviews shall smile, for him o'erflow
The patronage of Paternoster-row;
His book, with Longman's liberal aid, shall pass
(Who ne'er despises books that bring him brass);
Through three long weeks the taste of London lead,
And cross St. George's Channel and the Tweed.

But every thing has faults, nor is't unknown
That harps and fiddles often lose their tone,
And wayward voices, at their owner's call,
With all his best endeavors, only squall;
Dogs blink their covey, flints withhold the spark,[3]
And double-barrels (damn them!) miss their mark.[4]

Where frequent beauties strike the reader's view
We must not quarrel for a blot or two;
But pardon equally to books or men,
The slips of human nature and the pen.

Yet if an author, spite of foe or friend,
Despises all advice too much to mend,
But ever twangs the same discordant string,
Give him no quarter, howsoe'er he sing.
Let Havard's[5] fate o'ertake him, who, for once,
Produced a play too dashing for a dunce:
At first none deemed it his ; but when his name
Announced the fact — what then ? — it lost its fame.
Though all deplore when Milton deigns to doze,
In a long work 'tis fair to steal repose.

As pictures, so shall poems be ; some stand
The critic eye, and please when near at hand ;
But others at a distance strike the sight ;
This seeks the shade, but that demands the light,
Nor dreads the connoisseur's fastidious view,
But, ten times scrutinized, is ten times new.

Parnassian pilgrims! ye whom chance, or choice,
Hath led to listen to the Muse's voice,
Receive this counsel, and be timely wise ;
Few reach the summit which before you lies.
Our church and state, our courts and camps concede
Reward to very moderate heads indeed!
In these plain common sense will travel far ;
All are not Erskines who mislead the bar :
But poesy between the best and worst
No medium knows ; you must be last or first ;
For middling poets' miserable volumes
Are damned alike by gods, and men, and columns.[6]

---

[1] "Iro pauperior: " this is the same beggar who boxed with Ulysses for a pound of kid's fry, which he lost, and half a dozen teeth besides. — See *Odyssey*, b. 18.

[2] The Irish gold mine of Wicklow, which yields just ore enough to swear by, or gild a bad guinea.

[3] [This couplet is amusingly characteristic of that mixture of fun and bitterness with which their author sometimes spoke in conversation; so much so, that those who knew him might almost fancy they hear him utter the words. — *Moore*.]

[4] As Mr. Pope took the liberty of damning Homer, to whom he was under great obligations—"*And Homer (damn him!) calls*" — it may be presumed that anybody or any thing may be damned in verse by poetical license; and, in case of accident, I beg leave to plead so illustrious a precedent.

[5] For the story of Billy Havard's tragedy, see "Davies's Life of Garrick." I believe it is "Regulus," or "Charles the First." The moment it was known to be his the theatre thinned, and the bookseller refused to give the customary sum for the copyright. — [Charles the First was the name of Havard's tragedy.]

[6] [Here, in the original MS., we find the following couplet and note: —
"Though what 'Gods, men, and columns' interdict,
The Devil and Jeffrey pardon — in a Pict.*

* "The Devil and Jeffrey are here placed antithetically to gods and men, such being their usual position, and their due one — according to the facetious saying, 'If God won't take you, the Devil must;' and I am sure no one durst object to his taking the poetry which, rejected by Horace, is accepted by Jeffrey. That these gentlemen are in some cases kinder, — the one to countrymen, and the other from his odd propensity to prefer evil to good, — than the 'gods, men, and columns' of Horace, may be seen by a reference to the review of Campbell's 'Gertrude of Wyoming;' and in No. 31 of the Edinburgh Review (given to me the other day by the captain of an English frigate off Salamis), there is a similar concession to the mediocrity of Jamie Graham's 'British Georgics.' It is fortunate

Again, my Jeffrey! — as that sound inspires,
How wakes my bosom to its wonted fires!
Fires, such as gentle Caledonians feel
When Southrons writhe upon their critic wheel,
Or mild Eclectics,[1] when some, worse than
    Turks,
Would rob poor Faith to decorate "good
    works."

[1] To 'the Eclectic or Christian Reviewers I have to return thanks for the fervor of that charity which, in 1809, induced them to express a hope that a thing then published by me might lead to certain consequences, which, although natural enough, surely came but rashly from reverend lips. I refer them to their own pages, where they congratulated themselves on the prospect of a tilt between Mr. Jeffrey and myself, from which some great good was to accrue, provided one or both were knocked on the head. Having survived two years and a half, those "Elegies" which they were kindly preparing to review, I have no peculiar gusto to give them "so joyful a trouble," except, indeed, "upon compulsion, Hal;" but if, as David says in the "Rivals," it should come to "bloody sword and gun fighting," we "won't run, will we, Sir Lucius?" I do not know what I had done to these Eclectic gentlemen: my works are their lawful perquisite, to be hewn in pieces like Agag, if it seem meet unto them: but for Campbell, that his fame neither depends on his last poem, nor the puff of the Edinburgh Review. The catalogues of our English are also less fastidious than the pillars of the Roman librarians.—A word more with the author of 'Gertrude of Wyoming.' At the end of a poem, and even of a couplet, we have generally 'that unmeaning thing we call a thought;' so Mr. Campbell concludes with a thought in such a manner as to fulfil the whole of Pope's prescription, and be as 'unmeaning' as the best of his brethren:

    'Because I may not *stain* with grief
        The death-song of an Indian chief.'

When I was in the fifth form, I carried to my master the translation of a chorus in Prometheus, wherein was a pestilent expression about 'staining a voice,' which met with no quarter. Little did I think that Mr. Campbell would have adopted my fifth form 'sublime'—at least in so conspicuous a situation. 'Sorrow' has been 'dry' (in proverbs), and 'wet,' (in sonnets), this many a day; and now it '*stains*,' and stains a sound, of all feasible things! To be sure, death-songs might have been stained with that same grief to very good purpose, if Outalissi had clapped down his stanzas on wholesome paper for the Edinburgh Evening Post, or any other given hyperborean gazette; or if the said Outalissi had been troubled with the slightest second sight of his own notes embodied on the last proof of an overcharged quarto: but as he is supposed to have been an improvisatore on this occasion, and probably to the last tune he ever chanted in this world, it would have done him no discredit to have made his exit with a mouthful of common sense. Talking of '*staining*,' as (Caleb Quotem says) 'puts me in mind' of a certain couplet, which Mr. Campbell will find in a writer for whom he, and his school, have no small contempt:—

    'E'en copious Dryden wanted, or forgot,
        The last and greatest art — the art to *blot*!'"]

Such are the genial feelings thou canst claim.
My falcon flies not at ignoble game.
Mightiest of all Dunedin's beasts of chase!
For thee my Pegasus would mend his pace.
Arise, my Jeffrey! or my inkless pen
Shall never blunt its edge on meaner men;
Till thee or thine mine evil eye discerns,
"Alas! I cannot strike at wretched kernes.' [2]
Inhuman Saxon! wilt thou then resign
A muse and heart by choice so wholly thine?
Dear, d—d contemner of my schoolboy songs,
Hast thou no vengeance for my manhood's
    wrongs
If unprovoked thou once could bid me bleed,
Hast thou no weapon for my daring deed?
What! not a word!— and am I then so low?
Wilt thou forbear, who never spared a foe?
Hast thou no wrath, or wish to give it vent?
No wit for nobles, dunces by descent?
No jest on "minors," quibbles on a name,[3]
Nor one facetious paragraph of blame?
Is it for this on Ilion I have stood,
And thought of Homer less than Holyrood?
On shore of Euxine or Ægean sea,
My hate, untravelled, fondly turned to thee.
Ah! let me cease; in vain my bosom burns,
From Corydon unkind Alexis turns: [4]
Thy rhymes are vain; thy Jeffrey then forego,
Nor woo that anger which he will not show.
What then? — Edina starves some lanker son,
To write an article thou canst not shun;

why they should be in such a hurry to kill off their author, I am ignorant. "The race is not always to the swift, nor the battle to the strong:" and now, as these Christians have "smote me on one cheek," I hold them up the other; and, in return for their good wishes, give them an opportunity of repeating them. Had any other set of men expressed such sentiments, I should have smiled, and left them to the "recording angel;" but from the pharisees of Christianity decency might be expected. I can assure these brethren, that, publican and sinner as I am, I would not have treated "mine enemy's dog thus." To show them the superiority of my brotherly love, if ever the Reverend Messrs. Simeon or Ramsden should be engaged in such a conflict as that in which they requested me to fall, I hope they may escape with being "winged" only, and that Heaviside may be at hand to extract the ball.—[The following is the passage in the Eclectic Review of which Byron speaks:—
"If the noble lord and the learned advocate have the courage requisite to sustain their mutual insults, we shall probably soon hear the explosions of another kind of *paper*-war after the fashion of the ever memorable duel which the latter is said to have fought, or seemed to fight, with 'Little Moore.' We confess there is sufficient provocation, if not in the critique, at least in the satire, to urge a 'man of honor' to defy his assailant to mortal combat. Of this we shall no doubt hear more in due time."]
[2] [*Macbeth*.]
[3] [See the critique of the Edinburgh Review on "Hours of Idleness," vol. i. p. 188.]
[4] Invenies alium, si te hic fastidit Alexin.

Some less fastidious Scotchman shall be
found,
As bold in Billingsgate, though less renowned.

As if at table some discordant dish
Should shock our optics, such as frogs for fish;
As oil in lieu of butter men decry,
And poppies please not in a modern pie;
If all such mixtures then be half a crime,
We must have excellence to relish rhyme.
Mere roast and boiled no epicure invites;
Thus poetry disgusts, or else delights.

Who shoot not flying rarely touch a gun:
Will he who swims not to the river run?
And men unpractised in exchanging knocks
Must go to Jackson[1] ere they dare to box.
Whate'er the weapon, cudgel, fist, or foil,
None reach expertness without years of toil;
But fifty dunces can, with perfect ease,
Tag twenty thousand couplets, when they
please.
Why not?—shall I, thus qualified to sit
For rotten boroughs, never show my wit?
Shall I, whose fathers with the quorum sate,
And lived in freedom on a fair estate;
Who left me heir, with stables, kennels, packs,
To *all* their income, and to—*twice* its tax;
Whose form and pedigree have scarce a fault,
Shall I, I say, suppress my attic salt?

Thus think "the mob of gentlemen;" but
you,
Besides all this, must have some genius too.
Be this your sober judgment, and a rule,
And print not piping hot from Southey's school,
Who (ere another Thalaba appears),
I trust, will spare us for at least nine years.
And hark 'ye, Southey![2] pray—but don't be
vexed—
Burn all your last three works—and half the
next.

[1] [Byron's taste for boxing brought him acquainted, at an early period, with this distinguished professor of the pugilistic art: for whom, through-out life, he continued to entertain a sincere regard. In a note to the eleventh canto of Don Juan, he calls him "his old friend, and corporeal pastor and master."]

[2] Mr. Southey has lately tied another canister to his tail in the "Curse of Kehama," maugre the neglect of Madoc, etc., and has in one instance had a wonderful effect. A literary friend of mine, walking out one lovely evening last summer, on the eleventh bridge of the Paddington canal, was alarmed by the cry of "one in jeopardy:" he rushed along, collected a body of Irish haymakers (supping on butter-milk in an adjacent paddock), procured three rakes, one eel-spear, and a landing-net, and at last (horresco referens) pulled out—his own publisher. The unfortunate man was gone for ever, and so was a large quarto wherewith he had taken the leap, which proved, on inquiry, to have been Mr. Southey's last work. Its "alacrity of sinking" was so great, that it has never since been

But why this vain advice? once published,
books
Can never be recalled—from pastry-cooks!
Though "Madoc," with "Pucelle,"[3] instead
of punk,
May travel back to Quito—on a trunk![4]

heard of; though some maintain that it is at this moment concealed at Alderman Birch's pastry premises, Cornhill. Be this as it may, the coroner's inquest brought in a verdict of "Felo de bibliopolà" against a "quarto unknown;" and circumstantial evidence being since strong against the "Curse of Kehama" (of which the above words are an exact description), it will be tried by its peers next session, in Grub Street.—Arthur, Alfred, Davideis, Richard·Cœur de Lion, Exodus, Exodia, Epigoniad, Calvary, Fall of Cambria, Siege of Acre, Don Roderick, and Tom Thumb the Great, are the names of the twelve jurors. The judges are Pye, Bowles, and the bellman of St. Sepulchre's. The same advocates, pro and con, will be employed as are now engaged in Sir F. Burdett's celebrated cause in the Scotch courts. The public anxiously await the result, and all *live* publishers will be subpœnaed as witnesses.—But Mr. Southey has published the "Curse of Kehama,"—an inviting title to quibblers. By the by, it is a good deal beneath Scott and Campbell, and not much above Southey, to allow the booby Ballantyne to entitle them, in the Edinburgh Annual Register (of which, by the by, Southey is editor) "the grand poetical triumvirate of the day." But, on second thoughts, it can be no great degree f praise to be the one-eyed leaders of the blind, though they might as well keep to themselves "Scott's thirty thousand copies sold," which must sadly discomfit poor Southey's unsaleables. Poor Southey, it should seem, is the "Lepidus" of this poetical triumvirate. I am only surprised to see him in such good company.

"Such things, we know, are neither rich nor rare,
But wonder how the devil *he* came there."

The trio are well defined in the sixth proposition of Euclid: "Because, in the triangles DBC, ACB, DB is equal to AC, and BC common to both; the two sides DB, BC, are equal to the two AC, CB, each to each, and the angle DBC is equal to the angle ACB: therefore, the base DC is equal to the base AB, and the triangle DBC (Mr. Southey) is equal to the triangle ACB, the *less* to the *gre·ter*, which is *absurd*," etc.—The editor of the Edinburgh Register will find the rest of the theorem hard by his stabling; he has only to cross the river; 'tis the first turnpike t'other side "Pons Asinorum."[*]

[3] Voltaire's "Pucelle" is not quite so immaculate as Mr. Southey's "Joan of Arc," and yet I am afraid the Frenchman has both more truth and poetry too on his side—(they rarely go together)—than our patriotic minstrel, whose first essay was in praise of a fanatical French strumpet, whose title of witch would be correct with the change of the first letter.

[4] Like Sir Bland Burgess's "Richard;" the tenth book of which I read at Malta, on a trunk of Eyres, 19 Cockspur Street. If this be doubted, I shall buy a portmanteau to quote from.

[*] This Latin has sorely puzzled the University of

Orpheus, we learn from Ovid and Lem-
priere,
Led all wild beasts but women by the ear;
And had he fiddled at the present hour,
We'd seen the lions waltzing in the Tower;
And old Amphion, such were minstrels then,
Had built St. Paul's without the aid of Wren.
Verse too was justice, and the bards of Greece
Did more than constables to keep the peace;
Abolished cuckoldom with much applause,
Called county meetings, and enforced the laws,
Cut down crown influence with reforming
scythes,
And served the church — without demanding
tithes;
And hence, throughout all Hellas and the East,
Each poet was a prophet and a priest,
Whose old-established board of joint controls
Included kingdoms in the cure of souls.

Next rose the martial Homer, Epic's prince,
And fighting's been in fashion ever since;
And old Tyrtæus, when the Spartans warred,
(A limping leader, but a lofty bard,) [1]
Though walled Ithome had resisted long,
Reduced the fortress by the force of song.

When oracles prevailed, in times of old,
In song alone Apollo's will was told.
Then if your verse is what all verse should be,
And gods were not ashamed on't, why should
we?

The Muse, like mortal females, may be wooed;
In turns she'll seem a Paphian, or a prude;
Fierce as a bride when first she feels affright,
Mild as the same upon the second night;
Wild as the wife of alderman or peer,
Now for his grace, and now a grenadier!
Her eyes beseem, her heart belies, her zone,
Ice in a crowd, and lava when alone.

If verse be studied with some show of art,
Kind Nature always will perform her part;
Though without genius, and a native vein
Of wit, we loathe an artificial strain —
Yet art and nature joined will win the prize,
Unless they act like us and our allies.

The youth who trains to ride, or run a race,
Must bear privations with unruffled face,
Be called to labor when he thinks to dine,
And, harder still, leave wenching and his wine.
Ladies who sing, at least who sing at sight,
Have followed music through her farthest
flight;

[1] [Byron had originally written —
" As lame as I am, but a better bard."]

Edinburgh. Ballantyne said it meant the " Bridge
of Berwick," but Southey claimed it as half English;
Scott swore it was the " Brig o' Sterling; " he had
just passed two King James's and a dozen Doug-
lasses over it. At last it was decided by Jeffrey,
that it meant nothing more nor less than the " coun-
ter of Archy Constable's shop."

But rhymers tell you neither more nor less,
" I've got a pretty poem for the press; "
And that's enough; then write and print so
fast; —
If Satan take the hindmost, who'd be last?
They storm the types, they publish, one and all,
They leap the counter, and they leave the stall
Provincial maidens, men of high command,
Yea, baronets have inked the bloody hand! [2]
Cash cannot quell them; Pollio[3] played this
prank,
(Then Phœbus first found credit in a bank!)
Not all the living only, but the dead,
Fool on, as fluent as an Orpheus' head; [4]
Damned all their days, they posthumously
thrive —
Dug up from dust, though buried when alive!
Reviews record this epidemic crime,
Those Books of Martyrs to the rage for rhyme.
Alas! woe worth the scribbler! often seen
In Morning Post, or Monthly Magazine.
There lurk his earlier lays; but soon, hot-
pressed,
Behold a quarto! — Tarts must tell the rest.
Then leave, ye wise, the lyre's precarious
chords
To muse-mad baronets, or madder lords,
Or country Crispins, now grown somewhat
stale,
Twin Doric minstrels, drunk with Doric ale!
Hark to those notes, narcotically soft,
The cobbler-laureats[5] sing to Capel Lofft! [6]

[2] [The Red Hand of Ulster, introduced generally
in a canton, marks the shield of a baronet of the
United Kingdom.]
[3] [" *Pollio.*" — In the original MS. " *Rogers.*"]
[4] " Tum quoque, marmorea caput a cervice revulsum
Gurgite cum medio portans Œagrius Hebrus
Volveret, Eurydicen vox ipsa, et frigida lingua
Ah, miseram Eurydicen! anima fugiente voca-
bat;
Eurydicen toto referebant flumine ripæ." —
Georgic. iv. 523.
[5] I beg Nathaniel's pardon: he is not a cobbler;
it is a *tailor*, but begged Capel Lofft to sink the
profession in his preface to two pair of panta —
psha! — of cantos, which he wished the public to
try on; but the sieve of a patron let it out, and so
far saved the expense of an advertisement to his
country customers. — Merry's " Moorfields whine "
was nothing to all this. The " Della Cruscans "
were people of some education, and no profession
but these Arcadians (" Arcades ambo " — bumpkin:
both) send out their native nonsense without the
smallest alloy, and leave all the shoes and small-
clothes in the parish unrepaired, to patch up Ele-
gies on Enclosures and Pæans to Gunpowder. Sit-
ting on a shopboard, they describe fields of battle,
when the only blood they ever saw was shed from
the finger; and an " Essay on War " is produced
by the ninth part of a " poet."
" And own that *nine* such poets made a Tate."
Did Nathan ever read that line of Pope? and if he
did, why not take it as his motto?
[6] This well-meaning gentleman has spoiled some

Till, lo! that modern Midas, as he hears,
Adds an ell growth to his egregious ears!

There lives one druid, who prepares in time
'Gainst future feuds his poor revenge of rhyme;
Racks his dull memory, and his duller muse,
To publish faults which friendship should ex-
  cuse.
If friendship's nothing, self-regard might teach
More polished usage of his parts of speech.
But what is shame, or what is aught to him?
He vents his spleen, or gratifies his whim.
Some fancied slight has roused his lurking
  hate,
Some folly crossed, some jest, or some debate;
Up to his den Sir Scribbler hies, and soon
The gathered gall is voided in lampoon.
Perhaps at some pert speech you've dared to
  frown,
Perhaps your poem may have pleased the
  town:

If so, alas! 'tis nature in the man —
May Heaven forgive you, for he never can!
Then be it so; and may his withering bays
Bloom fresh in satire, though they fade in
  praise!
While his lost songs no more shall steep and
  stink,
The dullest, fattest weeds on Lethe's brink,
But springing upwards from the sluggish
  mould,
Be (what they never were before) be—sold!
Should some rich bard (but such a monster
  now,
In modern physics, we can scarce allow),
Should some pretending scribbler of the
  court,
Some rhyming peer[1] — there's plenty of the
  sort — [2]

[1] [In the original MS. —
"Some rhyming peer — Carlisle or Carysfort."
To which is subjoined this note: — "Of 'John Joshua, Earl of Carysfort' I know nothing at present, but from an advertisement in an old newspaper of certain Poems and Tragedies by his Lordship, which I saw by accident in the Morea. Being a rhymer himself, he will forgive the liberty I take with his name, seeing, as he must, how very commodious it is at the close of that couplet; and as for what follows and goes before, let him place it to the account of the other Thane; since I cannot, under these circumstances, augur pro or con the contents of his 'foolscap crown octavos.'" — John Joshua Proby, first Earl of Carysfort, was joint postmaster-general in 1805, envoy to Berlin in 1806, and ambassador to Petersburgh in 1807. Besides his poems, he published two pamphlets, to show the necessity of universal suffrage and short parliaments. He died in 1828.]

[2] Here will Mr. Gifford allow me to introduce once more to his notice the sole survivor, the "ultimus Romanorum," the last of the Cruscanti! — "Edwin" the "profound," by our Lady of Punishment! here he is, as lively as in the days of "well said Baviad the correct." I thought Fitzgerald had been the tail of poesy; but, alas! he is only the penultimate.

A FAMILIAR EPISTLE TO THE EDITOR OF THE
MORNING CHRONICLE.

"WHAT reams of paper, floods of ink,"
  Do some men spoil, who never think!
And so perhaps you'll say of me,
  In which your readers may agree.
Still I write on, and tell you why;
  Nothing's so bad, you can't deny,
But may instruct or entertain
  Without the risk of giving pain, etc. etc.

ON SOME MODERN QUACKS AND REFORMISTS

IN tracing of the human mind
  Through all its various courses,
Though strange, 'tis true, we often find
  It knows not its resources:

And men through life assume a part
  For which no talents they possess,

excellent shoemakers, and been accessary to the poetical undoing of many of the industrious poor. Nathaniel Bloomfield and his brother Bobby have set all Somersetshire singing; nor has the malady confined itself to one county. Pratt too (who once was wiser) has caught the contagion of patronage, and decoyed a poor fellow named Blackett into poetry; but he died during the operation, leaving one child and two volumes of "Remains" utterly destitute. The girl, if she don't take a poetical twist, and come forth as a shoemaking Sappho, may do well; but the "tragedies" are as rickety as if they had been the offspring of an Earl or a Seatonian prize poet. The patrons of this poor lad are certainly answerable for his end; and it ought to be an indictable offence. But this is the least they have done; for, by a refinement of barbarity, they have made the (late) man posthumously ridiculous, by printing what he would have had sense enough never to print himself. Certes these rakers of "Remains" come under the statute against "resurrection men." What does it signify whether a poor dear dead dunce is to be stuck up in Surgeons' or in Stationers' Hall? Is it so bad to unearth his bones as his blunders? Is it not better to gibbet his body on a heath, than his soul in an octavo? "We know what we are, but we know not what we may be;" and it is to be hoped we never shall know, if a man who has passed through life with a sort of éclat, is to find himself a mountebank on the other side of Styx, and made, like poor Joe Blackett, the laughing-stock of purgatory. The plea of publication is to provide for the child; now, might not some of this "Sutor ultra Crepidam's" friends and seducers have done a decent action without inveigling Pratt into biography? And then his inscription split into so many modicums! — "To the Duchess of Somuch, the Right Hon. So-and-So, and Mrs. and Miss Somebody, these volumes are, etc. etc." — why, this is doling out the "soft milk of dedication," in gills, — there is but a quart, and he divides it among a dozen. Why, Pratt, hadst thou not a puff left? Dost thou think six families of distinction can share this in quiet? There is a child, a book, and a dedication: send the girl to her grace, the volumes to the grocer, and the dedication to the devil.

All but one poor dependent priest withdrawn
(Ah! too regardless of his chaplain's yawn!)
Condemn the unlucky curate to recite
Their last dramatic work by candle-light,
How would the preacher turn each rueful leaf,
Dull as his sermons, but not half so brief!
Yet, since 'tis promised at the rector's death,
He'll risk no living for a little breath.
Then spouts and foams, and cries at every line,
(The Lord forgive him!) "Bravo! grand! di-
    vine!"
Hoarse with those praises (which, by flattery
    fed,
Dependence barters for her bitter bread),
He strides and stamps along with creaking
    boot,
Till the floor echoes his emphatic foot;
Then sits again, then rolls his pious eye,
As when the dying vicar will not die!
Nor feels, forsooth, emotion at his heart;—
But all dissemblers overact their part.

Ye, who aspire to "build the lofty rhyme,"[1]
Believe not all who laud your false "sublime;"
But if some friend shall hear your work, and
    say,
"Expunge that stanza, lop that line away,"
And, after fruitless efforts, you return
Without amendment, and he answers,
    "Burn!"
That instant throw your paper in the fire,
Ask not his thoughts, or follow his desire;
But (if true bard!) you scorn to condescend,
And will not alter what you can't defend,
If you will breed this bastard of your brains,—[2]
We'll have no words—I've only lost my pains.

Yet, if you only prize your favorite thought,
As critics kindly do, and authors ought;
If your cool friend annoy you now and then,
And cross whole pages with his plaguy pen;
No matter, throw your ornaments aside,—
Better let him than all the world deride.
Give light to passages too much in shade,
Nor let a doubt obscure one verse you've
    made;
Your friend's "a Johnson," not to leave one
    word,
However trifling, which may seem absurd;
Such erring trifles lead to serious ills,
And furnish food for critics,[3] or their quills.

As the Scotch fiddle, with its touching tune,
Or the sad influence of the angry moon,

Yet wonder that, with all their art,
    They meet no better with success, etc. etc.

[1] [Milton's Lycidas.]

[2] "*Bastard of your brains.*"—Minerva being
the first by Jupiter's headpiece, and a variety of
equally unaccountable parturitions upon earth, such
as Madoc, ete. etc. etc.

[3] "A crust for the critics."—*Bayes, in the "Re-
hearsal."*

All men avoid bad writers' ready tongues,
As yawning waiters fly[4] Fitzscribble's[5] lungs:
Yet on he mouths—ten minutes—tedious
    each
As prelate's homily, or placeman's speech;
Long as the last years of a lingering lease,
When riot pauses until rents increase.
While such a minstrel, muttering fustian, strays
O'er hedge and ditch, through unfrequented
    ways,
If by some chance he walks into a well,
And shouts for succor with stentorian yell,
"A rope! help Christians, as ye hope for
    grace!"
Nor woman, man, nor child will stir a pace;
For there his carcass he might freely fling,
From frenzy, or the humor of the thing.
Though this has happened to more bards
    than one;
I'll tell you Budgell's story,—and have done.

Budgell, a rogue and rhymester, for no good
(Unless his case be much misunderstood)
When teased with creditors' continual claims
"To die like Cato,"[6] leapt into the Thames!
And therefore be it lawful through the town
For any bard to poison, hang, or drown.
Who saves the intended suicide receives
Small thanks from him who loathes the life he
    leaves

---

[4] And the "waiters" are the only fortunate peo-
ple who can "fly" from them; all the rest, namely,
the sad subscribers to the "Literary Fund," being
compelled, by courtesy, to sit out the recitation
without a hope of exclaiming, "Sic" (that is, by
choking Fitz with bad wine, or worse poetry) "me
servavit Apollo!"

[5] ["Fitzscribble," originally "Fitzgerald."]

[6] On his table were found these words: "*What
Cato did, and Addison approved, cannot be
wrong.*" But Addison did not "approve;" and if
he had, it would not have mended the matter. He
had invited his daughter on the same water-party;
but Miss Budgell, by some accident, escaped this
last paternal attention. Thus fell the sycophant of
"Atticus," and the enemy of Pope!—[Eustace
Budgell, a friend and relative of Addison's, "leapt
into the Thames" to escape a prosecution, on ac-
count of forging the will of Dr. Tindal; in which
Eustace had provided himself with a legacy of two
thousand pounds. To this Pope alludes—
"Let Budgell charge low Grub Street on my quill,
  And write whate'er he please—except my will."
"We talked (says Boswell) of a man's drowning
himself.—*Johnson.* 'I should never think it time
to make away with myself.' I put the case of Eus-
tace Budgell, who was accused of forging a will, and
sunk himself in the Thames, before the trial of its
authenticity came on. 'Suppose, Sir,' said I, 'that
a man is absolutely sure that, if he lives a few days
longer, he shall be detected in a fraud, the conse-
quence of which will be utter disgrace, and expul-
sion from society.' *Johnson.* 'Then, Sir, let him
go abroad to a distant country; let him go to some
place where he is *not* known. Don't let him go to
the devil, where he *is* known.'"]

And, sooth to say, mad poets must not lose
The glory of that death they freely choose.

Nor is it certain that some sorts of verse
Prick not the poet's conscience as a curse;
Dosed[1] with vile drams on Sunday he was
found,

[1] If " dosed with," etc. be censured as low, I beg
leave to refer to the original for something still
lower; and if any reader will translate " Minxerit
in patrios cineres," etc. into a decent couplet, I will
nsert said couplet in lieu of the present.

Or got a child on consecrated ground!
And hence is haunted with a rhyming rage —
Feared like a bear just bursting from his
cage.
If free, all fly his versifying fit,
Fatal at once to simpleton or wit.
But *him*, unhappy! whom he seizes, — *him*
He flays with recitation limb by limb;
Probes to the quick where'er he makes his
breach,
And gorges like a lawyer — or a leech.

THE CURSE OF MINERVA.

——" Pallas te hoc vulnere, Pallas
Immolat, et pœnam scelerato ex sanguine sumit."
Æneid, lib. xii,

[The Curse of Minerva was written at Athens in 1811. It was prompted by Byron's indignation at
Lord Elgin, who had just carried from Greece a large collection of antique sculptures torn from the Par-
thenon and other edifices. This collection was purchased in 1816 by the British Government and placed
in the British Museum. In justice to Lord Elgin it may be said with truth that he rescued these precious
relics of ancient art from barbarism and decay, and placed them where they are likely to be preserved,
admired, and studied for ages to come.
The first authentic edition of The Curse of Minerva was published in 1828, but Byron speaks in a
letter, dated March, 1816, of a miserable and stolen copy printed in some magazine. The first four
paragraphs were, however, printed as the beginning of the third canto of the Corsair.]

ATHENS, Capuchin Convent,
March 17, 1811.

SLOW sinks, more lovely ere his race be run,
Along Morea's hills the setting sun;
Not, as in northern climes, obscurely bright,
But one unclouded blaze of living light;
O'er the hushed deep the yellow beam he
throws
Gilds the green wave that trembles as it glows;
On old Ægina's rock and Hydra's isle
The god of gladness sheds his parting smile;
O'er his own regions lingering loves to shine,
Though there his altars are no more divine.
Descending fast, the mountain-shadows kiss
Thy glorious gulf, unconquered Salamis!
Their azure arches through the long expanse,
More deeply purpled, meet his mellowing
glance,
And tenderest tints, along their summits driven,
Mark his gay course, and own the hues of
heaven;

Till, darkly shaded from the land and deep,
Behind his Delphian rock he sinks to sleep.

On such an eve his palest beam he cast
When, Athens! here thy wisest looked his last
How watched thy better sons his farewell ray,
That closed their murdered sage's[1] latest day!
Not yet — not yet — Sol pauses on the hill,
The precious hour of parting lingers still;
But sad his light to agonizing eyes,
And dark the mountain's once delightful dyes;
Gloom o'er the lovely land he seemed to pour,
The land where Phœbus never frowned be-
fore;
But ere he sunk below Citheron's head,
The cup of woe was quaffed — the spirit fled;
The soul of him that scorned to fear or fly,
Who lived and died as none can live or die.

[1] Socrates drank the hemlock a short time before
sunset (the hour of execution), notwithstanding the
entreaties of his disciples to wait till the sun went
down.

But, lo! from high Hymettus to the plain
The queen of night asserts her silent reign;[1]
No murky vapor, herald of the storm,
Hides her fair face, or girds her glowing form.
With cornice glimmering as the moonbeams play,
There the white column greets her grateful ray,
And bright around, with quivering beams beset,
Her emblem sparkles o'er the minaret:
The groves of olive scattered dark and wide,
Where meek Cephisus sheds his scanty tide,
The cypress saddening by the sacred mosque,
The gleaming turret of the gay kiosk,[2]
And sad and sombre mid the holy calm,
Near Theseus' fane, yon solitary palm;
All, tinged with varied hues, arrest the eye;
And dull were his that passed them heedless by.[3]

Again the Ægean, heard no more afar,
Lulls his chafed breast from elemental war;
Again his waves in milder tints unfold
Their long expanse of sapphire and of gold,
Mixed with the shades of many a distant isle,
That frown, where gentler ocean deigns to smile.

As thus, within the walls of Pallas' fane,
I marked the beauties of the land and main,
Alone, and friendless, on the magic shore,
Whose arts and arms but live in poets' lore;
Oft as the matchless dome I turned to scan,
Sacred to gods, but not secure from man,
The past returned, the present seemed to cease,
And Glory knew no clime beyond her Greece!

Hours rolled along, and Dian's orb on high
Had gained the centre of her softest sky;
And yet unwearied still my footsteps trod
O'er the vain shrine of many a vanished god:
But chiefly, Pallas! thine; when Hecate's glare,
Checked by thy columns, fell more sadly fair
O'er the chill marble, where the startling tread
Thrills the lone heart like echoes from the dead.
Long had I mused, and treasured every trace
The wreck of Greece recorded of her race,
When, lo! a giant form before me strode,
And Pallas hailed me in her own abode!

Yes, 'twas Minerva's self; but, ah! how changed
Since o'er the Dardan field in arms she ranged!
Not such as erst, by her divine command,
Her form appeared from Phidias' plastic hand:
Gone were the terrors of her awful brow,
Her idle ægis bore no Gorgon now;
Her helm was dinted, and the broken lance
Seemed weak and shaftless e'en to mortal glance;
The olive branch, which still she deigned to clasp,
Shrunk from her touch, and withered in her grasp;
And, ah! though still the brightest of the sky,
Celestial tears bedimmed her large blue eye;
Round the rent casque her owlet circled slow,
And mourned his mistress with a shriek of woe!

"Mortal!" — 'twas thus she spake — "that blush of shame
Proclaims thee Briton, once a noble name;
First of the mighty, foremost of the free,
Now honored less by all, and least by me:
Chief of thy foes shall Pallas still be found.
Seek'st thou the cause of loathing? — look around.
Lo! here, despite of war and wasting fire,
I saw successive tyrannies expire.
'Scaped from the ravage of the Turk and Goth,
Thy country sends a spoiler worse than both.[4]
Survey this vacant, violated fane;
Recount the relics torn that yet remain:
These Cecrops placed, *this* Pericles adorned,[5]
That Adrian reared when drooping Science mourned.
What more I owe let gratitude attest —
Know, Alaric and Elgin did the rest.
That all may learn from whence the plunderer came
The insulted wall sustains his hated name:
For Elgin's fame thus grateful Pallas pleads,
Below, his name — above, behold his deeds!
Be ever hailed with equal honor here
The Gothic monarch and the Pictish peer:
Arms gave the first his right, the last had none,
But basely stole what less barbarians won.
So when the lion quits his fell repast,
Next prowls the wolf, the filthy jackal last:
Flesh, limbs, and blood the former make their own,
The last poor brute securely gnaws the bone.

---

[1] The twilight in Greece is much shorter than in our own country; the days in winter are longer, but in summer of less duration.

[2] The kiosk is a Turkish summer-house; the palm is without the present walls of Athens, not far from the Temple of Theseus between which and the tree the wall intervenes. Cephisus' stream is indeed scanty, and Ilissus has no stream at all.

[3] [The Temple of Theseus is the most perfect ancient edifice in the world. In this fabric, the most enduring stability, and a simplicity of design peculiarly striking, are united with the highest elegance and accuracy of workmanship. — *Hobhouse*.]

[4] [In the original MS. —
"Ah, Athens! scarce escaped from Turk and Goth,
Hell sends a paltry Scotchman worse than both."]

[5] This is spoken of the city in general, and not of the Acropolis in particular. The temple of Jupiter Olympius, by some supposed the Pantheon, was finished by Hadrian: sixteen columns are standing, of the most beautiful marble and architecture.

Yet still the gods are just, and crimes are crossed:
See here what Elgin won, and what he lost!
Another name with *his* pollutes my shrine:
Behold where Dian's beams disdain to shine!
Some retribution still might Pallas claim,
When Venus half avenged Minerva's shame." [1]

She ceased awhile, and thus I dared reply,
To soothe the vengeance kindling in her eye:
" Daughter of Jove! in Britain's injured name,
A true-born Briton may the deed disclaim.
Frown not on England; England owns him not:
Athena, no! thy plunderer was a Scot.
Ask'st thou the difference? From fair Phyles' towers
Survey Bœotia; — Caledonia's ours.
And well I know within that bastard land [2]
Hath Wisdom's goddess never held command;
A barren soil, where Nature's germs, confined
To stern sterility, can stint the mind;
Whose thistle well betrays the niggard earth,
Emblem of all to whom the land gives birth;
Each genial influence nurtured to resist;
A land of meanness, sophistry, and mist.
Each breeze from foggy mount and marshy plain
Dilutes with drivel every drizzly brain,
Till, burst at length, each watery head o'er-flows,
Foul as their soil, and frigid as their snows.
Then thousand schemes of petulance and pride
Despatch her scheming children far and wide:
Some east, some west, some everywhere but north,
In quest of lawless gain, they issue forth.
And thus — accursed be the day and year! —
She sent a Pict to play the felon here.
Yet Caledonia claims some native worth,
As dull Bœotia gave a Pindar birth;
So may her few, the lettered and the brave,
Bound to no clime, and victors of the grave,
Shake off the sordid dust of such a land,
And shine like children of a happier strand;
As once, of yore, in some obnoxious place,
Ten names (if found) had saved a wretched race."

" Mortal!" the blue-eyed maid resumed, " once more
Bear back my mandate to thy native shore.

Though fallen, alas! this vengeance yet is mine,
To turn my counsels far from lands like thine.
Hear then in silence Pallas' stern behest;
Hear and believe, for Time will tell the rest.

" First on the head of him who did this deed
My curse shall light, — on him and all his seed,
Without one spark of intellectual fire,
Be all the sons as senseless as the sire:
If one with wit the parent brood disgrace,
Believe him bastard of a brighter race:
Still with his hireling artists let him prate,
And folly's praise repay for Wisdom's hate;
Long of their patron's gusto let them tell,
Whose noblest, *native* gusto is — to sell:
To sell, and make — may Shame record the day! —
The state receiver of his pilfered prey.
Meantime, the flattering, feeble dotard, West,
Europe's worst dauber, and poor Britain's best,
With palsied hand shall turn each model o'er,
And own himself an infant of fourscore. [3]
Be all the bruisers culled from all St. Giles'
That art and nature may compare their styles;
While brawny brutes in stupid wonder stare,
And marvel at his lordship's 'stone shop' [4] there.
Round the thronged gate shall sauntering cox-combs creep,
To lounge and lucubrate, to prate and peep;
While many a languid maid, with longing sigh,
On giant statues casts the curious eye;
The room with transient glance appears to skim,
Yet marks the mighty back and length of limb;
Mourns o'er the difference of *now* and *then;*
Exclaims, ' These Greeks indeed were proper men!'
Draws sly comparisons of *these* with *those*,
And envies Laïs all her Attic beaux.
When shall a modern maid have swains like these!
Alas! Sir Harry is no Hercules!
And last of all, amidst the gaping crew,
Some calm spectator, as he takes his view,
In silent indignation mixed with grief,
Admires the plunder, but abhors the thief.
Oh, loathed in life, nor pardoned in the dust,
May hate pursue his sacrilegious lust!
Linked with the fool that fired the Ephesian dome,
Shall vengeance follow far beyond the tomb,

---

[1] His lordship's name, and that of one who no longer bears it, are carved conspicuously on the Parthenon; above, in a part not far distant, are the torn remnants of the basso relievos, destroyed in a vain attempt to remove them.

[2] "Irish bastards," according to Sir Callaghan O'Brallaghan.

[3] Mr. West, on seeing the "Elgin Collection" (I suppose we shall hear of the "Abershaw" and "Jack Shephard" collection), declared himself "a mere tyro" in art.

[4] Poor Crib was sadly puzzled when the marbles were first exhibited at Elgin House; he asked if it was not "a stone shop?" — He was right; it *is* a shop.

And Eratostratus and Elgin shine
In many a branding page and burning line;
Alike reserved for aye to stand accursed,
Perchance the second blacker than the first.

" So let him stand, through ages yet unborn,
Fixed statue on the pedestal of Scorn;
Though not for him alone revenge shall wait,
But fits thy country for her coming fate:
Hers were the deeds that taught her lawless
    son
To do what oft Britannia's self had done.
Look to the Baltic — blazing from afar,
Your old ally yet mourns perfidious war. [1]
Not to such deeds did Pallas lend her aid,
Or break the compact which herself had
    made;
Far from such councils, from the faithless
    field
She fled — but left behind her Gorgon shield:
A fatal gift that turned your friends to stone,
And left lost Albion hated and alone.

" Look to the East, where Ganges' swarthy
    race
Shall shake your tyrant empire to its base;
Lo! there Rebellion rears her ghastly head,
And glares the Nemesis of native dead;
Till Indus rolls a deep purpureal flood,
And claims his long arrear of northern blood.
So may ye perish! — Pallas, when she gave
Your free-born rights, forbade ye to enslave.

" Look on your Spain! — she clasps the
    hand she hates,
But boldly clasps, and thrusts you from her
    gates.
Bear witness, bright Barossa! thou canst tell
Whose were the sons that bravely fought and
    fell.
But Lusitania, kind and dear ally,
Can spare a few to fight, and sometimes fly.
Oh glorious field! by Famine fiercely won,
The Gaul retires for once, and all is done!
But when did Pallas teach, that one retreat
Retrieved three long olympiads of defeat?

" Look last at home — ye love not to look
    there
On the grim smile of comfortless despair:
Your city saddens: loud though Revel howls,
Here Famine faints, and yonder Rapine
    prowls.
See all alike of more or less bereft;
No misers tremble when there's nothing left.
' Blest paper credit; '[2] who shall dare to sing?
It clogs like lead Corruption's weary wing.
Yet Pallas plucked each premier by the ear,
Who gods and men alike disdained to hear;

But one, repentant o'er a bankrupt state,
On Pallas calls, — but calls, alas! too late:
Then raves for * * ; to that Mentor bends,
Though he and Pallas never yet were friends
Him senates hear, whom never yet they heard,
Contemptuous once, and now no less absurd.
So, once of yore, each reasonable frog
Swore faith and fealty to·his sovereign ' log.'
Thus hailed your rulers their patrician clod,
As Egypt chose an onion for a god.

" Now fare ye well! enjoy your little hour;
Go, grasp the shadow of your vanished power;
Gloss o'er the failure of each fondest scheme;
Your strength a name, your bloated wealth a
    dream.
Gone is that gold, the marvel of mankind,
And pirates barter all that's left behind,[3]
No more the hirelings, purchased near and
    far,
Crowd to the ranks of mercenary war.
The idle merchant on the useless quay
Droops o'er the bales no bark may bear
    away;
Or, back returning, sees rejected stores
Rot piecemeal on his own encumbered
    shores:
The starved mechanic breaks his rusting loom,
And desperate mans him 'gainst the coming
    doom.
Then in the senate of your sinking state,
Show me the man whose counsels may have
    weight.
Vain is each voice where tones could once
    command;
E'en factions cease to charm a factious land:
Yet jarring sects convulse a sister isle,
And light with maddening hands the mutual
    pile.

" 'Tis done, 'tis past, since Pallas warns in
    vain;
The Furies seize her abdicated reign:
Wide o'er the realm they wave their kindling
    brands,
And wring her vitals with their fiery hands.
But one convulsive struggle still remains,
And Gaul shall weep ere Albion wear her
    chains.
The bannered pomp of war, the glittering files,
O'er whose gay trappings stern Bellona smiles;
The brazen trump, the spirit-stirring drum,
That bid the foe defiance ere they come;
The hero bounding at his country's call,
The glorious death that consecrates his fall,
Swell the young heart with visionary charms,
And bid it antedate the joys of arms.
But know, a lesson you may yet be taught,
With death alone are laurels cheaply bought:
Not in the conflict Havoc seeks delight,
His day of mercy is the day of fight.

[1] [The affair of Copenhagen.]
[2] " Blest paper credit! last and best supply,
    That lends Corruption lighter wings to fly!"
                                    Pobe.

[3] The Deal and Dover traffickers in specie.

But when the field is fought, the battle won,
Though drenched with gore, his woes are but
 begun.
His deeper deeds as yet ye know by name;
The slaughtered 'peasant and the ravished
 dame,
The rifled mansion and the foe-reaped field,
Ill suit with souls at home, untaught to yield.
Say with what eye along the distant down
Would flying burghers mark the blazing town?
How view the column of ascending flames
Shake his red shadow o'er the startled
 Thames ?
Nay, frown not, Albion! for the torch was
 thine
That lit such pyres from Tagus to the Rhine:
Now should they burst on thy devoted coast,
Go, ask thy bosom who deserves them most.
The law of heaven and earth is life for life,
And she who raised, in vain regrets, the
 strife." [1]

whole coast of Attica, her hills and mountains,
Pentelicus, Anchesmus, Philopapus, etc. etc. are
in themselves poetical; and would be so if the name
of Athens, of Athenians, and her very ruins, were
swept from the earth. But, am I to be told that
the "nature" of ·Attica would be *more* poetical
without the " art " of the Acropolis? of the Tem-
ple of Theseus? and of the still all Greek and glori-
ous monuments of her exquisitely artificial genius?
Ask the traveller what strikes him as most poetical,
the Parthenon, or the rock on.which it stands? The
COLUMNS of Cape Colonna, or the Cape itself? The
rocks at the foot of it, or the recollection that Fal-
coner's ship was bulged upon them? There are a
thousand rocks and capes far more picturesque than
those of the Acropolis and Cape Sunium in them-
selves. But it is the " *art*," the columns, the
temples, the wrecked vessel, which give them their
antique and their modern poetry, and not the spots
themselves. I opposed, and will ever oppose, the
robbery of ruins from Athens, to instruct the Eng-
lish in sculpture; but why did I do so? The *ruins*
are as poetical in Piccadilly as they were in the
Parthenon; but the Parthenon and its rock are less
so without them. Such is the poetry of art." --
Byron's Letters, 1821.]

[1] [" The beautiful but barren Hymettus, the

THE WALTZ: AN APOSTROPHIC HYMN.

" Qualis in Eurotæ tipis, aut per juga Cynthi,
 Exercet Diana choros."   VIRGIL.

" Such on Eurota's banks, or Cynthia's height,
 Diana seems: and so she charms the sight,
 When in the dance the graceful goddess leads
 The quire of nymphs, and overtops their heads."
                              DRYDEN'S VIRGIL.

[This trifle was written at Cheltenham in the autumn of 1812, and published anonymously in the
spring of the following year. It was not very well received at the time by the public: and Byron was
by no means anxious that it should be considered as his handiwork. " I hear," he says, in a letter to a
friend, " that a certain malicious publication on waltzing is attributed to me. This report, I suppose,
you will take care to contradict; as the author, I am sure, will not like that I should wear his cap and
bells."]

TO THE PUBLISHER.

SIR, — I AM a country gentleman of a midland county. I might have been a parliament-man for a
certain borough; having had the offer of as many votes as General T. at the general election in 1812.[1]
But I was all for domestic happiness; as, fifteen years ago, on a visit to London, I married a middle-aged
maid of honor. We lived happily at Hornem Hall till last season, when my wife and I were invited by
the Countess of Waltzaway (a distant relation of my spouse) to pass the winter in town. Thinking no
harm, and our girls being come to a marriageable (or, as they call it, *marketable*) age, and having
besides a Chancery suit inveterately entailed upon the family estate, we came up in our old chariot, — a

[1] State of the poll (last day), 5.

which, by the by, my wife grew so much ashamed in less than a week, that I was obliged to buy a second-hand barouche, of which I might mount the box, Mrs. H. says, if I could drive, but never see the inside — that place being reserved for the Honorable Augustus Tiptoe, her partner-general and opera-knight. Hearing great praises of Mrs. H.'s dancing (she was famous for birthnight minuets in the latter end of the last century), I unbooted, and went to a ball at the Countess's, expecting to see a country dance, or, at most, cotillions, reels, and all the old paces to the newest tunes. But, judge of my surprise, on arriving, to see poor dear Mrs. Hornem with her arms half round the loins of a huge hussar-looking gentleman I never set eyes on before; and his, to say truth, rather more than half round her waist, turning round, and round, and round, to a d———d see-saw up-and-down sort of a tune, that reminded me of the " Black joke," only more " *affettuoso*," till it made me quite giddy with wondering they were not so. By and by they stopped a bit, and I thought they would sit or fall down: — but no; with Mrs. H.'s hand on his shoulder, " *quam familiariter* "[1] (as Terence said, when I was at school), they walked about a minute, and then at it again, like two cockchafers spitted on the same bodkin. I asked what all this meant, when, with a loud laugh, a child no older than our Wilhelmina (a name I never heard but in the Vicar of Wakefield, though her mother *would* call her after the Princess of Swappenbach), said, " Lord! Mr. Hornem, can't you see they are valtzing?" or waltzing (I forget which); and then up she got, and her mother and sister, and away they went, and round-abouted it till supper time. Now, that I know what it is, I like it of all things, and so does Mrs. H. (though I have broken my shins, and four times overturned Mrs. Hornem's maid, in practising the preliminary steps in a morning). Indeed, so much do I like it, that having a turn for rhyme, tastily displayed in some election ballads, and songs in honor of all the victories (but till lately I have had little practice in that way), I sat down, and with the aid of William Fitzgerald, Esq.,[2] and a few hints from Dr. Busby (whose recitations I attend, and am monstrous fond of Master Busby's manner of delivering his father's late successful " Drury Lane Address,") I composed the following hymn, wherewithal to make my sentiments known to the public; whom, nevertheless, I heartily despise, as well as the critics.

I am, Sir, yours, etc. etc.

HORACE HORNEM.

[1] My Latin is all forgotten, if a man can be said to have forgotten what he never remembered; but I bought my title-page motto of a Catholic priest for a three-shilling bank token, after much haggling for the *even* sixpence. I grudged the money to a papist, being all for the memory of Perceval and " No popery," and quite regretting the downfall of the pope, because we can't burn him any more.
[2] [The " hoarse Fitzgerald " of the opening lines of " English Bards and Scotch Reviewers."]

MUSE of the many-twinkling feet![1] whose charms
Are now extended up from legs to arms;
Terpsichore! — too long misdeemed a maid —
Reproachful term — bestowed but to upbraid —
Henceforth in all the bronze of brightness shine,
The least a vestal of the virgin Nine.
Far be from thee and thine the name of prude;
Mocked, yet triumphant; sneered at, unsubdued;
Thy legs must move to conquer as they fly,
If but thy coats are reasonably high;
Thy breast — if bare enough — requires no shield;
Dance forth — *sans armour* thou shalt take the field,

And own — impregnable to *most* assaults,
Thy not too lawfully begotten " Waltz."

Hail, nimble nymph! to whom the young hussar,
The whiskered votary of waltz and war,
His night devotes, despite of spur and boots;
A sight unmatched since Orpheus and his brutes:
Hail, spirit-stirring Waltz! — beneath whose banners
A modern hero fought for modish manners;
On Hounslow's heath to rival Wellesley's[2] fame,

[1] " Glance their many-twinkling feet." — *Gray.*

[2] To rival Lord Wellesley's, or his nephew's, as the reader pleases: — the one gained a pretty woman, whom he deserved, by fighting for; and the other has been fighting in the Peninsula many a long day, " by Shrewsbury clock," without gaining any thing in *that* country but the title of " the Great

Cocked—fired—and missed his man—but
  gained his aim;
Hail, moving Muse! to whom the fair one's
  breast
Gives all it can, and bids us take the rest.
Oh! for the flow of Busby, or of Fitz,
The latter's loyalty, the former's wits,
To "energize the object I pursue,"[1]
And give both Belial and his dance their
  due!

Imperial Waltz! imported from the Rhine
(Famed for the growth of pedigrees and
  wine),
Long be thine import from all duty free,
And hock itself be less esteemed than thee;
In some few qualities alike—for hock
Improves our cellar—*thou* our living stock.
The head to hock belongs—thy subtler art
Intoxicates alone the heedless heart:
Through the full veins thy gentler poison
  swims,
And wakes to wantonness the willing limbs.

Oh, Germany! how much to thee we owe,
As heaven-born Pitt can testify below,

Lord," and "the Lord:" which savors of profana-
tion, having been hitherto applied only to that Be-
ing to whom "*Te Deums*" for carnage are the
rankest blasphemy. — It is to be presumed the gen-
eral will one day return to his Sabine farm; there
  "To tame the genius of the stubborn plain,
    Almost as quickly as he conquered Spain!"
The Lord Peterborough conquered continents in
a summer; we do more—we contrive both to con-
quer and lose them in a shorter season. If the
"great Lord's" *Cincinnatian* progress in agricul-
ture be no speedier than the proportional average
of time in Pope's couplet, it will, according to the
farmers' proverb, be "ploughing with dogs."
  By the by—one of this illustrious person's new
titles is forgotten—it is, however, worth remember-
ing—"*Salvador del mundo !*" *credite, posteri !*
If this be the appellation annexed by the inhabitants
of the Peninsula to the name of a *man* who has not
yet saved them—query—are they worth saving,
even in this world? for, according to the mildest
modifications of any Christian creed, those three
words make the odds much against them in the
next.—"Saviour of the world," quotha! —it were
to be wished that he, or any one else, could save a
corner of it—his country. Yet this stupid mis-
nomer, although it shows the near connection be-
tween superstition and impiety, so far has its use,
that it proves there can be little to dread from those
Catholics (inquisitorial Catholics too) who can con-
fer such an appellation on a *Protestant.* I suppose
next year he will be entitled the "Virgin Mary:"
if so, Lord George Gordon himself would have
nothing to object to such liberal bastards of our
Lady of Babylon.
  [1] [Among the addresses sent in to the Drury
Lane Committee (parodied in *Rejected Addresses*)
was one by Dr. Busby, which began by asking—
  "When energizing objects men pursue,
    What are the prodigies they cannot do?"]

Ere cursed confederation made thee France's
And only left us thy d—d debts and dances!
Of subsidies and Hanover bereft,
We bless thee still—for George the Third is
  left!
Of kings the best—and last, not least in worth,
For graciously begetting George the Fourth.
To Germany, and highnesses serene,
Who owe us millions—don't we owe the
  queen?
To Germany, what owe we not besides?
So oft bestowing Brunswickers and brides;
Who paid for vulgar, with her royal blood,
Drawn from the stem of each Teutonic stud:
Who sent us—so be pardoned all her faults—
A dozen dukes, some kings, a queen—and
  Waltz.

But peace to her—her emperor and diet,
Though now transferred to Buonaparte's
  "fiat!"
Back to my theme—O Muse of motion! say,
How first to Albion found thy Waltz her way?

Borne on the breath of hyperborean gales,
From Hamburg's port (while Hamburg yet
  had *mails*),
Ere yet unlucky Fame—compelled to creep
To snowy Gottenburg—was chilled to sleep;
Or, starting from her slumbers, deigned arise,
Heligoland! to stock thy mart with lies;
While unburnt Moscow[2] yet had news to
  send,
Nor owed her fiery exit to a friend,
She came—Waltz came—and with her cer-
  tain sets
Of true despatches, and as true gazettes;
Then flamed of Austerlitz the blest despatch,
Which Moniteur nor Morning Post can
  match;

---

[2] The patriotic arson of our amiable allies cannot
be sufficiently commended—nor subscribed for.
Amongst other details omitted in the various de-
spatches of our eloquent ambassador, he did not
state (being too much occupied with the exploits of
Colonel C——, in swimming rivers frozen, and gal-
loping over roads impassable,) that one entire prov-
ince perished by famine in the most melancholy
manner, as follows:—In General Rostopchin's
consummate conflagration, the consumption of
tallow and train oil was so great, that the market
was inadequate to the demand: and thus one hun-
dred and thirty-three thousand persons were starved
to death, by being reduced to wholesome diet! The
lamplighters of London have since subscribed a pint
(of oil) apiece, and the tallow-chandlers have unan-
imously voted a quantity of best moulds (four to
the pound), to the relief of the surviving Scythians;
—the scarcity will soon, by such exertions, and a
proper attention to the *quality* rather than the
quantity of provision, be totally alleviated. It is
said, in return, that the untouched Ukraine has
subscribed sixty thousand beeves for a day's meal
to our suffering manufacturers.

And—almost crushed beneath the glorious
  news—
Ten plays, and forty tales of Kotzebue's;
One envoy's letters, six composers' airs,
And loads from Frankfort and from Leipsic
  fairs;
Meiner's four volumes upon womankind,
Like Lapland witches to insure a wind;
Brunck's heaviest tome for ballast, and, to
  back it,
Of Heyné, such as should not sink the packet.

Fraught with this cargo—and her fairest
  freight,
Delightful Waltz, on tiptoe for a mate,
The welcome vessel reached the genial strand,
And round her flocked the daughters of the
  land.
Not decent David, when, before the ark,
His grand pas-seul excited some remark;
Not love-lorn Quixote, when his Sancho
  thought
The knight's fandango friskier than it ought;
Not soft Herodias, when, with winning tread,
Her nimble feet danced off another's head;
Not Cleopatra on her galley's deck,
Displayed so much of *leg*, or more of *neck*,
Than thou, ambrosial Waltz, when first the
  moon
Beheld thee twirling to a Saxon tune!

  To you, ye husbands of ten years! whose
  brows
Ache with the annual tributes of a spouse;
To you of nine years less, who only bear
The budding sprouts of those that you *shall*
  wear,
With added ornaments around them rolled
Of native brass, or law-awarded gold;
To you, ye matrons, ever on the watch
To mar a son's, or make a daughter's, match;
To you, ye children of—whom chance ac-
  cords —
Always the ladies, and *sometimes* their lords;
To you, ye single gentlemen, who seek
Torments for life, or pleasures for a week;
As Love or Hymen your endeavors guide,
To gain your own, or snatch another's bride;—
To one and all the lovely stranger came,
And every ball-room echoes with her name.

  Endearing Waltz!—to thy more melting tune
Bow Irish jig, and ancient rigadoon.
Scotch reels, avaunt! and country-dance, fore-
  go
Your future claims to each fantastic toe!
Waltz—Waltz alone—both legs and arms
  demands,
Liberal of feet, and lavish of her hands;
Hands which may freely range in public sight
Where ne'er before—but—pray " put out the
  light."
Methinks the glare of yonder chandelier

Shines much too far—or I am much too near;
And true, though strange—Waltz whispers
  this remark,
" My slippery steps are safest in the dark!"
But here the Muse with due decorum halts,
And lends her longest petticoat to Waltz.

  Observant travellers of every time!
Ye quartos published upon every clime!
O say, shall dull Romaika's heavy round,
Fandango's wriggle, or Bolero's bound;
Can Egypt's Almas[1]—tantalizing group—
Columbia's caperers to the warlike whoop—
Can aught from cold Kamschatka to Cape
  Horn
With Waltz compare, or after Waltz be borne?
Ah, no! from Morier's pages down to Galt's,
Each tourist pens a paragraph for " Waltz."

  Shades of those belles whose reign began
  of yore,
With George the Third's—and ended long
  before!—
Though in your daughters' daughters yet you
  thrive,
Burst from your lead, and be yourselves alive!
Back to the ball-room speed your spectred
  host:
Fool's Paradise is dull to that you lost.
No treacherous powder bids conjecture
  quake;
No stiff-starched stays make meddling fingers
  ache;
(Transferred to those ambiguous things that
  ape
Goats in their visage,[2] women in their shape;)
No damsel faints when rather closely pressed,
But more caressing seems when most ca-
  ressed;
Superfluous hartshorn, and reviving salts,
Both banished by the sovereign cordial
  " Waltz."

  Seductive Waltz!—though on thy native
  shore
Even Werter's self proclaimed thee half a
  whore;
Werter—to decent vice though much inclined,
Yet warm, not wanton; dazzled, but not blind—

---

[1] Dancing girls—who do for hire what Waltz
doth gratis.

[2] It cannot be complained now, as in the Lady
Baussière's time, of the " Sieur de la Croix," that
there be " no whiskers;" but how far these are in-
dications of valor in a field, or elsewhere, may *still*
be questionable. Much may be, and hath been,
avouched on both sides. In the olden time philoso-
phers had whiskers, and soldiers none—Scipio
himself was shaven—Hannibal thought his one
eye handsome enough without a beard; but Adrian,
the emperor, wore a beard (having warts on his
chin, which neither the Empress Sabina nor even
the courtiers could abide)—Turenne had whiskers,
Marlborough none—Buonaparte is unwhiskered.

Though gentle Genlis, in her strife with Stael,
Would even proscribe thee from a Paris ball;
The fashion hails—from countesses to queens,
And maids and valets waltz behind the scenes;
Wide and more wide thy witching circle
    spreads,
And turns—if nothing else—at least our
    heads;
With thee even clumsy cits attempt to bounce,
And cockneys practise what they can't pro-
    nounce.
Gods! how the glorious theme my strain exalts,
And rhyme finds partner rhyme in praise of
    "Waltz!"

Blest was the time Waltz chose for her *dé-*
    but;
The court, the Regent, like herself were new;[1]
New face for friends, for foes some new re-
    wards;
New ornaments for black and royal guards;
New laws to hang the rogues that roared for
    bread;
New coins (most new)[2] to follow those that
    fled;
New victories—nor can we prize them less,
Though Jenky wonders at his own success;
New wars, because the old succeed so well,
That most survivors envy those who fell;
New mistresses—no, old—and yet 'tis true,
Though they be *old*, the *thing* is something
    new;
Each new, quite new—(except some ancient
    tricks),[3]

New white-sticks, gold-sticks, broom-sticks, all
    new sticks!
With vests or ribands—decked alike in hue,
New troopers strut, new turncoats blush in
    blue:
So saith the muse: my——,[4] what say you?
Such was the time when Waltz might best
    maintain
Her new preferments in this novel reign;
Such was the time, nor ever yet was such;
Hoops are *no more*, and petticoats *not much;*
Morals and minuets, virtue and her stays,
And tell-tale powder—all have had their
    days.
The ball begins—the honors of the house
First duly done by daughter or by spouse,
Some potentate—or royal or serene—
With Kent's gay grace, or sapient Gloster's
    mien,
Leads forth the ready dame, whose rising flush
Might once have been mistaken for a blush.
From where the garb just leaves the bosom
    free,
That spot where hearts[5] were once supposed
    to be;
Round all the confines of the yielded waist,
The strangest hand may wander undisplaced;
The lady's in return may grasp as much
As princely paunches offer to her touch.
Pleased round the chalky floor how well they
    trip,
One hand reposing on the royal hip;
The other to the shoulder no less royal
Ascending with affection truly loyal!
Thus front to front the partners move or stand,
The foot may rest, but none withdraw the hand;
And all in turn may follow in their rank,
The Earl of—Asterisk—and Lady—Blank;

---

the Regent whiskered; "*argal*" greatness of mind and whiskers may or may not go together: but certainly the different occurrences, since the growth of the last mentioned, go further in behalf of whiskers than the anathema of Anselm did *against* long hair in the reign of Henry I.—Formerly, *red* was a favorite color. See Lodowick Barry's comedy of Ram Alley, 1661; Act I. Scene 1.
"*Taffeta.* Now for a wager—What colored beard comes next by the window?
"*Adriana.* A black man's, I think.
"*Taffeta.* I think not so: I think a *red*, for that is most in fashion."
There is "nothing new under the sun;" but *red*, then a *favorite*, has now subsided into a *favorite's* color.

[1] An anachronism—Waltz and the battle of Austerlitz are before said to have opened the ball together: the bard means (if he means any thing), Waltz was not so much in vogue till the Regent attained the acmé of his popularity. Waltz, the comet, whiskers, and the new government, illuminated heaven and earth, in all their glory, much about the same time: of these the comet only has disappeared; the other three continue to astonish us still.—*Printer's Devil.*

[2] Amongst others a new ninepence—a creditable coin now forthcoming, worth a pound, in paper, at the fairest calculation.

[3] "Oh that *right* should thus overcome *might!*" Who does not remember the "delicate investigation" in the "Merry Wives of Windsor"?—

"*Ford.* Pray you, come near: if I suspect without cause, why then make sport at me; then let me be your jest; I deserve it. How now? whither bear you this?
"*Mrs. Ford.* What have you to do whither they bear it?—you were best meddle with buck-washing.

[4] The gentle, or ferocious, reader may fill up the blank as he pleases—there are several dissyllabic names at *his* service (being already in the Regent's): it would not be fair to back any peculiar initial against the alphabet, as every month will add to the list now entered for the sweepstakes:—a distinguished consonant is said to be the favorite, much against the wishes of the *knowing ones.*

[5] "We have changed all that," says the Mock Doctor—'tis all gone—Asmodeus knows where. After all, it is of no great importance how women's hearts are disposed of; they have nature's privilege to distribute them as absurdly as possible. But there are also some men with hearts so thoroughly bad, as to remind us of those phenomena often mentioned in natural history; namely, a mass of solid stone—only to be opened by force—and when divided, you discover a *toad* in the centre lively, and with the reputation of being venomous.

Sir—Such-a-one—with those of fashion's host,
For whose blest surnames—vide "Morning Post"
(Or if for that impartial print too late,
Search Doctors' Commons six months from my date)—
Thus all and each, in movement swift or slow,
The genial contact gently undergo;
Till some might marvel, with the modest Turk,
If "nothing follows all this palming work?"[1]
True, honest Mirza!—you may trust my rhyme—
Something does follow at a fitter time;
The breast thus publicly resigned to man,
In private may resist him——if it can.

O ye who loved our grandmothers of yore,
Fitzpatrick, Sheridan, and many more!
And thou, my prince! whose sovereign taste and will
It is to love the lovely beldames still!
Thou ghost of Queensbury! whose judging sprite
Satan may spare to peep a single night,
Pronounce—if ever in your days of bliss
Asmodeus struck so bright a stroke as this;
To teach the young ideas how to rise,
Flush in the cheek, and languish in the eyes;
Rush to the heart, and lighten through the frame,
With half-told wish and ill-dissembled flame,

---

[1] In Turkey a pertinent, here an impertinent and superfluous question — literally put, as in the text, by a Persian to Morier on seeing a waltz in Pera. — *Vide Morier's Travels.*

For prurient nature still will storm the breast—
Who, tempted thus, can answer for the rest?

But ye—who never felt a single thought
For what our morals are to be, or ought;
Who wisely wish the charms you view to reap,
Say—would you make those beauties quite so cheap?
Hot from the hands promiscuously applied,
Round the slight waist, or down the glowing side,
Where were the rapture then to clasp the form
From this lewd grasp and lawless contact warm?
At once love's most endearing thought resign,
To press the hand so pressed by none but thine;
To gaze upon that eye which never met
Another's ardent look without regret;
Approach the lip which all, without restraint,
Come near enough—if not to touch—to taint;
If such thou lovest—love her then no more,
Or give—like her—caresses to a score;
Her mind with these is gone, and with it go
The little left behind it to bestow.

Voluptuous Waltz! and dare I thus blaspheme?
Thy bard forgot thy praises were his theme.
Terpsichore, forgive!—at every ball
My wife *now* waltzes—and my daughters *shall;*
My son—(or stop—'tis needless to inquire—
These little accidents should ne'er transpire;
Some ages hence our genealogic tree
Will wear as green a ough for him as me)—
Waltzing shall rear, to make our name amends,
Grandsons for me—in heirs to all his friends.

ODE TO NAPOLEON BUONAPARTE.

"Expende Annibalem: — quot libras in duce summo
Invenies?" JUVENAL, *Sat.* **X.**[1]

" The Emperor Nepos was acknowledged by the Senate, by the Italians, and by the Provincials of Gaul; his moral virtues, and military talents, were loudly celebrated; and those who derived any private benefit from his government announced in prophetic strains the restoration of public felicity.

*   *   *   *   *   *   *   *   *   *   *   *   *
*   *   *   *   *   *   *   *   *   *   *   *   *

By this shameful abdication, he protracted his life a few years, in a very ambiguous state, between an Emperor and an Exile, till ———" GIBBON'S *Decline and Fall*, vol. vi. p. 220.[2]

[Byron, when publishing "The Corsair," in January, 1814, announced an apparently quite serious resolution to withdraw, for some years at least, from poetry. His letters of the February and March following abound in repetitions of the same determination. On the morning of the *ninth* of April, he writes — "No more rhyme for — or rather *from* — me. I have taken my leave of that stage, and henceforth, will mountebank it no longer." In the evening, a Gazette Extraordinary announced the abdication of Fontainebleau, and the poet violated his vows next morning by composing this Ode, which he immediately published, though without his name. His diary says, "April 10. To-day I have boxed one hour — written an Ode to Napoleon Buonaparte — copied it — eaten six biscuits — drunk four bottles of soda water, and redde away the rest of my time."]

---

[1] ["Produce the urn that Hannibal contains,
And weigh the mighty dust which yet remains:
AND IS THIS ALL!" —
I know not that this was ever done in the old world; at least, with regard to Hannibal; but, in the Statistical Account of Scotland, I find that Sir John Paterson had the curiosity to collect, and weigh, the ashes of a person discovered a few years since in the parish of Eccles; which he was happily enabled to do with great facility, as "the inside of the coffin was smooth, and the whole body visible." Wonderful to relate, he found the whole did not exceed in weight one ounce and a half! AND IS THIS ALL! Alas! the *quot libras* itself is a satirical exaggeration. — *Gifford.*]

[2] ["I send you an additional motto from Gibbon, which you will find *singularly* appropriate." — *Byron to Mr. Murray*, April 12, 1814.]

I.

'TIS done — but yesterday a King!
  And armed with Kings to strive —
And now thou art a nameless thing:
  So abject — yet alive!
Is this the man of thousand thrones,
Who strewed our earth with hostile bones,
  And can he thus survive?[1]
Since he, miscalled the Morning Star,
Nor man nor fiend hath fallen so far.

[1] ["I don't know — but I think *I*, even *I* (an insect compared with this creature), have set my life on casts not a millionth part of this man's. But, after all, a crown may not be worth dying for. Yet, to outlive *Lodi* for this!!! Oh that Juvenal or

II.

Ill-minded man! why scourge thy kind
  Who bowed so low the knee?
By gazing on thyself grown blind,
  Thou taught'st the rest to see.

Johnson could rise from the dead! 'Expende — quot libras in duce summo invenies?' I knew they were light in the balance of mortality; but I thought their living dust weighed more *carats*. Alas! this imperial diamond hath a flaw in it, and is now hardly fit to stick in a glazier's pencil; — the pen of the historian won't rate it worth a ducat. Psha! 'something too much of this.' But I won't give him up even now; though all his admirers have, like the Thanes, fallen from him." — *Byron's Diary*, April 9, 1814.]

With might unquestioned,— power to save,—·
Thine only gift hath been the grave
  To those that worshipped thee;
Nor till thy fall could mortals guess
Ambition's less than littleness!

III.

Thanks for that lesson — it will teach
To after-warriors more
Than high Philosophy can preach,
  And vainly preached before.
That spell upon the minds of men
Breaks never to unite again,
  That led them to adore
Those Pagod things of sabre sway,
With fronts of brass, and feet of clay.

IV.

The triumph, and the vanity,
  The rapture of the strife [1] —
The earthquake voice of Victory,
  To thee the breath of life;
The sword, the sceptre, and that sway
Which man seemed made but to obey,
  Wherewith renown was rife —
All quelled! — Dark Spirit! what must be
The madness of thy memory!

V.

The Desolator desolate!
  The Victor overthrown!
The Arbiter of others' fate
  A Suppliant for his own!
Is it some yet imperial hope
That with such change can calmly cope?
  Or dread of death alone?
To die a prince — or live a slave —
Thy choice is most ignobly brave!

VI.

He who of old would rend the oak,[2]
  Dreamed not of the rebound;
Chained by the trunk he vainly broke —
  Alone — how looked he round?
Thou in the sternness of thy strength
An equal deed hast done at length,
  And darker fate hast found:
He fell, the forest prowlers' prey;
But thou must eat thy heart away!

VII.

The Roman,[3] when his burning heart
  Was slaked with blood of Rome,
Threw down the dagger — dared depart,
  ·In savage grandeur, home. —
He dared depart in utter scorn
Of men that such a yoke had borne,
  Yet left him such a doom!
His only glory was that hour
Of self-upheld abandoned power.

VIII.

The Spaniard,[4] when the lust of sway
  Had lost its quickening spell,[5]
Cast crowns for rosaries away,
  An empire for a cell;
A strict accountant of his beads,
A subtle disputant on creeds,
  His dotage trifled well:
Yet better had he neither known
A bigot's shrine, nor despot's throne.

IX.

But thou — from thy reluctant hand
  The thunderbolt is wrung —
Too late thou leav'st the high command
  To which thy weakness clung;
All Evil Spirit as thou art,
It is enough to grieve the heart
  To see thine own unstrung;
To think that God's fair world hath been
The footstool of a thing so mean;

X.

And Earth hath spilt her blood for him,
  Who thus can hoard his own!
And Monarchs bowed the trembling limb,
  And thanked him for a throne!
Fair Freedom! we may hold thee dear,
When thus thy mightiest foes their fear
  In humblest guise have shown.
Oh! ne'er may tyrant leave behind
A brighter name to lure mankind!

---

[1] "Certaminis *gaudia*" — the expression of Attila in his harangue to his army, previous to the battle of Chalons, given in Cassiodorus.

[2] ["Out of town six days. On my return, find my poor little pagod, Napoleon, pushed off his pedestal. It is his own fault. Like Milo, he would rend the oak; but it closed again, wedged his hands, and now the beasts — lion, bear, down to the dirtiest jackal — may all tear him. That Muscovite winter *wedged* his arms; — ever since, he has fought with his feet and teeth. The last may still leave their marks: and 'I guess now' (as the Yankees say), that he will yet play them a pass." — *Byron's Diary*, April 8.]

[3] Sylla. — [We find the germ of this stanza in the Diary of the evening before it was written: — "Methinks Sylla did better; for he revenged, and resigned in the height of his sway, red with the slaughter of his foes — the finest instance of glorious contempt of the rascals upon record. Dioclesian did well too — Amurath not amiss, had he become aught except a dervise — Charles the Fifth but so so; but Napoleon worst of all." — *Byron's Diary*, April 9.]

[4] Charles the Fifth.

[5] ["Alter '*potent* spell' to 'quickening spell:' the first (as Polonius says) 'is a vile phrase,' and means nothing, besides being commonplace and Rosa-Matildaish. After the resolution of not publishing, though our Ode is a thing of little length and less consequence, it will be better altogether that it is anonymous." — *Byron to Mr. Murray*, April 11.]

XI.

Thine evil deeds are writ in gore,
  Nor written thus in vain —
Thy triumphs tell of fame no more,
  Or deepen every stain:
If thou hadst died as honor dies,
Some new Napoleon might arise,
  To shame the world again —
But who would soar the solar height,
  To set in such a starless night ? [1]

XII.

Weighed in the balance, hero dust
  Is vile as vulgar clay;
Thy scales, Mortality! are just
  To all that pass away:
But yet methought the living great
Some higher sparks should animate,
  To dazzle and dismay:
Nor deemed Contempt could thus make mirth
Of these, the Conquerors of the earth.

XIII.

And she, proud Austria's mournful flower,
  Thy still imperial bride;
How bears her breast the torturing hour ?
  Still clings she to thy side ?
Must she too bend, must she too share
Thy late repentance, long despair,
  Thou throneless Homicide ?
If still she loves thee, hoard that gem,
'Tis worth thy vanished diadem ! [2]

XIV.

Then haste thee to thy sullen Isle,
  And gaze upon the sea;
That element may meet thy smile —
  It ne'er was ruled by thee!
Or trace with thine all idle hand
In loitering mood upon the sand
  That Earth is now as free!
That Corinth's pedagogue [3] hath now
Transferred his by-word to thy brow.

XV.

Thou Timour! in his captive's cage [4]
  What thoughts will there be thine,

While brooding in thy prisoned rage ?
  But one — " The world *was* mine ! "
Unless, like he of Babylon,
All sense is with thy sceptre gone,
  Life will not long confine
That spirit poured so widely forth —
So long obeyed — so little worth !

XVI.

Or, like the thief of fire from heaven, [5]
  Wilt thou withstand the shock ?
And share with him, the unforgiven,
  His vulture and his rock !
Foredoomed by God — by man accurst, [6]
And that last act, though not thy worst,
  The very Fiend's arch mock ; [7]
He in his fall preserved his pride,
And, if a mortal, had as proudly died !

XVII.

There was a day — there was an hour, [8]
  While earth was Gaul's — Gaul thine —
When that immeasurable power
  Unsated to resign
Had been an act of purer fame
Than gathers round Marengo's name
  And gilded thy decline,
Through the long twilight of all time,
Despite some passing clouds of crime.

XVIII.

But thou forsooth must be a king,
  And don the purple vest, —
As if that foolish robe could wring
  Remembrance from thy breast.
Where is that faded garment ? where
The gewgaws thou wert fond to wear,
  The star — the string — the crest ?
Vain froward child of empire ! say,
Are all thy playthings snatched away ?

---

[1] [In the original MS. —
  " But who would rise in brightest day
    To set without one parting ray ? "]

[2] [Count Neipperg, a gentleman in the suite of
the Emperor of Austria, who was first presented to
Maria Louisa within a few days after Napoleon's
abdication, became, in the sequel, her chamberlain,
and then her husband. He is said to have been a
man of remarkably plain appearance. He died in
1831.]

[3] [Dionysius the Younger, esteemed a greater ty-
rant than his father, on being for the second time
banished from Syracuse, retired to Corinth, where
he was obliged to turn schoolmaster for a subsist-
ence.]

[4] The cage of Bajazet, by order of Tamerlane.

[5] Prometheus.

[6] [In first draught —
    " He suffered for kind acts to men,
      Who have not seen his like again,
        At least of kingly stock;
    Since he was good, and thou but great,
      Thou canst not quarrel with thy fate."]

[7] —— " The very fiend's arch mock —
To lip a wanton, and suppose her chaste."
                Shakspeare.

[He alludes to the unworthy amour in which Napo-
leon engaged on the evening of his arrival at Fon-
tainebleau.]

[8] [The three last stanzas, which Byron had been
solicited by Mr. Murray to write, to avoid the stamp
duty then imposed upon publications not exceeding
a sheet, were not published with the rest of the
poem. "I don't like them at all," said Lord
Byron, "and they had better be left out. The fact
is, I can't do any thing I am asked to do, however
gladly I would; and at the end of a week my inter-
est in a composition goes off."]

XIX.

Where may the wearied eye repose
  When gazing on the Great;
Where neither guilty glory glows,
  Nor despieable state ?
Yes — one — the first — the last — the best —
The Cincinnatus of the West,
  Whom envy dared not hate,
Bequeathed the name of Washington,
To make men blush there was but one ! [1]

[1] On being reminded by a friend of his recent

promise not to write any more for years — "There was," replied Byron, " a mental reservation in my pact with the public, in behalf of *anonymes;* and, even had there not, the provocation was such as to make it physically impossible to pass over this epoch of triumphant tameness. 'Tis a sad business; and, after all, I shall think higher of rhyme and reason, and very humbly of your heroic people, till — Elba becomes a volcano, and sends him out again. I can't think it is all over yet."]

HEBREW MELODIES.

[Byron never alludes to his share in these Melodies with complacency. Moore having, on one occasion, rallied him a little on the manner in which some of them had been set to music, — " Sunburn Nathan," he exclaims, " why do you always twit me with his Ebrew nasalities? Have I not told you it was all Kinnaird's doing, and my own exquisite facility of temper?

ADVERTISEMENT.

The subsequent poems were written at the request of my friend, the Hon. D. Kinnaird, for a Selection of Hebrew Melodies, and have been published with the music, arranged by Mr. Braham and Mr. Nathan, January, 1815.

SHE WALKS IN BEAUTY.[1]

I.

SHE walks in beauty, like the night
  Of cloudless climes and starry skies;
And all that's best of dark and bright
  Meet in her aspect and her eyes:
Thus mellowed to that tender light
  Which heaven to gaudy day denies.

II.

One shade the more, one ray the less,
  Had half impaired the nameless grace,
Which waves in every raven tress,
  Or softly lightens o'er her face;
Where thoughts serenely sweet express
  How pure, how dear their dwelling-place.

[1] [These stanzas were written by Byron, on returning from a ball, where Lady Wilmot Horton had appeared in mourning with numerous spangles on her dress.]

III.

And on that cheek, and o'er that brow,
  So soft, so calm, yet eloquent,
The smiles that win, the tints that glow,
  But tell of days in goodness spent.
A mind at peace with all below,
  A heart whose love is innocent!

THE HARP THE MONARCH MINSTREL SWEPT.

I.

THE harp the monarch minstrel swept,
  The King of men, the loved of Heaven,
Which Music hallowed while she wept
  O'er tones her heart of hearts had given,
  Redoubled be her tears, its chords are riven
It softened men of iron mould,
  It gave them virtues not their own;
No ear so dull, no soul so cold.

That felt not, fired not to the tone,
Till David's lyre grew mightier than his
throne!

II.

It told the triumphs of our King,
It wafted glory to our God;
It made our gladdened valleys ring,
The cedars bow, the mountains nod;
Its sound aspired to Heaven and there
abode!
Since then, though heard on earth no more,
Devotion, and her daughter Love
Still bid the bursting spirit soar
To sounds that seem as from above,
In dreams that day's broad light cannot
remove.

IF THAT HIGH WORLD.

I.

IF that high world, which lies beyond
Our own, surviving Love endears;
If there the cherished heart be fond,
The eye the same, except in tears—
How welcome those untrodden spheres!
How sweet this very hour to die!
To soar from earth and find all fears
Lost in thy light—Eternity!

II.

It must be so: 'tis not for self
That we so tremble on the brink;
And striving to o'erleap the gulf,
Yet cling to Being's severing link.
Oh! in that future let us think
To hold each heart the heart that shares,
With them the immortal waters drink,
And soul in soul grow deathless theirs!

THE WILD GAZELLE.

I.

THE wild gazelle on Judah's hills
Exulting yet may bound,
And drink from all the living rills
That gush on holy ground;
Its airy step and glorious eye
May glance in tameless transport by:—

II.

A step as fleet, an eye more bright,
Hath Judah witnessed there;
And o'er her scenes of lost delight
Inhabitants more fair.
The cedars wave on Lebanon,
But Judah's statelier maids are gone!

III.

More blest each palm that shades those plains
Than Israel's scattered race;
For, taking root, it there remains
In solitary grace:
It cannot quit its place of birth,
It will not live in other earth.

IV.

But we must wander witheringly,
In other lands to die;
And where our fathers' ashes be,
Our own may never lie:
Our temple hath not left a stone,
And Mockery sits on Salem's throne.

OH! WEEP FOR THOSE.

I.

OH! weep for those that wept by Babel's
stream,
Whose shrines are desolate, whose land a
dream;
Weep for the harp of Judah's broken shell;
Mourn—where their God hath dwelt the God-
less dwell!

II.

And where shall Israel lave her bleeding feet?
And when shall Zion's songs again seem sweet?
And Judah's melody once more rejoice
The hearts that leaped before its heavenly
voice?

III.

Tribes of the wondering foot and weary breast,
How shall ye flee away and be at rest!
The wild-dove hath her nest, the fox his cave,
Mankind their country—Israel but the grave!

ON JORDAN'S BANKS.

I.

ON Jordan's banks the Arab's camels stray,
On Sion's hill the False One's votaries pray,
The Baal-adorer bows on Sinai's steep—
Yet there—even there—Oh God! thy thun-
ders sleep.

II.

There—where thy finger scorched the tablet
stone,
There—where thy shadow to thy people
shone!
Thy glory shrouded in its garb of fire:
Thyself—none living see and not expire!

III.

Oh! in the lightning let thy glance appear;
Sweep from his shivered hand the oppressor's
spear.

How long by tyrants shall thy land be trod!
How long thy temple worshipless, Oh God!

JEPHTHA'S DAUGHTER.

I.

SINCE our Country, our God — Oh, my Sire!
Demand that thy Daughter expire;
Since thy triumph was bought by thy vow —
Strike the bosom that's bared for thee now!

II.

And the voice of my mourning is o'er,
And the mountains behold me no more:
If the hand that I love lay me low,
There cannot be pain in the blow!

III.

And of this, oh, my Father! be sure—
That the blood of thy child is as pure
As the blessing I beg ere it flow,
And the last thought that soothes me below.

IV.

Though the virgins of Salem lament,
Be the judge and the hero unbent!
I have won the great battle for thee,
And my Father and Country are free!

V.

When this blood of thy giving hath gushed,
When the voice that thou lovest is hushed,
Let my memory still be thy pride,
And forget not I smiled as I died!

OH! SNATCHED AWAY IN BEAUTY'S BLOOM.

I.

OH! snatched away in beauty's bloom,
On thee shall press no ponderous tomb;
   But on thy turf shall roses rear
   Their leaves, the earliest of the year;
And the wild cypress wave in tender gloom:

II.

And oft by yon blue gushing stream
   Shall Sorrow lean her drooping head,
And feed deep thought with many a dream,
   And lingering pause and lightly tread;
   Fond wretch! as if her step disturbed the
      dead!

III.

Away! we know that tears are vain,
   That death nor heeds nor hears distress:
Will this unteach us to complain?
   Or make one mourner weep the less?
And thou — who tell'st me to forget,
Thy looks are wan, thine eyes are wet.

MY SOUL IS DARK.

I.

MY soul is dark — Oh! quickly string
   The harp I yet can brook to hear;
And let thy gentle fingers fling
   Its melting murmurs o'er mine ear.
If in this heart a hope be dear,
   That sound shall charm it forth again:
If in these eyes there lurk a tear,
   'Twill flow, and cease to burn my brain.

II.

But bid the strain be wild and deep,
   Nor let thy notes of joy be first:
I tell thee, minstrel, I must weep,
   Or else this heavy heart will burst;
For it hath been by sorrow nursed,
   And ached in sleepless silence long;
And now 'tis doomed to know the worst,
   And break at once — or yield to song.

I SAW THEE WEEP.

I.

I SAW thee weep — the big bright tear
   Came o'er that eye of blue;
And then methought it did appear
   A violet dropping dew:
I saw thee smile — the sapphire's blaze
   Beside thee ceased to shine;
It could not match the living rays
   That filled that glance of thine.

II.

As clouds from yonder sun receive
   A deep and mellow dye,
Which scarce the shade of coming eve
   Can banish from the sky,
Those smiles unto the moodiest mind
   Their own pure joy impart;
Their sunshine leaves a glow behind
   That lightens o'er the heart.

THY DAYS ARE DONE.

I.

THY days are done, thy fame begun;
   Thy country's strains record
The triumphs of her chosen Son,
   The slaughters of his sword!
The deeds he did, the fields he won,
   The freedom he restored!

II.

Though thou art fallen, while we are free
   Thou shalt not taste of death!
The generous blood that flowed from thee
   Disdained to sink beneath:
Within our veins its currents be,
   Thy spirit on our breath!

III.

Thy name, our charging hosts along,
  Shall be the battle-word!
Thy fall, the theme of choral song
  From virgin voices poured!
To weep would do thy glory wrong;
  Thou shalt not be deplored.

SONG OF SAUL BEFORE HIS LAST BATTLE.

I.

WARRIORS and chiefs! should the shaft or the sword
Pierce me in leading the host of the Lord,
Heed not the corse, though a king's, in your path:
Bury your steel in the bosoms of Gath!

II.

Thou who art bearing my buckler and bow,
Should the soldiers of Saul look away from the foe,
Stretch me that moment in blood at thy feet!
Mine be the doom which they dared not to meet.

III.

Farewell to others. but never we part,
Heir to my royalty, son of my heart!
Bright is the diadem, boundless the sway,
Or kingly the death, which awaits us to-day!

SAUL.

I.

THOU whose spell can raise the dead,
  Bid the prophet's form appear.
"Samuel, raise thy buried head!
  King, behold the phantom seer!"
Earth yawned; he stood the centre of a cloud:
Light changed its hue, retiring from his shroud.
Death stood all glassy in his fixed eye;
His hand was withered, and his veins were dry;
His foot, in bony whiteness, glittered there,
Shrunken and sinewless, and ghastly bare;
From lips that moved not and unbreathing frame,
Like caverned winds, the hollow accents came.
Saul saw, and fell to earth, as falls the oak,
At once, and blasted by the thunder-stroke.

II.

"Why is my sleep disquieted?
  Who is he that calls the dead?
Is it thou, O King? Behold,
  Bloodless are these limbs, and cold:

Such are mine; and such shall be
Thine to-morrow, when with me:
Ere the coming day is done,
Such shalt thou be, such thy son.
Fare thee well, but for a day,
Then we mix our mouldering clay.
Thou, thy race, lie pale and low,
Pierced by shafts of many a bow;
And the falchion by thy side
To thy heart thy hand shall guide;
Crownless, breathless, headless fall,
Son and sire, the house of Saul!"[1]

"ALL IS VANITY, SAITH THE PREACHER."

I.

FAME, wisdom, love, and power were mine,
  And health and youth possessed me;
My goblets blushed from every vine,
  And lovely forms caressed me;
I sunned my heart in beauty's eyes,
  And felt my soul grow tender;
All earth can give, or mortal prize,
  Was mine of regal splendor.

II.

I strive to number o'er what days
  Remembrance can discover,
Which all that life or earth displays
  Would lure me to live over.
There rose no day, there rolled no hour
  Of pleasure unembittered;
And not a trapping decked my power
  That galled not while it glittered.

III.

The serpent of the field, by art
  And spells, is won from harming;
But that which coils around the heart,
  Oh! who hath power of charming?
It will not list to wisdom's lore,
  Nor music's voice can lure it;
But there it stings for evermore
  The soul that must endure it.

---

1 ["Since we have spoken of witches," said Byron at Cephalonia, in 1823, "what think you of the witch of Endor? I have always thought this the finest and most finished witch-scene that ever was written or conceived; and you will be of my opinion, if you consider all the circumstances and the actors in the case, together with the gravity, simplicity, and dignity of the language. It beats all the ghost scenes I ever read. The finest conception on a similar subject is that of Goethe's Devil, Mephistopheles; and though, of course, you will give the priority to the former, as being inspired, yet the latter, if you know it, will appear to you — at least it does to me — one of the finest and most sublime specimens of human conception."]

WHEN COLDNESS WRAPS THIS SUFFERING CLAY.

I.

WHEN coldness wraps this suffering clay,
  Ah! whither strays the immortal mind?
It cannot die, it cannot stay,
  But leaves its darkened dust behind.
Then unembodied, doth it trace
  By steps each planet's heavenly way?
Or fill at once the realms of space,
  A thing of eyes, that all survey?

II.

Eternal, boundless, undecayed,
  A thought unseen, but seeing all,
All, all in earth, or skies displayed,
  Shall it survey, shall it recall:
Each fainter trace that memory holds
  So darkly of departed years,
In one broad glance the soul beholds,
  And all, that was, at once appears.

III.

Before Creation peopled earth,
  Its eye shall roll through chaos back;
And where the furthest heaven had birth,
  The spirit trace its rising track.
And where the future mars or makes,
  Its glance dilate o'er all to be,
While sun is quenched or system breaks,
  Fixed in its own eternity.

IV.

Above or Love, Hope, Hate, or Fear,
  It lives all passionless and pure:
An age shall fleet like earthly year;
  Its years as moments shall endure.
Away, away, without a wing,
  O'er all, through all, its thought shall fly;
A nameless and eternal thing,
  Forgetting what it was to die.

VISION OF BELSHAZZAR.

I.

THE King was on his throne,
  The Satraps thronged the hall;
A thousand bright lamps shone
  O'er that high festival.
A thousand cups of gold,
  In Judah deemed divine—
Jehovah's vessels hold
  The godless Heathen's wine.

II.

In that same hour and hall,
  The fingers of a hand
Came forth against the wall,
  And wrote as if on sand:
The fingers of a man;—
  A solitary hand
Along the letters ran,
  And traced them like a wand.

III.

The monarch saw, and shook,
  And bade no more rejoice;
All bloodless waxed his look,
  And tremulous his voice.
"Let the men of lore appear,
  The wisest of the earth,
And expound the words of fear,
  Which mar our royal mirth."

IV.

Chaldea's seers are good,
  But here they have no skill
And the unknown letters stood
  Untold and awful still.
And Babel's men of age
  Are wise and deep in lore;
But now they were not sage,
  They saw—but knew no more.

V.

A captive in the land,
  A stranger and a youth,
He heard the king's command,
  He saw that writing's truth.
The lamps around were bright,
  The prophecy in view;
He read it on that night,—
  The morrow proved it true.

VI.

"Belshazzar's grave is made,
  His kingdom passed away,
He, in the balance weighed,
  Is light and worthless clay.
The shroud, his robe of state,
  His canopy the stone;
The Mede is at his gate!
  The Persian on his throne!"

SUN OF THE SLEEPLESS!

SUN of the sleepless! melancholy star!
Whose tearful beam glows tremulously far,
That show'st the darkness thou canst not
  dispel,
How like art thou to joy remembered well!
So gleams the past, the light of other days,
Which shines, but warms not with its power-
  less rays;
A night-beam Sorrow watcheth to behold,
Distinct, but distant—clear—but, oh how
  cold!

WERE MY BOSOM AS FALSE AS THOU DEEM'ST IT TO BE.

I.

WERE my bosom as false as thou deem'st it
    to be,
I need not have wandered from far Galilee;
It was but abjuring my creed to efface
The curse which, thou say'st, is the crime of
    my race.

II.

If the bad never triumph, then God is with
    thee!
If the slave only sin, thou art spotless and
 . free!
If the Exile on earth is an Outcast on high,
Live on in thy faith, but in mine I will die.

III.

I have lost for that faith more than thou canst
    bestow,
As the God who permits thee to prosper doth
    know;
In his hand is my heart and my hope — and in
    thine
The land and the life which for him I resign.

HEROD'S LAMENT FOR MARI- AMNE.[1]

I.

OH, Mariamne! now for thee
    The heart for which thou bled'st is bleed-
    ing;
Revenge is lost in agony,
    And wild remorse to rage succeeding.
Oh, Mariamne! where art thou?
    Thou canst not hear my bitter pleading:
Ah! couldst thou — thou wouldst pardon
    now,
    Though Heaven were to my prayer un-
    heeding.

II.

And is she dead? — and did they dare
    Obey my frenzy's jealous raving?
My wrath but doomed my own despair:

[1] [Mariamne, the wife of Herod the Great, falling under the suspicion of infidelity, was put to death by his order. She was a woman of unrivalled beauty, and haughty spirit: unhappy in being the object of passionate attachment, which bordered on frenzy, to a man who had more or less concern in the murder of her grandfather, father, brother, and uncle, and who had twice commanded her death, in case of his own. Ever after, Herod was haunted by the image of the murdered Mariamne, until dis- order of the mind brought on disorder of body, which led to temporary derangement. — *Milman.*]

The sword that smote her's o'er me wav-
    ing. —
But thou art cold, my murdered love!
    And this dark heart is vainly craving
For her who soars alone above,
    And leaves my soul unworthy saving.

III.

She's gone, who shared my diadem;
    She sunk, with her my joys entombing;
I swept that flower from Judah's stem
    Whose leaves for me alone were blooming;
And mine's the guilt, and mine the hell,
    This bosom's desolation dooming;
And I have earned those tortures well,
    Which unconsumed are still consuming!

ON THE DAY OF THE DESTRUCTION OF JERUSALEM BY TITUS.

I.

FROM the last hill that looks on thy once holy
    dome
I beheld thee, oh Sion! when rendered to
    Rome:
'Twas thy last sun went down, and the flames
    of thy fall
Flashed back on the last glance I gave to thy
    wall.

II.

I looked for thy temple, I looked for my home,
And forgot for a moment my bondage to come;
I beheld but the death-fire that fed on thy fane,
And the fast-fettered hands that made ven-
    geance in vain.

III.

On many an eve, the high spot whence I gazed
Had reflected the last beam of day as it blazed;
While I stood on the height, and beheld the
    decline
Of the rays from the mountain that shone on
    thy shrine.

IV.

And now on that mountain I stood on that day,
But I marked not the twilight beam melting
    away;
Oh! would that the lightning had glared in its
    stead,
And the thunderbolt burst on the conqueror's
    head!

V.

But the Gods of the Pagan shall never profane
The shrine where Jehovah disdained not to
    reign;
And scattered and scorned as thy people may
    be,
Our worship, oh Father! is only for thee.

BY THE RIVERS OF BABYLON WE SAT DOWN AND WEPT.

I.

WE sate down and wept by the waters
  Of Babel, and thought of the day
When our foe, in the hue of his slaughters,
  Made Salem's high places his prey;
And ye, oh her desolate daughters!
  Were scattered all weeping away.

II.

While sadly we gazed on the river
  Which rolled on in freedom below,
They demanded the song; but, oh never
  That triumph the stranger shall know!
May this right hand be withered for ever,
  Ere it string our high harp for the foe!

III.

On the willow that harp is suspended,
  Oh Salem! its sounds should be free;
And the hour when thy glories were ended
  But left me that token of thee:
And ne'er shall its soft tones be blended
  With the voice of the spoiler by me.

THE DESTRUCTION OF SENNACH-ERIB.

I.

THE Assyrian came down like the wolf on the
  fold,
And his cohorts were gleaming in purple and
  gold;
And the sheen of their spears was like stars on
  the sea,
When the blue wave rolls nightly on deep Gal-
  ilee.

II.

Like the leaves of the forest when Summer is
  green,
That host with their banners at sunset were
  seen:
Like the leaves of the forest when Autumn hath
  blown,
That host on the morrow lay withered and
  strown.

III.

For the Angel of Death spread his wings on
  the blast,
And breathed in the face of the foe as he passed;

And the eyes of the sleepers waxed deadly and
  chill,
And their hearts but once heaved, and for ever
  grew still!

IV.

And there lay the steed with his nostril all wide,
But through it there rolled not the breath of
  his pride:
And the foam of his gasping lay white on the
  turf,
And cold as the spray of the rock-beating surf

V.

And there lay the rider distorted and pale,
With the dew on his brow, and the rust on his
  mail,
And the tents were all silent, the banners alone,
The lances uplifted, the trumpet unblown.

VI.

And the widows of Ashur are loud in their wail,
And the idols are broke in the temple of Baal;
And the might of the Gentile, unsmote by the
  sword,
Hath melted like snow in the glance of the
  Lord!

A SPIRIT PASSED BEFORE ME.

FROM JOB.

I.

A SPIRIT passed before me: I beheld
The face of immortality unveiled —
Deep sleep came down on every eye save
  mine —
And there it stood, — all formless — but divine:
Along my bones the creeping flesh did quake:
And as my damp hair stiffened, thus it spake:

II.

"Is man more just than God? Is man more
  pure
Than he who deems even Seraphs insecure?
Creatures of clay — vain dwellers in the dust!
The moth survives you, and are ye more just?
Things of a day! you wither ere the night,
Heedless and blind to Wisdom's wasted
  light!"[1]

[1] [The Hebrew Melodies, though obviously infe-
rior to Lord Byron's other works, display a skill in
versification, and a mastery in diction, which would
have raised an inferior artist to the very summit of
distinction. — *Jeffrey.*]

DOMESTIC PIECES — 1816.

[Of the six following poems, the first three were written immediately before Lord Byron's final departure from England; the others, during the earlier part of his residence in the neighborhood of Geneva. They all refer to the unhappy event, which will for ever mark the chief crisis of his personal story, — that separation from Lady Byron, of which, after all that has been said and written, the real motives and circumstances remain as obscure as ever.

Mr. Kennedy, in his account of Lord Byron's last residence in Cephalonia, represents him as saying, —" Lady Byron deserves every respect from me: I do not indeed know the cause of the separation, and I have remained, and ever will remain, ready for a reconciliation, whenever circumstances open and point out the way to it." Mr. Moore has preserved evidence of one attempt which Lord Byron made to bring about an explanation with his Lady, ere he left Switzerland for Italy. Whether he ever repeated the experiment we are uncertain: but *that* failed, — and the failure must be borne in mind, when the reader considers some of the smaller pieces included in this Section.]

FARE THEE WELL.[1]

"Alas! they had been friends in Youth;
But whispering tongues can poison truth;
And constancy lives in realms above;
And Life is thorny; and youth is vain:
And to be wroth with one we love,
Doth work like madness in the brain;

*　　*　　*　　*　　*　　*

But never either found another
To free the hollow heart from paining —
They stood aloof, the scars remaining,
Like cliffs, which had been rent asunder;
A dreary sea now flows between,
But neither heat, nor frost, nor thunder
Shall wholly do away, I ween,
The marks of that which once hath been."
　　　　　COLERIDGE's *Christabel.*

FARE thee well! and if for ever,
　Still for ever, fare thee well:
Even though unforgiving, never
　'Gainst thee shall my heart rebel.

Would that breast were bared before thee
　Where thy head so oft hath lain,
While that placid sleep came o'er thee
　Which thou ne'er canst know again:

Would that breast, by thee glanced over,
　Every inmost thought could show!
Then thou would'st at last discover
　'Twas not well to spurn it so.

Though the world for this commend thee —
　Though it smile upon the blow,
Even its praises must offend thee,
　Founded on another's woe:

Though my many faults defaced me,
　Could no other arm be found,
Than the one which once embraced me,
　To inflict a cureless wound?

---

ation ought to have placed her as much *beneath* his satire, as the undignified mode of his attack certainly raised her *above* it, with regard to the other poem, opinions were a good deal more divided. To many it appeared a strain of true conjugal tenderness, — a kind of appeal which no woman with a heart could resist; while, by others, on the contrary, it was considered to be a mere showy effusion of sentiment, as difficult for real feeling to have produced as it was easy for fancy and art, and altogether unworthy of the deep interests involved in the subject. To this latter opinion I confess my own to have, at first, strongly inclined, and suspicious as I could not help thinking the sentiment that could, at such a moment, indulge in such verses, the taste that prompted or sanctioned their publication appeared to me even still more questionable. On reading, however, his own account of all the circumstances in the Memoranda, I found that on both points I had, in common with a large portion of the public, done him injustice. He there described, and in a manner whose sincerity there was no doubting, the swell of tender recollections under the influence of which, as he sat one night musing in his study, these stanzas were produced, — the tears, as he said, falling fast over the paper as he wrote them. Neither did it appear from that account, to have been from any wish or intention of his own, but through the injudicious zeal of a friend whom he had suffered to take a copy, that the verses met the public eye. — *Moore.*]

[1] [It was about the middle of April that his two celebrated copies of verses, "Fare thee well," and "A Sketch," made their appearance in the newspapers; and while the latter poem was generally, and, it must be owned, justly condemned, as a sort of literary assault on an obscure female, whose situ-

Yet, oh yet, thyself deceive not;
　Love may sink by slow decay,
But by sudden wrench, believe not
　Hearts can thus be torn away:

Still thine own its life retaineth —
　Still must mine, though bleeding, beat;
And the undying thought which paineth
　Is — that we no more may meet.

These are words of deeper sorrow
　Than the wail above the dead;
Both shall live, but every morrow
　Wake us from a widowed bed.

And when thou would solace gather,
　When our child's first accents flow,
Wilt thou teach her to say " Father!"
　Though his care she must forego ?

When her little hands shall press thee,
　When her lip to thine is pressed,
Think of him whose prayer shall bless thee,
　Think of him thy love had blessed!

Should her lineaments resemble
　Those thou never more may'st see,
Then thy heart will softly tremble
　With a pulse yet true to me.

All my faults perchance thou knowest,
　All my madness none can know;
All my hopes, where'er thou goest,
　Wither, yet with *thee* they go.

Every feeling hath been shaken;
　Pride, which not a world could bow,
Bows to thee — by thee forsaken,
　Even my soul forsakes me now:

But 'tis done — all words are idle —
　Words from me are vainer still;
But the thoughts we cannot bridle
　Force their way without the will. —

Fare thee well! — thus disunited,
　Torn from every nearer tie,
Seared in heart, and lone, and blighted,
　More than this I scarce can die.

　　　　　　　　March 17, 1816.

A SKETCH.[1]

" Honest — honest Iago!
　If that thou be'st a devil, I cannot kill thee."
　　　　　　　　　　　　　SHAKSPEARE.

BORN in the garret, in the kitchen bred,
Promoted thence to deck her mistress' head;
Next — for some gracious service unexpressed,

---

[1] ["I send you my last night's dream, and request to have fifty copies struck off, for private distribution. I wish Mr. Gifford to look at them. They are from life." — *Byron to Mr. Murray,* March 30, 1816.]

And from its wages only to be guessed —
Raised from the toilet to the table, — where
Her wondering betters wait behind her chair.
With eye unmoved, and forehead unabashed,
She dines from off the plate she lately
　washed.
Quick with the tale, and ready with the lie —
The genial confidante, and general spy —
Who could, ye gods! her next employment
　guess —
An only infant's earliest governess!
She taught the child to read, and taught so
　well,
That she herself, by teaching, learned to spell.
An adept next in penmanship she grows,
As many a nameless slander deftly shows:
What she had made the pupil of her art,
None know — but that high Soul secured the
　heart,
And panted for the truth it could not hear,
With longing breast and undeluded ear.
Foiled was perversion by that youthful mind,
Which Flattery fooled not — Baseness could
　not blind,
Deceit infect not — near Contagion soil —
Indulgence weaken — nor Example spoil —
Nor mastered Science tempt her to look down
On humbler talents with a pitying frown —
Nor Genius swell — nor Beauty render vain —
Nor Envy ruffle to retaliate pain —
Nor Fortune change — Pride raise — nor
　Passion bow,
Nor Virtue teach austerity — till now.
Serenely purest of her sex that live,
But wanting one sweet weakness — to forgive,
Too shocked at faults her soul can never
　know,
She deems that all could be like her below:
Foe to all vice, yet hardly Virtue's friend,
For Virtue pardons those she would amend.

But to the theme: — now laid aside too long
The baleful burden of this honest song —
Though all her former functions are no more,
She rules the circle which she served before.
If mothers — none know why — before her
　quake;
If daughters dread her for the mothers' sake;
If early habits — those false links, which bind
At times the loftiest to the meanest mind —
Have given her power too deeply to instil
The angry essence of her deadly will;
If like a snake she steal within your walls,
Till the black slime betray her as she crawls;
If like a viper to the heart she wind,
And leave the venom there she did not find ·
What marvel that this hag of hatred works
Eternal evil latent as she lurks,
To make a Pandemonium where she dwells.
And reign the Hecate of domestic hells?
Skilled by a touch to deepen scandal's tint,
With all the kind mendacity of hints.·

While mingling truth with falsehood — sneers
  with smiles —
A thread of candor with a web of wiles ;
A plain blunt show of briefly-spoken seeming,
To hide her bloodless heart's soul-hardened
  scheming ;
A lip of lies — a face formed to conceal ;
And, without feeling, mock at all who feel :
With a vile mask the Gorgon would disown ;
A cheek of parchment — and an eye of stone.
Mark, how the channels of her yellow blood
Ooze to her skin, and stagnate there to mud,
Cased like the centipede in saffron mail,
Or darker greenness of the scorpion's scale —
(For drawn from reptiles only may we trace
Congenial colors in that soul or face) —
Look on her features ! and behold her mind
As in a mirror of itself defined :
Look on the picture ! deem it not o'er-
  charged —
There is no trait which might not be enlarged,
Yet true to " Nature's journeymen," who made
This monster when their mistress left off
  trade —
This female dog-star of her little sky,
Where all beneath her influence droop or die.

Oh ! wretch without a tear — without a
  thought,
Save joy above the ruin thou hast wrought —
The time shall come, nor long remote, when
  thou
Shalt feel far more than thou inflictest now ;
Feel for thy vile self-loving self in vain,
And turn thee howling in unpitied pain.
May the strong curse of crushed affections
  light
Back on thy bosom with reflected blight !
And make thee in thy leprosy of mind
As loathsome to thyself as to mankind !
Till all thy self-thoughts curdle into hate,
Black — as thy will for others would create :
Till thy hard heart be calcined into dust,
And thy soul welter in its hideous crust.
Oh, may thy grave be sleepless as the bed, —
The widowed couch of fire, that thou hast
  spread !
Then, when thou fain wouldst weary Heaven
  with prayer,
Look on thine earthly victims — and despair !
Down to the dust ! — and as thou rott'st away,
Even worms shall perish on thy poisonous
  clay.
But for the love I bore, and still must bear,
To her thy malice from all ties would tear —
Thy name — thy human name — to every eye
The climax of all scorn should hang on high,
Exalted o'er thy less abhorred compeers —
And festering [1] in the infamy of years.

                   March 29, 1816.

[1] [In first draught — " weltering." — " I doubt

STANZAS TO AUGUSTA.[2]

I.

WHEN all around grew drear and dark,
  And reason half withheld her ray —
And hope but shed a dying spark
  Which more misled my lonely way ;

II.

In that deep midnight of the mind,
  And that internal strife of heart,
When dreading to be deemed too kind,
  The weak despair — the cold depart ;

III.

When fortune changed — and love fled far,
  And hatred's shafts flew thick and fast,
Thou wert the solitary star
  Which rose and set not to the last.

IV.

Oh ! blest be thine unbroken light !
  That watched me as a seraph's eye,
And stood between me and the night,
  For ever shining sweetly nigh.

V.

And when the cloud upon us came,
  Which strove to blacken o'er thy ray —
Then purer spread its gentle flame,
  And dashed the darkness all away.

VI.

Still may thy spirit dwell on mine,
  And teach it what to brave or brook —
There's more in one soft word of thine
  Than in the world's defied rebuke.

VII.

Thou stood'st, as stands a lovely tree,
  That still unbroke, though gently bent,
Still waves with fond fidelity
  Its boughs above a monument.

VIII.

The winds might rend — the skies might pour,
  But there thou wert — and still would'st be
Devoted in the stormiest hour
  To shed thy weeping leaves o'er me.

about ' weltering.' We say ' weltering in blood ; '
but do not they also use ' weltering in the wind,'
' weltering on a gibbet ? ' I have no dictionary, so
look. In the mean time, I have put ' festering ; '
which perhaps, in any case, is the best word of the
two. Shakspeare has it often, and I do not think
it too strong for the figure in this thing. Quick !
quick ! quick ! " — *Byron to Mr. Murray,*
April 2, 1816.]
[2] [His sister, the Honorable Mrs. Leigh. —
These stanzas — the parting tribute to her, whose
tenderness had been his sole consolation during the
crisis of domestic misery — were the last verses
written by Byron in England.]

IX.

But thou and thine shall know no blight,
  Whatever fate on me may fall;
For heaven in sunshine will requite
  The kind — and thee the most of all.

X.

Then let the ties of baffled love
  Be broken — thine will never break;
Thy heart can feel — but will not move;
  Thy soul, though soft, will never shake.

XI.

And these, when all was lost beside,
  Were found and still are fixed in thee; —
And bearing still a breast so tried,
  Earth is no desert — even to me.

STANZAS TO AUGUSTA.[1]

I.

THOUGH the day of my destiny's over,
  And the star of my fate hath declined,[2]
Thy soft heart refused to discover
  The faults which so many could find;
Though thy soul with my grief was acquainted,
  It shrunk not to share it with me,
And the love which my spirit hath painted
  It never hath found but in *thee.*

II.

Then when nature around me is smiling,
  The last smile which answers to mine,
I do not believe it beguiling,
  Because it reminds me of thine;
And when winds are at war with the ocean,
  As the breasts I believed in with me,
If their billows excite an emotion,
  It is that they bear me from *thee.*

III.

Though the rock of my last hope is shivered,
  And its fragments are sunk in the wave,
Though I feel that my soul is delivered
  To pain — it shall not be its slave.
There is many a pang to pursue me:
  They may crush, but they shall not con-
    temn —
They may torture, but shall not subdue me —
  'Tis of *thee* that I think — not of them.[3]

---

[1] [These beautiful verses, so expressive of the
writer's wounded feelings at the moment, were
written in July, at the Campagne Diodati, near
Geneva. " Be careful," he says, " in printing the
stanzas beginning, ' Though the day of my destiny's,'
etc., which I think well of as a composition."]

[2] [In the original MS. —
  " Though the days of my glory are over,
    And the sun of my fame hath declined."]

[3] [Originally thus: —

There is many a pang to pursue me,
  And many a peril to stem:

IV.

Though human, thou did'st not deceive me,
  Though woman, thou did'st not forsake,
Though loved, thou forborest to grieve me,
  Though slandered, thou never could'st
    shake, —
Though trusted, thou didst not disclaim me,
  Though parted, it was not to fly,
Though watchful, 'twas not to defame me,
  Nor, mute, that the world might belie.[4]

V.

Yet I blame not the world, nor despise it,
  Nor the war of the many with one —
If my soul was not fitted to prize it,
  'Twas folly not sooner to shun:
And if dearly that error hath cost me,
  And more than I once could foresee,
I have found that, whatever it lost me,
  It could not deprive me of *thee.*

VI.

From the wreck of the past, which hath per-
    ished,
  Thus much I at least may recall,
It hath taught me that what I most cherished
  Deserved to be dearest of all:
In the desert a fountain is springing,
  In the wide waste there still is a tree,
And a bird in the solitude singing,
  Which speaks to my spirit of *thee.*

                              July 24, 1816.

EPISTLE TO AUGUSTA.[5]

I.

MY sister! my sweet sister! if a name
Dearer and purer were, it should be thine.
Mountains and seas divide us, but I claim
No tears, but tenderness to answer mine:
Go where I will, to me thou art the same —
A loved regret which I would not resign.
There yet are two things in my destiny, —
A world to roam through, and a home with
  thee.

II.

The first were nothing — had I still the last,
It were the haven of my happiness;

They may torture, but shall not subdue me;
  They may crush, but they shall not contemn."]

[4] [MS. —

" Though watchful, 'twas but to reclaim me,
  Nor, silent, to sanction a lie."]

[5] [These stanzas — " Than which," says the
Quarterly Review, for January, 1831, " there is,
perhaps, nothing more mournfully and desolately
beautiful in the whole range of Lord Byron's poe-
try " — were also written at Diodati; and sent home
at the time for publication, if Mrs. Leigh should
sanction it. She decided against it, and the Epistle
was not published till 1830.]

But other claims and other ties thou hast,
And mine is not the wish to make them less.
A strange doom is thy father's son's, and past
Recalling, as it lies beyond redress;
Reversed for him our grandsire's[1] fate of yore,—
He had no rest at sea, nor I on shore.

III.

If my inheritance of storms hath been
In other elements, and on the rocks
Of perils, overlooked or unforeseen,
I have sustained my share of worldly shocks,
The fault was mine; nor do I seek to screen
My errors with defensive paradox;
I have been cunning in mine overthrow,
The careful pilot of my proper woe.

IV.

Mine were my faults, and mine be their reward.
My whole life was a contest, since the day
That gave me being, gave me that which marred
The gift,—a fate, or will, that walked astray;
And I at times have found the struggle hard,
And thought of shaking off my bonds of clay:
But now I fain would for a time survive,
If but to see what next can well arrive.

V.

Kingdoms and empires in my little day
I have outlived, and yet I am not old;
And when I look on this, the petty spray
Of my own years of trouble, which have rolled
Like a wild bay of breakers, melts away:
Something—I know not what—does still uphold
A spirit of slight patience;—not in vain,
Even for its own sake, do we purchase pain.

VI.

Perhaps the workings of defiance stir
Within me,—or perhaps a cold despair,
Brought on when ills habitually recur,—
Perhaps a kinder clime, or purer air,
(For even to this may change of soul refer,
And with light armor we may learn to bear,)
Have taught me a strange quiet, which was not
The chief companion of a calmer lot.

[1] [Admiral Byron was remarkable for never making a voyage without a tempest. He was known to the sailors by the facetious name of "Foul-weather Jack."

"But, though it were tempest-tossed,
Still his bark could not be lost."

He returned safely from the wreck of the Wager (in Anson's voyage), and subsequently circumnavigated the world, many years after, as commander of a similar expedition.]

VII.

I feel almost at times as I have felt,
In happy childhood; trees, and flowers, and brooks,
Which do remember me of where I dwelt
Ere my young mind was sacrificed to books,
Come as of yore upon me, and can melt
My heart with recognition of their looks;
And even at moments I could think I see
Some living thing to love—but none like thee

VIII.

Here are the Alpine landscapes which create
A fund for contemplation;—to admire
Is a brief feeling of a trivial date;
But something worthier do such scenes inspire:
Here to be lonely is not desolate,
For much I view which I could most desire,
And, above all, a lake I can behold
Lovelier, not dearer, than our own of old.

IX.

Oh that thou wert but with me!—but I grow
The fool of my own wishes, and forget
The solitude which I have vaunted so
Has lost its praise in this but one regret;
There may be others which I less may show;—
I am not of the plaintive mood, and yet
I feel an ebb in my philosophy,
And the tide rising in my altered eye.

X.

I did remind thee of our own dear Lake,[2]
By the old Hall which may be mine no more.
Leman's is fair; but think not I forsake
The sweet remembrance of a dearer shore:
Sad havoc Time must with my memory make
Ere *that* or *thou* can fade these eyes before;
Though, like all things which I have loved, they are
Resigned for ever, or divided far.

XI.

The world is all before me; I but ask
Of Nature that with which she will comply—
It is but in her summer's sun to bask,
To mingle with the quiet of her sky,
To see her gentle face without a mask,
And never gaze on it with apathy.
She was my early friend, and now shall be
My sister—till I look again on thee.

XII.

I can reduce all feelings but this one;
And that I would not;—for at length I see
Such scenes as those wherein my life begun.

[2] [The Lake of Newstead Abbey which he has described minutely in the Thirteenth Canto of Don Juan.]

The earliest — even the only paths for me —
Had I but sooner learnt the crowd to shun,
I had been better than I now can be;
The passions which have torn me would
      have slept;
I had not suffered, and *thou* hadst not wept.

XIII.

With false Ambition what had I to do?
Little with Love, and least of all with Fame:
And yet they came unsought, and with me
      grew,
And made me all which they can make —
      a name.
Yet this was not the end I did pursue;
Surely I once beheld a nobler aim.
But all is over — I am one the more
To baffled millions which have gone before.

XIV.

And for the future, this world's future may
From me demand but little of my care;
I have outlived myself by many a day;
Having survived so many things that were;
My years have been no slumber, but the
      prey
Of ceaseless vigils; for I had the share
Of life which might have filled a century,
Before its fourth in time had passed me by.

XV.

And for the remnant which may be to come
I am content; and for the past I feel
Not thankless, — for within the crowded sum
Of struggles, happiness at times would steal,
And for the present, I would not benumb
My feelings further. — Nor shall I conceal
That with all this I still can look around
And worship Nature with a thought profound.

XVI.

For thee, my own sweet sister, in thy heart
I know myself secure, as thou in mine;
We were and are — I am, even as thou art —
Beings who ne'er each other can resign;
It is the same, together or apart,
From life's commencement to its slow de-
      cline
We are entwined — let death come slow or
      fast,
The tie which bound the first endures the last!

LINES

ON HEARING THAT LADY BYRON WAS ILL.

AND thou wert sad — yet I was not with thee;
   And thou wert sick, and yet I was not near;
Methought that joy and health alone could be

Where I was not — and pain and sorrow
      here!
And is it thus? — it is as I foretold,
   And shall be more so; for the mind recoils
Upon itself, and the wrecked heart lies cold,
   While heaviness collects the shattered spoils.
It is not in the storm nor in the strife
   We feel benumbed, and wish to be no more,
But in the after-silence on the shore,
When all is lost, except a little life.

I am too well avenged! — but 'twas my right;
   Whate'er my sins might be, *thou* wert not
      sent
To be the Nemesis who should requite —
   Nor did Heaven choose so near an instru-
      ment.
Mercy is for the merciful! — if thou
Hast been of such, 'twill be accorded now.
Thy nights are banished from the realms of
      sleep! —
Yes! they may flatter thee, but thou shalt
      feel
A hollow agony which will not heal,
For thou art pillowed on a curse too deep;
Thou hast sown in my sorrow, and must reap
   The bitter harvest in a woe as real!
I have had many foes, but none like thee;
   For 'gainst the rest myself I could defend,
   And be avenged, or turn them into friend;
But thou in safe implacability
Hadst nought to dread — in thy own weakness
      shielded,
And in my love, which hath but too much
      yielded,
And spared, for thy sake, some I should
      not spare —
And thus upon the world — trust in thy truth —
And the wild fame of my ungoverned youth —
   On things that were not, and on things that
      are —
Even upon such a basis hast thou built
A monument, whose cement hath been guilt!
   The moral Clytemnestra of thy lord,
And hewed down, with an unsuspected sword,
Fame, peace, and hope — and all the better
      life
   Which, but for this cold treason of thy heart,
Might still have risen from out the grave of
      strife,
And found a nobler duty than to part.
But of thy virtues didst thou make a vice,
   Trafficking with them in a purpose cold,
   For present anger, and for future gold —
And buying other's grief at any price.
And thus once entered into crooked ways,
The early truth, which was thy proper praise,
   Did not still walk beside thee — but at times,
   And with a breast unknowing its own crimes
Deceit, averments incompatible,
Equivocations, and the thoughts which dwell
   In Janus-spirits — the significant eye

Which learns to lie with silence — the pretext
Of Prudence, with advantages annexed —
The acquiescence in all things which tend,
No matter how, to the desired end —

All found a place in thy philosophy.
The means were worthy, and the end is won —
I would not do by thee as thou hast done!

September, 1816.

MONODY ON THE DEATH OF THE RIGHT HON. R. B. SHERIDAN,

SPOKEN AT DRURY-LANE THEATRE.

[Mr. Sheridan died the 7th of July, 1816, and this monody was written at Diodati on the 17th, at the request of Mr. Douglas Kinnaird. "I did as well as I could," says Byron, "but where I have not my choice, I pretend to answer for nothing." He told Lady Blessington, however, that his feelings were never more excited than while writing it, and that every word came direct from his heart.]

WHEN the last sunshine of expiring day
In summer's twilight weeps itself away,
Who hath not felt the softness of the hour
Sink on the heart, as dew along the flower ?
With a pure feeling which absorbs and awes
While Nature makes that melancholy pause,
Her breathing moment on the bridge where Time
Of light and darkness forms an arch sublime,
Who hath not shared that calm so still and deep,
The voiceless thought which would not speak but weep,
A holy concord — and a bright regret,
A glorious sympathy with suns that set ?
'Tis not harsh sorrow — but a tenderer woe,
Nameless, but dear to gentle hearts below,
Felt without bitterness — but full and clear,
A sweet dejection — a transparent tear,
Unmixed with worldly grief or selfish stain,
Shed without shame — and secret without pain.

Even as the tenderness that hour instils
When Summer's day declines along the hills,
So feels the fulness of our heart and eyes
When all of Genius which can perish dies.
A mighty Spirit is eclipsed — a Power
Hath passed from day to darkness — to whose hour
Of light no likeness is bequeathed — no name,
Focus at once of all the rays of Fame!

The flash of Wit — the bright Intelligence,
The beam of Song — the blaze of Eloquence,
Set with their Sun — but still have left behind
The enduring produce of immortal Mind;
Fruits of a genial morn, and glorious noon,
A deathless part of him who died too soon.
But small that portion of the wondrous whole,
These sparkling segments of that circling soul,
Which all embraced — and lightened over all,
To cheer — to pierce — to please — or to appall.
From the charmed council to the festive board,
Of human feelings the unbounded lord;
In whose acclaim the loftiest voices vied,
The praised — the proud — who made his praise their pride.
When the loud cry of trampled Hindostan [1]

[1] [See Fox, Burke, and Pitt's eulogy on Mr. Sheridan's speech on the charges exhibited against Mr. Hastings in the House of Commons. Mr. Pitt entreated the House to adjourn, to give time for a calmer consideration of the question than could then occur after the immediate effect of the oration. — " Before my departure from England," says Gibbon, " I was present at the august spectacle of Mr. Hastings's trial in Westminster Hall. It is not my province to absolve or condemn the governor of India; but Mr. Sheridan's eloquence demanded my applause; nor could I hear without emotion the personal compliment which he paid me in the presence of the British nation. This display of genius blazed four successive days," etc. On being asked

Arose to Heaven in her appeal from man,
His was the thunder — his the avenging rod,
The wrath — the delegated voice of God!
Which shook the nations through his lips —
    and blazed
Till vanquished senates trembled as they
    praised.[1]

And here, oh! here, where yet all young and
    warm
The gay creations of his spirit charm,
The matchless dialogue — the deathless wit,
Which knew not what it was to intermit;
The glowing portraits, fresh from life, that bring
Home to our hearts the truth from which they
    spring;
These wondrous beings of his Fancy, wrought
To fulness by the fiat of his thought,
Here in their first abode you still may meet,
Bright with the hues of his Promethean heat;
A halo of the light of other days,
Which still the splendor of its orb betrays.
But should there be to whom the fatal blight
Of failing Wisdom yields a base delight,
Men who exult when minds of heavenly tone
Jar in the music which was born their own,
Still let them pause — ah! little do they know
That what to them seemed Vice might be but
    Woe.
Hard is his fate on whom the public gaze
Is fixed for ever to detract or praise;
Repose denies her requiem to his name,
And Folly loves the martyrdom of Fame.
The secret enemy whose sleepless eye
Stands sentinel — accuser — judge — and spy,
The foe — the fool — the jealous — and the
    vain,
The envious who but breathe in others' pain,
Behold the host! delighting to deprave,
Who track the steps of Glory to the grave,
Watch every fault that daring genius owes
Half to the ardor which its birth bestows,
Distort the truth, accumulate the lie,
And pile the Pyramid of Calumny!

These are his portion — but if joined to these
Gaunt Poverty should league with deep Dis-
    ease,
If the high Spirit must forget to soar,
And stoop to strive with Misery at the door,[2]

To soothe Indignity — and face to face
Meet sorded Rage — and wrestle with Dis-
    grace,
To find in Hope but the renewed caress,
The serpent-fold of further Faithlessness : —
If such may be the Ills which men assail,
What marvel if at last the mightiest fail?
Breasts to whom all the strength of feeling
    given
Bear hearts electric — charged with fire from
    Heaven,
Black with the rude collision, inly torn,
By clouds surrounded, and on whirlwinds
    borne,
Driven o'er the lowering atmosphere that nurst
Thoughts which have turned to thunder —
    scorch — and burst.[3]

But far from us and from our mimic scene
Such things should be — if such have ever
    been;
Ours be the gentler wish, the kinder task,
To give the tribute Glory need not ask,
To mourn the vanished beam — and add our
    mite
Of praise in payment of a long delight.
Ye Orators! whom yet our councils yield,
Mourn for the veteran Hero of your field!
The worthy rival of the wondrous *Three!*[4]
Whose words were sparks of Immortality!
Ye Bards! to whom the Drama's Muse is dear,
He was your Master — emulate him *here!*
Ye men of wit and social eloquence![5]
He was your brother — bear his ashes hence!
While Powers of mind almost of boundless
    range,[6]

---

by a brother Whig, at the conclusion of the speech,
how he came to compliment Gibbon with the epi-
thet "luminous," Sheridan answered, in a half
whisper, "I said '*vo*luminous.'"]

[1] ["I heard Sheridan only once, and that briefly;
but I liked his voice, his manner, and his wit. He
is the only one of them I ever wished to hear at
greater length." — *Byron's Diary*, 1821.]

[2] [This was not fiction. Only a few days before
his death, Sheridan wrote thus to Mr. Rogers : —
"I am absolutely undone and broken-hearted.
They are going to put the carpets out of window,
and break into Mrs. S.'s room and *take me:* 150*l*.
will remove all difficulty. For God's sake let me

see you!" Mr. Moore was the immediate bearer
of the required sum. This was written on the 15th
of May. On the 14th of July, Sheridan's remains
were deposited in Westminster Abbey, — his pall-
bearers being the Duke of Bedford, the Earl of
Lauderdale, Earl Mulgrave, the Lord Bishop of
London, Lord Holland, and Earl Spencer.

[3] [In the original MS. —
"Abandoned by the skies, whose beams have nurst,
Their very thunders lighten — scorch — and burst."]

[4] Fox — Pitt — Burke.

[5] ["In society I have met Sheridan frequently.
He was superb! I have seen him cut up Whit-
bread, quiz Madame de Staël, annihilate Colman,
and do little less by some others of good fame and
ability. I have met him at all places and parties
and always found him convivial and delightful." —
Byron's Diary, 1821.]

[6] ["The other night we were all delivering our
respective and various opinions upon Sheridan, and
mine was this: — 'Whatever Sheridan has done or
chosen to do has been *par excellence* always the
best of its kind. He has written the best comedy
(School for Scandal), the best drama (in my mind,
far beyond that St. Giles's lampoon, the Beggars'
Opera), the best farce (the Critic — it is only too
good for a farce), and the best address (Monologue

Complete in kind — as various in their change,
While Eloquence — Wit — Poesy — and Mirth,

on Garrick) and, to crown all, delivered the very best oration (the famous Begum speech) ever conceived or heard in this country.' " — *Byron's Diary*, Dec. 17, 1813.]

That humbler Harmonist of care on Earth,
Survive within our souls — while lives our sense
Of pride in Merit's proud pre-eminence,
Long shall we seek his likeness — long in vain,
And turn to all of him which may remain,
Sighing that Nature formed but one such man,
And broke the die — in moulding Sheridan!

THE DREAM.

[" The Dream " — called in the first draught " *The Destiny* " — was written at Diodati, in July, 1816, and reflects the train of thought engendered by the recent quarrel with Lady Byron. The misery of his marriage led him to revert to his early passion for Miss Chaworth, whose union had proved no happier than his own.]

I.

OUR life is twofold : Sleep hath its own world,
A boundary between the things misnamed
Death and existence : Sleep hath its own world,
And a wide realm of wild reality,
And dreams in their development have breath,
And tears, and tortures, and the touch of joy;
They leave a weight upon our waking thoughts,
They take a weight from off our waking toils,
They do divide our being; they become
A portion of ourselves as of our time,
And look like heralds of eternity;
They pass like spirits of the past, — they speak
Like sibyls of the future; they have power —
The tyranny of pleasure and of pain;
They make us what we were not — what they will,
And shake us with the vision that's gone by,
The dread of vanished shadows — Are they so?
Is not the past all shadow? What are they?
Creations of the mind? — The mind can make
Substance, and people planets of its own
With beings brighter than have been, and give
A breath to forms which can outlive all flesh.
I would recall a vision which I dreamed
Perchance in sleep — for in itself a thought,
A slumbering thought, is capable of years,
And curdles a long life into one hour.

II.

I saw two beings in the hues of youth
Standing upon a hill, a gentle hill,
Green and of mild declivity, the last

As 'twere the cape of a long ridge of such,
Save that there was no sea to lave its base,
But a most living landscape, and the wave
Of woods and cornfields, and the abodes of men
Scattered at intervals, and wreathing smoke
Arising from such rustic roofs; — the hill
Was crowned with a peculiar diadem
Of trees, in circular array, so fixed,
Not by the sport of nature, but of man:
These two, a maiden and a youth, were there
Gazing — the one on all that was beneath
Fair as herself — but the boy gazed on her;
And both were young, and one was beautiful:
And both were young — yet not alike in youth.
As the sweet moon on the horizon's verge,
The maid was on the eve of womanhood;
The boy had fewer summers, but his heart
Had far outgrown his years, and to his eye
There was but one beloved face on earth,
And that was shining on him; he had looked
Upon it till it could not pass away;
He had no breath, no being, but in hers;
She was his voice; he did not speak to her,
But trembled on her words; she was his sight,[1]
For his eye followed hers, and saw with hers,
Which colored all his objects : — he had ceased
To live within himself; she was his life,
The ocean to the river of his thoughts,
Which terminated all : upon a tone,
A touch of hers, his blood would ebb and flow,

[1] [MS. : —   — " she was his sight,
For never did he turn his glance until
Her own had led by gazing on an object."]

And his cheek change tempestuously — his
   heart
Unknowing of its cause of agony.
But she in these fond feelings had no share:
Her sighs were not for him; to her he was
Even as a brother — but no more; 'twas much,
For brotherless she was, save in the name
Her infant friendship had bestowed on him;
Herself the solitary scion left
Of a time-honored race.[1] — It was a name
Which pleased him, and yet pleased him not —
   and why ?
Time taught him a deep answer — when she
   loved
Another; even *now* she loved another,
And on the summit of that hill she stood
Looking afar if yet her lover's steed
Kept pace with her expectancy, and flew.

III.

A change came o'er the spirit of my dream.
There was an ancient mansion, and before
Its walls there was a steed caparisoned:
Within an antique Oratory stood
The Boy of whom I spake; — he was alone,
And pale, and pacing to and fro: anon
He sate him down, and seized a pen, and traced
Words which I could not guess of; then he
   leaned
His bowed head on his hands, and shook as
   'twere
With a convulsion — then arose again,
And with his teeth and quivering hands did tear
What he had written, but he shed no tears.
And he did calm himself, and fix his brow
Into a kind of quiet: as he paused,
The Lady of his love reëntered there;
She was serene and smiling then, and yet
She knew she was by him beloved, — she knew,
For quickly comes such knowledge, that his
   heart
Was darkened with her shadow, and she saw
That he was wretched, but she saw not all.[2]
He rose, and with a cold and gentle grasp
He took her hand; a moment o'er his face
A tablet of unutterable thoughts
Was traced, and then it faded, as it came;
He dropped the hand he held, and with slow
   steps
Retired, but not as bidding her adieu,
For they did part with mutual smiles; he
   passed

From out the massy gate of that old Hall,
And mounting on his steed he went his way;
And ne'er repassed that hoary threshold more.

IV.

A change came o'er the spirit of my dream.
The boy was sprung to manhood: in the wilds
Of fiery climes he made himself a home,
And his Soul drank their sunbeams: he was
   girt
With strange and dusky aspects; he was not
Himself like what he had been; on the sea
And on the shore he was a wanderer;
There was a mass of many images
Crowded like waves upon me, but he was
A part of all; and in the last he lay
Reposing from the noontide sultriness,
Couched among fallen columns, in the shade
Of ruined walls that had survived the names
Of those who reared them; by his sleeping side
Stood camels grazing, and some goodly steeds
Were fastened near a fountain; and a man
Clad in a flowing garb did watch the while,
While many of his tribe slumber'd around:
And they were canopied by the blue sky,
So cloudless, clear, and purely beautiful,
That God alone was to be seen in Heaven.[3]

V.

A change came o'er the spirit of my dream.
The Lady of his love was wed with One
Who did not love her better: — in her home,
A thousand leagues from his, — her native
   home,
She dwelt, begirt with growing Infancy,
Daughters and sons of Beauty, — but behold !
Upon her face there was the tint of grief,
The settled shadow of an inward strife,
And an unquiet drooping of the eye
As if its lid were charged with unshed tears.
What could her grief be ? — she had all she
   loved,
And he who had so loved her was not there
To trouble with bad hopes, or evil wish, ·
Or ill-repress'd affliction, her pure thoughts.
What could her grief be ? — she had loved him
   not,
Nor given him cause to deem himself beloved,
Nor could he be a part of that which preyed
Upon her mind — a spectre of the past.

VI.

·A change came o'er the spirit of my dream.
The Wanderer was return'd. — I saw him stand

---

[1] ["Our union," said Byron in 1821, "would
have healed feuds in which blood had been shed by
our fathers — it would have joined lands, broad and
rich — it would have joined at least *one* heart and
two persons not ill-matched in years (she is two
years my elder) — and — and — and — what has
been the result!"]

[2] ["I had long been in love with M. A. C., and
never told it, though *she* had discovered it without.
I recollect my sensations, but cannot describe them,
and it is as well." — *Byron's Diary*, 1822.]

[3] [This is true *keeping* — an Eastern picture per-
fect in its foreground, and distance, and sky, and
no part of which is so dwelt upon or labored as to
obscure the principal figure. It is often in the
slight and almost imperceptible touches that the
hand of the master is shown, and that a single
spark, struck from his fancy, lightens with a long
train of illumination that of the reader. — *Sir
Walter Scott.*]

Before an Altar—with a gentle bride;
Her face was fair, but was not that which made
The Starlight of his Boyhood;—as he stood
Even at the altar, o'er his brow there came
The selfsame aspect, and the quivering shock
That in the antique Oratory shook
His bosom in its solitude; and then—
As in that hour—a moment o'er his face
The tablet of unutterable thoughts
Was traced,—and then it faded as it came,
And he stood calm and quiet, and he spoke
The fitting vows, but heard not his own words,
And all things reeled around him; he could see
Not that which was, nor that which should have been—
But the old mansion, and the accustomed hall,
And the remembered chambers, and the place,
The day, the hour, the sunshine, and the shade,
All things pertaining to that place and hour,
And her who was his destiny, came back
And thrust themselves between him and the light:
What business had they there at such a time?[1]

VII.

A change came o'er the spirit of my dream.
The Lady of his love;—Oh! she was changed
As by the sickness of the soul; her mind
Had wandered from its dwelling, and her eyes
They had not their own lustre, but the look
Which is not of the earth; she was become
The queen of a fantastic realm; her thoughts
Were combinations of disjointed things;
And forms impalpable and unperceived
Of others' sight familiar were to hers.
And this the world calls frenzy; but the wise
Have a far deeper madness, and the glance
Of melancholy is a fearful gift;

[1] [This touching picture agrees closely, in many of its circumstances, with Lord Byron's own prose account of the wedding in his Memoranda; in which he describes himself as waking, on the morning of his marriage, with the most melancholy reflections, on seeing his wedding-suit spread out before him. In the same mood, he wandered about the grounds alone, till he was summoned for the ceremony, and joined, for the first time, on that day, his bride and her family. He knelt down—he repeated the words after the clergyman; but a mist was before his eyes—his thoughts were elsewhere; and he was but awakened by the congratulations of the by-standers to find that he was—married.—*Moore.*]

What is it but the telescope of truth?
Which strips the distance of its fantasies,
And brings life near in utter nakedness,
Making the cold reality too real![2]

VIII.

A change came o'er the spirit of my dream.
The Wanderer was alone as heretofore,
The beings which surrounded him were gone,
Or were at war with him; he was a mark
For blight and desolation, compassed round
With Hatred and Contention; Pain was mixed
In all which was served up to him, until,
Like to the Pontic monarch of old days,[3]
He fed on poisons, and they had no power,
But were a kind of nutriment; he lived
Through that which had been death to many men,
And made him friends of mountains: with the stars
And the quick Spirit of the Universe
He held his dialogues; and they did teach
To him the magic of their mysteries;
To him the book of Night was open'd wide,
And voices from the deep abyss reveal'd
A marvel and a secret—Be it so.

IX.

My dream was past; it had no further change.
It was of a strange order, that the doom
Of these two creatures should be thus traced out
Almost like a reality—the one
To end in madness—both in misery.[4]

July, 1816.

[2] [MS.—   —" the glance
    Of melancholy is a fearful gift;
    For it becomes the telescope of truth,
    And shows us all things naked as they are."]

[3] Mithridates of Pontus.

[4] [This poem is written with great beauty and genius—but is extremely painful. We cannot maintain our accustomed tone of levity, or even speak like calm literary judges, in the midst of these agonizing traces of a wounded and distempered spirit. Even our admiration is swallowed up in a most painful feeling of pity and of wonder. It is impossible to mistake these for fictitious sorrows, conjured up for the purpose of poetical effect. There is a dreadful tone of sincerity, and an energy that cannot be counterfeited, in the expression of wretchedness, and alienation from human-kind, which occurs in every line of this poem.—*Jeffrey.*]

THE LAMENT OF TASSO.

At Ferrara, in the Library, are preserved the original MSS. of Tasso's Gierusalemme and of Guarini's Pastor Fido, with letters of Tasso, one from Titian to Ariosto; and the inkstand and chair, the tomb and the house of the latter. But, as misfortune has a greater interest for posterity, and little or none for the contemporary, the cell where Tasso was confined in the hospital of St. Anna attracts a more fixed attention, than the residence or the monument of Ariosto — at least it had this effect on me. There are two inscriptions, one on the outer gate, the second over the cell itself, inviting, unnecessarily, the wonder and the indignation of the spectator. Ferrara is much decayed, and depopulated: the castle still exists entire; and I saw the court where Parisina and Hugo were beheaded, according to the annal of Gibbon. — [The original MS. of this poem is dated, "The Apennines, April 20, 1817." It was written in consequence of Byron having visited Ferrara, for a single day, on his way to Florence. In a letter from Rome, he says, — "The 'Lament of Tasso,' which I sent from Florence, has, I trust, arrived. I look upon it as a ' These be good rhymes! ' as Pope's papa said to him when he was a boy."]

INTRODUCTION.

AFTER all that has been written upon the Duke of Ferrara's imprisonment of Tasso, a great deal continues to be left to conjecture. It seems certain that he was in love with the Princess Eleanora, and that he addressed her amatory poems. There are other pieces which probably refer to her, in which he boasts of a dishonorable success, and which are supposed to have fallen into the hands of her brother, the Duke. But the immediate cause of Tasso's arrest was a quarrel in the palace at Ferrara, when he threw a knife at a domestic. The affair ended in his being sent as a lunatic to the convent of St. Francis. This was on the 11th of July, 1577, and on the 20th he made his escape. In February, 1579, he returned to Ferrara, and the Duke and the Princess refusing to notice him, he uttered imprecations against them, was declared a madman, and was confined for seven years in the hospital of St. Anna. A miserable dungeon below the ground-floor, and lighted from a grated window, which looks into a small covert, is shown as the scene of his sufferings, but there is unlikelihood that it was so, and Tasso was at least removed to a spacious apartment before a twelvemonth had elapsed. The poet protested that the madness of 1577 was feigned to please the Duke, who hoped, according to modern inferences, that any imputations upon the name of the Princess would be ascribed to the hallucinations of a distempered mind. Whether the subsequent madness of 1579 was real or not, has been the subject of endless speculations, but if clouds obscured the mind of Tasso they broke away at intervals, and allowed him to continue his immortal compositions. Byron adopts the theory that he was imprisoned under a false pretence to avenge a pure but presumptuous love.

I.

LONG years! — It tries the thrilling frame to bear
And eagle-spirit of a Child of Song —
Long years of outrage, calumny, and wrong;
Imputed madness, prisoned solitude,
And the mind's canker in its savage mood,
When the impatient thirst of light and air
Parches the heart; and the abhorred grate,
Marring the sunbeams with its hideous shade,
Works through the throbbing eyeball to the brain
With a hot sense of heaviness and pain;
And bare, at once, Captivity displayed
Stands scoffing through the never-opened gate,
Which nothing through its bars admits, save day,
And tasteless food, which I have eat alone
Till its unsocial bitterness is gone;

And I can banquet like a beast of prey,
Sullen and lonely, couching in the cave
Which is my lair, and — it may be — my grave.
All this hath somewhat worn me, and may wear,
But must be borne. I stoop not to despair;
For I have battled with mine agony,
And made me wings wherewith to overfly
The narrow circus of my dungeon wall,
And freed the Holy Sepulchre from thrall;
And revelled among men and things divine,
And poured my spirit over Palestine,
In honor of the sacred war for Him,
The God who was on earth and is in heaven,
For he hath strengthened me in heart and limb.
That through this sufferance I might be forgiven,
I have employed my penance to record
How Salem's shrine was won, and how adored.

II.

But this is o'er — my pleasant task is done : — [1]
My long-sustaining friend of many years!
If I do blot thy final page with tears,
Know, that my sorrows have wrung from me none.
But, thou, my young creation! my soul's child!
Which ever playing round me came and smiled,
And wooed me from myself with thy sweet sight,
Thou too art gone — and so is my delight:
And therefore do I weep and inly bleed
With this last bruise upon a broken reed.
Thou too art ended — what is left me now?
For I have anguish yet to bear — and how?
I know not that — but in the innate force
Of my own spirit shall be found resource.
I have not sunk, for I had no remorse,
Nor cause for such: they called me mad — and why?
Oh Leonora! wilt not thou reply? [2]

I was indeed delirious in my heart
To lift my love so lofty as thou art;
But still my frenzy was not of the mind;
I knew my fault, and feel my punishment
Not less because I suffer it unbent.
That thou wert beautiful, and I not blind,
Hath been the sin which shuts me from mankind;
But let them go, or torture as they will,
My heart can multiply thine image still;
Successful love may sate itself away,
The wretched are the faithful; 'tis their fate
To have all feeling save the one decay,
And every passion into one dilate,
As rapid rivers into ocean pour;
But ours is fathomless, and hath no shore.

III.

Above me, hark! the long and maniac cry
Of minds and bodies in captivity.
And hark! the lash and the increasing howl,
And the half-inarticulate blasphemy!
There be some here with worse than frenzy foul,
Some who do still goad on the o'er-labored mind,
And dim the little light that's left behind
With needless torture, as their tyrant will
Is wound up to the lust of doing ill: [3]
With these and with their Victims am I classed,
'Mid sounds and sights like these long years have passed;
'Mid sights and sounds like these my life may close:
So let it be — for then I shall repose.

IV.

I have been patient, let me be so yet,
I had forgotten half I would forget,
But it revives — Oh! would it were my lot
To be forgetful as I am forgot! —
Feel I not wroth with those who bade me dwell
In this vast lazar-house of many woes?

[1] [The opening lines bring the poet before us at once. as if the door of the dungeon was thrown open. From this bitter complaint, how nobly the unconquered bard rises into calm, and serene, and dignified exultation over the beauty of "that young creation, his soul's child," the Gierusalemme Liberata. The exultation of conscious genius then dies away, and we behold him, "bound between distraction and disease," no longer in an inspired mood, but sunk into the lowest prostration of human misery. There is something terrible in this transition from divine rapture to degraded agony. — Wilson.]

[2] [In a letter written to his friend Scipio Gonzaga, shortly after his confinement, Tasso exclaims — "Ah, wretched me! I had designed to write, besides two epic poems of most noble argument, four tragedies, of which I had formed the plan. I had schemed, too, many works in prose, on subjects the most lofty, and most useful to human life; I had designed to write philosophy with eloquence, in such a manner that there might remain of me an

eternal memory in the world. Alas! I had expected to close my life with glory and renown; but now, oppressed with the burden of so many calamities, I have lost every prospect of reputation and of honor. The fear of perpetual imprisonment increases my melancholy: the indignities which I suffer augment it; and the squalor of my beard, my hair, and habit, the sordidness and filth, exceedingly annoy me. Sure am I, that, if she who so little has corresponded to my attachment — if she saw me in such a state, and in such affliction — she would have some compassion on me." — Opere, t. x. p. 387.]

[3] [For nearly the first year of his confinement Tasso was under the care of a gaoler whose chief virtue, although he was a poet and a man of letters, was a cruel obedience to the commands of his prince. His name was Agostino Mosti. Tasso says of him, in a letter to his sister, "he used me with every species of rigor and inhumanity."]

Where laughter is not mirth, nor thought the
  mind,
Nor words a language, nor ev'n men mankind;
Where cries reply to curses, shrieks to blows,
And each is tortured in his separate hell —
For we are crowded in our solitudes —
Many, but each divided by the wall,
Which echoes Madness in her babbling
  moods; —
While all can hear, none heed his neighbor's
  call—
None! save that One, the veriest wretch of all,
Who was not made to be the mate of these,
Nor bound between Distraction and Disease.
Feel I not wroth with those who placed me
  here?
Who have debased me in the minds of men,
Debarring me the usage of my own,
Blighting my life in best of its career,
Branding my thoughts as things to shun and
  fear?
Would I not pay them back these pangs again,
And teach them inward Sorrow's stifled groan?
The struggle to be calm, and cold distress,
Which undermines our Stoical success?
No! — still too proud to be vindictive — I
Have pardoned princes' insults, and would die.
Yes, Sister of my Sovereign! for thy sake
I weed all bitterness from out my breast,
It hath no business where *thou* art a guest;
Thy brother hates — but I cannot detest;[1]
Thou pitiest not — but I can not forsake.

V.

Look on a love which knows not to despair,[2]
But all unquenched is still my better part,
Dwelling deep in my shut and silent heart
As dwells the gathered lightning in its cloud,
Encompassed with its dark and rolling shroud,
Till struck, — forth flies the all-ethereal dart!

---

[1] [Not long after his imprisonment, Tasso appealed to the mercy of Alfonso, in a canzone of great beauty, couched in terms so respectful and pathetic, as must have moved, it might be thought, the severest bosom to relent. The heart of Alfonso was, however, impregnable to the appeal; and Tasso, in another ode to the princesses, whose pity he invoked in the name of their own mother, who had herself known, if not the like horrors, the like solitude of imprisonment, and bitterness of soul. "Considered merely as poems," says Black, "these canzoni are extremely beautiful; but, if we contemplate them as the productions of a mind diseased, they form important documents in the history of man." — *Life of Tasso,* vol. ii. p. 408.]

[2] [As to the indifference which the Princess is said to have exhibited for the misfortunes of Tasso, and the little effort she made to obtain his liberty, this is one of the negative arguments founded on an hypothesis that may be easily destroyed by a thousand others equally plausible. Was not the Princess anxious to avoid her own ruin? In taking too warm an interest for the poet, did she not risk destroying herself, without saving him? — *Foscolo.*]

And thus at the collision of thy name
The vivid thought still flashes through my
  frame,
And for a moment all things as they were
Flit by me; — they are gone — I am the same.
And yet my love without ambition grew;
I knew thy state, my station, and I knew
A Princess was no love-mate for a bard;
I told it not, I breathed it not, it was
Sufficient to itself, its own reward;
And if my eyes revealed it, they, alas!
Were punished by the silentness of thine,
And yet I did not venture to repine.
Thou wert to me a crystal-girded shrine,
Worshipped at holy distance, and around
Hallowed and meekly kissed the saintly
  ground;
Not for thou wert a princess, but that Love
Had robed thee with a glory, and arrayed
Thy lineaments in beauty that dismayed —
Oh! not dismayed — but awed, like One
  above;
And in that sweet severity there was
A something which all softness did surpass —
I know not how — thy genius mastered
  mine —
My star stood still before thee : — if it were
Presumptuous thus to love without design,
That sad fatality hath cost me dear;
But thou art dearest still, and I should be
Fit for this cell, which wrongs me — but for
  thee.
The very love which locked me to my chain
Hath lightened half its weight; and for the
  rest,
Though heavy, lent me vigor to sustain,
And look to thee with undivided breast,
And foil the ingenuity of Pain.[3]

VI.

It is no marvel — from my very birth
My soul was drunk with love, — which did
  pervade
And mingle with whate'er I saw on earth;
Of objects all inanimate I made
Idols, and out of wild and lonely flowers,
And rocks, whereby they grew, a paradise,
Where I did lay me down within the shade
Of waving trees, and dreamed uncounted
  hours,
Though I was chid for wandering; and the
  Wise
Shook their white aged heads o'er me, and
  said
Of such materials wretched men were made,
And such a truant boy would end in woe,

---

[3] [Tasso's profound and unconquerable love for Leonora, sustaining itself without hope throughout years of darkness and solitude, breathes a moral dignity over all his sentiments, and we feel the strength and power of his noble spirit in the unupbraiding devotedness of his passion. — *Wilson.*]

And that the only lesson was a blow; —
And then they smote me, and I did not weep,
But cursed them in my heart, and to my haunt
Returned and wept alone, and dreamed again
The visions which arise without a sleep.
And with my years my soul began to pant
With feelings of strange tumult and soft pain;
And the whole heart exhaled into One Want,
But undefined and wandering, till the day
I found the thing I sought — and that was
  thee;
And then I lost my being all to be
Absorbed in thine — the world was past
  away —
Thou didst annihilate the earth to me!

VII.

I loved all Solitude — but little thought
To spend I know not what of life, remote
From all communion with existence, save
The maniac and his tyrant; — had I been
Their fellow, many years ere this had seen
My mind like theirs corrupted to its grave,[1]
But who hath seen me writhe, or heard me
  rave?
Perchance in such a cell we suffer more
Than the wrecked sailor on his desert shore;
The world is all before him — *mine* is *here*
Scarce twice the space they must accord my
  bier.
What though *he* perish, he may lift his eye
And with a dying glance upbraid the sky —
I will not raise my own in such reproof,
Although 'tis clouded by my dungeon roof.

VIII.

Yet do I feel at times my mind decline,[2]
But with a sense of its decay: — I see
Unwonted lights along my prison shine,
And a strange demon, who is vexing me
With pilfering pranks and petty pains, below
The feeling of the healthful and the free;
But much to One, who long hath suffered so,
Sickness of heart, and narrowness of place,
And all that may be borne, or can debase.
I thought mine enemies had been but Man,

But Spirits may be leagued with them — all
  Earth
Abandons — Heaven forgets me; — in the
  dearth
Of such defence the Powers of Evil can,
It may be, tempt me further, — and prevail
Against the outworn creature they assail.
Why in this furnace is my spirit proved
Like steel in tempering fire? because I
  loved?
Because I loved what not to love, and see,
Was more or less than mortal, and than me.

IX.

I once was quick in feeling — that is o'er;
My scars are callous, or I should have dashed
My brain against these bars, as the sun
  flashed
In mockery through them; — if I bear and
  bore
The much I have recounted, and the more
Which hath no words, — 'tis that I would not
  die
And sanction with self-slaughter the dull lie
Which snared me here, and with the brand
  of shame
Stamp Madness deep into my memory,
And woo Compassion to a blighted name,
Sealing the sentence which my foes proclaim.
No — it shall be immortal! — and I make
A future temple of my present cell,
Which nations yet shall visit for my sake.[3]
While thou, Ferrara! when no longer dwell
The ducal chiefs within thee, shalt fall down,
And crumbling piecemeal view thy heartless
  halls,
A poet's wreath shall be thine only crown, —
A poet's dungeon thy most far renown,
While strangers wonder o'er thy unpeopled
  walls![4]
And thou, Leonora! — thou — who wert
  ashamed
That such as I could love — who blushed to
  hear
To less than monarchs that thou couldst be
  dear,
Go! tell thy brother, that my heart, untamed
By grief, years, weariness, — and it may be

---

[1] [MS. — "My mind like theirs adapted to its grave."]

[2] ["Nor do I lament," wrote Tasso, shortly after his confinement, "that my heart is deluged with almost constant misery, that my head is always heavy and often painful, that my sight and hearing are much impaired, and that all my frame is become spare and meagre; but, passing all this with a short sigh, what I would bewail is the infirmity of my mind. My mind sleeps, not thinks; my fancy is chill, and forms no pictures; my negligent senses will no longer furnish the images of things; my hand is sluggish in writing, and my pen seems as if it shrunk from the office. I feel as if I were chained in all my operations, and as if I were overcome by an unwonted numbness and oppressive stupor." — *Opere*, t. viii. p. 258.]

[3] [MS. —
"Which $\left\{ \begin{array}{l} \text{nations yet} \\ \text{after-days} \end{array} \right\}$ shall visit for my sake."]

[4] [Those who indulge in the dreams of earthly retribution will observe, that the cruelty of Alfonso was not left without its recompense, even in his own person. He survived the affection of his subjects and of his dependants, who deserted him at his death; and suffered his body to be interred without princely or decent honors. His last wishes were neglected; his testament cancelled. His kinsman, Don Cæsar, shrank from the excommunication of the Vatican, and, after a short struggle, or rather suspense, Ferrara passed away for ever from the dominion of the house of Este. — *Hobhouse.*]

A taint of that he would impute to me —
From long infection of a den like this,
Where the mind rots congenial with the abyss,
Adores thee still; — and add — that when the towers
And battlements which guard his joyous hours
Of banquet, dance, and revel, are forgot,
Or left untended in a dull repose,
This — this — shall be a consecrated spot!
But Thou — when all that Birth and Beauty throws
Of magic round thee is extinct — shalt have
One half the laurel which o'ershades my grave.
No power in death can tear our names apart,
As none in life could rend thee from my heart.[1]
Yes, Leonora! it shall be our fate
To be entwined for ever — but too late![2]

[1] [MS. — { "As none in { wring { thee from
                { life could { wrench { my heart."]
                          { rend

[2] [The "pleasures of imagination" have been explained and justified by Addison in prose, and by Akenside in verse; but there are moments of real life when its miseries and its necessities seem to overpower and destroy them. The history of mankind, however, furnishes proofs, that no bodily suffering, no adverse circumstances, operating on our material nature, will extinguish the spirit of imagination. Perhaps there is no instance of this so very affecting and so very sublime as the case of Tasso. They who have seen the dark horror-striking dungeon-hole at Ferrara, in which he was confined seven years under the imputation of madness, will have had this truth impressed upon their hearts in a manner never to be erased. In this vault, of which the sight makes the hardest heart shudder, the poet employed himself in finishing and correcting his immortal epic poem. Lord Byron's "Lament" on this subject is as sublime and profound a lesson in morality, and in the pictures of the recesses of the human soul, as it is a production most eloquent, most pathetic, most vigorous, and most elevating among the gifts of the Muse. The bosom which is not touched with it — the fancy which is not warmed, — the understanding which is not enlightened and exalted by it, is not fit for human intercourse. If Lord Byron had written nothing but this, to deny him the praise of a grand poet would have been flagrant injustice or gross stupidity. — *Sir Egerton Brydges.*]

ODE ON VENICE.

I.

Oh Venice! Venice! when thy marble walls
Are level with the waters, there shall be
A cry of nations o'er thy sunken halls,
A loud lament along the sweeping sea!
If I, a northern wanderer, weep for thee,
What should thy sons do? — any thing but weep;
And yet they only murmur in their sleep.
In contrast with their fathers — as the slime,
The dull green ooze of the receding deep,
Is with the dashing of the spring-tide foam,
That drives the sailor shipless to his home,
Are they to those that were; and thus they creep,
Crouching and crab-like, through their sapping streets.
Oh! agony — that centuries should reap
No mellower harvest! Thirteen hundred years
Of wealth and glory turned to dust and tears;
And every monument the stranger meets,
Church, palace, pillar, as a mourner greets;
And even the Lion all subdued appears,
And the harsh sound of the barbarian drum,
With dull and daily dissonance, repeats
The echo of thy tyrant's voice along
The soft waves, once all musical to song,
That heaved beneath the moonlight with the throng
Of gondolas — and to the busy hum
Of cheerful creatures, whose most sinful deeds
Were but the overbeating of the heart,
And flow of too much happiness, which needs
The aid of age to turn its course apart
From the luxuriant and voluptuous flood
Of sweet sensations, battling with the blood.
But these are better than the gloomy errors,
The weeds of nations in their last decay,
When Vice walks forth with her unsoftened terrors,
And Mirth is madness, and but smiles to slay;
And Hope is nothing but a false delay,
The sick man's lightning half an hour ere death,
When Faintness, the last mortal birth of Pain

And apathy of limb, the dull beginning
Of the cold staggering race which Death is
    winning,
Steals vein by vein and pulse by pulse away;
Yet so relieving the o'ertortured clay,
To him appears renewal of his breath,
And freedom the mere numbness of his
    chain; —
And then he talks of life, and how again
He feels his spirit soaring — albeit weak,
And of the fresher air, which he would seek;
And as he whispers knows not that he gasps,
That his thin finger feels not what it clasps,
And so the film comes o'er him — and the dizzy
Chamber swims round and round — and shad-
    ows busy,
At which he vainly catches, flit and gleam,
Till the last rattle chokes the strangled scream,
And all is ice and blackness, — and the earth
That which it was the moment ere our birth.

II.

There is no hope for nations! — Search the
    page
Of many thousand years — the daily scene,
The flow and ebb of each recurring age,
    The everlasting *to be* which *hath been*,
    Hath taught us nought or little : still we lean
On things that rot beneath our weight, and
    wear
Our strength away in wrestling with the air;
For 'tis our nature strikes us down : the beasts
Slaughtered in hourly hecatombs for feasts
Are of as high an order — they must go
Even where their driver goads them, though
    to slaughter.
Ye men, who pour your blood for kings as
    water,
What have they given your children in return ?
A heritage of servitude and woes,
A blindfold bondage, where your hire is blows.
What! do not yet the red-hot ploughshares
    burn,
O'er which you stumble in a false ordeal,
And deem this proof of loyalty the *real;*
Kissing the hand that guides you to your scars,
And glorying as you tread the glowing bars ?
All that your sires have left you, all that Time
Bequeathes of free, and History of sublime,
Spring from a different theme! — Ye see and
    read,
Admire and sigh, and then succumb and
    bleed!
Save the few spirits, who, despite of all,
And worse than all, the sudden crimes engen-
    dered
By the down-thundering of the prison-wall,
And thirst to swallow the sweet waters ten-
    dered,
Gushing from freedom's fountains — when the
    crowd,
Maddened with centuries of draught, are loud,

And trample on each other to obtain
The cup which brings oblivion of a chain
Heavy and sore, — in which long yoked they
    ploughed
The sand, — or if there sprung the yellow grain,
'Twas not for them, their necks were too much
    bowed,
And their dead palates chewed the cud of
    pain : —
Yes! the few spirits — who, despite of deeds
Which they abhor, confound not with the cause
Those momentary starts from Nature's laws,
Which, like the pestilence and earthquake,
    smite
But for a term, then pass, and leave the earth
With all her seasons to repair the blight
With a few summers, and again put forth
Cities and generations — fair, when free —
For, Tyranny, there blooms no bud for thee!

III.

Glory and Empire! once upon these towers
    With Freedom — godlike Triad! how ye
    sate!
The league of mightiest nations, in those hours
    When Venice was an envy, might abate,
    But did not quench, her spirit — in her fate
All were enwrapped : the feasted monarchs
    knew
    And loved their hostess, nor could learn to
    hate,
Although they humbled — with the kingly few
The many felt, for from all days and climes
She was the voyager's worship; — even her
    crimes
Were of the softer order — born of Love,
She drank no blood, nor fattened on the dead.
But gladdened where her harmless conquests
    spread;
For these restored the Cross, that from above
Hallowed her sheltering banners, which inces-
    sant
Flew between earth and the unholy Crescent,
Which, if it waned and dwindled, Earth may
    thank
The city it has clothed in chains, which clank
Now, creaking in the ears of those who owe
The name of Freedom to her glorious strug-
    gles!
Yet she but shares with them a common woe,
And called the "kingdom" of a conquering
    foe, —
But knows what all — and, most of all, *we*
    know —
With what set gilded terms a tyrant juggles!

IV.

The name of Commonwealth is past and gone
    O'er the three fractions of the groaning
    globe;
Venice is crushed, and Holland deigns to own
    A sceptre, and endures the purple robe;

If the free Switzer yet bestrides alone
His chainless mountains, 'tis but for a time,
For tyranny of late is cunning grown,
And in its own good season tramples down
The sparkles of our ashes. One great clime,
Whose vigorous offspring by dividing ocean
Are kept apart and nursed in the devotion
Of Freedom, which their fathers fought for, and
Bequeathed — a heritage of heart and hand,
And proud distinction from each other land,
Whose sons must bow them at a monarch's motion,
As if his senseless sceptre were a wand
Full of the magic of exploded science —
Still one great clime, in full and free defiance,
Yet rears her crest, unconquer'd and sublime,
Above the far Atlantic! — She has taught
Her Esau-brethren that the haughty flag,
The floating fence of Albion's feebler crag,
May strike to those whose red right hands have bought
Rights cheaply earned with blood. — Still, still, for ever
Better, though each man's life-blood were a river,
That it should flow, and overflow, than creep
Through thousand lazy channels in our veins,
Dammed like the dull canal with locks and chains,
And moving, as a sick man in his sleep,
Three paces, and then faltering : — better be
Where the extinguished Spartans still are free,
In their proud charnel of Thermopylæ,
Than stagnate in our marsh, — or o'er the deep
Fly, and one current to the ocean add,
One spirit to the souls our fathers had,
One freeman more, America, to thee !

BEPPO: A VENETIAN STORY.

Rosalind. Farewell, Monsieur Traveller: Look, you lisp, and wear strange suits; disable all the benefits of your own country; be out of love with your Nativity, and almost chide God for making you that countenance you are; or I will scarce think that you have swam in a *Gondola.*
                                                                As You Like It, Act IV. Sc. 1.

Annotation of the Commentators.

That is, been at *Venice*, which was much visited by the young English gentlemen of those times, and was then what *Paris* is *now* — the seat of all dissoluteness. — S. A.[1]

INTRODUCTION.

BEPPO was written at Venice, in October, 1817, and acquired great popularity immediately on its publication in the May of the following year. Byron's letters show that he attached very little importance to it at the time. He was not aware that he had opened a new vein, in which his genius was destined to work out some of his brightest triumphs. "I have written," he says to Mr. Murray, "a poem humorous, in or after the excellent manner of Mr. Whistlecraft, and founded on a Venetian anecdote which amused me. It is called *Beppo* — the short name for Giuseppo, — that is, the *Joe* of the Italian Joseph. It has politics and ferocity." Again — "Whistlecraft is my immediate model, but Berni is the father of that kind of writing; which, I think, suits our language, too, very well. We shall see by this experiment. It will, at any rate, show that I can write cheerfully, and repel the charge of monotony and mannerism." He wished Mr. Murray to accept of Beppo as a free gift, or, as he chose to express it, "as part of the contract for Canto Fourth of Childe Harold;" adding, however, — "if it pleases, you shall have more in the same mood: for I know the Italian *way of life*, and, as for the *verse* and the *passions*, I have them still in tolerable vigor."

[1] [Roger Ascham, Queen Elizabeth's tutor, says, in his "Schoolmaster," — "Although I was only nine days at Venice, I saw, in that little time, more liberty to sin, than ever I heard tell of in the city of London in nine years."]

John Hookham Frere has the merit of having introduced the *Bernesque* style into our language; but his performance, entitled " Prospectus and Specimen of an intended National Work, by William and Robert Whistlecraft, of Stowmarket, in Suffolk, Harness and Collar Makers, intended to comprise the most interesting Particulars relating to King Arthur and his Round Table," though it delighted all elegant and learned readers, obtained at the time little notice from the public at large, and is already almost forgotten. For the causes of this failure, it appears needless to look further than the last sentence we have been quoting from the letters of the author of the more successful *Beppo.* Whistlecraft had the *verse:* it had also the humor, the wit, and even the poetry of the Italian model; but it wanted the life of actual manners, and the strength of stirring passions. Mr. Frere had forgot, or was, with all his genius, to profit by remembering, that the poets, whose unfit style he was adopting, always made their style *appear* a secondary matter. They never failed to embroider their merriment on the texture of a really interesting story. Byron perceived this; and avoiding his immediate master's one fatal error, and at least equalling him in the excellences which he did display, engaged at once the sympathy of readers of every class, and became substantially the founder of a new species of English poetry.

I.

'Tis known, at least it should be, that throughout
  All countries of the Catholic persuasion,
Some weeks before Shrove Tuesday comes about,
  The people take their fill of recreation,
And buy repentance, ere they grow devout,
  However high their rank, or low their station,
With fiddling, feasting, dancing, drinking, masquing,
And other things which may be had for asking.

II.

The moment night with dusky mantle covers
  The skies (and the more duskily the better),
The time less liked by husbands than by lovers
  Begins, and prudery flings aside her fetter;
And gaiety on restless tiptoe hovers,
  Giggling with all the gallants who beset her;
And there are songs and quavers, roaring, humming,
Guitars, and every other sort of strumming.

III.

And there are dresses splendid, but fantastical,
  Masks of all times and nations, Turks and Jews,
And harlequins and clowns, with feats gymnastical,
  Greeks, Romans, Yankee-doodles, and Hindoos;
All kinds of dress, except the ecclesiastical,
  All people, as their fancies hit, may choose,
But no one in these parts may quiz the clergy, —
Therefore take heed, ye Freethinkers! I charge ye.

IV.

You'd better walk about begirt with briars,
  Instead of coat and smallclothes, than put on
A single stitch reflecting upon friars,
  Although you swore it only was in fun;
They'd haul you o'er the coals, and stir the fires
  Of Phlegethon with every mother's son,
Nor say one mass to cool the caldron's bubble
That boiled your bones, unless you paid them double.

V.

But saving this, you may put on whate'er
  You like by way of doublet, cape, or cloak,
Such as in Monmouth-street, or in Rag Fair,
  Would rig you out in seriousness or joke;
And even in Italy such places are,
  With prettier name in softer accents spoke,
For, bating Covent Garden, I can hit on
No place that's called " Piazza" in Great Britain.

VI.

This feast is named the Carnival,[1] which being
  Interpreted, implies " farewell to flesh:"
So called, because the name and thing agreeing,
  Through Lent they live on fish both salt and fresh.

---

[1] " The Carnival," says Mr. Rose, " though it is gayer or duller, according to the genius of the nations which celebrate it, is, in its general character, nearly the same all over the peninsula. The beginning is like any other season; towards the middle you begin to meet masques and murmurs in sunshine: in the last fifteen days the plot thickens; and during *the three last* all is hurly-burly. The shops are shut, all business is at a stand, and the drunken cries heard at night afford a clear proof of the pleasures to which these days of leisure are dedicated." — *Letters from the North of Italy.*]

But why they usher Lent with so much glee in,
  Is more than I can tell, although I guess
'Tis as we take a glass with friends at parting,
In the stage-coach or packet, just at starting.

VII.

And thus they bid farewell to carnal dishes,
  And solid meats, and highly spiced ragouts,
To live for forty days on ill-dressed fishes,
  Because they have no sauces to their stews,
A thing which causes many "poohs" and
    "pishes,"
And several oaths (which would not suit the
    Muse),
From travellers accustomed from a boy
To eat their salmon, at the least, with soy;

VIII.

And therefore humbly I would recommend
  "The curious in fish-sauce," before they
    cross
The sea, to bid their cook, or wife, or friend,
  Walk or ride to the Strand, and buy in gross
(Or if set out beforehand, these may send
  By any means least liable to loss),
Ketchup, Soy, Chili-vinegar, and Harvey,
Or, by the Lord! a Lent will well nigh starve
    ye;

IX.

That is to say, if your religion's Roman,
  And you at Rome would do as Romans do,
According to the proverb, — although no man,
  If foreign, is obliged to fast; and you,
If Protestant, or sickly, or a woman,
  Would rather dine in sin on a ragout —
Dine and be d—d! I don't mean to be coarse,
But that's the penalty, to say no worse.

X.

Of all the places where the Carnival
  Was most facetious in the days of yore,
For dance, and song, and serenade, and ball,
  And masque, and mime, and mystery, and
    more
Than I have time to tell now, or at all,
  Venice the bell from every city bore, —
And at the moment when I fix my story,
That sea-born city was in all her glory.

XI.

They've pretty faces yet, those same Venetians,
  Black eyes, arched brows, and sweet ex-
    pressions still;
Such as of old were copied from the Grecians,
  In ancient arts by moderns mimicked ill;
And like so many Venuses of Titian's
  (The best's at Florence 1 — see it, if ye will,)

They look when leaning over the balcony,
  Or stepped from out a picture by Giorgione,1

XII.

Whose tints are truth and beauty at their best·
  And when you to Manfrini's palace go,3
That picture (howsoever fine the rest)
  Is loveliest to my mind of all the show;
It may perhaps be also to *your* zest,
  And that's the cause I rhyme upon it so:
'Tis but a portrait of his son, and wife,
And self; but *such* a woman! love in life!

XIII.

Love in full life and length, not love ideal,
  No, nor ideal beauty, that fine name,
But something better still, so very real,
  That the sweet model must have been the
    same,
A thing that you would purchase, beg, or steal,
  Wer't not impossible, besides a shame:
The face recalls some face, as 'twere with pain,
You once have seen, but ne'er will see again;

XIV.

One of those forms which flit by us, when we
  Are young, and fix our eyes on every face;
And, oh! the loveliness at times we see
  In momentary gliding, the soft grace,
The youth, the bloom, the beauty which agree,
  In many a nameless being we retrace,

<hr>

1 [" At Florence I remained but a day, having a hurry for Rome. However, I went to the two galleries, from which one returns drunk with beauty; but there are sculpture and painting, which, for the first time, gave me an idea of what people mean by their *cant*, about those two most artificial of the arts. What struck me most were, — the mistress of Raphael, a portrait; the mistress of Titian, a portrait; a Venus of Titian, in the Medici gallery – *the* Venus; Canova's Venus, also in the other gallery," etc. — *Byron's Letters,* 1817.]

2 [" I know nothing of pictures myself, and care almost as little; but to me there are none like the Venetian — above all, Giorgione. I remember well his judgment of Solomon, in the Mariscalchi gallery in Bologna. The real mother is beautiful, exquisitely beautiful." — *Byron's Letters,* 1820.]

3 [The following is Byron's account of his visit to this palace, in April, 1817. — " To-day, I have been over the Manfrini palace, famous for its pictures. What struck most in the general collection, was the extreme resemblance of the style of the female faces in the mass of pictures, so many centuries or generations old, to those you see and meet every day among the existing Italians. The Queen of Cyprus and Giorgione's wife,* particularly the latter, are Venetians as it were·of yesterday; the same eyes and expression, and, to my mind, there is none finer. You must recollect, however, that I know nothing of painting, and that I detest it, unless it reminds me of something I have seen, or think it possible to see."]

<hr>

* [This appears to be an incorrect description of the picture; as, according to Vasari and others, Giorgione never was married, and died young.]

Whose course and home we knew not, nor
   shall know,
Like the lost Pleiad [1] seen no more below.

XV.

I said that like a picture by Giorgione
  Venetian women were, and so they *are*,
Particularly seen from a balcony,
  (For beauty's sometimes best set off afar)
And there, just like a heroine of Goldoni,
  They peep from out the blind, or o'er the
   bar;
And truth to say, they're mostly very pretty,
And rather like to show it, more's the pity!

XVI.

For glances beget ogles, ogles sighs,
  Sighs wishes, wishes words, and words a
   letter,
Which flies on wings of light-heeled Mercuries,
  Who do such things because they know no
   better,
And then, God knows, what mischief may
   arise,
  When love links two young people in one
   fetter,
Vile assignations, and adulterous beds,
Elopements, broken vows, and hearts, and
  heads.

XVII.

Shakspeare described the sex in Desdemona
  As very fair, but yet suspect in fame,[2]
And to this day from Venice to Verona
  Such matters may be probably the same,
Except that since those times was never
   known a
  Husband whom mere suspicion could in-
   flame
To suffocate a wife no more than twenty,
Because she had a " cavalier servente."

XVIII.

Their jealousy (if they are ever jealous)
  Is of a fair complexion altogether,
Not like that sooty devil of Othello's
  Which smothers women in a bed of feather,
But worthier of these much more jolly fellows,
  When weary of the matrimonial tether
His head for such a wife no mortal bothers,
But take at once another, or another's.[3]

XIX.

Didst ever see a Gondola ? For fear
  You should not, I'll describe it you exactly:
'Tis a long covered boat that's common here,
  Carved at the prow, built lightly, but com-
   pactly;
Rowed by two rowers, each called "Gon-
   dolier,"
  It glides along the water looking blackly,
Just like a coffin clapt in a canoe,
Where none can make out what you say or
  do.

XX.

And up and down the long canals they go,
  And under the Rialto [4] shoot along,
By night and day, all paces, swift or slow,
  And round the theatres, a sable throng,
They wait in their dusk livery of woe,—
  But not to them do woful things belong,
For sometimes they contain a deal of fun,
Like mourning coaches when the funeral's
  done.

XXI.

But to my story.— 'Twas some years ago,
  It may be thirty, forty, more or less,
The carnival was at its height, and so
  Were all kinds of buffoonery and dress;
A certain lady went to see the show,
  Her real name I know not, nor can guess,
And so we'll call her Laura, if you please,
Because it slips into my verse with ease.

XXII.

She was not old, nor young, nor at the years
  Which certain people call a "*certain age*,"
Which yet the most uncertain age appears,
  Because I never heard, nor could engage
A person yet by prayers, or bribes, or tears,
  To name, define by speech, or write on
   page,
The period meant precisely by that word,—
Which surely is exceedingly absurd.

XXIII.

Laura was blooming still, had made the best
  Of time, and time returned the compliment,
And treated her genteelly, so that, dressed,
  She looked extremely well where'er she
   went;
A pretty woman is a welcome guest,
  And Laura's brow a frown had rarely bent,

---

1 " Quæ septem dici sex tamen esse solent." —
Ovid.
2
           [" Look to't:
  In Venice they do let heaven see the pranks
  They dare not show their husbands; their best
    conscience
  Is — not to leave undone, but keep unknown."
                  Othello.]
3 [" Jealousy is not the order of the day in Venice,
and daggers are out of fashion, while duels on love
matters are unknown — at least, with the hus-
bands." — *Byron's Letters.*]

4 [An English abbreviation. Rialto is the name,
not of the bridge, but of the island from which it is
called; and the Venetians say, il ponte di Rialto, as
we say Westminster Bridge. In that island is the
Exchange. It was there that the Christian held
discourse with the Jew; and Shylock refers to it,
when he says,
  " Signor Antonio, many a time and oft,
    In the Rialto, you have rated me." — *Rogers.*]

Indeed she shone all smiles, and seemed to flatter
Mankind with her black eyes for looking at her.

XXIV.

She was a married woman; 'tis convenient,
  Because in Christian countries 'tis a rule
To view their little slips with eyes more lenient;
  Whereas if single ladies play the fool,
{ Unless within the period intervenient
  A well-timed wedding makes the scandal cool)
I don't know how they ever can get over it,
Except they manage never to discover it.

XXV.

Her husband sailed upon the Adriatic,
  And made some voyages, too, in other seas,
And when he lay in quarantine for pratique
  (A forty days' precaution 'gainst disease),
His wife would mount, at times, her highest attic,
  For thence she could discern the ship with ease:
He was a merchant trading to Aleppo,
His name Giuseppe, called more briefly, Beppo.

XXVI.

He was a man as dusky as a Spaniard,
  Sunburnt with travel, yet a portly figure;
Though colored, as it were, within a tanyard,
  He was a person both of sense and vigor —
A better seaman never yet did man yard:
  And *she*, although her manner showed no rigor,
Was deemed a woman of the strictest principle,
So much as to be thought almost invincible.

XXVII.

But several years elapsed since they had met;
  Some people thought the ship was lost, and some
That he had somehow blundered into debt,
  And did not like the thought of steering home;
And there were several offered any bet,
  Or that he would, or that he would not come,
For most men (till by losing rendered sager)
Will back their own opinions with a wager.

XXVIII.

'Tis said that their last parting was pathetic,
  As partings often are, or ought to be,
And their presentiment was quite prophetic
  That they should never more each other see,

(A sort of morbid feeling, half poetic,
  Which I have known occur in two or three,)
When kneeling on the shore upon her sad knee,
He left this Adriatic Ariadne.

XXIX.

And Laura waited long, and wept a little,
  And thought of wearing weeds, as well she might;
She almost lost all appetite for victual,
  And could not sleep with ease alone at night;
She deemed the window-frames and shutters brittle
  Against a daring housebreaker or sprite,
And so she thought it prudent to connect her
With a vice-husband, *chiefly to protect her.*

XXX.

She chose, (and what is there they will not choose,
  If only you will but oppose their choice?)
Till Beppo should return from his long cruise,
  And bid once more her faithful heart rejoice,
A man some women like, and yet abuse —
  A coxcomb was he by the public voice;
A Count of wealth, they said, as well as quality,
And in his pleasures of great liberality.[1]

XXXI.

And then he was a Count, and then he knew
  Music, and dancing, fiddling, French and Tuscan;
The last not easy, be it known to you,
  For few Italians speak the right Etruscan.
He was a critic upon operas, too,
  And knew all niceties of the sock and buskin;
And no Venetian audience could endure a
Song, scene, or air, when he cried " seccatura!"

XXXII.

His " bravo " was decisive, for that sound
  Hushed "Academie" sighed in silent awe;
The fiddlers trembled as he looked around,
  For fear of some false note's detected flaw.
The " prima donna's " tuneful heart would bound,
  Dreading the deep damnation of his " bah!"
Soprano, basso, even the contra-alto,
Wished him five fathom under the Rialto.

---

[1] [MS.—
"A Count of wealth inferior to his quality,
  Which somewhat limited his liberality."

XXXIII.

He patronized the Improvisatori,
  Nay, could himself extempórize some
    stanzas,
Wrote rhymes, sang songs, could also tell a
    story,
  Sold pictures, and was skilful in the dance
    as
Italians can be, though in this their glory
  Must surely yield the palm to that which
    France has;
In short, he was a perfect cavaliero,
And to his very valet seemed a hero.

XXXIV.

Then he was faithful too, as well as amorous;
  So that no sort of female could complain,
Although they're now and then a little clamor-
    ous,
  He never put the pretty souls in pain;
His heart was one of those which most
    enamour us,
  Wax to receive, and marble to retain.
He was a lover of the good old school,
Who still become more constant as they cool.

XXXV.

No wonder such accomplishments should
    turn
  A female head, however sage and steady —
With scarce a hope that Beppo could return,
  In law he was almost as good as dead, he
Nor sent, nor wrote, nor showed the least
    concern,
  And she had waited several years already;
And really if a man won't let us know
That he's alive, he's *dead*, or should be so.

XXXVI.

Besides, within the Alps, to every woman,
  (Although, God knows, it is a grievous
    sin,)
'Tis, I may say, permitted to have *two* men;
  I can't tell who first brought the custom in,
But "Cavalier Serventes" are quite common,
  And no one notices nor cares a pin;
And we may call this (not to say the worst)
A *second* marriage which corrupts the *first.*

XXXVII.

The word was formerly a "Cicisbeo,"
  But *that* is now grown vulgar and indecent;
The Spaniards call the person a "*Cortejo*," [1]
  For the same mode subsists in Spain, though
    recent;
In short it reaches from the Po to Teio,

---

[1] Cortejo is pronounced Corte*h*o, with an aspirate, according to the Arabesque guttural. It means what there is as yet no precise name for in England, though the practice is as common as in any tramon-tane country whatever.

And may perhaps at last be o'er the sea
    sent.
But Heaven preserve Old England from such
    courses!
Or what becomes of damage and divorces?

XXXVIII.

However, I still think, with all due deference
  To the fair *single* part of the Creation,
That married ladies should preserve the pre-
    ference
  In *tête-à-tête* or general conversation —
And this I say without peculiar reference
  To England, France, or any other nation —
Because they know the world, and are at ease,
And being natural, naturally please.

XXXIX.

'Tis true your budding Miss is very charm-
    ing,
  But shy and awkward at first coming out,
So much alarmed, that she is quite alarming,
  All Giggle, Blush; half Pertness, and half
    Pout;
And glancing at *Mamma*, for fear there's
    harm in
  What you, she, it, or they, may be about,
The Nursery still lisps out in all they utter —
Besides, they always smell of bread and but-
    ter.

XL.

But "Cavalier Servente" is the phrase
  Used in politest circles to express
This supernumerary slave, who stays
  Close to the lady as a part of dress,
Her word the only law which he obeys.
  He is no sinecure, as you may guess;
Coach, servants, gondola, he goes to call,
And carries fan and tippet, gloves and shawl.

XLI.

With all its sinful doings, I must say,
  That Italy's a pleasant place to me,
Who love to see the Sun shine every day,
  And vines (not nailed to walls) from tree to
    tree
Festooned, much like the back scene of a
    play,
  Or melodrame which people flock to see,
When the first act is ended by a dance
In vineyards copied from the south of France.

XLII.

I like on Autumn evenings to ride out,
  Without being forced to bid my groom be
    sure
My cloak is round his middle strapped about,
  Because the skies are not the most secure;
I know too that, if stopped upon my rout,
  Where the green alleys windingly allure,

Reeling with *grapes* red wagons choke the
    way, —
In England 'twould be dung, dust, or a dray.

XLIII.

I also like to dine on becaficas,
    To see the Sun set, sure he'll rise to-morrow,
Not through a misty morning twinkling weak
    as
    A drunken man's dead eye in maudlin sor-
    row,
But with all Heaven t' himself; that day will
    break as
    Beauteous as cloudless, nor be forced to
    borrow
That sort of farthing candlelight which glim-
    mers
While reeking London's smoky caldron sim-
    mers.

XLIV.

I love the language, that soft bastard Latin,
    Which melts like kisses from a female
    mouth,
And sounds as if it should be writ on satin,
    With syllables which breathe of the sweet
    South,
And gentle liquids gliding all so pat in,
    That not a single accent seems uncouth,
Like our harsh northern whistling, grunting
    guttural,
Which we're obliged to hiss, and spit, and
    sputter all.

XLV.

I like the women too (forgive my folly),
    From the rich peasant cheek of ruddy
    bronze,[1]
And large black eyes that flash on you a volley
    Of rays that say a thousand things at once,
To the high dama's brow, more melancholy,
    But clear, and with a wild and liquid glance,
Heart on her lips, and soul within her eyes,
Soft as her clime,[2] and sunny as her skies.

XLVI.

Eye of the land which still is Paradise!
    Italian beauty! didst thou not inspire
Raphael,[3] who died in thy embrace, and vies
    With all we know of Heaven, or can desire,
In what he hath bequeathed us? — in what
    guise,
    Though lashing from the fervor of the lyre,
Would *Words* describe thy past and present
    glow,
While yet Canova can create below?[4]

---

[1] [MS. — "From the tall peasant with her ruddy
bronze."]
[2] [MS. — "Like her own clime, all sun, and
bloom and skies."]
[3] For the received accounts of the cause of
Raphael's death, see his lives.
[4] (In talking thus, the writer, more especially
    Of women, would be understood to say,

XLVII.

"England! with all thy faults I love thee still,"
    I said at Calais, and have not forgot it;
I like to speak and lucubrate my fill;
    I like the government (but that is not it);
I like the freedom of the press and quill;
    I like the Habeas Corpus (when we've got
    it);
I like a parliamentary debate,
Particularly when 'tis not too late;

XLVIII.

I like the taxes, when they're not too many;
    I like a sea-coal fire, when not too dear;
I like a beef-steak, too, as well as any;
    Have no objection to a pot of beer;
I like the weather, when it is not rainy,
    That is, I like two months of every year.
And so God save the Regent, Church, and
    King!
Which means that I like all and every thing.

XLIX.

Our standing army, and disbanded seamen,
    Poor's rate, Reform, my own, the nation's
    debt,
Our little riots just to show we are free men,
    Our trifling bankruptcies in the Gazette,
Our cloudy climate, and our chilly women,
    All these I can forgive, and those forget,
And greatly venerate our recent glories,
And wish they were not owing to the Tories.

L.

But to my tale of Laura, — for I find
    Digression is a sin, that by degrees
Becomes exceeding tedious to the mind,
    And, therefore, may the reader too dis-
    please —
The gentle reader, who may wax unkind,
    And caring little for the author's ease,
Insist on knowing what he means, a hard
And hapless situation for a bard.

LI.

Oh that I had the art of easy writing
    What should be easy reading! could I scale
Parnassus, where the Muses sit inditing
    Those pretty poems never known to fail,
How quickly would I print (the world delight
    ing)
A Grecian, Syrian, or Assyrian tale;

He speaks as a spectator, not officially,
    And always, reader, in a modest way;
Perhaps, too, in no very great degree shall he
    Appear to have offended in this lay,
Since, as all know, without the sex, our son-
    nets
    Would seem unfinished, like their untrimmed
bonnets.)   (Signed) PRINTER'S DEVIL.

And sell you, mixed with western sentimen-
talism,
Some samples of the finest Orientalism.

LII.

But I am but a nameless sort of person,
  (A broken Dandy lately on my travels)
And take for rhyme, to hook my rambling
    verse on,
The first that Walker's Lexicon unravels,
And when I can't find that, I put a worse on,
  Not caring as I ought for critics' cavils;
I've half a mind to tumble down to prose,
But verse is more in fashion — so here goes.

LIII.

The Count and Laura made their new
    arrangement,
  Which lasted, as arrangements sometimes
    do,
For half a dozen years without estrangement;
  They had their little differences, too;
Those jealous whiffs, which never any change
    meant;
  In such affairs there probably are few
Who have not had this pouting sort of squab-
  ble,
From sinners of high station to the rabble.

LIV.

But on the whole, they were a happy pair,
  As happy as unlawful love could make
    them,
The gentleman was fond, the lady fair,
  Their chains so slight, 'twas not worth while
    to break them:
The world beheld them with indulgent air;
  The pious only wished "the devil take
    them!"
He took them not; he very often waits,
And leaves old sinners to be young ones'
  baits.

LV.

But they were young: Oh! what without our
    youth
  Would love be! What would youth be
    without love!
Youth lends it joy, and sweetness, vigor, truth,
  Heart, soul, and all that seems as from
    above;
But, languishing with years, it grows uncouth —
  One of few things experience don't improve,
Which is, perhaps, the reason why old fellows
Are always so preposterously jealous.

LVI.

It was the Carnival, as I have said
  Some six and thirty stanzas back, and
Laura the usual preparations made,
  Which you do when your mind's made up
    to go

To-night to Mrs. Boehm's masquerade,
  Spectator, or partaker in the show;
The only difference known between the cases
Is — *here*, we have six weeks of "varnished
  faces."

LVII.

Laura, when dressed, was (as I sang before)
  A pretty woman as was ever seen,
Fresh as the Angel o'er a new inn door,
  Or frontispiece of a new Magazine,
With all the fashions which the last month
    wore,
  Colored, and silver paper leaved between
That and the title-page, for fear the press
Should soil with parts of speech the parts of
  dress.

LVIII.

They went to the Ridotto; — 'tis a hall
  Where people dance, and sup, and dance
    again;
Its proper name, perhaps, were a masqued
    ball,
  But that's of no importance to my strain;
'Tis (on a smaller scale) like our Vauxhall,
  Excepting that it can't be spoilt by rain:
The company is "mixed" (the phrase I
    quote is
As much as saying, they're below your notice);

LIX.

For a "mixed company" implies that, save
  Yourself and friends, and half a hundred
    more,
Whom you may bow to without looking
    grave,
  The rest are but a vulgar set, the bore
Of public places, where they basely brave
  The fashionable stare of twenty score
Of well-bred persons, called "*the World;*"
  but I,
Although I know them, really don't know why.

LX.

This is the case in England; at least was
  During the dynasty of Dandies,[1] now
Perchance succeeded by some other class
  Of imitated imitators: — how
Irreparably soon decline, alas!
  The demagogues of fashion: all below
Is frail; how easily the world is lost
By love, or war, and now and then by frost!

---

[1] ["I liked the Dandies: they were always very
civil to me; though, in general, they disliked liter-
ary people, and persecuted and mystified Madame
De Stael, Lewis, Horace Twiss, and the like. The
truth is, that though I gave up the business early,
I had a tinge of Dandyism in my minority, and
probably retained enough of *it* to conciliate the
great ones, at four and twenty." —*Byron's Diary,*
1821.]

LXI.

Crushed was Napoleon by the northern Thor,
  Who knocked his army down with icy ham-
    mer,
Stopped by the *elements*,[1] li e a whaler, or
  A blundering novice ink his new French
    grammar,
Good cause had he to doubt the chance of
    war,
  And as for Fortune—but I dare not d—n her
Because, were I to ponder to infinity,
The more I should believe in her divinity.[2]

LXII.

She rules the present, past, and all to be yet,
  She gives us luck in lotteries, love, and
    marriage;
I cannot say that she's done much for me yet;
  Not that I mean her bounties to disparage,
We've not yet closed accounts, and we shall
    see yet
  How much she'll make amends for past
    miscarriage;
Meantime the goddess I'll no more importune,
Unless to thank her when she's made my for-
    tune.

LXIII.

To turn,—and to return;—the devil take it!
  This story slips forever through my fingers,
Because, just as the stanza likes to make it,
  It needs must be—and so it rather lingers;
This form of verse began, I can't well break it,
  But must keep time and tune like public
    singers;
But if I once get through my present measure,
I'll take another when I'm next at leisure.

LXIV.

They went to the Ridotto ('tis a place
  To which I mean to go myself to-morrow,[3]
Just to divert my thoughts a little space,

---

[1] ["When Brummell was obliged to retire to
France, he knew no French, and having obtained a
grammar for the purpose of study, our friend Scrope
Davies was asked what progress Brummell had
made in French: he responded, 'that Brummell
had been stopped, like Bonaparte in Russia, by the
elements.' I have put this pun into Beppo, which
is 'a fair exchange and no robbery;' for Scrope
made his fortune at several dinners (as he owned
himself), by repeating occasionally, as his own, some
of the buffooneries with which I had encountered
him in the morning."—*Byron's Diary*, 1821.]
[2] ["Like Sylla, I have always believed that all
things depend upon Fortune, and nothing upon our-
selves. I am not aware of any one thought or
action, worthy of being called good to myself or
others, which is not to be attributed to the good
goddess—Fortune!"—*Byron's Diary*, 1821.]
[3] [In the margin of the original MS. Byron has
written—"January 19th, 1818. To-morrow will be a
Sunday, and full Ridotto."]

Because I'm rather hippish, and may borrow
Some spirits, guessing at what kind of face
  May lurk beneath each mask; and as my
    sorrow
Slackens its pace sometimes, I'll make, or find
Something shall leave it half an hour behind).

LXV.

Now Laura moves along the joyous crowd,
  Smiles in her eyes, and simpers on her lips;
To some she whispers, other speaks aloud;
  To some she curtsies, and to some she dips,
Complains of warmth, and this complaint
    avowed,
  Her lover brings the lemonade, she sips;
She then surveys, condemns, but pities still
Her dearest friends for being dressed so ill.

LXVI.

One has false curls, another too much paint,
  A third—where did she buy that frightful
    turban?
A fourth's so pale she fears she's going to
    faint,
  A fifth's look's vulgar, dowdyish, and
    suburban,
A sixth's white silk has got a yellow taint,
  A seventh's thin muslin surely will be her
    bane,
And lo! an eighth appears,—" I'll see no
    more!"
For fear, like Banquo's kings, they reach a
    score.

LXVII.

Meantime, while she was thus at others gazing,
  Others were levelling their looks at her;
She heard the men's half-whispered mode of
    praising,
  And, till 'twas done, determined not to stir;
The women only thought it quite amazing
  That, at her time of life, so many were
Admirers still,—but men are so debased,
Those brazen creatures always suit their taste.

LXVIII.

For my part, now, I ne'er could understand
  Why naughty women—but I won't discuss
A thing which is a scandal to the land,
  I only don't see why it should be thus;
And if I were but in a gown and band,
  Just to entitle me to make a fuss,
I'd preach on this till Wilberforce and Romilly
Should quote in their next speeches from my
    homily.

LXIX.

While Laura thus was seen and seeing, smil-
    ing,
  Talking, she knew not why and cared not
    what,
So that her female friends, with envy broiling,

Beheld her airs and triumph, and all that;
And well-dressed males still kept before her
    filing,
    And passing bowed and mingled with her
    chat;
More than the rest one person seemed to stare
With pertinacity that's rather rare.

LXX.

He was a Turk, the color of mahogany;
    And Laura saw him, and at first was glad,
Because the Turks so much admire philogyny,
    Although their usage of their wives is sad;
'Tis said they use no better than a dog any
    Poor woman, whom they purchase like a
    pad:
They have a number, though they ne'er ex-
    bibit 'em,
Four wives by law, and concubines "ad libi-
    tum."

LXXI.

They lock them up, and veil, and guard them
    daily,
    They scarcely can behold their male rela-
    tions,
So that their moments do not pass so gaily
    As is supposed the case with northern na-
    tions;
Confinement, too, must make them look quite
    palely;
    And as the Turks abhor long conversations,
Their days are either passed in doing nothing,
Or bathing, nursing, making love, and cloth-
    ing.

LXXII.

They cannot read, and so don't lisp in criti-
    cism;
    Nor write, and so they don't affect the muse;
Were never caught in epigram or witticism,
    Have no romances, sermons, plays, re-
    views,—
In harams learning soon would make a pretty
    schism!
    But luckily these beauties are no "Blues,"
No bustling Botherbys have they to show 'em
"That charming passage in the last new
    poem."

LXXIII.

No solemn, antique gentleman of rhyme,
    Who having angled all his life for fame,
And getting but a nibble at a time,
    Still fussily keeps fishing on, the same
Small "Triton of the minnows," the sublime
    Of mediocrity, the furious tame,
The echo's echo, usher of the school
Of female wits, boy bards—in short, a fool!

LXXIV.

A stalking oracle of awful phrase,
    The approving "*Good!*" (by no means
    GOOD in law)

Humming like flies around the newest blaze,
    The bluest of bluebottles you e'er saw,
Teasing with blame, excruciating with praise,
    Gorging the little fame he gets all raw,
Translating tongues he knows not even by
    letter,
And sweating plays so middling, bad were
    better.

LXXV.

One hates an author that's *all author*, fellows
    In foolscap uniforms turned up with ink,
So very anxious, clever, fine, and jealous,
    One don't know what to say to them, or
    think,
Unless to puff them with a pair of bellows;
    Of coxcombry's worst coxcombs e'en the
    pink
Are preferable to these shreds of paper,
These unquenched snuffings of the midnight
    taper.

LXXVI.

Of these same we see several, and of others,
    Men of the world, who know the world like
    men,
Scott, Rogers, Moore, and all the better
    brothers,
    Who think of something else besides the
    pen;
But for the children of the "mighty mother's,"
    The would-be wits and can't-be gentlemen,
I leave them to their daily "tea is ready,"
Smug coterie, and literary lady.

LXXVII.

The poor dear Mussulwomen whom I men-
    tion
    Have none of these instructive pleasant
    people,
And *one* would seem to them a new invention,
    Unknown as bells within a Turkish steeple;
I think 'twould almost be worth while to pen-
    sion
    (Though best-sown projects very often reap
    ill)
A missionary author, just to preach
Our Christain usage of the parts of speech.

LXXVIII.

No chemistry for them unfolds her gases,
    No metaphysics are let loose in lectures,
No circulating library amasses
    Religious novels, moral tales, and strictures
Upon the living manners, as they pass us;
    No exhibition glares with annual pictures;
They stare not on the stars from out their
    attics,
Nor deal (thank God for that!) in mathe-
    matics.

LXXIX.

Why I thank God for that is no great matter,
    I have my reasons, you no doubt suppose.

And as, perhaps, they would not highly flatter,
  I'll keep them for my life (to come) in prose ;
I fear I have a little turn for satire,
  And yet methinks the older that one grows
Inclines us more to laugh than scold, though laughter
  Leaves us so doubly serious shortly after.

LXXX.

Oh, Mirth and Innocence! Oh, Milk and Water!
  Ye happy mixtures of more happy days!
In these sad centuries of sin and slaughter,
  Abominable Man no more allays
His thirst with such pure beverage. No matter,
  I love you both, and both shall have my praise.
Oh, for old Saturn's reign of sugar-candy! —
Meantime I drink to your return in brandy.

LXXXI.

Our Laura's Turk still kept his eyes upon her,
  Less in the Mussulman than Christian way,
Which seems to say, " Madam, I do you honor,
  " And while I please to stare, you'll please to stay : "
Could staring win a woman, this had won her,
  But Laura could not thus be led astray ;
She had stood fire too long and well, to boggle
Even at this stranger's most outlandish ogle.

LXXXII.

The morning now was on the point of breaking,
  A turn of time at which I would advise
Ladies who have been dancing, or partaking
  In any other kind of exercise,
To make their preparations for forsaking
  The ball-room ere the sun begins to rise,
Because when once the lamps and candles fail,
His blushes make them look a little pale.

LXXXIII.

I've seen some balls and revels in my time,
  And stayed them over for some silly reason,
And then I looked (I hope it was no crime)
  To see what lady best stood out the season ;
And though I've seen some thousands in their prime,
  Lovely and pleasing, and who still may please on,
I never saw but one (the stars withdrawn),
Whose bloom could after dancing dare the dawn.

LXXXIV.

The name of this Aurora I'll not mention,
  Although I might, for she was nought to me
More than that patent work of God's invention,
  A charming woman, whom we like to see ;
But writing names would merit reprehension,
  Yet if you like to find out this fair *she*,
At the next London or Parisian ball
You still may mark her cheek, out-blooming all.

LXXXV.

Laura, who knew it would not do at all
  To meet the daylight after seven hours' sitting
Among three thousand people at a ball,
  To make her curtsy thought it right and fitting ;
The Count was at her elbow with her shawl,
  And they the room were on the point of quitting,
When lo! those cursed gondoliers had got
Just in the very place where they *should not.*

LXXXVI.

In this they're like our coachmen, and the cause
  Is much the same — the crowd, and pulling, hauling,
With blasphemies enough to break their jaws,
  They make a never intermitting bawling.
At home, our Bow-street gemmen keep the laws,
  And here a sentry stands within your calling ;
But for all that, there is a deal of swearing,
And nauseous words past mentioning or bearing.

LXXXVII.

The Count and Laura found their boat at last,
  And homeward floated o'er the silent tide,
Discussing all the dances gone and past ;
  The dancers and their dresses, too, beside ;
Some little scandals eke : but all aghast
  (As to their palace stairs the rowers glide)
Sate Laura by the side of her Adorer,[1]
When lo! the Mussulman was there before her.

LXXXVIII.

"Sir," said the Count, with brow exceeding grave,
  "Your unexpected presence here will make
" It necessary for myself to crave
  " Its import ? But perhaps 'tis a mistake ;
" I hope it is so ; and at once to wave
  " All compliment, I hope so for *your* sake ;
"You understand my meaning, or you *shall*."
"Sir," (quoth the Turk) " 'tis no mistake at all.

[1] [MS. — " Sate Laura with a kind of comic horror."]

LXXXIX.

"That Lady is *my wife!*" Much wonder
  paints
The lady's changing cheek, as well it might;
But where an Englishwoman sometimes faints,
  Italian females don't do so outright;
They only call a little on their saints,
  And then come to themselves, almost or
    quite;
Which saves much hartshorn, salts, and
  sprinkling faces, ·
And cutting stays, as usual in such cases.

XC.

She said,—what could she say? Why, not a
  word:
But the Count courteously invited in
The stranger, much appeased by what he
  heard:
  " Such things, perhaps, we'd best discuss
    within,"
Said he; "don't let us make ourselves absurd
  " In public, by a scene, nor raise a din,
For then the chief and only satisfaction
Will be much quizzing on the whole trans-
  action."

XCI.

They entered, and for coffee called—it came,
  A beverage for Turks and Christians both,
Although the way they make it's not the same.
  Now Laura, much recovered, or less loth
To speak, cries, " Beppo! what's your pagan
  name?
  Bless me! your beard is of amazing growth!
And how came you to keep away so long?
Are you not sensible 'twas very wrong?

XCII.

And are you *really, truly,* now a Turk?
  With any other women did you wive?
Is't true they use their fingers for a fork?
  Well, that's the prettiest shawl—as I'm
    alive!
You'll give it me? They say you eat no pork.
  And how so many years did you contrive
To—Bless me! did I ever? No, I never
Saw a man grown so yellow! How's your
  liver?

XCIII.

Beppo! that beard of yours becomes you not;
  It shall be shaved before you're a day older:
Why do you wear it? Oh! I had forgot—
  Pray don't you think the weather here is
    colder?
How do I look? You shan't stir from this
  spot
  In that queer dress, for fear that some be-
    holder
Should find you out, and make the story known.
How short your hair is! Lord! how gray it's
  grown!"

XCIV.

What answer Beppo made to these demands
  Is more than I know. He was cast away
About where Troy stood once, and nothing
  stands,
  Became a slave of course, and for his pay
Had bread and bastinadoes, till some bands
  Of pirates landing in a neighboring bay,
He joined the rogues and prospered, and be-
    came
A renegado of indifferent fame.

XCV.

But he grew rich, and with his riches grew so
  Keen the desire to see his home again,
He thought himself in duty bound to do so,
  And not be always thieving on the main:
Lonely he felt, at times, as Robin Crusoe,
  And so he hired a vessel come from Spain,
Bound for Corfu: she was a fine polacca,
Manned with twelve hands, and laden with to-
  bacco.

XCVI.

Himself, and much (heaven knows how
  gotten!) cash,
  He then embarked with risk of life and
    limb,
And got clear off, although the attempt was
  rash;
  He said that *Providence* protected him—
For my part, I say nothing—lest we clash
  In our opinions:—well, the ship was trim,
Set sail, and kept her reckoning fairly on,
Except three days of calm when off Cape Bonn.

XCVII.

They reached the island, he transferred his
  lading,
  And self and live stock, to another bottom,
And passed for a true Turkey-merchant, trad-
  ing
  With goods of various names, but I've for-
    got 'em.
However, he got off by this evading,
  Or else the people would perhaps have shot
    him;
And thus at Venice landed to reclaim
His wife, religion, house, and Christian name.

XCVIII.

His wife received, the patriarch re-baptized
  him,
  (He made the church a present, by the way);
He then threw off the garments which dis-
  guised him,
  And borrowed the Count's smallclothes for
    a day:
His friends the more for his long absence
  prized him,
  Finding he'd wherewithal to make them
    gay,

With dinners, where he oft became the laugh
  of them,
For stories — but *I* don't believe the half of
  them.

          XCIX.

Whate'er his youth had suffered, his old
  age
With wealth and talking make him some
  amends;
Though Laura sometimes put him in a rage,
  I've heard the Count and he were always
  friends.
My pen is at the bottom of a page,
  Which being finished, here the story ends;
'Tis to be wished it had been sooner done,
But stories somehow lengthen when begun.[1]

---

[1] [This extremely clever and amusing perform-
ance affords a very curious and complete specimen
of a kind of diction and composition of which our
English literature has hitherto presented very few
examples. It is, in itself, absolutely a thing of noth-
ing — without story, characters, sentiments, or in-
telligible object; — a mere piece of lively and loqua-
cious prattling, in short, upon all kinds of frivolous
subjects, — a sort of gay and desultory babbling

about Italy and England, Turks, balls, literature,
and fish sauces. But still there is something very
engaging in the uniform gaiety, politeness, and good
humor of the author, and something still more strik-
ing and admirable in the matchless facility with
which he has cast into regular, and even difficult,
versification the unmingled, unconstrained, and un-
selected language of the most light, familiar, and
ordinary conversation. With great skill and felicity,
he has furnished us with an example of about one
hundred stanzas of good verse, entirely composed of
common words, in their common places: never pre-
senting us with one sprig of what is called poetical
diction, or even making use of a single inversion,
either to raise the style or assist the rhyme — but
running on in an inexhaustible series of good easy
colloquial phrases, and finding them fall into verse
by some unaccountable and happy fatality. In this
great and characteristic quality it is almost invari-
ably excellent. In some other respects, it is more
unequal. About one half is as good as possible, in
the style to which it belongs; the other half bears,
perhaps, too many marks of that haste with which
such a work must necessarily be written. Some
passages are rather too snappish, and some run too
much on the cheap and rather plebeian humor of out-
of-the-way-rhymes, and strange-sounding words and
epithets. But the greater part is extremely pleas-
ant, amiable, and gentlemanlike. — *Jeffrey.*]

THE PROPHECY OF DANTE.[1]

    " 'Tis the sunset of life gives me mystical lore,
    And coming events cast their shadows before."
                     CAMPBELL.

  [This poem, which Lord Byron, in sending it to Mr. Murray, called " the best thing he had ever done,
if not *unintelligible*," was written in the summer of 1819, at

        —— " that place
    Of old renown, once in the Adrian sea,
    Ravenna! — where from Dante's sacred tomb
    He had so oft, as many a verse declares,
    Drawn inspiration." — ROGERS.

The Prophecy, however, was first published in May, 1821. It is dedicated to the Countess Guiccioli,
who thus describes the origin of its composition: — " On my departure from Venice, Lord Byron had
promised to come and see me at Ravenna. Dante's tomb, the classical pine wood,[2] the relics of antiquity

---

[1] [Dante Alighieri was born in Florence in May, 1265, of an ancient and honorable family. In the
early part of his life he gained some credit in a military character, and distinguished himself by his brav-
ery in an action where the Florentines obtained a signal victory over the citizens of Arezzo. He became
still more eminent by the acquisition of court honors; and at the age of thirty-five he rose to be one o
the chief magistrates of Florence, when that dignity was conferred by the suffrages of the people. From
this exaltation the poet himself dated his principal misfortunes. Italy was at that time distracted by the
contending factions of the Ghibelines and Guelphs, — among the latter Dante took an active part. I—
one of the proscriptions he was banished, his possessions confiscated, and he died in exile in 1321.]

    [2] " 'Twas in a grove of spreading pines he strayed," etc.
                 DRYDEN's *Theodore and Honoria.*

which are to be found in that place, afforded a sufficient pretext for me to invite him to come, and for him to accept my invitation. He came in the month of June, 1819, arriving at Ravenna on the day of the festival of the Corpus Domini. Being deprived at this time of his books, his horses, and all that occupied him at Venice, I begged him to gratify me by writing something on the subject of Dante; and, with his usual facility and rapidity, he composed his Prophecy."]

DEDICATION.

LADY! if for the cold and cloudy clime
    Where I was born, but where I would not **die,**
    Of the great Poet-sire of Italy
I dare to build the imitative rhyme,
Harsh Runic copy of the South's sublime,
    THOU art the cause; and howsoever I
    Fall short of his immortal harmony,
Thy gentle heart will pardon me the crime.
Thou, in the pride of Beauty and of Youth,
    Spakest; and for thee to speak and be obeyed
Are one; but only in the sunny South
    Such sounds are uttered, and such charms displayed,
So sweet a language from so fair a mouth —
    Ah! to what effort would it not persuade?
RAVENNA, June 21, 1819.

• PREFACE.

IN the course of a visit to the city of Ravenna in the summer of 1819, it was suggested to the author that having composed something on the subject of Tasso's confinement, he should do the same on Dante's exile, — the tomb of the poet forming one of the principal objects of interest in that city, both to the native and to the stranger.

"On this hint I spake," and the result has been the following four cantos, in terza rima, now offered to the reader. If they are understood and approved, it is my purpose to continue the poem in various other cantos to its natural conclusion in the present age. The reader is requested to suppose that Dante addresses him in the interval between the conclusion of the Divina Commedia and his death, and shortly before the latter event, foretelling the fortunes of Italy in general in the ensuing centuries. In adopting this plan I have had in my mind the Cassandra of Lycophron, and the Prophecy of Nereus by Horace, as well as the Prophecies of Holy Writ. The measure adopted is the terza rima of Dante, which I am not aware to have seen hitherto tried in our language, except it may be by Mr. Hayley, of whose translation I never saw but one extract, quoted in the notes to Caliph Vathek; so that — if I do not err — this poem may be considered as a metrical experiment. The cantos are short, and about the same length of those of the poet, whose name I have borrowed, and most probably taken in vain.

Amongst the inconveniences of authors in the present day, it is difficult for any who have a name, good or bad, to escape translation. I have had the fortune to see the fourth canto of Childe Harold translated into Italian versi sciolti, — that is, a poem written in the *Spenserean stanza* into *blank verse*, without regard to the natural divisions of the stanza or of the sense. If the present poem, being on a national topic, should chance to undergo the same fate, I would request the Italian reader to remember that when I have failed in the imitation of his great "Padre Alighier," I have failed in imitating that which all study and few understand, since to this very day it is not yet settled what was the meaning of the allegory in the first canto of the Inferno, unless Count Marchetti's ingenious and probable conjecture may be considered as having decided the question.

He may also pardon my failure the more, as I am not quite sure that he would be pleased with my success, since the Italians, with a pardonable nationality, are particularly jealous of all that is left them as a nation — their literature; and in the present bitterness of the classic and romantic war, are but ill disposed to permit a foreigner even to approve or imitate them, without finding some fault with his ultra-montane presumption.   I can easily enter into all this, knowing what would be thought in England of an Italian imitator of Milton, or of a translation of Monti, or Pindemonte, or Arici, should be held up to the rising generation as a model for their future poetical essays.   But I perceive that I am deviating into an address to the Italian reader, when my business is with the English one; and be they few or many, I must take my leave of both.

CANTO THE FIRST.

ONCE more in man's frail world! which I had
  left
So long that 'twas forgotten; and I feel
The weight of clay again, — too soon bereft
Of the immortal vision which could heal
My earthly sorrows, and to God's own skies
Lift me from that deep gulf without repeal,
Where late my ears rung with the damned
  cries
Of souls in hopeless bale; and from that
  place
Of lesser torment, whence men may arise
Pure from the fire to join the angelic race;
  Midst whom my own bright Beatrice
  blessed [1]
My spirit with her light; and to the base
Of the eternal Triad! first, last, best,
Mysterious, three, sole, infinite, great God!
Soul universal! led the mortal guest,
Unblasted by the glory, though he trod
From star to star to reach the almighty
  throne.
Oh Beatrice! whose sweet limbs the sod
So long hath pressed, and the cold marble
  stone,
Thou sole pure seraph of my earliest love,
Love so ineffable, and so alone,
That nought on earth could more my bosom
  move,
And meeting thee in heaven was but to meet
That without which my soul, like the arkless
  dove,
Had wandered still in search of, nor her feet
Relieved her wing till found; without thy
  light
My paradise had still been incomplete. [2]

Since my tenth sun gave summer to my sight
Thou wert my life, the essence of my thought,
Loved ere I knew the name of love, [3] and
  bright
Still in these dim old eyes, now overwrought
With the world's war, and years, and banish-
  ment,
And tears for thee, by other woes untaught;
For mine is not a nature to be bent
By tyrannous faction, and the brawling
  crowd,
And though the long, long conflict hath been
  spent
In vain, and never more, save when the
  cloud
Which overhangs the Apennine, my mind's
  eye
Pierces to fancy Florence, once so proud
Of me, can I return, though but to die,
Unto my native soil, they have not yet
Quenched the old exile's spirit, stern and
  high.
But the sun, though not overcast, must set,
And the night cometh; I am old in days,
And deeds, and contemplation, and have met
Destruction face to face in all his ways.
The world hath left me, what it found me,
  pure,
And if I have not gathered yet its praise,
I sought it not by any baser lure;
Man wrongs, and Time avenges, and my
  name
May form a monument not all obscure,
Though such was not my ambition's end or
  aim,
To add to the vain-glorious list of those
Who dabble in the pettiness of fame,
And make men's fickle breath the wind that
  blows
Their sail, and deem it glory to be classed
With conquerors, and virtue's other foes,
In bloody chronicles of ages past.

---

[1] The reader is requested to adopt the Italian pronunciation of Beatrice, sounding all the sylla-bles.

[2] "Che sol per le belle opre
  Che fanno in cielo il sole e l' altre stelle,
  Dentro di lui *si crede il Paradiso,*
  Così se guardi fiso,
  . Pensar ben dei ch' ogni terren piacere
  Si trova dove tu non puoi vedere."
Canzone, in which Dante [?] describes the person of Beatrice, Strophe third.

[3] [According to Boccaccio, Dante was a lover long before he was a soldier, and his passion for the Beatrice whom he has immortalized commenced while he was in his ninth year, and she in her eighth year. — *Cary.*]

I would have had my Florence great and
  free : [1]
Oh Florence! Florence! unto me thou wast
Like that Jerusalem which the Almighty He,
  Wept over, " but thou wouldst not; " as the
  bird
Gathers its young, I would have gathered
  thee
Beneath a parent pinion, hadst thou heard
  My voice; but as the adder, deaf and fierce,
  Against the breast that cherished thee was
  stirred
Thy venom, and my state thou didst amerce,
  And doom this body forfeit to the fire.
Alas! how bitter is his country's curse
To him who *for* that could ry would expire,
  But did not merit to expire *by* her,
  And loves her, loves her even in her ire.
The day may come when she will cease to err,
  The day may come she would be proud to
  have
  The dust she dooms to scatter, and transfer [2]
Of him, whom she denied a home, the grave,
  But this shall not be granted; let my dust
  Lie where it falls; nor shall the soil which
  gave
Me breath, but in her sudden fury thrust
  Me forth to breathe elsewhere, so reassume
  My indignant bones, because her angry gust
Forsooth is over, and repealed her doom;
  No,—she denied me what was mine—my
  roof,
  And shall not have what is not hers—my
  tomb.
Too long her armed wrath hath kept aloof
  The breast which would have bled for her,
  the heart
That beat, the mind that was temptation
  proof,
The man who fought, toiled, travelled, and each
  part
Of a true citizen fulfilled, and saw

---

[1] L' Esilio che m' è dato onor mi tegno.
    *   *   *   *   *
Cader tra' buoni è pur di lode degno."
                     Sonnet of Dante,
in which he represents Right, Generosity, and Tem-
perance as banished from among men, and seeking
refuge from Love, who inhabits his bosom.

[2] "Ut si quis predictorum ullo tempore in fortiam
dicti communis pervenerit, *talis perveniens igne
comburatur, sic quod moriatur*." Second sen-
tence of Florence against Dante, and the fourteen
accused with him. The Latin is worthy of the sen-
tence. — [On the 27th of January, 1302, Dante was
mulcted eight thousand lire, and condemned to two
years' banishment; and in case the fine was not
paid, his goods were to be confiscated. On the
eleventh of March, the same year, he was sentenced
to a punishment due only to the most desperate of
malefactors. The decree, that he and his associates
in exile should be burned if they fell into the hands
of their enemies. was first discovered in 1772.]

For his reward the Guelf's ascendant art
Pass his destruction even into a law.
  These things are not made for forgetfulness,
  Florence shall be forgotten first; too raw
The wound, too deep the wrong, and the dis-
  tress
Of such endurance too prolonged to make
  My pardon greater, her injustice less,
Though late repented; yet—yet for her sake
  I feel some fonder yearnings, and for thine,
  My own Beatricë, I would hardly take
Vengeance upon the land which once was mine,
  And still is hallowed by thy dust's return,
  Which would protect the murderess like a
  shrine,
And save ten thousand foes by thy sole urn.
  Though, like old Marius from Minturnæ's
  marsh
And Carthage ruins, my lone breast may burn
At times with evil feelings hot and harsh,
  And sometimes the last pangs of a vile foe
  Writhe in a dream before me, and o'erarch
My brow with hopes of triumph, — let them go!
  Such are the last infirmities of those
  Who long have suffered more than mortal
  woe,
And yet being mortal still, have no repose
  But on the pillow of Revenge — Revenge,
  Who sleeps to dream of blood, and waking
  glows
With the oft-baffled, slakeless thirst of change,
  When we shall mount again, and they that
  trod
  Be trampled on, while Death and Atè range
O'er humbled heads and severed necks——
  Great God!
  Take these thoughts from me — to thy hands
  I yield
My many wrongs, and thine almighty rod
Will fall on those who smote me,—be my
  shield!
  As thou hast been in peril, and in pain,
  In turbulent cities, and the tented field—
In toil, and many troubles borne in vain
  For Florence. — I appeal from her to Thee!
  Thee, whom I late saw in thy loftiest reign,
Even in that glorious vision, which to see
  And live was never granted until now,
  And yet thou hast permitted this to me.
Alas! with what a weight upon my brow
  The sense of earth and earthly things come
  back,
  Corrosive passions, feelings dull and low.
The heart's quick throb upon the mental rack,
  Long day, and dreary night; the retrospect
  Of half a century bloody and black,
And the frail few years I may yet expect
  Hoary and hopeless, but less hard to bear,
  For I have been too long and deeply
  wrecked
On the lone rock of desolate Despair
  To lift my eyes more to the passing sail

Which shuns that reef so horrible and bare;
Nor raise my voice — for who would heed my
  wail?
I am not of this people, nor this age,
And yet my harpings will unfold a tale .
Which shall preserve these times when not a
  page
Of their perturbed annals could attract
An eye to gaze upon their civil rage,
Did not my verse embalm full many an act
Worthless as they who wrought it: 'tis the
  doom
Of spirits of my order to be racked
In life, to wear their hearts out, and consume
Their days in endless strife, and die alone;
Then future thousands crowd around their
  tomb,
And pilgrims come from climes where they
  have known
The name of him — who now is but a name,
And wasting homage o'er the sullen stone,
Spread his — by him unheard, unheeded —
  fame;
And mine at least hath cost me dear: to die
Is nothing; but to wither thus — to tame
My mind down from its own infinity —
To live in narrow ways with little men,
A common sight to every common eye,
A wanderer, while even wolves can find a den,
Ripped from all kindred, from all home, all
  things
That make communion sweet, and soften
  pain —
To feel me in the solitude of kings
Without the power that makes them bear a
  crown —
To envy every dove his nest and wings
Which waft him where the Apennine looks
  down
On Arno, till he perches, it may be,
Within my all inexorable town,
Where yet my boys are, and that fatal she,[1]

Their mother, the cold partner who hath
  brought
Destruction for a dowry [2] — this to see
And feel, and know without repair, hath taught
A bitter lesson; but it leaves me free ·
I have not vilely found, nor basely sought,
They made an Exile — not a slave of me.

---

[1] This lady, whose name was *Gemma*, sprung
from one of the most powerful Guelf families, named
Donati. Corso Donati was the principal adversary
of the Ghibelines. She is described as being " *Ad-
modum morosa, ut de Xantippe Socratis phi-
losophi conjuge scriptum esse legimus*," according
to Giannozzo Manetti. But Lionardo Aretino is
scandalized with Boccace, in his life of Dante, for
saying that literary men should not marry. " Qui
il Boccaccio non ha pazienza, e dice, le mogli esser
contrarie agli studj; e non si ricorda che Socrate il
più nobile filosofo che mai fosse, ebbe moglie e figli-
uoli e uffici della Repubblica nella sua Città; e
Aristotele che, etc. etc. ebbe due mogli in varj tempi,
ed ebbe figliuoli, e ricchezze as sai. — E Marco
Tullio — e Catone — e Varrone — e Seneca — eb-
bero moglie," etc. etc. It is odd that honest Lio-
nardo's examples, with the exception of Seneca, and,
for any thing I know, of Aristotle, are not the most
felicitous. Tully's Terentia, and Socrates' Xan-
tippe, by no means contributed to their husbands'
happiness, whatever they might as to their philoso-
phy — Cato gave away his wife — of Varro's we
know nothing — and of Seneca's, only that she was
disposed to die with him, but recovered, and lived
several years afterwards. But, says Lionardo,
" L' uomo è *animale civile*, secondo piace a tutti
i filosofi." And thence concludes that the greatest
proof of the *animal's civism* is " la prima congi
unzione, dalla quale multiplicata nasce la Città."

[2] [The violence of Gemma's temper proved a
source of the bitterest suffering to Dante; and in
that passage of the Inferno, where one of the char-
acters says —

  " La fiera moglie più ch' altro, mi nuoce,
       —— " me, my wife,
    Of savage temper, more than aught beside,
    Hath to this evil brought,"

his own conjugal unhappiness must have recurred
forcibly and painfully to his mind. — *Cary.*]

CANTO THE SECOND.

THE Spirit of the fervent days of Old,
When words were things that came to pass,
  and thought
Flashed o'er the future, bidding men behold
Their children's children's doom already
  brought
Forth from the abyss of time which is to be,
The chaos of events, where lie half-wrought
Shapes that must undergo mortality;
What the great Seers of Israel wore within,

That spirit was on them, and is on me.
And if, Cassandra-like, amidst the din
Of conflict none will hear, or hearing heed
This voice from out the Wilderness, the sin
Be theirs, and my own feelings be my meed.
The only guerdon I have ever known.
Hast thou not bled? and hast thou still
  bleed,
Italia? Ah! to me such things, foreshown
With dim sepulchral light, bid me forget

In thine irreparable wrongs my own:
We can have but one country, and even yet
  Thou'rt mine — my bones shall be within
    thy breast,
  My soul within thy language, which once
    set
With our old Roman sway in the wide West;
But I will make another tongue arise
As lofty and more sweet, in which expressed
The hero's ardor, or the lover's sighs,
Shall find alike such sounds for every theme
That every word, as brilliant as thy skies,
Shall realize a poet's proudest dream,
  And make thee Europe's nightingale of song;
So that all present speech to thine shall seem
The note of meaner birds, and every tongue
  Confess its barbarism when compared with
    thine.
This shalt thou owe to him thou didst so
  wrong,
Thy Tuscan bard, the banished Ghibeline.
Woe! woe! the veil of coming centuries
Is rent, — a thousand years which yet supine
Lie like the ocean waves ere winds arise,
  Heaving in dark and sullen undulation,
  Float from eternity into these eyes;
The storms yet sleep, the clouds still keep
    their station,
  The unborn earthquake yet is in the womb,
  The bloody chaos yet expects creation,
But all things are disposing for thy doom;
  The elements await but for the word,
  " Let there be darkness ! " and thou growest
    a tomb.
Yes! thou, so beautiful, shalt feel the sword,
  Thou, Italy! so fair that Paradise,
  Revived in thee, blooms forth to man re-
    stored:
Ah! must the sons of Adam lose it twice?
  Thou, Italy! whose ever golden fields,
  Ploughed by the sunbeams solely, would
    suffice
For the world's granary; thou, whose sky
    heaven gilds
  With brighter stars, and robes with deeper
    blue;
  Thou, in whose pleasant places Summer
    builds
Her palace, in whose cradle Empire grew,
  And formed the Eternal City's ornaments
  From spoils of kings whom freemen over-
    threw;
Birthplace of heroes, sanctuary of saints,
  Where earthly first, then heavenly glory
    made
  Her home; thou, all which fondest fancy
    paints,
And finds her prior vision but portrayed
  In feeble colors, when the eye — from the
    Alp
  Of horrid snow, and rock, and shaggy shade
Of desert-loving pine, whose emerald scalp

Nods to the storm — dilates and dotes o'er
  thee,
  And wistfully implores, as 'twere, for help;
To see thy sunny fields, my Italy,
  Nearer and nearer yet, and dearer still
  The more approached, and dearest were
    they free.
Thou — Thou must wither to each tyrant's
    will:
  The Goth hath been, — the German, Frank,
    and Hun
  Are yet to come, — and on the imperial hill
Ruin, already proud of the deeds done
  By the old barbarians, there awaits the new
  Throned on the Palatine, while lost and won
Rome at her feet lies bleeding; and the hue
  Of human sacrifice and Roman slaughter
  Troubles the clotted air, of late so blue,
And deepens into red the saffron water
  Of Tiber, thick with dead; the helpless
    priest,
  And still more helpless nor less holy daugh-
    ter,
Vowed to their God, have shrieking fled, and
    ceased
  Their ministry: the nations take their prey,
  Iberian, Almain, Lombard, and the beast
And bird, wolf, vulture, more humane than
    they
  Are; these but gorge the flesh and lap the
    gore
  Of the departed, and then go their way;
But those, the human savages, explore
  All paths of torture, and insatiate yet,
  With Ugolino hunger prowl for more.
Nine moons shall rise o'er scenes like this and
    set;[1]
  The chiefless army of the dead, which late
  Beneath the traitor Prince's banner met,
Hath left its leader's ashes at the gate;
  Had but the royal Rebel lived, perchance
  Thou hadst been spared, but his involved
    thy fate.
Oh! Rome, the spoiler or the spoil of France,
  From Brennus to the Bourbon, never, never
  Shall foreign standard to thy walls advance
But Tiber shall become a mournful river.
  Oh! when the strangers pass the Alps and
    Po,
  Crush them, ye rocks! floods whelm them,
    and for ever!
Why sleep the idle avalanches so,
  To topple on the lonely pilgrim's head?
  Why doth Eridanus but overflow
The peasant's harvest from his turbid bed?
  Were not each barbarous horde a nobler
    prey?
  Over Cambyses' host the desert spread

---

[1] See "Sacco di Roma," generally attributed to
Guicciardini. There is another written by a Jacopo
Buonaparte.

Her sandy ocean, and the sea waves' sway
  Rolled over Pharaoh and his thousands, —
    why,
Mountains and waters, do ye not as they?
And you, ye men! Romans, who dare not
    die,
  Sons of the conquerors who overthrew
  Those who overthrew proud Xerxes, where
    yet lie
The dead whose tomb Oblivion never knew,
  Are the Alps weaker than Thermopylæ?
  Their passes more alluring to the view
Of an invader? is it they, or ye,
  That to each host the mountain-gate unbar,
  And leave the march in peace, the passage
    free?
Why, Nature's self detains the victor's car,
  And makes your land impregnable, if earth
  Could be so; but alone she will not war,
Yet aids the warrior worthy of his birth
  In a soil where the mothers bring forth men;
  Not so with those whose souls are little
    worth;
For them no fortress can avail, — the den
  Of the poor reptile which preserves its sting

Is more secure than walls of adamant, when
  The hearts of those within are quivering.
  Are ye not brave? Yes, yet the Ausonian
    soil
Hath hearts, and hands, and arms, and
    hosts to bring
Against Oppression; but how vain the toil,
  While still Division sows the seeds of woe
  And weakness, till the stranger reaps the
    spoil.
Oh! my own beauteous land! so long laid
    low,
  So long the grave of thy own children's
    hopes,
  When there is but required a single blow
To break the chain, yet — yet the Avenger
    stops,
  And Doubt and Discord step 'twixt thine
    and thee,
  And join their strength to that which with
    thee copes;
What is there wanting then to set thee free,
  And show thy beauty in its fullest light?
  To make the Alps impassable; and we,
Her sons, may do this with *one* deed — Unite.

CANTO THE THIRD. '

FROM out the mass of never-dying ill,
  The Plague, the Prince, the Stranger, and
    the Sword,
  Vials of wrath but emptied to refill
And flow again, I cannot all record
  That crowds on my prophetic eye: the
    earth
  And ocean written o'er would not afford
Space for the annal, yet it shall go forth;
  Yes, all, though not by human pen, is
    graven,
  There where the furthest suns and stars
    have birth,
Spread like a banner at the gate of heaven,
  The bloody scroll of our millennial wrongs
  Waves, and the echo of our groans is driven
Athwart the sound of archangelic songs,
  And Italy, the martyred nation's gore,
  Will not in vain arise to where belongs
Omnipotence and mercy evermore:
  Like to a harpstring stricken by the wind,
  The sound of her lament shall, rising o'er
The seraph voices, touch the Almighty Mind.
  Meantime I, humblest of thy sons, and of
  Earth's dust by immortality refined
To sense and suffering, though the vain may
    scoff,
  And tyrants threat, and meeker victims bow

Before the storm because its breath is
    rough,
To thee, my country! whom before, as now,
  I loved and love, devote the mournful lyre
  And melancholy gift high powers allow
To read the future; and if now my fire
  Is not as once it shone o'er thee, forgive!
  I but foretell thy fortunes — then expire;
Think not that I would look on them and
    live.
A spirit forces me to see and speak,
  And for my guerdon grants *not* to survive;
My heart shall be poured over thee and
    break:
  Yet for a moment, ere I must resume
  Thy sable web of sorrow, let me take
Over the gleams that flash athwart thy gloom
  A softer glimpse; some stars shine through
    thy night,
  And many meteors, and above thy tomb
Leans sculptured Beauty, which Death cannot
    blight;
  And from thine ashes boundless spirits rise
  To give thee honor, and the earth delight;
Thy soil shall still be pregnant with the wise,
  The gay, the learned, the generous, and the
    brave,
  Native to thee as summer to thy skies,

Conquerors on foreign shores, and the far
  wave,[1]
Discoverers of new worlds, which take their
  name;[2]
For *thee* alone they have no arm to save,
And all thy recompense is in their fame,
  A noble one to them, but not to thee —
  Shall they be glorious, and thou still the
  same?
Oh! more than these illustrious far shall be
  The being — and even yet he may be born —
  The mortal savior who shall set thee free,
And see thy diadem so changed and worn
  By fresh barbarians, on thy brow replaced;
  And the sweet sun replenishing thy morn,
Thy moral morn, too long with clouds defaced
And noxious vapors from Avernus risen,
  Such as all they must breathe who are de-
  based
By servitude, and have the mind in prison.
  Yet through this centuried eclipse of woe
  Some voices shall be heard, and earth shall
  ·listen;
Poets shall follow in the path I show,
  And make it broader; the same brilliant sky
  Which cheers the birds to song shall bid
  them glow,
And raise their notes as natural and high;
  Tuneful shall be their numbers; they shall
  sing
Many of love, and some of liberty,
But few shall soar upon that eagle's wing,
  And look in the sun's face with eagle's gaze,
  All free and fearless as the feathered king,
But fly more near the earth; how many a phrase
  Sublime shall be lavished on some small
  prince
In all the prodigality of praise!
And language, eloquently false, evince
  The harlotry of genius, which, like beauty,
  Too oft forgets its own self-reverence,   .
And looks on prostitution as a duty.
He who once enters in a tyrant's hall[3]
  As guest is slave, his thoughts become a
  booty,
And the first day which sees the chain enthrall
  A captive, sees his half of manhood gone — [4]
  The soul's emasculation saddens all
His spirit; thus the Bard too near the throne
  Quails from his inspiration, bound to
  please, —
How servile is the task to please alone!
To smooth the verse to suit his sovereign's ease
  And royal leisure, nor too much prolong ·

Aught save his eulogy, and find, and seize,
Or force, or forge fit argument of song!
  Thus trammelled, thus condemned to Flat-
  tery's trebles,
He toils through all, still trembling to be
  wrong:
For fear some noble thoughts, like heavenly
  rebels,
  Should rise up in high treason to his brain,
  He sings, as the Athenian spoke, with peb`
  bles
In's mouth, lest truth should stammer through
  his strain.
  But out of the long file of sonneteers
  There shall be some who will not sing in
  vain,
And he, their prince, shall rank among my
  peers,[5]
  And love shall be his torment; but his grief
  Shall make an immortality of tears,
And Italy shall hail him as the Chief
  Of Poet-lovers, and his highest song
  Of Freedom wreathe him with as green a leaf.
But in a further age shall rise along
  The banks of Po two greater still than he;
  The world which smiled on him shall do
  them wrong
Till they are ashes, and repose with me.
  The first will make an epoch with his lyre,
  And fill the earth with feats of chivalry:
His fancy like a rainbow, and his fire,
  Like that of Heaven, immortal, and his
  thought
Borne onward with a wing that cannot tire:
Pleasure·shall, like a butterfly new caught,
  Flutter her lovely pinions o'er his theme,
  And Art itself seem into Nature wrought
By the transparency of his bright dream. —
  The second, of a tenderer, sadder mood,
  Shall pour his soul out o'er Jerusalem;
He, too, shall sing of arms, and Christian blood
  Shed where Christ bled for man; and his
  high harp
Shall, by the willow over Jordan's flood,
Revive a song of Sion, and the sharp
  Conflict, and final triumph of the brave
  And pious, and the strife of hell to warp
Their hearts from their great purpose, until
  wave
  The red-cross banners where the first red
  Cross
Was crimsoned from his veins who died to
  save,
Shall be his sacred argument; the loss
  Of years, of favor, freedom, even of fame
  Contested for a time, while the smooth gloss
Of courts would slide o'er his forgotten name,
  And call captivity a kindness, meant
  To shield him from insanity or shame,
Such shall be his meet guerdon! who was sent

---

[1] Alexander of Parma, Spinola, Pescara, Eugene
of Savoy, Montecucco.
[2] Columbus, Americus Vespucius, Sebastian
Cabot.
[3] A verse from the Greek tragedians, with which
Pompey took leave of Cornelia on entering the boat
in which he was slain.
[4] The verse and sentiment are taken from Homer.

[5] Petrarch.

To be Christ's Laureate — they reward him well.
Florence dooms me but death or banishment,
Ferrara him a pittance and a cell,
Harder to bear and less deserved, for I
Had stung the factions which I strove to quell;
But this meek man, who with a lover's eye
Will look on earth and heaven, and who will deign
To embalm with his celestial flattery
As poor a thing as e'er was spawned to reign,
What will *he* do to merit such a doom?
Perhaps he'll *love*, — and is not love in vain
Torture enough without a living tomb?
Yet it will be so — he and his compeer,
The Bard of Chivalry, will both consume
In penury and pain too many a year,
And, dying in despondency, bequeathe
To the kind world, which scarce will yield a tear,
A heritage enriching all who breathe
With the wealth of a genuine poet's soul,
And to their country a redoubled wreath,
Unmatched by time; not Hellas can unroll
Through her olympiads two such names, though one
Of hers be mighty; — and is this the whole
Of such men's destiny beneath the sun?
Must all the finer thoughts, the thrilling sense,
The electric blood with which their arteries run,
Their body's self turned soul with the intense
Feeling of that which is, and fancy of
That which should be, to such a recompense
Conduct? shall their bright plumage on the rough

Storm be still scattered? Yes, and it must be,
For, formed of far too penetrable stuff,
These birds of Paradise but long to flee
Back to their native mansion, soon they find
Earth's mist with their pure pinions not agree,
And die or are degraded, for the mind
Succumbs to long infection, and despair,
And vulture passions flying close behind,
Await the moment to assail and tear;
And when at length the winged wanderers stoop,
Then is the prey-birds' triumph, then they share
The spoil, o'erpowered at length by one fell swoop,
Yet some have been untouched who learned to bear,
Some whom no power could ever force to droop,
Who could resist themselves even, hardest care!
And task most hopeless; but some such have been,
And if my name amongst the number were,
That destiny austere, and yet serene,
Were prouder than more dazzling fame unblessed;
The Alp's snow summit nearer heaven is seen
Than the volcano's fierce eruptive crest,
Whose splendor from the black abyss is flung,
While the scorched mountain, from whose burning breast
A temporary torturing flame is wrung,
Shines for a night of terror, then repels
Its fire back to the hell from whence it sprung,
The hell which in its entrails ever dwells.

CANTO THE FOURTH.

MANY are poets who have never penned
Their inspiration, and perchance the best:
They felt, and loved, and died, but would not lend
Their thoughts to meaner beings; they compressed
The God within them, and rejoined the stars
Unlaurelled upon earth, but far more blessed
Than those who are degraded by the jars
Of passion, and their frailties linked to fame,
Conquerors of high renown, but full of scars.
Many are poets but without the name,
For what is poesy but to create
From overfeeling good or ill; and aim

At an external life beyond our fate,
And be the new Prometheus of new men,
Bestowing fire from heaven, and then, too late,
Finding the pleasure given repaid with pain,
And vultures to the heart of the bestower,
Who, having lavished his high gift in vain,
Lies chained to his lone rock by the seashore?
So be it: we can bear. — But thus all they
Whose intellect is an o'ermastering power
Which still recoils from its encumbering clay
Or lightens it to spirit, whatsoe'er
The form which their creations may essay,
Are bards; the kindled marble's bust may wear

More poesy upon its speaking brow
Than aught less than the Homeric page
  may bear;
One noble stroke with a whole life may glow,
  Or deify the canvas till it shine
~ With beauty so surpassing all below,
That they who kneel to idols so divine
  Break no commandment, for high heaven
    is there
Transfused, transfigurated: and the line
Of poesy, which peoples but the air
  With thought and beings of our thought re-
   - flected,
  Can do no more: then let the artist share
The palm, he shares the peril, and dejected
  Faints o'er the labor unapproved—Alas!
  Despair and Genius are too oft connected.
Within the ages which before me pass
  Art shall resume and equal even the sway
  Which with Apelles and old Phidias
She held in Hellas' unforgotten day.
  Ye shall be taught by Ruin to revive
  The Grecian forms at least from their decay,
And Roman souls at last again shall live
  In Roman works wrought by Italian hands,
  And temples, loftier than the old temples,
    give
New wonders to the world; and while still
    stands
  The austere Pantheon, into heaven shall soar
A dome,[1] its image, while the base expands
Into a fane surpassing all before,
  Such as all flesh shall flock to kneel in: ne'er
  Such sight hath been unfolded by a door
As this, to which all nations shall repair,
  And lay their sins at this huge gate of heaven.
  And the bold Architect unto whose care
The daring charge to raise it shall be given,
  Whom all arts shall acknowledge as their
    lord,
  Whether into the marble chaos driven
His chisel bid the Hebrew,[2] at whose word

---

[1] The cupola of St. Peter's.

[2] The statue of Moses on the monument of Julius II.

SONETTO.

Di Giovanni Battista Zappi.

Chi è costui, che in dura pietra scolto,
  Siede gigante; e le più illustre e conte
  Opre dell' arte avvanza, e ha vive e pronte
Le labbra sì, che le parole ascolto?
Quest' è Mosè; ben me 'l diceva il folto
  Onor del mento, e 'l doppio raggio in fronte.
Quest' è Mosè, quando scendea del monte,
  È gran parte del Nume avea nel volto.
Tal era allor, che le sonanti e vaste
  Acque ei sospese a se d' intorno, e tale
  Quando il mar chiuse, e ne fè tomba altrui.
E voi sue turbe un rio vitello alzaste?
  Alzata aveste imago a questa eguale!
  Ch' era men fallo l' adorar costui.

ᵛ And who is he that, shaped in sculptured stone,
  Sits giant-like? stern monument of art

Israel left Egypt, stop the waves in stone,
  Or hues of Hell be by his pencil poured
Over the damned before the Judgment throne,[3]
  Such as I saw them, such as all shall see,
  Or fanes be built of grandeur yet unknown,
The stream of his great thoughts shall spring
  .   from me,[4]
  The Ghibeline, who traversed the three
    realms
  Which form the empire of eternity.
Amidst the clash of swords, and clang of helms
  The age which I anticipate, no less
  Shall be the Age of Beauty, and while whelms
Calamity the nations with distress,
  The genius of my country shall arise,
  A Cedar towering o'er the Wilderness,
Lovely in all its branches to all eyes,
  Fragrant as fair, and recognized afar,
  Wafting its native incense through the skies.
Sovereigns shall pause amidst their sport of
    war,
  Weaned for an hour from blood, to turn
    and gaze
  On canvas or on stone; and they who mar
All beauty upon earth, compelled to praise,
  Shall feel the power of that which they de-
    stroy;
  And Art's mistaken gratitude shall raise
To tyrants who but take her for a toy
  Emblems and monuments, and prostitute
  Her charms to pontiffs proud,[5] who but
    employ

Unparalleled, while language seems to start
From his prompt lips, and we his precepts own?
—'Tis Moses; by his beard's thick honors known,
  And the twin beams that from his temples dart;
'Tis Moses; seated on the mount apart,
  Whilst yet the Godhead o'er his features shone.
Such once he looked, when ocean's sounding wave
  Suspended hung, and such amidst the storm,
  When o'er his foes the refluent waters roared.
An idol calf his followers did engrave;
  But had they raised this awe-commanding form,
  Then had they with less guilt their work adored.″
                Rogers

[3] The Last Judgment, in the Sistine Chapel.

[4] I have read somewhere (if I do not err, for I cannot recollect where), that Dante was so great a favorite of Michael Angelo's, that he had designed the whole of the Divina Commedia; but that the volume containing these studies was lost by sea.— ["Michael Angelo's copy of Dante," says Duppa, "was a large folio, with Landino's commentary; and upon the broad margin of the leaves he designed, with a pen and ink, all the interesting subjects. This book was possessed by Antonio Montauti, a sculptor and architect of Florence, who, being appointed architect to St. Peter's, removed to Rome, and shipped his effects at Leghorn for Civita Vecchia, among which was this edition of Dante: in the voyage the vessel foundered at sea, and it was unfortunately lost in the wreck."]

[5] See the treatment of Michael Angelo by Julius II., and his neglect by Leo X.—[Julius II. was no

The man of genius as the meanest brute
  To bear a burden, and to serve a need,
  To sell his labors, and his soul to boot.
Who toils for nations may be poor indeed,
  But free; who sweats for monarchs is no
     more
Than the gilt chamberlain, who, clothed and
    fee'd,
Stands sleek and slavish, bowing at his door.
  Oh, Power that rulest and inspirest! how
Is it that they on earth, whose earthly power
Is likest thine in heaven in outward show,
  Least like to thee in attributes divine,
  Tread on the universal necks that bow,
And then assure us that their rights are thine?
  And how is it that they, the sons of fame,
  Whose inspiration seems to them to shine
From high, they whom the nations oftest name,
  Must pass their days in penury or pain,
  Or step to grandeur through the paths of
    shame,
And wear a deeper brand and gaudier chain?
  Or if their destiny be born aloof
From lowliness, or tempted thence in vain,
In their own souls sustain a harder proof,
  The inner war of passions deep and fierce?
Florence! when thy harsh sentence razed
    my roof,

I loved thee; but the vengeance of my verse,
  The hate of injuries which every year
  Makes greater and accumulates my curse,
Shall live, outliving all thou holdest dear,
  Thy pride, thy wealth, thy freedom, and even
    that,
  The most infernal of all evils here,
The sway of petty tyrants in a state;
  For such sway is not limited to kings,
  And demagogues yield to them but in dark
As swept off sooner; in all deadly things
  Which make men hate themselves, and one
    another,
  In discord, cowardice, cruelty, all that
    springs
From Death the Sin-born's incest with his
    mother,
  In rank oppression in its rudest shape,
  The faction Chief is but the Sultan's brother,
And the worst despot's far less human ape:
  Florence! when this lone spirit, which so
    long
  Yearned, as the captive toiling at escape,
To fly back to thee in despite of wrong,
  An exile, saddest of all prisoners,
  Who has the whole world for a dungeon
    strong,
Seas, mountains, and the horizon's verge for
    bars,
  Which shut him from the sole small spot of
    earth
  Where — whatsoe'er his fate — he still were
    hers,
His country's, and might die where he had
    birth —
  Florence! when this lone spirit shall return
  To kindred spirits, thou wilt feel my worth,
And seek to honor with an empty urn
  The ashes thou shalt ne'er obtain [1] — Alas!

---

sooner seated on the papal throne than he was surrounded by men of genius, and Michael Angelo was among the first invited to his court. The pope had a personal attachment to him, and conversed with him upon every subject, as well as sculpture, with familiarity and friendship; and, that he might visit him frequently, and with perfect convenience, caused a covered bridge to be made from the Vatican palace to his study, to enable him to pass at all times without being observed. On paying his visit one morning, Michael Angelo was rudely interrupted by the person in waiting, who said, "I have an order not to let you enter." Michael felt with indignation this unmerited disgrace, and, in the warmth of resentment, desired him to tell the Pope, "from that time forward, if his Holiness should want him, he should have to seek him in another place." On his return home, he ordered his servants to sell the furniture in his house to the Jews, and to follow him to Florence. Himself, the same evening, took post, and arrived at Poggibonzi castle, in Tuscany, before he rested. The Pope despatched five couriers with orders to conduct him back: but he was not overtaken until he was in a foreign state. A reconciliation was, however, a few months after, effected at Bologna, through the mediation of the gonfaloniere. As Michael Angelo entered the presence chamber, the Pope gave him an askance look of displeasure, and after a short pause saluted him, "In the stead of your coming to us, you seem to have expected that we should wait upon you." Michael Angelo replied, with submission, that his error arose from too hastily feeling a disgrace that he was unconscious of meriting, and hoped his Holiness would pardon what was past. The Pope thereupon gave him his benediction, and restored him to his friendship. The whole reign of Leo X. was a blank in the life of Michael Angelo. — *Duppa.*]

---

[1] [In his "Convito," Dante speaks of his banishment, and the poverty and distress which attended it, in very decided terms. About the year 1316, his friends obtained his restoration to his country and his possessions, on condition that he should pay a certain sum of money, and, entering a church, there avow himself guilty, and ask pardon of the republic. "Far," he replied, "from the man who is familiar with philosophy, be the senseless baseness of a heart of earth, that could do like a little sciolist, and imitate the infamy of some others, by offering himself up as it were in chains. Far from the man who cries aloud for justice, this compromise, by his money, with his persecutors! No, my Father, this is not the way that shall lead me back to my country. But I shall return with hasty steps, if you or any other can open to me a way that shall not derogate from the fame and honor of Dante: but if by no such way Florence can be entered, then Florence I shall never enter. What! shall I not everywhere enjoy the sight of the sun and stars? and may I not seek and contemplate, in every corner of the earth under the canopy of heaven, consoling and delightful truth, without first rendering myself inglorious, nay infamous, to the

" What have I done to thee, my people ? [1]
Stern
Are all thy dealings, but in this they pass
The limits of man's common malice, for
All that a citizen could be I was;
Raised by thy will, all thine in peace or war,
And for this thou hast warred with me. —
'Tis done:
I may not overleap the eternal bar
Built up between us, and will die alone,
Beholding with the dark eye of a seer
The evil days to gifted souls foreshown,
Foretelling them to those who will not hear.

As in the old time, till the hour be come
When truth shall strike their eyes through
many a tear,
And make them own the Prophet in his tomb.[2]

people and republic of Florence? Bread, I hope, will not fail me."]

[1] " E scrisse più volte non solamente a particolari cittadini del reggimento, ma ancora al popolo, e intra l' altre una epistola assia lunga che comincia: — ' *Popule mi, quid feci tibi?* ' "
Vita di Dante scritta da Lionardo Aretino.

[2] [Dante died at Ravenna in 1321, in the palace of his patron, Guido Novello da Polenta, who testified his sorrow and respect by the sumptuousness of his obsequies, and by giving orders to erect a monument, which he did not live to complete. His countrymen showed, too late, that they knew the value of what they had lost. At the beginning of the next century, they entreated that the mortal remains of their illustrious citizen might be restored to them, and deposited among the tombs of their fathers. But the people of Ravenna were unwilling to part with the sad and honorable memorial of their own hospitality. No better success attended the subsequent negotiations of the Florentines for the same purpose, though renewed under the auspices of Leo X., and conducted through the powerful mediation of Michael Angelo.]

FRANCESCA OF RIMINI.

[THIS translation, of what is generally considered the most exquisitely pathetic episode in the Divina Commedia, was executed in March, 1820, at Ravenna, where, just five centuries before, and in the very house in which the unfortunate lady was born, Dante's poem had been composed.

In mitigation of the crime of Francesca, Boccaccio relates, that " Guido engaged to give his daughter in marriage to Lanciotto, the eldest son of his enemy, the master of Rimini. Lanciotto, who was hideously deformed in countenance and figure, foresaw that, if he presented himself in person, he should be rejected by the lady. He therefore resolved to marry her by proxy, and sent as his representative his younger brother, Paolo, the handsomest and most accomplished man in all Italy. Francesca saw Paolo arrive, and imagined she beheld her future husband. That mistake was the commencement of her passion. The friends of Guido addressed him in strong remonstrances, and mournful predictions of the dangers to which he exposed a daughter, whose high spirit would never brook to be sacrificed with impunity. But Guido was no longer in a condition to make war; and the necessities of the politician overcame the feelings of the father."

In transmitting his version to Mr. Murray, Lord Byron says — " Enclosed you will find, line for line, in third rhyme (terza rima), of which your British blackguard reader as yet understands nothing, Fanny of Rimini. You know that she was born here, and married, and slain, from Cary, Boyd, and such people. I have done it into *cramp* English, line for line, and rhyme for rhyme, to try the possibility. If it is published, publish it *with the original.*"

In one of the poet's MS. Diaries we find the following passage: — " January 29, 1821, past midnight — one of the clock. I have been reading Frederick Schlegel[1] till now, and I can make out nothing. He evidently shows a great power of words, but there is nothing to be taken hold of. He is like Hazlitt in English, who *talks pimples;* a red and white corruption rising up (in little imitation of mountains upon maps), but containing nothing, and discharging nothing, except their own humors. I like him the worse (that is, Schlegel), because he always seems upon the verge of meaning; and, lo! he goes down like sunset, or melts like a rainbow, leaving a rather rich confusion. Of Dante, he says, that ' at no time has the greatest and most national of all Italian poets ever been much the favorite of his countrymen!' 'Tis false. There have been more editors and commentators (and imitators ultimately) of Dante than of all their poets put together. *Not* a favorite! Why, they talk Dante — write Dante — and think and dream Dante,

[1] " Lectures on the History of Literature, Ancient and Modern."]

at this moment (1821), to an excess which would be ridiculous, but that he deserves it. He says also that Dante's 'chief defect is a want, in a word, of gentle feelings.' Of gentle feelings! — and Francesca of Rimini — and the father's feelings in Ugolino — and Beatrice — and ' La Pia! ' Why, there is a gentleness in Dante beyond all gentleness, when he is tender. It is true that, treating of the Christian Hades, or Hell, there is not much *scope* or site for gentleness: but who *but* Dante could have introduced any 'gentleness' at all into Hell? Is there any in Milton's? No — and Dante's Heaven is all love, and glory, and majesty."]

FRANCESCA DA RIMINI.[1]

DANTE L'INFERNO.

CANTO V.

SIEDE la terra dove nata fui
 Sulla marina, dove il Po discende,
 Per aver pace coi seguaci sui.
Amor, che al cor gentil ratto s' apprende,
 Prese costui della bella persona
 Che mi fu tolta ; e il modo ancor m' offende.
Amor, che a nullo amato amar perdona,
 Mi prese del costui piacer si forte,
 Che, come vedi, ancor non m' abbandona.
Amor condusse noi ad una morte :
 Caina attende chi in vita ci spense.
 Queste parole da lor ci fur porte.
Da ch' io intesi quell' anime offense,
 Chinai il viso, e tanto il tenni basso
 Fin chè il Poeta mi disse: Che pense ?
Quando risposi, incomminciai : Ahi lasso !
 Quanti dolci pensier, quanto desio
 Menò costoro al doloroso passo !
Poi mi rivolsi a loro, e parlai io,
 E cominciai : Francesca, i tuoi martiri

FRANCESCA OF RIMINI.

FROM THE INFERNO OF DANTE.

CANTO V.

" THE land where I was born [2] sits by the seas,
 Upon that shore to which the Po descends,
 With all his followers, in search of peace.
Love, which the gentle heart soon apprehends,
 Seized him for the fair person which was
  ta'en [3]
 From me, and me even yet the mode offends.
Love, who to none beloved to love again
 Remits, seized me with wish to please, so
  strong
 That, as thou seest, yet, yet it doth remain.
Love to one death conducted us along,
 But Cainà [4] waits for him our life who
  ended : "
 These were the accents uttered by her
  tongue. — ◆
Since I first listened to these souls offended,
 I bowed my visage, and so kept it till —
 " What think'st thou? " said the bard ; when
  I unbended,
And recommenced : " Alas ! unto such ill
 How many sweet thoughts, what strong
  ecstasies
 Led these their evil fortune to fulfil ! "
And then I turned unto their side my eyes,
 And said, " Francesca, thy sad destinies

---

[1] [Francesca, daughter of Guido da Polenta, Lord of Ravenna and of Cervia, was given by her father in marriage to Lanciotto, son of Malatesta, Lord of Rimini, a man of extraordinary courage, but deformed in his person. His brother Paolo, who unhappily possessed those graces which the husband of Francesca wanted, engaged her affections; and, being taken in adultery, they were both put to death by the enraged Lanciotto. The interest of this pathetic narrative is much increased, when it is recollected that the father of this unfortunate lady was the beloved friend and generous protector of Dante during his latter days.]

[2] Ravenna.

[3] [Among Byron's unpublished letters we find the following : — " Varied readings of the translation from Dante.
 Seized him for the fair person, which in its
 Bloom was ta'en from me, yet the mode offends.
   or,
 Seized him for the fair form, of which in its
 Bloom I was reft, and yet the mode offends.
Love, which to none beloved to love remits,
    (with mutual wish to please)
 Seized me { with wish of pleasing him } so strong,
    (with the desire to please)
 That, as thou see'st, not yet that passion quits, etc.
You will find these readings vary from the MS. I sent you. They are closer, but rougher: take which is liked best; or, if you like, print them as variations. They are all close to the text." — *Byron's Letters.*]

[4] [From Cain, the first fratricide. Cainà is that

A lagrimar mi fanno tristo e pio.
Ma dimmi: al tempo de' dolci sospiri,
  A che e come concedette Amore,
  Che conosceste i dubbiosi desiri?
Ed ella a me: Nessun maggior dolore
  Che ricordarsi del tempo felice
  Nella miseria;[1] e ciò sa il tuo dottore.
Ma se a conoscer la prima radice
  Del nostro amor tu hai cotanto affetto,
  Farò come colui che piange e dice.
Noi leggevamo un giorno per diletto
  Di Lancillotto,[2] come Amor lo strinse:
  Soli eravamo, e senza alcun sospetto.
Per più fiate gli occhi ci sospinse
  Quella lettura, e scolorocci il viso:
  Ma solo un punto fu quel che ci vinse.
Quando leggemmo il disiato riso
  Esser baciato da cotanto amante,
  Questi, che mai da me non fia diviso,
La bocca mi baciò tutto tremante:
  Galeotto fu il libro, e chi lo scrisse —
  Quel giorno più non vi leggemmo avante.
Mentre che l'uno spirto questo disse,
  L'altro piangeva sì, che di pietade
  Io venni men, così com' io morisse,
E caddi come corpo morto cade.

Have made me sorrow till the tears arise.
But tell me, in the season of sweet sighs,
  By what and how thy love to passion rose,
  So as his dim desires to recognize?"
Then she to me: "The greatest of all woes
  Is to remind us of our happy days[3]
  In misery, and that thy teacher knows.[4]
But if to learn our passion's first root preys
  Upon thy spirit with such sympathy,
  I will do even as he who weeps and says.[5]
We read one day for pastime, seated nigh,
  Of Lancelot, how love enchained him too.
  We were alone, quite unsuspiciously.
But oft our eyes met, and our cheeks in hue
  All o'er discolored by that reading were;
  But one point only wholly us o'erthrew;[6]
When we read the long-sighed-for smile of her,
  To be thus kissed by such devoted lover,[7]
  He who from me can be divided ne'er
Kissed my mouth, trembling in the act all over.
  Accursed was the book and he who wrote!
  That day no further leaf we did uncover."——
While thus one spirit told us of their lot,
  The other wept, so that with pity's thralls
  I swooned as if by death I had been smote,
And fell down even as a dead body falls.[8]

---

part of the Inferno to which murderers are condemned.]

[3] [MS. —
  "Is to { recall to mind / remind us of } our happy days."]

[4] [MS. —
  "In misery and { this / that } thy teacher knows."]

[5] [MS. —
  "I will { relate / do even } as he weeps and says."]

[6] [MS. — "But one point only us { overthrew / o'erthrew } ."]

[7] [MS. —
  "To be thus kissed by such { a fervent / devoted } lover."]

[8] [The "other spirit" is Francesca's lover, Paolo. It is the poet himself who swoons with pity, and his emotion will not be deemed exaggerated when we consider that he had known Francesca when a girl, blooming in innocence and beauty in the house of his friend, her father.]

---

[1] ["In omni adversitate fortunæ infelicissimum genus infortunii est fuisse felicem." — *Boetius*. Dante himself tells us, that Boetius and Cicero de Amicitiâ were the two first books that engaged his attention.]

[2] [One of the Knights of Arthur's Round Table, and the lover of Genevra, celebrated in romance.]

THE MORGANTE MAGGIORE OF PULCI.

ADVERTISEMENT.

The Morgante Maggiore, of the first canto of which this translation is offered, divides with the Orlando Innamorato the honor of having formed and suggested the style and story of Ariosto. The great defects of Boiardo were his treating too seriously the narratives of chivalry, and his harsh style. Ariosto, in his continuation, by a judicious mixture of the gaiety of Pulci, has avoided the one; and Berni, in his reformation of Boiardo's Poem, has corrected the other. Pulci may be considered as the precursor and model of Berni altogether, as he has partly been to Ariosto, however inferior to both his copyists. He is no less the founder of a new style of poetry very lately sprung up in England. I allude to that of the ingenious Whistlecraft. The serious poems on Roncesvalles in the same language, and more particularly the excellent one of Mr. Merivale, are to be traced to the same source It has never yet been decided entirely whether Pulci's intention was or was not to deride the religion which is one of his favorite topics. It appears to me, that such an intention would have been no less hazardous to the poet than to the priest, particularly in that age and country; and the permission to publish the poem, and its reception among the classics of Italy, prove that it neither was nor is so interpreted. That he intended to ridicule the monastic life, and suffered his imagination to play with the simple dulness of his converted giant, seems evident enough; but surely it were as unjust to accuse him of irreligion on this account, as to denounce Fielding for his Parson Adams, Barnabas, Thwackum, Supple, and the Ordinary in Jonathan Wild, — or Scott, for the exquisite use of his Covenanters in the "Tales of my Landlord."

In the following translation I have used the liberty of the original with the proper names; as Pulci uses Gan, Ganellon, or Ganellone; Carlo, Carlomagno, or Carlomano; Rondel, or Rondello, etc., as it suits his convenience; so has the translator. In other respects the version is faithful to the best of the translator's ability in combining his interpretation of the one language with the not very easy task of reducing it to the same versification in the other. The reader, on comparing it with the original, is requested to remember that the antiquated language of Pulci, however pure, is not easy to the generality of Italians themselves, from its great mixture of Tuscan proverbs; and he may therefore be more indulgent to the present attempt. How far the translator has succeeded, and whether or no he shall continue the work, are questions which the public will decide. He was induced to make the experiment partly by his love for, and partial intercourse with, the Italian language, of which it is so easy to acquire a slight knowledge, and with which it is so nearly impossible for a foreigner to become accurately conversant. The Italian language is like a capricious beauty, who accords her smiles to all, her favors to few, and sometimes least to those who have courted her longest. The translator wished also to present in an English dress a part at least of a poem never yet rendered into a northern language; at the same time that it has been the original of some of the most celebrated productions on this side of the Alps, as well as of those recent experiments in poetry in England which have been already mentioned.

INTRODUCTION.

The translation of the Morgante of Pulci was chiefly executed at Ravenna in 1820, and was first published in "The Liberal." Such was the care bestowed by Byron upon the task, that he only accomplished two stanzas a night, which was his principal time for composition, and such was his opinion of his success, that he always maintained that there was no such translation in the English language, and never would be such another. He appears to have thought that its merit consisted in the *verbum pro verbo* closeness of the version, rendered doubly difficult by the character of the poem, which, besides being humorous, is full of vulgar Florentine idioms, abrupt transitions, ungrammatical constructions, and sententious obscurity. The immense labor of mastering these accumulated obstacles[1] explains Byron's over-estimate of the piece. "Why," he wrote to Mr. Murray in 1821, "don't you publish my Pulci — the best thing I ever wrote?"

The first edition of the original Morgante was published at Venice in 1481. The characters are derived from some chivalrous romances of the thirteenth century. It is a question whether Pulci designed a burlesque or a serious poem — Ugo Foscolo maintaining that the air of ridicule arose from the contrast between the absurdity of the materials and the effort of the author to render them sublime; while Sismondi contends that the belief in the marvellous being much diminished, the adventures which formerly were heard with gravity could not be reproduced without a mixture of mockery. Hallam agrees with the latter, and thinks that Pulci meant to scoff at heroes whom duller poets held up to admiration.

There has been an equal difference of opinion upon the parts of the poem which touch on religion. Ugo Foscolo considers Pulci a devout Catholic who laughed at particular dogmas and divines; Sismondi doubts whether to charge him with gross bigotry or profane derision; and Hallam thinks that under pretence of ridiculing the intermixture of theology with romance, he had an intention of exposing religion to contempt. Whatever may have been his theoretical creed, he shows by his mode of treating sacred topics that he was entirely destitute of reverence. Byron was asked to allow some suppressions in his translation, to which he replied that Pulci must answer for his own impiety.

[1] [These difficulties are much exaggerated. — F. J. C.]

MORGANTE MAGGIORE.

CANTO PRIMO.

I.

IN principio era il Verbo appresso a Dio,
  Ed era Iddio il Verbo, e 'l Verbo lui:
Questo era nel principio, al parer mio;
  È nulla si può far sanza costui:
Però, giusto Signor benigno e pio,
  Mandami solo un de gli angeli tui,
Che m'accompagni, e rechimi a memoria
Una famosa antica e degna storia.

II.

E tu Vergine, figlia, e madre, e sposa
  Di quel Signor, che ti dette le chiave
Del cielo e dell' abisso, e d'ogni cosa,
  Quel dì che Gabriel tuo ti disse Ave!
Perchè tu se' de' tuo' servi pietosa,
  Con dolce rime, e stil grato e soave,
Ajuta i versi miei benignamente,
E'nfino al fine allumina la mente.

III.

Era nel tempo, quando Filomena
  Con la sorella si lamenta e plora,

THE MORGANTE MAGGIORE.

CANTO THE FIRST.

I.

IN the beginning was the Word next God;
  God was the Word, the Word no less was
    he:
This was in the beginning, to my mode
  Of thinking, and without him nought could
    be:
Therefore, just Lord! from out thy high abode,
  Benign and pious, bid an angel flee,
One only, to be my companion, who
Shall help my famous, worthy, old song·
  through.

II.

And thou, oh Virgin! daughter, mother, bride,
  Of the same Lord, who gave to you each key
Of heaven, and hell, and every thing beside,
  The day thy Gabriel said "All hail!" to thee,
Since to thy servants pity's ne'er denied,
  With flowing rhymes, a pleasant style and
    free,
Be to my verses then benignly kind,
And to the end illuminate my mind.

III.

'Twas in the season when sad Philomel
  Weeps with her sister, who remembers and

Che si ricorda di sua antica pena,
E pe' boschetti le ninfe innamora,
E Febo il carro temperato mena,
Che 'l suo Fetonte l'ammaestra ancora;
Ed appariva appunto all'orizzonte,
Tal che Titon si graffiava la fronte.

IV.

Quand'io varai la mia barchetta, prima
Per ubbidir chi sempre ubbidir debbe
La mente, e faticarsi in prosa e in rima,
E del mio Carlo Imperador m'increbbe;
Che so quanti la penna ha posto in cima,
Che tutti la sua gloria prevarrebbe:
E stata quella istoria, a quel ch' i' veggio,
Di Carlo male intesa, e scritta peggio.

V.

Diceva già Lionardo Aretino,
Che s' egli avesse avuto scrittor degno,
Com'egli ebbe un Ormanno il suo Pipino,
Ch'avesse diligenzia avuto e ingegno;
Sarebbe Carlo Magno un uom divino;
Però ch'egli ebbe gran vittorie e regno,
E fece per la chiesa e per la fede
Certo assai più, che non si dice o crede.

VI.

Guardisi ancora a san Liberatore
Quella badia là presso a Manoppello,
Giù ne gli Abbruzzi fatta per suo onore,
Dove fu la battaglia e 'l gran flaggello
D'un re pagan, che Carlo imperadore
Uccise, e tanto del suo popol fello:
E vedesi tante ossa, e tanto il sanno,
Che tutte in Giusaffà poi si vedranno.

VII.

Ma il mondo cieco e ignorante non prezza
Le sue virtù, com'io vorrei vedere:
E tu, Fiorenza, de la sua grandezza
Possiedi, e sempre potrai possedere
Ogni costume ed ogni gentilezza
Che si potesse acquistare o avere
Col senno col tesoro o con la lancia
Dal nobil sangue e venuto di Francia.

VIII.

Dodici paladini aveva in corte
Carlo; e'l più savio e famoso era Orlando:
Gan traditor lo condusse a la morte,
In Roncisvalle, un trattato ordinando;
Là dove il corno sonò tanto forte
Dopo la dolorosa rotta, quando

Deplores the ancient woes which both befell,
    And makes the nymphs enamoured, to the
        hand
Of Phaeton by Phœbus loved so well
    His car (but tempered by his sire's com-
        mand)
Was given, and on the horizon's verge just now
Appeared, so that Tithonus scratched his
    brow:

IV.

When I prepared my bark first to obey,
    As it should still obey, the helm, my mind,
And carry prose or rhyme, and this my lay
    Of Charles the Emperor, whom you will find
By several pens already praised; but they
    Who to diffuse his glory were inclined,
For all that I can see in prose or verse,
Have understood Charles badly, and wrote
    worse.

V.

Leonardo Aretino said already,
    That if like Pepin, Charles had had a writer
Of genius quick, and diligently steady,
    No hero would in history look brighter;
He in the cabinet being always ready,
    And in the field a most victorious fighter,
Who for the church and Christian faith had
    wrought,
Certes, far more than yet is said or thought.

VI.

You still may see at Saint Liberatore
    The abbey, no great way from Manopell,
Erected in the Abruzzi to his glory,
    Because of the great battle in which fell
A pagan king, according to the story,
    And felon people whom Charles sent to hell:
And there are bones so many, and so many,
Near them Giusaffa's would seem few, if any.

VII.

But the world, blind and ignorant, don't prize
    His virtues as I wish to see them: thou,
Florence, by his great bounty don't arise,
    And hast, and may have, if thou wilt allow,
All proper customs and true courtesies:
    Whate'er thou hast acquired from then till
        now,
With knightly courage, treasure, or the lance,
Is sprung from out the noble blood of France.

VIII.

Twelve paladins had Charles in court, of whom
    The wisest and most famous was Orlando;
Him traitor Gan conducted to the tomb
    In Roncesvalles, as the villain planned too,
While the horn rang so loud, and knelled the
    doom
    Of their sad rout, though he did all knight
        can do;

Ne la sua commedia Dante qui dice,
E mettelo con Carlo in ciel felice.

And Dante in his comedy has given
To him a happy seat with Charles in heaven.

IX.

Era per Pasqua quella dì natale:
Carlo la corte avea tutta in Parigi:
Orlando, com'io dico, il principale
Evvi, il Danese, Astolfo, e Ansuigi:
Fannosi feste e cose trionfale,
E molto celebravan San Dionigi;
Angiolin di Bajona, ed Ulivieri
V'era venuto, e'l gentil Berlinghieri:

IX.

'Twas Christmas-day; in Paris all his court
Charles held; the chief, I say, Orlando was,
The Dane; Astolfo there too did resort,
Also Ansuigi, the gay time to pass
In festival and in triumphal sport,
The much-renowned St. Dennis being the
cause;
Angiolin of Bayonne, and Oliver,
And gentle Belinghieri too came there:

X.

Eravi Avolio ed Avino ed Ottone,
Di Normandia, Riccardo Paladino,
E'l savio Namo, e'l vecchio Salamone,
Gualtier da Monlione, e Baldovino
Ch'era figliuol del tristo Ganellone.
Troppo lieto era il figliuol di Pipino;
Tanto che spesso d'allegrezza geme
Veggendo tutti i paladini insieme.

X.

Avolio, and Arino, and Othone
Of Normandy, and Richard Paladin,
Wise Hamo, and the ancient Salemone,
Walter of Lion's Mount and Baldovin,
Who was the son of the sad Ganellone,
Were there, exciting too much gladness in
The son of Pepin: — when his knights came
.hither,
He groaned with joy to see them altogether.

XI.

Ma la fortuna attenta sta nascosa,
Per guastar sempre ciascun nostro effetto;
Mentre che Carlo così si riposa,
Orlando governava in fatto e in detto
La corte e Carlo Magno ed ogni cosa:
Gan per invidia scoppia il maladetto,
E cominciava un dì con Carlo a dire:
Abbiam noi sempre Orlando ad ubbidire?

XI.

But watchful Fortune, lurking, takes good heed
Ever some bar 'gainst our intents to bring.
While Charles reposed him thus, in word and
deed,
Orlando ruled court, Charles, and every
thing;
Curst Gan, with envy bursting, had such need
To vent his spite, that thus with Charles the
king
One day he openly began to say,
" Orlando must we always then obey ?

XII.

Io ho creduto mille volte dirti:
Orlando ha in se troppa presunzione:
Noi siam qui conti, re, duchi a servirti,
E Namo, Ottone, Uggieri e Salamone,
Per onorarti ognun, per ubbidirti:
Che costui abbi ogni reputazione
Nol sofferrem; ma siam deliberati
Da un fanciullo non esser governati.

XII.

" A thousand times I've been about to say,
Orlando too presumptuously goes on;
Here are we, counts, kings, dukes, to own thy
sway,
Hamo, and Otho, Ogier, Solomon,
Each have to honor thee and to obey;
But he has too much credit near the throne,
Which we won't suffer, but are quite decided
By such a boy to be no longer guided.

XIII.

Tu cominciasti insino in Aspramonte
A dargli a intender che fusse gagliardo,
E facesse gran cose a quella fonte;
Ma se non fusse stato il buon Gherardo,
Io so che la vittoria era d'Almohte:
Ma egli ebbe sempre l'occhio a lo stendardo.
Che si voleva quel dì coronarlo:
Questo è colui ch'ha meritato, Carlo.

XIII. .

" And even at Aspramont thou didst begin
To let him know he was a gallant knight,
And by the fount did much the day to win;
But I know *who* that day had won the fight
If it had not for good Gherardo been:
The victory was Almonte's else; his sight
He kept upon the standard, and the laurels
In fact and fairness are his earning, Charles.

XIV.

Se ti ricorda già sendo in Guascogna,
Quando e'vi venne la gente di Spagna,

XIV.

" If thou rememberest being in Gascony,
When there advanced the nations out of
Spain,   .

Il popol de' cristiani avea vergogna,
Se non mostrava la sua forza magna.
Il ver convien pur dir, quando e'bisogna:
Sappi ch'ognuno imperador si lagna:
Quant'io per me, ripasserò que' monti
Ch'io passai 'n qua con sessantaduo conti.

The Christian cause had suffered shamefully,
Had not his valor driven them back again.
Best speak the truth when there's a reason why:
Know then, oh emperor! that all complain ·
As for myself, I shall repass the mounts
O'er which I crossed with two and sixty counts.

XV.

La tua grandezza dispensar si vuole,
E far che ciascun abbi la sua parte:
La corte tutta quanta se ne duole:
Tu credi che costui sia forse Marte?
Orlando un giorno udì queste parole,
Che si sedeva soletto in disparte:
Dispiacquegli di Gan quel che diceva;
Ma molto più che Carlo gli credeva.

XV.

" 'Tis fit thy grandeur should dispense relief,
So that each here may have his proper part,
For the whole court is more or less in grief:
Perhaps thou deem'st this lad a Mars in
heart?"
Orlando one day heard this speech in brief,
As by himself it chanced he sate apart:
Displeased he was with Gan because he said it,
But much more still that Charles should give
him credit.

XVI.

E volle con la spada uccider Gano;
Ma Ulivieri in quel mezzo si mise,
E Durlindana gli trasse di mano,
E cosi il me' che seppe gli divise.
Orlando si sdegnò con Carlo Mano,
E poco men che quivi non l'uccise;
E dipartissi di Parigi solo,
E scoppia e'mpazza di sdegno e di duolo.

XVI.

And with the sword he would have murdered
Gan,
But Oliver thrust in between the pair,
And from his hand extracted Durlindan,
And thus at length they separated were.
Orlando angry too with Carloman,
Wanted but little to have slain him there;
Then forth alone from Paris went the chief,
And burst and maddened with disdain and
grief.

XVII.

Ad Ermellina moglie del Danese
Tolse Cortana, e poi tolse Rondello;
E 'n verso Brara il suo cammin poi prese.
Alda la bella, come vide quello,
Per abbracciarlo le braccia distese.
Orlando, che ismarrito avea il cervello,
Com'ella disse: ben venga il mio Orlando:
Gli volle in su la testa dar col brando.

XVII.

From Ermellina, consort of the Dane,
He took Cortana, and then took Rondell,
And on towards Brara pricked him o'er the
plain;
And when she saw him coming, Aldabelle
Stretched forth her arms to clasp her lord
again:
Orlando, in whose brain all was not well,
As " Welcome, my Orlando, home," she said,
Raised up his sword to smite her on the head.

XVIII.

Come colui che la furia consiglia,
Egli pareva a Gan dar veramente:
Alda la bella si fe' maraviglia:
Orlando si ravvide prestamente:
E la sua sposa pigliava la briglia,
E scese dal caval subitamente:
Ed ogni cosa narrava a costei,
E riposossi alcun giorno con lei.

XVIII.

Like him a fury counsels; his revenge
On Gan in that rash act he seemed to take,
Which Aldabella thought extremely strange;
But soon Orlando found himself awake;
And his spouse took his bridle on this change,
And he dismounted from his horse, and
spake
Of every thing which passed without demur,
And then reposed himself some days with her.

XIX.

Poi si partì portato dal furore,
E terminò passare in Paganìa;
E mentre che cavalca, il traditore
Di Gan sempre ricorda per la via:
E cavalcando d'uno in altro errore,
In un deserto truova una badia

XIX.

Then full of wrath departed from the place,
And far as pagan countries roamed astray,
And while he rode, yet still at every pace
The traitor Gan remembered by the way;
And wandering on in error a long space,
An abbey which in a lone desert lay,

In luoghi oscuri e paesi lontani,
Ch'era a' confin' tra christiani e pagani.

XX.

L'abate si chiamava Chiaramonte,
  Era del sangue disceso d'Anglante:
  Di sopra a la badía v'era un gran monte,
  Dove abitava alcun fiero gigante,
  De'quali uno avea nome Passamonte,
  L'altro Alabastro, e'l terzo era Morgante:
  Con certe frombe gittavan da alto,
  Ed ogni dì facevan qualche assalto.

XXI.

I monachetti non potieno uscire
  Del monistero o per legne o per acque
  Orlando picchia, e non volieno aprire,
  Fin che a l'abate a la fine pur piacque;
  Entrato drento cominciava a dire,
  Come colui che di Maria già nacque,
  Adora, ed era cristian battezzato,
  E com' egli era a la badia arrivato.

XXII.

Disse l'abate: il ben venuto sia
  Di quel ch'io ho volentier ti daremo,
  Poi che tu credi al figliuol di Maria;
  E la cagion, cavalier, ti diremo,
  Acciò che non l'imputi a villania,
  Perchè a l'entrar resistenza facemo,
  E non ti volle aprir quel monachetto:
  Così intervien chi vive con sospetto.

XXIII.

Quando ci venni al principio abitare
  Queste montagne, benchè sieno oscure
  Come tu vedi; pur si potea stare
  Sanza sospetto, ch' ell' eran sicure:
  Sol da le fiere t'avevi a guardare;
  Fernoci spesso di brutte paure;
  Or ci bisogna, se vogliamo starci,
  Da le bestie dimestiche guardarci.

XXIV.

Queste ci fan piuttosto stare a segno:
  Sonci appariti tre fieri giganti,
  Non so di qual paese o di qual regno,
  Ma molto son feroci tutti quanti:
  La forza e 'l malvoler giunt' a lo' ngegno
  Sai che può 'l tutto; e noi non siam bastanti;

'Midst glens obscure, and distant lands, he found,
Which formed the Christian's and the pagan's bound.

XX.

The abbot was called Clermont, and by blood
  Descended from Angrante: under cover
Of a great mountain's brow the abbey stood,
  But certain savage giants looked him over
One Passamont was foremost of the brood,
  And Alabaster and Morgante hover
Second and third, with certain slings, and throw
In daily jeopardy the place below.

XXI.

The monks could pass the convent gate no more,
  Nor leave their cells for water or for wood;
Orlando knocked, but none would ope, before
  Unto the prior it at length seemed good;
Entered, he said that he was taught to adore
  Him who was born of Mary's holiest blood,
And was baptized a Christian; and then showed
How to the abbey he had found his road.

XXII.

Said the abbot, "You are welcome; what is mine
  We give you freely, since that you believe
With us in Mary Mother's Son divine;
  And that you may not, cavalier, conceive
The cause of our delay to let you in
  To be rusticity, you shall receive
The reason why our gate was barred to you:
Thus those who in suspicion live must do.

XXIII.

"When hither to inhabit first we came
  These mountains, albeit that they are obscure,
As you perceive, yet without fear or blame
  They seemed to promise an asylum sure:
From savage brutes alone, too fierce to tame,
  'Twas fit our quiet dwelling to secure;
But now, if here we'd stay, we needs must guard
Against domestic beasts with watch and ward.

XXIV.

"These make us stand, in fact, upon the watch;
  For late there have appeared three giants rough;
What nation or what kingdom bore the batch
  I know not, but they are all of savage stuff;
When force and malice with some genius match,
  You know, they can do all—*we* are not enough:

Questi perturban sì l'orazion nostra,
Che non so più che far, s'altri nol mostra.

And these so much our orisons derange,
I know not what to do, till matters change.

XXV.

Gli antichi padri nostri nel deserto, ˙
Se le lor opre sante erano e giuste,
Del ben servir da Dio n'avean buon merto;
Nè creder sol vivessin di locuste :
Piovea dal ciel la manna, questo è certo ;
Ma qui convien che spesso assaggi e guste
Sassi che piovon di sopra quel monte,
Che gettano Alabastro e Passamonte.

XXV.

" Our ancient fathers living the desert in,
  For just and holy works were duly fed ;
Think not they lived on locusts sole, 'tis
  certain
That manna was rained down from heaven
  instead :
But here 'tis fit we keep on the alert in
  Our bounds, or taste the stones showered
  down for bread,
From off yon mountain daily raining faster,
And flung by Passamont and Alabaster.

XXVI.

E 'l terzo ch'è Morgante, assai più fiero,
Isveglie e pini e faggi e cerri e gli oppi,
E gettagli infin qui : questo è pur vero ;
Non posso far che, d'ira non iscoppi.
Mentre che parlan così in cimitero,
Un sasso par che Rondel quasi sgroppi ;
Che da' giganti giù venne da alto
Tanto, ch'e' prese sotto il tetto un salto.

XXVI.

" The third, Morgante's savagest by far ; he
  Plucks up pines, beeches, poplar-trees, and
  oaks,
And flings them, our community to bury ;
  And all that I can do but more provokes."
While thus they parley in the cemetery, ˙
  A stone from one of their gigantic strokes,
Which nearly crushed Rondell, came tum-
  bling over,
So that he took a long leap under cover.

XXVII.

Tirati drento, cavalier, per Dio,
Disse l'abate, che la manna casca.
Risponde Orlando : caro abate mio,
Costui non vuol che'l mio caval più pasca ;
Veggo che lo guarrebbe del restio :
Quel sasso par che di buon braccio nasca.
Rispose il santo padre : io non t'inganno,
Credo che'l monte un giorno gitteranno.

XXVII.

" For God-sake, cavalier, come in with speed ;
  The manna's falling now," the abbot cried.
" This fellow does not wish my horse should
  feed,
  Dear abbot," Roland unto him replied.
" Of restiveness he'd cure him had he need ;
  That stone seems with good will and aim
  applied."
The holy father said, " I don't deceive ; ,
They'll one day fling the mountain, I believe."

XXVIII.

Orlando governar fece Rondello,
E ordinar per se da colazione :
Poi disse : abate, io voglio andare a quello
Che dette al mio caval con quel cantone.
Disse l'abate : come car fratello
Consiglierotti sanza passione :
Io ti sconforto, baron, di tal gita ;
Ch'io so che tu vi lascerai la vita.

XXVIII.

Orlando bade them take care of Rondello,
  And also made a breakfast of his own :
" Abbot," he said, " I want to find that fellow
  Who flung at my good horse yon corner-
  stone."
Said the abbot, " Let not my advice seem
  shallow ;   •
  As to a brother dear I speak alone ;
I would dissuade you, baron, from this strife,
As knowing 'sure that you will lose your life.

XXIX.

Quel Passamonte porta in man tre dardi :
Chi frombe, chi baston, chi mazzafrusti ;
Sai che giganti più di noi gagliardi
Son per ragion, che son anco più giusti ;
E pur se vuoi andar fa che ti guardi,
Che questi son villan molto e robusti.

XXIX.

" That Passamont has in his hand three
  darts —
  Such slings, clubs, ballast-stones, that yield
  you must ;
You know that giants have much stouter
  hearts
  Than us, with reason, in proportion just :
If go you will, guard well against their arts,
  For these are very barbarous and robust."

Rispose Orlando: io lo vedrò per certo;
Ed avviossi a piè su pel deserto.

Orlando answered, "This I'll see, be sure,
And walk the wild on foot to be secure."

XXX.

Disse l'abate col segnarlo in fronte:
Va, che da Dio e me sia benedetto.
Orlando, poi che salito ebbe il monte,
Si dirizzò, come l'abate detto
Gli avea, dove sta quel Passamonte;
Il quale Orlando veggendo soletto,
Molto lo squadra di drieto e davante;
Poi domandò, se star volea per fante.

XXX.

The abbot signed the great cross on his front,
  "Then go you with God's benison and
      mine:"
Orlando, after he had scaled the mount,
  As the abbot had directed, kept the line
Right to the usual haunt of Passamont;
  Who, seeing him alone in this design,
Surveyed him fore and aft with eyes observant,
Then asked him, "If he wished to stay as ser-
      vant?"

XXXI.

E' prometteva di farlo godere.
Orlando disse: pazzo saracino.
Io vengo a te, com'è di Dio volere,
Per darti morte, e non per ragazzino;
A'monaci suoi fatto hai dispiacere;
Non può più comportarti, can mastino.
Questo gigante armar si corse a furia,
Quando sentì ch'e'gli diceva ingiuria.

XXXI.

And promised him an office of great ease.
  But, said Orlando, "Saracen insane!
I come to kill you, if it shall so please
  God, not to serve as footboy in your train;
You with his monks so oft have broke the
      peace—
  Vile dog! 'tis past his patience to sustain."
The giant ran to fetch his arms, quite furious,
When he received an answer so injurious.

XXXII.

E ritornato ove aspettava Orlando,
Il qual non s'era partito da bomba;
Subito venne la corda girando,
E lascia un sasso andar fuor de la fromba,
Che in su la testa giugnea rotolando
Al conte Orlando, e l'elmetto rimbomba;
E' caddle per la pena tramortito;
Ma più che morto par, tanto è stordito.

XXXII.

And being returned to where Orlando stood,
  Who had not moved him from the spot, and
      swinging
The cord, he hurled a stone with strength so
      rude,
  As showed a sample of his skill in slinging;
It rolled on Count Orlando's helmet good
  And head, and set both head and helmet
      ringing,
So that he swooned with pain as if he died,
But more than dead, he seemed so stupefied.

XXXIII.

Passamonte pensò che fusse morto,
E disse: io voglio andarmi a disarmare:
Questo poltron per chi m'aveva scorto?
Ma Cristo i suoi non suole abbandonare,
Massime Orlando, ch'egli arebbe il torto,
Mentre il gigante l'arme va a spogliare,
Orlando in questo tempo si risente,
E rivocava e la forza e la mente.

XXXIII.

Then Passamont, who thought him slain out-
      ' right,
  Said, "I will go, and while he lies along,
Disarm me: why such craven did I fight?"
  But Christ his servants ne'er abandons long,
Especially Orlando, such a knight,
  As to desert would almost be a wrong.
While the giant goes to put off his defences,
Orlando has recalled his force and senses:

XXXIV.

E gridò forte: gigante, ove va?
Ben ti pensasti d'avermi ammazzato;
Volgiti a drieto, che, s'ale non hai,
Non puoi da me fuggir, can rinnegato:
A tradimento ingiuriato m'hai.
Donde il gigante allor maravigliato
Si volse a drieto, e riteneva il passo;
Poi si chinò per tor di terra un sasso.

XXXIV.

And loud he shouted, "Giant, where dost go?
  Thou thought'st me doubtless for the bier
      outlaid;
To the right about — without wings thou'rt
      too slow
  To fly my vengeance — currish renegade!
'Twas but by treachery thou laid'st me low."
  The giant his astonishment betrayed,
And turned about, and stopped his journey on,
And then he stooped to pick up a great stone.

XXXV.

Orlando avea Cortana ignuda in mano;
　Trasse a la testa: e Cortana tagliava:
Per mezzo il teschio parti del pagano,
　E Passamonte morto rovinava:
E nel cadere il superbo e villano
　Divotamente Macon bestemmiava;
Ma mentre che bestemmia il crudo e acerbo,
　Orlando ringraziava il Padre e'l Verbo.

XXXV.

Orlando had Cortana bare in hand;
　To split the head in twain was what he
　　schemed:—
Cortana clave the skull like a true brand,
　And pagan Passamont died unredeemed,
Yet harsh and haughty, as he lay he banned,
　And most devoutly Macon still blasphemed:
But while his crude, rude blasphemies he
　heard,
Orlando thanked the Father and the Word,—

XXXVI.

Dicendo: quanta grazia oggi m' ha' data!
　Sempre ti sono, o signor mio, tenuto;
Per te conosco la vita salvata;
　Però che dal gigante era abbattuto:
Ogni cosa a ragion fai misurata;
　Non val nostro poter sanza il tuo ajuto.
Priegoti, sopra me tenga la mano,
Tanto che ancor ritorni a Carlo Mano.

XXXVI.

Saying, "What grace to me thou'st this day
　given!
　And I to thee, oh Lord! am ever bound.
I know my life was saved by thee from heaven,
　Since by the giant I was fairly downed.
All things by thee are measured just and even;
　Our power without thine aid would nought
　　be found:
I pray thee take heed of me, till I can
At least return once more to Carloman."

XXXVII.

Poi ch'ebbe questo detto sen' andòe,
　Tanto che trouva Alabastro più basso
Che si sforzava, quando e'lo trovòe,
　Di sveglier d'una ripa fuori un masso.
Orlando, com'e' giunse a quel, gridòe:
　Che pensi tu, ghiotton, gittar quel sasso?
Quando Alabastro questo grido intende,
Subitamente la sua fromba prende.

XXXVII.

And having said thus much, he went his way;
　And Alabaster he found out below,
Doing the very best that in him lay
　To root from out a bank a rock or two.
Orlando, when he reached him, loud 'gan say,
　"How think'st thou, glutton, such a stone
　　to throw?"
When Alabaster heard his deep voice ring,
He suddenly betook him to his sling,

XXXVIII.

E trasse d'una pietra molto grossa,
　Tanto ch'Orlando bisognò schermisse;
Che se l'avesse giunto la percossa,
　Non bisognava il medico venisse.
Orlando adoperò poi la sua possa,
　Nel pettignon tutta la spada misse:
E morto cadde questo badalone,
E non dimenticò però Macone.

XXXVIII.

And hurled a fragment of a size so large,
　That if it had in fact fulfilled its mission,
And Roland not availed him of his targe,
　There would have been no need of a
　　physician.
Orlando set himself in turn to charge,
　And in his bulky bosom made incision
With all his sword. The lout fell; but o'er-
　thrown, he
However by no means forgot Macone.

XXXIX.

Morgante aveva al suo modo un palagio
　Fatto di frasche e di schegge e di terra:
Quivi, secondo lui, si posa ad agio;
　Quivi la notte si rinchiude e serra.
Orlando picchia, e daragli disagio,
　Perchè il gigante dal sonno si sferra;
Vennegli aprir come una cosa matta;
Ch'un aspra visione aveva fatta.

XXXIX.

Morgante had a palace in his mode,
　Composed of branches, logs of wood, and
　　earth,
And stretched himself at ease in this abode,
　And shut himself at night within his berth.
Orlando knocked, and knocked again, to goad
　The giant from his sleep; and he came
　　forth,
The door to open, like a crazy thing,
For a rough dream had shook him slumber-
　ing.

XL.

E' gli parea ch'un feroce serpente
L'avea assalito, e chiamar Macometto;
Ma Macometto non valea niente:
Ond'e' chiamava Gesù benedetto;
E liberato l'avea finalmente.
Venne alla porta, ed ebbe così detto;
Chi buzza qua? pur sempre borbottando.
Tu 'l saprai tosto, gli rispose Orlando.

XLI.

Vengo per farti, come a' tuo' fratelli,
Far de' peccati tuoi la penitènzia,
Da' monaci mandato, cattivelli,
Come stato è divina providenzia;
Pel mal ch'avete fatto a torto a quelli,
È dato in ciel così questa sentenzia;
Sappi, che freddo già più ch'un pilastro
Lasciato ho Passamonte e'l tuo Alabastro.

XLII.

Disse Morgante: o gentil cavaliere,
Per lo tuo Dio non midir villania:
Di grazia il nome tuo vorrei sapere;
Se se' Cristian, deh dillo in cortesia.
Rispose Orlando: di cotal mestiere
Contenterotti per la fede mia:
Adoro Cristo, ch'è Signor verace:
Epuoi tu adorarlo, se ti piace.

XLIII.

Rispose il saracin con umil voce:
Io ho fatto una strana visione,
Che m'assaliva un serpente feroce:
Non mi valeva per chiamar Macone;
Onde al tuo Dio che fu confitto in croce
Rivolsi presto la mia intenzione:
E' mi soccorse, e fui libero e sano,
E son disposto al tutto esser Cristiano,

XLIV.

Rispose Orlando: baron giusto e pio,
Se questo buon voler terrai nel core,
L'anima tua arà quel vero Dio
Che ci può sol gradir d'eterno onore:
E s'tu vorrai, sarai compagno mio,
E amerotti con perfetto amore:
Gl'idoli vostri son bugiardi e vani:
Il vero Dio è lo Dio de' Cristiani.

XLV.

Venne questo Signor sanza peccato
Ne la sua madre vergine pulzella:
Se conoscessi quel Signor beato,

XL.

He thought that a fierce serpent had attacked
  him;
And Mahomet he called; but Mahomet
Is nothing worth, and not an instant backed
  him;
But praying blessed Jesu, he was set
At liberty from all the fears which racked him;
And to the gate he came with great re-
  gret—
"Who knocks here?" grumbling all the while,
  said he.
"That," said Orlando, "you will quickly see.

XLI.

"I come to preach to you, as to your brothers,
  Sent by the miserable monks—repent-
  ance;
For Providence divine, in you and others,
  Condemns the evil done my new acquaint-
  ance.
'Tis writ on high—your wrong must pay an-
  other's;
  From heaven itself is issued out this sen-
  tence.
Know then, that colder now than a pilaster
I left your Passamont and Alabaster."

XLII.

Morgante said, "Oh gentle cavalier!
  Now by thy God say me no villany;
The favor of your name I fain would hear,
  And if a Christian, speak for courtesy."
Replied Orlando, "So much to your ear
  I by my faith disclose contentedly;
Christ I adore, who is the genuine Lord,
And, if you please, by you may be adored."

XLIII.

The Saracen rejoined in humble tone,
  "I have had an extraordinary vision;
A savage serpent fell on me alone,
  And Macon would not pity my condition;
Hence to thy God, who for ye did atone
  Upon the cross, preferred I my petition;
His timely succor set me safe and free,
And I a Christian am disposed to be."

XLIV.

Orlando answered, "Baron just and pious,
  If this good wish your heart can really move
To the true God, who will not then deny us
  Eternal honor, you will go above,
And, if you please, as friends we will ally us,
  And I will love you with a perfect love.
Your idols are vain liars, full of fraud:
The only true God is the Christian's God.

XLV.

"The Lord descended to the virgin breast
  Of Mary Mother, sinless and divine;
If you acknowledge the Redeemer blest,

Sanza'l qual non risplende sole o stella,
Aresti già Macon tuo rinnegato,
E la sua fede iniqua ingiusta e fella:
Battezzati al mio Dio di buon talento.
Morgante gli rispose: io son contento.

Without whom neither sun nor star can
    shine,
Abjure bad Macon's false and felon test,
    Your renegado god, and worship mine, ---
Baptize yourself with zeal, since you repent."
To which Morgante answered, " I'm content."

XLVI.

E corse Orlando subito abbracciare:
Orlando gran carezze gli facea,
E disse: a la badia ti vo' menare.
Morgante, andianci presto, respondea:
Co' monaci la pace ci vuol fare.
De la qual cosa Orlando in se godea,
Dicendo; fratel mio divoto e buono,
Io vò che chiegga a l' abate perdono,

XLVI.

And then Orlando to embrace him flew,
    And made much of his convert, as he cried,
" To the abbey I will gladly marshal you."
    To whom Morgante, " Let us go," replied;
" I to the friars have for peace to sue."
    Which thing Orlando heard with inward
        pride,
Saying, " My brother, so devout and good,
Ask the abbot pardon, as I wish you would:

XLVII.

Da poi che Dio ralluminato t'ha,
    Ed acettato per la sua umiltade;
Vuolsi che tu ancor usi umiltà.
Disse Morgante: per la tua bontade,
Poi che il tuo Dio mio sempre omai sarà,
Dimmio del nome tuo la veritade,
Poi di me dispor puoi al tuo comando;
Ond' e' gli disse, com 'egli era Orlando.

XLVII.

" Since God has granted your illumination,
    Accepting you in mercy for his own,
Humility should be your first oblation."
    Morgante said, " For goodness' sake, make
        known —
Since that your God is to be mine — your sta-
    tion,
    And let your name in verity be shown;
Then will I every thing at your command do."
On which the other said, he was Orlando.

XLVIII.

Disse il gigante: Gesù benedetto
    Per mille volte ringraziato sia; ·
Sentito t'ho nomar, baron perfetto,
Per tutti i tempi de la vita mia:
E, com'io dissi, sempremai suggetto
Esser ti vo' per la tua gagliardia.
Insieme molte cose ragionaro,
E'n verso la badia poi s'inviaro.

` XLVIII.

" Then," quoth the giant, " blessed be Jesu
    A thousand times with gratitude and praise !
Oft, perfect baron ! have I heard of you
    Through all the different periods of my days:
And, as I said, to be your vassal too
    I wish; for your great gallantry always."
Thus reasoning, they continued much to say,
And onwards to the abbey went their way.

XLIX.

E per la via da que' giganti morti
Orlando con Morgante sì ragiona:
De la lor morte vo' che ti conforti;
E poi che piace a Dio, a me perdona;
A' monaci avean fatto mille torti;
E la nostra scrittura aperto suona:
Il ben remunerato, e'l mal punito;
E mai non ha questo Signor fallito:

XLIX.

And by the way about the giants dead
    Orlando with Morgante reasoned: " Be,
For their decease, I pray you, comforted;
    And, since it is God's pleasure, pardon me,
A thousand wrongs unto the monks they bred.
    And our true Scripture soundeth openly.
Good is rewarded, and chastised the ill,
Which the Lord never faileth to fulfil:

L.

Però ch'egli ama la giustizia tanto,
    Che vuol, che sempre il suo giudicio morda
Ognun ch'abbi peccato tanto o quanto;
E cosi il ben ristorar si ricorda:
E non saria senza giustizia santo:
Adunque al suo voler presto t'accorda:
Che debbe ognun voler quel che vuol questo,
Ed accordarsi volentieri e presto.

• L.

" Because his love of justice unto all
    Is such, he wills his judgment should devou
All who have sin, however great or small:
    But good he well remembers to restore.
Nor without justice holy could we call
    Him, whom I now require you to adore.
All men must make his will their wishes sway,
And quickly and spontaneously obey.

LI.

E sonsi i nostri dottori accordati,
  Pigliando tutti una conclusione,
Che que' che son nel ciel glorificati,
  S'avessin nel pensier compassione
De' miseri parenti che dannati
  Son ne lo inferno in gran confusione,
La lor felicità nulla sarebbe;
E vedi che qui ingiusto Iddio parrebbe.

LII.

Ma egli anno posto in Gesù ferma spene;
  E tanto pare a lor, quanto a lui pare;
Afferman ciò ch'e'fa, che facci bene,
  E chenon possi in nessun.modo errare:
Se padre o madre è nell' eterne pene,
  Di questo non si posson contubare:
Che quel che piace a Dio, sol piace a loro:
Questo s'osserva ne l'eterno coro.

LIII.

Al savio suol bastar poche parole,
  Disse Morgante; tu il potrai vedere,
De' miei fratelli, Orlando, se mi duole,
  E s'io m'accorderò di Dio al volere,
Come tu di' che in ciel servar si suole:
  Morti co' morti; or pensiam di godere:
Io vo tagliar le mani a tutti quanti,
E porterolle a que' monaci santi,

LIV.

Acciò ch'ognun sia più sicuro e certo,
  Com' e' son morti, e non abbin paura
Andar soletti per questo deserto;
  E perchè veggan la mia mente pura
A quel Signor che m'ha il suo regno aperto,
  E tratto fuor di tenebre sì oscura.
E poi tagliò le mani a' due fratelli,
E lasciagli a le fiere ed agli uccelli.

LV.

A la badia insieme se ne vanno,
  Ove l'abate assai dubbioso aspetta:
I monaci che'l fatto ancor non sanno,
  Correvano a l'abate tutti·in fretta,
Dicendo paurosi e pien' d'affanno:
  Volete voi costui drente si metta?
Quando l'abate vedeva il gigante,
Sì turbò tutto nel primo sembiante.

LVI.

Orlando che turbato così il vede,
  Gli disse presto: abate, datti pace,

LI.

"And here our doctors are of one accord,
  Coming on this point to the same conclu-
    sion,—
That in their thoughts who praise in heaven
    the Lord,
  If pity e'er was guilty of intrusion
For their unfortunate relations stored
  In hell below, and damned in great confu-
    sion,—
Their happiness would be reduced to nought,
And thus unjust the Almighty's self be thought.

LII.

"But they in Christ have firmest hope, and all
  Which seems to him, to them too must ap-
    pear
Well done; nor could it otherwise befall:
  He never can in any purpose err.
If sire or mother suffer endless thrall,
  They don't disturb themselves for him or
    her;
What pleases God to them must joy inspire;—
Such is the observance of the eternal choir."

LIII.

"A word unto the wise," Morgante said,
  "Is wont to be enough, and you shall see
How much I grieve about my brethren dead;
  And if the will of God seem good to me,
Just, as you tell me, 'tis in heaven obeyed—
  Ashes to ashes,—merry let us be!
I will cut off the hands from both their trunks,
And carry them unto the holy monks.

LIV.

"So that all persons may be sure and certain
  That they are dead, and have no further fear
To wander solitary this desert in,
  And that they may perceive my spirit clear
By the Lord's grace, who hath withdrawn the
    curtain
  Of darkness, making his bright realm ap-
    pear."
He cut his brethren's hands off at these words,
And left them to the savage beasts and birds

LV.

Then to the abbey they went on together,
  Where waited them the abbot in great doubt.
The monks who knew not yet the fact, ran
    thither
  To their superior, all in breathless rout,
Saying with tremor, "Please to tell us whether
  You wish to have this person in or out?"
The abbot, looking through upon the giant,
Too greatly feared, at first, to be compliant.

LVI.

Orlando seeing him thus agitated,
  Said quickly, "Abbot, be thou of good
    cheer;

Questo è Cristiano, e in Cristo nostro crede,
  È rinnegato ha il suo Macon fallace.
Morgante i moncherin mostrò per fede,
Come i giganti ciascun morto giace;
Donde l'abate ringraziavia Iddio,
Dicendo; or m' hai contento, Signor mio!

He Christ believes, as Christian must be rated,
  And hath renounced his Macon false; "
  which here
Morgante with the hands corroborated,
  A proof of both the giants' fate quite clear:
Thence, with due thanks, the abbot God
  adored,
Saying, " Thou hast contented me, oh Lord!"

LVII.

E risguardava, e squadrava Morgante,
  La sua grandezza e una volta e due,
E poi gli disse : O famoso gigante,
Sappi ch'io non mi maraviglio più,
Che tu svegliessi e gittassi le piante,
Quand'io riguardo or le fattezze tue,
Tu sarai or perfetto e vero amico
A Cristo, quanto tu gli eri nimico.

LVII.

He gazed ; Morgante's height he calculated,
  And more than once contemplated his size :
And then he said, " Oh giant celebrated !
  Know, that no more my wonder will arise,
How you could tear and fling the trees you
  late did,
When I behold your form with my own eyes.
You now a true and perfect friend will show
Yourself to Christ, as once you were a foe.

LVIII.

Un nostro apostol, Saul già chiamato,
  Persegul molto la fede di Cristo :
Un giorno poi da lo spirto infiammato,
Perchè pur mi persegui ? disse Cristo :
E' si ravvide allor del suo peccato ;
Andò poi predicando sempre Cristo ;
E fatto è or de la fede una tromba,
La qual per tutto risuona e rimbomba.

LVIII.

" And one of our apostles, Saul once named,
  Long persecuted sore the faith of Christ,
Till, one day, by the Spirit being inflamed,
  ' Why dost thou persecute me thus? ' said
  Christ ;'
And then from his offence he was reclaimed,
  And went for ever after preaching Christ,
And of the faith became a trump, whose
  sounding
O'er the whole earth is echoing and rebound-
  ing.

LIX.

Così farai tu ancor, Morgante mio :
  E chi s'emenda, è scritto nel Vangelo,
Che maggior festa fa d'un solo Iddio,
Che di novantanove altri su in cielo :
Io ti conforto ch'ogni tuo disio
Rivolga a quel Signor con giusto zelo,
Che tu sarai felice in sempiterno,
Ch'eri perduto, e dannato all' inferno.

LIX.

" So, my Morgante, you may do likewise ;
  He who repents — thus writes the Evange-
  list —
Occasions more rejoicing in the skies
  Than ninety-nine of the celestial list.
You may be sure, should each desire arise
  With just zeal for the Lord, that you'll exist
Among the happy saints for evermore ;
But you were lost and damned to hell before !

LX.

E grande onore a Morgante faceva
  L'abate, e molti dì si son posati :
Un giorno, come ad Orlando piaceva,
A spasso in quà e in là si sono andati :
L'abate in una camera sua aveva
Molte armadure e certi archi appiccati :
Morgante gliene piacque un che ne vede ;
Onde e' sel cinse bench' oprar nol crede.

LX.

And thus great honor to Morgante paid
  The abbot : many days they did repose.
One day, as with Orlando they both strayed,
  And sauntered here and there, where'er they
  chose,
The abbot showed a chamber, where arrayed
  Much armor was, and hung up certain bows ;
And one of these Morgante for a whim
Girt on, though useless, he believed, to him.

LXI.

Avea quel luogo d'acqua carestia :
  Orlando disse come buon fratello,
Morgante, vo' che di piacer ti sia
Andar per l'acqua ; ond' e' rispose a quello :
Comanda ciò che vuoi che fatto sia ;

LXI.

There being a want of water in the place,
  Orlando, like a worthy brother, said,
" Morgante, I could wish you in this case
  To go for water." " You shall be obeyed
In all commands," was the reply, " straight-
  ways."

E posesi in ispalla un gran tinello,
Ed avviossi là verso una fonte
Dove solea ber sempre appiè del monte.

LXII.

Giunto a la fonte, sente un gran fracasso
  Di subito venir per la foresta:
Una saetta cavò del turcasso,
  Posela a l'arco, ed alzava la testa;
Ecco apparire un gran gregge al passo
  Di porci, e vanno con molta tempesta;
E arrivorno alla fontana appunto
Donde il gigante è da lor sopraggiunto.

LXIII.

Morgante a la ventura a un saetta;
  Appunto ne l'orecchio lo 'ncarnava;
Da l'altro lato passò la verretta;
  Onde il cinghial giù morto gambettava;
Un altro, quasi per farne vendetta,
  Addosso al gran gigante irato andava;
E perchè e' giunse troppo tosto al varco,
Non fu Morgante a tempo a trar con l'arco.

LXIV.

Vedendosi venuto il porco adosso,
  Gli dette in su la testa un gran punzone[1]
Per modo che gl'infranse insino a l'osso,
  E morto allato a quell'altro lo pone:
Gli altri porci veggendo quel percosso,
  Si misson tutti in fuga pel vallone;
Morgante si levò il tinello in collo,
Ch'era· pien d'acqua, e non si muove un
  crollo.

LXV.

Da l'una spalla il tinello avea posto,
  Da l'altra i porci, e spacciava il terreno;
E torna a la badia, ch'è pur discosto
  Ch' una gocciola d'acqua non va in seno.
Orlando che'l vedea tornar sì tosto
  Co' porci morti, e con quel vaso pieno,
Maravigliossi che sia tanto forte;
Così l'abate; e spalancan le porte.

LXVI.

`I monaci veggendo l'acqua fresca
  Si rallegrorno, ma più de' cinghiali;
Ch'ogni animal si rallegra de l'esca;
  E posano a dormire i breviali:
Ognun s'affanna, e non par che gl'incresca,
  Acciò che questa carne non s'insali,
E che poi secca sapesse di vieto:
E la digiune si restorno a drieto.

LXVII.

E ferno a scoppia corpo per un tratto,
  E scuffian, che parien de l'acqua usciti;

---

[1] "Gli dette in su la testa un gran punzone." It is strange that Pulci should have literally anticipated the technical terms of my old friend and master, Jackson, and the art which he has carried to its highest pitch. "*A punch on the head*," or "*a punch in the head*," —"un punzone in su la testa," —is the exact and frequent phrase of our best

---

Upon his shoulder a great tub he laid,
And went out on his way unto a fountain,
Where he was wont to drink below the mountain.

LXII.

Arrived there, a prodigious noise he hears,
  Which suddenly along the forest spread;
Whereat from out his quiver he prepares
  An arrow for his bow, and lifts his head;
And lo! a monstrous herd of swine appears,
  And onward rushes with tempestuous tread,
And to the fountain's brink precisely pours;
So that the giant's joined by all the boars.

LXIII.

Morgante at a venture shot an arrow,
  Which pierced a pig precisely in the ear,
And passed unto the other side quite thorough;
  So that the boar, defunct, lay tripped up near.
Another, to revenge his fellow farrow,
  Against the giant rushed in fierce career,
And reached the passage with so swift a foot,
Morgante was not now in time to shoot.

LXIV.

Perceiving that the pig was on him close,
  He gave him such a punch upon the head
As floored him so that he no more arose,
  Smashing the very bone; and he fell dead
Next to the other.   Having seen such blows,
  The other pigs along the valley fled;
Morgante on his neck the bucket took,
Full from the spring, which neither swerved
  nor shook.

LXV.

The ton was on one shoulder, and there were
  The hogs on t'other, and he brushed apace
On to the abbey, though by no means near,
  Nor spilt one drop of water in his race.
Orlando, seeing him so soon appear
  With the dead boars, and with that brimful
    vase,
Marvelled to see his strength so very great;
So did the abbot, and set wide the gate.

LXVI.

The monks, who saw the water fresh and good,
  Rejoiced, but much more to perceive the
    pork; —
All animals are glad at sight of food:
  They lay their breviaries to sleep, and work
With greedy pleasure, and in such a mood,
  That the flesh needs no salt beneath their
    fork.
Of rankness and of rot there is no fear,
For all the fasts are now left in arrear.

LXVII.

As though they wished to burst at once, they
    ate;
  And gorged so that, as if the bones had been

---

pugilists, who little dream that they are talking the purest Tuscan.

Tanto che'l cane sen doleva e 'l gatto,
Che gli ossi rimanean troppo puliti.
L'abate, poi che molto onoro ha fatto
A tutti, un dì dopo questi conviti
Dette a Morgante un destrier molto bello,
Che lungo tempo tenuto avea quello.

LXVIII.

Morgante in su 'n un prato il caval mena,
E vuol che corra, e che facci ogni pruova,
E pensa che di ferro abbi la schiena,
O forse non credeva schiacciar l'uova:
Questo caval s'accoscia per la pena,
E scoppia, e 'n su la terra si ritruova.
Dicea Morgante: lieva su, rozzone;
E va pur punzecchiando con lo sprone.

LXIX.

Ma finalmente convien ch' egli smonte,
E disse: io son pur leggier come penna,
Ed è scoppiato; che ne di' tu, conte?
Rispose Orlando: un arbore d'antenna
Mi par piuttosto, e la gaggia la fronte:
Lascialo andar, che la fortuna accenna
Che meco appiede ne venga, Morgante.
Ed io così verrò, disse il gigante.

LXX.

Quando sarà mestier, tu mi vedrai
Com'io mi proverò ne la battaglia.
Orlando disse: io credo tu farai
Come buon cavalier, se Dio mi vaglia;
Ed anco me dormir non mirerai:
Di questo tuo caval non te ne caglia:
Vorrebbesi portarlo in qualche bosco;
Ma il modo nè la via non ci conosco.

LXXI.

Disse il gigante: io il porterò ben io,
Da poi che portar me non ha voluto,
Per render ben per mal, come fa Dio;
Ma vo' che a porlo addosso mi dia ajuto.
Orlando gli dicea: Morgante mio,
S'al mio consiglio ti sarai attenuto,
Questo caval tu non ve 'l porteresti,
Che ti farà come tu a lui facesti,

LXXII.

Guarda che non facesse la vendetta,
Come fece già Nesso così morto:
Non so se la sua istoria hai inteso o letta:
E' ti farà scoppiar; datti conforto.
Disse Morgante: ajuta ch'io me 'l metta

In water, sorely grieved the dog and cat,
  Perceiving that they all were picked too
  clean.
The abbot, who to all did honor great,
  A few days after this convivial scene,
Gave to Morgante a fine horse, well trained,
Which he long time had for himself main-
  tained.

LXVIII.

The horse Morgante to a meadow led,
  To gallop, and to put him to the proof,
Thinking that he a back of iron had,
  Or to skim eggs unbroke was light enough;
But the horse, sinking with the pain, fell dead,
  And burst, while cold on earth lay head and
  hoof.
Morgante said, " Get up, thou sulky cur! "
And still continued pricking with the spur.

LXIX.

But finally he thought fit to dismount,
  And said, " I am as light as any feather,
And he has burst; — to this what say you,
  count? "
  Orlando answered, " Like a ship's mast
  rather
You seem to me, and with the truck for
  front: —
  Let him go; Fortune wills that we together
Should march, but you on foot Morgante still."
To which the giant answered, "So I will.

LXX.

" When there shall be occasion, you will see
  How I approve my courage in the fight."
Orlando said, " I really think you'll be,
  If it should prove God's will, a goodly knight;
Nor will you napping there discover me.
  But never mind your horse, though out of
  sight
'Twere best to carry him into some wood,
If but the means or way I understood."

LXXI.

The giant said, " Then carry him I will,
  Since that to carry me he was so slack —
To render, as the gods do, good for ill;
  But lend a hand to place him on my back."
Orlando answered, " If my counsel still
  May weigh, Morgante, do not undertake
To lift or carry this dead courser, who,
As you have done to him, will do to you.

LXXII.

" Take care he don't revenge himself, though
  dead,
  As Nessus did of old beyond all cure.
I don't know if the fact you've heard or read;
  But he will make you burst, you may be
  sure."
" But help him on my back," Morgante said,

Addosso, e poi vedrai s'io ve lo porto:
Io porterei, Orlando mio gentile,
Con le campane là quel campanile.

LXXIII.

Disse l'abate: il campanil v'è bene;
  Ma le campane voi l'avete rotte.
Dicea Morgante, e' ne porton le pene
  Color che' morti son là in quelle grotte;
E levossi il cavallo in su le schiene,
  E disse: guarda s'io sento di gotte,
Orlando, nelle gambe, e s' io lo posso;
E fe' duo salti col cavallo addosso.

LXXIV.

Era Morgante come una montagna:
  Se facea questo, non è maraviglia:
Ma pure Orlando con seco si lagna;
  Perchè pur era omai di sua famiglia,
Temenza avea non pigliasse magagna.
  Un' altra volta costui riconsiglia:
Posalo ancor, nol portare al deserto.
Disse Morgante: il porterò per certo.

LXXV.

E portollo, e gittollo in luogo strano,
  E tornò a la badìa subitamente.
Diceva Orlando: or che più dimoriano?
  Morgante, qui non facciam noi niente.
E prese un giorno l'abate per mano,
  E disse a quel molto discretamente,
Che vuol partir de la sua reverenzia,
E domandava e perdono e licenzia.

LXXVI.

E de gli onor ricevuti da questi,
  Qualche volta potendo, arà buon merito;
E dice: io intendo ristorare e presto
  I persi giorni del tempo preterito;
E' son più dì che licenzia arei chiesto,
  Benigno padre, se non ch' io mi perito;
Non so mostrarvi quel che drento sento;
Tanto vi veggo del mio star contento.

LXXVII.

Io me ne porto per sempre nel core
  L'abate, la badìa, questo deserto;
Tanto v'ho posto in picciol tempo amore:
  Rendavi su nel ciel per me buon merto
Quel vero Dio, quello eterno Signore
  Che vi serba il suo regno al fine aperto:
Noi aspettiam vostra benedizione,
Raccomandiamci a le vostre orazione.

"And you shall see what weight I can endure.
In place, my gentle Roland, of this palfrey,
With all the bells, I'd carry yonder belfry."

LXXIII.

The abbot said, "The steeple may do well,
  But, for the bells, you've broken them, I wot."
Morgante answered, "Let them pay in hell
  The penalty who lie dead in yon grot;"
And hoisting up the horse from where he fell,
He said, "Now look if I the gout have got,
Orlando, in the legs — or if I have force;" —
And then he made two gambols with the horse.

LXXIV.

Morgante was like any mountain framed·
  So if he did this, 'tis no prodigy;
But secretly himself Orlando blamed,
  Because he was one of his family;
And fearing that he might be hurt or maimed,
  Once more he bade him lay his burden by;
"Put down, nor bear him further the desert in."
Morgante said, "I'll carry him for certain."

LXXV.

He did; and stowed him in some nook away,
  And to the abbey then returned with speed.
Orlando said, "Why longer do we stay?
  Morgante, here is nought to do indeed."
The abbot by the hand he took one day,
  And said, with great respect, he had agreed
To leave his reverence; but for this decision
He wished to have his pardon and permission.

LXXVI.

The honors they continued to receive
  Perhaps exceeded what his merits claimed:
He said, "I mean, and quickly, to retrieve
  The lost days of time past, which may be blamed;
Some days ago I should have asked your leave,
  Kind father, but I really was ashamed,
And know not how to show my sentiment,
So much I see you with our stay content.

LXXVII.

"But in my heart I bear through every clime
  The abbot, abbey, and this solitude —
So much I love you in so short a time;
  For me, from heaven reward you with all good
The God so true, the eternal Lord sublime!
  Whose kingdom at the last hath open stood.
Meantime we stand expectant of your blessing,
And recommend us to your prayers with pressing."

LXXVIII.

Quando l'abate il conte Orlando intese,
Rintenerì nel cor per la dolcezza,
Tanto fervor nel petto se gli accese;
E disse: cavalier, se a tua prodezza
Non sono stato benigno e cortese,
Come conviensi a la gran gentillezza,
Che so che ciò ch'i'ho fatto è stato poco,
Incolpa la ignoranzia nostra e il loco.

LXXIX.

Noi ti potremo di messe onorare,
Di prediche, di laude, e paternostri,
Piuttosto che da cena o desinare,
O d'altri convenevol che da chiostri.
Tu m'hai di te sì fatto innamorare
Per mille alte excellenzie che tu mostri,
Ch'io me ne vengo ove tu andrai con teco
E d'altra parte tu resti quì meco.

LXXX.

Tanto ch'a questo par contraddizione;
Ma so che tu se' savio, e 'ntendi e gusti,
E intendi il mio parlar per discrizione.
De' beneficj tuoi pietosi e giusti
Renda il Signore a te munerazione,
Da cui mandato in queste selve fusti;
Per le virtù del qual liberi siamo,
E grazie a lui e a te noi ne rendiamo.

LXXXI.

Tu ci hai salvato l'anima e la vita:
Tanta perturbazion già que' giganti
Ci detton, che la strada era smarrita
Da ritrovar Gesù con gli altri santi.
Però troppo ci duol la tua partita,
E sconsolati restiam tutti quanti;
Nè ritener possiamti i mesi e gli anni:
Che tu non se' da vestir questi panni,

LXXXII.

Ma da portar la lancia e l' armadura:
E puossi meritar con essa, come
Con questa cappa; e leggi la scrittura:
Questo gigante al ciel drizzò le some
Per tua virtù; va in pace a tua ventura
Chi tu ti sia, ch'io non ricerco il nome;
Ma dirò sempre, s'io son domandato,
Ch' un angiol qui da Dio fussi mandato.

LXXXIII.

Se c'è armadura o cosa che tu voglia,
Vattene in zambra e pigliane tu stessi,
E cuopri a questo gigante le scoglia.
Rispose Orlando: se armadura avessi
Prima che noi uscissim de la soglia,
Che questo mio compagno difen dessi

LXXVIII.

Now when the abbot Count Orlando heard,
  His heart grew soft with inner tenderness,
Such fervor in his bosom bred each word;
  And, " Cavalier," he said, " if I have less
Courteous and kind to your great worth ap-
  peared,
Than fits me for such gentle blood to express,
I know I have done too little in this case;
But blame our ignorance, and this poor place.

LXXIX.

" We can indeed but honor you with masses,
  And sermons, thanksgivings, and pater-
  nosters,
Hot suppers, dinners (fitting other places
  In verity much rather than the cloisters);
But such a love for you my heart embraces,
  For thousand virtues which your bosom
  fosters,
That wheresoe'er you go I too shall be,
And, on the other part, you rest with me.

LXXX.

" This may involve a seeming contradiction;
  But you I know are sage, and feel, and taste,
And understand my speech with full conviction.
  For your just pious deeds may you be graced
With the Lord's great reward and benediction,
  By whom you were directed to this waste:
To his high mercy is our freedom due,
For which we render thanks to him and you.

LXXXI.

" You saved at once our life and soul: such fear
  The giants caused us, that the way was lost
By which we could pursue a fit career
  In search of Jesus and the saintly host;
And your departure breeds such sorrow here,
  That comfortless we all are to our cost;
But months and years you would not stay in
  sloth,
Nor are you formed to wear our sober cloth;

LXXXII.

" But to bear arms, and wield the lance; indeed,
  With these as much is done as with this cowl;
In proof of which the Scripture you may read.
  This giant up to heaven may bear his soul
By your compassion: now in peace proceed.
  Your state and name I seek not to unroll;
But, if I'm asked, this answer shall be given,
That here an angel was sent down from heaven.

LXXXIII.

" If you want armor or aught else, go in,
  Look o'er the wardrobe, and take what you
  choose,
And cover with it o'er this giant's skin."
  Orlando answered, " If there should lie loose
Some armor, ere our journey we begin,
  Which might be turned to my companion's
  use,

Questo accetto io, e sarammi piacere.
Disse l'abate: venite a vedere.

LXXXIV.

E in certa cameretta entrati sono,
Che d'armadure vecchie era copiosa;
Dice l'abate, tutte ve le dono.
Morgante va rovistando ogni cosa;
Ma solo un certo sbergo gli fu buono,
Ch'avea tutta la maglia rugginosa:
Maravigliossi che lo cuopra appunto:
Che mai più gnun forse glien' era aggiunto.

LXXXV.

Questo fu d'un gigante smisurato,
Ch'a la badia fu morto per antico
Dal gran Milon d'Angrante, ch' arrivato
V' era, s'appunto questa istoria dico;
Ed era ne le mura istoriato,
Come e' fu morto questo gran nimico,
Che fece a la badia già lunga guerra:
E Milon v'è com' e' l'abbatte in terra.

LXXXVI.

Veggendo questa istoria il conte Orlando,
Fra suo cor disse: o Dio, che sai sol tutto,
Come venne Milon quì capitando,
Che ha questo gigante quì distrutto?
E lesse certe letter lacrimando,
Che non potè tenir piu il viso asciutto,
Com'io dirò ne la seguente istoria.
Di mal vi guardi il Re de l'alta gloria.

The gift would be acceptable to me."
The abbot said to him, "Come in and see."

LXXXIV.

And in a certain closet, where the wall
  Was covered with old armor like a crust,
The abbot said to them, "I give you all."
  Morgante rummaged piecemeal from the
    dust
The whole, which save one cuirass, was too
    small,
  And that too had the mail inlaid with rust.
They wondered how it fitted him exactly,
Which ne'er has suited others so compactly.

LXXXV.

'Twas an immeasurable giant's, who
  By the great Milo of Agrante fell
Before the abbey many years ago.
  The story on the wall was figured well;
In the last moment of the abbey's foe,
  Who long had waged a war implacable:
Precisely as the war occurred they drew him,
And there was Milo as he overthrew him.

LXXXVI.

Seeing this history, Count Orlando said
  In his own heart, "Oh God, who in the sky
Know'st all things! how was Milo hither led?"
  Who caused the giant in this place to die?"
And certain letters, weeping, then he read,
  So that he could not keep his visage dry,—
As I will tell in the ensuing story.
From evil keep you the high King of glory.

THE BLUES; A LITERARY ECLOGUE.[1]

" Nimium ne crede colori." — VIRGIL.

O trust not, ye beautiful creatures, to hue,
Though your *hair* were as *red*, as your *stockings* are *blue.*

[This trifle, which Byron has himself designated as "a mere buffoonery, never meant for publication,"
was written in 1820, and first appeared in "The Liberal." The personal allusions in which it abounds
are, for the most part, sufficiently intelligible; and, with a few exceptions, so good-humored, that the
parties concerned may be expected to join in the laugh.]

[1] ["About the year 1781, it was much the fashion for several ladies to have evening assemblies, where
the fair sex might participate in conversation with literary and ingenious men, animated by a desire to
please. These societies were denominated *Blue-stocking Clubs;* the origin of which title being little
known, it may be worth while to relate it. One of the most eminent members of those societies, when

ECLOGUE FIRST.

London — Before the Door of a Lecture Room.

Enter TRACY, *meeting* INKEL.

Ink. YOU'RE too late.
Tra.   Is it over?
Ink.   Nor will be this hour.
But the benches are crammed, like a garden
   in flower,
With the pride of our belles, who have made
   it the fashion;
So, instead of "beaux arts," we may say "la
   belle passion"
For learning, which lately has taken the lead
   in
The world, and set all the fine gentlemen
   reading.
Tra. I know it too well, and have worn out
   my patience
With studying to study your new publica-
   tions.
There's Vamp, Scamp, and Mouthy, and
   Wordswords and Co.
With their damnable —
Ink.   Hold, my good friend, do you know
Whom you speak to?
Tra.   Right well, boy, and so does "the
   Row:"[1]
You're an author — a poet —
Ink.   And think you that I
Can stand tamely in silence, to hear you decry
The Muses?
Tra.   Excuse me: I meant no offence
To the Nine; though the number who make
   some pretence
To their favors is such —— but the subject to
   drop
I am just piping hot from a publisher's shop,
(Next door to the pastry-cook's; so that
   when I
Cannot find the new volume I wanted to buy
On the bibliopole's shelves, it is only two
   paces,
As one finds every author in one of those
   places;

Where I just had been skimming a charming
   critique,
So studded with wit, and so sprinkled with
   Greek!
Where your friend — you know who — has just
   got such a threshing,
That it is, as the phrase goes, extremely "*re
   freshing.*"[2]
What a beautiful word!
Ink.   Very true; 'tis so soft
And so cooling — they use it a little too oft;
And the papers have got it at last — but no
   matter.
So they've cut up our friend then?
Tra.   Not left him a tatter —
Not a rag of his present or past reputation,
Which they call a disgrace to the age and the
   nation.
Ink. I'm sorry to hear this! for friendship,
   you know ——
Our poor friend! — but I thought it would
   terminate so.
Our friendship is such, I'll read nothing to
   shock it.
You don't happen to have the Review in your
   pocket?
Tra. No; I left a round dozen of authors
   and others
(Very sorry, no doubt, since the cause is a
   brother's)
All scrambling and jostling, like so many
   imps,
And on fire with impatience to get the next
   glimpse.
Ink. Let us join them.
Tra. What, won't you return to the lecture?
Ink. Why, the place is so crammed, there's
   not room for a spectre.
Besides, our friend Scamp is to-day so
   absurd —
Tra. How can you know that till you hear
   him?
Ink.   I heard
Quite enough; and to tell you the truth, my
   retreat
Was from his vile nonsense, no less than the
   heat.
Tra. I have had no great loss then?
Ink.   Loss! — such a palaver!
I'd inoculate sooner my wife with the slaver

---

[1] [Paternoster-row — long and still celebrated as a very bazaar of booksellers. Sir Walter Scott "hitches into rhyme" one of the most important firms — that

  "Of Longman, Hurst, Rees, Orme, and Brown
    Our fathers of the Row."]

[2] [This cant phrase was first used in the Edinburgh Review — probably by Mr. Jeffrey.]

---

they first commenced, was Mr. Stillingfleet, whose dress was remarkably grave, and in particular it was observed that he wore blue stockings. Such was the excellence of his conversation, that his absence was felt as so great a loss, that it used to be said, '.We can do nothing without the *blue stockings;* ' and thus by degrees the title was established." — CROKER's *Boswell*, vol. iv. p. 480. — Sir William Forbes, in his Life of Dr. Beattie, says, that " a foreigner of distinction hearing the expression, translated it literally ' *Bas Bleu*,' by which these meetings came to be distinguished. Miss Hannah More, who was herself a member, has written a poem with the title of ' Bas Bleu,' in allusion to this mistake of the foreigner, in which she has characterized most of the eminent personages of which it was composed."]

Of a dog when gone rabid, than listen two
  hours
To the torrent of trash which around him he
  pours,
Pumped up with such effort, disgorged with
  such labor,
That —— come — do not make me speak ill of
  one's neighbor.
  Tra. I make you!
  Ink.   Yes, you! I said nothing until
You compelled me, by speaking the truth ——
  Tra.   *To speak ill*
Is that your deduction?
  Ink.   When speaking of Scamp ill,
I certainly *follow, not set* an example.
The fellow's a fool, an impostor, a zany.
  Tra. 'And the crowd of to-day shows that
  one fool makes many.
But we two will be wise.
  Ink.   Pray, then, let us retire.
  Tra. I would, but ——
  Ink. There must be attraction much higher
Than Scamp, or the Jews' harp he nicknames
  his lyre,
To call *you* to this hotbed.
  Tra.   I own it — 'tis true —
A fair lady ——
  Ink.   A spinster?
  Tra.   Miss Lilac!
  Ink.   The Blue!
The heiress?
  Tra.   The angel!
  Ink.   The devil! why, man!
Pray get out of this hobble as fast as you can.
You wed with Miss Lilac! 'twould be your
  perdition:
She's a poet, a chymist, a mathematician.
  Tra. I say she's an angel.
  Ink.   Say rather an *angle.*
If you and she marry, you'll certainly wrangle.
I say she's a Blue, man, as blue as the ether.
  Tra. And is that any cause for not coming
  together?
  Ink. Humph! I can't say I know any happy
  alliance
Which has lately sprung up from a wedlock
  with science.
She's so learned in all things, and fond of
  concerning
Herself in all matters connected with learning,
That ——
  Tra.   What?
  Ink. I perhaps may as well hold my tongue;
But there's five hundred people can tell you
  you're wrong.
  Tra. You forget Lady Lilac's as rich as a
  Jew.
  Ink. Is it miss or the cash of mamma you
  pursue?
  Tra. Why, Jack, I'll be frank with you —
  something of both.
The girl's a fine girl.

  Ink.   And you feel nothing loth
To her good lady-mother's reversion; and
  yet
Her life is as good as your own, I will bet.
  Tra. Let her live, and as long as she likes;
  I demand
Nothing more than the heart of her daughter
  and hand.
  Ink. Why, that heart's in the inkstand —
  that hand on the pen.
  Tra. A propos — Will you write me a song
  now and then?
  Ink. To what purpose?
  Tra. You know, my dear friend, that in
  prose
My talent is decent, as far as it goes;
But in rhyme ——
  Ink.   You're a terrible stick, to be sure.
  Tra. I own it; and yet in these times,
  there's no lure
For the heart of the fair like a stanza or two;
And so as I can't, will you furnish a few?
  Ink. In your name?
  Tra. In my name. I will copy them out,
To slip into her hand at the very next rout.
  Ink. Are you so far advanced as to hazard
  this?
  Tra.   Why,
Do you think me subdued by a Blue-stock-
  ing's eye,
So far as to tremble to tell her in rhyme
What I've told her in prose, at the least, as
  sublime?
  Ink. As sublime! If it be so, no need of
  my Muse.
  Tra. But consider, dear Inkel, she's one
  of the " Blues."
  Ink.   As sublime! — Mr. Tracy — I've
  nothing to say.
Stick to prose — As sublime!! — but I wish
  you good day.
  Tra. Nay, stay, my dear fellow - consider
  — I'm wrong;
I own it; but, prithee, compose me the song.
  Ink. As sublime!!
  Tra.   I but used the expression in haste.
  Ink. That may be, Mr. Tracy, but shows
  damned bad taste.
  Tra. I own it — know it — acknowledge it
  — what
Can I say to you more?
  Ink.   I see what you'd be at:
You disparage my parts with insidious abuse,
Till you think you can turn them best to your
  own use.
  Tra. And is that not a sign I respect them?
  Ink.   Why that
To be sure makes a difference.
  Tra.   I know what is what
And you, who're a man of the gay world, no
  less
Than a poet of t'other, may easily guess

That I never could mean, by a word, to offend
A genius like you, and moreover my friend.
Ink. No doubt; you by this time should know what is due
To a man of —— but come — let us shake hands.
Tra.   You knew,
And you *know*, my dear fellow, how heartily I, Whatever you publish, am ready to buy.
Ink. That's my bookseller's business; I care not for sale;
Indeed the best poems at first rather fail.
There were Renegade's epics, and Botherby's plays,[1]
And my own grand romance —
Tra.   Had its full share of praise.
I myself saw it puffed in the " Old Girl's Review." [2]
Ink. What Review?
Tra.   'Tis the English " Journal de Trevoux; " [3]
A clerical work of our jesuits at home.
Have you never seen it?
Ink.   That pleasure's to come.
Tra. Make haste then.
Ink.   Why so ?
Tra.   I have heard people say
That it threatened to give up the *ghost* t'other day.
Ink. Well, that is a sign of some *spirit.*
Tra.   No doubt.
Shall you be at the Countess of Fiddlecome's rout ?
Ink. I've a card, and shall go : but at present, as soon
As friend Scamp shall be pleased to step down from the moon
(Where he seems to be soaring in search of his wits),
And an interval grants from his lecturing fits,
I'm engaged to the Lady Bluebottle's collation,
To partake of a luncheon and learned conversation :
'Tis a sort of re-union for Scamp, on the days
Of his lecture, to treat him with cold tongue and praise.
And I own, for my own part, that 'tis not unpleasant.
Will you go ?   There's Miss Lilac will also be present.
Tra. That " metal's attractive."
Ink.   No doubt — to the pocket.

---

[1] [Messrs. Southey and Sotheby.]

[2] [" My Grandmother's Review, the British." Which has since been gathered to its grandmothers.]

[3] [The " Journal de Trevoux " (in fifty-six volumes) is one of the most curious collections of literary gossip in the world, — and the Poet paid the British Review an extravagant compliment, when he made this comparison.]

Tra. You should rather encourage my passion than shock it.
But let us proceed; for I think, by the hum ——
Ink. Very true; let us go, then, before they can come,
Or else we'll be kept here an hour at their levy,
On the rack of cross-questions, by all the blue bevy.
Hark! Zounds, they'll be on us; I know by the drone
Of old Botherby's spouting ex-cathedrâ tone.
Ay! there he is at it. Poor Scamp! better join
Your friends, or he'll pay you back in your own coin.
Tra. All fair; 'tis but lecture for lecture.
Ink.   That's clear.
But for God's sake let's go, or the Bore will be here.
Come, come; nay, I'm off.   [*Exit* INKEL.
Tra.   You are right, and I'll follow;
'Tis high time for a " *Sic me servavit Apollo.*" [4]
And yet we shall have the whole crew on our kibes,
Blues, dandies, and dowagers, and second-hand scribes,
All flocking to moisten their exquisite throttles
With a glass of Madeira at Lady Bluebottle's.
                        [*Exit* TRACY.

———

ECLOGUE SECOND.

An Apartment in the House of LADY BLUE-
BOTTLE. — *A Table prepared.*

SIR RICHARD BLUEBOTTLE *solus.*

WAS there ever a man who was married so sorry ?
Like a fool, I must needs do the thing in a hurry.
My life is reversed, and my quiet destroyed;

---

[4] [" Sotheby is a good man — rhymes well (if not wisely); but is a bore. He seizes you by the button. One night of a rout at Mrs. Hope's, he had fastened upon me —(something about Agamemnon, or Orestes, or some of his plays) notwithstanding my symptoms of manifest distress — (for I was in love, and just nicked a minute when neither mothers, nor husbands, nor rivals, nor gossips were near my then idol, who was beautiful as the statues of the gallery where we stood at the time). Sotheby, I say, had seized upon me by the button and the heart-strings, and spared neither. William Spencer, who likes fun, and don't dislike mischief, saw my case, and coming up to us both, took me by the hand, and pathetically bade me farewell; "for," said he, " I see it is all over with you." Sotheby then went away: ' *sic me servavit Apollo.*' " — *Byron's Diary*, 1821.]

My days, which once passed in so gentle a void,
Must now, every hour of the twelve, be em-
ployed:
The twelve, do I say? — of the whole twenty-
four,
Is there one which I dare call my own any
more?
What with driving and visiting, dancing and
dining,
What with learning, and teaching, and scrib-
bling, and shining,
In science and art, I'll be cursed if I know
Myself from my wife; for although we are two,
Yet she somehow contrives that all things
shall be done
In a style which proclaims us eternally one.
But the thing of all things which distresses
me more
Than the bills of the week (though they
trouble me sore)
Is the numerous, humorous, backbiting crew
Of scribblers, wits, lecturers, white, black, and
blue,
Who are brought to my house as an inn, to
my cost
— For the bill here, it seems, is defrayed by the
host—
No pleasure! no leisure! no thought for my
pains,
But to hear a vile jargon which addles my
brains;
A smatter and chatter, gleaned out of reviews,
By the rag, tag, and bobtail, of those they call
"BLUES;"
A rabble who know not —— But soft, here
they come!
Would to God I were deaf! as I'm not, I'll
be dumb.

Enter LADY BLUEBOTTLE, MISS LILAC,
LADY BLUEMOUNT, MR. BOTHERBY, IN-
KEL, TRACY, MISS MAZARINE, *and others,
with* SCAMP *the Lecturer, etc. etc.*

Lady Blueb. Ah! Sir Richard, good morn-
ing; I've brought you some friends.
Sir Rich. (*bows, and afterwards aside*). If
friends, they're the first.
Lady Blueb.   But the luncheon attends.
I pray ye be seated, "*sans cérémonie.*"
Mr. Scamp, you're fatigued; take your chair
there, next me.   [*They all sit.*
Sir Rich. (*aside*). If he does, his fatigue is
to come.
Lady Blueb.   Mr. Tracy—
Lady Bluemount — Miss Lilac — be pleased,
pray to place ye;
And you, Mr. Botherby—
Both.   Oh, my dear Lady,
I obey.
Lady Blueb. Mr. Inkel, I ought to upbraid
ye:
You were not at the lecture.

Ink.   Excuse me, I was;
But the heat forced me out in the best part—
alas!
And when ——
Lady Bleub. To be sure it was broiling;
but then
You have lost such a lecture!
Both.   The best of the ten.
Tra. How can you know that? there are
two more.
Both.   Because
I defy him to beat this day's wondrous ap-
plause.
The very walls shook.
Ink.   Oh, if that be the test,
I allow our friend Scamp has this day done
his best.
Miss Lilac, permit me to help you; — a
wing?
Miss Lil. No more, sir, I thank you. Who
lectures next spring?
Both. Dick Dunder.
Ink.   That is, if he lives.
Miss Lil.   And why not?
Ink. No reason whatever, save that he's a
sot.
Lady Bluemount! a glass of Madeira?
Lady Bluem.   With pleasure.
Ink. How does your friend Wordswords,
that Windermere treasure?
Does he stick to his lakes, like the leeches he
sings,
And their gatherers, as Homer sung warriors
and kings?
Lady Bleub. He has just got a place.
Ink.   As a footman?
Lady Bluem.   For shame!
Nor profane with your sneers so poetic a name.
Ink. Nay, I meant him no evil, but pitied
his master;
For the poet of pedlers 'twere, sure, no dis-
aster
To wear a new livery; the more, as 'tis not
The first time he has turned both his creed
and his coat.
Lady Bluem. For shame! I repeat. If
Sir George could but hear ——
Lady Blueb. Never mind our friend Inkel;
we all know, my dear,
'Tis his way.
Sir Rich. But this place ——
Ink.   Is perhaps like friend Scamp's,
A lecturer's.
Lady Blueb. Excuse me — 'tis one in "the
Stamps:"
He is made a collector.[1]
Tra.   Collector!
Sir Rich.   How?
Miss Lil.   What?

---

[1] [Wordsworth was collector of stamps for Cum-
berland and Westmoreland.]

Ink. I shall think of him oft when I buy
a new hat:
There his works will appear ——
Lady Bluem. Sir, they reach to the Ganges.
Ink. I sha'n't go so far — I can have them
at Grange's.[1]
Lady Blueb.   Oh fie!
Miss Lil.   And for shame!
Lady Bluem.   You're too bad.
Both.   Very good!
Lady Bluem. How good?
Lady Blueb. He means nought — 'tis his
phrase.
Lady Bluem.   He grows rude.
Lady Bleub. He means nothing; nay, ask
him.
Lady Bluem.   Pray, sir! did you mean
What you say?
Ink. Never mind if he did; 'twill be seen
That whatever he means won't alloy what he
says.
Both. Sir!
Ink. Pray be content with your portion of
praise;
'Twas in your defence.
Both.   If you please, with submission,
I can make out my own.
Ink.   It would be your perdition.
While you live, my dear Botherby, never de-
fend
Yourself or your works; but leave both to a
friend.
A propos — Is your play then accepted at last?
Both. At last?
Ink. Why I thought — that's to say — there
had passed
A few green-room whispers, which hinted —
you know
That the taste of the actors at best is so so.[2]
Both. Sir, the green-room's in rapture, and
so's the committee.
Ink. Ay — yours are the plays for exciting
our "pity
And fear," as the Greek says: for "purging
the mind,"
I doubt if you'll leave us an equal behind.
Both. I have written the prologue, and
meant to have prayed
For a spice of your wit in an epilogue's aid.
Ink. Well, time enough yet, when the
play's to be played.
Is it cast yet?
Both.   The actors are fighting for parts,
As is usual in that most litigious of arts.
Lady Blueb. We'll all make a party, and
go the *first* night.

---

[1] Grange is or was a famous pastry-cook and
fruiterer in Piccadilly.

[2] ["When I belonged to the Drury Lane Com-
mittee, the number of plays upon the shelves were
about five hundred. Mr. Sotheby obligingly offered
us ALL his tragedies, and I pledged myself, and —

Tra. And you promised the epilogue,
Inkel.
Ink.   Not quite.
However, to save my friend Botherby trouble,
I'll do what I can, though my pains must be
double.
Tra. Why so?
Ink.   To do justice to what goes before.
Both. Sir, I'm happy to say, I have no
fears on that score.
Your parts, Mr. Inkel, are ——
Ink.   Never mind *mine*;
Stick to those of your play, which is quite
your own line.
Lady Bluem. You're a fugitive writer, I
think, sir, of rhymes?
Ink. Yes, ma'am; and a fugitive reader
sometimes.
On Wordswords, for instance, I seldom alight,
Or on Mouthey, his friend, without taking to
flight.
Lady Bluem. Sir, your taste is too common;
but time and posterity
Will right these great men, and this age's
severity
Become its reproach.
Ink.   I've no sort of objection,
So I'm not of the party to take the infection.
Lady Blueb. Perhaps you have doubts
that they ever will *take?*
Ink. Not at all; on the contrary, those of
the lake
Have taken already, and still will continue
To take — what they can, from a groat to a
guinea,
Of pension or place; — but the subject's a
bore.
Lady Bluem. Well, sir, the time's coming.
Ink.   Scamp! don't you feel sore?
What say you to this?
Scamp.   They have merit, I own;
Though their system's absurdity keeps it un-
known.
Ink. Then why not unearth it in one of
your lectures?
Scamp. It is only time past which comes
under my strictures.
Lady Blueb. Come, a truce with all tart-
ness: — the joy of my heart
Is to see Nature's triumph o'er all that is art.
Wild nature! — Grand Shakspeare!
Both.   And down Aristotle!
Lady Bluem. Sir George[3] thinks exactly
with Lady Bluebottle;

---

notwithstanding many squabbles with my commit-
tee brethren — did get Ivan accepted, read, and the
parts distributed. But lo! in the very heart of the
matter, upon some *tepid*-ness on the part of Kean,
or warmth on that of the author, Sotheby withdrew
his play." — *Byron's Diary*, 1821.]

[3] [Sir George Beaumont — a constant friend of
Mr. Wordsworth.]

And my Lord Seventy-four,[1] who protects our
dear Bard,
And who gave him his place, has the greatest
regard
For the poet, who, singing of pedlers and
asses,
Has found out the way to dispense with
Parnassus.
Tra. And you, Scamp!—
Scamp. I needs must confess I'm embar-
rassed.
Ink. Don't call upon Scamp, who's already
so harassed
With old *schools,* and new *schools,* and no
schools, and all *schools.*
Tra. Well, one thing is certain, that *some*
must be fools.
I should like to know who.
Ink. And I should not be sorry
To know who are *not:*—it would save us
some worry.
Lady Blueb. A truce with remark, and let
nothing control
This "feast of our reason, and flow of the
soul."
Oh! my dear Mr. Botherby! sympathise!—I
Now feel such a rapture, I'm ready to fly,
I feel so elastic—"*so buoyant—so buoyant!*"[2]
Ink. Tracy! open the window.
Tra. I wish her much joy on't.
Both. For God's sake, my Lady Bluebottle,
check not
This gentle emotion, so seldom our lot
Upon earth. Give it way; 'tis an impulse
which lifts
Our spirits from earth; the sublimest of gifts;
For which poor Prometheus was chained to
his mountain.
'Tis the source of all sentiment—feeling's
true fountain:
'Tis the Vision of Heaven upon Earth: 'tis
the gas
Of the soul: 'tis the seizing of shades as they
pass,
And making them substance: 'tis something
divine:—

---

[1] [It was not the late Earl of Lonsdale; but
James, the first earl, who offered to build, and man,
a ship of seventy-four guns, towards the close of
the American war, for the service of his country, at
his own expense;—hence the *soubriquet* in the
text.]
[2] Fact from life, with the *words.*

Ink. Shall I help you, my friend, to a little
more wine?
Both. I thank you; not any more, sir, till I
dine.
Ink. A propos—Do you dine with Sir
Humphry[3] to-day?
Tra. I should think with *Duke* Humphry
was more in your way.
Ink. It might be of yore; but we authors
now look
To the knight, as a landlord, much more than
the Duke.
The truth is, each writer now quite at his
ease is,
And (except with his publisher) dines where
he pleases.
But 'tis now nearly five, and I must to the
Park.
Tra. And I'll take a turn with you there
till 'tis dark.
And you, Scamp—
Scamp. Excuse me; I must to my notes,
For my lectures next week.
Ink. He must mind whom he quotes
Out of "Elegant Extracts."
Lady Blueb. Well, now we break up;
But remember Miss Diddle[4] invites us to
sup.
Ink. Then at two hours past midnight we
all meet again,
For the sciences, sandwiches, hock, and
champagne!
Tra. And the sweet lobster salad!
Both. I honor that meal;
For 'tis then that our feelings most genu-
inely—feel.
Ink. True; feeling is truest *then,* far be-
yond question:
I wish to the gods 'twas the same with diges-
tion!
Lady Blueb. Pshaw!—never mind that;
for one moment of feeling
Is worth—God knows what.
Ink. 'Tis at least worth concealing
For itself, or what follows—— But here comes
your carriage.
Sir Rich. (aside). I wish all these people
were d——d with *my* marriage!
[*Exeunt.*

---

[3] [Sir Humphry Davy, President of the Royal
Society.]
[4] [Miss Lydia White, an accomplished, clever,
and truly amiable, but very eccentric lady.]

THE VISION OF JUDGMENT,

BY QUEVEDO REDIVIVUS.

SUGGESTED BY THE COMPOSITION SO ENTITLED BY THE AUTHOR OF "WAT TYLER."

"A Daniel come to judgment! yea, a Daniel!
I thank thee, Jew, for teaching me that word."

PREFACE.

IT hath been wisely said, that "One fool makes many;" and it hath been poetically observed,

"That fools rush in where angels fear to tread." — POPE.

If Mr. Southey had not rushed in where he had no business, and where he never was before, and never will be again, the following poem would not have been written. It is not impossible that it may be as good as his own, seeing that it cannot, by any species of stupidity, natural or acquired, be *worse*. The gross flattery, the dull impudence, the renegado intolerance and impious cant, of the poem by the author of "Wat Tyler," are something so stupendous as to form the sublime of himself — containing the quintessence of his own attributes.

So much for his poem — a word on his preface. In this preface it has pleased the magnanimous Laureate to draw the picture of a supposed "Satanic School," the which he doth recommend to the notice of the legislature; thereby adding to his other laurels the ambition of those of an informer. If there exists anywhere, excepting in his imagination, such a School, is he not sufficiently armed against it by his own intense vanity? The truth is, that there are certain writers whom Mr. S. imagines, like Scrub, to have "talked of *him ;* for they laughed consumedly."

I think I know enough of most of the writers to whom he is supposed to allude, to assert, that they, in their individual capacities, have done more good, in the charities of life, to their fellow-creatures in any one year, than Mr. Southey has done harm to himself by his absurdities in his whole life; and this is saying a great deal. But I have a few questions to ask.

1st. Is Mr. Southey the author of "Wat Tyler?"

2d. Was he not refused a remedy at law by the highest judge of his beloved England, because it was a blasphemous and seditious publication?[1]

---

[1] [In 1821, when Mr. Southey applied to the Court of Chancery for an injunction to restrain the publication of "Wat Tyler," Lord Chancellor Eldon pronounced the following judgment: — "I have looked into all the affidavits, and have read the book itself. The bill goes the length of stating, that the work was composed by Mr. Southey in the year 1794; that it is his own production, and that it has been published by the defendants without his sanction or authority; and therefore seeking an account of the profits which have arisen from, and an injunction to restrain, the publication. I have examined the cases that I have been able to meet with containing precedents for injunctions of this nature, and I find that they all proceed upon the ground of a title to the property in the plaintiff. On this head a distinction has been taken, to which a considerable weight of authority attaches, supported, as it is, by the opinion of Lord Chief Justice Eyre, who has expressly laid it down, that a person cannot recover in damages for a work which is, in its nature, calculated to do injury to the public. Upon the same principle this court refused an injunction in the case of Walcot " (Peter Pindar) " *v.* Walker, inasmuch as he could not have recovered damages in an action. After the fullest consideration, I remain of the same opinion as that which I entertained in deciding the case referred to. Taking all the circumstances into my consideration, it appears to me, that I cannot grant this injunction, until after Mr. Southey shall have established his right to the property by action." — Injunction refused.]

3d. Was he not entitled by William Smith, in full parliament, "a rancorous renegado ?"[1]

4th. Is he not poet laureate, with his own lines on Martin the regicide staring him in the face?[2]

And 5th. Putting the four preceding items together, with what conscience dare *he* call the attention of the laws to the publications of others, be they what they may?

I say nothing of the cowardice of such a proceeding; its meanness speaks for itself; but I wish to touch upon the *motive*, which is neither more nor less than that Mr. S. has been laughed at a little in some recent publications, as he was of yore in the "Anti-jacobin" by his present patrons.[3] Hence all this " skimble scamble stuff " about " Satanic " and so forth. However, it is worthy of him — "*qualis ab incepto.*"

If there is any thing obnoxious to the political opinions of a portion of the public in the following poem, they may thank Mr. Southey. He might have written hexameters, as he has written every thing else, for aught that the writer cared — had they been upon another subject. But to attempt to canonize a monarch, who, whatever were his household virtues, was neither a successful nor a patriot king, — inasmuch as several years of his reign passed in war with America and Ireland, to say nothing of the aggression upon France, — like all other exaggeration, necessarily begets opposition. In whatever manner he may be spoken of in this new " Vision," his *public* career will not be more favorably transmitted by history. Of his private virtues (although a little expensive to the nation) there can be no doubt.

With regard to the supernatural personages treated of, I can only say that I know as much about them, and (as an honest man) have a better right to talk of them than Robert Southey. I have also

[1] [Mr William Smith, M.P. for Norwich, made a virulent attack on Mr. Southey in the House of Commons on the 14th of March, 1817, and the Laureate replied by a letter in the *Courier*.]

[2] [Among the effusions of Mr. Southey's juvenile muse, we find this "Inscription for the Apartment in Chepstow Castle, where Henry Martin, the Regicide, was imprisoned thirty years: —

  " For thirty years secluded from mankind
  Here Martin lingered. Often have these walls
  Echoed his footsteps, as with even tread
  He paced around his prison. Not to him
  Did Nature's fair varieties exist;
  He never saw the sun's delightful beams;
  Save when through yon high bars he poured a sad
  And broken splendor. Dost thou ask his crime?
  He had rebelled against the King, and sat
  In judgment on him; for his ardent mind
  Shaped goodliest plans of happiness on earth,
  And peace and liberty. Wild dreams! but such
  As Plato loved; such as, with holy zeal,
  Our Milton worshipped. Blessed hopes! awhile
  From man withheld, even to the latter days
  When Christ shall come and all things be fulfilled."]

[3] [The following imitation of the Inscription on the Regicide's Apartment, written by Mr. Canning, appeared in the "*Anti-jacobin.*" —

" Inscription for the Door of the Cell in Newgate, where Mrs. Brownrigg, the 'Prentice-cide, was confined, previous to her Execution.

  " For one long term, or ere her trial came,
  Here Brownrigg lingered. Often have these cells
  Echoed her blasphemies, as with shrill voice
  She screamed for fresh geneva. Not to her
  Did the blithe fields of Tothill, or thy street,
  St. Giles, its fair varieties expand;
  Till at the last in slow-drawn cart she went
  To execution. Dost thou ask her crime?
  She whipped two female 'prentices to death,
  And hid them in the coal-hole. For her mind
  Shaped strictest plans of discipline. Sage schemes!
  Such as Lycurgus taught, when at the shrine
  Of the Orthyan goddess he bade flog
  The little Spartans; such as erst chastised
  Our Milton, when at college. For this act
  Did Brownrigg swing. Harsh laws! But time shall come
  When France shall reign, and laws be all repealed."]

treated them more tolerantly. The way in which that poor insane creature, the Laureate, deals about his judgments in the next world, is like his own judgment in this. If it was not completely ludicrous, it would be something worse. I don't think that there is much more to say at present.

QUEVEDO REDIVIVUS.

P. S. — It is possible that some readers may object, in these objectionable times, to the freedom with which saints, angels, and spiritual persons discourse in this "Vision." But, for precedents upon such points, I must refer him to Fielding's "Journey from this World to the next," and to the Visions of myself, the said Quevedo, in Spanish or translated. The reader is also requested to observe, that no, doctrinal tenets are insisted upon or discussed; that the person of the Deity is carefully withheld from sight, which is more than can be said for the Laureate, who hath thought proper to make him talk, not "like a school divine," but like the unscholarlike Mr. Southey. The whole action passes on the outside of heaven; and Chaucer's Wife of Bath, Pulci's Morgante Maggiore, Swift's Tale of a Tub, and the other works above referred to, are cases in point of the freedom with which saints, etc. may be permitted to converse in works not intended to be serious.   Q. R.

* Mr. Southey being, as he says, a good Christian and vindictive, threatens, I understand, a reply to this our answer. It is to be hoped that his visionary faculties will in the mean time have acquired a little more judgment, properly so called: otherwise he will get himself into new dilemmas. These apostate jacobins furnish rich rejoinders. Let him take a specimen. Mr. Southey laudeth grievously "one Mr. Landor," who cultivates much private renown in the shape of Latin verses; and not long ago, the poet laureate dedicated to him, it appeareth, one of his fugitive lyrics, upon the strength of a poem called *Gebir.* Who could suppose, that in this same Gebir the aforesaid Savage Landor (for such is his grim cognomen) putteth into the infernal regions no less a person than the hero of his friend Mr. Southey's heaven, — yea, even George the Third! See also how personal Savage becometh, when he hath a mind. The following is his portrait of our late gracious sovereign: —

(Prince Gebir having descended into the infernal regions, the shades of his royal ancestors are, at his request, called up to his view; and he exclaims to his ghostly guide) —

> "Aroar, what wretch that nearest us? what wretch
> Is that with eyebrows white and slanting brow?
> Listen! him yonder, who, bound down supine,
> Shrinks yelling from that sword there, engine-hung.
> He too amongst my ancestors! I hate
> The despot, but the dastard I despise.
> Was he our countryman?"
>   "Alas, O king!
> Iberia bore him, but the breed accurst
> Inclement winds blew blighting from north-east."
> "He was a warrior then, nor feared the gods?"
> "Gebir, he feared the demons, not the gods,
> Though them indeed his daily face adored;
> And was no warrior, yet the thousand lives
> Squandered, as stones to exercise a sling,
> And the tame cruelty and cold caprice—
> Oh madness of mankind! addressed, adored!" — *Gebir*, p. 28.

I omit noticing some edifying Ithyhallics of Savagius, wishing to keep the proper veil over them, if his grave but somewhat indiscreet worshipper will suffer it; but certainly these teachers of "great moral lessons" are apt to be found in strange company.

———

APPENDIX TO THE PREFACE.

[SOUTHEY, in 1821, published a poem in English hexameters, entitled "A Vision of Judgment;" in the preface to which, after some observations on the peculiar style of its versification, occurs the following remarks: —

" I am well aware that the public are peculiarly intolerant of such innovations; not less so than th populace are of any foreign fashion, whether of foppery or convenience. Would that this literary intoler ance were under the influence of a saner judgment, and regarded the morals more than the manner of a composition; the spirit rather than the form! Would that it were directed against those monstrous com binations of horrors and mockery, lewdness and impiety, with which English poetry has, in our days, first been polluted! For more than half a century English literature had been distinguished by its moral purity, the effect, and, in its turn, the cause of an improvement in national manners. A father might, without apprehension of evil, have put into the hands of his children any book which issued from the press, if it did not bear, either in its title-page or frontispiece, manifest signs that it was intended as fur niture for the brothel. There was no danger in any work which bore the name of a respectable publisher, or was to be procured at any respectable bookseller's. This was particularly the case with regard to our poetry. It is now no longer so: and woe to those by whom the offence cometh! The greater the talents of the offender, the greater is his guilt, and the more enduring will be his shame. Whether it be that the laws are in themselves unable to abate an evil of this magnitude, or whether it be that they are remissly administered, and with such injustice that the celebrity of an offender serves as a privilege whereby he obtains impunity, individuals are bound to consider that such pernicious works would neither be published nor written, if they were discouraged as they might, and ought to be, by public feeling: every person, therefore, who purchases such books, or admits them into his house, promotes the mischief, and thereby, as far as in him lies, becomes an aider and abettor of the crime.

" The publication of a lascivious book is one of the worst offences which can be committed against the well-being of society. It is a sin, to the consequences of which no limits can be assigned, and those con sequences no after-repentance in the writer can counteract. Whatever remorse of conscience he may feel when his hour comes (and come it must!) will be of no avail. The poignancy of a death-bed re pentance cannot cancel one copy of the thousands which are sent abroad; and as long as it continues to be read, so long is he the pander of posterity, and so long is he heaping up guilt upon his soul in per petual accumulation.

" These remarks are not more severe than the offence deserves, even when applied to those immoral writers who have not been conscious of any evil intention in their writings, who would acknowledge a little levity, a little warmth of coloring, and so forth, in that sort of language with which men gloss over their favorite vices, and deceive themselves. What then should be said of those for whom the thoughtlessness and inebriety of wanton youth can no longer be pleaded, but who have written in sober manhood and with deliberate purpose? — Men of diseased hearts and depraved imaginations, who, forming a system of opinions to suit their own unhappy course of conduct, have rebelled against the holiest ordi nances of human society, and hating that revealed religion which, with all their efforts and bravadoes, they are unable entirely to disbelieve, labor to make others as miserable as themselves, by infecting them with a moral virus that eats into the soul! The school which they have set up may properly be called the Satanic school; for though their productions breathe the spirit of Belial in their lascivious parts, and the spirit of Moloch in those loathsome images of atrocities and horrors which they delight to represent, they are more especially characterized by a Satanic spirit of pride and audacious impiety, which still betrays the wretched feeling of hopelessness wherewith it is allied.

" This evil is political as well as moral, for indeed moral and political evils are inseparably connected. Truly has it been affirmed by one of our ablest and clearest reasoners, that ' the destruction of govern ments may be proved and deduced from the general corruption of the subjects' manners, as a direct and natural cause thereof, by a demonstration as certain as any in the mathematics.' There is no maxim more frequently enforced by Machiavelli, than that where the manners of a people are generally corrupted, there the government cannot long subsist, — a truth which all history exemplifies; and there is no means whereby that corruption can be so surely and rapidly diffused, as by poisoning the waters of literature.

" Let rulers of the state look to this, in time! But, to use the words of Southey, if ' our physicians think the best way of curing a disease is to pamper it, — the Lord in mercy prepare the kingdom to suffer, what He by miracle only can prevent!'

" No apology is offered for these remarks. The subject led to them; and the occasion of introducing them was willingly taken, because it is the duty of every one, whose opinion may have any influence, to expose the drift and aim of those writers who are laboring to subvert the foundations of human virtue and of human happiness."

Byron rejoined as follows: —

" Mr. Southey, in his pious preface to a poem whose blasphemy is as harmless as the sedition of Wat Tyler, because it is equally absurd with that sincere production, calls upon the ' legislature to look to it,' as the toleration of such writings led to the French Revolution: not such writings as Wat Tyler, but as those of the ' Santanic School.' This is not true, and Mr. Southey knows it to be not true. Every French writer of any freedom was persecuted; Voltaire and Rousseau were exiles, Marmontel and Did erot were sent to the Bastile, and a perpetual war was waged with the whole class by the existing despot ism. In the next place, the French Revolution was not occasioned by any writings whatsoever, but must have occurred had no such writers ever existed. It is the fashion to attribute every thing to the French Revolution, and the French Revolution to every thing but its real cause. That cause is obvious — the government exacted too much, and the people could neither give nor bear more. Without this, the En cyclopedists might have written their fingers off without the occurrence of a single alteration. And the English revolution — (the first, I mean) — what was it occasioned by? The Puritans were surely as pious and moral as Wesley or his biographer? Acts — acts on the part of government, and not writings against them, have caused the past convulsions, and are tending to the future.

"I look upon such as inevitable, though no revolutionist: I wish to see the English constitution restored, and not destroyed. Born an aristocrat, and naturally one by temper, with the greater part of my present property in the funds, what have *I* to gain by a revolution? Perhaps I have more to lose in every way than Mr. Southey, with all his places and presents for panegyrics and abuse into the bargain. But that a revolution is inevitable, I repeat. The government may exult over the repression of petty tumults: these are but the receding waves repulsed and broken for a moment on the shore, while the great tide is still rolling on and gaining ground with every breaker. Mr. Southey accuses us of attacking the religion of the country; and is he abetting it by writing lives of *Wesley?* One mode of worship is merely destroyed by another. There never was, nor ever will be, a country without a religion. We shall be told of *France* again: but it was only Paris and a frantic party, which for a moment upheld their dogmatic nonsense of theo-philanthropy. The church of England, if overthrown, will be swept away by the sectarians and not by the sceptics. People are too wise, too well informed, too certain of their own immense importance in the realms of space, ever to submit to the impiety of doubt. There may be a few such diffident speculators, like water in the pale sunbeam of human reason, but they are very few; and their opinions, without enthusiasm or appeal to the passions, can never gain proselytes — unless, indeed, they are persecuted — *that*, to be sure, will increase any thing.

"Mr. Southey, with a cowardly ferocity, exults over the anticipated 'death-bed repentance' of the objects of his dislike; and indulges himself in a pleasant 'Vision of Judgment,' in prose as well as verse, full of impious impudence. What Mr. Southey's sensations or ours may be in the awful moment of leaving this state of existence, neither he nor we can pretend to decide. In common, I presume, with most men of any reflection, *I* have not waited for a 'death-bed' to repent of many of my actions, notwithstanding the 'di abolical pride' which this pitiful renegado in his rancor would impute to those who scorn *him*. Whether upon the whole the good or evil of my deeds may preponderate is not for me to ascertain; but as my means and opportunities have been greater, I shall limit my present defence to an assertion, (easily proved, if necessary,) that I, 'in my degree,' have done more real good in any one given year, since I was twenty, than Mr. Southey in the whole course of his shifting and turncoat existence. There are several actions to which I can look back with an honest pride, not to be damped by the calmness of a hireling. There are others to which I recur with sorrow and repentance; but the only *act* of *my* life of which Mr. Southey can have any real knowledge, as it was one which brought me in contact with a near connection of his own,[1] did no dishonor to that connection nor to me.

"I am not ignorant of Mr. Southey's calumnies on a different occasion, knowing them to be such, which he scattered abroad on his return from Switzerland against me and others: they have done him no good in this world; and if his creed be the right one, they will do him less in the next. What *his* 'death-bed' may be, it is not my province to predicate: let him settle with his Maker as I must do with mine. There is something at once ludicrous and blasphemous in this arrogant scribbler of all work sitting down to deal damnation and destruction upon his fellow-creatures, with Wat Tyler, the Apotheosis of George the Third, and the Elegy on Martin the regicide, all shuffled together in his writing-desk. One of his consolations appears to be a Latin note from a work of a Mr. Landor, the author of 'Gebir,' whose friendship for Robert Southey will, it seems, 'be an honor to him when the ephemeral disputes and ephemeral reputations of the day are forgotton.'[2] I for one neither envy him 'the friendship,' nor the glory in reversion which is to accrue from it, like Mr. Thelusson's fortune in the third and fourth generation. This friendship will probably be as memorable as his own epics, which (as I quoted to him ten or twelve years ago in 'English Bards') Porson said 'would be remembered when Homer and Virgil are forgotten, — and not till then.' For the present, I leave him."

Southey replied to this on the 5th of January, 1822, in a letter addressed to the Editor of the London Courier, of which we quote all that is of importance: —

"I come at once to his Lordship's charge against me, blowing away the abuse with which it is frothed, and evaporating a strong acid in which it is suspended. The residuum then appears to be, that 'Mr. Southey, on his return from Switzerland (in 1817), scattered abroad calumnies, knowing them to be such, against Lord Byron and others.' To this I reply with *a direct and positive denial.*

"If I had been told in that country that Lord Byron had turned Turk, or Monk of La Trappe, — that he had furnished a *harem*, or endowed an hospital, I might have thought the account, whichever it had been, possible, and repeated it accordingly; passing it, as it had been taken in the small change of conversation, for no more than 'it was worth. In this manner I might have spoken of him, as of Baron Geramb,[3] the Green Man,[4] the Indian Jugglers, or any other *figurante* of the time being. There was

----

[1] [Coleridge.]

[2] Southey, after quoting in a note to his preface a Latin passage from Mr. Landor, spoke thus of its author: — "I will only say in this place that to have obtained his approbation as a poet, and possessed his friendship as a man, will be remembered among the honors of my life, when the petty enmities of this generation will be forgotten, and its ephemeral reputations shall have passed away."

[3] [Baron Geramb, — a German Jew, who, for some time, excited much public attention in London, by the extravagance of his dress. Being very troublesome and menacing in demanding remuneration from Government, for a proposal he had made of engaging a body of Croat troops in the service of England, he was, in 1812, sent out of the country under the alien act.]

[4] [The "Green Man" was a popular afterpiece, so called from the hero, who wore every thing green, hat, gloves, etc. etc.]

no reason for any particular delicacy on my part in speaking of his Lordship: and, indeed, I should have thought any thing which might be reported of him, would have injured his character as little as the story which so greatly annoyed Lord Keeper Guilford, that he had ridden a rhinoceros. He may ride a rhinoceros, and though everybody would stare, no one would wonder. But making no inquiry concerning him when I was abroad, because I felt no curiosity, I heard nothing, and had nothing to repeat. When I spoke of wonders to my friends and acquaintance on my return, it was of the flying tree at Alpnacht, and the Eleven Thousand virgins at Cologne — not of Lord Byron. I sought for no staler subject than St. Ursula.

"Once, and only once, in connection with Switzerland, I have alluded to his Lordship; and as the passage was curtailed in the press, I take this opportunity of restoring it. In the 'Quarterly Review,' speaking incidentally of the Jungfrau, I said 'it was the scene where Lord Byron's Manfred met the Devil and bullied him — though the Devil must have won his cause before any tribunal in this world, or the next, if he had not pleaded more feebly for himself than his advocate, in a cause of canonization, ever pleaded for him.'

"With regard to the 'others,' whom his Lordship accuses me of calumniating, I suppose he alludes to a party of his friends, whose names I found written in the album at Mont-Anvert, with an avowal of Atheism annexed in Greek, and an indignant comment, in the same language, underneath it.[1] Those names, with that avowal and the comment, I transcribed in my note-book, and spoke of the circumstance on my return. If I had published it, the gentleman in question would not have thought himself slandered, by having that recorded of him which he has so often recorded of himself.

"The many opprobrious appellations which Lord Byron has bestowed upon me, I leave as I find them, with the praises which he has bestowed upon himself. ·

> 'How easily is a noble spirit discerned
> From harsh and sulphurous matter that flies out
> In contumelies, makes a noise, and stinks!'
> B. JONSON.

But I am accustomed to such things; and, so far from irritating me are the enemies who use such weapons, that, when I hear of their attacks, it is some satisfaction to think they have thus employed the malignity which must have been employed somewhere, and could not have been directed against any person whom it could possibly molest or injure less. The viper, however venomous in purpose, is harmless in effect, while it is biting at the file. It is seldom, indeed, that I waste a word, or a thought, upon those who are perpetually assailing me. But abhorring, as I do, the personalities which disgrace our current literature, and averse from controversy as I am, both by principle and inclination, I make no profession of non-resistance. When the offence and the offender are such as to call for the whip and the branding-iron, it has been both seen and felt that I can inflict them.

"Lord Byron's present exacerbation is evidently produced by an infliction of this kind — not by hearsay reports of my conversation, four years ago, transmitted him from England. The cause may be found in certain remarks upon the Satanic school of poetry, contained in my preface to the 'Vision of Judgment.' Well would it be for Lord Byron if he could look back upon any of his writings, with as much satisfaction as I shall always do upon what is there said of that flagitious school. Many persons, and parents especially, have expressed their gratitude to me for having applied the branding-iron where it was so richly deserved. The Edinburgh Reviewer, indeed, with that honorable feeling by which his criticisms are so peculiarly distinguished, suppressing the remarks themselves, has imputed them wholly to envy on my part. I give him, in this instance, full credit for sincerity: I believe he was equally incapable of comprehending a worthier motive, or of inventing a worse; and as I have never condescended to expose in any instance, his pitiful malevolence, I thank him for having, in this, stripped it bare himself, and exhibited it in its bald, naked, and undisguised deformity.

"Lord Byron, like his encomiast, has not ventured to bring the matter of those animadversions into view. He conceals the fact, that they are directed against the authors of blasphemous and lascivious books; against men who, not content with indulging their own vices, labor to make others the slaves of sensuality, like themselves; against public panders, who, mingling impiety with lewdness, seek at once to destroy the cement of social order, and to carry profanation and pollution into private families, and into the hearts of individuals.

"His Lordship has thought it not unbecoming in him to call me a scribbler of all work. Let the word *scribbler* pass; it is an appellation which will not stick, like that of the *Satanic school.* But, if a scribbler, how am I one of *all work?* I will tell Lord Byron what I have *not* scribbled — what kind of work I have *not* done. I have never published libels upon my friends and acquaintance, expressed my sorrow for those libels, and called them in during a mood of better mind — and then reissued them, when the evil spirit, which for a time had been cast out, had returned and taken possession, with seven others, more wicked than himself. I have never abused the power, of which every author is in some degree possessed, to wound the character of a man, or the heart of a woman. I have never sent into the world a book to which I did not dare to affix my name; or which I feared to claim in a court of justice, if it were pirated by a knavish bookseller. I have never manufactured furniture for the brothel. None of *these things* have I done; none of the foul work by which literature is perverted to the injury of mankind. My hands are clean; there is no 'damned spot' upon them — no taint, which 'all the perfumes of Arabia will not sweeten.'

[1] [Shelley signed his name, with the addition of $\dot{a}\theta\acute{e}os$, in this album.]

"Of the work which I *have* done, it becomes me not here to speak save only as relates to the Satanic School, and its Coryphæus, the author of 'Don Juan.' I have held up that school to public detestation, as enemies to the religion, the institutions, and the domestic morals of the country. I have given them a designation *to which their founder and leader answers.* I have sent a stone from my sling which has smitten their Goliath in the forehead. I have fastened his name upon the gibbet, for reproach and ignominy, as long as it shall endure. — Take it down who can!

"One word of advice to Lord Byron before I conclude. — When he attacks me again, let it be in rhyme. For one who has so little command of himself, it will be a great advantage that his temper should be obliged to *keep tune.* And while he may still indulge in the same rankness and virulence of insult, the metre will, in some degree, seem to lessen its vulgarity."

Byron, without waiting for the closing hint of the foregoing letter, had already "attacked" Southey 'in rhyme." On October 1, 1821, he says to Moore, —

"I have written about sixty stanzas of a poem, in octave stanzas (in the Pulci style, which the fools in England think was invented by Whistlecraft — it is as old as the hills, in Italy,) called 'The Vision of Judgment,' by Quevedo Redivivus. In this it is my intention to put the said George's Apothesis in a Whig point of view, not forgetting the Poet Laureate, for his preface and his other demerits."

Byron had proceeded some length in the performance thus announced, before Southey's letter to the "Courier" fell into his hands. On seeing it, his Lordship's feelings were so excited, that he could not wait for revenge in inkshed, but on the instant despatched a cartel of mortal defiance to the Poet Laureate, through the medium of Mr. Douglass Kinnaird, — to whom he thus writes, February 6, 1822: —

"I have got Southey's pretended reply: what remains to be done is to call him out. The question is, would he come? for, if he would not, the whole thing would appear ridiculous, if I were to take a long and expensive journey to no purpose. You must be my second, and, as such, I wish to consult you. I apply to you as one well versed in the duello, or monomachie. Of course I shall come to England as privately as possible, and leave it (supposing that I was the survivor) in the same manner; having no other object which could bring me to that country except to settle quarrels accumulated during my absence."

Mr. Kinnaird, justly appreciating the momentary exacerbation under which Byron had written the challenge which this letter inclosed, and fully aware how absurd the whole business would seem to his distant friend after the lapse of such a period as must intervene before the return of post from Keswick to Ravenna, put the warlike missive aside; and it never was heard of by Mr. Southey until after the death of its author. Meantime Byron had continued his "attack in rhyme" — and *his* "Vision of Judgment," after ineffectual negotiations with various publishers in London, at length saw the light in 1822, in the pages of the "Liberal."]

I.

SAINT PETER sat by the celestial gate:
  His keys were rusty, and the lock was dull,
So little trouble had been given of late;
  Not that the place by any means was full,
But since the Gallic era "eighty-eight"
  The devils had ta'en a longer, stronger pull,
And "a pull altogether," as they say
At sea — which drew most souls another way.

II.

The angels all were singing out of tune,
  And hoarse with having little else to do,
Excepting to wind up the sun and moon,
  Or curb a runaway young star or two,
Or wild colt of a comet, which too soon
  Broke out of bounds o'er the ethereal blue,
Splitting some planet with its playful tail,
As boats are sometimes by a wanton whale.

III.

The guardian seraphs had retired on high,
  Finding their charges past all care below;
Terrestrial business filled nought in the sky
  Save the recording angel's black bureau;
Who found, indeed, the facts to multiply
  With such rapidity of vice and woe,
That he had stripped off both his wings in quills,
And yet was in arrear of human ills.

IV.

His business so augmented of late years,
  That he was forced, against his will, no doubt,
(Just like those cherubs, earthly ministers,)
  For some resource to turn himself about
And claim the help of his celestial peers,
  To aid him ere he should be quite worn out

By the increased demand for his remarks;
Six angels and twelve saints were named his
  clerks.

v.

This was a handsome board — at least for
  heaven;
  And yet they had even then enough to do,
So many conquerors' cars were daily driven,
  So many kingdoms fitted up anew;
Each day too slew its thousands six or seven,
  Till at the crowning carnage, Waterloo,
They threw their pens down in divine disgust—
The page was so besmeared with blood and
  dust.

vi.

This by the way; 'tis not mine to record
  What angels shrink from: even the very
  devil
On this occasion his own work abhorred,
  So surfeited with the infernal revel:
Though he himself had sharpened every sword
  It almost quenched his innate thirst of evil.
(Here Satan's sole good work deserves inser-
  tion—
'Tis, that he has both generals in reversion.)

vii.

Let's skip a few short years of hollow peace,
  Which peopled earth no better, hell as wont,
And heaven none — they form the tyrant's
  lease,
  With nothing but new names subscribed
  upon't;
'Twill one day finish: meantime they increase,
  " With seven heads and ten horns," and all
  in front,
Like Saint John's foretold beast; but ours
  are born
Less formidable in the head than horn.

viii.

In the first year of freedom's second dawn [1]
  Died George the Third; although no tyrant,
  one
Who shielded tyrants, till each sense withdrawn
  Left him nor mental nor external sun:
A better farmer ne'er brushed dew from lawn,
  A worse king never left a realm undone!
He died — but left his subjects still behind,
One half as mad — and t'other no less blind.

ix.

He died! — his death made no great stir on
  earth;
  His burial made some pomp; there was
  profusion
Of velvet, gilding, brass, and no great dearth

---

[1] [George III. died the 29th of January, 1820, —
a year in which the revolutionary spirit broke out
all over the south of Europe.]

Of aught but tears — save those shed by
  collusion.
For these things may be bought at their true
  worth;
  Of elegy there was the due infusion —
Bought also; and the torches, cloaks, and
  banners,
Heralds, and relics of old Gothic manners,

x.

Formed a sepulchral melodrame. Of all
  The fools who flocked to swell or see the
  show,
Who cared about the corpse? The funeral
  Made the attraction, and the black the woe.
There throbbed not there a thought which
  pierced the pall;
  And when the gorgeous coffin was laid low,
It seemed the mockery of hell to fold
The rottenness of eighty years in gold.

xi.

So mix his body with the dust! It might
  Return to what it *must* far sooner, were
The natural compound left alone to fight
  Its way back into earth, and fire, and air;
But the unnatural balsams merely blight
  What nature made him at his birth, as bare
As the mere million's base unmummied clay —
Yet all his spices but prolong decay.

xii.

He's dead — and upper earth with him has
  done;
  He's buried; save the undertaker's bill,
Or lapidary scrawl, the world is gone
  For him, unless he left a German will;
But where's the proctor who will ask his son?
  In whom his qualities are reigning still,
Except that household virtue, most uncom-
  mon,
Of constancy to a bad, ugly woman.

xiii.

" God save the king! " It is a large economy
  In God to save the like; but if he will
Be saving, all the better; for not one am I
  Of those who think damnation better still:
I hardly know too if not quite alone am I
  In this small hope of bettering future ill
By circumscribing, with some slight restriction,
The eternity of hell's hot jurisdiction.

xiv.

I know this is unpopular; I know
  'Tis blasphemous; I know one may be
  damned
For hoping no one else may e'er be so;
  I know my catechism, I know we are
  crammed
With the best doctrines till we quite o'erflow;

I know that all save England's church have
  shammed,
And that the other twice two hundred churches
And synagogues have made a *damned* bad
  purchase.

XV.

God help us all! God help me too! I am,
  God knows, as helpless as the devil can
  wish,
And not a whit more difficult to damn
  Than is to bring to land a late-hooked fish,
Or to the butcher to purvey the lamb;
  Not that I'm fit for such a noble dish
As one day will be that immortal fry
Of almost everybody born to die.

XVI.

Saint Peter sat by the celestial gate,
  And nodded o'er his keys; when, lo! there
  came
A wondrous noise he had not heard of late —
  A rushing sound of wind, and stream, and
  flame;
In short, a roar of things extremely great,
  Which would have made aught save a saint
  exclaim;
But he, with first a start and then a wink,
Said, "There's another star gone out, I think!"

XVII.

But ere he could return to his repose,
  A cherub flapped his right wing o'er his
  eyes —
At which Saint Peter yawned, and rubbed his
  nose:
  "Saint porter," said the angel, "prithee
  rise!"
Waving a goodly wing, which glowed, as
  glows
  An earthly peacock's tail, with heavenly
  dyes:
To which the saint replied, "Well, what's the
  matter?
"Is Lucifer come back with all this clatter?"

XVIII.

"No," quoth the cherub; "George the Third
  is dead."
  "And who *is* George the Third?" replied
  the apostle:
"*What George? what Third?*" "The king
  of England," said
  The angel. "Well! he won't find kings to
  jostle
Him on his way; but does he wear his head?
  Because the last we saw here had a tussle,
And ne'er would have got into heaven's good
  graces,
Had he not flung his head in all our faces.

XIX.

"He was, if I remember, king of France;[1]
  That head of his, which could not keep a
  crown
On earth, yet ventured in my face to advance
  A claim to those of martyrs — like my own:
If I had had my sword, as I had once
  When I cut ears off, I had cut him down;
But having but my *keys*, and not my brand,
I only knocked his head from out his hand.

XX.

"And then he set up such a headless howl,
  That all the saints came out and took him in;
And there he sits by St. Paul, cheek by jowl;
  That fellow Paul — the parvenù! The skin
Of Saint Bartholomew, which makes his cowl
  In heaven, and upon earth redeemed his sin
So as to make a martyr, never sped
Better than did this weak and wooden head.

XXI.

"But had it come up here upon its shoulders
  There would have been a different tale to
  tell:
The fellow-feeling in the saints beholders
  Seems to have acted on them like a spell;
And so this very foolish head heaven solders
  Back on its trunk: it may be very well,
And seems the custom here to overthrow
Whatever has been wisely done below."

XXII.

The angel answered, "Peter! do not pout:
  The king who comes has head and all entire,
And never knew much what it was about —
  He did as doth the puppet — by its wire,
And will be judged like all the rest, no doubt:
  My business and your own is not to inquire
Into such matters, but to mind our cue —
Which is to act as we are bid to do."

XXIII.

While thus they spake, the angelic caravan,
  Arriving like a rush of mighty wind,
Cleaving the fields of space, as doth the swan
  Some silver stream (say Ganges, Nile, or
  Inde,
Or Thames, or Tweed), and 'midst them an
  old man
  With an old soul, and both extremely blind,
Halted before the gate, and in his shroud
Seated their fellow-traveller on a cloud.

XXIV.

But bringing up the rear of this bright host
  A Spirit of a different aspect waved
His wings, like thunder-clouds above some
  coast

---

[1] [Louis XVI., guillotined in January, 1793.]

Whose barren beach with frequent wrecks is
    paved;
His brow was like the deep when tempest-
    tossed;
Fierce and unfathomable thoughts engraved
Eternal wrath on his immortal face,
And *where* he gazed a gloom pervaded space.

XXV.

As he drew near, he gazed upon the gate
    Ne'er to be entered more by him or sin,
With such a glance of supernatural hate,
    As made Saint Peter wish himself within;
He pattered with his keys at a great rate,
    And sweated through his apostolic skin:
Of course his perspiration was but ichor,
Or some such other spiritual liquor.

XXVI.

The very cherubs huddled all together,
    Like birds when soars the falcon; and they
      felt
A tingling to the tip of every feather,
    And formed a circle like Orion's belt
Around their poor old charge; who scarce
      knew whither
    His guards had led him, though they gently
      dealt
With royal manes (for by many stories,
And true, we learn the angels all are Tories).

XXVII.

As things were in this posture, the gate flew
    Asunder, and the flashing of its hinges
Flung over space an universal hue
    Of many-colored flame, until its tinges
Reached even our speck of earth, and made a
      new
    Aurora borealis spread its fringes
O'er the North Pole; the same seen, when ice-
      bound,
By Captain Parry's crew, in Melville's
    Sound."[1]

XXVIII.

And from the gate thrown open issued beam-
    ing
A beautiful and mighty Thing of Light,
Radiant with glory, like a banner streaming
    Victorious from some world-o'erthrowing
      fight:
My poor comparisons must needs be teeming

[1] ["I believe it is almost impossible for words to
give an idea of the beauty and variety which this
magnificent phenomenon displayed. The luminous
arch had broken into irregular masses, streaming
with much rapidity in different directions, varying
continually in shape and interest, and extending
themselves from north, by the east, to north. The
usual pale light of the aurora strongly resembled
that produced by the combustion of phosphorus; a
very slight tinge of red was noticed on this occasion,
when the aurora was most vivid, but no other colors
were visible." — *Parry's Voyage in* 1819-20.]

With earthly likenesses, for here the night
Of clay obscures our best conceptions, saving,
Johanna Southcote,[2] or Bob Southey raving.

XXIX.

'Twas the archangel Michael: all men know
    The make of angels and archangels, since
There's scarce a scribbler has not one to
    show,
    From the fiends' leader to the angels' prince.
There also are some altar-pieces, though
    I really can't say that they much evince
One's inner notions of immortal spirits;
But let the connoisseurs explain *their* merits.

XXX.

Michael flew forth in glory and in good;
    A goodly work of him from whom all glory
And good arise; the portal past — he stood;
    Before him the young cherubs and saints
      hoary —
(I say *young*, begging to be understood
    By looks, not years; and should be very
     sorry
To state, they were not older than St. Peter,
But merely that they seemed a little sweeter).

XXXI.

The cherubs and the saints bowed down be-
    fore
That arch-angelic hierarch, the first
Of essences angelical, who wore
    The aspect of a god; but this ne'er nursed
Pride in his heavenly bosom, in whose core
    No thought, save for his Maker's service,
     durst
Intrude, however glorified and high;
He knew him but the Viceroy of the sky.

XXXII.

He and the sombre silent Spirit met —
    They knew each other both for good and
     ill;
Such was their power, that neither could forget
    His former friend and future foe; but still
There was a high, immortal, proud regret
    In either's eye, as if 'twere less their will
Than destiny to make the eternal years
Their date of war, and their " champ clos " the
    spheres.

XXXIII.

But here they were in neutral space: we know
    From Job that Satan hath the power to pay
A heavenly visit thrice a year or so;
    And that " the sons of God," like those of
     clay,
Must keep him company; and we might show

[2] [Johanna Southcote, the aged lunatic, who fan-
cied herself, and was believed by many followers
to be with child of a new Messiah, died in 1815.]

From the same book, in how polite a way
The dialogue is held between the Powers
Of Good and Evil — but 'twould take up hours.

XXXIV.

And this is not a theologic tract,
    To prove with Hebrew and with Arabic
If Job be allegory or a fact,
    But a true narrative; and thus I pick
From out the whole but such and such an act
    As sets aside the slightest thought of trick.
'Tis every tittle true, beyond suspicion,
And accurate as any other vision.

XXXV.

The spirits were in neutral space, before
    The gate of heaven; like eastern thresholds
        is
The place where Death's grand cause is argued
        o'er,
    And souls despatch to that world or to this;
And therefore Michael and the other wore
    A civil aspect: though they did not kiss,
Yet still between his Darkness and his Bright-
        ness
There passed a mutual glance of great polite-
        ness.

XXXVI.

The Archangel bowed, not like a modern beau,
    'But with a graceful oriental bend,
Pressing one radiant arm just where below
    The heart in good men is supposed to tend.
He turned as to an equal, not too low,
    But kindly; Satan met his ancient friend
With more hauteur, as might an old Castilian
Poor noble meet a mushroom rich civilian.

XXXVII.

He merely bent his diabolic brow
    An instant; and then raising it, he stood
In act to assert his right or wrong, and show
    Cause why King George by no means could
        or should
Make out a case to be exempt from woe
    Eternal, more than other kings, endued
With better sense and hearts, whom history
        mentions,
Who long have "paved hell with their good
        intentions."

XXXVIII.

Michael began: "What wouldst thou with
        this man,
    Now dead, and brought before the Lord?
        What ill
Hath he wrought since his mortal race began,
    That thou canst claim him? Speak! and
        do thy will,
If it be just: if in this earthly span
    He hath been greatly failing to fulfil
His duties as a king and mortal, say,
And he is thine; if not, let him have way"

XXXIX.

"Michael!" replied the Prince of Air, "even
        here
    Before the gate of him thou servest, must
I claim my subject: and will make appear
    That as he was my worshipper in dust,
So shall he be in spirit, although dear
    To thee and thine, because nor wine nor
        lust
Were of his weaknesses; yet on the throne
He reigned o'er millions to serve me alone.

XL.

"Look to *our* earth, or rather *mine*; it was,
    Once, more thy master's: but I triumph not
In this poor planet's conquest: nor, alas!
    Need he thou servest envy me my lot:
With all the myriads of bright worlds which
        pass
    In worship round him, he may have forgot
Yon weak creation of such paltry things:
I think few worth damnation save their
        kings, —

XLI.

"And these but as a kind of quit-rent, to
    Assert my right as lord; and even had
I such an inclination, 'twere (as you
    Well know) superfluous: they are grown
        so bad,
That hell has nothing better left to do
    Than leave them to themselves: so much
        more mad
And evil by their own internal curse,
Heaven cannot make them better, nor I worse.

XLII.

"Look to the earth, I said, and say again:
    When this old, blind, mad, helpless, weak,
        poor worm
Began in youth's first bloom and flush to reign,
    The world and he both wore a different form,
And much of earth and all the watery plain
    Of ocean called him king: through many a
        storm
His isles had floated on the abyss of time;
For the rough virtues chose them for their
        clime.

XLIII.

"He came to his sceptre young; he leaves it
        old:
    Look to the state in which he found his
        realm,
And left it; and his annals too behold,
    How to a minion first he gave the helm;
How grew upon his heart a thirst for gold,
    The beggar's vice, which can but over-
        whelm
The meanest hearts; and for the rest, but
        glance
Thine eye long America and France.

XLIV.

" 'Tis true, he was a tool from first to last
  (I have the workmen safe) ; but as a tool
So let him be consumed. From out the past
  Of ages, since mankind have known the rule
Of monarchs — from the bloody rolls amassed
  Of sin and slaughter — from the Cæsars'
    school,
Take the worst pupil ; and produce a reign
More drenched with gore, more cumbered
    with the slain.

XLV.

" He ever warred with freedom and the free :
  Nations as men, home subjects, foreign foes,
So that they uttered the word ' Liberty ! '
  Found George the Third their first opponent.
    Whose
History was ever stained as his will be
  With national and individual woes ?
I grant his household abstinence ; I grant
His neutral virtues, which most monarchs
    want ;

XLVI.

" I know he was a constant consort ; own
  He was a decent sire, and middling lord.
All this is much, and most upon a throne ;
  As temperance, if at Apicius' board,
Is more than at an anchorite's supper shown.
  I grant him all the kindest can accord ;
And this was well for him, but not for those
Millions who found him what oppression
    chose.

XLVII.

" The New World shook him off ; the Old
    yet groans
  Beneath what he and his prepared, if not
Completed : he leaves heirs on many thrones
  To all his vices, without what begot
Compassion for him — his tame virtues ;
    drones
  Who sleep, or despots who have now forgot
A lesson which shall be re-taught them, wake
Upon the thrones of earth ; but let them quake !

XLVIII.

" Five millions of the primitive, who hold
  The faith which makes ye great on earth,
    implored
A *part* of that vast *all* they held of old, —
  Freedom to worship — not alone your Lord,
Michael, but you, and you, Saint Peter ! Cold
  Must be your souls, if you have not abhorred
The foe to catholic participation
In all the license of a Christian nation.

XLIX.

" True ! he allowed them to pray God ; but as
  A consequence of prayer, refused the law
Which would have placed them upon the
    same base

With those who did not hold the saints in
    awe."
But here Saint Peter started from his place,
  And cried, " You may the prisoner with-
    draw :
Ere heaven shall ope her portals to this Guelph,
While I am guard, may I be damned myself !

L.

" Sooner will I with Cerberus exchange
  My office (and *his* is no sinecure)
Than see this royal Bedlam bigot range
  The azure fields of heaven, of that be sure !
" Saint ! " replied Satan, " you do well to
    avenge
  The wrongs he made your satellites endure ; [1]
And if to this exchange you should be given,
I'll try to coax *our* Cerberus up to heaven."

LI.

Here Michael interposed : " Good saint ! and
    devil !
  Pray, not so fast ; you both outrun discretion.
Saint Peter ! you were wont to be more civil :
  Satan ! excuse this warmth of his expression,
And condescension to the vulgar's level :
  Even saints sometimes forget themselves in
    session.
Have you got more to say ? " — " No." — " If
    you please,
I'll trouble you to call your witnesses." .

LII.

Then Satan turned and waved his swarthy
    hand,
  Which stirred with its electric qualities
Clouds further off than we can understand,
  Although we find him sometimes in our
    skies ;
Infernal thunder shook both sea and land
  In all the planets, and hell's batteries
Let off the artillery, which Milton mentions
As one of Satan's most sublime inventions.

LIII.

This was a signal unto such damned souls
  As have the privilege of their damnation
Extended far beyond the mere controls
  Of worlds past, present, or to come ; no
    station
Is theirs particularly in the rolls
  Of hell assigned ; but where their inclination
Or business carries them in search of game,
They may range freely — being damned the
    same.

LIV.

They are proud of this — as very well they may,
  It being a sort of knighthood, or gilt key

---

[1] [George III.'s opposition to the Catholic claims.]

Stuck in their loins;[1] or like to an " entré "
Up the back stairs, or such free-masonry.
I borrow my comparisons from clay,
Being clay myself. Let not those spirits be
Offended with such base low likenesses;
We know their posts are nobler far than these.

LV.

When the great signal ran from heaven to
hell —
About ten million times the distance reck-
oned
From our sun to its earth, as we can tell
How much time it takes up, even to a second,
For every ray that travels to dispel
The fogs of London, through which, dimly
beaconed,
The weathercocks are gilt some thrice a year,
If that the *summer* is not too severe : — [2]

LVI.

I say that I can tell — 'twas half a minute :
I know the solar beams take up more time
Ere, packed up for their journey, they begin it;
But then their telegraph is less sublime,
And if they ran a race, they would not win it
'Gainst Satan's couriers bound for their own
clime.
The sun takes up some years for every ray
To reach its goal — the devil not half a day.

LVII.

Upon the verge of space, about the size
Of half-a-crown, a little speck appeared
(I've seen a something like it in the skies
In the Ægean, ere a squall) ; it neared
And growing bigger, took another guise;
Like an aërial ship it tacked, and steered,
Or *was* steered (I am doubtful of the grammar
Of the last phrase, which makes the stanza
stammer; —

LVIII.

But take your choice) ; and then it grew a
cloud;
And so it was — a cloud of witnesses.
But such a cloud! No land e'er saw a crowd
Of locusts numerous as the heavens saw
these;
They shadowed with their myriads space;
their loud
And varied cries were like those of wild geese
(If nations may be likened to a goose),
And realized the phrase of " hell broke loose. "

LIX.

Here crashed a sturdy oath of stout John Bull,
Who damned away his eyes as heretofore :

---

[1] [A gold or gilt key, peeping from below the
skirts of the coat, marks a lord chamberlain.]
[2] [An allusion to Horace Walpole's expression
in a letter — " the summer has set in with *its usual
severity.*"]

There Paddy brogued " By Jasus ! "—
" What's your wull ? "
The temperate Scot exclaimed : the French
ghost swore
In certain terms I sha'n't translate in full,
As the first coachman will; and 'midst the
war,
The voice of Jonathan was heard to express,
" *Our* president is going to war, I guess. "

LX.

Besides there were the Spaniard, Dutch, and
Dane;
In short, an universal shoal of shades,
From Otaheite's isle to Salisbury Plain,
Of all climes and professions, years and
trades,
Ready to swear against the good king's reign,
Bitter as clubs in cards are against spades :
All summoned by this grand "subpœna," to
Try if kings mayn't be damned like me or you.

LXI.

When Michael saw this host, he first grew pale,
As angels can; next, like Italian twilight,
He turned all colors — as a peacock's tail,
Or sunset streaming through a Gothic sky-
light
In some old abbey, or a trout not stale,
Or distant lightning on the horizon *by* night,
Or a fresh rainbow, or a grand review
Of thirty regiments in red, green, and blue.

LXII.

Then he addressed himself to Satan : " Why —
My good old friend, for such I deem you,
though
Our different parties make us fight so shy,
I ne'er mistake you for a *personal* foe;
Our difference is *political*, and I
Trust that, whatever may occur below,
You know my great respect for you : and this
Makes me regret whate'er you do amiss —

LXIII.

" Why, my dear Lucifer, would you abuse
My call for witnesses ? I did not mean
That you should half of earth and hell produce ;
'Tis even superfluous, since two honest,
clean,
True testimonies are enough : we lose
Our time, nay, our eternity, between
The accusation and defence : if we
Hear both, 'twill stretch our immortality. "

LXIV.

Satan replied, " To me the matter is
Indifferent, in a personal point of view :
I can have fifty better souls than this
With far less trouble than we have gone
through
Already; and I merely argued his

Late majesty of Britain's case with you
Upon a point of form: you may dispose
Of him; I've kings enough below, God
knows!"

LXV.

Thus spoke the Demon (late called "multi-
faced"
By multo-scribbling Southey). " Then we'll
call
One or two persons of the myriads placed
Around our congress, and dispense with all
The rest," quoth Michael: " Who may be so
graced
As to speak first? there's choice enough—
who shall
It be?" Then Satan answered, "There are
many;
But you may choose Jack Wilkes as well as
any."

LXVI.

A merry, cock-eyed, curious looking sprite
Upon the instant started from the throng,
Dressed in a fashion now forgotten quite;
For all the fashions of the flesh stick long
By people in the next world; where unite
All the costumes since Adam's, right or
wrong,
From Eve's fig-leaf down to the petticoat,
Almost as scanty, of days less remote.

LXVII.

The spirit looked around upon the crowds
Assembled, and exclaimed, " My friends of
all
The spheres, we shall catch cold amongst these
clouds;
So let's to business: why this general call?
If those are freeholders I see in shrouds,
And 'tis for an election that they bawl,
Behold a candidate with unturned coat!
Saint Peter, may I count upon your vote?"

LXVIII.

"Sir," replied Michael, "you mistake; these
things
Are of a former life, and what we do
Above is more august; to judge of kings
Is the tribunal met: so now you know."
"Then I presume those gentlemen with
wings,"
Said Wilkes, "are cherubs; and that soul
below
Looks much like George the Third, but to my
mind
A good deal older — Bless me! is he blind?"

LXIX.

" He is what you behold him, and his doom
Depends upon his deeds," the Angel said.
" If you have aught to arraign in him, the tomb

Gives license to the humblest beggar's head
To lift itself against the loftiest."--"Some,"
Said Wilkes, " don't wait to see them laid in
lead,
For such a liberty — and I, for one,
Have told them what I thought beneath the
sun."

LXX.

" *Above* the sun repeat, then, what thou hast
To urge against him," said the Archangel.
" Why,"
Replied the spirit, " since old scores are past,
Must I turn evidence? In faith, not I.
Besides, I beat him hollow at the last,
With all his Lords and Commons : in the sky
I don't like ripping up old stories, since
His conduct was but natural in a prince.

LXXI.

" Foolish, no doubt, and wicked, to oppress
A poor unlucky devil without a shilling;
But then I blame the man himself much less
Than Bute and Grafton, and shall be un-
willing
To see him punished here for their excess,
Since they were both damned long ago, and
still in
Their place below : for me, I have forgiven,
And vote his ' habeas corpus' into heaven."

LXXII.

" Wilkes," said the Devil, " I understand all
this;
You turned to half a courtier ere you died,[1]
And seem to think it would not be amiss
To grow a whole one on the other side
Of Charon's ferry; you forget that *his*
Reign is concluded; whatsoe'er betide,
He won't be sovereign more : you've lost your
labor,
For at the best he will but be your neighbor.

LXXIII.

" However, I knew what to think of it,
When I beheld you in your jesting way
Flitting and whispering round about the spit
Where Belial, upon duty for the day,
With Fox's lard was basting William Pitt,
His pupil; I knew what to think, I say:
That fellow even in hell breathes further ills;
I'll have him *gagged* — 'twas one of his own
bills.

LXXIV.

" Call Junius!" From the crowd a shadow
stalked,
And at the name there was a general squeeze,

---

[1] [For the political history of John Wilkes, who
died chamberlain of the city of London, we must
refer to any history of the reign of George III.
His profligate personal character is abundantly dis

So that the very ghosts no longer walked
  In comfort, at their own aërial ease,
But were all rammed, and jammed (but to be
    balked,
  As we shall see), and jostled hands and
    knees,
Like wind compressed and pent within a blad-
    der,
Or like a human colic, which is sadder.

LXXV.

The shadow came — a tall, thin, gray-haired
    figure,
  That looked as it had been a shade on earth;
Quick in its motions, with an air of vigor,
  But nought to mark its breeding or its birth :
Now it waxed little, then again grew bigger,
  With now an air of gloom, or savage mirth;
But as you gazed upon its features, they
Changed every instant — to *what*, none could
  say.

LXXVI.

The more intently the ghosts gazed, the less
  Could they distinguish whose the features
    were ;
The Devil himself seemed puzzled even to
    guess ;
  They varied like a dream — now here, now
    there ;
And several people swore from out the press,
  They knew him perfectly ; and one could
    swear
He was his father : upon which another
Was sure he was his mother's cousin's brother :

LXXVII.

Another, that he was a duke, or knight,
  An orator, a lawyer, or a priest,
A nabob, a man-midwife ; [1] but the wight
  Mysterious changed his countenance at least
As oft as they their minds : though in full sight
  He stood, the puzzle only was increased ;
The man was a phantasmagoria in
Himself — he was so volatile and thin. [2]

LXXVIII.

The moment that you had pronounced him
    one,
  Presto ! his face changed, and he was
    another ;
And when that change was hardly well put on,
  It varied, till I don't think his own mother

(If that he had a mother) would her son
  Have known, he shifted so from one to
    t'other ;
Till guessing from a pleasure grew a task,
At this epistolary " Iron Mask." [3]

LXXIX.

For sometimes he like Cerberus would seem —
  " Three gentlemen at once " (as sagely says
Good Mrs. Malaprop) ; then you might deem
  That he was not even *one;* now many rays
Were flashing round him ; and now a thick
    steam
  Hid him from sight—like fogs on London
    days.
Now Burke, now Tooke, he grew to people's
    fancies,
And certes often like Sir Philip Francis. [4]

LXXX.

I've an hypothesis — 'tis quite my own ;
  I never let it out till now, for fear
Of doing people harm about the throne,
  And injuring some minister or peer,
On whom the stigma might perhaps be blown :
  It is — my gentle public, lend thine ear !
'Tis, that what Junius we are wont to call
Was *really, truly,* nobody at all.

LXXXI.

I don't see wherefore letters should not be
  Written without hands, since we daily view
Them written without heads ; and books, we
    see,
  Are filled as well without the latter too :
And really till we fix on somebody
  For certain sure to claim them as his due,
Their author, like the Niger's mouth, will
    bother
The world to say if *there* be mouth or author.

LXXXII.

" And who and what art thou ? " the Archangel
    said.
  " For *that* you may consult my title-page,"
Replied this mighty shadow of a shade :
  " If I have kept my secret half an age,
I scarce shall tell it now." — " Canst thou up
    braid,"

---

[1] [Among the various persons to whom the letters
of Junius have been attributed we find the Duke of
Portland, Lord George Sackville, Sir Philip Francis,
Mr. Burke, Mr. Dunning, the Rev. John Horne
Tooke, Mr. Hugh Boyd, Dr. Wilmot, etc.]

[2] [" I don't know what to think. Why should
Junius be dead? If suddenly apoplexed, would he

rest in his grave without sending his εἰδωλον to
shout in the ears of posterity, ' Junius was X. Y. Z.,
Esq. buried in the parish of * * * * *.' Repair his
monument, ye churchwardens ! Print a new edition
of his Letters, ye booksellers ! Impossible, — the
man *must be alive,* and will never die without the
disclosure. I like him ; — he was a good hater." —
Byron's Diary, Nov. 23, 1813.]

[3] [The mystery of " l'homme au masque de fer,"
the everlasting puzzle of the last century, has in the
opinion of some, been cleared up, by a French work
published in 1825, and which formed the basis of
an entertaining one in English by Lord Dover.]

[4] [That the work entitled " The Identity of Junius
with a distinguished Living Character established "

---

played in the collection of his letters, published by
his daughter ! since his death.]

Continued Michael, " George Rex, or allege
Aught further ? " Junius answered, " You had
better
First ask him for *his* answer to my letter:

LXXXIII.

" My charges upon record will outlast
 The brass of both his epitaph and tomb."
" Repent'st thou not," said Michael, " of some
 past
Exaggeration ? something which may doom
Thyself if false, as him if true ? Thou wast
Too bitter — is it not so ? — in thy gloom
Of passion ? " — " Passion ! " ·cried the phan-
 tom dim,
" I loved my country, and I hated him.

LXXXIV.

" What I have written, I have written ; let
 The rest be on his head or mine ! " So spoke
Old " Nominis Umbra ; " [1] and while speaking
 yet,
Away he melted in a celestial smoke.
Then Satan said to Michael, " Don't forget
 To call George Washington, and John
 Horne Tooke,
And Franklin ; " — but at this time there was
 heard
A cry for room, though not a phantom stirred.

LXXXV.

At length with jostling, elbowing, and the aid
 Of cherubim appointed to that post,
The devil Asmodeus to the circle made
 His way, and looked as if his journey cost
Some trouble. When his burden down he laid,
 " What's this ? " cried Michael ; " why, 'tis
 not a ghost ? "
" I know it," quoth the incubus ; " but he
Shall be one, if you leave the affair to me.

LXXXVI.

" Confound the renegado ! I have sprained
 My left wing, he's so heavy ; one would think
Some of his works about his neck were
 chained.
 But to the point ; while hovering o'er the
 brink
Of Skiddaw [2] (where as usual it still rained),
 I saw a taper, far below me, wink,

---

proves Sir Philip Francis to be Junius, we will not
affirm ; but this we can safely assert, that it accu-
mulates such a mass of circumstantial evidence, as
renders it extremely difficult to believe he is not,
and that, if so many coincidences shall be found to
have misled us in this case, our faith in all conclu-
sions drawn from proofs of a similar kind may
henceforth be shaken. — *Mackintosh.*]
 [1] [The well known motto of Junius is, " *stat
nominis umbra.*"]
 [2] [Southey's residence was on the shore of Der-
wentwater, near the mountain Skiddaw.]

And stooping, caught this fellow at a libel —
No less on history than the Holy Bible. ·

LXXXVII.

" The former is the devil's scripture, and
 The latter yours, good Michael ; so the affair
Belongs to all of us, you understand.
 I snatched him up just as you see him there,
And brought him off for sentence out of hand :
 I've scarcely been ten minutes in the air —
At least a quarter it can hardly be :
I dare say that his wife is still at tea."

LXXXVIII.

Here Satan said, " I know this man of old,
 And have expected him for some time here ;
A sillier fellow you will scarce behold,
 Or more conceited in his petty sphere :
But surely it was not worth while to fold
 Such trash below your wing, Asmodeus
 dear :
We had the poor wretch safe (without being
 bored
With carriage) coming of his own accord.

LXXXIX.

" But since he's here, let's see what he has
 done."
 " Done ! " cried Asmodeus, " he anticipates
The very business you are now upon,
 And scribbles as if head clerk to the Fates.
Who knows to what his ribaldry may run,
 When such an ass as this, like Balaam's,
 prates ? "
" Let's hear," quoth Michael, " what he has to
 say :
You know we're bound to that in every way."

XC.

Now the bard, glad to get an audience, which
 By no means often was his case below,
Began to cough, and hawk, and hem, and pitch
 His voice into that awful note of woe
To all unhappy hearers within reach
 Of poets when the tide of rhyme's in flow ;
But stuck fast with his first hexameter,
Not one of all whose gouty feet would stir.

XCI.

But ere the spavined dactyls could be spurred
 Into recitative, in great dismay
Both cherubim and seraphim were heard
 To murmur loudly through their long array ;
And Michael rose ere he could get a word
 Of all his foundered verses under way,
And cried, " For God's sake stop, my friend !
 'twere best —
Non Di, non homines — you know the rest." [3]

---

 [3] [Mediocribus esse poetis
Non Di, non homines, non concessere columnæ.
       Horace.]

XCII.

A general bustle spread throughout the throng,
  Which seemed to hold all verse in detesta-
    tion;
The angels had of course enough of song
  When upon service; and the generation
Of ghosts had heard too much in life, not long
  Before, to profit by a new occasion;
The monarch, mute till then, exclaimed,
    "What! what! [1]
Pye [2] come again? No more — no more of
    that!"

XCIII.

The tumult grew; an universal cough
  Convulsed the skies, as during a debate,
When Castlereagh has been up long enough
  (Before he was first minister of state,
I mean — the *slaves hear now*); some cried
    " Off, off!"
As at a farce; till, grown quite desperate,
The bard Saint Peter prayed to interpose
(Himself an author) only for his prose.

XCIV.

The varlet was not an ill-favored knave;
  A good deal like a vulture in the face,
With a hook nose and a hawk's eye, which
    gave
A smart and sharper-looking sort of grace
To his whole aspect, which, though rather
    grave,
  Was by no means so ugly as his case ;
But that indeed was hopeless as can be,
Quite a poetic felony " *de se.*"

XCV.

Then Michael blew his trump, and stilled
    the noise
  With one still greater, as is yet the mode
On earth besides; except some grumbling
    voice,
  Which now and then will make a slight in-
    road
Upon decorous silence, few will twice
  Lift up their lungs when fairly overcrowed;
And now the bard could plead his own bad
    cause,
With all the attitudes of self-applause.

XCVI.

He said — (I only give the heads) — he said,
  He meant no harm in scribbling; 'twas his
    way
Upon all topics; 'twas, besides, his bread,

Of which he buttered both sides; 'twould
    delay
Too long the assembly (he was pleased to
    dread),
  And take up rather more time than a day,
To name his works — he would but cite a
    few —
" Wat Tyler' —" Rhymes on Blenheim " —
  " Waterloo."

XCVII.

He had written praises of a regicide;
  He had written praises of all kings what-
    ever;
He had written for republics far and wide,
  And then against them bitterer than ever:
For pantisocracy he once had cried
  Aloud, a scheme less moral than 'twas
    clever;
Then grew a hearty anti-jacobin —
Had turned his coat — and would have
    turned his skin.

XCVIII.

He had sung against all battles, and again
  In their high praise and glory; he had
    called
Reviewing [3] " the ungentle craft," and then
  Become as base a critic as e'er crawled —
Fed, paid, and pampered by the very men
  By whom his muse and morals had been
    mauled :
He had written much blank verse, and blanker
    prose,
And more of both than anybody knows.[4]

XCIX.

He had written Wesley's life : — here turning
    round
To Satan, " Sir, I'm ready to write yours,
In two octavo volumes, nicely bound,
  With notes and preface, all that most
    allures
The pious purchaser; and there's no ground
  For fear, for I can choose my own re-
    viewers :

---

[1] [The king's trick of repeating his words in this
way was a fertile source of ridicule to Peter Pindar
(Dr. Wolcot).]

[2] [Henry James Pye, the predecessor of Southey
in the poet-laureateship, died in 1813. He was the
author of many works besides his official Odes,
among others " Alfred," an epic poem. Pye was

a man of good family in Berkshire, sat some time
in parliament, and was eminently respectable in
every thing but his poetry.]

[3] See " Life of Henry Kirke White."

[4] [This sarcasm about Southey's professional
authorship comes with a bad grace from a man
who, for several years, has been in the habit of re-
ceiving several thousand pounds per annum, all for
value received in Verse and Prose, from the mag-
nificent exchequer of Albemarle Street. What right
has Lord Byron to sneer at Southey as a " writer of
all work?" Has he not himself published, within
these two years, two volumes of tragic blank verse;
one volume of licentious *ottava rima ;* one pam-
phlet of clever polemical criticism, seasoned with
personalities against all sorts of men; besides writ-
ing an Armenian grammar? — *Blackwood,* 1822.]

So let me have the proper documents,
That I may add you to my other saints."

C.

Satan bowed, and was silent. " Well, if you,
  With amiable modesty, decline
My offer, what says Michael ? There are few
  Whose memoirs could be rendered more
    divine.
Mine is a pen of all work ; not so new
  As it was once, but I would make you shine
Like your own trumpet. By the way, my own
Has more of brass in it, and is as well blown.

CI.

" But talking about trumpets, here's my
    Vision !
  Now you shall judge, all people ; yes, you
    shall
Judge with my judgment, and by my decision
  Be guided who shall enter heaven or fall.
I settle all these things by intuition,
  Times present, past, to come, heaven, hell,
    and all,
Like King Alfonso.[1] When I thus see double,
I save the Deity some worlds of trouble."

CII.

He ceased, and drew forth an MS. ; and no
  Persuasion on the part of devils, or saints,
Or angels, now could stop the torrent ; so
  He read the first three lines of the contents ;
But at the fourth, the whole spiritual show
  Had vanished, with variety of scents,
Ambrosial and sulphureous, as they sprang,
Like lightning, off from his "melodious
    twang."[2]

CIII.

Those grand heroics acted as a spell ;
  The angels stopped their ears and plied
    their pinions ;
The devils ran howling, deafened, down to
    hell ;
  The ghosts fled, gibbering, for their own
    dominions —
(For 'tis not yet decided where they dwell,
  And I leave every man to his opinions) ;
Michael took refuge in his trump — but, lo !
His teeth were set on edge, he could not blow !

CIV.

Saint Peter, who has hitherto been known
  For an impetuous saint, upraised his keys,
And at the fifth line knocked the poet down ;
  Who fell like Phæton, but more at ease,
Into his lake, for there he did not drown ;
  A different web being by the Destinies
Woven for the Laureate's final wreath, when-
    e'er
Reform shall happen either here or there.

CV.

He first sank to the bottom — like his works,
  But soon rose to the surface — like himself ;
For all corrupted things are buoyed like corks,[3]
  By their own rottenness, light as an elf,
Or wisp that flits o'er a morass : he lurks,
  It may be, still, like dull books on a shelf,
In his own den, to scrawl some " Life " or
    " Vision,"[4]
As Welborn says — " the devil turned precis-
    ian."

CVI.

As for the rest, to come to the conclusion
  Of this true dream, the telescope is gone

---

[1] Alfonso, speaking of the Ptolomean system,
said, that " had he been consulted at the creation of
the world, he would have spared the Maker some
absurdities."

[2] See Aubrey's account of the apparition which
disappeared " with a curious perfume and a *most
melodious twang;*" or see the " *Antiquary,*"
vol. i. p. 225. — [" As the vision shut his. volume,
a strain of *delightful music* seemed to fill the apart-
ment." — " The usual time," says Grose, " at which
ghosts make their appearance is midnight, and sel-
dom before it is dark ; though some audacious spirits
have been said to appear even by day-light ; but of
this there are few instances, and those mostly ghosts
who had been laid, and whose terms of confinement
were expired. I cannot learn that ghosts carry
tapers in their hands, as they are sometimes de-
picted. Dragging chains is not the fashion of
English ghosts : chains and black vestments being
chiefly the accoutrements of foreign spectres seen
in arbitrary governments ; dead or alive, English
spirits are free. During the narration of its busi-
ness, a ghost must by no means be interrupted by
questions of any kind : its narration being com-
pleted, it vanishes away, frequently in a flash of
light ; in which case, some ghosts have been so
considerate as to desire the party to whom they
appeared to shut their eyes : — sometimes their depart-
ure is attended with *most delightful music.*" —
Provincial Glossary.]

[3] A drowned body lies at the bottom till rotten ;
it then floats, as most people know.

[4] [Southey's Vision of Judgment appears to us
to be an ill-judged, and not a well-executed work.
Milton alone has ever founded a fiction on the basis
of revelation, without degrading his subject ; but
Milton has been blamed by the most judicious
critics, and his warmest admirers, for expressing
the counsels of Eternal Wisdom, and the decrees of
Almighty Power, by words assigned to the Deity.
It is impossible to deceive ourselves into a momen-
tary and poetical belief that words proceeded from
the Holy Spirit, except on the warrant of inspira-
tion itself. It is here only that Milton fails, and
here Milton sometimes shocks. The blasphemies
of Milton's devils offend not a pious ear, because
they are devils who utter them. Nor are we dis-
pleased with the poet's presumption in feigning
language for heavenly spirits, because it is a lan-
guage that lifts the soul to heaven. The words are
human ; but the truths they express, and the doc-
trines they teach, are divine. — *Blackwood,* 1822.]

Which kept my optics free from all delusion,
And showed me what I in my turn have
  shown.
All I saw further, in the last confusion,

Was, that King George slipped into heaven
  for one;
And when the tumult dwindled to a calm,
I left him practising the hundredth psalm.

THE AGE OF BRONZE;

OR,

CARMEN SECULARE ET ANNUS HAUD MIRABILIS.

" Impar *Congressus* Achilli."

[This poem was written at Genoa, in the early part of the year 1823; and published in London, by Mr. John Hunt. Its authenticity was much disputed at the time.]

I.

THE "good old times "— all times when old
  are good —
Are gone; the present might be if they would;
Great things have been, and are, and greater
  still
Want little of mere mortals but their will:
A wider space, a greener field, is given
To those who play their "tricks before high
  heaven."
I know not if the angels weep, but men
Have wept enough — for what? — to weep
  again!

II.

All is exploded — be it good or bad.
Reader! remember when thou wert a lad,
Then Pitt was all; or, if not all, so much,
His very rival almost deemed him such.[1]
We, we have seen the intellectual race
Of giants stand, like Titans, face to face —
Athos and Ida, with a dashing sea
Of eloquence between, which flowed all free,
As the deep billows of the Ægean roar
Betwixt the Hellenic and the Phrygian shore.
But where are they — the rivals! — a few feet

Of sullen earth divide each winding sheet.[2]
How peaceful and how powerful is the grave
Which hushes all! a calm, unstormy wave
Which oversweeps the world.   The theme is
  old
Of " dust to dust; " but half its tale untold:
Time tempers not its terrors — still the worm
Winds its cold folds, the tomb preserves its
  form,
Varied above, but still alike below;
The urn may shine, the ashes will not glow,
Though Cleopatra's mummy cross the sea
O'er which from empire she lured Anthony;
Though Alexander's urn a show be grown
On shores he wept to conquer, though un-
  known —
How vain, how worse than vain, at length ap-
  pear
The madman's wish, the Macedonian's tear!
He wept for worlds to conquer — half the
  earth
Knows not his name, or but his death, and
  birth,
And desolation; while his native Greece
Hath all of desolation, save its peace.

---

[1] [Mr. Fox used to say — *I* never want *a* word, but Pitt never wants *the* word."]

[2] [The grave of Mr. Fox, in Westminster Abbey, is within eighteen inches of that of Mr. Pitt.]

He " wept for worlds to conquer!" he who
ne'er
Conceived the globe, he panted not to spare!
With even the busy Northern Isle unknown,
Which holds his urn, and never knew his
throne.[1]

III.

But,where is he, the modern, mightier far,
Who, born no king, made monarchs draw
his car;
The new Sesostris, whose unharnessed kings,[2]
Freed from the bit, believe themselves with
wings,
And spurn the dust o'er which they crawled
of late,
Chained to the chariot of the chieftain's state?
Yes! where is he, the champion and the child
Of all that's great or little, wise or wild?
Whose game was empires, and whose stakes
were thrones?
Whose table earth — whose dice were human
bones?
Behold the grand result in yon lone isle,[3]
And, as thy nature urges, weep or smile.
Sigh to behold the eagle's lofty rage
Reduced to nibble at his narrow cage;
Smile to survey the queller of the nations
Now daily squabbling o'er disputed rations;
Weep to perceive him mourning, as he dines,
O'er curtailed dishes and o'er stinted wines;
O'er petty quarrels upon petty things.
Is this the man who scourged or feasted kings?
Behold the scales in which his fortune hangs,
A surgeon's[4] statement, and an earl's[5] ha-
rangues!
A bust delayed,[6] a book refused, can shake
The sleep of him who kept the world awake.
Is this indeed the tamer of the great,
Now slave of all could tease or irritate —
The paltry gaoler[7] and the prying spy,
The staring stranger with his note-book nigh?[8]
Plunged in a dungeon, he had still been great;
How low, how little was this middle state,
Between a prison and a palace, where
How few could feel for what he had to bear!
Vain his complaint, — my lord presents his bill,
His food and wine were doled out duly still:

Vain was his sickness, never was a clime
So free from homicide — to doubt's a crime;
And the stiff surgeon, who maintained his
cause,
Hath lost his place, and gained the world's
applause,
But smile — though all the pangs of brain
and heart
Disdain, defy, the tardy aid of art;
Though, save the few fond friends and imaged
face
Of that fair boy his sire shall ne'er embrace,
None stand by his low bed — though even the
mind
Be wavering, which long awed and awes
mankind:
Smile — for the fettered eagle breaks his chain,
And higher worlds than this are his again.[9]

IV.

How, if that soaring spirit still retain
A conscious twilight of his blazing reign,
How must he smile, on looking down, to see
The little that he was and sought to be!
What though his name a wider empire found
Than his ambition, though with scarce a
bound;
Though first in glory, deepest in reverse,
He tasted empire's blessings and its curse;
Though kings rejoicing in their late escape
From chains, would gladly be *their* tyrant's ape;
How must he smile, and turn to yon lone
grave,
The proudest sea-mark that o'ertops the wave!
What though his gaoler, duteous to the last,
Scarce deemèd the coffin's lead could keep
him fast,
Refusing one poor line along the lid,
To date the birth and death of all it hid;
That name shall hallow the ignoble shore,
A talisman to all save him who bore:
The fleets that sweep before the eastern blast
Shall hear their sea-boys hail it from the mast;
When Victory's Gallic column shall but rise,
Like Pompey's pillar, in a desert's skies,
The rocky isle that holds or held his dust
Shall crown the Atlantic like the hero's bust,
And mighty nature o'er his obsequies
Do more than niggard envy still denies.
But what are these to him? Can glory's lust
Touch the freed spirit or the fettered dust?
Small care hath he of what his tomb consists;
Nought if he sleeps — nor more if he exists
Alike the better-seeing shade will smile
On the rude cavern of the rocky isle,
As if his ashes found their latest home
In Rome's Pantheon or Gaul's mimic dome.
He wants not this; but France shall feel the
want
Of this last consolation, though so scant;

[1] [The sarcophagus, of breccia, which is supposed to have contained the dust of Alexander, came into the possession of the English army, at the capitulation of Alexandria in 1802, and is now in the British Museum.]
[2] [Sesostris is said, by Diodorus, to have had his chariot drawn by eight vanquished sovereigns.]
[3] [St. Helena.]
[4] [Mr. Barry O'Meara.]
[5] [Earl Bathurst.]
[6] [The bust of his son.]
[7] [Sir Hudson Lowe.]
[8] [Captain Basil Hall's interesting account of his interview with the ex-emperor occurs in his "Voyage to Loo-choo."]
[9] [Buonaparte died the 5th of May, 1821.]

Her honor, fame, and faith demand his bones,
To rear above a pyramid of thrones;
Or carried onward in the battle's van,
To form, like Guesclin's [1] dust, her talisman.
But be it as it is — the time may come
His name shall beat the alarm, like Ziska's drum.[2]

V.

Oh heaven! of which he was in power a feature;
Oh Earth! of which he was a noble creature;
Thou isle! to be remembered long and well,
That saw'st the unfledged eaglet chip his shell!
Ye Alps, which viewed him in his dawning flights
Hover, the victor of a hundred fights!
Thou Rome, who saw'st thy Cæsar's deeds outdone!
Alas! why passed he too the Rubicon —
The Rubicon of man's awakened rights,
To herd with vulgar kings and parasites?
Egypt! from whose all dateless tombs arose
Forgotten Pharaohs from their long repose,
And shook within their pyramids to hear
A new Cambyses thundering in their ear;
While the dark shades of forty ages stood
Like startled giants by Nile's famous flood;
Or from the pyramid's tall pinnacle
Beheld the desert peopled, as from hell,
With clashing hosts, who strewed the barren sand
To re-manure the uncultivated land!
Spain! which, a moment mindless of the Cid,
Beheld his banner flouting thy Madrid!
Austria! which saw thy twice-ta'en capital
Twice spared to be the traitress of his fall!
Ye race of Frederic! — Frederics but in name
And falsehood — heirs to all except his fame;
Who, crushed at Jena, crouched at Berlin, fell
First, and but rose to follow! Ye who dwell
Where Kosciusko dwelt, remembering yet
The unpaid amount of Catherine's bloody debt!
Poland — o'er which the avenging angel past,
But left thee as he found thee, still a waste,
Forgetting all thy still enduring claim,
Thy lotted people and extinguished name,
Thy sigh for freedom, thy long-flowing tear,

That sound that crashes in the tyrant's ear—
Kosciusko! On — on — on — the thirst of war
Gasps for the gore of serfs and of their czar.
The half barbaric Moscow's minarets
Gleam in the sun, but 'tis a sun that sets!
Moscow! thou limit of his long career,
For which rude Charles had wept his frozen tear
To see in vain — *he* saw thee — how? with spire
And palace fuel to one common fire.
To this the soldier lent his kindling match,
To this the peasant gave his cottage thatch,
To this the merchant flung his hoarded store,
The prince his hall — and Moscow was no more!
Sublimest of volcanoes! Etna's flame
Pales before thine, and quenchless Hecla's tame;
Vesuvius shows his blaze, an usual sight
For gaping tourists, from his hackneyed height:
Thou stand'st alone unrivalled, till the fire
To come, in which all empires shall expire!

Thou other element! as strong and stern,
To teach a lesson conquerors will not learn! —
Whose icy wing flapped o'er the faltering foe,
Till fell a hero with each flake of snow;
How did thy numbing beak and silent fang
Pierce, till hosts perished with a single pang!
In vain shall Seine look up along his banks
For the gay thousands of his dashing ranks!
In vain shall France recall beneath her vines
Her youth — their blood flows faster than her wines;
Or stagnant in their human ice remains
In frozen mummies on the Polar plains.
In vain will Italy's broad sun awaken
Her offspring chilled; its beams are now forsaken.
Of all the trophies gathered from the war,
What shall return? — the conqueror's broken car!
The conqueror's yet unbroken heart! Again
The horn of Roland sounds, and not in vain,
Lutzen, where fell the Swede of victory,[3]
Beholds him conquer, but, alas! not die:
Dresden surveys three despots fly once more
Before their sovereign, — sovereign as before;
But there exhausted Fortune quits the field,
And Leipsic's treason bids the unvanquished yield;
The Saxon jackal leaves the lion's side
To turn the bear's, and wolf's, and fox's guide;
And backward to the den of his despair
The forest monarch shrinks, but finds no lair!

---

[1] [Guesclin, constable of France, died in the midst of his triumphs, before Châteauneuf de Randon, in 1380. The English garrison, which had conditioned to surrender at a certain time, marched out the day after his death; and the commander respectfully laid the keys of the fortress on the bier, so that it might appear to have surrendered to his ashes.]

[2] [John Ziska — a distinguished leader of the Hussites. It is recorded of him, that, in dying, he ordered his skin to be made the covering of a drum. The Bohemians hold his memory in superstitious veneration.]

[3] [Gustavus Adolphus fell at the great battle of Lutzen, in November, 1632.]

Oh ye! and each, and all! Oh France! who
found
Thy long fair fields, ploughed up as hostile
ground,
Disputed foot by foot, till treason, still
His only victor, from Montmartre's hill
Looked·d wn o'er trampled Paris! and thou
Isle,[1] 0
Which seest Etruria from thy ramparts smile,
Thou momentary shelter of his pride,
Till wooed by danger, his yet weeping bride!
Oh, France! retaken by a single march,
Whose path was through one long triumphal
arch!
Oh, bloody and most bootless Waterloo!
Which proves how fools may have their for-
tune too,
Won half by blunder, half by treachery:
Oh, dull Saint Helen! with thy gaoler nigh —
Hear! hear Prometheus[2] from his rock ap-
peal
To earth, air, ocean, all that felt or feel
His power and glory, all who yet shall hear
A name eternal as the rolling year;
He teaches them the lesson taught so long,
So oft, so vainly — learn to do no wrong!
A single step into the right had made
This man the Washington of worlds betrayed:
A single step into the wrong has given
His name a doubt to all the winds of
heaven;
The reed of Fortune, and of thrones the rod,
Of Fame the Moloch or the demigod;
His country's Cæsar, Europe's Hannibal,
Without their decent dignity of fall.
Yet Vanity herself had better taught
A surer path even to the fame he sought,
By pointing out on history's fruitless page
Ten thousand conquerors for a single sage.
While Franklin's quiet memory climbs to
heaven,
Calming the lightning which he thence hath
riven,
Or drawing from the no less kindled earth
Freedom and peace to that which boasts his
birth;[3]
While Washington's a watchword, such as
ne'er
Shall sink while there's an echo left to air:[4]

---

[1] [The Isle of Elba.]

[2] [I refer the reader to the first address of Prome-
theus in Æschylus, when he is left alone by his
attendants, and before the arrival of the Chorus of
Sea-nymphs.]

[3] [The celebrated motto on a French medal of
Franklin was —
" Eripuit cœlo fulmen, sceptrumque tyrannis."]

[4] [" To be the first man (*not* the Dictator), not
the Sylla, but the Washington, or Aristides, the
leader in talent and truth, is to be next to the Di-
vinity." — *Byron's Diary.*]

While even the Spaniard's thirst of gold and
war
Forgets Pizarro to shout Bolivar!·
Alas! why must the same Atlantic wave
Which wafted freedom gird a tyrant's grave —
The king of kings, and yet of slaves the slave,
Who bursts the chains of millions to renew
The very fetters which his arm broke through,
And crushed the rights of Europe and his
own,
To flit between a dungeon and a throne?

VI.

But 'twill not be — the spark's awakened —
lo!
The swarthy Spaniard feels his former glow;
The same high spirit which beat back the
Moor
Through eight long ages of alternate gore
Revives — and where? in that avenging clime
Where Spain was once synonymous with
crime,
Where Cortes' and Pizarro's banner flew,
The infant world redeems her name of *"New."*
'Tis the *old* aspiration breathed afresh,
To kindle souls within degraded flesh,
Such as repulsed the Persian from the shore
Where Greece *was* — No! she still is Greece
once more.   ·
One common cause makes myriads of one
breast,
Slaves of the east, or helots of the west;
On Andes' and on Athos' peaks unfurled,
The self-same standard streams o'er either
world;
The Athenian wears again Harmodius'
sword;[5]
The Chili chief abjures his foreign lord;
The Spartan knows himself once more a
Greek,
Young Freedom plumes the crest of each
cacique;
Debating despots, hemmed on either shore,
Shrink vainly from the roused Atlantic's roar;
Through Calpe's strait the rolling tides ad-
vance,
Sweep slightly by the half-tamed land of
France,
Dash o'er the old· Spaniard's cradle, and
would fain
Unite Ausonia to the mighty main:
But driven from thence awhile, yet not for aye,
Break o'er th' Ægean, mindful of the day
Of Salamis! — there, there the waves arise,
Not to be lulled by tyrant victories.

---

[5] [The famous hymn, ascribed to Callistratus: —
" Covered with myrtle-wreaths, I'll wear my sword
Like brave Harmodius, and his patriot friend
Aristogeiton, who the laws restored,
The tyrant slew, and bade oppression end,"
etc. etc.]

Lone, lost, abandoned in their utmost need
By Christians, unto whom they gave their
   creed.
The desolated lands, the ravaged isle,
The fostered feud encouraged to beguile,
The aid evaded, and the cold delay,
Prolonged but in the hope to make a prey; —
These, these shall tell the tale, and Greece can
   show
The false friend worse than the infuriate foe.
But this is well: Greeks only should free
   Greece,
Not the barbarian, with his mask of peace.
How should the autocrat of bondage be
The king of serfs, and set the nations free ?
Better still serve the haughty Mussulman,
Than swell the Cossaque's prowling caravan;
Better still toil for masters, than await,
The slave of slaves, before a Russian gate, —
Numbered by hordes, a human capital,
A live estate, existing but for thrall,
Lotted by thousands, as a meet reward
For the first courtier in the Czar's regard;
While their immediate owner never tastes
His sleep, *sans* dreaming of Siberia's wastes;
Better succumb even to their own despair,
And drive the camel than purvey the bear.

VII.

But not alone within the hoariest clime
Where Freedom dates her birth with that of
   Time,
And not alone where, plunged in night, a crown
Of Incas darkened to a dubious cloud,
The dawn revives : renowned, romantic Spain
Holds back the invader from her soil again.
Not now the Roman tribe nor Punic horde
Demand her fields as lists to prove the sword;
Not now the Vandal or the Visigoth
Pollute the plains, alike abhorring both;
Nor old Pelayo on his mountain rears
The warlike fathers of a thousand years.
That seed is sown and reaped, as oft the Moor
Sighs to remember on his dusky shore.
Long in the peasant's song or poet's page
Has dwelt the memory of Abencerrage;
The Zegri, and the captive victors, flung
Back to the barbarous realm from whence they
   sprung.
But these are gone — their faith, their swords,
   their sway,
Yet left more anti-christian foes than they:
The bigot monarch and the butcher priest,
The Inquisition, with her burning feast,
The faith's red "auto," fed with human fuel,
While sate the catholic Moloch, calmly cruel,
Enjoying, with inexorable eye,
That fiery festival of agony!
The stern or feeble sovereign, one or both
By turns; the haughtiness whose pride was
   sloth;
The long degenerate noble; the debased

Hidalgo, and the peasant less disgraced,
But more degraded; the unpeopled realm;
The once proud navy which forgot the helm;
The once impervious phalanx disarrayed;
The idle forge that formed Toledo's blade;
The foreign wealth that flowed on ev'ry shore,
Save hers who earned it with the natives' gore;
The very language which might vie with
   Rome's
And once was known to nations like their
   homes
Neglected or forgotten : — such was Spain;
But such she is not, nor shall be again.
These worst, these *home* invaders, felt and feel
The new Numantine soul of old Castile.
Up! up again! undaunted Tauridor!
The bull of Phalaris renews his roar;
Mount, chivalrous Hidalgo! not in vain
Revive the cry — " Iago! and close Spain! " [1]
Yes, close her with your armed bosoms round
And form the barrier which Napoleon found,
The exterminating war, the desert plain,
The streets without a tenant, save the slain;
The wild sierra, with its wilder troop
Of vulture-plumed guerrillas, on the stoop
For their incessant prey; the desperate wall
Of Saragossa, mightiest in her fall;
The man nerved to a spirit, and the maid
Waving her more than Amazonian blade;
The knife of Arragon,[2] Toledo's steel;
The famous lance of chivalrous Castile;
The unerring rifle of the Catalan;
The Andalusian courser in the van,
The torch to make a Moscow of Madrid;
And in each heart the spirit of the Cid : —
Such have been, such shall be, such are.
   Advance
And win — not Spain, but thine own freedom,
   France!

VIII.

But lo! a Congress! [3] What! that hallowed
   name
Which freed the Atlantic? May we hope the
   same
For outworn Europe? With the sound arise.
Like Samuel's shade to Saul's monarchic eyes,
The prophets of young Freedom, summoned
   far
From climes of Washington and Bolivar;
Henry, the forest-born Demosthenes,
Whose thunder shook the Philip of the seas;
And stoic Franklin's energetic shade,
Robed in the lightnings which his hand allayed;
And Washington, the tyrant-tamer, wake,

[1] [" Santiago, y serra España! " the old Spanish
war-cry.]

[2] The Arragonians are peculiarly dexterous in
the use of this weapon, and displayed it particularly
in former French wars.

[3] [The Congress of the Sovereigns of Russia, Aus-
tria, Prussia, etc. etc. etc., which assembled at Ve-
rona, in the autumn of 1822.]

To bid us blush for these old chains, or break.
But *who* compose this senate of the few
That should redeem the many ?   *Who* renew
This consecrated name, till now assigned
To councils held to benefit mankind ?
Who now assemble. at the holy call ?
The blest Alliance, which says three are all !
An earthly trinity ! which wears the shape
Of heaven's, as man is mimicked by the ape.
A pious unity ! in purpose one —
To melt three fools to a Napoleon.
Why, Egypt's gods were rational to these ;
Their dogs and oxen knew their own degrees,
And, quiet in their kennel or their shed,
Cared little, so that they were duly fed ;
But these, more hungry, must have something
    more,
The power to bark and bite, to toss and gore,
Ah ! how much happier were good Æsop's
    frogs
Than we ! for ours are animated logs,
With ponderous malice swaying to and fro,
And crushing nations with a stupid blow ;
All dully anxious to leave little work
Unto the revolutionary stork.

IX.

Thrice blest Verona ! since the holy three
With their imperial presence shine. on thee ;
Honored by them, thy treacherous site forgets
The vaunted tomb of " all the Capulets ; "[1]
Thy Scaligers — for what was " Dog the Great,"
" Can Grande,"[2] (which I venture to trans-
    late,)
To these sublimer pugs ?   Thy poet too,
Catullus, whose old laurels yield to new ;
Thine amphitheatre, where Romans sate ;
And Dante's exile sheltered by thy gate ;
Thy good old man, whose world was all within
Thy wall, nor knew the country held him in :[3]
Would that the royal guests it girds about
Were so far like, as never to get out !
Ay, shout !   inscribe !   rear monuments of
    shame,

---

[1] [" I have been over Verona.   The amphitheatre
is wonderful — beats even Greece.   Of the truth of
Juliet's story, they seem tenacious to a degree, insist-
ing on the fact — giving a date (1303), and showing
a tomb.   It is a plain, open, and partly decayed
sarcophagus, with withered leaves in it, in a wild
and desolate conventual garden, once a cemetery,
now ruined to the very graves.   The situation
struck me as very appropriate to the legend, being
blighted as their love.   I have brought away a few
pieces of the granite, to give to my daughter and
my nieces.   The Gothic monuments of the Scaliger
princess pleased me, but ' a poor virtuoso am I.' "
— *Byron's Letters*, Nov. 1816.]
[2] Cane I. Della Scala, surnamed the Great, died
in 1329: he was the protector of Dante, who cele-
brated him as " il Gran Lombardo."]
[3] [Claudian's famous old man of Verona, " qui
suburbium nunquam egressus est."]

To tell Oppression that the world is tame.
Crowd to the theatre with loyal rage,
The comedy is not upon the stage ;
The show is rich in ribandry and stars,
Then gaze upon it through thy dungeon bars ;
Clap thy permitted palms, kind Italy,
For thus much still thy fettered hands are free !

X.

Resplendent sight !   Behold the coxcomb
    Czar,[4]
The autocrat of waltzes and of war !
As eager for a plaudit as a realm,
And just as fit for flirting as the helm ;
A Calmuck beauty with a Cossack wit,
And generous spirit, when 'tis not frost-bit ;
Now half dissolving to a liberal thaw
But hardened back whene'er the morning's
    raw ;
With no objection to true liberty,
Except that it would make the nations free.
How well the imperial dandy prates of peace !
How fain, if Greeks would be his slaves, free
    Greece !
How nobly gave he back the Poles their Diet,
Then told pugnacious Poland to be quiet !
How kindly would he send the mild Ukraine,
With all her pleasant pulks, to lecture Spain !
How royally show off in proud Madrid
His goodly person, from the South long hid !
A blessing cheaply purchased, the world
    knows,
By having Muscovites for friends or foes.
Proceed, thou namesake of great Philips's son !
La Harpe, thine Aristotle, beckons on ;
And that which Scythia was to him of yore
Find with thy Scythians on Iberia's shore.
Yet think upon, thou somewhat aged youth,
Thy predecessor on the banks of Pruth ;
Thou hast to aid thee, should his lot be thine,
Many an old woman, but no Catherine.[5]
Spain, too, hath rocks, and rivers, and defiles —
The bear may rush into the lion's toils.
Fatal to Goths are Xeres' sunny fields ;
Think'st thou to thee Napoleon's victor yields ?
Better reclaim thy deserts, turn thy swords
To ploughshares, shave and wash thy Bashkir
    hordes,
Redeem thy realms from slavery and the knout,
Than follow headlong in the fatal route,
To infest the clime whose skies and laws are
    pure
With thy foul legions.   Spain wants no manure :
Her soil is fertile, but she feeds no foe ; ·
Her vultures, too, were gorged not long ago ;
And wouldst thou furnish them with fresher
    prey ?

---

[4] [The Emperor Alexander; who died in 1825.]
[5] The dexterity of Catherine extricated Peter
(called the Great by courtesy), when surrounded
by the Mussulmans on the banks of the river Pruth,

Alas! thou wilt not conquer, but purvey.
I am Diogenes, though Russ and Hun
Stand between mine and many a myriad's sun;
But were I not Diogenes, I'd wander
Rather a worm than *such* an Alexander!
Be slaves who will, the cynic shall be free;
His tub hath tougher walls than sinopè:
Still will he hold his lantern up to scan
The face of monarchs for an "honest man."

XI.

And what doth Gaul, the all-prolific land
Of *ne plus ultra* ultras and their band
Of mercenaries? and her noisy chambers
And tribune, which each orator first clambers
Before he finds a voice, and when 'tis found,
Hears "the lie" echo for his answer round?
Our British Commons sometimes deign to
     "hear!"
A Gallic senate hath more tongue than ear;
Even Constant, their sole master of debate,
Must fight next day his speech to vindicate.
But this costs little to true Franks, who had
     rather
Combat than listen, were it to their father.
What is the simple standing of a shot,
To listening long, and interrupting not?
Though this was not the method of old Rome,
When Tully fulmined o'er each vocal dome,
Demosthenes has sanctioned the transaction,
In saying eloquence meant "Action, action!"

XII.

But where's the monarch? hath he dined? or yet
Groans beneath indigestion's heavy debt?
Have revolutionary patés risen,
And turned the royal entrails to a prison?
Have discontented movements stirred the
     troops?
Or have *no* movements followed traitorous
     soups?
Have Carbonaro cooks not carbonadoed
Each course enough? or doctors dire dis-
     suaded
Repletion? Ah! in thy dejected looks
I read all France's treason in her cooks!
Good classic Louis! is it, canst thou say,
Desirable to be the "Desiré?"
Why wouldst thou leave calm Hartwell's
     green abode,[1]
Apician table, and Horatian ode,
To rule a people who will not be ruled,
And love much rather to be scourged than
     schooled?
Ah! thine was not the temper or the taste
For thrones; the table sees thee better placed:
A mild Epicurean, formed, at best,

To be a kind host and as good a guest,
To talk of letters, and to know by heart
One *half* the poet's, *all* the gourmand's art;
A scholar always, now and then a wit,
And gentle when digestion may permit; —
But not to govern lands enslaved or free;
The gout was martyrdom enough for thee.

XIII.

Shall noble Albion pass without a phrase
From a bold Briton in her wonted praise?
"Arts — arms — and George — and glory —
     and the isles —
And happy Britain — wealth — and Freedom's
     smiles —
White cliffs, that held invasion far aloof —
Contented subjects, all alike tax-proof —
Proud Wellington, with eagle beak so curled,
That nose, the hook where he suspends the
     world![2]
And Waterloo — and trade — and —— (hush!
     not yet
A syllable of imposts or of debt) ——
And ne'er (enough) lamented Castlereagh,
Whose penknife slit a goose-quill t'other day —
And 'pilots who have weathered every
     storm'—[3]
(But, no, not even for rhyme's sake, name
     Reform)."
These are the themes thus sung so oft before,
Methinks we need not sing them any more;
Found in so many volumes far and near,
There's no occasion you should find them
     here.
Yet something may remain perchance to
     chime
With reason, and, what's stranger still, with
     rhyme.
Even this thy genius, Canning! may permit,
Who, bred a statesman, still wast born a wit,
And never, even in that dull House, couldst
     tame
To unleavened prose thine own poetic flame;
Our last, our best, our only orator,[4]

---

[1] [Hartwell, in Buckinghamshire — the residence of Louis XVIII. during the latter years of the Emigration.]

[2] "Naso suspendit adunco." — *Horace.*
   The Roman applies it to one who merely was imperious to his acquaintance.

[3] ["The Pilot that weathered the storm," is the burden of a song in honor of Pitt, by Canning.]

[4] ["I have never heard any one who fulfilled my ideal of an orator. Grattan would have been near it, but for his harlequin delivery. Pitt I never heard — Fox but once; and then he struck me as a debater, which to me seems as different from an orator as an improvisatore or a versifier from a poet. Grey is great, but it is not oratory. Canning is sometimes very like one. Whitbread was the Demosthenes of bad taste and vulgar vehemence, but strong, and English. Holland is impressive from sense and sincerity. Burdett is sweet and silvery as Belial himself, and, I think, the greatest favorite in Pandemonium." — *Byron's Diary,* 1831.]

Even I can praise thee—Tories do no more:
Nay, not so much;—they hate thee, man, because
Thy spirit less upholds them than it awes.
The hounds will gather to their huntsman's hollo,
And where he leads the duteous pack will follow;
But not for love mistake their yelling cry;
Their yelp for game is not an eulogy;
Less faithful far than the four-footed pack,
A dubious scent would lure the bipeds back.
Thy saddle-girths are not yet quite secure,
Nor royal stallion's feet extremely sure; [1]
The unwieldy old white horse is apt at last
To stumble, kick, and now and then stick fast
With his great self and rider in the mud:
But what of that? the animal shows blood.

XIV.

Alas, the country! how shall tongue or pen
Bewail her now *un*country gentlemen?
The last to bid the cry of warfare cease,
The first to make a malady of peace.
For what were all these country patriots born?
To hunt, and vote, and raise the price of corn?
But corn, like every mortal thing, must fall,
Kings, conquerors, and markets most of all.
And must ye fall with every ear of grain?
Why would you trouble Buonaparte's reign?
He was your great Triptolemus; his vices
Destroyed but realms, and still maintained your prices;
He amplified to every lord's content
The grand agrarian alchymy, high *rent.*
Why did the tyrant stumble on the Tartars,
And lower wheat to such desponding quarters?
Why did you chain him on yon isle so lone?
The man was worth much more upon his throne.
True, blood and treasure boundlessly were spilt,
But what of that? the Gaul may bear the guilt:
But bread was high, the farmer paid his way,
And acres told upon the appointed day.
But where is now the goodly audit ale?
The purse-proud tenant, never known to fail?
The farm which never yet was left on hand?
The marsh reclaimed to most improving land?

[1] [On the suicide of Lord Londonderry, in August, 1822, Mr. Canning, who had prepared to sail for India as Governor-General, was made Secretary of State for Foreign Affairs,—not much, it was alleged, to the personal satisfaction of George the Fourth, or of the high Tories in the cabinet. He lived to verify some of the predictions of the poet—to abandon the *foreign* policy of his predecessor—to break up the Tory party by a coalition with the Whigs—and to prepare the way for *Reform* in Parliament.]

The impatient hope of the expiring lease?
The doubling rental? What an evil's peace!
In vain the prize excites the ploughman's skill,
In vain the Commons pass their patriot bill;
The *landed interest*—(you may understand
The phrase much better leaving out the *land*)—
The land self-interest groans from shore to shore,
For fear that plenty should attain the poor.
Up, up again, ye rents! exalt your notes,
Or else the ministry will lose their votes,
And patriotism, so delicately nice,
Her loaves will lower to the market price;
For ah! "the loaves and fishes," once so high,
Are gone—their oven closed, their ocean dry,
And nought remains of all the millions spent,
Excepting to grow moderate and content.
They who are not so, *had* their turn—and turn
About still flows from Fortune's equal urn;
Now let their virtue be its own reward,
And share the blessings which themselves prepared.
See these inglorious Cincinnati swarm,
Farmers of war, dictators of the farm;
Their ploughshare was the sword in hireling hands,
Their fields manured by gore of other lands;
Safe in their barns, these Sabine tillers sent
Their brethren out to battle—why? for rent!
Year after year they voted cent. per cent.,
Blood, sweat, and tear-wrung millions—why? for rent!
They roared, they dined, they drank, they swore they meant
To die for England—why then live?—for rent!
The peace has made one general malcontent
Of these high-market patriots; war was rent!
Their love of country, millions all mis-spent,
How reconcile? by reconciling rent!
And will they not repay the treasures lent?
No: down with every thing, and up with rent!
Their good, ill, health, wealth, joy, or discontent,
Being, end, aim, religion—rent, rent, rent!
Thou sold'st thy birthright, Esau! for a mess;
Thou shouldst have gotten more, or eaten less;
Now thou hast swilled thy pottage, thy demands
Are idle; Israel says the bargain stands.
Such, landlords! was your appetite for war,
And, gorged with blood, you grumble at a scar!
What! would they spread their earthquake even o'er cash?
And when land crumbles, bid firm paper crash?

So rent may rise, bid bank and nation fall,
And found on 'Change a *Fundling* Hospital ?
Lo, Mother Church, while all religion writhes,
Like Niobe, weeps o'er her offspring, Tithes ;
The prelates go to — where the saints have
   gone,
And proud pluralities subside to one ;
Church, state, and faction wrestle in the dark,
Tossed by the deluge in their common ark.
Shorn of her bishops, banks, and dividends,
Another Babel soars — but Britain ends.
And why ? to pamper the self-seeking wants,
And prop the hill of these agrarian ants.
" Go to these ants, thou sluggard, and be
   wise ; "
Admire their patience through each sacrifice,
Till taught to feel the lesson of their pride,
The price of taxes and of homicide ;
Admire their justice, which would fain deny
The debt of nations : — pray *who made it
   high ?*

XV.

Or turn to sail between those shifting rocks,
The new Symplegades — the crushing Stocks,
Where Midas might again his wish behold
In real paper or imagined gold.
That magic palace of Alcina shows
More wealth than Britain ever had to lose,
Were all her atoms of unleavened ore,
And all her pebbles from Pactolus' shore.
There Fortune plays, while Rumor holds the
   stake,
And the world trembles to bid brokers break.
How rich is Britain ! not indeed in mines,
Or peace or plenty, corn or oil, or wines ;
No land of Canaan, full of milk and honey,
Nor (save in paper shekels) ready money :
But let us not to own the truth refuse,
Was ever Christian land so rich in Jews ?
Those parted with their teeth to good King
   John,
And now, ye kings ! they kindly draw your
   own ;
All states, all things, all sovereigns they con-
   trol,
And waft a loan " from Indus to the pole."
The banker — broker — baron [1] — brethren,
   speed
To aid these bankrupt tyrants in their need.
Nor these alone ; Columbia feels no less
Fresh speculations follow each success ;
And philanthropic Israel deigns to drain
Her mild per-centage from exhausted Spain.
Not without Abraham's seed can Russia
   march ;
'Tis gold, not steel, that rears the conqueror's
   arch.
Two Jews, a chosen people, can command
In every realm their scripture-promised
   land : —

[1] [Baron Rothschild.]

Two Jews keep down the Romans, and up-
hold
The accursed Hun, more brutal than of old :
Two Jews — but not Samaritans — direct
The world, with all the spirit of their sect.
What is the happiness of earth to them ?
A congress forms their " New Jerusalem,"
Where baronies and orders both invite —
Oh, holy Abraham ! dost thou see the sight ?
Thy followers mingling with these royal swine
Who spit not " on their Jewish gaberdine,"
But honor them as portion of the show —
(Where now, oh pope ! is thy forsaken toe ?
Could it not favor Judah with some kicks ?
Or has it ceased to " kick against the pricks ? ")
On Shylock's shore behold them stand afresh,
To cut from nations' hearts their "pound of
flesh."

XVI.

Strange sight this Congress ! destined to unite
All that's incongruous, all that's opposite.
I speak not of the Sovereigns — they're alike,
A common coin as ever mint could strike :
But those who sway the puppets, pull the
   strings,
Have more of motley than their heavy kings.
Jews, authors, generals, charlatans, combine,
While Europe wonders at the vast design :
There Metternich, power's foremost parasite,
Cajoles ; there Wellington forgets to fight ;
There Chateaubriand forms new books of
   martyrs ; [2]
And subtle Greeks [3] intrigue for stupid Tar-
   tars ;
There Montmorenci, the sworn foe to
   charters, [4]
Turns a diplomatist of great eclat,
To furnish articles for the " Débats ; "
Of war so certain — yet not quite so sure
As his dismissal in the " Moniteur."
Alas ! how could his cabinet thus err ?
Can peace be worth an ultra-minister ?
He falls indeed, perhaps to rise again,
" Almost as quickly as he conquered Spain." [5]

XVII.

Enough of this — a sight more mournful woos
The averted eye of the reluctant muse.

[2] Monsieur Chateaubriand, who has not forgotten
the author in the minister, received a handsome
compliment at Verona from a literary sovereign :
" Ah ! Monsieur C., are you related to that Cha-
teaubriand who — who — who has written *some-
thing ?* " (écrit *quelque chose!*) It is said that the
author of Atala repented him for a moment of his
legitimacy.
[3] [Count Capo d'Istrias — afterwards President of
Greece. The Count was murdered, in September,
1831, by the brother and son of a Mainote chief
whom he had imprisoned.]
[4] [The Duke de Montmorenci-Laval.]
[5] [From Pope's verses on Lord Peterborough.]

The imperial daughter, the imperial bride,
The imperial victim — sacrifice to pride;
The mother of the hero's hope, the boy,
The young Astyanax of modern Troy;
The still pale shadow of the loftiest queen
That earth has yet to see, or e'er hath seen;
She flits amidst the phantoms of the hour,
The theme of pity, and the wreck of power.
Oh, cruel mockery! Could not Austria spare
A daughter? What did France's widow'
    there?
Her fitter place was by St. Helen's wave,
Her only throne is in Napoleon's grave.
But, no, — she still must hold a petty reign,
Flanked by her formidable chamberlain;
The martial Argus, whose not hundred eyes
Must watch her through these paltry pagean-
    tries.[1]
What though she share no more, and shared
    in vain,
A sway surpassing that of Charlemagne,
Which swept from Moscow to the southern
    seas!
Yet still she rules the pastoral realm of cheese,
Where Parma views the traveller resort
To note the trappings of her mimic court.
But she appears! Verona sees her shorn
Of all her beams — while nations gaze and
    mourn —
Ere yet her husband's ashes have had time
To chill in their inhospitable clime;
(If e'er those awful ashes can grow cold; —
But no, their embers soon will burst the
    mould;)
She comes! — the Andromache (but not
    Racine's,
Nor Homer's,) — Lo! on Pyrrhus' arm she
    leans!
Yes! the right arm, yet red from Waterloo,

Which cut her lord's half-shattered sceptre
    through,
Is offered and accepted! Could a slave
Do more? or less? — and *he* in his new
    grave!
Her eye, her cheek, betray no inward strife,
And the *ex*-empress grow as *ex* a wife!
So much for human ties in royal breasts!
Why spare men's feelings, when their own
    are jests?

XVIII.

But, tired of foreign follies, I turn home,
And sketch the group — the picture's yet to
    come.
My muse 'gan weep, but, ere a tear was spilt
She caught Sir William Curtis in a kilt!
While thronged the chiefs of every Highland
    clan
To hail their brother, Vich Ian Alderman!
Guildhall grows Gael, and echoes with Erse
    roar,
While all the Common Council cry "Clay-
    more!"
To see proud Albyn's tartans as a belt
Gird the gross sirloin of a city Celt,[2]
She burst into a laughter so extreme,
That I awoke — and lo! it was *no* dream!
Here, reader, will we pause: — if there's no
    harm in
This first — you'll have, perhaps, a second
    "Carmen."

---

[1] [Count Neipperg, chamberlain and second hus-
band to Maria Louisa, had but one eye. The count
died in 1831.]

[2] [George the Fourth is said to have been some-
what annoyed, on entering the levee-room at Holy-
rood (Aug. 1822) in full Stuart tartan, to see only
one figure similarly attired (and of similar bulk) —
that of Sir William Curtis. The city knight had
every thing complete — even the *knife* stuck in the
garter. He asked the King, if he did not think
him well dressed. "Yes!" replied his Majesty,
"only you have no *spoon* in your *hose*." The de-
vourer of turtle had a fine engraving executed of
himself in his Celtic attire.]

CHILDE HAROLD'S PILGRIMAGE:

A ROMAUNT.

L'univers est une espèce de livre, dont on n'a lu que la première page quand on n'a vu que son pays. J'en ai feuilleté un assez grand nombre, que j'ai trouvé également mauvaises. Cet examen ne m'a point été infructueux. Je haïssais ma patrie. Toutes les impertinences des peuples divers, parmi lesquels j'ai vécu, m'ont réconcilié avec elle. Quand je n'aurais tiré d'autre bénéfice de mes voyages que celui-là, je n'en regretterais ni les frais ni les fatigues. — *Le Cosmopolite.*[1]

PREFACE TO THE FIRST AND SECOND CANTOS.

The following poem was written, for the most part, amidst the scenes which it attempts to describe. It was begun in Albania; and the parts relative to Spain and Portugal were composed from the author's observations in those countries. Thus much it may be necessary to state for the correctness of the descriptions. The scenes attempted to be sketched are in Spain, Portugal, Epirus, Acarnania, and Greece. There, for the present, the poem stops: its reception will determine whether the author may venture to conduct his readers to the capital of the East, through Ionia and Phrygia: these two cantos are merely experimental.

A fictitious character is introduced for the sake of giving some connection to the piece; which, however, makes no pretension to regularity. It has been suggested to me by friends, on whose opinions I set a high value, that in this fictitious character, " Childe Harold," I may incur the suspicion of having intended some real personage: this I beg leave, once for all, to disclaim — Harold is the child of imagination, for the purpose I have stated. In some very trivial particulars, and those merely local, there might be grounds for such a notion; but in the main points, I should hope, none whatever.

It is almost superfluous to mention that the appellation " Childe," as " Childe Waters," " Childe Childers," etc. is used as more consonant with the old structure of versification which I have adopted. The " Good Night," in the beginning of the first canto, was suggested by " Lord Maxwell's Good Night," in the Border Minstrelsy, edited by Mr. Scott.

With the different poems which have been published on Spanish subjects, there may be found some slight coincidence in the first part which treats of the Peninsula; as, with the exception of a few concluding stanzas, the whole of this poem was written in the Levant.

The stanza of Spenser, according to one of our most successful poets, admits of every variety. Dr. Beattie makes the following observation: — " Not long ago I began a poem in the style and stanza of Spenser, in which I proposed to give full scope to my inclination, and be either droll or pathetic, descriptive or sentimental, tender or satirical, as the humor strikes me: for, if I mistake not, the measure which I have adopted admits equally of all these kinds of composition." [2] — Strengthened in my opinion by such authority, and by the example of some in the highest order of Italian poets, I shall make no apology for attempts at similar variations in the following composition; satisfied that, if they are unsuccessful, their failure must be in the execution, rather than in the design sanctioned by the practice of Ariosto, Thomson, and Beattie.

LONDON, February, 1812.

[1] [Par M. de Montbron, Paris, 1798. Byron somewhere calls it "an amusing little volume, full of French flippancy."]
[2] Beattie's Letters.

ADDITION TO THE PREFACE.

I HAVE now waited till almost all our periodical journals have distributed their usual portion of criti‑ cism. To the justice of the generality of their criticisms I have nothing to object: it would ill become me to quarrel with their very slight degree of censure, when, perhaps, if they had been less kind they had been more candid. Returning, therefore, to all and each my best thanks for their liberality, on one point alone shall I venture an observation. Amongst the many objections justly urged to the very indif‑ ferent character of the " vagrant Childe " (whom, notwithstanding many hints to the contrary, I still maintain to be a fictitious personage), it has been stated that, besides the anachronism, he is very *unknightly*, as the times of the Knights were times of Love, Honor, and so forth. Now, it so happens that the good old times, when " l'amour du bon vieux tems, l'amour antique " flourished, were the most profligate of all possible centuries. Those who have any doubts on this subject may consult Sainte‑ Palaye, *passim*, and more particularly vol. ii. p. 69. The vows of chivalry were no better kept than any other vows whatsoever; and the songs of the Troubadours were not more decent, and certainly were much less refined, than those of Ovid. The " Cours d'amour, parlemens d'amour, ou de courtésie et de gentilesse " had much more of love than of courtesy or gentleness. See Roland on the same subject with Sainte‑Palaye. Whatever other objection may be urged to that most unamiable personage, Childe Har‑ old, he was so far perfectly knightly in his attributes— " No waiter, but a knight templar." [1] By the by, I fear that Sir Tristrem and Sir Lancelot were no better than they should be, although very poetical personages and true knights " sans peur," though not " sans reproche." If the story of the institution of the " Garter" be not a fable, the knights of that order have for several centuries borne the badge of a Countess of Salisbury, of indifferent memory. So much for chivalry. Burke need not have regretted that its days are over, though Marie‑Antoinette was quite as chaste as most of those in whose honors lances were shivered, and knights unhorsed.

Before the days of Bayard, and down to those of Sir Joseph Banks [2] (the most chaste and celebrated of ancient and modern times), few exceptions will be found to this statement; and I fear a little investi‑ gation will teach us not to regret these monstrous mummeries of the middle ages.

I now leave " Childe Harold " to live his day, such as he is; it had been more agreeable, and certainly more easy, to have drawn an amiable character. It had been easy to varnish over his faults, to make him do more and express less, but he never was intended as an example, further than to show, that early perversion of mind and morals leads to satiety of past pleasures and disappointment in new ones, and that even the beauties of nature, and the stimulus of travel (except ambition, the most powerful of all excitements) are lost on a soul so constituted, or rather misdirected. Had I proceeded with the poem, this character would have deepened as he drew to the close; for the outline which I once meant to fill up for him was, with some exceptions, the sketch of a modern Timon, [3] perhaps a poetical Zeluco. [4]

LONDON, 1813.

---

[1] " The Rovers, or the Double Arrangement." *Anti‑jacobin.*

[2] [This compliment to Banks was ironical. His affairs with the women of Otaheite, during Cook's first voyage, had long been the subject of raillery in England.]

[3] [In one of his early poems— " Childish Recollections,"— Byron compares himself to the Athenian misanthrope: —

"Weary of Love, of Life, devoured with spleen, I rest a perfect Timon, not nineteen," etc.]

[4] [It was Dr. Moore's object, in this powerful romance, to trace the fatal effects resulting from a fond mother's unconditional compliance with the humors and passions of an only child. With high advan‑ tages of person, birth, fortune, and ability, Zeluco is represented as miserable, through every scene of life, owing to the spirit of unbridled self‑indulgence thus pampered in infancy.]

TO IANTHE.[1]

NOT in those climes where I have late been
    straying,
Though Beauty long hath there been match-
    less deemed;
Not in those visions to the heart displaying
Forms which it sighs but to have only
    dreamed,
Hath aught like thee in truth or fancy
    seemed:
Nor, having seen thee, shall I vainly seek
To paint those charms which varied as they
    beamed—
To such as see thee not my words were weak;
To those who gaze on thee what language
    could they speak?

Ah! may'st thou ever be what now thou art,
Nor unbeseem the promise of thy spring,
As fair in form, as warm yet pure in heart,
Love's image upon earth without his wing,
And guileless beyond Hope's imagining!
And surely she who now so fondly rears
Thy youth, in thee, thus hourly brightening,
Beholds the rainbow of her future years,
Before whose heavenly hues all sorrow disap-
    pears.

Young Peri of the West!—'tis well for me
My years already doubly number thine;
My loveless eye unmoved may gaze on thee,
And safely view thy ripening beauties shine;
Happy, I ne'er shall see them in decline;
Happier, that while all younger hearts shall
    bleed,

Mine shall escape the doom thine ey[...]
    assign
To those whose admiration shall succeed,
But mixed with pangs to Love's even loveli[...]
    hours decreed.

Oh! let that eye, which, wild as the G[...]
    zelle's,
Now brightly bold or beautifully shy,
Wins as it wanders, dazzles where it dwel[...]
Glance o'er this page, nor to my verse de[...]
That smile for which my breast might vain[...]
    sigh,
Could I to thee be ever more than friend[...]
This much, dear maid, accord; nor que[...]
    tion why
To one so young my strain I would con[...]
    mend,
But bid me with my wreath one matchless li[...]
    blend.

Such is thy name with this my verse e[...]
    twined;
And long as kinder eyes a look shall cast
On Harold's page, Ianthe's here enshrine[...]
Shall thus be first beheld, forgotten last:
My days once numbered, should this hon[...]
    age past,
Attract thy fairy fingers near the lyre
Of him who hailed thee, loveliest as tho[...]
    wast,
Such is the most my memory may desire;
Though more than Hope can claim, coul[...]
    Friendship less require?

[1] [Lady Charlotte Harley, afterwards Lady Charlotte Bacon, second daughter of the Earl of Oxfor[...]
in the autumn of 1812, when these lines were addressed to her, had not completed her eleventh yea[...]
Her juvenile beauty has been preserved in a portrait which Westall painted at Byron's request.]

CANTO THE FIRST.

I.

OH, thou! in Hellas deemed of heavenly
    birth,
Muse! formed or fabled at the minstrel's
    will!
Since shamed full oft by later lyres on earth,
Mine dares not call thee from thy sacred hill:
Yet there I've wandered by thy vaunted rill;
Yes! sighed o'er Delphi's long deserted
    shrine,[1]

Where, save that feeble fountain, all is still[...]
Nor mote my shell awake the weary Nine
To grace so plain a tale—this lowly lay of min[...]

[1] The little village of Castri stands partly on the
site of Delphi. Along the path of the mountain,
from Chrysso, are the remains of sepulchres hew[...]
in and from the rock. "One," said the guide, "[...]
a king who broke his neck hunting." His majest[...]
had certainly chosen the fittest spot for such a
achievement. A little above Castri is a cave, su[...]
posed the Pythian, of immense depth; the uppe[...]
part of it is paved, and now a cow-house. On th[...]
other side of Castri stands a Greek monastery[...]
some way above which is the cleft in the rock, wit[...]
a range of caverns difficult of ascent, and apparentl[...]

II.

Whilome in Albion's isle there dwelt a youth,
Who ne in virtue's ways did take delight;
But spent his days in riot most uncouth,
And vexed with mirth the drowsy ear of
   Night.
Ah, me! in sooth he was a shameless wight,
Sore given to revel and ungodly glee;
Few earthly things found favor in his sight,
Save concubines and carnal companie,
And flaunting wassailers of high and low
   degree.

III.

Childe Harold was he hight: — but whence
   his name
And lineage long, it suits me not to say;
Suffice it, that perchance they were of fame,
And had been glorious in another day,
But one sad losel soils a name for aye,
However mighty in the olden time;
Nor all that heralds rake from coffined clay,
Nor florid prose, nor honied lies of rhyme,
Can blazon evil deeds, or consecrate a crime.

IV.

Childe Harold basked him in the noontide
   sun,
Disporting there like any other fly,
Nor deemed before his little day was done
One blast might chill him into misery.
But long ere scarce a third of his passed by,
Worse than adversity the Childe befell;
He felt the fulness of satiety:
Then loathed he in his native land to dwell,
Which seemed to him more lone than Ere-
   mite's sad cell.

V.

For he through Sin's long labyrinth had run,
Nor made atonement when he did amiss,
Had sighed to many though he loved but
   one,
And that loved one, alas! could ne'er be his.
Ah, happy she! to 'scape from him whose
   kiss
Had been pollution unto aught so chaste;
Who soon had left her charms for vulgar
   bliss,
And spoiled her goodly lands to gild his
   waste,
Nor calm domestic peace had ever deigned
   to taste.

VI.

And now Childe Harold was sore sick at
   heart,
And from his fellow bacchanals would flee;
'Tis said, at times the sullen tear would start,
But Pride congealed the drop within his ee:
Apart he stalked in joyless reverie,
And from his native land resolved to go,
And visit scorching climes beyond the sea;
With pleasure drugged, he almost longed
   for woe,
And e'en for change of scene would seek the [1]
   shades below.

VII.

The Childe departed from his father's hall:
It was a vast and venerable pile;
So old, it seemed only not to fall,
Yet strength was pillared in each massy aisle.
Monastic dome! condemned to uses vile!
Where superstition once had made her den
Now Paphian girls were known to sing and
   smile;
And monks might deem their time was come
   agen,
If ancient tales say true, nor wrong these holy
   men.

VIII.

Yet oft-times in his maddest mirthful mood
Strange pangs would flash along Childe
   Harold's brow,
As if the memory of some deadly feud
Or disappointed passion lurked below:
But this none knew, nor haply cared to know;
For his was not that open, artless soul
That feels relief by bidding sorrow flow,
Nor sought he friend to counsel or condole,
Whate'er this grief mote be, which he could
   not control.

IX.

And none did love him.— though to hall and
   bower
He gathered revellers from far and near,
He knew them flatterers of the festal hour;

---

[1] [In these stanzas, and indeed throughout his
works, we must not accept too literally Byron's tes-
timony against himself — he took a morbid pleasure
in darkening every shadow of his self-portraiture.
His life at Newstead had, no doubt, been, in some
points loose and irregular enough; but it certainly
never exhibited any thing of the profuse and Sul-
tanic luxury which the language in the text might
seem to indicate. In fact, the narrowness of his
means at the time the verses refer to would alone
have precluded this. His household economy,
while he remained at the Abbey, is known to have
been conducted on a very moderate scale; and, be-
sides, his usual companions, though far from being
averse to convivial indulgences, were not only, as
Moore says, "of habits and tastes too intellectual
for mere vulgar debauchery," but, assuredly, quite
incapable of playing the parts of flatterers and
parasites.]

leading to the interior of the mountain; probably
to the Corycian Cavern mentioned by Pausanias.
From this part descend the fountain and the "Dews
of Castalie."— ["We were sprinkled," says Hob-
house, "with the spray of the immortal rill, and
here, if anywhere, should have felt the poetic inspi-
ration: we drank deep, too, of the spring; but —
(I can answer for myself) — without feeling sensi-
ble of any extraordinary effect."]

The heartless parasites of present cheer.
Yea! none did love him — not his lemans
    dear —
But pomp and power alone are woman's
    care,
And where these are light Eros finds a fere;
Maidens, like moths, are ever caught by
    glare,
And Mammon wins his way where Seraphs
    might despair.

X.

Childe Harold had a mother — not forgot,
Though parting from that mother he did
    shun;
A sister whom he loved, but saw her not
Before his weary pilgrimage begun:
If friends he had, he bade adieu to none.
Yet deem not thence his breast a breast of
    steel:
Ye, who have known what 'tis to dote upon
A few dear objects, will in sadness feel
Such partings break the heart they fondly
    hope to heal.

XI.

His house, his home, his heritage, his lands,
The laughing dames in whom he did delight,
Whose large blue eyes, fair locks, and snowy
    hands,
Might shake the saintship of an anchorite,
And long had fed his youthful appetite;
His goblets brimmed with every costly wine,
And all that mote to luxury invite,
Without a sigh he left, to cross the brine,
And traverse Paynim shores, and pass Earth's
    central line.[1]

XII.

The sails were filled, and fair the light winds
    blew,
As glad to waft him from his native home;
And fast the white rocks faded from his view,
And soon were lost in circumambient foam:
And then, it may be, of his wish to roam
Repented he, but in his bosom slept
The silent thought, nor from his lips did
    come
One word of wail, whilst others sate and
    wept,
And to the reckless gales unmanly moaning
    kept.

XIII.

But when the sun was sinking in the sea,
He seized his harp, which he at times could
    string,
And strike, albeit with untaught melody,
When deemed he no strange ear was listen-
    ing:
And now his fingers o'er it he did fling,
And tuned his farewell in the dim twilight.

[1] [Byron originally intended to visit India.]

While flew the vessel on her snowy win,
And fleeting shores receded from his sig
Thus to the elements he poured his l
    " Good Night."

I.

" ADIEU, adieu! my native shore
    Fades o'er the waters blue;
The Night-winds sigh, the breakers roa
    And shrieks the wild sea-mew.
Yon Sun that sets upon the sea
    We follow in his flight;
Farewell awhile to him and thee,
    My native Land — Good Night!

2.

" A few short hours and he will rise
    To give the morrow birth;
And I shall hail the main and skies,
    But not my mother earth.
Deserted is my own good hall,
    Its hearth is desolate;
Wild weeds are gathering on the wall,
    My dog howls at the gate.

3.

" Come hither, hither, my little page![2]
    Why dost thou weep and wail?
Or dost thou dread the billows' rage,
    Or tremble at the gale?
But dash the tear-drop from thine eye;
    Our ship is swift and strong:
Our fleetest falcon scarce can fly
    More merrily along."

4.

" Let winds be shrill, let waves roll high,
    I fear not wave nor wind;
Yet marvel not, Sir Childe, that I
    Am sorrowful in mind;
For I have from my father gone,
    A mother whom I love,
And have no friend, save these alone,
    But thee — and one above.

5.

" My father blessed me fervently,
    Yet did not much complain;
But sorely will my mother sigh
    Till I come back again." —
" Enough, enough, my little lad!
    Such tears become thine eye,
If I thy guileless bosom had,
    Mine own would not be dry.[3]

[2] [This " little page" was Robert Rushton, t'
son of one of Byron's tenants. " I take Rob
with me," says the poet, in a letter to his moth
" I like him, because, like myself, he seems a frien
less animal." The boy, being sickly, Byron,
reaching Gibraltar, sent him back to England.]

[3] [Here follows in the original MS. : —
    " My Mother is a high-born dame,
        And much misliketh me

6.

" Come hither, hither, my staunch yeoman,[1]
  Why dost thou look so pale ?
  Or dost thou dread a French foeman ?
  Or shiver at the gale ? "
" Deem'st thou I tremble for my life ?
  Sir Childe, I'm not so weak;
  But thinking on an absent wife
  Will blanch a faithful cheek.

7.

" My spouse and boys dwell near thy hall,
  Along the bordering lake,
  And when they on their father call,
  What answer shall she make ? "
" Enough, enough, my yeoman good,
  Thy grief let none gainsay;
  But I, who am of lighter mood,
  Will laugh to flee away.

8.

" For who would trust the seeming sighs
  Of wife or paramour ?
  Fresh feres will dry the bright blue eyes
  We late saw streaming o'er.
  For pleasures past I do not grieve,
  Nor perils gathering near;
  My greatest grief is that I leave
  No thing that claims a tear.

9.

" And now I'm in the world alone,
  Upon the wide, wide sea :
  But why should I for others groan,
  When none will sigh for me ?
  Perchance my dog will whine in vain,
  Till fed by stranger hands;
  But long ere I come back again
  He'd tear me where he stands.[2]

She saith my riot bringeth shame
  On all my ancestry :
I had a sister once I ween,
  Whose tears perhaps will flow;
But her fair face I have not seen
  For three long years and moe."]

[1] [William Fletcher, his faithful valet. This un-
sophisticated "yeoman" was a constant source of
pleasantry to his master: — *e.g.* "Fletcher," he
says, in a letter to his mother, "is not valiant: he
requires comforts that I can dispense with, and
sighs for beer, and beef, and tea, and his wife, and
the devil knows what besides. We were one night
lost in a thunder-storm, and since, nearly wrecked.
In both cases he was sorely bewildered; from
apprehensions of famine and banditti in the first,
and drowning in the second instance. His eyes
were a little hurt by the lightning, or crying, I don't
know which. I did what I could to console him,
but found him incorrigible. He sends six sighs to
Sally. I shall settle him in a farm; for he has
served me faithfully, and Sally is a good woman."]

[2] [Here follows in the original MS. : —
" Methinks it would my bosom glad,
  To change my proud estate,

10.

" With thee, my bark, I'll swiftly go
  Athwart the forming brine;
  Nor care what land thou bear'st me to,
  So not again to mine.
  Welcome, welcome, ye dark-blue waves !
  And when you fail my sight,
  Welcome, ye deserts, and ye caves !
  My native Land — Good Night ! "[3]

XIV.

On, on the vessel flies, the land is gone,
And winds are rude in Biscay's sleepless
  bay.
Four days are sped, but with the fifth, anon.
New shores descried make every bosom
  gay;
And Cintra's mountain greets them on their
  way,
And Tagus dashing onward to the deep,
His fabled golden tribute bent to pay;
And soon on board the Lusian pilots leap,
And steer 'twixt fertile shores where yet few
  rustics reap.

XV.

Oh, Christ ! it is a goodly sight to see
What Heaven hath done for this delicious
  land !
What fruits of fragrance blush on every tree !
What goodly prospects o'er the hills expand !
But man would mar them with an impious
  hand :
And when the Almighty lifts his fiercest
  scourge

And be again a laughing lad
  With one beloved playmate.
Since youth I scarce have passed an hour
  Without disgust or pain,
Except sometimes in Lady's bower,
  Or when the bowl I drain."]

[3] [Originally, the "little page" and the "yeo-
man" were introduced in the following stanzas : —

" And of his train there was a henchman page,
  A peasant boy, who served his master well;
  And often would his pranksome prate engage
  Childe Harold's ear, when his proud heart did
    swell
  With sable thoughts that he disdained to tell.
  Then would he smile on him, and Alwin smiled,
  When aught that from his young lips archly fell
  The gloomy film from Harold's eye beguiled;
And pleased for a glimpse appeared the woeful
    Childe.

" Him and one yeoman only did he take
  To travel eastward to a far countrie;
  And, though the boy was grieved to leave the lake
  On whose fair banks he grew from infancy,
  Eftsoons his little heart beat merrily
  With hope of foreign nations to behold,
  And many things right marvellous to see,
  Of which our vaunting voyagers oft have told,
In many a tome as true as Mandeville's of old."]

'Gainst those who most transgress his high
  command,
With treble vengeance will his hot shafts
  urge
Gaul's locust host, and earth from fellest foe-
  men purge.

XVI.

What beauties doth Lisboa[1] first unfold!
Her image floating on that noble tide,
Which poets vainly pave with sands of gold,
But now whereon a thousand keels did ride
Of mighty strength, since Albion was allied,
And to the Lusians did her aid afford:
A nation swoln with ignorance and pride,
Who lick yet loathe the hand that waves
  the sword
To save them from the wrath of Gaul's un-
  sparing lord.

XVII.

But whoso entereth within this town,
That, sheening far, celestial seems to be,
Disconsolate will wander up and down,
Mid many things unsightly to strange ee;
For hut and palace show like filthily:
The dingy denizens are reared in dirt;
Ne personage of high or mean degree '
Doth care for cleanness of surtout or shirt,
Though shent with Egypt's plague, unkempt,
  unwashed; unhurt.

XVIII.

Poor, paltry slaves! yet born 'midst noblest
  scenes —
Why, Nature, waste thy wonders on such
  men?
Lo! Cintra's[2] glorious Eden intervenes
In variegated maze of mount and glen.

Ah, me! what hand can pencil guide,
  pen,
To follow half on which the eye dilates
Through views more dazzling unto mor
  ken
Than those whereof such things the ba
  relates,
Who to the awe-struck world unlocked E
  sium's gates?

XIX.

The horrid crags, by toppling conve
  crowned,
The cork-trees hoar that clothe the shag
  steep,
The mountain-moss by scorching skies i
  browned,
The sunken glen, whose sunless shru
  must weep,
The tender azure of the unruffled deep,
The orange tints that gild the green
  bough,
The torrents that from cliff to valley leap
The vine on high, the willow branch belo
Mixed in one mighty scene, with varied beat
  glow.

XX.

Then slowly climb the many-winding wa
And frequent turn to linger as you go,
From loftier rocks new loveliness survey
And rest ye at " Our Lady's house of woe;
Where frugal monks their little relics sh
And sundry legends to the stranger tell:
Here impious men have punished been, a
  lo!
Deep in yon cave Honorius long did dw
In hope to merit Heaven by making cart
  Hell.

XXI.

And here and there, as up the crags y
  spring,
Mark many rude-carved crosses near t
  path:
Yet deem not these devotion's offering
These are memorials frail of murde
  wrath:
For wheresoe'er the shrieking victim ha

---

[1] [" A friend advises *Ulissipont;* but *Lisboa* is the Portuguese word, consequently the best. Ulissipont is pedantic; and as I had lugged in *Hellas* and *Eros* not long before, there would have been something like an affectation of Greek terms, which I wished to avoid. On the submission of *Lusitania* to the Moors, they changed the name of the capital, which till then had been Ulisipo, or Lispo; because, in the Arabic alphabet, the letter *p* is not used. Hence, I believe, Lisboa; whence again, the French Lisbonne, and our Lisbon, — God knows which the earlier corruption!" *Byron,* MS.]

[2] [" To make amends for the filthiness of Lisbon, and its still filthier inhabitants, the village of Cintra, about fifteen miles from the capital, is, perhaps, in every respect, the most delightful in Europe. It contains beauties of every description, natural and artificial: palaces and gardens rising in the midst of rocks, cataracts, and precipices; convents on stupendous heights; a distant view of the sea and the Tagus; and, besides (though that is a secondary consideration), is remarkable as the scene of Sir Hew Dalrymple's convention. It unites in itself all the wildness of the western Highlands, with the verdure of the south of France." — *B. to Mrs. Byron,* 1809.]

[3] The convent of " Our Lady of Punishmer *Nossa Señora de Pena,* on the summit of rock. Below, at some distance, is the Cork C vent, where St. Honorius dug his den, over wh is his epitaph. From the hills, the sea adds to beauty of the view. — [Since the publication of t poem, I have been informed of the misapprehens of the term *Nossa Señora de Pena.* It was ow to the want of the *tilde,* or mark over the *ñ,* wh alters the signification of the word: with it, *Pe* signifies a rock; without it, *Pena* has the sens adopted. I do not think it necessary to alter passage; as though the common acceptation affi to it is " Our Lady of the Rock," I may well sume the other sense from the severities practi there. — *Note to 2d Edition.*]

Poured forth his blood beneath the assas-
sin's knife,
Some hand erects a cross of mouldering
lath ;
And grove and glen with thousand such
are rife
Throughout this purple land, where law se-
cures not life.[1]

XXII.

On sloping mounds, or in the vale beneath,
Are domes where whilome kings did make
repair ;
But now the wild flowers round them only
breathe ;
Yet ruined splendor still is lingering there,
And yonder towers the Prince's palace fair :
There thou too, Vathek ![2] England's
wealthiest son,
Once formed thy Paradise, as not aware
When wanton Wealth her mightiest deeds
hath done,
Meek Peace voluptuous lures was ever wont
to shun.

XXIII.

Here didst thou dwell, here schemes of
pleasure plan,
Beneath yon mountain's ever beauteous
brow :
But now, as if a thing unblest by Man,
Thy fairy dwelling is as lone as thou !
Here giant weeds a passage scarce allow
To halls deserted, portals gaping wide ;
Fresh lessons to the thinking bosom, how
Vain are the pleasaunces on earth supplied ;
Swept into wrecks anon by Time's ungentle
tide !

---

[1] It is a well-known fact, that in the year 1809,
the assassinations in the streets of Lisbon and its
vicinity were not confined by the Portuguese to
their countrymen ; but that Englishmen were daily
butchered : and so far from redress being obtained,
we were requested not to interfere if we perceived
any compatriot defending himself against his allies.
I was once stopped in the way to the theatre at
eight o'clock in the evening, when the streets were
not more empty than they generally are at that
hour, opposite to an open shop, and in a carriage
with a friend : had we not fortunately been armed,
I have not the least doubt that we should have
" adorned a tale " instead of telling one. The crime
of assassination is not confined to Portugal : in Sicily
and Malta we are knocked on the head at a hand-
some average nightly, and not a Sicilian or Maltese
is ever punished !

[2] [" Vathek " (says Byron, in one of his diaries)
" was one of the tales I had a very early admiration
of. For correctness of costume, beauty of descrip-
tion, and power of imagination, it far surpasses all
European imitations ; and bears such marks of orig-
inality, that those who have visited the East will
find some difficulty in believing it to be more than
a translation. As an eastern tale, even Rasselas
must bow before it : his ' happy valley ' will not
bear a comparison with the ' Hall of Eblis.' "]

XXIV.

Behold the hall where chiefs were late con-
vened ![3]
Oh ! dome displeasing unto British eye !
With diadem hight foolscap, lo ! a fiend,
A little fiend that scoffs incessantly,
There sits in parchment robe arrayed, and
by
His side is hung a seal and sable scroll,
Where blazoned glare names known to
chivalry,
And sundry signatures adorn the roll,
Whereat the Urchin points and laughs with
all his soul.[4]

---

[3] The Convention of Cintra was signed in the
palace of the Marchese Marialva.—[Byron was
mistaken. " The armistice, the negotiations, the
convention itself, and the execution of its provisions,
were all commenced, conducted, and concluded, at
the distance of thirty miles from Cintra, with which
place they had not the slightest connection, politi-
cal, military, or local."—*Napier's History of the
Peninsular War.*]

[4] The passage stood differently in the original
MS. The following verses Byron omitted at the
entreaty of his friends : —

In golden characters right well designed,
First on the list appeareth one " Junot ; "
Then certain other glorious names we find,
Which rhyme compelleth me to place below :
Dull victors ! baffled by a vanquished foe,
Wheedled by conynge tongues of laurels due,
Stand, worthy of each other, in a row —
Sir Arthur, Harry, and the dizzard Hew
Dalrymple, seely wight, sore dupe of t'other tew.

Convention is the dwarfish demon styled
That foiled the knights in Marialva's dome :
Of brains (if brains they had) he them beguiled,
And turned a nation's shallow joy to gloom.
For well I wot, when first the news did come,
That Vimiera's field by Gaul was lost,
For paragraph ne paper scarce had room,
Such Pæans teemed for our triumphant host,
In Courier, Chronicle, and eke in Morning Post ;

But when Convention sent his handy-work,
Pens, tongues, feet, hands, combined in wild up-
roar ;
Mayor, aldermen, laid down the uplifted fork ;
The Bench of Bishops half forgot to snore ;
Stern Cobbett, who for one whole week forbore
To ues on aught, once more with transport
leapt;
And bit his devilish quill agen, and swore
Then burst the blatant* beast, and roared, and
raged, and — slept !

Thus unto Heaven appealed the people : Heaven,
Which loves the lieges of our gracious King,
Decreed, that, ere our generals were forgiven,
Inquiry should be held about the thing.
But Mercy cloaked the babes beneath her wing ;

---

* " Blatant beast "—a figure for the mob, I
think first used by Smollett in his " Adventures of
an Atom." Horace has the " bellua multorum capi-
tum : " in England fortunately enough, the illus-
trious mobility have not even *one.*

XXV.

Convention is the dwarfish demon styled
That foiled the knights in Marialva's dome:
Of brains (if brains they had) he them be-
  guiled,
And turned a nation's shallow joy to gloom.
Here Folly dashed to earth the victor's
  plume,
And Policy regained what arms had lost:
For chiefs like ours in vain may laurels
  bloom!
Woe to the conquering, not the conquered
  host,
Since baffled Triumph droops on Lusitania's
  coast!

XXVI.

And ever since that martial synod met,
Britannia sickens, Cintra! at thy name;
And folks in office at the mention fret,
And fain would blush, if blush they could,
  for shame.
How will posterity the deed proclaim!
Will not our own and fellow-nations sneer,
To view these champions cheated of their
  fame,
By foes in fight o'erthrown, yet victors here,
Where Scorn her finger points through many
  a coming year?

XXVII.

So deemed the Childe, as o'er the moun-
  tains he
Did take his way in solitary guise:
Sweet was the scene, yet soon he thought to
  flee,
More restless than the swallow in the skies:
Though here awhile he learned to moralize,
For Meditation fixed at times on him;
And conscious Reason whispered to despise
His early youth, misspent in maddest whim;
But as he gazed on truth his aching eyes grew
  dim.

XXVIII.

To horse! to horse! [1] he quits, for ever quits
A scene of peace, though soothing to his
  soul:

And as they spared our foes, so spared we them;
(Where was the pity of our sires for Byng?[*])
Yet knaves, not idiots, should the law condemn;
Then live, ye gallant knights' and bless your
  Judges' phlegm!

[1] [" After remaining ten days in Lisbon, we sent
our baggage and part of our servants by sea to Gi-
braltar, and travelled on horseback to Seville; a dis-
tance of nearly four hundred miles. The horses
are excellent: we rode seventy miles a day. Eggs

[*] By this query it is not meant that our foolish
generals should have been shot, but that Byng
might have been spared, though the one suffered
and the others escaped, probably for Candide's
reason, " pour encourager les autres."

Again he rouses from his moping fits,
But seeks not now the harlot and the bc
Onward he flies, nor fixed as yet the goa
Where he shall rest him on his pilgrima;
And o'er him many changing scenes m
  roll
Ere toil his thirst for travel can assuage,
Or he shall calm his breast, or learn exp
  ence sage.

XXIX.

Yet Mafra shall one moment claim dela>
Where dwelt of yore the Lusians' luckl
  queen; [2]
And church and court did mingle their
  ray,
And mass and revel were alternate seen
Lordlings and freres — ill-sorted fry I wee
But here the Babylonian whore hath bui
A dome, where flaunts she in such gloric
  sheen,
That men forget the blood which she h;
  spilt,
And bow the knee to Pomp that loves to v
  nish guilt.

XXX.

O'er vales that teem with fruits, roman
  hills,
(Oh, that such hills upheld a freeborn race
Whereon to gaze the eye with joyaunce fi
Childe Harold wends through many a plei
  ant place.
Though sluggards deem it but a fooli
  chase,
And marvel men should quit their ea
  chair,

and wine, and hard beds, are all the accommodati
we found, and, in such torrid weather, quite enougl
— *B. Letters*, 1809.]
[2] [" Her luckless Majesty went subsequeni
mad; and Dr. Willis, who so dexterously cudgell
kingly pericraniums, could make nothing of hers
—*Byron MS.* The Queen labored under a mela
choly kind of derangement, from which she nev
recovered. She died in Brazil in 1816.]
[3] The extent of Mafra is prodigious: it contai
a palace, convent, and most superb church. T
six organs are the most beautiful I ever beheld,
point of decoration: we did not hear them, but we
told that their tones were correspondent to the
splendor. Mafra is termed the Escurial of Portug;
[" About ten miles to the right of Cintra," sa
Byron, in a letter to his mother, " is the palace
Mafra, the boast of Portugal, as it might be of ai
country, in point of magnificence, without eleganc
There is a convent annexed: the monks, who pc
sess large revenues, are courteous enough, and u
derstand Latin, so that we had a long conversatio
They have a large library, and asked me if the En
lish had *any books* in their country."— Mafra w
erected by John V., in pursuance of a vow, ma
in a dangerous fit of illness, to found a convent f
the use of the poorest friary in the kingdom. Up
inquiry, this poorest was found at Mafra; whe
< twelve Franciscans lived together in a hut.]

The toilsome way, and long, long league to trace,
Oh! there is sweetness in the mountain air,
And life, that bloated Ease can never hope to share.

XXXI.

More bleak to view the hills at length recede,
And, less luxuriant, smoother vales extend;
Immense horizon-bounded plains succeed!
Far as the eye discerns, withouten end,
Spain's realms appear whereon her shep-
'herds tend
Flocks, whose rich fleece right well the trader knows—
Now must the pastor's arm his lambs de-
fend:
For Spain is compassed by unyielding foes,
And all must shield their all, or share Subjec-
tion's woes.

XXXII.

Where Lusitania and her Sister meet,
Deem ye what bounds the rival realms di-
vide?
Or ere the jealous queens of nations greet,
Doth Tayo interpose his mighty tide?
Or dark Sierras rise in craggy pride?
Or fence of art, like China's vasty wall?—
Ne barrier wall, ne river deep and wide,
Ne horrid crags, nor mountains dark and tall,
Rise like the rocks that part Hispania's land from Gaul:

XXXIII.

But these between a silver streamlet glides,
And scarce a name distinguisheth the brook,
Though rival kingdoms press its verdant sides.
Here leans the idle shepherd on his crook,
And vacant on the rippling waves doth look,
That peaceful still 'twixt bitterest foemen flow;
For proud each peasant as the noblest duke:
Well doth the Spanish hind the difference know
Twixt him and Lusian slave, the lowest of the low.[1]

XXXIV.

But ere the mingling bounds have far been passed,
Dark Guadiana rolls his power along
In sullen billows, murmuring and vast,
So noted ancient roundelays among.
Whilome upon his banks did legions throng
Of Moor and Knight, in mailed splendor drest:

Here ceased the swift their race, here sunk the strong;
The Paynim turban and the Christian crest
Mixed on the bleeding stream, by floating hosts oppressed.

XXXV.

Oh, lovely Spain! renowned, romantic land!
Where is that standard which Pelagio bore,
When Cava's traitor-sire first called the band
That dyed thy mountain streams with Gothic gore?[2]
Where are those bloody banners which of yore
Waved o'er thy sons, victorious to the gale,
And drove at last the spoilers to their shore?
Red gleamed the cross, and waned the cres-
cent pale,
While Afric's echoes thrilled with Moorish matrons' wail.

XXXVI.

Teems not each ditty with the glorious tale?
Ah! such, alas! the hero's amplest fate!
When granite moulders and when records fail,
A peasant's plaint prolongs his dubious date.
Pride! bend thine eye from heaven to thine estate,
See how the Mighty shrink into a song!
Can Volume, Pillar, Pile, preserve thee great?
Or must thou trust Tradition's simple tongue,
When Flattery sleeps with thee, and History does thee wrong?

XXXVII.

Awake, ye sons of Spain! awake! advance!
Lo! Chivalry, your ancient goddess, cries;
But wields not, as of old, her thirsty lance,
Nor shakes her crimson plumage in the skies:
Now on the smoke of blazing bolts she flies,

---

[1] As I found the Portuguese, so I have charac-
terized them. That they are since improved, at
least in courage, is evident. The late exploits of
Lord Wellington have effaced the follies of Cintra.
He has, indeed, done wonders: he has, perhaps,
changed the character of a nation, reconciled rival
superstitions, and baffled an enemy who never re-
treated before his predecessors.—1812. [In the
Peninsular War the "Lusian slave" proved greatly
superior to the "Spanish hind." When commanded
by English officers and brigaded with English
troops, the Portuguese made excellent soldiers.]

[2] Count Julian's daughter, the Helen of Spain.
Pelagius preserved his independence in the fast-
nesses of the Asturias, and the descendants of his
followers, after some centuries, completed their
struggle by the conquest of Granada.—[Count
Julian's daughter, called Cava by the Moors, is
called Florinda by the Spaniards. She is said to
have been violated by Roderick, the King of the
Goths, and her father in revenge invited the Moors
to invade Spain. The Goths were defeated (A.D.
711), Roderick was killed, and the Moors remained
masters of the greater part of the Peninsula; but
Pelagius in the north, kept them at bay, and even
recovered portions of the territory they had won.]

And speaks in thunder through yon engine's
  roar!
In every peal she calls — "Awake! arise!"
Say, is her voice more feeble than of yore,
When her war-song was heard on Andalusia's
  shore?

XXXVIII.

Hark! heard you not those hoofs of dread-
  ful note?
Sounds not the clang of conflict on the
  heath?
Saw ye not whom the reeking sabre smote;
Nor saved your brethren ere they sank be-
  neath
Tyrants and tyrants' slaves? — the fires of
  death,
The bale-fires flash on high: — from rock to
  rock
Each volley tells that thousands cease to
  breathe ·
Death rides upon the sulphury Siroc,
Red Battle stamps his foot, and nations feel
  the shock.

XXXIX.

Lo! where the Giant on the mountain
  stands,
His blood-red tresses deep'ning in the sun,
With death-shot glowing in his fiery hands,
And eye that scorcheth all it glares upon;
Restless it rolls, now fixed, and now anon
Flashing afar, — and at his iron feet
Destruction cowers, to mark what deeds are
  done;
For on this morn three potent nations
  meet,
To shed before his shrine the blood he deems
  most sweet.[1]

XL.

By Heaven! it is a splendid sight to see
(For one who hath no friend, no brother
  there)
Their rival scarfs of mixed embroidery,
Their various arms that glitter in the air!
What gallant war-hounds rouse them from
  their lair,
And gnash their fangs, loud yelling for the
  prey!
All join the chase, but few the triumph share;
The Grave shall bear the chiefest prize away,
And Havoc scarce for joy can number their
  array.

[1] ["A bolder prosopopœia," says a nameless
critic, "or one better imagined or expressed, can-
not easily be found in the whole range of ancient
and modern poetry. Unlike the 'plume of Horror,'
or the 'eagle-winged Victory,' described by our
great epic poet, this gigantic figure is a distinct ob-
ject, perfect in lineaments, tremendous in opera-
tion, and vested with all the attributes calculated to
excite terror and admiration."]

XLI.

Three hosts combine to offer sacrifice;
Three tongues prefer strange orisons (
  high;
Three gaudy standards flout the pale bl
  skies;
The shouts are France, Spain, Albion, Vi
  tory!
The foe, the victim, and the fond ally
That fights for all, but ever fights in vain,
Are met — as if at home they could n
  die —
To feed the crow on Talavera's plain,
And fertilize the field that each pretends
  gain.[2]

[2] [The following note Byron suppressed with
luctance, at the urgent request of a friend.
alludes, *inter alia*, to the then recent publicatic
of Sir Walter Scott's Vision of Don Roderick, t
profits of which had been given to the cause
Portuguese patriotism: — "We have heard wonde
of the Portuguese lately, and their gallantry. Pr
Heaven it continue; yet 'would it were bed-tim
Hal, and all were well!' They must fight a gre
many hours, by 'Shrewsbury clock,' before t
number of their slain equals that of our countrym
butchered by these kind creatures, now metamc
phosed into 'caçadores,' and what not. I mere
state a fact, not confined to Portugal; for in Sici
and Malta we are knocked on the head at a han
some average nightly, and not a Sicilian or Malte
is ever punished! The neglect of protection is di
graceful to our government and governors; for t
murders are as notorious as the moon that shin
upon them, and the apathy that overlooks ther
The Portuguese, it is to be hoped, are comp
mented with the 'Forlorn Hope,' — if the cowar
are become brave (like the rest of their kind, in
corner), pray let them display it. But there is
subscription for these 'θρασύ-δειλοι,' (they ne
not be ashamed of the epithet once applied to t
Spartans); and all the charitable patronymics, fro
ostentatious A. to diffident Z., and £1: 1: o fro
'An Admirer of Valor,' are in requisition for t
lists at Lloyd's, and the honor of British benev
lence. Well! we have fought, and subscribed, ar
bestowed peerages, and buried the killed by ou
friends and foes; and, lo! all this is to be done ove
again! Like Lien Chi (in Goldsmith's Citizen
the World), as 'we grow older, we grow never t
better.' It would be pleasant to learn who will su
scribe for us, in or about the year 1815, and what n
tion will send fifty thousand men, first to be decimate
in the capital, and then decimated again (in the I ris
fashion, *nine* out of *ten*), in the 'bed of honor;
which, as Sergeant Kite says, is considerably large
and more commodious than 'the bed of Ware
Then they must have a poet to write the 'Visio
of Don Perceval,' and generously bestow the profi
of the well and widely printed quarto, to rebuild th
'Backwynd' and the 'Canongate,' or furnish ne
kilts for the half-roasted Highlanders. Lord Wel
ington, however, has enacted marvels; and so di
his Oriental brother, whom I saw charioteering ove
the French flag, and heard clipping bad Spanis
after listening to the speech of a patriotic cobbler
Cadiz, on the event of his own entry into that cit

XLII.

There shall **they rot** — Ambition's honored
    fools!
Yes, Honor decks the turf that wraps their
    clay!
Vain Sophistry! in these behold the tools,
The broken tools, that tyrants cast away
By myriads, when they dare to pave their
    way
With human hearts—to what?—a dream
    alone.
Can despots compass aught that hails their
    sway?
Or call with truth one span of earth their
    own,
Save that wherein at last they crumble bone
    by bone?

XLIII.

Oh, Albuera, glorious field of grief!
As o'er thy plain the Pilgrim pricked his
    steed,
Who could foresee thee, in a space so brief,
A scene where mingling foes should boast
    and bleed!
Peace to the perished! may the warrior's
    meed
And tears of triumph their reward prolong!
Till others fall where other chieftains lead,
Thy name shall circle round the gaping
    throng,
And shine in worthless lays, the theme of
    transient song.

XLIV.

Enough of Battle's minions! let them play
Their game of lives, and barter breath for
    fame:
Fame that will scarce re-animate their clay,
Though thousands fall to deck some single
    name.
In sooth 'twere sad to thwart their noble aim
Who strike, blest hirelings! for their coun-
    try's good,

And die, that living might have proved her
    shame;
Perished, perchance, in some domestic feud,
Or in a narrower sphere wild Rapine's path
    pursued.

XLV.

Full swiftly Harold wends his lonely way
Where proud Sevilla[1] triumphs unsubdued:
Yet is she free—the spoiler's wished-for
    prey!
Soon, soon shall Conquest's fiery foot in-
    trude,
Blackening her lovely domes with traces
    rude.
Inevitable hour! 'Gainst fate to strive
Where Desolation plants her famished
    brood
Is vain, or Ilion, Tyre might yet survive,
And Virtue vanquish all, and Murder cease
    to thrive.

XLVI.

But all unconscious of the coming doom,
The feast, the song, the revel here abounds;
Strange modes of merriment the hours con-
    sume,
Nor bleed these patriots with their country's
    wounds:
Nor here War's clarion, but Love's rebeck[2]
    sounds;
Here Folly still his votaries inthralls;
And young-eyed Lewdness walks her mid-
    night rounds:
Girt with the silent crimes of Capitals,
Still to the last kind Vice clings to the totter-
    ing walls.

XLVII.

Not so the rustic—with his trembling mate
He lurks, nor casts his heavy eye afar,
Lest he should view his vineyard desolate,
Blasted below the dun hot breath of war.
No more beneath soft Eve's consenting star

---

and the exit of some five thousand bold Britons out
of this 'best of all possible worlds.' Sorely were
we puzzled how to dispose of that same victory of
Talavera; and a victory it surely was somewhere,
for everybody claimed it. The Spanish despatch and
mob called it Cuesta's, and made no great mention
of the Viscount; the French called it theirs (to my
great discomfiture,—for a French consul stopped
my mouth in Greece with a pestilent Paris gazette,
just as I had killed Sebastiani, 'in buckram,' and
King Joseph, 'in Kendal green'),—and we have
not yet determined *what* to call it, or *whose;* for,
certes, it was none of our own. Howbeit, Massena's
retreat is a great comfort; and as we have not been in
the habit of pursuing for some years past, no wonder
we are a little awkward at first. No doubt we shall
improve; or, if not, we have only to take to our
old way of retrograding, and there we are at
home."]

[1] ["At Seville, we lodged in the house of two
Spanish unmarried ladies, women of character, the
eldest a fine woman, the youngest pretty. The
freedom of manner, which is general here, aston-
ished me not a little; and, in the course of further
observation, I find that reserve is not the character-
istic of Spanish belles. The eldest honored your
unworthy son with very particular attention, em-
bracing him with great tenderness at parting (I was
there but three days), after cutting off a lock of his
hair, and presenting him with one of her own, about
three feet in length, which I send you, and beg you
will retain till my return. Her last words were,
' Adios, tu hermoso, me gusto mucho!' ' Adieu,
you pretty fellow, you please me much!'"—*Byron
to his Mother*, August, 1809.]

[2] [A kind of fiddle, with only two strings, played
on by a bow, said to have been brought by the
Moors into Spain. "The Spanish women," wrote
Byron in August, 1809, "are certainly fascinating,
but their minds have only one idea, and the busi-
ness of their lives is intrigue."]

Fandango twirls his jocund castanet:
Ah, monarchs! could ye taste the mirth ye
mar,
Not in the toils of Glory would ye fret;
The hoarse dull drum would sleep, and Man
be happy yet!

XLVIII.

How carols now the lusty muleteer?
Of love, romance, devotion is his lay,
As whilome he was wont the leagues to
cheer,
His quick bells wildly jingling on the way?
No! as he speeds, he chants "Vivā el
Rey!"[1]
And checks his song to execrate Godoy,
The royal wittol Charles, and curse the day
When first Spain's queen beheld the black-
eyed boy,
And gore-faced Treason sprung from her
adulterate joy.

XLIX.

On yon long, level plain, at distance crowned
With crags, whereon those Moorish turrets
rest,
Wide scattered hoof-marks dint the
wounded ground;
And, scathed by fire, the greensward's dark-
ened vest
Tells that the foe was Andalusia's guest:
Here was the camp, the watch-flame, and
the host,
Here the bold peasant stormed the dragon's
nest;
Still does he mark it with triumphant
boast,
And points to yonder cliffs, which oft were
won and lost.

L.

And whomsoe'er along the path you meet
Bears in his cap the badge of crimson hue,
Which tells you whom to shun and whom
to greet:[2]
Woe to the man that walks in public view
Without of loyalty this token true:
Sharp is the knife, and sudden is the stroke;
And sorely would the Gallic foeman rue,

[1] " Vivā el Rey Fernando! " Long live King
Ferdinand! is the chorus of most of the Spanish
patriotic songs. They are chiefly in dispraise of the
old king Charles, the Queen, and the Prince of
Peace. I have heard many of them: some of the
airs are beautiful. Don Manuel Godoy, the *Prin-
cipe de la Paz*, of an ancient but decayed family,
was born at Badajoz, on the frontiers of Portugal,
and was originally in the ranks of the Spanish
guards; till his person attracted the queen's eyes,
and raised him to the dukedom of Alcudia, etc. etc.
It is to this man that the Spaniards universally im-
pute the ruin of their country.
[2] The red cockade, with " Fernando VII.," in the
centre.

If subtle poniards, wrapt beneath the cloke
Could blunt the sabre's edge, or clear th
cannon's smoke.

LI.

At every turn Morena's dusky height
Sustains aloft the battery's iron load;
And, far as mortal eye can compass sight,,
The mountain-howitzer, the broken road,
The bristling palisade, the fosse o'erflowei
The stationed bands, the never-vacant watcl
The magazine in rocky durance stowed,
The holstered steed beneath the shed ι
thatch,
The ball-piled pyramid,[3] the ever-blazin
match,

LII.

Portend the deeds to come: — but he whos
nod
Has tumbled feebler despots from their swa:
A moment pauseth ere he lifts the rod;
A little moment deigneth to delay:
Soon will his legions sweep through thes
their way;
The West must own the Scourger of th
world.
Ah! Spain! how sad will be thy reckoning
day,
When soars Gaul's Vulture, with his wing
unfurled,
And thou shalt view thy sons in crowds to Ha
des hurled.

LIII.

And must they fall? the young, the proud
the brave,
To swell one bloated Chief's unwholesom
reign?
No step between submission and a grave?
The rise of rapine and the fall of Spain?
And doth the Power that man adores ordai
Their doom, nor heed the suppliant's ap
peal?
Is all that desperate Valor acts in vain?
And Counsel sage, and patriotic Zeal,
The Veteran's skill, Youth's fire, and Mar
hood's heart of steel?

LIV.

Is it for this the Spanish maid, aroused,
Hangs on the willow her unstrung guitar,
And, all unsexed, the anlace hath espoused
Sung the loud song, and dared the deed c
war?
And she, whom once the semblance of a sca
Appalled, an owlet's larum chilled wit
dread,

[3] All who have seen a battery will recollect th
pyramidal form in which shot and shells are piled
The Sierra Morena was fortified in every defil
through which I passed in my way to Seville.

Now views the column-scattering bayonet jar,
The falchion flash, and o'er the yet warm dead
Stalks with Minerva's step where Mars might quake to tread.

LV.

Ye who shall marvel when you hear her tale,
Oh! had you known her in her softer hour,
Marked her black eye that mocks her coal-black veil,
Heard her light, lively tones in Lady's bower,
Seen her long locks that foil the painter's power,
Her fairy form, with more than female grace,
Scarce would you deem that Saragoza's tower
Beheld her smile in Danger's Gorgon face,
Thin the closed ranks, and lead in Glory's fearful chase.

LVI.

Her lover sinks — she sheds no ill-timed tear;
Her chief is slain — she fills his fatal post;
Her fellows flee — she checks their base career;
The foe retires — she heads the sallying host:
Who can appease like her a lover's ghost?
Who can avenge so well a leader's fall?
What maid retrieve when man's flushed hope is lost?
Who hang so fiercely on the flying Gaul,
Foiled by a woman's hand, before a battered wall?[1]

LVII.

Yet are Spain's maids no race of Amazons,
But formed for all the witching arts of love:

[1] Such were the exploits of the Maid of Saragoza, who by her valor elevated herself to the highest rank of heroines. When the author was at Seville she walked daily on the Prado, decorated with medals and orders, by command of the Junta. — [The exploits of Augustina, the famous heroine of both the sieges of Saragoza, are recorded at length in Southey's History of the Peninsular War. At the time when she first attracted notice, by mounting a battery where her lover had fallen, and working a gun in his room, she was in her twenty-second year, exceedingly pretty, and in a soft feminine style of beauty. She has further had the honor to be painted by Wilkie, and alluded to in Wordsworth's Dissertation on the Convention of Cintra; where a noble passage concludes in these words: — "Saragoza has exemplified a melancholy, yea a dismal truth, — yet consolatory and full of joy, — that when a people are called suddenly to fight for their liberty, and are sorely pressed upon, their best field of battle is the floors upon which their children have played; the chambers where the family of each man has slept; upon or under the roofs by which they have been sheltered; in the gardens of their recreation; in the street, or in the market-place; before the altars of their temples, and among their congregated dwellings, blazing or uprooted."]

Though thus in arms they emulate her sons,
And in the horrid phalanx dare to move,
'Tis but the tender fierceness of a dove,
Pecking the hand that hovers o'er her mate:
In softness as in firmness far above
Remoter females, famed for sickening prate;
Her mind is nobler sure, her charms perchance as great.

LVIII.

The seal Love's dimpling finger hath impressed
Denotes how soft that chin which bears his touch:[2]
Her lips, whose kisses pout to leave their nest,
Bid man be valiant ere he merit such:
Her glance how wildly beautiful! how much
Hath Phœbus wooed in vain to spoil her cheek,
Which glows yet smoother from his amorous clutch!
Who round the North for paler dames would seek?
How poor their forms appear! how languid, wan, and weak!

LIX.

Match me, ye climes! which poets love to laud;
Match me, ye harams of the land! where now[3]
I strike my strain, far distant, to applaud
Beauties that e'en a cynic must avow;
Match me those Houries, whom ye scarce allow
To taste the gale lest Love should ride the wind,
With Spain's dark-glancing daughters[4] —
deign to know,
There your wise Prophet's paradise we find,
His black-eyed maids of Heaven, angelically kind.

LX.

Oh, thou Parnassus![5] whom I now survey,
Not in the phrensy of a dreamer's eye,
Not in the fabled landscape of a lay,
But soaring snow-clad through thy native sky,

[2] "Sigilla in mento impressa Amoris digitulo Vestigio demonstrant mollitudinem."
Aul. Gel.

[3] This stanza was written in Turkey.

[4] ["Long black hair, dark languishing eyes, clear olive complexions, and forms more graceful in motion than can be conceived by an Englishman, used to the drowsy, listless air of his countrywomen, added to the most becoming dress, and, at the same time, the most decent in the world, render a Spanish beauty irresistible." — *Byron to his Mother*, Aug. 1809.]

[5] These stanzas were written in Castri (Delphos), at the foot of Parnassus, now called Διάκουρα (Liakura), Dec. 1809.

In the wild pomp of mountain majesty!
What marvel if I thus essay to sing?
The humblest of thy pilgrims passing by
Would gladly woo thine Echoes with his
    string,
Though from thy heights no more one Muse
    will wave her wing.

LXI.

Oft have I dreamed of Thee! whose glori-
    ous name
Who knows not, knows not man's divinest
    lore:
And now I view thee, 'tis, alas! with shame
That I in feeblest accents must adore.
When I recount thy worshippers of yore
I tremble, and can only bend the knee;
Nor raise my voice, nor vainly dare to soar,
But gaze beneath thy cloudy canopy
In silent joy to think at last I look on Thee![1]

LXII.

Happier in this than mightiest bards have
    been,
Whose fate to distant homes confined their
    lot,
Shall I unmoved behold the hallowed scene,
Which others rave of, though they know it
    not?
Though here no more Apollo haunts his
    grot,
And thou, the Muses' seat, art now their
    grave,
Some gentle spirit still pervades the spot,
Sighs in the gale, keeps silence in the cave,
And glides with glassy foot o'er yon melodious
    wave.

LXIII.

Of thee hereafter. — Ev'n amidst my strain
I turned aside to pay my homage here;
Forgot the land, the sons, the maids of
    Spain;
Her fate, to every freeborn bosom dear;
And hailed thee, not perchance without a
    tear.
Now to my theme — but from thy holy haunt
Let me some remnant, some memorial bear;

---

[1] ["Upon Parnassus, going to the fountain of
Delphi (Castri), in 1809, I saw a flight of twelve
eagles (Hobhouse says they were vultures — at
least in conversation), and I seized the omen. On
the day before, I composed the lines to Parnassus
(in Childe Harold), and on beholding the birds,
had a hope that Apollo had accepted my homage.
I have at least had the name and fame of a poet,
during the poetical period of life (from twenty to
thirty); — whether it will last is another matter:
but I have been a votary of the deity and place, and
am grateful for what he has done in my behalf,
leaving the future in his hands, as I left the past."
— *Byron's Diary*, 1821.]

Yield me one leaf of Daphne's deathless
    plant,
Nor let thy votary's hope be deemed an idl
    vaunt.

LXIV.

But ne'er didst thou, fair Mount! whe
    Greece was young,
See round thy giant base a brighter choir,
Nor e'er dip Delphi, when her priestess sun
The Pythian hymn with more than mort:
    fire,
Behold a train more fitting to inspire
The song of love than Andalusia's maids,
Nurst in the glowing lap of soft desire:
Ah! that to these were given such peacefu
    shades
As Greece can still bestow, though Glory fl
    her glades.

LXV.

Fair is proud Seville; let her country boas
Her strength, her wealth, her site of ancien
    days;[2]
But Cadiz, rising on the distant coast,
Calls forth a sweeter, though ignobl
    praise.
Ah, Vice! how soft are thy voluptuou
    ways!
While boyish blood is mantling, who cal
    'scape
The fascination of thy magic gaze?
A Cherub-hydra round us dost thou gape,
And mould to every taste thy dear delusive
    shape.

LXVI.

When Paphos fell by time — accursec
    Time!
The Queen who conquers all must yield tc
    thee —
The Pleasures fled, but sought as warm a
    clime;
And Venus, constant to her native sea,
To nought else constant, hither deigned tc
    flee;
And fixed her shrine within these walls o:
    white;
Though not to one dome circumscribeth
    she
Her worship, but, devoted to her rite,
A thousand altars rise, for ever blazing
    bright.[3]

LXVII.

From morn till night, from night till startled
    Morn
Peeps blushing on the revel's laughing
    crew,

---

[2] Seville was the Hispalis of the Romans.
[3] ["Cadiz, sweet Cadiz! — it is the first spot in
the creation. The beauty of its streets and man·
sions is only excelled by the loveliness of its inhab
itants. It is a complete Cythera, full of the fines

The song is heard, the rosy garland worn;
Devices quaint, and frolics ever new,
Tread on each other's kibes. A long adieu
He bids to sober joy that here sojourns:
Nought interrupts the riot, though in lieu
Of true devotion monkish incense burns,
And love and prayer unite, or rule the hour
by turns.

LXVIII.

The Sabbath comes, a day of blessed rest;
What hallows it upon this Christian shore ?
Lo ! it is sacred to a solemn feast;
Hark ! heard you not the forest-monarch's
roar ?
Crashing the lance, he snuffs the spouting
gore
Of man and steed, o'erthrown beneath his
horn ;
The thronged arena shakes with shouts for
more ;
Yells the mad crowd o'er entrails freshly
torn,
Nor shrinks the female eye, nor even affects
to mourn.

LXIX.

The seventh day this; the jubilee of man.
London ! right well thou knowest the day
of prayer,
Then thy spruce citizen, washed artisan,
And smug apprentice gulp their weekly air :
Thy coach of hackney, whiskey, one-
horse chair,
And humblest gig through sundry suburbs
whirl ;
To Hampstead, Brentford, Harrow make
repair;
Till the tired jade the wheel forgets to
hurl,
Provoking envious gibe form each pedestrian
churl.[1]

LXX.

Some o'er thy Thamis row the ribboned
fair,
Others along the safer turnpike fly ;
Some Richmond-hill ascend, some scud to
Ware,

And many to the steep of Higïgate hie.
Ask ye Bœotian shades ! the reason why ?[2]
'Tis to the worship of the solemn Horn,
Grasped in the holy hand of Mystery,
In whose dread name both men and maids
are sworn,
And consecrate the oath with draught, and
dance till morn.[3]

LXXI.

All have their fooleries — not alike are
thine,
Fair Cadiz, rising o'er the dark blue sea !
Soon as the matin bell proclaimeth nine,
Thy saint adorers count the rosary :
Much is the VIRGIN teased to shrive them
free
(Well do I ween the only virgin there)
From crimes as numerous as her beadsmen
be ;
Then to the crowded circus forth they fare :
Young, old, high, low, at once the same
diversion share.

LXXII.

The lists are oped, the spacious area
cleared,
Thousands on thousands piled are seated
round
Long ere the first loud trumpet's note is
heard,
Ne vacant space for lated wight is found :
Here dons, grandees, but chiefly dames
abound,
Skilled in the ogle of a roguish eye,
Yet ever well inclined to heal the wound ;
None through their cold disdain are doomed
to die
As moon-struck bards complain, by Love's
sad archery.

LXXIII.

Hushed is the din of tongues — on gallant
steeds,
With milk-white crest, gold spur, and light-
poised lance,
Four cavaliers prepare for venturous deeds,
And lowly bending to the lists advance ;

---

women in Spain; the Cadiz belles being the Lan-
cashire witches of their land." — *Byron to his
Mother.* 1809.]
[1] [" In thus mixing up the light with the solemn,
it was the intention of the poet to imitate Ariosto.
But it is far easier to rise with grace, from the level
of a strain generally familiar, into an occasional
short burst of pathos or splendor, than to interrupt
thus a prolonged tone of solemnity by any descent
into the ludicrous or burlesque. In the former case,
the transition may have the effect of softening or
elevating; while, in the latter, it almost invariably
shocks: — for the same reason, perhaps, that a trait
of pathos or high feeling, in comedy, has a peculiar
charm; while the intrusion of comic scenes into
tragedy, however sanctioned among us by habit
and authority, rarely fails to offend. The poet was
himself convinced of the failure of the experiment,
and in none of the succeeding cantos of Childe
Harold repeated it." — *Moore.*]
[2] This was written at Thebes, and consequently
in the best situation for asking and answering such
a question; not as the birthplace of Pindar, but as
the capital of Bœotia, where the first riddle was pro-
pounded and solved.
[3] [Byron alludes to a ridiculous custom which
formerly prevailed at the public-houses in Highgate,
of administering a burlesque oath to all travellers
of the middling rank who stopped there. The party

Rich are their scarfs, their charges featly
  prance; '
If in the dangerous game they shine to-day,
The crowd's loud shout and ladies' lovely
  glance,
Best prize of better acts, they bear away,
And all that kings or chiefs e'er gain their
  toils repay.

LXXIV.

In costly sheen and gaudy cloak arrayed,
But all afoot, the light-limbed Matadore
Stands in the centre, eager to invade
The lord of lowing herds; but not before
The ground, with cautious tread, is trav-
  ersed o'er,
Lest aught unseen should lurk to thwart his
  speed:
His arms a dart, he fights aloof, nor more
Can man achieve without the friendly
  steed —
Alas! too oft condemned for him to bear and
  bleed.

LXXV.

Thrice sounds the clarion; lo! the signal
  falls,
The den expands, and Expectation mute
Gapes round the silent circle's peopled
  walls.
Bounds with one lashing spring the mighty
  brute,
And, wildly staring, spurns, with sounding
  foot,
The sand, nor blindly rushes on his foe:
Here, there, he points his threatening front,
  to suit
His first attack, wide waving to and fro
His angry tail; red rolls his eye's dilated glow.

LXXVI.

Sudden he stops; his eye is fixed: away,
Away, thou heedless boy! prepare the spear:
Now is thy time, to perish, or display
The skill that yet may check his mad career.
With well-timed croupe the nimble coursers
  veer;
On foams the bull, but not unscathed he
  goes;
Streams from his flank the crimson torrent
  clear:
He flies, he wheels, distracted with his
  throes;
Dart follows dart; lance lance; loud bellow-
  ings speak his woes.

LXXVII.

Again he comes; nor dart nor lance ava
Nor the wild plunging of the tortured hors
Though man and man's avenging arr
  assail,
Vain are his weapons, vainer is his force.
One gallant steed is stretched a mangl
  corse;
Another, hideous sight! unseamed appear
His gory chest unveils life's panting source
Though death-struck, still his feeble fram
  he rears;
Staggering, but stemming all, his lord u
  harmed he bears.

LXXVIII.

Foiled, bleeding, breathless, furious to th
  last,
Full in the centre stands the bull at bay,
Mid wounds, and clinging darts, and lanc
  brast,
And foes disabled in the brutal fray:
And now the Matadores around him play
Shake the red cloak, and poise the read
  brand.
Once more through all he bursts his thur
  dering way —
Vain rage! the mantle quits the conyng
  hand,
Wraps his fierce eye — 'tis past — he sink
  upon the sand![1]

LXXIX.

Where his vast neck just mingles with th
  spine,
Sheathed in his form the deadly weapo
  lies.
He stops — he starts — disdaining to de
  cline:
Slowly he falls, amidst triumphant cries,
Without a groan, without a struggle dies.
The decorated car appears — on high
The corse is piled — sweet sight for vulga
  eyes —
Four steeds that spurn the rein, as swift a
  shy,
Hurl the dark bulk along, scarce seen in dash
  ing by.

LXXX.

Such the ungentle sport that oft invites
  The Spanish maid, and cheers the Spanisl
  swain.

---

was sworn on a pair of horns, fastened, " never to
kiss the maid when he could the mistress; never to
eat brown bread when he could get white; never
to drink small beer when he could get strong;"
with many other injunctions of the like kind, — to
all which was added the saving clause, — "unless
you like it best."]

[1] [So inveterate was, at one time, the rage of th
Spanish people for this amusement, that even boy
mimicked its features in their play. In the slaugh
ter-house itself the professional bull-fighter gav
public lessons; and such was the force of deprave
custom, that ladies of the highest rank were nc
ashamed to appear amidst the filth and horror of th
shambles. The Spaniards received this sport fror
the Moors, among whom it was celebrated wit
great pomp and splendor.]

Nurtured in blood betimes, his heart delights
In vengeance, gloating on another's pain.
What private feuds the troubled village
   stain!
Though now one phalanxed host should
   meet the foe
Enough, alas! in humble homes remain,
To meditate 'gainst friends the secret blow,
For some slight cause of wrath, whence life's
   warm stream must flow.

LXXXI.

But Jealousy has fled: his bars, his bolts,
His withered centinel, Duenna sage!
And all whereat the generous soul revolts,
Which the stern dotard deemed he could
   encage
Have passed to darkness with the vanished
   age.
Who late so free as Spanish girls were seen,
(Ere War uprose in his volcanic rage,)
With braided tresses bounding o'er the
   green,
While on the gay dance shone Night's lover-
   loving Queen?

LXXXII.

Oh! many a time, and oft, had Harold loved,
Or dreamed he loved, since Rapture is a
   dream;
But now his wayward bosom was unmoved,
For not yet had he drunk of Lethe's stream;
And lately had he learned with truth to deem
Love has no gift so grateful as his wings:
How fair, how young, how soft soe'er he
   seem,
Full from the fount of Joy's delicious springs
Some bitter o'er the flowers its bubbling venom
   flings.[1]

LXXXIII.

Yet to the beauteous form he was not blind,
Though now it moved him as it moves the
   wise;
Not that Philosophy on such a mind
E'er deigned to bend her chastely-awful
   eyes:
But Passion raves itself to rest, or flies;
And Vice, that digs her own voluptuous
   tomb,
Had buried long his hopes, no more to rise:
Pleasure's palled victim! life-abhorring
   gloom
Wrote on his faded brow curst Cain's unrest-
   ing doom.

LXXXIV.

Still he beheld, nor mingled with the throng;
But viewed them not with misanthropic
   hate:

---

[1] "Medio de fonte leporum," etc. — *Lucret.*

Fain would he now have joined the dance,
   the song;
But who may smile that sinks beneath his
   fate?
Nought that he saw his sadness could abate:
Yet once he struggled 'gainst the demon's
   sway,
And as in Beauty's bower he pensive sate,
Poured forth this unpremeditated lay,
To charms as fair as those that soothed his
   happier day.

TO INEZ.

I.

Nay, smile not at my sullen brow;
   Alas! I cannot smile again:
Yet Heaven avert that ever thou
   Shouldst weep, and haply weep in vain.

2.

And dost thou ask, what secret woe
   I bear, corroding joy and youth?
And wilt thou vainly seek to know
   A pang, even thou must fail to soothe?

3.

It is not love, it is not hate,
   Nor low Ambition's honors lost,
That bids me loathe my present state,
   And fly from all I prized the most:

4.

It is that weariness which springs
   From all I meet, or hear, or see:
To me no pleasure Beauty brings;
   Thine eyes have scarce a charm for me.

5.

It is that settled, ceaseless gloom
   The fabled Hebrew wanderer bore;
That will not look beyond the tomb,
   But cannot hope for rest before.

6.

What Exile from himself can flee?
   To zones, though more and more remote,
Still, still pursues, where'er I be,
   The blight of life — the demon Thought.

7.

Yet others rapt in pleasure seem,
   And taste of all that I forsake;
Oh! may they still of transport dream,
   And ne'er at least like me, awake!

8.

Through many a clime 'tis mine to go,
   With many a retrospection curst;
And all my solace is to know,
   Whate'er betides, I've known the worst

9.

What is that worst? Nay do not ask —
In pity from the search forbear;
Smile on — nor venture to unmask
Man's heart, and view the Hell that's there.[1]

LXXXV.

Adieu, fair Cadiz! yea, a long adieu!
Who may forget how well thy walls have
　stood?
When all wert changing thou alone wert
　true,
First to be free and last to be subdued:
And if amidst a scene, a shock so rude,
Some native blood was seen thy streets to
　dye;

---

[1] In place of this song, which was written at
Athens, January 25, 1810, and which contains, as
Moore says, "some of the dreariest touches of sad-
ness that ever Byron's pen let fall," we find, in the
first draught of the Canto, the following: —

1.

Oh never talk again to me
　Of northern climes and British ladies;
It has not been your lot to see,
　Like me, the lovely girl of Cadiz.
Although her eye be not of blue,
　Nor fair her locks, like English lasses,
How far its own expressive hue
　The languid azure eye surpasses.

2.

Prometheus-like, from heaven she stole
　The fire, that through those silken lashes
In darkest glances seems to roll,
　From eyes that cannot hide their flashes:
And as along her bosom steal
　In lengthened flow her raven tresses,
You'd swear each clustering lock could feel,
　And curled to give her neck caresses.

3.

Our English maids are long to woo,
　And frigid even in possession;
And if their charms be fair to view,
　Their lips are slow at Love's confession:
But born beneath a brighter sun,
　For love ordained the Spanish maid is,
And who, — when fondly, fairly won,—
　Enchants you like the Girl of Cadiz?

4.

The Spanish maid is no coquette,
　Nor joys to see a lover tremble,
And if she love, or if she hate,
　Alike she knows not to dissemble.
Her heart can ne'er be bought or sold —
　Howe'er it beats, it beats sincerely;
And, though it will not bend to gold,
　'Twill love you long and love you dearly.

5.

The Spanish girl that meets your love
　Ne'er taunts you with a mock denial,
For every thought is bent to prove
　Her passion in the hour of trial.

A traitor only fell beneath the feud:[2]
Here all were noble, save Nobility;
None hugged a conqueror's chain, save fall[
Chivalry.

LXXXVI.

Such be the sons of Spain, and strange h
　fate!
They fight for freedom who were never fre
A Kingless people for a nerveless state,
Her vassals combat when their chieftai
　flee,
True to the veriest slaves of Treachery:
Fond of a land which gave them nought b
　life,
Pride points the path that leads to Libert
Back to the struggle, baffled in the strife,
War, war is still the cry, "War even to th
　knife!"[3]

LXXXVII.

Ye, who would more of Spain and Spaniar
　know
Go, read whate'er is writ of bloodiest strif
Whate'er keen Vengeance urged on foreig
　foe
Can act, is acting there against man's life
From flashing scimitar to secret knife,
War mouldeth there each weapon to h
　need —
So may he guard the sister and the wife,
So may he make each curst oppressor blee
So may such foes deserve the most remors
　less deed![4]

When thronging foemen menace Spain,
　She dares the deed and shares the danger;
And should her lover press the plain,
　She hurls the spear, her love's avenger.

6.

And when, beneath the evening star,
　She mingles in the gay Bolero,
Or sings to her attuned guitar
　Of Christian knight or Moorish hero,
Or counts her beads with fairy hand
　Beneath the twinkling rays of Hesper,
Or joins devotion's choral band,
　To chaunt the sweet and hallowed vesper; -

7.

In each her charms the heart must move
　Of all who venture to behold her;
Then let not maids less fair reprove
　Because her bosom is not colder:
Through many a clime 'tis mine to roam
　Where many a soft and melting maid is,
But none abroad, and few at home,
　May match the dark-eyed Girl of Cadiz.

---

[2] Alluding to the conduct and death of Solan
the governor of Cadiz, in May, 1800.

[3] "War to the knife." Palafox's answer to th
French general at the siege of Saragoza.

[4] The Canto, in the original MS., closes with th
following stanzas: —

LXXXVIII.

Flows there a tear of pity for the dead ?,
Look o'er the ravage of the reeking plain;
Look on the hands with female slaughter
   red;
Then to the dogs resign the unburied slain,
Then to the vulture let each corse remain,
Albeit unworthy of the prey-bird's maw;
Let their bleached bones, and blood's un-
   bleaching stain,
Long mark the battle-field with hideous awe :
Thus only may our sons conceive the scenes
   we saw !

LXXXIX.

Nor yet, alas ! the dreadful work is done;
Fresh legions pour adown the Pyrenees :
It deepens still, the work is scarce begun,
Nor mortal eye the distant end foresees.
Fallen nations gaze on Spain; if freed, she
   frees
More than her fell Pizarros once enchained :
Strange retribution ! now Columbia's ease
Repairs the wrongs that Quito's sons sus-
   tained,
While o'er the parent clime prowls Murder
   unrestrained.

Ye, who would more of Spain and Spaniards
   know,
Sights, Saints, Antiques, Arts, Anecdotes, and
   War,
Go! hie ye hence to Paternoster Row —
Are they not written in the Book of Carr,*
Green Erin's Knight and Europe's wandering
   star!
Then listen, Reader, to the Man of Ink,
Hear what he did, and sought, and wrote afar;
All these are cooped within one Quarto's brink,
This borrow, steal, — don't buy, — and tell us what
   you think.

There may you read, with spectacles on eyes,
How many Wellesleys did embark for Spain,
As if therein they meant to colonize,
How many troops y-crossed the laughing main
That ne'er beheld the said return again;
How many buildings are in such a place,
How many leagues from this to yonder plain,
How many relics each cathedral grace,
And where Giralda stands on her gigantic base.

There may you read (Oh, Phœbus, save Sir John!
That these my words prophetic may not err)
All that was said, or sung, or lost, or won,
By vaunting Wellesley or by blundering Frere,
He that wrote half the " Needy Knife-Grinder," †
Thus poesy the way to grandeur paves —

---

* Porphyry said that the prophecies of Daniel
were written after their completion, and such may
be my fate here; but it requires no second sight to
foretell a tome: the first glimpse of the knight was
enough.
  † [The " Needy Knife-grinder," in the Anti-
Jacobin, was a joint production of Frere and Can-
ning.]

XC.

Not all the blood at Talavera shed,
Not all the marvels of Barossa's fight,
Not Albuera lavish of the dead,
Have won for Spain her well-asserted right.
When shall her Olive-Branch be free from
   blight ?
When shall she breathe her from the blush-
   ing toil ?
How many a doubtful day shall sink in
   night,
Ere the Frank robber turn him from his
   spoil,
And Freedom's stranger-tree grow native of
   the soil !

XCI.

And thou, my friend! [1] — since unavailing
   woe
Bursts from my heart, and mingles with the
   strain —
Had the sword laid thee with the mighty low,
Pride might forbid e'en Friendship to com-
   plain :

Who would not such diplomatists prefer?
But cease, my Muse, thy speed some respite craves,
Leave Legates to their house, and armies to their
   graves.

Yet here of Vulpes mention may be made,
Who for the Junta modelled sapient laws,
Taught them to govern ere they were obeyed;
Certes, fit teacher to command, because
His soul Socratic no Xantippe awes;
Blest with a dame in Virtue's bosom nurst, —
With her let silent admiration pause! —
True to her second husband and her first:
On such unshaken fame let Satire do its worst.

[1] The Honorable John Wingfield, of the Guards,
who died of a fever at Coimbra. I had known him
ten years, the better half of his life, and the happiest
part of mine. In the short space of one month, I
have lost *her* who gave me being, and most of
those who had made that being tolerable. To me
the lines of Young are no fiction : —
" Insatiate archer! could not one suffice?
Thy shaft flew thrice, and thrice my peace was
   slain,
And thrice ere thrice yon moon had filled her horn."
I should have ventured a verse to the memory of
the late Charles Skinner Matthews, Fellow of
Downing College, Cambridge, were he not too
much above all praise of mine. His powers of
mind, shown in the attainment of greater honors,
against the ablest candidates, than those of any
graduate on record at Cambridge, have sufficiently
established his fame on the spot where it was ac-
quired; while his softer qualities live in the recol-
lection of friends who loved him too well to envy
his superiority. — [" To him all the men I ever
knew were pigmies. He was an intellectual giant.
It is true I loved Wingfield better; he was the earli-
est and the dearest, and one of the few one could
never repent of having loved: but in ability — Ah,
you did not know Matthews! " — *Byron to Dallas*,
1812.]

But thus unlaurelled to descend in vain,
By all forgotten, save the lonely breast,
And mix unbleeding with the boasted
    slain,
While Glory crowns so many a meaner
    crest!
What hadst thou done to sink so peacefully
    to rest?

XCII.

' Oh, known the earliest, and esteemed 'the
    most!
Dear to a heart where nought was left so
    dear!
Though to my hopeless days for ever lost,
In dreams deny me not to see thee here!
And Morn in secret shall renew the tear

Of Consciousness awaking to her woes,·
And Fancy hover o'er thy bloodless bier,
Till my frail frame return to whence it ros
And mourned and mourner lie united i
    repose.

XCIII.

Here is one fytte of Harold's pilgrimage:
Ye who of him may further seek to know,
Shall find some tidings in a future page,
If he that rhymeth now may scribble moe
Is this too much? stern Critic! say not s
Patience! and ye shall hear what he behe
In other lands, where he was doomed to g
Lands that contain the monuments of El(
Ere Greece and Grecian arts by barbaro
    hands were quelled.

CANTO THE SECOND.

I.

COME, blue-eyed maid of heaven!—but
    thou, alas,
Didst never yet one mortal song inspire—
Goddess of Wisdom! here thy temple was,
And is, despite of war and wasting fire,[1]
And years, that bade thy worship to expire.
But worse than steel, and flame, and ages
    slow,
Is the dread sceptre and dominion dire
Of men who never felt the sacred glow
That thoughts of thee and thine on polished
    breasts bestow.

II.

Ancient of days! august Athena![2] where,
Where are thy men of might? thy grand
    in soul?

Gone—glimmering through the dream
    things that were:
First in the race that led to Glory's goal,
They won, and passed away—is this th
    whole?
A schoolboy's tale, the wonder of an hour
The warrior's weapon and the sophist'
    stole

---

[1] Part of the Acropolis was destroyed by the explosion of a magazine during the Venetian siege. — [On the highest part of Lycabettus, as Chandler was informed by an eye-witness, the Venetians, in 1687, placed four mortars and six pieces of cannon, when they battered the Acropolis. One of the bombs was fatal to some of the sculpture on the west front of the Parthenon. "In 1667," says Hobhouse, "every antiquity of which there is now any trace in the Acropolis, was in a tolerable state of preservation. This great temple might, at that period, be called entire;—having been previously a Christian church, it was then a mosque, the most beautiful in the world."]

[2] We can all feel, or imagine, the regret with which the ruins of cities, once the capitals of empires, are beheld: the reflections suggested by such objects are too trite to require recapitulation. But never did the littleness of man, and the vanity of his very best virtues, of patriotism to exalt, and of

valor to defend his country, appear more conspicu ous than in the record of what Athens was, and th certainty of what she now is. This theatre of cor tention between mighty factions, of the struggles (orators, the exaltation and deposition of tyrant: the triumph and punishment of generals, is no become a scene of petty intrigue and perpetual di: turbance, between the bickering agents of certai British nobility and gentry. "The wild foxes, th owls and serpents in the ruins of Babylon," wer surely less degrading than such inhabitants. Th Turks have the plea of conquest for their tyranny and the Greeks have only suffered the fortune (war, incidental to the bravest; but how are th mighty fallen, when two painters contest the privi lege of plundering the Parthenon, and triumph i: turn, according to the tenor of each succeeding fil man! Sylla could but punish, Philip subdue, an Xerxes burn Athens: but it remained for the paltr antiquarian, and his despicable agents, to rende her contemptible as himself and his pursuits. Th Parthenon, before its destruction in part, by fir during the Venetian siege, had been a temple, church, and a mosque. In each point of view it i an object of regard: it changed its worshippers; bu still it was a place of worship thrice sacred to devo tion: its violation is a triple sacrilege. But—

        "Man, proud man,
Drest in a little brief authority,
Plays such fantastic tricks before high heaven
As make the angels weep."

Are sought in vain, and o'er each moulder-
  ing tower,
Dim with the mist of years, gray flits the shade
  of power.

III.

Son of the morning, rise I approach you
  here!
Come — but molest not yon defenceless
  urn:
Look on this spot — a nation's sepulchre!
Abode of gods, whose shrines no longer
  burn.
Even gods must yield — religions take their
  turn:
'Twas Jove's — 'tis Mahomet's — and other
  creeds
Will rise with other years, till man shall
  learn
Vainly his incense soars, his victim bleeds;
Poor child of Doubt and Death, whose hope
  is built on reeds. [1]

IV.

Bound to the earth, he lifts his eye to
  heaven —
Is't not enough, unhappy thing! to know
Thou art? Is this a boon so kindly given,
That being, thou would'st be again, and
  go,
Thou know'st not, reck'st not to what
  region, so
On earth no more, but mingled with the
  skies?

[1] [In the original MS. the following note to this stanza had been prepared for publication, but was afterwards withdrawn, " from a fear," says the poet, " that it might be considered rather as an attack, than a defence of religion:" — "In this age of bigotry, when the puritan and priest have changed places, and the wretched Catholic is visited with the 'sins of his fathers,' even unto generations far beyond the pale of the commandment, the cast of opinion in these stanzas will, doubtless, meet with many a contemptuous anathema. But let it be remembered, that the spirit they breathe is desponding, not sneering, scepticism; that he who has seen the Greek and Moslem superstitions contending for mastery over the former shrines of Polytheism — who has left in his own, 'Pharisees, thanking God that they are not like publicans and sinners,' and Spaniards in theirs, abhorring the heretics, who have holpen them in their need, — will be not a little bewildered, and begin to think, that as only one of them can be right, they may, most of them, be wrong. With regard to morals, and the effect of religion on mankind, it appears, from all historical testimony, to have had less effect in making them love their neighbors, than inducing that cordial Christian abhorrence between sectaries and schismatics. The Turks and Quakers are the most tolerant: if an Infidel pays his heratch to the former, he may pray how, when, and where he pleases; and the mild tenets, and devout demeanor of the latter, make their lives the truest commentary on the Sermon on the Mount."]

Still wilt thou dream on future joy and
  woe?
Regard and weigh yon dust before it flies:
That little urn saith more than thousand
  homilies.

V.

Or burst the vanished Hero's lofty mound;
Far on the solitary shore he sleeps: [2]
He fell, and falling nations mourned
  around;
But now not one of saddening thousands
  weeps,
Nor warlike-worshipper his vigil keeps
Where demi-gods appeared, as records
  tell.
Remove yon skull from out the scattered
  heaps:
Is that a temple where a God may dwell?
Why even the worm at last disdains her
  shattered cell!

VI.

Look on its broken arch, its ruined wall,
Its chambers desolate, and portals foul:
Yet, this was once Ambition's airy hall,
The dome of Thought, the palace of the
  Soul:
Behold through each lack-lustre, eyeless
  hole,
The gay recess of Wisdom and of Wit,
And Passion's host, that never brooked
  control.
Can all saint, sage, or sophist ever writ,
People this lonely tower, this tenement refit?

VII.

Well didst thou speak, Athena's wisest
  son!
"All that we know is, nothing can be
  known."
Why should we shrink from what we cannot
  shun?
Each hath his pang, but feeble sufferers
  groan
With brain-born dreams of evil all their
  own.
Pursue what Chance or Fate proclaimeth
  best;
Peace waits us on the shores of Acheron:
There no forced banquet claims the sated
  guest,
But Silence spreads the couch of ever welcome
  rest.

[2] It was not always the custom of the Greeks to burn their dead; the greater Ajax, in particular, was interred entire. Almost all the chiefs became gods after their decease; and he was indeed neglected, who had not annual games near his tomb, or festivals in honor of his memory by his countrymen, as Achilles, Brasidas, etc., and at last even Antinous, whose death was as heroic as his life was infamous.

VIII.

Yet if, as holiest men have deemed, there be
A land of souls beyond that sable shore,
To shame the doctrine of the Sadducee
And sophists, madly vain of dubious lore;
How sweet it were in concert to adore
With those who made our mortal labors
  light!
To hear each voice we feared to hear no
  more!
Behold each mighty shade revealed to
  sight,
The Bactrian, Samian sage, and all who
  taught the right! [1]

IX.

There, thou! — whose love and life together
  fled,
Have left me here to love and live in
  vain —
Twined with my heart, and can I deem thee
  dead
When busy Memory flashes on my brain?
Well — I will dream that we may meet
  again,
And woo the vision to my vacant breast:
If aught of young Remembrance then re-
  main,
Be as it may Futurity's behest,
For me 'twere bliss enough to know thy spirit
  blest! [2]

X.

Here let me sit upon this massy stone,
The marble column's yet unshaken base;
Here, son of Saturn! was thy fav'rite throne:
Mightiest of many such! Hence let me trace
The latent grandeur of thy dwelling-place.
It may not be: nor even can Fancy's eye
Restore what Time hath labored to deface.
Yet these proud pillars claim no passing
  sigh;
Unmoved the Moslem sits, the light Greek
  carols by.

XI.

But who, of all the plunderers of yon fane
On high, where Pallas lingered, loth to flee

The latest relic of her ancient reign;
The last, the worst, dull spoiler, who was he
Blush, Caledonia! such thy son could be
England! I joy no child he was of thine:
Thy free-born men should spare what onc
  was free;
Yet they could violate each saddenin
  shrine,
And bear these altars o'er the long-reluctar
  brine. [3]

XII.

But most the modern Pict's ignoble boast
To rive what Goth, and Turk, and Tim
  hath spared: [4]
Cold as the crags upon his native coast,
His mind as barren and his heart as hard,
Is he whose head conceived, whose han
  prepared,
Aught to displace Athena's poor remains:
Her sons too weak the sacred shrine t
  guard,
Yet felt some portion of their mother's pains,
And never knew, till then, the weight of De:
  pot's chains.

XIII.

What! shall it e'er be said by Britis
  tongue,
Albion was happy in Athena's tears?
Though in thy name the slaves her boso
  wrung,
Tell not the deed to blushing Europe's ears
The ocean queen, the free Britannia, bea
The last poor plunder from a bleeding land
Yes, she, whose gen'rous aid her name er
  dears,
Tore down those remnants with a harpy'
  hand,
Which envious Eld forbore, and tyrants le
  to stand. [6]

---

[1] [In the MS., instead of this stanza, was the following: —

"Frown not upon me, churlish Priest! that I
Look not for life, where life may never be;
I am no sneerer at thy phantasy;
Thou pitiest me, — alas! I envy thee,
Thou bold discoverer in an unknown sea,
Of happy isles and happier tenants there;
I ask thee not to prove a Sadducee;
Still dream of Paradise, thou know'st not where,
But lov'st too well to bid thine erring brother
  share."

[2] [Byron wrote this stanza at Newstead, in October, 1811, on hearing of the death of his Cambridge friend, young Eddlestone.]

[3] The temple of Jupiter Olympius, of which six teen columns, entirely of marble, yet survive: ori inally there were one hundred and fifty. Thes columns, however, are by many supposed to hav belonged to the Pantheon.

[4] See Appendix to this Canto [A], for a note to long to be placed here.

[5] I cannot resist availing myself of the permi sion of my friend Dr. Clarke, whose name requir no comment with the public, but whose sanctio will add tenfold weight to my testimony, to inse the following extract from a very obliging letter his to me, as a note to the above lines: — "Whe the last of the Metopes was taken from the Parthe non, and, in moving of it, great part of the supe structure with one of the triglyphs was thrown dow by the workmen whom Lord Elgin employed, th Disdar, who beheld the mischief done to the buildin took his pipe from his mouth, dropped a tear, an in a supplicating tone of voice, said to Lusier Τέλος! — I was present." The Disdar alluded was the father of the present Disdar.

[6] [After stanza xiii. the original MS. has th following: —

XIV.

Where was thine Ægis, Pallas! that appalled
Stern Alaric and Havoc on their way?[1]
Where Peleus' son? whom Hell in vain
enthralled,
His shade from Hades upon that dread day
Bursting to light in terrible array!
What! could not Pluto spare the chief once
more,
To scare a second robber from his prey?
Idly he wandered on the Stygian shore,
Nor now preserved the walls he loved to shield
before.

XV.

Cold is the heart, fair Greece! that looks on
thee,
Nor feels as lovers o'er the dust they loved;
Dull is the eye that will not weep to see
Thy walls defaced, thy mouldering shrines
removed
By British hands, which it had best behooved
To guard those relics ne'er to be restored.
Curst be the hour when from their isle they
roved,
And once again thy hapless bosom gored,
And snatched thy shrinking Gods to northern
climes abhorred!

XVI.

But where is Harold? shall I then forget
To urge the gloomy wanderer o'er the wave?
Little recked he of all that men regret;
No loved-one now in feigned lament could
rave;
No friend the parting hand extended gave,
Ere the cold stranger passed to other climes;
Hard is his heart whom charms may not
enslave;
But Harold felt not as in other times,
And left without a sigh the land of war and
crimes.

" Come, then, ye classic Thanes of each degree,
Dark Hamilton and sullen Aberdeen,
Come pilfer all the Pilgrim loves to see,
All that yet consecrates the fading scene:
Oh! better were it ye had never been,
Nor ye, nor Elgin, nor that lesser wight,
The victim sad of vase-collecting spleen,
House-furnisher withal, one Thomas hight,
Than ye should bear one stone from wronged
Athena's site.

" Or will the gentle Dilettanti crew
Now delegate the task to digging Gell,
That mighty limner of a birds'-eye view,
How like to Nature let his volumes tell;
Who can with him the folio's limits swell
With all the Author saw, or said he saw?
Who can topographize or delve so well?
No boaster he, nor impudent and raw,
His pencil, pen, and shade, alike without a flaw."]

[1] According to Zosimus, Minerva and Achilles
frightened Alaric from the Acropolis; but others

XVII.

He that has sailed upon the dark blue sea
Has viewed at times, I ween, a full fair sight;
When the fresh breeze is fair as breeze may
be,
The white sail set, the gallant frigate tight;
Masts, spires, and strand retiring to the right
The glorious main expanding o'er the bow.
The convoy spread like wild swans in their
flight,
The dullest sailer wearing bravely now,
So gaily curl the waves before each dashing
prow.

XVIII.

And oh, the little warlike world within!
The well-reeved guns, the netted canopy,[2]
The hoarse command, the busy humming
din,
When, at a word, the tops are manned on
high:
Hark, to the Boatswain's call, the cheering
cry!
While through the seaman's hand the tackle
glides,
Or schoolboy Midshipman that, standing by,
Strains his shrill pipe as good or ill betides,
And well the docile crew that skilful urchin
guides.

XIX.

White is the glassy deck, without a stain,
Where on the watch the staid Lieutenant
walks:
Look on that part which sacred doth remain
For the lone chieftain, who majestic stalks,
Silent and feared by all — not oft he talks
With aught beneath him, if he would pre-
serve
That strict restraint, which broken, ever
balks
Conquest and Fame: but Britons rarely
swerve
From law, however stern, which tends their
strength to nerve.

XX.

Blow! swiftly blow, thou keel-compelling
gale!
Till the broad sun withdraws his lessening
ray;
Then must the pennant-bearer slacken sail,
That lagging barks may make their lazy way.
Ah! grievance sore, and listless dull delay,
To waste on sluggish hulks the sweetest
breeze!
What leagues are lost, before the dawn of
day,

relate that the Gothic king was nearly as mischiev-
ous as the Scottish peer. — See *Chandler.*

[2] To prevent blocks or splinters from falling on
deck during action.

Thus loitering pensive on the willing seas,
The flapping sail hauled down to halt for logs
  like these!

XXI.

The moon is up; by Heaven, a lovely eve!
Long streams of light o'er dancing waves
  expand;
Now lads on shore may sigh, and maids
  believe:
Such be our fate when we return to land!
Meantime some rude Arion's restless hand
Wakes the brisk harmony that sailors love;
A circle there of merry listeners stand,
Or to some well-known measure featly move,
Thoughtless, as if on shore they still were free
  to rove.

XXII.

Through Calpe's straits survey the steepy
  shore:
Europe and Afric on each other gaze!
Lands of the dark-eyed Maid and dusky
  Moor
Alike beheld beneath pale Hecate's blaze:
How softly on the Spanish shore she plays,
Disclosing rock, and slope, and forest brown,
Distinct, though darkening with her waning
  phase;
But Mauritania's giant-shadows frown,
From mountain-cliff to coast descending
  sombre down.

XXIII.

'Tis night, when Meditation bids us feel
We once have loved, though love is at an
  end:
The heart, lone mourner of its baffled zeal,
Though friendless now, will dream it had a
  friend.
Who with the weight of years would wish
  to bend,
When Youth itself survives young Love
  and Joy?
Alas! when mingling souls forget to blend,
Death hath but little left him to destroy?
Ah! happy years! once more who would not
  be a boy?

XXIV.

Thus bending o'er the vessel's laving side,
To gaze on Dian's wave-reflected sphere,
The soul forgets her schemes of Hope and
  Pride,
And flies unconscious o'er each backward
  year.
None are so desolate but something dear,
Dearer than self, possesses or possessed
A thought, and claims the homage of a tear;
A flashing pang! of which the weary breast
Would still, albeit in vain, the heavy heart
  divest.

XXV.

To sit on rocks, to muse o'er flood and fell,
To slowly trace the forest's shady scene,

Where things that own not man's dominion
  dwell,
And mortal foot hath ne'er or rarely been;
To climb the trackless mountain all unseen
With the wild flock that never needs a fold
Alone o'er steeps and foaming falls to lean
This is not solitude; 'tis but to hold
Converse with Nature's charms, and view her
  stores unrolled.

XXVI.

But midst the crowd, the hum, the shock of
  men,
To hear, to see, to feel, and to possess,
And roam along, the world's tired denizen,
With none who bless us, none whom we
  can bless,
Minions of splendor shrinking from distress!
None that, with kindred consciousness en-
  dued,
If we were not, would seem to smile the less,
Of all that flattered, followed, sought, and
  sued;
This is to be alone; this, this is solitude!

XXVII.

More blest the life of godly eremite,
Such as on lonely Athos may be seen,[1]
Watching at eve upon the giant height,
Which looks o'er waves so blue, skies so
  serene,
That he who there at such an hour hath
  been,
Will wistful linger on that hallowed spot;
Then slowly tear him from the witching
  scene,
Sigh forth one wish that such had been his
  lot,
Then turn to hate a world he had almost for-
  got.

XXVIII.

Pass we the long, unvarying course, the
  track
Oft trod, that never leaves a trace behind;
Pass we the calm, the gale, the change, the
  tack,
And each well known caprice of wave and
  wind;
Pass we the joys and sorrows sailors find,

---

[1] [One of Byron's chief delights was, as he him-
self states in one of his journals, after bathing in
some retired spot, to seat himself on a high rock
above the sea, and there remain for hours, gazing
upon the sky and the waters. "He led the life,"
says Sir Egerton Brydges, "as he wrote the strains,
of a true poet. He could sleep, and very frequently
did sleep, wrapped up in his rough great coat, on
the hard boards of a deck, while the winds and the
waves were roaring round him on every side, and
could subsist on a crust and a glass of water. It
would be difficult to persuade me, that he who is a
coxcomb in his manners, and artificial in his habits
of life. could write good poetry."]

Cooped in their winged sea-girt citadel;
The foul, the fair, the contrary, the kind,
As breezes rise and fall and billows swell,
Till on some jocund morn — lo, land! and all
  is well.

XXIX.

But not in silence pass Calypso's isles,[1]
The sister tenants of the middle deep;
There for the weary still a haven smiles,
Though the fair goddess long hath ceased
  · to weep,
And o'er her cliffs a fruitless watch to keep
For him who dared prefer a mortal bride:
Here, too, his boy essayed the dreadful leap
Stern Mentor urged from high to yonder
  tide;
While thus of both bereft, the nymph-queen
  doubly sighed.

XXX.

Her reign is past, her gentle glories gone:
But trust not this; too easy youth, beware!
A mortal sovereign holds her dangerous
  throne,
And thou mayest find a new Calypso there.
Sweet Florence! could another ever share
This wayward, loveless heart, it would be
  · thine:
But checked by every tie, I may not dare
To cast a worthless offering at thy shrine,
Nor ask so dear a breast to feel one pang for
  mine.

XXXI.

Thus Harold deemed, as on that lady's eye
He looked, and met its beam without a
  · thought,
Save Admiration glancing harmless by:
Love kept aloof, albeit not far remote,
Who knew his votary often lost and caught,
But knew him as his worshipper no more,
And ne'er again the boy his bosom sought:
Since now he vainly urged him to adore,
Well deemed the little God his ancient sway
  was o'er.

XXXII.

Fair Florence[2] found, in sooth with some
  amaze,
One who, 'twas said, still sighed to all he
  saw,
Withstand, unmoved, the lustre of her gaze,
Which others hailed with real or mimic awe,
Their hope, their doom, their punishment,
  their law;
All that gay Beauty from her bondsmen
  claims:
And much she marvelled that a youth so raw

Nor felt, nor feigned at least, the oft-told
  flames,
Which, though sometimes they frown, yet
  rarely anger dames.

XXXIII.

Little knew she that seeming marble heart,
Now masked in silence or withheld by pride,
Was not unskilful in the spoiler's art,[3]
And spread its snares licentious far and
  wide;
Nor from the base pursuit had turned aside,
As long as aught was worthy to pursue:
But Harold on such arts no more relied;
And had he doted on those eyes so blue,
Yet never would he join the lover's whining
  crew.

XXXIV.

Not much he kens, I ween, of woman's
  breast,
Who thinks that wanton thing is won by
  sighs;
What careth she for hearts when once pos-
  sessed? ·
Do proper homage to thine idol's eyes;
But not too humbly, or she will despise
Thee and thy suit, though told in moving
  tropes:
Disguise even tenderness, if thou art wise;
Brisk Confidence still best with woman
  copes;
Pique her and soothe in turn, soon Passion
  crowns thy hopes.

XXXV.

'Tis an old lesson; Time approves it true,
And those who know it best, deplore it most;
When all is won that all desire to woo,
The paltry prize is hardly worth the cost:
Youth wasted, minds degraded, honor lost,
These are thy fruits, successful Passion!
  these!
If, kindly cruel, early Hope is crost,
Still to the last it rankles, a disease,
Not to be cured when Love itself forgets to
  please.

XXXVI.

Away! nor let me loiter in my song,
For we have many a mountain-path to
  tread,
And many a varied shore to sail along,
By pensive Sadness, not by Fiction, led —
Climes, fair withal as ever mortal head
Imagined in its little schemes of thought;
Or e'er in new Utopias were ared,

---

[1] Goza is said to have been the island of Calypso.
[2] [Mrs. Spencer Smith, an accomplished but eccentric lady, whose acquaintance the poet formed at Malta.]

[3] [Against this line it is sufficient to set the poet's own declaration, in 1821 — "I am not a Joseph, nor a Scipio, but I can safely affirm, that I never in my life seduced any woman."]

To teach man what he might be, or he
  ought;
If that corrupted thing could ever such be
  taught.

XXXVII.

Dear Nature is the kindest mother still,
Though alway changing, in her aspect mild;
From her bare bosom let me take my fill,
Her never-weaned, though not her favored
  child.
Oh! she is fairest in her features wild,
Where nothing polished dares pollute her
  path:
To me by day or night she ever smiled,
Though I have marked her when none other
  hath,
And sought her more and more, and loved
  her best in wrath.

XXXVIII.

Land of Albania! where Iskander rose,
Theme of the young, and beacon of the
  wise,
And he his namesake, whose oft-baffled foes
Shrunk from his deeds of chivalrous em-
  prize:
Land of Albania! [1] let me bend mine eyes
On thee, thou rugged nurse of savage men!
The cross decends, thy minarets arise,
And the pale crescent sparkles in the glen,
Through many a cypress grove within each
  city's ken.

XXXIX.

Childe Harold sailed, and passed the bar-
  ren spot
Where sad Penelope o'erlooked the wave; [2]
And onward viewed the mount, not yet for-
  got,
The lover's refuge, and the Lesbian's grave.
Dark Sappho! could not verse immortal
  save
That breast imbued with such immortal
  fire?
Could she not live who life eternal gave?
If life eternal may await the lyre,
That only heaven to which Earth's children
  may aspire.

XL.

'Twas on a Grecian autumn's gentle eve
Childe Harold hailed Leucadia's cape
  afar; [3]
A spot he longed to see, nor cared to leave:
Oft did he mark the scenes of vanished war,
Actium, Lepanto, fatal Trafalgar; [4]

---

[1] See Appendix to this Canto, Note [B].
[2] Ithaca.
[3] Leucadia, now Santa Maura. From the prom-
ontory (the Lover's Leap) Sappho is said to have
thrown herself.
[4] Actium and Trafalgar need no further mention.
The battle of Lepanto, equally bloody and consid-

Mark them unmoved, for he would not c
  light
(Born beneath some remote inglorious sta
In themes of bloody fray, or gallant fight,
But loathed the bravo's trade, and laughed
  martial wight.

XLI.

But when he saw the evening star above
Leucadia's far-projecting rock of woe,
And hailed the last resort f fruitless love
He felt, or deemed he felt, no common glo'
And as the stately vessel glided slow
Beneath the shadow of that ancient mou
He watched the billows' melancholy flow,
And, sunk albeit in thought as he was wor
More placid seemed his eye, and smooth h
  pallid front.

XLII.

Morn dawns; and with it stern Albania
  hills,
Dark Suli's rocks, and Pindus' inland pea
Robed half in mist, bedewed with snowy rill
Arrayed in many a dun and purple streak
Arise; and, as the clouds along them brea
Disclose the dwelling of the mountaineer
Here roams the wolf, the eagle whets h
  beak,
Birds, beasts of prey, and wilder men appea
And gathering storms around convulse th
  closing year.

XLIII.

Now Harold felt himself at length alone,
And bade to Christian tongues a long adieu
Now he adventured on a shore unknown,
Which all admire, but many dread to view :
His breast was armed 'gainst fate, his wan'
  were few;
Peril he sought not, but ne'er shrank to mee
The scene was savage, but the scene wa
  new;
This made the ceaseless toil of travel swee
Beat back keen winter's blast, and welcome
  summer's heat.

XLIV.

Here the red cross, for still the cross is her
Though sadly scoffed at by the circumcisec
Forgets that pride to pampered priesthoo
  dear;
Churchman and votary alike despised.
Foul superstition! howsoe'er disguised,
Idol, saint, virgin, prophet, crescent, cross,
For whatsoever symbol thou art prized,
Thou sacerdotal gain, but general loss!
Who from true worship's gold can separat
  thy dross?

---

erable, but less known, was fought in the Gulf c
Patras. Here the author of Don Quixote lost hi
left hand.

XLV.

Ambracia's gulf behold, where once was lost
A world for woman, lovely, harmless thing!
In yonder rippling bay, their naval host
Did many a Roman chief and Asian king[1]
To doubtful conflict, certain slaughter bring:
Look where the second Cæsar's trophies
    rose:[2]
Now, like the hands that reared them, wither-
    ing:
Imperial anarchs, doubling human woes!
GOD! was thy globe ordained for such to win
    and lose?

XLVI.

From the dark barriers of that rugged clime,
Even to the centre of Illyria's vales,
Childe Harold passed o'er many a mount
    sublime,
Through lands scarce noticed in historic
    tales;
Yet in famed Attica such lovely dales
Are rarely seen; nor can fair Tempe boast
A charm they know not; loved Parnassus
    fails,
Though classic ground and consecrated
    most,
To match some spots that lurk within this
    lowering coast.

XLVII.

He passed bleak Pindus, Acherusia's lake,[3]
And left the primal city of th land,
And onwards did his further journey take
To greet Albania's chief,[4] whose dread com-
    mand

Is lawless law; for with a bloody hand
He sways a nation, turbulent and bold:
Yet here and there some daring mountain-
    band
Disdain his power, and from their rocky hold
Hurl their defiance far, nor yield, unless to
    gold.[5]

XLVIII.

Monastic Zitza![6] from thy shady brow,
Thou small, but favored spot of holy ground!
Where'er we gaze, around, above, below,
What rainbow tints, what magic charms are
    found!
Rock, river, forest, mountain, all abound,
And bluest skies that harmonize the whole:
Beneath, the distant torrent's rushing sound
Tells where the volumed cataract doth roll
Between those hanging rocks, that shock yet
    please the soul.

XLIX.

Amidst the grove that crowns yon tufted hill,
Which, were it not for many a mountain nigh
Rising in lofty ranks, and loftier still,
Might well itself be deemed of dignity,
The convent's white walls glisten fair on
    high:
Here dwells the caloyer,[7] nor rude is he,
Nor niggard of his cheer; the passer by
Is welcome still; nor heedless will he flee
From hence, if he delight kind Nature's sheen
    to see.

L.

Here in the sultriest season let him rest,
Fresh is the green beneath those aged trees;
Here winds of gentlest wing will fan his
    breast,

---

[1] It is said, that, on th y previous to th battle of Actium, Antony had irteen kings at h.s levee. — ["To-day" (Nov. 12), "I s..w the remains of the town of Actium, near wh h Antony lost the world, in a small bay, wher t o frigates could hardly manœuvre: a broken wall is the sole remnant. On another part of the gulf stand the ruins of Nicopolis, built by Augustus, in hon r of his victory."]—*Byron to his Mother,* 1809.

[2] Nicopolis, whose ruins are most extensive, is at some distance from Actium, where the wall of the Hippodrome survives in a few fragments. These ruins are large masses of brickwork, the bricks of which are joined by intersticcs of mortar, as large as the bricks themselves, and equally durable.

[3] According to Pouqueville, the lake of Yanina! but Pouqueville is always out.

[4] The celebrated Ali Pacha. Of this extraordinary man there is an incorrect account in Fouqueville's Travels. — ["I left Malta in the Spider brig-of-war, on the 21st of September, and arrived in eight days at Prevesa. I thence have traversed the interior of the province of Albania, on a visit to the Pacha, as far as Tepaleen, his highness's coun t y palace, where I stayed three days. The name of the Pacha is Ali, and he is considercd a man of th first abilitic he governs the whole of Albania (the ancient Illyricum), Epirus, and part of Macedonia." — *Byron to his Mother.*]

[5] Five thousand Suliotes, among the rocks and in the castle of Suli, withstood thirty thousand Albanians for eighteen years; the castle at last was taken by bribery. In this contest there were several acts performed not unworthy of the better days of Greece.

[6] The convent and village of Zitza are four hours' journey from Joannina, or Yanina, the capital of the Pachalick. In the valley the river Halamas (once the Acheron) flows, and, not far from Zitza, forms a fine cataract. The situation is perhaps the finest in Greece, though the approach to Delvinachi and parts of Acarnania and Ætolia may contest the palm. Delphi, Parnassu-, and, in Attica, even Cape Colonna and Port Raphti, are very inferior; as also very scene in Ionia, or the Troad: I am almost inclined to add the approach to Constantinople; but, from the different features of the last, a comparison can hardly be made. ["Zitza," says the poet's companion, "is a village inhabited by Greek peasants. Perhaps there is not in the world a more romantic prospect than that which is viewed from the summit of the hill. The foreground is a gentle declivity, terminating on every side in an extensive landscape of green hills and dale, enriched with vineyards, and dotted with frequent flocks."]

The Greek monks are so called.

From heaven itself he may inhale the breeze :
The plain is far beneath — oh ! let him seize
Pure pleasure while he can ; the scorching
  ray
Here pierceth not, impregnate with disease :
Then let his length the loitering pilgrim lay,
And gaze, untired, the morn, the noon, the
  eve away.

LL

Dusky and huge, enlarging on the sight,
Nature's volcanic amphitheatre,[1]
Chimæra's alps extend from left to right :
Beneath, a living valley seems to stir ;
Flocks play, trees wave, streams flow, the
  mountain-fir
Nodding above ; behold black Acheron ![2]
Once consecrated to the sepulchre.
Pluto ! if this be hell I look upon,
Close shamed Elysium's gates, my shade shall
  seek for none.

LII.

No city's towers pollute the lovely view ;
Unseen is Yanina, though not remote,
Veiled by the screen of hills : here men are
  few,
Scanty the hamlet, rare the lonely cot :
But peering down each precipice, the goat
Browseth ; and, pensive o'er his scattered
  flock,
The little shepherd in his white capote[3]
Doth lean his boyish form along the rock,
Or in his cave awaits the tempest's short-lived
  shock.

LIII.

Oh ! where, Dodona ! is thine aged grove,
Prophetic fount, and oracle divine ?
What valley echoed the response of Jove ?
What trace remaineth of the Thunderer's
  shrine ?
All, all forgotten — and shall man repine
That his frail bonds to fleeting life are broke ?
Cease, fool ! the fate of gods may well be
  thine :
Wouldst thou survive the marble or the oak ?
When nations, tongues, and worlds must sink
  beneath the stroke !

LIV.

Epirus' bounds recede, and mountains fail ;
Tired of up-gazing still, the wearied eye
Reposes gladly on as smooth a vale
As ever Spring yclad in grassy dye :
Even on a plain no humble beauties lie,
Where some bold river breaks the long ex-
  panse,
And woods along the banks are waving high,

Whose shadows in the glassy waters dar
Or with the moonbeam sleep in midnig
  solemn trance.

LV.

The sun had sunk behind vast Tomerit,[4]
And Laos wide and fierce came roaring by
The shades of wonted night were gatheri
  yet,
When, down the steep banks winding war
Childe Harold saw, like meteors in the s
The glittering minarets of Tepalen,
Whose walls o'erlook the stream ; and dra
  ing nigh,
He heard the busy hum of warrior-men
Swelling the breeze that sighed along
  lengthening glen.[6]

LVI.

He passed the sacred Haram's silent tow
And underneath the wide o'erarching ga
Surveyed the dwelling of this chief of pow
Where all around proclaimed his high esta
Amidst no common pomp the despot sat
While busy preparation shook the court,
Slaves, eunuchs, soldiers, guests, and sa
  tons wait ;

---

[1] The Chimariot mountains appear to have been volcanic.
[2] Now called Kalamas.   [3] Albanese cloak.

[4] Anciently Mount Tomarus.
[5] The river Laos was full at the time the auth
passed it ; and immediately above Tepaleen, was
the eye as wide as the Thames at Westminster ;
least in the opinion of the author and his fellc
traveller. In the summer it must be much n
rower. It certainly is the finest river in the Leva
neither Achelous, Alpheus, Acheron, Scamand
nor Ca ster, approached it in breadth or beauty.
[6] ["Ali Pacha, hearing that an Englishman
rank was in his dominions, left orders, in Yanii
with the commandant, to provide a house, and s
ply me with every kind of necessary *gratis.*
rode out on the vizier's horses, and saw the pala
of himself and grandsons. I shall never forget t
singular scene on entering Tepaleen, at five in
afternoon (Oct. 11), as the sun was going dow
It brought to my mind (with some change of *dre*
however) Scott's description of Branksome Cas
in his Lay, and the feudal system. The Albania
in their dresses (the most magnificent in the wor
consisting of a long white kilt, gold-worked clo;
crimson velvet gold-laced jacket and waistcoat, ;
ver-mounted pistols and daggers) ; the Tarta
with their high caps ; the Turks in their vast pel
ses and turbans ; the soldiers and black slaves w
the horses, the former in groups, in an immer
large open gallery in front of the palace, the lat
placed in a kind of cloister below it ; two hundr
steeds ready caparisoned to move in a momer
couriers entering or passing out with despatche
the kettle-drums beating ; boys calling the ho
from the minaret of the mosque ; — altogether, wi
the singular appearance of the building itself, form
a new and delightful spectacle to a stranger. I w
conducted to a very handsome apartment, and r
health inquired after by the vizier's secretary, 'à
mode Turque.'" — *Byron's Letters.*]

Within, a palace, and without, a fort:
Here men of every clime appear to make resort.

LVII.

Richly caparisoned, a ready row
Of armed horse, and many a warlike store,
Circled the wide extending court below;
Above, strange groups adorned the corridore;
And oft-times through the area's echoing door,
Some high-capped Tartar spurred his steed away;
The Turk, the Greek, the Albanian, and the Moor,
Here mingled in their many-hued array,
While the deep war-drum's sound announced the close of day.

LVIII.

The wild Albanian kirtled to his knee,
With shawl-girt head and ornamented gun,
And gold-embroidered garments, fair to see:
The crimson-scarfed men of Macedon;
The Delhi with his cap of terror on,
And crooked glaive; the lively, supple Greek;
And swarthy Nubia's mutilated son;
The bearded Turk, that rarely deigns to speak,
Master of all around, too potent to be meek,

LIX.

Are mixed conspicuous: some recline in groups,
Scanning the motley scene that varies round;
There some grave Moslem to devotion stoops,
And some that smoke, and some that play, are found;
Here the Albanian proudly treads the ground;
Half whispering there the Greek is heard to prate;
Hark! from the mosque the nightly solemn sound,
The Muezzin's call doth shake the minaret,
There is no god but God! — to prayer — lo!
God is great!"[1]

LX.

Just at this season Ramazani's fast[2]
Through the long day its penance did maintain:
But when the lingering twilight hour was past,
Revel and feast assumed the rule again:
Now all was bustle, and the menial train
Prepared and spread the plenteous board within;
The vacant gallery now seemed made in vain,
But from the chambers came the mingling din,
As page and slave anon were passing out and in.

LXI.

Here woman's voice is never heard: apart,
And scarce permitted, guarded, veiled, to move,
She yields to one her person and her heart,
Tamed to her cage, nor feels a wish to rove:
For, not unhappy in her master's love,
And joyful in a mother's gentlest cares,
Blest cares! all other feelings far above!
Herself more sweetly rears the babe she bears,
Who never quits the breast, no meaner passion shares.

LXII.

In marble-paved pavilion, where a spring
Of living water from the centre rose,
Whose bubbling did a genial freshness fling,
And soft voluptuous couches breathed repose,
ALI reclined, a man of war and woes:[3]

---

[1] ["On our arrival at Tepaleen, we were lodged in the palace. During the night, we were disturbed by the perpetual carousal which seemed to be kept up in the gallery, and by the drum and the voice of the 'Muezzin,' or chanter, calling the Turks to prayers from the minaret of the mosque attached to the palace. The chanter was a boy, and he sang out his hymn in a sort of loud melancholy recitative. He was a long time repeating the purport of these few words: 'God most high! I bear witness, that there is no god but God, and Mahomet is his prophet: come to prayer; come to the asylum of salvation: great God! there is no god but God!'" —*Hobhouse*.]

[2] ["We were a little unfortunate in the time we chose for travelling, for it was during the Ramazan, or Turkish Lent, which fell this year in October, and was hailed at the rising of the new moon, on the evening of the 8th, by every demonstration of joy: but although, during this month, the strictest abstinence is observed in the daytime, yet with the setting of the sun the feasting commences: then is the time for paying and receiving visits, and for the amusements of Turkey, puppet-shows, jugglers, dancers, and story-tellers." —*Hobhouse*.]

[3] ["On the 12th, I was introduced to Ali Pacha. The vizier received me in a large room paved with marble; a fountain was playing in the centre. He received me standing, a wonderful compliment from a Mussulman, and made me sit down on his right hand. His first question was, why, at so early an age, I left my country. He then said, the English minister had told him I was of a great family, and desired his respects to my mother; which I now, in the name of Ali Pacha, present to you. He said he was certain I was a man of birth, because I had small ears, curling hair, and little white hands. He told me to consider him as a father, whilst I was in Turkey, and said he looked on me as his own son. Indeed, he treated me like a child, sending me almonds and sugared sherbet, fruit, and sweetmeats, twenty times a day. I then, after coffee and pipes, retired." — *Byron to his Mother*.]

Yet in his lineaments ye cannot trace,
While Gentleness her milder radiance throws
Along that aged venerable face,
The deeds that lurk beneath, and stain him
  with disgrace.

LXIII.

It is not that yon hoary lengthening beard
Ill suits the passions which belong to youth ;[1]
Love conquers age — so Hafiz hath averred,
So sings the Teian, and he sings in sooth —
But crimes that scorn the tender voice of
  Ruth,
Beseeming all men ill, but most the man
In years, have marked him with a tiger's
  tooth ;
Blood follows blood, and, through their mor-
  tal span,
In bloodier acts conclude those who with
  blood began.[2]

LXIV.

'Mid many things most new to ear and eye
The pilgrim rested here his weary feet,
And gazed around on Moslem luxury,
Till quickly wearied with that spacious seat
Of Wealth and Wantonness, the choice re-
  treat
Of sated Grandeur from the city's noise :
And were it humbler it in sooth were sweet ;
But Peace abhorreth artificial joys,
And Pleasure, leagued with Pomp, the zest of
  both destroys.

LXV.

Fierce are Albania's children, yet they lack
Not virtues, were those virtues more mature.
Where is the foe that ever saw their back ?
Who can so well the toil of war endure ?
Their native fastnesses not more secure
Than they in doubtful time of troublous
  need :

[1] [Hobhouse describes the vizier as "a short man, about five feet five inches in height, and very fat ; possessing a very pleasing face, fair and round, with blue quick eyes, not at all settled into a Turkish gravity." Dr. Holland happily compares the spirit which lurked under Ali's usual exterior, as "the fire of a stove, burning fiercely under a smooth and polished surface." When the doctor returned from Albania, in 1813, he brought a letter from the Pacha to Lord Byron. "It is," says the poet, "in Latin, and begins 'Excellentissime, *necnon* Carissime,' and ends about a gun he wants made for him. He tells me that, last spring, he took a town, a hostile town, where, forty-two years ago, his mother and sisters were treated as Miss Cunegunde was by the Bulgarian cavalry. He takes the town, selects all the survivors of the exploit — children, grand-children, etc. to the tune of six hundred, and has them shot before his face. So much for 'dearest friend.' "]

[2] [The fate of Ali was such as the poet anticipated. He was assassinated by order of the Sultan in February, 1822. His head was sent to Constantinople, and exhibited at the gates of the seraglio.]

Their wrath how deadly! but their fri
  ship sure,
When Gratitude or Valor bids them b
Unshaken rushing on where'er their
  may lead.

LXVI.

Childe Harold saw them in their chiefta
  tower
Thronging to war in splendor and succ
And after viewed them, when, within
  power,
Himself awhile the victim of distress ;
That saddening hour when bad men
  lier press :
But these did shelter him beneath their
When less barbarians would have che
  him less,
And fellow-countrymen have stood aloo
In aught that tries the heart how few withs
  the proof!

LXVII.

It chanced that adverse winds once d
  his bark
Full on the coast of Suli's shaggy shore
When all around was desolate and dar
To land was perilous, to sojourn more
Yet for a while the mariners forbore,
Dubious to trust where treachery m
  lurk :
At length they ventured forth, though do
  ing sore
That those who loathe alike the Frank
  Turk
Might once again renew their ancient butc
  work.

LXVIII.

Vain fear! the Suliotes stretched the
  come hand,
Led them o'er rocks and past the dange
  swamp,
Kinder than polished slaves though no
  bland,
And piled the hearth, and wrung their
  ments damp,
And filled the bowl, and trimmed the ch
  ful lamp,
And spread their fare ; though homely
  they had :
Such conduct bears Philanthropy's
  stamp —
To rest the weary and to soothe the sac
Doth lesson happier men, and shames at l
  the bad.

LXIX.

It came to pass, that when he did addr
Himself to quit at length this mountain-l
Combined   marauders   half-way   ba
  egress,

[3] Alluding to the wreckers of Cornwall.

And wasted far and near with glaive and
    brand;
And therefore did he take a trusty band
To traverse Acarnania's forest wide,
In war well seasoned, and with labors tanned,
Till he did greet white Achelous' tide,
And from his further bank Ætolia's wolds
    espied.

LXX.

Where lone Utraikey forms its circling cove,
And weary waves retire to gleam at rest,
How brown the foliage of the green hill's
    grove,
Nodding at midnight o'er the calm bay's
    breast,
As winds come lightly whispering from the
    west,
Kissing, not ruffling, the blue deep's se-
    rene:—
Here Harold was received a welcome guest;
Nor did he pass unmoved the gentle scene,
For many a joy could he from Night's soft
    presence glean.

LXXI.

On the smooth shore the night-fires brightly
    blazed,
The feast was done, the red wine circling
    fast,[1]
And he that unawares had there ygazed
With gaping wonderment had stared
    aghast;
For ere night's midmost, stillest hour was
    past,
The native revels of the troop began;
Each Palikar[2] his sabre from him cast,
And bounding hand in hand, man linked to
    man,
Yelling their uncouth dirge, long daunced the
    kirtled clan.[3]

---

[1] The Albanian Mussulmans do not abstain from wine, and indeed, very few of the others.

[2] Palikar, shortened when addressed to a single person, from Παλικαρι, a general name for a soldier amongst the Greeks and Albanese who speak Romaic: it means, properly, "a lad."

[3] ["In the evening the gates were secured, and preparations were made for feeding our Albanians. A goat was killed and roasted whole, and four fires were kindled in the yard, round which the soldiers seated themselves in parties. After eating and drinking, the greatest part of them assembled round the largest of the fires, and, whilst ourselves and the elders of the party were seated on the ground, danced round the blaze, to their own songs, with astonishing energy. All their songs were relations of some robbing exploits. One of them, which detained them more than an hour, began thus:— 'When we set out from Parga, there were sixty of us:' then came the burden of the verse,—

'Robbers all at Parga!
Robbers all at Parga!'

'Κλεφτεις ποτε Παργα!
Κλεφτεις ποτε Παργα!'

LXXII.

Childe Harold at a little distance stood
And viewed, but not displeased, the revelrie,
Nor hated harmless mirth, however rude:
In sooth, it was no vulgar sight to see
Their barbarous, yet their not indecent, glee;
And, as the flames along their faces gleamed,
Their gestures nimble, dark eyes flashing
    free,
The long wild locks that to their girdles
    streamed,
While thus in concert they this lay half sang,
    half screamed:—[4]

1.

TAMBOURGI! Tambourgi![5] thy 'larum afar
Gives hope to the valiant, and promise of war;
All the sons of the mountains arise at the note,
Chimariot, Illyrian, and dark Suliote![6]

2.

Oh! who is more brave than a dark Suliote,
In his snowy camese and his shaggy capote?
To the wolf and the vulture he leaves his wild
    flock,
And descends to the plain like the stream from
    the rock.

3.

Shall the sons of Chimari, who never forgive
The fault of a friend, bid an enemy live?
Let those guns so unerring such vengeance
    forego?
What mark is so fair as the breast of a foe?

4.

Macedonia sends forth her invincible race;
For a time they abandon the cave and the
    chase:

---

and, as they roared out this stave, they whirled round the fire, dropped, and rebounded from their knees, and again whirled round, as the chorus was again repeated. The rippling of the waves upon the pebbly margin where we were seated, filled up the pauses of the song with a milder, and not more monotonous music. The night was very dark; but, by the flashes of the fires, we caught a glimpse of the woods, the rocks, and the lake, which, together with the wild appearance of the dancers, presented us with a scene that would have made a fine picture in the hands of such an artist as the author of the Mysteries of Udolpho. As we were acquainted with the character of the Albanians, it did not at all diminish our pleasure to know, that every one of our guard had been robbers, and some of them a very short time before. It was eleven o'clock before we had retired to our room, at which time the Albanians, wrapping themselves up in their capotes, went to sleep round the fires." — *Hobhouse.*]

[4] [For a specimen of the Albanian or Arnaout dialect of the Illyric, see Appendix to this Canto, Note [C].]

[5] Drummer.

[6] These stanzas are partly taken from different Albanese songs, as far as I was able to make them

But those scarfs of blood-red shall be redder,
before
The sabre is sheathed and the battle is o'er.

5.

Then the pirates of Parga that dwell by the
waves,
And teach the pale Franks what it is to be
slaves,
Shall leave on the beach the long galley and
oar,
And track to his covert the captive on shore.

6.

I ask not the pleasures that riches supply,
My sabre shall win what the feeble must buy;
Shall win the young bride with her long flow-
ing hair
And many a maid from her mother shall tear.

7.

I love the fair face of the maid in her youth,
Her caresses shall lull me, her music shall
soothe;
Let her bring from the chamber her many-
toned lyre,
And sing us a song on the fall of her sire.

8.

Remember the moment when Previsa fell,[1]
The shrieks of the conquered, the conquerors'
yell;
The roofs that we fired, and the plunder we
shared,
The wealthy we slaughtered, the lovely we
spared.

9.

I talk not of mercy, I talk not of fear;
He neither must know who would serve the
Vizier:
Since the days of our prophet the Crescent
ne'er saw
A chief ever glorious like Ali Pashaw.

10.

Dark Muchtar his son to the Danube is sped,
Let the yellow-haired[2] Giaours[3] view his
horse-tail[4] with dread;
When his Delhis[5] come dashing in blood
o'er the banks,
How few shall escape from the Muscovite
ranks!

11.

Selictar![6] unsheathe then our chief's scimi
Tambourgi! thy 'larum gives promise of
Ye mountains, that see us descend to the sh
Shall view us as victors, or view us no mo

LXXIII.

Fair Greece! sad relic of departed wort
Immortal, though no more; though fal
great!
Who now shall lead thy scattered child
forth,
And long accustomed bondage uncreate
Not such thy sons who whilome did av
The hopeless warriors of a willing door
In bleak Thermopylæ's sepulchra. strait
Oh! who that gallant spirit shall resum
Leap from Eurotas' banks, and call thee f
the tomb?

LXXIV.

Spirit of freedom! when on Phyle's br
Thou sat'st with Thrasybulus and his tr
Couldst thou forebode the dismal h
which now
Dims the green beauties of thine Attic pla
Not thirty tyrants now enforce the chain
But every carle can lord it o'er thy land
Nor rise thy sons, but idly rail in vain,
Trembling beneath the scourge of Turl
hand.
From birth till death enslaved; in word
deed, unmanned.

LXXV.

In all save form alone, how changed!
who
That marks the fire still sparkling in e
eye,
Who but would deem their bosoms bur
anew
With thy unquenched beam, lost Libert
And many dream withal the hour is nig
That gives them back their fathers' berita
For foreign arms and aid they fondly si
Nor solely dare encounter hostile rage,
Or tear their name defiled from Slave
mournful page.

LXXVI.

Hereditary bondsmen! know ye not
Who would be free themselves must st
the blow?

---

out by the exposition of the Albanese in Romaic
and Italian.
[1] It was taken by storm from the French.
[2] Yellow is the epithet given to the Russians.
[3] Infidel.
[4] The insignia of a Pacha
[5] Horsemen, answering to our forlorn hope.

[6] Sword-bearer.
[7] Some thoughts on the present state of Gr
will be found in the Appendix to this Canto, N
[D].
[8] Phyle, which commands a beautiful view
Athens, has still considerable remains: it was se
by Thrasybulus, previous to the expulsion of
Thirty.

By their right arms the conquest must be
  wrought ?
Will Gaul or Muscovite redress ye ? no!
True, they may lay your proud despoilers
  low,
But not for you will freedom's altars flame.
Shades of the Helots! triumph o'er your
  foe!
Greece! change thy lords, thy state is still
  the same;
Thy glorious day is o'er, but not thine years
  of shame.

LXXVII.

The city won for Allah from the Giaour,
The Giaour from Othman's race again may
  wrest;
And the Serai's impenetrable tower
Receive the fiery Frank, her former guest; [1]
Or Wahab's rebel brood who dared divest
The prophet's [2] tomb of all its pious spoil,
May wind their path of blood along the
  West;
But ne'er will freedom seek this fated soil,
But slave succeed to slave through years of
  endless toil.

LXXVIII.

Yet mark their mirth — ere lenten days
  begin,
That penance which their holy rites prepare
To shrive from man his weight of mortal sin,
By daily abstinence and nightly prayer;
But ere his sackcloth garb Repentance wear,
Some days of joyaunce are decreed to all,
To take of pleasaunce each his secret share,
In motley robe to dance at masking ball,
And join the mimic train of merry Carnival.

LXXIX.

And whose more rife with merriment than
  thine,
Oh Stamboul! once the empress of their
  reign ?
Though turbans now pollute Sophia's
  shrine,
And Greece her very altars eyes in vain:
(Alas! her woes will still pervade my strain!)
Gay were her minstrels once, for free her
  throng,
All felt the common joy they now must feign,
Nor oft I've seen such sight, nor heard such
  song,
As wooed the eye, and thrilled the Bosphorus
  along. [3]

LXXX.

Loud was the lightsome tumult on the shore,
Oft Music changed, but never ceased her
  tone,
And timely echoed back the measured oar,
And rippling waters made a pleasant moan :
The Queen of tides on high consenting
  shone,
And when a transient breeze swept o'er the
  wave,
'Twas, as if darting from her heavenly
  throne,
A brighter glance her form reflected gave,
Till sparkling billows seemed to light the banks
  they lave.

LXXXI.

Glanced many a light caique along the foam,
Danced on the shore the daughters of the
  land,
Ne thought had man or maid of rest or
  home,
While many a languid eye and thrilling hand
Exchanged the look few bosoms may with-
  stand,
Or gently prest, returned the pressure still:
Oh Love! young Love! bound in thy rosy
  band,
Let sage or cynic prattle as he will,
These hours, and only these, redeem Life's
  years of ill!

LXXXII.

But, midst the throng in merry masquerade,
Lurk there no hearts that throb with secret
  pain,
Even through the closest searment half be-
  trayed ?
To such the gentle murmurs of the main
Seem to reëcho all they mourn in vain;
To such the gladness of the gamesome crowd
Is source of wayward thought and stern dis-
  dain:
How do they loathe the laughter idly loud,
And long to change the robe of revel for the
  shroud!

LXXXIII.

This must he feel, the true-born son of
  Greece,
If Greece one true-born patriot still can
  boast:
Not such as prate of war, but skulk in peace,
The bondsman's peace, who sighs for all he
  lost,
Yet with smooth smile his tyrant can accost,
And wield the slavish sickle, not the sword:
Ah! Greece! they love thee least who owe
  thee most;

---

[1] When taken by the Latins, and retained for several years.
[2] Mecca and Medina were taken some time ago by the Wahabees, a sect yearly increasing.
[3] [Of Constantinople Byron says, — "I have seen the ruins of Athens, of Ephesus, and Delphi; I have traversed great part of Turkey, and many other parts of Europe, and some of Asia; but I never beheld a work of nature or art which yielded an impression like the prospect on each side, from the Seven Towers to the end of the Golden Horn."]

Their birth, their blood, and that sublime
  record
Of hero sires, who shame thy now degenerate
  horde.
LXXXIV.

When riseth Lacedemon's hardihood,
When Thebes Epaminondas rears again,
When Athens' children are with hearts en-
  dued,
When Grecian mothers shall give birth to
  men,
Then may'st thou be restored; but not till
  then.
A thousand years scarce serve to form a
  state;
An houi may lay it in the dust: and when
Can man its shattered splendor renovate,
Recall its virtues back, and vanquish Time
  and Fate!
LXXXV.

And yet how lovely in thine age of woe,
Land of lost gods and godlike men! art
  thou!
Thy vales of evergreen, thy hills of snow,[1]
Proclaim thee Nature's varied favorite now;
Thy fanes, thy temples to thy surface bow,
Commingling slowly with heroic earth,
Broke by the share of every rustic plough:
So perish monuments of mortal birth,
So perish all in turn, save well-recorded Worth;

LXXXVI.

Save where some solitary column mourns
Above its prostrate brethren of the cave,[2]
Save where Tritonia's airy shrine adorns
Colonna's cliff,[3] and gleams along the wave;

---

[1] On many of the mountains, particularly Liakura,
the snow never is entirely melted, notwithstanding
the intense heat of the summer; but I never saw it
lie on the plains, even in winter.

[2] Of Mount Pentelicus, from whence the marble
was dug that constructed the public edifices of
Athens. The modern name is Mount Mendeli.
An immense cave, formed by the quarries, still re-
mains, and will till the end of time.

[3] In all Attica, if we except Athens itself and Mar-
athon, there is no scene more interesting than Cape
Colonna. To the antiquary and artist, sixteen col-
umns are an inexhaustible source of observation
and design; to the philosopher, the supposed scene
of some of Plato's conversations will not be unwel-
come: and the traveller will be struck with the
beauty of the prospect over " *Isles that crown the
Ægean deep:* " but for an Englishman, Colonna
has yet an additional interest, as the actual spot of
Falconer's Shipwreck. Pallas and Plato are for-
gotten, in the recollection of Falconer and Camp-
bell: —

  " Here in the dead of night by Lonna's steep,
  The seaman's cry was heard along the deep."

This temple of Minerva may be seen at sea from a
great distance. In two journeys which I made, and
one voyage to Cape Colonna, the view from either
side, by land, was less striking than the approach
from the isles. In our second land excursion, we

Save o'er some warrior's half-forgo
  grave,
Where the gray stones and unmolested g
Ages, but not oblivion, feebly brave,
While strangers only not regardless pas
Lingering like me, perchance, to gaze,
  sigh " Alas! "

LXXXVII.

Yet are thy skies as blue, thy crags as w
Sweet are thy groves, and verdant are
  fields,
Thine olive ripe as when Minerva smil
And still his honied wealth Hyme
  yields;
There the blithe bee his fragrant fort
  builds,
The freeborn wanderer of thy mountain-
Apollo still thy long, long summer gilds
Still in his beam Mendeli's marbles gla
Art, Glory, Freedom fail, but Nature sti
  fair.

LXXXVIII.

Where'er we tread 'tis haunted,
  ground;
No earth of thine is lost in vulgar moul
But one vast realm of wonder spre
  around,
And all the Muse's tales seem truly told,
Till the sense aches with gazing to beho
The scenes our earliest dreams have dv
  upon:
Each hill and dale, each deepening g
  and wold
Defies the power which crushed thy temp
  gone:
Age shakes Athena's tower, but spares g
  Marathon.

LXXXIX.

The sun, the soil, but not the slave, the san
Unchanged in all except its foreign lord
Preserves alike its bounds and boundl
  fame,

---

had a narrow escape from a party of Maino
concealed in the caverns beneath. We were
afterwards, by one of their prisoners, subseque
ransomed, that they were deterred from attack
us by the appearance of my two Albanians: con
turing very sagaciously, but falsely, that we
a complete guard of these Arnaouts at hand, t'
remained stationary, and thus saved our pa:
which was too small to have opposed any effec
resistance. Colonna is no less a resort of pain
than of pirates; there

  " The hireling artist plants his paltry desk,
  And makes degraded nature picturesque."
    (*See Hodgson's Lady Jane Grey, e*

But there Nature, with the aid of Art, has d
that for herself. I was fortunate enough to eng
a very superior German artist: and hope to ret
my acquaintance with this and many other Lev
tine scenes, by the arrival of his performances.

The Battle-field, where Persia's victim horde
First bowed beneath the brunt of Hellas'
    sword,
As on the morn to distant Glory dear,
When Marathon became a magic word; [1]
Which uttered, to the hearer's eye appear
The camp, the host, the fight, the conqueror's
    career.

XC.

The flying Mede, his shaftless broken bow;
The fiery Greek, his red pursuing spear;
Mountains above, Earth's, Ocean's plain
    below;
Death in the front, Destruction in the rear!
Such was the scene — what now remaineth
    here?
What sacred trophy marks the hallowed
    ground,
Recording Freedom's smile and Asia's tear?
The rifled urn, the violated mound,
The dust thy courser's hoof, rude stranger!
    spurns around.

XCI.

Yet to the remnants of thy splendor past
Shall pilgrims, pensive, but unwearied,
    throng;
Long shall the voyager, with th' Ionian blast,
Hail the bright clime of battle and of song;
Long shall thine annals and immortal
    tongue
Fill with thy fame the youth of many a
    shore;
Boast of the aged! lesson of the young!
Which sages venerate and bards adore,
As Pallas and the Muse unveil their awful lore.

XCII.

The parted bosom clings to wonted home,
If aught that's kindred cheer the welcome
    hearth;
He that is lonely, hither let him roam,
And gaze complacent on congenial earth.
Greece is no lightsome land of social mirth:
But he whom Sadness sootheth may abide,
And scarce regret the region of his birth,
When wandering slow by Delphi's sacred
    side,
Or gazing o'er the plains where Greek and
    Persian died.

[1] " Siste Viator — heroa calcas! " was the epitaph
on the famous Count Merci; — what then must be
our feelings when standing on the tumulus of the
two hundred (Greeks) who fell on Marathon? The
principal barrow has recently been opened by
Fauvel: few or no relics, as vases, etc. were found
by the excavator. The plain of Marathon was
offered to me for sale at the sum of sixteen thousand
piastres, about nine hundred pounds! Alas! —
" Expende — quot *libras* in duce summo — inven-
ies! " — was the dust of Miltiades worth no more?
It could scarcely have fetched less if sold by *weight*.

XCIII.

Let such approach this consecrated land,
And pass in peace along the magic waste;
But spare its relics — let no busy hand
Deface the scenes, already how defaced!
Not for such purpose were these altars
    placed:
Revere the remnants nations once revered:
So may our country's name be undisgraced,
So may'st thou prosper where thy youth
    was reared,
By every honest joy of love and life endeared!

XCIV.

For thee, who thus in too protracted song
Hast soothed thine idlesse with inglorious
    lays,
Soon shall thy voice be lost amid the throng
Of louder minstrels in these later days:
To such resign the strife for fading bays —
Ill may such contest now the spirit move
Which heeds nor keen reproach nor partial
    praise,
Since cold each kinder heart that might
    approve,
And none are left to please when none are left
    to love.

XCV.

Thou too art gone, thou loved and lovely
    one!
Whom youth and youth's affections bound
    to me;
Who did for me what none beside have
    done,
Nor shrank from one albeit unworthy thee.
What is my being? thou hast ceased to be!
Nor stayed to welcome here thy wanderer
    home,
Who mourns o'er hours which we no more
    shall see —
Would they had never been, or were to
    come!
Would he had ne'er returned to find fresh
    cause to roam!

XCVI.

Oh! ever loving, lovely, and beloved!
How selfish Sorrow ponders on the past,
And clings to thoughts now better far re-
    moved!
But Time shall tear thy shadow from me
    last.
All thou couldst have of mine, stern Death!
    thou hast;
The parent, friend, and now the more than
    friend:
Ne'er yet for one thine arrows flew so fast,
And grief with grief continuing still to blend,
Hath snatched the little joy that life had yet
    to lend.

XCVII.

Then must I plunge again into the crowd,
And follow all that Peace disdains to seek?
Where Revel calls, and Laughter, vainly
    loud,
False to the heart, distorts the hollow cheek,
To leave the flagging spirit doubly weak;
Still o'er the features, which perforce they
    cheer,
To feign the pleasure or conceal the pique;
Smiles form the channel of a future tear,
Or raise the writhing lip with ill-dissembled
    sneer.

XCVIII.

What is the worst of woes that wait on age?
What stamps the wrinkle deeper on the
    brow?
To view each loved one blotted from life's
    page,
And be alone on earth, as I am now.[1]

[1] [This stanza was written October 11, 1811;

Before the Chastener humbly let me b[
O'er hearts divided and o'er hopes,
    stroyed:
Roll on, vain days! full reckless may ye
Since Time hath reft whate'er my sou[
    joyed,
And with the ills of Eld mine earlier y
    alloyed.

upon which day the poet, in a letter to a f[
says, — " It seems as though I were to exper
in my youth the greatest misery of age. My fr
fall around me, and I shall be left a lonely
before I am withered. Other men can always
refuge in their families: I have no resource bu
own reflections, and they present no prospect
or hereafter, except the selfish satisfaction of
viving my friends. I am indeed very wretc[
In reference to this stanza, " Surely," said Pro[
Clarke to the author of the ' Pursuits of Litera
" Lord Byron cannot have experienced such
anguish as these exquisite allusions to what
men may have felt seem to denote." — " I f[
has," answered Matthias; — " *he could not o[*
wise have written such a poem."]

APPENDIX TO CANTO THE SECOND.

Note [A]. *See* p. 278.

" *To rive what Goth, and Turk, and Time hath*
spared." — Stanza xii. line 2.

AT this moment (January 3, 1810), besides what
has been already deposited in London, an Hydriot
vessel is in the Pyræus to receive every portable
relic. Thus, as I heard a young Greek observe, in
common with many of his countrymen — for, lost
as they are, they yet feel on this occasion — thus
may Lord Elgin boast of having ruined Athens.
An Italian painter of the first eminence, named
Lusieri, is the agent of devastation; and like the
Greek *finder* of Verres in Sicily, who followed the
same profession, he has proved the able instrument
of plunder. Between this artist and the French
Consul Fauvel, who wishes to rescue the remains
for his own government, there is now a violent dis-
pute concerning a car employed in their convey-
ance, the wheel of which — I wish they were both
broken upon it — has been locked up by the Consul,
and Lusieri has laid his complaint before the Way-
wode. Lord Elgin has been extremely happy in
his choice of Signor Lusieri. During a residence
of ten years in Athens, he never had the curiosity
to proceed as far as Sunium (now Caplonna), till
he accompanied us in our second excursion. How-
ever, his works, as far as they go, are most beauti-
ful: but they are almost all unfinished. While he
and his patrons confine themselves to tasting medals,
appreciating cameos, sketching columns, and cheap-
ening gems, their little absurdities are as harmless
as insect or fox hunting, maiden speechifying,
barouche-driving, or any such pastime; but when
they carry away three or four shiploads of the most

valuable and massy relics that time and barb,
have left to the most injured and most celebrat
cities; when they destroy, in a vain attempt t[
down, those works which have been the admit
of ages, I know no motive which can excus
name which can designate, the perpetrators o[
dastardly devastation. It was not the least c
crimes laid to the charge of Verres, that he
plundered Sicily, in the manner since imitat[
Athens. The most unblushing impudence [
hardly go further than to affix the name of its
derer to the walls of the Acropolis; while the
ton and useless defacement of the whole ran[
the basso-relievos, in one compartment of
temple, will never permit that name to be
nounced by an observer without execration.

On this occasion I speak impartially: I ar[
a collector or admirer of collections, consequ[
no rival; but I have some early prepossessi[
favor of Greece, and do not think the honor o[
land advanced by plunder, whether of Ind[
Attica.

Another noble Lord has done better, becau[
has done less: but some others, more or less n
yet " all honorable men," have done *best*, bec[
after a deal of excavation, and execration, br[
to the Waywode, mining and countermining,
have done nothing at all. We had such ink-[
and wine-shed, which almost ended in blood[
Lord E.'s " prig" — see Jonathan Wild fo[
definition of " priggism" — quarrelled with ano[
Gropius[1] by name (a very good name too fo[

[1] This Sr. Gropius was employed by a [
Lord for the sole purpose of sketching, in whi[

business), and muttered something about satisfaction, in a verbal answer to a note of the poor Prussian: this was stated at table to Gropius, who laughed, but could eat no dinner afterwards. The rivals were not reconciled when I left Greece. I have reason to remember their squabble, for they wanted to make me their arbitrator.

NOTE [B]. *See* p. 282.

" Land of Albania ! let me bend mine eyes
On thee, thou rugged nurse of savage men !"
            Stanza xxxvii. lines 5 and 6.

Albania comprises part of Macedonia, Illyria, Chaonia, and Epirus. Iskander is the Turkish word for Alexander; and the celebrated Scanderbeg (Lord Alexander) is alluded to in the third and fourth lines of the thirty-eighth stanza. I do not know whether I am correct in making Scanderbeg the countryman of Alexander, who was born at Pella in Macedon, but Mr. Gibbon terms him so, and adds Pyrrhus to the list, in speaking of his exploits.

Of Albania Gibbon remarks, that a country "within sight of Italy is less known than the interior of America." Circumstances, of little consequence to mention, led Mr. Hobhouse and myself into that country before we visited any other part of the Ottoman dominions; and with the exception of Major Leake, then officially resident at Joannina, no other Englishmen have ever advanced beyond the capital into the interior, as that gentleman very lately assured me. Ali Pacha was at that time (October, 1809) carrying on war against Ibrahim Pacha, whom he had driven to Berat, a strong fortress which he was then besieging; on our arrival at Joannina we were invited to Tepaleni, his highness's birthplace, and favorite Serai, only one day's distance from Berat; at this juncture the Vizier had made it his head-quarters. After some stay in the capital, we accordingly followed; but though furnished with every accommodation, and escorted by one of the Vizier's secretaries, we were nine days (on account of the rains) in accomplishing a journey which, on our return, barely occupied four. On our route we passed two cities, Argyrocastro and Libochabo, apparently little inferior to Yanina in size; and no pencil or pen can ever do justice to the scenery in the vicinity of Zitza and Delvinachi, the frontier village of Epirus and Albania Proper.

excels; but I am sorry to say, that he has, through the abused sanction of that most respectable name, been treading at humble distance in the steps of Sr. Lusieri.—A shipful of his trophies was detained, and I believe confiscated, at Constantinople, in 1810. I am most happy to be now enabled to state, that "this was not in his bond;" that he was employed solely as a painter, and that his noble patron disavows all connection with him, except as an artist. If the error in the first and second edition of this poem has given the noble Lord a moment's pain, I am very sorry for it: Sr. Gropius has assumed for years the name of his agent: and though I cannot much condemn myself for sharing in the mistake of so many, I am happy in being one of the first to be undeceived. Indeed, I have as much pleasure in contradicting this as I felt regret in stating it.—*Note to third edition.*

On Albania and its inhabitants I am unwilling to descant, because this will be done so much better by my fellow-traveller, in a work which may probably precede this in publication, that I as little wish to follow as I would to anticipate him. But some few observations are necessary to the text. The Arnaouts, or Albanese, struck me forcibly by their resemblance to the Highlanders of Scotland, in dress, figure, and manner of living. Their very mountains seemed Caledonian, with a kinder climate. The kilt, though white; the spare, active form; their dialect, Celtic in its sound, and their hardy habits, all carried me back to Morven. No nation are so detested and dreaded by their neighbors as the Albanese; the Greeks hardly regard them as Christians, or the Turks as Moslems; and in fact they are a mixture of both, and sometimes neither. Their habits are predatory—all are armed; and the red-shawled Arnaouts, the Montenegrins, Chimariots, and Gegdes, are treacherous; the other differ somewhat in garb, and essentially in character. As far as my own experience goes, I can speak favorably. I was attended by two, an Infidel and a Mussulman, to Constantinople and ever other part of Turkey which came within my observation; and more faithful in peril, or indefatigable in service, are rarely to be found. The Infidel was named Basilius, the Moslem, Dervish Tahiri; the former a man of middle age, and the latter about my own. Basili was strictly charged by Ali Pacha in person to attend us; and Dervish was one of fifty who accompanied us through the forests of Acarnania to the banks of Achelous, and onward to Messalonghi in Ætolia. There I took him into my own service, and never had occasion to repent it till the moment of my departure.

When in 1810, after the departure of my friend Mr. Hobhouse for England, I was seized with a severe fever in the Morea, these men saved my life by frightening away my physician, whose throat they threatened to cut if I was not cured within a given time. To this consolatory assurance of posthumous retribution, and a resolute refusal of Dr. Romanelli's prescriptions, I attributed my recovery. I had left my last remaining English servant at Athens; my dragoman was as ill as myself, and my poor Arnaouts nursed me with an attention which would have done honor to civilization. They had a variety of adventures; for the Moslem, Dervish, being a remarkably handsome man, was always squabbling with the husbands of Athens; insomuch that four of the principal Turks paid me a visit of remonstrance at the Convent, on the subject of his having taken a woman from the bath—whom he had lawfully bought however—a thing quite contrary to etiquette. Basili also was extremely gallant amongst his own persuasion, and had the greatest veneration for the church, mixed with the highest contempt of churchmen, whom he cuffed upon occasion in a most heterodox manner. Yet he never passed a church without crossing himself; and I remember the risk he ran in entering St. Sophia, in Stambol, because it had once been a place of his worship. On remonstrating with him on his inconsistent proceedings, he invariably answered, "Our church is holy, our priests are thieves;" and then he crossed himself as usual, and boxed the ears of the first "papas" who refused to assist in any required operation, as was always found to be necessary where a priest had any influence with the Cogia Bashi of his village. Indeed a more abandoned race of miscreants cannot exist than the lower orders of the Greek clergy.

When preparations were made for my return, my Albanians were summoned to receive their pay. Basili took his with an awkward show of regret at my intended departure, and marched away to his quarters with his bag of piastres. I sent for Dervish, but for some time he was not to be found; at last he entered, just as Signor Logotheti, father to the ci-devant Anglo-consul of Athens, and some other of my Greek acquaintances, paid me a visit. Dervish took the money, but on a sudden dashed it to the ground; and clasping his hands, which he raised to his forehead, rushed out of the room weeping bitterly. From that moment to the hour of my embarkation, he continued his lamentations, and all our efforts to console him only produced this answer, " Μ' αφεινει," " He leaves me." Signor Logotheti, who never wept before for any thing less than the loss of a part (about the fourth of a farthing), melted; the padre of the convent, my attendants, my visitors, — and I verily believe that even Sterne's " foolish, fat scullion " would have left her " fish-kettle," to sympathize with the unaffected and unexpected sorrow of this barbarian.

For my own part, when I remembered that, a short time before my departure from England, a noble and most intimate associate had excused himself from taking leave of me because he had to attend a relation " to a milliner's," I felt no less surprised than humiliated by the present occurrence and the past recollection. That Dervish would leave me with some regret was to be expected: when master and man have been scrambling over the mountains of a dozen provinces together, they are unwilling to separate; but his present feelings, contrasted with his native ferocity, improved my opinion of the human heart. I believe this almost feudal fidelity is frequent amongst them. One day, on our journey over Parnassus, an Englishman in my service gave him a push in some dispute about the baggage, which he unluckily mistook for a blow; he spoke not, but sat down leaning his head upon his hands. Foreseeing the consequences, we endeavored to explain away the affront, which produced the following answer: — " I *have been* a robber; I *am* a soldier; no captain ever struck me: *you* are my master, I have eaten your bread, but by *that* bread! (an usual oath) had it been otherwise, I would have stabbed the dog your servant, and gone to the mountains." So the affair ended, but from that day forward he never thoroughly forgave the thoughtless fellow who insulted him. Dervish excelled in the dance of his country, conjectured to be a remnant of the ancient Pyrrhic: be that as it may, it is manly, and requires wonderful agility. It is very distinct from the stupid Romaika, the dull round-about of the Greeks, of which our Athenian party had so many specimens.

The Albanians in general (I do not mean the cultivators of the earth in the provinces, who have also that appellation, but the mountaineers) have a fine cast of countenance; and the most beautiful women I ever beheld, in stature and in features, we saw *levelling* the *road* broken down by the torrents between Delvinachi and Libochabo. Their manner of walking is truly theatrical: but this strut is probably the effect of the capote, or cloak, depending from one shoulder. Their long hair reminds you of the Spartans, and their courage in desultory warfare is unquestionable. Though they have some

cavalry amongst the Gegdes, I never saw a Arnaout horseman; my own preferred the Er saddles, which, however, they could never But on foot they are not to be subdued by fatig

---

NOTE [C]. *See* p. 287.

" While thus in concert," etc.

Stanza lxxii. line la

As a specimen of the Albanian or Arnaout lect of the Illyric, I here insert two of their popular choral songs, which are generally cha in dancing by men or women indiscriminately. first words are merely a kind of chorus wit meaning, like some in our own and all other guages.

1.	1.
Bo, Bo, Bo, Bo, Bo, Bo, Naciarura, popuso.	Lo, Lo, I come, I c be thou silent.
2.	**2.**
Naciarura na civin Ha pen derini ti hin.	I come, I run, open door that I may e
3.	**3.**
Ha pe uderi escrotini Ti vin ti mar servetini.	Open the door by ha that I may take my ban.
4.	**4.**
Caliriote me surme Ea ha pe pse dua tive.	Caliriotes [1] with the eyes, open the gate I may enter.
5.	**5.**
Buo, Bo, Bo, Bo, Bo, Gi egem spirta esimiro.	Lo, Lo, I hear thee, soul.
6.	**6.**
Caliriote vu le funde Ede vete tunde tunde.	An Arnaout girl, in cc garb, walks with gr ful pride.
7.	**7.**
Caliriote me surme Ti mi put e poi mi le.	Caliriote maid of the eyes, give me a kis
8.	**8.**
Se ti puta citi mora Si mi ri ni veti udo gia.	If I have kissed thee, v hast thou gained? soul is consumed fire.
9.	**9.**
Va le ni il che cadale Celo more, more celo.	Dance lightly, more tly, and gently stil
10.	**10.**
Plu hari ti tirete Plu huron cia pra seti.	Make not so much du destroy your embt ered hose.

The last stanza would puzzle a commentator: men have certainly buskins of the most beau texture, but the ladies (to whom the above is

---

[1] The Albanese, particularly the women, are

posed to be addressed) have nothing under their little yellow boots and slippers but a well-turned and sometimes very white ankle. The Arnaout girls are much handsomer than the Greeks, and their dress is far more picturesque. They preserve their shape much longer also, from being always in the open air. It is to be observed, that the Arnaout is not a *written* language: the words of this song, therefore, as well as the one which follows, are spelt according to their pronunciation. They are copied by one who speaks and understands the dialect perfectly, and who is a native of Athens.

1.	1.
Ndi sefda tinde ulavossa	I am wounded by thy love,
Vettimi upri vi lofsa.	and have loved but to scorch myself.

2.	2.
Ah vaisisso mi privi lof- se	Thou hast consumed me! Ah, maid! thou hast
Si mi rini mi la vosse.	struck me to the heart.

3.	3.
Uti tasa roba stua	I have said I wish no dow-
Sitti eve tulati dua.	ry, but thine eyes and eye lashes.

4.	4.
Roba stinori ssidua	The accursed dowry I
Qu mi sini vetti dua.	want not, but thee only.

5.	5.
Qurmini dua civileni	Give me thy charms, and
Roba ti siarmi tildi eni.	let the portion feed the flames.

6.	6.
Utara pisa vaisisso me	I have loved thee, maid,
simi rin ti hapti	with a sincere soul, but
Eti mi bire a piste si gui	thou hast left me like a
dendroi tiltati.	withered tree.

7.	7.
Udi vura udorini udiri	If I have placed my hand
cicova cilti mora	on thy bosom, what
Udorini ָaָ hollna u	have I gained? my
ede caimoni mora.	hand is withdrawn, but retains the flame.

I believe the two last stanzas, as they are in a different measure, ought to belong to another ballad. An idea something similar to the thought in the last lines was expressed by Socrates, whose arm having come in contact with one of his ."ὑπο-κόλπιοι," Critobulus or Cleobulus, the philosopher complained of a shooting pain as far as his shoulder for some days after, and therefore very properly resolved to teach his disciples in future without touching them.

Note [D]. *See* p. 288.

*" Fair Greece! sad relic of departed worth!
Immortal, though no more; though fallen,
    great!"* — Stanza lxxiii. lines 1 and 2.

quently termed "Caliriotes;" for what reason I inquired in vain.

1.

Before I say any thing about a city of which everybody, traveller or not, has thought it necessary to say something, I will request Miss Owenson, when she next borrows an Athenian heroine for her four volumes, to have the goodness to marry her to somebody more of a gentleman than a "Disdar Aga" (who by the by is not an Aga), the most impolite of petty officers, the greatest patron of larceny Athens ever saw (except Lord E.), and the unworthy occupant of the Acropolis, on a handsome annual stipend of 150 piastres (eight pounds sterling), out of which he has only to pay his garrison, the most ill-regulated corps in the ill-regulated Ottoman Empire. I speak it tenderly, seeing I was once the cause of the husband of "Ida of Athens" nearly suffering the bastinado; and because the said "Disdar" is a turbulent husband, and beats his wife; so that I exhort and beseech Miss Owenson to sue for a separate maintenance in behalf of "Ida." Having premised thus much, on a matter of such import to the readers of romances, I may now leave Ida, to mention her birthplace.

Setting aside the magic of the name, and all those associations which it would be pedantic and superfluous to recapitulate, the very situation of Athens would render it the favorite of all who have eyes for art or nature. The climate, to me at least, appeared a perpetual spring; during eight months I never passed a day without being as many hours on horseback: rain is extremely rare, snow never lies in the plains, and a cloudy day is an agreeable rarity. In Spain, Portugal, and every part of the East which I visited, except Ionia and Attica, I perceived no such superiority of climate to our own; and at Constantinople, where I passed May, June, and part of July (1810), you might "damn the climate, and complain of spleen," five days out of seven.

The air of the Morea is heavy and unwholesome, but the moment you pass the isthmus in the direction of Megara the change is strikingly perceptible. But I fear Hesiod will still be found correct in his description of a Bœotian winter.

We found at Livadia an "esprit fort" in a Greek bishop, of all freethinkers! This worthy hypocrite rallied his own religion with great intrepidity (but not before his flock), and talked of a mass as a "coglioneria." It was impossible to think better of him for this: but, for a Bœotian, he was brisk with all his absurdity. This phenomenon (with the exception indeed of Thebes, the remains of Chæronea, the plain of Platea, Orchomenus, Livadia, and its nominal cave of Trophonius) was the only remarkable thing we saw before we passed Mount Cithæron.

The fountain of Dirce turns a mill: at least my companion (who, resolving to be at once cleanly and classical, bathed in it) pronounced it to be the fountain of Dirce, and anybody who thinks it worth while may contradict him. At Castri we drank of half a dozen streamlets, some not of the purest, before we decided to our satisfaction which was the true Castalian, and even that had a villanous twang, probably from the snow, though it did not throw us into an epic fever, like poor Dr. Chandler.

From Fort Phyle, of which large remains still exist, the Plain of Athens, Pentelicus, Hymettus, the Ægean, and the Acropolis, burst upon the eye at once; in my opinion, a more glorious prospect than even Cintra or Istambol. Not the view from the Troad, with Ida, the Hellespont, and the more distant Mount Athos, can equal it, though so superior in extent.

I heard much of the beauty of Arcadia, but excepting the view from the monastery of Megaspelion (which is inferior to Zitza in a command of country) and the descent from the mountains on the way from Tripolitza to Argos, Arcadia has little to recommend it beyond the name.

" *Sternitur,* et *dulces* moriens reminiscitur Argos."

Virgil could have put this into the mouth of none but an Argive, and (with reverence be it spoken) it does not deserve the epithet. And if the Polynices of Statius, " In mediis audit duo litora campis," did actually hear both shores in crossing the isthmus of Corinth, he had better ears than have ever been worn in such a journey since.

" Athens," says a celebrated topographer, " is still the most polished city of Greece." Perhaps it may of *Greece,* but not of the *Greeks ;* for Joannina in Epirus is universally allowed, amongst themselves, to be superior in the wealth, refinement, learning, and dialect of its inhabitants. The Athenians are remarkable for their cunning; and the lower orders are not improperly characterized in that proverb, which classes them with " the Jews of Salonica, and the Turks of the Negropont."

Among the various foreigners resident in Athens, French, Italians, Germans, Ragusans, etc., there was never a difference of opinion in their estimate of the Greek character, though on all other topics they disputed with great acrimony.

M. Fauvel, the French consul, who has passed thirty years principally at Athens, and to whose talents as an artist, and manners as a gentleman, none who have known him can refuse their testimony, has frequently declared in my hearing, that the Greeks do not deserve to be emancipated; reasoning on the grounds of their " national and individual depravity!" while he forgot that such depravity is to be attributed to causes which can only be removed by the measure he reprobates.

M. Roque, a French merchant of respectability long settled in Athens, asserted with the most amusing gravity, " Sir, they are the same *canaille* that existed *in the days of Themistocles!*" an alarming remark to the " Laudator temporis acti." The ancients banished Themistocles; the moderns cheat Monsieur Roque: thus great men have ever been treated!

In short, all the Franks who are fixtures, and most of the Englishmen, Germans, Danes, etc. of passage, came over by degrees to their opinion, on much the same grounds that a Turk in England would condemn the nation by wholesale, because he was wronged by his lacquey, and overcharged by his washerwoman.

Certainly it was not a little staggering when the Sieurs Fauvel and Lusieri, the two greatest demagogues of the day, who divide between them the power of Pericles and the popularity of Cleon, and puzzle the poor Waywode with perpetual differences, agreed in the utter condemnation, " nulla virtute redemptum," of the Greeks in general, and of the Athenians in particular.

For my own humble opinion, I am loth to hazard it, knowing as I do, that there be now in MS. no less than five tours of the first magnitude and of the most threatening aspect, all in typographical array, by persons of wit, and honor, and regular

common-place books: but, if I may say this w out offence, it seems to me rather hard to decla positively and pertinaciously, as almost everyb has declared, that the Greeks, because they very bad, will never be better.

Eton and Sonnini have led us astray by panegyrics and projects: but, on the other h De Pauw and Thornton have debased the Gr beyond their demerits.

The Greeks will never be independent; they never be sovereigns as heretofore, and God fo they ever should! but they may be subjects with being slaves. Our colonies are not independ but they are free and industrious, and such Greece be hereafter.

At present, like the Catholics of Ireland and Jews throughout the world, and such other moral and physical ills that can afflict human Their life is a struggle against truth; they vicious in their own defence. They are so un to kindness, that when they occasionally meet it they look upon it with suspicion, as a dog beaten snaps at your fingers if you attempt to ca him. " They are ungrateful, notoriously, ab nably ungrateful!"—this is the general cry. Nov the name of Nemesis! for what are they to be gr ful? Where is the human being that ever confe a benefit on Greek or Greeks? They are to grateful to the Turks for their fetters, and to Franks for their broken promises and lying co sels. They are to be grateful to the artist engraves their ruins, and to the antiquary who ries them away; to the traveller whose janiss flogs them, and to the scribbler whose jou abuses them! This is the amount of their obl tions to foreigners.

II.

FRANCISCAN CONVENT, ATHENS,
January 23, 1811.

Amongst the remnants of the barbarous polic the earlier ages, are the traces of bondage wh yet exist in different countries; whose inhabita however divided in religion and manners, alm all agree in oppression.

The English have at last compassionated t negroes, and under a less bigoted government, i probably one day release their Catholic brethi but the interposition of foreigners alone can ema pate the Greeks, who, otherwise, appear to have small a chance of redemption from the Turks the Jews have from mankind in general.

Of the ancient Greeks we know more t enough; at least the younger men of Europe vote much of their time to the study of the Gr writers and history, which would be more usef spent in mastering their own. Of the moderns, are perhaps more neglectful than they deserve; while every man of any pretensions to learnin tiring out his youth, and often his age, in the st of the language and of the harangues of the A nian demagogues in favor of freedom, the rea supposed descendants of these sturdy republic are left to the actual tyranny of their masters, though a very slight effort is required to strike their chains.

To talk, as the Greeks themselves do, of t rising again to their pristine superiority, woulc ridiculous: as the rest of the world must resume barbarism, after reasserting the sovereignty

Greece: but there seems to be no very great obstacle, except in the apathy of the Franks, to their becoming an useful dependency, or even a free state with a proper guarantee; — under correction, however, be it spoken, for many and well-informed men doubt the practicability even of this.

The Greeks have never lost their hope, though they are now more divided in opinion on the subject of their probable deliverers. Religion recommends the Russians; but they have twice been deceived and abandoned by that power, and the dreadful lesson they received after the Muscovite desertion in the Morea has never been forgotten. The French they dislike, although the subjugation of the rest of Europe will, probably, be attended by the deliverance of continental Greece. The islanders look to the English for succor, as they have very lately possessed themselves of the Ionian republic, Corfu excepted. But whoever appear with arms in their hands will be welcome; and when that day arrives, Heaven have mercy on the Ottomans, they cannot expect it from the Giaours.

But instead of considering what they have been, and speculating on what they may be, let us look at them as they are.

And here it is impossible to reconcile the contrariety of opinions: some, particularly the merchants, decrying the Greeks in the strongest language; others, generally travellers, turning periods in their eulogy, and publishing very curious speculations grafted on their former state, which can have no more effect on their present lot, than the existence of the Incas on the future fortunes of Peru.

One very ingenious person terms them the "natural allies of Englishmen;" another no less ingenious, will not allow them to be the allies of anybody, and denies their very descent from the ancients; a third, more ingenious than either, builds a Greek empire on a Russian foundation, and realizes (on paper) all the chimeras of Catharine II. As to the question of their descent, what can it import whether the Mainotes are the lineal Laconians or not? or the present Athenians as indigenous as the bees of Hymettus, or as the grasshoppers, to which they once likened themselves; what Englishman cares if he be of a Danish, Saxon, Norman, or Trojan blood? or who, except a Welshman, is afflicted with a desire of being descended from Caractacus?

The poor Greeks do not so much abound in the good things of this world, as to render even their claims to antiquity an object of envy; it is very cruel, then, in Mr. Thornton to disturb them in the possession of all that time has left them; viz. their pedigree, of which they are the more tenacious, as it is all they can call their own. It would be worth while to publish together, and compare, the works of Messrs. Thornton and De Pauw, Eton and Sonnini; paradox on one side, and prejudice on the other. Mr. Thornton conceives himself to have claims to public confidence from a fourteen years' residence at Pera; perhaps he may on the subject of the Turks, but can give him no more insight into the real state of Greece and her inhabitants, than as many years spent in Wapping into that of the Western Highlands.

The Greeks of Constantinople live in Fanal; and if Mr. Thornton did not oftener cross the Golden Horn than his brother merchants are accustomed to do, I should place no great reliance on his information. I actually heard one of these gentlemen boast of their little general intercourse with the

city, and assert of himself, with an air of triumph, that he had been but four times at Constantinople in as many years.

As to Mr. Thornton's voyages in the Black Sea with Greek vessels, they gave him the same idea of Greece as a cruise to Berwick in a Scotch smack would of Johnny Groat's house. Upon what grounds then does he arrogate the right of condemning by wholesale a body of men, of whom he can know little? It is rather a curious circumstance that Mr. Thornton, who so lavishly dispraises Fouqueville on every occasion of mentioning the Turks, has yet recourse to him as authority on the Greeks, and terms him an impartial observer. Now, Dr. Pouqueville is as little entitled to that appellation, as Mr. Thornton to confer it on him.

The fact is, we are deplorably in want of information on the subject of the Greeks, and in particular their literature; nor is there any probability of our being better acquainted, till our intercourse becomes more intimate, or their independence confirmed : the relations of passing travellers are as little to be depended on as the invectives of angry factors; but till something more can be attained, we must be content with the little to be acquired from similar sources.[1]

However defective these may be, they are preferable to the paradoxes of men who have read superficially of the ancients, and seen nothing of the moderns, such as De Pauw; who, when he asserts that the British breed of horses is ruined by Newmarket, and that the Spartans were cowards in the field, betrays an equal knowledge of English

[1] A word, *en passant*, with Mr. Thornton and Dr. Pouqueville, who have been guilty between them of sadly clipping the Sultan's Turkish. Dr. Pouqueville tells a long story of a Moslem who swallowed corrosive sublimate in such quantities that -he acquired the name of " *Suleyman Yeyen*," i.e. quoth the Doctor, " *Suleyman, the eater of corrosive sublimate*." " Aha," thinks Mr. Thornton, (angry with the Doctor for the fiftieth time,) " have I caught you? " — Then, in a note twice the thickness of the Doctor's anecdote, he questions the Doctor's proficiency in the Turkish tongue, and his veracity in his own. — " For," observes Mr. Thornton (after inflicting on us the tough participle of a Turkish verb), " it means nothing more than *Suleyman the eater*," and quite cashiers the supplementary " *sublimate*." Now both are right, and both are wrong. If Mr. Thornton, when he next resides " fourteen years in the factory," will consult his Turkish dictionary, or ask any of his Stamboline acquaintance, he will discover that " *Suleyma'n yeyen*," put together discreetly, mean the " *Swallower of sublimate*," without any " *Suleyman*" in the case : " *Suleyma*" signifying " *corrosive sublimate*," and not being a proper name on this occasion, although it be an orthodox name enough with the addition of *n*. After Mr. Thornton's frequent hints of profound Orientalism, he might have found this out before he sang such pæans over Dr. Pouqueville.

After this, I think " Travellers *versus* Factors " shall be our motto, though the above Mr. Thornton has condemned " hoc genus omne," for mistake and misrepresentation. " Ne Sutor ultra crepidam," " No merchant beyond his bales." N.B. For the benefit of Mr. Thornton, " Sutor " is not a proper name.

horses and Spartan men. His "philosophical observations" have a much better claim to the title of "poetical." It could not be expected that he who so liberally condemns some of the most celebrated institutions of the ancient, should have mercy on the modern Greeks; and it fortunately happens, that the absurdity of his hypothesis on their forefathers refutes his sentence on themselves.

Let us trust, then, that, in spite of the prophecies of De Pauw, and the doubts of Mr. Thornton, there is a reasonable hope of the redemption of a race of men, who, whatever may be the errors of their religion and policy, have been amply punished by three centuries and a half of captivity.

III.

ATHENS, FRANCISCAN CONVENT,
March 17, 1811.

" I must have some talk with this learned Theban."

Some time after my return from Constantinople to this city, I received the thirty-first number of the Edinburgh Review as a great favor, and certainly at this distance an acceptable one, from the captain of an English frigate off Salamis. In that number, Art. 3, containing the review of a French translation of Strabo, there are introduced some remarks on the modern Greeks and their literature, with a short account of Coray, a co-translator in the French version. On those remarks I mean to ground a few observations; and the spot where I now write will, I hope, be sufficient excuse for introducing them in a work in some degree connected with the subject. Coray, the most celebrated of living Greeks, at least among the Franks, was born at Scio (in the Review, Smyrna is stated, I have reason to think, incorrectly), and besides the translation of Beccaria and other works mentioned by the Reviewer, has published a lexicon in Romaic and French, if I may trust the assurance of some Danish travellers lately arrived from Paris; but the latest we have seen here in French and Greek is that of Gregory Zolikogloou.[1] Coray has recently been involved in an unpleasant controversy with M. Gail,[2] a Parisian commentator and editor of some translations from the Greek poets, in consequence of the Institute having awarded him the prize for his version of Hippocrates "Περὶ ὑδάτων," etc. to the disparagement, and consequently displeasure, of the said Gail. To his exertions, literary and patriotic, great praise is undoubtedly due, but a part of that praise ought not to be withheld from the two brothers Zosimado (merchants settled in Leghorn), who sent him to Paris, and maintained him, for the express purpose of elucidating the ancient, and adding to

the modern, researches of his countrymen. C(
however, is not considered by his countrymen e
to some who lived in the two last centuries;
particularly Dorotheus of Mitylene, whose Hel
writings are so much esteemed by the Greeks,
Meletius terms him " Μετὰ τὸν Θουκυδίδην
Ξενοφῶντα ἄριστος Ἑλλήνων." (P. 224. Ecc
astical History, vol. iv.)

Panagiotes Kodrikas, the translator of Fonten
and Kamarases, who translated Ocellus Luc
on the Universe into French, Christodoulus,
more particularly Psalida, whom I have conve
with in Joannina, are also in high repute an
their literati. The last mentioned has publishe
Romaic and Latin a work on "True Happine
dedicated to Catherine II. But Polyzois, wh
stated by the Reviewer to be the only mo
except Coray who has distinguished himself t
knowledge of Hellenic, if he be the Polyzois I
panitziotes of Yanina, who has published a nun
of editions in Romaic, was neither more nor
than an itinerant vender of books; with the
tents of which he had no concern beyond his n
on the title-page, placed there to secure his prop
in the publication; and he was, moreover, a
utterly destitute of scholastic acquirements.
the name, however, is not uncommon, some o
Polyzois may have edited the Epistles of Aristæne

It is to be regretted that the system of cc
mental blockade has closed the few channels thrc
which the Greeks received their publications,
ticularly Venice and Trieste. Even the comn
grammars for children are become too dear for
lower orders. Amongst their original works
Geography of Meletius, Archbishop of Athens,
a multitude of theological quartos and poet
pamphlets, are to be met with; their grammars
lexicons of two, three, and four languages are
merous and excellent. Their poetry is in rhy:
The most singular piece I have lately seen is a
ire in dialogue between a Russian, English,
French traveller, and the Waywode of Wallac
(or Blackbey, as they term him), an archbishop
merchant, and Cogia Bachi (or primate), in s
cession; to all of whom under the Turks the wr
attributes their present degeneracy. Their so
are sometimes pretty and pathetic, but their tu
generally unpleasing to the ear of a Frank;
best is the famous " Δεῦτε παῖδες τῶν Ἑλλήνω
by the unfortunate Riga. But from a catalogue
more than sixty authors, now before me, only fift
can be found who have touched on any theme
cept theology.

I am intrusted with a commission by a Greek
Athens named Marmarotouri to make arran
ments, if possible, for printing in London a tran:
tion of Barthelemi's Anacharsis in Romaic, as
has no other opportunity, unless he despatches
MS. to Vienna by the Black Sea and Danube.

The Reviewer mentions a school established
Hecatonesi, and suppressed at the instigation
Sebastiani: he means Cidonies, or, in Turki
Haivali; a town on the continent, where that in
tution for a hundred students and three profess
still exists. It is true that this establishment \
disturbed by the Porte, under the ridiculous pret
that the Greeks were constructing a fortress inst
of a college: but on investigation, and the paym
of some purses to the Divan, it has been permit
to continue. The principal professor, named U(
amin (i.e. Benjamin), is stated to be a man of

---

[1] I have in my possession an excellent lexicon "τριγλωσσον," which I received in exchange from S. G—, Esq. for a small gem: my antiquarian friends have never forgotten it, or forgiven me.

[2] In Gail's pamphlet against Coray, he talks of "throwing an insolent Hellenist out of the window." On this a French critic exclaims, "Ah, my God! throw an Hellenist out of the window! what sacrilege!" It certainly would be a serious business for those authors who dwell in the attics: but I have quoted the passage merely to prove the similarity of style among the controversialists of all polished countries; London or Edinburgh could hardly parallel this Parisian ebullition.

ent, but a freethinker. He was born in Lesbos, studied in Italy, and is master of Hellenic, Latin, and some Frank languages; besides a smattering of the sciences.

Though it is not my intention to enter further on this topic than may allude to the article in question, I cannot but observe that the Reviewer's lamentation over the fall of the Greeks appears singular, when he closes it with these words: "*The change is to be attributed to their misfortunes rather than to any 'physical degradation.'*" It may be true that the Greeks are not physically degenerated, and that Constantinople contained on the day when it changed masters as many men of six feet and upwards as in the hour of prosperity; but ancient history and modern politics instruct us that something more than physical perfection is necessary to preserve a state in vigor and independence; and the Greeks, in particular, are a melancholy example of the near connection between moral degradation and national decay.

The Reviewer mentions a plan "*we believe*" by Potemkin for the purification of the Romaic; and I have endeavored in vain to procure any tidings or traces of its existence. There was an academy in St. Petersburg for the Greeks; but it was suppressed by Paul, and has not been revived by his successor.

There is a slip of the pen, and it can only be a slip of the pen, in p. 58, No. 31, of the Edinburgh Review, where these words occur:—"We are told that when the capital of the East yielded to *Solyman*"—it may be presumed that this last word will, in a future edition, be altered to Mahomet II.[1] The "ladies of Constantinople," it seems, at that period spoke a dialect, "which would not have disgraced the lips of an Athenian." I do not know how that might be, but am sorry to say the ladies in general, and the Athenians in particular, are much altered; being far from choice either in their dialect or expressions, as the whole Attic race are barbarous to a proverb:—

"Ὦ Ἀθήνα, πρώτη χώρα,
Τί γαϊδάρους τρέφεις τώρα."

---

[1] In a former number of the Edinburgh Review, 1808, it is observed: "Lord Byron passed some of his early years in Scotland, where he might have learned that *pibroch* does not mean a *bagpipe*, any more than *duet* means a *fiddle*." Query,—Was it in Scotland that the young gentlemen of the Edinburgh Review *learned* that *Solyman* means *Mahomet II.* any more than *criticism* means *infallibility?*—but thus it is,

"Cædimus inque vicem præbemus crura sagittis."

The mistake seemed so completely a lapse of the pen (from the great *similarity* of the two words, and the *total absence of error* from the former pages of the literary leviathan) that I should have passed it over as in the text, had I not perceived in the Edinburgh Review much facetious exultation on all such detections, particularly a recent one, where words and syllables are subjects of disquisition and transposition; and the above-mentioned parallel passage in my own case irresistibly propelled me to hint how much easier it is to be critical than correct. The *gentlemen*, having enjoyed many a *triumph* on such victories, will hardly begrudge me a slight *ovation* for the present

In Gibbon, vol. x. p. 161, is the following sentence:—"The vulgar dialect of the city was gross and barbarous, though the compositions of the church and palace sometimes affected to copy the purity of the Attic models." Whatever may be asserted on the subject, it is difficult to conceive that the "ladies of Constantinople," in the reign of the last Cæsar, spoke a purer dialect than Anna Comnena wrote three centuries before: and those royal pages are not esteemed the best models of composition, although the princess γλῶτταν εἶχεν ΑΚΡΙΒΩΣ Ἀττικίζουσαν. In the Fanal, and in Yanina, the best Greek is spoken: in the latter there is a flourishing school under the direction of Psalida.

There is now in Athens a pupil of Psalida's, who is making a tour of observation through Greece: he is intelligent, and better educated than a fellow-commoner of most colleges. I mention this as a proof that the spirit of inquiry is not dormant among the Greeks.

The Reviewer mentions Mr. Wright, the author of the beautiful poem "Horæ Ionicæ," as qualified to give details of these nominal Romans and degenerate Greeks; and also of their language: but Mr. Wright, though a good poet and an able man, has made a mistake where he states the Albanian dialect of the Romaic to approximate nearest to the Hellenic: for the Albanians speak a Romaic as notoriously corrupt as the Scotch of Aberdeenshire, or the Italian of Naples. Yanina, (where, next to the Fanal, the Greek is purest,) although the capital of Ali Pacha's dominions, is not in Albania but Epirus; and beyond Delvinachi in Albania Proper up to Argyrocastro and Tepaleen (beyond which I did not advance) they speak worse Greek than even the Athenians. I was attended for a year and a half by two of these singular mountaineers, whose mother tongue is Illyric, and I never heard them or their countrymen (whom I have seen, not only at home, but to the amount of twenty thousand in the army of Veli Pacha) praised for their Greek, but often laughed at for their provincial barbarisms.

I have in my possession about twenty-five letters, amongst which some from the Bey of Corinth, written to me by Notaras, the Cogia Bachi, and others by the dragoman of the Caimacam of the Morea (which last governs in Vely Pacha's absence) are said to be favorable specimens of their epistolary style. I also received some at Constantinople from private persons, written in a most hyperbolical style, but in the true antique character.

The Reviewer proceeds, after some remarks on the tongue in its past and present state, to a paradox (page 59) on the great mischief the knowledge of his own language has done to Coray, who, it seems, is less likely to understand the ancient Greek, because he is perfect master of the modern! This observation follows a paragraph, recommending, in explicit terms, the study of the Romaic, as "a powerful auxiliary," not only to the traveller and foreign merchant, but also to the classical scholar; in short, to everybody except the only person who can be thoroughly acquainted with its uses; and by a parity of reasoning, our old language is conjectured to be probably more attainable by "foreigners" than by ourselves! Now, I am inclined to think, that a Dutch Tyro in our tongue (albeit himself of Saxon blood) would be sadly perplexed with "Sir Tristrem," or any other given "Auchinleck MS." with or without a grammar or glossary; and to most apprehensions it seems evident, that none but a native can acquire a competent, far less complete, knowledge of our obsolete idioms. We may give the critic credit for his ingenuity, but no more believe him than we do Smollett's Lismahago, who maintains that the purest English is spoken in Edinburgh. That Coray may err is very possible; but if he does, the fault is in the man rather than in his mother tongue, which is, as it ought to be, of the greatest aid to the native student. — Here the Reviewer proceeds to business on Strabo's translators, and here I close my remarks.

Sir W. Drummond, Mr. Hamilton, Lord Aberdeen, Dr. Clarke, Captain Leake, Mr. Gell, Mr. Walpole, and many others now in England, have all the requisites to furnish details of this fallen people. The few observations I have offered I should have left where I made them, had not the article in question, and above all the spot where I read it, induced me to advert to those pages, which the advantage of my present situation enabled me to clear, or at least to make the attempt.

I have endeavored to waive the personal feelings which rise in despite of me in touching upon any part of the Edinburgh Review; not from a wish to conciliate the favor of its writers, or to cancel the remembrance of a syllable I have formerly published, but simply from a sense of the impropriety of mixing up private resentments with a disquisition of the present kind, and more particularly at this distance of time and place.

Amongst an enslaved people, obliged to have recourse to foreign presses even for their books of religion, it is less to be wondered at that we find so few publications on general subjects than that we find any at all. The whole number of the Greeks, scattered up and down the Turkish empire and elsewhere, may amount, at most, to three millions; and yet, for so scanty a number, it is impossible to discover any nation with so great a proportion of books and their authors as the Greeks of the present century. "Ay, but," say the generous advocates of oppression, who, while they assert the ignorance of the Greeks, wish to prevent them from dispelling it, "ay, but these are mostly, if not all, ecclesiastical tracts, and consequently good for nothing." Well, and pray what else can they write about? It is pleasant enough to hear a Frank, particularly an Englishman, who may abuse the government of his own country; or a Frenchman, who may abuse every government except his own, and who may range at will over every philosophical, religious, scientific, or moral subject, sneering at the Greek legends. A Greek must not write on politics, and cannot touch on science for want of instruction; if he doubts he is excommunicated and damned; therefore his countrymen are not poisoned with modern philosophy; and as to morals, thanks to the Turks! there are no such things. What then is left him, if he has a turn for scribbling? Religion and holy biography; and it is natural enough that those who have so little in this life should look to the next. It is no great wonder, then, that in a catalogue now before me of fifty-five Greek writers, many of whom were lately living, not above fifteen should have touched on any thing but religion. The catalogue alluded to is contained in the twenty-sixth chapter of the fourth volume of Meletius's Ecclesiastical History.

ADDITIONAL NOTE, ON THE TURKS.

The difficulties of travelling in Turkey ha been much exaggerated, or rather have consid ably diminished of late years. The Mussulma have been beaten into a kind of sullen civility, ve comfortable to voyagers.

It is hazardous to say much on the subject Turks and Turkey; since it is possible to li amongst them twenty years without acquiring i formation, at least from themselves. As far as m own slight experience carried me, I have no com plaint to make; but am indebted for many civili ties (I might almost say for friendship), and muc hospitality, to Ali Pacha, his son Veli Pacha, of th Morea, and several others of high rank in th provinces. Suleyman Aga, late Governor o Athens, and now of Thebes, was a *bon vivant* and as social a being as ever sat cross-legged at tray or a table. During the carnival, when ou English party were masquerading, both himsel and his successor were more happy to "receiv masks" than any dowager in Grosvenor-square

On one occasion of his supping at the convent his friend and visitor, the Cadi of Thebes, was ca ried from table perfectly qualified for any club in Christendom; while the worthy Waywode himsel triumphed in his fall.

In all money transactions with the Moslems, ever found the strictest honor, the highest disinter estedness. In transacting business with them there are none of those dirty peculations, under th name of interest, difference of exchange, commis sion, etc. etc. uniformly found in applying to Greek consul to cash bills, even on the firs houses in Pera.

With regard to presents, an established custom in the East, you will rarely find yourself a loser; a one worth acceptance is generally returned by another of similar value — a horse, or a shawl.

In the capital and at court the citizens and court iers are formed in the same school with those o Christianity; but there does not exist a more hon orable, friendly, and high-spirited character than the true Turkish provincial Aga, or Moslem coun try gentleman. It is not meant here to designat the governors of towns, but those Agas who, by kind of feudal tenure, possess lands and houses, o more or less extent, in Greece and Asia Minor.

The lower orders are in as tolerable discipline a the rabble in countries with greater pretensions t civilization. A Moslem, in walking the streets o our country towns, would be more incommoded i England than a Frank in a similar situation in Tur key. Regimentals are the best travelling dress.

The best accounts of the religion and differen sects of Islamism, may be found in D'Ohsson' French; of their manners, etc. perhaps in Thorn ton's English. The Ottomans, with all their de fects, are not a people to be despised. Equal, a least, to the Spaniards, they are superior to th Portuguese. If it be difficult to pronounce wha they are, we can at least say what they are *not*. they are *not* treacherous, they are *not* cowardly they do *not* burn heretics, they are *not* assassins nor has an enemy advanced to *their* capital. The are faithful to their sultan till he becomes unfit t govern, and devout to their God without an inqui sition. Were they driven from St. Sophia to-mor row, and the French or Russians enthroned in thei stead, it would become a question whether Europ would gain by the exchange. England would certainly be the loser.

With regard to that ignorance of which they are so generally, and sometimes justly accused, it may be doubted, always excepting France and England, in what useful points of knowledge they are excelled by other nations. Is it in the common arts of life? In their manufactures? Is a Turkish sabre inferior to a Toledo? or is a Turk worse clothed or lodged or fed and taught than a Spaniard? Are their Pachas worse educated than a Grandee? or an Effendi than a Knight of St. Jago? I think not.

I remember Mahmout, the grandson of Ali Pacha, asking whether my fellow-traveller and myself were in the upper or lower House of Parliament. Now, this question from a boy of ten years old proved that his education had not been neglected. It may be doubted if an English boy at that age knows the difference of the Divan from a College of Dervises; but I am very sure are a Spaniard does not. How little Mahmout, surrounded, as he had been, entirely by his Turkish tutors, had learned that there was such a thing as a Parliament, it were useless to conjecture, unless we suppose that his instructors did not confine his studies to the Koran.

In all the mosques there are schools established, which are very regularly attended; and the poor are taught without the church of Turkey being put into peril. I believe the system is not yet printed (though there is such a thing as a Turkish press, and books printed on the late military institution of the Nizam Gedidd); nor have I heard whether the Mufti and the Mollas have subscribed, or the Caimacam and the Tefterdar taken the alarm, for fear the ingenuous youth of the turban should be taught not to "pray to God their way." The Greeks also — a kind of Eastern Irish papists -- have a college of their own at Maynooth — no, at Haivali; where the heterodox receive much the same kind of countenance from the Ottoman as the Catholic college from the English legislature. Who shall then affirm, that the Turks are ignorant bigots, when they thus evince the exact proportion of Christian charity which is tolerated in the most prosperous and orthodox of all possible kingdoms? But though they allow all this, they will not suffer the Greeks to participate in their privileges: no, let them fight their battles, and pay their haratch (taxes), be drubbed in this world, and damned in the next. And shall we then emancipate our Irish Helots? Mahomet forbid! We should then be bad Mussulmans, and worse Christians: at present we unite the best of both — jesuitical faith, and something not much inferior to Turkish toleration.

CANTO THE THIRD.

"Afin que cette application vous forçât de penser à autre chose; il n'y a en vérité de remède que celui-là et le temps." — *Lettre du Roi de Prusse à D'Alembert, September* 7, 1776.

I.

Is thy face like thy mother's, my fair child!
ADA![1] sole daughter of my house and
    heart?
When last I saw thy young blue eyes they
    smiled,
And then we parted, — not as now we part,
But with a hope.—
            Awaking with a start,
The waters heave around me; and on high
The winds lift up their voices: I depart,
Whither I know not; but the hour's gone by,
When Albion's lessening shores could grieve
    or glad mine eye.[2]

II.

Once more upon the waters! yet once more!
And the waves bound beneath me as a steed
That knows his rider. Welcome, to their
    roar!
Swift be their guidance, wheresoe'er it lead!
Though the strained mast should quiver as
    a reed,
And the rent canvas fluttering strew the gale,
Still must I on; for I am as a weed,
Flung from the rock, on Ocean's foam, to sail
Where'er the surge may sweep, the tempest's
    breath prevail.

III.

In my youth's summer I did sing of One,
The wandering outlaw of his own dark mind;
Again I seize the theme, then but begun,
And bear it with me, as the rushing wind
Bears the cloud onwards: in that Tale I find
The furrows of long thought, and dried-up
    tears,
Which, ebbing, leave a sterile track behind,
O'er which all heavily the journeying years
Plod the last sands of life, — where not a flower
    appears.

IV.

Since my young days of passion—joy, or
    pain,
Perchance my heart and harp have lost a
    string,

---

[1] [In a letter, dated Verona, November 6, 1816, Byron says — "By the way, *Ada's* name (which I found in our pedigree, under king John's reign), is the same with that of the sister of Charlemagne, as I redde, the other day, in a book treating of the Rhine."]

[2] [Byron quitted England, for the second and last time, on the 25th of April, 1816, attended by William Fletcher and Robert Rushton, the "yeoman" and "page" of Canto I.; his physician, Dr. Polidori; and a Swiss valet.]

And both may jar: it may be, that in vain
I would essay as I have sung to sing.
Yet, though a dreary strain, to this I cling —
So that it wean me from the weary dream
Of selfish grief or gladness — so it fling
Forgetfulness around me — it shall seem
To me, though to none else, a not ungrateful
theme.

V.

He, who grown aged in this world of woe,
In deeds, not years, piercing the depths of
life,
So that no wonder waits him; nor below
Can love, or sorrow, fame, ambition, strife,
Cut to his heart again with the keen knife
Of silent, sharp endurance: he can tell
Why thought seeks refuge in lone caves, yet
rife
With airy images, and shapes which dwell
Still unimpaired, though old, in the soul's
haunted cell.

VI.

'Tis to create, and in creating live
A being more intense, that we endow
With form our fancy, gaining as we give
The life we image, even as I do now.
What am I? Nothing: but not so art thou,
Soul of my thought! with whom I traverse
earth,
Invisible but gazing, as I glow
Mixed with thy spirit, blended with thy birth,
And feeling still with thee in my crushed feel-
ings dearth.

VII.

Yet must I think less wildly: — I *have*
thought
Too long and darkly, till my brain became,
In its own eddy boiling and o'erwrought,
A whirling gulf of phantasy and flame:
And thus, untaught in youth my heart to
tame,
My springs of life were poisoned. 'Tis too
late!
Yet am I changed; though still enough the
same
In strength to bear what time can not abate,
And feed on bitter fruits without accusing Fate.

VIII.

Something too much of this: — but now 'tis
past,
And the spell closes with its silent seal.
Long absent HAROLD reappears at last;
He of the breast which fain no more would
feel,
Wrung with the wounds which kill not, but
ne'er heal;
Yet Time, who changes all, had altered him
In soul and aspect as in age:[1] years steal

Fire from the mind as vigor from the limb,
And life's enchanted cup but sparkles near th
brim.

IX.

His had been quaffed too quickly, and h
found
The dregs were wormwood; but he fille
again,
And from a purer fount, on holier ground,
And deemed its spring perpetual; but i
vain!
Still round him clung invisibly a chain
Which galled for ever, fettering though un
seen,   .
And heavy though it clanked not; worn wit
pain,
Which pined although it spoke not, and grev
keen,
Entering with every step he took through man
a scene.

X.

Secure in guarded coldness, he had mixed
Again in fancied safety with his kind,
And deemed his spirit now so firmly fixed
And sheathed with an invulnerable mind,
That, if no joy, no sorrow lurked behind;

Pilgrimage" produced, on their appearance in 181
an effect upon the public, at least equal to any worl
which has appeared within this or the last century
and placed at once upon Lord Byron's head th
garland for which other men of genius have toile
long, and which they have gained late. He wa
placed preëminent among the literary men of hi
country by general acclamation. It was amids
such feelings of admiration that he entered the pub
lic stage. Every thing in his manner, person, an
conversation, tended to maintain the charm whicl
his genius had flung around him; and those ad
mitted to his conversation, far from finding that th
inspired poet sunk into ordinary mortality, fel
themselves attached to him, not only by many
noble qualities, but by the interest of a mysterious
undefined, and almost painful curiosity. A counte
nance exquisitely modelled to the expression o
feeling and passion, and exhibiting the remarkable
contrast of very dark hair and eyebrows, with ligh
and expressive eyes, presented to the physiogno
mist the most interesting subject for the exercise o
his art. The predominating expression was that o
deep and habitual thought, which gave way to the
most rapid play of features when he engaged in in
teresting discussion: so that a brother poet com
pared them to the sculpture of a beautiful alabaste
vase, only seen to perfection when lighted up from
within. The flashes of mirth, gaiety, indignation
or satirical dislike, which frequently animated Lorc
Byron's countenance, might, during an evening'
conversation, be mistaken, by a stranger, for the
habitual expression, so easily and so happily was h
formed for them all; but those who had an opportu
nity of studying his features for a length of time.
and upon various occasions, both of rest and emo
tion, will agree that their proper language was thai
of melancholy. Sometimes shades of this gloom
interrupted even his gayest and most happy mo
ments. — *Sir Walter Scott.*]

---

[1] [The first and second cantos of " Childe Harold's

And he, as one, might 'midst the many stand
Unheeded, searching through the crowd to find
Fit speculation; such as in strange land
He found in wonder-works of God and Nature's hand.

XI.

But who can view the ripened rose, nor seek
To wear it? who can curiously behold
The smoothness and the sheen of beauty's cheek,
Nor feel the heart can never all grow old?
Who can contemplate Fame through clouds unfold
The star which rises o'er her steep, nor climb?
Harold, once more within the vortex, rolled
On with the giddy circle, chasing Time,
Yet with a nobler aim than in his youth's fond prime.

XII.

But soon he knew himself the most unfit
Of men to herd with. Man; with whom he held
Little in common; untaught to submit
His thoughts to others, though his soul was quelled
In youth by his own thoughts; still uncompelled,
He would not yield dominion of his mind
To spirits against whom his own rebelled;
Proud though in desolation; which could find
A life within itself, to breathe without mankind.

XIII.

Where rose the mountains, there to him were friends;
Where rolled the ocean, thereon was his home;
Where a blue sky, and glowing clime, extends,
He had the passion and the power to roam;
The desert, forest, cavern, breaker's foam,
Were unto him companionship; they spake
A mutual language, clearer than the tome
Of his land's tongue, which he would oft forsake
For Nature's pages glassed by sunbeams on the lake.

XIV.

Like the Chaldean, he could watch the stars,
Till he had peopled them with beings bright
As their own beams; and earth, and earth-born jars,
And human frailties were forgotten quite:
Could he have kept his spirit to that flight
He had been happy; but this clay will sink
Its spark immortal, envying it the light
To which it mounts, as if to break the link
That keeps us from yon heaven which woos us to its brink.

XV.

But in Man's dwellings he became a thing
Restless and worn, and stern and wearisome,
Drooped as a wild-born falcon with clipt wing,
To whom the boundless air alone were home:
Then came his fit again, which to o'ercome,
As eagerly the barred-up bird will beat
His breast and beak against his wiry dome
Till the blood tinge his plumage, so the heat
Of his impeded soul would through his bosom eat.

XVI.

Self-exiled Harold [1] wanders forth again,
With nought of hope left, but with less of gloom;
The very knowledge that he lived in vain,
That all was over on this side the tomb,
Had made Despair a smilingness assume,
Which, though 'twere wild,—as on the plundered wreck
When mariners would madly meet their doom
With draughts intemperate on the sinking deck,—
Did yet inspire a cheer, which he forbore to check.[2]

[1] ["In the third canto of Childe Harold," says Sir Egerton Brydges, "there is much inequality. The thoughts and images are sometimes labored; but still they are a very great improvement upon the first two cantos. Lord Byron here speaks in his own language and character, not in the tone of others;—he is describing, not inventing; therefore he has not, and cannot have, the freedom with which fiction is composed. Sometimes he has a conciseness which is very powerful, but almost abrupt. From trusting himself alone, and working out his own deep-buried thoughts, he now, perhaps, fell into a habit of laboring, even where there was no occasion to labor. In the first sixteen stanzas there is yet a mighty but groaning burst of dark and appalling strength. It was unquestionably the unexaggerated picture of a most tempestuous and sombre, but magnificent soul!"]

[2] [These stanzas,—in which the author, adopting more distinctly the character of Childe Harold than in the original poem, assigns the cause why he has resumed his Pilgrim's staff when it was hoped he had sat down for life a denizen of his native country,—abound with much moral interest and poetical beauty. The commentary through which the meaning of this melancholy tale is rendered obvious, is still in vivid remembrance; for the errors of those who excel their fellows in gifts and accomplishments are not soon forgotten. Those scenes, ever most painful to the bosom, were rendered yet more so by public discussion; and it is at least possible that amongst those who exclaimed most loudly on this unhappy occasion, were some in whose eyes literary superiority exaggerated Lord Byron's of-

XVII.

Stop! — for 'thy tread is on an Empire's dust!
An Earthquake's spoil is sepulchred below!
Is the spot marked with no colossal bust?
Nor column trophied for triumphal show?
None; but the moral's truth tells simpler so,
As the ground was before, thus let it be; —
How that red rain hath made the harvest grow!
And is this all the world has gained by thee,
Thou first and last of fields! king-making Victory?

XVIII.

And Harold stands upon this place of skulls,
The grave of France, the deadly Waterloo;
How in an hour the power which gave annuls
Its gifts, transferring fame as fleeting too!
In "pride of place"[1] here last the eagle flew,
Then tore with bloody talon the rent plain,[2]
Pierced by the shaft of banded nations through;
Ambition's life and labors all were vain;
He wears the shattered links of the world's broken chain.

XIX.

Fit retribution! Gaul may champ the bit
And foam in fetters; — but is Earth more free?
Did nations combat to make *One* submit;

Or league to teach all kings true sov
eignty?
What! shall reviving Thraldom again b
The patched-up idol of enlightened days
Shall we, who struck the Lion down, sh
we
Pay the Wolf homage? proffering lov
gaze
And servile knees to thrones? No; *pr*
before ye praise!

XX.

If not, o'er one fallen despot boast no mor
In vain fair cheeks were furrowed with h
tears
For Europe's flowers long rooted up befc
The trampler of her vineyards; in vain yea
Of death, depopulation, bondage, fears,
Have all been borne, and broken by the a
cord
Of roused-up millions: all that most endea
Glory, is when the myrtle wreathes a swo
Such as Harmodius[3] drew on Athens' tyra
lord.

XXI.

There was a sound of revelry by night,[4]
And Belgium's capital had gathered then
Her Beauty and her Chivalry, and bright
The lamps shone o'er fair women and bra
men;
A thousand hearts beat happily; and wh
Music arose with its voluptuous swell,
Soft eyes looked love to eyes which spa
again,
And all went merry as a marriage-bell;[5]
But hush! hark! a deep sound strikes like
rising knell!

---

fence. The scene may be described in a few words: — the wise condemned — the good regretted — the multitude, idly or maliciously inquisitive, rushed from place to place, gathering gossip, which they mangled and exaggerated while they repeated it; and impudence, ever ready to hitch itself into noto- riety, *hooked on*, as Falstaff enjoins Bardolph, blustered, bullied, and talked of " pleading a cause," and " taking a side." — *Sir Walter Scott.*]

[1] "Pride of place" is a term of falconry, and means the highest pitch of flight. See Macbeth, etc.

"A falcon towering in his pride of place," etc.

[2] [In the original draught of this stanza (which, as well as the preceding one, was written after a visit to the field of Waterloo), the lines stood—

"Here his last flight the haughty eagle flew,
  Then tore with bloody beak the fatal plain."

On seeing these lines, Mr. Reinagle sketched an eagle, grasping the earth with his *talons*. The cir- cumstance being mentioned to Byron, he wrote thus to a friend at Brussels, — "Reinagle is a better poet and a better ornithologist than I am: eagles, and all birds of prey, attack with their talons, and not with their beaks; and I have altered the line thus: —

'Then tore with bloody talon the rent plain.'

This is, I think, a better line, besides its poetical justice."]

[3] See the famous song on Harmodius and Aris giton. The best English translation is in Blanc Anthology, by Mr. (since Lord Chief Justic Denman, —

"With myrtle my sword will I wreathe," etc.

[4] There can be no more remarkable proof of t greatness of Lord Byron's genius, than the spi and interest he has contrived to communicate to l picture of the often-drawn and difficult scene of t breaking up from Brussels before the great Batt It is a trite remark, that poets generally fail in t representation of great events, where the interest recent, and the particulars are consequently clea and commonly known. It required some coura to venture on a theme beset with so many dange and deformed with the wrecks of so many form adventurers. See, however, with what easy streng he enters upon it, and with how much grace gradually finds his way back to his own peculi vein of sentiment and diction! — *Jeffrey.*]

[5] On the night previous to the action, it is sa that a ball was given at Brussels.— [It is common] but erroneously asserted that Wellington was su prised by the French army while at a ball. T Duke had received intelligence of Napoleon's c cisive operations, and it was intended to put off t

XXII.

Did ye not hear it?—No; 'twas but the
    wind,
Or the car rattling o'er the stony street;
On with the dance! let joy be unconfined;
No sleep till morn, when Youth and Pleas-
    ure meet
To chase the glowing Hours with flying
    feet—
But, hark!—that heavy sound breaks in
    once more
As if the clouds its echo would repeat;
And nearer, clearer, deadlier than before!
Arm! Arm! it is—it is—the cannon's open-
    ing roar!

XXIII.

Within a windowed niche of that high hall
Sate Brunswick's fated chieftain; he did
    hear
That sound the first amidst the festival,
And caught its tone with Death's prophetic
    ear.
And when they smiled because he deemed
    it near,
His heart more truly knew that peal too well
Which stretched his father on a bloody
    bier,[1]
And roused the vengeance blood alone
    could quell:
He rushed into the field, and, foremost fight-
    ing, fell.[2]

XXIV.

Ah! then and there was hurrying to and fro,
And gathering tears, and tremblings of dis-
    tress,
And cheeks all pale, which but an hour ago
Blushed at the praise of their own loveli-
    ness;
And there were sudden partings, such as
    press
The life from out young hearts, and choking
    sighs
Which ne'er might be repeated; who could
    guess
If ever more should meet those mutual eyes,
Since upon night so sweet such awful morn
    could rise!

XXV.

And there was mounting in hot haste: the
    steed,
The mustering squadron, and the clattering
    car,
Went pouring forward with impetuous
    speed,
And swiftly forming in the ranks of war;
And the deep thunder peal on peal afar;
And near, the beat of the alarming drum
Roused up the soldier ere the morning star,
While thronged the citizens with terror
    dumb,
Or whispering, with white lips—"The foe!
    They come! they come!"

XXVI.

And wild and high the "Cameron's gather-
    ing" rose!
The war-note of Lochiel, which Albyn's hills
Have heard, and heard, too, have her
    Saxon foes:—
How in the noon of night that pibroch
    thrills,
Savage and shrill! But with the breath
    which fills
Their mountain-pipe, so fill the moun-
    taineers
With the fierce native daring which instils
The stirring memory of a thousand years,
And Evan's, Donald's[3] fame rings in each
    clansman's ears!

XXVII.

And Ardennes[4] waves above them her
    green leaves,
Dewy with nature's tear-drops, as they pass,
Grieving, if aught inanimate e'er grieves,
Over the unreturning brave,—alas!
Ere evening to be trodden like the grass
Which now beneath them, but above shall
    grow
In its next verdure, when this fiery mass
Of living valor, rolling on the foe
And burning with high hope, shall moulder
    cold and low.

XXVIII.

Last noon beheld them full of lusty life,
Last eve in Beauty's circle proudly gay,

---

ball; but, on reflection, thinking it important that
the people of Brussels should be kept in ignorance,
the Duke not only desired that the ball should pro-
ceed, but the general officers received his commands
to appear at it—each taking care to leave as quietly
as possible at ten o'clock, and join his respective
division.]
    [1] [The Duke of Brunswick fell at Quatre Bras.
His father received his death-wound at Jena.]
    [2] [This stanza is very grand, even from its total
unadornment. It is only a versification of the com-
mon narratives; but here may well be applied a
position of Johnson, that "where truth is sufficient
to fill the mind, fiction is worse than useless."—*Sir
E. Brydges.*]

---

[3] Sir Evan Cameron, and his descendant Donald,
the "gentle Lochiel" of the "forty-five."
    [4] The wood of Soignies is supposed to be a rem-
nant of the forest of Ardennes, famous in Boiardo's
Orlando, and immortal in Shakspeare's "As you
like it." It is also celebrated in Tacitus as being
the spot of successful defence by the Germans
against the Roman encroachments. I have ven-
tured to adopt the name connected with nobler
associations than those of mere slaughter.—[*Shak-
speare's Forest of Arden was in Warwickshire,
England.*]

The midnight brought the signal-sound of
    strife,
The morn the marshalling in arms, — the
    day
Battle's magnificently-stern array!
The thunder-clouds close o'er it, which
    when rent
The earth is covered thick with other clay,
Which her own clay shall cover, heaped
    and pent,
Rider and horse, — friend, foe, — in one red
    burial blent! [1]

XXIX.

Their praise is hymned by loftier harps than
    mine;
Yet one I would select from that proud
    throng,
Partly because they blend me with his line,
And partly that I did his sire some wrong,[2]
And partly that bright names will hallow
    song;
And his was of the bravest, and when show-
    ered
The death-bolts deadliest the thinned files
    along,
Even where the thickest of war's tempest
    lowered,
They reach no nobler breast than thine, young
    gallant Howard!

XXX.

There have been tears and breaking hearts
    for thee,
And mine were nothing, had I such to give;
But when I stood beneath the fresh green
    tree,
Which living waves where thou didst cease
    to live,
And saw around me the wide field revive
With fruits and fertile promise, and the
    Spring
Come forth her work of gladness to con-
    trive,
With all her reckless birds upon the wing,
I turned from all she brought to those she
    could not bring.[2]

XXXI.

I turned to thee, to thousands, of whom ea
And one as all a ghastly gap did make
In his own kind and kindred, whom to tea
Forgetfulness were mercy for their sake;
The Archangel's trump, not Glory's, mu
    awake
Those whom they thirst for; though t
    sound of Fame
May for a moment soothe, it cannot slake
The fever of vain longing, and the name
So honored but assumes a stronger, bitter
    claim.

XXXII.

They mourn, but smile at length; and, smi
    ing, mourn:
The tree will wither long before it fall;
The hull drives on, though mast and sa
    be torn;
The roof-tree sinks, but moulders on the h
In massy hoariness; the ruined wall
Stands when its wind-worn battlements a
    gone;
The bars survive the captive they enthrall
The day drags through though storms kee
    · out the sun;
And thus the heart will break, yet broken!
    live on:

XXXIII.

Even as a broken mirror, which the glass
In every fragment multiplies; and makes
A thousand images of one that was,
The same, and still the more, the more :
    breaks;
And thus the heart will do which not for
    sakes,
Living in shattered guise, and still, and cole

---

[1] [Childe Harold, though he shuns to celebrate the victory of Waterloo, gives us here a most beautiful description of the evening which preceded the battle of Quatre Bras, the alarm which called out the troops, and the hurry and confusion which preceded their march. I am not sure that any verses in our language surpass, in vigor and in feeling, this most beautiful description. — *Sir Walter Scott.*]

[2] [See note to English Bards and Scotch Reviewers, *ante*, p. 139.]

[3] My guide from Mont St. Jean over the field seemed intelligent and accurate. The place where Major Howard fell was not far from two tall and solitary trees (there was a third cut down, or shivered in the battle), which stand a few yards from each other at a pathway's side. Beneath these h died and was buried. The body has since been re moved to England. A small hollow for the pres ent marks where it lay, but will probably soon b effaced; the plough has been upon it, and the grai is. — After pointing out the different spots wher Picton and other gallant men had perished, th guide said, "Here Major Howard lay: I was nea him when wounded." I told him my relationshir and he seemed then still more anxious to point ou the particular spot and circumstances. The plac is one of the most marked in the field, from the pe culiarity of the two trees above mentioned. I wen on horseback twice over the field, comparing it wit my recollection of similar scenes. As a plain, Wa terloo seems marked out for the scene of some grea action, though this may be mere imagination: have viewed with attention those of Platea, Troy Mantinea, Leuctra, Chæronea, and Marathon; an the field around Mont St. Jean and Hougoumon appears to want little but a better cause, and tha undefinable but impressive halo which the lapse of ages throws around a celebrated spot, to vie in in terest with any or all of these, except, perhaps, th last mentioned.

And bloodless, with its sleepless sorrow
  aches,
Yet withers on till all without is cold,
Showing no visible sign, for such things are
  untold.[1]

XXXIV.

There is a very life in our despair,
Vitality of poison, — a quick root
Which feeds these deadly branches; for it
  were
As nothing did we die; but Life will suit
Itself to Sorrow's most detested fruit,
Like to the apples[2] on the Dead Sea's shore,
All ashes to the taste: Did man compute
Existence by enjoyment, and count o'er
Such hours 'gainst years of life, — say, would
  he name threescore?

XXXV.

The Psalmist numbered out the years of
  man:
They are enough; and if thy tale be *true,*
Thou, who didst grudge him even that fleet-
  ing span,
More than enough, thou fatal Waterloo!
Millions of tongues record thee, and anew
Their children's lips shall echo them, and
  say —
"Here, where the sword united nations
  drew,
Our countrymen were warring on that day!"
And this is much, and all which will not pass
  away.

XXXVI.

There sunk the greatest, nor the worst of
  men,
Whose spirit antithetically mixt
One moment of the mightiest, and again
On little objects with like firmness fixt,
Extreme in all things! hadst thou been be-
  twixt,
Thy throne had still been thine, or never
  been;
For daring made thy rise as fall: thou
  seek'st
Even now to re-assume the imperial mien,
And shake again the world, the Thunderer of
  the scene!

---

1 ["There is a richness and energy in this pas-
sage, which is peculiar to Lord Byron, among
all modern poets, — a throng of glowing images,
poured forth at once, with a facility and profusion
which must appear mere wastefulness to more eco-
nomical writers, and a certain negligence and harsh-
ness of diction which can belong only to an author
who is oppressed with the exuberance and rapidity
of his conceptions." — *Jeffrey.*]
2 The (fabled) apples on the brink of the lake
Asphaltites were said to be fair without, and, within,
ashes. Vide Tacitus, Histor. lib. v. 7.

XXXVII.

Conqueror and captive of the earth art thou!
She trembles at thee still, and thy wild name
Was ne'er more bruited in men's minds
  than now
That thou art nothing, save the jest of Fame,
Who wooed thee once, thy vassal, and be-
  came
The flatterer of thy fierceness, till thou wert
A god unto thyself; nor less the same
To the astounded kingdoms all inert,
Who deemed thee for a time whate'er thou
  didst assert.

XXXVIII.

Oh, more or less than man — in high or low,
Battling with nations, flying from the field;
Now making monarchs' necks thy footstool,
  now
More than thy meanest soldier taught to
  yield:
An empire thou couldst crush, command,
  rebuild,
But govern not thy pettiest passion, nor,
However deeply in men's spirits skilled,
Look through thine own, nor curb the lust
  of war,
Nor learn that tempted Fate will leave the
  loftiest star.

XXXIX.

Yet well thy soul hath brooked the turning
  tide
With that untaught innate philosophy,
Which, be it wisdom, coldness, or deep
  pride,
Is gall and wormwood to an enemy.
When the whole host of hatred stood hard
  by,
To watch and mock thee shrinking, thou
  hast smiled
With a sedate and all-enduring eye; —
When Fortune fled her spoiled and favorite
  child,
He stood unbowed beneath the ills upon him
  piled.

XL.

Sager than in thy fortunes; for in them
Ambition steeled thee on too far to show
That just habitual scorn, which could con-
  temn
Men and their thoughts; 'twas wise to feel,
  not so
To wear it ever on thy lip and brow,
And spurn the instruments thou wert to use
Till they were turned unto thine overthrow;
'Tis but a worthless world to win or lose;
So hath it proved to thee, and all such lot who
  choose.

XLI.

If, like a tower upon a headlong rock,
Thou hadst been made to stand or fall alone,

Such scorn of man had helped to brave the
   shock;
But men's thoughts were the steps which
   paved thy throne,
Their admiration thy best weapon shone;
The part of Philip's son was thine, not then
(Unless aside thy purple had been thrown)
Like stern Diogenes to mock at men;
For sceptred cynics earth were far too wide a
   den.[1]

XLII.

But quiet to quick bosoms is a hell,
And *there* hath been thy bane; there is a fire
And motion of the soul which will not dwell
In its own narrow being, but aspire
Beyond the fitting medium of desire;
And, but once kindled, quenchless evermore,
Preys upon high adventure, nor can tire
Of aught but rest; a fever at the core,
Fatal to him who bears, to all who ever bore.

XLIII.

This makes the madmen who have made
   men mad
By their contagion; Conquerors and Kings,
Founders of sects and systems, to whom add
Sophists, Bards, Statesmen, all unquiet
   things
Which stir too strongly the soul's secret
   springs,
And are themselves the fools to those they
   fool;
Envied, yet how unenviable! what stings
Are theirs! One breast laid open were a
   school
Which would unteach mankind the lust to
   shine or rule:

[1] The great error of Napoleon, "if we have writ
our annals true," was a continued obtrusion on
mankind of his want of all community of feeling
for or with them; perhaps more offensive to human
vanity than the active cruelty of more trembling
and suspicious tyranny. Such were his speeches to
public assemblies as well as individuals; and the
single expression which he is said to have used on
returning to Paris after the Russian winter had de-
stroyed his army, rubbing his hands over a fire,
"This is pleasanter than Moscow," would prob-
ably alienate more favor from his cause than the
destruction and reverses which led to the remark.
[Far from being deficient in that necessary branch
of the politician's art which soothes the passions
and conciliates the prejudices of those whom they
wish to employ as instruments, Bonaparte pos-
sessed it in exquisite perfection. He seldom missed
finding the very man that was fittest for his imme-
diate purpose; and he had, in a peculiar degree,
the art of moulding him to it. It was not, then,
because he despised the means necessary to gain
his end, that he finally fell short of attaining it, but
because, confiding in his stars, his fortune, and his
strength, the ends which he proposed were unat-
tainable even by the gigantic means which he pos-
sessed. — *Sir Walter Scott.*]

XLIV.

Their breath is agitation, and their life
A storm whereon they ride, to sink at la
And yet so nursed and bigoted to strife,
That should their days, surviving perils p
Melt to calm twilight, they feel overcast
With sorrow and supineness, and so die
Even as a flame unfed, which runs to wa
With its own flickering, or a sword laid
Which eats into itself, and rusts ingloriou

XLV.

He who ascends to mountain-tops, sl
   find
The loftiest peaks most wrapt in clouds a
   snow;
He who surpasses or subdues mankind,
Must look down on the hate of those bel
Though high *above* the sun of glory glov
And far *beneath* the earth and ocean spre
Round him are icy rocks, and loudly blo
Contending tempests on his naked head
And thus reward the toils which to th
   summits led.[2]

XLVI.

Away with these! true Wisdom's wo
   will be
Within its own creation, or in thine,
Maternal Nature! for who teems like th
Thus on the banks of thy majestic Rhin
There Harold gazes on a work divine,
A blending of all beauties; streams a
   dells,
Fruit, foliage, crag, wood, cornfield, mo
   tain, vine,
And chiefless castles breathing stern fa
   wells
From gray but leafy walls, where Ruin gre
   ly dwells.

XLVII.

And there they stand, as stands a lofty m
Worn, but unstooping to the baser crow
All tenantless, save to the crannying wir

[2] [This is certainly splendidly written, but
trust it is not true. From Macedonia's madma
the Swede — from Nimrod to Bonaparte, —
hunters of men have pursued their sport wit
much gaiety, and as little remorse, as the hur
of other animals: and have lived as cheerily in t
days of action, and as comfortably in their rep
as the followers of better pursuits. It would
strange, therefore, if the other active, but n
innocent spirits, whom Lord Byron has here pla
in the same predicament, and who share all t
sources of enjoyment, without the guilt and
hardness which they cannot fail of contract
should be more miserable or more unfriended
those splendid curses of their kind; and it w
be passing strange, and pitiful, if the most prec
gifts of Providence should produce only unha
ness, and mankind regard with hostility their g
est benefactors. — *Jeffrey.*]

Or holding dark communion with the cloud.
There was a day when they were young and
  proud,
Banners on high, and battles passed below;
But they who fought are in a bloody shroud,
And those which waved are shredless dust
  ere now,
And the bleak battlements shall bear no
  future blow.

XLVIII.

Beneath these battlements, within those
  walls,
Power dwelt amidst her passions; in
  proud state
Each robber chief upheld his armed halls,
Doing his evil will, nor less elate
Than mightier heroes of a longer date.
What want these outlaws[1] conquerors
  should have
But History's purchased page to call them
  great?
A wider space, an ornamented grave?
Their hopes were not less warm, their souls
  were full as brave.

XLIX.

In their baronial feuds and single fields,
What deeds of prowess unrecorded died!
And Love, which lent a blazon to their
  shields,
With emblems well devised by amorous
  pride,
Through all the mail of iron hearts would
  glide;
But still their flame was fierceness, and drew
  on
Keen contest and destruction near allied,
And many a tower for some fair mischief
  won,
Saw the discolored Rhine beneath its ruin run.

L.

But Thou, exulting and abounding river!
Making their waves a blessing as they flow
Through banks whose beauty would endure
  for ever
Could man but leave thy bright creation so,
Nor its fair promise from the surface mow
With the sharp scythe of conflict,— then to
  see
Thy valley of sweet waters, were to know
Earth paved like Heaven; and to seem
  such to me,
Even now what wants thy stream?—that it
  should Lethe be.

[1] "What wants that knave that a king should
have?" was King James's question on meeting
Johnny Armstrong and his followers in full accou-
trements. — See the Ballad.

LI.

A thousand battles have assailed thy
  banks,
But these and half their fame have passed
  away,
And Slaughter heaped on high his welter-
  ing ranks;
Their very graves are gone, and what are
  they?
Thy tide washed down the blood of yester
  day,
And all was stainless, and on thy clear
  stream
Glassed with its dancing light the sunny
  ray;
But o'er the blackened memory's blighting
  dream
Thy waves would vainly roll, all sweeping as
  they seem.

LII.

Thus Harold inly said, and passed along,
Yet not insensible to all which here
Awoke the jocund birds to early song
In glens which might have made even exile
  dear:
Though on his brow were graven lines aus-
  tere,
And tranquil sternness which had ta'en
  the place
Of feelings fierier far but less severe,
Joy was not always absent from his face,
But o'er it in such scenes would steal with
  transient trace.

LIII.

Nor was all love shut from him, though his
  days
Of passion had consumed themselves to dust.
It is in vain that we would coldly gaze
On such as smile upon us; the heart must
Leap kindly back to kindness, though dis-
  gust
Hath weaned it from all worldlings: thus
  he felt,
For there was soft remembrance, and sweet
  trust
In one fond breast, to which his own would
  melt,
And in its tenderer hour on that his bosom
  dwelt.

LIV.

And he had learned to love,— I know not
  why,
For this in such as him seems strange of
  mood,—
The helpless looks of blooming infancy,
Even in its earliest nurture; what subdued,
To change like this, a mind so far imbued
With scorn of man, it little boots to know;
But thus it was; and though in solitude

Small power the nipped affections have to
    grow,
In him this glowed when all beside had
    ceased to glow.

LV.

And there was one soft breast, as hath been
    said,
Which unto his was bound by stronger ties
Than the church links withal; and, though
    unwed,
That love was pure, and, far above disguise,
Had stood the test of mortal enmities
Still undivided, and cemented more
By peril, dreaded most in female eyes;
But this was firm, and from a foreign shore
Well to that heart might his these absent
    greetings pour!

I.

The castled crag of Drachenfels [1]
Frowns o'er the wide and winding Rhine,
Whose breast of waters broadly swells
Between the banks which bear the vine,
And hills all rich with blossomed trees,
And fields which promise corn and wine,
And scattered cities crowning these,
Whose far white walls along them shine,
Have strewed a scene, which I should see
With double joy wert *thou* with me.

2.

And peasant girls, with deep blue eyes,
And hands which offer early flowers,
Walk smiling o'er this paradise;
Above, the frequent feudal towers
Through green leaves lift their walls of gray,
And many a rock which steeply lowers,
And noble arch in proud decay,
Look o'er this vale of vintage-bowers;
But one thing want these banks of Rhine, —
Thy gentle hand to clasp in mine!

3.

I send the lilies given to me;
Though long before thy hand they touch,
I know that they must withered be,
But yet reject them not as such;
For I have cherished them as dear,
Because they yet may meet thine eye,

---

[1] The castle of Drachenfels stands on the highest summit of "the Seven Mountains," over the Rhine banks: it is in ruins, and connected with some singular traditions: it is the first in view on the road from Bonn, but on the opposite side of the river; on this bank, nearly facing it, are the remains of another, called the Jew's Castle, and a large cross commemorative of the murder of a chief by his brother. The number of castles and cities along the course of the Rhine on both sides is very great, and their situations remarkably beautiful. [These verses addressed to his sister, were written on the banks of the Rhine in May.]

And guide thy soul to mine even here,
When thou behold'st them drooping nigh
And know'st them gathered by the Rhine
And offered from my heart to thine!

4.

The river nobly foams and flows,
The charm of this enchanted ground,
And all its thousand turns disclose
Some fresher beauty varying round:
The haughtiest breast its wish might bou
Through life to dwell delighted here;
Nor could on earth a spot be found
To nature and to me so dear,
Could thy dear eyes in following mine
Still sweeten more these banks of Rhine!

LVI.

By Coblentz, on a rise of gentle ground,
There is a small and simple pyramid,
Crowning the summit of the verdant moun
Beneath its base are heroes' ashes hid,
Our enemy's — but let not that forbid
Honor to Marceau! o'er whose early ton
Tears, big tears, gushed from the rou
    soldier's lid,
Lamenting and yet envying such a doom
Falling for France, whose rights he battled
    resume.

LVII.

Brief, brave, and glorious was his your
    career, —
His mourners were two hosts, his frien
    and foes;
And fitly may the stranger lingering here
Pray for his gallant spirit's bright repose;
For he was Freedom's champion, one
    those,
The few in number, who had not o'erstep
The charter to chastise which she bestow
On such as wield her weapons; he had ke
The whiteness of his soul, and thus men o'
    him wept. [2]

---

[2] The monument of the young and lamented Ge eral Marceau (killed by a rifle-ball at Alterkirche on the last day of the fourth year of the Fren republic) still remains as described. The inscri tions on his monument are rather too long, and n required: his name was enough; France adore and her enemies admired; both wept over hii His funeral was attended by the generals and d tachments from both armies. In the same gra General Hoche is interred, a gallant man also every sense of the .word; but though he disti guished himself greatly in battle, *he* had not t good fortune to die there: his death was attend by suspicions of poison. A separate monume (not over his body, which is buried by Marceau' is raised for him near Andernach, opposite to whi one of his most memorable exploits was performe in throwing a bridge to an island on the Rhin The shape and style are different from that of Ma ceau's, and the inscription more simple and plea

LVIII.

Here Ehrenbreitstein,[1] with her shattered
  wall
Black with the miner's blast, upon her height
Yet shows of what she was, when shell and
  ball
Rebounding idly on her strength did light:
A tower of victory! from whence the flight
Of baffled foes was watched along the plain :
But Peace destroyed what War could never
  blight,
And laid those proud roofs bare to Sum-
  mer's rain —
On which the iron shower for years had
  poured in vain.

LIX.

Adieu to thee, fair Rhine! How long de-
  lighted
The stranger fain would linger on his way!
Thine is a scene alike where souls united
Or lonely Contemplation thus might stray;
And could the ceaseless vultures cease to
  prey
On self-condemning bosoms, it were here,
Where Nature, nor too sombre nor too gay,
Wild but not rude, awful yet not austere,
Is to the mellow Earth as Autumn to the year.

LX.

Adieu to thee again! a vain adieu!
There can be no farewell to scene like thine;
The mind is colored by thy every hue;
And if reluctantly the eyes resign
Their cherished gaze upon thee, lovely
  Rhine![2]

---

ing: — " The Army of the Sambre and Meuse to its
Commander-in-Chief Hoche." This is all, and as
it should be. Hoche was esteemed among the first
of France's earlier generals, before Bonaparte
monopolized her triumphs. He was the destined
commander of the invading army of Ireland.

[1] Ehrenbreitstein, *i.e.* " the broad stone of honor,"
one of the strongest fortresses in Europe, was dis-
mantled and blown up by the French at the truce
of Leoben. It had been, and could only be, reduced
by famine or treachery. It yielded to the former,
aided by surprise. After having seen the fortifica-
tions of Gibraltar and Malta, it did not much strike
by comparison; but the situation is commanding.
General Marceau besieged it in vain for some time,
and I slept in a room where I was shown a window
at which he is said to have been standing observing
the progress of the siege by moonlight, when a ball
struck immediately below it.

[2] [On taking Hockheim, the Austrians, in one
part of the engagement, got to the brow of the hill,
whence they had their first view of the Rhine.
They instantly halted — not a gun was fired — not
a voice heard: but they stood gazing on the river
with those feelings which the events of the last fif-
teen years at once called up. Prince Schwartzen-
berg rode up to know the cause of this sudden stop;
then they gave three cheers, rushed after the enemy,
and drove them into the water.]

'Tis with the thankful glance of parting
  praise;
More mighty spots may rise — more glar-
  ing shine,
But none unite in one attaching maze
The brilliant, fair, and soft, — the glories of
  old days,

LXI.

The negligently grand, the fruitful bloom
Of coming ripeness, the white city's sheen,
The rolling stream, the precipice's gloom,
The forest's growth, and Gothic walls be-
  tween,
The wild rocks shaped as they had turrets
  been
In mockery of man's art; and these withal
A race of faces happy as the scene,
Whose fertile bounties here extend to all,
Still springing o'er thy banks, though Em-
  pires near them fall.

LXII.

But these recede. Above me are the Alps,
The palaces of Nature, whose vast walls
Have pinnacled in clouds their snowy
  scalps,
And throned Eternity in icy halls
Of cold sublimity, where forms and falls
The avalanche — the thunderbolt of snow!
All that expands the spirit, yet appalls,
Gather around these summits, as to show
How Earth may pierce to Heaven, yet leave
  vain man below.

LXIII.

But ere these matchless heights I dare to
  scan,
There is a spot should not be passed in
  vain, —
Morat! the proud, the patriot field! where
  man
May gaze on ghastly trophies of the slain,
Nor blush for those who conquered on
  that plain;
Here Burgundy bequeathed his tombless
  host,
A bony heap, through ages to remain,
Themselves their monument; — the Stygian
  coast
Unsepulchred they roamed, and shrieked
  each wandering ghost.[3]

---

[3] The chapel is destroyed, and the pyramid of
bones diminished to a small number by the Burgun-
dian legion in the service of France; who anxiously
effaced this record of their ancestors' less successful
invasions. A few still remain, notwithstanding the
pains taken by the Burgundians for ages (all who
passed that way removing a bone to their own
country), and the less justifiable larcenies of the
Swiss postilions, who carried them off to sell for
knife-handles; a purpose for which the whiteness
imbibed by the bleaching of years had rendered

LXIV.

While Waterloo with Cannæ's carnage vies,
Morat and Marathon twin names shall
   stand;
They were true Glory's stainless victories,
Won by the unambitious heart and hand
Of a proud, brotherly, and civic band,
All unbought champions in no princely
   cause
Of vice-entailed Corruption; they no land
Doomed to bewail the blasphemy of laws
Making kings' rights divine, by some Dra-
   conic clause.

LXV.

By a lone wall a lonelier column rears
A gray and grief-worn aspect of old days;
'Tis the last remnant of the wreck of years,
And looks as with the wild-bewildered gaze
Of one to stone converted by amaze,
Yet still with consciousness; and there it
   stands
Making a marvel that it not decays,
When the coeval pride of human hands,
Levelled Aventicum,[1] hath strewed her sub-
   ject lands.

LXVI.

And there — oh! sweet and sacred be the
   name! —
Julia — the daughter, the devoted — gave
Her youth to Heaven; her heart, beneath a
   claim
Nearest to Heaven's, broke o'er a father's
   grave.
Justice is sworn 'gainst tears, and hers would
   crave
The life she lived in; but the judge was just,
And then she died on him she could not save.
Their tomb was simple, and without a bust,
And held within their urn one mind, one
   heart, one dust.[2]

them in great request. Of these relics I ventured
to bring away as much as may have made a quarter
of a hero, for which the sole excuse is, that if I had
not, the next passer by might have perverted them
to worse uses than the careful preservation which I
intend for them.

[1] Aventicum, near Morat, was the Roman capital
of Helvetia, where Avenches now stands.

[2] Julia Alpinula, a young Aventian priestess,
died soon after a vain endeavor to save her father,
condemned to death as a traitor by Aulus Cæcina.
Her epitaph was discovered many years ago; — it
is thus: — "Julia Alpinula: Hic jaceo. Infelicis
patris infelix proles. Deæ Aventiæ Sacerdos. Ex-
orare patris necem non potui: Male mori in fatis
illi erat. Vixi annos xxiii." — I know of no human
composition so affecting as this, nor a history of
deeper interest. These are the names and actions
which ought not to perish, and to which we turn
with a true and healthy tenderness, from the
wretched and glittering detail of a confused mass of
conquests and battles, with which the mind is
roused for a time to a false and feverish sympathy,

LXVII.

But these are deeds which should not p
   away,
And names that must not wither, thou
   the earth
Forgets her empires with a just decay,
The enslavers and the enslaved, their dea
   and birth;
The high, the mountain-majesty of worth
Should be, and shall, survivor of its woe,
And from its immortality look forth
In the sun's face, like yonder Alpine snov
Imperishably pure beyond all things below.

LXVIII.

Lake Leman woos me with its crystal fac
The mirror where the stars and mountai
   view
The stillness of their aspect in each trace
Its clear depth yields of their far height an
   hue:
There is too much of man here, to lo
   through
With a fit mind the might which I behol
But soon in me shall Loneliness renew
Thoughts hid, but not less cherished the
   of old,
Ere mingling with the herd had penned
   in their fold.

LXIX.

To fly from, need not be to hate, mankin
All are not fit with them to stir and toil,
Nor is it discontent to keep the mind
Deep in its fountain, lest it overboil
In the hot throng, where we become t
   spoil
Of our infection, till too late and long
We may deplore and struggle with the c
In wretched interchange of wrong for wrc
Midst a contentious world, striving wh
   none are strong.

LXX.

There, in a moment, we may plunge
   years
In fatal penitence, and in the blight
Of our own soul turn all our blood to tea
And color things to come with hues
   Night;
The race of life becomes a hopeless fligl
To those that walk in darkness: on the s

from whence it recurs at length with all the nau
consequent on such intoxication. [This inscrip
is a forgery. See *Quar. Rev.* vol. 68, p. 61, 62

[3] This is written in the eye of Mont Blanc (J
3d, 1816), which even at this distance dazzles m
— (July 20th.) I this day observed for some t
the distant reflection of Mont Blanc and M
Argentière in the calm of the lake, which I
crossing in my boat; the distance of these mo
tains from their mirror is sixty miles.

The boldest steer but where their ports in-
vite,
But there are wanderers o'er Eternity
Whose bark drives on and on, and anchored
ne'er shall be.

LXXI.

Is it not better, then, to be alone,
And love Earth only for its earthly sake ?
By the blue rushing of the arrowy Rhone,[1]
Or the pure bosom of its nursing lake,
Which feeds it as a mother who doth make
A fair but froward infant her own care,
Kissing its cries away as these awake ; —
Is it not better thus our lives to wear,
Than join the crushing crowd, doomed to in-
flict or bear ?

LXXII.

I live not in myself, but I become
Portion of that around me ; and to me
High mountains are a feeling,[2] but the hum
Of human cities torture : I can see
Nothing to loathe in nature, save to be
A link reluctant in a fleshly chain,
Classed among creatures, when the soul can
flee,
And with the sky, the peak, the heaving
plain
Of ocean, or the stars, mingle, and not in vain.

LXXIII.

And thus I am absorbed, and this is life ;
I look upon the peopled desert past,
As on a place of agony and strife,
Where, for some sin, to sorrow I was cast,
To act and suffer, but remount at last
With a fresh pinion ; which I feel to spring,
Though young, yet waxing vigorous, as the
blast
Which it would cope with, on delighted
wing,
Spurning the clay-cold bonds which round
our being cling.

LXXIV.

And when, at length, the mind shall be all
free
From what it hates in this degraded form,
Reft of its carnal life, save what shall be
Existent happier in the fly and worm, —

When elements to elements conform,
And dust is as it should be, shall I not
Feel all I see, less dazzling, but more warm ?
The bodiless thought ? the Spirit of each
spot ?
Of which, even now, I share at times the im-
mortal lot ?

LXXV.

Are not the mountains, waves, and skies, a
part
Of me and of my soul, as I of them ?
Is not the love of these deep in my heart
With a pure passion ? should I not con-
temn
All objects, if compared with these ? and
stem
A tide of suffering, rather than forego
Such feelings for the hard and worldly
phlegm
Of those whose eyes are only turned below,
Gazing upon the ground, with thoughts which
dare not glow ?

LXXVI.

But this is not my theme ; and I return
To that which is immediate, and require
Those who find contemplation in the urn,
To look on One, whose dust was once all fire,
A native of the land where I respire
The clear air for a while — a passing guest,
Where he became a being, — whose desire
Was to be glorious : 'twas a foolish quest,
The which to gain and keep, he sacrificed all
rest.

LXXVII.

Here the self-torturing sophist, wild Rous-
seau,[3]
The apostle of affliction, he who threw
Enchantment over passion, and from woe
Wrung overwhelming eloquence, first drew
The breath which made him wretched ; yet
he knew
How to make madness beautiful, and cast
O'er erring deeds and thoughts a heavenly
hue [4]

---

1 The color of the Rhone at Geneva is blue, to a
depth of tint which I have never seen equalled in
water, salt or fresh, except in the Mediterranean
and Archipelago.
2 [" Mr. Hobhouse and myself are just returned
from a journey of lakes and mountains. We have
been to the Grindelwald, and the Jungfrau, and
stood on the summit of the Wengen Alp: and seen
torrents of 900 feet in fall, and glaciers of all dimen-
sions: we have heard shepherds' pipes, and ava-
lanches, and looked on the clouds foaming up from
the valleys below us like the spray of the ocean of

hell. Chamouni, and that which it inherits, we
saw a month ago; but, though Mont Blanc is
higher, it is not equal in wildness to the Jungfrau,
the Eighers, the Shreckhorn, and the Rose Glaciers.
Besides this, I have been over all the Bernese Alps
and their lakes, and think many of the scenes
(some of which were not those usually frequented
by the English) finer than Chamouni. I have been
to Clarens again, and crossed the mountains behind
it." — *Byron's Letters, September,* 1816.]
3 [" I have traversed all Rousseau's ground with
the 'Héloïse' before me, and am struck to a
degree that I cannot express with the force and
accuracy of his descriptions, and the beauty of
their reality. Meillerie, Clarens, and Vevay, and
the Château de Chillon, are places of which I shall
say little: because all I could say must fall short of
the impressions they stamp." — *Byron's Letters.*]
4 [" It is evident that the impassioned parts of

Of words, like sunbeams, dazzling as they
   past
The eyes, which o'er them shed tears feelingly
   and fast.

LXXVIII.

His love was passion's essence — as a tree
On fire by lightning; with ethereal flame
Kindled he was, and blasted; for to be
Thus, and enamoured, were in him the
   same.
But his was not the love of living dame,
Nor of the dead who rise upon our dreams,
But of ideal beauty, which became
In him existence, and o'erflowing teems
Along his burning page, distempered though
   it seems.

LXXIX.

This breathed itself to life in Julie, *this*
Invested her with all that's wild and sweet;
This hallowed, too, the memorable kiss [1]
Which every morn his fevered lip would
   greet,
From hers, who but with friendship his
   would meet;

Rousseau's romance had made a deep impression upon the feelings of the noble poet. The enthusiasm expressed by Lord Byron is no small tribute to the power possessed by Jean Jacques over the passions: and, to say truth, we needed some such evidence; for, though almost ashamed to avow the truth, — still, like the barber of Midas, we must speak or die, — we have never been able to feel the interest or discover the merit of this far-famed performance. That there is much eloquence in the letters we readily admit: there lay Rousseau's strength. But his lovers, the celebrated St. Preux and Julie, have from the earliest moment we have heard the tale (which we well remember), down to the present hour, totally failed to interest us. There might be some constitutional hardness of heart; but like Lance's pebble-hearted cur, Crab, we remained dry-eyed while all wept around us. And still, on resuming the volume, even now, we can see little in the loves of these two tiresome pedants to interest our feelings for either of them. To state our opinion in language * much better than our own, we are unfortunate enough to regard this far-famed history of philosophical gallantry as an ' unfashioned, indelicate, sour, gloomy, ferocious medley of pedantry and lewdness: of metaphysical speculations, blended with the coarsest sensuality.' " — *Sir Walter Scott.*]

[1] This refers to the account in his "Confessions" of passion for the Comtesse d'Houdetot (the mistress of St. Lambert), and his long walk every morning, for the sake of the single kiss which was the common salutation of French acquaintance. Rousseau's description of his feelings on this occasion may be considered as the most passionate, yet not impure, description and expression of love that ever kindled into words; which, after all, must be felt, from their very force, to be inadequate to the delineation: a painting can give no sufficient idea of the ocean.

* See Burke's Reflections.

But to that gentle touch, through brain
   breast
Flashed the thrilled spirit's love-devou.
   heat;
In that absorbing sigh perchance more b
Than vulgar minds may be with all they s
   possest.[2]

LXXX.

His life was one long war with self-sou
   foes,
Or friends by him self-banished; for
   mind
Had grown Suspicion's sanctuary,
   chose
For its own cruel sacrifice, the kind
'Gainst whom he raged with fury stra
   and blind.
But he was phrensied,— wherefore,
   may know ?
Since cause might be which skill co
   never find;
But he was phrensied by disease or w
To that worst pitch of all, which wear
   reasoning show.

LXXXI.

For then he was inspired, and from
   came,
As from the Pythian's mystic cave of yor
Those oracles which set the world in flar
Nor ceased to burn till kingdoms were
   more :
Did he not this for France? which lay 1
   fore
Bowed to the inborn tyranny of years ?
Broken and trembling to the yoke she bo
Till by the voice of him and his compee
Roused up to too much wrath, which follo
   o'ergrown fears ?

LXXXII.

They made themselves a fearful monumer
The wreck of old opinions — things whi
   grew,
Breathed from the birth of time: the v
   they rent,
And what behind it lay all earth shall viev
But good with ill they also overthrew,
Leaving but ruins, wherewith to rebuild

[2] [" Lord Byron's character of Rousseau is dra with great force, great power of discrimination, a great eloquence. I know not that he says any thi which has not been said before, — but what he s issues, apparently, from the recesses of his o mind. It is a little labored, which, possibly, m be caused by the form of the stanza into which was necessary to throw it; but it cannot be doub that the poet felt a sympathy for the enthusias tenderness of Rousseau's genius, which he cot not have recognized with such extreme fervor. cept from a consciousness of having at least oc sionally experienced similar emotions." — *Sir Brydges.*]

Upon the same foundation, and renew
Dungeons and thrones, which the same hour
refilled,
As heretofore, because ambition was self-
willed.

LXXXIII.

But this will not endure, nor be endured!
Mankind have felt their strength, and made
it felt.
They might have used it better, but, allured
By their new vigor, sternly have they dealt
On one another; pity ceased to melt
With her once natural charities. But they,
Who in oppression's darkness caved had
dwelt,
They were not eagles, nourished with the day;
What marvel then, at times, if they mistook
their prey?

LXXXIV.

What deep wounds ever closed without a
scar?
The heart's bleed longest, and but heal to
wear
That which disfigures it; and they who war
With their own hopes, and have been van-
quished, bear
Silence, but not submission: in his lair
Fixed Passion holds his breath, until the hour
Which shall atone for years; none need
despair:
It came, it cometh, and will come, — the
power
To punish or forgive — in *one* we shall be
slower.

LXXXV.

Clear, placid Leman! thy contrasted lake,
With the wild world I dwelt in, is a thing
Which warns me, with its stillness, to forsake
Earth's troubled waters for a purer spring.
This quiet sail is as a noiseless wing
To waft me from distraction; once I loved
Torn ocean's roar, but thy soft murmuring
Sounds sweet as if a Sister's voice reproved,
That I with stern delights should e'er have
been so moved.

LXXXVI.

It is the hush of night, and all between
Thy margin and the mountains, dusk, yet
clear,
Mellowed and mingling, yet distinctly seen,
Save darkened Jura, whose capt heights
appear
Precipitously steep; and drawing near,
There breathes a living fragrance from the
shore,
Of flowers yet fresh with childhood; on the
ear
Drops the light drip of the suspended oar,
Or chirps the grasshopper one good-night
carol more;

LXXXVII.

He is an evening reveller, who makes
His life an infancy, and sings his fill;
At intervals, some bird from out the brakes
Starts into voice a moment, then is still.
There seems a floating whisper on the hill,
But that is fancy, for the starlight dews
All silently their tears of love instil,
Weeping themselves away, till they infuse
Deep into Nature's breast the spirit of her
hues.[1]

LXXXVIII.

Ye stars! which are the poetry of heaven,
If in your bright leaves we would read the
fate
Of men and empires, — 'tis to be forgiven,
That in our aspirations to be great,
Our destinies o'erleap their mortal state,
And claim a kindred with you; for ye are
A beauty and a mystery, and create
In us such love and reverence from afar,
That fortune, fame, power, life, have named
themselves a star.

LXXXIX.

All heaven and earth are still — though not
in sleep,
But breathless, as we grow when feeling
most;
And silent, as we stand in thoughts too
deep: —
All heaven and earth are still: From the
high host
Of stars, to the lulled lake and mountain-
coast,
All is concentred in a life intense,
Where not a beam, nor air, nor leaf is lost,
But hath a part of being, and a sense
Of that which is of all Creator and defence.

XC.

Then stirs the feeling infinite, so felt
In solitude, where we are *least* alone;
A truth, which through our being then doth
melt
And purifies from self: it is a tone,
The soul and source of music, which makes
known
Eternal harmony, and sheds a charm,
Like to the fabled Cytherea's zone,
Binding all things with beauty; — 'twould
disarm
The spectre Death, had he substantial power
to harm.

---

[1] [During Byron's stay in Switzerland, he took
up his residence at the Campagne-Diodati, in the
village of Coligny. It stands at the top of a rapidly
descending vineyard; the windows commanding,
one way, a noble view of the lake and of Geneva:
the other, up the lake. Every evening, the poet

XCI.

Not vainly did the early Persian make
His altar the high places and the peak
Of earth-o'ergazing mountains,[1] and thus take
A fit and unwalled temple, there to seek
The Spirit in whose honor shrines are weak,
Upreared of human hands. Come, and compare
Columns and idol-dwellings, Goth or Greek,
With Nature's realms of worship, earth and air,
Nor fix on fond abodes to circumscribe thy prayer!

XCII.

The sky is changed! — and such a change! Oh night,
And storm, and darkness, ye are wondrous strong,
Yet lovely in your strength, as is the light
Of a dark eye in woman! Far along,
From peak to peak, the rattling crags among
Leaps the live thunder! Not from one lone cloud,
But every mountain now hath found a tongue,
And Jura answers, through her misty shroud,
Back to the joyous Alps, who call to her aloud!

XCIII.

And this is in the night: — Most glorio
night!
Thou wert not sent for slumber! let me
A sharer in thy fierce and far delight, —
A portion of the tempest and of thee![2]
How the lit lake shines, a phosphoric sea
And the big rain comes dancing to the eart
And now again 'tis black, — and now, t
glee
Of the loud hills shakes with its mountai
mirth,
As if they did rejoice o'er a young eart
quake's birth.[3]

XCIV.

Now, where the swift Rhone cleaves his w
between
Heights which appear as lovers who ha
parted
In hate, whose mining depths so interven
That they can meet no more, though broke
hearted!
Though in their souls, which thus each oth
thwarted,
Love was the very root of the fond rage
Which blighted their life's bloom, and th
departed;
Itself expired, but leaving them an age
Of years all winters, — war within themselv
to wage.

XCV.

Now, where the quick Rhone thus hath cle
his way,
The mightiest of the storms hath ta'en h
stand:

embarked on the lake; and to the feelings created by these excursions we owe these delightful stanzas.]

[1] It is to be recollected, that the most beautiful and impressive doctrines of the divine Founder of Christianity were delivered, not in the *Temple*, but on the *Mount*. To waive the question of devotion, and turn to human eloquence, — the most effectual and splendid specimens were not pronounced within walls. Demosthenes addressed the public and popular assemblies. Cicero spoke in the forum. That this added to their effect on the mind of both orator and hearers, may be conceived from the difference between what we read of the emotions then and there produced, and those we ourselves experience in the perusal in the closet. It is one thing to read the Iliad at Sigæum and on the tumuli, or by the springs with Mount Ida, above, and the plain and rivers and Archipelago around you, and another to trim your taper over it in a snug library — *this* I know. Were the early and rapid progress of what is called Methodism to be attributed to any cause beyond the enthusiasm excited by its vehement faith, and doctrines (the truth or error of which I presume neither to canvass nor to question), I should venture to ascribe it to the practice of preaching in the *fields*, and the unstudied and extemporaneous effusions of its teachers. The Mussulmans, whose erroneous devotion (at least in the lower orders) is most sincere, and therefore impressive, are accustomed to repeat their prescribed orisons and prayers, wherever they may be, at the stated hours — of course, frequently in the open air, kneeling upon a light mat (which they carry for the purpose of a bed or cushion as required): the ceremony lasts some minutes, during which they are totally absorbed, and only living in their supplication: nothing can disturb them. On me the

simple and entire sincerity of these men, and th
spirit which appeared to be within and upon then
made a far greater impression than any gener.
rite which was ever performed in places of worshi
of which I have seen those of almost every persu;
sion under the sun: including most of our ow
sectaries, and the Greek, the Catholic, the Arm
nian, the Lutheran, the Jewish, and the Mahon
etan. Many of the negroes, of whom there a
numbers in the Turkish empire, are idolaters, an
have free exercise of their belief and its rites: son
of these I had a distant view of at Patras; and, fro
what I could make out of them, they appeared
be of a truly Pagan description, and not very agre
able to a spectator.

[2] The thunder-storm to which these lines ref
occurred on the 13th of June, 1816, at midnight.
have seen, among the Acroceraunian mountains
Chimari, several more terrible, but none more bea
tiful.

[3] ["This is one of the most beautiful passages
the poem. The 'fierce and far delight' of a thu
der-storm is here described in verse almost as viv
as its lightnings. The live thunder 'leaping amor
the rattling crags' — the voice of mountains, as
shouting to each other — the plashing of the b
rain — the gleaming of the wide lake, lighted like
phosphoric sea — present a picture of sublime terro

For here, not one, but many, make their play,
And fling their thunder-bolts from hand to
   hand,
Flashing and cast around: of all the band,
The brightest through these parted hills hath
   forked
His lightnings, — as if he did understand,
That in such gaps as desolation worked,
There the hot shaft should blast whatever
   therein lurked.

XCVI.

Sky, mountains, river, winds, lake, light-
   nings! ye!
With night, and clouds, and thunder, and
   a soul
To make these felt and feeling, well may be
Things that have made me watchful; the
   far roll
Of your departing voices, is the knoll
Of what in me is sleepless, — if I rest.[1]
But where of ye, oh tempests! is the goal?
Are ye like those within the human breast?
Or do ye find, at length, like eagles, some high
   nest?

XCVII.

Could I embody and unbosom now
That which is most within me, — could I
   wreak
My thoughts upon expression, and thus
   throw
Soul, heart, mind, passions, feelings, strong
   or weak,
All that I would have sought, and all I seek,
Bear, know, feel, and yet breathe — into *one*
   word,
And that one word were Lightning, I would
   speak;
But as it is, I live and die unheard,
With a most voiceless thought, sheathing it
   as a sword.

XCVIII.

The morn is up again, the dewy morn,
With breath all incense, and with cheek all
   bloom,
Laughing the clouds away with playful scorn,
And living as if earth contained no tomb, —
And glowing into day: we may resume
The march of our existence: and thus I,
Still on thy shores, fair Leman! may find
   room
And food for meditation, nor pass by
Much, that may give us pause, if pondered
   fittingly.

XCIX.

Clarens! sweet Clarens,[2] birthplace of deep
   Love,
Thine air is the young breath of passionate
   thought,
Thy trees take root in Love; the snows
   above
The very Glaciers have his colors caught,
And sunset into rose-hues sees them
   wrought
By rays which sleep there lovingly: the
   rocks,
The permanent crags, tell here of Love,
   who sought
In them a refuge from the worldly shocks,
Which stir and sting the soul with hope that
   woos, then mocks.

C.

Clarens! by heavenly feet thy paths are trod,—
Undying Love's, who here ascends a throne
To which the steps are mountains; where
   the god
Is a pervading life and light, — so shown
Not on those summits solely, nor alone
In the still cave and forest; o'er the flower

---

yet of enjoyment, often attempted, but never so well,
certainly never better brought out in poetry." —
Sir Walter Scott.]

  [1] [The Journal of his Swiss tour, which Byron
kept for his sister, closes with the following mourn-
ful passage: — "In the weather, for this tour, of thir-
teen days, I have been very fortunate — fortunate
in a companion" (Mr. Hobhouse) — "fortunate in
our prospects, and exempt from even the little petty
accidents and delays which often render journeys
in a less wild country disappointing. I was dis-
posed to be pleased. · I am a lover of nature, and
an admirer of beauty. I can bear fatigue, and wel-
come privation, and have seen some of the noblest
views in the world. But in all this, — the recollec-
tion of bitterness, and more especially of recent and
more home desolation, which must accompany me
through life, has preyed upon me here; and neither
the music of the shepherd, the crashing of the ava-
lanche, nor the torrent, the mountain, the glacier,
the forest, nor the cloud, have for one moment
lightened the weight upon my heart, nor enabled
me to lose my own wretched identity, in the ma-
jesty, and the power, and the glory, around, above,
and beneath me."]

  [2] [Stanzas xcix. to cxv. are exquisite. They
have every thing which makes a poetical picture of
local and particular scenery perfect. They exhibit
a miraculous brilliancy and force of fancy; but the
very fidelity causes a little constraint and labor of
language. The poet seems to have been so en-
grossed by the attention to give vigor and fire to
the imagery, that he both neglected and disdained
to render himself more harmonious by diffuser
words, which, while they might have improved the
effect upon the ear, might have weakened the im-
pression upon the mind. This mastery over new
matter — this supply of powers equal not only to an
untouched subject, but that subject one of peculiar
and unequalled grandeur and beauty — was suffi-
cient to occupy the strongest poetical faculties,
young as the author was, without adding to it all
the practical skill of the artist. The stanzas, too,
on Voltaire and Gibbon are discriminative, saga-
cious, and just. They are among the proofs of that
very great variety of talent which this Canto of
Lord Byron exhibits. — *Sir E. Brydges.*]

His eye is sparkling, and his breath hath
   blown .
His soft and summer breath, whose tender
   power
Passes the strength of storms in their most
   desolate hour.[1]

CI.

All things are here of *him;* from the black
   pines,
Which are his shade on high, and the loud
   roar
Of torrents, where he listeneth, to the vines
Which slope his green path downward to
   the shore,
Where the bowed waters meet him, and
   adore,
Kissing his feet with murmurs; and the
   wood,
The covert of old trees, with trunks all hoar,
But light leaves, young as joy, stands where
   it stood,
Offering to him, and his, a populous solitude.

CII.

A populous solitude of bees and birds,
And fairy-formed and many-colored thin
Who worship him with notes more sv
   than words,
And innocently open their glad wings,
Fearless and full of life : the gush of sprin
And fall of lofty fountains, and the bend
Of stirring branches, and the bud wh
   brings
The swiftest thought of beauty, here exte
Mingling, and made by Love, unto
   mighty end.

CIII.

He who hath loved not, here would le
   that lore,
And make his heart a spirit; he who kno
That tender mystery, will love the more,
For this is Love's recess, where vain me
   woes, .
And the world's waste, have driven him
   from those,
For 'tis his nature to advance or die ;
He stands not still, but or decays, or grc

---

[1] " Rousseau's Héloïse, Lettre 17, part. 4, note.
" Ces montagnes sont si hautes qu'une demi-heure
après le soleil couche, leurs sommets sont éclairés
de ses rayons; dont le rouge forme sur ces cimes
blanches *une belle couleur de rose,* qu'on apper-
çoit de fort loin." — This applies more particularly
to the heights over Meillerie. — " J'allai à Vevay lo-
ger à la Clef, et pendant deux jours que j'y restai sans
voir personne, je pris pour cette ville un amour qui
m'a suivi dans tous mes voyages, et qui m'y a fait établ-
lir enfin les héros de mon roman. Je dirois volontiers
à ceux qui ont du goût et qui sont sensibles: Allez à
Vevay — visitez le pays, examinez les sites, prome-
nez-vous sur le lac, et dites si la Nature n'a pas fait ce
beau pays pour une Julie, pour une Claire, et pour
un St. Preux: mais ne les y cherchez pas." — *Les
Confessions,* Livre iv. p. 306. Lyons, ed. 1796. —
In July, 1816, I made a voyage round the Lake of
Geneva; and, as far as my own observations have
led me in a not uninterested nor inattentive survey
of all the scenes most celebrated by Rousseau in his
" Héloïse," I can safely say, that in this there is no
exaggeration. It would be difficult to see Clarens
(with the scenes around it, Vevay, Chillon, Bôve-
ret, St. Gingo, Meillerie, Eivan, and the entrances
of the Rhone) without being forcibly struck with its
peculiar adaptation to the persons and events with
which it has been peopled. But this is not all : the
feeling with which all around Clarens, and the oppo-
site rocks of Meillerie, is invested, is of a still higher
and more comprehensive order than the mere sym-
pathy with individual passion; it is a sense of the
existence of love in its most extended and sublime
capacity, and of our own participation of its good
and of its glory: it is the great principle of the uni-
verse, which is there more condensed, but not less
manifested; and of which, though knowing our-
selves a part, we lose our individuality, and partake
in the beauty of the whole. — If Rousseau had never
written, nor lived, the same associations would not
less have belonged to such scenes. He has added
to the interest of his works by their adoption; he
has shown his sense of their beauty by the selection;
but they have done that for him which no human

being could do for them. — I had the fortune (g
or evil as it might be) to sail from Meillerie (wh
we landed for some time) to St. Gingo during a l
storm, which added to the magnificence of
around, although occasionally accompanied by d
ger to the boat which was small and overload
It was over this very part of the lake that Rouss
has driven the boat of St. Preux and Madame W
mar to Meillerie for shelter during a tempest.
gaining the shore at St. Gingo, I found that
wind had been sufficiently strong to blow dc
some fine old chestnut trees on the lower part
the mountains. On the opposite height of Clar
is a château. The hills are covered with vineya
and interspersed with some small but beaut
woods; one of these was named the " Bosquet
Julie; " and it is remarkable that, though long :
cut down by the brutal selfishness of the monk:
St. Bernard (to whom the land appertained), t
the ground might be inclosed into a vineyard
the miserable drones of an execrable superstiti
the inhabitants of Clarens still point out the s
where its trees stood, calling it by the name wh
consecrated and survived them. Rousseau has
been particularly fortunate in the preservation
the " local habitations " he has given to " a
nothings." The Prior of Great St. Bernard has
down some of his woods for the sake of a few ca
of wine, and Bonaparte has levelled part of
rocks of Meillerie in improving the road to
Simplon. The road is an excellent one, but I c
not quite agree with the remark which I he:
made, that " La route vaut mieux que les sou
nirs." [During the squall off Meillerie, of wh
Byron here makes mention, the danger of the pa
was considerable. At Ouchy, near Lausanne,
was detained two days, in a small inn, by
weather: and here it was that he wrote, in t
short interval, the " Prisoner of Chillon; " " a
ing," says Moore, " one more deathless associati
to the already immortalized localities of the Lake

Into a boundless blessing, which may vie
With the immortal lights, in its eternity!

CIV.

'Twas not for fiction chose Rousseau this
    spot,
Peopling it with affections; but he found
It was the scene which passion must allot
To the mind's purified beings; 'twas the
    ground
Where early Love his Psyche's zone un-
    bound,
And hallowed it with loveliness: 'tis lone,
And wonderful, and deep, and hath a sound,
And sense, and sight of sweetness; here the
    Rhone
Hath spread himself a couch, the Alps have
    reared a throne.

CV.

Lausanne! and Ferney! ye have been the
    abodes
Of names which unto you bequeathed a
    name;[1]
Mortals, who sought and found, by danger-
    ous roads
A path to perpetuity of fame:
They were gigantic minds, and their steep
    aim
Was, Titan-like, on daring doubts to pile
Thoughts which should call down thunder,
    and the flame
Of Heaven, again assailed, if Heaven the
    while
On man and man's research could deign do
    more than smile.

CVI.

The one was fire and fickleness, a child,
Most mutable in wishes, but in mind,
A wit as various, — gay, grave, sage, or
    wild, —
Historian, bard, philosopher, combined;
He multiplied himself among mankind,
The Proteus of their talents: But his own
Breathed most in ridicule, — which, as the
    wind,
Blew where it listed, laying all things prone,—
Now to o'erthrow a fool, and now to shake a
    throne.

CVII.

The other, deep and slow, exhausting
    thought,
And hiving wisdom with each studious year,
In meditation dwelt, with learning wrought,
And shaped his weapon with an edge severe,
Sapping a solemn creed with solemn sneer;
The lord of irony, — that master-spell,
Which stung his foes to wrath, which grew
    from fear,

---

[1] Voltaire and Gibbon.

And doomed him to the zealot's ready Hell,
Which answers to all doubts so eloquently well.

CVIII.

Yet, peace be with their ashes, — for by them,
If merited, the penalty is paid;
It is not ours to judge, — far less condemn;
The hour must come when such things shall
    be made
Known unto all, — or hope and dread al-
    layed
By slumber, on one pillow — in the dust,
Which, thus much we are sure, must lie de-
    cayed;
And when it shall revive, as is our trust,
'Twill be to be forgiven, or suffer what is just.

CIX.

But let me quit man's works, again to read
His Maker's, spread around me, and sus-
    pend
This page, which from my reveries I feed,
Until it seems prolonging without end;
The clouds above me to the white Alps tend,
And I must pierce them, and survey whate'er
May be permitted, as my steps I bend
To their most great and growing region,
    where
The earth to her embrace compels the powers
    of air.

CX.

Italia! too, Italia! looking on thee,
Full flashes on the soul the light of ages,
Since the fierce Carthaginian almost won
    thee,
To the last halo of the chiefs and sages
Who glorify thy consecrated pages;
Thou wert the throne and grave of empires;
    still,
The fount at which the panting mind as-
    suages
Her thirst of knowledge, quaffing there her
    fill,
Flows from the eternal source of Rome's im-
    perial hill.

CXI.

Thus far have I proceeded in a theme
Renewed with no kind auspices: — to feel
We are not what we have been, and to deem
We are not what we should be, — and to
    steel
The heart against itself; and to conceal,
With a proud caution, love, or hate, or
    aught, —
Passion or feeling, purpose, grief, or zeal, —
Which is the tyrant spirit of our thought,
Is a stern task of soul: — No matter, — it is
    taught.

CXII.

And for these words, thus woven into song
It may be that they are a harmless wile, —

The coloring of the scenes which fleet along,
Which I would seize, in passing, to beguile
My breast, or that of others, for a while.
Fame is the thirst of youth, — but I am not
So young as to regard men's frown or smile,
As loss or guerdon of a glorious lot;
I stood and stand alone, — remembered or
forgot.

CXIII.

I have not loved the world, nor the world me;
I have not flattered its rank breath, nor
bowed
To its idolatries a patient knee, —
Nor coined my cheek to smiles, — nor cried
aloud
In worship of an echo; in the crowd
They could not deem me one of such; I
stood
Among them, but not of them; in a shroud
Of thoughts which were not their thoughts,
and still could,
Had I not filed [1] my mind, which thus itself sub-
dued.

CXIV.

I have not loved the world, nor the world
me, —
But let us part fair foes; I do believe,
Though I have found them not, that there
may be
Words which are things, — hopes which will
not deceive,
And virtues which are merciful, nor weave
Snares for the failing: I would also deem
O'er others' griefs that some sincerely
grieve; [2]
That two, or one, are almost what they
seem, —
That goodness is no name, and happiness no
dream. [3]

---

[1] ———— "If it be thus,
For Banquo's issue have I *filed* my mind."
Macbeth.

[2] It is said by Rochefoucault, that "there is al-
ways something in the misfortunes of men's best
friends not displeasing to them."

[3] ["It is not the temper and talents of the poet,
but the use to which he puts them, on which his
happiness or misery is grounded. A powerful and
unbridled imagination is the author and architect
of its own disappointments. Its fascinations, its
exaggerated pictures of good and evil, and the
mental distress to which they give rise, are the
natural and necessary evils attending on that quick
susceptibility of feeling and fancy incident to the
poetical temperament. But the Giver of all talents,
while he has qualified them each with its separate
and peculiar alloy, has endowed the owner with the
power of purifying and refining them. But, as if to
moderate the arrogance of genius, it is justly and
wisely made requisite, that he must regulate and tame
the fire of his fancy, and descend from the heights to
which she exalts him, in order to obtain ease of
mind and tranquillity. The materials of happiness,

CXV.

My daughter! with thy name this song
gun —
My daughter! with thy name thus much
end —
I see thee not, — I hear thee not, — but ı
Can be so wrapt in thee; thou art the fr
To whom the shadows of far years ext
Albeit my brow thou never should'st bel
My voice shall with thy future visions b
And reach into thy heart, — when mir
cold, —
A token and a tone, even from thy fatl
mould.

CXVI.

To aid thy mind's development, — to w
Thy dawn of little joys, — to sit and see
Almost thy very growth, — to view thee c
Knowledge of objects, — wonders ye
thee!
To hold thee lightly on a gentle knee,
And print on thy soft cheek a parent's kis
This, it should seem, was not reserved
me;
Yet this was in my nature: — as it is,
I know not what is there, yet something lil
this.

CXVII.

Yet, though dull Hate as duty shoul
taught,
I know that thou wilt love me; thougl
name
Should be shut from thee, as a spell
fraught
With desolation, — and a broken clai
Though the grave closed between u
'twere the same,
I know that thou wilt love me; thoug
drain
My blood from out thy being were an a
And an attainment, — all would be in va
Still thou would'st love me, still that more
life retain.

CXVIII.

The child of love, — though born in b
ness
And nurtured in convulsion. Of thy si
These were the elements, — and thin
less.

that is, of such degree of happiness as is consi
with our present state, lie around us in profu
But the man of talents must stoop to gather t
otherwise they would be beyond the reach o
mass of society, for whose benefit, as well a
his, Providence has created them. There i
royal and no poetical path to contentment
heart's-ease: that by which they are attain
open to all classes of mankind, and lies withi
most limited range of intellect. To narro
wishes and desires within the scope of our p
of attainment; to consider our misfortunes,

As yet such are around thee, — but thy fire
Shall be more tempered, and thy hope far
  higher.
Sweet be thy cradled slumbers! O'er the
  sea,
And from the mountains where I now re-
  spire;·
Fain would I waft such blessing upon
  thee,
As, with a sigh, I deem thou might'st have been
  to me!

ever peculiar in their character, as our inevitable share in the patrimony of Adam; to bridle those irritable feelings, which ungoverned are sure to become governors; to shun that intensity of galling and self-wounding reflection which our poet has so forcibly described in his own burning language: —

                 ————— ' I have thought
  Too long and darkly, till my brain became,
  In its own eddy, boiling and o'erwrought,
  A whirling gulf of phantasy and flame ' ——

— to stoop, in short, to the realities of life; repent if we have offended, and pardon if we have been trespassed against; to look on the world less as our foe than as a doubtful and capricious friend, whose applause we ought as far as possible to deserve, but neither to court nor contemn — such seem the most obvious and certain means of keeping or regaining mental tranquillity.

               ————— ' Semita certe
  Tranquillæ per virtutem patet unica vitæ.' " —
Sir Walter Scott.]

CANTO THE FOURTH.

Visto ho Toscana, Lombardia, Romagna,
  Quel Monte che divide, e quel che serra
Italia, e un mare e l' altro, che la bagna.
             ARIOSTO, Satira iii.

TO JOHN HOBHOUSE, ESQ. A.M. F.R.S. ETC. ETC.

VENICE, January 2, 1818.

MY DEAR HOBHOUSE, — After an interval of eight years between the composition of the first and last cantos of Childe Harold, the conclusion of the poem is about to be submitted to the public. In parting with so old a friend, it is not extraordinary that I should recur to one still older and better, — to one who has beheld the birth and death of the other, and to whom I am far more indebted for the social advantages of an enlightened friendship, than — though not ungrateful — I can, or could be, to Childe Harold, for any public favor reflected through the poem on the poet, — to one, whom I have known long, and accompanied far, whom I have found wakeful over my sickness and kind in my sorrow, glad in my prosperity and firm in my adversity, true in counsel and trusty in peril, — to a friend often tried and never found wanting; — to yourself.

In so doing, I recur from fiction to truth; and in dedicating to you in its complete, or at least concluded state, a poetical work which is the longest, the most thoughtful and comprehensive of my compositions, I wish to do honor to myself by the record of many years' intimacy with a man of learning, of talent, of steadiness, and of honor. It is not for minds like ours to give or to receive flattery; yet the praises of sincerity have ever been permitted to the voice of friendship; and it is not for you, nor even for others, but to relieve a heart which has not elsewhere, or lately, been so much accustomed to the encounter of good-will as to withstand the shock firmly, that I thus attempt to commemorate your good qualities, or rather the advantages which I have derived from their exertion. Even the recurrence of the date of this letter, the anniversary of the most unfortunate day of my past existence,[1] but which cannot poison my future while I retain the resource of your friendship, and of my own faculties, will henceforth have a more agreeable recollection for both, inasmuch as it will remind us of this my attempt to thank you for an indefatigable regard, such as few men have experienced, and no one could experience without thinking better of his species and of himself.

It has been our fortune to traverse together, at various periods, the countries of chivalry, history, and fable — Spain, Greece, Asia Minor, and Italy; and what Athens and Constantinople were to us a few

[1] His marriage.

years ago, Venice and Rome have been more recently. The poem also, or the pilgrim, or both, accompanied me from first to last: and perhaps it may be a pardonable vanity which indu¿es reflect with complacency on a composition which in some degree connects me with the spot wnere i produced, and the objects it would fain describe; and however unworthy it may be deemed of magical and memorable abodes, however short it may fall of our distant conceptions and imme impressions, yet as a mark of respect for what is venerable, and of feeling for what is glorious, it has to me a source of pleasure in the production, and I part with it with a kind of regret, which I h suspected that events could have left me for imaginary objects.

With regard to the conduct of the last canto, there will be found less of the pilgrim than in any o preceding, and that little slightly, if at all, separated from the author speaking in his own person. fact is, that I had become weary of drawing a line which every one seemed determined not to perc like the Chinese in Goldsmith's "Citizen of the World," whom nobody would believe to be a Chine was in vain that I asserted, and imagined that I had drawn, a distinction between the author and th grim; and the very anxiety to preserve this difference, and disappointment at finding it unavailing, s crushed my efforts in the composition, that I determined to abandon it altogether — and have don The opinions which have been, or may be, formed on that subject, are *now* a matter of indifference work is to depend on itself and not on the writer; and the author, who has no resources in his own beyond the reputation, transient or permanent, which is to arise from his literary efforts, deserve fate of authors.

In the course of the following canto it was my intention, either in the text or in the notes, to touched upon the present state of Italian literature, and perhaps of manners. But the text, within limits I proposed, I soon found hardly sufficient for the labyrinth of external objects, and the conseq reflections; and for the whole of the notes, excepting a few of the shortest, I am indebted to yourself these were necessarily limited to the elucidation of the text.

It is also a delicate, and no very grateful task, to dissert upon the literature and manners of a nati dissimilar; and requires an attention and impartiality which would induce us — though perhaps no i tentive observers, nor ignorant of the language or customs of the people amongst whom we have rece abode — to distrust, or at least defer our judgment, and more narrowly examine our information. state of literary, as well as political party, appears to run, or to *have* run, so high, that for a strange steer impartially between them is next to impossible. It may be enough, then, at least for my purp to quote from their own beautiful language — "Mi pare che in un paese tutto poetico, che vante la li la più nobile ed insième la più dolce, tutte tutte la vie diverse si possono tentare, e che sinche la patr Alfieri e di Monti non ha perduto l' antico valore, in tutte essa dovrebbe essere la prima." Italy great names still — Canova, Monti, Ugo Foscolo, Pindemonte, Visconti, Morelli, Cicognara, Albi Mezzophanti, Mai, Mustoxidi, Aglietti, and Vacca, will secure to the present generation an honoi place in most of the departments of Art, Science, and Belles Lettres; and in some the very highe Europe — the World — has but one Canova.

It has been somewhere said by Alfieri, that "La pianta uomo nasce più robusta in Italia che in lunque altra terra — e che gli stessi atroci delitti che vi si commettono ne sono una prova." Witl subscribing to the latter part of his proposition, a dangerous doctrine, the truth of which may be disp on better grounds, namely that the Italians are in no respect more ferocious than their neighbors, man must be wilfully blind, or ignorantly heedless, who is not struck with the extraordinary capacit this people, or, if such a word be admissible, their *capabilities*, the facility of their acquisitions, rapidity of their conceptions, the fire of their genius, their sense of beauty, and, amidst all the disad tages of repeated revolutions, the desolation of battles, and the despair of ages, their still unquenc "longing after immortality," — the immortality of independence. And when we ourselves, in ri round the walls of Rome, heard the simple lament of the laborers' chorus, "Roma! Roma! Roma! R non è più come era prima," it was difficult not to contrast this melancholy dirge with the bacchanal of the songs of exultation still yelled from the London taverns, over the carnage of Mont St. Jean, the betrayal of Genoa, of Italy, of France, and of the world, by men whose conduct you yourself l exposed in a work worthy of the better days of our history. For me, —

> "Non movero mai corda
> Ove la turba di sue ciance assorda."

What Italy has gained by the late transfer of nations, it were useless for Englishmen to inquire, till it becomes ascertained that England has acquired something more than a permanent army and a suspended Habeas Corpus; it is enough for them to look at home. For what they have done abroad, and especially in the South, " Verily they *will have* their reward," and at no very distant period.

Wishing you, my dear Hobhouse, a safe and agreeable return to that country whose real welfare can be dearer to none than to yourself, I dedicate to you this poem in its completed state; and repeat once more how truly I am ever.

Your obliged and affectionate friend,

BYRON.

I.

I STOOD in Venice, on the Bridge of Sighs ; [1]
A palace and a prison on each hand :
I saw from out the wave her structures rise
As from the stroke of the enchanter's wand :
A thousand years their cloudy wings expand
Around me, and a dying Glory smiles
O'er the far times, when many a subject land
Looked to the winged Lion's marble piles,
Where Venice sate in state, throned on her hundred isles.

II.

She looks a sea Cybele, fresh from ocean,[2]
Rising with her tiara of proud towers
At airy distance, with majestic motion,
A ruler of the waters and their powers :
And such she was ; — her daughters had their dowers
From spoils of nations, and the exhaustless East
Poured in her lap all gems in sparkling showers.
In purple was she robed, and of her feast
Monarchs partook, and deemed their dignity increased.

III.

In Venice Tasso's echoes are no more,[3]
And silent rows the songless gondolier ;
Her palaces are crumbling to the shore,
And music meets not always now the ear :
Those days are gone — but Beauty still is here.
States fall, arts fade — but Nature doth not die,
Nor yet forget how Venice once was dear,
The pleasant place of all festivity,
The revel of the earth, the masque of Italy !

IV.

But unto us she hath a spell beyond
Her name in story, and her long array
Of mighty shadows, whose dim forms despond
Above the dogeless city's vanished sway ;
Ours is a trophy which will not decay
With the Rialto ; Shylock and the Moor,
And Pierre, cannot be swept or worn away —
The keystones of the arch ! though all were o'er,
For us repeopled were the solitary shore.

V.

The beings of the mind are not of clay ;
Essentially immortal, they create
And multiply in us a brighter ray
And more beloved existence : that which Fate
Prohibits to dull life, in this our state
Of mortal bondage, by these spirits supplied,
First exiles, then replaces what we hate ;
Watering the heart whose early flowers have died,
And with a fresher growth replenishing the void.

VI.

Such is the refuge of our youth and age,
The first from Hope, the last from Vacancy ;
And this worn feeling peoples many a page,
And, may be, that which grows beneath mine eye.
Yet there are things whose strong reality
Outshines our fairy-land ; in shape and hues
More beautiful than our fantastic sky,
And the strange constellations which the Muse
O'er her wild universe is skilful to diffuse :

VII.

I saw or dreamed of such, — but let them go, —
They came like truth, and disappeared like dreams ;
And whatsoe'er they were — are now but so :
I could replace them if I would ; still teems

---

[1] See " Historical Notes," at the end of this Canto, No. I.
[2] Sabellicus, describing the appearance of Venice, has made use of the above image, which would not be poetical were it not true. — " Quo fit ut qui superne urbem contempletur, turritam telluris imaginem medio Oceano figuratam se putet inspicere."
[3] See " Historical Notes," at the end of this Canto, No. II.

My mind with many a form which aptly seems
Such as I sought for, and at moments found;
Let these too go — for waking Reason deems
Such overweening phantasies unsound,
And other voices speak, and other sights sur-
round.

VIII.

I've taught me other tongues — and in strange eyes
Have made me not a stranger; to the mind
Which is itself, no changes bring surprise;
Nor is it harsh to make, nor hard to find
A country with — ay, or without mankind;
Yet was I born where men are proud to be,
Not without cause; and should I leave be-
hind
The inviolate island of the sage and free,
And seek me out a home by a remoter sea,

IX.

Perhaps I loved it well: and should I lay
My ashes in a soil which is not mine,
My spirit shall resume it — if we may
Unbodied choose a sanctuary. I twine
My hopes of being remembered in my line
With my land's language: if too fond and far
These aspirations in their scope incline, —
If my fame should be, as my fortunes are,
Of hasty growth and blight, and dull Oblivion bar

X.

My name from out the temple where the dead
Are honored by the nations — let it be —
And light the laurels on a loftier head!
And be the Spartan's epitaph on me —
" Sparta hath many a worthier son than he." [1]
Meantime I seek no sympathies, nor need;
The thorns which I have reaped are of the tree
I planted, — they have torn me, — and I bleed:
I should have known what fruit would spring from such a seed.

XI.

The spouseless Adriatic mourns her lord;
And, annual marriage now no more re-
newed,
The Bucentaur lies rotting unrestored,
Neglected garment of her widowhood!
St. Mark yet sees his lion where he stood [2]
Stand, but in mockery of his withered power,

Over the proud Place where an Emper
sued,
And monarchs gazed and envied in the ho
When Venice was a queen with an unequall
dower.

XII.

The Suabian sued, and now the Austri
reigns — [2]
An Emperor tramples where an Emper
knelt;
Kingdoms are shrunk to provinces, a chains
Clank over sceptred cities; nations melt
From power's high pinnacle, when th
have felt
The sunshine for a while, and downward
Like lauwine loosened from the mountai
belt;
Oh for one hour of blind old Dandolo ! [2]
Th' octogenarian chief, Byzantium's conqu
ing foe.

XIII.

Before St. Mark still glow his steeds of bra
Their gilded collars glittering in the sun;
But is not Doria's menace come to pass
Are they not *bridled?* — Venice, lost won,
Her thirteen hundred years of freedom d
Sinks, like a sea-weed, into whence she r
Better be whelmed beneath the waves,
shun,
Even in destruction's depth, her foreign f
From whom submission wrings an infam
repose.

XIV.

In youth she was all glory,— a new Tyre
Her very by-word sprung from victory,
The " Planter of the Lion," [4] which throu
fire
And blood she bore o'er subject e th
sea;
Though making many slaves, hersel
free,
And Europe's bulwark 'gainst the Ottom
Witness Troy's rival, Candia! Vouch it,
Immortal waves that saw Lepanto's figh
For ye are names no time nor tyranny
blight.

XV.

Statues of glass — all shivered — the l
file
Of her dead Doges are declined to dust
But where they dwelt, the vast and sump
ous pile
Bespeaks the pageant of their splendid tru

[1] The answer of the mother of Brasidas, the Lacedæmonian general, to the strangers who praised the memory of her son.
[2] See " Historical Notes," Nos. III., IV., V.
[3] See " Historical Notes," No. VI.
[4] That is, the Lion of St. Mark, the standar the republic, which is the origin of the word Pa loon — Piantaleone, Pantaleon, Pantaloon.

Their sceptre broken, and their sword in
. rust,
Have yielded to the stranger: empty halls,
Thin streets, and foreign aspects, such as
must
Too oft remind her who and what enthralls,[1]
Have flung a desolate cloud o'er Venice' lovely
walls.

XVI.

When Athens' armies fell at Syracuse,
And fettered thousands bore the yoke of war,
Redemption rose up in the Attic Muse,[2]
Her voice their only ransom from afar:
See! as they chant the tragic hymn, the car
Of the o'ermastered victor stops, the reins
Fall from his hands — his idle scimitar
Starts from its belt — he rends his captive's
chains,
And bids him thank the bard for freedom and
his strains.

XVII.

Thus, Venice, if no stronger claim were
thine,
Were all thy proud historic deeds forgot,
Thy choral memory of the Bard divine,
Thy love of Tasso, should have cut the knot
Which ties thee to thy tyrants; and thy lot
Is shameful to the nations, — most of all,
Albion! to thee: the Ocean queen should
not
Abandon Ocean's children; in the fall
Of Venice think of thine, despite thy watery
wall.

XVIII.

I loved her from my boyhood — she to me
Was as a fairy city of the heart,
Rising like water-columns from the sea,
Of joy the sojourn, and of wealth the mart;
And Otway, Radcliffe, Schiller, Shakspeare's
art,[3]
Had stamped her image in me, and even so,
Although I found her thus, we did not part,
Perchance even dearer in her day of woe,
Than when she was a boast, a marvel, and a
show.

XIX.

I can repeople with the past — and of
The present there is still for eye and thought,
And meditation chastened down, enough;
And more, it may be, than I hoped or
sought;
And of the happiest moments which were
wrought
Within the web of my existence, some

From thee, fair Venice! have their colors
caught:
There are some feelings Time cannot be-
numb,
Nor Torture shake, or mine would now be
cold and dumb.

XX.

But from their nature will the tannen grow[4]
Loftiest on loftiest and least sheltered rocks,
Rooted in barrenness, where nought below
Of soil supports them 'gainst the Alpine
shocks
Of eddying storms; yet springs the trunk,
and mocks
The howling tempest, till its height and
frame
Are worthy of the mountains from whose
blocks
Of bleak, gray granite, into life it came,
And grew a giant tree; — the mind may grow
the same.

XXI.

Existence may be born, and the deep root
Of life and sufferance make its firm abode
In bare and desolated bosoms: mute
The camel labors with the heaviest load,
And the wolf dies in silence, — not bestowed
In vain should such example be; if they,
Things of ignoble or of savage mood,
Endure and shrink not, we of nobler clay
May temper it to bear, — it is but for a day.

XXII.

All suffering doth destroy, or is destroyed,
Even by the sufferer; and, in each event,
Ends: — Some, with hope replenished and
rebuoyed,
Return to whence they came — with like in-
tent,
And weave their web again; some, bowed
and bent,
Wax gray and ghastly, withering ere their
time,
And perish with the reed on which they
leant;
Some seek devotion, toil, war, good or crime,
According as their souls were formed to sink
or climb:

XXIII.

But ever and anon of griefs subdued
There comes a token like a scorpion's sting,
Scarce seen, but with fresh bitterness im-
bued;
And slight withal may be the things which
bring

---

[1] See "Historical Notes," at the end of this
Canto, No. VII.
[2] The story is told in Plutarch's Life of Nicias.
[3] Venice Preserved; Mysteries of Udolpho; the
Ghost Seer, or Armenian; the Merchant of Venice;
Othello.

[4] *Tannen* is the plural of *tanne*, a species of fir
peculiar to the Alps, which only thrives in very
rocky parts, where scarcely soil sufficient for its
nourishment can be found. On these spots it
grows to a greater height than any other mountain
tree.

Back on the heart the weight which it would
   fling
Aside forever: it may be a sound —
A tone of music — summer's eve — or
   spring —
A flower — the wind — the ocean — which
   shall wound,
Striking the electric chain wherewith we are
   darkly bound;

XXIV.

And how and why we know not, nor can
   trace
Home to its cloud this lightning of the
   mind,
But feel the shock renewed, nor can efface
The blight and blackening which it leaves
   behind,
Which out of things familiar, undesigned,
When least we deem of such, calls up to
   view
The spectres whom no exorcism can bind,
The cold — the changed — perchance the
   dead — anew,
The mourned, the loved, the lost — too many!
   — yet how few!

XXV.

But my soul wanders; I demand it back
To meditate amongst decay, and stand
A ruin amidst ruins; there to track
Fallen states and buried greatness, o'er a
   land
Which *was* the mightiest in its old com-
   mand,
And *is* the loveliest, and must ever be
The master-mould of Nature's heavenly
   hand,
Wherein were cast the heroic and the free,
The beautiful, the brave — the lords of earth
   and sea.

XXVI.

The commonwealth of kings, the men of
   Rome!
And even since, and now, fair Italy!
Thou art the garden of the world, the home
Of all Art yields, and Nature [1] can decree;
Even in thy desert, what is like to thee?
Thy very weeds are beautiful, thy waste

[1] ['The whole of this canto is rich in description
of Nature. The love of Nature now appears as a
distinct passion in Byron's mind. It is a love that
does not rest in beholding, nor is satisfied with de-
scribing, what is before him. It has a power and
being, blending itself with the poet's very life.
Though Byron had, with his real eyes, perhaps,
seen more of Nature than ever was before per-
mitted to any great poet, yet he never before
seemed to open his whole heart to her genial im-
pulses. But in this he is changed: and in this and
the fourth Cantos of Childe Harold, he will stand
a comparison with the best descriptive poets, in
this age of descriptive poetry.—*Professor Wilson.*]

More rich than other climes' fertility;
Thy wreck of glory, and thy ruin grace̦
With an immaculate charm which can no̦
   defaced.

XXVII.

The moon is up, and yet it is not night-
Sunset divides the sky with her — a sea
Of glory streams along the Alpine heigl
Of blue Friuli's mountains; Heaven is
From clouds, but of all colors seems ț
Melted to one vast Iris of the West,
Where the Day joins the past Eternity;
While, on the other hand, meek Di̦
   crest
Floats through the azure air — an island of
  · blest![2]

XXVIII.

A single star is at her side, and reigns
With her o'er half the lovely heaven;
   still
Yon sunny sea heaves brightly, and rem̦
Rolled o'er the peak of the far Rhætian
As Day and Night contending were, un
Nature reclaimed her order: — gently fl
The deep-dyed Brenta, where their b
   instil
The odorous purple of a new-born rose
Which streams upon her stream,
   glassed within it glows,

XXIX.

Filled with the face of heaven, which, f̦
   afar
Comes down upon the waters; all its h̦
From the rich sunset to the rising star,
Their magical variety diffuse:
And now they change; a paler sha̦
   strews
Its mantle o'er the mountains; parting
Dies like the dolphin, whom each p
   imbues
With a new color as it gasps away,
The last still loveliest, till — 'tis gone —
   all is gray.

XXX.

There is a tomb in Arqua; — reared in
Pillared in their sarcophagus, repose
The bones of Laura's lover: here repai
Many familiar with his well-sung woeș
The pilgrims of his genius. He arose
To raise a language, and his land recla
From the dull yoke of her barbaric foe̦

[2] The above description may seem fantastic
exaggerated to those who have never seen
Oriental or an Italian sky, yet it is but a literal
hardly sufficient delineation of an August eve
(the eighteenth), as contemplated in one of n
rides along the banks of the Brenta, near La N

Watering the tree which bears his lady's
  name [1]
With his melodious tears, he gave himself to
  fame.

XXXI.

They keep his dust in Arqua, where he
  died; [1]
The mountain-village where his latter days
Went down the vale of years; and 'tis their
  pride —
An honest pride — and let it be their praise,
To offer to the passing stranger's gaze
His mansion and his sepulchre; both plain
And venerably simple, such as raise
A feeling more accordant with his strain
Than if a pyramid formed his monumental
  fane.

XXXII.

And the soft quiet hamlet where he dwelt [2]
Is one of that complexion which seems made
For those who their mortality have felt,
And sought a refuge from their hopes de-
  cayed
In the deep umbrage of a green hill's shade,
Which shows a distant prospect far away
Of busy cities, now in vain displayed,
For they can lure no further; and the ray
Of a bright sun can make sufficient holiday,

XXXIII.

Developing the mountains, leaves, and
  flowers,
And shining in the brawling brook, where-by,
Clear as its current, glide the sauntering
  hours
With a calm languor, which, though to the eye
Idlesse it seem, hath its morality.
If from society we learn to live,

---

[1] See " Historical Notes," Nos. VIII. and IX.

[2]   [" Half way up
He built his house, whence as by stealth he
    caught
Among the hills, a glimpse of busy life
That soothed, not stirred."

" I have built, among the Euganean hills, a
small house, decent and proper; in which I hope to
pass the rest of my days, thinking always of my
dead or absent friends." Among those still living
was Boccaccio, who is thus mentioned by him in his
will: — " To Don Giovanni of Certaldo, for a
winter gown at his evening studies, I leave fifty
golden florins; truly, little enough for so great a
man." When the Venetians overran the country,
Petrarch prepared for flight. " Write your Name
over your door," said one of his friends, " and you
will be safe." " I am not sure of that," replied
Petrarch, and fled with his books to Padua. His
books he left to the republic of Venice, laying, as it
were, a foundation for the library of St. Mark; but
they exist no longer. His legacy to Francis
Carrara, a Madonna painted by Giotto, is still pre-
served in the Cathedral of Padua. — *Rogers.*]

'Tis solitude should teach us how to die;
It hath no flatterers; vanity can give
No hollow aid; alone — man with his God
  must strive:

XXXIV.

Or, it may be, with demons, who impair [3]
The strength of better thoughts, and seek
  their prey
In melancholy bosoms, such as were
Of moody texture from their earliest day,
And loved to dwell in darkness and dismay,
Deeming themselves predestined to a doom
Which is not of the pangs that pass away;
Making the sun like blood, the earth a tomb,
The tomb a hell, and hell itself a murkier
  gloom.

XXXV.

Ferrara! [4] in thy wide and grass-grown
  streets,
Whose symmetry was not for solitude,
There seems as 'twere a curse upon the seats
Of former sovereigns, and the antique brood
Of Este, which for many an age made good
Its strength within thy walls, and was of
  yore
Patron or tyrant, as the changing mood
Of petty power impelled, of those who wore
The wreath which Dante's brow alone had
  worn before.

XXXVI.

And Tasso is their glory and their shame.
Hark to his strain! and then survey his cell!
And see how dearly earned Torquato's fame,
And where Alfonso bade his poet dwell:
The miserable despot could not quell
The insulted mind he sought to quench, and
  blend
With the surrounding maniacs, in the hell
Where he had plunged it. Glory without
  end
Scattered the clouds away — and on that name
  attend

XXXVII.

The tears and praises of all time; while thine
Would rot in its oblivion — in the sink
Of worthless dust, which from thy boasted
  line
Is shaken into nothing; but the link
Thou formest in his fortunes bids us think
Of thy poor malice, naming thee with scorn—
Alfonso! how thy ducal pageants shrink

---

[3] The struggle is to the full as likely to be with
demons as with our better thoughts. Satan chose
the wilderness for the temptation of our Saviour.
And our unsullied John Locke preferred the pres-
ence of a child to complete solitude.

[4] [In April, 1817, Byron visited Ferrara, went over
the castle, cell, etc., and wrote, a few days after, the
Lament of Tasso.]

From thee! if. in another station born,
Scarce fit to be the slave of him thou mad'st
  to mourn.

XXXVIII.

Thou! formed to eat, and be despised, and
  die,
Even as the beasts that perish, save that thou
Hadst a more splendid trough and wider sty:
He! with a glory round his furrowed brow,
Which emanated then, and dazzles now,
In face of all his foes, the Cruscan quire,
And Boileau, whose rash envy could allow [1]
No strain which shamed his country's
  creaking lyre,
That whetstone of the teeth — monotony in
  wire!

XXXIX.

Peace to Torquato's injured shade! 'twas
  his
In life and death to be the mark where
  Wrong
Aimed with her poisoned arrows; but to
  miss.
Oh, victor unsurpassed in modern song!
Each year brings forth its millions; but how
  long
The tide of generations shall roll on,
And not the whole combined and countless
  throng
Compose a mind like thine? though all in
  one
Condensed their scattered rays, they would
  not form a sun.

XL.

Great as thou art, yet paralleled by those,
Thy countrymen, before thee born to shine,
The Bards of Hell and Chivalry: first rose
The Tuscan father's comedy divine;
Then, not unequal to the Florentine,
The southern Scott,[2] the minstrel who called
  forth
A new creation with his magic line,
And, like the Ariosto of the North,
Sang ladye-love and war, romance and
  knightly worth.

XLI.

The lightning rent from Ariosto's bu:
The iron crown of laurel's mimicked]
Nor was the ominous element unjus
For the true laurel-wreath which
  weaves
Is of the tree no bolt of thunder clea
And the false semblance but disgrac
  brow;
Yet still, if fondly Superstition grieve
Know, that the lightning sanctifies be
Whate'er it strikes; — yon head is
  sacred now.

XLII.

Italia! oh Italia! thou who hast
The fatal gift of beauty, which becar
A funeral dower of present woes an
On thy sweet brow is sorrow ploug!
  shame,
And annals graved in characters of :
Oh, God! that thou wert in thy nake
Less lovely or more powerful, and
  claim
Thy right, and awe the robbers bac
  press
To shed thy blood, and drink the tears
  distress;

XLIII.

Then might'st thou more appall;
  desired,
Be homely and be peaceful, undeplo
For thy destructive charms; then, s
  tired,
Would not be seen the armed t
  poured
Down the deep Alps; nor would the
  horde
Of many-nationed spoilers from the
Quaff blood and water; nor the str
  sword
Be thy sad weapon of defence, and
Victor or vanquished, thou the slave c
  or foe.[4]

---

[1] See "Historical Notes," at the end of this
Canto, No. X.

[2] ["Scott," says Byron, in his MS. Diary, for
1821, "is certainly the most wonderful writer of the
day. His novels are a new literature in them-
selves, and his poetry as good as any — if not better
(only on an erroneous system), — and only ceased
to be so popular, because the vulgar were tired of
hearing 'Aristides called the Just,' and Scott the
best, and ostracized him. I know no reading to
which I fall with such alacrity as a work of his. I
love him, too, for his manliness of character, for the
extreme pleasantness of his conversation, and his
good nature towards myself, personally. May he
prosper! for he deserves it." In a letter, written
to Sir Walter, from Pisa, in 1822, he says — "I owe
to you far more than the usual obligation for the

courtesies of literature and common friends
you went out of your way, in 1817, to do n
vice, when it required not merely kindn
courage, to do so; to have been recorded b
such a manner, would have been a proud n
at any time, but at such a time, when '
world and his wife,' as the proverb goes, v
ing to trample upon me, was something sti
to my self-esteem. Had it been a comm
cism, however eloquent or panegyrical,]
have felt pleased and grateful, but not to th
which the extraordinary good-heartednes
whole proceeding must induce in any mind
of such sensations."]

[3] See "Historical Notes," at the end of thi
Nos. XI. XII. XIII.

[4] The two stanzas xlii. and xliii. are, wit
ception of a line or two, a translation of the
sonnet of Filicaja: — "Italia, Italia, O tu c
sorte!"

XLIV.

Wandering in youth, I traced the path of
  him,[1]
The Roman friend of Rome's least-mortal
  mind,
The friend of Tully: as my bark did skim
The bright blue waters with a fanning wind,
Came Megara before me, and behind
Ægina lay, Piræus on the right,
And Corinth on the left; I lay reclined
Along the prow, and saw all these unite
In ruin, even as he had seen the desolate sight;

XLV.

For Time hath not rebuilt them, but up-
  reared
Barbaric dwellings on their shattered site,
Which only make more mourned and more
  endeared
The few last rays of their far-scattered light,
And the crushed relics of their vanished
  night.
The Roman saw these tombs in his own age,
These sepulchres of cities, which excite
Sad wonder, and his yet surviving page
The moral lesson bears, drawn from such pil-
  grimage.

XLVI.

That page is now before me, and on mine
His country's ruin added to the mass
Of perished states he mourned in their de-
  cline,
And I in desolation: all that *was*
Of then destruction *is;* and now, alas!
Rome—Rome imperial, bows her to the
  storm,
In the same dust and blackness, and we pass
The skeleton of her Titanic form,[2]
Wrecks of another world, whose ashes still
  are warm.

[1] The celebrated letter of Servius Sulpicius to Cicero, on the death of his daughter, describes as it then was, and now is, a path which I often traced in Greece, both by sea and land, in different journeys and voyages. "On my return from Asia, as I was sailing from Ægina towards Megara, I began to contemplate the prospect of the countries around me: Ægina was behind, Megara before me; Piræus on the right, Corinth on the left: all which towns, once famous and flourishing, now lie overturned and buried in their ruins. Upon this sight, I could not but think presently within myself, Alas! how do we poor mortals fret and vex ourselves if any of our friends happen to die or be killed, whose life is yet so short, when the carcasses of so many noble cities lie here exposed before me in one view."— *See Middleton's Cicero,* vol. ii. p. 371.

[2] It is Poggio, who, looking from the Capitoline hill upon ruined Rome, breaks forth into the exclamation, "Ut nunc omni decore nudata, prostrata jacet, instar gigantei cadaveris corrupti atque undique exesi."

XLVII.

Yet, Italy! through every other land
Thy wrongs should ring, and shall, from side
  to side;
Mother of Arts! as once of arms; thy hand
Was then our guardian, and is still our
  guide;
Parent of our Religion! whom the wide
Nations have knelt to for the keys of heaven!
Europe, repentant of her parricide,
Shall yet redeem thee, and, all backward
  driven,
Roll the barbarian tide, and sue to be forgiven.

XLVIII.

But Arno wins us to the fair white walls,
Where the Etrurian Athens claims and
  keeps
A softer feeling for her fairy halls.
Girt by her theatre of hills, she reaps
Her corn, and wine, and oil, and Plenty leaps
To laughing life, with her redundant horn.
Along the banks where smiling Arno sweeps
Was modern Luxury of Commerce born,
And buried Learning rose, redeemed to a new
  morn.

XLIX.

There, too, the Goddess loves in stone, and
  fills[3]
The air around with beauty; we inhale
The ambrosial aspect, which, beheld, instils
Part of its immortality; the veil
Of heaven is half undrawn; within the pale
We stand, and in that form and face behold
What mind can make, when Nature's self
  would fail;
And to the fond idolaters of old
Envy the innate flash which such a soul could
  mould:

L.

We gaze and turn away, and know not where,
Dazzled and drunk with beauty, till the heart[4]
Reels with its fulness; there—for ever
  there—
Chained to the chariot of triumphal Art,
We stand as captives, and would not depart.
Away!—there need no words, nor terms
  precise,
The paltry jargon of the marble mart

[3] See "Historical Notes," at the end of this Canto, No. XIV.

[4] [In 1817, Byron visited Florence, on his way to Rome. "I remained," he says, "*but a day:* however, I went to the two galleries, from which one returns *drunk with beauty*. The Venus is more for admiration than love; but there are sculpture and painting, which, for the first time, at all gave me an idea of what people mean by their cant about those two most artificial of arts."]

Where Pedantry gulls Folly — we have eyes:
Blood — pulse — and breast, confirm the Dardan Shepherd's prize.

LI.

Appearedst thou not to Paris in this guise?
Or to more deeply blest Anchises? or,
In all thy perfect goddess-ship, when lies
Before thee thy own vanquished Lord of War?
And gazing in thy face as toward a star,
Laid on thy lap, his eyes to thee upturn,
Feeding on thy sweet cheek![1] while thy lips are
With lava kisses melting while they burn,
Showered on his eyelids, brow, and mouth, as
 from an urn![2]

LII.

Glowing, and circumfused in speechless love,
Their full divinity inadequate
That feeling to express, or to improve,
The gods become as mortals, and man's fate

---

[1]   'Οφθαλμοὺς ἑστιᾶν.
     " Atque oculos pascat uterque suos."
                 Ovid. Amor. lib. ii.

[2] [The delight with which the pilgrim contemplates the ancient Greek statues at Florence, and afterwards at Rome, is such as might have been expected from any great poet, whose youthful mind had, like his, been imbued with those classical ideas and associations which afford so many sources of pleasure through every period of life. He has gazed upon these masterpieces of art with a more susceptible, and, in spite of his disavowal, with a more learned eye, than can be traced in the effusions of any poet who had previously expressed, in any formal manner, his admiration of their beauty. It may appear fanciful to say so; — but we think the genius of Byron is, more than that of any other modern poet, akin to that peculiar genius which seems to have been diffused among all the poets and artists of ancient Greece; and in whose spirit, above all its other wonders, the great specimens of sculpture seem to have been conceived and executed. His creations, whether of beauty or of strength, are all single creations. He requires no grouping to give effect to his favorites, or to tell his story. His heroines are solitary symbols of loveliness, which require no foil; his heroes stand alone as upon marble pedestals, displaying the naked power of passion, or the wrapped up and reposing energy of grief. The artist who would illustrate, as it is called, the works of any of our other poets, must borrow the mimic splendors of the pencil. He who would transfer into another vehicle the spirit of Byron, must pour the liquid metal, or hew the stubborn rock. What he loses in ease, he will gain in power. He might draw from Medora, Gulnare, Lara, or Manfred, subjects for relievos, worthy of enthusiasm almost as great as Harold has himself displayed on the contemplation of the loveliest and the sternest relics of the inimitable genius of the Greeks. — *Professor Wilson.*]

Has moments like their brightest; bu weight
Of earth recoils upon us; — let it go!
We can recall such visions, and create
From what has been, or might be, th which grow
Into thy statue's form, and look like ; below.

LIII.

I leave to learned fingers, and wise han
The artist and his ape,[3] to teach and te
How well his connoisseurship understa
The graceful bend, and the volupt swell:
Let these describe the undescribable: |
I would not their vile breath should (the stream
Wherein that image shall for ever dwel
The unruffled mirror of the loveliest dr
That ever left the sky on the deep soul to be

LIV.

In Santa Croce's holy precincts lie[4] |
Ashes which make it holier, dust which
Even in itself an immortality,
Though there were nothing save the ; and this,
The particle of those sublimities
Which have relapsed to chaos: — her pose
Angelo's, Alfieri's bones, and his,[4]
The starry Galileo, with his woes;
Here Machiavelli's earth returned to wh it rose.[4]

LV.

These are four minds, which, like the ments,
Might furnish forth creation: — Italy!

---

[3] [Only a week before the poet visited the ence gallery, he wrote thus to a friend: — " I l nothing of painting. Depend upon it, of al arts, it is the most artificial and unnatural, and by which the nonsense of mankind is most imp upon. I never yet saw the picture or the s' which came a league within my conception o pectation; but I have seen many mountains, seas, and rivers, and views, and two or three wo who went as far beyond it." — *Byron's Letter*

[4] See " Historical Notes," at the end of this C: Nos. XV. XVI. XVII. — [" The church of S Croce contains much illustrious nothing. tombs of Machiavelli, Michael Angelo, Galileo, Alfieri, make it the Westminster Abbey of Italy did not admire any of these tombs — beyond contents. That of Alfieri is heavy; and all of t seem to me overloaded. What is necessary l bust and name? and perhaps a date? the las the unchronological, of whom I am one. Bu your allegory and eulogy is infernal, and w than the long wigs of English numskulls Roman bodies, in the statuary of the reign Charles the Second, William, and Anne." — *By Letters,* 1817.]

Time, which hath wronged thee with ten thousand rents
Of thine imperial garment, shall deny,
And hath denied, to every other sky,
Spirits which soar from ruin : — thy decay
Is still impregnate with divinity,
Which gilds it with revivifying ray;
Such as the great of yore, Canova is to-day.

LVI.

But where repose the all Etruscan three—
Dante, and Petrarch, and, scarce less than they,
The Bard of Prose, creative spirit! he
Of the Hundred Tales of love—where did they lay
Their bones, distinguished from our common clay
In death as life ? Are they resolved to dust,
And have their country's marbles nought to say ?
Could not her quarries furnish forth one bust ?
Did they not to her breast their filial earth intrust ?

LVII.

Ungrateful Florence ! Dante sleeps afar,[1]
Like Scipio, buried by the upbraiding shore;[1]
Thy factions, in their worse than civil war,
Proscribed the bard whose name for evermore
Their children's children would in vain adore
With the remorse of ages ; and the crown[1]
Which Petrarch's laureate brow supremely wore,
Upon a far and foreign soil had grown,
His life, his fame, his grave, though rifled — not thine own.

LVIII.

Boccaccio to his parent earth bequeathed[1]
His dust, — and lies it not her Great among,
With many a sweet and solemn requiem breathed
O'er him who formed the Tuscan's siren tongue ?
That music in itself, whose sounds are song,
The poetry of speech ? No ; — even his tomb
Uptorn, must bear the hyæna bigot's wrong,
No more amidst the meaner dead find room,
Nor claim a passing sigh, because it told for *whom!*

LIX.

And Santa Croce wants their mighty dust;
Yet for this want more noted, as of yore

The Cæsar's pageant, shorn of Brutus'bust,
Did but of Rome's best Son remind her more :
Happier Ravenna ! on thy hoary shore,
Fortress of falling empire ! honored sleeps
The immortal exile ; — Arqua, too, her store
Of tuneful relics proudly claims and keeps,
While Florence vainly begs her banished dead and weeps.

LX.

What is her pyramid of precious stones ?[2]
Of porphyry, jasper, agate, and all hues
Of gem and marble, to incrust the bones
Of merchant-dukes ? the momentary dews
Which, sparkling to the twilight stars, infuse
Freshness in the green turf that wraps the dead,
Whose names are mausoleums of the Muse,
Are gently prest with far more reverent tread
Than ever paced the slab which paves the princely head.

LXI.

There be more things to greet the heart and eyes
In Arno's dome of Art's most princely shrine,
Where Sculpture with her rainbow sister vies;
There be more marvels yet—but not for mine;
For I have been accustomed to entwine
My thoughts with Nature rather in the fields,
Than Art in galleries : though a work divine
Calls for my spirit's homage, yet it yields
Less than it feels, because the weapon which it wields

LXII.

Is of another temper, and I roam
By Thrasimene's lake, in the defiles
Fatal to Roman rashness, more at home;
For there the Carthaginian's warlike wiles
Come back before me, as his skill beguiles
The host between the mountains and the shore,
Where Courage falls in her despairing files,
And torrents, swollen to rivers with their gore,
Reek through the sultry plain, with legions scattered o'er,

LXIII.

Like to a forest felled by mountain winds;
And such the storm of battle on this day,
And such the frenzy, whose convulsion blinds
To all save carnage, that, beneath the fray,
An earthquake reeled unheededly away![3]

---

[1] See " Historical Notes," at the end of his Canto, Nos. XVIII. XIX. XX. and XXI.

[2] See " Historical Notes," at the end of this Canto, No. XXII.

[3] See " Historical Notes," at the end of this

None felt stern Nature rocking at his feet,
And yawning forth a grave for those who
  lay
Upon their bucklers for a winding-sheet;
Such is the absorbing hate when warring na-
  tions meet!

LXIV.

The Earth to them was as a rolling bark
Which bore them to Eternity; they saw
The Ocean round, but had no time to mark
The motions of their vessel; Nature's law,
In them suspended, recked not of the awe
Which reigns when mountains tremble, and
  the birds
Plunge in the clouds for refuge and with-
  draw
From their down-toppling nests; and bel-
  lowing herds
Stumble o'er heaving plains, and man's dread
  hath no words.

LXV.

Far other scene is Thrasimene now;
Her lake a sheet of silver, and her plain
Rent by no ravage save the gentle plough;
Her aged trees rise thick as once the slain
Lay where their roots are; but a brook hath
  ta'en —
A little rill of scanty stream and bed —
A name of blood from that day's sanguine
  rain;
And Sanguinetto tells ye where the dead
Made the earth wet, and turned the unwilling
  waters red.

LXVI.

But thou, Clitumnus! in thy sweetest wave [1]
Of the most living crystal that was e'er
The haunt of river nymph, to gaze and lave
Her limbs where nothing hid them, thou
  dost rear
Thy grassy banks whereon the milk-white
  steer
Grazes; the purest God of gentle waters!
And most serene of aspect, and most clear;
Surely that stream was unprofaned by
  slaughters —
A mirror and a bath for Beauty's youngest
  daughters!

LXVII.

And on thy happy shore a Temple still,
Of small and delicate proportion, keeps,

Upon a mild declivity of hill,
Its memory of thee; beneath it sweeps
Thy current's calmness; oft from out it leaps
The finny darter with the glittering scales,
Who dwells and revels in thy glassy deeps;
While, chance, some scattered water-lily
  sails
Down where the shallower wave still tells its
  bubbling tales.

LXVIII.

Pass not unblest the Genius of the place!
If through the air a zephyr more serene
Win to the brow, 'tis his; and if ye trace
Along his margin a more eloquent green,
If on the heart the freshness of the scene
Sprinkle its coolness, and from the dry dust
Of weary life a moment lave it clean
With Nature's baptism, — 'tis to him ye
  must
Pay orisons for this suspension of disgust.[2]

LXIX.

The roar of waters! — from the headlong
  height
Velino cleaves the wave-worn precipice;
The fall of waters! rapid as the light
The flashing mass foams shaking the abyss;
The hell of waters! where they howl and hiss,
And boil in endless torture; while the sweat
Of their great agony, wrung out from this
Their Phlegethon, curls round the rocks of
  jet
That gird the gulf around, in pitiless horror set,

LXX.

And mounts in spray the skies, and thence
  again
Returns in an unceasing shower, which
  round,
With its unemptied cloud of gentle rain,
Is an eternal April to the ground,

Canto, No. XXIII. — [An earthquake which shook all Italy occurred during the battle, and was unfelt by any of the combatants.]

[1] No book of travels has omitted to expatiate on the temple of the Clitumnus, between Foligno and Spoleto; and no site, or scenery, even in Italy, is more worthy a description. For an account of the dilapidation of this temple, the reader is referred to "Historical Illustrations of the Fourth Canto of Childe Harold," p. 35.

[2] ["Perhaps there are no verses in our language of happier descriptive power than the two stanzas which characterize the Clitumnus. In general poets find it so difficult to leave an interesting subject, that they injure the distinctness of the description by loading it so as to embarrass, rather than excite, the fancy of the reader; or else, to avoid that fault, they confine themselves to cold and abstract gener-alities. Byron has, in these stanzas, admirably steered his course betwixt these extremes: while they present the outlines of a picture as pure and as brilliant as those of Claude Lorraine, the task of filling up the more minute particulars is judiciously left to the imagination of the reader; and it must be dull indeed if it does not supply what the poet has left unsaid, or but generally and briefly inti-mated. While the eye glances over the lines, we seem to feel the refreshing coolness of the scene — we hear the bubbling tale of the more rapid streams, and see the slender proportions of the rural temple reflected in the crystal depth of the calm pool. — *Sir Walter Scott.*

Making it all one emerald : — how profound
The gulf! and how the giant element
From rock to rock leaps with delirious
    bound,
Crushing the cliffs, which, downward worn
    and rent
With his fierce footsteps, yield in chasms a
    fearful vent

LXXI.

To the broad column which rolls on, and
    shows
More like the fountain of an infant sea
Torn from the womb of mountains by the
    throes
Of a new world, than only thus to be
Parent of rivers, which flow gushingly,
With many windings, through the vale : —
    Look back!
Lo! where it comes like an eternity,
As if to sweep down all things in its track,
Charming the eye with dread, — a matchless
    cataract,[1]

LXXII.

Horribly beautiful! but on the verge,
From side to side, beneath the glittering
    morn,
An Iris sits, amidst the infernal surge,[2]
Like Hope upon a death-bed, and, unworn
Its steady dyes, while all around is torn
By the distracted waters, bears serene
Its brilliant hues with all their beams un-
    shorn :

---

[1] I saw the "Cascata del marmore" of Terni
twice, at different periods; once from the summit
of the precipice, and again from the valley below.
The lower view is far to be preferred, if the traveller
has time for one only; but in any point of view,
either from above or below, it is worth all the cas-
cades and torrents of Switzerland put together: the
Staubach, Reichenbach, Pisse Vache, fall of Ar-
penaz, etc. are rills in comparative appearance.
Of the fall of Schaffhausen I cannot speak, not yet
having seen it.
[2] Of the time, place, and qualities of this kind of
iris, the reader will see a short account, in a note
to *Manfred*. The fall looks so much like "the
hell of waters," that Addison thought the descent
alluded to by the gulf in which Alecto plunged into
the infernal regions. It is singular enough, that
two of the finest cascades in Europe should be arti-
ficial — this of the Velino, and the one at Tivoli.
The traveller is strongly recommended to trace the
Velino, at least as high as the little lake, called *Pie'
di Lup.* The Reatine territory was the Italian
Tempe,* and the ancient naturalist, amongst other
beautiful varieties, remarked the daily rainbows of
the lake Velinus.† A scholar of great name has
devoted a treatise to this district alone.‡

* Cicer. Epist. ad Attic. xv. lib. iv.
† Plin. Hist. Nat. lib. ii. cap. lxii.
‡ Ald. Manut. de Reatina Urbe Agroque, ap.
Sallengre, Thesaur. tom. i. p. 773.

Resembling, 'mid the torture of the scene,
Love watching Madness with unalterable
    mien.

LXXIII.

Once more upon the woody Apennine,
The infant Alps, which — had I not before
Gazed on their mightier parents, where the
    pine
Sits on more shaggy summits, and where
    roar[3]
The thundering lauwine — might be wor-
    shipped more;
But I have seen the soaring Jungfrau rear
Her never-trodden snow, and seen the hoar
Glaciers of bleak Mont Blanc both far and
    near,
And in Chimari heard the thunder-hills of fear,

LXXIV.

Th' Acroceraunian mountains of old name;
And on Parnassus seen the eagles fly
Like spirits of the spot, as 'twere for fame,
For still they soared unutterably high;
I've looked on Ida with a Trojan's eye;
Athos, Olympus, Ætna, Atlas, made
These hills seem things of lesser dignity,
All, save the lone Soracte's height, displayed
Not *now* in snow, which asks the lyric Roman's
    aid

LXXV.

For our remembrance, and from out the
    plain
Heaves like a long-swept wave about to
    break,
And on the curl hangs pausing: not in vain
May he, who will, his recollections rake
And quote in classic raptures, and awake
The hills with Latian echoes; I abhorred
Too much, to conquer for the poet's sake,
The drilled dull lesson, forced down word
    by word[4]
In my repugnant youth, with pleasure to record

---

[3] In the greater part of Switzerland, the ava-
lanches are known by the name of lauwine[n].
[4] These stanzas may probably remind the reader
of Ensign Northerton's remarks: "D—n Homo,"
etc.; but the reasons for our dislike are not exactly
the same. I wish to express, that we become tired
of the task before we can comprehend the beauty;
that we learn by rote before we can get by heart;
that the freshness is worn away, and the future
pleasure and advantage deadened and destroyed,
by the didactic anticipation, at an age when we can
neither feel nor understand the power of composi-
tions which it requires an acquaintance with life, as
well as Latin and Greek, to relish, or to reason
upon. For the same reason, we never can be aware
of the fulness of some of the finest passages of
Shakspeare ("To be, or not to be," for instance),
from the habit of having them hammered into us at
eight years old, as an exercise, not of mind, but of
memory: so that when we are old enough to enjoy
them, the taste is gone, and the appetite palled.

LXXVI.

Aught that recalls the daily drug which
    turned
My sickening memory; and, though Time
    hath taught
My mind to meditate what then it learned,
Yet such the fixed inveteracy wrought
By the impatience of my early thought,
That, with the freshness wearing out before
My mind could relish what it might have
    sought,
If free to choose, I cannot now restore
Its health; but what it then detested, still abhor.

LXXVII.

Then farewell, Horace; whom I hated so,
Not for thy faults, but mine; it is a curse
To understand, not feel thy lyric flow,
To comprehend, but never love thy verse;
Although no deeper Moralist rehearse
Our little life, nor Bard prescribe his art,
Nor livelier Satirist the conscience pierce,
Awakening without wounding the touched
    heart,
Yet fare thee well — upon Soracte's ridge we
    part.

LXXVIII.

Oh Rome! my country! city of the soul!
The orphans of the heart must turn to
    thee,
Lone mother of dead empires! and control
In their shut breasts their petty misery.
What are our woes and sufferance? Come
    and see
The cypress, hear the owl, and plod your
    way
O'er steps of broken thrones and temples,
    Ye!
Whose agonies are evils of a day —
A world is at our feet as fragile as our clay.

LXXIX.

The Niobe of nations! there she stands,[1]
Childless and crownless, in her voiceless
    woe;
An empty urn within her withered hands,
Whose holy dust was scattered long ago;
The Scipios' tomb contains no ashes now;[2]
The very sepulchres lie tenantless
Of their heroic dwellers: dost thou flow,
Old Tiber! through a marble wilderness?
Rise, with thy yellow waves, and mantle her
    distress.

LXXX.

The Goth, the Christian, Time, War, Flood,
    and Fire,
Have dealt upon the seven-billed city's
    pride;
She saw her glories star by star expire,
And up the steep barbarian monarchs ride,
Where the car climbed the capitol; far and
    wide
Temple and tower went down, nor left a
    site: —
Chaos of ruins! who shall trace the void,
O'er the dim fragments cast a lunar light,
And say, "here was, or is," where all is
    doubly night?

LXXXI.

The double night of ages, and of her,
Night's daughter, Ignorance, hath wrapt
    and wrap,'
All round us; we but feel our way to err:
The ocean hath his chart, the stars their map,
And Knowledge spreads them on her ample
    lap;
But Rome is as the desert, where we steer
Stumbling o'er recollections; now we clap
Our hands, and cry "Eureka!" it is clear —
When but some false mirage of ruin rises near.

LXXXII.

Alas! the lofty city! and alas!
The trebly hundred triumphs![3] and the day

In some parts of the continent, young persons are taught from more common authors, and do not read the best classics till their maturity. I certainly do not speak on this point from any pique or aversion towards the place of my education. I was not a slow, though an idle boy; and I believe no one could, or can be, more attached to Harrow than I have always been, and with reason; — a part of the time passed there was the happiest of my life; and my preceptor, the Rev. Dr. Joseph Drury, was the best and worthiest friend I ever possessed, whose warnings I have remembered but too well, though too late, when I have erred, — and whose counsels I have but followed when I have done well or wisely. If ever this imperfect record of my feelings towards him should reach his eyes, let it remind him of one who never thinks of him but with gratitude and veneration — of one who would more gladly boast of having been his pupil, if, by more closely following his injunctions he could reflect any honor upon his instructor.

[1] ["I have been some days in Rome the Wonderful. I am delighted with Rome. As a whole — ancient and modern, — it beats Greece, Constantinople, every thing — at least that I have ever seen. But I can't describe, because my first impressions are always strong and confused, and my memory *selects* and reduces them to order, like distance in the landscape, and blends them better, although they may be less distinct. I have been on horseback most of the day, all days since my arrival. I have been to Albano, its lakes, and to the top of the Alban Mount, and to Frescati, Aricia, etc. As for the Coliseum, Pantheon, St. Peter's, the Vatican, Palatine, etc. etc. — they are quite inconceivable, and must be *seen*." — *Byron's Letters*, May 1817.]

[2] For a comment on this and the two following stanzas, the reader may consult "Historical Illustrations," p. 46.

[3] Orosius gives 320 for the number of triumphs.

When Brutus made the dagger's edge sur-
pass
The conqueror's sword in bearing fame away!
Alas, for Tully's voice, and Virgil's lay,
And Livy's pictured page! — but these shall
be
Her resurrection; all beside — decay.
Alas, for Earth, for never shall we see
That brightness in her eye she bore when Rome
was free!

LXXXIII.

Oh thou, whose chariot rolled on Fortune's
wheel,
Triumphant Sylla! Thou, who didst subdue
Thy country's foes ere thou wouldst pause to
feel
The wrath of thy own wrongs, or reap the due
Of hoarded vengeance till thine eagles flew
O'er prostrate Asia; — thou, who with thy
frown
Annihilated senates — Roman, too,
With all thy vices, for thou didst lay down
With an atoning smile a more than earthly
crown —

LXXXIV.

The dictatorial wreath,[1] — couldst thou divine
To what would one day dwindle that which
made
Thee more than mortal ? and that so supine
By aught than Romans Rome should thus be
laid ?
She who was named Eternal, and arrayed
Her warriors but to conquer — she who veiled
Earth with her haughty shadow, and displayed,
Until the o'er-canopied horizon failed,
Her rushing wings — Oh! she who was Almighty
hailed!

LXXXV.

Sylla was first of victors; but our own
The sagest of usurpers, Cromwell; he
Too swept off senates while he hewed the
throne
Down to a block — immortal rebel! See

He is followed by Panvinius; and Panvinius by
Mr. Gibbon and the modern writers.
[1] Certainly, were it not for these two traits in the
life of Sylla, alluded to in this stanza, we should
regard him as a monster unredeemed by any admir-
able quality. The *atonement* of his voluntary res-
ignation of empire may perhaps be accepted by
us, as it seems to have satisfied the Romans, who
if they had not respected must have destroyed him.
There could be no mean, no division of opinion;
they must have all thought, like Eucrates, that
what had appeared ambition was a love of glory,
and that what had been mistaken for pride was a
real grandeur of soul.

What crimes it cost to be a moment free
And famous through all ages! but beneath
His fate the moral lurks of destiny;
His day of double victory and death
Beheld him win two realms, and, happier, yield
his breath.[2]

LXXXVI.

The third of the same moon whose former
course
Had all but crowned him, on the selfsame
day
Deposed him gently from his throne of force,
And laid him with the earth's preceding clay.
And showed not Fortune thus how fame and
sway,
And all we deem delightful, and consume
Our souls to compass through each arduous
way,
Are in her eyes less happy than the tomb ?
Were they but so in man's, how different were his
doom!

LXXXVII.

And thou, dread statue! yet existent in[3]
The austerest form of naked majesty,
Thou who beheldest, 'mid the assassins' din,
At thy bathed base the bloody Cæsar lie,
Folding his robe in dying dignity,
An offering to thine altar from the queen
Of gods and men, great Nemesis! did he die,
And thou, too, perish, Pompey ? have ye been
Victors of countless kings, or puppets of a scene ?

LXXXVIII.

And thou, the thunder-stricken nurse of Rome,[3]
She-wolf! whose brazen-imaged dugs impart
The milk of conquest yet within the dome
Where, as a monument of antique art,
Thou standest: — Mother of the mighty heart,
Which the great founder sucked from thy wild
teat,
Scorched by the Roman Jove's ethereal dart,
And thy limbs black with lightning — dost thou
yet
Guard thine immortal cubs, nor thy fond charge
forget ?

LXXXIX.

Thou dost; — but all thy foster-babes are dead —
The men of iron; and the world hath reared
Cities from out their sepulchres: men bled

[2] On the 3d of September Cromwell gained the
victory of Dunbar: a year afterwards he obtained
" his crowning mercy " of Worcester; and a few
years after, on the same day, which he had ever es-
teemed the most fortunate for him, died.
[3] See " Historical Notes," Nos. XXIV, XXV.

In imitation of the things they feared,
And fought and conquered, and the same
 course steered,
At apish distance; but as yet none have,
Nor could, the same supremacy have neared,
Save one vain man, who is not in the grave,
But, vanquished by himself, to his own slaves
 a slave —

XC.

The fool of false dominion — and a kind
Of bastard Cæsar, following him of old
With steps unequal; for the Roman's mind
Was modelled in a less terrestial mould,[1]
With passions fiercer, yet a judgment cold,
And an immortal instinct which redeemed
The frailties of a heart so soft, yet bold,
Alcides with the distaff now he seemed
At Cleopatra's feet, — and now himself he
 beamed,

XCI.

And came — and saw — and conquered!
 But the man
Who would have tamed his eagles down to
 flee,
Like a trained falcon, in the Gallic van,
Which he, in sooth, long led to victory,
With a deaf heart which never seemed to be
A listener to itself, was strangely framed;
With but one weakest weakness — vanity,
Coquettish in ambition — still he aimed —
At what? can he avouch — or answer what he
 claimed,

XCII.

And would be all or nothing — nor could
 wait
For the sure grave to level him; few years
Had fixed him with the Cæsars in his fate,
On whom we tread: For *this* the conqueror
 rears
The arch of triumph! and for this the tears
And blood of earth flow on as they have
 flowed,
An universal deluge, which appears
Without an ark for wretched man's abode,
And ebbs but to reflow! — Renew thy rainbow,
 God!

XCIII.

What from this barren being do we reap?
Our senses narrow, and our reason frail,
Life short, and truth a gem which loves the
 deep,
And all things weighed in custom's falsest
 scale;
Opinion an omnipotence, — whose veil
Mantles the earth with darkness, until right
And wrong are accidents, and men grow
 pale

---

[1] See "Historical Notes," at the end of this
Canto, No. XXVI.

Lest their own judgments should become
 too bright,
And their free thoughts be crimes, and earth
 have too much light.

XCIV.

And thus they plod in sluggish misery,
Rotting from sire to son, and age to age,
Proud of their trampled nature, and so die,
Bequeathing their hereditary rage
To the new race of inborn slaves, who wage
War for their chains, and rather than be free,
Bleed gladiator-like, and still engage
Within the same arena where they see
Their fellows fall before, like leaves of the
 same tree.

XCV.

I speak not of men's creeds — they rest
 between
Man and his Maker — but of things allowed,
Averred, and known, — and daily, hourly
 seen —
The yoke that is upon us doubly bowed,
And the intent of tyranny avowed,
The edict of Earth's rulers, who are grown
The apes of him who humbled once the
 proud,
And shook them from their slumbers on
 the throne;
Too glorious, were this all his mighty arm had
 done.

XCVI.

Can tyrants but by tyrants conquered be,
And freedom find no champion and no child
Such as Columbia saw arise when she
Sprung forth a Pallas, armed and undefiled?
Or must such minds be nourished in the
 wild,
Deep in the unpruned forest, 'midst the
 roar
Of cataracts, where nursing Nature smiled
On infant Washington? Has Earth no
 more
Such seeds within her breast, or Europe no
 such shore?

XCVII.

But France got drunk with blood to vomit
 crime,
And fatal have her Saturnalia been
To Freedom's cause, in every age and
 clime;
Because the deadly days which we have
 seen,
And vile Ambition, that built up between
Man and his hopes an adamantine wall,
And the base pageant last upon the scene,
Are grown the pretext for the eternal thrall
Which nips life's tree, and dooms man's
 worst — his second fall.

XCVIII.

Yet, Freedom! yet thy banner, torn, but
  flying,
Streams like the thunder-storm *against* the
  wind;
Thy trumpet voice, though broken now and
  dying,
The loudest still the tempest leaves behind;
Thy tree hath lost its blossoms, and the rind,
Chopped by the axe, looks rough and little
  worth,
But the sap lasts, and still the seed we find
Sown deep, even in the bosom of the North;
So shall a better spring less bitter fruit bring
  forth.

XCIX.

There is a stern round tower of other days,[1]
Firm as a fortress, with its fence of stone,
Such as an army's baffled strength delays,
Standing with half its battlements alone,
And with two thousand years of ivy grown,
The garland of eternity, where wave
The green leaves over all by time o'er-
  thrown; —
What was this tower of strength? within
  its cave
What treasure lay so locked, so hid? — A
  woman's grave.

C.

But who was she, the lady of the dead,
Tombed in a palace? Was she chaste and
  fair?
Worthy a king's — or more — a Roman's
  bed?
What race of chiefs and heroes did she
  bear?
What daughter of her beauties was the
  heir?
How lived — how loved — how died she?
Was she not
So honored — and conspicuously there,
Where meaner relics must not dare to rot,
Placed to commemorate a more than mortal
  lot?

CI.

Was she as those who love their lords, or
  they
Who love the lords of others? such have
  been
Even in the olden time, Rome's annals say.
Was she a matron of Cornelia's mien,
Or the light air of Egypt's graceful queen,
Profuse of joy — or 'gainst it did she war,
Inveterate in virtue? Did she lean
To the soft side of the heart, or wisely bar
Love from amongst her griefs? — for such the
  affections are.

[1] Alluding to the tomb of Cecilia Metella, called
Capo di Bove. See "Historical Illustrations," p.
200.

CII.

Perchance she died in youth: it may be,
  bowed
With woes far heavier than the ponderous
  tomb
That weighed upon her gentle dust, a cloud
Might gather o'er her beauty, and a gloom
In her dark eye, prophetic of the doom
Heaven gives its favorites — early death:
  yet shed
A sunset charm around her, and illume
With hectic light, the Hesperus of the dead,
Of her consuming cheek the autumnal leaf-
  like red.

CIII.

Perchance she died in age — surviving all,
Charms, kindred, children — with the silver
  gray
On her long tresses, which might yet recall,
It may be, still a something of the day
When they were braided, and her proud
  array
And lovely form were envied, praised, and
  eyed
By Rome — but whither would Conjecture
  stray?
Thus much alone we know — Metella died,
The wealthiest Roman's wife: Behold his
  love or pride!

CIV.

I know not why — but standing thus by thee
It seems as if I had thine inmate known,
Thou tomb! and other days come back on
  me
With recollected music, though the tone
Is changed and solemn, like the cloudy
  groan
Of dying thunder on the distant wind;
Yet could I seat me by this ivied stone
Till I had bodied forth the heated mind
Forms from the floating wreck which Ruin
  leaves behind;

CV.

And from the planks, far shattered o'er the
  rocks,
Built me a little bark of hope, once more
To battle with the ocean and the shocks
Of the loud breakers, and the ceaseless roar
Which rushes on the solitary shore
Where all lies foundered that was ever dear:
But could I gather from the wave-worn store
Enough for my rude boat, where should I
  steer?
There woos no home, nor hope, nor life, save
  what is here.

CVI.

Then let the winds howl on! their harmony
Shall henceforth be my music, and the night
The sound shall temper with the owlet's cry,
As I now hear them, in the fading light

Dim o'er the bird of darkness' native site,
Answering each other on the Palatine,
With their large eyes, all glistening gray
    and bright,
And sailing pinions. — Upon such a shrine
What are our petty griefs ? — let me not num-
    ber mine.

CVII.

Cypress and ivy, weed and wallflower grown
Matted and massed together, hillocks
    heaped
On what were chambers, arch crushed,
    column strown
In fragments, choked up vaults, and frescos
    steeped
In subterranean damps, where the owl
    peeped,
Deeming it midnight : — Temples, baths, or
    halls ?
Pronounce who can ; for all that Learning
    reaped
From her research hath been, that these are
    walls —
Behold the Imperial Mount ! 'tis thus the
    mighty falls.[1]

CVIII.

There is the moral of all human tales ; [2]
'Tis but the same rehearsal of the past.

---

[1] The Palatine is one mass of ruins, particularly
on the side towards the Circus Maximus. The very
soil s formed of crumbled brickwork. Nothing
has been told, nothing can be told, to satisfy the be-
lief of any but a Roman antiquar . See " Histori-
cal Illustrations," p. 206. — [The voice of Marius
could not sound more deep and solemn amid the
ruined arches of Carthage than the strains of the
pilgrim amid the broken shrines and fallen statues
of her subduer." — *Heber.*]

[2] The author of the Life of Cicero, speaking f the
opinion entertained of Britain by that orator and h
contemporary Romans has the fo owing loquent
passage : — " From their rai eries f this kind, o
the barbarity and misery of our island, one cannot
help reflecting on the surprising fate and revolutions
of kingdoms ; how Rome, once the mistress of t.
world, the seat of arts, empire, and glory, no' lies
sunk in sloth, ignorance, and poverty, enslaved to
the most cruel as well as to the most contemptible
of tyrants, superstition and religious imposture :
while this remote country, anciently the jest and
contempt of the polite Romans, is become the happy
seat of liberty, plenty, and letters ; flourishing in all
the arts and refinements of civil life ; yet running
perhaps the same course which Rome itself had run
before it, from virtuous industry to wealth ; from
wealth to luxury ; from luxury to an impatience of
discipline, and corruption of morals : till, by a total
degeneracy and loss of virtue, being grown ripe for
destruction, it fall a prey at last to some hardy op-
pressor, and, with the loss of liberty, losing every
thing that is valuable, sinks gradually again into its
original barbarism."*

---

* See History of the Life of M. Tullius Cicero,
sect. vi. vol. ii. p. 102.

First Freedom and then Glory — when that
    fails,
Wealth, vice, corruption, — barbarism a
    last.
And History, with all her volumes vast,
Hath but *one* page, — 'tis better written here,
Where gorgeous Tyranny hath thus amassed
All treasures, all delights, that eye or ear,
Heart, soul could seek, tongue ask — Away
    with words ! draw near,

CIX.

Admire, exult — despise — laugh, weep, —
    for here
There is such matter for all feeling : — Man !
Thou pendulum betwixt a smile and tear,
Ages and realms are crowded in this span,
This mountain, whose obliterated plan
The pyramid of empires pinnacled,
Of Glory's gewgaws shining in the van
Till the sun's rays with added flame were
    filled !
Where are its golden roofs ! where those who
    dared to build ?

CX.

Tully was not so eloquent as thou,
Thou nameless column with the buried
    base !
What are the laurels of the Cæsars' brow ?
Crown me with ivy from his dwelling-place.
Whose arch or pillar meets me in the face,
Titus or Trajan's ? No — 'tis that of Time :
Triumph, arch, pillar, all he doth displace
Scoffing ; and apostolic statues climb
To crush the imperial urn, whose ashes slept
    sublime,[3]

CXI.

Buried in air, the deep blue sky of Rome,
And looking to the stars : they had con-
    tained
A spirit which with these would find a
    home,
The last of those who o'er the whole earth
    r igned,
The Roman globe, for after none sustained,
But yielded back his conquests : — he was
    more
Than a mere Alexander, and, unstained
With household blood and wine, serenely
    wore
His sovereign virtues — still we Trajan's name
    adore.[4]

---

[3] The column of Trajan is surmounted by St
Peter ; that of Aurelius by St. Paul. See " Histori-
cal Illustrations," p. 214.

[4] Trajan was *proverbially* the best of the Roman
princes ; and it would be easier to find a sovereign
uniting exactly the opposite characteristics, than
one possessed of all the happy qualities ascribed to
this emperor. " When he mounted the throne,"
says the historian Dion, " he was strong in body,

CXII.

Where is the rock of Triumph, the high
place
Where Rome embraced her heroes ? where
the steep
Tarpeian ? fittest goal of Treason's race,
The promontory whence the Traitor's Leap
Cured all ambition. Did the conquerors
heap
Their spoils here ? Yes; and in yon field
below,
A thousand years of silenced factions sleep —
The Forum, where the immortal accents
glow,
And still the eloquent air breathes —burns
with Cicero !

CXIII.

The field of freedom, faction, fame, and
blood :
Here a proud people's passions were ex-
haled,
From the first hour of empire in the bud
To that when further worlds to conquer
failed;
But long before had Freedom's face been
veiled,
And Anarchy assumed her attributes;
Till every lawless soldier who assailed
Trod on the trembling senate's slavish mutes,
Or raised the venal voice of baser prostitutes.

CXIV.

Then turn we to her latest tribune's name,
From her ten thousand tyrants turn to thee,
Redeemer of dark centuries of shame—
The friend of Petrarch — hope of Italy —
Rienzi! last of Romans ![1] While the tree
Of freedom's withered trunk puts forth a
leaf,
Even for thy tomb a garland let it be —
The forum's champion, and the people's
chief—
Her new-born Numa thou — with reign, alas !
too brief.

CXV.

Egeria! sweet creation of some heart[2]
Which found no mortal resting-place so fair

he was vigorous in mind; age had impaired none
of his faculties; he was altogether free from envy
and from detraction; he honored all the good and he
advanced them; and on this account they could
not be the objects of his fear, or of his hate; he
never listened to informers; he gave not way to his
anger; he abstained equally from unfair exactions
and unjust punishments; he had rather be loved as
a man than honored as a sovereign; he was affable
with his people, respectful to the senate, and uni-
versally beloved by both; he inspired none with
dread but the enemies of his country."
[1] See "Historical Illustrations," p. 248.
[2] See "Historical Notes," at the end of this Can-
to, No. XXVII.

As thine ideal breast; whate'er thou art
Or wert, — a young Aurora of the air,
The nympholepsy of some fond despair;
Or, it might be, a beauty of the earth,
Who found a more than common votary
there
Too much adoring; whatsoe'er thy birth,
Thou wert a beautiful thought, and softly
bodied forth.

CXVI.

The mosses of thy fountain still are sprin-
kled
With thine Elysian water-drops; the face
Of thy cave-guarded spring, with years un-
wrinkled,
Reflects the meek-eyed genius of the place,
Whose green, wild margin now no more
erase
Art's works; nor must the delicate waters
sleep,
Prisoned in marble, bubbling from the base
Of the cleft statue, with a gentle leap
The rill runs o'er, and round, fern, flowers,
and ivy, creep,

CXVII.

Fantastically tangled; the green hills
Are clothed with early blossoms, through
the grass
The quick-eyed lizard rustles, and the bills
Of summer-birds sing welcome as ye pass;
Flowers fresh in hue, and many in their
class,
Implore the pausing step, and with their
dyes
Dance in the soft breeze in a fairy mass;
The sweetness of the violet's deep blue eyes,
Kissed by the breath of heaven· seems colored
by its skies.

CXVIII.

Here didst thou dwell, in this enchanted
cover,
Egeria! thy all heavenly bosom beating
For the far footsteps of thy mortal lover;
The purple Midnight veiled that mystic
meeting
With her most starry canopy, and seating
Thyself by thine adorer, what befell ?
This cave was surely shaped out for the
greeting
Of an enamoured Goddess, and the cell
Haunted by holy Love — the earliest oracle !

CXIX.

And didst thou not, thy breast to his reply-
ing,
Blend a celestial with a human heart·
And Love, which dies as it was born, in
sighing,
Share with immortal transports ? could thine
art

Make them indeed immortal, and impart
The purity of heaven to earthly joys,
Expel the venom and not blunt the dart —
The dull satiety which all destroys —
And root from out the soul the deadly weed
    which cloys ?

CXX.

Alas! our young affections run to waste,
Or water but the desert; whence arise
But weeds of dark luxuriance, tares of haste,
Rank at the core, though tempting to the
    eyes,
Flowers whose wild odors breathe but
    agonies,
And trees whose gums are poison; such the
    plants
Which spring beneath her steps as Passion
    flies
O'er the world's wilderness, and vainly pants
For some celestial fruit forbidden to our wants.

CXXI.

Oh Love! no habitant of earth thou art —
An unseen seraph, we believe in thee,
A faith whose martyrs are the broken heart,
But never yet hath seen, nor e'er shall see
The naked eye, thy form, as it should be;
The mind hath made thee, as it peopled
    heaven,
Even with its own desiring phantasy,
And to a thought such shape and image
    given,
As haunts the unquenched soul — parched —
    wearied — wrung — and riven.

CXXII.

Of its own beauty is the mind diseased,
And fevers into false creation : — where,
Where are the forms the sculptor's soul
    hath seized ?
In him alone. Can Nature show so fair ?
Where are the charms and virtues which we
    dare
Conceive in boyhood and pursue as men,
The unreached Paradise of our despair,
Which o'er-informs the pencil and the pen,
And overpowers the page where it would
    bloom again ?

CXXIII.

Who loves, raves — 'tis youth's frenzy — but
    the cure
Is bitterer still; as charm by charm unwinds
Which robed our idols, and we see too sure
Nor worth nor beauty dwells from out the
    mind's
Ideal shape of such; yet still it binds
The fatal spell, and still it draws us on,
Reaping the whirlwind from the oft-sown
    winds;

The stubborn heart, its alchemy begun,
Seems ever near the prize — wealthiest when
    most undone.

CXXIV.

We wither from our youth, we gasp away —
Sick — sick; unfound the boon — unslaked
    the thirst,
Though to the last, in verge of our decay,
Some phantom lures, such as we sought at
    first —
But all too late, — so are we doubly curst.
Love, fame, ambition, avarice — 'tis the
    same,
Each idle — and all ill — and none the
    worst —
For all are meteors with a different name,
And Death the sable smoke where vanishes
    the flame.

CXXV.

Few — none — find what they love or could
    have loved,
Though accident, blind contact, and the
    strong
Necessity of loving, have removed
Antipathies — but to recur, ere long,
Envenomed with irrevocable wrong;
And Circumstance, that unspiritual god
And miscreator, makes and helps along
Our coming evils with a crutch-like rod,
Whose touch turns Hope to dust, — the dust
    we all have trod.

CXXVI.

Our life is a false nature — 'tis not in
The harmony of things, — this hard decree,
This uneradicable taint of sin,
This boundless upas, this all-blasting tree,
Whose root is earth, whose leaves and
    branches be
The skies which rain their plagues on men
    like dew —
Disease, death, bondage — all the woes we
    see —
And worse, the woes we see not — which
    throb through
The immedicable soul, with heart-aches ever
    new.

CXXVII.

Yet let us ponder boldly — 'tis a base [1]
Abandonment of reason to resign
Our right of thought — our last and only
    place
Of refuge; this, at least, shall still be mine :

[1] "At all events," says the author of the Academical Questions, "I trust, whatever may be the fate of my own speculations, that philosophy will regain that estimation which it ought to possess. The free and philosophic spirit of our nation has been the theme of admiration to the world. This was the proud distinction of Englishmen, and the

Though from our birth the faculty divine
Is chained and tortured — cabined, cribbed, confined,
And bred in darkness, lest the truth should shine
Too brightly on the unprepared mind,
The beam pours in, for time and skill will couch the blind.

CXXVIII.

Arches on arches! as it were that Rome,
Collecting the chief trophies of her line,
Would build up all her triumphs in one dome,
Her Coliseum stands; the moonbeams shine
As 'twere its natural torches, for divine
Should be the light which streams here, to illume
This long-explored but still exhaustless mine
Of contemplation; and the azure gloom
Of an Italian night, where the deep skies assume

CXXIX.

Hues which have words, and speak to ye of heaven,
Floats o'er this vast and wondrous monument,
And shadows forth its glory. There is given
Unto the things of earth, which Time hath bent,
A spirit's feeling, and where he hath leant
His hand, but broke his scythe, there is a power
And magic in the ruined battlement,
For which the palace of the present hour
Must yield its pomp, and wait till ages are its dower.

CXXX.

Oh Time! the beautifier of the dead,
Adorner of the ruin, comforter
And only healer when the heart hath bled —
Time! the corrector where our judgments err,
The test of truth, love, — sole philosopher,
For all beside are sophists, from thy thrift,
Which never loses though it doth defer —
Time, the avenger! unto thee I lift
My hands, and eyes, and heart, and crave of thee a gift:

luminous source of all their glory. Shall we then forget the manly and dignified sentiments of our ancestors, to prate in the language of the mother or the nurse about our good old prejudices? This is not the way to defend the cause of truth. It was not thus that our fathers maintained it in the brilliant periods of our history. Prejudice may be trusted to guard the outworks for a short space of time, while reason slumbers in the citadel; but if the latter sink into a lethargy, the former will quickly erect a standard for herself. Philosophy, wisdom, and liberty support each other: he who will not reason is a bigot; he who cannot, is a fool; and he who dares not, is a slave."

CXXXI.

Amidst this wreck, where thou hast made a shrine
And temple more divinely desolate,
Among thy mightier offerings here are mine,
Ruins of years — though few, yet full of fate: —
If thou hast ever seen me too elate,
Hear me not; but if calmly I have borne
Good, and reserved my pride against the hate
Which shall not whelm me, let me not have worn
This iron in my soul in vain — shall *they* not mourn?

CXXXII.

And thou, who never yet of human wrong
Left the unbalanced scale, great Nemesis![1]
Here, where the ancient paid thee homage long —
Thou, who didst call the Furies from the abyss,
And round Orestes bade them howl and hiss
For that unnatural retribution — just,
Had it but been from hands less near — in this
Thy former realm, I call thee from the dust!
Dost thou not hear my heart? — Awake! thou shalt, and must.

CXXXIII.

It is not that I may not have incurred
For my ancestral faults or mine the wound
I bleed withal, and, had it been conferred
With a just weapon, it had flowed unbound;
But now my blood shall not sink in the ground;
To thee I do devote it — *thou* shalt take
The vengeance, which shall yet be sought and found,
Which if *I* have not taken for the sake ——
But let that pass — I sleep, but thou shalt yet awake.

CXXXIV.

And if my voice break forth, 'tis not that now
I shrink from what is suffered: let him speak
Who hath beheld decline upon my brow,
Or seen my mind's convulsion leave it weak;
But in this page a record will I seek.
Not in the air shall these my words disperse,
Though I be ashes; a far hour shall wreak
The deep prophetic fulness of this verse,
And pile on human heads the mountain of my curse!

CXXXV.

That curse shall be Forgiveness. — Have I not —
Hear me, my mother Earth! behold it, Heaven! —

[1] See "Historical Notes" at the end of this Canto, No. XXVIII.

Have I not had to wrestle with my lot!
Have I not suffered things to be forgiven?
Have I not had my brain seared, my heart
riven,
Hopes sapped, name blighted, Life's life
lied away?
And only not to desperation driven,
Because not altogether of such clay
As rots into the souls of those whom I survey.

CXXXVI.

From mighty wrongs to petty perfidy
Have I not seen what human things could
do?
From the loud roar of foaming calumny
To the small whisper of the as paltry few,
And subtler venom of the reptile crew,
The Janus glance of whose significant eye,
Learning to lie with silence, would *seem* true,
And without utterance, save the shrug or
sigh,
Deal round to happy fools its speechless oblo-
quy.[1]

CXXXVII.

But I have lived, and have not lived in vain:
My mind may lose its force, my blood its
fire,
And my flame perish even in conquering
pain;
But there is that within me which shall tire
Torture and Time, and breathe when I ex-
pire;
Something unearthly, which they deem not
of,
Like the remembered 'tone of a mute lyre,
Shall on their softened spirits sink, and
move
In hearts all rocky now the late remorse of love.

CXXXVIII.

The seal is set. — Now welcome, thou dread
power!
Nameless, yet thus omnipotent, which here
Walk'st in the shadow of the midnight hour
With a deep awe, yet all distinct from fear;
Thy haunts are ever where the dead walls
rear
Their ivy mantles, and the solemn scene
Derives from thee a sense so deep and clear

---

[1] [Between stanzas cxxxv. and cxxxvi. we find in
the original MS. the following: —
" If to forgive be heaping coals of fire —
As God hath spoken — on the heads of foes,
Mine should be a volcano, and rise higher
Than, o'er the Titans crushed, Olympus rose,
Or Athos soars, or blazing Etna glows: —
True they who stung were creeping things; but
what
Than serpents' teeth inflicts with deadlier throes?
The Lion may be goaded by the Gnat. —
Who sucks the slumberer's blood? — The Eagle? —
No: the Bat."]

That we become a part of what has been,
And grow unto the spot, all-seeing but unseen.

CXXXIX.

And here the buzz of eager nations ran,
In murmured pity, or loud-roared applause,
As man was slaughtered by his fellow man.
And wherefore slaughtered? wherefore, but
because
Such were the bloody Circus' genial laws,
And the imperial pleasure. — Wherefore
not?
What matters where we fall to fill the maws
Of worms — on battle-plains or listed spot?
Both are but theatres where the chief actors rot.

CXL.

I see before me the Gladiator lie:
He leans upon his hand — his manly brow
Consents to death, but conquers agony,
And his drooped head sinks gradually low
And through his side the last drops, ebbing
slow
From the red gash, fall heavy, one by one,
Like the first of a thunder-shower; and now
The arena swims around him — he is gone
Ere ceased the inhuman shout which hailed
the wretch who won.

CXLI.

He heard it, but he heeded not — his eyes
Were with his heart, and that was far away: [2]
He recked not of the life he lost nor prize,
But where his rude hut by the Danube lay,
There were his young barbarians all at play,
There was their Dacian mother — he, their
sire,
Butchered to make a Roman holiday — [3]

---

[2] Whether the wonderful statue which suggested
this image be a laquearian gladiator, which, in spite
of Winkelmann's criticism, has been stoutly main-
tained; or whether it be a Greek herald, as that
great antiquary positively asserted; [*] or whether it
is to be thought a Spartan or barbarian shield-
bearer, according to the opinion of his Italian
editor: it must assuredly seem *a copy* of that mas-
terpiece of Ctesilaus which represented " a wounded
man dying, who perfectly expressed what there re-
mained of life in him." Montfaucon and Maffei
thought it the identical statue: but that statue was
of bronze. The gladiator was once in the Villa
Ludovizi, and was bought by Clement XII. The
right arm is an entire restoration of Michael Angelo.
[3] See " Historical Notes " at the end of this Canto
Nos. XXIX. XXX.

---

[*] Either Polifontes, herald of Laius, killed by
Œdipus; or Cepreas, herald of Euritheus, killed
by the Athenians when he endeavored to drag the
Heraclidæ from the altar of mercy, and in whose
honor they instituted annual games, continued to
the time of Hadrian; or Anthemocritus, the Athe-
nian herald, killed by the Megarenses, who never
recovered the impiety. See Storia delle Arti, etc.
tom. ii. pag. 203, 204, 205, 206, 207, lib. ix. cap. ii.

All this rushed with his blood—Shall he expire
And unavenged?—Arise! ye Goths, and glut your ire!

CXLII.

But here, where Murder breathed her bloody steam,
And here, where buzzing nations choked the ways,
And roared or murmured like a mountain stream
Dashing or winding as its torrent strays;
Here, where the Roman millions' blame or praise
Was death or life, the playthings of a crowd,[1]
My voice sounds much—and fall the stars' faint rays
On the arena void—seats crushed—walls bowed—
And galleries, where my steps seem echoes strangely loud.

CXLIII.

A ruin—yet what ruin! from its mass
Walls, palaces, half-cities, have been reared;
Yet oft the enormous skeleton ye pass,
And marvel where the spoil could have appeared.
Hath it indeed been plundered, or but cleared?
Alas! developed, opens the decay,
When the colossal fabric's form is neared:
It will not bear the brightness of the day,
Which streams too much on all years, man, have reft away.

CXLIV.

But when the rising moon begins to climb
Its topmost arch, and gently pauses there;
When the stars twinkle through the loops of time,
And the low night-breeze waves along the air
The garland forest, which the gray walls wear,
Like laurels on the bald first Cæsar's hea ;[2]
When the light shines serene but doth not glare,
Then in this magic circle raise the dead:
Heroes have trod this spot—'tis on their dust ye tread.

[1] See "Historical Notes" at the end of this Canto, Nos. XXIX. XXX.

[2] Suetonius informs us that Julius Cæsar was particularly gratified by that decree of the senate which enabled him to wear a wreath of laurel on all occasions. He was anxious, not to show that he was the conqueror of the world, but to hide that he was bald. A stranger at Rome would hardly have guessed at the motive, nor should we without the help of the historian.

CXLV.

"While stands the Coliseum, Rome shall stand;[3]
"When falls the Coliseum, Rome shall fall;
"And when Rome falls—the World."
From our own land
Thus spake the pilgrims o'er this mighty wall
In Saxon times, which we are wont to call
Ancient; and these three mortal things are still
On their foundations, and unaltered all;
Rome and her Ruin past Redemption's skill,
The World, the same wide den—of thieves, or what ye will.

CXLVI.

Simple, erect, severe, austere, sublime—
Shrine of all saints and temple of all gods,
From Jove to Jesus—spared and blest by time;[4]
Looking tranquillity, while falls or nods
Arch, empire, each thing round thee, and man plods
His way through thorns to ashes—glorious dome!
Shalt thou not last? Time's scythe and tyrant's rods
Shiver upon thee—sanctuary and home
Of art and piety—Pantheon!—pride of Rome!

CXLVII.

Relic of nobler days, and noblest arts!
Despoiled yet perfect, with thy circle spreads
A holiness appealing to all hearts—
To art a model; and to him who treads
Rome for the sake of ages, Glory sheds
Her light through thy sole aperture; to those
Who worship, here are altars for their beads;
And they who feel for genius may repose
Their eyes on honored forms, whose busts around them close.[5]

[3] This is quoted in the "Decline and Fall of the Roman Empire," as a proof that the Coliseum was entire, when seen by the Anglo-Saxon pilgrims at the end of the seventh, or the beginning of the eighth, century. A notice on the Coliseum may be seen in the "Historical Illustrations," p. 263.

[4] "Though plundered of all its brass, except the ring which was necessary to preserve the aperture above; though exposed to repeated fires; though sometimes flooded by the river and always open to the rain, no monument of equal antiquity is so well preserved as this rotundo. It passed with little alteration from the Pagan into the present worship; and so convenient were its niches for the Christian altar, that Michael Angelo, ever studious of ancient beauty, introduced their design as a model in the Catholic church." — *Forsyth's Italy*, p. 137.

[5] The Pantheon has been made a receptacle for the busts of modern great, or, at least, distinguished, men. The flood of light which once fell

CXLVIII.

There is a dungeon, in whose dim drear
   light [1]
What do I gaze on? Nothing: Look again!
Two forms are slowly shadowed on my
   sight —
Two insulated phantoms of the brain:
It is not so; I see them full and plain —
An old man, and a female young and fair,
Fresh as a nursing mother, in whose vein
The blood is nectar: — but what doth she
   there,
With her unmantled neck, and bosom white
   and bare?

CXLIX.

Full swells the deep pure fountain of young
   life,
Where *on* the heart and *from* the heart we
   took
Our first and sweetest nurture, when the wife,
Blest into mother, in the innocent look,
Or even the piping cry of lips that brook
No pain and small suspense, a joy perceives
Man knows not, when from out its cradled
   nook
She sees her little bud put forth its leaves —
What may the fruit be yet? — I know not —
   Cain was Eve's.

CL.

But here youth offers to old age the food,
The milk of his own gift: — it is her sire
To whom she renders back the debt of blood
Born with her birth. No; he shall not ex-
   pire
While in those warm and lovely veins the
   fire
Of health and holy feeling can provide
Great Nature's Nile, whose deep stream
   rises higher
Than Egypt's river: — from that gentle side
Drink, drink and live, old man! Heaven's
   realm holds no such tide.

CLI.

The starry fable of the milky way
Has not thy story's purity; it is

through the large orb above on the whole ci.   of
divinities, now shines on a numerous a semblage of
mortals, some one or two of whom have been al-
most deified by the veneration of their countrymen.
For a notice of the Pantheon, see "Historical Illus-
trations," p. 287.

[1] "There is a dungeon, in whose dim drear light
   What do I gaze on?" etc.
This and the three next stanzas allude to the story
of the Roman daughter, which is recalled to the
traveller by the site, or pretended site, of that ad-
venture, now shown at the church of St. Nicholas
in Carcere. The difficulties attending the full be-
lief of the tale are stated in "Historical Illustra-
tions," p. 295.

A constellation of a sweeter ray,
And sacred Nature triumphs more in this
Reverse of her decree, than in the abyss
Where sparkle distant worlds: — Oh, ho-
   liest nurse!
No drop of that clear stream its way shall
   miss
To thy sire's heart, replenishing its source
With life, as our freed souls rejoin the universe.

CLII.

Turn to the Mole which Hadrian reared on
   high,[2]
Imperial mimic of old Egypt's piles,   ·
Colossal copyist of deformity,
Whose travelled phantasy from the far Nile's
Enormous model, doomed the artist's toils
To build for giants, and for his vain earth,
His shrunken ashes, raise this dome: How
   smiles
The gazer's eye with philosophic mirth,
To view the huge design which sprung from
   such a birth!

CLIII.

But lo! the dome — the vast and wondrous
   dome,[3]
To which Diana's marvel was a cell —
Christ's mighty shrine above his martyr's
   tomb!
I have beheld the Ephesian's miracle —
Its columns strew the wilderness, and dwell
The hyæna and the jackal in their shade;
I have beheld Sophia's bright roofs swell
Their glittering mass i' the sun, and have
   surveyed
Its sanctuary the while the usurping Moslem
   prayed;

CLIV.

But thou, of temples old, or altars new,
Standest alone — with nothing like to thee —
Worthiest of God, the holy and the true.
Since Zion's desolation, when that He
Forsook his former city, what could be,
Of earthly structures, in his honor piled,
Of a sublimer aspect? Majesty,
Power, Glory, Strength, and Beauty, all are
   aisled
In this eternal ark of worship undefiled.

CLV.

Enter: its grandeur overwhelms thee not;
And why? it is not lessened; but thy mind,
Expanded by the genius of the spot,
Has grown colossal, and can only find
A fit abode wherein appear enshrined
Thy hopes of immortality; and thou
Shalt one day, if found worthy, so defined,
See thy God face to face, as thou dost now
His Holy of Holies, nor be blasted by his brow.

[2] The castle of St. Angelo.
[3] The church of St. Peter's.

CLVI.

Thou movest — but increasing with the advance,
Like climbing some great Alp, which still doth rise,
Deceived by its gigantic elegance;
Vastness which grows — but grows to harmonize —
All musical in its immensities;
Rich marbles — richer painting — shrines where flame
The lamps of gold — and haughty dome which vies
In air with Earth's chief structures, though their frame
Sits on the firm-set ground — and this the clouds must claim.

CLVII.

Thou seest not all; but piecemeal thou must break,
To separate contemplation, the great whole;
And as the ocean many bays will make,
That ask the eye — so here condense thy soul
To more immediate objects, and control
Thy thoughts until thy mind hath got by heart
Its eloquent proportions, and unroll
In mighty graduations, part by part,
The glory which at once upon thee did not dart,

CLVIII.

Not by its fault — but thine: Our outward sense
Is but of gradual grasp — and as it is
That what we have of feeling most intense
Outstrips our faint expression; even so this
Outshining and o'erwhelming edifice
Fools our fond gaze, and greatest of the great
Defies at first our Nature's littleness,
Till, growing with its growth, we thus dilate
Our spirits to the size of that they contemplate.

CLIX.

Then pause, and be enlightened; there is more
In such a survey than the sating gaze
Of wonder pleased, or awe which would adore
The worship of the place, or the mere praise
Of art and its great masters, who could raise
What former time, nor skill, nor thought could plan;
The fountain of sublimity displays
Its depth, and thence may draw the mind of man
Its golden sands, and learn what great conceptions can.

CLX.

Or, turning to the Vatican, go see
Laocoon's torture dignifying pain —
A father's love and mortal's agony
With an immortal's patience blending: —
Vain
The struggle; vain, against the coiling strain
And gripe, and deepening of the dragon's grasp,
The old man's clench; the long envenomed chain
Rivets the living links, — the enormous asp
Enforces pang on pang, and stifles gasp on gasp.

CLXI.

Or view the Lord of the unerring bow,
The God of life, and poesy, and light —
The Sun in human limbs arrayed, and brow
All radiant from his triumph in the fight;
The shaft hath just been shot — the arrow bright
With an immortal's vengeance; in his eye
And nostril beautiful disdain, and might
And majesty, flash their full lightnings by,
Developing in that one glance the Deity.

CLXII.

But in his delicate form — a dream of Love,
Shaped by some solitary nymph, whose breast
Longed for a deathless lover from above,
And maddened in that vision — are exprest
All that ideal beauty ever blessed
The mind with in its most unearthly mood,
When each conception was a heavenly guest —
A ray of immortality — and stood,
Starlike, around, until they gathered to a god!

CLXIII.

And if it be Prometheus stole from Heaven
The fire which we endure, it was repaid
By him to whom the energy was given
Which this poetic marble hath arrayed
With an eternal glory — which, if made
By human hands, is not of human thought;
And Time himself hath hallowed it, nor laid
One ringlet in the dust — nor hath it caught
A tinge of years, but breathes the flame with which 'twas wrought.

CLXIV.

But where is he, the Pilgrim of my song,
The being who upheld it through the past?
Methinks he cometh late and tarries long.
He is no more — these breathings are his last;
His wanderings done, his visions ebbing fast,
And he himself as nothing: — if he was
Aught but a phantasy, and could be classed

With forms which live and suffer — let that
pass —
His shadow fades away into Destruction's
mass,

CLXV.

Which gathers shadow, substance, life, and
all
That we inherit in its mortal shroud,
And spreads the dim and universal pall
Through which all things grow phantoms;
and the cloud
Between us sinks and all which ever glowed,
Till Glory's self is twilight, and displays
A melancholy halo scarce allowed
To hover on the verge of darkness; rays
Sadder than saddest night, for they distract
the gaze,

CLXVI.

And send us prying into the abyss,
To gather what we shall be when the frame
Shall be resolved to something less than this
Its wretched essence; and to dream of fame,
And wipe the dust from off the idle name
We never more shall hear, — but never
more,
Oh, happier thought! can we be made the
same:
It is enough in sooth that *once* we bore
These fardels of the heart — the heart whose
sweat was gore.

CLXVII.

Hark! forth from the abyss a voice pro-
ceeds,
A long low distant murmur of dread sound,
Such as arises when a nation bleeds
With some deep and immedicable wound;
Through storm and darkness yawns the
rending ground,
The gulf is thick with phantoms, but the chief
Seems royal still, though with her head dis-
crowned,
And pale, but lovely, with maternal grief
She clasps a babe, to whom her breast yields
no relief.

CLXVIII.

Scion of chiefs and monarchs, where art
thou?
Fond hope of many nations, art thou dead?
Could not the grave forget thee, and lay low
Some less majestic, less beloved head?
In the sad midnight, while thy heart still
bled,
The mother of a moment, o'er thy boy,
Death hushed that pang for ever: with thee
fled
The present happiness and promised joy
Which filled the imperial isles so full it seemed
to cloy.

CLXIX.

Peasants bring forth in safety. — Can it be,
Oh thou that wert so happy, so adored!
Those who weep not for kings shall weep
for thee,
And Freedom's heart, grown heavy, cease
to hoard
Her many griefs for ONE; for she had poured
Her orisons for thee, and o'er thy head
Beheld her Iris. — Thou, too, lonely lord,
And desolate consort — vainly wert thou
wed!
The husband of a year! the father of the dead!

CLXX.

Of sackcloth was thy wedding garment
made;
Thy bridal's fruit is ashes: in the dust
The fair-haired Daughter of the Isles is laid,
The love of millions! How we did intrust
Futurity to her! and, though it must
Darken above our bones, yet fondly deemed
Our children should obey her child, and
blessed
Her and her hoped-for seed, whose prom-
ise seemed
Like stars to shepherds' eyes: — 'twas but a
meteor beamed.

CLXXI.

Woe unto us, not her; [1] for she sleeps well:
The fickle reek of popular breath, the tongue
Of hollow counsel, the false oracle,
Which from the birth of monarchy hath
rung
Its knell in princely ears, 'till the o'erstung
Nations have armed in madness, the strange
fate [2]
Which tumbles mightiest sovereigns, and
hath flung
Against their blind omnipotence a weight
Within the opposing scale, which crushes soon
or late, —

CLXXII.

These might have been her destiny; but no,
Our hearts deny it: and so young, so fair,
Good without effort, great without a foe;
But now a bride and mother — and now
there!

---

[1] ["The death of the Princess Charlotte has
been a shock even here (Venice), and must have
been an earthquake at home. The fate of this poor
girl is melancholy in every respect; dying at twenty
or so, in childbed — of a boy too, a present princess
and future queen, and just as she began to be
happy, and to enjoy herself, and the hopes which
she inspired. I feel sorry in every respect." — *By-
ron's Letters.*]
[2] Mary died on the scaffold; Elizabeth of a broken
heart; Charles V. a hermit; Louis XIV. a bank-
rupt in means and glory; Cromwell of anxiety

How many ties did that stern moment tear!
From thy Sire's to his humblest subject's
  breast
Is linked the electric chain of that despair,
Whose shock was as an earthquake's and
  opprest
The land which loved thee so that none could
  love thee best.

CLXXIII.

Lo, Nemi![1] navelled in the woody hills
So far, that the uprooting wind which tears
The oak from his foundation, and which
  spills
The ocean o'er its boundary, and bears
Its foam against the skies, reluctant spares
The oval mirror of thy glassy lake;
And, calm as cherished hate, its surface
  wears
A deep cold settled aspect naught can shake,
All coiled into itself and round, as sleeps the
  snake.

CLXXIV.

And near Albano's scarce divided waves
Shine from a sister valley; — and afar
The Tiber winds, and the broad ocean laves
The Latian coast where sprang the Epic war,
"Arms and the Man," whose re-ascending
  star
Rose o'er an empire: — but beneath thy
  right
Tully reposed from Rome; — and where
  yon bar
·Of girdling mountains intercepts the sight
The Sabine farm was tilled, the weary bard's
  delight.[2]

CLXXV.

But I forget. — My Pilgrim's shrine is won,
And he and I must part, — so let it be, —
His task and mine alike are nearly done;
Yet once more let us look upon the sea;
The midland ocean breaks on him and me,

and, "the greatest is behind," Napoleon lives a
prisoner. To these sovereigns a long but super-
fluous list might be added of names equally illus-
trious and unhappy.
  [1] The village of Nemi was near the Arician re-
treat of Egeria, and, from the shades which
embosomed the temple of Diana, has preserved to
this day its distinctive appellation of *The Grove.*
Nemi is but an evening's ride from the comfortable
inn of Albano.
  [2] The whole declivity of the Alban hill is of
unrivalled beauty, and from the convent on the
highest point, which has succeeded to the temple
of the Latian Jupiter, the prospect embraces all the
objects alluded to in this stanza; the Mediter-
ranean; the whole scene of the latter half of the
Æneid, and the coast from beyond the mouth of
the Tiber to the headland of Circæum and the Cape
of Terracina. — See "Historical Notes," at the
end of this Canto, No. XXXI.

And from the Alban Mount we now behold
Our friend of youth, that ocean, which when
  we
Beheld it last by Calpe's rock unfold
Those waves, we followed on till the dark
  Euxine rolled

CLXXVI.

Upon the blue Symplegades: long years —
Long, though not very many, since have
  done
Their work on both; some suffering and
  some tears
Have left us nearly where we had begun:
Yet not in vain our mortal race hath run,
We have had our reward — and it is here;
That we can yet feel gladdened by the sun,
And reap from earth, sea, joy almost as dear
As if there were no man to trouble what is
  clear.

CLXXVII.

Oh! that the Desert were my dwelling-place,
With one fair Spirit for my minister,
That I might all forget the human race,
And, hating no one, love but only her!
Ye Elements! — in whose ennobling stir
I feel myself exalted — Can ye not
Accord me such a being? Do I err
In deeming such inhabit many a spot?
Though with them to converse can rarely be
  our lot.

CLXXVIII.

There is a pleasure in the pathless woods,
There is a rapture on the lonely shore,
There is society, where none intrudes,
By the deep Sea, and music in its roar:
I love not Man the less, but Nature more,
From these our interviews, in which I steal
From all I may be, or have been before,
To mingle with the Universe, and feel
What I can ne'er express, yet cannot all con-
  ceal.

CLXXIX.

Roll on, thou deep and dark blue Ocean —
  roll!
Ten thousand fleets sweep over thee in vain;
Man marks the earth with ruin — his control
Stops with the shore; — upon the watery
  plain
The wrecks are all thy deed, nor doth
  remain
A shadow of man's ravage, save his own,
When, for a moment, like a drop of rain,
He sinks into thy depths with bubbling
  groan,
Without a grave, unknelled, uncoffined, and
  unknown.

CLXXX.

His steps are not upon thy paths, — thy
  fields
Are not a spoil for him, — thou dost arise

And shake him from thee; the vile strength
he wields
For earth's destruction thou dost all despise,
Spurning him from thy bosom to the skies,
And send'st him, shivering in thy playful
spray
And howling, to his Gods, where haply lies
His petty hope in some near port or bay,
And dashest him again to earth: — there let
him lay.

CLXXXI.

The armaments which thunderstrike the
walls
Of rock-built cities, bidding nations quake
And monarchs tremble in their capitals,
The oak leviathans, whose huge ribs make
Their clay creator the vain title take
Of lord of thee, and arbiter of war;
These are thy toys, and, as the snowy flake,
They melt into thy yeast of waves, which
mar
Alike the Armada's pride, or spoils of Trafal-
gar.

CLXXXII.

Thy shores are empires, changed in all save
thee —
Assyria, Greece, Rome, Carthage, what are
they? [1]
Thy waters washed them power while they
were free,[2]
And many a tyrant since; their shores obey
The stranger, slave, or savage; their decay
Has dried up realms to deserts: — not so
thou,
Unchangeable save to thy wild waves' play —
Time writes no wrinkle on thine azure
brow —
Such as creation's dawn beheld, thou rollest
now.

CLXXXIII.

Thou glorious mirror, where the Almighty's
form
Glasses itself in tempests; in all time,
Calm or convulsed — in breeze, or gale, or
storm,
Icing the pole, or in the torrid clime

Dark-heaving; — boundless, endless, and
sublime —
The image of Eternity — the throne
Of the Invisible; even from out thy slime
The monsters of the deep are made; each
zone
Obeys thee; thou goest forth, dread, fathom-
less, alone.

CLXXXIV.

And I have loved thee, Ocean![3] and my joy
Of youthful sports was on thy breast to be
Borne, like thy bubbles, onward: from a boy
I wantoned with thy breakers — they to me
Were a delight; and if the freshening sea
Made them a terror — 'twas a pleasing fear,
For I was as it were a child of thee,
And trusted to thy billows far and near,
And laid my hand upon thy mane — as I do
here.

CLXXXV.

My task is done [4] — my song hath ceased
— my theme
Has died into an echo; it is fit

---

[1] ["A man," said Johnson, "who has not been in Italy, is always conscious of an inferiority, from his not having seen what it is expected a man should see. The grand object of all travelling is to see the shores of the Mediterranean. On those shores were the four great empires of the world: the Assyrian, the Persian, the Grecian, and the Roman. All our religion, almost all our law, almost all our arts, almost all that sets us above savages, has come to us from the shores of the Mediterranean." — *Boswell's Johnson.*]

[2] [This line reads thus in Byron's MS. In all editions before that of London, 1853, it was printed — Thy waters wasted them while they were free.]

[3] [This passage would, perhaps, be read without emotion, if we did not know that Lord Byron was here describing his actual feelings and habits, and that this was an unaffected picture of his propensities and amusement even from childhood, — when he listened to the roar, and watched the bursts of the northern ocean on the tempestuous shores of Aberdeenshire. It was a fearful and violent change at the age of ten years to be separated from this congenial solitude, — this independence so suited to his haughty and contemplative spirit, — this rude grandeur of nature, — and thrown among the mere worldly-minded and selfish ferocity, the affected polish and repelling coxcombry, of a great public school. How many thousand times did the moody, sullen, and indignant boy wish himself back to the keen air and boisterous billows that broke lonely upon the simple and soul-invigorating haunts of his childhood. How did he prefer some ghost-story; some tale of second-sight; some relation of Robin Hood's feats; some harrowing narrative of buccaneer-exploits, to all of Horace, and Virgil, and Homer, that was dinned into his tepulsive spirit! To the shock of this change is, I suspect, to be traced much of the eccentricity of Lord Byron's future life. This fourth Canto is the fruit of a mind which had stored itself with great care and toil, and had digested with profound reflection and intense vigor what it had learned: the sentiments are not such as lie on the surface, but could only be awakened by long meditation. Whoever reads it, and is not impressed with the many grand virtues as well as gigantic powers of the mind that wrote it, seems to me to afford a proof both of insensibility of heart, and great stupidity of intellect." — *Sir E. Brydges.*]

[4] [It was a thought worthy of the great spirit of Byron, after exhibiting to us his Pilgrim amidst all the most striking scenes of earthly grandeur and earthly decay, — after teaching us, like him, to sicken over the mutability, and vanity, and emptiness of human greatness, to conduct him and us at

The spell should break of this protracted dream.

---

last to the borders of " the Great Deep." It is there that we may perceive an image of the awful and unchangeable abyss of eternity, into whose bosom so much has sunk, and all shall one day sink, — of that eternity wherein the scorn and the contempt of man, and the melancholy of great, and the fretting of little minds, shall be at rest for ever. No one, but a true poet of man and of nature, would have dared to frame such a termination for such a Pilgrimage. The image of the wanderer may well be associated, for a time, with the rock of Calpe, the shattered temples of Athens, or the gigantic fragments of Rome; but when we wish to think of this dark personification as of a thing which is, where can we so well imagine him to have his daily haunt as by the roaring of the waves? It was thus that Homer represented Achilles in his moments of ungovernable and inconsolable grief for the loss of Patroclus. It was thus he chose to depict the paternal despair of Chriseus—

" Βῆ δ' ἀκέων παρὰ θῖνα πολυφλοισβοιο θαλάσσης."

— *Professor Wilson.*]

The torch shall be extinguished which hath lit
My midnight lamp — and what is writ, is writ, —
Would it were worthier! but I am not now
That which I have been — and my visions flit
Less palpably before me — and the glow
Which in my spirit dwelt is fluttering, faint, and low.

CLXXXVI.

Farewell! a word that must be, and hath been —
A sound which makes us linger; — yet — farewell!
Ye! who have traced the Pilgrim to the scene
Which is his last, if in your memories dwell
A thought which once was his, if on ye swell
A single recollection, not in vain
He wore his sandal-shoon, and scallop-shell;
Farewell! with *him* alone may rest the pain,
If such there were — with *you*, the moral of his strain!

HISTORICAL NOTES TO CANTO THE FOURTH.

I. STATE DUNGEONS OF VENICE.

" I stood in Venice on the Bridge of Sighs;
A palace and a prison on each hand."

Stanza i. lines 1 and 2.

THE communication between the ducal palace and the prisons of Venice is by a gloomy bridge, or covered gallery, high above the water, and divided by a stone wall into a passage and a cell. The State dungeons, called "pozzi," or wells, were sunk in the thick walls of the palace; and the prisoner when taken out to die was conducted across the gallery to the other side, and being then led back into the other compartment, or cell, upon the bridge, was there strangled. The low portal through which the criminal was taken into this cell is now walled up; but the passage is still open, and is still known by the name of the Bridge of Sighs. The pozzi are under the flooring of the chamber at the foot of the bridge. They were formerly twelve, but on the first arrival of the French, the Venetians hastily blocked or broke up the deeper of these dungeons. You may still, however, descend by a trap-door, and crawl down through holes, halfchoked by rubbish, to the depth of two stories below the first range. If you are in want of consolation for the extinction of patrician power, perhaps you may find it there; scarcely a ray of light glimmers into the narrow gallery which leads to the cells, and the places of confinement themselves are totally dark. A small hole in the wall admitted the damp air of the passages, and served for the introduction of the prisoner's food. A wooden pallet raised a foot from the ground, was the only furniture. The conductors tell you that a light was not allowed. The cells are about five paces in length, two and a half in width, and seven feet in height. They are directly beneath one another, and respiration is somewhat difficult in the lower holes. Only one prisoner was found when the republicans descended into these hideous recesses, and he is said to have been confined sixteen years. But the inmates of the dungeons beneath had left traces of their repentance, or of their despair, which are still visible, and may, perhaps, owe something to recent ingenuity. Some of the detained appear to have offended against, and others to have belonged to, the sacred body, not only from their signatures, but from the churches and belfries which they have scratched upon the walls. The reader may not object to see a specimen of the records prompted by so terrific a solitude. As nearly as they could be copied by more than one pencil, three of them are as follows : —

1. NON TI FIDAR AD ALCUNO PENSA e TACI
   SE FUGIR VUOI DE SPIONI INSIDIE e LACCI
   IL PENTIRTI PENTIRTI NULLA GIOVA
   MA BEN DI VALOR TUO LA VERA PROVA
       1607. ADI 2. GENARO. FUI RE-
     TENTO P' LA BESTIEMMA P' AVER DATO
       DA MANZAR A UN MORTO
         IACOMO . GRITTI . SCRISSE.

2. UN PARLAR POCHO et
   NEGARE PRONTO et
   UN PENSAR AL FINE PUO DARE LA VITA
   A NOI ALTRI MESCHINI
         1605.
       EGO IOHN BAPTISTE AD
       ECCLESIAM CORTELLARIUS.

3. DE CHI MI FIDO GUARDAMI DIO
   DE CHI NON MI FIDO MI GUARDARO IO
   A   TA   H   A   NA
   V . LA S   . C .K . R .

The copyist has followed, not corrected, the solecisms; some of which are, however, not quite so decided, since the letters were evidently scratched in the dark. It only need be observed, that *bestemmia* and *mangiar* may be read in the first inscription, which was probably written by a prisoner confined for some act of impiety committed at a funeral; that *Cortellarius* is the name of a parish on terra firma, near the sea; and that the last initials evidently are put for *Viva la santa Chiesa Kattolica Romana.*

II. SONGS OF THE GONDOLIERS.

" In Venice Tasso's echoes are no more."
                              Stanza lii. line 1.

The well-known song of the gondoliers, of alternate stanzas from Tasso's Jerusalem, has died with the independence of Venice. Editions of the poem, with the original in one column, and the Venetian variations on the other, as sung by the boatmen, were once common, and are still to be found. The following extract will serve to show the difference between the Tuscan epic and the " Canta alla Barcarola."

ORIGINAL.

Canto l' arme pietose, e 'l capitano
   Che 'l gran Sepolcro liberò di Cristo.
Molto egli oprò col senno, o con la mano;
   Molto soffri nel glorioso acquisto;
E in van l' Inferno a lui s' oppose, o in vano
   S' armò d' Asia, e di Libia il popol misto
Che il Ciel gli diè favore, e sotto ai santi
Segni ridusse i suoi compagni erranti.

VENETIAN.

L' arme pietose de cantar gho vogia,
   E de Goffredo la immortal braura,
Che al fin l' ha libera co strassia, e dogia
   Del nostro buon Gesù la Sepoltura.
De mezo mondo unito, e de quel Bogia
   Missier Pluton non l' ha bu mai paura:
Dio l' ha agiutá, e i compagni sparpagnai
Tutti 'l gh' i ha messi insieme i di del Dai.

Some of the elder gondoliers will, however, take up and continue a stanza of their once familiar bard. On the 7th of last January, the author of Childe Harold, and another Englishman, the writer of this notice, rowed to the Lido with two singers, one of whom was a carpenter, and the other a gondolier. The former placed himself at the prow, the latter at the stern of the boat. A little after leaving the quay of the Piazzetta, they began to sing, and continued their exercise until we arrived at the island. They gave us, amongst other essays, the death of Clorinda, and the palace of Armida; and did not sing the Venetian, but the Tuscan verses. The carpenter, however, who was the cleverer of the two, and was frequently obliged to prompt his companion, told us that he could *translate* the original. He

added, that he could sing almost three hundred stanzas, but had not spirits (*morbin* was the word he used) to learn any more, or to sing what he already knew: a man must have idle time on his hands to acquire, or to repeat, and, said the poor fellow, " look at my clothes and at me ; I am starving." This speech was more affecting than his performance, which habit alone can make attractive. The recitative was shrill, screaming, and monotonous; and the gondolier behind assisted his voice by holding his hand to one side of his mouth. The carpenter used a quiet action, which he evidently endeavored to restrain; but was too much interested in his subject altogether to repress. From these men we learnt that singing is not confined to the gondoliers, and that, although the chant is seldom, if ever, voluntary, there are still several amongst the lower classes who are acquainted with a few stanzas.

It does not appear that it is usual for the performers to row and sing at the same time. Although the verses of the Jerusalem are no longer casually heard, there is yet much music upon the Venetian canals; and upon holydays, those strangers who are not near or informed enough to distinguish the words, may fancy that many of the gondolas still resound with the strains of Tasso. The writer of some remarks which appeared in the " Curiosities of Literature" must excuse his being twice quoted; for, with the exception of some phrases a little too ambitious and extravagant, he has furnished a very exact, as well as agreeable, description : —
" In Venice the gondoliers know by heart long passages from Ariosto and Tasso, and often chant them with a peculiar melody. But this talent seems at present on the decline: —at least, after taking some pains, I could find no more than two persons who delivered to me in this way a passage from Tasso. I must add, that the late Mr. Barry once chanted to me a passage in Tasso in the manner, as he assured me, of the gondoliers.
" There are always two concerned, who alternately sing the strophes. We know the melody eventually by Rousseau, to whose songs it is printed; it has properly no melodious movement, and is a sort of medium between the canto fermo and the canto figurato; it approaches to the former by recitativical declamation, and to the latter by passages and course, by which one syllable is detained and embellished.
" I entered a gondola by moonlight; one singer placed himself forwards and the other aft, and thus proceeded to St. Georgio. One began the song: when he had ended his strophe, the other took up the lay, and so continued the song alternately. Throughout the whole of it, the same notes invariably returned, but, according to the subject-matter of the strophe, they laid a greater or a smaller stress, sometimes on one, and sometimes on another note, and indeed changed the enunciation of the whole strophe as the object of the poem altered.
" On the whole, however, the sounds were hoarse and screaming: they seemed, in the manner of all rude uncivilized men, to make the excellency of their singing in the force of their voice: one seemed desirous of conquering the other by the strength of his lungs; and so far from receiving delight from this scene (shut up as I was in the box of the gondola), I found myself in a very unpleasant situation.
" My companion, to whom I communicated this

circumstance, being very desirous to keep up the credit of his countrymen, assured me that this singing was very delightful when heard at a distance. Accordingly we got out upon the shore, leaving one of the singers in the gondola, while the other went to the distance of some hundred paces. They now began to sing against one another, and I kept walking up and down between them both, so as always to leave him who was to begin his part. I frequently stood still and hearkened to the one and to the other.

"Here the scene was properly introduced. The strong declamatory, and, as it were, shrieking sound, met the ear from far, and called forth the attention; the quickly succeeding transitions, which necessarily required to be sung in a lower tone, seemed like plaintive strains succeeding the vociferations of emotion or of pain. The other, who listened attentively, immediately began where the former left off, answering him in milder or more vehement notes, according as the purport of the strophe required. The sleepy canals, the lofty buildings, the splendor of the moon, the deep shadows of the few gondolas that moved like spirits hither and thither, increased the striking peculiarity of the scene; and, amidst all these circumstances, it was easy to confess the character of this wonderful harmony.

"It suits perfectly well with an idle, solitary mariner, lying at length in his vessel at rest on one of these canals, waiting for his company, or for a fare, the tiresomeness of which situation is somewhat alleviated by the songs and poetical stories he has in memory. He often raises his voice as loud as he can, which extends itself to a vast distance over the tranquil mirror, and as all is still around, he is, as it were, in a solitude in the midst of a large and populous town. Here is no rattling of carriages, no noise of foot-passengers; a silent gondola glides now and then by him, of which the splashings of the oars are scarcely to be heard.

"At a distance he hears another, perhaps utterly unknown to him. Melody and verse immediately attach the two strangers; he becomes the responsive echo to the former, and exerts himself to be heard as he had heard the other. By a tacit convention they alternate verse for verse: though the song should last the whole night through, they entertain themselves without fatigue: the hearers, who are passing between the two, take part in the amusement.

"This vocal performance sounds best at a great distance, and is then inexpressibly charming, as it only fulfils its design in the sentiment of remoteness. It is plaintive, but not dismal in its sound, and at times it is scarcely possible to refrain from tears. My companion, who otherwise was not a very delicately organized person, said quite unexpectedly: E singolare come quel canto intenerisce, e molto più quando lo cantano meglio.

"I was told that the women of Libo, the long row of islands that divides the Adriatic from the Lagoons,[1] particularly the women of the extreme districts of Malamocco and Pelestrina, sing in like manner the works of Tasso to these and similar tunes.

"They have the custom, when their husbands are fishing out at sea, to sit along the shore in the evenings and vociferate these songs, and continue to do so with great violence, till each of them can distinguish the responses of her own husband at a distance."[2]

The love of music and of poetry distinguishes all classes of Venetians, even amongst the tuneful sons of Italy. The city itself can occasionally furnish respectable audiences for two and even three opera houses at a time; and there are few events in private life that do not call forth a printed and circulated sonnet. Does a physician or a lawyer take his degree, or a clergyman preach his maiden sermon, has a surgeon performed an operation, would a harlequin announce his departure or his benefit, are you to be congratulated on a marriage, or a birth, or a lawsuit, the Muses are invoked to furnish the same number of syllables, and the individual triumphs blaze abroad in virgin white or party-colored placards on half the corners of the capital. The last curtsy of a favorite "prima donna" brings down a shower of these poetical tributes from those upper regions, from which, in our theatres, nothing but cupids and snow-storms are accustomed to descend. There is a poetry in the very life of a Venetian, which, in its common course, is varied with those surprises and changes so recommendable in fiction, but so different from the sober monotony of northern existence: amusements are raised into duties, duties are softened into amusements, and every object being considered as equally making a part of the business of life, is announced and performed with the same earnest indifference and gay assiduity. The Venetian gazette constantly closes its columns with the following triple advertisement: —

Charade.

Exposition of the most Holy Sacrament in the church of St. ——.

Theatres.

St. Moses, opera.
St. Benedict, a comedy of characters.
St. Luke, repose.

When it is recollected what the Catholics believe their consecrated wafer to be, we may perhaps think it worthy of a more respectable niche than between poetry and the play-house.

III. THE LION AND HORSES OF ST. MARK'S.

"*St. Mark yet sees his lion where he stood Stand,*" —— Stanza xi. line 5.

The Lion has lost nothing by his journey to the Invalides but the gospel which supported the paw that is now on a level with the other foot. The Horses also are returned to the ill-chosen spot whence they set out, and are, as before, half hidden

---

[1] The writer meant *Lido*, which is not a long row of islands, but a long island: *littus*, the shore.

[2] Curiosities of Literature, vol. ii. p. 156, edit. 1807; and Appendix xxix. to Black's Life of Tasso.

under the porch window of St. Mark's church. Their history, after a desperate struggle, has been satisfactorily explored. The decisions and doubts of Erizzo and Zanetti, and lastly, of the Count Leopold Cicognara, would have given them a Roman extraction, and a pedigree not more ancient than the reign of Nero. But M. de Schlegel stepped in to teach the Venetians the value of their own treasures, and a Greek vindicated, at last and forever, the pretension of his countrymen to this noble production.[1] M. Mustoxidi has not been left without a reply; but, as yet, he has received no answer. It should seem that the horses are irrevocably Chian, and were transferred to Constantinople by Theodosius. Lapidary writing is a favorite play of the Italians, and has conferred reputation on more than one of their literary characters. One of the best specimens of Bodoni's typography is a respectable volume of inscriptions, all written by his friend Pacciaudi. Several were prepared for the recovered horses. It is to be hoped the best was not selected, when the following words were ranged in gold letters above the cathedral porch: —

QUATUOR · EQUORUM · SIGNA · A · VENETIS · BYZANTIO · CAPTA · AD · TEMP · D · MAR · A · R · S · MCCIV · POSITA · QUÆ · HOSTILIS · CUPIDITAS · A · MDCCCIIC · ABSTULERAT · FRANC · I · IMP · PACIS · ORBI · DATÆ · TROPHÆUM · A · MDCCCXV · VICTOR · REDUXIT.

Nothing shall be said of the Latin, but it may be permitted to observe, that the injustice of the Venetians in transporting the horses from Constantinople was at least equal to that of the French in carrying them to Paris, and that it would have been more prudent to have avoided all allusions to either robbery. An apostolic prince should, perhaps, have objected to affixing over the principal entrance of a metropolitan church an inscription having a reference to any other triumphs than those of religion. Nothing less than the pacification of the world can excuse such a solecism.

IV.   SUBMISSION OF BARBAROSSA TO POPE ALEXANDER III.

"*The Suabian sued, and now the Austrian reigns —*
An Emperor tramples where an Emperor knelt."
            Stanza xii. lines 1 and 2.

After many vain efforts on the part of the Italians entirely to throw off the yoke of Frederic Barbarossa, and as fruitless attempts of the Emperor to make himself absolute master throughout the whole of his Cisalpine dominions, the bloody struggles of four and twenty years were happily brought to a close in the city of Venice. The articles of a treaty had been previously agreed upon between Pope Alexander III. and Barbarossa; and the former having received a safe-conduct, had already arrived at Venice from Ferrara, in company with the ambassadors of the King of Sicily and the consuls of the Lombard

league. There still remained, however, many points to adjust, and for several days the peace was believed to be impracticable. At this juncture it was suddenly reported that the Emperor had arrived at Chioza, a town fifteen miles from the capital. The Venetians rose tumultuously, and insisted upor immediately conducting him to the city. The Lombards took the alarm, and departed towards Treviso. The Pope himself was apprehensive of some disaster if Frederic should suddenly advance upon him, but was reassured by the prudence and address of Sebastian Ziani, the Doge. Several embassies passed between Chioza and the capital, until, at last, the Emperor, relaxing somewhat of his pretensions, "laid aside his leonine ferocity, and put on the mildness of the lamb."[2]

On Saturday, the 23d of July, in the year 1177, six Venetian galleys transferred Frederic, in great pomp, from Chioza to the island of Lido, a mile from Venice. Early the next morning the Pope, accompanied by the Sicilian ambassadors, and by the envoys of Lombardy, whom he had recalled from the main land, together with a great concourse of people, repaired from the patriarchal palace to St. Mark's church, and solemnly absolved the Emperor and his partisans from the excommunication pronounced against him. The Chancellor of the Empire, on the part of his master, renounced the anti-popes and their schismatic adherents. Immediately the Doge, with a great suite both of the clergy and laity, got on board the galleys, and waiting on Frederic, rowed him in mighty state from the Lido to the capital. The Emperor descended from the galley at the quay of the Piazzetta. The Doge, the patriarch, his bishops and clergy, and the people of Venice with their crosses and their standards, marched in solemn procession before him to the Church of St. Mark. Alexander was seated before the vestibule of the basilica, attended by his bishops and cardinals, by the patriarch of Aquileja, by the archbishops and bishops of Lombardy, all of them in state, and clothed in their church robes. Frederic approached — "moved by the Holy Spirit, venerating the Almighty in the person of Alexander, laying aside his imperial dignity, and throwing off his mantle, he prostrated himself at full length at the feet of the Pope. Alexander, with tears in his eyes, raised him benignantly from the ground, kissed him, blessed him; and immediately the Germans of the train sang, with a loud voice, 'We praise thee, O Lord.' The Emperor then taking the Pope by the right hand, led him to the church, and having received his benediction, returned to the ducal palace."[3] The ceremony of humiliation was repeated the next day. The Pope himself, at the request of Frederic, said mass at St. Mark's. The Emperor again laid aside his imperial mantle, and taking a wand in his hand, officiated as *verger*, driving the laity from the choir, and preceding the pontiff to the altar. Alexander, after reciting the gospel, preached to the people. The Emperor put himself close to the pulpit in the attitude of listening; and the pontiff, touched by this mark of his attention (for he knew

---

[1] Su i quattro cavalli della Basilica di S. Marco in Venezia. Lettera di Andrea Mustoxidi Corcirese. Padua, per Bettoni e compag. . . . 1816

[2] "Quibus auditis, imperator, operante eo, qui corda principum sicut vult et quando vult humiliter inclinat, leonina feritate deposita, ovinam mansuetudinem induit." — Romualdi Salernitani Chronicon, apud Script. Rer. Ital. tom. vii. p. 229.

[3] Romualdi Salernitani Chronicon, apud Script Rer. Ital. tom. vii. p. 231.

that Frederic did not understand a word he said), commanded the patriarch of Aquileja to translate the Latin discourse into the German tongue. The creed was then chanted. Frederic made his oblation, and kissed the Pope's feet, and, mass being over, led him by the hand to his white horse. He held the stirrup, and would have led the horse's rein to the water side, had not the Pope accepted of the inclination for the performance, and affectionately dismissed him with his benediction. Such is the substance of the account left by the archbishop of Salerno, who was present at the ceremony, and whose story is confirmed by every subsequent narration. It would not be worth so minute a record, were it not the triumph of liberty as well as of superstition. The states of Lombardy owed to it the confirmation of their privileges; and Alexander had reason to thank the Almighty, who had enabled an infirm, unarmed old man to subdue a terrible and potent sovereign.[1]

V. HENRY DANDOLO.

" Oh, for one hour of blind old Dandolo !
Th' octogenarian chief, Byzantium's conquer-
ing foe."
Stanza xii. lines 8 and 9.

The reader will recollect the exclamation of the Highlander, *Oh for one hour of Dundee !* Henry Dandolo, when elected Doge, in 1192, was eighty-five years of age. When he commanded the Venetians at the taking of Constantinople, he was consequently ninety-seven years old. At this age he annexed the fourth and a half of the whole empire of Romania,[2] for so the Roman empire was then called, to the title and to the territories of the Venetian Doge. The three eighths of this empire were preserved in the diplomas until the dukedom of Giovanni Dolfino, who made use of the above designation in the year 1357.[3]

Dandolo led the attack on Constantinople in person: two ships, the Paradise and the Pilgrim, were

[1] See the above-cited Romuald of Salerno. In a second sermon which Alexander preached, on the first day of August, before the Emperor, he compared Frederic to the prodigal son, and himself to the forgiving father.

[2] Mr. Gibbon has omitted the important *æ*, and has written Romani instead of Romaniæ. Decline and Fall, chap. lxi. note 8. But the title acquired by Dandolo runs thus in the chronicle of his namesake, the Doge Andrew Dandolo. " Ducali titulo addidit, ' Quartæ partis et dimidiæ totius imperii Romaniæ.'" And. Dand. Chronicon, cap. iii. pars xxxvii. ap. Script. Rer. Ital. tom. xii. page 331. And the Romaniæ is observed in the subsequent acts of the Doge's. Indeed, the continental possessions of the Greek empire in Europe were then generally known by the name of Romania, and that appellation is still seen in the maps of Turkey as applied to Thrace.

[3] See the continuation of Dandolo's Chronicle, ibid. page 498. Mr. Gibbon appears not to include Dolfino, following Sanudo, who says, " il qual titolo si usò fin al Doge Giovanni Dolfino." See Vite de' Duchi di Venezia, ap. Script. Rer. Ital. tom. xxii. 530, 641.

tied together, and a drawbridge or ladder let down from their higher yards to the walls. The Doge was one of the first to rush into the city. Then was completed, said the Venetians, the prophecy of the Erythræan sibyl: — " A gathering together of the powerful shall be made amidst the waves of the Adriatic, under a blind leader; they shall beset the goat — they shall profane Byzantium — they shall blacken her buildings — her spoils shall be dispersed; a new goat shall bleat until they have measured out and run over fifty-four feet, nine inches, and a half."[4]

Dandolo died on the first day of June, 1205, having reigned thirteen years, six months, and five days, and was buried in the church of St. Sophia, at Constantinople. Strangely enough it must sound, that the name of the rebel apothecary who received the Doge's sword, and annihilated the ancient government, in 1796-7, was Dandolo.

VI. THE WAR OF CHIOZA.

" But is not Doria's menace come to pass;
Are they not bridled ? "
Stanza xiii. lines 3 and 4.

After the loss of the battle of Pola, and the taking of Chioza on the 16th of August, 1379, by the united armament of the Genoese and Francesco da Carrara, Signor of Padua, the Venetians were reduced to the utmost despair. An embassy was sent to the conquerors with a blank sheet of paper, praying them to prescribe what terms they pleased, and leave to Venice only her independence. The prince of Padua was inclined to listen to these proposals, but the Genoese, who, after the victory at Pola, had shouted, " To Venice, to Venice, and long live St. George ! " determined to annihilate their rival; and Peter Doria, their commander-in-chief, returned this answer to the suppliants: " On God's faith, gentlemen of Venice, ye shall have no peace from the Signor of Padua, nor from our commune of Genoa, until we have first put a rein upon those unbridled horses of yours, that are upon the porch of your evangelist St. Mark. When we have bridled them, we shall keep you quiet. And this is the pleasure of us and of our commune. As for these my brothers of Genoa, that you have brought with you to give up to us, I will not have them: take them back; for, in a few days hence, I shall come and let them out of prison myself, both these and all the others." In fact, the Genoese did advance as far as Malamocco, within five miles of the capital; but their own danger and the pride of their enemies gave courage to the Venetians, who made prodigious efforts and many individual sacrifices, all of them carefully recorded by their historians. Vettor Pisani was put at the head of thirty-four galleys. The Genoese broke up from Malamocco, and retired to Chioza in October; but they again threatened Venice, which was reduced to extremi-

[4] " Fiet potentium in aquis Adriaticis congregatio, cæco præduce Hircum ambigent, Byzantium profanabunt, ædificia denigrabunt; spolia dispergentur, Hircus novus balabit usque dum LIV pedea et IX pollices, et semis præmensurati discurrant." — Chronicon, Ibid. pars xxxiv.

ties. At this time, the first of January, 1380, arrived Carlo Zeno, who had been cruising on the Genoese coast with fourteen galleys. The Venetians were now strong enough to besiege the Genoese. Doria was killed on the 22d of January by a stone bullet 195 pounds weight, discharged from a bombard called the Trevisan. Chioza was then closely invested: 5,000 auxiliaries, amongst whom were some English condottieri, commanded by one Captain Ceccho, joined the Venetians. The Genoese, in their turn, prayed for conditions, but none were granted, until, at last, they surrendered at discretion; and, on the 24th of June, 1380, the Doge Contarini made his triumphal entry into Chioza. Four thousand prisoners, nineteen galleys, many smaller vessels and barks, with all the ammunition and arms, and outfit of the expedition, fell into the hands of the conquerors, who, had it not been for the inexorable answer of Doria, would have gladly reduced their dominion to the city of Venice. An account of these transactions is found in a work called the War of Chioza, written by Daniel Chinazzo, who was in Venice at the time.[1]

VII. VENICE UNDER THE GOVERN-MENT OF AUSTRIA.

" *Thin streets, and foreign aspects, such as must Too oft remind her who and what enthralls.*"

Stanza xv. lines 7 and 8.

The population of Venice at the end of the seventeenth century amounted to nearly two hundred thousand souls. At the last census, taken two years ago, it was no more than about one hundred and three thousand; and it diminishes daily. The commerce and the official employments, which were to be the unexhausted source of Venetian grandeur, have both expired.[2] Most of the patrician mansions are deserted, and would gradually disappear, had not the government, alarmed by the demolition of seventy-two, during the last two years, expressly forbidden this sad resource of poverty. Many remnants of the Venetian nobility are now scattered, and confounded with the wealthier Jews upon the banks of the Brenta, whose Palladian palaces have sunk, or are sinking, in the general decay. Of the "gentiluomo Veneto," the name is still known, and that is all. He is but the shadow of his former self, but he is polite and kind. It surely may be pardoned to him if he is querulous. Whatever may have been the vices of the republic, and although the natural term of its existence may be thought by foreigners to have arrived in the due course of mortality, only one sentiment can be expected from the Venetians themselves. At no time were the subjects of the republic so unanimous in their resolution to rally round the standard of St. Mark, as when it was for the last time unfurled;

and the cowardice and the treachery of the few patricians who recommended the fatal neutrality were confined to the persons of the traitors themselves. The present race cannot be thought to regret the loss of their aristocratical forms, and too despotic government; they think only on their vanished independence. They pine away at the remembrance, and on this subject suspend for a moment their gay good humor. Venice may be said, in the words of the Scripture, "to die daily;" and so general and so apparent is the decline, as to become painful to a stranger, not reconciled to the sight of a whole nation expiring as it were before his eyes. So artificial a creation, having lost that principle which called it into life and supported its existence, must fall to pieces at once, and sink more rapidly than it rose. The abhorrence of slavery which drove the Venetians to the sea, has, since their disaster, forced them to the land, where they may be at least overlooked amongst the crowd of dependents, and not present the humiliating spectacle of a whole nation loaded with recent chains. Their liveliness, their affability, and that happy indifference which constitution alone can give (for philosophy aspires to it in vain), have not sunk under circumstances: but many peculiarities of costume and manner have by degrees been lost, and the nobles, with a pride common to all Italians who have been masters, have not been persuaded to parade their insignificance. That splendor which was a proof and a portion of their power, they would not degrade into the trappings of their subjection. They retired from the space which they had occupied in the eyes of their fellow-citizens; their continuance in which would have been a symptom of acquiescence, and an insult to those who suffered by the common misfortune. Those who remained in the degraded capital might be said rather to haunt the scenes of their departed power, than to live in them. The reflection, " who and what enthralls," will hardly bear a comment from one who is, nationally, the friend and the ally of the conqueror. It may, however, be allowed to say thus much, that to those who wish to recover their independence, any masters must be an object of detestation; and it may be safely foretold that this unprofitable aversion will not have been corrected before Venice shall have sunk into the slime of her choked canals.

VIII. LAURA.

"Watering the tree which bears his lady's name With his melodious tears, he gave himself to fame."   Stanza xxx. lines 8 and o.

Thanks to the critical acumen of a Scotchman, we now know as little of Laura as ever.[3] The discoveries of the Abbé de Sade, his triumphs, his

---

[1] "Chronica della Guerra di Chioza," etc. Script. Rer. Italic. tom. xv. p. 699 to 804.

[2] "Nonnullorum è nobilitate immensæ sunt opes, adeo ut vix æstimari possint: id quod tribus è rebus oritur, parsimonia, commercio, atque iis emolumentis, quæ è repub. percipiunt, quæ hanc ob causam diuturna fore creditur." See De Principalibus Italiæ, Tractatus, edit. 1631.

[3] See An Historical and Critical Essay on the Life and Character of Petrarch; and a Dissertation on an Historical Hypothesis of the Abbé de Sade: the first appeared about the year 1784; the other is inserted in the fourth volume of the Transactions of the Royal Society of Edinburgh, and both have been incorporated into a work, published, under the first title, by Ballantyne, in 1810.

aneers, can no longer instruct or amuse.[1] We must not, however, think that these memoirs are as much a romance as Belisarius or the Incas, although we are told so by Dr. Beattie, a great name, but a little authority.[2] His "labor" has not been in vain, notwithstanding his "love" has, like most other passions, made him ridiculous.[3] The hypothesis which overpowered the struggling Italians, and carried along less interested critics in its current, is run out. We have another proof that we can be never sure that the paradox, the most singular, and therefore having the most agreeable and authentic air, will not give place to the reëstablished ancient prejudice.

It seems, then, first, that Laura was born, lived, died, and was buried not in Avignon, but in the country. The fountains of the Sorga, the thickets of Cabrieres, may resume their pretensions, and the exploded *de la Bastie* again be heard with complacency. The hypothesis of the Abbé had no stronger props than the parchment sonnet and medal found on the skeleton of the wife of Hugo de Sade, and the manuscript note to the Virgil of Petrarch, now in the Ambrosian library. If these proofs were both incontestable, the poetry was written, the medal composed, cast, and deposited within the space of twelve hours: and these deliberate duties were performed round the carcass of one who died of the plague, and was hurried to the grave on the day of her death. These documents, therefore, are too decisive: they prove not the fact, but the forgery. Either the sonnet or the Virgilian note must be a falsification. The Abbé cites both as incontestably true; the consequent deduction is inevitable — they are both evidently false.[4]

Secondly, Laura was never married, and was a haughty virgin rather than that *tender and prudent* wife who honored Avignon by making that town the theatre of an honest French passion, and played off for one and twenty years her *little machinery* of alternate favors and refusals[5] upon the first poet of the age. It was, indeed, rather too unfair that a female should be made responsible for eleven children upon the faith of a misinterpreted abbreviation, and the decision of a librarian.[6] It is,

however, satisfactory to think that the love of Petrarch was not platonic. The happiness which he prayed to possess but once and for a moment was surely not of the mind,[7] and something so very real as a marriage project, with one who has been idly called a shadowy nymph, may be, perhaps, detected in at least six places of his own sonnets.[8] The love of Petrarch was neither platonic nor poetical: and if in one passage of his works he calls it "amore veementeissimo ma unico ed onesto," he confesses, in a letter to a friend, that it was guilty and perverse, that it absorbed him quite, and mastered his heart.[9]

In this case, however, he was perhaps alarmed for the culpability of his wishes; for the Abbé de Sade himself, who certainly would not have been scrupulously delicate if he could have proved his descent from Petrarch as well as Laura, is forced into a stout defence of his virtuous grandmother. As far as relates to the poet, we have no security for the innocence, except perhaps in the constancy of his pursuit. He assures us in his epistle to posterity, that, when arrived at his fortieth year, he not only had in horror, but had lost all recollection and image of any "irregularity."[10] But the birth of his natural daughter cannot be assigned earlier than his thirty-ninth year; and either the memory or the morality of the poet must have failed him, when he forgot or was guilty of this *slip*.[11] The weakest argument for the purity of this love has been drawn from the permanence of its effects, which survived the object of his passion. The reflection of M. de la Bastie, that virtue alone is capable of making impressions which death cannot efface, is one of those which everybody applauds, and everybody finds not to be true, the moment he examines his own breast or the records of human feeling.[12] Such apophthegms can do nothing for Petrarch or for the cause of morality, except with the very weak and the very young. He that has made even a little progress beyond ignorance and pupilage cannot be edified

---

[1] Mémoires pour la Vie de Pétrarque.

[2] Life of Beattie, by Sir W. Forbes, vol. ii. p. 106.

[3] Mr. Gibbon called his Memoirs "a labor of love" (see Decline and Fall, chap. lxx. note 1), and followed him with confidence and delight. The compiler of a very voluminous work must take much criticism upon trust. Mr. Gibbon has done so, though not as readily as some other authors.

[4] The sonnet had before awakened the suspicions of Mr. Horace Walpole. See his letter to Warton in 1763.

[5] "Par ce petit manège, cette alternative de faveurs et de rigueurs bien ménagée, une femme tendre et sage amuse, pendant vingt et un ans, le plus grand poëte de son siècle, sans faire la moindre brèche à son honneur." Mém. pour la Vie de Pétrarque, Préface par François. The Italian editor of the London edition of Petrarch, who has translated Lord Woodhouselee, renders the "femme tendre et sage," "raffinata civetta." Riflessioni intorno a Madonna Laura, p. 234, vol. iii. ed. 1811.

[6] In a dialogue with St. Augustin, Petrarch has described Laura as having a body exhausted with repeated *ptubs*. The old editors read and printed

perturbationibus; but M. Capperonier, librarian to the French king in 1762, who saw the MS. in the Paris library, made an attestation that "on lit et qu'on doit lire, partubus exhaustum." De Sade joined the names of Messrs. Boudot and Bejot with M. Capperonier, and in the whole discussion on this *ptubs*, showed himself a downright literary dunce. See Riflessioni, etc. p. 267. Thomas Aquinas is called in to settle whether Petrarch's mistress was a *chaste* maid or a *continent* wife.

[7] "Pigmalion, quanto lodar ti dei
    Dell' immagine tua, se mille volte
    N' avesti quel ch' i' sol una vorrei."

Sonetto 58, *Quando giunse a Simon l'alto concetto Le Rime,* etc. par. i. p. 189, edit. Ven. 1756.

[8] See Riflessioni, etc. p. 291.

[9] "Quella rea e perversa passione che solo tutto mi occupava e mi regnava nel cuore."

[10] "Azion dishonesta" are his words.

[11] "A questa confessione così sincera diede forse occasione una nuova caduta ch' ei fece." Tiraboschi, Storia, etc. tom. v. lib. iv. par. ii. p. 492.

[12] "Il n'y a que la vertu seule qui soit capable de faire des impressions que la mort n'efface pas." M. de Bimard, Baron de la Bastie, in the Mémoires de l'Académie des Inscriptions et Belles Lettres for 1740 and 1751. See also Riflessioni, etc. p. 295.

with any thing but truth. What is called vindicating the honor of an individual or a nation, is the most futile, tedious, and uninstructive of all writing: although it will always meet with more applause than that sober criticism, which is attributed to the malicious desire of reducing a great man to the common standard of humanity. It is, after all, not unlikely that our historian was right in retaining his favorite hypothetic salvo, which secures the author, although it scarcely saves the honor of the still unknown mistress of Petrarch.[1]

IX. PETRARCH.

" They keep his dust in Arquà, where he died."
Stanza xxxi. line 1.

Petrarch retired to Arquà immediately on his return from the unsuccessful attempt to visit Urban V. at Rome, in the year 1370, and, with the exception of his celebrated visit to Venice in company with Francesco Novello de Carrara, he appears to have passed the four last years of his life between that charming solitude and Padua. For four months previous to his death he was in a state of continual languor, and in the morning of July the 19th, in the year 1374, was found dead in his library chair with his head resting upon a book. The chair is still shown amongst the precious relics of Arquà, which, from the uninterrupted veneration that has been attached to every thing relative to this great man from the moment of his death to the present hour, have, it may be hoped, a better chance of authenticity than the Shakspearian memorials of Stratford-upon-Avon.

Arquà (for the last syllable is accented in pronunciation, although the analogy of the English language has been observed in the verse) is twelve miles from Padua, and about three miles on the right of the high road to Rovigo, in the bosom of the Euganean hills. After a walk of twenty minutes across a flat well-wooded meadow, you come to a little blue lake, clear but fathomless, and to the foot of a succession of acclivities and hills, clothed with vineyards and orchards, rich with fir and pomegranate trees, and every sunny fruit shrub. From the banks of the lake the road winds into the hills, and the church of Arquà is soon seen between a cleft where two ridges slope towards each other, and nearly enclose the village. The houses are scattered at intervals on the steep sides of these summits: and that of the poet is on the edge of a little knoll overlooking two descents, and commanding a view, not only of the glowing gardens in the dales immediately beneath, but of the wide plains, above whose low woods of mulberry and willow, thickened into a dark mass by festoons of vines, tall single cypresses, and the spires of towns, are seen in the distance, which stretches to the mouths of the Po and the shores of the Adriatic. The climate of these volcanic hills is warmer, and the vintage begins a week sooner than in the plains of Padua. Petrarch is laid, for he cannot be said to be buried,

in a sarcophagus of red marble, raised on four pilasters on an elevated base, and preserved from an association with meaner tombs. It stands conspicuously alone, but will be soon overshadowed by four lately planted laurels. Petrarch's Fountain, for here every thing is Petrarch's, springs and expands itself beneath an artificial arch, a little below the church, and abounds plentifully, in the dryest season, with that soft water which was the ancient wealth of the Euganean hills. It would be more attractive, were it not, in some seasons, beset with hornets and wasps. No other coincidence could assimilate the tombs of Petrarch and Archilochus. The revolutions of centuries have spared these sequestered valleys, and the only violence which has been offered to the ashes of Petrarch was prompted, not by hate, but veneration. An attempt was made to rob the sarcophagus of its treasure, and one of the arms was stolen by a Florentine through a rent which is still visible. The injury is not forgotten, but has served to identify the poet with the country where he was born, but where he would not live. A peasant boy of Arquà being asked who Petrarch was, replied, " that the people of the parsonage knew all about him, but that he only knew that he was a Florentine."

Mr. Forsyth[2] was not quite correct in saying that Petrarch never returned to Tuscany after he had once quitted it when a boy. It appears he did pass through Florence on his way from Parma to Rome, and on his return in the year 1350, and remained there long enough to form some acquaintance with its most distinguished inhabitants. A Florentine gentleman, ashamed of the aversion of the poet for his native country, was eager to point out this trivial error in our accomplished traveller, whom he knew and respected for an extraordinary capacity, extensive erudition, and refined taste, joined to that engaging simplicity of manners which has been so frequently recognized as the surest, though it is certainly not an indispensable, trait of superior genius.

Every footstep of Laura's lover has been anxiously traced and recorded. The house in which he lodged is shown in Venice. The inhabitants of Arezzo, in order to decide the ancient controversy between their city and the neighboring Ancisa, where Petrarch was carried when seven months old, and remained until his seventh year, have designated by a long inscription the spot where their great fellow-citizen was born. A tablet has been raised to him at Parma, in the chapel of St. Agatha, at the cathedral, because he was archdeacon of that society, and was only snatched from his intended sepulture in their church by a *foreign* death. Another tablet, with a bust, has been erected to him at Pavia, on account of his having passed the autumn of 1368 in that city, with his son-in-law Brossano. The political condition which has for ages precluded the Italians from the criticism of the living, has concentrated their attention to the illustration of the dead.

X. TASSO.

" In face of all his foes, the Cruscan quire:
And Boileau, whose rash envy," etc.
Stanza xxxviii. lines 6 and 7.

---

[1] " And if the virtue or prudence of Laura was inexorable, he enjoyed, and might boast of enjoying, the nymph of poetry." Decline and Fall, chap. lxx. p. 327, vol. xii. 8vo. Perhaps the *if* is here meant for *although.*

[2] Remarks, etc. on Italy, p. 95, note, 2d edit.

Perhaps the couplet in which Boileau depreciates Tasso may serve as well as any other specimen to justify the opinion given of the harmony of French verse: —

A Malherbe, à Racan, préfère Théophile,
Et le clinquant du Tasse à tout l'or de Virgile.
                    Sat. ix. vers. 176.

The biographer Serassi,[1] out of tenderness to the reputation either of the Italian or the French poet, is eager to observe that the satirist recanted or explained away this censure, and subsequently allowed the author of the Jerusalem to be a " genius, sublime, vast, and happily born for the higher flights of poetry." To this we will add, that the recantation is far from satisfactory, when we examine the whole anecdote as reported by Olivet.[2] The sentence pronounced against him by Bohours[3] is recorded only to the confusion of the critic, whose *palinodia* the Italian makes no effort to discover, and would not, perhaps, accept. As to the opposition which the Jerusalem encountered from the Cruscan academy, who degraded Tasso from all competition with Ariosto, below Bojardo and Pulci, the disgrace of such opposition must also in some measure be laid to the charge of Alfonso, and the court of Ferrara. For Leonard Salviati, the principal and nearly the sole origin of this attack, was, there can be no doubt,[4] influenced by a hope to acquire the favor of the House of Este: an object which he thought attainable by exalting the reputation of a native poet at the expense of a rival, then a *prisoner of state*. The hopes and efforts of Salviati must serve to show the contemporary opinion as to the nature of the poet's imprisonment; and will fill up the measure of our indignation at the tyrant jailer.[5] In fact, the antagonist of Tasso was not disappointed in the reception given to his criticism; he was called to the court of Ferrara, where, having endeavored to heighten his claims to favor, by panegyrics on the family of his sovereign,[6] he was in turn abandoned, and expired in neglected

poverty. The opposition of the Cruscans was brought to a close in six years after the commencement of the controversy; and if the academy owed its first renown to having almost opened with such a paradox,[7] it is probable that, on the other hand, the care of his reputation alleviated rather than aggravated the imprisonment of the injured poet. The defence of his father and of himself, for both were involved in the censure of Salviati, found employment for many of his solitary hours, and the captive could have been but little embarrassed to reply to accusations, where, amongst other delinquencies, he was charged with invidiously omitting, in his comparison between France and Italy, to make any mention of the cupola of St. Maria del Fiore at Florence.[8] The late biographer of Ariosto seems as if willing to renew the controversy by doubting the interpretation of Tasso's self-estimation[9] related in Serassi's life of the poet. But Tiraboschi had before laid that rivalry at rest,[10] by showing, that between Ariosto and Tasso it is not a question of comparison, but of preference.

XL ARIOSTO.

" The lightning rent from Ariosto's bust,
The iron crown of laurel's mimicked leaves."
                    Stanza xli. lines 1 and 2.

Before the remains of Ariosto were removed from the Benedictine church to the library of Ferrara, his bust, which surmounted the tomb, was struck by lightning, and a crown of iron laurels melted away. The event has been recorded by a writer of the last century.[11] The transfer of these sacred ashes, on the 6th of June, 1801, was one of the most brilliant spectacles of the short-lived Italian Republic; and to consecrate the memory of the ceremony, the once famous fallen *Intrepidi* were revived and re-formed into the Ariostean academy. The large public place through which the procession paraded was then for the first time called Ariosto Square. The author of the Orlando is jealously claimed as the Homer, not of Italy, but Ferrara.[12] The mother of Ariosto was of Reggio, and

---

[1] La Vita del Tasso, lib. iii. p. 284, tom. ii. edit. Bergamo, 1790.

[2] Histoire de l'Académie Françoise depuis 1652 jusqu'à 1700, par l'Abbé d'Olivet, p. 181, edit. Amsterdam, 1730. " Mais, ensuite, venant à l'usage qu'il a fait de ses talens, j'aurais montré que le bon sens n'est pas toujours ce qui domine chez lui," p. 182. Boileau said, he had not changed his opinion. " J'en ai si peu changé, dit-il," etc. p. 181.

[3] La Manière de bien Penser dans les Ouvrages de l'Esprit, sec. dial. p. 39, edit. 1692. Philanthes is for Tasso, and says in the outset, " de tous les beaux esprits que l'Italie a portés, le Tasse est peut-être celui qui pense le plus noblement." But Bohours seems to speak in Eudoxus, who closes with the absurd comparison: " Faites valoir le Tasse tant qu'il vous plaira, je m'en tiens pour moi à Virgile," etc. Ibid. p. 102.

[4] La Vita, lib. iii. p. 90, tom. ii. The English reader may see an account of the opposition of the Crusca to Tasso, in Dr. Black, Life, etc. chap. xvii. vol. ii.

[5] For further, and, it is hoped, decisive proof, that Tasso was neither more nor less than a *prisoner of state*, the reader is referred to " Historical Illustrations of the IVth Canto of Childe Harold," p. 5, and following.

[6] Orazioni funebri . . . delle lodi di Don Luigi

Cardinal d'Este . . . delle lodi di Donno Alfonso d'Este. See La Vita, lib. iii. p. 117.

[7] It was founded in 1582, and the Cruscan answer to Pellegrino, *Caraffa*, or *Epica poesia*, was published in 1584.

[8] " Cotanto potè sempre in lui il veleno della sua pessima volontà contro alla nazion Fiorentina." La Vita, lib. iii. pp. 96, 98, tom. ii.

[9] La Vita di M. L. Ariosto, scritta dall' Abate Girolamo Baruffaldi Giuniore, etc. Ferrara, 1807, lib. iii. p. 262. See " Historical Illustrations," etc. p. 26.

[10] Storia della Lett. etc. lib. iii. tom. vii. par. iii. p. 1220, sect. 4.

[11] " Mi raccontarono que' monaci, ch' essendo caduto un fulmine nella loro chiesa schiantò esso dail tempie la corona di lauro a quell' immortale poeta." Op. di Bianconi, vol. iii. p. 176, ed. Milano, 1802; lettera al Signor Guido Savini Arcifisiocritico, sull' indole di un fulmine caduto in Dresda l'anno 1759.

[12] " Appassionato ammiratore ed invitto apologista dell' *Omero Ferrarese*." The title was first given

the house in which he was born is carefully distinguished by a tablet with these words: " Qui nacque Ludovico Ariosto, il giorno 8. di Settembre dell' anno 1474." But the Ferrarese make light of the accident by which their poet was born abroad, and claim him exclusively for their own. They possess his bones, they show his arm-chair, and his ink-stand, and his autographs.

> " . . . . . Hic illius arma,
> Hic currus fuit . . . . . ."

The house where he lived, the room where he died, are designated by his own replaced memorial,[1] and by a recent inscription. The Ferrarese are more jealous of their claims since the animosity of Denina, arising from a cause which their apologists mysteriously hint is not unknown to them, ventured to degrade their soil and climate to a Bœotian incapacity for all spiritual productions. A quarto volume has been called forth by the detraction, and this supplement to Barotti's Memoirs of the illustrious Ferrarese has been considered a triumphant reply to the " Quadro Storico Statistico dell' Alta Italia."

XII. ANCIENT SUPERSTITIONS RESPECTING LIGHTNING.

> "*For the true laurel - wreath which Glory weaves*
> *Is of the tree no bolt of thunder cleaves.*"
> Stanza xli. lines 4 and 5.

The eagle, the sea calf, the laurel,[2] and the white vine,[3] were amongst the most approved preservatives against lightning. Jupiter chose the first, Augustus Cæsar the second,[4] and Tiberius never failed to wear a wreath of the third when the sky threatened a thunder-storm.[5] These superstitions may be received without a sneer in a country where the magical properties of the hazel twig have not lost all their credit; and perhaps the reader may not be much surprised to find that a commentator on Suetonius has taken upon himself gravely to disprove the imputed virtues of the crown of Tiberius, by mentioning that a few years before he wrote, a laurel was actually struck by lightning at Rome.[6]

XIII.

> "*Know that the lightning sanctifies below.*"
> Stanza xli. line 8.

The Curtian lake and the Ruminal fig-tree in the Forum, having been touched by lightning, were held sacred, and the memory of the accident was preserved by a *puteal*, or altar resembling the mouth of a well, with a little chapel covering the cavity supposed to be made by the thunderbolt. Bodies scathed and persons struck dead were thought to be incorruptible;[7] and a stroke not fatal conferred perpetual dignity upon the man so distinguished by heaven.[8]

Those killed by lightning were wrapped in a white garment, and buried where they fell. The superstition was not confined to the worshippers of Jupiter: the Lombards believed in the omens furnished by lightning; and a Christian priest confesses that, by a diabolical skill in interpreting thunder, a seer foretold to Agilulf, duke of Turin, an event which came to pass, and gave him a queen and a crown.[9] There was, however, something equivocal in this sign, which the ancient inhabitants of Rome did not always consider propitious; and as the fears are likely to last longer than the consolations of superstition, it is not strange that the Romans of the age of Leo X. should have been so much terrified at some misinterpreted storms as to require the exhortations of a scholar, who arrayed all the learning on thunder and lightning to prove the omen favorable; beginning with the flash which struck the walls of Velitræ, and including that which played upon a gate at Florence, and foretold the pontificate of one of its citizens.[10]

XIV. THE VENUS OF MEDICIS.

> "*There, too, the Goddess loves in stone.*"
> Stanza xlix. line 1.

The view of the Venus of Medicis instantly suggests the lines in the *Seasons*, and the comparison of the object with the description proves, not only the correctness of the portrait, but the peculiar turn of thought, and, if the term may be used, the sexual imagination of the descriptive poet. The same conclusion may be deduced from another hint in the same episode of Musidora; for Thomson's notion of the privileges of favored love must have been either very primitive, or rather deficient in delicacy, when he made his grateful nymph inform her discreet Damon that in some happier moment he might perhaps be the companion of her bath: —

> "The time may come you need not fly."

The reader will recollect the anecdote told in the Life of Dr. Johnson. We will not leave the Florentine gallery without a word on the *Whetter.* It seems strange that the character of that disputed statue should not be entirely decided, at least in the mind of any one who has seen a sarcophagus in the vestibule of the Basilica of St. Paul without the walls, at Rome, where the whole group of the fable of Marsyas is seen in tolerable preservation: and the Scy-

---

[1] " Parva sed apta mihi, sed nulli obnoxia, sed non Sordida, parta meo sed tamen ære domus."

[2] Aquila, vitulus marinus, et laurus, fulmine non feriuntur. Plin. Nat. Hist. lib. ii. cap. 56.

[3] Columella, lib. x.

[4] Sueton. in Vit. August. cap. xc.

[5] Sueton. in Vit. Tiberii, cap. lxix.

[6] Note 2, p. 409, edit. Lugd. Bat. 1667.

[7] Vid. J. C. Bullenger, de Terræ Motu et Fulminib. lib. v. cap. xi.

[8] Οὐδεὶς κεραυνωθεὶς ἄτιμός ἐστι, ὅθεν καὶ ὡς θεὸς τιμᾶται. Plut. Sympos. vid. J. C. Bulieng. ut sup.

[9] Pauli Diaconi de Gestis Langobard. lib. iii. cap. xiv. fo. 15, edit. Taurin. 1527.

[10] I. P. Valeriani de fulminum significationibus declamatio, ap. Græv. Antiq. Rom. tom. v. p. 593. The declamation is addressed to Julian of Medicis

thian slave whetting the knife is represented exactly in the same position as this celebrated masterpiece. The slave is not naked; but it is easier to get rid of this difficulty than to suppose the knife in the hand of the Florentine statue an instrument for shaving, which it must be, if, as Lanzi supposes, the man is no other than the barber of Julius Cæsar. Winkelmann, illustrating a bas-relief of the same subject, follows the opinion of Leonard Agostini, and his authority might have been thought conclusive, even if the resemblance did not strike the most careless observer.[1] Amongst the bronzes of the same princely collection is still to be seen the inscribed tablet copied and commented upon by Mr. Gibbon.[2] Our historian found some difficulties, but did not desist from his illustration: he might be vexed to hear that his criticism has been thrown away on an inscription now generally recognized to be a forgery.

XV. MADAME DE STAËL.

" In Santa Croce's holy precincts lie."

Stanza liv. line 1.

This name will recall the memory, not only of those whose tombs have raised the Santa Croce into the centre of pilgrimage, the Mecca of Italy, but of her whose eloquence was poured over the illustrious ashes, and whose voice is now as mute as those she sung. CORINNA is no more; and with her should expire the fear, the flattery, and the envy, which threw too dazzling or too dark a cloud round the march of genius, and forbade the steady gaze of disinterested criticism. We have her picture embellished or distorted, as friendship or detraction has held the pencil: the impartial portrait was hardly to be expected from a contemporary. The immediate voice of her survivors will, it is probable, be far from affording a just estimate of her singular capacity. The gallantry, the love of wonder, and the hope of associated fame, which blunted the edge of censure, must cease to exist. — The dead have no sex; they can surprise by no new miracles ; they can confer no privilege : Corinna has ceased to be a woman — she is only an author : and it may be foreseen that many will repay themselves for former complaisance, by a severity to which the extravagance of previous praises may perhaps give the color of truth. The latest posterity, for to the latest posterity they will assuredly descend, will have to pronounce upon her various productions ; and the longer the vista through which they are seen, the more accurately minute will be the object, the more certain the justice, of the decision. She will enter into that existence in which the great writers of all ages and nations are, as it were, associated in a world of their own, and, from that superior sphere, shed their eternal influence for the control and consolation of mankind. But the individual will gradually disappear as the author is more distinctly seen : some one, therefore, of all those whom the charms of involuntary wit, and of easy hospitality, attracted within the friendly circles of Coppet, should rescue from oblivion those virtues which, although they are said to love the shade, are, in fact, more frequently chilled than excited by the domestic cares of private life. Some one should be found to portray the unaffected graces with which she adorned those dearer relationships, the performance of whose duties is rather discovered amongst the interior secrets, than seen in the outward management, of family intercourse ; and which, indeed, it requires the delicacy of genuine affection to qualify for the eye of an indifferent spectator. Some one should be found, not to celebrate, but to describe, the amiable mistress of an open mansion, the centre of a society, ever varied, and always pleased, the creator of which, divested of the ambition and the arts of public rivalry, shone forth only to give fresh animation to those around her. The mother tenderly affectionate and tenderly beloved, the friend unboundedly generous, but still esteemed, the charitable patroness of all distress, cannot be forgotten by those whom she cherished, and protected, and fed. Her loss will be mourned the most where she was known the best ; and, to the sorrows of very many friends, and more dependents, may be offered the disinterested regret of a stranger, who, amidst the sublimer scenes of the Leman lake, received his chief satisfaction from contemplating the engaging qualities of the incomparable Corinna.

XVI. ALFIERI.

" Here repose
Angelo's, Alfieri's bones."

Stanza liv. lines 6 and 7.

Alfieri is the great name of this age. The Italians, without waiting for the hundred years, consider him as " a poet good in law." — His memory is the more dear to them because he is the bard of freedom ; and because, as such, his tragedies can receive no countenance from any of their sovereigns. They are but very seldom, and but very few of them, allowed to be acted. It was observed by Cicero, that nowhere were the true opinions and feelings of the Romans so clearly shown as at the theatre.[3] In the autumn of 1816, a celebrated improvisatore exhibited his talents at the Opera-house of Milan. The reading of the theses handed in for the subjects of his poetry was received by a very

---

[1] See Monim. Ant. Ined. par. i. cap. xvii. n. xlii. p. 50.; and Storia telli Arti, etc. lib. xi. cap. i. tom. ii. p. 314, note B.

[2] Nomina gentesque Antiquæ Italiæ, p. 204, edit. oct.

[3] The free expression of their honest sentiments survived their liberties. Titius, the friend of Antony, presented them with games in the theatre of Pompey. They did not suffer into that existence to efface from their memory that the man who furnished them with the entertainment had murdered the son of Pompey: they drove him from the theatre with curses. The moral sense of a populace, spontaneously expressed, is never wrong. Even the soldiers of the triumvirs joined in the execration of the citizens, by shouting round the chariots of Lepidus and Plancus, who had proscribed their brothers, *De Germanis non de Gallis duo triumphant Consules;* a saying worth a record, were it nothing but a good pun. [C. Vell. Paterculi Hist. lib. ii. cap. lxxix. p. 78, edit. Elzevir. 1639. Ibid. lib. ii. cap. lxxvii.]

numerous audience, for the most part in silence, or with laughter; but when the assistant, unfolding one of the papers exclaimed, *The apotheosis of Victor Alfieri*, the whole theatre burst into a shout, and the applause was continued for some moments. The lot did not fall on Alfieri; and the Signor Sgricci had to pour forth his extemporary common-places on the bombardment of Algiers. The choice, indeed, is not left to accident quite so much as might be thought from a first view of the ceremony; and the police not only takes care to look at the papers beforehand, but, in case of any prudential after-thought, steps in to correct the blindness of chance. The proposal for deifying Alfieri was received with immediate enthusiasm, the rather because it was conjectured there would be no opportunity of carrying it into effect.

XVII. MACHIAVELLI.

" *Here Machiavelli's earth returned to whence it rose.*"
                              Stanza liv. line 9.

The affectation of simplicity in sepulchral inscriptions, which so often leaves us uncertain whether the structure before us is an actual depository, or a cenotaph, or a simple memorial not of death but life, has given to the tomb of Machiavelli no information as to the place or time of the birth or death, the age or parentage, of the historian.

TANTO NOMINI NVLLVM PAR ELOGIVM
NICCOLAVS MACHIAVELLI.

There seems at least no reason why the name should not have been put above the sentence which alludes to it.
It will readily be imagined that the prejudices which have passed the name of Machiavelli into an epithet proverbial of iniquity exist no longer at Florence. His memory was persecuted as his life had been for an attachment to liberty incompatible with the new system of despotism, which succeeded the fall of the free governments of Italy. He was put to the torture for being a "libertine," that is, for wishing to restore the republic of Florence; and such are the undying efforts of those who are interested in the perversion not only of the nature of actions, but the meaning of words, that what was once *patriotism*, has by degrees come to signify *debauch*. We have ourselves outlived the old meaning of "liberality," which is now another word for treason in one country and for infatuation in all. It seems to have been a strange mistake to accuse the author of "The Prince," as being a pander to tyranny; and to think that the Inquisition would condemn his work for such a delinquency. The fact is, that Machiavelli, as is usual with those against whom no crime can be proved, was suspected of and charged with atheism; and the first and last most violent opposers of "The Prince" were both Jesuits, one of whom persuaded the Inquisition "benchè fosse tardo," to prohibit the treatise, and the other qualified the secretary of the Florentine republic as no better than a fool. The father Possevin was proved never to have read the book, and the father Lucchesini not to have understood it. It is clear, however, that such critics must have objected not to the slavery of the doc

trines, but to the supposed tendency of a lesson which shows how distinct are the interests of a monarch from the happiness of mankind. The Jesuits are reëstablished in Italy, and the last chapter of "The Prince" may again call forth a particular refutation from those who are employed once more in moulding the minds of the rising generation, so as to receive the impressions of despotism. The chapter bears for title, "Esortazione a liberare la Italia dai Barbari," and concludes with a *libertine* excitement to the future redemption of Italy. " Non si deve adunque lasciar passare questa occasione, acciocche la Italia vegga dopo tanto tempo apparire un suo redentore. Nè posso esprimere con qual amore ei fusse ricevuto in tutte quelle provincie, che hanno patito per queste illuvioni esterne, con qual sete di vendetta, con che ostinata fede, con che lacrime. Quali porte se gli serrerebbono? Quali popoli gli negherebbono la obbedienza? Quale Italiano gli negherebbe l'ossequio? AD OGNUNO PUZZA QUESTO BAR-BARO DOMINIO." [1]

XVIII. DANTE.

" *Ungrateful Florence! Dante sleeps afar.*"
                              Stanza lvii. line 1.

Dante was born in Florence, in the year 1261. He fought in two battles, was fourteen times ambassador, and once prior of the republic. When the party of Charles of Anjou triumphed over the Bianchi, he was absent on an embassy to Pope Boniface VIII., and was condemned to two years' banishment, and to a fine of 8,000 lire; on the non-payment of which he was further punished by the sequestration of all his property. The republic, however, was not content with this satisfaction, for in 1772 was discovered in the archives at Florence a sentence in which Dante is the eleventh of a list of fifteen condemned in 1302 to be burnt alive; *Talis perveniens igne comburatur sic quod moriatur.* The pretext for this judgment was a proof of unfair barter, extortions, and illicit gains. *Baracteriarum iniquarum extorsionum, et illicitorum lucrorum*,[2] and with such an accusation it is not strange that Dante should have always protested his innocence, and the injustice of his fellow-citizens. His appeal to Florence was accompanied by another to the Emperor Henry; and the death of that sovereign in 1313 was the signal for a sentence of irrevocable banishment. He had before lingered near Tuscany with hopes of recall; then travelled into the north of Italy, where Verona had to boast of his longest residence; and he finally settled at Ravenna, which was his ordinary but not constant abode until his death. The refusal of the Venetians to grant him a public audience, on the part of Guido Novello da Polenta, his protector, is said to have been the principal cause of this event, which happened in 1321. He was buried ("in

---

[1] Il Principe di Niccolò Machiavelli, etc. con la prefazione e le note istoriche e politiche di M. Amelot de la Houssaye e l' esame e confutazione dell' opera. . . . Cosmopoli, 1769.
[2] Storia della Lett. Ital. tom. v. lib. iii. par. 2. p. 448. Tiraboschi is incorrect: the dates of the three decrees against Dante are A.D. 1302, 1314, and 1316.

sacra minorum æde") at Ravenna, in a handsome tomb, which was erected by Guido, restored by Bernardo Bembo in 1483, prætor for that republic which had refused to hear him, again restored by Cardinal Corsi, in 1692, and replaced by a more magnificent sepulchre, constructed in 1780 at the expense of the Cardinal Luigi Valenti Gonzaga. The offence or misfortune of Dante was an attachment to a defeated party, and, as his least favorable biographers allege against him, too great a freedom of speech and haughtiness of manner. But the next age paid honors almost divine to the exile. The Florentines, having in vain and frequently attempted to recover his body, crowned his image in a church,[1] and his picture is still one of the idols of their cathedral. They struck medals, they raised statues to him. The cities of Italy, not being able to dispute about his own birth, contended for that of his great poem, and the Florentines thought it for their honor to prove that he had finished the seventh Canto before they drove him from his native city. Fifty-one years after his death, they endowed a professorial chair for the expounding of his verses, and Boccaccio was appointed to this patriotic employment. The example was imitated by Bologna and Pisa, and the commentators, if they performed but little service to literature, augmented the veneration which beheld a sacred or moral allegory in all the images of his mystic muse. His birth and his infancy were discovered to have been distinguished above those of ordinary men: the author of the Decameron, his earliest biographer, relates that his mother was warned in a dream of the importance of her pregnancy: and it was found, by others, that at ten years of age he had manifested his precocious passion for that wisdom or theology, which, under the name of Beatrice, had been mistaken for a substantial mistress. When the Divine Comedy had been recognized as a mere mortal production, and at the distance of two centuries, when criticism and competition had sobered the judgment of the Italians, Dante was seriously declared superior to Homer;[2] and though the preference appeared to some casuists "an heretical blasphemy worthy of the flames," the contest was vigorously maintained for nearly fifty years. In later times it was made a question which of the Lords of Verona could boast of having patronized him,[3] and the jealous scepticism of one writer would not allow Ravenna the undoubted possession of his bones. Even the critical Tiraboschi was inclined to believe that the poet had foreseen and foretold one of the discoveries of Galileo. — Like the great originals of other nations, his popularity has not always maintained the same level. The last age seemed inclined to undervalue him as a model and a study; and Bettinelli one day rebuked his pupil Monti, for poring over the harsh and obsolete extravagances of the Commedia. The present generation having recovered from the Gallic idolatries of Cesarotti, has returned to the ancient worship, and the *Danteggiare* of the northern Italians is thought even indiscreet by the more moderate Tuscans.

There is still much curious information relative to the life and writings of this great poet, which has not as yet been collected even by the Italians; but the celebrated Ugo Foscolo meditates to supply this defect, and it is not to be regretted that this national work has been reserved for one so devoted to his country and the cause of truth.

---

xix. TOMB OF THE SCIPIOS.

"*Like Scipio, buried by the upbraiding shore;*
Thy factions, in their worse than civil war,
Proscribed," etc.
Stanza lvii. lines 2, 3, and 4.

The elder Scipio Africanus had a tomb if he was not buried at Liternum, whither he had retired to voluntary banishment. This tomb was near the sea-shore, and the story of an inscription upon it, *Ingrata Patria*, having given a name to a modern tower, is, if not true, an agreeable fiction. If he was not buried he certainly lived there.[4]

In così angusta e solitaria villa
Era 'l grand' uomo che d' Africa s' appella
Perchè prima col ferro al vivo aprilla.[5]

Ingratitude is generally supposed the vice peculiar to republics; and it seems to be forgotten that for one instance of popular inconstancy, we have a hundred examples of the fall of courtly favorites. Besides, a people have often repented — a monarch seldom or never. Leaving apart many familiar proofs of this fact, a short story may show the difference between even an aristocracy and the multitude.

Vettor Pisani, having been defeated in 1354 at Portolongo, and many years afterwards in the more decisive action of Pola, by the Genoese, was recalled by the Venetian government, and thrown into chains. The Avvogadori proposed to behead him, but the supreme tribunal was content with the sentence of imprisonment. Whilst Pisani was suffering this unmerited disgrace, Chioza, in the vicinity of the capital,[6] was by the assistance of the *Signor of Padua*, delivered into the hands of Pietro Doria. At the intelligence of that disaster, the great bell of St. Mark's tower tolled to arms, and the people and the soldiery of the galleys were summoned to the repulse of the approaching enemy; but they protested they would not move a step, unless Pisani were liberated and placed at their head. The great council was instantly assembled; the prisoner was called before them, and the Doge, Andrea Contarini, informed him of the demands of the people, and the necessities of the State, whose only hope of safety was reposed on his efforts, and who implored him to forget the indignities he had endured in her service. "I have submitted," replied the magnanimous republican, "I have submitted to your deliberations without complaint: I have supported

---

[1] So relates Ficino, but some think his coronation only an allegory. See Storia, etc. ut sup. p. 453.
[2] By Varchi, in his Ercolano. The controversy continued from 1570 to 1616. See Storia, etc. tom. vii. lib. iii. par. iii. p. 1280.
[3] Gio. Jacopo Dionisi Canonico di Verona. Serie

di Aneddoti, n. 2. See Storia, etc. tom. v. lib. i par. i. p. 24.
[4] Vitam Literni egit sine desiderio urbis. See T. Liv. Hist. lib. xxxviii. Livy reports that some said he was buried at Liternum, others at Roma. Ibid. cap. lvi.
[5] Trionfo della Castità.
[6] See Note VI., p. 319.

patiently the pains of imprisonment, for they were inflicted at your command: this is no time to inquire whether I deserved them — the good of the republic may have seemed to require it, and that which the republic resolves is always resolved wisely. Behold me ready to lay down my life for the preservation of my country." Pisani was appointed generalissimo, and by his exertions, in conjunction with those of Carlo Zeno, the Venetians soon recovered the ascendency over their maritime rivals.

The Italian communities were no less unjust to their citizens than the Greek republics. Liberty, both with the one and the other, seems to have been a national, not an individual object: and notwithstanding the boasted *equality before the laws,* which an ancient Greek writer[1] considered the great distinctive mark between his countrymen and the barbarians, the mutual rights of fellow-citizens seem never to have been the principal scope of the old democracies. The world may have not yet seen an essay by the author of the Italian Republics, in which the distinction between the liberty of former States, and the signification attached to that word by the happier constitution of England, is ingeniously developed. The Italians, however, when they had ceased to be free, still looked back with a sigh upon those times of turbulence, when every citizen might rise to a share of sovereign power, and have never been taught fully to appreciate the repose of a monarchy. Sperone Speroni, when Francis Maria II. Duke of Rovere proposed the question, "which was preferable, the republic or the principality — the perfect and not durable, or the less perfect and not so liable to change," replied, "that our happiness is to be measured by its quality, not by its duration; and that he preferred to live for one day like a man, than for a hundred years like a brute, a stock, or a stone." This was thought, and called, a *magnificent* answer, down to the last days of Italian servitude.[2]

XX. PETRARCH'S CROWN.

"And the crown
Which Petrarch's laureate brow supremely wore
Upon a far and foreign soil had grown."
Stanza lvii. lines 6, 7, and 8.

The Florentines did not take the opportunity of Petrarch's short visit to their city in 1350 to revoke the decree which confiscated the property of his father, who had been banished shortly after the exile of Dante. His crown did not dazzle them; but when in the next year they were in want of his assistance in the formation of their university, they repented of their injustice, and Boccaccio was sent to Padua to entreat the laureate to conclude his wanderings in the bosom of his native country, where he might finish his *immortal Africa,* and enjoy, with his recovered possessions, the esteem of

all classes of his fellow-citizens. They gave him the option of a book and the science he might condescend to expound: they called him the glory of his country, who was dear, and would be dearer to them; and they added, that if there was any thing unpleasing in their letter, he ought to return amongst them, were it only to correct their style.[3] Petrarch seemed at first to listen to the flattery and to the entreaties of his friend, but he did not return to Florence, and preferred a pilgrimage to the tomb of Laura and the shades of Vaucluse.

XXI. BOCCACCIO.

"Boccaccio to his parent earth bequeathed
His dust."   Stanza lviii. lines 1 and 2.

Boccaccio was buried in the church of St. Michael and St. James, at Certaldo, a small town in the Valdelsa, which was by some supposed the place of his birth. There he passed the latter part of his life in a course of laborious study, which shortened his existence; and there might his ashes have been secure, if not of honor, at least of repose. But the "hyæna bigots" of Certaldo tore up the tombstone of Boccaccio, and ejected it from the holy precincts of St. Michael and St. James. The occasion, and, it may be hoped, the excuse, of this ejectment was the making of a new floor for the church; but the fact is, that the tombstone was taken up and thrown aside at the bottom of the building. Ignorance may share the sin with bigotry. It would be painful to relate such an exception to the devotion of the Italians for their great names, could it not be accompanied by a trait more honorably conformable to the general character of the nation. The principal person of the district, the last branch of the house of Medicis, afforded that protection to the memory of the insulted dead which her best ancestors had dispensed upon all contemporary merit. The Marchioness Lenzoni rescued the tombstone of Boccaccio from the neglect in which it had some time lain, and found for it an honorable elevation in her own mansion. She has done more : the house in which the poet lived has been as little respected as his tomb, and is falling to ruin over the head of one indifferent to the name of its former tenant. It consists of two or three little chambers, and a low tower, on which Cosmo II. affixed an inscription. This house she has taken measures to purchase, and proposes to devote to it that care and consideration which are attached to the cradle and to the roof of genius.

This is not the place to undertake the defence of Boccaccio; but the man who exhausted his little patrimony in the acquirement of learning, who was amongst the first, if not the first, to allure the science and the poetry of Greece to the bosom of Italy; — who not only invented a new style, but founded, or certainly fixed, a new language; who, besides the esteem of every polite court of Europe, was thought worthy of employment by the pre-

---

[1] The Greek boasted that he was ἰσόνομος. See the last chapter of the first book of Dionysius of Halicarnassus.

[2] "E intorno *alla magnifica risposta,*" etc. Serassi, Vita del Tasso, lib. iii. p. 149, tom. ii. edit. 2, Bergamo.

[3] "Accingiti innoltre, se ci è lecito ancor l' esortarti, a compire l' immortal tua Africa . . . Se ti avviene d' incontrare nel nostro stile cosa che ti dispiaccia, ciò debb' essere un altro motivo ad esaudire i desiderj della tua patria." Storia della Lett. Ital. tom. v. par. i. lib. i. p. 76.

dominant republic of his own country, and, what is more, of the friendship of Petrarch, who lived the life of a philosopher and a freeman, and who died in the pursuit of knowledge, — such a man might have found more consideration than he has met with from the priest of Certaldo, and from a late English traveller, who strikes off his portrait as an odious, contemptible, licentious writer, whose impure remains should be suffered to rot without a record.[1] That English traveller, unfortunately for those who have to deplore the loss of a very amiable person, is beyond all criticism; but the mortality which did not protect Boccaccio from Mr. Eustace, must not defend Mr. Eustace from the impartial judgment of his successors. Death may canonize his virtues, not his errors; and it may be modestly pronounced that he transgressed, not only as an author, but as a man, when he evoked the shade of Boccaccio in company with that of Aretine, amidst the sepulchres of Santa Croce, merely to dismiss it with indignity. As far as respects

> " Il flagello de' Principi,
> Il divin Pietro Aretino,"

it is of little import what censure is passed upon a coxcomb who owes his present existence to the above burlesque character given to him by the poet, whose amber has preserved many other grubs and worms: but to classify Boccaccio with such a person, and to excommunicate his very ashes, must of itself make us doubt of the qualification of the classical tourist for writing upon Italian, or, indeed, upon any other literature; for ignorance on one point may incapacitate an author merely for that particular topic, but subjection to a professional prejudice must render him an unsafe director on all occasions. Any perversion and injustice may be made what is vulgarly called " a case of conscience," and this poor excuse is all that can be offered for the priest of Certaldo, or the author of the Classical Tour. It would have answered the purpose to confine the censure to the novels of Boccaccio; and gratitude to that source which supplied the muse of Dryden with her last and most harmonious numbers might, perhaps, have restricted that censure to the objectionable qualities of the hundred tales. At any rate the repentance of Boccaccio mght have arrested his exhumation, and it should have been recollected and told, that in his old age he wrote a letter entreating his friend to discourage the reading

[1] Classical Tour, chap. ix. vol. ii. p. 355, edit. 3d. " Of Boccaccio, the modern Petronius, we say nothing: the abuse of genius is more odious and more contemptible than its absence; and it imports little where the impure remains of a licentious author are consigned to their kindred dust. For the same reason the traveller may pass unnoticed the tomb of the malignant Aretino." This dubious phrase is hardly enough to save the tourist from the suspicion of another blunder respecting the burial-place of Aretine, whose tomb was in the church of St. Luke at Venice, and gave rise to the famous controversy of which some notice is taken in Bayle. Now the words of Mr. Eustace would lead us to think the tomb was at Florence, or at least was to be somewhere recognized. Whether the inscription so much disputed was ever written on the tomb cannot now be decided, for all memorial of this author has disappeared from the church of St. Luke.

of the Decameron, for the sake of modesty, and for the sake of the author, who would not have an apologist always at hand to state in his excuse that he wrote it when young, and at the command of his superiors.[2] It is neither the licentiousness of the writer, nor the evil propensities of the reader, which have given to the Decameron alone, of all the works of Boccaccio, a perpetual popularity. The establishment of a new and delightful dialect conferred an immortality on the works in which it was first fixed. The sonnets of Petrarch were, for the same reason, fated to survive his self-admired Africa, the " favorite of kings." The invariable traits of nature and feeling with which the novels, as well as the verses, abound, have doubtless been the chief source of the foreign celebrity of both authors; but Boccaccio, as a man, is no more to be estimated by that work, than Petrarch is to be regarded in no other light than as the lover of Laura. Even, however, had the father of the Tuscan prose been known only as the author of the Decameron, a considerate writer would have been cautious to pronounce a sentence irreconcilable with the unerring voice of many ages and nations. An irrevocable value has never been stamped upon any work solely recommended by impurity.

The true source of the outcry against Boccaccio, which began at a very early period, was the choice of his scandalous personages in the cloisters as well as the courts: but the princes only laughed at the gallant adventures so unjustly charged upon queen Thec delinda, whilst the priesthood cried shame upon the debauches drawn from the convent and the hermitage; and most probably for the opposite reason, namely, that the picture was faithful to the life. Two of the novels are allowed to be facts usefully turned into tales, to deride the canonization of rogues and laymen. Ser Ciappelletto and Marcellinus are cited with applause even by the decent Muratori.[3] The great Arnaud, as he is quoted in Bayle, states, that a new edition of the novels was proposed, of which the expurgation consisted in omitting the words " monk " and " nun " and tacking the immoralities to other names. The literary history of Italy particularizes no such edition: but it was not long before the whole of Europe had but one opinion of the Decameron; and the absolution of the author seems to have been a point settled at least a hundred years ago: " On se feroit siffler si l'on prétendoit convaincre Boccace de n'avoir pas été honnête homme, puis qu'il a fait le Décameron." So said one of the best men, and perhaps the best critic, that ever lived — the very martyr to impartiality.[4] But as this information, that in the beginning of the last century one would have been hooted at for pretending that Boccaccio was not a good man, may seem to come from one of those enemies who are to be suspected, even when they make us a present of truth, a more acceptable contrast with the proscription of the body, soul, and muse of

[2] " Non enim ubique est, qui in excusationem meam consurgens dicat, juvenis scripsit, et majoris coactus imperio." The letter was addressed to Maghinard of Cavalcanti, marshal of the kingdom of Sicily. See Tiraboschi, Storia, etc. tcm. v. par. ii. lib. iii. p. 525, ed. Ven. 1795.

[3] Dissertazioni sopra le Antichità Italiane, Diss. lviii. p. 253, tom. iii. edit. Milan, 1751.

[4] *Eclaircissement*, etc. etc. p. 638, edit. Basle, 1741, in the Supplement to Bayle's Dictionary.

Boccaccio may be found in a few words from the virtuous, the patriotic contemporary, who thought one of the tales of this impure writer worthy a Latin version from his own pen. "I have remarked elsewhere," says Petrarch, writing to Boccaccio, "that the book itself has been worried by certain dogs, but stoutly defended by your staff and voice. Nor was I astonished, for I have had proof of the vigor of your mind, and I know you have fallen on that unaccommodating incapable race of mortals, who, whatever they either like not, or know not, or cannot do, are sure to reprehend in others; and on those occasions only put on a show of learning and eloquence, but otherwise are entirely dumb."[1]

It is satisfactory to find that all the priesthood do not resemble those of Certaldo, and that one of them who did not possess the bones of Boccaccio would not lose the opportunity of raising a cenotaph to his memory. Bevius, canon of Padua, at the beginning of the sixteenth century, erected at Arquà, opposite to the tomb of the Laureate, a tablet, in which he associated Boccaccio to the equal honors of Dante and of Petrarch.

XXII. THE MEDICI.

"What is her pyramid of precious stones?"

Stanza lx. line 1.

Our veneration for the Medici begins with Cosmo and expires with his grandson; that stream is pure only at the source; and it is in search of some memorial of the virtuous republicans of the family that we visit the church of St. Lorenzo at Florence. The tawdry, glaring, unfinished chapel in that church, designed for the mausoleum of the Dukes of Tuscany, set round with crowns and coffins, gives birth to no emotions but those of contempt for the lavish vanity of a race of despots, whilst the pavement slab, simply inscribed to the Father of his Country, reconciles us to the name of Medici.[2] It was very natural for Corinna[3] to suppose that the statue raised to the Duke of Urbino in the *capella de' depositi* was intended for his great namesake; but the magnificent Lorenzo is only the sharer of a coffin half hidden in the niche of the sacristy. The decay of Tuscany dates from the sovereignty of the Medici. Of the sepulchral peace which succeeded to the establishment of the reigning families in Italy, our own Sidney has given us a glowing, but a faithful picture. "Notwithstanding all the seditions of Florence, and other cities of Tuscany, the horrid factions of Guelphs and Ghibelins, Neri and Bianchi, nobles and commons, they continued populous, strong, and exceeding rich; but in the space of less than a hundred and fifty years, the peaceable reign

[1] "Animadverti alicubi librum ipsum canum dentibus lacessitum, tuo tamen baculo egregiè tuâque voce defensum. Nec miratus sum: nam et vires ingenii tui novi, et scio expertus esses hominum genus insolens et ignavum, qui quicquid ipsi vel nolunt vel nesciunt, vel non possunt, in aliis reprehendunt; ad hoc unum docti et arguti, sed elingues ad reliqua." Epist. Joan. Boccatio, Opp. tom. i. p. 540, edit. Basil.
[2] Cosmus Medices, Decreto Publico, Pater Patriæ.
[3] Corinne, liv. xviii. chap. iii. vol. iii. p. 248.

of the Medices is thought to have destroyed nine parts in ten of the people of that province. Amongst other things, it is remarkable, that when Philip the Second of Spain gave Sienna to the Duke of Florence, his embassador then at Rome sent him word that he had given away more than 650,000 subjects; and it is not believed there are now 20,000 souls inhabiting that city and territory. Pisa, Pistoia, Arezzo, Cortona, and other towns, that were then good and populous, are in the like proportion, diminished, and Florence more than any. When that city had been long troubled with seditions, tumults, and wars, for the most part unprosperous, they still retained such strength, that when Charles VIII. of France, being admitted as a friend with his whole army, which soon after conquered the kingdom of Naples, thought to master them, the people, taking arms, struck such a terror into him, that he was glad to depart upon such conditions as they thought fit to impose. Machiavel reports, that in that time Florence alone, with the Val d'Arno, a small territory belonging to that city, could, in a few hours, by the sound of a bell, bring together 135,000 well-armed men; whereas now that city, with all the others in that province, are brought to such despicable weakness, emptiness, poverty, and baseness, that they can neither resist the oppressions of their own prince, nor defend him or themselves if they were assaulted by a foreign enemy. The people are dispersed or destroyed, and the best families sent to seek habitations in Venice, Genoa, Rome, Naples, and Lucca. This is not the effect of war or pestilence: they enjoy a perfect peace, and suffer no other plague than the government they are under."[4] From the usurper Cosmo down to the imbecile Gaston, we look in vain for any of those unmixed qualities which should raise a patriot to the command of his fellow-citizens. The Grand Dukes, and particularly the third Cosmo, had operated so entire a change in the Tuscan character, that the candid Florentines, in excuse for some imperfections in the philanthropic system of Leopold, are obliged to confess that the sovereign was the only liberal man in his dominions. Yet that excellent prince himself had no other notion of a national assembly, than of a body to represent the wants and wishes, not the will, of the people.

XXIII. BATTLE OF THRASIMENE.

"An earthquake reeled unheededly away."

Stanza lxiii. line 5.

"And such was their mutual animosity, so intent were they upon the battle, that the earthquake, which overthrew in great part many of the cities of Italy, which turned the course of rapid streams, poured back the sea upon the rivers, and tore down the very mountains, was not felt by one of the combatants."[5] Such is the description of Livy. It may be doubted

[4] On Government, chap. ii. sect. xxvi. p. 208, edit. 1751. Sidney is together with Locke and Hoadley, one of Mr. Hume's "despicable" writers.
[5] "Tantusque fuit ardor armorum, adeo intentus pugnæ animus, ut sum terræ motum qui multarum urbium Italiæ magnas partes prostravit, avertitque cursu rapidos amnes, mare fluminibus invexit, mor-

whether modern tactics would admit of such an abstraction.

The site of the battle of Thrasimene is not to be mistaken. The traveller from the village under Cortona to Casa di Piano, the next stage on the way to Rome, has for the first two or three miles, around him, but more particularly to the right, that flat land which Hannibal laid waste in order to induce the Consul Flaminius to move from Arezzo. On his left, and in front of him, is a ridge of hills bending down towards the lake of Thrasimene, called by Livy "montes Cortonenses," and now named the Gualandra. These hills he approaches at Ossaja, a village which the itineraries pretend to have been so denominated from the bones found there: but there have been no bones found there, and the battle was fought on the other side of the hill. From Ossaja the road begins to rise a little, but does not pass into the roots of the mountains until the sixty-seventh milestone from Florence. The ascent thence is not steep but perpetual, and continues for twenty minutes. The lake is soon seen below on the right, with Borghetto, a round tower, close upon the water; and the undulating hills partially covered with wood, amongst which the road winds, sink by degrees into the marshes near to this tower. Lower than the road, down to the right amidst these woody hillocks, Hannibal placed his horse,[1] in the jaws of, or rather above, the pass, which was between the lake and the present road, and most probably close to Borghetto, just under the lowest of the "tumuli."[2] On a summit to the left, above the road, is an old circular ruin, which the peasants call "the Tower of Hannibal the Carthaginian." Arrived at the highest point of the road, the traveller has a partial view of the fatal plain, which opens fully upon him as he descends the Gualandra. He soon finds himself in a vale inclosed to the left, and in front, and behind him by the Gualandra hills, bending round in a segment larger than a semicircle, and running down at each end to the lake, which obliques to the right and forms the chord of this mountain arc. The position cannot be guessed at from the plains of Cortona, nor appears to be so completely inclosed unless to one who is fairly within the hills. It then, indeed, appears "a place made as it were on purpose for a snare," *locus insidiis natus.* "Borghetto is then found to stand in a narrow marshy pass close to the hill, and to the lake, whilst there is no other outlet at the opposite turn of the mountains than through the little town of Passignano, which is pushed into the water by the foot of a high rocky acclivity."[3] There is a woody eminence branching down from the mountains into the upper end of the plain nearer to the side of Passignano, and on this stands a white village called Torre. Polybius seems to allude to this eminence as the one on which Hannibal encamped, and drew out his heavy-armed Africans and Spaniards in a conspicuous position.[4] From this spot he despatched his

Balearic and light-armed troops round through the Gualandra heights to the right, so as to arrive unseen and form an ambush amongst the broken acclivities which the road now passes, and to be ready to act upon the left flank and above the enemy, whilst the horse shut up the rear behind. Flaminius came to the lake near Borghetto at sunset; and, without sending any spies before him, marched through the pass the next morning before the day had quite broken, so that he perceived nothing of the horse and light troops above and about him, and saw only the heavy-armed Carthaginians in front on the hill of Torre.[5] The consul began to draw out his army in the flat, and in the mean time the horse in ambush occupied the pass behind him at Borghetto. Thus the Romans were completely inclosed, having the lake on the right, the main army on the hill of Torre in front, the Gualandra hills filled with the light-armed on their left flank, and being prevented from receding by the cavalry, who, the further they advanced, stopped up all the outlets in the rear. A fog rising from the lake now spread itself over the army of the consul, but the high lands were in the sunshine, and all the different corps in ambush looked towards the hill of Torre for the order of attack. Hannibal gave the signal, and moved down from his post on the height. At the same moment all his troops on the eminences behind and in the flank of Flaminius rushed forwards as it were with one accord into the plain. The Romans, who were forming their array in the mist, suddenly heard the shouts of the enemy amongst them, on every side, and before they could fall into their ranks, or draw their swords, or see by whom they were attacked, felt at once that they were surrounded and lost.

There are two little rivulets which run from the Gualandra into the lake. The traveller crosses the first of these at about a mile after he comes into the plain, and this divides the Tuscan from the Papal territories. The second, about a quarter of a mile further on, is called "the bloody rivulet;" and the peasants point out an open spot to the left between the "Sanguinetto," and the hills, which, they say, was the principal scene of slaughter. The other part of the plain is covered with thick-set olive-trees in corn grounds, and is nowhere quite level, except near the edge of the lake. It is, indeed, most probable that the battle was fought near this end of the valley, for the six thousand Romans, who, at the beginning of the action, broke through the enemy, escaped to the summit of an eminence which must have been in this quarter, otherwise they would have had to traverse the whole plain, and to pierce through the main army of Hannibal.

The Romans fought desperately for three hours; but the death of Flaminius was the signal for a general dispersion. The Carthaginian horse then burst in upon the fugitives, and the lake, the marsh about Borghetto, but chiefly the plain of the Sanguinetto and the passes of the Gualandra, were strewed with dead. Near some old walls on a bleak ridge to the

---

tes lapsu ingenti proruit, nemo pugnantium senserit." Tit. Liv. lib. xxii. cap. v.

[1] "Equites ad ipsas fauces saltus tumulis apte tegentibus locat." T. Livii, lib. xxii. cap. iv.

[2] "Ubi maxime montes Cortonenses Thrasimenus subit." T. Livii, lib. xxii. cap. iv.

[3] "Inde colles assurgunt." Ibid.

[4] Τὸν μὲν κατὰ πρόσωπον τῆς πορείας λόφον αὐτὸς κατελάβετο καὶ τοὺς Λίβυας καὶ τοὺς Ἴβηρας

ἔχων ἐπ᾽ αὐτοῦ κατεστρατοπέδευσε. Hist. lib. iii. cap. 83. The account in Polybius is not so easily reconcilable with present appearances as that in Livy: he talks of hills to the right and left of the pass and valley; but when Flaminius entered he had the lake at the right of both.

[5] "A tergo et super caput decepere insidiæ." T Liv. etc.

left above the rivulet many human bones have been repeatedly found, and this has confirmed the pretensions and the name of the " stream of blood."

Every district of Italy has its hero. In the north some painter is the usual genius of the place, and the foreign Julio Romano more than divides Mantua with her native Virgil.[1] To the south we hear of Roman names. Near Thrasimene tradition is still • faithful to the fame of an enemy, and Hannibal the Carthaginian is the only ancient name remembered on the banks of the Perugian lake. Flaminius is unknown; but the postilions on that road have been taught to show the very spot where *Il Console Romano* was slain. Of all who fought and fell in the battle of Thrasimene, the historian himself has, besides the generals and Maharbal, preserved indeed only a single name. You overtake the Carthaginian again on the same road to Rome. The antiquary, that is, the hostler of the posthouse at Spoleto, tells you that his town repulsed the victorious enemy, and shows you the gate still called *Porta di Annibale.* It is hardly worth while to remark that a French travel writer, well known by the name of the President Dupaty, saw Thrasimene in the lake of Bolsena, which lay conveniently on his way from Sienna to Rome.

XXIV. STATUE OF POMPEY.

" And thou, dread statue ! still existent in
The austerest form of naked majesty."
Stanza lxxxvii. lines 1 and 2.

The projected division of the Spada Pompey has already been recorded by the historian of the Decline and Fall of the Roman Empire. Mr. Gibbon found it in the memorials of Flaminius Vacca; and it may be added to his mention of it, that Pope Julius III. gave the contending owners five hundred crowns for the statue, and presented it to Cardinal Capo di Ferro, who had prevented the judgment of Solomon from being executed upon the image. In a more civilized age this statue was exposed to an actual operation; for the French, who acted the Brutus of Voltaire in the Coliseum, resolved that their Cæsar should fall at the base of that Pompey, which was supposed to have been sprinkled with the blood of the original dictator. The nine-foot hero was therefore removed to the arena of the amphitheatre, and, to facilitate its transport, suffered the temporary amputation of its right arm. The republican tragedians had to plead that the arm was a restoration: but their accusers do not believe that the integrity of the statue would have protected it. The love of finding every coincidence has discovered the true Cæsarean ichor in a stain near the right knee; but colder criticism has rejected not only the blood, but the portrait, and assigned the globe of power rather to the first of the emperors than to the last of the republican masters of Rome. Winkelmann[2] is loth

[1] About the middle of the twelfth century the coins of Mantua bore on one side the image and figure of Virgil. Zecca d' Italia, pl. xvii. i. 6. Voyage dans le Milanais, etc. par A. Z. Millin, tom. ii. p. 294, Paris, 1817.
[2] Storia delle Arti, etc. lib. ix. cap. i. p. 321, 322, tom. ii.

to allow an heroic statue of a Roman citizen, but the Grimani Agrippa, a contemporary almost, is heroic; and naked Roman figures were only very rare, not absolutely forbidden. The face accords much better with the " hominem integrum et castum et gravem,"[3] than with any of the busts of Augustus, and is too stern for him who was beautiful, says Suetonius, at all periods of his life. The pretended likeness to Alexander the Great cannot be discerned, but the traits resemble the medal of Pompey.[4] The objectionable globe may not have been an ill applied flattery to him who found Asia Minor the boundary, and left it the centre of the Roman empire. It seems that Winkelmann has made a mistake in thinking that no proof of the identity of this statue with that which received the bloody sacrifice can be derived from the spot where it was discovered.[5] Flaminius Vacca says *sotto una cantina*, and this cantina is known to have been in the Vicolo de' Leutari, near the Cancellaria; a position corresponding exactly to that of the Janus before the basilica of Pompey's theatre, to which Augustus transferred the statue after the *curia* was either burnt or taken down.[6] Part of the Pompeian shade,[7] the portico, existed in the beginning of the XVth century, and the *atrium* was still called *Satrum.* So says Blondus.[8] At all events, so imposing is the stern majesty of the statue, and so memorable is the story, that the play of the imagination leaves no room for the exercise of the judgment, and the fiction, if a fiction it is, operates on the spectator with an effect not less powerful than truth.

XXV. THE BRONZE WOLF.

" And thou, the thunder-stricken nurse of
Rome !"
Stanza lxxxviii. line 1.

Ancient Rome, like modern Sienna, abounded most probably with images of the foster-mother of her founder; but there were two she-wolves of whom history makes particular mention. One of these, *of brass in ancient work*, was seen by Dionysius[9] at the temple of Romulus, under the Palatine, and is universally believed to be that mentioned by the Latin historian, as having been made from the money collected by a fine on usurers, and as standing under the Ruminal fig-tree.[10] The other was that which Cicero[11] has celebrated both in prose

[3] Cicer. Epist. ad Atticum, xi. 6.
[4] Published by Causeus, in his Museum Romanum.
[5] Storia delle Arti, etc. lib. ix. cap. i. p. 321; 322, tom. ii.
[6] Sueton. in vit. August. cap. 31, and in vit. C. J. Cæsar. cap. 88. Appian says it was burnt down. See a note of Pitiscus to Suetonius, p. 324.
[7] " Tu modo Pompeia lentus spatiare sub umbra."
Ovid. Art. Am. 267.
[8] Roma Instaurata, lib. ii. fo. 31.
[9] Χάλκεα ποιήματα παλαιᾶς ἐργασίας. Antiq. Rom. lib. 1, c. 79.
[10] " Ad ficum Ruminalem simulacra infantium conditorum urbis sub uberibus lupæ posuerunt." Liv. Hist. lib. x. cap. xxiii. This was in the yea U.C. 455 or 457.
[11] " Tum statua Nattæ, tum simulacra Deorum,

and verse, and which the historian Dion also records as having suffered the same accident as is alluded to by the orator.[1] The question agitated by the antiquaries is, whether the wolf now in the Conservators' Palace is that of Livy and Dionysius, or that of Cicero, or whether it is neither one nor the other. The earlier writers differ as much as the moderns: Lucius Faunus[2] says, that it is the one alluded to by both, which is impossible, and also by Virgil, which may be. Fulvius Ursinus[3] calls it the wolf of Dionysius, and Marlianus[4] talks of it as the one mentioned by Cicero. To him Rycquius *tremblingly* assents.[5] Nardini is inclined to sup-

pose it may be one of the many wolves preserved in ancient Rome; but of the two rather bends to the Ciceronian statue.[6] Montfaucon[7] mentions it as a point without doubt. Of the latter writers the decisive Winkelmann[8] proclaims it as having been found at the church of Saint Theodore, where, or near where, was the temple of Romulus, and consequently makes it the wolf of Dionysius. His authority is Lucius Faunus, who, however, only says that it *was placed*, not *found*, at the Ficus Ruminalis, by the Comitium, by which he does not seem to allude to the church of Saint Theodore. Rycquius was the first to make the mistake, and Winkelmann followed Rycquius.

Flaminius Vacca tells quite a different story, and says he had heard the wolf with the twins was found[9] near the arch of Septimius Severus. The commentator on Winkelmann is of the same opinion with that learned person, and is incensed at Nardini for not having remarked that Cicero, in speaking of the wolf struck with lightning in the Capitol, makes use of the past tense. But, with the Abate's leave, Nardini does not positively assert the statue to be that mentioned by Cicero, and, if he had, the assumption would not perhaps have been so exceedingly indiscreet. The Abate himself is obliged to own that there are marks very like the scathing of lightning in the hinder legs of the present wolf; and, to get rid of this, adds, that the wolf seen by Dionysius might have been also struck by lightning, or otherwise injured.

Let us examine the subject by a reference to the words of Cicero. The orator in two places seems to particularize the Romulus and the Remus, especially the first, which his audience remembered to *have been* in the Capitol, as being struck with lightning. In his verses he records that the twins and wolf both fell, and that the latter left behind the marks of her feet. Cicero does not say that the wolf was consumed: and Dion only mentions that it fell down, without alluding, as the Abate has made him, to the force of the blow, or the firmness with which it had been fixed. The whole strength, therefore, of the Abate's argument hangs upon the past tense; which, however, may be somewhat diminished by remarking that the phrase only shows that the statue was not then standing in its former position. Winkelmann has observed, that the present twins are modern; and it is equally clear that there are marks of gilding on the wolf,

Romulus'que et Remus cum altrice bellua vi fulminis icti conciderunt." De Divinat. ii. 20.
" Tactus est ille etiam qui hanc urbem condidit Romulus, quem inauratum in Capitolio parvum atque lectentem, uberibus lupinis inhiantem fuisse meministis." In Catilin. iii. 8.

" Hic silvestris erat Romani nominis altrix
Martia, quæ parvos Mavortis semine natos
Uberibus gravidis vitali rore rigabat;
Quæ tum cum pueris flammato fulminis ictu
Concidit, atque avulsa pedum vestigia liquit."
De Consulatu, lib. ii. (lib. i. de Divinat. cap. xii.)

[1] 'Εν' γὰρ τῷ καπητολιῷ·ἀνδριάντες τε πολλοὶ ὑπὸ κεραυνῶν συνεχωνεύθησαν, καὶ ἀγάλματα ἄλλα τε, καὶ Διὸς ἐπὶ κίονος ἱδρυμένον, εἰκὼν τέ τις λυκαίνης σύν τε τῷ Ῥώμῳ καὶ σὺν τῷ Ῥωμύλῳ ἱδρυμένη ἔπεση. Dion. Hist. lib. xxxvii. p. 37, edit. Rob. Steph. 1548. He goes on to mention that the letters of the columns on which the laws were written were liquefied and become ἀμυδρά. All that the Romans did was to erect a large statue to Jupiter, looking towards the east: no mention is afterwards made of the wolf. This happened in A.U.C. 689. The Abate Fea, in noticing this passage of Dion (Storia delle Arti, etc. tom. i. p. 202, note x.), says, *Nonostante, aggiunge Dione, che fosse ben fermata* (the wolf) ; by which it is clear the Abate translated the Xylandro-Leunclavian version, which puts *quamvis stabilita* for the original ἱδρυμένη, a word that does not mean *ben fermata*, but only *raised*, as may be distinctly seen from another passage of the same Dion: Ἠβουλήθη μὲν οὖν ὁ Ἀγρίππας καὶ τὸν Αὔγουστον ἐνταῦθα ἱδρῦσαι. Hist. lib. lvi. Dion says that Agrippa " wished to *raise a statue* of Augustus in the Pantheon."

[2] " In eadem porticu ænea lupa, cujus uberibus Romulus ac Remus lactentes inhiant, conspicitur: de hac Cicero et Virgilius semper intellexere. Livius hoc signum ab Ædilibus ex pecuniis quibus mulctati essent fœneratores, positum innuit. Antea in Comitiis ad Ficum Ruminalem, quo loco pueri fuerant expositi locatum pro certo est." Luc. Fauni de Antiq. Urb. Rom. lib. ii. cap. vii. ap. Sallengre, tom. i. p. 217. In his xviith chapter he repeats that the statues were there, but not that they were *found* there.

[3] Ap. Nardini, Roma Vetus, lib. v. cap. iv.
[4] Marliani Urb. Rom. Topograph. lib. ii. cap. ix. He mentions another wolf and twins in the Vatican, lib. v. cap. xxi.
[5] " Non desunt qui hanc ipsam esse putent, quam adpinximus, quæ e con.itio in Basilicam Lateranam, cum nonnullis aliis antiquitatum reliquiis, atque hinc in Capitolium postea relata sit, quamvis Mar-

lianus antiquam Capitolinam esse maluit à Tullio descriptam, cui ut in re nimis dubia, trepidè adsentimur." Just. Rycquii de Capit. Roman. Comm. cap. xxiv. p. 250, edit. Lugd. Bat. 1696.
[6] Nardini, Roma Vetus, lib. v. cap. iv.
[7] " Lupa hodieque in capitolinis prostat ædibus, cum vestigio fulminis quo ictam narrat Cicero." Diarium Italic. tom. i. p. 174.
[8] Storia delle Arti, etc. lib. iii. cap. iii. § ii. note 10. Winkelmann has made a strange blunder in a note, by saying the Ciceronian wolf was *not* in the Capitol, and that Dion was wrong in saying so.
[9] " Intesi dire, che l' Ercolo di bronzo, che oggi si trova nella sala di Campidoglio, fu trovato nel foro Romano appresso l' arco di Settimio : e vi fu trovata anche la lupa di bronzo che allata Romolo e Remo, e stà nella Loggia de Conservatori." Flam. Vacca, Memorie, num. iii. p. i. ap. Montfaucon, Diar. Ital. tom. i.

which might therefore be supposed to make part of the ancient group. It is known that the sacred images of the Capitol were not destroyed when injured by time or accident, but were put into certain under-ground depositaries, called *favissæ*.[1] It may be thought possible that the wolf had been so deposited, and had been replaced in some conspicuous situation when the Capitol was rebuilt by Vespasian. Rycquius, without mentioning his authority, tells that it was transferred from the Comitium to the Lateran, and thence brought to the Capitol. If it was found near the arch of Severus, it may have been one of the images which Orosius[2] says was thrown down in the Forum by lightning when Alaric took the city. That it is of very high antiquity the workmanship is a decisive proof: and that circumstance induced Winkelmann to believe it the wolf of Dionysius. The Capitoline wolf, however, may have been of the same early date as that at the temple of Romulus. Lactantius[3] asserts that in his time the Romans worshipped a wolf; and it is known that the Lupercalia held out to a very late period[4] after every other observance of the ancient superstition had totally expired. This may account for the preservation of the ancient image longer than the other early symbols of Paganism.

It may be permitted, however, to remark, that the wolf was a Roman symbol, but that the worship of that symbol is an inference drawn by the zeal of Lactantius. The early Christian writers are not to be trusted in the charges which they make against the Pagans. Eusebius accused the Romans to their faces of worshipping Simon Magus, and raising a statue to him in the island of the Tyber. The Romans had probably never heard of such a person before who came, however, to play a considerable, though scandalous part in the church history, and has left several tokens of his aerial combat with St. Peter at Rome; notwithstanding that an inscription found in this very island of the Tyber showed the Simon Magus of Eusebius to be a certain indigenal god called Semo Sangus or Fidius.[5]

Even when the worship of the founder of Rome had been abandoned, it was thought expedient to humor the habits of the good matrons of the city,

by sending them with their sick infants to the church of Saint Theodore, as they had before carried them to the temple of Romulus.[6] The practice is continued to this day, and the site of the above church seems to be thereby identified with that of the temple : so that if the wolf had been really found there, as Winkelmann says, there would be no doubt of the present statue being that seen by Dionysius.[7] But Faunus, in saying that it was at the Ficus Ruminalis by the Comitium, is only talking of its ancient position as recorded by Pliny; and even if he had been remarking where it was found, would not have alluded to the church of Saint Theodore, but to a very different place, near which it was then thought the Ficus Ruminalis had been, and also the Comitium; that is, the three columns by the church of Santa Maria Liberatrice, at the corner of the Palatine looking on the Forum.

It is, in fact, a mere conjecture where the image was actually dug up:[8] and perhaps, on the whole, the marks of the gilding, and of the lightning, are a better argument in favor of its being the Ciceronian wolf, than any that can be adduced for the contrary opinion. At any rate, it is reasonably selected in the text of the poem as one of the most interesting relics of the ancient city,[9] and is certainly the figure, if not the very animal to which Virgil alludes in his beautiful verses: —

" Geminos huic ubera circum
Ludere pendentes pueros, et lambere matrem
Impavidos: illam tereti cervice reflexam
Mulcere alternos, et corpora fingere linguâ." [10]

---

[1] Luc. Faun. ibid.

[2] See note to stanza LXXX. in "Historical Illustrations."

[3] "Romuli nutrix Lupa honoribus est affecta divinis, et ferrem, si animal ipsum fuisset, cujus figuram gerit." Lactant. de Falsa Religione, lib. i. cap. xx. p. 101, edit. varior 1660; that is to say, he would rather adore a wolf than a prostitute. His commentator has observed that the opinion of Livy concerning Laurentia being figured in this wolf was not universal. Strabo thought so. Rycquius is wrong in saying that Lactantius mentions the wolf was in the Capitol.

[4] To A.D. 496, "Quis credere possit," says Baronius [Ann. Eccles. tom. viii. p. 602, in an. 496], " viguisse adhuc Romæ ad Gelasii tempora, quæ fuere ante exordia urbis allata in Italiam Lupercalia?" Gelasius wrote a letter which occupies four folio pages to Andromachus the senator, and others, to show that the rites should be given up.

[5] Eusebius has these words: καὶ ἀνδριάντι παρ' ὑμῖν ὡς θεὸς τετίμηται, ἐν τῷ Τιβερι ποταμῷ μεταξὺ τῶν δύο γεφυρῶν, ἔχων ἐπιγραφὴν Ῥωμαϊκὴν

ταύτην Σίμωνι δέω Σάγκτω. Eccles. Hist. lib. ii. cap. xiii. p. 40. Justin Martyr had told the story before: but Baronius himself was obliged to detect this fable. See Nardini, Roma Vet. lib. vii. cap. xii.

[6] "In esse gli antichi pontefici per toglier la memoria de' giuochi Lupercali istituiti in onore di Romolo, introdussero l' uso di portarvi bambini oppressi de infermità occulte, acciò si liberino per l' intercessione di questo santo, come di continuo si sperimenta." Rione xii. Ripa, accurata e succincta Descrizione, etc. di Roma Moderna, dell' Ab. Ridolf. Venuti, 1766.

[7] Nardini, lib. v. cap. 11, convicts Pomponius Lætus *crassi erroris*, in putting the Ruminal fig-tree at the church of Saint Theodore: but as Livy says the wolf was at the Ficus Ruminalis, and Dionysius at the temple of Romulus, he is obliged (cap. iv.) to own that the two were close together, as well as the Lupercal cave, shaded, as it were, by the fig-tree.

[8] "Ad comitium ficus olim Ruminalis germinabat, sub qua lupæ rumam, hoc est, mammam, docente Varrone, suxerant olim Romulus et Remus; non procul a templo hodie D. Mariæ Liberatricis appellato, ubi *forsan* inventa nobilis illa ænea statua lupæ geminos puerulos lactantis, quam hodie in Capitolio videmus." Olai Borrichii Antiqua Urbis Romanæ Facies, cap. x. See also cap. xii. Borrichius wrote after Nardini, in 1687. Ap. Græv. Antiq. Rom. tom. iv. p. 1522.

[9] Donatus, lib. xi. cap. 18, gives a medal representing on one side the wolf in the same position as that in the Capitol; and on the reverse the wolf with the head not reverted. It is of the time of Antoninus Pius.

[10] Æn. viii. 631. See Dr. Middleton, in his Letter from Rome, who inclines to the Ciceronian wolf, but without examining the subject.

XXVI. JULIUS CÆSAR.

" For the Roman's mind
Was modelled in a less terrestrial mould."

Stanza xc. lines 3 and 4.

It is possible to be a very great man and to be still very inferior to Julius Cæsar, the most complete character, so Lord Bacon thought, of all antiquity. Nature seems incapable of such extraordinary combinations as composed his versatile capacity, which was the wonder even of the Romans themselves. The first general — the only triumphant politician — inferior to none in eloquence — comparable to any in the attainments of wisdom, in an age made up of the greatest commanders, statesmen, orators, and philosophers that ever appeared in the world — an author who composed a perfect specimen of military annals in his travelling carriage — at one time in a controversy with Cato, at another writing a treatise on punning, and collecting a set of good sayings — fighting [1] and making love at the same moment, and willing to abandon both his empire and his mistress for a sight of the Fountains of the Nile. Such did Julius Cæsar appear to his contemporaries and to those of the subsequent ages who were the most inclined to deplore and execrate his fatal genius.

But we must not be so much dazzled with his surpassing glory, or with his magnanimous, his amiable qualities, as to forget the decision of his impartial countrymen: —

HE WAS JUSTLY SLAIN. [2]

XXVII. EGERIA.

" Egeria! sweet creation of some heart
Which found no mortal resting-place so fair
As thine ideal breast."

Stanza cxv. lines 1, 2, and 3.

The respectable authority of Flaminius Vacca would incline us to believe in the claims of the Egerian grotto. [3] He assures us that he saw an inscription in the pavement, stating that the fountain was that of Egeria, dedicated to the nymphs. The inscription is not there at this day; but Montfaucon quotes two lines [4] of Ovid from a stone in the Villa Giustiniani, which he seems to think had been brought from the same grotto.

This grotto and valley were formerly frequented in summer, and particularly the first Sunday in May, by the modern Romans, who attached a salubrious quality to the fountain which trickles from an orifice at the bottom of the vault, and, overflowing the little pools, creeps down the matted grass into the brook below. The brook is the Ovidian Almo, whose name and qualities are lost in the modern Aquataccio. The valley itself is called Valle di Caffarelli, from the dukes of that name who made over their fountain to the Pallavicini, with sixty *rubbia* of adjoining land.

There can be little doubt that this long dell is the Egerian valley of Juvenal, and the pausing place of Umbritius, notwithstanding the generality of his commentators have supposed the descent of the satirist and his friend to have been into the Arician grove, where the nymph met Hippolitus, and where she was more peculiarly worshipped.

The step from the Porta Capena to the Alban hill, fifteen miles distant, would be too considerable, unless we were to believe in the wild conjecture of Vossius, who makes that gate travel from its present station, where he pretends it was during the reign of the Kings, as far as the Arician grove, and then makes it recede to its old site with the shrinking city. [5] The tufo, or pumice, which the poet prefers to marble, is the substance composing the bank in which the grotto is sunk.

The modern topographers [6] find in the grotto the statue of the nymph, and nine niches for the Muses;

---

[1] In his tenth book, Lucan shows him sprinkled with the blood of Pharsalia in the arms of Cleopatra.

" Sanguine Thessalicæ cladis perfusus adulter
 Admisit Venerem curis, et miscuit armis."

After feasting with his mistress, he sits up all night to converse with the Egyptian sages, and tells Achoreus,

" Spes sit mihi certa videndi
 Niliacos fontes, bellum civile relinquam."
" Sic velut in tuta securi pace trahebant
 Noctis iter mediæ."

Immediately afterwards, he is fighting again, and defending every position.

" Sed adest defensor ubique
 Cæsar et hos aditu gladiis, hos ignibus arcet.
 . . . . cæca nocte carinis
 Insiluit Cæsar, semper feliciter usus
 Præcipiti cursu bellorum et tempore rapto."

[2] " Jure cæsus existimetur," says Suetonius, after a fair estimation of his character, and making use of a phrase which was a formula in Livy's time. " Mælium jure cæsum pronuntiavit, etiam si regni crimine insons fuerit:" [lib. iv. cap. 15,] and which was continued in the legal judgments pronounced in justifiable homicides, such as killing housebreakers. See Sueton. in Vit. C. J. Cæsar, with the commentary of Pitiscus, p. 184.

[3] " Poco lontano dal detto luogo si scende ad un casaletto, del quale ne sono padroni li Caffarelli, che con questo nome è chiamato il luogo; vi è una fontana sotto una gran volta antica, che al presente si gode, e i Romani vi vanno l'estate a ricrearsi; nel pavimento di essa fonte si egge in un epitaffio essere quella la fonte di Egeria, dedicata alle ninfe, e questa, dice l'epitaffio, essere la medesima fonte in cui fu convertita." Memorie, etc. ap. Nardini, p. 13. He does not give the inscription.

[4] " In villa Justiniana extat ingens lapis quadratus solidus, in quo sculpta hæc duo Ovidii carmina sunt: —

' Ægeria est quæ præbet aquas, dea grata Camœnis;
 Illa Numæ conjunx consiliumque fuit.'

Qui lapis videtur ex eodem Egeriæ fonte, aut ejus vicinia, isthuc comportatus." Diarium Italic. p. 153.

[5] De Magnit. Vet. Rom. ap. Græv. Ant. Rom. tom. iv. p. 1507.

[6] Echinard, Descrizione di Roma e dell' Agro Romano, corretto dall' Abate Venuti, in Roma, 1750. They believe in the grotto and nymph. " Simulacro di questo fonte, essendovi sculpite le acque a pie di esso."

and a late traveller[1] has discovered that the cave is restored to that simplicity which the poet regretted had been exchanged for injudicious ornament. But the headless statue is palpably rather a male than a nymph, and has none of the attributes ascribed to it at present visible. The nine Muses could hardly have stood in six niches; and Juvenal certainly does not allude to any individual cave.[2] Nothing can be collected from the satirist but that somewhere near the Porta Capena was a spot in which it was supposed Numa held nightly consultations with his nymph, and where there was a grove and a sacred fountain, and fanes once consecrated to the Muses; and that from this spot there was a descent into the valley of Egeria, where were several artificial caves. It is clear that the statues of the Muses made no part of the decoration which the satirist thought misplaced in these caves; for he expressly assigns other fanes (delubra) to these divinities above the valley, and moreover tells us that they had been ejected to make room for the Jews. In fact, the little temple, now called that of Bacchus, was formerly thought to belong to the Muses, and Nardini[3] places them in a poplar grove, which was in his time above the valley.

It is probable, from the inscription and position, that the cave now shown may be one of the "artificial caverns," of which, indeed, there is another a little way higher up the valley, under a tuft of alder bushes: but a *single* grotto of Egeria is a mere modern invention, grafted upon the application of the epithet Egerian to these nymphea in general, and which might send us to look for the haunts of Numa upon the banks of the Thames.

Our English Juvenal was not seduced into mistranslation by his acquaintance with Pope: he carefully preserves the correct plural —

"Thence slowly winding down the vale, we view
    The Egerian *grots :* oh, how unlike the true!"

The valley abounds with springs,[4] and over these springs, which the Muses might haunt from their neighboring groves, Egeria presided: hence she was said to supply them with water; and she was the nymph of the grottos through which the fountains were taught to flow.

The whole of the monuments in the vicinity of the Egerian valley have received names at will, which have been changed at will. Venuti[5] owns he can see no traces of the temples of Jove, Saturn,

Juno, Venus, and Diana, which Nardini found, or hoped to find. The mutatorium of Caracalla's circus, the temple of Honor and Virtue, the temple of Bacchus, and, above all, the temple of the god Rediculus, are the antiquaries' despair.

The circus of Caracalla depends on a medal of that Emperor cited by Fulvius Ursinus, of which the reverse shows a circus, supposed, however, by some to represent the Circus Maximus. It gives a very good idea of that place of exercise. The soil has been but little raised, if we may judge from the small cellular structure at the end of the Spina, which was probably the chapel of the god Consus. This cell is half beneath the soil, as it must have been in the circus itself; for Dionysius[6] could not be persuaded to believe that this divinity was the Roman Neptune, because his altar was under ground.

XXVIII. THE ROMAN NEMESIS.

" Great Nemesis!
Here, where the ancient paid thee homage long.'
                Stanza cxxxii. lines 2 and 3.

We read in Suetonius, that Augustus, from a warning received in a dream,[7] counterfeited, once a year, the beggar, sitting before the gate of his palace with his hand hollowed and stretched out for charity. A statue formerly in the Villa Borghese, and which should be now at Paris, represents the Emperor in that posture of supplication. The object of this self-degradation was the appeasement of Nemesis, the perpetual attendant on good fortune, of whose power the Roman conquerors were also reminded by certain symbols attached to their cars of triumph. The symbols were the whip and the *crotalo*, which were discovered in the Nemesis of the Vatican. The attitude of beggary made the above statue pass for that of Belisarius: and until the criticism of Winkelmann[8] had rectified the mistake, one fiction was called in to support another. It was the same fear of the sudden termination of prosperity that made Amasis king of Egypt warn his friend Polycrates of Samos, that the gods loved those whose lives were chequered with good and evil fortunes. Nemesis was supposed to lie in wait particularly for the prudent; that is, for those whose caution rendered them accessible to mere accidents: and her fatal altar was raised on the banks of the Phyrgian Æsepus by Adrastus, probably the prince of that name who killed the son of Crœsus by mistake. Hence the goddess was called Adrastea.[9]

---

[1] Classical Tour, chap. vi. p. 217, vol. ii.

[2] "Substitit ad veteres arcus, madidamque Capenam;

    Hic ubi nocturnæ Numa constituebat amicæ,
    Nunc sacri fontis nemus, et delubra locantur
    Judæis, quorum cophinus fœnumque supellex.
    Omnis enim populo mercedem pendere jussa
    .est
    Arbor, et ejectis mendicat silva Camœnis.
    In vallem Egeriæ descendimus, et speluncas
    Dissimiles veris: quanto præstantius esset
    Numen aquæ, viridi si margine clauderet
    undas
    Herba, nec ingenuum violarent marmora
    tophum." — Sat. III.

[3] Lib. iii. cap. iii.

[4] "Undique e solo aquæ scaturiunt." Nardini, lib. iii. cap. iii.

[5] Echinard, etc. Cic. cit. pp. 297, 298.

[6] Antiq. Rom. lib. ii. cap. xxxi.

[7] Sueton. in Vit. Augusti, cap. 91, Casaubon, in the note, refers to Plutarch's lives of Camillus and Æmilius Paulus, and also to his apophthegms, for the character of this deity. The hollowed hand was reckoned the last degree of degradation; and when the dead body of the præfect Rufinus was borne about in triumph by the people, the indignity was increased by putting his hand in that position.

[8] Storia delle Arti, etc. lib. xii. III. tom. ii. p. 422 Visconti calls the statue, however, a Cybele. It is given in the Museo Pio-Clement. tom. i, par. 40. The Abate Fea (Spiegazione dei Rami. Storia etc. tom. iii. p. 513,) calls it a Chrisippus.

[9] Dict. de Bayle, article Adrastea.

The Roman Nemesis was *sacred* and *august:* there was a temple to her in the Palatine under the name of Rhamnusia:[1] so great, indeed, was the propensity of the ancients to trust to the revolution of events, and to believe in the divinity of Fortune, that in the same Palatine there was a temple to the Fortune of the day.[2] This is the last superstition which retains its hold over the human heart; and, from concentrating in one object the credulity so natural to man, has always appeared strongest in those unembarrassed by other articles of belief. The antiquaries have supposed this goddess to be synonymous with Fortune and with Fate: but it was in her vindictive quality that she was worshipped under the name of Nemesis.

XXIX. GLADIATORS.

" He, their sire,
Butchered to make a Roman holiday."

Stanza cxli. lines 6 and 7.

Gladiators were of two kinds, compelled and voluntary; and were supplied from several conditions; — from slaves sold for that purpose; from culprits; from barbarian captives either taken in war, and, after being led in triumph, set apart for the games, or those seized and condemned as rebels: also from free citizens, some fighting for hire (*auctorati*), others from a depraved ambition: at last even knights and senators were exhibited, — a disgrace of which the first tyrant was naturally the first inventor.[3] In the end, dwarfs, and even women, fought; an enormity prohibited by Severus. Of these the most to be pitied undoubtedly were the barbarian captives; and to this species a Christian writer[4] justly applies the epithet "innocent," to distinguish them from the professional gladiators. Aurelian and Claudius supplied great numbers of these unfortunate victims; the one after his triumph, and the other on the pretext of a rebellion.[5] No war, says Lipsius,[6]

[1] It is enumerated by the regionary Victor.
[2] Fortunæ hujusce diei. Cicero mentions her, de Legib. lib. ii.

DEAE NEMESI
SIVE FORTVNAE
PISTORIVS
RVGIANVS
V. C. LEGAT.
LEG. XIII. G.
CORD.

See Questiones Romanæ, etc. ap. Græv. Antiq. Roman. tom. v. p. 942. See also Muratori, Nov. Thesaur. Inscrip. Vet. tom. i. pp. 88, 89, where there are three Latin and one Greek inscription to Nemesis, and others to Fate.
[3] Julius Cæsar, who rose by the fall of the aristocracy, brought Furius Leptinus and A. Calenus upon the arena.
[4] Tertullian, "certe quidem et innocentes gladiatores in ludum veniunt, et voluptatis publicæ hostiæ.fiant." Just. Lips. Saturn. Sermon. lib. ii. cap. iii.
[5] Vopiscus, in vit. Aurel. and in vit. Claud. ibid.
[6] "Credo, immo scio, nullum bellum tantam cladem vastitiemque generi humano intulisse, quam

was ever so destructive to the human race as these sports. In spite of the laws of Constantine and Constans, gladiatorial shows survived the old established religion more than seventy years; but they owed their final extinction to the courage of a Christian. In the year 404, on the kalends of January, they were exhibiting the shows in the Flavian amphitheatre before the usual immense concourse of people. Almachius, or Telemachus, an eastern monk, who had travelled to Rome intent on his holy purpose, rushed into the midst of the area, and endeavored to separate the combatants. The prætor Alypius, a person incredibly attached to these games,[7] gave instant orders to the gladiators to slay him; and Telemachus gained the crown of martyrdom, and the title of saint, which surely has never either before or since been awarded for a more noble exploit. Honorius immediately abolished the shows, which were never afterwards revived. The story is told by Theodoret[8] and Cassiodorus,[9] and seems worthy of credit notwithstanding its place in the Roman martyrology.[10] Besides the torrents of blood which flowed at the funerals, in the amphitheatres, the circus, the forums, and other public places, gladiators were introduced at feasts, and tore each other to pieces amidst the supper tables, to the great delight and applause of the guests. Yet Lipsius permits himself to suppose the loss of courage, and the evident degeneracy of mankind, to be nearly connected with the abolition of these bloody spectacles.[11]

XXX.

Here, where the Roman millions' blame or
praise
Was death or life, the playthings of a crowd.

Stanza cxlii. lines 5 and 6.

When one gladiator wounded another, he shouted, "he has it," "hoc habet," or "habet." The wounded combatant dropped his weapon, and advancing to the edge of the arena, supplicated the spectators. If he had fought well, the people saved him; if otherwise, or as they happened to be inclined, they turned down their thumbs, and he

hos ad voluptatem ludos." Just. Lips. ibid. lib. i. cap. xii.
[7] Augustinus (lib. vi. Confess. cap. viii.). "Alypium suum gladiatorii spectaculi inhiatu incredibiliter abreptum," scribit. ib. lib. i. cap. xii.
[8] Hist. Eccles. cap. xxvi. lib. v.
[9] Cassiod. Tripartita, l. x. c. xi. Saturn. ib. ib.
[10] Baronius, ad ann. et in notis ad Martyrol. Rom. I. Jan. See—Marangoni, Delle memorie sacre e profane dell' Anfiteatro Flavio, p. 25, edit. 1746.
[11] "Quod? non tu, Lipsi, momentum aliquod habuisse censes ad virtutem? Magnum. Tempora nostra, nosque ipsos, videamus. Oppidum ecce unum alterumve captum, direptum est; tumultus circa nos, non in nobis; et tamen concidimus et turbamur. Ubi robur, ubi tot per annos meditata sapientiæ studia? ubi ille animus qui possit dicere, si *fractus illabatur orbis ?*" etc. ibid. lib. ii. cap. xxv. The prototype of Mr. Windham's panegyric on bull-baiting.

vas slain. They were occasionally so savage that they were impatient if a combat lasted longer than ordinary without wounds or death. The emperor's presence generally saved the vanquished; and it is recorded as an instance of Caracalla's ferocity, that he sent those who supplicated him for life, in a spectacle, at Nicomedia, to ask the people; in other words, handed them over to be slain. A similar ceremony is observed at the Spanish bull-fights. The magistrate presides; and after the horsemen and piccadores have fought the bull, the matadore steps forward and bows to him for permission to kill the animal. If the bull has done his duty by killing two or three horses, or a man, which last is rare, the people interfere with shouts, the ladies wave their handkerchiefs, and the animal is saved. The wounds and death of the horses are accompanied with the loudest acclamations, and many gestures of delight, especially from the female portion of the audience, including those of the gentlest blood. Every thing depends on habit. The author of Childe Harold, the writer of this note, and one or two other Englishmen, who have certainly in other days borne the sight of a pitched battle, were, during the summer of 1809, in the governor's box at the great amphitheatre of Santa Maria, opposite to Cadiz. The death of one or two horses completely satisfied their curiosity. A gentleman present, observing them shudder and look pale, noticed that unusual reception of so delightful a sport to some young ladies, who stared and smiled, and continued their applauses as another horse fell bleeding to the ground. One bull killed three horses *off his own horns.* He was saved by acclamations, which were redoubled when it was known he belonged to a priest.

An Englishman who can be much pleased with seeing two men beat themselves to pieces, cannot bear to look at a horse galloping round an arena with his bowels trailing on the ground, and turns from the spectacle and the spectators with horror and disgust.

XXXI. THE ALBAN HILL.

"And afar
The Tiber winds, and the broad ocean laves
The Latian coast," etc. etc.

Stanza clxxiv. lines 2, 3, and 4.

The whole declivity of the Alban hill is of unrivalled beauty, and from the convent on the highest point, which has succeeded to the temple of the Latian Jupiter, the prospect embraces all the objects alluded to in the cited stanza; the Mediterranean; the whole scene of the latter half of the Æneid, and the coast from beyond the mouth of the Tiber to the headland of Circæum and the Cape of Terracina.

The site of Cicero's villa may be supposed either at the Grotta Ferrata, or at the Tusculum of Prince Lucien Buonaparte.

The former was thought some years ago the actual site, as may be seen from Middleton's Life of Cicero. At present it has lost something of its credit, except for the Domenichinos. Nine monks of the Greek order live there, and the adjoining villa is a cardinal's summer-house. The other villa, called Rufinella, is on the summit of the hill above Frascati, and many rich remains of Tuscu-

lum have been found there, besides seventy-two statues of different merit and preservation, and seven busts.

From the same eminence are seen the Sabine hills, embosomed in which lies the long valley of Rustica. There are several circumstances which tend to establish the identity of this valley with the *"Ustica"* of Horace; and it seems possible that the mosaic pavement which the peasants uncover by throwing up the earth of a vineyard may belong to his villa. Rustica is pronounced short, not according to our stress upon — *"Usticæ cubantis."* — It is more rational to think that we are wrong, than that the inhabitants of this secluded valley have changed their tone in this word. The addition of the consonant prefixed is nothing: yet it is necessary to be aware that Rustica may be a modern name which the peasants may have caught from the antiquaries.

The villa, or the mosaic, is in a vineyard on a knoll covered with chestnut trees. A stream runs down the valley; and although it is not true, as said in the guide books, that this stream is called Licenza, yet there is a village on a rock at the head of the valley which is so denominated, and which may have taken its name from the Digentia. Licenza contains 700 inhabitants. On a peak a little way beyond is Civitella, containing 300. On the banks of the Anio, a little before you turn up into Valle Rustica, to the left, about an hour from the *villa,* is a town called Vicovaro, another favorably coincidence with the *Varia* of the poet. At the end of the valley, towards the Anio, there is a bare hill, crowned with a little town called Bardela. At the foot of this hill the rivulet of Licenza flows, and is almost absorbed in a wide sandy bed before it reaches the Anio. Nothing can be more fortunate for the lines of the poet, whether in a metaphorical or direct sense: —

"Me quotiens reficit gelidus Digentia rivus,
Quem Mandela bibit rugosus frigore pagus."

The stream is clear high up the valley, but before it reaches the hill of Bardela looks green and yellow like a sulphur rivulet.

Rocca Giovane, a ruined village in the hills, half an hour's walk from the vineyard where the pavement is shown, does seem to be the site of the fane of Vacuna, and an inscription found there tells that this temple of the Sabine Victory, was repaired by Vespasian.[1] With these helps, and a position corresponding exactly to every thing which the poet has told us of his retreat, we may feel tolerably secure of our site.

The hill which should be Lucretilis is called Campanile, and by following up the rivulet to the pretended Bandusia, you come to the roots of the higher mountain Gennaro. Singularly enough, the only spot of ploughed land in the whole valley is on the knoll where this Bandusia rises.

". . . . tu frigus amabile
Fessis vomere tauris
Præbes, et pecori vago."

---

[1] IMP. CÆSAR VESPASIANVS
PONTIFEX MAXIMVS. TRIB.
POTEST. CENSOR. ÆDEM
VICTORIÆ. VETVSTATE ILLAPSAM.
SVA. IMPENSA. RESTITVIT.

The peasants show another spring near the mosaic pavement which they call "Oradina," and which flows down the hills into a tank, or mill-dam, and thence trickles over into the Digentia.

But we must not hope

" To trace the Muses upwards to their spring, "

by exploring the windings of the romantic valley in search of the Bandusian fountain. It seems strange that any one should have thought Bandusia a fountain of the Digentia — Horace has not let drop a word of it; and this immortal spring has in fact been discovered in possession of the holders of many good things in Italy, the monks. It was attached to the church of St. Gervais and Protais near Venusia, where it was most likely to be found.[1] We shall not be so lucky as a late traveller in finding the *occasional pine* still pendent on the poetic villa. There is not a pine in the whole valley, but there are two cypresses, which he evidently took, or mistook, for the tree in the ode.[2] The truth is, that the pine is now, as it was in the days of Virgil, a garden tree, and it was not at all likely to be found in the craggy acclivities of the valley of Rustica. Horace probably had one of them in the orchard close above his farm, immediately overshadowing his villa, not on the rocky heights at some distance from his abode. The tourist may have easily supposed himself to have seen this pine figured in the above cypresses; for the orange and lemon trees which throw such a bloom over his description of the royal gardens at Naples, unless they have been since displaced, were assuredly only acacias and other common garden shrubs.[3]

XXXII. EUSTACE'S CLASSICAL TOUR.

The extreme disappointment experienced by choosing the Classical Tourist as a guide in Italy must be allowed to find vent in a few observations, which, it is asserted without fear of contradiction, will be confirmed by every one who has selected the same conductor through the same country. This author is in fact one of the most inaccurate, unsatisfactory writers that have in our times attained a temporary reputation, and is very seldom to be trusted even when he speaks of objects which he must be presumed to have seen. His errors, from the simple exaggeration to the downright misstatement, are so frequent as to induce a suspicion that he had either never visited the spots described, or had trusted to the fidelity of former writers. Indeed, the Classical Tour has every characteristic of a mere compilation of former notices, strung together upon a very slender thread of personal observation, and swelled out by those decorations which are so easily supplied by a systematic adoption of all the common-places of praise, applied to every thing, and therefore signifying nothing.

[1] See — Historical Illustrations of the Fourth Canto, p. 43.

[2] See — Classical Tour, etc. chap. vii. p. 250, vol. ii.

[3] "Under our windows, and bordering on the beach, is the royal garden, laid out in parterres, and walks shaded by rows of orange trees." Classical Tour, etc. chap. xi. vol. ii. oct. 365.

The style which one person thinks cloggy and cumbrous, and unsuitable, may be to the taste of others, and such may experience some salutary excitement in ploughing through the periods of the Classical Tour. It must be said, however, that polish and weight are apt to beget an expectation of value. It is amongst the pains of the damned to toil up a climax with a huge round *stone*.

The tourist had the choice of his words, but there was no such latitude allowed to that of his sentiments. The love of virtue and of liberty, which must have distinguished the character, certainly adorns the pages of Mr. Eustace; and the gentlemanly spirit, so recommendatory either in an author or his productions, is very conspicuous throughout the Classical Tour. But these generous qualities are the foliage of such a performance, and may be spread about it so prominently and profusely, as to embarrass those who wish to see and find the fruit at hand. The unction of the divine, and the exhortations of the moralist, may have made this work something more and better than a book of travels, but they have not made it a book of travels; and this observation applies more especially to that enticing method of instruction conveyed by the perpetual introduction of the same Gallic Helot to reel and bluster before the rising generation, and terrify it into decency by the display of all the excesses of the revolution. An animosity against atheists and regicides in general, and Frenchmen specifically, may be honorable, and may be useful as a record; but that antidote should either be administered in any work rather than a tour, or, at least, should be served up apart, and not so mixed with the whole mass of information and reflection, as to give a bitterness to every page: for who would choose to have the antipathies of any man, however just, for his travelling companions? A tourist, unless he aspires to the credit of prophecy, is not answerable for the changes which may take place in the country which he describes; but his reader may very fairly esteem all his political portraits and deductions as so much waste paper, the moment they cease to assist, and more particularly if they obstruct, his actual survey.

Neither encomium nor accusation of any government, or governors, is meant to be here offered; but it is stated as an incontrovertible fact, that the change operated, either by the address of the late imperial system, or by the disappointment of every expectation by those who have succeeded to the Italian thrones, has been so considerable, and is so apparent, as not only to put Mr. Eustace's antigallican philippics entirely out of date, but even to throw some suspicion upon the competency and candor of the author himself. A remarkable example may be found in the instance of Bologna, over whose papal attachments, and consequent desolation, the tourist pours forth such strains of condolence and revenge, made louder by the borrowed trumpet of Mr. Burke. Now Bologna is at this moment, and has been for some years, notorious amongst the states of Italy for its attachment to revolutionary principles, and was almost the only city which made any demonstrations in favor of the unfortunate Murat. This change may, however, have been made since Mr. Eustace visited this country; but the traveller whom he has thrilled with horror at the projected stripping of the copper from the cupola of St. Peter's, must be much relieved to find that sacrilege out of the power of the French, or any other plunderers, the cupola being covered with *lead* [1]

If the conspiring voice of othewise rival critics had not given considerable currency to the Classical Tour, it would have been unnecessary to warn the reader, that however it may adorn his library, it will be of little or no service to him in his carriage; and if the judgment of those critics had hitherto been suspended, no attempt would have been made to anticipate their decision. As it is, those who stand in the relation of posterity to Mr. Eustace may be permitted to appeal from contemporary praises, and are perhaps more likely to be just in proportion as the causes of love and hatred are the further removed. This appeal had, in some measure, been made before the above remarks were written; for one of the most respectable of the Florentine publishers, who had been persuaded by the repeated inquiries of those on their journey southwards to reprint a cheap edition of the Classical Tour, was, by the concurring advice of returning travellers, induced to abandon his design, although he had already arranged his types and paper, and had struck off one or two of the first sheets.

The writer of these notes would wish to part (like Mr. Gibbon) on good terms with the Pope and the Cardinals, but he does not think it necessary to extend the same discreet silence to their humble partisans.

[1] " What, then, will be the astonishment, or rather the horror, of my reader, when I inform him . . . the French Committee turned its attention to Saint Peters, and employed a company of Jews to estimate and purchase the gold, silver, and bronze that adorn the inside of the edifice as well as the copper that covers the vaults and dome on the outside." Chap. iv. p. 130, vol. ii. The story about the Jews is positively denied at Rome.

<hr>

THE GIAOUR;

A FRAGMENT OF A TURKISH TALE.

" One fatal remembrance — one sorrow that throws
Its bleak shade alike o'er our joys and our woes —
To which Life nothing darker nor brighter can bring,
For which joy hath no balm — and affliction no sting.

MOORE.

TO SAMUEL ROGERS, ESQ.,

AS A SLIGHT, BUT MOST SINCERE TOKEN OF ADMIRATION OF HIS GENIUS,

RESPECT FOR HIS CHARACTER,

AND GRATITUDE FOR HIS FRIENDSHIP,

THIS PRODUCTION IS INSCRIBED

BY HIS OBLIGED AND AFFECTIONATE SERVANT,

LONDON, May, 1813.   BYRON.

ADVERTISEMENT.

THE tale which these disjointed fragments present is founded upon circumstances now less common in the East than formerly; either because the ladies are more circumspect than in the " olden time," or because the Christians have better fortune, or less enterprise. The story, when entire, contained the adventures of a female slave, who was thrown, in the Mussulman manner, into the sea for infidelity, and avenged by a young Venetian, her lover, at the time the Seven Islands were possessed by the Republic of Venice, and soon after the Arnauts were beaten back from the Morea, which they had ravaged for some time subsequent to the Russian invasion. The desertion of the Mainotes, on being refused the plunder of Misitra, led to the abandonment of that enterprise, and to the desolation of the Morea, during which the cruelty exercised on all sides was unparalleled even in the annals of the faithful.

INTRODUCTION.

THE " Giaour" was published in May, 1813, and abundantly sustained the impression created by the first two cantos of Childe Harold. It is obvious that in this, the first of his romantic narratives, Byron's versification reflects the admiration he always avowed for Coleridge's " Christabel," — the irregular rhythm of which had already been adopted in the " Lay of the Last Minstrel." The fragmentary style of the composition was suggested by the then new and popular " Columbus " of Mr. Rogers. As to the subject, it was not merely by recent travel that the author had familiarized himself with Turkish history. " Old Knolles," he said at Missolonghi, a few weeks before his death, " was one of the first books that gave me pleasure when a child; and I believe it had much influence on my future wishes to visit the Levant, and gave, perhaps, the oriental coloring which is observed in my poetry." In the margin of his copy of Mr. D'Israeli's essay on " The Literary Character," is the following note: — " Knolles, Cantemir, De Tott, Lady M. W. Montague, Hawkins's translation from Mignot's History of the Turks, the Arabian Nights. — All travels or histories, or books upon the East, I could meet with, I had read, as well as Ricaut, before I was *ten years old.*"

An incident which occurred while Byron was at Athens was the foundation of the Giaour. His Turkish servant tampered with a female slave, and on his return from bathing one day Byron met a party of men who were carrying the girl, sewn up in a sack, to throw her into the sea. He threatened to shoot the leader of the band unless they took back their victim to the governor's house, where by a combination of menaces, entreaties, and bribery, he obtained her release. He afterwards said, " that to describe the feelings of the situation was impossible, and that to recollect them even, was *icy.*"

No breath of air to break the wave
That rolls below the Athenian's grave,
That tomb [1] which, gleaming o'er the cliff,
First greets the homeward-veering skiff,
High o'er the land he saved in vain :
When shall such hero live again ?
*   *   *   *   *

Fair clime ! [2] where every season smiles
Benignant o'er those blessed isles,

Which, seen from far Colonna's height,
Make glad the heart that hails the sight,
And lend to loneliness delight.
There mildly dimpling, Ocean's cheek
Reflects the tints of many a peak
Caught by the laughing tides that lave
These Edens of the eastern wave :

---

[1] A tomb above the rocks on the promontory, by some supposed the sepulchre of Themistocles.

[2] [" Of the beautiful flow of Byron's fancy," says Moore, " when its sources were once opened on any subject, the Giaour affords one of the most remarkable instances : this poem having accumulated under his hand, both in printing and through successive editions, till from four hundred lines, of which it consisted in its first copy, it at present amounts to fourteen hundred. The plan, indeed, which he had adopted, of a series of fragments, — a set of ' orient pearls at random strung ' — left him free to introduce, without reference to more than the general complexion of his story, whatever sen-

timents or images his fancy, in its excursions, could collect; and, how little fettered he was by any regard to connection in these additions, appears from a note which accompanied his own copy of this paragraph, in which he says — ' I have not yet fixed the place of insertion for the following lines, but will, when I see you — as I have no copy.' Even into this new passage, rich as it was at first, his fancy afterwards poured a fresh infusion." — The value of these after-touches may be appreciated by comparing the following verses, from his original draft of this paragraph, with the form which they now wear : —

" Fair clime ! where *ceaseless summer* smiles,
   Benignant o'er those blessed isles,
   Which, seen from far Colonna's height,

And if at times a transient breeze
Break the blue crystal of the seas,
Or sweep one blossom from the trees,
How welcome is each gentle air
That wakes and wafts the odors there!
For there — the Rose o'er crag or vale,
Sultana of the Nightingale,[1]
   The maid for whom his melody,
His thousand songs are heard on high,
Blooms blushing to her lover's tale:
His queen, the garden queen, his Rose,
Unbent by winds, unchilled by snows,
Far from the winters of the west,
By every breeze and season blest,
Returns the sweets by nature given
In softest incense back to heaven;
And grateful yields that smiling sky
Her fairest hue and fragrant sigh.
And many a summer flower is there,
And many a shade that love might share,
And many a grotto, meant for rest,
That holds the pirate for a guest;
Whose bark in sheltering cove below
Lurks for the passing peaceful prow,
Till the gay mariner's guitar [2]
Is heard, and seen the evening star;
Then stealing with the muffled oar
Far shaded by the rocky shore,
Rush the night-prowlers on the prey,
And turn to groans his roundelay.
Strange — that where Nature loved to trace,
As if for Gods, a dwelling-place,
And every charm and grace hath mixed
Within the paradise she fixed,
There man, enamoured of distress,
Should mar it into wilderness,
And trample, brute-like, o'er each flower
That tasks not one laborious hour;
Nor claims the culture of his hand
To bloom along the fairy land,
But springs as to preclude his care,

Make glad the heart that hails the sight,
And *give* to loneliness delight.
There *shine the bright abodes ye seek,*
Like dimples upon Ocean's cheek,
So smiling round the waters lave
These Edens of the eastern wave.
Or if, at times, the transient breeze
Break the *smooth* crystal of the seas,
Or *brush* one blossom from the trees,
How *grateful* is the gentle air
That waves and wafts the *fragrance* there."
The whole of this passage, from line 7 down to line
167, " Who heard it first had cause to grieve," was
not in the first edition.

[1] The attachment of the nightingale to the rose is
a well-known Persian fable. If I mistake not, the
" Bulbul of a thousand tales " is one of his appel-
lations.

[2] The guitar is the constant amusement of the
Greek sailor by night: with a steady fair wind, and
during a calm, it is accompanied always by the
voice, and often by dancing.

And sweetly woos him — but to spare!
Strange — that where all is peace beside,
There passion riots in her pride,
And lust and rapine wildly reign
To darken o'er the fair domain.
It is as though the fiends prevailed
Against the seraphs they assailed,
And, fixed on heavenly thrones, should dwell
The freed inheritors of hell;
So soft the scene, so formed for joy,
So curst the tyrants that destroy!

   He who hath bent him o'er the dead
Ere the first day of death is fled,
The first dark day of nothingness,
The last of danger and distress,
(Before Decay's effacing fingers
Have swept the lines where beauty lingers,)
And marked the mild angelic air,
The rapture of repose that's there,
The fixed yet tender traits that streak
The languor of the placid cheek,
And — but for that sad shrouded eye,
   That fires not, wins not, weeps not, now,
   And but for that chill, changeless brow,
Where cold Obstruction's apathy [3]
Appalls the gazing mourner's heart,
As if to him it could impart
The doom he dreads, yet dwells upon;
Yes, but for these and these alone,
Some moments, ay, one treacherous hour,
He still might doubt the tyrant's power;
So fair, so calm, so softly sealed,
The first, last look by death revealed! [4]
Such is the aspect of this shore;
'Tis Greece, but living Greece no more! [5]
So coldly sweet, so deadly fair,
We start, for soul is wanting there.
Hers is the loveliness in death,
That parts not quite with parting breath;

[3] " Ay, but to die and go we know not where,
   To lie in cold obstruction — "
               Measure for Measure.
[4] I trust that few of my readers have ever had an
opportunity of witnessing what is here attempted
in description, but those who have will probably re-
tain a painful remembrance of that singular beauty
which pervades, with few exceptions, the features
of the dead, a few hours, and but for a few hours,
after " the spirit is not there." It is to be remarked
in cases of violent death by gun-shot wounds, the
expression is always that of languor, whatever the
natural energy of the sufferer's character: but in
death from a stab the countenance preserves its
traits of feeling or ferocity, and the mind its bias, to
the last.
[5] [In Dallaway's Constantinople, a book which
Lord Byron is not unlikely to have consulted, I find
a passage quoted from Gillies's History of Greece,
which contains, perhaps, the first seed of the thought
thus expanded into full perfection by genius: —
" The present state of Greece compared to the
ancient, is the silent obscurity of the grave con-
trasted with the vivid lustre of active life." —
Moore.]

But beauty with that fearful bloom,
That hue which haunts it to the tomb,
Expression's last receding ray,
A gilded halo hovering round decay,
The farewell beam of Feeling past away!
Spark of that flame, perchance of heavenly birth,
Which gleams, but warms no more its cherished earth! [1]

Clime of the unforgotten brave!
Whose land from plain to mountain-cave
Was Freedom's home or Glory's grave!
Shrine of the mighty! can it be,
That this is all remains of thee?
Approach, thou craven crouching slave:
Say, is not this Thermopylæ?
These waters blue that round you lave,
Oh servile offspring of the free—
Pronounce what sea, what shore is this?
The gulf, the rock of Salamis!
These scenes, their story not unknown,
Arise, and make again your own;
Snatch from the ashes of your sires
The embers of their former fires;
And he who in the strife expires
Will add to theirs a name of fear
That Tyranny shall quake to hear,
And leave his sons a hope, a fame,
They too will rather die than shame:
For Freedom's battle once begun,
Bequeathed by bleeding Sire to Son,
Though baffled oft is ever won.
Bear witness, Greece, thy living page,
Attest it many a deathless age!
While kings, in dusty darkness hid,
Have left a nameless pyramid,
Thy heroes, though the general doom
Hath swept the column from their tomb,
A mightier monument command,
The mountains of their native land!
There points thy Muse to stranger's eye
The graves of those that cannot die!
'Twere long to tell, and sad to trace,
Each step from splendor to disgrace;
Enough — no foreign foe could quell
Thy soul, till from itself it fell;
Yes! Self-abasement paved the way
To villain-bonds and despot sway.

What can he tell who treads thy shore?
No legend of thine olden time,
No theme on which the muse might soar
High as thine own in days of yore,

When man was worthy of thy clime.
The hearts within thy valleys bred,
The fiery souls that might have led
Thy sons to deeds sublime,
Now crawl from cradle to the grave,
Slaves — nay, the bondsmen of a slave,[2]
And callous, save to crime;
Stained with each evil that pollutes
Mankind, where least above the brutes;
Without even savage virtue blest,
Without one free or valiant breast,
Still to the neighboring ports they waft
Proverbial wiles, and ancient craft;
In this the subtle Greek is found,
For this, and this alone, renowned.
In vain might Liberty invoke
The spirit to its bondage broke,
Or raise the neck that courts the yoke:
No more her sorrows I bewail,
Yet this will be a mournful tale,
And they who listen may believe,
Who heard it first had cause to grieve.

* * * * *

Far, dark, along the blue sea glancing,
The shadows of the rocks advancing
Start on the fisher's eye like boat
Of island-pirate or Mainote;
And fearful for his light caique,
He shuns the near but doubtful creek
Though worn and weary with his toil,
And cumbered with his scaly spoil,
Slowly, yet strongly, plies the oar,
Till Port Leone's safer shore
Receives him by the lovely light
That best becomes an Eastern night.

* * * * *

Who thundering comes on blackest steed,[3]
With slackened bit and hoof of speed?
Beneath the clattering iron's sound
The caverned echoes wake around
In lash for lash, and bound for bound;
The foam that streaks the courser's side
Seems gathered from the ocean-tide:
Though weary waves are sunk to rest,
There's none within his rider's breast;
And though to-morrow's tempest lower,

---

[1] [There is infinite beauty and effect, though of a painful and almost oppressive character, in this extraordinary passage: in which the author has illustrated the beautiful, but still and melancholy aspect of the once busy and glorious shores of Greece, by an image more true, more mournful, and more exquisitely finished, than any that we can recollect in the whole compass of poetry. — *Jeffrey.*]

[2] Athens is the property of the Kislar Aga (the slave of the seraglio and guardian of the women), who appoints the Way-wode. A pander and eunuch — these are not polite, yet true appellations — now *governs* the *governor* of Athens!

[3] [The reciter of the tale is a Turkish fisherman, who has been employed during the day in the gulf of Ægina, and in the evening, apprehensive of the Mainote pirates who infest the coast of Attica, lands with his boat on the harbor of Port Leone, the ancient Piræus. He becomes the eye-witness of nearly all the incidents in the story, and in one of them is a principal agent. It is to his feelings, and particularly to his religious prejudices, that we are indebted for some of the most forcible and splendid parts of the poem. — *George Ellis.*]

'Tis calmer than thy heart, young Giaour![1]
I know thee not, I loathe thy race,
But in thine lineaments I trace
What time shall strengthen, not efface:
Though young and pale, that sallow front
Is scathed by fiery passion's brunt;
Though bent on earth thine evil eye,
As meteor-like thou glidest by,
Right well I view and deem thee one
Whom Othman's sons should slay or shun.

On — on he hastened, and he drew
My gaze of wonder as he flew:
Though like a demon of the night
He passed, and vanished from my sight,
His aspect and his air impressed
A troubled memory on my breast,
And long upon my startled ear
Rung his dark courser's hoofs of fear.
He spurs his steed; he nears the steep,
That, jutting, shadows o'er the deep;
He winds around; he hurries by;
The rock relieves him from mine eye;
For well I ween unwelcome he
Whose glance is fixed on those that flee;
And not a star but shines too bright
On him who takes such timeless flight.
He wound along; but ere he passed
One glance he snatched, as if his last,
A moment checked his wheeling steed,
A moment breathed him from his speed,
A moment on his stirrup stood —
Why looks he o'er the olive wood?
The crescent glimmers on the hill,
The Mosque's high lamps are quivering
    still:
Though too remote for sound to wake
In echoes of the far tophaike,[2]
The flashes of each joyous peal
Are seen to prove the Moslem's zeal,
To-night, set Rhamazani's sun;
To-night, the Bairam feast's begun;
To-night — but who and what art thou
Of foreign garb and fearful brow?
And what are these to thine or thee,
That thou should'st either pause or flee?

He stood — some dread was on his face,
Soon Hatred settled in its place:
It rose not with the reddening flush
Of transient Anger's hasty blush,
But pale as marble o'er the tomb,
Whose ghastly whiteness aids its gloom.
His brow was bent, his eye was glazed;

He raised his arm, and fiercely raised,
And sternly shook his hand on high,
As doubting to return or fly:
Impatient of his flight delayed,
Here loud his raven charger neighed —
Down glanced that hand, and grasped his
    blade.
That sound had burst his waking dream,
As Slumber starts at owlet's scream.
The spur hath lanced his courser's sides:
Away, away, for life he rides:
Swift as the hurled on high jerreed[3]
Springs to the touch his startled steed;
The rock is doubled, and the shore
Shakes with the clattering tramp no more;
The crag is won, no more is seen
His Christian crest and haughty mien.
'Twas but an instant he restrained
That fiery barb so sternly reined;
'Twas but a moment that he stood,
Then sped as if by death pursued:
But in that instant o'er his soul
Winters of Memory seemed to roll,
And gather in that drop of time
A life of pain, an age of crime.
O'er him who loves, or hates, or fears,
Such moment pours the grief of years:
What felt *he* then, at once opprest
By all that most distracts the breast?
That pause, which pondered o'er his fate,
Oh, who its dreary length shall date!
Though in Time's record nearly nought,
It was Eternity to Thought!
For infinite as boundless space
The thought that Conscience must embrace,
Which in itself can comprehend
Woe without name, or hope, or end.

The hour is past, the Giaour is gone;
And did he fly or fall alone?
Woe to that hour he came or went!
The curse for Hassan's sin was sent
To turn a palace to a tomb;
He came, he went, like the Simoom,[4]
That harbinger of fate and gloom,
Beneath whose widely-wasting breath
The very cypress droops to death —
Dark tree, still sad when others' grief is fled,
The only constant mourner o'er the dead!

The steed is vanished from the stall;
No serf is seen in Hassan's hall;
The lonely Spider's thin gray pall

---

[1] [In Dr. Clarke's Travels, this word, which means *Infidel*, is always written according to its English pronunciation, *Djour*. Byron adopted the Italian spelling usual among the Franks of the Levant.]
[2] "Tophaike," musket. — The Bairam is announced by the cannon at sunset; the illumination of the mosques, and the firing of all kinds of small arms, loaded with *ball*, proclaim it during the night.

[3] Jerreed, or Djerrid, a blunted Turkish javelin, which is darted from horseback with great force and precision. It is a favorite exercise of the Mussulmans; but I know not if it can be called a *manly* one, since the most expert in the art are the Black Eunuchs of Constantinople. I think, next to these, a Mamlouk at Smyrna was the most skilful that came within my observation.
[4] The blast of the desert, fatal to every thing living, and often alluded to in eastern poetry [The

Waves slowly widening o'er the wall;
The Bat builds in his Haram bower,
And in the fortress of his power
The Owl usurps the beacon-tower;
The wild-dog howls o'er the fountain's brim,
With baffled thirst, and famine, grim;
For the stream has shrunk from its marble
   bed,
Where the weeds and the desolate dust are
   spread.
'Twas sweet of yore to see it play
And chase the sultriness of day,
As springing high the silver dew
In whirls fantastically flew,
And flung luxurious coolness round
The air, and verdure o'er the ground.
'Twas sweet, when cloudless stars were
  . bright,
To view the wave of watery light,
And hear its melody by night.
And oft had Hassan's Childhood played
Around the verge of that cascade;
And oft upon his mother's breast
That sound had harmonized his rest;
And oft had Hassan's Youth along
Its bank been soothed by Beauty's song;
And softer seemed each melting tone
Of Music mingled with its own.
But ne'er shall Hassan's Age repose
Along the brink at Twilight's close:
The stream that filled that font is fled —
The blood that warmed his heart is shed!
And here no more shall human voice
Be heard to rage, regret, rejoice.
The last sad note that swelled the gale
Was woman's wildest funeral wail:
That quenched in silence, all is still,
But the lattice that flaps when the wind is
   shrill:
Though raves the gust, and floods the rain,
No hand shall close its clasp again.
On desert sands 'twere joy to scan
The rudest steps of fellow man,
So here the very voice of Grief
Might wake an Echo like relief —
At least 'twould say, " All are not gone " —
There lingers Life, though but in one " —
For many a gilded chamber's there,
Which Solitude might well forbear; [1]

effects of the Simoom have been grossly exag-
gerated.]

[1] [" I have just recollected an alteration you may
make in the proof. Among the lines on Hassan's
Serai, is this —
   ' Unmeet for solitude to share.'
Now, to share implies more than one, and Solitude
is a single gentleman; it must be thus —
   ' For many a gilded chamber's there,
    Which solitude might well forbear; '
and so on. Will you adopt this correction? and
pray accept a Stilton cheese from me for your
trouble. — P. S. I leave this to your discretion : if

Within that dome as yet Decay
Hath slowly worked her cankering way —
But gloom is gathered o'er the gate,
Nor there the Fakir's self will wait;
Nor there will wandering Dervise stay,
For bounty cheers not his delay;
Nor there will weary stranger halt
To bless the sacred " bread and salt." [2]
Alike must Wealth and Poverty
Pass heedless and unheeded by,
For Courtesy and Pity died
With Hassan on the mountain side.
His roof, that refuge unto men,
Is Desolation's hungry den.
The guest flies the hall, and the vassal from
   labor
Since his turban was cleft by the infidel's
   sabre! [3]
     *   *   *   *   *

I hear the sound of coming feet,
But not a voice mine ear to greet;
More near — each turban I can scan,
And silver-sheathed ataghan; [4]
The foremost of the band is seen
An Emir by his garb of green: [5]
" Ho! who art thou ? " — " this low salam [6]
Replies of Moslem faith I am." —
" The burden ye so gently bear
Seems one that claims your utmost care,
And, doubtless, holds some precious freight,
My humble bark would gladly wait."

" Thou speakest sooth : thy skiff unmoor,
And waft us from the silent shore;
Nay, jea₁ve the sail still furled, and ply
The nearest oar that's scattered by,
And midway to those rocks where sleep
The channelled waters dark and deep.

anybody thinks the old line a good one, or the cheese
a bad one, don't accept of either." — *Byron's Let-
ters*, Stilton, October 3, 1813.]
  [2] To partake of food, to break bread and salt
with your host, insures the safety of the guest: even
though an enemy, his person from that moment is
sacred.
  [3] I need hardly observe, that Charity and Hos-
pitality are the first duties enjoined by Mahomet;
and to say truth, very generally practised by his
disciples. The first praise that can be bestowed on
a chief, is a panegyric on his bounty; the next, on
his valor.
  [4] The ataghan, a long dagger worn with pistols
in the belt, in a metal scabbard, generally of silver;
and, among the wealthier, gilt, or of gold.
  [5] Green is the privileged color of the prophet's
numerous pretended descendants; with them, as
here, faith (the family inheritance) is supposed to
supersede the necessity of good works: they are
the worst of a very indifferent brood.
  [6] " Salam aleikoum! aleikoum salam! " peace be
with you; be with you peace — the salutation
reserved for the faithful : — to a Christian, " Urla-
rula," a good journey; or, " saban hiresem, saban
serula; " good morn, good even; and sometimes,
" may your end be happy; " are the usual salutes.

Rest from your task — so — bravely done,
Our course has been right swiftly run;
Yet 'tis the longest voyage, I trow,
That one of—   *   *   *
    *   *   *   *   * "

Sullen it plunged, and slowly sank,
The calm wave rippled to the bank;
I watched it as it sank, methought
Some motion from the current caught
Bestirred it more, — 'twas but the beam
That checkered o'er the living stream :
I gazed, till vanishing from view,
Like lessening pebble it withdrew;
Still less and less, a speck of white
That gemmed the tide, then mocked the
    sight;
And all its hidden secrets sleep,
Known but to Genii of the deep,
Which, trembling in their coral caves,
They dare not whisper to the waves.
    *   *   *   *   *

As rising on its purple wing
The insect queen [1] of eastern spring
O'er emerald meadows of Kashmeer
Invites the young pursuer near,
And leads him on from flower to flower
A weary chase and wasted hour,
Then leaves him, as it soars on high,
With panting heart and tearful eye :
So Beauty lures the full-grown child,
With hue as bright, and wing as wild;
A chase of idle hopes and fears,
Begun in folly, closed in tears.
If won, to equal ills betrayed,
Woe waits the insect and the maid;
A life of pain, the loss of peace,
From infant's play, and man's caprice :
The lovely toy so fiercely sought
Hath lost its charm by being caught,
For every touch that wooed its stay
Hath brushed its brightest hues away,
Till charm, and hue, and beauty gone,
'Tis left to fly or fall alone.
With wounded wing, or bleeding breast,
Ah! where shall either victim rest?
Can this with faded pinion soar
From rose to tulip as before?
Or Beauty, blighted in an hour,
Find joy within her broken bower?
No: gayer insects fluttering by
Ne'er droop the wing o'er those that die,
And lovelier things have mercy shown
To every failing but their own,
And every woe a tear can claim
Except an erring sister's shame.
    *   *   *   *   *

The Mind, that broods o'er guilty woes,
   Is like the Scorpion girt by fire,

In circle narrowing as it glows,
The flames around their captive close,
Till inly searched by thousand throes,
   And maddening in her ire,
One sad and sole relief she knows,
The sting she nourished for her foes,
Whose venom never yet was vain,
Gives but one pang, and cures all pain,
And darts into her desperate brain;
So do the dark in soul expire,
Or live like Scorpion girt by fire; [2]
So writhes the mind Remorse hath riven,
Unfit for earth, undoomed for heaven,
Darkness above, despair beneath,
Around it flame, within it death!
    *   *   *   *   *

Black Hassan from the Haram flies,
Nor bends on woman's form his eyes;
The unwonted chase each hour employs,
Yet shares he not the hunter's joys.
Not thus was Hassan wont to fly
When Leila dwelt in his Serai.
Doth Leila there no longer dwell?
That tale can only Hassan tell:
Strange rumors in our city say
Upon that eve she fled away
When Rhamazan's [3] last sun was set,
And flashing from each minaret
Millions of lamps proclaimed the feast
Of Bairam through the boundless East.
'Twas then she went as to the bath,
Which Hassan vainly searched in wrath;
For she was flown her master's rage
In likeness of a Georgian page,
And far beyond the Moslem's power
Had wronged him with the faithless Giaour.
Somewhat of this had Hassan deemed;
But still so fond, so fair she seemed,
Too well he trusted to the slave
Whose treachery deserved a grave:
And on that eve had gone to mosque,
And thence to feast in his kiosk.
Such is the tale his Nubians tell,
Who did not watch their charge too well;
But others say, that on that night,
By pale Phingari's [4] trembling light,
The Giaour upon his jet black steed

[1] The blue-winged butterfly of Kashmeer, the
most rare and beautiful of the species.

[2] Alluding to the dubious suicide of the scorpion,
so placed for experiment by gentle philosophers.
Some maintain that the position of the sting, when
turned towards the head, is merely a convulsive
movement; but others have actually brought in
the verdict " Felo de se." The scorpions are sure-
ly interested in a speedy decision of the question;
as, if once fairly established as insect Catos, they
will probably be allowed to live as long as they
think proper, without being martyred for the sake
of an hypothesis. [Byron told Mr. Dallas that this
simile of the scorpion was imagined by him in his
sleep.]
[3] The cannon at sunset close the Rhamazan.
See *ante*, p. 378, note.
[4] Phingari, the moon.

'Was seen, but seen alone to speed
With bloody spur along the shore,
Nor maid nor page behind him bore.

* * * * *

Her eyes' dark charm 'twere vain to tell,
But gaze on that of the Gazelle,
It will assist thy fancy well;
As large, as languishingly dark,
But Soul beamed forth in every spark
That darted from beneath the lid,
Bright as the jewel of Giamschid.[1]
Yea, *Soul*, and should our prophet say
That form was nought but breathing clay,
By Alla! I would answer nay;
Though on Al-Sirat's [2] arch I stood,
Which totters o'er the fiery flood,
With Paradise within my view,
And all his Houris [3] beckoning through.
Oh! who young Leila's glance could read
And keep that portion of his creed,
Which saith that woman is but dust,
A soulless toy for tyrant's lust? [4]
On her might Muftis gaze, and own
That through her eye the Immortal shone;
On her fair cheek's unfading hue

The young pomegranate's [5] blossoms strew
Their bloom in blushes ever new;
Her hair in hyacinthine [6] flow,
When left to roll its folds below,
As midst her handmaids in the hall
She stood superior to them all,
Hath swept the marble where her feet
Gleamed whiter than the mountain sleet
Ere from the cloud that gave it birth
It fell, and caught one stain of earth.
The cygnet nobly walks the water;
So moved on earth Circassia's daughter,
The loveliest bird of Franguestan! [7]
As rears her crest the ruffled Swan,
  And spurns the wave with wings of pride,
When pass the steps of stranger man
  Along the banks that bound her tide;
Thus rose fair Leila's whiter neck: —
Thus armed with beauty would she check
Intrusion's glance, till Folly's gaze
Shrunk from the charms it meant to praise.
Thus high and graceful was her gait;
Her heart as tender to her mate;
Her mate — stern Hassan, who was he?
Alas! that name was not for thee!

* * * * *

Stern Hassan hath a journey ta'en
With twenty vassals in his train,
Each armed, as best becomes a man,
With arquebuss and ataghan;
The chief before, as decked for war,
Bears in his belt the scimitar
Stained with the best of Arnaut blood,
When in the pass the rebels stood,
And few returned to tell the tale
Of what befell in Parne's vale.
The pistols which his girdle bore
Were those that once a pasha wore,
Which still, though gemmed and bosseo
    with gold,
Even robbers tremble to behold.
'Tis said he goes to woo a bride
More true than her who left his side;
The faithless slave that broke her bower,
And, worse than faithless, for a Giaour!

* * * * *

The sun's last rays are on the hill,
And sparkle in the fountain rill,
Whose welcome waters, cool and clear,
Draw blessings from the mountaineer:

---

[1] The celebrated fabulous ruby of Sultan Giamschid, the embellisher of Istakhar; from its splendor, named Schebgerag, "the torch of night;" also "the cup of the sun," etc. In the first edition, "Giamschid" was written as a word of three syllables, so D'Herbelot has it; but I am told Richardson reduces it to a dissyllable, and writes "Jamshid." I have left in the text the orthography of the one with the pronunciation of the other. — [In the first edition, Lord Byron had used this word as a trisyllable, — "Bright as the gem of Giamschid," — but, on my remarking to him, upon the authority of Richardson's Persian Dictionary, that this was incorrect, he altered it to "Bright as the ruby of Giamschid." On seeing this, however, I wrote to him, "that, as the comparison of his heroine's eye to a ruby might unluckily call up the idea of its being bloodshot, he had better change the line to 'Bright as the jewel of Giamschid;'" which he accordingly did, in the following edition. — *Moore.*]

[2] Al-Sirat, the bridge of breadth, narrower than the thread of a famished spider, and sharper than the edge of a sword, over which the Mussulmans must *skate* into Paradise, to which it is the only entrance; but this is not the worst, the river beneath being hell itself, into which, as may be expected, the unskilful and tender of foot contrive to tumble with a "facilis descensus Averni," not very pleasing in prospect to the next passenger. There is a shorter cut downwards for the Jews and Christians.

[3] [The virgins of Paradise, called from their large black eyes, *Hur al cyun.* An intercourse with these, according to the institution of Mahomet, is to constitute the principal felicity of the faithful. Not formed of clay, like mortal women, they are adorned with unfading charms, and deemed to possess the celestial privilege of an eternal youth.]

[4] A vulgar error: the Koran allots at least a third of Paradise to well-behaved women; but by far the greater number of Mussulmans interpret the text

their own way, and exclude their moities from heaven. Being enemies to Platonics, they cannot discern "any fitness of things" in the souls of the other sex, conceiving them to be superseded by the Houris.

[5] An oriental simile, which may, perhaps, though fairly stolen, be deemed "plus Arabe qu'en Arabie."

[6] Hyacinthine, in Arabic "Sunbul;" as common a thought in the eastern poets as it was among the Greeks.

[7] "Franguestan," Circassia.

Here may the loitering merchant Greek
Find that repose 'twere vain to seek
In cities lodged too near his lord,
And trembling for his secret hoard —
Here may he rest where none can see,
In crowds a slave, in deserts free;
And with forbidden wine may stain
The bowl a Moslem must not drain.
   *   *   *   *

The foremost Tartar's in the gap,
Conspicuous by his yellow cap;
The rest in lengthening line the while
Wind slowly through the long defile:
Above, the mountain rears a peak,
Where vultures whet the thirsty beak,
And theirs may be a feast to-night,
Shall tempt them down ere morrow's light;
Beneath, a river's wintry stream
Has shrunk before the summer beam,
And left a channel bleak and bare,
Save shrubs that spring to perish there:
Each side the midway path there lay
Small broken crags of granite gray,
By time, or mountain lightning, riven
From summits clad in mists of heaven;
For where is he that hath beheld
The peak of Liakura unveiled?
   *   *   *   *

They reach the grove of pine at last:
" Bismillah ! [1] now the peril's past;
For yonder view the opening plain,
And there we'll prick our steeds amain : "
The Chiaus spake, and as he said,
A bullet whistled o'er his head;
The foremost Tartar bites the ground!
  Scarce had they time to check the rein,
Swift from their steeds the riders bound;
  But three shall never mount again :
Unseen the foes that gave the wound,
  The dying ask revenge in vain.
With steel unsheathed, and carbine bent,
Some o'er their courser's harness leant,
  Half sheltered by the steed;
Some fly behind the nearest rock,
And there await the coming shock,
  Nor tamely stand to bleed
Beneath the shaft of foes unseen,
Who dare not quit their craggy screen.
Stern Hassan only from his horse
Disdains to light, and keeps his course,
Till fiery flashes in the van
Proclaim too sure the robber-clan
Have well secured the only way
Could now avail the promised prey;
Then curled his very beard [2] with ire,

And glared his eye with fiercer fire:
" Though far and near the bullets hiss,
I've scaped a bloodier hour than this."
And now the foe their covert quit,
And call his vassals to submit;
But Hassan's frown and furious word
Are dreaded more than hostile sword,
Nor of his little band a man
Resigned carbine or ataghan,
Nor raised the craven cry, Amaun! [3]
In fuller sight, more near and near,
The lately ambushed foes appear,
And, issuing from the grove, advance
Some who on battle-charger prance.
Who leads them on with foreign brand,
Far flashing in his red right hand?
" 'Tis he ! 'tis he ! I know him now;
I know him by his pallid brow;
I know him by the evil eye [4]
That aids his envious treachery;
I know him by his jet-black barb:
Though now arrayed in Arnaut garb,
Apostate from his own vile faith,
It shall not save him from the death:
'Tis he !, well met in any hour,
Lost Leila's love, accursed Giaour ! "

  As rolls the river into ocean,
In sable torrent wildly streaming;
  As the sea-tide's opposing motion,
In azure column proudly gleaming,
Beats back the current many a rood,
In curling foam and mingling flood,
While eddying whirl, and breaking wave,
Roused by the blast of winter, rave;
Through sparkling spray, in thundering
  clash,
The lightnings of the waters flash
In awful whiteness o'er the shore
That shines and shakes beneath the roar;
Thus — as the stream and ocean greet,
With waves that madden as they meet —
Thus join the bands, whom mutual wrong,
And fate, and fury, drive along.
The bickering sabres' shivering jar;
  And pealing wide or ringing near
  Its echoes on the throbbing ear,
The deathshot hissing from afar:
The shock, the shout, the groan of war,
  Reverberate along that vale,
  More suited to the shepherd's tale:
Though few the numbers — theirs the strife,

---

[1] Bismillah —" In the name of God;" the commencement of all the chapters of the Koran but one, and of prayer and thanksgiving.
[2] A phenomenon not uncommon with an angry Mussulman. In 1809, the Capitan Pacha's whiskers at a diplomatic audience were no less lively with indignation than a tiger cat's, to the horror of all the dragomans; the portentous mustachios twisted, they stood erect of their own accord, and were expected every moment to change their color, but at last condescended to subside, which, probably, saved more heads than they contained hairs.
[3] "Amaun," quarter, pardon.
[4] The " evil eye," a common superstition in the Levant, and of which the imaginary effects are yet very singular on those who conceive themselves affected.

That neither spares nor speaks for life!
Ah! fondly youthful hearts can press
To seize and share the dear caress:
But Love itself could never pant
For all that Beauty sighs to grant
With half the fervor Hate bestows
Upon the last embrace of foes,
When grappling in the fight they fold
Those arms that ne'er shall lose their hold:
Friends meet to part; Love laughs at faith;
True foes, once met, are joined till death!

* * * * *

With sabre shivered to the hilt,
Yet dripping with the blood he spilt;
Yet strained within the severed hand
Which quivers round that faithless brand;
His turban far behind him rolled,
And cleft in twain its firmest fold;
His flowing robe by falchion torn,
And crimson as those clouds of morn
That, streaked with dusky red, portend
The day shall have a stormy end;
A stain on every bush that bore
A fragment of his palampore, [1]
His breast with wounds unnumbered riven,
His back to earth, his face to heaven,
Fallen Hassan lies — his unclosed eye
Yet lowering on his enemy,
As if the hour that sealed his fate
Surviving left his quenchless hate;
And o'er him bends that foe with brow
As dark as his that bled below. —

* * * * *

"Yes, Leila sleeps beneath the wave,
But his shall be a redder grave;
Her spirit pointed well the steel
Which taught that felon heart to feel.
He called the Prophet, but his power
Was vain against the vengeful Giaour:
He called on Alla — but the word
Arose unheeded or unheard.
Thou Paynim fool! could Leila's prayer
Be passed, and thine accorded there?
I watched my time, I leagued with these,
The traitor in his turn to seize;
My wrath is wreaked, the deed is done,
And now I go — but go alone."

* * * * *

The browsing camels' bells are tinkling: [2]
His Mother looked from her lattice high,
She saw the dews of eve besprinkling

The pasture green beneath her eye,
She saw the planets faintly twinkling:
"'Tis twilight — sure his train is nigh."
She could not rest in the garden-bower,
But gazed through the grate of his steepest
    tower;
Why comes he not? his steeds are fleet,
Nor shrink they from the summer heat;
Why sends not the Bridegroom his prom-
    ised gift?
Is his heart more cold, or his barb less
    swift?
Oh, false reproach! yon Tartar now
Has gained our nearest mountain's brow,
And warily the steep decends,
And now within the valley bends; •
And he bears the gift at his saddle bow —
How could I deem his courser slow?
Right well my largess shall repay
His welcome speed, and weary way."

The Tartar lighted at the gate,
But scarce upheld his fainting weight:
His swarthy visage spake distress,
But this might be from weariness;
His garb with sanguine spots was dyed,
But these might be from his courser's side;
He drew the token from his vest —.
Angel of Death! 'tis Hassan's cloven crest!
His calpac [3] rent — his caftan red —
"Lady, a fearful bride thy Son hath wed:
Me, not from mercy, did they spare,
But this empurpled pledge to bear.
Peace to the brave! whose blood is spilt;
Woe to the Giaour! for his the guilt."

* * * * *

A turban [4] carved in coarsest stone,
A pillar with rank weeds o'ergrown,
Whereon can now be scarcely read
The Koran verse that mourns the dead,
Point out the spot where Hassan fell
A victim in that lonely dell.
There sleeps as true an Osmanlie
As e'er at Mecca bent the knee;
As ever scorned forbidden wine,
Or prayed with face towards the shrine,
In orisons resumed anew
At solemn sound of " Alla Hu! " [5]

---

[1] The flowered shawls generally worn by persons
of ....nk.

[2] [This beautiful passage first appeared in the
third edition. "If you send more proofs," writes
Byron to Mr. Murray (August 10th, 1813), "I
shall never finish this infernal story. *Ecce signum*
— thirty three more lines inclosed! — to the utter
discomfiture of the printer, and, I fear, not to your
advantage."]

[3] The " Calpac " is the solid cap or centre part of
the headdress; the shawl is wound round it, and
forms the turban.

[4] The turban, pillar, and inscriptive verse, deco-
rate the tombs of the Osmanlies, whether in the
cemetery or the wilderness. • In the mountains you
frequently pass similar mementos: and on inquiry
you are informed that they record some victim of
rebellion, plunder, or revenge.

[5] "Alla Hu!" the concluding words of the
Muezzin's call to prayer from the highest gallery '
on the exterior of the Minaret. On a still evening,
when the Muezzin has a fine voice, which is fre-
quently the case, the effect is solemn and beautiful
beyond all the bells in Christendom. — [Valid, the

Yet died he by a stranger's hand,
And stranger in his native land;
Yet died he as in arms he stood,
And unavenged, at least in blood.
But him the maids of Paradise
    Impatient to their halls invite,
And the dark Heaven of Houris' eyes
    On him shall glance for ever bright;
They come — their kerchiefs green they
        wave,[1]
And welcome with a kiss the brave!
Who falls in battle 'gainst a Giaour
Is worthiest an immortal bower.
        *   *   *   *   *

But thou, false Infidel! shalt writhe
Beneath avenging Monkir's[2] scythe;
And from its torment 'scape alone
To wander round lost Eblis'[3] throne;
And fire unquenched, unquenchable,
Around, within, thy heart shall dwell;
Nor ear can hear nor tongue can tell
The tortures of that inward hell!
But first, on earth as vampire[4] sent,
Thy corse shall from its tomb be rent:
Then ghastly haunt thy native place,
And suck the blood of all thy race;
There from thy daughter, sister, wife,
At midnight drain the stream of life;
Yet loathe the banquet which perforce

Must feed thy livid living corse:
Thy victims ere they yet expire
Shall know the demon for their sire,
As cursing thee, thou cursing them,
Thy flowers are withered on the stem.
But one that for thy crime must fall,
The youngest, most beloved of all,
Shall bless thee with a *father's* name —
That word shall wrap thy heart in flame!
Yet must thou end thy task, and mark
Her cheek's last tinge, her eye's last spark,
And the last glassy glance must view
Which freezes o'er its lifeless blue;
Then with unhallowed hand shall tear
The tresses of her yellow hair,
Of which in life a lock when shorn
Affection's fondest pledge was worn,
But now is borne away by thee,
Memorial of thine agony!
Wet with thine own best blood shall drip[5]
Thy gnashing tooth and haggard lip;
Then stalking to thy sullen grave,
Go — and with Ghouls and Afrits rave;
Till these in horror shrink away
From spectre more accursed than they![6]
        *   *   *   *   *

" How name ye yon lone Caloyer?
    His features I have scanned before
In mine own land: 'tis many a year,
    Since, dashing by the lonely shore,
I saw him urge as fleet a steed
As ever served a horseman's need.
But once I saw that face, yet then
It was so marked with inward pain,
I could not pass it by again;
It breathes the same dark spirit now,
As death were stamped upon his brow."

" 'Tis twice three years at summer tide
    Since first among our freres he came;
And here it soothes him to abide
    For some dark deed he will not name,
But never at our vesper prayer,
Nor e'er before confession chair
Kneels he, nor recks he when arise
Incense or anthem to the skies,
But broods within his cell alone,
His faith and race alike unknown.
The sea from Paynim land he crost,
And here ascended from the coast;
Yet seems he not of Othman race,
But only Christian in his face:
I'd judge him some stray renegade,

son of Abdalmalek, was the first who erected a
minaret or turret; and this he placed on the grand
mosque at Damascus, for the muezzin, or crier, to
announce from it the hour of prayer.]

[1] The following is part of a battle song of the
Turks: — " I see — I see a dark-eyed girl of Para-
dise, and she waves a handkerchief, a kerchief of
green: and cries aloud, ' Come, kiss me, for I love
thee,' " etc.

[2] Monkir and Nekir are the inquisitors of the
dead, before whom the corpse undergoes a slight
noviciate and preparatory training for damnation.
If the answers are none of the clearest, he is hauled
up with a scythe and thumped down with a red hot
mace till properly seasoned, with a variety of sub-
sidiary probations. The office of these angels is no
sinecure; there are but two, and the number of
orthodox deceased being in small proportion to the
remainder, their hands are always full. See *Relig.
Ceremon.* and Sale's *Koran.*

[3] Eblis, the Oriental Prince of Darkness. —
[D'Herbelot supposes this title to have been a cor-
ruption of the Greek Διαβολος.]

[4] The Vampire superstition is still general in the
Levant. Honest Tournefort tells a long story,
which Mr. Southey, in the notes on Thalaba, quotes,
about these " Vroucolochas," as he calls them.
The Romaic term is " Vardoulacha." I recollect a
whole family being terrified by the scream of a
child, which they imagined must proceed from such
a visitation. The Greeks never mention the word
without horror. I find that " Broucolocas " is an
old legitimate Hellenic appellation — at least is so
applied to Arsenius, who, according to the Greeks,
was after his death animated by the Devil. — The
moderns, however, use the word I mention.

[5] The freshness of the face, and the wetness of
the lip with blood, are the never-failing signs of a
Vampire. The stories told in Hungary and Greece
of these foul feeders are singular, and some of them
most *incredibly* attested.

[6] [The imprecations of the Turk, against the
" accursed Giaour," are introduced with great
judgment, and contribute much to the dramatic
effect of the narrative. — *George Ellis.*]

Repentant of the change he made,
Save that he shuns our holy shrine,
Nor tastes the sacred bread and wine.
Great largess to these walls he brought,
And thus our abbot's favor bought;
But were I Prior, not a day
Should brook such stranger's further stay,
Or pent within our penance cell
Should doom him there for aye to dwell.
Much in his visions mutters he
Of maiden whelmed beneath the sea;
Of sabres clashing, foemen flying,
Wrongs avenged, and Moslem dying.
On cliff he hath been known to stand,
And rave as to some bloody hand
Fresh severed from its parent limb,
Invisible to all but him,
Which beckons onward to his grave,
And lures to leap into the wave."

*   *   *   *   *
*   *   *   *   *

Dark and unearthly is the scowl [1]
That glares beneath his dusky cowl:
The flash of that dilating eye
Reveals too much of times gone by;
Though varying, indistinct its hue,
Oft will his glance the gazer rue,
For in it lurks that nameless spell,
Which speaks, itself unspeakable,
A spirit yet unquelled and high,
That claims and keeps ascendency:
And like the bird whose pinions quake,
But cannot fly the gazing snake,
Will others quail beneath his look,
Nor 'scape the glance they scarce can
    brook.
From him the half-affrighted Friar
When met alone would fain retire,
As if that eye and bitter smile
Transferred to others fear and guile:
Not oft to smile descendeth he,
And when he doth 'tis sad to see
That he but mocks at Misery.
How that pale lip will curl and quiver!
Then fix once more as if for ever;
As if his sorrow or disdain
Forbade him e'er to smile again.
Well were it so — such ghastly mirth
From joyaunce ne'er derived its birth.
But sadder still were it to trace
What once were feelings in that face;
Time hath not yet the features fixed,
But brighter traits with evil mixed;
And there are hues not always faded,
Which speak a mind not all degraded
Even by the crimes through which it
    waded:

---

[1] [The remaining lines, about five hundred in
number, were, with the exception of the last six-
teen, all added to the poem either during its first
progress through the press, or in subsequent edi-
tions.]

The common crowd but see the gloom
Of wayward deeds, and fitting doom;
The close observer can espy
A noble soul, and lineage high:
Alas! though both bestowed in vain,
Which Grief could change, and Guilt could
    stain,
It was no vulgar tenement
To which such lofty gifts were lent,
And still with little less than dread
On such the sight is riveted.
The roofless cot, decayed and rent,
    Will scarce delay the passer by;
The tower by war or tempest bent,
While yet may frown one battlement,
    Demands and daunts the stranger's eye;
Each ivied arch, and pillar lone,
Pleads haughtily for glories gone!

" His floating robe around him folding,
    Slow sweeps he through the columned
        aisle;
With dread beheld, with gloom beholding
    The rites that sanctify the pile.
But when the anthem shakes the choir,
And kneel the monks, his steps retire;
By yonder lone and wavering torch
His aspect glares within the porch;
There will he pause till all is done —
And hear the prayer, but utter none.
See — by the half-illumined wall
His hood fly back, his dark hair fall,
That pale brow wildly wreathing round,
As if the Gorgon there had bound
The sablest of the serpent-braid
That o'er her fearful forehead strayed:
For he declines the convent oath,
And leaves those locks unhallowed growth,
But wears our grab in all beside;
And, not from piety but pride,
Gives wealth to walls that never heard
Of his one holy vow nor word.
Lo! — mark ye, as the harmony
Peals louder praises to the sky,
That livid cheek, that stony air
Of mixed defiance and despair!
Saint Francis, keep him from the shrine!
Else may we dread the wrath divine
Made manifest by awful sign.
If ever evil angel bore
The form of mortal, such he wore:
By all my hope of sins forgiven,
Such looks are not of earth nor heaven!"

To love the softest hearts are prone,
But such can ne'er be all his own;
Too timid in his woes to share,
Too meek to meet, or brave despair;
And sterner hearts alone may feel
The wound that time can never heal.
The rugged metal of the mine
Must burn before its surface shine.

But plunged within the furnace-flame,
It bends and melts — though still the same;
Then tempered to thy want, or will,
'Twill serve thee to defend or kill;
A breast-plate for thine hour of need,
Or blade to bid thy foeman bleed;
But if a dagger's form it bear,
Let those who shape its edge, beware.
Thus passion's fire, and woman's art,
Can turn and tame the sterner heart;
From these its form and tone are ta'en,
And what they make it, must remain,
But break — before it bend again.
    *   *   *   *   *
    *   *   *   *   *

If solitude succeed to grief,
Release from pain is slight relief;
The vacant bosom's wilderness
Might thank the pang that made it less.
We loathe what none are left to share:
Even bliss — 'twere woe alone to bear;
The heart once left thus desolate
Must fly at last for ease — to hate.
It is as if the dead could feel
The icy worm around them steal,
And shudder, as the reptiles creep
To revel o'er their rotting sleep,
Without the power to scare away
The cold consumers of their clay!
It is as if the desert-bird,[1]
   Whose beak unlocks her bosom's stream
   To still her famished nestlings' scream,
Nor mourns a life to them transferred,
Should rend her rash devoted breast,
And find them flown her empty nest.
The keenest pangs the wretched find
   Are rapture to the dreary void,
The leafless desert of the mind,
   The waste of feelings unemployed.
Who would be doomed to gaze upon
A sky without a cloud or sun?
Less hideous far the tempest's roar
Than ne'er to brave the billows more —
Thrown, when the war of winds is o'er,
A lonely wreck on fortune's shore,
'Mid sullen calm, and silent bay,
Unseen to drop by dull decay; —
Better to sink beneath the shock
Than moulder piecemeal on the rock!
    *   *   *   *   *

"Father! thy days have passed in peace,
   'Mid counted beads, and countless prayer;
To bid the sins of others cease,
   Thyself without a crime or care,
Save transient ills that all must bear,
Has been thy lot from youth to age;
And thou wilt bless thee from the rage
Of passions fierce and uncontrolled,

---

[1] The pelican is, I believe, the bird so libelled, by the imputation of feeding her chickens with her blood.

Such as thy penitents unfold,
Whose secret sins and sorrows rest
Within thy pure and pitying breast.
My days, though few, have passed below
In much of joy, but more of woe;
Yet still in hours of love or strife,
I've 'scaped the weariness of life:
Now leagued with friends, now girt by foes,
I loathed the languor of repose.
Now nothing left to love or hate,
No more with hope or pride elate;
I'd rather be the thing that crawls
Most noxious o'er a dungeon's walls,
Than pass my dull, unvarying days,
Condemned to meditate and gaze.
Yet, lurks a wish within my breast
For rest — but not to feel 'tis rest.
Soon shall my fate that wish fulfil;
   And I shall sleep without the dream
Of what I was, and would be still,
   Dark as to thee my deeds may seem:
My memory now is but the tomb
Of joys long dead; my hope, their doom.
Though better to have died with those
Than bear a life of lingering woes.
My spirit shrunk not to sustain
The searching throes of ceaseless pain;
Nor sought the self-accorded grave
Of ancient fool and modern knave:
Yet death I have not feared to meet;
And in the field it had been sweet,
Had danger wooed me on to move
The slave of glory, not of love.
I've braved it — not for honor's boast;
I smile at laurels won or lost;
To such let others carve their way,
For high renown, or hireling pay:
But place again before my eyes
Aught that I deem a worthy prize,
The maid I love, the man I hate;
And I will hunt the steps of fate,
To save or slay, as these require,
Through rending steel, and rolling fire:
Nor needst thou doubt this speech from one
Who would but do — what he *hath* done.
Death is but what the haughty brave,
The weak must bear, the wretch must crave;
Then let Life go to him who gave:
I have not quailed to danger's brow
When high and happy — need I *now?*
    *   *   *   *

" I loved her, Friar! nay, adored —
   But these are words that all can use —
I proved it more in deed than word;
There's blood upon that dinted sword,
   A stain its steel can never lose:
'Twas shed for her, who died for me,
   It warmed the heart of one abhorred:
Nay, start not — no — nor bend thy knee,
   Nor midst my sins such act record;
Thou wilt absolve me from the deed.

For he was hostile to thy creed!
The very name of Nazarene
Was wormwood to his Paynim spleen.
Ungrateful fool! since but for brands
Well wielded in some hardy hands,
And wounds by Galileans given,
The surest pass to Turkish heaven,
For him his Houris still might wait
Impatient at the Prophet's gate.
I loved her — love will find its way
Through paths where wolves would fear to
      prey;
And if it dares enough, 'twere hard
If passion met not some reward —
No matter how, or where, or why,
I did not vainly seek, nor sigh :
Yet sometimes, with remorse, in vain
I wish she had not loved again.
She died — I dare not tell thee how;
But look 'tis written on my brow!
There read of Cain the curse and crime,
In characters unworn by time:
Still, ere thou dost condemn me, pause;
Not mine the act, though I the cause.
Yet did he but what I had done,
Had she been false to more than one.
Faithless to him, he gave the blow;
But true to me, I laid him low:
Howe'er deserved her doom might be,
Her treachery was truth to me;
To me she gave her heart, that all
Which tyranny can ne'er enthrall;
And I, alas! too late to save!
Yet all I then could give, I gave,
'Twas some relief, our foe a grave.
His death sits lightly; but her fate
Has made me — what thou well may'st hate.
   His doom was sealed — he knew it well,
Warned by the voice of stern Taheer,
Deep in whose darkly boding ear [1]

The deathshot pealed of murder near,
   As filed the troop to where they fell!
He died too in the battle broil,
A time that heeds nor pain nor toil;
One cry to Mahomet for aid,
One prayer to Alla all he made :
He knew and crossed me in the fray —
I gazed upon him where he lay,
And watched his spirit ebb away :
Though pierced like pard by hunters' steel,
He felt not half that now I feel.
I searched, but vainly searched, to find
The workings of a wounded mind;
Each feature of that sullen corse
Betrayed his rage, but no remorse.
Oh, what had Vengeance given to trace
Despair upon his dying face!
The late repentance of that hour,
When Penitence hath lost her power
To tear one terror from the grave,
And will not soothe, and cannot save.
   *   *   *   *   *

" The cold in clime are cold in blood,
   Their love can scarce deserve the name;
But mine was like the lava flood
   That boils in Ætna's breast of flame.

[1] This superstition of a second hearing (for I never met with downright second-sight in the East) fell once under my own observation. On my third journey to Cape Colonna, early in 1811, as we passed through the defile that leads from the hamlet between Keratia and Colonna, I observed Dervish Tahiri riding rather out of the path, and leaning his head upon his hand, as if in pain. I rode up and inquired. "We are in peril," he answered. "What peril? we are not now in Albania, nor in the passes to Ephesus Messalunghi, or Lepanto; there are plenty of us, well armed, and the Choriates have not courage to be thieves." — "True, Affendi, but nevertheless the shot is ringing in my ears." — "The shot! not a tophaike has been fired this morning." — "I hear it notwithstanding — Bom — Bom — as plainly as I hear your voice." — "Psha!" — "As you please, Affendi; if it is written, so will it be." — I left this quick-eared predestinarian, and rode up to Basili, his Christian compatriot, whose ears, though not at all prophetic, by no means relished the intelligence. We all arrived at Colonna, remained some hours, and returned leisurely, saying a variety of brilliant things, in more languages than spoiled the building of Babel, upon the mistaken seer. Romaic, Arnaout, Turkish, Italian, and English, were all exercised, in various conceits, upon the unfortunate Mussulman. While we were contemplating the beautiful prospect, Dervish was occupied about the columns. I thought he was deranged into an antiquarian, and asked him if he had become a " *Palaocastro* " man? "No," said he, "but these pillars will be useful in making a stand;" and added other remarks, which at least evinced his own belief in his troublesome faculty of *forehearing*. On our return to Athens we heard from Leoné (a prisoner set ashore some days after) of the intended attack of the Mainotes, mentioned, with the cause of its not taking place, in the notes to Childe Harold, Canto 2d. I was at some pains to question the man, and he described the dresses, arms, and marks of the horses of our party so accurately, that, with other circumstances, we could not doubt of *his* having been in "villanous company," and ourselves in a bad neighborhood. Dervish became a soothsayer for life, and I dare say is now hearing more musketry than ever will be fired, to the great refreshment of the Arnaouts of Berat, and his native mountains. — I shall mention one trait more of this singular race. In March, 1811, a remarkably stout and active Arnaout came (I believe the fiftieth on the same errand) to offer himself as an attendant, which was declined: ' Well, Affendi," quoth he, "may you live! — you would have found me useful. I shall leave the town for the hills tomorrow, in the winter I return, perhaps you will then receive me." — Dervish, who was present, remarked as a thing of course, and of no consequence, "in the meantime he will join the Klephtes" (robbers), which was true to the letter. If not cut off, they come down in the winter, and pass it unmolested in some town, where they are often as well known as their exploits.

I cannot prate in puling strain
Of ladye-love, and beauty's chain:
If changing cheek, and scorching vein,
Lips taught to writhe, but not complain,
If bursting heart, and maddening brain,
And daring deed, and vengeful steel,
And all that I have felt and feel,
Betoken love — that love was mine,
And shown by many a bitter sign.
'Tis true, I could not whine nor sigh,
I knew but to obtain or die.
I die — but first I have possessed,
And come what may, I *have been* blest.
Shall I the doom I sought upbraid ?
No — reft of all, yet undismayed
But for the thought of Leila slain,
Give me the pleasure with the pain,
So would I live and love again.
I grieve, but not, my holy guide!
For him who dies, but her who died:
She sleeps beneath the wandering wave —
Ah! had she but an earthly grave,
This breaking heart and throbbing head
Should seek and share her narrow bed.[1]
She was a form of life and light,
That, seen, became a part of sight;
And rose, where'er I turned mine eye,
The Morning-star of Memory!
  Yes, Love indeed is light from heaven;[2]
  A spark of that immortal fire
With angels shared, by Alla given,
  To lift from earth our low desire.
Devotion wafts the mind above,
But heaven itself descends in love;
A feeling from the Godhead caught,
To wean from self each sordid thought;
A Ray of him who formed the whole;
A Glory circling round the soul!
I grant *my* love imperfect, all
That mortals by the name miscall;

Then deem it evil, what thou wilt;
But say, oh say, *hers* was not guilt!
She was my life's unerring light:
That quenched, what beam shall break my
  night ?
Oh! would it shone to lead me still,
Although to death or deadliest ill!
Why marvel ye, if they who lose
This present joy, this future hope,
  No more with sorrow meekly cope;
In phrenzy then their fate accuse:
In madness do those fearful deeds
  That seem to add but guilt to woe ?
Alas! the breast that inly bleeds
  Hath nought to dread from outward blow
Who falls from all he knows of bliss,
Cares little into what abyss.
Fierce as the gloomy vulture's now
  To thee, old man, my deeds appear:
I read abhorrence on thy brow,
  And this too was I born to bear!
'Tis true, that, like that bird of prey,
With havoc have I marked my way:
But this was taught me by the dove,
To die — and know no second love.
This lesson yet hath man to learn,
Taught by the thing he dares to spurn:
The bird that sings within the brake,
The swan that swims upon the lake,
One mate, and one alone, will take.
And let the fool still prone to range,
And sneer on all who cannot change,
Partake his jest with boasting boys;
I envy not his varied joys,
But deem such feeble, heartless man,
Less than yon solitary swan;
Far, far beneath the shallow maid
He left believing and betrayed.
Such shame at least was never mine —
Leila! each thought was only thine!
My good, my guilt, my weal, my woe,
My hope on high — my all below.
Earth holds no other like to thee,
Or, if it doth, in vain for me:

---

[1] [These, in our opinion, are the most beautiful passages of the poem; and some of them of a beauty which it would not be easy to eclipse by many citations in the language. — *Jeffrey.*]

[2] [The hundred and twenty-six lines which follow, down to "Tell me no more of fancy's gleam," first appeared in the fifth edition. In returning the proof, Byron says: — "I have, but with some difficulty, *not* added any more to this snake of a poem, which has been lengthening its rattles every month. It is now fearfully long, being more than a canto and a half of 'Childe Harold.' The last lines Hodgson likes. It is not often he does; and when he don't, he tells me with great energy, and I fret, and alter. I have thrown them in to soften the ferocity of our Infidel; and, for a dying man, have given him a good deal to say for himself. Do you know anybody who can stop — I mean *point* — commas, and so forth? for I am, I hear, a sad hand at your punctuation." Among the Giaour MSS. is the first draught of this passage: —

" Yes } Love indeed { doth spring / descend / be born } from heaven;

A spark of that { immortal / eternal / celestial } fire,
To human hearts in mercy given,
  To lift from earth our low desire.
A feeling from the Godhead caught,
To wean from self { each / our } sordid thought;
Devotion sends the soul above,
  But Heaven itself descends to love.
Yet marvel not, if they who love
This present joy, this future hope,
  Which taught them with all ill to cope,
In madness, then, their fate accuse—
  In madness do those fearful deeds
That seem { to add but guilt to / but to augment their } woe.
  Alas! the { breast / heart } that inly bleeds,
Has nought to dread from outward foe," etc.]

For worlds I dare not view the dame
Resembling thee, yet not the same.
The very crimes that mar my youth,
This bed of death — attest my truth!
'Tis all too late — thou wert, thou art
The cherished madness of my heart!

"And she was lost — and yet I breathed,
  But not the breath of human life :
A serpent round my heart was wreathed,
  And stung my every thought to strife.
Alike all time, abhorred all place,
Shuddering I shrunk from Nature's face,
Where every hue that charmed before
The blackness of my bosom wore.
The rest thou dost already know,
And all my sins, and half my woe.
But talk no more of penitence ;
Thou see'st I soon shall part from hence :
And if thy holy tale were true,
The deed that's done canst *thou* undo ?
Think me not thankless — but this grief
Looks not to priesthood for relief.[1]
My soul's estate in secret guess :
But wouldst thou pity more, say less.
When thou canst bid my Leila live,
Then will I sue thee to forgive ;
Then plead my cause in that high place
Where purchased masses proffer grace.
Go, when the hunter's hand hath wrung
From forest-cave her shrieking young,
And calm the lonely lioness :
But soothe not — mock not *my* distress!

"In earlier days, and calmer hours,
  When heart with heart delights to blend,
Where bloom my native valley's bowers
  I had — Ah! have I now ? — a friend!
To him this pledge I charge thee send,
  Memorial of a youthful vow ;
I would remind him of my end :
  Though souls absorbed like mine allow
Brief thought to distant friendship's claim,
Yet dear to him my blighted name.
'Tis strange — he prophesied my doom,
  And I have smiled — I then could
    smile —
When Prudence would his voice assume,
  And warn — I recked not what — the
    while,
But now remembrance whispers o'er
Those accents scarcely marked before.
Say — that his bodings came to pass,
  And he will start to hear their truth,
  And wish his words had not been sooth :
Tell him, unheeding as I was,

Through many a busy bitter scene
Of all our golden youth had been,
In pain, my faltering tongue had tried
To bless his memory ere I died ;
But Heaven in wrath would turn away,
If Guilt should for the guiltless pray.
I do not ask him not to blame,
Too gentle he to wound my name ;
And what have I to do with fame ?
I do not ask him not to mourn,
Such cold request might sound like scorn ;
And what than friendship's manly tear
May better grace a brother's bier ?
But bear this ring, his own of old,
And tell him — what thou dost behold!
The withered frame, the ruined mind,
The wrack by passion left behind,
A shrivelled scroll, a scattered leaf,
Seared by the autumn blast of grief!
* * * * *

"Tell me no more of fancy's gleam,
No, father, no, 'twas not a dream ;
Alas! the dreamer first must sleep,
I only watched, and wished to weep ;
But could not, for my burning brow
Throbbed to the very brain as now :
I wished but for a single tear,
As something welcome, new, and dear ;
I wished it then, I wish it still ;
Despair is stronger than my will.
Waste not thine orison, despair
Is mightier than thy pious prayer :
I would not, if I might, be blest ;
I want no paradise, but rest.
'Twas then, I tell thee, father! then
I saw her ; yes, she lived again ;
And shining in her white symar,[2]
As through yon pale gray cloud the star
Which now I gaze on, as on her,
Who looked and looks far lovelier ;
Dimly I view its trembling spark ;
To-morrow's night shall be more dark ;
And I, before its rays appear,
That lifeless thing the living fear.
I wander, father! for my soul
Is fleeting towards the final goal.
I saw her, friar! and I rose
Forgetful of our former woes ;
And rushing from my couch, I dart,
And clasp her to my desperate heart ;
I clasp — what is it that I clasp ?
No breathing form within my grasp,
No heart that beats reply to mine,
Yet, Leila! yet the form is thine!
And art thou, dearest, changed so much,
As meet my eye, yet mock my touch ?
Ah! were thy beauties e'er so cold,
I care not ; so my arms enfold
The all they ever wished to hold.
Alas! around a shadow prest

[1] The monk's sermon is omitted. It seems to have had so little effect upon the patient, that it could have no hopes from the reader. It may be sufficient to say, that it was of a customary length (as may be perceived from the interruptions and uneasiness of the patient,) and was delivered in the usual tone of all orthodox preachers.

[2] "Symar," a shroud.

They shrink upon my lonely breast;
Yet still 'tis there! In silence stands,
And beckons with beseeching hands!
With braided hair, and bright-black eye —
I knew 'twas false — she could not die!
But he is dead! within the dell
I saw him buried where he fell;
He comes not, for he cannot break
From earth; why then art thou awake?
They told me wild waves rolled above
The face I view, the form I love;
They told me — 'twas a hideous tale!
I'd tell it, but my tongue would fail:
If true, and from thine ocean-cave
Thou com'st to claim a calmer grave,
Oh! pass thy dewy fingers o'er
This brow that then will burn no more;
Or place them on my hopeless heart:
But, shape or shade! whate'er thou art,
In mercy ne'er again depart!
Or further with thee bear my soul
Than winds can waft or waters roll!   •
          *   *   *   *   *

"Such is my name, and such my tale.
    Confessor! to thy secret ear
I breathe the sorrows I bewail,
    And thank thee for the generous tear
This glazing eye could never shed.
Then lay me with the humblest dead,
And, save the cross above my head,
Be neither name nor emblem spread,
By prying stranger to be read,
Or stay the passing pilgrim's tread." [1]

[1] The circumstance to which the above story relates was not very uncommon in Turkey. A few years ago the wife of Muchtar Pacha complained to

He passed — nor of his name and race
Hath left a token or a trace,
Save what the father must not say
Who shrived him on his dying day:
This broken tale was all we knew
Of her he loved, or him he slew.

his father of his son's supposed infidelity; he asked with whom, and she had the barbarity to give in a list of the twelve handsomest women in Yanina. They were seized, fastened up in sacks, and drowned in the lake the same night! One of the guards who was present informed me, that not one of the victims uttered a cry, or showed a symptom of terror at so sudden a "wrench from all we know, from all we love." The fate of Phrosine, the fairest of this sacrifice, is the subject of many a Romaic and Arnaout ditty. The story in the text is one told of a young Venetian many years ago, and now nearly forgotten. I heard it by accident recited by one of the coffee-house story-tellers who abound in the Levant, and sing or recite their narratives. The additions and interpolations by the translator will be easily distinguished from the rest, by the want of Eastern imagery; and I regret that my memory has retained so few fragments of the original. For the contents of some of the notes I am indebted partly to D'Herbelot, and partly to that most Eastern, and, as Mr. Weber justly entitles it, "sublime tale," the "Caliph Vathek." I do not know from what source the author of that singular volume may have drawn his materials: some of his incidents are to be found in the "Bibliothèque Orientale;" but for correctness of costume, beauty of description, and power of imagination, it far surpasses all European imitations; and bears such marks of originality, that those who have visited the East will find some difficulty in believing it to be more than a translation. As an Eastern tale, even Rasselas must bow before it; his "Happy Valley" will not bear a comparison with the "Hall of Eblis."

THE BRIDE OF ABYDOS:[1]

A TURKISH TALE.

"Had we never loved so kindly,
Had we never loved so blindly,
Never met or never parted,
We had ne'er been broken-hearted."
                                        BURNS.

[1] ["Murray tells me that Croker asked him why the thing is called the *Bride* of Abydos? It is an awkward question, being unanswerable: she is not a bride; only about to be one. I don't wonder at his finding out the *Bull;* but the detection is too late to do any good. I was a great fool to have made it, and am ashamed of not being an Irishman." — *Byron's Diary*, December 6, 1813.]

INTRODUCTION.

THE " Bride of Abydos" was published in the beginning of December, 1813. The mood of mind in which it was struck off is thus stated by Byron, in a letter to Mr. Gifford: — "You have been good enough to look at a thing of mine in MS. — a Turkish story — and I should feel gratified if you would do it the same favor in its probationary state of printing. It was written, I cannot say for amusement, nor ' obliged by hunger and request of friends,' but in a state of mind, from circumstances which occasionally occur to ' us youth,' that rendered it necessary for me to apply my mind to something, anything, but reality; and under this not very brilliant inspiration it was composed. Send it either to the flames, or

> ———' A hundred hawkers' load
> On wings of winds to fly or fall abroad.'

It deserves no better than the first, as the work of a week, and scribbled ' stans pede in uno ' (by the by, the only foot I have to stand on); and I promise never to trouble you again under forty cantos, and a voyage between each."

The opening lines of " The Bride " were supposed to have been imitated from a song of Goethe's —

> " Kennst du das Land wo die Citronen blühn ? "

But Byron could not read German, and if he borrowed the idea, he must, he said, have derived it from Madame de Staël who copied Goethe in some verses which Byron, however, was nearly confident he had never seen when he wrote his own.

TO THE RIGHT HONORABLE LORD HOLLAND,

THIS TALE IS INSCRIBED,

WITH EVERY SENTIMENT OF REGARD AND RESPECT,

BY HIS GRATEFULLY OBLIGED AND

SINCERE FRIEND,

BYRON.

CANTO THE FIRST.

I.

KNOW ye the land where the cypress and myrtle,
Are emblems of deeds that are done in their clime,
Where the rage of the vulture, the love of the turtle,
Now melt into sorrow, now madden to crime?
Know ye the land of the cedar and vine,
Where the flowers ever blossom, the beams ever shine;
Where the light wings of Zephyr, oppressed with perfume,
Wax faint o'er the gardens of Gúl[1] in her bloom;
Where the citron and olive are fairest of fruit,
And the voice of the nightingale never is mute:
Where the tints of the earth, and the hues of the sky,
In color though varied, in beauty may vie,
And the purple of Ocean is deepest in dye;
Where the virgins are soft as the roses they twine,
And all, save the spirit of man, is divine ?
'Tis the clime of the East; 'tis the land of the Sun —

---

[1] " Gúl," the rose.

Can he smile on such deeds as his children
    have done ? [1]
Oh! wild as the accents of lovers' farewell
Are the hearts which they bear, and the tales
    which they tell.

II.

Begirt with many a gallant slave,
Apparelled as becomes the brave,
Awaiting each his lord's behest
To guide his steps, or guard his rest,
Old Giaffir sate in his Divan:
    Deep thought was in his aged eye;
And though the face of Mussulman
    Not oft betrays to standers by
The mind within, well skilled to hide
All but unconquerable pride,
His pensive cheek and pondering brow
Did more than he was wont avow.

III.

" Let the chamber be cleared." — the train
    disappeared —
" Now call me the chief of the Haram
    guard."
With Giaffir is none but his only son,
And the Nubian awaiting the sire's award.
" Haroun — when all the crowd that wait
Are passed beyond the outer gate,
(Woe to the head whose eye beheld
My child Zuleika's face unveiled!)
Hence, lead my daughter from her tower;
Her fate is fixed this very hour:
Yet not to her repeat my thought;
By me alone be duty taught!"
" Pacha! to hear is to obey."
No more must slave to despot say —
Then to the tower had ta'en his way,
But here young Selim silence brake,
    First lowly rendering reverence meet;
And downcast looked, and gently spake,
    Still standing at the Pacha's feet:
For son of Moslem must expire,
Ere dare to sit before his sire!

" Father! for fear that thou shouldst chide
My sister, or her sable guide,
Know — for the fault, if fault there be,
Was mine, then fall thy frowns on me —
So lovelily the morning shone,
    That — let the old and weary sleep —
I could not; and to view alone
    The fairest scenes of land and deep,
With none to listen and reply
To thoughts with which my heart beat high
Were irksome — for whate'er my mood,
In sooth I love not solitude;
I on Zuleika's slumber broke,
    And, as thou knowest that for me

Soon turns the Haram's grating key,
Before the guardian slaves awoke
We to the cypress groves had flown,
And made earth, main, and heaven our own!
There lingered we, beguiled too long
With Mejnoun's tale, or Sadi's song; [2]
Till I, who heard the deep tambour [3]
Beat thy Divan's approaching hour,
To thee, and to my duty true,
Warned by the sound, to greet thee flew:
But there Zuleika wanders yet — .
Nay, Father, rage not — nor forget
That none can pierce that secret bower
But those who watch the women's tower."

IV.

" Son of a slave " — the Pacha said —
" From unbelieving mother bred,
Vain were a father's hope to see
Aught that beseems a man in thee.
Thou, when thine arm should bend the bow,
    And hurl the dart, and curb the steed,
    Thou, Greek in soul if not in creed,
Must pore where babbling waters flow,
And watch unfolding roses blow.
Would that yon orb, whose matin glow
Thy listless eyes so much admire,
Would lend thee something of his fire!
Thou, who would'st see this battlement
By Christian cannon piecemeal rent;
Nay, tamely view old Stambol's wall
Before the dogs of Moscow fall,
Nor strike one stroke for life and death
Against the curs of Nazareth!
Go — let thy less than woman's hand
Assume the distaff — not the brand.
But, Haroun! — to my daughter speed:
And hark — of thine own head take heed —
If thus Zuleika oft takes wing —
Thou see'st yon bow — it hath a string!"

V.

No sound from Selim's lip was heard,
    At least that met old Giaffir's ear,
But every frown and every word
Pierced keener than a Christian's sword.
    " Son of a slave! — reproached with fear!
    Those gibes had cost another dear.
Son of a slave! — and *who* my sire?"
    Thus held his thoughts their dark career;
And glances ev'n of more than ire
    Flash forth, then faintly disappear.
Old Giaffir gazed upon his son
    And started; for within his eye
He read how much his wrath had done;
He saw rebellion there begun:
    ." Come hither, boy — what, no reply?
I mark thee — and I know thee too;

---

[1] " Souls made of fire, and children of the Sun,
    With whom revenge is virtue."
               Young's Revenge.

[2] Mejnoun and Leila, the Romeo and Juliet of the
East. Sadi, the moral poet of Persia.
[3] Tambour. Turkish drum, which sounds at sun-
rise, noon, and twilight.

But there be deeds thou dar'st not do:
But if thy beard had manlier length,
And if thy hand had skill and strength,
I'd joy to see thee break a lance,
Albeit against my own perchance."

As sneeringly these accents fell,
On Selim's eye he fiercely gazed:
  That eye returned him glance for glance,
And proudly to his sire's was raised,
  Till Giaffir's quailed and. shrunk
    askance —
And why — he felt, but durst not tell.
" Much I misdoubt this wayward boy
Will one day work me more annoy:
I never loved him from his birth,
And — but his arm is little worth,
And scarcely in the chase could cope
With timid fawn or antelope,
Far less would venture into strife
Where man contends for fame and life —
I would not trust that look or tone:
No — nor the ,blood so near my own.
That blood — he hath not heard — no
  more —
I'll watch him closer than before.
He is an Arab [1] to my sight,
Or Christian crouching in the fight —
But hark! — I hear Zuleika's voice;
  Like Houris' hymn it meets mine ear:
She is the offspring of my choice;
  Oh! more than ev'n her mother dear,
With all to hope, and nought to fear —
My Peril ever welcome here!
Sweet as the desert fountain's wave
To lips just cooled in time to save —
  Such to my longing sight art thou;
Nor can they waft to Mecca's shrine
More· thanks for life, than I for thine,
  Who blest thy birth, and bless thee now."

VI.

Fair, as the first that fell of womankind,
  When on that dread yet lovely serpent
    smiling,
Whose image then was stamped upon her
  mind —
But once beguiled — and ever more beguil-
  ing;
Dazzling, as that, oh! too transcendent vision
To Sorrow's phantom-peopled slumber
  given,
When heart meets heart again in dreams
  Elysian,
And paints the lost on Earth revived in
  Heaven;
Soft, as the memory of buried love;
Pure, as the prayer which Childhood wafts
  above;

---

[1] The Turks abhor the Arabs (who return the compliment a hundred-fold) even more than they hate the Christians.

Was she — the daughter of that rude old Chief,
Who met the maid with tears — but not of
  grief.

Who hath not proved how feebly words essay
To fix one spark of Beauty's heavenly ray?
Who doth not feel, until his failing sight
Faints into dimness with its own delight,
His changing cheek, his sinking heart confess
The might — the majesty of Loveliness?
Such was Zuleika — such around her shone
The nameless charms unmarked by her
  alone;
The light of love, the purity of grace,
The mind, the Music [2] breathing from her
  face,[3]
The heart whose softness ·harmonized the
  whole —
And, oh! that eye was in itself a Soul!

---

[2] This expression has met with objections. I will not refer to " Him who hath not Music in his soul," but merely request the reader to recollect, for ten seconds, the features of the woman whom he believes to be the most beautiful; and if he then does not comprehend fully what is feebly expressed in the above line, I shall be sorry for us both. For an eloquent passage in the latest work of the first female writer of this, perhaps of any, age, on the analogy (and the immediate comparison excited · by that analogy) between "painting and music," see vol. iii. cap. 10, *De l'Allemagne.* And is not this connection still stronger with the original than the copy? With the coloring of Nature than of Art? After all, this is rather to be felt than described; still I think there are some who will understand it, at least they would have done had they beheld the countenance whose speaking harmony suggested the idea; for this passage is not drawn from imagination, but memory, that mirror which Affliction dashes to the earth, and looking down upon the fragments, only beholds the reflection multiplied! — [" This morning, a very pretty billet from the Staël. She has been pleased to be pleased with my slight eulogy in the note annexed to the ' Bride.' This is to be accounted for in several ways: — firstly, all women like all, or any praise; secondly, this was unexpected, because I have never courted her; and, thirdly, as Scrub says, those who have been all their lives regularly praised, by regular critics, like a little variety, and are glad when any one goes out of his way to say a civil thing; and, fourthly, she is a very good-natured creature, which is the best reason, after all, and, perhaps the only one." — *Byron's Diary,* Dec. 7, 1813.]

[3] [Among the imputed plagiarisms so industriously hunted out in his writings, this line has been with somewhat more plausibility than is frequent in such charges, included; the lyric poet Lovelace having, it seems, written " The melody and music of her face." Sir Thomas Browne, too, in his Religio Medici, says, " There is music even in beauty." The coincidence, no doubt, is worth observing, and the task of " tracking thus a favorite writer in the snow (as Dryden expresses it) of others," is sometimes not unamusing: but to those who found upon such resemblances a general charge of plagiarism, we may apply what Sir Walter Scott says: — " It is a favorite theme of laborious dulness to trace such

Her graceful arms in meekness bending
Across her gently-budding breast;
At one kind word those arms extending
To clasp the neck of him who blest
His child caressing and carest,
Zuleika came — and Giaffir felt
His purpose half within him melt:
Not that against her fancied weal
His heart though stern could ever feel;
Affection chained her to that heart;
Ambition tore the links apart.

VII.

" Zuleika! child of gentleness!
How dear this very day must tell,
When I forget my own distress,
. In losing what I love so well,
To bid thee with another dwell:
Another! and a braver man
Was never seen in battle's van.
We Moslem reck not much of blood;
But yet the line of Carasman [1]
Unchanged, unchangeable hath stood
First of the bold Timariot bands
That won and well can keep their lands.
Enough that he who comes to woo
Is kinsman of the Bey Oglou:
His years need scarce a thought employ;
I would not have thee wed a boy.
And thou shalt have a noble dower:
And his and my united power
Will laugh to scorn the death-firman,
Which others tremble but to scan,
And teach the messenger [2] what fate
The bearer of such boon may wait.
And now thou know'st thy father's will;
All that thy sex hath need to know:
'Twas mine to teach obedience still —
The way to love, thy lord may show."

VIII.

In silence bowed the Virgin's head;
And if her eye was filled with tears
That stifled feeling dare not shed,
And changed her cheek from pale to red,

And red to pale, as through her ears
Those winged words like arrows sped,
What could such be but maiden fears ?
So bright the tear in Beauty's eye,
Love half regrets to kiss it dry;
So sweet the blush of Bashfulness,
Even·Pity scarce can wish it less!
Whate'er it was the sire forgot;
Or if remembered, marked it not;
Thrice clapped his hands, and called his
　　steed,[3]
Resigned his gem-adorned chibouque,[4]
And mounting featly for the mead,
With Maugrabee [5] and Mamaluke,
His way amid his Delis took,[6]
To witness many an active deed
With sabre keen, or blunt jerreed.
The Kislar only and his Moors
Watch well the Haram's massy doors.

IX.

His head was leant upon his hand,
His eye looked o'er the dark blue water
That swiftly glides and gently swells
Between the winding Dardanelles;
But yet he saw nor sea nor strand,
Nor even his Pacha's turbaned band
Mix in the game of mimic slaughter,
Careering cleave the folded felt [7]
With sabre stroke right sharply dealt;
Nor marked the javelin-darting crowd,
Nor heard their Ollahs [8] wild and loud —
He thought but of old Giaffir's daughter!

X.

No word from Selim's bosom broke;
One sigh Zuleika's thought bespoke:

---

coincidences, because they appear to reduce genius of the higher order to the usual standard of humanity, and of course to bring the author nearer to a level with his critics." — *Moore.*]

[1] Carasman Oglou, or Kara Osman Oglou, is the principal landholder in Turkey; he governs Magnesia: those who, by a kind of feudal tenure, possess land on condition of service, are called Timariots: they serve as Spahis, according to the extent of territory, and bring a certain number into the field, generally cavalry.

[2] When a Pacha is sufficiently strong to resist, the single messenger, who is always the first bearer of the order for his death, is strangled instead, and sometimes five or six, one after the other on the same errand, by command of the refractory patient: if, on the contrary, he is weak or loyal, he bows, kisses the Sultan's respectable signature, and is bowstrung with great complacency. In 1810, sev-

eral of these presents were exhibited in the niche of the Seraglio gate; among others, the head of the Pacha of Bagdat, a brave young man, cut off by treachery after a desperate resistance.

[3] Clapping of the hands calls the servants. The Turks hate a superfluous expenditure of voice, and they have no bells.

[4] "Chibouque," the Turkish pipe of which the amber mouthpiece, and sometimes the ball which contains the leaf, is adorned with precious stones, if in possession of the wealthier orders.

[5] "Maugrabee," Moorish mercenaries.

[6] "Delis," bravos who form the forlorn hope of the cavalry, and always begin the action.

[7] A twisted fold of *felt* is used for scimitar practice by the Turks, and few but Mussulman arms can cut through it at a single stroke: sometimes a tough turban is used for the same purpose. The jerreed is a game of blunt javelins, animated and graceful.

[8] "Ollahs," Alla il Allah, the "Leilies," as the Spanish poets call them, the sound is Oliah; a cry of which the Turks, for a silent people, are somewhat profuse, particularly during the jerreed, or in the chase, but mostly in battle. Their animation in the field, and gravity in the chamber, with their pipes and comboloios, form an amusing contrast.

Still gazed he through the lattice grate,
Pale, mute, and mournfully sedate,
To him Zuleika's eye was turned,
But little from his aspect learned:
Equal her grief, yet not the same;
Her heart confessed a gentler flame:
But yet that heart alarmed or weak,
She knew not why, forbade to speak.
Yet speak she must — but when essay?
"How strange he thus should turn away!
Not thus we e'er before have met;
Not thus shall be our parting yet."
Thrice paced she slowly through the room,
    And watched his eye — it still was fixed:
    She snatched the urn wherein was mixed
The Persian Atar-gul's [1] perfume,
And sprinkled all its odors o'er
The pictured roof [2] and marble floor:
The drops, that through his glittering vest
The playful girl's appeal addressed,
Unheeded o'er his bosom flew,
As if that breast were marble too.
"What, sullen yet? it must not be —
Oh! gentle Selim, this from thee!"
She saw in curious order set
    The fairest flowers of eastern land —
" He loved them once; may touch them yet,
    If offered by Zuleika's hand."
The childish thought was hardly breathed
Before the Rose was plucked and wreathed;
The next fond moment saw her seat
Her fairy form at Selim's feet:
"This rose to calm my brother's cares
A message from the Bulbul [3] bears;
It says to-night he will prolong
For Selim's ear his sweetest song;
And though his note is somewhat sad,
He'll try for once a strain more glad,
With some faint hope his altered lay
May sing these gloomy thoughts away.

XI.

"What! not receive my foolish flower?
    Nay then I am indeed unblest:
On me can thus thy forehead lower?
    And know'st thou not who loves thee best?
Oh, Selim dear! oh, more than dearest!
Say, is it me thou hat'st or fearest?

[1] "Atar-gul," ottar of roses. The Persian is the finest.

[2] The ceiling and wainscots, or rather walls, of the Mussulman apartments are generally painted, in great houses, with one eternal and highly colored view of Constantinople, wherein the principal feature is a noble contempt of perspective: below, arms, scimitars, etc. are in general fancifully and not inelegantly disposed.

[3] It has been much doubted whether the notes of this " Lover of the rose " are sad or merry; and Mr. Fox's remarks on the subject have provoked some learned controversy as to the opinions of the ancients on the subject. I dare not venture a conjecture on the point, though a little inclined to the " errare mallem," etc. *if* Mr. Fox *was* mistaken.

Come, lay thy head upon my breast,
And I will kiss thee into rest,
Since words of mine, and songs must fail,
Ev'n from my fabled nightingale.
I knew our sire at times was stern,
But this from thee had yet to learn:
Too well I know he loves thee not;
But is Zuleika's love forgot?
Ah! deem I right? the Pacha's plan —
This kinsman Bey of Carasman
Perhaps may prove some foe of thine.
If so, I swear by Mecca's shrine,
If shrines that ne'er approach allow
To woman's step admit her vow,
Without thy free consent, command,
The Sultan should not have my hand!
Think'st thou that I could bear to part
With thee, and learn to halve my heart?
Ah! were I severed from thy side,
Where were thy friend — and who my
    guide?
Years have not seen, Time shall not see
The hour that tears my soul from thee:
Ev'n Azrael,[4] from his deadly quiver
When flies that shaft, and fly it must,
That parts all else, shall doom for ever
    Our hearts to undivided dust!"

XII.

He lived — he breathed — he moved — he
    felt.
He raised the maid from where she knelt:
His trance was gone — his keen eye shone
With thoughts that long in darkness dwelt;
With thoughts that burn — in rays that melt
As the stream late concealed
    By the fringe of its willows,
When it rushes revealed
    In the light of its billows;
As the bolt bursts on high
    From the black cloud that bound it,
Flashed the soul of that eye
    Through the long lashes round it.
A war-horse at the trumpet's sound,
A lion roused by heedless hound,
A tyrant waked to sudden strife
By graze of ill-directed knife,
Starts not to more convulsive life
Than he, who heard that vow, displayed,
And all, before repressed, betrayed:
"Now thou art mine, for ever mine,
With life to keep, and scarce with life resign;
Now thou art mine, that sacred oath,
Though sworn by one, hath bound us both.
Yes, fondly, wisely hast thou done;
That vow hath saved more heads than one;
But blench not thou — thy simplest tress
Claims more from me than tenderness;
I would not wrong the slenderest hair
That clusters round thy forehead fair,

[4] "Azrael," the angel of death.

For all the treasures buried far
Within the caves of Istakar,[1]
This morning clouds upon me lowered,
Reproaches on my head were showered,
And Giaffir almost called me coward!
Now I have motive to be brave,
The son of his neglected slave,
Nay, start not, 'twas the term he gave,
May show, though little apt to vaunt,
A heart his words nor deeds can daunt.
His son, indeed! — yet, thanks to thee,
Perchance I am, at least shall be;
But let our plighted secret vow
Be only known to us as now.
I know the wretch who dares demand
From Giaffir thy reluctant hand;
More ill-got wealth, a meaner soul
Holds not a Musselim's[2] control:
Was he not bred in Egripo?[3]
A viler race let Israel show;
But let that pass — to none be told
Our oath; the rest shall time unfold.
To me and mine leave Osman Bey;
I've partisans for peril's day:
Think not I am what I appear;
I've arms, and friends, and vengeance near."

XIII.

" Think not thou art what thou appearest!
　My Selim, thou art sadly changed:
This morn I saw thee gentlest, dearest;
　But now thou'rt from thyself estranged.
My love thou surely knew'st before,
It ne'er was less, nor can be more.
To see thee, hear thee, near thee stay,
　And hate the night I know not why,
Save that we meet not but by day;
　With thee to live, with thee to die,
　I dare not to my hope deny.
Thy cheek, thine eyes, thy lips to kiss,
Like this — and this — no more than this:
For, Alla! sure thy lips are flame:
　What fever in thy veins is flushing?
My own have nearly caught the same,
　At least I feel my cheek too blushing.
To soothe thy sickness, watch thy health,
Partake, but never waste thy wealth,
Or stand with smiles unmurmuring by,
And lighten half thy poverty;
Do all but close thy dying eye,
For that I could not live to try;
To these alone my thoughts aspire:
More can I do? or thou require?

---

[1] The treasures of the Pre-adamite Sultans. See D'Herbelot, article *Istakar*.

[2] " Musselim," a governor, the next in rank after a Pacha; a Waywode is the third; and then come the Agas.

[3] " Egripo," the Negropont. According to the proverb, the Turks of Egripo, the Jews of Salonica, and the Greeks of Athens, are the worst of their respective races.

But, Selim, thou must answer **why**
We need so much of mystery?
The cause I cannot dream nor tell,
But be it, since thou say'st 'tis well;
Yet what thou meanest by 'arms' and
　' friends,'
Beyond my weaker sense extends.
I meant that Giaffir should have heard
　The very vow I plighted thee;
His wrath would not revoke my word:
　But surely he would leave me free.
　Can this fond wish seem strange in me,
To be what I have ever been?
What other hath Zuleika seen
From simple childhood's earliest hour?
　What other can she seek to see
Than thee, companion of her bower,
　The partner of her infancy?
These cherished thoughts with life begun,
　Say, why must I no more avow?
What change is wrought to make me
　shun
　The truth; my pride, and thine till now?
To meet the gaze of stranger's eyes
Our law, our creed, our God denies;
Nor shall one wandering thought of mine
At such, our Prophet's will, repine:
No! happier made by that decree,
He left me all in leaving thee.
Deep were my anguish, thus compelled
To wed with one I ne'er beheld:
This wherefore should I not reveal?
Why wilt thou urge me to conceal?
I know the Pacha's haughty mood
To thee hath never boded good;
And he so often storms at nought,
Allah! forbid that e'er he ought!
And why, I know not, but within
My heart concealment weighs like sin.
If then such secrecy be crime,
　And such it feels while lurking here;
Oh, Selim! tell me yet in time,
　Nor leave me thus to thoughts of fear.
Ah! yonder see the Tchocadar,[4]
My father leaves the mimic war;
I tremble now to meet his eye —
Say, Selim, canst thou tell me **why?**"

XIV.

" Zuleika — to thy tower's retreat
Betake thee — Giaffir I can greet:
And now with him I fain must prate
Of firmans, impost, levies, state.
There's fearful news from Danube's banks,
Our Vizier nobly thins his ranks,
For which the Giaour may give him thanks!
Our Sultan hath a shorter way
Such costly triumph to repay.
But, mark me, when the twilight drum

---

[4] " Tchocadar " — one of the attendants who precedes a man of authority.

Hath warned the troops to food and sleep,
Unto thy cell will Selim come:
  Then softly from the haram creep
  Where we may wander by the deep:
  Our garden-battlements are steep;
Nor these will rash intruder climb
To list our words, or stint our time;
And if he doth, I want not steel
Which some have felt, and more may feel,
Then shalt thou learn of Selim more
Than thou hast heard or thought before.

Trust me, Zuleika — fear not me!
Thou knowest I hold a Haram key."

"Fear thee, my Selim! ne'er till now
Did word like this — "
       " Delay not thou;
I keep the key — and Haroun's guard
Have *some*, and hope of *more* reward.
To-night, Zuleika, thou shalt hear
My tale, my purpose, and my fear:
I am not, love! what I appear."

CANTO THE SECOND.

I.

THE winds are high on Helle's wave,
  As on that night of stormy water
When Love, who sent, forgot to save
  The young, the beautiful, the brave,
    The lonely hope of Sestos' daughter.
Oh! when alone along the sky
Her turret-torch was blazing high,
Though rising gale, and breaking foam,
And shrieking sea-birds warned him home;
And clouds aloft and tides below,
With signs and sounds, forbade to go,
He could not see, he would not hear,
Or sound or sign foreboding fear;
His eye but saw that light of love,
The only star it hailed above;
His ear but rang with Hero's song,
"Ye waves, divide not lovers long!" —
That tale is old, but love anew
May nerve young hearts to prove as true.

II.

The winds are high, and Helle's tide
  Rolls darkly heaving to the main;
And Night's descending shadows hide
  That field with blood bedewed in vain,
  The desert of old Priam's pride;
  The tombs, sole relics of his reign,
All — save immortal dreams that could be-
  guile
The blind old man of Scio's rocky isle!

III.

Oh! yet — for there my steps have been;
  These feet have pressed the sacred shore,
These limbs that buoyant wave hath borne—
Minstrel! with thee to muse, to mourn, ·
  To trace again those fields of yore,
Believing every hillock green
  Contains no fabled hero's ashes,
And that around the undoubted scene

Thine own "broad Hellespont"[1] still
  dashes,
Be long my lot! and cold were he
Who there could gaze denying thee!

IV.

The night hath closed on Helle's stream,
  Nor yet hath risen on Ida's hill
That moon, which shone on his high theme:
  No warrior chides her peaceful beam,
  But conscious shepherds bless it still.
Their flocks are grazing on the mound
  Of him wh felt the Dardan's arrow:
Tha. mighty heap of gathere ' ground
Which Ammon's son ran pr udly round,[2]
By nations raised, by monarchs crowned,
  Is ow a lone and nameless barrow!
Within — thy dwelling-place how narrow!
Without — cat. only strangers breathe
The nam of him that *was* beneath:
Dust long outlasts the storied stone;
But Thou — thy very dust is gone!

V.

Late, late to-night will Dian cheer
The swain, and chase the boatman's fear:

---

[1] The wrangling about this epithet, " the broad Hellespont" r the " boundless Hellespont," whether it means one or the other, or what it means at all, has been beyond all possibility of detail. I have even heard it disputed on the spot; and not foreseeing a speedy conclusion to the controversy, amused myself with swimming across it in the mean time; and probably may again, before the point is settled. Indeed, the question as to the truth of " the tale of Troy divine " still continues, much of it resting upon the talismanic word "απειρος: " probably Homer had the same notion of distance that a coquette has of time; and when he talks of boundless, means half a mile; as the latter, by a like figure, when she says *eternal* attachment, simply specifies three weeks.

[2] Before his Persian invasion, and crowned the altar with laurel, etc. He was afterwards imitated

Till then — no beacon on the cliff
May shape the course of struggling skiff;
The scattered lights that skirt the bay,
All, one by one, have died away;
The only lamp of this lone hour
Is glimmering in Zuleika's tower.
Yes! there is light in that lone chamber,
 And o'er her silken Ottoman
Are thrown the fragrant beads of amber,
 O'er which her fairy fingers ran; [1]
Near these, with emerald rays beset,
(How could she thus that gem forget ?)
Her mother's sainted amulet,[2]
Whereon engraved the Koorsee text,
Could smooth this life, and win the next;
And by her comboloio [3] lies
A Koran of illumined dyes;
And many a bright emblazoned rhyme
By Persian scribes redeemed from time;
And o'er those scrolls, not oft so mute,
Reclines her now neglected lute;
And round her lamp of fretted gold
Bloom flowers in urns of China's mould;
The richest work of Iran's loom,
And Sheeraz' tribute of perfume;
All that can eye or sense delight
 Are gathered in that gorgeous room:
 But yet it hath an air of gloom.
She, of this Peri cell the sprite,
What doth she hence,and on sorude anight?

VI.

Wrapt in the darkest sable vest,
 Which none save noblest Moslem wear,
To guard from winds of heaven the breast
As heaven itself to Selim dear,

---

by Caracalla in his race. It is believed that the
last also poisoned a friend, named Festus, for the
sake of new Patroclan games. I have seen the
sheep feeding on the tombs of Æsietes and Antilo-
chus : the first is in the centre of the plain.
 [1] When rubbed, the amber is susceptible of a
perfume, which is slight but *not* disagreeable. [On
discovering that, in some of the early copies, the
all-important monosyllable " *not* " had been omitted,
Byron wrote to Mr. Murray, — " There is a diabol-
ical mistake which must be corrected; it is the
omission of ' not ' before disagreeable, in the note
on the amber rosary. This is really horrible, and
nearly as bad as the stumble of mine at the threshold
— I mean the *misnomer* of Bride. Pray do not let
a copy go without the ' not:' it is nonsense, and
worse than nonsense. I wish the printer was sad-
dled with a vampire."]
 [2] The belief in amulets engraved on gems, or en-
closed in gold boxes, containing scraps from the
Koran, worn round the neck, wrist, or arm, is still
universal in the East. The Koorsee (throne) verse
in the second cap. of the Koran describes the attri-
butes of the Most High, and is engraved in this man-
ner, and worn by the pious, as the most esteemed
and sublime of all sentences.
 [3] " Comboloio "— a Turkish rosary. The MSS.,
particularly those of the Persians, are richly adorned
and illuminated. The Greek females are kept in

With cautious steps the thicket threading,
 And starting oft, as through the glade
The gust its hollow moanings made,
Till on the smoother pathway treading,
More free her timid bosom beat,
 The maid pursued her silent guide;
And though her terror urged retreat,
 How could she quit her Selim's side ?
 How teach her tender lips to chide ?

VII.

They reached at length a grotto, hewn
 By nature, but enlarged by art,
Where oft her lute she wont to tune,
 And oft her Koran conned apart;
And oft in youthful reverie
She dreamed what Paradise might be:
Where woman's parted soul shall go
Her Prophet had disdained to show;
But Selim's mansion was secure,
Nor deemed she, could he long endure
His bower in other worlds of bliss,
Without *her*, most beloved in this!
Oh! who so dear with him could dwell ?
What Houri soothe him half so well ?

VIII.

Since last she visited the spot
Some change seemed wrought within th
  grot:
It might be only that the night
Disguised things seen by better light:
That brazen lamp but dimly threw
A ray of no celestial hue;
But in a nook within the cell
Her eye on stranger objects fell.
There arms were piled, not such as wield
The turbaned Delis in the field;
But brands of foreign blade and hilt,
And one was red — perchance with guilt!
Ah! how without can blood be spilt ?
A cup too on the board was set
That did not seem to hold sherbet.
What may this mean ? she turned to see
Her Selim —" Oh! can this be he ? "

IX.

His robe of pride was thrown aside,
 His brow no high-crowned turban bore,
But in its stead a shawl of red,
 Wreathed lightly round,his temples wore.
That dagger, on whose hilt the gem
Were worthy of a diadem,
No longer glittered at his waist,
Where pistols unadorned were braced;
And from his belt a sabre swung,
And from his shoulder loosely hung
The cloak of white, the thin capote

---

utter ignorance; but many of the Turkish girls are
highly accomplished, though not actually qualified
for a Christian coterie. Perhaps some of our own
" *blues* " might not be the worse for *bleaching.*

That decks the wandering Candiote;
Beneath — his golden plated vest
Clung like a cuirass to his breast;
The greaves below his knee that wound
With silvery scales were sheathed and
    bound.
But were it not that high command
Spake in his eye, and tone, and hand,
All that a careless eye could see
In him was some young Galiongée.[1]

X.

"I said I was not what I seemed;
    And now thou see'st my words were true:
I have a tale thou hast not dreamed,
    If sooth — its truth must others rue.
My story now 'twere vain to hide,
I must not see thee Osman's bride:
But had not thine own lips declared
How much of that young heart I shared,
I could not, must not, yet have shown
The darker secret of my own.
In this I speak not now of love;
That, let time, truth, and peril prove:
But first — Oh! never wed another —
Zuleika! I am not thy brother!"

XI.

"Oh! not my brother! — yet unsay —
    God! am I left alone on earth
To mourn — I dare not curse — the day.
    That saw my solitary birth?
Oh! thou wilt love me now no more!
    My sinking heart foreboded ill;
But know *me* all I was before,
    Thy sister — friend — Zuleika still.
Thou led'st me here perchance to kill;
    If thou hast cause for vengeance, see!
My breast is offered — take thy fill!
    Far better with the dead to be
Than live thus nothing now to thee:
Perhaps far worse, for now I know
Why Giaffir always seemed thy foe;
And I, alas! am Giaffir's child,
For whom thou wert contemned, reviled.
If not thy sister — would'st thou save
My life, oh! bid me be thy slave!"

XII.

"My slave, Zuleika! — nay, I'm thine:
    But, gentle love, this transport calm,
Thy lot shall yet be linked with mine;

I swear it by our Prophet's shrine,
    And be that thought thy sorrow's balm.
So may the Koran [2] verse displayed
Upon its steel direct my blade,
In danger's hour to guard us both,
As I preserve that awful oath!
The name in which thy heart hath prided
    Must change; but, my Zuleika, know,
That tie is widened, not divided,
    Although thy Sire's my deadliest foe.
My father was to Giaffir all
    That Selim late was deemed to thee;
That brother wrought a brother's fall,
    But spared, at least, my infancy;
And lulled me with a vain deceit
That yet a like return may meet.
He reared me, not with tender help,
    But like the nephew of a Cain; [3]
He watched me like a lion's whelp,
    That gnaws and yet may break his chain.
My father's blood in every vein
Is boiling; but for thy dear sake
No present vengeance will I take;
    Though here I must no more remain.
But first, beloved Zuleika! hear
How Giaffir wrought this deed of fear.

XIII.

"How first their strife to rancor grew,
    If love or envy made them foes,

---

[1] "Galiongée" — or Galiongi, a sailor, that is, a Turkish sailor; the Greeks navigate, the Turks work the guns. Their dress is picturesque; and I have seen the Capitan Pacha more than once wearing it as a kind of *incog*. Their legs, however, are generally naked. The buskins described in the text are sheathed behind with silver are those of an Arnaut robber, who was my host (he had quitted the profession) at his Pyrgo, near Gastouni in the Morea; they were placed in scales one over the other like the back of an armadillo.

[2] The characters on all Turkish scimitars contain sometimes the name of the place of their manufacture, but more generally a text from the Koran, in letters of gold. Amongst those in my possession is one with a blade of singular construction; it is very broad, and the edge notched into serpentine curves like the ripple of water, or the wavering of flame. I asked the Arminian who sold it, what possible use such a figure could add: he said, in Italian, that he did not know; but the Mussulmans had an idea that those of this form gave a severer wound; and liked it because it was "piu feroce." I did not much admire the reason, but bought it for its peculiarity.

[3] It is to be observed, that every allusion to any thing or personage in the Old Testament, such as the Ark, or Cain, is equally the privilege of Mussulman and Jew: indeed, the former profess to be much better acquainted with the lives, true and fabulous, of the patriarchs, than is warranted by our own sacred writ; and not content with Adam, they have a biography of Pre-Adamites. Solomon is the monarch of all necromancy, and Moses a prophet inferior only to Christ and Mahomet. Zuleika is the Persian name of Potiphar's wife; and her amour with Joseph constitutes one of the finest poems in their language. It is, therefore, no violation of costume to put the names of Cain, or Noah, into the mouth of a Moslem. — [Some doubt having been expressed by Mr. Murray, as to the propriety of putting the name of Cain into the mouth of a Mussulman, Byron sent him the preceding note — "for the benefit of the ignorant." "I don't care one lump of sugar," he says, "for my poetry; but for my costume, and my correctness on those points, I will combat lustily."]

It matters little if I knew;
In fiery spirits, slights, though few
　And thoughtless, will disturb repose.
In war Abdallah's arm was strong,
Remembered yet in Bosniac song,
And Paswan's [1] rebel hordes attest
How little love they bore such guest:
His death is all I need relate,
The stern effect of Giaffir's hate;
And how my birth disclosed to me,
Whate'er beside it makes, hath made me
　　free.

XIV.

"When Paswan, after years of strife,
At last for power, but first for life,
In Widin's walls too proudly sate,
Our Pachas rallied round the state;
Nor last nor least in high command,
Each brother led a separate band;
They gave their horse-tails [2] to the wind,
　And mustering in Sophia's plain
Their tents were pitched, their post assigned;
　To one, alas! assigned in vain!
What need of words? the deadly bowl,
By Giaffir's order drugged and given,
With venom subtle as his soul,
　Dismissed Abdallah's hence to heaven.
Reclined and feverish in the bath,
　He, when the hunter's sport was up,
But little deemed a brother's wrath
　To quench his thirst had such a cup:
The bowl a bribed attendant bore;
He drank one draught [3] nor needed more!
If thou my tale, Zuleika, doubt,
Call Haroun — he can tell it out.

XV.

"The deed once done, and Paswan's feud
In part suppressed, though ne'er subdued,
　Abdallah's Pachalick was gained: —
Thou know'st not what in our Divan
Can wealth procure for worse than man —
　Abdallah's honors were obtained,
By him a brother's murder stained;
'Tis true, the purchase nearly drained
His ill got treasure, soon replaced.
Would'st question whence? Survey the
　　waste,
And ask the squalid peasant how

His gains repay his broiling brow! —
Why me the stern usurper spared,
Why thus with me his palace shared,
I know not. Shame, regret, remorse,
And little fear from infant's force;
Besides, adoption as a son
By him whom Heaven accorded none,
Or some unknown cabal, caprice,
Preserved me thus; — but not in peace:
He cannot curb his haughty mood,
Nor I forgive a father's blood.

XVI.

"Within thy father's house are foes;
　Not all who break his bread are true:
To these should I my birth disclose,
　His days, his very hours were few:
They only want a heart to lead,
A hand to point them to the deed.
But Haroun only knows or knew
　This tale, whose close is almost nigh:
He in Abdallah's palace grew,
　And held that post in his Serai
Which holds he here — he saw him die:
But what could single slavery do?
Avenge his lord? alas! too late;
Or save his son from such a fate?
He chose the last, and when elate
　With foes subdued, or friends betrayed,
Proud Giaffir in high triumph sate,
He led me helpless to his gate,
　And not in vain it seems essayed
To save the life for which he prayed.
The knowledge of my birth secured
　From all and each, but most from me:
Thus Giaffir's safety was insured.
Removed he too from Roumelie
To this our Asiatic side,
Far from our seats by Danube's tide,
　With none but Haroun, who retains
Such knowledge — and that Nubian feels
　A tyrant's secrets are but chains,
From which the captive gladly steals,
And this and more to me reveals:
Such still to guilt just Alla sends —
Slaves, tools, accomplices — no friends!

XVII.

"All this, Zuleika, harshly sounds;
　But harsher still my tale must be:
Howe'er my tongue thy softness wounds,
　Yet I must prove all truth to thee.
I saw thee start this garb to see,
Yet is it one I oft have worn,
　And long must wear: this Galiongée,
To whom thy plighted vow is sworn,
　Is leader of those pirate hordes,
Whose laws and lives are on their swords;
To hear whose desolating tale
Would make thy waning cheek more pale:
Those arms thou see'st my band have
　　brought,

---

[1] Paswan Oglou, the rebel of Widin; who, for
the last years of his life, set the whole power of the
Porte at defiance.
[2] "Horse-tail," the standard of a Pacha.
[3] Giaffir, Pacha of Argyro Castro, or Scutari, I
am not sure which, was actually taken off by the
Albanian Ali, in the manner described in the text.
Ali Pacha, while I was in the country, married the
daughter of his victim, some years after the event
had taken place at a bath in Sophia, or Adrianople.
The poison was mixed in the cup of coffee, which
is presented before the sherbet by the bath-keeper,
after dressing.

The hands that wield are not remote;
This cup too for the rugged knaves
　Is filled — once quaffed, they ne'er repine:
Our prophet might forgive the slaves;
　They're only infidels in wine.

XVIII.

"What could I be? Proscribed at home,
And taunted to a wish to roam;
And listless left — for Giaffir's fear
Denied the courser and the spear —
Though oft — Oh, Mahomet! how oft I —
In full Divan the despot scoffed,
As if *my* weak unwilling hand
Refused the bridle or the brand:
He ever went to war alone,
And pent me here untried — unknown;
To Haroun's care with women left,
By hope unblest, of fame bereft,
While thou — whose softness long endeared,
Though it unmanned me, still had cheered —
To Brusa's walls for safety sent,
Awaited'st there the field's event.
Haroun, who saw my spirit pining
　Beneath inaction's sluggish yoke,
His captive, though with dread resigning,
　My thraldom for a season broke,
On promise to return before
The day when Giaffir's charge was o'er.
'Tis vain — my tongue can not impart
My almost drunkenness of heart,
When first this liberated eye
Surveyed Earth, Ocean, Sun, and Sky,
As if my spirit pierced them through,
And all their inmost wonders knew!
One word alone can paint to thee
That more than feeling — I was Free!
E'en for thy presence ceased to pine;
The World — nay, Heaven itself was mine!

XIX.

"The shallop of a trusty Moor
Conveyed me from this idle shore;
I longed to see the isles that gem
Old Ocean's purple diadem:
I sought by turns, and saw them all;[1]
　But when and where I joined the crew,
With whom I'm pledged to rise or fall,
　When all that we design to do
Is done, 'twill then be time more meet
To tell thee, when the tale's complete.

XX.

'Tis true, they are a lawless brood,
But rough in form, nor mild in mood;
And every creed, and every race,
With them hath found — may find a place:
But open speech, and ready hand,
Obedience to their chief's command,

A soul for every enterprise,
That never sees with Terror's eyes;
Friendship for each, and faith to all,.
And vengeance vowed for those who fall,
Have made them fitting instruments
For more than ev'n my own intents.
And some — and I have studied all
　Distinguished from the vulgar rank,
But chiefly to my council call
　The wisdom of the cautious Frank —
And some to higher thoughts aspire,
　The last of Lambro's [2] patriots there
Anticipated freedom share;
And oft around the cavern fire
On visionary schemes debate,
To snatch the Rayahs [3] from their fate.
So let them ease their hearts with prate
Of equal rights, which man ne'er knew;
I have a love for freedom too.
Ay! let me like the ocean-Patriarch [4] roam,
Or only know on land the Tartar's home! [5]
My tent on shore, my galley on the sea,
Are more than cities and Serais to me:
Borne by my steed, or wafted by my sail,
Across the desert, or before the gale,
Bound where thou wilt, my barb! or glide,
　my prow,
But be the star that guides the wanderer,
　Thou!
Thou, my Zuleika, share and bless my bark;
The Dove of peace and promise to mine ark! [6]
Or, since that hope denied in worlds of strife,
Be thou the rainbow to the storms of life!
The evening beam that smiles the clouds away,
And tints to-morrow with prophetic ray!

---

[2] Lambro Canzani, a Greek, famous for his efforts, in 1789-90, for the independence of his country. Abandoned by the Russians, he became a pirate, and the Archipelago was the scene of his enterprises. He is said to be still alive at Petersburg. He and Riga are the two most celebrated of the Greek revolutionists.

[3] "Rayahs," — all who pay the capitation tax, called the "Haratch."

[4] The first of voyages is one of the few with which the Mussulmans profess much acquaintance.

[5] The wandering life of the Arabs, Tartars, and Turkomans, will be found well detailed in any book of Eastern travels. That it possesses a charm peculiar to itself, cannot be denied. A young French renegado confessed to Chateaubriand, that he never found himself alone, galloping in the desert, without a sensation approaching to rapture which was indescribable.

[6] [The longest, as well as most splendid, of those passages, with which the perusal of his own strains, during revision, inspired him, was that rich flow of eloquent feeling which follows the couplet, — "Thou, my Zuleika, share and bless my bark," etc. — a strain of poetry, which, for energy and tenderness of thought, for music of versification, and selectness of diction, has. throughout the greater portion of it, but few rivals in either ancient or modern song. — *Moore.*]

[1] The Turkish notions of almost all islands are confined to the Archipelago, the sea alluded to.

Blest — as the Muezzin's strain from Mecca's
  wall
To pilgrims pure and prostrate at his call;
Soft — as the melody of youthful days,
That steals the trembling tear of speechless
  praise;
Dear — as his native song to Exile's ears,
Shall sound each tone thy long-loved voice
  endears.
For thee in those bright isles is built a
  bower
Blooming as Aden [1] in its earliest hour.
A thousand swords, with Selim's heart and
  hand,
Wait—wave—defend—destroy — at thy com-
  mand!
Girt by my band, Zuleika at my side,
The spoil of nations shall bedeck my bride.
The Haram's languid years of listless ease
Are well resigned for cares — for joys like
  these:
Not blind to fate, I see, where'er I rove,
Unnumbered perils, — but one only love!
Yet well my toils shall that fond breast repay,
Though fortune frown, or falser friends betray.
How dear the dream in darkest hours of ill,
Should all be changed, to find thee faithful
  still!
Be but thy soul, like Selim's, firmly shown;
To thee be Selim's tender as thine own;
To soothe each sorrow, share in each delight,
Blend every thought, do all — but disunite!
Once free, 'tis mine our horde again to guide;
Friends to each other, foes to aught beside:
Yet there we follow but the bent assigned
By fatal Nature to man's warring kind:
Mark! where his carnage and his conquests
  cease!
He makes a solitude, and calls it — peace!
I like the rest must use my skill or strength,
But ask no land beyond my sabre's length:
Power sways but by division — her resource
The blest alternative of fraud or force!
Ours be the last; in time deceit may come
When cities cage us in a social home:
There even thy soul might err — how oft the
  heart
Corruption shakes which peril could not part!
And woman, more than man, when death or
  woe,
Or even Disgrace, would lay her lover low,
Sunk in the lap of Luxury will shame —
Away suspicion! — *not* Zuleika's name!
But life is hazard at the best; and here
No more remains to win, and much to fear:
Yes, fear! —the doubt, the dread of losing
  thee,
By Osman's power, and Giaffir's stern decree.
That dread shall vanish with the favoring gale,

Which love to-night hath promised to my
  sail:
No danger daunts the pair his smile hath
  blest,
Their steps still roving, but their hearts át rest.
With thee all toils are sweet, each clime hath
  charms,
Earth — sea alike—our world within our arms!
Ay! — let the loud winds whistle o'er the deck,
So that those arms cling closer round my
  neck:
The deepest murmur of this lip shall be
No sigh for safety, but a prayer for thee!
The war of elements no fears impart
To Love, whose deadliest bane is human Art:
There lie the only rocks our course can check;
Here moments menace — *there* are years of
  wreck!
But hence ye thoughts that rise in Horror's
  shape!
This hour bestows, or ever bars escape.
Few words remain of mine my tale to close:
Of thine but *one* to waft us from our foes;
Yea — foes — to me will Giaffir's hate decline ?
And is not Osman, who would part us, thine ?

XXI.

" His head and faith from doubt and death
  Returned in time my guard to save;
  Few heard, none told, that o'er the wave
From isle to isle I roved the while :
And since, though parted from my band,
Too seldom now I leave the land,
No deed they've done, nor deed shall do,
Ere I have heard and doomed it too:
I form the plan, decree the spoil,
'Tis fit I oftener share the toil.
But now too long I've held thine ear;
Time presses, floats my bark, and here
We leave behind but hate and fear.
To-morrow Osman with his train
Arrives — to-night must break thy chain:
And wouldst thou save that haughty Bey,
  Perchance, *his* life who gave thee thine,
With me, this hour away — away!
  But yet, though thou art plighted mine
Wouldst thou recall thy willing vow,
Appalled by truths imparted now,
Here rest I — not to see thee wed:
But be that peril on *my* head! "

XXII.

Zuleika, mute and motionless,
Stood like that statue of distress,
When, her last hope for ever gone,
The mother hardened into stone;
All in the maid that eye could see
Was but a younger Niobé.
But ere her lip, or even her eye,
Essayed to speak, or look reply,
Beneath the garden's wicket porch

---

[1] " Jannat al Aden," the perpetual abode, the
Mussulman paradise.

Far flashed on high a blazing torch!
Another — and another — and another —
" Oh! fly — no more — yet now my more
    than brother!"
Far, wide, through every thicket spread,
The fearful lights are gleaming red;
Nor these alone — for each right hand
Is ready with a sheathless brand.
They part, pursue, return, and wheel
With searching flambeau, shining steel;
And last of all, his sabre waving,
Stern Giaffir in his fury raving:
And now almost they touch the cave —
Oh! must that grot be Selim's grave?

XXIII.

Dauntless he stood — " 'Tis come — soon
    past —
One kiss, Zuleika! — 'tis my last:
  But yet my band not far from shore
May hear this signal, see the flash;
Yet now too few — the attempt were rash:
  No matter — yet one effort more."
Forth to the cavern mouth he stept;
  His pistol's echo rang on high,
Zuleika started not, nor wept,
  Despair benumbed her breast and eye! —
" They hear me not, or if they ply
Their oars, 'tis but to see me die;
That sound hath drawn my foes more nigh.
Then forth my father's scimitar,
Thou ne'er hast seen less equal war!
Farewell, Zuleika! — Sweet! retire:
  Yet stay within — here linger safe,
At thee his rage will only chafe.
Stir not — lest even to thee perchance
Some erring blade or ball should glance.
Fear'st thou for him? — may I expire
If in this strife I seek thy sire!
No — though by him that poison poured:
No — though again he call me coward!
But tamely shall I meet their steel?
No — as each crest save *his* may feel!"

XXIV.

One bound he made, and gained the sand.
  Already at his feet hath sunk
The foremost of the prying band,
  A gasping head, a quivering trunk:
Another falls — but round him close
A swarming circle of his foes;
From right to left his path he cleft,
  And almost met the meeting wave:
His boat appears — not five oars' length —
His comrades strain with desperate
    strength —
  Oh! are they yet in time to save?
His feet the foremost breakers lave;
His band are plunging in the bay,
Their sabres glitter through the spray;
Wet — wild — unwearied to the strand
They struggle — now they touch the land!

They come — 'tis but to add to slaughter —
His heart's best blood is on the water.

XXV.

Escaped from shot, unharmed by steel,
Or scarcely grazed its force to feel,
Had Selim won, betrayed, beset,
To where the strand and billows met;
There as his last step left the land,
And the last death-blow dealt his hand —
Ah! wherefore did he turn to look
  For her his eye but sought in vain?
That pause, that fatal gaze he took,
  Hath doomed his death, or fixed his chain.
Sad proof, in peril and in pain,
How late will Lover's hope remain!
His back was to the dashing spray;
Behind, but close, his comrades lay,
When, at the instant, hissed the ball —
" So may the foes of Giaffir fall!"
Whose voice is heard? whose carbine rang?
Whose bullet through the night-air sang,
Too nearly, deadly aimed to err?
'Tis thine — Abdallah's Murderer!
The father slowly rued thy hate,
The son hath found a quicker fate:
Fast from his breast the blood is bubbling,
The whiteness of the sea-foam troubling —
If aught his lips essayed to groan,
The rushing billows choked the tone!

XXVI.

Morn slowly rolls the clouds away;
  Few trophies of the fight are there:
The shouts that shook the midnight-bay
Are silent; but some signs of fray
  That strand of strife may bear,
And fragments of each shivered brand;
Steps stamped; and dashed into the sand
The print of many a struggling hand
  May there be marked; nor far remote
A broken torch, an oarless boat;
And tangled on the weeds that heap
The beach where shelving to the deep
  There lies a white capote!
'Tis rent in twain — one dark-red stain
The wave yet ripples o'er in vain:
  But where is he who wore?
Ye! who would o'er his relics weep,
Go, seek them where the surges sweep
Their burthen round Sigæum's steep
  And cast on Lemnos' shore:
The sea-birds shriek above the prey,
O'er which their hungry beaks delay,
As shaken on his restless pillow,
His head heaves with the heaving billow;
That hand, whose motion is not life,
Yet feebly seems to menace strife,
Flung by the tossing tide on high,
  Then levelled with the wave —
What recks it, though that corse shall lie
  Within a living grave?

The bird that tears that prostrate form
Hath only robbed the meaner worm;
The only heart, the only eye
Had bled or wept to see him die,
Had seen those scattered limbs composed,
  And mourned above his turban stone.[1]
That heart hath burst — that eye was
  closed —
    Yea — closed before his own!

XXVII.

By Helle's stream there is a voice of wail!
And woman's eye is wet — man's cheek is pale.
Zuleika! last of Giaffir's race,
Thy destined lord is come too late:
He sees not — ne'er shall see thy face!
    Can he not hear
The loud Wul-wulleh[2] warn his distant ear?
  Thy handmaids weeping at the gate,
  The Koran-chanters of the hymn of fate,
  The silent slaves with folded arms that wait,
Sighs in the hall, and shrieks upon the gale,
  Tell him thy tale!
Thou didst not view thy Selim fall!
  That fearful moment when he left the cave
    Thy heart grew chill:
He was thy hope — thy joy — thy love — thine
  all —
  And that last thought on him thou could'st
    not save
      Sufficed to kill;
Burst forth in one wild cry — and all was still.
Peace to thy broken heart, and virgin grave!
Ah! happy! but of life to lose the worst!
That grief — though deep — though fatal —
  was thy first!
Thrice happy! ne'er to feel nor fear the force
Of absence, shame, pride, hate, revenge, re-
  morse!
And, oh! that pang where more than Mad-
  ness lies!
The worm that will not sleep — and never
  dies;
Thought of the gloomy day and ghastly night,
That dreads the darkness, and yet loathes the
  light,
That winds around and tears the quivering
  heart!
Ah! wherefore not consume it — and depart!
Woe to thee, rash and unrelenting chief!
  Vainly thou heap'st the dust upon thy head,
  Vainly the sackcloth o'er thy limbs dost
    spread:
By that same hand Abdallah — Selim bled.
Now let it tear thy beard in idle grief:
Thy pride of heart, thy bride for Osman's bed,
She, whom thy sultan had but seen to wed,

Thy Daughter's dead!
Hope of thine age, thy twilight's lonely beam,
The Star hath set that shone on Helle's
  stream.
What quenched its ray? — the blood that thou
  hast shed!
Hark! to the hurried question of Despair:
" Where is my child?" — an Echo answers —
  " Where?"[3]

XXVIII.

Within the place of thousand tombs
  That shine beneath, while dark above
The sad but living cypress glooms,
  And withers not, though branch and leaf
Are stamped with an eternal grief,
  Like early unrequited Love,
One spot exists, which ever blooms,
  Ev'n in that deadly grove —
A single rose is shedding there
  Its lonely lustre, meek and pale:
It looks as planted by Despair —
  So white — so faint — the slightest gale
Might whirl the leaves on high;
  And yet, though storms and blight assail,
And hands more rude than wintry sky
  May wring it from the stem — in vain —
    To-morrow sees it bloom again!
The stalk some spirit gently rears,
And waters with celestial tears;
  For well may maids of Helle deem
That this can be no earthly flower,
Which mocks the tempest's withering hour,
And buds unsheltered by a bower;
Nor droops, though spring refuse her
  shower,
  Nor woos the summer beam:
To it the livelong night there sings
  A bird unseen — but not remote:
Invisible his airy wings,
But soft as harp that Houri strings
  His long entrancing note!
It were the Bulbul; but his throat,
  Though mournful, pours not such a strain;
For they who listen cannot leave
The spot, but linger there and grieve,
  As if they loved in vain!
And yet so sweet the tears they shed,
'Tis sorrow so unmixed with dread,
They scarce can bear the morn to break
  That melancholy spell,
And longer yet would weep and wake,

---

[1] A turban is carved in stone above the graves of *men* only.

[2] The death-song of the Turkish women. The " silent slaves " are the men, whose notions of decorum forbid complaint in *public.*

[3] " I came to the place of my birth, and cried, ' The friends of my youth, where are they?' and an Echo answered, ' Where are they?' " — *From an Arabic MS.* The above quotation (from which the idea in the text is taken) must be already familiar to every reader: it is given in the first annotation, p. 67, of " The Pleasures of Memory; " a poem so well known as to render reference almost superfluous; but to whose pages all will be delighted to recur.

He sings so wild and well!
But when the day-blush bursts from high
Expires that magic melody.
And some have been who could believe,
(So fondly youthful dreams deceive,
Yet harsh be they that blame,)
That note so piercing and profound
Will shape and syllable [1] its sound
Into Zuleika's name. [2]

---

[1] " And airy tongues that *syllable* men's names."
                                                    Milton.

For a belief that the souls of the dead inhabit the form of birds, we need not travel to the East. Lord Lyttleton's ghost story, the belief of the Duchess of Kendal, that George I. flew into her window in the shape of a raven (see Orford's Reminiscences), and many other instances, bring this superstition nearer home. The most singular was the whim of a Worcester lady, who, believing her daughter to exist in the shape of a singing bird, literally furnished her pew in the cathedral with cages full of the kind; and as she was rich, and a benefactress in beautifying the church, no objection was made to her harmless folly. For this anecdote, see Orford's Letters.

[2] [The heroine of this poem, the blooming Zuleika, is all purity and loveliness. Never was a faultless character more delicately or more justly delineated. Her piety, her intelligence, her strict sense of duty, and her undeviating love of truth, appear to have been originally blended in her mind, rather than inculcated by education. She is always natural, always attractive, always affectionate; and it must be admitted that her affections are not unworthily bestowed. Selim, while an orphan and dependant, is never degraded by calamity; when better hopes are presented to him, his buoyant spirit rises with his expectations: he is enterprising, with no more rashness than becomes his youth; and when disappointed in the success of a well concerted project, he meets, with intrepidity, the fate to which he is exposed through his own generous forbearance. To us, " The Bride of Abydos" appears to be, in every respect, superior to " The Giaour," though, in point of diction, it has been, perhaps, less warmly admired. We will not argue this point, but will simply ob-

'Tis from her cypress summit heard,
That melts in air the liquid word:
'Tis from her lowly virgin earth
That white rose takes its tender birth.
There late was laid a marble stone;
Eve saw it placed — the Morrow gone!
It was no mortal arm that bore
That deep fixed pillar to the shore;
For there, as Helle's legends tell,
Next morn 'twas found where Selim fell;
Lashed by the tumbling tide, whose wave
Denied his bones a holier grave:
And there by night, reclined, 'tis said,
Is seen a ghastly turbaned head:
    And hence extended by the billow,
    'Tis named the" Pirate-phantom's pillow !"
    Where first it lay that mourning flower
    Hath flourished; flourisheth this hour,
    Alone and dewy, coldly pure and pale;
    As weeping Beauty's cheek at Sorrow's tale ! [3]

---

serve, that what is read with ease is generally read with rapidity; and that many beauties of style which escape observation in a simple and connected narrative, would be forced on the reader's attention by abrupt and perplexing transitions. It is only when a traveller is obliged to stop on his journey, that he is disposed to examine and admire the prospect. — *George Ellis.*]

[3] [" The ' Bride,' such as it is, is my first *entire* composition of any length (except the Satire, and be d—d to it), for the 'Giaour' is, but a string of passages, and ' Childe Harold ' is, and I rather think always will be, unconcluded." " It was published on Thursday, the 2d of December; but how it is liked, I know not. Whether it succeeds or not, is no fault of the public, against whom I can have no complaint. But I am much more indebted to the tale than I can ever be to the most important reader; as it wrung my thoughts from reality to imagination; from selfish regrets to vivid recollections; and recalled me to a country replete with the brightest and darkest, but always most lively colors of my memory." — *Byron's Diary*, December 5, 1813.]

THE CORSAIR: A TALE.[1]

———

TO THOMAS MOORE, ESQ.

MY DEAR MOORE:—I dedicate to you the last production with which I shall trespass on public patience, and your indulgence, for some years; and I own that I feel anxious to avail myself of this late-est and only opportunity of adorning my pages with a name, consecrated by unshaken public principle, and the most undoubted and various talents. While Ireland ranks you among the firmest of her patriots; while you stand alone the first of her bards in her estimation, and Britain repeats and ratifies the decree, permit one, whose only regret, since our first acquaintance, has been the years he had lost before it com menced, to add the humble but sincere suffrage of friendship, to the voice of more than one nation. It will at least prove to you, that I have neither forgotten the gratification derived from your society, nor abandoned the prospect of its renewal, whenever your leisure or inclination allows you to atone to your friends for too long an absence. It is said among those friends, I trust truly, that you are engaged in the composition of a poem whose scene will be laid in the East; none can do those scenes so much justice. The wrongs of your own country,[2] the magnificent and fiery spirit of her sons, the beauty and feeling of her daughters, may there be found; and Collins, when he denominated his Oriental his Irish Eclogues was not aware how true, at least, was a part of his parallel. Your imagination will create a warmer sun, and less clouded sky; but wildness, tenderness, and originality, are part of your national claim of orien-tal descent, to which you have already thus far proved your title more clearly than the most zealous of your country's antiquarians.

May I add a few words on a subject on which all men are supposed to be fluent, and none agreeable, — Self? I have written much, and published more than enough to demand a longer silence than I now meditate; but, for some years to come, it is my intention to tempt no further the award of " Gods, men, nor columns." In the present composition I have attempted not the most difficult, but, perhaps, the best adapted measure to our language, the good old and now neglected heroic couplet. The stanza of Spen-ser is perhaps too slow and dignified for narrative; though, I confess, it is the measure most after my own

---

[1] The time in this poem may seem too short for the occurrences, but the whole of the Ægean isles are within a few hours' sail of the continent, and the reader must be kind enough to take the *wind* as I have often found it.

[2] [This political allusion having been objected to by a friend, Byron sent a second dedication to Mr. Moore, with a request that he would " take his choice." It ran as follows: —

January 7th, 1814.

" MY DEAR MOORE: — I had written to you a long letter of dedication, which I suppress, because, though it contained something relating to you, which every one had been glad to hear, yet there was too much about politics, and poesy, and all things whatsoever, ending with that topic on which most men are fluent, and none very amusing, — *one's self*. It might have been rewritten; but to what purpose? My praise could add nothing to your well-earned and firmly established fame; and with my most hearty admiration of your talents, and delight in your conversation, you are already acquainted. In availing myself of your friendly permission to inscribe this poem to you, I can only wish the offering were as worthy your acceptance, as your regard is dear to

" Yours, most affectionately and faithfully,
" BYRON."]

heart: Scott alone,[1] of the present generation, has hitherto completely triumphed over the fatal facility of the octo-syllabic verse; and this is not the least victory of his fertile and mighty genius: in blank verse, Milton, Thomson, and our dramatists, are the beacons that shine along the deep, but warn us from the rough and barren rock on which they are kindled. The heroic couplet is not the most popular measure certainly; but as I did not deviate into the other from a wish to flatter what is called public opinion, I shall quit it without further apology, and take my chance once more with that versification, in which I have hitherto published nothing but compositions whose former circulation is part of my present, and will be of my future regret.

With regard to my story, and stories in general, I should have been glad to have rendered my personages more perfect and amiable, if possible, inasmuch as I have been sometimes criticized, and considered no less responsible for their deeds and qualities than if all had been personal. Be it so—if I have deviated into the gloomy vanity of "drawing from self," the pictures are probably like, since they are unfavorable; and if not, those who know me are undeceived, and those who do not, I have little interest in undeceiving. I have no particular desire that any but my acquaintance should think the author better than the beings of his imagining; but I cannot help a little surprise, and perhaps amusement, at some odd critical exceptions in the present instance, when I see several bards (far more deserving, I allow) in very reputable plight, and quite exempted from all participation in the faults of those heroes, who, nevertheless, might be found with little more morality than "The Giaour," and perhaps—but no—I must admit Childe Harold to be a very repulsive personage; and as to his identity, those who like it must give him whatever "alias" they please.[2]

If, however, it were worth while to remove the impression, it might be of some service to me, that the man who is alike the delight of his readers and his friends, the poet of all circles, and the idol of his own, permits me here and elsewhere to subscribe myself

Most truly and affectionately, his obedient servant,

January 2, 1814. BYRON.

INTRODUCTION.

"THE Corsair" was begun on the 18th, and finished on the 31st, of December, 1813; a rapidity of composition seldom paralleled in literary history. Byron states it to have been written "*con amore*, and very much from *existence*." In the original MS. the chief female character was called *Francesca*, in whose person the author meant to delineate one of his acquaintance; but, while the work was at press, he changed the name to *Medora*. In his journal, soon after the publication of the poem, he made the following entry: "Hobhouse told me an odd report,—that *I* am the actual Conrad, the veritable Corsair, and that part of my travels are supposed to have passed in piracy. Um!—people sometimes hit near the truth, but never the whole truth. H. don't know what I was about the year after I left the Levant; nor does any one—nor—nor—nor—however, it is a lie—but 'I doubt the equivocation of the fiend that lies like truth!'" He mentioned the report to a female acquaintance, who replied, "'I don't wonder, Conrad is so *like*.'" Upon which Byron remarks that if *she* knew nothing, no one else could. These dark allusions are probably mere mystifications.

The success of the Corsair was immense. Fourteen thousand copies were sold in one day.

---

[1] [After the words of "Scott alone," Byron had inserted, in a parenthesis—"He will excuse the '*Mr.*'—we do not say *Mr.* Cæsar."]

[2] [It is difficult to say whether we are to receive this passage as an admission or a denial of the opinion to which it refers; but Lord Byron certainly did the public injustice, if he supposed it imputed to him the criminal actions with which many of his heroes were stained. Men no more expected to meet in Lord Byron the Corsair, who "knew himself a villain," than they looked for the hypocrisy of Kehama on the shores of the Derwent Water, or the profligacy of Marmion on the banks of the Tweed.—*Sir Walter Scott.*]

CANTO THE FIRST.

> " ———— nessun maggior dolore,
> Che ricordarsi del tempo felice
> Nella miseria, ———— "
>   DANTE.

I.

"O'ER the glad waters of the dark blue sea,
Our thoughts as boundless, and our souls as
     free,
Far as the breeze can bear, the billows foam,
Survey our empire, and behold our home !
These are our realms, no limits to their sway —
Our flag the sceptre all who meet obey.
Ours the wild life in tumult still to range
From toil to rest, and joy in every change.
Oh, who can tell ? not thou, luxurious slave !
Whose soul would sicken o'er the heaving
     wave ;
Not thou, vain lord of wantonness and ease !
Whom slumber soothes not — pleasure can-
     not please —
Oh, who can tell, save he whose heart hath
     tried,
And danced in triumph o'er the waters wide,
The exulting sense — the pulse's maddening
     play,
That thrills the wanderer of that trackless way ?
That for itself can woo the approaching fight,
And turn what some deem danger to delight ;
That seeks what cravens shun with more than
     zeal,
And where the feebler faint — can only feel —
Feel — to the rising bosom's inmost core,
Its hope awaken and its spirit soar ?
No dread of death — if with us die our foes —
Save that it seems even duller than repose :
Come when it will — we snatch the life of
     life —
When lost — what recks it — by disease or
     strife ?
Let him who crawls enamoured of decay
Cling to his couch, and sicken years away ;
Heave his thick breath, and shake his palsied
     head ;
Ours — the fresh turf, and not the feverish bed.
While gasp by gasp he falters forth his soul,
Ours with one pang — one bound — escapes
     control.
His corse may boast its urn and narrow cave,
And they who loathed his life may gild his
     grave :
Ours are the tears, though few, sincerely shed,
When Ocean shrouds and sepulchres our
     dead.
For us, even banquets fond regrets supply
In the red cup that crowns our memory ;
And the brief epitaph in danger's day,

When those who win at length divide the prey,
And cry, Remembrance saddening o'er each
     brow,
How had the brave who fell exulted *now !*"

II.

Such were the notes that from the Pirate's isle
Around the kindling watch-fire rang the while :
Such were the sounds that thrilled the rocks
     along,
And unto ears as rugged seemed a song !
In scattered groups upon the golden sand,
They game — carouse — converse — or whet
     the brand ;
Select the arms — to each his blade assign,
And careless eye the blood that dims its shine ;
Repair the boat, replace the helm or oar,
While others straggling muse along the shore ;
For the wild bird the busy springes set,
Or spread beneath the sun the dripping net ;
Gaze where some distant sail a speck supplies,
With all the thirsting eye of Enterprise ;
Tell o'er the tales of many a night of toil,
And marvel where they next shall seize a
     spoil :
No matter where — their chief's allotment this ;
Theirs, to believe no prey nor plan amiss.
But who that CHIEF ? his name on every
     shore
Is famed and feared — they ask and know no
     more.
With these he mingles not but to command ;
Few are his words, but keen his eye and hand.
Ne'er seasons he with mirth their jovial mess,
But they forgive his silence for success.
Ne'er for his lip the purpling cup they fill,
That goblet passes him untasted still —
And for his fare — the rudest of his crew
Would that, in turn, have passed untasted too ;
Earth's coarsest bread, the garden's homeliest
     roots,
And scarce the summer luxury of fruits,
His short repast in humbleness supply
With all a hermit's board would scarce deny.
But while he shuns the grosser joys of sense,
His mind seems nourished by that abstinence.
"Steer to that shore ! " — they sail. " Do
     this ! " 'tis done :
" Now form and follow me ! " — the spoil is
     won.
Thus prompt his accents and his actions still,
And all obey and few inquire his will ;

To such, brief answer and contemptuous eye
Convey reproof, nor further deign reply.

III.

"A sail!—a sail!"—a promised prize to
　　Hope!
Her nation—flag—how speaks the tele-
　　scope?
No prize, alas!—but yet a welcome sail:
The blood-red signal glitters in the gale.
Yes—she is ours—a home returning bark—
Blow fair, thou breeze!—she anchors ere the
　　dark.
Already doubled is the cape—our bay
Receives that prow which proudly spurns the
　　spray.
How gloriously her gallant course she goes!
Her white wings flying—never from her
　　foes—
She walks the water like a thing of life,
And seems to dare the elements to strife.
Who would not brave the battle-fire—the
　　wreck—
To move the monarch of her peopled deck?

IV.

Hoarse o'er her side the rustling cable rings;
The sails are furled; and anchoring round she
　　swings:
And gathering loiterers on the land discern
Her boat descending from the latticed stern.
'Tis manned—the oars keep concert to the
　　strand,
Till grates her keel upon the shallow sand.
Hail to the welcome shout!—the friendly
　　speech!
When hand grasps hand uniting on the beach;
The smile, the question, and the quick reply,
And the heart's promise of festivity!

V.

The tidings spread, and gathering grows the
　　crowd;
The hum of voices, and the laughter loud,
And woman's gentler anxious tone is heard—
Friends'—husbands'—lovers' names in each
　　dear word:
"Oh! are they safe? we ask not of success—
But shall we see them? will their accents
　　bless?
From where the battle roars—the billows
　　chafe—
They doubtless boldly did—but who are safe?
Here let them haste to gladden and surprise,
And kiss the doubt from these delighted eyes!"

VI.

"Where is our chief? for him we bear report—
And doubt that joy—which hails our com-
　　ing—short;
Yet thus sincere—'tis cheering, though so
　　brief;

But, Juan! instant guide us to our chief:
Our greeting paid, we'll feast on our return,
And all shall hear what each may wish to
　　learn."
Ascending slowly by the rock-hewn way,
To where his watch-tower beetles o'er the
　　bay,
By bushy brake, and wild flowers blossoming,
And freshness breathing from each silver
　　spring,
Whose scattered streams from granite basins
　　burst,
Leap into life, and sparkling woo your thirst;
From crag to cliff they mount—Near yonder
　　cave,
What lonely straggler looks along the wave?
In pensive posture leaning on the brand,
Not oft a resting-staff to that red hand?
"'Tis he—'tis Conrad—here—as wont—
　　alone;
On—Juan!—on—and make our purpose
　　known.
The bark he views—and tell him we would
　　greet
His ears with tidings he must quickly meet:
We dare not yet approach—thou know'st his
　　mood,
When strange or uninvited steps intrude."

VII.

Him Juan sought, and told of their intent;—
He spake not—but a sign expressed assent.
These Juan calls—they come—to their salute
He bends him slightly, but his lips are mute.
"These letters, Chief, are from the Greek—
　　the spy,
Who still proclaims our spoil or peril nigh:
Whate'er his tidings, we can well report,
Much that"—"Peace, peace!"—he cuts
　　their prating short.
Wondering they turn, abashed, while each to
　　each
Conjecture whispers in his muttering speech:
They watch his glance with many a stealing
　　look,
To gather how that eye the tidings took;
But, this as if he guessed, with head aside,
Perchance from some emotion, doubt, or
　　pride.
He read the scroll—"My tablets, Juan,
　　hark—
Where is Gonsalvo?"
　　　　　　　　"In the anchored bark."
"There let him stay—to him this order
　　bear—
Back to your duty—for my course prepare:
Myself this enterprise to-night will share."
"To-night, Lord Conrad?"
　　　　　　　　"Ay! at set of sun:
The breeze will freshen when the day is done.
My corslet—cloak—one hour—and we
　　are gone.

Sling on thy bugle — see that free from rust
My carbine-lock springs worthy of my trust;
Be the edge sharpened of my boarding-brand,
And give its guard more room to fit my hand.
This let the Armourer with speed dispose;
Last time, it more fatigued my arm than foes:
Mark that the signal-gun be duly fired,
To tell us when the hour of stay's expired."

VIII.

They make obeisance, and retire in haste,
Too soon to seek again the watery waste:
Yet they repine not — so that Conrad guides;
And who dare question aught that he decides?
That man of loneliness and mystery,
Scarce seen to smile, and seldom heard to
    sigh;
Whose name appalls the fiercest of his crew,
And tints each swarthy cheek with sallower
    hue;
Still sways their souls with that commanding
    art
That dazzles, leads, yet chills the vulgar heart.
What is that spell, that thus his lawless train
Confess and envy, yet oppose in vain?
What should it be, that thus their faith can
    bind?
The power of Thought — the magic of the
    Mind!
Linked with success, assumed and kept with
    skill,
That moulds another's weakness to its will;
Wields with their hands, but, still to these
    unknown
Makes even their mightiest deeds appear his
    own.
Such hath it been — shall be — beneath the
    sun
The many still must labor for the one!
'Tis Nature's doom — but let the wretch who
    toils,
Accuse not, hate not *him* who wears the spoils.
Oh! if he knew the weight of splendid chains,
How light the balance of his humbler pains!

IX.

Unlike the heroes of each ancient race,
Demons in act, but Gods at least in face,
In Conrad's form seems little to admire,
Though his dark eyebrow shades a glance of
    fire:
Robust but not Herculean — to the sight
No giant frame sets forth his common height;
Yet, in the whole, who paused to look again,
Saw more than marks the crowd of vulgar
    men;[1]

They gaze and marvel how — and still confess
That thus it is, but why they cannot guess.
Sun-burnt his cheek, his forehead high and
    pale
The sable curls in wild profusion veil;
And oft perforce his rising lip reveals
The haughtier thought it curbs, but scarce
    conceals.
Though smooth his voice and calm his gen-
    eral mien,
Still seems there something he would not
    have seen;
His features' deepening lines and varying hue
At times attracted, yet perplexed the view,
As if within that murkiness of mind
Worked feelings fearful, and yet undefined;
Such might it be — that none could truly tell —
Too close inquiry his stern glance would quell.
There breathe but few whose aspect might
    defy
The full encounter of his searching eye:
He had the skill, when Cunning's gaze would
    seek
To probe his heart and watch his changing
    cheek,
At once the observer's purpose to espy,
And on himself roll back his scrutiny,
Lest he to Conrad rather should betray
Some secret thought, than drag that chief's
    to-day.

[1] [In the features of Conrad, those who have looked upon Lord Byron will recognize some likeness; and the ascetic regimen which the noble poet himself observed, was no less marked in the preceding description of Conrad's fare. To what are we to ascribe the singular peculiarity which induced an author of such talent, and so well skilled in tracing the darker impressions which guilt and remorse leave on the human character, so frequently to affix features peculiar to himself to the robbers and corsairs which he sketched with a pencil as forcible as that of Salvator? More than one answer may be returned to this question; nor do we pretend to say which is best warranted by the facts. The practice may arise from a temperament which radical and constitutional melancholy had, as in the case of Hamlet, predisposed to identify its owner with scenes of that deep and amazing interest which arises from the stings of conscience contending with the stubborn energy of pride, and delighting to be placed in supposed situations of guilt and danger, as some men love instinctively to tread the giddy edge of a precipice, or holding by some frail twig, to stoop forward over the abyss into which the dark torrent discharges itself. Or, it may be that these disguises were assumed capriciously, as a man might choose the cloak, poniard, and dark lantern of a bravo, for his disguise at a masquerade. Or, feeling his own powers in painting the sombre and the horrible, Lord Byron assumed in his fervor the very semblance of the characters he describes; like an actor who presents on the stage at once his own person and the tragic character with which for the time he is invested. Nor, is it altogether incompatible with his character to believe that, in contempt of the criticisms which, on this account, had attended "Childe Harold" he was determined to show the public how little he was affected by them, and how effectually it was in his power to compel attention and respect, even when imparting a portion of his own likeness and his own peculiarities, to pirates and outlaws. — *Sir Walter Scott.*]

There was a laughing Devil in his sneer,
That raised emotions both of rage and fear;
And where his frown of hatred darkly fell,
Hope withering fled — and Mercy sighed farewell![1]

X.

Slight are the outward signs of evil thought,
Within — within — 'twas there the spirit wrought!
Love shows all changes — Hate, Ambition, Guile,
Betray no further than the bitter smile;
The lip's least curl, the lightest paleness thrown
Along the governed aspect, speak alone
Of deeper passions; and to judge their mien,
He, who would see, must be himself unseen.
Then — with the hurried tread, the upward eye,
The clenched hand, the pause of agony,
That listens, starting, lest the step too near
Approach intrusive on that mood of fear:
Then — with each feature working from the heart,
With feelings loosed to strengthen — not depart:
That rise — convulse — contend — that freeze or glow,
Flush in the cheek, or damp upon the brow;
Then — Stranger! if thou canst, and tremblest not,
Behold his soul — the rest that soothes his lot!
Mark — how that lone and blighted bosom sears
The scathing thought of execrated years!
Behold — but who hath seen, or e'er shall see,
Man as himself — the secret spirit free?

XI.

Yet was not Conrad thus by Nature sent
To lead the guilty — guilt's worst instrument —

[1] That Conrad is a character not altogether out of nature, I shall attempt to prove by some historical coincidences which I have met with since writing "The Corsair."
"Eccelin prisonnier," dit Rolandini, "s'enfermoit dans un silence menaçant, il fixoit sur la terre son visage féroce, et ne donnoit point d'essor à sa profonde indignation. De toutes partes cependant les soldats et les peuples accouroient; ils vouloient voir cet homme, jadis si puissant, et la joie universelle éclatoit de toutes partes." * * * "Eccelin étoit d'une petite taille; mais tout l'aspect de sa personne, tous ses mouvemens, indiquoient un soldat. — Son langage étoit amer, son déportement superbe — et par son seul regard, il faisoit trembler les plus hardis." — *Sismondi*, tome iii. p. 219.
Again, "Gizericus (Genseric, king of the Vandals, the conqueror of both Carthage and Rome), staturâ mediocris, et equi casu claudicans, animo profundus, sermone rarus, luxuriæ contemptor, irâ turbidus, habendi cupidus, ad solicitandas gentes providentissimus," etc. etc. — *Jornandes de Rebus Geticis*, c. 33.
I beg leave to quote these gloomy realities to keep in countenance my Giaour and Corsair.

His soul was changed, before his deeds had driven
Him forth to war with man and forfeit heaven.
Warped by the world in Disappointment's school,
In words too wise, in conduct *there* a fool;
Too firm to yield, and far too proud to stoop,
Doomed by his very virtues for a dupe,
He cursed those virtues as the cause of ill,
And not the traitors who betrayed him still;
Nor deemed that gifts bestowed on better men
Had left him joy, and means to give again.
Feared — shunned — belied — ere youth had lost her force,
He hated man too much to feel remorse,
And thought the voice of wrath a sacred call,
To pay the injuries of some on all.
He knew himself a villain — but he deemed
The rest no better than the thing he seemed;
And scorned the best as hypocrites who hid
Those deeds the bolder spirit plainly did.
He knew himself detested, but he knew
The hearts that loathed him, crouched and dreaded too.
Lone, wild, and strange, he stood alike exempt
From all affection and from all contempt:
His name could sadden, and his acts surprise;
But they that feared him dared not to despise:
Man spurns the worm, but pauses ere he wake
The slumbering venom of the folded snake:
The first may turn — but not avenge the blow;
The last expires — but leaves no living foe;
Fast to the doomed offender's form it clings,
And he may crush — not conquer — still it stings.

XII.

None are all evil — quickening round his heart
One softer feeling would not yet depart;
Oft could he sneer at others as beguiled
By passions worthy of a fool or child;
Yet 'gainst that passion vainly still he strove,
And even in him it asks the name of Love!
Yes, it was love — unchangeable — unchanged,
Felt but for one from whom he never ranged;
Though fairest captives daily met his eye,
He shunned, nor sought, but coldly passed them by;
Though many a beauty drooped in prisoned bower,
None ever soothed his most unguarded hour.
Yes — it was Love — if thoughts of tenderness,
Tried in temptation, strengthened by distress,
Unmoved by absence, firm in every clime,
And yet — Oh more than all! — untired by time;
Which nor defeated hope, nor baffled wile,
Could render sullen were she near to smile,
Nor rage could fire, nor sickness fret to vent
On her one murmur of his discontent;
Which still would meet with joy, with calmness part,

Lest that his look of grief should reach her
heart ;
Which nought removed, nor menaced to
remove —
If there be love in mortals — this was love!
He was a villain — ay — reproaches shower
On him — but not the passion, nor its power,
Which only proved, all other virtues gone,
Not guilt itself could quench this loveliest one !

XIII.

He paused a moment — till his hastening men
Passed the first winding downward to the glen.
"Strange tidings ! — many a peril have I past,
Nor know I why this next appears the last !
Yet so my heart forebodes, but must not fear,
Nor shall my followers find me falter here.
'Tis rash to meet, but surer death to wait
Till here they hunt us to undoubted fate ;
And, if my plan but hold, and Fortune smile,
We'll furnish mourners for our funeral pile.
Ay — let them slumber — peaceful be their
dreams,
Morn ne'er awoke them with such brilliant
beams
As kindle high to-night (but blow, thou
breeze !)
To warm these slow avengers of the seas.
Now to Medora — Oh! my sinking heart,
Long may her own be lighter than thou art!
Yet was I brave — mean boast where all are
brave !
Even insects sting for aught they seek to save.
This common courage which with brutes we
share,
That owes its deadliest efforts to despair,
Small merit claims — but 'twas my nobler hope
To teach my few with numbers still to cope ;
Long have I led them — not to vainly bleed ;
No medium now — we perish or succeed !
So let it be — it irks me not to die ;
But thus to urge them whence they cannot fly.
My lot hath long had little of my care,
But chafes my pride thus baffled in the snare :
Is this my skill ? my craft ? to set at last
Hope, power, and life upon a single cast ?
Oh, Fate ! — accuse thy folly, not thy fate —
She may redeem thee still — nor yet too late."

XIV.

Thus with himself communion held he, till
He reached the summit of his tower-crowned
hill :
There at the portal paused — for wild and soft
He heard those accents never heard too oft ;
Through the high lattice far yet sweet they
rung,
And these the notes his bird of beauty sung :

1.

Deep in my soul that tender secret dwells,
Lonely and lost to light for evermore,
Save when to thine my heart responsive swells
Then trembles into silence as before.

2.

"There, in its centre, a sepulchral lamp
Burns the slow flame, eternal — but unseen,
Which not the darkness of despair can damp,
Though vain its ray as it had never been.

3.

"Remember me — Oh! pass not thou my
grave
Without one thought whose relics there
recline,
The only pang my bosom dare not brave
Must be to find forgetfulness in thine.

4.

My fondest — faintest — latest accents hear —
Grief for the dead not Virtue can reprove ;
Then give me all I ever asked — a tear,
The first — last — sole reward of so much
love ! "

He passed the portal — crossed the corridore,
And reached the chamber as the strain gave
o'er :
"My own Medora! sure thy song is sad —"

"In Conrad's absence wouldst thou have it
glad ?
Without thine ear to listen to my lay,
Still must my song my thoughts, my soul
betray :
Still must each accent to my bosom suit,
My heart unhushed — although my lips were
mute.
Oh! many a night on this lone couch reclined,
My dreaming fear with storms hath winged
the wind
And deemed the breath that faintly fanned
thy sail
The murmuring prelude of the ruder gale ;
Though soft, it seemed the low prophetic dirge,
That mourned thee floating on the savage
surge :
Still would I rise to rouse the beacon fire,
Lest spies less true should let the blaze expire ;
And many a restless hour outwatched each
star,
And morning came — and still thou wert afar.
Oh! how the chill blast on my bosom blew,
And day broke dreary on my troubled view,
And still I gazed and gazed — and not a prow
Was granted to my tears — my truth — my
vow !
At length — 'twas noon — I hailed and blest
the mast
That met my sight — it neared — Alas! it past!
Another came — Oh God ! 'twas thine at last!
Would that those days were over! wilt thou
ne'er,

"My Conrad! learn the Joys of peace to share?
Sure thou hast more than wealth, and many
  a home
As bright as this invites us not to roam:
Thou know'st it is not peril that I fear,
I only tremble when thou art not here;
Then not for mine, but that far dearer life,
Which flies from love and languishes for
  strife —
How strange that heart, to me so tender still,
Should war with nature and its better will!"[1]

'Yea, strange indeed — that heart hath long
  been changed;
Worm-like 'twas trampled — adder-like
  avenged,
Without one hope on earth beyond thy love,
And scarce a glimpse of mercy from above.
Yet the same feeling which thou dost con-
  demn,
My very love to thee is hate to them,
So closely mingling here, that disentwined,
I cease to love thee when I love mankind:
Yet dread not this — the proof of all the past
Assures the future that my love will last;
But — Oh, Medora! nerve thy gentler heart,
This hour again — but not for long — we part."

"This hour we part! — my heart foreboded
  this:
Thus ever fade my fairy dreams of bliss.
This hour — it cannot be — this hour away!
Yon bark hath hardly anchored in the bay;
Her consort still is absent, and her crew
Have need of rest before they toil anew:
My love! thou mock'st my weakness; and
  wouldst steel
My breast before the time when it must feel;
But trifle now no more with my distress,
Such mirth hath less of play than bitterness.
Be silent, Conrad! — dearest! come and share
The feast these hands delighed to prepare;
Light toil! to cull and dress thy frugal fare!
See, I have plucked the fruit that promised
  best,
And where not sure, perplexed, but pleased,
  I guessed
At such as seemed the fairest; thrice the hill
My steps have wound to try the coolest rill;
Yes! thy sherbet to-night will sweetly flow,
See how it sparkles in its vase of snow!

[1] [Lord Byron has made a fine use of the gentle-
ness and submission of the females of these regions,
as contrasted with the lordly pride and martial
ferocity of the men: and though we suspect he has
lent them more *soul* than of right belongs to them,
as well as more delicacy and reflection; yet, there
is something so true to female nature in general, in
his representations of this sort, and so much of the
oriental softness and acquiescence in his particular
delineations, that it is scarcely possible to refuse
the picture the praise of being characteristic and
harmonious, as well as eminently sweet and beauti-
ful in itself. — *Jeffrey.*]

The grapes' gay juice thy bosom never cheers;
Thou more than Moslem when the cup ap-
  pears:
Think not I mean to chide — for I rejoice
What others deem a pennance is thy choice.
But come, the board is spread; our silver lamp
Is trimmed, and heeds not the sirocco's damp:
Then shall my handmaids while the time along;
And join with me the dance, or wake the song;
Or my guitar, which still thou lov'st to hear,
Shall soothe or lull — or, should it vex thine
  ear,
We'll turn the tale, by Ariosto told,
Of fair Olympia loved and left of old.[2]
Why — thou wert worse than he who broke
  his vow
To that lost damsel, shouldst thou leave me
  now;
Or even that traitor chief — I've seen thee
  smile,
When the clear sky showed Ariadne's Isle,
Which I have pointed from these cliffs the
  while:
And thus half sportive, half in fear, I said,
Lest Time should raise that doubt to more
  than dread,
Thus Conrad, too, will quit me for the main:
And he deceived me — for — he came again!

"Again — again — and oft again — my love!
If there be life below, and hope above,
He will return — but now, the moments bring
The time of parting with redoubled wing:
The why — the where — what boots it now to
  tell
Since all must end in that wild world — fare-
  well!
Yet would I fain — did time allow — disclose —
Fear not — these are no formidable foes;
And here shall watch a more than wonted
  guard,
For sudden siege and long defence prepared:
Nor be thou lonely — though thy lord's away,
Our matrons and thy handmaids with thee
  stay;
And this thy comfort — that, when next we
  meet,
Security shall make repose more sweet.
List! — 'tis the bugle — Juan shrilly blew —
One kiss — one more — another — Oh!
  Adieu!"

She rose — she sprung — she clung to his em-
  brace,
Till his heart heaved beneath her hidden face.
He dared not raise to his that deep-blue eye,
Which downcast drooped in tearless agony.
Her long fair hair lay floating o'er his arms,
In all the wildness of dishevelled charms;
Scarce beat that bosom where his image dwelt
So full — *that* feeling seemed almost unfelt!

[2] Orlando Furioso, Canto x.

Hark — peals the thunder of the signal-gun !
It told 'twas sunset — and he cursed that sun.
Again — again — that form he madly pressed,
Which mutely clasped, imploringly caressed !
And tottering to the couch his bride he bore,
One moment gazed — as if to gaze no more ;
Felt — that for him earth held but her alone,
Kissed her cold forehead — turned — is Conrad gone ?

XV.

"And is he gone? " — on sudden solitude
How oft that fearful question will intrude !
"'Twas but an instant past — and here he
    stood !
And now " — without the portal's porch she
    rushed,
And then at length her tears in freedom
    gushed ;
Big — bright — and fast, unknown to her they
    fell ;
But still her lips refused to send — "Farewell ! "
For in that word — that fatal word — howe'er
We promise — hope — believe — there breathes
    despair.
O'er every feature of that still, pale face,
Had sorrow fixed what time can ne'er erase :
The tender blue of that large loving eye
Grew frozen with its gaze on vacancy,
Till — Oh, how far l — it caught a glimpse of
    him,
And then it flowed — and phrenzied seemed
    to swim
Through those long, dark, and glistening
    lashes dewed
With drops of sadness oft to be renewed.
"He's gone ! " — against her heart that hand
    is driven,
Convulsed and quick — then gently raised to
    heaven ;
She looked and saw the heaving of the main ;
The white sail set — she dared not look again ;
But turned with sickening soul within the
    gate —
"It is no dream — and I am desolate ! "[1]

XVI.

From crag to crag descending — swiftly sped
Stern Conrad down, nor once he turned his
    head ;
But shrunk whene'er the windings of his way
Forced on his eye what he would not survey,
His lone, but lovely dwelling on the steep,
That hailed him first when homeward from
    the deep :
And she — the dim and melancholy star,
Whose ray of beauty reached him from afar,
On her he must not gaze, he must not think,

[1] [We do not know any thing in poetry ·more
beautiful or touching than this picture of their parting. — *Jeffrey.*]

There he might rest — but on D
    brink :
Yet once almost he stopped — and
His fate to chance, his projects to
But no — it must not be — a worth
May melt, but not betray to woma
He sees his bark, he notes how fail
And sternly gathers all his might o
Again he hurries on — and as he h
The clang of tumult vibrate on his
The busy sounds, the bustle of the
The shout, the signal, and the dash
As marks his eye the seaboy on the
The anchors rise, the sails unfurlin
The waving kerchiefs of the crowd
That mute adieu to those who stem
And more than all, his blood-red fl
He marvelled how his heart coul
    soft.
Fire in his glance, and wildne
    breast,
He feels of all his former self posse
He bounds — he flies — until his
    reach
The verge where ends the cliff,
    beach,
There checks his speed ; but pau
    breathe
The breezy freshness of the deep b
Than there his wonted statelier ste
Nor rush, distûrbed by haste, to vul
For well had Conrad learned to
    crowd,
By arts that veil, and oft preserved tl
His was the lofty port, the distant m
That seems to shun the sight — an
    seen :
The solemn aspect, and the high-bc
That checks low mirth, but lacks not
All these he wielded to command a:
But where he wished to win, so well
That kindness cancelled fear in t
    heard,
And others' gifts showed mean t
    word,
When echoed to the heart as from l
His deep yet tender melody of tone
But such was foreign to his wonted
He cared not what he softened, but
The evil passions of his youth had r
Him value less who loved — th
    obeyed.

XVII.

Around him mustering ranged I
    guard.
Before him Juan stands — "Are
    pared ? "
"They are — nay more — embarked:
    boat
Waits but my chief——"
        "My sword, and m¡

Soon firmly girded on, and lightly slung,
His belt and cloak were o'er his shoulders
  flung:
"Call Pedro here!" He comes — and Conrad
  bends,
With all the courtesy he deigned his friends;
"Receive · these tablets, and peruse with
  care,
Words of high trust and truth are graven
  there;
Double the guard, and when Anselmo's bark
Arrives, let him alike these orders mark:
In three days (serve the breeze) the sun shall
  shine
On our return — till then all peace be thine!"
This said, his brother Pirate's hand he wrung,
Then to his boat with haughty gesture sprung.
Flashed the dipt oars, and sparkling with the
  stroke,
Around the waves' phosphoric [1] brightness
  broke;
They gain the vessel — on deck he stands, —
Shrieks the shrill whistle — ply the busy
  hands —
He marks how well the ship her helm obeys,
How gallant all her crew — and deigns to
  praise.
His eyes of pride to young Gonsalvo turn —
Why doth he start, and inly seem to mourn?
Alas! those eyes beheld his rocky tower,
And live a moment o'er the parting hour;
She — his Medora — did she mark the prow?

[1] By night, particularly in a warm latitude, every
stroke of the oar, every motion of the boat or ship,
is followed by a slight flash like sheet lightning
from the water.

Ah! never loved he half so much as now!
But much must yet be done ere dawn of
  day —
Again he mans himself and turns away;
Down to the cabin with Gonsalvo bends,
And there unfolds his plan — his means —
  and ends;
Before them burns the lamp, and spreads the
  chart,
And all that speaks and aids the naval art;
They to the midnight watch protract debate;
To anxious eyes what hour is ever late?
Meantime, the steady breeze serenely blew,
And fast and falcon-like the vessel flew;
Passed the high headlands of each clustering
  isle
To gain their port — long — long ere morn-
  ing smile;
And soon the night-glass through the narrow
  bay
Discovers where the Pacha's galleys lay.
Count they each sail — and mark how there
  supine
The lights in vain o'er heedless Moslem
  shine.
Secure, unnoted, Conrad's prow passed by,
And anchored where his ambush meant to
  lie;
Screened from espial by the jutting cape,
That rears on high its rude fantastic shape.
Then rose his band to duty — not from sleep —
Equipped for deeds alike on land or deep;
While leaned their leader o'er the fretting
  flood,
And calmly talked — and yet he talked of
  blood!

CANTO THE SECOND.

"Conosceste i dubiosi desiri?"
    DANTE.

I.

In Coron's bay floats many a galley light,
Through Coron's lattices the lamps are bright,
For Seyd, the Pacha, makes a feast to-night:
A feast for promised triumph yet to come,
When he shall drag the fettered Rovers home;
This hath he sworn by Alla and his sword,
And faithful to his firman and his word,
His summoned prows collect along the coast,
And great the gathering crews, and loud the
  boast,
Already shared the captives and the prize.
Though far the distant foe they thus despise;
'Tis but to sail — no doubt to-morrow's Sun

Will see the Pirates bound — their haven won!
Meantime the watch may slumber, if they will,
Nor only wake to war, but dreaming kill.
Though all, who can, disperse on shore and
  seek
To flesh their glowing valor on the Greek;
How well such deed becomes the turbaned
  brave —
To bare the sabre's edge before a slave!
Infest his dwelling — but forbear to slay,
Their arms are strong, yet merciful to-day,
And do not deign to smite because they may!
Unless some gay caprice suggests the blow,
To keep in practice for the coming foe.

Revel and rout the evening hours beguiled,
And they who wish to wear a head must smile;
For Moslem mouths produce their choicest
  cheer,
And hoard their curses, till the coast is clear.

II.

High in his hall reclines the turbaned Seyd;
Around — the bearded chiefs he came to lead.
Removed the banquet, and the last pilaff —
Forbidden draughts, 'tis said, he dared to quaff,
Though to the rest the sober berry's juice [1]
The slaves bear round for rigid Moslems' use;
The long chibouque's [2] dissolving cloud sup-
  ply,
While dance the Almas [3] to wild minstrelsy.
The rising morn will view the chiefs embark;
But waves are somewhat treacherous in the
  dark;
And revellers may more securely sleep
On silken couch than o'er the rugged deep;
Feast there who can — nor combat till they
  must,
And less to conquest than to Korans trust;
And yet the numbers crowded in his host
Might warrant more than even the Pacha's
  boast.

III.

With cautious reverence from the outer gate
Slow stalks the slave, whose office there to wait,
Bows his bent head — his hand salutes the floor,
Ere yet his tongue the trusted tidings bore:
" A captive Dervise, from the pirate's nest
Escaped, is here — himself would tell the rest." [4]
He took the sign from Seyd's assenting eye,
And led the holy man in silence nigh.
His arms were folded on his dark-green vest,
His step was feeble, and his look deprest ;
Yet worn he seemed of hardship more than
  years,
And pale his cheek with penance, not from
  fears.
Vowed to his God — his sable locks he wore,
And these his lofty cap rose proudly o'er:
Around his form his loose long robe was
  thrown,

---

[1] Coffee.
[2] " Chibouque," pipe.
[3] Dancing girls.
[4] It has been observed, that Conrad's entering
disguised as a spy is out of nature. Perhaps so. I
find something not unlike it in history. — " Anxious
to explore with his own eyes the state of the Van-
dals, Majorian ventured, after disguising the color
of hair, to visit Carthage in the character of his
own ambassador; and Genseric was afterwards mor-
tified by the discovery, that he had entertained and
dismissed the Emperor of the Romans. Such an
anecdote may be rejected as an improbable fiction;
but it is a fiction which would not have been imag-
ined unless in the life of a hero." — See *Gibbon's
Decline and Fall*, vol. vi. p. 180.

And wrapt a breast bestowed on hea·
Submissive, yet with self-possession
He calmly met the curious eyes that
And question of his coming fain w·
Before the Pacha's will allowed to s

IV.

" Whence com'st thou, Dervise ? "
                    " From the ou
A fugitive — "
              " Thy capture where an
" From Scalanovo's port to Scio's i·
The Saick was bound; but Alla did
Upon our course — the Moslem 1
  gains
The Rovers won: our limbs have ·
  chains.
I had no death to fear, nor wealth t
Beyond the wandering freedom wh
At length a fisher's humble boat by
Afforded hope, and offered chance
I seized the hour, and find my safe[
With thee — most mighty Pacha!
  fear ?"
" How speed the outlaws ? stand
  prepared,
Their plundered wealth, and robł
  to guard.
Dream they of this our preparation,
To view with fire their scorpion
  sumed ? "
" Pacha! the fettered captive's mou
That weeps for flight, but ill can pla
I only heard the reckless waters roa
Those waves that would not bear m
  shore.
I only marked the glorious sun and
Too bright — too blue — for my caj
And felt — that all which Freedon
  cheers,
Must break my chain before it dried
This may'st thou judge, at least,
  escape,
They little deem of aught in peril's
Else vainly had I prayed or sought t
That leads me here — if eyed with
The careless guard that did not see
May watch as idly when thy power
Pacha! — my limbs are faint — ai
  craves
Food for my hunger, rest from tossi·
Permit my absence — peace be v
  Peace
With all around! — now grant reț
  lease."
" Stay, Dervise! I have more to q
  stay,
I do command thee — sit — dost
  obey!
More I must ask, and food the ala
  bring;

Thou shalt not pine where all are banqueting:
The supper done — prepare thee to reply,
Clearly and full — I love not mystery."
'Twere vain to guess what shook the pious man,
Who looked not lovingly on that Divan;
Nor showed high relish for the banquet prest,
And less respect for every fellow guest.
'Twas but a moment's peevish hectic past
Along his cheek, and tranquillized as fast:
He sate him down in silence, and his look
Resumed the calmness which before forsook:
The feast was ushered in — but sumptuous fare
He shunned as if some poison mingled there.
For one so long condemned to toil and fast,
Methinks he strangely spares the rich repast.
" What ails thee, Dervise? eat — dost thou suppose
This feast a Christian's? or my friends thy foes?
Why dost thou shun the salt? that sacred pledge,
Which, once partaken, blunts the sabre's edge,
Makes even contending tribes in peace unite,
And hated hosts seem brethren to the sight!"

" Salt seasons dainties — and my food is still
The humblest root, my drink the simplest rill;
And my stern vow and order's[1] laws oppose
To break or mingle bread with friend or foes:
It may seem strange — if there be aught to dread,
That peril rests upon my single head;
But for thy sway — nay more — thy Sultan's throne,
I taste nor bread nor banquet — save alone;
Infringed our orders rule, the Prophet's rage
To Mecca's dome might bar my pilgrimage."
" Well — as thou wilt — ascetic as thou art —
One question answer; then in peace depart.
How many? — Ha! it cannot sure be day?
What star — what sun is bursting on the bay?
It shines a lake of fire! — away — away!
Ho! treachery! my guards! my scimitar!
The galleys feed the flames — and I afar!
Accursed Dervise! — these thy tidings — thou
Some villain spy — seize — cleave him — slay him now!"

Up rose the Dervise with that burst of light,
Nor less his change of form appalled the sight:
Up rose that Dervise — not in saintly garb,
But like a warrior bounding on his barb,
Dashed his high cap, and tore his robe away —
Shone his mailed breast, and flashed his sabre's ray!
His close but glittering casque, and sable plume,

More glittering eye, and black brow's sabler gloom.
Glared on the Moslems' eyes some Afrit sprite,
Whose demon death-blow left no hope for fight.
The wild confusion, and the swarthy glow
Of flames on high, and torches from below;
The shriek of terror, and the mingling yell —
For swords began to clash, and shouts to swell —
Flung o'er that spot of earth the air of hell!
Distracted, to and fro, the flying slaves
Behold but bloody shore and fiery waves;
Nought heeded they the Pacha's angry cry,
They seize that Dervise! — seize on Zatanai![2]
He saw their terror — checked the first despair
That urged him but to stand and perish there,
Since far too early and too well obeyed,
The flame was kindled ere the signal made;
He saw their terror — from his baldric drew
His bugle — brief the blast — but shrilly blew;
'Tis answered — " Well ye speed, my gallant crew!
Why did I doubt their quickness of career?
And deem design had left me single here?"
Sweeps his long arm — that sabre's whirling sway
Sheds fast atonement for its first delay;
Completes his fury, what their fear begun,
And makes the many basely quail to one.
The cloven turbans o'er the chamber spread,
And scarce an arm dare rise to guard its head:
Even Seyd, convulsed, o'erwhelmed, with rage, surprise,
Retreats before him, though he still defies.
No craven he — and yet he dreads the blow,
So much Confusion magnifies his foe!
His blazing galleys still distract his sight,
He tore his beard, and foaming fled the fight;[3]
For now the pirates pass'd the Haram gate,
And burst within — and it were death to wait;
Where wild Amazement shrieking — kneeling — throws
The sword aside — in vain — the blood o'erflows!
The Corsairs pouring, haste to where within,
Invited Conrad's bugle, and the din
Of groaning victims, and wild cries for life,
Proclaimed how well he did the work of strife.
They shout to find him grim and lonely there,
A glutted tiger mangling in his lair!
But short their greeting — shorter his reply —

---

[1] The Dervises are in colleges, and of different orders, as the monks.

[2] " Zatanai," Satan.
[3] A common and not very novel effect of Mussulman anger. See Prince Eugene's Memoirs, p. 24. " The Seraskier received a wound in the thigh, he plucked up his beard by the roots, because he was obliged to quit the field."

" 'Tis well — but Seyd escapes — and he must die —
Much hath been done — but more remains to do —
Their galleys blaze — why not their city too?"

V.

Quick at the word — they seized him each a torch,
And fire the dome from minaret to porch.
A stern delight was fixed in Conrad's eye,
But sudden sunk — for on his ear the cry
Of women struck, and like a deadly knell
Knocked at that heart unmoved by battle's yell.
" Oh! burst the Haram — wrong not on your lives
One female form — remember — we have wives.
On them such outrage Vengeance will repay;
Man is our foe, and such 'tis ours to slay:
But still we spared — must spare the weaker prey.
Oh! I forgot — but Heaven will not forgive
If at my word the helpless cease to live:
Follow who will — I go — we yet have time
Our souls to lighten of at least a crime."
He climbs the crackling stair — he bursts the door,
Nor feels his feet glow scorching with the floor;
His breath choked gasping with the volumed smoke,
But still from room to room his way he broke.
They search — they find — they save: with lusty arms
Each bears a prize of unregarded charms;
Calm their loud fears; sustain their sinking frames
With all the care defenceless beauty claims:
So well could Conrad tame their fiercest mood,
And check the very hands with gore imbrued.
But who is she? whom Conrad's arms convey
From reeking pile and combat's wreck — away —
Who but the love of him he dooms to bleed?
The Haram queen — but still the slave of Seyd!

VI.

Brief time had Conrad now to greet Gulnare,[1]
Few words to reassure the trembling fair;
For in that pause compassion snatched from war,
The foe before retiring, fast and far,
With wonder saw their footsteps unpursued,
First slowlier fled — then rallied — then withstood.

[1] Gulnare, a female name; it means, literally, the flower of the pomegranate.

This Seyd perceives, then first p few,
Compared with his, the Corsair's
And blushes o'er his error, as he
The ruin wrought by panic and
Alla il Alla! Vengeance swells tl
Shame mounts to rage that must
And flame for flame and bloc must tell,
The tide of triumph ebbs tha well —
When wrath returns to renovate
And those who fought for conqu life.
Conrad beheld the danger — he
His followers faint by freshen pelled:
" One effort — one — to break host!"
They form — unite — charge — w lost!
Within a narrower ring compres
Hopeless, not heartless, strive yet —
Ah! now they fight in firmest fil
Hemmed in — cut off — cleft trampled o'er;
But each strikes singly, silently, ?
And sinks outwearied rather tha
His last faint quittance render breath
Till the blade glimmers in the gra

VII.

But first, ere came the rallying ho
And rank to rank, and hand to h?
Gulnare and all her Haram hand
Safe in the dome of one who helc
By Conrad's mandate safely were
And dried those tears for life ar flowed:
And when that dark-eyed lady, you
Recalled those thoughts late w despair,
Much did she marvel o'er the coi
That smoothed his accents; soft eye:
'Twas strange — that robber tht bedewed,
Seemed gentler then than Seyc mood.
The Pacha wooed as if he deeme
Must seem delighted with the hea
The Corsair vowed protection, fright,
As if his homage were a woman':
" The wish is wrong — nay, wors — vain:
Yet much I long to view that chie
If but to thank for, what my fear
The life — my loving lord remem

VIII.

And him she saw, where thickest carnage spread,
But gathered breathing from the happier dead;
Far from his band, and battling with a host
That deem right dearly won the field he lost,
Felled — bleeding — baffled of the death he sought,
And snatched to expiate all the ills he wrought;
Preserved to linger and to live in vain,
While Vengeance pondered o'er new plans of pain,
And stanched the blood she saves to shed again —
But drop for drop, for Seyd's unglutted eye
Would doom him ever dying — ne'er to die!
Can this be he? triumphant late she saw,
When his red hand's wild gesture waved, a law!
'Tis he indeed — disarmed but undeprest,
His sole regret the life he still possest;
His wounds too slight, though taken with that will,
Which would have kissed the hand that then could kill.
Oh were there none, of all the many given,
To send his soul — he scarcely asked 'to heaven?
Must he alone of all retain his breath,
Who more than all had striven and struck for death?
He deeply felt — what mortal hearts must feel,
When thus reversed on faithless fortune's wheel,
For crimes committed, and the Victor's threat,
Of lingering tortures to repay the debt —
He deeply, darkly felt; but evil pride
That led to perpetrate — now serves to hide.
Still in his stern and self-collected mien
A conqueror's more than captive's air is seen,
Though faint with wasting toil and stiffening wound,
But few that saw — so calmly gazed around:
Though the far shouting of the distant crowd,
Their tremors o'er, rose insolently loud,
The better warriors who beheld him near,
Insulted not the foe who taught them fear;
And the grim guards that to his durance led,
In silence eyed him with a secret dread.

IX.

The Leech was sent — but not in mercy — there,
To note how much the life yet left could bear;
He found enough to load with heaviest chain,
And promise feeling for the wrench of pain:
To-morrow — yea — to-morrow's evening sun
Will sinking see impalement's pangs begun,
And rising with the wonted blush of morn
Behold how well or ill those pangs are borne.
Of torments this the longest and the worst,
Which adds all other agony to thirst,
That day by day death still forbears to slake,
While famished vultures flit around the stake.
" Oh! water — water!" — smiling Hate denies
The victim's prayer — for if he drinks — he dies.
This was his doom; — the Leech, the guard, were gone,
And left proud Conrad fettered and alone.

X.

'Twere vain to paint to what his feelings grew —
It even were doubtful if their victim knew.
There is a war, à chaos of the mind,
When all its elements convulsed — combined —
Lie dark and jarring with perturbed force,
And gnashing with impenitent Remorse;
That juggling fiend — who never spake before —
But cries " I warned thee!" when the deed is o'er.
Vain voice! the spirit burning but unbent,
May writhe — rebel — the weak alone repent!
Even in that lonely hour when most it feels,
And, to itself, all — all that self reveals,
No single passion, and no ruling thought
That leaves the rest as once unseen, unsought;
But the wild prospect when the soul reviews —
All rushing through their thousand avenues,
Ambition's dreams expiring, love's regret,
Endangered glory, life itself beset;
The joy untasted, the contempt or hate
'Gainst those who fain would triumph in our fate;
The hopeless past, the hasting future driven
Too quickly on to guess if hell or heaven;
Deeds, thoughts, and words, perhaps remembered not
So keenly till that hour, but ne'er forgot;
Things light or lovely in their acted time,
But now to stern reflection each a crime;
The withering sense of evil unrevealed,
Not cankering less because the more concealed —
All, in a word, from which all eyes must start,
That opening sepulchre — the naked heart
Bares with its buried woes, till Pride awake,
To snatch the mirror from the soul — and break.
Ay — Pride can veil, and Courage brave it all,
All — all — before — beyond — the deadliest fall.
Each has some fear, and he who least betrays,
The only hypocrite deserving praise:
Not the loud recreant wretch who boasts and flies;
But he who looks on death — and silent dies.
So steeled by pondering o'er his far career,
He half-way meets him should he menace near!

XI.

In the high chamber of his highest tower
Sate Conrad, fettered in the Pacha's power.
His palace perished in the flame — this fort
Contained at once his captive and his court.
Not much could Conrad of his sentence blame,
His foe, if vanquished, had but shared the
   same : —
Alone he sate — in solitude had scanned
His guilty bosom, but that breast he manned :
One thought alone he could not — dared not
   meet —
" Oh, how these tidings will Medora greet ? "
Then — only then — his clanking hands he
   raised,
And strained with rage the chain on which he
   gazed :
But soon he found — or feigned — or dreamed
   relief,
And smiled in self-derision of his grief,
" And now come torture when it will — or
   may,
More need of rest to nerve me for the day ! "
This said, with languor to his mat he crept,
And, whatsoe'er his visions, quickly slept.
'Twas hardly midnight when that fray begun,
For Conrad's plans matured, at once were
   done ;
And Havoc loathes so much the waste of time,
She scarce had left an uncommitted crime.
One hour beheld him since the tide he
   stemmed —
Disguised — discovered — conquering — taken
   — condemned —
A chief on land — an outlaw on the deep —
Destroying — saving — prisoned— and asleep !

XII.

He slept in calmest seeming — for his breath
Was hushed so deep — Ah ! happy if in death !
He slept — Who o'er his placid slumber bends?
His foes are gone — and here he hath no
   friends ;
Is it some seraph sent to grant him grace ?
No, 'tis an earthly form with heavenly face !
Its white arm raised a lamp — yet gently hid,
Lest the ray flash abruptly on the lid
Of that closed eye, which opens but to pain,
And once unclosed — but once may close
   again.
That form, with eye so dark, and cheek so
   fair,
And auburn waves of gemmed and braided
   hair ;
With shape of fairy lightness — naked foot,
That shines like snow, and falls on earth as
   mute —
Through guards and dunnest night how came
   it there ?
Ah ! rather ask what will not woman dare ?
Whom youth and pity lead like thee, Gulnare !

She could not sleep — and while th
   rest
In muttering dreams yet saw his pi:
She left his side — his signet-ring sl
Which oft in sport adorned her hant
And with it, scarcely questioned, wo
Through drowsy guards that must
   obey.
Worn out with toil, and tired with
   blows,
Their eyes had envied Conrad his :
And chill and nodding at the turret
They stretch their listless limbs, a
   no more :
Just raised their heads to hail the s
Nor ask or what or who the sign m

XIII.

She gazed in wonder, " Can he calı
While other eyes his fall or ravage
And mine in restlessness are wander
What sudden spell hath made thi
   dear ?
True — 'tis to him my life, and mo
And me and mine he spared from \
   woe :
'Tis late to think — but soft — hi:
   breaks —
How heavily he sighs ! — he starts —

He raised his head — and dazzled
   light,
His eye seemed dubious if it saw aı
He moved his hand — the grating oʃ
Too harshly told him that he lived :
" What is that form ? if not a shape
Methinks, my jailor's face shows \
   fair ! "
" Pirate ! thou knowest me not — but
Grateful for deeds thou hast too rar
Look on me — and remember her,
Snatched from the flames, and thy ı
   ful band.
I come through darkness — and
   know why —
Yet not to hurt — I would not see tl
" If so, kind lady ! thine the only ey
That would not here in that gay hop
Theirs is the chance — and let them
   right.
But still I think their courtesy or thi
That would confess me at so fair a :
Strange though it seem — yet with
   grief
Is linked a mirth — it doth not brin
That playfulness of Sorrow ne'er be,
And smiles in bitterness — but still i
And sometimes with the wisest and
Till even the scaffold [1] echoes with (

---

[1] In Sir Thomas More, for instance, oı
fold, and Anne Boleyn, in the Tower, w

Yet not the joy to which it seems akin —
It may deceive all hearts, save that within.
Whate'er it was that flashed on Conrad, now
A laughing wildness half unbent his brow:
And these his accents had a sound of mirth,
As if the last he could enjoy on earth;
Yet 'gainst his nature — for through that short life,
Few thoughts had he to spare from gloom and strife.

XIV.

" Corsair! thy doom is named — but I have power
To soothe the Pacha in his weaker hour.
Thee would I spare — nay more — would save thee now,
But this — time — hope — nor even thy strength allow;
But all I can, I will: at least delay
The sentence that remits thee scarce a day.
More now were ruin — even thyself were loth
The vain attempt should bring but doom to both."

" Yes! — loth indeed : — my soul is nerved to all,
Or fall'n too low to fear a further fall:
Tempt not thyself with peril; me with hope
Of flight from foes with whom I could not cope:
Unfit to vanquish — shall I meanly fly,
The one of all my band that would not die?
Yet there is one — to whom my memory clings,
Till to these eyes her own wild softness springs.
My sole resources in the path I trod
Were these — my bark — my sword — my love — my God!
The last I left in youth — he leaves me now —
And Man but works his will to lay me low.
I have no thought to mock his throne with prayer
Wrung from the coward crouching of despair;
It is enough — I breathe — and I can bear.
My sword is shaken from the worthless hand
That might have better kept so true a brand;
My bark is sunk or captive — but my love —
For her in sooth my voice would mount above:
Oh! she is all that still to earth can bind —
And this will break a heart so more than kind,
And blight a form — till thine appeared, Gulnare!
Mine eye ne'er asked if others were as fair."

" Thou lov'st another then ? — but what to me
Is this — 'tis nothing — nothing e'er can be:

But yet — thou lov'st — and — Oh! I envy those
Whose hearts on hearts as faithful can repose,
Who never feel the void — the wandering thought
That sighs o'er visions — such as mine hath wrought."

"Lady—methought thy love was his, for whom
This arm redeemed thee from a fiery tomb."
" My love stern Seyd's! Oh — No — No — not my love —
Yet much this heart, that strives no more, once strove
To meet his passion — but it would not be,
I felt — I feel — love dwells with — with the free.
I am a slave, a favored slave at best,
To share his splendor, and seem very blest!
Oft must my soul the question undergo,
Of — ' Dost thou love ?' and burn to answer, ' No!'
Oh! hard it is that fondness to sustain,
And struggle not to feel averse in vain;
But harder still the heart's recoil to bear,
And hide from one — perhaps another there.
He takes the hand I give not — nor withhold —
Its pulse nor checked — nor quickened — calmly cold:
And when resigned, it drops a lifeless weight
From one I never loved enough to hate.
No warmth these lips return by his imprest,
And chilled remembrance shudders o'er the rest.
Yes — had I ever proved that passion's zeal,
The change to hatred were at least to feel:
But still — he goes unmourned — returns unsought —
And oft when present — absent from my thought.
Or when reflection comes — and come it must —
I fear that henceforth 'twill but bring disgust;
I am his slave — but, in despite of pride,
'Twere worse than bondage to become his bride.
Oh! that this dotage of his breast would cease!
Or seek another and give mine release,
But yesterday — I could have said, to peace!
Yes — if unwonted fondness now I feign,
Remember — captive! 'tis to break thy chain;
Repay the life that to thy hand I owe;
To give thee back to all endeared below,
Who share such love as I can never know.
Farewell — morn breaks — and I must now away:
'Twill cost me dear — but dread no death to-day!"

XV.

She pressed his fettered fingers to her heart,
And bowed her head, and turned her to depart,

And noiseless as a lovely dream is gone.
And was she here? and is he now alone?
What gem hath dropped and sparkles o'er
    his chain?
The tear most sacred, shed for others' pain,
That starts at once — bright — pure — from
    Pity's mine,
Already polished by the hand divine!

Oh! too convincing — dangerously dear —
In woman's eye the unanswerable tear!
That weapon of her weakness she can wield,
To save, subdue — at once her spear and
    shield:
Avoid it — Virtue ebbs and Wisdom errs,
Too fondly gazing on that grief of hers!
What lost a world, and bade a hero fly?

The timid tear in Cleopatra's eye.
Yet be the soft triumvir's fault forgi
By this — how many lose not e
    heaven!
Consign their souls to man's eterna
And seal their own to spare some wa;

XVI.

'Tis morn — and o'er his altered fe;
The beams — without the hope of ;
What shall he be ere night? percha
O'er which the raven flaps her fun(
By his closed eye unheeded and ui
While sets that sun, and dews of eve
Chill — wet — and misty round eac
    limb   .
Refreshing earth — reviving all but

CANTO THE THIRD.

"Come vedi — ancor non m' abbandona."
DANTE.

I.

SLOW sinks, more lovely ere his race be run,[1]
Along Morea's hills the setting sun;
Not, as in Northern climes, obscurely bright,
But one unclouded blaze of living light!
O'er the hushed deep the yellow beam he
    throws,
Gilds the green wave, that trembles as it glows.
On old Ægina's rock, and Idra's isle,
The god of gladness sheds his parting smile;
O'er his own regions lingering, loves to shine,
Though there his altars are no more divine.
Descending fast the mountain shadows kiss
Thy glorious gulf, unconquered Salamis!
Their azure arches through the long expanse
More deeply purpled meet his mellowing
    glance,
And tenderest tints, along their summits driven,
Mark his gay course, and own the hues of
    heaven,
Till, darkly shaded from the land and deep,
Behind his Delphian cliff he sinks to sleep.
On such an eve, his palest beam he cast,
When — Athens! here thy Wisest looked his
    last.
How watched thy better sons his farewell ray,

That closed their murdered sage's [2]
Not yet — not yet — Sol pauses on
The precious hour of parting linge
But sad his light to agonizing eyes,
And dark the mountain's once deli
Gloom o'er the lovely land he seem
The land, where Phœbus never f
    fore;
But ere he sank below Cithæron's
The cup of woe was quaffed — the
The soul of him who scorned to f(
Who lived and died, as none can

But lo! from high Hymettus to th
The queen of night asserts her sile
No murky vapor, herald of the sto
Hides her fair face, nor girds her glo
With cornice glimmering as the m
    play,
There the white column greets her
And, bright around with quiverin
    set,
Her emblem sparkles o'er the mi;
The groves of olive scattered dar
Where meek Cephisus pours his

---

[1] The opening lines, as far as section ii., have,
perhaps, little business here, and were annexed to
an unpublished (though printed) poem; but they
were written on the spot, in the Spring of 1811, and
— I scarce know why — the reader must excuse
their appearance here — if he can.

[2] Socrates drank the hemlock a shor
sunset (the hour of execution), notwith
entreaties of his disciples to wait till
down.

[3] The twilight in Greece is much sh
our own country: the days in winte
but in summer of shorter duration.

The cypress saddening by the sacred mosque,
The gleaming turret of the gay kiosk,[1]
And, dun and sombre 'mid the holy calm,
Near Theseus' fane yon solitary palm,
All tinged with varied hues arrest the eye—
And dull were his that passed them heedless
    by.
Again the Ægean, heard no more afar,
Lulls his chafed breast from elemental war;
Again his waves in milder tints unfold
Their long array of sapphire and of gold,
Mixed with the shades of many a distant isle,
That frown—where gentler ocean seems to
    smile.[2]

• II.

Not now my theme—why turn my thoughts
    to thee?
Oh! who can look along thy native sea,
Nor dwell upon thy name, whate'er the tale,
So much its magic must o'er all prevail?
Who that beheld that Sun upon thee set,
Fair Athens! could thine evening face forget?
Not he—whose heart nor time nor distance
    frees,
Spell-bound within the clustering Cyclades!
Nor seems this homage foreign to his strain,
His Corsair's isle was once thine own do-
    main.—
Would that with freedom it were thine again!

III.

The Sun hath sunk—and, darker than the
    night,
Sinks with its beam upon the beacon height
Medora's heart—the third day's come and
    gone—
With it he comes not—sends not—faithless
    one!
The wind was fair though light; and storms
    were none.
Last eve Anselmo's bark returned, and yet
His only tidings that they had not met!
Though wild, as now, far different were the
    tale

---

[1] The Kiosk is a Turkish summer-house: the
palm is without the present walls of Athens, not far
from the temple of Theseus, between which and the
tree the wall intervenes.—Cephisus' stream is in-
deed scanty, and Ilissus has no stream at all.
[2] [Of the brilliant skies and variegated land-
scapes of Greece every one has formed to himself a
general notion, from having contemplated them
through the hazy atmosphere of some prose narra-
tion; but, in Lord Byron's poetry, every image is
distinct and glowing, as if it were illuminated by its
native sunshine; and in the figures which people
the landscape we behold, not only the general form
and costume, but the countenance, and the attitude,
and the play of features and of gestures accompany-
ing, and indicating, the sudden impulses of momen-
tary feelings. The magic of coloring by which this
is effected is,.perhaps, the most striking evidence
of Lord Byron's talent.—*George Ellis.*]

Had Conrad waited for that single sail.
The night-breeze freshens—she that day had
    passed
In watching all that Hope proclaimed a mast;
Sadly she sate—on high—Impatience bore
At last her footsteps to the midnight shore,
And there she wandered, heedless of the spray
That dashed her garments oft, and warned
    away:
She saw not—felt not this—nor dared depart,
Nor deemed it cold—her chill was at her
    heart;
Till grew such certainty from that suspense—
His very Sight had shocked from life or sense!

It came at last—a sad and shattered boat,
Whose inmates first beheld whom first they
    sought;
Some bleeding—all most wretched—these
    the few—
Scarce knew they how escaped—*this* all they
    knew.
In silence, darkling, each appeared to wait
His fellow's mournful guess at Conrad's fate:
Something they would have said; but seemed
    to fear
To trust their accents to Medora's ear.
She saw at once, yet sunk not—trembled not—
Beneath that grief, that loneliness of lot,
Within that meek fair form, were feelings high,
That deemed not till they found their energy.
While yet was Hope—they softened—flut-
    tered—wept—
All lost—that softness died not—but it slept;
And o'er its slumber rose that Strength which
    said,
" With nothing left to love—there's nought to
    dread."
'Tis more than nature's; like the burning might
Delirium gathers from the fever's height.

"Silent you stand—nor would I hear you tell
What—speak not—breathe not—for I know
    it well—
Yet would I ask—almost my lip denies
The—quick your answer—tell me where he
    lies."

" Lady! we know not—scarce with life we
    fled;
But here is one denies that he is dead:
He saw him bound; and bleeding—but alive."

She heard no further—'twas in vain to
    strive—
So throbbed each vein—each thought—till
    then withstood;
Her own dark soul—these words at once sub-
    dued:
She totters—falls—and senseless had the
    wave
Perchance but snatched her from another
    grave;

But that with hands though rude, yet weeping
  eyes,
They yield such aid as Pity's haste supplies:
Dash o'er her deathlike cheek the ocean dew,
Raise — fan — sustain — till life returns anew;
Awake her handmaids, with the matrons leave
That fainting form o'er which they gaze and
  grieve;
Then seek Anselmo's cavern, to report
The tale too tedious — when the triumph short.

IV.

In that wild council words waxed warm and
  strange
With thoughts of ranson, rescue, and revenge;
All, save repose or flight: still lingering there
Breathed Conrad's spirit, and forbade despair;
Whate'er his fate — the breasts he formed and
  led
Will save him living, or appease him dead.
Woe to his foes! there yet survive a few,
Whose deeds are daring, as their hearts are
  true.

V.

Within the Haram's secret chamber sate
Stern Seyd, still pondering o'er his Captive's
  fate;
His thoughts on love and hate alternate dwell,
Now with Gulnare, and now in Conrad's cell;
Here at his feet the lovely slave reclined
Surveys his brow — would soothe his gloom
  of mind:
While many an anxious glance her large dark
  eye
Sends in its idle search for sympathy,
His only bends in seeming o'er his beads,[1]
But inly views his victim as he bleeds.

" Pacha! the day is thine; and on thy crest
Sits Triumph — Conrad taken — fallen the
  rest!
His doom is fixed — he dies: and well his fate
Was earned — yet much too worthless for thy
  hate:
Methinks, a short release, for ransom told
With all his treasure, not unwisely sold;
Report speaks largely of his pirate-hoard —
Would that of this my Pacha were the lord!
While baffled, weakened by this fatal fray —
Watched — followed — he were then an easier
  prey;
But once cut off — the remnant of his band
Embark their wealth, and seek a safer strand."

" Gulnare! — if for each drop of blood a gem
Were offered rich as Stamboul's diadem;
If for each hair of his a massy mine
Of virgin ore should supplicating shine;
If all our Arab tales divulge or dream

Of wealth were here — that gold
  redeem!
It had not now redeemed a single
But that I know him fettered, in m
And, thirsting for revenge, I pond
On pangs that longest rack, and la

" Nay, Seyd! — I seek not to restra
Too justly moved for mercy to ass
My thoughts were only to secure f
His riches — thus released, he wei
Disabled, shorn of half his might
His capture could but wait thy first

" His capture *could!* — and shall I
One day to him — the wretch alrea
Release my foe! — at whose remon
  thine,
Fair suitor! — to thy virtuous grati
That thus repays this Giaour's relen
Which thee and thine alone of all c
No doubt — regardless if the prize
My thanks and praise alike are
  hear!
I have a counsel for thy gentler ea
I do mistrust thee, woman! and ea
Of thine stamps truth on all Suspic
Borne in his arms through fire
  Serai —
Say, wert thou lingering there with .
Thou need'st not answer — thy
  speaks,
Already reddening on thy guilty ch
Then, lovely dame, bethink thee! ar
'Tis not *his* life alone may claim su
Another word and — nay — I need
Accursed was the moment when he
Thee from the flames, which bettei
  — no —
I then had mourned thee with a lov
Now 'tis thy lord that warns — dece.
Know'st thou that I can clip thy wai
In words alone I am not wont to cl
Look to thyself — nor deem thy
  safe ! "

He rose — and slowly, sternly thence
Rage in his eye and threats in his a
Ah! little recked that chief of wom
Which frowns ne'er quelled, nor me
  dued;
And little deemed he what thy heart
When soft could feel, and when
  could dare.
His doubts appeared to wrong — n
  knew
How deep the root from whence c
  grew —
She was a slave — from such ma
  claim
A fellow-feeling, differing but in na
Still half unconscious — heedless of

---

[1] The comboloio, or Mahometan rosary; the
beads are in number ninety-nine.

Again she ventured on the dangerous path,
Again his rage repelled ⋯ until arose
That strife of thought, the source of woman's
  woes!

VI.

Meanwhile — long anxious — weary — still —
  the same
Rolled day and night — his soul could never
  tame —
This fearful interval of doubt and dread,
When every hour might doom him worse than
  dead,
When every step that echoed by the gate
Might entering lead where axe and stake
  await;
When every voice that grated on his ear
Might be the last that he could ever hear;
Could terror tame — that spirit stern and high
Had proved unwilling as unfit to die;
'Twas worn — perhaps decayed — yet silent
  bore
That conflict, deadlier far than all before:
The heat of fight, the hurry of the gale,
Leave scarce one thought inert enough to
  quail;
But bound and fixed in fettered solitude,
To pine, the prey of every changing mood;
To gaze on thine own heart; and meditate
Irrevocable faults, and coming fate —
Too late the last to shun — the first to mend —
To count the hours that struggle to thine end,
With not a friend to animate, and tell
To other ears that death became thee well:
Around thee foes to forge the ready lie,
And blot life's latest scene with calumny;
Before thee tortures, which the soul can dare,
Yet doubts how well the shrinking flesh may
  bear;
But deeply feels a single cry would shame,
To valor's praise thy last and dearest claim;
The life thou leav'st below, denied above
By kind monopolists of heavenly love;
And more than doubtful paradise — thy heaven
Of earthly hope — thy loved one from thee
  riven.
Such were the thoughts that outlaw must sus-
  tain,
And govern pangs surpassing mortal pain:
And those sustained he — boots it well or ill?
Since not to sink beneath, is something still!

VII.

The first day passed — he saw not her — Gul-
  nare —
The second — third — and still she came not
  there;
But what her words avouched, her charms
  had done,
Or else he had not seen another sun.
The fourth day rolled along, and with the
  night · · ⋯

Came storm and darkness in their mingling
  might:
Oh! how he listened to the rushing deep,
That ne'er till now so broke upon his sleep:
And his wild spirit wilder wishes sent,
Roused by the roar of his own element!
Oft had he ridden on that winged wave,
And loved its roughness for the speed it gave;
And now its dashing echoed on his ear,
A long known voice — alas! too vainly near!
Loud sung the wind above; and, doubly loud,
Shook o'er his turret cell the thunder-cloud;
And flashed the lightning by the latticed bar,
To him more genial than the midnight star:
Close to the glimmering grate he dragged his
  chain,
And hoped *that* peril might not prove in vain.
He raised his iron hand to Heaven, and prayed
One pitying flash to mar the form it made:[1]
His steel and impious prayer attract alike —
The storm rolled onward, and disdained to
  strike;
Its peal waxed fainter — ceased — he felt alone,
As if some faithless friend had spurned his
  groan!

VIII.

The midnight passed — and to the massy door
A light step came — it paused — it moved once
  more;
Slow turns the grating bolt and sullen key:
'Tis as his heart foreboded — that fair she!
Whate'er her sins, to him a guardian saint,
And beauteous still as hermit's hope can
  paint;
Yet changed since last within that cell she
  came,
More pale her cheek, more tremulous her
  frame:
On him she cast her dark and hurried eye,
Which spoke before her accents — "Thou
  must die!

---

[1] ["By the way — I have a charge against you.
As the great Mr. Dennis roared out on a similar
occasion, 'By G—d, *that* is *my* thunder!' — so do
I exclaim, '*This* is *my* lightning!' I allude to a
speech of Ivan's, in the scene with Petrowna and
the Empress, where the thought and almost expres-
sion are similar to Conrad's in the third canto of
the 'Corsair.' I, however, do not say this to accuse
you, but to except myself from suspicion; as there
is a priority of six months' publication, on my
part, between the appearance of that composition
and of your tragedies." — *Lord B. to Mr. Sotheby*,
Sept. 25, 1815. — The following are the lines in Mr.
Sotheby's tragedy: —

———— "And I have leapt
In transport from my flinty couch, to welcome
The thunder as it burst upon my roof;
And beckoned to the lightning, as it flashed
And sparkled on these fetters.'

Notwithstanding Lord Byron's precaution, the coin-
cidence in question was cited against him, some
years after, in a periodical journal.]

Yes, thou must die — there is but one resource,
The last — the worst — if torture were not worse."
" Lady! I look to none — my lips proclaim
What last proclaimed they — Conrad still the same:
Why should'st thou seek an outlaw's life to spare,
And change the sentence I deserve to bear?
Well have I earned — nor here alone — the meed
Of Seyd's revenge, by many a lawless deed."

' Why should I seek? because — Oh! didst thou not
Redeem my life from worse than slavery's lot?
Why should I seek? — hath misery made thee blind
To the fond workings of a woman's mind!
And must I say? albeit my heart rebel
With all that woman feels, but should not tell —
Because — despite thy crimes — that heart is moved:
It feared thee — thanked thee — pitied — maddened — loved.
Reply not, tell not now thy tale again,
Thou lovest another — and I love in vain;
Though fond as mine her bosom, form more fair,
I rush through peril which she would not dare.
If that thy heart to hers were truly dear,
Were I thine own — thou wert not lonely here:
An outlaw's spouse — and leave her lord to roam!
What hath such gentle dame to do with home?
But speak not now — o'er thine and o'er my head
Hangs the keen sabre by a single thread;
If thou hast courage still, and wouldst be free,
Receive this poniard — rise — and follow me!"

"Ay — in my chains! my steps will gently tread,
With these adornments, o'er each slumbering head!
Thou hast forgot — is this a garb for flight?
Or is that instrument more fit for fight?"

"Misdoubting Corsair! I have gained the guard,
Ripe for revolt, and greedy for reward.
A single word of mine removes that chain:
Without some aid how here could I remain?
Well, since we met, hath sped my busy time,
If in aught evil, for thy sake the crime:
The crime — 'tis none to punish those of Seyd.
That hated tyrant, Conrad — he must bleed!
I see thee shudder — but my soul is changed —
Wronged, spurned, reviled — and it shall be avenged —
Accused of what till now my heart disdained —

Too faithful, though to bitte[r] chained.
Yes, smile! — but he had little cau[se]
I was not treacherous then — no[t] dear;
But he has said it — and the jealo[us]
Those tyrants, teasing, tempting t[o]
Deserve the fate their fretting lips
I never loved — he bought me — high —
Since with me came a heart he cou[ld]
I was a slave unmurmuring: he h[as]
But for his rescue I with thee had
'Twas false thou know'st — but augurs rue,
Their words are omens Insult rend[ered]
Nor was thy respite granted to my
This fleeting grace was only to pre[pare]
New torments for thy life, and my
Mine too he threatens; but his dot[age]
Would fain reserve me for his lord
When wearier of these fleeting c[harms] me,
There yawns the sack — and yonde[r] sea!
What, am I then a toy for dotard's
To wear but till the gilding frets aw[ay]
I saw thee — loved thee — owe
would save,
If but to show how grateful is a sla[ve]
But had he not thus menaced fame
(And well he keeps his oaths pron[e] strife,)
I still had saved thee — but the Pac[ha]
Now I am all thine own — for all p[?]
Thou lov'st me not — nor know'st the worst.
Alas! this love — that hatred are th[?]
Oh! couldst thou prove my tr[?] wouldst not start,
Nor fear the fire that lights an East[ern]
'Tis now the beacon of thy safety —
It points within the port a Mainote [?]
But in one chamber, where our [?] lead,
There sleeps — he must not wake- pressor Seyd!"

" Gulnare — Gulnare — I never fe[lt]
My abject fortune, withered fame so
Seyd is mine enemy: had swept my
From earth with ruthless but with o[?]
And therefore came I, in my bark o[?]
To smite the smiter with the scimita[r]
Such is my weapon — not the secre[t]
Who spares a woman's seeks not life.
Thine saved I gladly, Lady, not for
Let me not deem that mercy shown
Now fare thee well — more peace b[?] breast!
Night wears apace — my last of eart[h]

"Rest! rest! by sunrise must thy sinews
  shake,
And thy limbs writhe around the ready stake.
I heard the order — saw — I will not see —
If thou wilt perish, I will fall with thee.
My life — my love — my hatred — all below
Are on this cast — Corsair! 'tis but a blow!
Without it flight were idle — how evade
His sure pursuit ? my wrongs too unrepaid,
My youth disgraced — the long, long wasted
  years,
One blow shall cancel with our future fears;
But since the dagger suits thee less than brand,
I'll try the firmness of a female hand.
The guards are gained — one moment all
  were o'er —
Corsair! we meet in safety or no more;
If errs my feeble hand, the morning cloud
Will hover o'er thy scaffold, and my shroud."

IX.

She turned, and vanished ere he could reply,
But his glance followed far with eager eye;
And gathering, as he could, the links that
  bound
His form, to curl their length, and curb their
  sound,
Since bar and bolt no more his steps pre-
  clude,
He, fast as fettered limbs allow, pursued.
'Twas dark and winding, and he knew not
  where .
That passage led; nor lamp nor guard were
  there :
He sees a dusky glimmering — shall he seek
Or shun that ray so indistinct and weak ?
Chance guides his steps — a freshness seems
  to bear .
Full on his brow, as if from morning air —
He reached an open gallery — on his eye
Gleamed the last star of night, the clearing
  sky:
Yet scarcely heeded these — another light
From a lone chamber struck upon his sight.
Towards it he moved; a scarcely closing
  door
Revealed the ray within, but nothing more.
With hasty step a figure outward past,
Then paused — and turned — and paused —
  'tis She at last!
No poniard in that hand — nor sign of ill —
" Thanks to that softening heart — she could
  not kill ! "
Again he looked, the wildness of her eye
Starts from the day abrupt and fearfully.
She stopped — threw back her dark far-float-
  ing hair,
That nearly veiled her face and bosom fair :
As if she late had bent her leaning head
Above some object of her doubt or dread.
They meet — upon her brow — unknown —
  forgot —

Her hurrying hand had left — 'twas but a
  spot —
Its hue was all he saw, and scarce withstood —
Oh! slight but certain pledge of crime — 'tis
  blood!

X.

He had seen battle — he had brooded lone
O'er promised pangs to sentenced guilt fore-
  shown ;
He had been tempted — chastened — and the
  chain
Yet on his arms might ever there remain:
But ne'er from strife — captivity — remorse —
From all his feelings in their inmost force —
So thrilled — so shuddered every creeping
  vein,
As now they froze before that purple stain.
That spot of blood, that light but guilty
  streak,
Had banished all the beauty from her cheek!
Blood he had viewed — could view unmoved
  — but then
It flowed in combat, or was shed by men!

XI.

" 'Tis done — he nearly waked — but it is
  done.
Corsair! he perished — thou art dearly won.
All words would now be vain — away — away!
Our bark is tossing — 'tis already day.
The few gained over, now are wholly mine,
And these thy yet surviving band shall join :
Anon my voice shall vindicate my hand,
When once our sail forsakes this hated strand."

XII.

She clapped her hands — and through the
  gallery pour,
Equipped for flight, her vassals — Greek and
  Moor ;
Silent but quick they stoop, his chains un-
  bind ;
Once more his limbs are free as mountain
  wind !
But on his heavy heart such sadness sate,
As if they there transferred that iron weight.
No words are uttered — at her sign a door
Reveals the secret passage to the shore ;
The city lies behind — they speed, they reach
The glad waves dancing on the yellow beach ;
And Conrad following, at her beck, obeyed,
Nor cared he now if rescued or betrayed ;
Resistance were as useless as if Seyd
Yet lived to view the doom his ire decreed.

XIII.

Embarked, the sail unfurled, the light breeze
  blew —
How much had Conrad's memory to review !
Sunk he in Contemplation, till the cape
Where last he anchored reared its giant shape.

Ah! — since that fatal night, though brief the
   time,
Had swept an age of terror, grief, and crime,
As its far shadow frowned above the mast,
He veiled his face, and sorrowed as he passed;
He thought of all — Gonsalvo and his band,
His fleeting triumph and his failing hand;
He thought on her afar, his lonely bride:
He turned and saw — Gulnare, the homicide!

XIV.

She watched his features till she could not bear
Their freezing aspect and averted air,
And that strange fierceness foreign to her eye,
Fell quenched in tears, too late to shed or dry.
She knelt beside him and his hand she pressed,
" Thou may'st forgive though Allah's self de-
   test;
But for that deed of darkness what wert thou ?
Reproach me — but not yet — Oh! spare me
   now!
I am not what I seem — this fearful night
My brain bewildered — do not madden quite!
If I had never loved — though less my guilt,
Thou hadst not lived to — hate me — if thou
   wilt."

XV.

She wrongs his thoughts, they more himself
   upbraid
Than her, though undesigned, the wretch he
   made
But speechless all, deep, dark, and unexprest,
They bleed within that silent cell — his breast.
Still onward, fair the breeze, nor rough the
   surge,
The blue waves sport around the stern they
   urge;
Far on the horizon's verge appears a speck,
A spot — a mast — a sail — an armed deck!
Their little bark her men of watch descry,
And ampler canvas woos the wind from high;
She bears her down majestically near,
Speed on her prow, and terror in her tier;
A flash is seen — the ball beyond her bow
Booms harmless, hissing to the deep below.
Up rose keen Conrad from his silent trance,
A long, long absent gladness in his glance;
" 'Tis mine — my blood-red flag! again —
   again —·
I am not all deserted on the main!"
They own the signal, answer to the hail,
Hoist out the boat at once, and slacken sail.
" 'Tis Conrad! Conrad!" shouting from the
   deck,
Command nor duty could their transport
   check!
With light alacrity and gaze of pride,
They view him mount once more his vessel's
   side;
A smile relaxing in each rugged face,
Their arms can scarce forbear a rough em-
   brace.

He, half forgetting danger and defe
Returns their greeting as a chief m;
Wrings with a cordial grasp Anseln
And feels he yet can conquer and c

XVI.

These greetings o'er, the feelings tha
Yet grieve to win him back without
They sailed prepared for vengeat
   they known
A woman's hand secured that deed
She were their queen — less scru
   they
Than haughty Conrad how they win
With many an asking smile, and \
   stare,
They whisper round, and gaze upon
And her, at once above — beneath l
Whom blood appalled not, their re
   plex.
To Conrad turns her faint implorin
She drops her veil, and stands in s
Her arms are meekly folded on tha
Which — Conrad safe — to fate res
   rest.
Though worse than frenzy could th
   fill,
Extreme in love or hate, in good or
The worst of crimes had left her wo

XVII.

This Conrad marked, and felt — ah !
   less ? — [1]
Hate of that deed — but grief for her
What she has done no tears can w;
And Heaven must punish on its ang
But — it was done: he knew, wha
   guilt,
For him that poinard smote, that l
   spilt;
And he was free! — and she for him'
Her all on earth, and more than all ii
And now he turned him to that (
   slave
Whose brow was bowed beneath t
   he gave,
Who now seemed changed and hui
   faint and meek,
But varying oft the color of her chee
To deeper shades of paleness — all i
That fearful spot which stained it
   dead!
He took that hand — it trembled -
   late —
So soft in love — so wildly nerved in
He clasped that hand — it trembled -
   own

---

[1] [" I have added a section for *Guln*.
up the parting, and dismiss her more cerer
If Mr. Gifford or you dislike, 'tis but a s
another midnight." — *Lord Byron to*
January 11, 1814]

Had lost its firmness, and his voice its tone.
" Gulnare ! " — but she replied not — " dear
   Gulnare ! "
She raised her eye — her only answer there —
At once she sought and sunk in his embrace :
If he had driven her from that resting-place,
His had been more or less than mortal heart,
But — good or ill — it bade her not depart.
Perchance, but for the bodings of his breast,
His latest virtue then had joined the rest.
Yet even Medora might forgive the kiss
That asked from form so fair no more than
   this,
The first, the last that Frailty stole from Faith —
To lips where Love had lavished all his breath,
To lips — whose broken sighs such fragrance
   fling,
As he had fanned them freshly with his wing !

XVIII.

They gain by twilight's hour their lonely isle,
To them the very rocks appear to smile ;
The haven hums with many a cheering sound,
The beacons blaze their wonted stations round,
The boats are darting o'er the curly bay,
And sportive dolphins bend them through the
   spray ;
Even the hoarse sea-bird's shrill, discordant
   shriek,
Greets like the welcome of his tuneless beak !
Beneath each lamp that through its lattice
   gleams,
Their fancy paints the friends that trim the
   beams.
Oh ! what can sanctify the joys of home,
Like Hope's gay glance from Ocean's troub-
   led foam ?

XIX.

The lights are high on beacon and from
   bower,
And 'midst them Conrad seeks Medora's
   tower :
He looks in vain — 'tis strange — and all re-
   mark,
Amid so many, hers alone is dark.
'Tis strange — of yore its welcome never failed,
Nor now, perchance, extinguished, only veiled.
With the first boat descends he for the shore,
And looks impatient on the lingering oar.
Oh ! for a wing beyond the falcon's flight,
To bear him like an arrow to that height !
With the first pause the resting rowers gave,
He waits not — looks not — leaps into the
   wave,
Strives through the surge, bestrides the beach,
   and high
Ascends the path familiar to his eye.

He reached his turret door — he paused —
   no sound
Broke from within ; and all was night around.
He knocked, and loudly — footstep nor reply

Announced that any heard or deemed him
   nigh ;
He knocked — but faintly — for his trembling
   hand
Refused to aid his heavy heart's demand.
The portal opens — 'tis a well known face —
But not the form he panted to embrace.
Its lips are silent — twice his own essayed,
And failed to frame the question they delayed ;
He snatched the lamp — its light will answer
   all —
It quits his grasp, expiring in the fall.
He would not wait for that reviving ray —
As soon could he have lingered there for day ;
But, glimmering through the dusky corridore,
Another chequers o'er the shadowed floor ;
His steps the chamber gain — his eyes behold
All that his heart believed not — yet foretold !

XX.

He turned not — spoke not — sunk not — fixed
   his look,
And set the anxious frame that lately shook :
He gazed — how long we gaze despite of pain,
And know, but dare not own, we gaze in vain !
In life itself she was so still and fair,
That death with gentler aspect withered there ;
And the cold flowers [1] her colder hand con-
   tained,
In that last grasp as tenderly were strained
As if she scarcely felt, but feigned a sleep,
And made it almost mockery yet to weep :
The long dark lashes fringed her lids of snow,
And veiled — thought shrinks from all that
   lurked below —
Oh ! o'er the eye Death most exerts his might,
And hurls the spirit from her throne of light !
Sinks those blue orbs in that long last eclipse,
But spares, as yet, the charm around her lips —
Yet, yet they seem as they forbore to smile,
And wished repose — but only for a while ;
But the white shroud, and each extended tress,
Long — fair — but spread in utter lifelessness,
Which, late the sport of every summer wind,
Escaped the baffled wreath that strove to bind ;
These — and the pale pure cheek, became the
   bier —
But she is nothing — wherefore is he here ?

XXI.

He asked no question — all were answered
   now
By the first glance on that still — marble brow.
It was enough — she died — what recked it
   how ?
The love of youth, the hope of better years,
The source of softest wishes, tenderest fears,
The only living thing he could not hate,

---

[1] In the Levant it is the custom to strew flowers
on the bodies of the dead, and in the hands of young
persons to place a nosegay.

Was reft at once — and he deserved his fate,
But did not feel it less ; — the good explore,
For peace, those realms where guilt can never
 soar :
The proud — the wayward — who have fixed
 below
Their joy, and find this earth enough for woe,
Lose in that one their all — perchance a mite —
But who in patience parts with all delight ?
Full many a stoic eye and aspect stern
Mask hearts where grief hath little left to learn,
And many a withering thought lies hid, not lost,
In smiles that least befit who wear them most.

XXII.

By those, that deepest feel, is ill exprest
The indistinctness of the suffering breast ;
Where thousand thoughts begin to end in one,
Which seeks from all the refuge found in none ;
No words suffice the secret soul to show,
For Truth denies all eloquence to Woe.
On Conrad's stricken soul exhaustion prest,
And stupor almost lulled it into rest ;
So feeble now — his mother's softness crept
To those wild eyes, which like an infant's
 wept:
It was the very weakness of his brain,
Which thus confessed without relieving pain.
None saw his trickling tears — perchance, if
 seen,
That useless flood of grief had never been :
Nor long they flowed — he dried them to de-
 part,
In helpless — hopeless — brokenness of heart :
The sun goes forth — but Conrad's day is dim ;
And the night cometh — ne'er to pass from him.
There is no darkness like the cloud of mind,
On Grief's vain eye — the blindest of the blind !
Which may not — dare not see — but turns
 aside
To blackest shade — nor will endure a guide !

XXIII.

His heart was formed for softness — warped
 to wrong ; [1]
Betrayed too early, and beguiled too long ;
Each feeling pure — as falls the dropping dew
Within the grot ; like that had hardened too ;
Less clear, perchance, its earthly trials passed,
But sunk, and chilled, and pertified at last.
Yet tempests wear, and lightning cleaves the
 rock,

[1] [These sixteen lines are not in the original MS.]

If such his heart, so shattered it the
.There grew one flower beneath i
 brow,
Though dark the shade — it sheltere
 till now.   .
The thunder came — that bolt hat
 both,
The Granite's firmness, and the Lily'
The gentle plant hath left no leaf to
Its tale, but shrunk and withered wh
And of its cold protector, blacken rc
But shivered fragments on the barrei

xxiv.

'Tis morn — to venture on his lonel)
Few dare : though now Anselmo s
 tower.
He was not there — nor seen along t
Ere night, alarmed, their isle is travei
Another morn — another bids them
And shout his name till echo waxeth
Mount — grotto — cavern — valley se
 vain,
They find on shore a sea-boat's brok
Their hope revives — they follow o'er
'Tis idle all — moons roll on moons ε
And Conrad comes not — came not
 day :
Nor trace, nor tidings of his doom d
Where lives his grief, or perished his
Long mourned his band whom noı
 mourn beside ;
And fair the monument they gave his
For him they raise not the recording
His death yet dubious, deeds too
 known ;
He left a Corsair's name to other tim
Linked with one virtue, and a thousand

[1] [The "Corsair" is written in th
heroic couplet, with a spirit, freedom, an
of tone, of which, notwithstanding the e)
Dryden, we scarcely believed that measuı
tible. It was yet to be proved that this,
ponderous and stately verse in our languε
be accommodated to the variations of a ta
sion and of pity, and to all the breaks, s
transitions of an adventurous and drama
tion. This experiment Lord Byron has m
equal boldness and success ; and has sat
that the oldest and most respectable meε
is known amongst us, is at least as flexib
other, and capable, in the hands of a n
vibrations as strong and rapid as those of
structure. — *Jeffrey*.]

THAT the point of honor which is represented in one instance of Conrad's character haε
carried beyond the bounds of probability, may perhaps be in some degree confirmed by the
anecdote of a brother buccaneer in the year 1814 : — " Our readers have all seen the account of
prise against the pirates of Barrataria ; but few, we believe, were informed of the situation. ʰ
nature of that establishment. For the information of such as were unacquainted with it, we have

from a friend the following interesting narrative of the main 'facts, of which he has personal knowledge. and which cannot fail to interest some of our readers. — Barrataria is a bay, or a narrow arm of the Gulf of Mexico; it runs through a rich but very flat country, until it reaches within a mile of the Mississippi river, fifteen miles below the city of New Orleans. The bay has branches almost innumerable, in which persons can lie concealed from the severest scrutiny. It communicates with three lakes which lie on the south-west side, and these, with the lake of the same name, and which lies contiguous to the sea, where there is an island formed by the two arms of this lake and the sea. The east and west points of this island were fortified, in the year 1811, by a band of pirates under the command of one Monsieur La Fitte. A large majority of these outlaws are of that class of the population of the State of Louisiana who fled from the island of St. Domingo during the troubles there, and took refuge in the island of Cuba; and when the last war between France and Spain commenced, they were compelled to leave that island with the short notice of a few days. Without ceremony, they entered the United States, the most of them the State of Louisiana, with all the negroes they had possessed in Cuba. They were notified by the Governor of that State of the clause in the constitution which forbade the importation of slaves; but, at the same time, received the assurance of the Governor that he would obtain, if possible, the approbation of the General Government for their retaining this property. — The island of Barrataria is situated about lat. 29 deg. 15 min., lon. 92. 30.; and is as remarkable for its health as for the superior scale and shell fish with which its waters abound. The chief of this horde, like Charles de Moor, had mixed with his many vices some virtues. In the year 1813, this party had, from its turpitude and boldness, claimed the attention of the Governor of Louisiana; and to break up the establishment he thought proper to strike at the head. He therefore offered a reward of 500 dollars for the head of Monsieur La Fitte, who was well known to the inhabitants of the city of New Orleans, from his immediate connection, and his once having been a fencing-master in that city of great reputation, which art he learnt in Bonaparte's army, where he was a captain. The reward which was offered by the Governor for the head of La Fitte was answered by the offer of a reward from the latter of 15,000 for the head of the Governor. The Governor ordered out a company to march from the city to La Fitte's island, and to burn and destroy all the property, and to bring to the city of New Orleans all his banditti. This company, under the command of a man who had been the intimate associate of this bold Captain, approached very near to the fortified island, before he saw a man, or heard a sound, until he heard a whistle, not unlike a boatswain's call. Then it was he found himself surrounded by armed men who had emerged from the secret avenues which led into Bayou. Here it was that the modern Charles de Moor developed his few noble traits; for to this man, who had come to destroy his life and all that was dear to him, he not only spared his life, but offered him that which would have made the honest soldier easy for the remainder of his days; which was indignantly refused. He then, with the approbation of his captor, returned to the city. This circumstance, and some concomitant events, proved that this band of pirates was not to be taken by land. Our naval force having always been small in that quarter, exertions for the destruction of this illicit establishment could not be expected from them until augmented; for an officer of the navy, with most of the gun-boats on that station, had to retreat from an overwhelming force of La Fitte's. So soon as the augmentation of the navy authorized an attack, one was made; the overthrow of this banditti has been the result; and now this almost invulnerable point and key to New Orleans is clear of an enemy, it is to be hoped the government will hold it by a strong military force." — *American Newspaper.*

In Noble's continuation of Granger's Biographical History there is a singular passage in his account of Archbishop Blackbourne; and as in some measure connected with the profession of the hero of the foregoing poem, I cannot resist the temptation of extracting it. — " 'There is something mysterious in the history and character of Dr. Blackbourne. The former is but imperfectly known; and report has even asserted he was a buccaneer; and that one of his brethren in that profession having asked, on his arrival in England, what had become of his old chum, Blackbourne, was answered, he is Archbishop of York. We are informed that Blackbourne was installed sub-dean of Exeter in 1694, which office he resigned in 1702; but after his successor Lewis Barnet's death, in 1704, he regained it. In the following year he became dean; and in 1714 held with it the archdeanery of Cornwall. He was consecrated bishop of Exeter, February 24, 1716; and translated to York, November 28, 1724, as a reward, according to court scandal, for uniting George I. to the Duchess of Munster. This, however, appears to have been an unfounded calumny. As archbishop he behaved with great prudence, and was equally respectable as the guardian of the revenues of the see. Rumor whispered he retained the vices of his youth, and that a passion for the fair sex formed an item in the list of his weaknesses; but so far from being convicted by seventy witnesses, he does not appear to have been directly criminated by one. In short, I look upon these aspersions as the effects of mere malice. How is it possible a buccaneer should have been so good a scholar as Blackbourne certainly was? He who had so perfect a knowledge of the classics (particularly of the Greek tragedians), as to be able to read them with the same ease as he could Shakspeare, must have taken great pains to acquire the learned languages; and have had both leisure and good masters. But he was undoubtedly educated at Christ-church College, Oxford. He is allowed to have been a pleasant man; this however was turned against him, by its being said, 'he gained more hearts than souls.' "

" The only voice that could soothe the passions of the savage (Alphonso III.) was that of an amiable and virtuous wife, the sole object of his love; the voice of Donna Isabella, the daughter of the Duke of Savoy, and the grand-daughter of Philip II. King of Spain. — Her dying words sunk deep into his memory; his fierce spirit melted into tears; and after the last embrace, Alphonso retired into his chamber to bewail his irreparable loss, and to meditate on the vanity of human life."— *Gibbon's Miscellaneous Works,* vol. iii. p. 473.

LARA: A TALE.

INTRODUCTION.

LARA was published anonymously in August, 1814, in the same volume with the " Jacq
Rogers. It is obviously the sequel of " The Corsair." Lara is Conrad, and Kaled, Gulnare.
one of his letters says, " Lara I wrote while undressing, after coming home from balls and ma
in the year of revelry, 1814."

CANTO THE FIRST.

I.

THE Serfs [1] are glad through Lara's wide do-
   main,
And Slavery half forgets her feudal chain ;
He, their unhoped, but unforgotten lord,
The long self-exiled chieftain, is restored :
There be bright faces in the busy hall,
Bowls on the board, and banners on the wall ;
Far checkering o'er the pictured window, plays
The unwonted fagots' hospitable blaze ;
And gay retainers gather round the hearth,
With tongues all loudness, and with eyes all
   mirth.

II.

The chief of Lara is returned again :
And why had Lara crossed the bounding
   main ?
Left by his sire, too young such loss to know,
Lord of himself ; — that heritage of woe,
That fearful empire which the human breast
But holds to rob the heart within of rest ! —
With none to check, and few to point in time
The thousand paths that slope the way to
   crime ;
Then, when he most required commandment,
   then

[1] The reader is apprised, that the name of Lara
being Spanish, and no circumstance of local and
natural description fixing the scene or hero of the
poem to any country or age, the word ' Serf,' which
could not be correctly applied to the lower classes
in Spain, who were never vassals of the soil, has
nevertheless been employed to designate the follow-
ers of our fictitious chieftain. — [Byron elsewhere
intimates, that he meant Lara for a chief of the
Morea.]

Had Lara's daring boyhood govern
It skills not, boots not step by step t
His youth through all the mazes of j
Short was the course his restlessness
But long enough to leave him half u

III.

And Lara left in youth his father-lan
But from the hour he waved his part
Each trace waxed fainter of his cour:
Had nearly ceased his memory to re
His sire was dust, his vassals could c
'Twas all they knew, that Lara was nc
Nor sent, nor came he, till conjectur
Cold in the many, anxious in the few
His hall scarce echoes with his wont(
His portrait darkens in its fading fra
Another chief consoled his destined l
The young forgot him, and the old h
"Yet doth he live!" exclaims the i
   heir,
And sighs for sables which he must r
A hundred scutcheons deck with
   grace
The Laras' last and longest dwelling-
But one is absent from the moulderir
That now were welcome in that Goth

IV.

He comes at last in sudden loneliness.
And whence they know not, why th
   not guess ;
They more might marvel, when the g
   o'er,

[1] [Lord Byron's own tale is partly tol
section. — *Sir Walter Scott.*]

Not that he came, but came not long before:
No train is his beyond a single page,
Of foreign aspect, and of tender age.
Years had rolled on, and fast they speed away
To those that wander as to those that stay;
But lack of tidings from another clime
Had lent a flagging wing to weary Time.
They see, they recognize, yet almost deem
The present dubious, or the past a dream.

He lives, nor yet is past his manhood's prime,
Though seared by toil, and something touched
by time;
His faults, whate'er they were, if scarce forgot,
Might be untaught him by his varied lot;
Nor good nor ill of late were known, his name
Might yet uphold his patrimonial fame:
His soul in youth was haughty, but his sins
No more than pleasure from the stripling
wins;
And such, if not yet hardened in their course,
Might be redeemed, nor ask a long remorse.

V.

And they indeed were changed — 'tis quickly
seen,
Whate'er he be, 'twas not what he had been:
That brow in furrowed lines had fixed at last,
And spake of passions, but of passion past:
The pride, but not the fire, of early days,
Coldness of mien, and carelessness of praise;
A high demeanor, and a glance that took
Their thoughts from others by a single look;
And that sarcastic levity of tongue,
The stinging of a heart the world hath stung,
That darts in seeming playfulness around,
And makes those feel that will not own the
wound,
All these seemed his, and something more
beneath,
Than glance could well reveal, or accent
breathe.
Ambition, glory, love, the common aim,
That some can conquer, and that all would
claim,
Within his breast appeared no more to strive,
Yet seemed as lately they had been alive;
And some deep feeling it were vain to trace
At moments lightened o'er his livid face.

VI.

Not much he loved long question of the past,
Nor told of wondrous wilds, and deserts vast,
In those far lands where he had wandered
lone,
And — as himself would have it seem — un-
known:
Yet these in vain his eye could scarcely scan,
Nor glean experience from his fellow man;
But what he had beheld he shunned to show,
As bardly worth a stranger's care to know;
If still more prying such inquiry grew,
His brow fell darker, and his words more few.

VII.

Not unrejoiced to see him once again,
Warm was his welcome to the haunts of men;
Born of high lineage, linked in high com-
mand,
He mingled with the Magnates of his land;
Joined the carousals of the great and gay,
And saw them smile or sigh their hours
away;[1]
But still he only saw, and did not share,
The common pleasure or the general care;
He did not follow what they all pursued
With hope still baffled still to be renewed;
Nor shadowy honor, nor substantial gain,
Nor beauty's preference, and the rival's pain:
Around him some mysterious circle thrown
Repelled approach, and showed him still
alone;
Upon his eye sat something of reproof,
That kept at least frivolity aloof;
And things more timid that beheld him near,
In silence gazed, or whispered mutual fear;
And they the wiser, friendlier few confessed
They deemed him better than his air ex-
pressed.

VIII.

'Twas strange — in youth all action and all
life,
Burning for pleasure, not averse from strife;
Woman — the field — the ocean — all that
gave
Promise of gladness, peril of a grave,
In turn he tried — he ransacked all below,
And found his recompense in joy or woe,
No tame, trite medium; for his feelings sought
In that intenseness an escape from thought:
The tempest of his heart in scorn had gazed
On that the feebler elements hath raised;
The rapture of his heart had looked on high,
And asked if greater dwelt beyond the sky:
Chained to excess, the slave of each extreme,
How woke he from the wildness of that
dream?
Alas! he told not — but he did awake
To curse the withered heart that would not
break.

IX.

Books, for his volume heretofore was Man,
With eye more curious he appeared to scan,
And oft, in sudden mood, for many a day,
From all communion he would start away:
And then, his rarely called attendants said,
Through night's long hours would sound his
hurried tread

[1] [This description of Lara suddenly and unex-
pectedly returned from distant travels, and reassum-
ing his station in the society of his own country,
has strong points of resemblance to the part which
the author himself seemed occasionally to bear amid
the scenes where the great mingle with the fair. —
Sir Walter Scott.]

O'er the dark gallery, where his fathers frowned
In rude but antique portraiture around:
They heard, but whispered — "*that* must not
　　be known —
The sound of words less earthly than his own.
Yes, they who chose might smile, but some
　　had seen
They scarce knew what, but more than should
　　have been.
Why gazed he so upon the ghastly head
Which hands profane had gathered from the
　　dead,
That still beside his opened volume lay,
As if to startle all save him away?
Why slept he not when others were at rest?
Why heard no music, and received no guest?
All was not well, they deemed — but where
　　the wrong?
Some knew perchance — but 'twere a tale too
　　long;
And such besides were too discreetly wise,
To more than hint their knowledge in sur-
　　mise;
But if they would — they could " — around the
　　board,
Thus Lara's vassals prattled of their lord.

X.

It was the night — and Lara's glassy stream
The stars are studding, each with imaged
　　beam;
So calm, the waters scarcely seem to stray,
And yet they glide like happiness away;
Reflecting far and fairy-like from high
The immortal lights that live along the sky:
Its banks are fringed with many a goodly tree,
And flowers the fairest that may feast the bee;
Such in her chaplet infant Dian wove,
And Innocence would offer to her love.
These deck the shore; the waves their chan-
　　nel make
In windings bright and mazy like the snake.
All was so still, so soft in earth and air,
You scarce would start to meet a spirit there;
Secure that nought of evil could delight
To walk in such a scene, on such a night!
It was a moment only for the good:
So Lara deemed, nor longer there he stood,
But turned in silence to his castle-gate;
Such scene his soul no more could contem-
　　plate:
Such scene reminded him of other days,
Of skies more cloudless, moons of purer blaze,
Of nights more soft and frequent, hearts that
　　now —
No — no — the storm may beat upon his brow,
Unfelt — unsparing — but a night like this,
A night of beauty, mocked such breast as his.

XI.

He turned within his solitary hall,
And his high shadow shot along the wall:

There were the painted forms of oth
'Twas all they left of virtues or of cri
Save vague tradition; and the gloo
That hid their dust, their foibles,
　　faults;
And half a column of the pompous
That speeds the specious tale from ag
Where history's pen its praise or bla
　　plies,
And lies like truth, and still most trul
He wandering mused, and as the mo
　　shone
Through the dim lattice o'er the floor
And the high fretted roof, and saints, t
O'er Gothic windows knelt in picture
Reflected in fantastic figures grew,
Like life, but not like mortal life, to v
His bristling locks of sable, brow of
And the wide waving of his shaken [
Glanced like a spectre's attributes, a
His aspect all that terror gives the gr

XII.

'Twas midnight — all was slumber;
　　light
Dimmed in the lamp, as loath to b
　　night.
Hark! there be murmurs heard i
　　hall —
A sound — a voice — a shriek — a fea
A long, loud shriek — and silence —
　　hear
That frantic echo burst the sleeping e
They heard and rose, and, tremulous
Rush where the sound invoked thei
　　save;
They come with half-lit tapers in thei
And snatched in startled haste
　　brands.

XIII.

Cold as the marble where his length
Pale as the beam that o'er his feature
Was Lara stretched; his half-draw
　　near,
Dropped it should seem in more than
　　fear;
Yet he was firm, or had been firm till
And still defiance knit his gathered b
Though mixed with terror, senseless a
There lived upon his lip the wish to s
Some half-formed threat in utteranc
　　had died,
Some imprecation of despairing pride
His eye was almost sealed, but not fo
Even in its trance the gladiator's look
That oft awake his aspect could discl
And now was fixed in horrible repose
They raise him — bear him; — h
　　breathes, he speaks,
The swarthy blush recolors in his che
His lip resumes its red, his eye, thou[

Rolls wide and wild, each slowly quivering
limb
Recalls its function, but his words are strung
In terms that seem not of his native tongue;
Distinct but strange, enough they understand
To deem them accents of another land;
And such they were, and meant to meet an ear
That hears him not — alas! that cannot hear l

XIV.

His page approached, and he alone appeared
To know the import of the words they heard;
And, by the changes of his cheek and brow,
They were not such as Lara should avow,
Nor he interpret, — yet with less surprise
Than those around their chieftain's state he
eyes,
But Lara's prostrate form he bent beside,
And in that tongue which seemed his own
replied,
And Lara heeds those tones that gently seem
To soothe away the horrors of his dream —
If dream it were, that thus could overthrow
A breast that needed not ideal woe.

XV.

Whate'er his frenzy dreamed or eye beheld,
If yet remembered ne'er to be revealed,
Rests at his heart: the customed morning
came,
And breathed new vigor in his shaken frame;
And solace sought he none from priest nor
leech,
And soon the same in movement and in speech
As heretofore he filled the passing hours, —
Nor less he smiles, nor more his forehead
lowers,
Than these were wont; and if the coming
night
Appeared less welcome now to Lara's sight,
He to his marvelling vassals showed it not,
Whose shuddering proved *their* fear was less
forgot.
In trembling pairs (alone they dared not)
crawl
The astonished slaves, and shun the fated hall;
The waving banner, and the clapping door,
The rustling tapestry, and the echoing floor;
The long dim shadows of surrounding trees,
The flapping bat, the night song of the breeze;
Aught they behold or hear their thought
appalls,
As evening saddens o'er the dark gray walls.

XVI.

Vain thought! that hour of ne'er unravelled
gloom
Came not again, or Lara could assume
A seeming of forgetfulness, that made
His vassals more amazed nor less afraid —
Had memory vanished then with sense
restored?

Since word, nor look, nor gesture of their lord
Betrayed a feeling that recalled to these
That fevered moment of his mind's disease.
Was it a dream? was his the voice that spoke
Those strange wild accents; his the cry that
broke
Their slumber? his the oppressed, o'erlabored
heart
That ceased to beat, the look that made them
start?
Could he who thus had suffered so forget,
When such as saw that suffering shudder yet?
Or did that silence prove his memory fixed
Too deep for words, indelible, unmixed
In that corroding secrecy which gnaws
The heart to show the effect, but not the cause?
Not so in him; his breast had buried both,
Nor common gazers could discern the growth
Of thoughts that mortal lips must leave half
told;
They choke the feeble words that would unfold.

XVII.

In him inexplicably mixed appeared
Much to be loved and hated, sought and
feared;
Opinion varying o'er his hidden lot,
In praise or railing ne'er his name forgot:
His silence formed a theme for others' prate —
They guessed — they gazed — they fain would
know his fate.
What had he been? what was he, thus un-
known,
Who walked their world, his lineage only
known?
A hater of his kind? yet some would say,
With them he could seem gay amidst the gay;
But owned that smile, if oft observed and near,
Waned in its mirth, and withered to a sneer;
That smile might reach his lip, but passed not
by,
None e'er could trace its laughter to his eye:
Yet there was softness too in his regard,
At times, a heart as not by nature hard,
But once perceived, his spirit seemed to chide
Such weakness, as unworthy of its pride,
And steeled itself, as scorning to redeem
One doubt from others' half withheld esteem;
In self-inflicted penance of a breast
Which tenderness might once have wrung
from rest;
In vigilance of grief that would compel
The soul to hate for having loved too well.

XVIII.

There was in him a vital scorn of all:
As if the worst had fallen which could befall,
He stood a stranger in this breathing world,
An erring spirit from another hurled;
A thing of dark imaginings, that shaped
By choice the perils he by chance escaped;
But 'scaped in vain, for in their memory yet

His mind would half exult and half regret:
With more capacity for love than earth
Bestows on most of mortal mould and birth,
His early dreams of good outstripped the truth,
And troubled manhood followed baffled youth;
With thought of years in phantom chase mis-
    spent,
And wasted powers for better purpose lent;
And fiery passions that had poured their wrath
, In hurried desolation o'er his path,
And left the better feelings all at strife
In wild reflection o'er his stormy life;
But haughty still, and loth himself to blame,
He called on Nature's self to share the shame,
And charged all faults upon the fleshly form
She gave to clog the soul, and feast the worm;
Till he at last confounded good and ill,
And half mistook for fate the acts of will:
Too high for common selfishness, he could
At times resign his own for others' good,
But not in pity, not because he ought,
But in some strange perversity of thought,
That swayed him onward with a secret pride
To do what few or none would do beside;
And this same impulse would, in tempting time,
Mislead his spirit equally to crime;
So much he soared beyond, or sunk beneath,
The men with whom he felt condemned to
    breathe,
And longed by good or ill to separate
Himself from all who shared his mortal state;
His mind abhorring this had fixed her throne
Far from the world, in regions of her own:
Thus coldly passing all that passed below,
His blood in temperate seeming now would
    flow:
Ah! happier if it ne'er with guilt had glowed,
But ever in that icy smoothness flowed!
'Tis true, with other men their path he walked,
And like the rest in seeming did and talked,
Nor outraged Reason's rules by flaw nor start,
His madness was not of the head, but heart;
And rarely wandered in his speech, or drew
His thoughts so forth as to offend the view.

XIX.

With all that chilling mystery of mien,
And seeming gladness to remain unseen,
He had (if 'twere not nature's boon) an art
Of fixing memory on another's heart:
It was not love perchance — nor hate — nor
    aught
That words can image to express the thought;
But they who saw him did not see in vain,
And once beheld, would ask of him again:
And those to whom he spake remembered well,
And on the words, however light, would dwell:
None knew, nor how, nor why, but he entwined
Himself perforce around the hearer's mind;
There he was stamped, in liking, or in hate,
If greeted once; however brief the date

That friendship, pity, or aversion kn
Still there within the inmost thought
You could not penetrate his soul, bu
Despite your wonder, to your own he
His presence haunted still; and from t
He forced an all unwilling interest:
Vain was the struggle in that mental
His spirit seemed to dare you to forg

XX.

There is a festival, where knights an
And aught that wealth or lofty lineag
Appear — a highborn and a welcome
To Otho's hall came Lara with the r
The long carousal shakes the illumin
Well speeds alike the banquet and tl
And the gay dance of bounding Beau
Links grace and harmony in happies
Blest are the early hearts and gentle
That mingle there in well according
It is a sight the careful brow might s
And make Age smile, and dream itself
And Youth forget such hour was past
So springs the exulting bosom to tha

XXI.

And Lara gazed on these, sedately g
His brow belied him if his soul was
And his glance followed fast each :
    fair,
Whose steps of lightness woke no ec
He leaned against the lofty pillar ni
With folded arms and long attentive
Nor marked a glance so sternly fixed
Ill brooked high Lara scrutiny like
At length he caught it, 'tis a face un
But seems as searching his, and his
Prying and dark, a stranger's by his
Who still till now had gazed on him
At length encountering meets the m
Of keen inquiry, and of mute amaz
On Lara's glance emotion gathering
As if distrusting that the stranger th
Along the stranger's aspect, fixed a
Flashed more than thence the vulgar
    learn.

XXII.

" 'Tis he! " the stranger cried, and
    heard
Reëchoed fast and far the whispere
" 'Tis he! " — " 'Tis who ? " they qu
    and near,
Till louder accents rung on Lara's e
So widely spread, few bosoms well co
The general marvel, or that single l
But Lara stirred not, changed not, th
That sprung at first to his arrested e
Seemed now subsided, neither sunk n
Glanced his eye round, though still th
    gazed;

nigh, exclaimed, with haughty

how came he thence? — what
ere?"

XXIII.

uch for Lara to pass by
ıs, so repeated fierce and high:
llected, but with accent cold,
ïrm than petulantly bold,
ıd meţ the inquisitorial tone —
s Lara! — when thine own is

ᴣ fitting answer to requite
l for courtesy of such a knight.
·further wouldst thou mark or

estion, and I wear no mask."

n'st no question! Ponder — is
ıe
st answer, though thine ear would

thou me unknown too? Gaze

nemory was not given in vain.
ınst thou cancel half her debt,
ıds thee to forget."
d searching glance upon his face
:yes, but nothing there could trace
ır chose to know — with dubious

ıo answer, but his head he shook,
ıtemptuous turned to pass away;
stranger motioned him to stay.
I charge ţhee stay, and answer

, wert thou noble, were thy peer,
wast and art — nay, frown not,

asy to disprove the word —
vast and art, on thee looks down,
' smiles, but shakes not at thy

he? whose deeds ——"
            "Whate'er I be,
ıs these, accusers like to thee,
ırther; those with whom they

⁚ rest, nor venture to gainsay
us tale no doubt thy tongue can

ɔegins so courteously and well.
:rish here his polished guest,
hanks and thoughts shall be ex-

ıeir wondering host hath inter-

ıere be between you undisclosed,
ne nor fitting place to mar
meeting with a wordy war.
:zzelin, hast aught to show

Which it befits Count Lara's ear to know,
To-morrow, here, or elsewhere, as may best
Beseem your mutual judgment, speak the
    rest;
I pledge myself for thee, as not unknown,
Though, like Count Lara, now returned alone
From other lands, almost a stranger grown;
And if from Lara's blood and gentle birth
I augur right of courage and of worth,
He will not that untainted line belie,
Nor aught that knighthood may accord,
    deny."

"To-morrow be it," ·Ezzelin replied,
"And here our several worth and truth be
    tried.
I gage my life, my falchion to attest
My words, so may I mingle with the blest!"
What answers Lara? to its centre shrunk
His soul; in deep abstraction sudden sunk;
The words of many, and the eyes of all
That there were gathered, seemed on him to
    fall;
But his were silent, his appeared to stray
In far forgetfulness away — away —
Alas! that heedlessness of all around
Bespoke remembrance only too profound.

XXIV.

"To-morrow! — ay, to-morrow!" further word
Than those repeated none from Lara heard;
Upon his brow no outward passion spoke;
From his large eye no flashing anger broke;
Yet there was something fixed in that low
    tone,
Which showed resolve, determined, though
    unknown.
He seized his cloak — his head he slightly
    bowed,
And passing Ezzelin, he left the crowd;
And, as he passed him, smiling met the
    frown
With which that chieftain's brow would bear
    him down:
It was nor smile of mirth, nor struggling
    pride
That curbs to scorn the wrath it cannot hide;
But that of one in his own heart secure
Of all that he would do, or could endure.
Could this mean peace? the calmness of the
    good?
Or guilt grown old in desperate hardihood?
Alas! too like in confidence are each,
For man to trust to mortal look or speech;
From deeds, and deeds alone, may he discern
Truths which it wrings the unpractised heart
    to learn.

XXV.

And Lara called his page, and went his way —
Well could that stripling word or sign obey:
His only follower from those climes afar,
Where the soul glows beneath a brighter star;

For Lara left the shore from whence he
    sprung,
In duty patient, and sedate though young;
Silent as him he served, his faith appears
Above his station, and beyond his years.
Though not unknown the tongue of Lara's
    land,
In such from him he rarely heard command;
But fleet his step, and clear his tones would
    come,
When Lara's lip breathed forth the words of
    home:
Those accents, as his native mountains dear,
Awake their absent echoes in his ear,
Friends', kindreds', parents', wonted voice re-
    call,
Now lost, abjured, for one—his friend, his
    all:
For him earth now disclosed no other guide;
What marvel then he rarely left his side?

XXVI.

Light was his form, and darkly delicate
That brow whereon his native sun had sate,
But had not marred, though in his beams he
    grew,
The cheek where oft the unbidden blush shone
    through;
Yet not such blush as mounts when health
    would show
All the heart's hue in that delighted glow;
But 'twas a hectic tint of secret care
That for a burning moment fevered there;
And the wild sparkle of his eye seemed caught
From high, and lightened with electric thought,
Though its black orb those long low lashes'
    fringe
Had tempered with a melancholy tinge;
Yet less of sorrow than of pride was there,
Or, if 'twere grief, a grief that none should
    share:
And pleased not him the sports that please
    his age,
The tricks of youth, the frolics of the page;
For hours on Lara he would fix his glance,
As all-forgotten in that watchful trance;
And from his chief withdrawn, he wandered
    lone,
Brief were his answers, and his questions
    none;
His walk the wood, his sportsome foreign book;
His resting-place the bank that curbs the
    brook:
He seemed, like him he served, to live apart
From all that lures the eye, and fills the heart;
To know no brotherhood, and take from
    earth
No gift beyond that bitter boon—our birth.

XXVII.

If aught he loved, 'twas Lara; but was shown
His faith in reverence and in deeds alone;

In mute attention; and his ca
    guessed
Each wish, fulfilled it ere the to
    pressed.
Still there was haughtiness in all he
A spirit deep that brooked not to b
His zeal, though more than that
    hands,
In act alone obeys, his air comman
As if 'twas Lara's less than his desir
That thus he served, but surely not
Slight were the tasks enjoined hi
    lord,
To hold the stirrup, or to bear the
To tune his lute, or, if he willed it n
On tomes of other times and tongue
But ne'er to mingle with the menial
To whom he showed nor deferenc
    dain,
But that well-worn reserve which
    knew
No sympathy with that familiar crew
His soul, whate'er his station or his
Could bow to Lara, not descend to
Of higher birth he seemed, and bett
Nor mark of vulgar toil that hand b
So femininely white it might bespea
Another sex, when matched with th
    cheek,
But for his garb, and something in l
More wild and high than woman'
    trays;
A latent fierceness that far more bec
His fiery climate than his tender fra
True, in his words it broke not from l
But from his aspect might be m
    guessed.
Kaled his name, though rumor said
Another ere he left his mountain sh
For sometimes he would hear, howe
That name repeated loud without re
As unfamiliar, or, if roused again,
Start to the sound as but remember
Unless 'twas Lara's wonted voice th
For then, ear, eyes, and heart v
    awake.

XXVIII.

He had looked down upon the festi
And marked that sudden strife so r
    all;
And when the crowd around and
    told
Their wonder at the calmness of the
Their marvel how the high-born La
Such insults from a stranger, doubly
The color of young Kaled went and
The lip of ashes, and the cheek of fl
And o'er his brow the dampening he
    threw
The sickening iciness of that cold de
That rises as the busy bosom sinks

.vy thoughts from which reflection
ks.
:re be things which we must dream
lare,
ute ere thought be half aware:
might Kaled's be, it was enow
is lip, but agonize his brow.
. on Ezzelin till Lara cast
long smile upon the knight he past;
iled saw that smile his visage fell,
iomething recognized right well;
ory read in such a meaning more
ra's aspect unto others wore:
he sprung—a moment, both were

iithin that hall seemed left alone;
I so fixed his eye on Lara's mien,
) mixed their feelings with that scene,
in his long dark shadow through the
1
relieves the glare of yon high torch,
ise beats quicker, and all bosoms

i as doubting from too black a dream,
ve know is false, yet dread in sooth,
the worst is ever nearest truth.
are gone — but Ezzelin is there,
ughtful visage and imperious air;

But long remained not; ere an hour expired
He waved his hand to Otho, and retired.

XXIX.

The crowd are gone, the revellers at rest;
The courteous host, and all-approving guest,
Again to that accustomed couch must creep
Where joy subsides, and sorrow sighs to sleep,
And man, o'erlabored with his being's strife,
Shrinks to that sweet forgetfulness of life:
There lie love's feverish hope, and cunning's
    guile,
Hate's working brain, and lulled ambition's
    wile;
O'er each vain eye oblivion's pinions wave,
And quenched existence crouches in a grave.
What better name may slumber's bed become?
Night's sepulchre, the universal home,
Where weakness, strength, vice, virtue, sunk
    supine,
Alike in naked helplessness recline;
Glad for awhile to heave unconscious breath,
Yet wake to wrestle with the dread of death,
And shun, though day but dawn on ills in-
    creased,
That sleep, the loveliest, since it dreams the
    least.

* * * * *

CANTO THE SECOND.

I.

ranes — the vapors round the moun-
    curled
morn, and Light awakes the world.
another day to swell the past,
. him near to little, but his last;
ty Nature bounds as from her birth,
is in the heavens, and life on earth;
n the valley, splendor in the beam,
i the gale, and freshness in the stream.
l man! behold her glories shine,
exulting inly, " They are thine!"
while yet thy gladdened eye may see;
w comes when they are not for thee:
ie what may above thy senseless bier,
i nor sky will yield a single tear;
d shall gather more, nor leaf shall fall,
breathe forth one sigh for thee, for

ing things shall revel in their spoil,
iy clay to fertilize the soil.

II.

i —'tis noon — assembled in the hall,
ered chieftains come to Otho's call:

'Tis now the promised hour, that must pro-
    claim
The life or death of Lara's future fame;
When Ezzelin his charge may here unfold,
And whatsoe'er the tale, it must be told.
His faith was pledged, and Lara's promise
    given,
To meet it in the eye of man and heaven.
Why comes he not? Such truths to be di
    vulged,
Methinks the accuser's rest is long indulged.

III.

The hour is past, and Lara too is there,
With self-confiding, coldly patient air;
Why comes not Ezzelin? The hour is past,
And murmurs rise, and Otho's brow's o'ercast.
" I know my friend! his faith I cannot fear,
If yet he be on earth, expect him here;
The roof that held him in the valley stands
Between my own and noble Lara's lands;
My halls from such a guest had honor gained,
Nor had Sir Ezzelin his host disdained,
But that some previous proof forbade his stay,
And urged him to prepare against to-day;

The word I pledged for his I pledge again,
Or will myself redeem his knighthood's stain."

He ceased — and Lara answered, " I am
 here
To lend at thy demand a listening ear
To tales of evil from a stranger's tongue,
Whose words already might my heart have
 wrung,
But that I deemed him scarcely less than mad,
Or, at the worst, a foe ignobly bad.
I know him not — but me it seems he knew
In lands where — but I must not trifle too:
Produce this babbler — or redeem the pledge;
Here in thy hold, and with thy falchion's edge."

Proud Otho on the instant, reddening, threw
His glove on earth, and forth his sabre flew.
" The last alternative befits me best,
And thus I answer for mine absent guest."

With cheek unchanging from its sallow gloom,
However near his own or other's tomb;
With hand, whose almost careless coolness
 spoke
Its grasp well-used to deal the sabre-stroke;
With eye, though calm, determined not to
 spare,
Did Lara too his willing weapon bare.
In vain the circling chieftains round them
 closed,
For Otho's frenzy would not be opposed;
And from his lip those words of insult fell —
His sword is good who can maintain them
 well.

VI.

Short was the conflict; furious, blindly rash,
Vain Otho gave his bosom to the gash:
He bled, and fell; but not with deadly
 wound,
Stretched by a dextrous sleight along the
 ground.
" Demand thy life! " He answered not: and
 then
From that red floor he ne'er had risen again,
For Lara's brow upon the moment grew
Almost to blackness in its demon hue;
And fiercer shook his angry falchion now
Than when his foe's was levelled at his brow;
Then all was stern collectedness and art,
Now rose the unleavened hatred of his heart;
So little sparing to the foe he felled,
That when the approaching crowd his arm
 withheld,
He almost turned the thirsty point on those
Who thus for mercy dared to interpose;
But to a moment's thought that purpose bent;
Yet looked he on him still with eye intent,
As if he loathed the ineffectual strife
That left a foe, howe'er o'erthrown, with life;
As if to search how far the wound he gave
Had sent its victim onward to his grave.

V.

They raised the bleeding Otho, and
Forbade all present question, :
 speech;
The others met within a neighborin
And he, incensed and heedless of th
The cause and conqueror in this su
In haughty silence slowly strode aw
He backed his steed, his homeware
 took,
Nor cast on Otho's towers a single l

VI.

But where was he? that meteor of a
Who menaced but to disappear wit
Where was this Ezzelin? who came
To leave no other trace of his inten
He left the dome of Otho long ere i
In darkness, yet so well the path wa
He could not miss it: near his dwel
But there he was not, and with com
Came fast inquiry, which unfolded i
Except the absence of the chief it sc
A chamber tenantless, a steed at res
His host alarmed, his murmuring sc
 tressed
Their search extends along, around
In dread to meet the marks of prowle
But none are there, and not a brake h
Nor gout of blood, nor shred of m
Nor fall nor struggle hath defaced
Which still retains a mark where m
Nor dabbling fingers left to tell the
The bitter print of each convulsive
When agonized hands that ceased t
Wound in that pang the smoothn
 sward.
Some such had been, if here a life v
But these were not; and doubting h
And strange suspicion, whisperi
 name,
Now daily mutters o'er his blacken
Then sudden silent when his form
Awaits the absence of the thing it fe
Again its wonted wondering to rene
And dye conjecture with a darker h

VII.

Days roll along, and Otho's wounds
But not his pride; and hate no
 cealed:
He was a man of power, and Lara'
The friend of all who sought to worl
And from his country's justice now
Account of Ezzelin at Lara's hands
Who else than Lara could have ca
His presence? who had made him
If not the man on whom his menac
Had sate too deeply were he left at
The general rumor ignorantly loud,
The mystery dearest to the curious

seeming friendlessness of him who strove
win no confidence, and wake no love;
  sweeping fierceness which his soul be-
  trayed,
  skill with which he wielded his keen
  blade;
ere had his arm unwarlike caught that art?
ere had that fierceness grown upon his
  heart?
it was not the blind capricious rage
ord can kindle and a word assuage;
the deep working of a soul unmixed
h aught of pity where its wrath had fixed;
h as long power and overgorged success
centrates into all that's merciless:
se, linked with that desire which ever sways
nkind, the rather to condemn than praise,
inst Lara gathering raised at length a storm,
h as himself might fear, and foes would
  form,
d he must answer for the absent head
one that haunts him still, alive or dead.

VIII.

thin that land was many a malcontent,
o cursed the tyranny to which he bent;
it soil full many a wringing despot saw,
o worked his wantonness in form of law;
ng war without and frequent broil within
d made a path for blood and giant sin,
iat waited but a signal to begin
w havoc, such as civil discord blends,
hich knows no neuter, owns but foes or
  friends;
ced in his feudal fortress each was lord,
word and deed obeyed, in soul abhorred.
ius Lara had inherited his lands,
id with them pining hearts and sluggish
  hands;
t that long absence from his native clime
id left him stainless of oppression's crime,
id now, diverted by his milder sway,
l dread by slow degrees had worn away.
ie menials felt their usual awe alone,
t more for him than them that fear was
  grown;
iey deemed him now unhappy, though at
  first
teir evil judgment augured of the worst,
id each long restless night, and silent mood,
as traced to sickness, fed by solitude:
id though his lonely habits threw of late
oom o'er his chamber, cheerful was his
  gate;
r thence the wretched ne'er unsoothed
  withdrew,
r them, at least, his soul compassion knew.
ld to the great, contemptuous to the high,
e humble passed not his unheeding eye;
ich he would speak not, but beneath his
  roof
iey found asylum oft, and ne'er reproof.

And they who watched might mark that, day
  by day,
Some new retainers gathered to his sway;
But most of late, since Ezzelin was lost,
He played the courteous lord and bounteous
  host:
Perchance his strife with Otho made him
  dread
Some snare prepared for his obnoxious head:
Whate'er his view, his favor more obtains
With these, the people, than his fellow thanes.
If this were policy, so far 'twas sound,
The million judged but of him as they found:
From him by sterner chiefs to exile driven
They but required a shelter, and 'twas given.
By him no peasant mourned his rifled cot,
And scarce the Serf could murmur o'er his
  lot;
With him old avarice found its hoard secure,
With him contempt forbore to mock the poor;
Youth present cheer and promised recom-
  pense
Detained, till all too late to part from thence:
To hate he offered, with the coming change,
The deep reversion of delayed revenge;
To love, long baffled by the unequal match,
The well-won charms success was sure to
  snatch.
All now was ripe, he waits but to proclaim
That slavery nothing which was still a name.
The moment came, the hour when Otho
  thought
Secure at last the vengeance which he sought:
His summons found the destined criminal
Begirt by thousands in his swarming hall,
Fresh from their feudal fetters newly riven,
Defying earth, and confident of heaven.
That morning he had freed the soil-bound
  slaves
Who dig no land for tyrants but their graves!
Such is their cry — some watchword for the
  fight
Must vindicate the wrong, and warp the right;
Religion — freedom — vengeance — what you
  will,
A word's enough to raise mankind to kill;
Some factious phrase by cunning caught and
  spread,
That guilt may reign, and wolves and worms
  be fed!

IX.

Throughout that clime the feudal chiefs had
  gained
Such sway, their infant monarch hardly
  reigned;
Nor was the hour for faction's rebel growth,
The Serfs contemned the one, and hated both:
They waited but a leader, and they found
One to their cause inseparably bound;
By circumstance compelled to plunge again,
In self-defence, amidst the strife of men.

Cut off by some mysterious fate from those
Whom birth and nature meant not for his foes,
Had Lara from that night to him accurst,
Prepared to meet, but not alone, the worst:
Some reason urged, whate'er it was, to shun
Inquiry into deeds at distance done;
By mingling with his own the cause of all,
E'en if he failed, he still delayed his fall.
The sullen calm that long his bosom kept,
The storm that once had spent itself and
    slept,
Roused by events that seemed foredoomed to
    urge
His gloomy fortunes to their utmost verge,
Burst forth, and made him all he once had
    been,
And is again; he only changed the scene.
Light care had he for life, and less for fame,
But not less fitted for the desperate game:
He deemed himself marked out for others'
    hate,
And mocked at ruin so they shared his fate.
What cared he for the freedom of the
    crowd ?
He raised the humble but to bend the
    proud.
He had hoped quiet in his sullen lair,
But man and destiny beset him there :
Inured to hunters, he was found at bay;
And they must kill, they cannot snare the prey.
Stern, unambitious, silent, he had been
Henceforth a calm spectator of life's scene;
But dragged again upon the arena, stood
A leader not unequal to the feud;
In voice — mien — gesture — savage nature
    spoke,
And from his eye the gladiator broke.

X.

What boots the oft repeated tale of strife,
The feast of vultures, and the waste of life ?
The varying fortune of each separate field,
The fierce that vanquish, and the faint that
    yield ?
The smoking ruin, and the crumbled wall ?
In this the struggle was the same with all;
Save that distempered passions lent their
    force
In bitterness that banished all remorse.
None sued, for Mercy knew her cry was vain,
The captive died upon the battle-slain :
In either cause, one rage alone possessed
The empire of the alternate victor's breast;
And they that smote for freedom or for sway,
Deemed few were slain, while more remained
    to slay.
It was too late to check the wasting brand,
And Desolation reaped the famished land;
The torch was lighted, and the flame was
    spread,
And Carnage smiled upon her daily dead.

XI.

Fresh with the nerve the new-born
    strung,
The first success to Lara's numbers
But that vain victory hath ruined all ;
They form no longer to their leader'
In blind confusion on the foe they pr
And think to snatch is to secure succ
The lust of booty, and the thirst of hi
Lure on the broken brigands to their
In vain he doth whate'er a chief may
To check the headlong fury of that cr
In vain their stubborn ardor he woul
The hand that kindles cannot que
    flame ;
The wary foe alone hath turned their
And shown their rashness to tha
    brood :
The feigned retreat, the nightly ambu
The daily harass, and the fight delay
The long privation of the hoped sup
The tentless rest beneath the humid
The stubborn wall that mocks the leag
And palls the patience of his baffled
Of these they had not deemed : the b
They could encounter as a veteran m
But more preferred the fury of the str
And present death, to hourly sufferin
And famine wrings, and fever sweeps
His numbers melting fast from their
Intemperate triumph fades to discont
And Lara's soul alone seems still unbe
But few remain to aid his voice and h
And thousands dwindled to a scanty b
Desperate, though few, the last and l
    mained
To mourn the discipline they late dis
One hope survives, the frontier is not
And thence they may escape from nati
And bear within them to the neighbori
An exile's sorrows, or an outlaw's hate
Hard is the task their father-land to q
But harder still to perish or submit.

XII.

It is resolved — they march — con
    Night
Guides with her star their dim and to
    flight.
Already they perceive its tranquil bea
Sleep on the surface of the barrier str
Already they descry — Is yon the banl
Away! 'tis lined with many a hostile r
Return or fly ! — What glitters in the i
'Tis Otho's banner — the pursuer's spe
Are those the shepherds' fires up
    height ?
Alas ! they blaze too widely for the flig
Cut off from hope, and compassed
    toil,
Less blood perchance hath bought a
    spoil !

XIII.

moment's pause — 'tis but to breathe their
  band,
r shall they onward press, or here withstand ?
matters little — if they charge the foes
'ho by their border-stream their march op-
  pose,
me few, perchance, may break and pass
  the line,
owever linked to baffle such design.
he charge be ours! to wait for their
  assault
ere fate well worthy of a coward's halt."
orth flies each sabre, reined is every steed,
id the next word shall scarce outstrip the
  deed :
  the next tone of Lara's gathering breath
ow many shall but hear the voice of death !

XIV.

is blade is bared, — in him there is an air
s deep, but far too tranquil for despair;
something of indifference more than then
ecomes the bravest, if they feel for men.
e turned his eye on Kaled, ever near,
nd still too faithful to betray one fear;
erchance 'twas but the moon's dim twilight
  threw
long his aspect an unwonted hue
f mournful paleness, whose deep tint ex-
  pressed
he truth, and not the terror of his breast.
his Lara marked, and laid his hand on his :
t trembled not in such an hour as this ;
Iis lip was silent, scarcely beat his heart,
Iis eye alone proclaimed, "We will not part !
hy an may perish, or thy friends may
  flee, d
'arewell to life, but not adieu to thee !"

he word hath passed his lips, and onward
  driven,
'ours the linked band through ranks asunder
  riven ;
Vell has each steed obeyed the armed heel,
ind flash the scimitars, and rings the steel ;
)utnumbered, not outbraved, they still oppose
)espair to daring, and a front to foes ;
ind blood is mingled with the dashing stream,
Vhich runs all redly till the morning beam.

XV.

Commanding, aiding, animating all,
Vhere foe appeared to press, or friend to fall,
Cheers Lara's voice, and waves or strikes his
  steel,
nspiring hope himself had ceased to feel.
Jone fled, for well they knew that flight were
  vain
3ut those that waver turn to smite again,
Vhile yet they find the firmest of the foe
Recoil before their leader's look and blow.

Now girt with numbers, now almost alone,
He foils their ranks, or re-unites his own;
Himself he spared not — once they seemed
  to fly —
Now was the time, he waved his hand on
  high,
And shook — Why sudden droops that
  plumed crest ?
The shaft is sped — the arrow's in his breast !
That fatal gesture left the unguarded side,
And Death had stricken down yon arm of
  pride.
The word of triumph fainted from his tongue ;
That hand, so raised, how droopingly it hung !
But yet the sword instinctively retains,
Though from its fellow shrink the falling
  reins ;
These Kaled snatches : dizzy with the blow,
And senseless bending o'er his saddle-bow,
Perceives not Lara that his anxious page
Beguiles his charger from the combat's rage :
Meantime his followers charge, and charge
  again ;
Too mixed the slayers now to heed the slain !

XVI.

Day glimmers on the dying and the dead,
The cloven cuirass, and the helmless head ;
The war-horse masterless is on the earth,
And that last gasp hath burst his bloody girth ;
And near, yet quivering with what life re-
  mained,
The heel that urged him and the hand that
  reined ;
And some too near that rolling torrent lie,
Whose waters mock the lip of those that die ;
That panting thirst which scorches in the
  breath
Of those that die the soldier's fiery death,
In vain impels the burning mouth to crave
One drop — the last — to cool it for the grave ;
With feeble and convulsive effort swept,
Their limbs along the crimsoned turf have
  crept ;
The faint remains of life such struggles waste,
But yet they reach the stream and bend to
  taste :
They feel its freshness, and almost partake —
Why pause ? No further thirst have they to
  slake —
It is unquenched, and yet they feel it not ;
It was an agony — but now forgot !

XVII.

Beneath a lime, remoter from the scene,
Where but for him that strife had never been,
A breathing but devoted warrior lay :
'Twas Lara bleeding fast from life away.
His follower once, and now his only guide,
Kneels Kaled watchful o'er his welling side,
And with his scarf would stanch the tides that
  rush,

With each convulsion, in a blacker gush;
And then, as his faint breathing waxes low,
In feebler, not less fatal tricklings flow:
He scarce can speak, but motions him 'tis vain,
And merely adds another throb to pain.
He clasps the hand that pang which would assuage
And sadly smiles his thanks to that dark page,
Who nothing fears, nor feels, nor heeds, nor sees,
Save that damp brow which rests upon his knees;
Save that pale aspect, where the eye, though dim,
Held all the light that shone on earth for him.

XVIII.

The foe arrives, who long had searched the field,
Their triumph nought till Lara too should yield;
They would remove him, but they see 'twere vain,
And he regards them with a calm disdain,
That rose to reconcile him with his fate,
And that escape to death from living hate:
And Otho comes, and leaping from his steed,
Looks on the bleeding foe that made him bleed,
And questions of his state; he answers not,
Scarce glances on him as on one forgot,
And turns to Kaled: — each remaining word
They understood not, if distinctly heard;
His dying tones are in that other tongue,
To which some strange remembrance wildly clung.
They spake of other scenes, but what — is known
To Kaled, whom their meaning reached alone;
And he replied, though faintly, to their sound,
While gazed the rest in dumb amazement round:
They seemed even then — that twain — unto the last
To half forget the present in the past;
To share between themselves some separate fate,
Whose darkness none beside should penetrate.

XIX.

Their words though faint were many — from the tone
Their import those who heard could judge alone;
From this, you might have deemed young Kaled's death
More near than Lara's by his voice and breath,
So sad, so deep, and hesitating broke
The accents his scarce-moving pale lips spoke;
But Lara's voice, though low, at first was clear
And calm, till murmuring death gasped hoarsely near:
But from his visage little could we guess,
So unrepentant, dark, and passion
Save that when struggling nearer
Upon that page his eye was kind
And once, as Kaled's answeri ceased,
Rose Lara's hand, and pointed to
Whether (as then the breaking su
Rolled back the clouds) the mor his eye,
Or that 'twas chance, or some r scene,
That raised his arm to point whe been,
Scarce Kaled seemed to know, away,
As if his heart abhorred that comi
And shrunk his glance before th light,
To look on Lara's brow — whe night.
Yet sense seemed left, though be loss;
For when one near displayed th cross,
And proffered to his touch the ho
Of which his parting soul might ow
He looked upon it with an eye pr
And smiled — Heaven pardon! if disdain:
And Kaled, though he spoke no drew
From Lara's face his fixed despair
With brow repulsive, and with ges
Flung back the hand which held gift,
As if such but disturbed the expiri
Nor seemed to know his life but t
That life of Immortality, secure
To none, save them whose faith i sure.

XX.

But gasping heaved the breath that
And dull the film along his dim ey
His limbs stretched fluttering, an drooped o'er
The weak yet still untiring knee th
He pressed the hand he held upon
It beats no more, but Kaled will n
With the cold grasp, but feels, a vain,
For that faint throb which answers
" It beats! " — Away, thou drear gone —
It once was Lara which thou look

1 [The death of Lara is, by far, the fi in the poem, and is fully equal to ar which the author ever wrote. The ph of the event, though described with a and fidelity, is both relieved and enh: beautiful pictures of mental energy ; with which it is combined. The whc the poem is written with equal vigor

XXI.

Ie gazed, as if not yet had passed away
'he haughty spirit of that humble clay;
.nd those around have roused him from his
    trance,
:ut cannot tear from thence his fixèd glance;
.nd when, in raising him from where he bore
Within his arms the form that felt no more,
Ie saw the head his breast would still sustain,
:oll down like earth to earth upon the plain;
Ie did not dash himself thereby, nor tear
,'he glossy tendrils of his raven hair,
:ut strove to stand and gaze, but reeled and
    fell,
)carce breathing more than that he loved so
    well.
['han that *he* loved! Oh! never yet beneath
['he breast of man such trusty love may
    breathe!
['hat trying moment hath at once revealed
['he secret long and yet but half concealed;
'n baring to revive that lifeless brèast,
'ts grief seemed ended, but the sex confessed;
And life returned, and Kaled felt no shame —
What now to her was Womanhood or Fame?

XXII.

And Lara sleeps not where his fathers sleep,
But where he died his grave was dug as deep;
Nor is his mortal slumber less profound,
Though priest nor blessed nor marble decked
    the mound;
And he was mourned by one whose quiet grief,
Less loud, outlasts a people's for their chief.
Vain was all question asked her of the past,
And vain e'en menace — silent to the last;
She told nor whence, nor why she left behind
Her all for one who seemed but little kind.
Why did she love him? Curious fool! — be
    still —
Is human love the growth of human will?
To her he might be gentleness; the stern
Have deeper thoughts than your dull eyes
    discern,
And when they love, your smilers guess not
    how
Beats the strong heart, though less the lips
    avow.
They were not common links, that formed
    the chain
That bound to Lara Kaled's heart and brain;
But that wild tale she brooked not to unfold,
And sealed is now each lip that could have
    told.

XXIII.

They laid him in the earth, and on his breast,
Besides the wound that sent his soul to rest,

and may be put in competition with any thing that
poetry has produced, in point either of pathos or
energy. — *Jeffrey*.]

They found the scattered dints of many a scar,
Which were not planted there in recent war;
Where'er had passed his summer years of life,
It seems they vanished in a land of strife;
But all unknown his glory or his guilt,
These only told that somewhere blood was
    spilt,
And Ezzelin, who might have spoke the past,
Returned no more — that night appeared his
    last.

XXIV.

Upon that night (a peasant's is the tale)
A Serf that crossed the intervening vale,[1]

[1] The event in this section was suggested by the
description of the death, or rather burial, of the
Duke of Gandia. The most interesting and partic-
ular account of it is given by Burchard, and is in
substance as follows: — "On the eighth day of June,
the Cardinal of Valenza and the Duke of Gandia,
sons of the Pope, supped with their mother, Vanozza,
near the church of *S. Pietro ad vincula;* several
other persons being present at the entertainment.
A late hour approaching, and the cardinal having
reminded his brother, that it was time to return to
the apostolic palace, they mounted their horses or
mules, with only a few attendants, and proceeded
together as far as the palace of Cardinal Ascanio
Sforza, when the duke informed the cardinal that,
before he returned home, he had to pay a visit of
pleasure. Dismissing therefore all his attendants,
excepting his *staffiero*, or footman, and a person in
a mask, who had paid him a visit whilst at supper,
and who, during the space of a month or there-
abouts, previous to this time, had called upon him
almost daily, at the apostolic palace, he took this
person behind him on his mule, and proceeded to
the street of the Jews, where he quitted his servant,
directing him to remain there until a certain hour;
when, if he did not return, he might repair to the
palace. The duke then seated the person in the
mask behind him, and rode, I know not whither;
but in that night he was assassinated, and thrown
into the river. The servant, after having been dis-
missed, was also assaulted and mortally wounded;
and although he was attended with great care, yet
such was his situation, that he could give no intel-
ligible account of what had befallen his master. In
the morning, the duke not having returned to the
palace, his servants began to be alarmed; and one
of them informed the pontiff of the evening excur-
sion of his sons, and that the duke had not yet made
his appearance. This gave the pope no small anxi-
ety; but he conjectured that the duke had been at-
tracted by some courtesan to pass the night with
her, and, not choosing to quit the house in open
day, had waited till the following evening to return
home. When, however, the evening arrived, and
he found himself disappointed in his expectations,
he became deeply afflicted, and began to make in-
quiries from different persons, whom he ordered to
attend him for that purpose. Amongst these was a
mah named Giorgio Schiavoni, who, having dis-
charged some timber from a bark in the river, had
remained on board the vessel to watch it; and being
interrogated whether he had seen any one thrown
into the river on the night preceding, he replied,
that he saw two men on foot, who came down the
street, and looked diligently about, to observe

When Cynthia's light almost gave way to morn,
And nearly veiled in mist her waning horn;
A Serf, that rose betimes to thread the wood,
And hew the bough that bought his children's
    food,
Passed by the river that divides the plain
Of Otho's lands and Lara's broad domain:
He heard a tramp — a horse and horseman
    broke
From out the wood — before him was a cloak
Wrapt round some burden at his saddle-bow,
Bent was his head, and hidden was his brow.
Roused by the sudden sight at such a time,
And some foreboding that it might be crime,
Himself unheeded watched the stranger's
    course,
Who reached the river, bounded from his
    horse,

whether any person was passing. That seeing no
one, they returned, and a short time afterwards two
others came, and looked around in the same manner
as the former; no person still appearing, they gave
a sign to their companions, when a man came,
mounted on a white horse, having behind him a
dead body, the head and arms of which hung on
one side, and the feet on the other side of the horse;
the two persons on foot supporting the body, to pre-
vent its falling. They thus proceeded towards that
part where the filth of the city is usually discharged
into the river, and turning the horse, with his tail
towards the water, the two persons took the dead
body by the arms and feet, and with all their strength
flung it into the river. The person on horseback
then asked if they had thrown it in: to which they
replied, *Signor, si* (yes, sir). He then looked to-
wards the river, and seeing a mantle floating on the
stream, he inquired what it was that appeared black,
to which they answered, it was a mantle: and one
of them threw stones upon it, in consequence of
which it sunk. The attendants of the pontiff then
inquired from Giorgio, why he had not revealed
this to the governor of the city; to which he replied,
that he had seen in his time a hundred dead bodies
thrown into the river at the same place, without any
inquiry being made respecting them; and that he
had not, therefore, considered it as a matter of any
importance. The fishermen and seamen were then
collected, and ordered to search the river, where, on
the following evening, they found the body of the
duke, with his habit entire, and thirty ducats in his
purse. He was pierced with nine wounds, one of
which was in his throat, the others in his head, body,
and limbs. No sooner was the pontiff informed of the
death of his son, and that he had been thrown, like
filth, into the river, than, giving way to his grief, he
shut himself up in a chamber, and wept bitterly.
The Cardinal of Segovia, and other attendants on
the pope, went to the door, and after many hours
spent in persuasions and exhortations, prevailed
upon him to admit them. From the evening of
Wednesday till the following Saturday the pope took
no food; nor did he sleep from Thursday morning
till the same hour on the ensuing day. At length,
however, giving way to the entreaties of his attend-
ants, he began to restrain his sorrow, and to con-
sider the injury which his own health might sustain,
by the further indulgence of his grief."—*Roscoe's
Leo Tenth*; vol. i. p. 265.

And lifting thence the burden whic
Heaved up the bank, and dashed i
    shore,
Then paused, and looked, and tu
    seemed to watch,
And still another hurried glance wo|
And follow with his step the stream t|
As if even yet too much its surface
At once he started, stooped, around |
The winter floods had scattered heap
Of these the heaviest thence he gath
And slung them with a more tha|
    care.
Meantime the Serf had crept to wh
Himself might safely mark what |
    mean;
He caught a glimpse, as of a floatin
And something glittered starlike or
But ere he well could mark the
    trunk,
A massy fragment smote it, and it s
It rose again, but indistinct to view,
And left the waters of a purple hue,
Then deeply disappeared : the horse|
Till ebbed the latest eddy it had rai|
Then turning, vaulted on his pawin|
An instant spurred him into panting
His face was masked — the featur
    dead,
If dead it were, escaped the observer
But if in sooth a star its bosom bore,
Such is the badge that knighthood e
And such 'tis known Sir Ezzelin had
Upon the night that led to such a m|
If thus he perished, Heaven receive
His undiscovered limbs to ocean rol
And charity upon the hope would d|
It was not Lara's hand by which he

XXV.

And Kaled — Lara — Ezzelin, are g|
Alike without their monumental sto|
The first, all efforts vainly strove to |
From lingering where her chieftai|
    had been;
Grief had so tamed a spirit once too
Her tears were few, her wailing nev|
But furious would you tear her from
Where yet she scarce believed that h|
Her eye shot forth with all the living
That haunts the tigress in her whelp
But left to waste her weary moments
She talked all idly unto shapes of ai|
Such as the busy brain of Sorrow pa
And woos to listen to her fond comp
And she would sit beneath the very
Where lay his drooping head upon |
And in that posture where she saw |
His words, his looks, his dying gras|
And she had shorn, but saved her ra
And oft would snatch it from her bos|
And fold, and press it gently to the |

s if she stanched anew some phantom's
wound.
erself would question, and for him reply;
hen rising, start, and beckon him to fly
rom some imaginèd spectre in pursuit;

Then seat her down upon some linden's root,
And hide her visage with her meagre hand,
Or trace strange characters along the sand —
This could not last — she lies by him she loved;
Her tale untold — her truth too dearly proved.

THE SIEGE OF CORINTH.

TO JOHN HOBHOUSE, ESQ.,

THIS POEM IS INSCRIBED BY HIS

January 22, 1816.

FRIEND.

ADVERTISEMENT.

" THE grand army of the Turks (in 1715), under the Prime Vizier, to open to themselves a way into
he heart of the Morea, and to form the siege of Napoli di Romania, the most considerable place in all
hat country,[1] thought it best in the first place to attack Corinth, upon which they made several sotorms.
The garrison being weakened, and the governor seeing it was impossible to hold out against so mighty a
orce thought it fit to beat a parley : but while they were treating about the articles, one of the magazines
n the Turkish camp, wherein they had six hundred barrels of powder, blew up by accident, whereby six
r seven hundred men were killed; which so enraged the infidels, that they would not grant any capitu-
ation, but stormed the place with so much fury, that they took it, and put most of the garrison, with
ignior Minotti, the governor, to the sword.   The rest, with Antonio Bempo, proveditor extraordinary,
rere made prisoners of war." — *History of the Turks,* vol. iii. p. 151.

INTRODUCTION.

THE "Siege of Corinth," which appears, by the original MS., to have been begun in July, 1815,
nade its appearance in January, 1816. Mr. Murray having inclosed Byron a thousand guineas for the
opyright of this poem and of " Parisina," he replied — " Your offer is liberal in the extreme, and much
nore than the two poems can possibly be worth; but I cannot accept it, nor will not. You are most wel-
ome to them as additions to the collected volumes; but I cannot consent to their separate publication.

[1] Napoli di Romania is not now the most considerable place in the Morea, but Tripolitza, where the
'acha resides, and maintains his government. Napoli is near Argos. I visited all three in 1810-11;
nd, in the course of journeying through the country from my first arrival, in 1809, I crossed the Isthmus
ight times in my way from Attica to the Morea, over the mountains, or in the other direction, when pas-
ing from the Gulf of Athens to that of Lepanto. Both the routes are picturesque and beautiful, though
ery different: that by sea has more sameness: but the voyage being always within sight of land, and
ften very near it, presents many attractive views of the islands Salamis, Ægina, Poros, ect., and the
oast of the Continent.

THE SIEGE OF CORINTH.

I do not like to risk any fame (whether merited or not) which I have been favored with
tions which I do not feel to be at all equal to my own notions of what they should be; tho
do very well as things without pretension, to add to the publication with the lighter piece
closed your draft torn, for fear of accidents by the way — I wish you would not throw tempt
It is not from a disdain of the universal idol, nor from a present superfluity of his treasures
you, that I refuse to worship him; but what is right is right, and must not yield to circums
very glad that the *handwriting* was a favorable omen of the *morale* of the piece; but
trust to that, for my copyist would write out any thing I desired, in all the ignorance of
;hope, however, in this instance, with no great peril to either." The copyist was Lady B
gave Mr. Gifford *carte blanche* to strike out or alter any thing at his pleasure in this p
passing through the press; and the reader will be amused with the *variæ lectiones* which
gin in this extraordinary confidence.

IN the year since Jesus died for men,
Eighteen hundred years and ten,
We were a gallant company,
Riding o'er land, and sailing o'er sea.
Oh! but we went merrily!
We forded the river, and clomb the high hill,
Never our steeds for a day stood still;
Whether we lay in the cave or the shed,
Our sleep fell soft on the hardest bed;
Whether we couched in our rough capote,[1]
On the rougher plank of our gliding boat,
Or stretched on the beach, or our saddles
    spread
As a pillow beneath the resting head,
Fresh we woke upon the morrow:
  All our thoughts and words had scope,
We had health, and we had hope,
Toil and travel, but no sorrow.
We were of all tongues and creeds; —
Some were those who counted beads,
Some of mosque, and some of church,
  And some, or I mis-say, of neither;
Yet through the wide world might ye search,
  Nor find a motlier crew nor blither.

But some are dead, and some are gone,
And some are scattered and alone,
And some are rebels on the hills [2]

That look along Epirus' vall
  Where freedom still at mom
And pays in blood oppression'
  And some are in a far countr
And some all restlessly at hom
  But never more, oh! never, w
Shall meet to revel and to roam

But those hardy days flew chee
And when they now fall drearil
My thoughts, like swallows, ski
And bear my spirit back again
Over the earth, and through th
A wild bird and a wanderer.
'Tis this thåt ever wakes my str:
And oft, too oft, implores again
The few who may endure my la
To follow me so far away.
Stranger — wilt thou follow now
And sit with me on Acro-Corin

I.

Many a vanished year and age,
And tempest's breath, and battl(
Have swept o'er Corinth; yet s)
A fortress formed to Freedom's
The whirlwind's wrath, the e
    shock,
Have left untouched her hoary
The keystone of a land, which s
Though fall'n, looks proudly on
The landmark to the double tid
That purpling rolls on either sic
As if their waters chafed to mee
Yet pause and crouch beneath l
But could the blood before her :
Since first Timoleon's brother b

---

[1] [In one of his sea excursions, Byron was nearly
lost in a Turkish ship of war, owing to the igno-
rance of the captain and crew. "Fletcher," he
says, "yelled; the Greeks called on all the saints;
the Mussulmans on Alla; while the captain burst
into tears, and ran below deck. I did what I could
to console Fletcher; but finding him incorrigible,
I wrapped myself up in my Albanian capote, and
lay down to wait the worst." This instance of the
poet's coolness and courage is thus confirmed by
Mr. Hobhouse: — "Finding that, from his lame-
ness, he was unable to be of any service in the ex-
ertions which our very serious danger called for,
after a laugh or two at the panic of his valet, he not
only wrapped himself up and lay down, in the
manner he has described, but when our difficulties
were terminated was found fast asleep."]

[2] The last tidings recently heard of Dervish (one

of the Arnaouts who followed me) st
in revolt upon the mountains, at the l
of the bands common in that country
trouble.

[3] [In the original MS. —
  "A marvel from her Moslem ba

[4] [Timoleon, who had saved the
brother Timophanes in battle, afterwar

r baffled Persia's despot fled,
Arise from out the earth which drank
The stream of slaughter as it sank,
That sanguine ocean would o'erflow
Her isthmus idly spread below:
Or could the bones of all the slain,
Who perished there, be piled again,
That rival pyramid would rise
More mountain-like, through those clear
   skies,
Than yon tower-capped Acropolis,
Which seems the very clouds to kiss.

II.

On dun Cithæron's ridge appears
The gleam of twice ten thousand spears;
And downward to the Isthmian plain,
From shore to shore of either main,
The tent is pitched, the crescent shines
Along the Moslem's leaguering lines;
And the dusk Spahi's bands [1] advance
Beneath each bearded pacha's glance;
And far and wide as eye can reach
The turbaned cohorts throng the beach;
And there the Arab's camel kneels,
And there his steed the Tartar wheels;
The Turcoman hath left his herd,[2]
The sabre round his loins to gird;
And there the volleying thunders pour
Till waves grow smoother to the roar.
The trench is dug, the cannon's breath
Wings the far hissing globe of death;
Fast whirl the fragments from the wall,
Which crumbles with the ponderous ball;
And from that wall the foe replies,
O'er dusty plain and smoky skies,
With fires that answer fast and well
The summons of the Infidel.

III.

But near and nearest to the wall
Of those who wish and work its fall,
With deeper skill in war's black art,
Than Othman's sons, and high of heart
As any chief that ever stood
Triumphant in the fields of blood;
From post to post, and deed to deed,
Fast spurring on his reeking steed,
Where sallying ranks the trench assail,
And make the foremost Moslem quail;
Or where the battery, guarded well,
Remains as yet impregnable,

Alighting cheerly to inspire
The soldier slackening in his fire;
The first and freshest of the host
Which Stamboul's sultan there can boast,
To guide the follower o'er the field,
To point the tube, the lance to wield,
Or whirl around the bickering blade; —
Was Alp, the Adrian renegade!

IV.

From Venice — once a race of worth
His gentle sires — he drew his birth;
But late an exile from her shore,
Against his countrymen he bore
The arms they taught to bear; and now
The turban girt his shaven brow.
Through many a change had Corinth passed
With Greece to Venice' rule at last;
And here, before her walls, with those
To Greece and Venice equal foes,
He stood a foe, with all the zeal
Which young and fiery converts feel,
Within whose heated bosom throngs
The memory of a thousand wrongs.
To him had Venice ceased to be
Her ancient civic boast — " the Free;"
And in the palace of St. Mark
Unnamed accusers in the dark
Within the " Lion's mouth" had placed
A charge against him uneffaced:
He fled in time, and saved his life,
To waste his future years in strife,
That taught his land how great her loss
In him who triumphed o'er the Cross,
'Gainst which he reared the Crescent high,
And battled to avenge or die.

V.

Coumourgi [3] — he whose closing scene
Adorned the triumph of Eugene,
When on Carlowitz' bloody plain,
The last and mightiest of the slain,
He sank, regretting not to die,
But cursed the Christian's victory —
Coumourgi — can his glory cease,
That latest conqueror of Greece,
Till Christian hands to Greece restore

---

or aiming at the supreme power in Corinth, pre-
ferring his duty to his country to all the obligations
of blood. Dr. Warton says, that Pope once in-
tended to write an epic poem on the story, and that
Dr. Akenside had the same design.]

[1] [Turkish holders of military fiefs, which oblige
them to join the army, mounted at their own ex-
ense.]

[2] The life of the Turcomans is wandering and
patriarchal: they dwell in tents.

---

[3] Ali Coumourgi, the favorite of three sultans,
and Grand Vizier to Achmet III., after recovering
Peloponnesus from the Venetians in one campaign,
was mortally wounded in the next, against the
Germans, at the battle of Peterwaradin (in the
plain of Carlowitz), in Hungary, endeavoring to
rally his guards. He died of his wounds next day.
His last order was the decapitation of General
Breuner, and some other German prisoners; and
his last words, " Oh that I could thus serve all the
Christian dogs!" a speech and act not unlike one
of Caligula. He was a young man of great ambi-
tion and unbounded presumption: on being told
that Prince Eugene, then opposed to him, "was a
great general," he said, "I shall become a greater,
and at his expense."

The freedom Venice gave of yore ?
A hundred years have rolled away
Since he refixed the Moslem's sway,
And now he led the Mussulman,
And gave the guidance of the van
To Alp, who well repaid the trust
By cities levelled with the dust;
And proved, by many a deed of death,
How firm his heart in novel faith.

VI.

The walls grew weak; and fast and hot
Against them poured the ceaseless shot,
With unabating fury sent
From battery to battlement;
And thunder-like the pealing din
Rose from each heated culverin;
And here and there some crackling dome
Was fired before the exploding bomb.
And as the fabric sank beneath
The shattering shell's volcanic breath,
In red and wreathing columns flashed
The flame, as loud the ruin crashed,
Or into countless meteors driven,
Its earth-stars melted into heaven;
Whose clouds that day grew doubly dun,
Impervious to the hidden sun,
With volumed smoke that slowly grew
To one wide sky of sulphurous hue.

VII.

But not for vengeance, long delayed,
Alone, did Alp, the renegade,
The Moslem warriors sternly teach
His skill to pierce the promised breach:
Within these walls a maid was pent
His hope would win without consent
Of that inexorable sire,
Whose heart refused him in its ire,
When Alp, beneath his Christian name,
Her virgin hand aspired to claim.
In happier mood, and earlier time,
While unimpeached for traitorous crime,
Gayest in gondola or hall,
He glittered through the Carnival;
And tuned the softest serenade
That e'er on Adria's waters played
At midnight to Italian maid.[1]

VIII.

And many deemed her heart was won;
For sought by numbers, given to none,
Had young Francesca's hand remained
Still by the church's bonds unchained:
And when the Adriatic bore
Lanciotto to the Paynim shore,
Her wonted smiles were seen to fail,
And pensive waxed the maid and pale;
More constant at confessional,

---

[1] [MS. —

"In midnight courtship to Italian maid."]

More rare at masque and festi
Or seen at such, with downcas
Which conquered hearts the
    prize:
With listless look she seems to
With humbler care her form a
Her voice less lively in the son
Her step, though light, less fle
The pairs, on whom the Morn
Breaks, yet unsated with the d

IX.

Sent by the state to guard the l
(Which, wrested from the Mos
While Sobieski tamed his prid
By Buda's wall and Danube's s
The chiefs of Venice wrung aw
From Patra to Euboea's bay,)
Minotti held in Corinth's tower
The Doge's delegated powers,
While yet the pitying eye of Pe
Smiled o'er her long forgotten
And ere that faithless truce was
Which freed her from the unch
With him his gentle daughter c
Nor there, since Menelaus' dan
Forsook her lord and land, to
What woes await on lawless lo
Had fairer form adorned the sh
Than she, the matchless strang

X.

The wall is rent, the ruins yawn
And, with to-morrow's earliest d
O'er the disjointed mass shall v
The foremost of the fierce assau
The bands are ranked; the cho
Of Tartar and of Mussulman,
The full of hope, misnamed "fo
Who hold the thought of death
And win their way with falchion
Or pave the path with many a
O'er which the following brave
Their stepping-stone — the last

XI.

'Tis midnight : on the mountai
The cold, round moon shines de
Blue roll the waters, blue the sk
Spreads like an ocean hung on
Bespangled with those isles of li
So wildly, spiritually bright;
Who ever gazed upon them shi
And turned to earth without rep
Nor wished for wings to flee aw
And mix with their eternal ray ?
The waves on either shore lay t
Calm, clear, and azure as the ai
And scarce their foam the pebb
But murmured meekly as the br
The winds were pillowed on the
The banners drooped along thei

And, as they fell around them furling,
Above them shone the crescent curling;
And that deep silence was unbroke,
Save where the watch his signal spoke,
Save where the steed neighed oft and shrill,
And echo answered from the hill,
And the wide hum of that wild host
Rustled like leaves from coast to coast,
As rose the Muezzin's voice in air
In midnight call to wonted prayer;
It rose, that chanted mournful strain,
Like some lone spirit's o'er the plain:
'Twas musical, but sadly sweet,
Such as when winds and harp-strings meet,
And take a long unmeasured tone,
To mortal minstrelsy unknown.[1]
It seemed to those within the wall
A cry prophetic of their fall:
It struck even the besieger's ear
With something ominous and drear,
An undefined and sudden thrill,
Which makes the heart a moment still,
Then beat with quicker pulse, ashamed
Of that strange sense its silence framed;
Such as a sudden passing-bell
Wakes, though but for a stranger's knell.[2]

XII.

The tent of Alp was on the shore;
'The sound was hushed, the prayer was o'er;
The watch was set, the night-round made,
All mandates issued and obeyed:
'Tis but another anxious night,
His pains the morrow may requite
With all revenge and love can pay,
In guerdon for their long delay.
Few hours remain, and he hath need
Of rest, to nerve for many a deed
Of slaughter; but within his soul
The thoughts like troubled waters roll.
He stood alone among the host;
Not his the loud fanatic boast
To plant the crescent o'er the cross,
Or risk a life with little loss,
Secure in paradise to be
By Houris loved immortally:
Nor his, what burning patriots feel,
The stern exaltedness of zeal,
Profuse of blood, untired in toil,
When battling on the parent soil.
He stood alone—a renegade
Against the country he betrayed;
He stood alone amidst his band,
Without a trusted heart or hand:
They followed him, for he was brave,
And great the spoil he got and gave;
They crouched to him, for he had skill

To warp and wield the vulgar will:
But still his Christian origin
With them was little less than sin.
They envied even the faithless fame
He earned beneath a Moslem name;
Since he, their mightiest chief, had been
In youth a bitter Nazarene.
They did not know how pride can stoop,
When baffled feelings withering droop;
They did not know how hate can burn
In hearts once changed from soft to stern;
Nor all the false and fatal zeal
The convert of revenge can feel.
He ruled them—man may rule the worst,
By ever daring to be first;
So lions o'er the jackal sway;
The jackal points, he fells the prey,[8]
Then on the vulgar yelling press,
To gorge the relics of success.

XIII.

His head grows fevered, and his pulse
The quick successive throbs convulse;
In vain from side to side he throws
His form, in courtship of repose;[4]
Or if he dozed, a sound, a start
Awoke him with a sunken heart.
The turban on his hot brow pressed,
The mail weighed lead-like on his breast,
Though oft and long beneath its weight
Upon his eyes had slumber sate,
Without or couch or canopy,
Except a rougher field and sky
Than now might yield a warrior's bed,
Than now along the heaven was spread.
He could not rest, he could not stay
Within his tent to wait for day,
But walked him forth along the sand,
Where thousand sleepers strewed the strand.
What pillowed them? and why should he
More wakeful than the humblest be,
Since more their peril, worse their toil?
And yet they fearless dream of spoil;
While he alone, where thousands passed
A night of sleep, perchance their last,
In sickly vigil wandered on,
And envied all he gazed upon.

XIV.

He felt his soul become more light
Beneath the freshness of the night.
Cool was the silent sky, though calm,
And bathed his brow with airy balm.
Behind, the camp—before him lay,
In many a winding creek and bay,

---

[1] [MS.—" And make a melancholy moan,
    To mortal voice and ear unknown."]
[2] [MS.—" Which rings a deep, internal knell,.
    A visionary passing-bell."]

[8] [MS.—" As lions o'er the jackal sway
    By springing dauntless on the prey;
    They follow on, and yelling press
    To gorge the fragments of success."]
[4] [MS.—" He vainly turned from side to side,
    And each reposing posture tried."]

Lepanto's gulf; and, on the brow
Of Delphi's hill, unshaken snow,
High and eternal, such as shone
Through thousand summers brightly gone,
Along the gulf, the mount, the clime;
It will not melt, like man, to time:
Tyrant and slave are swept away,
Less formed to wear before the ray;
But that white veil, the lightest, frailest,
Which on the mighty mount thou hailest,
While tower and tree are torn and rent,
Shines o'er its craggy battlement;
In form a peak, in height a cloud,
In texture like a hovering shroud,
Thus high by parting Freedom spread,
As from her fond abode she fled,
And lingered on the spot, where long
Her prophet spirit spake in song.
Oh! still her step at moments falters
O'er withered fields, and ruined altars,
And fain would wake, in souls too broken,
By pointing to each glorious token:
But vain her voice, till better days
Dawn in those yet remembered rays
Which shone upon the Persian flying,
And saw the Spartan smile in dying.

XV.

Not mindless of these mighty times
Was Alp, despite his flight and crimes;
And through this night, as on he wandered
And o'er the past and present pondered,
And thought upon the glorious dead
Who there in better cause had bled,
He felt how faint and feebly dim
The fame that could accrue to him,
Who cheered the band, and waved the
     sword,
A traitor in a turbaned horde;
And led them to the lawless siege,
Whose best success were sacrilege.
Not so had those his fancy numbered,
The chiefs whose dust around him slum-
     bered;
Their phalanx marshalled on the plain,
Whose bulwarks were not then in vain.
They fell devoted, but undying;
The very gale their names seemed sighing:
The waters murmured of their name;
The woods were peopled with their fame;
The silent pillar, lone and gray,
Claimed kindred with their sacred clay;
Their spirits wrapped the dusky mountain,
Their memory sparkled o'er the fountain:
The meanest rill, the mightiest river
Rolled mingling with their fame forever.
Despite of every yoke she bears,
That land is glory's still and theirs![1]

[1] [Here follows, in MS. —
    " Immortal — boundless — undecayed —
     Their souls the very soil pervade."]

'Tis still a watch-word to the eartl
When man would do a deed of w
He points to Greece, and turns to
So sanctioned, on the tyrant's hea
He looks to her, and rushes on
Where life is lost, or freedom wor

XVI.

Still by the shore Alp mutely mused
And wooed the freshness Night diff[2]
There shrinks no ebb in that tideles
Which changeless rolls eternally;[3]
So that wildest of waves, in their angri
Scarce break on the bounds of the
     rood;
And the powerless moon beholds th
Heedless if she come or go:
Calm or high, in main or bay
On their course she hath no sway.
The rock unworn its base doth bar
And looks o'er the surf, but it comes
And the fringe of the foam may be s
On the line that it left long ages ag
A smooth short space of yellow san
Between it and the greener land.

He wandered on, along the beach,
Till within the range of a carbine's
Of the leaguered wall; but they saw
Or how could he 'scape from the host
Did traitors lurk in the Christians'
Were their hands grown stiff, or th[4]
     waxed cold?
I know not, in sooth; but from yon
There flashed no fire, and there
     ball,
Though he stood beneath the basti
That flanked the sea-ward gate of t
Though he heard the sound, and co
     tell
The sullen words of the sentinel,
As his measured step on the stone
Clanked, as he paced it to and fro;
And he saw the lean dogs beneath
Hold o'er the dead their carnival,[5]
Gorging and growling o'er carcass
They were too busy to bark at him
From a Tartar's skull they had str
     flesh,
As ye peel the fig when its fruit is fr
And their white tusks crunched o'er
     skull,[6]

[2] [MS. —
    " Where Freedom loveliest may be
[3] The reader need hardly be reminded
are no perceptible tides in the Mediterra
[4] [MS. — " Or would not waste on a si
       The ball on numbers bette
[5] [Omit the rest of this section. — *Gi*
[6] This spectacle I have seen, such as
beneath the wall of the Seraglio, at Cons
in the little cavities worn by the Bosph

As it slipped through their jaws, when their
    edge grew dull,
As they lazily mumbled the bones of the dead,
When they scarce could rise from the spot
    where they fed;
So well had they broken a lingering fast
With those who had fallen for that night's re-
    past.[1]
And Alp knew, by the turbans that rolled on
    the sand,
The foremost of these were the best of his band:
Crimson and green were the shawls of their
    wear,
And each scalp had a single long tuft of hair,[2]
All the rest was shaven and bare.
The scalps were in the wild dog's maw,
The hair was tangled round his jaw.
But close by the shore, on the edge of the gulf,
There sat a vulture flapping a wolf,
Who had stolen from the hills, but kept away,
Scared by the dogs, from the human prey;
But he seized on his share of a steed that lay,
Picked by the birds, on the sands of the bay.

XVII.

Alp turned him from the sickening sight:
Never had shaken his nerves in fight;
But he better could brook to behold the dying,
Deep in the tide of their warm blood lying,[3]
Scorched with the death-thirst, and writhing
    in vain,
Than the perishing dead who are past all
    pain.[4]
There is something of pride in the perilous
    hour,
Whate'er be the shape in which death may
    lower;
For Fame is there to say who bleeds,
And Honor's eye on daring deeds!
But when all is past, it is humbling to tread
O'er the weltering field of the tombless dead,[5]
And see worms of the earth, and fowls of the
    air,

Beasts of the forest, all gathering there;
All regarding man as their prey,
All rejoicing in his decay.[6]

XVIII.

There is a temple in ruin stands,
Fashioned by long forgotten hands;
Two or three columns, and many a stone,
Marble and granite, with grass o'ergrown!
Out upon Time! it will leave no more
Of the things to come than the things before!
Out upon Time! who for ever will leave
But enough of the past for the future to grieve
O'er that which hath been, and o'er that
    which must be:
What we have seen, our sons shall see;
Remnants of things that have passed away,
Fragments of stone, reared by creatures of
    clay![8]

XIX.

He sate him down at a pillar's base,[9]
And passed his hand athwart his face;
Like one in dreary musing mood,
Declining was his attitude;
His head was drooping on his breast,
Fevered, throbbing, and oppressed;
And o'er his brow, so downward bent,
Oft his beating fingers went,
Hurriedly, as you may see
Your own run over the ivory key
Ere the measured tone is taken
By the chords you would awaken.
There he sate all heavily,
As he heard the night-wind sigh.
Was it the wind through some hollow stone,
Sent that soft and tender moan?[10]

---

rock, a narrow terrace of which projects between
the wall and the water. I think the fact is also
mentioned in Hobhouse's Travels. The bodies
were probably those of some refractory Janizaries.

[1] [This passage shows the force of Lord Byron's
pencil. — *Jeffrey*.]

[2] This tuft, or long lock, is left from a supersti-
tion, that Mahomet will draw them into Paradise
by it.

[3] [Than the mangled corpse in its own blood
lying. — *Gifford*.]

[4] [Strike out—
"Scorched with the death-thirst, and writhing in
    vain,
Than the perishing dead who are past all pain."
What is a "perishing dead?" — *Gifford*.]

[5] [O'er the weltering *limbs* of the tombless dead.
— *Gifford*.]

[6] [MS. —
  "All that liveth on man will prey,
    All rejoice in his decay,
    All that can kindle dismay and disgust
    Follow his frame from the bier to the dust."]

[7] [Omit this couplet. — *Gifford*.]

[8] [After this follows in MS. —
"Monuments that the coming age
  Leaves to the spoil of the seasons' rage —
  Till Ruin makes the relics scarce,
  Then Learning acts her solemn farce,
  And, roaming through the marble waste,
  Prates of beauty, art, and taste.

        xix.
"That Temple was more in the midst of the plain:
  What of that shrine did yet remain
  Lay to his left ——"]

[9] [From this, all is beautiful to —
"He saw not, he knew not; but nothing is there."
                     Gifford.]

[10] I must here acknowledge a close, though unin-
tentional, resemblance in these twelve lines to a
passage in an unpublished poem of Mr. Coleridge,
called "Christabel." It was not till after these
lines were written that I heard that wild and singu-

He lifted his head, and he looked on the
    sea,
But it was unrippled as glass may be;
He looked on the long grass — it waved
    not a blade;
How was that gentle sound conveyed ?
He looked to the banners — each flag lay
    still,
So did the leaves on Cithæron's hill,
And he felt not a breath come over his
    cheek;
What did that sudden sound bespeak ?
He turned to the left — is he sure of sight ?
There sate a lady, youthful and bright!

XX.

He started up with more of fear
Than if an armed foe were near.
"God of my fathers! what is here ?
Who art thou, and wherefore sent
So near a hostile armament ?"
His trembling hands refused to sign
The cross he deemed no more divine:
He had resumed it in that hour,
But conscience wrung away the power.
He gazed, he saw: he knew the face
Of beauty, and the form of grace;
It was Francesca by his side,
The maid who might have been his bride!

The rose was yet upon her cheek,
But mellowed with a tenderer streak:
Where was the play of her soft lips fled ?
Gone was the smile that enlivened their
    red.
The ocean's calm within their view,
Beside her eye had less of blue;
But like that cold wave it stood still,
And its glance,[1] though clear, was chill.
Around her form a thin robe twining,
Nought concealed her bosom shining;

---

larly original and beautiful poem recited; and the
MS. of that production I never saw till very recently,
by the kindness of Mr. Coleridge himself, who, I
hope, is convinced that I have not been a wilful
plagiarist. The original idea undoubtedly pertains
to Mr. Coleridge, whose poem has been composed
above fourteen years. Let me conclude by a hope
that he will not longer delay the publication of a
production, of which I can only add my mite of
approbation to the applause of far more competent
judges. — [The lines in "Christabel" are these: —

> "The night is chill, the forest bare,
>   Is it the wind that moaneth bleak?
>   There is not wind enough in the air
>   To move away the ringlet curl
>   From the lovely lady's cheek —
>   There is not wind enough to twirl
>   The one red leaf, the last of its clan,
>   That dances as often as dance it can,
>   Hanging so light, and hanging so high,
>   On the topmost twig that looks at the sky."]

[1] [And its *thrilling* glance, etc. — *Gifford.*]

Through the parting of her hair,
Floating darkly downward there,
Her rounded arm showed white
And ere yet she made reply,
Once she raised her hand on high
It was so wan, and transparent of
You might have seen the m
    through.

XXI.

"I come from my rest to him I love
That I may be happy, and he may t
I have passed the guards, the gate,
Sought thee in safety through foes a
'Tis said the lion will turn and flee
From a maid in the pride of her pu
And the power on high, that can shiel
Thus from the tyrant of the wood,
Hath extended its mercy to guard
From the hands of the leaguering in
I come — and if I come in vain,
Never, oh never, we meet again!
Thou hast done a fearful deed
In falling away from thy father's cre
But dash that turban to earth, and s
The sign of the cross, and for ever
Wring the black drop from thy hea
And to-morrow unites us no more t

"And where should our bridal
    spread ?
In the midst of the dying and the d
For to-morrow we give to the slau
    flame
The sons and the shrines of the Chri
None, save thou and thine, I've sw
Shall be left upon the morn:
But thee will I bear to a lovely spo
Where our hands shall be joine
    sorrow forgot.
There thou yet shalt be my bride,
When once again I've quelled the
Of Venice; and her hated race
Have felt the arm they would deba
Scourge, with a whip of scorpions,
Whom vice and envy made my fo

Upon his hand she laid her own —
Light was the touch, but it thrilled t
And shot a chillness to his heart,
Which fixed him beyond the powe
Though slight was that grasp so n
He could not loose him from its h
But never did clasp of one so dear
Strike on the pulse with such feeli
As those thin fingers, long and whi
Froze through his blood by their
    night.
The feverish glow of his brow was
And his heart sank so still that
    stone,
As he looked on the face, and beh
So deeply changed from what he k

air but faint — without the ray
f mind, that made each feature play
ike sparkling waves on a sunny day;
nd her motionless lips lay still as death,
nd her words came forth without her breath,
nd there rose not a heave o'er her bosom's
    swell,
nd there seemed not a pulse in her veins to
    dwell.
hough her eye shone out, yet the lids were
    fixed,
nd the glance that it gave was wild and
    unmixed
/ith aught of change, as the eyes may seem
f the restless who walk in a troubled dream;
ike the figures on arras, that gloomily glare,
tirred by the breath of the wintry air,[1]
o seen by the dying lamp's fitful light,
ifeless, but life-like, and awful to sight;
s they seem, through the dimness, about to
    come down
rom the shadowy wall where their images
    frown;[2]
earfully flitting to and fro,
s the gusts on the tapestry come and go.
If not for love of me be given
hus much, then, for the love of heaven,—
gain I say — that turban tear
rom off thy faithless brow, and swear
hine injured country's sons to spare,
r thou art lost; and never shalt see —
Not earth — that's past — but heaven or me.
If this thou dost accord, albeit
A heavy doom 'tis thine to meet,
That doom shall half absolve thy sin,
And mercy's gate may receive thee within:
But pause one moment more, and take
The curse of Him thou didst forsake;
And look once more to heaven, and see
Its love for ever shut from thee.
There is a light cloud by the moon — [3]

'Tis passing, and will pass full soon —
If, by the time its vapory sail
Hath cased her shaded orb to veil,
Thy heart within thee is not changed,
Then God and man are both avenged;
Dark will thy doom be, darker still
Thine immortality of ill."

Alp looked to heaven, and saw on high
The sign she spake of in the sky;
But his heart was swollen, and turned aside,
By deep interminable pride.
This first false passion of his breast
Rolled like a torrent o'er the rest.
He sue for mercy! *He* dismayed
By wild words of a timid maid!
He, wronged by Venice, vow to save
Her sons, devoted to the grave!
No—though that cloud were thunder's worst,
And charge to crush him — let it burst!

He looked upon it earnestly,
Without an accent of reply;
He watched it passing; it is flown:
Full on his eye the clear moon shone,
And thus he spake — " Whate'er my fate,
I am no changeling — 'tis too late:
The reed in storms may bow and quiver,
Then rise again; the tree must shiver.
What Venice made me, I must be,
Her foe in all, save love to thee:
But thou art safe: oh, fly with me!"
He turned, but she is gone!
Nothing is there but the column stone.
Hath she sunk in the earth, or melted in air?
He saw not — he knew not — but nothing
    is there.

XXII.

The night is past, and shines the sun
As if that morn were a jocund one.[4]
Lightly and brightly breaks away
The Morning from her mantle gray,

---

[1] [MS.—
" Like a picture, that magic had charmed from its
    frame,
    Lifeless but life-like, and ever the same."]

[2] [In the summer of 1803, when in his sixteenth year, Byron, though offered a bed in Annesley, used at first to return every night to sleep at New-stead; alleging as a reason, that he was afraid of the family pictures of the Chaworths; that he fancied "they had taken a grudge to him on account of the duel." Moore thinks this passage may have been suggested by the recollection of these pictures.]

[3] I have been told that the idea expressed in this and the five following lines has been admired by those whose approbation is valuable. I am glad of it: but it is not original — at least not mine; it may be found much better expressed in pages 182-3-4 of the English version of "Vathek" (I forget the precise page of the French), a work to which I have before referred; and never recur to, or read, without a renewal of gratification. — [The following is the passage: — "' Deluded prince!' said the Genius, addressing the Caliph, ' to whom Providence hath confided the care of innumerable subjects; is it thus that thou fulfillest thy mission? Thy crimes are already completed; and art thou now hastening to thy punishment? Thou knowest that beyond those mountains Eblis and his accursed dives hold their infernal empire; and seduced by a malignant phantom, thou art proceeding to surrender thyself to them! This moment is the last of grace allowed thee: give back Nouronahar to her father, who still retains a few sparks of life; destroy thy tower, with all its abominations: drive Carathis from thy councils: be just to thy subjects: respect the ministers of the prophet: compensate for thy impieties by an exemplary life; and, instead of squandering thy days in voluptuous indulgence, lament thy crimes on the sepulchres of thy ancestors. Thou beholdest the clouds that obscure the sun: at the instant he recovers his splendor, if thy heart be not changed, the time of mercy assigned thee will be past for ever."]

[4] [Leave out this couplet. — *Gifford*.]

And the Noon will look on a sultry day,¹
Hark to the trump and the drum,
And the mournful sound of the barbarous horn,
And the flap of the banners, that flit as they're borne,
And the neigh of the steed, and the multitude's hum,
And the clash, and the shout, " They come! they come! "
The horsetails² are plucked from the ground, and the sword
From its sheath; and they form, and but wait for the word.
Tartar, and Spahi, and Turcoman,
Strike your tents, and throng to the van;
Mount ye, spur ye, skirr the plain,
That the fugitive may flee in vain,
When he breaks from the town; and none escape,
Aged or young, in the Christian shape;
While your fellows on foot, in a fiery mass,
Bloodstain the breach through which they pass.³
The steeds are bridled, and snort to the rein;
Curved is each neck, and flowing each mane;
White is the foam of their champ on the bit;
The spears are uplifted; the matches are lit;
The cannon are pointed, and ready to roar,
And crush the wall they have crumbled before:⁴
Forms in his phalanx each Janizar;
Alp at their head; his right arm is bare,
So is the blade of his scimitar;
The khan and the pachas are all at their post;
The vizier himself at the head of the host.
When the culverin's signal is fired, then on;
Leave not in Corinth a living one—
A priest at her altars, a chief in her halls,
A hearth in her mansions, a stone on her walls.
God and the prophet—Alla Hu!
Up to the skies with that wild halloo!
"There the breach lies for passage, the ladder to scale;
And your hands on your sabres, and how should ye fail?
He who first downs with the red cross may crave⁵

His heart's dearest wish; let him ? have! "
Thus uttered Coumourgi, the vizier;
The reply was the brandish of ? spear,
And the shout of fierce thousands ire:—
Silence—hark to the signal—fire!

XXIII.

As the wolves, that headlong go
On the stately buffalo,
Though with fiery eyes, and angry ?
And hoofs that stamp, and horns th?
He tramples on earth, or tosses on ?
The foremost, who rush on his stren?
die
Thus against the wall they went,
Thus the first were backward bent;
Many a bosom, sheathed in brass,
Strewed the earth like broken glass,
Shivered by the shot, that tore
The ground whereon they moved n?
Even as they fell, in files they lay,
Like the mower's grass at the close
When his work is done on the level
Such was the fall of the foremost sla?

XXIV.

As the spring-tides, with heavy plas?
From the cliffs invading dash
Huge fragments, sapped by the ceas?
Till white and thundering down the
Like the avalanche's snow
On the Alpine vales below;
Thus at length, outbreathed and wo?
Corinth's sons were downward born?
By the long and oft renewed
Charge of the Moslem multitude.
In firmness they stood, and in ma?
fell,
Heaped by the host of the infidel,
Hand to hand, and foot to foot:
Nothing there, save death, was mut?
Stroke, and thrust, and flash, and cr?
For quarter, or for victory,
Mingle there with the volleying thur?
Which makes the distant cities won?
How the sounding battle goes,
If with them, or for their foes;
If they must mourn, or may rejoice
In that annihilating voice,
Which pierces the deep hills thr?
through
With an echo dread and new:

---

¹ [Strike out—
"And the Noon will look on a sultry day."—*G.*]

² [The horsetails, fixed upon a lance, a pacha's standard.]

³ [Omit—
"While your fellows on foot, in a fiery mass,
Bloodstain the breach through which they pass."
Gifford.]

⁴ [" And crush the wall they have *shaken* before."
Gifford.]

⁵ [" He who first *downs* with the red cross may crave," etc.]   What vulgarism is this!—

" He who *lowers,*—or *plucks dow?*
Gifford.]

⁶ [Thus against the wall they *bent*,
Thus the first were backward *sent.*·

⁷ [Such was the fall of the foremost *tr?*

You might have heard it, on that day,
O'er Salamis and Megara;
(We have heard the hearers say,)
Even unto Piræus' bay.

XXV.

From the point of encountering blades to the
 hilt,
Sabres and swords with blood were gilt;
But the rampart is won, and the spoil begun,
And all but the after carnage done.
Shriller shrieks now mingling come
From within the plundered dome:
Hark to the haste of flying feet,
That splash in the blood of the slippery
 street;
But here and there, where 'vantage ground
Against the foe may still be found,
Desperate groups, of twelve or ten,
Make a pause, and turn again —
With banded backs against the wall,
Fiercely stand, or fighting fall.

There stood an old man [1] — his hairs were
 white,
But his veteran arm was full of might:
So gallantly bore he the brunt of the fray,
The dead before him, on that day,
In a semicircle lay; .
Still he combated unwounded,
Though retreating, unsurrounded.
Many a scar of former fight
Lurked [2] beneath his corslet bright;
But of every wound his body bore,
Each and all had been ta'en before:
 Though aged, he was so iron of limb,
 Few of our youth could cope with him;
 And the foes, whom he singly kept at bay,
 Outnumbered his thin hairs [3] of silver
  gray.
 From right to left his sabre swept:
 Many an Othman mother wept
 Sons that were unborn, when dipped [4]
 His weapon first in Moslem gore,
 Ere his years could count a score.
 Of all he might have been the sire [5]
 Who fell that day beneath his ire:
 For, sonless left long years ago,
 His wrath made many a childless foe;
 And since the day, when in the strait [6]
 His only boy had met his fate,
 His parent's iron hand did doom

More than a human hecatomb.[7]
If shades by carnage be appeased,
Patroclus' spirit less was pleased
Than his, Minotti's son, who died
Where Asia's bounds and ours divide.
Buried he lay, where thousands before
For thousands of years were inhumed on
 the shore;
What of them is left, to tell
Where they lie, and how they fell?
Not a stone on their turf, nor a bone in their
 graves
But they live in the verse that immortally
 saves.

XXVI.

Hark to the Allah shout! [8] a band
Of the Mussulman bravest and best is at
 hand:
Their leader's nervous arm is bare,
Swifter to smite, and never to spare —
Unclothed to the shoulder it waves them
 on;
Thus in the fight is he ever known:
Others a gaudier garb may show,
To tempt the spoil of the greedy foe;
Many a hand's on a richer hilt,
But none on a steel more ruddily gilt;
Many a loftier turban may wear, —
Alp is but known by the white arm bare;
Look through the thick of the fight, 'tis
 there!
There is not a standard on that shore
So well advanced the ranks before;
There is not a banner in Moslem war
Will lure the Delhis half so far;
It glances like a falling star!
Where'er that mighty arm is seen,
The bravest be, or late have been; [9]
There the craven cries for quarter
Vainly to the vengeful Tartar;
Or the hero, silent lying,
Scorns to yield a groan in dying;
Mustering his last feeble blow
'Gainst the nearest levelled foe,
Though faint beneath the mutual wound,
Grappling on the gory ground.

XXVII.

Still the old man stood erect,
And Alp's career a moment checked.
"Yield thee, Minotti; quarter take,
For thine own, thy daughter's sake."
"Never, renegado, never!
Though the life of thy gift would last for
 ever." [10]

---

[1] [There stood a man, etc. — *Gifford.*]
[2] ["*Lurked,*" a bad word — say "*Was hid.*"
— *Gifford.*]
[3] [Outnumbered his hairs, etc. — *G.*]
[4] [Sons that were unborn, when *he* dipped. — *G.*]
[5] [Bravo! — this is better than King Priam's fifty
sons. — *Gifford.*]
[6] In the naval battle at the mouth of the Darda-
nelles, between the Venetians and Turks.

[7] [There can be no such thing; but the whole of
this is poor and spun out. — *G.*]
[8] [Hark to the Alla Hu! etc. — *G.*]
[9] [Omit the remainder of the section. — *Gifford.*]
[10] [In the original MS. —
"Though the life of thy giving would last for ever."]

" Francesca! — Oh, my promised bride ! [1]
Must she too perish by thy pride ? "
" She is safe." — " Where ? where ? " — " In
    heaven ;
From whence thy traitor soul is driven —
Far from thee, and undefiled."
Grimly then Minotti smiled,
As he saw Alp staggering bow
Before his words, as with a blow.

" Oh God! when died she ? " — " Yester-
    night —
Nor weep I for her spirit's flight :
None of my pure race shall be
Slaves to Mahomet and thee —
Come on ! " — That challenge is in vain —
Alp's already with the slain !
While Minotti's words were wreaking
More revenge in bitter speaking
Than his falchion's point had found,
Had the time allowed to wound,
From within the neighboring porch
Of a long defended church,
Where the last and desperate few
Would the failing fight renew,
The sharp shot dashed Alp to the ground ;
Ere an eye could view the wound
That crashed through the brain of the infi-
    del,
Round he spun, and down he fell ;
A flash like fire within his eyes
Blazed, as he bent no more to rise,
And then eternal darkness sunk
Through all the palpitating trunk ; [2]
Nought of life left, save a quivering
Where his limbs were slightly shivering :
They turned him on his back ; his breast
And brow were stained with gore and dust,
And through his lips the life-blood oozed,
From its deep veins lately loosed ;
But in his pulse there was no throb,
Nor on his lips one dying sob ;
Sigh, nor word, nor struggling breath
Heralded his way to death :
Ere his very thought could pray,
Unanealed he passed away,
Without a hope from mercy's aid, —
To the last — a Renegade.

XXVIII.

Fearfully the yell arose
Of his followers, and his foes ;
These in joy, in fury those : [3]
Then again in conflict mixing,
Clashing swords, and spears transfixing,

Interchanged the blow and thrust
Hurling warriors in the dust.
Street by street, and foot by foot,
Still Minotti dares dispute
The latest portion of the land
Left beneath his high command ;
With him, aiding heart and hand
The remnant of his gallant band.
Still the church is tenable,
    Whence issued late the fated b
    That half avenged the city's fall
When Alp, her fierce assailant, fe
Thither bending sternly back,
They leave before a bloody track
And, with their faces to the foe,
Dealing wounds with every blow, [4]
The chief, and his retreating train
Join to those within the fane ;
There they yet may breathe awhil
Sheltered by the massy pile.

XXIX.

Brief breathing-time ! the turbane
With adding ranks and raging bo
Press onwards with such strength
Their numbers balk their own ret
For narrow the way that led to th
Where still the Christians yielded
And the foremost, if fearful, may
Through the massy column to turn
They perforce must do or die.
They die ; but ere their eyes could
Avengers o'er their bodies rose ;
Fresh and furious, fast they fill
The ranks unthinned, though sla
    still ;
And faint the weary Christians wa:
Before the still renewed attacks :
And now the Othmans gain the ga
Still resists its iron weight,
And still, all deadly aimed and ho
From every crevice comes the sho
From every shattered window pou
The volleys of the sulphurous sho
But the portal wavering grows anc
The iron yields, the hinges creak –
It bends — it falls — and all is o'er
Lost Corinth may resist no more !

XXX.

Darkly, sternly, and all alone, ,
Minotti stood o'er the altar stone :
Madonna's face upon him shone,
Painted in heavenly hues above,
With eyes of light and looks of lov
And placed upon that holy shrine
To fix our thoughts on things divi
When pictured there, we kneeling
Her, and the boy-God on her knee
Smiling sweetly on each prayer

---

[1] [MS. —
" Where's Francesca? — my promised bride ! "]
[3] [Here follows in MS. —
    " Twice and once he rolled a space,
    Then lead-like lay upon his face."]
[MS. — " These in rage, in triumph those:"]

[4] [Dealing *death* with every blow. — C

To heaven, as if to waft it there,
Still she smiled; even now she smiles,
Though slaughter streams along her aisles :
Minotti lifted his aged eye,
And made the sign of a cross with a sigh,
Then seized a torch which blazed thereby;
And still he stood, while, with steel and
    flame,
Inward and onward the Mussulman came.

XXXI.

The vaults beneath the mosaic stone
Contained the dead of ages gone;
Their names were on the graven floor,
But now illegible with gore;
The carved crests, and curious hues
The varied marble's veins diffuse,
Were smeared, and slippery — stained, and
    strown
With broken swords, and helms o'erthrown :
There were dead above, and the dead below
Lay cold in many a coffined row;
You might see them piled in sable state,
By a pale light through a gloomy grate;
But War had entered their dark caves,
And stored along the vaulted graves
Her sulphurous treasures, thickly spread
In masses by the fleshless dead :
Here, throughout the siege, had been
The Christians' chiefest magazine;
To these a late formed train now led,
Minotti's last and stern resource
Against the foe's o'erwhelming force.

XXXII.

The foe came on, and few remain
To strive, and those must strive in vain :
For lack of further lives, to slake
The thirst of vengeance now awake,
With barbarous blows they gash the dead,
And lop the already lifeless head,
And fell the statues from their niche,
And spoil the shrines of offerings rich,
And from each other's rude hands wrest
The silver vessels saints had blessed.
To the high altar on they go;
Oh, but it made a glorious show ! [1]
On its table still behold
The cup of consecrated gold;
Massy and deep, a glittering prize,
Brightly it sparkles to plunderers' eyes :
That morn it held the holy wine,
Converted by Christ to his blood so divine,
Which his worshippers drank at the break
    of day
To shrive their souls ere they joined in the
    fray.
Still a few drops within it lay;
And round the sacred table glow

[1] ["Oh, but it made a glorious show!!" Out. — Gifford.]

Twelve lofty lamps, in splendid row,
From the purest metal cast;
A spoil — the richest, and the last.

XXXIII.

So near they came, the nearest stretched
To grasp the spoil he almost reached,
    When old Minotti's hand
Touched with the torch the train —
    'Tis fired !
Spire, vaults, the shrine, the spoil, the slain,
    The turbaned victors, the Christian band,
All that of living or dead remain,
Hurled on high with the shivered fane,
    In one wild roar expired !
The shattered town — the walls thrown
    down —
The waves a moment backward bent —
The hills that shake, although unrent,
    As if an earthquake passed —
The thousand shapeless things all driven
In cloud and flame athwart the heaven,
    By that tremendous blast —
Proclaimed the desperate conflict o'er
On that too long afflicted shore : [2]
Up to the sky like rockets go
All that mingled there below :
Many a tall and goodly man,
Scorched and shrivelled to a span,
When he fell to earth again
Like a cinder strewed the plain :
Down the ashes shower like rain;
Some fell in the gulf, which received the
    sprinkles
With a thousand circling wrinkles;
Some fell on the shore, but, far away,
Scattered o'er the isthmus lay;
Christian or Moslem, which be they ?
Let their mothers see and say !
When in cradled rest they lay,
And each nursing mother smiled
On the sweet sleep of her child,
Little deemed she such a day
Would rend those tender limbs away.
Not the matrons that them bore
Could discern their offspring more:
That one moment left no trace
More of human form or face
Save a scattered scalp or bone:
And down came blazing rafters, strown
Around, and many a falling stone,
Deeply dinted in the clay,
All blackened there and reeking lay.
All the living things that heard
That deadly earth-shock disappeared :
The wild birds flew; the wild dogs fled,
And howling left the unburied dead; [3]

[2] [Strike out from "Up to the sky," etc. to "All blackened there and reeking lay." Despicable stuff. — Gifford.]
[3] [Omit the next six lines. — Gifford.]

The camels from their keepers broke;
The distant steer forsook the yoke —
The nearer steed plunged o'er the plain,
And burst his girth, and tore his rein;
The bull-frog's note, from out the marsh
Deep-mouthed arose, and doubly harsh;
The wolves yelled on the caverned hill
Where echo rolled in thunder still;
The jackal's troop, in gathered cry,[1]
Bayed from afar complainingly,
With a mixed and mournful sound,
Like crying babe, and beaten hound:[2]

[1] I believe I have taken a poetical license to transplant the jackal from Asia. In Greece I never saw nor heard these animals; but among the ruins of Ephesus I have heard them by hundreds. They haunt ruins, and follow armies.

[2] [Leave out this couplet. — *Gifford*.]

With sudden wing, and ruffle
The eagle left his rocky nest,
And mounted nearer to the su
The clouds beneath him seem
Their smoke assailed his start
And made him higher soar an
  Thus was Corinth lost an

[3] [The "Siege of Corinth," thou haps, with too visible an effect, anc harmonized in all its parts, cannot l as a magnificent composition. Ther is made up of alternate representati solemn scenes and emotions, and of terrors, and intoxication of war. pictures are, perhaps, too violently c in some parts, too harshly colored; general exquisitely designed, and ex utmost spirit and energy. — *Jeffrey*.

PARISINA.

TO SCROPE BERDMORE DAVIES, ESQ.

THE FOLLOWING POEM IS INSCRIBED

BY ONE WHO HAS LONG ADMIRED HIS TALENTS AND VALUED H
FRIENDSHIP.

January 22, 1816.

ADVERTISEMENT.

THE following poem is grounded on a circumstance mentioned in Gibbon's " Antiquitie: of Brunswick." I am aware, that in modern times the delicacy or fastidiousness of the rea such subjects unfit for the purposes of poetry. The Greek dramatists, and some of the l English writers, were of a different opinion: as Alfieri and Schiller have also been, more the Continent. The following extract will explain the facts on which the story is founded. *Azo* is substituted for Nicholas, as more metrical.

"Under the reign of Nicholas III. Ferrara was polluted with a domestic tragedy. By th an attendant, and his own observation, the Marquis of Este discovered the incestuous lo Parisina, and Hugo his bastard son, a beautiful and valiant youth. They were beheade by the sentence of a father and husband, who published his shame, and survived their e:

[1] [" Ferrara is much decayed and depopulated; but the castle still exists entire; and I where Parisina and Hugo were beheaded, according to the annal of Gibbon." — *B. Letter*.

as unfortunate, if they were guilty: if they were innocent, he was still more unfortunate; nor is there ay possible situation in which I can sincerely approve the last act of the justice of a parent." — *Gib-n's Miscellaneous Works*, vol. iii. p. 470.

INTRODUCTION

PARISINA was written in London in the autumn of 1815, and published in February, 1816. The his-rical facts on which it was founded are detailed in the following passage in Frizzi's History of 'errara.

"This turned out a calamitous year for the people of Ferrara; for there occurred a very tragical event 1 the court of their sovereign. Our annals, both printed and in manuscript, with the exception of the npolished and negligent work of Sardi, and one other, have given the following relation of it, — from hich, however, are rejected many details, and especially the narrative of Bandelli, who wrote a century fterwards, and who does not accord with the contemporary historians.

"By the above-mentioned Stella dell' Assassino, the Marquis, in the year 1405, had a son called Ugo, beautiful and ingenuous youth. Parisina Malatesta, second wife of Niccolo, like the generality of step-1others, treated him with little kindness, to the infinite regret of the Marquis, who regarded him with ɔnd partiality. One day she asked leave of her husband to undertake a certain journey, to which he onsented, but upon condition that Ugo should bear her company; for he hoped by these means to induce er, in the end, to lay aside the obstinate aversion which she had conceived against him. And indeed is intent was accomplished but too well, since, during the journey, she not only divested herself of all er hatred, but fell into the opposite extreme. After their return, the Marquis had no longer any occa-ion to renew his former reproofs. It happened one day that a servant of the Marquis, named Zoese, or, as some call him, Giorgio, passing before the apartments of Parisina, saw going out from them one of her chamber-maids, all terrified and in tears. Asking the reason, she told him that her mistress, for some slight offence, had been beating her; and, giving vent to her rage, she added, that she could easily be revenged, if she chose to make known the criminal familiarity which subsisted between Parisina and her step-son. The servant took note of the words, and related them to his master. He was astounded thereat, but, scarcely believing his ears, he assured himself of the fact, alas! too clearly, on the 18th of May, by looking through a hole made in the ceiling of his wife's chamber. Instantly he broke into a furious rage, and arrested both of them, together with Aldobrandino Rangoni, of Modena, her gentleman, and also as some say, two of the women of her chamber, as abettors of this sinful act. He ordered them to be brought to a hasty trial, desiring the judges to pronounce sentence, in the accustomed forms, upon the culprits. This sentence was death. Some there were that bestirred themselves in favor of the delin-quents, and, amongst others, Ugoccion Contrario, who was all powerful with Niccolo, and also his aged and much deserving minister Alberto dal Sale. Both of these, their tears flowing down their cheeks, and upon their knees, implored him for mercy; adducing whatever reasons they could suggest for sparing the offenders, besides those motives of honor and decency which might persuade him to conceal from the public so scandalous a deed. But his rage made him inflexible, and, on the instant, he commanded that the sentence should be put in execution.

"It was, then, in the prisons of the castle, and exactly in those frightful dungeons which are seen at :his day beneath the chamber called the Aurora, at the foot of the Lion's tower, at the top of the street Giovecca, that on the night of the 21st of May were beheaded, first, Ugo, and afterwards Parisina. Zoese, he that accused her, conducted the latter under his arm to the place of punishment. She, all along, fancied that she was to be thrown into a pit, and asked at every step, whether she was yet come to the spot? She was told that her punishment was the axe. She inquired what was become of Ugo, and received for answer, that he was already dead; at the which, sighing grievously, she exclaimed, 'Now, then, I wish not myself to live;' and, being come to the block, she stripped herself with her own hands of all her ornaments, and wrapping a cloth round her head, submitted to the fatal stroke, which termi-nated the cruel scene. The same was done with Rangoni, who, together with the others, according ɔ

two calendars in the library of St. Francesco, was buried in the cemetery of that convent.
is known respecting the women.

" The Marquis kept watch the whole of that dreadful night, and, as he was walking ba
forwards, inquired of the captain of the castle if Ugo was dead yet? who answered him, Ye
gave himself up to the most desperate lamentations, exclaiming, ' Oh! that I too were dead,
been hurried on to resolve thus against my own Ugo!' And then gnawing with his teeth a c
had in his hand, he passed the rest of the night in sighs and in tears, calling frequently u
dear Ugo. On the following day, calling to mind that it would be necessary to make public
tion, seeing that the transaction could not be kept secret, he ordered the narrative to be dra
paper, and sent it to all the courts of Italy.

" On receiving this advice, the Doge of Venice, Francesco Foscari, gave orders, but witho
his reasons, that stop should be put to the preparations for a tournament, which, under the
the Marquis, and at the expense of the city of Padua, was about to take place, in the square
in order to celebrate his advancement to the ducal chair.

"'The Marquis, in addition to what he had already done, from some unaccountable burst o
commanded that as many of the married women as were well known to him to be faithless, l
sina, should, like her, be beheaded. Amongst others, Barberina, or, as some call her, Laod
wife of the court judge, underwent this sentence, at the usual place of execution; that is t
quarter of St. Giacomo, opposite the present fortress, beyond St. Paul's. It cannot be told
appeared this proceeding in a prince, who, considering his own disposition, should, as it :
been in such cases most indulgent. Some, however, there were who did not fail to commen

The above passage of Frizzi was translated by Byron, and formed a closing note to the ori
of " Parisina."

I.

IT is the hour when from the boughs
  The nightingale's high note is heard;
It is the hour when lovers' vows
  Seem sweet in every whispered word
And gentle winds, and waters near,
Make music to the lonely ear.
Each flower the dews have lightly wet,
And in the sky the stars are met,
And on the wave is deeper blue,
And on the leaf a browner hue,
And in the heaven that clear obscure,
So softly dark, and darkly pure,
Which follows the decline of day,
As twilight melts beneath the moon away.[1]

II.

But it is not to list to the waterfall
That Parisina leaves her hall,
And it is not to gaze on the heavenly
  light
That the lady walks in the shadow of night;
And if she sits in Este's bower,
'Tis not for the sake of its full-blown flower —
She listens — but not for the nightingale —
Though her ear expects as soft a tale.

---

[1] The lines contained in this section were printed
as set to music some time since, but belonged to the
poem where they now appear: the greater part of
which was composed prior to " Lara."

There glides a step through the fo
And her cheek grows pale — and
  beats quick.
There whispers a voice through tl
  leaves,
And her blush returns, and h
  heaves   :
A moment more — and they shall :
'Tis past — her lover's at her feet.

III.

And what unto them is the world b
With all its change of time and tid
Its living things — its earth and sk
Are nothing to their mind and eye.
And heedless as the dead are they
  Of aught around, above, beneath
As if all else had passed away,
  They only for each other breathe
Their very sighs are full of joy
So deep, that did it not decay,
That happy madness would destro
  The hearts which feel its fiery sw
Of guilt, of peril, do they deem
In that tumultuous tender dream
Who that have felt that passion's
Or paused or feared in such an I
Or thought how brief such mom
But yet — they are already past!
Alas! we must awake before
We know such vision comes no

IV.

With many a lingering look they leave
  The spot of guilty gladness past;
And though they hope, and vow, they grieve,
  As if that parting were the last.
The frequent sigh — the long embrace —
The lip that there would cling for ever,
While gleams on Parisina's face
  The Heaven she fears will not forgive her,
As if each calmly conscious star
Beheld her frailty from afar —
The frequent sigh, the long embrace,
Yet binds them to their trysting-place.
But it must come, and they must part
In fearful heaviness of heart,
With all the deep and shuddering chill
Which follows fast the deeds of ill.

V.

And Hugo is gone to his lonely bed,
  To covet there another's bride;
But she must lay her conscious head
  A husband's trusting heart beside.
But fevered in her sleep she seems,
And red her cheek with troubled dreams,
  And mutters she in her unrest
A name she dare not breathe by day,
  And clasps her Lord unto the breast
Which pants for one away:
And he to that embrace awakes,
And, happy in the thought, mistakes
That dreaming sigh, and warm caress,
For such as he was wont to bless;
And could in very fondness weep
O'er her who loves him even in sleep.

VI.

He clasped her sleeping to his heart,
  And listened to each broken word:
He hears — Why doth Prince Azo start,
  As if the Archangel's voice he heard?
And well he may — a deeper doom
Could scarcely thunder o'er his tomb,
When he shall wake to sleep no more,
And stand the eternal throne before.
And well he may — his earthly peace
Upon that sound is doomed to cease.
That sleeping whisper of a name
Bespeaks her guilt and Azo's shame.
And whose that name? that o'er his pillow
Sounds fearful as the breaking billow,
Which rolls the plank upon the shore,
  And dashes on the pointed rock
The wretch who sinks to rise no more, —
  So came upon his soul the shock.
And whose that name? 'tis Hugo's, — his —
In sooth he had not deemed of this! —
'Tis Hugo's, — he, the child of one
He loved — his own all-evil son —
The offspring of his wayward youth,
When he betrayed Bianca's truth, .

The maid whose folly could confide
In him who made her not his bride.

VII.

He plucked his poniard in its sheath,
  But sheathed it ere the point was bare —
Howe'er unworthy now to breathe,
  He could not slay a thing so fair —
  At least, not smiling — sleeping — there — -
Nay more : — he did not wake her then,
  But gazed upon her with a glance
  Which, had she roused her from he'
    trance,
Had frozen her sense to sleep again — ·
And o'er his brow the burning lamp
Gleamed on the dew-drops big and damp.
She spake no more — but still she slum
    bered —
While, in his thought, her days are num-
    bered.

VIII.

And with the morn he sought, and found,
In many a tale from those around,
The proof of all he feared to know,
Their present guilt, his future woe;
The long-conniving damsels seek
  To save themselves, and would transfer
  The guilt — the shame — the doom — to
    her:
Concealment is no more — they speak
All circumstance which may compel
Full credence to the tale they tell:
And Azo's tortured heart and ear
Have nothing more to feel or hear.

IX.

He·was not one who brooked delay
  Within the chamber of his state,
The chief of Este's ancient sway
  Upon his throne of judgment sate;
His nobles and his guards are there, —
Before him is the sinful pair;
Both young, — and *one* how passing fair!
With swordless belt, and fettered hand,
Oh, Christ! that thus a son should stand
  Before a father's face!
Yet thus must Hugo meet his sire,
And hear the sentence of his ire,
  The tale of his disgrace!
And yet he seems not overcome,
Although, as yet, his voice be dumb.

X.

And still, and pale, and silently
  Did Parisina wait her doom;
How changed since last her speaking eye
  Glanced gladness round the glittering
    room,
Where high-born men were proud to wait —
Where Beauty watched to imitate
  Her gentle voice — her lovely mien —
And gather from her air and gait

The graces of its queen:
Then, — had her eye in sorrow wept,
A thousand warriors forth had leapt,
A thousand swords had sheathless shone,
And made her quarrel all their own.
Now, — what is she ? and what are they ?
Can she command, or these obey ?
All silent and unheeding now,
With downcast eyes and knitting brow,
And folded arms, and freezing air,
And lips that scarce their scorn forbear,
Her knights, and dames, her court — is
        there:
And he, the chosen one, whose lance
Had yet been couched before her glance,
Who — were his arm a moment free —
Had died or gained her liberty;
The minion of his father's bride, —
He, too, is fettered by her side;
Nor sees her swoln and full eye swim
Less for her own despair than him:
Those lids — o'er which the violet vein
Wandering, leaves a tender stain,
Shining through the smoothest white
That e'er did softest kiss invite —
Now seemed with hot and livid glow
To press, not shade, the orbs below ;
Which glance so heavily, and fill,
As tear on tear grows gathering still.

XI.

And he for her had also wept,
    But for the eyes that on him gazed:
His sorrow, if he felt it, slept;
    Stern and erect his brow was raised.
Whate'er the grief his soul avowed,
He would not shrink before the crowd;
But yet he dared not look on her:
Remembrance of the hours that were —
His guilt — his love — his present state —
His father's wrath — all good men's hate —
His earthly, his eternal fate —
And hers, — oh, hers ! — he dared not throw
One look upon that deathlike brow !
Else had his rising heart betrayed
Remorse for all the wreck it made.

XII.

And Azo spake : — " But yesterday
    I gloried in a wife and son;
That dream this morning passed away;
    Ere day declines, I shall have none.
My life must linger on alone;
Well, — let that pass, — there breathes not
        one
Who would not do as I have done:
Those ties are broken — not by me;
    Let that too pass ; — the doom's prepared !
Hugo, the priest awaits on thee,
    And then — thy crime's reward !
Away ! address thy prayers to Heaven,

Before its evening stars are
Learn if thou there canst be fo
    Its mercy may absolve thee
But here, upon the earth bene£
    There is no spot where thou
Together, for an hour, could b
    Farewell ! I will not see thee
But thou, frail thing ! shalt viev
    Away ! I cannot speak the r
    Go ! woman of the wanton b
Not I, but thou his blood dost
Go ! if that sight thou canst out
And joy thee in the life I give."

XIII.

And here stern Azo hid his fac
    For on his brow the swelling
    Throbbed as if back upon hi.
The hot blood ebbed and flov
And therefore bowed he for a s
And passed his shaking hand al
    His eye, to veil it from the th
While Hugo raised his chained
And for a brief delay demands
His father's ear: the silent sire
Forbids not what his words req

" It is not that I dread the de
    For thou hast seen me by thy si
All redly through the battle ride,
And that not once a useless brar
Thy slaves have wrested from m
Hath shed more blood in cause
Than e'er can stain the axe of m
    Thou gav'st, and may'st resume
A gift for which I thank thee no!
Nor are my mother's wrongs for
Her slighted love and ruined na\
Her offspring's heritage of sham
But she is in the grave, where h¢
Her son, thy rival, soon shall be.
Her broken heart — my severed
Shall witness for thee from the d
How trusty and how tender were
Thy youthful love — paternal car
'Tis true that I have done thee w
    But wrong for wrong : — this, c
        bride
The other victim of thy pride,
Thou knowest for me was destin
Thou saw'st, and coveted'st her ¢
    And with thy very crime — m}
    Thou taunted'st me — as little
A match ignoble for her arms,
Because, forsooth, I could not cl
The lawful heirship of thy name,
Nor sit on Este's lineal throne:
Yet, were a few short summers m
My name should more than Este
With honors all my own.
I had a sword — and have a bre£

That should have won as haught [1] a crest
As ever waved along the line
Of all these sovereign sires of thine.
Not always knightly spurs are worn
The brightest by the better born;
And mine have lanced my courser's flank
Before proud chiefs of princely rank,
When charging to the cheering cry
Of ' Este and of Victory ! '
I will not plead the cause of crime,
Nor sue thee to redeem from time
A few brief hours or days that must
At length roll o'er my reckless dust; —
Such maddening moments as my past,
They could not, and they did not, last.
Albeit my birth and name be base,
And thy nobility of race
Disdained to deck a thing like me —
  Yet in my lineaments they trace
Some features of my father's face,
And in my spirit — all of thee.
From thee — this tamelessness of heart —
From thee — nay, wherefore dost thou
    start ? —
From thee in all their vigor came
My arm of strength, my soul of flame —
Thou didst not give me life alone,
But all that made me more thine own.
See what thy guilty love hath done!
Repaid thee with too like a son!
I am no bastard in my soul,
For that, like thine, abhorred control:
And for my breath, that hasty boon
Thou gav'st and wilt resume so soon,
I valued it no more than thou,
When rose thy casque above thy brow,
And we, all side by side, have striven,
And o'er the dead our coursers driven:
The past is nothing — and at last
The future can but be the past;
Yet would I that I then had died:
  For though thou work'dst my mother's ill,
And made thy own my destined bride,
  I feel thou art my father still;
And, harsh as sounds thy hard decree,
'Tis not unjust, although from thee.
Begot in sin, to die in shame,
My life begun and ends the same:
As erred the sire, so erred the son,
And thou must punish both in one.
My crime seems worse to human view,
But God must judge between us too!"

XIV.

He ceased — and stood with folded arms,
On which the circling fetters sounded;
And not an ear but felt as wounded,
Of all the chiefs that there were ranked,

[1] Haught — haughty. — "Away, *haught* man, thou art insulting me." — *Shakspeare.*

When those dull chains in meeting
    clanked:
Till Parisina's fatal charms [2]
Again attracted every eye —
Would she thus hear him doomed to die!
She stood, I said, all pale and still,
The living cause of Hugo's ill:
Her eyes unmoved, but full and wide,
Not once had turned to either side —
Nor once did those sweet eyelids close
Or shade the glance o'er which they rose.
But round their orbs of deepest blue
The circling white dilated grew —
And there with glassy gaze she stood
As ice were in her curdled blood;
But every now and then a tear
  So large and slowly gathered slid
From the long dark fringe of that fair lid,
It was a thing to see, not hear!
And those who saw, it did surprise,
Such drops could fall from human eyes.
To speak she thought — the imperfect note
Was choked within her swelling throat,
Yet seemed in that low hollow groan
Her whole heart gushing in the tone.
It ceased — again she thought to speak,
Then burst her voice in one long shriek,
And to the earth she fell like stone
Or statue from its base o'erthrown,
More like a thing that ne'er had life, —
A monument of Azo's wife, —
Than her, that living guilty thing,
Whose every passion was a sting,
Which urged to guilt, but could not bear
That guilt's detection and despair.
But yet she lived — and all too soon
Recovered from that death-like swoon —
But scarce to reason — every sense
Had been o'erstrung by pangs intense;
And each frail fibre of her brain

[2] ["I sent for 'Marmion,' because it occurred to me, there might be a resemblance between part of 'Parisina,' and a similar scene in the second canto of 'Marmion.' I fear there is, though I never thought of it before, and could hardly wish to imitate that which is inimitable. I wish you would ask Mr. Gifford whether I ought to say any thing upon it. I had completed the story on the passage from Gibbon, which indeed leads to a like scene naturally, without a thought of- the kind: but it comes upon me not very comfortably." — *Lord Byron to Mr. M.*, February 3, 1816. — The scene referred to is the one in which Constance de Beverley appears before the conclave —
  "Her look composed, and steady eye,
  Bespoke a matchless constancy;
  And there she stood so calm and pale,
  That, but her breathing did not fail,
  And motion slight of eye and head,
  And of her bosom, warranted,
  That neither sense nor pulse she lacks,
  You must have thought a form of wax,
  Wrought to the very life, was there —
  So still she was, so pale, so fair."]

(As bowstrings, when relaxed by rain,
The erring arrow launch aside)
Sent forth her thoughts all wild and wide —
The past a blank, the future black,
With glimpses of a dreary track,
Like lightning on the desert path,
When midnight storms are mustering wrath.
She feared — she felt that something ill
Lay on her soul, so deep and chill —
That there was sin and shame she knew;
That some one was to die — but who ?
She had forgotten : — did she breathe ?
Could this be still the earth beneath,
The sky above, and men around ;
Or were they fiends who now so frowned
On one, before whose eyes each eye
Till then had smiled in sympathy ?
All was confused and undefined
To her all jarred and wandering mind ;
A chaos of wild hopes and fears :
And now in laughter, now in tears,
But madly still in each extreme,
She strove with that convulsive dream ;
For so it seemed on her to break:
Oh ! vainly must she strive to wake !

XV.

The Convent bells are ringing,
 But mournfully and slow;
In the gray square turret swinging,
 With a deep sound, to and fro.
Heavily to the heart they go !
Hark ! the hymn is singing —
 The song for the dead below,
 Or the living who shortly shall be so !
For a departing being's soul
The death-hymn peals and the hollow bells
 knoll :
He is near his mortal goal;
Kneeling at the Friar's knee:
Sad to hear — and piteous to see —
Kneeling on the bare cold ground,
With the block before and the guards
 around —
And the headsman with his bare arm ready,
That the blow may be both swift and steady,
Feels if the axe be sharp and true —
Since he set its edge anew :
While the crowd in a speechless circle gather
To see the Son fall by the doom of the
 Father !

XVI.

It is a lovely hour as yet
Before the summer sun shall set,
Which rose upon that heavy day,
And mocked it with his steadiest ray;
And his evening beams are shed
Full on Hugo's fated head,
As his last confession pouring
To the monk, his doom deploring.
In penitential holiness,

He bends to hear his accents bl
With absolution such as may
Wipe our mortal stains away.
That high sun on his head did
As he there did bow and listen
And the rings of chestnut hair
Curled half down his neck so b.
But brighter still the beam was
Upon the axe which near him s
With a clear and ghastly glitter
Oh ! that parting hour was bitte
Even the stern stood chilled witl
Dark the crime, and just the law
Yet they shuddered as they saw.

XVII.

The parting prayers are said an
Of that false son — and daring lc
His beads and sins are all recou
His hours to their last minute m
His mantling cloak before was s
His bright brown locks must now
'Tis done — all closely are they :
The vest which till this moment
The scarf which Parisina gave
Must not adorn him to the grave
Even that must now be thrown a
And o'er his eyes the kerchief tie
But no — that last indignity
Shall ne'er approach his haughty
All feelings seemingly subdued,
In deep disdain were half renewe
When headsman's hands prepare
Those eyes which would not b
 blind :
As if they dared not look on deat
" No — yours my forfeit blood anc
These hands are chained — but I
At least with an unshackled eye —
Strike : " — and as the word he sa
Upon the block he bowed his hea
These the last accents Hugo spol
" Strike " — and flashing fell the s
Rolled the head — and, gushing, :
Back the stained and heaving tru
In the dust, which each deep veii
Slaked with its ensanguined rain
His eyes and lips a moment quiv
Convulsed and quick — then fix f
He died, as erring man should di
 Without display, without parad
 Meekly had he bowed and pra
 As not disdaining priestly aid,
Nor desperate of all hope on higl
And while before the Prior kneeli
His heart was weaned from earth
His wrathful sire — his paramour
What were they in such an hour !
No more reproach — no more de:
No thought but heaven — no
 prayer —
Save the few which from him bro

When, bared to meet the headsman's
    stroke,
He claimed to die with eyes unbound,
His sole adieu to those around.

XVIII.

Still as the lips that closed in death,
Each gazer's bosom held his breath:
But yet, afar, from man to man,
A cold electric shiver ran,
As down the deadly blow descended
On him whose life and love thus ended;
And, with a hushing sound compressed,
A sigh shrunk back on every breast;
But no more thrilling noise rose there,
    Beyond the blow that to the block
    Pierced through with forced and sullen
       shock,
Save one: — what cleaves the silent air
So madly shrill, so passing wild?
That, as a mother's o'er her child,
Done to death by sudden blow,
To the sky these accents go,
Like a soul's in endless woe.
Through Azo's palace-lattice driven,
That horrid voice ascends to heaven,
And every eye is turned thereon;
But sound and sight alike are gone!
It was a woman's shriek — and ne'er
In madlier accents rose despair;
And those who heard it, as it passed,
In mercy wished it were the last.

XIX.

Hugo is fallen; and, from that hour,
No more in palace, hall, or bower,
Was Parisina heard or seen:
Her name — as if she ne'er had been —
Was banished from each lip and ear,
Like words of wantonness or fear;
And from Prince Azo's voice, by none
Was mention heard of wife or son;
No tomb — no memory had they;
Theirs was unconsecrated clay;
At least the knight's who died that day.
But Parisina's fate lies hid
Like dust beneath the coffin lid:
Whether in convent she abode,
And won to heaven her dreary road,
By blighted and remorseful years
Or scourge, and fast, and sleepless tears;
Or if she fell by bowl or steel,
For that dark love she dared to feel;
Or if, upon the moment smote,
She died by tortures less remote;
Like him she saw upon the block,
With heart that shared the headsman's
    shock,
In quickened brokenness that came,
In pity, o'er her shattered frame,
None knew — and none can ever know:

But whatsoe'er its end below,
Her life began and closed in woe!

XX.

And Azo found another bride,
And goodly sons grew by his side;
But none so lovely and so brave
As him who withered in the grave;
Or if they were — on his cold eye
Their growth but glanced unheeded by,
Or noticed with a smothered sigh.
But never tear his cheek descended,
And never smile his brow unbended;
And o'er that fair broad brow were wrough'
The intersected lines of thought;
Those furrows which the burning share
Of Sorrow ploughs untimely there;
Scars of the lacerating mind
Which the Soul's war doth leave behind.
He was past all mirth or woe:
Nothing more remained below
But sleepless nights and heavy days,
A mind all dead to scorn or praise,
A heart which shunned itself — and yet
That would not yield — nor could forget
Which, when it least appeared to melt,
Intensely thought — intensely felt:
The deepest ice which ever froze
Can only o'er the surface close —
The living stream lies quick below,
And flows — and cannot cease to flow.
Still was his sealed-up bosom haunted
By thoughts which Nature hath im-
    planted;
Too deeply rooted thence to vanish,
Howe'er our stifled tears we banish;
When, struggling as they rise to start,
We check those waters of the heart,
They are not dried — those tears unshed
But flow back to the fountain head,
And resting in their spring more pure,
For ever in its depth endure,
Unseen, unwept, but uncongealed,
And cherished most where least revealed.
With inward starts of feeling left,
To throb o'er those of life bereft;
Without the power to fill again
The desert gap which made his pain;
Without the hope to meet them where
United souls shall gladness share,
With all the consciousness that he
Had only passed a just decree;
That they had wrought their doom of ill;
Yet Azo's age was wretched still.
The tainted branches of the tree,
    If lopped with care, a strength may
      give,
By which the rest shall bloom and live
All greenly fresh and wildly free:
But if the lightning, in its wrath,
The waving boughs with fury scathe,

The massy trunk the ruin feels,
And never more a leaf reveals.[1]

of horror, perhaps, in the circumstances; but the writing is beautiful throughout, and the whole wrapped in a rich and redundant veil of poetry, where every thing breathes the pure essence of genius and sensibility. — *Jeffrey*.]

[1] [In Parisina there is no tumult or stir. It is all sadness, and pity, and terror. There is too much

THE PRISONER OF CHILLON: A FABLE.[1]

SONNET ON CHILLON.

ETERNAL Spirit of the chainless Mind![2]
  Brightest in dungeons, Liberty! thou art,
  For there thy habitation is the heart —
The heart which love of thee alone can bind;
And when thy sons to fetters are consigned —
  To fetters, and the damp vault's dayless gloom,
  Their country conquers with their martyrdom,
And Freedom's fame finds wings on every wind.
Chillon! thy prison is a holy place,
  And thy sad floor an altar — for 'twas trod,
Until his very steps have left a trace
  Worn, as if thy cold pavement were a sod,
By Bonnivard! — May none those marks efface!
  For they appeal from tyranny to God.

ADVERTISEMENT.

WHEN this poem was composed, I was not sufficiently aware of the history of Bonnivard, or I should have endeavored to dignify the subject by an attempt to celebrate his courage and his virtues. With some account of his life I have been furnished, by the kindness of a citizen of that republic, which is still proud of the memory of a man worthy of the best age of ancient freedom: —

"François de Bonnivard, fils de Louis de Bonnivard, originaire de Seyssel et Seigneur de Lunes, naquit en 1496. Il fit ses études à Turin : en 1510 Jean Aimé de Bonnivard, son oncle, lui résigna le Prieuré de St. Victor, qui aboutissoit aux murs de Genève, et qui formoit un bénéfice considérable.

[1] [Byron wrote this poem at a small inn, in the little village of Ouchy, near Lausanne, where he happened, in June, 1816, to be detained two days by stress of weather; "thereby adding," says Moore, "one more deathless association to the already immortalized localities of the Lake."]

[2] [In the first draught, the sonnet opens thus —
        " Beloved Goddess of the chainless mind!
          Brightest in dungeons, Liberty! thou art,
          Thy palace is within the Freeman's heart,
        Whose soul the love of thee alone can bind;
        And when thy sons to fetters are consigned —
          To fetters, and the damp vault's dayless gloom,
        Thy joy is with them still, and unconfined,
          Their country conquers with their martyrdom."]

"Ce grand homme — (Bonnivard mérite ce titre par la force des on âme, la droiture deson cœur, la noblesse de ses intentions. la sagesse de ses conseils, le courage de ses démarches, l'étendue de ses connaissances et la vivacité de son esprit), — ce grand homme, qui excitera l'admiration de tous ceux qu'une vertu héroïque peut encore émouvoir, inspirera encore la plus vive reconnaissance dans les cœurs des Génévois qui aiment Genève. Bonnivard en fut toujours un des plus fermes appuis: pour assurer la liberté de notre République, il ne craignit pas de perdre souvent la sienne; il oublia son repos; il méprisa ses richesses; il ne négligea rien pour affermir le bonheur d'une patrie qu'il honora de son choix: dès ce moment il la chérit comme le plus zélé de ses citoyens; il la servit avec l'intrépidité d'un héros, et il écrivit son Histoire avec la naïveté d'un philosophe et la chaleur d'un patriote.

"Il dit dans le commencement de son Histoire de Genève, que, *dès qu'il eut commencé de lire l'histoire des nations, il se entit entrainé par son goût pour les Républiques, dont il épousa toujours les intérêts : c'est* ce goût pour la liberté qui lui fit sans doute adopter Genève pour sa patrie.

"Bonnivard, encore jeune, s'annonça hautement comme le défenseur de Genève contre le Duc de Savoye et l'Evêque.

"En 1519, Bonnivard devient le martyr de sa patrie: Le Duc de Savoye étant entré dans Genève avec cinq cent hommes, Bonnivard craint le ressentiment du Duc; il volut se retirer à Fribourg pour en éviter les suites; mais il fut trahi par deux hommes qui l'accompagnoient, et conduit par ordre du Prince à Grolée, où il resta prisonnier pendant deux ans. Bonnivard étoit malheureux dans ses voyages: comme ses malheurs n'avoient point ralenti son zèle pour Genève, il étoit toujours un ennemi redoutable pour ceux qui la menaçoient, et par conséquent il devoit être exposé à leurs coups. Il fut rencontré en 1530 sur le Jura par des voleurs, qui le dépouillèrent, et qui le mirent encore entre les main du Duc de Savoye: ce prince le fit en fermer dans le Château de Chillon, où il resta sans être interrogé jusques en 1536; il fut alors delivré par les Bernois, qui s'emparèrent du Pays de Vaud.

"Bonnivard, en sortant de sa captivité, eut le plaisir de trouver Genève libre et réformée: la République s'empressa de lui témoigner sa reconnaissance, et de le dédommager des maux qu'il avoit soufferts; elle le reçut Bourgeois de la ville au mois de Juin, 1536; elle lui donna la maison habitée autrefois par le Vicaire-Général, et elle lui assigna une pension de deux cent écus d'or tant qu'il séjourneroit à Genève. Il fut admis dans le Conseil de Deux-Cent en 1537.

"Bonnivard n'a pas fini d'être utile: après avoir travaillé à rendre Genève libre, il réussit à la rendre tolérante. Bonnivard engagea le Conseil à accorder aux ecclésiastiques et aux paysans un tems suffisant pour examiner les propositions qu'on leur faisoit; il réussit par sa douceur: on prêche toujours le Christianisme avec succès quand on le prêche avec charité.

"Bonnivard fut savant: ses manuscrits, qui sont dans la Bibliothèque publique, prouvent qu'il avoit bien lu les auteurs classiques latins, et qu'il avoir approfondi la théologie et l'histoire. Ce grand homme aimoit les sciences, et il croyoit qu'elles pouvoient faire la gloire de Genève; aussi il ne négligea rien pour les fixer dans cette ville naissante; en 1551 il donna sa bibliothèque au publique; elle fut le commencement de notre bibliothèque publique; et ces livres sont en partie les rares et belles éditions du quinzième siècle qu'on voit dans notre collection. Enfin, pendant la même année, ce bon patriote institua la République son héritière, à condition qu'elle employeroit ses biens à entretenir le collège dont on projettoit la fondation.

"Il paroit que Bonnivard mourut en 1570; mais on ne peut l'assurer, parcequ'il y a une lacune dans le Nécrologe depuis le mois de Juillet, 1570, jusques en 1571."

I.

My hair is gray, but not with years,
　Nor grew it white
　In a single night,[1]
As men's have grown from sudden fears.

My limbs are bowed, though not with toil,
　But rusted with a vile repose,[2]
For they have been a dungeon's spoil,
　And mine has been the fate of those

[1] Ludovico Sforza, and others. — The same is asserted of Marie Antoinette's, the wife of Louis the Sixteenth, though not in quite so short a period.

[2] Grief is said to have the same effect: to such, and not to fear, this change in *hers* was to be attributed.

　[Original MS. —

　"But with the inward waste of grief."]

To whom the goodly earth and air
Are banned, and barred — forbidden fare;
But this was for my father's faith
I suffered chains and courted death;
That father perished at the stake
For tenets he would not forsake;
And for the same his lineal race
In darkness found a dwelling-place;
We were seven — who now are one,
  Six in youth and one in age,
Finished as they had begun,
  Proud of Persecution's rage; [1]
One in fire, and two in field,
Their belief with blood have sealed:
Dying as their father died,
For the God their foes denied;—
Three were in a dungeon cast,
Of whom this wreck is left the last.

II.

There are seven pillars of Gothic mould,
In Chillon's dungeons deep and old,
There are seven columns massy and gray,
Dim with a dull imprisoned ray,
A sunbeam which hath lost its way,
And through the crevice and the cleft
Of the thick wall is fallen and left:
Creeping o'er the floor so damp,
Like a marsh's meteor lamp:
And in each pillar there is a ring,
  And in each ring there is a chain;
That iron is a cankering thing,
  For in these limbs its teeth remain,
With marks that will not wear away,
Till I have done with this new day,
Which now is painful to these eyes,
Which have not seen the sun so rise
For years — I cannot count them o'er,
I lost their long and heavy score
When my last brother drooped and died,
And I lay living by his side.

III.

They chained us each to a column stone,
And we were three — yet, each alone:
We could not move a single pace,
We could not see each other's face,
But with that pale and livid light
That made us strangers in our sight:
And thus together — yet apart,
Fettered in hand, but joined in heart;
'Twas still some solace, in the dearth
Of the pure elements of earth,
To harken to each other's speech,
And each turn comforter to each
With some new hope or legend old,
Or song heroically bold;
But even these at length grew cold.
Our voices took a dreary tone,

An echo of the dungeon stone,
  A grating sound — not full and free
As they of yore were wont to be;
  It might be fancy — but to me
They never sounded like our own.

IV.

I was the eldest of the three,
  And to uphold and cheer the rest
  I ought to do — and did my best —
And each did well in his degree.
  The youngest, whom my father loved,
Because our mother's brow was given
To him — with eyes as blue as heaven,
  For him my soul was sorely moved:
And truly might it be distressed
To see such bird in such a nest;
For he was beautiful as day —
  (When day was beautiful to me
  As to young eagles being free) —
A polar day, which will not see
A sunset till its summer's gone,
  Its sleepless summer of long light,
The snow-clad offspring of the sun:
  And thus he was as pure and bright,
And in his natural spirit gay,
With tears for nought but others' ills,
And then they flowed like mountain rills,
Unless he could assuage the woe
Which he abhorred to view below.

V.

The other was as pure of mind,
But formed to combat with his kind;
Strong in his frame, and of a mood
Which 'gainst the world in war had stood,
And perished in the foremost rank
  With joy: — but not in chains to pine:
His spirit withered with their clank,
  I saw it silently decline —
  And so perchance in sooth did mine:
But yet I forced it on to cheer
Those relics of a home so dear.
He was a hunter of the hills,
  Had followed there the deer and wolf;
  To him this dungeon was a gulf,
And fettered feet the worst of ills.

VI.

Lake Leman lies by Chillon's walls.
A thousand feet in depth below
Its massy waters meet and flow;
Thus much the fathom-line was sent
From Chillon's snow-white battlement,[2]

---

[1] [MS. —
  " Braving rancour — chains — and rage."]

[2] The Château de Chillon is situated between Clarens and Villeneuve, which last is at one extremity of the Lake of Geneva. On its left are the entrances of the Rhone, and opposite are the heights of Meillerie and the range of Alps above Boveret and St. Gingo. Near it, on a hill behind, is a torrent: below it, washing its walls, the lake has been fathomed to the depth of 800 feet, French

Which round about the wave inthrals:
A double dungeon wall and wave
Have made — and like a living grave.
Below the surface of the lake
The dark vault lies wherein we lay,
We heard it ripple night and day;
  Sounding o'er our heads it knocked
And I have felt the winter's spray
Wash through the bars when winds were high
And wanton in the happy sky;
  And then the very rock hath rocked,
  And I have felt it shake, unshocked,
Because I could have smiled to see
The death that would have set me free.

VII.

I said my nearer brother pined,
I said his mighty heart declined,
He loathed and put away his food;
It was not that 'twas coarse and rude,
For we were used to hunter's fare,
And for the like had little care:
The milk drawn from the mountain goat
Was changed for water from the moat,
Our bread was such as captive's tears
Have moistened many a thousand years,
Since man first pent his fellow men
Like brutes within an iron den;
But what were these to us or him ?
These wasted not his heart or limb;
My brother's soul was of that mould
Which in a palace had grown cold,
Had his free breathing been denied
The range of the steep mountain's side;
But why delay the truth ? — he died.[1]
I saw, and could not hold his head,
Nor reach his dying hand — nor dead, —
Though hard I strove, but strove in vain,
To rend and gnash [2] my bonds in twain.
He died — and they unlocked his chain,
And scooped for him a shallow grave
Even from the cold earth of our cave.
I begged them, as a boon, to lay
His corse in dust whereon the day

measure: within it are a range of dungeons, in which
the early reformers, and subsequently prisoners of
state, were confined. Across one of the vaults is a
beam black with age, on which we were informed
that the condemned were formerly executed. In
the cells are seven pillars, or, rather, eight, one
being half merged in the wall; in some of these are
rings for the fetters and the fettered: in the pave-
ment the steps of Bonnivard have left their traces.
He was confined here several years. It is by this
castle that Rousseau has fixed the catastrophe of
his Héloïse, in the rescue of one of her children by
Julie from the water; the shock of which, and the
illness produced by the immersion, is the cause of
her death. The château is large, and seen along
the lake for a great distance. The walls are white.

[1] [MS. —
  " But why withhold the blow? — he died."]

[2] [MS. — " To break or bite."]

Might shine — it was a foolish thought,
But then within my brain it wrought,
That even in death his freeborn breast
In such a dungeon could not rest.
I might have spared my idle prayer —
They coldly laughed — and laid him there:
The flat and turfless earth above
The being we so much did love;
His empty chain above it leant,
Such murder's fitting monument!

VIII.

But he, the favorite and the flower,
Most cherished since his natal hour,
His mother's image in fair face,
The infant love of all his race,
His martyred father's dearest thought,
My latest care, for whom I sought
To hoard my life, that his might be
Less wretched now, and one day free;
He, too, who yet had held untired
A spirit natural or inspired —
He, too, was struck, and day by day
Was withered on the stalk away.
Oh, God! it is a fearful thing
To see the human soul take wing
In any shape, in any mood: —
I've seen it rushing forth in blood,
I've seen it on the breaking ocean
Strive with a swoln convulsive motion,
I've seen the sick and ghastly bed
Of Sin delirious with its dread :
But these were horrors — this was woe
Unmixed with such — but sure and slow:
He faded, and so calm and meek,
So softly worn, so sweetly weak,
So tearless, yet so tender — kind,
And grieved for those he left behind;
With all the while a cheek whose bloom
Was as a mockery of the tomb,
Whose tints as gently sunk away
As a departing rainbow's ray —
An eye of most transparent light,
That almost made the dungeon bright,
And not a word of murmur — not
A groan o'er his untimely lot, —
A little talk of better days,
A little hope my own to raise,
For I was sunk in silence — lost
In this last loss, of all the most;
And then the sighs he would suppress
Of fainting nature's feebleness,
More slowly drawn, grew less and less:
I listened, but I could not hear —
I called, for I was wild with fear;
I knew 'twas hopeless, but my dread
Would not be thus admonished;
I called, and thought I heard a sound —
I burst my chain with one strong bound,
And rushed to him : — I found him not,
I only stirred in this black spot,
I only lived — *I* only drew

The accursed breath of dungeon-dew;
The last — the sole — the dearest link
Between me and the eternal brink,
Which bound me to my failing race,
Was broken in this fatal place.[1]
One on the earth, and one beneath —
My brothers — both had ceased to breathe:
I took that hand which lay so still,
Alas! my own was full as chill;
I had not strength to stir, or strive,
But felt that I was still alive —
A frantic feeling, when we know
That what we love shall ne'er be so.
　　I know not why
　　I could not die,
I had no earthly hope — but faith,
And that forbade a selfish death.

IX.

What next befell me then and there
　I.know not well — I never knew —
First came the loss of light, and air,
　And then of darkness too:
I had no thought, no feeling — none —
Among the stones I stood a stone,
And was, scarce conscious what I wist,
As shrubless crags within the mist;
For all was blank, and bleak, and gray,
It was not night — it was not day,
It was not even the dungeon-light,
So hateful to my heavy sight,
But vacancy absorbing space,
And fixedness — without a place;
There were no stars — no earth — no time —
No　check — no　change — no　good — no
　crime —
But silence, and a stirless breath
Which neither was of life nor death;
A sea of stagnant idleness,
Blind, boundless, mute, and motionless!

X.

A light broke in upon my brain, —
　It was the carol of a bird;
It ceased, and then it came again,
　The sweetest song ear ever heard,
And mine was thankful till my eyes
Ran over with the glad surprise,
And they that moment could not see
I was the mate of misery;
But then by dull degrees came back
My senses to their wonted track,
I saw the dungeon walls and floor
Close slowly round me as before,
I saw the glimmer of the sun
Creeping as it before had done,
But through the crevice where it came
That bird was perched, as fond and tame,
　And tamer than upon the tree;

---

[1] [The gentle decay and gradual extinction of the
youngest life is the most tender and beautiful pas-
sage in the poem. — *Jeffrey*.]

A lovely bird, with azure wings,
And song that said a thousand things,
　And seemed to say them all for me!
I never saw its like before,
I ne'er shall see its likeness more:
It seemed like me to want a mate,
But was not half so desolate,
And it was come to love me when
None lived to love me so again,
And cheering from my dungeon's brink,
Had brought me back to feel and think.
I know not if it late were free,
　Or broke its cage to perch on mine,
But knowing well captivity,
　Sweet bird! I could not wish for thine!
Or if it were, in winged guise,
A visitant from Paradise;
For — Heaven forgive that thought! the while
Which made me both to weep and smile;
I sometimes deemed that it might be
My brother's soul come down to me;
But then at last away it flew,
And then 'twas mortal — well I knew,
For he would never thus have flown,
And left me twice so doubly lone, —
Lone — as the corse within its shroud,
Lone — as a solitary cloud,
　A single cloud on a sunny day,
While all the rest of heaven is clear,
A frown upon the atmosphere,
That hath no business to appear
　When skies are blue, and earth is gay.

XI.

A kind of change came in my fate,
My keepers grew compassionate;
I know not what had made them so,
They were inured to sights of woe,
But so it was: — my broken chain
With links unfastened did remain,
And it was liberty to stride
Along my cell from side to side,
And up and down, and then athwart,
And tread it over every part;
And round the pillars one by one,
Returning where my walk begun,
Avoiding only, as I trod,
My brothers' graves without a sod;
For if I thought with heedless tread
My step profaned their lowly bed,
My breath came gaspingly and thick,
And my crushed heart fell blind and sick.

XII.

I made a footing in the wall,
　It was not therefrom to escape,
For I had buried one and all
Who loved me in a human shape;
And the whole earth would henceforth be
A wider prison unto me:
No child — no sire — no kin had I,
No partner in my misery;

I thought of this, and I was glad,
For thought of them had made me mad;
But I was curious to ascend
To my barred windows, and to bend
Once more, upon the mountains high
The quiet of a loving eye.

XIII.

I saw them — and they were the same,
They were not changed like me in frame;
I saw their thousand years of snow
On high — their wide long lake below,[1]
And the blue Rhone in fullest flow;
I heard the torrents leap and gush
O'er channelled rock and broken bush;
I saw the white-walled distant town,
And whiter sails go skimming down;
And then there was a little isle,[2]
Which in my very face did smile,
    The only one in view;
A small green isle, it seemed no more,
Scarce broader than my dungeon floor,
But in it there were three tall trees,
And o'er it blew the mountain breeze,
And by it there were waters flowing,
And on it there were young flowers growing,
    Of gentle breath and hue.
The fish swam by the castle wall,
And tl , seemed joyous each and all;
The eagle rode the rising blast,
Methought he never flew so fast
As then to me he seemed to fly,
And then new tears came in my eye,
And I felt troubled — and would fain
I had not left my recent chain;
And when I did descend again,
The darkness of my dim abode
Fell on me as a heavy load;
It was as is a new-dug grave,

---

[1] [MS. —
    "I saw them with their lake below,
    And their three thousand years of snow."]

[2] Between the entrances of the Rhone and Ville-
neuve, not far from Chillon, is a very small island;
the only one I could perceive, in my voyage round
and over the lake, within its circumference. It
contains a few trees (I think not above three), and
from its singleness and diminutive size has a pecu-
liar effect upon the view.

Closing o'er one we sought to save, —
And yet my glance, too much oppressed,
Had almost need of such a rest.

XIV.

It might be months, or years, or days,
    I kept no count — I took no note,
I had no hope my eyes to raise,
    And clear them of their dreary mote;
At last men came to set me free,
    I asked not why, and recked not where,
It was at length the same to me,
    Fettered or fetterless to be,
    I learned to love despair.
And thus when they appeared at last,
And all my bonds aside were cast,
These heavy walls to me had grown
A hermitage — and all my own!
And half I felt as they were come
To tear me from a second home:
With spiders I had friendship made,
And watched them in their sullen trade,
Had seen the mice by moonlight play,
And why should I feel less than they?
We were all inmates of one place,
And I, the monarch of each race,
Had power to kill — yet, strange to tell!
In quiet we had learned to dwell — [3]
My very chains and I grew friends,
So much a long communion tends
To make us what we are : — even I
Regained my freedom with a sigh.[4]

---

[3] [Here follow in MS. —
"Nor slew I of my subjects one —
    What sovereign { hath so little } hath done?"]
                  { yet so much }

[4] [It will readily be allowed that this singular
poem is more powerful than pleasing. The dun-
geon of Bonnivard is, like that of Ugolino, a sub-
ject too dismal for even the power of the painter or
poet to counteract its horrors. It is the more dis-
agreeable as affording human hope no anchor to rest
upon, and describing the sufferer, though a man of
talents and virtues, as altogether inert and power-
less under his accumulated sufferings; yet, as a
picture, however gloomy the coloring, it may rival
any which Lord Byron has drawn; nor is it possible
to read it without a sinking of the heart, corre-
sponding with that which he describes the victim to
have suffered. — *Sir Walter Scott.*]

MAZEPPA.

ADVERTISEMENT.

"CELUI qui remplissait alors cette place était un gentilhomme Polonais, nommé Mazeppa, né dans le palatinat de Padolie: il avait été élevé page de Jean Casimir, et avait pris à sa cour quelque teinture des belles-lettres. Une intrigue qu'il eut dans sa jeunesse avec la femme d'un gentilhomme Polonais ayant été découverte, le mari le fit lier tout nu sur un cheval farouche, et le laissa aller en cet état. Le cheval, qui était du pays de l'Ukraine, y retourna, et y porta Mazeppa, demi-mort de fatigue et de faim. Quelques paysans le secoururent: il resta longtems parmi eux, et se signala dans plusieurs courses contre les Tartares. La supériorité de ses lumières lui donna une grande considération parmi les Cosaques: sa réputation s'augmentant de jour en jour, obligea le Czar à le faire Prince de l'Ukraine." — VOLTAIRE, *Hist. de Charles XII.* p. 196.

"Le roi fuyant, et poursuivi, eut son cheval tué sous lui; le Colonel Gieta, blessé, et perdant tout son sang, lui donna le sien. Ainsi on remit deux fois à cheval, dans la fuite, ce conquérant qui n'avait pu y monter pendant la bataille." — p. 216.

"Le roi alla par un autre chemin avec quelques cavaliers. Le carrosse, où il était, rompit dans la marche; on le remit à cheval. Pour comble de disgrace, il s'égara pendant la nuit dans un bois; là, son courage ne pouvant plus suppléer à ses forces épuisées, les douleurs de sa blessure devenues plus insupportables par la fatigue, son cheval étant tombé de lassitude, il se coucha quelques heures au pied d'un arbre, en danger d'être surpris à tout moment par les vainqueurs, qui le cherchaient de tous côtés." — p. 218.

INTRODUCTION.

MAZEPPA was written at Venice and Ravenna in the autumn of 1818. Mr. Gifford terms it on the margin of the MS., a "lively, spirited, and pleasant tale;" and M. Villemain, the eminent French critic, declares that sublime in its substance and finishing with a joke, it is at once the master-piece and symbol of Byron. An English reviewer says: — "Mazeppa is a very fine and spirited sketch of a very noble story, and is every way worthy of its author. The story is a well-known one; namely, that of the young Pole, who, being bound naked on the back of a wild horse, on account of an intrigue with the lady of a certain great noble of his country, was carried by his steed into the heart of the Ukraine, and being there picked up by some Cossacks, in a state apparently of utter hopelessness and exhaustion, recovered, and lived to be long after the prince and leader of the nation among whom he had arrived in this extraordinary manner. Lord Byron has represented the strange and wild incidents of this adventure, as being related in a half serious, half sportive way, by Mazeppa himself, to no less a person than Charles the Twelfth of Sweden, in some of whose last campaigns, the Cossack Hetman took a distinguished part. He tells it during the desolate bivouack of Charles and the few friends who fled with him towards Turkey, after the bloody overthrow of Pultowa. There is not a little of beauty and gracefulness in this way of setting the picture; — the age of Mazeppa — the calm, practised indifference with which he now submits to the worst of fortune's deeds — the heroic, unthinking coldness of the royal madman to whom he speaks — the dreary and perilous accompaniments of the scene around the speaker and the audience, — all contribute to throw a very striking charm both of preparation and of contrast over the wild story of the Hetman. Nothing can be more beautiful, in like manner, than the account of the love — the guilty love — the fruits of which had been so miraculous."

I.

'TWAS after dread Pultowa's day,
  When fortune left the royal Swede,
Around a slaughtered army lay,
  No more to combat and to bleed.
The power and glory of the war,
  Faithless as their vain votaries, men,
Had passed to the triumphant Czar,
  And Moscow's walls were safe again,
Until a day more dark and drear,
And a more memorable year,
Should give to slaughter and to shame
A mightier host and haughtier name;
A greater wreck, a deeper fall,
A shock to one—a thunderbolt to all.

II.

Such was the hazard of the die;
The wounded Charles was taught to fly
By day and night through field and flood,
Stained with his own and subjects' blood;
For thousands fell that flight to aid:
And not a voice was heard t' upbraid
Ambition in his humbled hour,
When truth had nought to dread from power.
His horse was slain, and Gieta gave
His own—and died the Russians' slave.
This too sinks after many a league
Of well sustained, but vain fatigue;
And in *y* ' depth of forests, darkling
The wat :-fires in the distance sparkling—
  The beacons of surrounding foes—
A king must lay his limbs at length.
  Are these the laurels and repose
For which the nations strain their strength?
They laid him by a savage tree,
In outworn nature's agony;
His wounds were stiff—his limbs were stark—
The heavy hour was chill and dark;
The fever in his blood forbade
A transient slumber's fitful aid:
And thus it was; but yet through all,
Kinglike the monarch bore his fall,
And made, in this extreme of ill,
His pangs the vassals of his will:
All silent and subdued were they,
As once the nations round him lay.

III.

A band of chiefs!—alas! how few,
  Since but the fleeting of a day
Had thinned it; but this wreck was true
  And chivalrous: upon the clay
Each sate him down, all sad and mute,
  Beside his monarch and his steed,
For danger levels man and brute,
  And all are fellows in their need.
Among the rest, Mazeppa made
His pillow in an old oak's shade—
Himself as rough, and scarce less old,
The Ukraine's hetman, calm and bold;
But first, outspent with this long course,

The Cossack prince rubbed down his horse,
And made for him a leafy bed,
  And smoothed his fetlocks and his mane,
  And slacked his girth, and stripped his rein,
And joyed to see how well he fed;
For until now he had the dread
His wearied courser might refuse
To browse beneath the midnight dews:
But he was hardy as his lord,
And little cared for bed and board;
But spirited and docile too;
Whate'er was to be done, would do.
Shaggy and swift, and strong of limb,
All Tartar-like he carried him;
Obeyed his voice, and came to call,
And knew him in the midst of all:
Though thousands were around,—and Night,
Without a star, pursued her flight,—
That steed from sunset until dawn
His chief would follow like a fawn.

IV.

This done, Mazeppa spread his cloak,
And laid his lance beneath his oak,
Felt if his arms in order good
The long day's march had well withstood—
If still the powder filled the pan,
  And flints unloosened kept their lock—
His sabre's hilt and scabbard felt,
And whether they had chafed his belt—
And next the venerable man,
From out his haversack and can,
  Prepared and spread his slender stock;
And to the monarch and his men
The whole or portion offered then
With far less of inquietude
Than courtiers at a banquet would.
And Charles of this his slender share
With smiles partook a moment there,
To force of cheer a greater show,
And seem above both wounds and woe,—
And then he said—" Of all our band,
Though firm of heart and strong of hand,
In skirmish, march, or forage, none
Can less have said or more have done
Than thee, Mazeppa! On the earth
So fit a pair had never birth,
Since Alexander's days till now,
As thy Bucephalus and thou:
All Scythia's fame to thine should yield
For pricking on o'er flood and field."
Mazeppa answered—" Ill betide
The school wherein I learned to ride!"
Quoth Charles—" Old Hetman, wherefore so
Since thou hast learned the art so well?"
Mazeppa said—" 'Twere long to tell;
And we have many a league to go,
With every now and then a blow,
And ten to one at least the foe,
Before our steeds may graze at ease,
Beyond the swift Borysthenes:
And, sire, your limbs have need of rest,

And I will be the sentinel
Of this your troop."—" But I request,"
Said Sweden's monarch, " thou wilt tell
This tale of thine, and I may reap,
Perchance, from this the boon of sleep;
For at this moment from my eyes
The hope of present slumber flies."

" Well, sire, with such a hope, I'll track
My seventy years of memory back:
I think 'twas in my twentieth spring,—
Ay, 'twas,—when Casimir was king—
John Casimir,—I was his page
Six summers, in my earlier age:
A learned monarch, faith! was he,
And most unlike your majesty:
He made no wars, and did not gain
New realms to lose them back again;
And (save debates in Warsaw's diet)
He reigned in most unseemly quiet;
Not that he had no cares to vex,
He loved the muses and the sex;
And sometimes these so froward are,
They made him wish himself at war;
But soon his wrath being o'er, he took
Another mistress, or new book:
And then he gave prodigious fêtes —
All Warsaw gathered round his gates
To gaze upon his splendid court,
And dames, and chiefs, of princely port:
He was the Polish Solomon,
So sung his poets, all but one,
Who, being unpensioned, made a satire,
And boasted that he could not flatter.
It was a court of jousts and mimes,
Where every courtier tried at rhymes;
Even I for once produced some verses,
And signed my odes ' Despairing Thyrsis.'
There was a certain Palatine,
　A count of far and high descent,
Rich as a salt or silver mine; [1]
And he was proud, ye may divine,
　As if from heaven he had been sent:
He had such wealth in blood and ore
　As few could match beneath the throne;
And he would gaze upon his store,
And o'er his pedigree would pore,
Until by some confusion led,
Which almost looked like want of head,
He thought their merits were is own.
His wife was not of his opinion —
　His junior she by thirty years —
Grew daily tired of his dominion;
　And, after wishes, hope:, and fears,
　To virtue a few farewell tears,
A restless dream or two, some glances
At Warsaw's youth, some songs, and dances
Awaited but the usual chances,

Those happy accidents which render
The coldest dames so very tender,
To deck her Count with titles given,
'Tis said, as passports into heaven;
But, strange to say, they rarely boast
Of these, who have deserved them most.

V.

" I was a goodly stripling then;
　At seventy years I so may say,
That there were few, or boys or men,
　Who, in my dawning time of day,
Of vassal or of knight's degree,
Could vie in vanities with me;
For I had strength, youth, gaiety,
A port, not like to this ye see,
But smooth, as all is rugged now;
　For time, and care, and war, have ploughed
My very soul from out my brow;
　And thus I should be disavowed
By all my kind and kin, could they
Compare my day and yesterday;
This change was wrought, too, long ere age
Had ta'en my features for his page:
With years, ye know, have not declined
My strength, my courage, or my mind,
Or at this hour I should not be
Telling old tales beneath a tree,
With starless skies my canopy.
But let me on: Theresa's form —
Methinks it glides before me now,
Between me and yon chestnut's bough,
The memory is so quick and warm;
And yet I find no words to tell
The shape of her I loved so well:
She had the Asiatic eye,
　Such as our Turkish neighborhood,
　Hath mingled with our Polish blood,
Dark as above us is the sky;
But through it stole a tender light,
Like the first moonrise of midnight;
Large, dark, and swimming in the stream,
Which seemed to melt to its own beam;
All love, half languor, and half fire,
Like saints that at the stake expire,
And lift their raptured looks on high,
As though it were a joy to die. [2]
A brow like a midsummer lake,
　Transparent with the sun therein,
When waves no murmur dare to make,
　And heaven beholds her face within.
A cheek and lip — but why proceed?
　I loved her then — I love her still;
And such as I am, love indeed
　In fierce extremes — in good and ill.
But still we love even in our rage,
And haunted to our very age
With the vain shadow of the past,
As is Mazeppa to the last.

---

[1] This comparison of a "*salt* mine" may, per-
haps, be permitted to a Pope, as the wealth of the
country consists greatly in the salt mines.

[2] [MS. — "Until it proves a joy to die."]

VI.

"We met—we gazed—I saw, and sighed,
She did not speak, and yet replied;
There are ten thousand tones and signs
We hear and see, but none defines—
Involuntary sparks of thought,
Which strike from out the heart o'erwrought,
And form a strange intelligence,
Alike mysterious and intense,
Which link the burning chain that binds,
Without their will, young hearts and minds;
Conveying, as the electric wire,
We know not how, the absorbing fire.—
I saw, and sighed—in silence wept,
And still reluctant distance kept,
Until I was made known to her,
And we might then and there confer
Without suspicion—then, even then,
   I longed, and was resolved to speak;
But on my lips they died again,
   The accents tremulous and weak,
Until one hour.—There is a game,
   A frivolous and foolish play,
   Wherewith we while away the day;
It is—I have forgot the name—
And we this, it seems, were set,
By some strange chance, which I forget:
I recked not if I won or lost,
   It was enough for me to be
   So near to hear, and oh! to see
The being whom I loved the most.—
I watched her as a sentinel,
(May ours this dark night watch as well!)
Until I saw, and thus it was,
That she was pensive, nor perceived
Her occupation, nor was grieved
Nor glad to lose or gain; but still
Played on for hours, as if her will
Yet bound her to the place, though not
That hers might be the winning lot.[1]
Then through my brain the thought did pass
Even as a flash of lightning there,
That there was something in her air
Which would not doom me to despair;
And on the thought my words broke forth,
   All incoherent as they were—
   Their eloquence was little worth,
But yet she listened—'tis enough—
   Who listens once will listen twice;
   Her heart, be sure, is not of ice,
And one refusal no rebuff.

VII.

"I loved, and was beloved again—
   They tell me, Sire, you never knew
   Those gentle frailties; if 'tis true,
I shorten all my joy or pain;
To you 'twould seem absurd as vain;

But all men are not born to reign,
Or o'er their passions, or as you
Thus o'er themselves and nations too.
I am—or rather *was*—a prince,
   A chief of thousands, and could lead
   Them on where each would foremost
      bleed
But could not o'er myself evince
The like control—But to resume:
   I loved and was beloved again;
In sooth, it is a happy doom,
   But yet where happiest ends in pain.—
We met in secret, and the hour
Which led me to that lady's bower
Was fiery expectation's dower.
My days and nights were nothing—all
Except that hour which doth recall
In the long lapse from youth to age
   No other like itself—I'd give
   The Ukraine back again to live
It o'er once more—and be a page,
The happy page, who was the lord
Of one soft heart, and his own sword,
And had no other gem nor wealth
Save nature's gift of youth and health.—
We met in secret—doubly sweet,
Some say, they find it so to meet;
I know not that—I would have given
   My life but to have called her mine
In the full view of earth and heaven;
   For I did oft and long repine
That we could only meet by stealth.

VIII.

"For lovers there are many eyes,
   And such there were on us;—the devil
   On such occasions should be civil—
The devil!—I'm loth to do him wrong,
   It might be some untoward saint,
Who would not be at rest too long,
   But to his pious bile gave vent—
But one fair night, some lurking spies
Surprised and seized us both.
The Count was something more than wroth—
I was unarmed; but if in steel,
All cap-à-pie from head to heel,
What 'gainst their numbers could I do?—
'Twas near his castle, far away
   From city or from succor near,
And almost on the break of day;
I did not think to see another,
   My moments seemed reduced to few;
And with one prayer to Mary Mother,
   And, it may be, a saint or two,
As I resigned me to my fate,
They led me to the castle gate:
   Theresa's doom I never knew,
Our lot was henceforth separate.—
An angry man, ye may opine,
Was he, the proud Count Palatine;
And he had reason good to be,

---

[1] [MS.—   —— "but not
For that which we had both forgot."]

But he was most enraged lest such
An accident should chance to touch
Upon his future pedigree;
Nor less amazed, that such a blot
His noble 'scutcheon should have got,
While he was highest of his line;
  Because unto himself he seemed
The first of men, nor less he deemed
In others' eyes, and most in mine.
'Sdeath! with a *page* — perchance a king
Had reconciled him to the thing;
But with a stripling of a page —
I felt — but cannot paint his rage.

        IX.

"'Bring forth the horse!'— the horse was
    brought
  In truth he was a noble steed,
  A Tartar of the Ukraine breed,
Who looked as though the speed of thought
Where in his limbs; but he was wild,
  Wild as the wild deer, and untaught,
With spur and bridle undefiled —
'Twas but a day he had been caught;
And snorting, with erected mane,
And struggling fiercely, but in vain,
In the full foam of wrath and dread
To me the desert-born was led:
They bound me on, that menial throng,
Upon his back with many a thong;
Then loosed him with a sudden lash —
Away! — away! — and on we dash! —
Torrents less rapid and less rash.

        X.

" Away! — away! — My breath was gone —
I saw not where he hurried on:
'Twas scarcely yet the break of day,
And on he foamed — away! — away! —
The last of human sounds which rose,
As I was darted from my foes,
Was the wild shout of savage laughter,
Which on the wind came roaring after
A moment from that rabble rout:
With sudden wrath I wrenched my head,
  And snapped the cord, which to the mane
  Had bound my neck in lieu of rein,
And, writhing half my form about,
Howled back my curse; but 'midst the tread,
The thunder of my courser's speed,
Perchance they did not hear nor heed:
It vexes me — for I would fain
Have paid their insult back again.
I paid it well in after days:
There is not of that castle gate,
Its drawbridge and portcullis' weight,
Stone, bar, moat, bridge, or barrier left;
Nor of its fields a blade of grass,
  Save what grows on a ridge of wall,
  Where stood the hearth-stone of the hall;
And many a time ye there might pass,
Nor dream that e'er that fortress was:

I saw its turrets in a blaze,
Their crackling battlements all (
  And the hot lead pour down 1
From off the scorched and blac|
Whose thickness was not venge!
  They little thought that day of
When launched, as on the lightı
They bade me to destruction da'
  That one day I should come {
With twice five thousand horse,|
  The Count for his uncourteou
They played me then a bitter pr;
  When, with the wild horse for
They bound me to his foaming |
At length I played them one as {
For time at last sets all things ev
  And if we do but watch the h(
There never yet was human p(
Which could evade, if unforgive
The patient search and vigil lon;
Of him who treasures up a wron;

        XI.

" Away, away, my steed and I,
  Upon the pinions of the wind,
  All human dwellings left behin
We sped like meteors through th
When with its crackling sound th
Is chequered with the northern li
Town — village — none were on (
  But a wild plain of far extent,
And bounded by a forest black;
And, save the scarce seen b.ttl(
On distant heights of some stron;
Against the Tartars built of old,
No trace of man. The year befo;
A Turkish army had marched o'(
And where the Spahi's hoof hath
The verdure flies the bloody sod
The sky was dull, and dim, and g
  And a low breeze crept moanir
I could have answered with a s
But fast we fled, away, away —
And I could neither sigh nor pra
And my cold sweat-drops fell lik(
Upon the courser's bristling man
But, snorting still with rage and f
He flew upon his far career:
At times I almost thought, indee(
He must have slackened in his sı
But no — my bound and slender
  Was nothing to his angry migh
And merely like a spur became:
Each motion which I made to fre
My swoln limbs from their agony
  Increased his fury and affright
I tried my voice, — 'twas faint an(
But yet he swerved as from a blo'
And, starting to each accent, spra
As from a sudden trumpet's clan;
Meantime my cords were wet wit
Which, oozing through my limbs

And in my tongue the thirst became
A something fierier far than flame.

XII.

" We neared the wild wood — 'twas so wide,
I saw no bounds on either side;
'Twas studded with old sturdy trees,
That bent not to the roughest breeze
Which howls down from Siberia's waste,
And strips the forest in its haste, —
But these were few, and far between
Set thick with shrubs more young and green,
Luxuriant with their annual leaves,
Ere strown by those autumnal eves
That nip the forest's foliage dead,
Discolored with a lifeless red,
Which stands thereon like stiffened gore
Upon the slain when battle's o'er,
And some long winter's night hath shed
Its frost o'er every tombless head,
So cold and stark the raven's beak
May peck ..pierced each frozen cheek:
'Twas a wild waste of underwood,
And here and there a chestnut stood,
The strong oak and the hardy pine;
  But far apart — and well it were,
Or else a different lot were mine —
  The boughs gave way, and did not tear
My limbs; and I found strength to bear
My wounds, already scarred with cold —
My bonds forbade to loose my hold.
We rustled through the leaves like wind,
Left shrubs, and trees, and wolves behind;
By night I heard them on the track,
Their troop came hard upon our back,
With their long gallop, which can tire
The hound's deep hate, and hunter's fire:
Where'er we flew they followed on,
Nor left us with the morning sun;
Behind I saw them, scarce a rood,
At day-break winding through the wood,
And through the night had heard their feet
Their stealing, rustling step repeat.
Oh! how I wished for spear or sword,
At least to die amidst the horde,
And perish — if it must be so —
At bay, destroying many a foe.
When first my courser's race begun,
I wished the goal already won;
But now I doubted strength and speed.
Vain doubt! his swift and savage breed
Had nerved him like the mountain-roe;
Nor faster falls the blinding snow
Which whelms the peasant near the door
Whose threshold he shall cross no more,
Bewildered with the dazzling blast,
Than through the forest-paths he past —
Untired, untamed, and worse than wild;
All furious as a favored child
Balked of its wish; or fiercer still —
A woman piqued — who has her will.

XIII.

" The wood was past; 'twas more than noon,
But chill the air, although in June;
Or it might be my veins ran cold —
Prolonged endurance tames the bold;
And I was then not what I seem,
But headlong as a wintry stream,
And wore my feelings out before
I well could count their causes o'er:
And what with fury, fear, and wrath,
The tortures which beset my path,
Cold, hunger, sorrow, shame, distress,
Thus bound in nature's nakedness;
Sprung from a race whose rising blood
When stirred beyond its calmer mood,
And trodden hard upon, is like
The rattle-snake's, in act to strike,
What marvel if this worn-out trunk
Beneath its woes a moment sunk ?
The earth gave way, the skies rolled round,
I seemed to sink upon the ground;
But erred, for I was fastly bound.
My heart turned sick, my brain grew sore,
And throbbed awhile, then beat no more:
The skies spun like a mighty wheel;
I saw the trees like drunkards reel,
And a slight flash sprang o'er my eyes,
Which saw no farther: he who dies
Can die no more than then I died.
O'ertortured by that ghastly ride,
I felt the blackness come and go,
  And strove to wake; but could not make
My senses climb up from below:
I felt as on a plank at sea,
When all the waves that dash o'er thee,
At the same time upheave and whelm,
And hurl thee towards a desert realm.
My undulating life was as
The fancied lights that flitting pass
Our shut eyes in deep midnight, when
Fever begins upon the brain;
But soon it passed, with little pain,
  But a confusion worse than such:
  I own that I should deem it much,
Dying, to feel the same again;
And yet I do suppose we must
Feel far more ere we turn to dust:
No matter; I have bared my brow
Full in Death's face — before — and now.

XIV.

" My thoughts came back; where was I?
  Cold,
And numb, and giddy: pulse by pulse
Life reassumed its lingering hold,
And throb by throb: till grown a pang
  Which for a moment would convulse,
My blood reflowed, though thick and chill;
My ear with uncouth noises rang,
  My heart began once more to thrill;
My sight returned, though dim; alas!

And thickened, as it were, with glass.
Methought the dash of waves was nigh;
There was a gleam too of the sky,
Studded with stars; — it is no dream;
The wild horse swims the wilder stream!
The bright broad river's gushing tide
Sweeps, winding onward, far and wide,
And we are half-way, struggling o'er
To yon unknown and silent shore.
The waters broke my hollow trance,
And with a temporary strength
; My stiffened limbs were rebaptized.
¡My courser's broad breast proudly braves,
And dashes off the ascending waves,
And onward we advance!
We reach the slippery shore at length,
A haven I but little prized,
For all behind was dark and drear
And all before was night and fear.
How many hours of night or day
In those suspended pangs I lay,
I could not tell; I scarcely knew
If this were human breath I drew.

XV.

" With glossy skin, and dripping mane,
And reeling limbs, and reeking flank,
The wild steed's sinewy nerves still strain
Up the repelling bank.
We gain the top: a boundless plain
Spreads through the shadow of the night,
And onward, onward, onward, seems,
Like precipices in our dreams,
To stretch beyond the sight;
And here and there a speck of white,
Or scattered spot of dusky green,
In masses broke into the light,
As rose the moon upon my right.
But nought distinctly seen
In the dim waste would indicate
The omen of a cottage gate;
No twinkling taper from afar   ..ut
Stood like a hospitable star;
Not even an ignis-fatuus rose
To make him merry with my woes:
That very cheat had cheered me then!
Although detected, welcome still,
Reminding me through every ill,
Of the abodes of men.

XVI.

" Onward we went — but slack and slow;
His savage force at length o'erspent,
The drooping courser, faint and low,
All feebly foaming went.
` A sickly infant had had power
To guide him forward in that hour;
But useless all to me.
His new-born tameness nought availed —
My limbs were bound; my force had failed,
Perchance, had they been free.
With feeble effort still I tried

To rend the bonds so starkly tie(
But still it was in vain;
My limbs were only wrung the m
And soon the idle strife gave o'e
Which but prolonged their pai
The dizzy race seemed almost d(
Although no goal was nearly wo
Some streaks announced the con
How slow, alas! he came!
Methought that mist of dawning
Would never dapple into day;
How heavily it rolled away —
Before the eastern flame
Rose crimson, and deposed the
And called the radiance from the
And filled the earth, from his de(
With lonely lustre, all his own.

XVII.

" Up rose the sun; the mists wer
Back from the solitary world
Which lay around — behind — b(
What booted it to traverse o'er
Plain, forest, river? Man nor b
Nor dint of hoof, nor print of fo(
Lay in the wild luxuriant soil;
No sign of travel — none of toil;
The very air was mute;
And not an insect's shrill small h
Nor matin bird's new voice was
From herb nor thicket. Many a
Panting as if his heart would bu
The weary brute still staggered (
And still we were — or seemed —
At length, while reeling on our w
Methought I heard a courser ne
From out yon tuft of blackening
Is it the wind those branches sti
No, no! from out the forest pran
A trampling troop; I see them
In one vast squadron they advar
I strove to cry — my lips were
The steeds rush on in plunging
But where are they the reins to g
A thousand horse — and none tc
With flowing tail, and flying ma
Wide nostrils — never stretched
Mouths bloodless to the bit or re
And feet that iron never shod,
And flanks unscarred by spur or
A thousand horse, the wild, the f
Like waves that follow o'er the s
Came thickly thundering on
As if our faint approach to meet
The sight re-nerved my courser'
A moment staggering, feebly flee
A moment, with a faint low neig
He answered, and then fell;
With gasps and glazing eyes he

---

1 [MS. — " Rose crimson, and for
To sparkle in their rad

And reeking limbs immovable,
His first and last career is done!
On came the troop — they saw him stoop,·
They saw me strangely bound along
His back with many a bloody thong:
They stop — they start — they snuff the air,
Gallop a moment here and there,
Approach, retire, wheel round and round,
Then plunging back with sudden bound,
Headed by one black mighty steed,
Who seemed the patriarch of his breed,
Without a single speck or hair
Of white upon his shaggy hide;
They snort — they foam — neigh — swerve
aside,
And backward to the forest fly,
By instinct, from a human eye. —
They left me there to my despair,
Linked to the dead and stiffening wretch,
Whose lifeless limbs beneath me stretch,
Relieved from that unwonted weight,
From whence I could not extricate
Nor him nor me — and there we lay
The dying on the dead!
I little deemed another day
Would see my houseless, helpless head.

"And there from morn till twilight bound,
I felt the heavy hours toil round,
With just enough of life to see
My last of suns go down on me,
In hopeless certainty of mind,
That makes us feel at length resigned
To that which our forboding years
Presents the worst and last of fears
Inevitable — even a boon,
Nor more unkind for coming soon;
Yet shunned and dreaded with such care,
As if it only were a snare
That prudence might escape:
At times both wished for and implored,
At times sought with self-pointed sword,
Yet still a dark and hideous close
To even intolerable woes,
And welcome in no shape.
And, strange to say, the sons of pleasure,
They who have revelled beyond measure
In beauty, wassail, wine, and treasure,
Die calm, or calmer, oft than he
Whose heritage was misery:
For he who hath in turn run through
All that was beautiful and new,
Hath nought to hope, and nought to leave;
And, save the future, (which is viewed
Not quite as men are base or good,
But as their nerves may be endued,)
With nought perhaps to grieve: —
The wretch still hopes his woes must end,
And Death, whom he should deem his friend,
Appears, to his distempered eyes,
Arrived to rob him of his prize,
The tree of his new Paradise.

To-morrow would have given him all,
Repaid his pangs, repaired his fall;
To-morrow would have been the first
Of days no more deplored or curst,
But bright, and long, and beckoning years,
Seen dazzling through the mist of tears,
Guerdon of many a painful hour;
To-morrow would have given him power
To rule, to shine, to smite, to save —
And must it dawn upon his grave ?

XVIII.

"The sun was sinking — still I lay
Chained to the chill and stiffening steed,
I thought to mingle there our clay;
And my dim eyes of death had need,
No hope arose of being freed :
I cast my last looks up the sky,
And there between me and the sun
I saw the expecting raven fly,
Who scarce would wait till both should die,
Ere his repast begun;
He flew, and perched, then flew once more,
And each time nearer than before;
I saw his wing through twilight flit,
And once so near me he alit
I could have smote, but lacked the strength;
But the slight motion of my hand,
And feeble scratching of the sand
The exerted throat's faint struggling noise,
Which scarcely could be called a voice,
Together scared him off at length. —
I know no more — my latest dream
Is something of a lovely star
Which fixed my dull eyes from afar,
And went and came with wandering beam,
And of the cold, dull, swimming, dense
Sensation of recurring sense,
And then subsiding back to death,
And then again a little breath,
A little thrill, a short suspense,
An icy sickness curdling o'er
My heart, and sparks that crossed my brain —
A gasp, a throb, a start of pain,
A sigh, and nothing more.

XIX.

"I woke — Where was I ? — Do I see
A human face look down on me ?
And doth a roof above me close ?
Do these limbs on a couch repose ?
Is this a chamber where I lie ?
And is it mortal yon bright eye,
That watches me with gentle glance ?
I closed my own again once more,
As doubtful that the former trance
Could not as yet be o'er.
A slender girl, long-haired, and tall,
Sate watching by the cottage wall:
The sparkle of her eye I caught,
Even with my first return of thought;
For ever and anon she threw

A prying, pitying glance on me
With her black eyes so wild and free:
I gazed, and gazed, until I knew
    No vision it could be,—
But that I lived, and was released
From adding to the vulture's feast:
And when the Cossack maid beheld
My heavy eyes at length unsealed,
She smiled — and I essayed to speak,
    But failed — and she approached, and made
    With lip and finger signs that said,
I must not strive as yet to break
The silence, till my strength should be
Enough to leave my accents free;
And then her hand on mine she laid,
And smoothed the pillow for my head,
And stole along on tiptoe tread,
    And gently oped the door, and spake
In whispers — ne'er was voice so sweet!
Even music followed her light feet; —
    But those she called were not awake,
And she went forth; but, ere she passed,
Another look on me she cast,
    Another sign she made, to say,
That I had nought to fear, that all
Were near, at my command or call,
    And she would not delay
Her due return : — while she was gone,
Methought I felt too much alone.

XX.

"She came with mother and with sire —
What need of more ? — I will not tire
With long recital of the rest,
Since I became the Cossack's guest.
They found me senseless on the plain —
    They bore me to the nearest hut —
They brought me into life again —
Me — one day o'er their realm to reign!

Thus the vain fool who strove to glut
His rage, refining on my pain,
    Sent me forth to the wilderness,
Bound, naked, bleeding, and alone,
To pass the desert to a throne,—
    What mortal his own doom may guess ? —
    Let none despond, let none despair!
To-morrow the Borysthenes   .
May see our coursers graze at ease
Upon his Turkish bank, — and never
Had I such welcome for a river
As I shall yield when safely there.[1]
Comrades, good night!" — the Hetman
        threw
His length beneath the oak-tree shade,
    With leafy couch already made,
A bed nor comfortless nor new
To him, who took his rest whene'er
The hour arrived, no matter where :
His eyes the hastening slumbers steep.
And if ye marvel Charles forgot
To thank his tale, *he* wondered not, —
    The king had been an hour asleep.

[1] ["Charles, having perceived that the day was lost, and that his only chance of safety was to retire with the utmost precipitation, suffered himself to be mounted on horseback, and with the remains of his army fled to a place called Perewolochna, situated in the angle formed by the junction of the Vorskla and the Borysthenes. Here, accompanied by Mazeppa and a few hundreds of his followers, Charles swam over the latter great river, and proceeding over a desolate country, in danger of perishing with hunger, at length reached the Bog, where he was kindly received by the Turkish pacha. The Russian envoy at the Sublime Porte demanded that Mazeppa should be delivered up to Peter, but the old Hetman of the Cossacks escaped this fate by taking a disease which hastened his death." — *Barrow's Peter the Great*, pp. 196-203.]

THE ISLAND;

OR,

CHRISTIAN AND HIS COMRADES.

THE foundation of the following story will be found partly in Lieutenant Bligh's "Narrative of the Mutiny and Seizure of the Bounty, in the South Seas, in 1789;" and partly in "Mariner's Account of the Tonga Islands."

Genoa, 1823.

INTRODUCTION.

ON the 28th of April, 1789, the Bounty was on its way from Otaheite with a cargo of bread fruit trees, which the English Government wished to naturalize in the West Indies, when the larger part of the crew, headed by Christian the mate, seized the commander, Captain Bligh, and launched him, together with eighteen others who remained faithful to their duty, in an open boat upon the wide ocean. The remainder, twenty-eight in number, of whom four were detained against their will, set sail for Toobonai, one of the Friendly Islands; thence they returned to Otaheite, where Christian landed the majority of the mutineers, while himself and eight of his comrades went back to Toobonai, with the intention of settling there. The natives regarding them as intruders, Christian and his company again put to sea, and established themselves, in 1790, upon Pitcairn's Island, which was then uninhabited. Captain Bligh, with twelve of his men, got safe to England, and the Pandora was despatched to Otaheite, to apprehend the mutineers. Fourteen were captured, and of these four were drowned on the voyage, and three executed in England. It was in anticipation of the search for them at Otaheite that Christian and his party sought a securer home, and they took the further precaution to burn the ship as soon as they were settled upon Pitcairn's Island. No one guessed what had become of them till the captain of an American vessel chanced, in 1809, to stop at their place of retreat, and learnt their curious story.

They had carried with them from Otaheite six Tahitian men and twelve women. Quarrels broke out, a war of races commenced, and ultimately the nine Englishmen were killed or died, with the exception of one Smith, who assumed the name of Adams, and was the patriarch of the colony, which amounted in all to thirty-five. Adams, touched by the tragedies he had witnessed, had trained up the half-caste children of himself and his countrymen in the way they should go, and they presented the singular spectacle of a moral, a united, and a happy family sprung from a colony of ferocious mutineers.

Such was the romance upon which the poet founded the tale of "The Island," though he has interwoven with the central narrative a marvellous incident from Mariner, which relates to an entirely different adventure.

The Island was written at Genoa, early in 1823, and published in June of that year.

CANTO THE FIRST.

I.

THE morning watch was come; the vessel lay
Her course, and gently made her liquid way;
The cloven billow flashed from off her prow
In furrows formed by that majestic plough;
The waters with their world were all before;
Behind, the South Sea's many an islet shore.
The quiet night, now dappling, 'gan to wane,
Dividing darkness from the dawning main;
The dolphins, not unconscious of the day,
Swam high, as eager of the coming ray;
The stars from broader beams began to creep,
And lift their shining eyelids from the deep;
The sail resumed its lately shadowed white,
And the wind fluttered with a freshening flight;
The purpling ocean owns the coming sun,
But ere he break — a deed is to be done.

II.

The gallant chief within his cabin slept,
Secure in those by whom the watch was kept:
His dreams were of Old England's welcome shore,
Of toils rewarded, and of dangers o'er;
His name was added to the glorious roll
Of those who search the storm-surrounded Pole.
The worst was over, and the rest seemed sure,[1]
And why should not his slumber be secure?
Alas! his deck was trod by unwilling feet,
And wilder hands would hold the vessel's sheet:
Young hearts, which languish for some sunny isle,
Where summer years and summer women smile;

---

[1] ["A few hours before, my situation had been peculiarly flattering. I had a ship in the most perfect order, stored with every necessary, both for health and service; the object of the voyage was attained, and two thirds of it now completed. The remaining part had every prospect of success."— *Bligh.*]

Men without country, who, too long estranged,
Had found no native home, or found it
   changed,
And, half uncivilized, preferred the cave
Of some soft savage to the uncertain wave —
The gushing fruits that nature gave untilled;
The wood without a path but where they
   willed;
The field o'er which promiscuous Plenty
   poured
Her horn; the equal land without a lord;
The wish — which ages have not yet subdued
In man — to have no master save his mood; [1]
The earth, whose mine was on its face, unsold,
The glowing sun and produce all its gold;
The freedom which can call each grot a home;
The general garden, where all steps may roam,
Where Nature owns a nation as her child,
Exulting in the enjoyment of the wild;
Their shells, their fruits, the only wealth they
   know
Their unexploring navy, the canoe;
Their sport, the dashing breakers and the
   chase;
Their strangest sight, an European face: —
Such was the country which these strangers
   yearned
To see again; a sight they dearly earned.

III.

Awake, bold Bligh! the foe is at the gate!
Awake! Awake! —— Alas! it is too late!
Fiercely beside thy cot the mutineer
Stands, and proclaims the reign of rage and
   fear.
Thy limbs are bound, the bayonet at thy
   breast;
The hands, which trembled at thy voice arrest;
Dragged o'er the deck, no more at thy com-
   mand
The obedient helm shall veer, the sail expand;
That savage spirit, which would lull by wrath
Its desperate escape from duty's path,
Glares round thee, in the scarce believing eyes
Of those who fear the chief they sacrifice:
For ne'er can man his conscience all assuage,
Unless he drain the wine of passion — rage.

IV.

In vain, not silenced by the eye of death,
Thou call'st the loyal with thy menaced
   breath: —
They come not; they are few, and, overawed,
Must acquiesce, while sterner hearts applaud.

In vain thou dost demand the cau[
Is all the answer, with the threat o[
Full in thine eyes is waved the glitte[
Close to thy throat the pointed bay[
The levelled muskets circle round]
In hands as steeled to do the dead
Thou darest them to their worst, ex[
   "Fire!"
But they who pitied not could yet [
Some lurking remnant of their for[
Restrained them longer than their b[
They would not dip their souls [
   blood,
But left thee to the mercies of the [

V.

"Hoist out the boat!" was now t[
   cry;
And who dare answer "No!" to [
In the first dawning of the drunker[
The Saturnalia of unhoped-for pov[
The boat is lowered with all the ha[
With its slight plank between thee a[
Her only cargo such a scant suppl[
As promises the death their hands[
And just enough of water and of b[
To keep, some days, the dying fron[
Some cordage, canvas, sails, and [
   twine,
But treasures all to hermits of the b[
Were added after, to the earnest p[

Of those who saw no hope, save sea and air;
And last, that trembling vassal of the Pole—
The feeling compass — Navigation's soul.[1]

VI.

And now the self-elected chief finds time
To stun the first sensation of his crime,
And raise it in his followers—" Ho! the bowl!"[2]
Lest passion should return to reason's shoal.
"Brandy for heroes!"[3] Burke could once exclaim—
No doubt a liquid path to epic fame;
And such the new-born heroes found it here,
And drained the draught with an applauding cheer.
"Huzza! for Otaheite!" was the cry.
How strange such shouts from sons of Mutiny!
The gentle island, and the genial soil,
The friendly hearts, the feasts without a toil,
The courteous manners but from nature caught,
The wealth unhoarded, and the love unbought;
Could these have charms for rudest sea-boys, driven
Before the mast by every wind of heaven?
And now, even now prepared with others' woes
To earn mild virtue's vain desire, repose?
Alas! such is our nature! all but aim
At the same end by pathways not the same;
Our means, our birth, our nation, and our name,
Our fortune, temper, even our outward frame,
Are far more potent o'er our yielding clay
Than aught we know beyond our little day.
Yet still there whispers the small voice within,
Heard through Gain's silence, and o'er Glory's din:
Whatever creed be taught or land be trod,
Man's conscience is the oracle of God.

VII.

The launch is crowded with the faithful few
Who wait their chief, a melancholy crew:
But some remained reluctant on the deck

Of that proud vessel — now a moral wreck —
And viewed their captain's fate with piteous eyes;
While others scoffed his augured miseries,
Sneered at the prospect of his pigmy sail,
And the slight bark so laden and so frail.
The tender nautilus, who steers his prow,
The sea-born sailor of his shell canoe,
The ocean Mab, the fairy of the sea,
Seems far less fragile, and, alas! more free.
He, when the lightning-winged tornadoes sweep
The surge, is safe — his port is in the deep —
And triumphs o'er the armadas of mankind,
Which shake the world, yet crumble in the wind.

VIII.

When all was now prepared, the vessel clear,
Which hailed her master in the mutineer—
A seaman, less obdurate than his mates,
Showed the vain pity which but irritates;
Watched his late chieftain with exploring eye,
And told, in signs, repentant sympathy;
Held the moist shaddock to his parched mouth,
Which felt exhaustion's deep and bitter drouth.
But soon observed, this guardian was withdrawn,
Nor further mercy clouds rebellion's dawn.[4]
Then forward stepped the bold and froward boy
His chief had cherished only to destroy,
And, pointing to the helpless prow beneath,
Exclaimed, "Depart at once! delay is death!"
Yet then, even then, his feelings ceased not all:
In that last moment could a word recall
Remorse for the black deed as yet half done,
And what he hid from many he showed to one:
When Bligh in stern reproach demanded where
Was now his grateful sense of former care?
Where all his hopes to see his name aspire,
And blazon Britain's thousand glories higher?
His feverish lips thus broke their gloomy spell,
" 'Tis that! 'tis that! I am in hell! in hell!"[5]

[1] [" The boatswain and those seamen who were to be put into the boat were allowed to collect twine, canvas, lines, sails, cordage, an eight-and-twenty-gallon cask of water; and Mr. Samuel got one hundred and fifty pounds of bread, with a small quantity of rum and wine: also a quadrant and compass."—*Bligh.*]

[2] [The mutineers having thus forced those of the seamen whom they wished to get rid of into the boat, Christian directed a dram to be served to each of his crew."— *Bligh.*]

[3] [It was Dr. Johnson who thus gave honor to Cognac. "He was persuaded," says Boswell, "to take one glass of claret. He shook his head, and said, 'Poor stuff! No, Sir, claret is the liquor for boys; port for men; but he who aspires to be a hero (smiling) must drink brandy.'"]

[4] [" Isaac Martin, I saw, had an inclination to assist me; and as he fed me with shaddock, my lips being quite parched, we explained each other's sentiments by looks. But this was observed, and he was removed. He then got into the boat, but was compelled to return."—*Bligh.*]

[5] [" Christian then said, 'Come, Captain Bligh, your officers and men are now in the boat: and you must go with them: if you attempt to make the least resistance, you will instantly be put to death, and, without further ceremony, I was forced over the side by a tribe of armed ruffians, where they untied my hands. Being in the boat we were veered astern by a rope. A few pieces of pork

No more he said; but urging to the bark
His chief, commits him to his fragile ark;
These the sole accents from his tongue that
  fell,
But volumes lurked below his fierce farewell.

IX.

The arctic sun rose broad above the wave;
The breeze now sank, now whispered from
  his cave;
As on the Æolian harp, his fitful wings
Now swelled, now fluttered o'er his ocean
  strings.
With slow, despairing oar, the abandoned
  skiff
Ploughs its drear progress to the scarce-seen
  cliff,
Which lifts its peak a cloud above the main.
That boat and ship shall never meet again!
But 'tis not mine to tell their tale of grief,
Their constant peril, and their scant relief;
Their days of danger, and their nights of
  pain;
Their manly courage even when deemed in
  vain;
The sapping famine, rendering scarce a son
Known to his mother in the skeleton;
The ills that lessened still their little store,
And starved even Hunger till he wrung no
  more;
The varying frowns and favors of the deep,
That now almost ingulfs, then leaves to creep
With crazy oar and shattered strength along
The tide that yields reluctant to the strong;
The incessant fever of that arid thirst
Which welcomes, as a well, the clouds that
  burst
Above their naked bones, and feels delight
In the cold drenching of the stormy night,
And from the outspread canvas gladly wrings
A drop to moisten life's all-gasping springs;
The savage foe escaped, to seek again
More hospitable shelter from the main;
The ghastly spectres which were doomed at
  last
To tell as true a tale of dangers past,

As ever the dark annals of the deep
Disclosed for man to dread or won

X.

We leave them to their fate, bu
  known
Nor unredressed.   Revenge may
  own:
Roused discipline aloud proclai
  cause,
And injured navies urge their brok
Pursue we on his track the mutinee
Whom distant vengeance had not
  fear.
Wide o'er the wave — away! away
Once more his eyes shall hail the
  bay;
Once more the happy shores witho
Receive the outlaws whom they late
Nature, and Nature's goddess —
  woos
To lands where, save their conscie
  accuse;
Where all partake the earth withou
And bread itself is gathered as a fru
Where none contest the fields, the
  streams: —
The goldless age, where gold di
  dreams,
Inhabits or inhabited the shore,
Till Europe taught them better tha
Bestowed her customs, and amend
But left her vices also to their heirs.
Away with this! behold them as the
Do good with Nature, or with Natu
" Huzza! for Otaheite! " was the c
As stately swept the gallant vessel b
The breeze springs up; the latel
  sail
Extends its arch before the growing
In swifter ripples stream aside the s
Which her bold bow flings off wit
  ease.
Thus Argo[2] ploughed the Euxin
  foam;
But those she wafted still looked
  home —
These spurn their country with tl
  bark,
And fly her as the raven fled the ar
And yet they seem to nestle with th
And tame their fiery spirits down to

---

were thrown to us, also the four cutlasses. After
having been kept some time to make sport for these
unfeeling wretches, and having undergone much
ridicule, we were at length cast adrift in the open
ocean. Eighteen persons were with me in the boat.
When we were sent away, ' Huzza for Otaheite!'
was frequently heard among the mutineers. Chris-
tian, the chief of them, was of a respectable family
in the north of England. While they were forcing
me out of the ship, I asked him whether this was a
proper return for the many instances he had expe-
rienced of my friendship? He appeared disturbed
at the question, and answered, with much emotion,

' That — Captain Bligh — that is the th
in hell — I am in hell! ' " — *Bligh.*]
  [1] The now celebrated bread-fruit, to
which Captain Bligh's expedition was t
  [2] [The vessel in which Jason embark
of the golden fleece.]

CANTO THE SECOND.

I.

How pleasant were the songs of Toobonai,[1]
When summer's sun went down the coral bay!
Come, let us to the islet's softest shade,
And hear the warbling birds! the damsels
    said:
The wood-dove from the forest depth shall coo,
Like voices of the gods from Bolotoo;
We'll cull the flowers that grow above the
    dead,
For these most bloom where rests the warrior's
    head;
And we will sit in twilight's face, and see
The sweet moon glancing through the tooa
    tree,
The lofty accents of whose sighing bough
Shall sadly please us as we lean below;
Or climb the steep, and view the surf in vain
Wrestle with rocky giants o'er the main,
Which spurn in columns back the baffled
    spray.
How beautiful are these! how happy they,
Who, from the toil and tumult of their lives,
Steal to look down where nought but ocean
    strives!
Even he too loves at times the blue lagoon,
And smoothes his ruffled mane beneath the
    moon.

II.

Yes — from the sepulchre we'll gather flowers,
Then feast like spirits in their promised bow-
    ers,
Then plunge and revel in the rolling surf,
Then lay our limbs along the tender turf,
And, wet and shining from the sportive toil,
Anoint our bodies with the fragrant oil,
And plait our garlands gathered from the
    grave,
And wear the wreaths that sprung from out
    the brave.
But lo! night comes, the Mooa woos us back,
The sound of mats are heard along our track;
Anon the torchlight dance shall fling its sheen
In flashing mazes o'er the Marly's green;
And we too will be there; we too recall
The memory bright with many a festival,
Ere Fiji blew the shell of war, when foes
For the first time were wafted in canoes.
Alas! for them the flower of mankind bleeds;

Alas! for them our fields are rank with weeds:
Forgotten is the rapture, or unknown,
Of wandering with the moon and love alone.
But be it so: — *they* taught us how to wield
The club, and rain our arrows o'er the field:
Now let them reap the harvest of their art!
But feast to-night! to-morrow we depart.
Strike up the dance! the cava bowl fill high!
Drain every drop! — to-morrow we may die.
In summer garments be our limbs arrayed;
Around our waists the tappa's white displayed;
Thick wreaths shall form our coronal, like
    spring's,
And round our necks shall glance the hooni
    strings;
So shall their brighter hues contrast the glow
Of the dusk bosoms that beat high below.

III.

But now the dance is o'er — yet stay awhile;
Ah, pause! nor yet put out the social smile.
To-morrow for the Mooa we depart,
But not to-night — to-night is for the heart.
Again bestow the wreaths we gently woo,
Ye young enchantresses of gay Licoo!
How lovely are your forms! how every sense
Bows to your beauties, softened, but intense,
Like to the flowers on Mataloco's steep,
Which fling their fragrance far athwart the
    deep! —
We too will see Licoo; but — oh! my heart! —
What do I say? — to-morrow we depart!

IV.

Thus rose a song — the harmony of times
Before the winds blew Europe o'er these climes.
True, they had vices — such are Nature's
    growth —
But only the barbarian's — we have both:
The sordor of civilization, mixed
With all the savage which man's fall hath
    fixed.
Who hath not seen Dissimulation's reign,
The prayers of Abel linked to deeds of Cain?
Who such would see may from his lattice view
The Old World more degraded than the
    New, —
Now *new* no more, save where Columbia rears
Twin giants, born by Freedom to her spheres,
Where Chimborazo, over air, earth, wave,
Glares with his Titan eye, and sees no slave.

V.

Such was this ditty of Tradition's days,
Which to the dead a lingering fame conveys:
In song, where fame as yet hath left no sign
Beyond the sound whose charm is half divine

---

[1] The first three sections are taken from an actual song of the Tonga Islanders, of which a prose translation is given in " Mariner's Account of the Tonga Islands." Toobonai is *not* however one of them; but was one of those where Christian and the mutineers took refuge. I have altered and added, but have retained as much as possible of the original.

Which leaves no record to the sceptic eye,
But yields young history all to harmony;
A boy Achilles, with the centaur's lyre
In hand, to teach him to surpass his sire.
For one long-cherished ballad's simple stave,
Rung from the rock, or mingled with the wave,
Or from the bubbling streamlet's grassy side,
Or gathering mountain echoes as they glide,
Hath greater power o'er each true heart and ear,
Than all the columns Conquest's minions rear;
Invites, when hieroglyphics are a theme
For the sages' labors or the student's dream;
Attracts, when History's volumes are a toil, —
The first, the freshest bud of Feeling's soil.
Such was this rude rhyme — rhyme is of the rude —
But such inspired the Norseman's solitude,
Who came and conquered; such, wherever rise,
Lands which no foes destroy or civilize,
Exist : and what can our accomplished art
Of verse do more than reach the awakened heart ?

VI.

And sweetly now those untaught melodies
Broke the luxurious silence of the skies,
The sweet siesta of a summer day,
The tropic afternoon of Toobonai,
When every flower was bloom, and air was balm,
And the first breath began to stir the palm,
The first yet voiceless wind to urge the wave
All gently to refresh the thirsty cave,
Where sat the songstress with the stranger boy,
Who taught her passion's desolating joy,
Too powerful over every heart, but most
O'er those who know not how it may be lost;
O'er those who, burning in the new-born fire,
Like martyrs revel in their funeral pyre,
With such devotion to their ecstasy,
That life knows no such rapture as to die :
And die they do; for earthly life has nought
Matched with that burst of nature, even in thought,
And all our dreams of better life above
But close in one eternal gush of love.

VII.

There sat the gentle savage of the wild,
In growth a woman, though in years a child,
As childhood dates within our colder clime,
Where nought is ripened rapidly save crime;
The infant of an infant world, as pure
From nature — lovely, warm, and premature;
Dusky like night, but night with all her stars;
Or cavern sparkling with its native spars;
With eyes that were a language and a spell,
A form like Aphrodite's in her shell,
With all her loves around her on the deep,

Voluptuous as the first approach
Yet full of life — for through her t
The blush would make its way, speak;
The sun-born blood suffused he threw
O'er her clear nut-brown skin a l
Like coral reddening through t wave,
Which draws the diver to the cri
Such was this daughter of the so
Herself a billow in her energies,
To bear the bark of others' happi
Nor feel a sorrow till their joy gr
Her wild and warm yet faithful b
No joy like what it gave; her hop
Aught from experience, that chill whose
Sad proof reduces all things from
She feared no ill, because she kne
Or what she knew was soon — forgot :
Her smiles and tears had pass winds pass
O'er lakes to ruffle, not destroy, t
Whose depths unsearched, and fo the hill,
Restore their surface, in itself so s
Until the earthquake tear the naia
Root up the spring, and trample o
And crush the living waters to a m
The amphibious desert of the dar
And must their fate be hers ? T change
But grasps humanity with quicker
And they who fall but fall as world
To rise, if just, a spirit o'er them a.

VIII.

And who is he ? the blue-eyed nort
Of isles more known to man, but wild;
The fair-haired offspring of the He
Where roars the Pentland with i seas;
Rocked in his cradle by the roarin
The tempest-born in body and in i
His young eyes opening on the oc
Had from that moment deemed th home,
The giant comrade of his pensive i
The sharer of his craggy solitudes,
The only Mentor of his youth, whe
His bark was borne; the sport of w

---

[1] [George Stewart. " He was," say
young man of creditable parents in tl
at which place, on the return of the
from the South Seas, in 1780, we receiv
civilities, that, on that account onl
gladly have taken him with me; but,
of this recommendation, he was a sean
always borne a good character."

A careless thing, who placed his choice in
  chance,
Nursed by the legends of his land's romance;
Eager to hope, but not less firm to bear,
Acquainted with all feelings save despair.
Placed in the Arab's clime, he would have been
As bold a rover as the sands have seen,
And braved their thirst with as enduring lip
As Ishmael, wafted on his desert-ship; [1]
Fixed upon Chili's shore, a proud cacique;
On Hellas' mountains, a rebellious Greek;
Born in a tent, perhaps a Tamerlane;
Bred to a throne, perhaps unfit to reign.
For the same soul that rends its path to sway,
If reared to such, can find no further prey
Beyond itself, and must retrace its way [2]
Plunging for pleasure into pain : the same
Spirit which made a Nero, Rome's worst
  shame,
A humbler state and discipline of heart,
Had formed his glorious namesake's counter-
  . part; [3]
But grant his vices, grant them all his own,
How small their theatre without a throne !

IX.

Thou smilest; — these comparisons seem high
To those who scan all things with dazzled eye;
Linked with the unkown name of one whose
  doom   .
Has nought to do with glory or with Rome,
With Chili, Hellas, or with Araby; —
Thou smilest ? — Smile ; 'tis better thus than
  sigh ;
Yet such he might have been; he was a man,
A soaring spirit, ever in the van,
A patriot hero or despotic chief,
To form a nation's glory or its grief,
Born under auspices which make us more
Or less than we delight to ponder o'er.
But these are visions ; say, what was he here ?

---

[1] The " ship of the desert " is the oriental figure
for the camel or dromedary; and they deserve the
metaphor well, — the former for his endurance,
the latter for his swiftness.

[2] " Lucullus, when frugality could charm,
  Had roasted turnips in the Sabine farm."
                         Pope.

[3] The consul Nero, who made the unequalled
march which deceived Hannibal, and defeated
Asdrubal; thereby accomplishing an achievement
almost unrivalled in military annals. The first
intelligence of his return, to Hannibal, was the
sight of Asdrubal's head, thrown into his camp.
When Hannibal saw this, he exclaimed with a
sigh, that " Rome would now be the mistress of
the world." And yet to this victory of Nero's
it might be owing that his imperial namesake
reigned at all. But the infamy of the one has
eclipsed the glory of the other. When the name of
" Nero " is heard, who thinks of the consul? — But
such are human things. . `.

A blooming boy, a truant mutineer.
The fair-haired Torquil, free as ocean's spray,
The husband of the bride of Toboonai.

X.

By Neuha's side he sate, and watched the
  waters, —
Neuha, the sun-flower of the island daughters,
High-born, (a birth at which the herald smiles,
Without a scutcheon for these secret isles,)
Of a long race, the valiant and the free,
The naked knights of savage chivalry,
Whose grassy cairns ascend along the shore ;
And thine — I've seen — Achilles ! do no more.
She, when the thunder-bearing strangers came,
In vast canoes, begirt with bolts of flame,
Topped with tall trees, which, loftier than the
  palm,
Seemed rooted in the deep amidst its calm :
But when the winds awakened, shot forth
  . wings
Broad as the cloud along the horizon flings,
And swayed the waves, like cities of the sea,
Making the very billows look less free ; —
She, with her paddling oar and dancing prow,
Shot through the surf, like reindeer through
  the snow,
Swift-gliding o'er the breaker's whitening edge,
Light as a nereid in her ocean sledge,
And gazed and wondered at the giant hulk,
Which heaved from wave to wave its tramp-
  ling bulk.
The anchor dropped; it lay along the deep,
Like a huge lion in the sun asleep,
While round it swarmed the proas' flitting
  chain,
Like summer bees that hum around his mane.

XI.

The white man landed ! — need the rest be
  told ?
The New World stretched its dusk hand to
  the Old.
Each was to each a marvel, and the tie
Of wonder warmed to better sympathy.
Kind was the welcome of the sun-born sires,
And kinder still their daughters' gentler fires.
Their union grew : the children of the storm
Found beauty linked with many a dusky form ;
While these in turn admired the paler glow,
Which seemed so white in climes that knew
  no snow.
The chase, the race, the liberty to roam,
The soil where every cottage showed a home ;
The sea-spread net, the lightly-launched
  canoe,
Which stemmed the studded archipelago,
O'er whose blue bosom rose the starry isles ;
The healthy slumber, earned by sportive toils ;
The palm, the loftiest dryad of the woods,
Within whose bosom infant Bacchus broods,

While eagles scarce build higher than the
  crest
Which shadows o'er the vineyard in her
  breast;
The cava feast, the yam, the cocoa's root,
Which bears at once the cup, and milk, and
  fruit;
The bread-tree, which, without the plough-
  share, yields
The unreaped harvest of unfurrowed fields,
And bakes its unadulterated loaves
Without a furnace in unpurchased groves,
And flings off famine from its fertile breast,
A priceless market for the gathering guest; —
These, with the luxuries of seas and woods,
The airy joys of social solitudes,
Tamed each rude wanderer to the sympathies
Of those who were more happy, if less wise,
Did more than Europe's discipline had done,
And civilized Civilization's son!

XII.

Of these, and there was many a willing pair,
Neuha and Torquil were not the least fair:
Both children of the isles, though distant far;
Both born beneath a sea-presiding star;
Both nourished amidst nature's native scenes,
Loved to the last, whatever intervenes
Between us and our childhood's sympathy,
Which still reverts to what first caught the eye.
He who first met the Highland's swelling blue
Will love each peak that shows a kindred hue,
Hail in each crag a friend's familiar face,
And clasp the mountain in his mind's embrace.
Long have I roamed through lands which are
  not mine,
Adored the Alp, and loved the Apennine,
Revered Parnassus, and beheld the steep
Jove's Ida and Olympus crown the deep;
But 'twas not all long ages' lore, nor all
Their nature held me in their thrilling thrall;
The infant rapture still survived the boy,
And Loch-na-gar with Ida looked o'er Troy,[1]
Mixed Celtic memories with the Phrygian
  mount,
And Highland linns with Castalie's clear fount.
Forgive me, Homer's universal shade!
Forgive me, Phœbus! that my fancy strayed;
The north and nature taught me to adore
Your scenes sublime, from those beloved be-
  fore.

XIII.

The love which maketh all things fond and
  fair,
The youth which makes one rainbow of the air,
The dangers past, that make even man enjoy
The pause in which he ceases to destroy,

The mutual beauty, which the ste
Strike to their hearts like lightning
United the half savage and the w
The maid and boy, in one absorb
No more the thundering memory
Wrapped his weaned bosom in its d
No more the irksome restlessnes
Disturbed him like the eagle in h
Whose whetted beak and far-per
Darts for a victim over all the sky
His heart was tamed to that volu
At once Elysian and effeminate,
Which leaves no laurels o'er the h
These wither when for aught save
  burn;
Yet when their ashes in their nook
Doth not the myrtle leave as swee
Had Cæsar known but Cleopatra'
Rome had been free, the world ha
  his;
And what have Cæsar's deeds a
  fame
Done for the earth? We feel t
  shame
The gory sanction of his glory sta
The rust which tyrants cherish on
Though Glory, Nature, Reason, F
Roused millions do what single B
Sweep these mere mock-birds of t
  song
From the tall bough where they ha
  so long, —
Still are we hawked at by such mo
And take for falcons those ignoble
When but a word of freedom wou
These bugbears, as their terrors sh

XIV.

Rapt in the fond forgetfulness of li
Neuha, the South Sea girl, was all
With no distracting world to call I
From love; with no society to sco
At the new transient flame; no babl
Of coxcombry in admiration loud,
Or with adulterous whisper to allo
Her duty, and her glory, and her j
With faith and feelings naked as I
She stood as stands a rainbow in a
Changing its hues with bright vari
But still expanding lovelier o'er th
Howe'er its arch may swell, its col
The cloud-compelling harbinger o

---

[1] When very young, about eight years of age, after an attack of the scarlet fever at Aberdeen, I was removed by medical advice into the High-lands. Here I passed occasionally some summers,

and from this period I date my love of. countries. I can never forget the years afterwards, in England, of the had long seen, even in miniature, of in the Malvern Hills. After I retur tenham, I used to watch them every sunset, with a sensation, which I can This was boyish enough, but I was th teen years of age, and it was in the l

XV.

Here, in this grotto of the wave-worn shore,
They passed the tropic's red meridian o'er;
Nor long the hours — they never paused o'er
    time,
Unbroken by the clock's funereal chime,
Which deals the daily pittance of our span,
And points and mocks with iron laugh at man.
What deemed they of the future or the past ?
The present, like a tyrant, held them fast :
Their hour-glass was the sea-sand, and the tide,
Like her smooth billow, saw their moments
    glide ;
Their clock the sun, in his unbounded tower ;
They reckoned not, whose day was but an
    hour ;
The nightingale, their only vesper-bell,
Sung sweetly to the rose the day's farewell ; [1]
The broad sun set, but not with lingering
    sweep,
As in the north he mellows o'er the deep ;
But fiery, full, and fierce, as if he left
The world for ever, earth of light bereft,
Plunged with red forehead down along the
    wave,
As dives a hero headlong to his grave.
Then rose they, looking first along the skies,
And then for light into each other's eyes,
Wondering that summer showed so brief a sun,
And asking if indeed the day were done.

XVI.

And let not this seem strange : the devotee
Lives not in earth, but in his ecstasy ;
Around him days and worlds are heedless
    driven,
His soul is gone before his dust to heaven.
Is love less potent ? No — his path is trod,
Alike uplifted gloriously to God ;
Or linked to all we know of heaven below,
The other better self, whose joy or woe
Is more than ours ; the all-absorbing flame
Which, kindled by another, grows the same,
Wrapt in one blaze ; the pure, yet funeral pile,
Where gentle hearts, like Bramins, sit and
    smile.
How often we forget all time, when lone,
Admiring Nature's universal throne,
Her woods, her wilds, her waters, the intense
Reply of *hers* to our intelligence !
Live not the stars and mountains ? Are the
    waves
Without a spirit ? Are the dropping caves
Without a feeling in their silent tears ?
No, no ; — they woo and clasp us to their
    spheres,
Dissolve this clog and clod of clay before

[1] The now well-known story of the loves of the
nightingale and rose need not be more than alluded
to, being sufficiently familiar to the Western as to
the Eastern reader.

Its hour, and merge our soul in the great shore.
Strip off this fond and false identity ! —
Who thinks of self, when gazing on the sky ?
And who, though gazing lower, ever thought
In the young moments ere the heart is taught
Time's lesson, of man's baseness or his own ?
All nature is his realm, and love his throne.

XVII.

Neuha arose, and Torquil : twilight's hour
Came sad and softly to their rocky bower,
Which, kindling by degrees its dewy spars,
Echoed their dim light to the mustering stars.
Slowly the pair, partaking nature's calm,
Sought out their cottage, built beneath the
    palm ;
Now smiling and now silent, as the scene ;
Lovely as Love — the spirit ! — when serene.
The Ocean scarce spoke louder with his
    swell,
Than breathes his mimic murmurer in the
    shell,[2]
As, far divided from his parent deep,
The sea-born infant cries, and will not sleep,
Raising his little plaint in vain, to rave
For the broad bosom of his nursing wave :

[2] If the reader will apply to his ear the seashell
on his chimney-piece, he will be aware of what is
alluded to. If the text should appear obscure, he
will find in " Gebir " the same idea better expressed
in two lines. The poem I never read, but have
heard the lines quoted by a more recondite reader
— who seems to be of a different opinion from the
editor of the Quarterly Review, who qualified it, in
his answer to the Critical Reviewer of his Juvenal,
as trash of the worst and most insane description.
It is to Mr. Landor, the author of " Gebir," so
qualified, and of some Latin poems, which vie with
Martial or Catullus in obscenity, that the immacu-
late Mr. Southey addresses his declamation against
impurity !
[Mr. Landor's lines above alluded to are —
  " For I have often seen her with both hands
    Shake a dry crocodile of equal height,
    And listen to the shells within the scales,
    And fancy there was life, and yet apply
    The jagged jaws wide open to the ear."
In the " Excursion " of Wordsworth occurs the
following exquisite passage : —
       —— " I have seen
A curious child, applying to his ear
The convolutions of a smooth-lipped shell.
To which, in silence hushed, his very soul,
Listened intensely, and his countenance soon
Brightened with joy ; for murmuring from within
Were heard sonorous cadences ! whereby,
To his belief, the monitor expressed
Mysterious union with its native sea.
Even such a shell the universe itself
Is to the ear of faith ; and doth impart
Authentic tidings of invisible things :
Of ebb and flow, and ever-during power ;
And central peace subsisting at the heart
Of endless agitation."]

The woods drooped darkly, as inclined to
    rest,
The tropic bird wheeled rockward to his
    nest,
And the blue sky spread round them like a
    lake
Of peace, where Piety her thirst might slake.

XVIII.

But through the palm and plantain, hark, a
    voice!
Not such as would have been a lover's choice,
In such an hour, to break the air so still;
No dying night-breeze, harping o'er the hill,
Striking the strings of nature, rock and tree,
Those best and earliest lyres of harmony,
With Echo for their chorus; nor the alarm
Of the loud war-whoop to dispel the charm;
Nor the soliloquy of the hermit owl,
Exhaling all his solitary soul,
The dim though large-eyed winged anchorite,
Who peals his dreary pæan o'er the night; —
But a loud, long, and naval whistle, shrill
As ever started through a sea-bird's bill;
And then a pause, and then a hoarse "Hillo!
Torquil! my boy! what cheer? Ho! brother,
    ho!"
"Who hails?" cried Torquil, following with
    his eye
The sound. "Here's one," was all the brief
    reply.

XIX.

But here the herald of the self-same mouth,
Came breathing o'er the aromatic south,
Not like a "bed of violets" on the gale,
But such as wafts its cloud o'er grog or ale,
Borne from a short frail pipe, which yet had
    blown
Its gentle odors over either zone,
And, puffed where'er winds rise or waters
    roll,
Had wafted smoke from Portsmouth to the
    Pole,
Opposed its vapor as the lightning flashed,
And reeked, 'midst mountain-billows una-
    bashed,
To Æolus a constant sacrifice,
Through every change of all the varying skies.
And what was he who bore it? — I may err,
But deem him sailor or philospher.[1]
Sublime tobacco! which from east to west
Cheers the tar's labor or the Turkman's rest,
Which on the Moslem's ottoman divides
His hours, and rivals opium and his brides;

Magnificent in Stamboul, but less grand,
Though not less loved, in Wapping or the
    Strand;
Divine in hookas, glorious in a pipe,
When tipped with amber, mellow, rich, and
    ripe;
Like other charmers, wooing the caress
More dazzlingly when daring in full dress;
Yet thy true lovers more admire by far
Thy naked beauties — Give me a cigar![2]

XX.

Through the approaching darkness of the
    wood
A human figure broke the solitude,
Fantastically, it may be, arrayed,
A seaman in a savage masquerade;
Such as appears to rise out from the deep
When o'er the line the merry vessels sweep,
And the rough saturnalia of the tar
Flock o'er the deck, in Neptune's borrowed
    car;[3]
And, pleased, the god of ocean sees his name
Revive once more, though but in mimic
    game
Of his true sons, who riot in the breeze
Undreamt of in his native Cyclades.
Still the old god delights, from out the main,
To snatch some glimpses of his ancient reign,
Our sailor's jacket, though in ragged trim,
His constant pipe, which never yet burned
    dim,
His foremast air, and somewhat rolling gait,
Like his dear vessel, spoke his former state;
But then a sort of kerchief round his head,
Not over-tightly bound, nor nicely spread;
And, 'stead of trousers (ah! too early torn!
For even the mildest woods will have their
    thorn)
A curious sort of somewhat scanty mat
Now served for inexpressibles and hat;

---

[1] Hobbes, the father of Locke's and other phil-
osophy, was an inveterate smoker, — even to pipes
beyond computation.
[Soon after dinner Mr. Hobbes retired to his
study, and had his candle, with ten or twelve pipes
of tobacco laid by him; then, shutting the door, he
fell to smoking, thinking, and writing for several
hours.]

[2] [We talked of change of manners (1773). Dr.
Johnson observed, that our drinking less than our
ancestors was owing to the change from ale to wine.
"I remember," said he, "when all the *decent* peo-
ple in Litchfield got drunk every night, and were
not the worse thought of. Smoking has gone out.
To be sure, it is a shocking thing, blowing smoke
out of our mouths into other people's mouths, eyes,
and noses, and having the same thing done to us.
Yet I cannot account, why a thing which requires
so little exertion, and yet preserves the mind from
total vacuity, should have gone out." — *Boswell.*
As an item in the history of manners, it may be
observed, that *drinking* to excess has diminished
greatly in the memory even of those who can
remember forty or fifty years. The taste for *smok-
ing*, however, has revived, probably from the mil-
itary habits of Europe during the French wars;
but, instead of the sober sedentary *pipe* the ambu-
latory *segar* is now chiefly used. — *Croker,* 1830.]
[3] This rough but jovial ceremony, used in cross-
ing the line, has been so often and so well described,
that it need not be more than alluded to.

His naked feet and ·neck, and sunburnt face,
Perchance might suit alike with either race.
His arms were· all his own, our Europe's
    growth,
Which two worlds bless for civilizing both;
The musket swung behind his shoulders
    broad, ·
And somewhat stooped by his marine abode,
But brawny as the boar's; and hung beneath,
His cutlass drooped, unconscious of a sheath,
Or lost or worn away; his pistols were
Linked to his belt, a matrimonial pair—
(Let not this metaphor appear a scoff,
Though one missed fire, the other would go
    off) ;
These, with a bayonet, not so free from rust
As when the arm-chest held its brighter trust,
Completed his accoutrements, as Night
Surveyed him in his garb heteroclite.

XXI.

"What cheer, Ben Bunting?" cried (when in
    full view
Our new acquaintance) Torquil. "Aught of
    new?"
"Ey, ey!" quoth Ben, "not new, but news
    enow ;
A·strange sail in the offing."—"Sail! and
    how?
What! could you make her out? It cannot
    be ;
I've seen no rag of canvas on the sea."
"Belike," said Ben, "you might not from the
    bay,
But from the bluff-head, where I watched to-
    day,
I saw her in the doldrums; for the wind .
Was light and baffling."—When the sun de-
    clined
Where lay she? had she anchored?"—"No,
    but still
She bore down on us, till the wind grew still."
"Her flag?"—"I had no glass: but fore and
    aft,
Egad! she seemed a wicked-looking craft."
"Armed?"—"I expect so;—sent on the
    look-out:
'Tis time, belike, to put our helm about."
"About?—Whate'er may have us now in
    chase,
We'll make no running fight, for that were
    base ;
We will die at our quarters, like true men."
"Ey, ey! for that 'tis all the same to Ben."
"Does Christian know this?"—"Ay; he has
    piped all hands
To quarters. They are furbishing the stands
Of arms; and we have got some guns to bear,
And scaled them: You are wanted."—"That's
    but fair ;
And if it were not, mine is not the soul
To leave my comrades helpless on the shoal.
My Neuha! ah! and must my fate pursue
Not me alone, but one so sweet and true?
But whatsoe'er betide, ah, Neuha! now ·
Unman me not; the hour will not allow
A tear; I am thine whatever intervenes!"
"Right," quoth Ben, "that will do for the
    marines."[1]

[1] "That will do for the marines, but the sailors won't believe it," is an old saying; and one of the few fragments of former jealousies which still survive (in jest only) between these gallant services.

CANTO THE THIRD.

I.

THE fight was o'er; the flashing through the
    gloom
Which robes the cannon as he wings a tomb,
Had ceased; and sulphury vapors upward
    driven
Had left the earth, and but polluted heaven :
The rattling roar which rung in every volley
Had left the echoes to their melancholy ;
No more they shrieked their horror, boom
    for boom ;
The strife was done, the vanquished had their
    doom ;
The mutineers were crushed, dispersed, or
    ta'en,
Or lived to deem the happiest were the slain.
Few, few escaped, and these were hunted o'er
The isle they loved beyond their native shore.
No further·home was theirs, it seemed, on earth,
Once renegades to that which gave them birth ;
Tracked like wild beasts, like them they sought
    the wild,
As to a mother's bosom flies the child;
But vainly wolves and lions seek their den,
And still more vainly men escape from men.

II.

Beneath a rock whose jutting base protrudes
Far over ocean in his fiercest moods,
When scaling his enormous crag the wave
Is hurled down headlong, like the foremost
    brave,

And falls back on the foaming crowd behind,
Which fight beneath the banners of the wind,
Bnt now at rest, a little remnant drew
Together, bleeding, thirsty, faint, and few;
But still their weapons in their hands, and still
With something of the pride of former will,
As men not all unused to meditate,
And strive much more than wonder at their
    fate.
Their present lot was what they had foreseen,
And dared as what was likely to have been ;
Yet still the lingering hope, which deemed
    their lot
Not pardoned, but unsought for or forgot,
Or trusted that, if sought, their distant caves
Might still be missed amidst the world of waves,
Had weaned their thoughts in part from what
    they saw
And felt, the vengeance of their country's law.
Their sea-green isle, their guilt-won paradise,
No more could shield their virtue or their vice :
Their better feelings, if such were, were thrown
Back on themselves, — their sins remained
    alone.
Proscribed even in their second country, they
Were lost ; in vain the world before them lay ;
All outlets seemed secured. Their new allies
Had fought and bled in mutual sacrifice ;
But what availed the club and spear, and arm
Of Hercules, against the sulphury charm,
The magic of the thunder, which destroyed
The warrior ere his strength could be em-
    ployed ?
Dug, like a spreading pestilence, the grave
No less of human bravery than the brave ![1]
Their own scant numbers acted all the few
Against the many oft will dare and do;
But though the choice seems native to die free,
Even Greece can boast but one Thermopylæ,
Till *now*, when she has forged her broken
    chain
Back to a sword, and dies and lives again !

III.

Beside the jutting rock the few appeared,
Like the last remnant of the red-deer's herd;
Their eyes were feverish, and their aspect worn,
But still the hunter's blood was on their horn,
A little stream came tumbling from the height,
And straggling into ocean as it might,
Its bounding crystal frolicked in the ray,
And gushed from cliff to crag with saltless
    spray:
Close on the wild, wide ocean, yet as pure
And fresh as innocence, and more secure,
Its silver torrent glittered o'er the deep,

---

[1] Archidamus, King of Sparta, and son of Age-
silaus, when he saw a machine invented for the
casting of stones and darts, exclaimed that it was
the "grave of valor." The same story has been
told of some knights on the first application of gun-
powder but the original anecdote is in Plutarch.

As the shy chamois' eye o'erlook
While far below the vast and su
Of ocean's alpine azure rose and
To this young spring they rushe
    ings first
Absorbed in passion's and in nat
Drank as they do who drink th
    threw
Their arms aside to revel in its d
Cooled their scorched throats,
    the gory stains
From wounds whose only band
    chains;
Then, when their drought wa
    looked sadly round,
As wondering how so many still
Alive and fetterless : — but silent
Each sought his fellow's eyes, as
On him for language which his l
As though their voices with the
    died.

IV.

Stern, and aloof a little from the
Stood Christian, with his arm
    chest.
The ruddy, reckless, dauntless
    spread
Along his cheek was livid now a
His light-brown locks, so grac
    flow,
Now rose like startled vipers o'er
Still as a statue, with his lips com
To stifle even the breath within h
Fast by the rock, all menacing, b
He stood ; and, save a slight beat
Which deepened now and the
    dint
Beneath his heel, his form seem
    flint.
Some paces further Torquil lean
Against a bank, and spoke not, bu
Not mortally ; — his worst wound
His brow was pale, his blue eyes
And blood-drops, sprinkled o'er hi
Showed that his faintness cam
    despair
But nature's ebb. Beside him w
Rough as a bear, but willing as a
Ben Bunting, who essayed to wa
And bind his wound — then c
    pipe,
A trophy which survived a hundr
A beacon which had cheered t
    nights.
The fourth and last of this desert
Walked up and down — at times
    then stoop
To pick a pebble up — then let it
Then hurry as in haste — then qu
Then cast his eyes on his compa
Half whistle half a tune, and pau

And then his former movements would re-
  double,
With something between carelessness and
  trouble.
This is a long description, but applies
To scarce five minutes passed before the eyes;
But yet *what* minutes! Moments like to these
Rend men's lives into immortalities.

V.

At length Jack Skyscrape, a mercurial man,
Who fluttered over all things like a fan,
More brave than firm and more disposed to
  dare
And die at once than wrestle with despair,
Exclaimed, "G—d damn!"—those syllables
  intense,—
Nucleus of England's native eloquence,
As the Turk's "Allah!" or the Roman's
  more
Pagan "Proh Jupiter!" was wont of yore
To give their first impressions such a vent,
By way of echo to embarrassment.
Jack was embarrassed,—never hero more,
And as he knew not what to say, he swore:
Nor swore in vain; the long congenial sound
Revived Ben Bunting from his pipe profound;
He drew it from his mouth, and looked full
  wise,
But merely added to the oath his *eyes;*
Thus rendering the imperfect phrase complete,
A peroration I need not repeat.

VI.

But Christian, of a higher order, stood
Like an extinct volcano in his mood;
Silent, and sad, and savage,— with the trace
Of passion reeking from his clouded face;
Till lifting up again his sombre eye,
It glanced on Torquil, who leaned faintly by.
"And is it thus?" he cried, "unhappy boy!
And thee, too, *thee*— my madness must de-
  stroy!"
He said, and strode to where young Torquil
  stood,
Yet dabbled with his lately flowing blood;
Seized his hand wistfully, but did not press,
And shrunk as fearful of his own caress;
Inquired into his state; and when he heard
The wound was slighter than he deemed or
  feared,
A moment's brightness passed along his brow,
As much as such a moment would allow.
"Yes," he exclaimed, "we are taken in the
  toil,
But not a coward or a common spoil;
Dearly they have bought us — dearly still may
  buy,—
And I mus fall; but have you strength to
  fly? t
'Twould be some comfort still, could you sur-
  vive;

Our dwindled band is now too few to strive.
Oh! for a sole canoe! though but a shell,
To bear you hence to where a hope may
  dwell!
For me, my lot is what I sought; to be,
In life or death, the fearless and the free."

VII.

Even as he spoke, around the promontory,
Which nodded o'er the billows high and
  hoary,
A dark speck dotted ocean: on it flew
Like to the shadow of a roused sea-mew;
Onward it came — and, lo! a second fol-
  lowed —
Now seen — now hid — where ocean's vale
  was hollowed;
And near, and nearer, till their dusky crew
Presented well-known aspects to the view,
Till on the surf their skimming paddles play,
Buoyant as wings, and flitting through the
  spray; —
Now perching on the wave's high curl, and
  now
Dashed downward in the thundering foam
  below,
Which flings it broad and boiling sheet on
  sheet,
And slings its high flakes, shivered into sleet:
But floating still through surf and swell, drew
  nigh
The barks, like small birds through a lower-
  ing sky;
Their art seemed nature — such the skill to
  sweep
The wave of these born playmates of the
  deep.

VIII.

And who the first that, springing on the strand,
Leaped like a nereid from her shell to land,
With dark but brilliant skin, and dewy eye
Shining with love, and hope, and constancy?
Neuha — the fond, the faithful, the adored —
Her heart on Torquil's like a torrent poured;
And smiled, and wept, and near, and nearer
  clasped,
As if to be assured 'twas *him* she grasped;
Shuddered to see his yet warm wound, and
  then,
To find it trivial, smiled and wept again.
She was a warrior's daughter, and could bear
Such sights, and feel, and mourn, but not
  despair.
Her lover lived, — nor foes nor fears could
  blight
That full-blown moment in its all delight:
Joy trickled in her tears, joy filled the sob
That rocked her heart till almost HEARD to
  throb;
And paradise was breathing in the sigh
Of nature's child in nature's ecstasy.

IX.

The sterner spirits who beheld that meeting
Were not unmoved; who are, when hearts
    are greeting?
Even Christian gazed upon the maid and
    boy
With tearless eye, but yet a gloomy joy
Mixed with those bitter thoughts the soul
    arrays
In hopeless visions of our better days,
When all's gone — to the rainbow's latest ray.
"And but for me!" he said, and turned
    away;
Then gazed upon the pair, as in his den
A lion looks upon his cubs again;
And then relapsed into his sullen guise,
As heedless of his further destinies.

X.

But brief their time for good or evil thought;
The billows round the promontory brought
The plash of hostile oars. — Alas! who made
That sound a dread? All round them
    seemed arrayed
Against them, save the bride of Toobonai:
She, as she caught the first glimpse o'er the
    bay

Of the armed boats, which hur
    plete
The remnant's ruin with their fl
Beckoned the natives round
    prows,
Embarked their guests and la
    light canoes;
In one placed Christian and
    twain;
But she and Torquil must not pa
She fixed him in her own. — Aw
They clear the breakers, dart al
And towards a group of islets, s
The sea-bird's nest and seal's
    lair,
They skim the blue tops of the
They flew, and fast their fie
    chased.
They gain upon them—now they
Again make way and menace o'
And now the two canoes in chas
And follow different courses o'e
To baffle the pursuit. — Away!
As life is on each paddle's flight
And more than life or lives to N
Freights the frail bark and urges
And now the refuge and the foe
Yet, yet a moment! — Fly, thou

CANTO THE FOURTH.

I.

WHITE as a white sail on a dusky sea,
When half the horizon's clouded and half
    free,
Fluttering between the dun wave and the sky,
Is hope's last gleam in man's extremity.
Her anchor parts; but still her snowy sail
Attracts our eye amidst the rudest gale:
Though every wave she climbs divides us
    more,
The heart still follows from the loneliest
    shore.

II.

Not distant from the isle of Toobonai,
A black rock rears its bosom o'er the spray,
The haunt of birds, a desert to mankind,
Where the rough seal reposes from the wind,
And sleeps unwieldy in his cavern dun,
Or gambols with huge frolic in the sun:
There shrilly to the passing oar is heard
The startled echo of the ocean bird,
Who rears on its bare breast her callow brood,
The feathered fishers of the solitude.
A narrow segment of the yellow sand
On one side forms the outline of a strand;

Here the young turtle, crawling fr
Steals to the deep wherein his pa
Chipped by the beam, a nursling
But hatched for ocean by the fos
The rest was one bleak precipice
Gave mariners a shelter and des
A spot to make the saved regret
Which late went down, and envy t
Such was the stern asylum Neuh
To shield her lover from his follo
But all its secret was not told; sh
In this a treasure hidden from th

III.

Ere the canoes divided, near the
The men that manned what held
    lot,
By her command removed, to stre
The skiff which wafted Christian fr
This he would have opposed; but
She pointed calmly to the craggy
And bade him "speed and prosper
    take
The rest upon herself for Torquil
They parted with this added aid;
The proa darted like a shooting s

And gained on the pursuers, who now steered
Right on the rock which she and Torquil
    neared.
They pulled; her arm, though delicate, was
    free
And firm as ever grappled with the sea,
And yielded scarce to Torquil's manlier
    strength.
The prow now almost lay within its length
Of the crag's steep, inexorable face,
With nought but soundless waters for its base;
Within a hundred boats' lengths was the foe,
And now what refuge but their frail canoe?
This Torquil asked with half upbraiding eye,
Which said—" Has Neuha brought me here
    to die?
Is this a place of safety, or a grave,
And yon huge rock the tombstone of the wave?"

IV.

They rested on their paddles, and uprose
Neuha, and pointing to the approaching foes,
Cried,"Torquil, follow me, and fearless follow!"
Then plunged at once into the ocean's hollow.
There was no time to pause—the foes were
    near—
Chains in his eye, and menace in his ear;
With vigor they pulled on, and as they came,
Hailed him to yield, and by his forfeit name.
Headlong he leapt—to him the swimmer's skill
Was native, and now all his hope from ill:
But how, or where? He dived, and rose no
    more;
The boat's crew looked amazed o'er sea and
    shore.
There was no landing on that precipice,
Steep, harsh, and slippery as a berg of ice.
They watched awhile to see him float again,
But not a trace rebubbled from the main:
The wave rolled on, no ripple on its face,
Since their first plunge recalled a single trace;
The little whirl which eddied, and slight foam,
That whitened o'er what seemed their latest
    home,
White as a sepulchre above the pair
Who left no marble (mournful as an heir)
The quiet proa wavering o'er the tide
Was all that told of Torquil and his bride;
And but for this alone the whole might seem
The vanished phantom of a seaman's dream.
They paused and searched in vain, then
    pulled away;
Even superstition now forbade their stay.
Some said he had not plunged into the wave,
But vanished like a corpse-light from a grave;
Others, that something supernatural
Glared in his figure, more than mortal tall;
While all agreed that in his cheek and eye
There was a dead hue of eternity.
Still as their oars receded from the crag,
Round every weed a moment would they lag,
Expectant of some token of their prey;

But no—he had melted from them like the
    spray.

V.

And where was he the pilgrim of the deep,
Following the nereid? Had they ceased to
    weep
For ever? or, received in coral caves,
Wrung life and pity from the softening waves?
Did they with ocean's hidden sovereigns dwell,
And sound with mermen the fantastic shell?
Did Neuha with the mermaids comb her hair
Flowing o'er ocean as it streamed in air?
Or had they perished, and in silence slept
Beneath the gulf wherein they boldly leapt?

VI.

Young Neuha plunged into the deep, and he
Followed: her track beneath her native sea
Was as a native's of the element,
So smoothly, bravely, brilliantly she went,
Leaving a streak of light behind her heel,
Which struck and flashed like an amphibious
    steel.
Closely, and scarcely less expert to trace
The depths where divers held the pearl in
    chase,
Torquil, the nursling of the northern seas,
Pursued her liquid steps with heart and ease.
Deep—deeper for an instant Neuha led
The way—then upward soared—and as she
    spread
Her arms, and flung the foam from off her
    locks,
Laughed, and the sound was answered by the
    rocks.
They had gained a central realm of earth
    again,
But looked for tree, and field, and sky, in vain.
Around she pointed to a spacious cave,
Whose only portal was the keyless wave,[1]
(A hollow archway by the sun unseen,
Save through the billows' glassy veil of green,
In some transparent ocean holiday,
When all the finny people are at play,)
Wiped with her hair the brine from Torquil's
    eyes,
And clapped her hands with joy at his sur-
    prise:
Led him to where the rock appeared to jut
And form a something like a Triton's hut;
For all was darkness for a space, till day,
Through clefts above let in a sobered ray;
As in some old cathedral's glimmering aisle
The dusty monuments from light recoil,
Thus sadly in their refuge submarine
The vault drew half her shadow from the scene.

[1] Of this cave (which is no fiction) the original
will be found in the ninth chapter of "Mariner's
Account of the Tonga Islands." I have taken the
poetical liberty to transplant it to Toobonai, the
last island where any distinct account is left of
Christian and his comrades.

VII.

Forth from her bosom the young savage drew
A pine torch, strongly girded with gnatoo;
A plantain-leaf o'er all, the more to keep
Its latent sparkle from the sapping deep.
This mantle kept it dry; then from a nook
Of the same plantain-leaf a flint she took,
A few shrunk withered twigs, and from the
    blade
Of Torquil's knife struck fire, and thus ar-
    rayed   .
The grot with torchlight.   Wide it was and
    high,
And showed a self-born Gothic canopy;
The arch upreared by nature's architect,
The architrave some earthquake might erect;
The buttress from some mountain's bosom
    hurled,
When the Poles crashed, and water was the
    world;
Or hardened from some earth-absorbing fire,
While yet the globe reeked from its funeral
    pyre;
The fretted pinnacle, the aisle, the nave,[1]
Were there, all scooped by Darkness from
    her cave.
There, with a little tinge of phantasy,
Fantastic faces moped and mowed on high,
And then a mitre or a shrine would fix
The eye upon its seeming crucifix.
Thus Nature played with the stalactites,
And built herself a chapel of the seas.

VIII.

And Neuha took her Torquil by the hand,
And waved along the vault her kindled brand,
And led him into each recess, and showed
The secret places of their new abode.
Nor these alone, for all had been prepared
Before, to soothe the lover's lot she shared:
The mat for rest; for dress the fresh gnatoo,
And sandal oil to fence against the dew;
For food the cocoa-nut, the yam, the bread
Borne of the fruit; for board the plantain
    spread
With its broad leaf, or turtle-shell which bore
A banquet in the flesh it covered o'er;
The gourd with water recent from the rill,
The ripe banana from the mellow hill;
A pine-torch pile to keep undying light,
And she herself, as beautiful as night,
To fling her shadowy spirit o'er the scene,
And make their subterranean world serene.

[1] This may seem too minute for the general out-
line (in Mariner's Account) from which it is taken.
But few men have travelled without seeing some-
thing of the kind — on *land*, that is. Without ad-
verting to Ellora, in Mungo Park's last journal, he
mentions having met with a rock or mountain so
exactly resembling a Gothic cathedral, that only
minute inspection could convince him that it was a
work of nature.

She had foreseen, since first th
    sail
Drew to their isle, that force or
    fail,
And formed a refuge of the rock
For Torquil's safety from his cou
Each dawn had wafted there her
Laden with all the golden fruits th
Each eve had seen her gliding
    hour
With all could cheer or deck t
    bower;
And now she spread her little
    smiles,
The happiest daughter of the lovi

IX.

She, as he gazed with grateful won
Her sheltered love to her impassio
And suited to her soft caresses, to
An olden tale of love, — for love i
Old as eternity, but not outworn
With each new being born or to
How a young chief, a thousand m
Diving for turtle in the depths bel
Had risen, in tracking fast his oce
Into the cave which round and o'e
How in some desperate feud of a
He sheltered there a daughter of
A foe beloved, and offspring of a
Saved by his tribe but for a captiv
How, when the storm of war wa
    led
His island clan to where the wate
Their deep-green shadow o'er the
Then dived — it seemed as if to ris
His wondering mates, amazed
    bark,
Or deemed him mad, or prey t
    shark;
Rowed round in sorrow the sea-gi
Then paused upon their paddle
    shock;
When, fresh and springing from
    they saw
A goddess rise — so deemed they i
And their companion, glorious by
Proud and exulting in his mermai
And how, when undeceived, the
    bore
With sounding conchs and joyou
    shore;
How they had gladly lived and cal
And why not also Torquil and his
Not mine to tell the rapturous car
Which followed wildly in that wil

[2] The reader will recollect the epi
Greek anthology, or its translation into
modern languages: —

    " Whoe'er thou art, thy master s
      He was, or is, or is to b<sup> "

This tale; enough that all within that cave
Was love, though buried strong as in the
   grave
Where Abelard,through twenty years of death,
When Eloïsa's form was lowered beneath
Their nuptial vault, his arms outstretched, and
   pressed
The kindling ashes to his kindled breast.[1]
The waves without sang round their couch,
   their roar
As much unheeded as if life were o'er;
Within, their hearts made all their harmony,
Love's broken murmur and more broken sigh.

X.

And they, the cause and sharers of the shock
Which left them exiles of the hollow rock,
Where were they ?   O'er the sea for life they
   plied,
To seek from Heaven the shelter men denied.
Another course had been their choice — but
   where ?
The wave which bore them still their foes
   would bear,
Who, disappointed of their former chase,
In search of Christian now renewed their race.
Eager with anger, their strong arms made way,
Like vultures baffled of their previous prey.
They gained upon them, all whose safety lay
In some bleak crag or deeply-hidden bay:
No further chance or choice remained; and
   right
For the first further rock which met their sight
They steered, to take their latest view of land,
And yield as victims, or die sword in hand;
Dismissed the natives and their shallop, who
Would still have battled for that scanty crew;
But Christian bade them seek their shore
   again,
Nor add a sacrifice which were in vain;
For what were simple bow and savage spear
Against the arms which must be wielded here ?

XI.

They landed on a wild but narrow scene,
Where few but Nature's footsteps yet had been ;
Prepared their arms, and with that gloomy eye,
Stern and sustained, of man's extremity,
When hope is gone, nor glory's self remains
To cheer resistance against death or chains, —
They stood, the three, as the three hundred
   stood
Who dyed Thermopylæ with holy blood.
But, ah! how different! 'tis the *cause* makes
   all,
Degrades or hallows courage in its fall.
O'er them no fame, eternal and intense,

---

[1] The tradition is attached to the story of Eloïsa,
that when her body was lowered into the grave of
Abelard, (who had been buried twenty years,) he
opened his arms to receive her.

Blazed through the clouds of death and beck-
   oned hence ;
No grateful country, smiling through her tears,
Begun the praises of a thousand years ;
No nation's eyes would on their tomb be
   bent,
No heroes envy them their monument;
However boldly their warm blood was spilt,
Their life was shame, their epitaph was guilt.
And this they knew and felt, at least the one,
The leader of the band he had undone ;
Who, born perchance for better things, had
   set
His life upon a cast which lingered yet.
But now the die was to be thrown, and all
The chances were in favor of his fall :
And such a fall !   But still he faced the shock,
Obdurate as a portion of the rock
Whereon he stood, and fixed his levelled gun,
Dark as a sullen cloud before the sun.

XII.

The boat drew nigh, well armed, and firm the
   crew
To act whatever duty bade them do ;
Careless of danger, as the onward wind
Is of the leaves it strews, nor looks behind.
And yet perhaps they rather wished to go
Against a nation's than a native foe,
And felt that this poor victim of self-will,
Briton no more, had once been Britain's still.
They hailed him to surrender — no reply ;
Their arms were poised, and glittered in the
   sky.
They hailed again — no answer; yet once
   more
They offered quarter louder than before.
The echoes only, from the rock's rebound,
Took their last farewell of the dying sound.
Then flashed the flint, and blazed the volley
   ing flame,
And the smoke rose between them and their
   aim,
While the rock rattled with the bullets' knell,
Which pealed in vain, and flattened as they
   fell ;
Then flew the only answer to be given
By those who had lost all hope in earth or
   heaven ;
After the first fierce peal, as they pulled nigher,
They heard the voice of Christian shout,
   " Now, fire ! "
And ere the word upon the echo died,
Two fell; the rest assailed the rock's rough
   side,
And, furious at the madness of their foes,
Disdained all further efforts, save to close.
But steep the crag, and all without a path,
Each step opposed a bastion to their wrath,
While, placed midst clefts the least accessible,
Which Christian's eye was trained to mark
   full well,

The three maintained a strife which must not
    yield,
In spots where eagles might have chosen to
    build.
Their every shot told; while the assailant fell,
Dashed on the shingles like the limpet shell;
But still enough survived, and mounted still,
Scattering their numbers here and there, until
Surrounded and commanded, though not nigh
Enough for seizure, near enough to die,
The desperate trio held aloof their fate
But by a thread, like sharks who have gorged
    the bait;
Yet to the very last they battled well,
And not a groan informed their foes *who* fell.
Christian died last — twice wounded; and
    once more
Mercy was offered when they saw his gore;
Too late for life, but not too late to die,
With, though a hostile hand, to close his eye.
A limb was broken, and he drooped along
The crag, as doth a falcon reft of young.
The sound revived him, or appeared to wake
Some passion which a weakly gesture spake:
He beckoned to the foremost, who drew nigh,
But, as they neared, he reared his weapon
    high —
His last ball had been aimed, but from his
    breast
He tore the topmost button from his vest,[1]
Down the tube dashed it, levelled, fired, and
    smiled
As his foe fell; then, like a serpent, coiled
His wounded, weary form, to where the steep
Looked desperate as himself along the deep;
Cast one glance back, and clenched his hand,
    and shook
His last rage 'gainst the earth which he for-
    sook;
Then plunged : the rock below received like
    glass
His body crushed into one gory mass,
With scarce a shred to tell of human form,
Or fragment for the sea-bird or the worm;
A fair-haired scalp, besmeared with blood and
    weeds,
Yet reeked, the remnant of himself and deeds;

---

[1] In Thibault's account of Frederic the Second
of Prussia, there is a singular relation of a young
Frenchman, who with his mistress appeared to be of
some rank. He enlisted and deserted at Schweid-
nitz; and after a desperate resistance was retaken,
having killed an officer, who attempted to seize him
after he was wounded, by the discharge of his mus-
ket loaded with a *button* of his uniform. Some
circumstances on his court martial raised a great
interest amongst his judges, who wished to discover
his real situation in life, which he offered to dis-
close, but to the *king* only, to whom he requested
permission to write. This was refused, and Frede-
ric was filled with the greatest indignation, from
baffled curiosity or some other motive, when he un-
derstood that his request had been denied.

Some splinters of his weapons (to
As long as hand could hold, he hel(
Yet glittered, but at distance — hu
To rust beneath the dew and dash
The rest was nothing — save a life
And soul — but who shall answe
    went ?
'Tis ours to bear, not judge the
    they
Who doom to hell, themselves are
Unless these bullies of eternal pair
Are pardoned their bad hearts for
    brains.

XIII.

The deed was over! All were go
The fugitive, the captive, or the sla
Chained on the deck, where onc
    crew,
They stood with honor, were the w:
Survivors of the skirmish on the is
But the last rock left no surviving
Cold lay they where they fell, and
While o'er them flapped the sea-l
    wing,
Now wheeling nearer from the n
    surge,
And screaming high their harsh a
    dirge :
But calm and careless heaved the v
Eternal with unsympathetic flow;
Far o'er its face the dolphins sport
And sprung the flying fish against
Till its dried wing relapsed from its b
To gather moisture for another fli

XIV.

'Twas morn; and Neuha, who by c
Swam smoothly forth to catch the
And watch if aught approach the a
    lair
Where lay her lover, saw a sail in
It flapped, it filled, and to the grov
Bent its broad arch : her breath be
With fluttering fear, her heart bea
    high,
While yet a doubt sprung where
    might lie.
But no! it came not; fast and far
The shadow lessened as it cleared
She gazed, and flung the sea-foar
    eyes,
To watch as for a rainbow in the s
On the horizon verged the distant
Diminished, dwindled to a very sp
Then vanished. All was ocean, a
Down plunged she through the ca
    her boy;
Told all she had seen, and all she ho
That happy love could augur or re
Sprung forth again, with Torquil fo
His bounding nereid over the brea

Swam round the rock, to where a shallow cleft
Hid the canoe that Neuha there had left
Drifting along the tide, without an oar,
That eve the strangers chased them from the
shore;
But when these vanished, she pursued her
prow, .
Regained, and urged to where they found it
now:
Nor ever did more love and joy embark,
Than now were wafted in that slender ark.

XV.

Again their own shore rises on the view,
No more polluted with a hostile hue;
No sullen ship lay bristling o'er the foam,
A floating dungeon:—all was hope and home!
A thousand proas darted o'er the bay,

With sounding shells, and heralded their way,
The chiefs came down, around the people
poured,
And welcomed Torquil as a son restored;
The women thronged, embracing and em,
braced
By Neuha, asking where they had been chased
And how escaped? The tale was told; and
then
One acclamation rent the sky again;
And from that hour a new tradition gave
Their sanctuary the name of " Neuha's Cave.'
A hundred fires, far flickering from the height
Blazed o'er the general revel of the night,
The feast in honor of the guest, returned
To peace and pleasure, perilously earned;
A night succeeded by such happy days
As only the yet infant world displays.

MANFRED: A DRAMATIC POEM.

"There are more things in heaven and earth, Horatio,
Than are dreamt of in your philosophy."

[THE following extracts from Byron's letters to Mr. Murray will sufficiently explain the history of the composition of Manfred:—

VENICE, February 15, 1817.—"I forgot to mention to you, that a kind of Poem in dialogue (in blank verse) or Drama, from which 'the Incantation' is an extract, begun last summer in Switzerland, is finished: it is in three acts, but of a very wild, metaphysical, and inexplicable kind. Almost all the persons —but two or three—are Spirits of the earth and air, or the waters; the scene is in the Alps; the hero a kind of magician, who is tormented by a species of remorse, the cause of which is left half unexplained. He wanders about invoking these Spirits, which appear to him, and are of no use; he at last goes to the very abode of the Evil Principle, *in propriâ personâ*, to evocate a ghost, which appears, and gives him an ambiguous and disagreeable answer; and, in the third act, he is found by his attendants dying in a tower where he had studied his art. You may perceive, by this outline, that I have no great opinion of this piece of fantasy; but I have at least rendered it *quite impossible* for the stage, for which my intercourse with Drury Lane has given me the greatest contempt. I have not even copied it off, and feel too lazy at present to attempt the whole; but when I have, I will send it you, and you may either throw it into the fire or not."

March 3.—"I sent you the other day, in two covers, the first act of 'Manfred,' a drama as mad as Nat. Lee's Bedlam tragedy, which was in twenty-five acts and some odd scenes: mine is but in three acts."

March 9.—"In remitting the third act of the sort of dramatic poem of which you will by this time have received the two first, I have little to observe, except that you must not publish it (if it ever is published) without giving me previous notice. I have really and truly no notion whether it is good or bad; and as this was not the case with the principal of my former publications, I am, therefore, inclined to rank it very humbly. You will submit it to Mr. Gifford, and to whomsoever you please besides. The thing you will see at a glimpse, could never be attempted or thought of for the stage; I much doubt if for publication even. It is too much in my old style; but I composed it actually with a *horror* of the stage, and with a view to render the thought of it impracticable, knowing the zeal of my friends that I should try that for which I have an invincible repugnance, viz., a representation. I certainly am a devil of a mannerist, and must leave off; but what could I do? Without exertion of some kind, I should have sunk under my imagination and reality."

March 25. — "With regard to the ' Witch Drama,' I repeat, that I have not an idea if it i
If bad, it must, on no account, be risked in publication; if good, it is at your service. I va
hundred guineas, or less, if you like it. Perhaps, if published, the best way will be to a
winter volume, and not publish separately. The price will show you I don't pique myse'
speak out. You may put it into the fire, if you like, and Gifford don't like."
April 9. — " As for ' Manfred,' the two first acts are the best; the third so so; but I w
the first and second heats. You may call it ' a Poem,' for it is no Drama, and I do not cl
it called by so d—d a name, — ' a Poem in dialogue,' or — Pantomime, if you will; any thin
room synonyme; and this is your motto —

> ' There are more things in heaven and earth, Horatio,
> Than are dreamt of in your philosophy.' "

The following passages are extracts from the ablest contemporary critiques upon Manfre

" In Manfred, we recognize at once the gloom and potency of that soul which burned an
fed upon itself, in Harold, and Conrad, and Lara — and which comes again in this piece, m
than in anger — more proud, perhaps, and more awful than ever — but with the fiercer trait
thropy subdued, as it were, and quenched in the gloom of a deeper despondency. Man
like Conrad and Lara, wreak the anguish of his burning heart in the dangers and daring of
predatory war — nor seek to drown bitter thoughts in the tumult of perpetual contention ;
Harold, does he sweep over the peopled scenes of the earth with high disdain and aversi
his survey of the business, and pleasures, and studies of man an occasion for taunts and
the food of an unmeasurable spleen. He is fixed by the genius of the poet in the majest
the central Alps — where, from his youth up, he has lived in proud but calm seclusion fro
men, conversing only with the magnificent forms and aspects of nature by which he is su
with the Spirits of the Elements over whom he has acquired dominion, by the secret an
studies of sorcery and magic. He is averse, indeed, from mankind, and scorns the low
nature to which he belongs; but he cherishes no animosity or hostility to that feeble race
cerns excite no interest — their pursuits no sympathy — their joys no envy. It is irksome
for him to be crossed by them in his melancholy musings, — but he treats them with gentler
and, except when stung to impatience by too importunate an intrusion, is kind and cons
comforts of all around him. — This piece is properly entitled a dramatic poem — for it is me
and is not at all a drama or play in the modern acceptation of the term. It has no action
no characters; Manfred merely muses and suffers from the beginning to the end. His distr
same at the opening of the scene and at its closing, and the temper in which they are borne
A hunter and a priest, and some domestics, are indeed introduced, but they have no connec
passions or sufferings on which the interest depends; and Manfred is substantially alone th
whole piece. He holds no communion but with the memory of the Being he had loved; and
Spirits whom he evokes to reproach with his misery, and their inability to relieve it. Th
beings approach nearer to the character of persons of the drama — but still they are but c
paniments to the performance; and Manfred is, in reality, the only actor and sufferer on th
delineate his character indeed — to render conceivable his feelings — is plainly the whole scor
of the poem; and the conception and execution are, in this respect, equally admirable. It i
terrific vision of a being invested with superhuman attributes, in order that he may be cap
than human sufferings, and be sustained under them by more than human force and pride.
the improbability of the fiction, is to mistake the end and aim of the author. Probabilities, w
did not enter at all into his consideration; his object was, to produce effect — to exalt a
character through whom he was to interest or appall us — and to raise our conception of
helps that could be derived from the majesty of nature, or the dread of superstition. It is e
fore, if the situation in which he has placed him is *conceivable*, and if the supposition
enhances our emotions and kindles our imagination; — for it is Manfred only that we are req
to pity, or admire. If we can once conceive of him as a real existence, and enter into the
height of his pride and his sorrows, we may deal as we please with the means that have
furnish us with this impression, or to enable us to attain to this conception. We may reg
as types, or metaphors, or allegories; but HE is the thing to be expressed, and the feeling
lect of which all these are but shadows." — JEFFREY.
" In this very extraordinary poem, Lord Byron has pursued the same course as in the
Childe Harold, and put out his strength upon the same objects. The action is laid among t
of the Alps — the characters are all, more or less, formed and swayed by the operations of th
scenery around them, and every page of the poem teems with imagery and passion, though
time, the mind of the poet is often overborne, as it were, by the strength and novelty of its
tions; and thus the composition, as a whole, is liable to many and fatal objections. But
more novel exhibition of Lord Byron's powers in this remarkable drama. He has here
world of spirits; and, in the wild delight with which the elements of nature seem to have
he has endeavored to embody and call up before him their ministering agents, and to empl
personifications, as he formerly employed the feelings and passions of man. We are not pre
that, in this daring attempt, he has completely succeeded. We are inclined to think, that th
conceived, and the principal character which he has wished to delineate, would require a fr
ment than is here given to them; and, accordingly, a sense of imperfection, incompletenes
sion accompanies the mind throughout the perusal of the poem, owing either to some failui

of the poet, or to the inherent mystery of the subject. But though, on that account, it is difficult to comprehend distinctly the drift of the composition, it unquestionably exhibits many noble delineations of mountain scenery, — many impressive and terrible pictures of passion, — and many wild and awful visions of imaginary horror."—Professor Wilson.]

DRAMATIS PERSONÆ.

Manfred.	Witch of the Alps.
Chamois Hunter.	Arimanes.
Abbot of St. Maurice.	Nemesis.
Manuel.	The Destinies.
Herman.	Spirits, etc.

The Scene of the Drama is amongst the Higher Alps—partly in the Castle of Manfred, and partly in the Mountains.

ACT I.

Scene I.—Manfred *alone.—Scene, a Gothic Gallery.— Time, Midnight.*

Man. The lamp must be replenished, but even then
It will not burn so long as I must watch:
My slumbers — if I slumber — are not sleep,
But a continuance of enduring thought,
Which then I can resist not: in my heart
There is a vigil, and these eyes but close
'To look within; and yet I live, and bear
The aspect and the form of breathing men.
But grief should be the instructor of the wise;
Sorrow is knowledge: they who know the most
Must mourn the deepest o'er the fatal truth,
The Tree of Knowledge is not that of Life.
Philosophy and science, and the springs
Of wonder, and the wisdom of the world,
I have essayed, and in my mind there is
A power to make these subject to itself—
But they avail not: I have done men good,
And I have met with good even among men—
But this availed not: I have had my foes,
And none have baffled, many fallen before me —
But this availed not: — Good, or evil, life,
Powers, passions, all I see in other beings,
Have been to me as rain unto the sands,
Since that all-nameless hour. I have no dread,
And feel the curse to have no natural fear,
Nor fluttering throb, that beats with hopes or wishes,
Or lurking love of something on the earth. —
Now to my task. —
                    Mysterious Agency!
Ye spirits of the unbounded Universe![1]

Whom I have sought in darkness and in light —
Ye, who do compass earth about, and dwell
In subtler essence — ye, to whom the tops
Of mountains inaccessible are haunts,[2]
And earth's and ocean's caves familiar things —
I call upon ye by the written charm
Which gives me power upon you——·Rise!
appear!   [A pause.
They come not yet.—Now by the voice of him
Who is the first among you— by this sign,
Which makes you tremble — by the claims of him
Who is undying,—Rise! appear!——Appear!
                                     [A pause.
If it be so. — Spirits of earth and air,
Ye shall not thus elude me: by a power,
Deeper than all yet urged, a tyrant-spell,
Which had its birthplace in a star condemned,
The burning wreck of a demolished world,
A wandering hell in the eternal space;
By the strong curse which is upon my soul,
The thought which is within me and around me,
I do compel ye to my will. — Appear!
    [A star is seen at the darker end of the gallery: it is stationary; and a voice is heard singing.

First Spirit.

Mortal! to thy bidding bowed,
From my mansion in the cloud,
Which the breath of twilight builds,
And the summer's sunset gilds
With the azure and vermilion,
Which is mixed for my pavilion;[3]

---

[1] [Original MS. —   " Eternal Agency!
              Ye spirits of the immortal Universe!

[2] [MS. —
" Of inaccessible mountains are the haunts."]
    [3] [MS. — " Which is fit for my pavilion "]

Though thy quest may be forbidden,
On a star-beam I have ridden;
To thine adjuration bowed,
Mortal — be thy wish avowed!

Voice of the SECOND SPIRIT.

Mont Blanc is the monarch of mountains;
　They crowned him long ago
On a throne of rocks, in a robe of clouds,
　With a diadem of snow.
Around his waist are forests braced,
　The Avalanche in his hand;
But ere it fall, that thundering ball
　Must pause for my command.
The Glacier's cold and restless mass
　Moves onward day by day;
But I am he who bids it pass,
　Or with its ice delay.[1]
I am the spirit of the place,
　Could make the mountain bow
And quiver to his caverned base —
And what with me wouldst *Thou?*

Voice of the THIRD SPIRIT.

In the blue depth of the waters,
　Where the wave hath no strife,
Where the wind is a stranger,
　And the sea-snake hath life,
Where the Mermaid is decking
　Her green hair with shells;
Like the storm on the surface
　Came the sound of thy spells;
O'er my calm Hall of Coral
　The deep echo rolled —
To the Spirit of Ocean
　Thy wishes unfold!

FOURTH SPIRIT.

Where the slumbering earthquake
　Lies pillowed on fire,
And the lakes of bitumen
　Rise boilingly higher;
Where the roots of the Andes
　Strike deep in the earth,
As their summits to heaven
　Shoot soaringly forth;
I have quitted my birthplace,
　Thy bidding to bide —
Thy spell hath subdued me,
　Thy will be my guide!

FIFTH SPIRIT.

I am the Rider of the wind,
　The Stirrer of the storm;
The hurricane I left behind
　Is yet with lightning warm;
To speed to thee, o'er shore and sea
　I swept upon the blast:
The fleet I met sailed well, and yet
　'Twill sink ere night be past.

　　' [MS. — " Or makes its ice delay."]

SIXTH SPIRIT.

My dwelling is the shadow of the night,
Why doth thy magic torture me with light?

SEVENTH SPIRIT.

The star which rules thy destiny
Was ruled, ere earth began, by me:
It was a world as fresh and fair
As e'er revolved round sun in air;
Its course was free and regular,
Space bosomed not a lovelier star.
The hour arrived — and it became
A wandering mass of shapeless flame,
A pathless comet, and a curse,
The menace of the universe;
Still rolling on with innate force,
Without a sphere, without a course,
A bright deformity on high,
The monster of the upper sky!
And thou! beneath its influence born —
Thou worm! whom I obey and scorn —
Forced by a power (which is not thine,
And lent thee but to make thee mine)
For this brief moment to descend,
Where these weak spirits round thee bend
And parley with a thing like thee —
What wouldst thou, Child of Clay! with me?

The SEVEN SPIRITS.

Earth, ocean, air, night, mountains, winds, thy
　　star,
　Are at thy beck and bidding, Child of Clay!
Before thee at thy quest their spirits are —
　What wouldst thou with us, son of mortals
　　— say?

Man.　Forgetfulness ——
First Spirit.　Of what — of whom — and
　why?
Man.　Of that which is within me; read it
　　there —
Ye know it, and I cannot utter it.
Spirit.　We can but give thee that which
　　we possess:
Ask of us subjects, sovereignty, the power
O'er earth, the whole, or portion, or a sign
Which shall control the elements, whereof
We are the dominators, each and all,
These shall be thine.
　Man.　　　　　Oblivion, self-oblivion —
Can ye not wring from out the hidden realms
Ye offer so profusely what I ask?
　Spirit.　It is not in our essence, in our skill;
But — thou mayst die.
　Man.　　　　　Will death bestow it on me?
　Spirit.　We are immortal, and do not for-·
　　get;
We are eternal; and to us the past
Is, as the future, present. Art thou answered?
　Man.　Ye mock me — but the power which
　　brought ye here

Hath made you mine. Slaves, scoff not at
    my will!
The mind, the spirit, the Promethean spark,
The lightning of my being, is as bright,
Pervading, and far darting as your own,
And shall not yield to yours, though cooped
    in clay.
Answer, or I will teach you what I am.
    Spirit. We answer as we answered; our
        reply
Is even in thine own words.
    Man.   Why say ye so?
    Spirit. If, as thou say'st, thine essence be
        as ours,
We have replied in telling thee, the thing
Mortals call death hath nought to do with us.
    Man. I then have called ye from your
        realms in vain;
Ye cannot, or ye will not, aid me.
    Spirit.   Say;
What we possess we offer; it is thine:
Bethink ere thou dismiss us, ask again —
Kingdom, and sway, and strength, and length
        of days——
    Man. Accursed! what have I to do with
        days?
They are too long already. — Hence — be-
        gone!
    Spirit. Yet pause: being here, our will
        would do thee service;
Bethink thee, is there then no other gift
Which we can make not worthless in thine
        eyes?
    Man. No, none: yet stay — one moment,
        ere we part —
I would behold ye face to face. I hear
Your voices, sweet and melancholy sounds,
As music.on the waters; and I see
The steady aspect of a clear large star;
But nothing more. Approach me as ye are,
Or one, or all, in your accustomed forms.
    Spirit. We have no forms, beyond the ele-
        ments
Of which we are the mind and principle:
But choose a form — in that we will appear.
    Man. I have no choice; there is no form
        on earth
Hideous or beautiful to me. Let him,
Who is most powerful of ye, take such aspect
As unto him may seem most fitting — Come!
    Seventh Spirit (*appearing in the shape of
        a beautiful female figure*). Behold!
    Man. Oh God! if it be thus, and *thou*
Art not a madness and a mockery,
I yet might be most happy. I will clasp thee,
And we again will be—— [*The figure vanishes.*
                    My heart is crushed!
            [MANFRED *falls senseless.*

(*A Voice is heard in the Incantation which
            follows.*) [1]

————————————————
[1] [These verses were written in Switzerland, in

When the moon is on the wave,
    And the glow-worm in the grass,
And the meteor on the grave,
    And the wisp on the morass; [2]
When the falling stars are shooting,
And the answered owls are hooting,
And the silent leaves are still
In the shadow of the hill,
Shall my soul be upon thine,
With a power and with a sign.

Though thy slumber may be deep,
Yet thy spirit shall not sleep;
There are shades which will not vanish.
There are thoughts thou canst not banish.
By a power to thee unknown,
Thou canst never be alone;
Thou art wrapt as with a shroud,
Thou art gathered in a cloud,
And for ever shalt thou dwell
In the spirit of this spell.

Though thou seest me not pass by,
Thou shalt feel me with thine eye
As a thing that, though unseen,
Must be near thee, and hath been;
And when in that secret dread
Thou hast turned around thy head,
Thou shalt marvel I am not
As thy shadow on the spot,
And the power which thou dost feel
Shall be what thou must conceal.

And a magic voice and verse
Hath baptized thee with a curse;
And a spirit of the air
Hath begirt thee with a snare;
In the wind there is a voice
Shall forbid thee to rejoice;
And to thee shall Night deny

————————————————
1816, and transmitted to England for publication
with the third canto of Childe Harold. "As they
were written," says Moore, "immediately after the
last fruitless attempt at reconciliation with Lady
Byron, it is needless to say who was in the poet's
thoughts while he penned some of the opening
stanzas."]

[2] ["And the *wisp* on the morass." Hearing, in
February, 1818, of a menaced version of Manfred
by some Italian, Byron wrote to his friend Mr.
Hoppner—"If you have any means of communi-
cating with the man, would you permit me to con-
vey to him the offer of any price he may obtain, or
think to obtain, for his project, provided he will
throw his translation into the fire, and promise not
to undertake any other of that, or any other of my
things? I will send him his money immediately, on
this condition." A negotiation was accordingly
set on foot, and the translator, on receiving two
hundred francs, delivered up his manuscript, and
engaged never to translate any other of the poet's
works. Of his qualifications for the task some
notion may be formed from the fact, that he had
turned the word "wisp," in this line, into "a
bundle of straw."]

All the quiet of her sky;
And the day shall have a sun,
Which shall make thee wish it done.

From thy false tears I did distil
An essence which hath strength to kill;
From thy own heart I then did wring
The black blood in its blackest spring;
From thy own smile I snatched the snake,
For there it coiled as in a brake;
From thy own lip I drew the charm
Which gave all these their chiefest harm;
In proving every poison known,
I found the strongest was thine own.

By thy cold breast and serpent smile,
By thy unfathomed gulfs of guile,
By that most seeming virtuous eye,
By thy shut soul's hypocrisy;
By the perfection of thine art
Which passed for human thine own heart;
By thy delight in others' pain,
And by thy brotherhood of Cain,
I call upon thee! and compel [1]
Thyself to be thy proper Hell!

And on thy head I pour the vial
Which doth devote thee to this trial;
Nor to slumber, nor to die,
Shall be in thy destiny;
Though thy death shall still seem near
To thy wish, but as a fear;
Lo! the spell now works around thee,
And the clankless chain hath bound thee;
O'er thy heart and brain together
Hath the word been passed — now wither!

SCENE II. — *The Mountain of the Jungfrau.
— Time, Morning.* — MANFRED *alone upon
the Cliffs.*

Man.   The spirits I have raised abandon
   me —
The spells which I have studied baffle me —
The remedy I recked of tortured me;
I lean no more on super-human aid,
It hath no power upon the past, and for
The future, till the past be gulfed in darkness,
It is not of my search. — My mother Earth!
And thou fresh breaking Day, and you, ye
   Mountains,
Why are ye beautiful? I cannot love ye.
And thou, the bright eye of the universe,
That openest over all, and unto all
Art a delight — thou shin'st not on my heart.
And you, ye crags, upon whose extreme
   edge
I stand, and on the torrent's brink beneath
Behold the tall pines dwindled as to shrubs
In dizziness of distance; when a leap,
A stir, a motion, even a breath, would bring
My breast upon its rocky bosom's bed

To rest for ever — wherefore do I pause?
I feel the impulse — yet I do not plunge;
I see the peril — yet do not recede;
And my brain reels — and yet my foot is firm:
There is a power upon me which withholds,
And makes it my fatality to live;
If it be life to wear within myself
This barrenness of spirit, and to be
My own soul's sepulchre, for I have ceased
To justify my deeds unto myself —
The last infirmity of evil. Ay,
Thou winged and cloud-cleaving minister,
                           [*An eagle passes.*
Whose happy flight is highest into heaven,
Well mayst thou swoop so near me — I should
   be
Thy prey, and gorge thine eaglets; thou art
   gone
Where the eye cannot follow thee; but thine
Yet pierces downward, onward, or above,
With a pervading vision. — Beautiful!
How beautiful is all this visible world!
How glorious in its action and itself!
But we, who name ourselves its sovereigns,
   we,
Half dust, half deity, alike unfit
To sink or soar, with our mixed essence make
A conflict of its elements, and breathe
The breath of degradation and of pride,
Contending with low wants and lofty will,
Till our mortality predominates,
And men are — what they name not to them-
   selves,
And trust not to each other. Hark! the note,
[*The Shepherd's pipe in the distance is heard.*
The natural music of the mountain reed —
For here the patriarchal days are not
A pastoral fable — pipes in the liberal air,
Mixed with the sweet bells of the sauntering
   herd; [2]

---

[1] [MS. — " I do adjure thee to this spell."]

---

[2] [The germs of this, and of several other pas-
sages in Manfred, may be found in the Journal of
his Swiss tour, which Byron transmitted to his
sister: *e.g.* "Sept. 19. — Arrived at a lake in the
very bosom of the mountains; left our quadrupeds,
and ascended further; came to some snow in patches,
upon which my forehead's perspiration fell like rain,
making the same dents as in a sieve; the chill of
the wind and the snow turned me giddy, but I
scrambled on and upwards. Hobhouse went to the
highest pinnacle. The whole of the mountains
superb. A shepherd on a steep and very high cliff
playing upon his *pipe;* very different from Arcadia.
The music of the cows' *bells* (for their wealth, like
the patriarchs', is cattle) in the pastures, which
reach to a height far above any mountains in Britain,
and the shepherds shouting to us from crag to crag,
and playing on their reeds where the steeps appeared
almost inaccessible, with the surrounding scenery,
realised all that I have ever heard or imagined of a
pastoral existence — much more so than Greece or
Asia Minor: for there we are a little too much of
the sabre and musket order, and if there is a crook
in one hand, you are sure to see a gun in the other:

My soul would drink those echoes.—Oh, that
    I were
The viewless spirit of a lovely sound,
A living voice, a breathing harmony,
A bodiless enjoyment—born and dying
With the blest tone which made me!

Enter from below a CHAMOIS HUNTER.

    Chamois Hunter.   Even so .
This way the chamois leapt: her nimble feet
Have baffled me; my gains to-day will scarce
Repay my break-neck travail.—What is here?
Who seems not of my trade, and yet hath
    reached
A height which none even of our mountaineers,
Save our best hunters, may attain: his garb
Is goodly, his mien manly, and his air
Proud as a free-born peasant's, at this dis-
    tance —
I will approach him nearer.

    Man. (not perceiving the other). To be
    thus —
Gray-haired with anguish,[1] like these blasted
    pines,
Wrecks of a single winter, barkless, branch-
    less,[2]
A blighted trunk upon a cursed root,
Which but supplies a feeling to decay —
And to be thus, eternally but thus,
Having been otherwise! Now furrowed o'er
With wrinkles, ploughed by moments, not by
    years
And hours — all tortured into ages — hours
Which I outlive! — Ye toppling crags of ice!
Ye avalanches, whom a breath draws down
In mountainous o'erwhelming, come and crush
    me!
I hear ye momently above, beneath,
Crash with a frequent conflict;[3] but ye pass,

And only fall on things that still would live;
On the young flourishing forest, or the hut
And hamlet of the harmless villager.

    C. Hun. The mists begin to rise up from
    the valley;
I'll warn him to descend, or he may chance
To lose at once his way and life together.

    Man. The mists boil up around the gla-
    ciers; clouds
Rise curling fast beneath me, white and sul-
    phury,
Like foam from the roused ocean of deep
    Hell,[4]
Whose every wave breaks on a living shore,
Heaped with the damned like pebbles.—I am
    giddy.[5]

    C. Hun. I must approach him cautiously;
    if near,
A sudden step will startle him, and he
Seems tottering already.

    Man.   Mountains have fallen,
Leaving a gap in the clouds, and with the shock
Rocking their Alpine brethren; filling up
The ripe green valleys with destruction's
    splinters;
Damming the rivers with a sudden dash,
Which crushed the waters into mist, and made
Their fountains find another channel — thus,
Thus, in its old age, did Mount Rosenberg —
Why stood I not beneath it ?

    C. Hun. .   Friend! have a care,
Your next step may be fatal! — for the love
Of him who made you, stand not on that
    brink!

    Man. (not hearing him). Such would have
    been for me a fitting tomb;
My bones had then been quiet in their depth;
They had not then been strewn upon the rocks
For the wind's pastime — as thus — thus they
    shall be —
In this one plunge. — Farewell, ye opening
    heavens!

---

but this was pure and unmixed — solitary, savage,
and *patriarchal*. As we went, they played the
'Ranz des Vaches' and other airs, by way of fare-
well. I have lately repeopled my mind with
nature."]

[1] [See the opening lines to the "Prisoner of
Chillon." Speaking of Marie Antoinette, "I was
struck," says Madame Campan, "with the aston-
ishing change misfortune had wrought upon her
features: her whole head of hair had turned almost
white, during her transit from Varennes to Paris."
The same thing occurred to the unfortunate Queen
Mary. "With calm but undaunted fortitude," says
her historian, "she laid her neck upon the block;
and while one executioner held her hands, the other,
at the second stroke, cut off her head, which, falling
out of its attire, discovered her hair, already grown
quite gray with cares and sorrows." The hair of
Mary's grandson, Charles I., turned quite gray, in
like manner, during his stay at Carisbrooke.]

[2] ["Passed whole woods of *withered pines*, all
withered, — trunks stripped and barkless, branches
lifeless, done by a *single winter:* their appearance
reminded me of me and my family." — *Swiss
Journal.*]

[3] ["Ascended the Wengern mountain; left the

horses, took off my coat, and went to the summit.
On one side, our view comprised the Jungfrau, with
all her glaciers; then the Dent d'Argent, shining
like truth; then the Little Giant, and the Great
Giant; and last, not least, the Wetterhorn. The
height of the Jungfrau is thirteen thousand feet above
the sea, and eleven thousand above the valley.
Heard the avalanches falling every five minutes.
nearly." — *Swiss Journal.*]

[4] [MS. —
"Like foam from the roused ocean of *old* Hell."]

[5] ["The clouds rose from the opposite valley,
curling up perpendicular precipices, like the *foam*
of the *ocean of hell* during a spring tide — it was
white and sulphury, and immeasurably deep in
appearance. The side we ascended was not of so
precipitous a nature; but, on arriving at the sum-
mit, we looked down upon the other side upon a
boiling sea of cloud, dashing against the crags on
which we stood — these crags on one side quite per-
pendicular. In passing the masses of snow, I made

Look not upon me thus reproachfully —
Ye were not meant for me —Earth! take these
    atoms!
    [*As Manfred is in act to spring from the
    cliff, the* CHAMOIS HUNTER *seizes and
    retains him with a sudden grasp.*
C. Hun. Hold, madman! — though aweary
    of thy life,
Stain not our pure vales with thy guilty blood—
Away with me —— I will not quit my hold.
    Man. I am most sick at heart — nay, grasp
    me not—
I am all feebleness — the mountains whirl
Spinning around me —— I grow blind ——
    What art thou?
    C. Hun. I'll answer that anon. — Away
    with me ——
The clouds grow thicker —— there — now
    lean on me—
Place your foot here — here, take this staff,
    and cling
A moment to that shrub — now give me your
    hand,
And hold fast by my girdle — softly — well —
The Chalet will be gained within an hour —
Come on, we'll quickly find a surer footing,
And something like a pathway, which the tor-
    rent
Hath washed since winter.—Come, 'tis bravely
    done—
You should have been a hunter.—Follow me.
    [*As they descend the rocks with difficulty,
    the scene closes.*

ACT II.

SCENE I.—*A Cottage amongst the Bernese
    Alps.*

MANFRED *and the* CHAMOIS HUNTER.

C. Hun. No, no — yet pause — thou must
    not yet go forth:
Thy mind and body are alike unfit
To trust each other, for some hours, at least;
When thou art better, I will be thy guide —
But whither?
    Man.   It imports not: I do know
My route full well, and need no further guid-
    ance.
    C. Hun. Thy garb and gait bespeak thee
    of high lineage —
One of the many chiefs, whose castled crags
Look o'er the lower valleys — which of these
May call thee lord? I only know their portals;
My way of life leads me but rarely down
To bask by the huge hearths of those old halls,
Carousing with the vassals; but the paths,
Which step from out our mountains to their
    doors,

a snowball and pelted Hobhouse with it." — *Swiss
Journal.*]

I know from childhood — which of these is
    thine?
    Man. No matter.
    C. Hun. Well, sir, pardon me the question
And be of better cheer. Come, taste my wine;
'Tis of an ancient vintage; many a day
'T has thawed my veins among our glaciers
    now
Let it do thus for thine — Come, pledge me
    fairly.
    Man. Away, away! there's blood upon the
    brim!
Will it then never — never sink in the earth?
    C. Hun. What dost thou mean? thy senses
    wander from thee.
    Man. I say 'tis blood—my blood! the pure
    warm stream
Which ran in the veins of my fathers, and in
    ours
When we were in our youth, and had one
    heart,
And loved each other as we should not love,
And this was shed: but still it rises up,
Coloring the clouds, that shut me out from
    heaven,
Where thou art not — and I shall never be.
    C. Hun. Man of strange words, and some
    half-maddening sin,
Which makes thee people vacancy, whate'er
Thy dread and sufferance be, there's comfort
    yet —   ʼ
The aid of holy men, and heavenly patience——
    Man. Patience and patience! Hence —
    that word was made
For brutes of burden, not for birds of prey;
Preach it to mortals of a dusk like thine, —
I am not of thine order.
    C. Hun.   Thanks to heaven!
I would not be of thine for the free fame
Of William Tell; but whatsoe'er thine ill,
Is must be borne, and these wild starts are
    useless.
    Man. Do I not bear it? — Look on me —
    I live.
    C. Hun. This is convulsion, and no health-
    ful life.
    Man. I tell thee, man! I have lived many
    years,
Many long years, but they are nothing now
To those which I must number: ages — ages—
Space and eternity — and consciousness,
With the fierce thirst of death — and still un-
    slaked!
    C. Hun. Why, on thy brow the seal of
    middle age
Hath scarce been set; I am thine elder far.
    Man. Think'st thou existence doth depend
    on time?
It doth; but actions are our epochs: mine
Have made my days and nights imperishable,
Endless, and all alike, as sands on the shore,
Innumerable atoms; and one desert,

Barren and cold, on which the wild waves
  break,
But nothing rests, save carcasses and wrecks,
Rocks, and the salt-surf weeds of bitterness.
  C. Hun. Alas! he's mad—but yet I must
    not leave him.
  Man. I would I were—for then the things
    I see
Would be but a distempered dream.
  C. Hun.   What is it
That thou dost see, or think thou look'st
    upon?
  Man. Myself, and thee—a peasant of the
    Alps—
Thy humble virtues, hospitable home,
And spirit patient, pious, proud, and free;
Thy self-respect, grafted on innocent thoughts;
Thy days of health, and nights of sleep; thy
    toils,
By danger dignified, yet guiltless; hopes
Of cheerful old age and a quiet grave,
With cross and garland over its green turf,
And thy grandchildren's love for epitaph;
This do I see—and then I look within—
It matters not—my soul was scorched al-
  · ready!
  C. Hun. And would'st thou then exchange
    thy lot for mine?
  Man. No, friend! I would not wrong thee,
    nor exchange
My lot with living being: I can bear—
However wretchedly, 'tis still to bear—
In life what others could not brook to
    dream,
But perish in their slumber.
  C. Hun.   And with this—
This cautious feeling for another's pain,
Canst thou be black with evil?—say not
    so.
Can one of gentle thoughts have wreaked re-
    venge   ·
Upon his enemies?
  Man.   Oh! no, no, no!
My injuries came down on those who loved
    me—
On those whom I best loved: I never
    quelled
An enemy, save in my just defence—
But my embrace was fatal.
  C. Hun.   Heaven give thee rest!
And penitence restore thee to thyself;
My prayers shall be for thee.
  Man.   I need them not,
But can endure thy pity. I depart—
'Tis time—farewell!—Here's gold, and thanks
    for thee—
No words—it is thy due.—Follow me
    not—
I know my path—the mountain peril's
    past: ·
And once again, I charge thee, follow not!
                            [*Exit* MANFRED.

SCENE II.—*A lower Valley in the Alps.—A
            Cataract.*[1]

            Enter MANFRED.

It is not noon—the sunbow's rays[2] still arch
The torrent with the many hues of heaven,
And roll the sheeted silver's waving column
O'er the crag's headlong perpendicular,
And fling its lines of foaming light along,
And to and fro, like the pale courser's tail,
The Giant steed, to be bestrode by Death,
As told in the Apocalypse.[3] No eyes
But mine now drink this sight of loveliness;
I should be sole in this sweet solitude,
And with the Spirit of the place divide
The homage of these waters.—I will call her.
  [MANFRED *takes some of the water into the
      palm of his hand, and flings it into the air,
      muttering the adjuration. After a pause
      the* WITCH OF THE ALPS *rises beneath
      the arch of the sunbow of the torrent.*
Beautiful Spirit! with thy hair of light,
And dazzling eyes of glory, in whose form
The charms of earth's least mortal daughters
    grow
To an unearthly stature, in an essence
Of purer elements; while the hues of youth,—
Carnationed like a sleeping infant's cheek,
Rocked by the beating of her mother's heart,
Or the rose tints, which summer's twilight
    leaves
Upon the lofty glacier's virgin snow,
The blush of earth embracing with her
    heaven,—

---

[1] [This scene is one of the most poetical and
most sweetly written in the poem. There is a still
and delicious witchery in the tranquillity and seclu-
sion of the place, and the celestial beauty of the
being who reveals herself in the midst of these
visible pleasures.—*Jeffrey.*]
[2] This iris is formed by the rays of the sun over
the lower part of the Alpine torrents: it is exactly
like a rainbow come down to pay a visit, and so
close that you may walk into it: this effect lasts till
noon.—["Before ascending the mountain, went to
the torrent; the sun upon it, forming a *rainbow* of
the lower part of all colors, but principally purple
and gold; the bow moving as you move. I never
saw any thing like this; it is only in the sunshine."
—*Swiss Journal.*]
[3] ["Arrived at the foot of the Jungfrau; glaciers;
torrents: one of these torrents nine hundred feet in
height of visible descent; heard an avalanche fall,
like thunder; glaciers enormous; storm came on—
thunder, lightning, hail; all in perfection, and
beautiful. The torrent is in shape curving over the
rock, like the tail of a white horse streaming in the
wind, such as it might be conceived would be that
of the '*pale horse*' on which Death is mounted in
the *Apocalypse*. It is neither mist nor water, but
a something between both; its immense height gives
it a wave or curve, a spreading here or condensa-
tion there wonderful and indescribable.—*Swiss
Journal.*]

Tinge thy celestial aspect, and make tame
The beauties of the sunbow which bends o'er
    thee.[1]
Beautiful Spirit! in thy calm clear brow,
Wherein is glassed serenity of soul,
Which of itself shows immortality,
I read that thou wilt pardon to a Son
Of Earth, whom the abstruser powers permit
At times to commune with them — if that he
Avail him of his spells — to call thee thus,
And gaze on thee a moment.
    Witch.   Son of Earth!
I know thee, and the powers which give thee
    power.
I know thee for a man of many thoughts,
And deeds of good and ill, extreme in both,
Fatal and fated in thy sufferings.
I have expected this — what would'st thou
 . with me ?
    Man. To look upon thy beauty — nothing
    further.[2]
The face of the earth hath maddened me, and I
Take refuge in her mysteries, and pierce
To the abodes of those who govern her —

---

[1] [In all Lord Byron's heroes we recognize, though
with infinite modifications, the same great charac-
teristics — a high and audacious conception of the
power of the mind, — an intense sensibility of pas-
sion, — an almost boundless capacity of tumultuous
emotion, — a haunting admiration of the grandeur
of disordered power, — and, above all, a soul-felt,
blood-felt delight in beauty. Parisina is full of it to
overflowing; it breathes from every page of the
" Prisoner of Chillon; " but it is in " Manfred "
that it riots and revels among the streams, and
waterfalls, and groves, and mountains, and heavens.
There is in the character of Manfred more of the
self-might of Byron than in all his previous produc-
tions.   He has therein brought, with wonderful
power, metaphysical conceptions into forms, — and
we know of no poem in which the aspect of external
nature is throughout lighted up with an expression
at once so beautiful, solemn, and majestic. It is the
poem, next to " Childe Harold," which we should
give to a foreigner to read, that he might know
something of Byron. Shakspeare has given to those
abstractions of human life and being, which are truth
in the intellect, forms as full, clear, glowing, as the
idealized forms of visible nature. The very words
of Ariel picture to us his beautiful being. In " Man-
fred," we see glorious but immature manifestations
of similar power. The poet there creates, with de-
light, thoughts and feelings and fancies into visible
forms, that he may cling and cleave to them, and
clasp them in his passion. The beautiful Witch of
the Alps seems exhaled from the luminous spray of
the cataract, — as if the poet's eyes, unsated with
the beauty of inanimate nature, gave spectral appa-
ritions of loveliness to feed the pure passion of the
poet's soul. —*Professor Wilson.*]
[2] [There is something exquisitely beautiful in all
this passage; and both the apparition and the dia-
logue are so managed, that the sense of their im-
probability is swallowed up in that of their beauty;
and without actually believing that such spirits exist
or communicate themselves, we feel for the moment
as if we stood in their presence. — *Jeffrey.*]

But they can nothing aid me. I have sought
From them what they could not bestow, and
    now
I search no further.
    Witch. What could be the quest
Which is not in the power of the most powerful,
The rulers of the invisible ?
    Man.   A boon;
But why should I repeat it ? 'twere in vain.
    Witch. I know not that; let thy lips utter
    it.
    Man. Well, though it torture me, 'tis but
    the same;
My pang shall find a voice. From my youth
    upwards
My spirit walked not with the souls of men,
Nor looked upon the earth with human eyes;
The thirst of their ambition was not mine,
The aim of their existence was not mine;
My joys, my griefs, my passions, and my
    powers,
Made me a stranger; though I wore the form,
I had no sympathy with breathing flesh,
Nor midst the creatures of clay that girded me
Was there but one who —— but of her anon.
I said with men, and with the thoughts of
    men,
I held but slight communion; but instead,
My joy was in the Wilderness, to breathe
The difficult air of the iced mountain's top,
Where the birds dare not build, nor insect's
    wing
Flit o'er the herbless granite; or to plunge
Into the torrent, and to roll along
On the swift whirl of the new breaking wave
Of river-stream, or ocean, in their flow.
In these my early strength exulted; or
To follow through the night the moving moon,
The stars and their development; or catch
The dazzling lightnings till my eyes grew dim;
Or to look, listening, on the scattered leaves,
While Autumn winds were at their evening
    song.
These were my pastimes, and to be alone;
For if the beings, of whom I was one, —
Hating to be so, — crossed me in my path,
I felt myself degraded back to them,
And was all clay again. And then I dived,
In my lone wanderings, to the caves of
    death,
Searching its cause in its effect; and drew
From withered bones, and skulls, and heaped
    up dust,
Conclusions most forbidden. Then I passed
The nights of years in sciences untaught,
Save in the old time; and with time and toil
And terrible ordeal, and such penance
As in itself hath power upon the air,
And spirits that do compass air and earth,
Space, and the peopled infinite, I made
Mine eyes familiar with Eternity,
Such as, before me, did the Magi, and

He who from out their fountain dwellings
　　raised
Eros and Anteros,[1] at Gadara,
As I do thee; — and with my knowledge grew
The thirst of knowledge, and the power and
　　joy
Of this most bright intelligence, until. ——
　Witch. 　Proceed.
　Man. 　Oh! I but thus prolonged my words,
Boasting these idle attributes, because
As I approach the core of my heart's grief—
But to my task.　I have not named to thee
Father, or mother, mistress, friend, or being,
With whom I wore the chain of human ties;
If I had such, they seemed not such to me—
Yet there was one ——
　Witch. 　　　　Spare not thyself—proceed.
　Man. 　She was like me in lineaments—
　　her eyes,
Her hair, her features, all, to the very tone
Even of her voice, they said were like to mine;
But softened all, and tempered into beauty;
She had the same lone thoughts and wander-
　　ings,
The quest of hidden knowledge, and a mind
To comprehend the universe: nor these
Alone, but with them gentler powers than
　　mine,
Pity, and smiles, and tears — which I had not;
And tenderness—but that I had for her;
Humility—and that I never had.
Her faults were mine — her virtues were her
　　own —
I loved her, and destroyed her!
　Witch. 　　　　　　With thy hand?
　Man. 　Not with my hand, but heart—which
　　broke her heart —
It gazed on mine, and withered.　I have shed
Blood, but not hers — and yet her blood was
　　shed —
I saw — and could not stanch it.

---

[1] The philosopher Jamblicus.　The story of the raising of Eros and Anteros may be found in his life by Eunapius.　It is well told. — ["It is reported of him," says Eunapius, "that while he and his schol-ars were bathing in the hot baths of Gadara in Syria, a dispute arising concerning the baths, he, smiling, ordered his disciples to ask the inhabitants by what names the two lesser springs, that were nearer and handsomer than the rest, were called.　To which the inhabitants replied, that 'the one was called Eros, and the other Anteros, but for what reason they knew not.'　Upon which Jamblicus, sitting by one of the springs, put his hand in the water, and muttering some few words to himself, called up a fair-complexioned boy, with gold-colored locks dan-gling from his back and breast, so that he looked like one that was washing: and then, going to the other spring, and doing as he had done before, called up another Cupid, with darker and more dis-hevelled hair: upon which both the Cupids clung about Jamblicus; but he presently sent them back to their proper places.　After this, his friends sub-mitted their belief to him in every thing."]

　Witch. 　　　　　　And for this —
A being of the race thou dost despise,
The order which thine own would rise above,
Mingling with us and ours, thou dost forego
The gifts of our great knowledge, and shrink'st
　　back
To recreant mortality —— Away!
　Man. 　Daughter of Air!　I tell thee, since
　　that hour—
But words are breath—look on me in my
　　sleep,
Or watch my watchings—Come and sit by
　　me!
My solitude is solitude no more,
But peopled with the Furies; — I have gnashed
My teeth in darkness till returning morn,
Then cursed myself till sunset; — I have
　　prayed
For madness as a blessing — 'tis denied me.
I have affronted death — but in the war
Of elements the waters shrunk from me,
And fatal things passed harmless — the cold
　　hand
Of an all-pitiless demon held me back,
Back by a single hair, which would not break.
In fantasy, imagination, all
The affluence of my soul—which one day was
A Crœsus in creation—I plunged deep,
But, like a ebbing wave, it dashed me back
Into the gulf of my unfathomed thought.
I plunged amidst mankind—Forgetfulness
I sought in all, save where 'tis to be found,
And that I have to learn — my sciences,
My long pursued and super-human art,
Is mortal here—I dwell in my despair —
And live—and live for ever.
　Witch. 　　　　　　It may be
That I can aid thee.
　Man. 　　　　To do this thy power
Must wake the dead, or lay me low with them.
Do so—in any shape—in any hour—
With any torture — so it be the last.
　Witch. 　That is not in my province; but
　　if thou
Wilt swear obedience to my will, and do
My bidding, it may help thee to thy wishes.
　Man. 　I will not swear—Obey! and whom?
　　the spirits
Whose presence I command, and be the slave
Of those who served me — Never!
　Witch. 　　　　　　Is this all?
Hast thou no gentler answer? — Yet bethink
　　thee,
And pause ere thou rejectest.
　Man. 　　　　　　I have said it.
　Witch. 　Enough! — I may retire then — say!
　Man. 　　　　　　　　Retire!
　　　　　　　　[*The* WITCH *disappears*
　Man. (*alone*).　We are the fools of time and
　　terror: Days
Steal on us and from us; yet we live,
Loathing our life, and dreading still to die.

In all the days of this detested yoke —
This vital weight upon the struggling heart,
Which sinks with sorrow, or beats quick with
    pain,
Or joy that ends in agony or faintness —
In all the days of past and future, for
In life there is no present, we can number
How few — how less than few — wherein the
    soul
Forbears to pant for death, and yet draws back
As from a stream in winter, though the chill
Be but a moment's. I have one resource
Still in my science — I can call the dead,
And ask them what it is we dread to be:
The sternest answer can but be the Grave,
And that is nothing — if they answer not —
The buried Prophet answered to the Hag
Of Endor; and the Spartan Monarch drew
From the Byzantine maid's unsleeping spirit
An answer and his destiny — he slew
That which he loved, unknowing what he
    slew,
And died unpardoned — though he called in
    aid
The Phyxian Jove, and in Phigalia roused
The Arcadian Evocators to compel
The indignant shadow to depose her wrath,
Or fix her term of vengeance — she replied
In words of dubious import, but fulfilled.[1]

---

[1] The story of Pausanias, king of Sparta (who
commanded the Greeks at the battle of Platea, and
afterwards perished for an attempt to betray the
Lacedæmonians), and Cleonice, is told in Plutarch's
life of Cimon; and in the Laconics of Pausanias
the sophist, in his description of Greece. — [The
following is the passage from Plutarch: — "It is
related, that when Pausanias was at Byzantium, he
cast his eyes upon a young virgin named Cleonice,
of a noble family there, and insisted on having her
for a mistress. The parents intimidated by his
power, were under the hard necessity of giving up
their daughter. The young woman begged that the
light might be taken out of his apartments, that she
might go to his bed in secrecy and silence. When
she entered he was asleep, and she unfortunately
stumbled upon the candlestick, and threw it down.
The noise waked him suddenly, and he, in his con-
fusion, thinking it was an enemy coming to assas-
sinate him, unsheathed a dagger that lay by him, and
plunged it into the virgin's heart. After this he
could never rest. Her image appeared to him every
night, and with a menacing tone repeated this he-
roic verse, —

' Go to the fate which pride and lust prepare! '

The allies, highly incensed at this infamous action,
joined Cimon to besiege him in Byzantium. But
he found means to escape thence; and, as he was
still haunted by the spectre, he is said to have ap-
plied to a temple at Heraclea, where the names of
the dead were consulted. There he invoked the
spirit of Cleonice, and entreated her pardon. She
appeared, and told him ' he would soon be delivered
from all his troubles, after his return to Sparta: ' in
which, it seems his death was enigmatically fore-
told. These particulars we have from many histo-

If I had never lived, that which I love
Had still been living; had I never loved,
That which I love would still be beautiful —
Happy and giving happiness. What is she?
What is she now? — a sufferer for my sins —
A thing I dare not think upon — or nothing.
Within few hours I shall not call in vain —
Yet in this hour I dread the thing I dare:
Until this hour I never shrunk to gaze
On spirit, good or evil — now I tremble,
And feel a strange cold thaw upon my heart.
But I can act even what I most abhor,
And champion human fears. — The night ap-
    proaches.
                     [Exit.

SCENE III. — *The Summit of the Jungfrau
Mountain.*

Enter FIRST DESTINY.

The moon is rising broad, and round, and
    bright,
And here on snows, where never human
    foot
Of common mortal trod, we nightly tread,
And leave no traces; o'er the savage sea,
The glassy ocean of the mountain ice,
We skim its rugged breakers, which put on
The aspect of a tumbling tempest's foam,
Frozen in a moment [2] — a dead whirlpool's
    image:
And this most steep fantastic pinnacle,
The fretwork of some earthquake — where
    the clouds
Pause to repose themselves in passing by —
Is sacred to our revels, or our vigils;
Here do I wait my sisters, on our way
To the Hall of Arimanes, for to-night
Is our great festival — 'tis strange they come
    not.

A Voice without, singing.

The Captive Usurper,
    Hurled down from the throne,
Lay buried in torpor,
    Forgotten and lone;
I broke through his slumbers,
    I shivered his chain,
I leagued him with numbers —
    He's Tyrant again!

---

rians." — *Langhorn's Plutarch*, vol. iii. p. 279.
" Thus we find," adds the translator, " that it was a
custom in the Pagan as well as in the Hebrew the-
ology, to conjure up the spirits of the dead; and
that the witch of Endor was not the only witch in
the world."]

[2] [" Came to a morass; Hobhouse dismounted to
get over well; I tried to pass my horse over; the
horse sunk up to the chin, and of course he and I
were in the mud together: bemired, but not hurt;
laughed and rode on. Arrived at the Grindenwald;
mounted again, and rode to the higher glacier —
like *a frozen hurricane.*" — *Swiss Journal.*]

He who from out their fountain dwellings raised
Eros and Anteros,[1] at Gadara,
As I do thee; — and with my knowledge grew
The thirst of knowledge, and the power and joy
Of this most bright intelligence, until ——
Witch. Proceed.
Man. Oh! I but thus prolonged my words,
Boasting these idle attributes, because
As I approach the core of my heart's grief—
But to my task. I have not named to thee
Father, or mother, mistress, friend, or being,
With whom I wore the chain of human ties;
If I had such, they seemed not such to me —
Yet there was one ——
Witch. Spare not thyself — proceed.
FIRST DESTINY, answering.

The city lies sleeping;
  The morn, to deplore it,
May dawn on it weeping:
  Sullenly, slowly,
The black plague flew o'er it —
  Thousands lie lowly;
Tens of thousands shall perish —
  The living shall fly from
The sick they should cherish;
  But nothing can vanquish
The touch that they die from.
  Sorrow and anguish,
And evil and dread,
  Envelope a nation —
The blest are the dead,
  Who see not the sight
Witch. .... With my hand?
Man. Not with my hand, but heart — which
broke her heart —
It gazed on mine, and withered. I have shed
Blood, but not hers — and yet her blood was shed —
I saw — and could not stanch it.

---

[1] The philosopher Jamblicus. The story of the raising of Eros and Anteros may be found in his life by Eunapius. It is well told. — [" It is reported of him," says Eunapius, "that while he and his scholars were bathing in the hot baths of Gadara in Syria, a dispute arising concerning the baths, he, smiling, ordered his disciples to ask the inhabitants by what names the two lesser springs, that were nearer and handsomer than the rest, were called. To which the inhabitants replied, that ' the one was called Eros, and the other Anteros, but for what reason they knew not.' Upon which Jamblicus, sitting by one of the springs, put his hand in the water, and muttering some few words to himself, called up a fair-complexioned boy, with gold-colored locks dangling from his back and breast, so that he looked like one that was washing: and then, going to the other spring, and doing as he had done before, called up another Cupid, with darker and more dishevelled hair: upon which both the Cupids clung about Jamblicus; but he presently sent them back to their proper places. After this, his friends submitted their belief to him in every thing."]

Witch.   And for this —
A being of the race thou dost despise,
The order which thine own would rise above,
Mingling with us and ours, thou dost forego
The gifts of our great knowledge, and shrink'st back
To recreant mortality —— Away!
Man. Daughter of Air! I tell thee, since that hour —
But words are breath — look on me in my sleep,
Or watch my watchings — Come and sit by me!
My solitude is solitude no more,
But peopled with the Furies; — I have gnashed
My teeth in darkness till returning morn,
Then cursed myself till sunset; — I have prayed
For madness as a blessing — 'tis denied me.
I have affronted death — but in the war
Of elements the waters shrunk from me,
And fatal things passed harmless — the cold hand
Of an all-pitiless demon held me back,
Back by a single hair, which would not break.
In fantasy, imagination, all
The affluence of my soul — which one day was
A Crœsus in creation — I plunged deep,
But, like a ebbing wave, it dashed me back
Into the gulf of my unfathomed thought.
I plunged amidst mankind — Forgetfulness
I sought in all, save where 'tis to be found,
And that I have to learn — my sciences,
My long pursued and super-human art,
Is mortal here — I dwell in my despair —
And live — and live for ever.
Witch.   It may be
That I can aid thee.
Man.   To do this thy power
Must wake the dead, or lay me low with them.
Do so — in any shape — in any hour —
With any torture — so it be the last.
Witch. That is not in my province; but if thou
Wilt swear obedience to my will, and do
My bidding, it may help thee to thy wishes.
Man. I will not swear — Obey! and whom? the spirits
Whose presence I command, and be the slave
Of those who served me — Never!
Witch.   Is this all?
Hast thou no gentler answer? — Yet bethink thee,
And pause ere thou rejectest.
Man.   I have said it.
Witch. Enough! — I may retire then — say!
Man.   Retire!
                    [*The* WITCH *disappears.*
Man. (*alone*). We are the fools of time and terror: Days
Steal on us and from us; yet we live,
Loathing our life, and dreading still to die.

In all the days of this detested yoke —
This vital weight upon the struggling heart,
Which sinks with sorrow, or beats quick with
     pain,
Or joy that ends in agony or faintness —
In all the days of past and future, for
In life there is no present, we can number
How few — how less than few — wherein the
     soul
Forbears to pant for death, and yet draws back
As from a stream in winter, though the chill
Be but a moment's.   I have one resource
Still in my science — I can call the dead,
And ask them what it is we dread to be:
The sternest answer can but be the Grave,
And that is nothing — if they answer not —
The buried Prophet answered to the Hag
Of Endor; and the Spartan Monarch drew
From the Byzantine maid's unsleeping spirit
An answer and his destiny — he slew
That which he loved, unknowing what he
     slew,
And died unpardoned — though he called in
     aid
The Phyxian Jove, and in Phigalia roused
The Arcadian Evocators to compel
The indignant shadow to depose her wrath,
Or fix her term of vengeance — she replied
In words of dubious import, but fulfilled.[1]

---

[1] The story of Pausanias, king of Sparta (who
commanded the Greeks at the battle of Platea, and
afterwards perished for an attempt to betray the
Lacedæmonians), and Cleonice, is told in Plutarch's
life of Cimon, and in the Laconics of Pausanias
the sophist, in his description of Greece. — [The
following is the passage from Plutarch: — "It is
related, that when Pausanias was at Byzantium, he
cast his eyes upon a young virgin named Cleonice,
of a noble family there, and insisted on having her
for a mistress.   The parents intimidated by his
power, were under the hard necessity of giving up
their daughter.   The young woman begged that the
light might be taken out of his apartments, that she
might go to his bed in secrecy and silence.   When
she entered he was asleep, and she unfortunately
stumbled upon the candlestick, and threw it down.
The noise waked him suddenly, and he, in his con-
fusion, thinking it was an enemy coming to assas-
sinate him, unsheathed a dagger that lay by him, and
plunged it into the virgin's heart.   After this he
could never rest.   Her image appeared to him every
night, and with a menacing tone repeated this he-
roic verse, —

' Go to the fate which pride and lust prepare! '

The allies, highly incensed at this infamous action,
joined Cimon to besiege him in Byzantium.   But
he found means to escape thence; and, as he was
still haunted by the spectre, he is said to have ap-
plied to a temple at Heraclea, where the names of
the dead were consulted.   There he invoked the
spirit of Cleonice, and entreated her pardon.   She
appeared, and told him ' he would soon be delivered
from all his troubles, after his return to Sparta: ' in
which, it seems his death was enigmatically fore-
told.   These particulars we have from many histo-

If I had never lived, that which I love
Had still been living; had I never loved
That which I love would still be beautiful —
Happy and giving happiness.   What is she?
What is she now? — a sufferer for my sins —
A thing I dare not think upon — or nothing.
Within few hours I shall not call in vain —
Yet in this hour I dread the thing I dare:
Until this hour I never shrunk to gaze
On spirit, good or evil — now I tremble,
And feel a strange cold thaw upon my heart,
But I can act even what I most abhor,
And champion human fears. — The night ap-
     proaches.   [*Exit.*

SCENE III. — *The Summit of the Jungfrau
               Mountain.*

Enter FIRST DESTINY.

The moon is rising broad, and round, and
     bright,
And here on snows, where never human
     foot
Of common mortal trod, we nightly tread,
And leave no traces; o'er the savage sea,
The glassy ocean of the mountain ice,
We skim its rugged breakers, which put on
The aspect of a tumbling tempest's foam,
Frozen in a moment[2] — a dead whirlpool's
     image:
And this most steep fantastic pinnacle,
The fretwork of some earthquake — where
     the clouds
Pause to repose themselves in passing by —
Is sacred to our revels, or our vigils;
Here do I wait my sisters, on our way
To the Hall of Arimanes, for to-night
Is our great festival — 'tis strange they come
     not. .

A Voice without, singing.

The Captive Usurper,
     Hurled down from the throne,
Lay buried in torpor,
     Forgotten and lone;
I broke through his slumbers,
     I shivered his chain,
I leagued him with numbers —
     He's Tyrant again!

rians." — *Langhorn's Plutarch*, vol. iii. p. 279.
"Thus we find," adds the translator, "that it was a
custom in the Pagan as well as in the Hebrew the-
ology, to conjure up the spirits of the dead; and
that the witch of Endor was not the only witch in
the world."]

[2] ["Came to a morass; Hobhouse dismounted to
get over well; I tried to pass my horse over; the
horse sunk up to the chin, and of course he and I
were in the mud together; bemired, but not hurt;
laughed and rode on.   Arrived at the Grindenwald;
mounted again, and rode to the higher glacier —
like *a frozen hurricane.*" — *Swiss Journal.*]

With the blood of a million he'll answer my
    care,
With a nation's destruction — his flight and
    despair.

Second Voice, without.

The ship sailed on, the ship sailed fast,
But I left not a sail, and I left not a mast;
There is not a plank of the hull or the deck,
And there is not a wretch to lament o'er his
    wreck;
Save one, whom I held, as he swam, by the
    hair,
And he was a subject well worthy my care;
A terror on land, and a pirate at sea —
But I saved him to wreak further havoc for
    me!

FIRST DESTINY, *answering.*

The city lies sleeping;
    The morn, to deplore it,
May dawn on it weeping:
    Sullenly, slowly,
The black plague flew o'er it —
    Thousands lie lowly;
Tens of thousands shall perish —
    The living shall fly from
The sick they should cherish;
    But nothing can vanquish
The touch that they die from.
    Sorrow and anguish,
And evil and dread,
    Envelope a nation —
The blest are the dead,
Who see not the sight
    Of their own desolation —
This work of a night —
This wreck of a realm — this deed of my
    doing —
For ages I've done, and shall still be renew-
    ing!

Enter the SECOND *and* THIRD DESTINIES.

The Three.

Our hands contain the hearts of men,
    Our footsteps are their graves;
We only give to take again
    The spirits of our slaves!

First Des. Welcome! — Where's Nemesis?
Second Des.   At some great work?
But what I know not, for my hands were full.
Third Des. Behold she cometh.

Enter NEMESIS.

First Des.   Say, where hast thou been?
My sisters and thyself are slow to-night.
Nem. I was detained repairing shattered
    thrones,
Marrying fools, restoring dynasties,
Avenging men upon their enemies,
And making them repent their own revenge;
Goading the wise to madness; from the dull

Shaping out oracles to rule the world
Afresh, for they were waxing out of date,
And mortals dared to ponder for themselves,
To weigh kings in the balance, and to speak
Of freedom, the forbidden fruit. — Away!
We have outstayed the hour — mount we our
    clouds!   [*Exeunt.*

SCENE IV.— *The Hall of Arimanes.— Ari-
manes on his Throne, a Globe of Fire, sur-
rounded by the Spirits.*

Hymn of the SPIRITS.

Hail to our Master! — Prince of Earth and
    Air!
Who walks the clouds and waters — in his
    hand
The sceptre of the elements, which tear
    Themselves to chaos at his high command!
He breatheth — and a tempest shakes the
    sea;
He speaketh — and the clouds reply in
    thunder;
He gazeth — from his glance the sunbeams
    flee;
He moveth — earthquakes rend the world
    asunder.
Beneath his footsteps the volcanoes rise;
    His shadow is the Pestilence; his path
The comets herald through the crackling
    skies;[1]
And planets turn to ashes at his wrath.
To him War offers daily sacrifice;
    To him Death pays his tribute; Life is
    his,
With all its infinite of agonies —
    And his the spirit of whatever is!

Enter the DESTINIES *and* NEMESIS.

First Des. Glory to Arimanes! on the earth
His power increaseth — both my sisters did
His bidding, nor did I neglect my duty!
Second Des. Glory to Arimanes! we who
    bow
The necks of men, bow down before his
    throne!
Third Des. Glory to Arimanes! we await
His nod!
Nem. Sovereign of Sovereigns! we are
    thine,
And all that liveth, more or less, is ours,
And most things wholly so; still to increase
Our power, increasing thine, demands our
    care,
And we are vigilant — Thy late commands
Have been fulfilled to the utmost.
Enter MANFRED.
A Spirit.   What is here?

---

[1] [MS. —

" The comets herald through the { crackling }
    skies."]   { burning }

A mortal! — Thou most rash and fatal wretch,
Bow down and worship!

Second Spirit.　　　I do know the man —
A Magian of great power, and fearful skill!

Third Spirit.　Bow down and worship,
　　slave! —
　　　　What, know'st thou not
Thine and our Sovereign? — Tremble, and
　obey!

All the Spirits.　Prostrate thyself, and thy
　condemned clay,
Child of the Earth! or dread the worst.

Man.　　　　　　　I know it;
And yet ye see I kneel not.

Fourth Spirit.　　'Twill be taught thee.

Man. 'Tis taught already; — many a night
　on the earth,
On the bare ground, have I bowed down my
　face,
And strewed my head with ashes; I have
　known
The fulness of humiliation, for
I sunk before my vain despair, and knelt
To my own desolation.

Fifth Spirit.　　　Dost thou dare
Refuse to Arimanes on his throne
What the whole earth accords, beholding not
The terror of his Glory? — Crouch! I say.

Man. Bid *him* bow down to that which is
　above him,
The overruling Infinite — the Maker
Who made him not for worship — let him
　kneel,
And we will kneel together.

The Spirits.　　　Crush the worm!
Tear him in pieces! —

First Des. Hence! Avaunt! — he's mine,
Prince of the Powers invisible! This man
Is of no common order, as his port
And presence here denote; his sufferings
Have been of an immortal nature, like
Our own; his knowledge, and his powers and
　will,
As far as is compatible with clay,
Which clogs the ethereal essence, have been
　such
As clay hath seldom borne; his aspirations
Have been beyond the dwellers of the earth,
And they have only taught him what we
　know —
That knowledge is not happiness, and
　science
But an exchange of ignorance for that
Which is another kind of ignorance.
This is not all — the passions, attributes
Of earth and heaven, from which no power,
　nor being,
Nor breath from the worm upwards is ex-
　empt,
Have pierced his heart; and in their conse-
　quence
Made him a thing, which I, who pity not,

Yet pardon those who pity. He is mine,
And thine, it may be — be it so, or not,
No other Spirit in this region hath
A soul like his — or power upon his soul.

Nem. What doth he here then?

First Des.　　　Let him answer that.

Man. Ye know what I have known; and
　without power
I could not be amongst ye: but there are
Powers deeper still beyond — I come in quest
Of such, to answer unto what I seek.

Nem. What would'st thou?

Man.　　　Thou canst not reply to me.
Call up the dead — my question is for them.

Nem. Great Arimanes, doth thy will avouch
The wishes of this mortal?

Ari.　　　Yea.

Nem.　　　　Whom would'st thou
Uncharnel?

Man.　　One without a tomb — call up
Astarte.

NEMESIS.

Shadow! or Spirit!
　•　Whatever thou art,
　Which still doth inherit
　　The whole or a part
Of the form of thy birth,
　Of the mould of thy clay,
　Which returned to the earth,
　　Reappear to the day!
Bear what thou borest,
　The heart and the form,
And the aspect thou worest
　Redeem from the worm.
Appear! — Appear! — Appear!
Who sent thee there requires thee here!

[*The Phantom of* ASTARTE *rises and stands
　in the midst.*

Man. Can this be death? there's bloom
　upon her cheek;
But now I see it is no living hue
But a strange hectic — like the unnatural red
Which Autumn plants upon the perished leaf.
It is the same! Oh, God! that I should dread
To look upon the same — Astarte! — No,
I cannot speak to her — but bid her speak —
Forgive me or condemn me.

NEMESIS.

By the power which hath broken
　The grave which enthralled thee,
Speak to him who hath spoken,
　Or those who have called thee!

Man.　　　She is silent,
And in that silence I am more than answered.

Nem. My power extends no further. Prince
　of air!
It rests with thee alone — command her voice.

Ari. Spirit — obey this sceptre!

Nem.　　　Silent still!

She is not of our order, but belongs
To the other powers. Mortal! thy quest is
vain,
And we are baffled also.
   Man.   Hear me, hear me—
Astarte! my beloved! speak to me:
I have so much endured—so much endured—
Look on me! the grave hath not changed
thee more
Than I am changed for thee. Thou lovedst
me
Too much, as I loved thee: we were not made
To torture thus each other, though it were
The deadliest sin to love as we have loved.
Say that thou loath'st me not—that I do bear
This punishment for both—that thou wilt be
One of the blessed—and that I shall die;
For hitherto all hateful things conspire
To bind me in existence—in a life
Which makes me shrink from immortality—
A future like the past. I cannot rest.
I know not what I ask, nor what I seek:
I feel but what thou art—and what I am;
And I would hear yet once before I perish
The voice which was my music—Speak to me!
For I have called on thee in the still night,
Startled the slumbering birds from the hushed
boughs,
And woke the mountain wolves, and made the
caves
Acquainted with thy vainly echoed name,
Which answered me—many things answered
me—
Spirits and men—but thou wert silent all.
Yet speak to me! I have outwatched the stars,
And gazed o'er heaven in vain in search of
thee.
Speak to me! I have wandered o'er the earth,
And never found thy likeness—Speak to me!
Look on the fiends around—they feel for me:
I fear them not, and feel for thee alone—
Speak to me! though it be in wrath;—but
say—
I reck not what—but let me hear thee once—
This once—once more!
   Phantom of Astarte. Manfred!
   Man.   Say on, say on—
I live but in the sound—it is thy voice!
   Phan. Manfred! To-morrow ends thine
earthly ills.
Farewell!
   Man. Yet one word more—am I forgiven?
   Phan. Farewell!
   Man. Say, shall we meet again?
   Phan.   Farewell!
   Man. One word for mercy! Say, thou
lovest me.
   Phan. Manfred!
        [*The Spirit of* ASTARTE *disappears.*1

¹ [Over this fine drama, a moral feeling hangs
like a sombrous thunder cloud. No other guilt but
that so darkly shadowed out could have furnished

Nem. She's gone, and will not be recalled;
Her words will be fulfilled. Return to the
earth.
   A Spirit. He is convulsed—This is to be
a mortal
And seek the things beyond mortality.
   Another Spirit. Yet, see, he mastereth him-
self, and makes
His torture tributary to his will.
Had he been one of us, he would have made
An awful spirit.
   Nem.   Hast thou further question
Of our great sovereign, or his worshippers?
   Man. None.
   Nem.   Then for a time farewell.
   Man. We meet then! Where? On the
earth?—
Even as thou wilt: and for the grace accorded
I now depart a debtor. Fare ye well!
                [*Exit* MANFRED.

   (*Scene closes.*)

ACT III.²

SCENE I.—*A Hall in the Castle of Manfred.*

MANFRED *and* HERMAN.

   Man. What is the hour?
   Her.   It wants but one till sunset,
And promises a lovely twilight.
   Man.   Say,
Are all things so disposed of in the tower
As I directed?
   Her.   All, my lord, are ready:
Here is the key and casket.

so dreadful an illustration of the hideous aberra-
tions of human nature, however noble and majestic,
when left a prey to its desires, its passions, and its
imagination. The beauty, at one time so inno-
cently adored, is at last soiled, profaned, and vio-
lated. Affection, love, guilt, horror, remorse, and
death, come in terrible succession, yet all darkly
linked together. We think of Astarte as young,
beautiful, innocent — guilty — lost — murdered—
buried — judged — pardoned; but still, in her per-
mitted visit to earth, speaking in a voice of sorrow,
and with a countenance yet pale with mortal
trouble. We had but a glimpse of her in her
beauty and innocence; but, at last, she rises up be-
fore us in all the mortal silence of a ghost, with
fixed, glazed, and passionless eyes, revealing death,
judgment, and eternity. The moral breathes and
burns in every word, — in sadness, misery, insan-
ity, desolation, and death. The work is ¹ instinct
with spirit,' — and in the agony and distraction, and
all its dimly imagined causes, we behold, though
broken up, confused, and shattered, the elements of
a purer existence. — *Professor Wilson.*]
  ² [The third Act, as originally written, being
shown to Mr. Gifford, he expressed his unfavorable
opinion of it very distinctly; and Mr. Murray
transmitted this to Byron. The result is told in
the following extracts from his letters:—

Man.   It is well:
Thou may'st retire.   [*Exit* HERMAN.
Man. (*alone*). There is a calm upon me —
Inexplicable stillness! which till now
Did not belong to what I knew of life.
If that I did not know philosophy
To be of all our vanities the motliest,
The merest word that ever fooled the ear
From out the schoolman's jargon, I should
    deem
The golden secret, the sought " Kalon," found,
And seated in my soul. It will not last,
But it is well to have known it, though but
    once:
It hath enlarged my thoughts with a new
    sense,
And I within my tablets would note down
That there is such a feeling. Who is there ?

       Reënter HERMAN.

Her. My lord, the abbot of St. Maurice
    craves
To greet your presence.

      Enter the ABBOT OF ST. MAURICE.

Abbot.   Peace be with Count Manfred!
Man. Thanks, holy father! welcome to
    these walls ;
Thy presence honors them, and blesseth those
Who dwell within them.
Abbot.   Would it were so, Count! —
But I would fain confer with thee alone.
Man. Herman, retire. — What would my
    reverend guest ?
Abbot. Thus, without prelude : — Age and
    zeal, my office,

" Venice, April 14, 1817. — The third Act is cer-
tainly d—d bad, and, like the Archbishop of Gre-
nada's homily (which savored of the palsy), has
the dregs of my fever, during which it was written.
It must *on no account* be published in its present
state. I will try and reform it, or rewrite it alto-
gether; but the impulse is gone, and I have no
chance of making any thing out of it. The speech
of Manfred to the Sun is the only part of this Act I
thought good myself; the rest is certainly as bad as
bad can be, and I wonder what the devil possessed
me. I am very glad, indeed, that you sent me Mr.
Gifford's opinion without *deduction*. Do you sup-
pose me such a booby as not to be very much
obliged to him? of that I was not, and am not, con-
vinced and convicted in my conscience of this same
overt act of nonsense? I shall try at it again : in
the mean time, lay it upon the shelf — the whole
Drama I mean. — Recollect *not* to publish, upon
pain of I know not what, until I have tried again at
the third act. I am not sure that I shall try, and
still less that I shall succeed if I do."

" Rome, May 5. — I have rewritten the greater
part, and returned what is not altered in the proof
you sent me. The Abbot is become a good man,
and the Spirits are brought in at the death. You
will find, I think, some good poetry in this new Act,
here and there: and if so, print it, without sending
me further proofs, *under Mr. Gifford's correction*,
if he will have the goodness to overlook it,"]

And good intent, must plead my privilege;
Our near, though not acquainted neighbor-
    hood,
May also be my herald. Rumors strange,
And of unholy nature, are abroad,
And busy with thy name ; a noble name
For centuries : may he who bears it now
Transmit it unimpaired !
Man.   Proceed, — I listen.
Abbot. 'Tis said thou holdest converse with
    the things
Which are forbidden to the search of man ;
That with the dwellers of the dark abodes,
The many evil and unheavenly spirits
Which walk the valley of the shade of death,
Thou communest. I know that with man-
    kind,
Thy fellows in creation, thou dost rarely
Exchange thy thoughts, and that thy solitude
Is as an anchorite's, were it but holy.
Man. And what are they who do avouch
    these things ?
Abbot. My pious brethren — the scared
    peasantry —
Even thy own vassals — who do look on thee
With most unquiet eyes. Thy life's in peril.
Man. Take it.
Abbot. I come to save, and not destroy —
I would not pry into thy secret soul ;
But if these things be sooth, there still is time
For penitence and pity : reconcile thee
With the true church, and through the church
    to heaven.
Man. I hear thee. This is my reply :
    whate'er
I may have been, or am, doth rest between
Heaven and myself. — I shall not choose a
    mortal
To be my mediator. Have I sinned
Against your ordinances ? prove and punish ! [1]

---

1 [Thus far the text stands as originally written:
this was the sequel of the scene as given in the first
MS. : —

" *Abbot.* Then, hear and tremble! For the
    headstrong wretch
Who in the mail of innate hardihood
Would shield himself, and battle for his sins,
There is the stake on earth, and beyond earth eter-
    nal —
Man. Charity, most reverend father,
Becomes thy lips so much more than this menace,
That I would call thee back to it: but say,
What wouldst thou with me?
Abbot.   It may be there are
Things that would shake thee — but I keep them
    back,
And give thee till to-morrow to repent,
Then if thou dost not all devote thyself
To penance, and with gift of all thy lands
To the monastery ——
Man.   I understand thee, — well !
Abbot. Expect no mercy ; I have warned thee.
Man. (*opening the casket*). Stop —
There is a gift for thee within this casket.

son! I did not speak of pun-
and pardon ; — with thyself
such remains — and for the last,
as and our strong belief
me power to smooth the path

*pens the casket, strikes a light,
some incense.*

!

ASHTAROTH *appears, singing as
follows : —*

stone,
ing flits
-white bone.
he night-winds blow,
f the assassin swings;
:, on the raven-stone,*
ps his dusky wings.

k —and his ebon beak
close of the hollow sound;
:une, by the light of the moon,
witches dance their round —
/, cheerily, cheerily,
ds the ball:
r shrouds, and the demons in clouds,
vitches' carnival.

hee not — hence — hence —
il one! — help, ho! without there!
y this man to the Shreckhorn — to

t peak — watch with him there
unrise; let him gaze, and know
will be so near to heaven.
ot; and, when the morrow breaks,
afe in his cell — away with him!
not better bring his brethren too,
, to bear him company?
is will serve for the present. Take

friar! now an exorcism or two,
' the lighter.

appears with the ABBOT, *singing
as follows : —*

son, and a maid undone,
low rewedded within the year;
lly monk, and a pregnant nun,
s which every day appear.

MANFRED *alone.*

ould this fool break in on me, and

s fantastical? — no matter,
' seeking. My heart sickens,
ced foreboding on my soul:
calm as a sullen sea
ane; the winds are still,
ves swell high and heavily,
iger in them. Such a rest
fy life hath been a combat,
ght a wound, till I am scarred
part of me. — What now? "]

ne (Rabenstein), a translation of
d for the gibbet, which in Germany
is permanent and made of stone."

To higher hope and better thoughts; the first
I leave to heaven, —' Vengeance is mine
alone!"
So saith the Lord, and with all humbleness
His servant echoes back the awful word.
    Man. Old man! there is no power in holy
men,
Nor charm in prayer — nor purifying form
Of penitence — nor outward look —nor fast -
Nor agony — nor, greater than all these,
The innate tortures of that deep despair,
Which is remorse without the fear of hell,
But all in all sufficient to itself
Would make a hell of heaven — can exorcise
From out the unbounded spirit the quick sense
Of its own sins, wrongs, sufferance, and re-
venge
Upon itself; there is no future pang
Can deal that justice on the self-condemned
He deals on his own soul.
    Abbot.   All this is well;
For this will pass away, and be succeeded
By an auspicious hope, which shall look up
With calm assurance to that blessed place,
Which all who seek may win, whatever be
Their earthly errors, so they be atoned :
And the commencement of atonement is
The sense of its necessity. — Say on —
And all our church can teach thee shall be
taught;
And all we can absolve thee shall be pardoned.
    Man. When Rome's sixth emperor[1] was
near his last,
The victim of a self-inflicted wound,
To shun the torments of a public death[2]
From senates once his slaves, a certain soldier,
With show of loyal pity, would have stanched
The gushing throat with his officious robe;
The dying Roman thrust him back, and
said —
Some empire still in his expiring glance,
"It is too late — is this fidelity?"
    Abbot. And what of this?
    Man.   I answer with the Roman —
"It is too late!"
    Abbot.   It never can be so,
To reconcile thyself with thy own soul,
And thy own soul with heaven. Hast thou
no hope?
'Tis strange — even those who do despair
above,

[1] [Otho, being defeated in a general engagement
near Brixelium, stabbed himself. Plutarch says,
that, though he lived full as badly as Nero, his last
moments were those of a philosopher. He com-
forted his soldiers who lamented his fortune, and
expressed his concern for their safety, when *they*
solicited to pay him the last friendly offices.]

[2] MS. —
"To shun { not loss of life, but } public death.
          { the torments of a }
Choose between them."]

Yet shape themselves some fantasy on earth,
To which frail twig they cling, like drowning
  men.
Man. Ay — father! I have had those earthly
    visions
And noble aspirations in my youth,
To make my own the mind of other men,
The enlightener of nations; and to rise
I knew not whither — it might be to fall;
But fall, even as the mountain-cataract,
Which having leaped from its more dazzling
    height,
Even in the foaming strength of its abyss,
(Which casts up misty columns that become
Clouds raining from the reascended skies,)
Lies low but mighty still. — But this is past,
My thoughts mistook themselves.
  Abbot.   And wherefore so?
Man. I could not tame my nature down;
    for he
Must serve who fain would sway — and soothe
    — and sue —
And watch all time — and pry into all place —
And be a living lie — who would become
A mighty thing amongst the mean, and such
The mass are; I disdained to mingle with
A herd, though to be leader — and of wolves.
The lion is alone, and so am I.
  Abbot. And why not live and act with other
    men?
Man. Because my nature was averse from
    life;
And yet not cruel; for I would not make,
But find a desolation : — like the wind,
The red-hot breath of the most lone Simoom,
Which dwells but in the desert, and sweeps
    o'er
The barren ·sands which bear no shrubs to
    blast,
And revels o'er their wild and arid waves,
And seeketh not, so that it is not sought,
But being met is deadly; such hath been
The course of my existence; but there came
Things in my path which are no more.
  Abbot.   Alas!
I 'gin to fear that thou art past all aid
From me and from my calling; yet so young,
I still would ——
Man.   Look on me! there is an order
Of mortals on the earth, who do become
Old in their youth, and die ere middle age,
Without the violence of warlike death;
Some perishing of pleasure—some of study—
Some worn with toil — some of mere weari-
    ness —
Some of disease — and some insanity — [1]

And some of withered, or of broken hearts;
For this last is a malady which slays
More than are numbered in the lists of Fate,
Taking all shapes, and bearing many names.
Look upon me! for even of all these things
Have I partaken; and of all these things,
One were enough; then wonder not that I
Am what I am, but that I ever was,
Or having been, that I am still on earth.
  Abbot. Yet, hear me still ——
Man.   Old man! I do respect
Thine order, and revere thine years; I deem
Thy purpose pious, but it is in vain:
Think me not churlish; I would spare thyself,
Far more than me, in shunning at this time
All further colloquy — and so — farewell.[2]
                    [*Exit* MANFRED.
  Abbot. This should have been a noble
    creature: [3] he
Hath all the energy which would have made

___

[1] [This speech has been quoted in more than one
of the sketches of the poet's own life. Much earlier,
when only twenty-three years of age, he had thus
prophesied: — "It seems as if I were to experience
in my youth the greatest misery of old age. My
friends fall around me, and I shall be left a lonely tree

before I am withered. Other men can always take
refuge in their families — *I* have no resource but my
own reflections, and they present no prospect, here
or hereafter, except the selfish satisfaction of sur-
viving my betters. I am, indeed, very wretched.
My days are listless, and my nights restless. I
have very seldom any society; and when I have, I
run out of it. I don't know that I sha'n't end in
insanity." — *Byron's Letters,* 1811.]

[2] ["Of the immortality of the soul, it appears to
me that there can be little doubt — if we attend for
a moment to the action of mind. It is in per-
petual activity. I used to doubt of it — but reflec-
tion has taught me better. How far our future state
will be individual; or, rather, how far it will at all
resemble our present existence, is another question;
but that the mind is eternal seems as probable as
that the body is not so." — *Byron's Diary,* 1821.
— "I have no wish to reject Christianity without
investigation; on the contrary, I am very desirous
of believing; for I have no happiness in my present
unsettled notions on religion." — *Byron's Conver-
sations with Kennedy,* 1823.]

[3] [There are three only, even among the great
poets of modern times, who have chosen to depict,
in their full shape and vigor, those agonies to which
great and meditative intellects are, in the present
progress of human history, exposed by the eternal
recurrence of a deep and discontented scepticism.
But there is only one who has dared to represent
himself as the victim of those nameless and unde-
finable sufferings. Goethe chose for his doubts
and his darkness the terrible disguise of the
mysterious Faustus. Schiller, with still greater
boldness, planted the same anguish in the restless,
haughty, and heroic bosom of Wallenstein. But
Byron has sought no external symbol in which to
embody the inquietudes of his soul. He takes the
world, and all that it inherit, for his arena and his
spectators; and he displays himself before their
gaze, wrestling unceasingly and ineffectually with
the demon that torments him. At times, there is
something mournful and depressing in his scepti-
cism; but oftener it is of a high and solemn character,
approaching to the very verge of a confiding faith.
Whatever the poet may believe, we, his readers,
always feel ourselves too much ennobled and ele-

ıe of glorious elements,
n wisely mingled; as it is,
chaos — light and darkness —
d dust — and passions and pure

ntending without end or order,
r destructive: he will perish,
ust not; I will try once more,
vorth redemption; and my duty
things for a righteous end.
— but cautiously, though surely.
[*Exit* ABBOT.

II. — *Another Chamber.*

FRED *and* HERMAN.

ord, you bade me wait on you
:
ind the mountain.
                    Doth he so?
him.
advances to the Window of the

          Glorious Orb! the idol
e, and the vigorous race
ı mankind, the giant sons[1]
ce of angels, with a sex
l than they, which did draw down
irits who can ne'er return. —
orb! that wert a worship, ere
f thy making was revealed!
minister of the Almighty,
ened, on their mountain tops,
s
ean shepherds, till they poured
n orisons! Thou material God!
tative of the Unknown —
ıee for his shadow! Thou chief

ny stars! which mak'st our earth
ıd temperest the hues

his melancholy, not to be confirmed
ef by the very doubts so majestically
uttered. His scepticism, if it ever
ı creed, carries with it its refutation
There is neither philosophy nor reli-
ıitter and savage taunts which have
thrown out, from many quarters,
ıoods of mind which are involuntary,
ss away; the shadows and spectres
ınt his imagination may once have
ıwn; — through his gloom there are
ı of illumination; — and the sublime
to him is breathed from the mysteries
ınce, is always joined with a longing
ty, and expressed in language that
— *Professor Wilson.*]
me to pass, that the *Sons of God* saw
of men, that they were fair," etc. —
ıdants in the earth in those days; and
vhen the *Sons of God* came in unto the
ın, and they bare children to them, the
nighty men which were of old, men
Genesis, ch. vi. verses 2 and 4.

And hearts of all who walk within thy rays!
Sire of the seasons! Monarch of the climes,
And those who dwell in them I for near or far,
Our inborn spirits have a tint of thee
Even as our outward aspects; — thou dost
    rise,
And shine, and set in glory. Fare thee well!
I ne'er shall see thee more. As my first glance
Of love and wonder was for thee, then take
My latest look: thou wilt not beam on one
To whom the gifts of life and warmth have
    been
Of a more fatal nature.[2] He is gone:
I follow. [*Exit* MANFRED.

SCENE III. — *The Mountains. — The Castle
of Manfred at some distance. — A Terrace
before a Tower. — Time, Twilight.*

HERMAN, MANUEL, *and other Dependants of*
MANFRED.

Her. 'Tis strange enough; night after night,
    for years,
He hath pursued long vigils in this tower,
Without a witness. I have been within it, —
So have we all been oft-times; but from it,
Or its contents, it were impossible
To draw conclusions absolute, of aught
His studies tend to. To be sure, there is
One chamber where none enter: I would give
The fee of what I have to come these three
    years,
To pore upon its mysteries.
    Manuel.   'Twere dangerous;
Content thyself with what thou know'st al-
    ready.
    Her. Ah! Manuel! thou art elderly and
    wise,
And couldst say much; thou hast dwelt with-
    in the castle —
How many years is't?
    Manuel.   Ere Count Manfred's birth,
I served him father, whom he nought resem-
    bles.
    Her. There be more sons in like predica-
    ment.
But wherein do they differ?
    Manuel.   I speak not
Of features or of form, but mind and habits;
Count Sigismund was proud, — but gay and
    free, —
A warrior and a reveller; he dwelt not
With books and solitude, nor made the night
A gloomy vigil, but a festal time,
Merrier than day; he did not walk the rocks
And forests like a wolf, nor turn aside
From men and their delights.
    Her.   Beshrew the hour,

2 ["Pray, was Manfred's speech to the Sun still
retained in Act third? I hope so: it was one of the
best in the thing, and better than the Coliseum." —
Byron's Letters, 1817.]

But those were jocund times! I would that
such
Would visit the old walls again; they look
As if they had forgotten them.
   Manuel.   These walls
Must change their chieftain first. Oh! I have
seen
Some strange things in them, Herman.[1]
   Her.   Come, be friendly;
Relate me some to while away our watch:
I've heard thee darkly speak of an event
Which happened hereabouts, by this same
tower.
   Manuel. That was a night indeed! I do
remember
'Twas twilight, as it may be now, and such
Another evening; — yon red cloud, which
rests
On Eigher's pinnacle, so rested then, —
So like that it might be the same; the wind
Was faint and gusty, and the mountain snows
Began to glitter with the climbing moon;
Count Manfred was, as now, within his
tower, —
How occupied, we knew not, but with him
The sole companion of his wanderings
And watchings — her, whom of all earthly
things
That lived, the only thing he seemed to
love, —
As he, indeed, by blood was bound to do,
The lady Astarte, his —— [2]
            Hush! who comes here?

        Enter the ABBOT.

---

[1] [MS. —

   " Some strange things in these few years."]

[2] [The remainder of the third Act, in its original
shape, ran thus : —

   Her. Look — look — the tower —
The tower's on fire. Oh, heavens and earth! what
sound,
What dreadful sound is that?
            [*A crash like thunder.*
   Manuel. Help, help, there! — to the rescue of
the Count, —
The Count's in danger, — what ho! there! approach!
   [*The Servants, Vassals, and Peasantry ap-
proach, stupefied with terror.*
If there be any of you who have heart
And love of human kind, and will to aid
Those in distress — pause not — but follow me —
The portal's open, follow.   [MANUEL *goes in.*
   Her. Come — who follows?
What, none of ye? — ye recreants! shiver then
Without. I will not see old Manuel risk
His few remaining years unaided. [HERMAN *goes in.*
   Vassal. Hark! —
No — all is silent — not a breath — the flame
Which shot forth such a blaze is also gone:
What may this mean? Let's enter!
   Peasant.   Faith, not I, —
Not that, if one, or two, or more, will join,
I then will stay behind; but, for my part,
I do not see precisely to what end.

Abbot. Where is your master?
   Her.   Yonder in the tower.
   Abbot. I must speak with him.
   Manuel.   'Tis impossible;
He is most private, and must not be thus
Intruded on.
   Abbot.   Upon myself I take
The forfeit of my fault, if fault there be —
But I must see him.
   Her.   Thou hast seen him once
This eve already.
   Abbot.   Herman! I command thee,
Knock, and apprise the Count of my approach.
   Her. We dare not.
   Abbot.   Then it seems I must be herald
Of my own purpose.
   Manuel.   Reverend father, stop —
I pray you pause.
   Abbot.   Why so?
   Manuel.   But step this way,
And I will tell you further.   [*Exeunt.*

    SCENE IV.[3] — *Interior of the Tower.*

        MANFRED *alone.*

The stars are forth, the moon above the tops
Of the snow-shining mountains. — Beautiful!
I linger yet with Nature, for the night
Hath been to me a more familiar face

   Vassal. Cease your vain prating — come.
   Manuel (speaking within). 'Tis all in vain —
He's dead.
   Her. (within). Not so — even now methought
he moved;
But it is dark — so bear him gently out —
Softly — how cold he is! take care of his temples
In winding down the staircase.

Reënter MANUEL *and* HERMAN, *bearing* MANFRED
in their Arms.

   Manuel. Hie to the castle, some of ye, and
bring
What aid you can. Saddle the barb, and speed
For the leech to the city — quick! some water there!
   Her. His cheek is black — but there is a faint
beat
Still lingering about the heart. Some water.
   [*They sprinkle* MANFRED *with water: after
a pause, he gives some signs of life.*
   Manuel. He seems to strive to speak — come —
cheerly, Count!
He moves his lips — canst hear him? I am old,
And cannot catch faint sounds.
   [HERMAN *inclining his head and listening.*
   Her.   I hear a word
Or two — but indistinctly — what is next?
What's to be done? let's bear him to the castle.
   [MANFRED *motions with his hand not to remove
him.*
   Manuel. He disapproves — and 'twere of no
avail —
He changes rapidly.
   Her.   'Twill soon be over.]

[3] [The opening of this scene is, perhaps, the finest
passage in the drama; and its solemn, calm, and
majestic character throws an air of grandeur over

man; and in her starry shade
solitary loveliness,
language of another world.
per me, that in my youth,
wandering, — upon such a night
n the Coliseum's wall,[1]
ief relics of almighty Rome;
which grew along the broken

k in the blue midnight, and the

gh the rents of ruin; from afar
g bayed beyond the Tiber; and
om out the Cæsars' palace came
ng cry, and, interruptedly,
ntinels the fitful song
lied upon the gentle wind.
ses beyond the time-worn breach
skirt the horizon, yet they stood
wshot — Where the Cæsars dwelt,
he tuneless birds of night, amidst
ch springs through levelled battle-

its roots with the imperial hearths,
he laurel's place of growth; —
iators' bloody Circus stands,
ck in ruinous perfection!
r's chambers, and the Augustan

rth in indistinct decay. —
didst shine, thou rolling moon,

cast a wide and tender light,
ned down the hoar austerity
esolation, and filled up,
ew, the gaps of centuries;
beautiful which still was so,
g that which was not, till the

zion, and the heart ran o'er
worship of the great of old! —
ut sceptred sovereigns, who still

om their urns. —
   'Twas such a night!
that I recall it at this time;
found our thoughts take wildest

---

e, which was in danger of appearing
nd somewhat too much in the style
and Dr. Faustus." — *Wilson.*]
at midnight to see the Coliseum by
it what can I say of the Coliseum?
een; to describe it I should have
ssible, if I had not read 'Manfred.'
it, as the Poet of the North tells us of
ie, one 'must see it by the pale moon-
llness of night, the whispering echoes,
 shadows, and the awful grandeur of
 ruins, form a scene of romantic sub-
is Byron alone could describe as it
s description is the very thing itself."
Diary of an Invalid.]

Even at the moment when they should array
Themselves in pensive order.

Enter the ABBOT.

Abbot.   My good lord!
I crave a second grace for this approach;
But yet let not my humble zeal offend
By its abruptness — all it hath of ill
Recoils on me; its good in the effect
May light upon your head — could I say
 heart —
Could I touch *that*, with words or prayers, I
 should
Recall a noble spirit which hath wandered;
But is not yet all lost.
Man.   Thou know'st me not;
My days are numbered, and my deeds re-
 corded:
Retire, or 'twill be dangerous — Away!
Abbot. Thou dost not mean to menace
 me?
Man.   Not I;
I simply tell thee peril is at hand,
And would preserve thee.
Abbot.   What dost thou mean?
Man.   Look there!
What dost thou see?
Abbot.   Nothing.
Man.   Look there, I say,
And steadfastly; — now tell me what thou
 seest?
Abbot. That which should shake me, — but
 I fear it not —
I see a dusk and awful figure rise,
Like an infernal god, from out the earth;
His face wrapt in a mantle, and his form
Robed as with angry clouds: he stands be-
 tween
Thyself and me — but I do fear him not.
Man. Thou hast no cause — he shall not
 harm thee — but
His sight may shock thine old limbs into palsy.
I say to thee — Retire!
Abbot.   And I reply —
Never — till I have battled with this fiend: —
What doth he here?
Man. Why — ay — what doth he here? —
I did not send for him, — he is unbidden.
Abbot. Alas! lost mortal! what with guests
 like these
Hast thou to do? I tremble for thy sake:
Why doth he gaze on thee, and thou on him?
Ah! he unveils his aspect: on his brow
The thunder-scars are graven; from his eye
Glares forth the immortality of hell —
Avaunt! ——
Man. Pronounce — what is thy mission?
Spirit.   Come!
Abbot. What art thou, unknown being? an-
 swer! — speak!
Spirit. The genius of this mortal. — Come!
 'tis time.

Man. I am prepared for all things, but deny
The power which summons me. Who sent thee here?
Spirit. Thou'lt know anon — Come! come!
Man. I have commanded
Things of an essence greater far than thine,
And striven with thy masters. Get thee hence!
Spirit. Mortal! thine hour is come — Away! I say.
Man. I knew, and know my hour is come, but not
To render up my soul to such as thee:
Away! I'll die as I have lived — alone.
Spirit. Then I must summon up my brethren. — Rise! [*Other Spirits rise up.*
Abbot. Avaunt! ye evil ones! — Avaunt! I say, —
Ye have no power where piety hath power,
And I do charge ye in the name ——
Spirit. Old man!
We know ourselves, our mission, and thine order;
Waste not thy holy words on idle uses,
It were in vain: this man is forfeited.
Once more I summon him — Away! away!
Man. I do defy ye, — though I feel my soul
Is ebbing from me, yet I do defy ye;
Nor will I hence, while I have earthly breath
To breathe my scorn upon ye — earthly strength
To wrestle, though with spirits; what ye take
Shall be ta'en limb by limb.
Spirit. Reluctant mortal!
Is this the Magian who would so pervade
The world invisible, and make himself
Almost our equal? — Can it be that thou
Art thus in love with life? the very life
Which made thee wretched!
Man. Thou false fiend, thou liest!
My life is in its last hour, — *that* I know,
Nor would redeem a moment of that hour;
I do not combat against death, but 'hee
And thy surrounding angels; my past power
Was purchased by no compact with thy crew,
But by superior science — penance — daring —
And length of watching — strength of mind — and skill
In knowledge of our fathers — when the earth
Saw men and spirits walking side by side,
And gave ye no supremacy: I stand
Upon my strength — I do defy — deny —
Spurn back, and scorn ye! —
Spirit. But thy many crimes
Have made thee ——
Man. What are they to such as thee?
Must crimes be punished but by other crimes,
And greater criminals? — Back to thy hell!
Thou hast no power upon me, *that* I feel ·

Thou never shalt possess me, *that* I know:
What I have done is done; I bear within
A torture which could nothing gain from thine:
The mind which is immortal makes itself
Requital for its good or evil thoughts —
Is its own origin of ill and end —
And its own place and time — its innate sense,
When stripped of this mortality, derives
No color from the fleeting things without;
But is absorbed in sufferance or in joy,
Born from the knowledge of its own desert.
Thou didst not tempt me, and thou couldst not tempt me;
I have not been thy dupe, nor am thy prey —
But was my own destroyer, and will be
My own hereafter. — Back, ye baffled fiends!
The hand of death is on me — but not yours!
[*The Demons disappear.*
Abbot. Alas! how pale thou art — thy lips are white —
And thy breast heaves — and in thy gasping throat
The accents rattle — Give thy prayers to Heaven —
Pray — albeit but in thought, — but die not thus.
Man. 'Tis over — my dull eyes can fix thee not;
But all things swim around me, and the earth
Heaves as it were beneath me Fare thee well —
Give me thy hand.
Abbot. Cold — cold — even to the heart —
But yet one prayer — Alas! how fares it with thee?
Man. Old man! 'tis not so difficult to die.[1]
[MANFRED *expires.*
Abbot. He's gone — his soul hath ta'en its earthless flight —
Whither? I dread to think — but he is gone.[2]

[1] [In the first edition, this line was accidentally left out. On discovering the omission, Byron wrote to Mr. Murray — "You have destroyed the whole effect and moral of the poem, by omitting the last line of Manfred's speaking."]

[2] In June, 1820, Byron thus writes to his publisher: — " Inclosed is something which will interest you; to wit, the opinion of the greatest man in Germany — perhaps in Europe — upon one of the great men of your advertisements (all 'famous hands,' as Jacob Tonson used to say of his ragamuffins) — in short, a critic of Goethe's upon *Manfred.* There is the original, an English translation, and an Italian one: keep them all in your archives; for the opinions of such a man as Goethe, whether favorable or not, are always interesting — and this is more so, as favorable. His Faust I never read, for I don't know German; but Matthew Monk Lewis, in 1816, at Coligny, translated most of it to me *vivâ voce*, and I was naturally much struck with it, but it was the Steinbach and the Jungfrau, and something else, much more than Faustus, that made me write Manfred. The first

and that of Faustus are very simi-

; is the extract from Goethe's *Kunst*
n (*i.e.* Art and Antiquity) which
inclosed: —
gedy, 'Manfred,' was to me a won-
non, and one that closely touched
ilarly intellectual poet has taken my
elf, and extracted from it the strong-
. for his hypochondriac humor. He
the impelling principles in his own
'n purposes, so that no one of them
ie; and it is particularly on this ac-
annot enough admire his genius.
in this way so completely formed
ould be an interesting task for the
out, not only the alterations he has
degree of resemblance with, or dis-
e original: in the course of which I
at the gloomy heat of an unbounded
despair becomes at last oppressive
the dissatisfaction we feel always
esteem and admiration.
is, in this tragedy, the quintessence
onishing talent born to be its own
e character of Lord Byron's life and
ermits a just and equitable appreci-
often enough confessed what it is
iim. He has repeatedly portrayed
y any one feels compassion for this
ering, over which he is ever labori-
ig. There are, properly speaking,
ose phantoms for ever haunt him,
this piece also, perform principal
ler the name of Astarte, the other
actual presence, and merely a voice.
occurrence which took place with
following is related: — When a bold
g young man, he won the affections
lady.* Her husband discovered
murdered his wife; but the mur-
ame night found dead in the street,
o one on whom any suspicion could
.ord Byron removed from Florence,
; haunted him all his life after.
tic incident is rendered highly prob-
rable allusions to it in his poems.

ye confidence with which the vener-
s the fancies of his brother poet to
i events, making no difficulty even
der at Florence to furnish grounds
affords an amusing instance of the
revalent throughout Europe, to pic-
man of marvels and mysteries, as
; his poetry. To these exaggerated,
iotions of him, the numerous fictions
ie world of his romantic tours and
itures, in places he never saw, and
at never existed, have, no doubt,
itributed; and the consequence is,
f truth and nature are the represen-
fe and character long current upon
:hat it may be questioned whether
and blood' hero of these pages, —
ical-minded, and, with all his faults
s, *English* Lord Byron, — may not,
ilted imaginations of most of his
s, appear but an ordinary, unro-
saic personage." — *Moore's Life of*

As, for instance, when turning his sad contempla-
tions inwards, he applies to himself the fatal history
of the king of Sparta. It is as follows: — Pausa-
nias, a Lacedæmonian general, acquires glory by
the important victory at Platæa but afterwards for-
feits the confidence of his countrymen through his
arrogance, obstinacy, and secret intrigues with the
enemies of his country. This man draws upon
himself the heavy guilt of innocent blood, which
attends him to his end; for, while commanding the
fleet of the allied Greeks, in the Black Sea, he is
inflamed with a violent passion for a Byzantine
maiden. After long resistance, he at length obtains
her from her parents, and she is to be delivered up
to him at night. She modestly desires the servant
to put out the lamp, and, while groping her way in
the dark, she overturns it. Pausanias is awakened
from his sleep — apprehensive of an attack from
murderers, he seizes his sword, and destroys his
mistress. The horrid sight never leaves him. Her
shade pursues him unceasingly, and he implores
for aid in vain from the gods and the exorcising
priests.

"That poet must have a lacerated heart who se-
lects such a scene from antiquity, appropriates it to
himself, and burdens his tragic image with it. The
following soliloquy, which is overladen with gloom
and a weariness of life, is, by this remark, rendered
intelligible. We recommend it as an exercise to all
friends of declamation. Hamlet's soliloquy appears
improved upon here." — Goethe here subjoins Man-
fred's soliloquy, beginning "We are the fools of
time and terror," in which the allusion to Pausanias
occurs. The reader will not be sorry to pass from
this German criticism to that of the Edinburgh Re-
view on Manfred. — "This is, undoubtedly, a work
of great genius and originality. Its worst fault,
perhaps, is that it fatigues and overawes us by the
uniformity of its terror and solemnity. Another,
is the painful and offensive nature of the circum-
stance on which its distress is ultimately founded.
The lyrical songs of the Spirits are too long, and
not all excellent. There is something of pedantry
in them now and then; and even Manfred deals in
classical allusions a little too much. If we were to
consider it as a proper drama, or even as a finished
poem, we should be obliged to add, that it is far too
indistinct and unsatisfactory. But this we take to
be according to the design and conception of the
author. He contemplated but a dim and magnifi-
cent sketch of a subject which did not admit of
more accurate drawing or more brilliant coloring.
Its obscurity is a part of its grandeur; — and the
darkness that rests upon it, and the smoky distance
in which it is lost, are all devices to increase its
majesty, to stimulate our curiosity, and to impress
us with deeper awe. — It is suggested, in an ingeni-
ous paper in a late number of the Edinburgh Mag-
azine, that the general conception of this piece, and
much of what is excellent in the manner of its exe-
cution, have been borrowed from 'The Tragical
History of Dr. Faustus,' of Marlow: † and a variety
of passages are quoted, which the author considers
as similar, and, in many respects superior to others
in the poem before us. We cannot agree in the
general terms of the conclusion: but there is no
doubt a certain resemblance, both in some of the

† [On reading this, Byron wrote from Venice: —
"Jeffrey is very kind about Manfred, and defends
its originality, which I did not know that anybody

topics that are suggested, and in the cast of the diction in which they are expressed. Thus, to induce Faustus to persist in his unlawful studies, he is told that the Spirits of the Elements will serve him, —

' Sometimes like women, or unwedded maids,
  Shadowing more beauty in their ayrie browes,
  Than have the white breasts of the Queene of Love.'

And again, when the amorous sorcerer commands Helen of Troy to revive again to be his paramour, he addresses her, on her first appearance, in these rapturous lines —

' Was this the face that launcht a thousand ships,
  And burned the topless towers of Ilium?
  Sweet Helen! make me immortal with a kiss,
  Her lips suck forth my soule! — see where it flies.
  Come Helen, come give me my soule againe,
  Here will I dwell, for heaven is on that lip,
  And all is dross that is not Helena.
  O! thou art fairer than the evening ayre,
  Clad in the beauty of a thousand starres;
  More lovely than the monarch of the skyes,
  In wanton Arethusa's azure arms!'

The catastrophe, too, is bewailed in verses of great elegance and classical beauty —

' Cut is the branch that might have growne full straight,
  And burned is Apollo's laurel bough
  That sometime grew within this learned man.
  Faustus is gone! — regard his hellish fall,
  Whose findful torture may exhort the wise,
  Only to wonder at unlawful things!'

But these, and many other smooth and fanciful

---

had attacked. As to the germs of it, they may be found in the Journal which I sent to Mrs. Leigh, shortly before I left Switzerland. I have the whole scene of Manfred before me, as if it was but yesterday, and could point it out, spot by spot, torrent and all."]

verses in this curious old drama, prove nothing, we think, against the originality of Manfred, for there is nothing to be found there of the pride, the abstraction, and the heart-rooted misery in which that originality consists. Faustus is a vulgar sorcerer, tempted to sell his soul to the devil for the ordinary price of sensual pleasure, and earthly power and glory; and who shrinks and shudders in agony when the forfeit comes to be exacted. The style, too, of Marlow, though elegant and scholarlike, is weak and childish compared with the depth and force of much of Lord Byron: and the disgusting buffoonery and low farce of which his piece is principally made up, place it more in contrast, than in any terms of comparison, with that of his noble successor. In the tone and pitch of the composition, as well as in the character of the diction in the more solemn parts, Manfred reminds us much more of the 'Prometheus' of Æschylus,* than of any more modern performance. The tremendous solitude of the principal person — the supernatural beings with whom alone he holds communion — the guilt — the firmness — the misery — are all points of resemblance, to which the grandeur of the poetic imagery only gives a more striking effect. The chief differences are, that the subject of the Greek poet was sanctified and exalted by the established belief of his country, and that his terrors are nowhere tempered with the sweetness which breathes from so many passages of his English rival." — *Jeffrey.*]

* [" Of the 'Prometheus' of Æschylus I was passionately fond as a boy (it was one of the Greek plays we read thrice a year at Harrow); indeed, that and the ▶Medea' were the only ones, except the 'Seven before Thebes,' which ever much pleased me. The Prometheus, if not exactly in my plan, has always been so much in my head, that I can easily conceive its influence over all or any thing that I have written: but I deny Marlow and his progeny, and beg that you will do the same." — *Byron's Letters,* 1817.]

MARINO FALIERO, DOGE OF VENICE;

AN HISTORICAL TRAGEDY, IN FIVE ACTS.

" Dux inquieti turbidus Adriæ." — HORACE.

[On the original MS. sent from Ravenna, Byron wrote: — " Begun April 4th, 1820 — completed July 16th, 1820 — finished copying August 16th-17th, 1820; the which copying makes ten times the toil of composing, considering the weather — thermometer 90 in the shade — and my domestic duties."]

[BYRON finished the composition of this tragedy on the 17th July, 1820. He at the time intended to keep it by him for six years before sending it to the press; but resolutions of this kind are, in modern days, very seldom adhered to. It was published in the end of the same year; and, to the poet's great disgust, and in spite of his urgent and repeated remonstrances, was produced on the stage of Drury Lane Theatre early in 1821.

ro was, greatly to his satisfaction, commended warmly for the truth of its adhesion to
r and manners, as well as the antique severity of its structure and language, by that emi-
Italian and classical literature, Ugo Foscolo. Mr. Gifford also delighted him by pro-
nglish—genuine English." It was, however, little favored by the contemporary critics.
ed, only one who spoke of it as quite worthy of Byron's reputation. "Nothing," said
ong time afforded us so much pleasure, as the rich promise of dramatic excellence un-
oduction of Lord Byron. Without question, no such tragedy as Marino Faliero has
lish, since the day when Otway also was inspired to his masterpiece by the interests of a
nd a Venetian conspiracy. The story of which Lord Byron has possessed himself is,
the finer of the two,—and we say *possessed*, because we believe he has adhered almost
ne transactions as they really took place."—The language of the Edinburgh and Quar-
, Mr. Jeffrey and Bishop Heber, was in a far different strain. The former says—
ero has undoubtedly considerable beauties, both dramatic and poetical; and might have
e of any young aspirant for fame: but the name of Byron raises expectations which are
sfied; and, judging of it by the lofty standard which he himself has established, we are
', that we cannot but regard it as a failure, both as a poem and a play. The story, in so
al in our drama, is extremely improbable, though, like most other very improbable sto-
n authentic sources: but, in the main, it is original; being, indeed, merely another 'Ven-
and continually recalling, though certainly without eclipsing, the memory of the first.
ier is driven to join the conspirators by the natural impulse of love and misery, and the
tment so outrageous as to exclude all sympathy,—and that the disclosure, which is pro-
a the old play, is here ascribed to mere friendship,—the general action and catastrophe
s are almost identical; while, with regard to the writing and management, it must be
ord Byron has most sense and vigor, Otway has by far the most passion and pathos; and
conspirators are better orators and reasoners than the gang of Pierre and Reynault, the
lvidere is as much more touching, as it is more natural, than the stoical and self-satisfied
iolina."
; is an extract from Bishop Heber's review in the Quarterly:—
iero has, we believe, been pretty generally pronounced a failure by the public voice, and
a to call for a revision of their sentence. It contains, beyond all doubt, many passages
eloquence, and some of genuine poetry; and the scenes, more particularly, in which Lord
cted the absurd creed of his pseudo-Hellenic writers, are conceived and elaborated with
:t and dexterity. But the subject is decidedly ill-chosen. In the main tissue of the plot,
isiest and most interesting parts of it, it is, in fact, no more than another 'Venice Pre-
h the author has had to contend (nor has he contended successfully) with our recollec-
: and deservedly popular play on the same subject. And the only respect in which it
e Jaffier of Lord Byron's plot is drawn in to join the conspirators, not by the natural and
ves of poverty, aggravated by the sufferings of a beloved wife, and a deep and well-
ent of oppression, but by his outrageous anger for a private wrong of no very atrocious
ge of Venice, to chastise the vulgar libel of a foolish boy, attempts to overturn that re-
ne is the first and most trusted servant; to massacre all of his ancient friends and fellow-
gistracy and nobility of the land. With such a resentment as this, thus simply stated
, who ever sympathized, or who but Lord Byron would have expected in such a cause
ken sympathy? It is little to the purpose to say that this is all historically true. A
e without being probable; and such a case of idiosyncrasy as is implied in a resentment
travagant, is no more a fitting subject for the poet, than an animal with two heads would
f a different description."
extract from a letter of January, 1821, will show the author's own estimate of the piece
After repeating his hope, that no manager would be so audacious as to trample on his
icing it on the stage, he thus proceeds:—
gular—the time, twenty-four hours—the change of place not frequent—nothing *melo-
rprises*—no starts, nor trap-doors, nor opportunities 'for tossing their heads and kicking
d no *love*, the grand ingredient of a modern play. I am persuaded that a great tragedy
uced by following the old dramatists—who are full of gross faults, pardoned only for the
anguage,—but by writing naturally and *regularly*, and producing regular tragedies,
; but not in imitation,—merely the outline of their conduct, adapted to our own times
es, and of course *no* chorus. You will laugh, and say, 'Why don't you do so?' I have,
sketch in Marino Faliero; but many people think my talent '*essentially undramatic*,'
all clear that they are not right. If Marino Faliero don't fail—in the perusal—I shall,
in (but not for the stage); and as I think that *love* is not the principal passion for tragedy
f ours turn upon it), you will not find me a popular writer. Unless it is love *furious*,
:apless, it ought not to make a tragic subject. When it is melting and maudlin, it *does*,
: to do; it is then for the gallery and second price boxes. If you want to have a notion
-ying, take up a *translation* of any of the Greek tragedians. If I said the original, it
pudent presumption of mine: but the translations are so inferior to the originals, that I
it. Then judge of the 'simplicity of plot,' and do not judge me by your old mad drama-
ike drinking usquebaugh, and then proving a fountain. Yet, after all, I suppose you do
spirits is a nobler element than a clear spring bubbling up in the sun? and this I take to
e between the Greeks and those turbid mountebanks—always excepting Ben Jonson,
lar and a classic. Or, take up a translation of Alfieri, and try the interest, etc. of these
s in the old line, by *him* in English: and then tell me fairly your opinion. But don't

measure me by YOUR OWN *old* or *new* tailor's yard. Nothing so easy as intricate confusion of plot and rant. Mrs. Centlivre, in comedy, has ten times the bustle of Congreve; but are they to be compared? and yet she drove Congreve from the theatre."

Again, February 16, he thus writes: —

"You say the Doge will not be popular: did I ever write for popularity? I defy you to show a work of mine (except a tale or two) of a popular style or complexion. It appears to me that there is room for a different style of the drama; neither a servile following of the old drama, which is a grossly erroneous one, nor yet *too* French, like those who succeeded the older writers. It appears to me that good English, and a severer approach to the rules, might combine something not dishonorable to our literature. I have also attempted to make a play without love; and there are neither rings, nor mistakes, nor starts, nor outrageous canting villains, nor melodrama in it. All this will prevent its popularity, but does not persuade me that it is *therefore* faulty. Whatever fault it has will arise from deficiency in the conduct, rather than in the conception, which is simple and severe.

"Reproach is useless always, and irritating — but my feelings were very much hurt, to be dragged like a gladiator to the fate of a gladiator by that '*retiarius*,' Mr. Elliston. As to his defence and offers of compensation, what is all this to the purpose? It is like Louis XIV. who insisted upon buying at any price Algernon Sydney's horse, and, on his refusal, on taking it by force, Sydney shot his horse. I could not shoot my tragedy, but I would have flung it into the fire rather than have had it represented."

The poet originally designed to inscribe this tragedy to his friend, Mr. Douglas Kinnaird; but the dedication he drew up remained in MS. till after the poet's death. It is in these words: —

"TO THE HONORABLE DOUGLAS KINNAIRD.

"MY DEAR DOUGLAS, — I dedicate to you the following tragedy, rather on account of your good opinion of it, than from any notion of my own that it may be worthy of your acceptance. But if its merits were ten times greater than they possibly can be, this offering would still be a very inadequate acknowledgment of the active and steady friendship with which, for a series of years, you have honored

"Your obliged and affectionate friend,

"BYRON."

At another moment, the poet resolved to dedicate the tragedy to Goethe, whose praises of "Manfred" had highly delighted him; but this dedication shared the fate of that to Mr. Kinnaird: — it did not reach the hands of Goethe till 1831, when it was presented to him at Weimar, by Mr. Murray, jun.; nor was it printed at all, until Moore included it in his Memoirs of Byron. In doing so, he omitted some passages, which, the MS. having since been lost, cannot be restored. "It is written," he says, "in the poet's most whimsical and mocking mood; and the unmeasured severity poured out in it upon the two favorite objects of his wrath and ridicule, compels me to deprive the reader of some of its most amusing passages."

Wordsworth and Southey were the persons ridiculed in these suppressed passages.

"TO BARON GOETHE,[1] ETC. ETC. ETC.

"Sir, — In the Appendix to an English work lately translated into German and published at Leipsic, a judgment of yours upon English poetry is quoted as follows: 'That in English poetry, great genius, universal power, a feeling of profundity, with sufficient tenderness and force, are to be found; but that *altogether these do not constitute poets*,' etc. etc.

"I regret to see a great man falling into a great mistake. This opinion of yours only proves, that the '*Dictionary of ten thousand living English Authors*' has not been translated into German. You will have read in your friend Schlegel's version, the dialogue in Macbeth —

> 'There are *ten thousand!*
> Macbeth. Geese, villain?
> Answer   Authors, sir.'

Now, of these 'ten thousand authors,' there are actually nineteen hundred and eighty-seven poets, all alive at this moment, whatever their works may be, as their booksellers well know: and amongst these there are several who possess a far greater reputation than mine, although considerably less than yours. It is owing to this neglect on the part of your German translators that you are not aware of the works of

* * * * * * * *

"There is also another, named * * * * * * * *

"I mention these poets by way of sample to enlighten you. They form but two bricks of our Babel (WINDSOR bricks, by the way), but may serve for a specimen of the building.

"It is, moreover, asserted that 'the predominant character of the whole body of the present English poetry is a *disgust* and *contempt* for life.' But I rather suspect that, by one single work of *prose, you* yourself have excited a greater contempt for life, than all the English volumes of poesy that ever were written. Madame de Staël says, that 'Werther has occasioned more suicides than the most beautiful woman;' and I really believe that he has put more individuals out of this world than Napoleon himself, — except in the way of his profession. Perhaps, Illustrious Sir, the acrimonious judgment passed by a celebrated northern journal upon you in particular, and the Germans in general, has rather indisposed you towards English poetry as well as criticism. But you must not regard our critics, who are at bottom

---

[1] [Goethe was ennobled, having the *Von* prefixed to his name, but never received the title of Baron.]

lows, considering their two professions, — taking up the law in court, and laying it down
ne can more lament their hasty and unfair judgment, in your particular, than I do; and
ryself to your friend Schlegel, in 1816, at Coppet.
" my 'ten thousand' living brethren, and of myself, I have thus far taken notice of an
:d with regard to ' English poetry' in general, and which merited notice, because it was

.l object in addressing you was to testify my sincere respect and admiration of a man,
entury, has led the literature of a great nation, and will go down to posterity as the first
r of his age.
een fortunate, Sir, not only in the writings which have illustrated your name, but in the
being sufficiently musical for the articulation of posterity. In this you have the advan-
your countrymen, whose names would perhaps be immortal also — if anybody could

haps, be supposed, by this apparent tone of levity, that I am wanting in intentional
you; but this will be a mistake: I am always flippant in prose. Considering you, as I
ly do, in common with all your own, and with most other nations, to be by far the first
r which has existed in Europe since the death of Voltaire, I felt, and feel, desirous to
the following work, — *not* as being either a tragedy or a *poem*, (for I cannot pronounce
:ions to be either one or the other, or both, or neither,) but as a mark of esteem and
a foreigner to the man who has been hailed in Germany ' THE GREAT GOETHE.'
onor to be, with the truest respect,

"Your most obedient and very humble servant,

bre 14°. 1820.   "BYRON.

:ceive that in Germany, as well as in Italy, there is a great struggle about what they call
' *Romantic*,' — terms which were not subjects of classification in England, at least when
ve years ago. Some of the English scribblers, it is true, abused Pope and Swift, but the
they themselves did not know how to write either prose or verse; but nobody thought
ing a sect of. Perhaps there may be something of the kind sprung up lately, but I have
about it, and it would be such bad taste that I shall be very sorry to believe it."

nuch gratified with this token of Byron's admiration.

PREFACE.

:y of the Doge Marino Faliero is one of the most remarkable events in the annals of the
vernment, city, and people of modern history. It occurred in the year 1355. Every thing
or was, extraordinary — her aspect is like a dream, and her history is like a romance.
s Doge is to be found in all her Chronicles, and particularly detailed in the "Lives of the
in Sanuto, which is given in the Appendix. It is simply and clearly related, and is per-
itic in itself than any scenes which can be founded upon the subject.
o appears to have been a man of talents and of courage. I find him commander-in-chief
s at the siege of Zara, where he beat the King of Hungary and his army of eighty thou-
ʒ eight thousand men, and keeping the besieged at the same time in check; an exploit to
ine similar in history, except that of Cæsar at Alesia, and of Prince Eugene at Belgrade.
ds commander of the fleet in the same war. He took Capo d'Istria. He was ambassa-
l Rome, — at which last he received the news of his election to the dukedom; his absence
iat he sought it by no intrigue, since he was apprised of his predecessor's death and his
it the same moment. But he appears to have been of an ungovernable temper. A story
:o, of his having, many years before, when podesta and captain at Treviso, boxed the
op, who was somewhat tardy in bringing the Host. For this, honest Sanuto "saddles
nent," as Thwackum did Square; but he does not tell us whether he was punished or
Senate for this outrage at the time of its commission. He seems, indeed, to have been
ace with the church, for we find him ambassador at Rome, and invested with the fief oi
n the march of Treviso, and with the title of Count, by Lorenzo Count-bishop of Ceneda.
ny authorities are Sanuto, Vettor Sandi, Andrea Navagero, and the account of the siege
ilished by the indefatigable Abate Morelli, in his "Monumenti Veneziani di varia Letter-
n 1796, all of which I have looked over in the original language. The moderns, Darù.

Sismondi, and Laugier, nearly agree with the ancient chroniclers. Sismondi attributes the conspiracy to his *jealousy;* but I find this nowhere asserted by the national historians. Vettor Sandi, indeed, says, that "Altri scrissero che . . . . . dalla gelosa suspizion di esso Doge siasi fatto (Michel Steno) staccar con viclenza," etc. etc.; but this appears to have been by no means the general opinion, nor is it alluded to by Sanuto or by Navagero; and Sandi himself adds, a moment after, that "per altre Veneziane memorie traspiri, che non il *solo* desiderio di vendetta lo dispose alla congiura, ma anche la innata abituale ambizion sua, per cui anelava a farsi principe independente." The first motive appears to have been excited by the gross affront of the words written by Michel Steno on the ducal chair, and by the light and inadequate sentence of the Forty on the offender, who was one of their "tre Capi." The attentions of Steno himself appear to have been directed towards one of her damsels, and not to the "Dogaressa" herself, against whose fame not the slightest insinuation appears, while she is praised for her beauty, and remarked for her youth. Neither do I find it asserted (unless the hint of Sandi be an assertion), that the Doge was actuated by jealousy of his wife; but rather by respect for her, and for his own honor, warranted by his past services and present dignity.

I know not that the historical facts are alluded to in English, unless by Dr. Moore in his View of Italy. His account is false and flippant, full of stale jests about old men and young wives, and wondering at so great an effect from so slight a cause. How so acute and severe an observer of mankind as the author of Zeluco could wonder at this is inconceivable. He knew that a basin of water spilt on Mrs. Masham's gown deprived the Duke of Marlborough of his command, and led to the inglorious peace of Utrecht — that Louis XIV. was plunged into the most desolating wars, because his minister was nettled at his finding fault with a window, and wished to give him another occupation — that Helen lost Troy — that Lucretia expelled the Tarquins from Rome — and that Cava brought the Moors to Spain — that an insulted husband led the Gauls to Clusium, and thence to Rome — that a single verse of Frederick II. of Prussia on the Abbé de Bernis, and a jest on Madame de Pompadour, led to the battle of Rosbach[1] — that the elopement of Dearbhorgil with Mac Murchad conducted the English to the slavery of Ireland — that a personal pique between Maria Antoinette and the Duke of Orleans precipitated the first expulsion of the Bourbons — and, not to multiply instances, that Commodus, Domitian, and Caligula fell victims not to their public tyranny, but to private vengeance — and that an order to make Cromwell disembark from the ship in which he would have sailed to America destroyed both king and commonwealth. After these instances, on the least reflection, it is indeed extraordinary in Dr. Moore to seem surprised that a man used to command, who had served and swayed in the most important offices, should fiercely resent, in a fierce age, an unpunished affront, the grossest that can be offered to a man, be he prince or peasant. The age of Faliero is little to the purpose, unless to favor it—

> "The young man's wrath is like straw on fire,
> *But like red-hot steel is the old man's ire.*"

> "Young men soon give and soon forget affronts,
> Old age is slow at both."

Laugier's reflections are more philosophical: — "Tale fù il fine ignominioso di un' uomo, che la sua nascità, la sua età, il suo carattere dovevano tener lontano dalle passioni produttrici di grandi delitti. I suoi *talenti* per lungo tempo esercitati ne' maggiori impieghi, la sua capacità sperimentata ne' governi e nelle ambasciate, gli avevano acquistato la stima e la fiducia de' cittadini, ed avevano uniti i suffragj per collocarlo alla testa della republica. Innalzato ad un grado che terminava gloriosamente la sua vita, il risentimento di un' ingiuria leggiera insinuò nel suo cuore tal veleno, che bastò a corrompere le antiche sue qualità, e a condurlo al termine dei scellerati; serio esempio, che prova *non esservi età, in cui la*

---

1 [The Abbé's biographer denies the correctness of this statement. — "Quelques écrivains," he says, "qui trouvaient sans doute piquant d'attribuer de grands effets à de petites causes, ont prétendus que l'Abbé avait insisté dans le conseil pour faire déclarer la guerre à la Prusse, par ressentiment contre Frédéric et pour venger sa vanité poëtique, humilié par le vers du monarque bel-esprit et poëte —

' Évitez de Bernis la stérile abondance.'

Je ne m'amuserai point à réfuter cette opinion ridicule; elle tombe par le fait, si l'abbé, comme dit Duclos, je déclara au contraire, dans le conseil, constamment pour l'alliance avec la Prusse, contre le sentiment même de Louis XV, et de Madame de Pompadour." — *Bib. Univ.*]

*na sia sicura, e che nell' uomo restano sempre 'passioni capaci a disonorarlo,
vigili sopra se stesso."* [1]

. Moore find that Marino Faliero begged his life? I have searched the chroniclers, and
he kind; it is true that he avowed all. He was conducted to the place of torture, but
ion made of any application for mercy on his part; and the very circumstance of their
ı to the rack seems to argue any thing but his having shown a want of firmness, which
have been also mentioned by those minute historians, who by no means favor him;
uld be contrary to his character as a soldier, to the age in which he lived, and *at* which
to the truth of history. I know no justification, at any distance of time, for calumni-
al character: surely truth belongs to the dead, and to the unfortunate; and they who
a scaffold have generally had faults enough of their own, without attributing to them
ery incurring of the perils which conducted them to their violent death renders, of all
improbable. The black veil which is painted over the place of Marino Faliero amongst
the Giants' Staircase where he was crowned, and discrowned, and decapitated, struck
ı imagination; as did his fiery character and strange story. I went, in 1819, in search
: than once to the church San Giovanni e San Paolo; and, as I was standing before the
other family, a priest came up to me and said, "I can show you finer monuments than
m that I was in search of that of the Faliero family, and particularly of the Doge
," said he, "I will show it you;" and conducting me to the outside, pointed out a sar-
wall with an illegible inscription. He said that it had been in a convent adjoining, but
er the French came, and placed in its present situation; that he had seen the tomb
moval; there were still some bones remaining, but no positive vestige of the decapi-
estrian statue, of which I have made mention in the third act, as before that church, is
a Faliero, but of some other now obsolete warrior, although of a later date. There were
of this family prior to Marino; Ordelafo, who fell in battle at Zara in 1117 (where his
wards conquered the Huns), and Vital Faliero, who reigned in 1082. The family,
ano, was of the most illustrious in blood and wealth in the city of once the most
the most ancient families in Europe. The length l have gone into on this subject will
I have taken in it. Whether I have succeeded or not in the tragedy, I have at least
ur language an historical fact worthy of commemoration.

years that I have meditated this work; and before I had sufficiently examined the
ther disposed to have made it turn on a jealousy in Faliero.[2] But, perceiving no foun-
historical truth, and aware that jealousy is an exhausted passion in the drama, I have
historical form. I was, besides, well advised by the late Matthew Lewis on that point,
m of my intention at Venice in 1817. "If you make him jealous," said he, "recollect
contend with established writers, to say nothing of Shakspeare, and an exhausted sub-
he old fiery Doge's natural character, which will bear you out, if properly drawn; and
s regular as you can." Sir William Drummond gave me nearly the same counsel.
followed these instructions, or whether they have availed me, is not for me to decide.
w to the stage; in its present state it is, perhaps, not a very exalted object of ambition;
en too much behind the scenes to have thought it so at any time.[3] And I cannot con-
irritable feeling putting himself at the mercies of an audience. The sneering reader,
ic, and the tart review, are scattered and distant calamities; but the trampling of an

. de la Répub. de Venise, Italian translation, vol. iv. p. 30.
1817, Byron wrote to Mr. Murray — "Look into Dr. Moore's 'View of Italy' for me:
ımes you will find an account of the Doge Valiero (it ought to be Falieri) and his con-
ɔtives of it. Get it transcribed for me, and send it in a letter to me soon. I want it,
good an account of that business here: though the veiled patriot, and the place where
ınd afterwards decapitated, still exist and are shown. I have searched all their his-
licy of the old aristocracy make their writers silent on his motives, which were a private
one of the patricians. I mean 'o write a tragedy on the subject, which appears to me
old man, jealous, and conspiring against the state, of which he was actually reigning
circumstance makes it the most remarkable, and only fact of the kind, in all history of

like being at the whole process of a woman's toilet — it disenchants."]

intelligent or of an ignorant audience on a production which, be it good or bad, has been a mental labor to the writer, is a palpable and immediate grievance, heightened by a man's doubt of their competency to judge, and his certainty of his own imprudence in electing them his judges. Were I capable of writing a play which could be deemed stage-worthy, success would give me no pleasure, and failure great pain. It is for this reason that, even during the time of being one of the committee of one of the theatres, I never made the attempt, and never will.[1] But surely there is dramatic power somewhere, where Joanna Baillie, and Millman, and John Wilson exist. The " City of the Plague " and the " Fall of Jerusalem " are full of the best " *matériel* " for tragedy that has been seen since Horace Walpole, except passages of Ethwald and De Montfort. It is the fashion to underate Horace Walpole: firstly, because he was a nobleman, and secondly, because he was a gentleman; but, to say nothing of the composition of his incomparable letters, and of the Castle of Otranto, he is the " Ultimus Romanorum," the author of the Mysterious Mother, a tragedy of the highest order, and not a puling love-play. He is the father of the first romance and of the last tragedy in our language, and surely worthy of a higher place than any living writer, be he who he may.

In speaking of the drama of Marino Faliero, I forgot to mention, that the desire of preserving, though still too remote, a nearer approach to unity than the irregularity, which is the approach of the English theatrical compositions, permits, has induced me to represent the conspiracy as already formed, and the Doge acceding to it: whereas, in fact, it was of his own preparation and that of Israel Bertuccio. The other characters (except that of the Duchess), incidents, and almost the time, which was wonderfully short for such a design in real life, are strictly historical, except that all the consultations took place in the palace. Had I followed this, the unity would have been better preserved; but I wished to produce the Doge in the full assembly of the conspirators, instead of monotonously placing him always in dialogue with the same individuals.[2] For the real facts, I refer to the Appendix.

[1] While I was in the sub-committee of Drury Lane Theatre, I can vouch for my colleagues, and I hope for myself, that we did our best to bring back the legitimate drama. I tried what I could to get " De Montfort " revived, but in vain, and equally in vain in favor of Sotheby's " Ivan," which was thought an acting play; and I endeavored also to wake Mr. Coleridge to write a tragedy. Those who are not in the secret will hardly believe that the " School for Scandal " is the play which has brought *least money*, averaging the number of times it has been acted since its production; so Manager Dibdin assured me. Of what has occurred since Maturin's " Bertram " I am not aware; so that I may be traducing, through ignorance, some excellent new writers: if so, I beg their pardon. I have been absent from England nearly five years, and, till last year, I never read an English newspaper since my departure, and am now only aware of theatrical matters through the medium of the Parisian Gazette of Galignani, and only for the last twelve months. Let me then deprecate all offence to tragic or comic writers, to whom I wish well, and of whom I know nothing. The long complaints of the actual state of the drama arise, however, from no fault of the performers. I can conceive nothing better than Kemble, Cooke, and Kean in their very different manners, or than Elliston in *gentleman's* comedy, and in some parts of tragedy. Miss O'Neill I never saw, having made and kept a determination to see nothing which should divide or disturb my recollection of Siddons. Siddons and Kemble were the *ideal* of tragic action; I never saw any thing at all resembling them even in *person:* for this reason, we shall never see again Coriolanus or Macbeth. When Kean is blamed for want of dignity, we should remember that it is a grace, and not an art, and not to be attained by study. In all, *not* SUPER-natural parts, he is perfect; even his very defects belong, or seem to belong, to the parts themselves, and appear truer to nature. But of Kemble we may say, with reference to his acting, what the Cardinal de Retz said of the Marquis of Montrose, " that he was the only man he ever saw who reminded him of the heroes of Plutarch."
[2] [" We cannot conceive a greater instance of the efficacy of system to blind the most acute perception, than the fact that Lord Byron, in works exclusively intended for the closet, has piqued himself on the observance of rules which are evidently, *off* the stage, a matter of perfect indifference. The only object of adhering to the unities is to preserve the illusion of the scene. To the reader they are obviously useless." — *Heber*.]

DRAMATIS PERSONÆ.

MEN.	
MARINO FALIERO, *Doge of Venice.*	BENINTENDE, *Chief of the Council cf Ten.*
BERTUCCIO FALIERO, *Nephew of the Doge.*	MICHEL STENO, *One of the three Capi of the Forty.*
LIONI, *a Patrician and Senator.*	

RTUCCIO, *Chief*
Arsenal,
LENDARO, } *Conspirators.*
,

he Night, { *" Signore di Notte," one*
of the Officers belong-
ing to the Republic.
n.
zen.
:en.

VINCENZO, }
PIETRO,   } *Officers belonging to the Ducal*
BATTISTA, }   *Palace.*
Secretary of the Council of Ten.
Guards, Conspirators, Citizens, The Council
of Ten, The Giunta, etc. etc.

WOMEN.

ANGIOLINA, *Wife to the Doge.*
MARIANNA, *her Friend.*
Female Attendants, etc.

Scene Venice — in the year 1355.

ACT I.

— *An Antechamber in the Ducal*
Palace.

peaks, *in entering, to* BATTISTA.

not the messenger returned ?
Not yet;
frequently, as you commanded,
Signory is deep in council,
ebate on Steno's accusation.
long—at least so thinks the Doge.
How bears he
ients of suspense ?
With struggling patience
ie ducal table, covered o'er
e apparel of the state ; petitions,
, judgments, acts, reprieves, re-

apt in duty ; but whene'er
ie jarring of a distant door,
iat intimates a coming step,
of a voice, his quick eye wanders,
ll start up from his chair, then

mself again, and fix his gaze
edict ; but I have observed
hour he has not turned a leaf.
s said he is much moved, — and
ss 'twas
in Steno to offend so grossly.
if a poor man : Steno's a patrician,
iard, gay, and haughty.
Then you think
be judged hardly ?
'Twere enough
ed justly ; but 'tis not for us
ie the sentence of the Forty.
d here it comes. — What news,
zo ?

Enter VINCENZO.

'Tis
ut as yet his doom's unknown :
resident in act to seal

The parchment which will bear the Forty's
judgment
Unto the Doge, and hasten to inform him.
[*Exeunt.*

SCENE II. — *The Ducal Chamber.*

MARINO FALIERO, *Doge ; and his Nephew,*
BERTUCCIO FALIERO.

Ber. F. It cannot be but they will do you
justice.
Doge. Ay, such as the Avogadori[1] did,
Who sent up my appeal unto the Forty
To try him by his peers, his own tribunal.
Ber. F. His peers will scarce protect him ;
such an act
Would bring contempt on all authority.
Doge. Know you not Venice ? Know you
not the Forty ?
But we shall see anon.
Ber. F. (*addressing* VINCENZO, *then enter-*
ing).   How now — what tidings ?
Vin. I am charged to tell his highness that
the court
Has passed its resolution, and that, soon
As the due forms of judgment are gone through,
The sentence will be sent up to the Doge ;
In the mean time the Forty doth salute
The Prince of the Republic, and entreat
His acceptation of their duty.
Doge.   Yes —
They are wond'rous dutiful, and ever humble.
Sentence is passed, you say ?
Vin.   It is, your highness :
The president was sealing it, when I
Was called in, that no moment might be lost
In forwarding the intimation due
Not only to the Chief of the Republic,
But the complainant, both in one united.

---

[1] [The Avogadori, three in number, were the
conductors of criminal prosecutions on the part of
the state ; and no act of the councils was valid, un-
less sanctioned by the presence of one of them.]

Ber. F. Are you aware, from aught you
  have perceived,
Of their decision?
Vin.   No, my lord; you know
The secret custom of the courts in Venice.
Ber. F. True; but there still is something
  given to guess,
Which a shrewd gleaner and quick eye would
  catch at;
A whisper, or a murmur, or an air
More or less solemn spread o'er the tribunal.
The Forty are but men — most worthy men,
And wise, and just, and cautious — this I
  grant —
And secret as the grave to which they doom
The guilty; but with all this, in their aspects—
At least in some, the juniors of the number—
A searching eye, an eye like yours, Vincenzo,
Would read the sentence ere it was pro-
  nounced.
Vin. My lord, I came away upon the mo-
  ment,
And had no leisure to take note of that
Which passed among the judges, even in
  seeming;
My station near the accused too, Michel Steno,
Made me —
Doge. (*abruptly*). And how looked *he?*
  deliver that.
Vin. Calm, but not overcast, he stood re-
  signed
To the decree, whate'er it were : — but lo!
It comes, for the perusal of his highness.
      Enter the SECRETARY *of the Forty.*
Sec. The high tribunal of the Forty sends
Health and respect to the Doge Faliero,
Chief magistrate of Venice, and requests
His highness to peruse and to approve
The sentence passed on Michel Steno, born
Patrician, and arraigned upon the charge
Contained, together with its penalty,
Within the rescript which I now present.
Doge. Retire, and wait without.
      [*Exeunt* SECRETARY *and* VINCENZO.
          Take thou this paper,
The misty letters vanish from my eyes;
I cannot fix them.
Ber. F.   Patience, my dear uncle :
Why do you tremble thus? — Nay, doubt not,
  all
Will be as could be wished.
Doge.   Say on.
Ber. F. (*reading*).   "Decreed
In council, without one dissenting voice,
That Michel Steno, by his own confession,
Guilty on the last night of Carnival
Of having graven on the ducal throne
The following words ——" [1]
Doge.   Would'st thou repeat them?

Would'st *thou* repeat them — *thou*, a Faliero,
Harp on the deep dishonor of our house,
Dishonored in its chief — that chief the prince
Of Venice, first of cities? — To the sentence.
Ber. F. Forgive me, my good lord; I will
  obey —
(*Reads.*) "That Michel Steno be detained a
  month
In close arrest."
Doge.   Proceed.
Ber. F.   My lord, 'tis finished.
Doge. How, say you? — finished! Do I
  dream? — 'tis false —
Give me the paper — (*Snatches the paper and
  reads.*) — " 'Tis decreed in council
That Michel Steno "—— Nephew, thine arm!
Ber. F.   Nay,
Cheer up, be calm; this transport is uncalled
  for —
Let me seek some assistance.
Doge.   Stop, sir — Stir not —
'Tis past.
Ber. F. I cannot but agree with you
The sentence is too slight for the offence —
It is not honorable in the Forty
To affix so slight a penalty to that
Which was a foul affront to you, and even
To them, as being your subjects; but 'tis not
Yet without remedy : you can appeal
To them once more, or to the Avogadori,
Who, seeing that true justice is withheld,
Will now take up the cause they once de-
  clined,
And do you right upon the bold delinquent.
Think you not thus, good uncle? why do you
  stand
So fixed? You heed me not : — I pray you,
  hear me!
Doge (*dashing down the ducal bonnet, and
  offering to trample upon it, exclaims, as
  he is withheld by his nephew*).
Oh! that the Saracen were in Saint Mark's!
Thus would I do him homage.
Ber. F.   For the sake
Of Heaven and all its saints, my lord ——
Doge.   Away!
Oh, that the Genoese were in the port!
Oh, that the Huns whom I o'erthrew at Zara
Were ranged around the palace!
Ber. F.   'Tis not well
In Venice' Duke to say so.
Doge.   Venice' Duke!
Who now is Duke in Venice? let me see him,
That he may do me right.
Ber. F.   If you forget
Your office, and its dignity and duty,
Remember that of man, and curb this passion.
The Duke of Venice ——
Doge (*interrupting him*). There is no such
  thing —
It is a word — nay, worse — a worthless by-
  word :

---

[1] ["Marino Faliero dalla bella moglie — altrì la
gode, ed egli la mantiene." — *Sanuto.*

spised, wronged, outraged, help-
:h.
; bread, if 'tis refused by one,
om another kinder heart;
s denied his right by those
it is to do no wrong, is poorer
:cted beggar — he's a slave —
I, and thou, and all our house,
is hour; the meanest artisan
e finger, and the haughty noble
n us : — where is our redress ?
he law, my prince ? ——
rupting him). You see what it
—
:medy but from the law —
engeance but redress by law —
dges but those named by law —
I appealed unto my subjects,
ectswho had made me sovereign,
thus a double right to be so.
place and choice, of birth and

years, these scars, these hoary

il, the perils, the fatigues,
:d sweat of almost eighty years,
d i' the balance, 'gainst the foul-

insult, most contemptuous crime
h patrician—and found wanting !
: borne !
I say not that : —
fresh appeal should be rejected,
ther means to make all even.
:al again ! art thou my brother's

house of Faliero ?
f a Doge ? and of that blood
already given three dukes to

'st well — we must be humble

y princely uncle ! you are too
ved : —
a gross offence, and grossly
tting punishment : but still
exceed the provocation,
:ation : if we are wronged,
istice ; if it be denied,
; but may do all this in calm-

nce is the daughter of deep Si-

rce a third part of your years,
se, I honor you, its chief,
of my youth, and its instructor —
understand your grief, and enter
r disdain, it doth appall me
nger, like our Adrian waves,
bounds, and foam itself to air.
l thee — *must* I tell thee — what

Would have required no words to compre-
hend ?
Hast thou no feeling save the external sense
Of torture from the touch ? hast thou no
soul —
No pride — no passion — no deep sense of
honor ?
Ber. F. 'Tis the first time that honor has
been doubted,
And were the last, from any other sceptic.
Doge. You know the full offence of this
born villain,
This creeping, coward, rank, acquitted felon,
Who threw his sting into a poisonous libel,
And on the honor of — Oh God ! — my wife,
The nearest, dearest part of all men's honor,
Left a base slur to pass from mouth to mouth
Of loose mechanics, with all coarse foul com-
ments,
And villanous jests, and blasphemies obscene ;
While sneering nobles, in more polished guise,
Whispered the tale, and smiled upon the lie
Which made me look like them — a courteous
wittol,
Patient — ay, proud, it may be, of dishonor.
Ber. F. But still it was a lie — you knew
it false,
And so did all men.
Doge.   Nephew, the high Roman
Said, "Cæsar's wife must not even be sus-
pected,"
And put her from him.
Ber. F.   True — but in those days ——
Doge. What is it that a Roman would not
suffer,
That a Venetian prince must bear ? Old Dan-
dolo
Refused the diadem of all the Cæsars,
And wore the ducal cap I trample on,
Because 'tis now degraded.
Ber. F.   'Tis even so.
Doge. It is — it is ; — I did not visit on
The innocent creature thus most vilely slan-
dered
Because she took an old man for her lord,
For that he had been long her father's friend
And patron of her house, as if there were
No love in woman's heart but lust of youth
And beardless faces ; — I did not for this
Visit the villain's infamy on her,
But craved my country's justice on his head,
The justice due unto the humblest being
Who hath a wife whose faith is sweet to him,
Who hath a home whose hearth is dear to him,
Who hath a name whose honor's all to him,
When these are tinted by the accursing breath
Of calumny and scorn.
Ber. F.   And what redress
Did you expect as his fit punishment ?
Doge. Death ! Was I not the sovereign
of the state —
Insulted on his very throne, and made

A mockery to the men who should obey me?
Was I not injured as a husband? scorned
As man? reviled, degraded, as a prince?
Was not offence like his a complication
Of insult and of treason?—and he lives!
Had he instead of on the Doge's throne
Stamped the same brand upon a peasant's
    stool,
His blood had gilt the threshold; for the carl
Had stabbed him on the instant.
    Ber. F.   Do not doubt it,
He shall not live till sunset—leave to me
The means, and calm yourself.
    Doge.   Hold, nephew: this
Would have sufficed but yesterday; at present
I have no further wrath against this man.
    Ber. F.   What mean you? is not the of-
fence redoubled
By this most rank—I will not say—acquittal;
For it is worse, being full acknowledgment
Of the offence, and leaving it unpunished?
    Doge.   It is *redoubled*, but not now by him:
The Forty hath decreed a month's arrest—
We must obey the Forty.
    Ber. F.   Obey *them!*
Who have forgot their duty to the sovereign?
    Doge. Why yes;—boy, you perceive it
then at last:
Whether as fellow-citizen who sues
For justice, or as sovereign who commands it,
They have defrauded me of both my rights
(For here the sovereign is a citizen);
But, notwithstanding, harm not thou a hair
Of Steno's head—he shall not wear it long.
    Ber. F. Not twelve hours longer, had you
left to me
The mode and means: if you had calmly heard
    me,
I never meant this miscreant should escape,
But wished you to suppress such gusts of pas-
    sion,
That we more surely might devise together
His taking off.
    Doge.   No, nephew, he must live;
At least, just now—a life so vile as his
Were nothing at this hour; in th' olden time
Some sacrifices asked a single victim,
Great expiations had a hecatomb.
    Ber. F. Your wishes are my law: and yet
I fain
Would prove to you how near unto my heart
The honor of our house must ever be.
    Doge. Fear not; you shall have time and
place of proof,
But be not thou too rash, as I have been.
I am ashamed of my own anger now;
I pray you, pardon me.
    Ber. F.   Why that's my uncle!
The leader, and the statesman, and the chief
Of commonwealths, and sovereign of him-
    self!
I wondered to perceive you so forget

All prudence in your fury at these years,
Although the cause——
    Doge.   Ay, think upon the cause—
Forget it not:—When you lie down to rest,
Let it be black among your dreams; and when
The morn returns, so let it stand between
The sun and you, as an ill-omened cloud
Upon a summer-day of festival:
So will it stand to me;—but speak not, stir
not,—
Leave all to me;—we shall have much to
do,
And you shall have a part.—But now retire,
'Tis fit I were alone.
    *Ber. F. (taking up and placing the ducal
bonnet on the table).* Ere I depart,
I pray you to resume what you have spurned,
Till you can change it haply for a crown.
And now I take my leave, imploring you
In all things to rely upon my duty
As doth become your near and faithful kins-
    man,
And not less loyal citizen and subject.
             [*Exit* BERTUCCIO FALIERO.
    Doge (solus). Adieu, my worthy nephew.—
Hollow bauble! [*Taking up the ducal cap.*
Beset with all the thorns that line a crown,
Without investing the insulted brow
With the all-swaying majesty of kings;
Thou idle, gilded, and degraded toy,
Let me resume thee as I would a vizor.
                  [*Puts it on.*
How my brain aches beneath thee! and my
    temples
Throb feverish under thy dishonest weight.
Could I not turn thee to a diadem?
Could I not shatter the Briarean sceptre
Which in this hundred-handed senate rules,
Making the people nothing, and the prince
A pageant? In my life I have achieved
Tasks not less difficult—achieved for them,
Who thus repay me!—Can I not requite them?
Oh for one year! Oh but for even a day
Of my full youth, while yet my body served
My soul as serves the generous steed his lord
I would have dashed amongst them, asking few
In aid to overthrow these swoln patricians;
But now I must look round for other hands
To serve this hoary head;—but it shall plan
In such a sort as will not leave the task
Herculean, though as yet 'tis but a chaos
Of darkly brooding thoughts: my fancy is
In her first work, more nearly to the light
Holding the sleeping images of things
For the selection of the pausing judgment.—
The troops are few in——

          Enter VINCENZO.

    Vin.   There is one without
Craves audience of your highness.
    Doge.   I'm unwell—
I can see no one, not even a patrician—

his business to the council.
ord, I will deliver your reply;
ch import — he's a plebeian,
f a galley, I believe.
w! did you say the patron of a

ıean — a servant of the state:
e may be on public service.
    [*Exit* VINCENZO.
:). This patron may be sounded;
him.
ɛople to be discontented:
:ause, since Sapienza's adverse

ı conquered: they have further

e nothing in the state, and in
e than nothing — mere machines,
nobles' most patrician pleasure.
ıve long arrears of pay, oft prom-

deeply — any hope of change
hem forward: they shall pay
es
r: — but the priests — I doubt
:hood
'ith us; they have hated me
,sh hour, when, maddened with
ɛ,
ırdy bishop at Treviso,[1]
is holy march; yet, ne'ertheless
won, at least their chief at Rome,
l-timed concessions; but, above
nust be speedy: at my hour
tle light of life remains.
Venice, and avenge my wrongs,
o long, and willingly would sleep
. with my sires; and, wanting this,
tty of my four-score years
ready where — how soon, I care

ıst be extinguished; — better that
ıd been, than drag me on 'to be
ese arch-oppressors fain would
:.
der — of efficient troops
ee thousand posted at ——

:NZO *and* ISRAEL BERTUCCIO.

                May it please
s, the same patron whom I spake

ve your patience.
        Leave the chamber,
            [*Exit* VINCENZO.
y advance — what would you?
:dress.

al fact. See Marin Sanuto's Lives
- ["Sanuto says that Heaven took
; for this buffet, and induced him to
erò fu permesso che il Faliero per-
)," " etc. — *Byron's Letters.*]

Doge.   Of whom?
I. Ber.   Of God and of the Doge.
Doge. Alas! my friend, you seek it of the
    twain
Of least respect and interest in Venice.
You must address the council.
    I. Ber.   'Twere in vain;
For he who injured me is one of them.
    Doge. There's blood upon thy face — how
        came it there?
    I. Ber. 'Tis mine, and not the first I've
        shed for Venice,
But the first shed by a Venetian hand:
A noble smote me.
    Doge.   Doth he live?
    I. Ber.   Not long —
But for the hope I had and have, that you,
My prince, yourself a soldier, will redress
Him, whom the laws of discipline and Venice
Permit not to protect himself; — if not —
I say no more.
    Doge.   But something you would do —
Is it not so?
    I. Ber.   I am a man, my lord.
    Doge. Why so is he who smote you.
    I. Ber.   He is called so;
Nay, more, a noble one — at least, in Venice:
But since he hath forgotten that I am one,
And treats me like a brute, the brute may
        turn —
'Tis said the worm will.
    Doge.   Say — his name and lineage?
    I. Ber. Barbaro.
    Doge. What was the cause? or the pre-
        text?
    I. Ber. I am the chief of the arsenal,[1]
        employed
At present in repairing certain galleys
But roughly used by the Genoese last year.
This morning comes the noble Barbaro
Full of reproof, because our artisans
Had left some frivolous order of his house,
To execute the state's decree; I dared
To justify the men — he raised his hand; —
Behold my blood! the first time it e'er flowed
Dishonorably.
    Doge.   Have you long time served?
    I. Ber. So long as to remember Zara's
        siege,
And fight beneath the chief who beat the Huns
        there,
Sometime my general, now the Doge Faliero.—
    Doge. How! are we comrades? — the
        state's ducal robes
Sit newly on me, and you were appointed

[1] [This officer was chief of the artisans of the
arsenal, and commanded the Bucentaur, for the
safety of which, even if an accidental storm should
arise, he was responsible with his life. He mounted
guard at the ducal palace during an interregnum,
and bore the red standard before the new Doge on
his inauguration. — *Amelot de la Houssaye,* 79.]

Chief of the arsenal ere I came from Rome;
So that I recognized you not. Who placed
 you?
I. Ber. The late Doge; keeping still my
 old command
As patron of a galley: my new office
Was given as the reward of certain scars
(So was your predecessor pleased to say):
I little thought his bounty would conduct me
To his successor as a helpless plaintiff;
At least, in such a cause.
Doge.   Are you much hurt?
I. Ber. Irreparably in my self-esteem.
Doge. Speak out; fear nothing: being
 stung at heart,
What would you do to be revenged on this
 man?
I. Ber. That which I dare not name, and
 yet will do.
Doge. Then wherefore came you here?
I. Ber.   I come for justice.
Because my general is Doge, and will not
See his old soldier trampled on. Had any,
Save Faliero, filled the ducal throne,
This blood had been washed out in other
 blood.
Doge. You come to me for justice — unto
 me!
The Doge of Venice, and I cannot give it;
I cannot even obtain it — 'twas denied
To me most solemnly an hour ago!
I. Ber. How says your highness?
Doge.   Steno is condemned
To a month's confinement.
I. Ber.   What! the same who dared
To stain the ducal throne with those foul
 words,
That have cried shame to every ear in Venice?
Doge. Ay, doubtless they have echoed
 o'er the arsenal,
Keeping due time with every hammer's clink
As a good jest to jolly artisans;
Or making chorus to the creaking oar,
In the vile tune of every galley-slave,
Who, as he sung the merry stave, exulted
He was not a shamed dotard like the Doge.
I. Ber. Is't possible? a month's imprison-
 ment!
No more for Steno?
Doge.   You have heard the offence,
And now you know his punishment; and
 then
You ask redress of *me!* Go to the Forty,
Who passed the sentence upon Michel Steno;
They'll do as much by Barbaro, no doubt.
I. Ber. Ah! dared I speak my feelings!
Doge.   Give them breath.
Mine have no further outrage to endure.
I. Ber. Then, in a word, it rests but on
 your word
To punish and avenge — I will not say
My petty wrong, for what is a mere blow

However vile, to such a thing as I am? —
But the base insult done your state and
 person.
Doge. You overrate my power, which is a
 pageant.
This cap is not the monarch's crown; these
 robes
Might move compassion, like a beggar's rags;
Nay, more, a beggar's are his own, and these
But lent to the poor puppet, who must play
Its part with all its empire in this ermine.
I. Ber. Wouldst thou be king?
Doge. Yes — of a happy people.
I. Ber. Wouldst thou be sovereign lord of
 Venice?
Doge.   Ay,
If that the people shared that sovereignty,
So that nor they nor I were further slaves
To this o'ergrown aristocratic Hydra,
The poisonous heads of whose envenomed
 body
Have breathed a pestilence upon us all.
I. Ber. Yet, thou wast born, and still hast
 lived, patrician.
Doge. In evil hour was I so born; my birth
Hath made me Doge to be insulted: but
I lived and toiled a soldier and a servant
Of Venice and her people, not the senate;
Their good and my own honor were my guer-
 don.
I have fought and bled; commanded, ay, and
 conquered;
Have made and marred peace oft in em-
 bassies,
As it might chance to be our country's 'van-
 tage;
Have traversed land and sea in constant duty,
Through almost sixty years, and still for
 Venice,
My fathers' and my birthplace, whose dear
 spires,
Rising at distance o'er the blue Lagoon,
It was reward enough for me to view
Once more; but not for any knot of men,
Nor sect, nor faction, did I bleed or sweat!
But would you know why I have done all this?
Ask of the bleeding pelican why she
Hath ripped her bosom? Had the bird a
 voice,
She'd tell thee 'twas for *all* her little ones.
I. Ber. And yet they made thee duke.
Doge.   *They made* me so;
I sought it not, the flattering fetters met me
Returning from my Roman embassy,
And never having hitherto refused
Toil, charge, or duty for the state, I did not,
At these late years, decline what was the
 highest
Of all in seeming, but of all most base
In what we have to do and to endure:
Bear witness for me thou, my injured subject,
When I can neither right myself nor thee.

ou shall do both, if you possess

ousands more not less oppressed,
it for a signal — will you give it?
u speak in riddles.
　　　　Which shall soon be read
iy life; if you disdain not
tient ear.
　　　　Say on.
　　　　　　Not thou,
, are injured and abused,
and trampled on; but the whole

the strong conception of their
:
soldiers in the senate's pay
nted for their long arrears;
ariners, and civic troops,
ir friends; for who is he amongst

ren, parents, children, wives, or

rtook oppression, or pollution,
tricians? And the hopeless war
Genoese, which is still maintained
beian blood, and treasure wrung
ard earnings, has inflamed them

but, I forget that speaking thus,
ass the sentence of my death!
nd suffering what thou hast done
it thou death?
n, and live on, to be beaten
whom thou hast bled.
　　　　　No, I will speak
zard; and if Venice' Doge
. delator, be the shame on him,
too; for he will lose far more

om me fear nothing; out with it!
now then, that there are met and
n secret
brethren, valiant hearts and true;
ive proved all fortunes, and have

r that of Venice, and have right
iaving served her in all climes,
rescued her from foreign foes,
the same from those within her

it numerous, nor yet too few
eat purpose; they have arms, and

and hopes, and faith, and patient
:.
or what then do they pause?
　　　　　An hour to strike.
de). Saint Mark's shall strike that

---

of San Marco were never rung but
the Doge. One of the pretexts for

I. Ber.　　　　　I now have placed
My life, my honor, all my earthly hopes
Within thy power, but in the firm belief
That injuries like ours, sprung from one
　　cause,
Will generate one vengeance: should it be so,
Be our chief now — our sovereign hereafter.
　　Doge. How many are ye?
　　I. Ber.　　　　　I'll not answer that
Till I am answered.
　　Doge.　　　　How, sir! do you menace?
　　I. Ber. No; I affirm. I have betrayed my-
　　self;
But there's no torture in the mystic wells
Which undermine your palace, nor in those
Not less appalling cells, the "leaden roofs,"
To force a single name from me of others.
The Pozzi[2] and the Piombi were in vain;
They might wring blood from me, but treach-
　　ery never.
And I would pass the fearful "Bridge of
　　Sighs,"
Joyous that mine must be the last that e'er
Would echo o'er the Stygian wave which flows
Between the murderers and the murdered,
　　washing
The prison and the palace walls: there are
Those who would live to think on't, and
　　avenge me.
　　Doge. If such your power and purpose,
　　why come here
To sue for justice, being in the course
To do yourself due right?
　　I. Ber.　　　　　Because the man,
Who claims protection from authority,
Showing his confidence and his submission
To that authority, can hardly be
Suspected of combining to destroy it.
Had I sate down too humbly with this blow,
A moody brow and muttered threats had
　　made me
A marked man to the Forty's inquisition;
But loud complaint, however angrily
It shapes its phrase, is little to be feared,
And less distrusted. But, besides all this,
I had another reason.
　　Doge.　　　　What was that?
　　I. Ber. Some rumors that the Doge was
　　greatly moved
By the reference of the Avogadori

---

ringing this alarm was to have been an announce-
ment of the appearance of a Genoese fleet off the
Lagune.
　2 [The state dungeons, called Pozzi, or wells,
were sunk in the thick walls of the palace; and the
prisoner, when taken out to die, was conducted
across the gallery to the other side, and being then
led back into the other compartment, or cell, upon
the bridge, was there strangled. The low portal
through which the criminal was taken into this cell
is now walled up; but the passage is open, and is
still known by the name of the Bridge of Sighs. —
Hobhouse.]

Of Michel Steno's sentence to the Forty
Had reached me. I had served you, honored
  you,
And felt that you were dangerously insulted,
Being of an order of such spirits, as
Requite tenfold both good and evil: 'twas
My wish to prove and urge you to redress.
Now you know all; and that I speak the truth,
My peril be the proof.
Doge.   You have deeply ventured;
But all must do so who would greatly win:
Thus far I'll answer you—your secret's safe.
I. Ber. And is this all?
Doge.   Unless with all intrusted,
What would you have me answer?
I. Ber.   I would have you
Trust him who leaves his life in trust with you.
Doge. But I must know your plan, your
  names, and numbers;
The last may then be doubled, and the former
Matured and strengthened.
I. Ber.   We're enough already;
You are the sole ally we covet now.
Doge. But bring me to the knowledge of
  your chiefs.
I. Ber. That shall be done upon your
  formal pledge
To keep the faith that we will pledge to you.
Doge. When? where?
I. Ber. This night I'll bring to your apart-
  ment
Two of the principals; a greater number
Were hazardous.
Doge.   Stay, I must think of this.
What if I were to trust myself amongst you,
And leave the palace?
I. Ber.   You must come alone.
Doge. With but my nephew.
I. Ber.   Not were he your son.
Doge. Wretch! darest thou name my son?
He died in arms
At Sapienza for this faithless state.
Oh! that he were alive, and I in ashes!
Or that he were alive ere I be ashes!
I should not need the dubious aid of strangers.
I. Ber. Not one of all those strangers whom
  thou doubtest,
But will regard thee with a filial feeling,
So that thou keep'st a father's faith with them.
Doge. The die is cast. Where is the place
  of meeting?
I. Ber. At midnight I will be alone and
  masked
Where'er your highness pleases to direct me,
To wait your coming, and conduct you where
You shall receive our homage, and pronounce
Upon our project.
Doge.   At what hour arises
The moon?
I. Ber. Late, but the atmosphere is thick
  and dusky,
Tis a sirocco.

Doge.   At the midnight hour, then,
Near to the church where sleep my sires;[1]
  the same,
Twin-named from the apostles John and
  Paul,
A gondola,[2] with one oar only, will
Lurk in the narrow channel which glides by.
Be there.
I. Ber. I will not fail.
Doge.   And now retire —
I. Ber. In the full hope your highness will
  not falter
In your great purpose. Prince, I take my
  leave.   [*Exit* ISRAEL BERTUCCIO.
Doge (solus). At midnight, by the church
  Saints John and Paul,
Where sleep my noble fathers, I repair—
To what? to hold a council in the dark
With common ruffians leagued to ruin states!
And will not my great sires leap from the
  vault,
Where lie two doges who preceded me,
And pluck me down amongst them? Would
  they could!
For I should rest in honor with the honored.
Alas! I must not think of them, but those
Who have made me thus unworthy of a name
Noble and brave as aught of consular
On Roman marbles; but I will redeem it
Back to its antique lustre in our annals,
By sweet revenge on all that's base in Venice,
And freedom to the rest, or leave it black
To all the growing calumnies of time,
Which never spare the fame of him who fails,
But try the Cæsar or the Catiline,
By the true touchstone of desert — success.

ACT II.

SCENE I. — *An Apartment in the Ducal
  Palace.*

ANGIOLINA (*wife of the* DOGE) *and* MARI-
  ANNA.

Ang. What was the Doge's answer?
Mar.   That he was
That moment summoned to a conference;

---

[1] [The Doges were all buried in St. Mark's *be-
fore* Faliero. It is singular that when his prede-
cessor, Andrea Dandolo, died, the Ten made a law
that all the future Doges should be buried with their
families in their own churches — one would think,
by a kind of presentiment. So that all that is said
of his *ancestral Doges*, as buried at St. John's
and Paul's, is altered from the fact, they being
in St. Mark's. Make a note of this, and put *Editor*
as the subscription to it. As I make such preten-
sions to accuracy, I should not like to be twitted
even with such trifles on that score. Of the play
they may say what they please, but not so of my
costume and *dram. pers.* — they having been real
existences. — *Byron's Letters*, Oct. 1820.]
[2] A gondola is not like a common boat, but is as

, time ended. I perceived
the senators embarking;
ondola may now be seen
ιe throng of barks which stud
waters.
  Would he were returned!
nuch disquieted of late;
·hich has not tamed his fiery

эled even his mortal frame,
to be more nourished by a soul
restless that it would consume
ιy — Time has but little power
nents or his griefs. Unlike
ts of his order, who,
rst of passion, pour away
r sorrow, all things wear in him
ιternity: his thoughts,
assions, good or evil, all
of old age; and his bold brow
scars of mind, the thoughts of

epitude: and he of late
e agitated than his wont.
e come! for I alone have power
bled spirit.
                It is true,
ιas of late been greatly moved
of Steno, and with cause:
.er doubtless even now
expiate his rash insult with
nent as will enforce respect
ue, and to noble blood.
s a gross insult; but I heed it

corner's falsehood in itself,
ect, the deadly deep impression
nade upon Faliero's soul,
e fiery, the austere — austere
ι: I tremble when I think
y conduct.
               Assuredly
, not suspect you ?
               Suspect *me!*
.red not: when he scrawled his

stealth in the moon's glimmer-

onscious smote him for the act,
Jow on the walls frowned shame
ιrd calumny.
            'Twere fit
punished grievously.
            He is so.
t! is the sentence passed ? is he
:d ?
ιw not that, but he has been de-

___

·h one oar as with two (though of
ɹiftly), and often is so from motives
ιd, since the decay of Venice, of

  Mar. And deem you this enough for such
    foul scorn ?
  Ang. I would not be a judge in my own
    cause,
Nor do I know what sense of punishment
May reach the soul of ribalds such as Steno;
But if his insults sink no deeper in
The minds of the inquisitors than they
Have ruffled mine, he will, for all acquittance,
Be left to his own shamelessness or shame.
  Mar. Some sacrifice is due to slandered
    virtue.
  Ang. Why, what is virtue if it needs a
    victim ?
Or if it must depend upon men's words ?
The dying Roman said, " 'twas but a name : "
It were indeed no more, if human breath
Could make or mar it.
  Mar.   Yet full many a dame,
Stainless and faithful, would feel all the wrong
Of such a slander; and less rigid ladies,
Such as abound in Venice, would be loud
And all-inexorable in their cry
For justice.
  Ang.   This but proves it is the name
And not the quality they prize: the first
Have found it a hard task to hold their honor,
If they require it to be blazoned forth;
And those who have not kept it, seek its
    seeming
As they would look out for an ornament
Of which they feel the want, but not because
They think it so; they live in others' thoughts,
And would seem honest as they must seem
    fair.
  Mar. You have strange thoughts for a
    patrician dame.
  Ang. And yet they were my father's; with
    his name,
The sole inheritance he left.
  Mar.   You want none;
Wife to a prince, the chief of the Republic.
  Ang. I should have sought none though a
    peasant's bride,
But feel not less the love and gratitude
Due to my father, who bestowed my hand
Upon his early, tried, and trusted friend,
The Count Val di Marino, now our Doge.
  Mar. And with that hand did he bestow
    your heart ?
  Ang. He did so, or it had not been bestowed.
  Mar. Yet this strange disproportion in
    your years,
And, let me add, disparity of tempers,
Might make the world doubt whether such an
    union
Could make you wisely, permanently happy.
  Ang. The world will think with worldlings;
    but my heart
Has still been in my duties, which are many,
But never difficult.
  Mar.   And do you love him ?

Ang. I love all noble qualities which merit
Love, and I loved my father, who first taught
    me
To single out what we should love in others,
And to subdue all tendency to lend
The best and purest feelings of our nature
To baser passions. He bestowed my hand
Upon Faliero : he had known him noble,
Brave, generous ; rich in all the qualities
Of soldier, citizen, and friend ; in all
Such have I found him as my father said.
His faults are those that dwell in the high
    bosoms
Of men who have commanded ; too much
    pride,
And the deep passions fiercely fostered by
The uses of patricians, and a life
Spent in the storms of state and war ; and also
From the quick sense of honor, which be-
    comes
A duty to a certain sign, a vice
When overstrained, and this I fear in him. ·
And then he has been rash from his youth
    upwards,
Yet tempered by redeeming nobleness
In such sort, that the wariest of republics
Has lavished all its chief employs upon him,
From his first fight to his last embassy,
From which on his return the dukedom met
    him.
  Mar. But previous to this marriage, had
    your heart
Ne'er beat for any of the noble youth,
Such as in years had been more meet to match
Beauty like yours ? or since have you ne'er
    seen
One, who, if your fair hand were still to give,
Might now pretend to Loredano's daughter ?
  Ang. I answered your first question when
    I said
I married.
  Mar. And the second ?
  Ang.   Needs no answer.
  Mar. I pray your pardon, if I have of-
    fended.
  Ang. I feel no wrath, but some surprise :
    I knew not
That wedded bosoms could permit themselves
To ponder upon what they *now* might choose,
Or aught save their past choice.
  Mar.   'Tis their past choice
That far too often makes them deem they
    would
Now choose more wisely, could they cancel it.
  Ang. It may be so. I knew not of such
    thoughts.
  Mar. Here comes the Doge — shall I re-
    tire ?
  Ang.   It may
Be better you should quit me ; he seems rapt
In thought. — How pensively he takes his way !
                  [Exit MARIANNA.

        · *Enter the* DOGE *and* PIETRO.

  Doge (musing). There is a certain Philip
    Calendaro
Now in the Arsenal, who holds command
Of eighty men, and has great influence
Besides on all the spirits of his comrades :
This man, I hear, is bold and popular,
Sudden and daring, and yet secret ; 'twould
Be well that he were won : I needs must hope
That Isreal Bertuccio has secured him,
But fain would be——
  Pie.   My lord, pray pardon me
For breaking in upon your meditation ;
The Senator Bertuccio, your kinsman,
Charged me to follow and inquire your pleasure
To fix an hour when he may speak with you.
  Doge. At sunset. — Stay a moment — let
    me see —
Say in the second hour of night.
                  [Exit PIETRO.
  Ang.   My lord !
  Doge. My dearest child, forgive me — why
    delay
So long approaching me ? — I saw you not.
  Ang. You were absorbed in thought, and
    he who now
Has parted from you might have words of
    weight
To bear you from the senate.
  Doge.   ,   From the senate ? [1]
  Ang. I would not interrupt him in his duty
And theirs.
  Doge.   The senate's duty ! you mistake ;
'Tis we who owe all service to the senate.

  [1] [This scene is, perhaps, the finest in the whole
play. The character of the calm, pure-spirited
Angiolina is developed in it most admirably ; — the
great difference between her temper and that of her
fiery husband is vividly portrayed ; — but not less
vividly touched is that strong bond of their union
which exists in the common nobleness of their
deeper natures. There is no spark of jealousy in
the old man's thoughts, — he does not expect the
fervors of youthful passion in his wife, nor does
he find them : but he finds what is far better, — the
fearless confidence of one, who, being to the heart's
core innocent, can scarcely be a believer in the ex-
istence of such a thing as guilt. He finds every
charm which gratitude, respect, anxious and deep-
seated affection can give to the confidential lan-
guage of a lovely, and a modest, and a pious woman
She has been extremely troubled by her observance
of the countenance and gesture of the Doge, ever
since the discovery of Steno's guilt ; and she does
all she can to soothe him from his proud irritation.
Strong in her consciousness of purity, she has
brought herself to regard without anger the insult
offered to herself ; and the yet uncorrected instinct
of a noble heart makes her try to persuade her lord,
as she is herself persuaded, that Steno, whatever
be the sentence of his judges, *must* be punished —
more even than they would wish him to be — by the
secret suggestions of his own guilty conscience. —
Lockhart.]

ught the Duke had held com-
Venice.
shall. — But let that pass. — We
cund.
·ith you ? have you been abroad?
·ercast, but the calm wave
ndolier's light skimming oar ;
·eld a levee of your friends ?
nusic made you solitary ?
aught that you would will within
y now left the Duke ? or aught
ndor, or of honest pleasure,
ly, that would glad your heart,
te for many a dull hour, wasted
n oft moved with many cares ?
·s done.
    You're ever kind to me.
g to desire, or to request,
you oftener and calmer.
mer ?
almer, my good lord. — Ah, why
eep apart, and walk alone,
trong emotions stamp your brow,
ing their full import, yet
much ?
  Disclose too much ! — of what ?
to disclose ?
    A heart so ill
nothing, child. — But in the state
hat daily cares oppress all those
this precarious commonwealth ;
g from the Genoese without,
·tents within — 'tis this which
·e
· and less tranquil than my wont.
this existed long before, and never
late days did I see you thus.
there is something at your heart
·e mere discharge of public duties,
use and a talent like to yours
ed light, nay, a necessity,
· mind from stagnating. 'Tis not
tes, nor perils, thus to shake you ;
·e stood all storms and never sunk,
·p to the pinnacle of power
·inted by the way, and stand
can look down steadily
·pth beneath, and ne'er feel dizzy.
·'s galleys riding in the port,
·ry raging in Saint Mark's,
·o be wrought on, but would fall,
risen, with an unaltered brow —
· now are of a different kind ;
·s stung your pride, not patriotism.
·de l Angiolina ? Alas! none is
— the same sin that overthrew
·ls,
·s most easily besets
·earest to the angelic nature :
only vain ; the great are proud.

Doge. I *had* the pride of honor, of *your*
  honor,
Deep at my heart —— But let us change the
  theme.
  Ang. Ah no ! — As I have ever shared your
  kindness
In all things else, let me not be shut out
From your distress : were it of public import,
You know I never sought, would never seek
To win a word from you ; but feeling now
Your grief is private, it belongs to me
To lighten or divide it. Since the day
When foolish Steno's ribaldry detected
Unfixed your quiet, you are greatly changed,
And I would soothe you back to what you
  were.
  Doge. To what I was ! — Have you heard
  Steno's sentence ?
  Ang. No.
  Doge.   A month's arrest.
  Ang.   Is it not enough ?
  Doge. Enough ! — yes, for a drunken gal-
  ley slave,
Who, stung by stripes, may murmur at his
  master,
But not for a deliberate, false, cool villain,
Who stains a lady's and a prince's honor
Even on the throne of his authority.
  Ang. There seems to be enough in the con-
  viction
Of a patrician guilty of a falsehood :
All other punishment were light unto
His loss of honor.
  Doge.   Such men have no honor ;
They have but their vile lives — and these are
  spared.
  Ang. You would not have him die for this
  offence ?
  Doge. Not *now :* — being still alive, I'd
  have him live
Long as *he* can ; he has ceased to merit death ;
The guilty saved hath damned his hundred
  judges,
And he is pure, for now his crime is theirs.
  Ang. Oh! had this false and flippant li-
  beller
Shed his young blood for his absurd lampoon,
Ne'er from that moment could this breast have
  known
A joyous hour, or dreamless slumber more.
  Doge. Does not the law of Heaven say
  blood for blood ?
And he who *taints* kills more than he who
  sheds it.
Is it the *pain* of blows, or *shame* of blows,
That make such deadly to the sense of man ?
Do not the laws of man say blood for honor ?
And, less than honor, for a little gold ?
Say not the laws of nations blood for treason ?
Is't nothing to have filled these veins with
  poison
For their once healthful current ? is it nothing

To have stained your name and mine — the
noblest names ?
Is't nothing to have brought into contempt
A prince before his people ? to have failed
In the respect accorded by mankind
To youth in woman, and old age in man ?
To virtue in your sex, and dignity
In ours ? — But let them look to it who have
saved him.[1]
Ang. Heaven bids us to forgive our enemies.
Doge. Doth Heaven forgive her own ? Is
Satan saved
From wrath eternal ?[2]
Ang. Do not speak thus wildly —
Heaven will alike forgive you and your foes.
Doge Amen! May Heaven forgive them!
Ang. And will you?
Doge. Yes, when they are in heaven!
Ang. And not till then ?
Doge. What matters my forgiveness ? an
old man's,
Worn out, scorned, spurned, abused; what
matters then
My pardon more than my resentment, both
Being weak and worthless ? I have lived too
long. —
But let us change the argument. — My child!
My injured wife, the child of Loredano,
The brave, the chivalrous, how little deemed
Thy father, wedding thee unto his friend,
That he was linking thee to shame! — Alas!
Shame without sin, for thou art faultless.
Hadst thou
But had a different husband, *any* husband
In Venice save the Doge, this blight, this brand,
This blasphemy had never fallen upon thee.
So young, so beautiful, so good, so pure,
To suffer this, and yet be unavenged!
Ang. I am too well avenged, for you still
love me,
And trust, and honor me; and all men know
That you are just, and I am true: what more
Could I require, or you command ?
Doge. 'Tis well,
And may be better; but whate'er betide,
Be thou at least kind to my memory.
Ang. Why speak you thus ?
Doge. It is no matter why;
But I would still, whatever others think,
Have your respect both now and in my grave.

---

[1] [This scene between the Doge and Angiolina,
though intolerably long, has more force and beauty
than any thing that goes before it. She endeavors
to soothe the furious mood of her aged partner; while
he insists that nothing but the libeller's death could
make fitting expiation for his offence. This speech
of the Doge is an elaborate, and, after all, ineffectual
attempt, by rhetorical exaggerations, to give some
color to the insane and unmeasured resentment on
which the piece hinges. — *Jeffrey.*]

[2] MS. —
" Doth Heaven forgive her own ? is there not Hell ? "

Ang. Why should you doubt it ? has it ever
failed ?
Doge. Come hither, child; I would a word
with you.
Your father was my friend; unequal fortune
Made him my debtor for some courtesies
Which bind the good more firmly: when, op-
pressed
With his last malady, he willed our union,
It was not to repay me, long repaid
Before by his great loyalty in friendship;
His object was to place your orphan beauty
In honorable safety from the perils,
Which, in this scorpion nest of vice, assail
A lonely and undowered maid. I did not
Think with him, but would not oppose the
thought
Which soothed his death-bed.
Ang. I have not forgotten
The nobleness with which you bade me speak
If my young heart held any preference
Which would have made me happier; nor
your offer
To make my dowry equal to the rank
Of aught in Venice, and forego all claim
My father's last injunction gave you.
Doge. Thus,
'Twas not a foolish dotard's vile caprice,
Nor the false edge of aged appetite,
Which made me coveteous of girlish beauty,
And a young bride : for in my fieriest youth
I swayed such passions; nor was this my
age
Infected with that leprosy of lust
Which taints the hoariest years of vicious men,
Making them ransack to the very last
The dregs of pleasure for their vanished joys;
Or buy in selfish marriage some young victim,
Too helpless to refuse a state that's honest,
Too feeling not to know herself a wretch.
Our wedlock was not of this sort; you had
Freedom from me to choose, and urged in
answer
Your father's choice.
Ang. I did so; I would do so
In face of earth and heaven; for I have never
Repented for my sake; sometimes for yours.
In pondering o'er your late disquietudes.
Doge. I knew my heart would never treat
you harshly;
I knew my days could not disturb you long;
And then the daughter of my earliest friend,
His worthy daughter, free to choose again,
Wealthier and wiser, in the ripest bloom
Of womanhood, more skilful to select
By passing these probationary years
Inheriting a prince's name and riches,
Secured, by the short penance of enduring
An old man for some summers, against all
That law's chicane or envious kinsmen might
Have urged against her right; my best
friend's child

Would choose more fitly in respect of years,
And not less truly in a faithful heart.
  Ang.   My lord, I looked but to my father's
    wishes,
Hallowed by his last words, and to my heart
For doing all its duties, and replying
With faith to him with whom I was affianced.
Ambitious hopes ne'er crossed my dreams;
    and should
The hour you speak of come, it will be seen
    so.
  Doge.   I do believe you; and I know you
    true:
For love, romantic love, which in my youth
I knew to be illusion, and ne'er saw
Lasting, but often fatal, it had been
No lure for me, in my most passionate days,
And could not be so now, did such exist.
But such respect, and mildly paid regard
As a true feeling for your welfare, and
A free compliance with all honest wishes;
A kindness to your virtues, watchfulness
Not shown, but shadowing o'er such little
    failings
As youth is apt in, so as not to check
Rashly, but win you from them ere you knew
You had been won, but thought the change
    your choice;
A pride not in your beauty, but your con-
    duct,—
A trust in you—a patriarchal love,
And not a doting homage—friendship,
    faith—
Such estimation in your eyes as these
Might claim, I hoped for.
  Ang.   And have ever had.
  Doge.   I think so. For the difference in
    our years
You knew it, choosing me, and chose: I
    trusted
Not to my qualities, nor would have faith
In such, nor outward ornaments of nature,
Were I still in my five and twentieth spring;
I trusted to the blood of Loredano
Pure in your veins; I trusted to the soul
God gave you—to the truths your father
    taught you—
To your belief in heaven—to your mild vir-
    tues—
To your own faith and honor, for my own.
  Ang.   You have done well.—I thank you
    for that trust,
Which I have never for one moment ceased
To honor you the more for.
  Doge.   Where is honor,
Innate and precept-strengthened, 'tis the rock
Of faith connubial: where it is not—where
Light thoughts are lurking, or the vanities
Of worldly pleasure rankle in the heart,
Or sensual throbs convulse it, well I know
'Twere hopeless for humanity to dream
Of honesty in such infected blood,

Although 'twere wed to him it covets most:
An incarnation of the poet's god
In all his marble-chiselled beauty, or
The demi-deity, Alcides, in
His majesty of superhuman manhood,
Would not suffice to bind where virtue is not;
It is consistency which forms and proves it:
Vice cannot fix, and virtue cannot change.
The once fallen woman must for ever fall;
For vice must have variety, while virtue
Stands like the sun, and all which rolls around
Drinks life, and light, and glory from her
    aspect.
  Ang.   And seeing, feeling thus this truth in
    others,
(I pray you pardon me;) but wherefore
    yield you
To the most fierce of fatal passions, and
Disquiet your great thoughts with restless hate
Of such a thing as Steno?
  Doge.   You mistake me,
It is not Steno who could move me thus;
Had it been so, he should —— but let that pass,
  Ang.   What is't you feel so deeply, then,
    even now?
  Doge.   The violated majesty of Venice,
At once insulted in her lord and laws.
  Ang.   Alas! why will you thus consider it?
  Doge.   I have thought on't till —— but let
    me lead you back
To what I urged; all these things being noted,
I wedded you; the world then did me justice
Upon the motive, and my conduct proved
They did me right, while yours was all to
    praise:
You had all freedom —all respect — all trust
From me and mine; and, born of those who
    made
Princes at home, and swept kings from their
    thrones
On foreign shores, in all things you appeared
Worthy to be our first of native dames.
  Ang.   To what does this conduct?
  Doge.   To thus much — that
A miscreant's angry breath may blast it all—
A villain, whom for his unbridled bearing,
Even in the midst of our great festival,
I caused to be conducted forth, and taught
How to demean himself in ducal chambers;
A wretch like this may leave upon the wall
The blighting venom of his sweltering heart,
And this shall spread itself in general poison;
And woman's innocence, man's honor, pass
Into a by-word; and the doubly felon
(Who first insulted virgin modesty
By a gross affront to your attendant damsels
Amidst the noblest of our dames in public)
Requite himself for his most just expulsion
By blackening publicly his sovereign's consort,
And be absolved by his upright compeers.
  Ang.   But he has been condemned into
    captivity.

Doge. For such as him a dungeon were
  acquittal ;
And his brief term of mock-arrest will pass
Within a palace. But I've done with him ;
The rest must be with you.
  Ang.   With me, my lord?
Doge. Yes Angiolina. Do not marvel ; I
Have let this prey upon me till I feel
My life cannot be long ; and fain would have
  you
¦Regard the injunctions you will find within
⸱This scroll (*Giving her a paper.*) ──── Fear
  not ; they are for your advantage :
Read them hereafter at the fitting hour.
  Ang. My lord, in life, and after life, you
  ⸱shall
Be honored still by me : but may your days
Be many yet — and happier than the present !
This passion will give way, and you will be
Serene, and what you should be — what you
  were.
  Doge. I will be what I should be, or be
  nothing ;
But never more — oh ! never, never more,
O'er the few days or hours which yet await
The blighted old age of Faliero, shall
Sweet Quiet shed her sunset ! Never more
Those summer shadows rising from the past
Of a not ill-spent nor inglorious life,
Mellowing the last hours as the night ap-
  proaches,
Shall soothe me to my moment of long rest.
I had but little more to ask, or hope,
Save the regards due to the blood and sweat,
And the soul's labor through which I had
  toiled
To make my country honored. As her ser-
  vant —
Her servant, though her chief — I would have
  gone
Down to my fathers with a name serene
And pure as theirs ; but this has been denied
  me. —
Would I had died at Zara !
  Ang.   There you saved
The state ; then live to save her still. A
  day,
Another day like that would be the best
Reproof to them, and sole revenge for you.
  Doge. But one such day occurs within an
  age ;
My life is little less than one, and 'tis
Enough for Fortune to have granted *once*,
That which scarce one more favored citizen
May win in many states and years. But why
⸱ Thus speak I ? Venice has forgot that day —
Then why should I remember it ? — Farewell,
Sweet Angiolina ! I must to my cabinet ;
There's much for me to do — and the hour
  hastens.
  Ang. Remember what you were.
  Doge.   It were in vain !

Joy's recollection is no longer joy,
While Sorrow's memory is a sorrow still.
  Ang. At least, whate'er may urge, let me
  implore
That you will take some little pause of rest :
Your sleep for many nights has been so tur-
  bid,
That it had been relief to have awaked you,
Had I not hoped that Nature would o'er-
  power
At length the thoughts which shook your
  slumbers thus.
An hour of rest will give you to your toils
With fitter thoughts and freshened strength.
  Doge.   I cannot —
I must not, if I could ; for never was
Such reason to be watchful : yet a few —
Yet a few days and dream-perturbed nights,
And I shall slumber well — but where ? — no
  matter.
Adieu, my Angiolina.
  Ang.   Let me be
An instant — yet an instant your companion !
I cannot bear to leave you thus.
  Doge.   Come then,
My gentle child — forgive me ; thou wert made
For better fortunes than to share in mine,
Now darkling in their close toward the deep
  vale
Where Death sits robed in his all-sweeping
  shadow. ⸱
When I am gone — it may be sooner than
Even these years warrant, for there is that
  stirring
Within — above — around, that in this city
Will make the cemeteries populous
As e'er they were by pestilence or war, —
When I *am* nothing, let that which I *was*
Be still sometimes a name on thy sweet lips,
A shadow in thy fancy, of a thing
Which would not have thee mourn it, but re-
  member ; —
Let us begone, my child — the time is pressing.
                          [*Exeunt.*

SCENE II. — *A retired Spot near the Arsenal.*
  ISRAEL BERTUCCIO *and* PHILIP CALEN-
                    DARO.

  Cal. How sped you, Israel, in your late
  complaint ?
  I. Ber. Why, well.
  Cal. Is't possible ! will he be punished ?
  I. Ber.   Yes.
  Cal. With what ? a mulct or an arrest ?
  I. Ber.   With death ! —
  Cal. Now you rave, or must intend revenge,
  Such as I counselled you, with your own hand.
  I. Ber. Yes ; and for one sole draught of
  hate, forego
The great redress we meditate for Venice,
And change a life of hope for one of exile ;

Leaving one scorpion crushed, and thousands
  stinging
My friends, my family, my countrymen!
No, Calendaro; these same drops of blood,
Shed shamefully, shall have the whole of his
For their requital —— But not only his;
We will not strike for private wrongs alone:
Such are for selfish passions and rash men,
But are unworthy a tyrannicide.

Cal. You have more patience than I care
  to boast.
Had I been present when you bore this insult,
I must have slain him, or expired myself
In the vain effort to repress my wrath.

I. Ber. Thank Heaven, you were not — all
  had else been marred:
As 'tis, our cause looks prosperous still.

Cal. You saw
The Doge — what answer gave he?

I. Ber. That there was
No punishment for such as Barbaro.

Cal. I told you so before, and that 'twas
  idle
To think of justice from such hands.

I. Ber. At least,
It lulled suspicion, showing confidence.
Had I been silent, not a sbirro but
Had kept me in his eye, as meditating
A silent, solitary, deep revenge.

Cal. But wherefore not address you to the
  Council?
The Doge is a mere puppet, who can scarce
Obtain right for himself. Why speak to him?

I. Ber. You shall know that hereafter.

Cal. Why not now?

I. Ber. Be patient but till midnight. Get
  your musters,
And bid our friends prepare their com-
  panies: —
Set all in readiness to strike the blow,
Perhaps in a few hours; we have long waited
For a fit time — that hour is on the dial,
It may be, of to-morrow's sun: delay
Beyond may breed us double danger. See
That all be punctual at our place of meeting,
And armed, excepting those of the Sixteen,
Who will remain among the troops to wait
The signal.

Cal. These brave words have breathed
  new life
Into my veins; I am sick of these protracted
And hesitating councils: day on day
Crawled on, and added but another link
To our long fetters, and some fresher wrong
Inflicted on our brethren or ourselves,
Helping to swell our tyrants' bloated strength.
Let us but deal upon them, and I care not
For the result, which must be death or free-
  dom!
I'm weary to the heart of finding neither.

I. Ber. We will be free in life or death! the
  grave

Is chainless. Have you all the musters ready?
And are the sixteen companies completed
To Sixty?

Cal. All save two, in which there are
Twenty-five wanting to make up the number.

I. Ber. No matter; we can do without.
  Whose are they?

Cal. Bertram's and old Soranzo's, both of
  whom
Appear less forward in the cause than we are.

I. Ber. Your fiery nature makes you deem
  all those
Who are not restless cold: but there exists
Oft in concentred spirits not less daring
Than in more loud avengers. Do not doubt
  them.

Cal. I do not doubt the elder; but in Ber-
  tram
There is a hesitating softness, fatal
To enterprise like ours: I've seen that man
Weep like an infant o'er the misery
Of others, heedless of his own, though greater;
And in a recent quarrel I beheld him
Turn sick at sight of blood, although a villain's.

I. Ber. The truly brave are soft of heart
  and eyes,
And feel for what their duty bids them do.
I have known Bertram long; there doth not
  breathe
A soul more full of honor.

Cal. It may be so:
I apprehend less treachery than weakness;
Yet as he has no mistress, and no wife
To work upon his milkiness of spirit,
He may go through the ordeal; it is well
He is an orphan, friendless save in us:
A woman or a child had made him less
Than either in resolve.

I. Ber. Such ties are not
For those who are called to the high destinies
Which purify corrupted commonwealths;
We must forget all feelings save the *one* —
We must resign all passions save our pur-
  pose —
We must behold no object save our country —
And only look on death as beautiful,
So that the sacrifice ascend to heaven,
And draw down freedom on her evermore.

Cal. But if we fail ——

I. Ber. They never fail who die
In a great cause: the block may soak their
  gore;
Their heads may sodden in the sun; their limbs
Be strung to city gates and castle walls —
But still their spirit walks abroad. Though
  years
Elapse, and others share as dark a doom,
They but augment the deep and sweeping
  thoughts
Which overpower all others, and conduct
The world at last to freedom: What were we,
If Brutus had not lived? He died in giving

Rome liberty, but left a deathless lesson —
A name which is a virtue, and a soul
Which multiplies itself throughout all time
When wicked men wax mighty, and a state
Turns servile: he and his high friend were
    styled
" The last of Romans ! " Let us be the first
Of true Venetians, sprung from Roman sires.
   Cal. Our fathers did not fly from Attila
Into these isles, where palaces have sprung
On banks redeemed from the rude ocean's
    ooze,
To own a thousand despots in his place.
Better bow down before the Hun, and call
A Tartar lord, than these swoln silkworms
   masters.
The first at least was man, and used his sword
As sceptre : these unmanly creeping things
Command our swords, and rule us with a word
As with a spell.
   I. Ber.   It shall be broken soon.
You say that all things are in readiness :
To-day I have not been the usual round,
And why thou knowest; but thy vigilance
Will better have supplied my care : these
    orders
In recent council to redouble now
Our efforts to repair the galleys, have
Lent a fair color to the introduction
Of many of our cause into the arsenal,
As new artificers for their equipment,
Or fresh recruits obtained in haste to man
The hoped-for fleet. — Are all supplied with
    arms ?
   Cal. All who were deemed trustworthy :
    there are some
Whom it were well to keep in ignorance
Till it be time to strike, and then supply them ;
When in the heat and hurry of the hour
They have no opportunity to pause,
But needs must on with those who will sur-
    round them.
   I. Ber. You have said well. Have you re-
    marked all such ?
   Cal. I've noted most; and caused the
    other chiefs
To use like caution in their companies.
As far as I have seen, we are enough
To make the enterprise secure, if 'tis
Commenced to-morrow ; but, till 'tis begun,
Each hour is pregnant with a thousand perils.
   I. Ber. Let the Sixteen meet at the wonted
    hour,
Except Soranzo, Nicoletto Blondo,
And Marco Giuda, who will keep their watch
Within the arsenal, and hold all ready
Expectant of the signal we will fix on.
   Cal. We will not fail.
   I. Ber.   Let all the rest be there ;
I have a stranger to present to them.
   Cal. A stranger ! doth he know the secret ?
   I. Ber.   Yes.

   Cal. And have you dared to peril your
    friends' lives
On a rash confidence in one we know not ?
   I. Ber. I have risked no man's life except
    my own —
Of that be certain : he is one who may
Make our assurance doubly sure, according
His aid ; and if reluctant, he no less
Is in our power : he comes alone with me,
And cannot 'scape us ; but he will not swerve.
   Cal. I cannot judge of this until I know
    him :
Is he one of our order ?
   I. Ber.   Ay, in spirit,
Although a child of greatness ; he is one
Who would become a throne, or overthrow
    one —
One who has done great deeds, and seen
    great changes ;
No tyrant, though bred up to tyranny ;
Valiant in war, and sage in council ; noble
In nature, although haughty ; quick, yet wary :
Yet for all this, so full of certain passions,
That if once stirred and baffled, as he has
    been
Upon the tenderest points, there is no Fury
In Grecian story like to that which wrings
His vitals with her burning hands, till he
Grows capable of all things for revenge ;
And add too, that his mind is liberal,
He sees and feels the people are oppressed,
And shares their sufferings. Take him all in
    all,
We have need of such, and such have need
    of us.
   Cal. And what part would you have him
    take with us ?
   I. Ber. It may be, that of chief.
   Cal.   What ! and resign
Your own command as leader ?
   I. Ber.   Even so.
My object is to make your cause end well,
And not to push myself to power. Experi-
    ence,
Some skill, and your own choice, had marked
    me out
To act in trust as your commander, till
Some worthier should appear : if I have found
    such
As you yourselves shall own more worthy.
    think you
That I would hesitate from selfishness,
And, covetous of brief authority,
Stake our deep interest on my single thoughts,
Rather than yield to one above me in
All leading qualities ? No, Calendaro,
Know your friend better ; but you all shall
    judge. —
Away ! and let us meet at the fixed hour.
Be vigilant, and all will yet go well.
   Cal. Worthy Bertuccio, I have known you
    ever

Trusty and brave, with head and heart to plan
What I have still been prompt to execute.
For my own part, I seek no other chief;
What the rest will decide I know not, but
I am with YOU, as I have ever been,
In all our undertakings. Now farewell,
Until the hour of midnight sees us meet.

                      [Exeunt.

ACT III.

SCENE I.— *Scene, the Space between the Canal
and the Church of San Giovanni e San
Paolo. An equestrian Statue before it.— A
Gondola lies in the Canal at some distance.*

     Enter the DOGE *alone, disguised.*

Doge (*solus*). I am before the hour, the
    hour whose voice,
Pealing into the arch of night, might strike
These palaces with ominous tottering,
And rock their marbles to the corner-stone,
Waking the sleepers from some hideous
    dream
Of indistinct but awful augury
Of that which will befall them. Yes, proud
    city!
Thou must be cleansed of the black blood
    which makes thee
A lazar-house of tyranny: the task
Is forced upon me, I have sought it not;
And therefore was I punished, seeing this
Patrician pestilence spread on and on,
Until at length it smote me in my slumbers,
And I am tainted, and must wash away
The plague-spots in the healing wave. Tall
    fane!
Where sleep my fathers, whose dim statues
    shadow
The floor which doth divide us from the dead,
Where all the pregnant hearts of our bold
    blood,
Mouldered into a mite of ashes, hold
In one shrunk heap what once made many
    heroes,
When what is now a handful shook the
    earth —
Fane of the tutelar saints who guard our
    house!
Vault where two Doges rest — my sires! who
    died
The one of toil, the other in the field,
With a long race of other lineal chiefs
And sages, whose great labors, wounds, and
    state
I have inherited, — let the graves gape,
Till all thine aisles be peopled with the dead,
And pour them from thy portals to gaze on
    me!
I call them up, and them and thee to witness
What it hath been which put me to this
    task —

Their pure high blood, their blazon-roll of
    glories,
Their mighty name dishonored all *in* me,
Not *by* me, but by the ungrateful nobles
We fought to make our equals, not our
    lords : —
And chiefly thou, Ordelafo the brave,
Who perished in the field, where I since con-
    quered,
Battling at Zara, did the hecatombs
Of thine and Venice' foes, there offered up
By thy descendant, merit such acquittance?
Spirits! smile down upon me; for my cause
Is yours, in all life now can be of yours,—
Your fame, your name, all mingled up in
    mine,
And in the future fortunes of our race!
Let me but prosper, and I make this city
Free and immortal, and our house's name
Worthier of what you were, now and here-
    after! [1]

     Enter ISRAEL BERTUCCIO.

I. Ber. Who goes there?
Doge.   A friend to Venice.
I. Ber.   'Tis he.
Welcome, my lord,— you are before the time.
Doge. I am ready to proceed to your as-
    sembly.
I. Ber. Have with you.— I am proud and
    pleased to see
Such confident alacrity. Your doubts
Since our last meeting, then, are all dispelled?
Doge. Not so — but I have set my little left
Of life upon this cast: the die was thrown
When I first listened to your treason — Start
    not!
That is the word; I cannot shape my tongue
To syllable black deeds into smooth names,
Though I be wrought on to commit them.
    When
I heard you tempt your sovereign, and forbore
To have you dragged to prison, I became
Your guiltiest accomplice : now you may,
If it so please you, do as much by me.
I. Ber. Strange words, my lord, and most
    unmerited;
I am no spy, and neither are we traitors.
Doge. We— We!— no matter— you have
    earned the right
To talk of *us.* — But to the point. — If this
Attempt succeeds, and Venice, rendered free
And flourishing, when we are in our graves,
Conducts her generations to our tombs,
And makes her children with their little hands
Strew flowers o'er her deliverers' ashes, then
The consequence will sanctify the deed,
And we shall be like the two Bruti in

---

[1] [The Doge, true to his appointment, is waiting
for his conductor before the church of San Paolo e
Giovanni. There is great loftiness, both of feeling
and diction, in this passage. — *Jeffrey.*]

The annals of hereafter; but if not,
If we should fail, employing bloody means
And secret plot, although to a good end,
Still we are traitors, honest Israel; — thou
No less than he who was tny sovereign
Six hours ago, and now thy brother rebel.
I. Ber. 'Tis not the moment to consider
thus,
Else I could answer. — Let us to the meeting,
Or we may be observed in lingering here.
Doge. We *are* observed, and have been.
I. Ber. We observed!
Let me discover — and this steel ——
Doge. Put up;
Here are no human witnesses; look there —
What see you?
I. Ber. Only a tall warrior's statue
Bestriding a proud steed, in the dim light
Of the dull moon.
Doge. That warrior was the sire
Of my sire's fathers, and that statue was
Decreed to him by the twice rescued city : —
Think you that he looks down on us or no?
I. Ber. My lord, these are mere fantasies;
there are
No eyes in marble.
Doge. But there are in Death.
I tell thee, man, there is a spirit in
Such things that acts and sees, unseen, though
felt;
And, if there be a spell to stir the dead,
'Tis in such deeds as we are now upon.
Deem'st thou the souls of such a race as mine
Can rest, when he, their last descendant chief,
Stands plotting on the brink of their pure
graves
With stung plebeians? [1]
I. Ber. It had been as well

---

[1] [There is a great deal of natural struggle in the breast of the high-born and haughty Doge, between the resentment with which he burns on the one hand, and the reluctance with which he considers the meanness of the associates with whom he has leagued himself, on the other. The conspiring Doge is not, we think, meant to be ambitious for himself, as he is sternly, proudly, a Venetian noble; and it is impossible for him to tear from his bosom the scorn for every thing plebeian which has been implanted there by birth, education, and a long life of princely command. There are other thoughts, too, and of a gentler kind, which cross from time to time his perturbed spirit. He remembers — he cannot entirely forget — the days and nights of old companionship, by which he had long been bound to those whose sentence he has consented to seal. He has himself been declaiming against the folly of mercy, and arguing valiantly the necessity of total extirpation, — and that, too, in the teeth even of some of the plebeian conspirators themselves: yet the poet, with profound insight into the human heart, makes him shudder when his own impetuosity has brought himself, and all who hear him, to the brink. He cannot look upon the bloody resolution, no not even after he himself has been the chief nstrument of its formation. — *Lockhart.*]

To have pondered this before, — ere you embarked
In our great enterprise. — Do you repent?
Doge. No — but I *feel*, and shall do to the
last.
I cannot quench a glorious life at once,
Nor dwindle to the thing I now must be, [2]
And take men's lives by stealth, without some
pause :
Yet doubt me not; it is this very feeling,
And knowing *what* has wrung me to be thus,
Which is your best security. There's not
A roused mechanic in your busy plot
So wronged as I, so fallen, so loudly called
To his redress : the very means I am forced
By these fell tyrants to adopt is such,
That I abhor them doubly for the deeds
Which I must do to pay them back for theirs.
I. Ber. Let us away — hark — the hour
strikes.
Doge. On — on —
It is our knell or that of Venice — On.
I. Ber. Say rather, 'tis her freedom's rising
peal
Of triumph —— This way — we are near the
place. [*Exeunt.*

SCENE II. — *The House where the Conspirators meet.*

DAGOLINO, DORO, BERTRAM, FEDELE
TREVISANO, CALENDARO, ANTONIO
DELLE BENDE, etc. etc.

Cal. (entering). Are all here?
Dag. All with you; except the three
On duty, and our leader Israel,
Who is expected momently.
Cal. Where's Bertram?
Ber. Here!
Cal. Have you not been able to complete
The number wanting in your company?
Ber. I had marked out some : but I have
not dared
To trust them with the secret, till assured
That they were worthy faith.
Cal. There is no need
Of trusting to their faith : *who*, save ourselves
And our more chosen comrades, is aware
Fully of our intent? they think themselves
Engaged in secret to the Signory, [3]
To punish some more dissolute young nobles
Who have defied the law in their excesses :
But once drawn up, and their new swords
well fleshed
In the rank hearts of the more odious senators,
They will not hesitate to follow up
Their blow upon the others, when they see

---

[2] [MS. —
"Nor dwindle to a cut-throat without shuddering."]
[3] An historical fact. See Appendix, Note A.

The example of their chiefs, and I for one
Will set them such, that they for very shame
And safety will not pause till all have perished.
  Ber. How say you? *all!*
  Cal.   Whom wouldst thou spare?
  Ber. -   *I spare?*
I have no power to spare. I only questioned,
Thinking that even amongst these wicked
    men
There might be some, whose age and qualities
Might mark them out for pity.
  Cal.   Yes, such pity
As when the viper hath been cut to pieces,
The separate fragments quivering in the sun,
In the last energy of venomous life,
Deserve and have. Why, I should think as
    soon
Of pitying some particular fang which made
One in the jaw of the swoln serpent, as
Of saving one of these: they form but links
Of one long chain; one mass, one breath, one
    body,
They eat, and drink, and live, and breed to-
    gether,
Revel, and lie, oppress, and kill in concert, —
So let them die as *one!*
  Dag.   Should *one* survive,
He would be dangerous as the whole; it is not
Their number, be it tens or thousands, but
The spirit of this aristocracy
Which must be rooted out; and if there were
A single shoot of the old tree in life,
'Twould fasten in the soil, and spring again
To gloomy verdure and to bitter fruit.
Bertram, we must be firm!
  Cal.   Look to it well,
Bertram; I have an eye upon thee.
  Ber.   Who
Distrusts me?
  Cal.   Not I; for if I did so,
Thou wouldst not now be there to talk of
    trust:
It is thy softness, not thy want of faith,
Which makes thee to be doubted.
  Ber.   You should know
Who hear me, who and what I am; a man
Roused like yourselves to overthrow oppres-
    sion;
A kind man, I am apt to think, as some
Of you have found me; and if brave or no,
You, Calendaro, can pronounce, who have
    seen me
Put to the proof; or, if you should have doubts,
I'll clear them on your person!
  Cal.   You are welcome
When once our enterprise is o'er, which must
    not
Be interrupted by a private brawl.
  Ber. I am no brawler; but can bear myself
As far among the foe as any he
Who hears me; else why have I been selected
To be of your chief comrades? but no less

I own my natural weakness; I have not
Yet learned to think of indiscriminate murder
Without some sense of shuddering; and the
    sight
Of blood which spouts through hoary scalps
    is not
To me a thing of triumph, nor the death
Of man surprised a glory. Well — too well
I know that we must do such things on those
Whose acts have raised up such avengers; but
If there were some of these who could be saved
From out this sweeping fate, for our own sakes
And for our honor, to take off some stain
Of massacre, which else pollutes it wholly,
I had been glad; and see no cause in this
For sneer, nor for suspicion!
  Dag.   Calm thee, Bertram,
For we suspect thee not, and take good heart;
It is the cause, and not our will, which asks
Such actions from our hands: we'll wash away
All stains in Freedom's fountain!

Enter ISRAEL BERTUCCIO, *and the* DOGE,
    disguised.

  Dag.   Welcome, Israel.
  Consp. Most welcome. — Brave Bertuccio,
    thou art late —
Who is this stranger?
  Cal.   It is time to name him.
Our comrades are even now prepared to greet
    him
In brotherhood, as I have made it known
That thou wouldst add a brother to our cause,
Approved by thee, and thus approved by all,
Such is our trust in all thine actions. Now
Let him unfold himself.
  I. Ber.   Stranger, step forth!
                        [*The* DOGE *discovers himself.*
  Consp. To arms! — we are betrayed — it
    is the Doge!
Down with them both! our traitorous captain,
    and
The tyrant he hath sold us to.
  Cal. (*drawing his sword*).   Hold! hold!
Who moves a step against them dies. Hold!
    hear
Bertuccio — What! are you appalled to see
A lone, unguarded, weaponless old man
Amongst you? — Israel, speak! what means
    this mystery?
  I. Ber. Let them advance and strike at
    their own bosoms,
Ungrateful suicides! for on our lives
Depend their own, their fortunes, and their
    hopes.
  Doge. Strike! — If I dreaded death, a
    death more fearful
Than any your rash weapons can inflict,
I should not now be here: — Oh, noble Cour-
    age!
The eldest born of Fear, which makes you
    brave

Against this solitary hoary head!
See the bold chiefs, who would reform a state
And shake down senates, mad with wrath and
    dread
At sight of one patrician! — Butcher me,
You can; I care not. — Israel, are these men
The mighty hearts you spoke of? look upon
    them!
  Cal. Faith! he hath shamed us, and de-
servedly.
Was this your trust in your true chief Bertuc-
    cio,
To turn your swords against him and his guest?
Sheathe them, and hear him.
  I. Ber.   I disdain to speak.
They might and must have known a heart like
    mine
Incapable of treachery; and the power
They gave me to adopt all fitting means
To further their design was ne'er abused.
They might be certain that whoe'er was
    brought
By me into this council had been led
To take his choice — as brother or as victim.
  Doge. And which am I to be? your ac-
tions leave
Some cause to doubt the freedom of the choice.
  I. Ber. My lord, we would have perished
    here together,
Had these rash men proceeded; but, behold,
They are ashamed of that mad moment's im-
    pulse,
And droop their heads; believe me, they are
    such
As I described them — Speak to them.
  Cal.   Ay, speak;
We are all listening in wonder.
  I. Ber. (*addressing the Conspirators*). You
    are safe,
Nay, more, almost triumphant — listen then,
And know my words for truth.
  Doge.   You see me here,
As one of you hath said, an old, unarmed,
Defenceless man; and yesterday you saw me
Presiding in the hall of ducal state,
Apparent sovereign of our hundred isles,
Robed in official purple, dealing out
The edicts of a power which is not mine,
Nor yours, but of our masters — the patricians.
Why I was there you know, or think you know;
Why I am *here*, he who hath been most
    wronged,
He who among you hath been most insulted,
Outraged and trodden on, until he doubt
If he be worm or no, may answer for me,
Asking of his own heart what brought him
    here?
You know my recent story, all men know it,
And judge of it far differently from those
Who sate in judgment to heap scorn on scorn.
But spare me the recital — it is here,
Here at my heart the outrage — but my words,

Already spent in unavailing plaints,
Would only show my feebleness the more,
And I come here to strengthen even the strong,
And urge them on to deeds, and not to war
With woman's weapons; but I need not urge
    you.
Our private wrongs have sprung from public
    vices
In this — I cannot call it commonwealth
Nor kingdom, which hath neither prince nor
    people,
But all the sins of the old Spartan state [1]
Without its virtues — temperance and valor. '
The Lords of Lacedæmon were true soldiers,
But ours are Sybarites, while we are Helots,
Of whom I am the lowest, most enslaved;
Although dressed out to head a pageant, as
The Greeks of yore made drunk their slaves
    to form
A pastime for their children. You are met
To overthrow this monster of a state,
This mockery of a government, this spectre,
Which must be exorcised with blood, — and
    then
We will renew the times of truth and justice,
Condensing in a fair free commonwealth
Not rash equality but equal rights,
Proportioned like the columns to the temple,
Giving and taking strength reciprocal,
And making firm the whole with grace and
    beauty, •
So that no part could be removed without
Infringement of the general symmetry.
In operating this great change, I claim
To be one of you — if you trust in me;
If not, strike home, — my life is compromised,
And I would rather fall by freemen's hands
Than live another day to act the tyrant
As delegate of tyrants: such I am not,
And never have been — read it in our annals;
I can appeal to my past government
In many lands and cities; they can tell you
If I were an oppressor, or a man
Feeling and thinking for my fellow men.
Haply had I been what the senate sought,
A thing of robes and trinkets, dizened out
To sit in state as for a sovereign s picture;
A popular scourge, a ready sentence-signer,
A stickler for the Senate and "the Forty,"
A sceptic of all measures which had not
The sanction of "the Ten," a council-fawner,
A tool, a fool, a puppet, — they had ne'er
Fostered the wretch who stung me. What I
    suffer
Has reached me through my pity for the peo-
    ple;
That many know, and they who know not yet
Will one day learn: meantime I do devote,
Whate'er the issue, my last days of life —

1 [MS. —
"But all the worst sins of the Spartan state."]

My present power such as it is, not that
Of Doge, but of a man who has been great
Before he was degraded to a Doge,
And still has individual means and mind;
I stake my fame (and I had fame) — my
  breath—
(The least of all, for its last hours are nigh)
My heart — my hope — my soul — upon this
  cast!
Such as I am, I offer me to you
And to your chiefs, accept me or reject me,
A Prince who fain would be a citizen
Or nothing, and who has left his throne to be
  so.
  Cal. Long live Faliero! — Venice shall be
  free!
  Consp. Long live Faliero!
  I. Ber.   Comrades! did I well?
Is not this man a host in such a cause?
  Doge. This is no time for eulogies, nor
  place
For exultation. Am I one of you?
  Cal. Ay, and the first amongst us, as thou
  hast been
Of Venice — be our general and chief.
  Doge. Chief! — general! — I was general at
  Zara,
And chief in Rhodes and Cyprus, prince in
  Venice:
I cannot stoop —— that is, I am not fit
To lead a band of —— patriots: when I lay
Aside the dignities which I have borne,
'Tis not to put on others, but to be
Mate to my fellows — but now to the point:
Israel has stated to me your whole plan —
'Tis bold, but feasible if I assist it,
And must be set in motion instantly.
  Cal. E'en when thou wilt. Is it not so, my
  friends?
I have disposed all for a sudden blow;
When shall it be then?
  Doge.   At sunrise.
  Ber.   So soon?
  Doge. So soon? — so late — each hour
  accumulates
Peril on peril, and the more so now
Since I have mingled with you; — know you not
The Council, and "the Ten?" the spies, the
  eyes
Of the patricians dubious of their slaves,
And now more dubious of the prince they
  have made one?
I tell you, you must strike, and suddenly,
Full to the Hydra's heart — its heads will
  follow.
  Cal. With all my soul and sword, I yield
  assent.
Our companies are ready, sixty each,
And all now under arms by Israel's order;
Each at their different place of rendezvous,
And vigilant, expectant of some blow;
Let each repair for action to his post!

And now, my lord, the signal?
  Doge.   When you hear
The great bell of Saint Mark's, which may not
  be
Struck without special order of the Doge
(The last poor privilege they leave their
  prince),
March on Saint Mark's!
  I. Ber.   And there? —
  Doge.   By different routes
Let your march be directed, every sixty
Entering a separate avenue, and still
Upon the way let your cry be of war
And of the Genoese fleet, by the first dawn
Discerned before the port; form round the
  palace,
Within whose court will be drawn out in arms
My nephew and the clients of our house,
Many and martial; while the bell tolls on,
Shout ye, "Saint Mark! — the foe is on our
  waters!"
  Cal. I see it now — but on, my noble lord.
  Doge. All the patricians flocking to the
  Council,
(Which they dare not refuse, at the dread
  signal
Pealing from out their patron saint's proud
  tower,)
Will then be gathered in unto the harvest,
And we will reap them with the sword for
  sickle.
If some few should be tardy or absent them,
'Twill be but to be taken faint and single,
When the majority are put to rest.
  Cal. Would that the hour were come! we
  will not scotch,
But kill.
  Ber. Once more, sir, with your pardon, I
Would now repeat the question which I asked
Before Bertuccio added to our cause
This great ally who renders it more sure,
And therefore safer, and as such admits
Some dawn of mercy to a portion of
Our victims — must all perish in this slaughter?
  Cal. All who encounter me and mine, be
  sure,
The mercy they have shown, I show.
  Consp.   All! all!
Is this a time to talk of pity? when
Have they e'er shown, or felt, or feigned it?
  I. Ber.   Bertram,
This false compassion is a folly, and
Injustice to thy comrades and thy cause!
Dost thou not see, that if we single out
Some for escape, they live but to avenge
The fallen? and how distinguish now the
  innocent
From out the guilty? all their acts are *one* —
A single emanation from one body,
Together knit for our oppression! 'Tis
Much that we let their children live; I doubt
If all of these even should be set apart:

The hunter may reserve some single cub
From out the tiger's litter, but who e'er
Would seek to save the spotted sire or dam,
Unless to perish by their fangs? however,
I will abide by Doge Faliero's counsel:
Let him decide if any should be saved.

Doge. Ask me not — tempt me not with
  such a question —
Decide yourselves.

I. Ber.   You know their private virtues
Far better than we can, to whom alone
Their public vices, and most foul oppression,
Have made them deadly; if there be amongst
  them
One who deserves to be repealed, pronounce.

Doge. Dolfino's father was my friend, and
  Lando
Fought by my side, and Marc Cornaro
  shared[1]
My Genoese embassy: I saved the life
Of Veniero — shall I save it twice?
Would that I could save them and Venice
  also!
All these men, or their fathers, were my
  friends
Till they became my subjects; then fell from
  me
As faithless leaves drop from the o'erblown
  flower,
And left me a lone blighted thorny stalk,
Which, in its solitude, can shelter nothing;
So, as they let me wither, let them perish!

Cal. They cannot coexist with Venice' free-
  dom!

Doge. Ye, though you know and feel our
  mutual mass
Of many wrongs, even ye are ignorant[2]
What fatal poison to the springs of life,
To human ties, and all that's good and dear,
Lurks in the present institutes of Venice:
All these men were my friends; I loved them,
  they
Requited honorably my regards;
We served and fought; we smiled and wept
  in concert;
We revelled or we sorrowed side by side;
We made alliances of blood and marriage;
We grew in years and honors fairly, — till
Their own desire, not my ambition, made
Them choose me for their prince, and then
  farewell!
Farewell all social memory! all thoughts

In common! and sweet bonds which link old
  friendships,
When the survivors of long years and actions,
Which now belong to history, soothe the
  days
Which yet remain by treasuring each other,
And never meet, but each beholds the mirror
Of half a century on his brother's brow,
And sees a hundred beings, now in earth,
Flit round them whispering of the days gone
  by,
And seeming not all dead, as long as two
Of the brave, joyous, reckless, glorious band,
Which once were one and many, still retain
A breath to sigh for them, a tongue to speak
Of deeds that else were silent, save on
  marble ——
Oime! Oime! — and must I do this deed?[3]

I. Ber. My lord, you are much moved: it
  is not now
That such things must be dwelt upon.

Doge.   Your patience
A moment — I recede not: mark with me
The gloomy vices of this government.
From the hour that made me Doge, the *Doge*
THEY *made* me —
Farewell the past! I died to all that had
  been,
Or rather they to me: no friends, no kind-
  ness,
No privacy of life — all were cut off:
They came not near me, such approach gave
  umbrage.
They could not love me, such was not the law;
They thwarted me, 'twas the state's policy;
They baffled me, 'twas a patrician's duty;
They wronged me, for such was to right the
  state;
They could not right me, that would give
  suspicion;
So that I was a slave to my own subjects;
So that I was a foe to my own friends;
Begirt with spies for guards — with robes for
  power —
With pomp for freedom — gaolers for a
  council —

---

[1] [MS. —

"Fought by my side, and { Marc Cornaro / John Grimani } shared.

My { Genoese embassy; / mission to the Pope; } I saved the life," etc.]

[2] [MS. —

"Bear witness with me! ye who hear and know,
And feel our mutual mass of many wrongs."]

[3] [The Doge is at last ushered into the presence of the conspirators, who are at first disposed to sacrifice both him and his introducer; but are pacified and converted by a speech of three pages, which is not very good: and then they put it to him to say, whether any of the devoted senate shall be spared in the impending massacre. He says —

"Ask me not — tempt me not with such a question — Decide yourselves." —

But, on being further pressed, he, in these passages, gives way to feelings most natural to his own condition, but by no means calculated to recommend him to his new associates: and afterwards, when he is left alone with the chief conspirator, the contrast of their situation is still more finely and forcibly elicited. — *Jeffrey.*]

Inquisitors for friends — and hell for life!
I had one only fount of quiet left,
And *that* they poisoned! My pure household
    gods[1]
Were shivered on my hearth, and o'er their
    shrine
Sate grinning Ribaldry and sneering Scorn.
    I. Ber. You have been deeply wronged, and
    now shall be
Nobly avenged before another night.
    Doge. I had borne all — it hurt me, but I
    bore it —
Till this last running over of the cup
Of bitterness — until this last loud insult,
Not only unredressed, but sanctioned; then,
And thus, I cast all further feelings from me —
The feelings which they crushed for me, long,
    long
Before, even in their oath of false allegiance!
Even in that very hour and vow, they abjured
Their friend and made a sovereign, as boys
    make
Playthings, to do their pleasure — and be
    broken!
I from that hour have seen but senators
In dark suspicious conflict with the Doge,
Brooding with him in mutual hate and fear;
They dreading he should snatch the tyranny
From out their grasp, and he abhorring tyrants.
To me, then, these men have no *private* life,
Nor claim to ties they have cut off from others;
As senators for arbitrary acts
Amenable, I look on them — as such
Let them be dealt upon.[2]
    Cal.   And now to action!
Hence, brethren, to our posts, and may this be
The last night of mere words: I'd fain be do-
    ing!
Saint Mark's great bell at dawn shall find me
    wakeful!
    I. Ber. Disperse then to your posts: be
    firm and vigilant;
Think on the wrongs we bear, the rights we
    claim.

---

[1] ["I could have forgiven the dagger or the bowl, any thing, but the deliberate desolation piled upon me, when I stood alone upon my hearth, with my household gods shivered around me. Do you suppose I have forgotten or forgiven it? It has, comparatively, swallowed up in me every other feeling, and I am only a spectator upon earth till a tenfold opportunity offers. It may come yet." — *Byron's Letters*, 1819.]

[2] [The struggle of feelings with which the Doge undertakes the conspiracy is admirably contrasted with the ferocious eagerness of his low-born associates; and only loses its effect because we cannot but be sensible that the man who felt thus, could not have gone on with his guilty project, unless stimulated by some greater and more accumulated injuries than are, in the course of the tragedy, brought before the perception of the reader. — *Hobhr.*]

This day and night shall be the last of peril!
Watch for the signal, and then march   I go
To join my band; let each be prompt to
    marshal
His separate charge: the Doge will now re-
    turn
To the palace to prepare all for the blow.
We part to meet in freedom and in glory!
    Cal. Doge, when I greet you next, my
    homage to you
Shall be the head of Steno on this sword!
    Doge. No; let him be reserved unto the
    last,
Nor turn aside to strike at such a prey,[3]
Till nobler game is quarried: his offence
Was a mere ebullition of the vice,
The general corruption generated
By the foul aristocracy: he could not —
He dared not in more honorable days
Have risked it. I have merged all private
    wrath
Against him in the thought of our great pur-
    pose.
A slave insults me — I require his punish-
    ment
From his proud master's hands; if he refuse it,
The offence grows his, and let him answer it.
    Cal. Yet, as the immediate cause of the
    alliance
Which consecrates our undertaking more,
I owe him such deep gratitude, that fain
I would repay him as he merits; may I?
    Doge. You would but lop the hand, and I
    the head;
You would but smite the scholar, I the mas-
    ter;
You would but punish Steno, I· the senate.
I cannot pause on individual hate,
In the absorbing, sweeping, whole revenge,
Which, like the sheeted fire from heaven,
    must blast
Without distinction, as it fell of yore,
Where the Dead Sea hath quenched two
    cities' ashes.
    I. Ber. Away, then, to your posts! I but
    remain
A moment to accompany the Doge
To our late place of tryst, to see no spies
Have been upon the scout, and thence I
    hasten
To where my allotted band is under arms.
    Cal. Farewell, then, — until dawn!
    I. Ber.   Success go with you!
    Consp. We will not fail — Away! My
    lord, farewell![4]

---

[3] [MS.—

"Nor turn aside to strike at such a wretch."]

[4] [The great defect of Marino Faliero is, that the nature and character of the conspiracy excite no interest. It matters little that Lord Byron has been faithful to history, if the event is destitute of a

[*The Conspirators salute the* DOGE *and*
ISRAEL BERTUCCIO, *and retire, headed
by* PHILIP CALENDARO.   *The* DOGE
and ISRAEL BERTUCCIO *remain.*
I. Ber. We have them in the toil — it can-
not fail!
Now thou'rt indeed a sovereign, and wilt
make
A name immortal greater than the greatest:
Free citizens have struck at kings ere now;
Cæsars have fallen, and even patrician hands
Have crushed dictators, as the popular steel
Has reached patricians: but, until this hour,
What prince has plotted for his people's free-
dom ?
Or risked a life to liberate his subjects ?
For ever, and for ever, they conspire
Against the people, to abuse their hands
To chains, but laid aside to carry weapons
Against the fellow nations, so that yoke
On yoke, and slavery and death may whet,
Not glut, the never-gorged Leviathan!
Now, my lord, to our enterprise; — 'tis great,
And greater the reward; why stand you rapt ?
A moment back, and you were all impa-
tience!
Doge. And is it then decided! must they
die ?
I. Ber. Who ?
Doge. My own friends by blood and cour-
tesy,
And many deeds and days — the senators ?
I. Ber. You passed their sentence, and it
is a just one.
Doge. Ay, so it seems, and so it is to *you;*
You are a patriot, plebeian Gracchus —
The rebel's oracle, the people's tribune —
I blame you not — you act in your vocation;

poetic character. Like Alfieri, to whom, in many
points, his genius approximates, he is fettered by
an intractable story, which is wholly remote from
the instincts and feelings of mankind. How ele-
vated soever may be his diction, how vivid soever
his coloring, a moral truth is wanting. That
charm, so difficult to define, so easy to apprehend,
which, diffused over the scene, excites in generous
bosoms an exalted enthusiasm for the great in-
terests of humanity. This is the poesy of history.
It is the charm of the William Tell of Schiller; it
is felt in the awful plot of Brutus, and, to a certain
degree, in the conspiracy of Pierre and Jaffier; for
the end and purpose of these conspiracies were, to
redeem their country from insult and oppression.
But in Marino Faliero's attempt against the state,
we contemplate nothing but the project of a san-
guinary ruffian, seeking to grasp unlimited author-
ity, and making, after the established precedents of
all usurpers, the wrongs and sufferings of the
commonalty his pretence; while, in another aspect
of his character, we see him goaded, by an imag-
ined injury, into an enterprise which would have
inundated Venice with her best blood. Is this a
sublime spectacle, calculated to purge the mind,
according to the aphorism of Aristotle, by means of
terror or pity ? — *Ecl. Rev.*]

They smote you, and oppressed you, and
despised you;
So they have *me :* but *you* ne'er spake with
them ;
You never broke their bread, nor shared their
salt ;
You never had their wine-cup at your lips;
You grew not up with them, nor laughed, nor
wept,
Nor held a revel in their company;
Ne'er smiled to see them smile, nor claimed
their smile
In social interchange for yours, nor trusted
Nor wore them in your heart of hearts, as I
have:
These hairs of mine are gray, and so are
theirs,
The elders of the council: I remember
When all our locks were like the raven's wing,
As we went forth to take our prey around
The isles wrung from the false Mahometan;
And can I see them dabbled o'er with blood?
Each stab to them will seem my suicide.[1]
I. Ber. Doge! Doge! this vacillation is
unworthy
A child; if you are not in second childhood,
Call back your nerves to your own purpose,
nor
Thus shame yourself and me. By heavens!
I'd rather
Forego even nôw, or fail in our intent,
Than see the man I venerate subside
From high resolves into such shallow weak-
ness!
You have seen blood in battle, shed it, both
Your own and that of others ; can you shrink
then
From a few drops from veins of hoary vam-
pires,
Who but give back what they have drained
from millions ?

---

[1] [The unmixed selfishness of the motives with
which the Doge accedes to the plot perpetually
escapes him. Not that he is wholly untouched by
the compunctious visitings of nature. But the
fearful unity of such a character is broken by assign-
ing to it the throbbings and the pangs of human
feelings, and by making him recoil with affright
from slaughter and desolation. In the roar and
whirlwind of the mighty passions which precede
the acting of a dreadful plot, it is wholly unreason-
able and out of keeping to put into his mouth the
sentimental effusions of affectionate pity for his
friends, whom he thinks of rather too late to give
these touches of remorse and mercy any other char-
acter than that of hypocritical whining. The senti-
ments are certainly good, but lamentably out of
time and place, and remind us of Scarron's remark
upon the moralizing Phlegyas in the infernal re-
gions, —
    " Cette sentence est vrai et belle,
      Mais dans enfer de quoi sert-elle? "
Yet though wholly repugnant to dramatic congruity,
the passage has great poetic power. — *Ecl. Rev.*]

Doge. Bear with me! Step by step, and
blow on blow,
I will divide with you; think not I waver:
Ah! no; it is the *certainty* of all
Which I must do doth make me tremble thus.
But let these last and lingering thoughts have
way
To which you only and the Night are con-
scious,
And both regardless; when the hour arrives,
'Tis mine to sound the knell, and strike the
blow,
Which shall unpeople many palaces,
And hew the highest genealogic trees
Down to the earth, strewed with their bleed-
ing fruit,
And crush their blossoms into barrenness:
This will I — must I — have I sworn to do,
Nor aught can turn me from my destiny;
But still I quiver to behold what I
Must be, and think what I have been! Bear
with me.
I. Ber. Re-man your breast; I feel no such
remorse,
I understand it not: why should you change?
You acted, and you act, on your free will.
Doge. Ay, there it is —*you* feel not, nor
do I,
Else I should stab thee on the spot, to save
A thousand lives, and, killing, do no murder;
You *feel* not —*you* go to this butcher-work
As if these high-born men were steers for
shambles!
When all is over, you'll be free and merry,
And calmly wash those hands incarnadine;
But I, outgoing thee and all thy fellows
In this surpassing massacre, shall be,
Shall see and feel — oh God! oh God! 'tis true,
And thou dost well to answer that it was
" My own free will and act," and yet you err,
For I *will* do this! Doubt not — fear not; I
Will be your most unmerciful accomplice!
And yet I act no more on my free will,
Nor my own feelings — both compel me back;
But there is *hell* within me and around,
And like the demon who believes and trem-
bles,
Must I abhor and do. Away! away!
Get thee unto thy fellows, I will hie me
To gather the retainers of our house.
Doubt not, Saint Mark's great bell shall wake
all Venice,
Except her slaughtered senate: ere the sun
Be broad upon the Adriatic there
Shall be a voice of weeping, which shall
drown
The roar of waters in the cry of blood!
I am resolved — come on.
I. Ber. With all my soul!
Keep a firm rein upon these bursts of passion;
Remember what these men have dealt to
thee,

And that this sacrifice will be succeeded
By ages of prosperity and freedom
To this unshackled city: a true tyrant
Would have depopulated empires, nor
Have felt the strange compunction which
hath wrung you
To punish a few traitors to the people.
Trust me, such were a pity more misplaced
Than the late mercy of the state to Steno.
Doge. Man, thou hast struck upon the
chord which jars
All nature from my heart. Hence to our task!
[*Exeunt.*

ACT IV.

SCENE I.[1]— *Palazzo of the patrician* LIONI.
LIONI *laying aside the mask and cloak
which the Venetian Nobles wore in public,
attended by a Domestic.*

Lioni. I will to rest, right weary of this
revel,
The gayest we have held for many moons,
And yet, I know not why, it cheered me not;
There came a heaviness across my heart,
Which, in the lightest movement of the
dance,
Though eye to eye, and hand in hand united
Even with the lady of my love, oppressed me,
And through my spirit chilled my blood, until
A damp like death rose o'er my brow; I
strove
To laugh the thought away, but 'twould not
be;
Through all the music ringing in my ears
A knell was sounding as distinct and clear,
Though low and far, as e'er the Adrian wave
Rose o'er the city's murmur in the night,
Dashing against the outward Lido's bulwark:
So that I left the festival before
It reached its zenith, and will woo my pillow
For thoughts more tranquil, or forgetfulness.
Antonio, take my mask and cloak, and light
The lamp within my chamber.
Ant. Yes, my lord;
Command you no refreshment?

---

[1] [The fourth act opens with the most poetical
and brilliantly written scene in the play — though
it is a soliloquy, and altogether alien from the busi-
ness of the piece. Lioni, a young nobleman, returns
home from a splendid assembly, rather out of spirits;
and, opening his palace window for air, contrasts the
tranquillity of the night scene which lies before him,
with the feverish turbulence and glittering enchant-
ments of that which he has just quitted. Nothing can
be finer than this picture, in both its compartments.
There is a truth and a luxuriance in the description
of the rout, which mark at once the hand of a
master, and raise it to a very high rank as a piece
of poetical painting; — while the moonlight view
from the window is equally grand and beautiful. —
Jeffrey.]

Lioni.   Nought, save sleep,
Which will not be commanded. Let me hope
     it,   [*Exit* ANTONIO.
Though my breast feels too anxious; I will try
Whether the air will calm my spirits : 'tis
A goodly night; the cloudy wind which blew
From the Levant hath crept into its cave,
And the broad moon has brightened. What
     a stillness!   [*Goes to an open lattice.*
And what a contrast with the scene I left,
Where the tall torches' glare, and silver
     lamps'
More pallid gleam along the tapestried walls,
Spread over the reluctant gloom which haunts
Those vast and dimly-latticed galleries
A dazzling mass of artificial light,
Which showed all things, but nothing as they
     were.
There age essaying to recall the past,
After long striving for the hues of youth
At the sad labor of the toilet, and
Full many a glance at the too faithful mirror,
Pranked forth in all the pride of ornament,
Forgot itself, and trusting to the falsehood
Of the indulgent beams, which show, yet hide,
Believed itself forgotten, and was fooled.
There Youth, which needed not, nor thought
     of such
Vain adjuncts, lavished its true bloom, and
     health,
And bridal beauty, in the unwholesome press
Of flushed and crowded wassailers, and wasted
Its hours of rest in dreaming this was pleasure,
And so shall waste them till the sunrise streams
On sallow cheeks and sunken eyes, which
     should not
Have worn this aspect yet for many a year.
The music, and the banquet, and the wine —
The garlands, the rose odors, and the flow-
     ers —
The sparkling eyes, and flashing ornaments —
The white arms and the raven hair — the
     braids
And bracelets; swanlike bosoms, and the
     necklace,
An India in itself, yet dazzling not
The eye like what it circled ; the thin robes,
Floating like light clouds 'twixt our gaze and
     heaven ;
The many-twinkling feet so small and sylph-
     like,
Suggesting the more secret symmetry
Of the fair forms which terminate so well —
All the delusion of the dizzy scene,
Its false and true enchantments — art and
     nature,
Which swam before my giddy eyes, that drank
The sight of beauty as the parched pilgrim's
On Arab sands the false mirage, which offers
A lucid lake to his eluded thirst,
Are gone. Around me are the stars and
     waters —

Worlds mirrored in the ocean, goodlier sight
Than torches glared back by a gaudy glass ;
And the great element, which is to space
What ocean is to earth, spreads its blue depths,
Softened with the first breathings of the
     spring ;
The high moon sails upon her beauteous way,
Serenely smoothing o'er the lofty walls
Of those tall piles and sea-girt palaces,
Whose porphyry pillars, and whose costly
     fronts,
Fraught with the orient spoil of many marbles,
Like altars ranged along the broad canal,
Seem each a trophy of some mighty deed
Reared up from out the waters, scarce less ·
     strangely
Than those more massy and mysterious giants
Of architecture, those Titanian fabrics,
Which point in Egypt's plains to times that
     have
No other record. All is gentle : nought
Stirs rudely ; but, congenial with the night,
Whatever walks is gliding like a spirit.
The tinklings of some vigilant guitars
Of sleepless lovers to a wakeful mistress,
And cautious opening of the casement, show-
     ing
That he is not unheard ; while her young
     hand,
Fair as the moonlight of which it seems part,
So delicately white, it trembles in
The act of opening the forbidden lattice,
To let in love through music, makes his heart
Thrill like his lyre-strings at the sight ; the dash
Phosphoric of the oar, or rapid twinkle
Of the far lights of skimming gondolas,
And the responsive voices of the choir
Of boatmen answering back with verse for
     verse ;
Some dusky shadow checkering the Rialto ;
Some glimmering palace roof, or tapering
     spire,
Are all the sights and sounds which here per-
     vade
The ocean-born and earth-commanding city —
How sweet and soothing is this hour of calm !
I thank thee, Night ! for thou hast chased
     away
Those horrid bodements which, amidst the
     throng,
I could not dissipate : and with the blessing
Of thy benign and quiet influence, —
Now will I to my couch, although to rest
Is almost wronging such a night as this ——
     [*A knocking is heard from without.*
Hark ! what is that ? or who at such a mo-
     ment ?

Enter ANTONIO.

Ant. My lord, a man without, on urgent
     business,
Implores to be admitted.

Lioni.   Is he a stranger?
Ant. His face is muffled in his cloak, but
    both   ·
    .tis voice and gestures seem familiar to me;
    I craved his name, but this he seemed reluc-
    tant
To trust, save to yourself; most earnestly
He sues to be permitted to approach you.
Lioni. 'Tis a strange hour, and a sus-
    picious bearing!
And yet there is slight peril: 'tis not in
Their houses noble men are struck at; still,
Although I know not that I have a foe
In Venice, 'twill be wise to use some caution.
Admit him, and retire; but call up quickly
Some of thy fellows, who may wait without. —
Who can this man be? —
    [*Exit* ANTONIO, *and returns with* BER-
    TRAM *muffled.*
Ber.   My good lord Lioni,
I have no time to lose, nor thou — dismiss
This menial hence; I would be private with
    you.
Lioni. It seems the voice of Bertram —
    Go, Antonio.   [*Exit* ANTONIO.
Now, stranger, what would you at such an
    hour?
Ber. (*discovering himself*). A boon, my
    noble patron; you have granted
Many to your poor client, Bertram; add
This one, and make him happy.
Lioni.   Thou hast known me
From boyhood, ever ready to assist thee
In all fair objects of advancement, which
Beseem one of thy station; I would promise
Ere thy request was heard, but that the hour,
Thy bearing, and this strange and hurried
    mode
Of suing, gives me to suspect this visit
Hath some mysterious import — but say on —
What has occurred, some rash and sudden
    broil? —
A cup too much, a scuffle, and a stab? —
Mere things of every day; so that thou hast not
Spilt noble blood, I guarantee thy safety;
But then thou must withdraw, for angry friends
And relatives, in the first burst of vengeance,
Are things in Venice deadlier than the laws.
Ber. My lord, I thank you; but —
Lioni.   But what? You have not
Raised a rash hand against one of our order?
If so, withdraw and fly, and own it not;
I would not slay — but then I must not save
    thee!
He who has shed patrician blood —
Ber.   I come
To save patrician blood, and not to shed it!
And thereunto I must be speedy, for
Each minute lost may lose a life; since Time
Has changed his slow scythe for the two-
    edged sword,
And is about to take, instead of sand,

The dust from sepulchres to fill his hour-
    glass! —
Go not *thou* forth to-morrow!
Lioni.   Wherefore not? —
What means this menace?
Ber.   Do not seek its meaning,
But do as I implore thee; — stir not forth,
Whate'er be stirring; though the roar of
    crowds —
The cry of women, and the shrieks of babes —
The groans of men — the clash of arms —
    the sound
Of rolling drum, shrill trump, and hollow bell,
Peal in one wide alarum! — Go not forth
Until the tocsin's silent, nor even then
Till I return!
Lioni.   Again, what does this mean?
Ber. Again, I tell thee, ask not; but by all
Thou holdest dear on earth or heaven — by all
The souls of thy great fathers, and thy hope
To emulate them, and to leave behind
Descendants worthy both of them and thee —
By all thou hast of blessed in hope or mem-
    ory —
By all thou hast to fear here or hereafter —
By all the good deeds thou hast done to me,
Good I would now repay with greater good,
Remain within — trust to thy household gods,
And to my word for safety, if thou dost
As I now counsel — but if not, thou art lost!
Lioni. I am indeed already lost in wonder;
Surely thou ravest! what have *I* to dread?
Who are my foes? or if there be such, *why*
Art *thou* leagued with them? — *thou!* or if so
    leagued,
Why comest thou to tell me at this hour,
And not before?
Ber.   I cannot answer this.
Wilt thou go forth despite of this true warning?
Lioni. I was not born to shrink from idle
    threats,
The cause of which I know not: at the hour
Of council, be it soon or late, I shall not
Be found among the absent.
Ber.   Say not so!
Once more, art thou determined to go forth?
Lioni. I am. Nor is there aught which
    shall impede me!
Ber. Then Heaven have mercy on thy
    soul! — Farewell!   [*Going.*
Lioni. Stay — there is more in this than
    my own safety
Which makes me call thee back; we must
    not part thus:
Bertram I have known thee long.
Ber.   From childhood, signor,
You have been my protector: in the days
Of reckless infancy, when rank forgets,
Or, rather, is not yet taught to remember
Its cold prerogative, we played together;
Our sports, our smiles, our tears, were min-
    gled oft;

My father was your father's client, I
His son's scarce less than foster-brother; years
Saw us together — happy, heart-full hours!
Oh God! the difference 'twixt those hours and
   this!
Lioni. Bertram, 'tis thou who hast forgot-
ten them.
!er. Nor now, nor ever; whatsoe'er be-
   tide,
would have saved you: when to manhood's
   growth
we sprung, and you, devoted to the state,
As suits your station, the more humble Ber-
   tram
Was left unto the labors of the humble,
Still you forsook me not; and if my fortunes
Have not been towering, 'twas no fault of him
Who ofttimes rescued and supported me
When struggling with the tides of circum-
   stance
Which bear away the weaker: noble blood
Ne'er mantled in a nobler heart than thine
Has proved to me, the poor plebeian Bertram.
Would that thy fellow senators were like thee!
Lioni. Why, what hast thou to say against
   the senate?
Ber. Nothing.
Lioni. I know that there are angry spirits
And turbulent mutterers of stifled treason,
Who lurk in narrow places, and walk out
Muffled to whisper curses to the night;
Disbanded soldiers, discontented ruffians,
And desperate libertines who brawl in taverns;
Thou herdest not with such: 'tis true, of late,
I have lost sight of thee, but thou wert wont
To lead a temperate life, and break thy bread
With honest mates, and bear a cheerful aspect.
What hath come to thee? in thy hollow eye
And hueless cheek, and thine unquiet motions,
Sorrow and shame and conscience seem at
   war
To waste thee.
Ber. Rather shame and sorrow light
On the accursed tyranny which rides[1]
The very air in Venice, and makes men
Madden as in the last hours of the plague
Which sweeps the soul deliriously from life!
Lioni. Some villains have been tampering
   with thee, Bertram;
This is not thy old language, nor own thoughts;
Some wretch has made thee drunk with dis-
affection,
But thou must not be lost so; thou *wert* good
And kind, and art not fit for such base acts
As vice and villany would put thee to:
Confess — confide in me — thou know'st my
   nature —
What is it thou and thine are bound to do,
Which should prevent thy friend, the only son

---

[1] [MS. —
   " On the accursed tyranny which taints."]

Of him who was a friend unto thy father,
So that our good-will is a heritage
We should bequeathe to our posterity
Such as ourselves received it, or augmented;
I say, what is it thou must do, that I
Should deem thee dangerous, and keep the
   house
Like a sick girl?
Ber. Nay, question me no further:
I must be gone. ——
Lioni. And I be murdered! — say,
Was it not thus thou said'st, my gentle Ber-
   tram?
Ber. Who talks of murder? what said I
   of murder? —
'Tis false! I did not utter such a word.
Lioni. Thou didst not; but from out thy
   wolfish eye,
So changed from what I knew it, there glares
   forth
The gladiator. If *my* life's thine object,
Take it — I am unarmed, — and then away!
I would not hold my breath on such a tenure
As the capricious mercy of such things
As thou and those who have set thee to thy
   task-work.
Ber. Sooner than spill thy blood, I peril
   mine;
Sooner than harm a hair of thine, I place
In jeopardy a thousand heads, and some
As noble, nay, even nobler than thine own.
Lioni. Ay, is it even so? Excuse me,
   Bertram;
I am not worthy to be singled out
From such exalted hecatombs — who are they
That *are* in danger, and that *make* the dan-
   ger?
Ber. Venice, and all that she inherits, are
Divided like a house against itself,
And so will perish ere to-morrow's twilight!
Lioni. More mysteries, and awful ones!
   But now
Or thou, or I, or both, it may be, are
Upon the verge of ruin; speak once out,
And thou art safe and glorious; for 'tis more
Glorious to save than slay, and slay i' the dark
   too —
Fie, Bertram! that was not a craft for thee!
How would it look to see upon a spear
The head of him whose heart was open to
   thee,
Borne by thy hand before the shuddering
   people?
And such may be my doom; for here I swear,
Whate'er the peril or the penalty
Of thy denunciation, I go forth,
Unless thou dost detail the cause, and show
The consequence of all which led thee here!
Ber. Is there no way to save thee? min-
   utes fly,
And thou art lost! — *thou!* my sole benefactor,
The only being who was constant to me

Through every change. Yet, make me not a
    traitor!
Let me save thee—but spare my honor!
    Lioni.   Where
Can lie the honor in a league of murder?
And who are traitors save unto the state?
    Ber. A league is still a compact, and more
        binding
In honest hearts when words must stand for
        law;
And in my mind, there is no traitor like
He whose domestic treason plants the poniard
Within the breast which trusted to his truth.
    Lioni. And *who* will strike the steel to
        mine?
    Ber.   Not I;
I could have wound my soul up to all things
Save this. *Thou* must not die! and think
        how dear
Thy life is, when I risk so many lives,
Nay, more, the life of lives, the liberty
Of future generations, *not* to be
The assassin thou miscall'st me;—once,
        once more
I do adjure thee, pass not o'er thy threshold!
    Lioni. It is in vain—this moment I go
        forth.
    Ber. Then perish Venice rather than my
        friend!
I will disclose—ensnare—betray—destroy—
Oh, what a villain I become for thee!
    Lioni. Say, rather thy friend's savior and
        the state's!—
Speak—pause not—all rewards, all pledges
        for
Thy safety and thy welfare; wealth such as
The state accords her worthiest servants; nay,
Nobility itself I guarantee thee,
So that thou art sincere and penitent.
    Ber. I have thought again: it must not be
        —I love thee—
Thou knowest it—that I stand here is the
        proof,
Not least though last; but having done my
        duty
By thee, I now must do it by my country!
Farewell—we meet no more in life!—fare-
        well!
    Lioni. What, ho!—Antonio—Pedro—
        to the door!
See that none pass—arrest this man!——

Enter ANTONIO *and other armed Domestics,*
        who seize BERTRAM.

    Lioni (continues).   Take care
He hath no harm; bring me my sword and
        cloak,
And man the gondola with four oars—
        quick—   [*Exit* ANTONIO.
We will unto Giovanni Gradenigo's,
And send for Marc Cornaro:—fear not, Ber-
        tram;

This needful violence is for thy safety,
No less than for the general weal.
    Ber.   Where wouldst thou
Bear me a prisoner?
    Lioni.   Firstly to "the Ten;"
Next to the Doge.
    Ber.   To the Doge?
    Lioni.   Assuredly:
Is he not chief of the state?
    Ber.   Perhaps at sunrise—
    Lioni. What mean you?—but we'll know
        anon.
    Ber.   Art sure?
    Lioni. Sure as all gentle means can make;
        and if
They fail, you know "the Ten" and their
        tribunal,
And that St. Mark's has dungeons, and the
        dungeons
A rack.
    Ber. Apply it then before the dawn
Now hastening into heaven.—One more such
        word
And you shall perish piecemeal, by the death
You think to doom to me.

            Reënter ANTONIO.

    Ant.   The bark is ready,
My lord, and all prepared.
    Lioni.   Look to the prisoner.
Bertram, I'll reason with thee as we go
To the Magnifico's, sage Gradenigo. [*Exeunt.*

SCENE II.—*The Ducal Palace.—The*
        Doge's Apartment.

    The DOGE *and his nephew* BERTUCCIO
        FALIERO.

    Doge. Are all the people of our house in
        muster?
    Ber. F. They are arrayed, and eager for
        the signal,
Within our palace precincts at San Polo.[1]
I come for your last orders.
    Doge.   It had been
As well had there been time to have got to-
        gether,
From my own fief, Val di Marino, more
Of our retainers—but it is too late.
    Ber. F. Methinks, my lord, 'tis better as it
        is:
A sudden swelling of our retinue
Had waked suspicion; and, though fierce
        and trusty,
The vassals of that district are too rude
And quick in quarrel to have long maintained
The secret discipline we need for such
A service, till our foes are dealt upon.
    Doge. True; but when once the signal has
        been given,
These are the men for such an enterprise;

────────────────
[1] The Doge's family palace.

These city slaves have all their private bias,
Their prejudice *against* or *for* this noble,
Which may induce them to o'erdo or spare
Where mercy may be madness; the fierce
　　peasants,
Serfs of my county of Val di Marino,
Would do the bidding of their lord without
Distinguishing for love or hate his foes;
Alike to them Marcello or Cornaro,
A Gradenigo or a Foscari;
They are not used to start at those vain names,
Nor bow the knee before a civic senate;
A chief in armor is their Suzerain,
And not a thing in robes.
Ber. F.　　　　　　　We are enough;
And for the dispositions of our clients
Against the senate I will answer.
　　Doge.　　　　　　　　Well,
The die is thrown; but for a warlike service,
Done in the field, commend me to my peas-
　　ants:
They made the sun shine through the host of
　　Huns
When sallow burghers slunk back to their
　　tents,
And cowered to hear their own victorious
　　trumpet.
If there be small resistance, you will find
These citizens all lions, like their standard;
But if there's much to do, you'll wish with me,
A band of iron rustics at our backs.
　　Ber. F.　Thus thinking, I must marvel you
　　resolve
To strike the blow so suddenly.
　　Doge.　　　　　　　Such blows
Must be struck suddenly or never.　When
I had o'ermastered the weak false remorse
Which yearned about my heart, too fondly
　　yielding
A moment to the feelings of old days,
I was most fain to strike; and, firstly, that
I might not yield again to such emotions;
And, secondly, because of all these men,
Save Israel and Philip Calendaro,
I know not well the courage or the faith:
To-day might find 'mongst them a traitor to
　　us,
As yesterday a thousand to the senate;
But once in, with their hilts hot in their hands,
They must *on* for their own sakes; one stroke
　　struck,
And the mere instinct of the first-born Cain,
Which ever lurks somewhere in human
　　hearts,
Though circumstance may keep it in abey-
　　ance,
Will urge the rest on like to wolves; the sight
Of blood to crowds begets the thirst of more,
As the first wine-cup leads to the long revel;
And you will find a harder task to quell
Than urge them when they *have* commenced,
　　but *till*

That moment, a mere voice, a straw, a
　　shadow,
Are capable of turning them aside. —
How goes the night?
　　Ber. F.　　　　　Almost upon the dawn.
　　Doge.　Then it is time to strike upon the
　　bell.
Are the men posted?
　　Ber. F.　　　　　By this time they are,
But they have orders not to strike, until
They have command from you through me in
　　person.
　　Doge.　'Tis well. — Will the morn never
　　put to rest
These stars which twinkle yet o'er all the
　　heavens?
I am settled and bound up, and being so,
The very effort which it cost me to
Resolve to cleanse this commonwealth with
　　fire,
Now leaves my mind more steady.　I have
　　wept,
And trembled at the thought of this dread
　　duty; .
But now I have put down all idle passion,
And look the growing tempest in the face,
As doth the pilot of an admiral galley:
Yet (wouldst thou think it, kinsman?) it hath
　　been
A greater struggle to me, than when nations
Beheld their fate merged in the approaching
　　fight,
Where I was leader of a phalanx, where
Thousands were sure to perish — Yes, to
　　spill
The rank polluted current from the veins
Of a few bloated despots needed more
To steel me to a purpose such as made
Timoleon immortal, than to face
The toils and dangers of a life of war.
　　Ber. F.　It gladdens me to see your former
　　wisdom
Subdue the furies which so wrung you ere
You were decided.
　　Doge.　　　　It was ever thus
With me; the hour of agitation came
In the first glimmerings of a purpose, when
Passion had too much room to sway; but in
The hour of action I have stood as calm
As were the dead who lay around me: this
They knew who made me what I am, and
　　trusted
To the subduing power which I preserved
Over my mood, when its first burst was spent.
But they were not aware that there are things
Which make revenge a virtue by reflection,
And not an impulse of mere anger; though
The laws sleep, justice wakes, and injured
　　souls
Oft do a public right with private wrong,
And justify their deeds unto themselves. —
Methinks the day breaks — is it not so? look

Thine eyes are clear with youth; — the air
 puts on
A morning freshness, and, at least to me,
The sea looks grayer through the lattice.
 Ber. F.   True,
The morn is dappling in the sky.[1]
 Doge.   Away then!
See that they strike without delay, and with
The first toll from Saint Mark's, march on the
 palace
With all our house's strength; here I will
 meet you —
The Sixteen and their companies will move
In separate columns at the self-same moment—
Be sure you post yourself at the great gate:
I would not trust "the Ten" except to us —
The rest, the rabble of patricians, may
Glut the more careless swords of those leagued
 with us.
Remember that the cry is still "Saint Mark!
The Genoese are come — ho! to the rescue!
Saint Mark and Liberty!"— Now — now to
 action!
 Ber. F. Farewell then, noble uncle! we
 will meet
In freedom and true sovereignty, or never!
 Doge. Come hither, my Bertuccio — one
 embrace —
Speed, for the day grows broader — Send me
 soon
A messenger to tell me how all goes
When you rejoin our troops, and then sound
 — sound
The storm-bell from Saint Mark's!
           [*Exit* BERTUCCIO FALIERO.
 Doge (*solus*).   He is gone,[2]
And on each footstep moves a life,—'Tis done.
Now the destroying angel hovers o'er
Venice, and pauses ere he pours the vial,
Even as the eagle overlooks his prey,
And for a moment, poised in middle air,
Suspends the motion of his mighty wings,
Then swoops with his unerring beak. — Thou
 day!
That slowly walk'st the waters! march —
 march on —
I would not smite i' the dark, but rather see
That no stroke errs. And you, ye blue sea-
 waves!
I have seen you dyed ere now, and deeply too,
With Genoese, Saracen, and Hunnish gore,
While that of Venice flowed too, but victorious;

Now thou must wear an unmixed crimson; no
Barbaric blood can reconcile us now
Unto that horrible incarnadine,
But friend or foe will roll in civic slaughter.
And have I lived to fourscore years for this?
I, who was named Preserver of the City?
I, at whose name the million's caps were flung
Into the air, and cries from tens of thousands
Rose up, imploring Heaven to send me bless-
 ings,
And fame, and length of days — to see this
 day?
But this day, black within the calendar,
Shall be succeeded by a bright millennium.
Doge Dandolo survived to ninety summers
To vanquish empires, and refuse their crown;
I will resign a crown, and make the state
Renew its freedom — but oh! by what means?
The noble end must justify them — What
Are a few drops of human blood? 'tis false,
The blood of tyrants is not human; they,
Like to incarnate Molochs, feed on ours,
Until 'tis time to give them to the tombs
Which they have made so populous. — Oh
 world!
Oh men! what are ye, and our best designs,
That we must work by crime to punish crime?
And slay as if Death had but this one gate,
When a few years would make the sword su-
 perfluous?
And I, upon the verge of th' unknown realm,
Yet send so many heralds on before me? —
I must not ponder this.   [*A pause.*
                   Hark! was there not
A murmur as of distant voices, and
The tramp of feet in martial unison?
What phantoms even of sound our wishes
 raise!
It cannot be — the signal hath not rung —
Why pauses it? My nephew's messenger
Should be upon his way to me, and he
Himself perhaps even now draws grating back
Upon its ponderous hinge the steep tower
 portal,
Where swings the sullen huge oracular bell,[3]
Which never knells but for a princely death,
Or for a state in peril, pealing forth
Tremendous bodements; let it do its office
And be this peal its awfullest and last
Sound till the strong tower rock! — What!
 silent still?
I would go forth, but that my post is here,
To be the centre of re-union to
The oft discordant elements which form
Leagues of this nature, and to keep compact
The wavering of the weak, in case of conflict;
For if they should do battle, 'twill be here,
Within the palace, that the strife will thicken:

---

[1] [MS. — "The night is clearing from the sky."]

[2] [At last the moment arrives when the bell is to
be sounded, and the whole of the conspiring bands
are watching in impatience for the signal. The
nephew of the Doge, and the heir of his house (for
he is childless), leaves Faliero in his palace, and
goes to strike with his own hand the fatal summons.
The Doge is left alone: and English poetry, we
think, contains few passages superior to that which
follows. — *Lockhart.*]

[3] [MS. —
 "Where swings the sullen { iron oracle.
                          { huge oracular bell."]

Then here must be my station, as becomes
The master-mover.—— Hark! he comes—he
comes,
My nephew, brave Bertuccio's messenger.—
What tidings? Is he marching? hath he
sped?—
They here!—all's lost—yet will I make an
effort.[1]

Enter a SIGNOR OF THE NIGHT,[2] *with
Guards, etc. etc.*

Sig.   Doge, I arrest thee of high treason!
Doge.   Me!
Thy prince, of treason?—Who are they that
dare
Cloak their own treason under such an order?
Sig. (*showing his order*). Behold my order
from the assembled Ten.
Doge. And *where* are they, and *why* assem-
bled? no
Such council can be lawful, till the prince
Preside there, and that duty's mine: on thine
I charge thee, give me way, or marshal me
To the council chamber.
Sig.   Duke! it may not be:
Nor are they in the wonted Hall of Council,
But sitting in the convent of Saint Saviour's.
Doge. You dare to disobey me, then?
Sig.   I serve
The state, and needs must serve it faithfully;
My warrant is the will of those who rule it.
Doge. And till that warrant has my signa-
ture
It is illegal, and, as *now* applied,
Rebellious—Hast thou weighed well thy life's
worth,
That thus you dare assume a lawless function?
Sig. 'Tis not my office to reply, but act—
I am placed here as guard upon thy person,
And not as judge to hear or to decide.
Doge (*aside*). I must gain time—So that
the storm-bell sound
All may be well yet.—Kinsman, speed—
speed—speed!—
Our fate is trembling in the balance, and
Woe to the vanquished! be they prince and
people,
Or slaves and senate—
            [*The great bell of Saint Mark's tolls.*
            Lo! it sounds—it tolls!
Dog (*aloud*). Hark, Signor of the Night!
and you, ye hirelings,
Who wield your mercenary staves in fear,

It is your knell—Swell on, thou lusty peal!
Now, knaves, what ransom for your lives?
Sig.   Confusion
Stand to your arms, and guard the door—
all's lost
Unless that fearful bell be silenced soon.
The officer hath missed his path or purpose,
Or met some unforeseen and hideous obstacle.
Anselmo, with thy company proceed
Straight to the tower; the rest remain with me.
                        [*Exit part of the Guard.*
Doge. Wretch! if thou wouldst have thy
vile life, implore it;
It is not now a lease of sixty seconds.
Ay, send thy miserable ruffians forth;
They never shall return.
Sig.   So let it be!
They die then in their duty, as wiff I.
Doge. Fool! the high eagle flies at nobler
game
Than thou and thy base myrmidons,—live on,
So thou provok'st not peril by resistance,
And learn (if souls so much obscured can
bear
To gaze upon the sunbeams) to be free.
Sig. And learn thou to be captive—It hath
ceased,   [*The bell ceases to toll.*
The traitorous signal, which was to have set
The bloodhound mob on their patrician prey—
The knell hath rung, but it is not the senate's!
Doge (*after a pause*). All's silent, and all's
lost!
Sig.   Now, Doge, denounce me
As rebel slave of a revolted council!
Have I not done my duty?
Doge.   Peace, thou thing!
Thou hast done a worthy deed, and earned
the price
Of blood, and they who use thee will reward
thee.   ..
But thou wert sent to watch, and not to prate,
As thou said'st even now—then do thine
office,
But let it be in silence, as behooves thee,
Since, though thy prisoner, I am thy prince.
Sig. I did not mean to fail in the respect
Due to your rank: in this I shall obey you.
Doge (*aside*). There now is nothing left
me save to die;
And yet how near success! I would have
fallen,
And proudly, in the hour of triumph, but
To miss it thus!——

Enter other SIGNORS OF THE NIGHT, *with*
BERTUCCIO FALIERO *prisoner.*

2d Sig.   We took him in the act
Of issuing from the tower, where, at his order,
As delegated from the Doge, the signal
Had thus begun to sound.
1st Sig.   Are all the passes
Which lead up to the palace well secured?

---

[1] [A relenting conspirator, whom the contem-
plative Lioni had formerly befriended, calls to warn
him of his danger; and is gradually led to betray
his associates. The plot is crushed in the moment
of its development, and the Doge arrested in his
palace. The scene immediately preceding this
catastrophe is noble and thrilling.—*Jeffrey.*]
[2] [" I Signori di Notte " held an important charge
in the old republic.]

2d Sig. They are — besides, it matters not;
the chiefs
Are all in chains, and some even now on
trial —
Their followers are dispersed, and many taken.
Ber. F. Uncle!
Doge.   It is in vain to war with Fortune;
The glory hath departed from our house.
Ber. F. Who would have deemed it? —
Ah! one moment sooner!
Doge. That moment would have changed
the face of ages;
This gives us to eternity — We'll meet it
As men whose triumph is not in success,
But who can make their own minds all in all,
Equal to every fortune. Droop not, 'tis
But a brief passage — I would go alone,
Yet if they send us, as 'tis like, together,
Let us go worthy of our sires and selves.
Ber F. I shall not shame you, uncle.
1st Sig.   Lords, our orders
Are to keep guard on both in separate cham-
bers,
Until the council call ye to your trial.
Doge. Our trial! will they keep their
mockery up
Even to the last? but let them deal upon us,
As we had dealt on them, but with less pomp.
'Tis but a game of mutual homicides,
Who have cast lots for the first death, and they
Have won with false dice. — Who hath been
our Judas?
1st Sig. I am not warranted to answer that.
Ber. F. I'll answer for thee — 'tis a certain
Bertram,
Even now deposing to the secret giunta.
Doge. Bertram, the Bergamask! With
what vile tools
We operate to slay or save! This creature,
Black with a double treason, now will earn
Rewards and honors, and be stamped in story
With the geese in the Capitol, which gabbled
Till Rome awoke, and had an annual triumph,
While Manlius, who hurled down the Gauls,
was cast [1]
From the Tarpeian.
1st Sig.   He aspired to treason,
And sought to rule the state.
Doge.   He saved the state,
And sought but to reform what he revived —
But this is idle —— Come, sirs, do your work.
1st Sig. Noble Bertuccio, we must now
remove you
Into an inner chamber.
Ber. F.   Farewell, uncle!
If we shall meet again in life I know not,
But they perhaps will let our ashes mingle.
Doge. Yes, and our spirits, which shall yet
go forth,

[1] [MS.—

"While Manlius, who hurled back the Gauls," etc.]

And do what our frail clay, thus clogged, hath
failed in!
They cannot quench the memory of those
Who would have hurled them from their
guilty thrones,
And such examples will find heirs, though
distant.

·ACT V.

SCENE I.— *The Hall of the Council of Ten
assembled with the additional Senators, who,
on the Trials of the Conspirators for the Trea-
son of* MARINO FALIERO, *composed what
was called the Giunta, — Guards, Officers,
etc. etc.—*ISRAEL BERTUCCIO *and* PHILIP
CALENDARO *as prisoners.—*BERTRAM,
LIONI, *and Witnesses, etc.*[2]

The Chief of the Ten, BENINTENDE.[3]

Ben. There now rests, after such conviction
of
Their manifold and manifest offences,
But to pronounce on these obdurate men
The sentence of the law : — a grievous task
To those who hear, and those who speak.
Alas!
That it should fall to me! and that my days
Of office should be stigmatized through all
The years of coming time, as bearing record
To this most foul and complicated treason
Against a just and free state, known to all
The earth as being the Christian bulwark
'gainst
The Saracen and the schismatic Greek,
The savage Hun, and not less barbarous
Frank;
A city which has opened India's wealth
To Europe; the last Roman refuge from
O'erwhelming Attila; the ocean's queen;
Proud Genoa's prouder rival! 'Tis to sap
The throne of such a city, these lost men
Have risk'd and forfeited their worthless
lives —
So let them die the death.
I. Ber.   We are prepared;
Your racks have done that for us. Let us die.
Ben. If ye have that to say which would
obtain
Abatement of your punishment, the Giunta
Will hear you; if you have aught to confess,
Now is your time, perhaps it may avail ye.

[2] [The fifth Act, which begins with the arraign-
ment of the original conspirators, is much in the
style of that of Pierre and his associates in the old
play. After them, the Doge is brought in : his
part is very forcibly written throughout. — *Jef-
frey.*]
[3] [" In the notes to Marino Faliero, it may be as
well to say, that Benintende was not really of the
Ten, but merely Grand Chancellor—a separate
office, though an important one. It was an arbi-
trary alteration of mine." — *Byron's Letters.*]

Ber. F. We stand to hear, and not to speak.
Ben.   Your crimes
Are fully proved by your accomplices,
And all which circumstance can add to aid
    them;
Yet we would hear from your own lips com-
    plete
Avowal of your treason: on the verge
Of that dread gulf which none repass, the truth
Alone can profit you on earth or heaven —
Say, then, what was your motive?
    I. Ber.   Justice!
    Ben.   What
Your object?
    I. Ber.   Freedom!
    Ben.   You are brief, sir.
    I. Ber. So my life grows: I
Was bred a soldier, not a senator.
    Ben. Perhaps you think by this blunt
        brevity
To brave your judges to postpone the sen-
    tence?
    I. Ber. Do you be brief as I am, and be-
        lieve me,
I shall prefer that mercy to your pardon.
    Ben. Is this your sole reply to the tribunal?
    I. Ber. Go, ask your racks what they have
        wrung from us,
Or place us there again; we have still some
    blood left,
And some slight sense of pain in these
    wrenched limbs:
But this ye dare not do; for if we die there —
And you have left us little life to spend
Upon your engines, gorged with pangs
    already —
Ye lose the public spectacle, with which
You would appall your slaves to further slav-
    ery!
Groans are not words, nor agony assent,
Nor affirmation truth, if nature's sense
Should overcome the soul into a lie,
For a short respite — must we bear or die?
    Ben. Say, who were your accomplices?
    I. Ber.   The Senate!
    Ben. What do you mean?
    I. Ber.   Ask of the suffering people,
Whom your patrician crimes have driven to
    crime.
    Ben. You know the Doge?
    I. Ber.   I served with him at Zara
In the field, when *you* were pleading here your
    way
To present office; we exposed our lives,
While you but hazarded the lives of others,
Alike by accusation or defence;
And, for the rest, all Venice knows her
    Doge,
Through his great actions, and the Senate's
    insults.
    Ben. You have held conference with him?
    I. Ber.   I am weary —

Even wearier of your questions than your
    tortures.
I pray you pass to judgment.
    Ben.   It is coming. —
And you, too, Philip Calendaro, what
Have you to say why you should not be
    doomed?
    Cal. I never was a man of many words,
And now have few left worth the utterance.
    Ben. A further application of yon engine
May change your tone.
    Cal.   Most true, it *will* do so;
A former application did so; but
It will not change my words, or, if it did —
    Ben. What then?
    Cal.   Will my avowal on yon rack
Stand good in law?
    Ben.   Assuredly.
    Cal.   Whoe'er
The culprit be whom I accuse of treason?
    Ben. Without doubt, he will be brought
        up to trial.
    Cal. And on this testimony would he per-
        ish?
    Ben. So your confession be detailed and
        full,
He will stand here in peril of his life.
    Cal. Then look well to thy proud self,
        President!
For by the eternity which yawns before me,
I swear that *thou*, and only thou, shalt be
The traitor I denounce upon that rack,
If I be stretched there for the second time.
    One of the Giunta. Lord President, 'twere
        best proceed to judgment;
There is no more to be drawn from these
    men.
    Ben. Unhappy men! prepare for instant
        death.
The nature of your crime — our law — and
    peril
The state now stands in, leave not an hour's
    respite —
Guards! lead them forth, and upon the bal-
    cony
Of the red columns, where, on festal Thurs-
    day,[1]
The Doge stands to behold the chase of bulls,
Let them be justified: and leave exposed
Their wavering relics, in the place of judg-
    ment,
To the full view of the assembled people! —
And Heaven have mercy on their souls!
    The Giunta.   Amen!
    I. Ber. Signors, farewell! we shall not all
        again
Meet in one place.
    Ben.   And lest they should essay
To stir up the distracted multitude —

---

[1] "Giovedì grasso," — "fat or greasy Thurs-
day," — which I cannot literally translate in the
text, was the day.

Guards! let their mouths be gagged [1] even in
the act
Of execution.—Lead them hence!
  Cal.   What! must we
Not even say farewell to some fond friend,
Nor leave a last word with our confessor?
  Ben. A priest is waiting in the antechamber;
But, for your friends, such interviews would be
Painful to them, and useless all to you.
  Cal. I knew that we were gagged in life;
at least
All those who had not heart to risk their
lives
Upon their open thoughts; but still I deemed
That in the last few moments, the same idle
Freedom of speech accorded to the dying,
Would not now be denied to us; but since——
  I. Ber. Even let them have their way,
brave Calendaro!
What matter a few syllables? let's die
Without the slightest show of favor from
them;
So shall our blood more readily arise
To heaven against them, and more testify
To their atrocities, than could a volume
Spoken or written of our dying words!
They tremble at our voices—nay, they dread
Our very silence—let them live in fear!—
Leave them unto their thoughts, and let us
now
Address our own above!—Lead on; we are
ready.
  Cal. Israel, hadst thou but hearkened unto
me
It had not now been thus; and yon pale villain,
The coward Bertram, would——
  I. Ber.   Peace, Calendaro.
What brooks it now to ponder upon this?
  Bert. Alas! I fain you died in peace with
me:
I did not seek this task; 'twas forced upon
me:
Say, you forgive me, though I never can
Retrieve my own forgiveness—frown not
thus!
  I. Ber. I die and pardon thee!
  Cal. (spitting at him).[2] I die and scorn
thee!

[*Exeunt* ISRAEL BERTUCCIO *and* PHILIP
CALENDARO, *Guards, etc.*

  Ben. Now that these criminals have been
disposed of,
'Tis time that we proceed to pass our sentence
Upon the greatest traitor upon record

In any annals, the Doge Faliero!
The proofs and process are complete; the
time
And crime require a quick procedure: shall
He now be called in to receive the award?
  The Giunta. Ay, ay.
  Ben. Avogadori, order that the Doge
Be brought before the council.
  One of the Giunta.   And the rest,
When shall they be brought up?
  Ben.   When all the chiefs
Have been disposed of. Some have fled to
Chiozza;
But there are thousands in pursuit of them,
And such precaution ta'en on terra firma,
As well as in the islands, that we hope
None will escape to utter in strange lands
His libellous tale of treasons 'gainst the sen-
ate.

Enter the DOGE *as Prisoner, with Guards,
etc. etc.*

  Ben. Doge—for such still you are, and
by the law
Must be considered, till the hour shall come
When you must doff the ducal bonnet from
That head, which could not wear a crown
more noble
Than empires can confer, in quiet honor,
But it must plot to overthrow your peers,
Who made you what you are, and quench in
blood
A city's glory—we have laid already
Before you in your chamber at full length,
By the Avogadori, all the proofs
Which have appeared against you; and more
ample
Ne'er reared their sanguinary shadows to
Confront a traitor. What have you to say
In your defence?
  Doge.   What shall I say to ye,
Since my defence must be your condemna-
tion?
You are at once offenders and accusers,
Judges and executioners!—Proceed
Upon your power.
  Ben.   Your chief accomplices
Having confessed, there is no hope for you.
  Doge. And who be they?
  Ben.   In number many; but
The first now stands before you in the court,
Bertram, of Bergamo,—would you question
him?
  Doge (looking at him contemptuously). No.
  Ben.   And two others, Israel Bertuccio,

---

[1] Historical fact.
[2] ["I know what Foscolo means, about Calen-
daro's *spitting* at Bertram; *that's* national—the
objection, I mean. The Italians and French, with
those 'flags of abomination' their pocket handker-
chiefs, spit there, and here, and everywhere else—
in your face almost, and therefore *object* to it on

the stage as *too familiar.* But we who spit no-
where—but in a man's face when we grow savage
—are not likely to feel this. Remember Mas-
singer, and Kean's Sir Giles Overreach—
'Lord! *thus* I *spit* at thee and at thy counsel!'"
                                   Byron's Letters.]

And Philip Calendaro, have admitted
Their fellowship in treason with the Doge!
Doge.   And where are they?
Ben.   Gone to their place, and now
Answering to Heaven for what they did on
   earth.
Doge. Ah! the plebeian Brutus, is he gone?
And the quick Cassius of the arsenal? —
How did they meet their doom?
Ben.   Think of your own:
It is approaching. You decline to plead, then?
Doge. I cannot plead to my inferiors, nor
Can recognize your legal power to try me.
Show me the law!
Ben.   On great emergencies,
The law must be remodelled or amended:
Our fathers had not fixed the punishment
Of such a crime, as on the old Roman tables
The sentence against parricide was left
In pure forgetfulness; they could not render
That penal, which had neither name nor
   thought
In their great bosoms: who would have fore-
   seen
That nature could be filed to such a crime
As sons 'gainst sires, and princes 'gainst their
   realms?
Your sin hath made us make a law which will
Become a precedent 'gainst such haught trai-
   tors,
As would with treason mount to tyranny;
Not even contented with a sceptre, till
They can convert it to a two-edged sword!
Was not the place of Doge sufficient for ye?
What's nobler than the signory of Venice?
Doge. The signory of Venice! You betrayed
   me —
You — you, who sit there, traitors as ye are!
From my equality with you in birth,
And my superiority in action,
You drew me from my honorable toils
In distant lands — on flood — in field — in
   cities —
You singled me out like a victim to
Stand crowned, but bound and helpless, at the
   altar
Where you alone could minister. I knew
   not —
I sought not — wished not — dreamed not the
   election,
Which reached me first at Rome, and I
   obeyed;
But found on my arrival, that, besides
The jealous vigilance which always led you
To mock and mar your sovereign's best in-
   tents,
You had, even in the interregnum of
My journey to the capital, curtailed
And mutilated the few privileges
Yet left the duke: all this I bore, and would
Have borne, until my very hearth was stained
By the pollution of your ribaldry,

And he, the ribald, whom I see amongst you —
Fit judge in such tribunal! ——
Ben. (interrupting him).   Michel Steno
Is here in virtue of his office, as
One of the Forty; "the Ten" having craved
A Giunta of patricians from the senate
To aid our judgment in a trial arduous
And novel as the present: he was set
Free from the penalty pronounced upon him,
Because the Doge, who should protect the law
Seeking to abrogate all law, can claim
No punishment of others by the statutes
Which he himself denies and violates!
Doge. His PUNISHMENT! I rather see him
   there,
Where he now sits, to glut him with my death,
Than in the mockery of castigation,
Which your foul, outward, juggling show of
   justice
Decreed as sentence! Base as was his crime
'Twas purity compared with your protection.
Ben. And can it be, that the great Doge of
   Venice,
With three parts of a century of years
And honors on his head, could thus allow
His fury, like an angry boy's, to master
All feeling, wisdom, faith, and fear, on such
A provocation as a young man's petulance?
Doge. A spark creates the flame — tis the
   last drop
Which makes the cup run o'er, and mine was
   full
Already: you oppressed the prince and peo-
   ple;
I would have freed both, and have failed in
   both:
The price of such success would have been
   glory,
Vengeance, and victory, and such a name
As would have made Venetian history
Rival to that of Greece and Syracuse
When they were freed, and flourished ages
   after,
And mine to Gelon and to Thrasybulus: —
Failing, I know the penalty of failure
Is present infamy and death — the future
Will judge, when Venice is no more, or free;
Till then, the truth is in abeyance. Pause not;
I would have shown no mercy, and I seek
   none;
My life was staked upon a mighty hazard,
And being lost, take what I would have taken!
I would have stood alone amidst your tombs:
Now you may flock round mine, and trample
   on it,
As you have done upon my heart while living.
Ben. You do confess then, and admit the
   justice
Of our tribunal?
Doge.   I confess to have failed;
Fortune is female: from my youth her favors
Were not withheld, the fault was mine to hope

Her former smiles again at this late hour.
Ben. You do not then in aught arraign our
equity ?
Doge. Noble Venetians! stir me not with
questions.
I am resigned to the worst; but in me still
Have something of the blood of brighter days,
And am not over-patient. Pray you, spare me
Further interrogation, which boots nothing,
Except to turn a trial to debate.
I shall but answer that which will offend you,
And please your enemies — a host already;
'Tis true, these sullen walls should yield no
echo:
But walls have ears — nay, more, they have
tongues; and if
There were no other way for truth to o'erleap
them,[1]
You who condemn me, you who fear and slay
me,
Yet could not bear in silence to your graves .
What you would hear from me of good or evil;
The secret were too mighty for your souls :
Then let it sleep in mine, unless you court
A danger which would double that you escape.
Such my defence would be, had I full scope
To make it famous; for true *words* are *things*,
And dying men's are things which long outlive,
And oftentimes avenge them; bury mine,
If ye would fain survive me; take this counsel,
And though too oft ye made me live in wrath,
Let me die calmly; you may grant me this; —
I deny nothing — defend nothing — nothing
I ask of you, but silence for myself,
And sentence from the court!
Ben.   This full admission
Spares us the harsh necessity of ordering
The torture to elicit the whole truth.[2]
Doge. The torture! you have put me there
already,
Daily since I was Doge; but if you will
Add the corporeal rack, you may: these limbs
Will yield with age to crushing iron; but
There's that within my heart shall strain your
engines.

Enter an OFFICER.

Officer. Noble Venetians! Duchess Fa-
liero[3]
Requests admission to the Giunta's presence.
Ben. Say, conscript fathers,[4] shall she be
admitted ?

---

[1] [MS. — "There were no other way for truth to
pierce them."]

[2] [MS. — "The torture for the exposure of the
truth."]

[3] [MS. —

"Noble Venetians! { Doge Faliero's consort.
                  { with respect the Duchess."]

[4] The Venetian senate took the same title as the
Roman, of "conscript fathers."

One of the Giunta. She may have reve-
lations of importance
Unto the state, to justify compliance
With her request.
Ben.   Is this the general will ?
All. It is.
Doge.   Oh, admirable laws of Venice!
Which would admit the wife, in the full hope
That she might testify against the husband,
What glory to the chaste Venetian dames!
But such blasphemers 'gainst all honor, as
Sit here, do well to act in their vocation.
Now, villain Steno! if this woman fail,
I'll pardon thee thy lie, and thy escape,
And my own violent death, and thy vile life.

The DUCHESS *enters.*[5]

Ben. Lady! this just tribunal has resolved,
Though the request be strange, to grant it, and
Whatever be its purport, to accord
A patient hearing with the due respect
Which fits your ancestry, your rank, and vir-
tues :
But you turn pale — ho! there, look to the
lady!
Place a chair instantly.
Ang.   A moment's faintness —
'Tis past; I pray you pardon me, — I sit not
In presence of my prince and of my husband,
While he is on his feet.
Ben.   Your pleasure, lady ?
Ang. Strange rumors, but most true, if all I
hear
And see be sooth, have reached me, and I
come
To know the worst, even at the worst; forgive
The abruptness of my entrance and my bear-
ing.
Is it —— I cannot speak — I cannot shape
The question — but you answer it ere spoken,

---

[5] [The drama, which has the merit, uncommon in
modern performances, of embodying no episodical
deformity whatever, now hurries in full career to
its close. Every thing is despatched with the stern
decision of a tyrannical aristocracy. There is no
hope of mercy on any side, — there is no petition,
— nay, there is no wish for mercy. Even the ple-
beian conspirators have too much Venetian blood in
them to be either scared by the approach, or shaken
in the moment, of death: and, as for the Doge, he
bears himself as becomes a warrior of sixty years, and
a deeply insulted prince. At the moment, however,
which immediately precedes the pronouncing of the
sentence, admission is asked and obtained by one
from whom less of the Spartan firmness might have
been expected. This is Angiolina. She indeed haz-
ards one fervent prayer to the unbending senate; but
she sees in a moment that it is in vain, and she re-
covers herself on the instant; and turning to her
lord, who stands calm and collected at the foot of
the council table, speaks words worthy of him and
of her. Nothing can be more unexpected, or more
beautiful, than the behavior of the young patrician
who interrupts their conversation. — *Lockhart.*]

With eyes averted, and with gloomy brows —
Oh God! this is the silence of the grave!
Ben.(after a pause). Spare us, and spare
   thyself the repetition .
Of our most awful, but inexorable
Duty to heaven and man!
Ang.   Yet speak; I cannot —
I cannot — no — even now believe these things.
Is *he* condemned?
Ben.   Alas!
Ang.   And was he guilty?
Ben. Lady! the natural distraction of
Thy thoughts at such a moment makes the
   question
Merit forgiveness; else a doubt like this
Against a just and paramount tribunal
Were deep offence. But question even the
   Doge,
And if he can deny the proofs, believe him
Guiltless as thy own bosom.
Ang.   Is it so?
My lord — my sovereign — my poor father's
   friend —
The mighty in the field, the sage in council;
Unsay the words of this man! — Thou art si-
   lent!
Ben. He hath already owned to his own
   guilt,[1]
Nor, as thou see'st, doth he deny it now.
Ang. Ay, but he must not die! Spare his
   few years,
Which grief and shame will soon cut down
   to days!
One day of baffled crime must not efface
Near sixteen lustres crowded with brave acts.
Ben. His doom must be fulfilled without
   remission
Of time or penalty — 'tis a decree.
Ang. He hath been guilty, but there may
   be mercy.
Ben. Not in this case with justice.
Ang.   Alas! signor,
He who is only just is cruel; who
Upon the earth would live were all judged
   justly?
Ben. His punishment is safety to the state.
Ang. He was a subject, and hath served
   the state;
He was your general, and hath saved the state;
He is your sovereign, and hath ruled the state.
One of the Council. He is a traitor, and be-
   trayed the state.
Ang. And, but for him, there now had
   been no state
To save or to destroy; and you who sit
There to pronounce the death of your deliv-
   erer,
Had now been groaning at a Moslem oar,
Or digging in the Hunnish mines in fetters!

---

[1] [MS. —
    " He hath already granted his own guilt."]

One of the Council. No, lady, there are
   others who would die
Rather than breathe in slavery!
Ang.   If there are so
Within *these* walls, *thou* art not of the number.
The truly brave are generous to the fallen! —
Is there no hope?
Ben.   Lady, it cannot be.
Ang. (turning to the Doge). Then die, Fa-
   liero, since it must be so;
But with the spirit of my father's friend.
Thou hast been guilty of a great offence,
Half-cancelled by the harshness of these men.
I would have sued to them — have prayed to
   them —
Have begged as famished mendicants for
   bread —
Have wept as they will cry unto their God
For mercy, and be answered as they answer —
Had it been fitting for thy name or mine,
And if the cruelty in their cold eyes
Had not announced the heartless wrath
   within.
Then, as a prince, address thee to thy doom!
Doge. I have lived too long not to know
   how to die!
Thy suing to these men were but the bleating
Of the lamb to the butcher, or the cry
Of seamen to the surge: I would not take
A life eternal, granted at the hands
Of wretches, from whose monstrous villanies
I sought to free the groaning nations!
Michel Steno.   Doge,
A word with thee, and with this noble lady,
Whom I have grievously offended. Would
Sorrow, or shame, or penance on my part,
Could cancel the inexorable past!
But since that cannot be, as Christians let us
Say farewell, and in peace: with full contrition
I crave, not pardon, but compassion from you,
And give, however weak, my prayers for
   both.
Ang. Sage Benintende, now chief judge of
   Venice,
I speak to thee in answer to yon signor.
Inform the ribald Steno, that his words
Ne'er weighed in mind with Loredano's
   daughter
Further than to create a moment's pity
For such as he is: would that others had
Despised him as I pity! I prefer
My honor to a thousand lives, could such
Be multiplied in mine, but would not have
A single life of others lost for that
Which nothing human can impugn — the
   sense
Of virtue, looking not to what is called
A good name for reward, but to itself.
To me the scorner's words were as the wind
Unto the rock: but as there are — alas!
Spirits more sensitive, on which such things
Light as the whirlwind on the waters; souls

To whom dishonor's shadow is a substance
More terrible than death, here and hereafter;
Men whose vice is to start at vice's scoffing,
And who, though proof against all blandish-
ments
Of pleasure, and all pangs of pain, are feeble
When the proud name on which they pinna-
cled
Their hopes is breathed on, jealous as the
eagle
Of her high aiery; let what we now
Behold, and feel, and suffer, be a lesson
To wretches how they tamper in their spleen
With beings of a higher order. Insects
Have made the lion mad ere now; a shaft
I' the heel o'erthrew the bravest of the brave;
A wife's dishonor was the bane of Troy;
A wife's dishonor unkinged Rome for ever;
An injured husband brought the Gauls to
Clusium,
And thence to Rome, which perished for a
time;
An obscene gesture cost Caligula
His life, while Earth yet bore his cruelties;
A virgin's wrong made Spain a Moorish
province;
And Steno's lie, couched in two worthless lines,
Hath decimated Venice, put in peril
A senate which hath stood eight hundred
years,
Discrowned a prince, cut off his crownless
head,
And forged new fetters for a groaning people!
Let the poor wretch, like to the courtesan
Who fired Persepolis, be proud of this,
If it so please him — 'twere a pride fit for him!
But let him not insult the last hours of
Him, who, whate'er he now is, *was* a hero,
By the intrusion of his very prayers;
Nothing of good can come from such a
source,
Nor would we aught with him, nor now, nor
ever.
We leave him to himself, that lowest depth
Of human baseness. Pardon is for men,
And not for reptiles — we have none for
Steno,
And no resentment: things like him must
sting,
And higher beings suffer; 'tis the charter
Of life. The man who dies by the adder's
fang
May have the crawler crushed, but feels no
anger:
'Twas the worm's nature; and some men are
worms
In soul, more than the living things of tombs.[1]

Doge (to Ben.). Signor! complete that
which you deem your duty.
Ben. Before we can proceed upon that duty,
We would request the princess to withdraw;
'Twill move her too much to be witness to it.
Ang. I know it will, and yet I must endure
it,
For 'tis a part of mine — I will not quit,
Except by force, my husband's side. — Pro-
ceed!
Nay, fear not either shriek, or sigh, or tear;
Though my heart burst, it shall be silent. —
Speak!
I have that within which shall o'ermaster all.
Ben. Marino Faliero, Doge of Venice,
Count of Val di Marino, Senator,
And some time General of the Fleet and
Army,
Noble Venetian, many times and oft
Intrusted by the state with high employ-
ments,
Even to the highest, listen to the sentence.
Convict by many witnesses and proofs,
And by thine own confession, of the guilt
Of treachery and treason, yet unheard of
Until this trial — the decree is death.
Thy goods are confiscate unto the state,
Thy name is razed from out her records, save
Upon a public day of thanksgiving
For this our most miraculous deliverance,
When thou art noted in our calendars
With earthquakes, pestilence, and foreign foes,
And the great enemy of man, as subject
Of grateful masses for Heaven's grace in
snatching
Our lives and country from thy wickedness.
The place wherein as Doge thou shouldst be
painted
With thine illustrious predecessors, is
To be left vacant, with a death-black veil
Flung over these dim words engraved be-
neath, —
" This place is of Marino Faliero,
Decapitated for his crimes."
Doge.   " His crimes!"
But let it be so: — it will be in vain.
The veil which blackens o'er this blighted
name,

[1] [The Duchess is formal and cold, without even
that degree of love for her old husband which a child
might have for her parent, or a pupil for her in-
structor. Even in this her longest and best speech,
at the most touching moment of the catastrophe, she
can moralize, in a strain of pedantry less natural to
a woman than to any other person similarly circum-
stanced, on lions stung by gnats, Achilles, Helen,
Lucretia, the siege of Clusium, Caligula, Caaba, and
Persepolis! The lines are fine in themselves, in-
deed; and if they had been spoken by Benintende
as a funeral oration over the Duke's body, or still
more, perhaps, if they had been spoken by the
Duke's counsel on his trial, they would have been
perfectly in place and character. But that is not
the highest order of female intellect which is dis-
posed to be long-winded in distress; nor does any
one, either male or female, who is really and deeply
affected, find time for wise saws and instances an-
cient and modern. — *Heber.*]

And hides, or seems to hide, these lineaments,
Shall draw more gazers than the thousand
    portraits
Which glitter round it in their pictured trap-
    pings —
Your delegated slaves—the people's tyrants !
" Decapita!ed   for   his   crimes ! " — *What*
    crimes ?
Were it not better to record the facts,
So that the contemplator might approve,
Or at the least learñ *whence* the crimes arose ?
When the beholder knows a Doge conspired,
Let him be told the cause — it is your history.
    Ben.   Time must reply to that; our sons
        will judge
Their fathers' judgment, which I now pro-
    nounce.
As Doge, clad in the ducal robes and cap,
Thou shalt be led hence to the Giants', Stair-
    case,
Where thou and all our princes are invested ;
And there, the ducal crown being first resumed
Upon the spot where it was first assumed,
Thy head shall be struck off; and Heaven
    have mercy
Upon thy soul !
    Doge.   Is this the Giunta's sentence ?
    Ben.   It is.
    Doge.   I can endure it. — And the time ?
    Ben.   Must be immediate. — Make thy
        peace with God :
Within an hour thou must be in His presence.
    Doge.   I am already ; and my blood will
        rise
To Heaven before the souls of those who shed
    it. —
Are all my lands confiscated ?
    Ben.   They are ;
And goods, and jewels, and all kind of treasure,
Except two thousand ducats— these dispose
    of.
    Doge.   That's harsh. — I would have fain
        reserved the lands
Near to Treviso, which I hold by investment
From Laurence the Count-bishop of Ceneda,
In fief perpetual to myself and heirs,
To portion them (leaving my city spoil,
My palace and my treasures, to your forfeit)
Between my consort and my kinsmen.
    Ben.   These
Lie under the state's ban; their chief, thy
    nephew,
In peril of his own life; but the council
Postpones his trial for the present.   If
Thou will'st a state unto thy widowed princess,
Fear not, for we will do her justice.
    Ang.   Signors,
I share not in your spoil ! From henceforth,
    know
I am devoted unto God alone,
And take my refuge in the cloister.
    Doge.   Come !

The hour may be a hard one, but 'twill end.
Have I aught else to undergo save death ?
    Ben.   You have nought to do, except con-
        fess and die.
The priest is robed, the scimitar is bare,
And both await without. — But, above all,
Think not to speak unto the people ; they
Are now by thousands swarming at the gates,
But these are closed : the Ten, the Avogadori,
The Giunta, and the chief men of the Forty,
Alone will be beholders of thy doom,
And they are ready to attend the Doge.
    Doge.   The Doge !
    Ben.   Yes, Doge, thou hast lived and thou
        shalt die
A sovereign ; till the moment which precedes
The separation of that head and trunk,
That ducal crown and head shall be united.
Thou hast forgot thy dignity in deigning
To plot with petty traitors ; not so we,
Who in the very punishment acknowledge
The prince.   Thy vile accomplices have died
The dog's death, and the wolf's ; but thou
    shalt fall
As falls the lion by the hunters, girt
By those who feel a proud compassion for thee,
And mourn even the inevitable death
Provoked by thy wild wrath, and regal fierce-
    ness.
Now we remit thee to thy preparation :
Let it be brief, and we ourselves will be
Thy guides unto the place where first we were
United to thee as thy subjects, and
Thy senate ; and must now be parted from thee
As such for ever, on the self-same spot. —
Guards ! form the Doge's escort to his cham-
    ber.   [*Exeunt.*

SCENE II.— *The Doge's Apartment.*

The DOGE *as Prisoner, and the* DUCHESS *at-
    tending him.*

    Doge.   Now, that the priest is gone, 'twere
        useless all
To linger out the miserable minutes ;
But one pang more, the pang of parting from
    thee,
And I will leave the few last grains of sand,
Which yet remain of the accorded hour,
Still falling — I have done with Time.
    Ang.   Alas !
And I have been the cause, the unconscious
    cause ;
And for this funeral marriage, this black union,
Which thou, compliant with my father's wish,
Didst promise at *his* death, thou hast sealed
    thine own.
    Doge.   Not so : there was that in my spirit
        ever
Which shaped out for itself some great re-
    verse ;

The marvel is, it came not until now —
And yet it was foretold me.
 Ang.   How foretold you ?
 Doge. Long years ago — so long, they are
  a doubt
In memory, and yet they live in annals :
When I was in my youth, and served the sen-
  ate
And signory as podesta and captain
Of the town of Treviso, on a day
Of festival, the sluggish bishop who
Conveyed the Host aroused my rash young
  anger
By strange delay, and arrogant reply
To my reproof; I raised my hand and smote
  him
Until he reeled beneath his holy burden ;
And as he rose from earth again, he raised
His tremulous hands in pious wrath towards
  Heaven,
Thence pointing to the Host, which had fallen
  from him,
He turned to me, and said, " The hour will
  come
When he thou hast o'erthrown shall overthrow
  thee :
The glory shall depart from out thy house,
The wisdom shall be shaken from thy soul,
And in thy best maturity of mind
A madness of the heart shall seize upon thee ; [1]
Passion shall tear thee when all passions cease
In other men, or mellow into virtues ;
And majesty, which decks all other heads,
Shall crown to leave thee headless ; honors
  shall
But prove to thee the heralds of destruction,
And hoary hairs of shame, and both of death,
But not such death as fits an aged man."
Thus saying, he passed on. — That hour is
  come.
 Ang. And with this warning couldst thou
  not have striven
To avert the fatal moment, and atone,
By penitence for that which thou hadst done ?
 Doge. I own the words went to my heart,
  so much
That I remembered them amid the maze
Of life, as if they formed a spectral voice,
Which shook me in a supernatural dream;
And I repented ; but 'twas not for me
To pull in resolution : what must be
I could not change, and would not fear. — Nay
  more,
Thou canst not have forgot, what all remem-
  ber,
That on my day of landing here as Doge,
On my return from Rome, a mist of such
Unwonted density went on before
The bucentaur, like the columnar cloud

Which ushered Israel out of Egypt, till
The pilot was misled, and disembarked us
Between the pillars of Saint Mark's, where 'tis
The custom of the state to put to death
Its criminals, instead of touching at
The Riva della Paglia, as the wont is, —
So that all Venice shuddered at the omen.
 Ang. Ah! little boots it now to recollect
  Such things.
 Doge. And yet I find a comfort in
The thought that these things are the work of
  Fate ;
For I would rather yield to gods than men,
Or cling to any creed of destiny,
Rather than deem these mortals, most of whom
I know to be as worthless as the dust,
And weak as worthless, more than instruments
Of an o'erruling power; they in themselves
Were all incapable — they could not be
Victors of him who oft had conquered for
  them !
 Ang. Employ the minutes left in aspira-
  tions
Of a more healing nature, and in peace
Even with these wretches take thy flight to
  Heaven.
 Doge. I *am* at peace : the peace of certainty
That a sure hour will come, when their sons'
  sons,
And this proud city, and these azure waters,
And all which makes them eminent and
  bright,
Shall be a desolation and a curse,
A hissing and a scoff unto the nations,
A Carthage, and a Tyre, an Ocean Babel !
 Ang. Speak not thus now; the surge of
  passion still
Sweeps o'er thee to the last ; thou dost deceive
Thyself, and canst not injure them — be
  calmer.
 Doge. I stand within eternity, and see
Into eternity, and I behold —
Ay, palpable as I see thy sweet face
For the last time — the days which I denounce
Unto all time against these wave-girt walls,
And they who are indwellers.
 Guard (*coming forward*). Doge of Venice,
The Ten are in attendance on your highness.
 Doge. Then farewell, Angiolina ! — one em-
  brace —
Forgive the old man who hath been to thee
A fond but fatal husband — love my mem-
  ory —
I would not ask so much for me still living,
But thou canst judge of me more kindly now,
Seeing my evil feelings are at rest.
Besides, of all the fruit of these long years,
Glory, and wealth, and power, and fame, and
  name,
Which generally leave some flowers to bloom
Even o'er the grave, I have nothing left, not
  even

A little love, or friendship, or esteem,
No, not enough to extract an epitaph
From ostentatious kinsmen; in one hour
I have uprooted all my former life,
And outlived every thing, except thy heart,
The pure, the good, the gentle, which will oft
With unimpaired but not a clamorous grief [1]
Still keep —— Thou turn'st so pale l — Alas,
    she faints,
She has no breath, no pulse! — Guards! lend
    your aid —
I cannot leave her thus, and yet 'tis better,
Since every lifeless moment spares a pang.
When she shakes off this temporary death,
I shall be with the Eternal. — Call her
    .women —
One look! — how cold her hand! — as cold as
    mine
Shall be ere she recovers. — Gently tend her,
And take my last thanks —— I am ready now.
[*The Attendants of* ANGIOLINA *enter and
    surround their mistress, who has fainted.
    —Exeunt the* DOGE, *Guards, etc. etc.*

SCENE III.— *The Court of the Ducal Palace :
the outer gates are shut against the people.
— The* DOGE *enters in his ducal robes, in
procession with the Council of Ten and other
Patricians, attended by the Guards, till they
arrive at the top of the " Giants' Staircase"
(where the Doges took the oaths) ; the Ex-
ecutioner is stationed there with his sword.
— On arriving, a Chief of the Ten takes off
the ducal cap from the Doge's head.*

Doge. So now the Doge is nothing, and
    at last
I am again Marino Faliero :
'Tis well to be so, though but for a moment.
Here was I crowned, and here, bear witness,
    Heaven!
With how much more contentment I resign
That shining mockery, the ducal bauble,
Than I received the fatal ornament.
One of the Ten. Thou tremblest, Faliero!
Doge.   'Tis with age, then.[2]
Ben. Faliero! hast thou aught further to
    commend,
Compatible with justice, to the senate ?

---

[1] [MS. —
"With unimpaired but not outrageous grief."]

[2] This was the actual reply of Bailli, maire of
Paris, to a Frenchman who made him the same re-
proach on his way to execution, in the earliest part
of their revolution. I find in reading over (since
the completion of this tragedy), for the first time
these six years, "Venice Preserved," a similar re-
ply on a different occasion by Renault, and other
coincidences arising from the subject. I need hardly
remind the gentlest reader, that such coincidences
must be accidental, from the very facility of their
detection by reference to so popular a play on the
stage and in the closet as Otway's chef-d'œuvre.

Doge. I would commend my nephew t«
    their mercy,
My consort to their justice; for methinks
My death, and such a death, might settle all
Between the state and me.
Ben.   They shall be cared for:
Even notwithstanding thine unheard-of crime.
Doge. Unheard of! ay, there's not a his-
    tory
But shows a thousand crowned conspirators
Against the people; but to set them free
One sovereign only died, and one is dying.
Ben. And who were they who fell in such
    a cause ?
Doge. The King of Sparta, and the Doge
    of Venice —
Agis and Faliero !
Ben.   Hast thou more
To utter or to do ?
Doge.   May I speak ?
Ben.   Thou may'st;
But recollect the people are without,
Beyond the compass of the human voice.
Doge. I speak to Time and to Eternity,[3]
Of which I grow a portion, not to man.
Ye elements! in which to be resolved
I hasten, let my voice be as a spirit
Upon you! ye blue waves! which bore my
    banner,
Ye winds! which fluttered o'er as if you loved
    it,   ,
And filled my swelling sails as they were wafted
To many a triumph! Thou, my native earth,
Which I have bled for, and thou foreign earth,
Which drank this willing blood from many a
    wound!
Ye stones, in which my gore will not sink, but
Reek up to Heaven! Ye skies, which will re-
    ceive it!
Thou sun! which shinest on these things, and
    Thou!
Who kindlest and who quenchest suns! [4] —
    Attest!
I am not innocent — but are these guiltless ?
I perish, but not unavenged; far ages
Float up from the abyss of time to be,
And show these eyes, before they close, the
    doom
Of this proud city, and I leave my curse
On her and hers for ever! —— Yes, the hours
Are silently engendering of the day,
When she, who built 'gainst Attila a bulwark,
Shall yield, and bloodlessly and basely yield
Unto a bastard Attila, without
Shedding so much blood in her last defence

---

[3] [The last speech of the Doge is a grand pro-
phetic rant, something strained and elaborate—but
eloquent and terrible. — *Jeffrey.*]

[4] [In MS. —
—— " and Thou!
Who makest and destroyest suns! "]

As these old veins, oft drained in shielding her,
Shall pour in sacrifice. — She shall be bought
And sold, and be an appanage to those
Who shall despise her! [1] — She shall stoop
   to be
A province for an empire, petty town
In lieu of capital, with slaves for senates,
Beggars for nobles, [2] panders for a people!
Then when the Hebrew's in thy palaces, [3]
The Hun in thy high places, and the Greek
Walks o'er thy mart, and smiles on it for his!
When thy patricians beg their bitter bread

In narrow streets, and in their shameful need
Make their nobility a plea for pity!
Then, when the few who still retain a wreck
Of their great fathers' heritage shall fawn
Round a barbarian Vice of Kings' Vice-gerent,
Even in the palace where they swayed as sov-
   ereigns,
Even in the palace where they slew their sov-
   ereign,
Proud of some name they have disgraced, or
   sprung
From an adulteress boastful of her guilt
With some large gondolier or foreign soldier,
Shall bear about their bastardy in triumph
To the third spurious generation; — when
Thy sons are in the lowest scale of being,
Slaves turned o'er to the vanquished by the
   victors,
Despised by cowards for greater cowardice,
And scorned even by the vicious for such vices
As in the monstrous grasp of their conception
Defy all codes to image or to name them;
Then, when of Cyprus, now thy subject king-
   dom,
All thine inheritance shall be her shame
Entailed on thy less virtuous daughters, grown
A wider proverb for worse prostitution; —
When all the ills of conquered states shall
   cling thee,
Vice without splendor, sin without relief
Even from the gloss of love to smoothe it o'er
But in its stead, coarse lusts of habitude,
Prurient yet passionless, cold studied lewdness,
Depraving nature's frailty to an art; —
When these and more are heavy on thee, when
Smiles without mirth, and pastimes without
   pleasure,
Youth without honor, age without respect,
Meanness and weakness, and a sense of woe
'Gainst which thou wilt not strive, and dar'st not
   murmur, [4]
Have made thee last and worst of peopled
   deserts,
Then, in the last gasp of thine agony,
Amidst thy many murders, think of *mine!*

---

[1] Should the dramatic picture seem harsh, let the reader look to the historical, of the period prophesied, or rather of the few years preceding that period. Voltaire calculated their "nostre bene merite meretrici" at 12,000 of regulars, without including volunteers and local militia, on what authority I know not; but it is, perhaps, the only part of the population not decreased. Venice once contained two hundred thousand inhabitants: there are now about ninety thousand; and THESE!! few individuals can conceive, and none could describe, the actual state into which the more than infernal tyranny of Austria has plunged this unhappy city. From the present decay and degeneracy of Venice under the Barbarians, there are some honorable individual exceptions. There is Pasqualigo, the last, and, alas! *posthumous* son of the marriage of the Doges with the Adriatic, who fought his frigate with far greater gallantry than any of his French coadjutors in the memorable action off Lissa. I came home in the squadron with the prizes in 1811, and recollect to have heard Sir William Hoste, and the other officers engaged in that glorious conflict, speak in the highest terms of Pasqualigo's behavior. There is the Abbate Morelli. There is Alvise Querini, who, after a long and honorable diplomatic career, finds some consolation for the wrongs of his country, in the pursuits of literature with his nephew, Vittor Benzon, the son of the celebrated beauty, the heroine of "La Biondina in Gondoletta." There are the patrician poet Morosini, and the poet Lamberti, the author of the "Biondina," etc. and many other estimable productions; and not least in an Englishman's estimation, Madame Michelli, the translator of Shakspeare. There are the young Dandolo and the improvvisatore Carrer, and Giuseppe Albrizzi, the accomplished son of an accomplished mother. There is Aglietti, and were there nothing else, there is the immortality of Canova, Cicognara, Mustoxithi, Bucati, etc. etc. I do not reckon, because the one is a Greek, and the others were born at least a hundred miles off, which, throughout Italy, constitutes, if not a *foreigner,* at least a *stranger (forestiere).*

[2] [MS. —
   "Beggars for nobles, { lazars / lepers / wretches } for a people! "]

[3] The chief palaces on the Brenta now belong to the Jews; who in the earlier times of the republic were only allowed to inhabit Mestri, and not to enter the city of Venice. The whole commerce is in the hands of the Jews and Greeks, and the Huns form the garrison.

[4] If the Doge's prophecy seem remarkable, look to the following, made by Alamanni two hundred and seventy years ago: — "There is one very singular prophecy concerning Venice: 'If thou dost not change,' it says to that proud republic, 'thy liberty, which is already on the wing, will not reckon a century more than the thousandth year.' If we carry back the epocha of Venetian freedom to the establishment of the government under which the republic flourished, we shall find that the date of the election of the first doge is 697; and if we add one century to a thousand, that is, eleven hundred years, we shall find the sense of the prediction to be literally this: 'Thy liberty will not last till 1797.' Recollect that Venice ceased to be free in the year 1796, the fifth year of the French republic; and you will perceive, that there never was prediction more pointed, or more exactly followed by the

Thou den of drunkards with the blood of
   princes![1]
Gehenna of the waters! thou sea Sodom![2]
Thus I devote thee to the infernal gods!
Thee and thy serpent seed![3]
   [*Here the* DOGE *turns and addresses the
   Executioner.*
           Slave, do thine office!
Strike as I struck the foe! Strike as I would
Have struck those tyrants! Strike deep as
   my curse!
Strike—and but once!
   [*The* DOGE *throws himself upon his knees,
   and as the Executioner raises his sword
   the scene closes.*

event. You will, therefore, note as very remark-
able the three lines of Alamanni addressed to Venice;
which, however, no one has pointed out: —

  ' Se non cangi pensier, un secol solo
    Non conterà sopra 'l millesimo anno
    Tua libertà, che-va fuggendo a volo.'

Many prophecies have passed for such, and many
men have been called prophets for much less." —
Ginguené, Hist. Lit. de l'Italie, t. ix. p. 144.

[1] Of the first fifty Doges, *five* abdicated —*five*
were banished with their eyes put out —*five* were
MASSACRED — and *nine* deposed; so that *nineteen*
out of fifty lost the throne by violence, besides two
who fell in battle: this occurred long previous to
the reign of Marino Faliero. One of his more im-
mediate predecessors, Andrea Dandolo, died of
vexation. Marino Faliero himself perished as re-
lated. Amongst his successors, *Foscari,* after
seeing his son repeatedly tortured and banished,
was deposed, and died of breaking a blood-vessel,
on hearing the bell of Saint Mark's toll for the elec-
tion of his successor. Morosini was impeached
for the loss of Candia; but this was previous to his
dukedom, during which he conquered the Morea,
and was styled the Peloponnesian. Faliero might
truly say,
  " Thou den of drunkards with the blood of princes! "

[2] [MS. —
" Thou brothel of the waters! thou sea Sodom!"]

[3] [The sentence is pronounced, a brief hour is
permitted for the last devotions, and then, — still
robed in his ducal gown, and wearing the diadem,
— preceded with all the pomp of his station, from
which he is to be degraded in the moment only be-
fore the blow be struck, — Marino Faliero is led sol-
emnly to the Giants' Staircase, at the summit of
which he had been crowned. On that spot he is to
expiate his offence against the majesty of the Vene-
tian state. His wife struggles to accompany him
to the dreadful spot, but she faints, and he leaves
her on the marble pavement, forbidding them to
raise her, until all had been accomplished with
himself. Lord Byron breaks out with all his power
in the curse with which he makes this old man take
leave of the scene of his triumphs and his sorrows.
The present abject condition of her that " once did
hold the gorgeous East in fee " — the barbarian
sway under which she is bowed down to the dust
— the profligacy of manners, which ought rather,
perhaps, to have been represented as the cause than
the consequence of the loss of Venetian liberty: —

SCENE IV.— *The Piazza and Piazzetta of Saint
  Mark's.— The People in crowds gathered
  round the grated gates of the Ducal Palace,
  which are shut.*

First Citizen. I have gained the gate, and
  can discern the Ten,
Robed in their gowns of state, ranged round
  the Doge.
Second Cit. I cannot reach thee with mine
  utmost effort.
How is it? let us hear at least, since sight
Is thus prohibited unto the people,
Except the occupiers of those bars.
  First Cit. One has approached the Doge,
  and now they strip
The ducal bonnet from his head — and now
He raises his keen eyes to heaven; I see
Them glitter, and his lips move — Hush!
  Hush! — no,
'Twas but a murmur — Curse upon the dis-
  tance!
His words are inarticulate, but the voice
Swells up like muttered thunder; would we
  could
But gather a sole sentence!
  Second Cit. Hush! we perhaps may catch
  the sound.
  First Cit. 'Tis vain,
I cannot hear him.— How his hoary hair
Streams on the wind like foam upon the wave!
Now — now — he kneels — and now they form
  a circle
Round him, and all is hidden — but I see
The lifted sword in air ——Ah! hark! it
  falls!   [*The People murmur.*
  Third Cit. Then they have murdered him
  who would have freed us.
  Fourth Cit. He was a kind man to the com-
  mons ever.
  Fifth Cit. Wisely they did to keep their
  portals barred.
Would we had known the work they were
  preparing
Ere we were summoned here — we would have
  brought
Weapons, and forced them!
  Sixth Cit. Are you sure he's dead?
  First Cit. I saw the sword fall — Lo! what
  have we here?

*Enter on the Balcony of the Palace which fronts
  Saint Mark's Place a* CHIEF OF THE TEN,[4]
  *with a bloody sword. He waves it thrice be-
  fore the People and exclaims,*

" Justice hath dealt upon the mighty Traitor! "
  [*The gates are opened; the populace rush in*

all these topics are handled — and handled as no
writer but Byron could have dared to handle them.
—*Lockhart.*]

[4] " Un Capo de' Dieci " are the words of Sanu-
to's Chronicle.

*towards the " Giants' Staircase," where the
execution has taken place. The foremost
of them exclaims to those behind,*
The gory head [1] rolls down the Giants' Steps!
                                    [*The curtain falls.* [2]

[1] [MS. —
{ " The gory head is rolling down the steps! }
{ " The head is rolling down the gory steps! " }

[2] [As a play, Marino Faliero is deficient in the
attractive passions, in probability, and in depth and
variety of interest; and revolts throughout, by the
extravagant disproportion which the injury bears
to the unmeasured resentment with which it is pur-
sued. As a poem, though it occasionally displays
great force and elevation, it obviously wants both
grace and facility. The diction is often heavy and
cumbrous, and the versification without sweetness
or elasticity. It is generally very verbose, and
sometimes exceedingly dull. Altogether, it gives
us the impression of a thing worked out against the
grain, and not poured forth from the fulness of the
heart or the fancy; — the ambitious and elaborate
work of a powerful mind engaged with an unsuit-
able task — not the spontaneous effusion of an exu-
berant imagination, sporting in the fulness of its
strength. Every thing is heightened and enforced
with visible effort and design; and the noble author
is often contented to be emphatic by dint of exag-
geration, and eloquent by the common topics of
declamation. Lord Byron is, undoubtedly, a poet
of the very first order, and has talents to reach the
very highest honors of the drama. But he must
not again disdain love, and ambition, and jealousy:

he must not substitute what is merely *bizarre* and
extraordinary, for what is naturally and universally
interesting, nor expect, by any exaggerations, so to
rouse and rule our sympathies by the senseless
anger of an old man, and the prudish proprieties
of an untempted woman, as by the agency of the
great and simple passions with which, in some of
their degrees, all men are familiar, and by which
alone the Dramatic Muse has hitherto wrought her
miracles. — *Jeffrey.*

On the whole, the Doge of Venice is the effect
of a powerful and cultivated mind. It has all the
requisites of tragedy, sublimity, terror, and pathos
— all but that without which the rest are unavail-
ing, interest! With many detached passages which
neither derogate from Lord Byron's former fame,
nor would have derogated from the reputation of
our best ancient tragedians, it is, as a whole, nei-
ther sustained nor impressive. The poet, except in
the soliloquy of Lioni, scarcely ever seems to have
written with his own thorough good liking. He
may be suspected throughout to have had in his
eye some other model than nature; and we rise
from his work with the same feeling as if we had
been reading a translation. For this want of inter-
est the subject itself is, doubtless, in some measure
to blame; though, if the same subject had been
differently treated, we are inclined to believe a very
different effect would have been produced. But for
the constraint and stiffness of the poetry, we have
nothing to blame but the apparent resolution of it«
author to set (at whatever risk) an example o
classical correctness to his uncivilized countrymet
and rather to forego success than to succeed aft
the manner of Shakspeare. — *Heber.*]

APPENDIX.

NOTE A.

I AM obliged for the following excellent transla-
tion of the old Chronicle to Mr. F. Cohen,[1] to
whom the reader will find himself indebted for a
version that I could not myself — though after
many years' intercourse with Italian — have given
by any means so purely and so faithfully.[2]

[1] [Mr. Francis Cohen, now Sir Francis Palgrave,
K. H., the learned author of the " Rise and Prog-
ress of the English Constitution," " History of the
Anglo-Saxons," etc. etc.]
[2] [In a letter to Mr. Murray, dated Ravenna,
July 30, 1821, Byron says: — " Enclosed is the
best account of the Doge Faliero, which was only
sent to me, from an old MS., the other day. Get it
translated, and append it as a note to the next
edition. You will, perhaps, be pleased to see, that
my conceptions of his character were correct, though
I regret not having met with the extract before.
You will perceive that he himself said exactly what
he is made to say about the Bishop of Treviso.
You will see also that he spoke little, and those
only words of rage and disdain AFTER his arrest;
which is the case in the play, except when he

STORY OF MARINO FALIERO, DOGE XLIX. MCCCLIV.

On the eleventh day of September, in the year
of our Lord 1354, Marino Faliero was elected and
chosen to be the Duke of the Commonwealth of
Venice. He was Count of Valdemarino, in the
Marches of Treviso, and a Knight, and a wealthy
man to boot. As soon as the election was com-
pleted, it was resolved in the Great Council, that a
deputation of twelve should be despatched to Ma-
rino Faliero the Duke, who was then on his way
from Rome; for when he was chosen, he was em-
bassador at the court of the Holy Father, at Rome,
— the Holy Father himself held his court at Avig-
non. When Messer Marino Faliero the Duke was
about to land in this city, on the 5th day of October,
1354, a thick haze came on, and darkened the air;
and he was enforced to land on the place of Saint
Mark, between the two columns, on the spot where
evil doers are put to death; and all thought that
this was the worst of tokens. — Nor must I forget
to write that which I have read in a chronicle.
When Messer Marino Faliero was Podesta and

breaks out at the close of Act fifth. But his speech
to the conspirators is better in the MS. than in the
play. I wish I had met with it in time."]

Captain of Treviso, the Bishop delayed coming in with the holy sacrament, on a day when a procession was to take place. Now, the said Marino Faliero was so very proud and wrathful, that he buffeted the Bishop, and almost struck him to the ground: and, therefore, Heaven allowed Marino Faliero to go out of his right senses, in order that he might bring himself to an evil death.

When this Duke had held the dukedom during nine months and six days, he, being wicked and ambitious, sought to make himself Lord of Venice, in the manner which I have read in an ancient chronicle. When the Thursday arrived upon which they were wont to hunt the bull, the bull hunt took place as usual; and, according to the usage of those times, after the bull hunt had ended, they all proceeded unto the palace of the Duke, and assembled together in one of his halls; and they disported themselves with the women. And until the first bell tolled they danced, and then a banquet was served up. My Lord the Duke paid the expenses thereof, provided he had a Duchess, and after the banquet they all returned to their homes.

Now to this feast there came a certain Ser Michele Steno, a gentleman of poor estate and very young, but crafty and daring, and who loved one of the damsels of the Duchess. Ser Michele stood amongst the women upon the solajo; and he behaved indiscreetly, so that my Lord the Duke ordered that he should be kicked off the solajo; and the esquires of the Duke flung him down from the solajo accordingly. Ser Michele thought that such an affront was beyond all bearing; and when the feast was over, and all other persons had left the palace, he, continuing heated with anger, went to the hall of audience, and wrote certain unseemly words relating to the Duke and the Duchess upon the chair in which the Duke was used to sit; for in those days the Duke did not cover his chair with cloth of sendal but he sat in a chair of wood. Ser Michele wrote thereon — "*Marin Falier, the husband of the fair wife; others kiss her, but he keeps her.*" In the morning the words were seen, and the matter was considered to be very scandalous; and the Senate commanded the Avogadori of the Commonwealth to proceed therein with the greatest diligence. A largess of great amount was immediately proffered by the Avogadori, in order to discover who had written these words. And at length it was known that Michele Steno had written them. It was resolved in the Council of Forty that he should be arrested; and he then confessed that in the fit of vexation and spite, occasioned by his being thrust off the solajo in the presence of his mistress, he had written the words. Therefore the Council debated thereon. And the Council took his youth into consideration, and that he was a lover; and therefore they adjudged that he should be kept in close confinement during two months, and that afterwards he should be banished from Venice and the state during one year. In consequence of this merciful sentence the Duke became exceedingly wroth, it appearing to him, that the Council had not acted in such a manner as was required by the respect due to his ducal dignity; and he said they ought to have condemned Ser Michele to be hanged by the neck, or at least to be banished for life.

Now it was fated that my Lord Duke Marino was to have his head cut off. And as it is necessary when any effect is to be brought about, that the cause of

such effect must happen, it therefore came to pass, that on the very day after sentence had been pronounced on Ser Michele Steno, being the first day of Lent, a gentleman of the house of Barbaro, a choleric gentleman, went to the arsenal, and required certain things of the masters of the galleys. This he did in the presence of the Admiral of the arsenal, and he, hearing the request, answered, — No, it cannot be done. High words arose between the gentleman and the Admiral, and the gentleman struck him with his fist just above the eye; and as he happened to have a ring on his finger, the ring cut the Admiral and drew blood. The Admiral, all bruised and bloody, ran straight to the Duke to complain, and with the intent of praying him to inflict some heavy punishment upon the gentleman of Cà Barbaro. — "What wouldst thou have me do for thee?" answered the Duke: "think upon the shameful gibe which hath been written concerning me; and think on the manner in which they have punished that ribald Michele Steno, who wrote it; and see how the Council of Forty respect our person." — Upon this the Admiral answered, — "My Lord Duke, if you would wish to make yourself a prince, and to cut all those cuckoldy gentlemen to pieces, I have the heart, if you do but help me, to make you prince of all this state; and then you may punish them all." — Hearing this, the Duke said, — "How can such a matter be brought about?" — and so they discoursed thereon.

The Duke called for his nephew, Ser Bertuccio Faliero, who lived with him in the palace, and they communed about this plot. And without leaving the place, they sent for Philip Calendaro, a seaman of great repute, and for Bertuccio Israello, who was exceedingly wily and cunning. Then taking counsel amongst themselves, they agreed to call in some others; and so, for several nights successively, they met with the Duke at home in his palace. And the following men were called in singly; to wit; — Niccolò, Fagiuolo, Giovanni da Corfu, Stefano Fagione, Niccolo dalle Bende, Niccolo Biondo, and Stefano Trivisano. — It was concerted that sixteen or seventeen leaders should be stationed in various parts of the city, each being at the head of forty men, armed and prepared: but the followers were not to know their destination. On the appointed day they were to make affrays amongst themselves here and there, in order that the Duke might have a pretence for tolling the bells of San Marco: these bells are never rung but by the order of the Duke. And at the sound of the bells, these sixteen or seventeen, with their followers, were to come to San Marco, through the streets which open upon the Piazza. And when the noble and leading citizens should come into the Piazza, to know the cause of the riot, then the conspirators were to cut them in pieces, and this work being finished, my Lord Marino Faliero the Duke was to be proclaimed the Lord of Venice. Things having been thus settled, they agreed to fulfil their intent on Wednesday, the 15th day of April, in the year 1355. So covertly did they plot, that no one ever dreamt of their machinations.

But the Lord, who hath always helped this most glorious city, and who, loving its righteousness and holiness, hath never forsaken it, inspired one Beltramo Bergamasco to be the cause of bringing the plot to light, in the following manner. This Beltramo, who belonged to Ser Niccolo Liono of Santo Stefano, had heard a word or two of what was to take place; and so, in the before-mentioned month of April, he went to the house of the aforesaid Ser Niccolo Liono, and told him all the particulars of the plot. Ser Niccolo, when 'he heard all these things, was struck dead, as it were, with affright. He heard all the particulars; and Beltramo prayed him to keep it all secret; and if he told Ser Niccolo, it was in order that Ser Niccolo might stop at home on the 15th of April, and thus save his life. Beltramo was going, but Ser Niccolo ordered his servants to lay hands upon him, and lock him up. Ser Niccolo then went to the house of Messer Giovanni Gradenigo Nasoni, who afterwards became Duke, and who also lived at Santo Stefano, and told him all. The matter seemed to him to be of the very greatest importance, as indeed it was; and they two went to the house of Ser Marco Cornaro, who lived at San Felice; and, having spoken with him, they all three then determined to go back to the house of Ser Niccolo Lioni, to examine the said Beltramo; and having questioned him, and heard all that he had to say, they left him in confinement. And then they all three went into the sacristy of San Salvatore, and sent their men to summon the Councillors, the Avogadori, the Capi de' Dieci, and those of the Great Council.

When all were assembled, the whole story was told to them. They were struck dead, as it were, with affright. They determined to send for Beltramo. He was brought in before them. They examined him, and ascertained that the matter was true; and, although they were exceedingly troubled, yet they determined upon their measures. And they sent for the Capi de' Quarante, the Signori di Notte, the Capi de' Sestieri, and the Cinque della Pace; and they were ordered to associate to their men other good men and true, who were to proceed to the houses of the ringleaders of the conspiracy, and secure them. And they secured the foreman of the arsenal, in order that the conspirators might not do mischief. Towards nightfall they assembled in the palace. When they were assembled in the palace, they caused the gates of the quadrangle of the palace to be shut. And they sent to the keeper of the Bell-tower, and forbade the tolling of the bells. All this was carried into effect. The before-mentioned conspirators were secured, and they were brought to the palace; and, as the Council of Ten saw that the Duke was in the plot, they resolved that twenty of the leading men of the state should be associated to them for the purpose of consultation and deliberation, but that they should not be allowed to ballot.

The counsellors were the following: — Ser Giovanni Mocenigo, of the Sestiero of San Marco; Ser Almoro Veniero da Santa Marina, of the Sestiero of Castello; Ser Tomaso Viadro, of the Sestiero of Canaregio; Ser Giovanni Sanudo, of the Sestiero of Santa Croce; Ser Pietro Trivisano, of the Sestiero of San Paolo; Ser Pantalione Barbo il Grando, of the Sestiero of Ossoduro. The Avogadori of the Commonwealth were Zufredo Morosini, and Ser Orio Pasqualigo; and these did not ballot. Those of the Council of Ten were Ser Giovanni Marcello, Ser Tommaso Sanudo, and Ser Micheletto Dolfino, the heads of the aforesaid Council of Ten. Ser Luca da Legge, and Ser Pietro da Mosto, inquisitors of the aforesaid Council. And Ser Marco Polani, Ser Marino Veniero, Ser Lando Lombardo, and Ser Nicoletto Trivisano, of Sant' Angelo.

Late in the night, just before the dawning, they chose a junta of twenty noblemen of Venice from amongst the wisest, and the worthiest, and the oldest. They were to give counsel, but not to ballot. And they would not admit any one of Cà Faliero. And Niccolo Faliero, and another Niccolo Faliero, of San Tomaso, were expelled from the Council, because they belonged to the family of the Doge. And this resolution of creating the junta of twenty was much praised throughout the state. The following were the members of the junta of twenty: — Ser Marco Giustiniani, Procuratore, Ser Andrea Erizzo, Procuratore, Ser Lionardo Giustiniani, Procuratore, Ser Andrea Contarini, Ser Simone Dandolo, Ser Nicolo Volpe, Ser Giovanni Loredano, Ser Marco Diedo, Ser Giovanni Gradenigo, Ser Andrea Cornaro, Cavaliere, Ser Marco Soranzo, Ser Rinieri du Mosto, Ser Gazano Marcello, Ser Marino Morosini, Ser Stefano Belegno, Ser Nicolo Lioni, Ser Filippo Orio, Ser Marco Trivisano, Ser Jacopo Bragadino, Ser Giovanni Foscarini.

These twenty were accordingly called in to the Council of Ten; and they sent for My Lord Marino Faliero the Duke: and My Lord Marino was then consorting in the palace with people of great estate, gentlemen, and other good men, none of whom knew yet how the fact stood.

At the same time Bertucci Israello, who, as one of the ring-leaders, was to head the conspirators in Santa Croce, was arrested and bound, and brought before the Council. Zanello del Bria, Nicoletto di Rosa, Nicoletto Alberto, and the Guardiaga, were also taken, together with several seamen, and people of various ranks. These were examined, and the truth of the plot was ascertained.

On the 16th of April judgment was given in the Council of Ten, that Filippo Calendaro and Bertuccio Israello should be hanged upon the red pillars of the balcony of the palace, from which the Duke is wont to look at the bull hunt: and they were hanged with gags in their mouths.

The next day the following were condemned: — Niccolo Zuccuolo, Nicoletto Blondo, Nicoletto Doro, Marco Giuda, Jacomello Dagolino, Nicoletto Fidele, the son of Filippo Calendaro, Marco Torello, called Israello, Stefano Trivisano, the money changer of Santa Margherita, and Antonio dalle Bende. These were all taken at Chiozza, for they were endeavoring to escape. Afterwards, by virtue of the sentence which was passed upon them in the Council of Ten, they were hanged on successive days; some singly and some in couples, upon the columns of the palace, beginning from the red columns, and so going onwards towards the canal. And other prisoners were discharged, because, although they had been involved in the conspiracy, yet they had not assisted in it: for they were given to understand by some of the heads of the plot, that they were to come armed and prepared for the service of the state, and in order to secure certain criminals; and they knew nothing else. Nicoletto Alberto, the Guardiaga, and Bartolommeo Ciricolo and his son, and several others, who were not guilty, were discharged.

On Friday, the 16th day of April, judgment was also given, in the aforesaid Council of Ten, that my Lord Marino Faliero, the Duke, should have his head cut off; and that the execution should be done on the landing-place of the stone staircase, where the Dukes take their oath when they first enter the palace. On the following day, the 17th of April, the doors of the palace being shut, the Duke had his head cut off, about the hour of noon. And the cap of estate was taken from the Duke's head before he came down stairs. When the execution was over, it is said that one of the Council of Ten went to the columns of the palace over against the place of St. Mark, and that he showed the bloody sword unto the people, crying out with a loud voice — "The terrible doom hath fallen upon the traitor!" — and the doors were opened, and the people all rushed in, to see the corpse of the Duke, who had been beheaded.

It must be known that Ser Giovanni Sanudo, the councillor, was not present when the aforesaid sentence was pronounced; because he was unwell and remained at home. So that only fourteen balloted; that is to say, five councillors, and nine of the Council of Ten. And it was adjudged, that all the lands and chattels of the Duke, as well as of the other traitors, should be forfeited to the state. And as a grace to the Duke, it was resolved in the Council of Ten, that he should be allowed to dispose of two thousand ducats out of his own property. And it was resolved, that all the councillors and all the Avogadori of the Commonwealth, those of the Council of Ten, and the members of the junta, who had assisted in passing sentence on the Duke and the other traitors, should have the privilege of carrying arms both by day and by night in Venice, and from Grado to Cavazere. And they were also to be allowed two footmen carrying arms, the aforesaid footmen living and boarding with them in their own houses. And he who did not keep two footmen might transfer the privilege to his sons or his brothers; but only to two. Permission of carrying arms was also granted to the four Notaries of the Chancery, that is to say, of the Supreme Court, who took the depositions: and they were, Amedio, Nicoletto di Lorino, Steffanello, and Pietro de Compostelli, the secretaries of the Signori di Notte.

After the traitors had been hanged, and the Duke had had his head cut off, the state remained in great tranquillity and peace. And, as I have read in a Chronicle, the corpse of the Duke was removed in a barge, with eight torches, to his tomb in the church of San Giovanni e Paolo, where it was buried. The tomb is now in that aisle in the middle of the little church of Santa Maria della Pace, which was built by Bishop Gabriel of Bergamo. It is a coffin of stone, with these words engraven thereon: — "*Heic jacet Dominus Marinus Faletro Dux.*" — And they did not paint his portrait in the hall of the Great Council: — but in the place where it ought to have been, you see these words: — "*Hic est locus Marini Faletro, decapitati pro criminibus.*" — And it is thought that his house was granted to the church of Sant' Apostolo; it was that great one near the bridge. Yet this could not be the case, or else the family bought it back from the church; for it still belongs to Cà Faliero. I must not refrain from noting, that some wished to write the following words in the place where his portrait ought to have been, as aforesaid: — "*Marinus Faletro Dux, temeritas me cepit. Pœnas lui, decapitatus pro criminibus.*" — Others, also, indited a couplet, worthy of being inscribed upon his tomb.

"*Dux Venetum jacet heic, patriam qui prodere tentans,*
Sceptra, decus, censum perdidit. atque caput."

NOTE B.

PETRARCH ON THE CONSPIRACY OF MARINO FALIERO.[1]

"AL giovane Doge Andrea Dandolo succedette un vecchio, il quale tardi si pose al timone della repubblica, ma sempre prima di quel che facea d' uopo a lui, ed alla patria: egli è Marino Faliero, personaggio a me noto per antica dimestichezza. Falsa era l' opinione intorno a lui, giacchè egli si mostrò fornito più di corraggio, che di senno. Non pago della prima dignità, entrò con sinistro piede nel pubblico Palazzo: imperciocchè questo Doge dei Veneti, magistrato sacro in tutti i secoli, che dagli antichi fù sempre venerato qual nume in quella città, l' altr' jeri fu decollato nel vestibolo dell' istesso Palazzo. Discorrerei fin dal principio le cause di un tale evvento, se così vario ed ambiguo non ne fosse il grido. Nessuno però lo scusa, tutti affermano, che egli abbia voluto cangiar qualche cosa nell' ordine della repubblica a lui tramandato dai maggiori. Che desiderava egli di più? Io son d' avviso, che egli abbia ottenuto ciò che non si concedette a nessun altro: mentre adempiva gli uffcj di legato presso il Pontefice, e sulle rive del Rodano trattava la pace, che io prima di lui aveva indarno tentato di conchiudere, gli fù conferito l' onore del Ducato, che ne chiedeva, ne s' aspettava. Tornato in patria, pensò a quello cui nessuno non pose mente giammai, e soffrì quello che a niuno accadde mai di soffrire: giacchè in quel luogo celeberrimo, e chiarissimo, e bellissimo infra tutti quelli che io vidi, ove i suoi antenati avevano ricevuti grandissimi onori in mezzo alle pompe trionfali, ivi egli fù trascinato in modo servile, e spogliato delle insegne ducali, perdette la testa, e macchiò col proprio sangue le soglie del tempio, l' atrio del Palazzo, e le scale marmoree rendute spesse volte illustri, o dalle solenni festività, o dalle ostili spoglie. Hò notato il luogo, ora noto il tempo: è l' anno del Natale di Cristo 1355, fù il giorno 18 d' Aprile. Si alto è il grido sparso, che se alcuno esaminerà la disciplina, e le costumanze di quella città, e quanto mutamento di cose venga minacciato dalla morte di un sol uomo (quantunque molti altri, come narrano, essendo complici, o subirono l' istesso supplicio, o lo aspettano) si accorgerà, che nulla di più grande avvenne ai nostri tempi nella Italia. Tu forse qui attendi il mio giudizio: assolvo il popolo, se credere alla fama, benchè abbia potuto e castigare più mitemente, e con maggior dolcezza vendicare il suo dolore: ma non così facilmente si modera un' ira giusta insieme e grande, in un numeroso popolo volgo aguzza gli stimoli dell' irracondia con rapidi e sconsigliati clamori. Compatisco, e nell' istesso tempo mi adiro con quell' infelice uomo, il quale adorno di un' insolito onore, non so che cosa si volesse negli estremi anni della sua vita: la calamità di lui diviene sempre più grave, perchè dalla sentenza contradi esso promulgata aperirà, che egli fù non solo misero, ma insano, e demente, e che con vane arti si

[1] [" Had a copy taken of an extract from Petrarch's Letters, with reference to the conspiracy of the Doge Marino Faliero, containing the poet's opinion of the matter." — *Byron's Diary*, February 11, 1821.]

usurpò per tanti anni una falsa fama di sapienza. Ammonisco i Dogi, i quali gli succederano, che questo è un' esempio posto inanzi ai loro occhj, quale specchio, nel quale veggano d' essere non Signori, ma Duci, anzi nemmeno Duci, ma onorati servi della Repubblica. Tu sta sano; e giacchè fluttuano le pubbliche cose, sforsiamosi di governar modestissimamente i privati nostri affari."—LE-VATI, *Viaggi di Petrarca*, vol. iv. p. 323.

The above Italian translation from the Latin epistles of Petrarch proves —

1stly, That Marino Faliero was a personal friend of Petrarch's; "antica dimestichezza," old intimacy, is the phrase of the poet.

2dly, That Petrarch thought that he had more courage than conduct, "più di *corraggio* che di senno."

3dly, That there was some jealousy on the part of Petrarch; for he says that Marino Faliero was treating of the peace which he himself had "vainly attempted to conclude."

4thly. That the honor of the Dukedom was conferred upon him, which he neither sought nor expected, "che nè chiedeva nè aspettava," and which had never been granted to any other in like circumstances, "ciò che non si concedette a nessun altro," a proof of the high esteem in which he must have been held.

5thly, That he had a reputation for *wisdom, only* forfeited by the last enterprise of his life, "si usurpò per tanti anni una falsa fama di sapienza." —"He had usurped for so many years a false fame of wisdom," rather a difficult task, I should think. People are generally found out before eighty years of age, at least in a republic.

From these and the other historical notes which I have collected, it may be inferred, that Marino Faliero possessed many of the qualities, but not the success of a hero; and that his passions were too violent. The paltry and ignorant account of Dr. Moore falls to the ground. Petrarch says, "that there had been no greater event in his times" (*our times* literally), "nostri tempi," in Italy. He also differs from the historian in saying that Faliero was "on the banks of the *Rhone*," instead of at Rome, when elected; the other accounts say, that the deputation of the Venetian senate met him at R venna. How this may have been, it is not for me to decide, and is of no great importance. Had the man succeeded, he would have changed the face of Venice, and perhaps of Italy. As it is, what *are* they both?

NOTE C.

VENETIAN SOCIETY AND MANNERS.

"Vice without splendor, sin without relief
Even from the gloss of love to smoothe it o'er;
But, in its stead, coarse lusts of habitude," etc.
— (*See* p. 173.)

"To these attacks so frequently pointed by the government against the clergy, — to the continual struggles between the different constituted bodies, — to these enterprises carried on by the mass of the nobles against the depositaries of power, — to all those projects of innovation, which always ended by a stroke of state policy; we must add a cause not less fitted to spread contempt for ancient doctrines; *this was the excess of corruption.*

"That freedom of manners, which had been long boasted of as the principal charm of Venetian society, had degenerated into scandalous licentiousness: the tie of marriage was less sacred in that Catholic country, than among those nations where the laws and religion admit of its being dissolved. Because they could not break the contract, they feigned that it had not existed; and the ground of nullity, immodestly alleged by the married pair, was admitted with equal facility by priests and magistrates, alike corrupt. These divorces, veiled under another name, became so frequent, that the most important act of civil society was discovered to be amenable to a tribunal of exceptions; and to restrain the open scandal of such proceedings became the office of the police. In 1782, the Council of Ten decreed, that every woman who should sue for a dissolution of her marriage should be compelled to await the decision of the judges in some convent, to be named by the court.[1] Soon afterwards the same council summoned all causes of that nature before itself.[2] This infringement on ecclesiastical jurisdiction having occasioned some remonstrance from Rome, the council retained only the right of rejecting the petition of the married persons, and consented to refer such causes to the holy office as it should not previously have rejected.[3]

"There was a moment in which, doubtless, the destruction of private fortunes, the ruin of youth, the domestic discord occasioned by these abuses, determined the government to depart from its established maxims concerning the freedom of manners allowed the subject. All the courtesans were banished from Venice; but their absence was not enough to reclaim and bring back good morals to a whole people brought up in the most scandalous licentiousness. Depravity reached the very bosoms of private families, and even into the cloister; and they found themselves obliged to recall, and even to indemnify[4] women who sometimes gained possession of important secrets, and who might be usefully employed in the ruin of men whose fortunes might have rendered them dangerous. Since that time licentiousness has gone on increasing; and we have seen mothers, not only selling the innocence of their daughters, but selling it by a contract, authenticated by the signature of a public officer, and the performance of which was secured by the protection of the laws.[5]

"The parlors of the convents of noble ladies, and the houses of the courtesans, though the police carefully kept up a number of spies about them, were the only assemblies for society in Venice; and in these two places, so different from each other, there was equal freedom. Music, collations, gallantry, were not more forbidden in the parlors than at the casinos. There were a number of casinos for the purpose of public assemblies, where gaming was the principal pursuit of the company. It was

[1] Correspondence of M. Schlick, French chargé d'affaires. Despatch of 24th August, 1782.
[2] *Ibid.* Despatch, 31st August.
[3] *Ibid.* Despatch of 3d September, 1785.
[4] The decree for their recall designates them as *nostre bènemerite meretrici:* a fund and some houses, called *Case rampane*, were assigned to them; hence the opprobrious appellation of *Carampane.*
[5] Mayer, Description of Venice, vol. ii., and M. Archenholz, Picture of Italy, vol. i. ch. 2.

a strange sight to see persons of either sex masked, or grave in their magisterial robes, round a table, invoking chance, and giving way at one instant to the agonies of despair, at the next to the illusions of hope, and that without uttering a single word. "The rich had private casinos, but they lived *incognito* in them; and the wives whom they abandoned found compensation in the liberty they enjoyed. The corruption of morals had deprived them of their empire. We have just reviewed the whole history of Venice, and we have not once seen them exercise the slightest influence." — *Daru: Hist. de la Répub. a. vénise,* vol. **v.** p. 95.

SARDANAPALUS:[1] A TRAGEDY.

TO THE ILLUSTRIOUS GOETHE

A STRANGER PRESUMES TO OFFER THE HOMAGE OF A

LITERARY VASSAL TO HIS LIEGE LORD, THE FIRST OF EXISTING WRITERS,

WHO HAS CREATED THE LITERATURE OF HIS OWN COUNTRY,

AND ILLUSTRATED THAT OF EUROPE.

THE UNWORTHY PRODUCTION

WHICH THE AUTHOR VENTURES TO INSCRIBE TO HIM IS ENTITLED

SARDANAPALUS.[2]

[1] [Sardanapalus is, beyond all doubt, a work of great beauty and power; and though the heroine has many traits in common with the Medoras and Gulnares of Lord Byron's undramatic poetry, the hero must be allowed to be a new character in his hands. He has, indeed, the scorn of war, and glory, and priestcraft, and regular morality, which distinguishes the rest of his lordship's favorites; but he has no misanthropy, and very little pride — and may be regarded, on the whole, as one of the most truly good-humored, amiable, and respectable voluptuaries to whom we have ever been presented. In this conception of his character, the author has very wisely followed nature and fancy rather than history. *His* Sardanapalus is not an effeminate, worn-out debauchee, with shattered nerves and exhausted senses, the slave of indolence and vicious habits; but a sanguine votary of pleasure, a princely epicure, indulging, revelling in boundless luxury while he can, but with a soul so inured to voluptuousness, so saturated with delights, that pain and danger, when they come uncalled for, give him neither concern nor dread; and he goes forth from the banquet to the battle, as to a dance or measure, attired by the Graces, and with youth, joy, and love for his guides. He dallies with Bellona as bridegroom — for his sport and pastime; and the spear or fan, the shield or shining mirror, become his hands equally well. He enjoys life, in short, and triumphs in death; and whether in prosperous or adverse circumstances, his soul smiles out superior to evil. — *Jeffrey.*

The Sardanapalus of Lord Byron is pretty nearly such a person as the Sardanapalus of history may be supposed to have been. Young, thoughtless, spoiled by flattery and unbounded self-indulgence, but with a temper naturally amiable, and abilities of a superior order, he affects to undervalue the sanguinary renown of his ancestors as an excuse for inattention to the most necessary duties of his rank; and flatters himself, while he is indulging his own sloth, that he is making his people happy. Yet, even in his fondness for pleasure, there lurks a love of contradiction. Of the whole picture, selfishness is the prevailing feature — selfishness admirably drawn indeed; apologized for by every palliating circumstance of education and habit, and clothed in the brightest colors of which it is susceptible from youth, talents, and placability. But it is selfishness still; and we should have been tempted to quarrel with the art which made vice and frivolity thus amiable, if Lord Byron had not at the same time pointed out with much skill the bitterness and weariness of spirit which inevitably wait on such a character; and if he had not given a fine contrast to the picture in the accompanying portraits of Salemenes and of Myrrha. — *Bishop Heber.*]

[2] ["Well knowing myself and my labors, in my old age, I could not but reflect with gratitude and diffidence on the expressions contained in this dedication, nor interpret them but as the generous tribute of a superior genius, no less original in the choice than inexhaustible in the materials of his subjects." — *Goethe.*]

INTRODUCTION.

On the original MS. Byron wrote: —"*Mem.* Ravenna, May 27, 1821. — I began this drama on the 13th of January, 1821; and continued the two first acts very slowly, and by intervals. The three last acts were-written since the 13th of May, 1821 (this present month); that is to say, in a fortnight." The following are extracts from Byron's diary and letters: —

" January 13, 1821. Sketched the outline and Dram. Pers. of an intended tragedy of Sardanapalus, which I have for some time meditated. Took the names from Diodorus Siculus, (I know the history of Sardanapalus, and have known it since I was twelve years old,) and read over a passage in the ninth volume of Mitford's Greece, where he rather vindicates the memory of this last of the Assyrians. Carried Teresa the Italian translation of Grillparzer's Sappho. She quarrelled with me, because I said that love was *not the loftiest* theme for a tragedy; and, having the advantage of her native language, and natural female eloquence, she overcame my fewer arguments. I believe she was right. I must put more love into ' Sardanapalus ' than I intended."

" May 25. I have completed four acts. I have made Sardanapalus brave, (though voluptuous, as history represents him,) and also as amiable as my poor powers could render him. I have strictly pre-served all the unities hitherto, and mean to continue them in the fifth, if possible; but NOT for *the stage.*"

" May 30. By this post I send you the tragedy. You will remark that the unities are all strictly pre-served. The scene passes in the same hall always: the time, a summer's night, about nine hours or less; though it begins before sunset, and ends after sunrise. It is not for the stage, any more than the other was intended for it; and I shall take better care this time that they don't get hold on't."

" July 14. I trust that ' Sardanapalus ' will not be mistaken for a political play; which was so far from my intention, that I thought of nothing but Asiatic history. My object has been to dramatize, like the Greeks (a *modest* phrase), striking passages of history and mythology. You will find all this very unlike Shakspeare; and so much the better in one sense, for I look upon him to be the worst of models, though the most extraordinary of writers. It has been my object to be as simple and severe as Alfieri, and I have broken down the poetry as nearly as I could to common language. The hardship is that, in these times, one can neither speak of kings nor queens without suspicion of politics or personalities. I intended neither.

" July 22. Print away, and publish. I think they must own that I have more styles than one. ' Sar-danapalus ' is, however, almost a comic character; but, for that matter, so is Richard the Third. Mind the *unities*, which are my great object of research. I am glad Gifford likes it: as for the million, you see I have carefully consulted any thing but the taste of the day for extravagant ' coups de théâtre.' "

Sardanapalus was published in December, 1821, and was received with very great approbation.

The following is an extract from The Life of Dr. Parr: —" In the course of the evening the Doctor tried out —' Have you read Sardanapalus?' —' Yes, Sir.' —' Right; and you couldn't sleep a wink after it?' —' No.' —' Right, right — now don't say a word more about it to-night.' —The memory of that fine poem seemed to act like a spell of horrible fascination upon him."

DRAMATIS PERSONÆ.

MEN.	WOMEN.
SARDANAPALUS, *King of Nineveh and As-syria, etc.*	ZARINA, *the Queen.*
ARBACES, *the Mede who aspired to the Throne.*	MYRRHA, *an Ionian female Slave, and the Favorite of* SARDANAPALUS.
BELESES, *a Chaldean and Soothsayer.*	*Women composing the Harem of* SARDA-NAPALUS, *Guards, Attendants, Chaldean Priests, Medes, etc. etc.*
SALEMENES, *the King's Brother-in-law.*	
ALTADA, *an Assyrian Officer of the Palace.*	
PANIA. ZAMES. SFERO. BALEA.	

Scene — a Hall in the Royal Palace of Nineveh.

ACT I.

SCENE I. — *A Hall in the Palace.*

Salemenes (solus). He hath wronged his
   queen, but still he is her lord;
He hath wronged my sister, still he is my
   brother;
He hath wronged his people, still he is their
   sovereign,
And I must be his friend as well as subject:
He must not perish thus. I will not see
The blood of Nimrod and Semiramis
Sink in the earth, and thirteen hundred years
Of empire ending like a shepherd's tale;
He must be roused. In his effeminate heart
There is a careless courage which corruption
Has not all quenched, and latent energies,
Repressed by circumstance, but not de-
   stroyed—
Steeped, but not drowned, in deep voluptu-
   ousness.
If born a peasant, he had been a man
To have reached an empire: to an empire
   born,
He will bequeathe none; nothing but a name,
Which his sons will not prize in heritage:—
Yet, not all lost, even yet he may redeem
His sloth and shame, by only being that
Which he should be, as easily as the thing
He should not be and is. Were it less toil
To sway his nations than consume his life?
To head an army than to rule a harem?
He sweats in palling pleasures, dulls his soul,[1]
And saps his goodly strength, in toils which
   yield not
Health like the chase, nor glory like the war—
He must be roused. Alas! there is no sound
   [*Sound of soft music heard from within.*
To rouse him short of thunder. Hark! the
   lute,
The lyre, the timbrel; the lascivious tinklings
Of lulling instruments, the softening voices
Of women, and of beings less than women,
Must chime in to the echo of his revel,
While the great king of all we know of earth
Lolls crowned with roses, and his diadem
Lies negligently by to be caught up
By the first manly hand which dares to snatch
   it.
Lo, where they come! already I perceive
The reeking odors of the perfumed trains,
And see the bright gems of the glittering girls,[2]
At once his chorus and his council, flash
Along the gallery, and amidst the damsels,
As femininely garbed, and scarce less female,
The grandson of Semiramis, the man-
   queen.—

He comes! Shall I await him? yes, and
   front him,
And tell him what all good men tell each
   other,
Speaking of him and his. They come, the
   slaves,
Led by the monarch subject to his slaves.[3]

SCENE II.— *Enter* SARDANAPALUS *effemi-
nately dressed, his Head crowned with
Flowers, and his Robe negligently flowing,
attended by a Train of Women and young
Slaves.*

Sar. (speaking to some of his attendants).
Let the pavilion over the Euphrates
Be garlanded, and lit, and furnished forth
For an especial banquet; at the hour
Of midnight we will sup there: see nought
   wanting,
And bid the galley be prepared. There is
A cooling breeze which crisps the broad clear
   river:
We will embark anon. Fair nymphs, who
   deign
To share the soft hours of Sardanapalus,
We'll meet again in that the sweetest hour,
When we shall gather like the stars above us,
And you will form a heaven as bright as
   theirs;
Till then, let each be mistress of her time,
And thou, my own Ionian Myrrha,[4] choose,
Wilt thou along with them or me?

---

[1] [MS.—
  "He sweats in dreary, dulled effeminacy."]

[2] [MS.—
  "And see the gewgaws of the glittering girls."]

[3] [Salemenes is the direct opposite to selfishness;
and the character, though slightly sketched, dis-
plays little less ability than that of Sardanapalus.
He is a stern, loyal, plain-spoken soldier and sub-
ject; clear-sighted, just, and honorable in his ulti-
mate views, though not more punctilious about the
means of obtaining them than might be expected
from a respectable satrap of ancient Nineveh, or a
respectable vizier of the modern Turkish empire.
To his king, in spite of personal neglect and family
injuries, he is, throughout, pertinaciously attached
and punctiliously faithful. To the king's rebels he
is inclined to be severe, bloody, and even treacher-
ous; an imperfection, however, in his character,
to want which would, in his situation, be almost
unnatural, and which is skilfully introduced as a
contrast to the instinctive perception of virtue and
honor which flashes out from the indolence of his
master. Of the satrap, however, the faults as well
as the virtues are alike the offspring of disinterested
loyalty and patriotism. It is for his country and
king that he is patient of injury; for them he is
valiant; for them cruel. He has no ambition of
personal power, no thirst of individual fame. In
battle and in victory, "Assyria!" is his only war-
cry. When he sends off the queen and princes, he
is less anxious for his nephews and sister than for
the preservation of the line of Nimrod; and, in his
last moments, it is the supposed flight of his sov-
ereign which alone distresses and overcomes him.—
Heber.]

[4] "The Ionian name had been still more com-
prehensive, having included the Achaians and the

Myr.   My lord——
Sar. My lord, my life! why answerest
  thou so coldly?
It is the curse of kings to be so answered.
Rule thy own hours, thou rulest mine — say,
  wouldst thou
Accompany our guests, or charm away
The moments from me?
  Myr.   The king's choice is mine.[1]
Sar. I pray thee say not so: my chiefest
  joy
Is to contribute to thine every wish.
I do not dare to breathe my own desire,
Lest it should clash with thine; for thou art
  still
Too prompt to sacrifice thy thoughts for
  others.[2]
  Myr. I would remain: I have no happiness
Save in beholding thine; yet——
  Sar.   Yet! what YET?
Thy own sweet will shall be the only barrier
Which ever rises betwixt thee and me.
  Myr. I think the present is the wonted hour
Of council; it were better I retire.
Sal. (*comes forward and says*). The Ionian
  slave says well: let her retire.
Sar. Who answers? How now, brother?
Sal.   The *queen's* brother,
And your most faithful vassal, royal lord.
Sar. (*addressing his train*). As I have
  said, let all dispose their hours
Till midnight, when again we pray your pres-
  ence.   [*The court retiring.*

Bœotians, who, together with those to whom it was
afterwards confined, would make nearly the whole
of the Greek nation; and among the orientals it was
always the general name for the Greeks." — *Mit-
ford's Greece*, vol. i. p. 199.
  [1] [The chief charm and vivifying angel of the
piece is Myrrha, the Greek slave of Sardanapalus
— a beautiful, heroic, devoted, and ethereal being —
in love with the generous and infatuated monarch —
ashamed of loving a barbarian — and using all her
influence over him to ennoble as well as to adorn
his existence, and to arm him against the terrors of
his close. Her voluptuousness is that of the heart
— her heroism of the affections. If the part she
takes in the dialogue be sometimes too subdued
and submissive for the lofty daring of her character,
it is still such as might become a Greek slave — a
lovely Ionian girl, in whom the love of liberty and
the scorn of death were tempered by the conscious-
ness of what she regarded as a degrading passion,
and an inward sense of fitness and decorum with
reference to her condition. — *Jeffrey.*]
  [2] [Myrrha is a female Salemenes, in whom, with
admirable skill, attachment to the individual Sar-
danapalus is substituted for the gallant soldier's
loyalty to the descendant of kings; and whose
energy of expostulation, no less than the natural
high tone of her talents, her courage, and her
Grecian pride, is softened into a subdued and win-
ning tenderness by the constant and painful recol-
lection of her abasement as a slave in the royal
harem; and still more by the lowliness of perfect

(*To* MYRRHA,[3] *who is going*.) Myrrha! I
  thought *thou* wouldst remain.
  Myr.   Great king,
Thou didst not say so.
  Sar.   But *thou* lookedst it
I know each glance of those Ionic eyes,[4]
Which said thou wouldst not leave me.
  Myr.   Sire! your brother——
Sal. His *consort's* brother, minion of Ionia!
How darest *thou* name *me* and not blush?
  Sar.   Not blush!
Thou hast no more eyes than heart to make
  her crimson
Like to the dying day on Caucasus,
Where sunset tints the snow with rosy shadows,
And then reproach her with thine own cold
  blindness,
Which will not see it. What, in tears, my
  Myrrha?
Sal. Let them flow on; she weeps for
  more than one,
And is herself the cause of bitterer tears.
Sar. Cursed be he who caused those tears
  to flow!
Sal. Curse not thyself — millions do that
  already.
Sar. Thou dost forget thee: make me not
  remember
I am a monarch.
Sal.   Would thou couldst!
Myr.   My sovereign,
I pray, and thou, too, prince, permit my ab-
  sence.
Sar. Since it must be so, and this churl
  has checked
Thy gentle spirit, go; but recollect
That we must forthwith meet: I had rather lose
An empire than thy presence.
                    [*Exit* MYRRHA.
Sal.   It may be,
Thou wilt lose both, and both for ever!
Sar.   Brother,
I can at least command myself, who listen
To language such as this: yet urge me not
Beyond my easy nature.
Sal.   'Tis beyond
That easy, far too easy, idle nature,
Which I would urge thee. O that I could
  rouse thee!
Though 'twere against myself.

---

womanly love in the presence of and towards the
object of her passion. No character can be drawn
more natural than hers; few ever have been drawn
more touching and amiable. Of course she is not,
nor could be, a Jewish or a Christian heroine; but
she is a model of Grecian piety and nobility of spirit,
and she is one whom a purer faith would have
raised to the level of a Rebecca or a Miriam. —
Heber.]
  [3] [In the original draught, " *Byblis.*"]
  [4] [MS. — " I know each glance of those deep
          Greek-souled eyes."]

Sar.   By the god Baal!
The man would make me tyrant.
Sal.   So thou art.
Think'st thou there is no tyranny but that
Of blood and chains? The despotism of
    vice —
The weakness and the wickedness of luxury —
The negligence — the apathy — the evils
Of sensual sloth — produce ten thousand ty-
    rants,
Whose delegated cruelty surpasses
The worst acts of one energetic master,
However harsh and hard in his own bearing.
The false and fond examples of thy lusts
Corrupt no less than they oppress, and sap
In the same moment all thy pageant power
And those who should sustain it; so that
    whether
A foreign foe invade, or civil broil
Distract within, both will alike prove fatal:
The first thy subjects have no heart to con-
    quer;
The last they rather would assist than van-
    quish.
Sar. Why, what makes thee the mouth-
    piece of the people?
Sal. Forgiveness of the queen, my sister's
    wrongs;
A natural love unto my infant nephews;
Faith to the king, a faith he may need shortly,
In more than words; respect for Nimrod's
    line;
Also, another thing thou knowest not.
Sar. What's that?
Sal.   To thee an unknown word.
Sar.   Yet speak it;
I love to learn.
Sal.   Virtue.
Sar.   Not know the word!
Never was word yet rung so in my ears —
Worse than the rabble's shout, or splitting
    trumpet:
I've heard thy sister talk of nothing else.
Sal. To change the irksome theme, then,
    hear of vice.
Sar. From whom?
Sal. Even from the winds, if thou couldst
    listen
Unto the echoes of the nation's voice.
Sar. Come, I'm indulgent, as thou know-
    est, patient,
As thou hast often proved — speak out, what
    moves thee?
Sal. Thy peril.
Sar.   Say on.
Sal.   Thus, then: all the nations,
For they are many, whom thy father left
In heritage, are loud in wrath against thee.
Sar. 'Gainst *me!* What would the slaves?
Sal.   A king.
Sar.   And what
Am I then?

Sal.   In their eyes a nothing; but
In mine a man who might be something still.
Sar. The railing drunkards! why, what
    would they have?
Have they not peace and plenty?
Sal.   Of the first
More than is glorious; of the last, far less
Than the king recks of.
Sar.   Whose then is the crime,
But the false satraps, who provide no better?
Sal. And somewhat in the monarch who
    ne'er looks
Beyond his palace walls, or if he stirs
Beyond them, 'tis but to some mountain palace,
Till summer heats wear down. O glorious
    Baal!
Who built up this vast empire, and wert made
A god, or at the least shinest like a god
Through the long centuries of thy renown,
This, thy presumed descendant, ne'er beheld
As king the kingdoms thou didst leave as
    ·   hero,
Won with thy blood, and toil, and time, and
    peril!
For what? to furnish imposts for a revel,
Or multiplied extortions for a minion.
Sar. I understand thee — thou wouldst
    have me go
Forth as a conqueror. By all the stars
Which the Chaldeans read — the restless
    slaves [1]   •
Deserve that I should curse them with their
    wishes,
And lead them forth to glory.
Sal.   Wherefore not?
Semiramis — a woman only — led
These our Assyrians to the solar shores
Of Ganges.
Sar. 'Tis most true. And *how* returned?
Sal. Why, like a *man* — a hero; baffled,
    but
Not vanquished. With but twenty guards,
    she made
Good her retreat to Bactria.
Sar.   And how many
Left she behind in India to the vultures?
Sal. Our annals say not.
Sar.   Then I will say for them —
That she had better woven within her palace
Some twenty garments, than with twenty
    guards
Have fled to Bactria, leaving to the ravens,
And wolves, and men — the fiercer of the three
Her myriads of fond subjects. Is *this* glory?
Then let me live in ignominy ever.
Sal. All warlike spirits have not the same
    fate.
Semiramis, the glorious parent of
A hundred kings, although she failed in India,

---

[1] [MS.   — " I have a mind
To curse the restless slaves with their own wishes."]

Brought Persia, Media, Bactria, to the realm
Which she once swayed — and thou *might'st*
  sway.
  Sar.   I *sway* them —
She but subdued them.
  Sal.   It may be ere long
That they will need her sword more than your
  sceptre.
  Sar. There was a certain Bacchus, was
  there not ?
I've heard my Greek girls speak of such —
  they say
He was a god, that is, a Grecian god,
An idol foreign to Assyria's worship,
Who conquered this same golden realm of
  Ind
Thou prat'st of, where Semiramis was van-
  quished.
  Sal. I have heard of such a man; and
  thou perceiv'st
That he is deemed a god for what he did.
  Sar. And in his godship I will honor
  him —
Not much as man. What, ho! my cup-
  bearer!
  Sal. What means the king?
  Sar.   To worship your new god
And ancient conqueror. Some wine, I say.

Enter Cupbearer.

  Sar. (*addressing the Cupbearer*). Bring me
  the golden goblet thick with gems,
Which bears the name of Nimrod's chalice.
  Hence,
Fill full, and bear it quickly. [*Exit Cupbearer.*
  Sal.   In this moment
A fitting one for the resumption of
Thy yet unslept-off revels?

Re-enter Cupbearer, with wine.

  Sar. (*taking the cup from him*). Noble
  kinsman,
If these barbarian Greeks of the far shores
And skirts of these our realms lie not, this
  Bacchus
Conquered the whole of India, did he not?
  Sal. He did, and thence was deemed a
  deity.[1]
  Sar. Not so : — of all his conquests a few
  columns,
Which may be his, and might be mine, if I
Thought them worth purchase and convey-
  ance, are
The landmarks of the seas of gore he shed,
The realms he wasted, and the hearts he
  broke.
But here, here in this goblet is his title
To immortality — the immortal grape
From which he first expressed the soul, and
  gave

____
[1] [MS. —
'He did, and thence was deemed a god in story.'']

To gladden that of man, as some atonement
For the victorious mischiefs he had done.
Had it not been for this, he would have been
A mortal still in name as in his grave;
And, like my ancestor Semiramis,
A sort of semi-glorious human monster.
Here's that which deified him — let it now
Humanize thee; my surly, chiding brother,
Pledge me to the Greek god!
  Sal.   For all thy realms
I would not so blaspheme our country's
  creed.
  Sar. That is to say, thou thinkest him a
  hero,
That he shed blood by oceans; and no god,
Because he turned a fruit to an enchantment,
Which cheers the sad, revives the old, in-
  spires
The young, makes weariness forget his toil,
And fear her danger; opens a new world
When this, the present, palls. Well, then *I*
  pledge thee
And *him* as a true man, who did his utmost
In good or evil to surprise mankind. [*Drinks.*
  Sal. Wilt thou resume a revel at this hour?
  Sar. And if I did, 'twere better than a
  trophy,
Being bought without a tear. But that is not
My present purpose: since thou wilt not
  pledge me,
Continue what thou pleasest.
  (*To the Cupbearer.*)   Boy, retire.
                            [*Exit Cupbearer.*
  Sal. I would but have recalled thee from
  thy dream;
Better by me awakened than rebellion.
  Sar. Who should rebel ? or why ? what
  cause ? pretext ?
I am the lawful king, descended from
A race of kings who knew no predecessors.
What have I done to thee, or to the people,
That thou shouldst rail, or they rise up against
  me ?
  Sal. Of what thou hast done to me, I
  speak not.
  Sar.   But
Thou think'st that I have wronged the queen:
  is't not so ?
  Sal. *Think!* Thou hast wronged her![2]
  Sar.   Patience, prince, and hear me.
She has all power and splendor of her sta-
  tion,
Respect, the tutelage of Assyria's heirs,
The homage and the appanage of sovereignty.
I married her as monarchs wed — for state,

____
[2] [In many parts of this play, it strikes me that
Lord Byron has more in his eye the case of a
sinful Christian that has but one wife, and a sly
business or so which she and her kin do not ap-
prove of, than a bearded Oriental, like Sardanapa-
lus, with three hundred wives and seven hundred
concubines. — *Hogg.*]

And loved her as most husbands love their
  wives.
If she or thou supposedst I could link me
Like a Chaldean peasant to his mate,
Ye knew nor me, nor monarchs, nor mankind.
  Sal. I pray thee, change the theme: my
  blood disdains
Complaint, and Salemenes' sister seeks not
Reluctant love even from Assyria's lord!
Nor would she deign to accept divided pas-
  sion
With foreign strumpets and Ionian slaves.
The queen is silent.
  Sar.   And why not her brother?
  Sal. I only echo thee the voice of empires,
Which he who long neglects not long will gov-
  ern.
  Sar. The ungrateful and ungracious slaves!
  they murmur
Because I have not shed their blood, nor led
  them
To dry into the desert's dust by myriads,
Or whiten with their bones the banks of
  Ganges;
Nor decimated them with savage laws,
Nor sweated them to build up pyramids,
Or Babylonian walls.
  Sal.   Yet these are trophies
More worthy of a people and their prince
Than songs, and lutes, and feasts, and concu-
  bines,
And lavished treasures, and contemned vir-
  tues.
  Sar. Oh, for my trophies I have founded
  cities:
There's Tarsus and Anchialus, both built
In one day — what could that blood-loving
  beldame,
My martial grandam, chaste Semiramis,
Do more, except destroy them?
  Sal.   'Tis most true;
I own thy merit in those founded cities,
Built for a whim, recorded with a verse
Which shames both them and thee to coming
  ages.
  Sar. Shame me! By Baal, the cities, though
  well built,
Are not more goodly than the verse! Say
  what
Thou wilt 'gainst me, my mode of life or rule,
But nothing 'gainst the truth of that brief
  record.
Why, those few lines contain the history
Of all things human: hear — "Sardanapalus,
The king, and son of Anacyndaraxes,
In one day built Anchialus and Tarsus.
Eat, drink, and love; the rest's not worth a
  fillip."[1]

  Sal. A worthy moral, and a wise inscrip-
  tion,
For a king to put up before his subjects!
  Sar. Oh, thou wouldst have me doubtless
  set up edicts —
"Obey the king — contribute to his treasure —
Recruit his phalanx — spill your blood at bid-
  ding —
Fall down and worship, or get up and toil."
Or thus — "Sardanapalus on this spot
Slew fifty thousand of his enemies.
These are their sepulchres, and this his tro-
  phy."
I leave such things to conquerors; enough
For me, if I can make my subjects feel
The weight of human misery less, and glide
Ungroaning to the tomb: I take no license
Which I deny to them. We all are men.
  Sal. Thy sires have been revered as gods —
  Sar.   In dust
And death, where they are neither gods nor
  men.
Talk not of such to me! the worms are gods;

---

[1] "For this expedition he took only a small chosen body of the phalanx, but all his light troops. In the first day's march he reached Anchialus, a town said to have been founded by the king of Assyria, Sardanapalus. The fortifications, in their magnitude and extent, still in Arrian's time, bore the character of greatness, which the Assyrians appear singularly to have affected in works of the kind. A monument representing Sardanapalus was found there, warranted by an inscription in Assyrian characters, of course in the old Assyrian language, which the Greeks, whether well or ill, interpreted thus: 'Sardanapalus, son of Anacyndaraxes, in one day founded Anchialus and Tarsus. Eat, drink, play: all other human joys are not worth a fillip.' Supposing this version nearly exact (for Arrian says it was not quite so), whether the purpose has not been to invite to civil order a people disposed to turbulence, rather than to recommend immoderate luxury, may perhaps reasonably be questioned. What, indeed, could be the object of a king of Assyria in founding such towns in a country so distant from his capital, and so divided from it by an immense extent of sandy deserts and lofty mountains, and, still more, how the inhabitants could be at once in circumstances to abandon themselves to the intemperate joys which their prince has been supposed to have recommended, is not obvious: but it may deserve observation that, in that line of coast, the southern of Lesser Asia, ruins of cities, evidently of an age after Alexander, yet barely named in history, at this day astonish the adventurous traveller by their magnificence and elegance. Amid the desolation which, under a singularly barbarian government, has for so many centuries been daily spreading in the finest countries of the globe, whether more from soil and climate, or from opportunities for commerce, extraordinary means must have been found her communities to flourish there; whence it may seem that the measures of Sardanapalus were directed by juster views than have been commonly ascribed to him: but that monarch having been the last of a dynasty, ended by a revolution, obloquy on his memory would follow of course from the policy of his successors and their partisans. The inconsistency of traditions concerning Sardanapalus is striking in Diodorus's account of him." — *Mitford's Greece,* vol. x. p. 311.

At least they banqueted upon your gods,
And died for lack of farther nutriment.
Those gods were merely men; look to their
  issue —
I feel a thousand mortal things about me,
But nothing godlike, — unless it may be
The thing which you condemn, a disposition
To love and to be merciful, to pardon
The follies of my species, and (that's human)
To be indulgent to my own.
  Sal.   Alas!
The doom of Nineveh is sealed. — Woe —
  woe
To the unrivalled city!
  Sar.   What dost dread?
  Sal. Thou art guarded by thy foes: in a
  few hours
The tempest may break out which overwhelms
  thee,
And thine and mine; and in another day
What *is* shall be the past of Belus' race.
  Sar. What must we dread?
  Sal.   Ambitious treachery,
Which has environed thee with snares; but
  yet
There is resource: empower me with thy
  signet
To quell the machinations, and I lay
The heads of thy chief foes before thy feet.
  Sar. The heads — how many?
  Sal.   Must I stay to number
When even thine own's in peril? Let me go;
Give me thy signet — trust me with the rest.
  Sar. I will trust no man with unlimited
  lives.
When we take those from others, we nor know
What we have taken, nor the thing we give.
  Sal. Wouldst thou not take their lives who
  seek for thine?
  Sar. That's a hard question — But I an-
  swer, Yes.
Cannot the thing be done without? Who are
  they
Whom thou suspectest? — Let them be ar-
  rested.
  Sal. I would thou wouldst not ask me;
  the next moment
Will send my answer through thy babbling
  troop
Of paramours, and thence fly o'er the palace,
Even to the city, and so baffle all. —
Trust me.
  Sar. Thou knowest I have done so ever:
Take thou the signet. [*Gives the signet.*
  Sal.   I have one more request. —
  Sar. Name it.
  Sal. That thou this night forbear the ban-
  quet
In the pavilion over the Euphrates.
  Sar. Forbear the banquet! Not for all
  the plotters
That ever shook a kingdom! Let them come,

And do their worst: I shall not blench for
  them;
Nor rise the sooner; nor forbear the goblet;
Nor crown me with a single rose the less;
Nor lose one joyous hour. — I fear them not.
  Sal. But thou wouldst arm thee, wouldst
  thou not, if needful?
  Sar. Perhaps. I have the goodliest armor,
A sword of such a temper; and a bow
And javelin, which might furnish Nimrod
  forth:
A little heavy, but yet not unwieldy.
And now I think on't, 'tis long since I've used
  them,
Even in the chase. Hast ever seen them,
  brother?
  Sal. Is this a time for such fantastic tri-
  fling? —
If need be, wilt thou wear them?
  Sar.   Will I not?
Oh! if it must be so, and these rash slaves
Will not be ruled with less, I'll use the sword
Till they shall wish it turned into a distaff.
  Sal. They say thy sceptre's turned to that
  already.
  Sar. That's false! but let them say so: the
  old Greeks,
Of whom our captives often sing, related
The same of their chief hero, Hercules,
Because he loved a Lydian queen: thou seest
The populace of all the nations seize
Each calumny they can to sink their sover-
  eigns.
  Sal. They did not speak thus of thy fathers.
  Sar.   No;
They dared not. They were kept to toil and
  combat;
And never changed their chains but for their
  armor.
Now they have peace and pastime, and the
  license
To revel and to rail; it irks me not.
I would not give the smile of one fair girl
For all the popular breath that e'er divided
A name from nothing. What are the rank
  tongues
Of this vile herd, grown insolent with feeding,
That I should prize their noisy praise, or dread
Their noisome clamor?
  Sal.   You have said they are men;
As such their hearts are something.
  Sar.   So my dogs' are;
And better, as more faithful: — but, proceed;
Thou hast my signet: — since they are tumul-
  tuous,
Let them be tempered, yet not roughly, till
Necessity enforce it. I hate all pain,
Given or received; we have enough within us,
The meanest vassal as the loftiest monarch,
Not to add to each other's natural burden
Of mortal misery, but rather lessen,

By mild reciprocal alleviation,
The fatal penalties imposed on life:
But this they know not, or they will not know.
I have, by Baal! done all I could to soothe
them:
I made no wars, I added no new imposts,
I interfered not with their civic lives,
I let them pass their days as best might suit
them,
Passing my own as suited me.

Sal. Thou stopp'st
Short of the duties of a king; and therefore
They say thou art unfit to be a monarch.

Sar. They lie. — Unhappily, I am unfit
To be aught save a monarch; else for me
The meanest Mede might be the king instead.

Sal. There is one Mede, at least, who seeks
to be so.

Sar. What mean'st thou? — 'tis thy secret;
thou desirest
Few questions, and I'm not of curious nature.
Take the fit steps; and, since necessity
Requires, I sanction and support thee. Ne'er
Was man who more desired to rule in peace
The peaceful only: if they rouse me, better
They had conjured up stern Nimrod from his
ashes,
"The mighty hunter." I will turn these realms
To one wide desert chase of brutes, who *were*,
But *would* no more, by their own choice, be
human.
What they have found me, they belie; *that
which*
They yet may find me—shall defy their wish
To speak it worse; and let them thank them-
selves.

Sal Then thou at last canst feel?

Sar. Feel! who feels not
Ingratitude?

Sal. I will not pause to answer
With words, but deeds. Keep thou awake
that energy
Which sleeps at times, but is not dead within
thee,
And thou may'st yet be glorious in thy reign,
As powerful in thy realm. Farewell!
[*Exit* SALEMENES.

Sar. (*solus*). Farewell!
He's gone; and on his finger bears my signet,
Which is to him a sceptre. He is stern
As I am heedless; and the slaves deserve
To feel a master. What may be the danger,
I know not: he hath found it, let him quell it.
Must I consume my life — this little life —
In guarding against all may make it less? [1]
It is not worth so much! It were to die

---

[1] [The epicurean philosophy of Sardanapalus
gives him a fine opportunity, in his conferences
with his stern and confidential adviser, Salemenes,
to contrast his own imputed and fatal vices of ease
and love of pleasure with the boasted virtues of his
predecessors, war and conquest. — *Jeffrey.*]

Before my hour, to live in dread of death,
Tracing revolt; suspecting all about me,
Because they are near; and all who are remote;
Because they are far. But if it should be so —
If they should sweep me off from earth and
empire,
Why, what is earth or empire of the earth?
I have loved, and lived, and multiplied my
image:
To die is no less natural than those
Acts of this clay! 'Tis true I have not shed
Blood as I might have done, in oceans, till
My name became the synonyme of death —
A terror and a trophy. But for this
I feel no penitence; my life is love:
If I must shed blood, it shall be by force.
Till now, no drop from an Assyrian vein
Hath flowed for me, nor hath the smallest coin
Of Nineveh's vast treasures e'er been lavished
On objects which could cost her sons a tear:
If then they hate me, 'tis because I hate not:
If they rebel, 'tis because I oppress not.
Oh, men! ye must be ruled with scythes, not
sceptres,
And mowed down like the grass, else all we
reap
Is rank abundance, and a rotten harvest
Of discontents infecting the fair soil,
Making a desert of fertility. —
I'll think no more. —— Within there, ho!

Enter an ATTENDANT.

Sar. Slave, tell
The Ionian Myrrha we would crave her pres-
ence.

Attend. King, she is here.

MYRRHA *enters.*

Sar. (*apart to Attendant*). Away!
(*Addressing* MYRRHA.) Beautiful being!
Thou dost almost anticipate my heart;
It throbbed for thee, and here thou comest:
let me
Deem that some unknown influence, some
sweet oracle,
Communicates between us, though unseen,
In absence, and attracts us to each other.

Myr. There doth.

Sar. I know there doth, but not its name:
What is it?

Myr. In my native land a God,
And in my heart a feeling like a God's,
Exalted; yet I own 'tis only mortal;
For what I feel is humble, and yet happy—
That is, it would be happy; but ——
[MYRRHA *pauses.*

Sar. There comes
For ever some thing between us and what
We deem our happiness: let me remove
The barrier which that hesitating accent
Proclaims to thine, and mine is sealed.

Myr. My lord!—

Sar. My lord — my king — sire — sovereign; thus it is —
For ever thus, addressed with awe. I ne'er
Can see a smile, unless in some broad banquet's
Intoxicating glare, when the buffoons
Have gorged themselves up to equality,
Or I have quaffed me down to their abasement.
Myrrha, I can hear all these things, these names,
Lord — king — sire — monarch — nay, time was I prized them;
That is, I suffered them — from slaves and nobles;
But when they falter from the lips I love,
The lips which have been pressed to mine, a chill
Comes o'er my heart, a cold sense of the falsehood
Of this my station, which represses feeling
In those for whom I have felt most, and makes me
Wish that I could lay down the dull tiara,
And share a cottage on the Caucasus
With thee, and wear no crowns but those of flowers.
Myr. Would that we could!
Sar. And dost *thou* feel this ? — Why ?
Myr. Then thou wouldst know what thou canst never know.
Sar. And that is ——
Myr. The true value of a heart;
At least, a woman's.
Sar. I have proved a thousand —
A thousand, and a thousand.
Myr. Hearts ?
Sar. I think so.
Myr. Not one! the time may come thou may'st.
Sar. It will.
Here, Myrrha; Salemenes has declared —
Or why or how he hath divined it, Belus,
Who founded our great realm, knows more than I —
But Salemenes hath declared my throne
In peril.
Myr. He did well.
Sar. And say'st *thou* so ?
Thou whom he spurned so harshly, and now dared[1]
Drive from our presence with his savage jeers,
And made thee weep and blush ?
Myr. I should do both
More frequently, and he did well to call me
Back to my duty. But thou spakest of peril —
Peril to thee ——
Sar. Ay, from dark plots and snares
From Medes — and discontented troops and nations.

I know not what — a labyrinth of things —
A maze of muttered threats and mysteries:
Thou know'st the man — it is his usual custom.
But he is honest. Come, we'll think no more on't —
But of the midnight festival.
Myr. 'Tis time
To think of aught save festivals. Thou hast not
Spurned his sage cautions ?
Sar. What ? — and dost thou fear ?
Myr. Fear ? — I'm a Greek, and how should I fear death ?
Sar. Then wherefore dost thou turn so pale ?
Myr. I love.
Sar. And do not I ? I love thee far —
far more
Than either the brief life or the wide realm,
Which, it may be, are menaced ; — yet I blench not.
Myr. That means thou lovest not thyself nor me;
For he who loves another loves himself,
Even for that other's sake. This is too rash :
Kingdoms and lives are not to be so lost.
Sar. Lost ! — why, who is the aspiring chief who dared
Assume to win them ?
Myr. Who is he should dread
To try so much ? When he who is their ruler
Forgets himself, will they remember him ?
Sar. Myrrha!
Myr. Frown not upon me: you have smiled
Too often on me not to make those frowns
Bitterer to bear than any punishment
Which they may augur. — King, I am your subject !
Master, I am your slave ! Man, I have loved you ! —
Loved you, I know not by what fatal weakness,
Although a Greek, and born a foe to monarchs —
A slave, and hating fetters — an Ionian,
And, therefore, when I love a stranger, more
Degraded by that passion than by chains !
Still I have loved you. If that love were strong
Enough to overcome all former nature,
Shall it not claim the privilege to save you ?
Sar. Save me, my beauty ! Thou art very fair,
And what I seek of thee is love — not safety.
Myr. And without love where dwells security ?
Sar. I speak of woman's love.
Myr. The very first
Of human life must spring from woman's breast,
Your first small words are taught you from her lips,
Your first tears quenched by her, and your last sighs

Too often breathed out in a woman's hearing,
When men have shrunk from the ignoble care
Of watching the last hour of him who led
them.
Sar. My eloquent Ionian! thou speak'st
music,
The very chorus of the tragic song [1]
I have heard thee talk of as the favorite pas-
time
Of thy far father-land. Nay, weep not — calm
thee.
Myr. I weep not. — But I pray thee, do not
speak
About my fathers or their land.
Sar.   Yet oft
Thou speakest of them.
Myr.   True — true : constant thought
Will overflow in words unconsciously ;
But when another speaks of Greece, it wounds
me.
Sar. Well, then, how wouldst thou *save*
me, as thou saidst ?
Myr. By teaching thee to save thyself, and
not
Thyself alone, but these vast realms, from all
The rage of the worst war — the war of
brethren.
Sar. Why, child, I loathe all war, and
warriors ;
I live in peace and pleasure : what can man
Do more ?
Myr. Alas! my lord, with common men
There needs too oft the show of war to keep
The substance of sweet peace ; and, for a king,
'Tis sometimes better to be feared than loved.
Sar. And I have never sought but for the
last.
Myr. And now art neither.
Sar.   Dost *thou* say so, Myrrha ?
Myr. I speak of civic popular love, *self*-love,
Which means that men are kept in awe and
law,
Yet not oppressed — at least they must not
think so ;
Or if they think so, deem it necessary,
To ward off worse oppression, their own
passions.
A king of feasts, and flowers, and wine, and
revel,
And love, and mirth, was never king of glory.
Sar. Glory! what's that ?
Myr.   Ask of the gods thy fathers.
Sar. They cannot answer ; when the priests
speak for them,
'Tis for some small addition to the temple.

Myr. Look to the annals of thine empire's
founders.
Sar. They are so blotted o'er with blood,
I cannot.
But what wouldst have ? the empire *has been*
founded.
I cannot go on multiplying empires.
Myr. Preserve thine own.
Sar.   At least, I will enjoy it,
Come, Myrrha, let us go on to the Euphrates :
The hour invites, the galley is prepared,
And the pavilion, decked for our return,
In fit adornment for the evening banquet,
Shall blaze with beauty and with light, until
It seems unto the stars which are above us
Itself an opposite star ; and we will sit
Crowned with fresh flowers like ——
Myr.   Victims.
Sar.   No, like sovereigns,
The shepherd kings of patriarchal times,
Who knew no brighter gems than summer
wreaths, [2]
And none but tearless triumphs. Let us on.

Enter PANIA.

Pan. May the king live for ever !
Sar.   Not an hour
Longer than he can love. How my soul hates
This language, which makes life itself a lie,
Flattering dust with eternity. [3] Well, Pania!
Be brief.
Pan.   I am charged by Salemenes to
Reiterate his prayer unto the king,
That for this day, at least, he will not quit
The palace : when the general returns,
He will adduce such reasons as will warrant
His daring, and perhaps obtain the pardon
Of his presumption.
Sar.   What? am I then cooped ?
Already captive ? can I not even breathe
The breath of heaven ? Tell prince Salemenes,
Were all Assyria raging round the walls
In mutinous myriads, I would still go forth.
Pan. I must obey, and yet —
Myr.   Oh, monarch, listen. —
How many a day and moon thou hast reclined
Within these palace walls in silken dalliance,
And never shown thee to thy people's longing;
Leaving thy subjects' eyes ungratified,
The satraps uncontrolled, the gods unwor-
shipped,
And all things such as render thee inglorious
Till all, save evil, slumbered through the
realm !
And wilt thou not now tarry for a day, —
A day which may redeem thee ? Wilt thou
not
Yield to the few still faithful for a few hours,

---

[1] [To speak of " the tragic song " as the favorite
pastime of Greece, two hundred years before Thes-
pis, is an anachronism. Nor could Myrrha, at so
early a period of her country's history, have spoken
of their national hatred of kings, or of that which
was equally the growth of a later age, — their con-
tempt for " barbarians." — *Heber.*]

[2] [MS. —
" Who loved no gems so well as those of nat're.']

[3] [MS. — " Wishing eternity to dust."]

For them, for thee, for thy past father's race,
And for thy son's inheritance?
 Pan. .   'Tis true!
From the deep urgency with which the prince
Despatched me to your sacred presence, I
Must dare to add my feeble voice to that
Which now has spoken.
 Sar.   No, it must not be.
 Myr. For the sake of thy realm!
 Sar.   Away!
 Pan.   For that
Of all thy faithful subjects, who will rally
Round thee and thine.
 Sar. These are mere fantasies;
There is no peril: — 'tis a sullen scheme
Of Salemenes, to approve his zeal,
And show himself more necessary to us.
 Myr. By all that's good and glorious take
 this counsel.
 Sar. Business to-morrow.
 Myr.   Ay, or death to-night.
 Sar. Why let it come then unexpectedly
'Midst joy and gentleness, and mirth and love;
So let me fall like the plucked rose! — far
 better
Thus than be withered.
 Myr. Then thou wilt not yield,
Even for the sake of all that ever stirred
A monarch into action, to forego
A trifling revel.
 Sar. No.
 Myr.   Then yield for *mine;*
For my sake!
 Sar. Thine, my Myrrha!
 Myr.   'Tis the first
Boon which I ever asked Assyria's king.
 Sar. That's true, and wer't my kingdom
 must be granted.
Well, for thy sake, I yield me. Pania, hence!
Thou hear'st me.
 Pan. And obey. [*Exit* PANIA.
 Sar.   I marvel at thee.
What is thy motive, Myrrha, thus to urge me?
 Myr. Thy safety; and the certainty that
 nought
Could urge the prince thy kinsman to require
Thus much from thee, but some impending
 danger.
 Sar. And if I do not dread it, why shouldst
 thou?
 Myr. Because *thou* dost not fear, I fear
 for *thee.*
 Sar. To-morrow thou wilt smile at these
 vain fancies.
 Myr. If the worse come, I shall be where
 none weep,
And that is better than the power to smile.
And thou?
 Sar. I shall be king, as heretofore.
 Myr. Where?
 Sar. With Baal, Nimrod, and Semiramis,
Sole in Assyria, or with them elsewhere.

Fate made me what I am — may make me
 nothing —
But either that or nothing must I be:
I will not live degraded.
 Myr.   Hadst thou felt
Thus always, none would ever dare degrade
 thee.
 Sar. And who will do so now?
 Myr.   Dost thou suspect none?
 Sar. Suspect! — that's a spy's office. Oh!
 we lose
Ten thousand precious moments in vain
 words,
And vainer fears. Within there! — ye slaves,
 deck
The hall of Nimrod for the evening revel:
If I must make a prison of our palace,
At least we'll wear our fetters jocundly;
If the Euphrates be forbid us, and
The summer dwelling on its beauteous border,
Here we are still unmenaced. Ho! within
 there! [*Exit* SARDANAPALUS.
 Myr. (*sola*). Why do I love this man?
 My country's daughters
Love none but heroes. But I have no coun-
 try!
The slave hath lost all save her bonds. I love
 him;
And that's the heaviest link of the long chain —
To love whom we esteem not. Be it so:
The hour is coming when he'll need all love,
And find none. To fall from him now were
 baser
Than to have stabbed him on his throne when
 highest
Would have been noble in my country's
 creed:
I was not made for either. Could I save him,
I should not love *him* better, but myself;
And I have need of the last, for I have
 fallen
In my own thoughts, by loving this soft stran-
 ger:
And yet methinks I love him more, perceiv-
 ing
That he is hated of his own barbarians,
The natural foes of all the blood of Greece.
Could I but wake a single thought like those
Which even the Phrygians felt when battling
 long
'Twixt Ilion and the sea, within his heart,
He would tread down the barbarous crowds,
 and triumph.
He loves me, and I love him; the slave
 loves
Her master, and would free him from his
 vices.
If not, I have a means of freedom still,
And if I cannot teach him how to reign,
May show him how alone a king can leave
His throne. I must not lose him from my
 sight. [*Exit.*

ACT II.

SCENE I.— *The Portal of the same Hall of the Palace.*

Beleses (solus). The sun goes down: methinks he sets more slowly,
Taking his last look of Assyria's empire.
How red he glares amongst those deepening clouds,
Like the blood he predicts. If not in vain,
Thou sun that sinkest, and ye stars which rise,
I have outwatched ye, reading ray by ray
The edicts of your orbs, which make Time tremble
For what he brings the nations, 'tis the furthest
Hour of Assyria's years. And yet how calm!
An earthquake should announce so great a fall —
A summer's sun discloses it. Yon disk,
To the star-read Chaldean, bears upon
Its everlasting page the end of what
Seemed everlasting; but oh! thou true sun!
The burning oracle of all that live,
As fountain of all life, and symbol of
Him who bestows it, wherefore dost thou limit
Thy lore unto calamity? Why not
Unfold the rise of days more worthy thine
All-glorious burst from ocean? why not dart
A beam of hope athwart the future years,
As of wrath to its days? Hear me! oh, hear me!
I am thy worshipper, thy priest, thy servant —
I have gazed on thee at thy rise and fall,
And bowed my head beneath thy mid-day beams,
When my eye dared not meet thee. I have watched
For thee, and after thee, and prayed to thee,
And sacrificed to thee, and read, and feared thee,
And asked of thee, and thou hast answered — but
Only to thus much: while I speak, he sinks —
Is gone — and leaves his beauty, not his knowledge,
To the delighted west, which revels in
Its hues of dying glory. Yet what is
Death, so it be but glorious? 'Tis a sunset;
And mortals may be happy to resemble
The gods but in decay.

Enter ARBACES, *by an inner door.*

Arb.   Beleses, why
So rapt in thy devotions? Dost thou stand
Gazing to trace thy disappearing god
Into some realm of undiscovered day?
Our business is with night — 'tis come.
Bel.   But not
Gone.
Arb. Let it roll on — we are ready.

Bel.   Yes.
Would it were over!
Arb.   Does the prophet doubt,
To whom the very stars shine victory?
Bel. I do not doubt of victory — but the victor.
Arb. Well, let thy science settle that.
  Meantime
I have prepared as many glittering spears
As will out-sparkle our allies — your planets.
There is no more to thwart us. The she-king,
That less than woman, is even now upon
The waters with his female mates. The order
Is issued for the feast in the pavilion.
The first cup which he drains will be the last
Quaffed by the line of Nimrod.
Bel.   'Twas a brave one.
Arb. And is a weak one — 'tis worn out —
  we'll mend it.
Bel. Art sure of that?
Arb.   Its founder was a hunter —
I am soldier — what is there to fear?
Bel. The soldier.
Arb.   And the priest, it may be: but
If you thought thus, or think, why not retain
Your king of concubines? why stir me up?
Why spur me to this enterprise? your own
No less than mine?
Bel.   ,   Look to the sky!
Arb.   I look.
Bel. What seest thou?
Arb.   A fair summer's twilight, and
The gathering of the stars.
Bel.   And midst them, mark
Yon earliest, and the brightest, which so quivers,
As it would quit its place in the blue ether.
Arb. Well?
Bel. 'Tis thy natal ruler — thy birth planet.
Arb. (touching his scabbard). My star is in
  this scabbard: when it shines,
It shall out-dazzle comets. Let us think
Of what is to be done to justify
Thy planets and their portents. When we conquer,
They shall have temples — ay, and priests — and thou
Shalt be the pontiff of — what gods thou wilt;
For I observe that they are ever just,
And own the bravest for the most devout.
Bel. Ay, and the most devout for brave —
  thou hast not
Seen me turn back from battle.
Arb.   No; I own thee
As firm in fight as Babylonia's captain,
As skilful in Chaldea's worship: now,
Will it but please thee to forget the priest,
And be the warrior?
Bel.   Why not both?
Arb.   The better;
And yet it almost shames me, we shall have
So little to effect. This woman's warfare

Degrades the very conqueror. To have
plucked
A bold and bloody despot from his throne,
And grappled with him, clashing steel with
steel,
That were heroic or to win or fall ;
But to upraise my sword against this silk-
worm,
And hear him whine, it may be——
  Bel.   Do not deem it :
He has that in him which may make you strife
yet ;
And were he all you think, his guards are
hardy,
And headed by the cool, stern Salemenes.
  Arb. They'll not resist.
  Bel.   Why not ? they are soldiers.
  Arb.   True,
And therefore need a soldier to command
them.
  Bel. That Salemenes is.
  Arb.   But not their king.
Besides, he hates the effeminate thing that
governs,
For the queen's sake, his sister. Mark you not
He keeps aloof from all the revels ?
  Bel.   But
Not from the council — there he is ever con-
stant.
  Arb. And ever thwarted : what would you
have more
To make a rebel out of ? A fool reigning,
His blood dishonored, and himself disdained :
Why, it is *his* revenge we work for.
  Bel.   Could
He but be brought to think so : this I doubt of.
  Arb. What, if we sound him ?
  Bel.   Yes — if the time served.

         Enter BALEA.

  Bal. Satraps ! The king commands your
presence at
The feast to-night.
  Bel.   To hear is to obey.
In the pavilion ?
  Bal.   No ; here in the palace.
  Arb. How ! in the palace ? it was not thus
ordered.
  Bal. It is so ordered now.
  Arb.   And why ?
  Bal.   I know not :
May I retire ?
  Arb.   Stay.
  Bel. (*to Arb. aside*). Hush ! let him go his
way.
(*Alternately to Bal.*) Yes, Balea, thank the
monarch, kiss the hem
Of his imperial robe, and say, his slaves
Will take the crumbs he deigns to scatter
from
His royal table at the hour — was't mid-
night ?

  Bal. It was : the place, the hall of Nimrod.
Lords,
I humble me before you, and depart.
                   [*Exit* BALEA.
  Arb. I like not this same sudden change of
place ;
There is some mystery : wherefore should he
change it ?
  Bel. Doth he not change a thousand times
a day ?
Sloth is of all things the most fanciful —
And moves more parasangs in its intents
Than generals in their marches, when they
seek
To leave their foe at fault. — Why dost thou
muse ?
  Arb. He loved that gay pavilion, — it was
ever
His summer dotage.
  Bel.   And he loved his queen —
And thrice a thousand harlotry besides —
And he has loved all things by turns, except
Wisdom and glory.
  Arb.   Still — I like it not.
If he has changed — why, so must we : the
attack
Were easy in the isolated bower,
Beset with drowsy guards and drunken cour-
tiers ;
But in the hall of Nimrod——
  Bel.   Is it so ?
Methought the haughty soldier feared to mount
A throne too easily — does it disappoint thee
To find there is a slipperier step or two
Than what was counted on ?
  Arb.   When the hour comes,
Thou shalt perceive how far I fear or no.
Thou hast seen my life at stake — and gaily
played for :
But here is more upon the die — a kingdom.
  Bel. I have foretold already — thou wilt
win it :
Then on, and prosper.
  Arb.   Now were I a soothsayer,
I would have boded so much to myself.
But be the stars obeyed — I cannot quarrel
With them, nor their interpreter. Who's here ?

        Enter SALEMENES.

  Sal. Satraps !
  Bel.   My prince !
  Sal.   Well met — I sought ye both,
But elsewhere than the palace.
  Arb.   Wherefore so ?
  Sal. 'Tis not the hour.
  Arb.   The hour ! — what hour ?
  Sal.   Of midnight.
  Bel. Midnight, my lord !
  Sal.   What, are you not invited ?
  Bel. Oh ! yes — we had forgotten.
  Sal.   Is it usual
Thus to forget a sovereign's invitation ?

Arb. Why —we but now received it.
Sal.   Then why here?
Arb. On duty.
Sal.   On what duty?
Bel.   On the state's.
We have the privilege to approach the pres-
   ence;
But found the monarch absent.[1]
Sal.   And I too
Am upon duty.
Arb.   May we crave its purport?
Sal. To arrest two traitors. Guards! With-
   in there!

               Enter Guards.

Sal. (*continuing*).   Satraps,
Your swords.
   Bel. (*delivering his*). My lord, behold my
   scimitar.
Arb. (*drawing his sword*). Take mine.
Sal. (*advancing*).   I will.
Arb.   But in your heart the blade —
The hilt quits not this hand.[2]
   Sal. (*drawing*). How! dost thou brave me?
'Tis well — this saves a trial, and false mercy.
Soldiers, hew down the rebel!
   Arb.   Soldiers! Ay —
Alone you dare not.
Sal.   Alone! foolish slave —
What is there in thee that a prince should
   shrink from
Of open force? We dread thy treason, not
Thy strength: thy tooth is nought without its
   venom —
The serpent's, not the lion's. Cut him down.
   Bel. (*interposing*). Arbaces! Are you mad?
Have I not rendered
My sword? Then trust like me our sover-
   eign's justice.
Arb. No — I will sooner trust the stars
   thou prat'st of,
And this slight arm, and die a king at least
Of my own breath and body — so far that
None else shall claim them.
   Sal. (*to the Guards*). You hear *him* and *me*.
   Take him not, — kill.
   [*The Guards attack* ARBACES, *who defends
   himself valiantly and dexterously till they
   waver.*
Sal.   Is it even so; and must
I do the hangman's office? Recreants! See
How you should fell a traitor.
            [SALEMENES *attacks* ARBACES.

            Enter SARDANAPALUS *and Train.*

Sar.   Hold your hands —
Upon your lives, I say. What, deaf or
   drunken?

---

¹ [MS. —
   " But found the monarch claimed his privacy."]
² [MS.   — " not else
      It quits this living hand."]

My sword! Oh fool, I wear no sword; here,
   fellow,
Give me thy weapon.   [*To a Guard.*
   [SARDANAPALUS *snatches a sword from one
   of the soldiers, and rushes between the com-
   batants — they separate.*
Sar.   In my very palace!
What hinders me from cleaving you in twain,
Audacious brawlers?
   Bel.   Sire, your justice.
Sal.   Or —
Your weakness.
   Sar. (*raising the sword*). How!
   Sal.   Strike! so the blow's repeated
Upon yon traitor — whom you spare a mo-
   ment,
I trust, for torture — I'm content.
   Sar.   What — him!
Who dares assail Arbaces?
   Sal.   I!
   Sar.   Indeed!
Prince, you forget yourself. Upon what war-
   rant?
   Sal. (*showing the signet*). Thine.
   Arb. (*confused*).   The king's!
   Sal.   Yes! and let the king confirm it.
   Sar. I parted not from this for such a pur-
   pose.
   Sal. You parted with it for your safety — I
Employed it for the best. Pronounce in per-
   son.
Here I am but your slave — a moment past
I was your representative.
   Sar.   Then sheathe
Your swords.
   [ARBACES *and* SALEMENES *return their
   swords to the scabbards.*
Sal. Mine's sheathed; I pray you sheathe
   not yours:
'Tis the sole sceptre left you now with safety.
   Sar. A heavy one; the hilt, too, hurts my
   hand.
(*To a Guard.*) Here, fellow, take thy weapon
   back.
            Well, sirs,
What doth this mean?
   Bel.   The prince must answer that.
   Sal. Truth upon my part, treason upon
   theirs.
   Sar. Treason — Arbaces! treachery and
   Beleses!
That were an union I will not believe.
   Bel. Where is the proof?
   Sal.   I'll answer that, if once
The king demands your fellow-traitor's sword.
   Arb. (*to Sal.*). A sword which hath been
   drawn as 'oft as thine
Against his foes.
   Sal.   And now against his brother,
And in an hour or so against himself.
   Sar. That is not possible: he dared not;
   no —

No — I'll not hear of such things. These vain
  bickerings
Are spawned in courts by base intrigues, and
  baser
Hirelings, who live by lies on good men's lives.
You must have been deceived, my brother.
  Sal.   First
Let him deliver up his weapon, and
Proclaim himself your subject by that duty,
And I will answer all.
  Sar.   Why, if I thought so —
But no, it cannot be: tne Mede Arbaces —
The trusty, rough, true soldier — the best cap-
  tain
Of all who discipline our nations —— No,
I'll not insult him thus, to bid him render
The scimitar to me he never yielded
Unto our enemies. Chief, keep your weapon.
  Sal. (delivering back the signet). Monarch,
  take back your signet.
  Sar.   No, retain it;
But use it with more moderation.
  Sal.   Sire,
I used it for your honor, and restore it
Because I cannot keep it with my own.
Bestow it on Arbaces.
  Sar.   So I should:
He never asked it.
  Sal.   Doubt not, he will have it,
Without that hollow semblance of respect.
  Bel. I know not what hath prejudiced the
  prince
So strongly 'gainst two subjects, than whom
  none
Have been more zealous for Assyria's weal.
  Sal. Peace, factious priest, and faithless
  soldier! thou
Unit'st in thy own person the worst vices
Of the most dangerous orders of mankind.
Keep thy smooth words and juggling homilies
For those who know thee not. Thy fellow's
  sin
Is, at the least, a bold one, and not tempered
By the tricks taught thee in Chaldea.
  Bel.   Hear him,
My liege — the son of Belus! he blasphemes
The worship of the land, which bows the knee
Before your fathers.
  Sar.   Oh! for that I pray you
Let him have absolution. I dispense with
The worship of dead men; feeling that I
Am mortal, and believing that the race
From whence I sprung are — what I see them
  — ashes.
  Bel. King! Do not deem so: they are
  with the stars,
And ——
  Sar. You shall join them there ere they
  will rise,
If you preach further — Why, *this* is rank
  treason.
  Sal. My lord!

  Sar.   To school me in the worship of
Assyria's idols! Let him be released —
Give him his sword.
  Sal.   My lord, and king, and brother,
I pray ye pause.
  Sar.   Yes, and be sermonized,
And dinned, and deafened with dead men and
  Baal,
And all Chaldea's starry mysteries.
  Bel. Monarch! respect them.
  Sar.   Oh! for that — I love them,
I love to watch them in the deep blue vault,
And to compare them with my Myrrha's eyes;
I love to see their rays redoubled in
The tremulous silver of Euphrates' wave,
As the light breeze of midnight crisps the
  broad
And rolling water, sighing through the sedges
Which fringe his banks: but whether they
  may be
Gods, as some say, or the abodes of gods,
As others hold, or simply lamps of night,
Worlds, or the lights of worlds, I know not
  care not.
There's something sweet in my uncertainty
I would not change for your Chaldean lore;
Besides, I know of these all clay can know
Of aught above it, or below it — nothing.
I see their brilliancy and feel their beauty — [1]
When they shine on my grave I shall know
  neither.
  Bel. For *neither*, sire, say *better*.
  Sar.   I will wait,
If it so please you, pontiff, for that knowledge.
In the mean time receive your sword, and
  know
That I prefer your service militant
Unto your ministry — not loving either.
  Sal. (aside). His lusts have made him mad.
  Then must I save him,
Spite of himself.
  Sar.   Please you to hear me, Satraps!
And chiefly thou, my priest, because I doubt
  thee
More than the soldier; and would doubt thee
  all
Wert thou not half a warrior: let us part
In peace — I'll not say pardon — which must
  be
Earned by the guilty; this I'll not pronounce
  ye,
Although upon this breath of mine depends
Your own; and, deadlier for ye, on my fears.
But fear not — for that I am soft, not fearful —
And so live on. Were I the thing some think
  me,
Your heads would now be dripping the last
  drops
Of their attainted gore from the high gates

---

[1] [MS. —

"I know them beautiful, and see them brilliant."]

Of this our palace, into the dry dust,
Their only portion of the coveted kingdom
They would be crowned to reign o'er — let
    that pass.
As I have said, I will not *deem* ye guilty,
Nor *doom* ye guiltless. Albeit better men
Than ye or I stand ready to arraign you ;
And should I leave your fate to sterner judges,
And proofs of all kinds, I might sacrifice
Two men, who, whatsoe'er they now are, were
O:ice honest. Ye are free, sirs.
   Arb.   Sire, this clemency ——
   Bel. (*interrupting him*). Is worthy of
yourself and, although innocent,
We thank ——
   Sar. Priest! keep your thanksgivings for
Belus;
His offspring needs none.
   Bel.   But being innocent ——
   Sar. Be silent — Guilt is loud. If ye are
loyal,
Ye are injured men, and should be sad, not
grateful.
   Bel. So we should be, were justice always
done
By earthly power omnipotent ; but innocence
Must oft receive her right as a mere favor.
   Sar. That's a good sentence for a homily,
Though not for this occasion. Prithee keep it
To plead thy sovereign's cause before his
people.
   Bel. I trust there is no cause.
   Sar.   No *cause*, perhaps ;
But many causers : — if ye meet with such
In the exercise of your inquisitive function
On earth, or should you read of it in heaven
In some mysterious twinkle of the stars,
Which are your chronicles, I pray you note,
That there are worse things betwixt earth and
heaven
Than him who ruleth many and slays none ;
And, hating not himself, yet loves his fellows
Enough to spare even those who would not
spare him
Were they once masters — but that's doubtful.
Satraps !
Your swords and persons are at liberty
To use them as ye will — but from this hour
I have no call for either. Salemenes,
Follow me.[1]
   [*Exeunt* SARDANAPALUS, SALEMENES,
     and the Train, etc. leaving ARBACES *and*
     BELESES.
   Arb.   Beleses !

---

[1] [The second Act is, we think, a failure. The
conspirators have a tedious dialogue, which is in-
terrupted by Salemenes with a guard. Salemenes
is followed by the king, who reverses all his meas-
ures, pardons Arbaces, because he will not believe
him guilty, and Beleses, in order to escape from
his long speeches about the national religion. This
incident only is well managed. — *Heber*.]

   Bel.   Now, what think you ?
   Arb. That we are lost.
   Bel.   That we have won the kingdom.
   Arb. What ? thus suspected — with the
sword slung o'er us
But by a single hair, and that still wavering,
To be blown down by his imperious breath
Which spared us — why, I know not.
   Bel.   Seek not why;
But let us profit by the interval.
The hour is still our own — our power the
    same —
The night the same we destined. He hath
changed
Nothing except our ignorance of all
Suspicion into such a certainty
As must make madness of delay.
   Arb.   And yet ——
   Bel. What, doubting still ?
   Arb.   He spared our lives, nay, more,
Saved them from Salemenes.
   Bel.   And how long
Will he so spare? till the first drunken minute.
   Arb. Or sober, rather. Yet he did it nobly ;
Gave royally what we had forfeited
Basely ——
   Bel. Say bravely.
   Arb.   Somewhat of both, perhaps.
But it has touched me, and, whate'er betide,
I will no further on.
   Bel.   ,   And lose the world !
   Arb. Lose any thing except my own esteem.
   Bel. I blush that we should owe our lives
to such
A king of distaffs !
   Arb.   But no less we owe them ;
And I should blush far more to take the
grantor's
   Bel. Thou may'st endure whate'er thou
wilt — the stars
Have written otherwise.
   Arb.   Though they came down,
And marshalled me the way in all their bright-
ness,
I would not follow.
   Bel.   This is weakness — worse
Than a scared beldam's dreaming of the dead,
And waking in the dark. — Go to — go to.
   Arb. Methought he looked like Nimrod as
he spoke,
Even as the proud imperial statue stands
Looking the monarch of the kings around it,
And sways, while they but ornament, the tem-
ple.
   Bel. I told you that you had too much
despised him,
And that there was some royalty within him —
What then ? he is the nobler foe.
   Arb.   But we
The meaner. — Would he had not spared us !
   Bel.   So —
Wouldst thou be sacrificed thus readily ?

Arb. No — but it had been better to have died
Than live ungrateful.

Bel.   Oh, the souls of some men!
Thou wouldst digest what some call treason, and
Fools treachery — and, behold, upon the sudden,
Because for something or for nothing, this
Rash reveller steps, ostentatiously,
'Twixt thee and Salemenes, thou art turned
Into — what shall I say ? — Sardanapalus!
I know no name more ignominious.

Arb.   But
An hour ago, who dared to term me such
Had held his life but lightly — as it is,
I must forgive you, even as he forgave us —
Semiramis herself would not have done it.

Bel. No — the queen liked no sharers of the kingdom,
Not even a husband.

Arb.   I must serve him truly ——

Bel. And humbly ?

Arb.   No, sir, proudly — being honest.
I shall be nearer thrones than you to heaven;
And if not quite so haughty, yet more lofty.
You may do your own deeming — you have codes,
And mysteries, and corollaries of
Right and wrong, which I lack for my direction,
And must pursue but what a plain heart teaches.
And now you know me.

Bel.   Have you finished ?

Arb.   Yes —
With you.

Bel. And would, perhaps, betray as well
As quit me ?

Arb.   That's a sacerdotal thought
And not a soldier's.

Bel.   Be it what you will —
Truce with these wranglings, and but hear me.

Arb.   No —
There is more peril in your subtle spirit
Than in a phalanx.

Bel.   If it must be so —
I'll on alone.

Arb.   Alone!

Bel.   Thrones hold but one.

Arb. But this is filled.

Bel.   With worse than vacancy —
A despised monarch. Look to it, Arbaces:
I have still aided, cherished, loved, and urged you;
Was willing even to serve you, in the hope
To serve and save Assyria. Heaven itself
Seemed to consent, and all events were friendly,
Even to the last, till that your spirit shrunk
Into a shallow softness; but now, rather
Than see my country languish, I will be
Her savior or the victim of her tyrant,

Or one or both, for sometimes both are one;
And if I win, Arbaces is my servant.

Arb. Your servant!

Bel.   Why not ? better than be slave,
The *pardoned* slave of *she* Sardanapalus!

Enter PANIA.

Pan. My lords, I bear an order from the king.

Arb. It is obeyed ere spoken.

Bel.   Notwithstanding
Let's hear it.

Pan.   Forthwith, on this very night,
Repair to your respective satrapies
Of Babylon and Media.

Bel.   With our troops ?

Pan. My order is unto the satraps and
Their household train.

Arb.   But ——

Bel.   It must be obeyed:
Say, we depart.

Pan.   My order is to see you
Depart, and not to bear your answer.

Bel (*aside*).   Ay!
Well, sir, we will accompany you hence.

Pan. I will retire to marshal forth the guard
Of honor which befits your rank, and wait
Your leisure, so that it the hour exceeds not.
                                   [*Exit* PANIA.

Bel. *Now* then obey!

Arb.   Doubtless.

Bel.   Yes, to the gates
That grate the palace, which is now our prison —
No further.

Arb. Thou hast harped the truth indeed!
The realm itself, in all its wide extension,
Yawns dungeons at each step for thee and me.

Bel. Graves?

Arb. If I thought so, this good sword should dig
One more than mine.

Bel.   It shall have work enough.
Let me hope better than thou augurest;
At present, let us hence as best we may.
Thou dost agree with me in understanding
This order as a sentence ?

Arb.   Why, what other
Interpretation should it bear ? it is
The very policy of orient monarchs —
Pardon and poison — favors and a sword —
A distant voyage, and an eternal sleep.
How many satraps in his father's time —
For he I own is, or at least *was*, bloodless —

Bel. But *will* not, *can* not be so now.

Arb.   I doubt it
How many satraps have I seen set out
In his sire's day for mighty vice-royalties,
Whose tombs are on their path! I know not how,
But they all sickened by the way, it was
So long and heavy.

Bel.   Let us but regain
The free air of the city, and we'll shorten
The journey.
   Arb.   'Twill be shortened at the gates,
It may be.
   Bel.   No; they hardly will risk that.
They mean us to die privately, but not
Within the palace or the city walls,
Where we are known, and may have partisans:
If they had meant to slay us here, we were
No longer with the living. Let us hence.
   Arb.   If I but thought he did not mean my
   life —
   Bel.   Fool! hence — what else should des-
   potism alarmed
Mean? Let us but rejoin our troops and
   march.
   Arb.   Towards our provinces?
   Bel.   No; towards your kingdom.
There's time, there's heart, and hope, and
   power and means,
Which their half measures leave us in full
   scope.—
Away!
   Arb.   And I even yet repenting must
Relapse to guilt!
   Bel.   Self-defence is a virtue,
Sole bulwark of the right. Away, I say!
Let's leave this place, the air grows thick and
   choking,
And the walls have a scent of night-shade —
   hence!
Let us not leave them time for further counsel.
Our quick departure proves our civic zeal;
Our quick departure hinders our good escort,
The worthy Pania, from anticipating
The orders of some parasangs from hence:
Nay, there's no other choice, but —— hence, I
   say.
[*Exit with* ARBACES, *who follows reluctantly.*[1]

Enter SARDANAPALUS *and* SALEMENES.

   Sar.   Well, all is remedied, and without
   bloodshed,
That worst of mockeries of a remedy;
We are now secure by these men's exile.
   Sal.   Yes,
As he who treads on flowers is from the adder
Twined round their roots.
   Sar.   Why, what wouldst have me do?
   Sal.   Undo what you have done. ·
   Sar.   Revoke my pardon?
   Sal.   Replace the crown now tottering on
   your temples.
   Sar.   That were tyrannical.·
   Sal.   But sure.
   Sar.   We are so.
What danger can they work upon the frontier?
   Sal.   They are not there yet — never should
   they be so,
Were I well listened to.
   Sar.   Nay, I *have* listened
Impartially to thee — why not to them?
   Sal.   You may know that hereafter; as it is,
I take my leave to order forth the guard.
   Sar.   And you will join us at the banquet?
   Sal.   Sire,
Dispense with me — I am no wassailer:
Command me in all service save the Bac-
   chant's.
   Sar.   Nay, but 'tis fit to revel now and then.
   Sal.   And fit that some should watch for
   those who revel
Too oft. Am I permitted to depart?
   Sar.   Yes —— Stay a moment, my good
   Salemenes.
My brother, my best subject, better prince
Than I am king. You should have been the
   monarch,
And I — I know not what, and care not; but

---

[1] [Arbaces is a mere common-place warrior; and
Beleses, on whom, we suspect, Lord Byron has
bestowed more than usual pains, is a very ordinary
and uninteresting villain. Sardanapalus, indeed,
and Salemenes, are both made to speak of the wily
Chaldean as the master-mover of the plot, as a
politician in whose hands Arbaces is but a " war-
like puppet; " and Diodorus Siculus has repre-
sented him, in fact, as the first instigator of Arbaces
to his treason, and as making use of his priestly
character, and his supposed power of foretelling
future events, to inflame the ambition, to direct the
measures, to sustain the hopes, and to reprove the
despondency of his comrade. But of all this noth-
ing appears in the tragedy. Lord Byron has
been so anxious to show his own contempt for the
priest, that he has not even allowed him that share
of cunning and evil influence which was necessary
for the part which he had to fill. Instead of being
the original, the restless and unceasing prompter to
bold and wicked measures, we find him, on his first
appearance, hanging back from the enterprise, and
chilling the energy of Arbaces by an enumeration
of the real or possible difficulties which might yet
impede its execution. Instead of exercising that
power over the mind of his comrade which a re-
ligious imposter may well possess over better and
more magnanimous souls than his own, Beleses is
made to pour his predictions into incredulous
ears; and Arbaces is as mere an epicurean in his
creed as Sardanapalus. When we might have ex-
pected to find him gazing with hope and reverence
on the star which the Chaldean points out as his
natal planet, the Median warrior speaks, in the
language of Mezentius, of the sword on which *his*
confidence depends, and instead of being a tool in
the hand of the pontiff, he says almost every thing
which is likely to affront him. Though Beleses
is introduced to us as engaged in devotion, and as
a fervent worshipper of the Sun, he is nowhere
made either to feel or to counterfeit that *profes-
sional* zeal against Sardanapalus which his open
contempt of the gods would naturally call for; and
no reason appears, throughout the play, why
Arbaces should follow, against his own conscience
and opinion the counsels of a man of whom he
speaks with dislike and disgust, and whose pre-
tences to inspiration and sanctity he treats with
unmingled ridicule. — *Heber.*]

Think not I am insensible to all
Thine honest wisdom, and thy rough yet
    kind,   .
Though oft reproving, sufferance of my follies.
If I have spared these men against thy counsel,
That is, their lives — it is not that I doubt
The advice was sound ; but, let them live : we
    will not   •
Cavil about their lives — so let them mend
    them.
Their banishment will leave me still sound
    sleep,
Which their death had not left me.
    Sal.   Thus you run
The risk to sleep for ever, to save traitors —
A moment's pang now changed for years of
    crime.
Still let them be made quiet.
    Sar.   Tempt me not :
My word is past.
    Sal.   But it may be recalled.
    Sar.   'Tis royal.
    Sal.   And should therefore be decisive.
This half indulgence of an exile serves
But to provoke — a pardon should be full,
Or it is none.
    Sar.   And who persuaded me
After I had repealed them, or at least
Only dismissed them from our presence, who
Urged me to send them to their satrapies ?
    Sal. True ; that I had forgotten ; that is,
    sire,
If they e'er reached their satrapies — why,
    then,
Reprove me more for my advice.
    Sar.   And if
They do not reach them — look to it ! — in
    safety,
In safety, mark me — and security —
Look to thine own.
    Sal.   Permit me to depart ;
Their *safety* shall be cared for.
    Sar.   Get thee hence, then ;
And, prithee, think more gently of thy brother.
    Sal. Sire, I shall ever duly serve my sover-
    eign.   [*Exit* SALEMENES.
    Sar. (*solus*). That man is of a temper too
    severe ;
Hard but as lofty as the rock, and free
From all the taints of common earth — while I
Am softer clay, impregnated with flowers :
But as our mould is, must the produce be.
If I have erred this time, 'tis on the side
Where error sits most lightly on that sense,
I know not what to call it ; but it reckons
With me ofttimes for pain, and sometimes
    pleasure.
A spirit which seems placed about my heart
To count its throbs, not quicken them, and
    ask
Questions which mortal never dared to ask
    me,

Nor Baal, though an oracular deity —[1]
Albeit his marble face majestical
Frowns as the shadows of the evening dim.
His brows to changed expression, till at times
I think the statue looks in act to speak.
Away with these vain thoughts, I will be joy-
    ous —
And here comes Joy's true herald.

          Enter MYRRHA.

    Myr.   King ! the sky
Is overcast, and musters muttering thunder,
In clouds that seem approaching fast, and
    show
In forked flashes a commanding tempest.[2]
Will you then quit the palace ?
    Sar.   Tempest, say'st thou ?
    Myr. Ay, my good lord.
    Sar.   For my own part, I should be
Not ill content to vary the smooth scene,
And watch the warring elements ; but this
Would little suit the silken garments and
Smooth faces of our festive friends. Say,
    Myrrha,
Art thou of those who dread the roar of
    clouds ?
    Myr. In my own country we respect their
    voices
As auguries of Jove.[3]
    Sar.   Jove ! — ay, your Baal —
Ours also has a property in thunder,
And ever and anon some falling bolt
Proves his divinity, — and yet sometimes
Strikes his own altars.
    Myr.   That were a dread omen.
    Sar. Yes — for the priests. Well, we will
    not go forth
Beyond the palace walls to-night, but make
Our feast within.
    Myr.   Now, Jove be praised ! that he
Hath heard the prayer thou wouldst not hear.
    The gods
Are kinder to thee than thou to thyself,
And flash this storm between thee and thy
    foes,
To shield thee from them.
    Sar.   Child, if there be peril,
Methinks it is the same within these walls
As on the river's brink.
    Myr.   Not so ; these walls
Are high and strong, and guarded. Treason
    has
To penetrate through many a winding way,

---

[1] [MS. —

"Nor silent Baal, our imaged deity,
  Although his marble face looks frowningly
  As the dull shadows," etc.]

[2] [MS. —

"In distant flashes { a wide-spreading } tempest."]
              { the approaching }

[3] [MS. — " As from the gods to augur."]

And massy portal; but in the pavilion
There is no bulwark.
Sar. No, nor in the palace,
Nor in the fortress, nor upon the top
Of cloud-fenced Caucasus, where the eagle
sits
Nested in pathless clefts, if treachery be :
Even as the arrow finds the airy king,
The steel will reach the earthly. But be calm :
The men, or innocent or guilty, are
Banished, and far upon their way.
Myr. They live, then?
Sar. So sanguinary? *Thou !*
Myr. I would not shrink
From just infliction of due punishment
On those who seek your life : wer't otherwise,
I should not merit mine. Besides, you heard
The princely Salemenes.
Sar. This is strange;
The gentle and the austere are both against
me,
And urge me to revenge.
. *Myr.* 'Tis a Greek virtue.
Sar. But not a kingly one — I'll none on't;
or
If ever I indulge in't, it shall be
With kings — my equals.
Myr. These men sought to be so.
Sar. Myrrha, this is too feminine, and
springs
From fear——
Myr. For you.
Sar. No matter, still 'tis fear.
I have observed your sex, once roused to
wrath,
Are timidly vindictive to a pitch
Of perseverance, which I would not copy.
I thought you were exempt from this, as from
The childish helplessness of Asian women.[1]
Myr. My lord, I am no boaster of my
love,
Nor of my attributes; I have shared your
splendor
And will partake your fortunes. You may
live
To find one slave more true than subject
myriads :
But this the gods avert! I am content
To be beloved on trust for what I feel,
Rather than prove it to you in your griefs,[2]
Which might not yield to any cares of mine.
Sar. Grief cannot come where perfect love
exists,
Except to heighten it, and vanish from
That which it could not scare away. Let's
in —

The hour approaches, and we must prepare
To meet the invited guests who grace our
feast. [*Exeunt.*[3]

ACT III.

SCENE I.— *The Hall of the Palace illumi-
nated.* —SARDANAPALUS *and his Guests at
Table. — A Storm without, and Thunder
occasionally heard during the Banquet.*

Sar. Fill full! why this is as it should be :
here
Is my true realm, amidst bright eyes and faces
Happy as fair! Here sorrow cannot reach.
Zam. Nor elsewhere — where the king is,
pleasure sparkles.
Sar. Is not this better now than Nimrod's
huntings,
Or my wild grandam's chase in search of king-
doms
She could not keep when conquered?
Alt. Mighty though
They were, as all thy royal line have been,
Yet none of those who went before have
reached
The acmé of Sardanapalus, who
Has placed his joy in peace — the sole true
glory.
Sar. And pleasure, good Altada, to which
glory
Is but the path. What is it that we seek?
Enjoyment! We have cut the way short to
it,
And not gone tracking it through human
ashes,
Making a grave with every footstep.
Zam. No;
All hearts are happy, and all voices bless
The king of peace, who holds a world in jubi-
lee.
Sar. Art sure of that? I have heard other-
wise;
Some say that there be traitors.
Zam. Traitors they
Who dare to say so! — 'Tis impossible.
What cause?
Sar. What cause? true, — fill the goblet
up;
We will not think of them : there are none
such,
Or if there be, they are gone.
Alt. Guests, to my pledge!
Down on your knees, and drink a measure to
The safety of the king — the monarch, say I?
The god Sardanapalus!

---

[3] [The second Act, which contains the details of
the conspiracy of Arbaces, its detection by the vigi-
lance of Salemenes, and the too rash and hasty for-
giveness of the rebels by the king, is, on the whole,
heavy and uninteresting. — *Jeffrey.*]

[ZAMES *and the Guests kneel and exclaim —*
. Mightier than
His father Baal, the god Sardanapalus!
[*It thunders as they kneel; some start up
in confusion.*

Zam. Why do you rise, my friends? in
that strong peal
His father gods consented.

Myr. Menaced, rather.
King, wilt thou bear this mad impiety?

Sar. Impiety! — nay, if the sires who
reigned
Before me can be gods, I'll not disgrace
Their lineage. But arise, my pious friends;
Hoard your devotion for the thunderer there.
I seek but to be loved, not worshipped.

Alt. Both —
Both you must ever be by all true subjects.

Sar. Methinks the thunders still increase:
it is
An awful night.

Myr. Oh yes, for those who have
No palace to protect their worshippers.

Sar. That's true, my Myrrha; and could I
convert
My realm to one wide shelter for the wretched,
I'd do it.

Myr. . Thou'rt no god, then, not to be
Able to work a will so good and general,
As thy wish would imply.

Sar. And your gods, then,
Who can, and do not?

Myr. Do not speak of that,
Lest we provoke them.

Sar. True, they love not censure
Better than mortals. Friends, a thought has
struck me:
Were there no temples, would there, think ye,
be
Air worshippers? that is, when it is angry,
And pelting as even now.

Myr. The Persian prays
Upon his mountain.

Sar. Yes, when the sun shines.

Myr. And I would ask if this your palace
were
Unroofed and desolate, how many flatterers
Would lick the dust in which the king lay low?

Alt. The fair Ionian is too sarcastic
Upon a nation whom she knows not well;
The Assyrians know no pleasure but their
king's,
And homage is their pride.

Sar. Nay, pardon, guests,
The fair Greek's readiness of speech.

Alt. Pardon! sire:
We honor her of all things next to thee.
Hark! what was that?

Zam. That! nothing but the jar
Of distant portals shaken by the wind.

Alt. It sounded like the clash of — hark
again!

Zam. The big rain pattering on the roof.

Sar. No more.
Myrrha, my love, hast thou thy shell in order?
Sing me a song of Sappho, her, thou know'st,
Who in thy country threw ——

Enter PANIA, *with his sword and garments
bloody, and disordered. The Guests rise in
confusion.*[1]

Pan. (to the Guards). Look to the portals;
And with your best speed to the walls without.
Your arms! To arms! The king's in danger.
Monarch!
Excuse this haste, — 'tis faith.

Sar. Speak on.

Pan. It is
As Salemenes feared; the faithless satraps——

Sar. You are wounded — give some wine.
Take breath, good Pania.

Pan. 'Tis nothing — a mere flesh wound.
I am worn
More with my speed to warn my sovereign,
Than hurt in his defence.

Myr. Well, sir, the rebels?

Pan. Soon as Arbaces and Beleses reached
Their stations in the city, they refused
To march; and on my attempt to use the power
Which I was delegated with, they called
Upon their troops, who rose in fierce defiance.

Myr. All?

Pan. Too many.

Sar. Spare not of thy free speech,
To spare mine ears the truth.

Pan. . My own slight guard
Were faithful, and what's left of it is still so.

Myr. And are these all the force still faithful?

Pan. No —
The Bactrians, now led on by Salemenes,
Who even then was on his way, still urged
By strong suspicion of the Median chiefs,
Are numerous, and make strong head against
The rebels, fighting inch by inch, and forming
An orb around the palace, where they mean
To centre all their force, and save the king.
(*He hesitates.*) I am charged to ——

Myr. 'Tis no time for hesitation.

Pan. Prince Salemenes doth implore the
king
To arm himself, although but for a moment,
And show himself unto the soldiers: his
Sole presence in this instant might do more
Than hosts can do in his behalf.

Sar. What, ho!
My armor there.

Myr. And wilt thou?

Sar. Will I not?
Ho, there! — but seek not for the buckler: 'tis

---

[1] [Early in the third Act, the royal banquet is disturbed by sudden tidings of treason and revolt; and then the reveller blazes out into the hero, and the Greek blood of Myrrha mounts to its proper office! — *Jeffrey.*]

Too heavy: — a light cuirass and my sword.
Where are the rebels?

Pan.   Scarce a furlong's length
From the outward wall the fiercest conflict
  rages.

Sar.   Then I may charge on horseback.
  Sfero, ho!
Order my horse out. — There is space enough
Even in our courts, and by the outer gate,
To marshal half the horsemen of Arabia.
                    [*Exit* SFERO *for the armor.*

Myr. How I do love thee!

Sar.   I ne'er doubted it.

Myr. But now I know thee.

Sar. (*to his Attendant*). Bring down my
  ·spear too.—
Where's Salemenes?

Pan.   Where a soldier should be,
In the thick of the fight.

Sar.   Then hasten to him —— Is
The path still open, and communication
Left 'twixt the palace and the phalanx?

Pan.   'Twas
When I late left him, and I have no fear:
Our troops were steady, and the phalanx
  formed.

Sar. Tell him to spare his person for the
  present,
And that I will not spare my own — and say,
I come.

Pan. There's victory in the very word.
                                  [*Exit* PANIA.

Sar. Altada — Zames — forth, and arm ye!
  There
Is all in readiness in the armory.
See that the women are bestowed in safety
In the remote apartments: let a guard
Be set before them, with strict charge to quit
The post but with their lives — command it,
  Zames.
Altada, arm yourself, and return here;
Your post is near our person.
          [*Exeunt* ZAMES, ALTADA, *and all save*
          MYRRHA.

Enter SFERO *and others with the King's*
              Arms, etc.

Sfe.   King! your armor.

Sar. (*arming himself*). Give me the cui-
  rass — so my baldric; now
My sword: I had forgot the helm — where is
  it?
That's well — no, 'tis too heavy: you mistake,
  too —
It was not this I meant, but that which bears
A diadem around it.

Sfe.   Sire, I deemed
That too conspicuous from. the precious
  stones
To risk your sacred brow beneath — and trust
  me,
This is of better metal, though less rich.

Sar. You deemed! · Are you too turned a
  rebel? Fellow!
Your part is to obey: return, and — no —
It is too late — I will go forth without it.

Sfe. At least, wear this.

Sar.   Wear Caucasus! why, 'tis
A mountain on my temples.

Sfe.   Sire, the meanest
Soldier goes not forth thus exposed to battle.
All men will recognize you — for the storm
Has ceased, and the moon breaks forth in her
  brightness.

Sar. I go forth to be recognized, and
  thus
Shall be so sooner. Now — my spear! I'm
  armed.
          [*In going stops short, and turns to* SFERO.
Sfero — I had forgotten — bring the mirror.[1]

Sfe. The mirror, sire?

Sar.   Yes, sir, of polished brass,
Brought from the spoils of India — but be
  speedy.[2]   [*Exit* SFERO.

Sar. Myrrha, retire unto a place of safety.
Why went you not forth with the other dam-
  sels?

Myr. Because my place is here.

Sar.   And when I am gone ——

Myr. I follow.

Sar.   You / to battle?

Myr.   ●   If it were so,
'Twere not the first Greek girl had trod the
  path.
I will await here your *return*.

Sar.   The place
Is spacious, and the first to be sought out,
If they prevail; and, if it be so,
And I return not ——

Myr.   Still we meet again.

Sar. How?

----

[1] ["In the third Act, where Sardanapalus calls
for a mirror to look at himself in his armor, recol-
lect to quote the Latin passage from Juvenal upon
Otho (a similar character, who did the same thing).
Gifford will help you to it. The trait is, perhaps,
too familiar, but it is historical (of Otho, at least),
and natural in an effeminate character." — *Byron*
to Mr. M.]

[2] ["Ille tenet speculum pathici gestamen Othonis,
      Actoris Arunci spolium, quo se ille videbat
      Armatum, cum jam tolli vexilla juberet.
      Res memoranda novis annalibus, atque
        recenti
      Historia, speculum civilis farcina belli."
                                  Juv. Sat. ii.

  "This grasps a mirror — pathic Otho's boast
    (Auruncan Actor's spoil), where, while his
        host,
  With shouts, the signal of the fight required,
  He viewed his mailed form; viewed, and
        admired!
  Lo, ▪ new subject for the historic page.
  A MIRROR, midst the arms of civil rage,"
                                  Gifford.]

Myr. In the spot where all must meet at last—
In Hades! if there be, as I believe,
A shore beyond the Styx: and if there be not,
In ashes.

Sar.　　Darest thou so much?

Myr.　　　　　　　I dare all things
Except survive what I have loved, to be
A rebel's booty: forth, and do your bravest.

Re-enter SFERO *with the mirror.*

Sar. (*looking at himself*). This cuirass
fits me well, the baldric better;
And the helm not at all. Methinks I seem
[*Flings away the helmet after trying it again.*
Passing well in these toys; and now to prove them.
Altada! Where's Altada?

Sfe.　　　　　　　　Waiting, sire,
Without: he has your shield in readiness.

Sar. True; I forgot he is my shield-bearer
By right of blood, derived from age to age.
Myrrha, embrace me; — yet once more—
once more—
Love, me, whate'er betide. My chiefest glory
Shall be to make me worthier of your love.

Myr. Go forth, and conquer!
[*Exeunt* SARDANAPALUS *and* SFERO.[1]
Now, I am alone.
All are gone forth, and of that all how few
Perhaps return. Let him but vanquish, and
Me perish! If he vanquish not, I perish;
For I will not outlive him. He has wound
About my heart, I know not how nor why.
Not for that he is king; for now his kingdom
Rocks underneath his throne, and the earth yawns
To yield him no more of it than a grave;
And yet I love him more. Oh, mighty Jove!
Forgive this monstrous love for a barbarian,
Who knows not of Olympus! yes, I love him
Now, now, far more than—— Hark—to the
war shout!
Methinks it nears me. If it should be so,
[*She draws forth a small vial.*
This cunning Colchian poison, which my father
Learned to compound on Euxine shores, and taught me
How to preserve, shall free me! It had freed me
Long ere this hour, but that I loved, until

I half forgot I was a slave: — where all
Are slaves save one, and proud of servitude,
So they are served in turn by something lower
In the degree of bondage, we forget
That shackles worn like ornaments no less
Are chains. Again that shout! and now the clash
Of arms — and now — and now——

Enter ALTADA.

Alt.　　　　　　　　Ho Sfero, ho!

Myr. He is not here; what wouldst thou with him? How
Goes on the conflict?

Alt.　　　　　Dubiously and fiercely.

Myr. And the king?

Alt.　　　　　Like a king. I must find Sfero
And bring him a new spear and his own helmet.
He fights till now bare-headed, and by far
Too much exposed. The soldiers knew his face,
And the foe too; and in the moon's broad light,
His silk tiara and his flowing hair
Make him a mark too royal. Every arrow
Is pointed at the fair hair and fair features,
And the broad fillet which crowns both.

Myr.　　　　Ye gods,
Who fulminate o'er my father's land, protect him!
Were you sent by the king?

Alt.　　　　　　By Salemenes,
Who sent me privily upon this charge,
Without the knowledge of the careless sovereign.
The king! the king fights as he revels! ho!
What, Sfero! I will seek the armory —
He must be there.　　　　[*Exit* ALTADA.

Myr.　　'Tis no dishonor— no—
'Tis no dishonor to have loved this man.
I almost wish now, what I never wished
Before, that he were Grecian. If Alcides
Were shamed in wearing Lydian Omphale's
She-garb, and wielding her vile distaff; surely
He, who springs up a Hercules at once,
Nursed in effeminate arts from youth to manhood,
And rushes from the banquet to the battle,
As though it were a bed of love, deserves
That a Greek girl should be his paramour,
And a Greek bard his minstrel, a Greek tomb
His monument. How goes the strife, sir?

Enter an Officer.

Officer.　　　　　　　Lost,
Lost almost past recovery. Zames! Where
Is Zames?

Myr.　　　　Posted with the guard appointed
To watch before the apartment of the women.
[*Exit Officer.*

Myr. (*sola*). He's gone; and told no more
than that all's lost!

---

[1] [In the third Act, the king and his courtiers are disturbed at their banquet by the breaking out of the conspiracy. The battle which follows, if we overlook the absurdity, which occurs during one part of it, of hostile armies drawn up against each other in a dining-room, is extremely well told; and Sardanapalus displays the precise mixture of effeminacy and courage, levity and talent, which belongs to his character. — *Heber.*]

What need have I to know more? In those
  words,
Those little words, a kingdom and a king,
A line of thirteen ages, and the lives
Of thousands, and the fortune of all left
With life, are merged; and I, too, with the great,
Like a small bubble breaking with the wave
Which bore it, shall be nothing. At the least,
My fate is in my keeping: no proud victor
Shall count me with his spoils.

Enter PANIA.

Pan.   Away with me,
Myrrha, without delay; we must not lose
A moment—all that's left us now.

Myr.   The king?

Pan. Sent me here to conduct you hence,
  beyond
The river, by a secret passage.

Myr.   Then
He lives——

Pan. And charged me to secure your life,
And beg you to live on for his sake, till
He can rejoin you.

Myr.   Will he then give way?

Pan. Not till the last. Still, still he does
  whate'er
Despair can do; and step by step disputes
The very palace.

Myr.   They are here, then:—ay,
Their shouts come ringing through the ancient
  halls,
Never profaned by rebel echoes till
This fatal night. Farewell, Assyria's line!
Farewell to all of Nimrod! Even the name
Is now no more.

Pan.   Away with me—away!

Myr. No: I'll die here!—Away, and tell
  your king
I loved him to the last.

Enter SARDANAPALUS *and* SALEMENES *with
Soldiers.* PANIA *quits* MYRRHA, *and
ranges himself with them.*

Sar.   Since it is thus,
We'll die where we were born—in our own
  halls.
Serry your ranks—stand firm. I have
  despatched
A trusty satrap for the guard of Zames,
All fresh and faithful; they'll be here anon.
All is not over.—Pania, look to Myrrha.
            [PANIA *returns towards* MYRRHA.

Sal. We have breathing time; yet once
  more charge, my friends—
One for Assyria!

Sar. Rather say for Bactria!
My faithful Bactrians, I will henceforth be
King of your nation, and we'll hold together
This realm as province.

Sal.   Hark! they come—they come.

Enter BELESES *and* ARBACES *with the Rebels.*

Arb. Set on, we have them in the toil.
  Charge! charge!

Bel. On! on!—Heaven fights for us and
  with us—On!
  [*They charge the King and* SALEMENES
    *with their Troops, who defend themselves
    till the Arrival of* ZAMES, *with the Guard
    before mentioned. The Rebels are then
    driven off, and pursued by* SALEMENES, *etc.
    As the King is going to join the pursuit,*
    BELESES *crosses him.*

Bel. Ho! tyrant—*I* will end this war.

Sar. •   Even so,
My warlike priest, and precious prophet, and
Grateful and trusty subject:—yield, I pray
  thee.
I would reserve thee for a fitter doom,
Rather than dip my hands in holy blood.

Bel. Thine hour is come.

Sar.   No, thine.—I've lately read,
Though but a young astrologer, the stars;
And ranging round the zodiac, found thy fate
In the sign of the Scorpion, which proclaims
That thou wilt now be crushed.

Bel.   But not by thee.
  [*They fight;* BELESES *is wounded and dis-
    armed.*

Sar. (*raising his sword to dispatch him, ex-
  claims*)—
Now call upon thy planets, will they shoot
From the sky to preserve their seer and credit?
  [*A party of Rebels enter and rescue* BELESES.
    *They assail the King, who, in turn, is res-
    cued by a Party of his Soldiers, who drive
    the Rebels off.*
The villain was a prophet after all.
Upon them—ho! there—victory is ours.
            [*Exit in pursuit.*

Myr. (*to Pan.*). Pursue! Why stand'st thou
  here, and leavest the ranks
Of fellow soldiers conquering without thee?

Pan. The king's command was not to quit
  thee.

Myr.   Me!
Think not of me—a single soldier's arm
Must not be wanting now. I ask no guard,
I need no guard: what, with a world at stake,
Keep watch upon a woman? Hence, I say,
Or thou art shamed! Nay, then, *I* will go forth,
A feeble female, 'midst their desperate strife,
And bid thee guard me *there*—where thou
  shouldst shield
Thy sovereign.   [*Exit* MYRRHA.

Pan.   Yet stay, damsel! She is gone,
If aught of ill betide her, better I
Had lost my life. Sardanapalus holds her
Far dearer than his kingdom, yet he fights
For that too; and can I do less than he,
Who never flashed a scimitar till now?
Myrrha, return, and I obey you, though
In disobedience to the monarch.
            [*Exit* PANIA.

Enter ALTADA *and* SFERO *by an opposite door.*

Alt.   Myrrha!
What, gone? yet she was here when the fight
     raged,
And Pania also. Can aught have befallen
     them?
Sfe. I saw both safe, when late the rebels
     fled:
They probably are but retired to made
Their way back to the harem.
     Alt.   If the king
Prove victor, as it seems even now he must,
And miss his own Ionian, we are doomed
To worse than captive rebels.
  Sfe.   Let us trace them;
She cannot be fled far; and, found, she makes
A richer prize to our soft sovereign
Than his recovered kingdom.
     Alt.   Baal himself
Ne'er fought more fiercely to win empire, than
His silken son to save it: he defies
All augury of foes or friends; and like
The close and sultry summer's day, which
     bodes
A twilight tempest, bursts forth in such thunder
As sweeps the air and deluges the earth.
The man's inscrutable.
     Sfe.   Not more than others.
All are the sons of circumstance: away —
Let's seek the slave out, or prepare to be
Tortured for his infatuation, and
Condemned without a crime.   [*Exeunt.*

Enter SALEMENES *and Soldiers, etc.*

Sal.   The triumph is
Flattering: they are beaten backward from
     the palace,
And we have opened regular access
To the troops stationed on the other side
Euphrates, who may still be true; nay, must
     be,
When they hear of our victory. But where
Is the chief victor? where's the king.

Enter SARDANAPALUS, *cum suis, etc. and*
                MYRRHA.

Sar.   Here, brother.[1]
Sal. Unhurt, I hope.
Sar.   Not quite; but let it pass.
We've cleared the palace ——
  Sal.   And I trust the city.
Our numbers gather: and I've ordered on-
     ward
A cloud of Parthians, hitherto reserved,
All fresh and fiery, to be poured upon them
In their retreat, which soon will be a flight.
Sar. It is already, or at least they marched
Faster than I could follow with my Bactrians,

---

[1] [The king, by his daring valor, restores the
fortune of the fight, and returns, with all his train,
to the palace. The scene that ensues is very mas-
terly and characteristic. — *Jeffrey.*]·

Who spared no speed. I am spent: give me
     a seat.
Sal. There stands the throne, sire.
Sar.   'Tis no place to rest on,
For mind nor body: let me have a couch,
                      [*They place a seat.*
A peasant's stool, I care not what: so — now
I breathe more freely.
Sal.   This great hour has proved
The brightest and most glorious of your life.
Sar. And the most tiresome. Where's
     my cupbearer?
Bring me some water.
Sal. (*smiling*).   'Tis the first time he
Ever had such an order: even I,
Your most austere of counsellors, would now
Suggest a purpler beverage.
Sar.   Blood — doubtless.
But there's enough of that shed; as for wine,
I have learned to-night the price of the pure
     element:
Thrice have I drank of it, and thrice renewed,
With greater strength than the grape ever gave
     me,
My charge upon the rebels. Where's the sol-
     dier
Who gave me water in his helmet?
One of the Guards.   Slain, sire!
An arrow pierced his brain, while, scattering
The last drops from his helm, he stood in act
To place it on his brows.
  Sar.   Slain! unrewarded!
And slain to serve my thirst: that's hard, poor
     slave.
Had he but lived, I would have gorged him
     with
Gold: all the gold of earth could ne'er repay
The pleasure of that draught; for I was
     parched
As I am now. [*They bring water — he drinks.*
             I live again — from henceforth
The goblet I reserve for hours of love,
But war on water.
Sal.   And that bandage, sire,
Which girds your arm?
Sar.   A scratch from brave Beleses.
Myr. Oh! he is wounded!
Sar.   Not too much of that;
And yet it feels a little stiff and painful,
Now I am cooler.
Myr.   You have bound it with ——
Sar. The fillet of my diadem: the first time
That ornament was ever aught to me,
Save an incumbrance.
Myr. (*to the attendants*). Summon speed-
     ily
A leech of the most skilful: pray, retire:
I will unbind your wound and tend it.
Sar.   Do so;
For now it throbs sufficiently: but what
Know'st thou of wounds? yet wherefore do
     I ask?

Know'st thou, my brother, where I lighted
   on
This minion?
   Sal.   Herding with the other females,
Like frightened antelopes.
   Sar.   No: like the dam
Of the young lion, femininely raging,
(And femininely meaneth furiously,
Because all passions in excess are female,)
Against the hunter flying with her cub,
She urged on with her voice and gesture, and
Her floating hair and flashing eyes, the sol-
   diers,
In the pursuit.
   Sal.   Indeed!
   Sar.   You see, this night
Made warriors of more than me. I paused
To look upon her, and her kindled cheek;
Her large black eyes, that flashed through her
   long hair
As it streamed o'er her; her blue veins that
   rose
Along her most transparent brow; her nos-
   tril
Dilated from its symmetry; her lips
Apart; her voice that clove through all the din,
As a lute's pierceth through the cymbal's
   clash,
Jarred but not drowned by the loud brattling;
   her
Waved arms, more dazzling with their own
   born whiteness
Than the steel her hand held, which she
   caught up
From a dead soldier's grasp; — all these
   things made
Her seem unto the troops a prophetess
Of victory, or Victory herself,
Come down to hail us hers.
   Sal. (*aside*).   This is too much.
Again the love fit's on him, and all's lost,
Unless we turn his thoughts.
   (*Aloud.*)   But pray thee, sire,
Think of your wound — you said even now
   'twas painful.
   Sar. That's true, too; but I must not
   think of it.
   Sal. I have looked to all things needful,
   and will now
Receive reports of progress made in such
Orders as I had given, and then return
To hear your further pleasure.
   Sar.   Be it so.
   Sal. (*in retiring*). Myrrha!
   Myr.   Prince!
   Sal.   You have shown a soul to-night,
Which, were he not my sister's lord —— But
   now
I have no time: thou lovest the king?
   Myr.   I love
Sardanapalus.
   Sal. But wouldst have him king still?

   Myr. I would not have him less than what
   he should be.
   Sal. Well then, to have him king, and
   yours, and all
He should, or should not be; to have him
   live,
Let him not sink back into luxury.
You have more power upon his spirit than
Wisdom within these walls, or fierce rebellion
Raging without: look well that he relapse not.
   Myr. There needed not the voice of Sale-
   menes
To urge me on to this: I will not fail.
All that a woman's weakness can ——
   Sal.   Is power
Omnipotent o'er such a heart as his:
Exert it wisely.   [*Exit* SALEMENES.
   Sar.   Myrrha! what, at whispers
With my stern brother? I shall soon be
   jealous.[1]
   Myr. (*smiling*). You have cause, sire; for
   on the earth there breathes not
A man more worthy of a woman's love —
A soldier's trust — a subject's reverence —
A king's esteem — the whole world's admira-
   tion![2]
   Sar. Praise him, but not so warmly. I
   must not
Hear those sweet lips grow eloquent in aught
That throws me into shade; yet you speak
   truth. *
   Myr. And now retire, to have your wound
   looked to.
Pray, lean on me.
   Sar.   Yes, love! but not from pain.
                    [*Exeunt omnes.*

ACT IV.

SCENE I. — SARDANAPALUS *discovered sleep-*
ing upon a Couch, and occasionally disturbed
in his Slumbers, with MYRRHA *watching.*

   Myr. (*sola, gazing*). I have stolen upon his
   rest, if rest it be,
Which thus convulses slumber: shall I wake
   him?
No, he seems calmer. Oh, thou God of
   Quiet!

---

[1] ['The rebels are at length repulsed. The king
reënters wounded, and retires to rest, after a short
and very characteristic conversation between Sale-
menes and Myrrha, in which the two kindred spir-
its show their mutual understanding of each other,
and the loyal warrior, postponing all the selfish
domestic feelings which led him to dislike the fair
Ionian, exhorts her to use her utmost power to
keep her lover from relaxing into luxury. The
transient effect which their whispers produce on
Sardanapalus is well imagined. — *Heber.*]

[2] [MS. —   { admiration
"A king's esteem — the whole world's { veneration
                             { reverence."]

Whose reign is o'er sealed eyelids and soft
  dreams,
Or deep, deep sleep, so as to be unfathomed,
Look like thy brother, Death, — so still — so
  stirless —
For then we are happiest, as it may be, we
Are happiest of all within the realm
Of thy stern, silent, and unwakening twin.
Again he moves — again the play of pain
Shoots o'er his features, as the sudden gust
Crisps the reluctant lake that lay so calm [1]
Beneath the mountain shadow; or the blast
Ruffles the autumn leaves, that drooping cling
Faintly and motionless to their loved boughs.
I must awake him — yet not yet: who knows
From what I rouse him? It seems pain;
  but if
I quicken him to heavier pain? The fever
Of this tumultuous might, the grief too of
His wound, though slight, may cause all this,
  and shake
Me more to see than him to suffer. No:
Let Nature use her own maternal means, —
And I await to second, not disturb her.[2]
  Sar. (*awakening*). Not so — although ye
  multiplied the stars,
And gave them to me as a realm to share
From you and with you! I would not so
  purchase
The empire of eternity. Hence — hence —
Old hunter of the earliest brutes! and ye,
Who hunted fellow-creatures as if brutes!
Once bloody mortals — and now bloodier
  idols,
If your priests lie not! And thou, ghastly
  beldame!
Dripping with dusky gore, and trampling on
The carcasses of Inde — away! away!
Where am I? Where the spectres? Where
     — No — that
Is no false phantom: I should know it 'midst
All that the dead dare gloomily raise up
From their black gulf to daunt the living.
  Myrrha!
  Myr. Alas! thou art pale, and on thy brow
  the drops
Gather like night dew. My beloved, hush —
Calm thee. Thy speech seems of another
  world,
And thou art lord of this. Be of good cheer;
All will go well.
  Sar.   Thy *hand* — so — 'tis thy hand;
'Tis flesh; grasp — clasp — yet closer, till I feel
Myself that which I was.

  Myr.   At least know me
For what I am, and ever must be — thine.
  Sar. I know it now. I know this life again.
Ah, Myrrha! I have been where we shall be.
  Myr. My lord!
  Sar. I've been i' the grave — where worms
  are lords,
And kings are —— But I did not deem it so;
I thought 'twas nothing.
  Myr.   So it is; except
Unto the timid, who anticipate
That which may never be.[3]
  Sar.   Oh, Myrrha! if

[1] [MS. — "Crisps the unswelling wave," etc.]
[2] [The fourth Act opens with Myrrha watching over the slumbers of Sardanapalus. He wakens and tells a horrid dream, which we do not much admire, except that part of it which describes the form of his warlike ancestress Semiramis, with whom, and the rest of his regal predecessors, he had fancied himself at a ghostly banquet. — *Heber.*]

[3] [The general tone of Myrrha's character (in perfect consistency with the manners of her age and nation, and with her own elevated but pure and feminine spirit,) is that of a devout worshipper of her country's gods. She reproves, with dignity, the impious flattery of the Assyrian courtiers and the libertine scoffs of the king. She does not forget, while preparing for death, that libation which was the latest and most solemn act of Grecian piety; and she, more particularly, expresses her belief in a future state of existence. Yet this very Myrrha, when Sardanapalus is agitated by his evil dream, and by the natural doubt as to what worse visions death may bring, is made to console him, in the strain of his own Epicurean philosophy, with the doctrine that death is really nothing, except

  "Unto the timid who anticipate
    That which may never be,"

and with the insinuation that all which remains of "the dead is the dust we tread upon." We do not wish to ask, we do not like to conjecture, *whose* sentiments these are, but they are certainly not the sentiments of an ancient Grecian heroine. They are not the sentiments which Myrrha might have learned from the heroes of her native land, or from the poems whence those heroes derived their heroism, their contempt of death, " and their love of virtue." Myrrha would rather have told her lover of those happy islands where the benevolent and the brave reposed after the toils of their mortal existence; of that venerable society of departed warriors and sages to which, if he renounced his sloth and lived for his people and for glory, he might yet expect admission. She would have told him of that joy with which his warlike ancestors would move along their meads of asphodel, when the news reached them of their descendant's prowess; she would have anticipated those songs which denied that " Harmodius was dead," however he might be removed from the sphere of mortality; which told her countrymen of the " roses and the golden-fruited bowers, where beneath the light of a lower sun, departed warriors reined their shadowy cars, or struck their harps amid altars steaming with frankincense." * Such were the doctrines which naturally led men to a contempt for life and a thirst for glory: but the opposite opinions were the doubts of a later day, and of those sophists under whose influence Greece soon ceased to be free, or valiant, or virtuous." — *Heber.*]

* Hom. Odyss. λ. 539. Callistratus ap. Athenæum, l. xv. Pindar Fragm. Heyne, vol. iii. p. 31.

Sleep shows such things, what may not death
    disclose ?
Myr. I know no evil death can show, which
    life
Has not already shown to those who live
Embodied longest. If there be indeed
A shore where mind survives, 'twill be as
    mind,
All unincorporate: or if there flits
A shadow of this cumbrous clog of clay,
Which stalks, methinks, between our souls
    and heaven,
And fetters us to earth — at least the phantom,
Whate'er it have to fear, will not fear death.
    Sar. I fear it not; but I have felt — have
    seen —
A legion of the dead.
    Myr.   And so have I.
The dust we tread upon was once alive,
And wretched. But proceed: what hast thou
    seen ?
Speak it, 'twill lighten thy dimmed mind.
    Sar.   Methought —
    Myr. Yet pause, thou art tired — in pain —
    exhausted; all
Which can impair both strength and spirit:
    seek
Rather to sleep again.
    Sar.   Not now — I would not
Dream; though I know it now to be a dream
What have I dreamt: — and canst thou bear
    to hear it ?
    Myr. I can bear all things, dreams of life or
    death,
Which I participate with you in semblance
Or full reality.
    Sar.   And this looked real,
I tell you: after that these eyes were open,
I saw them in their flight — for then they fled.
    Myr. Say on.
    Sar.   I saw, that is, I dreamed myself
Here — here — even where we are, guests as
    we were,
Myself a host that deemed himself but guest,
Willing to equal all in social freedom;
But, on my right hand and my left, instead
Of thee and Zames, and our customed meeting,
Was ranged on my left hand a haughty, dark,
And deadly face — I could not recognize it,
Yet I had seen it, though I knew not where:
The features were a giant's, and the eye
Was still, yet lighted; his long locks curled
    down
On his vast bust, whence a hugh quiver rose
With shaft-heads feathered from the eagle's
    wing,[1]
That peeped up bristling through his serpent
    hair.
I invited him to fill the cup which stood

---

[1] [MS. —
    " With arrows peeping through his falling hair."]

Between us, but he answered not — I filled it —
He took it not, but stared upon me, till
I trembled at the fixed glare of his eye:
I frowned upon him as a king should frown —
He frowned not in his turn, but looked upon me
With the same aspect, which appalled me
    more,
Because it changed not; and I turned for refuge
To milder guests, and sought them on the
    right,
Where thou wert wont to be. But —
                        [*He pauses.*
    Myr.   What instead ?
    Sar. In thy own chair — thy own place in
    the banquet —
I sought thy sweet face in the circle — but
Instead — a gray-haired, withered, bloody-
    eyed,
And bloody-handed, ghastly, ghostly thing,
Female in garb, and crowned upon the brow,
Furrowed with years, yet sneering with the
    passion
Of vengeance, leering too with that of lust,
Sate: — my veins curdled.
    Myr.   Is this all ?
    Sar.   Upon
Her right hand — her lank, bird-like right
    hand — stood
A goblet, bubbling o'er with blood; and on
Her left, another, filled with — what I saw not,
But turned from it and her. But all along
The table sate a range of crowned wretches,
Of various aspects, but of one expression.
    Myr. And felt you not this a mere vision ?
    Sar.   No:
It was so palpable, I could have touched
    them.
I turned from one face to another, in
The hope to find at last one which I knew
Ere I saw theirs: but no — all turned upon
    me,
And stared, but neither ate nor drank, but
    stared,
Till I grew stone, as they seemed half to be,
Yet breathing stone, for I felt life in them,
And life in me: there was a horrid kind
Of sympathy between us, as if they
Had lost a part of death to come to me,
And I the half of life to sit by them.
We were in an existence all apart
From heaven or earth —— And rather let me
    see
Death all than such a being!
    Myr.   And the end ?
    Sar. At last I sate, marble, as they, when
    rose
The hunter and the crone; and smiling on
    me —
Yes, the enlarged but noble aspect of
The hunter smiled upon me — I should say,
His lips, for his eyes moved not — and the
    woman's

Thin lips relaxed to something like a smile.
Both rose, and the crowned figures on each
   hand
Rose also, as if aping their chief shades —
Mere mimics even in death — but I sate still:
A desperate courage crept through every
   limb,
And at the last I feared them not, but laughed
Full in their phantom faces. But then — then
The hunter laid his hand on mine: I took it,
And grasped it — but it melted from my own;
While he too vanished, and left nothing but
The memory of a hero, for he looked so.
   Myr.   And was: the ancestor of heroes, too,
And thine no less.
   Sar.   Ay, Myrrha, but the woman,
The female who remained, she flew upon me,
And burnt my lips up with her noisome kisses;
And, flinging down the goblets on each hand,
Methought their poisons flowed around us, till
Each formed a hideous river. Still she clung;
The other phantoms, like a row of statues,
Stood dull as in our temples, but she still
Embraced me, while I shrunk from her, as if,
In lieu of her remote descendant, I
Had been the son who slew her for her incest.
Then — then — a chaos of all loathsome things
Thronged thick and shapeless: I was dead,
   yet feeling —
Buried and raised again — consumed by
   worms,
Purged by the flames, and withered in the air!
I can fix nothing further of my thoughts,
Save that I longed for thee, and sought for
   thee,
In all these agonies, — and woke and found
   thee.
   Myr. So shalt thou find me ever at thy
   side,
Here and hereafter, if the last may be.
But think not of these things — the mere crea-
   tions
Of late events, acting upon a frame
Unused to toil, yet over-wrought by toil
Such as might try the sternest.
   Sar.   I am better.
Now that I see *thee once* more, *what was seen*
Seems nothing.

Enter SALEMENES.

   Sal.   Is the king so soon awake?
   Sar. Yes, brother, and I would I had not
   slept;
For all the predecessors of our line
Rose up, methought, to drag me down to
   them.
My father was amongst them, too; but he,
I know not why, kept from me, leaving me
Between the hunter-founder of our race,
And her, the homicide and husband-killer,
Whom you call glorious.
   Sal.   So I term you also,

Now you have shown a spirit like to hers.
By day-break I propose that we set forth,
And charge once more the rebel crew, who still
Keep gathering head, repulsed, but not quite
   quelled.
   Sar. How wears the night?
   Sal.   There yet remain some hours
Of darkness: use them for your further rest.
   Sar. No, not to-night, if 'tis not gone: me-
   thought I passed hours in that vision.
   Myr.   Scarcely one;
I watched by you: it was a heavy hour,
But an hour only.
   Sar.   Let us then hold council;
To-morrow we set forth.
   Sal.   But ere that time,
I had a grace to seek.
   Sar.   'Tis granted.
   Sal.   Hear it
Ere you reply too readily; and 'tis
For *your* ear only.
   Myr.   Prince, I take my leave.
                  [Exit MYRRHA.
   Sal. That slave deserves her freedom.
   Sar.   Freedom only!
That slave deserves to share a throne.
   Sal.   Your patience —
'Tis not yet vacant, and 'tis of its partner
I come to speak with you.
   Sar.   How! of the queen?
   Sal. Even so. I judged it fitting for their
   safety,
That, ere the dawn, she sets forth with her
   children
For Paphlagonia, where our kinsman Cotta
Governs; and there at all events secure
My nephews and your sons their lives, and
   with them
Their just pretensions to the crown in case——
   Sar. I perish — as is probable: well
   thought —
Let them set forth with a sure escort.
   Sal.   That
Is all provided, and the galley ready
To drop down the Euphrates;[1] but ere they
Depart, will you not see ——
   Sar.   My sons? It may
Unman my heart, and the poor boys will
   weep;
And what can I reply to comfort them,
Save with some hollow hopes, and ill-worn
   smiles?
You know I cannot feign.
   Sal.   But you can feel;

---

[1] [We hardly know why Lord Byron, who has
not in other respects shown a slavish deference for
Diodorus Siculus, should thus follow him in the
manifest geographical blunder of placing Nineveh
on the *Euphrates* instead of the *Tigris*, in opposi-
tion not only to the uniform tradition of the East,
but to the express assertions of Herodotus- Pliny,
and Ptolemy. — *Heber.*]

At least, I trust so: in a word, the queen
Requests to see you ere you part — for ever.
  Sar. Unto what end? what purpose? I
    will grant
Aught — all that she can ask — but such a
    meeting.
  Sal. You know, or ought to know, enough
    of women,
Since you have studied them so steadily,
That what they ask in aught that touches on
The heart, is dearer to their feelings or
Their fancy, than the whole external world.
I think as you do of my sister's wish;
But 'twas her wish — she is my sister — you
Her husband — will you grant it?
  Sar.   'Twill be useless:
But let her come.
  Sal.   I go. [*Exit* SALEMENES.
  Sar.   We have lived asunder
Too long to meet again — and *now* to meet!
Have I not cares enow, and pangs enow,
To bear alone, that we must mingle sorrows,
Who have ceased to mingle love?

    Re-enter SALEMENES *and* ZARINA.

  Sal.   My sister! Courage:
Shame not our blood with trembling, but re-
    member
From whence we sprung. The queen is pres-
    ent, sire.
  Zar. I pray thee, brother, leave me.
  Sal.   Since you ask it.
                  [*Exit* SALEMENES.
  Zar. Alone with him! How many a year
    has passed,
Though we are still so young, since we have
    met,
Which I have worn in widowhood of heart.
He loved me not: yet he seems little
    changed —
Changed to me only — would the change were
    mutual!
He speaks not — scarce regards me — not a
    word —
Nor look — yet he *was* soft of voice and as-
    pect,
Indifferent, not austere. My lord!
  Sar.   Zarina!
  Zar. No, *not* Zarina — do not say Zarina.
That tone — that word — annihilate long years,
And things which make them longer.
  Sar.   'Tis too late
To think of these past dreams. Let's not
    reproach —
That is, reproach me not — for the *last*
    time ——
  Zar. And *first*. I ne'er reproached you.
  Sar.   'Tis most true;
And that reproof comes heavier on my heart
Than —— But our hearts are not in our
    own power.
  Zar. Nor hands· but I gave both.

  Sar.   Your brother said
It was your will to see me, ere you went
From Nineveh with —— (*He hesitates.*)
  Zar.   Our children: it is true.
I wished to thank you that you have not
    divided
My heart from all that's left it now to love —
Those who are yours and mine, who look
    like you,
And look upon me as you looked upon me
Once —— But they have not changed.
  Sar.   Nor ever will.
I fain would have them dutiful.
  Zar.   I cherish
Those infants, not alone from the blind love
Of a fond mother, but as a fond woman.
They are now the only tie between us.
  Sar.   Deem not
I have not done you justice: rather make
    them
Resemble your own line than their own sire.
I trust them with you — to you: fit them for
A throne, or, if that be denied —— You have
    heard
Of this night's tumults?
  Zar.   I had half forgotten,
And could have welcomed any grief save
    yours,
Which gave me to behold your face again.
  Sar. The throne — I say it not in fear —
    but 'tis *
In peril; they perhaps may never mount it:
But let them not for this lose sight of it.
I will dare all things to bequeathe it them;
But if I fail, then they must win it back
Bravely — and, won, wear it wisely, not as I
Have wasted down my royalty.
  Zar.   They ne'er
Shall know from me of aught but what may
    honor
Their father's memory.
  Sar.   Rather let them hear
The truth from you than from a trampling
    world.
If they be in adversity, they'll learn
Too soon the scorn of crowds for crownless
    princes,
And find that all their father's sins are theirs.
My boys! — I could have borne it were I
    childless.
  Zar. Oh! do not say so — do not poison
    all
My peace left, by unwishing that thou wert
A father. If thou conquerest, they shall reign,
And honor him who saved the realm for them,
So little cared for as his own; and if ——
  Sar. 'Tis lost, all earth will cry out, thank
    your father!
And they will swell the echo with a curse.
  Zar. That they shall never do; but rather
    honor
The name of him, who, dying like a king,

In his last hours did more for his own mem-
ory
Than many monarchs in a length of days,
Which date the flight of time, but make no
annals.
   Sar. Our annals draw perchance unto
their close;
But at the least, whate'er the past, their end
Shall be like their beginning — memorable.
   Zar. Yet, be not rash — be careful of your
life,
Live but for those who love.
   Sar.   And who are they ?
A slave, who loves from passion — I'll not say
Ambition — she has seen thrones shake, and
loves;
A few friends who have revelled till we are
As one, for they are nothing if I fall;
A brother I have injured — children whom
I have neglected, and a spouse ——
   Zar.   Who loves.
   Sar. And pardons ? ·
   Zar.   I have never thought of this,
And cannot pardon till I have condemned.
   Sar. My wife !
   Zar. Now blessings on thee for that word !
I never thought to hear it more — from thee.
   Sar. Oh! thou wilt hear it from my sub-
jects. Yes —
These slaves whom I have nurtured, pam-
pered, fed,
And swoln with peace, and gorged with plen-
ty, till
They reign themselves — all monarchs in
their mansions —
Now swarm forth in rebellion, and demand
His death, who made their lives a jubilee;
While the few upon whom I have no claim
Are faithful! This is true, yet monstrous.
   Zar.   'Tis
Perhaps too natural; for benefits
Turn poison in bad minds.
   Sar.   And good ones make
Good out of evil. Happier than the bee,
Which hives not but from wholesome flowers.
   Zar.   Then reap
The honey, nor inquire whence 'tis derived.
Be satisfied — you are not all abandoned.
   Sar. My life insures me that. How long,
bethink you,
Were not I yet a king, should I be mortal;
That is, where mortals *are*, not where they
must be ?
   Zar. I know not. But yet live for my —
that is,
Your children's sake !
   Sar.   My gentle, wronged Zarina ! [1]
I am the very slave of circumstance

And impulse — borne away with every
breath !
Misplaced upon the throne — misplaced in
life.
I know not what I could have been, but feel
I am not what I should be — let it end.
But take this with thee : if I was not formed
To prize a love like thine, a mind like thine,
Nor dote even on thy beauty — as I've doted
On lesser charms, for no cause save that such
Devotion was a duty, and I hated
All that looked like a chain for me or others
(This even rebellion must avouch) ; yet hear
These words, perhaps among my last — that
none
E'er valued more thy virtues, though he knew
not
To profit by them — as the miner lights
Upon a vein of virgin ore, discovering
That which avails him nothing : he hath
found it,
But 'tis not his — but some superior's, who
Placed him to dig, but not divide the wealth
Which sparkles at his feet; nor dare he lift
Nor poise it, but must grovel on, upturning
The sullen earth.
   Zar.   Oh! if thou hast at length
Discovered that my love is worth esteem,
I ask no more — but let us hence together,·
And *I* — let me say *we* — shall yet be happy.
Assyria is not all the earth — we'll find
A world out of our own — and be more blessed
Than I have ever been, or thou, with all
An empire to indulge thee.

Enter SALEMENES.

   Sal.   I must part ye —
The moments, which must not be lost, are
passing.
   Zar. Inhuman brother ! wilt thou thus
weigh out
Instants so high and blest ?
   Sal.   Blest!
   Zar.   He hath been
So gentle with me, that I cannot think
Of quitting.
   Sal.   So — this feminine farewell
Ends as such partings end, in *no* departure.

---

[1] [We are not sure, whether there is not a con-
siderable violation of costume in the sense of degra-
dation with which Myrrha seems to regard her sit-
uation in the harem, no less than in the resentment
of Salemenes, and the remorse of Sardanapalus on
the score of his infidelity to Zarina. Little as we
know of the domestic habits of Assyria, we have
reason to conclude, from the habits of contempo-
rary nations, and from the manners of the East in
every age, that polygamy was neither accounted a
crime in itself, nor as a measure of which the prin-
cipal wife was justified in complaining. And even
in Greece, in those times when Myrrha's character
must have been formed — to be a captive, and sub-
ject to the captor's pleasure, was accounted a mis-
fortune indeed, but could hardly be regarded as an
infamy. But where is the critic who would object
to an inaccuracy which has given occasion to such
sentiments and such poetry? — *Heber.*]

I thought as much, and yielded against all
My better bodings. But it must not be.
Zar. Not be ?
Sal. Remain, and perish ——
Zar. With my husband ——
Sal. And children.
Zar. Alas !
Sal. Hear me, sister, like
My sister :— all's prepared to make your
safety
Certain, and of the boys too, our last hopes ;
'Tis not a single question of mere feeling,
Though that were much — but 'tis a point of
state :
The rebels would do more to seize upon
The offspring of their sovereign, and so
crush ——
Zar. Ah ! do not name it.
Sal. Well, then, mark me : when
They are safe beyond the Median's grasp, the
rebels
Have missed their chief aim — the extinction of
The line of Nimrod. Though the present king
Fall, his sons live for victory and vengeance.
Zar. But could not I remain, alone ?
Sal. What ! leave
Your children, with two parents and yet or-
phans —
In a strange land — so young, so distant ?
Zar. No —
My heart will break.
Sal. Now you know all — decide.
Sar. Zarina, he hath spoken well, and we
Must yield awhile to this necessity.
Remaining here, you may lose all ; departing,
You save the better part of what is left,
To both of us, and to such loyal hearts
As yet beat in these kingdoms.
Sal. The time presses.
Sar. Go, then. If e'er we meet again,
perhaps
I may be worthier of you — and, if not,
Remember that my faults, though not atoned
for,
Are *ended.* Yet, I dread thy nature will
Grieve more above the blighted name and
ashes
Which once were mightiest in Assyria —
than ——
But I grow womanish again, and must not ;
I must learn sternness now. My sins have all
Been of the softer order —— *hide* thy tears —
I do not bid thee *not* to shed them — 'twere
Easier to stop Euphrates at its source
Than one tear of a true and tender heart —
But let me not behold them ; they unman
me
Here when I had remanned myself. My
brother,
Lead her away.
Zar. Oh, God ! I never shall
Behold him more !

Sal. (*striving to conduct her*). Nay, sister,
I *must* be obeyed.
Zar. I must remain — away ! you shall not
hold me.
What, shall he die alone ? — *I* live alone ?
Sal. He shall *not die alone ;* but lonely you
Have lived for years.
Zar. That's false ! I knew *he* lived,
And lived upon his image — let me go !
Sal. (*conducting her off the stage*). Nay,
then, I must use some fraternal force,
Which you will pardon.
Zar. Never. Help me ! Oh !
Sardanapalus, wilt thou thus behold me
Torn from thee ?
Sal. Nay — then all is lost again,
If that this moment is not gained.
Zar. My brain turns —
My eyes fail — where is he ? [*She faints.*
Sar. (*advancing*). No — set her down —
She's dead — and you have slain her.
Sal. 'Tis the mere
Faintness of o'erwrought passion : in the air
She will recover. Pray, keep back. — [*Aside.*]
I must
Avail myself of this sole moment to
Bear her to where her children are embarked,
I' the royal galley on the river.
[SALEMENES *bears her off.*[1]
Sar. (*solus*). This, too —
And this too must I suffer — I, who never
Inflicted purposely on human hearts
A voluntary pang ! But that is false —
She loved me, and I loved ·her. — Fatal pas-
sion !
Why dost th·ou not expire *at once* in hearts
Which thou hast lighted up at once ? Zarina !
I must pay dearly for the desolation
Now brought upon thee. Had I never loved
But thee, I should have been an unopposed
Monarch of honoring nations. To what gulfs
A single deviation from the track
Of human duties leads even those who claim
The homage of mankind as their born due,
And find it, till they forfeit it themselves !

Enter MYRRHA.

---

[1] [This scene has been, we know not why, called
"useless," "unnatural," and "tediously written." *
For ourselves, we are not ashamed to own that we
have read it with emotion. It is an interview be-
tween Sardanapalus and his neglected wife, whom,
with her children, he is about to send to a place of
safety. Here, too, however, he is represented, with
much poetical art and justice of delineation, as, in
the midst of his deepest regrets for Zarina, chiefly
engrossed with himself and his own sorrows, and
inclined, immediately afterwards, to visit on poor
Myrrha the painful feelings which his own re·
proaches of himself have occasioned. — *Heber.*]

* [These expressions occurred in the Edinburgh·
Review.]

Sar. `You` here! Who called you?
Myr.   No one — but I heard
Far off a voice of wail and lamentation,
And thought——
Sar.   It forms no portion of your duties
To enter here till sought for.
Myr.   Though I might,
Perhaps, recall some softer words of yours
(Although they *too were chiding*), which re-
    proved me,
Because I ever dreaded to intrude;
Resisting my own wish and your injunction
To heed no time nor presence, but approach
    you
Uncalled for: — I retire.
Sar.   Yet stay — being here.
I pray you pardon me : events have soured
    me
Till I wax peevish — heed it not : I shall
Soon be myself again.
Myr.   I wait with patience,
What I shall see with pleasure.
Sar.   Scarce a moment
Before your entrance in this hall, Zarina,
Queen of Assyria, departed hence.
Myr. Ah!
Sar.   Wherefore do you start?
Myr.   Did I do so?
Sar. 'Twas well you entered by another
    portal,
Else you had met. That pang at least is spared
    her.
Myr. I know to feel for her.
Sar.   That is too much
And beyond nature — 'tis nor mutual [1]
Nor possible. You cannot pity her,
Nor she aught but——
Myr.   Despise the favorite slave?
Not more than I have ever scorned myself.
Sar. Scorned! what, to be the envy of
    your sex,
And lord it o'er the heart of the world's lord?
Myr. Were you the lord of twice ten thou-
    sand worlds —
As you are like to lose the one you swayed —
I did abase myself as much in being
Your paramour, as though you were a peas-
    ant —
Nay, more, if that the peasant were a Greek.
Sar. You talk it well——
Myr.   And truly.
Sar.   In the hour
Of man's adversity all things grow daring
Against the falling; but as I am not
Quite fallen, nor now disposed to bear re-
    proaches,
Perhaps because I merit them too often,
Let us then part while peace is still between us.
Myr. Part!

---

[1] [For *mutual* the MS. has *natural;* which certainly seems better.]

Sar. Have not all past human beings
    parted,
And must not all the present one day part?
Myr. Why?
Sar. For your safety, which I will have
    looked to,
With a strong escort to your native land;
And such gifts, as, if you had not been all
A queen, shall make your dowry worth ●
    kingdom.
Myr. I pray you talk not thus.
Sar.   The queen is gone
You need not shame to follow. I would fall
Alone — I seek no partners but in pleasure.
Myr. And I no pleasure but in parting not.
You shall not force me from you.
Sar.   Think well of it —
It soon may be too late.
Myr.   So let it be;
For then you cannot separate me from you.
Sar. And will not; but I thought you
    wished it.
Myr. I!
Sar. You spoke of your abasement.
Myr.   And I feel it
Deeply — more deeply than all things but love.
Sar. Then fly from it.
Myr.   'Twill not recall the past —
'Twill not restore my honor, nor my heart.
No — here I stand or fall. If that you conquer,
I live to joy in your great triumph : should
Your lot be different, I'll not weep, but share it,
You did not doubt me a few hours ago.
Sar. Your courage never — nor your love
    till now,
And none could make me doubt it save your-
    self.
Those words——
Myr. Were words. I pray you, let the
    proofs
Be in the past acts you were pleased to praise
This very night, and in my further bearing,
Beside, wherever you were borne by fate.
Sar. I am content: and, trusting in my
    cause,
Think we may yet be victors and return
To peace — the only victory I covet.
To me war is no glory — conquest no
Renown. To be forced thus to uphold my right
Sits heavier on my heart than all the wrongs
These men would bow me down with. Never,
    never
Can I forget this night, even should I live
To add it to the memory of others.
I thought to have made mine inoffensive rule
An era of sweet peace 'midst bloody annals,
A green spot amidst desert centuries,
On which the future would turn back and
    smile,
And cultivate, or sigh when it could not
Recall Sardanapalus' golden reign.
I thought to have made my realm a paradise,

And every moon an epoch of new pleasures.
I took the rabble's shouts for love — the breath
Of friends for truth — the lips of woman for
My only guerdon — so they are, my Myrrha:
                              [*He kisses her.*
Kiss me. Now let them take my realm and
    life!
They shall have both, but never thee!
Myr.   No, never!
Man may despoil his brother man of all
That's great or glittering — kingdoms fall —
    hosts yield —
Friends fail — slaves fly — and all betray —
    and more
Than all, the most indebted — but a heart
That loves without self-love! 'Tis here — now
    prove it.

Enter SALEMENES.

Sal. I sought you — How? *she* here again?
Sar.   Return not
Now to reproof: methinks your aspect speaks
Of higher matter than a woman's presence.
Sal. The only woman whom it much im-
    ports me
At such a moment now is safe in absence —
The queen's embarked.
Sar.   And well? say that much.
Sal.   Yes.
Her transient weakness has passed o'er; at
    least,
It settled into tearless silence: her
Pale face and glittering eye, after a glance
Upon her sleeping children, were still fixed
Upon the palace towers as the swift galley
Stole down the hurrying stream beneath the
    starlight;
But she said nothing.
Sar.   Would I felt no more
Than she has said!
Sal.   'Tis now too late to feel!
Your feelings cannot cancel a sole pang:
To change them, my advices bring sure tidings
That the rebellious Medes and Chaldees, mar-
    shalled
By their two leaders, are already up
In arms again; and, serrying their ranks,
Prepare to attack: they have apparently
Been joined by other satraps.
Sar.   What! more rebels?
Let us be first, then.
Sal.   That were hardly prudent
Now, though it was our first intention. If
By noon to-morrow we are joined by those
I've sent for by sure messengers, we shall be
In strength enough to venture an attack,
Ay, and pursuit too; but till then, my voice
Is to await the onset.
Sar.   I detest
That waiting; though it seems so safe to fight
Behind high walls, and hurl down foes into
Deep fosses, or behold them sprawl on spikes

Strewed to receive them, still I like it not —
My soul seems lukewarm; but when I set on
    them,
Though they were piled on mountains, I would
    have
A pluck at them, or perish in hot blood! —
Let me then charge.
Sal.   You talk like a young soldier.
Sar. I am no soldier, but a man: speak not
Of soldiership, I loathe the word, and those
Who pride themselves upon it; but direct me
Where I may pour upon them.
Sal.   You must spare
To expose your life too hastily; 'tis not
Like mine or any other subject's breath.
The whole war turns upon it — with it; this
Alone creates it, kindles, and may quench it —
Prolong it — end it.
Sar.   Then let us end both!
'Twere better thus, perhaps, than prolong
    either;
I'm sick of one, perchance of both.
                        [*A trumpet sounds without.*
Sal.   Hark!
Sar.   Let us
Reply, not listen.
Sal.   And your wound!
Sar.   'Tis bound —
'Tis healed — I had forgotten it. Away!
A leech's lancet would have scratched me
    deeper;[1]
The slave that gave it might be well ashamed
To have struck so weakly.
Sal.   Now, may none this hour
Strike with a better aim!
Sar.   Ay, if we conquer;
But if not, they will only leave to me
A task they might have spared their king.
Upon them! [*Trumpet sounds again.*
Sal. I am with you.
Sar.   Ho, my arms! again, my arms!
                              [*Exeunt.*

———

ACT V.

SCENE I. — *The same Hall in the Palace.*

MYRRHA *and* BALEA.

Myr. (*at a window*). The day at last has
    broken. What a night
Hath ushered it! How beautiful in heaven!
Though varied with a transitory storm,
More beautiful in that variety!
How hideous upon earth! where peace and
    hope,
And love and revel, in an hour were trampled
By human passions to a human chaos,
Not yet resolved to separate elements —

———

[1] [MS. —

"A leech's lancet would have done as much."]

And can the sun so rise,
ıg back the clouds into
ly than the unclouded sky,
acles, and snowy mountains,
ler than the ocean's, making
ous mockery of the earth,
t deem it permanent;
n scarcely call it aught
'tis so transiently
he eternal vault: [1] and yet
e soul and soothes the soul,
into the soul, until
t form the haunted epoch
love; which they who mark

lms where those twin genii [2]
d who purify our hearts,
ld not change their sweet

ous joys that ever shook
or) build the palaces
votaries repose and breathe
that brief cool calm inhale
ı to enable them to bear
ıon, heavy, human hours,
hrough in placid sufferance;
y employed like all the rest
rs in allotted tasks [3]
re, *two* names for *one* feeling,
al, restless agony
ıe sound, although the sense
,est efforts to be happy.
e right calmly: and can you

h may be our last?
                    It is
so watch it, and reproach
h never may behold it more,
d upon it oft, too oft,
rence and the rapture due
eps all earth from being as

ırm. Come, look upon it,
ıd, which, when I gaze upon,
convert to your Baal.

---

on of the sun rolling back the
ly imitated from a magnificent
i book of Wordsworth's Excur-
Round them and above,
: recesses interposed,
ıttage-roof, and stems of trees
poring cloud, the silver steam
ing on their leafy boughs
ıbeams smitten.'']

et form the epoch of
; and they who mark them now
ınverse with," etc.]

etches in allotted tasks."]

Bal. As now he reigns in heaven, so once
  on earth
He swayed.
Myr. He sways it now far more, then;
  never
Had earthly monarch half the power and glory [4]
Which centres in a single ray of his.
Bal. Surely he is a god!
Myr.   So we Greeks deem too;
And yet I sometimes think that gorgeous orb
Must rather be the abode of gods than one
Of the immortal sovereigns. Now he breaks
Through all the clouds, and fills my eyes with
  light
That shuts the world out. I can look no more.
. *Bal.* Hark! heard you not a sound?
Myr.   No, 'twas mere fancy;
They battle it beyond the wall, and not
As in late midnight conflict in the very
Chambers: the palace has become a fortress
Since that insidious hour; and here, within
The very centre, girded by vast courts
And regal halls of pyramid proportions,
Which must be carried one by one before
They penetrate to where they then arrived,
We are as much shut in even from the
  sound
Of peril as from glory.
Bal.   But they reached
Thus far before.
Myr.   Yes, by surprise, and were
Beat back by valor: now at once we have
Courage and vigilance to guard us.
Bal.   May they
Prosper!
Myr.   That is the prayer of many, and
The dread of more: it is an anxious hour;
I strive to keep it from my thoughts. Alas!
How vainly!
Bal.   It is said the king's demeanor
In the late action scarcely more appalled
The rebels than astonished his true subjects.
Myr. 'Tis easy to astonish or appall
The vulgar mass which moulds a horde of
  slaves;
But he did bravely.
Bal.   Slew he not Beleses?
I heard the soldiers say he struck him down.
Myr. The wretch was overthrown, but res-
  cued to
Triumph, perhaps, o'er one who vanquished
  him
In fight, as he had spared him in his peril;
And by that heedless pity risked a crown.
Bal. Hark!
Myr. You are right; some steps approach,
  but slowly.
Enter Soldiers, bearing in SALEMENES *wound-
  ed, with a broken Javelin in his Side: they*

---

[4] [Misprinted hitherto—
" Had earthly monarch half the *peace* and glory."]

*seat him upon one of the Couches which fur-
nish the Apartment.*

Myr. Oh, Jove!

Bal.   Then all is over.

Sal.   That is false.
Hew down the slave who says so, if a soldier.

Myr. Spare him — he's none: a mere
    court butterfly,
That flutters in the pageant of a monarch.

Sal. Let him live on, then.

Myr.   So wilt thou, I trust.

Sal. I fain would live this hour out, and
    the event,
But doubt it. Wherefore did ye bear me here?

Sol. By the king's order. When the jave-
    lin struck you,
You fell and fainted: 'twas his strict command
To bear you to this hall.

Sal.   'Twas not ill done :
For seeming slain in that cold dizzy trance,
The sight might shake our soldiers — but —
    'tis vain,
I feel it ebbing!

Myr.   Let me see the wound;
I am not quite skilless : in my native land
'Tis part of our instruction. War being con-
    stant,
We are nerved to look on such things.[1]

Sol.   Best extract
The javelin.

Myr.   Hold! no, no, it cannot be.

Sal. I am sped, then!

Myr.   With the blood that fast must
follow
The extracted weapon, I do fear thy life.

Sal. And I *not* death. Where was the king
    when you
Conveyed me from the spot where I was
    stricken?

Sol. Upon the same ground, and encour-
    aging
With voice and gesture the dispirited troops
Who had seen you fall, and faltered back.

Sal.   Whom heard ye
Named next to the command?

Sol.   I did not hear.

Sal. Fly, then, and tell him, 'twas my last
    request
That Zames take my post until the junction,
So hoped for, yet delayed, of Ofratanes,
Satrap of Susa. Leave me here: our troops
Are not so numerous as to spare your absence.

Sol. But prince ——

Sal.   Hence, I say! Here's a cour-
    tier and
A woman, the best chamber company.
As you would not permit me to expire .
Upon the field, I'll have no idle soldiers
About my sick couch. Hence! and do my
    bidding.   [*Exeunt the Soldiers.*

─────────
[1] [MS. — "We are used to such inflictions."]

Myr. Gallant and glorious spirit! must the
    earth
So soon resign thee?

Sal.   Gentle Myrrha, 'tis
The end I would have chosen, had I saved
The monarch or the monarchy by this;
As 'tis, I have not outlived them.

Myr.   You wax paler.

Sal. Your hand; this broken weapon but
    prolongs
My pangs, without sustaining life enough
To make me useful: I would draw it forth
And my life with it, could I but hear how
The fight goes.

Enter SARDANAPALUS *and Soldiers.*

Sar.   My best brother!

Sal.   And the battle
Is lost?

Sar. (despondingly). You see *me* here.

Sal.   I'd rather see you *thus!*
    [*He draws out the weapon from the wound,
    and dies.*

Sar. And *thus* I will be seen; unless the
    succor,
The last frail reed of our beleaguered hopes,
Arrive with Ofratanes.

Myr.   Did you not
Receive a token from your dying brother,
Appointing Zames chief?

Sar.   I did.

Myr.   Where's Zames?

Sar. Dead.

Myr.   And Altada?

Sar.   Dying.

Myr. Pania? Sfero?

Sar. Pania yet lives: but Sfero's fled or
    captive.
I am alone.

Myr.   And is all lost?

Sar.   Our walls,
Though thinly manned, may still hold out
    against
Their present force, or aught save treachery:
But i' the field ——

Myr.   I thought 'twas the intent
Of Salemenes not to risk a sally
Till ye were strengthened by the expected
    succors.

Sar. *I* over-ruled him.

Myr.   Well, the fault's a brave one.

Sar. But fatal. Oh, my brother! I would
    give
These realms, of which thou wert the orna-
    ment,
The sword and shield, the sole-redeeming
    honor,
To call back —— But I will not weep for thee;
Thou shalt be mourned for as thou wouldst
    be mourned.
It grieves me most that thou couldst quit this
    life

could survive what thou
our long royalty of race.
will give thee blood
rs of millions, for atonement
the good are thine already).
gain soon, — if the spirit
eyond : — thou readest mine,
tice now. Let me once clasp
and, and fold that throbless
    [*Embraces the body.*
ats so bitterly. Now, bear
.
    Where?
        To my proper chamber.
my canopy, as though
re : when this is done, we will
the rites due to such ashes.
s with the body of SALEMENES.

nter PANIA.

ania! have you placed the
issued
on ?
    Sire, I have obeyed.
the soldiers keep their hearts

swered! When a king asks
as
    answer to *his* question,
hat! they are disheartened ?
eath of Salemenes, and the

rebels on his fall,
m ——
-not droop — it should have

teans to rouse them.
        Such a loss
ven a victory.   Alas!
l it as I feel ? but yet,
l within these walls, they are
we
ithout will break their way
sts,
sovereign's dwelling what it

: prison, nor a fortress.
r an Officer, hastily.
:e seems ominous. Speak!
    I dare not.
        Dare not ?
lare revolt with sword in hand !
I pray thee break that loyal

o shock its sovereign; we can

u hast to tell.
    Proceed, thou hearest.
ll which skirted near the river's

Is thrown down by the sudden inundation
Of the Euphrates, which now rolling, swoln
From the enormous mountains where it rises,
By the late rains of that tempestuous region,
O'erfloods its banks, and hath destroyed the
  bulwark.
Pan. That's a black augury! it has been
  said
For ages, "That the city ne'er should yield
To man, until the river grew its foe."
Sar. I can forgive the omen, not the ravage.
How much is swept down of the wall?
Offi.   About
Some twenty stadii.[1]
Sar.   And all this is left
Pervious to the assailants ?
Offi.   For the present
The river's fury must impede the assault;
But when he shrinks into his wonted channel,
And may be crossed by the accustomed barks,
The palace is their own.
Sar.   That shall be never.
Though men, and gods, and elements, and
  omens,
Have risen up 'gainst one who ne'er pro-
  voked them,
My father's house shall never be a cave
For wolves to horde and howl in.
Pan.   With your sanction,
I will proceed to the spot, and take such meas-
  ures
For the assurance of the vacant space
As time and means permit.
Sar.   About it straight
And bring me back, as speedily as full
And fair investigation may permit,
Report of the true state of this irruption
Of waters.   [*Exeunt* PANIA *and the Officer.*
Myr. Thus the very waves rise up
Against you.
Sar.   They are not my subjects, girl,
And may be pardoned, since they can't be
  punished.
Myr. I joy to see this portent shakes you
  not.
Sar. I am past the fear of portents: they
  can tell me
Nothing I have not told myself since mid-
  night:
Despair anticipates such things.
Myr.   Despair!
Sar. No; not despair precisely. When
  we know
All that can come, and how to meet it, our
Resolves, if firm, may merit a more noble
Word than this is to give it utterance.
But what are words to us ? we have wellnigh
  done
With them and all things.
Myr.   Save *one deed* — the last

---

[1] About two miles and a half.

And greatest to all mortals; crowning act
Of all that was — or is — or is to be —
The only thing common to all mankind,
So different in their births, tongues, sexes,
natures,
Hues, features, climes, times, feelings, intel-
lects,[1]
Without one point of union save in this,
To which we tend, for which we're born, and
thread
The labyrinth of mystery, called life.
   Sar. Our clew being wellnigh wound out,
let's be cheerful.
They who have nothing more to fear may well
Indulge a smile at that which once appalled;
As children at discovered bugbears.

       Reënter PANIA.

   Pan.   'Tis
As was reported: I have ordered there
A double guard, withdrawing from the wall
Where it was strongest the required addition
To watch the breach occasioned by the waters.
   Sar. You have done your duty faithfully,
and as
My worthy Pania! further ties between us
Draw near a close. I pray you take this key:
                   [*Gives a key.*
It opens to a secret chamber, placed
Behind the couch in my own chamber. (Now
Pressed by a nobler weight than e'er it bore —
Though a long line of sovereigns have lain
down
Along its golden frame — as bearing for
A time what late was Salemenes). Search
The secret covert to which this will lead you;
'Tis full of treasure;[2] take it for yourself
And your companions: there's enough to
load ye
Though ye be many.[3] Let the slaves be
freed, too;
And all the inmates of the palace, of
Whatever sex, now quit it in an hour.
Thence launch the regal barks, once formed
for pleasure,
And now to serve for safety, and embark.
The river's broad and swoln, and uncom-
manded

---

[1] [MS. —
 "Complexions, climes, eras, and intellects."]

[2] [" Athenæus makes these treasures amount to
a thousand myriads of talents of gold, and ten
times as many talents of silver, which is a sum that
exceeds all credibility. A man is lost if he attempts
to sum up the whole value; which induces me to
believe, that Athenæus must have very much ex-
aggerated; however, we may be assured, from his
account, that the treasures were immensely great."
— *Rollin.*]

[3] [MS.   —" Ye will find the crevice
 To which the key fits, with a little care."]

(More potent than a king) by these besiegers.
Fly! and be happy!
   Pan.   Under your protection!
So you accompany your faithful guard.
   Sar. No, Pania! that must not be; get
thee hence,
And leave me to my fate.
   Pan.   'Tis the first time
I ever disobeyed: but now——
   Sar.   So all men
Dare beard me now, and Insolence within
Apes Treason from without. Question no
further;
'Tis my command, my last command. Wilt
thou
Oppose it? *thou!*
   Pan.   But yet — not yet.
   Sar.   Well, then,
Swear that you will obey when I shall give
The signal.
   Pan.   With a heavy but true heart,
I promise.
   Sar.   'Tis enough. Now order here
Fagots, pine-nuts, and withered leaves, and
such[4]
Things as catch fire and blaze with one sole
spark;
Bring cedar, too, and precious drugs, and
spices,
And mighty planks, to nourish a tall pile;
Bring frankincense and myrrh, too, for it is
For a great sacrifice I build the pyre;
And heap them round yon throne.
   Pan.   My lord!
   Sar.   I have said it,
And *you* have *sworn.*
   Pan.   And could keep my faith
Without a vow.   [*Exit* PANIA.
   Myr. What mean you?
   Sar.   You shall know
Anon — what the whole earth shall ne'er forget.

    PANIA, *returning with a Herald.*

   Pan. My king, in going forth upon my duty
This herald has been brought before me
craving
An audience
   Sar.   Let him speak.
   Her.   The *King* Arbaces —
   Sar What, crowned already? — But, pro
ceed.
   Her.   Beleses,
The anointed high-priest——
   Sar.   Of what god or demon?
With new kings rise new altars. But, proceed;
You are sent to prate your master's will, and
not
Reply to mine.
   Her.   And Satrap Ofratanes ——

---

[4] [MS.   .——" Now order here
 Enough of dry wood," etc.]

he is *ours.*
ving a ring). Be sure that he

f the conquerors; behold
ʒ.
'Tis his. A worthy triad!
es! thou hast died in time
achery the less: this man
friend and my most trusted sub-

offer thee thy life, and freedom
ingle out a residence
further provinces,
watched, but not confined in

halt pass thy days in peace; but

t the three young princes are
ostages.
:ally). The generous victors!
it the answer.
Answer, slave! How long
ecided on the doom of kings?
e they were free.
Mouthpiece of mutiny!
east shalt learn the penalty
ough its proxy only. Pania!
be thrown from our walls within
nes, his carcass down the river.
m!
NIA *and the Guards seizing him.*
I never yet obeyed
with more pleasure than the pres-

im, soldiers! do not soil this hall
th treasonable gore;
st without.
A single word;
ng, is sacred.
And what's *mine?*
uldst come and dare to ask of me
n?
I but obeyed my orders,
peril if refused, as now
my obedience.
So there are
hs of an hour's growth as despotic
ns swathed in purple, and
d
manhood!
My life waits your breath.
ak humbly) — but it may be —

in danger scarce less imminent:
n suit the last hours of a line
at of Nimrod, to destroy
erald, unarmed, in his office;
not only all that man
l between man and man — but

which links us with the gods?

Sar. He's right. — Let him go free. — My life's last act
Shall not be one of wrath. Here, fellow, take
[*Gives him a golden cup from a table near.*
This golden goblet, let it hold your wine,
And think of *me;* or melt it into ingots,
And think of nothing but their weight and value.

Her. I thank you doubly for my life, and this
Most gorgeous gift, which renders it more precious.
But must I bear no answer?

Sar. Yes, — I ask
An hour's truce to consider.

Her. But an hour's?

Sar. An hour's: if at the expiration of
That time your masters hear no further from me,
They are to deem that I reject their terms,
And act befittingly.

Her. I shall not fail
To be a faithful legate of your pleasure.

Sar. And hark! a word more.

Her. I shall not forget it,
Whate'er it be.

Sar. Commend me to Beleses;
And tell him, ere a year expire, I summon
Him hence to meet me.

Her. Where?

Sar. At Babylon.
At least from thence he will depart to meet me.

Her. I shall obey you to the letter.
[*Exit Herald.*

Sar. Pania! —
Now, my good Pania! — quick — with what I ordered.

Pan. My lord, — the soldiers are already charged.
And see! they enter.
[*Soldiers enter, and form a Pile about the Throne, etc.*

Sar. Higher, my good soldiers,
And thicker yet; and see that the foundation
Be such as will not speedily exhaust
Its own too subtle flame; nor yet be quenched
With aught officious aid would bring to quell it.
Let the throne form the *core* of it; I would not
Leave that, save fraught with fire unquenchable,
To the new comers. Frame the whole as if
'Twere to enkindle the strong tower of our
Inveterate enemies. Now it bears an aspect!
How say you, Pania, will this pile suffice
For a king's obsequies?

Pan. Ay, for a kingdom's.
I understand you, now.

Sar. And blame me?

Pan. No —
Let me but fire the pile, and share it with you.

Myr. That duty's mine.

Pan.   A woman's!
Myr.   'Tis the soldier's
Part to die *for* his sovereign, and why not
The woman's with her lover?
  Pan.   'Tis most strange!
  Myr. But not so rare, my Pania, as thou
    think'st it.
In the mean time, live thou.— Farewell! the
    pile
Is ready.
  Pan. I should shame to leave my sovereign
With but a single female to partake
His death.
  Sar.   Too many far have heralded
Me to the dust, already. Get thee hence;
Enrich thee.
  Pan.   And live wretched!
  Sar.   Think upon
Thy vow:— 'tis sacred and irrevocable.
  Pan. Since it is so, farewell.
  Sar.   Search well my chamber,
Feel no remorse at bearing off the gold;
Remember what you leave you leave the slaves
Who slew me: and when you have borne away
All safe oft to your boats, blow one long blast
Upon the trumpet as you quit the palace.
The river's brink is too remote, its stream
Too loud at present to permit the echo
To reach distinctly from its banks. Then fly,—
And as you sail, turn back; but still keep on
Your way along the Euphrates: if you reach
The land of Paphlagonia, where the queen
Is safe with my three sons in Cotta's court,
Say, what you *saw* at parting, and request
That she remember what I *said* at one
Parting more mournful still.
  Pan.   That royal hand!
Let me then once more press it to my lips;
And these poor soldiers who throng round
    you, and
Would fain die with you!
    [*The soldiers and* PANIA *throng round him,
      kissing his hand and the hem of his robe.*
  Sar.   My best! my last friends!
Let's not unman each other: part at once:
All farewells should be sudden, when for ever,
Else they make an eternity of moments,
And clog the last sad sands of life with tears.
Hence, and be happy: trust me, I am not
Now to be pitied; or far more for what
Is past than present;— for the future, 'tis
In the hands of the deities, if such
There be: I shall know soon. Farewell —
    Farewell.   [*Exeunt* PANIA *and Soldiers.*
  Myr. These men were honest: it is com-
    fort still
That our last looks should be on loving faces.
  Sar. And *lovely* ones, my beautiful!— but
    hear me!
If at this moment,— for we now are on
The brink,— thou feel'st an inward shrinking
    from

This leap through flame into the future, say it:
I shall not love thee less; nay, perhaps more,
For yielding to thy nature: and there's time
Yet for thee to escape hence.
  Myr.   Shall I light
One of the torches which lie heaped beneath
The ever-burning lamp that burns without,
Before Baal's shrine, in the adjoining hall?
  Sar. Do so. Is that thy answer?
  Myr.   Thou shalt see.
    [*Exit* MYRRHA.
  Sar. (*solus*). She's firm. My fathers!
    whom I will rejoin,
It may be, purified by death from some
Of the gross stains of too material being,
I would not leave your ancient first abode
To the defilement of usurping bondmen;
If I have not kept your inheritance
As ye bequeathed it, this bright part of it,
Your treasure, your abode, your sacred relics
Of arms, and records, monuments, and spoils,
In which *they* would have revelled, I bear with
    me
To you in that absorbing element,
Which most personifies the soul as leaving
The least of matter unconsumed before
Its fiery workings:— and the light of this
Most royal of funereal pyres shall be
Not a mere pillar formed of cloud and flame,
A beacon in the horizon for a day,
And then a mount of ashes, but a light
To lesson ages, rebel nations, and
Voluptuous princes. Time shall quench full
    many
A people's records, and a hero's acts;
Sweep empire after empire, like this first
Of empires, into nothing; but even then
Shall spare this deed of mine, and hold it up
A problem few dare imitate, and none
Despise— but, it may be, avoid the life
Which led to such a consummation.

MYRRHA *returns with a lighted Torch in one
    Hand, and a Cup in the other.*

  Myr.   Lo!
I've lit the lamp which lights us to the stars.
  Sar. And the cup?
  Myr.   'Tis my country's custom to
Make a libation to the gods.
  Sar.   And mine
To make libations amongst men. I've not
Forgot the custom; and although alone,
Will drain one draught in memory of many
A joyous banquet past.
    [SARDANAPALUS *takes the cup, and after
      drinking and tinkling the reversed cup, as
      a drop falls, exclaims—*
                And this libation
Is for the excellent Beleses.
  Myr.   Why
Dwells thy mind rather upon that man's name
That on his mate's in villany?

The one
dier, a mere tool, a kind
ord in a friend's-hand; the other
ver of his warlike puppet:
ss them from my mind.—Yet

dost thou truly follow me,
arlessly?
        And dost thou think
dare not do for love, that which
'dow braves for custom?¹
               Then
t the signal.
      It is long

ow, farewell; one last embrace.
brace, but *not* the last; there is
e.
, the commingling fire will mix
s.
   pure as is my love to thee, shall

the dross of earth, and earthly

th thine. A single thought yet

it.
    It is that no kind hand will

both into one urn.
           The better:
lem be borne abroad upon
f heaven, and scattered into air,
luted more by human hands
d traitors. In this blazing palace,
:mous walls of reeking ruin,
nobler monument than Egypt
in her brick mountains, o'er dead

none know whether those proud

monarch, or their ox-god Apis:

——" And what is there
in widow dares for custom, which
girl dare not do for love?"]
nes are in bad taste enough, from
i *kings* and *kine,* down to the absurd-
ig that Sardanapalus at such a mo-
e likely to discuss a point of antiqua-
. But they involve also an anachro-
:h as, whatever date be assigned to
of the earlier pyramids, there can be
r apprehending that, at the fall of
while the kingdom and hierarchy of
ed in their full splendor, the destina-
immense fabrics could have been a
bt to any who might inquire concern-
:erodotus, three hundred years later,
n misinformed of these points; but,
ipalus lived, the erection of pyramids
irobability, have not been still of un-
irrence, and the nature of their con-
ct of mistake or mystery.—*Heber.*]

So much for monuments that have forgotten
Their very record!
  Myr.   Then farewell, thou earth!
And loveliest spot of earth! farewell, Ionia!
Be thou still free and beautiful, and far
Aloof from desolation! My last prayer
Was for thee, my last thoughts, save *one,*
      were of thee!
  Sar. And that?
  Myr.   Is yours.
      [*The trumpet of* PANIA *sounds without.*
  Sar.   Hark!
  Myr.   *Now!*
  Sar.   Adieu, Assyria!
I loved thee well, my own, my fathers' land,
And better as my country than my kingdom.
I sated thee with peace and joys; and this
Is my reward! and now I owe thee nothing,
Not even a grave.   [*He mounts the pile.*
                Now, Myrrha!
  Myr.   Art thou ready?
  Sar. As the torch in thy grasp.
              [MYRRHA *fires the pile.*
  Myr.   'Tis fired! I come.
  [*As* MYRRHA *springs forward to throw
    herself into the flames, the Curtain falls.*³

³ [In "Sardanapalus" Lord Byron has been far
more fortunate than in the "Doge of Venice," inas-
much as his subject is one eminently adapted not
only to tragedy in general, but to that peculiar kind
of tragedy which Lord Byron is anxious to recom-
mend. The history of the last of the Assyrian kings
is at once sufficiently well known to awaken that
previous interest which belongs to illustrious names
and early associations; and sufficiently remote and
obscure to admit of any modification of incident or
character which a poet may find convenient. All
that we know of Nineveh and its sovereigns is
majestic, indistinct, and mysterious. We read of
an extensive and civilized monarchy erected in the
ages immediately succeeding the deluge, and exist-
ing in full might and majesty while the shores of
Greece and Italy were unoccupied, except by roving
savages. We read of an empire whose influence
extended from Samarcand to Troy, and from the
mountains of Judah to those of Caucasus, subverted,
after a continuance of thirteen hundred years, and a
dynasty of thirty generations, in an almost incredi-
bly short space of time, less by the revolt of two
provinces than by the anger of Heaven and the pre-
dicted fury of natural and inanimate agents. And
the influence which both the conquests and the mis-
fortunes of Assyria appear to have exerted over the
fates of the people for whom, of all others in ancient
history, our strongest feelings are (from religious
motives) interested, throws a sort of sacred pomp
over the greatness and the crimes of the descend-
ants of Nimrod, and a reverence which no other
equally remote portion of profane history is likely
to obtain with us. At the same time, all which we
know is so brief, so general, and so disjointed, that
we have few of those preconceived notions of the
persons and facts represented which in classical
dramas, if servilely followed, destroy the interest,
and if rashly departed from offend the prejudices, of
the reader or the auditor. An outline is given of

the most majestic kind; but it is an outline only, which the poet may fill up at pleasure; and in ascribing, as Lord Byron has done for the sake of his favorite unities, the destruction of the Assyrian empire to the treason of one night, instead of the war of several years, he has neither shocked our better knowledge, nor incurred any conspicuous improbability. . . . Still, however, the development of Sardanapalus's character is incidental only to the plot of Lord Byron's drama, and though the unities have confined his picture within far narrower limits than he might otherwise have thought advisable, the character is admirably sketched; nor is there any one of the portraits of this great master which gives us a more favorable opinion of his talents, his force of conception, his delicacy and vigor of touch, or the richness and harmony of his coloring. He had, indeed, no unfavorable ground-work, even in a few hints supplied by the ancient historians, as to the conduct and history of the last and most unfortunate of the line of Belus. Though accused (whether truly or falsely), by his triumphant enemies, of the most revolting vices, and an effeminacy even beyond what might be expected from the last dregs of Asiatic despotism, we find Sardanapalus, when roused by the approach of danger, conducting his armies with a courage, a skill, and, for some time at least, with a success not inferior to those of his most warlike ancestors. We find him retaining to the last the fidelity of his most trusted servants, his nearest kindred, and no small proportion of his hardiest subjects. We see him providing for the safety of his wife, his children, and his capital city, with all the calmness and prudence of an experienced captain. We see him at length subdued, not by man, but by Heaven and the elements, and seeking his death with a mixture of heroism and ferocity which little accords with our notions of a weak or utterly degraded character. And even the strange story, variously told, and without further explanation scarcely intelligible, which represents him as building (or fortifying) two cities in a single day, and then deforming his exploits with an indecent image and inscription, would seem to imply a mixture of energy with his folly not impossible, perhaps, to the madness of absolute power, and which may lead us to impute his fall less to weakness than to an injudicious and ostentatious contempt of the opinions and prejudices of mankind. Such a character, — luxurious, energetic, misanthropical, — affords, beyond a doubt, no common advantages to the work of poetic delineation; and it is precisely the character which Lord Byron most delights to draw, and which he has succeeded best in drawing. — *Heber.*

I remember Lord Byron's mentioning, that the story of Sardanapalus had been working in his brain for seven years before he commenced it. — *Trelawney.*]

THE TWO FOSCARI: AN HISTORICAL TRAGEDY.[1]

The *father* softens, but the *governor's* resolved. — CRITIC.

["THE Two Foscari" was composed at Ravenna, between the 11th of June and the 10th of July, 1821, and published with "Sardanapalus" in the following December. "The Venetian story," Byron wrote to Mr. Murray, "is strictly historical. I am much mortified that Gifford don't take to my new dramas. To be sure, they are as opposite to the English drama as one thing can be to another; but I have a notion that, if understood, they will, in time, find favor (though *not* on the stage) with the reader. The simplicity of plot is intentional, and the avoidance of *rant* also, as also the compression of the speeches in the more severe situations. What I seek to show in 'the Foscaris' is the *suppressed* passions, rather than the rant of the present day. For that matter —

'Nay, if thou'lt mouth,
I'll rant as well as thou —'

would not be difficult, as I think I have shown in my younger productions — not *dramatic* ones, to be sure." The best English account of the incidents on which this play is founded, is in Smedley's "Sketches of Venetian History:" —

"The reign of Francesco Foscari had now been prolonged to the unusual period of thirty-four years, and these years were marked by almost continual warfare; during which, however, the courage, the firmness, and the sagacity of the illustrious Doge had won four rich provinces for his country, and increased her glory not less than her dominion. Ardent, enterprising, and ambitious of the glory of conquest, it was not without much opposition that Foscari had obtained the Dogeship; and he soon discovered that

[1] [MS. — "Begun June the 12th, completed July the 9th, Ravenna, 1821. — *Byron.*]

ι he had coveted with so great earnestness was far from being a seat of repose. Accord-
ace of Ferrara, which in 1433 succeeded a calamitous war, foreseeing the approach of
reater troubles, and wearied by the factions which ascribed all disasters to the Prince, he
dication to the senate, and was refused. A like offer was renewed by him when nine
‹perience of sovereignty had confirmed his former estimate of its cares; and the Council,
)ccasion, much more from adherence to existing institutions than from any attachment to
ιe Doge, accompanied their negative with the exaction of an oath that he would retain
dignity for life. Too early, alas! was he to be taught that life, on such conditions, was
curses! Three out of his four sons were already dead: to Giacopo, the survivor, ḥe
ontinuation of his name and the support of his declining age; and, from that youth's
ith the illustrious house of Contarini, and the popular joy with which his nuptials were
Doge drew favorable auspices for future happiness. Four years, however, had scarcely
e conclusion of that well-omened marriage, when a series of calamities began, from which
ς to relieve either the son or his yet more wretched father. In 1445, Giacopo Foscari was
he Ten, as having received presents from foreign potentates, and especially from Filippo-
. The offence, according to the law, was one of the most heinous which a noble could
if Giacopo were guiltless of infringing that law, it was not easy to establish innocence
ian tribunal. Under the eyes of his own father, compelled to preside at the unnatural
confession was extorted from the prisoner, on the rack; and, from the lips of that father,
sentence which banished him for life to Napoli di Romania. On his passage, severe ill-
m at Trieste; and, at the special prayer of the Doge, a less remote district was assigned
ent; he was permitted to reside at Treviso, and his wife was allowed to participate his

commencement of the winter of 1450, while Giacopo Foscari rested, in comparative tran-
the bounds to which he was restricted, that an assassination occurred in the streets of
olao Donato, the Chief of the Ten, was murdered on his return from a sitting of that
own door, by unknown hands. The magnitude of the offence and the violation of the
f the Ten demanded a victim; and the coadjutors of the slain magistrate caught with
the slightest clue which suspicion could afford. A domestic in the service of Giacopo
εn seen in Venice on the evening of the murder, and on the following morning, when met
estre by a Chief of the Ten, and asked, 'What news?' he had answered by reporting the
several hours before it was generally known. It might seem that such frankness of
ḍ all participation in the crime; for the author of it was not likely thus unseasonably and
disclose its committal. But the Ten thought differently, and matters which to others bore
innocence, to them savored strongly of guilt. The servant was arrested, examined, and
)rtured; but even the eightieth application of the strappado failed to elicit one syllable
ιstify condemnation. That Giacopo Foscari had experienced the severity of the Council's
ḷ that its jealous watchfulness was daily imposing some new restraint upon his father's
ᵣerfully operated to convince the Ten that they must themselves in return be objects of his
ᵣ. Who else, they said, could be more likely to arm the hand of an assassin against a
'en, than one whom the Ten have visited with punishment? On this unjust and unsup-
:, the young Foscari was recalled from Treviso, placed on the rack which his servant had
ortured again in his father's presence, and not absolved even after he resolutely persisted
the end.
ḷ, however, which Giacopo Foscari endured had by no means chilled the passionate love
continued to regard his ungrateful country. He was now excluded from all communica-
ιmily, torn from the wife of his affections, debarred from the society of his children, hopeless
acing those parents who had already far outstripped the natural term of human existence;
gination, for ever centering itself on the single desire of return, life presented no other
ιg pursuit; till, for the attainment of this wish, life itself at length appeared to be scarcely
adequate sacrifice. Preyed upon by this fever of the heart, after six years' unavailing suit
ι of punishment, in the summer of 1456, he addressed a letter to the Duke of Milan, implor-
ffices with the senate. That letter, purposely left open in a place obvious to the spies by
ι his exile, he was surrounded, and afterwards entrusted to an equally treacherous hand for
ᵣza, was conveyed, as the writer intended, to the Council of Ten; and the result, which
:d his expectation, was a hasty summons to Venice to answer for the heavy crime of
gn intercession with his native government.
time, Francesco Foscari listened to the accusation of his son; for the first time he heard
ow the charge of his accusers, and calmly state that his offence, such as it was, had been
ιignedly and aforethought, with the sole object of detection, in order that he might be
even as a malefactor, to Venice. This prompt and voluntary declaration, however, was
o decide the nice hesitation of his judges. Guilt, they said, might be too easily admitted
pertinaciously denied; and the same process therefore by which, at other times, confession
om the hardened criminal might now compel a too facile self-accuser to retract his ac-
. The father again looked on while his son was raised on the accursed cord no less than
ι order that, under his agony he might be induced to utter a lying declaration of innocence.
ty was exercised in vain; and, when nature gave way, the sufferer was carried to the
the Doge, torn, bleeding, senseless, and dislocated, but firm in his original purpose. Nor
:utors relaxed in *theirs;* they renewed his sentence of exile, and added that its first year
ṣed in prison. Before he embarked, one interview was permitted with his family. The
ιto, perhaps unconscious of the pathos of his simplicity, has narrated, was an aged and

decrepit man, who walked with the support of a crutch, and when he came into the chamber, he spake with great firmness, so that it might seem it was not his son whom he was addressing, but it was his son — his only son. 'Go, Giacopo,' was his reply, when prayed for the last time to solicit mercy; 'Go, Giacopo, submit to the will of your country, and seek nothing further.' This effort of self-restraint was beyond the powers, not of the old man's enduring spirit, but of his exhausted frame; and when he retired, he swooned in the arms of his attendants. Giacopo reached his Candian prison, and was shortly afterwards released by death.

Francesco Foscari, far less happy in his survival, continued to live on, but it was in sorrow and feebleness which prevented attention to the duties of his high office: he remained secluded in his chamber, never went abroad, and absented himself even from the sittings of the councils. No practical inconvenience could result from this want of activity in the chief magistrate; for the constitution sufficiently provided against any accidental suspension of his personal functions, and his place in council, and on state occasions, was supplied by an authorized deputy. Some indulgence, moreover, might be thought due to the extreme age and domestic griefs of Foscari; since they appeared to promise that any favor which might be granted would be claimed but for a short period. But yet further trials were in store. Giacopo Loredano, who in 1467 was appointed one of the Chiefs of the Ten, belonged to a family between which and that of Foscari an hereditary feud had long existed. His uncle Pietro, after gaining high distinction in active service, as Admiral of Venice, on his return to the capital, headed the political faction which opposed the warlike projects of the Doge; divided applause with him by his eloquence in the councils; and so far extended his influence as frequently to obtain majorities in their divisions. In an evil moment of impatience, Foscari once publicly avowed in the senate, that so long as Pietro Loredano lived he should never feel himself really to be Doge. Not long afterwards, the Admiral engaged as Provveditore with one of the armies opposed to Filippo-Maria, died suddenly at a military banquet given during a short suspension of arms; and the evil-omened words of Foscari were connected with his decease. It was remarked, also, that his brother Marco Loredano, one of the Avvogadori, died in a somewhat similar manner, while engaged in instituting a legal process against a son-in-law of the Doge, for peculation upon the state. The foul rumors partially excited by these untoward coincidences, for they appear in truth to have been no more, met with little acceptation, and were rejected or forgotten except by a single bosom. Giacopo, the son of one, the nephew of the other deceased Loredano, gave full credit to the accusation, inscribed on his father's tomb at Sta. Elena, that he died by poison, bound himself by a solemn vow to the most deadly and unrelenting pursuit of revenge, and fulfilled that vow to the uttermost.

During the lifetime of Pietro Loredano, Foscari, willing to terminate the feud by a domestic alliance, had tendered the hand of his daughter to one of his rival's sons. The youth saw his proffered bride, openly expressed dislike of her person, and rejected her with marked discourtesy; so that, in the quarrel thus heightened, Foscari might now conceive himself to be the most injured party. Not such was the impression of Giacopo Loredano: year after year he grimly awaited the season most fitted for his unbending purpose; and it arrived at length when he found himself in authority among the Ten. Relying upon the ascendency belonging to that high station, he hazarded a proposal for the deposition of the aged Doge, which was at first, however, received with coldness; for those who had twice before refused a voluntary abdication, shrank from the strange contradiction of now demanding one on compulsion. A junta was required to assist in their deliberations, and among the assessors elected by the Great Council, in complete ignorance of the purpose for which they were needed, was Marco Foscari, a Procuratore of St. Mark, and brother of the Doge himself. The Ten perceived that to reject his assistance might excite suspicion, while to procure his apparent approbation would give a show of impartiality to their process· his nomination, therefore, was accepted, but he was removed to a separate apartment, excluded from the debate, sworn to keep that exclusion secret, and yet compelled to assent to the final decree in the discussion of which he had not been allowed to participate. The council sat during eight days and nearly as many nights; and, at the close of their protracted meetings, a committee was deputed to request the abdication of the Doge. The old man received them with surprise, but with composure, and replied that he had sworn not to abdicate, and therefore must maintain his faith. It was not possible that he could resign; but if it appeared fit to their wisdom that he should cease to be Doge, they had it in their power to make a proposal to that effect to the Great Council. It was far, however, from the intention of the Ten to subject themselves to the chances of debate in that larger body, and, assuming to their own magistracy a prerogative not attributed to it by the constitution, they discharged Foscari from his oath, declared his office vacant, assigned to him a pension of two thousand ducats, and enjoined him to quit the palace within three days, on pain of confiscation of all his property. Loredano, to whom the right belonged, according to the weekly routine of office, enjoyed the barbarous satisfaction of presenting this decree with his own hand. 'Who are you, Signor?' inquired the Doge of another Chief of the Ten who accompanied him, and whose person he did not immediately recognize. 'I am a son of Marco Memmo.' 'Ah, your father,' replied Foscari, 'is my friend.' Then declaring that he yielded willing obedience to the most excellent Council of Ten, and laying aside the ducal bonnet and robes, he surrendered his ring of office, which was broken in his presence. On the morrow, when he prepared to leave the palace, it was suggested to him that he should retire by a private staircase, and thus avoid the concourse assembled in the court-yard below. With calm dignity he refused the proposition: he would descend, he said, by no other than the self-same steps by which he had mounted thirty years before. Accordingly, supported by his brother, he slowly traversed the Giant's Stairs, and, at their foot, leaning on his staff and turning round to the palace, he accompanied his last look to it with these parting words, 'My services established me within your walls; it is the malice of my enemies which tears me from them!'

It was to the Oligarchy alone that Foscari was obnoxious; by the populace he had always been beloved, and strange indeed would it have been had he now failed to excite their sympathy. But even the regrets of the people of Venice were fettered by their tyrants; and whatever pity they might secretly

cherish for their wronged and humiliated prince, all expression of it was silenced by a per-
'ee of the Council, forbidding any mention of his name, and annexing death as a penalty to
. On the fifth day after Foscari's deposition, Pascale Malipieri was elected Doge. The de-
ce heard the announcement of his successor by the bell of the campanile, suppressed his
t ruptured a blood vessel in the exertion, and died in a few hours."]

DRAMATIS PERSONÆ.

MEN.	Other Senators, The Council of Ten, Guards
OSCARI, *Doge of Venice.*	*Attendants, etc. etc.*
'SCARI, *Son of the Doge.*	
REDANO, *a Patrician.*	WOMAN.
EMMO, *a Chief of the Forty.*	MARINA, *Wife of young* FOSCARI.
), *a Senator.*	

Scene— the Ducal Palace, Venice.

ACT I.

.— *A Hall in the Ducal Palace.*

LOREDANO[1] *and* BARBARIGO,
meeting.

ere is the prisoner?
            Reposing from
on.
The hour's past—fixed yesterday
imption of his trial.—Let us
colleagues in the council, and
call.
        Nay, let him profit by
minutes for his tortured limbs;
wrought by the Question yesterday,
e under it if now repeated.
ell?
yield not to you in love of justice,
he ambitious Foscari,
son, and all their noxious race;
or wretch has suffered beyond
s
l endurance.
                Without owning

---

racter of Loredano is well conceived
gic. The deep and settled principle of
animates him, and which impels him
ssion of the most atrocious cruelties,
at first, unnatural and overstrained.
' is it historically true; but, when the
: hatred (the supposed murder of his
cles), and when the atrocious maxims
venge, and that habitual contempt of
feelings are taken into consideration
tuted the glory of a Venetian patriot,
eive how such a principle might be not
but exulted in by a Venetian who re-
ouse of Foscari as, at once, the ene-
mily and his country.—*Heber.*]

Bar.   Perhaps without committing any.
But he avowed the letter to the Duke
Of Milan, and his sufferings half atone for
Such weakness.
Lor.   We shall see.
Bar.   You, Loredano,
Pursue hereditary hate too far.
Lor.   How far?
Bar.   To extermination.
Lor.   When they are
Extinct, you may say this.—Let's in to council.
Bar.   Yet pause—the number of our col-
        leagues is not
Complete yet; two are wanting ere we can
Proceed.
Lor.   And the chief judge, the Doge?
Bar.   No—he,
With more than Roman fortitude, is ever
First at the board in this unhappy process
Against his last and only son.
Lor.   True—true—
His *last.*
Bar.   Will nothing move you?
Lor.   *Feels he,* think you?
Bar.   He shows it not.
Lor.   I have marked *that*—the wretch!
Bar.   But yesterday, I hear, on his return
To the ducal chambers, as he passed the
        threshold.
The old man fainted.
Lor.   It begins to work, then.
Bar.   The work is half your own.
Lor.   And should be *all* mine—
My father and my uncle are no more.
Bar.   I have read their epitaph, which says
        they died
By poison.[2]

---

[2] [" *Veneno sublatus.*" The tomb is in the
church of Santa Elena.]

Lor.   When the Doge declared that he
Should never deem himself a sovereign till
The death of Peter Loredano, both
The brothers sickened shortly : — he *is* sover-
eign.
Bar.   A wretched one.
Lor.   What should they be who make
Orphans ?
Bar.   But *did* the Doge make you so ?
Lor.   Yes.
Bar.   What solid proofs ?
Lor.   When princes set themselves
To work in secret, proofs and process are
Alike made difficult; but I have such
Of the first, as shall make the second need-
·less.
Bar.   But you will move by law ?
Lor.   By all the laws
Which he would leave us.
Bar.   They are such in this
Our state as render retribution easier
Than 'mongst remoter nations. Is it true
That you have written in your books of com-
merce,
(The wealthy practice of our highest nobles)
" Doge Foscari, my debtor for the deaths
Of Marco aud Pietro Loredano,
My sire and uncle ? "
Lor.   It is written thus.
Bar.   And will you leave it unerased ?
Lor.   Till balanced.
Bar.   And how ?
    [*Two Senators pass over the stage, as in
    their way to " the Hall of the Council of
    Ten.*"
Lor.   You see the number is complete.
Follow me.   [*Exit* LOREDANO.
Bar. (*solus*). Follow *thee /* I have followed
        long [1]
Thy path of desolation, as the wave
Sweeps after that before it, alike whelming
·The wreck that creaks to the wild winds, and
        wretch
Who shrieks within its riven ribs, as gush
The waters through them; but this son and
        sire
Might move the elements to pause, and yet
Must I. on hardily like them — Oh! would
I could as blindly and remorselessly ! —
Lo, where he comes ! — Be still, my heart !
        they are

---

[1] [Loredano is accompanied, upon all emergen-
cies, by a senator called Barbarigo — a sort of con-
ꜰdant or chorus — who comes for no end that we
can discover, but to twit him with conscientious
cavils and objections, and then to second him by
his personal countenance and authority. *Jeffrey.* —
Loredano is the only personage above mediocrity.
The remaining characters are all unnatural, or fee-
ble. Barbarigo is as tame and insignificant a con-
fidant, as ever swept after the train of his principal
over the Parisian stage. — *Heber.*]

Thy foes, must be thy victims : wilt thou beat
For those who almost broke thee ?

Enter Guards, with young FOSCARI *as pris-
    oner, etc.*

Guard.   Let him rest.
Signor, take time.
Jac. Fos. I thank thee, friend, I'm feeble;
But thou may'st stand reproved.
Guard.   I'll stand the hazard.
Jac. Fos. That's kind : — I meet some pity,
    but no mercy;
This is the first.
Guard.   And might be last, did they
Who rule behold us.
Bar. (*advancing to the Guard*). There is
    one who does :
Yet fear not ; I will neither be thy judge
Nor thy accuser; though the hour is past,
Wait their last summons — I am of "the
    Ten,"
And waiting for that summons, sanction you
Even by my presence: when the last call
    sounds,
We'll in together. — Look well to the prisoner !
Jac. Fos. What voice is that ? — 'Tis Bar-
    barigo's! Ah!
Our house's foe, and one of my few judges.
Bar. To balance such a foe, if such there
    be,
Thy father sits⸱amongst thy judges.
Jac. Fos.   True,
He judges.
Bar.   Then deem not the laws too harsh
Which yield so much indulgence to a sire
As to allow his voice in such high matter
As the state's safety —
Jac. Fos.   And his son's. I'm faint;
Let me approach, I pray you, for a breath
Of air, yon window which o'erlooks the waters.

Enter an Officer, who whispers BARBARIGO.

Bar. (*to the Guard*). Let him approach.
    I must not speak with him
Further than thus : I have transgressed my
    duty
In this brief parley, and must now redeem it
Within the Council Chamber.
                    [*Exit* BARBARIGO.
    [*Guard conducting* JACOPO FOSCARI *to the
    window.*
Guard.   There, sir, 'tis
Open — How feel you ?
Jac. Fos.   Like a boy — Oh Venice !
Guard. And your limbs ?
Jac. Fos. Limbs! how often have they
    borne me
Bounding o'er yon blue tide, as I have
    skimmed
The gondola along in childish race.
And, masqued as a young gondolier, amidst
My gay competitors, noble as I.

our pleasure, in the pride of
th ;
fair populace of crowding beauties,
s patrician, cheered us on
ling smiles, and wishes audible,
g kerchiefs, and applauding hands,
e goal ! — how many a time have I
h arm still lustier, breast most dar-

all roughened ; with a swimmer's

he billows back from my drenched

hing from my lip the audacious

sed it like a wine-cup, rising o'er
as they arose, and prouder still
they uplifted me ; and oft,
ness of spirit, plunging down
green and glassy gulfs, and making
shells and sea-weed, all unseen
bove, till they waxed fearful ; then
with my grasp full of such tokens
d that I had searched the deep :
ng,
-dashing stroke, and drawing deep
uspended breath, again I spurned
which broke around me, and pur-

like a sea-bird. — I war a boy then.
Be a man now : there never was
need
od's strength.
s. (*looking from the lattice*). My
ful, my own,
Venice — *this is breath!* Thy
,
ian sea-breeze, how it fans my face !
vinds feel native to my veins,
them into calmness ! How unlike
ales of the horrid Cyclades,
wled about my Candiote dungeon,

heart sick.
                        I see the color comes
your cheek : Heaven send you
th to bear
re may be imposed ! — I dread to
on't.
. They will not banish me again ?
— no,
vring on ; I am strong yet.
                                Confess,
ick will be spared you.
.   I confessed
'ice before : both times they exiled

And the third time will slay you.
:.   Let them do so,
tried in my birth-place : better
here than aught that lives else-
.

Guard. And can you so much love the
    soil which hates you ?
Jac. Fos. The soil ! — Oh no, it is the
    seed of the soil
Which persecutes me ; but my native earth
Will take me as a mother to her arms.
I ask no more than a Venetian grave,
A dungeon, what they will, so it be here.[1]

Enter an Officer.

Offi. Bring in the prisoner !
Guard.   Signor, you hear the order.
Jac. Fos. Ay, I am used to such a sum-
    mons ; 'tis
The third time they have tortured me : —
    then lend me
Thine arm.   [*To the Guard.*
Offi.   Take mine, sir ; 'tis my duty to
Be nearest to your person.
Jac. Fos.   You ! — you are he
Who yesterday presided o'er my pangs —
Away ! — I'll walk alone.
Offi.   As you please, signor ;
The sentence was not of my signing, but
I dared not disobey the Council when
They ——
Jac. Fos. Bade thee stretch me on their
    horrid engine.
I pray thee touch me not — that is, just now ;
The time will come they will renew that order,
But keep off from me till 'tis issued. As
I look upon thy hands, my curdling limbs

---

1 [And the hero himself, what is he ? If there
ever existed in nature a case so extraordinary as
that of a man who gravely preferred tortures and a
dungeon at home, to a temporary residence in a
beautiful island and a fine climate, at the distance
of three days' sail, it is what few can be made to
believe, and still fewer to sympathize with ; and
which is, therefore, no very promising subject for
dramatic representation. For ourselves, we have
little doubt that Foscari wrote the fatal letter with
the view, which was imputed to him by his accus-
ers, of obtaining an honorable recall from banish-
ment, through foreign influence ; and that the color
which, when detected, he endeavored to give to the
transaction, was the evasion of a drowning man,
who is reduced to catch at straws and shadows.
But, if Lord Byron chose to assume this alleged
motive of his conduct as the real one, it behooved
him, at least, to set before our eyes the intolerable
separation from a beloved country, the lingering
home-sickness, the gradual alienation of intellect,
and the fruitless hope that his enemies had at length
relented, which were necessary to produce a conduct
so contrary to all usual principles of action as that
which again consigned him to the racks and dun-
geons of his own country. He should have shown
him to us, first, taking leave of Venice, a con-
demned and banished man ; next pining in Candia ;
next tampering with the agents of government ; by
which time, and not till then, we should have been
prepared to listen with patience to his complaints,
and to witness his sufferings with interest as well as
horror. — *Heber.*]

Quiver with the anticipated wrenching,
And the cold drops strain through my brow,
   as if ——
But onward — I have borne it — I can bear
   it. —
How looks my father?
   Off.   With his wonted aspect.
   Jac. Fos. So does the earth, and sky, the
      blue of ocean,
The brightness of our city, and her domes,
The mirth of her Piazza, even now
Its merry hum of nations pierces here,
Even here, into these chambers of the unknown
Who govern, and the unknown and the un-
   numbered
Judged and destroyed in silence, — all things
   wear
The self-same aspect, to my very sire!
Nothing can sympathize with Foscari,
Not even a Foscari. — Sir, I attend you.
   [*Exeunt* JACOPO FOSCARI, *Officer, etc.*

   Enter MEMMO *and another Senator.*

   Mem. He's gone — we are too late: —
      think you "the Ten"
Will sit for any length of time to-day?
   Sen. They say the prisoner is most obdu-
      rate,
Persisting in his first avowal; but
More I know not.
   Mem.   And that is much; the
      secrets
Of yon terrific chamber are as hidden
From us, the premier nobles of the state,
As from the people.
   Sen.   Save the wonted rumors,
Which — like the tales of spectres, that are rife
Near ruined buildings — never have been
   proved,
Nor wholly disbelieved: men know as little
Of the state's real acts as of the grave's
Unfathomed mysteries.
   Mem.   But with length of time
We gain a step in knowledge, and I look
Forward to be one day of the decemvirs.
   Sen. Or Doge?
   Mem.   Why, no; not if I can avoid it.
   Sen. 'Tis the first station of the state, and
      may
Be lawfully desired, and lawfully
Attained by noble aspirants.
   Mem.   To such
I leave it; though born noble, my ambition
Is limited: I'd rather be an unit
Of an united and imperial "Ten,"
Than shine a lonely, though a gilded cipher. —
Whom have we here? the wife of Foscari?

   Enter MARINA, *with a female Attendant.*

   Mar. What, no one? — I am wrong, there
      still are two;
But they are senators.

   Mem.   Most noble lady,
Command us.
   Mar.   *I command!* — Alas! my life
Has been one long entreaty, and a vain one.
   Mem. I understand thee, but I must not
      answer.
   Mar. (*fiercely*). True — none dare answer
      here save on the rack,
Or question save those ——
   Mem. (*interrupting her*). High-born dame![1]
      bethink thee
Where thou now art.
   Mar.   Where I now am! — It was
My husband's father's palace.
   Mem.   The Duke's palace.
   Mar. And his son's prison; — true, I have
      not forgot it;
And if there were no other nearer, bitterer
Remembrances, would thank the illustrious
      Memmo
For pointing out the pleasures of the place.
   Mem. Be calm!
   Mar. (*looking up towards heaven*). I am;
      but oh, thou eternal God!
Canst *thou* continue so, with such a world?
   Mem. Thy husband yet may be absolved.
   Mar.   He is,
In heaven. I pray you, signor senator,
Speak not of that; you are a man of office,
So is the Doge; he has a son at stake
Now, at this moment, and I have a husband,
Or had; they are there within, or were at
      least
An hour since, face to face, as judge and
      culprit:
Will *he* condemn *him?*
   Mem.   I trust not.
   Mar.   But if
He does not, there are those will sentence
      both.
   Mem. They can.
   Mar. And with them power and will are
      one
In wickedness: — my husband's lost!
   Mem.   Not so;
Justice is judge in Venice.
   Mar.   If it were so,
There now would be no Venice. But let it
Live on, so the good die not, till the hour
Of nature's summons; but "the Ten's" is
      quicker,

---

1 [She was a Contarini —
   " A daughter of the house that now among
      Its ancestors in monumental brass
      Numbers eight Doges." — *Rogers.*
On the occasion of her marriage with the younger
Foscari, the Bucentaur came out in his splendor;
and a bridge of boats was thrown across the Canal
Grande for the bridegroom, and his retinue of three
hundred horse. According to Sanuto, the tourna-
ments in the place of St. Mark lasted three days,
and were attended by thirty thousand people.]

ıst wait on't. Ah! a voice of wail!
　　　　　[*A faint cry within.*
·k!
　'Twas a cry of—
　　No, no; not my husband's—
i's.
　The voice was—
　　　　　　Not his : no.
No; that should be his father's

ıot his—he'll die in silence.
　　　[*A faint groan again within.*
　　　　　　　　What!

ʀ voice! it seemed so: I will not
　Should he shrink, I cannot cease
ut—no—no—no—it must have

ʌang, which wrung a groan from

l, feeling for thy husband's wrongs,
ıt thou
　bear more than mortal pain, in
?
ᴇ all must bear our tortures. I
ot
, the great house of Foscari,
ᴇy sweep both the Doge and son
fe;
ured as much in giving life
ʾho will succeed them, as they can
it: but mine were joyful pangs:
ıey wrung me till I *could* have
:d,
ᴛ; for my hope was to bring forth
.d would not welcome them with

l's silent now.
　　　　Perhaps all's over; but
eem it: he hath nerved himself,
efies them.

Enter an Officer hastily.

　How now, friend, what seek you?
ᴇech. The prisoner has fainted.
　　　　　　[*Exit Officer.*
　　　　　　　　Lady,
ᴛer to retire.
ʾering to assist her*). I pray thee do

f! *I* will tend him.
　　　You! Remember, lady!
ʒiven to none within those cham-

ᴇ Ten," and their familiars.
　　　　　　　　Well,
ᴛ none who enter there return
ve entered—many never; but
　not balk my entrance.
　　　　　　　Alas! this
ᴄpose yourself to harsh repulse,
suspense.

Mar.　　　Who shall oppose me?
Mem.　　　　　　　　They
Whose duty 'tis to do so.
Mar.　　　　　　'Tis *their* duty
To trample on all human feelings, all
Ties which bind man to man, to emulate
The fiends who will one day requite them in
Variety of torturing! Yet I'll pass.
Mem. It is impossible.
Mar.　　　　　That shall be tried.
Despair defies even despotism: there is
That in my heart would make its way through
　hosts
With levelled spears; and think you a few
　jailors
Shall put me from my path? Give me, then,
　way.
This is the Doge's palace; I am wife
Of the Duke's son, the *innocent* Duke's son,
And they shall hear this!
Mem.　　　　　It will only serve
More to exasperate his judges.
Mar.　　　　　　What
Are *judges* who give way to anger? they
Who do so are assassins. Give me way.
　　　　　　　[*Exit* MARINA.
Sen. Poor lady!
Mem.　　　　'Tis mere desperation: she
Will not be admitted o'er the threshold.
Sen.　　　　　　And
Even if she be so, cannot save her husband.
But, see, the officer returns.
　[*The Officer passes over the stage with an-
　other person.*
Mem.　　　　　I hardly
Thought that "the Ten" had even this touch
　of pity,
Or would permit assistance to this sufferer.
Sen. Pity! Is't pity to recall to feeling
The wretch too happy to escape to death
By the compassionate trance, poor nature's
　last
Resource against the tyranny of pain?
Mem. I marvel they condemn him not at
　once.
Sen. That's not their policy: they'd have
　him live,
Because he fears not death; and banish him,
Because all earth, except his native land,
To him is one wide prison, and each breath
Of foreign air he draws seems a slow poison,
Consuming but not killing.
Mem.　　　　　Circumstance
Confirms his crimes, but he avows them not.
Sen. None, save the Letter, which he says
　was written,
Addressed to Milan's duke, in the full knowl-
　edge
That it would fall into the senate's hands,
And thus he should be reconveyed to Venice.
Mem. But as a culprit.
Sen.　　　　Yes, but to his country

And that was all he sought, — so he avouches.
Mem. The accusation of the bribes was
proved.
Sen. Not clearly, and the charge of homi-
cide
Has been annulled by the death-bed confession
Of Nicolas Erizzo, who slew the late
Chief of " the Ten." [1]
Mem.   Then why not clear him ?
Sen.   That
They ought to answer; for it is well known
That Almoro Donato, as I said,
Was slain by Erizzo for private vengeance.
Mem. There must be more in this strange
process than
The apparent crimes of the accused disclose —
But here come two of " the Ten ; " let us re-
tire.   [*Exeunt* MEMMO *and Senator.*

Enter LOREDANO *and* BARBARIGO.

Bar. (addressing LOR.). That were too
much : believe me, 'twas not meet
The trial should go further at this moment.
Lor. And so the Council must break up,
and Justice
Pause in her full career, because a woman
Breaks in on our deliberations ?
Bar.   No,
That's not the cause; you saw the prisoner's
state.
Lor. And had he not recovered ?
Bar.   To relapse
Upon the least renewal.
Lor.   'Twas not tried.
Bar. 'Tis vain to murmur ; the majority
In council were against you.
Lor.   Thanks to you, sir,
And the old ducal dotard, who combined
The worthy voices which o'er-ruled my own.
Bar. I am a judge; but must confess that
part
Of our stern duty, which prescribes the Ques-
tion,

---

[1] [The extraordinary sentence pronounced against
him, still existing among the archives of Venice,
runs thus: — " Giacopo Foscari, accused of the
murder of Hermolao Donato, has been arrested and
examined; and, from the testimony, evidence, and
documents exhibited, *it distinctly appears* that he
is guilty of the aforesaid crime; nevertheless, on
account of his obstinacy, and of *enchantments and
spells*, in his possession, of which there are manifest
proofs, it has not been possible to extract from him
the truth, which is clear from parol and written
evidence; for, while he was on the cord, he uttered
neither word nor groan, but only murmured some-
thing to himself indistinctly and under his breath;
therefore *as the honor of the state requires*, he is
condemned to a more distant banishment in Candia."
Will it be credited, that a distinct proof of his inno-
cence, obtained by the discovery of the real assassin,
wrought no change in his unjust and cruel sen-
tence ? " — *Smedley.*]

And bids us sit and see its sharp infliction,
Makes me wish ——
Lor.   What ?
Bar.   That *you* would *sometimes* feel,
As I do always.
Lor.   Go to, you're a child,
Infirm of feeling as of purpose, blown
About by every breath, shook by a sigh,
And melted by a tear — a precious judge
For Venice! and a worthy statesman to
Be partner in my policy.
Bar.   He shed
No tears.
Lor.   He cried out twice.
Bar.   A saint had done so,
Even with the crown of glory in his eye,
At such inhuman artifice of pain
As was forced on him ; but he did not cry
For pity; not a word nor groan escaped him,
And those two shrieks were not in supplica-
tion,
But wrung from pangs, and followed by no
prayers.
Lor. He muttered many times between
his teeth,
But inarticulately.
Bar.   That I heard not;
You stood more near him.
Lor.   I did so.
Bar.   ,   Methought,
To my surprise too, you were touched with
mercy,
And were the first to call out for assistance
When he was failing.
Lor.   I believed that swoon
His last.
Bar. And have I not oft heard thee name
His and his father's death your nearest wish ?
Lor. If he dies innocent, that is to say,
With his guilt unavowed, he'll be lamented.
Bar. What, wouldst thou slay his memory ?
Lor.   Wouldst thou have
His state descend to his children, as it must,
If he die unattainted ?
Bar.   War with *them* too ?
Lor. With all their house, till theirs or
mine are nothing.
Bar. And the deep agony of his pale wife,
And the repressed convulsion of the high
And princely brow of his old father, which
Broke forth in a slight shuddering, though
rarely,
Or in some clammy drops, soon wiped away
In stern serenity ; these moved you not ?
                              [*Exit* LOREDANO.
He's silent in his hate, as Foscari
Was in his suffering ; and the poor wretch
moved me
More by his silence than a thousand outcries
Could have effected. 'Twas a dreadful sight
When his distracted wife broke through into
The hall of our tribunal, and beheld

ould scarcely look upon, long used
ghts. I must think no more of this,
et in this compassion for
ieir former injuries, and lose
f vengeance Loredano plans
id me; but mine would be content
r retribution than he thirsts for,
ld mitigate his deeper hatred
· thoughts; but for the present,
:i
:t hourly respite, granted at
ce of the elders of the Council,
abtless by his wife's appearance in
nd his own sufferings. — Lo! they
:
e and forlorn! I cannot bear
n them again in this extremity:
and try to soften Loredano.
　　　　　　　　[*Exit* BARBARIGO.

ACT II.

. — *A Hall in the* DOGE'S *Palace.*

he DOGE *and a* SENATOR.

it your pleasure to sign the report
ostpone it till to-morrow?
　　　　　　　　　　　　Now;
ed it yesterday: it wants
e signature. Give me the pen —
DOGE *sits down and signs the paper.*
;nor.
oking at the paper). You have for-
it is not signed.
Not signed? Ah, I perceive my eyes

iore weak with age. I did not see
d dipped the pen without effect.[1]
ipping the pen into the ink, and plac-
he paper before the DOGE). Your
. too, shakes, my lord: allow me,

'Tis done, I thank you.
　　　　　　Thus the act confirmed
nd by "the Ten" gives peace to
:e.
'Tis long since she enjoyed it: may

re she resume her arms!
　　　　　　　　　　'Tis almost
ir years of nearly ceaseless warfare
Turk, or the powers of Italy;
had need of some repose.
　　　　　　　　No doubt:
;r Queen of Ocean, and I leave her
.ombardy;[2] it is a comfort

---

had dipped the pen too heedlessly."]

; of Lombardy — it is some comfort."]

That I have added to her diadem
The gems of Brescia and Ravenna; Crema
And Bergamo no less are hers; her realm
By land has grown by thus much in my reign,
While her sea-sway has not shrunk.
　Sen.　　　　　　　'Tis most true,
And merits all our country's gratitude.
　Doge. Perhaps so.
　Sen.　　　Which should be made manifest.
　Doge. I have not complained, sir.
　Sen.　　My good lord, forgive me.
　Doge. For what?
　Sen.　　　　My heart bleeds for you.
　Doge.　　　　　For me, signor?
　Sen. And for your ——
　Doge.　　　　　Stop!
　Sen.　　　It must have way, my lord;
I have too many duties towards you
And all your house, for past and present kind-
　　　　ness,
Not to feel deeply for your son.
　Doge.　　　　　Was this
In your commission?
　Sen.　　　What, my lord?
　Doge.　　　　　This prattle
Of things you know not: but the treaty's
　　signed;
Return with it to them who sent you.
　Sen.　　　　　　　　I
Obey. I had in charge, too, from the Council
That you would fix an hour for their reunion.
　Doge. Say, when they will — now, even at
　　this moment,
If it so please them: I am the state's servant.
　Sen. They would accord some time for
　　your repose.
　Doge. I have no repose, that is, none which
　　shall cause
The loss of an hour's time unto the state.
Let them meet when they will, I shall be found
Where I should be, and *what* I have been ever.
　　　　　　　　[*Exit* SENATOR.
　　　　[*The* DOGE *remains in silence.*

Enter an Attendant.

　Att. Prince!
　Doge.　　Say on.
　Att.　　The illustrious lady Foscari
Requests an audience.
　Doge.　　　　Bid her enter. Poor
Marina!　　　　　[*Exit Attendant.*
　　　[*The* DOGE *remains in silence as before.*

Enter MARINA.

　Mar. I have ventured, father, on
Your privacy.
　Doge.　　I have none from you, my child.
Command my time, when not commanded by
The state.
　Mar.　　I wished to speak to you of *him.*
　Doge. Your husband?
　Mar.　　　　　And your son.

Doge. Proceed, my daughter!

Mar. I had obtained permission from " the
    Ten "
To attend my husband for a limited number
Of hours.

Doge.   You had so.

Mar.   'Tis revoked.

Doge.   By whom ?

Mar. " The Ten." — When we had reached
    " the Bridge of Sighs,"
Which I prepared to pass with Foscari,
The gloomy guardian of that passage first
Demurred : a messenger was sent back to
" The Ten ; " but as the court no longer sate,
And no permission had been given in writing,
I was thrust back, with the assurance that
Until that high tribunal re-assembled
The dungeon walls must still divide us.

Doge.   True,
The form has been omitted in the haste
With which the court adjourned ; and till it
    meets,
'Tis dubious.

Mar.   Till it meets ! and when it meets,
They'll torture him again ; and he and *I*
Must purchase by renewal of the rack
The interview of husband and of wife,
The holiest tie beneath the heavens ! — Oh
    God !
Dost thou see this ?

Doge.   Child — child ——

Mar. (*abruptly*).   Call *me* not " child ! "
You soon will have no children — you deserve
    none —
You, who can talk thus calmly of a son
In circumstances which would call forth tears
Of blood from Spartans ! Though these did
    not weep
Their boys who died in battle, is it written
That they beheld them perish piecemeal, nor
Stretched forth a hand to save them ?

Doge.   You behold me :
I cannot weep — I would I could ; but if
Each white hair on this head were a young life,
This ducal cap the diadem of earth,
This ducal ring with which I wed the waves
A talisman to still them — I'd give all
For him.

Mar. With less he surely might be saved.

Doge. That answer only shows you know
    not Venice.
Alas ! how should you ? she knows not her-
    self,
In all her mystery. Hear me — they who aim
At Foscari, aim no less at his father ;
The sire's destruction would not save the son ;
They work by different means to the same
    end,
And that is —— but they have not conquered
    yet.

Mar. But they have crushed.

Doge.   Nor crushed as yet — I live.

Mar. And your son, — how long will he
    live ?

Doge.   I trust,
For all that yet is past, as many years
And happier than his father. The rash boy,
With womanish impatience to return,
Hath ruined all by that detected letter :
A high crime, which I neither can deny
Nor palliate, as parent or as Duke :
Had he but borne a little, little longer
His Candiote exile, I had hopes —— he has
    quenched them —
He must return.

Mar.   To exile ?

Doge.   I have said it.

Mar. And can I not go with him ?

Doge.   You well know
This prayer of yours was twice denied before
By the assembled " Ten," and hardly now
Will be accorded to a third request,
Since aggravated errors on the part
Of your lord renders them still more austere.

Mar. Austere ? Atrocious ! The old hu-
    man fiends,
With one foot in the grave, with dim eyes,
    strange
To tears save drops of dotage, with long white
And scanty hairs, and shaking hands, and
    heads
As palsied as their hearts are hard, they coun-
    sel,
Cabal, and put men's lives out, as if life
Were no more than the feelings long extin-
    guished
In their accursed bosoms.

Doge.   You know not ——

Mar. I do — I do — and so should you,
    methinks —
That these are demons : could it be else that
Men, who have been of women born and
    suckled —
Who have loved, or talked at least of love —
    have given
Their hands in sacred vows — have danced
    their babes
Upon their knees, perhaps have mourned
    above them —
In pain, in peril, or in death — who are,
Or were at least in seeming, human, could
Do as they have done by yours, and you your-
    self,
You, who abet them ?

Doge.   I forgive this, for
You know not what you say.

Mar.   *You* know it well,
And feel it nothing.

Doge.   I have borne so much,
That words have ceased to shake me.

Mar.   Oh, no doubt !
You have seen your son's blood flow, and
    your flesh shook not :
And after that, what are a woman's words ?

than woman's tears, that they should
e you.
  Woman, this clamorous grief of
, I tell thee,
re in the balance weighed with that
but I pity thee, my poor Marina!
Pity my husband, or I cast it from

son! *Thou* pity! — 'tis a word
o thy heart — how came it on thy lips?
I must bear these reproaches, though
wrong me.
thou but read ——
       'Tis not upon thy brow,
ine eyes, nor in thine acts, — where

behold this sympathy? or shall?
(*pointing downwards*). There.
          In the earth?
    To which I am tending: when
on this heart, far lightlier, though
with marble, than the thoughts which
s it
u will know me better.
          Are you, then,
thus to be pitied?
          Pitied! None
r use that base word, with which men
eir soul's hoarded triumph, as a fit

₃le with my name; that name shall be,
s *I* have borne it, what it was
received it.
        But for the poor children
thou canst not, or thou wilt not save,
re the last to bear it.
        Would it were so!
or him he never had been born;
or me. — I have seen our house dis-
iored.
    That's false! A truer, nobler, trustier
rt,
ving, or more loyal, never beat
a human breast. I would not change
ed, persecuted, mangled husband,
sed but not disgraced, crushed, over-
elmed,
r dead, for prince or paladin
or in fable, with a world
ck his suit. Dishonored! — *he* dis-
tored!
ee, Doge, 'tis Venice is dishonored;
ne shall be her foulest, worst reproach,
at he suffers, not for what he did.
who are all traitors, tyrant! — ye!
ı but love your country like this victim
tters back in chains to tortures, and
s to all things rather than to exile,
ing yourselves before him, and implore
ce for your enormous guilt.
          He was
all you have said. I better bore

The deaths of the two sons Heaven took from
  me,
Than Jacopo's disgrace.
  Mar.   That word again?
  Doge. Has he not been condemned?
  Mar.   Is none but guilt so?
  Doge. Time may restore his memory — I
  would hope so.
He was my pride, my —— but 'tis useless
  now —
I am not given to tears, but wept for joy
When he was born: those drops were ominous.
  Mar. I say he's innocent! And were he
  not so,
Is our own blood and kin to shrink from us
In fatal moments?
  Doge.   I shrank not from him ı
But I have other duties than a father's;
The state would not dispense me from those
  duties;
Twice I demanded it, but was refused:
They must then be fulfilled.[1]

        Enter an Attendant.

  Att.   A message from
" The Ten."
  Doge.   Who bears it?
  Att.   Noble Loredano.
  Doge. He! — but admit him.
          [*Exit Attendant.*
  Mar.   Must I then retire?
  Doge. Perhaps it is not requisite, if this
Concerns your husband, and if not —— Well,
  signor,
Your pleasure!   [*To* LOREDANO *entering.*
  Lor.   I bear that of " the Ten."
  Doge.   They
Have chosen well their envoy.
  Lor.   'Tis *their* choice
Which leads me here.
  Doge.   It does their wisdom honor,
And no less to their courtesy. — Proceed.

---

[1] [The interest of this play is founded upon feel-
ings so peculiar or overstrained, as to engage no
sympathy; and the whole story turns on incidents
that are neither pleasing nor natural. The younger
Foscari undergoes the rack twice (once in the hear-
ing of the audience), merely because he has chosen
to feign himself a traitor, that he might be brought
back from undeserved banishment, and dies at last
of pure dotage on this sentiment; while the elder
Foscari submits, in profound and immovable silence,
to this treatment of his son, lest, by seeming to feel
for his unhappy fate, he should be implicated in his
guilt — though he is supposed guiltless. He, the
Doge, is afraid to stir hand or foot, to look or speak,
while these inexplicable horrors are transacting, on
account of the hostility of one Loredano, who lords
it in the council of " the Ten," nobody knows why
or how; and who at last " enmeshes " both father
and son in his toils, in spite of their passive obedi-
ence and non-resistance to his plans. They are
silly flies for this spider to catch, and " feed fat his
ancient grudge upon." — *Jeffrey.*]

Lor. We have decided.
Doge. We?
Lor. "The Ten" in council.
Doge. What! have they met again, and met without
Apprising me?
Lor. They wished to spare your feelings,
No less than age.
Doge. That's new — when spared they either?
I thank them, notwithstanding.
Lor. You know well
That they have power to act at their discretion,
With or without the presence of the Doge.
Doge. 'Tis some years since I learned this, long before
I became Doge, or dreamed of such advancement.
You need not school me, signor; I sate in
That council when you were a young patrician.
Lor. True, in my father's time; I have heard him and
The admiral, his brother, say as much.
Your highness may remember them; they both
Died suddenly.
Doge. And if they did so, better
So die than live on lingeringly in pain.
Lor. No doubt; yet most men like to live their days out.
Doge. And did not they?
Lor. The grave knows best: they died,
As I said, suddenly.
Doge. Is that so strange,
That you repeat the word emphatically?
Lor. So far from strange, that never was there death
In my mind half so natural as theirs.
Think *you* not so?
Doge. What should I think of mortals?
Lor. That they have mortal foes.
Doge. I understand you;
Your sires were mine, and you are heir in all things.
Lor. You best know if I should be so.
Doge. I do.
Your fathers were my foes, and I have heard
Foul rumors were abroad; I have also read
Their epitaph, attributing their deaths
To poison. 'Tis perhaps as true as most
Inscriptions upon tombs, and yet no less
A fable.
Lor. Who dares say so?
Doge. I! — 'Tis true
Your fathers were mine enemies, as bitter
As their son e'er can be, and I no less
Was theirs; but I was *openly* their foe:
I never worked by plot in council, nor
Cabal in commonwealth, nor secret means
Of practice against life by steel or drug.
The proof is, your existence.
Lor. I fear not.

Doge. You have no cause, being what I am; but were I
That you would have me thought, you long ere now
Were past the sense of fear. Hate on; I care not.
Lor. I never yet knew that a noble's life
In Venice had to dread a Doge's frown,
That is, by open means.
Doge. But I, good signor,
Am, or at least *was*, more than a mere duke,
In blood, in mind, in means; and that they know
Who dreaded to elect me, and have since
Striven all they dare to weigh me down : be sure,
Before or since that period, had I held you
At so much price as to require your absence,
A word of mine had set such spirits to work
As would have made you nothing. But in all things
I have observed the strictest reverence;
Not for the laws alone, for those *you* have strained
(I do not speak of *you* but as a single
Voice of the many) somewhat beyond what
I could enforce for my authority,
Were I disposed to brawl; but, as I said,
I have observed with veneration, like
A priest's for the high altar, even unto
The sacrifice of my own blood and quiet,
Safety, and all save honor, the decrees,
The health, the pride, and welfare of the state.
And now, sir, to your business.
Lor. 'Tis decreed,
That, without further repetition of
The Question, or continuance of the trial,
Which only tends to show how stubborn guilt is,
("The Ten," dispensing with the stricter law
Which still prescribes the Question till a full
Confession, and the prisoner partly having
Avowed his crime in not denying that
The letter to the Duke of Milan's his),
James Foscari, return to banishment,
And sail in the same galley which conveyed him.
Mar. Thank God! At least they will not drag him more
Before that horrible tribunal. Would he
But think so, to my mind the happiest doom,
Not he alone, but all who dwell here, could
Desire, were to escape from such a land.
Doge. That is not a Venetian thought, my daughter.
Mar. No, 'twas too human. May I share his exile?
Lor. Of this "the Ten' said nothing.
Mar. So I thought'
That were too human, also. But it was not
Inhibited?
Lor. It was not named.

(*to the* DOGE). Then, father,
ou can obtain or grant me thus much:
[*To* LOREDANO.
, sir, not oppose my prayer to be
d to accompany my husband.
　　　　　　　　　I will endeavor.
　　　　　　And you, signor?
　　　　　　　　　　Lady!
for me to anticipate the pleasure
·ibunal.
　　　　　　Pleasure! what a word
or the decrees of——
　　　　　　　Daughter, know you
a presence you pronounce these things?
A prince's and his subject's.
　　　　　　　　　Subject!
　　　　　　　　　　　　Oh!
ou:— well, you are his equal, as
k; but that you are not, nor would be,
ᵤ a peasant:— well, then, you're a
ce,
ly noble; and what then am I?
The offspring of a noble house.
　　　　　　　　　And wedded
as noble. What, or whose, then, is
esence that should silence my free
ghts?
he presence of your husband's judges.
　　　　　　　　　　　　And
erence due even to the lightest word
ls from those who rule in Venice.
　　　　　　　　　　　Keep
maxims for your mass of scared me-
.nics,
ᵤerchants, your Dalmatian and Greek
ᵤes,
.butaries, your dumb citizens,
tsked nobility, your sbirri, and
·ies, your galley and your other slaves,
ᵤm your midnight carryings off and
·wnings,
ingeons next the palace roofs, or under
ter's level; your mysterious meetings,
known dooms, and sudden executions,
Bridge of Sighs,"[1] your strangling
.mber, and
ᵤrturing instruments, have made ye
m
.ngs of another and worse world!
ᵤch for them: I fear ye not. I know ye;
ᵤown and proved your worst, in the in-
ᵤal
of my poor husband! Treat me as
ᵤed him:— you did so, in so dealing
m. Then what have I to fear *from* you,
I were of fearful nature, which
ᵤ am not?
　　　　　You hear, she speaks wildly.
Not wisely, yet not wildly.
　　　　　　　　Lady! words

[1] [See *ante*, p. 537.]

Uttered within these walls I bear no further
Than to the threshold, saving such as pass
Between the Duke and me on the state's ser-
vice.
Doge! have you aught in answer?
　Doge.　　　　　　Something from
The Doge; it may be also from a parent.
　Lor. My Mission *here* is to the *Doge.*
　Doge.　　　　　　Then say
The Doge will choose his own ambassador,
Or state in person what is meet; and for
The father——
　Lor.　　I remember *mine.* — Farewell!
I kiss the hands of the illustrious lady,
And bow me to the Duke. [*Exit* LOREDANO.
　Mar.　　　　Are you content?
　Doge. I am what you behold.
　Mar. ·　　　And that's a mystery.
　Doge. All things are so to mortals; who
　　can read them
Save he who made? Or, if they can, the few
And gifted spirits, who have studied long
That loathsome volume — man, and pored
　upon
Those black and bloody leaves, his heart and
　brain,[2]
But learn a magic which recoils upon
The adept who pursues it: all the sins
We find in others, nature made our own;
All our advantages are those of fortune;
Birth, wealth, health, beauty, are her accidents,
And when we cry out against Fate 'twere well
We should remember Fortune can take nought
Save what she *gave* — the rest was nakedness,
And lusts, and appetites, and vanities,
The universal heritage, to battle
With as we may, and least in humblest stations,
Where hunger swallows all in one low want,[3]
And the original ordinance, that man
Must sweat for his poor pittance, keeps al.
　passions
Aloof, save fear of famine! All is low,
And false, and hollow — clay from first to last,
The prince's urn no less than potter's vessel.
Our fame is in men's breath, our lives upon
Less than their breath; our durance upon days,
Our days on seasons; our whole being on
Something which is not *us!* — So, we are
　slaves,
The greatest as the meanest — nothing rests
Upon our will; the will itself no less
Depends upon a straw than on a storm;[4]
And when we think we lead, we are most led,

[2] [MS. — "The blackest leaf, his heart, and
　　　　　　blankest his brain."]

[3] [MS. —
" Where hunger swallows all — wherever was
The monarch who could bear a three days' fast?"]

[4] [MS. —
　　　　" the will itself dependent
　　　Upon a storm, a straw, and both alike
　　　Leading to death."]

And still towards death, a thing which comes
as much
Without our act or choice as birth, so that
Methinks we must have sinned in some old
world,
And *this* is hell: the best is, that it is not
Eternal.

Mar. These are things we cannot judge
On earth.

Doge. And how then shall we judge each
other,
Who are all earth, and I, who am called upon
To judge my son ? I have administered
My country faithfully — victoriously —
I dare them to the proof, the *chart* of what
She was and is : my reign has doubled realms ;
And, in reward, the gratitude of Venice
Has left, or is about to leave, *me* single.

Mar. And Foscari ? I do not think of such
things,
So I be left with him.

Doge. You shall be so ;
Thus much they cannot well deny.

Mar. And if
They should, I will fly with him.

Doge. That can ne'er be.
And whither would you fly ?

Mar. I know not, reck not —
To Syria, Egypt, to the Ottoman —
Anywhere, where we might respire unfettered,
And live nor girt by spies, nor liable
To edicts of inquisitors of state.

Doge. What, wouldst thou have a renegade
for husband,
And turn him into traitor ?

Mar. He is none !
The country is the traitress, which thrusts forth
Her best and bravest from her. Tyranny
Is far the worst of treasons. Dost thou deem
None rebels except subjects ? The prince
who
Neglects or violates his trust is more
A brigand than the robber-chief.

Doge. I cannot
Charge me with such a breach of faith.

Mar. No ; thou
Observ'st, obey'st, such laws as make old
Draco's
A code of mercy by comparison.

Doge. I found the law ; I did not make it.
Were I
A subject, still I might find parts and portions
Fit for amendment ; but as prince, I never
Would change, for the sake of my house, the
charter
Left by our fathers.

Mar. Did they make it for
The ruin of their children ?

Doge. Under such laws, Venice
Has risen to what she is — a state to rival
In deeds, and days, and sway, and, let me add,
In glory (for we have had Roman spirits

Amongst us), all that history has bequeathed
Of Rome and Carthage in their best times,
when
The people swayed by senates.

Mar. Rather say,
Groaned under the stern oligarchs.

Doge. Perhaps so ;
But yet subdued the world : in such a state
An individual, be he richest of
Such rank as is permitted, or the meanest,
Without a name, is alike nothing, when
The policy, irrevocably tending
To one great end, must be maintained in
vigor.

Mar. This means that you are more
Doge than father.

Doge. It means, I am more citizen than
either.
If we had not for many centuries
Had thousands of such citizens, and shall,
I trust, have still such, Venice were no city.

Mar. Accursed be the city where the laws
Would stifle nature's !

Doge. Had I as many sons
As I have years, I would have given them all,
Not without feeling, but I would have given
them
To the state's service, to fulfil her wishes
On the flood, in the field, or, if it must be,
As it, alas ! has been, to ostracism,
Exile, or chains, or whatsoever worse
She might decree.

Mar. And this is patriotism ?
To me it seems the worst barbarity.
Let me seek out my husband : the sage
"Ten,"
With all its jealousy, will hardly war
So far with a weak woman as deny me
A moment's access to his dungeon.

Doge. I'll
So far take on myself, as order that
You may be admitted.

Mar. And what shall I say
To Foscari from his father !

Doge. That he obey
The laws.

Mar. And nothing more ? Will you not
see him
Ere he depart ? It may be the last time.

Doge. The last ! — my boy ! — the last time
I shall see
My last of children ! Tell him I will come.
[*Exeunt.*

ACT III.

SCENE I. — *The Prison of* JACOPO FOSCARI.

Jac. Fos. (solus). No light, save yon faint
gleam which shows me walls
Which never echoed but to sorrow's sounds,
The sigh of long imprisonment, the step

on which the iron clanked, the groan
th, the imprecation of despair !
ɛt for this I have returned to Venice,
ome faint hope, 'tis true, that time, which
ars
arble down, had worn away the hate
n's hearts; but I knew them not, and
re
consume my own, which never beat
ɛnice but with such a yearning as
ove has for her distant nest, when
ʒeeling
n the air on her return to greet
allow brood.   What letters are these
ɪich   [*Approaching the wall.*
rawled along the inexorable wall ?
he gleam let me trace them ?   Ah ! the
mes
sad predecessors in this place,
ates of their despair, the brief words of
f too great for many.   This stone page
like an epitaph their history;
e poor captive's tale is graven on
ngeon barrier, like the lover's record
the bark of some tall tree, which bears
vn and his beloved's name.   Alas,
gnize some names familiar to me,
lighted like to mine, which I will add,
for such a chronicle as this,
only can be read, as writ, by wretches.[1]
          [*He engraves his name.*

Enter a Familiar of " the Ten." [2]

ɪ.   I bring you food.
ʾ. *Fos.*   I pray you set it down;
ʒast hunger : but my lips are parched —
ɪater !
ɪ.   There.
ʾ. *Fos.* (*after drinking*).   I thank you :
am better.
ɪ.   I am commanded to inform you that
further trial is postponed.
ʾ. *Fos.*   Till when ?
ɪ.   I know not. — It is also in my orders
your illustrious lady be admitted.
ʾ. *Fos.*   Ah ! they relent, then — I had
eased to hope it :
ɪ time.

Enter MARINA.

IS. —
ɪich never can be read but, as 'twas written,
wretched beings."]
ɔrd Byron, in this tragedy, has not ventured
ʋrther deviation from historical truth than is
ɪuthorized by the license of the drama.   We
ːmark, however, that after Giacopo had been
ːd, he was removed to the Ducal apartments,
one of the *Pozzi;* that his death occurred, not
ɪice, but at Canea; that fifteen months elapsed
n his last condemnation and his father's dep-
ɪ; and that the death of the Doge took place,
the palace, but in his own house. — *Smed-*

Mar.   My best beloved !
Jac. Fos. (*embracing her*).   My true wife,
And only friend !   What happiness !
. *Mar.*   We'll part
No more.
Jac. Fos.   How !   wouldst thou share a dun-
geon ?
Mar.   Ay,
The rack, the grave, all — any thing with thee,
But the tomb last of all, for there we shall
Be ignorant of each other, yet I will
Share that — all things except new separa-
tion;
It is too much to have survived the first.
How dost thou ?   How are those worn limbs ?
Alas !
Why do I ask ?   Thy paleness ——
Jac. Fos.   'Tis the joy
Of seeing thee again so soon, and so
Without expectancy, has sent the blood
Back to my heart, and left my cheeks like
thine.
For thou art pale too, my Marina !
Mar.   'Tis
The gloom of this eternal cell, which never
Knew sunbeam, and the sallow sullen glare
Of the familiar's torch, which seems akin [3]
To darkness more than light, by lending to
The dungeon vapors its bituminous smoke,
Which cloud whate'er we gaze on, even thine
eyes ——
No, not thine eyes — they sparkle — how they
sparkle !
Jac. Fos.   And thine ! — but I am blinded
by the torch.
Mar.   As I have been without it.   Couldst
thou see here ?
Jac. Fos.   Nothing at first; but use and
time had taught me
Familiarity with what was darkness;
And the gray twilight of such glimmerings as
Glide through the crevices made by the winds
Was kinder to mine eyes than the full sun,
When gorgeously o'ergilding any towers
Save those of Venice; but a moment ere
Thou camest hither I was busy writing.
Mar.   What ?
Jac. Fos.   My name : look, 'tis there — re-
corded next
The name of him who here preceded me,
If dungeon dates say true.
Mar.   And what of him ?
Jac. Fos.   These walls are silent of men's
ends; they only
Seem to hint shrewdly of them.   Such stern
walls
Were never piled on high save o'er the dead
Or those who soon must be so. — *What of
him ?*

[3] [MS. —
" Of the familiar's torch, which seems to love
Darkness far more than light."]

Thou askest.— What of me? may soon be
  asked,
With the like answer — doubt and dreadful
  surmise —
Unless thou tell'st my tale.
   Mar.   *I speak* of thee!
   Jac. Fos. And wherefore not? All then
  shall speak of me :
The tyranny of silence is not lasting,
And, though events be hidden, just men's
  groans
Will burst all cerement, even a living grave's !
I do not *doubt* my memory, but my life ;
And neither do I fear.
   Mar.   Thy life is safe.
   Jac. Fos. And liberty ?
   Mar.   The mind should make its own.
   Jac. Fos. That has a noble sound; but
  'tis a sound,
A music most impressive, but too transient :
The mind is much, but is not all. The
  mind
Hath nerved me to endure the risk of death,
And torture positive, far worse than death
[If death be a deep sleep), without a groan,
Or with a cry which rather shamed my judges
Than me, but 'tis not all, for there are things
More woful — such as this small dungeon,
  where
I may breathe many years.
   Mar.   Alas ! and this
Small dungeon is all that belongs to thee
Of this wide realm, of which thy sire is prince.
   Jac. Fos. That thought would scarcely aid
  me to endure it.
My doom is common, many are in dungeons,
But none like mine, so near their father's
  palace ;
But then my heart is sometimes high, and hope
Will stream along those moted rays of light
Peopled with dusty atoms, which afford
Our only day ; for, save the gaoler's torch,
And a strange firefly, which was quickly caught
Last night in yon enormous spider's net,
I ne'er saw aught here like a ray. Alas !
I know if mind may bear us up, or no,
For I have such, and shown it before men ;
It sinks in solitude : my soul is social.
   Mar   I will be with thee.
   Jac. Fos.   Ah! if it were so!
But *that* they never granted — nor will grant,
And I shall be alone : no men — no books —
Those lying likenesses of lying men.
I asked for even those outlines of their kind,
Which they term annals, history, what you
  will,
Which men bequeathe as portraits, and they
  were
Refused me, — so these walls have been my
  study,
More faithful pictures of Venetian story,
With all their blank, or dismal stains, than is

The Hall not far from hence, which bears on
  high
Hundreds of doges, and their deeds and dates.
   Mar. I come to tell thee the result of their
Last council on thy doom.
   Jac. Fos.   I know it — look!
   [*He points to his limbs, as referring to the
  question which he had undergone.*
   Mar. No — no — no more of that : even
  they relent
From that atrocity.
   Jac. Fos.   What then ?
   Mar.   That you
Return to Candia.
   Jac. Fos.   Then my last hope's gone.
I could endure my dungeon, for 'twas Venice ;
I could support the torture, there was some-
  thing
In my native air that buoyed my spirits up
Like a ship on the ocean tossed by storms,
But proudly still bestriding the high waves,
And holding on its course ; but *there,* afar,
In that accursed isle of slaves and captives,
And unbelievers, like a stranded wreck,
My very soul seemed mouldering in my
  bosom,
And piecemeal I shall perish, if remanded.
   Mar. And *here?*
   Jac. Fos. At once — by better means, as
  briefer.
What ! would they even deny me my sire's
  sepulchre,
As well as home and heritage ?
   Mar.   My husband !
I have sued to accompany thee hence,
And not so hopelessly. This love of thine
For an ungrateful and tyrannic soil
Is passion, and not patriotism ; for me,
So I could see thee with a quiet aspect,
And the sweet freedom of the earth and air,
I would not cavil about climes or regions.
This crowd of palaces and prisons is not
A paradise ; its first inhabitants
Were wretched exiles.
   Jac. Fos.   Well I know *how* wretched.
   Mar. And yet you see how from their
  banishment
Before the Tartar into these salt isles,
Their antique energy of mind, all that
Remained of Rome for their inheritance,
Created by degrees an ocean-Rome ;[1]
And shall an evil, which so often leads
To good, depress thee thus ?
   Jac. Fos.   Had I gone forth
From my own land, like the old patriarchs,
  seeking

---

[1] In Lady Morgan's fearless and excellent work
upon Italy, I perceive the expression of " Rome of
the Ocean" applied to Venice. The same phrase
occurs in the " Two Foscari." My publisher can
vouch for me, that the tragedy was written and sent
to England some time before I had seen Lady Mor-

her region, with their flocks and herds;
I been cast out like the Jews from Zion,
ke our fathers, driven by Attila
a fertile Italy, to barren islets,
uld have given some tears to my late
country,
many thoughts; but afterwards addressed
lf, with those about me, to create
w home and fresh state: perhaps I could
borne this — though I know not.
ar.   Wherefore not?
s the lot of millions, and must be
fate of myriads more.
c. Fos.   Ay — we but hear
e survivors' toil in their new lands,
r numbers and success; but who can
umber
hearts which broke in silence of that
parting,
fter their departure; of that malady[1]
ch calls up green and native fields to view
the rough deep, with such identity
e poor exile's fevered eye, that he
scarcely be restrained from treading
hem?
melody,[2] which out of tones and tunes
cts such pasture for the longing sorrow
e sad mountaineer, when far away

work, which I only received on the 16th of
st. I hasten, however, to notice the coinci-
, and to yield the originality of the phrase to
ho first placed it before the public. I am the
anxious to do this, as I am informed (for I
seen but few of the specimens, and those
entally) that there have been lately brought
st me charges of plagiarism.

he calenture. — [A distemper peculiar to sai-
n hot climates. —

' So by a calenture misled
    The mariner with rapture sees
On the smooth ocean's azure bed
    Enamelled fields and verdant trees:
With eager haste he longs to rove,
    In that fantastic scene, and thinks
It must be some enchanted grove,
    And in he leaps, and down he sinks."
                                    Swift.]

lluding to the Swiss air and its effects. — [The
des Vaches, played upon the bagpipe by the
g cow-keepers on the mountains: — "An air,"
Rousseau, "so dear to the Swiss, that it was
lden, under the pain of death, to play it to the
s, as it immediately drew tears from them, and
those who heard it desert, or die of what is
l *la maladie du païs*, so ardent a desire did it
to return to their country. It is in vain to
in this air for energetic accents capable of pro-
g such astonishing effects, for which strangers
nable to account from the music, which is in
uncouth and wild. But it is from habit, recol-
ns, and a thousand circumstances, retraced in
une by those natives who hear it, and remind-
em of their country, former pleasures of their
, and all their ways of living, which occasion
er reflection at having lost them."]

From his snow canopy of cliffs and clouds,
That he feeds on the sweet, but poisonous
    thought,
And dies. You call this *weakness!* It is
    strength,
I say, — the parent of all honest feeling.
He who loves not his country, can love nothing.
  Mar. Obey her, then: 'tis she that puts
    thee forth.
  Jac. Fos. Ay, there it is; 'tis like a mother's
    curse
Upon my soul — the mark is set upon me.
The exiles you speak of went forth by nations,
Their hands upheld each other by the way,
Their tents were pitched together — I'm alone.
  Mar. You shall be so no more — I will go
    with thee.
  Jac. Fos. My best Marina! — and our
    children?
  Mar.   They,
I fear, by the prevention of the state's
Abhorrent policy, (which holds all ties
As threads, which may be broken at her
    pleasure,)
Will not be suffered to proceed with us.
  Jac. Fos. And canst thou leave them?
  Mar.   Yes. With many a pang.
But — I *can* leave them, children as they are,
To teach you to be less a child. From this
Learn you to sway your feelings, when ex-
    acted
By duties paramount; and 'tis our first
On earth to bear.
  Jac. Fos.   Have I not borne?
  Mar.   Too much
From tyrannous injustice, and enough
To teach you not to shrink now from a lot,
Which, as compared with what you have un-
    dergone
Of late is mercy.
  Jac. Fos.   Ah! you never yet
Were far away from Venice, never saw
Her beautiful towers in the receding distance,
While every furrow of the vessel's track
Seemed ploughing deep into your heart; you
    never
Saw day go down upon your native spires
So calmly with its gold and crimson glory,
And after dreaming a disturbed vision
Of them and theirs, awoke and found them
    not.
  Mar. I will divide this with you. Let us
    think
Of our departure from this much-loved city,
(Since you must *love* it, as it seems,) and this
Chamber of state, her gratitude allots you.
Our children will be cared for by the Doge,
And by my uncles; we must sail ere night.
  Jac. Fos. That's sudden. Shall I not
    behold my father?
  Mar. You will.
  Jac. Fos.   Where?

Mar.   Here, or in the ducal chamber —
He said not which. I would that you could bear
Your exile as he bears it.

Jac. Fos.   Blame him not.
I sometimes murmur for a moment; but
He could not now act otherwise. A show
Of feeling or compassion on his part
Would have but drawn upon his aged head
Suspicion from " the Ten," and upon mine
Accumulated ills.

Mar.   Accumulated!
What pangs are those they have spared you?

Jac. Fos.   That of leaving
Venice with out beholding him or you,
Which might have been forbidden now, as
   'twas
Upon my former exile.

Mar.   That is true,
And thus far I am also the state's debtor,
And shall be more so when I see us both
Floating on the free waves — away — away —
Be it to the earth's end, from this abhorred,
Unjust and ——

Jac. Fos. Curse it not. If I am silent,
Who dares accuse my country?

Mar.   Men and angels,
The blood of myriads reeking up to heaven,
The groans of slaves in chains, and men in
   dungeons,
Mothers, and wives, and sons, and sires, and
   subjects,
Held in the bondage of ten bald-heads; and
Though last, not least, *thy silence. Couldst thou*
   say
Aught in its favor, who would praise like *thee ?*

Jac. Fos. Let us address us then, since so
   it must be,
To our departure. Who comes here?

Enter LOREDANO, *attended by Familiars.*

Lor. (*to the Familiars*).   Retire,
But leave the torch.
       [*Exeunt the two Familiars.*

Jac. Fos.   Most welcome, noble signor.
I did not deem this poor place could have
   drawn
Such presence hither.

Lor.   'Tis not the first time
I have visited these places.

Mar.   Nor would be
The last, were all men's merits well rewarded.
Came you here to insult us, or remain
As spy upon us, or as hostage for us?

Lor. Neither are of my office, noble lady!
I am sent hither to your husband, to
Announce " the Ten's " decree.

Mar.   That tenderness
Has been anticipated: it is known.

Lor. As how?

Mar. I have informed him, not so gently,
Doubtless, as your nice feelings would pre-
   scribe,

The indulgence of your colleagues; but he
   knew it.
If you come for our thanks, take them, and
   hence!
The dungeon gloom is deep enough without
   you,
And full of reptiles, not less loathsome, though
Their sting is honester.

Jac. Fos.   I pray you, calm you:
What can avail such words?

Mar.   To let him know
That he is known.

Lor. Let the fair dame preserve
Her sex's privilege.

Mar.   I have some sons, sir,
Will one day thank you better.

Lor.   You do well
To nurse them wisely. Foscari — you know
Your sentence, then?

Jac. Fos.   Return to Candia?

Lor.   True —
For life.

Jac. Fos. Not long.

Lor.   I said — for *life.*

Jac. Fos.   And I
Repeat — not long.

Lor.   A year's imprisonment
In Canea — afterwards the freedom of
The whole isle.

Jac. Fos. Both the same to me: the after
Freedom as is the first imprisonment
Is't true my wife accompanies me?

Lor.   Yes,
If she so wills it.

Mar.   Who obtained that justice?

Lor. One who wars not with women.

Mar.   But oppresses
Men: howsoever let him have *my* thanks
For the only boon I would have asked or
   taken
From him or such as he is.

Lor.   He receives them
As they are offered.

Mar.   May they thrive with him
So much! — no more.

Jac. Fos. Is this, sir, your whole mis-
   sion?
Because we have brief time for preparation,
And you perceive your presence doth dis-
   quiet
This lady, of a house noble as yours.

Mar. Nobler!

Lor.   How nobler?

Mar.   As more generous!
We say the " generous steed " to express the
   purity
Of his high blood. Thus much I've learnt,
   although
Venetian (who see few steeds save of bronze),
From those Venetians who have skimmed the
   coasts
Of Egypt, and her neighbor Araby:

why not say as soon the "*generous
ian?"*
e be aught, it is in qualities
than in years; and mine, which is as
ld
urs, is better in its product, nay—
not so stern—but get you back, and
ore
your genealogic tree's most green
ves and most mature of fruits, and there
to find ancestors, who would have
lushed
ich a son—thou cold inveterate hater!
. Fos. Again, Marina!
r. Again, *still*, Marina.
ou not, he comes here to glut his hate
a last look upon our misery?
im partake it!
:. Fos. That were difficult.
r. Nothing more easy. He partakes it
ow—
e may veil beneath a marble brow
sneering lip the pang, but he partakes it.
' brief words of truth shame the devil's
ervants
ss than master; I have probed his soul
ment, as the eternal fire, ere long,
reach it always. See how he shrinks
om me!
death, and chains, and exile in his hand
catter o'er his kind as he thinks fit;
' are his weapons, not his armor, for
ve pierced him to the core of his cold
heart.
'e not for his frowns! We can but die,
he but live, for him the very worst
estinies: each day secures him more
tempter's.
tc. Fos. This is mere insanity.
ar. It may be so; and *who* hath made
us *mad?*
r. Let her go on; it irks not me.
ar. That's false.
came here to enjoy a heartless triumph
:old looks upon manifold griefs! You
came
'e sued to in vain—to mark our tears,
hoard our groans—to gaze upon the
wreck
ch you have made a prince's son—my
husband;
iort, to trample on the fallen—an office
hangman shrinks from, as all men from
him!
' have you sped? We are wretched, sig-
nor, as
: plots could make, and vengeance could
desire us,
how *feel you?*
'r. As rocks.
ar. By thunder blasted:
' feel not, but no less are shivered. Come,

Foscari; now let us go, and leave this felon,
The sole fit habitant of such a cell,
Which he has peopled often, but ne'er fitly
Till he himself shall brood in it alone.[1]

Enter the DOGE.

Jac. Fos. My father!
Doge (embracing him). Jacopo! my son
—my son!
Jac. Fos. My father still! How long it is
since I
Have heard thee name my name—*our* name!
Doge. My boy!
Couldst thou but know——
Jack. Fos. I rarely, sir, have murmured.
Doge. I feel too much thou hast not.
Mar. Doge, look there!
[*She points to* LOREDANO.
Doge. I see the man—what mean'st thou?
Mar. Caution!
Lor. Being
The virtue which this noble lady most
May practise, she doth well to recommend it.
Mar. Wretch! 'tis no virtue, but the policy
Of those who fain must deal perforce with
vice:
As such I recommend it, as I would
To one whose foot was on an adder's path.
Doge. Daughter, it is superfluous; I have
long
Known Loredano.
Lor. You may know him better.
Mar. Yes; *worse* he could not.
Jac. Fos. Father, let not these
Our parting hours be lost in listening to
Reproaches, which boot nothing. Is it—
• is it,
Indeed, our last of meetings?
Doge. You behold
These white hairs!
Jac. Fos. And I feel, besides, that mine
Will never be so white. Embrace me, father!
I loved you ever—never more than now.
Look to my children—to your last child's
children;
Let them be all to you which he was once,
And never be to you what I am now.
May I not see *them* also?
Mar. No—not *here.*
Jac. Fos. They might behold their parent
any where.
Mar. I would that they beheld their father
in
A place which would not mingle fear with
love,

[1] [If the two Foscari do nothing to defeat the machinations of their remorseless foe, Marina, the wife of the younger, at least revenges them, by letting loose the venom of her tongue upon their hateful oppressor, which she does without stint or measure; and in a strain of vehemence not inferior to that of the old queen Margaret in Richard the Third. — *Jeffrey.*]

To freeze their young blood in its natural cur-
rent.
They have fed well, slept soft, and knew not
that
Their sire was a mere hunted outlaw. Well,
I know his fate may one day be their heritage,
But let it only be their *heritage,*
And not their present fee. Their senses,
though
Alive to love, are yet awake to terror,
And these vile damps, too, and yon *thick
green* wave
Which floats above the place where we now
stand —
A cell so far below the water's level,
Sending its pestilence through every crevice,
Might strike them: *this is not their* atmos-
phere,
However you — and you — and, most of all,
As worthiest — *you,* sir, noble Loredano!
May breathe It without prejudice.
Jac. Fos.   I have not
Reflected upon this, but acquiesce.
I shall depart, then, without meeting them?
    Doge. Not so: they shall await you in my
chamber.
    Jac. Fos. And must I leave them — *all?*
Lor.   You must.
    Jac. Fos.   Not one?
Lor. They are the state's.
    Mar. I thought they had been mine.
    Lor. They are, in all maternal things.
    Mar.   That is,
In all things painful. If they're sick, they will
Be left to me to tend them; should they die,
To me to bury and to mourn; but if
They live, they'll make you soldiers, senators,
Slaves, exiles — what *you* will; or if they are
Females with portions, brides and *bribes* for
nobles!
Behold the state's care for its sons and
mothers!
    Lor. The hour approaches, and the wind
is fair.
    Jac. Fos. How know you that here, where
the genial wind
Ne'er blows in all its blustering freedom?
    Lor.   'Twas so
When I came here. The galley floats within
A bow-shot of the " Riva di Schiavoni."
    Jac. Fos. Father! I pray you to precede
me, and
Prepare my children to behold their father.
    Doge. Be firm, my son!
    Jac. Fos. I will do my endeavor.
    Mar. Farewell! at least to this detested
dungeon,
And him to whose good offices you owe
In part your past imprisonment.
    Lor.   And present
Liberation.
    Doge. He speaks truth.

Jac. Fos.   No doubt! but 'tis
Exchange of chains for heavier chains I owe
him.
He knows this, or he had not sought to
change them.
But I reproach not.
    Lor.   The time narrows, signor.
    Jac. Fos. Alas! I little thought so linger-
ingly
To leave abodes like this: but when I feel
That every step I take, even from this cell,
Is one away from Venice, I look back
Even on these dull damp walls, and ——
    Doge.   Boy! no tears.
    Mar. Let them flow on: he wept not on
the rack
To shame him, and they cannot shame him
now.
They will relieve his heart — that too kind
heart —
And I will find an hour to wipe away
Those tears, or add my own. I could weep
now,
But would not gratify yon wretch so far.
Let us proceed. Doge, lead the way.
    Lor. (to the Familiar). The torch, there!
    Mar. Yes, light us on, as to a funeral pyre,
With Loredano mourning like an heir.
    Doge. My son, you are feeble; take this
hand.
    Jac. Fos. Alas!
Must youth support itself on age, and I
Who ought to be the prop of yours?
    Lor.   Take mine.
    Mar. Touch it not, Foscari; 'twill sting
you. Signor,
Stand off! be sure, that if a grasp of yours
Would raise us from the gulf wherein we are
plunged,
No hand of ours would stretch itself to meet it.
Come, Foscari, take the hand the altar gave
you;
It could not save, but will support you ever.
            [*Exeunt.*

————

ACT IV.

SCENE I. — *A Hall in the Ducal Palace.*

Enter LOREDANO *and* BARBARIGO.

    Bar. And have you confidence in such a
project?
    Lor. I have.
    Bar.   'Tis hard upon his years.
    Lor.   Say rather
Kind to relieve him from the cares of state.
    Bar. 'Twill break his heart.
    Lor.   Age has no heart to break.
He has seen his son's half-broken, and, except
A start of feeling in his dungeon, never
Swerved.

Bar. In his countenance, I grant you,
   never;
t I have seen him sometimes in a calm
desolate, that the most clamorous grief
d nought to envy him within. Where is he?
Lor. In his own portion of the palace,
   with
s son, and the whole race of Foscaris.
Bar. Bidding farewell.
Lor.   A last. As soon he shall
l to his dukedom.
Bar.   When embarks the son?
Lor. Forthwith — when this long leave is
   taken. 'Tis
ne to admonish them again.
Bar.   Forbear;
trench not from their moments.
Lor.   Not I, now
: have higher business for our own. This
   day
ill be the last of the old Doge's reign,
the first of his son's last banishment,
d that is vengeance.
Bar.   In my mind, too deep.
Lor. 'Tis moderate — not even life for life,
   the rule
nounced of retribution from all time;
ey owe me still my father's and my uncle's.
Bar. Did not the Doge deny this strongly?
Lor.   Doubtless.
Bar. And did not this shake your suspi-
   cion?
Lor. No.
Bar. But if this deposition should take
   place
our united influence in the Council,
nust be done with all the deference
e to his years, his station, and his deeds.
Lor. As much of ceremony as you will,
   that the thing be done. You may, for
   aught
are, depute the Council on their knees,
ke Barbarossa to the Pope,) to beg him
have the courtesy to abdicate.
Bar. What, if he will not?
Lor.   We'll elect another,
d make him null.
Bar.   But will the laws uphold us?
Lor. What laws? — "The Ten" are laws;
   and if they were not,
ill be legislator in this business.
Bar. At your own peril?
Lor.   There is none, I tell you,
r powers are such.
Bar.   But he has twice already
icited permission to retire,
d twice it was refused.
Lor.   The better reason
grant it the third time.
Bar.   Unasked?
Lor.   It shows
e impression of his former instances:

If they were from his heart, he may be thank-
   ful:
If not, 'twill punish his hypocrisy.
Come, they are met by this time; let us join
   them,
And be *thou* fixed in purpose for this once.
I have prepared such arguments as will not
Fail to move them, and to remove him: since
Their thoughts, their objects, have been
   sounded, do not
You, with your wonted scruples, teach us
   pause,
And all will prosper.
Bar.   Could I but be certain
This is no prelude to such persecution
Of the sire as has fallen upon the son,
I would support you.
Lor.   He is safe, I tell you;
His fourscore years and five may linger on
As long as he can drag them: 'tis his throne
Alone is aimed at.
Bar.   But discarded princes
Are seldom long of life.
Lor.   And men of eighty
More seldom still.
Bar. And why not wait these few years?
Lor. Because we have waited long enough,
   and he
Lived longer than enough. Hence! in to
   council!
   [*Exeunt* LOREDANO *and* BARBARIGO.

Enter MEMMO *and a Senator.*

Sen. A summons to "the Ten!" Why so?
Mem.   "The Ten"
Alone can answer; they are rarely wont
To let their thoughts anticipate their purpose
By previous proclamation. We are sum-
   moned —
That is enough.
Sen.   For them, but not for us;
I would know why.
Mem.   You will know why anon,
If you obey; and if not, you no less
Will know why you should have obeyed.
Sen.   I mean not
To oppose them, *but* ——
Mem.   In Venice "*but*" 's a traitor.
But me no "*buts*," unless you would pass o'er
The Bridge which few repass.
Sen.   I am silent.
Mem.   Why
Thus hesitate? "The Ten" have called in
   aid
Of their deliberation five and twenty
Patricians of the senate — you are one,
And I another; and it seems to me
Both honored by the choice or chance which
   leads us
To mingle with a body so august.
Sen. Most true. I say no more.
Mem.   As we hope, Signor

And all may honestly, (that is, all those
Of noble blood may,) one day hope to be
Decemvir, it is surely for the senate's
Chosen delegates, a school of wisdom, to
Be thus admitted, though as novices,
To view the mysteries.
Sen.   Let us view them : they,
No doubt, are worth it.
Mem.   Being worth our lives
If we divulge them, doubtless they are worth
Something, at least to you or me.
Sen.   I sought not
A place within the sanctuary ; but being
Chosen, however reluctantly so chosen,
I shall fulfil my office.
Mem.   Let us not
Be latest in obeying " the Ten's " summons.
Sen. All are not met, but I am of your
thought
So far — let's in.
Mem.   The earliest are most welcome
In earnest councils — we will not be least so.
                    [*Exeunt.*

Enter the DOGE, JACOPO FOSCARI, *and*
                    MARINA.

Jac. Fos. Ah, father! though I must and
will depart,
Yet — yet — I pray you to obtain for me
That I once more return unto my home,
Howe'er remote the period. Let there be
A point of time, as beacon to my heart,
With any penalty annexed they please,
But let me still return.
Doge.   Son Jacopo,
Go and obey our country's will : 'tis not
For us to look beyond.
Jac. Fos.   But still I must
Look back. I pray you think of me.
Doge.   Alas !
You ever were my dearest offspring, when
They were more numerous, nor can be less so
Now you are last ; but did the state demand
The exile of the disinterred ashes
Of your three goodly brothers, now in earth,
And their desponding shades came flitting
round
To impede the act, I must no less obey
A duty, paramount to every duty.
Mar. My husband! let us on : this but
prolongs
Our sorrow.
Jac. Fos. But we are not summoned yet ;
The galley's sails are not unfurled : — who
knows ?
The wind may change.
Mar.   And if it do, it will not
Change *their* hearts, or your lot : the galley's
oar
Will quickly clear the harbor.
Jac. Fos.   O, ye elements !
Where are your storms ?

Mar.   In human breasts. Alas !
Will nothing calm you ?
Jac. Fos.   Never yet did mariner
Put up to patron saint such prayers for pros-
perous
And pleasant breezes, as I call upon you,
Ye tutelar saints of my own city ! which
Ye love not with more holy love than I
To lash up from the deep the Adrian waves,
And waken Auster, sovereign of the tempest!
Till the sea dash me back on my own shore,
A broken corse upon the barren Lido,
Where I may mingle with the sands which
skirt
The land I love, and never shall see more !
Mar. And wish you this with *me* beside
you ?
Jac. Fos. No —
No — not for thee, too good, too kind ! May'st
thou
Live long to be a mother to those children
Thy fond fidelity for a time deprives
Of such support ! But for myself alone,
May all the winds of heaven howl down the
Gulf,
And tear the vessel, till the mariners,
Appalled, turn their despairing eyes on me,
As the Phenicians did on Jonah, then
Cast me out from amongst them, as an offer-
ing
To appease the waves. The billow which de-
stroys me
Will be more merciful than man, and bear me,
Dead, but *still bear* me to a native grave,
From fishers' hands upon the desolate strand,
Which, of its thousand wrecks, hath ne'er re-
ceived
One lacerated like the heart which then
Will be — But wherefore breaks it not ? why
live I ?
Mar. To man thyself, I trust, with time, to
master
Such useless passion. Until now thou wert
A sufferer, but not a loud one : why,
What is this to the things thou hast borne in
silence —
Imprisonment and actual torture ?
Jac. Fos.   Double,
Triple, and tenfold torture ! But you are right,
It must be borne. Father, your blessing.
Doge.   Would
It could avail thee ! but no less thou hast it.
Jac. Fos. Forgive ——
Doge.   What ?
Jac. Fos. My poor mother, for my birth,
And me for having lived, and you yourself
(As I forgive you), for the gift of life,
Which you bestowed upon me as my sire.
Mar. What hast thou done ?
Jac. Fos.   Nothing. I cannot charge
My memory with much save sorrow : but
I have been so beyond the common lot

ıstened and visited, I needs must think
ıt I was wicked. If it be so, may
at I have undergone here keep me from
ke hereafter!
far.   Fear not: *that's* reserved
your oppressors.
ac. Fos.   Let me hope not.
far.   Hope not?
ac. Fos. I cannot wish them *all* they have
inflicted.
   ar. All! the consummate fiends! A
thousand fold
· the worm which ne'er dieth feed upon
them!
ıc. Fos. They may repent.
   ar.   And if they do, Heaven will not
ept the tardy penitence of demons.

   Enter an Officer and Guards.

ffi. . Signor! the boat is at the shore—
the wind
ısing—we are ready to attend you.
ac. Fos. And I to be attended. Once
more, father,
r hand!
oge. Take it. Alas! how thine own
trembles!
ac. Fos. No—you mistake; 'tis yours
that shakes, my father.
rewell!
Doge. Farewell! Is there aught else?
Jac. Fos.   No—nothing.
                                 [*To the Officer.*
nd me your arm, good signor.
Offi.   You turn pale—
t me support you — paler — ho! some aid
there!
me water!
Mar.   Ah, he is dying!
Jac. Fos.   Now, I'm ready—
ı eyes swim strangely—where's the door?
Mar.   Away!
t me support him—my best love! Oh,
God!
ıw faintly beats this heart—this pulse!
Jac. Fos.   The·light!
it the light?—I am faint.
             [*Officer presents him with water.*
Offi.   He will be better,
rhaps, in the air.
Jac. Fos. I doubt not. Father—wife—
ıur hands!
Mar. There's death in that damp clammy
grasp.
ı, God!—My Foscari, how fare you?
Jac. Fos.   Well!
                                 [*He dies.*
Offi. He's gone!
Doge.   He's free.
Mar.   No—no, he is not dead;
ıere must be life yet in that heart—he
could **not**

Thus leave me.
Doge.   Daughter!
Mar.   Hold thy peace, old man!
I am no daughter now—thou hast no son.
Oh, Foscari!
   Offi.   We must remove the body.
   Mar. Touch it not, dungeon miscreants!
your base office
Ends with his life, and goes not beyond
murder,
Even by your murderous laws. Leave his
remains
To those who know to honor them.
   Offi.   I must
Inform the signory, and learn their pleasure.
   Doge. Inform the signory, from *me*, the
Doge,
They have no further power upon those ashes:
While he lived, he was theirs, as fits a subject—
Now he is *mine*—my broken-hearted boy!
                                 [*Exit Officer.*

   Mar. And I must live!
   Doge.   Your children live, Marina.
   Mar. My children! true—they live, and I
must live
To bring them up to serve the state, and die
As died their father. Oh! what best of
blessings
Were barrenness in Venice! Would my
mother
Had been so!
   Doge.   My unhappy children!
   Mar.   What!
You feel it then at last—*you!*—Where is now
The stoic of the state?
   Doge (*throwing himself down by the body*).
Here!
   Mar.   Ay, weep on!
I thought you had no tears—you hoarded
them
Until they are useless; but weep on! he
never
Shall weep more—never, never more.

   Enter LOREDANO *and* BARBARIGO.

   Lor.   What's here?
   Mar. Ah! the devil come to insult the dead!
Avaunt!
Incarnate Lucifer! 'tis holy ground.
A martyr's ashes now lie there, which make it
A shrine. Get thee back to thy place of tor-
ment!
   Bar. Lady, we knew not of this sad event,
But passed here merely on our path from
council.   ·
   Mar. Pass on.
   Lor.   We sought the Doge.
   Mar. (*pointing to the Doge, who is still on
the ground by his son's body*). He's busy,
look,
About the business *you* provided for him.
Are ye content?

Bar.　　　　　　We will not interrupt
A parent's sorrows.
Mar.　　　　　　No, ye only make them,
Then leave them.
Doge (rising). Sirs, I am ready.
Bar.　　　　　　No — not now.
Lor. Yet 'twas important.
Doge.　　　　　If 'twas so, I can
Only repeat — I am ready.
Bar.　　　　　　It shall not be
Just now, though Venice tottered o'er the
　deep
Like a frail vessel. I respect your griefs.
Doge. I thank you. If the tidings which
　. you bring
Are evil, you may say them; nothing further
Can touch me more than him thou look'st on
　there;
If they be good, say on; you need not *fear*
That they can *comfort* me.
Bar.　　　　　　I would they could!
Doge. I spoke not to *you*, but to Loredano.
He understands me.
Mar.　　　Ah! I thought it would be so.
Doge. What mean you?
Mar.　　　Lo! there is the blood beginning
To flow through the dead lips of Foscari —
The body bleeds in presence of the assassin.
　　　　　　　　　　[*To* LOREDANO.
Thou cowardly murderer by law, behold
How death itself bears witness to thy deeds!
Doge. My child! this is a phantasy of
　grief.
Bear hence the body. [*To his attendants.*]
　Signors, if it please you,
Within an hour I'll hear you.
　[*Exeunt* DOGE, MARINA, *and attendants
　　with the body. Manent* LOREDANO *and*
　　BARBARIGO.
Bar.　　　　　　He must not
Be troubled now.
Lor.　　　He said himself that nought
Could give him trouble further.
Bar.　　　　　These are words.
But grief is lonely, and the breaking in
Upon it barbarous.
Lor.　　　　Sorrow preys upon
Its solitude, and nothing more diverts it
From its sad visions of the other world
Than calling it at moments back to this.
The busy have no time for tears.
Bar.　　　　　And therefore
You would deprive this old man of all busi-
　ness?
Lor. The thing's decreed. The Giunta and
　"the Ten"
Have made it law — who shall oppose that
　law?
Bar. Humanity!
Lor.　　　　Because his son is dead?
Bar. And yet unburied.
Lor.　　　　Had we known this when

The act was passing, it might have suspended
Its passage, but impedes it not — once past.
Bar. I'll not consent.
Lor.　　　　You have consented to
All that's essential — leave the rest to me.
Bar. Why press his abdication now?
Lor.　　　　　The feelings
Of private passion may not interrupt
The public benefit; and what the state
Decides to-day must not give way before
To-morrow for a natural accident.
Bar. You have a son.
Lor.　　　　I *have* — and *had* a father.
Bar. Still so inexorable?
Lor.　　　　　Still.
Bar.　　　　　　But let him
Inter his son before we press upon him
This edict.
Lor.　　　Let him call up into life
My sire and uncle — I consent. Men may,
Even aged men, be, or appear to be,
Sires of a hundred sons, but cannot kindle
An atom of their ancestors from earth.
The victims are not equal; he has seen
His sons expire by natural deaths, and I
My sires by violent and mysterious maladies.
I used no poison, bribed no subtle master
Of the destructive art of healing, to
Shorten the path to the eternal cure.
His sons — and he had four — are dead, with-
　out
My dabbling in vile drugs.
Bar　　　　　And art thou sure
He dealt in such?
Lor.　　　Most sure.
Bar.　　　　　And yet he seems
All openness.
Lor.　　　And so he seemed not long
Ago to Carmagnuola.
Bar.　　　　　The attainted
And foreign traitor?
Lor.　　　　Even so: when *he*,
After the very night in which " the Ten "
(Joined with the Doge) decided his destruc-
　tion,
Met with the great Duke at daybreak with a
　jest,
Demanding whether he should augur him
" The good day or good night? " his Doge-
　ship answered,
" That he in truth had passed a night of vigil,
" In which (he added with a gracious smile),
" There often has been question about you."[1]
'Twas true; the question was the death re-
　solved
Of Carmagnuola, eight months ere he died,
And the old Doge, who knew him doomed,
　smiled on him
With deadly cozenage, eight long months
　before-hand —

---

[1] An historical fact. See *Daru*, tom. ii.

ght months of such hypocrisy as is
:arnt but in eighty years. Brave Carmag-
   nuola
  dead; so is young Foscari and his breth-
   ren —
 never *smiled* on *them*.
Bar.   Was Carmagnuola
ur friend ?
Lor.   He was the safeguard of the city.
  early life its foe, but in his manhood,
  saviour first, then victim.
Bar.   Ah! that seems
e penalty of saving cities. He
  hom we now act against not only saved
r own, but added others to her sway.
Lor. The Romans (and we ape them)
  gave a crown
 him who took a city; and they gave
 crown to him who saved a citizen
  battle: the rewards are equal. Now,
we should measure forth the cities taken
 the Doge Foscari, with citizens
stroyed by him, or *through* him, the
  account
ere fearfully against him, although narrowed
 private havoc, such as between him
nd my dead father.
Bar.   Are you then thus fixed ?
Lor. Why, what should change me !
Bar.   That which changes me.
t you, I know, are marble to retain
  feud. But when all is accomplished, when
e old man is deposed, his name degraded,
s sons all dead, his family depressed,
 d you and yours triumphant, shall you
  sleep?
or.   More soundly.
ar.   That's an error, and you'll find it
  you sleep with your fathers.
or.   They sleep not
  their accelerated graves, nor will
 l Foscari fills his. Each night I see them
  lk frowning round my couch, and, point-
   ing towards
e ducal palace, marshal me to vengeance.
ar. Fancy's distemperature! There is no
  passion
re spectral or fantastical than Hate;
t even its opposite, Love, so peoples air
th phantoms, as this madness of the heart.

Enter an Officer.

or. Where go you, sirrah ?
ff.   By the ducal order
 forward the preparatory rites
 the late Foscari's interment.
ar.   Their
lt has been often opened of late years.
or. 'Twill be full soon, and may be closed
  for ever.
ff.   May I pass on ?
or.   You may.

Bar.   How bears the Doge
This last calamity ?
Off.   With desperate firmness.
In presence of another he says little,
But I perceive his lips move now and then;
And once or twice I heard him, from the ad-
  joining
Apartment mutter forth the words —"My
  son!"
Scarce audibly. I must proceed. [*Exit Officer.*
Bar.   This stroke
Will move all Venice in his favor.
Lor.   Right!
We must be speedy: let us call together
The delegates appointed to convey
The council's resolution.
Bar.   I protest
Against it at this moment.
Lor.   As you please —
I'll take their voices on it ne'ertheless,
And see whose most may sway them, yours
  or mine.
    [*Exeunt* BARBARIGO *and* LOREDANO.

ACT V.

SCENE I. — *The* DOGE'S *Apartment.*

The DOGE *and Attendants.*

Att. My lord, the deputation is in waiting;
But add, that if another hour would better
Accord with your will, they will make it theirs.
Doge. To me all hours are like. Let them
  approach.   [*Exit Attendant.*
An Officer. Prince! I have done your
  bidding.
Doge.   What command ?
Off. A melancholy one — to call the at-
  tendance
Of——
Doge. True — true — true: I crave you
  pardon. I
Begin to fail in apprehension, and
Wax very old — old almost as my years.
Till now I fought them off, but they begin
To overtake me.

*Enter the Deputation consisting of six of the
Signory and the Chief of the Ten.*

          Noblemen, your pleasure !
Chief of the Ten. In the first place, the
  Council doth condole
With the Doge on his late and private grief.
Doge. No more — no more of that.
Chief of the Ten.   Will not the Duke
Accept the homage of respect ?
Doge.   I do
Accept it as 'tis given — proceed.
Chief of the Ten.   " The Ten,"
With a selected giunta from the senate

Of twenty-five of the best born patricians,
Having deliberated on the state
Of the republic, and the o'erwhelming cares
Which, at this moment, doubly must oppress
Your years, so long devoted to your country,
Have judged it fitting, with all reverence,
Now to solicit from your wisdom (which
Upon reflection must accord in this),
The resignation of the ducal ring,
Which you have worn so long and venerably:
And to prove that they are not ungrateful, nor
Cold to your years and services, they add
An appanage of twenty hundred golden
Ducats to make retirement not less splendid
Than should become a sovereign's retreat.
   Doge Did I hear rightly?
   Chief of the Ten.   Need I say again?
   Doge. No. — Have you done?
   Chief of the Ten. I have spoken. Twenty-
four
Hours are accorded you to give an answer.
   Doge. I shall not need so many seconds.
   Chief of the Ten.   We
Will now retire.
   Doge.   Stay! Four and twenty hours
Will alter nothing which I have to say.
   Chief of the Ten. Speak!
   Doge.   When I twice before reiterated
My wish to abdicate, it was refused me:
And not alone refused, but ye exacted
An oath from me that I would never more
Renew this instance. I have sworn to die
In full exertion of the functions, which
My country called me here to exercise,
According to my honor and my conscience —
I cannot break *my* oath.
   Chief of the Ten.   Reduce us not
To the alternative of a decree,
Instead of your compliance.
   Doge.   Providence
Prolongs my days to prove and chasten me;
But ye have no right to reproach my length
Of days, since every hour has been the coun-
   try's.
I am ready to lay down my life for her,
As I have laid down dearer things than life:
But for my dignity — I hold it of
The *whole* republic; when the *general* will
Is manifest, then you shall all be answered.
   Chief of the Ten. We grieve for such an
   answer, but it cannot
Avail you aught.
   Doge.   I can submit to all things,
But nothing will advance; no, not a moment.
What you decree — decree.
   Chief of the Ten. With this, then, must we
Return to those who sent us?
   Doge.   You have heard me.
   Chief of the Ten. With all due reverence
   we retire.   [*Exeunt the Deputation. etc.*

      Enter an Attendant.

   Att.   My lord,
The noble dame Marina craves an audience.
   Doge. My time is hers.

       Enter MARINA.

   Mar.   My lord, if I intrude —
Perhaps you fain would be alone?
   Doge.   Alone,
Alone, come all the world around me, I
Am now and evermore. But we will bear it.
   Mar. We will, and for the sake of those
   who are,
Endeavor —— Oh my husband!
   Doge.   Give it way;
I cannot comfort thee.
   Mar.   He might have lived,
So formed for gentle privacy of life,
So loving, so beloved; the native of
Another land, and who so blest and blessing
As my poor Foscari? Nothing was wanting
Unto his happiness and mine save not
To be Venetian.
   Doge.   Or a prince's son.
   Mar. Yes; all things which conduce to
   other men's
Imperfect happiness or high ambition,
By some strange destiny, to him proved deadly.
The country and the people whom he loved,
The prince of whom he was the elder born,
And ——   *
   Doge. Soon may be a prince no longer.
   Mar.   How?
   Doge. They have taken my son from me,
   and now aim
At my too long worn diadem and ring.
Let them resume the gewgaws!
   Mar.   Oh the tyrants!
In such an hour too!
   Doge.   'Tis the fittest time;
An hour ago I should have felt it.
   Mar.   And
Will you not now resent it? — Oh for ven-
   geance!
But he, who, had he been enough protected,
Might have repaid protection in this moment,
Cannot assist his father.
   Doge.   Nor should do so
Against his country, had he a thousand lives
Instead of that ——
   Mar.   They tortured from him. This
May be pure patriotism. I am a woman:
To me my husband and my children were
Country and home. I loved *him* — how I
   loved him!
I have seen him pass through such an ordeal
   as
The old martyrs would have shrunk from: he
   is gone,
And I, who would have given my blood for
   him,
Have nought to give but tears! But could I
   compass

The retribution of his wrongs! — Well, well;
I have sons, who shall be men.
   Doge.   Your grief distracts you.
   Mar.   I thought I could have borne it,
     when· I saw him
Bowed down by such oppression; yes, I
     thought
That I would rather look upon his corse
Than his prolonged captivity: — I am pun-
     ished
For that thought now. Would I were in his
     grave!
   Doge. I must look on him once more.
   Mar.   Come with me!
   Doge. Is he——
   Mar.   Our bridal bed is now his bier.
   Doge. And he is in his shroud!
   Mar.   Come, come, old man!
              [*Exeunt the* DOGE *and* MARINA.

   Enter BARBARIGO *and* LOREDANO.

   Bar. (*to an Attendant*). Where is the
     Doge?
   Att.   This instant retired hence
With the illustrious lady, his son's widow.
   Lor. Where?
   Att. To the chamber where the body lies.
   Bar. Let us return, then.
   Lor.   You forget, you cannot.
We have the implicit order of the Giunta
To await their coming here, and join them in
Their office: they'll be here soon after us.
   Bar. And will they press their answer on
     the Doge?
   Lor. 'Twas his own wish that all should be
     done promptly.
He answered quickly, and must so be an-
     swered;
His dignity is looked to, his estate
Cared for — what would he more?
   Bar.   Die in his robes:
He could not have lived long; but I have
     done
My·best to save his honors, and opposed
This proposition to the last, though vainly.
Why would the general vote compel me
     hither?
   Lor. 'Twas fit that some one of such differ-
     ent thoughts
From ours should be a witness, lest false
     tongues
Should whisper that a harsh majority
Dreaded to have its acts beheld by others.
   Bar. And not less, I must needs think, for
     the sake
Of humbling me for my vain opposition.
You are ingenious, Loredano, in
Your modes of vengeance, nay, poetical,
A very Ovid in the art of *hating;*
'Tis thus (although a secondary object,
Yet hate has microscopic eyes), to you
I owe, by way of foil to the more zealous,

This undesired association in
Your Giunta's duties.
   Lor.   How! — *my* Giunta!
   Bar.   *Yours !*
They speak your language, watch your nod,
     approve
Your plans, and do your work. Are they not
     yours?
   Lor. You talk unwarily. 'Twere best they
     hear not
This from you.
   Bar.   Oh! they'll hear as much one day
From louder tongues than mine; they have
     gone beyond
Even their exorbitance of power: and when
This happens in the most contemned and
     abject
States, stung humanity will rise to check it.
   Lor. You talk but idly.
   Bar.   That remains for proof.
Here come our colleagues.

   Enter the Deputation as before.

   Chief of the Ten.   Is the Duke aware
We seek his presence?
   Att.   He shall be informed.
              [*Exit Attendant.*
   Bar. The Duke is with his son.
   Chief of the Ten.   If it be so,
We will remit him till the rites are over.
Let us return. 'Tis time enough to-morrow.
   Lor. (*aside to Bar.*). Now the rich man's
     hell-fire upon thy tongue,
Unquenched, unquenchable! I'll have it torn
From its vile babbling roots, till you shall utter
Nothing but sobs through blood, for this!
     Sage signors,
I pray ye be not hasty. [*Aloud to the others.*
   Bar.   But be human!
   Lor. See, the Duke comes!

   Enter the DOGE.

   Doge.   I have obeyed your summons.
   Chief of the Ten. We come once more to
     urge our past request.
   Doge. And I to answer.
   Chief of the Ten.   What?
   Doge.   My only answer.
You have heard it.
   Chief of the Ten. Hear *you* then the last
     decree,
Definitive and absolute!
   Doge.   To the point —
To the point! I know of old the forms of
     office,
And gentle preludes to strong acts — Go on!
   Chief of the Ten. You are no longer Doge;
     you are released
From your imperial oath as sovereign;
Your ducal robes must be put off; but for
Your services, the state allots the appanage
Already mentioned in our former congress.

Three days are left you to remove from hence,
Under the penalty to see confiscated
All your own private fortune.
 Doge.   That last clause,
I am proud to say, would not enrich the treas-
  ury.
 Chief of the Ten. Your answer, Duke!
 Lor.   Your answer, Francis Foscari!
 Doge. If I could have foreseen that my old
  age
Was prejudicial to the state, the chief
Of the republic never would have shown
Himself so far ungrateful, as to place
His own high dignity before his country;
But this *life* having been so many years
Not useless to that country, I would fain
Have consecrated my last moments to her.
But the decree being rendered, I obey.[1]
 Chief of the Ten. If you would have the
  three days named extended,
We willingly will lengthen them to eight,
As sign of our esteem.
 Doge.   Not eight hours, signor,
Nor even eight minutes — There's the ducal
  ring, [*Taking off his ring and cap.*
And there the ducal diadem. And so
The Adriatic's free to wed another.
 Chief of the Ten. Yet go not forth so
  quickly.
 Doge. I am old, sir,
And even to move but slowly must begin
To move betimes. Methinks I see amongst
  you
A face I know not — Senator! your name,
You, by your garb, Chief of the Forty!
 Mem.   Signor,
I am the son of Marco Memmo.
 Doge.   Ah!
Your father was my friend. — But *sons* and *fa-*
  thers! —
What, ho! my servants there!
 Atten.   My prince!
 Doge.   No prince —
There are the princes of the prince! [*Point-
ing to the Ten's Deputation.*] — Prepare
To part from hence upon the instant.
 Chief of the Ten.   Why
So rashly? 'twill give scandal.
 Doge.   Answer that;
        [*To the Ten.*
It is your province. — Sirs, bestir yourselves:
        [*To the Servants.*
There is one burden which I beg you bear
With care, although 'tis past all further
  harm —
But I will look to that myself.
 Bar.   He means
The body of his son.
 Doge.   And call Marina,
My daughter!

<hr/>

Enter MARINA.

 Doge. Get thee ready, we must mourn
Elsewhere.
 Mar. And everywhere.
 Doge.   True; but in freedom,
Without these jealous spies upon the great.
Signors, you may depart: what would you
  more?
We are going: do you fear that we shall
  bear
The palace with us? Its *old* walls, ten times
As *old* as I am, and I'm very old,
Have served you, so have I, and I and they
Could tell a tale; but I invoke them not
To fall upon you! else they would, as erst
The pillars of stone Dagon's temple on
The Israelite and his Philistine foes.
Such power I do believe there might exist
In such a curse as mine, provoked by such
As you; but I curse not. Adieu, good sig-
  nors!
May the next duke be better than the present.
 Lor. The *present* duke is Paschal Mali-
  piero.
 Doge. Not till I pass the threshold of these
  doors.
 Lor. Saint Mark's great bell is soon about
  to toll
For his inauguration.
 Doge.   Earth and heaven!
Ye will reverberate this peal; and I
Live to hear this! — the first doge who e'er
  heard
Such sound for his successor: happier he,
My attainted predecessor, stern Faliero —
This insult at the least was spared him.
 Lor.   What!
Do you regret a traitor?
 Doge.   No — I merely
Envy the dead.
 Chief of the Ten. My lord, if you indeed
Are bent upon this rash abandonment
Of the state's palace, at the least retire
By the private staircase, which conducts you
  towards
The landing-place of the canal.
 Doge.   No. I
Will now descend the stairs by which I
  mounted
To sovereignty — the Giants' Stairs, on whose
Broad eminence I was invested duke.
My services have called me up those steps,
The malice of my foes will drive me down
  them.
There five and thirty years ago was I
Installed, and traversed these same halls, from
  which
I never thought to be divorced except
A corse — a corse, it might be, fighting for
  them —
But not pushed brace by fellow-citizens.

But come; my son and I will go together —
He to his grave, and I to pray for mine.
    Chief of the Ten. What! thus in public?
    Doge.   I was publicly
Elected, and so will I be deposed.
Marina! art thou willing?
    Mar.   Here's my arm!
    Doge. And here my *staff*: thus propped
will I go forth.
    Chief of the Ten. It must not be — the
people will perceive it.
    Doge. The people! — There's no people,
    you well know it,
Else you dare not deal thus by them or me.
There is a *populace*, perhaps, whose looks
May shame you; but they dare not groan nor
    curse you,
Save with their hearts and eyes.
    Chief of the Ten.   You speak in passion,
Else ——
    Doge. You have reason. I have spoken
    much
More than my wont: it is a foible which
Was not of mine, but more excuses you,
Inasmuch as it shows that I approach
A dotage which may justify this deed
Of yours, although the law does not, nor will.
Farewell, sirs!
    Bar.   You shall not depart without
An escort fitting past and present rank.
We will accompany, with due respect,
The Doge unto his private palace. Say!
My brethren, will we not?
    Different voices.   Ay! — Ay!
    Doge.   You shall not
Stir — in my train, at least. I entered here
As sovereign — I go out as citizen
By the same portals, but as citizen.
All these vain ceremonies are base insults,
Which only ulcerate the heart the more,
Applying poisons there as antidotes.
Pomp is for princes — I am *none!* — That's
    false,
I *am*, but only to these gates. — Ah!
    Lor.   Hark!
           [*The great bell of Saint Mark's tolls.*
    Bar. The bell!
    Chief of the Ten. St. Mark's, which tolls
for the election
Of Malipiero.
    Doge.   Well I recognize
The sound! I heard it once, but once before,
And that is five and thirty years ago;
Even *then* I *was not young.*
    Bar.   Sit down, my lord!
You tremble.
    Doge.   'Tis the knell of my poor boy!
My heart aches bitterly.
    Bar.   I pray you sit.
    Doge. No; my seat here has been a throne
till now.
Marina! let us go.

    Mar.   Most readily.
    Doge (*walks a few steps, then stops*). I feel
athirst — will no one bring me here
A cup of water?
    Bar.   I ——
    Mar.   And I ——
    Lor.   And I ——
    [*The* DOGE *takes a goblet from the hand of*
    LOREDANO.
    Doge. I take *yours*, Loredano, from the
hand
Most fit for such an hour as this.[1]
    Lor.   Why so?
    Doge. 'Tis said that our Venetian crystal
    has
Such pure antipathy to poisons as
To burst, if aught of venom touches it.
You bore this goblet, and it is not broken.
    Lor. Well, sir!
    Doge.   Then it is false, or you are true.
For my own part, I credit neither; 'tis
An idle legend.
    Mar.   You talk wildly, and
Had better now be seated, nor as yet
Depart. Ah! now you look as looked my
    husband!
    Bar. He sinks! — support him! — quick —
a chair — support him!
    Doge. The bell tolls on! — let's hence —
my brain's on fire!
    Bar. I do beseech you, lean upon us!
    Doge.   No!
A sovereign should die standing. My poor
boy!
Off with your arms! — *That bell!*
         [*The* DOGE *drops down and dies.*[2]
    Mar.   My God! My God!
    Bar. (*to Lor.*). Behold! your work's com-
pleted!
    Chief of the Ten.   Is there then
No aid? Call in assistance!
    Att.   'Tis all over.
    Chief of the Ten. If it be so, at least his
obsequies
Shall be such as befits his name and nation,
His rank and his devotion to the duties
Of the realm, while his age permitted him
To do himself and them full justice. Breth-
ren,
Say, shall it not be so?
    Bar.   He has not had
The misery to die a subject where
He reigned: then let his funeral rites be
princely.[3]

---

[1] [MS. —
  "I take yours, Loredano — 'tis the draught
    Most fitting such an hour as this."]
[2] [The death of the elder Foscari took place not
at the palace, but in his own house; not immedi-
ately on his descent from the Giants' Stairs, but
five days afterwards. — *Smedley.*]
[3] [By a decree of the Council, the trappings of

Chief of the Ten. We are agreed, then ?
All, except Lor., answer.   Yes.
Chief of the Ten. Heaven's peace be with
   him !
Mar. Signors, your pardon: this is
   mockery.
Juggle no more with that poor remnant,
   which,
A moment since while yet it had a soul,
(A soul by whom you have increased your
   empire,
And made your power as proud as was his
   glory,)
You banished from his palace, and tore down
From his high place, with such relentless
   coldness;
And now, when he can neither know these
   honors,
Nor would accept them if he could, you,
   signors,
Purpose, with idle and superfluous pomp,
To make a pageant over what you tram-
   pled.
A princely funeral will be your reproach,
And not his honor.
Chief of the Ten.   Lady, we revoke not
Our purposes so readily.
Mar.   I know it,
As far as touches torturing the living.
I thought the dead had been beyond even
   you,
Though (some, no doubt) consigned to
   powers which may
Resemble that you exercise on earth.
Leave him to me ; you would have done so for
His dregs of life, which you have kindly
   shortened:
It is my last of duties, and may prove
A dreary comfort in my desolation.
Grief is fantastical, and loves the dead,
And the apparel of the grave.
Chief of the Ten.   Do you
Pretend still to this office ?
Mar.   I do, signor.
Though his possessions have been all con-
   sumed
In the state's service, I have still my dowry,
Which shall be consecrated to his rites,
And those of——   [*She stops with agitation.*
Chief of the Ten. Best retain it for your
   children.
Mar. Ay, they are fatherless, I thank you.
Chief of the Ten.   We
Cannot comply with your request. His relics
Shall be exposed with wonted pomp, and fol-
   lowed
Unto their home by the new Doge, not clad

---

supreme power of which the Doge had divested
himself while living, were restored to him when
dead; and he was interred, with ducal magnificence,
in the church of the Minorites, the new Doge attend-
ing as a mourner. — See *Daru.*]

As *Doge,* but simply as a senator.
Mar. I have heard of murderers, who have
   interred
Their victims; but ne'er heard until this
   hour,
Of so much splendor in hypocrisy
O'er those they slew.[1] I have heard of
   widow's tears —
Alas ! I have shed some — always thanks to
   you !
I've heard of *heirs* in sables — you have left
   none
To the deceased, so you would act the part
Of such. Well, sirs, your will be done! as
   one day, '
I trust, Heaven's will be done too !
Chief of the Ten.   Know, you, lady,
To whom ye speak, and perils of such
   speech ?
Mar. I know the former better than your-
   selves ;
The latter—like yourselves; and can face
   both.
Wish you more funerals ?
Bar.   Heed not her rash words;
Her circumstances must excuse her bearing.
Chief of the Ten. We will not note them
   down.
Bar. (*turning to Lor. who is writing upon
   his tablets*).   What art thou writing,
With such an earnest brow, upon thy tab-
   lets ?
Lor. (*pointing to the Doge's body*). That *he*
   has paid me![2]
Chief of the Ten. What debt did he owe
   you ?
Lor. A long and just one ; Nature's debt
   and *mine.*   [*Curtain falls.*

[1] The Venetians appear to have had a particular
turn for breaking the hearts of their Doges. The
following is another instance of the kind in the
Doge Marco Barbarigo: he was succeeded by his
brother Agostino Barbarigo, whose chief merit is
here mentioned. — " Le doge, blessé de trouver
constamment un contradicteur et un censeur si
amer dans son frère, lui dit un jour en plein conseil :
' Messire Augustin, vous faites tout votre possible
pour hâter ma mort; vous vous flattez de me suc-
céder, mais, si les autres vous connaissent aussi-
bien que je vous connais, ils n'auront garde de vous
élire.' La-dessus il se leva, ému de colère, rentra
dans son appartement, et mourut quelques jours
apres. Ce frere, contre lequel il s'etait emporté,
fut précisément le successeur qu'on lui donna.
C'était un mérite dont on aimait à tenir compte;
surtout à un parent, de s'être mis en opposition
avec le chef de la république." — *Daru, Hist. de
Venise,* vol. ii. p. 533.
[2] " *L' ha pagata.*" An historical fact. See *Hist.
de Venise,* par P. Daru, t. ii. p. 411. — [Here the
original MS. ends. The two lines which follow,
were added by Mr. Gifford. In the margin of the
MS., Byron has written, — " If the last line should
appear obscure to those who do not recollect the

historical fact mentioned in the first act of Lore-
dar.o's inscription in his book, of 'Doge Foscari,
debtor for the deaths of my father and uncle,' you
may add the following lines to the conclusion of the
last act:—

Chief of the Ten. For what has he repaid thee?
Lor. For my father's
And father's brother's death—by his son's and own!
Ask Gifford about this."]

[Considered as poems, we confess that "Sardanapalus" and "The Two Foscari" appear to us to be
rather heavy, verbose, and inelegant—deficient in the passion and energy which belongs to Lord Byron's
other writings—and still more in the richness of imagery, the originality of thought, and the sweetness
of versification for which he used to be distinguished. They are for the most part solemn, prolix, and
ostentatious—lengthened out by large preparations for catastrophes that never arrive, and tantalizing us
with slight specimens and glimpses of a higher interest scattered thinly up and down many weary pages
of pompous declamation. Along with the concentrated pathos and homestruck sentiments of his former
poetry, the noble author seems also—we cannot imagine why—to have discarded the spirited and melo-
dious versification in which they were embodied, and to have formed to himself a measure equally remote
from the spring and vigor of his former compositions, and from the softness and inflexibility of the ancient
masters of the drama. There are some sweet lines, and many of great weight and energy; but the gen-
eral march of the verse is cumbrous and unmusical. His lines do not vibrate like polished lances, at
once strong and light, in the hands of his persons, but are wielded like clumsy batons in a bloodless
affray. Instead of the graceful familiarity and idiomatical melodies of Shakspeare, it is apt, too, to fall
into clumsy prose, in its approaches to the easy and colloquial style; and, in the loftier passages, is
occasionally deformed by low and common images that harmonize but ill with the general solemnity of
the diction.—*Jeffrey.*]

CAIN: A MYSTERY.

"Now the serpent was more subtile than any beast of the field which the LORD God had made."—
Gen. ch. iii. ver. 1.

["CAIN" was begun at Ravenna, on the 16th of July, 1821—completed (in three acts, and without the
chorus) on the 9th of September—and published, in the same volume with "Sardanapalus" and "The
Two Foscari," in December.]

TO SIR WALTER SCOTT, BART.,

THIS MYSTERY OF CAIN IS INSCRIBED,

BY HIS OBLIGED FRIEND, AND FAITHFUL SERVANT,

THE AUTHOR.[1]

·· Sir Walter Scott announced his acceptance of this dedication in the following letter to Mr. Murray:—

"EDINBURGH, 4th December, 1821.

"MY DEAR SIR,—I accept, with feelings of great obligation, the flattering proposal of Lord Byron to
prefix my name to the very grand and tremendous drama of 'Cain.' I may be partial to it, and you will
allow I have cause; but I do not know that his Muse has ever taken so lofty a flight amid her former
soarings. He has certainly matched Milton on his own ground. Some part of the language is bold, and
may shock one class of readers, whose line will be adopted by others out of affectation or envy. But
then they must condemn the 'Paradise Lost,' if they have a mind to be consistent. The fiend-like rea-
soning and bold blasphemy of the fiend and of his pupil lead exactly to the point which was to be expected,
—the commission of the first murder, and the ruin and despair of the perpetrator.

"I do not see how any one can accuse the author himself of Manicheism. The devil talks the lan-
guage of that sect, doubtless; because, not being able to deny the existence of the Good Principle, he
endeavors to exalt himself—the Evil Principle—to a seeming equality with the Good; but such argu-
ments, in the mouth of such a being, can only be used to deceive and to betray. Lord Byron might

PREFACE.

THE following scenes are entitled "A Mystery," in conformity with the ancient title annexed to dramas upon similar subjects, which were styled "Mysteries, or Moralities." The author has by no means taken the same liberties with his subject which were common formerly, as may be seen by any reader curious enough to refer to those very profane productions, whether in English, French, Italian, or Spanish. The author has endeavored to preserve the language adapted to his characters; and where it is (and this is but rarely) taken from actual *Scripture*, he has made as little alteration, even of words, as the rhythm would permit. The reader will recollect that the book of Genesis does not state that Eve was tempted by a demon, but by " the Serpent; " and that only because he was " the most subtile of all the beasts of the field." Whatever interpretation the Rabbins and the Fathers may have put upon this, I take the words as I find them, and reply, with Bishop Watson upon similar occasions, when the Fathers were quoted to him, as Moderator in the schools of Cambridge, " Behold the book! " — holding up the Scripture.[1] It is to be recollected, that my present subject has nothing to do with the *New Testament*, to which no reference can be here made without anachronism. With the poems upon similar topics I have not been recently familiar. Since I was twenty, I have never read Milton; but I had read him so frequently before, that this may make little difference. Gesner's " Death of Abel " I have never read since I was eight years of age, at Aberdeen. The general impression of my recollection is delight; but of the contents I remember only that Cain's wife was called Mahala, and Abel's Thirza: in the following pages I have called them "Adah" and " Zillah, " the earliest female names which occur in Genesis; they were those of Lamech's wives: those of Cain and Abel are not called by their names. Whether, then, a coincidence of subject may have caused the same in expression, I know nothing, and care as little.[2]

The reader will please to bear in mind (what few choose to recollect), that there is no allusion to a future state in any of the books of Moses, nor indeed in the Old Testament.[3] For a reason for this extraordinary omission he may consult Warburton's " Divine Legation; " whether satisfactory or not,

have made this more evident, by placing in the mouth of Adam, or of some good and protecting spirit, the reasons which render the existence of moral evil consistent with the general benevolence of the Deity. The great key to the mystery is, perhaps, the imperfection of our own faculties, which see and feel strongly the partial evils which press upon us, but know too little of the general system of the universe, to be aware how the existence of these is to be reconciled with the benevolence of the great Creator.

" To drop these speculations, you have much occasion for some mighty spirit, like Lord Byron, to come down and trouble the waters; for, excepting ' The John Bull,'* you seem stagnating strangely in London.   '' Yours, my dear Sir, very truly,

" To John Murray, Esq.   " WALTER SCOTT."

[1] [" I never troubled myself with answering any arguments which the opponents in the divinity schools brought against the Articles of the Church, nor ever admitted their authority as decisive of a difficulty; but I used on such occasions to say to them, holding up the New Testament in my hand: ' En sacrum codicem! Here is the fountain of truth; why do you follow the streams derived from it by the sophistry, or polluted by the passions, of man?' " — *Bishop Watson's Life*, vol. i. p. 63.]

[2] [Here follows, in the original draft, — "I am prepared to be accused of Manicheism, or some other hard name ending in *ism*, which make a formidable figure and awful sound in the *eyes* and ears of those who would be as much puzzled to explain the terms so bandied about, as the liberal and pious indulgers in such epithets. Against such I can defend myself, or, if necessary, I can attack in turn."]

[3] [There *are* numerous passages dispersed throughout the Old Testament which import something more than " an allusion to a future state." In truth, the Old Testament abounds in phrases which imply the immortality of the soul, and which would be insignificant and hardly intelligible, but upon that supposition. " Then shall the dust return to the earth as it was, and the spirit return unto God who gave it." — *Eccl.* xii. 7. " And many of them that sleep in the dust of the earth shall awake, some to everlasting life, and some to shame: and they that be wise shall shine as the brightness of the firmament; and they that turn many to righteousness as the stars for ever and ever." — *Dan.* x. 2. " I know that my Redeemer liveth, and that he shall stand in the latter days upon the earth: and though after my skin worms shall destroy my body, yet in my flesh shall I see God." — *Job* xix. 25. — *Brit. Rev.*]

* [The pungent Sunday newspaper of that name had been lately established, and had excited an immense sensation.]

no better has yet been assigned. I have therefore supposed it new to Cain, without, I hope, any perversion of Holy Writ.

With regard to the language of Lucifer, it was difficult for me to make him talk like a clergyman upon the same subjects; but I have done what I could to restrain him within the bounds of spiritual politeness. If he disclaims having tempted Eve in the shape of the Serpent, it is only because the book of Genesis has not the most distant allusion to any thing of the kind, but merely to the Serpent in his serpentine capacity.

Note. — The reader will perceive that the author has partly adopted in this poem the notion of Cuvier, that the world had been destroyed several times before the creation of man. This speculation, derived from the different strata and the bones of enormous and unknown animals found in them, is not contrary to the Mosaic account, but rather confirms it; as no human bones have yet been discovered in those strata, although those of many known animals are found near the remains of the unknown. The assertion of Lucifer, that the pre-Adamite world was also peopled by rational beings much more intelligent than man, and proportionably powerful to the mammoth, etc. etc. is, of course, a poetical fiction to help him to make out his case.

I ought to add, that there is a "tramelogedia" of Alfieri, called "Abele."—I have never read that, nor any other of the posthumous works of the writer, except his Life.

RAVENNA, September 20, 1821.

DRAMATIS PERSONÆ.

MEN.	SPIRITS.	WOMEN.
ADAM.	ANGEL OF THE LORD.	EVE.
CAIN.	LUCIFER.	ADAH.
ABEL.		ZILLAH.

ACT I.

SCENE I. — *The Land without Paradise. — Time, Sunrise.*

ADAM, EVE, CAIN, ABEL, ADAH, ZILLAH, *offering a Sacrifice.*

Adam. God, the Eternal! Infinite! All-wise! —
Who out of darkness on the deep didst make
Light on the waters with a word — all hail!
Jehovah, with returning light, all hail!

Eve. God! who didst name the day, and separate
Morning from night, till then divided never —
Who didst divide the wave from wave, and call
Part of thy work the firmament — all hail!

Abel. God! who didst call the elements into
Earth — ocean — air — and fire, and with the day
And night, and worlds which these illuminate,
Or shadow, madest beings to enjoy them,
And love both them and thee — all hail! all hail!

Adah. God, the Eternal! Parent of all things!
Who didst create these best and beauteous beings,

To be beloved, more than all, save thee —
Let me love thee and them : — All hail! all hail!

Zillah. Oh, God! who loving, making, blessing all,
Yet didst permit the Serpent to creep in,
And drive my father forth from Paradise,
Keep us from further evil : — Hail! all hail!

Adam. Son Cain, my first-born, wherefore art thou silent?

Cain. Why should I speak?

Adam. To pray.[1]

Cain. Have ye not prayed?

---

[1] ["Prayer," said Lord Byron, at Cephalonia, "does not consist in the act of kneeling, nor in repeating certain words in a solemn manner. Devotion is the affection of the heart, and this I feel; for when I view the wonders of creation, I bow to the majesty of heaven; and when I feel the enjoyment of life, health, and happiness, I feel grateful to God for having bestowed these upon me." — "All this is well," I said, "so far as it goes, but to be a Christian you must go further." — "I read more of the Bible than you are aware," he said : "I have a Bible which my sister gave me, who is an excellent woman, and I read it very often." He went into his bedroom on saying this, and brought out a pocket Bible, finely bound, and showed it to me. — *Kennedy's Conversations with Lord B.*, p. 135.]

Adam. We have, most fervently.
Cain.   And loudly: I
Have heard you.
Adam.   So will God, I trust.
Abel.   Amen!
Adam. But thou, my eldest born, art silent
  still.
Cain. 'Tis better I should be so.
Adam.   Wherefore so?
Cain. I have nought to ask.
Adam.   Nor aught to thank for?
Cain.   No.
Adam. Dost thou not live?
Cain.   Must I not die?
Eve.   Alas!
The fruit of our forbidden tree begins
To fall.[1]
Adam. And we must gather it again.
Oh, God! why didst thou plant the tree of
  knowledge?
Cain. And wherefore plucked ye not the
  tree of life?
Ye might have then defied him.
Adam.   Oh! my son,
Blaspheme not: these are serpent's words.
Cain.   Why not?
The snake spoke *truth:* it *was* the tree of
  knowledge;
It *was* the tree of life: knowledge is good,
And life is good; and how can both be
  evil?
Eve. My boy! thou speakest as I spoke, in
  sin,
Before thy birth: let me not see renewed
My misery in thine. I have repented.
Let me not see my offspring fall into
The snares beyond the walls of Paradise,
Which e'en in Paradise destroyed his parents.
Content thee with what *is.* Had we been so,
Thou now hadst been contented. — Oh, my
  son!
Adam. Our orisons completed, let us hence,
Each to his task of toil — not heavy, though
Needful: the earth is young, and yields us
  kindly
Her fruits with little labor.
Eve.   Cain, my son,
Behold thy father cheerful and resigned,
And do as he doth. [*Exeunt* ADAM *and* EVE.
Zillah. Wilt thou not, my brother?

---

[1] [This passage affords a key to the temper and frame of mind of Cain throughout the piece. He disdains the limited existence allotted to him; he has a rooted horror of death, attended with a vehement curiosity as to his nature; and he nourishes a sullen anger against his parents, to whose misconduct he ascribes his degraded state. Added to this, he has an insatiable thirst for knowledge beyond the bounds prescribed to mortality; and this part of the poem bears a strong resemblance to Manfred, whose counterpart, indeed, in the main points of character, Cain seems to be. — *Campbell's Magazine.*]

Abel. Why wilt thou wear this gloom upon
  thy brow,
Which can avail thee nothing, save to rouse
The Eternal anger?
Adah.   My beloved Cain,
Wilt thou frown even on me?
Cain.   No, Adah! no,
I fain would be alone a little while.
Abel, I'm sick at heart; but it will pass.
Precede me, brother — I will follow shortly.
And you, too, sisters, tarry not behind;
Your gentleness must not be harshly met:
I'll follow you anon.
Adah.   If not, I will
Return to seek you here.
Abel.   The peace of God
Be on your spirit, brother!
                [*Exeunt* ABEL, ZILLAH, *and* ADAH.
Cain. (*solus*).   And this is
Life! — Toil! and wherefore should I toil? —
  because
My father could not keep his place in Eden.
What had *I* done in this? — I was unborn:
I sought not to be born; nor love the state
To which that birth has brought me. Why
  did he
Yield to the serpent and the woman? or,
Yielding, why suffer? What was there in this?
The tree was planted, and why not for him?
If not, why place him near it, where it grew,
The fairest in the centre? They have but
One answer to all questions, " 'Twas *his* will,
And *he* is good." How know I that? Because
He is all-powerful, must all-good, too, follow?
I judge but by the fruits — and they are bitter—
Which I must feed on for a fault not mine.
Whom have we here? — A shape like to the
  angels,
Yet of a sterner and a sadder aspect
Of spiritual essence: why do I quake?
Why should I fear him more than other spirits,
Whom I see daily wave their fiery swords
Before the gates round which I linger oft,
In twilight's hour, to catch a glimpse of those
Gardens which are my just inheritance,
Ere the night closes o'er the inhibited walls
And the immortal trees which overtop
The cherubim-defended battlements?
If I shrink not from these, the fire-armed an-
  gels,
Why should I quail from him who now ap-
  proaches?
Yet he seems mightier far than them, nor less
Beauteous, and yet not all as beautiful
As he hath been, and might be: sorrow seems
Half of his immortality.[2] And is it
So? and can aught grieve save humanity?
He cometh.

---

[2] [Cain's description of the approach of Lucifer would have shown in the " Paradise Lost." There is something spiritually fine in this conception of the terror of presentiment of coming evil. — *Jeffrey*]

Enter LUCIFER. [1]

Lucifer. Mortal!
Cain. Spirit, who art thou?
Lucifer. Master of spirits.
Cain. And being so, canst thou
Leave them, and walk with dust?
Lucifer. I know the thoughts
Of dust, and feel for it, and with you.
Cain. How!
You know my thoughts?
Lucifer. They are the thoughts of all
Worthy of thought;— 'tis your immortal part
Which speaks within you.
Cain. What immortal part?
This has not been revealed: the tree of life
Was withheld from us by my father's folly,
While that of knowledge, by my mother's haste,
Was plucked too soon; and all the fruit is
death!

[1] [Milton, with true tact and feeling, put no metaphysics into Satan's mouth. There is no querulousness, no sneaking doubts, no petty reasoning in "the Archangel fallen." It is a fine, blunt, sublime, characteristic defiance, that reigns throughout, and animates his character; the spirit is still of celestial birth; and all the evil of his speech and act is utterly neutralized by the impossibility of *man's* feeling any sympathy with it. The Satan of Milton is no half-human devil, with enough of earth about him to typify the malignant sceptic, and enough of heaven to throw a shade of sublimity on his very malignity. The Lucifer of Byron is neither a noble-fiend, nor yet a villain-fiend,— he does nothing, and he seems nothing — there is no poetry either of character or description about him — he is a poor, sneaking, talking devil — a most wretched metaphysician, without wit enough to save him even from the damnation of criticism — he speaks neither poetry nor common sense. Thomas Aquinas would have flogged him more for his bad logic than his unbelief — and St. Dunstan would have caught him by the nose ere the purblind fiend was aware. — *Blackwood.*

The impiety chargeable on this mystery consists mainly in this — that the purposeless and gratuitous blasphemies put into the mouth of Lucifer and Cain are left unrefuted, so that they appear introduced for their own sake, and the design of the writer seems to terminate in them. There is no attempt made to prevent their leaving the strongest possible impression on the reader's mind. On the contrary, the arguments, if such they can be called, levelled against the wisdom and goodness of the Creator are put forth with the utmost ingenuity. And it has been the noble poet's endeavor to palliate as much as possible the characters of the Evil Spirit and of the first Murderer; the former of whom is made an elegant, poetical, philosophical sentimentalist, a sort of Manfred,— the latter an ignorant, proud, and self-willed boy. Lucifer, too, is represented as denying all share in the temptation of Eve, which he throws upon the serpent "in his serpentine capacity;" the author pleading, that he does so, *only* because the book of Genesis has not the most distant allusion to any thing of the kind, and that a reference to the New Testament would be an anachronism. — *Ecl. Rev.*]

Lucifer. They have deceived thee; thou
shalt live.
Cain. I live,
But live to die: and, living, see nothing
To make death hateful, save an innate cling-
ing,
A loathsome, and yet all invincible
Instinct of life, which I abhor, as I
Despise myself, yet cannot overcome —
And so I live. Would I had never lived!
Lucifer. Thou livest, and must live for ever:
The earth, which is thine outward cov'ring, is
Existence— it will cease, and thou wilt be
No less than thou art now.
Cain. No *less!* and why
No more?
Lucifer. It may be thou shalt be as we.
Cain. And ye?
Lucifer. Are everlasting.
Cain. Are ye happy?
Lucifer. We are mighty.
Cain. Are ye happy?
Lucifer. No: art thou?
Cain. How should I be so? Look on me!
Lucifer. Poor clay!
And thou pretendest to be wretched! Thou!
Cain. I am: — and thou, with all thy
might, what art thou?
Lucifer. One who aspired to be what made
thee, and
Would not have made thee what thou art.
Cain. Ah!
Thou look'st almost a god; and ——
Lucifer. I am none:
And having failed to be one, would be nought
Save what I am. He conquered; let him
reign!
Cain. Who?
Lucifer. Thy sire's Maker, and the
earth's.
Cain. And heaven's,
And all that in them is. So I have heard
His seraphs sing; and so my father saith.
Lucifer. They say — what they must sing
and say, on pain
Of being that which I am — and thou art —
Of spirits and of men.
Cain. And what is that?
Lucifer. Souls who dare use their immor-
tality — [2]

[2] [In this long dialogue, the tempter tells Cain (who is thus far supposed to be ignorant of the fact) that the soul is immortal, and that "souls who dare use their immortality" are condemned by God to be wretched everlastingly.* This sentiment, which

* "There is nothing against the immortality or the soul in 'Cain' that I recollect. I hold no such opinions; — but, in a drama, the first rebel and the first murderer must be made to talk according to their characters." — *Byron's Letters.*]

Souls who dare look the Omnipotent tyrant in
His everlasting face, and tell him that
His evil is not good! If he has made,
As he saith — which I know not, nor believe —
But, if he made us — he cannot unmake:
We are immortal! — nay, he'd *have* us so,
That he may torture: — let him! He is
  great —
But, in his greatness, is no happier than
We in our conflict! Goodness would not
  make
Evil; and what else hath he made? But let
  him
Sit on his vast and solitary throne,
Creating worlds, to make eternity
Less burdensome to his immense existence
And unparticipated solitude;
Let him crowd orb on orb: he is alone
Indefinite, indissoluble tyrant; [1]
Could he but crush himself, 'twere the best
  boon
He ever granted: but let him reign on,
And multiply himself in misery!
Spirits and Men, at least we sympathize —
And, suffering in concert, make our pangs
Innumerable, more endurable,
By the unbounded sympathy of all
With all! But *He!* so wretched in his height,
So restless in his wretchedness, must still
Create, and recreate —— [2]
  Cain. Thou speak'st to me of things which
    long have swum
In visions through my thought: I never could
Reconcile what I saw with what I heard.
My father and my mother talk to me
Of serpents, and of fruits and trees: I see
The gates of what they call their Paradise
Guarded by fiery-sworded cherubim,
Which shut them out, and me: I feel the
  weight
Of daily toil, and constant thought: I look
Around a world where I seem nothing, with
Thoughts which arise within me, as if they
Could master all things — but I thought alone

is the pervading *moral* (if we may call it so) of the play, is developed in the lines which follow. — *Heber.*]

[1] [The poet rises to the sublime in making Lucifer first inspire Cain with the knowledge of his immortality — a portion of truth which hath the efficacy of falsehood upon the victim; for Cain, feeling himself already unhappy, knowing that his being cannot be abridged, has the less scruple to desire to be as Lucifer, "mighty." The whole of this speech is truly Satanic; a daring and dreadful description given by everlasting despair of the Deity. — *Galt.*]

[2] [In MS. —
  " Create and recreate — perhaps he'll make
    One day a Son unto himself — as he
    Gave you a Father — and if he so doth,
    Mark me! that Son will be a sacrifice!"]

This misery was *mine.* — My father is
Tamed down; my mother has forgot the mind
Which made her thirst for knowledge at the
  risk
Of an eternal curse; my brother is
A watching shepherd boy, who offers up
The firstlings of the flock to him who bids
The earth yield nothing to us without sweat;
My sister Zillah sings an earlier hymn
Than the birds' matins; and my Adah, my
Own and beloved, she, too, understands not
The mind which overwhelms me: never till
Now met I aught to sympathize with me.
'Tis well — I rather would consort with spirits,
  Lucifer. And hadst thou not been fit by
    thine own soul
For such companionship, I would not now
Have stood before thee as I am: a serpent
Had been enough to charm ye, as before. [3]
  Cain. Ah! didst *thou* tempt my mother?
  Lucifer.   I tempt none,
Save with the truth: was not the tree, the tree
Of knowledge? and was not the tree of life
Still fruitful? Did *I* bid her pluck them not?
Did *I* plant things prohibited within
The reach of beings innocent, and curious
By their own innocence? I would have made
  ye
Gods; and even He who thrust ye forth, so
  thrust ye '
Because "ye should not eat the fruits of life,
And become gods as we." Were those his
  words?
  Cain. They were, as I have heard from
    those who heard them,
In thunder.
  Lucifer.   Then who was the demon? He
Who would not let ye live, or he who would
Have made ye live for ever in the joy
And power of knowledge?
  Cain.   Would they had snatched both
The fruits, or neither!
  Lucifer.   One is yours already,
The other may be still.
  Cain.   How so?
  Lucifer.   By being
Yourselves, in your resistance. Nothing can
Quench the mind, if the mind will be itself
And centre of surrounding things — 'tis made
To sway.
  Cain. But didst thou tempt my parents?
  Lucifer.   I?
Poor clay! what should I tempt them for, or
  how?
  Cain. They say the serpent was a spirit.
  Lucifer.   Who
Saith that? It is not written so on high:
The proud One will not so far falsify,

[3] [MS. —
  " Have stood before thee as I am; but chosen
    The serpent's charming symbol, as before."]

Though man's vast fears and little vanity
Would make him cast upon the spiritual
    nature
His own low failing. The snake *was* the
    snake —
No more; and yet not less than those he
    tempted
In nature being earth also — *more* in *wisdom*,
Since he could overcome them, and foreknew
The knowledge fatal to their narrow joys.
Think'st thou I'd take the shape of things
    that die ?
    Cain. But the thing had a demon ?
    Lucifer.   He but woke one
In those he spake to with his forky tongue.
I tell thee that the serpent was no more
Than a mere serpent: ask the cherubim
Who guard the tempting tree. When thou-
    sand ages
Have rolled o'er your dead ashes, and your
    seed's,
The seed of the then world may thus array
Their earliest fault in fable, and attribute
To me a shape I scorn, as I scorn all
That bows to him, who made things but to
    bend
Before his sullen, sole eternity;
But we who see the truth, must speak it. Thy
Fond parents listened to a creeping thing,
And fell. For what should spirits tempt
    them ? What
Was there to envy in the narrow bounds
Of Paradise, that spirits who pervade
Space —— but I speak to thee of what thou
    know'st not,
With all thy tree of knowledge.
    Cain.   But thou canst not
Speak aught of knowledge which I would not
    know,
And do not thirst to know, and bear a mind
To know.
    Lucifer. And heart to look on ?
    Cain.   Be it proved.
    Lucifer. Darest thou to look on Death ?
    Cain.   He has not yet
Been seen.
    Lucifer. But must be undergone.
    Cain.   My father
Says he is something dreadful, and my
    mother
Weeps when he's named; and Abel lifts his
    eyes
To heaven, and Zillah casts hers to the earth,
And sighs a prayer; and Adah looks on me,
And speaks not.
    Lucifer.   And thou ?
    Cain.   Thoughts unspeakable
Crowd in my breast to burning, when I hear
Of this almighty Death, who is, it seems,
Inevitable. Could I wrestle with him ?
I wrestled with the lion, when a boy,
In play, till he ran roaring from my gripe.

    Lucifer. It has no shape; but will absorb
    all things
That bear the form of earth-born being.
    Cain.   Ah!
I thought it was a being: who could do
Such evil things to beings save a being ?
    Lucifer. Ask the Destroyer.
    Cain.   Who ?
    Lucifer.   The Maker — call him
Which name thou wilt: he makes but to de-
    stroy.
    Cain. I knew not that, yet thought it, since
    I heard
Of death: although I know not what it is,
Yet it seems horrible. I have looked out
In the vast desolate night in search of him;
And when I saw gigantic shadows in
The umbrage of the walls of Eden, chequered
By the far-flashing of the cherubs' swords,
I watched for what I thought his coming; for
With fear rose longing in my heart to know
What 'twas which shook us all — but nothing
    came.
And then I turned my weary eyes from off
Our native and forbidden Paradise,
Up to the lights above us, in the azure,
Which are so beautiful: shall they, too, die ?
    Lucifer. Perhaps — but long outlive both
    thine and thee.
    Cain. I'm glad of that: I would not have
    them die —
They are so lovely. What is death ? I fear,
I feel, it is a dreadful thing; but what,
I cannot compass: 'tis denounced against us,
Both them who sinned and sinned not, as an
    ill —
What ill ?
    Lucifer. To be resolved into the earth.
    Cain. But shall I know it ?
    Lucifer.   As I know not death,
I cannot answer.
    Cain.   Were I quiet earth,
That were no evil: would I ne'er had been
Aught else but dust!
    Lucifer.   That is a grovelling wish,
Less than thy father's, for he wished to know.
    Cain. But not to live, or wherefore plucked
    he not
The life-tree ?
    Lucifer. ·   He was hindered.
    Cain.   Deadly error!
Not to snatch first that fruit: — but ere he
    plucked

---

[1] [It may appear a very prosaic, but it is cer-
tainly a very obvious criticism on these passages,
that the young family of mankind had, long ere
this, been quite familiar with the *death of animals*
— some of whom Abel was in the habit of offering
up as sacrifices; so that it is not quite conceivable
that they should be so much at a loss to conjecture
what *Death* was. — *Jeffrey.*]

The knowledge, he was ignorant of death.
Alas! I scarcely now know what it is,
And yet I fear it — fear I know not what!
  Lucifer. And I, who know all things, fear
      nothing, see
What is true knowledge.
  Cain.   Wilt thou teach me all?
  Lucifer. Ay, upon one condition.
  Cain.   Name it.
  Lucifer.   That
Thou dost fall down and worship me — thy
    Lord.
  Cain. Thou art not the Lord my father
    worships.
  Lucifer.   No.
  Cain.   His equal?
  Lucifer. No; — I have nought in common
    with him!
Nor would: I would be aught above — be-
    neath —
Aught save a sharer or a servant of
His power. I dwell apart; but I am great: —
Many there are who worship me, and more
Who shall — be thou amongst the first.
  Cain.   I never
As yet have bowed unto my father's God,
Although my brother Abel oft implores
That I would join with him in sacrifice: —
Why should I bow to thee?
  Lucifer.   Hast thou ne'er bowed
To him?
  Cain. Have I not said it? — need I say it?
Could not thy mighty knowledge teach thee
    that?
  Lucifer. He who bows not to him has
    bowed to me!
  Cain. But I will bend to neither.
  Lucifer.   Ne'er the less
Thou art my worshipper: not worshipping
Him makes thee mine the same.
  Cain.   And what is that?
  Lucifer. Thou'lt know here — and here-
    after.
  Cain   Let me but
Be taught the mystery of my being.
  Lucifer.   Follow
Where I will lead thee.
  Cain.   But I must retire
To till the earth — for I had promised —
  Lucifer.   What?
  Cain. To cull some first-fruits.
  Lucifer.   Why?
  Cain.   To offer up
With Abel on an altar.
  Lucifer.   Saidst thou not
Thou ne'er hadst bent to him who made
    thee?
  Cain.   Yes —
But Abel's earnest prayer has wrought upon
    me;
The offering is more his than mine — and
    Adah —

  Lucifer. Why dost thou hesitate?
  Cain.   She is my sister,
Born on the same day, of the same womb; and
She wrung from me, with tears, this promise;
    and
Rather than see her weep, I would, methinks,
Bear all — and worship aught.
  Lucifer.   Then follow me!
  Cain. I will.[1]

Enter ADAH.

  Adah.   My brother, I have come for thee;
It is our hour of rest and joy — and we
Have less without thee. Thou hast labored
    not
This morn; but I have done thy task: the
    fruits
Are ripe, and glowing as the light which
    ripens:
Come away.
  Cain.   See'st thou not?
  Adah.   I see an angel;
We have seen many: will he share our hour
Of rest? — he is welcome.
  Cain.   But he is not like
The angels we have seen.
  Adah.   Are there, then, others?
But he is welcome, as they were: they deigned
To be our guests — will he?
  Cain (*to* LUCIFER).   Wilt thou?
  Lucifer.   I ask
Thee to be mine.
  Cain.   I must away with him.
  Adah. And leave us?
  Cain.   Ay.
  Adah.   And me?
  Cain.   Beloved Adah!
  Adah. Let me go with thee.
  Lucifer.   No, she must not.
  Adah.   Who
Art thou that steppest between heart and
    heart?
  Cain. He is a god.
  Adah.   How know'st thou?
  Cain.   He speaks like
A god.
  Adah. So did the serpent, and it lied.
  Lucifer. Thou errest, Adah! — was not
    the tree that
Of knowledge?
  Adah.   Ay — to our eternal sorrow.
  Lucifer. And yet that grief is knowledge —
    so he lied not:
And if he did betray you, 'twas with truth;
And truth in its own essence cannot be
But good.
  Adah. But all we know of it has gathered
Evil on ill: expulsion from our home,
And dread, and toil, and sweat, and heavi-
    ness;

---

[1] [The first interview of Lucifer with Cain is full of sublimity. — *Jeffrey.*]

:emorse of that which was — and hope of that
Vhich cometh not. Cain! walk not with this spirit,
ear with what we have borne, and love me — I
ove thee.
Lucifer. More than thy mother, and thy sire?
Adah. I do. Is that a sin, too?
Lucifer. No, not yet,
: one day will be in your children.
Adah. What!
Iust not my daughter love her brother Enoch?
Lucifer. Not as thou lovest Cain.
Adah. Oh, my God!
hall they not love and bring forth things that love
ut of their love? have they not drawn their milk
ut of this bosom? was not he, their father,
orn of the same sole womb, in the same hour
Vith me? did we not love each other? and
n multiplying our being multiply
hings which will love each other as we love
hem? — And as I love thee, my Cain! go not
orth with this spirit; he is not of ours.
Lucifer. The sin I speak of is not of my making,
nd cannot be a sin in you — whate'er
: seem in those who will replace ye in
ortality.[1]
Adah. What is the sin which is not
n in itself? Can circumstance make sin
r virtue? — if it doth, we are the slaves
f ——
Lucifer. Higher things than ye are slaves: and higher
han them or ye would be so, did they not
efer an independency of torture
o the smooth agonies of adulation,
hymns and harpings, and self-seeking prayers,
o that which is omnipotent, because
is omnipotent, and not from love,
t terror and self-hope.
Adah. Omnipotence
ust be all goodness.
Lucifer. Was it so in Eden?
Adah. Fiend! tempt me not with beauty; thou art fairer
an was the serpent, and as false.
Lucifer. As true.
k Eve, your mother: bears she not the knowledge
good and evil?
Adah. Oh, my mother! thou
ast plucked a fruit more fatal to thine offspring
Than to thyself; thou at the least hast passed
Thy youth in Paradise, in innocent
And happy intercourse with happy spirits:
But we, thy children, ignorant of Eden,
Are girt about by demons, who assume
The words of God, and tempt us with our own
Dissatisfied and curious thoughts — as thou
Wert worked on by the snake, in thy most flushed
And heedless, harmless wantonness of bliss.
I cannot answer this immortal thing
Which stands before me; I cannot abhor him;
I look upon him with a pleasing fear,
And yet I fly not from him: in his eye
There is a fastening attraction which
Fixes my fluttering eyes on his; my heart
Beats quick; he awes me, and yet draws me near,
Nearer and nearer: — Cain — Cain — save me from him!
Cain. What dreads my Adah? This is no ill spirit.
Adah. He is not God — nor God's: I have beheld
The cherubs and the seraphs; he looks not
Like them.
Cain. But there are spirits loftier still —
The archangels.
Lucifer. And still loftier than the archangels.
Adah. Ay — but not blessed.
Lucifer. If the blessedness
Consists in slavery — no.
Adah. I have heard it said,
The seraphs *love most* — cherubim *know most* —
And this should be a cherub — since he loves not.
Lucifer. And if the higher knowledge quenches love,
What must *he be* you cannot love when known?[1]
Since the all-knowing cherubim love least,
The seraphs' love can be but ignorance:
That they are not compatible, the doom
Of thy fond parents, for their daring, proves.
Choose betwixt love and knowledge — since there is
No other choice: your sire hath chosen already;
His worship is but fear.
Adah. Oh, Cain! choose love.
Cain. For thee, my Adah, I choose not — it was
Born with me — but I love nought else.
Adah. Our parents?
Cain. Did they love us when they snatched from the tree

[It is impossible not to be struck with the re-
blance between many of these passages and
ers in *Manfred.*]

[1] [MS. —
"What can *he be* who places love in ignorance?"]

That which hath driven us all from Para-
dise ?
 Adah. We were not born then — and if
we had been,
Should we not love them and our children,
Cain ?
 Cain. My little Enoch! and his lisping
sister!
Could I but deem them happy, I would half
Forget —— but it can never be forgotten
Through thrice a thousand generations! never
Shall men love the remembrance of the man
Who sowed the seed of evil and mankind
In the same hour! They plucked the tree of
science
And sin — and, not content with their own
sorrow,
Begot *me — thee* — and all the few that are,
And all the unnumbered and innumerable
Multitudes, millions, myriads, which may be,
To inherit agonies accumulated
By ages! — and *I* must be sire of such things!
Thy beauty and thy love — my love and joy,
The rapturous moment and the placid hour,
All we love in our children and each other,
But lead them and ourselves through many
years
Of sin and pain — or few, but still of sorrow,
Interchecked with an instant of brief pleasure,
To Death — the unknown! Methinks the tree
of knowledge
Hath not fulfilled its promise: — if they sinned,
At least they ought to have known all things
that are
Of knowledge — and the mystery of death.
What do they know? — that they are miserable.
What need of snakes and fruits to teach us
that ?
 Adah. I am not wretched, Cain, and if thou
Wert happy ——
 Cain. Be thou happy, then, alone —
I will have nought to do with happiness,
Which humbles me and mine.
 Adah. Alone I could not,
Nor *would* be happy: but with those around
us
I think I could be so, despite of death,
Which, as I know it not, I dread not, though
It seems an awful shadow — if I may
Judge from what I have heard.
 Lucifer. And thou couldst not
Alone, thou say'st, be happy ?
 Adah. Alone! Oh, my God!
Who could be happy and alone, or good ?
To me my solitude seems sin; unless
When I think how soon I shall see my brother,
His brother, and our children, and our parents.
 Lucifer. Yet thy God is alone; and is he
happy,
Lonely, and good ?
 Adah. He is not so; he hath
The angels and the mortals to make happy,

And thus becomes so in diffusing joy;
What else can joy be, but the spreading joy ?
 Lucifer. Ask of your sire, the exile fresh
from Eden;
Or of his first-born son: ask your own heart;
It is not tranquil.
 Adah. Alas! no! and you —
Are you of heaven ?
 Lucifer. If I am not, inquire
The cause of this all-spreading happiness
(Which you proclaim) of the all-great and
good
Maker of life and living things; it is
His secret, and he keeps it. *We* must bear,
And some of us resist, and both in vain,
His seraphs say: but it is worth the trial,
Since better may not be without: there is
A wisdom in the spirit, which directs
To right, as in the dim blue air the eye
Of you, young mortals, lights at once upon
The star which watches, welcoming the morn.
 Adah. It is a beautiful star; I love it for
Its beauty.
 Lucifer. And why not adore ?
 Adah. Our father
Adores the Invisible only.
 Lucifer. But the symbols
Of the Invisible are the loveliest
Of what is visible; and yon bright star
Is leader of the host of heaven.
 Adah. Our father
Saith that he has beheld the God himself
Who made him and our mother.
 Lucifer. Hast *thou* seen him ?
 Adah. Yes — in his works.
 Lucifer. But in his being ?
 Adah. No —
Save in my father, who is God's own image;
Or in his angels, who are like to thee —
And brighter, yet less beautiful and powerful
In seeming: as the silent sunny noon,
All light, they look upon us; but thou seem'st
Like an ethereal night, where long white clouds
Streak the deep purple, and unnumbered stars
Spangle the wonderful mysterious vault
With things that look as if they would be suns;
So beautiful, unnumbered, and endearing,
Not dazzling, and yet drawing us to them,
They fill my eyes with tears, and so dost thou.
Thou seem'st unhappy: do not make us so,
And I will weep for thee.[1]

---

[1] [In the drawing of Cain himself, there is much
vigorous expression. It seems, however, as if, in
the effort to give to Lucifer that " spiritual polite-
ness" which the poet professes to have in view, he
has reduced him rather below the standard of dia-
bolic dignity, which was necessary to his dramatic
interest. He has scarcely "given the devil his
due." We thought Lord Byron knew better. Mil-
ton's Satan, with his faded majesty, and blasted but
not obliterated glory, holds us suspended between
terror and amazement, with something like awe of
his spiritual essence and lost estate; but Lord Byron

Lucifer.   Alas! those tears!
Could'st thou but know what oceans will be
     shed ——
    Adah.   By me?
    Lucifer.   By all.
    Adah.   What all?
    Lucifer.   The million millions —
The myriad myriads — the all-peopled earth —
The unpeopled earth — and the o'er-peopled
     Hell,
Of which thy bosom is the germ.
    Adah.   O Cain!
This spirit curseth us.
    Cain.   Let him say on;
Him will I follow.
    Adah.   Whither?
    Lucifer.   To a place
Whence he shall come back to thee in an hour;
But in that hour see things of many days.
    Adah.   How can that be?
    Lucifer.   Did not your Maker make
Out of old worlds this new one in few days?
And cannot I, who aided in this work,
Show in an hour what he hath made in many,
Or hath destroyed in few?
    Cain.   Lead on.
    Adah.   Will he,
In sooth, return within an hour?
    Lucifer.   He shall.
With us acts are exempt from time, and we
Can crowd eternity into an hour,
Or stretch an hour into eternity:
We breathe not by a mortal measurement —
But that's a mystery. Cain, come on with
     me.
    Adah.   Will he return?
    Lucifer.   Ay, woman! he alone
Of mortals from that place (the first and last
Who shall return, save ONE), shall come back
     to thee,
To make that silent and expectant world
As populous as this : at present there
Are few inhabitants.
    Adah.   Where dwellest thou?
    Lucifer.   Throughout all space. Where
     should I dwell?   Where are
Thy God or Gods — there am I : all things are
Divided with me ; life and death — and time —
Eternity — and heaven and earth — and that
Which is not heaven nor earth, but peopled
     with
Those who once peopled or shall people
     both —
These are my realms! So that I do divide
His, and possess a kingdom which is not
His. If I were not that which I have said,

has introduced him to us as elegant, pensive, and
beautiful, with an air of sadness and suffering that
ranks him with the oppressed, and bespeaks our
pity. Thus, in this dialogue with Adah, he comes
forth to our view so qualified as to engage our sym-
pathies. — *Brit. Crit.*]

Could I stand here? His angels are within
Your vision.
    Adah.   So they were when the fair serpent
Spoke with our mother first.
    Lucifer.   Cain! thou hast heard.
If thou dost long for knowledge, I can satiate
That thirst ; nor ask thee to partake of fruits
Which shall deprive thee of a single good
The conqueror has left thee. Follow me.
    Cain.   Spirit, I have said it.
                [*Exeunt* LUCIFER *and* CAIN.
    Adah (*follows, exclaiming*). Cain! my
     brother! Cain!

——

ACT II.

   SCENE I.— *The Abyss of Space.*

    Cain.   I tread on air, and sink not; yet I
     fear to sink.
    Lucifer.   Have faith in me, and thou shalt
     be
Borne on the air, of which I am the prince.
    Cain.   Can I do so without impiety?
    Lucifer.   Believe — and sink not! doubt —
     and perish! thus
Would run the edict of the other God,
Who names me demon to his angels ; they
Echo the sound to miserable things,
Which, knowing nought beyond their shall
     low senses,
Worship the word which strikes their ear, and
     deem
Evil or good what is proclaimed to them
In their abasement. I will have none such :
Worship or worship not, thou shalt behold
The worlds beyond thy little world, nor be
Amerced for doubts beyond thy little life,
With torture of *my* dooming. There will
     come
An hour, when, tossed upon some water-
     drops,[1]
A man shall say to a man, " Believe in me,
And walk the waters ; " and the man shall
     walk
The billows and be safe. *I* will not say,
Believe in *me,* as a conditional creed
To save thee ; but fly with me o'er the gulf
Of space an equal flight, and I will show
What thou dar'st not deny, — the history
Of past, and present, and of future worlds.
    Cain.   Oh, god, or demon, or whate'er
     thou art,
Is yon our earth?
    Lucifer.   Dost thou not recognize
The dust which formed your father?
    Cain.   Can it be?
Yon small blue circle, swimming in far ether,
With an inferior circlet near it still,

   [1] [MS. —

    " An hour, when, walking on a pretty lake."]

Which looks like that which lit our earthly
   night ?
Is this our Paradise ? Where are its walls,
And they who guard them ?
Lucifer.   Point me out the site
Of Paradise.
Cain.   How should I ? As we move
Like sunbeams onward, it grows small and
   smaller,
And as it waxes little, and then less,
Gathers a halo round it, like the light
Which shone the roundest of the stars, when I
Beheld them from the skirts of Paradise :
Methinks they both, as we recede from them,
Appear to join the innumerable stars
Which are around us ; and, as we move on,
Increase their myriads.
Lucifer.   And if there should be
Worlds greater than thine own, inhabited
By greater things, and they themselves far
   more
In number than the dust of thy dull earth,
Though multiplied to animated atoms,
All living, and all doomed to death, and
   wretched,
What wouldst thou think ?
Cain.   I should be proud of thought
Which knew such things.
Lucifer.   But if that high thought were
Linked to a servile mass of matter, and,
Knowing such things, aspiring to such things,
And science still beyond them, were chained
   down
To the most gross and petty paltry wants,
All foul and fulsome, and the very best
Of thine enjoyments a sweet degradation,
A most enervating and filthy cheat
To lure thee on to the renewal of
Fresh souls and bodies, all foredoomed to be
As frail, and few so happy —[1]

Cain.   Spirit ! I
Know nought of death, save as a dreadful
   thing
Of which I have heard my parents speak,
   as of
A hideous heritage I owe to them
No less than life ; a heritage not happy,
If I may judge, till now. But, spirit ! if
It be as thou hast said (and I within
Feel the prophetic torture of its truth),
Here let me die : for to give birth to those
Who can but suffer many years, and die,
Methinks is merely propagating death,
And multiplying murder.
Lucifer.   Thou canst not
All die — there is what must survive.
Cain.   The Other
Spake not of this unto my father, when
He shut him forth from Paradise, with death
Written upon his forehead. But at least
Let what is mortal of me perish, that
I may be in the rest as angels are.
Lucifer. *I* am angelic : wouldst thou be as
   I am ?
Cain. I know not what thou art : I see
   thy power
And see thou show'st me things beyond *my*
   power,
Beyond all power of my born faculties,
Although inferior still to my desires
And my conceptions.
Lucifer.   What are they which dwell
So humbly in their pride, as to sojourn
With worms in clay ?
Cain.   And what art thou who dwellest
So haughtily in spirit, and canst range
Nature and immortality — and yet
Seem'st sorrowful ?
Lucifer.   I seem that which I am ;

[1] [It is nothing less than absurd to suppose, that Lucifer cannot well be expected to talk like an orthodox divine, and that the conversation of the first Rebel and the first Murderer was not likely to be very unexceptionable ; or to plead the authority of Milton, or the authors of the old mysteries, for such offensive colloquies. The fact is, that *here* the whole argument — and a very *elaborate** and specious argument it is — is directed against the goodness or the power of the Deity ; and there is no answer so much as attempted to the offensive doctrines that are so strenuously inculcated. The Devil and his pupil have the field entirely to themselves, and are encountered with nothing but feeble obtestations and unreasoning horrors. Nor is this argumentative blasphemy a mere incidental deformity that arises in the course of an action directed to the common sympathies of our nature. It forms, on the contrary, the great staple of the piece, and occupies, we should think, not less than two thirds of it ; so that it is really difficult to believe that it was written for any other purpose than to inculcate these doctrines ; or, at least, to discuss the question upon which they bear. Now, we can certainly have no objection to Lord Byron writing an essay on the origin of evil, and sifting the whole of that vast and perplexing subject, with the force and the freedom that would be expected and allowed in a fair philosophical discussion ; but we do not think it fair thus to argue it partially and *con amore*, in the name of Lucifer and Cain, without the responsibility or the liability to answer, that would attach to a philosophical disputant ; and in a form which bo,b doubles the danger, if the sentiments are pernicious, and almost precludes his opponents from the possibility of a reply. — *Jeffrey.*]

* "What does Jeffrey mean by *elaborate ?* Why ! they were written as fast as I could put pen to paper, in the midst of evolutions, and revolutions, and persecutions, and proscriptions of all who interested me in Italy. They said the same of 'Lara,' which I wrote while undressing, after coming home from balls and masquerades. Of all I have ever written, they are perhaps the most carelessly composed ; and their faults, whatever they may be, are those of negligence, and not of labor. I do not think this is a merit, but it is a fact." — *Byron's Letters.*

And therefore do I ask of thee, if thou
Wouldst be immortal?
    Cain.   Thou hast said, I must be
Immortal in despite of me. I knew not
This until lately — but since it must be,
Let me, or happy or unhappy, learn
To anticipate my immortality.
    Lucifer. Thou didst before I came upon
    thee.
    Cain. How?
    Lucifer. By suffering.
    Cain.   And must torture be immortal?
    Lucifer. We and thy sons will try. But
    now, behold!
Is it not glorious?
    Cain.   Oh, thou beautiful
And unimaginable ether! and
Ye multiplying masses of increased
And still increasing lights! what are ye? what
Is this blue wilderness of interminable
Air, where ye roll along, as I have seen
The leaves along the limpid streams of Eden?
Is your course measured for ye? Or do ye
Sweep on in your unbounded revelry
Through an aërial universe of endless
Expansion — at which my soul aches to think—
Intoxicated with eternity?
Oh God! Oh Gods! or whatsoe'er ye are!
How beautiful ye are! how beautiful
Your works, or accidents, or whatsoe'er
They may be! Let me die, as atoms die,
(If that they die) or know ye in your might
And knowledge! My thoughts are not in this
    hour
Unworthy what I see, though my dust is;
Spirit! let me expire, or see them nearer.
    Lucifer. Art thou not nearer? look back
    to thine earth!
    Cain. Where is it? I see nothing save a
    mass
Of most innumerable lights.
    Lucifer.   Look there!
    Cain. I cannot see it.
    Lucifer.   Yet it sparkles still.
    Cain. That! — yonder!
    Lucifer.   Yea.
    Cain.   And wilt thou tell me so?
Why, I have seen the fire-flies and fire-worms
Sprinkle the dusky groves and the green banks
In the dim twilight, brighter than yon world
Which bears them.
    Lucifer. Thou hast seen both worms and
    worlds,
Each bright and sparkling — what dost think
    of them?
    Cain. That they are beautiful in their own
    sphere,
And that the night, which makes both beautiful,
The little shining fire-fly in its flight,
And the immortal star in its great course,
Must both be guided.
    Lucifer.   But by whom or what?

    Cain. Show me.
    Lucifer.   Dar'st thou behold?
    Cain.   How know I what
I *dare* behold? As yet, thou hast shown
    nought
I dare not gaze on further.
    Lucifer.   On, then, with me,
Wouldst thou behold things mortal or im-
    mortal?
    Cain. Why, what are things?
    Lucifer.   Both partly: but what doth
Sit next thy heart?
    Cain.   The things I see.
    Lucifer.   But what
Sate nearest it?
    Cain.   The things I have not seen,
Nor ever shall — the mysteries of death.
    Lucifer. What, if I show to thee things
    which have died,
As I have shown thee much which cannot die?
    Cain. Do so.
    Lucifer. Away, then! on our mighty wings.
    Cain. Oh! how we cleave the blue! the
    stars fade from us!
The earth! where is my earth? Let me look
    on it,
For I was made of it.
    Lucifer.   'Tis now beyond thee,
Less, in the universe, than thou in it;
Yet deem not that thou canst escape it; thou
Shalt soon return to earth, and all its dust;
'Tis part of thy eternity, and mine.
    Cain. Where dost thou lead me?
    Lucifer.   To what was before thee!
The phantasm of the world; of which thy
    world
Is but the wreck.
    Cain.   What! is it not then new?
    Lucifer. No more than life is; and that
    was ere thou
Or *I* were, or the things which seem to us
Greater than either: many things will have
No end; and some, which would pretend to
    have
Had no beginning, have had one as mean
As thou; and mightier things have been ex-
    tinct
To make way for much meaner than we can
Surmise; for *moments* only and the *space*
Have been and must be all *unchangeable.*
But changes make not death, except to clay;
But thou art clay — and canst but comprehend
That which was clay, and such thou shalt be-
    hold.
    Cain. Clay, spirit! what thou wilt, I can
    survey.
    Lucifer. Away, then!
    Cain.   But the lights fade from me fast
And some till now grew larger as we ap-
    proached,
And wore the look of worlds.
    Lucifer.   And such they are,

Cain. And Edens in them?
Lucifer.   It may be.
Cain.   And men?
Lucifer. Yea, or things higher.
Cain.   Ay? and serpents too?
Lucifer. Wouldst thou have men without
them? must no reptiles ·
Breathe, save the erect ones?
Cain.   How the lights recede!
Where fly we?
Lucifer. To the world of phantoms, which
Are beings past, and shadows still to come.
Cain. But it grows dark, and dark — the
stars are gone!
Lucifer. And yet thou seest.
Cain.   'Tis a fearful light!
No sun, no moon, no lights innumerable.
The very blue of the empurpled night
Fades to a dreary twilight, yet I see
Huge dusky masses; but unlike the worlds
We were approaching, which, begirt with light,
Seemed full of life even when their atmosphere
Of light gave way, and showed them taking
. shapes
Unequal, of deep valleys and vast mountains;
And some emitting sparks, and some display-
ing   •   .
Enormous liquid plains, and some begirt
With luminous belts, and floating moons,
which took,
Like them, the features of fair earth: — instead,
All here seems dark and dreadful.
Lucifer.   But distinct.
Thou seekest to behold death, and dead
things?
Cain. I seek it not; but as I know there
are
Such, and that my sire's sin makes him and me,
And all that we inherit, liable
To such, I would behold at once, what I
Must one day see perforce.
Lucifer.   Behold!
Cain.   'Tis darkness.
Lucifer. And so it shall be ever; but we will
Unfold its gates!
Cain.   Enormous vapors roll
Apart — what's this?
Lucifer.   Enter!
Cain.   Can I return?
Lucifer. Return! be sure: how else should
death be peopled?
Its present realm is thin to what it will be,
Through thee and thine.
Cain.   The clouds still open wide
And wider, and make widening circles round
us.
Lucifer. Advance!
Cain.   And thou!
Lucifer.   Fear not — without me thou
Couldst not have gone beyond thy world.
On! on!
          [*They disappear through the clouds.*

SCENE II. — *Hades.*

Enter LUCIFER *and* CAIN.

Cain. How silent and how vast are these
dim worlds!
For they seem more than one, and yet more
peopled
Than the huge brilliant luminous orbs which
swung
So thickly in the upper air, that I
Had deemed them rather the bright populace
Of some all unimaginable Heaven,
Than things to be inhabited themselves,
But that on drawing near them I beheld
Their swelling into palpable immensity
Of matter, which seemed made for life to dwell
on
Rather than life itself. But here, all is
So shadowy and so full of twilight, that
It speaks of a day past.
Lucifer.   It is the realm
Of death. — Wouldst have it present?
Cain.   Till I know
That which it really is, I cannot answer.
But if it be as I have heard my father
Deal out in his long homilies, 'tis a thing —
Oh God! I dare not think on't! Cursed be
He who invented life that leads to death!
Or the dull mass of life, that, being life,
Could not retain, but needs must forfeit it —
Even for the innocent!
Lucifer.   Dost thou curse thy father?
Cain. Cursed he not me in giving me my
birth?
Cursed he not me before my birth, in daring
To pluck the fruit forbidden?
Lucifer.   Thou say'st well:
The curse is mutual 'twixt thy sire and thee —
But for thy sons and brother?
Cain.   Let them share it
With me, their sire and brother! What else is
Bequeathed to me? I leave them my inher-
itance.
Oh, ye interminable gloomy realms
Of swimming shadows and enormous shapes,
Some fully shown, some indistinct, and all
Mighty and melancholy — what are ye?
Live ye, or have ye lived?
Lucifer.   Somewhat of both.
Cain. Then what is death?
Lucifer. What? Hath not he who made ye
Said 'tis another life?
Cain.   Till now he hath
Said nothing, save that all shall die.
Lucifer.   Perhaps
He one day will unfold that further secret.
Cain. Happy the day!
Lucifer.   Yes; happy! when unfolded,
Through agonies unspeakable, and clogged
With agonies eternal, to innumerable
Yet unborn myriads of unconscious atoms
All to be animated for this only!

Cain. What are these mighty phantoms
  which I see
Floating around me? — They wear not the
  form
Of the intelligences I have seen
Round our regretted and unentered Eden,
Nor wear the form of man as I have viewed it
In Adam's and in Abel's, and in mine,
Nor in my sister-bride's, nor in my children's;
And yet they have an aspect, which, though not
Of man nor angels, looks like something, which
If not the last, rose higher than the first,
Haughty, and high, and beautiful, and full
Of seeming strength, but of inexplicable
Shape; for I never saw such. They bear not
The wing of seraph, nor the face of man,
Nor form of mightiest brute, nor aught that is
Now breathing; mighty yet and beautiful
As the most beautiful and mighty which
Live, and yet so unlike them, that I scarce
Can call them living.
  Lucifer.   Yet they lived.
  Cain.   Where?
  Lucifer.   Where
Thou livest.
  Cain.   When?
  Lucifer.   On what thou callest earth
They did inhabit.
  Cain.   Adam is the first.
  Lucifer. Of thine, I grant thee — but too
    mean to be
The last of these.
  Cain.   And what are they?
  Lucifer.   That which
Thou shalt be.
  Cain.   But what *were* they?
  Lucifer.   Living, high,
Intelligent, good, great, and glorious things,
As much superior unto all thy sire,
Adam, could e'er have been in Eden, as
The sixty-thousandth generation shall be,
In its dull damp degeneracy, to
Thee and thy son; — and how weak they are,
    judge
By thy own flesh.
  Cain.   Ah me! and did *they* perish?
  Lucifer. Yes, from their earth, as thou wilt
    fade from thine.
  Cain. But was *mine* theirs?
  Lucifer.   It was.
  Cain.   But not as now.
It is too little and too lowly to
Sustain such creatures.[1]

  Lucifer.   True, it was more glorious.
  Cain. And wherefore did it fall?
  Lucifer.   Ask him who fells.
  Cain. But how?
  Lucifer. By a most crushing and inexorable
Destruction and disorder of the elements,
Which struck a world to chaos, as a chaos
Subsiding has struck out a world: such things,
Though rare in time, are frequent in eternity. —
Pass on, and gaze upon the past.
  Cain.   'Tis awful!
  Lucifer. And true. Behold these phantoms!
    they were once
Material as thou art.
  Cain.   And must I be
Like them?
  Lucifer. Let He who made thee answer
    that.
I show thee what thy predecessors are,.
And what they *were* thou feelest, in degree
Inferior as thy petty feelings and
Thy pettier portion of the immortal part
Of high intelligence and earthly strength.
What ye in common have with what they had
Is life, and what ye *shall* have — death: the
    rest
Of your poor attributes is such as suits
Reptiles engendered out of the subsiding
Slime of a mighty universe, crushed into
A scarcely-yet shaped planet, peopled with
Things whose enjoyment was to be in blind-
    ness —
A Paradise of Ignorance, from which
Knowledge was barred as poison. But behold
What these superior beings are or were;
Or, if it irk thee, turn thee back and till
The earth, thy task — I'll waft thee there in
    safety.
  Cain. No: I'll stay here.
  Lucifer.   How long?
  Cain.   Forever! Since
I must one day return here from the earth,
I rather would remain; I am sick of all
That dust has shown me — let me dwell in
    shadows.
  Lucifer. It cannot be: thou now beholdest
    as
A vision that which is reality.
To make thyself fit for this dwelling, thou
Must pass through what the things thou see'st
    have passed —
The gates of death.

---

[1] [" If, according to some speculations, you could prove the world many thousand years older than the Mosaic chronology — or if you could knock up Adam and Eve, and the Apple and Serpent — still, what is to be put up in their stead? — or how is the difficulty removed? Things must have had a beginning: and what matters it *when*, or *how?* I sometimes think that man may be the relic of some higher material being wrecked in a former world, and degenerated in the hardship and struggle through chaos into conformity, or something like it — as we see Laplanders, Esquimaux, etc., inferior, in the present date, as the elements become more inexorable. But even then, this higher pre-Adamite supposititious creation must have had an origin and a Creator; for a Creator is a more natural imagination than a fortuitous concourse of atoms: all things remount to a fountain, though they may flow to an ocean." — *Byron's Diary*, 1821.]

Cain.   By what gate have we entered
Even now?
   Lucifer.   By mine! But, plighted to return,
Mv spirit buoys thee up to breathe in regions
Where all is breathless save thyself. Gaze on,
But do not think to dwell here till thine hour
Is come.
   Cain.   And these, too; can they ne'er repass
To earth again?
   Lucifer.   *Their* earth is gone for ever —
So changed by its convulsion, they would not
Be conscious to a single present spot
Of its new scarcely hardened surface — 'twas —
Oh, what a beautiful world it *was!* [1]
   Cain.   And is.
It is not with the earth, though I must till it,
I feel at war, but that I may not profit
By what it bears of beautiful, untoiling,
Nor gratify my thousand swelling thoughts
With knowledge, nor allay my thousand fears
Of death and life.
   Lucifer.   What thy world is, thou see'st,
But canst not comprehend the shadow of
That which it was.
   Cain.   And those enormous creatures,
Phantoms inferior in intelligence
(At least so seeming) to the things we have
passed,
Resembling somewhat the wild habitants

---

[1] [Mr. Gifford having, through Mr. Murray, suggested the propriety of omitting a portion of this dialogue, Byron replied: — "The two passages cannot be altered without making Lucifer talk like the Bishop of London, which would not be in the character of the former. The notion is from Cuvier (that of the *old worlds*). The other passage is also in character; if *nonsense*, so much the better, because then it can do no harm; and the sillier Satan is made, the safer for everybody. As to 'alarms,' etc., do you really think such things ever led anybody astray? Are these people more impious than Milton's Satan? or the Prometheus of Æschylus? or even than the 'Sadducees,' the 'Fall of Jerusalem' of Milman, etc.? Are not Adam, Eve, Adah, and Abel, as pious as the Catechism? Gifford is too wise a man to think that such things can have any serious effect: who was ever altered by a poem? I beg leave to observe, that there is no creed or personal hypothesis of mine in all this; but I was obliged to make Cain and Lucifer talk consistently, and surely this has always been permitted to poesy. Cain is a proud man: if Lucifer promised him kingdom, etc., it would *elate* him: the object of the demon is to *depress* him still further in his own estimation than he was before, by showing him infinite things and his own abasement, till he falls into the frame of mind that leads to the catastrophe, from mere *internal* irritation, not premeditation, or envy of *Abel* (which would have made him contemptible), but from rage and fury against the inadequacy of his state to his conceptions, and which discharges itself rather against life, and the Author of life, than the mere living. His subsequent remorse is the natural effect of looking on his sudden deed. Had the deed been *premeditated*, his repentance would have been tardier."]

Of the deep woods of earth, the hugest which
Roar nightly in the forest, but ten-fold
In magnitude and terror; taller than
The cherub-guarded walls of Eden, with
Eyes flashing like the fiery swords which fence
   them,
And tusks projecting like the trees stripped of
Their bark and branches — what were they?
   Lucifer.   That which
The Mammoth is in thy world; — but these
   lie
By myriads underneath its surface.
   Cain.   But
None on it?
   Lucifer.   No: for thy frail race to war
With them would render the curse on it use-
   less —
'Twould be destroyed so early.
   Cain.   But why *war?*
   Lucifer.   You have forgotten the denuncia-
tion
Which drove your race from Eden — war
   with all things,
And death to all things, and disease to most
   things,
And pangs, and bitterness; these were the
   fruits
Of the forbidden tree.
   Cain.   ,   But animals —
Did they, too, eat of it, that they must die?
   Lucifer.   Your Maker told ye, *they* were
made for you
As you for him. — You would not have their
   doom
Superior to your own? Had Adam not
Fallen, all had stood.
   Cain.   Alas! the hopeless wretches!
They too must share my sire's fate, like his
   sons;
Like them, too, without having shared the
   apple;
Like them, too, without the so dear-bought
   knowledge!
It was a lying tree — for we *know* nothing.
At least it *promised knowledge* at the *price*
Of death — but *knowledge* still : but what *knows*
   man?
   Lucifer.   It may be death leads to the *high-*
   est knowledge;
And being of all things the sole thing certain,
At least leads to the *surest* science: therefore
The tree was true, though deadly.
   Cain.   These dim realms!
I see them, but I know them not.
   Lucifer.   Because
Thy hour is yet afar, and matter cannot
Comprehend spirit wholly — but 'tis some-
   thing
To know there are such realms.
   Cain.   We knew already
That there was death.
   Lucifer.   But not what was beyond it.

_J

Cain. Nor know I now.
Lucifer. Thou knowest that there is
A state, and many states beyond thine own —
And this thou knewest not this morn.
Cain. But all
Seems dim and shadowy.
Lucifer. Be content; it will
Seem clearer to thine immortality.
Cain. And yon immeasurable liquid space
Of glorious azure which floats on beyond us,
Which looks like water, and which I should
deem
The river which flows out of Paradise
Past my own dwelling, but that it is bankless
And boundless, and of an ethereal hue —
What is it?
Lucifer. There is still some such on earth,
Although inferior, and thy children shall
Dwell near it — 'tis the phantasm of an ocean.
Cain. 'Tis like another world; a liquid
sun —
And those inordinate creatures sporting o'er
Its shining surface?
Lucifer. Are its habitants,
The past leviathans.
Cain. And yon immense
Serpent, which rears his dripping mane and
vasty
Head ten times higher than the haughtiest
cedar
Forth from the abyss, looking as he could coil
Himself around the orbs we lately looked on —
Is he not of the kind which basked beneath
The tree in Eden?
Lucifer. Eve, thy mother, best
Can tell what shape of serpent tempted her.
Cain. This seems too terrible. No doubt
the other
Had more of beauty.
Lucifer. Hast thou ne'er beheld him?
Cain. Many of the same kind (at least so
called),
But never that precisely which persuaded
The fatal fruit, nor even of the same aspect.
Lucifer. Your father saw him not?
Cain. No: 'twas my mother
Who tempted him — she tempted by the ser-
pent.
Lucifer. Good man! whene'er thy wife,
or thy sons' wives,
Tempt thee or them to aught that's new or
strange,
Be sure thou see'st first who hath tempted *them.*
Cain. Thy precept comes too late: there
is no more
For serpents to tempt women to.
Lucifer. But there
Are some things still which woman may tempt
man to,
And man tempt woman: — let thy sons look
to it!
My counsel is a kind one; for 'tis even

Given chiefly at my own expense; 'tis true,
'Twill not be followed, so there's little lost.
Cain. I understand not this.
Lucifer. The happier thou! —
Thy world and thou are still too young! Thou
thinkest
Thyself most wicked and unhappy: is it
Not so?
Cain. For crime, I know not; but for pain,
I have felt much.
Lucifer. First-born of the first man!
Thy present state of sin — and thou art evil,
Of sorrow — and thou sufferest, are both Eden
In all its innocence compared to what
Thou shortly may'st be; and that state again,
In its redoubled wretchedness, a Paradise
To what thy sons' sons' sons, accumulating
In generations like to dust (which they
In fact but add to), shall endure and do. —
Now let us back to earth!
Cain. And wherefore didst thou
Lead me here only to inform me this?
Lucifer. Was not thy quest for knowledge?
Cain. Yes: as being
The road to happiness.
Lucifer. If truth be so,
Thou hast it.
Cain. Then my father's God did well
When he prohibited the fatal tree.
Lucifer. But had done better in not plant-
ing it.
But ignorance of evil doth not save
From evil; it must still roll on the same,
A part of all things.
Cain. Not of all things. No:
I'll not believe it — for I thirst for good.
Lucifer. And who and what doth not?
Who covets evil
For its own bitter sake? — *none* — nothing! 'tis
The leaven of all life, and lifelessness.
Cain. Within those glorious orbs which
we behold,
Distant and dazzling, and innumerable,
Ere we came down into this phantom realm,
Ill cannot come: they are too beautiful.
Lucifer. Thou hast seen them from afar —
Cain. And what of that?
Distance can but diminish glory — they,
When nearer, must be more ineffable.
Lucifer. Approach the things of earth most
beautiful,
And judge their beauty near.
Cain. I have done this —
The loveliest thing I know is loveliest nearest.
Lucifer. Then there must be delusion. —
What is that,
Which being nearest to thine eyes is still
More beautiful than beauteous things remote?
Cain. My sister Adah. — All the stars of
heaven,
The deep blue noon of night, lit by an orb
Which looks a spirit, or a spirit's world —

The hues of twilight — the sun's gorgeous
   coming —
His setting indescribable, which fills
My eyes with pleasant tears as I behold
Him sink, and feel my heart float softly with
   him
Along that western paradise of clouds —
The forest shade — the green bough — the
   bird's voice —
The vesper bird's, which seems to sing of love,
And mingles with the song of cherubim,
As the day closes over Eden's walls ; —
All these are nothing, to my eyes and heart,
Like Adah's face : I turn from earth and
   heaven
To gaze on it.
   Lucifer. 'Tis fair as frail mortality,
In the first dawn and bloom of young creation
And earliest embraces of earth's parents,
Can make its offspring ; still it is delusion.
   Cain. You think so, being not her brother.
   Lucifer.   Mortal !
My brotherhood's with those who have no
   children.
   Cain. Then thou canst have no fellowship
   with us.
   Lucifer. It may be that thine own shall be
   for me.
But if thou dost possess a beautiful
Being beyond all beauty in thine eyes,
Why art thou wretched ?
   Cain.   Why do I exist ?
Why art *thou* wretched ? why are all things so ?
Ev'n he who made us must be, as the maker
Of things unhappy ! To produce destruction
Can surely never be the task of joy,
And yet my sire says he's omnipotent :
Then why is evil — he being good ? I asked
This question of my father ; and he said,
Because this evil only was the path
To good. Strange good, that must arise
   from out
Its deadly opposite.[1] I lately saw
A lamb stung by a reptile : the poor suckling
Lay foaming on the earth, beneath the vain
And piteous bleating of its restless dam ;
My father plucked some herbs, and laid them to
The wound ; and by degrees the helpless wretch
Resumed its careless life, and rose to drain
The mother's milk, who o'er it tremulous
Stood licking its reviving limbs with joy.

---

[1] [" God Almighty !
There is some soul of goodness in things evil,
Would men observingly distil it out :
For our bad neighbors make us early stirrers,
Which is both healthful and good husbandry ;
Besides, they are our outward consciences,
And preachers to us all ; admonishing,
That we should dress us fairly for our end.
Thus may we gather honey from the weed,
And make a moral of the devil himself."
                  Shakspeare.]

Behold, my son ! said Adam, how from evil
Springs good !
   Lucifer. What didst thou answer?
   Cain.   Nothing ; for
He is my father : but I thought, that 'twere
A better portion for the animal
Never to have been *stung at all*, than to
Purchase renewal of its little life
With agonies unutterable, though
Dispelled by antidotes.
   Lucifer. ·   But as thou saidst
Of all beloved things thou lovest her
Who shared thy mother's milk, and giveth hers
Unto thy children ——
   Cain.   Most assuredly :
What should I be without her ?
   Lucifer.   What am I ?
   Cain. Dost thou love nothing ?
   Lucifer.   What does thy God love ?
   Cain. All things, my father says ; but I
   confess
I see it not in their allotment here.
   Lucifer. And, therefore, thou canst not see
   if *I* love
Or no, except some vast and general purpose,
To which particular things must melt like snows.
   Cain. Snows ! what are they ?
   Lucifer. Be happier in not knowing
What thy remoter offspring must encounter :
But bask beneath the clime which knows no
   winter.
   Cain. But dost thou not love something
   like thyself ?
   Lucifer. And dost thou love *thyself ?*
   Cain.   Yes, but love more
What makes my feelings more endurable,
And is more than myself, because I love it.
   Lucifer. Thou lovest it, because 'tis beau-
   tiful,
As was the apple in thy mother's eye ;
And when it ceases to be so, thy love
Will cease, like any other appetite.
   Cain. Cease to be beautiful ! how can that
   be ?
   Lucifer. With time.
   Cain. But time has past, and hitherto
Even Adam and my mother both are fair :
Not fair like Adah and the seraphim —
But very fair.
   Lucifer. All that must pass away
In them and her.
   Cain. I'm sorry for it ; but
Cannot conceive my love for her the less.
And when her beauty disappears, methinks
He who creates all beauty will lose more
Than me in seeing perish such a work.
   Lucifer. I pity thee who lovest what must
   perish.
   Cain. And I thee who lov'st nothing.
   Lucifer.   And thy brother —
Sits he not near thy heart ?
   Cain.   Why should he not ?

Lucifer. Thy father loves him well — so does thy God.

Cain. And so do I.

Lucifer. 'Tis well and meekly done.

Cain. Meekly!

Lucifer. He is the second born of flesh, And is his mother's favorite.

Cain. Let him keep Her favor, since the serpent was the first To win it.

Lucifer. And his father's?

Cain. What is that To me? should I not love that which all love?

Lucifer. And the Jehovah — the indulgent Lord,
And bounteous planter of barred Paradise —
He, too, looks smilingly on Abel.

Cain. I Ne'er saw him, and I know not if he smiles.

Lucifer. But you have seen his angels.

Cain. Rarely.

Lucifer. But Sufficiently to see they love your brother: *His* sacrifices are acceptable.

Cain. So be they! wherefore speak to me of this?

Lucifer. Because thou hast thought of this ere now.

Cain. And if I *have* thought, why recall a thought that —— (*He pauses, as agitated.*) — Spirit!
Here we are in *thy* world; speak not of *mine.*
Thou hast shown me wonders; thou hast shown me those
Mighty pre-Adamites who walked the earth
Of which ours is the wreck; thou hast pointed out
Myriads of starry worlds, of which our own
Is the dim and remote companion, in
Infinity of life: thou hast shown me shadows
Of that existence with the dreaded name
Which my sire brought us — Death; [1] thou hast shown me much —
But not all: show me where Jehovah dwells,
In his especial Paradise — or *thine:*
Where is it?

Lucifer. *Here,* and o'er all space.

Cain. But ye Have some allotted dwelling — as all things; Clay has its earth, and other worlds their tenants;
All temporary breathing creatures their
Peculiar element; and things which have
Long ceased to breathe *our* breath, have theirs, thou say'st;
And the Jehovah and thyself have thine —
Ye do not dwell together?

Lucifer. No, we reign Together; but our dwellings are asunder.

Cain. Would there were only one of ye! perchance
An unity of purpose might make union
In elements which seem now jarred in storms.
How came ye, being spirits, wise and infinite,
To separate? Are ye not as brethren in
Your essence, and your nature, and your glory?

Lucifer. Art thou not Abel's brother?

Cain. We are brethren, And so we shall remain; but were it not so,
Is spirit like to flesh? can it fall out?
Infinity with Immortality?
Jarring and turning space to misery—
For what?

Lucifer. To reign.

Cain. Did ye not tell me that Ye are both eternal?

Lucifer. Yea!

Cain. And what I have seen, Yon blue immensity, is boundless?

Lucifer. Ay.

Cain. And cannot ye both *reign* then? — is there not
Enough? — why should ye differ?

Lucifer. We *both* reign.

Cain. But one of you makes evil.

Lucifer. Which?

Cain. Thou! for If thou canst do man good, why dost thou not?

Lucifer. And why not he who made? *I* made ye not;
Ye are *his* creatures, and not mine.

Cain. Then leave us *His* creatures, as thou say'st we are, or show me
Thy dwelling, or *his* dwelling.

Lucifer. I could show thee Both; but the time will come thou shalt see one
Of them for evermore. [2]

Cain. And why not now?

Lucifer. Thy human mind hath scarcely grasp to gather
The little I have shown thee into cam
And clear thought; and *thou* wouldst go on aspiring
To the great double Mysteries! the *two Principles!*
And gaze upon them on their secret thrones.

---

[1] [MS. —

"Which my sire shrinks from — Death."]

[2] [In Byron's Diary for January 28, 1821, is the following entry: —

"*Thought for a speech of Lucifer, in the Tragedy of Cain.*

'Were *Death* an *evil*, would *I* let thee *live?*
Fool! live as I live — as thy father lives,
And thy sons' sons shall live for evermore!' "]

Dust! limit thy ambition; for to see
Either of these, would be for thee to perish!
Cain. And let me perish, so I see them!
Lucifer.   There
The son of her who snatched the apple spake!
But thou wouldst only perish, and not see
them;
That sight is for the other state.
Cain.   Of death?
Lucifer. That is the prelude.
¹ *Cain.*   Then I dread it less,
Now that I know it leads to something definite.
Lucifer. And now I will convey thee to thy
world,
Where thou shalt multiply the race of Adam,
Eat, drink, toil, tremble, laugh, weep, sleep,
and die.
Cain. And to what end have I beheld these
things
Which thou hast shown me?
Lucifer.   Didst thou not require
Knowledge? And have I not, in what I
showed,
Taught thee to know thyself?
Cain.   Alas! I seem
Nothing.
Lucifer. And this should be the human sum
Of knowledge, to know mortal nature's noth-
ingness;
Bequeathe that science to thy children, and
'Twill spare them many tortures.
Cain.   Haughty spirit!
Thou speak'st it proudly; but thyself, though
proud,
Hast a superior.
Lucifer.   No! By heaven, which He
Holds, and the abyss, and the immensity
Of worlds and life, which I hold with him—
No!
I have a victor—true; but no superior.
Homage he has from all—but none from me:
I battle it against him, as I battled
In highest heaven. Through all eternity,
And the unfathomable gulfs of Hades,
And the interminable realms of space,
And the infinity of endless ages,
All, all, will I dispute! And world by world,
And star by star, and universe by universe,
Shall tremble in the balance, till the great
Conflict shall cease, if ever it shall cease,
Which it ne'er shall, till he or I be quenched!
And what can quench our immortality,
Or mutual and irrevocable hate?
He as a conqueror will call the conquered
Evil; but what will be the *good* he gives?
Were I the victor, *his* works would be deemed
The only evil ones. And you, ye new
And scarce-born mortals, what have been his
gifts
To you already, in your little world?
Cain. But few; and some of those but bit-
ter.

Lucifer.   Back
With me, then, to thine earth, and try the rest
Of his celestial boons to you and yours.
Evil and good are things in their own essence,
And not made good or evil by the giver;
But if he gives you good—so call him; if
Evil springs from *him,* do not name it *mine,*
Till ye know better its true fount; and judge
Not by words, though of spirits, but the fruits
Of your existence, such as it must be.
One good gift has the fatal apple given—
Your *reason :*— let it not be over-swayed
By tyrannous threats to force you into faith
'Gainst all external sense and inward feeling:
Think and endure,—and form an inner world
In your own bosom—where the outward fails;
So shall you nearer be the spiritual
Nature, and war triumphant with your own.¹
                              [*They disappear.*

ACT III.

SCENE I.— *The Earth, near Eden, as in*
Act I.

Enter CAIN *and* ADAH.

Adah. Hush! tread softly, Cain.
Cain.   I will; but wherefore?
Adah. Our little Enoch sleeps upon yon
bed
Of leaves, beneath the cypress.
Cain.   Cypress! 'tis
A gloomy tree, which looks as if it mourned

¹ [As to the question of the origin of evil, which
is the burden of this misdirected verse, Lord Byron
has neither thrown any new light upon it, nor
darkened the previous knowledge which we pos-
sessed. It remains just where it was, in its mighty,
unfathomed obscurity. His Lordship may, it is
true, have recapitulated some of the arguments with
a more concise and cavalier air than the old school-
men or fathers; but the result is the same. There
is no poetical road to metaphysics. In one view,
however, which our rhapsodist has taken of the
subject, we conceive he has done well. He repre-
sents the temptations held out to Cain by Satan, as
constantly succeeding and corresponding to some
previous discontent and gloomy disposition in his
own mind; so that Lucifer is little more than the per-
sonified demon of his imagination: and further, the
acts of guilt and folly into which Cain is hurried are
not treated as accidental, or as occasioned by pass-
ing causes, but as springing from an internal fury,
a morbid state akin to phrensy, a mind dissatisfied
with itself and all things, and haunted by an insati-
able, stubborn longing after knowledge rather than
happiness, and a fatal proneness to dwell on the evil
side of things rather than the good. We here see
the dreadful consequences of not curbing this dis-
position (which is, after all, perhaps, the sin that
most easily besets humanity), exemplified in a
striking point of view; and we so far think, that the
moral to be derived from a perusal of this Mystery
is a valuable one. — *Jeffrey.*]

O'er what it shadows; wherefore didst thou
  choose it
For our child's canopy ?
  Adah.   Because its branches
Shut out the sun like night, and therefore
  seemed
Fitting to shadow slumber.
  Cain.   Ay, the last—
And longest; but no matter — lead me to him.
                [*They go up to the child.*
How lovely he appears! his little cheeks,
In their pure incarnation, vying with
The rose leaves strewn beneath them.
  Adah.   And his lips, too,
How beautifully parted! No; you shall not
Kiss him, at least not now: he will awake
  soon—
His hour of mid-day rest is nearly over;
But it were pity to disturb him till
'Tis closed.
  Cain.   You have said well; I will contain
My heart till then. He smiles, and sleeps!—
  Sleep on
And smile, thou little, young inheritor
Of a world scarce less young: sleep on, and
  smile!
Thine are the hours and days when both are
  cheering
And innocent! *thou* hast not plucked the
  fruit —
Thou know'st not thou art naked! Must the
  time
Come thou shalt be amerced for sins un-
  known,
Which were not thine nor mine? But now
  sleep on!
His cheeks are reddening into deeper smiles,
And shining lids are trembling o'er his long
Lashes, dark as the cypress which waves o'er
  them;
Half open, from beneath them the clear blue
Laughs out, although in slumber. He must
  dream—
Of what? Of Paradise!—Ay! dream of it,
My disinherited boy! 'Tis but a dream;
For never more thyself, thy sons, nor fathers,
Shall walk in that forbidden place of joy! [1]
  Adah.   Dear Cain! Nay, do not whisper
  o'er our son
Such melancholy yearnings o'er the past:
Why wilt thou always mourn for Paradise?
Can we not make another?
  Cain.   Where ?
  Adah.   Here, or
Where'er thou wilt: where'er thou art, I feel
  not
The want of this so much regretted Eden.

Have I not thee, our boy, our sire, and
  brother,
And Zillah — our sweet sister, and our Eve,
To whom we owe so much besides our birth ?
  Cain.   Yes — death, too, is amongst the
  debts we owe her.
  Adah.   Cain! that proud spirit, who with-
  drew thee hence,
Hath saddened thine still deeper. I had hoped
The promised wonders which thou hast be-
  held,
Visions, thou say'st, of past and present worlds,
Would have composed thy mind into the calm
Of a contented knowledge; but I see
Thy guide hath done thee evil: still I thank
  him,
And can forgive him all, that he so soon
Hath given thee back to us.
  Cain.   So soon ?
  Adah.   'Tis scarcely
Two hours since ye departed: two *long* hours
To *me*, but only *hours* upon the sun.
  Cain.   And yet I have approached that sun,
  and seen
Worlds which he once shone on, and never
  more
Shall light; and worlds he never lit: methought
Years had rolled o'er my absence.
  Adah.   Hardly hours.
  Cain.   The mind then hath capacity of time,
And measures it by that which it beholds,
Pleasing or painful; little or almighty.
I had beheld the immemorial works
Of endless beings; [2] skirred extinguished
  worlds;
And, gazing on eternity, methought
I had borrowed more by a few drops of ages
From its immensity: but now I feel
My littleness again. Well said the spirit,
That I was nothing!
  Adah.   Wherefore said he so ?
Jehovah said not that.
  Cain.   No: *he* contents him
With making us the *nothing* which we are;
And after flattering dust with glimpses of
Eden and Immortality, resolves
It back to dust again — for what ?
  Adah.   Thou know'st—
Even for our parents' error.
  Cain.   What is that
To us ? they sinned, then *let them* die !
  Adah.   Thou hast not spoken well, nor is
  that thought
Thy own, but of the spirit who was with thee.
Would *I* could die for them, so *they* might live !
  Cain.   Why, so say I — provided that one
  victim
Might satiate the insatiable of life,
And that our little rosy sleeper there

---

[1] [The censorious may say what they will, but
there are speeches in the mouth of Cain and Adah,
especially regarding their child, which nothing in
English poetry but the "wood-notes wild" of Shak-
speare ever equalled. — *Sir Egerton Brydges.*]

[2] [MS. — "I had beheld the works of ages and
  Immortal beings."]

Might never taste of death nor human sorrow,
Nor hand it down to those who spring from
    him.
Adah. How know we that some such atone-
ment one day
May not redeem our race?
Cain.   By sacrificing
The harmless for the guilty? what atonement
Were there? why, *we* are innocent: what
    have we
Done that we must be victims for a deed
Before our birth, or need have victims to
Atone for this mysterious, nameless sin —
If it be such a sin to seek for knowledge?
Adah. Alas! thou sinnest now, my Cain:
    thy words
Sound impious in mine ears.
Cain.   Then leave me!
Adah.   Never
Though thy God left thee.
Cain.   Say, what have we here?
Adah. Two altars, which our brother Abel
    made
During thine absence, whereupon to offer
A sacrifice to God on thy return.
Cain. And how knew *he*, that *I* would be
    so ready
With the burnt offerings, which he daily brings
With a meek brow, whose base humility
Shows more of fear than worship, as a bribe
To the Creator?
Adah.   Surely, 'tis well done.
Cain. One altar may suffice; *I* have no
    offering.
Adah. The fruits of the earth, the early,
    beautiful
Blossom and bud, and bloom of flowers, and
    fruits;
These are a goodly offering the Lord,
Given with a gentle and a contrite spirit.
Cain. I have toiled, and tilled, and sweaten
    in the sun
According to the curse: — must I do more?
For what should I be gentle? for a war
With all the elements ere they will yield
The bread we eat? For what must I be
    grateful?
For being dust, and grovelling in the dust,
Till I return to dust? If I am nothing —
For nothing shall I be an hypocrite,
And seem well-pleased with pain? For what
    should I
Be contrite? for my father's sin, already
Expiate with what we all have undergone,
And to be more than expiated by
The ages prophesied, upon our seed.
Little deems our young blooming sleeper,
    there,
The germs of an eternal misery
To myriads is within him! better 'twere
I snatched him in his sleep, and dashed him
    'gainst

The rocks, than let him live to ——
Adah.   Oh, my God!
Touch not the child — my child! *thy* child!
    Oh Cain!
Cain. Fear not! for all the stars, and all
    the power .
Which sways them, I would not accost yon
    infant
With ruder greeting than a father's kiss.
Adah. Then, why so awful in thy speech?
Cain.   I said,
'Twere better that he ceased to live, than give
Life to so much of sorrow as he must
Endure, and, harder still, bequeathe; but since
That saying jars you, let us only say —
'Twere better that he never had been born.
Adah. Oh, do not say so! Where were
    then the joys,
The mother's joys of watching, nourishing,
And loving him? Soft! he awakes. Sweet
    Enoch!   [*She goes to the child.*
Oh Cain! look on him; see how full of life,
Of strength, of bloom, of beauty, and of joy,
How like to me — how like to thee, when
    gentle,
For *then* we are *all* alike; is't not so, Cain?
Mother, and sire, and son, our features are
Reflected in each other; as they are
In the clear waters, when *they* are *gentle*, and
When *thou* art *gentle*. Love us, then, my
    Cain!
And love thyself for our sakes, for we love
    thee.
Look! how he laughs and stretches out his
    arms,
And opens wide his blue eyes upon thine,
To hail his father; while his little form
Flutters as winged with joy. Talk not of pain!
The childless cherubs well might envy thee
The pleasures of a parent! Bless him, Cain!
As yet he hath no words to thank thee, but
His heart will, and thine own too.[1]
Cain.   Bless thee, boy!
If that a mortal blessing may avail thee,
To save thee from the serpent's curse!
Adah.   It shall.
Surely a father's blessing may avert
A reptile's subtlety.
Cain.   Of that I doubt;
But bless him ne'er the less.
Adah.   Our brother comes.
Cain. Thy brother Abel.

                Enter ABEL.

[1] [The third Act shows us Cain gloomily lament-
ing over the future fortunes of his infant son, and
withstanding all the consolation and entreaties of
Adah, who is anxious to soften him to the task of
submission and to a participation in the sacrifice
which his brother is about to offer. Here are some
passages of no common beauty. That which strikes
us most is when the parents are hanging over their
sleeping boy. — *Bishop Heber.*]

Abel.   Welcome, Cain! My brother.
The peace of God be on thee!
Cain.   Abel, hail!
Abel. Our sister tells me that thou hast
      been wandering,
In high communion with a spirit, far
Beyond our wonted range. Was he of
      those
We have seen and spoken with, like to our
      father ?
Cain. No.
Abel. Why then commune with him ? he
      may be
A foe to the Most High.
Cain.   And friend to man.
Has the Most High been so — if so you term
      him ?
Abel. Term him! your words are strange
      to-day, my brother.
My sister Adah, leave us for awhile —
We mean to sacrifice.
Adah.   Farewell, my Cain;
But first embrace thy son. May his soft
      spirit,
And Abel's pious ministry, recall thee
To peace and holiness !
                   [*Exit* ADAH, *with her child.*
Abel.   Where hast thou been ?
Cain. I know not.
Abel. Nor what thou hast seen ?
Cain.   The dead,
The immortal, the unbounded, the omnipo-
      tent,
The overpowering mysteries of space —
The innumerable worlds that were and are —
A whirlwind of such overwhelming things,
Suns, moons, and earths, upon their loud-
      voiced spheres
Singing in thunder round me, as have made
      me
Unfit for mortal converse : leave me, Abel.
   Abel. Thine eyes are flashing with un-
      natural light —
Thy cheek is flushed with an unnatural hue —
Thy words are fraught with an unnatural
      sound —
What may this mean ?
   Cain. It means —— I pray thee, leave me.
   Abel. Not till we have prayed and sacri-
      ficed together.
   Cain. Abel, I pray thee, sacrifice alone —
Jehovah loves thee well.
   Abel.   *Both* well, I hope.
   Cain. But thee the better : I care not for
      that;
Thou art fitter for his worship than I am;
Revere him, then — but let it be alone —
At least, without me.
   Abel.   Brother, I should ill
Deserve the name of our great father's son,
If, as my elder, I revered thee not,
And in the worship of our God called not

On thee to join me, and precede me in
Our priesthood — 'tis thy place.
   Cain.   But I have ne'er
Asserted it.
   Abel. The more my grief; I pray thee
To do so now : thy soul seems laboring in
Some strong delusion; it will calm thee.
   Cain.   •   No;
Nothing can calm me more. *Calm!* say I ?
      Never
Knew I what calm was in the soul, although
I have seen the elements stilled. My Abel,
      leave me!
Or let me leave thee to thy pious purpose.
   Abel. Neither; we must perform our task
      together.
Spurn me not.
   Cain.   If it must be so —— well, then,
What shall I do ?
   Abel. Choose one of those two altars.
   Cain. Choose for me : they to me are so
      much turf
And stone.
   Abel. Choose thou!
   Cain.   I have chosen.
   Abel.   'Tis the highest,
And suits thee, as the elder. Now prepare
Thine offerings.
   Cain.   Where are thine ?
   Abel.   Behold them here —
The firstlings of the flock, and fat thereof—
A shepherd's humble offering.
   Cain.   I have no flocks;
I am a tiller of the ground, and must
Yield what it yieldeth to my toil — its fruit:
                 •   [*He gathers fruits.*
Behold them in their various bloom and ripe-
      ness.
   [*They dress their altars, and kindle a flame
      upon them.*
   Abel. My brother, as the elder, offer first
Thy prayer and thanksgiving with sacrifice.
   Cain. No — I am new to this; lead thou
      the way,
And I will follow — as I may.
   Abel (*kneeling*).   Oh God!
Who made us, and who breathed the breath
      of life
Within our nostrils, who hath blessed us,
And spared, despite our father's sin, to
      make [1]
His children all lost, as they might have
      been,
Had not thy justice been so tempered with
The mercy which is thy delight, as to
Accord a pardon like a Paradise,
Compared with our great crimes: — Sole
      Lord of light !
Of good, and glory, and eternity;

---

[1] [MS. —
"And despised not for our father's sin to make."]

Without whom all were evil, and with whom
Nothing can err, except to some good end
Of thine omnipotent benevolence —
Inscrutable, but still to be fulfilled —
Accept from out thy humble first of shep-
herd's
First of the first-born flocks — an offering,
In itself nothing — as what offering can be
Aught unto thee ? — but yet accept it for
The thanksgiving of him who spreads it in
The face of thy high heaven, bowing his own
Even to the dust, of which he is, in honor
Of thee, and of thy name, for evermore !
Cain (standing erect during this speech).
Spirit ! whate'er or whosoe'er thou art,
Omnipotent, it may be — and, if good, .
Shown in the exemption of thy deeds from
evil ;
Jehovah upon earth ! and God in heaven !
And it may be with other names, because
Thine attributes seem many, as thy works : —
If thou must be propitiated with prayers,
Take them ! If thou must be induced with
altars,
And softened with a sacrifice, receive them !
Two beings here erect them unto thee.
If thou lov'st blood, the shepherd's shrine,
which smokes
On my right hand, hath shed it for thy service
In the first of his flock, whose limbs now reek
In sanguinary incense to thy skies ;
Or if the sweet and blooming fruits of earth,
And milder seasons, which the unstained turf
I spread them on now offers in the face
Of the broad sun which ripened them, may
seem   .
Good to thee, inasmuch as they have not
Suffered in limb or life, and rather form
A sample of thy works, than supplication
To look on ours ! If a shrine without victim,
And altar without gore, may win thy favor,
Look on it ! and for him who dresseth it,
He is — such as thou madest him ; and seeks
nothing
Which must be won by kneeling : if he's evil,
Strike him ! thou art omnipotent, and may'st —
For what can he oppose ? If he be good,
Strike him, or spare him, as thou wilt ! since all
Rests upon thee ; and good and evil seem
To have no power themselves, save in thy
will :
And whether that be good or ill I know not,
Not being omnipotent, nor fit to judge
Omnipotence, but merely to endure
Its mandate ; which thus far I have endured.
[*The fire upon the altar of* ABEL *kindles
into a column of the brightest flame, and
ascends to heaven ; while a whirlwind
throws down the altar of* CAIN, *and scat-
ters the fruits abroad upon the earth.*
Abel (kneeling). Oh. 'brother, pray ! Je-
hovah's wroth with thee.

Cain. Why so ?
Abel. Thy fruits are scattered on the earth,
Cain. From earth they came, to earth let
them return ;
Their seed will bear fresh fruit there ere the
summer.
Thy burnt flesh-offering prospers better ; see
How heaven licks up the flames, when thick
with blood !
Abel. Think not upon my offering's ac-
ceptance,
But make another of thine own before
It is too late.
Cain.   I will build no more altars,
Nor suffer any. —
Abel (rising). Cain ! what meanest thou ?
Cain. To cast down yon vile flatterer of the
clouds,
The smoky harbinger of thy dull prayers —
Thine altar, with its blood of lambs and kids,
Which fed on milk, to be destroyed in blood.
Abel (opposing him). Thou shalt not : —
add not impious works to impious
Words ! let that altar stand — 'tis hallowed
now
By the immortal pleasure of Jehovah,
In his acceptance of the victims.
Cain.   .   *His !*
His pleasure ! what was his high pleasure in
The fumes of scorching flesh and smoking
blood,
To the pain of the bleating mothers, which
Still yearn for their dead offspring ? or the
pangs
Of the sad ignorant victims underneath
Thy pious knife ? Give way ! this bloody
record
Shall not stand in the sun, to shame creation !
Abel. Brother, give back ! thou shalt not
touch my altar
With violence : if that thou wilt adopt it,
To try another sacrifice, 'tis thine.
Cain. Another sacrifice ! Give way, or
else
That sacrifice may be ——
Abel.   What mean'st thou ?
Cain.   Give —
Give way ! — thy God loves blood ! — then
look to it : —
Give way, ere he hath *more !*
Abel.   In *his* great name,
I stand between thee and the shrine which
hath
Had his acceptance.
Cain.   If thou lov'st thyself,
Stand back till I have strewed this turf along
Its native soil : — else ——
Abel (opposing him). I love God far more
Than life.[1]

---

[1] [It is evident that Lord Byron had studied his
subject very deeply ; and, though he has varied a

Cain (striking him with a brand, on the temples, which he snatches from the altar).
   Then take thy life unto thy God,
Since he loves lives.
   Abel (falls). What hast thou done, my
      brother?
   Cain. Brother!
   Abel.   Oh, God! receive thy servant,
      and
Forgive his slayer, for he knew not what
He did.— Cain, give me — give me thy hand;
      and tell
Poor Zillah——
   Cain (after a moment's stupefaction). My
      hand! 'tis all red, and with —
What?
      [*A long pause.— Looking slowly round.*
   Where am I? alone! Where's Abel?
      where
Cain? Can it be that I am he? My brother,
Awake! — why liest thou so on the green
      earth?
'Tis not the hour of slumber: — why so pale?
What, hast thou!——thou wert full of life
      this morn!
Abel! I pray thee, mock me not! I smote
Too fiercely, but not fatally. Ah, why [1]
Wouldst thou oppose me? This is mockery;
And only done to daunt me : — 'twas a blow —
And but a blow. Stir — stir — nay, only stir!
Why, so — that's well! — thou breath'st!
      breathe upon me!
Oh, God! Oh, God!
   Abel (very faintly). What's he who speaks
      of God?
   Cain. Thy murderer.
   Abel. Then may God forgive him! Cain,
Comfort poor Zillah: — she has but one
      brother
Now.   [ABEL *dies.*[2]

little from, or gone a little beyond, the letter of
Scripture, which is very concise, yet he has appar-
ently entered with great exactness into the minds
of Cain and Abel in this most interesting scene:
and were it allowable to ascribe to the author of a
dramatic work the principles or feelings of all or
any of his characters, except as adopting them for
his particular purpose, one would be at a loss to
say, whether Lord Byron ought most to be identi-
fied with Cain, or with Abel; so appropriately has
he maintained the character of each. — *Grant's
'Notes on Cain,"* p. 401.]

[1] [MS.—
   " Too hard, but it was not my purpose — why."]

[2] [The sacrifices of Abel and Cain follow: the
first is accepted, the second rejected by Jehovah.
Cain, in wrath, attempts to throw down the altars,
is opposed by Abel, and strikes him with a half-
burnt brand. As a whole, this scene is heavy and
clumsily managed. It can hardly fail to strike the
reader as a defect in poetry, no less than a depart-
ure from history, that the event which is the catas-
trophe of the drama, is no otherwise than inciden-

   Cain. And I none! — Who makes me
      brotherless?
His eyes are open! then he is not dead!
Death is like sleep; and sleep shuts down our
      lids.
His lips, too, are apart; why then he breathes;
And yet I feel it not.— His heart! — his
      heart!—
Let me see, doth it beat? Methinks——No!
      — no!
This is a vision, else I am become
The native of another and worse world.
The earth swims round me : — what is this?—
      'tis wet;
      [*Puts his hand to his brow, and then looks at
      it.*
And yet there are no dews! 'Tis blood — my
      blood —
My brother's and my own; and shed by me!
Then what have I further to do with life,
Since I have taken life from my own flesh?
But he can not be dead! — is silence death?
No; he will wake; then let me watch by him.
Life cannot be so slight, as to be quenched
Thus quickly! — he hath spoken to me since —
What shall I say to him? — my brother! — No:
He will not answer to that name; for brethren
Smite not each other. Yet — yet — speak to
      me.
Oh! for a word more of that gentle voice,
That I may bear to hear my own again!

                  Enter ZILLAH.

   Zillah. I heard a heavy sound; what can
      it be?
'Tis Cain; and watching by my husband.
      What
Dost thou there, brother? Doth he sleep?
      Oh, heaven!
What means this paleness, and yon stream?
      — No, no!
It is not blood; for who would shed his blood?
Abel! what's this? — who hath done this? He
      moves not;
He breathes not: and his hands drop down
      from mine

tally, we may say accidentally, produced by those
which precede it. Cain, whose whole character is
represented in Scripture as envious and malicious,
rather than impious; — this Cain, as painted by
Lord Byron, has no quarrel with his brother what-
ever, nor, except in a single word, does he intimate
any jealousy of him. Two acts, and half the third,
are passed without our advancing a single step
towards the conclusion; and Abel at length falls by
a random blow given in a struggle of which the
object is not his destruction, but the overthrow of
Jehovah's altar. If we could suppose a reader to
sit down to a perusal of the drama in ignorance of
its catastrophe, he could scarcely be less surprised
by its termination in such a stroke of chance-medley,
than if Abel had been made to drop down in an
apoplexy, or Cain to die of grief over his body. —
Bishop Heber.]

With stony lifelessness! Ah! cruel Cain!
Why cam'st thou not in time to save him
  from
This violence? Whatever hath assailed him,
Thou wert the stronger, and should'st have
  stepped in
Between him and aggression! Father!—
  Eve!—
Adah!—come hither! Death is in the world!
  [*Exit* ZILLAH, *calling on her Parents, etc.*
Cain (*solus*). And who hath brought him
  there?—I—who abhor
The name of Death so deeply, that the thought
Empoisoned all my life, before I knew
His aspect—I have led him here, and giv'n
My brother to his cold and still embrace,
As if he would not have asserted his
Inexorable claim without my aid.
I am awake at last—a dreary dream
Had maddened me;—but *he* shall ne'er
  awake!

   Enter ADAM, EVE, ADAH, *and* ZILLAH.

  Adam. A voice of woe from Zillah brings
  me here.—
What do I see?—'Tis true!—My son!
  my son!
Woman, behold the serpent's work, and thine!
                 [*To* EVE.
  Eve. Oh! speak not of it now: the serpent's
  fangs
Are in my heart. My best beloved, Abel!
Jehovah! this is punishment beyond
A mother's sin, to take *him* from me!
  Adam. Who,
Or what hath done this deed?—speak, Cain,
  since thou
Wert present; was it some more hostile angel,
Who walks not with Jehovah? or some wild
Brute of the forest?
  Eve. Ah! a livid light
Breaks through, as from a thunder-cloud! yon
  brand,
Massy and bloody! snatched from off the altar,
And black with smoke, and red with——
  Adam. Speak, my son!
Speak, and assure us, wretched as we are,
That we are not more miserable still.
  Adah. Speak, Cain! and say it was not *thou!*
  Eve. It was.
I see it now—he hangs his guilty head,
And covers his ferocious eye with hands
Incarnadine.
  Adah. Mother, thou dost him wrong—
Cain! clear thee from this horrible accusal,
Which grief wrings from our parent.
  Eve. Hear, Jehovah!
May the eternal serpent's curse be on him!
For he was fitter for his seed than ours
May all his days be desolate! May——
  Adah. Hold!
Curse him not, mother, for he is thy son—

Curse him not, mother, for he is my brother,
And my betrothed.
  Eve. He hath left thee no brother—
Zillah no husband—me *no son!*—for thus
I curse him from my sight for evermore!
All bonds I break between us, as he broke
That of his nature, in yon——Oh death!
  death!
Why didst thou not take *me,* who first incurred
  thee?
Why dost thou not so now?
  Adam. Eve! let not this,
Thy natural grief, lead to impiety!
A heavy doom was long forespoken to us;
And now that it begins, let it be borne
In such sort as may show our God, that we
Are faithful servants to his holy will.
  Eve (pointing to Cain). His will!! the will
  of yon incarnate spirit
Of death, whom I have brought upon the earth
To strew it with the dead. May all the curses
Of life be on him! and his agonies
Drive him forth o'er the wilderness, like us,[1]
From Eden, till his children do by him
As he did by his brother! May the swords
And wings of fiery cherubim pursue him
By day and night—snakes spring up in his
  path—
Earth's fruits be ashes in his mouth—the
  leaves
On which he lays his head to sleep be strewed
With scorpions! May his dreams be of his
  victim!
His waking a continual dread of death!
May the clear rivers turn to blood as he
Stoops down to stain them with his raging lip!
May every element shun or change to him!
May he live in the pangs which others die
  with!
And death itself wax something worse than
  death
To him who first acquainted him with man!
Hence, fratricide! henceforth that word is
  Cain,
Through all the coming myriads of mankind,
Who shall abhor thee, though thou wert their
  sire!
May the grass wither from thy feet! the woods
Deny thee shelter! earth a home! the dust
A grave! the sun his light! and heaven her
  God![2]   [*Exit* EVE.
  Adam. Cain! get thee forth: we dwell no
  more together.
Depart! and leave the dead to me—I am
Henceforth alone—we never must meet more.

---

[1] [MS.—" Drive him forth o'er the world, as we
  were driven."]

[2] [The three last lines were not in the original
MS. In forwarding them to Mr. Murray, to be
added to Eve's speech, Byron says—"There's as
pretty a piece of imprecation for you, when joined
to the lines already sent, as you may wish to meet

Adah. Oh, part not with him thus, my
father: do not
Add thy deep curse to Eve's upon his head!
Adam. I curse him not: his spirit be his
curse.
Come, Zillah!
Zillah. I must watch my husband's corse.
Adam. We will return again, when he is
gone
Who hath provided for us this dread office.
Come, Zillah!
Zillah.   Yet one kiss on yon pale clay,
And those lips once so warm — my heart!
my heart!
          [*Exeunt* ADAM *and* ZILLAH *weeping.*
Adah. Cain! thou hast heard, we must go
forth. I am ready,
So shall our children be. I will bear Enoch,
And you his sister. Ere the sun declines
Let us depart, nor walk the wilderness
Under the cloud of night. — Nay, speak to me.
To *me — thine own.*
Cain.   Leave me!
Adah.   Why, all have left thee.
Cain. And wherefore lingerest thou? Dost
thou not fear
To dwell with one who hath done this?
Adah.   I fear
Nothing except to leave thee, much as I
Shrink from the deed which leaves thee
brotherless.
I must not speak of this — it is between thee
And the great God.
A Voice from within exclaims, Cain! Cain!
Adah.   Hear'st thou that voice?
The Voice within. Cain! Cain!
Adah.   It soundeth like an angel's tone.

          Enter the ANGEL *of the Lord.*

Angel. Where is thy brother Abel?
Cain.   Am I then
My brother's keeper?
Angel.   Cain! what hast thou done?
The voice of thy slain brother's blood cries
out,
Even from the ground, unto the Lord! — Now
art thou
Cursed from the earth, which opened late her
mouth
To drink thy brother's blood from thy rash
hand.
Henceforth, when thou shalt till the ground,
it shall not
Yield thee her strength; a fugitive shalt thou
Be from this day, and vagabond on earth!

with in the course of your business. But don't
forget the addition of these three lines, which are
clinchers to Eve's speech. Let me know what
Gifford thinks, for I have a good opinion of the
piece, as poetry: it is in my gay metaphysical style,
and in the Manfred line."]

Adah. This punishment is more than he
can bear.
Behold, thou drivest him from the face of
earth,
And from the face of God shall he be hid.
A fugitive and vagabond on earth,
'Twill come to pass, that whoso findeth him
Shall slay him.
Cain. Would they could! but who are
they
Shall slay me? Where are these on the lone
earth
As yet unpeopled?
Angel.   Thou hast slain thy brother,
And who shall warrant thee against thy son?
Adah. Angel of Light! be merciful, nor say
That this poor aching breast now nourishes
A murderer in my boy, and of his father.
Angel. Then he would but be what his
father is.
Did not the milk of Eve give nutriment
To him thou now see'st so besmeared with
blood?
The fratricide might well engender parri-
cides. —
But it shall not be so — the Lord thy God
And mine commandeth me to set his seal
On Cain, so that he may go forth in safety.
Who slayeth Cain, a sevenfold vengeance
shall
Be taken on his head. Come hither!
Cain. .   What
Wouldst thou with me?
Angel.   To mark upon thy brow
Exemption from such deeds as thou hast
done.
Cain. No, let me die!
Angel.   It must not be.
          [*The* ANGEL *sets the mark on* CAIN'S *brow.*
Cain.   It burns
My brow, but nought to that which is within it.
Is there more? let me meet it as I may.
Angel. Stern hast thou been and stubborn
from the womb,
As the ground thou must henceforth till; but
he
Thou slew'st was gentle as the flocks he
tended.
Cain. After the fall too soon was I begotten;
Ere yet my mother's mind subsided from
The serpent, and my sire still mourned for
Eden.
That which I am, I am; I did not seek
For life, nor did I make myself; but could I
With my own death redeem him from the
dust —
And why not so? let him return to-day,
And I lie ghastly! so shall be restored
By God the life to him he loved; and taken
From me a being I ne'er loved to bear.
Angel. Who shall heal murder? What is
done is done!

Go forth! fulfil thy days! and be thy deeds
Unlike the last! [*The* ANGEL *disappears.*
Adah. He's gone, let us go forth;
I hear our little Enoch cry within
Our bower.
   Cain. Ah! little knows he what he weeps
   for!
And I who have shed blood cannot shed
   tears!
But the four rivers [1] would not cleanse my
   soul.
Think'st thou my boy will bear to look on me?
   Adah. If I thought that he would not, I
   would —
   Cain (*interrupting her*). No,
No more of threats: we have had too many
   of them:
Go to our children; I will follow thee.
   Adah. I will not leave thee lonely with
   the dead;
Let us depart together.[2]
   Cain.   Oh! thou dead
And everlasting witness! whose unsinking
Blood darkens earth and heaven! what thou
   now art
I know not! but if *thou* see'st what *I* am,
I think thou wilt forgive him, whom his God
Can ne'er forgive, nor his own soul. — Fare-
   well!
I must not, dare not touch what I have made
   thee.
I, who sprung from the same womb with thee,
   drained
The same breast, clasped thee often to my own,
In fondness brotherly and boyish, I
Can never meet thee more, nor even dare
To do that for thee, which thou shouldst have
   done
For me — compose thy limbs into their grave —
The first grave yet dug for mortality.
But who hath dug that grave? Oh, earth!
   Oh, earth!
For all the fruits thou hast rendered to me, I
Give thee back this. — Now for the wilderness.
   [ADAH *stoops down and kisses the body of*
   ABEL.
   Adah. A dreary, and an early doom, my
   brother,
Has been thy lot! Of all who mourn for thee,
I alone must not weep. My office is
Henceforth to dry up tears, and not to shed
   them;

---

[1] The "four rivers" which flowed round Eden,
and consequently the only waters with which Cain
was acquainted upon earth.
[2] ['The catastrophe is brought about with great
dramatic skill and effect. The murderer is sorrow-
ful and confounded, — his parents reprobate and
renounce him, — his wife clings to him with eager
and unhesitating affection; and they wander forth
together into the vast solitude of the universe. —
Jeffrey.]

But yet of all who mourn, none mourn like me,
Not only for thyself, but him who slew thee.
Now, Cain! I will divide thy burden with thee.
   Cain. Eastward from Eden will we take
   our way;
'Tis the most desolate, and suits my steps.
   Adah. Lead! thou shalt be my guide, and
   may our God
Be thine! Now let us carry forth our children.
   Cain. And *he* who lieth there was child-
   less. I
Have dried the fountain of a gentle race,
Which might have graced his recent mar-
   riage couch,
And might have tempered this stern blood of
   mine,
Uniting with our children Abel's offspring!
O Abel!
   Adah. Peace be with him!
   Cain.   But with *me!* ——
                       [*Exeunt.*[3]

---

[3] [The reader has seen what Sir Walter Scott's
general opinion of "Cain" was, in the letter ap-
pended to the dedication, *ante*, p. 653. Moore's
was conveyed to Byron in these words: —
   "I have read Foscari and Cain. The former
does not please me so highly as Sardanapalus. It
has the fault of all those violent Venetian stories;
being unnatural and improbable, and therefore, in
spite of all your fine management of them, appeal-
ing but remotely to one's sympathies. But Cain is
wonderful — terrible — never to be forgotten. If I
am not mistaken, it will sink deep into the world's
heart; and while many will shudder at its blas-
phemy, all must fall prostrate before its grandeur.
Talk of Æschylus and his Prometheus! — here is
the true spirit both of the Poet — and the Devil."
   Byron's answer to Moore on this occasion
contains the substance of all that he ever thought
fit to advance in defence of the assaulted points in
his "Mystery:" —
   "With respect to religion," he says, "can I never
convince you that *I* hold no such opinions as the
characters in that drama, which seems to have
frightened everybody? My ideas of a character
may run away with me: like all imaginative men,
I, of course, embody myself with the character
while I draw it, but not a moment after the pen is
from off the paper."
   He thus alludes to the effects of the critical tem-
pest excited by "Cain," in the eleventh canto of
"Don Juan." —

"In twice five years the 'greatest living poet,'
   Like to the champion in the fisty ring,
Is called on to support his claim, or show it,
   Although 'tis an imaginary thing.
Even I — albeit I'm sure I did not know it,
   Nor sought of foolscap subjects to be king —
The Grand Napoleon of the realms of rhyme.

"But Juan was my Moscow, and Faliero
   My Leipsic, and my Mont Saint Jean seems
   Cain."

   We shall now present the reader with a few of
the most elaborate summaries of the contemporary

critics, — favorable and unfavorable, — beginning with the Edinburgh Review.

Mr. Jeffrey says, — "Though 'Cain' abounds in beautiful passages, and shows more *power*, perhaps, than any of the author's dramatical compositions, we regret very much that it should ever have been published. It will give very great scandal and offence to pious persons in general, and may be the means of suggesting the most painful doubts and distressing perplexities to hundreds of minds that might never otherwise have been exposed to such dangerous disturbance. Lord Byron has no priestlike cant or priestlike reviling to apprehend from us. We do not charge him with being either a disciple or an apostle of Lucifer; nor do we describe his poetry as a mere compound of blasphemy and obscenity. On the contrary, we are inclined to believe that he wishes well to the happiness of mankind, and are glad to testify that his poems abound with sentiments of great dignity and tenderness, as well as passages of infinite sublimity and beauty."

The Reviewer in the Quarterly was Bishop Heber. His article ends as follows: —

"We do not think, that there is much vigor or poetical propriety in any of the characters of Lord Byron's Mystery. Eve, on one occasion, and one only, expresses herself with energy, and not even then with any great depth of that maternal feeling which the death of her favorite son was likely to excite in her. Adam moralizes without dignity. Abel is as dull as he is pious. Lucifer, though his first appearance is well conceived, is as sententious and sarcastic as a Scotch metaphysician; and the gravamina which drive Cain into impiety are circumstances which could only produce a similar effect on a weak and sluggish mind, — the necessity of exertion and the fear of death! Yet, in the happiest climate of earth, and amid the early vigor of nature, it would be absurd to describe (nor has Lord Byron so described it) the toil to which Cain can have been subject as excessive or burdensome. And he is made too happy in his love, too extravagantly fond of his wife and child, to have much leisure for those gloomy thoughts which belong to disappointed ambition and jaded licentiousness. Nor, though there are some passages in this drama of no common power, is the general tone of its poetry so excellent as to atone for these imperfections of design. The dialogue is cold and constrained. The descriptions are like the shadows of a phantasmagoria, at once indistinct and artificial. Except Adah, there is no person in whose fortunes we are interested; and we close the book with no distinct or clinging recollection of any single passage in it, and with the general impression only that Lucifer has said much and done little, and that Cain has been unhappy without grounds and wicked without an object. But if, as a poem, Cain is little qualified to add to Lord Byron's reputation, we are unfortunately constrained to observe that its poetical defects are the very smallest of its demerits. It is not, indeed, as some both of its admirers and its enemies appear to have supposed, a direct attack on Scripture and on the authority of Moses. The expressions of Cain and Lucifer are not more offensive to the ears of piety than such discourses must necessarily be, or than Milton, without offence, has put into the mouths of beings similarly situated."

The following extract is from Mr. Campbell's Magazine: —

"'Cain,' is altogether of a higher order than 'Sardanapalus' and the 'Two Foscari.' Lord Byron has not, indeed, fulfilled our expectations of a gigantic picture of the first murderer; for there is scarcely any passion, except the immediate agony of rage, which brings on the catastrophe; and Cain himself is little more than the subject of supernatural agency. This piece is essentially nothing but a vehicle for striking allusions to the mighty abstractions of Death and Life, Eternity and Time; for vast but dim descriptions of the regions of space, and for daring disputations on that great problem, the origin of evil. The groundwork of the arguments on the awful subjects handled is very common-place; but they are arrayed in great majesty of language, and conducted with a frightful audacity. The direct attacks on the goodness of God are not, perhaps, taken apart, bolder than some passages of Milton; but they inspire quite a different sensation; because, in thinking of Paradise Lost, we never regard the Deity, or Satan, as other than great adverse powers, created by the imagination of the poet. The personal identity which Milton has given to his spiritual intelligences, — the local habitations which he has assigned them, — the material beauty with which he has invested their forms, — all these remove the idea of impurity from their discourses. But we know nothing of Lord Byron's Lucifer, except his speeches: he is invented only that he may utter them; and the whole appears an abstract discussion, held for its own sake, not maintained in order to serve the dramatic consistency of the persons. He has made no attempt to imitate Milton's plastic power; — that power by which our great poet has made his Heaven and Hell, and the very regions of space, sublime realities, palpable to the imagination, and has traced the lineaments of his angelic messengers with the precision of a sculptor. The Lucifer of 'Cain' is a mere bodiless abstraction, — the shadow of a dogma; and all the scenery over which he presides is dim, vague, and seen only in faint outline. There is, no doubt, a very uncommon power displayed, even in this shadowing out of the ethereal journey of the spirit and his victim, and in the vast sketch of the world of phantasms at which they arrive: but they are utterly unlike the massive grandeurs of Milton's creation. We are far from imputing intentional impiety to Lord Byron for this Mystery: nor, though its language occasionally shocks, do we apprehend any danger will arise from its perusal."

So much for the professed Reviewers. We shall conclude with a passage from Sir Egerton Brydges's "Letters on the Character and Genius of Lord Byron:" —

"I remember, when I first read 'Cain,' I thought it, as a composition, the most enchanting and irresistible of all Lord Byron's works; and I think so still. Some of the sentiments, taken detachedly, and left unanswered, are no doubt dangerous, and therefore ought not to have been so left; but the class of readers whom this poem is likely to interest are of so very elevated a cast, and the effect of the poetry is to refine, spiritualize, and illumine the imagination with such a sort of unearthly sublimity, that the mind of these, I am persuaded, will become too strong to incur any taint thus predicted, from the defect which has been so much insisted on."

HEAVEN AND EARTH; A MYSTERY,

FOUNDED ON THE FOLLOWING PASSAGE IN GENESIS, CHAP. VI.: "AND IT CAME TO PASS . . . THAT THE SONS OF GOD SAW THE DAUGHTERS OF MEN THAT THEY WERE FAIR; AND THEY TOOK THEM WIVES OF ALL WHICH THEY CHOSE."

"And woman wailing for her demon lover."—COLERIDGE.

INTRODUCTION.

"HEAVEN and Earth," was written at Ravenna, in October, 1821. In forwarding it to Mr. Murray, in the following month, Lord Byron says:—"Enclosed is a lyrical drama, entitled 'A Mystery.' You will find it pious enough, I trust—at least some of the chorus might have been written by Sternhold and Hopkins themselves for that, and perhaps for melody. As it is longer, and more lyrical and Greek than I intended at first, I have not divided it into acts, but called what I have sent *Part First;* as there is a suspension of the action which may either close there without impropriety, or be continued in a way that I have in view. I wish the first part to be published before the second; because, if it don't succeed, it is better to stop there, than to go on in a fruitless experiment."

Though without delay revised by Mr. Gifford, and printed, this "First Part" was not published till 1822, when it appeared in the second number of the "Liberal." The "Mystery" was never completed.

DRAMATIS PERSONÆ.

ANGELS.	MEN.	WOMEN.
SAMIASA.	NOAH and his Sons.	ANAH.
AZAZIEL.	IRAD.	AHOLIBAMAH.
RAPHAEL the Archangel.	JAPHET.	

Chorus of Spirits of the Earth.—*Chorus of Mortals.*

PART I.

SCENE I.[1]—*A woody and mountainous district near Mount Ararat.*—*Time, midnight.*

Enter ANAH *and* AHOLIBAMAH.

Anah. Our father sleeps: it is the hour when they
Who love us are accustomed to descend
Through the deep clouds o'er rocky Ararat:—
How my heart beats!

Aho. 　　　　Let us proceed upon
Our invocation.

Anah. 　　　But the stars are hidden.
I tremble.

Aho. 　　So do I, but not with fear
Of aught save their delay.

Anah. 　　　　　My sister, though

He seeks for nothing, but it rises before him in its death-doomed magnificence. Man, or angel, or demon, the being who mourns, or laments, or ex-

---

[1] [The great power of this "Mystery" is in its fearless and daring simplicity. Lord Byron faces at once all the grandeur of his sublime subject

I love Azaziel more than —— oh, too much!
What was I going to say? my heart grows
impious.
Aho. And where is the impiety of loving
Celestial natures?
Anah. But, Aholibamah,
I love our God less since his angel loved me:
This cannot be of good; and though I know
not
That I do wrong, I feel a thousand fears
Which are not ominous of right.
Aho. Then wed thee
Unto some son of clay, and toil and spin!
There's Japhet loves thee well, hath loved thee
long:
Marry, and bring forth dust!
Anah. I should have loved
Azaziel not less were he mortal; yet
I am glad he is not. I can not outlive him.
And when I think that his immortal wings
Will one day hover o'er the sepulchre
Of the poor child of clay which so adored him,
As he adores the Highest, death becomes
Less terrible; but yet I pity him:
His grief will be of ages, or at least
Mine would be such for him, were I the
seraph,
And he the perishable.
Aho. Rather say,
That he will single forth some other daughter
Of Earth, and love her as he once loved Anah.
Anah. And if it should be so, and she loved
him,
etter thus than that he should weep for me.
Aho. If I thought thus of Samiasa's love,
ll seraph as he is, I'd spurn him from me.
ut to our invocation! — 'Tis the hour.
Anah. Seraph!
From thy sphere!
Whatever star contain thy glory;
In the eternal depths of heaven
Albeit thou watchest with "the seven,"[1]
Though through space infinite and hoary

lts, is driven to speak by his own soul. The
ngels deign not to use many words, even to their
eautiful paramours: and they scorn Noah and his
entious sons. The first scene is a woody and
ountainous district, near Mount Ararat; and the
ime midnight. Mortal creatures, conscious of
heir own wickedness, have heard awful predictions
f the threatened flood, and all their lives are dark-
ned with terror. But the sons of God have been
wellers on earth, and women's hearts have been
tirred by the beauty of these celestial visitants.
nah and Aholibamah, two of these angel-stricken
aidens, come wandering along while others sleep,
 pour forth their invocations to their demon lov-
s. They are of very different characters: Anah,
ft, gentle, and submissive; Aholibamah, proud,
npetuous, and aspiring — the one loving in fear,
nd the other in ambition. — *Wilson.*
1 The archangels, said to be seven in number,
nd to occupy the eighth rank in the celestial hier-
rchy.

Before thy bright wings worlds be
driven,
Yet hear!
Oh! think of her who holds thee dear!
And though she nothing is to thee,
Yet think that thou art all to her.
Thou canst not tell — and never be
Such pangs decreed to aught save me,—
The bitterness of tears.
Eternity is in thine years,
Unborn, undying beauty in thine eyes;
With me thou canst not sympathize,
Except in love, and there thou must
Acknowledge that more loving dust
Ne'er wept beneath the skies.
Thou walk'st thy many worlds, thou see'st
The face of him who made thee great,
As he hath made me of the least
Of those cast out from Eden's gate:
Yet, Seraph dear!
Oh hear!
For thou hast loved me, and I would not die
Until I know what I must die in knowing,
That thou forget'st in thine eternity
Her whose heart death could not keep
from o'erflowing
For thee, immortal essence as thou art!
Great is their love who love in sin and fear;
And such, I feel, are waging in my heart
A war unworthy: to an Adamite
Forgive, my Seraph! that such thoughts
appear,
For sorrow is our element;
Delight
An Eden kept afar from sight,
Though sometimes with our visions
blent.
The hour is near
Which tells me we are not abandoned
quite. —
Appear! Appear!
Seraph!
My own Azaziel! be but here,
And leave the stars to their own light.
Aho. Samiasa!
Wheresoe'er
Thou rulest in the upper air —
Or warring with the spirits who may dare
Dispute with Him
Who made all empires, empire; or recalling
Some wandering star, which shoots through
the abyss,
Whose tenants dying, while their world is
falling,
Share the dim destiny of clay in this;
Or joining with the inferior cherubim,
Thou deignest to partake their hymn —
Samiasa!
I call thee, I await thee, and I love thee.
Many may worship thee, that will I not:
If that thy spirit down to mine may move
thee.

Descend and share my lot!
Though I be formed of clay,
   And thou of beams
More bright than those of day
   On Eden's streams,
Thine immortality can not repay
With love more warm than mine
My love. There is a ray
In me, which, though forbidden yet to
   shine,
I feel was lighted at thy God's and thine.
It may be hidden long: death and decay
  Our mother Eve bequeathed us — but
   my heart
Defies it: though this life must pass away
Is *that* a cause for thee and me to part?
Thou art immortal — so am I: I feel —
I feel my immortality o'ersweep
All pains, all tears, all time, all fears, and
   peal,
Like the eternal thunders of the deep,
Into my ears this truth —" Thou liv'st for
   ever! "
   But if it be in joy
I know not, nor would know;
That secrets rest with the Almighty giver
Who folds in clouds the fonts of bliss and
   woe,
   But thee and me he never can de-
   stroy;
Change us he may, but not o'erwhelm; we
   are
Of as eternal essence, and must war
With him if he will war with us: with *thee*
   I can share all things, even immortal
   sorrow;
For thou hast ventured to share life with *me*,
And shall *I* shrink from thine eternity?
No! though the serpent's sting should pierce
   me through,
And thou thyself wert like the serpent, coil
Around me still! and I will smile,
   And curse thee not; but hold
   Thee in as warm a fold
   As —— but descend; and prove
   A mortal's love
For an immortal. If the skies contain
More joy than thou canst give and take, re-
   main! [1]
Anah. Sister! sister! I view them winging
Their bright way through the parted night.
Aho. The clouds from off their pinions
   flinging,
As though they bore to-morrow's light.
Anah. But if our father see the sight!

Aho. He would but deem it was the moon
Rising unto some sorcerer's tune
An hour too soon.
  Anah. They come! *he* comes! — Azaziel!
  Aho.   Haste
To meet them! Oh! for wings to bear
My spirit, while they hover there,
To Samiasa's breast!
  Anah. Lo! they have kindled all the west,
Like a returning sunset; — lo!
  On Ararat's late secret crest
A mild and many-colored bow,
The remnant of their flashing path,
Now shines! and now, behold! it hath
Returned to night, as rippling foam,
  Which the leviathan bath lashed
From his unfathomable home,
When sporting on the face of the calm deep,
  Subsides soon after he again hath dashed
Down, down, to where the ocean's fountains
   sleep.[2]
  Aho. They have touched earth! Samiasa!
  Anah.   My Azaziel!
                         [*Exeunt*

SCENE II.[3] — *Enter* IRAD *and* JAPHET.

  Irad. Despond not: wherefore wilt thou
   wander thus
To add thy silence to the silent night,
And lift thy tearful eye unto the stars?
They cannot aid thee.
  Japh.   But they soothe me — now
Perhaps she looks upon them as I look.
Methinks a being that is beautiful
Becometh more so as it looks on beauty,
The eternal beauty of undying things.
Oh, Anah!
  Irad.   But she loves thee not.
  Japh.   Alas!
  Irad. And proud Aholibamah spurns me
   also.
  Japh. I feel for thee too.
  Irad.   Let her keep her pride,
Mine hath enabled me to bear her scorn:
It may be, time too will avenge it.
  Japh.   Canst thou
Find joy in such a thought?
  Irad.   Nor joy nor sorrow.
I loved her well; I would have loved her bet-
   ter,

---

[1] [This invocation is extremely beautiful: its chief beauty lies in the continuous and meandering flow of its impassioned versification. At its *close,* — and it might well win down to earth erring angels from heaven, — the maidens disappear in the midnight darkness, hoping the presence of their celestial lovers. — *Wilson.*]

[2] [Lord Byron here takes a wide career, and is sometimes obscure and confused; but the flashes of fire continually break through, and illumine the clouds of smoke and vapor. The extravagance is dictated by passion. His muse, even in her riddles and digressions, has a sybil-like, prophetic fury. — *Jeffrey.*]

[3] [In the second scene, Japhet, Noah's son, and Irad — the earthly and despised lovers of the two maidens — appear. Their talk is somewhat dull; which, we presume, is natural in such circumstances. — *Wilson.*]

Had love been met with love : as 'tis, I leave her
To brighter destinies, if so she deems them.
  Japh. What destinies ?
  Irad. ~   I have some cause to think
She loves another.
  Japh.   Anah !
  Irad.   No ; her sister.
  Japh. What other ?
  Irad.   That I know not; but her air,
If not her words, tells me she loves another.
  Japh. Ay, but not Anah : she but loves her
  God.
  Irad. Whate'er she loveth, so she loves
  thee not,
What can it profit thee ? [1]
  Japh.   True, nothing ; but
I love.
  Irad. And so did I.
  Japh.   And now thou lov'st not,
Or think'st thou lov'st not, art thou happier ?
  Irad.   Yes.
  Japh. I pity thee.
  Irad.   Me ! why ?
  Japh.   For being happy
Deprived of that which makes my misery.
  Irad. I take thy taunt as part of thy dis-
  temper,
And would not feel as thou dost for more
  shekels
Than all our father's herds would bring if
  weighed
Against the metal of the sons of Cain —
The yellow dust they try to barter with us,
As if such useless and discolored trash,
The refuse of the earth, could be received
For milk, and wool, and flesh, and fruits, and
  all
Our flocks and wilderness afford. — Go, Ja-
  phet,
Sigh to the stars, as wolves howl to the
  moon —
I must back to my rest.
  Japh.   And so would I
If I could rest.
  Irad.   Thou wilt not to our tents then ?
  Japh. No, Irad ; I will to the cavern, whose
Mouth they say opens from the internal world
To let the inner spirits of the earth
Forth when they walk its surface.
  Irad.   Wherefore so ?
What wouldst thou there ?
  Japh.   Soothe further my sad spirit
With gloom as sad : it is a hopeless spot,
And I am hopeless.

---

[1] [This is one of those bitter, taunting sarcasms
that escape Lord Byron's pen, in spite of himself.
Japhet is afterwards introduced alone in a moun-
tainous cave ; and his soliloquy, bemoaning his
own fate, and the approaching destruction of man-
kind, is interrupted by a laugh of demons, rejoic-
ing over the event. This scene is terrific. — *Jeff-
rey.*]

  Irad.   But 'tis dangerous ;
Strange sounds and sights have peopled it
  with terrors.
I must go with thee.
  Japh.   Irad, no ; believe me
I feel no evil thought, and fear no evil.
  Irad. But evil things will be thy foe the
  more
As not being of them : turn thy steps aside,
Or let mine be with thine.
  Japh.   No, neither, Irad ;
I must proceed alone.
  Irad.   Then peace be with thee !
                        [*Exit* IRAD.
  Japh. (*solus*). Peace ! I have sought it
  where it should be found,
In love — with love, too, which perhaps de-
  served it ;
And, in its stead, a heaviness of heart —
A weakness of the spirit — listless days,
And nights inexorable to sweet sleep —
Have come upon me. Peace ! what peace ?
  the calm
Of desolation, and the stillness of
The untrodden forest, only broken by
The sweeping tempest through its groaning
  boughs ;
Such is the sullen or the fitful state
Of my mind overworn. The earth's grown
  wicked,
And many signs and portents have proclaimed
A change at hand, and an o'erwhelming doom,
To perishable beings. Oh, my Anah !
When the dread hour denounced shall open
  wide
The fountains of the deep, how mightest thou
Have lain within this bosom, folded from
The elements ; this bosom, which in vain
Hath beat for thee, and then will beat more
  vainly,
While thine —— Oh, God ! at least remit to
  her
Thy wrath ! for she is pure amidst the failing
As not a star in the clouds, which cannot quench,
Although they obscure it for an hour. My
  Anah !
How would I have adored thee, but thou
  wouldst not,
And still would I redeem thee — see thee live
When ocean is earth's grave, and, unopposed
By rock or shallow, the leviathan,
Lord of the shoreless sea and watery world,
Shall wonder at his boundlessness of realm.
                      [*Exit* JAPHET.

Enter NOAH *and* SHEM.

  Noah. Where is thy brother Japhet ?
  Shem.   He went forth,
According to his wont, to meet with Irad,
He said ; but, as I fear, to bend his steps
Towards Anah's tents, round which he hovers
  nightly,

Like a dove round and round its pillaged nest;
Or else he walks the wild up to the cavern
Which opens to the heart of Ararat.
   Noah. What doth he there ? It is an evil
     spot
Upon an earth all evil; for things worse
Than even wicked men resort there: he
Still loves this daughter of a fated race,
Although he could not wed her if she loved
     him,
And that she doth not. Oh, the unhappy
     hearts
Of men! that one of my blood, knowing well
The destiny and evil of these days,
And that the hour approacheth, should in-
     dulge
In such forbidden yearnings! Lead the way —
He must be sought for!
   Shem.   Go not forward, father:
I will seek Japhet.
   Noah.   Do not fear for me:
All evil things are powerless on the man
Selected by Jehovah. — Let us on.
   Shem. To the tents of the father of the sis-
     ters ?
   Noah. No; to the cavern of the Caucasus.
                [*Exeunt* NOAH *and* SHEM.

SCENE III. — *The mountains. — A cavern,
    and the rocks of Caucasus.*

   Japh. (*solus*). Ye wilds, that look eternal;
     and thou cave,
Which seem'st unfathomable; and ye moun-
     tains,
So varied and so terrible in beauty;
Here, in your rugged majesty of rocks
And toppling trees that twine their roots with
     stone
In perpendicular places, where the foot
Of man would tremble, could he reach them
     — yes,
Ye look eternal! Yet, in a few days,
Perhaps even hours, ye will be changed, rent,
     hurled
Before the mass of waters; and yon cave,
Which seems to lead into a lower world,
Shall have its depths searched by the sweeping
     wave,
And dolphins gambol in the lion's den!
And man — Oh, men! my fellow-beings! Who
Shall weep above your universal grave,
Save I ? Who shall be left to weep? My kins-
     men,
Alas! what am I better than ye are,
That I must live beyond ye ? Where shall be
The pleasant places where I thought of Anah
While I had hope ? or the more savage haunts,
Scarce less beloved, where I despaired for her ?
And can it be! — Shall yon exulting peak,
Whose glittering top is like a distant star,
Lie low beneath the boiling of the deep ?

No more to have the morning sun break forth,
And scatter back the mists in floating folds
From its tremendous brow ? no more to have
Day's broad orb drop behind its head at even,
Leaving it with a crown of many hues ?
No more to be the beacon of the world,
For angels to alight on, as the spot
Nearest the stars ? And can those words "*no
    more*"
Be meant for thee, for all things, save for us,
And the predestined creeping things reserved
By my sire to Jehovah's bidding ? May
He preserve *them*, and *I not* have the power
To snatch the loveliest of earth's daughters
    from
A doom which even some serpent, with his
    mate,
Shall 'scape to save his kind to be prolonged,
To hiss and sting through some emerging
    world,
Reeking and dank from out the slime, whose
    ooze
Shall slumber o'er the wreck of this until
The salt morass subside into a sphere
Beneath the sun, and be the monument,
The sole and undistinguished sepulchre,
Of yet quick myriads of all life ? How much
Breath will be stilled at once! All beauteous
    world   *
So young, so marked out for destruction, I
With a cleft heart look on thee day by day,
And night by night, thy numbered days and
    nights:
I cannot save thee, cannot save even her
Whose love had made me love thee more;
    but as
A portion of thy dust, I cannot think
Upon thy coming doom without a feeling
Such as — Oh God! and canst thou —
                    [*He pauses.*[1]

*A rushing sound from the cavern is heard, and
   shouts of laughter — afterwards a Spirit
   passes.*

   Japh.   In the name
Of the Most High, what art thou ?
   Spirit (*laughs*).   Ha! ha! ha!
   Japh. By all that earth holds holiest, speak!
   Spirit (*laughs*).   Ha! ha!
   Japh. By the approaching deluge! by the
     earth
Which will be strangled by the ocean! by
The deep which will lay open all her foun-
    tains!
The heaven which will convert her clouds to
    seas,

---

[1] [This soliloquy has the fault of being too long
and wire-drawn. At its close, spirits rush from the
cavern, and exult in the approaching calamity of
the world: a dialogue ensues between Japhet and
one of them, and a chorus is sung by a body of
them, part of which is truly noble. — *Campbell.*]

id the Omnipotent who makes and crushes!
ıou unknown, terrible, and indistinct,
:t awful Thing of Shadows, speak to me!
hy dost thou laugh that horrid laugh?
Spirit.   Why weep'st thou?
Japh.   For earth and all her children.
Spirit.   Ha! ha! ha!   [*Spirit vanishes.*
Japh.   How the fiend mocks the tortures of
    a world,
ıe coming desolation of an orb,
ı which the sun shall rise and warm no life!
ɔw the earth sleeps! and all that in it is
ɛep too upon the very eve of death!
hy should they wake to meet it?   What is
    here,
hich look like death in life, and speak like
    things
ɔrn ere this dying world?   They come like
    clouds!
        [*Various Spirits pass from the cavern.*
Spirit.   Rejoice!
    The abhorred race
hich could not keep in Eden their high place,
    But listened to the voice
: knowledge without power,
    Are nigh the hour
        Of death!
ɔt slow, not single, not by sword, nor sorrow,
    Nor years, nor heart-break, nor time's
        sapping motion,
tall they drop off.   Behold their last to-mor-
        ·row!
    Earth shall be ocean!
        And no breath,
ıve of the winds, be on the unbounded wave!
ɪgels shall tire their wings, but find no spot:
ɔt even a rock from out the liquid grave
    Shall lift its point to save,
r show the place where strong Despair hath
    died,
After long looking o'er the ocean wide
    For the expected ebb which cometh not:
    .   All shall be void,
        Destroyed!
nother element shall be the lord
Of life, and the abhorred
hildren of dust be quenched; and of each hue
f earth nought left but the unbroken blue;
And of the variegated mountain
    Shall nought remain
    Unchanged, or of the level plain;
    Cedar and pine shall lift their tops in vain:
ll merged within the universal fountain,
    Man, earth, and fire, shall die,
        And sea and sky
ɔok vast and lifeless in the eternal eye.
    Upon the foam
Who shall erect a home?
aph. (*coming forward*).   My sire!
Earth's seed shall not expire;
    Only the evil shall be put away
        From day.

Avaunt! ye exulting demons of the waste!
Who howl your hideous joy
When God destroys whom you dare not
    destroy;
            Hence! haste!
    Back to your inner caves!
    Until the waves
Shall search you in your secret place,
    And drive your sullen race
Forth, to be rolled upon the tossing winds
    In restless wretchedness along all space!
Spirit.   Son of the saved!
    When thou and thine have braved
    The wide and warring element;
    When the great barrier of the deep is rent,
Shall thou and thine be good or happy? — No!
    Thy new world and new race shall be of
        woe —
. Less goodly in their aspect, in their years
    Less than the glorious giants, who
    Yet walk the world in pride,
The Sons of Heaven by many a mortal bride.
Thine shall be nothing of the past, save tears.
        ' And art thou not ashamed
        Thus to survive,
    And eat, and drink, and wive?
With a base heart so far subdued and tamed,
As even to hear this wide destruction named,
Without such grief and courage, as should
    rather
Bid thee await the world-dissolving wave,
Than seek a shelter with thy favored father,
    And build thy city o'er the drowned earth's
        grave?
        Who would outlive their kind,
        Except the base and blind?
            Mine
        Hateth thine
As of a different order in the sphere,
        But not our own.
There is not one who hath not left a throne
Vacant in heaven to dwell in darkness here
Rather than see his mates endure alone.
        Go, wretch! and give
A life like thine to other wretches — live!
    And when the annihilating waters roar
        Above what they have done,
Envy the giant patriarchs then no more,
And scorn thy sire as the surviving one!
        Thyself for being his son!

Chorus of Spirits issuing from the cavern.
        Rejoice!
No more the human voice
Shall vex our joys in middle air
        With prayer;
    No more
        Shall they adore;
And we, who ne'er for ages have adored
    The prayer-exacting Lord,
To whom the omission of a sacrifice
        Is vice;

We, we shall view the deep's salt sources
    poured
Until one element shall do the work
        Of all in chaos; until they,
    The creatures proud of their poor clay,
Shall perish, and their bleached bones shall
    lurk
In caves, in dens, in clefts of mountains, where
The deep shall follow to their latest lair;
    Where even the brutes, in their despair,
Shall cease to prey on man and on each other,
    And the striped tiger shall lie down to die
Beside the lamb, as though he were his
    brother;
    Till all things shall be as they were,
    Silent and uncreated, save the sky:
        While a brief truce
    Is made with Death, who shall forbear
The little remnant of the past creation,
To generate new nations for his use;
    This remnant, floating o'er the undulation
    Of the subsiding deluge, from its slime,
    When the hot sun hath baked the reeking
        soil
Into a world, shall give again to Time
New beings — years — diseases — sorrow —
    crime —
With all companionship of hate and toil,
        Until ——
Japh. (*interrupting them*). The eternal will
    Shall deign to expound this dream
    Of good and evil; and redeem
    Unto himself all times, all things;
        And, gathered under his almighty winge,
            Abolish hell!
And to the expiated Earth
Restore the beauty of her birth,
    Her Eden in an endless paradise,
Where man no more can fall as once he fell,
And even the very demons shall do well!
Spirits.   And when shall take effect this
    wondrous spell?
Japh.   When the Redeemer cometh; first
    in pain,
        And then in glory.
Spirit.   Meantime still struggle in the mor-
    tal chain,
        Till earth wax hoary;
War with yourselves, and hell, and heaven, in
    vain,
        Until the clouds look gory
With the blood reeking from each battle plain;
New times, new climes, new arts, new men;
    but still,
The same old tears, old crimes, and oldest ill,
Shall be amongst your race in different forms;
        But the same moral storms
Shall oversweep the future, as the waves
In a few hours the glorious giants' graves.[1]

Chorus of Spirits.

        Brethren, rejoice!
        Mortal, farewell!
Hark! hark! already we can hear the voice
Of growing ocean's gloomy swell;
    The winds, too, plume their piercing wings;
    The clouds have nearly filled their springs;
The fountains of the great deep shall be
    broken,
    And heaven set wide her windows;[2] while
        mankind
View, unacknowledged, each tremendous to-
    ken —
    Still, as they were from the beginning, blind,
    We hear the sound they cannot hear,
        The mustering thunders of the threaten-
            ing sphere;
    Yet a few hours their coming is de-
        layed —
        Their flashing banners, folded still on
            high,
            Yet undisplayed,
Save to the Spirit's all-pervading eye.
        Howl! howl! oh Earth!
Thy death is nearer than thy recent birth:
Tremble, ye mountains, soon to shrink below
        The ocean's overflow!
The wave shall break upon your cliffs; and
        shells,
    The little shells, of ocean's least things be
Deposed where now the eagle's offspring
        dwells —
How shall he shriek o'er the remorseless sea!
And call his nestlings up with fruitless yell,
Unanswered, save by the encroaching swell; —
While man shall long in vain for his broad
    wings,
    The wings which could not save: —
Where could he rest them, while the whole
        space brings
    Nought to his eye beyond the deep, his
        grave?
        Brethren, rejoice!
And loudly lift each superhuman voice —
        All die;
Save the slight remnant of Seth's seed —
        The seed of Seth,
Exempt for future sorrow's sake from death.
        But of the sons of Cain
        None shall remain;
    And all his goodly daughters
Must lie beneath the desolating waters —
Or, floating upward, with their long hair laid
Along the wave, the cruel heaven upbraid,
        Which would not spare
    Beings even in death so fair.
        It is decreed,
        All die!

---

[1] "And there were giants in the earth in those days, and after; mighty men, which were of old, men of renown." — *Genesis.*

[2] "The same day were all the fountains of the great deep broken up, and the windows of heaven were opened." — *Ibid.*

And to the universal human cry
The universal silence shall succeed!
    Fly, brethren, fly!
    But still rejoice!
        We fell!
        They fall!
    So perish all
These petty foes of Heaven who shrink from
        hell!
[*The Spirits disappear, soaring upwards.*
Japh. (*solus*). God hath proclaimed the destiny of earth;
My father's ark of safety hath announced it;
The very demons shriek it from their caves;
The scroll [1] of Enoch prophesied it long
In silent books, which, in their silence, say
More to the mind than thunder to the ear:
And yet men listened not, nor listen; but
Walk darkling to their doom; which, though
        so nigh,
Shakes them no more in their dim disbelief,
Than their last cries shall shake the Almighty
        purpose,
Or deaf obedient ocean, which fulfils it.
No sign yet hangs its banner in the air;
The clouds are few, and of their wonted texture;
The sun will rise upon the earth's last day
As on the fourth day of creation, when
God said unto him, "Shine!" and he broke
        forth
to the dawn, which lighted not the yet
Informed forefather of mankind — but roused
Before the human orison the earlier
Made and far sweeter voices of the birds,
Which in the open firmament of heaven
Have wings like angels, and like them salute
Heaven first each day before the Adamites:
Their matins now draw nigh — the east is
        kindling —
And they will sing! and day will break! Both
        near,
    near the awful close! For these must drop
Their outworn pinions on the deep; and day,
After the bright course of a few brief morrows, —
Ay, day will rise; but upon what? — a chaos,
Which was ere day; and which, renewed,
        makes time
Nothing! for, without life, what are the
        hours ?
No more to dust than is eternity
Unto Jehovah, who created both.
Without him, even eternity would be
Void: without man, time, as made for man,
Dies with man, and is swallowed in that deep
Which has no fountain; as his race will be
Devoured by that which drowns his infant
        world. —

The book of Enoch, preserved by the Ethiops, is said by them to be anterior to the flood.

What have we here ? Shapes of both earth
        and air ?
No — *all* of heaven, they are so beautiful.
I cannot trace their features; but their forms,
How lovelily they move along the side
Of the gray mountain, scattering its mist!
And after the swart savage spirits, whose
Infernal immortality poured forth
Their impious hymn of triumph, they shall be
Welcome as Eden. It may be they come
To tell me the reprieve of our young world,
For which I have so often prayed — They
        come!
Anah! oh, God! and with her [2] ——

Enter SAMIASA, AZAZIEL, ANAH, *and* AHOLIBAMAH.

    Anah.   Japhet!
    Sam.   Lo!
A son of Adam!
    Aza.   What doth the earth-born here,
While all his race are slumbering?
    Japh.   Angel! what
Dost thou on earth when thou shouldst be on
        high ?
    Aza. Know'st thou not, or forget'st thou,
        that a part
Of our great function is to guard thine
        earth ?
    Japh. But all good angels have forsaken
        earth,
Which is condemned; nay, even the evil fly
The approaching chaos. Anah! Anah! my
In vain, and long, and still to be beloved!
Why walk'st thou with this spirit, in those
        hours
When no good spirit longer lights below ?
    Anah. Japhet, I cannot answer thee; yet,
        yet
Forgive me ——
    Japh. May the Heaven, which soon no
        more
Will pardon, do so! for thou art greatly
        tempted.
    Aho. Back to thy tents, insulting son of
        Noah! —
We know thee not.
    Japh.   The hour may come when thou
May'st know me better; and thy sister know
Me still the same which I have ever been.

---

[2] [The spirits disappear soaring upwards, and Japhet has again recourse to a very fine soliloquy. He is now joined by Anah and Aholibamah, who are accompanied by the two angels, Samiasa and Azaziel. The angels seem somewhat sulky, and are extremely laconic; they look like Quakers yet unmoved by the spirit — dull dogs. But Japhet takes them to task very severely. Noah and Shem now join the party, and a conversation ensues between them all, neither very spirited nor very edifying — when enters Raphael the Archangel, who holds a highly poetical dialogue with Samiasa. — *Wilson.*]

Sam. Son of the patriarch, who hath ever
been
Upright before his God, whate'er thy gifts,
And thy words seem of sorrow, mixed with
wrath,
How have Azaziel, or myself, brought on thee
Wrong?
Japh. Wrong! the greatest of all wrongs;
but thou
Say'st well, though she be dust, I did not,
could not,
Deserve her. Farewell, Anah! I have said
That word so often! but now say it, ne'er
To be repeated. Angel! or whate'er
Thou art, or must be soon, hast thou the
power
To save this beautiful —*these* beautiful
Children of Cain?
Aza.   From what?
Japh.   And is it so,
That ye too know not? Angels! angels! ye
Have shared man's sin, and, it may be, now
must
Partake his punishment; or, at the least,
My sorrow.
Sam.   Sorrow! I ne'er thought till now
To hear an Adamite speak riddles to me.
Japh. And hath not the Most High ex-
pounded them?
Then ye are lost, as they are lost.
Aho.   So be it!
If they love as they are loved, they will not
shrink
More to be mortal, than I would to dare
An immortality of agonies
With Samiasa!
Anah.   Sister! Sister! speak not
Thus.
Aza. Fearest thou, my Anah?
Anah.   Yes, for thee:
I would resign the greater remnant of
This little life of mine, before one hour
Of thine eternity should know a pang.
Japh. It is for *him*, then! for the seraph
thou
Hast left me! That is nothing, if thou hast
not
Left thy God too! for unions like to these,
Between a mortal and an immortal, cannot
Be happy or be hallowed. We are sent
Upon the earth to toil and die; and they
Are made to minister on high unto
The Highest: but if he can *save* thee, soon
The hour will come in which celestial aid
Alone can do so.
Anah.   Ah! he speaks of death.
Sam. Of death to *us!* and those who are
with us;
But that the man seems full of sorrow, I
Could smile.
Japh.   I grieve not for myself, nor fear;
I am safe, not for my own deserts, but those

Of a well-doing sire, who hath been found
Righteous enough to save his children. Would
His power was greater of redemption! or
That by exchanging my own life for hers,
Who could alone have made mine happy,
she,
The last and loveliest of Cain's race, could
share
The ark which shall receive a remnant of
The seed of Seth!
Aho.   And dost thou think that we,
With Cain's, the eldest born of Adam's, blood
Warm in our veins, — strong Cain! who
was begotten
In Paradise — would mingle with Seth's chil-
dren?
Seth, the last offspring of old Adam's dotage?
No, not to save all earth, were earth in peril!
Our race hath always dwelt apart from thine
From the beginning, and shall do so ever.
Japh. I did not speak to thee, Aholi-
bamah!
Too much of the forefather whom thou vaunt-
est
Has come down in that haughty blood which
springs
From him who shed the first, and that a
brother's!
But thou, my Anah! let me call thee mine,
Albeit thou art not; 'tis a word I cannot
Part with, although I must from thee. My
Anah!
Thou who dost rather make me dream that
Abel
Had left a daughter, whose pure pious race
Survived in thee, so much unlike thou art
The rest of the stern Cainites, save in beauty,
For all of them are fairest in their favor ——
Aho. (*interrupting him*). And wouldst
thou have her like our father's foe
In mind, in soul? If *I* partook thy thought,
And dreamed that aught of *Abel* was in *her!* —
Get thee hence, son of Noah; thou makest
strife.
Japh. Offspring of Cain, thy father did so!
Aho.   But
He slew not Seth: and what hast thou to do
With other deeds between his God and him?
Japh. Thou speakest well: his God hath
judged him, and
I had not named his deed, but that thyself
Didst seem to glory in him, nor to shrink
From what he had done.
Aho.   He was our father's father:
The eldest born of man, the strongest, bravest,
And most enduring: — Shall I blush for him
From whom we had our being? Look upon
Our race; behold their stature and their
beauty,
Their courage, strength, and length of
days ——
Japh.   They are numbered.

Aho. Be it so! but while yet their hours
endure,
I glory in my brethren and our fathers.
  Japh. My sire and race but glory in their
God,
Anah! and thou? ——
  Anah.   Whate'er our God decrees,
The God of Seth as Cain, I must obey,
And will endeavor patiently to obey.
But could I dare to pray in his dread hour
Of universal vengeance (if such should be),
It would not be to live, alone exempt
Of all my house. My sister! oh, my sister!
What were the world, or other worlds, or all
The brightest future, without the sweet past—
Thy love—my father's—all the life, and all
The things which sprang up with me, like the
  · stars,
Making my dim existence radiant with
Soft lights which were not mine? Aholi-
  bamah!
Oh! if there should be mercy—seek it, find
  it:
I abhor death, because that thou must die.
  Aho. What, hath this dreamer, with his
father's ark,
The bugbear he hath built to scare the world,
Shaken *my* sister? Are *we* not the loved
Of seraphs? and if we were not, must we
Cling to a son of Noah for our lives?
Rather than thus —— But the enthusiast
  dreams
The worst of dreams, the fantasies engendered
By hopeless love and heated vigils. Who
Shall shake these solid mountains, this firm
  earth,
And bid those clouds and waters take a shape
Distinct from that which we and all our sires
Have seen them wear on their eternal way?
Who shall do this?
  Japh. He whose one word produced them.
  Aho. Who *heard* that word?
  Japh.   The universe, which leaped
To life before it. Ah! smilest thou still in
  scorn?
Turn to thy seraphs: if they attest it not,
They are none.
  Sam.   Aholibamah, own thy God!
  Aho. I have ever hailed our Maker, Sa-
  miasa,
As thine, and mine: a God of love, not sorrow.
  Japh. Alas! what else is love but sorrow?
  Even
He who made earth in love had soon to grieve
Above its first and best inhabitants.
  Aho. 'Tis said so.
  Japh.   It is even so.

Enter NOAH and SHEM.

  Noah.   Japhet! What
Dost thou here with these children of the
  wicked?

Dread'st thou not to partake their coming
  doom?
  Japh. Father, it cannot be a sin to seek
To save an earth-born being; and behold,
These are not of the sinful, since they have
The fellowship of angels.
  Noah.   These are they, then,
Who leave the throne of God, to take them
  wives
From out the race of Cain; the sons of
  heaven,
Who seek earth's daughters for their beauty?
  Aza.   Patriarch!
Thou hast said it.
  Noah. Woe, woe, woe to such communion!
Has not God made a barrier between earth
And heaven, and limited each, kind to kind?
  Sam. Was not man made in high Jeho-
  vah's image?
Did God not love what he had made? And
  what
Do we but imitate and emulate
His love unto created love? •
  Noah.   I am
But man, and was not made to judge mankind,
Far less the sons of God; but as our God
Has deigned to commune with me, and reveal
His judgments, I reply, that the descent
Of seraphs from their everlasting seat
Unto a perishable and perishing,
Even on the very *eve* of *perishing*, world,
Cannot be good.
  Aza.   What! though it were to save?
  Noah. Not ye in all your glory can redeem
What he who made you glorious hath con-
  demned.
Were your immortal mission safety, 'twould
Be general, not for two, though beautiful;
And beautiful they are, but not the less
Condemned.
  Japh.   Oh, father! say it not.
  Noah.   Son! son!
If that thou wouldst avoid their doom, forget
That they exist: they soon shall cease to be;
While thou shalt be the sire of a new world,
And better.
  Japh.   Let me die with *this*, and *them!*
  Noah. Thou *shouldst* for such a thought,
  but shalt not; he
Who *can* redeems thee.
  Sam.   And why him and thee,
More than what he, thy son, prefers to both?
  Noah. Ask him who made thee greater
  than myself
And mine, but not less subject to his own
Almightiness. And lo! his mildest and
Least to be tempted messenger appears!

Enter RAPHAEL[1] the Archangel.

[In the original MS. "Michael." "I return
you," says Byron to Mr. M., " the revise. I have
softened the part to which Gifford objected, and

Raph.   Spirits!
    Whose seat is near the throne,
        What do ye here?
    Is thus a seraph's duty to be shown,
        Now that the hour is near
    When earth must be alone?
            Return!
        Adore and burn
In glorious homage with the elected "seven."
        Your place is heaven.
Sam.   Raphael!
The first and fairest of the sons of God,
    How long hath this been law,
That earth by angels must be left untrod?
    Earth! which oft saw
Jehovah's footsteps not disdain her sod!
    The world he loved, and made
    For love; and oft have we obeyed
His frequent mission with delighted pinions:
    Adoring him in his least works displayed;
Watching this youngest star of his dominions;
    And, as the latest birth of his great word,
    Eager to keep it worthy of our Lord.
        Why is thy brow severe?
And wherefore speak'st thou of destruction
        near?
Raph. Had Samiasa and Azaziel been
In their true place, with the angelic choir,
        Written in fire
        They would have seen
        Jehovah's late decree,
And not inquired their Maker's breath of me:
    But ignorance must ever be
        A part of sin;
And even the spirits' knowledge shall grow
        less
        As they wax proud within;
For Blindness is the first-born of Excess.
    When all good angels left the world, ye
        stayed
Stung with strange passions, and debased
By mortal feelings for a mortal maid:
But ye are pardoned thus far, and replaced
With your pure equals. Hence! away! away!
        Or stay,
And lose eternity by that delay.
Aza. And thou! if earth be thus forbidden
        In the decree
    To us until this moment hidden,
        Dost thou not err as we
        In being here?
Raph. I came to call ye back to your fit
    sphere,
In the great name and at the word of God.
Dear, dearest in themselves, and scarce less
    dear
That which I came to do: till now we trod
Together the eternal space; together

---

ohanged the name of Michael to Raphael, who was
an angel of gentler sympathies." — *Byron Letters*,
July 6, 1822.]

Let us still walk the stars.   True, earth must
    die!
Her race, returned into her womb, must wither,
    And much which she inherits: but oh! why
Cannot this earth be made, or be destroyed,
    Without involving ever some vast void
In the immortal ranks? immortal still
    In their immeasurable forfeiture.
Our brother Satan fell; his burning will
    Rather than longer worship dared endure!
But ye who still are pure!
Seraphs! less mighty than that mightiest one,
    Think how he was undone!
And think if tempting man can compensate
    For heaven desired too late?
        Long have I warred,
        Long must I war
    With him who deemed it hard
    To be created, and to acknowledge him
    Who midst the cherubim
Made him as suns to a dependent star,
Leaving the archangels at his right hand dim.
    I loved him — beautiful he was: oh
        heaven!
Save *his* who made, what beauty and what
        power
Was ever like to Satan's! Would the hour
    In which he fell could ever be forgiven!
The wish is impious: but, oh ye!
Yet undestroyed, be warned! Eternity
    With him, or with his God, is in your choice:
He hath not tempted you; he cannot tempt
The angels, from his further snares exempt:
    But man hath listened to his voice,
And ye to woman's — beautiful she is,
The serpent's voice less subtle than her kiss.
The snake but vanquished dust; but she will
    draw
A second host from heaven, to break heaven's
    law.
        Yet, yet, oh fly!
        Ye cannot die;
        But they
        Shall pass away,
While ye shall fill with shrieks the upper sky
    For perishable clay,
Whose memory in your immortality
    Shall long outlast the sun which gave
        them day.
Think how your essence differeth from theirs
In all but suffering! why partake
The agony to which they must be heirs —
Born to be ploughed with years, and sown
    with cares,
And reaped by Death, lord of the human soil?
Even had their days been left to toil their
    path
Through time to dust, unshortened by God's
    wrath,
Still they are Evil's prey and Sorrow's spoil.
Aho.   Let them fly!
I hear the voice which says that all must die

Sooner than our white-bearded patriarchs
  died;
           And that on high
       An ocean is prepared,
         While from below
The deep shall rise to meet heaven's overflow.
      Few shall be spared,
It seems; and, of that few, the race of Cain
Must lift their eyes to Adam's God in vain.
        Sister! since it is so,
      And the eternal Lord
     In vain would be implored
For the remission of one hour of woe,
Let us resign even what we have adored,
And meet the wave, as we would meet the
    sword,
  If not unmoved, yet undismayed,
And wailing less for us than those who shall
Survive in mortal or immortal thrall,
  And, when the fatal waters are allayed,
Weep for the myriads who can weep no more.
Fly, seraphs! to your own eternal shore,
Where winds nor howl nor waters roar.
      Our portion is to die,
    And yours to live for ever:
  But which is best, a dead eternity,
Or living, is but known to the great Giver.
     Obey him, as we shall obey;
  I would not keep this life of mine in clay
    An hour beyond his will;
Nor see ye lose a portion of his grace,
For all the mercy which Seth's race
        Find still.
        Fly!
And as your pinions bear ye back to heaven,
Think that my love still mounts with thee on
    high,
      Samiasa!
And if I look up with a tearless eye,
  'Tis that an angel's bride disdains to weep,—
Farewell! Now rise, inexorable deep!
  Anah.   And must we die?
     And must I lose thee too,
      Azaziel?
     Oh, my heart! my heart!
      Thy prophecies were true!
  And yet thou wert so happy too!
The blow, though not unlooked for, falls as
  new:
      But yet depart!
     Ah! why?
    Yet let me not retain thee—fly!
My pangs can be but brief; but thine would be
Eternal, if repulsed from heaven for me.
    Too much already hast thou deigned
     To one of Adam's race!
Our doom is sorrow: not to us alone,
But to the spirits who have not disdained
To love us, cometh anguish with disgrace.
The first who taught us knowledge hath been
  hurled
  From his once archangelic throne

Into some unknown world:
      And thou, Azaziel! No—
     Thou shalt not suffer woe
For me. Away! nor weep!
  Thou canst not weep; but yet
  May'st suffer more, not weeping: then forget
Her, whom the surges of the all-strangling deep
  Can bring no pang like this. Fly! fly!
Being gone, 'twill be less difficult to die.
  Japh. Oh say not so!
    Father! and thou, archangel, thou!
Surely celestial mercy lurks below
That pure severe serenity of brow:
Let them not meet this sea without a shore.
Save in our ark, or let me be no more!
  Noah. Peace, child of passion, peace!
If not within thy heart, yet with thy tongue
Do God no wrong!
Live as he wills it—die, when he ordains,
A righteous death, unlike the seed of Cain's.
Cease, or be sorrowful in silence; cease
To weary Heaven's ear with thy selfish plaint.
Wouldst thou have God commit a sin for
  thee?
      Such would it be
     To alter his intent
For a mere mortal sorrow. Be a man!
And bear what Adam's race must bear, and
  can.
  Japh. Ay, father! but when they are gone,
And we are all alone,
Floating upon the azure desert, and
The depth beneath us hides our own dear
  land,
  And dearer, silent friends and brethren, all
Buried in its immeasurable breast,
Who, who, our tears, our shrieks, shall then
  command?
Can we in desolation's peace have rest?
    Oh God! be thou a God, and spare
     Yet while 'tis time!
Renew not Adam's fall:
  Mankind were then but twain,
But they are numerous now as are the waves
    And the tremendous rain,
Whose drops shall be less thick than would
    their graves,
  Were graves permitted to the seed of Cain.
  Noah. Silence, vain boy! each word of
  thine's a crime.
Angel! forgive this stripling's fond despair.
  Raph. Seraphs! these mortals speak in
    passion! Ye!
Who are, or should be, passionless and pure,
May now return with me.
  Sam.   It may not be:
We have chosen, and will endure.
  Raph. Say'st thou?
  Aza.   He hath said it, and I say, Amen.
  Raph.   Again!
      Then from this hour,
Shorn as ye are of all celestial power,

And aliens from your God,
　　　　　　Farewell!
Japh.　　　　Alas! where shall they dwell?
Hark, hark! Deep sounds, and deeper still,
　Are howling from the mountain's bosom:
There's not a breath of wind upon the hill,
　Yet quivers every leaf, and drops each blos-
　　som:
Earth groans as if beneath a heavy load.
Noah.　Hark, hark! the sea-birds cry!
In clouds they overspread the lurid sky,
And hover round the mountain, where before
　Never a white wing, wetted by the wave,
　　Yet dared to soar,
　Even when the waters waxed too fierce to
　　brave.
Soon it shall be their only shore,
　And then, no more!
Japh.　　　　The sun! the sun!
He riseth, but his better light is gone;
　And a black circle, bound
　　His glaring disk around,
Proclaims earth's last of summer days hath
　　shone!
The clouds return into the hues of night,
Save where their brazen-colored edges streak
The verge where brighter morns were wont
　to break.
Noah.　And lo! yon flash of light,
The distant thunder's harbinger, appears!
　It cometh! hence, away!
Leave to the elements their evil prey!
Hence to where our all-hallowed ark uprears
　　　　　Its safe and wreckless sides!
Japh.　Oh, father, stay!
Leave not my Anah to the swallowing tides!
Noah.　Must we not leave all life to such?
　Begone!
Japh.　　　Not I.
Noah.　　　　　　Then die
　With them!
How darest thou look on that prophetic sky,
And seek to save what all things now con-
　demn,
　In overwhelming unison
　　With just Jehovah's wrath!
Japh.　Can rage and justice join in the
　　same path?
Noah.　Blasphemer! darest thou murmur
　　even now?
Raph.　Patriarch, be still a father! smoothe
　　thy brow:
Thy son, despite his folly, shall not sink:
He knows not what he says, yet shall not drink
　With sobs the salt foam of the swelling
　　waters;
But be, when passion passeth, good as thou,
　Nor perish like heaven's children with man's
　　daughters.
Aho.　The tempest cometh; heaven and
　　earth unite
　For the annihilation of all life.

Unequal is the strife
Between our strength and the Eternal Might!
Sam.　But ours is with thee; we will bear
　ye far
To some untroubled star,
Where thou and Anah shalt partake our lot:
　And if thou dost not weep for thy lost earth,
Our forfeit heaven shall also be forgot.
Anah.　Oh! my dear father's tents, my
　　place of birth,
And mountains, land, and woods! when ye
　are not,
Who shall dry up my tears!
Aza.　　　　Thy spirit-lord.
Fear not; though we are shut from heaven,
Yet much is ours, whence we cannot be
　driven.
Raph.　Rebel! thy words are wicked, as
　thy deeds
Shall henceforth be but weak: the flaming
　sword,
Which chased the first-born out of Paradise,
Still flashes in the angelic hands.
Aza.　It cannot slay us: threaten dust with
　death,
And talk of weapons unto that which bleeds.
What are thy swords in our immortal eyes?
Raph.　The moment cometh to approve
　thy strength;
　And learn at length
How vain to war with what thy God com-
　mands!
Thy former force was in thy faith.

　　　　Enter Mortals, flying for refuge.

　　　　　Chorus of Mortals.

The heavens and earth are mingling — God,
　oh God!
What have we done? Yet spare!
Hark! even the forest beasts howl forth their
　prayer!
　The dragon crawls from out his den,
　To herd, in terror, innocent with men;
And the birds scream their agony through air
Yet, yet, Jehovah! yet withdraw thy rod
Of wrath, and pity thine own world's despair!
Hear not man only but all nature plead!
Raph.　Farewell, thou earth! ye wretched
　sons of clay,
I cannot, must not, aid you. 'Tis decreed!
　　　　　　　　　[*Exit* RAPHAEL.
Japh.　Some clouds sweep on as vultures
　for their prey,
While others, fixed as rocks, await the word
At which their wrathful vials shall be poured.
No azure more shall robe the firmament,
Nor spangled stars be glorious: Death hath
　risen:
In the sun's place a pale and ghastly glare
Hath wound itself around the dying air.[2]

---

[1] [In his description of the deluge, which is a

Aza. Come, Anah! quit this chaos-founded prison,
To which the elements again repair,
To turn it into what it was: beneath
The shelter of these wings thou shalt be safe,
As was the eagle's nestling once within
Its mother's.— Let the coming chaos chafe
With all its elements! Heed not their din!
A brighter world than this, where thou shalt breathe
Ethereal life, will we explore:
These darkened clouds are not the only skies.
[AZAZIEL *and* SAMIASA *fly off, and disappear with* ANAH *and* AHOLIBAMAH.
Japh. They are gone! They have disappeared amidst the roar
Of the forsaken world; and never more,
Whether they live, or die with all earth's life,
Now near its last, can aught restore
Anah unto these eyes.[1]

Chorus of Mortals.

Oh son of Noah! mercy on thy kind!
What! wilt thou leave us all—all—*all* behind?
While safe amidst the elemental strife,
Thou sitt'st within thy guarded ark?
A Mother (offering her infant to JAPHET).
Oh let this child embark!
I brought him forth in woe,
But thought it joy
To see him to my bosom clinging so.
Why was he born?
What hath he done—
My unweaned son—
To move Jehovah's wrath or scorn?
What is there in this milk of mine, that death
Should stir all heaven and earth up to destroy
My boy,
And roll the waters o'er his placid breath?
Save him, thou seed of Seth!
Or cursed be — with him who made
Thee and thy race, for which we are betrayed!
Japh. Peace! 'tis no hour for curses, but for prayer.

Chorus of Mortals.

For prayer!!!
And where

Shall prayer ascend,
When the swoln clouds unto the mountains bend
And burst,
And gushing oceans every barrier rend,
Until the very deserts know no thirst?
Accursed
Be he who made thee and thy sire!
We deem our curses vain; we must expire;
But as we know the worst,
Why should our hymn be raised, our knees be bent
Before the implacable Omnipotent,
Since we must fall the same?
If he hath made earth, let it be his shame,
To make a world for torture.— Lo! they come,
The loathsome waters, in their rage!
And with their roar make wholesome nature dumb
The forest's trees (coeval with the hour
When Paradise upsprung,
Ere Eve gave Adam knowledge for her dower,
Or Adam his first hymn of slavery sung),
So massy, vast, yet green in their old age,
Are overtopped,
Their summer blossoms by the surges lopped,
Which rise, and rise, and rise.
Vainly we look up to the lowering skies—
They meet the seas,
And shut out God from our beseeching eyes.
Fly, son of Noah, fly! and take thine ease
In thine allotted ocean-tent;
And view, all floating o'er the element,
The corpses of the world of thy young days:
Then to Jehovah raise
Thy song of praise!
A Mortal. Blessed are the dead
Who die in the Lord!
And though the waters be o'er earth outspread,
Yet, as *his* word,
Be the decree adored!
He gave me life — he taketh but
The breath which is his own:
And though these eyes should be for ever shut,
Nor longer this weak voice before his throne,
Be heard in supplicating tone,
Still blessed be the Lord
For what is past,
For that which is;
For all are his,
From first to last —
Time — space — eternity — life — death —
The vast known and immeasurable unknown,
He made, and can unmake;
And shall *I*, for a little gasp of breath,
Blaspheme and groan?
No; let me die, as I have lived, in faith,
Nor quiver, though the universe may quake!

---

varied and recurring masterpiece,—(we hear it foretold, and we see it come,)— Lord Byron appears to us to have had an eye to Poussin's celebrated picture, with the sky hanging like a weight of lead upon the waters, the sun quenched and lurid, the rocks and trees upon them gloomily watching their fate, and a few figures struggling vainly with the overwhelming waves.— *Jeffrey.*]
[1] [The despair of the mortal lovers for the loss of their mortal mistresses is well and pathetically expressed. — *Jeffrey.*]

Chorus of Mortals.

Where shall we fly ?
Not to the mountains high;
For now their torrents rush, with double roar,
To meet the ocean, which, advancing still,
Already grasps each drowning hill,
Nor leaves an unsearched cave.

Enter a Woman.

Woman. Oh, save me, save !
Our valley is no more :
My father and my father's tent,
My brethren and my brethren's herds,
The pleasant trees that o'er our noonday
    bent,
And sent forth evening songs from sweetest
    birds,
The little rivulet which freshened all
    Our pastures green,
No more are to be seen.
When to the mountain cliff I climbed this morn,
I turned to bless the spot,
And not a leaf appeared about to fall ; —
    And now they are not ! —
Why was I born ?
Japh.   To die ! in youth to die ;
And happier in that doom,
Than to behold the universal tomb
    Which I
Am thus condemned to weep above in vain.
Why, when all perish, why must I remain ? [1]

    [*The waters rise : Men fly in very direction ;
    many are overtaken by the waves; the Cho-
    rus of Mortals disperses in search of safety
    up the mountains; Japhet remains upon a
    rock, while the Ark floats towards him in
    the distance.*

---

[1] [This poem, or rather first part of a poem, for so it is stated to be, carries with it the peculiar impress of the writer's genius. It displays great vigor, and even a severity of style, throughout; which is another proof, if proof were needed, that elevation of writing is to be obtained only by a rigid regard to simplicity. It may be perused without shocking the feelings of the sensitive, or furnishing an object for the discriminating morality of the Lord Chancellor. Lord Byron has evidently endeavored to sustain the interest of this poem, by depicting natural, but deep drawn thoughts, in all their freshness and intensity, with as little fictitious aid as possible. Nothing is circumlocutory: there is no going about and about to enter at length upon his object, but he impetuously rushes into it at once. All over the poem there is a gloom cast suitable to the subject: an ominous fearful hue, like that which Poussin has flung over his inimitable picture of the Deluge. We see much evil, but we dread more. All is out of earthly keeping, as the events of the time are out of the course of nature. Man's wickedness, the perturbed creation, fear-struck mortals, demons passing to and fro in the earth, an overshadowing solemnity, and unearthly loves, form together the materials. That it has faults is obvious: prosaic passages, and too much tedious soliloquizing: but there is the vigor and force of Byron to fling into the scale against these : there is much of the sublime in description, and the beautiful in poetry. Prejudice, or ignorance, or both, may condemn it; but, while true poetical feeling exists amongst us, it will be pronounced not unworthy of its distinguished author. — *Campbell.*

It appears that this is but the first part of a poem: but it is likewise a poem, and a fine one too, within itself. We confess that we see little or nothing objectionable in it, either as to theological orthodoxy, or general human feeling. It is solemn, lofty, fearful, wild, tumultuous, and shadowed all over with the darkness of a dreadful disaster. Of the angels who love the daughters of men we see little, and know less — and not too much of the love and passion of the fair lost mortals. The inconsolable despair preceding and accompanying an incomprehensible catastrophe pervades the whole composition; and its expression is made sublime by the noble strain of poetry in which it is said or sung. Sometimes there is heaviness — dulness — as if it were pressed in on purpose; intended, perhaps, to denote the occasional stupefaction, drowsiness, and torpidity of soul produced by the impending destruction upon the latest of the Antediluvians. But, on the whole, it is not unworthy of Lord Byron. — *Wilson.*

Lord Byron's " Mystery," with whatever crudeness and defects it is chargeable, certainly has more poetry and music in it than any of his dramatic writings since " Manfred; " and has also the peculiar merit of throwing us back, in a great degree, to the strange and preternatural time of which it professes to treat. It is truly, and in every sense of the word, a meeting of " heaven and earth; " angels are seen ascending and descending, and the windows of the sky are opened to deluge the face of nature. We have an impassioned picture of the strong and devoted attachment inspired into the daughters of men by angel forms, and have placed before us the emphatic picture of " woman wailing for her demon lover." There is a like conflict of the passions as of the elements — all wild, chaotic, uncontrollable, fatal; but there is a discordant harmony in all this — a keeping in the coloring and the time. In handling the unpolished page, we look upon the world before the flood, and gaze upon a doubtful blank, with only a few straggling figures, part human and part divine; while, in the expression of the former, we read the fancies, ethereal and lawless, that lifted the eye of beauty to the skies, and, in the latter, the human passions that " drew angels down to earth." — *Jeffrey.*]

THE DEFORMED TRANSFORMED; A DRAMA.

AUTHOR'S PREFACE.

THIS production is founded partly on the story of a novel called "The Three Brothers,"[1] published many years ago, from which M. G. Lewis's "Wood Demon" was also taken — and partly on the "Faust" of the great Goethe. The present publication contains the two first Parts only, and the opening chorus of the third. The rest may perhaps appear hereafter.

INTRODUCTION.

THIS drama was begun at Pisa in 1821, but was not published till January, 1824. Mr. Medwin says: — "On my calling on Lord Byron one morning, he produced the 'Deformed Transformed.' Handing it to Shelley, as he was in the habit of doing his daily compositions, he said — 'Shelley, I have been writing a Faustish kind of drama. tell me what you think of it.' After reading it attentively, Shelley returned it. 'Well,' said Lord B., 'how do you like it?' 'Least,' replied he, of 'any thing I ever saw of yours. It is a bad imitation of "Faust," and besides, there are two entire lines of Southey's in it.' Lord Byron changed color immediately, and asked hastily, 'what lines?' Shelley repeated,

> 'And water shall see thee,
> And fear thee, and flee thee.'

They are in the Curse of Kehama.' His Lordship instantly threw the poem into the fire. He seemed to feel no chagrin at seeing it consume — at least his countenance betrayed none, and his conversation became more gay and lively than usual. Whether it was hatred of Southey, or respect for Shelley's opinion, which made him commit the act that I considered a sort of suicide, was always doubtful to me. _ vas never more surprised than to see, two years afterwards, 'The Deformed Transformed' announced (supposing it to have perished at Pisa); but it seems that he must have had another copy of the manuscript, or that he had rewritten it perhaps, without changing a word, except omitting the Kehama lines. His memory was remarkably retentive of his own writings. I believe he could have quoted almost every line he ever wrote."

Mrs. Shelley says: — "This had long been a favorite subject with Lord Byron. I think that he mentioned it also in Switzerland. I copied it — he sending a portion of it at a time, as it was finished, to me. At this time he had a great horror of its being said that he plagiarized, or that he studied for ideas, and wrote with difficulty. Thus, he gave Shelley Aiken's edition of the British Poets, that it might not be found in his house by some English lounger, and reported home: thus, too, he always dated when he began and when he ended a poem, to prove hereafter how quickly it was done. I do not think that he altered a line in this drama after he had once written it down. He composed and corrected in his mind. I do not know how he meant to finish it; but he said himself that the whole conduct of the story was already conceived. It was at this time that a brutal paragraph alluding to his lameness appeared, which he repeated to me; lest I should hear it first from some one else. No action of Lord Byron's life — scarce a line he has written — but was influenced by his personal defect."

[1] [The "Three Brothers" is a romance, published in 1803, the work of a Joshua Pickersgill, junior.]

DRAMATIS PERSONÆ.

STRANGER. *afterwards* CÆSAR.
ARNOLD.
BOURBON.
PHILIBERT.

CELLINI.
BERTHA.
OLIMPIA.

Spirits, Soldiers, Citizens of Rome, Priests, Peasants, etc.

PART I.

SCENE I. — *A Forest.*

Enter ARNOLD *and his mother* BERTHA.

Bert. Out, hunchback!
Arn. I was born so, mother![1]
Bert. Out,
Thou incubus! Thou nightmare! Of seven sons,
The sole abortion!
Arn. Would that I had been so,
And never seen the light!
Bert. I would so too!
But as thou *hast* — hence, hence — and do thy best!
That back of thine may bear its burden; 'tis
More high, if not so broad as that of others.
Arn. It *bears* its burden; — but, my heart! Will it
Sustain that which you lay upon it, mother?
I love, or, at the least, I loved you: nothing
Save you, in nature, can love aught like me.
You nursed me — do not kill me!
Bert. Yes — I nursed thee,
Because thou wert my first-born, and I knew not
If there would be another unlike thee,
That monstrous sport of nature. But get hence,
And gather wood!
Arn. I will: but when I bring it,
Speak to me kindly. Though my brothers are
So beautiful and lusty, and as free
As the free chase they follow, do not spurn me:
Our milk has been the same.
Bert. As is the hedgehog's,
Which sucks at midnight from the wholesome dam
Of the young bull, until the milkmaid finds
The nipple next day sore and udder dry.[2]
Call not thy brothers brethren! Call me not

Mother; for if I brought thee forth, it was
As foolish hens at times hatch vipers, by
Sitting upon strange eggs. Out, urchin, out!
[*Exit* BERTHA.
Arn. (*solus*). Oh Mother! —— She is gone,
and I must do
Her bidding; — wearily but willingly
I would fulfil it, could I only hope
A kind word in return. What shall I do?
[ARNOLD *begins to cut wood : in doing this*
he wounds one of his hands.
My labor for the day is over now.
Accursed be this blood that flows so fast;
For double curses will be my meed now
At home — What home? I have no home,
no kin,
No kind — not made like other creatures, or
To share their sports or pleasures. Must I
bleed too
Like them? Oh that each drop which falls to
earth
Would rise a snake to sting them, as they have
stung me!
Or that the devil, to whom they liken me,
Would aid his likeness! If I must partake
His form, why not his power? Is it because
I have not his will too? For one kind word
From her that bore me would still reconcile me
Even to this hateful aspect. Let me wash
The wound.
[ARNOLD *goes to a spring, and stoops to wash*
his hand : he starts back.
They are right; and Nature's mirror shows me,
What she hath made me. I will not look on it
Again, and scarce dare think on't. Hideous
wretch
That I am! The very waters mock me with
My horrid shadow — like a demon placed
Deep in the fountain to scare back the cattle
From drinking therein. [*He pauses.*
And shall I live on,
A burden to the earth, myself, and shame
Unto what brought me into life! Thou blood,
Which flowest so freely from a scratch, let me
Try if thou wilt not in a fuller stream
Pour forth my woes for ever with thyself
On earth, to which I will restore at once
This hateful compound of her atoms, and
Resolve back to her elements, and take
The shape of any reptile save myself,

---

[1] [Lord Byron's own mother, when in ill humor with him, used to make the deformity in his foot the subject of taunts and reproaches. She would (we quote from a letter written by one of her relations in Scotland) pass from passionate caresses to the repulsion of actual disgust; then devour him with kisses again, and swear his eyes were as beautiful as his father's. — *Quar. Rev.*]

[2] [This is now believed to be a vulgar error; the smallness of the animal's mouth rendering it incapable of the mischief laid to its charge.]

And make a world for myriads of new worms!
This knife! now let me prove if it will sever
This withered slip of nature's nightshade—my
Vile form—from the creation, as it hath
The green bough from the forest.

[ARNOLD *places the knife in the ground, with
the point upwards.*

               Now 'tis set,
And I can fall upon it. Yet one glance
On the fair day, which sees no foul thing like
Myself, and the sweet sun which warmed me,
   but
In vain. The birds—how joyously they sing!
So let them, for I would not be lamented:
But let their merriest notes be Arnold's knell;
The fallen leaves my monument; the murmur
Of the near fountain my sole elegy.
Now, knife, stand firmly, as I fain would fall!
  [*As he rushes to throw himself upon the knife,
    his eye is suddenly caught by the fountain,
    which seems in motion.*
The fountain moves without a wind: but shall
The ripple of a spring change my resolve?
No. Yet it moves again! The waters stir,
Not as with air, but by some subterrane
And rocking power of the internal world.
What's here? A mist! No more?—
  [*A cloud comes from the fountain. He stands
    gazing upon it; it is dispelled, and a tall
    black man comes towards him.*
  Arn.   What would you? Speak!
Spirit or man?
  Stran.   As man is both, why not
Say both in one?
  Arn.   Your form is man's, and yet
You may be devil.
  Stran.   So many men are that
Which is so called or thought, that you may
  add me
To which you please, without much wrong to
  either.
But come: you wish to kill yourself;—pursue
Your purpose.
  Arn.   You have interrupted me.
  Stran. What is that resolution which can
  e'er
Be interrupted? If I be the devil
You deem, a single moment would have made
  you
Mine, and for ever, by your suicide;
And yet my coming saves you.
  Arn.   I said not
You *were* the demon, but that your approach
Was like one.
  Stran.   Unless you keep company
With him (and you seem scarce used to such
  high
Society) you can't tell how he approaches;
And for his aspect, look upon the fountain,
And then on me, and judge which of us twain
Looks likest what the boors believe to be
Their cloven-footed terror.   .

  Arn.   Do you — dare *you*
To taunt me with my born deformity?
  Stran. Were I to taunt a buffalo with this
Cloven foot of thine, or the swift dromedary
With thy sublime of humps, the animals
Would revel in the compliment. And yet
Both beings are more swift, more strong, more
  mighty
In action and endurance than thyself,
And all the fierce and fair of the same kind
With thee. Thy form is natural: 'twas only
Nature's mistaken largess to bestow
The gifts which are of others upon man.
  Arn. Give me the strength then of the buf-
  falo's foot,
When he spurs high the dust, beholding his
Near enemy; or let me have the long
And patient swiftness of the desert-ship,
The helmless dromedary!—and I'll bear
Thy fiendish sarcasm with a saintly patience.
  Stran. I will.
  Arn. (*with surprise*). Thou canst?
  Stran. Perhaps. Would you aught else?
  Arn. Thou mockest me.
  Stran.   Not I. Why should I mock
What all are mocking? That's poor sport,
  methinks.
To talk to thee in human language (for
Thou canst not yet speak mine), the forester
Hunts not the wretched coney, but the boar
Or wolf, or lion, leaving paltry game
To petty burghers, who leave once a year
Their walls, to fill their household caldrons with
Such scullion prey. The meanest gibe at
  thee,—
Now *I* can mock the mightiest.
  Arn.   Then waste not
Thy time on me: I seek thee not.
  Stran.   Your thoughts
Are not far from me. Do not send me back:
I am not so easily recalled to do
Good service.
  Arn.   What wilt thou do for me?
  Stran.   Change
Shapes with you, if you will, since yours so irks
  you;
Or form you to your wish in any shape.
  Arn. Oh! then you are indeed the demon,
  for
Nought else would wittingly wear mine.
  Stran.   I'll show thee
The brightest which the world e'er bore, and
  give thee
Thy choice.
  Arn.   On what condition?
  Stran.   There's a question!
An hour ago you would have given your soul
To look like other men, and now you pause
To wear the form of heroes.
  Arn.   No; I will not.
I must not compromise my soul.
  Stran.   What soul

Worth naming so, would dwell in such a car-
   cass?
Arn. 'Tis an inspiring one, whate'er the
   tenement
In which it is mislodged. But name your
   compact:
Must it be signed in blood?
Stran.   Not in your own.
Arn. Whose blood then?
Stran.   We will talk of that hereafter.
But I'll be moderate with you, for I see
Great things within you. You shall have no
   bond
But your own will, no contract save your
   deeds.
Are you content?
Arn.   I take thee at thy word.
Stran. Now then! —
[*The Stranger approaches the fountain, and*
   turns to ARNOLD.
              A little of your blood.
Arn.   For what?
Stran. To mingle with the magic of the
   waters,
And make the charm effective.
Arn. (*holding out his wounded arm*). Take
   it all.
Stran. Not now. A few drops will suffice
   for this.
[*The Stranger takes some of* ARNOLD'S *blood*
   in his hand, and casts it into the fountain.
Stran. Shadows of beauty!
              Shadows of power!
   Rise to your duty —
      This is the hour!
   Walk lovely and pliant
      From the depth of this fountain,
   As the cloud-shapen giant
      Bestrides the Hartz Mountain.[1]
   Come as ye were,
      That our eyes may behold
   The model in air
      Of the form I will mould,
   Bright as the Iris
      When ether is spanned; —
   Such *his* desire is, [*Pointing to* ARNOLD.
      Such my command!
   Demons heroic —
      Demons who wore
   The form of the stoic
      Or sophist of yore —
   Or the shape of each victor,
      From Macedon's boy

---

[1] This is a well-known German superstition — a
gigantic shadow produced by reflection on the
Brocken. [The Brocken is the name of the loftiest
of the Hartz mountains, in the kingdom of Hano-
ver. From the earliest periods of authentic history,
the Brocken has been the seat of the marvellous.
The spectres are merely shadows of the observer
projected on dense vapor or thin fleecy clouds
which have the power of reflecting much light.]

   To each high Roman's picture,
      Who breathed to destroy —
   Shadows of beauty!
      Shadows of power!
   Up to your duty —
      This is the hour!
[*Various Phantoms arise from the waters,*
   and pass in succession before the Stranger
   and ARNOLD.
Arn. What do I see?
Stran.   The black-eyed Roman, with
The eagle's beak between those eyes which
   ne'er
Beheld a conqueror, or looked along
The land he made not Rome's, while Rome
   became
His, and all theirs who heired his very name.
Arn. The phantom's bald; my quest is
   beauty. Could I
Inherit but his fame with his defects!
Stran. His brow was girt with laurels more
   than hairs.
You see his aspect — choose it, or reject.
I can but promise you his form; his fame
Must be long sought and fought for.
Arn.   I will fight too,
But not as a mock Cæsar. Let him pass;
His aspect may be fair, but suits me not.
Stran. Then you are far more difficult to
   please
Than Cato's sister, or than Brutus' mother,
Or Cleopatra at sixteen — an age
When love is not less in the eye than heart.
But be it so! Shadow, pass on!
[*The phantom of Julius Cæsar disappears.*
Arn.   And can it
Be, that the man who shook the earth is gone,
And left no footstep?
Stran.   There you err. His substance
Left graves enough, and woes enough, and fame
More than enough to track his memory;
But for his shadow, 'tis no more than yours,
Except a little longer and less crooked
I' the sun. Behold another!
              [*A second phantom passes.*
Arn.   Who is he?
Stran. He was the fairest and the bravest of
Athenians. Look upon him well.
Arn.   He is
More lovely than the last. How beautiful![2]
Stran. Such was the curled son of Cli-
   nias; — wouldst thou
Invest thee with his form?
Arn.   Would that I had
Been born with it! But since that I may choose
   further,
I will *look* further.
          [*The shade of Alcibiades disappears.*
Stran.   Lo! behold again!

---

[2] ["Upon the whole, it may be doubted whether
there be a name of antiquity which comes down

Arn. What! that low, swarthy, short-nosed,
    round-eyed satyr,
With the wide nostrils and Silenus' aspect,
The splay feet and low stature![1] I had better
Remain that which I am.
    Stran.   And yet he was
The earth's perfection of all mental beauty,
And personification of all virtue.
But you reject him?
    Arn.   If his form could bring me
That which redeemed it — no.
    Stran.   I have no power
To promise that; but you may try, and find it
Easier in such a form, or in your own.
    Arn. No. I was not born for philosophy,
Though I have that about me which has need
    on't.
Let him fleet on.

----

with such a general charm as that of Alcibiades.
Why? I cannot answer. Who can?"*— *Byron's
Diary.*]
    [1] ["The outside of Socrates was that of a satyr
and buffoon, but his soul was all virtue, and from
within him came such divine and pathetic things,
as pierced the heart, and drew tears from the hear-
ers." — *Plato.*]

* One cannot help being struck with Lord By-
ron's choice of a favorite among the heroic names
of antiquity. The man who was educated by Peri-
cles, and who commanded the admiration as well
as the affection of Socrates; whose gallantry and
boldness were always as undisputed as the pre-emi-
nent graces of his person and manners; who died
at *forty-five*, after having been successively the
delight and hero of Athens, of Sparta, of Persia; —
this most versatile of great men has certainly left to
the world a very splendid reputation. But his
fame is stained with the recollections of a most
profligate and debauched course of private life, and
of the most complete and flagrant contempt of pub-
lic principle; and it is to be hoped that there are
not many men who could gravely give to the name
of Alcibiades a preference, on the whole, over such
an one as that of an Epaminondas or a Leonidas,
or even of a Miltiades or a Hannibal. But the
career of Alcibiades was *romantic:* every great
event in which he had a share has the air of a per-
sonal adventure; and, whatever might be said of
his want of principle, moral and political, nobody
ever doubted the greatness of his powers and the
brilliancy of his accomplishments. By the gift of
nature, the handsomest creature of his time, and
the possessor of a very extraordinary genius, he
was by accidents or by fits, a soldier, — a hero, —
an orator, — and even, it should seem, a philoso-
pher; but he played these parts only because he
wished it to be thought that there was no part
which he could not play. He thought of nothing
but himself. His vanity entirely commanded the
direction of his genius, and could even make him
abandon occasionally his voluptuousness for the
very opposite extreme; which last circumstance,
by the way, was probably one of those that had hit
Lord Byron's fancy — as indeed it may be sus-
pected to have influenced his behavior. — *Lock-
hart.*

Stran.   Be air, thou hemlock-drinker!
    [*The shadow of Socrates disappears: another
    rises.*
Arn. What's here? whose broad brow and
    whose curly beard
And manly aspect look like Hercules,
Save that his jocund eye hath more of Bacchus
Than the sad purger of the infernal world,
Leaning dejected on his club of conquest,
As if he knew the worthlessness of those
For whom he had fought.
    Stran.   It was the man who lost
The ancient world for love.
    Arn.   I cannot blame him,
Since I have risked my soul because I find
    not
That which he exchanged the earth for.
    Stran.   Since so far
You seem congenial, will you wear his features?
    Arn. No. As you leave me choice, I am
    difficult,
If but to see the heroes I should ne'er
Have seen else on this side of the dim shore
Whence they float back before us.
    Stran.   Hence, triumvir!
Thy Cleopatra's waiting.
    [*The shade of Antony disappears: another
    rises.*
    Arn.   Who is this?
Who truly looketh like a demigod,
Blooming and bright, with golden hair, and
    stature,
If not more high than mortal, yet immortal
In all that nameless bearing of his limbs,
Which he wears as the sun his rays — a some-
    thing
Which shines from him, and yet is but the
    flashing
Emanation of a thing more glorious still.
Was *he e'er human only?*[2]
    Stran.   Let the earth speak,
If there be atoms of him left, or even
Of the more solid gold that formed his urn.
    Arn. Who was this glory of mankind?
    Stran.   The shame
Of Greece in peace, her thunderbolt in war—
Demetrius the Macedonian, and
Taker of cities.
    Arn.   Yet one shadow more.
    Stran. (*addressing the shadow*). Get thee
    to Lamia's lap!
    [*The shade of Demetrius Poliorcetes van-
    ishes: another rises.*
                    I'll fit you still,
Fear not, my hunchback: if the shadows of

----

[2] [The beauty and mien of Demetrius Poliorcetes
were so inimitable, that no statuary or painter
could hit off a likeness. His countenance had a
mixture of grace and dignity, and was at once
amiable and awful, and the unsubdued and eager
air of youth was blended with the majesty of the
hero and the king.—*Plutarch.*]

That which existed please not your nice taste,
I'll animate the ideal marble, till
Your soul be reconciled to her new garment.
Arn. Content! I will fix here.
Stran. I must commend
Your choice. The godlike son of the sea-
goddess,
The unshorn boy of Peleus, with his locks
As beautiful and clear as the amber waves
Of rich Pactolus, rolled o'er sands of gold,
Softened by intervening crystal, and
Rippled like flowing waters by the wind,
All vowed to Sperchius as they were — be-
hold them!
And *him* — as he stood by Polixena,
With sanctioned and with softened love, be-
fore
The altar, gazing on his Trojan bride,
With some remorse within for Hector slain
And Priam weeping, mingled with deep pas-
sion
For the sweet downcast virgin, whose young
hand
Trembled in *his* who slew her brother. So
He stood i' the temple! Look upon him as
Greece looked her last upon her best, the
instant
Ere Paris' arrow flew.
Arn. I gaze upon him
As if I were his soul, whose form shall soon
Envelop mine.
Stran. You have done well. The greatest
Deformity should only barter with
The extremest beauty, if the proverb's true
Of mortals, that extremes meet.
Arn. Come! Be quick!
I am impatient.
Stran. As a youthful beauty
Before her glass. *You both* see what is not,
But dream it is what must be.
Arn. Must I wait?
Stran. No; that were a pity. But a word
or two:
His stature is twelve cubits; would you so
far
Outstep these times, and be a Titan? Or
(To talk canonically) wax a son
Of Anak?
Arn. Why not?
Stran. Glorious ambition!
I love thee most in dwarfs! A mortal of
Philistine stature would have gladly pared
His own Goliath down to a slight David:
But thou, my manikin, wouldst soar a show
Rather than hero. Thou shalt be indulged,
If such be thy desire; and yet, by being
A little less removed from present men
In figure, thou canst sway them more; for all
Would rise against thee now, as if to hunt
A new-found mammoth; and their cursed
engines,
Their culverins, and so forth, would find way

Through our friend's armor there, with greater
ease
Than the adulterer's arrow through his heel,
Which Thetis had forgotten to baptize
In Styx.
Arn. Then let it be as thou deem'st best.
Stran. Thou shalt be beauteous as the
thing thou seest,
And strong as what it was, and ——
Arn. I ask not
For valor, since deformity is daring.
It is its essence to o'ertake mankind
By heart and soul, and make itself the equal —
Ay, the superior of the rest. There is
A spur in its halt movements, to become
All that the others cannot, in such things
As still are free to both, to compensate
For stepdame Nature's avarice at first.
They woo with fearless deeds the smiles of
fortune,
And oft, like Timour the lame Tartar, win
them.
Stran. Well spoken! And thou doubtless
wilt remain
Formed as thou art. I may dismiss the mould
Of shadow, which must turn to flesh, to in-
case
This daring soul, which could achieve no less
Without it.
Arn. Had no power presented me
The possibility of change, I would
Have done the best which spirit may to make
Its way with all deformity's dull, deadly,
Discouraging weight upon me, like a moun-
tain,
In feeling, on my heart as on my shoulders —
An hateful and unsightly molehill to
The eyes of happier men. I would have
looked
On beauty in that sex which is the type
Of all we know or dream of beautiful
Beyond the world they brighten, with a sigh —
Not of love, but despair; nor sought to win,
Though to a heart all love, what could not
love me
In turn, because of this vile crooked clog,
Which makes me lonely. Nay, I could have
borne
It all, had not my mother spurned me from
her.
The she-bear licks her cubs into a sort
Of shape; — my dam beheld my shape was
hopeless.
Had she exposed me, like the Spartan, ere
I knew the passionate part of life, I had
Been a clod of the valley, — happier nothing
Than what I am. But even thus, the lowest,
Ugliest, and meanest of mankind, what cour-
age
And perseverance could have done, perchance
Had made me something — as it has made
heroes

Of the same mould as mine.   You lately saw
   me
Master of my own life, and quick to quit it;
And he who is so is the master of
Whatever dreads to die.
   Stran.   Decide between
What you have been, or will be.
   Arn.   I have done so.
You have opened brighter prospects to my
   eyes,
And sweeter to my heart.   As I am now,
I might be feared, admired, respected, loved
Of all save those next to me, of whom I
Would be beloved.   As thou showest me
A choice of forms, I take the one I view.
Haste! haste!
   Stran.   And what shall *I* wear?
   Arn.   Surely he
Who can command all forms will choose the
   highest,
Something superior even to that which was
Pelides now before us.   Perhaps *his*
Who slew him, that of Paris : or — still
   higher —
The poet's god, clothed in such limbs as are
Themselves a poetry.
   Stran.   Less will content me;
For I, too, love a change.
   Arn.   Your aspect is
Dusky, but not uncomely.
   Stran.   If I chose,
I might be whiter; but I have a penchant
For black — it is so honest, and besides
Can neither blush with shame nor pale with
   fear;
But I have worn it long enough of late,
And now I'll take your figure.
   Arn.   Mine!
   Stran.   Yes.   You
Shall change with Thetis' son, and I with
   Bertha,
Your mother's offspring.   People have their
   tastes;
You have yours — I mine.
   Arn.   Despatch! despatch!
   Stran.   Even so.
   [*The Stranger takes some earth and moulds
   it along the turf, and then addresses the
   phantom of Achilles.*
      Beautiful shadow
        Of Thetis's boy!
      Who sleeps in the meadow
        Whose grass grows o'er Troy:
      From the red earth, like Adam,[1]
        Thy likeness I shape,
      As the being who made him,
        Whose actions I ape.
      Thou clay, be all glowing,
        Till the rose in his cheek

---

[1] Adam means "*red earth*," from which the
first man was formed.

      Be as fair as, when blowing,
        It wears its first streak!
      Ye violets, I scatter,
        Now turn into eyes!
      And thou, sunshiny water,
        Of blood take the guise!
      Let these hyacinth boughs
        Be his long flowing hair,
      And wave o'er his brows,
        As thou wavest in air!
      Let his heart be this marble
        I tear from the rock!
      But his voice as the warble
        Of birds on yon oak!
      Let his flesh be the purest
        Of mould, in which grew
      The lily-root surest,
        And drank the best dew!
      Let his limbs be the lightest
        Which clay can compound,
      And his aspect the brightest
        On earth to be found!
      Elements, near me,
        Be mingled and stirred,
      Know me, and hear me,
        And leap to my word!
      Sunbeams, awaken
        This earth's animation!
      'Tis done!   He hath taken
        His stand in creation!
   [ARNOLD *falls senseless; his soul passes in-
   to the shape of Achilles, which rises from
   the ground; while the phantom has dis-
   appeared, part by part, as the figure was
   formed from the earth.*
   Arn. (*in his new form*).   I love, and I shall
   be beloved!   Oh life!
At last I feel thee!   Glorious spirit!
   Stran.   Stop!
What shall become of your abandoned gar-
   ment,
Your hump, and lump, and clod of ugliness,
Which late you wore, or were?
   Arn.   Who cares?   Let wolves
And vultures take it, if they will.
   Stran.   And if
They do, and are not scared by it, you'll say
It must be peace-time, and no better fare
Abroad i' the fields.
   Arn.   Let us but leave it there;
No matter what becomes on't.
   Stran.   That's ungracious,
If not ungrateful.   Whatsoe'er it be,
It hath sustained your soul full many a day.
   Arn.   Ay, as the dunghill may conceal a
   gem
Which is now set in gold, as jewels should be.
   Stran.   But if I give another form, it must be
By fair exchange, not robbery.   For they
Who make men without women's aid have
   long
Had patents for the same, and do not love

Your interlopers. The devil may take men,
Not make them, — though he reaped the ben-
   efit
Of the original workmanship: — and therefore
Some one must be found to assume the
   shape
You have quitted.

   Arn.   Who would do so?

   Stran.   That I know not,
And therefore I must.

   Arn.   You!

   Stran.   I said it ere
You inhabited your present dome of beauty.

   Arn.   True. I forget all things in the new
   joy
Of this immortal change.

   Stran.   In a few moments
I will be as you were, and you shall see
Yourself for ever by you, as your shadow.

   Arn.   I would be spared this.

   Stran.   But it cannot be.
What! shrink already, being what you are,
From seeing what you were?

   Arn.   Do as thou wilt.

   Stran. (*to the late form of* ARNOLD, *ex-
tended on the earth*).
Clay! not dead, but soul-less!
   Though no man would choose thee,
An immortal no less
   Deigns not to refuse thee.
Clay thou art; and unto spirit
All clay is of equal merit.
Fire! *without* which nought can live;
Fire! but *in* which nought can live,
   Save the fabled salamander,
   Or immortal souls, which wander,
Praying what doth not forgive,
Howling for a drop of water,
   Burning in a quenchless lot:
Fire! the only element
   Where nor fish, beast, bird, nor worm,
   Save the worm which dieth not,
   Can preserve a moment's form,
But must with thyself be blent:
Fire! man's safeguard and his slaughter:
Fire! Creation's first-born daughter,
   And Destruction's threatened son,
   When heaven with the world hath done:
Fire! assist me to renew
Life in what lies in my view
   Stiff and cold!
His resurrection rests with me and you!
One little, marshy spark of flame —
And he again shall seem the same;
   But I his spirit's place shall hold!

[*An ignis-fatuus flits through the wood and
rests on the brow of the body. The Stran-
ger disappears: the body rises.*

   Arn. (*in his new form*). Oh! horrible!

   Stran. (*in* ARNOLD'S *late shape*). What!
   tremblest thou?

   Arn.   Not so—

I merely shudder. Where is fled the shape
Thou lately worest?

   Stran.   To the world of shadows.
But let us thread the present. Whither wilt
   thou?

   Arn.   Must thou be my companion?

   Stran.   Wherefore not?
Your betters keep worse company.

   Arn.   *My* betters!

   Stran. Oh! you wax proud, I see, of your
   new form:
I'm glad of that. Ungrateful too! That's well;
You improve apace; — two changes in an
   instant,
And you are old in the world's ways already.
But bear with me: indeed you'll find me useful
Upon your pilgrimage. But come, pronounce
Where shall we now be errant?

   Arn.   Where the world
Is thickest, that I may behold it in
Its workings.

   Stran.   That's to say, where there is war
And woman in activity. Let's see!
Spain — Italy — the new Atlantic world —
Afric, with all its Moors. In very truth,
There is small choice: the whole race are
   just now
Tugging as usual at each other's hearts.

   Arn.   I have heard great things of Rome.

   Stran.   A goodly choice —
And scarce a better to be found on earth,
Since Sodom was put out. The field is wide
   too;
For now the Frank, and Hun, and Spanish ·
   scion
Of the old Vandals, are at play along
The sunny shores of the world's garden.

   Arn.   How
Shall we proceed?

   Stran.   Like gallants, on good coursers.
What ho! my chargers! Never yet were
   better,
Since Phaeton was upset into the Po.
Our pages too!

Enter two Pages, with four coal-black horses.

   Arn.   A noble sight!

   Stran.   And of
A nobler breed. Match me in Barbary,
On your Kochlini race of Araby,
With these!

   Arn. The mighty steam, which volumes high
From their proud nostrils, burns the very
   air;
And sparks of flame, like dancing fire-flies,
   wheel
Around their manes, as common insects
   swarm
Round common steeds towards sunset.

   Stran.   Mount, my lord·
They and I are your servitors.

   Arn.   And these

Our dark-eyed pages — what may be their
names ?

Stran. You shall baptize them.

Arn. What! in holy water ?

Stran. Why not ? The deeper sinner, bet-
ter saint.

Arn. They are beautiful, and cannot, sure,
be demons.

Stran. True; the devil's always ugly; and
your beauty
In never diabolical.

Arn. I'll call him
Who bears the golden horn, and wears such
bright
And blooming aspect, *Huon;* for he looks
Like to the lovely boy lost in the forest,
And never found till now. And for the other
And darker, and more thoughtful, who smiles
not,
But looks as serious though serene as night,
He shall be *Memnon,* from the Ethiop king
Whose statue turns a harper once a day.
And you ?

Stran. I have ten thousand names, and
twice
As many attributes; but as I wear
A human shape, will take a human name.

Arn. More human than the shape (though
it was mine once)
I trust.

Stran. Then call me Cæsar.

Arn. Why, that name
Belongs to empires, and has been but borne
By the world's lords.

Stran. And therefore fittest for
The devil in disguise — since so you deem me,
Unless you call me pope instead.

Arn. Well, then,
Cæsar thou shalt be. For myself, my name
Shall be plain Arnold still.

Cæs. We'll add a title —
' Count Arnold :" it hath no ungracious sound,
And will look well upon a billet-doux.

Arn. Or in an order for a battle-field.

Cæs. (*sings*). To horse! to horse! my
coal-black steed
Paws the ground and snuffs the air!
There's not a foal of Arab's breed
More knows whom he must bear;
On the hill he will not tire,
Swifter as it waxes higher,
In the marsh he will not slacken,
On the plain be overtaken;
In the wave he will not sink,
Nor pause at the brook's side to drink;
In the race he will not pant,
In the combat he'll not faint;
On the stones he will not stumble,
Time nor toil shall make him humble;
In the stall he will not stiffen,
But be winged as a griffin,
Only flying with his feet :

And will not such a voyage be sweet ?
Merrily! merrily! never unsound,
Shall our bonny black horses skim over the
ground!
From the Alps to the Caucasus, ride we, or
fly!
For we'll leave them behind in the glance of
an eye.
[*They mount their horses, and disappear.*

SCENE II. — *A Camp before the Walls of Rome.*

ARNOLD *and* CÆSAR.

Cæs. You are well entered now.

Arn. Ay; but my path
Has been o'er carcasses : mine eyes are full
Of blood.

Cæs. Then wipe them, and see clearly.
Why!
Thou art a conqueror; the chosen knight
And free companion of the gallant Bourbon,
Late constable of France : and now to be
Lord of the city which hath been earth's lord
Under its emperors, and — changing sex,
Not sceptre, an hermaphrodite of empire —
Lady of the old world.

Arn. How *old ?* What! are there
New worlds ?

Cæs. To *you.* You'll find there are such
shortly,
By its rich harvests, new disease, and gold ;
From one *half* of the world named a *whole* new
one,
Because you know no better than the dull
And dubious notice of your eyes and ears.

Arn. I'll trust them.

Cæs. Do! They will deceive you sweetly,
And that is better than the bitter truth.

Arn. Dog!

Cæs. Man!

Arn. Devil!

Cæs. Your obedient humble servant.

Arn. Say *master* rather. Thou has lured
me on,
Through scenes of blood and lust, till I am
here.

Cæs. And where wouldst *thou* be ?

Arn. Oh, at peace — in peace.

Cæs. And where is that which is so ? From
the star
To the winding worm, all life is motion; and
In life *commotion* is the extremest point
Of life. The planet wheels till it becomes
A comet, and destroying as it sweeps
The stars, goes out. The poor worm winds
its way,
Living upon the death of other things,
But still, like them, must live and die, the subject
Of something which has made it live and die.
You must obey what all obey, the rule
Of fixed necessity : against her edict
Rebellion prospers not.

Arn.   And when it prospers——
Cæs. 'Tis no rebellion.   .
Arn.   Will it prosper now?
Cæs. The Bourbon hath given orders for the assault,
And by the dawn there will be work.
Arn.   Alas!
And shall the city yield? I see the giant
Abode of the true God, and his true saint,
Saint Peter, rear its dome and cross into
That sky whence Christ ascended from the cross,
Which his blood made a badge of glory and
Of joy (as once of torture unto him,
God and God's Son, man's sole and only refuge).
Cæs. 'Tis there, and shall be.
Arn.   What?
Cæs.   The crucifix
Above, and many altar shrines below.
Also some culverins upon the walls,
And harquebusses, and what not; besides
The men who are to kindle them to death
Of other men.
Arn. And those scarce mortal arches,
Pile above pile of everlasting wall,
The theatre where emperors and their subjects
(Those subjects *Romans*) stood at gaze upon
The battles of the monarchs of the wild
And wood, the lion and his tusky rebels
Of the then untamed desert, brought to joust
In the arena (as right well they might,
When they had left no human foe unconquered);
Made even the forest pay its tribute of
Life to their amphitheatre, as well
As Dacia men to die the eternal death
For a sole instant's pastime, and "Pass on
To a new gladiator!"——Must it fall?
Cæs. The city, or the amphitheatre?
The church, or one, or all? for you confound
Both them and me.
Arn. To-morrow sounds the assault
With the first cock-crow.
Cæs.   Which, if it end with
The evening's first nightingale, will be
Something new in the annals of great sieges;
For men must have their prey after long toil.
Arn. The sun goes down as calmly, and perhaps
More beautifully, than he did on Rome
On the day Remus leapt her wall.
Cæs.   I saw him.
Arn. You!
Cæs.   Yes, sir. You forget I am or was
Spirit, till I took up with your cast shape
And a worse name. I'm Cæsar and a bunchback
Now. Well! the first of Cæsars was a baldhead,
And loved his laurels better as a wig

(So history says) than as a glory.[1] Thus
The world runs on, but we'll be merry still.
I saw your Romulus (simple as I am)
Slay his own twin, quick-born of the same womb,
Because he leapt a ditch ('twas then no wall,
Whate'er it now be); and Rome's earliest cement
Was brother's blood; and if its native blood
Be spilt till the choked Tiber be as red
As e'er 'twas yellow, it will never wear
The deep hue of the ocean and the earth,
Which the great robber sons of fratricide
Have made their never-ceasing scene of slaughter
For ages.
Arn.   But what have these done, their far
Remote descendants, who have lived in peace,
The peace of heaven, and in her sunshine of
Piety?
Cæs. And what had *they* done, whom the old
Romans o'erswept? — Hark!
Arn.   They are soldiers singing
A reckless roundelay, upon the eve
Of many deaths, it may be of their own.
Cæs. And why should they not sing as well as swans?
They are black ones, to be sure.
Arn.   So, you are learned,
I see, too?
Cæs.   In my grammar, certes. I
Was educated for a monk of all times,
And once I was well versed in the forgotten
Etruscan letters, and — were I so minded —
Could make their hieroglyphics plainer than
Your alphabet.
Arn.   And wherefore do you not?
Cæs. It answers better to resolve the alphabet
Back into hieroglyphics. Like your statesman,
And prophet, pontiff, doctor, alchemist,
Philospher, and what not, they have built
More Babels, without new dispersion, than
The stammering young ones of the flood's dull ooze,
Who failed and fled each other. Why? why, marry,
Because no man could understand his neighbor.
They are wiser now, and will not separate
For nonsense. Nay, it is their brotherhood,

---

[1] [Suetonius relates of Julius Cæsar, that his baldness gave him much uneasiness, having often found himself, upon that account, exposed to the ridicule of his enemies; and that, therefore, of all the honors conferred upon him by the senate and people, there was none which he either accepted or used with so much pleasure as the right of wearing constantly a laurel crown.]

Their Shibboleth, their Koran, Talmud, their
Cabala; their best brick-work, wherewithal
They build more——
　　Arn. (*interrupting him*). Oh, thou ever-
　　　lasting sneerer!
Be silent! How the soldiers' rough strain
　seems
Softened by distance to a hymn-like ca-
dence!
Listen!
　Cæs. Yes. I have heard the angels sing.
　Arn. And demons howl.
　Cæs.　　　　And man too. Let us listen;
I love all music.

　　　Song of the Soldiers within.

The black bands came over
　The Alps and their snow;
With Bourbon, the Rover,
　They passed the broad Po.
We have beaten all foemen,
　We have captured a king,
We have turned back on no men,
　And so let us sing!
Here's the Bourbon for ever!
　Though pennyless all,
We'll have one more endeavor
　At yonder old wall.
With the Bourbon we'll gather
　At day-dawn before
The gates, and together
　Or break or climb o'er
The wall: on the ladder
　As mounts each firm foot,
Our shouts shall grow gladder,
　And death only be mute.
With the Bourbon we'll mount o'er
　The walls of old Rome,
And who then shall count o'er
　The spoils of each dome?
Up! up with the lily!
　And down with the keys!
In old Rome, the seven-hilly,
　We'll revel at ease.
Her streets shall be gory,
　Her Tiber all red,
And her temples so hoary
　Shall clang with our tread.
Oh, the Bourbon! the Bourbon!
　The Bourbon for aye!
Of our song bear the burden!
　And fire, fire away!
With Spain for the vanguard,
　Our varied host comes;
And next to the Spaniard
　Beat Germany's drums;
And Italy's lances
　Are couched at their mother;
But our leader from France is,
　Who warred with his brother.
Oh, the Bourbon! the Bourbon!
　Sans country or home,

We'll follow the Bourbon,
　To plunder old Rome.
　Cæs.　　　　An indifferent song
For those within the walls, methinks, to hear.
　Arn. Yes, if they keep to their chorus. But
　　here comes
The general with his chiefs and men of trust.
A goodly rebel!

Enter the Constable BOURBON [1] "*cum suis,*"
　　　　etc. etc.

　Phil. 　　　How now, noble prince,
You are not cheerful?
　Bourb.　　　　Why should I be so?
　Phil. Upon the eve of conquest, such as
　　ours,
Most men would be so.
　Bourb.　　　　If I were secure!
　Phil. Doubt not our soldiers. Were the
　　walls of adamant,
They'd crack them. Hunger is a sharp artil-
　lery.
　Bourb. That they will falter is my least of
　　fears.
That they will be repulsed, with Bourbon for
Their chief, and all their kindled appetites
To marshal them on — were those hoary walls
Mountains, and those who guard them like
　the gods
Of the old fables, I would trust my Titans; —
But now——
　Phil. They are but men who war with
　　mortals.
　Bourb. True: but those walls have girded
　　in great ages,
And sent forth mighty spirits. The past earth
And present phantom of imperious Rome
Is peopled with those warriors; and methinks
They flit along the eternal city's rampart,
And stretch their glorious, gory, shadowy
　hands,
And beckon me away!
　Phil.　　　　So let them! Wilt thou
Turn back from shadowy menaces of shadows?
　Bourb. They do not menace me. I could
　　have faced,
Methinks, a Sylla's menace; but they clasp,
And raise, and wring their dim and deathlike
　hands,
And with their thin aspen faces and fixed
　eyes
Fascinate mine. Look there!
　Phil.　　　　I look upon
A lofty battlement.
　Bourb.　　　And there!
　Phil.　　　　Not even

---

[1] [Charles of Bourbon was cousin to Francis I.
and Constable of France. Being bitterly perse-
cuted by the queen-mother for having declined the
honor of her hand, and also by the king, he trans-
ferred his services to the Emperor Charles V.]

A guard in sight; they wisely keep below,
Sheltered by the gray parapet from some
Stray bullet of our lansquenets, who might
Practise in the cool twilight.

Bourb.   You are blind.

Phil. If seeing nothing more than may be
       seen
Be so.

Bourb. A thousand years have manned
       the walls
With all their heroes, — the last Cato stands
And tears his bowels, rather than survive
The liberty of that I would enslave.
And the first Cæsar with his triumphs flits
From battlement to battlement.

Phil.   Then conquer
The walls for which he conquered,· and be
       greater!

Bourb. True: so I will, or perish.

Phil.   You can *not.*
In such an enterprise to die is rather
The dawn of an eternal day, than death.

       [*Count* ARNOLD *and* CÆSAR *advance.*

Cæs. And the mere men — do they too
       sweat beneath
The noon of this same ever-scorching glory?

Bourb.   Ah!
Welcome the bitter hunchback! and his
       master,
The beauty of our host, and brave as beau-
       teous,
And generous as lovely. We shall find
Work for you both ere morning.

Cæs.   .   You will find,
So please your highness, no less for yourself.

Bourb. And if I do, there will not be a
       laborer
More forward, hunchback!

Cæs.   You may well say so,
For *you* have seen that back — as general,
Placed in the rear in action — but your foes
Have never seen it.

Bourb.   That's a fair retort,
For I provoked it : — but the Bourbon's breast
Has been, and ever shall be, far advanced
In danger's face as yours, were you the
       devil.

Cæs. And if I were, I might have saved
       myself
The toil of coming here.

Phil.   Why so?

Cæs.   One half
Of your brave bands of their own bold accord
Will go to him, the other half be sent,
More swiftly, not less surely.

Bourb.   Arnold, your
Slight crooked friend's as snake-like in his
       words
As his deeds.

Cæs.   Your highness much mistakes me.
The first snake was a flatterer — I am none;
And for my deeds, I only sting when stung.

Bourb. You are brave, and that's enough
       for me; and quick
In speech as sharp in action —and that's
       more.
I am not alone a soldier, but the soldiers'
Comrade.

Cæs. They are but bad company, your
       highness,
And worse even for their friends than foes, as
       being
More permanent acquaintance.

Phil.   How now, fellow!
Thou waxest insolent, beyond the privilege
Of a buffoon.

Cæs.   You mean I speak the truth.
I'll lie — it is as easy: then you'll praise me
For calling you a hero.

Bourb.   Philibert!
Let him alone; he's brave, and ever has
Been first, with that swart face and mountain
       shoulder
In field or storm, and.patient in starvation;
And for his tongue, the camp is full of
       license,
And the sharp stinging of a lively rogue
Is, to my mind, far preferable to
The gross, dull, heavy, gloomy execration
Of a mere famished, sullen, grumbling slave,
Whom nothing can convince save a full meal,
And wine, and sleep, and a few maravedis,
With which he deems him rich.

Cæs.   It would be well
If the earth's princes asked no more.

Bourb.   Be silent!

Cæs. Ay, but not idle. Work yourself
       with words!
You have few to speak.

Phil. What means the audacious prater?

Cæs. To prate, like other prophets.

Bourb.   Philibert!
Why will you vex him? Have we not enough
To think on? Arnold! I will lead the attack
To-morrow.

Arn.   I have heard as much, my lord.

Bourb. And you will follow?

Arn.   Since I must not lead.

Bourb. 'Tis necessary for the further daring
Of our too needy army, that their chief
Plant the first foot upon the foremost ladder's
First step.

Cæs. Upon its topmost, let us hope:
So shall he have his full deserts.

Bourb.   The world's
Great capital perchance is ours to-morrow.
Through every change the seven-billed city
       hath
Retained her sway o'er nations, and the
       Cæsars,
But yielded to the Alarics, the Alarics
Unto the pontiffs. Roman, Goth, or priest,
Still the world's masters. Civilized, barbarian,
Or saintly, still the walls of Romulus

Have been the circus of an empire. Well!
'Twas *their* turn — now 'tis ours; and let us
  hope
That we will fight as well, and rule much
  better.
   Cæs. No doubt, the camp's the school of
  civic rights.
What would you make of Rome ?
   Bourb.   That which it was.
   Cæs. In Alaric's time ?
   Bourb.   No, slave ! in the first Cæsar's,
Whose name you bear like other curs ——
   Cæs.   And kings !
Tis a great name for blood-hounds.
   Bourb.   There's a demon
In that fierce rattlesnake thy tongue. Wilt
  never
Be serious ?
   Cæs.   On the eve of battle, no ; —
That were not soldier-like. 'Tis for the gen-
  eral
To be more pensive : we adventurers
Must be more cheerful. Wherefore should
  we think
Our tutelar deity, in a leader's shape,
Takes care of us. Keep thought aloof from
  hosts !
If the knaves take to thinking, you will have
To crack those walls alone.
   Bourb.   You may sneer, since
Tis lucky for you that you fight no worse
  for't.
   Cæs. I thank you for the freedom ; 'tis the
  only
Pay I have taken in your highness' service.
   Bourb. Well, sir, to-morrow you shall pay
  yourself.
Look on those towers ; they hold my treasury :
But, Philibert, we'll in to council. Arnold,
We would request your presence.
   Arn.   Prince ! my service
Is yours, as in the field.
   Bourb.   In both we prize it,
And yours will be a post of trust at daybreak.
   Cæs. And mine ?
   Bourb. To follow glory with the Bourbon.
Good night !
   Arn. (*to* CÆSAR). Prepare our armor for
  the assault,
And wait within my tent.
   [*Exeunt* BOURBON, ARNOLD, PHILIBERT,
    etc.
   Cæs. (*solus*).   Within thy tent !
Think'st thou that I pass from thee with my
  presence ?
Or that this crooked coffer, which contained
Thy principle of life, is aught to me
Except a mask ? And these are men, for-
  sooth !
Heroes and chiefs, the flower of Adam's
  bastards !
This is the consequence of giving matter

The power of thought. It is a stubborn sub-
  stance,
And thinks chaotically, as it acts,
Ever relapsing into its first elements.
Well ! I must play with these poor puppets :
  'tis
The spirit's pastime in his idler hours.
When I grow weary of it, I have business
Amongst the stars, which these poor creatures
  deem
Were made for them to look at. 'Twere a
  jest now
To bring one down amongst them, and set fire
Unto their anthill : how the pismires then
Would scamper o'er the scalding soil, and,
  ceasing
From tearing down each other's nests, pipe
  forth
One universal orison ! Ha! ha!
                 [*Exit* CÆSAR.

PART II.

SCENE I. — *Before the walls of Rome. — The
  assault : the army in motion, with ladders to
  scale the walls ;* BOURBON, *with a white
  scarf over his armor, foremost.*

    Chorus of Spirits in the air.

               1.

'Tis the morn, but dim and dark.
Whither flies the silent lark ?
Whither shrinks the clouded sun ?
Is the day indeed begun ?
Nature's eye is melancholy
O'er the city high and holy :
But without there is a din
Should arouse the saints within,
And revive the heroic ashes
Round which yellow Tiber dashes.
Oh ye seven hills ! awaken,
Ere your very base be shaken !

               2.

Hearken to the steady stamp !
Mars is in their every tramp !
Not a step is out of tune,
As the tides obey the moon !
On they march, though to self-slaughter,
Regular as rolling water,
Whose high waves o'ersweep the border
Of huge moles, but keep their order,
Breaking only rank by rank.
Hearken to the armor's clank !
Look down o'er each frowning warrior,
How he glares upon the barrier :
Look on each step of each ladder,
As the stripes that streak an adder.

               3.

Look upon the bristling wall,
Manned without an interval !

Round and round, and tier on tier,
Cannon's black mouth, shining spear,
Lit match, bell-mouthed musquetoon,
Gaping to be murderous soon;
All the warlike gear of old,
Mixed with what we now behold,
In this strife 'twixt old and new,
Gather like a locusts' crew.
Shade of Remus! 'tis a time
Awful as thy brother's crime!
Christians war against Christ's shrine:—
Must its lot be like to thine?

4.

Near—and near—and nearer still,
As the earthquake saps the hill,
First with trembling, hollow motion,
Like a scarce-awakened ocean,
Then with stronger shock and louder,
Till the rocks are crushed to powder,—
Onward sweeps the rolling host!
Heroes of the immortal boast!
Mighty chiefs! eternal shadows!
First flowers of the bloody meadows
Which encompass Rome, the mother
Of a people without brother!
Will you sleep when nations' quarrels
Plough the root up of your laurels?
Ye who weep o'er Carthage burning,
Weep not—*strike!* for Rome is mourning![1]

5.

Onward sweep the varied nations!
Famine long hath dealt their rations.
To the wall, with hate and hunger,
Numerous as wolves, and stronger,
On they sweep. Oh! glorious city,
Must thou be a mother for pity?
Fight, like your first sire, each Roman!
Alaric was a gentle foeman,
Matched with Bourbon's black banditti!
Rouse thee, thou eternal city;
Rouse thee! Rather give the torch
With thine own hand to thy porch,
Than behold such hosts pollute
Your worst dwelling with their foot.

6.

Ah! behold yon bleeding spectre!
Ilion's children find no Hector;
Priam's offspring loved their brother;
Rome's great sire forgot his mother,
When he slew his gallant twin,
With inexpiable sin.
See the giant shadow stride
O'er the ramparts high and wide!
When the first o'erleapt thy wall,

1 Scipio, the second Africanus, is said to have repeated a verse of Homer, and wept over the burning of Carthage. He had better have granted it a capitulation.

Its foundation mourned thy fall.
Now, though towering like a Babel,
Who to stop his steps are able?
Stalking o'er thy highest dome,
Remus claims his vengeance, Rome!

7.

Now they reach thee in their anger:
Fire and smoke and hellish clangor
Are around thee, thou world's wonder!
Death is in thy walls and under.
Now the meeting steel first clashes,
Downward then the ladder crashes,
With its iron load all gleaming,
Lying at its foot blaspheming!
Up again! for every warrior
Slain, another climbs the barrier.
Thicker grows the strife: thy ditches
Europe's mingling gore enriches.
Rome! although thy wall may perish,
Such manure thy fields will cherish,
Making gay the harvest home;
But thy hearths, alas! oh, Rome!—
Yet be Rome amidst thine anguish,
Fight as thou wast wont to vanquish!

8.

Yet once more, ye old Penates!
Let not your quenched hearths be Até's!
Yet again ye shadowy heroes,
Yield not to these stranger Neros!
Though the son who slew his mother
Shed Rome's blood, he was your brother:
'Twas the Roman curbed the Roman;—
Brennus was a baffled foeman.
Yet again, ye saints and martyrs,
Rise! for yours are holier charters!
Mighty gods of temples falling,
Yet in ruin still appalling!
Mightier founders of those altars,
True and Christian,—strike the assaulters!
Tiber! Tiber! let thy torrent
Show even nature's self abhorrent.
Let each breathing heart dilated
Turn, as doth the lion baited!
Rome be crushed to one wide tomb,
But be still the Roman's Rome!

BOURBON, ARNOLD, CÆSAR, *and others, ar-
rive at the foot of the wall.* ARNOLD *is
about to plant his ladder.*

Bourb. Hold, Arnold! I am first.
Arn.   Not so, my lord.
Bourb. Hold, sir, I charge you! Follow!
I am proud
Of such a follower, but will brook no leader.
[BOURBON *plants his ladder, and begins to
mount.*
Now, boys! On! on!
[*A shot strikes him, and* BOURBON *falls.*
Cæs.   And off!
Arn.   Eternal powers!

The host will be appalled, — but vengeance!
vengeance!
Bourb. 'Tis nothing — lend me your hand.
[BOURBON *takes* ARNOLD *by the hand, and
rises; but as he puts his foot on the step,
falls again.*
                              Arnold! I am sped.
Conceal my fall — all will go well — conceal
it!
Fling my cloak o'er what will be dust anon;
Let not the soldiers see it.
Arn.   You must be
Removed; the aid of ——
Bourb.   No, my gallant boy;
Death is upon me. But what is *one* life?
The Bourbon's spirit shall command them
still.
Keep them yet ignorant that I am but clay,
Till they are conquerors — then do as you
may.
Cæs. Would not your highness choose to
kiss the cross?
We have no priest here, but the hilt of sword
May serve instead : — it did the same for Bay-
ard.[1]
Bourb. Thou bitter slave! to name *him*
at this time!
But I deserve it.
Arn. (*to* CÆSAR).   Villain, hold your
peace!
Cæs. What, when a Christian dies? Shall
I not offer
Christian " Vade in pace ? "
Arn.   Silence! Oh!
Those eyes are glazing which o'erlooked the
world,
And saw no equal.
Bourb.   Arnold, should'st thou see
France —— But hark! hark! the assault grows
warmer — Oh!
For but an hour, a minute more of life
To die within the wall! Hence, Arnold, hence!
You lose time — they will conquer Rome
without thee.
Arn. And without *thee!*
Bourb.   Not so; I'll lead them still
In spirit. Cover up my dust, and breathe not
That I have ceased to breathe. Away! and
be
Victorious!

Arn.   But I must not leave thee thus.
Bourb. You must — farewell — Up! up!
the world is winning.   [BOURBON *dies.*[2]
Cæs. (*to* ARNOLD). Come, count, to busi-
ness.
Arn.   True. I'll weep hereafter.
[ARNOLD *covers* BOURBON'S *body with a
mantle, and mounts the ladder, crying,*
The Bourbon! Bourbon! On, boys! Rome is
ours!
Cæs. Good night, lord constable! thou
wert a man.
[CÆSAR *follows* ARNOLD; *they reach the
battlement;* ARNOLD *and* CÆSAR *are
struck down.*
Cæs. A precious somerset! Is your count-
ship injured?
Arn. No.   [*Remounts the ladder.*
Cæs. A rare blood-hound, when his own is
heated!
And 'tis no boy's play. Now he strikes them
down!
His hand is on the battlement — he grasps it
As though it were an altar; now his foot
Is on it, and —— What have we here ? — a
Roman?   [*A man falls.*
The first bird of the covey! he has fallen
On the outside of the nest. Why, how now,
fellow?
Wounded Man. A drop of water!
Cæs.   Blood's the only liquid
Nearer than Tiber.
Wounded Man. I have died for Rome.
                                     [*Dies.*
Cæs. And so did Bourbon, in another sense.
Oh these immortal men! and their great
motives!
But I must after my young charge. Come
By this time i' the forum. Charge! charge!
[CÆSAR *mounts the ladder; the scene closes.*

SCENE II. — *The City. — Combats between the
Besiegers and Besieged in the streets. In-
habitants flying in confusion.*

Enter CÆSAR.

Cæs. I cannot find my hero; he is mixed
With the heroic crowd that now pursue

---

[1] [Finding himself mortally wounded, Bayard
ordered one of his attendants to place him under a
tree with his face towards the enemy; then fixing
his eyes on the guard of his sword, which he held
up instead of a cross, he addressed his prayers to
God, and in this posture he calmly waited the ap-
roach of death. — *Robertson's Charles V.*
   Just before Bayard's death Bourbon passing by
with the victorious Imperialists, expressed his
compassion. " Pity not me," said Bayard, " for I
die like an honest man; but I pity you who are
serving against your king, your country, and your
oath." Hence the dying Bourbon exclaims against

Cæsar for bringing to his mind the rebuke of the
dying Bayard.]
   [2] [On the 1st of May, 1527, the Constable and
his army came in sight of Rome; and the next
morning commenced the attack. Bourbon wore a
white vest over his armor, in order, he said, to be
more conspicuous both to his friends and foes. He
led on to the walls, and commenced a furious as-
sault, which was repelled with equal violence. See-
ing that his army began to waver, he seized a scal-
ing-ladder from a soldier standing, and was in the
act of ascending, when he was pierced by a mus-
ket-ball, and fell. Feeling that his wound was
mortal, he desired that his body might be concealed
from his soldiers, and instantly expired. — *Robert-
son.*]

The fugitives, or battle with the desperate.
What have we here? A cardinal or two
That do not seem in love with martyrdom.
How the old red-shanks scamper! Could
        they doff
Their hose as they have doffed their hats,
        'twould be
A blessing, as a mark the less for plunder.
But let them fly; the crimson kennels now
Will not much stain their stockings, since the
        mire
Is of the self-same purple hue.

Enter a Party fighting — ARNOLD *at the head
        of the Besiegers.*
                                He comes,
Hand in hand with the mild twins Gore and
        Glory.
Holla! hold, count!
    Arn.   Away! they must not rally.
    Cæs. I tell thee, be not rash; a golden
        bridge
Is for a flying enemy. I gave thee
A form of beauty, and an
Exemption from some maladies of body,
But not of mind, which is not mine to give.
But though I gave the form of Thetis' son,
I dipt thee not in Styx; and 'gainst a foe
I would not warrant thy chivalric heart
More than Pelides' heel; why then, be cau-
        tious,
And know thyself a mortal still.
    Arn.   And who
With aught of soul would combat if he were
Invulnerable? That were pretty sport.
Think'st thou I beat for hares when lions roar?
        [ARNOLD *rushes into the combat.*
    Cæs. A precious sample of humanity!
Well, his blood's up; and if a little's shed,
'Twill serve to curb his fever.
        [ARNOLD *engages with a Roman, who re-
        tires towards a portico.*
    Arn.   Yield thee, slave!
I promise quarter.
    Rom.   That's soon said.
    Arn.   And done —
My word is known.
    Rom.   So shall be my deeds.
        [*They reëngage.* CÆSAR *comes forward.*
    Cæs. Why, Arnold! hold thine own: thou
        hast in hand
A famous artísan, a cunning sculptor;
Also a dealer in the sword and dagger.
Not so, my musqueteer; 'twas he who slew
The Bourbon from the wall.
    Arn.   Ay, did he so?
Then he hath carved his monument.
    Rom.   I yet
May live to carve your betters.
    Cæs. Well said, my man of marble! Ben-
        venuto,
Thou hast some practice in both ways; and he

Who slays Cellini will have worked as hard
As e'er thou didst upon Carrara's blocks.[1]
    [ARNOLD *disarms and wounds* CELLINI,
        *but slightly: the latter draws a pistol, and
        fires; then retires, and disappears through
        the portico.*
    Cæs. How farest thou? Thou hast a taste,
        methinks,
Of red Bellona's banquet.
    Arn. (*staggers*).   'Tis a scratch.
Lend me thy scarf. He shall not 'scape me
        thus.
    Cæs. Where is it?
    Arn. In the shoulder, not the sword arm —
And that's enough. I am thirsty: would I had
A helm of water!
    Cæs.   That's a liquid now
In requisition, but by no means easiest
To come at.
    Arn.   And my thirst increases; — but
I'll find a way to quench it.
    Cæs.   Or be quenched
Thyself?
    Arn.   The chance is even; we will throw
The dice thereon. But I lose time in prating;
Prithee be quick. [CÆSAR *binds on the scarf.*
                        And what dost thou so idly?
Why dost not strike?
    Cæs.   Your old philosophers
Beheld mankind, as mere spectators of
The Olympic games. When I behold a prize
Worth wrestling for, I may be found a Milo.
    Arn. Ay, 'gainst an oak.
    Cæs.   A forest, when it suits me:
I combat with a mass, or not at all.
Meantime, pursue thy sport as I do mine;
Which is just now to gaze, since all these la-
        borers
Will reap my harvest gratis.
    Arn.   Thou art still
A fiend!
    Cæs. And thou — a man.
    Arn. Why, such I fain would show me.
    Cæs.   True — as men are.
    Arn. And what is that?
    Cæs.   Thou feelest and thou see'st.
        [*Exit* ARNOLD, *joining in the combat which
        still continues between detached parties.
        The scene closes.*

SCENE III. — *St. Peter's.* — *The Interior of
    the Church.* — *The Pope at the Altar.* —
    *Priests, etc., crowding in confusion, and Cit-
    izens flying for refuge, pursued by soldiery.*

            Enter CÆSAR.

A Spanish Soldier. Down with them, com-
        rades! seize upon those lamps!

---

[1] ["Levelling my arquebuse," says Benvenuto
Cellini, "I discharged it with a deliberate aim at a
person who seemed to be lifted above the rest. I

Cleave yon bald-pated shaveling to the chine!
His rosary's of gold!

Lutheran Soldier. Revenge! revenge!
Plunder hereafter, but for vengeance now —
Yonder stands Anti-Christ!

Cæs. (*interposing*). How now, schismatic?
What wouldst thou?

Luth. Sold. In the holy name of Christ,
Destroy proud Anti-Christ. I am a Christian.

Cæs. Yea, a disciple that would make the
founder
Of your belief renounce it, could he see
Such proselytes. Best stint thyself to plunder.

Luth. Sold. I say he is the devil.

Cæs. Hush! keep that secret,
Lest he should recognize you for his own.

Luth. Sold. Why would you save him? I
repeat he is
The devil, or the devil's vicar upon earth.

Cæs. And that's the reason: would you
make a quarrel
With your best friends? You had far best be
quiet;
His hour is not yet come.

Luth. Sold. That shall be seen!

[*The Lutheran Soldier rushes forward; a
shot strikes him from one of the Pope's
Guards, and he falls at the foot of the Al-
tar.*

Cæs. (*to the Lutheran*). I told you so.

Luth. Sold. And will you not avenge me?

Cæs. Not I! You know that "Vengeance
is the Lord's:"
You see he loves no interlopers.

Luth. Sold. (*dying*). Oh!
Had I but slain him, I had gone on high,
Crowned with eternal glory! Heaven, forgive
My feebleness of arm that reached him not,
And take thy servant to thy mercy. 'Tis
A glorious triumph still; proud Babylon's
No more; the Harlot of the Seven Hills
Hath changed her scarlet raiment for sack-
cloth
And ashes!   [*The Lutheran dies.*

Cæs.   Yes, thine own amidst the rest.
Well done, old Babel!

[*The Guards defend themselves desperately,
while the Pontiff escapes, by a private pas-
sage, to the Vatican and the Castle of St.
Angelo.*

Cæs.   Ha! right nobly battled!
Now, priest! now, soldier! the two great pro-
fessions,
Together by the ears and hearts! I have not

cautiously approached the walls, and perceived that
there was an extraordinary confusion among the
assailants, occasioned by our having shot the duke
of Bourbon: he was, as I understood afterwards,
that chief personage whom I saw raised above the
rest."—Vol. i. p. 120. This, however, is one of
the many stories in Cellini's amusing autobiogra-
phy which nobody credits.]

Seen a more comic pantomime since Titus
Took Jewry. But the Romans had the best
then;
Now they must take their turn.

Soldiers.   He hath escaped!
Follow!

Another Sold. They have barred the nar-
row passage up,
And it is clogged with dead even to the door.

Cæs. I am glad he hath escaped: he may
thank me for't
In part. I would not have his bulls abolished—
'Twere worth one half our empire: his indul-
gences
Demand some in return; — no, no, he must not
Fall; — and besides, his now escape may fur-
nish
A future miracle, in future proof
Of his infallibility. [*To the Spanish Soldiery.*
Well, cut-throats!
What do you pause for? If you make not
haste,
There will not be a link of pious gold left.
And *you*, too, catholics! Would ye return
From such a pilgrimage without a relic?
The very Lutherans have more true devotion:
See how they strip the shrines!

Soldiers.   By Holy Peter!
He speaks the truth; the heretics will bear
The best away.

Cæs.   And that were shame! Go to!
Assist in their conversion.

[*The Soldiers disperse; many quit the
Church, others enter.*

Cæs.   They are gone,
And others come: so flows the wave on wave
Of what these creatures call eternity,
Deeming themselves the breakers of the ocean,
While they are but its bubbles, ignorant
That foam is their foundation. So, another!

Enter OLIMPIA, *flying from the pursuit. She
springs upon the Altar.*

Sold. She's mine!

Another Sold. (*opposing the former*). You
lie, I tracked her first; and were she
The Pope's niece, I'll not yield her.
                              [*They fight.*

3d Sold. (*advancing towards* OLIMPIA).
You may settle
Your claims; I'll make mine good.

Olimp.   Infernal slave!
You touch me not alive.

3d Sold.   Alive or dead!

Olimp. (*embracing a massive crucifix*). Re-
spect your God!

3d Sold.   Yes, when he shines in gold.
Girl, you but grasp your dowry.

[*As he advances,* OLIMPIA, *with a strong
and sudden effort, casts down the crucifix:
it strikes the Soldier, who falls.*

3d Sold.   Oh, great God!

Olimp. Ah! now you recognize him.

· 3*d Sold.*   My brain's crushed!
Comrades, help, ho! All's darkness!

[*He dies.*

Other Soldiers (coming up). Slay her, al-
though she had a thousand lives:
She hath killed our comrade.

Olimp.   Welcome such a death!
You have no life to give, which the worst slave
Would take. Great God! through thy re-
deeming Son,
And thy Son's Mother, now receive me as
I would approach thee, worthy her, and him,
and thee!

Enter ARNOLD.

Arn. What do I see? Accursed jackals!
Forbear!

Cæs. (*aside and laughing*). Ha! ha! here's
equity! The dogs
Have as much right as he. But to the issue!

Soldiers. Count, she hath slain our com-
rade.

Arn.   With what weapon?

Sold. The cross, beneath which he is
crushed; behold him
Lie there, more like a worm than man; she
cast it
Upon his head.

Arn.   Even so; there is a woman
Worthy a brave man's liking. Were ye such,
Ye would have honored her. But get ye hence,
And thank your meanness, other God you
have none
For your existence. Had you touched a hair
Of those dishevelled locks, I would have
thinned
Your ranks more than the enemy. Away!
Ye jackals! gnaw the bones the lion leaves,
But not even these till he permits.

A Sold. (*murmuring*).   The lion
Might conquer for himself then.

Arn. (*cuts him down*).   Mutineer!
Rebel in hell — you shall obey on earth!

[*The Soldiers assault* ARNOLD.

Arn. Come on! I'm glad on't! I will show
you, slaves,
How you should be commanded, and who led
you
First o'er the wall you were so shy to scale,
Until I waved my banners from its height,
As you are bold within it.

[ARNOLD *mows down the foremost; the rest
throw down their arms.*

Soldiers.   Mercy! mercy!

Arn. Then learn to grant it. Have I
taught you *who*
Led you o'er Rome's eternal battlements?

Soldiers. We saw it, and we know it; yet
forgive
A moment's error in the heat of conquest —
The conquest which you led to.

Arn.   Get you hence!
Hence to your quarters! you will find them
fixed
In the Colonna palace.

Olimp. (*aside*).   In my father's
House!

Arn. (*to the Soldiers*). Leave your arms;
ye have no further need
Of such: the city's rendered. And mark well
You keep your hands clean, or I'll find out a
stream
As red as Tiber now runs, for your baptism.

Soldiers (*deposing their arms and depart-
ing*). We obey!

Arn. (*to* OLIMPIA). Lady, you are safe.

Olimp.   I should be so,
Had I a knife even; but it matters not —
Death hath a thousand gates; and on the
marble,
Even at the altar foot, whence I look down
Upon destruction, shall my head be dashed,
Ere thou ascend it. God forgive thee, man!

Arn. I wish to merit his forgiveness, and
Thine own, although I have not injured thee.

Olimp. No! Thou hast only sacked my
native land, —
No injury! — and made my father's house
A den of thieves! No injury! — this temple —
Slippery with Roman and with holy gore.
No injury! And now thou would'st preserve me
To be —— but that shall never be!

[*She raises her eyes to Heaven, folds her
robe round her, and prepares to dash her-
self down on the side of the Altar opposite
to that where* ARNOLD *stands.*

Arn.   Hold! hold!
I swear.

Olimp. Spare thine already forfeit soul
A perjury for which even hell would loathe thee,
I know thee.

Arn.   No, thou know'st me not; I am not
Of these men, though ——

Olimp.   I judge thee by thy mates;
It is for God to judge thee as thou art.
I see thee purple with the blood of Rome;
Take mine, 'tis all thou e'er shalt have of me,
And here, upon the marble of this temple,
Where the baptismal font baptized me God's,
I offer him a blood less holy
But not less pure (pure as it left me then,
A redeemed infant) than the holy water
The saints have sanctified!

[OLIMPIA *waves her hand to* ARNOLD *with
disdain, and dashes herself on the pave-
ment from the Altar.*

Arn.   .   Eternal God!
I feel thee now! Help! help! She's gone.

Cæs. (*approaches*).   I am here.

Arn. Thou! but oh, save her!

Cæs. (*assisting him to raise* OLIMPIA!
hath done it well!
The leap was serious.

Arn.   Oh! she is lifeless!
Cæs.   If
She be so, I have nought to do with that:
The resurrection is beyond me.
    Arn.   Slave!
    Cæs.   Ay, slave or master, 'tis all one: me-
thinks
Good words, however, are as well at times.
    Arn.   Words!—Canst thou aid her?
    Cæs.   I will try. A sprinkling
Of that same holy water may be useful.
[*He brings some in his helmet from the font.*
    Arn.   'Tis mixed with blood.
    Cæs.   There is no cleaner now
In Rome.
    Arn.   How pale! how beautiful! how life-
less!
Alive or dead, thou essence of all beauty,
I love but thee!
    Cæs.   Even so Achilles loved
Penthesilea: with his form it seems
You have his heart, and yet it was no soft one.
    Arn.   She breathes! But no, 'twas nothing
or the last
Faint flutter life disputes with death.
    Cæs.   She breathes.
    Arn.   *Thou* say'st it? Then 'tis truth.
    Cæs.   You do me right—
The devil speaks truth much oftener than he's
deemed:
He hath an ignorant audience.
    Arn. (*without attending to him*). Yes! her
heart beats.
Alas! that the first beat of the only heart
I ever wished to beat with mine should vibrate
To an assassin's pulse.
    Cæs.   A sage reflection,
But somewhat late i' the day. Where shall
we bear her?
I say she lives.
    Arn.   And will she live?
    Cæs.   As much
As dust can.
    Arn.   Then she is dead!
    Cæs.   Bah! bah! You are so,
And do not know it. She will come to life—
Such as you think so, such as you now are;
But we must work by human means.
    Arn.   We will
Convey her unto the Colonna palace,
Where I have pitched my banner.
    Cæs.   Come then! raise her up!
    Arn.   Scftly!
    Cæs.   As softly as they bear the dead.
Perhaps because they cannot feel the jolting.
    Arn.   But doth she live indeed r
    Cæs.   Nay, never fear!
But, if you rue it after, blame not me.
    Arn.   Let her but live!
    Cæs.   The spirit of her life
Is yet within her breast, and may revive.
Count! count! I am your servant in all things.

And this is a new office: — 'tis not oft
I am employed in such; but you perceive
How stanch a friend is what you call a fiend.
On earth you have often only fiends for friends;
Now *I* desert not mine. Soft! bear her hence,
The beautiful half-clay, and nearly spirit!
I am almost enamoured of her, as
Of old the angels of her earliest sex.
    Arn.   Thou!
    Cæs.   I! But fear not. I'll not be your
rival.
    Arn.   Rival!
    Cæs.   I could be one right formidable;
But since I slew the seven husbands of
Tobias' future bride (and after all
Was smoked out by some incense), I have laid
Aside intrigue: 'tis rarely worth the trouble
Of gaining, or—what is more difficult—
Getting rid of your prize again; for there's
The rub! at least to mortals.
    Arn.   Prithee, peace!
Softly! methinks her lips move, her eyes open!
    Cæs.   Like stars, no doubt; for that's a
metaphor
For Lucifer and Venus.
    Arn.   To the palace
Colonna, as I told you!
    Cæs.   Oh! I know
My way through Rome.
    Arn.   Now onward, onward! Gently!
[*Exeunt, bearing* OLIMPIA.   *The scene
closes.*

PART III.

SCENE I.— *A Castle in the Apennines, sur-
rounded by a wild but smiling country.
Chorus of Peasants singing before the Gates.*

CHORUS.

I.

The wars are over,
    The spring is come;
    The bride and her lover
    Have sought their home:
They are happy, we rejoice;
Let their hearts have an echo in every voice!

2.

The spring is come; the Violet's gone,
The first-born child of the early sun:
With us she is but a winter's flower,
The snow on the hills cannot blast her bower,
And she lifts up her dewy eye of blue
To the youngest sky of the self-same hue.

3.

And when the spring comes with her host
Of flowers, that flower beloved the most
Shrinks from the crowd that may confuse
Her heavenly odor and virgin hues.

4.

Pluck the others, but still remember
Their herald out of dim December —
The morning star of all the flowers,
The pledge of daylight's lengthened hours;
Nor, midst the roses, e'er forget
The virgin, virgin violet.

Enter CÆSAR.

Cæs. (singing). The wars are all over,
  Our swords are all idle,
  The steed bites the bridle,
  The casque's on the wall.
  There's rest for the rover;
  But his armor is rusty,
  And the veteran grows crusty,
As he yawns in the hall.
  He drinks — but what's drinking?
  A mere pause from thinking! '
No bugle awakes him with life-and-death call.

CHORUS.

But the hound bayeth loudly,
  The boar's in the wood,.
And the falcon longs proudly
  To spring from her hood:
On the wrist of the noble
  She sits like a crest,
And the air is in trouble
  With birds from their nest.

Cæs. Oh! shadow of glory!
  Dim image of war!
But the chase hath no story,
  Her hero no star,
Since Nimrod, the founder
  Of empire and chase,
Who made the woods wonder
  And quake for their race;
When the lion was young,
  In the pride of his might,
Then 'twas sport for the strong
  To embrace him in fight;
To go forth, with a pine
  For a spear, 'gainst the mammoth,
Or strike through the ravine
  At the foaming behemoth;
While man was in stature
  As towers in our time,
The first-born of Nature,
  And, like her, sublime!

CHORUS.

But the wars are over,
  The spring is come;
The bride and her lover
  Have sought their home:
They are happy, and we rejoice;
Let their hearts have an echo from every voice!
    [*Exeunt the Peasantry, singing.*

WERNER; OR, THE INHERITANCE.

A TRAGEDY.

PREFACE.

THE following drama is taken entirely from the " *German's Tale, Kruitzner,*" published many years ago in *Lee's Canterbury Tales;* written (I believe) by two sisters, of whom one furnished only this story and another, both of which are considered superior to the remainder of the collection.[1] I have adopted the characters, plan, and even the language, of many parts of this story. Some of the characters are modified or altered, a few of the names changed, and one character (Ida of Stralenheim) added by myself: but in the rest the original is chiefly followed. When I was young (about fourteen, I think), I first read this tale, which made a deep impression upon me; and may, indeed, be said to contain the germ of much that I have since written. I am not sure that it ever was very popular; or, at any rate, its popularity has since been eclipsed by that of other great writers in the same department. But I have

---

[1] [This is not correct. "The Young Lady's Tale, or the Two Emily's," and " the Clergyman's Tale, or Pembroke," were contributed by Sophia Lee. The "German's Tale," and all the others in the Canterbury Collection, were written by Harriet, the younger of the sisters.]

generally found that those who *had* read it, agreed with me in their estimate of the singular power of mind and conception which it develops. I should also add *conception*, rather than execution; for the story might, perhaps, have been developed with greater advantage. Amongst those whose opinions agreed with mine upon this story, I could mention some very high names: but it is not necessary, not indeed of any use; for every one must judge according to his own feelings. I merely refer the reader to the original story, that he may see to what extent I have borrowed from it; and am not unwilling that he should find much greater pleasure in perusing it than the drama which is founded upon its contents.

I had begun a drama upon this tale so far back as 1815, (the first I ever attempted, except one at thirteen years old, called " *Ulric and Ilvina*," which I had sense enough to burn,) and had nearly completed an act, when I was interrupted by circumstances. This is somewhere amongst my papers in England; but as it has not been found, I have re-written the first, and added the subsequent acts.

The whole is neither intended, nor in any shape adapted, for the stage.[1]

Pisa, February, 1822.

INTRODUCTION.

The tragedy of " Werner " was begun at Pisa, December the 18th, 1821, completed January the 20th, 1822, and published in London in the November after. The contemporary reviews of " Werner " were, without exception, unfavorable. The critique in Blackwood begins thus: —

" Who could be so absurd as to think, that a dramatist has no right to make free with other people's fables? On the contrary, we are quite aware that that particular species of genius which is exhibited in the construction of plots, never at any period flourished in England. We all know that Shakspeare himself took his stories from Italian novels, Danish sagas, English chronicles, Plutarch's Lives — from anywhere rather than from his own invention. But did he take *the whole* of Hamlet, or Juliet, or Richard the Third, or Antony and Cleopatra, from any of these foreign sources? Did he not *invent*, in the noblest sense of the word, all the *characters* of his pieces? Who dreams that any old Italian novelist, or ballad-maker, could have formed the imagination of such a creature as Juliet? Who dreams that the Hamlet of Shakspeare, the princely enthusiast, the melancholy philosopher, that spirit refined even to pain, that most incomprehensible and unapproachable of all the creations of human genius, is the same being, in any thing but the name, with the rough, strong-hearted, bloody-handed Amlett of the north? Who is there that supposes Goethe to have taken the character of *his* Faust from the nursery rhymes and penny pamphlets about the Devil and Doctor Faustus? Or who, to come nearer home, imagines that Lord Byron himself found *his* Sardanapalus in Dionysius of Halicarnassus?

" But *here* Lord Byron has *invented* nothing — absolutely nothing. There is not one incident in his play, not even the most trivial, that is not to be found in Miss Lee's novel, occurring exactly in the same manner, brought about by exactly the same agents, and producing exactly the same effects on the plot. And then as to the characters, — not only is every one of them to be found in ' Kruitzner,' but every one is to be found there more fully and powerfully developed. Indeed, but for the preparation which we had received from our old familiarity with Miss Lee's own admirable work, we rather incline to think that we should have been unable to comprehend the gist of her noble imitator, or rather copier, in several of what seem to be meant for his most elaborate delineations. The fact is, that this undeviating closeness, this humble fidelity of *imitation*, is a thing so perfectly new in any thing worthy of the name of *literature*, that we are sure no one, who has not read the Canterbury Tales, will be able to form the least conception of what it amounts to.

" Those who have never read Miss Lee's book, will, however, be pleased with this production; for, in truth, the story is one of the most powerfully conceived, one of the most picturesque, and at the same time instructive stories, that we are acquainted with. Indeed, thus led as we are to name Harriet Lee, we cannot allow the opportunity to pass without saying, that we have always considered her works as standing upon the verge of *the very first rank* of excellence; that is to say, as inferior to no English novels

---

[1] [Werner, however, has been produced on the stage with tolerable success since Byron's death.]

whatever, excepting those of Fielding, Sterne, Smollett, Richardson, Defoe, Radcliffe, Godwin, Edge-
worth, and the author of Waverley. It would not, perhaps, be going too far to say, that the Canterbury
Tales exhibit more of that species of invention which, as we have already remarked, was never common
in English literature, than any of the works even of those first-rate novelists we have named, with the
single exception of Fielding.

"'Kruitzner, or the German's Tale,' possesses mystery, and yet clearness, as to its structure;
strength of characters, and admirable contrast of characters; and, above all, the most lively interest,
blended with and subservient to the most affecting of moral lessons. The main idea which lies at the
root of it is, the horror of an erring father, who, having been detected in vice by his son, has dared to
defend his own sin, and so to perplex the son's notions of moral rectitude, on finding that the son, in his
turn, has pushed the false principles thus instilled to the last and worst extreme — on hearing his own
sophistries flung in his face by a — Murderer."

The reader will find a minute analysis, introduced by the above remarks, in Blackwood, vol. xii.
p. 710.

TO THE ILLUSTRIOUS GOETHE,

BY ONE OF HIS HUMBLEST ADMIRERS, THIS TRAGEDY IS DEDICATED.

DRAMATIS PERSONÆ.

MEN.	ARNHEIM.
WERNER.	MEISTER.
ULRIC.	RODOLPH.
STRALENHEIM.	LUDWIG.
IDENSTEIN.	
GABOR.	WOMEN.
FRITZ.	JOSEPHINE.
HENRICK.	IDA STRALENHEIM.
ERIC.	

Scene — Partly on the Frontier of Silesia, and partly in Siegendorf Castle, near Prague.

Time — the Close of the Thirty Years' War.

ACT I.

SCENE I.— *The Hall of a decayed Palace
near a small Town on the Northern Frontier
of Silesia — the Night tempestuous.*

WERNER *and* JOSEPHINE *his wife.*

Jos. My love, be calmer!
Wer.   I am calm.
Jos.   To me —
Yes, but not to thyself: thy pace is hurried,
And no one walks a chamber like to ours
With steps like thine when his heart is at rest.
Were it a garden, I should deem thee happy,

And stepping with the bee from flower to
      flower;
But *here!*
Wer.   'Tis chill; the tapestry lets through
The wind to which it waves: my blood is
      frozen.
Jos. Ah, no!
Wer. (*smiling*). Why! wouldst thou have
      it so?
Jos.   I would
Have it a healthful current.
Wer.   Let it flow
Until 'tis spilt or checked — how soon, I care
      not.

Jos. And am I nothing in thy heart?
Wer.　　　　　　　　　　　　All—all.
Jos. Then canst thou wish for that which
must break mine?
Wer. (*approaching her slowly*). But for
thee I had been — no matter what,
But much of good and evil; what I am,
Thou knowest; what I might or should have
been,
Thou knowest not: but still I love thee, nor
Shall aught divide us.
　　　　[WERNER *walks on abruptly, and then ap-*
　　　　proaches JOSEPHINE.
　　　　　　　　　The storm of the night
Perhaps affects me; I'm a thing of feelings,
And have of late been sickly, as, alas!
Thou know'st by sufferings more than mine,
my love!
In watching me.
Jos.　　　　　To see thee well is much —
To see thee happy ——
Wer.　　　　　Where hast thou seen such?
Let me be wretched with the rest!
Jos.　　　　　　　　　But think
How many in this hour of tempest shiver
Beneath the biting wind and heavy rain,
Whose every drop bows them down nearer
earth
Which hath no chamber for them save be-
neath
Her surface.
Wer. And that's not the worst: who cares
For chambers? rest is all. The wretches whom
Thou namest—ay, the wind howls round them,
and
The dull and dropping rain saps in their
bones
The creeping marrow. I have been a soldier,
A hunter, and a traveller, and am
A beggar, and should know the thing thou
talk'st of.
Jos. And art thou not now sheltered from
them all?
Wer. Yes. And from these alone.
Jos.　　　　　　　　And that is something.
Wer. True — to a peasant.
Jos.　　　　　Should the nobly born
Be thankless for that refuge which their
habits
Of early delicacy render more
Needful than to the peasant, when the ebb
Of fortune leaves them on the shoals of life?
Wer. It is not that, thou know'st it is not;
we
Have borne all this, I'll not say patiently,
Except in thee — but we have borne it.
Jos.　　　　　　　　　Well?
Wer. Something beyond our outward suf-
ferings (though
These were enough to gnaw into our souls)
Hath stung me oft, and, more than ever, *now*.
When, but for this untoward sickness, which

Seized me upon this desolate frontier, and [1]
Hath wasted, not alone my strength, but
means,
And leaves us—no! this is beyond me! [2]—
but
For this I had been happy—*thou* been happy—
The splendor of my rank sustained—my
name—
My father's name—been still upheld; and,
more
Than those ——
Jos. (*abruptly*). My son—our son—our
Ulric,
Been clasped again in these long-empty arms,
And all a mother's hunger satisfied.
Twelve years! he was but eight then: — beau-
tiful
He was, and beautiful he must be now,
My Ulric! my adored!
Wer.　　　　　　I have been full oft
The chase of Fortune; now she hath o'ertaken
My spirit where it cannot turn at bay, —
Sick, poor, and lonely.
Jos.　　　　Lonely! my dear husband?
Wer. Or worse—involving all I love, in
this
Far worse than solitude. *Alone*, I had died,
And all been over in a nameless grave.
Jos. And I had not outlived thee; but
pray take
Comfort! We have struggled long; and they
who strive
With Fortune win or weary her at last,
So that they find the goal or cease to feel
Further. Take comfort, — we shall find our
boy.
Wer. We were in sight of him, of every
thing

[1] [In this play, Lord Byron adopts the same
nerveless and pointless kind of blank verse, which
was a sorrow to everybody in his former dramatic
essays. It is, indeed, "most unmusical, most mel-
ancholy." — "Ofs," "tos," "ands," "fors," "bys,"
"buts," and the like, are the most common conclu-
sions of a line; there is no ease, no flow, no har-
mony, "in linked sweetness long drawn out:"
neither is there any thing of abrupt fiery vigor to
compensate for these defects. — *Blackwood.*]

[2] [This is, indeed, beyond us. If this be poetry,
then we were wrong in taking his Lordship's pref-
ace for prose. It will run on ten feet as well as the
rest — (See p. 716, *antè*.)
"Some of the characters are modified
Or altered, a few of the names changed, and
One character (Ida of Stralenheim)
Added by myself; but in the rest the
Original is chiefly followed. When
I was young (about fourteen, I think) I
First read this tale, which made a deep impression
Upon me" —
Nor is there a line in these so lame and halting, but
we could point out many in the drama as bad.—
Campbell.]

Which could bring compensation for past
  sorrow —
And to be baffled thus!
Jos.   We are not baffled.
Wer.   Are we not penniless?
Jos.   We ne'er were wealthy.
Wer.   But I was born to wealth, and rank,
  and power;
Enjoyed them, loved them, and, alas! abused
  them,
And forfeited them by my father's wrath,
In my o'er-fervent youth; but for the abuse
Long sufferings have atoned. My father's
  death
Left the path open, yet not without snares.
This cold and creeping kinsman, who so long
Kept his eye on me, as the snake upon
The fluttering bird, hath ere this time outstept
  me,
Become the master of my rights, and lord
Of that which lifts him up to princes in
Dominion and domain.
Jos.   Who knows? our son
May have returned back to his grandsire, and
Even now uphold thy rights for thee?
Wer.   'Tis hopeless.
Since his strange disappearance from my
  father's,
Entailing, as it were, my sins upon
Himself, no tidings have revealed his course.
I parted with him to his grandsire, on
The promise that his anger would stop short
Of the third generation; but Heaven seems
To claim her stern prerogative, and visit
Upon my boy his father's faults and follies.
Jos.   I must hope better still, — at least we
  have yet
Baffled the long pursuit of Stralenheim.
Wer.   We should have done, but for this
  fatal sickness;
More fatal than a mortal malady,
Because it takes not life, but life's sole solace:
Even now I feel my spirit girt about
By the snares of this avaricious fiend; —
How do I know he hath not tracked us here?
Jos.   He does not know thy person; and
  his spies,
Who so long watched thee, have been left
  at Hamburgh.
Our unexpected journey, and this change
Of name, leaves all discovery far behind:
None hold us here for aught save what we
  seem.
Wer.   Save what we seem! save what we
  are — sick beggars,
Even to our very hopes. — Ha! ha!
Jos.   Alas!
That bitter laugh!
Wer.   Who would read in this form
The high soul of the son of a long line?
Who, in this garb, the heir of princely lands?
Who, in this sunken, sickly eye, the pride

Of rank and ancestry? In this worn cheek
And famine-hollowed brow, the lord of halls
Which daily feast a thousand vassals?
Jos.   You
Pondered not thus upon these worldly things,
My Werner! when you deigned to choose for
  bride
The foreign daughter of a wandering exile.
Wer.   An exile's daughter with an outcast
  son
Were a fit marriage; but I still had hopes
To lift thee to the state we both were born for.
Your father's house was noble, though de-
  cayed;
And worthy by its birth to match with ours.
Jos.   Your father did not think so, though
  'twas noble;
But had my birth been all my claim to match
With thee, I should have deemed it what it is.
Wer.   And what is that in thine eyes?
Jos.   All which it
Has done in our behalf, — nothing.
Wer.   How, — nothing?
Jos.   Or worse; for it has been a canker in
Thy heart from the beginning: but for this,
We had not felt our poverty but as
Millions of myriads feel it, cheerfully;
But for these phantoms of thy feudal fathers,
Thou mightst have earned thy bread, as thou-
  sands earn it;
Or, if that seem too humble, tried by commerce,
Or other civic means, to amend thy fortunes.
Wer. (*ironically*). And been an Hanse-
  atic burgher. Excellent!
Jos.   Whate'er thou mightst have been, to
  me thou art
What no state high or low can ever change,
My heart's first choice; — which chose thee,
  knowing neither
Thy birth, thy hopes, thy pride; nought, save
  thy sorrows:
While they last, let me comfort or divide them;
When they end, let mine end with them, or
  thee![1]
Wer.   My better angel! such I have ever
  found thee;
This rashness, or this weakness of my temper,
Ne'er raised a thought to injure thee or
  thine.
Thou didst not mar my fortunes: my own
  nature
In youth was such as to unmake an empire,
Had such been my inheritance; but now,

---

[1] [Werner's wife, Josephine, with the exception
of Ida, the only female in the drama, is an example
of true and spotless virtue. A true woman, she not
only well maintains the character of her sex by gen-
eral integrity, but equally displays the endearing,
soft, and unshaken affection of a wife; cherishing
and comforting a suffering husband throughout all
the adversities of his fate, and all the errors of his
own conduct. — *Monthly Rev.*]

Chastened, subdued, out-worn, and taught to
    know
Myself, — to lose this for our son and thee!
Trust me, when, in my two-and-twentieth
    spring,
My father barred me from my father's house,
The last sole scion of a thousand sires,
(For I was then the last,) it hurt me less
Than to behold my boy and my boy's mother
Excluded in their innocence from what
My faults deserved — exclusion ; although then
My passions were all living serpents, and
Twined like the gorgon's round me.
                [A loud knocking is heard.
    Jos.   Hark!
    Wer.   A knocking!
    Jos. Who can it be at this lone hour ? We
    have
Few visitors.
    Wer.   And poverty hath none,
Save those who come to make it poorer still.
Well, I am prepared.
    [WERNER *puts his hand into his bosom, as
    if to search for some weapon.*
    Jos.   Oh! do not look so. I
Will to the door. It cannot be of import
In this lone spot of wintry desolation : —
The very desert saves man from mankind.
                   [She goes to the door.

        Enter IDENSTEIN.[1]

    Iden. A fair good evening to my fairer
    hostess
And worthy — What's your name, my friend ?
    Wer.   Are you
Not afraid to demand it ?
    Iden.   Not afraid ?
Egad! I am afraid. You look as if
I asked for something better than your name,
By the face you put on it.
    Wer.   Better, sir!
    Iden. Better or worse, like matrimony:
    what
Shall I say more ? You have been a guest
    this month
Here in the prince's palace — (to be sure,
His highness had resigned it to the ghosts
And rats these twelve years — but 'tis still a
    palace) —
I say you have been our lodger, and as yet
We do not know your name.
    Wer.   My name is Werner.
    Iden. A goodly name, a very worthy name
As e'er was gilt upon a trader's board :
I have a cousin in the lazaretto
Of Hamburgh, who has got a wife who bore
The same. He is an officer of trust,

        [1] [The most amusing fellow in the drama is
Monsieur Idenstein; who makes the finest speech,
too, beyond comparison, of any of the personages.
The only wonder is, where he got it. — *Ecl. Rev.*]

Surgeon's assistant (hoping to be surgeon),
And has done miracles i' the way of business.
Perhaps you are related to my relative ?
    Wer. To yours ?
    Jos.   Oh, yes; we are, but distantly.
                     [Aside to WERNER.
Cannot you humor the dull gossip till
We learn his purpose ?
    Iden.   Well, I am glad of that;
I thought so all along, such natural yearnings
Played round my heart : — blood is not water,
    cousin;
And so let's have some wine, and drink unto
Our better acquaintance : relatives should be
Friends.
    Wer. You appear to have drank enough
    already;
And if you had not, I've no wine to offer,
Else it were yours: but this you know, or
    should know :
You see I am poor, and sick, and will not see
That I would be alone; but to your business!
What brings you here ?
    Iden. Why, what should bring me here ?
    Wer. I know not, though I think that I
    could guess
That which will send you hence.
    Jos. (*aside*).   Patience, dear Werner!
    Iden. You don't know what has happened,
    then ?
    Jos.   How should we ?
    Iden. The river has o'erflowed.
    Jos.   Alas! we have known
That to our sorrow for these five days ; since
It keeps us here.
    Iden.   But what you don't know is,
That a great personage, who fain would cross
Against the stream and three postilions'
    wishes,
Is drowned below the ford, with five post-
    horses,
A monkey, and a mastiff, and a valet.
    Jos. Poor creatures! are you sure ?
    Iden.   Yes, of the monkey,
And the valet, and the cattle; but as yet
We know not if his excellency's dead
Or no; your noblemen are hard to drown,
As it is fit that men in office should be;
But what is certain is, that he has swallowed
Enough of the Oder to have burst two peas-
    ants;
And now a Saxon and Hungarian traveller,
Who, at their proper peril, snatched him from
The whirling flood, have sent on to crave
A lodging, or a grave, according as
It may turn out with the live or dead body.
    Jos. And where will you receive him ?
    here, I hope,
If we can be of service — say the word.
    Iden. Here ? no; but in the prince's own
    apartment,
As fits a noble guest : — 'tis damp, no doubt,

Not having been inhabited these twelve years;
But then he comes from a much damper place,
So scarcely will catch cold in't, if he be
Still liable to cold — and if not, why
He'll be worse lodged to-morrow : ne'ertheless,
I have ordered fire and all appliances
To be got ready for the worst — that is,
In case he should survive.
 Jos.   Poor gentleman !
I hope he will, with all my heart.
 Wer.   Intendant,
Have you not learned his name ? My
 Josephine,   [*Aside to his wife.*
Retire : I'll sift this fool. [*Exit* JOSEPHINE.
 Iden.   His name ? oh Lord !
Who knows if he hath now a name or no ?
Tis time enough to ask it when he's able
To give an answer ; or if not, to put
His heir's upon his epitaph. Methought
Just now you chid me for demanding names ?
 Wer. True, true, I did so ; you say well
and wisely.

    Enter GABOR.

 Gab. If I intrude, I crave ——
 Iden.   Oh, no intrusion !
This is the palace ; this a stranger like
Yourself ; I pray you make yourself at home :
But where's his excellency ? and how fares he ?
 Gab. Wetly and wearily, but out of peril :
He paused to change his garments in a cot-
 tage,
(Where I doffed mine for these, and came
 on hither)
And has almost recovered from his drenching.
He will be here anon.
 Iden.   What ho, there ! bustle !
Without there, Herman, Weilburg, Peter,
 Conrad !
 [*Gives directions to different servants who
 enter.*
A nobleman sleeps here to-night — see that
All is in order in the damask chamber —
Keep up the stove — I will myself to the
 cellar —
And Madame Idenstein (my consort,stranger)
Shall furnish forth the bed-apparel ; for,
To say the truth, they are marvellous scant of
 this
Within the palace precincts, since his highness
Left it some dozen years ago. And then
His excellency will sup, doubtless?
 Gab.   Faith !
I cannot tell ; but I should think the pillow
Would please him better than the table after
His soaking in your river : but for fear
Your viands should be thrown away, I mean
To sup myself, and have a friend without
Who will do honor to your good cheer with
A traveller's appetite. .
 Id·n.   But are you sure
His excellency —— But his name : what is it ?

 Gab. I do not know.
 Iden. And yet you saved his life.
 Gab. I helped my friend to do so.
 Iden.   Well, that's strange,
To save a man's life whom you do not know.
 Gab. Not so ; for there are some I know
 so well,
I scarce should give myself the trouble.
 Iden.   Pray,
Good friend, and who may you be ?
 Gab.   By my family,
Hungarian.
 Iden. Which is called ?
 Gab.   It matters little.
 Iden. (*aside*). I think that all the world are
 grown anonymous,
Since no one cares to tell me what he's called !
Pray, has his excellency a large suite ?
 Gab.   Sufficient.
 Iden. How many ?
 Gab.   I did not count them.
We came up by mere accident, and just
In time to drag him through his carriage
 window.
 Iden. Well, what would I give to save a
 great man !
No doubt you'll have a swinging sum as
 recompense.
 Gab. Perhaps.
 Iden. Now, how much do you reckon on ?
 Gab. I have not yet put up myself to sale :
In the mean time, my best reward would be
A glass of your Hockcheimer — a *green* glass,
Wreathed with rich grapes and Bacchanal
 devices,
O'erflowing with the oldest of your vintage ;
For which I promise you, in case you e'er
Run hazard of being drowned, (although I own
It seems, of all deaths, the least likely for you,)
I'll pull you out for nothing. Quick, my
 friend,
And think, for every bumper I shall quaff,
A wave the less may roll above your head.
 Iden. (*aside*). I don't much like this fellow
 — close and dry
He seems, two things which suit me not ;
 however
Wine he shall have ; if that unlocks him not,
I shall not sleep to-night for curiosity.
      [*Exit* IDENSTEIN.
 Gab. (*to* WERNER). This master of the
 ceremonies is
The intendant of the palace, I presume :
'Tis a fine building, but decayed.
 Wer.   The apartment
Designed for him you rescued will be found
In fitter order for a sickly guest.
 Gab. I wonder then you occupied it not,
For you seem delicate in health.
 Wer. (*quickly*).   Sir !
 Gab.   Pray
Excuse me : have I said aught to offend you?

Wer. Nothing: but we are strangers to each other.

Gab. And that's the reason I would have us less so:
I thought our bustling guest without had said
You were a chance and passing guest, the counterpart
Of me and my companions.

Wer.   Very true.

Gab. Then, as we never met before, and never,
It may be, may again encounter, why,
I thought to cheer up this old dungeon here
(At least to me) by asking you to share
The fare of my companions and myself.

Wer. Pray, pardon me; my health ——

Gab.   Even as you please.
I have been a soldier, and perhaps am blunt
In bearing.

Wer.   I have also served, and can
Requite a soldier's greeting.

Gab.   In what service?
The Imperial?

Wer. (*quickly, and then interrupting himself*). I commanded — no — I mean
I served; but it is many years ago,
When first Bohemia raised her banner 'gainst
The Austrian.

Gab.   Well, that's over now, and peace
Has turned some thousand gallant hearts adrift
To live as they best may; and, to say truth,
Some take the shortest.

Wer.   What is that?

Gab.   Whate'er
They lay their hands on. All Silesia and
Lusatia's woods are tenanted by bands
Of the late troops, who levy on the country
Their maintenance: the Chatelains must keep
Their castle walls — beyond them 'tis but doubtful
Travel for your rich count or full-blown baron.
My comfort is that, wander where I may,
I've little left to lose now.

Wer.   And I — nothing.

Gab. That's harder still. You say you were a soldier.

Wer. I was.

Gab. You look one still. All soldiers are
Or should be comrades, even though enemies.
Our swords when drawn must cross, our engines aim
(While levelled) at each other's hearts; but when
A truce, a peace, or what you will, remits
The steel into its scabbard, and lets sleep
The spark which lights the matchlock, we are brethren.
You are poor and sickly — I am not rich but healthy,
I want for nothing which I cannot want;
You seem devoid of this — wilt share it?

                    [GABOR *pulls out his purse.*

Wer.   Who
Told you I was a beggar?

Gab.   You yourself,
In saying you were a soldier during peace-time.

Wer. (*looking at him with suspicion*). You know me not?

Gab.   I know no man, not even
Myself: how should I then know one I ne'er
Beheld till half an hour since?

Wer.   Sir, I thank you.
Your offer's noble were it to a friend,
And not unkind to an unknown stranger,
Though scarcely prudent; but no less I thank you.
I am a beggar in all save his trade;
And when I beg of any one, it shall be
Of him who was the first to offer what
Few can obtain by asking. Pardon me.
                    [*Exit* WERNER.

Gab. (*solus*). A goodly fellow by his looks, though worn,
As most good fellows are, by pain or pleasure,
Which tear life out of us before our time;
I scarce know which most quickly: but he seems
To have seen better days, as who has not
Who has seen yesterday? — But here approaches
Our sage intendant, with the wine: however,
For the cup's sake I'll bear the cupbearer.

                    Enter IDENSTEIN.

Iden. 'Tis here! the supernaculum! twenty years,
Of age, if 'tis a day.

Gab.   Which epoch makes
Young women and old wine; and 'tis great pity,
Of two such excellent things, increase of years,
Which still improves the one, should spoil the other.
Fill full — Here's to our hostess! — your fair wife!   [*Takes the glass.*

Iden. Fair! — Well, I trust your taste in wine is equal
To that you show for beauty; but I pledge you
Nevertheless.

Gab.   Is not the lovely woman
I met in the adjacent hall, who, with
An air, and port, and eye, which would have better
Beseemed this palace in its brightest days
(Though in a garb adapted to its present
Abandonment), returned my salutation —
Is not the same your spouse?

Iden.   I would she were!
But you're mistaken: — that's the stranger's wife.

Gab. And by her aspect she might be a prince's:

Though time hath touched her too, she still
    retains
Much beauty, and more majesty.
    Iden.   And that
Is more than I can say for Madame Iden-
    stein,
At least in beauty : as for majesty,
She has some of its properties which might
Be spared — but never mind !
    Gab.   I don't. But who
May be this stranger ? He too hath a bearing
Above his outward fortunes.
    Iden.   There I differ.
He's poor as Job, and not so patient ; but
Who he may be, or what, or aught of him,
Except his name (and that I only learned
To-night), I know not.
    Gab.   But how came he here ?
    Iden. In a most miserable old caleche,
About a month since, and immediately
Fell sick, almost to death. He should have
    died.
    Gab. Tender and true ! — but why ?
    Iden.   Why, what is life
Without a living ? He has not a stiver.
    Gab. In that case, I much wonder that a
        person
Of your apparent prudence should admit
Guests so forlorn into this noble mansion.
    Iden. That's true ; but pity, as you know,
        does make
One's heart commit these follies ; and besides,
They had some valuables left at that time,
Which paid their way up to the present hour ;
And so I thought they might as well be
    lodged
Here as at the small tavern, and I gave them
The run of some of the oldest palace rooms.
They served to air them, at the least as long
As they could pay for fire-wood.
    Gab.   Poor souls !
    Iden.   Ay,
Exceeding poor.
    Gab.   And yet unused to poverty,
If I mistake not. Whither were they going ?
    Iden. Oh ! Heaven knows where, unless to
        heaven itself.
Some days ago that looked the likeliest jour-
    ney
For Werner.
    Gab. Werner ! I have heard the name :
But it may be a feigned one.
    Iden.   Like enough !
But hark ! a noise of wheels and voices, and
A blaze of torches from without. As sure
As destiny, his excellency's come.
I must be at my post : will you not join me,
To help him from his carriage, and present
Your humble duty at the door ?
    Gab.   I dragged him
From out that carriage when he would have
    given

His barony or county to repel
The rushing river from his gurgling throat.
He has valets now enough : they stood aloof
    then,
Shaking their dripping ears upon the shore,
All roaring "Help ! " but offering none ; and
    as
For *duty* (as you call it) — I did mine *then*,
Now do *yours*. Hence, and bow and cringe
    him here !
    Iden. *I* cringe ! — but I shall lose the op-
        portunity —
Plague take it ! he'll be *here*, and I *not there !*
                    [*Exit* IDENSTEIN *hastily*.

                Reënter WERNER.

    Wer. (*to himself*). I heard a noise of
        wheels and voices. How
All sounds now jar me !
Still here ! Is he not   [*Perceiving* GABOR.
A spy of my pursuer's ? His frank offer
So suddenly, and to a stranger, wore
The aspect of a secret enemy ;
For friends are slow at such.
    Gab.   Sir, you seem rapt ;
And yet the time is not akin to thought,
These old walls will be noisy soon. The
    baron,
Or count (or whatsoe'er this half-drowned
    noble
May be), for whom this desolate village and
Its lone inhabitants show more respect
Than did the elements, is come.
    Iden. (*without*).   This way —
This way, your excellency : — have a care,
The staircase is a little gloomy, and
Somewhat decayed ; but if we had expected
So high a guest — Pray take my arm, my
    lord !

Enter STRALENHEIM, IDENSTEIN, *and At-*
    tendants — partly his own, and partly Re-
    tainers of the Domain of which IDENSTEIN
    is Intendant.

    Stral. I'll rest me here a moment.
    Iden. (*to the servants*).   Ho ! a chair !
Instantly, knaves ! [STRALENHEIM *sits down*.
    Wer. (*aside*).   'Tis he !
    Stral.   I'm better now.
Who are these strangers ?
    Iden.   Please you, my good lord,
One says he is no stranger.
    Wer. (*aloud and hastily*). *Who* says that ?
                [*They look at him with surprise*.
    Iden. Why, no one spoke *of you* or *to you*
    — but
Here's one his excellency may be pleased
To recognize.   [*Pointing to* GABOR.
    Gab.   I seek not to disturb
His noble memory.
    Stral.   I apprehend
This is one of the strangers to whose aid

I owe my rescue. Is not that the other?
　　　　　　　　[*Pointing to* WERNER.
My state when I was succored must excuse
My uncertainty to whom I owe so much.
　Iden. He!—no, my lord! he rather wants
　　for rescue
Than can afford it. 'Tis a poor sick man,
Travel-tired, and lately risen from a bed
From whence he never dreamed to rise.
　Stral.　　　　　　　　　Methought
That there were two.
　Gab.　　　　There were, in company;
But, in the service rendered to your lordship,
I needs must say but *one*, and he is absent.
The chief part of whatever aid was rendered
Was *his*: it was his fortune to be first.
My will was not inferior, but his strength
And youth outstripped me; therefore do not
　waste
Your thanks on me. I was but a glad second
Unto a nobler principal.
　Stral.　　　　　　　Where is he?
　An Atten. My lord, he tarried in the cot-
　　tage where
Your excellency rested for an hour,
And said he would be here to-morrow.
　Stral.　　　　　　　　　　　Till
That hour arrives, I can but offer thanks,
And then ——
　Gab. I seek no more, and scarce deserve
So much. My comrade may speak for him-
　self.
　Stral. (*fixing his eyes upon* WERNER: *then
　aside*).
It cannot be! and yet he must be looked to.
'Tis twenty years since I beheld him with
These eyes; and, though my agents still have
　kept
Theirs on him, policy has held aloof
My own from his, not to alarm him into
Suspicion of my plan. Why did I leave
At Hamburgh those who would have made
　assurance
If this be he or no? I thought, ere now,
To have been lord of Siegendorf, and parted
In haste, though even the elements appear
To fight against me, and this sudden flood
May keep me prisoner here till ——
　　[*He pauses, and looks at* WERNER; *then
　　resumes.*
　　　　　　　　This man must
Be watched. If it is he, he is so changed,
His father, rising from his grave again,
Would pass him by unknown. I must be wary:
An error would spoil all.
　Iden.　　　　　Your lordship seems
Pensive. Will it not please you to pass on?
　Stral. 'Tis past fatigue which gives my
　　weighed-down spirit
An outward show of thought. I will to rest.
　Iden. The prince's chamber is prepared,
　　with all

The very furniture the prince used when
Last here, in its full splendor.
　　　(*Aside.*) Somewhat tattered,
And devilish damp, but fine enough by torch-
　　light;
And that's enough for your right noble blood
Of twenty quarterings upon a hatchment;
So let their bearer sleep 'neath something like
　one
Now, as he one day will forever lie.
　Stral. (*rising and turning to* GABOR).
　　Good night, good people! Sir, I trust
　　to-morrow
Will find me apter to requite your service.
In the mean time I crave your company
A moment in my chamber.
　Gab.　　　　　　I attend you.
　Stral. (*after a few steps, pauses, and calls*
　　WERNER). Friend!
　Wer.　　　　　　　Sir!
　Iden. Sir! Lord—oh Lord! Why don't
　　you say
His lordship, or his excellency? Pray,
My lord, excuse this poor man's want of breed-
　　ing.
He hath not been accustomed to admission
To such a presence.
　Stral. (*to* IDENSTEIN). Peace, intendant!
　Iden.　　　　　　　　　　　Oh!
I am dumb.
　Stral. (*to* WERNER). Have you been long
　　here?
　Wer. Long?
　Stral.　　　　　　I sought
An answer, not an echo.
　Wer. You may seek
Both from the walls. I am not used to answer
Those whom I know not.
　Stral.　　　　Indeed! Ne'er the less,
You might reply with courtesy to what
Is asked in kindness.
　Wer.　　　　When I know it such,
I will requite — that is, *reply* — in unison.
　Stral. The intendant said, you had been
　　detained by sickness —
If I could aid you — journeying the same way?
　Wer. (*quickly*). I am not journeying the
　　same way!
　Stral.　　　　How know ye
That, ere you know my route?
　Wer.　　　　　　Because there is
But one way that the rich and poor must tread
Together. You diverged from that dread path
Some hours ago, and I some days: hence-
　forth
Our roads must lie asunder, though they tend
All to one home.
　Stral.　　　　Your language is above
Your station.
　Wer. (*bitterly*). Is it?
　Stral.　　　　　Or, at least, beyond
Your garb.

Wer. 'Tis well that it is not beneath it,
As sometimes happens to the better clad.
But, in a word, what would you with me?
Stral. (*startled*).   I?
Wer. Yes — you! You know me not, and
question me,
And wonder that I answer not — not knowing
My inquisitor. Explain what you would have,
And then I'll satisfy yourself, or me.
Stral. I knew not that you had reasons
for reserve.
Wer. Many have such : — Have you none?
Stral.   None which can
Interest a mere stranger.
Wer.   Then forgive
The same unknown and humble stranger, if
He wishes to remain so to the man
Who can have nought in common with him.
Stral.   Sir,
I will not balk your humor, though untoward:
I only meant you service — but good night!
Intendant, show the way! (*To* GABOR.) Sir,
you will with me?
[*Exeunt* STRALENHEIM *and attendants;*
IDENSTEIN *and* GABOR.
Wer. (*solus*). 'Tis he! I am taken in the
toils. Before
I quitted Hamburgh, Giulio, his late steward,
Informed me that he had obtained an order
From Brandenburg's elector, for the arrest
Of Kruitzner (such the name I then bore)
when
I came upon the frontier; the free city
Alone preserved my freedom — till I left
Its walls — fool that I was to quit them! But
I deemed this humble garb, and route obscure,
Had baffled the slow hounds in their pursuit.
What's to be done? He knows me not by
person
Nor could aught, save the eye of apprehen-
sion,
Have recognized *him*, after twenty years,
We met so rarely and so coldly in
Our youth. But those about him! Now I
can
Divine the frankness of the Hungarian, who
No doubt is a mere tool and spy of Stralen-
heim's,
To sound and to secure me. Without
means!
Sick, poor — begirt too with the flooding riv-
ers,
Impassable even to the wealthy, with
All the appliances which purchase modes
Of overpowering peril with men's lives,—
How can I hope! An hour ago methought
My state beyond despair; and now, 'tis such,
The past seems paradise. Another day,
And I'm detected,— on the very eve
Of honors, rights, and my inheritance,
When a few drops of gold might save me still
In favoring an escape.

Enter IDENSTEIN *and* FRITZ *in conver-
sation.*
Fritz.   Immediately.
Iden. I tell you, 'tis impossible.
Fritz.   It must
Be tried, however; and if one express
Fail, you must send on others, till the answer
Arrives from Frankfort, from the command-
dant.
Iden. I will do what I can.
Fritz.   And recollect
To spare no trouble; you will be repaid
Tenfold.
Iden. The baron is retired to rest?
Fritz. He hath thrown himself into an
easy chair
Beside the fire, and slumbers; and has or-
dered
He may not be disturbed until eleven,
When he will take himself to bed.
Iden.   Before
An hour is past I'll do my best to serve him.
Fritz. Remember!   [*Exit* FRITZ.
Iden. The devil take these great men! they
Think all things made for them. Now here
must I
Rouse up some half a dozen shivering vassals
From their scant pallets, and, at peril of
Their lives, despatch them o'er the river
towards
Frankfort. Methinks the baron's own ex-
perience
Some hours ago might teach him fellow-
feeling:
But no, " it *must*," and there's an end. How
now?
Are you there, Mynheer Werner?
Wer.   You have left
Your noble guest right quickly.
Iden.   Yes — he's dozing,
And seems to like that none should sleep be-
sides.
Here is a packet for the commandant
Of Frankfort, at all risks and all expenses;
But I must not lose time: Good night!
[*Exit* IDEN.
Wer.   " To Frankfort!"
So, so, it thickens! Ay, " the commandant."
This tallies well with all the prior steps
Of this cool, calculating fiend, who walks
Between me and my father's house. No doubt
He writes for a detachment to convey me
Into some secret fortress. — Sooner than
This ——
[WERNER *looks around, and snatches up a
knife lying on a table in a recess.*
Now I am master of myself at least.
Hark, — footsteps! How do I know that
Stralenheim
Will wait for even the show of that authority
Which is to overshadow usurpation?
That he suspects me's certain. I'm alone;

He with a numerous train. I weak; he strong
In gold, in numbers, rank, authority.
I nameless, or involving in my name
Destruction, till I reach my own domain;
He full-blown with his titles, which impose
Still further on these obscure petty burghers
Than they could do elsewhere. Hark! nearer
  still.
⌐'ll to the secret passage, which communicates
With the —— No! all is silent — 'twas my
  fancy! —
Still as the breathless interval between
The flash and thunder: — I must hush my soul
Amidst its perils. Yet I will retire,
To see if still be unexplored the passage
I wot of: it will serve me as a den
Of secrecy for some hours, at the worst.
  [WERNER *draws a panel, and exit, closing
    it after him.*

    Enter GABOR *and* JOSEPHINE.

  Gab. Where is your husband?
  Jos.   *Here*, I thought: I left him
Not long since in his chamber. But these
  rooms
Have many outlets, and he may be gone
To accompany the intendant.
  Gab.   Baron Stralenheim
Put many questions to the intendant on
The subject of your lord, and, to be plain,
I have my doubts if he means well.
  Jos.   · Alas!
What can there be in common with the proud
And wealthy baron, and the unknown Werner?
  Gab. That you know best.
  Jos.   Or, if it were so, how
Come you to stir yourself in his behalf,
Rather than that of him whose life you saved?
  Gab. I helped to save him, as in peril; but
I did not pledge myself to serve him in
Oppression. I know well these nobles, and
Their thousand modes of trampling on the
  poor.
I have proved them; and my spirit boils up
  when
I find them practising against the weak: —
This is my only motive.
  Jos.   It would be
Not easy to persuade my consort of
Your good intentions.
  Gab.   Is he so suspicious?
  Jos. He was not once; but time and trou-
  bles have
Made him what you beheld.
  Gab.   I'm sorry for it.
Suspicion is a heavy armor, and
With its own weight impedes more than pro-
  tects.
Good night! I trust to meet with him at day-
  break.   [*Exit* GABOR.
  Reënter IDENSTEIN *and some Peasants.*
  JOSEPHINE *retires up the Hall.*

  First Peasant. But if I'm drowned?
  Iden. Why, you will be well paid for 't,
And have risked more than drowning for as
  much,
I doubt not.
  Second Peasant. But our wives and families?
  Iden. Cannot be worse off than they are,
  and may
Be better.
  Third Peasant. I have neither, and will
  venture.
  Iden. That's right. A gallant carle, and
  fit to be
A soldier. I'll promote you to the ranks
In the prince's body-guard — if you succeed;
And you shall have besides, in sparkling coin,
Two thalers.
  Third Peasant. No more!
  Iden.   Out upon your avarice!
Can that low vice alloy so much ambition?
I tell thee, fellow, that two thalers in
Small change will subdivide into a treasure.
Do not five hundred thousand heroes daily
Risk lives and souls for the tithe of one
  thaler?
When had you half the sum?
  Third Peasant.   Never — but ne'er
The less I must have three.
  Iden.   Have you forgot
Whose vassal you were born, knave?
  Third Peasant.   No — the prince's.
And not the stranger's.
  Iden.   Sirrah! in the prince's
Absence, I'm sovereign; and the baron is
My intimate connection; "Cousin Idenstein!
(Quoth he) you'll order out a dozen villains."
And so, you villains! troop — march — march,
  I say;
And if a single dog's-ear of this packet
Be sprinkled by the Oder — look to it!
For every page of paper, shall a hide
Of yours be stretched as parchment on a
  drum,
Like Ziska's skin, to beat alarm to all
Refractory vassals, who cannot effect
Impossibilities — Away, ye earth worms!
              [*Exit, driving them out.*
  Jos. (*coming forward*). I fain would shun
these scenes, too oft repeated,
Of feudal tyranny o'er petty victims;
I cannot aid, and will not witness such.
Even here, in this remote, unnamed, dull spot,
The dimmest in the district's map, exist
The insolence of wealth in poverty
O'er something poorer still — the pride of
  rank
In servitude, o'er something still more ser-
  vile;
And vice in misery affecting still
A tattered splendor. What a state of being!
In Tuscany, my own dear sunny land,
Our nobles were but citizens and merchants,

Like Cosmo. We had evils, but not such
As these; and our all-ripe and gushing
  valleys
Made poverty more cheerful, where each
  herb
Was in itself a meal, and every vine
Rained, as it were, the beverage which makes
  glad
The heart of man; and the ne'er unfelt sun
(But rarely clouded, and when clouded, leav-
  ing
His warmth behind in memory of his beams)
Makes the worn mantle, and the thin robe, less
Oppressive than an emperor's jewelled purple.
But, here! the despots of the north appear
To imitate the ice-wind of their clime,
Searching the shivering vassal through his
  rags,
To wring his soul—as the bleak elements
His form. And 'tis to be amongst these sov-
  ereigns
My husband pants! and such his pride of
  birth—
That twenty years of usage, such as no
Father born in a humble state could nerve
His soul to persecute a son withal,
Hath changed no atom of his early nature;
But I, born nobly also, from my father's
Kindness was taught a different lesson.
  Father!
May thy long-tried and now rewarded spirit
Look down on us and our so long desired
Ulric! I love my son, as thou didst me!
What's that? Thou, Werner! can it be? and
  thus?

Enter WERNER *hastily, with the knife in his
  hand, by the secret panel, which he closes
  hurriedly after him.*

  Wer. (*not at first recognizing her*).   Dis-
    covered! then I'll stab——(*Recognizing
    her.*)
                        Ah! Josephine,
Why art thou not at rest?
  Jos.   What rest? My God!
What doth this mean?
  Wer. (*showing a rouleau*). Here's gold
    —gold, Josephine,
Will rescue us from this detested dungeon.
  Jos. And how obtained?—that knife!
  Wer.   'Tis bloodless—yet.
Away—we must to our chamber.
  Jos.   But whence comest thou?
  Wer. Ask not! but let us think where we
    shall go—
This—this will make us way—(*showing the
  gold*)—I'll fit them now.
  Jos. I dare not think thee guilty of dis-
    honor.
  Wer. Dishonor!
  Jos.   I have said it.
  Wer   Let us hence;

'Tis the last night, I trust, that we need pass
  here.
  Jos. And not the worst, I hope.
  Wer.   Hope! I make sure
But let us to our chamber.
  Jos.   Yet one question—
What hast thou *done?*
  Wer. (*fiercely*).   Left one thing *undone,*
    which
Had made all well: let me not think of it!
Away!
  Jos. Alas, that I should doubt of thee!
                              [*Exeunt*
                    ———

ACT II.

SCENE I.—*A Hall in the same Palace.*

Enter IDENSTEIN *and Others.*

  Iden. Fine doings! goodly doings! honest
    doings!
A baron pillaged in a prince's palace!
Where, till this hour, such a sin ne'er was
  heard of.
  Fritz. It hardly could, unless the rats de-
    spoiled
The mice of a few shreds of tapestry.
  Iden. Oh! that I e'er should live to see
    this day!
The honor of our city's gone for ever.
  Fritz. Well, but now to discover the de-
    linquent.
The baron is determined not to lose
This sum without a search.
  Iden.   And so am I.
  Fritz. But whom do you suspect?
  Iden.   Suspect! all people
Without—within—above—below—Heaven
  help me!
  Fritz. Is there no other entrance to the
    chamber?
  Iden. None whatsoever.
  Fritz.   Are you sure of that?
  Iden. Certain. I have lived and served
    here since my birth,
And if there were such must have heard of
  such,
Or seen it.
  Fritz.   Then it must be some one who
Had access to the antechamber.
  Iden.   Doubtless.
  Fritz. The man called *Werner's* poor!
  Iden.   Poor as a miser.
But lodged so far off, in the other wing,
By which there's no communication with
The baron's chamber, that it can't be he.
Besides, I bade him "good night" in the hall
Almost a mile off, and which only leads
To his own apartment, about the same time
When this burglarious, larcenous felony
Appears to have been committed.

Fritz.　　　　　　There's another,
The stranger——
　Iden.　　　　The Hungarian?
　Fritz.　　　　　He who helped
To fish the baron from the Oder.
　Iden.　　　　　Not
Unlikely. But, hold — might it not have been
One of the suite?
　Fritz.　　How?　*We*, sir!
　Iden.　　　　　No — not *you*,
But some of the inferior knaves. You say
The baron was asleep in the great chair—
The velvet chair — in his embroidered night-
　gown;
His toilet spread before him, and upon it
A cabinet with letters, papers, and
Several rouleaux of gold; of which *one* only
Has disappeared: — the door unbolted, with
No difficult access to any.
　Fritz.　　　　Good sir,
Be not so quick; the honor of the corps
Which forms the baron's household's unim-
　peached
From steward to scullion, save in the fair way
Of peculation; such as in accompts,
Weights, measures, larder, cellar, buttery,
Where all men take their prey; as also in
Postage of letters, gathering of rents,
Purveying feasts, and understanding with
The honest trades who furnish noble masters:
But for your petty, picking, downright thiev-
　ery,
We scorn it as we do board-wages. Then
Had one of our folks done it, he would not
Have been so poor a spirit as to hazard
His neck for *one* rouleau, but have swooped
　all;
Also the cabinet, if portable.
　Iden. There is some sense in that——
　Fritz.　　　　No, sir, be sure
'Twas none of our corps; but some petty, tri-
　vial
Picker and stealer, without art or genius.
The only question is — who else could have
Access, save the Hungarian and yourself?
　Iden. You don't mean me?
　Fritz.　　　No, sir; I honor more
Your talents——
　Iden.　　　And my principles, I hope.
　Fritz. Of course. But to the point: What's
to be done?
　Iden. Nothing — but there's a good deal
to be said.
We'll offer a reward; move heaven and earth.
And the police (though there's none nearer
　than
Frankfort); post notices in manuscript
(For we've no printer); and set by my clerk
To read them (for few can, save he and I).
We'll send out villains to strip beggars, and
Search empty pockets; also, to arrest
All gipsies, and ill-clothed and sallow people.

Prisoners we'll have at least, if not the culprit;
And for the baron's gold — if 'tis not found,
At least he shall have the full satisfaction
Of melting twice its substance in the raising
The ghost of this rouleau. Here's alchemy
For your lord's losses!
　Fritz.　　　He hath found a better.
　Iden. Where?
　Fritz.　　In a most immense inheritance.
The late Count Siegendorf, his distant kins-
　man,
Is dead near Prague, in his castle, and my lord
Is on his way to take possession.
　Iden.　　　　　Was there
No heir?
　Fritz. Oh, yes; but he has disappeared
Long from the world's eye, and perhaps the
　world.
A prodigal son, beneath his father's ban
For the last twenty years; for whom his sire
Refused to kill the fatted calf; and, therefore,
If living, he must chew the husks still. But
The baron would find means to silence him,
Were he to reappear: he's politic,
And has much influence with a certain court.
　Iden. He's fortunate.
　Fritz.　　'Tis true, there is a grandson,
Whom the late count reclaimed from his son's
　hands
And educated as his heir; but then
His birth is doubtful.
　Iden.　　　How so?
　Fritz.　　　　　His sire made
A left-hand, love, imprudent sort of marriage,
With an Italian exile's dark-eyed daughter:
Noble, they say, too; but no match for such
A house as Siegendorf's. The grandsire ill
Could brook the alliance; and could ne'er be
　brought
To see the parents, though he took the son.
　Iden. If he's a lad of mettle, he may yet
Dispute your claim, and weave a web that
　may
Puzzle your baron to unravel.
　Fritz.　　　　　Why,
For mettle, he has quite enough: they say,
He forms a happy mixture of his sire
And grandsire's qualities, — impetuous as
The former, and deep as the latter; but
The strangest is, that he too disappeared
Some months ago.
　Iden.　　The devil he did!
　Fritz.　　　　　Why, yes;
It must have been at his suggestion, at
An hour so critical as was the eve
Of the old man's death, whose heart was
　broken by it.
　Iden. Was there no cause assigned?
　Fritz.　　　　Plenty, no doubt,
And none perhaps the true one. Some averred
It was to seek his parents; some because
The old man held his spirit in so strictly

(But that could scarce be, for he doted on
  him);
A third believed he wished to serve in war,
But peace being made soon after his departure,
He might have since returned, were that the
  motive;
A fourth set charitably have surmised,
As there was something strange and mystic in
  him,
That in the wild exuberance of his nature
He had joined the black bands, who lay waste
  . Lusatia,
The mountains of Bohemia and Silesia,
Since the last years of war had dwindled into
A kind of general condottiero system
Of bandit warfare; each troop with its chief,
And all against mankind.
  Iden.   That cannot be.
A young heir, bred to wealth and luxury,
To risk his life and honors with disbanded
Soldiers and desperadoes!
  Fritz.   Heaven best knows!
But there are human natures so allied
Unto the savage love of enterprise,
That they will seek for peril as a pleasure.
I've heard that nothing can reclaim your In-
  dian,
Or tame the tiger, though their infancy
Were fed on milk and honey. After all,
Your Wallenstein, your Tilly and Gustavus,
Your Bannier, and your Torstenson and Wei-
  mar,
Were but the same thing upon a grand scale;
And now that they are gone, and peace pro-
  claimed,
They who would follow the same pastime must
Pursue it on their own account. Here comes
The baron, and the Saxon stranger, who
Was his chief aid in yesterday's escape,
But did not leave the cottage by the Öder
Until this morning.

        Enter STRALENHEIM *and* ULRIC.

  Stral.   Since you have refused
All compensation, gentle stranger, save
Inadequate thanks, you almost check even
  them,
Making me feel the worthlessness of words,
And blush at my own barren gratitude,
They seem so niggardly, compared with what
Your courteous courage did in my behalf ——
  Ulr. I pray you press the theme no further.
  Stral.   But
Can I not serve you? You are young, and of
That mould which throws out heroes; fair in
  favor,
Brave, I know, by my living now to say so;
And doubtlessly, with such a form and heart,
Would look into the fiery eyes of war,
As ardently for glory as you dared
An obscure death to save an unknown stran-
  ger

In an as perilous, but opposite, element.
You are made for the service: I have served;
Have rank by birth and soldiership, and
  friends,
Who shall be yours. 'Tis true this pause of
  peace
Favors such views at present scantily;
But 'twill not last, men's spirits are too stirring;
And, after thirty years of conflict, peace
Is but a petty war, as the times show us
In every forest, or a mere armed truce.
War will reclaim his own; and, in the mean
  time,
You might obtain a post, which would insure
A higher soon, and, by my influence, fail not
To rise. I speak of Brandenburg, wherein
I stand well with the elector; in Bohemia,
Like you, I am a stranger, and we are now
Upon its frontier.
  Ulr.   You perceive my garb
Is Saxon, and of course my service due
To my own sovereign. If I must decline
Your offer, 'tis with the same feeling which
Induced it.
  Stral.   Why, this is mere usury!
I owe my life to you, and you refuse
The acquittance of the interest of the debt,
To heap more obligations on me, till
I bow beneath them.
  Ulr.   You shall say so when
I claim the payment.
  Stral.   Well, sir, since you will not —
You are nobly born?
  Ulr.   I have heard my kinsman say so.
  Stral. Your actions show it. Might I ask
  your name?
  Ulr. Ulric.
  Stral.   Your house's?
  Ulr.   When I'm worthy of it,
I'll answer you.
  Stral. (aside). Most probably an Austrian,
Whom these unsettled times forbid to boast
His lineage on these wild and dangerous fron-
  tiers,
Where the name of his country is abhorred.
               [*Aloud to* FRITZ *and* IDENSTEIN.
So, sirs! how have ye sped in your researches?
  Iden. Indifferent well, your excellency.
  Stral.   Then
I am to deem the plunderer is caught?
  Iden. Humph! — not exactly.
  Stral.   Or at least suspected?
  Iden. Oh! for that matter, very much sus-
  pected.
  Stral. Who may he be?
  Iden. Why, don't *you* know, my lord?
  Stral. How should I? I was fast asleep.
  Iden.   And so
Was I, and that's the cause I know no more
Than does your excellency.
  Stral.   Dolt!
  Iden.   Why, ?]

Your lordship, being robbed, don't recognize
The rogue; how should I, not being robbed,
   identify
The thief among so many ? In the crowd,
May it please your excellency, your thief looks
Exactly like the rest, or rather better :
'Tis only at the bar and in the dungeon
That wise men know your felon by his fea-
   tures;
But I'll engage, that if seen there but once,
Whether he be found criminal or no,
His face shall be so.   '
   Stral. (*to* FRITZ). Prithee, Fritz, inform me
What hath been done to trace the fellow ?
   Fritz.   Faith !
My lord, not much as yet, except conjecture.
   Stral. Besides the loss (which, I must
   own, affects me
Just now materially), I needs would find
The villain out of public motives ; for
So dexterous a spoiler, who could creep
Through my attendants, and so many peopled
And lighted chambers, on my rest, and snatch
The gold before my scarce-closed eyes, would
   soon
Leave bare your borough, Sir Intendant !
   Iden.   True ;
If there were aught to carry off, my lord.
   Ulr. What is all this ?
   Stral.   You joined us but this morning,
And have not heard that I was robbed last
   night.
   Ulr. Some rumor of it reached me as I
   passed
The outer chambers of the palace, but
I know no further.
   Stral.   It is a strange business ;
The intendant can inform you of the facts.
   Iden. Most willingly. You see——
   Stral. (*impatiently*).   Defer your tale,
Till certain of the hearer's patience.
   Iden.   That
Can only be approved by proofs. You
   see——
   Stral. (*again interrupting him, and ad-
   dressing* ULRIC).
In short, I was asleep upon a chair,
My cabinet before me, with some gold
Upon it (more than I much like to lose,
Though in part only) : some ingenious person
Contrived to glide through all my own attend-
   ants,
Besides those of the place, and bore away
A hundred golden ducats, which to find
I would be fain, and there's an end. Perhaps
You (as I still am rather faint) would add
To yesterday's great obligation, this,
Though slighter, yet not slight, to aid these men
(Who seem but lukewarm) in recovering it ?
   Ulr. Most willingly, and without loss of
   time—
[*To* IDENSTEIN.) Come hither, mynheer !

   Iden.   But so much haste bodes
Right little speed, and——
   Ulr.   Standing motionless
None ; so let's march : we talk as we go on.
   Iden. But——
   Ulr. Show the spot, and then I'll answer
   you.
   Fritz. I will, sir, with his excellency's leave.
   Stral. Do so, and take yon old ass with you.
   Fritz.   Hence !
   Ulr. Come on, old oracle, expound thy
   riddle !
                  [*Exit with* IDENSTEIN *and* FRITZ.
   Stral. (*solus*). A stalwart, active, soldier- .
   looking stripling,
Handsome as Hercules ere his first labor,
And with a brow of thought beyond his years
When in repose, till his eye kindles up
In answering yours. I wish I could engage
   him :
I have need of some such spirits near me now,
For this inheritance is worth a struggle. ,
And though I am not the man to yield with-
   out one,
Neither are they who now rise up between me
And my desire. The boy, they say, 's a bold
   one ;
But he hath played the truant in some hour
Of freakish folly, leaving fortune to
Champion his claims. That's well. The
   father, whom
For years I've tracked, as does the blood-
   hound, never
In sight, but constantly in scent, had put me
To fault ; but *here* I *have* him, and that's better.
It must be *he !* All circumstance proclaims it ;
And careless voices, knowing not the cause
Of my inquiries, still confirm it. — Yes !
The man, his bearing, and the mystery
Of his arrival, and the time ; the account, too,
The intendant gave (for I have not beheld
   her)
Of his wife's dignified but foreign aspect ;
Besides the antipathy with which we met,
As snakes and lions shrink back from each
   other
By secret instinct that both must be foes
Deadly, without being natural prey to either ;
All — all — confirm it to my mind. However,
We'll grapple, ne'ertheless. In a few hours
The order comes from Frankfort, if these
   waters
Rise not the higher (and the weather favors
Their quick abatement), and I'll have him safe
Within a dungeon, where he may avouch
His real estate and name ; and there's no
   harm done,
Should he prove other than I deem. This
   robbery
(Save for the actual loss) is lucky also :
He's poor, and that's suspicious — he's un-
   known,

And that's defenceless. — True, we have no
    proofs
Of guilt, — but what hath he of innocence ?
Were he a man indifferent to my prospects,
In other bearings, I should rather lay
The inculpation on the Hungarian, who
Hath something which I like not; and alone
Of all around, except the intendant, and
The prince's household and my own, had in-
    gress
Familiar to the chamber.

Enter GABOR.

                        Friend, how fare you ?
    Gab. As those who fare well everywhere,
        when they
Have supped and slumbered, no great matter
    how —
And you, my lord ?
    Stral.   Better in rest than purse :
Mine inn is like to cost me dear.
    Gab.   I heard
Of your late loss; but 'tis a trifle to
One of your order.
    Stral.   You would hardly think so,
Were the loss yours.
    Gab.   I never had so much
(At once) in my whole life, and therefore am
    not
Fit to decide.   But I came here to seek you.
Your couriers are turned back — I have out-
    stripped them,
In my return.
    Stral.   You ! — Why ?
    Gab.   I went at daybreak,
To watch for the abatement of the river,
As being anxious to resume my journey.
Your messengers were all checked like myself;
And, seeing the case hopeless, I await
The current's pleasure.
    Stral.   Would the dogs were in it !
Why did they not, at least, attempt the pas-
    sage ?
I ordered this at all risks.
    Gab.   Could you order
The Oder to divide, as Moses did
The Red Sea (scarcely redder than the flood
Of the swoln stream), and be obeyed, perhaps
They might have ventured.
    Stral.   I must see to it :
The knaves! the slaves! — but they shall
    smart for this.   [*Exit* STRALENHEIM.
    Gab. (*solus*). There goes my noble, feudal,
    self-willed baron !
Epitomè of what brave chivalry
The preux chevaliers of the good old times
Have left us.   Yesterday he would have given
His lands (if he hath any), and, still dearer,
His sixteen quarterings, for as much fresh air
As would have filled a bladder, while he lay
Gurgling and foaming half way through the
    window

Of his o'erset and water-logged conveyance.
And now he storms at half a dozen wretches
Because they love their lives too !   Yet, he's
    right :
'Tis strange they should, when such as he may
    put them
To hazard at his pleasure.   Oh ! thou world !
Thou art indeed a melancholy jest !
                              [*Exit* GABOR.

SCENE II. — *The Apartment of* WERNER, *in
                the Palace.*

        Enter JOSEPHINE *and* ULRIC.

    Jos.   Stand back, and let me look on thee
        again !
My Ulric ! — my beloved ! — can it be —
After twelve years ?
    Ulr.   My dearest mother !
    Jos.   Yes !
My dream is realized — how beautiful ! —
How more than all I sighed for !   Heaven
    receive
A mother's thanks ! — a mother's tears of joy !
This is indeed thy work ! — At such an hour,
    too,
He comes not only as a son, but saviour.
    Ulr.   If such a joy await me, it must double
What I now feel, and lighten from my heart
A part of the long debt of duty, not
Of love (for that was ne'er withheld) — forgive
    me !
This long delay was not my fault.
    Jos.   I know it,
But cannot think of sorrow now, and doubt
If I e'er felt it, 'tis so dazzled from
My memory by this oblivious transport ! —
My son !

            Enter WERNER.

    Wer.   What have we here, — more stran-
        gers ?
    Jos.   No !
Look upon him !   What do you see ?
    Wer.   A stripling,
For the first time ——
    Ulr. (*kneeling*).   For twelve long years, my
        father !
    Wer.   Oh, God !
    Jos.   He faints !
    Wer.   No — I am better now —
Ulric !   [*Embraces him.*
    Ulr.   My father, Siegendorf !
    Wer. (*starting*).   Hush ! boy —
The walls may hear that name !
    Ulr.   What then ?
    Wer.   Why, then —
But we will talk of that anon.   Remember,
I must be known here but as Werner.   Come !
Come to my arms again !   Why, thou look'st
    all

I should have been, and was not. Josephine!
Sure 'tis no father's fondness dazzles me;
But, had I seen that form amid ten thousand
Youth of the choicest, my heart would have chosen
This for my son!
    Ulr.   And yet you knew me not!
    Wer. Alas! I have had that upon my soul
Which makes me look on all men with an eye
That only knows the evil at first glance.
    Ulr. My memory served me far more fondly: I
Have not forgotten aught; and oft-times in
The proud and princely halls of — (I'll not name them,
As you say that 'tis perilous) — but i' the pomp
Of your sire's feudal mansion, I looked back
To the Bohemian mountains many a sunset,
And wept to see another day go down
O'er thee and me, with those huge hills between us.
They shall not part us more.
    Wer.   I know not that.
Are you aware my father is no more ?
    Ulr. Oh, heavens! I left him in a green old age,
And looking like the oak, worn, but still steady
Amidst the elements, whilst younger trees
Fell fast around him. 'Twas scarce three months since.
    Wer. Why did you leave him ?
    Jos. (embracing ULRIC). Can you ask that question ?
is he not *here* ?
    Wer. True; he hath sought his parents,
nd found them; but, oh! *how*, and in what state!
    Ulr. All shall be bettered. What we have to do
s to proceed, and to assert our rights,
r rather yours; for I waive all, unless
our father has disposed in such a sort
f his broad lands as to make mine the foremost,
o that I must prefer my claim for form:
ut I trust better, and that all is yours.
    Wer. Have you not heard of Stralenheim ?
    Ulr.   I saved
is life but yesterday : he's here.
    Wer.   You saved
he serpent who will sting us all!
    Ulr. You speak riddles : what is this *Stralenheim* to us ?
    Wer. Every thing. One who claims our father's lands;
ur distant kinsman, and our nearest foe.
    Ulr. I never heard his name till now. The count,
ndeed, spoke sometimes of a kinsman, who,
f his own line should fail, might be remotely
nvolved in the succession; but his titles

Were never named before me — and what then ?
His right must yield to ours.
    Wer.   Ay, if at Prague :
But here he is all-powerful; and has spread
Snares for thy father, which, if hitherto
He hath escaped them, is by fortune, not
By favor.
    Ulr.   Doth he personally know you ?
    Wer. No; but he guesses shrewdly at my person,
As he betrayed last night; and I, perhaps,
But owe my temporary liberty
To his uncertainty.
    Ulr.   I think you wrong him
(Excuse me for the phrase) ; but Stralenheim
Is not what you prejudge him, or, if so,
He owes me something both for past and present.
I saved his life, he therefore trusts in me.
He hath been plundered, too, since he came hither :
Is sick; a stranger; and as such not now
Able to trace the villain who hath robbed him :
I have pledged myself to do so; and the business
Which brought me here was chiefly that :[1] but I
Have found, in searching for another's dross,
My own whole treasure, — you, my parents!
    Wer. (agitatedly).   Who
Taught you to mouth that name of "villain?"
    Ulr.   What
More noble name belongs to common thieves ?
    Wer. Who taught you thus to brand an unknown being
With an infernal stigma ?
    Ulr.   My own feelings
Taught me to name a ruffian from his deeds.
    Wer. Who taught you, long-sought and ill-found boy! that
It would be safe for my own son to insult me ?
    Ulr. I named a villain. What is there in common
With such a being and my father ?
    Wer.   Every thing!
That ruffian is thy father![2]

---

[1] [The following is the original passage in the novel: — "Stralenheim," said Conrad, "does not appear to be altogether the man you take him for: but were it even otherwise, he owes me gratitude not only for the past, but for what he supposes to be my present employment. I saved his life, and he therefore places confidence in me. He hath been robbed last night — is sick — a stranger — and in no condition to discover the villain who has plundered him; and the business on which I sought the intendant was chiefly that," etc. — *Miss Lee.*]

[2] ["'And who,' said he, starting furiously from his seat, ' has entitled you to brand thus with ignominious epithets ? being you do not know? Who,' he added, with increasing agitation, 'has taught

Jos. . Oh, my son!
Believe him not — and yet! —— (*Her voice
falters.*)
Ulr. (*starts, looks earnestly at* WERNER, *and
then says slowly*). And you avow it?
Wer. Ulric, before you dare despise your
father,
Learn to divine and judge his actions. *Young,*
Rash, new to life, and reared in luxury's lap,
Is it for you to measure passion's force,
Or misery's temptation? Wait — (not long,
It cometh like the night, and quickly) —
Wait! —
Wait till, like me, your hopes are blighted [1] —
till
Sorrow and shame are handmaids of your
cabin;
Famine and poverty your guests at table;
Despair your bed-fellow — then rise, but not
From sleep, and judge! Should that day e'er
arrive —
Should you see then the serpent, who hath
coiled
Himself around all that is dear and noble
Of you and yours, lie slumbering in your path,
With but *his* folds between your steps and
happiness,
When *he*, who lives but to tear from you name,
Lands, life itself, lies at your mercy, with
Chance your conductor; midnight for your
mantle;
The bare knife in your hand, and earth asleep,
Even to your deadliest foe; and he as 'twere
Inviting death, by looking like it, while
His death alone can save you: — Thank your
God!
If then, like me, content with petty plunder,
You turn aside —— I did so.
Ulr. But ——

you that it would be even safe for my son to insult
me?' — 'It is not necessary to know the person of
a ruffian,' replied Conrad indignantly, ' to give him
the appellation he merits: — and what is there in
common between my father and such a character?'
— 'Every thing,' said Siegendorf, bitterly, — 'for
that ruffian was your father!' " — *Miss Lee.*]
[1] [" Conrad, before you thus presume to chastise
me with your eye, learn to understand my actions.
Young, and inexperienced in the world — reposing
hitherto in the bosom of indulgence and luxury, is
it for you to judge of the force of the passions, or
the temptations of misery? Wait till, like me, you
have blighted your fairest hopes — have endured
humiliation and sorrow — poverty and famine —
before you pretend to judge of their effects on you!
Should that miserable day ever arrive — should you
see the being at your mercy who stands between
you and every thing that is dear or noble in life!
who is ready to tear from you your name — your
inheritance — your very life itself — congratulate
your own heart, if, like me, you are content with
petty plunder, and are not tempted to exterminate
a serpent, who now lives, perhaps, to sting us all!"
— *Ibid.*]

Wer. (*abruptly*). Hear me!
I will not brook a human voice — scarce dare
Listen to my own (if that be human still) —
Hear me! You do not know this man — I
do.[2]
He's mean, deceitful, avaricious. You
Deem yourself safe, as young and brave; but
learn
None are secure from desperation, few
From subtilty. My worst foe, Straleiheim,
Housed in a prince's palace, couched within
A prince's chamber, lay below my knife!
An instant — a mere motion — the least im-
pulse —
Had swept him and all fears of mine from
earth.
He was within my power — my knife was
raised —
Withdrawn — and I'm in his: — are you not
so?
Who tells you that he knows you *not?* Who
says
He hath not lured you here to end you? or
To plunge you with your parents, in a dun-
geon? [*He pauses.*
Ulr. Proceed — proceed!
Wer. *Me* he hath ever known,
And hunted through each change of time —
name — fortune —
And why not *you?* Are you more versed in
men?
He wound snares round me; flung along my
path
Reptiles, whom, in my youth, I would have
spurned
Even from my presence; but, in spurning
now,
Fill only with fresh venom. Will you be
More patient? Ulric! — Ulric! — there are
crimes
Made venial by the occasion, and temptations
Which nature cannot master or forbear.[3]
Ulr. (*looks first at him, and then at Jose-
phine*). My mother!

[2] [" You do not know this man," continued he:
"I do! I believe him to be mean, sordid, deceit-
ful! You will conceive yourself safe, because you
are young and brave! Learn, however, none are
so secure but desperation or subtilty may reach
them! Stralenheim, in the palace of a prince, was
in my power! My knife was held over him — I
forbore — and I am now in his," etc. etc. — *Ibid.*]
[3] [" Me he has known invariably through every
change of fortune or name — and why not you?
Me he has entrapped — are you more discreet? He
has wound the snares of Idenstein around me; — of
a reptile whom, a few years ago, I would have
spurned from my presence, and whom, in spurning
now, I have furnished with fresh venom. Will you
be more patient? Conrad, Conrad, there are crimes
rendered venial by the occasion, and temptations
too exquisite for human fortitude to master or for
bear," etc. etc. — *Ibid.*]

Wer.　　Ay! I thought so: you have now
Only one parent. I have lost alike
Father and son, and stand alone.
　Ulr.　　　　　　　　　　　But stay!
　　　[WERNER *rushes out of the chamber.*
　Jos. (*to* ULRIC). Follow him not, until this
　　storm of passion
Abates. Think'st thou, that were it well for
　him,
I had not followed?
　Ulr.　　　　　　I obey you, mother,
Although reluctantly. My first act shall not
Be one of disobedience.
　Jos.　　　　　　　Oh! he is good!
Condemn him not from his own mouth, but
　trust
To me, who have borne so much with him,
　and for him,
That this is but the surface of his soul,
And that the depth is rich in better things.
　Ulr. These then are but my father's prin-
　ciples?
My mother thinks not with him?
　Jos.　　　　　　　　Nor doth he
Think as he speaks. Alas! long years of
　grief
Have made him sometimes thus.
　Ulr.　　　　　　　Explain to me
More clearly, then, these claims of Stralen-
　heim,
That, when I see the subject in its bearings,
I may prepare to face him, or at least
To extricate you from your present perils.
I pledge myself to accomplish this — but
　would
I had arrived a few hours sooner!
　Jos.　　　　　　　　　　Ay!
Hadst thou but done so!

Enter GABOR *and* IDENSTEIN, *with Attend-
ants.*

　Gab. (*to* ULRIC). I have sought you, com-
　rade.
So this is my reward!
　Ulr.　　　　　What do you mean?
　Gab. 'Sdeath! have I lived to these years,
　and for this!
　(*To* IDENSTEIN.) But for your age and folly,
　I would ——
　Iden.　　　　　　Help!
Hands off! Touch an intendant!
　Gab.　　　　　　　Do not think
I'll honor you so much as save your throat
From the Ravenstone[1] by choking you
　myself.
　Iden. I thank you for the respite: but there
　are
Those who have greater need of it than me.

---

[1] Ravenstone, "Rabenstein," is the *stone gibbet*
of Germany, and so called from the ravens perch-
ing on it.

　Ulr. Unriddle this vile wrangling, or ——
　Gab.　　　　　　　At once, then,
The baron has been robbed, and upon me
This worthy personage has deigned to fix
His kind suspicions — me! whom he ne'er
　saw
Till yester' evening.
　Iden.　　　Wouldst have me suspect
My own acquaintances? You have to learn
That I keep better company.
　Gab.　　　　　　You shall
Keep the best shortly, and the last for all men,
The worms! you hound of malice!
　　　　　　　[GABOR *seizes on him.*
　Ulr. (*interfering*).　　Nay, no violence:
He's old, unarmed — be temperate, Gabor!
　Gab. (*letting go* IDENSTEIN).　　True:
I am a fool to lose myself because
Fools deem me knave: it is their homage.
　Ulr. (*to* IDENSTEIN).　　　　How
Fare you?
　Iden.　　Help!
　Ulr.　　　　I *have* helped you.
　Iden.　　　　　Kill him! then
I'll say so.
　Gab. I am calm — live on!
　Iden.　　　　　　That's more
Than you shall do, if there be judge or judg-
　ment
In Germany. The baron shall decide!
　Gab. Does *he* abet you in your accusation?
　Iden. Does he not?
　Gab.　　　Then next time let him go sink
Ere I go hang for snatching him from drown-
　ing.
But here he comes!

Enter STRALENHEIM.

　Gab. (*goes up to him*). My noble lord, I'm
　here!
　Stral. Well, sir!
　Gab.　　　　Have you aught with me?
　Stral.　　　　　　What should I
Have with you?
　Gab.　　　　You know best, if yesterday's
Flood has not washed away your memory;
But that's a trifle. I stand here accused,
In phrases not equivocal, by yon
Intendant, of the pillage of your person
Or chamber : — is the charge your own or his?
　Stral. I accuse no man.
　Gab.　　　Then you acquit me, baron?
　Stral. I know not whom to accuse, or to
　acquit,
Or scarcely to suspect.
　Gab.　　　　　But you at least
Should know whom *not* to suspect. I am in-
　sulted —
Oppressed here by these menials, and I look
To you for remedy — teach them their duty!
To look for thieves at home were part of it.
If duly taught; but, in one word, if I

Have an accuser, let it be a man
Worthy to be so of a man like me.
I am your equal.
   Stral.   You!
   Gab.   Ay, sir; and, for
Aught that you know, superior; but proceed —
I do not ask for hints, and surmises,
And circumstance, and proofs; I know enough
Of what I have done for you, and what you
   owe me,
To have at least waited your payment rather
Than paid myself, had I been eager of
Your gold. I also know, that were I even
The villain I am deemed, the service rendered
So recently would not permit you to
Pursue me to the death, except through shame,
Such as would leave your scutcheon but a
   blank.
But this is nothing: I demand of you
Justice upon your unjust servants, and
From your own lips a disavowal of
All sanction of their insolence: thus much
You owe to the unknown, who asks no more,
And never thought to have asked so much.
   Stral.   This tone
May be of innocence.
   Gab.   'Sdeath! who dare doubt it
Except such villains as ne'er had it?
   Stral.   You
Are hot, sir.
   Gab.   Must I turn an icicle
Before the breath of menials, and their master?
   Stral. Ulric! you know this man; I found
   him in
Your company.
   Gab.   We found *you* in the Oder;
Would we had left you there!
   Stral.   I give you thanks, sir.
   Gab. I've earned them; but might have
   earned more from others,
Perchance, if I had left you to your fate.
   Stral. Ulric! you know this man?
   Gab.   No more than you do,
If he avouches not my honor.
   Ulr.   I
Can vouch your courage, and, as far as my
Own brief connection led me, honor.
   Stral.   Then
I'm satisfied.
   Gab. (*ironically*). Right easily, methinks.
What is the spell in his asseveration
More than in mine?
   Stral.   I merely said that *I*
Was satisfied — not that you are absolved.
   Gab. Again! Am I accused or no?
   Stral.   Go to!
You wax too insolent. If circumstance
And general suspicion be against you,
Is the fault mine? Is't not enough that I
Decline all question of your guilt or innocence?
   Gab. My lord, my lord, this is mere cozen-
   age,

A vile equivocation; you well know
Your doubts are certainties to all around
   you —
Your looks a voice — your frowns a sentence;
   you
Are practising your power on me — because
You have it; but beware! you know not whom
You strive to tread on.
   Stral.   Threat'st thou?
   Gab.   Not so much
As you accuse. You hint the basest injury,
And I retort it with an open warning.
   Stral. As you have said, 'tis true I owe you
   something,
For which you seem disposed to pay yourself.
   Gab. Not with your gold.
   Stral.   With bootless insolence.
   [*To his Attendants and* IDENSTEIN.
You need not further to molest this man,
But let him go his way. Ulric, good morrow!
   [*Exit* STRALENHEIM, IDENSTEIN, *and At-*
   tendants.
   Gab. (*following*). I'll after him and ——
   Ulr. (*stopping him*).   Not a step.
   Gab.   Who shall
Oppose me?
   Ulr. Your own reason, with a moment's
Thought.
   Gab.   Must I bear this?
   Ulr.   Pshaw! we all must bear
The arrogance of something higher than
Ourselves — the highest cannot temper Satan,
Nor the lowest his vicegerents upon earth.
I've seen you brave the elements, and bear
Things which had made this silkworm cast
   his skin —
And shrink you from a few sharp sneers and
   words?
   Gab. Must I bear to be deemed a thief?
   If 'twere
A bandit of the woods, I could have borne
   it —
There's something daring in it; — but to steal
The moneys of a slumbering man! —
   Ulr.   It seems, then,
You are *not* guilty?
   Gab.   Do I hear aright?
You too!
   Ulr. I merely asked a simple question.
   Gab. If the judge asked me, I would
   answer "No" —
To you I answer *thus.*   [*He draws.*
   Ulr. (*drawing*). With all my heart!
   Jos. Without there! Ho! help! help! —
Oh, God! here's murder!
          [*Exit* JOSEPHINE, *shrieking.*
[GABOR *and* ULRIC *fight.* GABOR *is dis-*
   armed just as STRALENHEIM, JOSEPHINE,
   IDENSTEIN, *etc. reënter.*
   Jos. Oh! glorious heaven! He's safe!
   Stral. (*to* JOSEPHINE). Who's safe?
   Jos.   My —

rupting her with a stern look,
ning afterwards to STRALEN-
Both !
eat harm done.
   What hath caused all this ?
u, baron, I believe; but as the

, let it not disturb you. — Gabor!
ur sword; and when you bare it

e against your *friends.*
onounces the last words slowly and
ically in a low voice to GABOR.
     I thank you
life than for your counsel.
      These
t end here.
ing his sword). They *shall.* You
ronged me, Ulric,
our unkind thoughts than sword :

re in my bosom rather than
 yours. I could have borne yon

nuations — ignorance
spicion are a part of his
ast him longer than his lands. —
t *him* yet : — you have vanquished

ol of passion to conceive
uld cope with you, whom I had

oved by greater perils than
is arm. We may meet by and by,
-but in friendship.
    [*Exit* GABOR.
    I will brook
 This outrage following up his
,
s guilt, has cancelled all the little
1 heretofore for the so-vaunted
he added to your abler succor.
are not hurt ? —
    Not even by a scratch.
'o IDENSTEIN). Intendant! take
neasures to secure
: I revoke my former lenity.
e sent to Frankfort with an escort
t that the waters have abated.
cure him ! He hath got his sword
—
s to know the use on't; 'tis his

I'm a civilian.
    Fool! are not
of vassals dogging at your heels
o seize a dozen such ? Hence!
im !
aron, I do beseech you !
     I must be
No words!
   Well, if it must be so —

March, vassals! I'm your leader, and will
 bring
The rear up : a wise general never should
Expose his precious life — on which all rests.
I like that article of war.
   [*Exit* IDENSTEIN *and Attendants.*
 Stral.   Come hither,
Ulric : what does that woman here ? Oh!
 now
I recognize her, 'tis the stranger's wife
Whom they *name* " Werner."
 Ulr.   'Tis his name.
 Stral.   Indeed!
Is not your husband visible, fair dame ? —
 Jos. Who seeks him ?
 Stral. No one — for the present : but
I fain would parley, Ulric, with yourself
Alone.
 Ulr. I will retire with you.
 Jos.   Not so :
You are the latest stranger, and command
All places here.
(*Aside to* ULRIC, *as she goes out.*) O Ulric!
 have a care —
Remember what depends on a rash word !
 Ulr. (*to* JOSEPHINE). Fear not! —
     [*Exit* JOSEPHINE.
 Stral. Ulric, I think that I may trust you :
You saved my life — and acts like these beget
Unbounded confidence.
 Ulr.   Say on.
 Stral.   Mysterious
And long-engendered circumstances (not
To be now fully entered on) have made
This man obnoxious — perhaps fatal to me.
 Ulr. Who ? Gabor, the Hungarian ?
 Stral. No — this " Werner " —
With the false name and habit.
 Ulr.   How can this be ?
He is the poorest of the poor — and yellow
Sickness sits caverned in his hollow eye :
The man is helpless.
 Stral.   He is — 'tis no matter; —
But if he be the man I deem (and that
He is so, all around us here — and much
That is not here — confirm my apprehension)
He must be made secure ere twelve hours
 further.
 Ulr. And what have I to do with this ?
 Stral.   I have sent
To Frankfort, to the governor, my friend
(I have the authority to do so by
An order of the house of Brandenburgh),
For a fit escort — but this cursed flood
Bars all access, and may do for some hours.
 Ulr. It is abating.
 Stral.   That is well.
 Ulr.   But how
Am I concerned ?
 Stral. As one who did so much
For me, you cannot be indifferent to
That which is of more import to me than

The life you rescued. — Keep your eye on *him!*
The man avoids me, knows that I now know
him. —
Watch him! — as you would watch the wild
boar when
He makes against you in the hunter's gap —
Like him he must be speared.
Ulr.   Why so ?
Stral.   He stands
Between me and a brave inheritance!
Oh! could you see it! But you shall.
Ulr.   I hope so.
  Stral. It is the richest of the rich Bohemia,
Unscathed by scorching war. It lies so near
The strongest city, Prague, that fire and sword
Have skimmed it lightly : so that now, besides
Its own exuberance, it bears double value
Confronted with whole realms far and near
Made deserts.
Ulr.   You describe it faithfully.
Stral. Ay — could you see it, you would
say so — but,
As I have said, you shall.
Ulr.   I accept the omen.
Stral. Then claim a recompense from it
and me,
Such as *both* may make worthy your accep-
tance
And services to me and mine for ever.
Ulr. And this sole, sick, and miserable
wretch —
This way-worn stranger — stands between you
· and
This Paradise ? — (As Adam did between
The devil and his) — [*Aside.*]
Stral.   He doth.
Ulr.   Hath he no right ?
Stral. Right! none. A disinherited prod-
igal,
Who for these twenty years disgraced his
lineage
In all his acts — but chiefly by his marriage, '
And living amidst commerce-fetching burgh-
ers,
And dabbling merchants, in a mart of Jews.
Ulr. He has a wife, then ?
Stral.   You'd be sorry to
Call such your mother. You have seen the
woman
He *calls* his wife.
Ulr.   Is she not so ?
Stral.   No more
Than he's your father : — an Italian girl,
The daughter of a banished man, who lives
On love and poverty with this same Werner.
Ulr. They are childless, then ?
Stral.   There is or was a bastard,
Whom the old man — the grandsire (as old age
Is ever doting) took to warm his bosom,
As it went chilly downward to the grave :
Bu. the imp stands not in my path — he has fled,
No one knows whither; and if he had not,

His claims alone were too contemptible
To stand. — Why do you smile ?
Ulr.   At your vain fears :
A poor man almost in his grasp — a child
Of doubtless birth — can startle a grandee !
Stral. All's to be feared, where all is to be
gained.
Ulr. True ; and aught done to save or to
obtain it.
Stral. You have harped the very string
next to my heart.
I may depend upon you ?
Ulr.   'Twere too late
To doubt it.
Stral.   Let no foolish pity shake
Your bosom (for the appearance of the mar.
Is pitiful) — he is a wretch, as likely
To have robbed me as the fellow more sus-
pected,
Except that circumstance is less against him ;
He being lodged far off, and in a chamber
Without approach to mine : and, to say truth,
I think too well of blood allied to mine,
To deem he would descend to such an act :
Besides, he was a soldier, and a brave one
Once — though too rash.
Ulr.   ˌ   And they, my lord, we know
By our experience, never plunder till
They knock the brains out first — which makes
them heirs,
Not thieves. The dead, who feel nought, can
lose nothing,
Nor e'er be robbed : their spoils are a be-
quest —
No more.
Stral. Go to! you are a wag. But say
I may be sure you'll keep an eye on this man,
And let me know his slightest movement
towards
Concealment or escape ?
Ulr.   You may be sure
You yourself could not watch him more than I
Will be his sentinel.
Stral.   By this you make me
Yours, and for ever.
Ulr.   Such is my intention. [*Exeunt.*

ACT III.

SCENE I. — *A Hall in the same Palace, from
whence the secret passage leads.*

Enter WERNER *and* GABOR.

Gab. Sir, I have told my tale : if it so please
you
To give me refuge for a few hours, well —
If not, I'll try my fortune elsewhere.
Wer.   How
Can I, so wretched, give to Misery
A shelter ? — wanting such myself as much
As e'er the hunted deer a covert ——

Gab.   Or
The wounded lion his cool cave. Methinks
You rather look like one would turn at bay,
And rip the hunter's entrails.
Wer.   Ah! ·
Gab.   I care not
If it be so, being much disposed to do
The same myself. But will you shelter me?
I am oppressed like you — and poor like you —
Disgraced ——
   Wer. (*abruptly*). Who told you that I was
     disgraced?
Gab. No one; nor did I say *you* were so:
     with
Your poverty my likeness ended; but
said *I* was so — and would add, with truth,
As undeservedly as *you.*
Wer.   Again!
As *I?*
Gab. Or any other honest man.
What the devil would you have? You don't
     believe me
Guilty of this base theft?
Wer.   No, no — I cannot.
Gab. Why that's my heart of honor! yon
     young gallant —
Your miserly and dense noble —
All — all suspected me; and why? because
I am the worst-clothed, and least named
     amongst them;
Although, were Momus' lattice in your breasts,
My soul might brook to open it more widely
Than theirs: but thus it is — you poor and
     helpless —
Both still more than myself.
Wer.   How know you that?
Gab. You're right: I ask for shelter at the
     hand
Which I call helpless; if you now deny it,
I were well paid. But you, who seem to have
     proved
The wholesome bitterness of life, know well,
By sympathy, that all the outspread gold
Of the New World the Spaniard boasts about
Would never tempt the man who knows its
     worth,
Weighed at its proper value in the balance,
Have in such guise (and there I grant its power,
Because I feel it) as may leave no nightmare
Upon his heart o' nights.
Wer.   What do you mean?
Gab. Just what I say; I thought my speech
     was plain:
You are no thief — nor I — and, as true men,
Should aid each other.
Wer.   It is a damned world, sir.
Gab. So is the nearest of the two next, as
The priests say (and no doubt they should
     know best),
Therefore I'll stick by this — as being loth
To suffer martyrdom, at least with such
An epitaph as larceny upon my tomb.

It is but a night's lodging which I crave;
To-morrow I will try the waters, as
The dove did, trusting that they have abated.
Wer. Abated? Is there hope of that?
Gab.   There was
At noontide.
Wer.   Then we may be safe.
Gab.   Are *you*
In peril?
Wer.   Poverty is ever so.
Gab. That I know by long practice. Will
     you not
Promise to make mine less?
Wer.   Your poverty?
Gab. No — you don't look a leech for that
     disorder;
I meant my peril only: you've a roof,
And I have none; I merely seek a covert.
 Wer. Rightly; for how should such a
     wretch as I
Have gold?
Gab. Scarce honestly, to say the truth on't,
Although I almost wish you had the baron's.
Wer. Dare you insinuate?
Gab.   What?
Wer.   Are you aware
To whom you speak?
Gab.   No; and I am not used
Greatly to care. (*A noise heard without.*) But
     hark! they come!
Wer.   Who come?
Gab. The intendant and his man-hounds
     after me:
I'd face them — but it were in vain to expect
Justice at hands like theirs. Where shall I
     go?
But show me any place. I do assure you,
If there be faith in man, I am most guilt-
     less!
Think if it were your own case!
Wer. (*aside*).   Oh, just God!
Thy hell is not hereafter! Am I dust still?
Gab. I see you're moved; and it shows
     well in you:
I may live to requite it.
Wer.   Are you not
A spy of Stralenheim's?
Gab.   Not I! and if
I were, what is there to espy in you?
Although I recollect his frequent question
About you and your spouse might lead to
     some
Suspicion; but you best know — what — and
     why
I am his deadliest foe.
Wer.   You?
Gab.   After such
A treatment for the service which in part
I rendered him, I am his enemy:
If you are not his friend, you will assist me.
Wer. I will.
Gab.   But how?

Wer. (*showing the panel*). There is a secret
   spring.
Remember, I discovered it by chance,
And used it but for safety.
   Gab.   Open it,
And I will use it for the same.
   Wer.   I found it,
As I have said: it leads through winding
   walls,
(So thick as to bear paths within their ribs,
Yet lose no jot of strength or stateliness,)
And hollow cells, and obscure niches, to
I know not whither; you must not advance:
Give me your word.
   Gab.   It is unnecessary:
How should I make my way in darkness
   through
A Gothic labyrinth of unknown windings?
   Wer. Yes, but who knows to what place it
   may lead?
I know not — (mark you!) — but who knows
   it might not
Lead even into the chamber of your foe?
So strangely were contrived these galleries
By our Teutonic fathers in old days,
When man built less against the elements
Than his next neighbor. You must not ad-
   vance
Beyond the two first windings; if you do
(Albeit I never passed them), I'll not answer
For what you may be led to.
   Gab.   But I will.
A thousand thanks!
   Wer. You'll find the spring more obvious
On the other side; and, when you would re-
   turn,
It yields to the least touch.
   Gab.   I'll in — farewell!
      [GABOR *goes in by the secret panel.*
   Wer. (*solus*). What have I done? Alas!
   what *had* I done
Before to make this fearful? Let it be
Still some atonement that I save the man,
Whose sacrifice had saved perhaps my
   own —
They come! to seek elsewhere what is before
   them!

     Enter IDENSTEIN *and Others.*

   Iden. Is he not here? He must have van-
   ished then
Through the dim Gothic glass by pious aid
Of pictured saints upon the red and yellow
Casements, through which the sunset streams
   like sunrise
On long pearl-colored beards and crimson
   crosses,
And gilded crosiers, and crossed arms, and
   cowls,
And helms, and twisted armor, and long
   swords,
All the fantastic furniture of windows

Dim with brave knights and holy hermits,
   whose
Likeness and fame alike rest in some panes
Of crystal, which each rattling wind proclaims
As frail as any other life or glory.
He's gone, however.
   Wer.   Whom do you seek?
   Iden.   A villain.
   Wer. Why need you come so far, then?
   Iden.   In the search
Of him who robbed the baron. ·
   Wer.   Are you sure
You have divined the man?
   Iden.   As sure as you
Stand there: but where's he gone?
   Wer.   Who?
   Iden.   He we sought.
   Wer. You see he is not here.
   Iden.   And yet we traced him
Up to this hall. Are you accomplices?
Or deal you in the black art?
   Wer.   I deal plainly,
To many men the blackest.
   Iden.   It may be
I have a question or two for yourself
Hereafter; but we must continue now
Our search for t'other.
   Wer.   You had best begin
Your inquisition now: I may not be
So patient always.
   Iden.   I should like to know,
In good sooth, if you really are the man
That Stralenheim's in quest of.
   Wer.   Insolent!
Said you not that he was not here?
   Iden.   Yes, *one;*
But there's another whom he tracks more
   keenly,
And soon, it may be, with authority
Both paramount to his and mine. But, come!
Bustle, my boys! we are at fault.
     [*Exit* IDENSTEIN *and Attendants.*
   Wer.   In what
A maze hath my dim destiny involved me!
And one base sin hath done me less ill than
The leaving undone one far greater. Down,
Thou busy devil, rising in my heart!
Thou art too late! I'll nought to do with
   blood.

     Enter ULRIC.

   Ulr. I sought you, father.
   Wer.   Is't not dangerous?
   Ulr. No; Stralenheim is ignorant of all
Or any of the ties between us: more —
He sends me here a spy upon your actions,
Deeming me wholly his.
   Wer.   I cannot think it:
'Tis but a snare he winds about us both,
To swoop the sire and son at once.
   Ulr.   I cannot
Pause in each petty fear, and stumble at

The doubts that rise like briers in our path,
But must break through them, as an unarmed
  carle
Would, though with naked limbs, were the
  wolf rustling
In the same thicket where he hewed for bread.
Nets are for thrushes, eagles are not caught so:
We'll overfly or rend them.
Wer.   Show me *how?*
Ulr. Can you not guess?
Wer.   I cannot.
Ulr.   That is strange.
Came the thought ne'er into your mind *last
  night?*
Wer. I understand you not.
Ulr.   Then we shall never
More understand each other. But to change
The topic ——
Wer.   You mean to *pursue* it, as
'Tis of our safety.
Ulr.   Right; I stand corrected.
I see the subject now more clearly, and
Our general situation in its bearings.
The waters are abating; a few hours
Will bring his summoned myrmidons from
  Frankfort,
When you will be a prisoner, perhaps worse,
And I an outcast, bastardized by practice
Of this same baron to make way for him.
Wer. And now your remedy! I thought
  to escape
By means of this accursed gold; but now
I dare not use it, show it, scarce look on it.
Methinks it wears upon its face my guilt
For motto, not the mintage of the state;
nd for the sovereign's head, my own begirt
With hissing snakes, which curl around my
  temples,
And cry to all beholders, Lo! a villain!
Ulr. You must not use it, at least now;
  but take
his ring.   [*He gives* WERNER *a jewel.*
Wer. A gem! It was my father's!
Ulr.   And
s such is now your own. With this you must
ribe the intendant for his old caleche
nd horses to pursue your route at sunrise,
ogether with my mother.
Wer.   And leave you,
o lately found, in peril too?
Ulr.   Fear nothing!
he only fear were if we fled together,
or that would make our ties beyond all doubt.
he waters only lie in flood between
his burgh and Frankfort; so far's in our favor.
he route on to Bohemia, though encum-
  bered,
i not impassable; and when you gain
few hours' start, the difficulties will be
he same to your pursuers. Once beyond
he frontier, and you're safe.
Wer.   My noble boy!

Ulr. Hush! hush! no transports: we'll
  indulge in them
In Castle Siegendorf! Display no gold:
Show Idenstein the gem (I know the man,
And have looked through him): it will an-
  swer thus
A double purpose. Stralenheim lost *gold*—
No jewel: therefore it could *not* be his;
And then the man who was possest of this
Can hardly be suspected of abstracting
The baron's coin, when he could thus cou
  vert
This ring to more than Stralenheim has lost
By his last night's slumber. Be not over
  timid
In your address, nor yet too arrogant,
And Idenstein will serve you.
Wer.   I will follow
In all things your direction.
Ulr.   I would have
Spared you the trouble; but had I appeared
To take an interest in you, and still more
By dabbling with a jewel in your favor,
All had been known at once.
Wer.   My guardian angel!
This overpays the past. But how wilt thou
Fare in our absence?
Ulr.   Stralenheim knows nothing
Of me as aught of kindred with yourself.
I will but wait a day or two with him
To lull all doubts, and then rejoin my father.
Wer. To part no more!
Ulr.   I know not that; but at
The least we'll meet again once more.
Wer.   My boy!
My friend! my only child, and sole preserver!
Oh, do not hate me!
Ulr.   Hate my father!
Wer.   Ay,
My father hated me. Why not my son?
Ulr. Your father knew you not as I do.
Wer.   Scorpions
Are in thy words! Thou know me? in this
  guise
Thou canst not know me, I am not myself;
Yet (hate me not) I will be soon.
Ulr.   I'll *wait!*
In the mean time be sure that all a son
Can do for parents shall be done for mine.
Wer. I see it, and I feel it; yet I feel
Further—that you despise me.
Ulr.   Wherefore should I?
Wer. Must I repeat my humiliation?
Ulr.   No!
I have fathomed it and you. But let us talk
Of this no more. Or, if it must be ever,
Not *now.* Your error has redoubled all
The present difficulties of our house,
At secret war with that of Stralenheim:
All we have now to think of is to baffle
HIM. I have shown *one* way.
Wer.   The only one,

And I embrace it, as I did my son,
Who showed *himself* and father's *safety* in
One day.
　Ulr.　　　You *shall* be safe; let that suffice.
Would Stralenheim's appearance in Bohemia
Disturb your right, or mine, if once we were
Admitted to our lands?
　Wer.　　　Assuredly,
Situate as we are now, although the first
Possessor might, as usual, prove the strongest,
Especially the next in blood.
　Ulr.　　　*Blood!* 'tis
A word of many meanings; in the veins,
And out of them, it is a different thing —
And so it should be, when the same in blood
(As it is called) are aliens to each other,
Like Theban brethren: when a part is bad,
A few spilt ounces purify the rest.
　Wer.　I do not apprehend you.
　Ulr.　　　That may be —
And should, perhaps — and yet —— but get
　ye ready;
You and my mother must away to-night.
Here comes the intendant: sound him with
　the gem;
'Twill sink into his venal soul like lead
Into the deep, and bring up slime and mud,
And ooze too, from the bottom, as the lead
　doth
With its greased understratum; but no less
Will serve to warn our vessels through these
　shoals.
The freight is rich, so heave the line in time!
Farewell! I scarce have time, but yet your
　hand,
My father! ——
　Wer.　　Let me embrace thee!
　Ulr.　　　We may be
Observed: subdue your nature to the hour!
Keep off from me as from your foe!
　Wer.　　　Accursed
Be he who is the stifling cause which smothers
The best and sweetest feeling of our hearts;
At such an hour too!
　Ulr.　　Yes, curse — it will ease you!
Here is the intendant.

　　　Enter IDENSTEIN.

　　　Master Idenstein,
How fare you in your purpose? Have you
　caught
The rogue?
　Iden.　No, faith!
　Ulr.　　Well, there are plenty more:
You may have better luck another chase.
Where is the baron?
　Iden.　　Gone back to his chamber:
And now I think on't, asking after you
With nobly-born impatience.
　Ulr.　　　Your great men
Must be answered on the instant, as the
　bound

Of the stung steed replies unto the spur:
'Tis well they have horses, too; for if they had
　not,
I fear that men must draw their chariots, as
They say kings did Sesostris.
　Iden.　　　Who was he?
　Ulr.　An old Bohemian — an imperial
　gipsy.
　Iden.　A gipsy or Bohemian, 'tis the same,
For they pass by both names. And was he
　one?
　Ulr.　I've heard so; but I must take leave.
　Intendant,
Your servant! — Werner (*to* WERNER *slight-
ly*), if that be your name,
Yours.　　　　　　　　　　[*Exit* ULRIC.
　Iden.　A well-spoken, pretty-faced young
　man!
And prettily behaved! He knows his station.
You see, sir: how he gave to each his due
Precedence!
　Wer.　　I perceived it, and applaud
His just discernment and your own.
　Iden.　　　That's well —
That's very well. You also know your place,
　too;
And yet I don't know that I know your
　place.
　Wer. (*showing the ring*). Would this as-
　sist your knowledge?
　Iden.　　　How! — What! — Eh!
A jewel!
　Wer.　'Tis your own on one condition.
　Iden.　Mine! — Name it!
　Wer.　　That hereafter you permit me
At thrice its value to redeem it: 'tis
A family ring.
　Iden.　　A family! — *yours!* — a gem!
I'm breathless!
　Wer.　　You must also furnish me
An hour ere daybreak with all means to quit
This place.
　Iden.　But is it real? Let me look on it:
Diamond, by all that's glorious!
　Wer.　　　Come, I'll trust you:
You have guessed, no doubt, that I was born
　above
My present seeming.
　Iden.　　I can't say I did,
Though this looks like it: this is the tru"
　breeding
Of gentle blood!
　Wer.　　I have important reason-
For wishing to continue privily
My journey hence.
　Iden.　　So then *you are* the man,
Whom Stralenheim's in quest of?
　Wer.　　　I am no';
But being taken for him might conduct
So much embarrassment to me just now,
And to the baron's self hereafter — 'tis
To spare both that I would avoid all bustle.

Iden. Be you the man or no, 'tis not my
business.
Besides, I never should obtain the half
From this proud, niggardly noble, who would
raise
The country for some missing bits of coin,
And never offer a precise reward —
But *this !* —another look !
  Wer.   Gaze on it freely ;
t day-dawn it is yours.
  Iden.   Oh, thou sweet sparkler !
Thou more than stone of the philosopher !
Thou touchstone of Philosophy herself !
Thou bright eye of the Mine ! thou loadstar of
The soul ! the true magnetic Pole to which
All hearts point duly north, like trembling
needles !
  hou flaming Spirit of the Earth ! which, sit-
ting
High on the monarch's diadem, attractest
More worship than the majesty who sweats
Beneath the crown which makes his head
ache, like
Millions of hearts which bleed to lend it lustre !
halt thou be mine ? I am, methinks, already
little king, a lucky alchemist ! —
wise magician, who has bound the devil
ithout the forfeit of his soul. But come,
erner, or what else ?
  Wer.   Call me Werner still.
You may yet know me by a loftier title.
  Iden. I do believe in thee ! thou art the
spirit
Of whom I long have dreamed in a low
garb.—
But come, I'll serve thee ; thou shalt be as free
As air, despite the waters ; let us hence :
I'll show thee I am honest — (oh, thou jewel !)
Thou shalt be furnished, Werner, with such
means
Of flight, that if thou wert a snail, not birds
Should overtake thee. — Let me gaze again !
I have a foster-brother in the mart
Of Hamburgh skilled in precious stones.
How many
Carats may it weigh ? — Come, Werner, I
will wing thee.   [*Exeunt.*

    SCENE II.—STRALENHEIM'S *Chamber.*

      STRALENHEIM *and* FRITZ.

Fritz. All's ready, my good lord !
  Stral.   I am not sleepy,
And yet I must to bed ; I fain would say
To rest, but something heavy on my spirit,
Too dull for wakefulness, too quick for
slumber,
Sits on me as a cloud along the sky,
Which will not let the sunbeams through, nor
yet
Descend in rain and end, but spreads itself

'Twixt earth and heaven, like envy between
man
And man, an everlasting mist ; — I will
Unto my pillow.
  Fritz.   May you rest there well !
  Stral. I feel, and fear, I shall.
  Fritz.   And wherefore fear ?
  Stral. I know not why, and therefore do
fear more,
Because an undescribable —— but 'tis
All folly. Were the locks (as I desired)
Changed, to-day, of this chamber ? for last
night's
Adventure makes it needful.
  Fritz.   Certainly,
According to your order, and beneath
The inspection of myself and the young Saxon
Who saved your life. I think they call him
" Ulric."
  Stral. You *think !* you supercilious slave !
what right
Have you to *tax your* memory, which should
be
Quick, proud, and happy to retain the *name*
Of him who saved your master, as a litany
Whose daily repetition marks your duty.—
Get hence ! " *You think,*" indeed ! you who
stood still
Howling and drippling on the bank, whilst I
Lay dying, and the stranger dashed aside
The roaring torrent, and restored me to
Thank him — and despise you. "*You think !*"
and scarce
Can recollect his name ! I will not waste
More words on you. Call me betimes.
  Fritz.   Good night !
I trust to-morrow will restore your lordship
To renovated strength and temper.
                       [*The scene closes.*

    SCENE III.— *The Secret Passage.*

  Gab. (*solus*).   Four —
Five — six hours have I counted, like the
guard
Of outposts on the never-merry clock :
That hollow tongue of time, which, even when
It sounds for joy, takes something from en-
joyment
With every clang. 'Tis a perpetual knell,
Though for a marriage-feast it rings : each
stroke
Peals for a hope the less ; the funeral note
Of Love deep-buried without resurrection
In the grave of Possession ; while the knoll
Of long-lived parents finds a jovial echo
To triple Time in the son's ear.
                    I'm cold —
I'm dark ; — I've blown my fingers — num-
bered o'er
And o'er my steps — and knocked my head
against

Some fifty buttresses — and roused the rats
And bats in general insurrection, till
Their cursed pattering feet and whirling wings
Leave me scarce hearing for another sound.
A light! It is at distance (if I can
Measure in darkness distance) : but it blinks
As through a crevice or a key-hole, in
The inhibited direction : I must on,
Nevertheless, from curiosity.
A distant lamp-light is an incident
In such a den as this. Pray Heaven it lead
     me
To nothing that may tempt me! Else —
     Heaven aid me
To obtain or to escape it! Shining still!
Were it the star of Lucifer himself,
Or he himself girt with its beams, I could
Contain no longer. Softly! mighty well!
That corner's turned — so — ah! no ; — right!
     it draws
Nearer. Here is a darksome angle — so,
That's weathered. — Let me pause. — Sup-
     pose it leads
Into some greater danger than that which
I have escaped — no matter, 'tis a new one ;
And novel perils, like fresh mistresses,
Wear more magnetic aspects : — I will on,
And be it where it may — I have my dagger,
Which may protect me at a pinch. — Burn
     still,
Thou little light! Thou art my *ignis fatuus!*
My stationary Will-o'-the-wisp! — So! so!
He hears my invocation, and fails not.
                              [*The scene closes.*

SCENE IV. — *A Garden.*

Enter WERNER.

Wer. I could not sleep — and now the
     hour's at hand ;
All's ready. Idenstein has kept his word ;
And stationed in the outskirts of the town,
Upon the forest's edge, the vehicle
Awaits us. Now the dwindling stars begin
To pale in heaven ; and for the last time I
Look on these horrible walls. Oh! never,
     never
Shall I forget them. Here I came most poor,
But not dishonored : and I leave them with
A stain, — if not upon my name, yet in
My heart! — a never-dying canker worm,
Which all the coming splendor of the lands,
And rights, and sovereignty of Siegendorf
Can scarcely lull a moment. I must find
Some means of restitution, which would ease
My soul in part ; but how without discovery ? —
It must be done, however ; and I'll pause
Upon the method the first hour of safety.
The madness of my misery led to this
Base infamy ; repentance must retrieve it :
I will have nought of Stralenheim's upon

My spirit, though he would grasp all of mine ;
Lands, freedom, life, — and yet he sleeps! as
     soundly,
Perhaps, as infancy, with gorgeous curtains
Spread for his canopy, o'er silken pillows,
Such as when —— Hark! what noise is that ?
     Again!
The branches shake ; and some loose stones
     have fallen
From yonder terrace.
          [ULRIC *leaps down from the terrace.*
                              Ulric! ever welcome!
Thrice welcome now! this filial ——
Ulr.   Stop! Before
We approach, tell me ——
Wer.   Why look you so?
Ulr.   Do I
Behold my father, or ——
Wer.   What ?
Ulr.   An assassin?
Wer. Insane or insolent!
Ulr.   Reply, sir, as
You prize your life, or mine!
Wer.   To what must I
Answer ?
Ulr. Are you or are you not the assassin
Of Stralenheim ?
Wer.   I never was as yet
The murderer of any man. What mean you ?
     Ulr. Did not you *this* night (as the night
          before)
Retrace the secret passage ? Did you not
Again revisit Stralenheim's chamber? and ——
                              [ULRIC *pauses.*
     Wer. Proceed.
     Ulr.   *Died* he not by your hand ?
     Wer.   Great God!
     Ulr. You are innocent, then! my father's
          innocent!
Embrace me! Yes, — your tone — your
     look — yes, yes, —
Yet *say* so.
     Wer.   If I e'er, in heart or mind,
Conceived deliberately such a thought,
But rather strove to trample back to hell
Such thoughts — if e'er they glared a moment
     through
The irritation of my oppressed spirit —
May heaven be shut forever from my hopes
As from mine eyes!
     Ulr.   But Stralenheim is dead.
     Wer. 'Tis horrible! 'tis hideous, as 'tis
          hateful! —
But what have I to do with this ?
     Ulr.   No bolt
Is forced ; no violence can be detected,
Save on his body. Part of his own household
Have been alarmed ; but as the intendant is
Absent, I took upon myself the care
Of mustering the police. His chamber has,
Past doubt, been entered secretly. Excuse me
If nature ——

Wer. Oh, my boy! what unknown woes
˙dark fatality, like clouds, are gathering
ɔove our house!
Ulr. My father! I acquit you!
ɪt will the world do so? will even the judge,
—— But you must away this instant.
Wer. No!
l face it. Who shall dare suspect me?
Ulr. Yet
ɔu had *no* guests — *no* visitors — no life
˙eathing around you, save my mother's?
Wer. Ah!
ɪe Hungarian!
Ulr. He is gone! he disappeared
:e sunset.
Wer. No; I hid him in that very
ɔncealed and fatal gallery.
Ulr. *There* I'll find him.
[ULRIC *is going*.
Wer. It is too late: he had left the palace
ere
ʔuitted it. I found the secret panel
ɔen, and the doors which lead from that hall
'hich masks it: I but thought he had
snatched the silent
ɪd favorable moment to escape
ɪe myrmidons of Idenstein, who were
ɔgging him yester-even.
Ulr. You reclosed
ɪe panel?
Wer. Yes; and not without reproach
nd inner trembling for the avoided peril)
his dull heedlessness, in leaving thus
s shelterer's asylum to the risk
a discovery.
Ulr. You are sure you closed it?
Wer. Certain.
Ulr. That's well; but had been better, if
u ne'er had turned it to a den for——
[*He pauses.*
Wer. Thieves!
ou wouldst say: I must bear it and de-
serve it;
t not——
Ulr. No, father; do not speak of this:
ɪis is no hour to think of petty crimes,
ɪt to prevent the consequence of great ones.
hy would you shelter this man?
Wer. Could I shun it?
man pursued by my chief foe; disgraced
r my own crime; a victim to *my* safety,
ploring a few hours' concealment from
e very wretch who was the cause he needed
ch refuge. Had he been a wolf, I could not
ve in such circumstances thrust him forth.
Ulr. And like the wolf he hath repaid you.
But
is too late to ponder thus: — you must
t out ere dawn. I will remain here to
˙ace the murderer, if 'tis possible.
Wer. But this my sudden flight will give
the Moloch

Suspicion: two new victims in the lieu
Of one, if I remain. The fled Hungarian,
Who seems the culprit, and ——
Ulr. Who *seems?* *Who* else
Can be so?
Wer. Not *I,* though just now you
doubted —
You, my *son* / — doubted ——
Ulr. And do you doubt of him
The fugitive?
Wer. Boy! since I fell into
The abyss of crime (though not of *such*
crime), I,
Having seen the innocent oppressed for me,
May doubt even of the guilty's guilt. Your
heart
Is free, and quick with virtuous wrath to accuse
Appearances; and views a criminal
In Innocence's shadow, it may be,
Because 'tis dusky.
Ulr. And if I do so,
What will mankind, who know you not, or
knew   .
But to oppress? You must not stand the
hazard.
Away! — I'll make all easy. Idenstein
Will for his own sake and his jewel's hold
His peace — he also is a partner in
Your flight — moreover ——
Wer. Fly! and leave my name
Linked with the Hungarian's, or preferred as
poorest,
To bear the brand of bloodshed?
Ulr. Pshaw! leave anything
Except our father's sovereignty and castles,
For which you have so long panted and in
vain! ·
What *name?* You have *no* name since that   ·
you bear
Is feigned.
Wer. Most true; but still I would not
have it
Engraved in crimson in men's memories,
Though in this most obscure abode of men —
Besides, the search ——
Ulr. I will provide against
Aught that can touch you. No one knows
you here
As heir of Siegendorf: if Idenstein
Suspects, 'tis *but suspicion,* and he is
A fool: his folly shall have such employment,
Too, that the unknown Werner shall give way
To nearer thoughts of self. The laws (if e'er
Laws reached this village) are all in abeyance
With the late general war of thirty years,
Or crushed, or rising slowly from the dust,
To which the march of armies trampled them.
Stralenheim, although noble, is unheeded
Here, save as *such* — without lands, influence,
Save what hath perished with him. Few pro-
long
A week beyond their funeral rites their sway

O'er men, unless by relatives, whose interest
Is roused: such is not here the case; he died
Alone, unknown, — a solitary grave,
Obscure as his deserts, without a scutcheon,
Is all he'll have, or wants. If *I* discover
The assassin, 'twill be well — if not, believe me
None else; though all the full-fed train of
menials
May howl above his ashes (as they did
Around him in his danger on the Oder),
Will no more stir a finger *now* than *then*.
Hence! hence! I must not hear your answer.
— Look!
The stars are almost faded, and the gray
Begins to grizzle the black hair of night.
You shall not answer: — Pardon me that I
Am peremptory; 'tis your son that speaks,
Your long-lost, late-found son. — Let's call
my mother!
Softly and swiftly step, and leave the rest
To me: I'll answer for the event as far
As regards *you*, and that is the chief point,
As my first duty, which shall be observed.
We'll meet in Castle Siegendorf — once more
Our banners shall be glorious! Think of that
Alone, and leave all other thoughts to me,
Whose youth may better battle with them.—
Hence!
And may your age be happy! — I will kiss
My mother once more, then Heaven's speed
be with you!
   Wer. This counsel's safe — but is it honor-
able?
   Ulr. To save a father is a child's chief
honor.   [*Exeunt.*

ACT IV.

SCENE I.— *A Gothic Hall in the Castle of
Siegendorf, near Prague.*

Enter ERIC *and* HENRICK, *Retainers of the
Count.*

   Eric. So better times are come at last; to
these
Old walls new masters and high wassail —
both
A long desideratum.
   Hen.   Yes, for *masters*,
It might be unto those who long for novelty,
Though made by a new grave: but as for
wassail,
Methinks the old Count Siegendorf main-
tained
His feudal hospitality as high
As e'er another prince of the empire.
   Eric.   Why,
For the mere cup and trencher, we no doubt
Fared passing well; but as for merriment
And sport, without which salt and sauces
season

The cheer but scantily, our sizings were
Even of the narrowest.
   Hen.   The old count loved not
The roar of revel; are you sure that *this* does?
   Eric. As yet he hath been courteous as
he's bounteous,
And we all love him.
   Hen.   His reign is as yet
Hardly a year o'erpast its honey-moon,
And the first year of sovereigns is bridal:
Anon, we shall perceive his real sway
And moods of mind.
   Eric. Pray Heaven he keep the present!
Then his brave son, Count Ulric — there's a
knight.
Pity the wars are o'er!
   Hen.   Why so?
   Eric.   Look on him!
And answer that yourself.
   Hen.   He's very youthful,
And strong and beautiful as a young tiger.
   Eric. That's not a faithful vassal's likeness.
   Hen.   But
Perhaps a true one.
   Eric.   Pity, as I said,
The wars are over: in the hall, who like
Count Ulric for a well-supported pride,
Which awes, but yet offends not? in the field,
Who like him with his spear in hand, when,
gnashing
His tusks, and ripping up from right to left
The howling hounds, the boar makes for the
thicket?
Who backs a horse, or bears a hawk, or
wears
A sword like him? Whose plume nods
knightlier?
   Hen. No one's, I grant you. Do not fear,
if war
Be long in coming, he is of that kind
Will make it for himself, if he hath not
Already done as much.
   Eric.   What do you mean?
   Hen. You can't deny his train of followers
(But few our native fellow vassals born
On the domain) are such a sort of knaves
As —— (*Pauses.*)
   Eric.   What?
   Hen. The war (you love so much) leaves
living.
Like other parents, she spoils her worst
children.
   Eric. Nonsense! they are all brave iron-
visaged fellows,
Such as old Tilly loved.
   Hen.   And who loved Tilly?
Ask that at Magdebourg — or for that matter
Wallenstein either; — they are gone to ——
   Eric.   Rest;
But what beyond 'tis not ours to pronounce.
   Hen. I wish they had left us something of
their rest:

The country (nominally now at peace)
Is over-run with — God knows who: they fly
By night, and disappear with sunrise; but
Leave us no less desolation, nay, even more,
Than the most *open* warfare.
Eric.   But Count Ulric —
What has all this to do with him?
Hen.   With *him!*
He —— might prevent it. As you say he's fond
Of war, why makes he it not on those ma-
rauders?
Eric. You'd better ask himself.
Hen.   I would as soon
Ask the lion why he laps not milk.
Eric. And here he comes!
Hen. The devil! you'll hold your tongue?
Eric. Why do you turn so pale?
Hen.   'Tis nothing — but
Be silent.
Eric.   I will, upon what you have said.
Hen. I assure you I meant nothing — a
mere sport
Of words, no more; besides, had it been
otherwise,
He is to espouse the gentle Baroness
Ida of Stralenheim, the late baron's heiress;
And she, no doubt, will soften whatsoever
Of fierceness the late long intestine wars
Hath given all natures, and most unto those
Who were born in them, and bred up upon
The knees of Homicide; sprinkled, as it were,
With blood even at their baptism. Prithee,
peace
n all that I have said!

Enter ULRIC *and* RODOLPH.

                    Good morrow, count.
Ulr. Good morrow, worthy Henrick. Eric, is
ll ready for the chase?
Eric.   The dogs are ordered
'own to the forest, and the vassals out
o beat the bushes, and the day looks prom-
ising.
Shall I call forth your excellency's suite?
What courser will you please to mount?
Ulr.   The dun,
Walstein.
Eric.   I fear he scarcely has recovered
The toils of Monday: 'twas a noble chase:
ou speared *four* with your own hand.
Ulr.   True, good Eric;
I had forgotten — let it be the gray, then,
Old Ziska: he has not been out this fortnight.
Eric. He shall be straight caparisoned.
How many
Of your immediate retainers shall
Escort you?
Ulr.   I leave that to Weilburgh, our
Master of the horse.   [*Exit* ERIC.
            Rodolph!
Rod.   My lord!
Ulr.   The news

Is awkward from the — (RODOLPH *points to*
HENRICK.)
                    How now, Henrick? why
Loiter you here?
Hen.   For your commands, my lord.
Ulr. Go to my father, and present my duty,
And learn if he would aught with me before
I mount.   [*Exit* HENRICK.
      Rodolph, our friends have had a check
Upon the frontiers of Franconia, and
'Tis rumored that the column sent against them
Is to be strengthened. I must join them soon.
Rod. Best wait for further and more sure
advices.
Ulr. I meant it — and indeed it could not
well
Have fallen out at a time more opposite
To all my plans.
Rod.   It will be difficult
To excuse your absence to the count your
father.
Ulr. Yes, but the unsettled state of our
domain
In high Silesia will permit and cover
My journey. In the mean time, when we are
Engaged in the chase, draw off the eighty men
Whom Wolffe leads — keep the forests on
your route:
You know it well?
Rod.   As well as on that night
When we ——
Ulr.   We will not speak of that until
We can repeat the same with like success:
And when you have joined, give Rosenberg
this letter.   [*Gives a letter.*
Add further, that I have sent this slight addi-
tion
To our force with you and Wolffe, as herald of
My coming, though I could but spare them ill
At this time, as my father loves to keep
Full numbers of retainers round the castle,
Until this marriage, and its feasts and fooleries,
Are rung out with its peal of nuptial nonsense.
Rod. I thought you loved the lady Ida?
Ulr.   Why,
I do so — but it follows not from that
I would bind in my youth and glorious years,
So brief and burning, with a lady's zone,
Although 'twere that of Venus; — but I love
her,
As woman should be loved, fairly and solely.
Rod. And constantly?
Ulr.   I think so; for I love
Nought else. — But I have not the time to
pause
Upon these gewgaws of the heart. Great things
We have to do ere long. Speed! speed! good
Rodolph!
Rod. On my return, however, I shall find
The Baroness Ida lost in Countess Siegen-
dorf?
Ulr. Perhaps my father wishes it; and sooth

'Tis no bad policy; this union with
The last bud of the rival branch at once
Unites the future and destroys the past.
  Rod. Adieu.
  Ulr. Yet hold — we had better keep together
Until the chase begins; then draw thou off,
And do as I have said.
  Rod.   I will. But to
Return — 'twas a most kind act in the count
Your father to send up to Konigsberg
For this fair orphan of the baron, and
To hail her as his daughter.
  Ulr.   Wondrous kind!
Especially as little kindness till
Then grew between them.
  Rod.   The late baron died
Of a fever, did he not?
  Ulr.   How should I know?
  Rod. I have heard it whispered there was
    something strange
About his death — and even the place of it
Is scarcely known.
  Ulr.   Some obscure village on
The Saxon or Silesian frontier.
  Rod.   He
Has left no testament — no farewell words?
  Ulr. I am neither confessor nor notary,
So cannot say.
  Rod.   Ah! here's the lady Ida.

Enter IDA STRALENHEIM.[1]

  Ulr. You are early, my sweet cousin!
  Ida.   Not *too* early,
Dear Ulric, if I do not interrupt you.
Why do you call me "*cousin?*"
  Ulr. (*smiling*).   Are we not so?
  Ida. Yes, but I do not like the name; me-
thinks
It sounds so cold, as if you thought upon
Our pedigree, and only weighed our blood.
  Ulr. (*starting*).   Blood!
  Ida. Why does yours start from your
    cheeks?
  Ulr.   Ay! doth it?
  Ida. It doth — but no! it rushes like a tor-
rent
Even to your brow again.
  Ulr. (*recovering himself*). And if it fled,
It only was because your presence sent it
Back to my heart, which beats for you, sweet
    cousin!
  Ida. "Cousin" again.
  Ulr.   Nay, then, I'll call you sister.
  Ida. I like that name still worse. — Would
we had ne'er
Been aught of kindred!

---

[1] [Ida, the *new* personage, is a precocious girl
of fifteen, in a great hurry to be married; and who
has very little to do in the business of the play, but
to produce an effect by fainting at the discovery of
the villany of her beloved, and partially touching
on it in a previous scene. — *Ecl. Rev.*]

  Ulr. (*gloomily*).   Would we never had!
  Ida. Oh heavens! and can *you wish that?*
  Ulr.   Dearest Ida!
Did I not echo your own wish?
  Ida.   Yes, Ulric,
But then I wished it not with such a glance,
And scarce knew what I said; but let me be
Sister, or cousin, what you will, so that
I still to you am something.
  Ulr.   You shall be
All — all ——
  Ida.   And you to *me are* so already;
But I can wait.
  Ulr.   Dear Ida!
  Ida.   Call me Ida,
Your Ida, for I would be yours, none else's —
Indeed I have none else left, since my poor
    father —   [*She pauses.*
  Ulr. You have *mine* — you have *me.*
  Ida.   Dear Ulric, how I wish
My father could but view my happiness,
Which wants but this!
  Ulr.   Indeed!
  Ida.   You would have loved him,
He you; for the brave ever love each other:
His manner was a little cold, his spirit
Proud (as is birth's prerogative); but under
This grave exterior —— Would you had known
    each other!
Had such as you been near him on his jour-
ney,
He had not died without a friend to soothe
His last and lonely moments.
  Ulr.   Who says *that?*
  Ida. What?
  Ulr.   That he *died alone.*
  Ida.   The general rumor,
And disappearance of his servants, who
Have ne'er returned: that fever was most
    deadly
Which swept them all away.
  Ulr.   If they were near him,
He could not die neglected or alone.
  Ida. Alas! what is a menial to a deathbed,
When the dim eye rolls vainly round for what
It loves? — They say he died of a fever.
  Ulr.   Say!
It *was* so.
  Ida.   I sometimes dream otherwise.
  Ulr. All dreams are false.
  Ida.   And yet I see him as
I see you.
  Ulr.   *Where?*
  Ida.   In sleep — I see him lie
Pale, bleeding, and a man with a raised knife
Beside him.
  Ulr.   But you do not see his *face?*
  Ida (*looking at him*). No! Oh, my God!
    do *you?*
  Ulr.   Why do you ask?
  Ida. Because you look as if you *saw* a
    murderer!

Ulr. (*agitatedly*). Ida, this is mere child-
ishness; your weakness
fects me, to my shame; but as all feelings
yours are common to me, it affects me.
ithee, sweet child, change ——
Ida.   Child, indeed! I have
ll fifteen summers!   [*A bugle sounds.*
Rod.   Hark, my lord, the bugle!
Ida (*peevishly to* RODOLPH). Why need
you tell him that? Can he not hear it
ithout your echo?
Rod.   Pardon me, fair baroness!
Ida. I will not pardon you, unless you earn
it
aiding me in my dissuasion of
unt Ulric from the chase to-day.
Rod.   You will not,
dy, need aid of mine.
Ulr.   I must not now
rego it.
Ida.   But you shall!
Ulr.   Shall!
Ida.   Yes, or be
 true knight. — Come, dear Ulric! yield to
me
this, for this one day: the day looks heavy,
d you are turned so pale and ill.
Ulr.   You jest.
Ida. Indeed I do not: — ask of Rodolph.
Rod.   Truly,
y lord, within this quarter of an hour
u have changed more than e'er I saw you
change
years.
Ulr.   'Tis nothing; but if 'twere, the air
ould soon restore me. I'm the true cha-
meleon,
d live but on the atmosphere; your feasts
castle halls, and social banquets, nurse not
y spirit — I'm a forester and breather
the steep mountain-tops, where I love all
e eagle loves.
Ida.   Except his prey, I hope.
Ulr. Sweet Ida, wish me a fair chase, and I
ill bring you six boars' heads for trophies
home.
Ida. And will you not stay, then? You
shall not go!
me! I will sing to you.   .
Ulr.   Ida, you scarcely
ill make a soldier's wife.
Ida.   I do not wish
 be so; for I trust these wars are over,
d you will live in peace on your domains.

Enter WERNER *as* COUNT SIEGENDORF.

Ulr. My father, I salute you, and it grieves
me
ith such brief greeting. — You have heard
our bugle;
e vassals wait.
Sieg.   So let them. — You forget

To-morrow is the appointed festival
In Prague for peace restored. You are apt
to follow
The chase with such an ardor as will scarce
Permit you to return to-day, or if
Returned, too much fatigued to join to-morrow
The nobles in our marshalled ranks.
Ulr.   You, count,
Will well supply the place of both — I am not
A lover of these pageantries.
Sieg.   No, Ulric:
It were not well that you alone of all
Our young nobility ——
Ida.   And far the noblest
In aspect and demeanor.
Sieg. (*to* IDA).   True, dear child,
Though somewhat frankly said for a fair dam-
sel. —
But, Ulric, recollect too our position,
So lately reinstated in our honors.
Believe *me*, 'twould be marked in any house,
But most in *ours*, that ONE should be found
wanting
At such a time and place. Besides, the Heaven
Which gave us back our own, in the same
moment
It spread its peace o'er all, hath double
claims
On us for thanksgiving: first, for our country;
And next, that we are here to share its bless-
ings.
Ulr. (*aside*). Devout, too! Well, sir, I
obey at once.
                    (*Then aloud to a Servant.*)
Ludwig, dismiss the train without!
                        [*Exit* LUDWIG.
Ida.   And so
You yield at once to him what I for hours
Might supplicate in vain.
Sieg. (*smiling*).   You are not jealous
Of me, I trust, my pretty rebel! who
Would sanction disobedience against all
Except thyself? But fear not; thou shalt
rule him
Hereafter with a fonder sway and firmer.
Ida. But I should like to govern *now*.
Sieg.   You shall,
Your *harp*, which by the way awaits you with
The countess in her chamber. She com-
plains
That you are a sad truant to your music:
She attends you.
Ida. Then good morrow, my kind kins-
men!
Ulric, you'll come and hear me?
Ulr.   By and by.
Ida. Be sure I'll sound it better than your
bugles;
Then pray you be as punctual to its notes:
I'll play you King Gustavus' march.
Ulr.   And why not
Old Tilly's?

WERNER.

Ida. Not that monster's! I should think
My harp-strings rang with groans, and not
  with music,
Could aught of *his* sound on it : — but come
  quickly!
Your mother will be eager to receive you.
                 [*Exit* IDA.
Sieg. Ulric, I wish to speak with you
  alone.
Ulr. My time's your vassal.
(*Aside to* RODOLPH.) Rodolph, hence! and
  do
As I directed : and by his best speed
And readiest means let Rosenberg reply.
  Rod. Count Siegendorf, command you
  aught? I am bound
Upon a journey past the frontier.
  Sieg. (*starts*).   Ah! —
Where? on *what* frontier?
  Rod.   The Silesian, on
My way — (*Aside to* ULRIC.) — *Where* shall
  I say?
  Ulr. (*aside to* RODOLPH). To Hamburgh.
        (*Aside to himself.*) That
Word will, I think, put a firm padlock on
His further inquisition.
  Rod.   Count, to Hamburgh.
  Sieg. (*agitated*). Hamburgh! No, I have
  nought to do there, nor
Am aught connected with that city. Then
God speed you!
  Rod.   Fare ye well, Count Siegendorf!
               [*Exit* RODOLPH.
  Sieg. Ulric, this man, who has just de-
  parted, is
One of those strange companions whom I
  fain
Would reason with you on.
  Ulr.   My lord, he is
Noble by birth, of one of the first houses
In Saxony.
  Sieg.   I talk not of his birth,
But of his bearing. Men speak lightly of him.
  Ulr. So they will do of most men. Even
  the monarch
Is not fenced from his chamberlain's slander,
  or
The sneer of the last courtier whom he has
  made
Great and ungrateful.
  Sieg.   If I must be plain,
The world speaks more than lightly of this
  Rodolph :
They say he is leagued with the " black bands "
  who still
Ravage the frontier.
  Ulr.   And will you believe
The world?
  Sieg.   In this case — yes.
  Ulr.   In *any* case,
I thought you knew it better than to take
An accusation for a sentence.

Sieg.   Son!
I understand you : you refer to —— but
My Destiny has so involved about me
Her spider web, that I can only flutter
Like the poor fly, but break it not. Take heed,
Ulric ; you have seen to what the passions led
  me :
Twenty long years of misery and famine
Quenched them not — twenty thousand more,
  perchance,
Hereafter (or even here in *moments* which
Might date for years, did Anguish make the
  dial)
May not obliterate or expiate
The madness and dishonor of an instant.
Ulric, be warned by a father! — I was not
By mine, and you behold me!
  Ulr.   I behold
The prosperous and beloved Siegendorf,
Lord of a prince's appanage, and honored
By those he rules and those he ranks with.
  Sieg.   Ah!
Why wilt thou call me prosperous, while I fear
For thee? Beloved, when thou lovest me not!
All hearts but one may beat in kindness for
  me — ,
But if my son's is cold! ——
  Ulr.   Who *dare* say that?
  Sieg. None else but I, who see it — *feel* it
  — keener
Than would your adversary, who dared say so,
Your sabre in his heart! But mine survives
The wound.
  Ulr.   You err. My nature is not given
To outward fondling : how should it be so,
After twelve years' divorcement from my
  parents?
  Sieg. And did not *I* too pass those twelve
  torn years
In a like absence? But 'tis vain to urge you —
Nature was never called back by remon-
  strance.
Let's change the theme. I wish you to con-
  sider
That these young violent nobles of high name,
But dark deeds (ay, the darkest, if all Rumor
Reports be true), with whom thou consortest,
Will lead thee ——
  Ulr. (*impatiently*). I'll be *led* by no man.
  Sieg.   Nor
Be leader of such, I would hope : at once
To wean thee from the perils of thy youth
And haughty spirit, I have thought it well
That thou shouldst wed the lady Ida — more
As thou appear'st to love her.
  Ulr.   I have said
I will obey your orders, were they to
Unite with Hecate — can a son say more?
  Sieg. He says too much in saying this. It
  is not
The nature of thine age, nor of thy blood,
Nor of thy temperament, to talk so coolly,

act so carelessly, in that which is
.e bloom or blight of all men's happiness,
or Glory's pillow is but restless if
ve lay not down his cheek there) : some
  strong bias,
me master fiend is in thy service to
srule the mortal who believes him slave,
,d makes his every thought subservient ; else
,ou'dst say at once — " I love young Ida, and
ill wed her ; " or, " I love her not, and all
,e powers of earth shall never make me." —
  So
ould I have answered.
Ulr.   Sir, *you wed* for love ?
Sieg. I did, and it has been my only refuge
  many miseries.
Ulr.   Which miseries
,d never been but for this love-match.
Sieg.   Still
;ainst your age and nature ! Who at twenty
,r answered thus till now ?
Ulr.   Did you not warn me
;ainst your own example ?
Sieg.   Boyish sophist !
, a word, do you love, or love not, Ida ?
Ulr. What matters it, if I am ready to
,ey you in espousing her ?
Sieg.   As far
, you feel, nothing, but all life for her.
,e's young — all beautiful — adores you — is
,dowed with qualities to give happiness,
,ch as rounds common life into a dream
' something which your poets cannot paint,
,d (if it were not wisdom to love virtue)
,r which Philosophy might barter Wisdom ;
,d giving so much happiness, deserves
little in return. I would not have her
eak her heart for a man who has none to
  break ;
' wither on her stalk like some pale rose
,serted by the bird she thought a nightin-
  gale,
,cording to the Orient tale. She is ——
Ulr. The daughter of dead Stralenheim,
  your foe.
l wed her, ne'ertheless ; though, to say truth,
st now I am not violently transported
favor of such unions.
Sieg.   But she loves you.
Ulr. And I love her, and therefore would
  think *twice.*
Sieg. Alas! Love never *did* so.
Ulr.   Then 'tis time
,e should begin, and take the bandage from
,s eyes, and look before he leaps: till now
,e hath ta'en a jump i' the dark.
Sieg.   But you consent?
Ulr. I did, and do.
Sieg.   Then fix the day.
Ulr.   'Tis usual,
,d certes courteous, to leave that to the lady.
Sieg. I will engage for *her.*

Ulr.   So will not *I*
For any woman ; and as what I fix,
I fain would see unshaken, when she gives
Her answer, I'll give mine.
Sieg.   But 'tis your office
To woo.
Ulr. Count, 'tis a marriage of your making,
So be it of your wooing ; but to please you
I will now pay my duty to my mother,
With whom, you know, the lady Ida is. —
What would you have ? You have forbid my
  stirring
For manly sports beyond the castle walls,
And I obey ; you bid me turn a chamberer,
To pick up gloves, and fans, and knitting-
  needles,
And list to songs and tunes, and watch for
  smiles,
And smile at pretty prattle, and look into
The eyes of feminine, as though they were
The stars receding early to our wish
Upon the dawn of a world-winning battle —
What can a son or man do more ?
                    [*Exit* ULRIC.
Sieg. (*solus*).   Too much ! —
Too much of duty and too little love !
He pays me in the coin he owes me not :
For such hath been my wayward fate, I could
  not
Fulfil a parent's duties by his side
Till now ; but love he owes me, for my thoughts
Ne'er left him, nor my eyes longed without
  tears
To see my child again, and now I have found
  him !
But how ! — obedient, but with coldness ;
  duteous
In my sight, but with carelessness ; mysteri-
  ous —
Abstracted — distant — much given to long
  absence,
And where — none know — in league with the
  most riotous
Of our young nobles ; though, to do him
  justice,
He never stoops down to their vulgar pleas-
  ures ;
Yet there's some tie between them which ,
  cannot
Unravel. They look up to him — consult
  him —
Throng round him as a leader : but with me
He hath no confidence ! Ah ! can I hope it
After — what ! doth my father's curse descend
Even to my child ? Or is the Hungarian
  near
To shed more blood ? or — Oh ! if it should
  be !
Spirit of Stralenheim, dost thou walk these
  walls
To wither him and his — who, though they
  slew not,

Unlatched the door of death ,or thee ? 'Twas
  not
Our fault, nor is our sin : thou wert our foe,
And yet I spared thee when my own destruction
Slept with thee, to awake with thine awak-
  ening!
And only took — Accursed gold! thou liest
Like poison in my hands; I dare not use
  thee,
Nor part from thee; thou camest in such a
  guise,
Methinks thou wouldst contaminate all hands
Like mine. Yet I have done, to atone for
  thee,
Thou villanous gold! and thy dead master's
  doom,
Though he died not by me or mine, as much
As if he were my brother! I have ta'en
His orphan Ida — cherished her as one
Who will be mine.

Enter an ATTENDANT.

Atten.   The abbot, if it please
Your excellency, whom you sent for, waits
Upon you.   [*Exit* ATTENDANT.

Enter the PRIOR ALBERT.

Prior.   Peace be with these walls, and all
Within them!
Sieg.   Welcome, welcome, holy father!
And may thy prayer be heard! — all men have
  need
Of such, and I ——
Prior.   ·Have the first claim to all
The prayers of our community. Our convent,
Erected by your ancestors, is still
Protected by their children.
Sieg.   Yes, good father;
Continue daily orisons for us
In these dim days of heresies and blood,
Though the schismatic Swede, Gustavus, is
Gone home.
Prior.   To the endless home of unbelievers,
Where there is everlasting wail and woe,
Gnashing of teeth, and tears of blood, and
  fire
Eternal, and the worm which dieth not!
Sieg.   True, father: and to avert those
  pangs from one,
Who, though of our most faultless holy church,
Yet died without its last and dearest offices,
Which smooth the soul through purgatorial
  pains,
I have to offer humbly this donation
In masses for his spirit.
    [SIEGENDORF *offers the gold which he had*
    taken from STRALENHEIM.
Prior.   Count, if I
Receive it, 'tis because I· know too well
Refusal would offend you. Be assured
The largess shall be only dealt in alms,
And every mass no less sung for the dead.

Our house needs no donations, thanks to
  yours,
Which has of old endowed it; but from you
And yours in all meet things 'tis fit we obey.
For whom shall mass be said ?
Sieg. (*faltering*).   For — for — the dead.
Prior.   His name ?
Sieg.   'Tis from a soul, and not a name
I would avert perdition.
Prior.   I meant not
To pry into your secret. We will pray
For one unknown, the same as for the
  proudest.
Sieg.   Secret! I have none; but, father, he
  who's gone
Might *have* one; or, in short, he did be-
  queathe —
No, not bequeathe — but I bestow this sum
For pious purposes.
Prior.   A proper deed
In the behalf of our departed friends.
Sieg. But he who's gone was not my friend,
  but foe,
The deadliest and the stanchest.
Prior.   Better still!
To employ our means to obtain heaven for
  the souls
Of our dead enemies is worthy those
Who can forgive them living.
Sieg.   But I did not
Forgive this man. I loathed him to the last,
As he did me. I do not love him now,
But ——
Prior.   Best of all! for this is pure religion!
You fain would rescue him you hate from
  hell —
An evangelical compassion — with
Your own gold too!
Sieg.   Father, 'tis not my gold.
Prior. Whose then ? You said it was no
  legacy.
Sieg.   No matter whose — of this be sure,
  that he
Who owned it never more will need it, save
In that which it may purchase from your altars:
'Tis yours, or theirs.
Prior.   Is there no blood upon it ?
Sieg.   No; but there's worse than blood —
  eternal shame!
Prior.   Did he who owned it die in kis
  bed?
Sieg.   Alas!
He did.
Prior. Son! you relapse into revenge,
If you regret your enemy's bloodless death.
Sieg. His death was fathomlessly deep in
  blood.
Prior. You said he died in bed, not battle.
Sieg.   He
Died, I scarce know — but — he was stabbed
  i' the dark,
And now you have it — perished on his pillow

y a cut-throat! — Ay! — you may look upon me!

am *not* the man. I'll meet your eye on that point,

s I can one day God's.

Prior.   Nor did he die
y means, or men, or instrument of yours?

Sieg. No! by the God who sees and strikes!

Prior.   Nor know you
/ho slew him?

Sieg.   I could only guess at *one*,
nd he to me a stranger, unconnected,
s unemployed. Except by one day's knowl-
    edge,
never saw the man who was suspected.

Prior. Then you are free from guilt.

Sieg. (*eagerly*).   Oh! am I? — say.

Prior. You have said so, and know best.

Sieg.   Father! I have spoken
he truth, and nought but truth, if *not* the
    whole :
et say I am *not* guilty! for the blood
f this man weighs on me, as if I shed it,
hough, by the Power who abhorreth hu-
    man blood,
    did not! — nay, once spared it, when
    I might
nd *could* — ay, perhaps, *should* (if our self-
    safety
e e'er excusable in such defences
.gainst the attacks of over-potent foes) :
ut pray for him, for me, and all my
    house;
or, as I said, though I be innocent,
know not why, a like remorse is on me,
.s if he had fallen by me or mine. Pray for
    me,
ather! I have prayed myself in vain.

Prior.   I will.
e comforted!   You are innocent, and
    should
e calm as innocence.

Sieg.   But calmness is not
lways the attribute of innocence.
feel it is not.

Prior.   But it will be so,
/hen the mind gathers up its truth within
    it.
emember the great festival to-morrow,
ı which you rank amidst our chiefest no-
    bles,
s well as your brave son; and smooth your
    aspect,
or in the general orison of thanks
ɔr bloodshed stopt, let blood you shed not
    rise,
cloud upon your thoughts. This were
    to be
ɔo sensitive. Take comfort, and forget
ıch things, and leave remorse unto the
    guilty.   [*Exeunt.*

ACT V.

SCENE I. — *A large and magnificent Gothic
    Hall in the Castle of Siegendorf, decorated
    with Trophies, Banners, and Arms of that
    Family.*

Enter ARNHEIM *and* MEISTER, *attendants of*
    COUNT SIEGENDORF.

Arn. Be quick! the count will soon return :
    the ladies
Already are at the portal. Have you sent
The messengers in search of him he seeks
    for?

Meis. I have, in all directions, over
    Prague,
As far as the man's dress and figure could
By your description track him. The devil take
These revels and processions! All the pleasure
(If such there be) must fall to the spectators.
I'm sure none doth to us who make the show.

Arn. Go to! my lady countess comes.

Meis.   I'd rather
Ride a day's hunting on an outworn jade,
Than follow in the train of a great man
In these dull pageantries.

Arn.   Begone! and rail
Within.   [*Exeunt.*

Enter the COUNTESS JOSEPHINE SIEGEN-
    DORF *and* IDA STRALENHEIM.

Jos. Well, Heaven be praised, the show is
    over.

Ida. How can you say so! never have I
    dreamt
Of aught so beautiful. The flowers, the
    boughs,
The banners, and the nobles, and the knights,
The gems, the robes, the plumes, the happy
    faces,
The coursers, and the incense, and the sun
Streaming through the stained windows, even
    the *tombs*,
Which looked so calm, and the celestial
    hymns,
Which seemed as if they rather came from
    heaven
Than mounted there. The bursting organ's
    peal
Rolling on high like an harmonious thunder;
The white robes and the lifted eyes; the world
At peace! and all at peace with one another!
Oh, my sweet mother!
                [*Embracing* JOSEPHINE.

Jos.   My beloved child!
For such, I trust, thou shalt be shortly.

Ida.   Oh!
I am so already. Feel how my heart beats!

Jos. It does, my love; and never may it
    throb
With aught more bitter.

Ida.   Never shall it do so!

How should it?　What should make us
　grieve?　I hate
To hear of sorrow: how can we be sad,
Who love each other so entirely?　You,
The count, and Ulric, and your daughter Ida.
Jos.　Poor child!
Ida.　　　　Do you pity me?
Jos.　　　　　　No; I but envy.
And that in sorrow, not in the world's sense
Of the universal vice, if one vice be
More general than another.
Ida.　　　　I'll not hear
A word against a world which still contains
You and my Ulric.　Did you ever see
Aught like him?　How he towered amongst
　them all!
How all eyes followed him!　The flowers fell
　faster—
Rained from each lattice at his feet, me-
　thought,
Than before all the rest; and where he trod
I dare be sworn that they grow still, nor e'er
Will wither.
Jos.　　You will spoil him, little flatterer,
If he should hear you.
Ida.　　　　But he never will.
I dare not say so much to him—I fear him.
Jos.　Why so? he loves you well.
Ida.　　　　But I can never
Shape my thoughts *of* him into words *to* him.
Besides, he sometimes frightens me.
Jos.　　　　　　How so?
Ida.　A cloud comes o'er his blue eyes
　suddenly,
Yet he says nothing.
Jos.　　　　It is nothing: all men,
Especially in these dark troublous times,
Have much to think of.
Ida.　　　　But I cannot think
Of aught save him.
Jos.　　　Yet there are other men,
In the world's eye, as goodly.　There's, for in-
　stance,
The young Count Waldorf, who scarce once
　withdrew
His eyes from yours to-day.
Ida.　　　　I did not see him,
But Ulric.　Did you not see at the moment
When all knelt, and I wept? and yet me-
　thought,
Through my fast tears, though they were thick
　and warm,
I saw him smiling on me.
Jos.　　　　I could not
See aught save heaven, to which my eyes
　were raised
Together with the people's.
Ida.　　　　I thought too
Of heaven, although I looked on Ulric.
Jos.　　　　　　Come,
Let us retire; they will be here anon
Expectant of the banquet.　We will lay

Aside these nodding plumes and dragging
　trains.
Ida.　And, above all, these stiff and heavy
　jewels,
Which make my head and heart ache, as
　both throb
Beneath their glitter o'er my brow and zone.
Dear mother, I am with you.

Enter COUNT SIEGENDORF, *in full dress,*
　from the solemnity, and LUDWIG.

Sieg.　　　　　Is he not found?
Lud.　Strict search is making everywhere;
　and if
The man be in Prague, be sure he will be
　found.
Sieg.　Where's Ulric?
Lud.　　　He rode round the other way
With some young nobles; but he left them
　soon;
And, if I err not, not a minute since
I heard his excellency, with his train,
Gallop o'er the west drawbridge.

Enter ULRIC, *splendidly dressed.*

Sieg. (*to* LUDWIG).　　See they cease not
Their quest of him I have described.
　　　　　　　　　[*Exit* LUDWIG.
　Oh, Ulric!
How have I longed for thee!
Ulr.　　　　Your wish is granted—
Behold me!
Sieg.　　　I have seen the murderer.
Ulr.　Whom?　Where?
Sieg.　The Hungarian, who slew Stralen-
　heim.
Ulr.　You dream.
Sieg.　I live! and as I live, I saw him—
Heard him! he dared to utter even my name.
Ulr.　What name?
Sieg.　　Werner!　'twas mine.
Ulr.　　　　It must be so
No more: forget it.
Sieg.　　　Never! never! all
My destinies were woven in that name:
It will not be engraved upon my tomb,
But it may lead me there.
Ulr.　　To the point—the Hungarian?
Sieg. Listen!—The church was thronged;
　the hymn was raised;
" *Te Deum* " pealed from nations, rather than
From choirs, in one great cry of " God be
　praised "
For one day's peace, after thrice ten dread
　years,
Each bloodier than the former: I arose,
With all the nobles, and as I looked down
Along the lines of lifted faces,—from
Our bannered and escutcheoned gallery, I
Saw, like a flash of lightning (for I saw
A moment and no more), what struck me
　sightless

⊃ all else — the Hungarian's face! I grew
ck; and when I recovered from the mist
ᵗhich curled about my senses, and again
⊃oked down, I saw him not. The thanks-
  giving
ᵗas over, and we marched back in pro-
  cession.
Ulr. Continue.
Sieg.   When we reached the Muldau's
  bridge,
ʰe joyous crowd above, the numberless
ᵘrks manned with revellers in their best
  garbs,
ᵗhich shot alone the glancing tide below,
ᵗe decorated street, the long array,
ᵗe clashing music, and the thundering
ᶠ far artillery, which seemed to bid
 long and loud farewell to its great doings,
ʰe standards o'er me and the tramplings
  round,   ·
ʰe roar of rushing thousands, — all — all
  could not
ʰase this man from my mind, although my
  senses
⊃ longer held him palpable.
Ulr.   You saw him
⊃ more, then?
Sieg.   I looked, as a dying soldier
⊃oks at a draught of water, for this man:
ᵘt still I saw him not; but in his stead ——
Ulr. What in his stead?
Sieg.   My eye for ever fell
 on your dancing crest; the loftiest,
 on the loftiest and the loveliest head
 rose the highest of the stream of plumes,
ʰich overflowed the glittering streets of
  Prague.
Ulr. What's this to the Hungarian?
Sieg.   Much; for I
 d almost then forgot him in my son;
ʰen just as the artillery ceased, and paused
 e music, and the crowd embraced in lieu
  shouting, I heard in a deep, low voice,
 stinct and keener far upon my ear
 an the late cannon's volume, this word —
  "*Werner!*"
Ulr. Uttered by ——
ⁱeg. HIM! I turned — and saw — and fell.
·*lr.* And wherefore? Were you seen?
ⁱeg.   The officious care
 those around me dragged me from the spot,
 ᵉing my faintness, ignorant of the cause;
 u, too, were too remote in the procession
ʰe old nobles being divided from their
  children)
  aid me.
Ulr.   But I'll aid you now.
ⁱeg.   In what?
lr. In searching for this man, or ——
  When he's found,
 at shall we do with him?
ⁱeg.   I know not that.

Ulr. Then wherefore seek?
Sieg.   Because I cannot rest
Till he is found. His fate, and Stralenheim's,
And ours, seem intertwisted! nor can be
Unravelled, till ——

Enter an ATTENDANT.

Atten.   A stranger to wait on
Your excellency.
Sieg.   Who?
Atten.   He gave no name.
Sieg. Admit him, ne'ertheless.
[*The* ATTENDANT *introduces* GABOR, *and
  afterwards exit.*
                                   Ah!
Gab.   'Tis, then, Werner!
Sieg. (*haughtily*). The same you knew, sir,
  by that name; and *you!*
Gab. (*looking round*). I recognize you
  both: father and son,
It seems. Count, I have heard that you, or
  yours,
Have lately been in search of me: I am here.
Sieg. I have sought you, and have found
  you: you are charged
(Your own heart may inform you why) with
  such
A crime as ——   [*He pauses.*
Gab. ·   Give it utterance, and then
I'll meet the consequences.
Sieg.   You shall do so —
Unless ——
Gab.   First, who accuses me?
Sieg.   All things,
If not all men: the universal rumor —
My own presence on the spot — the place —
  the time —
And every speck of circumstance unite
To fix the blot on you.
Gab.   And on *me only?*
Pause ere you answer: is no other name,
Save mine, stained in this business?
Sieg.   Trifling villain!
Who play'st with thine own guilt! Of all
  that breathe
Thou best dost know the innocence of him
'Gainst whom thy breath would blow thy
  bloody slander.
But I will talk no further with a wretch,
Further than justice asks. Answer at once
And without quibbling, to my charge.
Gab.   'Tis false!
Sieg. Who says so?
Gab.   I.
Sieg.   And how disprove it?
.*Gab.*   By
The presence of the murderer.
Sieg.   Name him!
Gab.   He
May have more names than one. Your lord-
  ship had so
Once on a time.

Sieg.   If you mean me, I dare
Your utmost.
Gab.   You may do so, and in safety;
I know the assassin.
    Sieg.   Where is he?
Gab. (*pointing to* ULRIC).   Beside you!
[ULRIC *rushes forward to attack* GABOR;
   SIEGENDORF *interposes.*
Sieg.   Liar and fiend! but you shall not be
  slain;
These walls are mine, and you are safe within
  them.   [*He turns to* ULRIC.
Ulric, repel this calumny, as I
Will do.   I avow it is a growth so monstrous,
I could not deem it earth-born: but be
  calm;
It will refute itself.   But touch him not.
       [ULRIC *endeavors to compose himself.*
Gab.   Look at *him*, count, and then *hear me.*
Sieg. (*first to* GABOR, *and then looking at*
  ULRIC).
             I hear thee.
My God! you look ——
    Ulr.   How?
Sieg.   As on that dread night
When we met in the garden.
    Ulr. (*composes himself*).   It is nothing.
Gab.   Count, you are bound to hear me.   I
  came hither
Not seeking you, but sought.   When I knelt
  down
Amidst the people in the church, I dreamed
  not
To find the beggared Werner in the seat
Of senators and princes; but you have called
  me,
And we have met.
    Sieg.   Go on, sir.
    Gab.   Ere I do so,
Allow me to inquire who profited
By Stralenheim's death?   Was't I — as poor
  as ever;
And poorer by suspicion on my name!
The baron lost in that last outrage neither
Jewels nor gold; his life alone was sought,—
A life which stood between the claims of others
To honors and estates scarce less than princely.
    Sieg.   These hints, as vague as vain, attach
  no less
To me than to my son.
    Gab.   I can't help that.
But let the consequence alight on him
Who feels himself the guilty one amongst us.
I speak to you, Count Siegendorf, because
I know you innocent, and deem you just.
But ere I can proceed — *dare* you protect
  me?
Dare you command me?
    [SIEGENDORF *first looks at the Hungarian,*
  and then at ULRIC, *who has unbuckled*
  his sabre, and is drawing lines with it on
  the floor — still in its sheath.

Ulr. (*looks at his father and says*).
            Let the man go on!
Gab.   I am unarmed, count — bid your son
  lay down
His sabre.
    Ulr. (*offers it to him contemptuously*).
            Take it.
    Gab.   No, sir, 'tis enough
That we are both unarmed — I would not
  choose
To wear a steel which may be stained with
  more
Blood than came there in battle.
    Ulr. (*casts the sabre from him in contempt*).
             It — or some
Such other weapon, in my hands — spared
  yours
Once when disarmed and at my mercy.
    Gab.   True —
I have not forgotten it: you spared me for
Your own especial purpose — to sustain
An ignominy not my own.
    Ulr.   Proceed.
The tale is doubtless worthy the relater.
But is it of my father to hear further?
            [*To* SIEGENDORF.
    Sieg. (*takes his son by the hand*).
My son, I know my own innocence, and doubt
  not
Of yours — but I have promised this man pa-
  tience.
Let him continue.
    Gab.   I will not detain you
By speaking of myself much; I began
Life early — and am what the world has made
  me.
At Frankfort on the Oder, where I passed
A winter in obscurity, it was
My chance at several places of resort
(Which I frequented sometimes but not often)
To hear related a strange circumstance
In February last.   A martial force,
Sent by the state, had, after strong resistance,
Secured a band of desperate men, supposed
Marauders from the hostile camp. — They
  proved,
However, not to be so — but banditti,
Whom either accident or enterprise
Had carried from their usual haunt — the
  forests
Which skirt Bohemia — even into Lusatia.
Many amongst them were reported of
High rank — and martial law slept for a time.
At last they were escorted o'er the frontiers,
And placed beneath the civil jurisdiction
Of the free town of Frankfort.   Of *their* fate,
I know no more.
    Sieg.   And what is this to Ulric?
    Gab.   Amongst them there was said to be
  one man
Of wonderful endowments: — birth and for-
  tune,

outh, strength, and beauty, almost super-
   human,
nd courage as unrivalled, were proclaimed
is by the public rumor; and his sway,
ot only over his associates, but
is judges, was attributed to witchcraft.
ich was his influence : — I have no great faith
ı any magic save that of the mine —
therefore deemed him wealthy. — But my soul
ʃas roused with various feelings to seek out
his prodigy, if only to behold him.
Sieg. And did you so ?
Gab.   You'll hear. Chance favored me:
popular affray in the public square
rew crowds together — it was one of those
ccasions where men's souls look out of
   them,
nd show them as they are — even in their
   faces :
he moment my eye met his, I exclaimed,
This is the man ! " though he was then, as
   since,
ʃith the nobles of the city. I felt sure
had not erred, and watched him long and
   nearly.
noted down his form — his gesture — fea-
   tures,
ature, and bearing — and amidst them all,
idst every natural and acquired distinction,
could discern, methought, the assassin's eye
nd gladiator's heart.
Ulr. (*smiling*).   The tale sounds well.
Gab. And may sound better. — He ap-
   peared to me
ne of those beings to whom Fortune bends
; she doth to the daring — and on whom
he fates of others oft depend ; besides,
ı indescribable sensation drew me
ear to this man, as if my point of fortune
ʃas to be fixed by him. — There I was wrong.
Sieg. And may not be right now.
Gab.   I followed him,
ɔlicited his notice — and obtained it —
ɪough not his friendship : — it was his inten-
   tion
ɔ leave the city privately — we left it
ɔgether — and together we arrived
. the poor town where Werner was con-
   cealed,
ɪd Stralenheim was succored —— Now we
   are on
ɪe verge — *dare* you hear further ?
Sieg.   I must do so —
: I have heard too much.
Gab.   I saw in you
man above his station — and if not
ɪ high, as now I find you, in my then
ɔnceptions, 'twas that I had rarely seen
en such as you appeared in height of mind
the most high of worldly rank ; you were
ɔor, even to all save rags : I would have
   shared

My purse, though slender, with you — you
   refused it.
Sieg. Doth my refusal make a debt to you,
That thus you urge it ?
Gab.   Still you owe me something,
Though not for that; and I owed you my
   safety,
At least my seeming safety, when the slaves
Of Stralenheim pursued me on the grounds
That *I* had robbed him.
Sieg.   *I* concealed you — I,
Whom and whose house you arraign, reviving
   viper ! .
Gab. I accuse no man — save in my de-
   fence.
You, count, have made yourself accuser —
   judge :
Your hall's my court, your heart is my tribunal.
Be just, and *I*'ll be merciful !
Sieg.   You merciful !
You ! Base calumniator !
Gab.   I.   'Twill rest
With me at last to be so. You concealed me —
In secret passages known to yourself,
You said, and to none else. At dead of night,
Weary with watching in the dark, and dubious
Of tracing back my way, I saw a glimmer,
Through distant crannies, of a twinkling light :
I followed it, and reached a door — a secret
Portal — which opened to the chamber, where,
With cautious hand and slow, having first
   undone
As much as made a crevice of the fastening,
I looked through and beheld a purple bed,
And on it Stralenheim ! —
Sieg.   Asleep ! And yet
You slew him ! — Wretch !
Gab.   He was already slain,
And bleeding like a sacrifice. My own
Blood became ice.
Sieg.   But he was all alone !
You saw none else ? You did not see the ——
      [*He pauses from agitation.*
Gab.   No,
He, whom you dare not name, nor even I
Scarce dare to recollect, was not then in
The chamber.
Sieg. (*to* ULRIC). Then, my boy ! thou
   art guiltless still —
Thou bad'st me say *I* was so once — Oh ! now
Do thou as much !
Gab.   Be patient ! I can *not*
Recede now, though it shake the very walls
Which frown above us. You remember, — or
If not, your son does, — that the locks were
   changed
Beneath *his* chief inspection on the morn
Which led to this same night : how he had
   entered
He best knows — but within an antechamber,
The door of which was half ajar, I saw
A man who washed his bloody hands, and oft

With stern and anxious glance gazed back
  upon
The bleeding body — but it moved no more.
  Sieg. Oh! God of fathers!
  Gab. I beheld his features
As I see yours — but yours they were not,
  though
Resembling them — behold them in Count
  Ulric's!
Distinct as I beheld them, though the expres-
  sion
Is not now what it then was; — but it was so
When I first charged him with the crime — so
  lately.
  Sieg. This is so ——
  Gab. (*interrupting him*). Nay — but hear
me to the end!
Now you must do so. — I conceived myself
Betrayed by you and *him* (for now I saw
There was some tie between you) into this
Pretended den of refuge, to become
The victim of your guilt; and my first thought
Was vengeance: but though armed with a
  short poniard
(Having left my sword without) I was no match
For him at any time, as had been proved
That morning — either in address or force.
I turned, and fled — i' the dark: chance rather
  than
Skill made me gain the secret door of the hall,
And thence the chamber where you slept: if I
Had found you *waking*, Heaven alone can tell
What vengeance and suspicion might have
  prompted;
But ne'er slept guilt as Werner slept that night.
  Sieg. And yet I had horrid dreams! and
  such brief sleep,
The stars had not gone down when I awoke.
Why didst thou spare me? I dreamt of my
  father —
And now my dream is out!
  Gab. 'Tis not my fault,
If I have read it. — Well! I fled and hid me —
Chance led me here after so many moons —
And showed me Werner in Count Siegendorf!
Werner, whom I had sought in huts in vain,
Inhabited the palace of a sovereign!
You sought me and have found me — now
  you know
My secret, and may weigh its worth.
  Sieg. (*after a pause*). Indeed!
  Gab. Is it revenge or justice which inspires
Your meditation?
  Sieg. Neither — I was weighing
The value of your secret.
  Gab. You shall know it
At once: — When you were poor, and I,
  though poor,
Rich enough to relieve such poverty
As might have envied mine, I offered you
My purse — yóu would not share it: — I'll
  be franker

With you: you are wealth*y*, noble, trusted by
The imperial powers — you understand me?
  Sieg. Yes.
  Gab. Not quite. You think me venal,
  and scarce true:
'Tis no less true, however, that my fortunes
Have made me both at present. You shall
  aid me:
I would have aided you — and also have
Been somewhat damaged in my name to save
Yours and your son's. Weigh well what I
  have said.
  Sieg. Dare you await the event of a few
  minutes'
Deliberation?
  Gab. (*casts his eyes on* ULRIC, *who is lean-
  ing against a pillar*). If I should do so?
  Sieg. I pledge my life for yours. With-
  draw into
This tower. [*Opens a turret door.*
  Gab. (*hesitatingly*). This is the second *safe*
  asylum
You have offered me.
  Sieg. And was not the first so?
  Gab. I know not that even now — but will
  approve·
The second. I have still a further shield. —
I did not enter Prague alone; and should I
Be put to rest with Stralenheim, there are
Some tongues without will wag in my behalf.
Be brief in your decision! [1]
  Sieg. I will be so. —
My word is sacred and irrevocable
Within *these* walls, but it extends no further.
  Gab. I'll take it for so much.
  Sieg. (*points to* ULRIC'S *sabre still upon
  the ground*). Take also *that* —
I saw you eye it eagerly, and him
Distrustfully.
  Gab. (*takes up the sabre*). I will; and so
  provide
To sell my life — not cheaply.
  [GABOR *goes into the turret, which* SIEGEN-
  DORF *closes.*
  Sieg. (*advances to* ULRIC). Now, Count
  Ulric!
For son I dare not call thee — What say'st
  thou?
  Ulr. His tale is true.
  Sieg. True, monster!
  Ulr. Most true, father!
And you did well to listen to it: what
We know, we çan provide against. He must
Be silenced.

[1] ["*Gab.* I have yet an additional security — I
did not enter Prague a solitary individual; and
there are tongues without that will speak for me,
although I should even share the fate of Stralen-
heim. Let your deliberation be short." — "*Sieg.*
My promise is solemn, sacred, irrevocable: It ex-
tends not, however, beyond these walls." — *Min.
Lee.*]

Sieg. ⸻ Ay, with half of my domains;
nd with the other half, could he and thou
nsay this villany.

Ulr.   It is no time
or trifling or dissembling. I have said
is story's true; and he too must be silenced.

Sieg. How so?

Ulr. As Stralenheim is. Are you so dull
s never to have hit on this before?
/hen we met in the garden, what except
iscovery in the act could make me know
is death? Or had the prince's household
been
hen summoned, would the cry for the police
een left to such a stranger? Or should I
ave loitered on the way? Or, could you,
    Werner,
he object of the baron's hate and fears,
ave fled, unless by many an hour before
spicion woke? I sought and fathomed you,
oubting if you were false or feeble: I
erceived you were the latter; and yet so
onfiding have I found you, that I doubted
t times your weakness.[1]

Sieg.   Parricide! no less
han common stabber! What deed of my
    life,
r thought of mine, could make you deem
    me fit
or your accomplice?

Ulr.   Father, do not raise
he devil you cannot lay between us. This
 time for union and for action, not
or family disputes. While *you* were tortured,

---

[1] [I am ready to allow every fair license to dra-
atic verse; but still it must have more than the
re typographic impress of metre. Ten syllables,
unted by finger and thumb, will not do. None
us imagine—

        Day and Martin
To prevent fraud, request purchasers to
Look on the signature on the patent Blacking
Bottles, etc. —

be versification, and the great majority of the
es in this tragedy are just as harmonious:—*e.g.*
" Ul. He too must be silenced.— *Wer.* How
?— *Ul.* As Stralenheim is. Are you so dull
 never to have hit on this before? When we
 t in the garden, what except discovery in the
 t could make me know his death? Or had the
ince's household been then summoned, would the
y for the police been left to such a stranger? [Pretty
glish this last sentence by the by!] Or should
have loitered on the way? Or could you, Wer-
r, the object of the baron's hate and fears, have
d—unless by many an hour before suspicion
ke? I sought and fathomed you, doubting if
u were false or feeble: I perceived you were
e latter; and yet so confiding have I found you,
at I doubted at times your weakness," etc etc.
ere are other passages still more prosaic. Why
ey are printed for verse, I cannot for the life of
 conjecture: they are as plain prose as a turn-
ke act. — *Dr. Maginn.*]

Could *I* be calm? Think you that I have
    heard
This fellow's tale without some feeling? —
    You
Have taught me feeling for *you* and myself;
For whom or what else did you ever teach it?

Sieg. Oh! my dead father's curse! 'tis
    working now.

Ulr. Let it work on! the grave will keep
    it down!
Ashes are feeble foes: it is more easy
To baffle such, than countermine a mole,
Which winds its blind but living path beneath
    you.
Yet hear me still!—If *you* condemn me, yet
Remember *who* hath taught me once too often
To listen to him! *Who* proclaimed to me
That *there were crimes* made venial by the
    occasion?
That passion was our nature? that the goods
Of Heaven waited on the goods of fortune?
Who showed me his humanity secured
By his *nerves* only? *Who* deprived me of
All power to vindicate myself and race
In open day? By his disgrace which stamped
(It might be) bastardy on me, and on
Himself—a *felon's* brand! The man who is
At once both warm and weak invites to deeds
He longs to do, but dare not. Is it strange
That I should *act* what you could *think?* We
    have done
With right and wrong; and now must only
    ponder
Upon effects, not causes. Stralenheim,
Whose life I saved from impulse, as *unknown,*
I would have saved a peasant's or a dog's, I
    slew
Known as our foe—but not from vengeance.
    He
Was a rock in our way which I cut through,
As doth the bolt, because it stood between us
And our true destination—but not idly.
As stranger I preserved him, and he *owed me*
His *life:* when due, I but resumed the debt.
He, you, and I stood o'er a gulf wherein
I have plunged our enemy.[2] *You* kindled first

---

[2] [" *Ulr.* We stood on a precipice down which
one of three must inevitably have plunged; for I
will not deny that I knew my own situation to be
as critical as yours. I therefore precipitated Stra-
lenheim! You held the torch! You pointed out
the path! Show me now that of safety; or let me
show it you!—

Sieg.   I have done with life!

Ulr. Let us have done with retrospection. We
have nothing more either to learn or to conceal
from each other. I have courage and partisans;
they are even within the walls, though you do not
know them. Keep your own secret. Preserve an
unchanged countenance. Without your further
interference I will forever secure you from the in-
discretion of a *third* person," etc. etc.,—*Miss
\ Lee.*]

The torch — *you* showed the path ; now trace
me that
Of safety — or let me !
Sieg. I have done with life !
Ulr. Let us have done with that which
cankers life —
Familiar feuds and vain recriminations
Of things which cannot be undone. We have
No more to learn or hide : I know no fear,
And have within these very walls men who
(Although you know them not) dare venture
all things.
You stand high with the state ; what passes here
Will not excite her too great curiosity :
Keep your own secret, keep a steady eye,
Stir not, and speak not ; — leave the rest to
me :
We must have no *third* babblers thrust be-
tween us. [*Exit* ULRIC.
Sieg. (*solus*). Am I awake ? are these my
father's halls ?
And *you* — my son ? *My* son ! *mine !* who
have ever
Abhorred both mystery and blood, and yet
Am plunged into the deepest hell of both !
I must be speedy, or more will be shed —
The Hungarian's ! — Ulric — he hath partisans,
It seems : I might have guessed as much.
Oh fool !
Wolves prowl in company. He hath the key
(As I too) of the opposite door which leads
Into the turret. Now then ! or once more
To be the father of fresh crimes, no less
Than of the criminal ! Ho ! Gabor ! Gabor !
[*Exit into the turret, closing the door after
him.*

SCENE II. — *The Interior of the Turret.*

GABOR *and* SIEGENDORF.

Gab. Who calls ?
Sieg. I — Siegendorf ! Take these, and fly !
Lose not a moment !
[*Tears off a diamond star and other jewels,
and thrusts them into* GABOR'S *hand.*
Gab. What am I to do
With these ?
Sieg. Whate'er you will : sell them, or hoard,
And prosper ; but delay not, or you are lost !
Gab. You pledged your honor for my safety !
Sieg. And
Must thus redeem it. Fly ! I am not master,
It seems, of my own castle — of my own
Retainers — nay, even of these very walls,
Or I would bid them fall and crush me !· Fly !
Or you will be slain by——
Gab. Is it even so ?
Farewell, then ! Recollect, however, Count,
You sought this fatal interview !
Sieg. I did :
Let it not be more fatal still ! — Begone !
Gab. By the same path I entered ?

Sieg. Yes ; that's safe still
But loiter not in Prague ; — you do not know
With whom you have to deal.
Gab. I know too well —
And knew it ere yourself, unhappy sire !
Farewell ! [*Exit* GABOR.
Sieg. (*solus and listening*). He hath cleared
the staircase. Ah ! I hear
The door sound loud behind him ! He is safe !
Safe ! — Oh, my father's spirit ! — I am faint — —
[*He leans down upon a stone seat, near the
wall of the tower, in a drooping posture.*

Enter ULRIC, *with others armed, and with
weapons drawn.*

Ulr. Despatch ! — he's there !
Lud. The count, my lord !
Ulr. (*recognizing* SIEGENDORF). *You* here,
sir !
Sieg. Yes : if you want another victim,
strike !
Ulr. (*seeing him stript of his jewels*). Where
is the ruffian who hath plundered you ?
Vassals, despatch in search of him ! You see
'Twas as I said — the wretch hath stript my
father
Of jewels which might form a prince's heir-
loom !
Away ! I'll follow you forthwith.
[*Exeunt all but* SIEGENDORF *and* ULRIC.
What's this ?
Where is the villain ?
Sieg. There are *two*, sir : which
Are you in quest of ?
Ulr. Let us hear no more
Of this : he must be found. You have not let
him escape ?
Sieg. He's gone.
Ulr. With your connivance ?
Sieg. With
My fullest, freest aid.
Ulr. Then fare you well !
[ULRIC *is going.*
Sieg. Stop ! I command — entreat — im-
plore ! Oh, Ulric !
Will you then leave me ?
Ulr. What ! remain to be
Denounced — dragged, it may be, in chains ;
and all
By your inherent weakness, half-humanity,
Selfish remorse, and temporizing pity,
That sacrifices your whole race to save
A wretch to profit by our ruin ! No, count,
Henceforth you have no son !
Sieg. I never had one ;
And would you ne'er had borne the useless
name !
Where will you go ? I would not send you
forth
Without protection.
Ulr. Leave that unto me.
I am not alone ; nor merely the vain heir

our domains; a thousand, ay, ten thousand
rds, hearts, and hands, are mine.
ieg.   The foresters!
th whom the Hungarian found you first at
  Frankfort!
?lr. Yes — men — who are worthy of the
  name! Go tell
ir senators that they look well to Prague;
ir feast of peace was early for the times;
re are more spirits abroad than have been
  laid
th Wallenstein!

Enter JOSEPHINE *and* IDA.

'os. What is't we hear? My Siegendorf,
nk Heaven, I see you safe!
ieg.   Safe!
ia.   Yes, dear father!
ieg. No, no; I have no children: never
  more
l me by that worst name of parent.
'os.   What
ans my good lord!

Sieg.   That you have given birth
To a demon!
Ida. (*taking* ULRIC'S *hand*). Who shall
  dare say this of Ulric?
Sieg. Ida, beware! there's-blood upon that
  hand.
Ida. (*stooping to kiss it*). I'd kiss it off,
  though it were mine.
Sieg.   It is so!
Ulr. Away! it is your father's!
                                [Exit ULRIC.
Ida.   Oh, great God!
And I have loved this man!
  [IDA *falls senseless —* JOSEPHINE *stands
  speechless with horror.*
Sieg.   The wretch hath slain
Them both! — My Josephine! we are now
  alone!
Would we had ever been so! — All is over
For me! — Now open wide, my sire, thy
  grave;
Thy curse hath dug it deeper for thy son
In mine! — The race of Siegendorf is past.

DON JUAN.

OULD to heaven that I were so much clay,
s I am blood, bone, marrow, passion,
  feeling —
ause at least the past were passed away —
nd for the future — (but I write this reel-
  ing,
ing got drunk exceedingly to-day,
) that I seem to stand upon the ceiling)
y — the future is a serious matter —
l so — for God's sake — hock and soda-
  water!

DEDICATION.

I.

SOUTHEY! You're a Poet — Poet-
laureate,
nd representative of all the race,
ough 'tis true that you turned out a Tory at

Last, — yours has lately been a common
  case, —
And now, my Epic Renegade! what are ye at?
  With all the Lakers, in and out of place?
A nest of tuneful persons, to my eye
Like "four and twenty Blackbirds in a pye;

II.

"Which pye being opened they began to sing"
  (This old song and new simile holds good),
"A dainty dish to set before the King,"
  Or Regent, who admires such kind of
  food; —
And Coleridge, too, has lately taken wing,
  But like a hawk encumbered with his
  hood, —
Explaining metaphysics to the nation —
I wish he would explain his Explanation.

III.

You, Bob! are rather insolent, you know,
  At being disappointed in your wish
To supersede all warblers here below,
  And be the only Blackbird in the dish;

And then you overstrain yourself, or so,
    And tumble downward like the flying fish
Gasping on deck, because you soar too high,
    Bob,
And fall, for lack of moisture quite a-dry, Bob!

IV.

And Wordsworth, in a rather long "Excur-
    sion"
    (I think the quarto holds five hundred
    pages),
Has given a sample from the vasty version
    Of his new system to perplex the sages;
'Tis poetry—at least by his assertion,
    And may appear so when the dog-star
    rages—
And he who understands it would be able
To add a story to the Tower of Babel.

V.

You—Gentlemen! by dint of long seclusion
    From better company, have kept your own
At Keswick, and, through still continued
    fusion
Of one another's minds, at last have grown
To deem as a most logical conclusion,
    That Poesy has wreaths for you alone:
There is a narrowness in such a notion,
Which makes me wish you'd change your
    lakes for ocean.

VI.

I would not imitate the petty thought,
    Nor coin my self-love to so base a vice,
For all the glory your conversion brought,
    Since gold alone should not have been its
    price.
You have your salary; was't for that you
    wrought?
    And Wordsworth has his place in the Ex-
    cise.
You're shabby fellows—true—but poets still,
And duly seated on the immortal hill.

VII.

Your bays may hide the boldness of your
    brows—
    Perhaps some virtuous blushes;—let them
    go—
To you I envy neither fruit nor boughs—
    And for the fame you would engross below,
The field is universal, and allows
    Scope to all such as feel the inherent glow:
Scott, Rogers, Campbell, Moore, and Crabbe,
    will try
'Gainst you the question with posterity.

VIII.

For me, who, wandering with pedestrian
    Muses,
    Contend not with you on the winged steed.

I wish your fate may yield ye, when she
    chooses,
    The fame you envy, and the skill you need;
And recollect a poet nothing loses
    In giving to his brethren their full meed
Of merit, and complaint of present days
Is not the certain path to future praise.

IX.

He that reserves his laurels for posterity
    (Who does not often claim the bright re-
    version)
Has generally no great crop to spare it, he
    Being only injured by his own assertion;
And although here and there some glorious
    rarity
    Arise like Titan from the sea's immersion,
The major part of such appellants go
To—God knows where—for no one else can
    know.

X.

If fallen in evil days on evil tongues,
    Milton appealed to the Avenger, Time,
If Time, the Avenger, execrates his wrongs,
    And makes the word "Miltonic" mean
    "*sublime*,"
He deigned not to belie his soul in songs,
    Nor turn his very talent to a crime;
He did not loathe the Sire to laud the Son,
But closed the tyrant-hater he begun.

XI.

Think'st thou, could he—the blind Old
    Man—arise
Like Samuel from the grave, to freeze once
    more
The blood of monarchs with his prophecies,
    Or be alive again—again all hoar
With time and trials, and those helpless eyes,
    And heartless daughters—worn—and pale
    —and poor;
Would *he* adore a sultan? *he* obey
The intellectual eunuch Castlereagh?

XII.

Cold-blooded, smooth-faced, placid miscreant!
    Dabbling its sleek young hands in Erin's
    gore,
And thus for wider carnage taught to pant,
    Transferred to gorge upon a sister shore,
The vulgarest tool that Tyranny could want,
    With just enough of talent, and no more,
To lengthen fetters by another fixed,
And offer poison long already mixed.

XIII.

An orator of such set trash of phrase
    Ineffably—legitimately vile,
That even its grossest flatterers dare not praise,
    Nor foes—all nations—condescend to
    smile,—

ot even a sprightly blunder's spark can blaze
From that Ixion grindstone's ceaseless toil,
hat turns and turns to give the world a notion
f endless torments and perpetual motion.

XIV.

bung,er even in its disgusting trade,
And botching, patching, leaving still behind
ɔmething of which its masters are afraid,
States to be curbed, and thoughts to be
confined,
ɔnspiracy or Congress to be made —
Cobbling at manacles for all mankind —
tinkering slave-maker, who mends old
chains,
ʰith God and man's abhorrence for its gains.

XV.

we may judge of matter by the mind,
Emasculated to the marrow *It*
ath but two objects, how to serve, and bind,
Deeming the chain it wears even men may
fit,
utropius of its many masters, — blind
To worth as freedom, wisdom as to wit,
ɛarless — because *no* feeling dwells in ice,
s very courage stagnates to a vice.

XVI.

Where shall I turn me not to *view* its
bonds,
For I will never *feel* them ; — Italy !
Thy late reviving Roman soul desponds
Beneath the lie this State-thing breathed
o'er thee —
Thy clanking chain, and Erin's yet green
wounds,
Have voices — tongues to cry aloud for
me.
Europe has slaves — allies — kings — armies
still,
And Southey lives to sing them very ill.

XVII.

Meantime — Sir Laureate — I proceed to
dedicate,
In honest simple verse, this song to you.
And, if in flattering strains I do not predi-
cate,
'Tis that I still retain my " buff and blue ; "
My politics as yet are all to educate :
Apostasy's so fashionable, too,
To keep *one* creed's a task grown quite Her-
culean ;
Is it not so, my Tory, ultra-Julian ?
VENICE, September 16, 1818.

CANTO THE FIRST.

I.

WANT a hero : an uncommon want,
When every year and month sends forth a
new one,
ll, after cloying the gazettes with cant,
The age discovers he is not the true one ;
f such as these I should not care to vaunt,
I'll therefore take our ancient friend Don
Juan —
ʼe all have seen him, in the pantomime,
ɪnt to the devil somewhat ere his time.

II.

ɛrnon, the butcher Cumberland, Wolfe,
Hawke,
Prince Ferdinand, Granby, Burgoyne, Kep-
pel, Howe,
ʾil and good have had their tithe of talk,
And filled their sign-posts then, like Welles-
ley now,
ıch in their turñ like Banquo's monarchs
stalk,
Followers of fame, " nine farrow " of thaʰ
sow :
ʾance, too, had Buonaparté anɗ Dɪɪ·
mourier
ɛcorded in the Moniteur and Courier.

III.

Barnave, Brissot, Condorcet, Mirabeau,
Petion, Clootz, Danton, Marat, La Fayette,
Were French, and famous people, as we know ;
And there were others, scarce forgotten yet,
Joubert, Hoche, Marceau, Lannes, Desaix,
Moreau,
With many of the military set,
Exceedingly remarkable at times,
But not at all adapted to my rhymes.

IV.

Nelson was once Britannia's god of war,
And still should be so, but the tide is turned :
There's no more to be said of Trafalgar,
'Tis with our hero quietly inurned ;
Because the army's grown more popular,
At which the naval people are concerned ;
Besides, the prince is all for the land-service,
Forgetting Duncan, Nelson, Howe, and Jervis.

V.

Brave men were living before Agamemnon
And since, exceeding valorous and sage,
A good deal like him too, though quite the
same none ;
But then they shone not on the poet's page

And so have been forgotten: — I condemn
　none,
But can't find any in the present age
Fit for my poem (that is, for my new one) ;
So, as I said, I'll take my friend Don Juan.

VI.

Most epic poets plunge " in medias res "
　(Horace makes this the heroic turnpike
　. road),
And then your hero tells, whene'er you please,
　What went before — by way of episode,
While seated after dinner at his ease,
　Beside his mistress in some soft abode,
Palace, or garden, paradise, or cavern,
Which serves the happy couple for a tavern.

VII.

That is the usual method, but not mine —
　My way is to begin with the beginning ;
The regularity of my design
　Forbids all wandering as the worst of sin-
　　ning,
And therefore I shall open with a line
　(Although it cost me half an hour in spin-
　　ning)
Narrating somewhat of Don Juan's father,
And also of his mother, if you'd rather.

VIII.

In Seville was he born, a pleasant city,
　Famous for oranges and women — he
Who has not seen it will be much to pity,
　So says the proverb — and I quite agree ;
Of all the Spanish towns is none more pretty,
　Cadiz perhaps — but that you soon may
　　see : —
Don Juan's parents lived beside the river,
A noble stream, and called the Guadalquivir.

IX.

His father's name was Jóse — *Don,* of course,
　A true Hidalgo, free from every stain
Of Moor or Hebrew blood, he traced his source
　Through the most Gothic gentlemen of
　　Spain ;
A better cavalier ne'er mounted horse,
　Or, being mounted, e'er got down again,
Than Jóse, who begot our hero, who
Begot — but that's to come —— Well, to re-
　new :

X.

His mother was a learned lady, famed
　For every branch of every science known —
In every Christian language ever named,
　With virtues equalled by her wit alone
She made the cleverest people quite ashamed,
　And even the good with inward envy groan,
Finding themselves so very much exceeded
In their own way by all the things that she did.

XI.

Her memory was a mine : she knew by heart
　All Calderon and greater part of Lopé,
So that if any actor missed his part
　She could have served him for the promp-
　　ter's copy ;
For her Feinagle's were an useless art,
　And he himself obliged to shut up shop — he
Could never make a memory so fine as
That which adorned the brain of Donna Inez.

XII.

Her favorite science was the mathematical,
　Her noblest virtue was her magnanimity,
Her wit (she sometimes tried at wit) was At-
　tic all,
　Her serious sayings darkened to sublimity ;
In short, in all things she was fairly what I call
　A prodigy — her morning dress was dimity,
Her evening silk, or, in the summer, muslin,
And other stuffs, with which I won't stay puz-
　zling.

XIII.

She knew the Latin — that is, " the Lord's
　prayer," ₹
And Greek — the alphabet — I'm nearly
　sure ;
She read some French romances here and
　there,
　Although her mode of speaking was not
　　pure ;
For native Spanish she had no great care,
　At least her conversation was obscure ;
Her thoughts were theorems, her words a
　problem,
As if she deemed that mystery would ennoble
　'em.

XIV.

She liked the English and the Hebrew tongue,
　And said there was analogy between 'em ;
She proved it somehow out of sacred song,
　But I must leave the proofs to those who've
　　seen 'em,
But this I heard her say, and can't be wrong,
　And all may think which way their judg-
　　ments lean 'em,
" 'Tis strange — the Hebrew noun which
　means ' I am,'
The English always used to govern d — n."

XV.

Some women use their tongues — she *looked*
　a lecture,
　Each eye a sermon, and her brow a homily,
An all-in-all-sufficient self-director,
　Like the lamented late Sir Samuel Romilly,
The Law's expounder, and the State's correc
　tor,
　Whose suicide was almost an anomaly —
One sad example more, that " All is vanity," —
(The jury brought their verdict in " Insanity.")

XVI.

short, she was a walking calculation,
Miss Edgeworth's novels stepping from their
    covers,
Mrs. Trimmer's books on education,
Or "Cœlebs' Wife" set out in quest of
    lovers,
Morality's prim personification,
In which not Envy's self a flaw discovers;
    others' share let "female errors fall,"
For she had not even one — the worst of all.

XVII.

If she was perfect past all parallel —
Of any modern female saint's comparison;
So far above the cunning powers of hell,
Her guardian angel had given up his gar-
    rison;
Even her minutest motions went as well
As those of the best time-piece made by
    Harrison:
In virtues nothing earthly could surpass her,
Save thine "incomparable oil," Macassar!

XVIII.

Perfect she was, but as perfection is
Insipid in this naughty world of ours,
Where our first parents never learned to kiss
Till they were exiled from their earlier
    bowers,
Where all was peace, and innocence, and
    bliss
(I wonder how they got through the twelve
    hours)
Don José, like a lineal son of Eve,
Went plucking various fruit without her leave.

XIX.

He was a mortal of the careless kind,
With no great love for learning, or the
    learned,
Who chose to go where'er he had a mind,
And never dreamed his lady was concerned;
The world, as usual, wickedly inclined
To see a kingdom or a house o'erturned,
Whispered he had a mistress, some said two,
But for domestic quarrels one will do.

XX.

Now Donna Inez had, with all her merit,
A great opinion of her own good qualities;
Neglect, indeed, requires a saint to bear it,
And such, indeed, she was in her moralities;
But then she had a devil of a spirit,
And sometimes mixed up fancies with real-
    ities,
And let few opportunities escape
Of getting her liege lord into a scrape.

XXI.

This was an easy matter with a man
Oft in the wrong, and never on his guard;
And even the wisest, do the best they can,
    Have moments, hours, and days, so unpre-
    pared,
That you might "brain them with their lady's
    fan;"
    And sometimes ladies hit exceeding hard,
And fans turn into falchions in fair hands,
And why and wherefore no one understands.

XXII.

'Tis pity learned virgins ever wed
    With persons of no sort of education,
Or gentlemen, who, though well born and bred,
    Grow tired of scientific conversation:
I don't choose to say much upon this head,
    I'm a plain man, and in a single station, ·
But — Oh! ye lords of ladies intellectual,
Inform us truly, have they not hen-pecked
    you all?

XXIII.

Don José and his lady quarrelled — why,
    Not any of the many could divine,
Though several thousand people chose to try,
    'Twas surely no concern of theirs nor mine;
I loathe that low vice — curiosity;
    But if there's any thing in which I shine,
'Tis in arranging all my friends' affairs,
Not having, of my own, domestic cares.

XXIV.

And so I interfered, and with the best
    Intentions, but their treatment was not kind;
I think the foolish people were possessed,
    For neither of them could I ever find,
Although their porter afterwards confessed —
    But that's no matter, and the worst's behind,
For little Juan o'er me threw, down stairs,
A pail of housemaid's water unawares.

XXV.

A little curly-headed, good-for-nothing,
    And mischief-making monkey from his
    birth;
His parents ne'er agreed except in doting
    Upon the most unquiet imp on earth;
Instead of quarrelling, had they been but
    both in
    Their senses, they'd have sent young mas-
    ter forth
To school, or had him soundly whipped at
    home,
To teach him manners for the time to come.

XXVI.

Don José and the Donna Inez led
    For some time an unhappy sort of life,
Wishing each other, not divorced, but dead;
    They lived respectably as man and wife,
Their conduct was exceedingly well-bred,
    And gave no outward signs of inward strife
Until at length the smothered fire broke out,
And put the business past all kind of doubt.

XXVII.

For Inez called some druggists and physicians,
  And tried to prove her loving lord was *mad*,
But as he had some lucid intermissions,
  She next decided he was only *bad ;*
Yet when they asked her for her depositions,
  No sort of explanation could be had,
Save that her duty both to man and God
Required this conduct—which seemed very
  odd.

XXVIII.

She kept a journal, where his faults were noted,
  And opened certain trunks of books and
  letters,
All which might, if occasion served, be
  quoted ;
  And then she had all Seville for abettors,
Besides her good old grandmother (who
  doted) ;
  The hearers of her case became repeaters,
Then advocates, inquisitors, and judges,
Some for amusement, others for old grudges.

XXIX.

And then this best and meekest woman bore
  With such serenity her husband's woes,
Just as the Spartan ladies did of yore,
  Who saw their spouses killed, and nobly
  chose
Never to say a word about them more—
  Calmly she heard each calumny that rose,
And saw *his* agonies with such sublimity,
That all the world exclaimed, "What magna-
  nimity !"

XXX.

No doubt this patience, when the world is
  damning us,
  Is philosophic in our former friends ;
'Tis also pleasant to be deemed magnani-
  mous,
  The more so in obtaining our own ends ;
And what the lawyers call a " *malus animus* "
  Conduct like this by no means compre-
  hends :
Revenge in person's certainly no virtue,
But then 'tis not *my* fault, if *others* hurt you.

XXXI.

And if our quarrels should rip up old stories,
  And help them with a lie or two additional,
I'm not to blame, as you well know—no
  more is
  Any one else.—they were become tradi-
  tional ;
Besides, their resurrection aids our glories
  By contrast, which is what we just were
  wishing all :
And science profits by this resurrection—
Dead scandals form good subjects for dis-
  section.

XXXII.

Their friends had tried at reconciliation,
  Then their relations, who made matters
  worse,
('Twere hard to tell upon a like occasion
  To whom it may be best to have recourse—
I can't say much for friend or yet relation) :
  The lawyers did their utmost for divorce ;
But scarce a fee was paid on either side
Before, unluckily, Don Jóse died.

XXXIII.

He died : and most unluckily, because,
  According to all hints I could collect
From counsel learned in those kinds of laws,
  (Although their talk's obscure and circum-
  spect)
His death contrived to spoil a charming cause ;
  A thousand pities also with respect
To public feeling, which on this occasion
Was manifested in a great sensation.

XXXIV.

But ah ! he died ; and buried with him lay
  The public feeling and the lawyers' fees :
His house was sold, his servants sent away,
  A Jew took one of his two mistresses,
A priest the other—at least so they say :
  I asked the doctors after his disease—
He died of the slow fever called the tertian,
And left his widow to her own aversion.

XXXV.

Yet Jóse was an honorable man,
  That I must say, who knew him very well ;
Therefore his frailties I'll no further scan,
  Indeed there were not many more to tell :
And if his passions now and then outran
  Discretion, and were not so peaceable
As Numa's (who was also named Pom-
  pilius),
He had been ill brought up, and was born
  bilious.

XXXVI.

Whate'er might be his worthlessness or worth,
  Poor fellow ! he had many things to wound
  him.
Let's own—since it can do no good on
  earth—
  It was a trying moment that which found him
Standing alone beside his desolate hearth,
  Where all his household gods lay shivered
  round him.
No choice was left his feelings or his pride,
Save death or Doctors' Commons—so he
  died.

XXXVII.

Dying intestate, Juan was sole heir
  To a chancery suit, and messuages. and
  lands,

.ich, with a long minority and care,
romised to turn out well in proper hands :
z became sole guardian, which was fair,
.nd answered but to nature's just demands ;
only son left with an only mother
rought up much more wisely than another.

XXXVIII.

est of women, even of widows, she
.esolved that Juan should be quite a
  paragon,
i worthy of the noblest pedigree:
His sire was of Castile, his dam from
  Aragon.)
:n for accomplishments of chivalry,
n case our lord the king should go to war
  again,
learned the arts of riding, fencing, gun-
  nery,
i how to scale a fortress — or a nunnery.

XXXIX.

that which Donna Inez most desired,
.nd saw into herself each day before all
: learned tutors whom for him she hired,
Vas, that his breeding should be strictly
  moral :
ch into all his studies she inquired,
.nd so they were submitted first to her, all,
;, sciences, no branch was made a mystery
Juan's eyes, excepting natural history.

XL.

: languages, especially the dead,
he sciences, and most of all the abstruse,
: arts, at least all such as could be said
o be the most remote from common use,
ill these he was much and deeply read ;
ut not a page of anything that's loose,
aints continuation of the species,
s ever suffered, lest he should grow vicious.

XLI.

classic studies made a little puzzle,
:cause of filthy loves of gods and goddesses,
o in the earlier ages raised a bustle,
ut never put on pantaloons or bodices ;
reverend tutors had at times a tussle,
nd for their Æneids, Iliads, and Odysseys,
'e forced to make an odd sort of apology,
Donna Inez dreaded the Mythology.

XLII.

l's a rake, as half his verses show him,
nacreon's morals are a still worse sample,
illus scarcely has a decent poem,
lon't think Sappho's Ode a good example,
ough Longinus tells us there is no hymn
'here the sublime soars forth on wings
  more ample ;

But Virgil's songs are pure, except that horrid
  one
Beginning with " Formosum Pastor Corydon."

XLIII.

Lucretius' irreligion is too strong
  For early stomachs, to prove wholesome
    food ;
I can't help thinking Juvenal was wrong,
  Although no doubt his real intent was good,
For speaking out so plainly in his song,
  So much indeed as to be downright rude ;
And then what proper person can be partial
To all those nauseous epigrams of Martial ?

XLIV.

Juan was taught from out the best edition,
  Expurgated by learned men, who place,
Judiciously, from out the schoolboy's vision,
  The grosser parts ; but fearful to deface
Too much their modest bard by this omission,
  And pitying sore his mutilated case,
They only add them all in an appendix,
Which saves, in fact, the trouble of an index ;

XLV.

For there we have them all " at one fell swoop,"
  Instead of being scattered through the
    pages ;
They stand forth marshalled in a handsome
    troop,
  To meet the ingenuous youth of future ages,
Till some less rigid editor shall stoop
  To call them back into their separate cages,
Instead of standing staring altogether,
Like garden gods — and not so decent either.

XLVI.

The Missal too (it was the family Missal)
  Was ornamented in a sort of way
Which ancient mass-books often are, and this
  all
  Kinds of grotesques illumined ; and how
    they,
Who saw those figures on the margin kiss all,
  Could turn their optics to the text and pray,
Is more than I know — but Don Juan's mother
Kept this herself, and gave her son another.

XLVII.

Sermons he read, and lectures he endured,
  And homilies, and lives of all the saints ;
To Jerome and to Chrysostom inured,
  He did not take such studies for restraints ;
But how faith is acquired, and then insured,
  So well not one of the aforesaid paints
As Saint Augustine in his fine Confessions,
Which makes the reader envy his transgres-
  sions.

XLVIII.

This, too, was a sealed book to little Juan —
  I can't but say that his mamma was right,

If such an education was the true one.
   She scarcely trusted him from out her sight;
Her maids were old, and if she took a new one,
   You might be sure she was a perfect fright,
She did this during even her husband's life —
   I recommend as much to every wife.

XLIX.

Young Juan waxed in goodliness and grace;
   At six a charming child, and at eleven
With all the promise of as fine a face
   As e'er to man's maturer growth was given:
He studied steadily, and grew apace,
   And seemed, at least, in the right road to heaven,
For half his days were passed at church, the other
Between his tutors, confessor, and mother.

L.

At six, I said, he was a charming child,
   At twelve he was a fine, but quiet boy;
Although in infancy a little wild,
   They tamed him down amongst them: to destroy
His natural spirit not in vain they toiled.
   At least it seemed so; and his mother's joy
Was to declare how sage, and still, and steady,
Her young philosopher was grown already.

LI.

I had my doubts, perhaps I have them still,
   But what I say is neither here nor there:
I knew his father well, and have some skill
   In character — but it would not be fair
From sire to son to augur good or ill:
   He and his wife were an ill-sorted pair,
But scandal's my aversion — I protest
Against all evil speaking, even in jest.

LII.

For my part I say nothing — nothing — but
   This I will say — my reasons are my own —
That if I had an only son to put
   To school (as God be praised that I have none),
'Tis not with Donna Inez I would shut
   Him up to learn his catechism alone,
No — no — I'd send him out betimes to college,
For there it was I picked up my own knowledge.

LIII.

For there one learns — 'tis not for me to boast,
   Though I acquired — but I pass over *that*,
As well as all the Greek I since have lost:
   I say that there's the place — but " *Verbum sat,*"
I think I picked up too, as well as most,
   Knowledge of matters — but no matter *what*—

I never married — but, I think, I know
That sons should not be educated so.

LIV.

Young Juan now was sixteen years of age
   Tall, handsome, slender, but well knit: he seemed
Active, though not so sprightly, as a page;
   And every body but his mother deemed
Him almost man; but she flew in a rage
   And bit her lips (for else she might have screamed)
If any said so, for to be precocious
Was in her eyes a thing the most atrocious.

LV.

Amongst her numerous acquaintance, all
   Selected for discretion and devotion,
There was the Donna Julia, whom to call
   Pretty were but to give a feeble notion
Of many charms in her as natural
   As sweetness to the flower, or salt to ocean,
Her zone to Venus, or his bow to Cupid,
(But this last simile is trite and stupid).

LVI.

The darkness of her Oriental eye
   Accorded with her Moorish origin;
(Her blood was not all Spanish, by the by;
   In Spain, you know, this is a sort of sin).
When proud Granada fell, and, forced to fly,
   Boabdil wept, of Donna Julia's kin
Some went to Africa, some stayed in Spain,
Her great great grandmamma chose to remain.

LVII.

She married (I forget the pedigree)
   With an Hidalgo, who transmitted down
His blood less noble than such blood should be;
   At such alliances his sires would frown,
In that point so precise in each degree
   That they bred *in and in*, as might be shown,
Marrying their cousins — nay, their aunts, and nieces,
Which always spoils the breed, if it increases.

LVIII.

This heathenish cross restored the breed again,
   Ruined its blood, but much improved its flesh;
For from a root the ugliest in Old Spain
   Sprung up a branch as beautiful as fresh;
The sons no more were short, the daughters plain;
   But there's a rumor which I fain would hush,
'Tis said that Donna Julia's grandmamma
Produced her Don more heirs at love than law.

LIX.

:ver this might be, the race went on
proving still through every generation,
  it centred in an only son,
10 left an only daughter; my narration
have suggested that this single one
uld be but Julia (whom on this occasion
ll have much to speak about), and she
married, charming, chaste, and twenty-
hree.

LX.

:ye (I'm very fond of handsome eyes)
is large and dark, suppressing half its
.re
 she spoke, then through its soft disguise
shed an expression more of pride than
:e,
iove than either; and there would arise
.omething in them which was not desire,
/ould have been, perhaps, but for the soul
:h struggled through and chastened down
he whole.

LXI.

jlossy hair was clustered o'er a brow
ght with intelligence, and fair, and
mooth;
:yebrow's shape was like the aërial bow,
r cheek all purple with the beam of youth,
iting, at times, to a transparent glow,
if her veins ran lightning; she, in sooth,
:ssed an air and grace by no means
.ommon:
itature tall — I hate a dumpy woman.

LXII.

ded she was some years, and to a man
fifty, and such husbands are in plenty;
yet, I think, instead of such a ONE
vere better to have TWO of five-and-
.wenty,
:ially in countries near the sun:
d now I think on't, "mi vien in mente,"
:s even of the most uneasy virtue
r a spouse whose age is short of
airty.

LXIII.

. sad thing, I cannot choose but say,
1 all the fault of that indecent sun,
cannot leave alone our helpless clay,
· will keep baking, broiling, burning on,
howsoever people fast and pray,
2 flesh is frail, and so the soul undone:
 men call gallantry, and gods adultery,
ich more common where the climate's
altry.

LXIV.

y the nations of the moral North!
iere all is virtue, and the winter season
: sin, without a rag on, shivering forth

('Twas snow that brought St. Anthony to
  reason);
Where juries cast up what a wife is worth,
  By laying whate'er sum, in mulct, they
  please on
The lover, who must pay a handsome price,
Because it is a marketable vice.

LXV.

Alfonso was the name of Julia's lord,
  A man well looking for his years, and who
Was neither much beloved nor yet abhorred;
  They lived together, as most people do,
Suffering each other's foibles by accord,
  And not exactly either *one* or *two;*
Yet he was jealous, though he did not show it,
For jealousy dislikes the world to know it.

LXVI.

Julia was — yet I never could see why —
  With Donna Inez quite a favorite friend;
Between their tastes there was small sympathy,
  For not a line had Julia ever penned:
Some people whisper (but, no doubt, they lie,
  For malice still imputes some private end)
That Inez had, ere Don Alfonso's marriage,
Forgot with him her very prudent carriage;

LXVII.

And that still keeping up the old connection,
  Which time had lately rendered much more
  chaste,
She took his lady also in affection,
  And certainly this course was much the
  best:
She flattered Julia with her sage protection,
  And complimented Don Alfonso's taste;
And if she could not (who can?) silence
  scandal,
At least she left it a more slender handle.

LXVIII.

I can't tell whether Julia saw the affair
  With other people's eyes, or if her own
Discoveries made, but none could be aware
  Of this, at least no symptom e'er was shown;
Perhaps she did not know, or did not care,
  Indifferent from the first, or callous grown:
I'm really puzzled what to think or say,
She kept her counsel in so close a way.

LXIX.

Juan she saw, and, as a pretty child,
  Caressed him often — such a thing might be
Quite innocently done, and harmless styled,
  When she had twenty years, and thirteen he;
But I am not so sure I should have smiled
  When he was sixteen, Julia twenty-three;
These few short years make wondrous altera-
  tions
Particularly amongst sun-burn nations.

LXX.

Whate'er the cause might be, they had become
  Changed; for the dame grew distant, the
    youth shy,
Their looks cast down, their greetings almost
    dumb,
  And much embarrassment in either eye;
There surely will be little doubt with some
  That Donna Julia knew the reason why,
But as for Juan, he had no more notion
Than he who never saw the sea of ocean.

LXXI.

Yet Julia's very coldness still was kind,
  And tremulously gentle her small hand
Withdrew itself from his, but left behind
  A little pressure, thrilling, and so bland
And slight, so very slight, that to the mind
  'Twas but a doubt; but ne'er magician's
    wand
Wrought change with all Armida's fairy art
Like what this light touch left on Juan's heart.

LXXII.

And if she met him, though she smiled no
    more,
  She looked a sadness sweeter than her smile,
As if her heart had deeper thoughts in store
  She must not own, but cherished more the
    while
For that compression in its burning core;
  Even innocence itself has many a wile,
And will not dare to trust itself with truth,
And love is taught hypocrisy from youth.

LXXIII.

But passion most dissembles, yet betrays
  Even by its darkness; as the blackest sky
Foretells the heaviest tempest, it displays
  Its workings through the vainly guarded
    eye,
And in whatever aspect it arrays
  Itself, 'tis still the same hypocrisy;
Coldness or anger, even disdain or hate,
Are masks it often wears, and still too late.

LXXIV.

Then there were sighs, the deeper for sup-
    pression,
  And stolen glances, sweeter for the theft,
And burning blushes, though for no trans-
    gression,
  Tremblings when met, and restlessness
    when left,
All these are little preludes to possession,
  Of which young passion cannot be bereft,
And merely tend to show how greatly love is
Embarrassed at first starting with a novice.

LXXV.

Poor Julia's heart was in an awkward state;
  She felt it going, and resolved to make

The noblest efforts for herself and mate,
  For honor's, pride's, religion's, virtue's sake
Her resolutions were most truly great,
  And almost might have made a Tarquin
    quake:
She prayed the Virgin Mary for her grace,
As being the best judge of a lady's case.

LXXVI.

She vowed she never would see Juan more,
  And next day paid a visit to his mother,
And looked extremely at the opening door,
  Which, by the Virgin's grace, let in another;
Grateful she was, and yet a little sore —
  Again it opens, it can be no o, her,
'Tis surely Juan now — No! I'm afraid
That night the Virgin was no further prayed.

LXXVII.

She now determined that a virtuous woman
  Should rather face and overcome tempta-
    tion,
That flight was base and dastardly, and no
    man
  Should ever give her heart the least sensa-
    tion;
That is to say, a thought beyond the common
  Preference, that we must feel upon occasion,
For people who are pleasanter than others,
But then they only seem so many brothers.

LXXVIII.

And even if by chance — and who can tell ?
  The devil's so very sly — she should dis-
    cover
That all within was not so very well,
  And, if still free, that such or such a lover
Might please perhaps, a virtuous wife can
    quell
  Such thoughts, and be the better when
    they're over;
And if the man should ask, 'tis but denial:
I recommend young ladies to make trial.

LXXIX.

And then there are such things as love divine,
  Bright and immaculate, unmixed and pure,
Such as the angels think so very fine,
  And matrons, who would be no less secure,
Platonic, perfect, "just such love as mine:"
  Thus Julia said — and thought so, to be
    sure;
And so I'd have her think, were I the man
On whom her reveries celestial ran.

LXXX.

Such love is innocent, and may exist
  Between young persons without any danger.
A hand may first, and then a lip be kist;
  For my part, to such doings I'm a stranger,
But *hear* these freedoms form the utmost
    list

Of all o'er which such love may be a
  ranger:
If people go beyond, 'tis quite a crime,
But not my fault — I tell them all in time.

LXXXI.

Love, then, but love within its proper limits,
  Was Julia's innocent determination
In young Don Juan's favor, and to him its
  Exertion might be useful on occasion ;
And, lighted at too pure a shrine to dim its
  Ethereal lustre, with what sweet persuasion
He might be taught, bv love and her to-
    gether —
  really don't know what, nor Julia either.

LXXXII.

Fraught with this fine intention, and well
    fenced
  In mail of proof — her purity of soul,
She, for the future of her strength convinced,
  And that her honor was a rock, or mole,
Exceeding sagely from that hour dispensed
  With any kind of troublesome control ;
But whether Julia to the task was equal
Is that which must be mentioned in the
    sequel.

LXXXIII.

Her plan she deemed both innocent and feas-
    ible,
  And, surely, with a stripling of sixteen
Not scandal's fangs could fix on much that's
    seizable,
  Or if they did so, satisfied to mean
Nothing but what was good, her breast was
    peaceable —
  A quiet conscience makes one so serene !
Christians have burnt each other, quite per-
    suaded
That all the Apostles would have done as they
    did.

LXXXIV.

And if in the mean time her husband died,
  But Heaven forbid that such a thought
    should cross
Her brain, though in a dream ! (and then she
    sighed)
  Never could she survive that common loss ;
But just suppose that moment should betide,
  I only say suppose it — *inter nos.*
This should be *entre nous,* for Julia thought
French, but then the rhyme would go for
    nought.)

LXXXV.

Only say suppose this supposition :
  Juan being then grown up to man's estate
Would fully suit a widow of condition,
  Even seven years hence it would not be too
    late ;
And in the interim (to pursue this vision)
  The mischief, after all, could not be great,

For he would learn the rudiments of love,
I mean the seraph way of those above.

LXXXVI.

So much for Julia. Now we'll turn to Juan,
  Poor little fellow ! he had no idea
Of his own case, and never hit the true one ;
  In feelings quick as Ovid's Miss Medea,
He puzzled over what he found a new one,
  But not as yet imagined it could be a
Thing quite in course, and not at all alarming,
Which, with a little patience, might grow
    charming.

LXXXVII.

Silent and pensive, idle, restless, slow,
  His home deserted for the lonely wood,
Tormented with a wound he could not know,
  His, like all deep grief, plunged in solitude :
I'm fond myself of solitude or so,
  But then, I beg it may be understood,
By solitude I mean a sultan's, not
A hermit's, with a haram for a grot.

LXXXVIII.

" Oh Love ! in such a wilderness as this,
  Where transport and security entwine,
Here is the empire of thy perfect bliss,
  And here thou art a god indeed divine."
The bard I quote from does not sing amiss,
  With the exception of the second line,
For thatsame twining " transport and security "
Are twisted to a phrase of some obscurity.

LXXXIX.

The poet meant, no doubt, and thus appeals
  To the good sense and senses of mankind,
The very thing which everybody feels,
  As all have found on trial, or may find,
That no one likes to be disturbed at meals
  Or love. — I won't say more about " en-
    twined "
Or " transport," as we knew all that before,
But beg " Security " will bolt the door.

XC.

Young Juan wandered by the glassy brooks
  Thinking unutterable things ; he threw
Himself at length within the leafy nooks
  Where the wild branch of the cork forest
    grew ;
There poets find materials for their books,
  And every now and then we read them
    through,
So that their plan and prosody are eligible,
Unless, like Wordsworth, they prove unintel-
ligible.

XCI.

He, Juan, (and not Wordsworth) so pursued
  His self-communion with his own high soul,
Until his mighty heart, in its great mood,
  Had mitigated part, though not the whole

Of its disease; he did the best he could
  With things not very subject to control,
And turned, without perceiving his condition,
  Like Coleridge, into a metaphysician.

XCII.

He thought about himself, and the whole earth,
  Of man the wonderful, and of the stars,
And how the deuce they ever could have birth;
  And then he thought of earthquakes, and
    of wars,
How many miles the moon might have in
    girth,
  Of air-balloons, and of the many bars
To perfect knowledge of the boundless skies;—
And then he thought of Donna Julia's eyes.

XCIII.

In thoughts like these true wisdom may dis-
    cern
  Longings sublime, and aspirations high,
Which some are born with, but the most part
    learn
  To plague themselves withal, they know not
    why:
'Twas strange that one so young should thus
    concern
  His brain about the action of the sky;
If *you* think 'twas philosophy that this did,
I can't help thinking puberty assisted.

XCIV.

He pored upon the leaves, and on the flowers,
  And heard a voice in all the winds; and then
He thought of wood-nymphs and immortal
    bowers,
  And how the goddesses came down to men:
He missed the pathway, he forgot the hours,
  And when he looked upon his watch again,
He found how much old Time had been a
    winner —
He also found that he had lost his dinner.

XCV.

Sometimes he turned to gaze upon his book,
  Boscan, or Garcilasso; — by the wind
Even as the page is rustled while we look,
  So by the poesy of his own mind
Over the mystic leaf his soul was shook,
  As if 'twere one whereon magicians bind
Their spells, and give them to the passing gale,
According to some good old woman's tale.

XCVI.

Thus would he while his lonely hours away
  Dissatisfied, nor knowing what he wanted;
Nor glowing reverie, nor poet's lay,
  Could yield his spirit that for which it panted,
A bosom whereon he his head might lay,
  And hear the heart beat with the love it
    granted.

With —— several other things, which I forget,
Or which, at least, I need not mention yet.

XCVII.

Those lonely walks, and lengthening reveries,
  Could not escape the gentle Julia's eyes;
She saw that Juan was not at his ease;
  But that which chiefly may, and must sur-
    prise,
Is, that the Donna Inez did not tease
  Her only son with question or surmise;
Whether it was she did not see, or would not,
Or, like all very clever people, could not.

XCVIII.

This may seem strange, but yet 'tis very com-
    mon;
  For instance — gentlemen, whose ladies take
Leave to o'erstep the written rights of woman,
  And break the —— Which commandment
    is't they break?
(I have forgot the number, and think no man
  Should rashly quote, for fear of a mistake.)
I say, when these same gentlemen are jealous,
They make some blunder, which their ladies
    tell us.

XCIX.

A real husband always is suspicious,
  But still no less suspects in the wrong place,
Jealous of some one who had no such wishes,
  Or pandering blindly to his own disgrace,
By harboring some dear friend extremely
    vicious;
  The last indeed's infallibly the case:
And when the spouse and friend are gone off
    wholly,
He wonders at their vice, and not his folly.

C.

Thus parents also are at times short-sighted;
  Though watchful as the lynx, they ne'er dis-
    cover,
The while the wicked world beholds delighted,
  Young Hopeful's mistress, or Miss Fanny's
    lover,
Till some confounded escapade has blighted
  The plan of twenty years, and all is over;
And then the mother cries, the father swears,
And wonders why the devil he got heirs.

CI.

But Inez was so anxious, and so clear
  Of sight, that I must think, on this occa-
    sion,
She had some other motive much more near
  For leaving Juan to this new temptation;
But what that motive was, I sha'n't say here;
  Perhaps to finish Juan's education,
Perhaps to open Don Alfonso's eyes,
In case he thought his wife too great a prize

CII.

t was upon a day, a summer's day;—
  Summer's indeed a very dangerous season,
ınd so is spring about the end of May;
  The sun, no doubt, is the prevailing reason;
ʟut whatsoe'er the cause is, one may say,
  And stand convicted of more truth than
    treason,
ʼhat there are months which nature grows
  mɔre merry in,—
ʀarch has its hares, and May must have its
  ʜeroine.

CIII.

ʈwɔs on a summer's day — the sixth of
  June:—
I like to be particular in dates,
ʃot only of the age, and year, but moon;
  They are a sort of post-house, where the
    Fates
ʒhange horses, making history change its
  tune,
  Then spur away o'er empires and o'er states,
ʟeaving at last not much besides chronology,
ʾxcepting the post-obits of theology.

CIV.

ʈwas on the sixth of June, about the hour
  Of half-past six — perhaps still nearer
    seven—
ʃhen Julia sate within as pretty a bower
  As e'er held houri in that heathenish heaven
ʿescribed by Mahomet, and Anacreon
    Moore,
  To whom the lyre and laurels have been
    given,
ʃith all the trophies of triumphant song—
ʜe won them well, and may he wear them
  long!

CV.

ʜe sate, but not alone; I know not well
  How this same interview had taken place,
ɪnd even if I knew, I should not tell—
  People should hold their tongues in any
    case;
ɪo matter how or why the thing befell,
  But there were she and Juan, face to face—
ʃhen two such faces are so, 'twould be wise,
ʙut very difficult, to shut their eyes.

CVI.

ɪow beautiful she looked! her conscious heart
  Glowed in her cheek, and yet she felt no
    wrong.
ʏh Love! how perfect is thy mystic art,
  Strengthening the weak, and trampling on
    the strong,
ʜow self-deceitful is the sagest part
  Oɪ mortals whom thy lure hath led along—
ʈhe precipice she stood on was immense,
ᴏ was heɪ creed in her own innocence.

CVII.

She thought of her own strength, and Juan's
  youth,
  And of the folly of all prudish fears,
Victorious virtue, and domestic truth,
  And then of Don Alfonso's fifty years:
I wish these last had not occurred, in sooth,
  Because that number rarely much endears,
And through all climes, the snowy and the
  sunny,
Sounds ill in love, whate'er it may in money.

CVIII.

When people say, "I've told you *fifty* times,"
  They mean to scold, and very often do;
When poets say, "I've written *fifty* rhymes,"
  They make you dread that they'll recite
    them too;
In gangs of *fifty*, thieves commit their crimes;
  At *fifty* love for love is rare, 'tis true,
But then, no doubt, it equally as true is,
A good deal may be bought for *fifty* Louis.

CIX.

Julia had honor, virtue, truth, and love,
  For Don Alfonso; and she inly swore,
By all the vows below to powers above,
  She never would disgrace the ring she wore,
Nor leave a wish which wisdom might reprove;
  And while she pondered this, besides much
    more,
One hand on Juan's carelessly was thrown,
Quite by mistake — she thought it was her
  own;

CX.

Unconsciously she leaned upon the other,
  Which played within the tangles of her hair;
And to contend with thoughts she could not
    smother
  She seemed, by the distraction of her air.
'Twas surely very wrong in Juan's mother
  To leave together this imprudent pair,
She who for many years had watched her son
  so—
I'm very certain *mine* would not have done so.

CXI.

The hand which still held Juan's by degrees
  Gently, but palpably confirmed its grasp,
As if it said, "Detain me, if you please;"
  Yet there's no doubt she only meant to clasp
His fingers with a pure Platonic squeeze;
  She would have shrunk as from a toad or asp,
Had she imagined such a thing could rouse
A feeling dangerous to a prudent spouse.

* * * * *

CXX.

Here my chaste Muse a liberty must take·--
  Start not! still chaster reader—she'll bʜ
    nice hence-

Forward, and there is no great cause to quake;
　This liberty is a poetic license,
Which some irregularity may make
　In the design, and as I have a high sense
Of Aristotle and the Rules, 'tis fit
To beg his pardon when I err a bit.

CXXI.

This license is to hope the reader will
　Suppose from June the sixth (the fatal day,
Without whose epoch my poetic skill
　For want of facts would all be thrown away),
But keeping Julia and Don Juan still
　In sight, that several months have passed;
　　we'll say
'Twas in November, but I'm not so sure
About the day — the era's more obscure.

CXXII.

We'll talk of that anon. — 'Tis sweet to hear
　At midnight on the blue and moonlit deep
The song and oar of Adria's gondolier,
　By distance mellowed, o'er the water's
　　sweep;
'Tis sweet to see the evening star appear;
　'Tis sweet to listen as the night-winds creep
From leaf to leaf; 'tis sweet to view on high
The rainbow, based on ocean, span the sky.

CXXIII.

'Tis sweet to hear the watch-dog's honest
　bark
Bay deep-mouthed welcome as we draw
　near home;
'Tis sweet to know there is an eye will mark
　Our coming, and look brighter when we
　　come;
'Tis sweet to be awakened by the lark,
　Or lulled by falling waters; sweet the hum
Of bees, the voice of girls, the song of birds,
The lisp of children, and their earliest words.

CXXIV.

Sweet is the vintage, when the showering
　grapes
In Bacchanal profusion reel to earth
Purple and gushing: sweet are our escapes
　From civic revelry to rural mirth;
Sweet to the miser are his glittering heaps,
　Sweet to the father is his first-born's birth,
Sweet is revenge — especially to women,
Pillage to soldiers, prize-money to seamen.

CXXV.

Sweet is a legacy, and passing sweet
　The unexpected death of some old lady
Or gentlemen of seventy years complete,
　Who've made "us youth" wait too — too
　　long already
For an estate, or cash, or country-seat,
　Still breaking, but with stamina so steady,

That all the Israelites are fit to mob its
Next owner for their double-damned post
　obits.

CXXVI.

'Tis sweet to win, no matter how, one's laurels
　By blood or ink; 'tis sweet to put an end
To strife; 'tis sometimes sweet to have our
　quarrels,
Particularly with a tiresome friend:
Sweet is old wine in bottles, ale in barrels;
　Dear is the helpless creature we defend
Against the world; and dear the schoolboy
　spot
We ne'er forget, though there we are forgot.

CXXVII.

But sweeter still than this, than these, than
　all,
　Is first and passionate love — it stands alone,
Like Adam's recollection of his fall;
　The tree of knowledge has been plucked —
　　all's known —
And life yields nothing further to recall
　Worthy of this ambrosial sin, so shown,
No doubt in fable, as the unforgiven
Fire which Prometheus filched for us from
　heaven.

CXXVIII.

Man's a strange animal, and makes strange
　use
　Of his own nature, and the various arts,
And likes particularly to produce
　Some new experiment to show his parts;
This is the age of oddities let loose,
　Where different talents find their different
　　marts;
You'd best begin with truth, and when you've
　lost your
Labor, there's a sure market for imposture.

CXXIX.

What opposite discoveries we have seen!
　(Signs of true genius, and of empty
　pockets.)
One makes new noses, one a guillotine,
　One breaks your bones, one sets them in
　their sockets;
But vaccination certainly has been
　A kind antithesis to Congreve's rockets,
With which the Doctor paid off an old pox,
By borrowing a new one from an ox.

* 　 * 　 * 　 * 　 *

CXXXII.

This is the patent age of new inventions
For killing bodies, and for saving souls,
All propagated with the best intentions:
　Sir Humphry Davy's lantern, by which
　　coals
Are safely mined for in the mode he mentions,
　Tombuctoo travels, voyages to the Poles,

Are ways to benefit mankind, as true,
Perhaps, as shooting them at Waterloo.

CXXXIII.

Man's a phenomenon, one knows not what,
  And wonderful beyond all wondrous measure;
'Tis pity though, in this sublime world, that
  Pleasure's a sin, and sometimes sin's a pleasure;
Few mortals know what end they would be at,
  But whether glory, power, or love, or treasure,
The path is through perplexing ways, and when
The goal is gained, we die, you know — and then —

CXXXIV.

What then ? — I do not know, no more do you —
  And so good-night. — Return we to our story:
'Twas in November, when fine days are few,
  And the far mountains wax a little hoary,
And clap a white cape on their mantles blue;
  And the sea dashes round the promontory,
And the loud breaker boils against the rock,
And sober suns must set at five o'clock.

CXXXV.

'Twas, as the watchmen say, a cloudy night;
  No moon, no stars, the wind was low or loud
By gusts, and many a sparkling hearth was bright
  With the piled wood, round which the family crowd;
There's something cheerful in that sort of light,
  Even as a summer sky's without a cloud;
I'm fond of fire, and crickets, and all that,
A lobster salad, and champagne, and chat.

CXXXVI.

'Twas midnight — Donna Julia was in bed,
  Sleeping, most probably, — when at her door
Arose a clatter might awake the dead,
  If they had never been awoke before,
And that they have been so we all have read,
  And are to be so, at the least, once more ; —
The door was fastened, but with voice and fist
First knocks were heard, then "Madam — Madam — hist!

*   *   *   *   *

CXXXVIII.

By this time Don Alfonso was arrived,
  With torches, friends, and servants in great number;
The major part of them had long been wived,
  And therefore paused not to disturb the slumber

Of any wicked woman, who contrived
  By stealth her husband's temples to encumber:
Examples of this kind are so contagious,
Were *one* not punished, *all* would be outrageous.

CXXXIX.

I can't tell how, or why, or what suspicion
  Could enter into Don Alfonso's head;
But for a cavalier of his condition
  It surely was exceedingly ill-bred,
Without a word of previous admonition,
  To hold a levee round his lady's bed,
And summon lackeys, armed with fire and sword,
To prove himself the thing he most abhorred.

*   *   *   *   *

CXLIII.

He searched, *they* searched, and rummaged everywhere,
  Closet and clothes' press, chest and window-seat,
And found much linen, lace, and several pair
  Of stockings, slippers, brushes, combs, complete,
With other articles of ladies fair,
  To keep them beautiful, or leave them neat:
Arras they pricked and curtains with their swords,
And wounded several shutters, and some boards.

*   *   *   *   *

CXLV.

During this inquisition Julia's tongue
  Was not asleep — "Yes, search and search," she cried,
"Insult on insult heap, and wrong on wrong!
  It was for this that I became a bride!
For this in silence I have suffered long
  A husband like Alfonso at my side;
But now I'll bear no more, nor here remain,
If there be law or lawyers, in all Spain.

CXLVI.

"Yes, Don Alfonso! husband now no more,
  If ever you indeed deserved the name,
Is't worthy of your years ? — you have threescore —
  Fifty, or sixty, it is all the same —
Is't wise or fitting, causeless to explore
  For facts against a virtuous woman's fame?
Ungrateful, perjured, barbarous Don Alfonso,
How dare you think your lady would go on so ?

*   *   *   *   *

CLXI.

But Don Alfonso stood with downcast looks,
  And, truth to say, he made a foolish figure;
When, after searching in five hundred nooks,

And treating a young wife with so much
    rigor,   .
He gained no point, except some self-rebukes,
    Added to those his lady with such vigor
Had poured upon him for the last half-hour,
    Quick, thick, and heavy — as a thunder-
        shower.

CLXII.

At first he tried to hammer an excuse,
    To which the sole reply was tears, and
        sobs,
And indications of hysterics, whose
    Prologue is always certain throes, and
        throbs,
Gasps, and whatever else the owners choose:
    Alfonso saw his wife, and thought of Job's;
He saw too, in perspective, her relations,
And then he tried to muster all his patience.

CLXIII. ·

He stood in act to speak, or rather stammer,
    But sage Antonia cut him short before
The anvil of his speech received the hammer,
    With " Pray, sir, leave the room and say no
        more,
Or madam dies." — Alfonso muttered, " D — n
        her,"
    But nothing else, the time of words was
        o'er;
He cast a rueful look or two, and did,
He knew not wherefore, that which he was bid.

CLXIV.

With him retired his " *posse comitatus*,"
    The attorney last, who lingered near the
        door,
Reluctantly, still tarrying there as late as
    Antonia let him — not a little sore
At this most strange and unexplained " *hiatus* "
    In Don Alfonso's facts, which just now wore

An awkward look; as he revolved the case,
    The door was fastened in his legal face.

*   *   *   *   *

CLXXXVIII.

Here ends this canto. — Need I sing, or say,
    How Juan, naked, favored by the night,
Who favors what she should not, found his
        way,
    And reached his home in an unseemly
        plight ?
The pleasant scandal which arose next day,
    The nine days' wonder which was brought
        to light,
And how Alfonso sued for a divorce,
    Were in the English newspapers, of course.

CLXXXIX.

If you would like to see the whole proceed-
        ings,
    The depositions, and the cause at full,
The names of all the witnesses, the pleadings
    Of counsel to nonsuit, or to annul,
There's more than one edition, and the read-
        ings
    Are various, but they none of them are dull;
The best is that in short-hand ta'en by Gur-
        ney,
Who to Madrid on purpose made a journey.

CXC.

But Donna Inez, to divert the train
    Of one of the most circulating scandals
That had for centuries been known in Spain,
    At least since the retirement of the Vandals,
First vowed (and never had she vowed in vain)
    To Virgin Mary several pounds of candles;
And then, by the advice of some old ladies,
She sent her son to be shipped off from Cadiz.

*   *   *   *   *

CANTO THE SECOND.

I.

OH ye! who teach the ingenuous youth of
        nations,
    Holland, France, England, Germany or
        Spain,
I pray ye flog them upon all occasions,
    It mends their morals, never mind the
        pain:
The best of mothers and of educations
    In Juan's case were but employed in vain,
Since, in a way that's rather of the oddest,
    he
Became divested of his native modesty.

II.

Had he but been placed at a public school,
    In the third form, or even in the fourth,
His daily task had kept his fancy cool,
    At least, had he been nurtured in the north;
Spain may prove an exception to the rule,
    But then exceptions always prove its worth —
A lad of sixteen causing a divorce
Puzzled his tutors very much, of course.

III.

I can't say that it puzzles me at all,
    If all things be considered : first, there was

is lady-mother, mathematical,
A —— never mind; — his tutor, an old ass;
pretty woman — (that's quite natural,
Or else the thing had hardly come to pass)
husband rather old, not much in unity
'ith his young wife — a time, and opportunity.

IV.

'ell — well, the world must turn upon its
   axis,
And all mankind turn with it, heads or tails,
ıd live and die, make love, and pay our
   taxes,
And as the veering wind shifts, shift our
   sails;
ıe king commands us, and the doctor
   quacks us,
The priest instructs, and so our life exhales,
little breath, love, wine, ambition, fame,
ghting, devotion, dust, — perhaps a name.

V.

ʒaid that Juan had been sent to Cadiz —
A pretty town, I recollect it well —
is there the mart of the colonial trade is
(Or was, before Peru learned to rebel),
ıd such sweet girls — I mean, such graceful
   ladies,
Their very walk would make your bosom
   swell;
ʒan't describe it, though so much it strike,
or liken it — I never saw the like:

VI.

ı Arab horse, a stately stag, a barb
New broke, a camelopard, a gazelle,
o — none of these will do; — and then their
   garb!
Their veil and petticoat — Alas! to dwell
ɔon such things would very near absorb
A canto — then their feet and ankles, —
   well,
ıank Heaven I've got no metaphor quite
   ready,
ınd so, my sober Muse — come, let's be
   steady —

VII.

ıaste Muse! — well, if you must, you must)
   — the veil
Thrown back a moment with the glancing
   hand,
hile the o'erpowering eye, that turns you
   pale,
Flashes into the heart: — all sunny land
ˑlove! when I forget you, may I fail
To —— say my prayers — but never was
   there planned
dress through which the eyes give such a
   volley,
cepting the Venetian Fazzioli

VIII.

But to our tale: the Donna Inez sent
   Her son to Cadiz only to embark;
To stay there had not answered her intent,
   But why? — we leave the reader in the
   dark —
'Twas for a voyage that the young man was
   meant,
As if a Spanish ship were Noah's ark,
To wean him from the wickedness of earth,
And send him like a dove of promise forth.

IX.

Don Juan bade his valet pack his things
   According to direction, then received
A lecture and some money: for four springs
   He was to travel; and though Inez grieved
(As every kind of parting has its stings),
   She hoped he would improve — perhaps
   believed
A letter, too, she gave (he never read it)
Of good advice — and two or three of credit.

X.

In the mean time, to pass her hours away,
   Brave Inez now set up a Sunday school
For naughty children, who would rather play
   (Like truant rogues) the devil, or the fool;
Infants of three years old were taught that day,
   Dunces were whipt, or set upon a stool:
The great success of Juan's education,
Spurred her to teach another generation.

XI.

Juan embarked — the ship got under way,
   The wind was fair, the water passing rough;
A devil of a sea rolls in that bay,
   As I, who've crossed it oft, know well
   enough;
And, standing upon deck, the dashing spray
   Flies in one's face, and makes it weather-
   tough;
And there he stood to take, and take again,
His first — perhaps his last — farewell of Spain.

XII.

I can't but say it is an awkward sight
   To see one's native land receding through,
The growing waters; it unmans one quite,
   Especially when life is rather new:
I recollect Great Britain's coast looks white,
   But almost every other country's blue,
When gazing on them, mystified by distance,
We enter on our nautical existence.

XIII.

So Juan stood, bewildered on the deck:
   The wind sung, cordage strained, and sail-
   ors swore,
And the ship creaked, the town became a
   speck,

From which away so fair and fast they bore.
The best of remedies is a beef-steak
Against sea-sickness: try it, sir, before
You sneer, and I assure you this is true,
For I have found it answer — so may you.

XIV.

Don Juan stood, and, gazing from the stern,
  Beheld his native Spain receding far:
First partings form a lesson hard to learn,
  Even nations feel this when they go to war;
There is a sort of unexprest concern,
  A kind of shock that sets one's heart ajar:
At leaving even the most unpleasant people
And places, one keeps looking at the steeple.

XV.

But Juan had got many things to leave,
  His mother, and a mistress, and no wife,
So that he had much better cause to grieve
  Than many persons more advanced in life;
And if we now and then a sigh must heave
  At quitting even those we quit in strife,
No doubt we weep for those the heart en-
  dears —
That is, till deeper griefs congeal our tears.

XVI.

So Juan wept, as wept the captive Jews
  By Babel's waters, still remembering Sion:
I'd weep, — but mine is not a weeping Muse,
  And such light griefs are not a thing to
  die on;
Young men should travel, if but to amuse
  Themselves; and the next time their ser-
  vants tie on
Behind their carriages their new portmanteau,
Perhaps it may be lined with this my canto.

XVII.

And Juan wept, and much he sighed and
  thought,
  While his salt tears dropped into the salt
  sea,
"Sweets to the sweet;" (I like so much to
  quote;
  You must excuse this extract, — 'tis where she,
The Queen of Denmark, for Ophelia brought
  Flowers to the grave;) and, sobbing often,
  he
Reflected on his present situation,
And seriously resolved on reformation.

XVIII.

"Farewell, my Spain! a long farewell!" he
  cried,
  "Perhaps I may revisit thee no more,
But die, as many an exiled heart hath died,
  Of its own thirst to see again thy shore:
Farewell, where Guadalquivir's waters glide!
  Farewell, my mother! and, since all is o'er,

Farewell, too, dearest Julia! — (here he drew
  Her letter out again, and read it through).

XIX.

"And oh! if e'er I should forget, I swear —
  But that's impossible, and cannot be—
Sooner shall this blue ocean melt to air,
  Sooner shall earth resolve itself to sea,
Than I resign thine image, oh, my fair!
  Or think of any thing excepting thee;
A mind diseased no remedy can physic —
(Here the ship gave a lurch and he grew sea
  sick).

XX.

"Sooner shall heaven kiss earth — (here he
  fell sicker)
  Oh, Julia! what is every other woe? —
(For God's sake let me have a glass of liquor
  Pedro, Battista, help me down below).
Julia, my love! — (you rascal, Pedro
  quicker) —
  Oh, Julia! — (this curst vessel pitches so) —
Beloved Julia, hear me still beseeching!"
(Here he grew inarticulate with retching).

XXI.

He felt that chilling heaviness of heart,
  Or rather stomach, which, alas! attends,
Beyond the best apothecary's art,
  The loss of love, the treachery of friends,
Or death of those we dote on, when a part
  Of us dies with them as each fond hope ends:
No doubt he would have been much more pa
  thetic,
But the sea acted as a strong emetic.

XXII.

Love's a capricious power: I've known it hold
  Out through a fever caused by its own heat,
But be much puzzled by a cough and cold
  And find a quinsy very hard to treat;
Against all noble maladies he's bold,
  But vulgar illnesses don't like to meet,
Nor that a sneeze should interrupt his sigh
Nor inflammations redden his blind eye.

XXIII.

But worst of all is nausea, or a pain
  About the lower region of the bowels;
Love, who heroically breathes a vein,
  Shrinks from the application of hot towels,
And purgatives are dangerous to his reign,
  Sea-sickness death: his love was perfect,
  how else
Could Juan's passion, while the billows roar,
Resist his stomach, ne'er at sea before?

XXIV.

The ship, called the most holy "Trinidada,"
  Was steering duly for the port Leghorn;
For there the Spanish family Moncada

Were settled long ere Juan's sire was born:
They were relations, and for them he had a
Letter of introduction, which the morn
Of his departure had been sent him by
His Spanish friends for those in Italy.

XXV.

His suite consisted of three servants and
A tutor, the licentiate Pedrillo,
Who several languages did understand,
But now lay sick and speechless on his pil-
low,
And, rocking in his hammock, longed for land,
His headache being increased by every bil-
low;
And the waves oozing through the port-hole
made
His berth a little damp, and him afraid.

XXVI.

Twas not without some reason, for the wind
Increased at night, until it blew a gale;
And though 'twas not much to a naval mind,
Some landsmen would have looked a little
pale,
For sailors are, in fact, a different kind:
At sunset they began to take in sail,
For the sky showed it would come on to blow,
And carry away, perhaps, a mast or so.

XXVII.

At one o'clock the wind with sudden shift
Threw the ship right into the trough of the
sea,
Which struck her aft, and made an awkward
rift,
Started the stern-post, also shattered the
Whole of her stern-frame, and, ere she could
lift
Herself from out her present jeopardy,
The rudder tore away: 'twas time to sound
The pumps, and there were four feet water
found.

XXVIII.

One gang of people instantly was put
Upon the pumps, and the remainder set
To get up part of the cargo, and what not;
But they could not come at the leak as yet;
At last they did get at it really, but
Still their salvation was an even bet:
The water rushed through in a way quite
puzzling,
While they thrust sheets, shirts, jackets, bales
of muslin,

XXIX.

Into the opening; but all such ingredients
Would have been vain, and they must have
gone down,
Despite of all their efforts and expedients,
But for the pumps: I'm glad to make them
known

To all the brother tars who may have need
hence,
For fifty tons of water were upthrown
By them per hour, and they had all been un-
done,
But for the maker, Mr. Mann, of London.

XXX.

As day advanced, the weather seemed to
abate,
And then the leak they reckoned to reduce,
And keep the ship afloat, though three feet
yet
Kept two hand and one chain-pump still in
use.
The wind blew fresh again: as it grew late
A squall came on, and while some guns
broke loose,
A gust — which all descriptive power tran-
scends —
Laid with one blast the ship on her beam
ends.

XXXI.

There she lay, motionless, and seemed upset;
The water left the hold, and washed the
decks,
And made a scene men do not soon forget;
For they remember battles, fires, and
wrecks,
Or any other thing that brings regret,
Or breaks their hopes, or hearts, or heads,
or necks:
Thus drownings are much talked of by the
divers,
And swimmers, who may chance to be sur-
vivors.

XXXII.

Immediately the masts were cut away,
Both main and mizzen; first the mizzen
went,
The main-mast followed: but the ship still
lay
Like a mere log, and baffled our intent.
Foremast and bowsprit were cut down, and
they
Eased her at last (although we never meant
To part with all till every hope was blighted),
And then with violence the old ship righted.

*　　*　　*　　*　　*

XXXVIII.

But now there came a flash of hope once
more;
Day broke and the wind lulled: the masts
were gone,
The leak increased; shoals round her, but
no shore;
The vessel swam, yet still she held her own.
They tried the pumps again, and though be-
fore

Their desperate efforts seemed all useless
  grown,
A glimpse of sunshine set some hands to
  bale —
The stronger pumped, the weaker thrummed
  a sail.

XXXIX.

Under the vessel's keel the sail was past,
  And for the moment it had some effect;
But with a leak, and not a stick of mast,
  Nor rag of canvas, what could they ex-
  · pect?
But still 'tis best to struggle to the last,
  'Tis never too late to be wholly wrecked:
And though 'tis true that man can only die
  once,
'Tis not so pleasant in the Gulf of Lyons.

XL.

There winds and waves had hurled them, and
  from thence,
  Without their will, they carried them away;
For they were forced with steering to dis-
  pense,
  And never had as yet a quiet day
On which they might repose, or even com-
  mence
  A jurymast or rudder, or could say
The ship would swim an hour, which, by good
  luck,
Still swam — though not exactly like a duck.

XLI.

The wind, in fact, perhaps, was rather less,
  But the ship labored so, they scarce could
  hope
To weather out much longer; the distress
  Was also great with which they had to
  cope
For want of water, and their solid mess
  Was scant enough: in vain the telescope
Was used — nor sail nor shore appeared in
  sight,
Nought but the heavy sea, and coming night.

XLII.

Again the weather threatened, — again blew
  A gale, and in the fore and after hold
Water appeared; yet, though the people knew
  All this, the most were patient, and some
  bold,
Until the chains and leathers were worn
  through
  Of all our pumps: — a wreck complete she
  rolled,
At mercy of the waves, whose mercies are
Like human beings during civil war.

XLIII.

Then came the carpenter, at last, with tears
  In his rough eyes, and told the captain, he

Could do no more : he was a man in years,
  And long had voyaged through many a
  stormy sea,
And if he wept at length, they were not fears
  That made his eyelids as a woman's be,
But he, poor fellow, had a wife and children,
Two things for dying people quite bewildering.

XLIV.

The ship was evidently settling now
  Fast by the head; and, all distinction gone,
Some went to prayers again, and made a vow
  Of candles to their saints — but there were
  none
To pay them with; and some looked o'er the
  bow,
  Some hoisted out the boats; and there was
  one
That begged Pedrillo for an absolution,
Who told him to be damned — in his confu-
  sion.

XLV.

Some lashed them in their hammocks; some
  put on
  Their best clothes, as if going to a fair;
Some cursed the day on which they saw the
  sun,
  And gnashed their teeth, and, howling, tore
  their hair;
And others went on as they had begun,
  Getting the boats out, being well aware
That a tight boat will live in a rough sea,
Unless with breakers close beneath her lee.

XLVI.

The worst of all was, that in their condition,
  Having been several days in great distress,
'Twas difficult to get out such provision
  As now might render their long suffering less:
Men, even when dying, dislike inanition;
  Their stock was damaged by the weather's
  stress:
Two casks of biscuit, and a keg of butter,
Were all that could be thrown into the cutter

XLVII.

But in the long-boat they contrived to stow,
  Some pounds of bread, though injured by
  the wet;
Water, a twenty-gallon cask or so;
  Six flasks of wine; and they contrived to get
A portion of their beef up from below,
  And with a piece of pork, moreover, met
But scarce enough to serve them for a lunch
  eon —
Then there was rum, eight gallons in a
  puncheon.

XLVIII.

The other boats, the yawl and pinnace, had
  Been stove in the beginning of the gale;

And the long-boat's condition was but bad,
  As there were but two blankets for a sail,
And one oar for a mast, which a young lad
  Threw in by good luck over the ship's rail;
And two boats could not hold, far less be
    stored,
To save one half the people then on board.

XLIX.

'Twas twilight, and the sunless day went down
  Over the waste of waters; like a veil,
Which, if withdrawn, would but disclose the
    frown,
  Of one whose hate is masked but to assail.
Thus to their hopeless eyes the night was
    shown,
  And grimly darkled o'er the faces pale,
And the dim desolate deep: twelve days had
    Fear
Been their familiar, and now Death was here.

L.

Some trial had been making at a raft,
  With little hope in such a rolling sea,
A sort of thing at which one would have
    laughed,
  If any laughter at such times could be,
Unless with people who too much have
    quaffed,
  And have a kind of wild and horrid glee,
Half epileptical, and half hysterical:—
Their preservation would have been a miracle.

LI.

At half-past eight o'clock, booms, hencoops,
    spars,
  And all things, for a chance, had been cast
    loose,
That still could keep afloat the struggling
    tars,
  For yet they strove, although of no great
    use:
There was no light in heaven but a few
    stars,
  The boats put off o'ercrowded with their
    crews:
She gave a heel, and then a lurch to port,
And, going down head foremost—sunk, in
    short.

LII.

Then rose from sea to sky the wild farewell—
  Then shrieked the timid, and stood still the
    brave,—
Then some leaped overboard with dreadful yell,
  As eager to anticipate their grave;
And the sea yawned around her like a hell,
  And down she sucked with her the whirl-
    ing wave,
Like one who grapples with his enemy,
And strives to strangle him before he die.

LIII.

And first one universal shriek there rushed,
  Louder than the loud ocean, like a crash
Of echoing thunder; and then all was hushed,
  Save the wild wind and the remorseless dash
Of billows; but at intervals there gushed,
  Accompanied with a convulsive splash,
A solitary shriek, the bubbling cry
Of some strong swimmer in his agony.

LIV.

The boats, as stated, had got off before,
  And in them crowded several of the crew;
And yet their present hope was hardly more
  Than what it had been, for so strong it blew
There was slight chance of reaching any
    shore;
  And then they were too many, though so
    few—
Nine in the cutter, thirty in the boat,
Were counted in them when they got afloat.

LV.

All the rest perished; near two hundred souls
  Had left their bodies; and what's worse,
    alas!
When over Catholics the ocean rolls,
  They must wait several weeks before a mass
Takes off one peck of purgatorial coals,
  Because, till people know what's come to
    pass,
They won't lay out their money on the dead—
It costs three francs for every mass that's said.

LVI.

Juan got into the long-boat, and there
  Contrived to help Pedrillo to a place;
It seemed as if they had exchanged their care,
  For Juan wore the magisterial face
Which courage gives, while poor Pedrillo's
    pair
  Of eyes were crying for their owner's case:
Battista, though (a name called shortly Tita),
Was lost by getting at some aqua-vita.

LVII.

Pedro, his valet, too, he tried to save,
  But the same cause, conducive to his loss,
Left him so drunk, he jumped into the wave
  As o'er the cutter's edge he tried to cross,
And so he found a wine-and-watery grave;
  They could not rescue him although so close,
Because the sea ran higher every minute,
And for the boat—the crew kept crowding
    in it.

LVIII.

A small old spaniel,—which had been Don
    Jóse's,
  His father's, whom he loved, as ye may think,
For on such things the memory reposes

With tenderness — stood howling on the
brink,
Knowing, (dogs have intellectual noses!)
No doubt, the vessel was about to sink;
And Juan caught him up, and e'er he stepped
Off, threw him in, then after him he leaped.

LIX.

He also stuffed his money where he could
About his person, and Pedrillo's too,
Who let him do, in fact, whate'er he would,
'Not knowing what himself to say, or do,
As every rising wave his dread renewed;
But Juan, trusting they might still get
through,
And deeming there were remedies for any ill,
Thus reëmbarked his tutor and his spaniel.

LX.

'Twas a rough night, and blew so stiffly yet,
That the sail was becalmed between the seas,
Though on the wave's high top too much to
set,
They dared not take it in for all the breeze;
Each sea curled o'er the stern, and kept them
wet,
And made them bale without a moment's
ease,
So that themselves as well as hopes were
damped,
And the poor little cutter quickly swamped.

LXI.

Nine souls more went in her: the long-boat still
Kept above water, with an oar for mast,
Two blankets stitched together, answering ill
Instead of sail, were to the oar made fast:
Though every wave rolled menacing to fill,
And present peril all before surpassed,
They grieved for those who perished with the
cutter
And also for the biscuit-casks and butter.

LXII.

The sun rose red and fiery, a sure sign
Of the continuance of the gale : to run
Before the sea until it should grow fine,
Was all that for the present could be done:
A few tea-spoonfuls of their rum and wine
Were served out to the people, who begun
To faint, and damaged bread wet through the
bags,
And most of them had little clothes but rags.

LXIII.

They counted thirty, crowded in a space
Which left scarce room for motion or ex-
ertion;
They did their best to modify their case,
One half sate up though numbed with the
immersion

While t'other half were laid down in their
place,
At watch and watch; thus, shivering like the
tertian
Ague in its cold fit, they filled their boat,
With nothing but the sky for a great coat.

LXIV.

'Tis very certain the desire of life
Prolongs it : this is obvious to physicians,
When patients, neither plagued with friends
nor wife,
Survive through very desperate conditions,
Because they still can hope, nor shines the knife
Nor shears of Atropos before their visions :
Despair of all recovery spoils longevity,
And makes men's miseries of alarming brevity.

LXV.

'Tis said that persons living on annuities
Are longer lived than others, — God knows
why,
Unless to plague the granters, — yet so it is,
That some, I really think, do never die;
Of any creditors the worst a Jew it is,
And that's their mode of furnishing supply:
In my young days they lent me cash that way,
Which I found very troublesome to pay.

LXVI.

'Tis thus with people in an open boat,
They live upon the love of life, and bear
More than can be believed, or even thought,
And stand like rocks the tempest's wear and
tear;
And hardship still has been the sailor's lot,
Since Noah's ark went cruising here and
there;
She had a curious crew as well as cargo,
Like the first old Greek privateer, the Argo.

LXVII.

But man is a carnivorous production,
And must have meals, at least one meal a
day;
He cannot live, like woodcocks, upon suction,
But, like the shark and tiger, must have
prey;
Although his anatomical construction
Bears vegetables, in a grumbling way,
Your laboring people think beyond all ques-
tion,
Beef, veal, and mutton, better for digestion.

LXVIII.

And thus it was with this our hapless crew;
For on the third day there came on a calm,
And though at first their strength it might re-
new,
And lying on their weariness like balm,
Lulled them like turtles sleeping on the blue

Of ocean, when they woke they felt a qualm,
And fell all ravenously on their provision,
Instead of hoarding it with due precision.

LXIX.

The consequence was easily foreseen —
They ate up all they had, and drank their
  wine,
In spite of all remonstrances, and then
On what, in fact, next day were they to dine ?
They hoped the wind would rise, these foolish
  men !
And carry them to shore; these hopes were
  fine,
But as they had but one oar, and that brittle,
It would have been more wise to save their
  victual.

LXX.

The fourth day came, but not a breath of air,
And Ocean slumbered like an unweaned
  child :
The fifth day, and their boat lay floating there,
The sea and sky were blue, and clear, and
  mild —
With their one oar (I wish they had a pair)
What could they do ? and hunger's rage
  grew wild :
So Juan's spaniel, spite of his entreating,
Was killed, and portioned out for present
  eating.

LXXI.

On the sixth day they fed upon his hide,
And Juan, who had still refused, because
The creature was his father's dog that died,
Now feeling all the vulture in his jaws,
With some remorse received (though first de-
  nied)
As a great favor one of the fore-paws,
Which he divided with Pedrillo, who
Devoured it, longing for the other too.

LXXII.

The seventh day, and no wind — the burning
  sun
Blistered and scorched, and, stagnant on
  the sea,
They lay like carcasses; and hope was none,
Save in the breeze that came not; savagely
They glared upon each other — all was done,
Water, and wine, and food, — and you might
  see
The longings of the cannibal arise
(Although they spoke not) in their wolfish eyes.

LXXIII.

At length one whispered his companion, who
Whispered another, and thus it went round,
And then into a hoarser murmur grew,
An ominous, and wild, and desperate sound;

And when his comrade's thought each suf-
  ferer knew,
'Twas but his own, suppressed till now, he
  found :
And out they spoke of lots for flesh and blood,
And who should die to be his fellow's food.

* * * * *

LXXV.

The lots were made, and marked, and mixed,
  and handed,
In silent horror, and their distribution
Lulled even the savage hunger which de-
  manded,
Like the Promethean vulture, this pollution ;
None in particular had sought or planned it,
'Twas nature gnawed them to this resolution,
By which none were permitted to be neuter —
And the lot fell on Juan's luckless tutor.

* * * * *

C.

The land appeared a high and rocky coast,
And higher grew the mountains as they
  drew,
Set by a current, toward it : they were lost
In various conjectures, for none knew
To what part of the earth they had been tost,
So changeable had been the winds that
  blew ;
Some thought it was Mount Ætna, some the
  highlands
Of Candia, Cyprus, Rhodes, or other islands.

CI.

Meantime the current, with a rising gale,
Still set them onwards to the welcome shore,
Like Charon's bark of spectres, dull and pale :
Their living freight was now reduced to
  four,
And three dead, whom their strength could
  not avail
To heave into the deep with those before,
Though the two sharks still followed them,
  and dashed
The spray into their faces as they splashed.

CII.

Famine, despair, cold, thirst, and heat, had
  done
Their work on them by turns, and thinned
  them to
Such things a mother had not known her son
Amidst the skeletons of that gaunt crew ;
By night chilled, by day scorched, thus one
  by one
They perished, until withered to these few.
But chiefly by a species of self-slaughter,
In washing down Pedrillo with salt water.

CIII.

As they drew nigh the land, which now was
   seen
Unequal in its aspect here and there,
They felt the freshness of its growing green,
   That waved in forest-tops, and smoothed
   the air,
And fell upon their glazed eyes like a screen
   From glistening waves, and skies so hot
   and bare —
Lovely seemed any object that should sweep
Away the vast, salt, dread, eternal deep.

CIV.

The shore looked wild, without a trace of man,
   And girt by formidable waves; but they
Were mad for land, and thus their course they
   ran,
   Though right ahead the roaring breakers
   lay:
A reef between them also now began
   To show its boiling surf and bounding spray,
But finding no place for their landing better,
They ran the boat for shore, — and overset
   her.

CV.

But in his native stream, the Guadalquivir,
   Juan to lave his youthful limbs was wont;
And having learnt to swim in that sweet river,
   Had often turned the art to some account:
A better swimmer you could scarce see ever,
   He could, perhaps, have passed the Helles-
   pont,
As once (a feat on which ourselves we prided)
Leander, Mr. Ekenhead, and I did.

CVI.

So here, though faint, emaciated, and stark,
   He buoyed his boyish limbs, and strove to
   ply
With the quick wave, and gain, ere it was
   dark,
   The beach which lay before him, high and
   dry:
The greatest danger here was from a shark,
   That carried off his neighbor by the thigh;
As for the other two, they could not swim,
So nobody arrived on shore but him.

CVII.

Nor yet had he arrived but for the oar,
   Which, providentially for him, was washed
Just as his feeble arms could strike no more,
   And the hard wave o'erwhelmed him as
   'twas dashed
Within his grasp; he clung to it, and sore
   The waters beat while he thereto was
   lashed;
At last, with swimming, wading, scrambling, he
Rolled on the beach, half senseless, from the
   sea:

CVIII.

There, breathless, with his digging nails he
   clung
Fast to the sand, lest the returning wave,
From whose reluctant roar his life he wrung,
   Should suck him back to her insatiate
   grave:
And there he lay, full length, where he was
   flung,
   Before the entrance of a cliff-worn cave,
With just enough of life to feel its pain,
And deem that it was saved, perhaps, in vain.

CIX.

With slow and staggering effort he arose,
   But sunk again upon his bleeding knee
And quivering hand; and then he looked for
   those
   Who long had been his mates upon the sea;
But none of them appeared to share his woes,
   Save one, a corpse from out the famished
   three,
Who died two days before, and now had
   found
An unknown barren beach for burial ground.

CX.

And as he gazed, his dizzy brain spun fast,
   And down he sunk; and as he sunk, the
   sand
Swam round and round, and all his senses
   passed:
   He fell upon his side, and his stretched hand
Drooped dripping on the oar (their jury-mast),
   And, like a withered lily, on the land
His slender frame and pallid aspect lay,
As fair a thing as e'er was formed of clay.

CXI.

How long in his damp trance young Juan lay
   He knew not, for the earth was gone for him,
And Time had nothing more of night nor day
   For his congealing blood, and senses dim;
And how this heavy faintness passed away
   He knew not, till each painful pulse and
   limb,
And tingling vein, seemed throbbing back to
   life,
For Death, though vanquished, still retired
   with strife.

CXII.

His eyes he opened, shut, again unclosed,
   For all was doubt and dizziness; he thought
He still was in the boat, and had but dozed,
   And felt again with his despair o'erwrought,
And wished it death in which he had reposed,
   And then once more his feelings back were
   brought,
And slowly by his swimming eyes was seen
A lovely female face of seventeen.

CXIII.

vas bending close o'er his, and the small
   mouth
Seemed almost prying into his for breath;
d chafing him, the soft warm hand of youth
Recalled his answering spirits back from
   death;
d, bathing his chill temples, tried to soothe
Each pulse to animation, till beneath
   gentle touch and trembling care, a sigh
these kind efforts made a low reply.

CXIV.

en was the cordial poured, and mantle flung
Around his scarce-clad limbs; and the fair
   arm
ised higher the faint head which o'er it
   hung;
And her transparent cheek, all pure and
   warm,
lowed his death-like forehead; then she
   wrung
His dewy curls, long drenched by every
   storm;
d watched with eagerness each throb that
   drew
igh from his heaved bosom — and hers, too.

CXV.

d lifting him with care into the cave,
The gentle girl, and her attendant, — one
ung, yet her elder, and of brow less grave,
And more robust of figure, — then begun
kindle fire, and as the new flames gave
Light to the rocks that roofed them, which
   the sun
d never seen, the maid, or whatsoe'er
: was, appeared distinct, and tall, and fair.

CXVI.

r brow was overhung with coins of gold,
'hat sparkled o'er the auburn of her hair,
r clustering hair, whose longer locks were
   rolled
n braids behind; and though her stature
   were
n of the highest for a female mould,
'hey nearly reached her heel; and in her air
:re was something which bespoke com-
   mand,
one who was a lady in the land.

CXVII.

· hair, I said, was auburn; but her eyes
7ere black as death, their lashes the same
   hue,
Lowncast length, in whose silk shadow lies
eepest attraction; for when to the view
h from its raven fringe the full glance flies,
e'er with such force the swiftest arrow flew:

'Tis as the snake late coiled, who pours his
   length,
And hurls at once his venom and his strength.

CXVIII.

Her brow was white and low, her cheek's pure
   dye
Like twilight rosy still with the set sun;
Short upper lip — sweet lips! that make us
   sigh
Ever to have seen such; for she was one
Fit for the model of a statuary,
(A race of mere imposters, when all's done—
I've seen much finer women, ripe and real,
Than all the nonsense of their stone ideal).

CXIX.

I'll tell you why I say so, for 'tis just
   One should not rail without a decent cause:
There was an Irish lady, to whose bust
   I ne'er saw justice done, and yet she was
A frequent model; and if e'er she must
   Yield to stern Time and Nature's wrinkling
   laws
They will destroy a face which mortal thought
Ne'er compassed, nor less mortal chisel
   wrought.

CXX.

And such was she, the lady of the cave:
   Her dress was very different from the Span-
   ish,
Simpler, and yet of colors not so grave;
   For, as you know, the Spanish women ban-
   ish
Bright hues when out of doors, and yet, while
   wave
Around them (what I hope will never vanish)
The basquina and the mantilla, they
Seem at the same time mystical and gay.

CXXI.

But with our damsel this was not the case:
   Her dress was many-colored, finely spun;
Her locks curled negligently round her face,
   But through them gold and gems profusely
   shone:
Her girdle sparkled, and the richest lace
   Flowed in her veil, and many a precious
   stone
Flashed on her little hand; but, what was
   shocking
Her small snow feet had slippers, but no stock-
   ing.

CXXII.

The other female's dress was not unlike,
   But of inferior materials: she
Had not so many ornaments to strike,
   Her hair had silver only, bound to be
Her dowry; and her veil, in form alike,
   Was coarser; and her air, 'hough firm,
   less free;

Her hair was thicker, but less long; her eyes
As black, but quicker, and of smaller size.

CXXIII.

And these two tended him, and cheered him
   both
   With food and raiment, and those soft
      attentions,
Which are — (as I must own) — of female
   growth,
 And have ten thousand delicate inventions:
They made a most superior mess of broth,
   A thing which poesy but seldom mentions,
But the best dish that e'er was cooked since
   Homer's
Achilles ordered dinner for new comers.

CXXIV.

I'll tell you who they were, this female pair,
   Lest they should seem princesses in dis-
      guise;
Besides, I hate all mystery, and that air
   Of clap-trap, which your recent poets prize;
And so, in short, the girls they really were
   They shall appear before your curious eyes,
Mistress and maid; the first was only daughter
Of an old man, who lived upon the water.

CXXV.

A fisherman he had been in his youth,
   And still a sort of fisherman was he;
But other speculations were, in sooth,
   Added to his connection with the sea,
Perhaps not so respectable, in truth:
   A little smuggling, and some piracy,
Left him, at last, the sole of many masters
Of an ill-gotten million of piastres.

CXXVI.

A fisher, therefore, was he, — though of men,
 . Like Peter the Apostle, — and he fished
For wandering merchant-vessels, now and
   then,
   And sometimes caught as many as he
      wished;
The cargoes he confiscated, and gain
   He sought in the slave-market too, and
      dished
Full many a morsel for that Turkish trade,
By which, no doubt, a good deal may be made.

CXXVII.

He was a Greek, and on his isle had built
   (One of the wild and smaller Cyclades)
A very handsome house from out his guilt,
   And there he lived exceedingly at ease;
Heaven knows, what cash he got or blood he
   spilt,
   A sad old fellow was he, if you please;
But this I know, it was a spacious building,
Full of barbaric carving, paint, and gilding.

CXXVIII.

He had an only daughter, called Haidée,
   The great heiress of the Eastern Isles;
Besides, so very beautiful was she,
   Her dowry was as nothing to her smiles:
Still in her teens, and like a lovely tree
   She grew to womanhood, and between
      whiles
Rejected several suitors, just to learn
How to accept a better in his turn.

CXXIX.

And walking out upon the beach, below
   The cliff, towards sunset, on that day she
      found,
Insensible, — not dead, but nearly so, —
   Don Juan, almost famished, and half
      drowned;
But being naked, she was shocked, you know,
   Yet deemed herself in common pity bound,
As far as in her lay, "to take him in,
A stranger" dying, with so white a skin.

CXXX.

But taking him into her father's house
   Was not exactly the best way to save,
But like conveying to the cat the mouse,
   Or people in a trance into their grave;
Because the good old man had so much
   "*vous,*"
Unlike the honest Arab thieves so brave,
He would have hospitably cured the stranger,
And sold him instantly when out of danger.

CXXXI.

And therefore, with her maid, she thought it
   best
   (A virgin always on her maid relies)
To place him in the cave for present rest:
   And when, at last, he opened his black eyes,
Their charity increased about their guest;
   And their compassion grew to such a size,
It opened half the turnpike-gates to heaven —
(St. Paul says, 'tis the toll which much must
   be given).

CXXXII.

They made a fire, — but such a fire as they
   Upon the moment could contrive with such
Materials as were cast up round the bay, —
   Some broken planks, and oars, that to the
      touch
Were nearly tinder, since so long they lay,
   A mast was almost crumbled to a crutch;
But, by God's grace, here wrecks were in such
   plenty,
That there was fuel to have furnished twenty.

CXXXIII.

He had a bed of furs, and a pelisse,
   For Haidée stripped her sables off to make
His couch; and, that he might be more at ease,

nd warm, in case by chance he should awake,
y also gave a petticoat apiece,
he and her maid, — and promised by day-
break
pay him a fresh visit, with a dish
breakfast, of eggs, coffee, bread, and fish.

CXXXIV.

l thus they left him to his lone repose:
ian slept like a top, or like the dead,
o sleep at last, perhaps (God only knows),
ist for the present; and in his lulled head
even a vision of his former woes
hrobbed in accursed dreams, which some-
times spread
velcome visions of our former years,
the eye, cheated, opens thick with tears.

CXXXV.

ng Juan slept all dreamless: — but the
maid,
'ho smoothed his pillow, as she left the
den
ked back upon him, and a moment stayed,
nd turned, believing that he called again.
slumbered; yet she thought, at least she
said
fhe heart will slip, even as the tongue and
pen),
iad pronounced her name — but she forgot
t at this moment Juan knew it not.

CXXXVI.

pensive to her father's house she went,
ijoining silence strict to Zoe, who
:r than she knew what, in fact, she·meant,
ie being wiser by a year or two:
ar or two's an age when rightly.spent,
id Zoe spent hers, as most women do,
iining all that useful sort of knowledge
ch is acquired in Nature's good ōld col-
lege.

CXXXVII.

morn broke, and found Juan slumbering
still
st in his cave, and nothing clashed upon
·est; the rushing of the neighboring rill,
id the young beams of the excluded .sun,
bled him not, and he might sleep his fill;
d need he had of slumber yet, for none
suffered more — his hardships were com-
)arative
hose related in my grand-dad's " Narra-
ive."

*   *   *   *   *

CXLI.

Haidée met the morning face to face;
r own was freshest, though a feverish
lush

Had dyed it with the headlong blood, whose
race
From heart to cheek is curbed into a blush,
Like to a torrent which a mountain's base,
That overpowers some Alpine river's rush,
Checks to a lake, whose waves in circles spread,
Or the Red Sea — but the sea is not red.

CXLII.

And down the cliff the island virgin came,
And near the cave her quick light footsteps
drew,
While the sun smiled on her with his first
flame,
And young Aurora kissed her lips with dew,
Taking her for a sister; just the same
Mistake you would have made on seeing
the two,
Although the mortal, quite as fresh and fair,
Had all the advantage, too, of not being air.

CXLIII.

And when into the cavern Haidée stepped
All timidly, yet rapidly, she saw
That like an infant Juan sweetly slept;
And then she stopped, and stood as if in
awe
(For sleep is awful), and on tiptoe crept
And wrapt him closer, lest the air, too raw,
Should reach his blood, then o'er him still as
death
Bent, with hushed lips, that drank his scarce-
drawn breath.

*   *   *   *   *

CXLIX.

He woke and gazed, and would have slept
again,
But the fair face which met his eyes forbade
Those eyes to close, though weariness and pain
Had further sleep a further pleasure made;
For woman's face was never formed in vain
For Juan, so that even when he prayed
He turned from grisly saints, and martyrs
hairy,
To the sweet portraits of the Virgin Mary.

CL.

And thus upon his elbow he arōse,
And looked upon the lady, in whose cheek
The pale contended with the purple rose,
As with an effort she began to speak;
Her eyes were eloquent, her words would pose
Although she told him, in good modern
Greek,
With an Ionian accent, low and sweet,
That he was faint, and must not talk, but eat.

CLI.

Now Juan could not understand a word,
Being no Grecian; but he had an ear,

And her voice was the warble of a bird,
  So soft, so sweet, so delicately clear,
That finer, simpler music ne'er was heard;
  The sort of sound we echo with a tear,
Without knowing why — an overpowering
    tone,
Whence Melody descends as from a throne.

CLII.

, And Juan gazed as one who is awoke
  By a distant organ, doubting if he be
Not yet a dreamer, till the spell is broke
  By the watchman, or some such reality,
Or by one's early valet's cursed knock;
  At least it is a heavy sound to me,
Who like a morning slumber — for the night
Shows stars and women in a better light.

*   *   *   *   *

CLVII.

But to resume. The languid Juan raised
  His head upon his elbow, and he saw
A sight on which he had not lately gazed,
  As all his latter meals had been quite raw,
Three or four things, for which the Lord he
    praised,
  And, feeling still the famished vulture gnaw,
He fell upon whate'er was offered, like
A priest, a shark, an alderman, or pike.

CLVIII.

He ate, and he was well supplied: and she,
  Who watched him like a mother, would
    have fed
Him past all bounds, because she smiled to
    see
  Such appetite in one she had deemed dead:
But Zoe, being older than Haidée,
  Knew (by tradition, for she ne'er had read)
That famished people must be slowly nurst,
And fed by spoonfuls, else they always burst.

*   *   *   *   *

CLX.

Next they — he being naked, save a tattered
  Pair of scarce decent trousers — went to
    work,
And in the fire his recent rags they scattered,
  And dressed him, for the present, like a
    Turk,
Or Greek — that is, although it not much
    mattered, · - ·
Omitting turban, slippers, pistols, dirk, —
They furnished him, entire, except some
    stitches,
With a clean shirt, and very spacious breeches.

CLXI.

And then fair Haidée tried her tongue at
  speaking,
  But not a word could Juan comprehend,

Although he listened so that the young Greek
  in
  Her earnestness would ne'er have made an
    end;
And, as he interrupted not, went eking
  Her speech out to her protégé and friend,
Till pausing at the last her breath to take,
She saw he did not understand Romaic.

CLXII.

And then she had recourse to nods, and
  signs,
  And smiles, and sparkles of the speaking
    eye,
And read (the only book she could) the
  lines
  Of his fair face, and found, by sympathy,
The answer eloquent, where the soul shines
  And darts in one quick glance a long reply;
And thus in every look she saw exprest
A world of words, and things at which she
  guessed.

CLXIII.

And now, by dint of fingers and of eyes,
  And words repeated after her, he took
A lesson in her tongue; but by surmise,
  No doubt, less of her language than her
    look:
As he who studies fervently the skies
  Turns oftener to the stars than to his book,
Thus Juan learned his alpha beta better
From Haidée's glance than any graven letter.

CLXIV.

'Tis pleasing to be schooled in a strange
  tongue
  By female lips and eyes — that is, I mean,
When both the teacher and the taught are
  young,
  As was the case, at least, where I have
    been;
They smile so when one's right, and when
  one's wrong
  They smile still more, and then there inter-
    vene
Pressure of hands, perhaps even a chaste
  kiss; —
I learned the little that I know by this:

CLXV.

That is, some words of Spanish, Turk, and
  Greek,
  Italian not at all, having no teachers;
Much English I cannot pretend to speak,
  Learning that language chiefly from its
    preachers,
Barrow, South, Tillotson, whom every week
  I study, also Blair, the highest reachers
Of eloquence in piety and prose —
I hate your poets, so read none of those

CLXVI.

r the ladies, I have nought to say,
wanderer from the British world of
ashion,
re I, like other "dogs, have had my day,"
ke other men, too, may have had my
passion —
hat, like other things, has passed away,
d all her fools whom I *could* lay the lash
on :
, friends, men, women, now are nought
o me
dreams of what has been, no more to be.

CLXVII.

rn we to Don Juan. He begun
, hear new words, and to repeat them ;
out
e feelings, universal as the sun,
ere such as could not in his breast be
shut
e than within the bosom of a nun :
e was in love, — as you would be, no
doubt,
a young benefactress, — so was she,
in the way we very often see.

*   *   *   *   *

CLXXIV.

thus a moon rolled on, and fair Haidée
id daily visits to her boy, and took
plentiful precautions, that still he
mained unknown within his craggy nook ;
st her father's prows put out to sea,
r certain merchantmen upon the look,
as of yore to carry off an Io,
three Ragusan vessels, bound for Scio.

CLXXV.

came her freedom, for she had no
mother,
that, her father being at sea, she was
as a married woman, or such other
male, as where she likes may freely pass,
out even the incumbrance of a brother,
e freest she that ever gazed on glass :
eak of Christian lands in this comparison,
re wives, at least, are seldom kept in gar-
rison.

CLXXVI.

she prolonged her visits and her talk
or they must talk), and he had learnt to
say
uch as to propose to take a walk, —
r little had he wandered since the day
hich, like a young flower snapped from
he stalk,
ooping and dewy on the beach he lay, —
thus they walked out in the afternoon,
saw the sun set opposite the moon.

CLXXVII.

It was a wild and breaker-beaten coast
  With cliffs above, and a broad sandy shore,
Guarded by shoals and rocks as by an host,
  With here and there a creek, whose aspect
    wore
A better welcome to the tempest-tost ;
  And rarely ceased the haughty billow's roar,
Save on the dead long summer days, which
    make
The outstretched ocean glitter like a lake.

*   *   *   *   *

CLXXXI.

The coast — I think it was the coast that I
  Was just describing — Yes, it *was* the
    coast —
Lay at this period quiet as the sky,
  The sands untumbled, the blue waves untost,
And all was stillness, save the sea-bird's cry,
  And dolphin's leap, and little billow crost
By some low rock or shelve, that made it fret
Against the boundary it scarcely wet.

CLXXXII.

And forth they wandered, her sire being gone,
  As I have said, upon an expedition ;
And mother, brother, guardian, she had none,
  Save Zoe, who, although with due precision
She waited on her lady with the sun,
  Thought daily service was her only mission,
Bringing warm water, wreathing her long
    tresses,
And asking now and then for cast-off dresses.

CLXXXIII.

It was the cooling hour, just when the rounded
  Red sun sinks down behind the azure hill,
Which then seems as if the whole earth it
    bounded,
  Circling all nature, hushed, and dim, and
    still,
With the far mountain-crescent half surround-
    ed
  On one side, and the deep sea calm and chill
Upon the other, and the rosy sky,
With one star sparkling through it like an eye.

CLXXXIV.

And thus they wandered forth, and hand in
    hand,
  Over the shining pebbles and the shells,
Glided along the smooth and hardened sand,
  And in the worn and wild receptacles
Worked by the storms, yet worked as it were
    planned,
  In hollow halls, with sparry roof and cells,
They turned to rest ; and, each clasped by an
    arm,
Yielded to the deep twilight's purple charm.

CLXXXV.

They looked up to the sky, whose floating glow
  Spread like a rosy ocean, vast and bright;
They gazed upon the glittering sea below,
  Whence the broad moon rose circling into sight;
They heard the waves splash, and the wind so low,
  And saw each other's dark eyes darting light
Into each other — and, beholding this,
Their lips drew near, and clung into a kiss;

*   *   *   *   *

CXCIX.

Alas! the love of women! it is known
  To be a lovely and a fearful thing;
For all of theirs upon that die is thrown,
  And if 'tis lost, life hath no more to bring

To them but mockeries of the past alone,
  And their revenge is as the tiger's spring,
Deadly, and quick, and crushing; yet, as real
Torture is theirs, what they inflict they feel.

CC.

They are right; for man, to man so oft un-
  just,
  Is always so to women; one sole bound
Awaits them, treachery is all their trust;
  Taught to conceal, their bursting hearts despond
Over their idol, till some wealthier lust
  Buys them in marriage — and what rests beyond?
A thankless husband, next a faithless lover,
Then dressing, nursing, praying, and all's over.

*   *   *   *   *

CANTO THE THIRD.

I.

HAIL, Muse! *et cetera.* — We left Juan sleeping,
  Pillowed upon a fair and happy breast,
And watched by eyes that never yet knew weeping,
  And loved by a young heart, too deeply blest
To feel the poison through her spirit creeping,
  Or know who rested there, a foe to rest,
Had soiled the current of her sinless years,
And turned her pure heart's purest blood to tears!

II.

Oh, Love! what is it in this world of ours
  Which makes it fatal to be loved? Ah why
With cypress branches hast thou wreathed thy bowers,
  And made thy best interpreter a sigh?
As those who dote on odors pluck the flowers,
  And place them on their breast — but place to die —
Thus the frail beings we would fondly cherish
Are laid within our bosoms but to perish.

*   *   *   *   *

V.

Omitting turban, slippers, pistols, dirk, —
  They furnished him, entire, except some stitches,
With a clean shirt, and very spacious breeches.

CLXI.

And then fair Haidée tried her tongue at speaking,
  But not a word could Juan comprehend,

VI.

No doubt, less of her language than her look:
As he who studies fervently the skies
  Turns oftener to the stars than to his book,
Thus Juan learned his alpha beta better
From Haidée's glance than any graven letter.

CLXIV.

'Tis pleasing to be schooled in a strange tongue
  By female lips and eyes — that is, I mean,
When both the teacher and the taught are young,
  As was the case, at least, where I have been;
They smile so when one's right, and when one's wrong
  They smile still more, and then there intervene
Pressure of hands, perhaps even a chaste kiss; —
I learned the little that I know by this:

CLXV.

That is, some words of Spanish, Turk, and Greek,
  Italian not at all, having no teachers;
Much English I cannot pretend to speak,
  Learning that language chiefly from its preachers,
Barrow, South, Tillotson, whom every week
  I study, also Blair, the highest reachers
Of eloquence in piety and prose —
I hate your poets, so read none of those

₂ future states of both are left to faith,
'or authors fear description might disparage
₂ worlds to come of both, or fall beneath,
ₐnd then both worlds would punish their
  miscarriage;
leaving each their priest and prayer-book
  ready,
₂y say no more of Death or of the Lady.

X.

₂ only two that in my recollection
Iave sung of heaven and hell, or marriage,
  are
ₙte and Milton, and of both the affection
Vas hapless in their nuptials, for some bar
  fault or temper ruined the connection
Such things, in fact, it don't ask much to
  mar);
₂ Dante's Beatrice and Milton's Eve
₂re not drawn from their spouses, you con-
  ceive.

XI.

ₙe persons say that Dante meant theology
₂y Beatrice, and not a mistress — I,
ₕough my opinion may require apology,
₂eem this a commentator's phantasy,
less indeed it was from his own knowledge
  he
₂ecided thus, and showed good reason
  why;
ₐink that Dante's more abtruse ecstatics
ant to personify the mathematics.

*　　*　　*　　*　　*

XV.

₂ good old gentleman had been detained
₂y winds and waves, and some important
  captures;
₂, in the hope of more, at sea remained,
ₐlthough a squall or two had damped his
  raptures,
swamping one of the prizes; he had
  chained
ₕis prisoners, dividing them like chapters
ₙumbered lots; they all had cuffs and col-
  lars,
₂ averaged each from ten to a hundred
  dollars.

XVI.

ₙe he disposed of off Cape Matapan,
ₐmong his friends the Mainots; some he
  sold
ₕis Tunis correspondents, save one man
ₒssed overboard unsalable (being old);
  rest — save here and there some richer
  one,
ₑserved for future ransom in the hold,
₂e linked alike, as for the common people
ₙe
₂ a large order from the Dey of Tripoli.

XVII.

The merchandise was served in the same
  way,
  Pieced out for different marts in the Levant,
Except some certain portions of the prey,
  Light classic articles of female want,
French stuffs, lace, tweezers, toothpicks, tea-
  pot, tray,
  Guitars and castanets from Alicant,
All which selected from the spoil he gathers,
Robbed for his daughter by the best of fathers.

XVIII.

A monkey, a Dutch mastiff, a mackaw,
  Two parrots, with a Persian cat and kittens,
He chose from several animals he saw —
  A terrier, too, which once had been a Bri-
  ton's,
Who dying on the coast of Ithaca,
  The peasants gave the poor dumb thing a
  pittance;
These to secure in this strong blowing weather,
He caged in one huge hamper altogether.

XIX.

Then having settled his marine affairs,
  Despatching single cruisers here and there,
His vessel having need of some repairs,
  He shaped his course to where his daugh-
  ter fair
Continued still her hospitable cares;
  But that part of the coast being shoal and
  bare,
And rough with reefs which ran out many a
  mile,
His port lay on the other side o' the isle.

XX.

And there he went ashore without delay,
  Having no custom-house nor quarantine
To ask him awkward questions on the way
  About the time and place where he had
  been:
He left his ship to be hove down next day,
  With orders to the people to careen;
So that all hands were busy beyond measure,
In getting out goods, ballast, guns, and treas-
  ure.

XXI.

Arriving at the summit of a hill
  Which overlooked the white walls of his
  home,
He stopped. — What singular emotions fill
  Their bosoms who have been induced to
  roam!
With fluttering doubts if all be well or ill —
  With love for many, and with fears for some;
All feelings which o'erleap the years long lost,
And bring our hearts back to their starting-
  post.

*　　*　　*　　*　　*

XXVII.

He saw his white walls shining in the sun,
  His garden trees all shadowy and green;
He heard his rivulet's light bubbling run,
  The distant dog-bark; and perceived be-
    tween
The umbrage of the wood so cool and dun
  The moving figures, and the sparkling sheen
Of arms (in the East all arm) — and various
    dyes
Of colored garbs, as bright as butterflies.

XXVIII.

And as the spot where they appear he nears,
  Surprised at these unwonted signs of idling,
He hears — alas! no music of the spheres,
  But an unhallowed, earthly sound of fid-
    dling!
A melody which made him doubt his ears,
  The cause being past his guessing or un-
    riddling;
A pipe, too, and a drum, and shortly after,
A most unoriental roar of laughter.

XXIX.

And still more nearly to the place advancing,
  Descending rather quickly the declivity,
Through the waved branches, o'er the green-
    sward glancing,
  'Midst other indications of festivity,
Seeing a troop of his domestics dancing
  Like dervises, who turn as on a pivot, he
Perceived it was the Pyrrhic dance so martial,
To which the Levantines are very partial.

XXX.

And further on a group of Grecian girls,
  The first and tallest her white kerchief wav-
    ing,
Were strung together like a row of pearls,
  Linked hand in hand, and dancing; each
    too having
Down her white neck long floating auburn
    curls —
  (The least of which would set ten poets
    raving);
Their leader sang — and bounded to her song,
With choral step and voice, the virgin throng.

XXXI.

And here, assembled cross-legged round their
    trays,
  Small social parties just begun to dine;
Pilaus and meats of all sorts met the gaze,
  And flasks of Samian and of Chian wine,
And sherbet cooling in the porous vase;
  Above them their dessert grew on its vine,
The orange and pomegranate nodding o'er
Dropped in their laps, scarce plucked, their
    mellow store.

XXXII.

A band of children, round a snow-white ram,
  There wreathe his venerable horns with
    flowers;
While peaceful as if still an unweaned lamb,
  The patriarch of the flock all gently cowers
His sober head, majestically tame,
  Or eats from out the palm, or playful lowers
His brow, as if in act to butt, and then
Yielding to their small hands, draws back
    again.

XXXIII.

Their classical profiles, and glittering dresses,
  Their large black eyes, and soft seraphic
    cheeks,
Crimson as cleft pomegranates, their long
    tresses,
  The gesture which enchants, the eye that
    speaks
The innocence which happy childhood
    blesses,
  Made quite a picture of these little Greeks;
So that the philosophical beholder
Sighed, for their sakes — that they should e'er
    grow older.

XXXIV.

Afar, a dwarf buffoon stood telling tales
  To a sedate gray circle of old smokers
Of secret treasures found in hidden vales,
  Of wonderful replies from Arab jokers,
Of charms to make good gold and cure bad
    ails,
  Of rocks bewitched that open to the knock-
    ers,
Of magic ladies who, by one sole act,
Transformed their lords to beasts (but that's
  a fact).

XXXV.

Here was no lack of innocent diversion
  For the imagination or the senses,
Song, dance, wine, music, stories from the
    Persian,
  All pretty pastimes in which no offence is;
But Lambro saw all these things with aver-
    sion,
  Perceiving in his absence such expenses,
Dreading that climax of all human ills,
The inflammation of his weekly bills.

XXXVI.

Ah! what is man? what perils still environ
  The happiest mortals even after dinner —
A day of gold from out an age of iron
  Is all that life allows the luckiest sinner;
Pleasure (whene'er she sings, at least) 's a
    siren,
  That lures, to flay alive, the young beginner;
Lambro's reception at his people's banquet
Was such as fire accords to a wet blanket.

XXXVII.

 — being a man who seldom used a word
Too much, and wishing gladly to surprise
n general he surprised men with the sword)
His daughter — had not sent before to ad-
  vise
his arrival, so that no one stirred;
And long he paused to re-assure his eyes,
 fact much more astonished than delighted,
 find so much good company invited.

XXXVIII.

 did not know (alas! how men will lie)
That a report (especially the Greeks)
rouched his death (such people never die),
And put his house in mourning several
  weeks, —
it now their eyes and also lips were dry;
The bloom, too, had returned to Haidée's
  cheeks.
er tears, too, being returned into their fount,
 e now kept house upon her own account.

XXXIX.

ence all this rice, meat, dancing, wine, and
  fiddling,
Which turned the isle into a place of plea-
  sure,
 e servants all were getting drunk or
  idling,
A life which made them happy beyond
  measure.
 er father's hospitality seemed middling,
Compared with what Haidée did with his
  treasure;
was wonderful how things went on improv-
  ing,
hile she had not one hour to spare from
  loving.

XL.

rhaps you think in stumbling on this feast
He flew into a passion, and in fact
 ere was no mighty reason to be pleased;
Perhaps you prophesy some sudden act,
 e whip, the rack, or dungeon at the least,
To teach his people to be more exact,
 d that, proceeding at a very high rate,
 : showed the royal *penchants* of a pirate.

XLI.

u're wrong. — He was the mildest man-
  nered man
That ever scuttled ship or cut a throat;
th such true breeding of a gentleman,
 ou never could divine his real thought;
 courtier could, and scarcely woman can
 iird more deceit within a petticoat;
 y he loved adventurous life's variety,
 was so great a loss to good society.

XLII.

Advancing to the nearest dinner tray,
  Tapping the shoulder of the nighest guest,
With a peculiar smile, which, by the way,
  Boded no good, whatever it expressed,
He asked the meaning of this holiday;
  The vinous Greek to whom he had ad-
  dressed
His question, much too merry to divine
The questioner, filled up a glass of wine,

XLIII.

And without turning his facetious head,
  Over his shoulder, with a Bacchant air,
Presented the o'erflowing cup, and said,
  "Talking's dry work, I have no time to
  spare."
A second hiccuped, "Our old master's dead,
  You'd better ask our mistress who's his heir."
"Our mistress!" quoth a third: "Our mis-
  tress! — pooh! —
You mean our master — not the old, but new."

XLIV.

These rascals, being new comers, knew not
  whom
  They thus addressed — and Lambro's vis-
  age fell —
And o'er his eye a momentary gloom
  Passed, but he strove quite courteously to
  quell
The expression, and endeavoring to resume
  His smile, requested one of them to tell
The name and quality of his new patron,
Who seemed to have turned Haidée into a
  matron.

XLV.

"I know not," quoth the fellow, "who or what
  He is, nor whence he came — and little care;
But this I know, that this roast capon's fat,
  And that good wine ne'er washed down
  better fare;
And if you are not satisfied with that,
  Direct your questions to my neighbor
  there;
He'll answer all for better or for worse,
For none likes more to hear himself con-
  verse."

XLVI.

I said that Lambro was a man of patience,
  And certainly he showed the best of breed-
  ing,
Which scarce even France, the paragon of
  nations,
  E'er saw her most polite of sons exceeding;
He bore these sneers against his near relations,
  His own anxiety, his heart, too, bleeding,
The insults, too, of every servile glutton,
Who all the time was eating up his mutton.

*   *   *   *   *

XLIX.

He asked no further questions, and proceeded
  On to the house, but by a private way,
So that the few who met him hardly heeded,
  So little they expected him that day;
If love paternal in his bosom pleaded
  For Haidée's sake, is more than I can say,
But certainly to one deemed dead returning,
This revel seemed a curious mode of mourning.

* * * * *

LII.

He entered in the house — his home no more,
  For without hearts there is no home; — and felt
The solitude of passing his own door
  Without a welcome: *there* he long had dwelt,
There his few peaceful days Time had swept o'er,
  There his worn bosom and keen eye would melt
Over the innocence of that sweet child,
His only shrine of feelings undefiled.

* * * * *

LXI.

Old Lambro passed unseen a private gate,
  And stood within his hall at eventide;
Meantime the lady and her lover sate
  At wassail in their beauty and their pride:
An ivory inlaid table spread with state
  Before them, and fair slaves on every side;
Gems, gold, and silver, formed the service mostly,
Mother of pearl and coral the less costly.

LXII.

The dinner made about a hundred dishes;
  Lamb and pistachio nuts — in short, all meats,
And saffron soups, and sweetbreads; and the fishes
  Were of the finest that e'er flounced in nets,
Drest to a Sybarite's most pampered wishes;
  The beverage was various sherbets
Of raisin, orange, and pomegranate juice,
Squeezed through the rind, which makes it best for use.

LXIII.

These were ranged round, each in its crystal ewer,
  And fruits, and date-bread loaves closed the repast,
And Mocha's berry, from Arabia pure,
  In small fine China cups, came in at last;
Gold cups of filigree made to secure
  The hand from burning underneath them placed,
Cloves, cinnamon, and saffron too were boiled
Up with the coffee, which (I think) they spoiled.

LXIV.

The hangings of the room were tapestry, made
  Of velvet panels, each of different hue,
And thick with damask flowers of silk inlaid;
  And round them ran a yellow border too;
The upper border, richly wrought, displayed,
  Embroidered delicately o'er with blue,
Soft Persian sentences, in lilac letters,
From poets, or the moralists their betters.

* * * *

LXVII.

Haidée and Juan carpeted their feet
  On crimson satin, bordered with pale blue;
Their sofa occupied three parts complete
  Of the apartment — and appeared quite new;
The velvet cushions (for a throne more meet) —
  Were scarlet, from whose glowing centre grew
A sun embossed in gold, whose rays of tissue,
Meridian-like, were seen all light to issue.

LXVIII.

Crystal and marble, plate and porcelain,
  Had done their work of splendor; Indian mats
And Persian carpets, which the heart bled to stain,
  Over the floors were spread; gazelles and cats,
And dwarfs and blacks, and such like things, that gain
  Their bread as ministers and favorites — (that's
To say, by degradation) — mingled there
As plentiful as in a court, or fair.

LXIX.

There was no want of lofty mirrors, and
  The tables, most of ebony inlaid
With mother of pearl or ivory, stood at hand,
  Or were of tortoise-shell or rare woods made,
Fretted with gold or silver: — by command,
  The greater part of these were ready spread
With viands and sherbets in ice — and wine —
Kept for all comers, at all hours to dine.

LXX.

Of all the dresses I select Haidée's:
  She wore two jelicks — one was of pale yellow;
Of azure, pink, and white was her chemise —

'Neath which her breast heaved like a little
   billow;
With buttons formed of pearls as large as peas,
   All gold and crimson shone her jelick's fel-
   low,
And the striped white gauze baracan that
   bound her,
Like fleecy clouds about the moon, flowed
   round her.

LXXI.

One large gold bracelet clasped each lovely
   arm,
   Lockless — so pliable from the pure gold
That the hand stretched and shut it without
   harm,
   The limb which it adorned its only mould;
So beautiful — its very shape would charm,
   And clinging as if loath to lose its hold,
The purest ore inclosed the whitest skin
That e'er by precious metal was held in.

LXXII.

Around, as princess of her father's land,
   A like gold bar above her instep rolled,
Announced her rank; twelve rings were on
   her hand;
   Her hair was starred with gems; her veil's
   fine fold
Below her breast was fastened with a band
   Of lavish pearls, whose worth could scarce
   be told;
Her orange silk full Turkish trowsers furled
About the prettiest ankle in the world.

LXXIII.

Her hair's long auburn waves down to her heel
   Flowed like an Alpine torrent which the sun
Dyes with his morning light, — and would con-
   ceal
   Her person if allowed at large to run,
And still they seem resentfully to feel
   The silken fillet's curb, and sought to shun
Their bonds whene'er some Zephyr caught
   began
To offer his young pinion as her fan.

LXXIV.

Round her she made an atmosphere of life,
   The very air seemed lighter from her eyes,
They were so soft and beautiful, and rife
   With all we can imagine of the skies,
And pure as Psyche e'er she grew a wife —
   Too pure even for the purest human ties;
Her overpowering presence made you feel
It would not be idolatry to kneel.

LXXV.

Her eyelashes, though dark as night, were
   tinged
   (It is the country's custom), but in vain;

For those large black eyes were so blackly
   fringed,
   The glossy rebels mocked the jetty stain,
And in their native beauty stood avenged:
   Her nails were touched with henna; but
   again
The power of art was turned to nothing, for
They could not look more rosy than before.

LXXVI.

The henna should be deeply dyed to make
   The skin relieved appear more fairly fair;
She had no need of this, day ne'er will break
   On mountain tops more heavenly white than
   her.
The eye might doubt if it were well awake,
   She was so like a vision; I might err,
But Shakspeare also says 'tis very silly
" To gild refined gold, or paint the lily."

LXXVII.

Juan had on a shawl of black and gold,
   But a white baracan, and so transparent
The sparkling gems beneath you might behold,
   Like small stars through the milky way ap-
   parent:
His turban, furled in many a graceful fold,
   An emerald aigrette with Haidée's hair in't
Surmounted, as its clasp, a glowing crescent,
Whose rays shone ever trembling, but inces-
   sant.

LXXVIII.

And now they were diverted by their suite,
   Dwarfs, dancing girls, black eunuchs, and a
   poet,
Which made their new establishment com-
   plete;
   The last was of great fame, and liked to show
   it;
His verses rarely wanted their due feet —
   And for his theme — he seldom sung below
   it,
He being paid to satirize or flatter,
As the psalm says, " inditing a good matter."

LXXIX.

He praised the present, and abused the past,
   Reversing the good custom of old days,
An Eastern anti-jacobin at last
   He turned, preferring pudding to *no* praise—
For some few years his lot had been o'ercast
   By his seeming independent in his lays,
But now he sung the Sultan and the Pacha
With truth like Southey, and with verse like
   Crashaw.

LXXX.

He was a man who had seen many changes,
   And always changed as true as any needle;
His polar star being one which rather ranges,
   And not the fixed — he knew the way to
   wheedle:

So vile he 'scaped the doom which oft avenges;
And being fluent (save indeed when fee'd
    ill),
He lied with such a fervor of intention —
There was no doubt he earned his laureate
    pension.

LXXXI.

But he had genius, — when a turncoat has it,
    The " Vates irritabilis " takes care
That without notice few full moons shall pass it;
    Even good men like to make the public
    stare : —
But to my subject — let me see — what was
    it ? —
Oh! — the third canto — and the pretty
    pair —
Their loves, and feasts, and house, and dress,
    and mode
Of living in their insular abode.

LXXXII.

Their poet, a sad trimmer, but no less
    In company a very pleasant fellow,
Had been the favorite of full many a mess
    Of men, and made them speeches when half
    mellow;
And though his meaning they could rarely
    guess,
Yet still they deigned to hiccup or to bellow
The glorious meed of popular applause,
Of which the first ne'er knows the second
    cause.

LXXXIII.

But now being lifted into high society,
    And having picked up several odds and ends
Of free thoughts in his travels for variety,
    He deemed, being in a lone isle, among
    friends,
That without any danger of a riot, he
    Might for long lying make himself amends;
And singing as he sung in his warm youth,
Agree to a short armistice with truth.

LXXXIV.

He had travelled 'mongst the Arabs, Turks,
    and Franks,
    And knew the self-loves of the different na-
    tions;
And having lived with people of all ranks,
    Had something ready upon most occa-
    sions —
Which got him a few presents and some
    thanks.
He varied with some skill his adulations;
To " do at Rome as Romans do," a piece
Of conduct was which he observed in Greece.

LXXXV.

Thus, usually, when he was asked to sing,
    He gave the different nations something
    national;

'Twas all the same to him — " God save the
    king,"
    Or " *Ça ira*," according to the fashion all :
His muse made increment of any thing,
    From the high lyric down to the low
    rational :
If Pindar sang horse-races, what should hinder
Himself from being as pliable as Pindar ?

LXXXVI.

In France, for instance, he would write a
    chanson;
    In England a six canto quarto tale;
In Spain, he'd make a ballad or romance on
    The last war — much the same in Portugal;
In Germany, the Pegasus he'd prance on
    Would be old Goethe's — (See what says
    de Staël) :
In Italy, he'd ape the " Trecentisti ; "
In Greece, he'd sing some sort of hymn like
    this t'ye :

1.

The isles of Greece, the isles of Greece !
    Where burning Sappho loved and sung,
Where grew the arts of war and peace, —
    Where Delos rose, and Phœbus sprung!
Eternal summer gilds them yet,
But all, except their sun, is set.

2.

The Scian and the Teian muse,
    The hero's harp, the lover's lute,
Have found the fame your shores refuse;
    Their place of birth alone is mute
To sounds which echo further west
Than your sires' " Islands of the Blest."

3.

The mountains look on Marathon —
    And Marathon looks on the sea;
And musing there an hour alone,
    I dreamed that Greece might still be free·
For standing on the Persians' grave,
I could not deem myself a slave.

4.

A king sate on the rocky brow
    Which looks o'er sea-born Salamis;
And ships, by thousands, lay below,
    And men in nations; — all were his!
He counted them at break of day —
And when the sun set where were they ?

5.

And where are they ? and where art thou,
    My country ? On thy voiceless shore
The heroic lay is tuneless now —
    The heroic bosom beats no more!
And must thy lyre, so long divine,
Degenerate into hands like mine ?

6.

'Tis something, in the dearth of fame,
 Though linked among a fettered race,
To feel at least a patriot's shame,
 Even as I sing, suffuse my face;
For what is left the poet here?
For Greeks a blush — for Greece a tear.

7.

Must *we* but weep o'er days more blest?
 Must *we* but blush? — Our fathers bled.
Earth! render back from out thy breast
A remnant of our Spartan dead!
Of the three hundred grant but three,
To make a new Thermopylæ!

8.

What, silent still? and silent all?
 Ah! no; — the voices of the dead
Sound like a distant torrent's fall,
 And answer, "Let one living head,
But one arise, — we come, we come!"
Tis but the living who are dumb.

9.

In vain — in vain: strike other chords;
 Fill high the cup with Samian wine!
Leave battles to the Turkish hordes,
 And shed the blood of Scio's vine!
Hark! rising to the ignoble call —
How answers each bold Bacchanal!

10.

You have the Pyrrhic dance as yet,
 Where is the Pyrrhic phalanx gone?
Of two such lessons, why forget
 The nobler and the manlier one?
You have the letters Cadmus gave —
Think ye he meant them for a slave?

11.

Fill high the bowl with Samian wine!
 We will not think of themes like these!
It made Anacreon's song divine:
 He served — but served Polycrates —
A tyrant; but our masters then
Were still, at least, our countrymen.

12.

The tyrant of the Chersonese
 Was freedom's best and bravest friend;
That tyrant was Miltiades!
 Oh! that the present hour would lend
Another despot of the kind!
Such chains as his were sure to bind.

13.

Fill high the bowl with Samian wine!
 On Suli's rock, and Parga's shore,
Exists the remnant of a line
 Such as the Doric mothers bore;

And there, perhaps, some seed is sown,
The Heracleidan blood might own.

14.

Trust not for freedom to the Franks —
 They have a king who buys and sells:
In native swords, and native ranks,
 The only hope of courage dwells;
But Turkish force, and Latin fraud,
Would break your shield, however broad.

15.

Fill high the bowl with Samian wine!
 Our virgins dance beneath the shade —
I see their glorious black eyes shine;
 But gazing on each glowing maid,
My own the burning tear-drop laves,
To think such breasts must suckle slaves.

16.

Place me on Sunium's marbled steep,
 Where nothing, save the waves and I,
May hear our mutual murmurs sweep;
 There, swan-like, let me sing and die:
A land of slaves shall ne'er be mine —
Dash down yon cup of Samian wine!

* * * * *

CI.

T'our tale. — The feast was over, the slaves
 gone,
 The dwarfs and dancing girls had all re-
 tired;
The Arab lore and poet's song were done,
 And every sound of revelry expired;
The lady and her lover, left alone,
 The rosy flood of twilight's sky admired; —
Ave Maria! o'er the earth and sea,
That heavenliest hour of Heaven is worthiest
 thee!

CII.

Ave Maria! blessed be the hour!
 The time, the clime, the spot, where I so
 oft
Have felt that moment in its fullest power
 Sink o'er the earth so beautiful and soft,
While swung the deep bell in the distant
 tower,
 Or the faint dying day-hymn stole aloft,
And not a breath crept through the rosy air,
And yet the forest leaves seemed stirred with
 prayer.

CIII.

Ave Maria! 'tis the hour of prayer!
 Ave Maria! 'tis the hour of love!
Ave Maria! may our spirits dare
 Look up to thine and to thy Son's above!
Ave Maria! oh that face so fair!
 Those downcast eyes beneath the Almighty
 dove —

What though 'tis but a pictured image ? —
  strike —
That painting is no idol, — 'tis too like.

CIV.

Some kinder casuists are pleased to say,
  In nameless print — that I have no devotion;
But set those persons down with me to pray,
  And you shall see who has the properest notion
Of getting into heaven the shortest way;
  My altars are the mountains and the ocean,
Earth, air, stars, — all that springs from the great Whole,
Who hath produced, and will receive the soul.

CV.

Sweet hour of twilight! — in the solitude
  Of the pine forest, and the silent shore
Which bounds Ravenna's immemorial wood,
  Rooted where once the Adrian wave flowed o'er,
To where the last Cæsarean fortress stood,
  Evergreen forest! which Boccaccio's lore
And Dryden's lay made haunted ground to me,
How have I loved the twilight hour and thee!

CVI.

The shrill cicalas, people of the pine,
  Making their summer lives one ceaseless song,
Were the sole echoes, save my steed's and mine,
  And vesper bell's that rose the boughs along;
The spectre huntsman of Onesti's line,
  His hell-dogs, and their chase, and the fair throng
Which learned from this example not to fly
From a true lover, — shadowed my mind's eye.

CVII.

Oh, Hesperus! thou bringest all good things —
  Home to the weary, to the hungry cheer,
To the young bird the parent's brooding wings,
  The welcome stall to the o'erlabored steer;
Whate'er of peace about our hearthstone clings,
  Whate'er our household gods protect of dear,
Are gathered round us by thy look of rest;
Thou bring'st the child, too, to the mother's breast.

CVIII.

Soft hour! which wakes the wish and melts the heart
  Of those who sail the seas, on the first day
When they from their sweet friends are torn apart;
  Or fills with love the pilgrim on his way
As the far bell of vesper makes him start,
  Seeming to weep the dying day's decay;
Is this a fancy which our reason scorns ?
Ah! surely nothing dies but something mourns !

CIX.

When Nero perished by the justest doom
  Which ever the destroyer yet destroyed,
Amidst the roar of liberated Rome,
  Of nations freed, and the world overjoyed,
Some hands unseen strewed flowers upon his tomb;
  Perhaps the weakness of a heart not void
Of feeling for some kindness done, when power
Had left the wretch an uncorrupted hour.

CX.

But I'm digressing; what on earth has Nero,
  Or any such like sovereign buffoons,
To do with the transactions of my hero,
  More than such madmen's fellow man — the moon's ?
Sure my invention must be down at zero,
  And I grown one of many " wooden spoons "
Of verse (the name with which we Cantabs please
To dub the last of honors in degrees).

CXI.

I feel this tediousness will never do —
  'Tis being *too* epic, and I must cut down
(In copying) this long canto into two;
  They'll never find it out, unless I own
The fact, excepting some experienced few;
  And then as an inprovement 'twill be shown
I'll prove that such the opinion of the critic is
From Aristotle *passim.* — See Ποιητικης.

CANTO THE FOURTH.

I.

NOTHING so difficult as a beginning
  In poesy, unless perhaps the end;
For oftentimes when Pegasus seems winning
  The race, he sprains a wing, and down we tend,
Like Lucifer when hurled from heaven for sinning;

Our sin the same, and hard as his to mend,
Being pride, which leads the mind to soar too
    far,
Till our own weakness shows us what we are.

II.

But Time, which brings all beings to their
    level,
And sharp Adversity, will teach at last·
Man,— and, as we hope,— perhaps the devil,
    That neither of their intellects are vast:
While youth's hot wishes in our red veins
    revel,
We know not this — the blood flows on too
    fast;
But as the torrent widens towards the ocean,
We ponder deeply on each past emotion.

III.

As boy, I thought myself a clever fellow,
    And wished that others held the same
    opinion;
They took it up when my days grew more
    mellow,
    And other minds acknowledged my domin-
    ion:
Now my sere fancy "falls into the yellow
    Leaf," and Imagination droops her pinion,
And the sad truth which hovers o'er my desk
Turns what was once romantic to burlesque.

IV.

And if I laugh at any mortal thing,
    'Tis that I may not weep; and if I weep,
'Tis that our nature cannot always bring
    Itself to apathy, for we must steep
Our hearts first in the depths of Lethe's spring,
    Ere what we least wish to behold will sleep :
Thetis baptized her mortal son in Styx ;
A mortal mother would on Lethe fix.

V.

Some have accused me of a strange design
    Against the creed and morals of the land,
And trace it in this poem every line :
    I don't pretend that I quite understand
My own meaning when I would be *very* fine;
    But the fact is that I have nothing planned,
Unless it were to be a moment merry,
A novel word in my vocabulary.

VI.

To the kind reader of our sober clime
    This way of writing will appear exotic;
Pulci was sire of the half-serious rhyme,
    Who sang when chivalry was more Quix-
    otic,
And revelled in the fancies of the time,
    True knights, chaste dames, huge giants,
    kings despotic:
But all these, save the last, being obsolete,
I choose a modern subject as more meet.

VII.

How I have treated it, I do not know;
    Perhaps no better than they have treated me
Who have imputed such designs as show
    Not what they saw, but what they wished to
    see :
But if it gives them pleasure, be it so;
    This is a liberal age, and thoughts are free.
Meantime Apollo plucks me by the ear,
And tells me to resume my story here.

VIII.

Young Juan and his lady-love were left
    To their own hearts' most sweet society;
Even Time the pitiless in sorrow cleft
    With his rude scythe such gentle bosoms;
    he
Sighed to behold them of their hours bereft
    Though foe to love; and yet they could not
    be
Meant to grow old, but die in happy spring,
Before one charm or hope had taken wing.

IX.

Their faces were not made for wrinkles, their
    Pure blood to stagnate, their great hearts to
    fail;
The blank gray was not made to blast their
    hair,
    But like the climes that know nor snow nor
    hail
They were all summer: lightning might as-
    sail
    And shiver them to ashes, but to trail
A long and snake-like life of dull decay
Was not for them — they had too little clay.

X.

They were alone once more; for them to be
    Thus was another Eden; they were never
Weary, unless when separate : the tree
    Cut from its forest root of years — the river
Dammed from its fountain — the child from
    the knee
    And breast maternal weaned at once for
    ever,—
Would wither less than these two torn apart;
Alas! there is no instinct like the heart —

XI.

The heart — which may be broken: happy
    they !
Thrice fortunate! who of that fragile mould,
The precious porcelain of human clay,
    Break with the first fall: they can ne'er be-
    hold
The long year linked with heavy day on day,
    And all which must be borne, and never
    told;
While life's strange principle will often lie
Deepest in those who long the most to die.

XII.

"Whom the gods love die young," was said
    of yore,
And many deaths do they escape by this :
The death of friends, and that which slays
    even more—
    The death of friendship, love, youth, all
    that is,
Except mere breath ; and since the silent shore
    Awaits at last even those who longest miss
The old archer's shafts, perhaps the early
    grave
Which men weep over may be meant to save.

XIII.

Haidée and Juan thought not of the dead.
    The heavens, and earth, and air, seemed
    made for them :
They found no fault with Time, save that he
    fled.
    They saw not in themselves aught to con-
    demn.
Each was the other's mirror, and but read
    Joy sparkling in their dark eyes like a gem,
And knew such brightness was but the re-
    flection
Of their exchanging glances of affection.

XIV.

The gentle pressure, and the thrilling touch,
    The least glance better understood than
    words,
Which still said all, and ne'er could say too
    much ;
    A language, too, but like to that of birds,
Known but to them, at least appearing such
    As but to lovers a true sense affords ;
Sweet playful phrases, which would seem
    absurd
To those who have ceased to hear such, or
    ne'er heard.

XV.

All these were theirs, for they were children
    still,
    And children still they should have ever
    been ;
They were not made in the real world to fill
    A busy character in the dull scene,
But like two beings born from out a rill,
    A nymph and her beloved, all unseen
To pass their lives in fountains and on flowers,
And never know the weight of human hours.

*   *   *   *   **

XXVIII.

They should have lived together deep in
    woods,
    Unseen as sings the nightingale ; they were
Unfit to mix in these thick solitudes
    Called social, haunts of Hate, and Vice,
    and Care :

How lonely every freeborn creature broods !
    The sweetest song-birds nestle in a pair ;
The eagle soars alone ; the gull and crow
Flock o'er their carrion, just like men below.

*   *   *   *   **

XXX.

Or as the stirring of a deep clear stream
    Within an Alpine hollow, when the wind
Walks o'er it, was she shaken by the dream,
    The mystical usurper of the mind—
O'erpowering us to be whate'er may seem
    Good to the soul which we no more can
    bind ;
Strange state of being ! (for 'tis still to be)
Senseless to feel, and with sealed eyes to see.

XXXI.

She dreamed of being alone on the sea-shore,
    Chained to a rock ; she knew not how, but
    stir
She could not from the spot, and the loud roar
    Grew, and each wave rose roughly, threat-
    ening her ;
And o'er her upper lip they seemed to pour,
    Until she sobbed for breath, and soon they
    were
Foaming o'er her lone head, so fierce and
    high—
Each broke to drown her, yet she could not
    die.

XXXII.

Anon—she was released, and then she strayed
    O'er the sharp shingles with her bleeding feet,
And stumbled almost every step she made ;
    And something rolled before her in a sheet,
Which she must still pursue howe'er afraid :
    'Twas white and indistinct, nor stopped to
    meet
Her glance nor grasp, for still she gazed and
    grasped,
And ran, but it escaped her as she clasped.

XXXIII.

The dream changed :—in a cave she stood,
    its walls
    Were hung with marble icicles ; the work
Of ages on its water-fretted halls,
    Where waves might wash, and seals might
    breed and lurk ;
Her hair was dripping, and the very balls
    Of her black eyes seemed turned to tears,
    and mirk
The sharp rocks looked below each drop
    they caught,
Which froze to marble as it fell,—she thought.

XXXIV.

And wet, and cold, and lifeless at her feet,
    Pale as the foam that frothed on his dead
    brow

Which she essayed in vain to clear, (how
sweet
Were once her cares, how idle seemed they
now!)
Lay Juan, nor could aught renew the beat
Of his quenched heart; and the sea dirges
low
Rang in her sad ears like a mermaid's song,
And that brief dream appeared a life too long.

XXXV.

And gazing on the dead, she thought his face
Faded, or altered into something new—
Like to her father's features, till each trace
More like and like to Lambro's aspect
grew—
With all his keen worn look and Grecian
grace;
And starting, she awoke, and what to view?
Oh! Powers of Heaven! what dark eye meets
she there?
'Tis—'tis her father's—fixed upon the pair!

XXXVI.

Then shrieking, she arose, and shrieking fell,
With joy and sorrow, hope and fear, to see
Him whom she deemed a habitant where
dwell
The ocean-buried, risen from death, to be
Perchance the death of one she loved too
well:
Dear as her father had been to Haidée,
It was a moment of that awful kind ——
I have seen such — but must not call to mind.

XXXVII.

Up Juan sprung to Haidée's bitter shriek,
And caught her falling, and from off the wall
Snatched down his sabre, in hot haste to wreak
Vengeance on him who was the cause of all:
Then Lambro, who till now forbore to speak,
Smiled scornfully, and said, "Within my
call,
A thousand scimitars await the word;
Put up, young man, put up your silly sword."

XXXVIII.

And Haidée clung around him; "Juan, 'tis—
'Tis Lambro—'tis my father! Kneel with
me—
He will forgive us—yes—it must be—yes.
Oh! dearest father, in this agony
Of pleasure and of pain—even while I kiss
Thy garment's hem with transport, can it be
That doubt should mingle with my filial joy?
Deal with me as thou wilt, but spare this boy."

XXXIX.

High and inscrutable the old man stood,
Calm in his voice, and calm within his eye—
Not always signs with him of calmest mood:
He looked upon her, but gave no reply;
Then turned to Juan, in whose cheek the
blood
Oft came and went, as there resolved to die;
In arms, at least, he stood, in act to spring
On the first foe whom Lambro's call might
bring.

XL.

"Young man, your sword;" so Lambro once
more said:
Juan replied, "Not while this arm is free."
The old man's cheek grew pale, but not with
dread,
And drawing from his belt a pistol, he
Replied, "Your blood be then on your own
head."
Then looked close to the flint, as if to see
'Twas fresh—for he had lately used the lock—
And next proceeded quietly to cock.

XLI.

It has a strange quick jar upon the ear,
That cocking of a pistol, when you know
A moment more will bring the sight to bear
Upon your person, twelve yards off, or so;
A gentlemanly distance, not too near,
If you have got a former friend or foe;
But after being fired at once or twice,
The ear becomes more Irish, and less nice.

XLII.

Lambro presented, and one instant more
Had stopped this Canto, and Don Juan's
breath,
When Haidée threw herself her boy before;
Stern as her sire: "On me," she cried, "let
death
Descend—the fault is mine; this fatal shore
He found—but sought not. I have pledged
my faith;
I love him—I will die with him: I knew
Your nature's firmness—know your daughter's
too."

XLIII.

A minute past, and she had been all tears,
And tenderness, and infancy; but now
She stood as one who championed human
fears—
Pale, statue-like, and stern, she wooed the
blow;
And tall beyond her sex, and their compeers,
She drew up to her height, as if to show
A fairer mark; and with a fixed eye scanned
Her father's face—but never stopped his hand.

XLIV.

He gazed on her, and she on him; 'twas strange
How like they looked! the expression was
the same;
Serenely savage, with a little change
In the large dark eye's mutual-darted flame;
For she, too, was as one who could avenge,

If cause should be — a lioness, though tame,
  Her father's blood before her father's face
Boiled up, and proved her truly of his race.

XLV.

I said they were alike, their features and
  Their stature, differing but in sex and years;
Even to the delicacy of their hand
  There was resemblance, such as true blood
    wears;
And now to see them, thus divided, stand
  In fixed ferocity, when joyous tears,
And sweet sensations, should have welcomed
    both,
Show what the passions are in their full growth.

XLVI.

The father paused a moment, then withdrew
  His weapon, and replaced it; but stood still,
And looking on her, as to look her through,
  " Not *I*," he said, " have sought this stranger's
    ill;
Not *I* have made this desolation: few
  Would bear such outrage, and forbear to
    kill;
But I must do my duty — how thou hast
Done thine, the present vouches for the past.

XLVII.

'' Let him disarm; or, by my father's head,
  His own shall roll before you like a ball! ''
He raised his whistle, as the word he said,
  And blew, another answered to the call,
And rushing in disorderly, though led,
  And armed from boot to turban, one and all,
Some twenty of his train came, rank on rank;
He gave the word, — " Arrest or slay the
    Frank."

XLVIII.

Then, with a sudden movement, he withdrew
  His daughter; while compressed within his
    clasp,
'Twixt her and Juan interposed the crew;
  In vain she struggled in her father's grasp —
His arms were like a serpent's coil: then flew
  Upon their prey, as darts an angry asp,
The file of pirates; save the foremost, who
Had fallen, with his right shoulder half cut
    through.

XLIX.

The second had his cheek laid open; but
  The third, awary, cool old sworder, took
The blows upon his cutlass, and then put
  His own well in; so well, ere you could
    look,
His man was floored, and helpless at his
    foot,
  With the blood running like a little brook
From two smart sabre gashes, deep and red —
One on the arm, the other on the head.

L.

And then they bound him where he fell, and
    bore
  Juan from the apartment: with a sign
Old Lambro bade them take him to the shore,
  Where lay some ships which were to sail at
    nine.
They laid him in a boat, and plied the oar
  Until they reached some galliots, placed in
    line;
On board of one of these, and under hatches,
They stowed him, with strict orders to the
    watches.

LI.

The world is full of strange vicissitudes,
  And here was one exceedingly unpleasant:
A gentleman so rich in the world's goods,
  Handsome and young, enjoying all the
    present,
Just at the very time when he least broods
  On such a thing is suddenly to sea sent,
Wounded and chained so that he cannot
    move,
And all because a lady fell in love.

LII.

Here I must leave him, for I grow pathetic,
  Moved by the Chinese nymph of tears,
    green tea!
Than whom Cassandra was not more pro-
    phetic;
  For if my pure libations exceed three,
I feel my heart become so sympathetic,
  That I must have recourse to black Bohea:
'Tis pity wine should be so deleterious,
For tea and coffee leave us much more serious,

LIII.

Unless when qualified with thee, Cogniac!
  Sweet Naïad of the Phlegethontic rill!
Ah! why the liver wilt thou thus attack,
  And make, like other nymphs, thy lovers ill?
I would take refuge in weak punch, but *rack*
  (In each sense of the word), whene'er I fill
My mild and midnight beakers to the brim,
Wakes me next morning with its synonym.

LIV.

I leave Don Juan for the present, safe —
  Not sound, poor fellow, but severely
    wounded;
Yet could his corporal pangs amount to half
  Of those with which his Haidée's bosom
    bounded!
She was not one to weep, and rave, and
    chafe,
  And then give way, subdued because sur-
    rounded;
Her mother was a Moorish maid, from Fez,
Where all is Eden, or a wilderness.

LV.

There the large olive rains its amber store
  In marble fonts; there grain, and flower,
    and fruit,
Gush from the earth until the land runs o'er;
  But there, too, many a poison-tree has root,
And midnight listens to the lion's roar,
  And long, long deserts scorch the camel's
    foot,
Or heaving whelm the helpless caravan;
And as the soil is, so the heart of man.

LVI.

Afric is all the sun's, and as her earth
  Her human clay is kindled; full of power
For good or evil, burning from its birth,
  The Moorish blood partakes the planet's
    hour,
And like the soil beneath it will bring forth:
  Beauty and love were Haidée's mother's
    dower;
But her large dark eye showed deep Passion's
    force,
Though sleeping like a lion near a source.

LVII.

Her daughter, tempered with a milder ray,
  Like summer clouds all silvery, smooth, and
    fair,
Till slowly charged with thunder they display
  Terror to earth, and tempest to the air,
Had held till now her soft and milky way;
  But overwrought with passion and despair,
The fire burst forth from her Numidian veins,
Even as the simoom sweeps the blasted plains.

LVIII.

The last sight which she saw was Juan's gore,
  And he himself o'ermastered and cut down;
His blood was running on the very floor
  Where late he trod, her beautiful, her own;
Thus much she viewed an instant and no
    more,—
  Her struggles ceased with one convulsive
    groan;
On her sire's arm, which until now scarce held
Her writhing, fell she like a cedar felled.

LIX.

A vein had burst, and her sweet lips' pure dyes
  Were dabbled with the deep blood which
    ran o'er;
And her head drooped as when the lily lies
  O'ercharged with rain: her summoned
    handmaids bore
Their lady to her couch with gushing eyes;
  Of herbs and cordials they produced their
    store,
But she defied all means they could employ,
Like one life could not hold, nor death destroy.

LX.

Days lay she in that state unchanged, though
    chill—
  With nothing livid, still her lips were red;
She had no pulse, but death seemed absent
    still;
  No hideous sign proclaimed her surely
    dead;
Corruption came not in each mind to kill
  All hope; to look upon her sweet face bred
New thoughts of life, for it seemed full of
    soul—
She had so much, earth could nor claim the
    whole.

LXI.

The ruling passion, such as marble shows
  When exquisitely chiselled, still lay there,
But fixed as marble's unchanged aspect throws
  O'er the fair Venus, but for ever fair;
O'er the Laocoon's all eternal throes,
  And ever-dying Gladiator's air,
Their energy like life forms all their fame,
Yet looks not life, for they are still the same.

LXII.

She woke at length, but not as sleepers wake,
  Rather the dead, for life seemed something
    new,
A strange sensation which she must partake
  Perforce, since whatsoever met her view
Struck not on memory, though a heavy ache
  Lay at her heart, whose earliest beat still
    true
Brought back the sense of pain without the
    cause,
For, for a while, the furies made a pause.

LXIII.

She looked on many a face with vacant eye,
  On many a token without knowing what;
She saw them watch her without asking why,
  And recked not who around her pillow
    sat;
Not speechless, though she spoke not; not a
    sigh
  Relieved her thoughts; dull silence and
    quick chat
Were tried in vain by those who served; she
    gave
No sign, save breath, of having left the grave.

LXIV.

Her handmaids tended, but she heeded not;
  Her father watched, she turned her eyes
    away;
She recognized no being, and no spot
  However dear or cherished in their day;
They changed from room to room, but all
    forgot,
  Gentle, but without memory she lay;

At length those eyes, which they would fain
 be weaning
Back to old thoughts, waxed full of fearful
 meaning.

LXV.

And then a slave bethought her of a harp;
 The harper came, and tuned his instru-
  ment;
At the first notes, irregular and sharp,
 On him her flashing eyes a moment bent,
Then to the wall she turned as if to warp
 Her thoughts from sorrow through her heart
  re-sent;
And he begun a long low island song
Of ancient days, ere tyranny grew strong.

LXVI.

Anon her thin wan fingers beat the wall
 In time to his old tune; he changed the
  theme,
And sung of love; the fierce name struck
 through all
Her recollection; on her flashed the dream
 Of what she was, and is, if ye could call
 To be so being; in a gushing stream
The tears rushed forth from her o'erclouded
 brain,
Like mountain mists at length dissolved in
 rain.

LXVII.

Short solace, vain relief! — thought came too
 quick,
 And whirled her brain to madness; she
  arose
As one who ne'er had dwelt among the sick,
 And flew at all she met, as on her foes;
But no one ever heard her speak or shriek,
 Although her paroxysm drew towards its
  close; —
Hers was a phrensy which disdained to rave,
Even when they smote her, in the hope to save.

LXVIII.

Yet she betrayed at times a gleam of sense;
 Nothing could make her meet her father's
  face,
Though on all other things with looks intense
 She gazed, but none she ever could retrace;
Food she refused, and raiment; no pretence
 Availed for either; neither change of place,
Nor time, nor skill, nor remedy, could give her
Senses to sleep — the power seemed gone for
 ever.

LXIX.

Twelve days and nights she withered thus; at
 last,
 Without a groan, or sigh, or glance, to show
A parting pang, the spirit from her past:
 And they who watched her nearest could
  not know
The very instant, till the change that cast

Her sweet face into shadow, dull and
 slow,
Glazed o'er her eyes — the beautiful, the
 black —
Oh! to possess such lustre — and then lack!

LXX.

She died, but not alone; she held within
 A second principle of life, which might
Have dawned a fair and sinless child of sin;
 But closed its little being without light,
And went down to the grave unborn, wherein
 Blossom and bough lie withered with one
  blight;
In vain the dews of heaven descend above
The bleeding flower and blasted fruit of love.

LXXI.

Thus lived — thus died she; never more on
 her
 Shall sorrow light, or shame. She was not
  made
Through years or moons the inner weight to
 bear,
 Which colder hearts endure till they are laid
By age in earth: her days and pleasures were
 Brief, but delightful — such as had not staid
Long with her destiny; but she sleeps well
By the sea-shore, whereon she loved to dwell.

LXXII.

That isle is now all desolate and bare,
 Its dwellings down, its tenants passed away;
None but her own and father's grave is there,
 And nothing outward tells of human clay;
Ye could not know where lies a thing so fair,
 No stone is there to show, no tongue to say
What was; no dirge, except the hollow sea's,
Mourns o'er the beauty of the Cyclades.

LXXIII.

But many a Greek maid in a loving song
 Sighs o'er her name; and many an islander
With her sire's story makes the night less long;
 Valor was his, and beauty dwelt with her:
If she loved rashly, her life paid for wrong —
 A heavy price must all pay who thus err,
In some shape; let none think to fly the dan-
 ger,
For soon or late Love is his own avenger.

LXXIV.

But let me change this theme, which grows
 too sad,
 And lay this sheet of sorrows on the shelf;
I don't much like describing people mad,
 For fear of seeming rather touched myself—
Besides, I've no more on this head to add;
 And as my Muse is a capricious elf,
We'll put about, and try another tack
With Juan, left half-killed some stanzas back.

LXXV.

Wounded and fettered, "cabined, cribbed,
confined,"
Some days and nights elapsed before that he
Could altogether call the past to mind;
And when he did, he found himself at sea,
Sailing six knots an hour before the wind;
The shores of Ilion lay beneath their lee—
Another time he might have liked to see 'em,
But now was not much pleased with Cape
Sigæum.

LXXVI.

There, on the green and village-cotted hill, is
(Flanked by the Hellespont, and by the sea)
Entombed the bravest of the brave, Achilles;
They say so— (Bryant says the contrary) :
And further downward, tall and towering still,
is
The tumulus—of whom ? Heaven knows;
't may be
Patroclus, Ajax, or Protesilaus;
All heroes, who if living still would slay us.

LXXVII.

High barrows, without marble, or a name,
A vast, untilled, and mountain-skirted plain,
And Ida in the distance, still the same,
And old Scamander, (if 'tis he) remain ;
The situation seems still formed for fame—
A hundred thousand men might fight again
With ease; but where I sought for Ilion's
walls,
The quiet sheep feeds, and the tortoise crawls ;

LXXVIII.

Troops of untended horses; here and there
Some little hamlets, with new names un-
couth ;
Some shepherds, (unlike Paris,) led to stare
A moment at the European youth
Whom to the spot their school-boy feelings
bear ;
A Turk, with beads in hand, a pipe in
mouth,
Extremely taken with his own religion,
Are what I found there—but the devil a
Phrygian.

LXXIX.

Don Juan, here permitted to emerge
From his dull cabin, found himself a slave ;
Forlorn, and gazing on the deep blue surge,
O'ershadowed there by many a hero's
grave ;
Weak still with loss of blood, he scarce
could urge
A few brief questions; and the answers
gave
To very satisfactory information
About his past or present situation.

LXXX.

He saw some fellow captives, who appeared
To be Italians, as they were in fact;
From them, at least, *their* destiny he heard,
Which was an odd one ; a troop going to act
In Sicily—all singers, duly reared
In their vocation; had not been attacked
In sailing from Livorno by the pirate,
But sold by the impresario at no high rate.

LXXXI.

By one of these, the buffo of the party,
Juan was told about their curious case ;
For although destined to the Turkish mart, he
Still kept his spirits up—at least his face ;
The little fellow really looked quite hearty,
And bore him with some gaiety and grace,
Showing a much more reconciled demeanor
Than did the prima donna and the tenor.

LXXXII.

In a few words he told their hapless story,
Saying, " Our Machiavelian impresario,
Making a signal off some promontory,
Hailed a strange brig; Corpo di Caio
Mario !
We were transferred on board her in a hurry,
Without a single scudo of salario ;
But if the Sultan has a taste for song,
We will revive our fortunes before long."

*　　*　　*　　*　　*

XC.

Here Raucocanti's eloquent recital
Was interrupted by the pirate crew,
Who came at stated moments to invite all
The captives back to their sad berths ; each
threw
A rueful glance upon the waves, (which bright
all
From the blue skies derived a double blue,
Dancing all free and happy in the sun,)
And then went down the hatchway one by one.

XCI.

They heard next day—that in the Darda-
nelles,
Waiting for his Sublimity's firmān,
The most imperative of sovereign spells,
Which everybody does without who can,
More to secure them in their naval cells,
Lady to lady, well as man to man,
Were to be chained and lotted out per couple,
For the slave market of Constantinople.

*　　*　　*　　*　　*

XCIV.

Juan's companion was a Romagnole,
But bred within the March of old Ancona
With eyes that looked into the very soul

(And other chief points of a " bella donna "),
Bright — and as black and burning as a coal;
  And through her clear brunette complexion
  shone a
Great wish to please — a most attractive dower,
Especially when added to the power.

XCV.

But all that power was wasted upon him,
  For sorrow o'er each sense held stern com-
  mand;
Her eye might flash on his, but found it dim;
  And though thus chained, as natural her
  hand
Touched his, nor that — nor any handsome
  limb
(And she had some not easy to withstand)
Could stir his pulse, or make his faith feel
  brittle;
Perhaps his recent wounds might help a little.

XCVI.

No matter; we should ne'er too much inquire,
  But facts are facts: no knight could be more
  true,
And firmer faith no ladye-love desire;
  We will omit the proofs, save one or two:
'Tis said no one in hand " can hold a fire
  By thought of frosty Caucasus; " but few,
I really think; yet Juan's then ordeal
Was more triumphant, and not much less real.

XCVII.

Here I might enter on a chaste description,
  Having withstood temptation in my youth,
But hear that several people take exception
  At the first two books having too much truth;
Therefore I'll make Don Juan leave the ship
  soon,
Because the publisher declares, in sooth,
Through needles' eyes it easier for the camel
  is
To pass, than those two cantos into families.

XCVIII.

'Tis all the same to me; I'm fond of yielding,
  And therefore leave them to the purer page
Of Smollett, Prior, Ariosto, Fielding,
  Who say strange things for so correct an
  age;
I once had great alacrity in wielding
  My pen, and liked poetic war to wage,
And recollect the time when all this cant
Would have provoked remarks which now it
  shan't.

⁕　⁕　⁕　⁕　⁕

CXIII.

But to the narrative: — The vessel bound
  With slaves to sell off in the capital,
After the usual process, might be found
  At anchor under the seraglio wall;
Her cargo, from the plague being safe and
  sound,
  Were landed in the market, one and all,
And there with Georgians, Russians, and Cir-
  cassians,
Bought up for different purposes and passions.

CXIV.

Some went off dearly; fifteen hundred dollars
  For one Circassian, a sweet girl, were given,
Warranted virgin; beauty's brightest colors
  Had decked her out in all the hues of
  heaven:
Her sale sent home some disappointed
  bawlers,
  Who bade on till the hundreds reached
  eleven;
But when the offer went beyond, they knew
'Twas for the Sultan, and at once withdrew.

CXV.

Twelve negresses from Nubia brought a price
  Which the West Indian market scarce
  would bring;
Though Wilberforce, at last has made it twice
  What 'twas ere Abolition; and the thing
Need not seem very wonderful, for vice
  Is always much more splendid than a king:
The virtues, even the most exalted, Charity,
Are saving — vice spares nothing for a rarity.

CXVI.

But for the destiny of this young troop,
  How some were bought by pachas, some by
  Jews,
How some to burdens were obliged to stoop,
  And others rose to the command of crews
As renegadoes; while in hapless group,
  Hoping no very old vizier might choose,
The females stood, as one by one they picked
  'em,
To make a mistress, or fourth wife, or victim:

CXVII.

All this must be reserved for further song;
  Also our hero's lot, howe'er unpleasant
(Because this Canto has become too long),
  Must be postponed discreetly for the present;
I'm sensible redundancy is wrong,
  But could not for the muse of me put less in't
And now delay the progress of Don Juan,
Till what is called in Ossian the fifth Duan.

CANTO THE FIFTH.

I.

WHEN amatory poets sing their loves
In liquid lines mellifluously bland,
And pair their rhymes as Venus yokes her
  doves,
They little think what mischief is in hand;
The greater their success the worse it proves,
As Ovid's verse may give to understand;
Even Petrarch's self, if judged with due
  severity,
Is the Platonic pimp of all posterity.

II.

I therefore do denounce all amorous writing,
  Except in such a way as not to attract;
Plain — simple — short, and by no means in-
  viting,
  But with a moral to each error tacked,
Formed rather for instructing than delighting,
  And with all passions in their turn attacked:
Now, if my Pegasus should not be shod ill,
This poem will become a moral model.

III.

The European with the Asian shore
  Sprinkled with palaces; the ocean stream
Here and there studded with a seventy-four;
  Sophia's cupola with golden gleam;
The cypress groves; Olympus high and hoar;
  The twelve isles, and the more than I could
  dream,
Far less describe, present the very view
Which charmed the charming Mary Montagu.

IV.

I have a passion for the name of "Mary,"
  For once it was a magic sound to me;
And still it half calls up the realms of fairy,
  Where I beheld what never was to be;
All feelings changed, but this was last to vary,
  A spell from which even yet I'm not quite
  free:
But I grow sad — and let a tale grow cold,
Which must not be pathetically told.

V.

The wind swept down the Euxine, and the wave
  Broke foaming o'er the blue Symplegades;
'Tis a grand sight from off "the Giant's
  Grave"
  To watch the progress of those rolling seas
Between the Bosphorus, as they lash and lave
  Europe and Asia, you being quite at ease;
There's not a sea the passenger e'er pukes in,
Turns up more dangerous breakers than the
  Euxine.

VI.

'Twas a raw day of Autumn's bleak beginning,
  When nights are equal, but not so the days;
The Parcæ then cut short the further spin-
  ning
  Of seamen's fates, and the loud tempests
  raise
The waters, and repentance for past sinning
  In all, who o'er the great deep take their
  ways:
They vow to amend their lives, and yet they
  don't;
Because if drowned, they can't — if spared,
  they won't.

VII.

A crowd of shivering slaves of every nation,
  And age, and sex, were in the market
  ranged:
Each bevy with the merchant in his station:
  Poor creatures! their good looks were sadly
  changed.
All save the blacks seemed jaded with vexa-
  tion,
  From friends, and home, and freedom far
  estranged;
The negroes more philosophy displayed, —
Used to it, no doubt, as eels are to be flayed.

VIII

Juan was juvenile, and thus was full,
  As most at his age are, of hope, and health;
Yet I must own, he looked a little dull,
  And now and then a tear stole down by
  stealth;
Perhaps his recent loss of blood might pull
  His spirit down; and then the loss of
  wealth,
A mistress, and such comfortable quarters,
To be put up for auction amongst Tartars,

IX.

Were things to shake a stoic; ne'ertheless,
  Upon the whole his carriage was serene:
His figure, and the splendor of his dress,
  Of which some gilded remnants still were
  seen,
Drew all eyes on him, giving them to guess
  He was above the vulgar by his mien;
And then, though pale, he was so very hand-
  some;
And then — they calculated on his ransom.

X.

Like a backgammon board the place was
  dotted
  With whites and blacks, in groups on show
  for sale,

Though rather more irregularly spotted :
  Some bought the jet, while others chose the
    pale.
It chanced amongst the other people lotted,
  A man of thirty, rather stout and hale,
With resolution in his dark gray eye,
Next Juan stood, till some might choose to
    buy.

XI.

He had an English look ; that is, was square
  In make, of a complexion white and ruddy,
Good teeth, with curling rather dark brown
    hair,
  And, it might be from thought, or toil, or
    study,
An open brow a little marked with care :
  One arm had on a bandage rather bloody ;
And there he stood with such *sang-froid*, that
    greater
Could scarce be shown even by a mere spec-
    tator.

XII.

But seeing at his elbow a mere lad,
  Of a high spirit evidently, though
At present weighed down by a doom which
    had
  O'erthrown even men, he soon began to
    show
A kind of blunt compassion for the sad
  Lot of so young a partner in the woe,
Which for himself he seemed to deem no
    worse
Than any other scrape, a thing of course.

XIII.

" My boy ! " — said he, " amidst this motley
    crew
Of Georgians, Russians, Nubians, and what
    not,
All ragamuffins differing but in hue,
  With whom it is our luck to cast our lot,
The only gentlemen seem I and you ;
  So let us be acquainted as we ought :
If I could yield you any consolation,
'Twould give me pleasure. — Pray, what is
    your nation ? "

XIV.

When Juan answered — ' Spanish ! " he re-
    plied,
" I thought, in fact, you could not be a
    Greek ;
Those servile dogs are not so proudly eyed :
  Fortune has played you here a pretty freak,
But that's her way with all men, till they're
    tried ;
  But never mind, — she'll turn, perhaps, next
    week ;
She has served me also much the same as
    you,
Except that I have found it nothing new."

XV.

" Pray, sir," said Juan, " if I may presume,
  What brought you here ? " — " Oh ! nothing
    very rare —
Six Tartars and a drag-chain —— " — " To
    this doom
  But what conducted, if the question's fair,
Is that which I would learn." — " I served for
    some
Months with the Russian army here and
    there,
And taking lately, by Suwarrow's bidding,
A town, was ta'en myself instead of Widdin."

XVI.

" Have you no friends ? " — " I had — but, by
  God's blessing,
Have not been troubled with them lately.
    Now
I have answered all your questions without
    pressing,
  And you an equal courtesy should show."
" Alas ! " said Juan, " 'twere a tale distressing,
  And long besides." — " Oh ! if 'tis really so,
You're right on both accounts to hold your
    tongue ;
A sad tale saddens doubly, when 'tis long.

XVII.

" But droop not : Fortune at your time of life,
  Although a female moderately fickle,
Will hardly leave you (as she's not your wife)
  For any length of days in such a pickle.
To strive, too, with our fate were such a strife
  As if the corn-sheaf should oppose the
    sickle :
Men are the sport of circumstances, when
The circumstances seem the sport of men."

*   *   *   *

XXV.

" But after all, what *is* our present state ?
  'Tis bad, and may be better — all men's lot :
Most men are slaves, none more so than the
    great,
  To their own whims and passions, and what
    not ;
Society itself, which should create
  Kindness, destroys what little we have got.
To feel for none is the true social art
Of the world's stoics — men without a heart."

XXVI.

Just now a black old neutral personage
  Of the third sex stept up, and peering over
The captives seemed to mark their looks and
    age,
  And capabilities, as to discover
If they were fitted for the purposed cage :
  No lady e'er is ogled by a lover,
Horse by a blackleg, broadcloth by a tailor,
Fee by a counsel, felon by a jailor

XXVII.

As is a slave by his intended bidder.
　'Tis pleasant purchasing our fellow-crea-
　　tures;
And all are to be sold, if you consider
　Their passions, and are dext'rous; some
　　by features
Are bought up, others by a warlike leader,
　Some by a place — as tend their years or
　　natures;
The most by ready cash — but all have prices,
From crowns to kicks, according to their vices.

XXVIII.

The eunuch having eyed them o'er with care,
　Turned to the merchant, and begun to bid
First but for one, and after for the pair;
　They haggled, wrangled, swore, too — so
　　they did!
As though they were in a mere Christian fair
　Cheapening an ox, an ass, a lamb, or kid;
So that their bargain sounded like a battle
For this superior yoke of human cattle.

XXIX.

At last they settled into simple grumbling,
　And pulling out reluctant purses, and
Turning each piece of silver o'er, and tumbling
　Some down, and weighing others in their
　　hand,
And by mistake sequins with paras jumbling,
　Until the sum was accurately scanned,
And then the merchant giving change, and
　signing
Receipts in full, began to think of dining.

*　　*　　*　　*　　*

XL.

The purchaser of Juan and acquaintance
　Bore off his bargains to a gilded boat,
Embarked himself and them, and off they
　went thence
　As fast as oars could pull and water float;
They looked like persons being led to sentence,
　Wondering what next, till the caïque was
　　brought
Up in a little creek below a wall
O'ertopped with cypresses, dark-green and tall.

XLI.

Here their conductor tapping on the wicket
　Of a small iron door, 'twas opened, and
He led them onward, first through a low
　thicket
　Flanked by large groves, which towered on
　　either hand:
They almost lost their way, and had to pick
　it —
　For night was closing ere they came to land.
The eunuch made a sign to those on board,
Who rowed off, leaving them without a word.

*　　*　　*　　*　　*

LIV.

As the black eunuch entered with his brace
　Of purchased Infidels, some raised their eyes
A moment without slackening from their pace;
　But those who sate, ne'er stirred in any wise:
One or two stared the captives in the face,
　Just as one views a horse to guess his price;
Some nodded to the negro from their station,
But no one troubled him with conversation.

LV.

He leads them through the hall, and, without
　stopping,
　On through a further range of goodly rooms,
Splendid but silent, save in *one*, where drop-
　ping,
　A marble fountain echoes through the
　　glooms
Of night, which robe the chamber, or where
　popping
　Some female head most curiously presumes
To thrust its black eyes through the door or
　lattice,
As wondering what the devil noise that is.

*　　*　　*　　*　　*

LXIV.

At last they reached a quarter most retired,
　Where echo woke as if from a long slumber;
Though full of all things which could be de-
　sired,
　One wondered what to do with such a
　　number
Of articles which nobody required;
　Here wealth had done its utmost to en-
　　cumber
With furniture an exquisite apartment,
Which puzzled Nature much to know what
　Art meant.

LXV.

It seemed, however, but to open on
　A range or suite of further chambers, which
Might lead to heaven knows where; but in
　this one
　The movables were prodigally rich:
Sofas 'twas half a sin to sit upon,
　So costly were they; carpets every stitch
Of workmanship so rare, they made you wish
You could glide o'er them like a golden fish.

LXVI.

The black, however, without hardly deigning
　A glance at that which wrapt the slaves in
　　wonder,
Trampled what they scarce trod for fear of
　staining,
　As if the milky way their feet was under
With all its stars; and with a stretch attaining
　A certain press or cupboard niched in yon-
　　der —

In that remote recess which you may see —
Or if you don't the fault is not in me, —

LXVII.

I wish to be perspicuous; and the black,
  I say, unlocking the recess, pulled forth
A quantity of clothes fit for the back
  Of any Mussulman, whate'er his worth ;
And of variety there was no lack —
  And yet, though I have said there was no
    dearth, —
He chose himself to point out what he thought
Most proper for the Christians he had bought.

LXVIII.

The suit he thought most suitable to each
  Was, for the elder and the stouter, first
A Candiote cloak, which to the knee might
    reach,
  And trousers not so tight that they would
    burst,
But such as fit an Asiatic breech ;
  A shawl, whose folds in Cashmere had been
    nurst,
Slippers of saffron, dagger rich and handy ;
In short, all things which form a Turkish
    Dandy.

*   *   *   *   *

LXXIII.

Baba eyed Juan, and said, " Be so good
  As dress yourself — " and pointed out a suit
In which a Princess with great pleasure would
  Array her limbs ; but Juan standing mute,
As not being in a masquerading mood,
  Gave it a slight kick with his Christian foot ;
And when the old negro told him to " Get
    ready,"
Replied, " Old gentleman, I'm not a lady."

LXXIV.

" What you may be, I neither know nor care,"
  Said Baba ; " but pray do as I desire."
I have no more time nor many words to spare."
  " At least," said Juan, " sure I may inquire
The cause of this odd travesty ? " — " Forbear,"
  Said Baba, " to be curious ; 'twill transpire,
No doubt, in proper place, and time, and sea-
    son :
I have no authority to tell the reason."

*   *   *   *   *

LXXX.

And now being femininely all arrayed,
  With some small aid from scissors, paint,
    and tweezers,
He looked in almost all respects a maid,
  And Baba smilingly exclaimed, " You see,
    sirs,
A perfect transformation here displayed ;
  And now, then, you must come along with
    me, sirs,

That is — the Lady : " clapping his hands
    twice,
Four blacks were at his elbow in a trice.

LXXXI.

" You, sir," said Baba, nodding to the one,
  " Will please to accompany those gentlemen
To supper ; but you, worthy Christian nun,
  Will follow me : no trifling, sir ; for when
I say a thing, it must at once be done.
  What fear you ? think you this a lion's den?
Why, 'tis a palace ; where the truly wise
Anticipate the Prophet's paradise.

*   *   *   *   *

XCV.

In this imperial hall, at distance lay
  Under a canopy, and there reclined
Quite in a confidential queenly way,
  A lady ; Baba stopped, and kneeling signed
To Juan, who though not much used to pray,
  Knelt down by instinct, wondering in his
    mind
What all this meant : while Baba bowed and
    bended
His head, until the ceremony ended.

XCVI.

The lady rising up with such an air
  As Venus rose with from the wave, on them
Bent like an antelope a Paphian pair
  Of eyes, which put out each surrounding
    gem ;
And raising up an arm as moonlight fair,
  She signed to Baba, who first kissed the hem
Of her deep purple robe, and speaking low,
Pointed to Juan, who remained below.

*   *   *   *   *

CVII.

The lady eyed him o'er and o'er, and bade
  Baba retire, which he obeyed in style,
As if well-used to the retreating trade ;
  And taking hints in good part all the while,
He whispered Juan not to be afraid,
  And looking on him with a sort of smile,
Took leave with such a face of satisfaction,
As good men wear who have done a virtuous
    action.

CVIII.

When he was gone, there was a sudden
    change :
  I know not what might be the lady's thought;
But o'er her bright brow flashed a tumult
    strange,
  And into her clear cheek the blood was
    brought,
Blood-red as sunset summer clouds which
    range
  The verge of Heaven ; and in her large
    eyes wrought

A mixture of sensations, might be scanned,
Of half-voluptuousness and half command.

CIX.

Her form had all the softness of her sex,
  Her features all the sweetness of the devil,
When he put on the cherub to perplex
  Eve, and paved (God knows how) the road
    to evil;
The sun himself was scarce more free from
    specks
  Than she from aught at which the eye could
    cavil;
Yet, somehow, there was something some-
    where wanting,
As if she rather *ordered* than was *granting.* —

CX.

Something imperial, or imperious, threw
  A chain o'er all she did; that is, a chain
Was thrown as 'twere about the neck of you, —
  And rapture's self will seem almost a pain
With aught which looks like despotism in
    view:
  Our souls at least are free, and 'tis in vain
We would against them make the flesh obey —
The spirit in the end will have its way.

CXI.

Her very smile was haughty, though so sweet;
  Her very nod was not an inclination;
There was a self-will in her small feet,
  As though they were quite conscious of her
    station —
They trod as upon necks; and to complete
  Her state (it is the custom of her nation),
A poniard decked her girdle, as the sign
She was a sultan's bride (thank Heaven not
    mine!).

CXII.

" To hear and to obey " had been from birth
  The law of all around her; to fulfil
All phantasies which yielded joy or mirth,
  Had been her slave's chief pleasure, as her
    will;
Her blood was high, her beauty scarce of earth:
  Judge, then, if her caprices e'er stood still;
Had she but been a Christian, I've a notion
We should have found out the "perpetual
    motion."

CXIII.

Whate'er she saw and coveted was brought;
  Whate'er she did *not* see, if she supposed
It might be seen, with diligence was sought,
  And when 'twas found straightway the bar-
    gain closed:
There was no end unto the things she bought,
  Nor to the trouble which her fancies caused;
Yet even her tyranny had such a grace,
The women pardoned all except her face.

CXIV.

Juan, the latest of her whims, had caught
  Her eye in passing on his way to sale;
She ordered him directly to be bought,
  And Baba, who had ne'er been known to fail
In any kind of mischief to be wrought,
  At all such auctions knew how to prevail:
She had no prudence, but he had; and this
Explains the garb which Juan took amiss.

CXV.

His youth and features favored the disguise,
  And, should you ask how she, a sultan's
    bride,
Could risk or compass such strange phanta-
    sies,
  This I must leave sultanas to decide:
Emperors are only husbands in wives' eyes,
  And kings and consorts oft are mystified,
As we may ascertain with due precision,
Some by experience, others by tradition.

CXVI.

But to the main point, where we have been
    tending: —
  She now conceived all difficulties past,
And deemed herself extremely condescending
  When, being made her property at last,
Without more preface, in her blue eyes blend-
    ing
  Passion and power, a glance on him she
    cast,
And merely saying, " Christian, canst thou
    love ?"
Conceived that phrase was quite enough to
    move.

* * * * *

CXXVII.

" Thou ask'st, if I can love ? be this the proof
  How much I *have* loved — that I love not
    thee!
In this vile garb, the distaff, web, and woof,
  Were fitter for me: Love is for the free!
I am not dazzled by this splendid roof;
  Whate'er thy power, and great it seems to
    be,
Heads bow, knees bend, eyes watch around a
    throne,
And hands obey — our hearts are still our
    own."

* * * * *

CXXXIV.

If I said fire flashed from Gulbeyaz' eyes,
  'Twere nothing — for her eyes flashed
    always fire;
Or said her cheeks assumed the deepest dyes,
  I should but bring disgrace upon the dyer,
So supernatural was her passion's rise;
  For ne'er till now she knew a checked
    desire :

Even ye who know what a checked woman is
(Enough, God knows!) would fall short of this.

CXXXV.

Her rage was but a minute's, and 'twas well —
A moment's more had slain her; but the while
It lasted 'twas like a short glimpse of hell :
Nought's more sublime than energetic bile,
Though horrible to see yet grand to tell,
Like ocean warring 'gainst a rocky isle ;
And the deep passions flashing though her form
Made her a beautiful embodied storm.

CXXXVI.

A vulgar tempest 'twere to a typhoon
To match a common fury with her rage,
And yet she did not want to reach the moon,
Like moderate Hotspur on the immortal page,
Her anger pitched into a lower tune,
Perhaps the fault of her soft sex and age —
Her wish was but to " kill, kill, kill," like Lear's,
And then her thirst for blood was quenched in tears.

*   *   *   *   *

CLV.

His Highness cast around his great black eyes,
And looking, as he always looked, perceived
Juan amongst the damsels in disguise,
At which he seemed no whit surprised nor grieved,
But just remarked with air sedate and wise,
While still a fluttering sigh Gulbeyaz heaved,
" I see you've bought another girl ; 'tis pity
That a mere Christian should be half so pretty."

CLVI.

This compliment, which drew all eyes upon
The new-bought virgin, made her blush and shake ;

Her comrades, also, thought themselves undone :
Oh ! Mahomet ! that his Majesty should take
Such notice of a giaour, while scarce to one
Of them his lips imperial ever spake !
There was a general whisper, toss, and wriggle,
But etiquette forbade them all to giggle.

CLVII.

The Turks do well to shut — at least, some times —
The women up — because, in sad reality,
Their chastity in these unhappy climes
Is not a thing of that astringent quality
Which in the North prevents precocious crimes,
And makes our snow less pure than our morality.
The sun, which yearly melts the polar ice,
Has quite the contrary effect on vice.

CLVIII.

Thus in the East they are extremely strict,
And *Wedlock* and a *Padlock* mean the same ;
Excepting only when the former's picked
It ne'er can be replaced in proper frame ;
Spoilt, as a pipe of claret is when pricked :
But then their own Polygamy's to blame ;
Why don't they knead two virtuous souls for life
Into that moral centaur, man and wife ?

CLIX.

Thus far our chronicle ; and now we pause
Though not for want of matter ; but 'tis time,
According to the ancient epic laws,
To slacken sail, and anchor with our rhyme.
Let this fifth canto meet with due applause,
The sixth shall have a touch of the sublime ;
Meanwhile, as Homer sometimes sleeps, perhaps
You'll pardon to my muse a few short naps.

CANTO THE SIXTH.

I.

" THERE is a tide in the affairs of men
Which, taken at the flood," — you know the rest,
And most of us have found it now and then ;
At least we think so, though but few have guessed

The moment, till too late to come again.
But no doubt every thing is for the best —
Of which the surest sign is in the end :
When things are at the worst they sometimes mend.

II.

There is a tide in the affairs of women
 Which, taken at the flood, leads — God
  knows where :
Those navigators must be able seamen
 Whose charts lay down its current to a hair ;
Not all the reveries of Jacob Behmen
 With its strange whirls and eddies can
  compare ;
Men with their heads reflect on this and that —
But women with their hearts on heaven knows
  what.

III.

And yet a headlong, headstrong, downright
  she,
 Young, beautiful, and daring — who would
  risk
A throne, the world, the universe, to be
 Beloved in her own way, and rather whisk
The stars from out the sky, than not be free
 As are the billows when the breeze is
  brisk —
Though such a she's a devil (if that there be
  one)
Yet she would make full many a Manichean.

IV.

Thrones, worlds, et cetera, are so oft upset
 By commonest ambition, that when passion
O'erthrows the same, we readily forget,
 Or at the least forgive, the loving rash one.
If Anthony be well remembered yet,
 'Tis not his conquests keep his name in
  fashion,
But Actium, lost for Cleopatra's eyes,
Outbalances all Cæsar's victories.

V.

He died at fifty for a queen of forty ;
 I wish their years had been fifteen and
  twenty,
For then wealth, kingdoms, worlds are but a
  sport — I
 Remember when, though I had no great
  plenty
Of worlds to lose, yet still, to pay my court, I
 Gave what I had — a heart : as the world
  went, I
Gave what was worth a world ; for worlds
  could never
Restore me those pure feelings, gone for ever.

VI.

'Twas the boy's "mite," and, like the "widow's,"
  may
 Perhaps be weighed hereafter, if not now ;
But whether such things do or do not weigh,
 All who have loved, or love, will still allow
Life has nought like it. God is love, they
  say,
 And Love's a God, or was before the brow

Of earth was wrinkled by the sins and tears
Of — but Chronology best knows the years.

VII.

We left our hero and third heroine in
 A kind of state more awkward than uncom-
  mon,
For gentlemen must sometimes risk their skin
 For that sad tempter, a forbidden woman :
Sultans too much abhor this sort of sin,
 And don't agree at all with the wise Roman,
Heroic, stoic Cato, the sententious,
Who lent his lady to his friend Hortensius.

VIII.

I know Gulbeyaz was extremely wrong ;
 I own it, I deplore it, I condemn it ;
But I detest all fiction even in song,
 And so must tell the truth, howe'er you
  blame it.
Her reason being weak, her passions strong,
 She thought that her lord's heart (even
  could she claim it)
Was scarce enough ; for he had fifty-nine
Years, and a fifteen-hundredth concubine.

  * * * * *

XCVII.

Meantime Gulbeyaz, when her king was gone,
 Retired into her boudoir, a sweet place
For love or breakfast ; private, pleasing, lone,
 And rich with all contrivances which grace
Those gay recesses : — many a precious stone
 Sparkled along its roof, and many a vase
Of porcelain held in the fettered flowers,
Those captive soothers of a captive's hours.

XCVIII.

Mother of pearl, and porphyry, and marble,
 Vied with each other on this costly spot ;
And singing birds without were heard to
  warble ;
 And the stained glass which lighted this fair
  grot
Varied each ray ; — but all descriptions garble
 The true effect, and so we had better not
Be too minute ; an outline is the best, —
A lively reader's fancy does the rest.

XCIX.

And here she summoned Baba, and required
 Don Juan at his hands, and information
Of what had passed since all the slaves retired,
 And whether he had occupied their station ;
If matters had been managed as desired,
 And his disguise with due consideration
Kept up ; and above all, the where and how
He had passed the night, was what she wished
  to know.

C.

Baba, with some embarrassment, replied
 To this long catechism of questions, asked

More easily than answered, — that he had tried
His best to obey in what he had been tasked;
But there seemed something that he wished
 to hide,
Which hesitation more betrayed than
 masked;
He scratched his ear, the infallible resource
To which embarrassed people have recourse.

CI.

Gulbeyaz was no model of true patience,
 Nor much disposed to wait in word or deed;
She liked quick answers in all conversations;
 And when she saw him stumbling like a
 steed
In his replies, she puzzled him for fresh ones;
 And as his speech grew still more broken-
 kneed,
Her cheek began to flush, her eyes to sparkle,
And her proud brow's blue veins to swell and
 darkle.

CII.

When Baba saw these symptoms, which he
 knew
 To bode him no great good, he deprecated
Her anger, and beseeched she'd hear him
 through —
 He could not help the thing which he re-
 lated:
Then out it came at length, that to Dudù
 Juan was given in charge, as hath been
 stated;
But not by Baba's fault, he said, and swore on
The holy camel's hump, besides the Koran.

CIII.

The chief dame of the Oda, upon whom
 The discipline of the whole haram bore
As soon as they reëntered their own room,
 For Baba's function stopt short at the door,
Had settled all; nor could he then presume
 (The aforesaid Baba) just then to do more,
Without exciting such suspicion as
Might make the matter still worse than it was.

CIV.

He hoped, indeed he thought, he could be sure
 Juan had not betrayed himself; in fact
'Twas certain that his conduct had been pure,
 Because a foolish or imprudent act
Would not alone have made him insecure,
 But ended in his being found out and *sacked*,
And thrown into the sea. — Thus Baba spoke
Of all save Dudu's dream, which was no joke.

CV.

This he discreetly kept in the back ground,
 And talked away — and might have talked
 till now
For any further answer that he found,
 So deep an anguish wrung Gulbeyaz' brow;

Her cheek turned ashes, ears rung, brain
 whirled round,
 As if she had received a sudden blow,
And the heart's dew of pain sprang fast and
 chilly
O'er her fair front, like Morning's on a lily.

CVI.

Although she was not of the fainting sort,
 Baba thought she would faint, but there he
 erred —
It was but a convulsion, which though short
 Can never be described; we all have heard,
And some of us have felt thus " *all amort*,"
 When things beyond the common have oc-
 curred; —
Gulbeyaz proved in that deep agony
What she could ne'er express — then how
 should I ?

CVII.

She stood a moment as a Pythoness
 Stands on her tripod, agonized, and full
Of inspiration gathered from distress,
 When all the heart-strings like wild horses
 pull
The heart asunder; — then, as more or less
 Their speed abated or their strength grew
 dull,
She sunk down on her seat by slow degrees,
And bowed her throbbing head o'er trem-
 bling knees.

CVIII.

Her face declined and was unseen; her hair
 Fell in long tresses like the weeping willow,
Sweeping the marble underneath her chair,
 Or rather sofa, (for it was all pillow,
A low soft ottoman,) and black despair
 Stirred up and down her bosom like a bil-
 low,
Which rushes to some shore whose shingles
 check
Its further course, but must receive its wreck.

CIX.

Her head hung down, and her long hair in
 stooping
 Concealed her features better than a veil;
And one hand o'er the ottoman lay drooping,
 White, waxen, and as alabaster pale:
Would that I were a painter! to be grouping
 All that a poet drags into detail!
Oh that my words were colors! but their tints
May serve perhaps as outlines or slight hints.

CX.

Baba, who knew by experience when to talk
 And when to hold his tongue, now held it till
This passion might blow o'er, nor dared to balk
 Gulbeyaz' taciturn or speaking will.
At length she rose up, and began to walk
 Slowly along the room, but silent still,

And her brow cleared, but not her troubled eye;
The wind was down, but still the sea ran high.

CXI.

She stopped, and raised her head to speak
— but paused,
And then moved on again with rapid pace;
Then slackened it, which is the march most
    caused
By deep emotion: — you may sometimes
    trace
A feeling in each footstep, as disclosed
By Sallust in his Catiline, who, chased
By all the demons of all passions, showed
Their work even by the way in which he trode.

CXII.

Gulbeyaz stopped and beckoned Baba: —
    " Slave!
Bring the two slaves! " she said in a low tone,
But one which Baba did not like to brave,
    And yet he shuddered, and seemed rather
    prone
To prove reluctant, and begged leave to crave
    (Though he well knew the meaning) to be
    shown
What slaves her highness wished to indicate,
For fear of any error, like the late.

CXIII.

'The Georgian and her paramour," replied
    The imperial bride — and added, " Let the
    boat
Be ready by the secret portal's side:
    You know the rest." The words stuck in her
    throat,
Despite her injured love and fiery pride;
    And of this Baba willingly took note,
And begged by every hair of Mahomet's
    beard
She would revoke the order he had heard.

CXIV.

'To hear is to obey," he said; " but still,
    Sultana, think upon the consequence:
It is not that I shall not all fulfil
    Your orders, even in their severest sense;
But such precipitation may end ill,
    Even at your own imperative expense:
I do not mean destruction and exposure,
In case of any premature disclosure;

CXV.

But your own feelings. Even should all the
    rest
Be hidden by the rolling waves, which hide
Already many a once love-beaten breast
    Deep in the caverns of the deadly tide —
You love this boyish, new, seraglio guest,
    And if this violent remedy be tried —

Excuse my freedom, when I here assure you,
That killing him is not the way to cure you."

CXVI.

" What dost thou know of love or feeling ? —
    Wretch!
Begone! " she cried, with kindling eyes —
    " and do
My bidding! " Baba vanished, for to stretch
    His own remonstrance further he well knew
Might end in acting as his own " Jack Ketch ; "
    And though he wished extremely to get
    through
This awkward business without harm to others,
He still preferred his own neck to another's.

CXVII.

Away he went then upon his commission,
    Growling and grumbling in good Turkish
    phrase
Against all women of whate'er condition,
    Especially sultanas and their ways;
Their obstinacy, pride, and indecision,
    Their never knowing their own mind two
    days,
The trouble that they gave, their immorality,
Which made him daily bless his own neu-
    trality.

CXVIII.

And then he called his brethren to his aid,
    And sent one on a summons to the pair,
That they must instantly be well arrayed,
    And above all be combed even to a hair,
And brought before the empress, who had
    made
Inquiries after them with kindest care:
At which Dudù looked strange, and Juan silly;
But go they must at once, and will I — nill I.

CXIX.

And here I leave them at their preparation
    For the imperial presence, wherein whether
Gulbeyaz showed them both commiseration,
    Or got rid of the parties altogether,
Like other angry ladies of her nation, —
    Are things the turning of a hair or feather
May settle; but far be't from me to anticipate
In what way feminine caprice may dissipate.

CXX.

I leave them for the present with good wishes,
    Though doubts of their well doing, to ar-
    range
Another part of history; for the dishes
    Of this our banquet we must sometimes
    change;
And trusting Juan may escape the fishes,
    Although his situation now seems strange,
And scarce secure, as such digressions *are* fair,
The Muse will take a little touch at warfare.

CANTO THE SEVENTH.

I.

O LOVE! O Glory! what are ye who fly
　Around us ever, rarely to alight?
There's not a meteor in the polar sky
　Of such transcendent and more fleeting
　　flight.
Chill, and chained to cold earth, we lift on high
　Our eyes in search of either lovely light;
A thousand and a thousand colors they
Assume, then leave us on our freezing way.

II.

And such as they are, such my present tale is,
　A non-descript and ever-varying rhyme,
A versified Aurora Borealis,
　Which flashes o'er a waste and icy clime.
When we know what all are, we must bewail
　us,
　But ne'ertheless I hope it is no crime
To laugh at *all* things — for I wish to know
What, after *all*, are *all* things — but a *show?*

III.

They accuse me — *Me* — the present writer of
　The present poem — of — I know not
　　what —
A tendency to under-rate and scoff
　At human power and virtue, and all that;
And this they say in language rather rough.
　Good God! I wonder what they would be
　　at!
I say no more than has been said in Dante's
Verse, and by Solomon and Cervantes;

IV.

By Swift, by Machiavel, by Rochefoucault,
　By Fénélon, by Luther, and by Plato;
By Tillotson, and Wesley, and Rousseau,
　Who knew this life was not worth a potato.
'Tis not their fault, nor mine, if this be so —
　For my part, I pretend not to be Cato,
Nor even Diogenes. — We live and die,
But which is best, you know no more than I.

V.

Socrates said, our only knowledge was
　"To know that nothing could be known;"
　　a pleasant
Science enough, which levels to an ass
　Each man of wisdom, future, past, or present.
Newton (that proverb of the mind), alas!
　Declared, with all his grand discoveries re-
　　cent,
That he himself felt only "like a youth
Picking up shells by the great ocean — Truth."

VI.

Ecclesiastes said, "that all is vanity" —
　Most modern preachers say the same, or
　　show it
By their examples of true Christianity:
　In short, all know, or very soon may know
　　it;
And in this scene of all-confessed inanity,
　By saint, by sage, by preacher, and by poet,
Must I restrain me, through the fear of strife,
From holding up the nothingness of life?

VII.

Dogs, or men! — for I flatter you in saying
　That ye are dogs — your betters far — ye
　　may
Read, or read not, what I am now essaying
　To show ye what ye are in every way.
As little as the moon stops for the baying
　Of wolves, will the bright muse withdraw
　　one ray
From out her skies — then howl your idle
　wrath!
While she still silvers o'er your gloomy path.

VIII.

"Fierce loves and faithless wars" — I am not
　　sure
　If this be the right reading — 'tis no matter;
The fact's about the same, I am secure;
　I sing them both, and am about to batter
A town which did a famous siege endure,
　And was beleaguered both by land and
　　water
By Souvaroff, or Anglicè Suwarrow,
Who loved blood as an alderman loves mar-
　row.

IX.

The fortress is called Ismail, and is placed
　Upon the Danube's left branch and left
　　bank,
With buildings in the Oriental taste,
　But still a fortress of the foremost rank,
Or was at least, unless 'tis since defaced,
　Which with your conquerors is a common
　　prank.
It stands some eighty versts from the high
　sea,
And measures round of toises thousands three.

X.

Within the extent of this fortification
　A borough is comprised along the height
Upon the left, which from its loftier station
　Commands the city, and upon its site
A Greek had raised around this elevation

A quantity of palisades *upright*,
  So placed as to *impede* the fire of those
Who held the place, and to *assist* the foe's.

XI.

This circumstance may serve to give a notion
  Of the high talents of this new Vauban:
But the town ditch below was deep as ocean,
  The rampart higher than you'd wish to hang:
But then there was a great want of precaution
  (Prithee, excuse this engineering slang),
Nor work advanced, nor covered way was there,
To hint at least " Here is no thoroughfare."

XII.

But a stone bastion, with a narrow gorge,
  And walls as thick as most skulls born as yet:
Two batteries, cap-à-pie, as our St. George,
  Case-mated one, and t'other "à barbette,"
Of Danube's bank took formidable charge;
  While two and twenty cannon duly set
Rose over the town's right side, in bristling tier,
Forty feet high, upon a cavalier

XIII.

But from the river the town's open quite,
  Because the Turks could never be persuaded
A Russian vessel e'er would heave in sight;
  And such their creed was, till they were invaded,
When it grew rather late to set things right.
  But as the Danube could not well be waded,
They looked upon the Muscovite flotilla,
And only shouted, "Allah!" and "Bis Millah!"

XIV.

The Russians now were ready to attack;
  But oh, ye goddesses of war and glory!
How shall I spell the name of each Cossacque
  Who were immortal, could one tell their story?
Alas! what to their memory can lack?
  Achilles' self was not more grim and gory
Than thousands of this new and polished nation,
Whose names want nothing but — pronunciation.

    *   *   *   *   *

XXXVIII.

While things were in abeyance, Ribas sent
  A courier to the prince, and he succeeded
In ordering matters after his own bent;
  I cannot tell the way in which he pleaded,
But shortly he had cause to be content.
  In the mean time, the batteries proceeded,

And fourscore cannon on the Danube's border
Were briskly fired and answered in due order.

XXXIX.

But on the thirteenth, when already part
  Of the troops were embarked, the siege to raise,
A courier on the spur inspired new heart
  Into all panters for newspaper praise,
As well as dilettanti in war's art,
  By his despatches couched in pithy phrase;
Announcing the appointment of that lover of
Battles to the command, Field-Marshal Souvaroff.

XL.

The letter of the prince to the same marshal
  Was worthy of a Spartan, had the cause
Been one to which a good heart could be partial —
  Defence of freedom, country, or of laws;
But as it was mere lust of power to o'er-arch all
  With its proud brow, it merits slight applause,
Save for its style, which said, all in a trice,
" You will take Ismail at whatever price."

    *   *   *   *

XLIX.

The whole camp rung with joy; you would have thought
  That they were going to a marriage feast
(This metaphor, I think, holds good as aught,
  Since there is discord after both at least):
There was not now a luggage boy but sought
  Danger and spoil with ardor much increased;
And why? because a little — odd — old man,
Stript to his shirt, was come to lead the van.

L.

But so it was; and every preparation
  Was made with all alacrity: the first
Detachment of three columns took its station,
  And waited but the signal's voice to burst
Upon the foe: the second's ordination
  Was also in three columns, with a thirst
For glory gaping o'er a sea of slaughter:
The third, in columns two, attacked by water.

    *   *   *   *

LVI.

The day before the assault, while upon drill —
  For this great conqueror played the corporal —
Some Cossacques, hovering like hawks round a hill,
  Had met a party towards the twilight's fall,
One of whom spoke their tongue — or well or ill,
  'Twas much that he was understood at all;

But whether from his voice, or speech, or manner,
They found that he had fought beneath their
    banner.

LVII.

Whereon immediately at his request
    They brought him and his comrades to
        headquarters;
Their dress was Moslem, but you might have
        guessed
    That these were merely masquerading Tartars,
And that beneath each Turkish-fashioned vest
    Lurked Christianity; which sometimes barters
Her inward grace for outward show, and makes
It difficult to shun some strange mistakes.

LVIII.

Suwarrow, who was standing in his shirt
    Before a company of Calmucks, drilling,
Exclaiming, fooling, swearing at the inert,
    And lecturing on the noble art of killing,—
For deeming human clay but common dirt,
    This great philosopher was thus instilling
His maxims, which to martial comprehension
Proved death in battle equal to a pension;—

LIX.

Suwarrow, when he saw this company
    Of Cossacques and their prey, turned round
        and cast
Upon them his slow brow and piercing eye:—
    "Whence come ye?"—"From Constantinople last,
Captives just now escaped," was the reply.
    "What are ye?"—"What you see us."
        Briefly passed
This dialogue; for he who answered knew
To whom he spoke, and made his words but few.

LX.

"Your names?"—"Mine's Johnson, and my
        comrade's Juan;
The other two are women, and the third
Is neither man nor woman." The chief threw on
    The party a slight glance, then said, "I have
        heard
Your name before, the second is a new one:
    To bring the other three here was absurd:
But let that pass:—I think I have heard your
        name
In the Nikolaiew regiment?"—"The same."

LXI.

"You served at Widdin?"—"Yes."—"You
        led the attack?"
    "I did."—"What next?"—"I really hardly
        know."
"You were the first i' the breach?"—"I was
    not slack

At least to follow those who might be so.
"What followed?"—"A shot laid me on my
        back,
    And I became a prisoner to the foe."
"You shall have vengeance, for the town surrounded
Is twice as strong as that where you were
        wounded."

LXII.

"Where will you serve?"—"Where'er you
        please."—"I know
You like to be the hope of the forlorn,
And doubtless would be foremost on the foe
    After the hardships you've already borne.
And this young fellow—say what can he do?
    He with the beardless chin and garments
        torn?"
"Why, general, if he hath no greater fault
In war than love, he had better lead the
        assault."

LXIII.

"He shall if that he dare." Here Juan bowed
    Low as the compliment deserved. Suwarrow
Continued: "Your old regiment's allowed,
    By special providence, to lead to-morrow,
Or it may be to-night, the assault: I have
        vowed
    To several saints, that shortly plough or
        harrow
Shall pass o'er what was Ismail, and its tusk
Be unimpeded by the proudest mosque.

LXIV.

"So now, my lads, for glory!"—Here he
        turned
    And drilled away in the most classic Russian,
Until each high, heroic bosom burned
    For cash and conquest, as if from a cushion
A preacher had held forth (who nobly spurned
    All earthly goods save tithes) and bade
        them push on
To slay the Pagans who resisted, battering
The armies of the Christian Empress Catherine.

LXV.

Johnson, who knew by this long colloquy
    Himself a favorite, ventured to address
Suwarrow, though engaged with accents high
    In his resumed amusement. "I confess
My debt in being thus allowed to die
    Among the foremost; but if you'd express
Explicitly our several posts, my friend
And self would know what duty to attend."

LXVI.

"Right! I was busy, and forgot. Why, you
    Will join your former regiment, which
        should be
Now under arms. Ho! Katskoff, take him
    to—

(Here he called up a Polish orderly)
His post, I mean the regiment Nikolaiew:
  The stranger stripling may remain with me;
He's a fine boy. The women may be sent
To the other baggage, or to the sick tent."

* * * * *

LXX.

He said,—and in the kindest Calmuck tone,—
  "Why, Johnson, what the devil do you
    mean
By bringing women here? They shall be
    shown
All the attention possible, and seen
In safety to the wagons, where alone
  In fact they can be safe. You should have
    been
Aware this kind of baggage never thrives:
Save wed a year, I hate recruits with wives."

LXXI.

"May it please your excellency," thus replied
  Our British friend, "these are the wives of
    others,
And not our own. I am too qualified
  By service with my military brothers
To break the rules by bringing one's own
    bride
  Into a camp: I know that nought so bothers
The hearts of the heroic on a charge,
As leaving a small family at large.

LXXII.

"But these are but two Turkish ladies, who
  With their attendant aided our escape,
And afterwards accompanied us through
  A thousand perils in this dubious shape.
To me this kind of life is not so new;
  To them, poor things, it is an awkward
    scrape.
I therefore, if you wish me to fight freely,
Request that they may both be used genteelly."

* * * * *

LXXVI.

And then with tears, and sighs, and some
    slight kisses,
  They parted for the present—these to await,
According to the artillery's hits or misses,
  What sages call Chance, Providence, or
    Fate—
(Uncertainty is one of many blisses,
  A mortgage on Humanity's estate)—
While their beloved friends began to arm,
To burn a town which never did them harm.

* * * * *

LXXX.

Oh, thou eternal Homer! I have now
  To paint a siege, wherein more men were
    slain

With deadlier engines and a speedier blow,
  Than in my Greek gazette of that campaign;
And yet, like all men else, I must allow,
  To vie with thee would be about as vain
As for a brook to cope with ocean's flood;
But still we moderns equal you in blood;

LXXXI.

If not in poetry, at least in fact;
  And fact is truth, the grand desideratum!
Of which, howe'er the Muse describes each
    act,
  There should be ne'ertheless a slight sub-
    stratum.
But now the town is going to be attacked;
  Great deeds are doing—how shall I relate
    'em?
Souls of immortal generals! Phœbus watches
To color up his rays from your despatches.

LXXXII.

Oh, ye great bulletins of Bonaparte!
  Oh, ye less grand long lists of killed and
    wounded!
Shade of Leonidas, who fought so hearty,
  When my poor Greece was once, as now,
    surrounded!
Oh, Cæsar's Commentaries! now impart, ye
  Shadows of glory! (lest I be confounded)
A portion of your fading twilight hues,
So beautiful, so fleeting, to the Muse.

LXXXIII.

When I call "fading" martial immortality,
  I mean, that every age and every year,
And almost every day in sad reality,
  Some sucking hero is compelled to rear,
Who, when we come to sum up the totality
  Of deeds to human happiness most dear,
Turns out to be a butcher in great business,
Afflicting young folks with a sort of dizziness.

LXXXIV.

Medals, rank, ribands, lace, embroidery,
    scarlet,
  Are things immortal to immortal man,
As purple to the Babylonian harlot:
  An uniform to boys is like a fan
To women; there is scarce a crimson varlet
  But deems himself the first in Glory's van.
But Glory's glory; and if you would find
What that is—ask the pig who sees the wind!

LXXXV.

At least *he feels it*, and some say he *sees*,
  Because he runs before it like a pig;
Or, if that simple sentence should displease,
  Say, that he scuds before it like a brig,
A schooner, or—but it is time to ease
  This Canto, ere my Muse perceives fatigue.
The next shall ring a peal to shake all people,
Like a bob-major from a village steeple.

LXXXVI.

Hark! through the silence of the cold, dull
  night,
  The hum of armies gathering rank on rank!
Lo! dusky masses steal in dubious sight
  Along the leaguered wall and bristling bank
Of the armed river, while with straggling light
  The stars peep through the vapors dim and
  dank,
,Which curl in curious wreaths :—how soon
  the smoke
Of Hell shall pall them in a deeper cloak!

LXXXVII.

Here pause we for the present—as even then
  That awful pause, dividing life from death,
Struck for an instant on the hearts of men,
  Thousands of whom were drawing their
  last breath!
A moment—and all will be life again!
  The march! the charge! the shouts of
  either faith!
Hurra! and Allah! and—one moment
  more—
The death-cry drowning in the battle's roar.

CANTO THE EIGHTH.

I.

OH blood and thunder! and oh blood and
  wounds!
  These are but vulgar oaths, as you may
  deem,
Too gentle reader! and most shocking sounds:
  And so they are; yet thus is Glory's dream
Unriddled, and as my true Muse expounds
  At present such things, since they are her
  theme,
So be they her inspirers! Call them Mars,
Bellona, what you will—they mean but wars.

II.

All was prepared—the fire, the sword, the men
  To wield them in their terrible array.
The army, like a lion from his den,
  Marched forth with nerve and sinews bent
  to slay,—
A human Hydra, issuing from its fen
  To breathe destruction on its winding way,
Whose heads were heroes, which cut off in
  vain
Immediately in others grew again.

III.

History can only take things in the gross;
  But could we know them in detail, perchance
In balancing the profit and the loss,
  War's merit it by no means might enhance,
To waste so much gold for a little dross,
  As hath been done, mere conquest to ad-
  vance.
The drying up a single tear has more
Of honest fame, than shedding seas of gore.

IV.

And why?—because it brings self-approba-
  tion;
  Whereas the other, after all its glare,
Shouts, bridges, arches, pensions from a na-
  tion,

Which (it may be) has not much left to
  spare,
A higher title, or a loftier station,
  Though they may make Corruption gape
  or stare,
Yet, in the end, except in Freedom's battles,
Are nothing but a child of Murder's rattles.

V.

And such they are—and such they will be
  found;
  Not so Leonidas and Washington,
Whose every battle-field is holy ground,
  Which breathes of nations saved, not worlds
  undone.
How sweetly on the ear such echoes sound!
  While the mere victor's may appal or stun
The servile and the vain, such names will be
A watchword till the future shall be free.

VI.

The night was dark, and the thick mist allowed
  Nought to be seen save the artillery's flame,
Which arched the horizon like a fiery cloud,
  And in the Danube's waters shone the
  same—
A mirrored hell! the volleying roar, and loud
  Long booming of each peal on peal, o'er-
  came
The ear far more than thunder; for heaven's
  flashes,
Spare, or smite rarely—man's make millions
  ashes!

VII.

The column ordered on the assault scarce
  passed
  Beyond the Russian batteries a few toises,
When up the bristling Moslem rose at last,
  Answering the Christian thunders with like
  voices:
Then one vast fire, air, earth, and stream em-
  braced,

Which rocked as 'twere beneath the mighty
  noises;
While the whole rampart blazed like Etna,
  when
The restless Titan hiccups in his den.

VIII.

And one enormous shout of " Allah!" rose
  In the same moment, loud as even the roar
Of war's most mortal engines, to their foes
  Hurling defiance: city, stream, and shore
Resounded "Allah!" and the clouds which
  close
With thick'ning canopy the conflict o'er,
Vibrate to the Eternal name. Hark! through
All sounds it pierceth "Allah! Allah! Hu!"

*   *   *   *   *

XIX.

Juan and Johnson joined a certain corps,
  And fought away with might and main, not
    knowing
The way which they had never trod before,
  And still less guessing where they might be
    going;
But on they marched, dead bodies trampling
  o'er,
  Firing, and thrusting, slashing, sweating,
    glowing,
But fighting thoughtlessly enough to win,
To their *two* selves, *one* whole bright bulletin.

XX.

Thus on they wallowed in the bloody mire
  Of dead and dying thousands,—sometimes
    gaining
A yard or two of ground, which brought them
  nigher
  To some odd angle for which all were strain-
    ing;
At other times, repulsed by the close fire,
  Which really poured as if all hell were raining
Instead of heaven, they stumbled backwards
  o'er
A wounded comrade, sprawling in his gore.

XXI.

Though 'twas Don Juan's first of fields, and
  though
  The nightly muster and the silent march
In the chill dark, when courage does not glow
  So much as under a triumphal arch,
Perhaps might make him shiver, yawn, or
  throw
  A glance on the dull clouds (as thick as
    starch,
Which stiffened heaven) as if he wished for
  day;—
Yet for all this he did not run away.

*   *   *   *   *

XXVII.

Juan, by some strange chance, which oft divides
  Warrior from warrior in their grim career,
Like chastest wives from constant husbands'
  sides
  Just at the close of the first bridal year,
By one of those odd turns of Fortune's tides,
  Was on a sudden rather puzzled here,
When, after a good deal of heavy firing,
He found himself alone, and friends retiring.

*   *   *   *   *

XXXII.

Perceiving nor commander nor commanded,
  And left at large, like a young heir, to make
His way to—where he knew not—single
  handed
  As travellers follow over bog and brake
An "ignis fatuus;" or as sailors stranded
  Unto the nearest hut themselves betake;
So Juan, following honor and his nose,
Rushed where the thickest fire announced
  most foes.

*   *   *   *   *

XXXIV.

And as he rushed along, it came to pass he
  Fell in with what was late the second column,
Under the orders of the General Lascy,
  But now reduced, as is a bulky volume
Into an elegant extract (much less massy)
  Of heroism, and took his place with solemn
Air 'midst the rest, who kept their valiant
  faces
And levelled weapons still against the glacis.

XXXV.

Just at this crisis up came Johnson too;
  Who had " retreated," as the phrase is when
Men run away much rather than go through
  Destruction's jaws into the devil's den;
But Johnson was a clever fellow, who
  Knew when and how " to cut and come
    again,"
And never ran away, except when running
Was nothing but a valorous kind of cunning.

XXXVI.

And so, when all his corps were dead or
  dying,
  Except Don Juan, a mere novice, whose
More virgin valor never dreamt of flying,
  From ignorance of danger, which indues
Its votaries, like innocence relying
  On its own strength, with careless nerves and
    thews,—
Johnson retired a little, just to rally
Those who catch cold in " shadows of Death's
  valley."

XXXVII.

And there, a little sheltered from the shot,
  Which rained from bastion, battery, parapet,
Rampart, wall, casement, house — for there
    was not
  In this extensive city, sore beset
By Christian soldiery, a single spot
  Which did not combat like the devil, as
    yet, —
He found a number of Chasseurs, all scattered
By the resistance of the chase they battered.

XXXVIII.

And these he called on; and, what's strange,
  · they came
Unto his call, unlike "the spirits from
The vasty deep," to whom you may exclaim,
  Says Hotspur, long ere they will leave their
    home.
Their reasons were uncertainty, or shame
  At shrinking from a bullet or a bomb,
And that odd impulse, which in wars or creeds
Makes men, like cattle, follow him who leads.

*   *   *   *   *

XLIII.

They fell as thick as harvests beneath hail,
  Grass before scythes, or corn below the
    sickle,
Proving that trite old truth, that life's as frail
  As any other boon for which men stickle.
The Turkish batteries thrashed them like a flail
  Or a good boxer, into a sad pickle.
Putting the very bravest, who were knocked
Upon the head, before their guns were cocked.

XLIV.

The Turks behind the traverses and flanks
  Of the next bastion, fired away like devils,
And swept, as gales sweep foam away, whole
    ranks:
  However, Heaven knows how, the Fate who
    levels
Towns, nations, worlds, in her revolving
    pranks,
  So ordered it, amidst these sulphury revels,
That Johnson and some few who had not
    scampered,
Reached the interior talus of the rampart.

XLV.

First one or two, then five, six, and a dozen
  Came mounting quickly up, for it was now
All neck or nothing, as, like pitch or rosin,
  Flame was showered forth above, as well's
    below,
So that you scarce could say who best had
    chosen,
  The gentlemen that were the first to show
Their martial faces on the parapet,
Or those who thought it brave to wait as yet.

XLVI.

But those who scaled, found out that their ad
    vance
  Was favored by an accident or blunder:
The Greek or Turkish Cohorn's ignorance
  Had pallisadoed in a way you'd wonder
To see in forts of Netherlands or France —
  (Though these to our Gibraltar must knock
    under) —
Right in the middle of the parapet
Just named, these palisades were primly set.

*   *   *   *   *

XLVIII.

Among the first, — I will not say the *first,*
  For such precedence upon such occasions
Will oftentimes make deadly quarrels burst
  Out between friends as well as allied nations:
The Briton must be bold who really durst
  Put to such trial John Bull's partial pa-
    tience,
As say that Wellington at Waterloo
Was beaten, — though the Prussians say so
    too.

*   *   *   *   *

LII.

But to continue : — I say not *the* first,
  But of the first, our little friend Don Juan
Walked o'er the walls of Ismail, as if nursed
  Amidst such scenes — though this was quite
    a new one
To him, and I should hope to *most.* The
    thirst   ♪
  Of glory, which so pierces through and
    through one,
Pervaded him — although a generous creature,
As warm in heart as feminine in feature.

*   *   *   *   *

LVI.

The General Lascy, who had been hard
    pressed,
  Seeing arrive an aid so opportune
As were some hundred youngsters all abreast,
  Who came as if just dropped down from
    the moon,
To Juan, who was nearest him, addressed
  His thanks, and hopes to take the city soon,
Not reckoning him to be a "base Bezonian,"
(As Pistol calls it) but a young Livonian.

*   *   *   *   *

LX.

The town was entered.   Oh eternity! —
  "God made the country, and man made
    the town,"
So Cowper says — and I begin to be
  Of his opinion, when I see cast down
Rome, Babylon, Tyre, Carthage, Nineveh,
  All walls men know, and many never known;

And pondering on the present and the past,
To deem the woods shall be our home at
    last : —

LXI.

Of all men, saving Sylla the man-slayer,
    Who passes for in life and death most
    lucky,
Of the great names which in our faces stare,
    The general Boone, back-woodsman of
    Kentucky
Was happiest amongst mortals anywhere ;
    For killing nothing but a bear or buck, he
Enjoyed the lonely, vigorous, harmless days
Of his old age in wilds of deepest maze.

LXII.

Crime came not near him — she is not the
    child
    Of solitude ; Health shrank not from him —
    for
Her home is in the rarely trodden wild,
    Where if men seek her not, and death be
    more
Their choice than life, forgive them, as be-
    guiled
    By habit to what their own hearts abhor —
In cities caged. The present case in point I
Cite is, that Boone lived hunting up to ninety ;

LXIII.

And what's still stranger, left behind a name
    For which men vainly decimate the throng,
Not only famous, but of that *good* fame,
    · Without which glory's but a tavern song —
Simple, serene, the antipodes of shame,
    Which hate nor envy e'er could tinge with
    wrong.
An active hermit, even in age the child
Of Nature, or the man of Ross run wild.

LXIV.

'Tis true he shrank from men even of his
    nation,
    When they built up unto his darling trees, —
He moved some hundred miles off, for a
    station
    Where there were fewer houses and more
    ease ;
The inconvenience of civilization
    Is, that you neither can be pleased nor
    please ;
But where he met the individual man,
He showed himself as kind as mortal can.

LXV.

He was not all alone : around him grew
    A sylvan tribe of children of the chase,
Whose young, unwakened world was ever
    new,
    Nor sword nor sorrow yet had left a trace
On her unwrinkled brow, nor could you view

A frown on Nature's or on human face ; —
The free-born forest found and kept them free,
And fresh as is a torrent or a tree.

LXVI.

And tall, and strong, and swift of foot were
    they,
    Beyond the dwarfing city's pale abortions,
Because their thoughts had never been the
    prey
    Of care or gain : the green woods were their
    portions ;
No sinking spirits told them they grew gray,
    No fashion made them apes of her dis-
    tortions ;
Simple they were, not savage ; and their rifles,
Though very true, were not yet used for trifles.

LXVII.

Motion was in their days, rest in their slum-
    bers,
    And cheerfulness the handmaid of their toil ;
Nor yet too many nor too few their numbers,
    Corruption could not make their hearts her
    soil ;
The lust which stings, the splendor which en-
    cumbers,
    With the free foresters divide no spoil ;
Serene, not sullen, were the solitudes
Of this unsighing people of the woods.

LXVIII.

So much for Nature : — by way of variety,
    Now back to thy great joys, Civilization !
And the sweet consequence of large society,
    War, pestilence, the despot's desolation,
The kingly scourge, the lust of notoriety,
    The millions slain by soldiers for their ra-
    tion,
The scenes like Catherine's boudoir at three-
    score,
With Ismail's storm to soften it the more.

LXIX.

The town was entered : first one column made
    Its sanguinary way good — then another ;
The reeking bayonet and the flashing blade
    Clashed 'gainst the scimitar, and babe and
    mother
With distant shrieks were heard Heaven to
    upbraid : —
    Still closer sulphury clouds began to smother
The breath of morn and man, where foot by
    foot
The maddened Turks their city still dispute.

*   *   *   *   *

LXXXVII.

The city's taken, but not rendered ! — No !
    There's not a Moslem that hath yielded
    sword :

The blood may gush out, as the Danube's flow
  Rolls by the city wall; but deed nor word
Acknowledge aught of dread of death or foe:
  In vain the yell of victory is roared
By the advancing Muscovite — the groan
Of the last foe is echoed by his own.

LXXXVIII.

The bayonet pierces and the sabre cleaves,
  And human lives are lavished everywhere,
As the year closing whirls the scarlet leaves
  When the stripped forest bows to the bleak
    air,
And groans; and thus the peopled city grieves,
  Shorn of its best and loveliest, and left
  · bare;
But still it falls with vast and awful splinters,
As oaks blown down with all their thousand
  winters.

LXXXIX.

It is an awful topic — but 'tis not
  My cue for any time to be terrific:
For checkered as is seen our human lot
  With good, and bad, and worse, alike pro-
  · lific
Of melancholy merriment, to quote
  Too much of one sort would be soporific; —
Without, or with offence to friends or foes,
I sketch your world exactly as it goes.

XC.

And one good action in the midst of crimes
  Is "quite refreshing," in the affected phrase
Of these ambrosial, Pharisaic ways,
  With all their pretty milk-and-water ways,
And may serve therefore to bedew these
  rhymes,
  A little scorched at present with the blaze
Of conquest and its consequences, which
Make epic poesy so rare and rich.

XCI.

Upon a taken bastion, where there lay
  Thousands of slaughtered men, a yet warm
    group
Of murdered women, who had found their
    way
  To this vain refuge, made the good heart
    droop
And shudder; — while, as beautiful as May,
  A female child of ten years tried to stoop
And hide her little palpitating breast
Amidst the bodies lulled in bloody rest.

XCII.

Two villanous Cossacques pursued the child
  With flashing eyes and weapons: matched
    with them,
The rudest brute that roams Siberia's wild,
  Has feelings pure and polished as a gem, —
The bear is civilized, the wolf is mild;

And whom for this at last must we con-
  demn ?
Their natures ? or their sovereigns, who em-
  ploy
All arts to teach their subjects to destroy ?

XCIII.

Their sabres glittered o'er her little head,
  Whence her fair hair rose twining with
    affright,
Her hidden face was plunged amidst the dead:
  When Juan caught a glimpse of this sad
    sight,
I shall not say exactly what he *said*,
  Because it might not solace "ears polite;"
But what he *did*, was to lay on their backs,
The readiest way of reasoning with Cos-
  sacques.

XCIV.

One's hip he slashed, and split the other's
    shoulder,
  And drove them with their brutal yells to
    seek
If there might be chirurgeons who could solder
  The wounds they richly merited, and shriek
Their baffled rage and pain; while waxing
    colder
  As he turned o'er each pale and gory cheek,
Don Juan raised his little captive from
The heap a moment more had made her
    tomb.

XCV.

And she was chill as they, and on her face
  A slender streak of blood announced how
    near
Her fate had been to that of all her race;
  For the same blow which laid her mother
    here
Had scarred her brow, and left its crimson
    trace
  As the last link which all she had held dear;
But else unhurt, she opened her large eyes,
And gazed on Juan with a wild surprise.

XCVI.

Just at this instant, while their eyes were fixed
  Upon each other, with dilated glance,
In Juan's look, pain, pleasure, hope, fear,
    mixed
  With joy to save, and dread of some mis-
    chance
Unto his protégée; while hers, transfixed
  With infant terrors, glared as from a trance,
A pure, transparent, pale, yet radiant face,
Like to a lighted alabaster vase; —

XCVII.

Up came John Johnson (I will not say
    "*Jack*,"
  For that were vulgar, cold, and common
    place

On great occasions, such as an attack
  On cities, as hath been the present case) :
Up Johnson came, with hundreds at his back,
  Exclaiming: — "Juan! Juan! On, boy! brace
Your arm, and I'll bet Moscow to a dollar
That you and I will win St. George's collar.

XCVIII.

" The Seraskier is knocked upon the head,
  But the stone bastion still remains, wherein
The old Pacha sits among some hundreds
  dead,
  Smoking his pipe quite calmly 'midst the din
Of our artillery and his own : 'tis said
  Our killed, already piled up to the chin,
Lie round the battery; but still it batters,
And grape in volleys, like a vineyard, scatters.

XCIX.

" Then up with me!" — but Juan answered,
  "Look
Upon this child — I saved her — must not
  leave
Her life to chance; but point me out some
  nook
Of safety, where she less may shrink and
  grieve,
And I am with you." — Whereon Johnson
  took
A glance around — and shrugged — and
  twitched his sleeve
And black silk neckcloth — and replied,
  "You're right;
Poor thing! what's to be done? I'm puzzled
  quite."

*   *   *   *   *

CII.

But Juan was immovable; until
  Johnson, who really loved him in his way,
Picked out amongst his followers with some
  skill
  Such as he thought the least given up to
  prey;
And swearing if the infant came to ill
  That they should all be shot on the next day;
But if she were delivered safe and sound,
They should at least have fifty rubles round,

CIII.

And all allowances besides of plunder
  In fair proportion with their comrades; —
  then
Juan consented to march on through thunder,
  Which thinned at every step their ranks of
  men :
And yet the rest rushed eagerly — no wonder,
  For they were heated by the hope of gain,
A thing which happens everywhere each day —
No hero trusteth wholly to half pay.

*   *   *   *   *

CXXVII.

But let me put an end unto my theme;
  There was an end of Ismail — hapless town!
Far flashed her burning towers o'er Danube's
  stream,
  And redly ran his blushing waters down.
The horrid war-whoop and the shriller scream
  Rose still; but fainter were the thunders
  grown
Of forty thousand who had manned the wall,
Some hundreds breathed — the rest were si-
  lent all!

*   *   *   *   *

CXXXVIII.

Reader! I have kept my word, — at least so
  far
As the first Canto promised. You have now
  Had sketches of love, tempest, travel, war —
All very accurate, you must, allow,
  And *epic*, if plain truth should prove no bar;
For I have drawn much less with a long bow
  Than my forerunners. Carelessly I sing,
But Phœbus lends me now and then a string,

CXXXIX.

With which I still can harp, and carp, and fid-
  dle.
  What further hath befallen or may befall
The hero of this grand poetic riddle,
  I by and by may tell you, if at all :
But now I choose to break off in the middle,
  Worn out with battering Ismail's stubborn
  wall,
While Juan is sent off with the despatch,
For which all Petersburgh is on the watch.

CXL.

This special honor was conferred, because
  He had behaved with courage and human-
  ity —
Which *last* men like, when they have time to
  pause
  From their ferocities produced by vanity.
His little captive gained him some applause
  For saving her amidst the wild insanity
Of carnage, — and I think he was more glad
  in her
Safety, than his new order of St. Vladimir.

CXLI.

The Moslem orphan went with her protector,
  For she was homeless, houseless, helpless;
  all
Her friends, like the sad family of Hector,
  Had perished in the field or by the wall:
Her very place of birth was but a spectre
  Of what it had been; there the Muezzin's
  call
To prayer was heard no more! — and Juan
  wept,
And made a vow to shield her, which he kept.

CANTO THE NINTH.

I.

OH, Wellington! (or " Vilainton "— for Fame
  Sounds the heroic syllables both ways;
France could not even conquer your great
    name,
  But punned it down to this facetious
    phrase —
Beating or beaten she will laugh the same,)
  You have obtained great pensions and
    much praise:
Glory like yours should any dare gainsay,
Humanity would rise, and thunder " Nay!"

II.

I don't think that you used Kinnaird quite
    well
  In Marinèt's affair — in fact, 'twas shabby,
And like some other things won't do to
    tell
  Upon your tomb in Westminster's old
    abbey.
Upon the rest 'tis not worth while to dwell,
  Such tales being for the tea-hours of some
    tabby;
But though your years as *man* tend fast to
    zero,
In fact your grace is still but a *young hero.*

III.

Though Britain owes (and pays you too) so
    much,
  Yet Europe doubtless owes you greatly
    more:
You have repaired Legitimacy's crutch,
  A prop not quite so certain as before:
The Spanish, and the French, as well as
    Dutch,
  Have seen, and felt, how strongly you
    restore;
And Waterloo has made the world your
    debtor
(I wish your bards could sing it rather better).

IV.

You are " the best of cut-throats:" — do not
    start;
  The phrase is Shakspeare's, and not mis-
    applied; —
War's a brain-spattering, windpipe-slitting
    art,
  Unless her cause by right be sanctified.
If you have acted *once* a generous part,
  The world, not the world's masters, will
    decide,
And I shall be delighted to learn who,
Save you and yours, have gained by Waterloo?

V.

I am no flatterer — you've supped full of flat-
    tery;
  They say you like it too — 'tis no great won-
    der.
He whose whole life has been assault and
    battery,
  At last may get a little tired of thunder;
And swallowing eulogy much more than sat-
    ire, he
  May like being praised for every lucky
    blunder,
Called " Saviour of the Nations " — not yet
    saved,
And " Europe's Liberator " — still enslaved.

VI.

I've done. Now go and dine from off the
    plate
  Presented by the Prince of the Brazils,
And send the sentinel before your gate
  A slice or two from your luxurious meals:
He fought, but has not fed so well of late.
  Some hunger, too, they say the people
    feels: —
There is no doubt that you deserve your
    ration,
But pray give back a little to the nation.

VII.

I don't mean to reflect — a man so great as
  You, my lord duke! is far above reflection:
The high Roman fashion, too, of Cincinnatus,
  With modern history has but small connec-
    tion:
Though as an Irishman you love potatoes,
  You need not take them under your direc-
    tion;
And half a million for your Sabine farm
Is rather dear! — I'm sure I mean no harm.

VIII.

Great men have always scorned great recom-
    penses:
  Epaminondas saved his Thebes, and died,
Not leaving even his funeral expenses:
  George Washington had thanks and nought
    beside,
Except the all-cloudless glory (which few
    men's is)
  To free his country: Pitt too had his pride,
And as a high-souled minister of state is
Renowned for ruining Great Britain gratis.

IX.

Never had mortal man such opportunity,
  Except Napoleon, or abused it more·

You might have freed fallen Europe from the
  unity
  Of tyrants, and been blest from shore to
    shore:
And *now*—what *is* your fame? Shall the
  Muse tune it ye?
  Now—that the rabble's first vain shouts are
    o'er?
Go! hear it in your famished country's cries!
Behold the world! and curse your victories!

X.

As these new cantos touch on warlike feats,
  To *you* the unflattering Muse deigns to
    inscribe
Truths, that you will not read in the Gazettes,
  But which 'tis time to teach the hireling tribe
Who fatten on their country's gore, and debts,
  Must be recited, and—without a bribe.
You *did great* things; but not being *great* in
  mind,
Have left *undone* the *greatest*—and mankind.

XI.

Death laughs—Go ponder o'er the skeleton
  With which men image out the unknown
    thing
That hides the past world, like to a set sun
  Which still elsewhere may rouse a brighter
    spring—
Death laughs at all you weep for:—look upon
  This hourly dread of all! whose *threatened*
    sting
Turns life to terror, even though in its sheath:
Mark! how its lipless mouth grins without
  breath!

XII.

Mark! how it laughs and scorns at all you
  are!
  And yet *was* what you are: from *ear* to *ear*
It *laughs not*—there is now no fleshy bar
  So called; the Antic long hath ceased to
    hear,
But still he *smiles;* and whether near or far
  He strips from man that mantle (far more
    dear
Than even the tailor's), his incarnate skin,
White, black, or copper—the dead bones
  will grin.

XIII.

And thus Death laughs,—it is sad merriment,
  But still it *is* so; and with such example
Why should not Life be equally content
  With his superior, in a smile to trample
Upon the nothings which are daily spent
  Like bubbles on an ocean much less ample
Than the eternal deluge, which devours
Suns as rays—worlds like atoms—years like
  hours?

*   *   *   *   *

XXII.

'Tis time we should proceed with our good
  poem,—
  For I maintain that it is really good,
Not only in the body but the proem,
  However little both are understood.
Just now,—but by and by the Truth will show
  'em
  Herself in her sublimest attitude:
And till she doth, I fain must be content
To share her beauty and her banishment.

XXIII.

Our hero (and, I trust, kind reader! yours—)
  Was left upon his way to the chief city
Of the immortal Peter's polished boors,
  Who still have shown themselves more
    brave than witty.
I know its mighty empire now allures
  Much flattery—even Voltaire's, and that's
    a pity.
For me, I deem an absolute autocrat
Not a barbarian, but much worse than that.

*   *   *   *

XXIX.

Don Juan, who had shone in the late slaughter,
  Was left upon his way with the despatch,
Where blood was talked of as we would of
  water;
  And carcasses that lay as thick as thatch
O'er silenced cities, merely served to flatter
  Fair Catherine's pastime—who looked on
    the match
Between these nations as a main of cocks,
Wherein she liked her own to stand like
  rocks.

XXX.

And there in a *kibitka* he rolled on,
  (A cursed sort of carriage without springs,
Which on rough roads leaves scarcely a whole
  bone,)
  Pondering on glory, chivalry, and kings,
And orders, and on all that he had done—
  And wishing that post-horses had the wings
Of Pegasus, or at the least post-chaises
Had feathers, when a traveller on deep ways is.

XXXI.

At every jolt—and there were many—still
  He turned his eyes upon his little charge,
As if he wished that she should fare less ill
  Than he, in these sad highways left at large
To ruts, and flints, and lovely Nature's skill,
  Who is no pavior, nor admits a barge
On *her* canals, where God takes sea and land,
Fishery and farm, both into his own hand.

XXXII.

At least he pays no rent, and has best right
  To be the first of what we used to call

"Gentlemen farmers" — a race worn out quite,
  Since lately there have been no rents at all,
And "gentlemen" are in a piteous plight,
  And "farmers" can't raise Ceres from her fall:
She fell with Buonaparte — What strange thoughts
Arise, when we see emperors fall with oats!

XXXIII.

But Juan turned his eyes on the sweet child
  Whom he had saved from slaughter — what a trophy!
Oh! ye who build up monuments, defiled
  With gore, like Nadir Shah, that costive sophy,
Who, after leaving Hindostan a wild,
  And scarce to the Mogul a cup of coffee
To soothe his woes withal, was slain, the sinner!
Because he could no more digest his dinner; —

XXXIV.

Oh ye! or we! or he! or she! reflect,
  That *one* life saved, especially if young
Or pretty, is a thing to recollect
  Far sweeter than the greenest laurels sprung
From the manure of human clay, though decked
  With all the praises ever said or sung:
Though hymned by every harp, unless within
Your heart joins chorus, Fame is but a din.

* * * * *

XLII.

So on I ramble, now and then narrating,
  Now pondering: — it is time we should narrate.
I left Don Juan with his horses baiting —
  Now we'll get o'er the ground at a great rate.
I shall not be particular in stating
  His journey, we've so many tours of late:
Suppose him then at Petersburgh; suppose
That pleasant capital of painted snows;

XLIII.

Suppose him in a handsome uniform;
  A scarlet coat, black facings, a long plume,
Waving, like sails new shivered in a storm,
  Over a cocked hat in a crowded room,
And brilliant breeches, bright as a Cairn Gorme,
  Of yellow casimire we may presume,
White stockings drawn uncurdled as new milk
O'er limbs whose symmetry set off the silk;

XLIV.

Suppose him sword by side, and hat in hand,
  Made up by youth, fame, and an army tailor —
That great enchanter, at whose rod's command
  Beauty springs forth, and Nature's self turns paler,
Seeing how Art can make her work more grand
  (When she don't pin men's limbs in like a gaoler), —
Behold him placed as if upon a pillar! He
Seems Love turned a lieutenant of artillery!

XLV.

His bandage slipped down into a cravăt;
  His wings subdued to epaulettes; his quiver
Shrunk to a scabbard, with his arrows at
  His side as a small sword, but sharp as ever;
His bow converted into a cocked hat;
  But still so like, that Psyche were more clever
Than some wives (who make blunders no less stupid),
If she had not mistaken him for Cupid.

XLVI.

The courtiers stared, the ladies whispered, and
  The empress smiled: the reigning favorite frowned —
I quite forget which of them was in hand
  Just then; as they are rather numerous found,
Who took by turns that difficult command
  Since first her majesty was singly crowned:
But they were mostly nervous six-foot fellows,
All fit to make a Patagonian jealous.

XLVII.

Juan was none of these, but slight and slim,
  Blushing and beardless; and yet ne'ertheless
There was a something in his turn of limb,
  And still more in his eye, which seemed to express,
That though he looked one of the seraphim,
  There lurked a man beneath the spirit's dress.
Besides, the empress sometimes liked a boy,
And had just buried the fair-faced Lanskoi.

* * * * *

LIII.

Juan, I said, was a most beauteous boy,
  And had retained his boyish look beyond
The usual hirsute seasons which destroy,
  With beards and whiskers, and the like, the fond
Parisian aspect which upset old Troy
  And founded Doctors' Commons: — I have conned
The history of divorces, which, though chequered,
Calls Ilion's the first damages on record.

LIV.

And Catherine, who loved all things, (save her lord,
  Who was gone to his place,) and passed for much,

Admiring those (by dainty dames abhorred)
　Gigantic gentlemen, yet had a touch
Of sentiment; and he she most adored
　Was the lamented Lanskoi, who was such
A lover as had cost her many a tear,
And yet but made a middling grenadier.

*　　*　　*　　*　　*

LVII.

Catherine, who was the grand epitome
　Of that great cause of war, or peace, or
　　what
You please (it causes all the things which
　　be,
　So you may take your choice of this or
　　that) —
Catherine, I say, was very glad to see
　The handsome herald, on whose plumage
　　sat
Victory; and, pausing as she saw him kneel
With his despatch, forgot to break the seal.

LVIII.

Then recollecting the whole empress, nor
　Forgetting quite the woman (which com-
　　posed
At least three parts of this great whole), she
　　tore
The letter open with an air which posed
　The court, that watched each look her visage
　　wore,
Until a royal smile at length disclosed
Fair weather for the day. Though rather
　　spacious,
Her face was noble, her eyes fine, mouth gra-
　　cious.

LIX.

Great joy was hers, or rather joys: the first
　Was a ta'en city, thirty thousand slain.
Glory and triumph o'er her aspect burst,
　As an East Indian sunrise on the main.
These quenched a moment her ambition's
　　thirst —
　So Arab deserts drink in summer's rain:
In vain! — As falls the dews on quenchless
　　sands,
Blood only serves to wash Ambition's hands!

LX.

Her next amusement was more fanciful;
　She smiled at mad Suwarrow's rhymes,
　　who threw
Into a Russian couplet rather dull
　The whole gazette of thousands whom he
　　slew,
Her third was feminine enough to annul
　The shudder which runs naturally through
Our veins, when things called sovereigns think
　　it best
To kill, and generals turn it into jest.

LXI.

The two first feelings ran their course com-
　　plete,
　And lighted first her eye, and then her
　　mouth:
The whole court looked immediately most
　　sweet,
　Like flowers well watered after a long
　　drouth: —
But when on the lieutenant at her feet
　Her majesty, who liked to gaze on youth
Almost as much as on a new despatch,
Glanced mildly, all the world was on the watch.

*　　*　　*　　*　　*

LXXVIII.

The whole court melted into one wide whisper,
　And all lips were applied unto all ears!
The elder ladies' wrinkles curled much crisper
　As they beheld; the younger cast some leers
On one another, and each lovely lisper
　Smiled as she talked the matter o'er; but
　　tears
Of rivalship rose in each clouded eye
Of all the standing army who stood by.

LXXIX.

All the ambassadors of all the powers
　Inquired, Who was this very new young
　　man,
Who promised to be great in some few hours?
　Which is full soon (though life is but a
　　span).
Already they beheld the silver showers
　Of rubles rain, as fast as specie can,
Upon his cabinet, besides the presents
Of several ribands, and some thousand peas-
　　ants.

LXXX.

Catherine was generous, — all such ladies are:
　Love, that great opener of the heart and all
The ways that lead there, be they near or far,
　Above, below, by turnpikes great or small, —
Love — (though she had a cursed taste for war,
　And was not the best wife, unless we call
Such Clytemnestra, though perhaps 'tis better
That one should die, than two drag on the
　　fetter) —

LXXXI.

Love had made Catherine make each lover's
　　fortune,
　Unlike our own half-chaste Elizabeth,
Whose avarice all disbursements did impor-
　　tune,
　If history, the grand liar, ever saith
The truth; and though grief her old age
　　might shorten,
　Because she put a favorite to death,
Her vile, ambiguous method of flirtation,
And stinginess, disgrace her sex and station.

LXXXII.

But when the levee rose, and all was bustle
In the dissolving circle, all the nations'
Ambassadors began as 'twere to hustle
Round the young man with their congratu-
lations.
Also the softer silks were heard to rustle
Of gentle dames, among whose recreations
It is to speculate on handsome faces,
Especially when such lead to high places.

LXXXIII.

Juan, who found himself, he knew not how,
A general object of attention, made
His answers with a very graceful bow,
As if born for the ministerial trade.
Though modest, on his unembarrassed brow
Nature had written "gentleman." He said
Little, but to the purpose; and his manner
Flung hovering graces o'er him like a banner.

LXXXIV.

An order from her majesty consigned
Our young lieutenant to the genial care
Of those in office: all the world looked kind,
(As it will look sometimes with the first stare,
Which youth would not act ill to keep in
mind,)
As also did Miss Protasoff then there,
Named from her mystic office "l'Eprouveuse,"
A term inexplicable to the Muse.

LXXXV.

With *her* then, as in humble duty bound,
Juan retired,—and so will I, until
My Pegasus shall tire of touching ground.
We have just lit on a "heaven-kissing hill,"
So lofty that I feel my brain turn round,
And all my fancies whirling like a mill;
Which is a signal to my nerves and brain,
To take a quiet ride in some green lane.

CANTO THE TENTH.

I.

WHEN Newton saw an apple fall, he found
In that slight startle from his contempla-
tion—
'Tis *said* (for I'll not answer above ground
For any sage's creed or calculation)—
A mode of proving that the earth turned
round
In a most natural whirl, called "gravita-
tion;"
And this is the sole mortal who could grapple,
Since Adam, with a fall, or with an apple.

II.

Man fell with apples, and with apples rose,
If this be true; far be it we must deem the mode
In which Sir Isaac Newton could disclose
Through the then unpaved stars the turn-
pike road,
A thing to counterbalance human woes:
For ever since immortal man hath glowed
With all kinds of mechanics, and full soon
Steam-engines will conduct him to the moon.

III.

And wherefore this exordium?—Why, just
now,
In taking up this paltry sheet of paper,
My bosom underwent a glorious glow,
And my internal spirit cut a caper:
And though so much inferior, as I know,
To those who, by the dint of glass and vapor,
Discover stars, and sail in the wind's eye,
I wish to do as much by poesy.

IV.

In the wind's eye I have sailed, and sail; but
for
The stars, I own my telescope is dim;
But at the least I have shunned the common
shore,
And leaving land far out of sight, would skim
The ocean of eternity: the roar
Of breakers has not daunted my slight, trim,
But *still* sea-worthy skiff; and she may float
Where ships have foundered, as doth many a
boat.

V.

We left our hero, Juan, in the *bloom*
Of favoritism, but not yet in the *blush;*—
And far be it from my *Muses* to presume
(For I have more than one Muse at a push)
To follow him beyond the drawing-room:
It is enough that Fortune found him flush
Of youth, and vigor, beauty, and those things
Which for an instant clip enjoyment's wings.

* * * * *

XXI.

Don Juan grew a very polished Russian—
How we won't mention, *why* we need not
say:
Few youthful minds can stand the strong con-
cussion
Of any slight temptation in their way;
But *his* just now were spread as is a cushion
Smoothed for a monarch's seat of honor: gay
Damsels, and dances, revels, ready money,
Made ice seem paradise, and winter sunny.

XXII.

The favor of the empress was agreeable;
   And though the duty waxed a little hard,
Young people at his time of life should be able
   To come off handsomely in that regard.
He was now growing up like a green tree, able
   For love, war, or ambition, which reward
Their luckier votaries, till old age's tedium
Make some prefer the circulating medium.

XXIII.

About this time, as might have been antici-
   pated,
   Seduced by youth and dangerous examples,
Don Juan grew, I fear, a little dissipated;
   Which is a sad thing, and not only tramples
On our fresh feelings, but — as being partici-
   pated
   With all kinds of incorrigible samples
Of frail humanity — must make us selfish,
And shut our souls up in us like a shell-fish.

     *   *   *   *   **

XXXVII.

The gentle Juan flourished, though at times
   He felt like other plants called sensitive,
Which shrink from touch, as monarchs do
   from rhymes,
   Save such as Southey can afford to give.
Perhaps he longed in bitter frosts for climes
   In which the Neva's ice would cease to live
Before May-day: perhaps, despite his duty,
In royalty's vast arms he sighed for beauty:

XXXVIII.

Perhaps — but, sans perhaps, we need not
   seek
   For causes young or old: the canker-worm
Will feed upon the fairest, freshest cheek,
   As well as further drain the withered form:
Care, like a housekeeper, brings every week
   His bills in, and however we may storm,
They must be paid: though six days smoothly
   run,
The seventh will bring blue devils or a dun.

XXXIX.

I don't know how it was, but he grew sick:
   The empress was alarmed, and her physi-
   cian
(The same who physicked Peter) found the
   tick
   Of his fierce pulse betoken a condition
Which augured of the dead, however *quick*
   Itself, and showed a feverish disposition;
At which the whole court was extremely
   troubled,
The sovereign shocked, and all his medicines
   doubled.

     *   *   *   *   **

XLIII.

Juan demurred at this first notice to
   Quit; and though death had threatened an
   ejection,
His youth and constitution bore him through,
   And sent the doctors in a new direction.
But still his state was delicate: the hue
   Of health but flickered with a faint reflection
Along his wasted cheek, and seemed to gravel
The faculty — who said that he must travel.

XLIV.

The climate was too cold, they said, for him,
   Meridian-born, to bloom in. This opinion
Made the chaste Catherine look a little grim,
   Who did not like at first to lose her minion:
But when she saw his dazzling eye wax dim,
   And drooping like an eagle's with clipt pin-
   ion,
She then resolved to send him on a mission,
But in a style becoming his condition.

XLV.

There was just then a kind of a discussion,
   A sort of treaty or negotiation
Between the British cabinet and Russian,
   Maintained with all the due prevarication
With which great states such things are apt to
   push on;
   Something about the Baltic's navigation,
Hides, train-oil, tallow, and the rights of Thetis,
Which Britons deem their "uti possidetis."

XLVI.

So Catherine, who had a handsome way
   Of fitting out her favorites, conferred
This secret charge on Juan, to display
   At once her royal splendor, and reward
His services. He kissed hands the next day,
   Received instructions how to play his card,
Was laden with all kinds of gifts and honors,
Which showed what great discernment was
   the donor's.

     *   *   *   *   **

LVIII.

They journeyed on through Poland and
   through Warsaw,
   Famous for mines of salt and yokes of
   iron:
Through Courland also, which that famous
   farce saw
   Which gave her dukes the graceless name
   of "Biron."
'Tis the same landscape which the modern
   Mars saw,
   Who marched to Moscow, led by Fame, the
   siren!
To lose by one month's frost some twenty
   years
Of conquest, and his guard of grenadiers.

LIX.

Let this not seem an anti-climax : — " Oh !
　My guard ! my old guard ! " exclaimed that
　　god of clay.
Think of the Thunderer's falling down below
　Carotid-artery-cutting Castlereagh !
Alas ! that glory should be chilled by snow !
　But should we wish to warm us on our way
Through Poland, there is Koscuisko's name
Might scatter fire through ice, like Hecla's
　　flame.

LX.

From Poland they came on through Prussia
　· Proper,
　And Königsberg the capital, whose vaunt,
Besides some veins of iron, lead, or copper,
　Has lately been the great Professor Kant.
Juan, who cared not a tobacco-stopper
　About philosophy, pursued his jaunt
To Germany, whose somewhat tardy millions
Have princes who spur more than their pos-
　　tillons.

LXI.

And thence through Berlin, Dresden, and the
　like,
　Until he reached the castellated Rhine : —
Ye glorious Gothic scenes ! how much ye
　　strike
　All phantasies, not even excepting mine ;
A gray wall, a green ruin, rusty pike,
　Make my soul pass the equinoctial line
Between the present and ·past worlds, and
　　hover
Upon their airy confine, half-seas-over.

LXII.

But Juan posted on through Manheim, Bonn,
　Which Drachenfels frowns over like a spec-
　　tre
Of the good feudal times for ever gone,
　On which I have not time just now to lec-
　　ture.
From thence he was drawn onwards to Cologne,
　A city which presents to the inspector
Eleven thousand maidenheads of bone,
The greatest number flesh hath ever known.

LXIII.

From thence to Holland's Hague and Hel-
　voetsluys,
　That water-land of Dutchmen and of
　　ditches,
Where juniper expresses its best juice,
　The poor man's sparkling substitute for
　　riches.
Senates and sages have condemned its use —
　But to deny the mob a cordial, which is
Too often all the clothing, meat, or fuel,
Good government has left them, seems but
　　cruel.·　　　　　　*

LXIV.

Here he embarked, and with a flowing sail
　Went bounding for the island of the free,
Towards which the impatient wind blew half
　　a gale ;
High dashed the spray, the bows dipped in
　　the sea,
And sea-sick passengers turned somewhat
　　pale ;
　But Juan, seasoned, as he well might be,
By former voyages, stood to watch the skiffs
Which passed, or catch the first glimpse of
　　the cliffs.

LXV.

At length they rose, like a white wall along
　The blue sea's border ; and Don Juan felt —
What even young strangers feel a little strong
　At the first sight of Albion's chalky belt —
A kind of pride that he should be among
　Those haughty shopkeepers, who sternly
　　' dealt
Their goods and edicts out from pole to
　　pole,
And made the very billows pay them toll.

LXVI.

I've no great cause to love that spot of earth,
　Which holds what *might have been* the
　　noblest nation ;
But though I owe it little but my birth,
　I feel a mixed regret and veneration
For its decaying fame and former worth.
　Seven years (the usual term of transporta
　　tion)
Of absence lay one's old resentments level,
When a man's country's going to the devil.

LXVII.

Alas ! could she but fully, truly, know
　How her great name is now throughout
　　abhorred,
How eager all the earth is for the blow
　Which shall lay bare her bosom to the
　　sword ;
How all the nations deem her their worst foe,
　That worse than *worst of foes*, the once
　　adored
False friend, who held out freedom to man-
　　kind,
And now would chain them, to the very
　　mind ; —

LXVIII.

Would she be proud, or boast herself the free,
　Who is but first of slaves ? The nations are
In prison, — but the gaoler, what is he ?
　No less a victim to the bolt and bar.
Is the poor privilege to turn the key
　Upon the captive, freedom ?　He's as far
From the enjoyment of the earth and air
Who watches o'er the chain, as they who wear.

LXIX.

Don Juan now saw Albion's earliest beauties,
  Thy cliffs, *dear* Dover! harbor, and hotel;
Thy custom-house, with all its delicate du-
    ties;
  Thy waiters running mucks at every bell;
Thy packets, all whose passengers are booties
  To those who upon land or water dwell;
And last, not least, to strangers uninstructed,
Thy long, long bills, whence nothing is de-
    ducted.

* * * * *

CANTO THE ELEVENTH.

I.

WHEN Bishop Berkeley said "there was no
    matter,"
  And proved it — 'twas no matter what he
    said:
They say his system 'tis in vain to batter,
  Too subtle for the airiest human head;
And yet who can believe it ? I would shatter
  Gladly all matters down to stone or lead,
Or adamant, to find the world a spirit,
And wear my head, denying that I wear it.

II.

What a sublime discovery 'twas to make the
  Universe universal egotism,
That all's ideal — *all ourselves:* I'll stake the
  World (be it what you will) that *that's* no
    schism.
Oh Doubt! — if thou be'st Doubt, for which
    some take thee,
  But which I doubt extremely — thou sole
    prism
Of the Truth's rays, spoil not my draught of
    spirit!
Heaven's brandy, though our brain can hardly
    bear it.

III.

For ever and anon comes Indigestion,
  (Not the most "dainty Ariel") and pre-
    plexes
Our soarings with another sort of question:
  And that which after all my spirit vexes,
Is, that I find no spot where man can rest eye
    on,
  Without confusion of the sorts and sexes,
Of beings, stars, and this unriddled wonder,
  The world, which at the worst's a glorious
    blunder —

IV.

If it be chance; or if it be according
  To the old text, still better: — lest it should
Turn out so, we'll say nothing 'gainst the
    wording,
  As several people think such hazards rude.
They're right; our days are too brief for af-
    fording
  Space to dispute what *no one* ever could
Decide, and *everybody one day* will
Know very clearly — or at least lie still.

V.

And therefore will I leave off metaphysical
  Discussion, which is neither here nor there:
If I agree that what is, is; then this I call
  Being quite perspicuous and extremely fair;
The truth is, I've grown lately rather phthisical:
  I don't know what the reason is — the air
Perhaps; but as I suffer from the shocks
Of illness, I grow much more orthodox.

VI.

The first attack at once proved the Divinity
  (But *that* I never doubted, nor the Devil) ;
The next, the Virgin's mystical virginity ;
  The third, the usual Origin of Evil;
The fourth at once established the whole
    Trinity
  On so uncontrovertible a level,
That I devoutly wished the three were four,
On purpose to believe so much the more.

VII.

To our theme. — The man who has stood on
    the Acropolis,
  And looked down over Attica; or he
Who has sailed where picturesque Constan-
    tinople is,
  Or seen Timbuctoo, or hath taken tea
In small-eyed China's crockery-ware metropo-
    lis,
  Or sat amidst the bricks of Nineveh,
May not think much of London's first appear-
    ance —
But ask him what he thinks of it a year hence ?

* * * * *

XXIX.

Over the stones still rattling, up Pall Mall,
  Through crowds and carriages, but waxing
    thinner
As thundered knockers broke the long sealed
    spell
  Of doors 'gainst duns, and to an early din-
    ner

Admitted a small party as night fell, —
　Don Juan, our young diplomatic sinner,
Pursued his path, and drove past some hotels,
St. James's Palace and St. James's "Hells."

XXX.

They reached the hotel : forth streamed from
　the front door
A tide of well-clad waiters, and around
The mob stood, and as usual several score
Of those pedestrian Paphians who abound
In decent London when the daylight's o'er;
　Commodious but immoral, they are found
Useful, like Malthus, in promoting marriage.—
But Juan now is stepping from his carriage

XXXI.

Into one of the sweetest of hotels,
　Especially for foreigners — and mostly
For those whom favor or whom fortune swells,
　And cannot find a bill's small items costly.
There many an envoy either dwelt or dwells
　(The den of many a diplomatic lost lie),
Until to some conspicuous square they pass,
And blazon o'er the door their names in brass.

XXXII.

,uan, whose was a delicate commission,
　Private, though publicly important, bore
No title to point out with due precision
　The exact affair on which he was sent o'er.
'Twas merely known that on a secret mission,
　A foreigner of rank had graced our shore,
Young, handsome, and accomplished, who
　was said
(In whispers) to have turned his sovereign's
　head.

XXXIII.

Some rumor also of some strange adventures
　Had gone before him, and his wars and
　loves ;
And as romantic heads are pretty painters,
　And, above all, an Englishwoman's roves
Into the excursive, breaking the indentures
　Of sober reason, wheresoe'er it moves,
He found himself extremely in the fashion,
Which serves our thinking people for a pas-
　sion.

XXXIV.

I don't mean that they are passionless, but quite
　The contrary ; but then 'tis in the head ;
Yet as the consequences are as bright
　As if they acted with the heart instead,
What after all can signify the site
　Of ladies' lucubrations ? So they lead
In safety to the place from which you start,
What matters if the road be head or heart ?

XXXV.

Juan presented in the proper place,
　To proper placemen, every Russ credential ;

And was received with all the due grimace,
　By those who govern in the mood potential,
Who, seeing a handsome stripling with
　smooth face,
Thought (what in state affairs is most es-
　sential)
That they as easily might *do* the youngster,
As hawks may pounce upon a woodland song-
　ster.

＊　＊　＊　＊　＊

XLVIII.

Fair virgins blushed upon him ; wedded
　dames
Bloomed also in less transitory hues ;
For both commodities dwell by the Thames,
　The painting and the painted ; youth, ceruse,
Against his heart preferred their usual claims,
　Such as no gentleman can quite refuse :
Daughters admired his dress, and pious
　mothers
Inquired his income, and if he had brothers.

＊　＊　＊　＊　＊

LXIII.

My Juan, whom I left in deadly peril
　Amongst live poets and blue ladies, past
With some small profit through that field so
　sterile.
Being tired in time, and neither least nor
　last
Left it before he had been treated very ill;
　And henceforth found himself more gaily
　classed
Amongst the higher spirits of the day,
The sun's true son, no vapor, but a ray.

LXIV.

His morns he passed in business — which
　dissected,
　Was like all business, a laborious nothing
That leads to lassitude, the most infected
　And Centaur Nessus garb of mortal clothing,
And on our sofas makes us lie dejected,
　And talk in tender horrors of our loathing
All kinds of toil, save for our country's good —
Which grows no better, though 'tis time it
　should.

LXV.

His afternoons he passed in visits, luncheons,
　Lounging, and boxing ; and the twilight hour
In riding round those vegetable puncheons
　Called "Parks," where there is neither fruit
　nor flower
Enough to gratify a bee's slight munchings ;
　But after all it is the only "bower,"
(In Moore's phrase) where the fashionable
　fair
Can form a slight acquaintance with fresh air

LXVI.

Then dress, then dinner, then awakes the world!
  Then glare the lamps, then whirl the wheels,
    then roar
Through street and square fast flashing
    chariots hurled
  Like harnessed meteors; then along the floor
Chalk mimics painting; then festoons are
    twirled;
  Then roll the brazen thunders of the door,
Which opens to the thousand happy few
  An earthly Paradise of "Or Molu."

*   *   *   *   *

LXXXVI.

But how shall I relate in other cantos
  Of what befell our hero in the land,
Which 'tis the common cry and lie to vaunt as
  A moral country? But I hold my hand —
For I disdain to write an Atalantis;
  But 'tis as well at once to understand
You are *not* a moral people, and you know it
Without the aid of too sincere a poet.

LXXXVII.

What Juan saw and underwent shall be
  My topic, with of course the due restriction
Which is required by proper courtesy;
  And recollect the work is only fiction,

And that I sing of neither mine nor me,
  Though every scribe, in some slight turn of
    diction,
Will hint allusions never *meant.* Ne'er doubt
This — when I speak, I *don't hint,* but *speak
  out.*

LXXXVIII.

Whether he married with the third or fourth
  Offspring of some sage husband-hunting
    countess,
Or whether with some virgin of more worth
  (I mean in Fortune's matrimonial bounties)
He took to regularly peopling Earth,
  Of which your lawful awful wedlock fount
    is, —
Or whether he was taken in for damages,
For being too excursive in his homages, —

LXXXIX.

Is yet within the unread events of time
  Thus far, go forth, thou lay, which I will
    back
Against the same given quantity of rhyme,
  For being as much the subject of attack
As ever yet was any work sublime,
  By those who love to say that white is black.
So much the better! — I may stand alone,
But would not change my free thoughts for a
  throne.

CANTO THE TWELFTH.

I.

Of all the barbarous middle ages, that
  Which is most barbarous is the middle age
Of man; it is — I really scarce know what;
  But when we hover between fool and sage,
And don't know justly what we would be at —
  A period something like a printed page,
Black letter upon foolscap, while our hair
Grows grizzled, and we are not what we
  were; —

II.

Too old for youth, — too young, at thirty-five,
  To herd with boys, or hoard with good
    three-score, —
I wonder people should be left alive;
  But since they are, that epoch is a bore:
Love lingers still, although 'twere late to wive;
  And as for other love, the illusion's o'er;
And money, that most pure imagination,
Gleams only through the dawn of its creation.

III.

O Gold! Why call we misers miserable?
  Theirs is the pleasure that can never pall;

Theirs is the best bower anchor, the chain
    cable
  Which holds fast other pleasures great and
    small.
Ye who but see the saving man at table,
  And scorn his temperate board, as none at
    all,
And wonder how the wealthy can be sparing,
Know not what visions spring from each
  cheese-paring.

IV.

Love or lust makes man sick, and wine much
    sicker;
  Ambition rends, and gaming gains a loss;
But making money, slowly first, then quicker,
  And adding still a little through each
    cross
(Which *will* come over things), beats love or
    liquor,
  The gamester's counter, or the statesman's
    dross.
O Gold! I still prefer thee unto paper
Which makes bank credit like a bark of
  vapor.

v.

Who hold the balance of the world ?   Who
    reign
O'er congress, whether royalist or liberal ?
Who rouse the shirtless patriots of Spain ?
    (That make old Europe's journals squeak
    and gibber all.)
Who keep the 'world, both old and new, in
    pain
    Or pleasure ?   Who make politics run
    glibber all ?
The shade of Buonaparte's noble daring ? —
Jew Rothschild, and his fellow-Christian, Bar-
    ing.

*   *   *   *   *

XIII.

" Love rules the camp, the court, the grove," —
    " for love
    Is heaven, and heaven is love : " — so sings
    the bard ;
Which it were rather difficult to prove
    (A thing with poetry in general hard).
Perhaps there may be something in " the
    grove,"
    At least it rhymes to " love : " but I'm pre-
    pared
To doubt (no less than landlords of their
    rental)
If " courts " and " camps " be quite so senti-
    mental.

XIV.

But if Love don't, *Cash* does, and Cash
    alone :
    Cash rules the grove, and fells it too be-
    sides ;
Without cash, camps were thin, and courts
    were none ;
    Without cash, Malthus tells you — " take no
    brides."
So Cash rules Love the ruler, on his own
    High ground, as virgin Cynthia sways the
    tides :
And as for " Heaven being Love," why not
    say honey
Is wax ? Heaven is not Love, 'tis Matrimony.

*   *   *   *   *

XXIII.

And now to business. — O my gentle Juan !
    Thou art in London — in that pleasant
    place
Where every kind of mischief's daily brew-
    ing,
    Which can await warm youth in its wild
    race.
'Tis true, that thy career is not a new one ;
    Thou art no novice in the headlong chase
Of early life ; but this is a new land,
Which foreigners can never understand.

XXIV.

What with a small diversity of climate,
    Of hot or cold, mercurial or sedate,
I could send forth my mandate like a primate
    Upon the rest of Europe's social state ;
But thou art the most difficult to rhyme at,
    Great Britain, which the Muse may pene-
    trate.
All countries have their " Lions," but in thee
There is but one superb menagerie.

XXV.

But I am sick of politics. Begin,
    " Paulo Majora." Juan, undecided
Amongst the paths of " being taken in,"
    Above the ice had like a skater glided :
When tired of play, he flirted without sin
    With some of those fair creatures who have
    prided
Themselves on innocent tantalization,
And hate all vice except its reputation.

*   *   *   *   *

XXVII.

The little Leila, with her orient eyes,
    And taciturn Asiatic disposition,
(Which saw all western things with small sur-
    prise
    To the surprise of people of condition,
Who think that novelties are butterflies
    To be pursued as food for inanition,)
Her charming figure and romantic history
Became a kind of fashionable mystery.

XXVIII.

The women much divided — as is usual
    Amongst the sex in little things or great.
Think not, fair creatures, that I mean to abuse
    you all —
I have always liked you better than I state :
Since I've grown moral, still I must accuse
    you all
Of being apt to talk at a great rate ;
And now there was a general sensation
Amongst you, about Leila's education.

*   *   *   *   *

XXX.

So first there was a generous emulation,
    And then there was a general competition
To undertake the orphan's education.
    As Juan was a person of condition,
It had been an affront on this occasion
    To talk of a subscription or petition ;
But sixteen dowagers, ten unwed she sages,
    Whose tale belongs to " Hallam's Middle
    Ages,"

XXXI.

And one or two sad, separate wives, without
    A fruit to bloom upon their withering
    bough —

Begged to bring *up* the little girl, and "*out*," —
  For that's the phrase that settles all things
    now,
Meaning a Virgin's first blush at a rout,
  And all her points as thorough-bred to
    show :
And I assure you, that like virgin honey
Tastes their first season (mostly if they have
    money).

   *   *   *   *   *

XLI.

But first of little Leila we'll dispose ;
  For like a day-dawn she was young and
    pure,
Or like the old comparison of snows,
  Which are more pure than pleasant to be
    sure.
Like many people everybody knows,
Don Juan was delighted to secure
A goodly guardian for his infant charge,
Who might not profit much by being at large.

XLII.

Besides, he had found out he was no tutor
  (I wish that others would find out the
    same) ;
And rather wished in such things to stand
    neuter,
  For silly wards will bring their guardians
    blame :
So when he saw each ancient dame a suitor
  To make his little wild Asiatic tame,
Consulting " the Society for Vice
Suppression," Lady Pinchbeck was his
    choice.

XLIII.

Olden she was — but had been very young ;
  Virtuous she was — and had been, I believe ;
Although the world has such an evil tongue
  That —— but my chaster ear will not re-
    ceive
An echo of a syllable that's wrong :
  In fact, there's nothing makes me so much
    grieve,
As that abominable tittle-tattle,
Which is the cud eschewed by human cattle.

   *   *   *   *   *

XLVIII.

High in high circles, gentle in her own,
  She was the mild reprover of the young
Whenever — which means every day — they'd
    shown
  An awkward inclination to go wrong.
The quantity of good she did's unknown,
  Or at the least would lengthen out my
    song :
In brief, the little orphan of the East
Had raised an interest in her, which in-
    creased.

XLIX.

Juan, too, was a sort of favorite with her,
  Because she thought him a good heart at
    bottom,
A little spoiled, but not so altogether ;
  Which was a wonder, if you think who got
    him,
And how he had been tossed, he scarce knew
    whither,
  Though this might ruin others, it did *not*
    him,
At least entirely — for he had seen too many
Changes in youth, to be suprised at any.

   *   *   *   *   *

LIV.

But now I will begin my poem. 'Tis
  Perhaps a little strange, if not quite new,
That from the first of Cantos up to this
  I've not begun what we have to go through.
These first twelve books are merely flourishes,
  Preludios, trying just a string or two
Upon my lyre, or making the pegs sure ;
And when so, you shall have the overture.

LV.

My Muses do not care a pinch of rosin
  About what's called success, or not succeed-
    ing :
Such thoughts are quite below the strain they
    have chosen ;
  'Tis a " great moral lesson" they are reading.
I thought, at setting off, about two dozen
  Cantos would do ; but at Apollo's plead-
    ing,
If that my Pegasus should not be foundered,
I think to canter gently through a hundred.

LVI.

Don Juan saw that microcosm on stilts,
  Yclept the Great World ; for it is the least,
Although the highest : but as swords have
    hilts
  By which their power of mischief is in-
    creased,
When man in battle or in quarrel tilts,
  Thus the low world, north, south, or west,
    or east,
Must still obey the high — which is their
    handle,
Their moon, their sun, their gas, their far-
    thing candle.

LVII.

He had many friends who had many wives,
    and was
  Well looked upon by both, to that extent
Of friendship which you may accept or pass,
  It does nor good nor harm ; being merely
    meant
To keep the wheels going of the higher class,

And draw them nightly when a ticket's
    sent:
And what with masquerades, and fêtes, and
    balls,
For the first season such a life scarce palls.

     ✱   ✱   ✱   ✱   ✱

LXXXII.

He also had been busy seeing sights —
    The Parliament and all the other houses;
Had sat beneath the gallery at nights,
    To hear debates whose thunder *roused* (not
    rouses)
The world to gaze upon those northern lights
    Which flashed as far as where the musk-
    bull browses;
He had also stood at times behind the
    throne —
But Grey was not arrived, and Chatham gone.

LXXXIII.

He saw, however, at the closing session,
    That noble sight, when *really* free the
    nation,
A king in constitutional possession
    Of such a throne as is the proudest station,
Though despots know it not — till the pro-
    gression
    Of freedom shall complete their education.
'Tis not mere splendor makes the show
    august
To eye or heart — it is the people's trust.

LXXXIV.

There, too, he saw (whate'er he may be now)
    A Prince, the prince of princes at the time,
With fascination in his very bow,
    And full of promise, as the spring of prime.
Though royalty was written on his brow,
    He had *then* the grace, too, rare in every
    clime,
Of being, without alloy of fop or beau,
A finished gentleman from top to toe.

LXXXV.

And Juan was received, as hath been said,
    Into the best society: and there
Occurred what often happens, I'm afraid,
    However disciplined and debonnaire: —
The talent and good humor he displayed,
    Besides the marked distinction of his air,

Exposed him, as was natural, to temptation,
    Even though himself avoided the occasion.

LXXXVI.

But what, and where, with whom, and when
    and why,
    Is not to be put hastily together;
And as my object is morality
    (Whatever people say), I don't know
    whether
I'll leave a single reader's eyelid dry,
    But harrow up his feelings till they wither,
And hew out a huge monument of pathos,
As Philip's son proposed to do with Athos.

LXXXVII.

Here the twelfth Canto of our introduction
    Ends. When the body of the book's begun,
You'll find it of a different construction
    From what some people say 'twill be when
    done:
The plan at present's simply in concoction.
    I can't oblige you, reader, to read on;
That's your affair, not mine: a real spirit
Should neither court neglect, nor dread to
    bear it.

LXXXVIII.

And if my thunderbolt not always rattles,
    Remember, reader! you have had before
The worst of tempests and the best of battles
    That e'er were brewed from elements or
    gore,
Besides the most sublime of— Heaven knows
    what else:
    An usurer could scarce expect much
    more —
But my best canto, save one on astronomy,
Will turn upon " political economy."

LXXXIx.

That is your present theme for popularity:
    Now that the public hedge hath scarce a
    stake,
It grows an act of patriotic charity,
    To show the people the best way to break.
My plan (but I, if but for singularity,
    Reserve it) will be very sure to take.
Meantime, read all the national debt-sinkers,
    And tell me what you think of our great
    thinkers.

CANTO THE THIRTEENTH.

1.

I NOW mean to be serious; — it is time,
    Since laughter now-a-days is deemed too
    serious,

A jest at Vice by Virtue's called a crime,
    And critically held as deleterious:
Besides, the sad's a source of the sublime,
    Although when long a little apt to weary us.

And therefore shall my lay soar high and
  solemn,
As an old temple dwindled to a column.

II.

The Lady Adeline Amundeville
  ('Tis an old Norman name, and to be
    found
In pedigrees by those who wander still
Along the last fields of that Gothic ground)
Was high-born, wealthy by her father's will,
  And beauteous, even where beauties most
    abound,
In Britain — which of course true patriots find
The goodliest soil of body and of mind.

III.

I'll not gainsay them; it is not my cue;
  I'll leave them to their taste, no doubt the
    best:
An eye's an eye, and whether black or blue,
  Is no great matter, so 'tis in request,
'Tis nonsense to dispute about a hue —
  The kindest may be taken as a test.
The fair sex should be always fair; and no
  man,
Till thirty, should perceive there's a plain
  woman.

IV.

And after that serene and somewhat dull
  Epoch, that awkward corner turned for days
More quiet, when our moon's no more at
  full,
We may presume to criticise or praise;
Because indifference begins to lull
  Our passions, and we walk in wisdom's
    ways;
Also because the figure and the face
Hint, that 'tis time to give the younger place.

V.

I know that some would fain postpone this
  era,
  Reluctant as all placemen to resign
Their post; but theirs is merely a chimera,
  For they have passed life's equinoctial line:
But then they have their claret and Madeira
  To irrigate the dryness of decline;
And county meetings, and the parliament,
And debt, and what not, for their solace sent.

VI.

And is there not religion, and reform,
  Peace, war, the taxes, and what's called
    the " Nation? "
The struggle to be pilots in a storm?
  The landed and the moneyed speculation?
The joys of mutual hate to keep them warm,
  Instead of love, that mere hallucination?
Now hatred is by far the longest pleasure;
Men love in haste, but they detest at leisure.

VII.

Rough Johnson, the great moralist, professed,
  Right honestly, " he liked an honest
    hater! " —
The only truth that yet has been confest
  Within these latest thousand years or later.
Perhaps the fine old fellow spoke in jest: —
  For my part, I am but a mere spectator,
And gaze where'er the palace or the hovel is,
Much in the mode of Goethe's Mephis-
  topheles;

VIII.

But neither love nor hate in much excess;
  Though 'twas not once so. If I sneer
    sometimes,
It is because I cannot well do less,
  And now and then it also suits my rhymes.
I should be very willing to redress
  Men's wrongs, and rather check than punish
    crimes,
Had not Cervantes, in that too true tale
Of Quixote, shown how all such efforts fail.

IX.

Of all tales 'tis the saddest — and more sad,
  Because it makes us smile: his hero's right,
And still pursues the right; — to curb the bad
  His only object, and 'gainst odds to fight
His guerdon: 'tis his virtue makes him mad!
  But his adventures form a sorry sight; —
A sorrier still is the great moral taught
By that real epic unto all who have thought.

X.

Redressing injury, revenging wrong,
  To aid the damsel and destroy the caitiff;
Opposing singly the united strong,
  From foreign yoke to free the helpless
    native: —
Alas! must noblest views, like an old song,
  Be for mere fancy's sport a theme creative,
A jest, a riddle, Fame through thick and thin
  sought!
And Socrates himself but Wisdom's Quixote?

XI.

Cervantes smiled Spain's chivalry away;
  A single laugh demolished the right arm
Of his own country; — seldom since that day
  Has Spain had heroes. While Romance
    could charm,
The world gave ground before her bright
  array;
  And therefore have his volumes done such
    harm,
That all their glory, as a composition,
Was dearly purchased by his land's perdition.

XII.

I'm " at my old lunes " — digression, and
  forget
  The Lady Adeline Amundeville·

The fair most fatal Juan ever met,
  Although she was not evil nor meant ill;
But Destiny and Passion spread the net
  (Fate is a good excuse for our own will),
And caught them; — what do they *not* catch,
    methinks ?
But I'm not Œdipus, and life's a Sphinx.

XIII.

I tell the tale as it is told, nor dare
  To venture a solution : " Davus sum ! "
And now I will proceed upon the pair.
  Sweet Adeline, amidst the gay world's hum,
Was the Queen-Bee, the glass of all that's fair;
  Whose charms made all men speak, and
    women dumb.
That last's a miracle, and such was reckoned,
And since that time there has not been a
    second.

XIV.

Chaste was she, to detraction's desperation,
  And wedded unto one she had loved well —
A man known in the councils of the nation,
  Cool, and quite English, imperturbable,
Though apt to act with fire upon occasion,
  Proud of himself and her : the world could
    tell
Nought against either, and both seemed
    secure —
She in her virtue, he in his hauteur.

XV.

It chanced some diplomatical relations,
  Arising out of business, often brought
Himself and Juan in their mutual stations
  Into close contact. Though reserved, nor
    caught
By specious seeming, Juan's youth, and
    patience,
  And talent, on his haughty spirit wrought,
And formed a basis of esteem, which ends
In making men what courtesy calls friends.

XVI.

And thus Lord Henry, who was cautious as
  Reserve and pride could make him, and full
    slow
In judging men — when once his judgment
    was
Determined, right or wrong, on friend or foe,
  Had all the pertinacity pride has,
  Which knows no ebb to its imperious flow,
And loves or hates, disdaining to be guided,
Because its own good pleasure hath decided.

*   *   *   *   *

XXII.

He liked the gentle Spaniard for his gravity;
  He almost honored him for his docility,
Because, though young, he acquiesced with
    suavity,

Or contradicted but with proud humility.
He knew the world, and would not see de-
    pravity
  In fault which sometimes show the soil's
    fertility,
If that the weeds o'erlive not the first crop —
For then they are very difficult to stop.

XXIII.

And then he talked with him about Madrid,
  Constantinople, and such distant places;
Where people always did as they were bid,
  Or did what they should not with foreign
    graces.
Of coursers also spake they : Henry rid
  Well, like most Englishmen, and loved the
    races,
And Juan, like a true-born Andalusian,
Could back a horse, as despots ride a Russian.

XXIV.

And thus acquaintance grew, at noble routs,
  And diplomatic dinners, or at other —
For Juan stood well both with Ins and Outs,
  As in freemasonry a higher brother.
Upon his talent Henry had no doubts;
  His manner showed him sprung from a
    high mother;
And all men like to show their hospitality
To him whose breeding matches with his
    quality.

*   *   *   *   *

XLVIII.

The London winter and the country summer
  Were well nigh over. 'Tis perhaps a pity,
When nature wears the gown that doth be-
    come her,
  To lose those best months in a sweaty city,
And wait until the nightingale grows dumber,
  Listening debates not very wise or witty,
Ere patriots their true *country* can remem-
    ber ; —
But there's no shooting (save grouse) till Sep-
    tember.

XLIX.

I've done my tirade. The world was gone :
  The twice two thousand, for whom earth
    was made,
Were vanished to be what they call alone —
  That is, with thirty servants for parade,
As many guests, or more ; before whom groan
  As many covers, duly, daily laid.
Let none accuse old England's hospitality —
Its quantity is but condensed to quality.

L.

Lord Henry and the Lady Adeline
  Departed like the rest of their compeers,
The peerage, to a mansion very fine ;
  The Gothic Babel of a thousand years.

None than themselves could boast a longer
  line,
  Where time through heroes and through
    beauties steers;
And oaks as olden as their pedigree
Told of their sires, a tomb in every tree.

LI.

A paragraph in every paper told
  Of their departure: such is modern fame:
'Tis pity that it takes no further hold
  Than an advertisement, or much the same;
When, ere the ink be dry, the sound grows
  cold,
    The Morning Post was foremost to pro-
    claim—
"Departure, for his country seat, to-day,
Lord H. Amundeville and Lady A.

LII.

"We understand the splendid host intends
  To entertain, this autumn, a select
And numerous party of his noble friends;
  Midst whom we have heard, from sources
    quite correct,
The Duke of D——the shooting season
  spends,
  With many more by rank and fashion
    decked;
Also a foreigner of high condition,
The envoy of the secret Russian mission."

    *   *   *   *   *

LV.

To Norman Abbey whirled the noble pair,—
  An old, old monastery once, and now
Still older mansion,—of a rich and rare
  Mixed Gothic, such as artists all allow
Few specimens yet left us can compare
  Withal: it lies perhaps a little low,
Because the monks preferred a hill behind,
To shelter their devotions from the wind.

LVI.

It stood embosomed in a happy valley,
  Crowned by high woodlands, where the
    Druid oak
Stood like Caractacus in act to rally
  His host, with broad arms 'gainst the thun-
    der-stroke;
And from beneath his boughs were seen to
  sally
  The dappled foresters—as day awoke,
The branching stag swept down with all his
  herd,
To quaff a brook which murmured like a bird.

LVII.

Before the mansion lay a lucid lake,
  Broad as transparent, deep, and freshly fed
By a river, which its softened way did take

In currents through the calmer water spread
Around: the wildfowl nestled in the brake
  And sedges, brooding in their liquid bed:
The woods sloped downwards to its brink,
  and stood
With their green faces fixed upon the flood.

LVIII.

Its outlet dashed into a deep cascade,
  Sparkling with foam, until again subsiding,
Its shriller echoes—like an infant made
  Quiet—sank into softer ripples, gliding
Into a rivulet; and thus allayed,
  Pursued its course, now gleaming, and now
    hiding
Its windings through the woods; now clear,
    now blue,
According as the skies their shadows threw.

LIX.

A glorious remnant of the Gothic pile
  (While yet the church was Rome's) stood
    half apart
In a grand arch, which once screened many
  an aisle.
  These last had disappeared—a loss to art:
The first yet frowned superbly o'er the soil,
  And kindled feelings in the roughest heart,
Which mourned the power of time's or tem-
    pest's march
In gazing on that venerable arch.

LX.

Within a niche, nigh to its pinnacle,
  Twelve saints had once stood sanctified in
    stone;
But these had fallen, not when the friars fell,
  But in the war which struck Charles from
    his throne,
When each house was a fortalice—as tell
  The annals of full many a line undone,—
The gallant cavaliers, who fought in vain
For those who knew not to resign or reign.

LXI.

But in a higher niche, alone, but crowned,
  The Virgin Mother of the God-born Child,
With her Son in her blessed arms, looked
    round,
  Spared by some chance when all beside
    was spoiled;
She made the earth below seem holy ground.
  This may be superstition, weak or wild,
But even the faintest relics of a shrine
Of any worship wake some thoughts divine.

LXII.

A mighty window, hollow in the centre,
  Shorn of its glass of thousand colorings,
Through which the deepened glories once
  could enter,

Streaming from off the sun like seraph's
  wings,
Now yawns all desolate: now loud, now
  fainter,
The gale sweeps through its fretwork, and
  oft sings
The owl his anthem, where the silenced quire
Lie with their hallelujahs quenched like fire.

LXIII.

But in the noontide of the moon, and when
  The wind is winged from one point of
  heaven,
There moans a strange unearthly sound, which
  then
  Is musical — a dying accent driven
Through the huge arch, which soars and sinks
  again.
  Some deem it but the distant echo given
Back to the night wind by the waterfall,
And harmonized by the old choral wall:

LXIV.

Others, that some original shape, or form
  Shaped by decay, perchance, hath given the
  power
(Though less than that of Memnon's statue,
  warm
  In Egypt's rays, to harp at a fixed hour)
To this gray ruin, with a voice to charm;
  Sad, but serene, it sweeps o'er tree or
  tower;
The cause I know not, nor can solve; but
  such
The fact: — I've heard it, — once perhaps too
  much.

LXV.

Amidst the court a Gothic fountain played,
  Symmetrical, but decked with carvings
  quaint —
Strange faces, like to men in masquerade,
  And here perhaps a monster, there a saint:
The spring gushed through grim mouths of
  granite made,
  And sparkled into basins, where it spent
Its little torrent in a thousand bubbles,
Like man's vain glory, and his vainer troubles.

LXVI.

The mansion's self was vast and venerable,
  With more of the monastic than has been
Elsewhere preserved: the cloisters still were
  stable,
  The cells, too, and refectory, I ween:
An exquisite small chapel had been able,
  Still unimpaired, to decorate the scene;
The rest had been reformed, replaced, or
  sunk,
And spoke more of the baron than the
  monk.

LXVII.

Huge halls, long galleries, spacious chambers,
  joined
  By no quite lawful marriage of the arts,
Might shock a connoisseur; but when com-
  bined,
  Formed a whole which, irregular in parts,
Yet left a grand impression on the mind,
  At least of those whose eyes are in their
  hearts.
We gaze upon a giant for his stature,
Nor judge at first if all be true to nature.

LXVIII.

Steel barons, molten the next generation
  To silken rows of gay and gartered earls,
Glanced from the walls in goodly preservation:
  And Lady Marys blooming into girls,
With fair long locks, had also kept their sta-
  tion:
  And countesses mature in robes and pearls:
Also some beauties of Sir Peter Lely,
  Whose drapery hints we may admire them
  freely.

LXIX.

Judges in very formidable ermine
  Were there, with brows that did not much
  invite
The accused to think their lordships would
  determine
  His cause by leaning much from might to
  right:
Bishops, who had not left a single sermon:
  Attorney-generals, awful to the sight,
As hinting more (unless our judgments warp
  us)
Of the "Star Chamber" than of "Habeas
  Corpus."

LXX.

Generals, some all in armor, of the old
  And iron time, ere lead had ta'en the lead;
Others in wigs of Marlborough's martial fold,
  Huger than twelve of our degenerate breed:
Lordlings, with staves of white or keys of gold:
  Nimrods, whose canvas scarce contained
  the steed;
And here and there some stern high patriot
  stood,
Who could not get the place for which he sued.

LXXI.

But ever and anon, to soothe your vision,
  Fatigued with these hereditary glories,
There rose a Carlo Dolce or a Titian,
  Or wilder group of savage Salvatore's.
Here danced Albano's boys, and here the sea
  shone
  In Vernet's ocean light; and there the sto-
  ries
Of martyrs awed, as Spagnoletto tainted
His brush with all the blood of all the sainted.

LXXII.

Here sweetly spread a landscape of Lorraine;
 There Rembrandt made his darkness equal
 light,
Or gloomy Caravaggio's gloomier stain
 Bronzed o'er some lean and stoic ancho-
 rite: —
But, lo! a Teniers woos, and not in vain,
 Your eyes to revel in a livelier sight:
His bell-mouthed goblet makes me feel quite
 Danish
Or Dutch with thirst — What, ho! a flask of
 Rhenish.

LXXIII.

O reader! if that thou canst read, — and know,
 'Tis not enough to spell, or even to read,
To constitute a reader; there must go
 Virtues of which both you and I have need.
Firstly, begin with the beginning — (though
 That clause is hard); and secondly, pro-
 ceed;
Thirdly, commence not with the end — or,
 sinning
In this sort, end at least with the beginning.

LXXIV.

But, reader, thou hast patient been of late,
 While I, without remorse of rhyme, or fear,
Have built and laid out ground at such a rate,
 Dan Phœbus takes me for an auctioneer.
That poets were so from the earliest date,
 By Homer's "Catalogue of ships" is clear;
But a mere modern must be moderate —
I spare you then the furniture and plate.

LXXV.

The mellow autumn came, and with it came
 The promised party, to enjoy its sweets.
The corn is cut, the manor full of game;
 The pointer ranges, and the sportsman beats
In russet jacket: — lynx-like is his aim;
 Full grows his bag, and wonder*ful* his feats.
Ah, nutbrown partridges! Ah, brilliant pheas-
 ants!
And ah, ye poachers! — 'Tis no sport for
 peasants.

LXXVI.

An English autumn, though it hath no vines,
 Blushing with Bacchant coronals along
The paths, o'er which the far festoon entwines
 The red grape in the sunny lands of song,
Hath yet a purchased choice of choicest wines;
 The claret light, and the Madeira strong.
If Britain mourn her bleakness, we can tell her,
The very best of vineyards is the cellar.

LXXVII.

Then, if she hath not that serene decline
 Which makes the southern autumn's day
 appear
As if 'twould to a second spring resign
 The season, rather than to winter drear, —
Of indoor comforts still she hath a mine, —
 The sea-coal fires, the "earliest of the year;"
Without doors, too, she may complete in
 mellow,
As what is lost in green is gained in yellow.

*   *   *   *   *

CANTO THE FOURTEENTH.

I.

IF from great nature's or our own abyss
 Of thought we could but snatch a certainty,
Perhaps mankind might find the path they
 miss —
 But then 'twould spoil much good philosophy.
One system eats another up, and this
 Muoh as old Saturn ate his progeny;
For when his pious consort gave him stones
In lieu of sons, of these he made no bones.

II.

But System doth reverse the Titan's breakfast,
 And eats her parents, albeit the digestion
'Is difficult. Pray tell me, can you make fast,
 After due search, your faith to any question?
Look back o'er ages, ere unto the stake fast
 You bind yourself, and call some mode the
 best one.
Nothing more true than *not* to trust your
 senses;
And yet what are your other evidences?

III.

For me, I know nought; nothing I deny,
 Admit, reject, contemn; and what know
 you,
Except perhaps that you were born to die?
 And both may after all turn out untrue.
An age may come, Font of Eternity,
 When nothing shall be either old or new.
Death, so called, is a thing which makes men
 weep,
And yet a third of life is passed in sleep.

IV.

A sleep without dreams, after a rough day
 Of toil, is what we covet most; and yet

How clay shrinks back from more quiescent
   clay!
The very Suicide that pays his debt
At once without instalments (an old way
   Of paying debts, which creditors regret)
Lets out impatiently his rushing breath,
Less from disgust of life than dread of death.

V.

'Tis round him, near him, here, there, every-
   where;
   And there's a courage which grows out of
      fear,
Perhaps of all most desperate, which will dare
   The worst to _know_ it:— when the moun-
      tains rear
Their peaks beneath your human foot, and
      there
You look down o'er the precipice, and drear
The gulf of rock yawns,— you can't gaze a
      minute
Without an awful wish to plunge within it.

VI.

'Tis true, you don't — but, pale and struck
   with terror,
   Retire: but look into your past impression!
And you will find, though shuddering at the
   mirror
   Of your own thoughts, in all their self-con-
      fession,
The lurking bias, be it truth or error,
   To the _unknown;_ a secret prepossession,
To plunge with all your fears — but where?
   You know not,
And that's the reason why you do — or do not.

VII.

But what's this to the purpose? you will say.
   Gent. reader, nothing; a mere speculation,
For which my sole excuse is — 'tis my way,
   Sometimes _with_ and sometimes without oc-
      casion
I write what's uppermost, without delay;
   This narrative is not meant for narration,
But a mere airy and fantastic basis,
To build up common things with common
   places.

VIII.

You know, or don't know, that great Bacon
   saith,
   "Fling up a straw, 'twill show the way the
      wind blows;"
And such a straw, borne on by human breath,
   Is poesy, according as the mind glows;
A paper kite which flies 'twixt life and death,
   A shadow which the onward soul behind
      throws,
And mine's a bubble, not blown up for
   praise,
But just to play with, as an infant plays.

IX.

The world is all before me — or behind;
   For I have seen a portion of that same,
And quite enough for me to keep in mind;—
   Of passions, too, I have proved enough to
      blame,
To the great pleasure of our friends, mankind,
   Who like to mix some slight alloy with fame;
For I was rather famous in my time,
Until I fairly knocked it up with rhyme.

X.

I have brought this world about my ears, and
   eke
   The other; that's to say, the clergy — who
Upon my head have bid their thunders break
   In pious libels by no means a few.
And yet I can't help scribbling once a week,
   Tiring old readers, nor discovering new.
In youth I wrote because my mind was full,
And now because I feel it growing dull.

    *   *   *   *   *

LXXXV.

Our gentle Adeline had one defect —
   Her heart was vacant, though a splendid
      mansion;
Her conduct had been perfectly correct,
   As she had seen nought claiming its expan-
      sion.
A wavering spirit may be easier wrecked,
   Because 'tis frailer, doubtless, than a stanch
      one;
But when the latter works its own undoing,
Its inner crash is like an earthquake's ruin.

LXXXVI.

She loved her lord, or thought so; but _that_
   love
   Cost her an effort, which is a sad toil,
The stone of Sisyphus, if once we move
   Our feelings 'gainst the nature of the soil.
She had nothing to complain of, or reprove,
   No bickerings, no connubial turmoil:
Their union was a model to behold,
Serene and noble, — conjugal, but cold.

LXXXVII.

There was no great disparity of years,
   Though much in temper; but they never
      clashed;
They moved like stars united in their spheres,
   Or like the Rhone by Leman's waters
      washed,
Where mingled and yet separate appears
   The river from the lake, all bluely dashed
Through the serene and placid glassy deep,
Which fain would lull its river-child to sleep.

LXXXVIII.

Now when she once had ta'en an interest
   In any thing, however she might flatter

Herself that her intentions were the best,
  Intense intentions are a dangerous matter:
Impressions were much stronger than she
  guessed,
And gathered as they run like growing
  water
Upon her mind; the more so, as her breast
Was not at first too readily impressed.

LXXXIX.

But when it was, she had that lurking demon
  Of double nature, and thus doubly named —
Firmness yclept in heroes, kings, and seamen,
  That is, when they succeed; but greatly
  blamed
As *obstinacy*, both in men and women,
  Whene'er their triumph pales, or star is
  tamed : —
And 'twill perplex the casuist in morality
To fix the due bounds of this dangerous qual-
  ity.

XC.

Had Buonaparté won at Waterloo,
  It had been firmness; now 'tis pertinacity:
Must the event decide between the two ?
  I leave it to your people of sagacity
To draw the line between the false and true,
  If such can e'er be drawn by man's capacity.
My business is with Lady Adeline,
Who in her way too was a heroine.

XCI.

She knew not her own heart; then how
  should I ?
I think not she was *then* in love with Juan :
If so, she would have had the strength to fly
  The wild sensation, unto her a new one :
She merely felt a common sympathy
  (I will not say it was a false or true one)
In him, because she thought he was in dan-
  ger, —
Her husband's friend, her own, young, and a
  stranger.

XCII.

She was, or thought she was, his friend — and
  this
  Without the farce of friendship, or ro-
  mance;
Platonism, which leads so oft amiss
  Ladies who have studied friendship but in
  France
Or Germany, where people *purely* kiss.
  To thus much Adeline would not advance;
But of such friendship as man's may to man
  be
She was as capable as woman can be.

XCIII.

No doubt the secret influence of the sex
  Will there, as also in the ties of blood,

An innocent predominance annex,
  And tune the concord to a finer mood.
If free from passion, which all friendship
  checks,
  And your true feelings fully understood,
No friend like to a woman earth discovers,
So that you have not been nor will be lovers.

XCIV.

Love bears within its breast the very germ
  Of change; and how should this be other-
  wise ?
That violent things more quickly find a term
  Is shown through nature's whole analogies ;
And how should the most fierce of all be firm ?
  Would you have endless lightning in the
  skies ?
Methinks Love's very title says enough :
How should " the *tender* passion " e'er be
  tough ?

XCV.

Alas ! by all experience, seldom yet
  (I merely quote what I have heard from
  many)
Had lovers not some reason to regret
  The passion which made Solomon a zany.
I've also seen some wives (not to forget
  The marriage state, the best or worst of
  any)
Who were the very paragons of wives,
Yet made the misery of at least two lives.

XCVI.

I've also seen some female *friends* ('tis odd,
  But true — as, if expedient, I could prove)
That faithful were through thick and thin,
  abroad,
At home, far more than ever yet was
  Love —
Who did not quit me when Oppression trod
  Upon me; whom no scandal could re-
  move;
Who fought, and fight, in absence, too, my
  battles,
Despite the snake Society's loud rattles.

XCVII.

Whether Don Juan and chaste Adeline
  Grew friends in this or any other sense
Will be discussed hereafter, I opine :
  At present I am glad of a pretence
To leave them hovering, as the effect is fine,
  And keeps the atrocious reader in *suspense;*
The surest way for ladies and for books
To bait their tender or their tenter hooks.

XCVIII.

Whether they rode, or walked, or studied
  Spanish
  To read Don Quixote in the original,

DON JUAN.

A pleasure before which all others vanish;
  Whether their talk was of the kind called
  "small,"
Or serious, are the topics I must banish
  To the next Canto; where perhaps I shall
Say something to the purpose, and display
Considerable talent in my way.

XCIX.

Above all, I beg all men to forbear
  Anticipating aught about the matter:
They'll only make mistakes about the fair,
  And Juan too, especially the latter.
And I shall take a much more serious air
  Than I have yet done, in this epic satire.
It is not clear that Adeline and Juan
Will fall; but if they do, 'twill be their ruin.

C.

But great things spring from little: — Would
  you think,
  That in our youth, as dangerous a passion
As e'er brought man and woman to the
  brink
  Of ruin, rose from such a slight occasion,
As few would ever dream could form the
  link
  Of such a sentimental situation?

You'll never guess, I'll bet you millions, mil-
  liards —
It all sprung from a harmless game at billiards.

CI.

'Tis strange, — but true; for truth is always
  strange;
  Stranger than fiction: if it could be told,
How much would novels gain by the ex-
  change;
  How differently the world would men be-
  hold!
How oft would vice and virtue places change!
  The new world would be nothing to the
  old,
If some Columbus of the moral seas
Would show mankind their souls' antipodes.

CII.

What "antres vast and deserts idle" then
  Would be discovered in the human soul!
What icebergs in the hearts of mighty men,
  With self-love in the centre as their pole!
What Anthropophagi are nine of ten
  Of those who hold the kingdoms in control!
Were things but only called by their right
  name,
Cæsar himself would be ashamed of fame.

CANTO THE FIFTEENTH.

I.

AH! — What should follow slips from my
  reflection!
  Whatever follows ne'ertheless may be
As à-propos of hope or retrospection,
  As though the lurking thought had followed
  free.
All present life is but an interjection,
  An "Oh!" or "Ah!" of joy or misery,
Or a "Ha! ha!" or "Bah!" — a yawn, or
  "Pooh!"
Of which perhaps the latter is most true.

II.

But, more or less, the whole's a syncopé
  Or a singultus — emblems of emotion,
The grand antithesis to great ennui,
  Wherewith we break our bubbles on the
  ocean,
That watery outline of eternity,
  Or miniature at least, as is my notion,
Which ministers unto the soul's delight,
In seeing matters which are out of sight.

III.

But all are better than the sigh supprest,
  Corroding in the cavern of the heart,

Making the countenance a masque of rest,
  And turning human nature to an art.
Few men dare show their thoughts of worst
  or best;
  Dissimulation always sets apart
A corner for herself; and therefore fiction
Is that which passes with least contradiction.

IV.

Ah! who can tell? Or rather, who can not
  Remember, without telling, passion's errors?
The drainer of oblivion, even the sot,
  Hath got blue devils for his morning mir-
  rors:
What though on Lethe's stream he seem to
  float,
  He cannot sink his tremors or his terrors;
The ruby glass that shakes within his hand
Leaves a sad sediment of Time's worst sand.

V.

And as for love — O love! —— We will pro-
  ceed.
  The Lady Adeline Amundeville,
A pretty name as one would wish to read,
  Must perch harmonious on my tuneful quill
There's music in the sighing of a reed;

There's music in the gushing of a rill;
There's music in all things, if men had ears;
Their earth is but an echo of the spheres.

VI.

The Lady Adeline, right honorable,
  And honored, ran a risk of growing less so;
For few of the soft sex are very stable
  In their resolves — alas! that I should say so!
They differ as wine differs from its label,
  When once decanted; — I presume to guess
    so,
But will not swear: yet both upon occasion,
'Till old, may undergo adulteration.

VII.

But Adeline was of the purest vintage,
  The unmingled essence of the grape; and
    yet
Bright as a new Napoleon from its mintage,
  Or glorious as a diamond richly set;
A page where Time should hesitate to print
    age,
  And for which Nature might forego her
    debt —
Sole creditor whose process doth involve in't
The luck of finding everybody solvent.

VIII.

O Death! thou dunnest of all duns! thou daily
  Knockest at doors, at first with modest tap,
Like a meek tradesman when, approaching
    palely,
  Some splendid debtor he would take by sap:
But oft denied, as patience 'gins to fail, he
  Advances with exasperated rap,
And (if let in) insists, in terms unhandsome,
On ready money or " a draft on Ransom."

IX.

Whate'er thou takest, spare a while poor
    Beauty!
  She is so rare, and thou hast so much prey.
What though she now and then may slip from
    duty,
  The more's the reason why you ought to
    stay.
Gaunt Gourmand! with whole nations for
    your booty,
  You should be civil in a modest way:
Suppress, then, some slight feminine diseases,
And take as many heroes as Heaven pleases.

X.

Fair Adeline, the more ingenuous
  Where she was interested (as was said),
Because she was not apt, like some of us,
  To like too readily, or too high bred
To show it — (points we need not now dis-
    cuss) —
  Would give up artlessly both heart and head,

Unto such feelings as seemed innocent,
For objects worthy of the sentiment.

XI.

Some parts of Juan's history, which Rumor,
  That live gazette, had scattered to disfigure,
She had heard; but women hear with more
    good humor
  Such aberrations than we men of rigor:
Besides, his conduct, since in England, grew
    more
  Strict, and his mind assumed a manlier
    vigor;
Because he had, like Alcibiades,
The art of living in all climes with ease.

XII.

His manner was perhaps the more seductive,
  Because he ne'er seemed anxious to seduce;
Nothing affected, studied, or constructive
  Of coxcombry or conquest: no abuse
Of his attractions marred the fair perspective,
  To indicate a Cupidon broke loose,
And seemed to say, " Resist us if you can " —
Which makes a dandy while it spoils a man.

XIII.

They are wrong — that's not the way to set
    about it;
  As, if they told the truth, could well be
    shown.
But, right or wrong, Don Juan was without it;
  In fact, his manner was his own alone:
Sincere he was — at least you could not doubt
    it,
  In listening merely to his voice's tone.
The devil hath not in all his quiver's choice
An arrow for the heart like a sweet voice.

XIV.

By nature soft, his whole address held off
  Suspicion: though not timid, his regard
Was such as rather seemed to keep aloof,
  To shield himself than put you on your
    guard:
Perhaps 'twas hardly quite assured enough,
  But modesty's at times its own reward,
Like virtue; and the absence of pretension
Will go much further than there's need to
    mention.

XV.

Serene, accomplished, cheerful but not loud;
  Insinuating without insinuation;
Observant of the foibles of the crowd,
  Yet ne'er betraying this in conversation;
Proud with the proud, yet courteously proud,
  So as to make them feel he knew his sta-
    tion
And theirs: — without a struggle for priority,
He neither brooked nor claimed superiority.

XVI.

That is, with men : with women he was what
  They pleased to make or take him for; and
    their
Imagination's quite enough for that:
  So that the outline's tolerably fair,
They fill the canvas up—and " verbum sat."
  If once their phantasies be brought to bear
Upon an object, whether sad or playful,
They can transfigure brighter than a Raphael.

XVII.

Adeline, no deep judge of character,
  Was apt to add a coloring from her own.
'Tis thus the good will amiably err,
  And eke the wise, as has been often shown.
Experience is the chief philosopher,
  But saddest when his science is well known :
And persecuted sages teach the schools
Their folly in forgetting there are fools.

XVIII.

Was it not so, great Locke ? and greater
    Bacon ?
  Great Socrates ? And thou, Diviner still,
Whose lot it is by man to be mistaken,
  And thy pure creed made sanction of all ill?
Redeeming worlds to be by bigots shaken,
  How was thy toil rewarded ? We might fill
Volumes with similar sad illustrations,
But leave them to the conscience of the nations.

XIX.

I perch upon an humbler promontory,
  Amidst life's infinite variety :
With no great care for what is nicknamed
    glory,
  But speculating as I cast mine eye
On what may suit or may not suit my story,
  And never straining hard to versify,
I rattle on exactly as I'd talk
With anybody in a ride or walk.

XX.

I don't know that there may be much ability
  Shown in this sort of desultory rhyme ;
But there's a conversational facility,
  Which may round off an hour upon a time.
Of this I'm sure at least, there's no servility
  In mine irregularity of chime,
Which rings what's uppermost of new or hoary
Just as I feel the " Improvvisatore."

*   *   *   *   *

XXVIII.

When Adeline, in all her growing sense
  Of Juan's merits and his situation,
Felt on the whole an interest intense, —
  Partly perhaps because a fresh sensation,
Or that he had an air of innocence,
  Which is for innocence a sad temptation, —

As women hate half measures, on the whole,
She 'gan to ponder how to save his soul.

XXIX.

She had a good opinion of advice,
  Like all who give and eke receive it gratis,
For which small thanks are still the market
    price,
  Even where the article at highest rate is :
She thought upon the subject twice or thrice,
  And morally decided, the best state is
For morals, marriage ; and this question car·
    ried,
She seriously advised him to get married.

XXX.

Juan replied, with all becoming deference,
  He had a predilection for that tie ;
But that, at present, with immediate reference
  To his own circumstances, there might lie
Some difficulties, as in his own preference,
  Or that of her to whom he might apply :
That still he'd wed with such or such a lady,
If that they were not married all already.

XXXI.

Next to the making matches for herself,
  And daughters, brothers, sisters, kith or kin,
Arranging them like books on the same shelf,
  There's nothing women love to dabble in
More (like a stockholder in growing pelf)
  Than match-making in general : 'tis no sin,
Certes, but a preventative, and therefore
That is, no doubt, the only reason wherefore.

*   *   *   *   *

XL.

But Adeline determined Juan's wedding
  In her own mind, and that's enough for
    woman :
But then, with whom ? There was the sage
    Miss Reading,
  Miss Raw, Miss Flaw, Miss Showman, and
    Miss Knowman,
And there two fair co-heiresses Giltbedding.
  She deemed his merits something more than
    common :
All these were unobjectionable matches,
And might go on, if well wound up, like
    watches.

XLI.

There was Miss Millpond, smooth as sum·
    mer's sea,
  That usual paragon, an only daughter,
Who seemed the cream of equanimity,
  Till skimmed—and then there was some
    milk and water,
With a slight shade of blue too, it might be,
  Beneath the surface ; but what did it matter?
Love's riotous, but marriage should have quiet,
And being consumptive, live on a milk diet.

XLII.

And then there was the Miss Audacia Shoe-
string,
  A dashing demoiselle of good estate,
Whose heart was fixed upon a star or blue
    string;
  But whether English dukes grew rare of late,
Or that she had not harped upon the true
    string,
  By which such sirens can attract our great,
She took up with some foreign younger
    brother,
A Russ or Turk—the one's as good as t'other.

XLIII.

And then there was — but why should I go on,
  Unless the ladies should go off ? — there was
Indeed a certain fair and fairy one,
  Of the best class, and better than her class,—
Aurora Raby, a young star who shone
  O'er life, too sweet an image for such glass,
A lovely being, scarcely formed or moulded,
A rose with all its sweetest leaves yet folded;

XLIV.

Rich, noble, but an orphan; left an only
  Child to the care of guardians good and
    kind;
But still her aspect had an air so lonely;
  Blood is not water; and where shall we find
Feelings of youth like those which overthrown
    lie
  By death, when we are left, alas! behind,
To feel, in friendless palaces, a home
Is wanting, and our best ties in the tomb?

XLV.

Early in years, and yet more infantine
  In figure, she had something of sublime
In eyes which sadly shone, as seraphs' shine.
  All youth — but with an aspect beyond time;
Radiant and grave—as pitying man's decline;
  Mournful—but mournful of another's crime,
She looked as if she sat by Eden's door,
And grieved for those who could return no
    more.

XLVI.

She was a Catholic, too, sincere, austere,
  As far as her own gentle heart allowed,
And deemed that fallen worship far more dear
  Perhaps because 'twas fallen : her sires were
    proud
Of deeds and days when they had filled the ear
  Of nations, and had never bent or bowed
To novel power; and as she was the last,
She held their old faith and old feelings fast.

XLVII.

She gazed upon a world she scarcely knew
  As seeking not to know it; silent, lone,
As grows a flower, thus quietly she grew,

And kept her heart serene within its zone.
There was awe in the homage which she
    drew;
  Her spirit seemed as seated on a throne
Apart from the surrounding world, and strong
In its own strength — most strange in one so
    young!

XLVIII.

Now it so happened, in the catalogue
  Of Adeline, Aurora was omitted,
Although her birth and wealth had given her
    vogue
  Beyond the charmers we have already cited;
Her beauty also seemed to form no clog
  Against her being mentioned as well fitted,
By many virtues, to be worth the trouble
Of single gentlemen who would be double.

XLIX.

And this omission, like that of the bust
  Of Brutus at the pageant of Tiberius,
Made Juan wonder, as no doubt he must,
  This he expressed half smiling and half
    serious;
When Adeline replied with some disgust,
  And with an air, to say the least, impe-
    rious,
She marvelled " what he saw in such a baby
As that prim, silent, cold Aurora Raby ? "

L.

Juan rejoined — " She was a Catholic,
  And therefore fittest, as of his persuasion;
Since he was sure his mother would fall sick,
  And the Pope thunder excommunication,
If——" But here Adeline, who seemed to
    pique
  Herself extremely on the inoculation
Of others with her own opinions, stated —
As usual — the same reason which she late did.

LI.

And wherefore not ? A reasonable reason,
  If good, is none the worse for repetition;
If bad, the best way's certainly to teaze on,
  And amplify : you lose much by concision,
Whereas insisting in or out of season
  Convinces all men, even a politician;
Or — what is just the same — it wearies out.
So the end's gained, what signifies the route !

LII.

Why Adeline had this slight prejudice —
  For prejudice it was — against a creature
As pure as sanctity itself from vice,
  With all the added charm of form and feat-
    ure,
For me appears a question far too nice,
  Since Adeline was liberal by nature;
But nature's nature, and has more caprices
Than I have time, or will, to take to pieces.

LIII.

Perhaps she did not like the quiet way
　With which Aurora on those baubles looked,
Which charm most people in their earlier day:
　For there are few things by mankind less
　　brooked,
And womankind too, if we so may say,
　Than finding thus their genius stand re-
　　buked,
Like " Antony's by Cæsar," by the few
Who look upon them as they ought to do.

LIV.

It was not envy — Adeline had none;
　Her place was far beyond it, and her mind.
It was not scorn — which could not light on
　　one
　Whose greatest *fault* was leaving few to find.
It was not jealousy, I think : but shun
　Following the " ignes fatui " of mankind.
It was not —— but 'tis easier far, alas !
To say what it was not than what it was.

LV.

Little Aurora deemed she was the theme
　Of such discussion.　She was there a guest;
A beauteous ripple of the brilliant stream
　Of rank and youth, though purer than the
　　rest,
Which flowed on for a moment in the beam
　Time sheds a moment o'er each sparkling
　　crest.
Had she known this, she would have calmly
　　smiled —
She had so much, or little, of the child.

LVI.

The dashing and proud air of Adeline
　Imposed not upon her: she saw her blaze
Much as she would have seen a glow-worm
　　shine,
　Then turned unto the stars for loftier rays.
Juan was something she could not divine,
　Being no sibyl in the new world's ways;
Yet she was nothing dazzled by the meteor,
Because she did not pin her faith on feature.

LVII.

His fame too, — for he had that kind of fame
　Which sometimes plays the deuce with
　　womankind,
A heterogeneous mass of glorious blame,
　Half virtues and whole vices being com-
　　bined;
Faults which attract because they are not tame;
　Follies tricked out so brightly that they
　　blind ——

These seals upon her wax made no impres-
　　sion,
Such was her coldness or her self-possession.

LVIII.

Juan knew nought of such a character —
　High, yet resembling not his lost Haidée;
Yet each was radiant in her proper sphere:
　The island girl, bred up by the lone sea,
More warm, as lovely, and not less sincere,
　Was Nature's all : Aurora could not be,
Nor would be thus : — the difference in them
Was such as lies between a flower and gem.

LIX.

Having wound up with this sublime compari-
　　son,
　Methinks we may proceed upon our narra-
　　tive,
And, as my friend Scott says, " I sound my
　　warison ; "
　Scott, the superlative of my comparative —
Scott, who can paint your Christian knight or
　　Saracen,
　Serf, lord, man, with such skill as none would
　　share it, if
There had not been one Shakspeare and Vol-
　　taire,
Of one or both of whom he seems the heir.

LX.

I say, in my slight way I may proceed
　To play upon the surface of humanity.
I write the world, nor care if the world
　　read,
　At least for this I cannot spare its vanity.
My Muse hath bred, and still perhaps may
　　breed
　More foes by this same scroll: when I be-
　　gan it, I
Thought that it might turn out so — *now* I
　know it,
But still I am, or was, a pretty poet.

LXI.

The conference or congress (for it ended
　As congresses of late do) of the Lady
Adeline and Don Juan rather blended
　Some acids with the sweets — for she was
　　heady;
But, ere the matter could be marred or mended,
　The silvery bell rang, not for " dinner ready,"
But for that hour, called *half-hour*, given to
　dress,
Though ladies' robes seem scant enough for
　less.

　　　*　　*　　*　　*　　*

CANTO THE SIXTEENTH.

I.

THE antique Persians taught three useful things,
  To draw the bow, to ride, and speak the truth.
This was the mode of Cyrus, best of kings —
  A mode adopted since by modern youth.
Bows have they, generally with two strings;
  Horses they ride without remorse or ruth;
At speaking truth perhaps they are less clever,
But draw the long bow better now than ever.

II.

The cause of this effect, or this defect, —
  "For this effect defective comes by cause,"—
Is what I have not leisure to inspect;
  But this I must say in my own applause,
Of all the Muses that I recollect,
  What'er may be her follies or her flaws
In some things, mine's beyond all contradic-
  tion
The most sincere that ever dealt in fiction.

III.

And as she treats all things, and ne'er retreats
  From any thing, this epic will contain
A wilderness of the most rare conceits,
  Which you might elsewhere hope to find in
  vain.
'Tis true there be some bitters with the
  sweets,
  Yet mixed so slightly, that you can't com-
  plain,
But wonder they so few are, since my tale is
De rebus cunctis et quibusdam aliis."

IV.

But of all truths which she has told, the most
  True is that which she is about to tell.
I said it was a story of a ghost —
  What then ? I only know it so befell.
Have you explored the limits of the coast,
  Where all the dwellers of the earth must
  dwell ?
'Tis time to strike such puny doubters dumb as
The sceptics who would not believe Columbus.

V.

Some people would impose now with author-
  ity,
Turpin's or Monmouth Geoffry's Chronicle;
  On whose historical superiority
Is always greatest at a miracle.
  But Saint Augustine has the great priority,
Who bids all men believe the impossible,
  Because 'tis so. Who nibble, scribble, quibble,
he
Sets at once with " *quia* impossibile."

VI.

And therefore, mortals, cavil not at all;
  Believe : — if 'tis improbable, you *must;*
And if it is impossible, you *shall :*
  'Tis always best to take things upon trust.
I do not speak profanely, to recall
  Those holier mysteries which the wise and
  just
Receive as gospel, and which grow more
  rooted,
As all truths must, the more they are disputed :

VII.

I merely mean to say what Johnson said,
  That in the course of some six thousand
  years,
All nations have believed that from the dead
  A visitant at intervals appears;
And what is strangest upon this strange head,
  Is, that whatever bar the reason rears
'Gainst such belief, there's something stronger
  still
In its behalf, let those deny who will.

VIII.

The dinner and the soirée too were done,
  The supper too discussed, the dames ad-
  mired,
The banqueteers had dropped off one by
  one —
  The song was silent, and the dance expired :
The last thin petticoats were vanished, gone
  Like fleecy clouds into the sky retired,
And nothing brighter gleamed through the
  saloon
Than dying tapers — and the peeping moon.

IX.

The evaporation of a joyous day
  Is like the last glass of champagne, without
The foam which made its virgin bumper gay;
  Or like a system coupled with a doubt;
Or like a soda bottle when its spray
  Has sparkled and let half its spirit out;
Or like a billow left by storms behind,
Without the animation of the wind;

X.

Or like an opiate, which brings troubled
  rest,
  Or none; or like — like nothing that I know
Except itself; — such is the human breast;
  A thing, of which similitudes can show
No real likeness, — like the old Tyrian vest
  Dyed purple, none at present can tell how,
If from a shell-fish or from cochineal.
So perish every tyrant's robe piece-meal!

Lightning Source UK Ltd.
Milton Keynes UK
UKHW010329281218
334537UK00007B/224/P